Oxford STUDENT'S Dictionary

for learners using English to study other subjects

OXFORD
UNIVERSITY PRESS

Great Clarendon Street, Oxford OX2 6DP

Oxford University Press is a department of the University of Oxford. It furthers the University's objective of excellence in research, scholarship, and education by publishing worldwide in

Oxford New York

Auckland Cape Town Dar es Salaam Hong Kong Karachi Kuala Lumpur Madrid Melbourne Mexico City Nairobi New Delhi Shanghai Taipei Toronto

With offices in

Argentina Austria Brazil Chile Czech Republic France Greece Guatemala Hungary Italy Japan Poland Portugal Singapore South Korea Switzerland Thailand Turkey Ukraine Vietnam

First published 2007

2011 2010 2009 2008
8 7 6 5 4 3 2

The British National Corpus is a collaborative project involving Oxford University Press, Longman, Chambers, the Universities of Oxford and Lancaster and the British Library

The Academic Word List was developed by Averil Coxhead, Massey University, New Zealand. The list is available at language.massey.ac.nz/staff/awl

ISBN: 978 0 19 431746 7 (DICTIONARY)
ISBN: 978 0 19 431747 4 (BOOK AND CD-ROM PACK)
ISBN: 978 0 19 430645 4 (BOOK IN PACK)
ISBN: 978 0 19 431748 1 (CD-ROM IN PACK)

Acknowledgements

Edited by: Alison Waters, assisted by Victoria Bull

Advisory Board: Dr Keith Brown; Prof Guy Cook; Dr Alan Cruse; Ms Ruth Gairns; Ms Moira Runcie; Prof. Gabriele Stein; Dr Norman Whitney; Prof. Henry Widdowson

Illustrations: Oxford Revision Guides GCSE series: Biology, W R Pickering; Chemistry, Michael Lewis; Geography,Garrett Nagel; Physics, Brian Arnold; Science, George Bethell. All illustrations by Hardlines, Charlbury, Oxford except 'cloud', which was originally published in Skills and Techniques in Geography, Nagle and Spencer, 1997, reproduced in the Geography Revision Guide with the permission of Stanley Thornes (Publishers) Ltd. Other illustrations by Lorna Barnard; Jeremy Bays; Mark Dunn; David Eaton; Gay Galsworthy; Karen Hiscock; Richard Lewington; Jason Lewis; Technical Graphics Department OUP; Graham White; Colin Woolf; Michael Woods

Text capture, processing and typesetting by Oxford University Press
Printed in China

CONTENTS

List of illustrations

At or near the words in **bold** you will find pictures to help you to understand words, or diagrams with labels and text to help you to describe processes.

List of notes to build your vocabulary

Look at these words to find **synonyms** in **THESAURUS** boxes:

action	care	effect	make	structure
ad	certain	essential	mention	successful
admit	claim	examine	product	sure
agree	clear	example	purpose	target
artificial	collect	factory	reason	think
ask	comment	fall	recommend	true
basis	declare	income	regard	trust
bill	demand	injure	rise	zero
build	difficult	language	sign	
building	disease	limit	situation	
campaign	economic	main	statement	

Look at these words to find **COLLOCATIONS AND PATTERNS** boxes:

agriculture	Agriculture
art	Works of art
compass	Points of the compass
crime	Crime
criminal	Types of criminal
currency	Currency
directions	Asking for and giving directions
disasters	Natural disasters
job	Jobs
language	Speaking a foreign language
law court	Law courts
measure	Weights and measures
medical	Medical practitioners
meetings	Formal meetings
opinion	Giving your opinion
organization	Organizations
performing arts	Performing arts
professional	Professionals
religion	Religion
study	Studying and exams
subject	Studying subjects at college and university
trends	Describing economic trends
water	The water cycle

Look at these words to find **WORD FAMILY** boxes:

able	defy	grateful	pronounce
accuse	deny	inhabit	prove
ally	destroy	intend	rely
clear	discreet	marry	repeat
conceive	divide	perceive	stable
deceive	explain	pity	true
decide	explode	produce	wit

GUIDE TO THE DICTIONARY

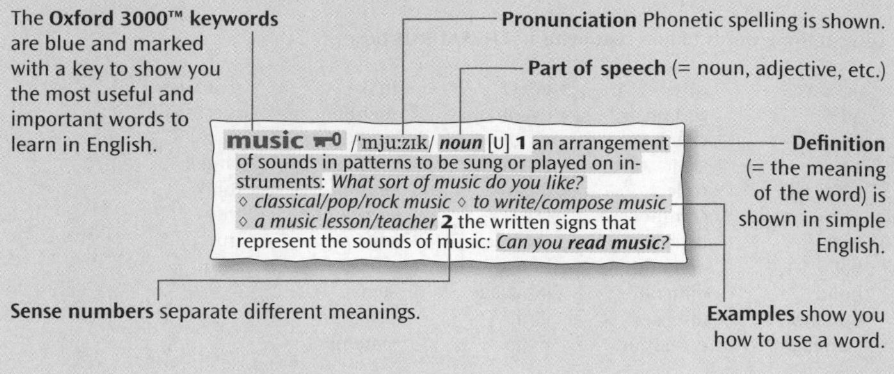

Stress marks show pronunciation in compounds.

Headwords are listed in alphabetical order whether they are written with one word or two or with a hyphen.

'sound effect *noun* [C, usually pl.] (ARTS AND MEDIA) a sound that is made artificially, for example the sound of the wind, and used in a play, film or computer game to make it more realistic

soundly /'saʊndli/ ***adv.*** completely or deeply: *The children were sleeping soundly.*

soundproof /'saʊndpru:f/ ***adj.*** made so that no sound can get in or out: *a soundproof room*

soundtrack /'saʊndtræk/ ***noun*** [C] (ARTS AND MEDIA, MUSIC) the recorded sound and music from a film or computer game ➲ look at **track**

Subject labels show the words that relate to a particular subject.

A **cross-reference** directs you to related vocabulary.

Academic Words from the *Academic Word List*, developed by Averil Coxhead of Massey University, New Zealand, are clearly marked.

professionally AW /prə'feʃənəli/ ***adv.*** **1** in a way that shows great skill and experience **2** for money; by a professional person: *Rob plays the saxophone professionally.*

Abbreviations of the main word are shown in brackets.

professor 🗝 /prə'fesə(r)/ ***noun*** [C] (*abbr.* Prof.) (EDUCATION) **1** (*BrE*) a university teacher of the highest level: *She's professor of English at Bristol University.* **2** (*AmE*) a teacher at a college or university

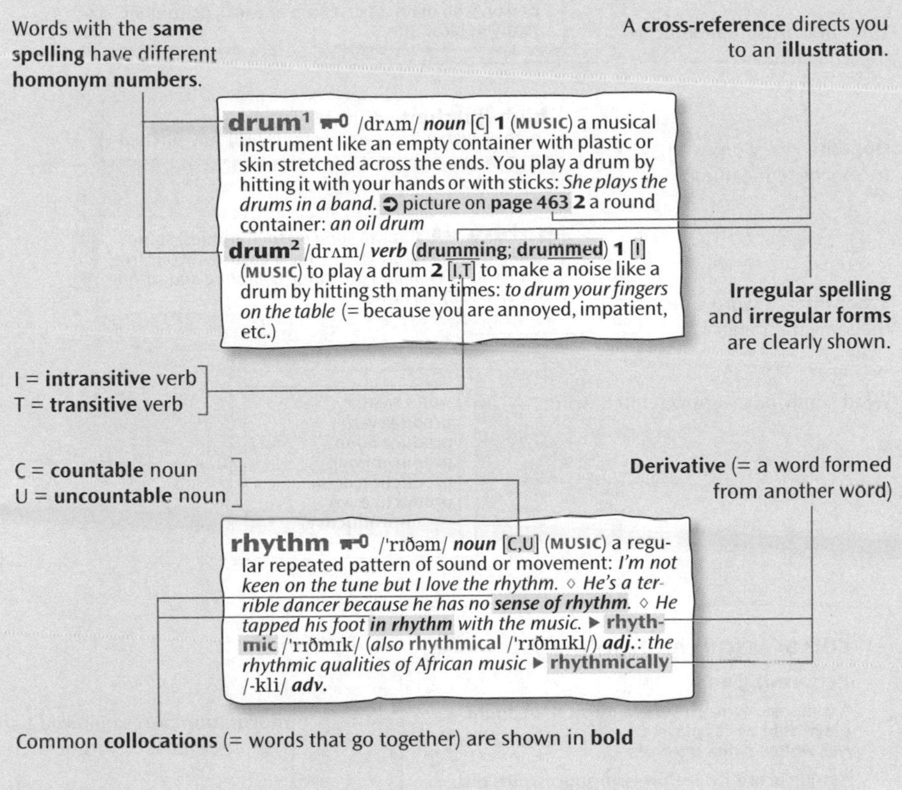

drum[1] /drʌm/ *noun* [C] **1** (MUSIC) a musical instrument like an empty container with plastic or skin stretched across the ends. You play a drum by hitting it with your hands or with sticks: *She plays the drums in a band.* ➲ picture on **page 463** **2** a round container: *an oil drum*

drum[2] /drʌm/ *verb* (**drumming**; **drummed**) **1** [I] (MUSIC) to play a drum **2** [I,T] to make a noise like a drum by hitting sth many times: *to drum your fingers on the table* (= because you are annoyed, impatient, etc.)

rhythm /ˈrɪðəm/ *noun* [C,U] (MUSIC) a regular repeated pattern of sound or movement: *I'm not keen on the tune but I love the rhythm.* ◇ *He's a terrible dancer because he has no* ***sense of rhythm***. ◇ *He tapped his foot* ***in rhythm*** *with the music.* ► **rhythmic** /ˈrɪðmɪk/ (*also* **rhythmical** /ˈrɪðmɪkl/) ***adj.***: *the rhythmic qualities of African music* ► **rhythmically** /-kli/ ***adv.***

Common **collocations** (= words that go together) are shown in **bold**

Idioms are shown in a separate section.

An arrow → shows that the meaning of an idiom is explained at the word following the arrow.

tune[1] /tjuːn/ *noun* [C,U] (MUSIC) a series of musical notes that are sung or played to form a piece of music: *The children* ***played us a tune*** *on their recorders.*

IDM **call the shots/tune** → CALL[1]

change your tune → CHANGE[1]

in/out of tune **1** (MUSIC) at/not at the correct musical level (**pitch**): *You're singing out of tune.* **2** having/not having the same opinions, interests, feelings, etc. as sb/sth

tune[2] /tjuːn/ *verb* **1** [I] (MUSIC) to make small changes to the sound a musical instrument makes so that it is at the correct musical level (**pitch**): *to tune a piano/guitar* **2** [T] to make small changes to an engine so that it runs well **3** [T] (usually passive) **~ sth (in) (to sth)** to move the controls on a radio or television so that you can receive a particular station: *The radio was tuned (in) to the BBC World Service.* ◇ (*spoken*) ***Stay tuned*** *for the latest news.*

PHR V **tune in (to sth)** to listen to a radio programme or watch a television programme

tune (sth) up (MUSIC) to make small changes to a group of musical instruments so that they sound pleasant when played together

sb = **somebody**
sth = **something**

Register (= words used in particular situations, for example *formal*, *informal*, *spoken*, *written*, etc.)

Words to **extend your vocabulary** appear in brackets in **bold**.

Phrasal verbs are shown in a separate section after idioms.

American and other **different spellings** are shown in brackets.

flautist /ˈflɔːtɪst/ (*AmE* **flutist**) ***noun*** [C] (MUSIC) a person who plays a FLUTE (= a musical instrument that you blow into)

Difficult words in definitions are explained.

ˌhigh-ˈpitched ***adj.*** (used about sounds) very high: *a high-pitched voice/whistle* OPP **low-pitched**

Opposite (= a word with the opposite meaning)

hobby /ˈhɒbi/ ***noun*** [C] (*pl.* **hobbies**) something that you do regularly for pleasure in your free time: *Barry's hobbies are stamp collecting and surfing the net.* SYN **pastime**

Synonym (= a word with the same meaning)

Word family boxes show related words.

WORD FAMILY
produce *verb*
produce *noun*
producer *noun*
production *noun*
productive *adj.*
(≠ **unproductive**)

COLLOCATIONS AND PATTERNS

Performing arts

A **composer** writes **a song/a musical/an opera.** A **playwright** writes **plays.**
He's written a new musical.

A group **presents/performs/produces/puts on/stages** a play, show, etc.
The drama group is putting on a show at the local school.
We are proud to present Arthur Miller's 'The Crucible'.

A **director directs** a play, show, etc.
The theatre has got a new director.
She is directing Mozart's 'Figaro' at La Scala.

A performer, actor, etc. **acts/appears/performs/sings/stars in** a play, show, etc..
She's appearing in 'The Seagull' at the New Theatre.
He starred in the musical 'Guys and Dolls'.

A performer, actor, etc. **rehearses (for)** a play, show, etc..
She had 3 weeks to rehearse for the concert.

Information boxes help you to extend your vocabulary.

THESAURUS

ask

enquire • demand • query
All these words mean to say or write sth in the form of a question, in order to get information.
ask: *Can I ask you a question?*
enquire/inquire (*rather formal*): *I rang the station to enquire about train times.*
demand: *'Where have you been?' he demanded angrily.*
query (*formal*): *'Why ever not?' she queried.*

DICTIONARY QUIZ

This quiz shows how your dictionary can help you.
You'll find the answers to all these questions by looking up the words in dark type.

1 What is **mincemeat** made of?
2 Who would use a **stethoscope**?
3 What does a **narrator** do?

Meanings
The dictionary explains what words mean in language that is easy to understand. The example sentences show you how to use the word correctly.

4 What's the first thing you do when you make a **telephone** call?
5 What's the opposite of **honest**?
6 What's another word for **pursue**?

Vocabulary
There are notes that give extra vocabulary associated with a word. Opposites and synonyms are marked with the symbols **OPP** and **SYN**.

7 Which word in this sentence would you **not** use in an informal situation: - *What time does the meeting commence?*

Style
The dictionary tells you if a word is formal or informal, spoken, written, slang, figurative or old-fashioned.

8 Is the word **meek** a noun, a verb or an adjective?
9 Is the word **luggage** countable or uncountable?
10 What's the past tense form of the word **broadcast**?

Grammar
The dictionary tells you whether a word is a noun, verb, adjective, etc. and whether nouns are countable or uncountable. It also gives irregular forms (e.g. irregular past tenses of verbs).

11 How do you spell the plural of **factory**?
12 How do you spell the -ing form of the word **occur**?

Spelling
You can use the dictionary to check how a word is spelled. It also tells you about small spelling changes in other forms of the word (e.g. irregular plurals).

13 Which letter is silent in the word **receipt**?
14 Which part of the compound **tourist board** receives the main stress?

Pronunciation
This dictionary gives the pronunciation of words and at the end of the dictionary there is a key that tells you how to read the phonetic spelling. Look also at the stress marks (') that show you where the main stress of the word is.

15 How many idioms are there that have the word **kill** in them?
16 How many phrasal verbs can you make with the word **burn**?

Idioms and phrasal verbs
These are given in two separate sections after the main meanings of the word.

17 What's the noun formed from **elegant**?
18 What's the adverb formed from **jealous**?

Words formed from other words
Derivatives (**loudly** and **loudness** are derivatives of **loud**) are given after the main meanings of the word.

19 What do you call a person who comes from **Norway**?
20 What number does the prefix **mega-** indicate?

Extra information
In the Reference section in the middle of the dictionary you will find helpful information, lists and exercises, including a list of geographical names and a list of prefixes and suffixes.

Answers on page 801

LABELS, SYMBOLS AND SHORT FORMS

Subject labels

These show which subject area a word belongs to

AGRICULTURE
ANATOMY
ARCHITECTURE
ART
ARTS AND MEDIA
ASTRONOMY
BIOLOGY
BUSINESS
CHEMISTRY
COMPUTING
EDUCATION
ECONOMICS
ENVIRONMENT
FINANCE
GEOGRAPHY
GEOLOGY
HEALTH
HISTORY
LANGUAGE
LAW
LITERATURE
MATHEMATICS
MUSIC
PHYSICS
POLITICS
PSYCHOLOGY
RELIGION
SCIENCE
SOCIAL STUDIES
SPORT
TOURISM

Labels used in the dictionary

formal used in serious or official language

informal used between friends, or in a relaxed or an unofficial situation

written used in books, letters, reports, etc.

spoken used especially in informal conversation

slang very informal language, sometimes used only by a particular group of people, such as teenagers

figurative not used with its exact meaning, but in an imaginative way to give a special effect, for example: *She was exploding with anger.*

old-fashioned usual in the past, but not now

Abbreviations used in the dictionary

abbr.	abbreviation
adj.	adjective
adv.	adverb
AmE	American English
BrE	British English
conj.	conjunction
det.	determiner
etc.	and so on
pl.	plural
pp	past participle
prep.	preposition
pres.	present tense
pres. part.	present participle
pt	past tense
sb	somebody
sing.	singular
sth	something
3rd pers. sing.	third person singular
[C]	countable noun
[U]	uncountable noun
[I]	intransitive verb
[T]	transitive verb

Symbols used in the dictionary

🔑 Oxford 3000™ word
For more information about the Oxford 3000™ and to download a copy of the list, visit the website: **www.oup.com/elt/oxford3000**

AW Word from the Academic Word List
For the list of headwords from the Academic Word List, see Reference Pages R12–14

IDM idiom

PHR V phrasal verb

SYN synonym

OPP opposite

▶ derivative

A a

A *abbr.* (*written*) = AMP (1)

A, a¹ /eɪ/ ***noun*** [C,U] (*pl.* **A's; a's** /eɪz/) **1** the first letter of the English alphabet: *'Andy' begins with (an) 'A'.* **2** (**EDUCATION**) the highest mark given for an exam or piece of work: *I got an 'A' for my essay.*
IDM **from A to B** from one place to another: *All I need is a car that gets me from A to B.*

a² ⊶ /ə strong form eɪ/ (*also* **an** /ən strong form æn/) ***indef. article*** ❶ The form **an** is used before a vowel sound. **1** one: *A cup of coffee, please.* ◇ *We've got an apple, a banana and two oranges.* **2** used when you talk about one example of sth for the first time: *I saw a dog chasing a cat this morning. The cat climbed up a tree.* ◇ *Have you got a dictionary* (= any dictionary)? **3** used for saying what kind of person or thing sb/sth is: *He's a doctor.* ◇ *She's a Muslim.* ◇ *You are a clever boy.* ◇ *'Is that an eagle?' 'No, it's a falcon.'* **4** (used with prices, rates, measurements) each: *I usually drink two litres of water a day.* ◇ *twice a week* ◇ *He was travelling at about 80 miles an hour.* **5** used with some expressions of quantity: *a lot of money* ◇ *a few cars* **6** used when you are talking about a typical example of sth: *An elephant can live for up to eighty years.* HELP You can also use the plural in this sense: *Elephants can live for up to eighty years.*

a- /eɪ/ ***prefix*** (in nouns, adjectives and adverbs) not; without: *atheist* ◇ *amoral*

A & E /ˌeɪ ənd 'iː/ ***abbr.*** → ACCIDENT AND EMERGENCY

aback /ə'bæk/ ***adv.***
PHR V **take sb aback** to surprise or shock sb

abacus /'æbəkəs/ ***noun*** [C] (*pl.* **abacuses**) (**MATHEMATICS**) a frame containing wires with small balls that move along them. It is used as a tool or toy for counting.

abandon ⊶ AW /ə'bændən/ ***verb*** [T] **1** to leave sb/sth that you are responsible for, usually permanently: *The bank robbers abandoned the car just outside the city.* **2** to stop doing sth without finishing it or without achieving what you wanted to do: *The search for the missing sailors was abandoned after two days.* ▶ **abandonment** ***noun*** [U]

abandoned ⊶ AW /ə'bændənd/ ***adj.*** left and no longer wanted, used or needed: *an abandoned car/house*

abashed /ə'bæʃt/ ***adj.*** feeling guilty and embarrassed because of sth that you have done: *'I'm sorry', said Ali, **looking abashed**.*

abate /ə'beɪt/ ***verb*** [I,T] (*formal*) to become less strong; to make sth less strong

abattoir /'æbətwɑː(r)/ (*BrE*) (**AGRICULTURE**) = SLAUGHTERHOUSE

abbess /'æbes/ ***noun*** [C] (**RELIGION**) a woman who is the head of a religious community for NUNS (= a religious group of women who live together in a building called a convent, away from other people)

abbey /'æbi/ ***noun*** [C] (**RELIGION**) a large church together with a group of buildings where religious communities of MONKS or NUNS live or used to live

abbot /'æbət/ ***noun*** [C] (**RELIGION**) a man who is the head of a religious community for MONKS

abbr. (*also* **abbrev.**) ***abbr.*** abbreviation

abbreviate /ə'briːvieɪt/ ***verb*** [T] to make sth shorter, especially a word or phrase: *'Kilometre' is usually abbreviated to 'km'.* ➲ look at **abridge**

abbreviation /əˌbriːvi'eɪʃn/ ***noun*** [C] (**LANGUAGE**) a short form of a word or phrase: *In this dictionary 'sth' is the abbreviation for 'something'.*

ABC /ˌeɪ biː 'siː/ ***noun*** [sing.] **1** (**LANGUAGE**) the alphabet; the letters of English from A to Z **2** the simple facts about sth: *an ABC of Gardening*

abdicate /'æbdɪkeɪt/ ***verb*** **1** [I] (**POLITICS, HISTORY**) to give up being King or Queen: *The Queen abdicated in favour of her son* (= her son became king). **2** [T] to give sth up, especially power or a position: *to **abdicate responsibility*** (= to refuse to be responsible for sth) ▶ **abdication** /ˌæbdɪ'keɪʃn/ ***noun*** [C,U]

abdomen /'æbdəmən/ ***noun*** [C] **1** (**ANATOMY**) a part of your body below the chest that contains the stomach, BOWELS, etc. **2** (**BIOLOGY**) the end part of an insect's body ➲ look at **thorax** ▶ **abdominal** /æb'dɒmɪnl/ ***adj.***: *abdominal pains*

abdominals /æb'dɒmɪnlz/ ***noun*** [pl.] (also *informal* **abs**) (**ANATOMY**) the muscles of the ABDOMEN

abduct /æb'dʌkt/ ***verb*** [T] (**LAW**) to take hold of sb and take them away illegally ▶ **abduction** ***noun*** [C,U]

aberration /ˌæbə'reɪʃn/ ***noun*** [C,U] (*formal*) a fact, an action or a way of behaving that is not typical, and that may be unacceptable

abet /ə'bet/ ***verb*** [T] (**abetting; abetted**)
IDM **aid and abet** → AID²

abhor /əb'hɔː(r)/ ***verb*** [T] (**abhorring; abhorred**) (*formal*) (not used in the progressive tenses) to hate sth very much

abhorrence /əb'hɒrəns/ ***noun*** [U] (*formal*) a strong feeling of hate; disgust

abhorrent /əb'hɒrənt/ ***adj.*** (*formal*) that makes you feel hate or disgust: *The idea of slavery is **abhorrent to** us nowadays.*

abide /ə'baɪd/ ***verb***
IDM **can't/couldn't abide sb/sth/doing sth** to hate sb/sth; to not like sb/sth at all
PHR V **abide by sth** to obey a law, etc.; to do what sb has decided

ability ⊶ /ə'bɪləti/ ***noun*** [C,U] (*pl.* **abilities**) **(an) ~ to do sth** the mental or physical power or skill that makes it possible to do sth: *an ability to make decisions* ◇ *A person of his ability should have no difficulty at all in getting a job.*

abject /'æbdʒekt/ ***adj.*** (*formal*) **1** terrible and without hope: *abject poverty/misery/failure* **2** without any pride or respect for yourself: *an abject apology*

ablation /æb'leɪʃn/ ***noun*** [U] (**GEOGRAPHY**) the loss of material from a large mass of ice, snow or rock as a result of the action of the sun, wind or rain ➲ picture at **glacial**

ablaze /ə'bleɪz/ ***adj.*** (not *before* a noun) burning strongly; completely on fire: *Soldiers used petrol to **set the building ablaze**.*

able ⊶ /'eɪbl/ ***adj.*** **1 ~ to do sth** (used as a modal verb) to have the ability, power, opportunity, time, etc. to do sth: *Will you be able to come to a meeting next week?* ◇ *I was able to solve the problem quickly.* ◇ *Many men don't **feel able** to express their emotions.*

> WORD FAMILY
> **able** *adj.* (≠ **unable**)
> **ability** *noun* (≠ **inability**)
> **disabled** *adj.*

2 (*comparative* **abler** /ˈeɪblə(r)/; *superlative* **ablest** /ˈeɪblɪst/) clever; doing your job well: *one of the ablest students in the class* ◇ *an able politician* ▶ **ably** /ˈeɪbli/ *adv.*

ˌable-ˈbodied *adj.* (**HEALTH**) physically healthy and strong; having full use of your body

abnormal AW /æbˈnɔːml/ *adj.* different from what is normal or usual, in a way that worries you or that is unpleasant OPP **normal** ▶ **abnormally** *adv.*: *abnormally high temperatures*

abnormality /ˌæbnɔːˈmæləti/ *noun* [C,U] (*pl.* **abnormalities**) (**HEALTH**) something that is not normal, especially in a person's body: *He was born with an abnormality of the heart.*

aboard /əˈbɔːd/ *adv.*, *prep.* on or onto a train, ship, aircraft or bus: *We climbed aboard the train and found a seat.* ◇ *Welcome aboard this flight to Caracas.*

abode /əˈbəʊd/ *noun* [sing.] (*written*) the place where you live

IDM **(of) no fixed abode/address** → FIXED

abolish /əˈbɒlɪʃ/ *verb* [T] (**LAW**) to end a law or system officially: *When was capital punishment abolished here?*

abolition /ˌæbəˈlɪʃn/ *noun* [U] (**LAW**) the act of ending a law or system officially: *the abolition of slavery*

abominable /əˈbɒmɪnəbl/ *adj.* very bad; shocking ▶ **abominably** /-əbli/ *adv.*

aboriginal /ˌæbəˈrɪdʒənl/ *noun* [C] (usually **Aboriginal**) (**SOCIAL STUDIES**) a member of a race of people who were the original people living in a country, especially Australia ▶ **Aboriginal** *adj.*: *Aboriginal traditions*

aborigine /ˌæbəˈrɪdʒəni/ *noun* [C] (**SOCIAL STUDIES**) **1** a member of a race of people who were the original people living in a country **2 Aborigine** a member of the race of people who were the original people of Australia

abort /əˈbɔːt/ *verb* [T] **1** (**HEALTH**) to end a PREGNANCY early in order to prevent a baby from developing and being born alive **2** to end sth before it is complete, especially because it is likely to fail: *The company aborted the project when they realized it was costing too much.*

abortion /əˈbɔːʃn/ *noun* [C,U] (**HEALTH**) a medical operation that causes a baby to die inside its mother before it is fully developed: *to have an abortion* ◇ *Abortion is illegal in that country.* ➲ look at **miscarriage**

abortionist /əˈbɔːʃənɪst/ *noun* [C] a person who performs a medical operation, especially illegally, that causes a baby to die while it is still inside its mother

abortive /əˈbɔːtɪv/ *adj.* (*formal*) (used about an action) not completed successfully; failed: *He made two abortive attempts to escape from prison.*

abound /əˈbaʊnd/ *verb* [I] to exist in large numbers: *Animals abound in the forest.*

PHRV **abound with/in sth** to contain large numbers of sth: *The lake abounds with fish.*

about¹ 🔑 /əˈbaʊt/ *adv.* **1** (*especially AmE* **around**) a little more or less than; approximately: *It's about three miles from here to the city centre.* ◇ *I got home at about half past seven.* **2** (*informal*) almost; nearly: *Dinner's just about ready.* **3** (*also* **around**) in many directions or places: *I could hear people moving about upstairs.* ◇ *Don't leave your clothes lying about all over the floor.* **4** (*also* **around**) (used after certain verbs) without doing anything in particular: *The kids spend most evenings **sitting about**, bored.* **5** (*also* **around**) present in a place; existing: *It was very late and there were few people about.* ◇ *There isn't much good music about these days.*

IDM **be about to do sth** to be going to do sth very soon: *The film's about to start.* ◇ *I was just about to explain when she interrupted me.*

about² 🔑 /əˈbaʊt/ *prep.* **1** on the subject of: *Let's talk about something else.* ◇ *What's your book about?* ◇ *He told me **all about** his family.* ◇ *I don't like it, but there's nothing I can do about it.* **2** (*also* **around**) in many directions or places; in different parts of sth: *We wandered about the town for an hour or two.* ◇ *Lots of old newspapers were scattered about the room.* **3** in the character of sb/sth: *There's something about him that I don't quite trust.* ◇ *I like the food, the climate, and everything else about this country.*

IDM **how/what about...?** **1** (used when asking for information about sb/sth or for sb's opinion or wish): *How about Ruth? Have you heard from her lately?* ◇ *I'm going to have chicken. What about you?* **2** (used when making a suggestion): *What about going to a film tonight?*

aˌbout-ˈturn (*AmE* **aˌbout-ˈface**) *noun* [C] a complete change of opinion, plan or behaviour: *The government did an about-turn over tax.*

above 🔑 /əˈbʌv/ *prep.*, *adj.*, *adv.* **1** in a higher place: *The people in the flat above make a lot of noise.* ◇ *The coffee is in the cupboard above the sink.* **2** in an earlier part (of sth written): *Contact me at the above address/the address above.* HELP The opposite is **below**, but note that **below** is not used before a noun: *Contact me at the address below.*

3 more than a number, amount, price, etc.: *children aged 11 and above* ◇ *A score of 70 and above will get you a grade B.* ◇ *You must get above 50% to pass.* ◇ *above-average temperatures* OPP **below** ➲ look at **over** **4** with a higher position in an organization, etc.: *The person above me is the department manager.* OPP **below** **5** too proud to do sth: *He seems to think he's above helping with the cleaning.*

IDM **above all** (used to emphasize the main point) most importantly: *Above all, stay calm!*

(be) above board (used especially about a business deal, etc.) honest and open

aˌbove-ˈmentioned *adj.* (only *before* a noun) (*written*) mentioned or named earlier in the same letter, book, etc.

aˌbove-the-ˈline *adj.* **1** (**FINANCE**) relating to the normal business costs and money earned that form a company's total profit: *Raw materials are recorded as **above-the-line costs**.* **2** (**BUSINESS**) relating to advertising that uses the MASS MEDIA (= newspapers, television and radio): *above-the-line promotion* ➲ look at **below-the-line**

abrasion /əˈbreɪʒn/ *noun* **1** [C] (**HEALTH**) a damaged area of the skin where it has been rubbed against sth hard and rough **2** [U] (**GEOGRAPHY**) damage to a surface caused by rubbing sth very hard against it

abrasive /əˈbreɪsɪv/ *adj.* **1** rough and likely to scratch: *Do not use abrasive cleaners on the bath.* **2** (used about a person) rude and rather aggressive

abreast /əˈbrest/ *adv.* ~ **(of sb/sth)** next to or level with sb/sth and going in the same direction: *The soldiers marched two abreast.*

IDM **be/keep abreast of sth** to have all the most recent information about sth

abridge /ə'brɪdʒ/ ***verb*** [T] (**LITERATURE**) to make a book, play, etc. shorter by removing parts of it ➲ look at **abbreviate**

abroad 🔑 /ə'brɔːd/ ***adv.*** in or to another country or countries: *They found it difficult to get used to living abroad.* ◇ *My mother has never been abroad.* ◇ *She often **goes abroad** on business.*

abrupt /ə'brʌpt/ ***adj.*** **1** sudden and unexpected: *an abrupt change of plan* **2** seeming rude and unfriendly ▶ **abruptly** ***adv.*** ▶ **abruptness** ***noun*** [U]

abs /æbz/ ***noun*** [pl.] (*informal*) = ABDOMINALS

ABS /ˌeɪ biː 'es/ ***abbr.*** anti-lock braking system

abscess /'æbses/ ***noun*** [C] (**HEALTH**) a swelling on or in the body, containing PUS (= a poisonous yellow liquid)

abscond /əb'skɒnd/ ***verb*** [I] (*formal*) ~ **(from sth) (with sth)** to run away from a place where you should stay, sometimes with sth that you should not take: *to abscond from prison* ◇ *She absconded with all the company's money.*

abseil /'æbseɪl/ (*AmE* **rappel**) ***verb*** [I] (**SPORT**) to go down a steep CLIFF or rock while you are fastened to a rope, pushing against the rock with your feet

absence 🔑 /'æbsəns/ ***noun*** **1** [C,U] a time when sb is away from somewhere; the fact of being away from somewhere: *Frequent absences due to illness meant he was behind with his work.* ◇ *I have to make all the decisions in my boss's absence.* **2** [U] the fact of sth/sb not being there; lack: ***In the absence of** a doctor, try to help the injured person yourself.* OPP **presence**

absent 🔑 /'æbsənt/ ***adj.*** **1** ~ (from sth) not present somewhere: *He was absent from work because of illness.* OPP **present** **2** showing that you are not really looking at or thinking about what is happening around you: *an absent expression/stare* ▶ **absently** ***adv.***

absentee /ˌæbsən'tiː/ ***noun*** [C] a person who is not in the place where they should be

absenteeism /ˌæbsən'tiːɪzəm/ ***noun*** [U] the problem of workers or students often not going to work or school

ˌabsent-'minded ***adj.*** often forgetting or not noticing things, because you are thinking about sth else ▶ **ˌabsent-'mindedly** ***adv.***

absolute 🔑 /'æbsəluːt/ ***adj.*** **1** complete; total: *The trip was an absolute disaster.* **2** not measured in comparison with sth else: *Spending on the Health Service has increased **in absolute terms**.*

absolutely 🔑 ***adv.*** **1** /'æbsəluːtli/ completely; totally. *It's absolutely freezing outside!* ◇ *I absolutely refuse to believe that.* ◇ *He made absolutely no effort* (= no effort at all) *to help me.* **2** /ˌæbsə'luːtli/ (used when you are agreeing with sb) yes; certainly: *'It is a good idea, isn't it?' 'Oh, absolutely!'*

ˌabsolute ma'jority ***noun*** [C] (**POLITICS**) (in an election) more than half of the total number of votes or winners: *280 seats are needed for an absolute majority in the National Assembly.*

ˌabsolute 'zero ***noun*** [U] (**PHYSICS**) the lowest temperature that is thought to be possible

absolution /ˌæbsə'luːʃn/ ***noun*** [U] (**RELIGION**) (especially in the Christian Church) a formal statement that a person is forgiven for what he or she has done wrong

absolve /əb'zɒlv/ ***verb*** [T] ~ **sb (from/of sth)** **1** to say formally that sb does not have to take responsibility for sth: *The driver was absolved of any blame for the train crash.* **2** (**RELIGION**) to give ABSOLUTION to sb

absorb 🔑 /əb'zɔːb; əb'sɔːb/ ***verb*** [T] **1** ~ **sth (into sth)** to take in and hold sth (a liquid, heat, etc.): *a drug that is quickly absorbed into the bloodstream* **2** to take sth into the mind and understand it: *I found it impossible to absorb so much information so quickly.* **3** ~ **sth (into sth)** to take sth into sth larger, so that it becomes part of it: *Over the years many villages have been absorbed into the city.* **4** to hold sb's attention completely or interest sb very much: *History is a subject that absorbs her.* **5** to reduce the effect of a sudden violent knock, hit, etc.: *The front of the car is designed to absorb most of the impact of a crash.* ➲ noun **absorption**

absorbed /əb'zɔːbd; əb'sɔːbd/ ***adj.*** ~ **(in sth)** giving all your attention to sth: *He was absorbed in his work and didn't hear me come in.*

absorbent /əb'zɔːbənt; əb'sɔːbənt/ ***adj.*** able to take in and hold liquid: *an absorbent cloth*

absorbing /əb'zɔːbɪŋ; əb'sɔːbɪŋ/ ***adj.*** holding all your interest and attention: *an absorbing book*

absorption /əb'sɔːpʃn; -zɔːpʃn/ ***noun*** [U] **1** the process of a liquid, gas or other substance being taken in: *Vitamin D is necessary to aid the absorption of calcium from food.* **2** (**SOCIAL STUDIES**) the process of a smaller group, country, etc., becoming part of a larger group or country: *the absorption of immigrants into the host country* **3** ~ **(in sth)** the fact of sb being very interested in sth so that it takes all their attention: *His work suffered because of his total absorption in sport.*

abstain /əb'steɪn/ ***verb*** [I] **1** (*formal*) ~ **(from sth/doing sth)** to stop yourself from doing sth that you enjoy: *The doctor said I should abstain from (drinking) alcohol until I'm better.* ➲ noun **abstinence** **2** (**POLITICS**) (in a vote) to say that you are not voting either for or against sth: *Two people voted in favour, two voted against and one abstained.* ➲ noun **abstention**

abstainer /əb'steɪnə(r)/ ***noun*** [C] **1** (**POLITICS**) a person who chooses not to vote either in favour of or against sth **2** a person who never drinks alcohol

abstention /əb'stenʃn/ ***noun*** [C,U] (**POLITICS**) an act of choosing not to vote either for or against sth

abstinence /'æbstɪnəns/ ***noun*** [U] (*formal*) stopping yourself from having or doing sth that you enjoy: *The doctor advised total abstinence from alcohol.* ➲ verb **abstain**

abstract[1] AW /'æbstrækt/ ***adj.*** existing only as an idea, not as a physical thing: *It is hard to imagine an abstract idea like 'eternity'.* OPP **concrete**

abstract[2] AW /'æbstrækt/ ***noun*** [C] **1** (**ART**) an example of ABSTRACT ART **2** (**LITERATURE**) a short piece of writing that tells you the main contents of a book, speech, etc. SYN **summary**

IDM **in the abstract** only as an idea, not in real life

abstract[3] AW /æb'strækt/ ***verb*** [T] ~ **sth (from sth)** to remove sth from somewhere: *She abstracted the main points from the argument.*

ˌabstract 'art ***noun*** [U] (**ART**) art that does not show people or things as they really look, but which shows the artist's feelings about them

ˌabstract ex'pressionism ***noun*** [U] (**ART**) a style and movement in ABSTRACT ART that developed in New York in the middle of the 20th century and tries to express the feelings of the artist rather than showing a physical object

▶ ˌabstract exˈpressionist *noun* [C]: *abstract expressionists like Jackson Pollock* ▶ ˌ**abstract exˈpressionist** *adj.*: *abstract expressionist art*

abstraction AW /æbˈstrækʃn/ **noun 1** [C,U] (*formal*) a general idea not based on any particular real person, thing or situation **2** [U] (*formal*) the state of thinking deeply about sth and not paying attention to what is around you **3** [U, C] the act of removing sth from sth else: *water abstraction from rivers*

ˌ**abstract ˈnoun** *noun* [C] (LANGUAGE) a noun, for example 'goodness' or 'freedom', that refers to an idea or a general quality, not to a physical object

absurd /əbˈsɜːd/ *adj.* not at all logical or sensible; ridiculous: *It would be absurd to spend all your money on one book.* ◇ *Don't be absurd! I can't possibly do all this work in one day.* ▶ **absurdity** *noun* [C,U] (*pl.* **absurdities**) ▶ **absurdly** *adv.*

abundance /əˈbʌndəns/ *noun* [U, C, sing.] a very large quantity of sth: *These flowers grow here* ***in abundance***. ◇ *There is an abundance of wildlife in the forest.*

abundant /əˈbʌndənt/ *adj.* existing in very large quantities; more than enough ▶ **abundantly** *adv.*

abuse¹ 🔑 /əˈbjuːs/ **noun 1** [U, sing.] using sth in a bad or dishonest way: *an abuse of power* ◇ *the dangers of drug abuse* **2** [U] (LAW) bad, usually violent treatment of sb: *He subjected his children to verbal and physical abuse.* ◇ *a victim of sexual abuse* **3** [U] rude words, used to insult another person SYN **insults**: *The other driver leaned out of the car and* ***hurled abuse*** *at me.* ◇ *racial abuse*

abuse² 🔑 /əˈbjuːz/ **verb** [T] **1** to use sth in a bad or dishonest way: *to abuse alcohol/drugs* ◇ *The politician was accused of abusing his position in order to enrich himself.* **2** to say rude things to sb **3** (LAW) to treat sb badly, often violently: *The victim had been sexually abused.*

abusive /əˈbjuːsɪv/ *adj.* using rude language to insult sb: *an abusive remark*

abysmal /əˈbɪzməl/ *adj.* very bad; of very poor quality ▶ **abysmally** *adv.*

abyss /əˈbɪs/ *noun* [C] (GEOGRAPHY) a very deep hole that seems to have no bottom

abyssal /əˈbɪsəl/ *adj.* (GEOGRAPHY) connected with the deepest parts of the ocean or the ocean floor

AC /ˌeɪ ˈsiː/ *abbr.* **1** = AIR CONDITIONING **2** = ALTERNATING CURRENT

a/c *abbr.* **1** (FINANCE) account **2** air conditioning

acacia /əˈkeɪʃə/ (*also* **aˈcacia tree**) *noun* [C] a tree with yellow or white flowers. There are several types of **acacia** tree, some of which produce a sticky liquid.

academic¹ 🔑 AW /ˌækəˈdemɪk/ *adj.* **1** (EDUCATION) connected with education, especially in schools and universities: *The academic year begins in September.* **2** (EDUCATION) connected with subjects of interest to the mind rather than technical or practical subjects: *academic subjects such as History* OPP **non-academic 3** not connected with reality; not affecting the facts of a situation: *It's academic which one I prefer because I can't have either of them.* ▶ **academically** /-kli/ *adv.*

academic² AW /ˌækəˈdemɪk/ *noun* [C] (EDUCATION) a person who teaches and/or does research at a university or college

academician /əˌkædəˈmɪʃn/ *noun* [C] (ARTS AND MEDIA) a member of an official group of people who are important in art, science or literature

academy AW /əˈkædəmi/ *noun* [C] (*pl.* **academies**) **1** (EDUCATION) a school for special training: *a military academy* **2** (*also* **Academy**) (ARTS AND MEDIA) an official group of people who are important in art, science or literature: *the Royal Academy of Arts*

accede /əkˈsiːd/ *verb* [I] ~ **(to sth)** (*formal*) **1** to agree to a request, demand, etc.: *He acceded to demands for his resignation.* **2** (POLITICS, HISTORY) to achieve a high position, especially to become king or queen ➲ noun **accession**

accelerando /ækˌseləˈrændəʊ/ *adv., adj.* (MUSIC) gradually increasing in speed ▶ **accelerando** *noun* [C] (*pl.* **accelerandos**)

accelerate /əkˈseləreɪt/ *verb* [I,T] to go faster; to make sth go faster or happen more quickly: *The driver slowed down for the bend then accelerated away.* ◇ *The government plans to accelerate the pace of reform.* ▶ **acceleration** /əkˌseləˈreɪʃn/ *noun* [U]

accelerator /əkˈseləreɪtə(r)/ *noun* [C] the control in a vehicle that you press with your foot in order to make it go faster

accent 🔑 /ˈæksənt; -sent/ *noun* **1** [C,U] (SOCIAL STUDIES) a particular way of pronouncing words that is connected with the country, area or social class that you come from: *He speaks with a strong Scottish accent.* **2** [C] (LANGUAGE) the greater force that you give to a particular word or part of a word when you speak: *In the word 'because' the accent is on the second syllable.* **3** [C] (LANGUAGE) (in writing) a mark, usually above a letter, that shows that it has to be pronounced in a certain way **4** [C, usually sing.] the particular importance that is given to sth: *In all our products the accent is on quality.*

accentuate /əkˈsentʃueɪt/ *verb* [T] to make sth easier to notice: *She uses make-up to accentuate her beautiful eyes.*

accept 🔑 /əkˈsept/ *verb* **1** [I,T] to agree to take sth that sb offers you: *Please accept this small gift.* ◇ *Do I have to pay in cash or will you accept a cheque?* ◇ *Why won't you accept my advice?* **2** [I,T] to say yes to sth or to agree to sth: *Thank you for your invitation. I am happy to accept.* ◇ *He asked her to marry him and she accepted.* ◇ *She has accepted the job.* **3** [I,T] to admit or recognize that sth unpleasant is true: *They refused to accept responsibility for the accident.* **4** [T] to allow sb to join a group, etc.: *The university has accepted me on the course.*

acceptable 🔑 /əkˈseptəbl/ *adj.* **1** that can be allowed: *One or two mistakes are acceptable but no more than that.* **2** good enough; SATISFACTORY: *We hope that you will consider our offer acceptable.* OPP **unacceptable** ▶ **acceptability** /əkˌseptəˈbɪləti/ *noun* [U] ▶ **acceptably** /-bli/ *adv.*

acceptance /əkˈseptəns/ *noun* [C,U] the act of accepting or being accepted: *His ready acceptance of the offer surprised me.* ◇ *He quickly* ***gained acceptance*** *in the group* (= the other people thought of him as equal to them).

access¹ 🔑 AW /ˈækses/ *noun* [U] **1** ~ **(to sth)** a way of entering or reaching a place: *Access to the garden is through the kitchen.* **2** ~ **(to sth)** the chance or right to use or have sth: *Do you have access to a computer?* **3** ~ **(to sb)** (LAW) permission, especially legal or official, to see sb: *They are divorced, but he has regular access to the children.*

access² AW /ˈækses/ *verb* [T] (COMPUTING) to find information on a computer: *Click on the icon to access a file.*

accessible AW /ək'sesəbl/ ***adj.*** **1** possible to be reached or entered: *The island is only accessible by boat.* **2** easy to get, use or understand: *This television programme aims to make history more accessible to children.* OPP **inaccessible** ▶ **accessibility** /əkˌsesə'bɪləti/ ***noun*** [U]: *Computers have given people greater accessibility to information.*

accession /æk'seʃn/ ***noun*** [U] (POLITICS, HISTORY) the act of taking a very high position, especially as ruler of a country or head of sth: *the accession of Queen Elizabeth to the throne in 1952* ➲ verb **accede**

accessory /ək'sesəri/ ***noun*** [C] (*pl.* **accessories**) **1** an extra item that is added to sth and is useful or attractive but not of great importance: *The car has accessories such as an electronic alarm.* **2** [usually pl.] a thing that you wear or carry that matches your clothes, for example a piece of jewellery, a bag, etc. **3 an ~ (to sth)** (LAW) a person who helps sb to do sth illegal: *He was charged with being an accessory to murder.*

accident 🔑 /'æksɪdənt/ ***noun*** [C] an unpleasant event that happens unexpectedly and causes damage, injury or death: *I hope they haven't* ***had an accident.*** ◇ *a car accident* ◇ *a fatal accident* (= when sb is killed) ◇ *I didn't mean to kick you; it was an accident.*

IDM **by accident** by chance; without intending to: *I knocked the vase over by accident as I was cleaning.*

accidental[1] 🔑 /ˌæksɪ'dentl/ ***adj.*** happening by chance; not planned: *Police do not know if the explosion was accidental or caused by a bomb.* ▶ **accidentally** /-təli/ ***adv.***: *She accidentally took the wrong coat.*

accidental[2] /ˌæksɪ'dentl/ ***noun*** [C] (MUSIC) a sign meaning that a note in a piece of music should be made higher or lower

ˌaccident and e'mergency (*abbr.* **A & E**) (*AmE* **e'mergency room**) ***noun*** [U] (HEALTH) the part of a hospital where people who need urgent treatment are taken: *the hospital accident and emergency department* ➲ look at **casualty**

'accident-prone ***adj.*** often having accidents

acclaim /ə'kleɪm/ ***verb*** [T] to express a very high opinion of sth/sb: *a* ***highly acclaimed*** *new film* ◇ *The novel has been* ***acclaimed as*** *a modern classic.* ▶ **acclaim** ***noun*** [U]

acclamation /ˌæklə'meɪʃn/ ***noun*** [U] (*formal*) loud and enthusiastic approval or welcome

acclimatize (also **-ise**) /ə'klaɪmətaɪz/ ***verb*** [I,T] **~ (yourself/sb/sth) (to sth)** to get used to a new climate, a new situation, etc. so that it is not a problem any more ▶ **acclimatization** (also **-isation**) /əˌklaɪmətaɪ'zeɪʃn/ ***noun*** [U] ▶ **acclimatized** (also **-ised**) ***adj.***

accolade /'ækəleɪd/ ***noun*** [C] a comment, prize, etc. that you receive that shows people's high opinion of sth that you have done

accommodate AW /ə'kɒmədeɪt/ ***verb*** [T] **1** to have enough space for sb/sth, especially for a certain number of people: *Each apartment can accommodate up to six people.* **2** to provide sb with a place to stay, live or work: *During the conference, you will be accommodated in a nearby hotel.* **3** (*formal*) to do or provide what sb wants or needs

accommodating /ə'kɒmədeɪtɪŋ/ ***adj.*** (used about a person) agreeing to do or provide what sb wants

accommodation 🔑 AW /əˌkɒmə'deɪʃn/ ***noun*** **1** [U] (*BrE*) a place for sb to live or stay: *We lived in rented accommodation before buying this house.* ◇ *The price of the holiday includes flights and accommodation.* **2 accommodations** [pl.] (*AmE*) somewhere to live or stay, often also providing food or other services **3** [U] the way in which the LENS (= a part of your eye) automatically becomes flatter or thicker in order to create a clear image of the object that you want to look at

accommodation

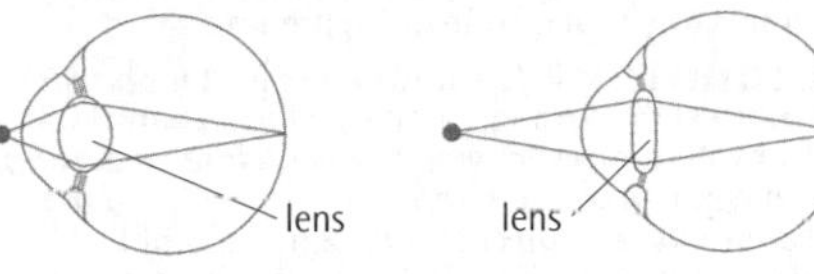

viewing a close object   viewing a distant object

accompaniment AW /ə'kʌmpənimənt/ ***noun*** **~ (to sth) 1** [C,U] (MUSIC) music that is played to support singing or another instrument: *traditional songs with piano accompaniment* **2** [C] something that goes together with another more important thing

accompanist /ə'kʌmpənɪst/ ***noun*** [C] (MUSIC) a person who plays the piano, or another instrument, while sb else plays or sings the main part of the music

accompany 🔑 AW /ə'kʌmpəni/ ***verb*** [T] (*pres. part.* **accompanying**; *3rd person sing. pres.* **accompanies**; *pt, pp* **accompanied**) **1** to go together with sb/sth: *He went to America accompanied by his wife and three children.* ◇ *Massive publicity accompanied the film's release.* **2 ~ sb (on sth)** (MUSIC) to play music for a singer or another instrument: *She accompanied him on the guitar.*

accomplice /ə'kʌmplɪs/ ***noun*** [C] **an ~ (to/in sth)** (LAW) a person who helps sb to do sth bad, especially a crime

accomplish /ə'kʌmplɪʃ/ ***verb*** [T] to succeed in doing sth difficult that you planned to do: *I managed to accomplish my goal of writing ten letters a day.*

accomplished /ə'kʌmplɪʃt/ ***adj.*** highly skilled at sth: *an accomplished actor*

accomplishment /ə'kʌmplɪʃmənt/ ***noun*** **1** [U] the act of completing sth successfully: *the accomplishment of a plan* **2** [C] something difficult that sb has succeeded in doing or learning

accord[1] /ə'kɔːd/ ***noun*** [C] (POLITICS) an agreement, especially between countries: *the Helsinki Accords on human rights*

IDM **in accord** in agreement about sth

of your own accord without being forced or asked: *He wasn't sacked from his job – he left of his own accord.*

accord[2] /ə'kɔːd/ ***verb*** (*formal*) **1** [T] to give sth to sb **2** [I] **~ (with sth)** to match; to agree with

accordance /ə'kɔːdns/ ***noun***

IDM **in accordance with sth** in a way that follows or obeys sth: *to act in accordance with instructions*

accordingly /ə'kɔːdɪŋli/ ***adv.*** **1** in a way that is suitable: *I realized that I was in danger and acted accordingly.* **2** (*formal*) therefore; for that reason

according to 🔑 /ə'kɔːdɪŋ tə before vowels tu/ ***prep.*** **1** as stated by sb; as shown by sth: *According to Mick, it's a brilliant film.* ◇ *More people now have a high standard of living, according to the statistics.* **2** in a way that matches, follows or depends on sth: *Everything went off* ***according to plan*** (= as we had planned it). ◇ *The salary will be fixed according to age and experience.*

accordion /ə'kɔːdiən/ *noun* [C] a musical instrument that you hold in both hands and play by pulling the two sides apart and then pushing them together, while pressing the keys and/or buttons with your fingers

accost /ə'kɒst/ *verb* [T] to go up and talk to a stranger in a way that is rude or frightening

account[1] /ə'kaʊnt/ *noun* [C] **1** (*abbr.* a/c) (FINANCE) the arrangement by which a bank looks after your money for you: *to **open/close an account** ◇ I have an **account with/at** Barclays. ◇ I paid the cheque into my bank account.* **2** [usually pl.] (BUSINESS) a record of all the money that a person or business has received or paid out: *If you are self-employed you have to **keep** your own **accounts**.* ➲ note at **bill**[1] **3** an arrangement with a shop, etc. that allows you to pay for goods or services at a later date: *Most customers **settle/pay** their **account** in full at the end of each month.* **4** an arrangement that sb has with a company that allows them to use the Internet, send and receive messages by email, etc.: *an **Internet/email account*** **5** somebody's report or description of sth that has happened: *She gave the police a full account of the robbery.*

IDM **by all accounts** according to what everyone says: *By all accounts, she's a very good doctor.*

by your own account according to what you say yourself: *By his own account, Peter was not very good at his job.*

on account of because of: *Our flight was delayed on account of bad weather.*

on no account; not on any account not for any reason: *On no account should you walk home by yourself.*

take account of sth; take sth into account to consider sth, especially when deciding or judging sth: *We'll take account of your comments. ◇ We'll take your comments into account.*

account[2] /ə'kaʊnt/ *verb*

PHR V **account for sth 1** to explain or give a reason for sth: *How can we account for these changes?* **2** to form the amount that is mentioned: *Sales to Europe accounted for 80% of our total sales last year.*

accountable /ə'kaʊntəbl/ *adj.* expected to give an explanation of your actions, etc.; responsible: *She is too young to **be held accountable** for what she did.* ▶ **accountability** /-ə'bɪləti/ *noun* [U]

accountancy /ə'kaʊntənsi/ *noun* [U] (FINANCE) the work or profession of an ACCOUNTANT

accountant /ə'kaʊntənt/ *noun* [C] (FINANCE) a person whose job is to keep or examine the financial accounts of a business, etc.

accounting /ə'kaʊntɪŋ/ *noun* [U] (FINANCE) the process or work of keeping financial accounts: *a career in accounting ◇ accounting methods*

ac,counts 'payable *noun* [pl.] (FINANCE) money that is owed by a company

accreditation /ə,kredɪ'teɪʃn/ *noun* [U] official approval given by an organization when sb/sth achieves a certain standard

accredited /ə'kredɪtɪd/ *adj.* officially recognized or approved: *a fully accredited course*

accrue /ə'kruː/ *verb* (*formal*) (FINANCE) **1** [I] ~ **(to sb) (from sth)** to increase over a period of time: *interest accruing to savers from their bank accounts* **2** [T] to allow a sum of money or debts to grow over a period of time SYN **accumulate**

accumulate AW /ə'kjuːmjəleɪt/ *verb* **1** [T] to collect a number or quantity of sth over a period of time SYN **amass**: *Over the years, I've accumulated hundreds of books.* ➲ note at **collect**[1] **2** [I] to increase over a period of time ▶ **accumulation** /ə,kjuːmjə'leɪʃn/ *noun* [C,U] ▶ **accumulative** /ə'kjuːmjələtɪv/ *adj.*

accurate AW /'ækjərət/ *adj.* exact and correct; without mistakes: *He managed to give the police an accurate description of the robbers. ◇ That clock isn't very accurate.* ➲ note at **true** OPP **inaccurate** ▶ **accuracy** AW /'ækjərəsi/ *noun* [U] OPP **inaccuracy** ▶ **accurately** *adv.*

accusation /,ækju'zeɪʃn/ *noun* [C,U] a statement saying that sb has done sth wrong

accusative /ə'kjuːzətɪv/ *noun* [C] (LANGUAGE) the form of a noun, a pronoun, or an adjective in some languages when it is, or is connected with, the DIRECT OBJECT of a verb: *In the sentence 'I bought them', 'them' is in the accusative.* ➲ look at **dative**, **genitive**, **nominative**, **vocative** ▶ **accusative** *adj.*

accusatory /ə'kjuːzətəri; ,ækju'zeɪtəri/ *adj.* (*formal*) suggesting that you think sb has done sth wrong

accuse /ə'kjuːz/ *verb* [T] ~ **sb (of sth/doing sth)** to say that sb has done sth wrong or broken the law: *I accused her of cheating. ◇ He was accused of murder and sent for trial.* ▶ **accuser** *noun* [C]

> **WORD FAMILY**
> **accuse** *verb*
> **accusation** *noun*
> **accusing** *adj.*
> **accusatory** *adj.*

the accused /ə'kjuːzd/ *noun* [C] (*pl.* **the accused**) (LAW) (used in a court of law) the person who is said to have broken the law: *The jury found the accused not guilty of murder.*

accusing /ə'kjuːzɪŋ/ *adj.* showing that you think sb has done sth wrong: *He gave me an **accusing look**.* ▶ **accusingly** *adv.*

accustom /ə'kʌstəm/ *verb* [T] ~ **yourself/sb/sth to sth** to make yourself/sb/sth get used to sth: *It took me a while to accustom myself to working nights.*

accustomed /ə'kʌstəmd/ *adj.* **1** ~ **to sth** if you are **accustomed** to sth, you are used to it and it is not strange for you: *She's accustomed to travelling a lot in her job. ◇ It took a while for my eyes to get accustomed to the dark room.* **2** (*formal*) usual; regular

ace /eɪs/ *noun* [C] **1** a playing card which has a single shape on it. An **ace** has either the lowest or the highest value in a game of cards: *the ace of spades* **2** (SPORT) (in TENNIS) a SERVICE (= the first hit of the ball) that the person playing against you cannot hit back: *to serve an ace*

acetate /'æsɪteɪt/ *noun* [U] **1** (CHEMISTRY) a chemical COMPOUND that is made from ACETIC ACID and that is used in making plastics **2** a smooth type of artificial cloth

acetic acid /ə,siːtɪk 'æsɪd/ *noun* [U] a type of acid that is in VINEGAR (= a liquid with a bitter taste that we use to add flavour to food)

acetone /'æsɪtəʊn/ *noun* [U] a colourless liquid with a strong smell used for cleaning things, making paint thinner and producing various chemicals

acetylene /ə'setəliːn/ *noun* [U] (*symbol* C_2H_2) a gas that burns with a very hot bright flame, used for cutting or joining metal

ache[1] /eɪk/ *noun* [C] (HEALTH) a pain that lasts for a long time: *to have toothache/earache/stomach-ache*

GRAMMAR

Ache is often used in compounds. In British English it is usually used without 'a' or 'an': *I've got toothache.* But we always use 'a' with 'headache': *I've got a bad headache.* In American English, ache is usually used with 'a' or 'an', especially when talking about a particular attack of pain: *I have an awful toothache.*

ache[2] /eɪk/ *verb* [I] (HEALTH) to feel a continuous pain: *His legs ached after playing football.* ◇ *She was aching all over.*

achieve 🔑 AW /ə'tʃiːv/ *verb* [T] **1** to complete sth by hard work and skill: *They have achieved a lot in a short time.* **2** to gain sth, usually by effort or skill: *You have achieved the success you deserve.*
▶ **achievable** *adj.*: *Profits of $20m look achievable.* ◇ *achievable goals*

achievement 🔑 AW /ə'tʃiːvmənt/ *noun* [C,U] something that you have done successfully, especially through hard work or skill: *She felt that winning the gold medal was her greatest achievement.* ◇ *He enjoys climbing mountains because it gives him **a sense of achievement**.*

Achilles heel /əˌkɪliːz 'hiːl/ *noun* [C] a weak point or fault in sb/sth

Achilles tendon /əˌkɪliːz 'tendən/ *noun* [C] (ANATOMY) the strong thin material inside your leg that connects the muscles at the CALF (= the back of the lower part of your leg) to the HEEL (= the back part of your foot)

acid[1] 🔑 /'æsɪd/ *noun* [C,U] (CHEMISTRY) a liquid substance that can dissolve metal and may burn your skin or clothes. **Acids** have a pH value of less than 7: *sulphuric acid* ➲ look at **alkali**, **base**

acid[2] /'æsɪd/ *adj.* **1** (used about a fruit, etc.) with a sour taste **2** (*also* **acidic** /ə'sɪdɪk/) (CHEMISTRY) containing an acid: *an acid solution* ➲ look at **alkaline**

acidify /ə'sɪdɪfaɪ/ *verb* [I,T] (*3rd person sing. pres.* **acidifies**; *pres. part.* **acidifying**; *pt, pp* **acidified**) (CHEMISTRY) to become or make sth become an acid

acidity /ə'sɪdəti/ *noun* [U] (CHEMISTRY) the quality of being acid: *to measure the acidity of soil*

ˌacid 'rain *noun* [U] (ENVIRONMENT) rain that has chemicals in it from factories, etc. and that causes damage to trees, buildings and rivers

ˌacid 'test *noun* [sing.] a way of deciding whether sth is successful or true: *The acid test of a good driver is whether he or she remains calm in an emergency.*

acknowledge 🔑 AW /ək'nɒlɪdʒ/ *verb* [T] **1** to accept or admit that sth is true or exists: *He **acknowledged (the fact) that** he had made a mistake.* ◇ *He is acknowledged to be the country's greatest writer.* ➲ note at **admit** **2** to show that you have seen or noticed sb/sth or received sth: *The manager sent a card to all the staff to acknowledge their hard work.*

acknowledgement (also **acknowledgment**) AW /ək'nɒlɪdʒmənt/ *noun* **1** [U] the act of showing that you have seen or noticed sb/sth: *The president gave a smile of acknowledgement to the photographers.* **2** [C,U] a letter, etc. that says that sth has been received or noticed: *I haven't received (an) acknowledgement of my job application yet.* **3** [C, usually pl.] (LITERATURE) a few words of thanks that an author writes at the beginning or end of a book to the people who have helped them

acne /'ækni/ *noun* [U] (HEALTH) a skin disease that usually affects young people. When you have **acne** you get a lot of spots on your face.

acid rain

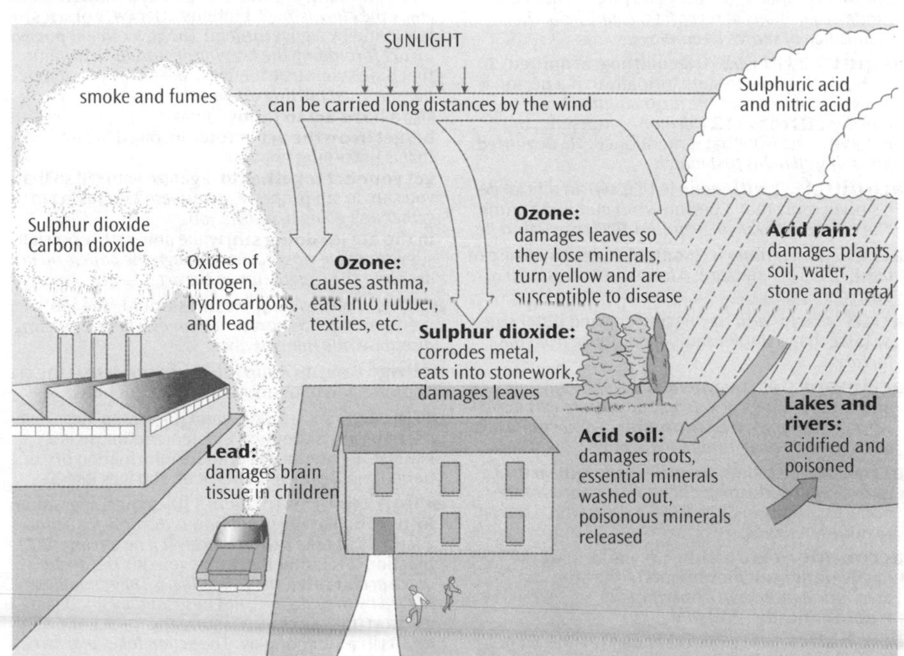

acorn /ˈeɪkɔːn/ ***noun*** [C] the small nut of the OAK tree, that grows in a base shaped like a cup

acoustic /əˈkuːstɪk/ ***adj.*** **1** (**PHYSICS**) connected with sound or the sense of hearing **2** (**MUSIC**) (of a musical instrument) not electric: *an acoustic guitar* ➲ picture on **page 465**

acoustics /əˈkuːstɪks/ ***noun*** [pl.] (**PHYSICS**) the qualities of a room, etc. that make it good or bad for you to hear music, etc. in: *The theatre has excellent acoustics.*

acquaint /əˈkweɪnt/ ***verb*** [T] **~ sb/yourself with sth** (*formal*) to make sb or yourself become familiar with sth: *I spent several hours acquainting myself with the new computer system.*

acquaintance /əˈkweɪntəns/ ***noun*** **1** [C] a person that you know but who is not a close friend **2** [U] **~ with sb/sth** a slight knowledge of sb/sth

acquainted /əˈkweɪntɪd/ ***adj.*** (*formal*) **1 ~ with sth** knowing sth: *I went for a walk to **get acquainted** with my new neighbourhood.* **2 ~ (with sb)** knowing sb, but usually not very closely

acquiesce /ˌækwiˈes/ ***verb*** [I] (*written*) **~ in/to sth** to accept sth without argument, although you may not agree with it ➲ note at **agree** ▶ **acquiescence** /ˌækwiˈesns/ ***noun*** [U]

acquire AW /əˈkwaɪə(r)/ ***verb*** [T] (*formal*) to obtain or buy sth: *She acquired an American accent while living in New York.* ◇ *The company has acquired shares in a rival business.*

acquisition AW /ˌækwɪˈzɪʃn/ ***noun*** (*formal*) **1** [U] the act of getting sth, especially knowledge, a skill, etc.: *a study of language acquisition in children* **2** [C] something that sb buys to add to what they already own, usually sth valuable: *This sculpture is the museum's latest acquisition.* **3** [C,U] (**BUSINESS**) a company, piece of land, etc. bought by sb, especially another company; the act of buying it: *They have made acquisitions in several EU countries.* ◇ *the acquisition of shares by employees*

acquit /əˈkwɪt/ ***verb*** [T] (**acquitting**; **acquitted**) **1 ~ sb (of sth)** (**LAW**) to state formally that a person is not guilty of a crime: *The jury acquitted her of murder.* OPP **convict** **2** (*formal*) **~ yourself...** to behave in the way that is mentioned: *He **acquitted himself well** in his first match.*

acquittal /əˈkwɪtl/ ***noun*** [C,U] (**LAW**) an official decision in court that a person is not guilty of a crime: *The case resulted in an acquittal.* OPP **conviction**

acre /ˈeɪkə(r)/ ***noun*** [C] (**AGRICULTURE**) a measure of land; 0.405 of a hectare: *a farm of 20 acres/a 20-acre farm*

acrid /ˈækrɪd/ ***adj.*** having a strong and bitter smell or taste that is unpleasant: *acrid smoke from the factory*

acrimony /ˈækrɪməni/ ***noun*** [U] (*formal*) angry and bitter feelings or words: *The dispute was settled without acrimony.* ▶ **acrimonious** /ˌækrɪˈməʊniəs/ ***adj.*** (*formal*): *an acrimonious divorce*

acrobat /ˈækrəbæt/ ***noun*** [C] (**ARTS AND MEDIA**) a person who performs difficult movements of the body, especially in a CIRCUS (= a show which travels to different towns)

acrobatic /ˌækrəˈbætɪk/ ***adj.*** performing or involving difficult movements of the body: *an acrobatic dancer* ◇ *an acrobatic leap* ▶ **acrobatically** /-kli/ ***adv.***

acrobatics /ˌækrəˈbætɪks/ ***noun*** [U] (the art of performing) difficult movements of the body

acronym /ˈækrənɪm/ ***noun*** [C] **an ~ (for sth)** (**LANGUAGE**) a short word that is made from the first letters of a group of words: *TEFL is an acronym for Teaching English as a Foreign Language.*

acropolis /əˈkrɒpəlɪs/ ***noun*** [C] (**HISTORY**) (in an ancient Greek city) a castle, or an area that is designed to resist attack, especially one on top of a hill

across /əˈkrɒs/ ***adv., prep.*** **1** from one side of sth to the other: *The stream was too wide to jump across.* ◇ *He walked across the field.* ◇ *A smile spread across his face.* ◇ *The river was about 20 metres across.* ◇ *The bank has 800 branches across* (= in all parts of) *the country.* **2** on the other side of sth: *There's a bank just across the road.* ◇ *The house **across** the road **from** us is for sale.*

IDM **across the board** involving or affecting all groups, members, cases, etc.

acrylic /əˈkrɪlɪk/ ***noun*** [C,U] (**ART**) an artificial material that is used in making clothes and paint

act[1] /ækt/ ***verb*** **1** [I] **~ (on sth)** to do sth; to take action: *The doctor knew he had to act quickly to save the child.* ◇ *I'm always giving my brother advice but he never acts on* (= as a result of) *it.* **2** [I] **~ as sth** to perform a particular function: *The man we met on the plane to Tokyo was kind enough to act as our guide.* ◇ *The elephant's trunk acts as a nose, a hand and an arm.* **3** [I] to behave in the way that is mentioned: *Stop **acting like** a child!* ◇ *Although she was trying to act cool, I could see she was really upset.* ◇ *He hasn't really hurt himself – he's just acting!* ◇ *Ali's acting strangely today – what's wrong with him?* **4** [I,T] (**ARTS AND MEDIA**) to perform in a play or film: *I acted in a play at school.*

act[2] /ækt/ ***noun*** [C] **1** a thing that you do: *In a typical act of generosity they refused to accept any money.* ◇ *to commit a violent act* ➲ note at **action[1]** **2** (often **Act**) (**ARTS AND MEDIA**) one of the main divisions of a play or an OPERA: *How many scenes are there in Act 4?* **3** (**ARTS AND MEDIA**) a short piece of entertainment, especially as part of a show: *Did you enjoy the clowns' act?* **4** (often **Act**) (**LAW, POLITICS**) a law made by a government: *The government **passed an act** forbidding the keeping of guns.* **5** behaviour that hides your true feelings: *She seems very happy but she's just **putting on an act**.*

IDM **a hard act to follow** → HARD[1]

be/get in on the act become involved in an activity that is becoming popular

get your act together to organize yourself so that you can do sth properly: *If he doesn't get his act together he's going to lose his job.*

in the act (of doing sth) while doing sth, especially sth wrong: *He was looking through the papers on her desk and she caught him in the act.*

acting[1] /ˈæktɪŋ/ ***adj.*** (**BUSINESS**) doing the job mentioned for a short time: *James will be the acting director while Henry is away.*

acting[2] /ˈæktɪŋ/ ***noun*** [U] (**ARTS AND MEDIA**) the art or profession of performing in plays or films

actinium /ækˈtɪniəm/ ***noun*** [U] (*symbol* **Ac**) (**CHEMISTRY**) a chemical element. **Actinium** is a RADIOACTIVE metal. ❶ For more information on the periodic table of elements, look at pages R34-5.

action[1] /ˈækʃn/ ***noun*** **1** [U] doing things, often for a particular purpose: *Now is the time for action.* ◇ *If we don't **take action** quickly it'll be too late!* OPP **inaction** **2** [C] something that you do: *The doctor's quick action saved the child's life.* ◇ *They should be judged by their actions, not by what they say.* **3** [sing.] (**LITERATURE, ARTS AND MEDIA**) the most important events in a story or play: *The action takes place in London.* **4** [U] exciting things that happen: *There's*

THESAURUS

action

move • act • gesture • deed • feat

These are all words for a thing that sb does.

action: *Her quick action saved the child's life.*

move: *What's your next move?*

act: *a heroic act of bravery*

gesture: *They sent me some flowers as a gesture of sympathy.*

deed (*formal*): *heroic/evil deeds*

feat: *The tunnel is a brilliant feat of engineering.*

not much action in this boring town. ◇ *I like films with lots of action.* ◇ *an **action-packed** film* **5** [U] fighting in a war: *Their son was **killed in action**.* **6** [sing.] (CHEMISTRY) the effect that one substance has on another: *They're studying the **action of** alcohol **on** the brain.* **7** [C,U] (LAW) the process of settling an argument in a court of law. *He is **going to take legal action** against the hospital.*

IDM **in action** in operation; while working or doing sth: *We shall have a chance to see their new team in action next week.*

into action into operation: *We'll put the plan into action immediately.*

out of action not able to do the usual things; not working: *The coffee machine's out of action again.*

action² /ˈækʃn/ ***verb*** [T] to make sure that sth is done or dealt with: *Your request will be actioned.*

ˈaction painting ***noun*** [U, C] (ART) a style of painting in which paint is thrown or poured onto paper in a way that is not planned or organized; a painting done in this way

ˌaction ˈreplay ***noun*** [C] (SPORT) (*AmE* **ˌinstant ˈreplay**) part of sth, for example a sports game on television, that is immediately repeated, often more slowly, so that you can see a goal or another exciting or important moment again

activate /ˈæktɪveɪt/ ***verb*** [T] to make sth start working: *A slight movement can activate the car alarm.*

activation energy /ˌæktɪˌveɪʃn ˈenədʒi/ ***noun*** [U] (CHEMISTRY) the minimum amount of necessary energy for a chemical reaction to happen

active ⊶ /ˈæktɪv/ ***adj.*** **1** involved in activity; lively: *My grandfather is very active for his age.* ◇ *I have a very active social life.* ◇ *I was at the meeting but I didn't **take an active part** in the discussion.* OPP **inactive** **2** that produces an effect; that is in operation: *an **active volcano*** (= one that can still erupt) **3** (LANGUAGE) used about the form of a verb or a sentence when the subject of the sentence performs the action of the verb: *In the sentence 'The dog bit him', the verb is active.* ▸ **actively** ***adv.***: *She was actively looking for a job.*

activist /ˈæktɪvɪst/ ***noun*** [C] (POLITICS) a person who takes action to cause political or social change, usually as a member of a group

activity ⊶ /ækˈtɪvəti/ ***noun*** (*pl.* **activities**) **1** [U] a situation in which there is a lot of action or movement: *The house was full of activity on the morning of the wedding.* OPP **inactivity** **2** [C] something that you do, usually regularly and for enjoyment: *The hotel offers a range of leisure activities.*

actor ⊶ /ˈæktə(r)/ ***noun*** [C] (ARTS AND MEDIA) a man or woman whose job is to act in a play or film or on television

actress ⊶ /ˈæktrəs/ ***noun*** [C] (ARTS AND MEDIA) a woman whose job is to act in a play or film or on television

actual ⊶ /ˈæktʃuəl/ ***adj.*** real; that happened: *The actual damage to the car was not as great as we had feared.* ◇ *They seemed to be good friends but **in actual fact** they hated each other.*

actually ⊶ /ˈæktʃuəli/ ***adv.*** **1** really; in fact: *You don't actually believe her, do you?* ◇ *I can't believe that I'm actually going to America!* **2** although it may seem strange: *He actually expected me to cook his meal for him!*

actuary /ˈæktʃuəri/ ***noun*** [C] (*pl.* **actuaries**) (FINANCE) a person whose job involves calculating insurance risks and payments for insurance companies by studying how frequently accidents, fires, deaths, etc. happen

acumen /ˈækjəmən/ ***noun*** [U] the ability to understand and judge things quickly and clearly: *business/financial acumen*

acupuncture /ˈækjupʌŋktʃə(r)/ ***noun*** [U] (HEALTH) a way of treating an illness or stopping pain by putting thin needles into parts of the body

acupuncturist /ˈækjupʌŋktʃərɪst/ ***noun*** [C] (HEALTH) a person who is trained to perform ACUPUNCTURE

acute /əˈkjuːt/ ***adj.*** **1** very serious; very great: *an acute shortage of food* ◇ *acute pain* **2** (HEALTH) (used about an illness) becoming dangerous very quickly: *acute appendicitis* ➲ look at **chronic** **3** (used about feelings or the senses) very strong: *Dogs have an acute sense of smell.* **4** showing that you are able to understand things easily: *The report contains some acute observations on the situation.* ▸ **acutely** ***adv.***

aˌcute ˈaccent ***noun*** [C] (LANGUAGE) the mark placed over a vowel to show how it should be pronounced, as over the *e* in *fiancé* ➲ look at **circumflex**, **grave³**, **tilde**, **umlaut**

aˌcute ˈangle ***noun*** [C] (MATHEMATICS) an angle of less than 90° ➲ look at **obtuse angle**, **reflex angle**, **right angle** ➲ picture at **angle**

AD (*AmE* **A.D.**) /ˌeɪ ˈdiː/ ***abbr.*** (HISTORY, RELIGION) from the Latin 'anno domini'; used in dates for showing the number of years after the time when Jesus Christ was born: *AD 44* ➲ look at **BC**

THESAURUS

ad

advertisement • commercial • promotion • advert • trailer

These are all words for a notice, picture or film telling people about a product, job or service.

ad: *an ad for a new chocolate bar*

advertisement: *an advertisement for a job*

commercial: *a commercial on TV for a new car*

promotion: *a special promotion of our products*

advert (*BrE, informal*): *I think there are too many adverts on TV.*

trailer: *The cinema usually shows three or four trailers before the main film.*

ad ⊶ /æd/ ***noun*** [C] (*informal*) = ADVERTISEMENT: *I saw your ad in the local paper.*

adage /ˈædɪdʒ/ ***noun*** [C] (LANGUAGE) a well-known phrase expressing sth that is always true about people or the world

adagio /ə'dɑːdʒiəʊ/ *noun* [C] (*pl.* **adagios**) (MUSIC) a piece of music that you should play slowly ▶ **adagio** *adj., adv.* ➲ look at **allegro, andante**

adamant /'ædəmənt/ *adj.* (*formal*) very sure; refusing to change your mind ▶ **adamantly** *adv.*

Adam's apple /ˌædəmz 'æpl/ *noun* [C] (ANATOMY) the part at the front of the throat which moves up and down when a man talks or swallows

adapt 🔑 AW /ə'dæpt/ *verb* **1** [I,T] ~ **(yourself) (to sth)** to change your behaviour because the situation you are in has changed: *He was quick to adapt (himself) to the new system.* **2** [T] ~ **sth (for sth)** to change sth so that you can use it in a different situation: *The bus was adapted for disabled people.* ◇ *The teacher adapts the coursebook to suit the needs of her students.*

adaptable AW /ə'dæptəbl/ *adj.* able to change to suit new situations ▶ **adaptability** /əˌdæptə'bɪləti/ *noun* [U]

adaptation AW /ˌædæp'teɪʃn/ *noun* **1** [C] (ARTS AND MEDIA) a play or film that is based on a novel, etc. **2** [U] the state or process of changing to suit a new situation

adaptive /ə'dæptɪv/ *adj.* (TECHNICAL) concerned with changing; able to change when necessary in order to deal with different situations

adaptor (also **adapter**) /ə'dæptə(r)/ *noun* [C] **1** (PHYSICS) a device for connecting pieces of electrical equipment that were not designed to be fitted together **2** (*BrE*) a device that allows you to connect more than one piece of electrical equipment to a SOCKET (= an electricity supply point)

add 🔑 /æd/ *verb* **1** [I,T] ~ **(sth) (to sth)** to put sth together with sth else, so that you increase the size, number, value, etc.: *I added a couple more items to the list.* ◇ *The noise of the crowd added to the excitement of the race.* ◇ *The juice contains no added sugar.* **2** (MATHEMATICS) [I,T] to put numbers or amounts together so that you get a total: *If you* ***add*** *3* ***and*** *3* ***together****, you get 6.* ◇ ***Add*** *$8* ***to*** *the total, to cover postage and packing.* ◇ *Ronaldo cost more than all the other players added together.* OPP **subtract** **3** [T] to say sth more: *'By the way, please don't tell anyone I phoned you,' she added.*

PHR V **add sth on (to sth)** to include sth: *10% will be added on to your bill as a service charge.*

add up to seem to be a true explanation: *I'm sorry, but your story just doesn't add up.*

add (sth) up to find the total of several numbers: *The waiter hadn't added up the bill correctly.*

add up to sth to have as a total: *How much does all the shopping add up to?*

'added to *prep.* in addition to sth; as well as

addendum /ə'dendəm/ *noun* [C] (*pl.* **addenda** /-də/) (*formal*) (LITERATURE) an item of extra information that is added to sth, especially to a book

adder /'ædə(r)/ *noun* [C] a small poisonous snake

addict /'ædɪkt/ *noun* [C] (HEALTH) a person who cannot stop taking or doing sth harmful: *a drug addict* ▶ **addicted** /ə'dɪktɪd/ *adj.* ~ **(to sth)**: *He is addicted to heroin.* SYN **hooked on** ▶ **addiction** *noun* [C,U]: *the problem of teenage drug addiction*

addictive /ə'dɪktɪv/ *adj.* difficult to stop taking or doing: *a highly addictive drug* ◇ *an addictive game*

addition 🔑 /ə'dɪʃn/ *noun* **1** [U] (MATHEMATICS) adding sth, especially two or more numbers ➲ look at **subtraction** **2** [C] **an** ~ **(to sth)** a person or thing that is added to sth

IDM **in addition (to sth)** as well as: *She speaks five foreign languages in addition to English.*

additional 🔑 /ə'dɪʃənl/ *adj.* added; extra: *a small additional charge for the use of the swimming pool* ▶ **additionally** /-ʃənəli/ *adv.*

additive /'ædətɪv/ *noun* [C] (CHEMISTRY) a substance that is added to sth in small amounts for a special purpose: *food additives* (= to add colour or flavour)

address[1] 🔑 /ə'dres/ *noun* [C] **1** the number of the building and the name of the street and place where sb lives or works: *my home/business address* ◇ *She no longer lives at this address.* ◇ *Please inform the office of any* ***change of address****.* **2** (COMPUTING) a series of words and/or numbers that tells you where you can find sb/sth using a computer: *What's your email address?* **3** a formal speech that is given to an audience

address[2] 🔑 /ə'dres/ *verb* [T] **1** ~ **sth (to sb/sth)** to write the name and address of the person you are sending a letter, etc. to: *The parcel was returned because it had been wrongly addressed.* **2** to make an important speech to an audience **3** (*formal*) ~ **(yourself to) sth** to try to deal with a problem, etc.: *The government is finally addressing the question of corruption.* **4** ~ **sb as sth** to talk or write to sb using a particular name or title: *She prefers to be addressed as 'Ms'.* **5** (*formal*) ~ **sth to sb** make a comment, etc. to sb: *Would you kindly address any complaints you have to the manager.*

ad'dress book *noun* [C] **1** a book in which you keep addresses, phone numbers, etc. **2** (COMPUTING) a computer file where you store email and Internet addresses

adenine /'ædəniːn/ *noun* [U] (*technical*) (BIOLOGY) one of the four COMPOUNDS that make up NUCLEIC ACIDS ➲ picture at **DNA**

adenoids /'ædənɔɪdz/ *noun* [pl.] (ANATOMY) soft areas at the back of the nose and throat that can swell up and cause breathing difficulties, especially in children

adept /ə'dept/ *adj.* ~ **(at sth)** very good or skilful at sth OPP **inept**

adequate 🔑 AW /'ædɪkwət/ *adj.* **1** enough for what you need: *Make sure you take an adequate supply of water with you.* **2** just good enough; acceptable: *Your work is adequate but I'm sure you could do better.* OPP **inadequate** ▶ **adequacy** /'ædɪkwəsi/ *noun* [U] ▶ **adequately** *adv.*: *The mystery has never been adequately explained.*

adhere /əd'hɪə(r)/ *verb* [I] (*formal*) **1** ~ **(to sth)** to stick firmly to sth: *Make sure that the paper adheres firmly to the wall.* **2** ~ **to sth** to continue to support an idea, etc.; to follow a rule

adherent /əd'hɪərənt/ *noun* [C] somebody who supports a particular idea ▶ **adherence** *noun* [U]

adhesion /əd'hiːʒn/ *noun* [U] **1** (TECHNICAL) the ability to stick or become attached to sth **2** (HEALTH) the sticking together of surfaces inside the body in a way that is not normal, caused by injury

adhesive[1] /əd'hiːsɪv/ *noun* [C] a substance that makes things stick together

adhesive[2] /əd'hiːsɪv/ *adj.* that can stick, or can cause two things to stick together: *He sealed the parcel with adhesive tape.* SYN **sticky**

ad hoc /ˌæd 'hɒk/ *adj.* made or done suddenly for a particular purpose: *They set up an ad hoc committee to discuss the matter.* ◇ *Staff training takes place occasionally* ***on an ad hoc basis****.*

ad infinitum /ˌæd ˌɪnfɪˈnaɪtəm/ *adv.* for ever; again and again: *We can't stay ad infinitum.* ◇ *and so on, ad infinitum*

adipose /ˈædɪpəʊs; ˈædɪpəʊz *adj.*/ (BIOLOGY) (used about body TISSUE) used for storing fat ➲ picture at **skin**

adjacent AW /əˈdʒeɪsnt/ *adj.* ~ **(to sth)** (used about an area, a building, a room, etc.) next to or near sth: *She works in the office adjacent to mine.*

aˌdjacent ˈangle *noun* [C] (MATHEMATICS) one of the two angles formed on the same side of a straight line when another line meets it ➲ picture at **angle**

adjectival /ˌædʒekˈtaɪvl/ *adj.* (LANGUAGE) that contains or is used like an adjective: *The adjectival form of 'smell' is 'smelly'.*

adjective /ˈædʒɪktɪv/ *noun* [C] (LANGUAGE) a word that tells you more about a noun: *The adjective 'reserved' is often applied to British people.* ◇ *What adjective would you use to describe my sister?*

adjoining /əˈdʒɔɪnɪŋ/ *adj.* next to or nearest to sth: *A scream came from the adjoining room.*

adjourn /əˈdʒɜːn/ *verb* [I,T] (often passive) to stop a meeting, a trial, etc. for a short time and start it again later: *The meeting adjourned for lunch.* ◇ *The trial was adjourned until the following week.* ▸ **adjournment** *noun* [C]

adjudicate /əˈdʒuːdɪkeɪt/ *verb* [I,T] (*written*) to act as an official judge in a competition or to decide who is right when two people or groups disagree about sth

adjudicator /əˈdʒuːdɪkeɪtə(r)/ *noun* [C] a person who acts as a judge, especially in a competition

adjunct /ˈædʒʌŋkt/ *noun* [C] **1** (LANGUAGE) an adverb or a phrase that adds meaning to the verb in a sentence or part of a sentence: *In the sentence 'He ran away in a panic', 'in a panic' is an adjunct.* **2** (*formal*) a thing that is added or joined to sth larger or more important

adjust ⊶ AW /əˈdʒʌst/ *verb* **1** [T] to change sth slightly, especially because it is not in the right position: *The seat can be adjusted to different positions.* **2** [I] ~ **(to sth)** to get used to new conditions or a new situation: *She found it hard to adjust to working at night.* ▸ **adjustment** *noun* [C,U]: *We'll just* ***make a few minor adjustments*** *and the room will look perfect.*

adjustable /əˈdʒʌstəbl/ *adj.* that can be adjusted: *an adjustable mirror*

ˌadjustable ˈspanner (*BrE*) (*especially AmE* **ˈmonkey wrench**) *noun* [C] a tool that can be adjusted to hold and turn things of different widths ➲ look at **spanner**, **wrench** ➲ picture at **tool**

ad lib /ˌæd ˈlɪb/ *adj.*, *adv.* done or spoken without preparation: *She had to speak ad lib because she couldn't find her notes.* ▸ **ad lib** *verb* [I] (**ad libbing**; **ad libbed**): *He forgot his notes so he had to ad lib.*

admin = ADMINISTRATION

administer /ədˈmɪnɪstə(r)/ *verb* [T] (*formal*) **1** (*also* **administrate**) to control or manage sth **2** (HEALTH) to give sb sth, especially medicine

administrate AW /ədˈmɪnɪstreɪt/ = ADMINISTER (1)

administration AW /ədˌmɪnɪˈstreɪʃn/ *noun* **1** (*also* **admin** /ˈædmɪn/) [U] the control or the act of managing sth, for example a system, an organization or a business: *The administration of a large project like this is very complicated.* ◇ *A lot of the teachers' time is taken up by admin.* **2** (*also* **admin** /ˈædmɪn/) [sing.] (BUSINESS) the group of people or part of a company that organizes or controls sth: *the hospital administration* ◇ *She works in admin, on the second floor.* **3** (often **the Administration**) [C] (POLITICS) the government of a country, especially the US: *the Kennedy Administration*

administrative AW /ədˈmɪnɪstrətɪv/ *adj.* connected with the organization of a country, business, etc., and the way in which it is managed

administrator /ədˈmɪnɪstreɪtə(r)/ *noun* [C] (BUSINESS) a person whose job is to organize or manage a system, a business, etc.

admirable /ˈædmərəbl/ *adj.* (*formal*) that you admire; excellent ▸ **admirably** /-əbli/ *adv.*: *She dealt with the problem admirably.*

admiral /ˈædmərəl/ *noun* [C] the most important officer in the navy

admiration ⊶ /ˌædməˈreɪʃn/ *noun* [U] ~ **(for/of sb/sth)** a feeling of liking and respecting sb/sth very much: *I have great admiration for what he's done.*

admire ⊶ /ədˈmaɪə(r)/ *verb* [T] ~ **sb/sth (for sth/doing sth)** to respect or like sb/sth very much; to look at sb/sth with pleasure: *Everyone admired the way he dealt with the problem.* ◇ *I've always admired her for being such a wonderful mother.* ◇ *We stopped at the top of the hill to admire the view.*

admirer /ədˈmaɪərə(r)/ *noun* [C] a person who admires sb/sth: *I've always been a great admirer of her work.*

admiring /ədˈmaɪərɪŋ/ *adj.* feeling or expressing admiration ▸ **admiringly** *adv.*

admissible /ədˈmɪsəbl/ *adj.* (LAW) that can be allowed or accepted, especially in a court of law: *The judge ruled the tapes to be admissible as evidence.*

admission /ədˈmɪʃn/ *noun* **1** [C,U] ~ **(to sth)** the act of allowing sb to enter a school, club, public place, etc.: *Admissions to British universities have increased by 15% this year.* ➲ look at **entrance** **2** [C] (LAW) a statement in which sb admits that sth is true, especially sth wrong or bad that they have done: *an admission of guilt/failure/defeat* **3** [U] the amount of money that you have to pay to enter a place: *The museum charges half-price admission on Mondays.*

THESAURUS

admit

acknowledge • concede • confess • grant

These words all mean to agree, often unwillingly, that sth is true.

admit: *It was a stupid thing to do, I admit.*

acknowledge (*formal*): *to acknowledge the need for reform*

concede (*formal*): *He conceded that there might be difficulties.*

confess: *She confessed that she'd scratched his car.*

grant: *It's a fine painting, I grant you, but is it worth the money?*

admit ⊶ /ədˈmɪt/ *verb* (**admitting**; **admitted**) **1** [I,T] ~ **sth**; ~ **to sth/doing sth**; ~ **(that...)** to agree that sth unpleasant is true or that you have done sth wrong: *He refused to admit to the theft.* ◇ *You should admit your mistake.* ◇ *After trying four times to pass the exam, I finally* ***admitted defeat.*** ◇ *I have to admit (that) I was wrong.* ◇ *She admitted having broken the computer.* OPP **deny** **2** [T] ~ **sb/sth (into/to sth)** to allow sb/sth to enter; to take sb into a place: *He was* ***admitted to hospital*** *with suspected appendicitis.*

admittance /əd'mɪtns/ ***noun*** [U] (*formal*) being allowed to enter a place; the right to enter: *The journalist tried to **gain admittance** to the minister's office.*

admittedly /əd'mɪtɪdli/ ***adv.*** it must be admitted (that...): *The work is very interesting. Admittedly, I do get rather tired.*

admonish /əd'mɒnɪʃ/ ***verb*** [T] (*formal*) **1 ~ sb (for sth/for doing sth)** to tell sb firmly that you do not approve of sth that they have done: *He was admonished for arriving late at work.* **2** to strongly advise sb to do sth: *She admonished the staff to call off the strike.*

ad nauseam /ˌæd 'nɔːziæm/ ***adv.*** if a person does or says sth **ad nauseam**, they do or say it again and again until it becomes boring and annoying

ado /ə'duː/ ***noun***

IDM **without further/more ado** (*old-fashioned*) without delaying; immediately

adobe /ə'dəʊbi/ ***noun*** [U] mud that is dried in the sun and used as a building material

adolescence /ˌædə'lesns/ ***noun*** [U] the period of a person's life between being a child and becoming an adult, between the ages of about 13 and 17

adolescent /ˌædə'lesnt/ ***noun*** [C] a young person who is no longer a child and not yet an adult, between the ages of about 13 and 17: *the problems of adolescents* ◇ *an adolescent daughter* ➲ look at **teenager**

adopt ⊶ /ə'dɒpt/ ***verb*** **1** [I,T] (SOCIAL STUDIES) to take a child into your family and treat them as your own child by law: *They couldn't have children so they adopted.* ◇ *They're hoping to adopt a child.* **2** [T] to take and use sth: *What approach did you adopt when dealing with the problem?* ▶ **adopted *adj.***: *an adopted child* ▶ **adoption *noun*** [C,U]: *The number of adoptions has risen in the past year* (= the number of children being adopted).

adoptive /ə'dɒptɪv/ ***adj.*** (SOCIAL STUDIES) (used about parents) having legally taken a child to live with them as part of their family: *the baby's adoptive parents*

adorable /ə'dɔːrəbl/ ***adj.*** very attractive and easy to feel love for: *an adorable child* SYN **lovely**

adore /ə'dɔː(r)/ ***verb*** [T] **1** to love and admire sb/sth very much: *Kim adores her older sister.* **2** to like sth very much: *She adores Italy.* ▶ **adoration** /ˌædə'reɪʃn/ ***noun*** [U] ▶ **adoring *adj.***: *his adoring fans*

adorn /ə'dɔːn/ ***verb*** [T] **~ sth (with sth)** (*formal*) to add sth in order to make a thing or person more attractive or beautiful ▶ **adornment *noun*** [C,U]

adrenal /ə'driːnl/ ***adj.*** (BIOLOGY) connected with the production of ADRENALIN

adrenalin (also **adrenaline**) /ə'drenəlɪn/ ***noun*** [U] (BIOLOGY) a substance that your body produces when you are very angry, frightened or excited and that makes your heart go faster: *The excitement at the start of a race can really **get the adrenalin flowing**.*

adrift /ə'drɪft/ ***adj.*** (not *before* a noun) (used about a boat) not tied to anything or controlled by anyone

adroit /ə'drɔɪt/ ***adj.*** (*written*) **~ (at sth)** skilful and clever, especially in dealing with people: *She is adroit at avoiding awkward questions.*

ADSL /ˌeɪ diː es 'el/ ***abbr.*** (COMPUTING) **asymmetric digital subscriber line**; a system for connecting a computer to the Internet using a telephone line

adulation /ˌædju'leɪʃn/ ***noun*** [U] (*formal*) extreme admiration: *The band learned to deal with the adulation of their fans.*

adult ⊶ AW /'ædʌlt; ə'dʌlt/ ***noun*** [C] a person or an animal that is fully grown: *This film is suitable for both adults and children.* ▶ **adult *adj.***

ˌadult eduˈcation (*also* **conˌtinuing eduˈcation**) ***noun*** [U] (EDUCATION) education for adults that is available outside the formal education system, for example at evening classes

adulterate /ə'dʌltəreɪt/ ***verb*** [T] (often passive) **~ sth (with sth)** to make food or drink less pure or of lower quality by adding sth to it SYN **contaminate**

adulterer /ə'dʌltərə(r)/ ***noun*** [C] (*formal*) a person who commits ADULTERY

adultery /ə'dʌltəri/ ***noun*** [U] (*formal*) sex between a married person and sb who is not their wife/husband: *to commit adultery* ▶ **adulterous** /ə'dʌltərəs/ ***adj.***: *an adulterous relationship*

adulthood /'ædʌlthʊd; ə'dʌlt-/ ***noun*** [U] the time in your life when you are an adult

advance[1] ⊶ /əd'vɑːns/ ***verb*** **1** [I] to move forward: *The army advanced towards the city.* OPP **retreat** **2** [I,T] to make progress or help sth make progress: *Our research has not advanced much recently.*

advance[2] ⊶ /əd'vɑːns/ ***noun*** **1** [C, usually sing.] forward movement: *the army's advance towards the border* OPP **retreat** **2** [C,U] progress in sth: *advances in computer technology* **3** [C] (FINANCE) an amount of money that is paid to sb before the time when it is usually paid

IDM **in advance (of sth)** before a particular time or event: *You should book tickets for the concert well in advance.*

advance[3] /əd'vɑːns/ ***adj.*** (only *before* a noun) that happens before sth: *There was no advance warning of the earthquake.*

advanced /əd'vɑːnst/ ***adj.*** **1** of a high level: *an advanced English class* **2** highly developed: *a country that is not very advanced industrially*

ad'vanced level = A LEVEL

advancement /əd'vɑːnsmənt/ ***noun*** (*formal*) **1** [U, C] the process of helping sth to make progress and succeed: *the advancement of knowledge/science* **2** [U] progress in a job, social class, etc.: *There is good opportunity for advancement if you have the right skills.*

advantage ⊶ /əd'vɑːntɪdʒ/ ***noun*** **1** [C] an **~ (over sb)** something that may help you to do better than other people: *Her experience gave her a big advantage over the other people applying for the job.* ◇ *Living abroad means he **has the advantage of** being fluent in two languages.* ◇ *Some runners try to gain an unfair advantage by taking drugs.* **2** [C,U] something that helps you or that will bring you a good result: *the advantages and disadvantages of a plan* ◇ *The traffic is so bad here that **there is no advantage in** having a car.* OPP **disadvantage**

IDM **take advantage of sb/sth** **1** to make good or full use of sth: *We should take full advantage of these low prices while they last.* **2** to make unfair use of sb or of sb's kindness, etc. in order to get what you want: *Don't let him take advantage of you like this.*

turn sth to your advantage to use or change a bad situation so that it helps you

advantageous /ˌædvənˈteɪdʒəs/ *adj.* that will help you or bring you a good result

advent /ˈædvent/ *noun* [sing.] **1** (*formal*) the fact of sb/sth arriving **2 Advent** (RELIGION) (in the Christian year) the four weeks before Christmas

adventure /ədˈventʃə(r)/ *noun* [C,U] an experience or event that is very unusual, exciting or dangerous: *She left home to travel, hoping for excitement and adventure.* ◇ *Our journey through the jungle was quite an adventure!*

adˈventure holiday (*AmE* **adˈventure vacation**) *noun* [C] (TOURISM) a holiday in which you spend all your time outdoors doing activities such as climbing a mountain or cycling in a wild part of a country

adventurer /ədˈventʃərə(r)/ *noun* [C] **1** a person who enjoys exciting new experiences, especially going to unusual places **2** a person who is capable of taking risks and perhaps acting dishonestly in order to gain money or power

adventurous /ədˈventʃərəs/ *adj.* **1** (used about a person) liking to try new things or have adventures **2** involving adventure: *For a more adventurous holiday try mountain climbing.*

adverb /ˈædvɜːb/ *noun* [C] (LANGUAGE) a word that adds more information about place, time, manner, cause or degree to a verb, an adjective, a phrase or another adverb: *In 'speak slowly', 'extremely funny', 'arrive late' and 'I know her well', 'slowly', 'extremely', 'late' and 'well' are adverbs.* ▶ **adverbial** /ædˈvɜːbiəl/ *adj.*: *'Very quickly indeed' is an adverbial phrase.*

adversary /ˈædvəsəri/ *noun* [C] (*pl.* **adversaries**) (*formal*) an enemy, or an opponent in a competition

adverse /ˈædvɜːs/ *adj.* (*formal*) making sth difficult for sb: *Our flight was cancelled because of adverse weather conditions.* OPP **favourable** ➲ look at **unfavourable** ▶ **adversely** *adv.*

adversity /ədˈvɜːsəti/ *noun* [C,U] (*pl.* **adversities**) (*formal*) difficulties or problems

advert /ˈædvɜːt/ (*BrE, informal*) = ADVERTISEMENT ➲ note at **ad**

advertise /ˈædvətaɪz/ *verb* **1** [I,T] to put information in a newspaper, on television, on a picture on the wall, etc. in order to persuade people to buy sth, to interest them in a new job, etc.: *a poster advertising a new car* ◇ *The job was advertised in the local newspapers.* ◇ *It's very expensive to advertise on television.* **2** [I] ~ **for sb/sth** to say publicly in a newspaper, on a sign, etc. that you need sb to do a particular job, want to buy sth, etc.: *The shop is advertising for a sales assistant.*

advertisement /ədˈvɜːtɪsmənt/ (also *informal* **advert; ad**) *noun* [C] a piece of information in a newspaper, on television, a picture on a wall, etc. that tries to persuade people to buy sth, to interest them in a new job, etc.: *an advertisement for a new brand of washing powder* ◇ *to put an advertisement in a newspaper* ➲ note at **ad**

advertiser /ˈædvətaɪzə(r)/ *noun* [C] a person or company that pays to put an advertisement in a newspaper, etc.

advertising /ˈædvətaɪzɪŋ/ *noun* [U] the activity and industry of advertising things to people on television, in newspapers, on the Internet, etc.: *an **advertising campaign*** ◇ ***radio/TV advertising*** ◇ *Val works for an **advertising agency***

advertorial /ˌædvəˈtɔːriəl/ *noun* [C] an advertisement that is designed to look like an article in the newspaper or magazine in which it appears

advice /ədˈvaɪs/ *noun* [U] an opinion that you give sb about what they should do: *She **took** her doctor's **advice** and gave up smoking.* ◇ *Let me **give** you some **advice** ...*

advisable /ədˈvaɪzəbl/ *adj.* (*formal*) that is a good thing to do; sensible: *It is advisable to reserve a seat.* OPP **inadvisable**

advise /ədˈvaɪz/ *verb* **1** [I,T] ~ **sb (to do sth)**; ~ **(sb) (against sth/against doing sth)**; ~ **(sb) on sth** to tell sb what you think they should do: *I would strongly advise you to take the job.* ◇ *They advised us not to travel on a Friday.* ◇ *The newspaper article advised against eating too much meat.* ◇ *He did what the doctor advised.* ◇ *She advises the Government on economic affairs.* ➲ note at **recommend** **2** [T] (*formal*) ~ **sb (of sth)** to officially tell sb sth; to inform sb

adviser (*AmE* **advisor**) /ədˈvaɪzə(r)/ *noun* [C] (BUSINESS, POLITICS) a person who gives advice to a company, government, etc.: *an adviser on economic affairs*

advisory /ədˈvaɪzəri/ *adj.* having the role of giving professional advice

advocacy AW /ˈædvəkəsi/ *noun* [U] **1** ~ **(of sth)** (*formal*) the giving of public support to an idea, a course of action or a belief **2** (LAW) the work of lawyers who speak about cases in courts of law

advocate[1] AW /ˈædvəkeɪt/ *verb* [T] (*formal*) to recommend or say that you support a particular plan or action ➲ note at **recommend**

advocate[2] AW /ˈædvəkət/ *noun* [C] **1** an ~ **(of/for sth/sb)** a person who supports or speaks in favour of sb or of a public plan or action **2** (LAW) a lawyer who defends sb in a court of law

adze (*AmE* **adz**) /ædz/ *noun* [C] a heavy tool with a curved edge at 90° to the handle, used for cutting or shaping large pieces of wood

aeolian (*AmE* **eolian**) /iˈəʊliən/ *adj.* (GEOGRAPHY) connected with or caused by the action of the wind

aeon (*BrE*) (also **eon**) /ˈiːən/ *noun* [C] (*formal*) an extremely long period of time; thousands of years

aerate /ˈeəreɪt/ *verb* [T] **1** (AGRICULTURE) to make it possible for air to become mixed with soil, water, etc. **2** (CHEMISTRY) to add a gas to a liquid under pressure: *aerated water*

aerial[1] /ˈeəriəl/ (*AmE* **antenna**) *noun* [C] a long metal stick on a building, car, etc. that receives radio or television signals

aerial[2] /ˈeəriəl/ *adj.* from or in the air: *an aerial photograph of the town*

aerobic /eəˈrəʊbɪk/ *adj.* **1** (BIOLOGY) connected with or needing OXYGEN (= the gas that we need in order to live) ➲ picture at **respiration** **2** (SPORT) (used about physical exercise) that we do to improve the way our bodies use OXYGEN ➲ look at **anaerobic**

aerobics /eəˈrəʊbɪks/ *noun* [U] (SPORT) physical exercises that people do to music: ***I do aerobics** twice a week to keep fit.*

aerodrome /ˈeərədrəʊm/ (*AmE* **airdrome**) *noun* [C] a small airport, used mainly by private planes

aerodynamics /ˌeərəʊdaɪˈnæmɪks/ *noun* [U] (PHYSICS) the scientific study of the way that things move through the air ▶ **aerodynamic** *adj.*: *the aerodynamic design of a racing car* ▶ **aerodynamically** /-kli/ *adv.*

aeronautics /ˌeərəˈnɔːtɪks/ ***noun*** [U] (PHYSICS) the science or practice of building and flying aircraft ▸ **aeronautical** /-ˈnɔːtɪkl/ ***adj.***: *an aeronautical engineer*

aeroplane /ˈeərəpleɪn/ (*also* **plane**, *AmE* **airplane**) ***noun*** [C] a vehicle that can fly through the air, with wings and one or more engines ➲ picture at **plane**

aerosol /ˈeərəsɒl/ ***noun*** [C] a container in which a liquid substance is kept under pressure. When you press a button the liquid comes out in a fine spray.

aerospace /ˈeərəʊspeɪs/ ***noun*** [U] (often used as an adjective) the industry of building aircraft, and vehicles and equipment to be sent into space

aesthete (*AmE also* **esthete**) /ˈiːsθiːt; ˈesθiːt/ ***noun*** [C] (*formal*) a person who has a love and understanding of art and beautiful things

aesthetic (*AmE also* **esthetic**) /iːsˈθetɪk; esˈθetɪk/ ***adj.*** (ART) concerned with beauty or art and the understanding of beautiful things: *The columns are there for purely aesthetic reasons* (= only to look beautiful). ▸ **aesthetically** (*AmE also* **esthetically**) /-kli/ ***adv.***: *The design is **aesthetically pleasing** as well as practical.*

aesthetics (*AmE also* **esthetics**) /iːsˈθetɪks; esˈθetɪks/ ***noun*** [U] (ART) the branch of philosophy that studies the principles of beauty, especially in art ▸ **aestheticism** (*AmE* **estheticism**) /iːsˈθetɪsɪzəm; es-/ ***noun*** [U]

aetiology (*AmE* **etiology**) /ˌiːtiˈɒlədʒi/ ***noun*** [U] (HEALTH) the scientific study of the causes of disease

afar /əˈfɑː(r)/ ***adv.*** (*written*)
IDM **from afar** from a long distance away

affable /ˈæfəbl/ ***adj.*** pleasant, friendly and easy to talk to ▸ **affability** /ˌæfəˈbɪləti/ ***noun*** [U] ▸ **affably** /ˈæfəbli/ ***adv.***

affair ⊶ /əˈfeə(r)/ ***noun*** **1 affairs** [pl.] (POLITICS) events that are of public interest or political importance: *an expert on **foreign affairs*** (= political events in other countries) ◇ *affairs of state* ◇ ***current affairs*** (= the political and social events that are happening at the present time) **2** [C] an event that people are talking about or describing in a particular way: *The newspapers exaggerated the whole affair wildly.* **3** [C] a sexual relationship between two people, usually when at least one of them is married to sb else: *She's **having an affair with** her boss.* **4 affairs** [pl.] matters connected with a person's private business and financial situation: *I looked after my father's financial affairs.* **5** [sing.] a thing that sb is responsible for (and that other people should not be concerned with)
IDM **state of affairs** → STATE[1]

affect ⊶ AW /əˈfekt/ ***verb*** [T] **1** make sb/sth change in a particular way; to influence sb/sth: *Her personal problems seem to be affecting her work.* ◇ *This disease affects the brain.* **2** to make sb feel very sad, angry, etc.: *The whole community was affected by the terrible tragedy.*

affected /əˈfektɪd/ ***adj.*** (used about a person or their behaviour) not natural or sincere OPP **unaffected** ▸ **affectation** /ˌæfekˈteɪʃn/ ***noun*** [C,U]

affection ⊶ /əˈfekʃn/ ***noun*** [C,U] (an) ~ (**for/towards sb/sth**) a feeling of loving or liking sb/sth

affectionate /əˈfekʃənət/ ***adj.*** showing that you love or like sb very much ▸ **affectionately** ***adv.***

affective /əˈfektɪv/ ***adj.*** (PSYCHOLOGY) connected with emotions and attitudes: *affective disorders*

affidavit /ˌæfəˈdeɪvɪt/ ***noun*** [C] (LAW) a written statement that you say officially is true, and that can be used as evidence in a court of law: *to make/swear/sign an affidavit*

affiliate[1] /əˈfɪlieɪt/ ***verb*** [T] (usually passive) **~ sth (to sth)** (BUSINESS) to connect an organization to a larger organization: *Our local club is affiliated to the national association.* ▸ **affiliated** ***adj.*** ▸ **affiliation** /əˌfɪliˈeɪʃn/ ***noun*** [C,U]

affiliate[2] /əˈfɪliət/ ***noun*** [C] (BUSINESS) a company, an organization, etc. that is connected with or controlled by another larger one

afˌfiliate ˈmarketing ***noun*** [U] (BUSINESS) the use of other websites to advertise and sell the products and services of your website. The other websites receive a payment for this.

affinity /əˈfɪnəti/ ***noun*** [C,U] (*pl.* **affinities**) **1** (**an**) **~ (for/with sb/sth)** a strong feeling that you like and understand sb/sth, usually because you feel similar to them or it in some way: *He had always had an affinity for wild and lonely places.* **2** (**an**) **~ (with sb/sth)**; (**an**) **~ (between A and B)** a similar quality in two or more people or things

affirm /əˈfɜːm/ ***verb*** [T] (*formal*) to say formally or clearly that sth is true or that you support sth strongly ▸ **affirmation** /ˌæfəˈmeɪʃn/ ***noun*** [C,U]

affirmative[1] /əˈfɜːmətɪv/ ***adj.*** (*formal*) (LANGUAGE) an **affirmative** word or reply means 'yes' or expresses agreement OPP **negative** ▸ **affirmatively** ***adv.***: *90% voted affirmatively.*

affirmative[2] /əˈfɜːmətɪv/ ***noun*** [C] (*formal*) (LANGUAGE) a word or statement that means 'yes'; an agreement or a CONFIRMATION: *She answered **in the affirmative*** (= said 'yes'). OPP **negative**

afˌfirmative ˈaction ***noun*** [U] (*especially AmE*) = POSITIVE DISCRIMINATION

affix[1] /əˈfɪks/ ***verb*** [T] (often passive) (*formal*) **~ sth (to sth)** to stick or join sth to sth else: *The label should be firmly affixed to the package.*

affix[2] /ˈæfɪks/ ***noun*** [C] (LANGUAGE) a letter or group of letters that are added to the beginning or end of a word and that change its meaning: *The 'un-' in 'unhappy' and the '-less' in 'painless' are affixes.* ➲ look at **prefix**, **suffix**

afflict /əˈflɪkt/ ***verb*** [T] (usually passive) (*formal*) **~ sb/sth (with sth)** to cause sb/sth to suffer pain, sadness, etc. ▸ **affliction** ***noun*** [C,U]

affluent /ˈæfluənt/ ***adj.*** having a lot of money ▸ **affluence** ***noun*** [U]: *Increased exports have brought new affluence.*

afford ⊶ /əˈfɔːd/ ***verb*** [T] (usually after *can, could* or *be able to*) **~ sth/to do sth 1** to have enough money or time to be able to do sth: *We couldn't afford a television in those days.* ◇ *I've spent more money than I can afford.* **2** to not be able to do sth or let sth happen because it would have a bad result for you: *The other team was very good so we couldn't afford to make any mistakes.* ▸ **affordable** ***adj.***: *affordable prices*

afforestation /əˌfɒrɪˈsteɪʃn/ ***noun*** [U] (ENVIRONMENT) planting trees on an area of land in order to form a forest OPP **deforestation**

affront /əˈfrʌnt/ ***noun*** [C] **an ~ (to sb/sth)** something that you say or do that is insulting to sb/sth

afield /əˈfiːld/ ***adv.***
IDM **far afield** → FAR[2]

afloat /əˈfləʊt/ ***adj.*** (not *before* a noun) **1** on the surface of the water; not sinking: *A life jacket helps you **stay afloat** if you fall in the water.* **2** (BUSINESS) (used about a business, an economy, etc.) having enough money to survive

afoot /əˈfʊt/ ***adj.*** (not *before* a noun) being planned or prepared

aforementioned /əˌfɔːˈmenʃənd/ (*also* **afore-said** /əˈfɔːsed/; *also* **said**) ***adj.*** (only *before* a noun) (*formal* or LAW) mentioned before, in an earlier sentence: *The aforementioned person was seen acting suspiciously.*

aforethought /əˈfɔːθɔːt/ ***adj.***
IDM **with malice aforethought** → MALICE

afraid ⊶ /əˈfreɪd/ ***adj.*** (not *before* a noun) **1** ~ (**of sb/sth**); ~ (**of doing sth/to do sth**) having or showing fear; frightened: *Are you afraid of dogs?* ◇ *Ben is afraid of going out after dark.* ◇ *I was too afraid to answer the door.* **2** ~ (**that...**); ~ (**of doing sth**) worried about sth: *We were afraid that you would be angry.* ◇ *to be afraid of offending sb* **3** ~ **for sb/sth** worried that sb/sth will be harmed, lost, etc.: *When I saw the gun I was afraid for my life.*
IDM **I'm afraid (that...)** used for saying politely that you are sorry about sth: *I'm afraid I can't come on Sunday.* ◇ *'Is the factory going to close?' 'I'm afraid so.'* ◇ *'Is this seat free?' 'I'm afraid not/it isn't.'*

afresh /əˈfreʃ/ ***adv.*** (*formal*) again, in a new way: *to start afresh*

ˌ**African Aˈmerican** ***noun*** [C] an American citizen whose family was originally from Africa ▶ **African American *adj.***

Afrikaans /ˌæfrɪˈkɑːns/ ***noun*** [U] (LANGUAGE) a language that has developed from Dutch, spoken in South Africa

Afro-Caribbean /ˌæfrəʊ kærəˈbiːən/ ***noun*** [C] a person whose family came originally from Africa, and who was born or whose parents were born in the Caribbean ▶ **Afro-Caribbean *adj.***

aft /ɑːft/ ***adv.***, ***adj.*** at, near or towards the back of a ship or an aircraft ➲ look at **fore**

after ⊶ /ˈɑːftə(r)/ ***prep.***, ***conj.***, ***adv.*** **1** later than sth; at a later time: *Ian phoned just after six o'clock.* ◇ *the week after next* ◇ *I hope to arrive some time after lunch.* ◇ *They arrived at the station after the train had left.* ◇ *After we had finished our dinner, we went into the garden.* ◇ *I went out yesterday morning, and **after that** I was at home all day.* ◇ *That was in April. Soon after, I heard that he was ill.* **2** ... **after** ... repeated many times or continuing for a long time: ***day after day** of hot weather* ◇ *I've told them **time after time** not to do that.* **3** following or behind sb/sth: *Shut the door after you.* ◇ *C comes after B in the alphabet.* **4** looking for or trying to catch or get sb/sth: *The police were after him.* ◇ *Nicky is after a job in advertising.* **5** because of sth: *After the way he behaved I won't invite him here again.* **6** used when sb/sth is given the name of another person or thing: *We called our son Bill after his grandfather.*
IDM **after all 1** used when sth is different in reality to what sb expected or thought: *So you decided to come after all!* (= I thought you weren't going to come) **2** used for reminding sb of a certain fact: *She can't understand. After all, she's only two.*

afterbirth /ˈɑːftəbɜːθ/ ***noun*** [sing.] (BIOLOGY) the material that comes out of a woman or female animal's body after a baby has been born, and which was necessary to feed and protect the baby
SYN **placenta**

ˈ**after-effect** ***noun*** [C] an unpleasant result of sth that comes some time later ➲ look at **effect, side effect**

afterlife /ˈɑːftəlaɪf/ ***noun*** [sing.] (RELIGION) a life that some people believe exists after death

aftermath /ˈɑːftəmæθ/ ***noun*** [sing.] a situation that is the result of an important or unpleasant event

afternoon ⊶ /ˌɑːftəˈnuːn/ ***noun*** [C,U] the part of a day between midday and about six o'clock: *I'll see you tomorrow afternoon.* ◇ *What are you doing this afternoon?* ◇ *I studied all afternoon.* ◇ *I usually go for a walk **in the afternoon**.* ◇ *He goes swimming every afternoon.* ◇ *She arrived at four o'clock in the afternoon.* ◇ *Tom works two afternoons a week.* ◇ *Are you busy **on Friday afternoon**?* ❶ When we are talking about a particular afternoon we say **on Monday, Tuesday, Wednesday, etc. afternoon**, but when we are talking generally about doing sth at the time of day we say **in the afternoon**.
IDM **good afternoon** used when you see sb for the first time in the afternoon

aftershave /ˈɑːftəʃeɪv/ ***noun*** [C,U] a liquid with a pleasant smell that men put on their faces after shaving

aftershock /ˈɑːftəʃɒk/ ***noun*** [C] (GEOGRAPHY) a smaller EARTHQUAKE (= movement of the earth's surface), that happens after a bigger one

aftertaste /ˈɑːftəteɪst/ ***noun*** [sing.] a taste (usually an unpleasant one) that stays in your mouth after you have eaten or drunk sth

afterthought /ˈɑːftəθɔːt/ ***noun*** [C, usually sing.] something that you think of or add to sth else at a later time

afterwards ⊶ /ˈɑːftəwədz/ (*AmE also* **after-ward**) ***adv.*** at a later time: *He was taken to hospital and died shortly afterwards.* ◇ *Afterwards, I realized I'd made a terrible mistake.*

again ⊶ /əˈgen; əˈgeɪn/ ***adv.*** **1** once more; another time: *Could you say that again, please?* ◇ *Don't ever do that again!* **2** in the place or condition that sb/sth was in before: *It's great to be home again.* ◇ *I hope you'll soon be well again.* **3** in addition to sth: *'Is that enough?' 'No, I'd like half as much again, please.'* (= one-and-a-half times the original amount)
IDM **again and again** many times: *He said he was sorry again and again, but she wouldn't listen.*
then/there again used to say that sth you have just said may not happen or be true: *She might pass her test, but then again she might not.*
yet again → YET

against ⊶ /əˈgenst; əˈgeɪnst/ ***prep.*** **1** being an opponent to sb/sth in a game, competition, etc., or an enemy of sb/sth in a war or fight: *We played football against a school from another district.* **2** not agreeing with or supporting sb/sth: *Are you for or against the plan?* ◇ *She felt that everybody was against her.* **3** what a law, rule, etc. says you must not do: *It's **against the law** to buy cigarettes before you are sixteen.* **4** to protect yourself from sb/sth: *Take these pills as a precaution against malaria.* **5** in the opposite direction to sth: *We had to cycle against the wind.* **6** touching sb/sth for support: *I put the ladder against the wall.*

agar /ˈeɪgɑː(r)/ (*also* ˌ**agar-ˈagar**) ***noun*** [U] (BIOLOGY) a substance like jelly, used by scientists for growing CULTURES (= a group of cells or bacteria, grown for medical or scientific study)

agate /ˈægət/ ***noun*** [U, C] a hard stone with bands or areas of colour, used in jewellery

age[1] ⊶ /eɪdʒ/ ***noun*** **1** [C,U] the length of time that sb has lived or that sth has existed: *Ali is 17 **years of age**.* ◇ *She left school **at the age of** 16.* ◇ *Children of* all ages will enjoy this film. ◇ He needs some friends of his own age. **2** [C,U] a particular period in sb's life: *a problem that often develops in* ***middle age*** ◇ *Her sons will look after her in her* ***old age.*** **3** [U] the state of being old: *a face lined with age* ◇ *The doctor said she* ***died of old age.*** ➲ look at **youth 4** [C] (**HISTORY**) a particular period of history: *the computer age* ◇ *the history of art through the ages* **5 ages** [pl.] (*informal*) a very long time: *We had to wait (for) ages at the hospital.* ◇ *It's ages since I've seen her.*

IDM **come of age** (**LAW**) to become an adult in law
feel your age → FEEL[1]
under age (**LAW**) not old enough by law to do sth

age[2] /eɪdʒ/ ***verb*** [I,T] (*pres. part.* **ageing** or **aging**; *pt, pp* **aged** /eɪdʒd/) to become or look old; to cause sb to look old: *My father seems to have aged a lot recently.* ◇ *I could see her illness had aged her.* ◇ *an ageing aunt*

aged 🔑 **1** /eɪdʒd/ ***adj.*** (not *before* a noun) of the age mentioned: *The woman, aged 26, was last seen at the central station.* **2 the aged** /ˈeɪdʒɪd/ ***noun*** [pl.] very old people

ˈage group ***noun*** [C] people of about the same age: *This club is very popular with the 20-30 age group.*

ageism (*also* **agism**) /ˈeɪdʒɪzəm/ ***noun*** [U] (**SOCIAL STUDIES**) unfair treatment of people because they are considered too old ▸ **ageist** /ˈeɪdʒɪst/ ***adj.***

ageless /ˈeɪdʒləs/ ***adj.*** (*written*) **1** never seeming to grow old **2** existing for ever; impossible to give an age to: *the ageless mystery of the universe*

ˈage limit ***noun*** [C] (**LAW**) the oldest or youngest age at which you are allowed to do sth: *to be over/under the age limit*

agency 🔑 /ˈeɪdʒənsi/ ***noun*** [C] (*pl.* **agencies**) **1** (**BUSINESS**) a business that provides a particular service: *an advertising agency* **2** (*AmE*) (**POLITICS**) a government department

agenda /əˈdʒendə/ ***noun*** [C] a list of items to be discussed at a meeting: *The first item* ***on the agenda*** *at the meeting will be security.* ◇ *The government have* ***set an agenda*** *for reform over the next ten years.*

agent 🔑 /ˈeɪdʒənt/ ***noun*** [C] **1** (**BUSINESS**) a person whose job is to do business for a company or for another person: *Our company's agent in Rio will meet you at the airport.* ◇ *Most actors and musicians have their own agents.* ◇ *a travel agent* ◇ *an estate agent* **2** = SECRET AGENT **3** (**TECHNICAL**) a chemical or a substance that produces an effect or a change or is used for a particular purpose: *cleaning/oxidizing agents*

the ˌage of conˈsent ***noun*** [sing.] (**LAW**) the age at which sb is legally old enough to agree to have a sexual relationship

ˌage-ˈold ***adj.*** that has existed for a very long time: *an age-old custom/problem*

agglomeration /əˌglɒməˈreɪʃn/ ***noun*** [C,U] (*formal*) a group of things put together in no particular order or arrangement

aggravate /ˈægrəveɪt/ ***verb*** [T] **1** to make sth worse or more serious **2** (*informal*) to make sb angry or annoyed ▸ **aggravation** /ˌægrəˈveɪʃn/ ***noun*** [C,U]

aggregate[1] AW /ˈægrɪgət/ ***noun*** **1** [C] a total number or amount made up of smaller amounts that are collected together **2** [U,C] (**TECHNICAL**) sand or broken stone that is used to make concrete or for building roads, etc.

IDM **on aggregate** (*BrE*) (**SPORT**) when the scores of a number of games are added together: *Our team won 3-1 on aggregate.*

aggregate[2] AW /ˈægrɪgət/ ***adj.*** (only *before* a noun) made up of several amounts that are added together to form a total number: ***aggregate demand/investment/turnover*** ◇ *an aggregate win over their rivals*

aggregate[3] AW /ˈægrɪgeɪt/ ***verb*** [T] (usually passive) **~ sth (with sth)** (*formal* or *technical*) to put together different items, amounts, etc. into a single group or total: *The scores were aggregated with the first round totals to decide the winner.*

aggression /əˈgreʃn/ ***noun*** [U] **1** angry feelings or behaviour that make you want to attack other people: *People often react to this kind of situation with fear or aggression.* **2** the act of starting a fight or war without reasonable cause

aggressive 🔑 /əˈgresɪv/ ***adj.*** **1** ready or likely to fight or argue: *an aggressive dog* ◇ *Some people get aggressive after drinking alcohol.* **2** using or showing force or pressure in order to succeed: *an aggressive salesman* ▸ **aggressively** ***adv.***: *The boys responded aggressively when I asked them to make less noise.*

aggressor /əˈgresə(r)/ ***noun*** [C] a person or country that attacks sb/sth or starts fighting first

aggrieved /əˈgriːvd/ ***adj.*** (*formal*) upset or angry

aghast /əˈgɑːst/ ***adj.*** (not *before* a noun) (*written*) **~ (at sth)** filled with horror and surprise when you see or hear sth: *He stood aghast at the sight of so much blood.*

agile /ˈædʒaɪl/ ***adj.*** able to move quickly and easily ▸ **agility** /əˈdʒɪləti/ ***noun*** [U]: *This sport is a test of both physical and mental agility.*

agitate /ˈædʒɪteɪt/ ***verb*** [I] **~ (for/against sth)** to make other people feel very strongly about sth so that they want to help you achieve it: *to agitate for reform*

agitated /ˈædʒɪteɪtɪd/ ***adj.*** worried or excited ▸ **agitation** /ˌædʒɪˈteɪʃn/ ***noun*** [U]

agitator /ˈædʒɪteɪtə(r)/ ***noun*** [C] (**POLITICS**) a person who tries to persuade people to take part in political protest

aglow /əˈgləʊ/ ***adj.*** (*written*) (not *before* a noun) shining with warmth or happiness: *The children's faces were aglow with excitement.*

AGM /ˌeɪ dʒiː ˈem/ ***abbr.*** (*BrE*) (**BUSINESS**) **Annual General Meeting**; an important meeting which the members of an organization hold once a year in order to elect officers, discuss past and future activities and examine the accounts

agnostic /ægˈnɒstɪk/ ***noun*** [C] (**RELIGION**) a person who is not sure if God exists or not

ago 🔑 /əˈgəʊ/ ***adv.*** in the past; back in time from now: *Patrick left ten minutes ago* (= if it is twelve o'clock now, he left at ten to twelve). ◇ *That was* ***a long time ago.*** ◇ ***How long ago*** *did this happen?*

agog /əˈgɒg/ ***adj.*** (not *before* a noun) very excited while waiting to hear sth: *We were all agog when she said she had good news.*

agonize (also **-ise**) /ˈægənaɪz/ ***verb*** [I] to worry or think about sth for a long time: *to agonize over a difficult decision*

agonized (also **-ised**) /ˈægənaɪzd/ ***adj.*** showing extreme pain or worry: *an agonized cry*

agonizing (also **-ising**) /ˈægənaɪzɪŋ/ ***adj.*** causing extreme worry or pain: *an agonizing choice* ◇ *an agonizing headache*

agony /ˈægəni/ ***noun*** [C,U] (*pl.* **agonies**) great pain or suffering: *to be/scream* ***in agony***

'agony aunt (*masculine* **'agony uncle**) (*AmE* **ad'vice columnist**) ***noun*** [C] (**ARTS AND MEDIA**) a person who writes in a newspaper or magazine giving advice in reply to people's letters about their personal problems

agoraphobia /ˌæɡərə'fəʊbiə/ ***noun*** [U] (**HEALTH**) fear of being in public places where there are a lot of people ▸ **agoraphobic** ***adj.***

agrarian /ə'ɡreəriən/ ***adj.*** (*formal*) (**AGRICULTURE**) connected with farming and the use of land for farming

THESAURUS

agree

approve • consent • acquiesce

These words all mean to say that you will do what somebody wants or that you will allow something to happen.

agree: *He agreed to let me go early.*

approve: *The committee approved the plans.*

consent (*formal*): *He finally consented to answer our questions.*

acquiesce (*formal*): *Senior politicians must have acquiesced in the cover-up.*

agree 🔑 /ə'ɡriː/ ***verb*** **1** [I] ~ (**with sb/sth**); ~ (**that...**) to have the same opinion as sb/sth: *'I think we should leave now.' 'Yes, I agree.'* ◇ *I agree with Paul.* ◇ *Do you agree that we should travel by train?* ◇ *I'm afraid I don't agree.* OPP **disagree** **2** [I] ~ (**to sth/ to do sth**) to say yes to sth: *I asked my boss if I could go home early and she agreed.* ◇ *Alkis has agreed to lend me his car for the weekend.* OPP **refuse** **3** [I,T] ~ (**to do sth**); ~ (**on**) (**sth**) to make an arrangement or decide sth with sb: *They agreed to meet again the following day.* ◇ *Can we agree on a price?* ◇ *We agreed a price of £500.* **4** [I] ~ **with sth** to think that sth is right: *I don't agree with experiments on animals.* **5** [I] to be the same as sth: *The two accounts of the accident do not agree.*

agreeable /ə'ɡriːəbl/ ***adj.*** **1** pleasant; nice OPP **disagreeable** **2** (*formal*) ready to agree: *If you are agreeable, we would like to visit your offices on 21 May.* ▸ **agreeably** /-əbli/ ***adv.***: *I was agreeably surprised by the film.*

COLLOCATIONS AND PATTERNS

Agriculture

Fruit and vegetables **grow** or **are grown.**
Pineapples grow in tropical climates.
We have been growing strawberries for many years.

When fruit is almost ready to pick and eat, it **ripens** or becomes **ripe.**
Peaches ripen in the sun.
Those pears are not quite ripe yet.

A plant **produces** fruit or vegetables.
The tree produces very sweet plums.

The amount of fruit/vegetables collected is the **harvest/crop.**
Growers are expecting a plentiful harvest this year.
Hereford enjoyed a bumper crop of apples.

Fruit that grows on trees grows in **orchards** or **groves.** Nuts grow in **groves.**
apple/cherry orchards
almond/citrus/lemon/olive/orange groves

Plantations are large areas of land where fruit and other crops grow.
banana/coffee/rice/sugar/tea plantations

agricultural tools

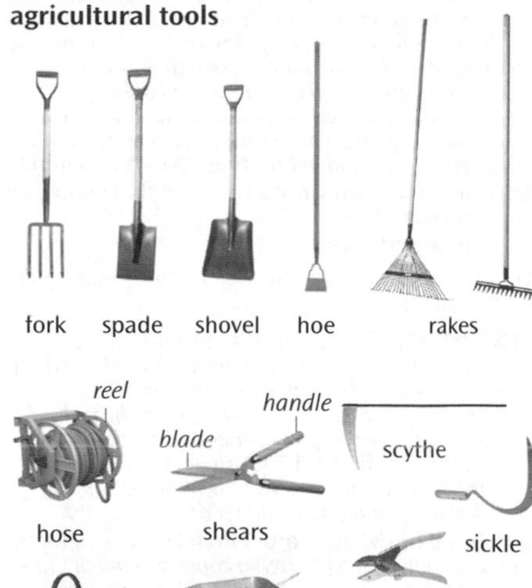

agreement 🔑 /ə'ɡriːmənt/ ***noun*** **1** [U] the state of agreeing with sb/sth: *She nodded her head in agreement.* ◇ *We* ***are totally in agreement with*** *what you have said.* OPP **disagreement** **2** [C] a contract or decision that two or more people have made together: *Please sign the agreement and return it to us.* ◇ *The leaders* ***reached an agreement*** *after five days of talks.* ◇ *We never* ***break an agreement.***

agribusiness /'æɡrɪbɪznəs/ ***noun*** [U] (**AGRICULTURE**) the industry concerned with making and selling farm products, especially involving large companies

agriculture /'æɡrɪkʌltʃə(r)/ ***noun*** [U] keeping animals and growing crops for food; farming: *the Minister of Agriculture* ▸ **agricultural** /ˌæɡrɪ'kʌltʃərəl/ ***adj.***

agritourism /'æɡrɪtʊərɪzəm; -tɔːr-/ ***noun*** [U] (**TOURISM**) holidays in which tourists visiting a country stay with local people who live in the countryside

agrochemical /'æɡrəʊkemɪkl/ ***noun*** [C] (**AGRICULTURE**) a chemical used in farming, especially for killing insects or for making plants grow better

agronomist /ə'ɡrɒnəmɪst/ ***noun*** [C] (**AGRICULTURE, ENVIRONMENT**) a scientist who studies the relationship between the plants that farmers grow and the environment ▸ **agronomy** ***noun*** [U]

aground /ə'ɡraʊnd/ ***adv.*** if a ship **runs/goes aground**, it touches the ground in water that is not deep enough and it cannot move: *The oil tanker ran/ went aground off the Spanish coast.* ▸ **aground** ***adj.***

ah /ɑː/ ***exclamation*** used for expressing surprise, pleasure, understanding, etc.: *Ah, there you are.*

aha /ɑː'hɑː/ ***exclamation*** used when you suddenly find or understand sth: *Aha! Now I understand.*

ahead 🔑 /ə'hed/ ***adv., adj.*** ~ (**of sb/sth**) **1** in front of sb/sth: *I could see the other car about half a mile ahead of us.* ◇ *The path ahead looked narrow and steep.* ◇ *Look* ***straight ahead*** *and don't turn* *round!* **2** before or more advanced than sb/sth: *Inga and Nils arrived a few minutes ahead of us.* ◇ *London is about five hours ahead of New York.* ◇ *The Japanese are **way ahead** of us in their research.* **3** into the future: *He's got a difficult time ahead of him.* ◇ *We must **think ahead** and make a plan.* **4** (SPORT) winning in a game, competition, etc.: *The goal **put** Argentina 2-1 **ahead** at half-time.* ➲ look at **behind**

IDM **ahead of your time** so modern that people do not understand you

streets ahead → STREET

AI /ˌeɪ ˈaɪ/ ***abbr.*** **1** = ARTIFICIAL INSEMINATION **2** = ARTIFICIAL INTELLIGENCE

aid¹ 🔑 AW /eɪd/ ***noun*** **1** [U] money, food, etc. that is sent to a country or to people in order to help them: *We sent aid to the earthquake victims.* ◇ *economic aid* **2** [U] help: *to walk **with the aid of** a stick* ◇ *He had to **go to the aid of** a child in the river.* ➲ look at **first aid** **3** [C] an object, a machine, etc. that you use to help you do sth: *a hearing aid* ◇ *dictionaries and other study aids*

IDM **in aid of sb/sth** in order to collect money for sb/sth, especially for a charity: *a concert in aid of Children in Need*

aid² 🔑 AW /eɪd/ ***verb*** [T] (*formal*) to help sb/sth: *Sleep aids recovery from illness.*

IDM **aid and abet** to help sb to do sth that is not allowed by law

AIDA /ˌeɪ aɪ diː ˈeɪ/ ***abbr.*** (BUSINESS) **awareness/attention, interest, desire, action**; a description used in advertising to try to explain how people make decisions about buying products and services

aide /eɪd/ ***noun*** [C] (POLITICS) a person who helps sb important in the government, etc.; an assistant

AIDS (*BrE also* **Aids**) /eɪdz/ ***noun*** [U] (HEALTH) **Acquired Immune Deficiency Syndrome**; an illness which destroys the body's ability to fight infection and which usually causes death: *He was HIV positive for three years before developing **full-blown AIDS**.* ◇ *to contract AIDS* ◇ *the AIDS virus*

aileron /ˈeɪlərɒn/ ***noun*** [C] (*technical*) a part of the wing of a plane that moves up and down to control the plane's balance ➲ picture at **plane**

ailing /ˈeɪlɪŋ/ ***adj.*** not in good health; weak: *an ailing economy*

ailment /ˈeɪlmənt/ ***noun*** [C] (*formal*) (HEALTH) any illness that is not very serious ➲ note at **disease**

aim¹ 🔑 /eɪm/ ***noun*** **1** [C] something that you intend to do; a purpose: *Our main aim is to increase sales in Europe.* ◇ *His only aim in life is to make money.* ➲ note at **purpose** **2** [U] the act of pointing sth at sb/sth before trying to hit them or it with it: *She picked up the gun, **took aim** and fired.* ◇ *Jo's aim was good and she hit the target.*

aim² 🔑 /eɪm/ ***verb*** **1** [I] **~ to do sth; ~ at/for sth** to intend to do or achieve sth: *We aim to leave after breakfast.* ◇ *The company is aiming at a 25% increase in profit.* ◇ *You should always aim for perfection in your work.* **2** [T] **~ sth at sb/sth** to direct sth at a particular person or group: *The advertising campaign is aimed at young people.* **3** [I,T] **~ (sth) (at sb/sth)** to point sth at sb/sth before trying to hit them or it with it: *She aimed (the gun) at the target and fired.*

IDM **be aimed at sth/doing sth** to be intended to achieve sth: *The new laws are aimed at reducing heavy traffic in cities.*

aimless /ˈeɪmləs/ ***adj.*** having no purpose: *an aimless discussion* ▶ ***aimlessly adv.***

ain't /eɪnt/ (*informal*) short for AM NOT, IS NOT, ARE NOT, HAS NOT, HAVE NOT

air¹ 🔑 /eə(r)/ ***noun*** **1** [U] the mixture of gases that surrounds the earth and that people, animals and plants breathe: *the pure mountain air* ◇ *Open a window – I need some **fresh air**.* ◇ *The air was polluted by smoke from the factory.* **2** [U] the space around and above things: *to throw a ball high **into the air*** ◇ ***in the open air*** (= outside) **3** [U] travel or transport in an aircraft: *to travel **by air*** ◇ *an air ticket* **4** [sing.] **an ~ (of sth)** the particular feeling or impression that is given by sb/sth: *She has a confident air.*

IDM **a breath of fresh air** → BREATH

clear the air → CLEAR³

in the air probably going to happen soon: *A feeling of change was in the air.*

in the open air → OPEN¹

on (the) air sending out programmes on the radio or television: *This radio station is on the air 24 hours a day.*

vanish, etc. into thin air → THIN¹

air² /eə(r)/ ***verb*** **1** [I,T] to put clothes, etc. in a warm place or outside in the fresh air to make sure they are completely dry; to become dry in this way **2** [I,T] to make a room, etc. fresh by letting air into it; to become fresh in this way **3** [T] to tell people what you think about sth: *The discussion gave people a chance to **air their views**.*

airbag /ˈeəbæg/ ***noun*** [C] a safety device in a car that fills with air if there is an accident. It protects the people sitting in the front.

airbase /ˈeəbeɪs/ ***noun*** [C] an airport for military aircraft

airborne /ˈeəbɔːn/ ***adj.*** **1** (used about a plane or passengers) flying in the air: *Five minutes after getting on the plane we were airborne.* **2** (only *before* a noun) carried through the air ➲ look at **water-borne**

airbrush¹ /ˈeəbrʌʃ/ ***noun*** [C] (ART) an artist's tool for spraying paint onto a surface, that works by air pressure

airbrush² /ˈeəbrʌʃ/ ***verb*** [T] **~ sth (out)** (ART) to paint sth with an **airbrush**; to change a detail in a photograph using this tool: *Somebody had been airbrushed out of the picture.*

Airbus™ /ˈeəbʌs/ ***noun*** [C] (TOURISM) a large plane that carries passengers over short and medium distances

ˈair conditioner ***noun*** [C] a machine that cools and dries air

ˈair conditioning ***noun*** [U] (*abbr.* **a/c**) the system that keeps the air in a room, building, etc. cool and dry ▶ **ˈair-conditioned** ***adj.***: *air-conditioned offices*

aircraft 🔑 /ˈeəkrɑːft/ ***noun*** [C] (*pl.* **aircraft**) any vehicle that can fly in the air, for example a plane

ˈaircraft carrier ***noun*** [C] a ship that carries military aircraft and that has a long flat area where they can take off and land

aircrew /ˈeəkruː/ ***noun*** [C, with sing. or pl. verb] the pilot and other people who fly a plane, especially in the air force

airdrome /ˈeədrəʊm/ (*AmE*) = AERODROME

airdrop /ˈeədrɒp/ ***noun*** [C] the act of dropping supplies, equipment, soldiers, etc. from an aircraft using a PARACHUTE (= a thing that helps them fall to the ground slowly)

airfield /ˈeəfiːld/ ***noun*** [C] an area of land where aircraft can land or take off. An **airfield** is smaller than an airport.

'air force *noun* [C, with sing. or pl. verb] the part of a country's military organization that fights in the air ➲ look at **army**, **navy**

'air gun (*also* **'air rifle**) *noun* [C] a gun that uses air pressure to fire PELLETS (= small metal balls)

'air hostess (*also* **hostess**) *noun* [C] (TOURISM) a woman who looks after the passengers on a plane SYN **stewardess** ➲ look at **steward**

'airing cupboard *noun* [C] a warm cupboard that you put clothes, etc. in to make sure they are completely dry after being washed

airless /'eələs/ *adj.* not having enough fresh air: *The room was hot and airless.*

airlift /'eəlɪft/ *noun* [C] an operation to take people, soldiers, food, etc. to or from an area by plane, especially in an emergency or when roads are closed or dangerous ▶ **airlift** *verb* [T]: *Two casualties were **airlifted to safety**.*

airline /'eəlaɪn/ *noun* [C] (TOURISM) a company that provides regular flights for people or goods in aircraft: *international airlines* ◇ *an airline pilot*

airliner /'eəlaɪnə(r)/ *noun* [C] (TOURISM) a large plane that carries passengers

airlock /'eəlɒk/ *noun* [C] (PHYSICS) **1** a small room with a tightly closed door at each end, which you go through to reach another area at a different air pressure, for example on a SPACECRAFT or SUBMARINE (= a type of ship that can travel under the water) **2** a bubble of air that blocks the flow of liquid in a pipe or PUMP (= a machine used for forcing a gas or liquid in a particular direction)

airmail /'eəmeɪl/ *noun* [U] the system for sending letters, packages, etc. by plane: *I sent the parcel (by) airmail.*

airplane /'eəpleɪn/ (*AmE*) = AEROPLANE

'air pocket *noun* [C] **1** a closed area that becomes filled with air: *Make sure there are no air pockets around the roots of the plant.* **2** an area of low air pressure that makes a plane suddenly drop while flying

airport ⊶ /'eəpɔːt/ *noun* [C] a place where aircraft can land and take off and that has buildings for passengers to wait in

'air raid *noun* [C] an attack by military aircraft

'air rifle = AIR GUN

airship /'eəʃɪp/ *noun* [C] a large aircraft without wings, filled with gas that is lighter than air, and driven by engines

airsick /'eəsɪk/ *adj.* feeling ill or sick when you are travelling on a plane ➲ look at **carsick**, **seasick**, **travel-sick** ▶ **airsickness** *noun* [U]

airspace /'eəspeɪs/ *noun* [U] the part of the sky that is above a country and that belongs to that country by law

airstrip /'eəstrɪp/ (*also* **'landing strip**) *noun* [C] a narrow piece of land where aircraft can take off and land

airtight /'eətaɪt/ *adj.* that air cannot get into or out of

airtime /'eətaɪm/ *noun* [U] **1** (ARTS AND MEDIA) the amount of time that is given to a subject on radio or television **2** the amount of time that is paid for when you use a mobile phone: *This deal gives you 90 minutes free airtime a week.*

ˌair-to-'air *adj.* (usually before a noun) from one aircraft to another while they are both flying: *an air-to-air missile*

ˌair ˌtraffic con'troller *noun* [C] a person whose job is to organize routes for aircraft, and to tell pilots by radio when they can land and take off

airwaves /'eəweɪvz/ *noun* [pl.] (ARTS AND MEDIA) radio waves that are used in sending out radio and television programmes: *A well-known voice came **over the airwaves**.*

airway /'eəweɪ/ *noun* [C] (ANATOMY) the passage from your nose and throat down into your lungs, through which you breathe ➲ picture at **lung**

airworthy /'eəwɜːði/ *adj.* (used about aircraft) safe to fly ▶ **airworthiness** *noun* [U]

airy /'eəri/ *adj.* having a lot of fresh air inside

aisle /aɪl/ *noun* [C] a passage between the rows of seats in a church, theatre, plane, etc.

ajar /ə'dʒɑː(r)/ *adj.* (not *before* a noun) (used about a door) slightly open

akin /ə'kɪn/ *adj.* **~ to sth** (*formal*) similar to sth

alabaster /'æləbɑːstə(r)/ *noun* [U] a type of white stone that is often used to make statues and decorative objects: *an alabaster tomb* ◇ (*figurative*) *her pale, alabaster* (= white and smooth) *skin*

à la carte /ˌɑː lɑː 'kɑːt/ *adj.*, *adv.* (used about a meal in a restaurant) where each dish on the MENU (= a list of available dishes) has a separate price and there is not a fixed price for a complete meal

alarm¹ ⊶ /ə'lɑːm/ *noun* **1** [U] a sudden feeling of fear or worry: *She jumped up **in alarm**.* **2** [sing.] a warning of danger: *A small boy saw the smoke and **raised the alarm**.* **3** [C] a machine that warns you of danger, for example by ringing a loud bell: *The burglars **set off the alarm** when they broke the window.* ◇ *The **fire alarm** went off in the middle of the night.* **4** [C] = ALARM CLOCK

IDM **a false alarm** → FALSE

alarm² ⊶ /ə'lɑːm/ *verb* [T] to make sb/sth feel suddenly frightened or worried

a'larm call *noun* [C] a telephone call which is intended to wake you up SYN **wake-up call**: *Could I have an alarm call at 5.30 tomorrow morning, please?*

a'larm clock (*also* **alarm**) *noun* [C] a clock that you can set to make a noise at a particular time to wake you up: *She set the alarm clock for half past six.*

alarmed ⊶ /ə'lɑːmd/ *adj.* **~ (at/by sth)** feeling frightened or worried

alarming ⊶ /ə'lɑːmɪŋ/ *adj.* that makes you frightened or worried ▶ **alarmingly** *adv.*

alarmist /ə'lɑːmɪst/ *adj.* causing unnecessary fear and worry: *The reports of a flu epidemic were alarmist.* ▶ **alarmist** *noun* [C]

alas /ə'læs/ *exclamation* (*written*, *old-fashioned*) used for expressing sadness about sth

albatross /'ælbətrɒs/ *noun* [C] **1** a very large white bird with long wings that lives in the Pacific and Southern Oceans ➲ picture on **page 29** **2** [usually sing.] (*formal*) a thing that causes problems or that prevents you from doing sth: *The national debt is an albatross around the President's neck.*

albeit AW /ˌɔːl'biːɪt/ *conj.* (*formal*) although: *He finally agreed to come, albeit unwillingly.*

albino /æl'biːnəʊ/ *noun* [C] (*pl.* **albinos**) a person or an animal with very white skin, white hair and pink eyes

album /'ælbəm/ ***noun*** [C] **1** (MUSIC) a collection of songs on one CD, tape, etc.: *The band are about to release their third album.* ➲ look at **single 2** a book in which you can keep stamps, photographs, etc. that you have collected

albumen /'ælbjumɪn/ ***noun*** [U] (BIOLOGY, TECHNICAL) the clear inside part of an egg that turns white when you cook it SYN **white**

alchemist /'ælkəmɪst/ ***noun*** [C] a person who studied ALCHEMY

alchemy /'ælkəmi/ ***noun*** [U] **1** (HISTORY) a form of chemistry in the Middle Ages which involved trying to discover how to change ordinary metals into gold **2** (*written*) magic power that can change things

alcohol 🔑 /'ælkəhɒl/ ***noun*** **1** [U] drinks such as beer, wine, etc. that can make people drunk: *He never drinks alcohol.* ◇ *alcohol abuse* **2** [U, C] (CHEMISTRY) the colourless liquid that is found in drinks such as beer, wine, etc. and is used in medicines, cleaning products, etc.: *Wine contains about 12% alcohol.* ◇ ***alcohol-free*** *beer*

alcoholic[1] 🔑 /ˌælkə'hɒlɪk/ ***adj.*** containing alcohol: *alcoholic drinks* OPP **non-alcoholic**

alcoholic[2] 🔑 /ˌælkə'hɒlɪk/ ***noun*** [C] a person who cannot stop drinking large amounts of alcohol

alcoholism /'ælkəhɒlɪzəm/ ***noun*** [U] (HEALTH) a medical condition that is caused by regularly drinking a large amount of alcohol and not being able to stop

alcove /'ælkəʊv/ ***noun*** [C] a small area in a room where one part of the wall is further back than the rest of the wall

alderman /'ɔːldəmən/ ***noun*** [C] (*pl.* **-men** /-mən/) (HISTORY, POLITICS) (in England and Wales in the past) an important member of the town or county council, chosen by other members of the council

ale /eɪl/ ***noun*** [U, C] a type of beer

alert[1] /ə'lɜːt/ ***adj.*** ~ **(to sth)** watching, listening, etc. for sth with all your attention: *Security guards must be alert at all times.* ◇ *to be alert to possible changes*

alert[2] /ə'lɜːt/ ***noun*** [C] a warning of possible danger: *a bomb alert*

IDM **on the alert (for sth)** ready or prepared for danger or an attack

alert[3] /ə'lɜːt/ ***verb*** [T] ~ **sb (to sth)** to warn sb of danger or a problem

'A level (also *formal* **ad'vanced level**) ***noun*** [C,U] (EDUCATION) an exam that schoolchildren in England, Wales and Northern Ireland take when they are about 18. You usually take **A levels** in two or three subjects and you need good GRADES (= results) if you want to go to university: *How many A levels have you got?* ◇ *I'm doing my A levels this summer.* ➲ look at **AS level**, **A2 level**, **GCSE**

alfalfa /æl'fælfə/ ***noun*** [U] (AGRICULTURE) a plant with small divided leaves and purple flowers, grown as food for farm animals and as a salad vegetable

algae /'ældʒiː; 'ælgiː/ ***noun*** [pl., with sing. or pl. verb] (BIOLOGY) very simple plants that grow mainly in water

algebra /'ældʒɪbrə/ ***noun*** [U] (MATHEMATICS) a type of mathematics in which letters and symbols are used to represent numbers ▶ **algebraic** /ˌældʒɪ'breɪɪk/ ***adj.***: *an algebraic equation*

algorithm /'ælgərɪðəm/ ***noun*** [C] (MATHEMATICS, COMPUTING) a set of rules that must be followed when solving a particular problem

alias[1] /'eɪliəs/ ***noun*** [C] a false name, for example one that is used by a criminal

alias[2] /'eɪliəs/ ***adv.*** used for giving sb's false name: *Norma Jean Baker, alias Marilyn Monroe*

alibi /'æləbaɪ/ ***noun*** [C] (*pl.* **alibis**) **an ~ (for sth)** (LAW) a statement by sb that says you were in a different place at the time of a crime and so cannot be guilty of the crime

alien[1] /'eɪliən/ ***adj.*** **1** ~ **(to sb)** strange and frightening; different from what you are used to **2** from another country or society; foreign: *an alien land* **3** connected with creatures from another world

alien[2] /'eɪliən/ ***noun*** [C] **1** (LAW) a person who is not a citizen of the country in which they live or work: *an illegal alien* **2** a creature that comes from another planet: *aliens from outer space*

alienate /'eɪliəneɪt/ ***verb*** [T] **1** to make people feel that they cannot share your opinions any more: *The Prime Minister's new policies on defence have alienated many of his supporters.* **2** ~ **sb (from sb/sth)** to make sb feel that they do not belong somewhere or are not part of sth ▶ **alienation** /ˌeɪliə'neɪʃn/ ***noun*** [U]

alight[1] /ə'laɪt/ ***adj.*** (not *before* a noun) on fire; burning: *A cigarette* ***set*** *the petrol* ***alight***.

alight[2] /ə'laɪt/ ***verb*** [I] (*formal*) **1** ~ **(in/on/upon sth)** (used about a bird or an insect) to land in or on sth after flying to it SYN **land 2** ~ **(from sth)** to get out of a bus, train or other vehicle SYN **get off**

align /ə'laɪn/ ***verb*** [T] **1** ~ **sth (with sth)** to arrange things in a straight line or so that they are parallel to sth else: *to align the wheels of a car* **2** ~ **yourself with sb** (POLITICS) to say that you support the opinions of a particular group, country, etc.

alignment /ə'laɪnmənt/ ***noun*** **1** [U] arrangement in a straight line or parallel to sth else **2** [C,U] (POLITICS) an agreement between political parties, countries, etc. to support the same thing

alike /ə'laɪk/ ***adj.***, ***adv.*** (not *before* a noun) **1** very similar: *The two boys are very alike.* **2** in the same way: *We try to treat women and men alike in this company.* ◇ *The book is popular with adults and children alike.*

alimentary canal /ˌælɪmentəri kə'næl/ ***noun*** [sing.] (ANATOMY) the long passage inside your body which food moves along, from the mouth to the opening where it leaves your body as waste

alimony /'ælɪməni/ ***noun*** [U] (LAW) money that you have to pay by law to your former wife or husband after getting divorced

'A-list ***adj.*** (ARTS AND MEDIA) used to describe a group of people who are famous, successful or important: *He only invited* ***A-list*** *celebrities to his party.*

alive 🔑 /ə'laɪv/ ***adj.*** **1** not dead; living: *The young woman was still alive when the ambulance reached the hospital.* ◇ *The quick action of the doctors* ***kept*** *the child* ***alive***. **2** continuing to exist: *Many old traditions are very much alive in this area of the country.* **3** full of life: *In the evening the town really* ***comes alive***.

alkali /'ælkəlaɪ/ ***noun*** [C,U] (CHEMISTRY) a chemical substance that can burn skin when it is dissolved in water. An **alkali** has a pH value of more than 7. ➲ look at **acid**, **base** ➲ picture at **pH** ▶ **alkaline** ***adj.***

alkaloid /'ælkəlɔɪd/ ***noun*** [C] (BIOLOGY, HEALTH) a poisonous substance that is found in some plants. Some **alkaloids** are used in drugs.

alkane /'ælkeɪn/ ***noun*** [C] (CHEMISTRY) any of a series of gases that contain HYDROGEN and CARBON: *Methane and propane are alkanes.*

alkene /'ælki:n/ *noun* [C] (CHEMISTRY) any of a series of gases that contain HYDROGEN and CARBON and that have a double BOND (= force of attraction) holding atoms together

all[1] /ɔ:l/ *det., pronoun* **1** the whole of a thing or of a period of time: *All (of) the food has gone.* ◇ *They've eaten all of it.* ◇ *They've eaten it all.* ◇ *This money is all yours.* ◇ *All of it is yours.* ◇ *all week/month/year* ◇ *He worked hard all his life.* **2** every one of a group: *All (of) my children can swim.* ◇ *My children can all swim.* ◇ *She's read all (of) these books.* ◇ *She's read them all.* ◇ *The people at the meeting all voted against the plan.* ◇ *All of them voted against the plan.* **3** everything that; the only thing that: *I wrote down all I could remember.* ◇ *All I've eaten today is one banana.*
IDM **above all** → ABOVE
after all → AFTER
for all 1 in spite of: *For all her wealth and beauty, she was never very happy.* **2** used to show that sth is not important or of no interest or value to you: ***For all I know**, he's probably remarried by now.*
in all in total: *There were ten of us in all.*
not all that... not very: *The film wasn't all that good.*
(not) at all (not) in any way: *I didn't enjoy it at all.*
not at all used as a polite reply when sb thanks you for something

all[2] /ɔ:l/ *adv.* **1** completely; very: *He has lived all alone since his wife died.* ◇ *I didn't watch that programme – I forgot all about it.* ◇ *They got all excited about it.* **2** (SPORT) for each side: *The score was two all.*
IDM **all along** from the beginning: *I knew you were joking all along.*
all the better, harder, etc. even better, harder, etc. than before: *It will be all the more difficult with two people missing.*

all- /ɔ:l/ *prefix* (used in adjectives and adverbs) **1** completely: *an all-American show* ◇ *an all-inclusive price* **2** in the highest degree: *all-important* ◇ *all-powerful*

Allah /'ælə/ *noun* [sing.] (RELIGION) the name of God among Muslims

allay /ə'leɪ/ *verb* [T] (*formal*) to make sth, especially a feeling, less strong: *to allay fears/concern/suspicion*

the ˌall-'clear *noun* [sing.] a signal telling you that a situation is no longer dangerous

allege /ə'ledʒ/ *verb* [T] (*formal*) (LAW) to say that sb has done sth wrong, but without having any proof that this is true: *The woman alleged that Williams had attacked her with a knife.* ▶ **allegation** /ˌælə'geɪʃn/ *noun* [C]: *to **make allegations** of police corruption* ➲ note at **claim**[2] ▶ **alleged** /ə'ledʒd/ *adj.* (only *before* a noun) ▶ **allegedly** /ə'ledʒɪdli/ *adv.*: *The man was allegedly shot while trying to escape.*

allegiance /ə'li:dʒəns/ *noun* [U, C] (*formal*) (POLITICS) support for a leader, government, belief, etc.: *Many people **switched allegiance** and voted against the government.*

allegory /'æləgəri/ *noun* [C,U] (*pl.* **allegories**) (LITERATURE, ART) a story, play, picture, etc. in which each character or event is a symbol representing an idea or a quality, such as truth, evil, death, etc.; the use of such symbols ▶ **allegorical** /ˌælə'gɒrɪkl/ *adj.*

allegro /ə'legrəʊ/ *noun* [C] (*pl.* **allegros**) (MUSIC) a piece of music that you should play quickly and with energy ▶ **allegro** *adj., adv.* ➲ look at **adagio, andante**

allele /ə'li:l/ *noun* [C] (BIOLOGY) one of two or more possible forms of a GENE (= one of the units of information that control what a living thing will be like) that are found at the same place on a CHROMOSOME (= one of the parts of every cell of a living thing that contains a particular combination of genes)

allergen /'ælədʒən/ *noun* [C] (HEALTH) any substance that causes an ALLERGY in some people when they eat, touch or breathe it

allergenic /ˌælə'dʒenɪk/ *adj.* (HEALTH) **allergenic** substances and materials are likely to cause an ALLERGIC reaction in the person who uses them.

allergic /ə'lɜ:dʒɪk/ *adj.* (HEALTH) **1** ~ **(to sth)** having an ALLERGY: *I can't drink cow's milk. I'm allergic to it.* **2** caused by an ALLERGY: *an allergic reaction to house dust*

allergy /'ælədʒi/ *noun* [C] (*pl.* **allergies**) **an ~ (to sth)** (HEALTH) a medical condition that makes you ill when you eat, touch or breathe sth that does not normally make other people ill

alleviate /ə'li:vieɪt/ *verb* [T] to make sth less strong or bad SYN **ease**: *The doctor gave me an injection to alleviate the pain.* ▶ **alleviation** /əˌli:vi'eɪʃn/ *noun* [U]

alley /'æli/ (*also* **alleyway** /'æliweɪ/) *noun* [C] a narrow passage between buildings

alliance /ə'laɪəns/ *noun* [C] (POLITICS) an agreement between groups, countries, etc. to work together and support each other: *The two parties **formed an alliance**.* ➲ look at **ally**

allied *adj.* **1** /'ælaɪd/ (often **Allied**) (only *before* a noun) (POLITICS) connected with countries that unite to fight a war together, especially the countries that fought together against Germany in the First and Second World Wars: *Italy joined the war on the Allied side in 1915.* ◇ *allied forces/troops* **2** /ə'laɪd; 'ælaɪd/ ~ **(to sth)** (*formal*) (used about two or more things) similar or existing together; connected with sth: *medicine, nursing, physiotherapy and other allied professions*

alligator /'ælɪgeɪtə(r)/ *noun* [C] a large REPTILE similar to a CROCODILE with a long tail and a big mouth with sharp teeth. **Alligators** live in the lakes and rivers of America and China.

'alligator clip *noun* [C] (*especially AmE*) = CROCODILE CLIP

ˌall-'in *adj.* including everything: *an all-in price*

ˌall-in'clusive *adj.* (BUSINESS, TOURISM) including everything or everyone: *Our trips are all-inclusive — there are no hidden costs.*

alliteration /əˌlɪtə'reɪʃn/ *noun* [U] (LITERATURE) the use of the same letter or sound at the beginning of words that are close together, as in '*he built a big boat*'

allocate AW /'æləkeɪt/ *verb* [T] ~ **sth (to/for sb/sth)** to give sth to sb as their share or to decide to use sth for a particular purpose: *The government has allocated half the budget for education.* ▶ **allocation** /ˌælə'keɪʃn/ *noun* [C,U]

allot /ə'lɒt/ *verb* [T] (**allotting**; **allotted**) ~ **sth (to sb/sth)** to give a share of work, time, etc. to sb/sth: *Different tasks were allotted to each member of the class.* ◇ *We all finished the exam in the allotted time.*

allotment /ə'lɒtmənt/ *noun* [C] (*BrE*) (AGRICULTURE) a small area of land in a town that you can rent for growing vegetables on

allotropy /ə'lɒtrəpi/ *noun* [U] (CHEMISTRY) the ability that certain substances have to exist in more than one physical form

'all out *adj., adv.* using all your strength, etc.: *an all-out effort*

allow ⊶ /əˈlaʊ/ ***verb*** [T] **1** ~ **sb/sth to do sth;** ~ **sth** to give permission for sb/sth to do sth or for sth to happen: *Children under eighteen are not allowed to buy alcohol.* ◇ *I'm afraid we don't allow people to bring dogs into this restaurant.* ◇ *Photography is not allowed inside the cathedral.* **2** to give permission for sb/sth to be or go somewhere: *No dogs allowed.* ◇ *I'm only allowed out on Friday and Saturday nights.* **3** ~ **sb sth** to let sb have sth: *My contract allows me four weeks' holiday a year.* **4** ~ **sb/sth to do sth** to make it possible for sb/sth to do sth: *Working part-time would allow me to spend more time with my family.* **5** ~ **sth (for sb/sth)** to provide money, time, etc. for sb/sth: *You should allow about 30 minutes for each question.*

PHR V **allow for sb/sth** to think about possible problems when you are planning sth and include extra time, money, etc. for them: *The journey should take about two hours, allowing for heavy traffic.*

allowable /əˈlaʊəbl/ ***adj.*** that is allowed, especially by law or by the rules

allowance /əˈlaʊəns/ ***noun*** [C] **1** an amount of sth that you are allowed: *Most flights have a 20 kg* ***baggage allowance****.* **2** an amount of money that you receive regularly to help you pay for sth that you need

IDM **make allowances for sb/sth** to judge a person or their actions in a kinder way than usual because they have a particular problem or disadvantage

alloy /ˈælɔɪ/ ***noun*** [C,U] (CHEMISTRY) a metal made by mixing two types of metal together: *Brass is an alloy of copper and zinc.*

ˌall ˈright (also *informal* **alright**) ***exclamation, adv., adj.*** (not *before* a noun) **1** good enough; OK: *Is everything all right?* **2** (HEALTH) safe; not hurt; well; OK: *I hope the children are all right.* ◇ *Do you feel all right?* **3** showing you agree to do what sb has asked; OK: *'Can you get me some stamps?' 'Yes, all right.'*

SPEAKING

You say 'That's all right,' when sb thanks you for sth or when sb says sorry for sth he/she has done: *'Thanks for the lift home.' 'That's (quite) all right.'* ◇ *'I'm so sorry I'm late.' 'That's all right. We haven't started yet anyway.'*

ˈall-round ***adj.*** (only *before* a noun) able to do many different things well; good in many different ways: *a superb all-round athlete* ◇ *The school aims at the all-round development of the child.*

ˌall-ˈrounder ***noun*** [C] a person who can do many different things well

allspice /ˈɔːlspaɪs/ ***noun*** [U] the dried BERRIES of a West Indian tree, used in cooking as a spice

ˌall-terrain ˈvehicle = ATV

ˈall-time ***adj.*** (only *before* a noun) (used when you are comparing things or saying how good or bad sb/sth is) of any time: *It's my all-time favourite song.* ◇ *He's one of the all-time great athletes.* ◇ *Unemployment is at an all-time high.*

allude /əˈluːd/ ***verb*** [I] (*formal*) ~ **to sb/sth** to speak about sb/sth in an indirect way ➲ note at **mention** ▶ **allusion** /əˈluːʒn/ ***noun*** [C,U]: *He likes to* ***make allusions to*** *the size of his salary.*

allure /əˈlʊə(r)/ ***noun*** [U] (*written*) the quality of being attractive and exciting: *sexual allure* ◇ *the allure of the big city*

alluring /əˈlʊərɪŋ/ ***adj.*** attractive and exciting in a way that is not easy to understand or explain: *an alluring smile* ▶ **alluringly** ***adv.***

alluvial /əˈluːviəl/ ***adj.*** (GEOGRAPHY) made of sand and earth that is left by rivers or floods: *alluvial deposits/soil/plains*

alluvium /əˈluːviəm/ ***noun*** [U] (GEOGRAPHY) sand and earth that is left by rivers or floods

ally[1] ⊶ /ˈælaɪ/ ***noun*** [C] (*pl.* **allies**) (POLITICS) **1** a country that has an agreement to support another country, especially in a war: *France and its European allies* ➲ look at **alliance** **2** a person who helps and supports you, especially when other people are against you: *the Prime Minister's political allies*

> **WORD FAMILY**
> **ally** *verb, noun*
> **allied** *adj.*
> **alliance** *noun*

ally[2] /əˈlaɪ/ ***verb*** [T] (*3rd person sing. pres.* **allies**; *pres. part.* **allying**; *pt, pp* **allied**) ~ **(yourself) with sb/sth** to give your support to another group or country: *The prince allied himself with the Scots.*

almanac (also **almanack**) /ˈɔːlmənæk; ˈæl-/ ***noun*** [C] **1** a book that is published every year giving information for that year about a particular subject or activity **2** a book that gives information about the sun, moon, times of the TIDES (= the rise and fall of the sea level), etc. for each day of the year

almighty /ɔːlˈmaɪti/ ***adj.*** **1** having the power to do anything: *Almighty God* **2** (only *before* a noun) (*informal*) very great: *Suddenly we heard the most almighty crash.*

almond /ˈɑːmənd/ ***noun*** [C] a flat pale nut

almost ⊶ /ˈɔːlməʊst/ ***adv.*** very nearly; not quite: *By nine o'clock almost everybody had arrived.* ◇ *The film has almost finished.* ◇ *She almost always cycles to school.* ◇ *There's almost nothing left.* ◇ *Almost all the students passed the exam.*

aloft /əˈlɒft/ ***adv.*** (*formal*) high in the air

alone ⊶ /əˈləʊn/ ***adj., adv.*** **1** without any other person: *The old man lives alone.* ◇ *Are you alone? Can I speak to you for a moment?* ◇ *I don't like walking home alone after dark.* **2** (after a noun or pronoun) only: *You alone can help us.* ◇ *The rent alone takes up most of my salary.*

IDM **go it alone** to start working on your own without the usual help

leave sb/sth alone → LEAVE[1]

let alone → LET

along ⊶ /əˈlɒŋ/ ***prep., adv.*** **1** from one end to or towards the other end of sth: *I walked slowly along the road.* ◇ *David looked along the corridor to see if anyone was coming.* **2** on or beside sth long: *Wild flowers grew along both sides of the river.* ◇ *Our house is about halfway along the street.* **3** forward: *We moved along slowly with the crowd.* **4** (*informal*) with sb: *We're going for a walk. Why don't you* ***come along*** *too?*

IDM **all along** → ALL[2]

along with sb/sth together with sb/sth

go along with sb/sth to agree with sb's ideas or plans

alongside ⊶ /əˌlɒŋˈsaɪd/ ***adv., prep.*** **1** next to sb/sth or at the side of sth **2** together with sb/sth: *the opportunity to work alongside experienced musicians*

aloof /əˈluːf/ ***adj.*** **1** not friendly to other people; DISTANT: *Her shyness made her seem aloof.* **2** ~ **(from sb/sth)** not involved in sth; apart

aloud /ə'laʊd/ (*also* ˌout 'loud) *adv.* in a normal speaking voice that other people can hear: *The teacher listened to the children* ***reading aloud****.*

alpaca /æl'pækə/ *noun* **1** [C] a South American animal whose long hair makes good quality wool **2** [U] the wool of the **alpaca**

alpha /'ælfə/ *noun* [C] (LANGUAGE) the first letter of the Greek alphabet (α)

alphabet /'ælfəbet/ *noun* [C] (LANGUAGE) a set of letters in a fixed order that you use when you are writing a language: *There are 26 letters in the English alphabet.*

alphabetical /ˌælfə'betɪkl/ *adj.* arranged in the same order as the letters of the alphabet: *The names are listed* ***in alphabetical order****.* ▶ **alphabetically** /-kli/ *adv.*

alphanumeric /ˌælfənju:'merɪk/ *adj.* containing or using both numbers and letters: *alphanumeric data*

'alpha particle *noun* [C] (PHYSICS) a very small piece of matter with a positive electric charge passing through it, that is produced in a nuclear reaction

alpine /'ælpaɪn/ *adj.* (GEOGRAPHY) of or found in high mountains: *alpine flowers*

ˌAlpine 'skiing *noun* [U] (SPORT) the sport of SKIING down mountains ➲ look at **Nordic skiing**

already /ɔ:l'redi/ *adv.* **1** used for talking about sth that has happened before now or before a particular time in the past: *'Would you like some lunch?' 'No, I've already eaten, thanks.'* ◇ *We got there at 6.30 but Marsha had already left.* ◇ *Sita was already awake when I went into her room.* **2** (used in negative sentences and questions for expressing surprise) so early; as soon as this: *Have you finished already?* ◇ *Surely you're not going already!*

alright /ɔ:l'raɪt/ (*informal*) = ALL RIGHT

Alsatian /æl'seɪʃn/ (*also* **ˌGerman 'shepherd**) *noun* [C] a large dog, often trained to help the police or to guard buildings

also /'ɔ:lsəʊ/ *adv.* (not with negative verbs) in addition; too: *He plays several instruments and also writes music.* ◇ *Bring summer clothing and also something warm to wear in the evenings.* ◇ *The food is wonderful, and also very cheap.*

IDM **not only ... but also** → ONLY

'also-ran *noun* [C] (SPORT, POLITICS) a person who is not successful, especially in a competition or an election

altar /'ɔ:ltə(r)/ *noun* [C] (RELIGION) a high table that is the centre of a religious ceremony

altarpiece /'ɔ:ltəpi:s/ *noun* [C] (ART, RELIGION) a painting or other piece of art, found near the ALTAR in a church

alter AW /'ɔ:ltə(r)/ *verb* [I,T] to make sth different in some way, but without changing it completely; to become different: *We've altered our plan, and will now arrive at 7.00 instead of 8.00.* ◇ *The village seems to have altered very little in the last twenty years.*

alteration AW /ˌɔ:ltə'reɪʃn/ *noun* [C,U] **(an) ~ (to/in sth)** a small change in sb/sth: *We want to* ***make a*** *few* ***alterations*** *to the house before we move in.*

altercation /ˌɔ:ltə'keɪʃn/ *noun* [C,U] (*formal*) a noisy argument or disagreement

alternate¹ AW /ɔ:l'tɜ:nət/ *adj.* **1** (used about two types of events, things, etc.) happening or following regularly one after the other: *alternate periods of sun and showers* **2** one of every two: *He works alternate weeks* (= he works the first week, he doesn't work the second week, he works again the third week, etc.). ▶ **alternately** *adv.*: *The bricks were painted alternately white and red.*

alternate² AW /'ɔ:ltənəɪt/ *verb* **1** [I] **~ with sth; ~ between A and B** (used about two types of events, things, etc.) to happen or follow regularly one after the other: *Busy periods at work alternate with times when there is not much to do.* ◇ *She seemed to alternate between hating him and loving him.* **2** [T] **~ A with B** to cause two types of events or things to happen or follow regularly one after the other: *He alternated periods of work with periods of rest.*
▶ **alternation** /ˌɔ:ltə'neɪʃn/ *noun* [C,U]

alˌternate 'angles *noun* [pl.] (MATHEMATICS) two angles, formed on opposite sides of a line that crosses two other lines. If the two lines that are crossed are PARALLEL (= always the same distance apart), the **alternate angles** are equal. ➲ picture at **angle**

ˌalternating 'current *noun* [C,U] (*abbr.* AC) (PHYSICS) a flow of electricity that changes direction regularly many times a second ➲ look at **direct current**

alternative¹ AW /ɔ:l'tɜ:nətɪv/ *adj.* (only *before* a noun) **1** that you can use, do, etc. instead of sth else: *The motorway was closed so we had to find an alternative route.* **2** different to what is usual or traditional: *alternative medicine*

alternative² AW /ɔ:l'tɜ:nətɪv/ *noun* [C] **an ~ (to sth)** one of two or more things that you can choose between: *What can I eat as an alternative to meat?* ◇ *There are several alternatives open to us at the moment.*

alternatively /ɔ:l'tɜ:nətɪvli/ *adv.* used to introduce a suggestion that is a second choice or possibility: *The agency will make travel arrangements for you. Alternatively, you can organize your own transport.*

alˌternative 'medicine *noun* [C, U] (HEALTH) any type of treatment that does not use the usual scientific methods of Western medicine, for example one using plants instead of artificial drugs

alternator /'ɔ:ltəneɪtə(r)/ *noun* [C] (PHYSICS) a device, used especially in a car, that produces electrical current that moves in different directions

although /ɔ:l'ðəʊ/ *conj.* **1** in spite of the fact that: *Although she was tired, she stayed up late watching television.* **2** and yet; but: *I love dogs, although I wouldn't have one as a pet.*

altimeter /'æltɪmi:tə(r)/ *noun* [C] (PHYSICS) an instrument for showing height above sea level, used especially in an aircraft

altitude /'æltɪtju:d/ *noun* (GEOGRAPHY) **1** [sing.] the height of sth above sea level: *The plane climbed to an altitude of 10 000 metres.* **2** [C, usually pl.] a place that is high above sea level: *You need to carry oxygen when you are climbing at high altitudes.*

alto /'æltəʊ/ *noun* [C] (*pl.* **altos**) (MUSIC) the lowest normal singing voice for a woman, the highest for a man; a woman or man with this voice

altogether /ˌɔ:ltə'geðə(r)/ *adv.* **1** completely: *I don't altogether agree with you.* ◇ *At the age of 55 he stopped working altogether.* ◇ *This time the situation is altogether different.* **2** including everything; in total: *How much money will I need altogether?* ◇ *Altogether there were six of us.* **3** when you consider everything; generally: *Altogether, this town is a pleasant place to live.*

altostratus /ˌæltəʊˈstrɑːtəs; -ˈstreɪtəs/ **noun** [U] (GEOGRAPHY) a layer of cloud of equal thickness that is formed at a height of between 2 and 7 kilometres ➲ picture at **cloud**

altruism /ˈæltruɪzəm/ **noun** [U] (SOCIAL STUDIES) (*formal*) the fact of caring about the needs and happiness of other people more than your own ▸ **altruistic** /ˌæltruˈɪstɪk/ **adj.**: *altruistic behaviour*

aluminium /ˌæləˈmɪniəm/ (*AmE* **aluminum** /əˈluːmɪnəm/) (*symbol* **Al**) **noun** [U] (CHEMISTRY) a light silver-coloured metal that is used for making cooking equipment, etc.: *aluminium foil* ❶ For more information on the periodic table of elements, look at pages R34-5.

alumna /əˈlʌmnə/ **noun** [C] (*pl.* **alumnae** /-niː/) (*especially AmE, formal*) (EDUCATION) a former female student of a school, college or university

alumnus /əˈlʌmnəs/ **noun** [C] (*pl.* **alumni** /-naɪ/) (*especially AmE, formal*) (EDUCATION) a former male student of a school, college or university

alveolus /ælˈviːələs/ (*BrE also* /ˌælviˈəʊləs/) **noun** [C] (*pl.* **alveoli** /ælˈviːəlaɪ; -liː/ (*BrE also* /ˌælviˈəʊlaɪ; -liː/) (ANATOMY) one of the many small spaces in each lung where gases can pass into or out of the blood ➲ picture at **lung**

always ⊷ /ˈɔːlweɪz/ **adv.** **1** at all times; regularly: *I always get up at 6.30.* ◇ *Why is the train always late when I'm in a hurry?* **2** all through the past until now: *Tony has always been shy.* **3** for ever: *I shall always remember this moment.* **4** (only used with continuous tenses) again and again, usually in an annoying way: *She's always complaining about something.* **5** used with 'can' or 'could' for suggesting sth that sb could do, especially if nothing else is possible: *If you haven't got enough money, I could always lend you some.*

Alzheimer's disease /ˈæltshaɪməz dɪziːz/ **noun** [sing.] (HEALTH) a disease that affects the brain and makes some people become more and more confused as they get older

AM /ˌeɪ ˈem/ (PHYSICS) **amplitude modulation**; one of the main methods of broadcasting sound by radio

a.m. ⊷ /ˌeɪ ˈem/ **abbr.** (*AmE* A.M.) before midday: *10 a.m. (= 10 o'clock in the morning)*

am → BE[1]

amalgam /əˈmælgəm/ **noun** **1** [C, usually sing.] (*formal*) a mixture or combination of things **2** [U] (CHEMISTRY, HEALTH) a mixture of MERCURY (= a heavy silver-coloured metal) and another metal, used especially to fill holes in teeth

amalgamate /əˈmælgəmeɪt/ **verb** [I,T] (BUSINESS) (used especially about organizations, groups, etc.) to join together to form a single organization, group, etc. ▸ **amalgamation** /əˌmælgəˈmeɪʃn/ **noun** [C,U]

amass /əˈmæs/ **verb** [T] to collect or put together a large quantity of sth SYN **accumulate**: *We've amassed a lot of information on the subject.* ➲ note at **collect**[1]

amateur[1] /ˈæmətə(r)/ **noun** [C] **1** (SPORT) a person who takes part in a sport or an activity for pleasure, not for money as a job OPP **professional 2** (usually used when being critical) a person who does not have skill or experience when doing sth

amateur[2] /ˈæmətə(r)/ **adj.** **1** done, or doing sth, for pleasure (not for money as a job): *an amateur production of a play* ◇ *an amateur photographer* OPP **professional 2** (*also* **amateurish** /-rɪʃ/) done without skill or experience: *The painting was an amateurish fake.*

ˌamateur draˈmatics **noun** [U] (*BrE*) (ARTS AND MEDIA) the activity of producing and acting in plays for the theatre by people who do it as a hobby, not as a job

amaze ⊷ /əˈmeɪz/ **verb** [T] to surprise sb very much; to be difficult for sb to believe: *Sometimes your behaviour amazes me!* ◇ *It amazes me that anyone could be so stupid!*

amazed ⊷ /əˈmeɪzd/ **adj.** ~ (**at/by sb/sth**); ~ (**to do sth/that...**) very surprised: *I was amazed by the change in his attitude.* ◇ *She was amazed to discover the truth about her husband.*

amazement /əˈmeɪzmənt/ **noun** [U] a feeling of great surprise: *He looked at me **in amazement**.* ◇ ***To my amazement**, I passed the test easily.*

amazing ⊷ /əˈmeɪzɪŋ/ **adj.** very surprising and difficult to believe SYN **incredible**: *She has shown amazing courage.* ◇ *I've got an amazing story to tell you.* ▸ **amazingly** **adv.**

ambassador /æmˈbæsədə(r)/ **noun** [C] (POLITICS) an important person who represents their country in a foreign country: *the Spanish Ambassador to Britain* ❶ An ambassador lives and works in an **embassy**. ➲ Look also at **consul**.

amber /ˈæmbə(r)/ **noun** [U] **1** a hard clear yellow-brown substance used for making jewellery or objects for decoration **2** a yellow-brown colour: *The three colours in traffic lights are red, amber and green.* ▸ **amber** **adj.**

ambi- /ˈæmbi/ **prefix** (in nouns, adjectives and adverbs) referring to both of two: *ambivalent*

ambidextrous /ˌæmbiˈdekstrəs/ **adj.** able to use the left hand and the right hand equally well

ambience (*also* **ambiance**) /ˈæmbiəns/ **noun** [sing.] the character and atmosphere of a place

ambient /ˈæmbiənt/ **adj.** (only *before* a noun) **1** (TECHNICAL) relating to the surrounding area; on all sides: *ambient temperature/conditions* **2** (used especially about music) creating a relaxed atmosphere: *ambient music/lighting*

ambiguity AW /ˌæmbɪˈgjuːəti/ **noun** [C,U] (*pl.* **ambiguities**) the possibility of being understood in more than one way; sth that can be understood in more than one way

ambiguous AW /æmˈbɪgjuəs/ **adj.** having more than one possible meaning ▸ **ambiguously** **adv.**

ambition ⊷ /æmˈbɪʃn/ **noun** **1** [C] ~ (**to do/be sth**); ~ (**of doing sth**) something that you very much want to have or do: *It has always been her ambition to travel the world.* ◇ *He finally **achieved** his **ambition** of becoming a doctor.* **2** [U] a strong desire to be successful, to have power, etc.: *One problem of young people today is their lack of ambition.*

ambitious /æmˈbɪʃəs/ **adj.** **1** ~ (**to be/do sth**) having a strong desire to be successful, to have power, etc.: *I'm not particularly ambitious – I'm content with my life the way it is.* ◇ *We are ambitious to succeed.* **2** difficult to achieve or do because it takes a lot of work or effort: *The company have announced ambitious plans for expansion.*

ambivalent /æmˈbɪvələnt/ **adj.** having or showing a mixture of feelings or opinions about sth or sb ▸ **ambivalence** **noun** [C,U]

amble /ˈæmbl/ **verb** [I] to walk at a slow relaxed speed SYN **stroll**: *We ambled down to the beach.*

ambulance 🔑 /'æmbjələns/ ***noun*** [C] a special vehicle for taking ill or injured people to and from hospital

ambush /'æmbʊʃ/ ***noun*** [C,U] a surprise attack from a hidden position: *He was killed in an enemy ambush.* ◇ *The robbers were waiting* ***in ambush****.* ▶ **ambush** ***verb*** [T]

ameba (*AmE*) = AMOEBA

ameliorate /ə'mi:liəreɪt/ ***verb*** [T] (*formal*) to make sth better: *Steps have been taken to ameliorate the situation.*

amen /ɑ:'men; eɪ'men/ ***exclamation*** (**RELIGION**) a word used at the end of prayers by Christians and Jews

amenable /ə'mi:nəbl/ ***adj.*** happy to accept sth: *I'm amenable to any suggestions you may have.*

amend AW /ə'mend/ ***verb*** [T] (**LAW, POLITICS**) to change a law, document, statement, etc. slightly in order to correct a mistake or to improve it: *He asked to see the amended version.*

amendment AW /ə'mendmənt/ ***noun*** **1** [C,U] (**LAW**) a small change or improvement that is made to a law or a document; the process of changing a law or a document **2 Amendment** (**POLITICS**) a statement of a change to the CONSTITUTION of the US: *The 19th Amendment gave women the right to vote.*

amends /ə'mendz/ ***noun*** [pl.]
IDM **make amends** to do sth for sb, that shows that you are sorry for sth bad that you have done before

amenity /ə'mi:nəti/ ***noun*** [C] (*pl.* **amenities**) something that makes a place pleasant or easy to live in: *Among the town's amenities are two cinemas and a sports centre.*

Amerasian /ˌæmə'reɪʃn/ ***noun*** [C] a person with one American and one Asian parent ▶ **Amerasian** ***adj.***

American /ə'merɪkən/ ***adj.*** from or connected with the US: *Have you met Bob? He's American.* ◇ *an American accent* ▶ **American** ***noun*** [C]: *Millions of Americans visit Britain each year.*

Aˌmerican 'football (*AmE* **football**) ***noun*** [U] (**SPORT**) a game played in the US by two teams of eleven players with a ball that is not round. The players wear HELMETS (= hard hats) and other protective clothing and try to carry the ball to the end of the field.

Aˌmerican 'Indian = NATIVE AMERICAN

Americanism /ə'merɪkənɪzəm/ ***noun*** [C] (**LANGUAGE**) a word, phrase or spelling that is typical of American English, used in another variety of English

Americanize (also **-ise**) /ə'merɪkənaɪz/ ***verb*** [T] to make sb/sth American in character

americium /ˌæmə'rɪsiəm; -'rɪʃi-/ ***noun*** [U] (*symbol* **Am**) (**CHEMISTRY**) a chemical element. **Americium** is a RADIOACTIVE metal. ❶ For more information on the periodic table of elements, look at pages R34-5.

amethyst /'æməθɪst/ ***noun*** [C,U] a purple precious stone, used in making jewellery

amiable /'eɪmiəbl/ ***adj.*** friendly and pleasant ▶ **amiably** /-əbli/ ***adv.***

amicable /'æmɪkəbl/ ***adj.*** made or done in a friendly way, without argument ▶ **amicably** /-əbli/ ***adv.***

amid /ə'mɪd/ (*also* **amidst** /ə'mɪdst/) ***prep.*** (*written*) in the middle of; among

amino acid /əˌmi:nəʊ 'æsɪd/ ***noun*** [C] (**BIOLOGY**) any of the substances that are found in animals and plants and that combine to form a PROTEIN that is necessary for a healthy body and for growth

amir – EMIR

amiss /ə'mɪs/ ***adj., adv.*** wrong; not as it should be: *When I walked into the room I could sense that something was amiss.*
IDM **not come/go amiss** to be useful or pleasant: *Things are fine, although a bit more money wouldn't come amiss.*
take sth amiss to be upset by sth, perhaps because you have understood it in the wrong way: *Please don't take my remarks amiss.*

ammeter /'æmi:tə(r)/ ***noun*** [C] (**PHYSICS**) an instrument for measuring the strength of an electric current

ammonia /ə'məʊniə/ ***noun*** [U] (*symbol* NH_3) (**CHEMISTRY**) a colourless gas with a strong smell; a clear liquid containing **ammonia** used for cleaning

ammonite /'æmənaɪt/ ***noun*** [C] (**GEOLOGY**) a type of FOSSIL (= an animal that lived thousands of years ago which has turned into rock)

ammonium /ə'məʊniəm/ ***noun*** [sing.] (*symbol* NH_4) (**CHEMISTRY**) a chemical substance with a positive electrical charge that is found in liquids and salts that contain AMMONIA

ammunition /ˌæmju'nɪʃn/ ***noun*** [U] **1** the supply of bullets, etc. that you need to fire from a weapon: *The troops surrendered because they had run out of ammunition.* **2** facts or information that can be used against sb/sth

amnesia /æm'ni:ziə/ ***noun*** [U] (**HEALTH**) a medical condition in which sb partly or completely loses their memory

amnesty /'æmnəsti/ ***noun*** [C] (*pl.* **amnesties**) **1** (**POLITICS**) a time when a government forgives political crimes **2** (**LAW**) a time when people can give in illegal weapons without being arrested

ˌAmnesty Inter'national ***noun*** [sing.] (**POLITICS**) an international human rights organization that works to help people who have been put in prison for their beliefs or race and not because they have committed a crime. It also works to prevent TORTURE (= the action of causing sb great pain either as a punishment or to make them say or do sth)

amniocentesis /ˌæmniəʊsen'ti:sɪs/ ***noun*** [U, sing.] (**HEALTH**) a medical test in which some liquid is taken from a pregnant woman's WOMB (= the part where a baby grows before it is born) to find out if the baby has particular illnesses or health problems

amnion ***noun*** [C] (**BIOLOGY**) the thin skin that is around a baby when it is inside its mother's body and filled with AMNIOTIC FLUID ➲ picture at **fertilization**

amniotic fluid /ˌæmniɒtɪk 'flu:ɪd/ ***noun*** [U] (**BIOLOGY**) the liquid that is around a baby when it is inside its mother's body ➲ picture at **embryo**

amoeba (*AmE* **ameba**) /ə'mi:bə/ ***noun*** [C] (*pl.* **amoebas** or **amoebae** /-bi:/) (**BIOLOGY**) a very small living creature that consists of only one cell

amoeba

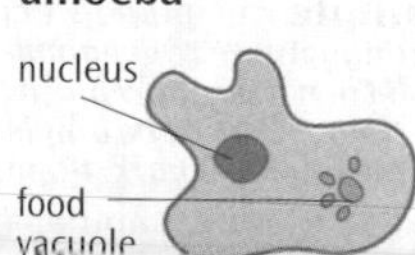

amok /ə'mɒk/ ***adv.***
IDM **run amok** to suddenly start behaving

violently, especially in a public place: *Football fans ran amok in the centre of Brussels last night.*

among 🔑 /ə'mʌŋ/ (*also* **amongst** /ə'mʌŋst/) ***prep.* 1** surrounded by; in the middle of: *I often feel nervous when I'm among strangers.* ◇ *I found the missing letter amongst a heap of old newspapers.* **2** in or concerning a particular group of people or things: *Discuss it* ***amongst yourselves*** *and let me know your decision.* ◇ *There is a lot of anger among students about the new law.* ◇ ***Among other things****, the drug can cause headaches and sweating.* **3** to each one (of a group): *On his death, his money will be divided among his children.*

amoral /ˌeɪ'mɒrəl/ ***adj.*** (used about people or their behaviour) not following any moral rules; not caring about right or wrong ➲ look at **moral**, **immoral**

amorous /'æmərəs/ ***adj.*** showing sexual desire and love for sb: *She rejected his amorous advances.* ▶ **amorously** ***adv.***

amorphous /ə'mɔːfəs/ ***adj.*** (*formal*) having no definite shape, form or structure: *an amorphous mass of cells with no identity at all*

amount[1] 🔑 /ə'maʊnt/ ***noun*** [C] **1** the amount of sth is how much of it there is; a quantity of sth: *I spent an enormous amount of time preparing for the exam.* ◇ *I have a certain amount of sympathy with her.* ◇ *a large amount of money* **2** a total or sum of money: *You are requested to pay the full amount within seven days.*

amount[2] 🔑 /ə'maʊnt/ ***verb***

PHR V **amount to sth 1** to add up to sth; to make sth as a total: *The cost of the repairs amounted to £5 000.* **2** to be equal to or the same as sth: *Whether I tell her today or tomorrow, it amounts to the same thing.*

amp /æmp/ ***noun*** [C] **1** (also *formal* **ampere** /'æmpeə(r)/) (*abbr.* **A**) (**PHYSICS**) a unit for measuring electric current: *a 13 amp fuse/plug* **2** (**MUSIC**) (*informal*) = AMPLIFIER

ampersand /'æmpəsænd/ ***noun*** [C] (*symbol* **&**) (**LANGUAGE**) the symbol used to mean 'and'

amphetamine /æm'fetəmiːn/ ***noun*** [C,U] (**HEALTH**) a drug that makes you feel excited and full of energy. **Amphetamines** are sometimes taken illegally.

amphibian /æm'fɪbiən/ ***noun*** [C] (**BIOLOGY**) an animal that can live both on land and in water: *frogs, toads and other amphibians* ➲ picture on **page 29**

amphibious /æm'fɪbiəs/ ***adj.*** able to live or be used both on land and in water: *Frogs are amphibious.* ◇ *amphibious vehicles*

amphitheatre (*AmE* **amphitheater**) /'æmfɪθɪətə(r)/ ***noun*** [C] (**ARCHITECTURE**, **HISTORY**) a circular building without a roof and with rows of seats that rise in steps around an open space. **Amphitheatres** were used in ancient Greece and Rome.

amphora /'æmfərə/ ***noun*** [C] (*pl.* **amphorae** /'æmfəriː/ or **amphoras**) (**HISTORY**) a tall ancient Greek or Roman container with two handles and a narrow neck

ample /'æmpl/ ***adj.* 1** enough or more than enough: *We've got ample time to make a decision.* ◇ *I'm not sure how much the trip will cost, but I should think £500 will be ample.* **2** large: *There is space for an ample car park.* ▶ **amply** /'æmpli/ ***adv.***

amplifier /'æmplɪfaɪə(r)/ (also *informal* **amp**) ***noun*** [C] an electrical device or piece of equipment that makes sounds or radio signals louder

amplify /'æmplɪfaɪ/ ***verb*** (*pres. part.* **amplifying**; *3rd person sing. pres.* **amplifies**; *pt, pp* **amplified**) **1** [T] to increase the strength of a sound, using electrical equipment: *to amplify a guitar/an electric current/a signal* **2** [I,T] (*formal*) to add details to a story, statement, etc. in order to explain it more fully ▶ **amplification** /ˌæmplɪfɪ'keɪʃn/ ***noun*** [U]

amplitude

loud sound

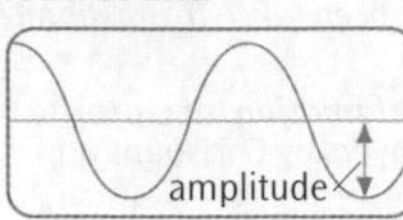

quiet sound

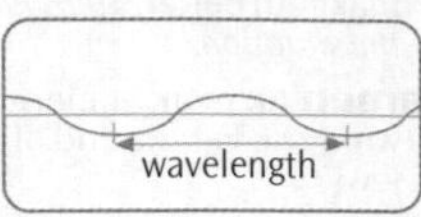

amplitude /'æmplɪtjuːd/ ***noun*** [U, C] (**PHYSICS**) the greatest distance that a wave, especially a sound or radio wave, moves up and down

ampoule /'æmpuːl/ ***noun*** [C] (**HEALTH**) a small container, usually made of glass, containing a drug that will be INJECTED into sb (= put into sb's body through a thin needle)

amputate /'æmpjuteɪt/ ***verb*** [I,T] (**HEALTH**) to cut off a person's arm, leg, etc. for medical reasons ▶ **amputation** /ˌæmpju'teɪʃn/ ***noun*** [C,U]

amputee /ˌæmpju'tiː/ ***noun*** [C] (**HEALTH**) a person who has had an arm or a leg AMPUTATED (= cut off)

amulet /'æmjʊlət/ ***noun*** [C] a piece of jewellery that some people wear because they think it protects them from bad luck, illness, etc.

amuse 🔑 /ə'mjuːz/ ***verb*** [T] **1** to make sb laugh or smile; to seem funny to sb: *Everybody laughed but I couldn't understand what had amused them.* **2** to make time pass pleasantly for sb; to stop sb from getting bored: *I did some crosswords to amuse myself on the journey.* ◇ *I've brought a few toys to amuse the children.*

amused 🔑 /ə'mjuːzd/ ***adj.*** thinking that sth is funny and wanting to laugh or smile: *I was amused to hear his account of what happened.*

IDM **keep sb/yourself amused** to do sth in order to pass time pleasantly and stop sb/yourself getting bored

amusement /ə'mjuːzmənt/ ***noun* 1** [U] the feeling caused by sth that makes you laugh or smile, or by sth that entertains you: *Much to the pupils' amusement, the teacher fell off his chair.* **2** [C] something that makes time pass pleasantly; an entertainment: *The holiday centre offers a wide range of amusements, including golf and tennis.*

a'musement arcade ***noun*** [C] a place where you can play games on machines which you use coins to operate

a'musement park ***noun*** [C] (**TOURISM**) a large park which has a lot of things that you can ride and play on and many different activities to enjoy

amusing 🔑 /ə'mjuːzɪŋ/ ***adj.*** causing you to laugh or smile: *He's a very amusing person.* ◇ *The story was quite amusing.*

amylase /'æmɪleɪz/ ***noun*** [U] (**BIOLOGY**) an ENZYME (= a substance that helps a chemical change take place) that allows the body to change some substances into simple sugars

an 🔑 → A[2]

anabolic steroid /ˌænəbɒlɪk 'sterɔɪd/ ***noun*** [C] (**CHEMISTRY**) a chemical substance that increases the size of the muscles. It is sometimes taken illegally by people who play sports. ➲ look at **steroid**

anachronism /ə'nækrənɪzəm/ *noun* [C] **1** a person, a custom, etc. that seems old-fashioned and does not belong in the present **2** something that does not belong in the period of history in which it appears, for example in a book or a film: *The movie, which is set in Ancient Rome, is full of anachronisms and inaccuracies.* ▶ **anachronistic** /əˌnækrə'nɪstɪk/ *adj.*

anaemia (*AmE* **anemia**) /ə'ni:miə/ *noun* [U] (HEALTH) a medical condition in which there are not enough red cells in the blood ▶ **anaemic** (*AmE* **anemic**) /ə'ni:mɪk/ *adj.*

anaerobic /ˌæneə'rəʊbɪk/ *adj.* **1** (BIOLOGY) not needing OXYGEN (= the gas that people and animals need in order to live): *anaerobic bacteria* ➲ picture at **respiration** **2** (SPORT) (used about physical exercise) not especially designed to improve the function of the heart and lungs OPP **aerobic**

anaesthesia (*AmE* **anesthesia**) /ˌænəs'θi:ziə/ *noun* [U] (HEALTH) the use of drugs that make you unable to feel pain during medical operations

anaesthetic (*AmE* **anesthetic**) /ˌænəs'θetɪk/ *noun* [C,U] (HEALTH) a substance that stops you feeling pain, for example when a doctor is performing a medical operation on you: *You'll need to be* ***under anaesthetic*** *for the operation.* ◇ *The dentist gave me a* ***local anaesthetic*** (= one that only affects part of the body and does not make you unconscious). ◇ *Did you have a* ***general anaesthetic*** (= one that makes you unconscious) *for your operation?*

anaesthetist (*AmE* **anesthetist**) /ə'ni:sθətɪst/ *noun* [C] (HEALTH) a person with the medical training necessary to give an ANAESTHETIC to patients

anaesthetize (also -ise; *AmE* **anesthetize**) /ə'ni:sθətaɪz/ *verb* [T] (HEALTH) to make a person unable to feel pain, etc., especially by giving them an ANAESTHETIC

anagram /'ænəgræm/ *noun* [C] (LANGUAGE) a word or phrase that is made by arranging the letters of another word or phrase in a different order: *'Worth' is an anagram of 'throw'.*

anal /'eɪnl/ → ANUS

analgesia /ˌænəl'dʒi:ziə/ *noun* [U] (HEALTH) the loss of the ability to feel pain while still conscious; medicine that makes you unable to feel pain

analgesic /ˌænəl'dʒi:zɪk/ *noun* [C] (HEALTH) a substance that reduces pain ▶ **analgesic** *adj.*

analogous AW /ə'næləgəs/ *adj.* (*formal*) ~ **(to/with sth)** similar in some way; that you can compare

analogue (*AmE* **analog**) /'ænəlɒg/ *adj.* **1** (TECHNICAL) (used about an electronic process) using a continuously changing range of physical quantities to measure or store data: *an analogue circuit/computer/signal* **2** (used about a clock or watch) showing information using hands that move around a DIAL (= twelve numbers or marks arranged in a circle) ➲ look at **digital**

analogy AW /ə'nælədʒi/ *noun* [C] (*pl.* **analogies**) **an ~ (between A and B)** a comparison between two things that shows a way in which they are similar: *You could make an analogy between the human body and a car engine.*

IDM **by analogy** by comparing sth to sth else and showing how they are similar

analyse 🔑 AW (*AmE* analyze) /'ænəlaɪz/ *verb* [T] to look at or think about the different parts or details of sth carefully in order to understand or explain it. *The water samples are now being analysed in a laboratory.* ◇ *to analyse statistics* ◇ *She analysed the situation and then decided what to do.*

analysis 🔑 AW /ə'næləsɪs/ *noun* (*pl.* **analyses** /-si:z/) **1** [C,U] the careful examination of the different parts or details of sth: *Some samples of the water were sent to a laboratory* ***for analysis.*** **2** [C] the result of a careful examination of sth: *Your analysis of the situation is different from mine.*

analyst AW /'ænəlɪst/ *noun* [C] a person whose job is to examine sth carefully as an expert: *a food analyst* ◇ *a political analyst*

analytical AW /ˌænə'lɪtɪkl/ (*also* **analytic** /ˌænə'lɪtɪk/) *adj.* **1** using a logical method of thinking about sth in order to understand it, especially by looking at all the parts separately: *She has a clear analytical mind.* **2** using scientific analysis in order to find out about sth: *analytical methods of research* ▶ **analytically** AW /-kli/ *adv.*

anarchism /'ænəkɪzəm/ *noun* [U] (POLITICS) the political belief that there should be no government or laws in a country ▶ **anarchist** *noun* [C]

anarchy /'ænəki/ *noun* [U] (POLITICS) a situation in a country, an organization, etc. in which there is no government, order or control: *The overthrow of the military regime was followed by a period of anarchy.* ▶ **anarchic** /ə'nɑ:kɪk/**anarchical** /-kl/ *adj.*

anathema /ə'næθəmə/ *noun* [U, C, usually sing.] (*formal*) a thing or an idea which you hate because it is the opposite of what you believe: *Racial prejudice is (an) anathema to me.*

anatomist /ə'nætəmɪst/ *noun* [C] a scientist who studies ANATOMY

anatomy /ə'nætəmi/ *noun* (*pl.* **anatomies**) (BIOLOGY) **1** [U] the scientific study of the structure of human or animal bodies **2** [C] the structure of a living thing: *the anatomy of the frog* ▶ **anatomical** /ˌænə'tɒmɪkl/ *adj.*

ancestor /'ænsestə(r)/ *noun* [C] (HISTORY) a person in your family who lived a long time before you: *My ancestors settled in this country a hundred years ago.* ➲ look at **descendant** SYN **forebear** ▶ **ancestral** /æn'sestrəl/ *adj.*: *her ancestral home* (= that had belonged to her ancestors)

ancestry /'ænsestri/ *noun* [C,U] (*pl.* **ancestries**) all of a person's ANCESTORS: *He is* ***of*** *Irish* ***ancestry.***

anchor¹ /'æŋkə(r)/ *noun* [C] **1** a heavy metal object at the end of a chain that you drop into the water from a boat in order to stop the boat moving **2** (*especially AmE*) = ANCHORMAN, ANCHORWOMAN

anchor² /'æŋkə(r)/ *verb* **1** [I,T] to drop an **anchor** down from a boat or a ship to prevent it from moving away: *They anchored off the coast of Spain.* **2** [T] to fix sth firmly so that it cannot move

anchorage /'æŋkərɪdʒ/ *noun* [C,U] **1** a place where boats or ships can ANCHOR **2** a place where sth can be fastened to sth else: *anchorage points for a baby's car seat*

anchorman /'æŋkəmæn/ **anchorwoman** /'æŋkəwʊmən/ *noun* [C] (*pl.* **-men** /-men/) (*pl.* **-women** /-wɪmɪn/) (*especially AmE* **anchor**) (ARTS AND MEDIA) a person who presents a radio or television programme and introduces reports by other people

anchovy /'æntʃəvi/ *noun* [C,U] (*pl.* **anchovies**) a small fish with a strong salty flavour

ancient 🔑 /'eɪnʃənt/ *adj.* **1** (HISTORY) belonging to a period of history that is thousands of years in the past: *ancient history/civilization* ◇ *the ancient world* ◇ *ancient Rome/Greece* **2** very old: *I can't believe he's only 30 – he looks ancient!*

The animal kingdom
birds
beak/bill
wing
tail
claw
webbed foot
talons
finch
crest
feather
egg
nest
poultry and game
pheasant
duck
turkey
chicken
birds of prey
carrion
eagle
vulture
owl
seabirds
gull
albatross
puffin
mammals
coat
mane
muzzle
tail
snout
paw
claw
lion
whisker
antlers
horn
hooves
cetacean
blowhole
whale
tusk
trunk
fish
tail
dorsal fin
ventral fin
scales
gill
trout
bat
primates
prehensile tail
chimpanzee (also chimp)
monkey
rodents
squirrel
beaver
marsupials
eucalyptus tree
joey
pouch
koala
kangaroo

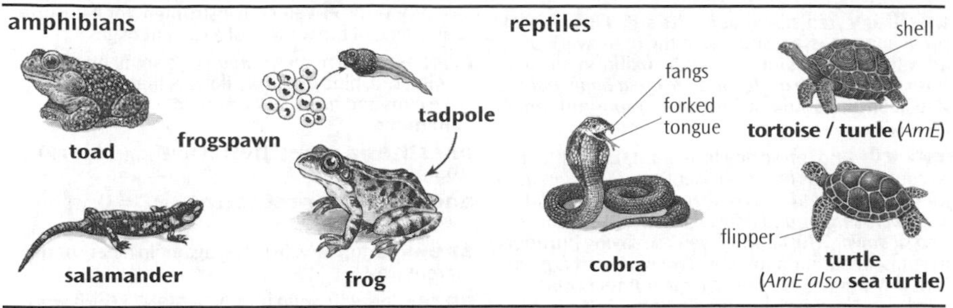

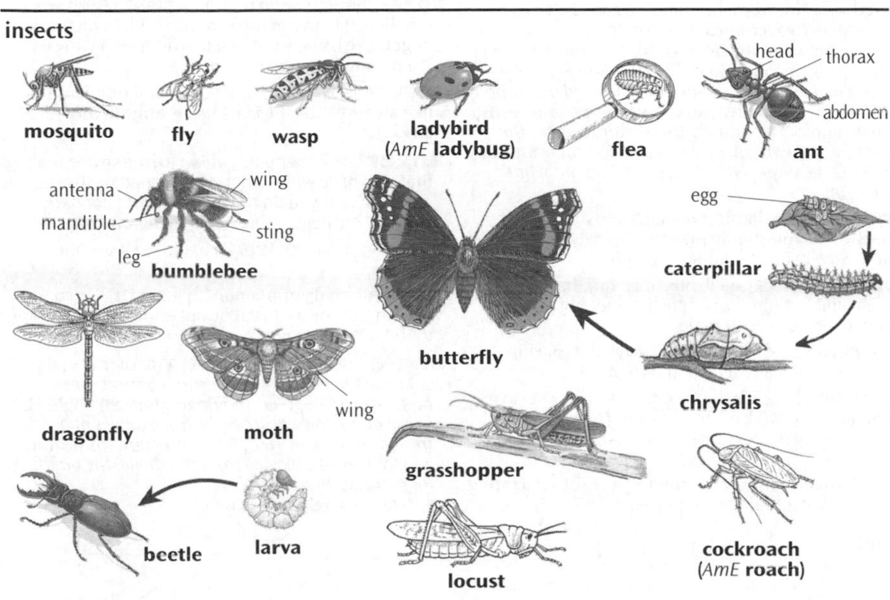

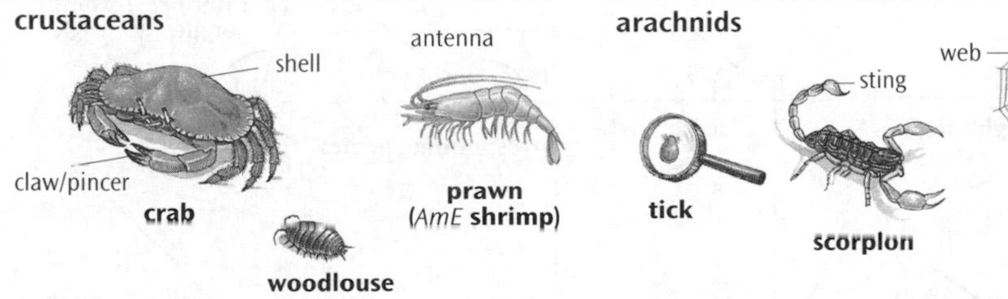

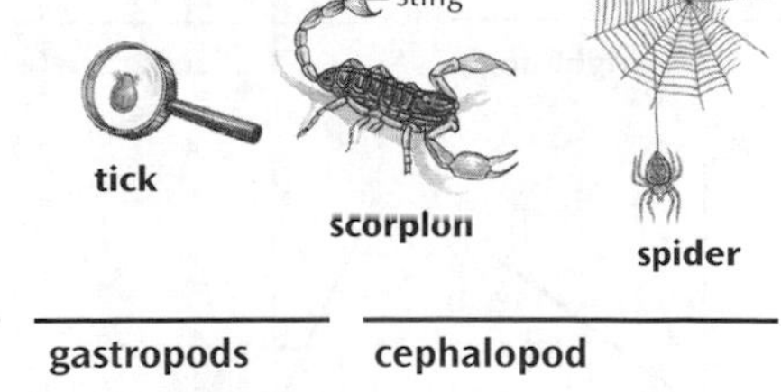

Taxonomy
Living things are grouped on the basis of their similarities and differences into smaller and smaller groups. This scientific process of classification is called **taxonomy**. The main groups, from the largest to the smallest, are:

- **kingdom** (animal or plant)
- **phylum** (*plural* **phyla**) (e.g. mollusc, arthropod)
- **class** (e.g. mammal, gastropod)
- **order** (e.g. primate, marsupial)
- **family**
- **genus** (*plural* **genera**)
- **species**

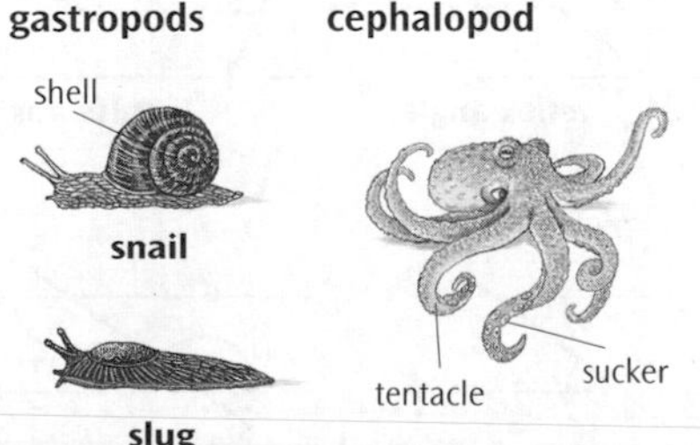

ancillary /æn'sɪləri/ *adj.* ~ (to sth) **1** (BUSINESS) providing necessary support to the main work or activities of an organization SYN **auxiliary**: *Ancillary hospital staff such as cleaners are often badly paid.* **2** in addition to sth else but not as important: *ancillary rights*

and ⊶ /ənd; ən strong form ænd/ *conj.* **1** (used to connect words or parts of sentences) also; in addition to: *a boy and a girl* ◇ *Do it slowly and carefully.* ◇ *We were singing and dancing all evening.* ◇ *Come in and sit down.* **2** (used when you are saying numbers in sums) in addition to; plus: *Twelve and six is eighteen.* ❶ When you are saying large numbers *and* is used after the word 'hundred': *We say 2 264 as two thousand, two hundred and sixty-four.*
3 used between repeated words to show that sth is increasing or continuing: *The situation is getting worse and worse.* ◇ *I shouted and shouted but nobody answered.* **4** used instead of 'to' after certain verbs, for example 'go', 'come', 'try': *Go and answer the door for me, will you?* ◇ *Why don't you come and stay with us one weekend?* ◇ *I'll try and find out what's going on.*

andante /æn'dænteɪ/ *noun* [C] (MUSIC) a piece of music that you should play fairly slowly ▶ **andante** *adj.*, *adv.* ➲ look at **adagio**, **allegro**

androgynous /æn'drɒdʒənəs/ *adj.* having both male and female characteristics; looking neither very male nor very female

android /'ændrɔɪd/ *noun* [C] a type of machine that looks like a real person SYN **robot**

anecdotal /ˌænɪk'dəʊtl/ *adj.* based on ANECDOTES and possibly not true or accurate: *The newspaper's 'monster shark' story was based on anecdotal evidence.*

anecdote /'ænɪkdəʊt/ *noun* [C] a short interesting story about a real person or event

anemia, anemic (*AmE*) = ANAEMIA, ANAEMIC

anemometer /ænɪ'mɒmɪtə(r)/ *noun* [C] (GEOGRAPHY, PHYSICS) an instrument for measuring the speed of the wind or of a current of gas

anemone /ə'neməni/ *noun* [C] a small plant with white, red, blue or purple flowers that are shaped like cups and have dark centres ➲ look at **sea anemone**

anesthesia, anesthetic (*AmE*) = ANAESTHESIA, ANAESTHETIC

anesthetist, anesthetize (*AmE*) = ANAESTHETIST, ANAESTHETIZE

anew /ə'nju:/ *adv.* (*written*) again; in a new or different way

angel /'eɪndʒl/ *noun* [C] **1** (RELIGION) a spirit who is believed to live in heaven with God. In pictures **angels** are usually dressed in white, with wings. **2** a person who is very kind

angelic /æn'dʒelɪk/ *adj.* good, kind or beautiful; like an ANGEL: *an angelic smile* ▶ **angelically** /-kli/ *adv.*

anger¹ ⊶ /'æŋgə(r)/ *noun* [U] the strong feeling that you have when sth has happened or sb has done sth that you do not like: *He could not hide his anger at the news.* ◇ *She was shaking with anger.*

anger² /'æŋgə(r)/ *verb* [T] to make sb become angry

angina /æn'dʒaɪnə/ *noun* [U] (HEALTH) very bad pain in the chest caused by not enough blood going to the heart during exercise

angle¹ ⊶ /'æŋgl/ *noun* [C] **1** (GEOMETRY) the space between two lines or surfaces that meet, measured in degrees: *a **right angle*** (= an angle of 90°) ◇ *at an angle of 40°* ◇ *The three angles of a triangle add up to 180°.* **2** the direction from which you look at sth: *Viewed from this angle, the building looks bigger than it really is.*
IDM **at an angle** not straight

angles

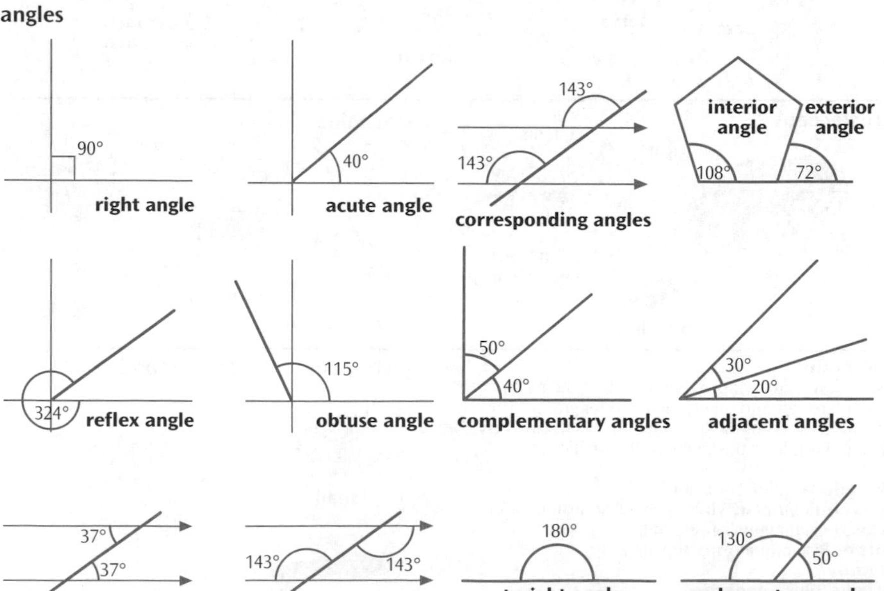

angle² /'æŋgl/ *verb* **1** [I,T] to put sth in a position that is not straight; to be in this position: *Angle the lamp towards the desk.* **2** [T] ~ **sth (at/to/towards sb)** to show sth from a particular point of view; to aim sth at a particular person or group: *The new magazine is angled at young professional people.*
PHR V **angle for sth** to try to make sb give you sth, without asking for it in a direct way: *She was angling for an invitation to our party.*

angler /'æŋglə(r)/ *noun* [C] a person who catches fish as a hobby ➲ look at **fisherman**

Anglican /'æŋglɪkən/ *noun* [C] (RELIGION) a member of the Church of England or of a related church in another English-speaking country ▶ **Anglican** *adj.*

Anglicism /'æŋglɪsɪzm/ *noun* [C] (LANGUAGE) a word, phrase or spelling that is typical of British English, used in another variety of English or another language

anglicize (also **-ise**) /'æŋglɪsaɪz/ *verb* [T] (LANGUAGE) to make sb/sth English in character: *Gutmann anglicized his name to Goodman.*

angling /'æŋglɪŋ/ *noun* [U] (SPORT) the art or sport of catching fish with a **fishing rod**, usually in rivers and lakes rather than in the sea: *He* ***goes angling*** *at weekends.* ➲ look at **fishing**

Anglo- /'æŋgləʊ/ (in compounds) connected with England or Britain (and another country or countries): *Anglo-American relations*

anglophone /'æŋgləʊfəʊn/ *noun* [C] (LANGUAGE) a person who speaks English, especially in countries where English is not the only language spoken ▶ **anglophone** *adj.*: *anglophone communities*

Anglo-Saxon /,æŋgləʊ 'sæksn/ *noun* **1** [C] (SOCIAL STUDIES) a person whose family originally came from England **2** [C] (HISTORY) a person who lived in England before the Norman Conquest (1066) **3** (*also* **Old English**) [U] (LANGUAGE) the English language before about 1150 ▶ **Anglo-Saxon** *adj.*

angora /æŋ'gɔːrə/ *noun* [U] a type of soft wool or cloth

angry 🔑 /'æŋgri/ *adj.* (**angrier**; **angriest**) ~ **(with sb) (at/about sth)** feeling or showing anger: *Calm down, there's no need to get angry.* ◇ *My parents will be angry with me if I get home late.* ◇ *He's always getting angry about something.* ▶ **angrily** *adv.*

angst /æŋst/ *noun* [U] a feeling of worry about a situation or about your life: *songs full of teenage angst*

anguish /'æŋgwɪʃ/ *noun* [U] (*written*) great mental pain or suffering ▶ **anguished** *adj.*

angular /'æŋgjələ(r)/ *adj.* with sharp points or corners

animal 🔑 /'ænɪml/ *noun* [C] (BIOLOGY) **1** a living creature that is not a bird, a fish, a REPTILE, an insect or a human: *the animals and birds of South America* ◇ *a small furry animal* ◇ *farm animals* **2** any living thing that is not a plant or a human: *the animal kingdom* ◇ *This product has not been tested on animals.* **3** any living creature, including humans: *Humans are the only animals to have developed speech.*

animate¹ /'ænɪmeɪt/ *verb* [T] **1** to make sth have more life and energy: *Her enthusiasm animated the whole room.* **2** (usually passive) (ARTS AND MEDIA) to make a model, toy, etc. seem to move by taking a series of pictures of it in very slightly different positions and then showing the pictures as a continuous film

animate² /'ænɪmət/ *adj.* (*formal*) living; having life: *animate beings* OPP **inanimate**

animated /'ænɪmeɪtɪd/ *adj.* **1** interesting and full of energy: *an animated discussion* **2** (ARTS AND MEDIA) (used about films) using a process or method which makes pictures or models appear to move: *an animated cartoon*

animation /,ænɪ'meɪʃn/ *noun* **1** [U] the state of being full of energy and enthusiasm **2** [U] (ARTS AND MEDIA) the method of making films, computer games, etc. with pictures or models that appear to move: *computer animation* **3** [C] (ARTS AND MEDIA) a film in which drawings of people and animals seem to move: *The electronic dictionary includes some animations.*

animosity /,ænɪ'mɒsəti/ *noun* [U, C] (*pl.* **animosities**) ~ **(toward(s) sb/sth)**; ~ **(between A and B)** a strong feeling of anger and of not liking sb/sth: *There is still animosity between these two teams after last year's match.* SYN **hostility**

anion /'ænaɪən/ *noun* [C] (CHEMISTRY, PHYSICS) an ION with a negative electrical charge ➲ look at **cation**

anise /'ænɪs/ *noun* [U] a plant with seeds that smell sweet

aniseed /'ænəsiːd/ *noun* [U] the dried seeds of the ANISE plant that are used to give flavour to sweets and alcoholic drinks

ankle 🔑 /'æŋkl/ *noun* [C] the part of your body where your foot joins your leg: *The water only came up to my ankles.* ➲ picture on **page 80**

anklet /'æŋklət/ *noun* [C] a piece of jewellery worn around the ankle

annals /'ænlz/ *noun* [pl.] (HISTORY) an official record of events or activities year by year; historical records: *The battle went down* ***in the annals of*** *British* ***history***.

anneal /ə'niːl/ *verb* [T] (TECHNICAL) to heat metal or glass and allow it to cool slowly, in order to make it harder

annex /ə'neks/ *verb* [T] (POLITICS) to take control of another country or region by force SYN **occupy**: *Germany annexed Austria in 1938.* ▶ **annexation** /,ænek'seɪʃn/ *noun* [C,U]

annexe (*especially AmE* **annex**) /'æneks/ *noun* [C] a building that is joined to a larger one

annihilate /ə'naɪəleɪt/ *verb* [T] to destroy or defeat sb/sth completely ▶ **annihilation** /ə,naɪə'leɪʃn/ *noun* [U]

anniversary 🔑 /,ænɪ'vɜːsəri/ *noun* [C] (*pl.* **anniversaries**) a day that is exactly a year or a number of years after a special or important event: *the hundredth anniversary of the country's independence* ◇ *a wedding anniversary* ➲ look at **birthday**

annotate /'ænəteɪt/ *verb* [T] (LITERATURE) to add notes to a book or text, giving explanations or comments ▶ **annotated** *adj.* ▶ **annotation** /,ænə'teɪʃn/ *noun* [C,U]

announce 🔑 /ə'naʊns/ *verb* [T] **1** to make sth known publicly and officially: *They announced that our train had been delayed.* ◇ *The winners will be announced in next week's paper.* **2** to say sth in a firm or serious way: *She stormed into my office and announced that she was leaving.* ➲ note at **declare**

announcement /ə'naʊnsmənt/ *noun* **1** [C] a statement that tells people about sth: *Ladies and gentlemen, I'd like to* ***make an announcement***.

➲ note at **statement** **2** [U] an act of telling people about sth

announcer /ə'naʊnsə(r)/ ***noun*** [C] (ARTS AND MEDIA) a person who introduces or gives information about programmes on radio or television

annoy ⊶ /ə'nɔɪ/ ***verb*** [T] to make sb angry or slightly angry: *It really annoys me when you say things like that.* ◇ *Close the door if the noise is annoying you.*

annoyance /ə'nɔɪəns/ ***noun*** **1** [U] the feeling of being annoyed **2** [C] something that annoys sb

annoyed ⊶ /ə'nɔɪd/ ***adj.*** feeling angry or slightly angry: *I shall be extremely annoyed if he turns up late again.* ◇ *She's annoyed with herself for making such a stupid mistake.* ◇ *He's annoyed that nobody believes him.*

annoying ⊶ /ə'nɔɪɪŋ/ ***adj.*** making you feel angry or slightly angry: *It's so annoying that there's nobody here to answer questions.* ◇ *His most annoying habit is always arriving late.*

annual¹ ⊶ AW /'ænjuəl/ ***adj.*** **1** happening or done once a year or every year: *the company's annual report* ◇ *an annual festival* **2** relating to a period of one year: *a person's annual salary* ◇ *the annual sales figures* ◇ *annual rainfall*

annual² /'ænjuəl/ ***noun*** [C] **1** (LITERATURE) a book, especially one for children, that is published once each year: *a football annual* **2** (BIOLOGY) any plant that grows and dies within one year or season ➲ look at **biennial**, **perennial**

annually ⊶ /'ænjuəli/ ***adv.*** once a year: *The exhibition is held annually.*

annuity /ə'nju:əti/ ***noun*** [C] (*pl.* **annuities**) (FINANCE) a fixed amount of money that is paid to sb each year, usually for the rest of their life

annul /ə'nʌl/ ***verb*** [T] (*pres. part.* **annulling**; *pt, pp* **annulled**) (usually passive) (LAW) to state officially that sth is no longer legally valid or recognized: *Their marriage was annulled after just six months.* ▸ **annulment** ***noun*** [C, U]

anode /'ænəʊd/ ***noun*** [C] (PHYSICS, CHEMISTRY) an ELECTRODE in an electrical device; the positive ELECTRODE in an ELECTROLYTIC CELL and the negative ELECTRODE in a battery ➲ look at **cathode**

anoint /ə'nɔɪnt/ ***verb*** [T] **~ sb (with sth)** (RELIGION) to put oil or water on sb's head as part of a religious ceremony

anomalous /ə'nɒmələs/ ***adj.*** different from what is normal

anomaly /ə'nɒməli/ ***noun*** [C] (*pl.* **anomalies**) something that is different from what is normal or usual: *We discovered an anomaly in the sales figures for August.*

anon. /ə'nɒn/ ***abbr.*** (LITERATURE) **anonymous**; used to show that the writer's name is not known

anonymity /ˌænə'nɪməti/ ***noun*** [U] the situation where a person's name is not known

anonymous /ə'nɒnɪməs/ ***adj.*** **1** (used about a person) whose name is not known or made public: *An anonymous caller told the police that a robbery was being planned.* **2** (*abbr.* **anon.**) done, written, etc. by sb whose name is not known or made public: *He received an anonymous letter.* ▸ **anonymously** ***adv.***

aˌnonymous FT'P ***noun*** [U] (COMPUTING) a system that allows anybody to DOWNLOAD files from the Internet without having to give their name

anorak /'ænəræk/ ***noun*** [C] (*BrE*) **1** a short coat with a covering for your head that protects you from rain, wind and cold **2** (*slang*) a person who enjoys learning boring facts

anorexia /ˌænə'reksiə/ (*also* **anorexia nervosa** /ˌænəˌreksiə nɜ:'vəʊsə/) ***noun*** [U] (HEALTH) an illness, especially affecting young women. It makes them afraid of being fat and so they do not eat. ➲ look at **bulimia** ▸ **anorexic** ***adj.***, ***noun*** [C]

another ⊶ /ə'nʌðə(r)/ ***det.***, ***pronoun*** **1** one more person or thing of the same kind: *Would you like another drink?* ◇ *They've got three children already and they're having another.* **2** a different thing or person: *I'm afraid I can't see you tomorrow. Could we arrange another day?* ◇ *If you've already seen that film, we can go and see another.*

IDM **one after another/the other** → ONE¹

yet another → YET

answer¹ ⊶ /'ɑ:nsə(r)/ ***noun*** [C] **an ~ (to sb/sth) 1** something that you say, write or do as a reply: *The answer to your question is that I don't know.* ◇ *They've made me an offer and I have to* ***give them an answer*** *by Friday.* ◇ *I wrote to them two weeks ago and I'm still waiting for an answer.* ◇ *I knocked on the door and waited but there was no answer.* **2** a solution to a problem: *I didn't have any money so the only answer was to borrow some.* **3** (EDUCATION) a reply to a question in a test or exam: *My answer to question 5 was wrong.* ◇ *How many answers did you get right?* **4** (EDUCATION) the correct reply to a question in a test or exam: *What was the answer to question 4?*

IDM **in answer (to sth)** as a reply (to sth)

answer² ⊶ /'ɑ:nsə(r)/ ***verb*** [I,T] **1** to say or write sth back to sb who has asked you sth or written to you: *I asked her what the matter was but she didn't answer.* ◇ *I've asked you a question, now please answer me.* ◇ *Answer all the questions on the form.* ◇ *He hasn't answered my letter yet* (= written a letter back to me). ◇ *When I asked him how much he earned, he answered that it was none of my business.* ◇ *'No!' he answered angrily.* **2** to do sth as a reply: *Can you* ***answer the phone*** (= pick up the receiver) *for me, please?* ◇ *I rang their doorbell but nobody answered.*

PHR V **answer back** to defend yourself against sth bad that has been written or said about you

answer (sb) back to reply rudely to sb

answer for sb/sth 1 to accept responsibility for sth/sb: *Somebody will have to answer for all the damage that has been caused.* **2** to speak in support of sb/sth

answerable /'ɑ:nsərəbl/ ***adj.*** **~ to sb (for sth)** having to explain and give good reasons for your actions to sb; responsible to sb

'answering machine (*BrE also* **answerphone** /'ɑ:nsəfəʊn/) ***noun*** [C] a machine that answers the telephone and records messages from the people who call: *I rang him and left a message on his answering machine.*

ant /ænt/ ***noun*** [C] a very small insect that lives in large groups (**colonies**) and works very hard ➲ picture on **page 29**

antacid /ænt'æsɪd/ ***noun*** [C] (HEALTH) a medicine that reduces the amount of acid in the stomach

antagonism /æn'tæɡənɪzəm/ ***noun*** [C,U] **~ (towards sb/sth)**; **~ (between A and B)** a feeling of hate and of being against sb/sth ▸ **antagonistic** /ænˌtæɡə'nɪstɪk/ ***adj.***

antagonist /æn'tæɡənɪst/ ***noun*** [C] (*formal*) a person who is strongly against sb/sth

antagonize (also -ise) /æn'tæɡənaɪz/ ***verb*** [T] to make sb angry or to annoy sb

Antarctic /æn'tɑːktɪk/ ***adj.*** (**GEOGRAPHY**) connected with the coldest, most southern parts of the world: *an Antarctic expedition* ➲ look at **Arctic**

the Antarctic /æn'tɑːktɪk/ ***noun*** [sing.] (**GEOGRAPHY**) the most southern part of the world ➲ look at **the Arctic** ➲ picture at **earth**

the ˌAntarctic 'Circle ***noun*** [sing.] (**GEOGRAPHY**) the line of LATITUDE 66° 33'S ➲ look at **the Arctic Circle** ➲ picture at **earth**

ante- /'ænti/ ***prefix*** (in nouns, adjectives and verbs) before; in front of: *antenatal* ◇ *ante-room* ➲ look at **post-**, **pre-**

anteater /'æntiːtə(r)/ ***noun*** [C] an animal with a long nose and tongue that eats ANTS (= small insects)

antecedent /ˌæntɪ'siːdnt/ ***noun*** [C] **1** (*formal*) a thing or an event that exists or comes before another, and may have influenced it **2 antecedents** [pl.] the people in sb's family who lived a long time ago **SYN ancestors 3** (**LANGUAGE**) a word or phrase to which the following word, especially a pronoun, refers: *In 'He grabbed the ball and threw it in the air', 'ball' is the antecedent of 'it'.*

antelope /'æntɪləʊp/ ***noun*** [C] (*pl.* **antelope** or **antelopes**) an African animal with horns and long, thin legs that can run very fast

antenatal /ˌænti'neɪtl/ ***adj.*** (**HEALTH**) connected with the care of pregnant women: *an antenatal clinic* ◇ *antenatal care* ➲ look at **post-natal**

antenna /æn'tenə/ ***noun*** [C] **1** (*pl.* **antennae** /-niː/) (**BIOLOGY**) one of the two long thin parts on the heads of insects and some animals that live in shells. **Antennae** are used for feeling things with. **SYN feelers** ➲ picture on **page 29 2** (*pl.* **antennas**) (*AmE*) = AERIAL[1]

anterior /æn'tɪəriə(r)/ ***adj.*** (only *before* a noun) (**ANATOMY**) (used about a part of the body) at or near the front

anthem /'ænθəm/ ***noun*** [C] (**MUSIC**) a song, especially one that is sung on special occasions: *the national anthem* (= the special song of a country)

anther /'ænθə(r)/ ***noun*** [C] (**BIOLOGY**) the part of a flower at the top of a STAMEN (= the male part in the middle of a flower) that produces POLLEN (= the powder which makes other flowers of the same type produce seeds) ➲ picture at **flower**

anthology /æn'θɒlədʒi/ ***noun*** [C] (*pl.* **anthologies**) (**LITERATURE**) a book that contains pieces of writing or poems, often on the same subject, by different authors

anthracite /'ænθrəsaɪt/ ***noun*** [U] a very hard type of coal that burns slowly without producing a lot of smoke or flames

anthrax /'ænθræks/ ***noun*** [U] (**AGRICULTURE**, **HEALTH**) a serious disease that affects sheep and cows and sometimes people, and can cause death

anthropo- /'ænθrəpəʊ/ ***prefix*** (in nouns, adjectives and adverbs) connected with humans

anthropology /ˌænθrə'pɒlədʒi/ ***noun*** [U] (**SOCIAL STUDIES**) the study of humans, especially of their origin, development, customs and beliefs
▶ **anthropological** /ˌænθrəpə'lɒdʒɪkl/ ***adj.***
▶ **anthropologist** /ˌænθrə'pɒlədʒɪst/ ***noun*** [C]

anti- /'ænti/ ***prefix*** (in nouns, adjectives and adverbs) **1** against: *anti-war* ◇ *antiperspirant* ◇ *anticlockwise* **2** the opposite of: *anticlimax*

ˌanti-'aircraft ***adj.*** (only *before* a noun) designed to destroy enemy aircraft: ***anti-aircraft fire/guns/*** *missiles*

antibacterial /ˌæntibæk'tɪəriəl/ ***adj.*** (**HEALTH**) that kills bacteria that can cause disease: *antibacterial treatments*

antibiotic /ˌæntibaɪ'ɒtɪk/ ***noun*** [C] (**HEALTH**) a medicine which is used for destroying bacteria and curing infections

antibody /'æntibɒdi/ ***noun*** [C] (*pl.* **antibodies**) (**HEALTH**) a substance that the body produces in the blood to fight disease, or as a reaction when certain substances are put in the body

anticipate 🔑 **AW** /æn'tɪsɪpeɪt/ ***verb*** [T] to expect sth to happen (and prepare for it): *to anticipate a problem* ◇ *I anticipate that the situation will get worse.*

anticipation **AW** /ænˌtɪsɪ'peɪʃn/ ***noun*** [U] **1** the state of expecting sth to happen (and preparing for it): *The government has reduced tax* ***in anticipation of*** *an early general election.* **2** excited feelings about sth that is going to happen: *They queued outside the stadium* ***in excited anticipation.***

anticlimax /ˌænti'klaɪmæks/ ***noun*** [C,U] an event, etc. that is less exciting than you had expected or than what has already happened

anticline /'æntiklaɪn/ ***noun*** [C] (**GEOLOGY**) an area of ground where layers of rock in the earth's surface have been folded into a curve that is higher in the middle than at the ends ➲ look at **syncline**

anticlockwise /ˌænti'klɒkwaɪz/ (*AmE* **'counterclockwise**) ***adv.***, ***adj.*** in the opposite direction to the movement of the hands of a clock: *Turn the lid anticlockwise/in an anticlockwise direction.* **OPP clockwise**

anticoagulant /ˌæntikəʊ'ægjələnt/ ***noun*** [C] (**HEALTH**) a substance that stops the blood from becoming thick and forming CLOTS (= lumps)

antics /'æntɪks/ ***noun*** [pl.] funny, strange or silly ways of behaving

anticyclone /ˌænti'saɪkləʊn/ ***noun*** [C] (**GEOGRAPHY**) an area of high air pressure that produces calm weather conditions with clear skies ➲ look at **depression**

antidepressant /ˌæntidɪ'presnt/ ***noun*** [C] (**HEALTH**) a drug that is used to treat DEPRESSION

antidote /'æntidəʊt/ ***noun*** [C] **1** (**HEALTH**) a medical substance that is used to prevent a poison or a disease from having an effect **2** anything that helps you to deal with sth unpleasant

antifreeze /'æntifriːz/ ***noun*** [U] a chemical that is added to the water in the RADIATOR of cars and other vehicles to stop it from freezing

antigen /'æntɪdʒən/ ***noun*** [C] (**HEALTH**) a substance that enters the body and starts a process that can cause disease. The body then usually produces ANTIBODIES to fight the **antigens**.

'anti-hero ***noun*** [C] (**ARTS AND MEDIA**, **LITERATURE**) the main character in a film, story or play who does not have the qualities that a HERO normally has, such as courage. An **anti-hero** is more like an ordinary person or is very unpleasant. ➲ look at **hero**, **villain**

antihistamine /ˌænti'hɪstəmiːn/ ***noun*** [C,U] (**HEALTH**) a drug used to treat an ALLERGY (= a medical condition that makes you ill when you touch, eat or breathe sth): ***antihistamine cream/ injections*** ➲ look at **histamine**

'anti-lock *adj.* (only *before* a noun) **anti-lock** BRAKES stop the wheels of a vehicle locking if you have to stop suddenly, and so make the vehicle easier to control: *an anti-lock braking system or ABS*

antimony /'æntɪməni/ ***noun*** [U] (*symbol* **Sb**) a silver-white metal that breaks easily ❶ For more information on the periodic table of elements, look at pages R34-5.

antioxidant /ænti'ɒksɪdənt/ ***noun*** [C] **1** (**BIOLOGY, HEALTH**) a substance such as VITAMIN C or E that removes dangerous MOLECULES, etc., such as FREE RADICALS from the body **2** (**CHEMISTRY**) a substance that helps prevent OXIDATION (= oxygen combining with other substances and damaging them), especially one used to help prevent stored food products from going bad

antipathy /æn'tɪpəθi/ ***noun*** [C,U] **~ (to/towards sb/sth)** a strong feeling of not liking sb/sth; dislike

antiperspirant /ˌænti'pɜːspərənt/ ***noun*** [C,U] a liquid that you use to reduce sweating, especially under your arms

antiphony /æn'tɪfəni/ ***noun*** [U] (**MUSIC**) music, especially church music, that is sung or played by two groups taking turns

the Antipodes /æn'tɪpədiːz/ ***noun*** [pl.] (*BrE*) (**GEOGRAPHY**) a way of referring to Australia and New Zealand ▶ **Antipodean** /ˌæntɪpə'diːən/ ***adj.***

antiquated /'æntɪkweɪtɪd/ ***adj.*** old-fashioned and not suitable for the modern world

antique /æn'tiːk/ ***adj.*** (used about furniture, jewellery, etc.) old and therefore often valuable: *an antique vase/table* ◇ *antique furniture/jewellery* ▶ **antique** ***noun*** [C]: *That vase is an antique.* ◇ *an antique shop* (= one that sells antiques)

antiquity /æn'tɪkwəti/ ***noun*** (*pl.* **antiquities**) **1** [U] (**HISTORY**) the ancient past, especially the times of the Ancient Greeks and Romans: *The statue was brought to Rome* ***in antiquity***. **2** [U] the state of being very old or ancient **2** [C, usually pl.] (**HISTORY**) a building or object from ancient times: *Egyptian/Roman antiquities*

antiretroviral /ˌænti'retrəʊvaɪrəl/ ***adj.*** (**HEALTH**) of or connected with a class of drugs designed to stop viruses such as HIV from damaging the body: *Antiretroviral drugs are the only way to treat HIV.*

anti-Semitism /ˌænti 'semətɪzəm/ ***noun*** [U] (**POLITICS, SOCIAL STUDIES**) unfair treatment of Jewish people ▶ **anti-Semitic** /ˌænti sə'mɪtɪk/ ***adj.***

antiseptic /ˌænti'septɪk/ ***noun*** [C,U] (**HEALTH**) a liquid or cream that prevents a cut, etc. from becoming infected: *Put an antiseptic/some antiseptic on that scratch.* ▶ **antiseptic** ***adj.***: *antiseptic cream*

antisocial /ˌænti'səʊʃl/ ***adj.*** **1** harmful or annoying to other people: *antisocial behaviour* **2** not liking to be with other people

antithesis /æn'tɪθəsɪs/ ***noun*** [C,U] (*pl.* **antitheses** /æn'tɪθəsiːz/) (*formal*) **1** the opposite of sth: *Love is the antithesis of hate.* **2** a difference between two things

antiviral /ˌænti'vaɪrəl/ ***adj.*** (**HEALTH**) (used about a drug or treatment) effective against diseases caused by viruses

antler /'æntlə(r)/ ***noun*** [C, usually pl.] (**BIOLOGY**) a horn on the head of a STAG (= an adult male deer): *a pair of antlers*

antonym /'æntənɪm/ ***noun*** [C] (**LANGUAGE**) a word that means the opposite of another word ➲ look at **synonym**

anus /'eɪnəs/ ***noun*** [C] (**ANATOMY**) the hole through which solid waste substances leave the body ➲ picture at **digestive system** ▶ **anal** /'eɪnl/ ***adj.***

anvil /'ænvɪl/ ***noun*** [C] **1** an iron block on which a BLACKSMITH (= a person who works with iron) puts hot pieces of metal before shaping them with a hammer **2** (also *technical* **incus**) (**ANATOMY**) a very small bone inside the ear

anxiety 🔑 /æŋ'zaɪəti/ ***noun*** [C,U] (*pl.* **anxieties**) a feeling of worry or fear, especially about the future: *a feeling/state of anxiety* ◇ *There are anxieties over the effects of unemployment.*

anxious 🔑 /'æŋkʃəs/ ***adj.*** **1 ~ (about/for sb/sth)** worried and afraid: *I began to get anxious when they still hadn't arrived at 9 o'clock.* ◇ *an anxious look/expression* **2** causing worry and fear: *For a few anxious moments we thought we'd missed the train.* **3 ~ to do sth; ~ for sth** wanting sth very much ▶ **anxiously** ***adv.***

any 🔑 /'eni/ ***det., pronoun, adv.*** **1** (used instead of *some* in negative sentences and in questions): *We didn't have any lunch.* ◇ *I speak hardly any* (= almost no) *Spanish.* ◇ *Do you have any questions?* ◇ *I don't like any of his books.* **2** used for saying that it does not matter which thing or person you choose: *Take any book you want.* ◇ *Come round any time – I'm usually in.* ◇ *I'll take any that you don't want.* **3** (used in negative sentences and questions) at all; to any degree: *I can't run any faster.* ◇ *Is your father any better?*

IDM **any moment/second/minute/day (now)** very soon: *She should be home any minute now.*

anybody 🔑 /'enibɒdi/ (*also* **anyone**) ***pronoun*** **1** (usually in questions or negative statements) any person: *I didn't know anybody at the party.* ◇ *Is there anybody here who can speak Japanese?* ◇ *Would* ***anybody else*** (= any other person) *like to come with me?* **2** any person, it does not matter who: *Anybody* (= all people) *can learn to swim.* ◇ *Can anybody come, or are there special invitations?*

anyhow /'enihaʊ/ ***adv.*** **1** = ANYWAY **2** in a careless way; not arranged in any order: *She threw the clothes down onto the bed, just anyhow.*

ˌany 'more (*BrE*) (*also* **anymore**) ***adv.*** often used at the end of negative sentences and at the end of questions, to mean 'any longer': *She doesn't live here any more.* ◇ *Why doesn't he speak to me any more?*

anyone 🔑 /'eniwʌn/ = ANYBODY

anyplace /'enipleɪs/ (*AmE*) = ANYWHERE

anything 🔑 /'eniθɪŋ/ ***pronoun*** **1** (usually in negative sentences and in questions) one thing (of any kind): *It was so dark that I couldn't see anything at all.* ◇ *There isn't anything interesting in the newspaper today.* ◇ *Did you buy anything?* ◇ *'I'd like a kilo of apples please.'* ***'Anything else?'*** (= any other thing?) **2** any thing or things: it does not matter what: *I'm very hungry – I'll eat anything!* ◇ *I'll do anything you say.*

IDM **anything but** not at all: *Their explanation was anything but clear.*

anything like sb/sth at all similar to sb/sth; nearly: *She isn't anything like her sister, is she?* ◇ *This car isn't anything like as fast as mine.*

as happy, quick, etc. as anything (*spoken*) very happy, quick, etc.

like anything → LIKE[2]

not come to anything → COME

anyway 🔑 /'eniweɪ/ (*also* **anyhow**) ***adv.*** **1** (used to add an extra point or reason) in any case: *It's too late now, anyway.* ◇ *I don't want to go out* *tonight, and anyway I haven't got any money.* SYN **besides 2** in spite of sth; even so: *I'm afraid I can't come to your party, but thanks anyway.* **3** used after a pause in order to change the subject or go back to a subject being discussed before: *Anyhow, that's enough about my problems. How are you?* ◇ *Anyhow, as I was saying...* **4** used to correct or slightly change what you have said: *He works in a bank. He did when I last saw him, anyway.*

anywhere 🔑 /'eniweə(r)/ (*AmE also* **anyplace**) *adv.* **1** (usually in negative sentences or in questions) in, at or to any place: *I can't find my keys anywhere.* ◇ *Is there a post office anywhere near here?* ◇ *You can't buy the book* ***anywhere else*** (= in another place). **2** any place; it does not matter where: *You can sit anywhere you like.*

AOB /ˌeɪ əʊ 'biː/ *abbr.* (BUSINESS) **any other business**; the things that are discussed at the end of an official meeting that are not on the AGENDA (= list of things to discuss)

aorta /eɪ'ɔːtə/ *noun* [C] (ANATOMY) the main ARTERY (= tube) that carries blood from the heart to the rest of the body ➲ picture at **heart**

apart 🔑 /ə'pɑːt/ *adv.* **1** away from sb/sth or each other; not together: *The doors slowly slid apart.* ◇ *Stand with your feet apart.* ◇ *The houses are ten metres apart.* ◇ *I'm afraid our ideas are too far apart.* **2** into pieces: *The material was so old that it just* ***fell/came apart*** *in my hands.*

IDM **take sth apart** to separate sth into pieces: *He took the whole bicycle apart.*

tell A and B apart to see the difference between A and B: *It's very difficult to tell the twins apart.*

a'part from (*especially AmE* **a'side from**) *prep.* **1** except for: *I've answered all the questions apart from the last one.* ◇ *There's nobody here apart from me.* **2** as well as; in addition to: *Apart from music, she also loves sport and reading.*

apartheid /ə'pɑːthaɪt/ *noun* [U] (POLITICS) the former official government policy in South Africa of separating people of different races and making them live apart

apartment 🔑 /ə'pɑːtmənt/ *noun* [C] **1** (*especially AmE*) = FLAT² (1) **2** (TOURISM) a set of rooms rented for a holiday: *a self-catering apartment*

a'partment block *noun* [C] (*especially AmE*) a large building containing several apartments

apathetic /ˌæpə'θetɪk/ *adj.* lacking interest or desire to act

apathy /'æpəθi/ *noun* [U] the feeling of not being interested in or enthusiastic about anything

ape¹ /eɪp/ *noun* [C] a type of animal like a large MONKEY with no tail or only a very short tail: *Chimpanzees and gorillas are apes.*

ape² /eɪp/ *verb* [T] to copy sb/sth, especially in a ridiculous way: *The children were aping the teacher's way of walking.*

aperitif /əˌperə'tiːf/ *noun* [C] (*especially BrE*) a drink, usually one containing alcohol, that people sometimes have just before a meal

aperture /'æpətʃə(r)/ *noun* [C] **1** (*formal*) a small opening in sth **2** (TECHNICAL) a small opening that allows light to reach a LENS (= the small curved piece of glass or plastic that light passes through inside a camera) ➲ picture at **camera**

apex /'eɪpeks/ *noun* [C, usually sing.] (*pl.* **apexes**) the top or highest part of sth: *the apex of a roof/triangle*

aphid /'eɪfɪd/ *noun* [C] a very small insect that is harmful to plants. There are several different types of **aphid**.

aphorism /'æfərɪzəm/ *noun* [C] (*formal*) (LANGUAGE) a short phrase that expresses in a clever way sth that is true

aphrodisiac /ˌæfrə'dɪziæk/ *noun* [C] a food or drug that is said to make people have a desire to have sex ▶ **aphrodisiac** *adj.*

apiece /ə'piːs/ *adv.* each: *Coates and Winterbotham scored a goal apiece.*

apocalypse /ə'pɒkəlɪps/ *noun* **1** [sing., U] the total destruction of the world **2 the Apocalypse** [sing.] (RELIGION) the end of the world, as described in the Bible **3** [sing.] a situation causing very serious damage and destruction: *an environmental apocalypse* ▶ **apocalyptic** /əˌpɒkə'lɪptɪk/ *adj.*

apocryphal /ə'pɒkrɪfl/ *adj.* (used about a story) well known, but probably not true: *Most of the stories about him are apocryphal.*

apolitical /ˌeɪpə'lɪtɪkl/ *adj.* (POLITICS) **1** (used about a person) not interested in politics; not thinking politics are important **2** not connected with a political party: *an apolitical organization*

apologetic /əˌpɒlə'dʒetɪk/ *adj.* feeling or showing that you are sorry for sth you have done: *He was most apologetic about his son's bad behaviour.* ◇ *I wrote him an apologetic letter.* ▶ **apologetically** /-kli/ *adv.*

apologize 🔑 (also -ise) /ə'pɒlədʒaɪz/ *verb* [I] ~ **(to sb) (for sth)** to say that you are sorry for sth that you have done: *You'll have to apologize to your teacher for being late.*

apology /ə'pɒlədʒi/ *noun* [C,U] (*pl.* **apologies**) **(an)** ~ **(to sb) (for sth)** a spoken or written statement that you are sorry for sth you have done, etc.: *Please accept our apologies for the delay.* ◇ *a letter of apology*

apostle /ə'pɒsl/ *noun* [C] (RELIGION) one of the twelve men chosen by Christ to spread his teaching

apostrophe /ə'pɒstrəfi/ *noun* [C] (LANGUAGE) **1** the sign (') used for showing that you have left a letter or letters out of a word as in 'I'm', 'can't' or 'we'll' **2** the sign (') used for showing who or what sth belongs to as in 'John's chair', 'the boys' room' or 'Russia's President'.

app /æp/ *abbr.* = APPLICATION (4)

appal (*AmE* **appall**) /ə'pɔːl/ *verb* [T] (**appalling**; **appalled**) (usually passive) to shock sb very much ▶ **appalling** /ə'pɔːlɪŋ/ *adj.* ▶ **appallingly** *adv.*

appalled /ə'pɔːld/ *adj.* ~ **(at sth)** feeling disgust at sth unpleasant or wrong

apparatus /ˌæpə'reɪtəs/ *noun* [U] the set of tools, instruments or equipment used for doing a job or an activity ➲ picture at **laboratory**

apparent 🔑 AW /ə'pærənt/ *adj.* **1** (*only before* a noun) that seems to be real or true but may not be **2** ~ **(to sb)** clear; easy to see: *It quickly became apparent to us that our teacher could not speak French.* ➲ verb **appear** ➲ note at **clear¹**

apparently 🔑 /ə'pærəntli/ *adv.* according to what people say or to how sth appears, but perhaps not true: *Apparently, he's already been married twice.* ◇ *He was apparently undisturbed by the news.*

apparition /ˌæpə'rɪʃn/ *noun* [C] a GHOST or an image of a person who is dead

appeal[1] /ə'pi:l/ ***noun*** **1** [C,U] ~ **against sth** (LAW) a formal request to a court or to sb in authority for a judgement or a decision to be changed: *an appeal court/judge* ➲ look at **court of appeal** **2** [U] the attraction or interesting quality of sth/sb: *The Beatles have never really* ***lost their appeal.*** **3** [C] an urgent and deeply felt request for money, help or information, especially one made by a charity or by the police: *The police have made an urgent appeal for witnesses to come forward.* **4** [C] **an ~ to sth** a suggestion that tries to influence sb's feelings or thoughts so that they will do what you want

appeal[2] /ə'pi:l/ ***verb*** [I] **1** ~ **(against/for sth)** (LAW) to make a formal request to a court or to sb in authority for a judgement or a decision to be changed: *He decided to appeal against his conviction.* ◇ *The player fell down and appealed for a penalty.* **2** ~ **(to sb)** to be attractive or interesting to sb: *The idea of living in the country doesn't appeal to me at all.* **3** ~ **to sb (for sth)**; ~ **for sth** to make a serious request for sth you need or want very much: *Relief workers in the disaster area are appealing for more supplies.* ◇ *She appealed to the kidnappers to let her son go.* **4** ~ **to sth** to try to influence sb's feelings or thoughts so that they will do sth you want: *We aim to appeal to people's generosity.*

appealing /ə'pi:lɪŋ/ ***adj.*** **1** attractive or interesting: *The idea of a lying on a beach sounds very appealing!* **2** showing that you need help, etc.: *an appealing look* ▶ **appealingly** ***adv.***

appear /ə'pɪə(r)/ ***verb*** **1** ***linking verb*** ~ **to be/do sth**; ~ **(that)...** to seem: *She appears to be very happy in her job.* ◇ *It appears that you were given the wrong information.* ➲ adjective **apparent**
2 [I] to suddenly be seen; to come into sight: *The bus appeared from round the corner.* OPP **disappear** **3** [I] to begin to exist: *When did mammals appear on the earth?* **4** [I] (ARTS AND MEDIA) to be published or printed: *The article appeared in this morning's paper.* **5** [I] (ARTS AND MEDIA) to perform or speak where you are seen by a lot of people: *to appear on television/in a play*

appearance /ə'pɪərəns/ ***noun*** **1** [U] the way that sb/sth looks or seems: *A different hairstyle can completely change your appearance.* ◇ *He gives the appearance of being extremely confident.* **2** [sing.] the coming of sb/sth: *the appearance of television in the home in the 1950s* **3** [C] (ARTS AND MEDIA) an act of appearing in public, especially on stage, television, etc.

appease /ə'pi:z/ ***verb*** [T] (*formal*) **1** to make sb calmer or less angry by agreeing to what they want **2** (POLITICS) to give a country what it wants in order to avoid war ▶ **appeasement** ***noun*** [U]: *a policy of appeasement*

append AW /ə'pend/ ***verb*** [T] ~ **sth (to sth)** (*formal*) to add sth to the end of a piece of writing: *Footnotes have been appended to the document.*

appendage /ə'pendɪdʒ/ ***noun*** [C] (*formal*) a smaller or less important part of sth larger

appendicitis /əˌpendə'saɪtɪs/ ***noun*** [U] (HEALTH) an illness in which your APPENDIX becomes extremely painful and usually has to be removed

appendix AW /ə'pendɪks/ ***noun*** [C] **1** (*pl.* **appendixes**) (ANATOMY) a small organ inside your body near your stomach. In humans, the **appendix** has no real function. ➲ picture at **digestive system** **2** (*pl.* **appendices** /-dɪsi:z/) (LITERATURE) a section at the end of a book, etc. that gives extra information

appertain /ˌæpə'teɪn/ ***verb***
PHR V **appertain to sb/sth** (*formal*) to belong or refer to sb/sth: *These figures appertain to last year's sales.*

appetite /'æpɪtaɪt/ ***noun*** [C,U] a strong desire for sth, especially food: *Some fresh air and exercise should* ***give you an appetite*** (= make you hungry). ◇ *He has a great* ***appetite for*** *work/life.* ◇ *loss of appetite*
IDM **whet sb's appetite** → WHET

appetizer (also **-iser**) /'æpɪtaɪzə(r)/ (*especially AmE*) = STARTER

appetizing (also **-ising**) /'æpɪtaɪzɪŋ/ ***adj.*** (used about food, etc.) that looks or smells attractive; making you feel hungry

applaud /ə'plɔ:d/ ***verb*** **1** [I,T] to hit your hands together noisily (**clap**) in order to show that you like sb/sth: *The audience applauded loudly.* ◇ *The team was applauded as it left the field.* **2** [T] (usually passive) to express approval of sth: *The decision was applauded by everybody.*

applause /ə'plɔ:z/ ***noun*** [U] the noise made by a group of people hitting their hands together (**clapping**) to show their approval and enjoyment: *Give her a big* ***round of applause!*** ◇ *The audience broke into rapturous applause.*

apple /'æpl/ ***noun*** [C,U] a hard, round fruit with a smooth green, red or yellow skin: *apple juice*

applet /'æplət/ ***noun*** [C] (COMPUTING) a simple program that can make one thing or a few simple things happen, for example on a page on the Internet

appliance /ə'plaɪəns/ ***noun*** [C] a piece of equipment for a particular purpose in the house: *washing machines and other* ***domestic appliances***

applicable /'æplɪkəbl; ə'plɪkəbl/ ***adj.*** (not *before* a noun) ~ **(to sb/sth)** that concerns sb/sth; relevant to sb/sth: *This part of the form is only applicable to married women.*

applicant /'æplɪkənt/ ***noun*** [C] a person who makes a formal request for sth (**applies for sth**), especially for a job, a place at a college, university, etc.: *There were over 200 applicants for the job.*

application /ˌæplɪ'keɪʃn/ ***noun*** **1** [C,U] **(an) ~ (to sb) (for sth)** a formal written request, especially for a job or a place in a school, club, etc.: *Applications for the job should be made to the Personnel Manager.* ◇ *To become a member, fill in the* ***application form.*** **2** [C,U] the practical use (of sth) **3** [U] hard work; effort **4** [C] (*abbr.* **app**) (COMPUTING) a program that is designed to do a particular job; a piece of software: *a database application*

applied /ə'plaɪd/ ***adj.*** (EDUCATION) (used about a subject) studied in a way that has a practical use: *You have to study applied mathematics as part of the engineering course.* ➲ look at **pure**

apply /ə'plaɪ/ ***verb*** (*pres. part.* **applying**; *3rd person sing. pres.* **applies**; *pt, pp* **applied**) **1** [I] ~ **(to sb) (for sth)** to ask for sth in writing: *I've applied to that company for a job.* ◇ *She's applying for a place at university.* **2** [I] ~ **(to sb/sth)** to concern or involve sb/sth: *This information applies to all children born after 2000.* **3** [T] ~ **sth (to sth)** to make practical use of sth: *new technology which can be applied to solving problems in industry* **4** [T] (usually passive) to use a word, a name, etc. to describe sb/sth: *I don't think the term 'music' can be applied to that awful noise.* **5** [T] ~ **sth (to sth)** to put or spread sth onto sth: *Apply the cream to the infected area twice a day.* **6** [T] ~ **yourself/sth (to sth/doing sth)** to make yourself give all your attention to sth: *to apply your mind to sth*

appoint ⊶ /ə'pɔɪnt/ *verb* [T] **1** ~ **sb (to sth)** (BUSINESS) to choose sb for a job or position: *She has recently been appointed to the committee.* ◇ *The committee have appointed a new chairperson.* ◇ *He's been appointed (as) assistant to Dr Beale.* **2** (*formal*) ~ **sth (for sth)** to arrange or decide on sth

appointment ⊶ /ə'pɔɪntmənt/ *noun* **1** [C,U] an ~ **(with sb)** an arrangement to see sb at a particular time: *I have an appointment with Dr Sula at 3 o'clock.* ◇ *I'd like to* ***make an appointment*** *to see the manager.* ◇ *I realized I wouldn't be able to keep the appointment so I cancelled it.* ◇ *Visits are* ***by appointment only*** (= at a time that has been arranged in advance). **2** [C] (BUSINESS) a job or a position of responsibility: *a temporary/permanent appointment* **3** [C,U] ~ **(to sth)** the act of choosing sb for a job

apportion /ə'pɔːʃn/ *verb* [T] (*written*) ~ **sth (among/between/to sb)** to divide sth among people; to give a share of sth to sb: *The land was apportioned between members of the family.* ◇ *The programme gives the facts but does not* ***apportion blame***.

apposition /ˌæpə'zɪʃn/ *noun* [U] (LANGUAGE) the use of a noun phrase immediately after another noun phrase which refers to the same person or thing: *In the phrase 'Paris, the capital of France', 'the capital of France' is in apposition to 'Paris'.*

appraisal /ə'preɪzl/ *noun* [C,U] (*formal*) **1** a judgement about the value or quality of sb/sth **2** (*BrE*) (BUSINESS) a meeting in which an employee discusses with their manager how well they have been doing their job; the system of holding such meetings

appraise /ə'preɪz/ *verb* [T] (*formal*) **1** to judge the value or quality of sb/sth **2** (BUSINESS) to make a formal judgement about the value of a person's work, usually after a discussion with them about it: *Managers must appraise all staff.*

appreciable AW /ə'priːʃəbl/ *adj.* large enough to be noticed or thought important SYN **considerable**: *an appreciable effect/increase/amount*

appreciate ⊶ AW /ə'priːʃieɪt/ *verb* **1** [T] to enjoy sth or to understand the value of sb/sth: *My boss doesn't appreciate me.* ◇ *I don't appreciate good coffee – it all tastes the same to me.* **2** [T] to understand a problem, situation, etc.: *I appreciate your problem but I'm afraid I can't help you.* **3** [T] to be grateful for sth: *Thanks very much. I really appreciate your help.* **4** [I] (FINANCE) to increase in value: *Their investments have appreciated over the years.*

appreciation AW /əˌpriːʃi'eɪʃn/ *noun* **1** [U] understanding and enjoyment of the value of sth: *I'm afraid I have little appreciation of modern architecture.* **2** [U] the feeling of being grateful for sth: *We bought him a present to show our appreciation for all the work he had done.* **3** [U, sing.] understanding of a situation, problem, etc. **4** [U, sing.] (FINANCE) an increase in value over a period of time

appreciative /ə'priːʃətɪv/ *adj.* **1** feeling or showing pleasure or admiration: *an appreciative audience* **2** ~ **(of sth)** grateful for sth: *He was very appreciative of our efforts to help.*

apprehend /ˌæprɪ'hend/ *verb* [T] (*formal*) (LAW) (used about the police) to catch sb and arrest them

apprehensive /ˌæprɪ'hensɪv/ *adj.* worried or afraid that sth unpleasant may happen: *I'm feeling apprehensive about tomorrow's exam.*
▸ **apprehension** /-ʃn/ *noun* [C,U]

apprentice /ə'prentɪs/ *noun* [C] a person who works for low pay, in order to learn the skills needed in a particular job: *an apprentice electrician/chef/plumber*

apprenticeship /ə'prentɪʃɪp/ *noun* [C,U] the state or time of being an APPRENTICE

approach[1] ⊶ AW /ə'prəʊtʃ/ *verb* **1** [I,T] to come near or nearer to sb/sth: *The day of the exam approached.* ◇ *When you approach the village you will see a garage on your left.* **2** [T] to begin to deal with a problem, a situation, etc.: *What is the best way to approach this problem?* **3** [T] to speak to sb usually in order to ask for sth: *I'm going to approach them about a loan.*

approach[2] ⊶ AW /ə'prəʊtʃ/ *noun* **1** [C] a way of dealing with sb/sth: *Parents don't always know what approach to take with teenage children.* **2** [sing.] the act of coming nearer (to sb/sth): *the approach of winter* **3** [C] a request for sth: *The company has* ***made an approach to*** *us for financial assistance.* **4** [C] a road or path leading to sth: *the approach to the village*

approachable /ə'prəʊtʃəbl/ *adj.* **1** friendly and easy to talk to **2** (not before a noun) that can be reached SYN **accessible**

appropriate[1] ⊶ AW /ə'prəʊpriət/ *adj.* ~ **(for/to sth)** suitable or right for a particular situation, person, use, etc.: *The matter will be dealt with by the appropriate authorities.* ◇ *I don't think this film is appropriate for children.* OPP **inappropriate** ▸ **appropriately** *adv.*

appropriate[2] AW /ə'prəʊprieɪt/ *verb* [T] (*formal*) to take sth to use for yourself, usually without permission: *He appropriated the money from the company's pension fund.* ▸ **appropriation** /əˌprəʊpri'eɪʃn/ *noun* [U, sing.]

approval ⊶ /ə'pruːvl/ *noun* [U] feeling, showing or saying that you think sth is good; agreement: *Everybody* ***gave their approval to*** *the proposal.*

approve ⊶ /ə'pruːv/ *verb* **1** [I] ~ **(of sb/sth)** to be pleased about sth; to like sb/sth: *His father didn't approve of him becoming a dancer.* ◇ *Her parents don't approve of her friends.* OPP **disapprove** **2** [T] to agree formally to sth or to say that sth is correct: *We need to get an accountant to approve these figures.*
➲ note at **agree**

approving ⊶ /ə'pruːvɪŋ/ *adj.* showing support or admiration for sth: *'Good,' he said with an approving smile.* ▸ **approvingly** *adv.*

approx *abbr.* (*written*) approximate; approximately

approximate[1] ⊶ AW /ə'prɒksɪmət/ *adj.* almost correct but not completely accurate: *The approximate time of arrival is 3 o'clock.* ◇ *I can only give you an approximate idea of the cost.*

approximate[2] AW /ə'prɒksɪmeɪt/ *verb* (*formal*) [T] **1** ~ **(to) sth** to be similar or close to sth in nature, quality, amount, etc., but not exactly the same: *The animals were reared in conditions which approximated the wild as closely as possible.* ◇ *The total cost will approximate £15 billion.* ◇ *His story approximates to the facts that we already know.* **2** to calculate or estimate sth fairly accurately: *a formula for approximating the weight of a horse*

approximately ⊶ /ə'prɒksɪmətli/ *adv.* about; roughly: *It's approximately fifty miles from here.*

approximation AW /əˌprɒksɪˈmeɪʃn/ ***noun*** [C] an estimate of a number or an amount that is almost correct, but not exact: *That's just an approximation, you understand.*

Apr. ***abbr.*** April: *24 Apr. 2007*

apricot /ˈeɪprɪkɒt/ ***noun*** [C] a small, round, yellow or orange fruit with a large STONE inside

April /ˈeɪprəl/ ***noun*** [U, C] (*abbr.* **Apr.**) the fourth month of the year, coming after March

ˌApril ˈFool's Day ***noun*** [sing.] 1 April

CULTURE

On this day it is traditional for people to play tricks on each other, especially by inventing silly stories and trying to persuade other people that they are true. If somebody believes such a story he/she is called an **April Fool**.

a priori /ˌeɪ praɪˈɔːraɪ/ ***adj., adv.*** (*formal*) using facts or principles that we know are true in order to decide what the probable effects or results of sth will be, for example saying 'They haven't eaten anything all day so they must be hungry.': *an a priori assumption*

apron /ˈeɪprən/ ***noun*** [C] a piece of clothing that you wear over the front of your usual clothes in order to keep them clean, especially when cooking

apropos /ˌæprəˈpəʊ/ (*also* **apropos of**) ***prep.*** on the subject of sth/sb: *Apropos (of) what you were just saying...*

apse /æps/ ***noun*** [C] (ARCHITECTURE) a small area, often in the shape of a HALF-CIRCLE, usually at the east end of a church

apt /æpt/ ***adj.*** **1** suitable in a particular situation: *I thought 'complex' was an apt description of the book.* **2** **~ to do sth** often likely to do sth ▶ **aptly** ***adv.***: *The winner of the race was aptly named Alan Speedy.*

aptitude /ˈæptɪtjuːd/ ***noun*** [U, C] ~ **(for sth/for doing sth)** natural ability or skill: *She has an aptitude for learning languages.* ◇ *an* ***aptitude test*** (= one designed to show whether sb has the natural ability for a particular job or educational course)

aqualung /ˈækwəlʌŋ/ ***noun*** [C] (SPORT) a piece of breathing equipment that a DIVER wears on his or her back when swimming underwater

aquamarine /ˌækwəməˈriːn/ ***noun*** **1** [C, U] a pale greenish-blue precious stone **2** [U] a pale greenish-blue colour ▶ **aquamarine** ***adj.***

aquarium /əˈkweəriəm/ ***noun*** [C] (*pl.* **aquariums** or **aquaria** /-riə/) **1** a glass container filled with water, in which fish and water animals are kept **2** a building where people can go to see fish and other water animals

Aquarius /əˈkweəriəs/ ***noun*** [U] the eleventh sign of the ZODIAC, the Water Carrier

aquatic /əˈkwætɪk/ ***adj.*** (BIOLOGY) living or taking place in, on or near water: *aquatic plants* ◇ *windsurfing and other aquatic sports*

aqueduct /ˈækwɪdʌkt/ ***noun*** [C] a structure like a bridge for carrying water across a valley or low ground

aqueous /ˈeɪkwiəs/ ***adj.*** (SCIENCE) containing water; like water

aquifer /ˈækwɪfə(r)/ ***noun*** [C] (GEOLOGY) a layer of rock or soil that can take in and hold water ➲ picture at **water**

Arab /ˈærəb/ ***noun*** [C] (SOCIAL STUDIES) a member of a people who lived originally in Arabia and who now live in many parts of the Middle East and North Africa ▶ **Arab** ***adj.***: *Arab countries*

Arabic /ˈærəbɪk/ ***noun*** [U] (LANGUAGE) the language of Arab people

arable /ˈærəbl/ ***adj.*** (AGRICULTURE) connected with growing crops for sale, not keeping animals: *arable land/farmers*

arachnid /əˈræknɪd/ ***noun*** [C] (BIOLOGY) any of the CLASS (= group) of small creatures with eight legs that includes spiders ➲ picture on **page 29**

arbitrage /ˈɑːbɪtrɑːʒ; -trɪdʒ/ ***noun*** [U] (FINANCE) the practice of buying sth, for example foreign money, in one place and selling it in another place where the price is higher

arbitrageur /ˌɑːbɪtrɑːˈʒɜː(r)/ (also **arbitrager** /ˈɑːbɪtrɪdʒə(r)/) ***noun*** [C] (FINANCE) a person whose job is to buy sth, for example foreign money, in one place and sell it in another place where the price is higher

arbitrary AW /ˈɑːbɪtrəri/ ***adj.*** not seeming to be based on any reason or plan: *The choice of players for the team seemed completely arbitrary.* ▶ **arbitrarily** ***adv.***

arbitrate /ˈɑːbɪtreɪt/ ***verb*** [I,T] to officially settle an argument between two people or groups by finding a solution that both can accept: *to arbitrate in a dispute* ▶ **arbitration** /ˌɑːbɪˈtreɪʃn/ ***noun*** [U]: *The union and the management decided to* ***go to arbitration.***

arbitrator /ˈɑːbɪtreɪtə(r)/ ***noun*** [C] a person who is chosen to settle an argument between two people or two groups of people

arc /ɑːk/ ***noun*** [C] (GEOMETRY) a curved line, part of a circle ➲ picture at **circle**

arcade /ɑːˈkeɪd/ ***noun*** **1** (ARCHITECTURE) a covered passage with ARCHES along one or both sides **2** a covered passage between streets, with shops on either side **3** (*also* **ˈshopping arcade**) a large building with a number of shops in it ➲ look at **shopping centre** **4** = AMUSEMENT ARCADE: *arcade games*

arcane /ɑːˈkeɪn/ ***adj.*** (*formal*) known to very few people and therefore difficult to understand: *the arcane rules of cricket*

arch[1] /ɑːtʃ/ ***noun*** [C] **1** a curved structure that supports the weight of sth above it, such as a bridge or the upper part of a building ➲ look at **archway** ➲ picture at **erode** **2** (ARCHITECTURE) a structure with a curved top that is supported by straight sides, sometimes forming an entrance or built as a MONUMENT: *Marble Arch is a famous London landmark.* **3** the curved bottom part of your foot

arch

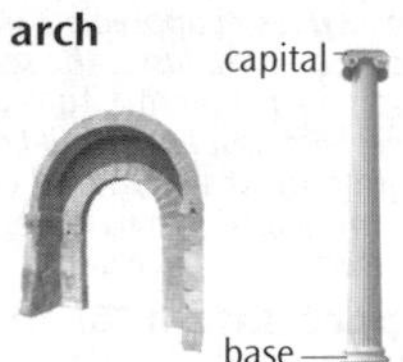

arch[2] /ɑːtʃ/ ***verb*** [I,T] if you **arch** part of your body, or if it **arches**, it moves and forms a curved shape: *The cat arched its back and hissed.*

arch- /ɑːtʃ/ ***prefix*** (in nouns) main, most important or most extreme: *archbishop* ◇ *arch-rival*

archaeological (*AmE* **archeological**) /ˌɑːkiəˈlɒdʒɪkl/ ***adj.*** connected with ARCHAEOLOGY

archaeologist (*AmE* **archeologist**) /ˌɑːkiˈɒlədʒɪst/ ***noun*** [C] an expert in ARCHAEOLOGY

archaeology (*AmE* **archeology**) /ˌɑːki'ɒlədʒi/ ***noun*** [U] the study of the past, based on objects or parts of buildings that are found in the ground

archaic /ɑː'keɪɪk/ ***adj.*** very old-fashioned; no longer used

archbishop /ˌɑːtʃ'bɪʃəp/ ***noun*** [C] (**RELIGION**) a priest with a very high position, in some branches of the Christian Church, who is responsible for all the churches in a large area of a country: *the Archbishop of Canterbury* (= the head of the Church of England) ➲ look at **bishop**

arched /ɑːtʃt/ ***adj.*** in the shape of an ARCH: *a chair with an arched back*

archer /'ɑːtʃə(r)/ ***noun*** [C] (**HISTORY, SPORT**) a person who shoots ARROWS (= pieces of wood or metal with a sharp point) through the air by pulling back a tight string on a curved piece of wood (**a bow**) and letting go. In past times this was done in order to kill people, but it is now done as a sport.

archery /'ɑːtʃəri/ ***noun*** [U] (**SPORT**) the sport of shooting arrows

archetypal /ˌɑːki'taɪpl/ ***adj.*** (*written*) having all the qualities that make sb/sth a typical example of a particular kind of person or thing: *He lived an archetypal rock star's lifestyle.*

archetype /'ɑːkitaɪp/ ***noun*** [C] (*written*) the most typical example of a particular kind of person or thing

archipelago /ˌɑːkɪ'peləgəʊ/ ***noun*** [C] (*pl.* **archipelagos** or **archipelagoes**) (**GEOGRAPHY**) a group of islands and the sea around them

architect /'ɑːkɪtekt/ ***noun*** [C] a person whose job is to design buildings

architectural /ˌɑːkɪ'tektʃərəl/ ***adj.*** connected with the design of buildings

architecture /'ɑːkɪtektʃə(r)/ ***noun*** [U] **1** the study of designing and making buildings **2** the style or design of a building or buildings: *modern architecture* **3** (**COMPUTING**) the design and structure of a computer system

architrave /'ɑːkɪtreɪv/ ***noun*** [C] (**ARCHITECTURE**) the frame around a door or window

archive[1] /'ɑːkaɪv/ ***noun*** [C] (also **archives** [pl.]) (**HISTORY**) a collection of historical documents, etc. which show the history of a place or an organization; the place where they are kept: *archive material on the First World War*

archive[2] /'ɑːkaɪv/ ***verb*** [T] **1** to put a document or other material in an ARCHIVE[1] **2** (**COMPUTING**) to move information that you do not often need to a tape or disk to store it

archway /'ɑːtʃweɪ/ ***noun*** [C] (**ARCHITECTURE**) a passage or entrance with an ARCH over it

Arctic /'ɑːktɪk/ ***adj.*** **1** (**GEOGRAPHY**) connected with the region around the North Pole (the most northern point of the world) ➲ look at **Antarctic** **2** **arctic** extremely cold

the Arctic /'ɑːktɪk/ ***noun*** [sing.] (**GEOGRAPHY**) the area around the North Pole ➲ look at **the Antarctic** ➲ picture at **earth**

the ˌArctic 'Circle ***noun*** [sing.] (**GEOGRAPHY**) the line of LATITUDE 66° 33′N ➲ look at **the Antarctic Circle** ➲ picture at **earth**

ardent /'ɑːdnt/ ***adj.*** showing strong feelings, especially a strong liking for sb/sth: *He was an ardent supporter of the Government.* ▶ **ardently** ***adv.***

arduous /'ɑːdjuəs; -dʒu-/ ***adj.*** full of difficulties; needing a lot of effort: *an arduous journey* ◇ *arduous work*

are → BE

area 🔑 AW /'eəriə/ ***noun*** **1** [C] a part of a town, a country or the world: *Housing is very expensive in the Tokyo area.* ◇ *The wettest areas are in the West of the country.* ◇ *built-up areas* (= where there are a lot of buildings) ◇ *Forests cover a large area of the country.* **2** [C,U] (**MATHEMATICS**) the size of a surface, that you can calculate by multiplying the length by the width: *The area of the office is 35 square metres.* ◇ *The office is 35 square metres **in area**.* ➲ look at **volume** **3** [C] a space used for a particular activity: *The restaurant has a non-smoking area.* **4** [C] a particular part of a subject or activity: *Training is one area of the business that we could improve.*

arena /ə'riːnə/ ***noun*** [C] **1** an area with seats around it where public entertainments (sporting events, concerts, etc.) are held **2** an area of activity that concerns the public

aren't short for ARE NOT

arête /ə'ret/ ***noun*** [C] (**GEOGRAPHY**) a long sharp piece of high land (**a ridge**) along the top of mountains ➲ picture at **glacial**

argon /'ɑːgɒn/ ***noun*** [U] (*symbol* **Ar**) (**CHEMISTRY**) a colourless gas that does not react with chemicals and is used in electric lights ❶ **Argon** is a **noble gas**. ❶ For more information on the periodic table of elements, look at pages R34-5.

argot /'ɑːgəʊ/ ***noun*** [U] (**LANGUAGE**) informal words and phrases that are used by a particular group of people and that other people do not easily understand

arguable /'ɑːgjuəbl/ ***adj.*** **1** probably true; that you can give reasons for: *It is arguable that all hospital treatment should be free.* **2** probably not true; that you can give reasons against ▶ **arguably** /-əbli/ ***adv.***: *'King Lear' is arguably Shakespeare's best play.*

argue 🔑 /'ɑːgjuː/ ***verb*** **1** [I] ~ **(with sb) (about/over sth)** to say things, often angrily, that show that you do not agree with sb about sth: *The couple next door are always arguing.* ◇ *I never argue with my husband about money.* ➲ look at **fight[1]** (4), **quarrel[2]** (1) **2** [I,T] ~ **that...**; ~ **(for/against sth)** to give reasons that support your opinion about sth: *He argued against buying a new computer.*

argument 🔑 /'ɑːgjumənt/ ***noun*** **1** [C,U] **an** ~ **(with sb) (about/over sth)** an angry discussion between two or more people who disagree with each other: *Sue **had an argument** with her father about politics.* ◇ *He accepted the decision without argument.* **2** [C] the reason(s) that you give to support your opinion about sth: *What are the **arguments for/against** lower taxes?*

argumentation /ˌɑːgjumən'teɪʃn/ ***noun*** [U] logical arguments used to support a theory, an action or an idea

argumentative /ˌɑːgju'mentətɪv/ ***adj.*** often involved in or enjoying arguments

aria /'ɑːriə/ ***noun*** [C] (**MUSIC**) a song for one voice, especially in an OPERA

arid /'ærɪd/ ***adj.*** (**GEOGRAPHY**) (used about land or climate) very dry; with little or no rain

Aries /'eəriːz/ ***noun*** [U] the first of the twelve signs of the ZODIAC, the Ram

arise 🔑 /ə'raɪz/ ***verb*** [I] (*pt* **arose** /ə'rəʊz/; *pp* **arisen** /ə'rɪzn/) to begin to exist, to appear: *If any problems arise, let me know.*

aristocracy /ˌærɪˈstɒkrəsi/ *noun* [C, with sing. or pl. verb] (*pl.* **aristocracies**) (SOCIAL STUDIES) the people of the highest social class who often have special titles SYN **nobility**

aristocrat /ˈærɪstəkræt/ *noun* [C] (SOCIAL STUDIES) a member of the highest social class, often with a special title ▸ **aristocratic** /ˌærɪstəˈkrætɪk/ *adj.*

arithmetic /əˈrɪθmətɪk/ *noun* [U] (MATHEMATICS) the kind of mathematics which involves counting with numbers (adding, SUBTRACTING, MULTIPLYING and dividing): *I'm not very good at* ***mental arithmetic****.*

arithˌmetic ˈmean *noun* [C] (MATHEMATICS) = MEAN³ (1)

arithˌmetic proˈgression (*also* **arithˌmetical proˈgression**) *noun* [C] (MATHEMATICS) a series of numbers that decrease or increase by the same amount each time, for example 2, 4, 6, 8 ➲ look at **geometric progression**

the ark /ɑːk/ *noun* [sing.] (RELIGION) (in the Bible) a large boat which Noah built to save his family and two of every type of animal from the flood

arm

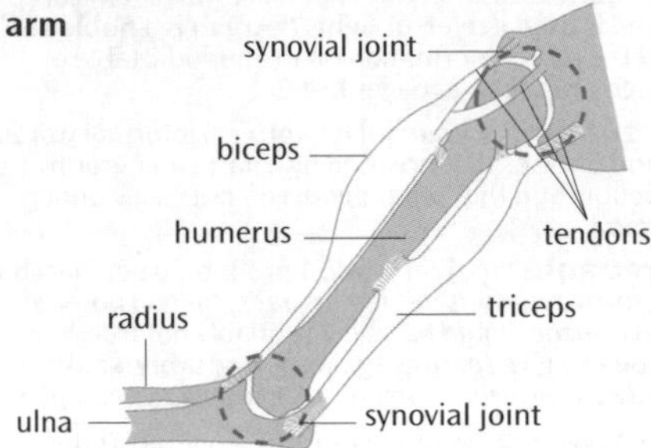

arm¹ ⊶ /ɑːm/ *noun* [C] **1** the long part at each side of your body connecting your shoulder to your hand: *He was carrying a newspaper under his arm.* **2** the part of a piece of clothing that covers your arm; a sleeve **3** the part of a chair where you rest your arms

IDM **arm in arm** with your arm folded around sb else's arm: *The two friends walked arm in arm.*

cross/fold your arms to cross your arms in front of your chest: *She folded her arms and waited.* ◇ *James was sitting with his arms crossed.*

twist sb's arm → TWIST¹

with open arms → OPEN¹

arm² ⊶ /ɑːm/ *verb* [I,T] to prepare sb/yourself to fight by supplying or getting weapons ➲ look at **armed**, **arms**

armadillo /ˌɑːməˈdɪləʊ/ *noun* [C] (*pl.* **armadillos**) an American animal with a hard shell, that eats insects and rolls into a ball if sth attacks it

armament /ˈɑːməmənt/ *noun* **1** [C, usually pl.] weapons, especially large guns, bombs, tanks, etc. **2** [U] (POLITICS) the process of increasing the amount of weapons an army or a country has, especially to prepare for war ➲ look at **disarmament**

armband /ˈɑːmbænd/ *noun* [C] **1** a piece of material that you wear around your arm: *The captain of the team wears an armband.* **2** a plastic ring filled with air which you can wear on each of your arms when you are learning to swim

armchair /ˈɑːmtʃeə(r)/ *noun* [C] a soft comfortable chair with sides which support your arms

armed ⊶ /ɑːmd/ *adj.* carrying a gun or other weapon; involving weapons: *All the terrorists were armed.* ◇ *armed robbery* OPP **unarmed**

the ˌarmed ˈforces (*BrE also* **the ˌarmed ˈservices**) *noun* [pl.] (POLITICS) a country's army, navy and air force

armful /ˈɑːmfʊl/ *noun* [C] the amount that you can carry in your arms

armhole /ˈɑːmhəʊl/ *noun* [C] the opening in a piece of clothing where your arm goes through

armistice /ˈɑːmɪstɪs/ *noun* [C] (POLITICS) an agreement between two countries who are at war that they will stop fighting

armour (*AmE* **armor**) /ˈɑːmə(r)/ *noun* [U] (HISTORY) clothing, often made of metal, that soldiers wore in earlier times to protect themselves: *a suit of armour*

armoured (*AmE* **armored**) /ˈɑːməd/ *adj.* (used about a vehicle) covered with metal to protect it in an attack

armpit /ˈɑːmpɪt/ *noun* [C] the part of the body under the arm at the point where it joins the shoulder ➲ picture on **page 80**

arms ⊶ /ɑːmz/ *noun* [pl.] **1** weapons, especially those that are used in war **2** = COAT OF ARMS

IDM **up in arms** protesting angrily about sth: *The workers were up in arms over the news that the factory was going to close.*

army ⊶ /ˈɑːmi/ *noun* [C, with sing. or pl. verb] (*pl.* **armies**) **1** the military forces of a country which are trained to fight on land: *the British Army* ◇ *She* ***joined the army*** *at the age of eighteen.* ◇ *The army is/are advancing towards the border.* ◇ *an army officer* ➲ look at **air force**, **navy** **2** a large number of people, especially when involved in an activity together

ˈA-road *noun* [C] (in Britain) a main road, usually not as wide as a motorway

aroma /əˈrəʊmə/ *noun* [C] a smell, especially a pleasant one ▸ **aromatic** /ˌærəˈmætɪk/ *adj.*

aromatherapy /əˌrəʊməˈθerəpi/ *noun* [U] (HEALTH) the use of natural oils that smell pleasant for controlling pain or for MASSAGE (= rubbing into the body) ▸ **aromatherapist** *noun* [C]

aromatic /ˌærəˈmætɪk/ *adj.* having a pleasant noticeable smell SYN **fragrant**: *aromatic oils/herbs*

arose past tense of **arise**

around ⊶ /əˈraʊnd/ *adv.*, *prep.* **1** (*also* **about**) in or to various places or directions: *This is our office – David will show you around* (= show you the different parts of it). ◇ *They wandered around the town, looking at the shops.* **2** moving so as to face in the opposite direction: *Turn around and go back the way you came.* **3** on all sides; forming a circle: *The park has a wall all around.* ◇ *Gather around so that you can all see.* ◇ *We sat down around the table.* **4** near a place: *Is there a bank around here?* **5** (*also* **about**) present or available: *I went to the house but there was nobody around.* **6** (*also* **about**) approximately: *I'll see you around seven* (= at about 7 o'clock). **7** (*also* **about**) used for activities with no real purpose: *'What are you doing?' 'Nothing, just lazing around.'*

arouse /əˈraʊz/ *verb* [T] to cause a particular reaction in people: *to arouse sb's curiosity/interest* ▸ **arousal** *noun* [U]

arpeggio /ɑːˈpedʒiəʊ/ *noun* [C] (*pl.* **arpeggios**) (MUSIC) the notes of a CHORD played quickly one after the other

arr. *abbr.* arrives: *arr. York 07.15*

arraign /ə'reɪn/ *verb* [T] (usually passive) (LAW) ~ **sb (for sth)** to bring a person to a court of law in order to formally accuse them of a crime ▸ **arraignment** *noun* [C,U]

arrange ⊶ /ə'reɪndʒ/ *verb* **1** [T] to put sth in order or in a particular pattern: *The books were arranged in alphabetical order.* ◇ *Arrange the chairs in a circle.* ◇ *She arranged the flowers in a vase.* **2** [I,T] ~ **(for) sth**; ~ **to do sth**; ~ **(sth) with sb** to make plans and preparations so that sth can happen in the future: *We're arranging a surprise party for Aisha.* ◇ *She arranged to meet Stuart after work.* ◇ *She arranged for her mother to look after the baby.*

arˌranged 'marriage *noun* [C] (SOCIAL STUDIES) a marriage in which the parents choose the husband or wife for their child

arrangement ⊶ /ə'reɪndʒmənt/ *noun* **1** [C, usually pl.] plans or preparations for sth that will happen in the future: *Come round this evening and we'll* ***make arrangements for*** *the party.* **2** [C,U] an agreement with sb to do sth: *They* ***have an arrangement*** *to share the cost of the food.* ◇ *We both need to use the computer so we'll have to* ***come to*** *some* ***arrangement****.* **3** [C] a group of things that have been placed in a particular pattern: *a flower arrangement*

arranger /ə'reɪndʒə/ *noun* [C] (MUSIC) a person who arranges music that has been written by sb different

array /ə'reɪ/ *noun* [C] **1** a large collection of things, especially one that is impressive and is seen by other people **2** (COMPUTING) a way of organizing and storing related data in a computer memory **3** (MATHEMATICS) a set of numbers, signs or values arranged in rows and columns

arrears /ə'rɪəz/ *noun* [pl.] (FINANCE) money that sb owes that they should have paid earlier
IDM **be in arrears; fall/get into arrears** to be late in paying money that you owe
be paid in arrears to be paid for work after you have done the work

arrest¹ ⊶ /ə'rest/ *verb* [T] (LAW) when the police **arrest** sb, they take them prisoner in order to question them about a crime

arrest² ⊶ /ə'rest/ *noun* [C,U] (LAW) the act of arresting sb: *The police* ***made*** *ten* ***arrests*** *after the riot.* ◇ *The wanted man is now* ***under arrest*** (= has been arrested).

arrival ⊶ /ə'raɪvl/ *noun* **1** [C,U] reaching the place to which you were travelling: *On our arrival we were told that our rooms had not been reserved.* OPP **departure 2** [C] people or things that have arrived: *We brought in extra chairs for the late arrivals.*

arrive ⊶ /ə'raɪv/ *verb* [I] **1** ~ **(at/in...)** to reach the place to which you were travelling: *We arrived home at about midnight.* ◇ *What time does the train arrive in Newcastle?* ◇ *They arrived at the station ten minutes late.* **2** to come or happen: *The day of the wedding had finally arrived.*
PHR V **arrive at** to reach sth: *We finally arrived at a decision.*

arrogant /'ærəgənt/ *adj.* thinking that you are better and more important than other people ▸ **arrogance** *noun* [U] ▸ **arrogantly** *adv.*

arrow ⊶ /'ærəʊ/ *noun* [C] **1** a thin piece of wood or metal, with one pointed end and feathers at the other end, that is shot by pulling back the string on a curved piece of wood (**a bow**) and letting go: ***a bow and arrow*** ◇ *to fire/shoot an arrow* ➲ look at **archer 2** the sign (→) which is used to show direction or position: *Follow the arrows.* ◇ *Use the arrow keys to move the cursor.*

arsenal /'ɑːsənl/ *noun* [C] **1** a collection of weapons such as guns and EXPLOSIVES **2** a building where military weapons and EXPLOSIVES are made or stored

arsenic /'ɑːsnɪk/ *noun* [U] (*symbol* **As**) (CHEMISTRY) a type of very strong poison ℹ For more information on the periodic table of elements, look at pages R34-5.

arson /'ɑːsn/ *noun* [U] (LAW) the crime of setting fire to a building on purpose

arsonist /'ɑːsənɪst/ *noun* [C] (LAW) a person who deliberately sets fire to a building

COLLOCATIONS AND PATTERNS

Works of art

An **artist** works in a **studio.**
A **painter** paints **pictures** , for example **portraits** (= pictures of people), **landscapes** (= pictures of the countryside) or **abstract paintings.**
Constable was a famous landscape painter.
Velazquez painted many portraits of King Philip IV of Spain.

A picture might be a **watercolour**, an **acrylic** or an **oil painting.**
A **sculptor** makes **sculptures** of figures or objects in materials such as **marble** (= a type of stone) or **bronze** (= a type of metal).
Some people collect **works of art.**
She collects 19th century watercolours.

An **exhibition** is a **collection** of **works of art** which is **on display/show** for a short time in an **art gallery.**
Cezanne's landscapes will be on display at the Musée d'Orsay from 8th May.
Kandinsky's abstract paintings were on show at MOMA last year.

Many **public galleries** have **permanent collections.**
A great work of art is called a **masterpiece.**
The National Gallery has a fine collection of Impressionist masterpieces.

art ⊶ /ɑːt/ *noun* **1** [U] the activity or skill of producing things such as paintings, designs, etc.; the objects that are produced: *an art class* ◇ *modern art* ◇ *I've never been good at art.* ➲ look at **work of art 2** [C] a skill or sth that needs skill: *There's an art* ***to*** *writing a good letter.* **3 the arts** [pl.] activities which involve creating things such as paintings, literature or music **4 arts** [pl.] (EDUCATION) subjects such as history or languages that you study at school or university ➲ look at **sciences**

art deco (also **Art Deco**) /ˌɑːt 'dekəʊ/ *noun* [U] (ART) a popular style of decorative art in the 1920s and 1930s that has GEOMETRIC (= regular) shapes with clear outlines and bright strong colours

artefact /'ɑːtɪfækt/ *noun* [C] (TECHNICAL) an object that is made by a person, especially sth of historical or cultural interest

arteriosclerosis /ɑːˌtɪəriəʊsklə'rəʊsɪs/ *noun* [U] (HEALTH) a condition in which the walls of the ARTERIES (= the tubes that carry blood from the heart to the other parts of the body) become thick and hard, making it difficult for blood to flow

artery /'ɑːtəri/ *noun* [C] (*pl.* **arteries**) (ANATOMY) one of the tubes which take blood from the heart to other parts of the body ➲ look at **carotid artery**, vein ➲ picture at **circulation** ▸ **arterial** /ɑːˈtɪəriəl/ *adj.*: *arterial blood/disease*

artesian well /ɑːˌtiːziən ˈwel/ *noun* [C] (GEOGRAPHY) a hole made in the ground through which water rises to the surface by natural pressure

artful /ˈɑːtfl/ *adj.* clever at getting what you want, perhaps by not telling the truth

ˈart gallery (*also* **gallery**) *noun* [C] (ART) a building where paintings and other works of art are shown to the public

arthritis /ɑːˈθraɪtɪs/ *noun* [U] (HEALTH) a disease which causes swelling and pain in the joints (= places where the bones are connected) ▸ **arthritic** /ɑːˈθrɪtɪk/ *adj.*

arthropod /ˈɑːθrəpɒd/ *noun* [C] (BIOLOGY) any of the PHYLUM (= group) of animals that have a hard body without a BACKBONE in it. **Arthropods** have legs that are made of more than one part and that can bend where the parts join together: *Spiders, insects and crustaceans are arthropods.*

artichoke /ˈɑːtɪtʃəʊk/ *noun* [C] a green vegetable with a lot of thick pointed leaves. You can eat the bottom part of the leaves and its centre

article ⊶ /ˈɑːtɪkl/ *noun* **1** [C] (ARTS AND MEDIA) a piece of writing in a newspaper or magazine: *Have you seen that article about young fashion designers?* **2** [C] (LAW) a separate item in an agreement or a contract: *Article 10 of the European Convention guarantees free speech.* **3** [C] (*formal*) an object, especially one of a set SYN **item**: *articles of clothing* **4** [C] (LANGUAGE) the words 'a/an' (**the indefinite article**) or 'the' (**the definite article**) **5 articles** [pl.] (*BrE*) (*old-fashioned*) (LAW) a period of training with a firm in certain professions: *Toby is **in articles** with a city law firm.*

articled clerk *noun* [C] (*BrE*) (*old-fashioned*) (LAW) a person who is employed by a group of lawyers while being trained in the job

articulate[1] /ɑːˈtɪkjələt/ *adj.* good at expressing your ideas clearly OPP **inarticulate**

articulate[2] /ɑːˈtɪkjuleɪt/ *verb* [I,T] to say sth clearly or to express your ideas or feelings ▸ **articulation** /ɑːˌtɪkjuˈleɪʃn/ *noun* [U]

articulated /ɑːˈtɪkjuleɪtɪd/ *adj.* (*BrE*) (used about a large vehicle such as a lorry) with two or more sections joined together in a way that makes it easier to turn corners

artifice /ˈɑːtɪfɪs/ *noun* [U, C] (*formal*) the use of clever methods to trick sb

THESAURUS

artificial

synthetic • false • man-made • fake • imitation

These words all describe things that are not real, or not naturally produced or grown.

artificial: *artificial flowers*
synthetic: *synthetic drugs*
false: *false teeth*
man-made: *man-made fibres such as nylon*
fake: *a fake-fur jacket*
imitation: *imitation pearls*

artificial ⊶ /ˌɑːtɪˈfɪʃl/ *adj.* **1** made or produced to copy sth natural; not real: *artificial limb/flower/sweetener/fertilizer* **2** created by people; not happening naturally: *A job interview is a very artificial situation.* ▸ **artificially** /-ʃəli/ *adv.*

ˌartificial inseminˈation *noun* [U] (*abbr.* **AI**) (BIOLOGY) the scientific process of making a woman or a female animal pregnant by putting male SPERM inside her so that babies or young can be produced without sexual activity

ˌartificial inˈtelligence *noun* [U] (*abbr.* **AI**) (COMPUTING) (the study of) the way in which computers can be made to copy the way humans think

ˌartificial ˈlanguage *noun* [C] (LANGUAGE) a language invented for international communication or for use with computers

ˌartificial respiˈration *noun* [U] (HEALTH) the process of helping a person who has stopped breathing begin to breathe again, usually by blowing into their mouth or nose

artillery /ɑːˈtɪləri/ *noun* [U] large, heavy guns that are moved on wheels; the part of the army that uses them

artisan /ˌɑːtɪˈzæn/ *noun* [C] a person who makes things skilfully, especially with their hands SYN **craftsman**

artist ⊶ /ˈɑːtɪst/ *noun* [C] (ART) somebody who produces art, especially paintings or drawings

artiste /ɑːˈtiːst/ *noun* [C] (ARTS AND MEDIA) a person whose job is to entertain people, by singing, dancing, etc.

artistic ⊶ /ɑːˈtɪstɪk/ *adj.* (ART) **1** connected with art: *the artistic director of the theatre* **2** showing a skill in art ▸ **artistically** /-kli/ *adv.*

artistry /ˈɑːtɪstri/ *noun* [U] the skill of an artist

art nouveau (also **Art Nouveau**) /ˌɑː(t) nuːˈvəʊ/ *noun* [U] (ART) a style of decorative art and ARCHITECTURE popular in Europe and the US at the end of the 19th century and beginning of the 20th century that uses complicated designs and curved patterns based on natural shapes like leaves and flowers

ˌarts and ˈcrafts *noun* [pl.] (ART) activities that need both artistic and practical skills, such as making cloth, jewellery and furniture

the ˌArts and ˈCrafts Movement *noun* [sing.] (HISTORY, ART) a group of people in England at the end of the 19th century who wanted to show the importance and value of ARTS AND CRAFTS at a time when machines were being used more and more

artwork /ˈɑːtwɜːk/ *noun* **1** [U] (ARTS AND MEDIA) photographs, drawings, etc. that have been prepared for a book or magazine: *a piece of artwork* **2** (ART) [C] a work of art, especially one in a museum or an EXHIBITION

arty /ˈɑːti/ *adj.* (*informal*) pretending or wanting to be very artistic or interested in the arts: *He can't really like all those boring arty films.*

as ⊶ /əz strong form æz/ *conj.*, *prep.*, *adv.* **1** while sth else is happening: *The phone rang just as I was leaving the house.* ◇ *As she walked along the road, she thought about her father.* **2 as ...as** used for comparing people or things: *Todor's almost as tall as me.* ◇ *Todor's almost as tall as I am.* ◇ *It's not as cold as it was yesterday.* ◇ *I'd like an appointment **as soon as possible**.* ◇ *She earns **twice as much as** her husband.* ◇ *I haven't got as many books as you have.* **3** used for talking about sb/sth's job, role or function: *He works as a train driver.* ◇ *Think of me as your friend, not as your boss.* ◇ *You could use this white sheet as a tablecloth.* **4** in a particular way, state, etc.; like: *Please do as I tell you.* ◇ *Leave the room **as it is**. Don't move anything.* **5** used at the beginning of a comment about what you are saying: ***As you know**, I've decided to leave at the end of the month.* **6** because: *I didn't buy the dress, as I decided it was too expensive.*

IDM **as for** used when you are starting to talk about a different person or thing: *Gianni's upstairs. As for Andreas, I've no idea where he is.*
as if; **as though** used for saying how sb/sth appears: *She looks as if/though she's just got out of bed.*
as it were used for saying that sth is only true in a certain way: *She felt, as it were, a stranger in her own house.*
as of; **as from** starting from a particular time: *As from next week, Tim Shaw will be managing this department.*
as to about a particular thing; concerning: *I was given no instructions as to how to begin.*

ASA /ˌeɪ es ˈeɪ/ ***abbr.*** **1 Advertising Standards Authority**; an organization in Britain which controls the standard of advertising **2 American Standards Association**; used for indicating the speed of a camera film

asap /ˌeɪ es eɪ ˈpiː/ ***abbr.*** as soon as possible

asbestos /æsˈbestəs/ ***noun*** [U] a soft grey material that does not burn and is used to protect against heat

ASBO /ˈæzbəʊ/ ***noun*** [C] (LAW) **antisocial behaviour order**; in the UK, an order made by a court which says that sb must stop behaving in a harmful or annoying way to other people

ascend /əˈsend/ ***verb*** [I,T] (*formal*) to go up
OPP **descend** ▶ **ascending** ***adj.***: *The questions are arranged **in ascending order** of difficulty* (= the most difficult ones are at the end).

Ascension Day /əˈsenʃn deɪ/ ***noun*** [U,C] (RELIGION) the 40th day after Easter when Christians remember Christ leaving the earth and going to heaven

ascent /əˈsent/ ***noun*** [C, usually sing.] **1** the act of climbing or going up: *the ascent of Everest* **2** a path or hill leading upwards: *There was a steep ascent before the path became flat again.* OPP **descent**

ascertain /ˌæsəˈteɪn/ ***verb*** [T] (*formal*) to find sth out

ascetic /əˈsetɪk/ ***adj.*** (RELIGION) not allowing yourself physical pleasures, especially for religious reasons ▶ **ascetic *noun*** [C]

ASCII /ˈæski/ ***noun*** [U] (COMPUTING) **American Standard Code for Information Interchange**; a system that allows data to be moved between computers that use different programs

ascorbic acid /əˌskɔːbɪk ˈæsɪd/ (*also* **ˌvitamin ˈC**) ***noun*** [U] (HEALTH) a natural substance that is found in fruit such as lemons and oranges and in green vegetables. Humans and some animals need **ascorbic acid** in order to stay healthy.

ascribe /əˈskraɪb/ ***verb*** [T] **~ sth to sb/sth** to say that sth was written by or belonged to sb; to say what caused sth: *Many people ascribe this play to Shakespeare.*

ASEAN /ˈæsiæn/ ***abbr.*** Association of South East Asian Nations

aseptic /ˌeɪˈseptɪk/ ***adj.*** (HEALTH) not having any harmful bacteria

asexual /ˌeɪˈsekʃuəl/ ***adj.*** **1** (BIOLOGY) not involving sex; not having sexual organs: *asexual reproduction* **2** not having sexual qualities; not interested in sex ▶ **asexually *adv.***: *to reproduce asexually*

ash /æʃ/ ***noun*** **1** [U] (*also* **ashes** [pl.]) the grey or black powder which is left after sth has burned: *cigarette ash* ◇ *the ashes of a fire* ➲ picture at **volcano** **2 ashes** [pl.] what is left after a dead person has been CREMATED (= burned after death) **3** [C] a type of forest tree that grows in cool countries

ashamed ⊶ /əˈʃeɪmd/ ***adj.*** (not *before* a noun) **~ (of sth/sb/yourself)**; **~ (that...)**; **~ (to do sth)** feeling guilty or embarrassed about sb/sth or because of sth you have done: *She was ashamed of her old clothes.* ◇ *How could you be so rude? I'm ashamed of you!* ◇ *She felt ashamed that she hadn't helped him.*
OPP **unashamed**

ashen /ˈæʃn/ ***adj.*** (used about sb's face) very pale; without colour because of illness or fear

ashore /əˈʃɔː(r)/ ***adv.*** onto the land from the sea, a river, etc.: *The passengers went ashore for an hour while the ship was in port.* ➲ look at **shore**

ashram /ˈæʃrəm/ ***noun*** [C] (RELIGION) **1** a place where Hindus live together in a religious community **2** a place where a Hindu religious man lives alone

ashtray /ˈæʃtreɪ/ ***noun*** [C] a small dish for collecting the powder (**ash**) made when a cigarette burns

Asian /ˈeɪʒn; ˈeɪʃn/ ***noun*** [C] a person from Asia or whose family was originally from Asia ▶ **Asian *adj.***

aside ⊶ /əˈsaɪd/ ***adv.*** **1** on or to one side; out of the way: *We stood aside to let the man go past.* **2** to be kept separately, for a special purpose: *I try to **set aside** a little money each month.*

aˈside from ***prep.*** (*especially AmE*) = APART FROM

THESAURUS

ask

enquire • demand • query

All these words mean to say or write sth in the form of a question, in order to get information.

ask: *Can I ask you a question?*

enquire/inquire (*rather formal*): *I rang the station to enquire about train times.*

demand: *'Where have you been?' he demanded angrily.*

query (*formal*): *'Why ever not?' she queried.*

ask ⊶ /ɑːsk/ ***verb*** **1** [I,T] **~ (sb) (about sb/sth)**; **~ sb sth** to put a question to sb in order to find out some information: *We need to ask about tickets.* ◇ *Ask him how old he is.* ◇ *She asked if I wanted tea or coffee.* ◇ *'What's the time?' he asked.* ◇ *He asked what the time was.* ◇ *He asked me the time.* **2** [I,T] **~ (sb) for sth**; **~ sth (of sb)**; **~ sb to do sth** to request that sb gives you sth or does sth for you: *She sat down and asked for a cup of coffee.* ◇ *Don't ask Joe for money – he hasn't got any.* ◇ *You are asking too much of him – he can't possibly do all that!* ◇ *Ring this number and ask for Mrs Khan.* ◇ *I asked him if he would drive me home.* ◇ *I asked him to drive me home.* ➲ note at **demand**[2] **3** [I,T] to request permission to do sth: *I'm sure she'll let you go if you ask.* ◇ *He asked to use our phone.* ◇ *We asked if we could go home early.* **4** [T] **~ sb (to sth)** to invite sb **5** [T] to say the price that you want for sth: *How much are they asking for their car?*
IDM **ask for trouble/it** to behave in a way that will almost certainly cause you problems: *Driving when you're tired is just asking for trouble.*
if you ask me if you want my opinion
PHRV **ask after sb** to ask about sb's health or to ask for news of sb: *Tina asked after you today.*
ask sb out to invite sb to go out with you, especially as a way of starting a romantic relationship: *Harry's too shy to ask her out.*

askew /əˈskjuː/ ***adv.***, ***adj.*** (not *before* a noun) not in a straight or level position

'asking price *noun* [C] (BUSINESS) the price that sb wants to sell sth for ➲ look at **cost price**, **selling price**

asleep 🔑 /ə'sli:p/ *adj.* (not before a noun) not awake; sleeping: *The baby is fast/sound asleep.* ◇ *It didn't take me long to* ***fall asleep*** *last night.*

AS (level) /eɪ 'es levl/ *noun* [C,U] (EDUCATION) **Advanced Subsidiary (level)**; a British exam usually taken in Year 12 of school or college (= the year before the final year) when students are aged 17. Together with A2 EXAMS, **AS levels** form A LEVELS, which are needed for entrance to universities: *She's doing an AS (level) in French.* ➲ look at **A2 (level)**

asp /æsp/ *noun* [C] a small poisonous snake found especially in North Africa

asparagus /ə'spærəgəs/ *noun* [U] a plant with long green or white STEMS that you can cook and eat as a vegetable

aspect 🔑 AW /'æspekt/ *noun* **1** [C] one of the qualities or parts of a situation, idea, problem, etc.: *the most important aspect of the debate* **2** [U, sing.] (*formal*) the appearance of a place, a situation or a person: *Events began to take on a more sinister aspect.*

asphalt /'æsfælt/ *noun* [U] a thick black substance that is used for making the surface of roads

asphyxia /æs'fɪksiə; əs'f-/ *noun* [U] the state of being unable to breathe, which causes sb to die or to become unconscious

asphyxiate /əs'fɪksieɪt/ *verb* [T] to make sb become unconscious or die by preventing them from breathing: *He was asphyxiated by the smoke while he was asleep.* ▸ **asphyxiation** /əsˌfɪksi'eɪʃn/ *noun* [U]

aspic /'æspɪk/ *noun* [U] clear JELLY (= a soft, solid substance), which food is sometimes put into when it is being served cold

aspire /ə'spaɪə(r)/ *verb* [I] (*formal*) ~ **to sth/to do sth** to have a strong desire to have or do sth: *an aspiring actor* ▸ **aspiration** /ˌæspə'reɪʃn/ *noun* [C,U]

aspirin /'æsprɪn; 'æspərɪn/ *noun* [C,U] (HEALTH) a drug used to reduce pain and a high temperature

ass /æs/ = DONKEY

assailant /ə'seɪlənt/ *noun* [C] (*formal*) (LAW) a person who attacks sb

assassin /ə'sæsɪn/ *noun* [C] a person who kills a famous or important person for money or for political reasons ▸ **assassinate** /ə'sæsɪneɪt/ *verb* [T] ➲ note at **kill** ▸ **assassination** /əˌsæsɪ'neɪʃn/ *noun* [C,U]

assault /ə'sɔ:lt/ *noun* [C,U] ~ **(on sb/sth)** a sudden attack on sb/sth ▸ **assault** *verb* [T]: *He was charged with assaulting a police officer.*

as'sault course (*AmE* **'obstacle course**) *noun* [C] (SPORT) an area of land with many objects that are difficult to climb, jump over or go through, which is used, especially by soldiers, for improving physical skills and strength

assemble AW /ə'sembl/ *verb* **1** [I,T] to come together or bring sb/sth together in a group: *I've assembled all the information I need for my essay.* **2** [T] to fit the parts of sth together: *We spent hours trying to assemble our new bookshelves.* ➲ note at **build**[1]

assembly AW /ə'sembli/ *noun* (*pl.* **assemblies**) **1** (also **Assembly**) [C] (POLITICS) a group of people who have been elected to meet together regularly and make decisions or laws for a particular region or country: *State/legislative/federal/local assemblies* ◇ *the UN General Assembly* **2** [U,C] a large group of people who come together for a particular purpose: ***school assembly*** (= a regular meeting for all the students and teachers of a school) **3** [U] the process of putting together the parts of sth such as a vehicle or piece of furniture

as'sembly line *noun* [C] a line of people and machines in a factory that fit the parts of sth together in a fixed order

assemblyman /ə'semblimən/ **assemblywoman** /ə'sembliwʊmən/ *noun* [C] (*pl.* **-men** /-mən/, **-women** /-wɪmɪn/) (POLITICS) a person who is an elected representative in a state ASSEMBLY in the US

assent /ə'sent/ *noun* [U] (*formal*) ~ **(to sth)** official agreement to sth: *The committee* ***gave their assent*** *to the proposed changes.* ▸ **assent** *verb* [I] ~ **(to sth)**: *Nobody would assent to the terms he proposed.*

assert /ə'sɜ:t/ *verb* [T] **1** to say sth clearly and firmly **2** to behave in a determined and confident way to make people listen to you or to get what you want: *You ought to assert yourself more.* ◇ *to assert your authority*

assertion /ə'sɜ:ʃn/ *noun* **1** [C] a statement that says you strongly believe that sth is true ➲ note at **claim**[2] **2** [U] the action of showing, using or stating sth strongly

assertive /ə'sɜ:tɪv/ *adj.* expressing your opinion clearly and firmly so that people listen to you or do what you want ▸ **assertively** *adv.* ▸ **assertiveness** *noun* [U]

assess AW /ə'ses/ *verb* [T] **1** to judge or form an opinion about sth: *It's too early to assess the effects of the price rises.* **2** ~ **sth (at sth)** to guess or decide the amount or value of sth: *to assess the cost of repairs* ▸ **assessment** AW *noun* [C,U]: *I made a careful assessment of the risks involved.*

assessor /ə'sesə(r)/ *noun* [C] **1** (LAW) an expert in a particular subject who is asked by a court of law or other official group to give advice **2** (FINANCE) a person who calculates the value or cost of sth or the amount of money to be paid: *an insurance/a tax assessor* **3** a person who judges how well sb has done in an exam, a competition, etc.: *Marks are awarded by an external assessor.*

asset /'æset/ *noun* [C] **1 an** ~ **(to sb/sth)** a person or thing that is useful to sb/sth: *She's a great asset to the organization.* **2** [usually pl.] (FINANCE) something of value that a person, company, etc. owns

assiduous /ə'sɪdjuəs/ *adj.* (*formal*) working very hard and taking great care that everything is done as well as it can be SYN **diligent** ▸ **assiduously** *adv.*

assign AW /ə'saɪn/ *verb* [T] **1** ~ **sth to sb/sth** to give sth to sb for a particular purpose: *We have assigned 20% of our budget to the project.* **2** ~ **sb to sth** to give sb a particular job to do

assignment AW /ə'saɪnmənt/ *noun* [C,U] a job or type of work that you are given to do: *The reporter disappeared while on (an) assignment in the war zone.*

assimilate /ə'sɪməleɪt/ *verb* **1** [I,T] ~ **(sb/sth) (into sth)** (SOCIAL STUDIES) to become or allow sb/sth to become part of a country, a social group, etc. **2** [T] to learn and understand sth: *to assimilate new facts/information/ideas* ▸ **assimilation** /əˌsɪmə'leɪʃn/ *noun* [U]

assist 🔑 AW /ə'sɪst/ *verb* [I,T] (*formal*) ~ **(sb) in/with sth**; ~ **(sb) in doing sth** to help: *Volunteers assisted in searching for the boy.*

assistance ⊶ AW /ə'sɪstəns/ ***noun*** [U] (*formal*) help or support: *financial assistance for poorer families* ◇ *She shouted for help but nobody came to her assistance.*

assistant[1] ⊶ /ə'sɪstənt/ ***noun*** [C] **1** a person who helps or supports sb, usually in their job: *My assistant will now demonstrate the machine in action.* ➲ look at **PDA**, **personal assistant** **2** = SHOP ASSISTANT: *a sales assistant in a department store*

assistant[2] ⊶ /ə'sɪstənt/ ***adj.*** (*abbr.* Asst) (often used in titles) having a rank below a senior person and helping them in their work: *the assistant manager* ◇ *Assistant Attorney General William Weld*

Assoc. ***abbr.*** association

associate[1] ⊶ /ə'səʊʃieɪt/ ***verb*** **1** [T] ~ **sb/sth (with sb/sth)** to make a connection between people or things in your mind: *I always associate the smell of the sea with my childhood.* **2** [I] ~ **with sb** to spend time with sb **3** [T] ~ **yourself with sth** to say that you support sth or agree with sth OPP **disassociate**

associate[2] /ə'səʊʃiət; -siət/ ***adj.*** **1** (often used in titles) of a lower rank or having fewer rights in a particular profession or organization: *associate membership of the European Union* ◇ *an* ***associate member/director*** **2** (BUSINESS) joined to or connected with a profession or an organization: *an associate company in Japan*

associate[3] /ə'səʊsiət/ ***noun*** [C] (BUSINESS) a person that you meet and get to know through your work: *a business associate*

association ⊶ /əˌsəʊsi'eɪʃn/ ***noun*** **1** [U] joining or working with another person or group: *We work* ***in association with*** *our New York office.* **2** [C] a group of people or organizations who work together for a particular purpose: *the National Association of Language Teachers* **3** [C,U] the act of connecting one person or thing with another in your mind

assonance /'æsənəns/ ***noun*** [U] (LITERATURE, LANGUAGE) the effect created when two SYLLABLES in words that are close together have the same VOWEL sound, but different CONSONANTS, or the same CONSONANTS but different VOWELS, for example, 'seen' and 'beat' or 'cold' and 'killed'

assorted /ə'sɔːtɪd/ ***adj.*** of different types; mixed

assortment /ə'sɔːtmənt/ ***noun*** [C] a group of different things or of different types of the same thing; a mixture

Asst (*also* **asst**) ***abbr.*** assistant

assuage /ə'sweɪdʒ/ ***verb*** [T] (*formal*) to make an unpleasant feeling less strong: *He hoped that by confessing he could assuage his guilt.*

assume ⊶ AW /ə'sjuːm/ ***verb*** [T] **1** to accept or believe that sth is true even though you have no proof; to expect sth to be true: *I assume that you have the necessary documents.* ◇ *Everyone assumed Ralph was guilty.* ◇ *Everyone assumed Ralph to be guilty.* **2** to pretend to have or be sb/sth: *to assume a false name* **3** to begin to use power or to have a powerful position: *to assume control of sth*

assuming AW /ə'sjuːmɪŋ/ ***conj.*** ~ **(that)** used to suppose that sth is true so that you can talk about what the results might be: *Assuming (that) he's still alive, how old would he be now?*

assumption AW /ə'sʌmpʃn/ ***noun*** **1** [C] something that you accept is true even though you have no proof: *We'll work* ***on the assumption that*** *the guests will be hungry when they arrive.* ◇ *It's unfair to* ***make assumptions about*** *a person's character before you know them.* ◇ *a reasonable/false assumption* **2** [U] **the ~ of sth** (*formal*) the act of taking power or of starting an important job

assurance AW /ə'ʃɔːrəns/ ***noun*** **1** [C] a promise that sth will certainly happen or be true: *They gave me* ***an assurance that*** *the work would be finished by Friday.* **2** (*also* **self-assurance**) [U] the belief that you can do or succeed at sth; confidence

assure ⊶ AW /ə'ʃɔː(r)/ ***verb*** [T] **1** to promise sb that sth will certainly happen or be true, especially if they are worried: *I assure you that it is perfectly safe.* ◇ *Let me assure you of my full support.* **2** to make sth sure or certain: *The success of the new product assured the survival of the company.*

assured /ə'ʃɔːd/ (*also* ˌ**self-as'sured**) ***adj.*** believing that you can do sth or succeed at sth; confident ➲ note at **certain**

astatine /'æstətiːn/ ***noun*** [U] (*symbol* **At**) (CHEMISTRY) a chemical element. **Astatine** is a RADIOACTIVE element which is found in small amounts in nature, and is produced artificially for use in medicine. ❶ For more information on the periodic table of elements, look at pages R34-5.

asterisk /'æstərɪsk/ ***noun*** [C] the sign (*) that you use to make people notice sth in a piece of writing

asteroid /'æstərɔɪd/ ***noun*** [C] (ASTRONOMY) any of the many small planets that go around the sun ➲ picture at **solar system**

asthma /'æsmə/ ***noun*** [U] (HEALTH) a medical condition that makes breathing difficult

asthmatic /æs'mætɪk/ ***noun*** [C] (HEALTH) a person who has ASTHMA ▶ **asthmatic** ***adj.***

astigmatism /ə'stɪgmətɪzəm/ ***noun*** [C] (HEALTH) a fault in the shape of a person's eye that prevents them from seeing clearly

astonish /ə'stɒnɪʃ/ ***verb*** [T] to surprise sb very much: *She astonished everybody by announcing her engagement.* ▶ **astonished** ***adj.***: *I was astonished by the decision.*

astonishing /ə'stɒnɪʃɪŋ/ ***adj.*** very surprising ▶ **astonishingly** ***adv.***

astonishment /ə'stɒnɪʃmənt/ ***noun*** [U] very great surprise: *He dropped his book* ***in astonishment***.

astound /ə'staʊnd/ ***verb*** [T] (usually passive) to surprise sb very much: *We were astounded by how well he performed.*

astounded /ə'staʊndɪd/ ***adj.*** feeling or showing great surprise

astounding /ə'staʊndɪŋ/ ***adj.*** causing sb to feel extremely surprised

astray /ə'streɪ/ ***adv.***
IDM **go astray** to become lost or be stolen
lead sb astray → LEAD[1]

astride /ə'straɪd/ ***adv.***, ***prep.*** with one leg on each side of sth: *to sit astride a horse*

astringent /ə'strɪndʒənt/ ***adj.*** **1** (HEALTH) (used about a liquid or a cream) able to stop the loss of blood from a cut, or to make the skin tighter so that it feels less OILY: *an astringent cream* **2** (*formal*) critical in a severe or clever way: *astringent comments* **3** (*formal*) slightly bitter but fresh in taste or smell ▶ **astringent** ***noun*** [U]

astrolabe /'æstrəleɪb/ ***noun*** (ASTRONOMY) a device used in the past for measuring the distances of stars, planets etc. and for calculating the position of a ship

astrologer /ə'strɒlədʒə(r)/ ***noun*** [C] a person who is an expert in ASTROLOGY

astrology /ə'strɒlədʒi/ ***noun*** [U] the study of the positions and movements of the stars and planets and the way that some people believe they affect people and events ➲ look at **horoscope**, **zodiac**

astronaut /'æstrənɔːt/ ***noun*** [C] a person who travels in a SPACECRAFT

astronomer /ə'strɒnəmə(r)/ ***noun*** [C] (ASTRONOMY) a person who studies ASTRONOMY

astronomical /ˌæstrə'nɒmɪkl/ ***adj.*** **1** (ASTRONOMY) connected with ASTRONOMY **2** (*also* **astronomic**) (*informal*) (used about an amount, a price, etc.) extremely high: *astronomical house prices*

astronomy /ə'strɒnəmi/ ***noun*** [U] the scientific study of the sun, moon, stars, etc.

astrophysics /ˌæstrəʊ'fɪzɪks/ ***noun*** [U] (ASTRONOMY, PHYSICS) the scientific study of the physical and chemical structure of the stars, planets, etc.

astute /ə'stjuːt/ ***adj.*** very clever; good at judging people or situations

asylum /ə'saɪləm/ ***noun*** **1** [U] (also *formal* **poˌlitical a'sylum**) (POLITICS, SOCIAL STUDIES) protection that a government gives to people who have left their own country, usually because they were in danger for political reasons: *to seek/apply for/be granted asylum* **2** [C] (*old-fashioned*) (HEALTH) a hospital where people who were mentally ill could be cared for, often for a long time

a'sylum ˌseeker ***noun*** [C] (POLITICS, SOCIAL STUDIES) a person who has been forced to leave their own country because they are in danger and who arrives in another country asking to be allowed to stay there

asymmetric /ˌeɪsɪ'metrɪk/ (*also* **asymmetrical** /ˌeɪsɪ'metrɪkl/) ***adj.*** having two sides or parts that are not the same in size or shape OPP **symmetrical** ▶ **asymmetrically** /-ɪkli/ ***adv.*** ▶ **asymmetry** /ˌeɪ'sɪmətri/ ***noun*** [U]

asymmetric bars

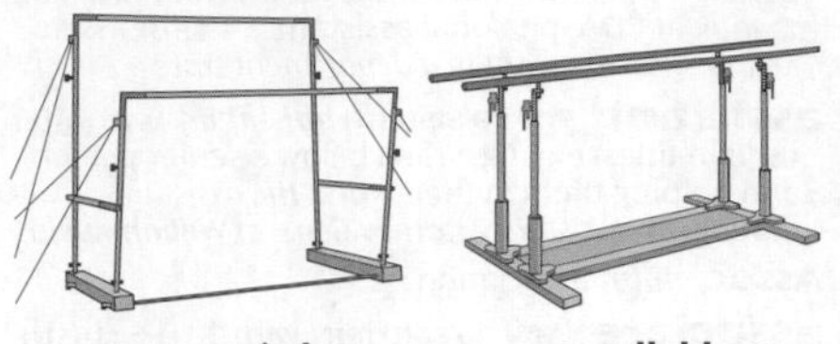

asymˌmetric 'bars (*BrE*) (*AmE* **unˌeven 'bars**) ***noun*** [pl.] (SPORT) two bars on posts of different heights that are used by women for doing GYMNASTIC exercises on

at ⊶ /ət strong form æt/ ***prep.*** **1** used to show where sb/sth is or where sth happens: *at the bottom/top of the page* ◇ *He was standing at the door.* ◇ *Change trains at Chester.* ◇ *We were at home all weekend.* ◇ *Are the children at school?* ◇ *'Where's Peter?' 'He's at Sue's.'* (= at Sue's house) **2** used to show when sth happens: *I start work at 9 o'clock.* ◇ *at the weekend* ◇ *at night* ◇ *at Easter* ◇ *She got married at 18* (= when she was 18). **3** in the direction of sb/sth: *What are you looking at?* ◇ *He pointed a gun at the policeman.* ◇ *Don't shout at me!* **4** because of sth: *I was surprised at her behaviour.* ◇ *We laughed at his jokes.* **5** used to show what sb is doing or what is happening: *They were* ***hard at work***. ◇ *The two countries were* ***at war***. **6** used to show the price, rate, speed, etc. of sth: *We were travelling at about 50*

atmosphere

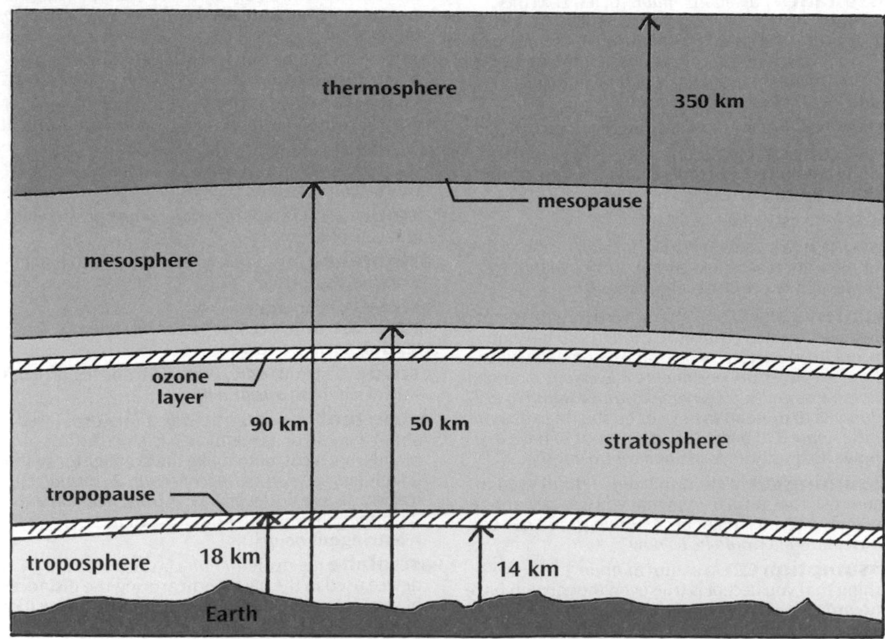

layers of the Earth's atmosphere

miles per hour. **7** used with adjectives that show how well sb/sth does sth: *She's not very **good at** French.* **8** (COMPUTING) the symbol (@) used in email addresses

ate past tense of **eat**

atheism /ˈeɪθiɪzəm/ *noun* [U] (RELIGION) the belief that there is no God ▶ **atheist** *noun* [C]

athlete /ˈæθliːt/ *noun* [C] (SPORT) a person who can run, jump, etc. very well, especially one who takes part in sports competitions, etc.

athletic /æθˈletɪk/ *adj.* **1** (SPORT) connected with ATHLETES or ATHLETICS: *athletic ability* **2** (HEALTH) (used about a person) having a fit, strong, and healthy body

athletics /æθˈletɪks/ *noun* [U] (SPORT) sports such as running, jumping, throwing, etc.

atishoo /əˈtɪʃuː/ *exclamation* used to represent the sound that you make when you SNEEZE (= suddenly blow air out of your nose)

atlas /ˈætləs/ *noun* [C] (*pl.* **atlases**) (GEOGRAPHY) a book of maps: *a road atlas of Europe*

ATM /ˌeɪ tiː ˈem/ = CASH MACHINE

atm *abbr.* = ATMOSPHERE (4)

atmosphere 🔑 /ˈætməsfɪə(r)/ *noun* **1** [C, usually sing.] (SCIENCE) the mixture of gases that surrounds the earth or any other star, planet, etc.: *the earth's atmosphere* ◊ *Saturn's atmosphere* **2** [sing.] the air in a place: *a smoky atmosphere* **3** [sing.] the mood or feeling of a place or situation: *The atmosphere of the meeting was relaxed.* **4** (*abbr.* atm) [C] (PHYSICS) a unit for measuring pressure

atmospheric /ˌætməsˈferɪk/ *adj.* **1** (SCIENCE) connected with the earth's atmosphere: ***atmospheric pollution/conditions/pressure*** **2** creating a particular feeling or emotion: *atmospheric music*

atoll /ˈætɒl/ *noun* [C] (GEOGRAPHY, GEOLOGY) an island made of CORAL (= a hard red, pink or white substance that forms in the sea from the bones of very small sea animals) and shaped like a ring with a lake of salt water (**a lagoon**) in the middle

atom 🔑 /ˈætəm/ *noun* [C] (PHYSICS, CHEMISTRY) the smallest part of a chemical element that can take part in a chemical reaction: *the splitting of the atom* ◊ *Two atoms of hydrogen combine with one atom of oxygen to form a molecule of water.* ➲ look at **molecule**

ˈatom bomb (*also* **aˌtomic ˈbomb**) *noun* [C] a bomb that explodes using the energy that is produced when an atom or atoms are split

atomic /əˈtɒmɪk/ *adj.* (PHYSICS, CHEMISTRY) **1** connected with atoms or an atom: *atomic structure* **2** related to the energy that is produced when atoms are split; related to weapons that use this energy: *atomic energy/power*

aˌtomic ˈenergy *noun* [U] (SCIENCE) the energy that is produced when an atom or atoms are split

aˌtomic ˈmass *noun* [C] (CHEMISTRY) the mass of an atom of a particular chemical substance: *Oxygen has an atomic mass of 16.*

aˌtomic ˈnumber *noun* [C] (CHEMISTRY) the number of PROTONS (= very small things with a positive electric charge) that a chemical element has in its centre (**nucleus**) ❶ Elements are arranged in the **periodic table** according to their **atomic number**. ❶ For more information on the periodic table of elements, look at pages R34-5.

atonal /eɪˈtəʊnl/ *adj.* (MUSIC) (used about a piece of music) not written in any particular KEY (= set of musical notes based on one note)

atone /əˈtəʊn/ *verb* [I] (*formal*) ~ **(for sth)** to show that you are sorry for doing sth wrong: *to atone for your crimes* ▶ **atonement** *noun* [U]

atrium /ˈeɪtriəm/ *noun* [C] (*pl.* **atria** /-triə/ or **atriums**) **1** (ARCHITECTURE) a large high open space in the centre of a modern building **2** (HISTORY) an open space in the centre of an ancient Roman VILLA (= a large house) **3** (ANATOMY) either of the two upper spaces in the heart ➲ picture at **heart** ➲ look at **ventricle**

atrocious /əˈtrəʊʃəs/ *adj.* extremely bad: *atrocious weather* ▶ **atrociously** *adv.*

atrocity /əˈtrɒsəti/ *noun* [C,U] (*pl.* **atrocities**) (an act of) very cruel treatment of sb/sth: *Both sides were accused of committing atrocities during the war.*

atrophy /ˈætrəfi/ *noun* [U] (HEALTH) the medical condition of losing flesh, muscle, strength, etc. in a part of the body because it does not have enough blood

attach 🔑 AW /əˈtætʃ/ *verb* [T] **1** ~ **sth (to sth)** to fasten or join sth to sth: *I attach a copy of the spreadsheet* (= send it with an email) ◊ *I attached a label to each bag.* OPP **detach** **2** (usually passive) ~ **sb/sth to sb/sth** to make sb/sth join or belong to sb/sth: *The research centre is attached to the university.* **3** ~ **sth to sb/sth** to think that sth has a particular quality: *Don't attach too much importance to what they say.*

IDM **(with) no strings attached; without strings** → STRING[1]

attaché /əˈtæʃeɪ/ *noun* [C] (POLITICS) a person who works in an EMBASSY and who usually has special responsibility for a particular area of activity: *a cultural/military attaché*

attached 🔑 /əˈtætʃt/ *adj.* **1** ~ **to sb/sth** liking sb/sth very much **2** ~ **to sth** working for or forming part of an organization: *The research unit is attached to the university.* **3** ~ **(to sth)** joined to sth: *Please complete the attached application form.*

attachment AW /əˈtætʃmənt/ *noun* **1** [C] something that you can fit on sth else to make it do a different job: *an electric drill with a range of attachments* **2** [C,U] ~ **(to/for sb/sth)** the feeling of liking sb/sth very much: *emotional attachment* **3** [C] (COMPUTING) a document that you send to sb using email

attack[1] 🔑 /əˈtæk/ *noun* **1** [C,U] (an) ~ **(on sb/sth)** trying to hurt or defeat sb/sth by using force: *The town was **under attack from** all sides.* **2** [C,U] (an) ~ **(on sb/sth)** an act of saying strongly that you do not like or agree with sb/sth: *an outspoken attack on government policy* **3** [C] (HEALTH) a sudden, short period of illness, usually severe, especially an illness that you have often: *an **attack of** asthma/flu* ➲ look at **heart attack** **4** [C] (SPORT) the act of trying to score a point in a game of sport

attack[2] 🔑 /əˈtæk/ *verb* **1** [I,T] to try to hurt or defeat sb/sth by using force: *The child was attacked by a dog.* **2** [T] to say strongly that you do not like or agree with sb/sth **3** [T] to have a harmful effect on sth: *a virus that attacks the nervous system* **4** [I,T] (SPORT) to try to score a point in a game of sport: *This team attacks better than it defends.*

attacker /əˈtækə(r)/ *noun* [C] a person who tries to hurt sb using force: *The victim of the assault didn't recognize his attackers*

attain AW /əˈteɪn/ ***verb*** **1** [I,T] to succeed in getting sth, usually after a lot of effort: *Most of our students attained five 'A' grades in their exams.* **2** (*formal*) to reach a particular age, level or condition

attainable /əˈteɪnəbl/ ***adj.*** that can be achieved: *realistically attainable targets*

attainment AW /əˈteɪnmənt/ ***noun*** **1** [U] success in achieving sth: *the attainment of the government's objectives* **2** [C] a skill or sth you have achieved

attempt[1] /əˈtempt/ ***verb*** [T] ~ **(to do)** sth to try to do sth that is difficult: *Don't attempt to make him change his mind.* ◇ *Don't attempt to repair this yourself.*

attempt[2] /əˈtempt/ ***noun*** [C] **1** an ~ **(to do sth/at doing sth)** an act of trying to do sth: *The thief* ***made no attempt*** *to run away.* ◇ *I failed the exam once but passed* ***at the*** *second* ***attempt***. ◇ *They failed* ***in*** *their* ***attempt*** *to reach the North Pole.* **2** an ~ **(on sb/sth)** trying to attack or beat sb/sth: *an attempt on sb's life* (= to kill sb)

IDM **a last-ditch attempt** → LAST[1]

attempted /əˈtemptɪd/ (only *before* a noun) (LAW) (used about a crime, etc.) that sb has tried to do but without success: *attempted rape/murder/robbery*

attend /əˈtend/ ***verb*** **1** [T] to go to or be present at a place: *The children attend the local school.* **2** [I] (*formal*) ~ **to sb/sth** to give your care, thought or attention to sb/sth or look after sb/sth: *Please attend to this matter immediately.*

attendance /əˈtendəns/ ***noun*** **1** [U] being present somewhere: *Attendance at lectures is compulsory.* **2** [C,U] the number of people who go to or are present at a place: *There was a poor attendance at the meeting.*

attendant[1] /əˈtendənt/ ***noun*** [C] a person whose job is to serve or help people in a public place: *a car park attendant*

attendant[2] /əˈtendənt/ ***adj.*** (only *before* a noun) (*formal*) that goes together with or results from sth: *unemployment and all its attendant social problems*

attention[1] /əˈtenʃn/ ***noun*** [U] **1** watching, listening to or thinking about sb/sth carefully: *I shouted in order to* ***attract*** *her* ***attention***. ◇ *Shy people hate to be* ***the centre of attention*** (= the person that everybody is watching). ◇ *to hold sb's attention* (= to keep them interested in sth) **2** special care or action: *The hole in the roof needs urgent attention.* ◇ *to require* ***medical attention*** **3** a position in which a soldier stands up straight and still: *to* ***stand/come to attention***

IDM **catch sb's attention/eye** → CATCH[1]
draw (sb's) attention to sth → DRAW[1]
pay attention → PAY[1]

attention[2] /əˈtenʃn/ ***exclamation*** used for asking people to listen to sth carefully

attentive /əˈtentɪv/ ***adj.*** ~ **(to sb/sth)** watching, listening to or thinking about sb/sth carefully OPP **inattentive** ▸ **attentively** ***adv.***: *to listen attentively to sth*

attest /əˈtest/ ***verb*** [I,T] (*formal*) **1** ~ **(to sth)** to show that sth is true: *Her long fight against cancer attested to her courage.* **2** (LAW) to state that you believe that sth is true or genuine, for example in a court of law: *The signature was attested by two witnesses.*

attic /ˈætɪk/ ***noun*** [C] the space or room under the roof of a house ➲ look at **loft**

attire /əˈtaɪə(r)/ ***noun*** [U] (*formal*) clothes

attitude AW /ˈætɪtjuːd/ ***noun*** [C] an ~ **(to/towards sb/sth)** the way that you think, feel or behave: *She has a very positive attitude to her work.*

attn ***abbr.*** (used in writing) for the attention of: *Sales Dept, attn M Holland*

attorney /əˈtɜːni/ ***noun*** [C] (LAW) **1** (*especially AmE*) a lawyer, especially one who can act for sb in court ➲ look at **district attorney** ➲ note at **lawyer** **2** a person who is given the power to act on behalf of another in business or legal matters: *She was made her father's attorney when he became ill.* ➲ look at **power of attorney**

At,torney 'General ***noun*** [C] (*pl.* **Attorneys General** or **Attorney Generals**) (LAW, POLITICS) **1** the most senior legal officer in some countries or states, for example the UK or Canada, who advises the government or head of state on legal matters **2 the At,torney 'General** the head of the US Department of Justice and a member of the President's CABINET (= a group of senior politicians who advise the President)

attract /əˈtrækt/ ***verb*** [T] **1** to cause sb/sth to go to sth or give attention to sth: *I waved to attract the waiter's attention.* ◇ *Moths are attracted to light.* ◇ *The new film has attracted a lot of publicity.* **2** (usually passive) to cause sb to like sb/sth: *She's attracted to older men.* **3** (PHYSICS) if a MAGNET or GRAVITY **attracts** sth, it makes it move towards it. OPP **repel**

attraction /əˈtrækʃn/ ***noun*** **1** [U] a feeling of liking sb/sth: *sexual attraction* **2** [C] sth that is interesting or enjoyable: *The city offers all kinds of tourist attractions.* **3** [U] (PHYSICS) a force which pulls things towards each other: *gravitational/magnetic attraction* ➲ look at **repulsion** ➲ picture at **magnet**

attractive /əˈtræktɪv/ ***adj.*** **1** that pleases or interests you; that you like: *an attractive part of the country* ◇ *an attractive idea* **2** (used about a person) beautiful or nice to look at ▸ **attractively** ***adv.*** ▸ **attractiveness** ***noun*** [U]

attributable AW /əˈtrɪbjətəbl/ ***adj.*** (not *before* a noun) (*written*) ~ **to sb/sth** probably caused by the thing mentioned: *Their illnesses are attributable to poor diet.*

attribute[1] AW /əˈtrɪbjuːt/ ***verb*** [T] ~ **sth to sb/sth** to believe that sth was caused or done by sb/sth: *Mustafa attributes his success to hard work.* ◇ *a poem attributed to Shakespeare*

attribute[2] AW /ˈætrɪbjuːt/ ***noun*** [C] a quality of sb/sth; a feature: *physical attributes*

attributive /əˈtrɪbjətɪv/ ***adj.*** (LANGUAGE) (used about adjectives or nouns) used before a noun to describe it: *In 'the blue sky' and 'a family business', 'blue' and 'family' are attributive.* ➲ look at **predicative** ▸ **attributively** ***adv.***

attrition /əˈtrɪʃn/ ***noun*** [U] **1** (*formal*) a process of making sb/sth, especially your enemy, weaker by attacking them or it or causing problems for them or it over a period of time: *It was a* ***war of attrition***. **2** (SCIENCE) the gradual removal of material from a mass by moving against it over a long period of time: *The teeth show signs of attrition.* ➲ picture at **erode**

ATV /ˌeɪ tiː ˈviː/ ***abbr.*** **all-terrain vehicle**; a small open motor vehicle with one seat and four wheels with very thick tyres, designed especially for use on rough ground without roads ➲ look at **four-wheel drive**

A2 (level) /eɪ ˈtuː levl/ ***noun*** [C,U] (EDUCATION) a British exam usually taken in Year 13 of school or college (= the final year) when students are aged 18. Students must first have studied a subject at **AS level** before they can take an **A2** exam. Together, **AS** and

A2 level exams form **A levels**, which are needed for entrance to universities ➲ look at **AS (level)**

atypical /ˌeɪˈtɪpɪkl/ ***adj.*** (*formal*) not typical of a particular type, group, etc. **OPP typical**

aubergine /ˈəʊbəʒiːn/ (*especially AmE* **eggplant**) ***noun*** [C,U] a long vegetable with dark purple skin

auburn /ˈɔːbən/ ***adj.*** (used about hair) reddish-brown

auction¹ /ˈɔːkʃn/ ***noun*** [C,U] a public sale at which items are sold to the person who offers to pay the most money: *The house was sold **at /by auction**.*

auction² /ˈɔːkʃn/ ***verb*** [T] ~ **sth (off)** to sell sth at an AUCTION

auctioneer /ˌɔːkʃəˈnɪə(r)/ ***noun*** [C] a person who organizes the selling at an AUCTION

audacious /ɔːˈdeɪʃəs/ ***adj.*** (*written*) not afraid to take risks or do sth shocking: *an audacious decision* ▶ **audaciously** ***adv.***

audacity /ɔːˈdæsəti/ ***noun*** [U] behaviour that risks being shocking: *He **had the audacity to** tell me I was fat!*

audible /ˈɔːdəbl/ ***adj.*** that can be heard: *Her speech was **barely audible**.* **OPP inaudible** ▶ **audibly** /-əbli/ ***adv.***

audience ⊶ /ˈɔːdiəns/ ***noun*** [C] **1** [with sing. or pl. verb] (**ARTS AND MEDIA**) all the people who are watching or listening to a play, concert, speech, the television, etc.: *The audience was/were wild with excitement.* ◇ *There were only about 200 people in the audience.* **2** a formal meeting with a very important person: *He was granted an audience with the Pope.*

audio /ˈɔːdiəʊ/ ***adj.*** connected with the recording of sound: *audio equipment* ◇ *audio tape*

audio- /ˈɔːdiəʊ/ ***prefix*** (in nouns, adjectives and adverbs) connected with hearing or sound: *an audio book* (= a recording of a book that has been read aloud)

ˌ**audio-ˈvisual** ***adj.*** using both sound and pictures

audit ⊶ /ˈɔːdɪt/ ***noun*** [C] (**FINANCE**) an official examination of the present state of sth, especially of a company's financial records: *to carry out an audit* ▶ **audit** ***verb*** [T]: *We have just had our accounts audited.*

audition¹ /ɔːˈdɪʃn/ ***noun*** [C] (**ARTS AND MEDIA**) a short performance by a singer, actor, etc. to find out if they are good enough to be in a play, show, etc.

audition² /ɔːˈdɪʃn/ ***verb*** [I,T] ~ **(sb) (for sth)** (**ARTS AND MEDIA**) to do or to watch sb do an AUDITION: *I auditioned for a part in the play.*

auditor /ˈɔːdɪtə(r)/ ***noun*** [C] (**FINANCE**) a person whose job is to examine a company's financial records

auditorium /ˌɔːdɪˈtɔːriəm/ ***noun*** [C] (*pl.* **auditoriums** or **auditoria** /-riə/) (**ARTS AND MEDIA**) the part of a theatre, concert hall, etc. where the audience sits

auditory /ˈɔːdətri/ ***adj.*** (**TECHNICAL**) connected with hearing ➲ picture at **ear**

au fait /ˌəʊ ˈfeɪ/ ***adj.*** (not *before* a noun) completely familiar with sth: *Are you au fait with this type of computer system?*

Aug. ***abbr.*** August: *10 Aug. 1957*

augment /ɔːgˈment/ ***verb*** [T] (*formal*) to increase the amount, value, size, etc. of sth

augur /ˈɔːgə(r)/ ***verb***
IDM augur well/ill for sb/sth (*formal*) to be a good/bad sign of what will happen in the future

August /ˈɔːgəst/ ***noun*** [U, C] (*abbr.* **Aug.**) the eighth month of the year, coming after July

aunt ⊶ /ɑːnt/ (also *informal* **auntie**; **aunty** /ˈɑːnti/) ***noun*** [C] the sister of your father or mother; the wife of your uncle: *Aunt Ellen*

au pair /ˌəʊ ˈpeə(r)/ ***noun*** (*BrE*) [C] a person, usually a girl, from another country who comes to live with a family in order to learn the language. An au pair helps to clean the house and looks after the children.

aura /ˈɔːrə/ ***noun*** [C] (*formal*) the particular quality that sb/sth seems to have: *These hills have a magical aura.*

aural /ˈɔːrəl/ ***adj.*** (**TECHNICAL**) connected with hearing and listening: *an aural comprehension test* ➲ look at **oral** ▶ **aurally** ***adv.***

auricle /ˈɔːrɪkl/ ***noun*** [C] (**ANATOMY**) **1** either of the two upper spaces in the heart used to send blood around the body **SYN atrium** ➲ look at **ventricle** **2** the outer part of the ear

aurora australis /ɔːˌrɔːrə ɒsˈtrɑːlɪs; ɔːsˈt-/ ***noun*** [sing.] (**ASTRONOMY**) = THE SOUTHERN LIGHTS

aurora borealis /ɔːˌrɔːrə ˌbɔːriˈeɪlɪs/ ***noun*** [sing.] (**ASTRONOMY**) = THE NORTHERN LIGHTS

auspices /ˈɔːspɪsɪz/ ***noun*** [pl.]
IDM under the auspices of sb/sth with the help and support of sb/sth

auspicious /ɔːˈspɪʃəs/ ***adj.*** that seems likely to be successful in the future **OPP inauspicious**

austere /ɒˈstɪə(r)/ ***adj.*** **1** very simple; without decoration **2** (used about a person) very strict and serious **3** not having anything that makes your life more comfortable: *The nuns lead simple and austere lives.* ▶ **austerity** /ɒˈsterəti/ ***noun*** [U]

Australasian /ˌɒstrəˈleɪʒn; -ˈleɪʃn/ ***adj.*** (**GEOGRAPHY**) of or from Australia and the islands of the south west Pacific

authentic /ɔːˈθentɪk/ ***adj.*** **1** that you know is real or genuine: *an authentic Van Gogh painting* **2** true or accurate: *an authentic model of the building* ▶ **authenticity** /ˌɔːθenˈtɪsəti/ ***noun*** [U]

authenticate /ɔːˈθentɪkeɪt/ ***verb*** [T] to produce evidence to show that sth is genuine, real or true: *The picture has been authenticated as a genuine Picasso.*

author¹ ⊶ **AW** /ˈɔːθə(r)/ ***noun*** [C] a person who writes a book, play, etc.: *a well-known author of detective novels* ▶ **authorship AW** ***noun*** [U]

author² **AW** /ˈɔːθə(r)/ ***verb*** [T] (*formal*) to be the author of a book, report, etc.

authoritarian /ɔːˌθɒrɪˈteəriən/ ***adj.*** not allowing people the freedom to decide things for themselves: *authoritarian parents*

authoritative **AW** /ɔːˈθɒrətətɪv/ ***adj.*** **1** having authority; demanding or expecting that people obey you: *an authoritative tone of voice* **2** that you can trust and respect as true and correct: *the most authoritative book on the subject*

authority ⊶ **AW** /ɔːˈθɒrəti/ ***noun*** (*pl.* **authorities**) **1** [U] the power and right to give orders and make others obey: *Children often begin to question their parents' authority at a very early age.* ◇ *You must get this signed by a person **in authority*** (= who has a position of power). **2** [U] ~ **(to do sth)** the right or permission to do sth: *The police **have the authority** to question anyone they wish.* ◇ *He was sacked for using a company vehicle **without authority**.* **3** [C] (often plural) a person, group or government department that has the power to give orders, make official decisions, etc.: *I have to report this to the authorities.* **4** [U] a quality that sb has which makes it possible to influence and control other people: *He spoke with authority and everybody listened.* **5** [C] an ~ **(on sth)** a person with special knowledge: *He's an authority on criminal law.*

authorize (also **-ise**) /'ɔːθəraɪz/ ***verb*** [T] to give official permission for sth or for sb to do sth: *He authorized his secretary to sign letters in his absence.* ▸ **authorization** (also **-isation**) /ˌɔːθəraɪ'zeɪʃn/ ***noun*** [U]

autism /'ɔːtɪzəm/ ***noun*** [U] (HEALTH) a mental condition in which a person finds it difficult to communicate or form relationships with other people ▸ **autistic** /ɔː'tɪstɪk/ ***adj.***: *autistic behaviour/children*

auto- /'ɔːtəʊ/ (*also* **aut-**) ***prefix*** (in nouns, adjectives and adverbs) **1** about or by yourself: *an autobiography* **2** by itself without a person to operate it: *automatic*

autobiography /ˌɔːtəbaɪ'ɒgrəfi/ ***noun*** [C,U] (*pl.* **autobiographies**) (LITERATURE) the story of a person's life written by that person ➲ look at **biography** ▸ **autobiographical** /ˌɔːtəˌbaɪə'græfɪkl/ ***adj.***

autoclave /'ɔːtəʊkleɪv; 'ɔːtə-/ ***noun*** [C] (SCIENCE) a strong closed container, used for processes that involve high temperatures or pressure

autocracy /ɔː'tɒkrəsi/ ***noun*** (POLITICS) **1** [U] a system of government of a country in which one person has complete power **2** [C] (*pl.* **autocracies**) a country that is ruled by one person who has complete power

autocrat /'ɔːtəkræt/ ***noun*** [C] **1** (POLITICS) a ruler who has complete power ➲ look at **despot** **2** a person who expects to be obeyed by other people and does not care about their opinions or feelings ▸ **autocratic** /ˌɔːtə'krætɪk/ ***adj.***

Autocue™ /'ɔːtəʊkjuː/ (*AmE* and *BrE also* **teleprompter**) ***noun*** [C] (ARTS AND MEDIA) a device used by people who are speaking in public, especially on television, which shows them the words they have to say

autograph /'ɔːtəgrɑːf/ ***noun*** [C] the signature of a famous person: *The players stopped outside the stadium to* ***sign autographs.*** ▸ **autograph** ***verb*** [T]: *The whole team have autographed the football.*

autoimmune /ˌɔːtəʊɪ'mjuːn/ ***adj.*** (only *before* a noun) (HEALTH) an **autoimmune** disease or medical condition is one which is caused by substances that usually prevent illness: *an autoimmune response*

automate AW /'ɔːtəmeɪt/ ***verb*** [T] (usually passive) to make sth operate by machine, without needing people

automatic¹ 🔑 AW /ˌɔːtə'mætɪk/ ***adj.*** **1** (used about a machine) that can work by itself without direct human control: *an automatic washing machine* **2** done without thinking **3** always happening as a result of a particular action or situation: *All the staff have an automatic right to a space in the car park.* ▸ **automatically** /-kli/ ***adv.***: *The lights will come on automatically when it gets dark.*

automatic² /ˌɔːtə'mætɪk/ ***noun*** [C] an **automatic** machine, gun or car: *This car is an automatic* (= has automatic gears).

ˌautomatic 'pilot (*also* **autopilot**) ***noun*** [C, usually sing.] a device in an aircraft or a ship that keeps it on a fixed course without the need for a person to control it

IDM **be on automatic pilot** to do sth without thinking because you have done the same thing many times before: *I tidied up and made the dinner on automatic pilot.*

automation AW /ˌɔːtə'meɪʃn/ ***noun*** [U] the use of machines instead of people to do work

automobile /'ɔːtəməbiːl/ (*especially AmE*) = CAR (1)

autonomy /ɔː'tɒnəmi/ ***noun*** [U] **1** (POLITICS) the freedom for a country, a region or an organization to govern itself independently **2** the ability to act and make decisions without being controlled by anyone else: *giving learners greater autonomy in the classroom* ▸ **autonomous** /ɔː'tɒnəməs/ ***adj.***

autopilot /'ɔːtəʊpaɪlət/ = AUTOMATIC PILOT

autopsy /'ɔːtɒpsi/ ***noun*** [C] (*pl.* **autopsies**) (HEALTH) an examination of a dead body to find out the cause of death SYN **post-mortem**

ˌauto-su'ggestion ***noun*** [U] (PSYCHOLOGY) a process that makes you believe sth or do sth according to ideas that come from within yourself without you realizing it

autotroph /'ɔːtətrəʊf/ ***noun*** [C] (BIOLOGY) a living thing that is able to feed itself using simple chemical substances such as CARBON DIOXIDE ▸ **autotrophic** /ˌɔːtə'trɒfɪk/ ***adj.***

autumn 🔑 /'ɔːtəm/ (*AmE usually* **fall**) ***noun*** [C,U] the season of the year that comes between summer and winter: *In autumn the leaves on the trees begin to fall.* ➲ picture at **season** ▸ **autumnal** /ɔː'tʌmnəl/ ***adj.***

auxiliary¹ /ɔːg'zɪliəri/ ***adj.*** (only *before* a noun) **1** (used about workers) giving help or support to the main group of workers: *auxiliary nurses/troops/staff* SYN **ancillary** **2** (used about a piece of equipment) used if there is a problem with the main piece of equipment: *an auxiliary pump*

auxiliary² /ɔːg'zɪliəri/ ***noun*** [C] (*pl.* **auxiliaries**) **1** (*also* **auˌxiliary 'verb**) (LANGUAGE) a verb such as *be, do* and *have* that is used with a main verb to show tense, etc. or to form questions and negatives **2** a worker who gives help or support to the main group of workers: *nursing auxiliaries*

auxin /'ɔːksɪn/ ***noun*** [U] (BIOLOGY) a chemical substance in plants that helps control their growth

avail /ə'veɪl/ ***noun*** [U]

IDM **of little/no avail** not helpful; having little or no effect

to little/no avail without success: *They searched everywhere, but to no avail.*

availability /əˌveɪlə'bɪləti/ ***noun*** [U] the state of being available: *You will receive the colour you order, subject to availability* (= if it is available).

available 🔑 AW /ə'veɪləbl/ ***adj.*** **1** ~ **(to sb)** (used about things) that you can get, buy, use, etc.: *This information is easily available to everyone at the local library.* ◇ *Refreshments are available at the snack bar.* **2** (used about people) free to be seen, talked to, etc.: *The minister was not available for comment.*

avalanche /'ævəlɑːnʃ/ ***noun*** [C] (GEOGRAPHY) a very large amount of snow that slides quickly down the side of a mountain ➲ picture at **glacial**

the avant-garde /ˌævɒ̃ 'gɑːd/ ***noun*** [sing.] (ARTS AND MEDIA) extremely modern works of art, music or literature, or the artists who create these ▸ **avant-garde** ***adj.***

avarice /ˈævərɪs/ *noun* [U] (*formal*) extreme desire for money SYN **greed** ▸ **avaricious** /ˌævəˈrɪʃəs/ *adj.*

avatar /ˈævətɑː(r)/ *noun* [C] **1** (RELIGION) (in Hinduism and Buddhism) a god appearing in a physical form **2** (COMPUTING) a picture of a person or an animal which represents a person, on a computer screen, especially in a computer game or CHAT ROOM

Ave. *abbr.* AVENUE: *26 Elm Ave.*

avenge /əˈvendʒ/ *verb* [T] ~ **sth**; ~ **yourself on sb** to punish sb for hurting you, your family, etc. in some way: *He wanted to avenge his father's murder.* ◇ *He wanted to avenge himself on his father's murderer.* ➲ look at **revenge**

avenue /ˈævənjuː/ *noun* [C] **1** (*abbr.* **Ave.**) a wide street, especially one with trees or tall buildings on each side: *I live on Tennyson Avenue.* **2** a way of doing or getting sth: *We must explore every avenue open to us* (= try every possibility).

average[1] 🔑 /ˈævərɪdʒ/ *noun* **1** [C] (MATHEMATICS) the number you get when you add two or more figures together and then divide the total by the number of figures you added: *The average of 14, 3 and 1 is 6* (= 18 divided by 3 is 6). ◇ *He has scored 93 goals at **an average of** 1.55 per game.* **2** [sing., U] the normal standard, amount or quality: ***On average**, I buy a newspaper about twice a week.*

average[2] 🔑 /ˈævərɪdʒ/ *adj.* **1** (only *before* a noun) (MATHEMATICS) (used about a number) found by calculating the average[1](1): *What's the average age of your students?* **2** normal or typical: *children of **above /below average** intelligence*

average[3] /ˈævərɪdʒ/ *verb* [T] to do, get, etc. a certain amount as an average: *If we average 50 miles an hour we should arrive at about 4 o'clock.*

PHR V **average out (at sth)** to result in an average (of sth)

averse /əˈvɜːs/ *adj.* (*formal*) ~ **to sth** (often with a negative) against or not in favour of sth: *He is not averse to trying out new ideas.*

aversion /əˈvɜːʃn/ *noun* [C] **1** [usually sing.] **an** ~ **(to sb/sth)** a strong feeling of not liking sb/sth: *Some people **have an aversion** to spiders.* **2** a thing that you do not like

avert /əˈvɜːt/ *verb* [T] to prevent sth unpleasant: *The accident could have been averted.*

avian /ˈeɪviən/ *adj.* (BIOLOGY) relating to or connected with birds

ˈ**avian flu** *noun* [U] (*formal*) = BIRD FLU

aviary /ˈeɪviəri/ *noun* [C] (*pl.* **aviaries**) a large CAGE or area in which birds are kept

aviation /ˌeɪviˈeɪʃn/ *noun* [U] the designing, building and flying of aircraft

avid /ˈævɪd/ *adj.* **1** very enthusiastic about sth (usually a hobby): *an avid collector of antiques* **2** ~ **for sth** wanting to get sth very much: *Journalists crowded round the entrance, avid for news.* ▸ **avidly** *adv.*: *He read avidly as a child.*

avocado /ˌævəˈkɑːdəʊ/ *noun* [C] (*pl.* **avocados**) a tropical fruit that is wider at one end than the other, with a hard green skin and a large seed (**stone**) inside

avoid 🔑 /əˈvɔɪd/ *verb* [T] **1** ~ **sth/doing sth** to prevent sth happening or to try not to do sth: *He always tried to avoid an argument if possible.* ◇ *She has to avoid eating fatty food.* **2** to keep away from sb/sth: *I leave home at 7 o'clock in order to avoid the rush hour.* ▸ **avoidance** *noun* [U]

avoidable /əˈvɔɪdəbl/ *adj.* that can be prevented; unnecessary OPP **unavoidable**

avow /əˈvaʊ/ *verb* [I,T] (*formal*) to say firmly and often publicly what your opinion is, what you think is true, etc. ▸ **avowal** /əˈvaʊəl/ *noun* [C] (*formal*)

await /əˈweɪt/ *verb* [T] (*formal*) to wait for sb/sth: *We sat down to await the arrival of the guests.*

awake[1] 🔑 /əˈweɪk/ *adj.* (not before a noun) not sleeping: *I was sleepy this morning but I'm **wide awake** now.* ◇ *They were so tired that they found it difficult to **stay awake**.* ◇ *I hope our singing didn't **keep you awake** last night.* OPP **asleep**

awake[2] /əˈweɪk/ *verb* (*pt* **awoke** /əˈwəʊk/; *pp* **awoken** /əˈwəʊkən/) [I,T] to wake up; to make sb/sth wake up: *I awoke to find that it was already 9 o'clock.* ◇ *A sudden loud noise awoke us.*

awaken /əˈweɪkən/ *verb* **1** [I,T] (*written*) to wake up; to make sb/sth wake up: *We were awakened by a loud knock at the door.* **2** [T] (*formal*) to produce a particular feeling, attitude, etc. in sb: *The film awakened memories of her childhood.*

PHR V **awaken sb to sth** to make sb notice or realize sth for the first time

awakening /əˈweɪkənɪŋ/ *noun* [sing.] **1** the act of starting to feel or understand sth; the start of a feeling, etc.: *the awakening of an interest in the opposite sex* **2** a moment when sb notices or realizes sth for the first time: *It was a rude* (= unpleasant) *awakening when I suddenly found myself unemployed.*

award[1] 🔑 /əˈwɔːd/ *noun* [C] **1** a prize, etc. that sb gets for doing sth well: *This year the awards for best actor and actress went to two Americans.* **2** (LAW) an amount of money given to sb as the result of a court decision: *She **received an award of** £5 000 for damages.*

award[2] 🔑 /əˈwɔːd/ *verb* [T] ~ **sth (to sb)** to give sth to sb as a prize, payment, etc.: *She was awarded first prize in the gymnastics competition.* ◇ *The court awarded £10 000 each to the workers injured in the accident.*

aware 🔑 AW /əˈweə(r)/ *adj.* **1** ~ **(of sb/sth)**; ~ **(that)** knowing about or realizing sth; conscious of sb/sth: *I am **well aware** of the problems you face.* ◇ *I suddenly **became aware** that someone was watching me.* ◇ *There is no other entrance, **as far as I am aware**.* OPP **unaware** **2** interested and informed: *Many young people are very politically aware.*

awareness AW /əˈweənəs/ *noun* [U, sing.] ~ **(of sth)**; ~ **(that...)** knowing sth; knowing that sth exists and is important; being interested in sth: *People's awareness of healthy eating has increased in recent years.* ◇ *There was an almost complete **lack of awareness** of the issues involved.*

awash /əˈwɒʃ/ *adj.* (not *before* a noun) ~ **(with sth)** covered with water; flooded: (*figurative*) *The city was awash with rumours.*

away 🔑 /əˈweɪ/ *adv.*, *adj.* **1** ~ **(from sb/sth)** to a different place or in a different direction: *Go away! I'm busy!* ◇ *I asked him a question, but he just looked away.* **2** ~ **(from sth)** at a particular distance from a place: *The village is two miles away from the sea.* ◇ *My parents live five minutes away.* **3** ~ **(from sth)** (used about people) not present; absent: *My neighbours are away on holiday at the moment.* ◇ *Aki was away from school for two weeks with measles.* **4** in the future: *Our summer holiday is only three weeks away.* **5** into a place where sth is usually kept: *Put your books away now.* ◇ *They cleared the dishes away* (= off the table). ➲ look at **throw sth away** **6** continuously, without stopping: *They chatted away for* *hours.* **7** (SPORT) (used about a football, etc. match) on the other team's ground: *Our team's playing away on Saturday.* ◇ *an away match/game* OPP (at) **home 8** until sth disappears: *The crash of thunder slowly died away.*

IDM **right/straight away** immediately; without any delay: *I'll phone the doctor right away.*

PHR V **do away with sb/yourself** (*informal*) to kill sb/yourself

do away with sb/sth (*informal*) to stop doing or having sth; to make sth end SYN **abolish**: *He thinks it's time we did away with the monarchy.*

awe /ɔː/ ***noun*** [U] feelings of respect and either fear or admiration: *As a young boy he was very much in awe of his uncle.*

IDM **be in awe of sb/sth** to admire sb/sth and be slightly frightened of them or it

'awe-inspiring ***adj.*** causing a feeling of respect and fear or admiration

awesome /'ɔːsəm/ ***adj.*** **1** impressive and sometimes frightening: *an awesome task* **2** (*AmE, slang*) very good; excellent

awful ⊶ /'ɔːfl/ ***adj.*** **1** very bad or unpleasant: *We had an awful holiday. It rained every day.* ◇ *I feel awful – I think I'll go to bed.* ◇ *What an awful thing to say!* **2** terrible; very serious: *I'm afraid there's been some awful news.* **3** (only *before* a noun) (*informal*) very great: *We've got* ***an awful lot*** *of work to do.*

awfully ⊶ /'ɔːfli/ ***adv.*** (*informal*) very; very much: *I'm awfully sorry.*

awkward ⊶ /'ɔːkwəd/ ***adj.*** **1** difficult to deal with: *That's an awkward question.* ◇ *You've put me in an awkward position.* ◇ *an awkward customer* ◇ *The box isn't heavy but it's awkward to carry.* **2** not convenient, difficult: *My mother always phones at an awkward time.* ◇ *This tin-opener is very awkward to clean.* **3** embarrassed or embarrassing: *I often feel awkward in a group of people.* ◇ *There was an awkward silence.* **4** not using the body in the best way; not elegant or comfortable: *I was sitting with my legs in an awkward position.* ▶ **awkwardness** ***noun*** [U] ▶ **awkwardly** ***adv.***

awning /'ɔːnɪŋ/ ***noun*** [C] a sheet of cloth or other material that stretches out from above a door or window to keep off the sun or rain

awoke past tense of **awake**[1]

awoken past participle of **awake**[1]

AWOL /'eɪwɒl/ ***abbr.*** **absent without leave**; used especially when sb in the army, etc. has left their group without permission: *He's* ***gone AWOL*** *from his base.*

awry /ə'raɪ/ ***adv.***, ***adj.*** (not *before* a noun) wrong, not in the way that was planned; untidy

axe[1] (*especially AmE* **ax**) /æks/ ***noun*** [C] a tool with a wooden handle and a heavy metal head with a sharp edge, used for cutting wood, etc.

axe (*AmE* **ax**)

pickaxe **axe** **hatchet**

axe[2] (*especially AmE* **ax**) /æks/ ***verb*** [T] **1** to remove sb/sth: *Hundreds of jobs have been axed.* **2** to reduce sth by a great amount: *School budgets are to be axed.*

axiom /'æksiəm/ ***noun*** [C] a rule or principle that most people believe to be true

axiomatic /ˌæksiə'mætɪk/ ***adj.*** (*formal*) true in such an obvious way that you do not need evidence to show that it is true

axis

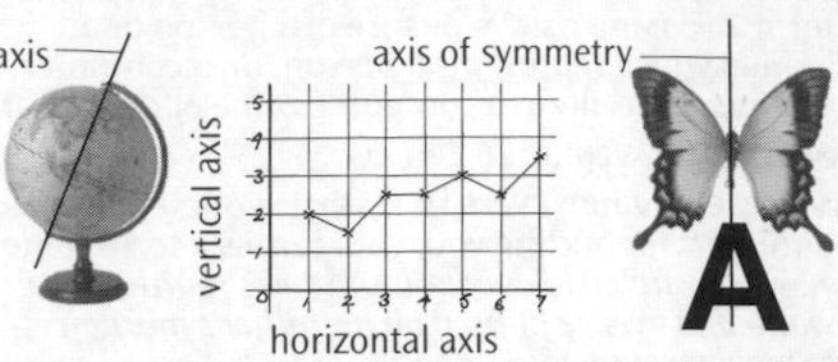

axis /'æksɪs/ ***noun*** [C] (*pl.* **axes** /'æksiːz/) **1** (PHYSICS) a line we imagine through the middle of an object, around which the object turns: *The earth rotates on its axis.* **2** (MATHEMATICS) a fixed line used for marking measurements on a GRAPH: *the* ***horizontal/vertical axis*** **3** (MATHEMATICS) a line that divides a shape into two equal parts: *an* ***axis of symmetry*** ◇ *The axis of a circle is its diameter.*

axle /'æksl/ ***noun*** [C] a bar that connects a pair of wheels on a vehicle

ayatollah /ˌaɪə'tɒlə/ ***noun*** [C] (RELIGION) a religious leader of Shiite Muslims in Iran

azalea /ə'zeɪliə/ ***noun*** [C] a plant or bush with large flowers that may be pink, purple, white or yellow

azure /'æʒə(r)/ (*BrE also* 'æzjʊə(r)/) ***adj.*** (*written*) bright blue in colour like the sky ▶ **azure** ***noun*** [U]

B b

B, b /biː/ ***noun*** [C,U] (*pl.* **B's**; **b's** /biːz/) the second letter of the English alphabet: *'Billy' begins with (a) 'B'.*

b. ***abbr.*** born: *J S Bach, b. 1685*

B2B (also **b2b**, **B-to-B**) /ˌbiː tə 'biː/ ***adj.*** (only *before* a noun) (BUSINESS) **business-to-business**; used to describe the buying, selling and exchanging over the Internet of products, services or information between companies: *B2B transactions*

B2C (also **b2c**, **B-to-C**) /ˌbiː tə 'siː/ ***adj.*** (only *before* a noun) (BUSINESS) **business-to-consumer/customer**; used to describe the selling of products, services or information to consumers over the Internet: *B2C e-commerce*

BA (*AmE* **B.A.**) /ˌbiː 'eɪ/ ***abbr.*** **Bachelor of Arts**; the degree that you receive when you complete a university or college course in an arts subject ➲ look at **BSc**, **MA**

baa /bɑː/ ***noun*** [C] the sound that a sheep makes

B & B /ˌbiː ən 'biː/ ***abbr.*** (TOURISM) = BED AND BREAKFAST

babble[1] /'bæbl/ ***noun*** [sing.] **1** the sound of many voices talking at the same time **2** the sound of water running over stones

babble[2] /'bæbl/ ***verb*** [I] **1** to talk quickly or in a way that is difficult to understand **2** to make the sound of water running over stones

babe /beɪb/ ***noun*** [C] **1** (*especially AmE, slang*) used when talking to sb, especially a girl or young woman: *It's OK, babe.* **2** (*slang*) an attractive young woman **3** (*old-fashioned*) a baby

baboon /bə'buːn/ ***noun*** [C] a large African or Asian MONKEY with a long face like a dog's

baby ⊶ /ˈbeɪbi/ ***noun*** [C] (*pl.* **babies**) **1** a very young child: *I'm going to **have a baby**.* ◇ *She's **expecting a baby** early next year.* ◇ *When's the **baby due**?* (= when will it be born?) ◇ *a baby boy/girl* **2** a very young animal or bird **3** (*AmE, slang*) a person, especially a girl or young woman, that you like or love

ˈbaby boom ***noun*** [C, usually sing.] (**SOCIAL STUDIES**) a time when more babies are born than usual, for example after a war

ˈbaby boomer ***noun*** [C] (**SOCIAL STUDIES**) a person born during a BABY BOOM

ˈbaby carriage (*AmE*) = PRAM

babyhood /ˈbeɪbihʊd/ ***noun*** [U] the time of your life when you are a baby

babyish /ˈbeɪbiɪʃ/ ***adj.*** suitable for or behaving like a baby

babysit /ˈbeɪbisɪt/ ***verb*** [I] (**babysitting**; *pt, pp* **babysat**) to look after a child for a short time while the parents are out ▸ **babysitter** ***noun*** [C]

baccalaureate /ˌbækəˈlɔːriət/ ***noun*** [C] (**EDUCATION**) the last SECONDARY SCHOOL exam in France and other countries, and in some international schools: *to sit/take/pass/fail your baccalaureate* ➲ look at **international baccalaureate**

bachelor /ˈbætʃələ(r)/ ***noun*** [C] **1** (**SOCIAL STUDIES**) a man who has not yet married **2 Bachelor** (**EDUCATION**) a person who has a **Bachelor's** degree (= a first university degree): *a Bachelor of Arts/Science*

bacillus /bəˈsɪləs/ ***noun*** [C] (*pl.* **bacilli** /bəˈsɪlaɪ/) (**BIOLOGY**) a type of very small living creature (**bacterium**). There are several types of **bacillus**, some of which cause diseases.

back[1] ⊶ /bæk/ ***noun*** **1** [C] the part of a person's or animal's body between the neck and the bottom: *Do you sleep **on your back** or on your side?* ◇ *She was standing **with her back to** me so I couldn't see her face.* ◇ *A camel has a hump on its back.* **2** [C, usually sing.] the part or side of sth that is furthest from the front: *I sat **at the back of** the class.* ◇ *The answers are **in the back of** the book.* ◇ *Write your address **on the back of** the cheque.* **3** [C] the part of a chair that supports your upper body when you sit down

IDM **at/in the back of your mind** if sth is at the back of your mind, it is in your thoughts but is not the main thing that you are thinking about

back to front with the back where the front should be: *Wait a minute – you've got your jumper on back to front.* ➲ look at **way[1]** (3)

behind sb's back without sb's knowledge or agreement: *They criticized her behind her back.* OPP **to sb's face**

get off sb's back (*informal*) to stop annoying sb, for example when you keep asking them to do sth: *I've told her I'll do the job by Monday, so I wish she'd get off my back!*

know sth like the back of your hand → KNOW[1]

a pat on the back → PAT[2]

turn your back on sb/sth to refuse to be involved with sb/sth

back[2] ⊶ /bæk/ ***adj.*** (only *before* a noun) **1** furthest from the front: *Have you locked the back door?* ◇ *the back row of the theatre* ◇ *back teeth* **2** owed from a time in the past: *back pay/rent/taxes*

IDM **on the back burner** (*informal*) (used about an idea, a plan, etc.) left for the present time, to be done or considered later

take a back seat to allow sb to play a more important or active role than you do in a particular situation

back[3] ⊶ /bæk/ ***adv.*** **1** in or to a place or state that sb/sth was in before: *I'm going out now – I'll **be back** about six o'clock.* ◇ *It started to rain so I **came back** home.* ◇ ***Go back** to sleep.* ◇ *Could I **have** my pen **back**, please?* ◇ *I've got to **take** these books **back** to the library.* **2** away from the direction you are facing or moving in: *She walked away without **looking back**.* ◇ *Could everyone **move back** a bit, please?* OPP **forward** **3** away from sth; under control: *The police were unable to **keep** the crowds **back**.* ◇ *She tried to **hold back** her tears.* **4** in return or in reply: *He said he'd **phone** me **back** in half an hour.* **5** in or into the past; ago: *I met him a few years back, in Madrid.* ◇ ***Think back** to your first day at school.*

IDM **back and forth** from one place to another and back again, all the time: *Travelling back and forth to work takes up quite a bit of time.*

back[4] ⊶ /bæk/ ***verb*** **1** [I,T] to move backwards or to make sth move backwards: *I'll have to back into that parking space.* ◇ *He backed the car into the garage.* **2** [I] to face sth at the back: *Many of the colleges back onto the river.* **3** [T] to give help or support to sb/sth: *We can go ahead with the scheme if the bank will agree to back us.* **4** [T] (**SPORT**) to bet money that a particular horse, team, etc. will win in a race or game: *Which horse are you backing in the 2 o'clock race?*

PHR V **back away (from sb/sth)** to move backwards because you are afraid, shocked, etc.

back down to stop saying that you are right: *I think you are right to demand an apology. Don't back down now.*

back out (of sth) to decide not to do sth that you had promised to do: *You promised you would come with me. You can't back out of it now!*

back sb/sth up to support sb; to say or show that sth is true: *I'm going to say exactly what I think at the meeting. Will you back me up?* ◇ *All the evidence backed up what the woman had said.*

back (sth) up to move backwards, especially in a vehicle: *Back up a little so that the other cars can get past.*

back sth up (**COMPUTING**) to make a copy of a computer program, etc. in case the original one is lost or damaged

backache /ˈbækeɪk/ ***noun*** [U] (**HEALTH**) a pain in your back ➲ note at **ache**

ˌback ˈbench ***noun*** [C, usually pl.] (**POLITICS**) (in British and certain other parliaments) any of the seats for Members of Parliament who do not have senior positions in the government or the other parties: *He resigned as Home Secretary and returned to the back benches.*

backbencher /ˌbækˈbentʃə(r)/ ***noun*** [C] (**POLITICS**) (in British and certain other parliaments) a member who sits in the rows of seats at the back, and who does not have an important position in the government or the opposition

backbone /ˈbækbəʊn/ ***noun*** **1** [C] (**ANATOMY**) the row of small bones that are connected together down the middle of your back SYN **spine** ➲ picture on **page 80** **2** [sing.] the most important part of sth: *Agriculture is the backbone of the country's economy.*

ˈback-breaking ***adj.*** (used about physical work) very hard and tiring

backcloth /ˈbækklɒθ/ = BACKDROP

backdate /ˌbækˈdeɪt/ ***verb*** [T] to make a document, cheque or a payment take effect from an earlier date: *The pay rise will be backdated to 1 April.*

backdrop /ˈbækdrɒp/ (*also* **backcloth**) ***noun*** [C] (**ARTS AND MEDIA**) a painted piece of material that is hung behind the stage in a theatre as part of the SCENERY

backer /ˈbækə(r)/ ***noun*** [C] (**FINANCE**) a person, organization or company that gives support to sb, especially financial support

backfire /ˌbækˈfaɪə(r)/ ***verb*** [I] to have an unexpected and unpleasant result, often the opposite of what was intended

backgammon /ˈbækgæmən/ ***noun*** [U] a game for two people played by moving pieces around a board marked with long thin triangles

background 🗝 /ˈbækgraʊnd/ ***noun*** **1** [sing.] the part of a view, scene, picture, etc. which is furthest away from the person looking at it: *You can see the mountains **in the background** of the photo.* OPP **foreground 2** [sing.] a position where sb/sth can be seen/heard, etc. but is not the centre of attention: *The film star's husband prefers to stay in the background.* ◇ *All the time I was speaking to her, I could hear a child crying **in the background**.* ◇ *I like to have **background music** when I'm studying.* **3** [sing., U] the facts or events that are connected with a situation: *The talks are taking place against a background of increasing tension.* ◇ *I need some background information.* **4** [C] the type of family and social class you come from and the education and experience you have: *We get on very well together in spite of our different backgrounds.*

backhand /ˈbækhænd/ ***noun*** [sing.] (**SPORT**) a way of hitting the ball in TENNIS, etc. that is made with the back of your hand facing forward OPP **forehand**

backing /ˈbækɪŋ/ ***noun*** **1** [U] help or support to do sth, especially financial support: *The police gave the proposals their full backing.* **2** [U,C, usually sing.] (**MUSIC**) (in pop songs) music that accompanies the main singer or tune: ***a backing group/singer/track***

backlash /ˈbæklæʃ/ ***noun*** [sing.] a strong reaction against a political or social event or development

backlog /ˈbæklɒg/ ***noun*** [C, usually sing.] an amount of work, etc. that has not yet been done and should have been done already

backpack[1] /ˈbækpæk/ ***noun*** [C] a large bag, often on a metal frame, that you carry on your back when travelling SYN **rucksack** ➲ picture at **luggage**

backpack[2] /ˈbækpæk/ ***verb*** [I] (**TOURISM**) to go walking or travelling with your clothes, etc. in a BACKPACK: *We **went backpacking** round Europe last summer.* ▶ **backpacker** ***noun*** [C]

ˌ**back-ˈpedal** *verb* [I] (*pres. part.* **back-pedalling**; *pt, pp* **back-pedalled**: *AmE* **back-pedaling**; **back-pedaled**) **1 back-pedal (on sth)** to change an earlier statement or opinion; to not do sth that you promised to do: *The protests have forced the government to back-pedal on plans to introduce a new tax.* **2** to move your feet backwards when you are riding a bicycle in order to go backwards or slow down

backside /ˈbæksaɪd/ ***noun*** [C] (*informal*) the part of your body that you sit on; your bottom

backslash /ˈbækslæʃ/ ***noun*** [C] (**COMPUTING**) a mark (\) used in computer COMMANDS (= instructions) ➲ look at **forward slash**

backstage /ˌbækˈsteɪdʒ/ ***adv.*** (**ARTS AND MEDIA**) in the part of a theatre where the actors get dressed, wait to perform, etc.

backstroke /ˈbækstrəʊk/ ***noun*** [U] (**SPORT**) a style of swimming that you do on your back: ***Can you do backstroke?*** ➲ picture at **swim**

backtrack /ˈbæktræk/ ***verb*** [I] **1** to go back the same way you came **2** ~ **(on sth)** to change your mind about a plan, promise, etc. that you have made: *The union forced the company to backtrack on its plans to close the factory.*

backup /ˈbækʌp/ ***noun*** **1** [U] extra help or support that you can get if necessary **2** [C] (**COMPUTING**) a copy of a computer disk that you can use if the original one is lost or damaged: *Always make a backup of your files.*

backward 🗝 /ˈbækwəd/ ***adj.*** **1** (only *before* a noun) directed towards the back: *a backward step/glance* OPP **forward 2** slow to develop or learn: *Our teaching methods are backward compared to some countries.*

backwards 🗝 /ˈbækwədz/ (*also* **backward**) ***adv.*** **1** towards a place or a position that is behind: *Could everybody take a step backwards?* **2** in the opposite direction to usual: *Can you say the alphabet backwards?* OPP **forwards**

IDM **backward(s) and forward(s)** first in one direction and then in the other, all the time: *The dog ran backwards and forwards, barking loudly.*

backwash /ˈbækwɒʃ/ ***noun*** [U] (**GEOGRAPHY**) the movement of water back into the sea after a wave has hit the beach ➲ look at **swash** ➲ picture at **wave**

backwater /ˈbækwɔːtə(r)/ ***noun*** [C] a place that is away from where most things happen and so it is not affected by new ideas or outside events

backyard /ˌbækˈjɑːd/ ***noun*** [C] **1** (*BrE*) an area behind a house, usually with a hard surface made of stone or CONCRETE, with a wall or fence around it **2** (*AmE*) the whole area behind the house including the grass area and the garden

bacon /ˈbeɪkən/ ***noun*** [U] thin pieces of SALTED or smoked meat from the back or sides of a pig ➲ note at **meat**

bacteria 🗝 /bækˈtɪəriə/ ***noun*** [pl.] (*sing.* **bacterium** /-iəm/) (**BIOLOGY**) very small living things that can only be seen with special equipment (**a microscope**). Bacteria exist in large numbers in air, water, soil, plants and the bodies of people and animals. Some **bacteria** cause disease. ➲ look at **germ** (1), **virus** ▶ **bacterial** /-riəl/ ***adj.***: *bacterial infections/growths*

bad 🗝 /bæd/ ***adj.*** (**worse** /wɜːs/, **worst** /wɜːst/) **1** not good; unpleasant: *Our family's had a bad time recently.* ◇ *bad weather* ◇ *I'm afraid I've got some bad news for you.* **2** of poor quality; of a low standard: *Many accidents are caused by bad driving.* ◇ *Some of the company's problems are the result of bad management.* **3** ~ **(at sth/at doing sth)** not able to do sth well or easily; not skilful: *a bad teacher/driver/cook* ◇ *I've always been bad at sport.* **4** serious; severe: *The traffic was very bad on the way to work.* ◇ *She went home with a bad headache.* ◇ *That was a bad mistake!* **5** (used about food) not fresh or fit to eat: *These eggs will **go bad** if we don't eat them soon.* **6** (**HEALTH**) (used about parts of the body) not healthy; painful: *He's always had a bad heart.* ◇ *Keith's off work with a bad back.* **7** (used about a person or behaviour) not good; morally wrong: *He was not a bad man, just rather weak.* **8** (not *before* a noun) ~ **for sb/sth** likely to damage or hurt sb/sth: *Sugar is bad for your teeth.* **9** ~ **(for sth/to do sth)** difficult or not suitable: *This is a bad time to phone – everyone's out to lunch.*

IDM **not bad** (*informal*) quite good: *'What was the film like?' 'Not bad.'*

too bad (*informal*) used to show that nothing can be

done to change a situation: *'I'd much rather stay at home.' 'Well that's just too bad. We've said we'll go.'*

baddy (also **baddie**) /'bædi/ ***noun*** [C] (*pl.* **baddies**) (*informal*) (ARTS AND MEDIA) a bad person in a film, book, etc. OPP **goody**

badge /bædʒ/ ***noun*** [C] a small piece of metal, cloth or plastic with a design or words on it that you wear on your clothing: *The players all have jackets with the club badge on.*

badger /'bædʒə(r)/ ***noun*** [C] an animal with black and white lines on its head that lives in holes in the ground and comes out at night

ˌbad 'language ***noun*** [U] (LANGUAGE) words that are used for swearing

badly 🔑 /'bædli/ ***adv.*** (**worse** /wɜːs/, **worst** /wɜːst/) **1** in a way that is not good enough; not well: *She did badly in the exams.* **2** seriously; severely: *He was badly hurt in the accident.* **3** very much: *He badly needed a holiday.*

IDM **badly off** poor; not having enough of sth OPP **well off**

badminton /'bædmɪntən/ ***noun*** [U] (SPORT) a game for two or four people in which players hit a type of light ball with feathers (**a shuttlecock**) over a high net, using a piece of equipment (**a racket**), which is held in the hand

ˌbad-'tempered 🔑 ***adj.*** often angry or impatient

baffle /'bæfl/ ***verb*** [T] to be impossible to understand; to confuse sb very much: *His illness baffled the doctors.* ▶ **baffled** ***adj.***: *The instructions were so complicated that I was completely baffled.* ▶ **baffling** ***adj.***

bag¹ 🔑 /bæg/ ***noun*** **1** [C] a container made of paper or thin plastic that opens at the top: *She brought some sandwiches in a plastic bag.* **2** [C] a strong container made from cloth, plastic, leather, etc., usually with one or two handles, used to carry things in when travelling, shopping, etc.: *a shopping bag* ◇ *Have you packed your bags yet?* ◇ *She took her purse out of her bag* (= handbag). **3** [C] the amount contained in a bag: *She's eaten a whole bag of sweets!* ◇ *a bag of crisps/sugar/flour* **4 bags** [pl.] (HEALTH) folds of skin under the eyes, often caused by lack of sleep **5 bags** [pl.] (*BrE, informal*) **bags (of sth)** a lot (of sth); plenty (of sth): *There's no hurry, we've got bags of time.*

bag² /bæg/ ***verb*** [T] (**bagging**; **bagged**) (*informal*) to try to get sth for yourself so that other people cannot have it: *Somebody's bagged the seats by the pool!*

bagel /'beɪgl/ ***noun*** [C] a type of bread roll in the shape of a ring

baggage 🔑 /'bægɪdʒ/ ***noun*** [U] (TOURISM) bags, suitcases, etc. used for carrying a person's clothes and things on a journey: ***excess baggage*** (= baggage weighing more than the airline's permitted limit) ◇ ***baggage handlers*** (= people employed to load and unload baggage at airports) SYN **luggage**

'baggage reclaim (*BrE*) (*AmE* **'baggage claim**) ***noun*** [U] (TOURISM) the place at an airport where you get your bags, suitcases, etc. again after you have flown

'baggage room (*AmE*) = LEFT-LUGGAGE OFFICE

baggy /'bægi/ ***adj.*** (used about a piece of clothing) big; hanging loosely on the body

bagpipes /'bægpaɪps/ ***noun*** [pl.] a musical instrument, popular in Scotland, that is played by blowing air through a pipe into a bag and then pressing the bag so that the air comes out of other pipes

baguette /bæ'get/ ***noun*** [C] a type of bread in the shape of a long thick stick

bail¹ /beɪl/ ***noun*** [U] (LAW) money that sb agrees to pay if a person accused of a crime does not appear in front of the court on the day they are called. When **bail** has been arranged, the accused person can go free until that day: *She was **released on bail** of £2 000.* ◇ *The judge **set bail** at £10 000.* ◇ *The judge felt that he was a dangerous man and **refused** him **bail**.* ◇ *She was **granted bail**.*

bail² /beɪl/ ***verb*** [T] (LAW) to let sb go free on BAIL

PHR V **bail sb out 1** (LAW) to obtain sb's freedom by paying money to the court: *Her parents went to the police station and bailed her out.* **2** to rescue sb from a difficult situation (especially by providing money)

bailey /'beɪli/ ***noun*** [C] (HISTORY) the outer wall of a castle or the area inside the wall ➲ look at **motte and bailey castle**

bailiff /'beɪlɪf/ ***noun*** [C] **1** (*BrE*) (LAW) a law officer whose job is to take the possessions and property of people who cannot pay their debts **2** (*BrE*) (AGRICULTURE) a person employed to manage land or a large farm for sb else **3** (*AmE*) (LAW) an official who keeps order in court, takes people to their seats, watches prisoners, etc.

bait /beɪt/ ***noun*** [U] **1** food or sth that looks like food that is put onto a hook to catch fish, animals or birds **2** something that is used for persuading or attracting sb: *Free offers are often used as bait to attract customers.*

baize /beɪz/ ***noun*** [U] a type of thick cloth made of wool that is usually green, used especially for covering card tables and BILLIARD, SNOOKER or POOL tables

bake 🔑 /beɪk/ ***verb*** [I,T] **1** to cook or be cooked in an oven in dry heat: *I could smell bread baking in the oven.* ◇ *On his birthday she baked him a cake.* ➲ note at **cook 2** to become or to make sth hard by heating it: *The hot sun baked the earth.*

ˌbaked 'beans ***noun*** [pl.] small white BEANS, usually cooked in a sauce and sold in cans

baker /'beɪkə(r)/ ***noun*** **1** [C] a person who bakes bread, cakes, etc. to sell in a shop **2 the baker's** [sing.] a shop that sells bread, cakes, etc.: *Get a loaf at the baker's.*

bakery /'beɪkəri/ ***noun*** [C] (*pl.* **bakeries**) a place where bread, cakes, etc. are baked to be sold

baking /'beɪkɪŋ/ (*also* **ˌbaking 'hot**) ***adj.*** very hot: *The workers complained of the baking heat in the office in the summer.*

'baking powder ***noun*** [U] a mixture of powders used to make cakes rise and become light as they are baked

'baking soda = SODIUM BICARBONATE

balance¹ 🔑 /'bæləns/ ***noun*** **1** [sing.] (a) ~ (**between A and B**) a situation in which different or opposite things are of equal importance, size, etc.: *The course provides a good balance between academic and practical work.* ◇ *Tourism has upset **the** delicate **balance of nature** on the island.* **2** [U] the ability to keep steady with an equal amount of weight on each side of the body: *to **lose** your **balance*** ◇ *It's very difficult to **keep** your **balance** when you start learning to ski.* ◇ *You need a good **sense of balance** to ride a motorbike.* **3** [C, sing.] (FINANCE) the amount that still has to be paid; the amount that is left after some has been used, taken, etc.: *You can pay a 10% deposit now, with **the balance** due in one month.* ◇ *to check your **bank balance*** (= to find out how much money you have in your account) **4** [C] an instrument used for weighing things

IDM **in the balance** uncertain: *Following poor results, the company's future hangs in the balance.*

(catch/throw sb) off balance (to find or put sb) in a position that is not safe and from which it is easy to fall

on balance having considered all sides, facts, etc.: *On balance, I've had a pretty good year.*

strike a balance (between A and B) → STRIKE²

balance² /'bæləns/ ***verb*** **1** [I,T] to be or to put sb/sth in a steady position so that their/its weight is not heavier on one side than on the other: *I had to balance on the top step of the ladder to paint the ceiling.* ◇ *Carefully, she balanced a glass on top of the pile of plates.* **2** [I,T] (FINANCE) to have equal totals of money spent and money received: *I must have made a mistake – the accounts don't balance.* ◇ *She is always very careful to balance her weekly budget.* **3** [I,T] ~ **(sth) (out) (with sth)** to have or give sth equal value, importance, etc. in relation to other parts: *The loss in the first half of the year was balanced out by the profit in the second half.* **4** [T] ~ **sth against sth** to consider and compare one matter in relation to another: *In planning the new road, we have to balance the benefit to motorists against the damage to the environment.*

'balance beam ***noun*** (*AmE*) (SPORT) = BEAM¹ (4)

balanced /'bælənst/ ***adj.*** keeping or showing a balance so that different things, or different parts of things exist in equal or correct amounts: *I like this newspaper because it gives a balanced view.* ◇ *A* ***balanced diet*** *plays an important part in good health.* OPP **unbalanced**

ˌbalance of 'payments ***noun*** [sing.] (ECONOMICS) the difference between the amount of money one country receives from other countries from exports, etc. and the amount it pays to them for imports and services in a particular period of time

ˌbalance of 'power ***noun*** [sing.] (POLITICS) **1** a situation in which political power or military strength is divided between two countries or groups of countries **2** the power that a smaller political party has when the larger parties need its support because they do not have enough votes on their own

ˌbalance of 'trade (*also* **'trade balance**) ***noun*** [sing.] (ECONOMICS) the difference in value between the amount that a country buys from other countries (**imports**) and the amount that it sells to them (**exports**)

'balance sheet ***noun*** [C] (FINANCE) a written statement showing the amount of money and property that a company has, and how much has been received and paid out

balcony /'bælkəni/ ***noun*** [C] (*pl.* **balconies**) **1** a platform built on an upstairs outside wall of a building, with a wall or rail around it **2** (*especially AmE*) (ARTS AND MEDIA) an area of seats upstairs in a theatre

bald /bɔːld/ ***adj.*** **1** (used about people) having little or no hair on your head: *I hope I don't* ***go bald*** *like my father did.* ◇ *He has a* ***bald patch*** *on the top of his head.* **2** (used about sth that is said) simple; without extra words: *the bald truth*

balding /'bɔːldɪŋ/ ***adj.*** starting to lose the hair on your head: *a balding man in his fifties*

baldly /'bɔːldli/ ***adv.*** in a few words with nothing extra or unnecessary: *He told us baldly that he was leaving.*

bale /beɪl/ ***noun*** [C] a large quantity of sth pressed tightly together and tied up: *a bale of hay/cloth/paper*

balk (*especially AmE*) = BAULK

ball /bɔːl/ ***noun*** [C] **1** a round object that you hit, kick, throw, etc. in games and sports: *a tennis/golf/rugby ball* ◇ *a football* ➲ picture at **sport** **2** a round object or a thing that has been formed into a round shape: *a ball of wool* ◇ *The children threw* ***snowballs*** *at each other.* ◇ *We had meatballs and pasta for dinner.* **3** one throw, kick, etc. of the ball in some sports: *That was a great ball from the defender.* **4** a large formal party at which people dance

IDM **be on the ball** (*informal*) to always know what is happening and be able to react to or deal with it quickly

set/start the ball rolling to start sth (an activity, conversation, etc.) that involves or is done by a group

ballad /'bæləd/ ***noun*** [C] (LITERATURE, MUSIC) a long song or poem that tells a story, often about love

ballast /'bæləst/ ***noun*** [U] heavy material placed in a ship or HOT-AIR BALLOON to make it heavier and keep it steady

ˌball 'bearing ***noun*** [C] (PHYSICS) one of a number of metal balls put between parts of a machine to make them move smoothly

ballboy /'bɔːlbɔɪ/ **ballgirl** /'bɔːlgɜːl/ ***noun*** [C] (SPORT) a young person who picks up the balls for the players in a TENNIS match

ballerina /ˌbælə'riːnə/ ***noun*** [C] (ARTS AND MEDIA) a woman who dances in BALLETS

ballet /'bæleɪ/ ***noun*** (ARTS AND MEDIA) **1** [U] a style of dancing that tells a story with music but without words: *He wants to be a* ***ballet dancer***. **2** [C] a performance or work that consists of this type of dancing

'ballet dancer ***noun*** [C] a person who dances in ballets

'ball game ***noun*** [C] (SPORT) **1** any game played with a ball **2** (*AmE*) a BASEBALL match

IDM **a (whole) new/different ball game** something completely new or different

ballistic /bə'lɪstɪk/ ***adj.*** connected with BALLISTICS

IDM **go ballistic** (*informal*) to become very angry: *He went ballistic when I told him.*

balˌlistic 'missile ***noun*** [C] a MISSILE (= a powerful exploding weapon that can be sent long distances) that is fired into the air at a particular speed and angle in order to fall in the right place

ballistics /bə'lɪstɪks/ ***noun*** [U] (SCIENCE) the scientific study of things that are shot or fired through the air, for example bullets

balloon /bə'luːn/ ***noun*** [C] **1** a small coloured object that you blow air into and use as a toy or for decoration: *to blow up/burst/pop a balloon* **2** (*also* **hot-'air balloon**) a large **balloon** made of material that is filled with gas or hot air so that it can fly through the sky, carrying people in a BASKET underneath it

ballot /'bælət/ ***noun*** (POLITICS) **1** [U, C] a secret written vote: *The union will* ***hold a ballot*** *on the new pay offer.* ◇ *The committee are elected by ballot every year.* **2** (*BrE also* **'ballot paper**) [C] the piece of paper on which sb marks who they are voting for: *What percentage of eligible voters* ***cast*** *their* ***ballots****?*

▶ **ballot** *verb* [T] ~ sb (on sth): *The union is balloting its members on strike action.*

ˈballot box *noun* (POLITICS) **1** [C] the box into which people put the piece of paper with their vote on **2 the ballot box** [sing.] the system of voting in an election: *People will express their opinion through the ballot box.*

ˈballot paper (*BrE*) (POLITICS) = BALLOT (2)

ballpark /ˈbɔːlpɑːk/ *noun* [C] a place where BASEBALL is played
IDM **a ballpark estimate/figure** a number, amount, etc. that is approximately correct
in the ballpark (*informal*) (used about figures or amounts) that are within the same limits: *All the bids for the contract were in the same ballpark.*

ballpoint /ˈbɔːlpɔɪnt/ (*also* ˌ**ballpoint ˈpen**) *noun* [C] a pen with a very small metal ball at the end that rolls ink onto paper ➲ look at **Biro**

ballroom /ˈbɔːlruːm; -rʊm/ *noun* [C] a large room used for dancing on formal occasions

ˌ**ballroom ˈdancing** *noun* [U] a formal type of dance in which couples dance together using particular steps and movements

balm /bɑːm/ *noun* [U, C] (HEALTH) cream that is used to make your skin feel better if you have hurt it or if it is very dry

baloney /bəˈləʊni/ *noun* [U] (*AmE, spoken*) nonsense; lies: *Don't give me that baloney!*

balsa /ˈbɔːlsə/ (*also* ˈ**balsa wood**) *noun* [U] the light wood of the tropical American **balsa** tree, used especially for making models

balustrade /ˌbæləˈstreɪd/ *noun* [C] (ARCHITECTURE) a row of posts, joined together at the top, built along the edge of a bridge, etc.

bamboo /ˌbæmˈbuː/ *noun* [C,U] (*pl.* **bamboos**) a tall tropical plant of the grass family. Young **bamboo** plants (**bamboo shoots**), can be eaten and the hard parts of the plant are used for making furniture, etc.: *a bamboo chair*

ban ⊶ /bæn/ *verb* [T] (**banning**; **banned**) ~ **sth**; ~ **sb (from sth/from doing sth)** (LAW) to officially say that sth is not allowed, often by law: *The government has banned the import of products from that country.* ◇ *He was fined £500 and banned from driving for a year.* ▶ **ban** *noun* [C] a ~ (**on sth**): *There is a ban on smoking in this office.* ◇ *to impose/lift a ban*

banal /bəˈnɑːl/ *adj.* not original or interesting: *a banal comment*

banana /bəˈnɑːnə/ *noun* [C] a curved fruit with yellow skin that grows in hot countries: *a bunch of bananas*

band ⊶ /bænd/ *noun* [C] **1** [with sing. or pl. verb] (MUSIC) a small group of musicians who play popular music together, often with a singer or singers: *a rock/jazz band* ◇ *He plays the drums in a band.* ◇ *The band has/have released a new CD.*
2 [with sing. or pl. verb] a group of people who do sth together or have the same ideas: *A small band of rebels is/are hiding in the hills.* **3** a thin, flat, narrow piece of material used for fastening sth, or to put round sth: *She rolled up the papers and put an* ***elastic band*** *round them.* **4** a line of colour or material on sth that is different from what is around it: *She wore a red pullover with a green band across the middle.*
5 = WAVEBAND

bandage ⊶ /ˈbændɪdʒ/ *noun* [C] (HEALTH) a long piece of soft white material that you tie round a wound or injury ➲ picture at **health** ▶ **bandage** *verb* [T] ~ **sth (up)**: *The nurse bandaged my hand up.*

bandanna /bænˈdænə/ *noun* [C] a piece of brightly coloured cloth worn around the neck or head

bandit /ˈbændɪt/ *noun* [C] a member of an armed group of thieves, who attack travellers

bandwagon /ˈbændwægən/ *noun*
IDM **climb/jump on the bandwagon** to copy what other people are doing because it is fashionable or successful

bandwidth /ˈbændwɪdθ; -wɪtθ/ *noun* [C,U]
1 (PHYSICS) a band of FREQUENCIES used for sending electronic signals **2** (COMPUTING) a measurement of the amount of information that a particular computer NETWORK or Internet connection can send in a particular time. It is often measured in BITS per second.

bandy[1] /ˈbændi/ *adj.* (used about a person's legs) curving towards the outside so that the knees are wide apart

bandy[2] /ˈbændi/ *verb* (*pres. part.* **bandying**; *3rd person sing. pres.* **bandies**; *pt, pp* **bandied**)
PHRV **bandy sth about/around** (usually passive) (used about a name, word, story, etc.) to mention sth frequently

bang[1] /bæŋ/ *verb* [I,T] **1** to make a loud noise by hitting sth hard; to close sth or to be closed with a loud noise: *Somewhere in the house, I heard a door bang.* ◇ *He banged his fist on the table and started shouting.* **2** to knock against sth by accident; to hit a part of the body against sth by accident: *Be careful not to bang your head on the ceiling. It's quite low.* ◇ *As I was crossing the room in the dark I banged into a table.*

bang[2] /bæŋ/ *noun* [C] **1** a sudden, short, very loud noise: *There was an enormous bang when the bomb exploded.* **2** a short, strong knock or hit, especially one that causes pain and injury: *a nasty bang on the head*
IDM **with a bang** in a successful or exciting way: *Our team's season started with a bang when we won our first five matches.*

bang[3] /bæŋ/ *adv.* (*especially BrE, informal*) exactly; directly; right: *Our computers are* ***bang up to date.*** ◇ *The shot was bang on target.*
IDM **bang goes sth** (*informal*) used for expressing the idea that sth is now impossible: *'It's raining!' 'Ah well, bang goes our picnic!'*

bang[4] /bæŋ/ *exclamation* used to sound like the noise of a gun, etc.

banger /ˈbæŋə(r)/ *noun* [C] (*BrE, informal*) **1** a SAUSAGE **2** an old car that is in very bad condition **3** a small device (**firework**) that explodes with a short loud noise and is used for fun

bangle /ˈbæŋgl/ *noun* [C] a circular metal band that is worn round the arm or wrist for decoration

bangs /bæŋz/ (*AmE*) = FRINGE[1] (1)

banish /ˈbænɪʃ/ *verb* [T] (*formal*) **1** (LAW) to send sb away (especially out of the country), usually as a punishment **2** to make sb/sth go away; to get rid of sb/sth: *She banished all hope of winning from her mind.*

banister (also **bannister**) /ˈbænɪstə(r)/ *noun* [C] (often plural) the posts and rail which you can hold for support when going up or down stairs: *The children loved sliding down the banister at the old house.*

banjo /ˈbændʒəʊ/ *noun* [C] (*pl.* **banjos**) (MUSIC) a musical instrument like a GUITAR, with a long thin neck, a round body and four or more strings
➲ picture on **page 465**

bank[1] 🔑 /bæŋk/ ***noun*** [C] **1** an organization which keeps money safely for its customers; the office or building of such an organization. You can take money out, save, borrow or exchange money at a **bank**: *My salary is paid directly into my bank.* ◇ *I need to go to the bank to get some money out.* ◇ *a bank loan* ➲ look at **bank account** **2** a store of things, which you keep to use later: *a databank* ◇ *a blood bank in a hospital* **3** (GEOGRAPHY) the ground along the side of a river or CANAL: *People were fishing along the banks of the river.* **4** (GEOGRAPHY) a higher area of ground that goes down or up at an angle, often at the edge of sth or dividing sth: *There were grassy banks on either side of the road.* **5** a mass of cloud, snow, etc.: *The sun disappeared behind a bank of clouds.*

bank[2] /bæŋk/ ***verb*** [I] **1** ~ **(with/at...)** (FINANCE) to have an account with a particular bank: *I've banked with Lloyds for years.* **2** to travel with one side higher than the other when turning: *The plane banked steeply to the left.*

PHR V **bank on sb/sth** to expect and trust sb to do sth, or sth to happen: *Our boss might let you have the morning off but I wouldn't bank on it.*

'bank account ***noun*** [C] (FINANCE) an arrangement that you have with a bank that allows you to keep your money there, to pay in or take out money, etc.: *to **open/close** a bank account*

banker /'bæŋkə(r)/ ***noun*** [C] (BUSINESS, FINANCE) a person who owns or has an important job in a bank

bank 'holiday ***noun*** [C] (*BrE*) a public holiday (not a Saturday or Sunday)

banking /'bæŋkɪŋ/ ***noun*** [U] (BUSINESS, FINANCE) the type of business done by banks: *a career in banking*

banknote /'bæŋknəʊt/ = NOTE[1] (4)

bankrupt[1] /'bæŋkrʌpt/ ***adj.*** (FINANCE) not having enough money to pay your debts: *The company must cut its costs or it will **go bankrupt**.* ▶ **bankrupt** ***verb*** [T]: *The failure of the new product almost bankrupted the firm.*

bankrupt[2] /'bæŋkrʌpt/ ***noun*** [C] (LAW) a person who has been judged by a court to be unable to pay his or her debts

bankruptcy /'bæŋkrʌptsi/ ***noun*** [C,U] (*pl.* **bankruptcies**) (FINANCE) the state of being BANKRUPT: *The company **filed for bankruptcy*** (= asked to be officially declared bankrupt) *in 2005.*

'bank statement (*also* **statement**) ***noun*** [C] (FINANCE) a printed list of all the money going into or out of your bank account during a certain period

banner /'bænə(r)/ ***noun*** [C] a long piece of cloth with words or signs on it, which can be hung up or carried on two poles: *The demonstrators carried banners saying 'Stop the War'.*

'banner ad ***noun*** [C] (BUSINESS) an advertisement across the top or bottom or down the side of a page on the Internet

bannister = BANISTER

banquet /'bæŋkwɪt/ ***noun*** [C] a formal dinner for a large number of people, usually as a special event at which speeches are made

banter /'bæntə(r)/ ***noun*** [U] friendly comments and jokes ▶ **banter** ***verb*** [I]

baobab /'beɪəbæb/ ***noun*** [C] an African tree with a very thick central part (**trunk**)

baptism /'bæptɪzəm/ ***noun*** [C,U] (RELIGION) a ceremony in which a person becomes a member of the Christian Church by being held under water for a short time or having drops of water put onto their head. Often they are also formally given a name. ➲ look at **christening** ▶ **baptize** (also **-ise**) /bæp'taɪz/ ***verb*** [T]: *She was baptized a Catholic.* ➲ look at **christen**

Baptist /'bæptɪst/ ***noun, adj.*** (RELIGION) (a member) of a Protestant Church that believes that BAPTISM should only be for people who are old enough to understand the meaning of the ceremony and should be done by placing the person fully under water

bar[1] 🔑 /bɑː(r)/ ***noun*** [C] **1** a place where you can buy and drink (especially alcoholic) drinks and sometimes have sth to eat: *a wine/coffee/snack bar* **2** a long, narrow, high surface where drinks are served: *She went to the bar and ordered a drink.* ◇ *We sat on stools **at the bar**.* **3** a ~ **(of sth)** a small block of solid material, longer than it is wide: *a **bar of soap/ chocolate*** **4** a long, thin, straight piece of metal, often placed across a window or door, etc. to stop sb from getting through it **5** a ~ **(to sth)** a thing that prevents you from doing sth: *Lack of education is not always a bar to success in business.* **6** (*AmE* **measure**) (MUSIC) one of the short sections of equal length that a piece of music is divided into, and the notes that are in it: *If you sing a few bars of the song I might recognize it.* ➲ picture at **music** **7 the Bar** [sing.] (*BrE*) (LAW) the profession of a BARRISTER (= a lawyer in a higher court): *to **be called to the Bar*** (= allowed to work as a qualified barrister) **8 the Bar** (*AmE*) [sing.] (LAW) the profession of any kind of lawyer **9** (GEOGRAPHY) a line of sand or mud that forms in the sea parallel to the beach **10** (PHYSICS) a unit for measuring the pressure of the atmosphere, equal to a hundred thousand NEWTONS per square metre ➲ look at **millibar**

IDM **behind bars** (*informal*) in prison: *The criminals are now safely behind bars.*

bar[2] /bɑː(r)/ ***verb*** [T] (**barring**; **barred**) **1** (usually passive) to close sth with a bar or bars[1](4): *All the windows were barred.* **2** to block a road, path, etc. so that nobody can pass: *A line of police officers barred the entrance to the embassy.* **3** ~ **sb from sth/from doing sth** to say officially that sb is not allowed to do, use or enter sth: *He was barred from the club for fighting.*

bar[3] /bɑː(r)/ ***prep.*** except: *All the seats were taken, bar one.*

barb /bɑːb/ ***noun*** [C] **1** the point of an arrow or a hook that is curved backwards to make it difficult to pull out **2** something that sb says that is intended to hurt another person's feelings

barbarian /bɑː'beəriən/ ***noun*** [C] a wild person with no culture, who behaves very badly

barbaric /bɑː'bærɪk/ ***adj.*** very cruel and violent: *barbaric treatment of prisoners* ▶ **barbarism** /'bɑːbərɪzəm/ ***noun*** [U]: *acts of barbarism committed in war*

barbarity /bɑː'bærəti/ ***noun*** [U, C] (*pl.* **barbarities**) extremely cruel and violent behaviour

barbecue /'bɑːbɪkjuː/ (*abbr.* **BBQ**) ***noun*** [C] **1** a metal frame on which food is cooked outdoors over an open fire **2** an outdoor party at which food is cooked in this way: *Let's **have a barbecue** on the beach.* ➲ look at **roast**[2] (2) ▶ **barbecue** ***verb*** [T]: *barbecued steak*

barbed wire /ˌbɑːbd 'waɪə(r)/ ***noun*** [U] strong wire with sharp points on it: *a barbed wire fence*

barber /ˈbɑːbə(r)/ *noun* **1** [C] a person whose job is to cut men's hair and sometimes to shave them ➲ look at **hairdresser** **2 the barber's** [sing.] (*BrE*) a shop where men go to have their hair cut

barbed wire

barbiturate /bɑːˈbɪtʃʊrət/ *noun* [C] (HEALTH) a powerful drug that makes people sleep or become calmer

ˈbar chart (*also* **ˈbar graph**) *noun* [C] (MATHEMATICS) a diagram that uses narrow bands of different heights to show different amounts so that they can be compared ➲ picture at **chart**

ˈbar code *noun* [C] (COMPUTING) a pattern of thick and thin lines that is printed on things you buy. It contains information that a computer can read.

bar code

bard /bɑːd/ *noun* [C] (*written*) (LITERATURE) a person who writes poems

bare /beə(r)/ *adj.* **1** (used about part of the body) not covered by clothing: *bare arms/feet/shoulders* ➲ look at **naked**, **nude** **2** without anything covering it or in it: *They had taken the painting down, so the walls were all bare.* **3** just enough; the most basic or simple: *You won't get good marks if you just do* ***the bare minimum***. ◇ *I don't take much luggage when I travel, just* ***the bare essentials***.

IDM **with your bare hands** without weapons or tools: *She killed him with her bare hands.*

bareback /ˈbeəbæk/ *adj., adv.* riding a horse without a seat (**saddle**): *bareback riders in the circus*

barefoot /ˈbeəfʊt/ (*also* **barefooted**) *adj., adv.* not wearing anything on your feet: *We walked barefoot along the beach.*

bareheaded /ˌbeəˈhedɪd/ *adj., adv.* not wearing anything to cover your head

barely /ˈbeəli/ *adv.* (used especially after 'can' and 'could' to emphasize that sth is difficult to do) only just; almost not: *I was so tired I could barely stand up.* ◇ *I earn barely enough money to pay my rent.* ➲ look at **hardly**

bargain¹ ⊶ /ˈbɑːgən/ *noun* [C] **1** something that is cheaper or at a lower price than usual: *At that price, it's an absolute bargain!* ◇ *I found a lot of bargains in the sale.* **2** an agreement between people or groups about what each of them will do for the other or others: *Let's* ***make a bargain*** *– I'll lend you the money if you'll help me with my work.* ◇ *I lent him the money but he didn't* ***keep*** *his* ***side of the bargain***.

IDM **into the bargain** (used for emphasizing sth) as well; in addition; also: *They gave me free tickets and a free meal into the bargain.*

strike a bargain (with sb) → STRIKE²

bargain² /ˈbɑːgən/ *verb* [I] ~ **(with sb) (about/over/for sth)** (BUSINESS) to discuss prices, conditions, etc. with sb in order to reach an agreement that suits each person: *They bargained over the price.*

PHRV **bargain for/on sth** (usually in negative sentences) to expect sth to happen and be ready for it: *When I agreed to help him I didn't bargain for how much it would cost me.*

barge¹ /bɑːdʒ/ *noun* [C] a long narrow boat with a flat bottom that is used for carrying goods or people on a CANAL or river

barge² /bɑːdʒ/ *verb* [I,T] to push people out of the way in order to get past them: *He barged (his way) angrily through the crowd.*

ˈbar graph (MATHEMATICS) = BAR CHART

baritone /ˈbærɪtəʊn/ *noun* [C] (MUSIC) a male singing voice that is fairly low; a man with this voice ❶ Baritone is between **tenor** and **bass**.

barium /ˈbeəriəm/ *noun* [U] (*symbol* **Ba**) (CHEMISTRY) a soft silver-white metal ❶ For more information on the periodic table of elements, look at pages R34-5.

bark¹ /bɑːk/ *noun* **1** [U] the hard outer covering of a tree ➲ picture at **tree** **2** [C] the short, loud noise that a dog makes

bark² /bɑːk/ *verb* **1** [I] ~ **(at sb/sth)** (used about dogs) to make a loud, short noise or noises **2** [T] ~ **sth (out) (at sb)** to give orders, ask questions, etc. in a loud unfriendly way: *The boss came in, barked out some orders and left again.*

barley /ˈbɑːli/ *noun* [U] (AGRICULTURE) **1** a plant that produces grain that is used for food or for making beer and other drinks **2** the grain produced by this plant ➲ picture at **cereal**

barmaid /ˈbɑːmeɪd/ *noun* [C] (*AmE* **bartender**) a woman who serves drinks from behind a bar in a pub, etc.

barman /ˈbɑːmən/ *noun* [C] (*pl.* **-men** /-mən/) (*AmE* **bartender**) a man who serves drinks from behind a bar in a pub, etc.

bar mitzvah /ˌbɑː ˈmɪtsvə/ *noun* [C] (RELIGION) a ceremony in the Jewish religion for a boy who has reached the age of 13. After the ceremony, he is considered an adult. ➲ look at **bat mitzvah**

barn /bɑːn/ *noun* [C] (AGRICULTURE) a large building on a farm in which crops or animals are kept

barometer /bəˈrɒmɪtə(r)/ *noun* [C] **1** (GEOGRAPHY) an instrument that measures air pressure and indicates changes in weather **2** something that indicates the state of sth (a situation, a feeling, etc.): *Results of local elections are often a barometer of the government's popularity.*

baron /ˈbærən/ *noun* [C] **1** a NOBLEMAN of the lowest rank. In Britain, **barons** use the title *Lord*; in other countries they use the title *Baron*. **2** (BUSINESS) a person who controls a large part of a particular industry or type of business: *drug/oil barons*

baroness /ˈbærənəs/ *noun* [C] **1** a woman who has the same rank as a BARON. In Britain, **baronesses** use the title *Lady* or *Baroness*: *Baroness Thatcher* **2** the wife of a BARON

baroque (also **Baroque**) /bəˈrɒk/ *adj.* (HISTORY, ARTS AND MEDIA) used to describe a highly decorated style of European ARCHITECTURE, art and music of the 17th and early 18th centuries

barracks /ˈbærəks/ *noun* [C, with sing. or pl. verb] (*pl.* **barracks**) a building or group of buildings in which soldiers live: *Guards were on duty at the gate of the barracks.*

barrage /ˈbærɑːʒ/ *noun* [C] **1** the continuous firing of a large number of guns in a particular direction, especially to protect soldiers while they are attacking or moving towards the enemy **2** a large number of questions, comments, etc., directed at a person very quickly: *The minister faced a barrage of questions from reporters.* **3** a wall or barrier built across a river to store water, prevent a flood, etc.

barrel /ˈbærəl/ *noun* [C] **1** a large, round, wooden, plastic or metal container for liquids, that has a flat top and bottom and is wider in the middle: *a beer/wine barrel* **2** a unit of measurement in the oil industry equal to approximately 159 litres: *The price of oil is usually given per barrel.* **3** the long metal part of a gun like a tube through which the bullets are fired

barrel

ˈ**barrel vault** *noun* [C] (ARCHITECTURE) a roof in a church, etc. that is made from a number of arches side by side to form the shape of half a tube

barren /ˈbærən/ *adj.* (AGRICULTURE) **1** (used about land or soil) not good enough for plants to grow on **2** (used about trees or plants) not producing fruit or seeds

barricade /ˌbærɪˈkeɪd/ *noun* [C] an object or line of objects that is placed across a road, entrance, etc. to stop people getting through: *The demonstrators **put up barricades** to keep the police away.* ▶ **barricade** *verb* [T]

PHR V **barricade yourself in** to defend yourself by building a BARRICADE: *Demonstrators took over the building and barricaded themselves in.*

barrier 🔑 /ˈbæriə(r)/ *noun* [C] **1** an object that keeps people or things separate or prevents them moving from one place to another: *The crowd were all kept behind barriers.* ◇ *The mountains form a natural barrier between the two countries.* ➲ look at **crash barrier** **2** a ~ (**to sth**) something that causes problems or makes it impossible for sth to happen: *When you live in a foreign country, the **language barrier** is often the most difficult problem to overcome.*

barring /ˈbɑːrɪŋ/ *prep.* except for; unless there is/are: *Barring any unforeseen problems, we'll be moving house in a month.*

barrister /ˈbærɪstə(r)/ *noun* [C] (LAW) (in English law) a lawyer who is trained to speak for you in the higher courts ➲ note at **lawyer**

barrow /ˈbærəʊ/ *noun* [C] **1** (*BrE*) a small thing on two wheels on which fruit, vegetables, etc. are moved or sold in the street, especially in markets **2** = WHEELBARROW

ˈ**bar staff** *noun* [U, with pl. verb] the people who serve drinks from behind a bar in a pub, etc.: *The bar staff are very friendly here.* ➲ look at **barmaid**, **barman**

bartender /ˈbɑːtendə(r)/ (*AmE*) = BARMAID or BARMAN

barter /ˈbɑːtə(r)/ *verb* [I,T] ~ **sth** (**for sth**); ~ (**with sb**) (**for sth**) (BUSINESS) to exchange goods, services, property, etc. for other goods, etc., without using money: *The farmer bartered his surplus grain for machinery.* ◇ *The prisoners bartered with the guards for writing paper and books.* ▶ **barter** *noun* [U]

basalt /ˈbæsɔːlt/ *noun* [U] (GEOLOGY) a type of dark rock that comes from VOLCANOES (= mountains that sometimes produce melted rock, fire, etc.)

base¹ 🔑 /beɪs/ *noun* [C] **1** the lowest part of sth, especially the part on which it stands or at which it is fixed or connected to sth: *I felt a terrible pain **at the base of** my spine.* ◇ *the base of a column/glass/box* ➲ picture at **arch** **2** an idea, fact, etc. from which sth develops or is made: *With these ingredients **as a base**, you can create all sorts of interesting dishes.* ◇ *The country needs a strong economic base.* ➲ note at **basis** **3** a place used as a centre from which activities are done or controlled: *This hotel is an ideal base for touring the region.* **4** a military centre from which the armed forces operate: *an army base* **5** (SPORT) (in BASEBALL) one of the four points that a runner must touch **6** (CHEMISTRY) a chemical substance with a pH value of more than 7 ➲ look at **acid**, **alkali** **7** (MATHEMATICS) a number on which a system of counting and expressing numbers is built up, for example 10 in the DECIMAL system and 2 in the BINARY system

base² 🔑 /beɪs/ *verb* [T] (usually passive) ~ **sb/sth in...** to make one place the centre from which sb/sth can work or move around: *I'm based in New York, although my job involves a great deal of travel.* ◇ *a Cardiff-based company*

PHR V **base sth on sth** to form or develop sth from a particular starting point or source: *This film is based on a true story.*

baseball /ˈbeɪsbɔːl/ *noun* [U] (SPORT) a team game that is popular in the US in which players hit the ball with a BAT (= a piece of wood with a handle) and run round four points (**bases**). They have to touch all four bases in order to score a point (**run**).

baseboard /ˈbeɪsbɔːd/ (*AmE*) = SKIRTING BOARD

baseline /ˈbeɪslaɪn/ *noun* [C, usually sing.] **1** (SPORT) a line that marks each end of the court in games such as TENNIS or the edge of the area where a player can run in BASEBALL **2** (TECHNICAL) a line or measurement that is used as a starting point when comparing facts: *The figures for 2006 were used as a baseline for the study.*

basement /ˈbeɪsmənt/ *noun* [C] a room or rooms in a building, partly or completely below ground level: *a basement flat* ➲ look at **cellar**

ˌ**base** ˈ**metal** *noun* [C] (CHEMISTRY) a metal that is not a precious metal such as gold

ˈ**base rate** *noun* [C] (ECONOMICS, FINANCE) a rate of interest, set by a central bank, that all banks in Britain use when calculating the amount of interest that they charge on the money they lend

bases **1** plural of **basis** **2** plural of **base¹**

bash¹ /bæʃ/ *verb* (*informal*) **1** [I,T] to hit sb/sth very hard: *I didn't stop in time and bashed into the car in front.* **2** [T] to criticize sb/sth strongly: *The candidate continued to bash her opponent's policies.*

bash² /bæʃ/ *noun* [C] (*informal*) **1** a hard hit: *He gave Alex a bash on the nose.* **2** a large party or celebration

IDM **have a bash (at sth/at doing sth)** (*BrE*, *spoken*) to try: *I'll get a screwdriver and have a bash at mending the light.*

bashful /ˈbæʃfl/ *adj.* shy and embarrassed

basic 🔑 /ˈbeɪsɪk/ *adj.* **1** forming the part of sth that is most necessary and from which other things develop: *The basic question is, can we afford it?* ◇ *basic information/facts/ideas* **2** of the simplest kind or level; including only what is necessary without anything extra: *This course teaches basic computer skills.* ◇ *The **basic pay** is £200 a week – with extra for overtime.*

BASIC /ˈbeɪsɪk/ *noun* [U] (COMPUTING) a simple language, using familiar English words, for writing computer programs

basically 🔑 /ˈbeɪsɪkli/ *adv.* used to say what the most important or most basic aspect of sb/sth is: *The new design is basically the same as the old one.*

basics /ˈbeɪsɪks/ ***noun*** [pl.] the simplest or most important facts or aspects of sth; things that you need the most: *So far, I've only learnt the basics of computing.*

basil /ˈbæzl/ ***noun*** [C] a plant with shiny green leaves that smell sweet and are used in cooking as a HERB

basilica /bəˈzɪlɪkə/ ***noun*** [C] (**ARCHITECTURE**) a large church or hall with a curved end and two rows of columns inside

basin /ˈbeɪsn/ ***noun*** [C] **1** = WASHBASIN **2** a round open bowl often used for mixing or cooking food **3** (**GEOGRAPHY**) an area of land from which water flows into a river: *the Amazon Basin*

THESAURUS

basis

foundation • base

These are all words for ideas or facts that sth is based on.

basis: *the basis for a discussion*

foundation: *He laid the foundation of Japan's modern economy.*

base: *a sound economic base*

basis /ˈbeɪsɪs/ ***noun*** (*pl.* **bases** /ˈbeɪsiːz/) **1** [sing.] the principle or reason which lies behind sth: *We made our decision* ***on the basis of*** *the reports which you sent us.* **2** [sing.] the way sth is done or organized: *They meet* ***on a regular basis.*** ◇ *to employ sb* ***on a*** *temporary/part-time* ***basis*** **3** [C] a starting point, from which sth can develop: *She used her diaries as a basis for her book.*

bask /bɑːsk/ ***verb*** [I] ~ **(in sth) 1** to sit or lie in a place where you can enjoy the warmth: *The snake basked in the sunshine on the rock.* **2** to enjoy the good feelings you have when other people admire you, give you a lot of attention, etc.: *The team was still* ***basking in the glory*** *of winning the cup.*

basket /ˈbɑːskɪt/ ***noun*** [C] **1** a container for carrying or holding things, made of thin pieces of material such as wood, plastic or wire that bends easily: *a* ***waste-paper basket*** ◇ *a* ***shopping basket*** ◇ *a* ***clothes/laundry basket*** (= in which you put dirty clothes before they are washed) **2** (**SPORT**) a net that hangs from a metal ring high up at each end of a BASKETBALL court ➲ picture at **sport** **3** (**SPORT**) a score of one, two or three points in BASKETBALL, made by throwing the ball through one of the nets

IDM **put all your eggs in one basket** → EGG[1]

basketball /ˈbɑːskɪtbɔːl/ ***noun*** [U] (**SPORT**) a game for two teams of five players. There is a net (**basket**) fixed to a metal ring high up at each end of the court and the players try to throw a ball through the other team's net in order to score points (**baskets**).

basketry /ˈbɑːskɪtri/ ***noun*** [U] the skill of making BASKETS

bas-relief /ˌbæs rɪˈliːf/ ***noun*** [U,C] (**ART**) a form of SCULPTURE in which the shapes are cut so that they are slightly raised from the background; a SCULPTURE made in this way

bass /beɪs/ ***noun*** (**MUSIC**) **1** [U] the lowest tone or part in music, for instruments or voices ➲ look at **treble 2** [C] the lowest male singing voice; a singer with this kind of voice ➲ look at **tenor**, **baritone** **3** = DOUBLE BASS **4** [C] (*also* ˌ**bass guiˈtar**) an electric GUITAR which plays very low notes ▶ **bass** ***adj.*** (only *before* a noun): *a bass drum* ◇ *Can you sing the bass part in this song?*

bassoon /bəˈsuːn/ ***noun*** [C] (**MUSIC**) a musical instrument that you blow which makes a very deep sound ➲ picture on **page 165**

bastard /ˈbɑːstəd; ˈbæs-/ ***noun*** [C] (*old-fashioned, taboo*) a person whose parents were not married to each other when he or she was born

baste /beɪst/ ***verb*** [T] to pour liquid fat or juices over meat, etc. while it is cooking

bat[1] /bæt/ ***noun*** [C] **1** (**SPORT**) a piece of wood for hitting the ball in sports such as TABLE TENNIS, CRICKET or BASEBALL: *a cricket bat* ➲ picture at **sport** **2** a small animal, like a mouse with wings, which flies and hunts at night ➲ picture on **page 29**

IDM **off your own bat** without anyone asking you or helping you

bat[2] /bæt/ ***verb*** [I] (**batting**; **batted**) (**SPORT**) (used about one player or a whole team) to have a turn hitting the ball in sports such as CRICKET or BASEBALL

IDM **not bat an eyelid**; (*AmE*) **not bat an eye** to show no surprise or embarrassment when sth unusual happens

batch[1] /bætʃ/ ***noun*** [C] **1** a number of things or people which belong together as a group: *The bus returned to the airport for the next batch of tourists.* **2** (**COMPUTING**) a set of jobs that are done together on a computer: *to process a batch job* ◇ *a batch file/program*

batch[2] /bætʃ/ ***verb*** [T] to put things into groups in order to deal with them: *The service will be improved by batching and sorting enquiries.*

bated /ˈbeɪtɪd/ ***adj.***

IDM **with bated breath** excited or afraid, because you are waiting for sth to happen

bath[1] /bɑːθ/ ***noun*** (*pl.* **baths** /bɑːðz/) **1** [C] (*also* **bathtub**) a large container for water in which you sit to wash your body: *Can you answer the phone? I'm in the bath!* **2** [sing.] an act of washing the whole of your body when you sit or lie in a bath filled with water: *to* ***have a bath*** ◇ (*especially AmE*) *Would you prefer to* ***take a bath*** *or a shower?* **3** **baths** [pl.] (*BrE, old-fashioned*) a public building where you can go to swim **4** [C, usually pl.] (**HISTORY**) a public place where people went in past times to wash or have a bath: *Roman baths*

bath[2] /bɑːθ/ ***verb*** **1** [T] to give sb a bath: *to bath the baby* **2** [I] (*old-fashioned*) to have a bath

bathe /beɪð/ ***verb*** **1** [T] to wash or put part of the body in water, often for medical reasons: *She bathed the wound with antiseptic.* **2** [I] (*old-fashioned*) to swim in the sea or in a lake or river ➲ look at **sunbathe**

bathed /beɪðd/ ***adj.*** (*written*) ~ **in sth** (not *before* a noun) covered with sth: *The room was bathed in moonlight.*

bathing /ˈbeɪðɪŋ/ ***noun*** [U] the act of swimming in the sea, a river or a lake (not in a swimming pool): *Bathing is possible at a number of beaches along the coast.*

bathos /ˈbeɪθɒs/ ***noun*** [U] (*formal*) (**LITERATURE**) a sudden change, which is not usually deliberate, from a serious subject or feeling to sth ridiculous or unimportant

bathrobe /ˈbɑːθrəʊb/ ***noun*** [C] **1** a loose piece of clothing worn before and after taking a bath **2** (*AmE*) = DRESSING GOWN

bathroom /ˈbɑːθruːm; -rʊm/ ***noun*** [C] **1** a room where there is a bath, a place to wash your hands (**a washbasin**), and sometimes a toilet **2** (*AmE*) a room with a toilet

bathtub /ˈbɑːθtʌb/ = BATH[1] (1)

batik /bə'ti:k/ ***noun*** [U, C] (**ART**) a method of printing patterns on cloth by putting WAX (= the solid substance used to make candles) on the parts of the cloth that will not have any colour; a piece of cloth that is printed in this way

bat mitzvah /ˌbæt 'mɪtsvə/ ***noun*** [C] (**RELIGION**) a ceremony in the Jewish religion for a girl who has reached the age of 12 ➲ look at **bar mitzvah**

baton /'bætɒn/ ***noun*** [C] **1** = TRUNCHEON **2** (**MUSIC**) a short thin stick used by the leader of an ORCHESTRA (**the conductor**) **3** (**SPORT**) a stick which a runner in a race (**a relay race**) passes to the next person in the team

batsman /'bætsmən/ ***noun*** [C] (*pl.* **-men** /-mən/) (**SPORT**) (in CRICKET) one of the two players who hit the ball to score points (**runs**).

battalion /bə'tæliən/ ***noun*** [C] a large unit of soldiers that forms part of a larger unit in the army

batter[1] /'bætə(r)/ ***verb*** [I,T] to hit sb/sth hard, many times: *The wind battered against the window.* ◇ *He battered the door down.*

batter[2] /'bætə(r)/ ***noun*** [U] a mixture of flour, eggs and milk used to cover food such as fish, vegetables, etc. before frying them, or to make PANCAKES

battered /'bætəd/ ***adj.*** no longer looking new; damaged or out of shape: *a battered old hat*

battery 🔑 ***noun*** (*pl.* **batteries**) **1** /'bætri/ [C] (**PHYSICS**) a device which provides electricity for a toy, radio, car, etc.: *to recharge **a flat battery*** (= no longer producing electricity) **2** /'bætri/ [C] (*BrE*) (often used as an adjective) (**AGRICULTURE**) a large number of very small CAGES in which chickens, etc. are kept on a farm: *a battery hen/farm* ➲ look at **free-range 3** /'bætəri/ [U] (**LAW**) the crime of attacking sb physically: *He was charged with **assault and battery**.*

battle[1] 🔑 /'bætl/ ***noun*** **1** [C,U] (**POLITICS, HISTORY**) a fight, especially between armies in a war: *the battle of Trafalgar* ◇ *to die/be killed **in battle*** **2** [C] **a ~ (with sb) (for sth)** a competition, argument or fight between people or groups of people trying to win power or control: *a legal battle for custody of the children* **3** [C, usually sing.] **a ~ (against/for sth)** a determined effort to solve a difficult problem or to succeed in a difficult situation: *After three years she lost her battle against cancer.* ➲ note at **campaign**[1]
IDM **a losing battle** → LOSE

battle[2] /'bætl/ ***verb*** [I] **~ (with/against sb/sth) (for sth); ~ (on)** to try very hard to achieve sth difficult or to deal with sth unpleasant or dangerous: *Mark is battling with his maths homework.* ◇ *The two brothers were battling for control of the family business.* ◇ *Life is hard at the moment but we're battling on.*

battlefield /'bætlfi:ld/ (*also* **battleground** /'bætlgraʊnd/) ***noun*** [C] the place where a battle is fought

battlements /'bætlmənts/ ***noun*** [pl.] (**HISTORY**) a low wall around the top of a castle with spaces in it that people inside could shoot through ➲ picture at **drawbridge**, **castle**

battleship /'bætlʃɪp/ ***noun*** [C] the largest type of ship used in war

bauble /'bɔ:bl/ ***noun*** [C] **1** a piece of cheap jewellery **2** a decoration in the shape of a ball that is hung on a Christmas tree

Bauhaus /'baʊhaʊs/ ***noun*** [U] (**ARCHITECTURE**) a style and movement in German ARCHITECTURE and design in the early 20th century that was influenced by the methods and materials used in industry and placed emphasis on how things would be used

baulk (*especially AmE* **balk**) /bɔ:k/ ***verb*** [I] **~ (at sth)** to not want to do or agree to sth because it seems too difficult, dangerous or unpleasant

bauxite /'bɔ:ksaɪt/ ***noun*** [U] (**GEOLOGY**) a soft rock from which we get a light metal (**aluminium**)

bawdy /'bɔ:di/ ***adj.*** (**bawdier**; **bawdiest**) (*old-fashioned*) (**LITERATURE**) (used about songs, plays, etc.) loud, and dealing with sex in an amusing way

bawl /bɔ:l/ ***verb*** [I,T] to shout or cry loudly

bay 🔑 /beɪ/ ***noun*** [C] **1** (**GEOGRAPHY**) a part of the coast where the land goes in to form a curve: *the Bay of Bengal* ◇ *The harbour was in a sheltered bay.* **2** a part of a building, aircraft or area which has a particular purpose: *a parking/loading bay*
IDM **hold/keep sb/sth at bay** to stop sb/sth dangerous from getting near you; to prevent a situation or problem from getting worse

bayonet /'beɪənət/ ***noun*** [C] a knife that can be fixed to the end of a gun

ˌbay 'window ***noun*** [C] (**ARCHITECTURE**) a window in a part of a room that sticks out from the wall of a house

bazaar /bə'zɑ:(r)/ ***noun*** [C] **1** (in some eastern countries) a market **2** (*BrE*) a sale where the money that is made goes to charity: *The school held a bazaar to raise money for the homeless.*

bazooka /bə'zu:kə/ ***noun*** [C] a long gun, shaped like a tube, which is held on the shoulder and used to fire ROCKETS (= weapons that travel through the air)

BBC /ˌbi: bi: 'si:/ ***abbr.*** (**ARTS AND MEDIA**) the British Broadcasting Corporation; one of the national radio and television companies in Britain: *a BBC documentary* ◇ *watch a programme on BBC1*

BBQ ***abbr.*** = BARBECUE

BC (*AmE* **B.C.**) /ˌbi: 'si:/ ***abbr.*** (**RELIGION, HISTORY**) before Christ; used in dates to show the number of years before the time when Christians believe Jesus Christ was born: *300 BC* ➲ look at **AD**

be[1] 🔑 /bi; *strong form* bi:/ ***verb*** ❶ For the forms of 'be', look at the irregular verbs section at the back of this dictionary. **1** ***linking verb* there is/are** to exist; to be present: *I tried phoning them but there was no answer.* ◇ *There are some people outside.* ◇ *There are a lot of trees in our garden.* **2** [I] used to give the position of sb/sth or the place where sb/sth is SITUATED: *Katrina's in her office.* ◇ *Where are the scissors?* ◇ *The bus stop is five minutes' walk from here.* ◇ *St Tropez is on the south coast.* **3** ***linking verb*** used to give the date or age of sb/sth or to talk about time: *My birthday is on April 24th.* ◇ *It's 6 o'clock.* ◇ *It was Tuesday yesterday.* ◇ *Sue'll be 21 in June.* ◇ *He's older than Miranda.* ◇ *It's ages since I last saw him.* **4** ***linking verb*** used when you are giving the name of people or things, describing them or giving more information about them: *This is my father, John.* ◇ *I'm Alison.* ◇ *He's Italian. He's from Milan.* ◇ *He's a doctor.* ◇ *What's that?* ◇ *A lion is a mammal.* ◇ *'What colour is your car?' 'It's green.'* ◇ *How much was your ticket?* ◇ *The film was excellent.* ◇ *She's very friendly.* ◇ *'How is your wife?' 'She's fine, thanks.'* **5** [I] (only used in the perfect tenses) to go to a place (and return): *Have you ever **been to** Japan?*
IDM **be yourself** to act naturally: *Don't be nervous; just be yourself and the interview will be fine.*
-to-be (used to form compound nouns) future: *his bride-to-be* ◇ *mothers-to-be* (= pregnant women)

be² ⊶ /bi; *strong form* biː/ ***aux. verb*** **1** used with a past participle to form the passive; used with a present participle to form the continuous tenses **2** ~ **to do sth** used to show that sth must happen or that sth has been arranged: *You are to leave here at 10 o'clock at the latest.* **3 if sb/sth were to do sth** used to show that sth is possible but not very likely: *If they were to offer me the job, I'd probably take it.*

be- /bi/ ***prefix*** **1** (in verbs) to make or treat sb/sth as: *They befriended him.* **2** (in adjectives ending in -ed) wearing or covered with: *bejewelled*

beach ⊶ /biːtʃ/ ***noun*** [C] (GEOGRAPHY) an area of sand or small stones beside the sea: *to sit* ***on the beach***

beacon /ˈbiːkən/ ***noun*** [C] a fire or light on a hill or tower, often near the coast, which is used as a signal

bead /biːd/ ***noun*** [C] **1** a small round piece of wood, glass or plastic with a hole in the middle for putting a string through to make jewellery, etc. **2 beads** [pl.] a circular piece of jewellery (**a necklace**) made of **beads 3** a drop of liquid: *There were* ***beads of sweat*** *on his forehead.*

beady /ˈbiːdi/ ***adj.*** (used about a person's eyes) small round and bright; watching everything closely or with suspicion

beak ⊶ /biːk/ ***noun*** [C] the hard pointed part of a bird's mouth ➲ picture on **page 29**

beaker /ˈbiːkə(r)/ ***noun*** [C] **1** a plastic or paper drinking cup, usually without a handle **2** (CHEMISTRY) a glass container used in scientific experiments, etc. for pouring liquids ➲ picture at **laboratory**

beam¹ /biːm/ ***noun*** [C] **1** (PHYSICS) a line of light, electric waves or PARTICLES: *the beam of a torch* ◇ *The car's headlights were* ***on full beam*** (= giving the most light possible and not directed downwards). ◇ *a laser beam* **2** (ARCHITECTURE) a long piece of wood, metal, etc. that is used to support weight, for example in the floor or ceiling of a building **3** a happy smile **4** (*AmE* **'balance beam**) (SPORT) a wooden bar that is used in the sport of GYMNASTICS for people to move and balance on: *The gymnast performed a somersault on the beam.*

beam² /biːm/ ***verb*** **1** [I] ~ **(at sb)** to smile happily: *I looked at Sam and he beamed back at me.* **2** [T] to send out radio or television signals: *The programme was beamed live by satellite to many different countries.* **3** [I] to send out light and warmth: *The sun beamed down on them.*

bean /biːn/ ***noun*** [C] **1** the seeds or seed containers (**pods**) from a climbing plant which are eaten as vegetables: *soya beans* ◇ *a tin of* ***baked beans*** (= beans in a tomato sauce) ◇ ***green beans*** **2** similar seeds from some other plants: ***coffee beans***

IDM **full of beans/life** → FULL¹

spill the beans → SPILL

'bean sprouts ***noun*** [pl.] BEAN seeds that are just beginning to grow, often eaten without being cooked

bear¹ ⊶ /beə(r)/ ***verb*** (*pt* **bore** /bɔː(r)/; *pp* **borne** /bɔːn/) **1** [T] (used with *can/could* in negative sentences or in questions) to be able to accept and deal with sth unpleasant: *I can't bear spiders.* ◇ *She couldn't bear the thought of anything happening to him.* ◇ *How can you bear to listen to that music?* ◇ *The pain was almost more than he could bear.* SYN **stand, endure 2** [T] **not bear sth/doing sth** to not be suitable for sth; to not allow sth: *These figures won't bear close examination* (= when you look closely you will find mistakes). ◇ *What I would do if I lost my job* ***doesn't bear thinking about*** (= is too unpleasant to think about). **3** [T] (*formal*) to take responsibility for sth: *Customers will bear the full cost of the improvements.* **4** [T] to have a feeling, especially a negative feeling: *Despite what they did, she* ***bears no resentment*** *towards them.* ◇ *He's not the type to* ***bear a grudge*** *against anyone.* **5** [T] to support the weight of sth: *Twelve pillars bear the weight of the roof.* **6** [T] (*formal*) to show sth; to carry sth so that it can be seen: *The waiters came in bearing trays of food.* ◇ *He still* ***bears the scars*** *of his accident.* ◇ *She* ***bore a*** *strong* ***resemblance*** *to her mother* (= she looked like her). **7** [T] (*written*) to give birth to children: *She bore him four children, all sons.* **8** [I] to turn or go in the direction that is mentioned: *Where the road forks, bear left.*

IDM **bear the brunt of sth** to suffer the main force of sth: *Her sons usually bore the brunt of her anger.*

bear fruit to be successful; to produce results

bear in mind (that); bear/keep sb/sth in mind → MIND¹

bear witness (to sth) to show evidence of sth: *The burning buildings and empty streets bore witness to a recent attack.*

PHR V **bear down (on sb/sth) 1** to move closer to sb/sth in a frightening way: *We could see the hurricane bearing down on the town.* **2** to push down hard on sb/sth

bear sb/sth out to show that sb is correct or that sth is true

bear up to be strong enough to continue at a difficult time: *How is he bearing up after his accident?*

bear with sb/sth to be patient with: *Bear with me – I won't be much longer.*

bear² /beə(r)/ ***noun*** [C] **1** a large, heavy wild animal with thick fur and sharp teeth: *a polar/grizzly/brown bear* ➲ look at **teddy 2** (FINANCE) a person who sells shares in a company, hoping to buy them back later at a lower price: ***a bear market*** (= in which prices are falling) ➲ look at **bull**

bearable /ˈbeərəbl/ ***adj.*** that you can accept or deal with, although unpleasant: *It was extremely hot but the breeze made it more bearable.* OPP **unbearable**

beard ⊶ /bɪəd/ ***noun*** [C,U] the hair which grows on a man's cheeks and chin: *I'm going to* ***grow a beard.*** ◇ *a week's growth of beard* ➲ look at **goatee, moustache**

bearded /ˈbɪədɪd/ ***adj.*** with a beard

bearer /ˈbeərə(r)/ ***noun*** [C] a person who carries or brings sth: *I'm sorry to be the bearer of bad news.*

bearing /ˈbeərɪŋ/ ***noun*** **1** [U, sing.] **(a) ~ on sth** a relation or connection to the subject being discussed: *Her comments* ***had no bearing*** *on our decision.* **2** [U, sing.] the way in which sb stands or moves: *a man of dignified bearing* **3** [C] (GEOGRAPHY) a direction measured from a fixed point using a special instrument (**a compass**) **4** [C] (PHYSICS) a part of a machine that supports a moving part, especially one that is turning ➲ look at **ball bearing**

IDM **get/find your bearings** to become familiar with where you are

lose your bearings → LOSE

beast /biːst/ ***noun*** [C] (*formal*) an animal, especially a large one: *a wild beast*

beat¹ ⊶ /biːt/ ***verb*** (*pt* **beat**; *pp* **beaten** /ˈbiːtn/) **1** [T] ~ **sb (at sth)**; ~ **sth** to defeat sb; to be better than sth: *He always beats me at tennis.* ◇ *We're hoping to beat the world record.* ◇ *If you want to keep fit, you can't beat swimming.* **2** [I,T] to hit sb/sth many times, usually very hard: *The man was beating the* donkey with a stick. ◇ *The rain was beating on the roof of the car.* **3** [I,T] to make a regular sound or movement: *Her **heart beat** faster as she ran to pick up her child.* ◇ *We could hear the drums beating in the distance.* ◇ *The bird **beat its wings*** (= moved them up and down quickly). **4** [T] to mix sth quickly with a fork, etc.: *Beat the eggs and sugar together.*

IDM **beat about the bush** to talk about sth for a long time without mentioning the main point

(it) beats me (*spoken*) I do not know: *It beats me where he's gone.* ◇ *'Why is she angry?' 'Beats me!'*

beat time (to sth) (MUSIC) to mark or follow the rhythm of music, by waving a stick, tapping your foot, etc.: *She beat time with her fingers.*

off the beaten track in a place where people do not often go

PHR V **beat sb/sth off** to fight until sb/sth goes away: *The thieves tried to take his wallet but he beat them off.*

beat sb to sth to get somewhere or do sth before sb else: *She beat me back to the house.* ◇ *I wanted to get there first but Aisha beat me to it.*

beat sb up to attack sb by hitting or kicking them many times

beat² ⊶ /biːt/ ***noun*** **1** [C] a single hit on sth such as a drum or the movement of sth, such as your heart; the sound that this makes: *several loud beats on the drum* ◇ *Her heart skipped a beat when she saw him.* **2** [sing.] a series of regular hits on sth such as a drum, or of movements of sth; the sound that this makes: *the beat of the drums* ➲ look at **heartbeat** **3** [C] (MUSIC) the strong rhythm that a piece of music has **4** [sing.] the route along which a police officer regularly walks: *Having more policemen **on the beat** helps reduce crime.*

beating /ˈbiːtɪŋ/ ***noun*** [C] **1** a punishment that you give to sb by hitting them **2** (SPORT) a defeat

IDM **take a lot of/some beating** to be so good that it would be difficult to find sth better: *Mary's cooking takes some beating.*

the Beaufort scale /ˈbəʊfət skeɪl/ ***noun*** [sing.] (GEOGRAPHY) a scale used to measure the speed of the wind, from FORCE 0 (= calm) to FORCE 12 (= a very strong wind) (**a hurricane**)

beautician /bjuːˈtɪʃn/ ***noun*** [C] a person whose job is to improve the way people look with beauty treatments, etc.

beautiful ⊶ /ˈbjuːtɪfl/ ***adj.*** very pretty or attractive; giving pleasure to the senses: *The view from the top of the hill was really beautiful.* ◇ *What a beautiful day – the weather's perfect!* ◇ *He has a beautiful voice.* ◇ *A beautiful perfume filled the air.* ◇ *a beautiful woman*

beautifully ⊶ /ˈbjuːtɪfli/ ***adv.*** **1** in a beautiful way: *a beautifully decorated house* ◇ *He plays the piano beautifully.* ◇ *She was beautifully dressed.* **2** very well; in a pleasing way: *It's all working out beautifully.*

beautify /ˈbjuːtɪfaɪ/ ***verb*** [T] (**beautifies**; **beautifying**; **beautified**) to make sb/sth beautiful or more beautiful ▶ **beautification** /ˌbjuːtɪfɪˈkeɪʃn/ ***noun*** [U]

beauty ⊶ /ˈbjuːti/ ***noun*** (*pl.* **beauties**) **1** [U] the quality which gives pleasure to the senses; the state of being beautiful: *I was amazed by the beauty of the mountains.* ◇ *music of great beauty* **2** [C] a beautiful woman: *She grew up to be a beauty.* **3** [C] a particularly good example of sth: *Look at this tomato – it's a beauty!*

ˈbeauty contest (*AmE* **pageant**) ***noun*** [C] a competition to choose the most beautiful from a group of women

ˈbeauty queen ***noun*** [C] a woman who is judged to be the most beautiful in a competition (**a beauty contest**)

ˈbeauty salon (*also* **ˈbeauty parlour**, *AmE also* **ˈbeauty shop**) ***noun*** [C] a place where you can pay for treatment to your face, hair, nails, etc., which is intended to make you more beautiful

ˈbeauty spot ***noun*** [C] (*BrE*) a place in the countryside which is famous for its attractive SCENERY

beaver /ˈbiːvə(r)/ ***noun*** [C] an animal with brown fur, a wide, flat tail and sharp teeth. It lives in water and on land and uses branches to build DAMS (= walls across rivers to hold back the water.) ➲ picture on **page 29**

became past tense of **become**

because ⊶ /bɪˈkɒz/ ***conj.*** for the reason that: *They didn't go for a walk because it was raining.*

beˈcause of ***prep.*** as a result of; on account of: *They didn't go for a walk because of the rain.*

beck /bek/ ***noun***

IDM **at sb's beck and call** always ready to obey sb's orders

beckon /ˈbekən/ ***verb*** [I,T] to show sb with a movement of your finger or hand that you want them to come closer: *She beckoned me over to speak to her.*

become ⊶ /bɪˈkʌm/ ***linking verb*** (*pt* **became** /bɪˈkeɪm/; *pp* **become**) to begin to be sth: *Mr Saito became Chairman in 2000.* ◇ *She wants to become a pilot.* ◇ *They became friends.* ◇ *She became nervous as the exam date came closer.* ◇ *He is becoming more like you every day.*

PHR V **become of sb/sth** to happen to sb/sth: *What became of Alima? I haven't seen her for years!*

BEd /ˌbiː ˈed/ ***abbr.*** (EDUCATION) **Bachelor of Education**; a degree in education for people who want to be teachers and do not already have a degree in a particular subject

bed¹ ⊶ /bed/ ***noun*** **1** [C,U] a piece of furniture that you lie on when you sleep: *to **make the bed*** (= to arrange the sheets, etc. so that the bed is tidy and ready for sb to sleep in) ◇ *What time do you usually **go to bed**?* ◇ *She was lying **on the bed*** (= on top of the covers). ◇ *When he rang I was already **in bed*** (= under the covers). ◇ *It's late. **It's time for bed.*** ◇ *to get into/out of bed* **2 -bedded** having the type or number of beds mentioned: *a twin-bedded room* **3** [C] (GEOGRAPHY) the bottom of a river, the sea, etc.: *the ocean bed* **4** = FLOWER BED **5** [C] (GEOLOGY) a layer of rock in the earth's surface

IDM **go to bed with sb** (*informal*) to have sex with sb

bed² /bed/ ***verb*** [T] (**be<u>dd</u>ing**; **be<u>dd</u>ed**) to fix sth firmly in sth

PHR V **bed down** to sleep in a place where you do not usually sleep: *We couldn't find a hotel so we bedded down for the night in the van.*

ˌbed and ˈbreakfast ***noun*** [C] (*abbr.* **B&B**) (TOURISM) a place to stay in a private house or small hotel that consists of a room for the night and breakfast; a place that provides this

ˈbed bath (HEALTH) = BLANKET BATH

bedclothes /ˈbedkləʊðz/ (*BrE also* **ˈbedcovers**) ***noun*** [pl.] the sheets, covers, etc. that you put on a bed

bedding /ˈbedɪŋ/ ***noun*** [U] everything that you put on a bed and need for sleeping

bedpan /ˈbedpæn/ ***noun*** [C] (HEALTH) a container used as a toilet by sb in hospital who is too ill to get out of bed

bedraggled /bɪˈdræɡld/ ***adj.*** very wet and untidy or dirty: *bedraggled hair*

bedridden /ˈbedrɪdn/ ***adj.*** (HEALTH) being too old or ill to get out of bed

bedrock /ˈbedrɒk/ ***noun*** **1** [sing.] a strong base for sth, especially the facts or principles on which it is based: *The poor suburbs traditionally* ***formed the bedrock of*** *the party's support.* **2** [U] (GEOLOGY) the solid rock in the ground below the soil and sand ➲ picture at **flood plain**

bedroom ⊶ /ˈbedruːm; -rʊm/ ***noun*** [C] a room which is used for sleeping in: *You can sleep in the* ***spare bedroom***. ◇ *a three-bedroom house*

bedside /ˈbedsaɪd/ ***noun*** [sing.] the area that is next to a bed: *She sat* ***at*** *his* ***bedside*** *all night long.* ◇ *A book lay open on the* ***bedside table***.

bedsit /ˈbedsɪt/ (*also* **ˈbedsitter**) ***noun*** [C] (*BrE*) a rented room which is used for both living and sleeping in

bedsore /ˈbedsɔː(r)/ ***noun*** [C] (HEALTH) a painful place on a person's skin that is caused by lying in bed for a long time

bedspread /ˈbedspred/ ***noun*** [C] an attractive cover for a bed that you put on top of the sheets and other covers

bedtime /ˈbedtaɪm/ ***noun*** [U] the time that you normally go to bed

bee /biː/ ***noun*** [C] a black and yellow insect that lives in large groups and that makes a sweet substance that we eat (**honey**)

beech /biːtʃ/ ***noun*** **1** (*also* **ˈbeech tree**) [C] a large tree that produces small nuts **2** [U] the wood from this tree

beef ⊶ /biːf/ ***noun*** [U] the meat from a cow: *a slice of* ***roast beef*** ➲ note at **meat**

beefburger /ˈbiːfbɜːɡə(r)/ ***noun*** [C] beef that has been cut up small and pressed into a flat round shape ➲ look at **hamburger**

beefeater /ˈbiːfiːtə(r)/ ***noun*** [C] a guard who dresses in a traditional red uniform at the Tower of London

beefy /ˈbiːfi/ ***adj.*** (**beefier**; **beefiest**) having a strong body with big muscles

beehive /ˈbiːhaɪv/ (*also* **hive**) ***noun*** [C] a type of box that people use for keeping BEES in

ˈbee-keeper ***noun*** [C] a person who owns and takes care of BEES ▶ **ˈbee-keeping** ***noun*** [U]

been past participle of **be, go**[1]

beep[1] /biːp/ ***noun*** [C] a short high noise, for example made by the horn of a car

beep[2] /biːp/ ***verb*** **1** [I] (used about an electronic machine) to make a short high noise: *The microwave beeps when the food is cooked.* **2** [I,T] when a car horn **beeps**, or when you **beep** it, it makes a short noise: *I beeped my horn at the dog, but it wouldn't get off the road.* **3** [T] (*AmE*) = BLEEP[2] (2)

beeper /ˈbiːpə(r)/ (*AmE*) → BLEEPER

beer ⊶ /bɪə(r)/ ***noun*** **1** [U] a type of alcoholic drink that is made from grain **2** [C] a type or glass of beer

beeswax /ˈbiːzwæks/ ***noun*** [U] a yellow sticky substance that is produced by BEES. We use it to make CANDLES and polish for wood.

beet /biːt/ ***noun*** **1** (*BrE*) = SUGAR BEET **2** (*AmE*) = BEETROOT

beetle /ˈbiːtl/ ***noun*** [C] an insect, often large, shiny and black, with a hard case on its back covering its wings. There are many different types of **beetle**. ➲ picture on **page 29**

beetroot /ˈbiːtruːt/ (*AmE* **beet**) ***noun*** [C,U] a dark red vegetable which is the root of a plant. **Beetroot** is cooked and can be eaten hot or cold.

befall /bɪˈfɔːl/ ***verb*** [T] (*pt* **befell** /bɪˈfel/; *pp* **befallen** /bɪˈfɔːlən/) (*written*) (used about sth bad) to happen to sb

before[1] ⊶ /bɪˈfɔː(r)/ ***prep., conj.*** **1** earlier than sb/sth; earlier than the time that: *You can call me any time before 10 o'clock.* ◇ *the week before last* ◇ *They should be here before long* (= soon). ◇ *Turn the lights off before you leave.* **2** in front of sb/sth (in an order): *'H' comes before 'N' in the alphabet.* ◇ *A very difficult task lies before us.* ◇ *a company that puts profit before safety* (= thinks profit is more important than safety) **3** (*formal*) in a position in front of sb/sth: *They knelt before the altar.* ◇ *You will appear before the judge tomorrow.* **4** rather than: *I'd die before I apologized to him!*

before[2] ⊶ /bɪˈfɔː(r)/ ***adv.*** at an earlier time; already: *I think we've met somewhere before.* ◇ *It was fine yesterday but it rained the day before.*

beforehand /bɪˈfɔːhænd/ ***adv.*** at an earlier time than sth: *If you visit us, phone beforehand to make sure we're in.*

befriend /bɪˈfrend/ ***verb*** [T] (*written*) to become sb's friend; to be kind to sb

beg /beɡ/ ***verb*** [I,T] (**begging**; **begged**) **1** ~ **(sb) for sth**; ~ **sth (of/from sb)**; ~ **(sb) to do sth** to ask sb for sth strongly, or with great emotion: *He begged for forgiveness.* ◇ *We begged him to lend us the money.* **SYN** **entreat, implore** **2** ~ **(for) sth (from sb)** to ask people for food, money, etc. because you are very poor: *There are people begging for food in the streets.*

IDM **I beg your pardon** (*formal*) **1** I am sorry: *I beg your pardon. I picked up your bag by mistake.* **2** used for asking sb to repeat sth because you did not hear it properly

began past tense of **begin**

beggar /ˈbeɡə(r)/ ***noun*** [C] a person who lives by asking people for money, food, etc. on the streets

begin ⊶ /bɪˈɡɪn/ ***verb*** (*pres. part.* **beginning**; *pt* **began** /bɪˈɡæn/; *pp* **begun** /bɪˈɡʌn/) **1** [I,T] to start doing sth; to do the first part of sth: *Shall I begin or will you?* ◇ *I began* (= started reading) *this novel last month and I still haven't finished it.* ◇ *When did he begin his lesson?* ◇ *When do you begin work?* ◇ *We began writing to each other in 1980.* ◇ *The carpet is beginning to look dirty.* **2** [I] to start to happen or exist, especially from a particular time: *What time does the concert begin?* **3** [I] ~ **(with sth)** to start in a particular way, with a particular event, or in a particular place: *My name begins with 'W' not 'V'.* ◇ *The fighting began with an argument about money.* ◇ *This is where the footpath begins.* ▶ **beginner** ***noun*** [C]

IDM **to begin with 1** at first: *To begin with, they were very happy.* **2** used for giving your first reason for sth or to introduce your first point: *We can't possibly go. To begin with, it's too far and we can't afford it either.*

beginning ⊶ /bɪˈɡɪnɪŋ/ ***noun*** [C] the first part of sth; the time when or the place where sth starts: *I've read the article* ***from beginning to end***. ◇ *We're going away* ***at the beginning of*** *the school holidays.*

begrudge /bɪˈɡrʌdʒ/ ***verb*** [T] ~ **(sb) sth** **1** to feel angry or upset because sb has sth that you think that they should not have: *He's worked hard. I don't begrudge him his success.* **2** to be unhappy that you have to do sth: *I begrudge paying so much money in tax each month.*

begun past participle of **begin**

behalf ⊶ AW /bɪˈhɑːf/ ***noun***
IDM **on behalf of sb; on sb's behalf** for sb; as the representative of sb: *Emma couldn't be present so her husband accepted the prize on her behalf.* ◇ *I would like to thank you all on behalf of my colleagues and myself.*

behave ⊶ /bɪˈheɪv/ ***verb*** **1** [I] ~ **well, badly, etc. (towards sb)** to act in a particular way: *Don't you think that Ellen has been behaving very strangely recently?* ◇ *I think you behaved very badly towards your father.* ◇ *He **behaves as if/though** he was the boss.* **2** [I,T] ~ **(yourself)** to act in the correct or appropriate way: *I want you to behave yourselves while we're away.* OPP **misbehave** **3 -behaved** (used to form compound adjectives) behaving in the way mentioned: *a well-behaved child* ◇ *a badly-behaved class*

behaviour ⊶ (*AmE* **behavior**) /bɪˈheɪvjə(r)/ ***noun*** [U] the way that you act or behave: *He was sent out of the class for bad behaviour.*

behead /bɪˈhed/ ***verb*** [T] to cut off sb's head, especially as a punishment

behind ⊶ /bɪˈhaɪnd/ ***prep., adv.*** **1** in, at or to the back of sb/sth: *There's a small garden behind the house.* ◇ *The sun went behind a cloud.* ◇ *You go on ahead. I'll follow on behind.* ◇ *Look behind you before you drive off.* ◇ *He ran off but the police were close behind.* **2** ~ **(in/with) (sth)** later or less good than sb/sth; making less progress than sb/sth: *The train is twenty minutes behind schedule.* ◇ *Jane is behind the rest of the class in maths.* ◇ *We are a month behind with the rent.* ➲ look at **ahead** **3** supporting or agreeing with sb/sth: *Whatever she decides, her family will be behind her.* **4** responsible for causing or starting sth: *What is the reason behind his sudden change of opinion?* **5** used to say that sth is in sb's past: *It's time you **put** your problems **behind you*** (= forgot about them). **6** in the place where sb/sth is or was: *Oh no! I've **left** the tickets **behind*** (= at home).

beige /beɪʒ/ ***adj., noun*** [U] (of) a light brown colour

being[1] → BE

being[2] /ˈbiːɪŋ/ ***noun*** **1** [U] the state of existing; existence: *When did the organization **come into being**?* **2** [C] a living person or thing: *a human being*

belated /bɪˈleɪtɪd/ ***adj.*** coming late: *a belated apology* ▶ **belatedly** ***adv.***: *They have realized, rather belatedly, that they have made a mistake.*

belch /beltʃ/ ***verb*** **1** [I] to let gas out from your stomach through your mouth with a sudden noise SYN **burp** **2** [T] to send out a lot of smoke, etc.: *The volcano belched smoke and ashes.* ▶ **belch** ***noun*** [C]

belie /bɪˈlaɪ/ ***verb*** [T] (*pres. part.* **belying**; *3rd person sing. pres.* **belies**; *pt, pp* **belied**) (*formal*) to give an idea of sth that is false or not true: *His smiling face belied his true feelings.*

belief ⊶ /bɪˈliːf/ ***noun*** **1** [sing., U] ~ **in sb/sth** a feeling that sb/sth is true, morally good or right, or that sb/sth really exists: *She has lost her belief in God.* ➲ look at **disbelief** **2** [sing., U] (*formal*) ~ **(that...)** something you accept as true; what you believe: *It's my belief that people are basically good.* ◇ *There is a general belief that things will soon get better.* ◇ ***Contrary to popular belief*** (= in spite of what many people think), *the north of the country is not poorer than the south.* **3** [C] an idea about religion, politics, etc.: *Divorce is contrary to their religious beliefs.*
IDM **beyond belief** (in a way that is) too great, difficult, etc. to be believed

believable /bɪˈliːvəbl/ ***adj.*** that can be believed OPP **unbelievable**

believe ⊶ /bɪˈliːv/ ***verb*** (not used in the continuous tenses) **1** [T] to feel sure that sth is true or that sb is telling the truth: *He said he hadn't taken any money but I didn't believe him.* ◇ *Nobody believes a word she says.* ➲ note at **think** OPP **disbelieve** **2** [T] ~ **(that)...** to think that sth is true or possible, although you are not certain: *I believe they have moved to Italy.* ◇ *'Does Pat still work there?' '**I believe so.**'* ◇ *The escaped prisoner is believed to be in this area.* ◇ *Four people are still missing, believed drowned.* **3 don't/can't ~ sth** used to show anger or surprise at sth: *I can't believe (that) you're telling me to do it again!* **4** [I] to have religious beliefs
IDM **believe it or not** it may be surprising but it is true: *Believe it or not, English food is often quite good.*
give sb to believe/understand (that) (often passive) to give sb the impression or idea that sth is true: *I was given to believe that I had got the job.*
PHR V **believe in sb/sth** to be sure that sb/sth exists: *Do you believe in God?* ◇ *Most young children believe in Father Christmas.*
believe in sb/sth to feel that you can trust sb and/or that they will be successful: *They need a leader they can believe in.* ➲ note at **trust**[2]
believe in doing sth to think that sth is good, right or acceptable: *He doesn't believe in killing animals for their fur.*

believer /bɪˈliːvə(r)/ ***noun*** [C] (**RELIGION**) a person who has religious beliefs
IDM **be a (great/firm) believer in sth** to think that sth is good or right: *He is a great believer in getting things done on time.*

belittle /bɪˈlɪtl/ ***verb*** [T] to make sb or the things they do, seem unimportant or not very good

bell ⊶ /bel/ ***noun*** [C] **1** a metal object, often shaped like a cup, that makes a ringing sound when it is hit by a small piece of metal inside it: *the sound of church bells* ◇ *Her voice came back **clear as a bell**.* ➲ picture at **goat** **2** an electrical device that makes a ringing sound when the button on it is pushed; the sound that it makes: *Ring the bell and see if they're at home.*
IDM **ring a bell** → RING[2]

bellboy /ˈbelbɔɪ/ (*AmE also* **bellhop**) ***noun*** [C] (**TOURISM**) a person whose job is to carry people's cases to their rooms in a hotel

bellhop /ˈbelhɒp/ ***noun*** [C] (*AmE*) = BELLBOY

belligerent /bəˈlɪdʒərənt/ ***adj.*** **1** unfriendly and aggressive SYN **hostile** **2** (only *before* a noun) (*formal*) (**POLITICS**) (used about a country) fighting a war

bellow /ˈbeləʊ/ ***verb*** **1** [I,T] to shout in a loud deep voice, especially because you are angry **2** [I] to make a deep low sound, like a BULL (= a male cow) ▶ **bellow** ***noun*** [C]

belly /ˈbeli/ ***noun*** [C] (*pl.* **bellies**) the part of the body below the chest SYN **stomach**

ˈ**belly button** (*informal*) = NAVEL

belong ⊶ /bɪˈlɒŋ/ ***verb*** [I] **1** ~ **to sb** to be owned by sb: *Who does this pen belong to?* ◇ *Don't take anything that doesn't belong to you.* **2** ~ **to sth** to be a member of a group or organization: *Do you belong to any political party?* **3** to have a right or usual place: *The plates belong in the cupboard over there.* ◇ *It took quite a long time before we felt we belonged in the village* (= until we felt comfortable).

belongings /bɪˈlɒŋɪŋz/ ***noun*** [pl.] the things that you own that can be moved, that is, not land and buildings

beloved /bɪˈlʌvd; bɪˈlʌvɪd/ ***adj.*** (*formal*) much loved: *They had always intended to return to their beloved Ireland.* ❶ When 'beloved' comes before a noun, the pronunciation is /bɪˈlʌvɪd/.

below ⊶ /bɪˈləʊ/ ***prep., adv.*** at or to a lower position or level than sb/sth: *Do not write below this line.* ◇ *The temperature fell below freezing during the night.* ◇ *Her marks in the exam were below average.* ◇ *I don't live on the top floor. I live on the floor below.* ◇ *temperatures of 30° and below* OPP **above**

beˌlow-the-ˈline ***adj.*** **1** (FINANCE) relating to unusual costs or money earned after a company's total profit has been calculated that show its final profit **2** (BUSINESS) relating to advertising activities that do not involve the MASS MEDIA (= newspapers, television and radio), such as DIRECT MAIL (= advertisements sent to people through the post) ➲ look at **above-the-line**

belt¹ ⊶ /belt/ ***noun*** [C] **1** a thin piece of cloth, leather, etc. that you wear around your waist: *I need a belt to keep these trousers up.* ➲ look at **seat belt** **2** a continuous band of material that moves round and is used to carry things along or to drive machinery: *The suitcases were carried round on a **conveyor belt**.* ◇ *the **fan belt** of a car* (= that operates the machinery that cools a car engine) **3** (GEOGRAPHY) an area of land that has a particular quality or where a particular group of people live: ***the green belt*** *around London* (= an area of countryside where you are not allowed to build houses, factories, etc.) ◇ *a country's **corn/industrial belt*** ◇ *the **commuter belt***

IDM **below the belt** (*informal*) unfair or cruel: *That remark was rather below the belt.*

tighten your belt → TIGHTEN

under your belt (*informal*) that you have already done or achieved: *She's already got four tournament wins under her belt.*

belt² /belt/ ***verb*** (*informal*) **1** [T] to hit sb hard **2** [I] to run or go somewhere very fast: *I was belting along on my bicycle.*

PHRV **belt sth out** to sing, shout or play sth loudly

belt up (*slang*) used to tell sb rudely to be quiet: *Belt up! I can't think with all this noise.*

bemused /bɪˈmjuːzd/ ***adj.*** confused and unable to think clearly

bench /bentʃ/ ***noun*** **1** [C] a long wooden or metal seat for two or more people, often outdoors: *a park bench* **2 the bench** [sing.] (LAW) a judge in court or the seat where he/she sits; the position of being a judge or MAGISTRATE: *His lawyer turned to address the bench.* **3** [C, usually pl.] (POLITICS) (in the British Parliament) a seat where a particular group of politicians sit: *the Government **front bench*** ◇ *There was cheering from the Opposition benches.* ➲ look at **back bench** **4 the bench** [sing.] (SPORT) the seats where players sit when they are not playing in the game **5** [C] a long narrow table that people work at; for example, in a factory: *a carpenter's bench* ➲ look at **workbench**

benchmark /ˈbentʃmɑːk/ ***noun*** [C] a standard that other things can be compared to: *These new safety features **set a benchmark** for other manufacturers to follow.*

bend¹ ⊶ /bend/ ***verb*** (*pt, pp* **bent** /bent/) **1** [T] to make sth that was straight into a curved shape: *to bend a piece of wire into an S shape* ◇ *It hurts when I bend my knee.* **2** [I] to be or become curved: *The road bends to the left here.* **3** [I] to move your body forwards and downwards: *He **bent down** to tie up his shoelaces.*

IDM **bend the rules** to do sth that is not normally allowed by the rules

bend² ⊶ /bend/ ***noun*** [C] a curve or turn, for example in a road: *a sharp bend in the road*

IDM **round the bend** (*informal*) crazy; mad: *His behaviour is **driving me round the bend*** (= annoying me very much).

beneath ⊶ /bɪˈniːθ/ ***prep., adv.*** **1** in, at or to a lower position than sb/sth; under: *The ship disappeared beneath the waves.* ◇ *He seemed a nice person but there was a lot of anger beneath the surface.* **2** not good enough for sb: *She felt that cleaning for other people was beneath her.*

benefactor /ˈbenɪfæktə(r)/ ***noun*** [C] (*formal*) a person who helps or gives money to a person or an organization

beneficial AW /ˌbenɪˈfɪʃl/ ***adj.*** ~ **(to sb/sth)** improving a situation; having a helpful or useful effect SYN **advantageous**: *a good diet is beneficial to health* OPP **detrimental**

beneficiary AW /ˌbenɪˈfɪʃəri/ ***noun*** [C] (*pl.* **beneficiaries**) (LAW) a person who gains as a result of sth, especially money or property when sb dies

benefit¹ ⊶ AW /ˈbenɪfɪt/ ***noun*** **1** [U, C] an advantage or useful effect that sth has: *A change in the law would be **to everyone's benefit**.* ◇ *I can't see **the benefit of** doing things this way.* ◇ *the benefits of modern technology* **2** [U] (*BrE*) (POLITICS) money that the government gives to people who are ill, poor, unemployed, etc.: ***child/sickness/housing benefit*** ◇ *I'm not entitled to **unemployment benefit**.* **3** [C, usually pl.] (BUSINESS) advantages that you get from your company in addition to the money you earn: *a company car and other benefits*

IDM **for sb's benefit** especially to help, please, etc. sb: *For the benefit of the newcomers, I will start again.*

give sb the benefit of the doubt to believe what sb says although there is no proof that it is true

benefit² ⊶ AW /ˈbenɪfɪt/ ***verb*** (**benefiting**; **benefited** or **benefitting**; **benefitted**) **1** [T] to produce a good or useful effect: *The new tax laws will benefit people on low wages.* **2** [I] ~ **(from sth)** to receive an advantage from sth: *Small businesses have benefited from the changes in the law.*

benevolent /bəˈnevələnt/ ***adj.*** (*formal*) kind, friendly and helpful to others OPP **malevolent**

▸ **benevolence** ***noun*** [U]

benign /bɪˈnaɪn/ ***adj.*** **1** (used about people) kind or gentle **2** (HEALTH) (used about a disease, etc.) not dangerous: *a benign tumour* OPP **malignant**

bent¹ past tense, past participle of **bend¹**

bent² ⊶ /bent/ ***adj.*** **1** not straight: *Do this exercise with your knees bent.* ◇ *This knife is bent.* ◇ *It was so funny we were **bent double** with laughter.* **2** (*BrE, informal*) (used about a person in authority) dishonest SYN **corrupt**: *a bent policeman*

IDM **bent on sth/on doing sth** wanting to do sth very much; determined

bent³ /bent/ ***noun*** [sing.] **a ~ for sth/for doing sth** a natural skill at sth or interest in sth: *She has a bent for music.*

benzene /ˈbenziːn/ ***noun*** [U] (CHEMISTRY) a colourless liquid obtained from PETROLEUM and used in making plastics and many chemical products

ˈbenzene ring *noun* [C] (CHEMISTRY) a ring of six CARBON atoms in BENZENE and many other COMPOUNDS

bequeath /bɪˈkwiːð/ *verb* [T] (*formal*) ~ **sth (to sb)** (LAW) to say in a WILL (= a legal document) that you want sb to have your property, money, etc. after you die SYN **leave**: *He bequeathed £1 000 to his favourite charity.*

bequest /bɪˈkwest/ *noun* [C] (*formal*) (LAW) money or property that you ask to be given to a particular person when you die: *He left a bequest to each of his grandchildren.*

bereaved /bɪˈriːvd/ *adj.* (*formal*) **1** having lost a relative or close friend who has recently died **2 the bereaved** *noun* [pl.] the people whose relative or close friend has died recently

bereavement /bɪˈriːvmənt/ *noun* (*formal*) **1** [U] the state of having lost a relative or close friend who has recently died **2** [C] the death of a relative or close friend: *There has been a bereavement in the family.*

bereft /bɪˈreft/ *adj.* (not *before* a noun) (*formal*) **1** ~ **of sth** completely lacking sth; having lost sth: *bereft of ideas/hope* **2** (used about a person) sad and lonely because you have lost sb/sth: *He was utterly bereft when his wife died.*

beret /ˈbereɪ/ *noun* [C] a soft flat round hat

bergschrund /ˈbɜːgʃrʊnd/ *noun* [C] (GEOGRAPHY) a deep crack formed where a GLACIER (= a large moving mass of ice) meets the side of a mountain

berkelium /bɜːˈkiːliəm; ˈbɜːkliəm/ *noun* [U] (*symbol* **Bk**) (CHEMISTRY) a chemical element. **Berkelium** is a RADIOACTIVE metal that is produced artificially from AMERICIUM and HELIUM. ❶ For more information on the periodic table of elements, look at pages R34-5.

berry /ˈberi/ *noun* [C] (*pl.* **berries**) a small soft fruit with seeds: *Those berries are poisonous.* ◇ *a raspberry/strawberry/blueberry*

berserk /bəˈzɜːk/ *adj.* (not *before* a noun) very angry; crazy: *If the teacher finds out what you've done he'll* ***go berserk***.

berth /bɜːθ/ *noun* [C] **1** a place to sleep on a ship or train, or in a CARAVAN SYN **bunk**: *a cabin with four berths* **2** a place where a ship or boat can stop and stay, usually in a HARBOUR

beryllium /bəˈrɪliəm/ *noun* [U] (*symbol* **Be**) (CHEMISTRY) a hard white metal that is used in making mixtures of other metals (**alloys**) ❶ For more information on the periodic table of elements, look at pages R34-5.

beseech /bɪˈsiːtʃ/ *verb* [T] (*pt, pp* **besought** /bɪˈsɔːt/ or *pt, pp* **beseeched**) (*formal*) to ask sb for sth in a worried way because you want or need it very much

beset /bɪˈset/ (*pres. part.* **besetting**; *pt, pp* **beset**) *verb* [T] (*written*) to affect sb/sth in a bad way: *The team has been beset by injuries all season.*

beside ⊸ /bɪˈsaɪd/ *prep.* at the side of, or next to sb/sth: *Come and sit beside me.* ◇ *He kept his bag close beside him at all times.*

IDM **beside the point** not connected with the subject you are discussing

beside yourself (with sth) not able to control yourself because of a very strong emotion: *Emily was almost beside herself with grief.*

besides /bɪˈsaɪdz/ *prep., adv.* in addition to or as well as sb/sth; also: *There will be six people coming, besides you and David.* ◇ *I don't want to go out tonight. Besides, I haven't got any money.*

besiege /bɪˈsiːdʒ/ *verb* [T] **1** (HISTORY) to surround a place with an army **2** (usually passive) (used about sth unpleasant or annoying) to surround sb/sth in large numbers: *The actor was besieged by fans and reporters.*

besotted /bɪˈsɒtɪd/ *adj.* (not *before* a noun) ~ **(with/by sb/sth)** so much in love with sb/sth that you cannot think or behave normally

besought past tense, past participle of **beseech**

bespectacled /bɪˈspektəkld/ *adj.* (*formal*) wearing glasses

best[1] ⊸ /best/ *adj.* (the superlative of *good*) of the highest quality or level; most suitable: *His latest book is by far his best.* ◇ *I'm going to wear my best shirt to the interview.* ◇ *Who in the class is* ***best at*** *maths?* ◇ ***It's best to*** *arrive early if you want a good seat.* ◇ *What's the best way to get to York from here?* ◇ *Who's your* ***best friend***?

IDM **your best bet** (*informal*) the most sensible or appropriate thing for you to do in a particular situation: *There's nowhere to park in the city centre. Your best bet is to go in by bus.*

the best/better part of sth → PART[1]

best[2] ⊸ /best/ *adv.* (the superlative of *well*) to the greatest degree; most: *He works best in the morning.* ◇ *Which of these dresses do you like best?* ◇ *one of Britain's best-loved TV stars*

IDM **as best you can** as well as you can even if it is not perfectly

best[3] ⊸ /best/ *noun* [sing.] **the best** the person or thing that is of the highest quality or level or better than all others: *When you pay that much for a meal you expect the best.* ◇ *Even the best of us make mistakes sometimes.* ◇ *I think James is the best!* ◇ *They are the best of friends.* ◇ *The best we can hope for is that the situation doesn't get any worse.* ➲ look at **second-best**

IDM **all the best** (*informal*) used when you are saying goodbye to sb and wishing them success: *All the best! Keep in touch, won't you?*

at best if everything goes as well as possible; taking the most HOPEFUL view: *We won't be able to deliver the goods before March, or, at best, the last week in February.*

at its/your best in its/your best state or condition: *This is an example of Beckett's work at its best.* ◇ *No one is at their best first thing in the morning.*

be (all) for the best to be good in the end even if it does not seem good at first: *I didn't get the job, but I'm sure it's all for the best.*

bring out the best/worst in sb to show sb's best/worst qualities: *The crisis really brought out the best in Tony.*

do/try your best to do all or the most that you can

look your best to look as beautiful or attractive as possible

make the best of sth/a bad job to accept a difficult situation and try to be as happy as possible

ˌbest ˈman *noun* [sing.] a man who helps and supports the man who is getting married (**the bridegroom**) at a wedding

bestow /bɪˈstəʊ/ *verb* [T] ~ **sth (on/upon sb)** (*formal*) to give sth to sb, especially to show how much they are respected: *The title was bestowed on him by the king.*

ˌbest-ˈseller *noun* [C] (ARTS AND MEDIA) a book or other product that is bought by large numbers of people ► **ˈbest-selling** *adj.*: *a best-selling novel*

bet[1] ⊸ /bet/ *verb* [I,T] (*pres. part.* **betting**; *pt, pp* **bet** or **betted**) **1** ~ **(sth) (on sth)** to risk money on a race or an event by trying to predict the result. If you are right, you win money: *I wouldn't bet on them*

winning the next election. ◇ *I bet him £10 he couldn't stop smoking for a week.* SYN **gamble**, **put money on sth** **2** (*spoken*) used to say that you are almost certain that sth is true or that sth will happen: *I bet he arrives late – he always does.* ◇ *I bet you're worried about your exam, aren't you?*
IDM **you bet** (*spoken*) a way of saying 'Yes, of course!': *'Are you coming too?' 'You bet (I am)!'*

bet² ⊶ /bet/ ***noun*** [C] **1** an act of betting: *Did you **have a bet on** that race?* ◇ *to **win/lose a bet*** **2** an opinion: *My bet is that he's missed the train.*
IDM **your best bet** → BEST¹
hedge your bets → HEDGE²

beta /ˈbiːtə/ ***noun*** [C] (LANGUAGE) the second letter of the Greek alphabet (β)

ˈ**beta decay** ***noun*** [sing.] (PHYSICS) the breaking up of an atom in which an ELECTRON (= a very small part of the atom with a negative electrical charge) is given off

ˈ**beta particle** ***noun*** [C] (PHYSICS) a fast-moving ELECTRON (= a very small part of the atom with a negative electrical charge) that is given off when an atom breaks up

betide /bɪˈtaɪd/ ***verb***
IDM **woe betide sb** → WOE

betray /bɪˈtreɪ/ ***verb*** [T] **1** to give information about sb/sth to an enemy; to make a secret known: *She betrayed all the members of the group to the secret police.* ◇ *He refused to betray their plans.* ◇ *to betray your country* ➲ note at **traitor** **2** to hurt sb who trusts you, especially by not being loyal or faithful to them: *If you take the money you'll **betray** her **trust**.* ◇ *When parents get divorced the children often **feel betrayed**.* **3** to show a feeling or quality that you would like to keep hidden: *Her steady voice did not betray the emotion she was feeling.* ▶ **betrayal** /bɪˈtreɪəl/ ***noun*** [C,U]

betrothal /bɪˈtrəʊðl/ ***noun*** [C] (*formal* or *old-fashioned*) an agreement to marry sb SYN **engagement**

betrothed /bɪˈtrəʊðd/ ***adj.*** ~ **(to sb)** (*formal* or *old-fashioned*) having promised to marry sb SYN **engaged**

better¹ ⊶ /ˈbetə(r)/ ***adj.*** **1** (the comparative of *good*) ~ **than sb/sth** of a higher quality or level or more suitable than sb/sth: *I think her second novel was much better than her first.* ◇ *He's far better at English than me.* ◇ *It's a long way to drive. It would be better to take the train.* ◇ *You'd be better getting the train than driving.* **2** (HEALTH) (the comparative of *well*) less ill; fully recovered from an illness: *You can't go swimming until you're better.*

better² ⊶ /ˈbetə(r)/ ***adv.*** (the comparative of *well*) in a better way; to a greater or higher degree: *I think you could have done this better.* ◇ *Sylvie speaks English better than I do.*
IDM **(be) better off** **1** to be in a more pleasant or suitable situation: *You look terrible. You'd be better off at home in bed.* **2** (comparative of *well off*) with more money: *We're much better off now I go out to work too.*
the best/better part of sth → PART¹
you, etc. had better you should; you ought to: *I think we'd better go before it gets dark.*
know better (than that/than to do sth) → KNOW¹
think better of (doing) sth → THINK

better³ ⊶ /ˈbetə(r)/ ***noun*** [sing., U] something that is of higher quality: *The hotel wasn't very good. I must say we'd expected better.*
IDM **get the better of sb/sth** to defeat or be stronger than sb/sth: *When we have an argument she always gets the better of me.*

ˈ**betting shop** ***noun*** [C] a shop where you can go to put money on a race or an event ➲ look at **bookmaker** (2)

between ⊶ /bɪˈtwiːn/ ***prep.***, ***adv.*** **1** ~ **A and B**; **in** ~ in the space in the middle of two things, people, places etc.: *I was sitting between Sam and Charlie.* ◇ *a village between Girona and Palamos* ◇ *She was standing **in between** the desk **and** the wall.* **2** ~ **A and B**; **in** ~ (used about two amounts, distances, ages, times, etc.) at a point that is greater or later than the first and smaller or earlier than the second; somewhere in the middle: *They said they would arrive between 4 and 5 o'clock.* ◇ *They've got this shirt in size 10 and size 16, but nothing in between.* **3** from one place to another and back again: *There aren't any direct trains between here and Manchester.* **4** involving or connecting two people, groups or things: *There's some sort of disagreement between them.* ◇ *There may be a connection between the two crimes.* **5** choosing one and not the other (of two things): *to choose between two jobs* ◇ *What's the difference between 'some' and 'any'?* **6** by putting together the actions, efforts, etc. of two or more people: *Between us we saved up enough money to buy a car.* **7** giving each person a share: *The money was divided equally between the two children.* ◇ *We ate all the chocolates between us.*

bevel /ˈbevl/ ***noun*** [C] **1** an edge or a surface that is cut at an angle, for example at the side of a picture frame or sheet of glass **2** a tool for cutting edges or surfaces at an angle on wood or stone

beverage /ˈbevərɪdʒ/ ***noun*** [C] (*formal*) any type of drink except water

beware /bɪˈweə(r)/ ***verb*** [I] (only in the imperative or infinitive) ~ **(of sb/sth)** (used for giving a warning) to be careful: *Beware of the dog!* (= written on a sign) ◇ *We were told to beware of strong currents in the sea.*

bewilder /bɪˈwɪldə(r)/ ***verb*** [T] to confuse and surprise sb: *I was completely bewildered by his sudden change of mood.* ▶ **bewildered** ***adj.***: *a bewildered expression* ▶ **bewildering** ***adj.***: *a bewildering experience* ▶ **bewilderment** ***noun*** [U]: *to stare at sb **in bewilderment***

bewitch /bɪˈwɪtʃ/ ***verb*** [T] to attract and interest sb very much

beyond ⊶ /bɪˈjɒnd/ ***prep.***, ***adv.*** **1** on or to the other side of: *beyond the distant mountains* ◇ *We could see the mountains and the sea beyond.* **2** further than; later than: *Does the motorway continue beyond Birmingham?* ◇ *Most people don't go on working beyond the age of 65.* **3** more than sth: *The house was **far beyond** what I could afford.* ◇ *I haven't heard anything beyond a few rumours.* **4** used to say that sth is not possible: *The car was completely **beyond repair*** (= too badly damaged to repair). ◇ *The situation is **beyond** my **control**.* **5** too far or too advanced for sb/sth: *The activity was beyond the students' abilities.*
IDM **be beyond sb** (*informal*) to be impossible for sb to understand or imagine: *Why she wants to go and live there is quite beyond me.*

bhangra /ˈbɑːŋgrə/ ***noun*** [U] (MUSIC) a type of popular music that combines traditional Punjabi music from India and Pakistan with Western pop music

bi- /baɪ/ ***prefix*** (in nouns and adjectives) two; twice; double: *bicentenary* ◇ *bilingual*

bias¹ AW /ˈbaɪəs/ ***noun*** (*pl.* **biases**) **1** [U, C, usually sing.] a strong feeling of favour towards or against one group of people, or on one side in an argument, often not based on fair judgement or facts: *a bias against women drivers* ◇ *The BBC has been accused of* ***political bias****.* **2** [C, usually sing.] an interest in one thing more than others; a special ability: *a course with a strong scientific bias*

bias² AW /ˈbaɪəs/ ***verb*** [T] (**biasing**; **biased** or **biassing**; **biassed**) to influence sb/sth, especially unfairly; to give an advantage to one group, etc.: *Good newspapers should not be biased towards a particular political party.* ▶ **biased** AW ***adj.***: *a biased report*

bib /bɪb/ ***noun*** [C] a piece of cloth or plastic that a baby or small child wears under the chin to protect its clothes while it is eating

the Bible /ˈbaɪbl/ ***noun*** [sing.] (RELIGION) **1** the holy book of the Christian religion, consisting of the Old Testament and the New Testament **2** the holy book of the Jewish religion, consisting of the Torah (or Law), the PROPHETS, and the Writings ▶ **biblical** /ˈbɪblɪkl/ ***adj.***

bibliography /ˌbɪbliˈɒɡrəfi/ ***noun*** [C] (*pl.* **bibliographies**) (LITERATURE, EDUCATION) **1** a list of the books and articles that a writer used when they were writing a particular book or article **2** a list of books on a particular subject

bicameral /ˌbaɪˈkæmərəl/ ***adj.*** (POLITICS) (used about a parliament) having two main parts, such as the Senate and the House of Representatives in the US, and the House of Commons and the House of Lords in Britain: *a bicameral assembly/legislature/congress*

bicarbonate /ˌbaɪˈkɑːbənət/ ***noun*** [U] (CHEMISTRY) a salt made from CARBONIC ACID containing CARBON, HYDROGEN and OXYGEN together with another element

biˌcarbonate of ˈsoda ***noun*** [U] = SODIUM BICARBONATE

bicentenary /ˌbaɪsenˈtiːnəri/ ***noun*** [C] (*pl.* **bicentenaries**) (*AmE* **bicentennial** /ˌbaɪsenˈteniəl/) the day or the year two hundred years after sth happened or began: *the bicentenary of the French Revolution*

bicentennial /ˌbaɪsenˈteniəl/ (*AmE*) = BICENTENARY

biceps /ˈbaɪseps/ ***noun*** [C] (*pl.* **biceps**) (ANATOMY) the large muscle at the front of the top part of your arm ➲ look at **triceps** ➲ picture at **arm**

bicker /ˈbɪkə(r)/ ***verb*** [I] to argue about unimportant things: *My parents are always bickering about money.*

bicycle 🔑 /ˈbaɪsɪkl/ (*also* **bike**) ***noun*** [C] a vehicle with two wheels, which you sit on and ride by moving your legs

ˈbicycle lane ***noun*** [C] (*AmE*) = CYCLE LANE

bid¹ 🔑 /bɪd/ ***verb*** (**bidding**; *pt, pp* **bid**) [I,T] ~ (sth) (for sth) (FINANCE) to offer to pay a particular price for sth, especially at an AUCTION (= a public sale where things are sold to the person who offers most money): *I wanted to buy the vase but another man was* ***bidding against*** *me.* ◇ *Somebody bid £5 000 for the painting.*

bid² 🔑 /bɪd/ ***noun*** [C] **1** a ~ (for sth); a ~ (to do sth) an effort to do, obtain, etc. sth; an attempt: *His bid for freedom had failed.* ◇ *Tonight the Ethiopian athlete will* ***make a bid*** *to break the world record.* **2** (BUSINESS, FINANCE) an offer by a person or a business company to pay a certain amount of money for sth: *Granada mounted a hostile* ***takeover bid*** (= when one company tries to buy another company) *for Forte.* ◇ *At the auction we* ***made a bid*** *of £100 for the chair.* **3** (*especially AmE*) (BUSINESS) an offer to do work or provide a service for a particular price, in competition with other companies, etc. SYN **tender** ▶ **bidder** ***noun*** [C]: *The house was sold to the highest bidder* (= the person who offered the most money).

bide /baɪd/ ***verb***

IDM **bide your time** to wait for a good opportunity: *I'll bide my time until the situation improves.*

bidet /ˈbiːdeɪ/ ***noun*** [C] a low bowl in the bathroom that you fill with water and sit on to wash your bottom

biennial¹ /baɪˈeniəl/ ***adj.*** happening once every two years ➲ look at **annual**

biennial² /baɪˈeniəl/ ***noun*** [C] (BIOLOGY) any plant that lives for two years, producing flowers in the second year ➲ look at **annual**, **perennial**

bifocals /ˌbaɪˈfəʊklz/ ***noun*** [pl.] a pair of glasses with each piece of glass (**lens**) made in two parts. The top part is for looking at things at a distance, and the bottom part is for reading or for looking at things close to you. ▶ **bifocal** ***adj.***

big 🔑 /bɪɡ/ ***adj.*** (**bigger**; **biggest**) **1** large; not small: *a big house/town/salary* ◇ *This dress is too big for me.* **2** great or important: *They had a big argument yesterday.* ◇ *That was the biggest decision I've ever had to make.* ◇ *some of the big names in Hollywood* **3** (only *before* a noun) (*informal*) older: *a big brother/sister*

IDM **Big deal!** (*informal*) used to say that you think sth is not important or interesting: *'Look at my new bike!' 'Big deal! It's not as nice as mine.'*

a big deal/no big deal (*informal*) something that is (not) very important or exciting: *Birthday celebrations are a big deal in our family.* ◇ *We may lose, I suppose, but it's no big deal.*

give sb a big hand → HAND¹

bigamy /ˈbɪɡəmi/ ***noun*** [U] (LAW) the crime of being married to two people at the same time ➲ look at **monogamy**, **polygamy** ▶ **bigamist** ***noun*** [C]

the ˌbig ˈbang ***noun*** [sing.] (PHYSICS) the single large explosion that some scientists believe created the universe

ˈbig-head (*informal*) ***noun*** [C] a person who thinks they are very important or clever because of sth they have done ▶ **ˌbig-ˈheaded** ***adj.***

ˈbig mouth (*informal*) ***noun*** [C] a person who talks too much and cannot keep a secret

bigot /ˈbɪɡət/ ***noun*** [C] a person who has very strong and unreasonable opinions and refuses to change them or listen to other people: *a religious/racial bigot* ▶ **bigoted** ***adj.*** ▶ **bigotry** /ˈbɪɡətri/ ***noun*** [U]

ˈbig time¹ ***noun*** [sing.] **the big time** (ARTS AND MEDIA) great success in a profession, especially the entertainment business: *This is the role that could help her make it to the big time in Hollywood.*

ˈbig time² ***adv.*** (*especially AmE, slang*) very much: *You screwed up big time, Wayne!*

ˌbig ˈtoe ***noun*** [C] the largest toe on a person's foot ➲ picture on **page 80**

bike 🔑 /baɪk/ ***noun*** [C] a bicycle or a motorbike: *Hasan's just learnt to* ***ride a bike****.* ◇ *We went* ***by bike****.* ◇ *He came* ***on his bike****.*

ˈbike lane ***noun*** [C] (*AmE, informal*) = CYCLE LANE

bikini /bɪˈkiːni/ ***noun*** [C] a piece of clothing, in two pieces, that women wear for swimming

bilateral /ˌbaɪˈlætərəl/ ***adj.*** **1** (**POLITICS**) involving two groups of people or two countries: *bilateral trade/talks* **2** (**HEALTH**) involving both sides of the body or brain ▶ **bilaterally** ***adv.***

bile /baɪl/ ***noun*** [U] (**BIOLOGY**) the greenish-brown liquid with a bitter unpleasant taste that comes into your mouth when you VOMIT with an empty stomach

bilge /bɪldʒ/ ***noun*** **1** [C] (*also* **bilges** [pl.]) the almost flat part of the bottom of a boat or a ship, inside or outside **2** (*also* ˈ**bilge water**) [U] dirty water that collects in a ship's **bilge**

bilharzia /bɪlˈhɑːtsiə/ ***noun*** [U] (**HEALTH**) a serious disease, common in parts of Africa and S America, caused by small WORMS (= small animals with long bodies) that get into the blood

bilingual /ˌbaɪˈlɪŋgwəl/ ***adj.*** (**LANGUAGE**) **1** having or using two languages: *a bilingual dictionary* ➲ look at **monolingual** **2** able to speak two languages equally well: *Our children are* ***bilingual in*** *English and Spanish.* ➲ look at **monolingual, multilingual**

THESAURUS

bill

statement • account • invoice

These are all words for a record of how much you owe for goods or services you have bought or used.

bill: *The waiter brought us our bill.*

statement: *a credit card statement*

account: *Put it on my account please.*

invoice: *The builders sent an invoice for £750.*

bill[1] 🔑 /bɪl/ ***noun*** [C] **1** (**BUSINESS**) a piece of paper that shows how much money you owe sb for goods or services: *the electricity/gas/telephone bill* ◇ *to pay a bill* **2** (*AmE* **check**) a piece of paper that shows how much you have to pay for the food and drinks that you have had in a restaurant: *Can I have the bill, please?* **3** (*AmE*) = NOTE[1] (4): *a ten-dollar bill* **4** (**POLITICS**) a plan for a possible new law: *The bill was passed/defeated.* **5** (**ARTS AND MEDIA**) a programme of entertainment offered in a show, concert, etc.: ***Topping the bill*** (= the most important performer) *is Robbie Williams.* **6** a bird's beak ➲ picture on **page 29**

IDM **foot the bill** → FOOT[2]

bill[2] /bɪl/ ***verb*** [T] (usually passive) ~ **sb/sth as sth** to describe sb/sth to the public in an advertisement, etc.: *This young player is being billed as 'the new Pele'.*

billboard /ˈbɪlbɔːd/ (*BrE* also **hoarding**) ***noun*** [C] a large board near a road where advertisements are put

billet /ˈbɪlɪt/ ***noun*** [C] a place, often in a private house, where soldiers live temporarily ▶ **billet** ***verb*** [T] (usually passive): *The troops were billeted in the town with local families.*

billfold /ˈbɪlfəʊld/ (*AmE*) = WALLET

billiards /ˈbɪliədz/ ***noun*** [U] (**SPORT**) a game played on a big table covered with cloth. You use a long stick (**a cue**) to hit three balls against each other and into pockets at the corners and sides of the table: *to have a game of/play billiards* ➲ look at **snooker, pool**[1] (5)

billion /ˈbɪljən/ ***number*** 1 000 000 000 HELP Notice that when you are counting you use **billion** without 's'. You use **billions** when you mean 'a lot': *three billion yen* ◇ *billions of dollars*. Formerly, 'billion' was used with the meaning 'one million million'. We now say **trillion** for this. HELP For more information about numbers look at the special section on numbers on page R36.

ˌ**bill of exˈchange** ***noun*** [C] (*pl.* **bills of exchange**) (**BUSINESS, FINANCE**) a written order to pay a sum of money to a particular person on a particular date

bill of lading /ˌbɪl əv ˈleɪdɪŋ/ ***noun*** [C] (*pl.* **bills of lading**) (**BUSINESS**) a list giving details of the goods that a ship, etc. is carrying

ˌ**bill of ˈsale** ***noun*** [C] (*pl.* **bills of sale**) (**BUSINESS**) an official document showing that sth has been bought

billow /ˈbɪləʊ/ ***verb*** [I] **1** to fill with air and move in the wind: *curtains billowing in the breeze* **2** to move in large clouds through the air: *Smoke billowed from the chimneys.*

billy goat /ˈbɪli gəʊt/ ***noun*** [C] a male GOAT(= a farm animal like a sheep that often lives wild in mountain areas) ➲ look at **nanny goat**

bimetallic strip /ˌbaɪmətælɪk ˈstrɪp/ ***noun*** [C] (**PHYSICS**) a strip made of two different types of metal which bends when it is heated, used in THERMOSTATS (= a device that controls the temperature in a house or machine by switching the heat on and off as necessary)

bin 🔑 /bɪn/ ***noun*** [C] **1** a container that you put rubbish in: *to throw sth in the bin* ◇ *a litter bin* ◇ *The dustmen come to empty the bins on Wednesdays.* **2** a container, usually with a lid, for storing bread, flour, etc.: *a bread bin*

binary /ˈbaɪnəri/ ***adj.*** **1** (**COMPUTING, MATHEMATICS**) using only 0 and 1 as a system of numbers: *the* ***binary system*** ◇ *binary arithmetic* **2** (**TECHNICAL**) based on only two numbers; consisting of two parts: ***binary code/numbers*** ▶ **binary** ***noun*** [U]: *The computer performs calculations* ***in binary*** *and converts the results to decimal.*

bind[1] /baɪnd/ ***verb*** [T] (*pt, pp* **bound** /baʊnd/) **1** ~ **sb/sth (to sb/sth)**; ~ **A and B (together)** to tie or fasten with string or rope: *They bound the prisoner's hands behind his back.* **2** ~ **A to B**; ~ **A and B (together)** to unite people, organizations, etc. so that they live or work together more happily or with better effect: *The two countries are bound together by a common language.* **3** ~ **sb (to sth)** to force sb to do sth by making them promise to do it or by making it their duty to do it: *to be bound by a law/an agreement* ◇ *The contract binds you to completion of the work within two years.* **4** (usually passive) to fasten sheets of paper into a cover to form a book: *The book was bound in leather.*

bind[2] /baɪnd/ ***noun*** [sing.] (*BrE, informal*) something that you find boring or annoying; a NUISANCE

binder /ˈbaɪndə(r)/ ***noun*** [C] a hard cover for holding loose sheets of paper together: *a ring binder*

binding[1] /ˈbaɪndɪŋ/ ***adj.*** (**LAW**) making it necessary for sb to do sth they have promised or to obey a law, etc.: *This contract is* ***legally binding****.*

binding[2] /ˈbaɪndɪŋ/ ***noun*** **1** [C] a cover that holds the pages of a book together **2** [C,U] material that you fasten to the edge of sth to protect or decorate it **3 bindings** [pl.] (**SPORT**) (used in SKIING) a device that fastens your boot to your SKI

binge[1] /bɪndʒ/ ***noun*** [C] (*informal*) a period of eating or drinking too much: *to* ***go on a binge***

binge[2] /bɪndʒ/ ***verb*** [I] (*pres. part.* **bingeing**) (*informal*) ~ **(on sth)** to eat or drink too much, especially without being able to control yourself

bingo /ˈbɪŋgəʊ/ ***noun*** [U] a game in which each player has a different card with numbers on it. The person in charge of the game calls numbers out and the winner is the first player to have all the numbers on their card called out.

binoculars /bɪˈnɒkjələz/ *noun* [pl.] an instrument with two glass parts (**lenses**) which you look through in order to make objects in the distance seem nearer: *a pair of binoculars* ➲ look at **telescope**

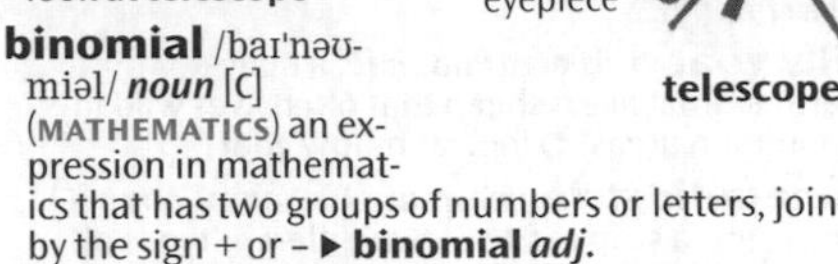

binomial /baɪˈnəʊmiəl/ *noun* [C] (MATHEMATICS) an expression in mathematics that has two groups of numbers or letters, joined by the sign + or – ▶ **binomial** *adj.*

bio- /ˈbaɪəʊ/ *prefix* (in nouns, adjectives and adverbs) connected with living things or human life: *biology* ◇ *biodegradable*

biochemist /ˌbaɪəʊˈkemɪst/ *noun* [C] (BIOLOGY, CHEMISTRY) a scientist who studies the chemistry of living things

biochemistry /ˌbaɪəʊˈkemɪstri/ *noun* (BIOLOGY, CHEMISTRY) **1** [U] the scientific study of the chemistry of living things **2** [C,U] the chemical structure of a living thing ▶ **biochemical** /ˌbaɪəʊˈkemɪkl/ *adj.*

biodegradable /ˌbaɪəʊdɪˈgreɪdəbl/ *adj.* (BIOLOGY, ENVIRONMENT) that can be taken back into the earth naturally and so not harm the environment OPP **non-biodegradable**

biodiversity /ˌbaɪəʊdaɪˈvɜːsəti/ *noun* [U] (BIOLOGY, ENVIRONMENT) the existence of a number of different kinds of animals and plants which together make a good and healthy environment

biofuel /ˈbaɪəʊfjuːəl/ *noun* [C,U] (BIOLOGY, ENVIRONMENT) a fuel that is produced by living matter, such as plants or waste matter from animals: *Ministers are promoting the use of biofuels for transport to reduce greenhouse gas emissions.*

biogas /ˈbaɪəʊgæs/ *noun* [U] (BIOLOGY, CHEMISTRY) gas such as METHANE that is produced by dead plants, etc. and that we can burn to produce heat

biographer /baɪˈɒgrəfə(r)/ *noun* [C] (LITERATURE) a person who writes the story of sb else's life

biography /baɪˈɒgrəfi/ *noun* [C,U] (*pl.* **biographies**) (LITERATURE) the story of a person's life written by sb else: *a biography of Napoleon* ◇ *I enjoy reading science fiction and biography.* ➲ look at **autobiography** ▶ **biographical** /ˌbaɪəˈgræfɪkl/ *adj.*

biological /ˌbaɪəˈlɒdʒɪkl/ *adj.* **1** (BIOLOGY) connected with the scientific study of animals, plants and other living things: *biological research* **2** involving the use of living things to destroy or damage other living things: *biological weapons*

ˌbiological ˈwarfare (*also* **ˌgerm ˈwarfare**) *noun* [U] the use of harmful bacteria as weapons of war

ˌbioˌlogical ˈweapon *noun* [C] a weapon of war that uses harmful bacteria to kill and injure people ➲ look at **chemical weapon**

biologist /baɪˈɒlədʒɪst/ *noun* [C] a scientist who studies biology

biology ⊶ /baɪˈɒlədʒi/ *noun* [U] the scientific study of living things ➲ look at **botany**, **zoology**

biomass /ˈbaɪəʊmæs/ *noun* [U, sing.] (BIOLOGY) the total quantity or weight of plants and animals in a particular area or volume

biome /ˈbaɪəʊm/ *noun* [C] (ENVIRONMENT) the characteristic plants and animals that exist in a particular type of environment, for example in a forest or desert

biometric /ˌbaɪəʊˈmetrɪk/ *adj.* (BIOLOGY) using measurements of human features, such as fingers or eyes, in order to identify people: *Biometric systems have several advantages over conventional identification methods.*

bionic /baɪˈɒnɪk/ (SCIENCE) having parts of the body that are electronic, and therefore able to do things that are not possible for normal humans

biophysicist /ˌbaɪəʊˈfɪzɪsɪst/ *noun* [C] (SCIENCE) a scientist who uses the laws and methods of PHYSICS to study BIOLOGY

biophysics /ˌbaɪəʊˈfɪzɪks/ *noun* [U] (SCIENCE) the science which uses the laws and methods of PHYSICS to study BIOLOGY ▶ **biophysical** /ˌbaɪəʊˈfɪzɪkl/ *adj.*

biopsy /ˈbaɪɒpsi/ *noun* [C] (*pl.* **biopsies**) (HEALTH) the removal of some cells from sb's body in order to find out about a disease that they may have

biorhythm /ˈbaɪəʊrɪðəm/ *noun* [C, usually pl.] a regular series of changes in the life of a living creature, for example sleeping and waking

BIOS /ˈbaɪɒs/ *abbr.* (COMPUTING) **Basic Input Output System**; a set of basic instructions in a computer which controls how it starts up when you first switch it on

biosphere /ˈbaɪəʊsfɪə(r)/ *noun* [sing.] (BIOLOGY) the part of the earth's surface and atmosphere in which plants and animals can live

biotechnology /ˌbaɪəʊtekˈnɒlədʒi/ (also *informal* **biotech** /ˈbaɪəʊtek/) *noun* [U] (TECHNICAL) the use of living cells and bacteria in industrial and scientific processes ▶ **biotechnological** /ˌbaɪəʊteknəˈlɒdʒɪkl/ *adj.*: *biotechnological research*

bipartisan /ˌbaɪpɑːtɪˈzæn/ *adj.* (POLITICS) involving two political parties: *a bipartisan policy*

biped /ˈbaɪped/ *noun* [C] (BIOLOGY) any creature with two feet ➲ look at **quadruped**

bipolar /ˌbaɪˈpəʊlə(r)/ (*also* **ˌmanic-deˈpressive**) *adj.* (PSYCHOLOGY, HEALTH) suffering from or connected with BIPOLAR DISORDER

ˌbiˌpolar disˈorder (*also* **ˌbiˌpolar afˌfective disˈorder**) *noun* [U,C] (*also* **ˌmanic-deˈpression** [U]) (PSYCHOLOGY, HEALTH) a mental illness causing sb to change suddenly from being extremely depressed to being extremely happy

birch /bɜːtʃ/ *noun* **1** (*also* **ˈbirch tree**) [C] a type of tree with smooth thin branches **2** [U] the wood from this tree

bird ⊶ /bɜːd/ *noun* [C] a creature with feathers and wings which can (usually) fly: *I could hear the birds singing outside.* ◇ *There was a bird's nest in the hedge with four eggs in it.* ➲ picture on **page 29**
IDM **kill two birds with one stone** → KILL[1]

ˈbird flu (*also* **ˈavian flu**; **ˈchicken flu**) *noun* [U] (HEALTH) a serious illness that affects birds, especially chickens, that can be spread from birds to humans and that can cause death: *Ten new cases of bird flu were reported yesterday.*

ˌbird of ˈprey *noun* [C] (*pl.* **birds of prey**) a bird that kills and eats other animals and birds ➲ picture on **page 29**

birdsong /ˈbɜːdsɒŋ/ *noun* [U] the musical sounds made by birds

birdwatcher /ˈbɜːdwɒtʃə(r)/ ***noun*** [C] a person who studies birds in their natural surroundings **SYN** **ornithologist** ▶ **birdwatching** ***noun*** [U]

Biro™ /ˈbaɪrəʊ/ ***noun*** [C] (*pl.* **Biros**) a type of pen in which ink comes out of a small metal ball at the end ➲ look at **ballpoint**

birth ⊶ /bɜːθ/ ***noun*** **1** [C,U] being born; coming out of a mother's body: *It was a difficult birth.* ◇ *The baby weighed 3 kilos* ***at birth*** (= when it was born). ◇ *What's your* ***date of birth*** (= the date on which you were born)? **2** [U] the country you belong to: *She's lived in England since she was four but she's German* ***by birth***. **3** [sing.] the beginning of sth: *the birth of an idea*
IDM **give birth (to sb)** to produce a baby: *She gave birth to her second child at home.*

ˈ**birth certificate** ***noun*** [C] an official document that states the date and place of a person's birth and the names of their parents

ˈ**birth control** ***noun*** [U] ways of limiting the number of children you have ➲ look at **contraception**, **family planning**

birthday ⊶ /ˈbɜːθdeɪ/ ***noun*** [C] the day in each year which is the same date as the one when you were born: *My birthday's on November 15th.* ◇ *my eighteenth birthday* ◇ *a birthday present/card/cake*

birthmark /ˈbɜːθmɑːk/ ***noun*** [C] a red or brown mark on a person's body that has been there since they were born

birthplace /ˈbɜːθpleɪs/ ***noun*** **1** [C] the house or town where a person was born **2** [sing.] the place where sth began: *Greece is the birthplace of the Olympic Games.*

ˈ**birth rate** ***noun*** [C] (SOCIAL STUDIES) the number of babies born in a particular group of people during a particular period of time

biscuit ⊶ /ˈbɪskɪt/ ***noun*** [C] **1** (*AmE* **cookie**) a type of small cake that is thin, hard and usually sweet: *a chocolate biscuit* ◇ *a packet of biscuits*
2 (*AmE*) a type of small simple cake that is not sweet

bisect /baɪˈsekt/ ***verb*** [T] (MATHEMATICS) to divide sth into two equal parts ▶ **bisection** /-ˈsekʃn/ ***noun*** [C, U]

bisexual /ˌbaɪˈsekʃuəl/ ***adj.*** sexually attracted to both men and women ➲ look at **heterosexual**, **homosexual**

bishop /ˈbɪʃəp/ ***noun*** [C] **1** (RELIGION) a priest with a high position in some branches of the Christian Church, who is responsible for all the churches in a city or a district ➲ look at **archbishop** **2** a piece used in the game of CHESS that can move any number of squares in a DIAGONAL line

bismuth /ˈbɪzməθ/ ***noun*** [U] (*symbol* **Bi**) (CHEMISTRY) a chemical element. **Bismuth** is a reddish-white metal that breaks easily and is used in medicine. ❶ For more information on the periodic table of elements, look at pages R34-5.

bison /ˈbaɪsn/ ***noun*** [C] a large wild animal that looks like a cow with long curved horns. There are two types of **bison**, the North American (also called BUFFALO) and the European.

bistro /ˈbiːstrəʊ/ ***noun*** [C] (*pl.* **bistros**) a small informal restaurant

bit¹ ⊶ /bɪt/ ***noun*** **1** **a bit** [sing.] slightly, a little: *I was a bit annoyed with him.* ◇ *I'm afraid I'll be a little bit late tonight.* ◇ *Could you be a bit quieter, please?*
2 **a bit** [sing.] a short time or distance: *Could you move forward a bit?* ◇ *I'm just going out for a bit.* **3** **a bit** [sing.] (*informal*) a lot: *It must have rained* ***quite a bit*** *during the night.* **4** [C] **a ~ of sth** a small piece, amount or part of sth: *There were bits of broken glass all over the floor.* ◇ *Could you give me a bit of advice?* ◇ *Which bit of the film did you like best?* **5** [C] (COMPUTING) the smallest unit of information that is stored in a computer's memory **6** [C] a metal bar that you put in a horse's mouth when you ride it
IDM **bit by bit** slowly or a little at a time: *Bit by bit we managed to get the information we needed.*
a bit much (*informal*) annoying or unpleasant: *It's a bit much expecting me to work on Sundays.*
a bit of a (*informal*) rather a: *I've got a bit of a problem.*
bits and pieces (*informal*) small things of different kinds: *I've finished packing except for a few bits and pieces.*
do your bit (*informal*) to do your share of sth; to help with sth: *It won't take long to finish if we all do our bit.*
not a bit not at all: *The holiday was not a bit what we had expected.*
to bits **1** into small pieces: *She angrily tore the letter to bits.* **2** very; very much: *I was* ***thrilled to bits*** *when I won the competition.*

bit² past tense of **bite¹**

bitch¹ /bɪtʃ/ ***verb*** [I] (*informal*) **~ (about sb/sth)** to say unkind and critical things about sb, especially when they are not there

bitch² /bɪtʃ/ ***noun*** [C] a female dog

bitchy /ˈbɪtʃi/ ***adj.*** talking about other people in an unkind way: *a bitchy remark*

bite¹ ⊶ /baɪt/ ***verb*** (*pt* **bit** /bɪt/; *pp* **bitten** /ˈbɪtn/)
1 [I,T] **~ (into sth)**; **~ (sb/sth)** to cut or attack sb/sth with your teeth: *Don't worry about the dog – she never bites.* ◇ *The cat bit me.* ◇ *He picked up the bread and bit into it hungrily.* **2** [I,T] (used about some insects and animals) to push a sharp point into your skin and cause pain: *He was bitten by a snake/mosquito/spider.* ❶ Wasps, bees and jellyfish do not **bite** you. They **sting** you.
3 [I] to begin to have an unpleasant effect: *In the South the job losses are starting to bite.*
IDM **bite sb's head off** to answer sb in a very angry way

bite² ⊶ /baɪt/ ***noun*** **1** [C] a piece of food that you can put into your mouth: *She took a big bite of the apple.* **2** (HEALTH) [C] a painful place on the skin made by an insect, snake, dog, etc.: *I'm covered in mosquito bites.* **3** [sing.] (*informal*) a small meal; a SNACK: *Would you like* ***a bite to eat*** *before you go?*

ˈ**bit rate** ***noun*** [C] (COMPUTING) the average number of BITS (= the smallest units of information that are stored in a computer's memory) that can be sent along a network in one second

bitten past participle of **bite¹**

bitter¹ ⊶ /ˈbɪtə(r)/ ***adj.*** **1** caused by anger or hatred: *a bitter quarrel* **2** **~ (about sth)** (used about a person) very unhappy or angry about sth that has happened because you feel you have been treated unfairly: *She was very bitter about not getting the job.*
3 causing unhappiness or anger for a long time; difficult to accept: *Failing the exam was* ***a bitter disappointment*** *to him.* ◇ *I've learnt* ***from bitter experience*** *not to trust him.* **4** having a sharp, unpleasant taste; not sweet: *bitter coffee* **5** (used about the weather) very cold: *a bitter wind*
▶ **bitterness** ***noun*** [U]: *The pay cut caused bitterness among the staff.*

bitter² /ˈbɪtə(r)/ ***noun*** [U] (*BrE*) a type of dark beer that is popular in Britain: *A pint of bitter, please.*

bitterly 🔑 /ˈbɪtəli/ ***adv.*** **1** (used for describing strong negative feelings or cold weather) extremely: *bitterly disappointed/resentful* ◇ *a bitterly cold winter/wind* **2** in an angry and disappointed way: *'I've lost everything,' he said bitterly.*

bitty /ˈbɪti/ ***adj.*** made up of lots of parts which do not seem to be connected: *Your essay is rather bitty.*

bitumen /ˈbɪtʃəmən/ ***noun*** [U] (**CHEMISTRY**) a black substance made from petrol, used for covering roads or roofs ➲ picture at **fractional distillation**

bivalve /ˈbaɪvælv/ ***noun*** [C] (**BIOLOGY**) any SHELLFISH with a shell in two parts: *Mussels and clams are bivalves.*

bizarre /bɪˈzɑː(r)/ ***adj.*** very strange: *The story had a most bizarre ending.*

bk (*pl.* **bks**) ***abbr.*** book

black[1] 🔑 /blæk/ ***adj.*** **1** of the darkest colour, like night or coal **2** belonging to a race of people with dark skins: *the black population of Britain* ◇ *black culture* **3** (used about coffee or tea) without milk or cream: *black coffee with sugar* **4** very angry: *to give sb* ***a black look*** **5** (used about a situation) without hope; depressing: *The economic outlook for the coming year is rather black.* **6** funny in a cruel or unpleasant way: *The film was* ***a black comedy****.*

IDM **black and blue** covered with blue, brown or purple marks on the body (**bruises**) because you have been hit by sb/sth

black and white (used about television, photographs, etc.) showing no colours except black, white and grey

black[2] 🔑 /blæk/ ***noun*** **1** [U] the darkest colour, like night or coal: *People often* ***wear black*** (= black clothes) *at funerals.* **2** (usually **Black**) [C] a person who belongs to a race of people with dark skins ▸ **blackness** ***noun*** [U]

IDM **be in the black** (**FINANCE**) to have some money in the bank OPP **be in the red**

in black and white in writing or in print: *I won't believe we've got the contract till I see it in black and white.*

black[3] /blæk/ ***verb***

PHR V **black out** to become unconscious for a short time

ˌ**black ˈbelt** ***noun*** [C] (**SPORT**) **1** a belt that you can earn in some fighting sports such as JUDO or KARATE which shows that you have reached a very high standard **2** a person who has gained a black belt

blackberry /ˈblækbəri/ ***noun*** [C] (*pl.* **blackberries**) **1** a small black fruit that grows wild on bushes **2 Blackberry™** (**COMPUTING**) a very small computer that can be held in the hand and that can send emails and often contains a mobile phone ➲ look at **PDA**

blackbird /ˈblækbɜːd/ ***noun*** [C] a common European bird. The male is black with a yellow beak and the female is brown.

blackboard /ˈblækbɔːd/ (*AmE* **chalkboard**) ***noun*** [C] a large board with a smooth black or dark green surface that teachers write on with a piece of CHALK ➲ look at **whiteboard**

blackcurrant /ˌblækˈkʌrənt/ ***noun*** [C] a small round black fruit that grows on bushes

blacken /ˈblækən/ ***verb*** [T] **1** to make sth black **2** to make sth seem bad, by saying unpleasant things about it: *to blacken sb's name*

ˌ**black ˈeye** ***noun*** [C] an area of dark-coloured skin around sb's eye where they have been hit: *He got a black eye in the fight.*

blackhead /ˈblækhed/ ***noun*** [C] a small spot on the skin with a black centre

ˌ**black ˈhole** ***noun*** [C] (**ASTRONOMY**) an area in space that nothing, not even light, can escape from, because GRAVITY (= the force that pulls objects in space towards each other) is so strong there

ˌ**black ˈice** ***noun*** [U] ice in a thin layer on the surface of a road

blackleg /ˈblækleg/ ***noun*** [C] (*BrE*) a person who continues to work when the people they work with are on strike; a person who is employed to work instead of those who are on strike

blacklist /ˈblæklɪst/ ***noun*** [C] a list of people, companies, etc. who are considered bad or dangerous ▸ **blacklist** ***verb*** [T]: *She was blacklisted by all the major Hollywood studios.*

ˌ**black ˈmagic** ***noun*** [U] a type of magic that is used for evil purposes

blackmail /ˈblækmeɪl/ ***noun*** [U] (**LAW**) the crime of forcing a person to give you money or do sth for you, usually by threatening to make known sth which they want to keep secret ▸ **blackmail** ***verb*** [T] **~ sb (into doing sth)** ▸ **blackmailer** ***noun*** [C]

ˌ**black ˈmark** ***noun*** [C] a note, either in writing on an official record, or in sb's mind, of sth you have done or said that makes people think badly of you: *He earned a black mark for turning up late to the meeting.*

ˌ**black ˈmarket** ***noun*** [C, usually sing.] (**ECONOMICS**) the buying and selling of goods or foreign money in a way that is not legal: *to buy/sell sth* ***on the black market***

blackout /ˈblækaʊt/ ***noun*** [C] **1** a period of time during a war, when all lights must be turned off or covered so that the enemy cannot see them **2** (**HEALTH**) a period when you become unconscious for a short time: *to have a blackout*

blacksmith /ˈblæksmɪθ/ ***noun*** [C] a person whose job is to make and repair things made of iron

bladder /ˈblædə(r)/ ***noun*** [C] (**ANATOMY**) the part of your body where waste liquid (**urine**) collects before leaving your body ➲ picture on **page 80**

blade 🔑 /bleɪd/ ***noun*** [C] **1** the flat, sharp part of a knife, etc. ➲ picture at **agriculture** **2** one of the flat parts that turn around in an engine or on a HELICOPTER: *the blades of a propeller* **3** the flat wide part of an OAR (= one of the long poles that are used to make a boat move through water) that goes in the water ➲ picture at **canoe** **4** a long, thin leaf of grass: *a blade of grass* ➲ look at **shoulder blade**

blag /blæg/ ***verb*** [T] (**blagging**; **blagged**) (*BrE, informal*) to persuade sb to give you sth, or to let you do sth, by talking to them in a clever or amusing way: *I blagged some tickets for the game.*

blame[1] 🔑 /bleɪm/ ***verb*** [T] **1 ~ sb (for sth)**; **~ sth on sb/sth** to think or say that a certain person or thing is responsible for sth bad that has happened: *The teacher blamed me for the accident.* ◇ *Some people blame the changes in the climate on pollution.* **2 not ~ sb (for sth)** to think that sb is not wrong to do sth; to understand sb's reason for doing sth: *I don't blame you for feeling fed up.*

IDM **be to blame (for sth)** to be responsible for sth bad: *The police say that careless driving was to blame for the accident.*

shift the blame/responsibility (for sth) (onto sb) → SHIFT[1]

blame² ⊶ /bleɪm/ ***noun*** [U] ~ **(for sth)** responsibility for sth bad: *The government must* ***take the blame*** *for the economic crisis.* ◇ *The report* ***put the blame on*** *rising prices.* ◇ *Why do I always* ***get the blame****?*

blameless /ˈbleɪmləs/ ***adj.*** (*written*) not guilty; that should not be blamed: *He insisted that his wife was blameless and hadn't known about his crimes.*

blanch /blɑːntʃ/ ***verb*** **1** [I] (*written*) ~ **(at sth)** to become pale because you are shocked or frightened **2** [T] to prepare food, especially vegetables, by putting it into boiling water for a short time

bland /blænd/ ***adj.*** **1** ordinary or not very interesting: *a rather bland style of writing* **2** (used about food) mild or lacking in taste **3** not showing any emotion ▶ **blandly** ***adv.***

blank¹ ⊶ /blæŋk/ ***adj.*** **1** empty, with nothing written, printed or recorded on it: *a blank video/cassette/piece of paper/page* **2** without feelings, understanding or interest: *a blank expression on his face* ◇ *My mind* ***went blank*** *when I saw the exam questions* (= I couldn't think properly or remember anything). ▶ **blankly** ***adv.***: *She stared at me blankly, obviously not recognizing me.*

blank² ⊶ /blæŋk/ ***noun*** [C] an empty space: ***Fill in the blanks*** *in the following exercise.* ◇ (*figurative*) *I couldn't remember his name – my mind was a complete blank.*
IDM **draw a blank** → DRAW¹

ˌ**blank ˈcheque** ***noun*** [C] (**FINANCE**) a cheque that has been signed but that has an empty space so that the amount to be paid can be written in later

blanket¹ /ˈblæŋkɪt/ ***noun*** [C] **1** a cover made of wool, etc. that is put on beds to keep people warm **2** a thick layer or covering of sth: *a blanket of snow* ▶ **blanket** ***verb*** [T] ~ **sth (in/with sth)**: *The countryside was blanketed in snow.*
IDM **a wet blanket** → WET¹

blanket² /ˈblæŋkɪt/ ***adj.*** (only *before* a noun) affecting everyone or everything: *There is a* ***blanket ban*** *on journalists reporting the case.*

ˈ**blanket bath** (*BrE also* ˈ**bed bath**, *AmE* ˈ**sponge bath**) ***noun*** [C] (**HEALTH**) an act of washing a person who cannot get out of bed because they are sick or old

ˌ**blank ˈverse** ***noun*** [U] (**LITERATURE**) poetry that has a regular rhythm but whose lines do not end with the same sound ➲ look at **free verse**

blare /bleə(r)/ ***verb*** [I,T] ~ **(sth) (out)** to make a loud, unpleasant noise: *Car horns were blaring in the street outside.* ◇ *The loudspeaker blared out pop music.* ▶ **blare** ***noun*** [U, sing.]: *the blare of a siren*

blasphemy /ˈblæsfəmi/ ***noun*** [U] (**RELIGION**) writing or speaking about God in a way that shows a lack of respect ▶ **blasphemous** /ˈblæsfəməs/ ***adj.***

blast¹ /blɑːst/ ***noun*** [C] **1** an explosion, especially one caused by a bomb **2** a sudden strong current of air: *a blast of cold air* **3** a loud sound made by a musical instrument, etc.: *The driver gave a few blasts on his horn.*

blast² /blɑːst/ ***verb*** [T] **1** to make a hole, a tunnel, etc. in sth with an explosion: *They blasted a tunnel through the mountainside.* **2** to criticize sth very strongly
PHR V **blast off** (used about a SPACECRAFT) to leave the ground SYN **lift off, take off**

ˈ**blast furnace** ***noun*** [C] (**CHEMISTRY**) a large structure like an oven in which rock containing iron (**iron ore**) is melted in order to take out the metal

ˈ**blast-off** ***noun*** [U] the time when a SPACECRAFT leaves the ground

blatant /ˈbleɪtnt/ ***adj.*** very clear or obvious: *a blatant lie* ▶ **blatantly** ***adv.***

blaze¹ /bleɪz/ ***noun*** **1** [C] a large and often dangerous fire: *It took firefighters four hours to put out the blaze.* **2** [sing.] **a ~ of sth** a very bright show of light or colour: *The garden was a blaze of colour.* ◇ *The new theatre was opened in* ***a blaze of publicity*** (= the media gave it a lot of attention).

blaze² /bleɪz/ ***verb*** [I] **1** to burn with bright strong flames **2** ~ **(with sth)** to be extremely bright; to shine brightly: *I woke up to find that the room was blazing with sunshine.* ◇ (*figurative*) *'Get out!' she shouted, her eyes blazing with anger.*

blazer /ˈbleɪzə(r)/ ***noun*** [C] a jacket, especially one that has the colours or sign (**badge**) of a school, club or team on it: *a school blazer*

bleach¹ /bliːtʃ/ ***verb*** [T] to make sth white or lighter in colour by using a chemical or by leaving it in the sun

bleach² /bliːtʃ/ ***noun*** [C,U] a strong chemical substance used for making clothes, etc. whiter or for cleaning things

bleachers /ˈbliːtʃəz/ ***noun*** [pl.] (*AmE*) (**SPORT**) rows of seats at a sports ground

bleak /bliːk/ ***adj.*** **1** (used about a situation) not encouraging or giving any reason to have hope: *a bleak future for the next generation* **2** (used about a place) cold, empty and grey: *the bleak Arctic landscape* **3** (used about the weather) cold and grey: *a bleak winter's day* ▶ **bleakly** ***adv.*** ▶ **bleakness** ***noun*** [U]

bleary /ˈblɪəri/ ***adj.*** (used about the eyes) red, tired and unable to see clearly: *We were all rather bleary-eyed after the journey.* ▶ **blearily** ***adv.***

bleat /bliːt/ ***verb*** **1** [I] to make the sound of a sheep **2** [I,T] to speak in a weak or complaining voice ▶ **bleat** ***noun*** [C]

bleed /bliːd/ ***verb*** [I] (*pt, pp* **bled** /bled/) to lose blood ▶ **bleeding** ***noun*** [U]: *He wrapped a scarf around his arm to stop the bleeding.*

bleep¹ /bliːp/ ***noun*** [C] a short, high sound made by a piece of electronic equipment

bleep² /bliːp/ ***verb*** **1** [I] (used about machines) to make a short high sound **2** (*AmE also* **beep**) [T] to attract a person's attention using an electronic machine: *Please bleep the doctor on duty immediately.*

bleeper /ˈbliːpə(r)/ (*AmE* **beeper**) ***noun*** [C] a small piece of electronic equipment that BLEEPS to let a person (for example a doctor) know when sb is trying to contact them SYN **pager**

blemish /ˈblemɪʃ/ ***noun*** [C] a mark that spoils the way sth looks ▶ **blemish** ***verb*** [T] (*figurative*): *The defeat has blemished the team's perfect record.*

blend¹ /blend/ ***verb*** **1** [T] ~ **A with B**; ~ **A and B (together)** to mix two or more substances together: *First blend the flour and the melted butter together.* **2** [I] ~ **(in) with sth** to combine with sth in an attractive or suitable way: *The new room is decorated to blend in with the rest of the house.* **3** [I] ~ **(into sth)** to match or be similar to the surroundings sb/sth is in: *These animals' ability to blend into their surroundings provides a natural form of defence.*

blend² /blend/ ***noun*** [C] a mixture: *He had the right blend of enthusiasm and experience.*

ˌblended ˈlearning *noun* [U] (EDUCATION) a way of studying a subject that combines being taught in class with the use of the Internet

blender /ˈblendə(r)/ (*BrE also* **liquidizer**) *noun* [C] an electric machine that is used for making food into liquid

bless /bles/ *verb* [T] (RELIGION) to ask for God's help and protection for sb/sth

IDM **be blessed with sth/sb** to be lucky enough to have sth/sb: *The West of Ireland is an area blessed with many fine sandy beaches.*

Bless you! what you say to a person who has just SNEEZED (= made a noise through their nose)

blessed /ˈblesɪd/ *adj.* **1** (RELIGION) holy; having God's help and protection: *the Blessed Virgin Mary* **2** (RELIGION) (in religious language) lucky: *Blessed are the pure in heart.* **3** (*formal*) giving great pleasure: *The cool breeze brought* ***blessed relief*** *from the heat.*

blessing /ˈblesɪŋ/ *noun* [C] **1** a thing that you are grateful for or that brings happiness: *It's a great blessing that we have two healthy children.* ◇ *Not getting that job was* ***a blessing in disguise*** (= something which seems unlucky but turns out to be a good thing). **2** [usually sing.] approval or support: *They got married without their parents' blessing.* **3** [usually sing.] (RELIGION) (a prayer asking for) God's help and protection: *The priest said a blessing.*

blew past tense of **blow**[1]

blight[1] /blaɪt/ *verb* [T] to spoil or damage sth, especially by causing a lot of problems: *an area blighted by unemployment*

blight[2] /blaɪt/ *noun* **1** [U, C] (AGRICULTURE) any disease that kills plants, especially crops that are grown for food: *potato blight* **2** [sing., U] ~ **(on sb/sth)** something that has a bad effect on a situation, a person's life or the environment

blimp /blɪmp/ *noun* [C] (*especially AmE*) a small AIRSHIP (= an aircraft without wings that is filled with gas)

blind[1] ⊶ /blaɪnd/ *adj.* **1** unable to see: *a blind person* ◇ *to be completely/partially blind* **2** ~ **(to sth)** not wanting to notice or understand sth: *He was completely blind to her faults.* **3** without reason or thought: *He drove down the motorway in* ***a blind panic.*** **4** impossible to see round: *You should never overtake on* ***a blind corner.*** ▶ **blindly** *adv.* ▶ **blindness** *noun* [U]

IDM **turn a blind eye (to sth)** to pretend not to notice sth bad is happening so that you do not have to do anything about it

blind[2] /blaɪnd/ *verb* [T] **1** to make sb unable to see: *Her grandfather had been blinded in an accident* (= permanently). ◇ *Just for a second I was blinded by the sun* (= for a short time). **2** ~ **sb (to sth)** to make sb unable to think clearly or behave in a sensible way

blind[3] /blaɪnd/ *noun* **1** [C] a piece of cloth or other material that you pull down to cover a window **2 the blind** [pl.] people who are unable to see

ˌblind ˈdate *noun* [C] an arranged meeting between two people who have never met before to see if they like each other enough to begin a romantic relationship

blinders /ˈblaɪndəz/ (*AmE*) = BLINKERS

blindfold /ˈblaɪndfəʊld/ *noun* [C] a piece of cloth, etc. that is used for covering sb's eyes ▶ **blindfold** *verb* [T]

ˈblind spot *noun* [C] **1** the part of the road just behind you that you cannot see when driving a car **2** if you have a blind spot about sth, you cannot understand or accept it **3** (ANATOMY) the part of the RETINA in the eye that is not sensitive to light

bling-bling /ˌblɪŋ ˈblɪŋ/ (*also* **bling**) *noun* [U] (*informal*) expensive shiny jewellery ▶ **bling-bling** (also **bling**) *adj.*

blink /blɪŋk/ *verb* **1** [I,T] to shut your eyes and open them again very quickly: *Oh dear! You blinked just as I took the photograph!* ➲ look at **wink** **2** [I] (used about a light) to come on and go off again quickly ▶ **blink** *noun* [C]

blinkered /ˈblɪŋkəd/ *adj.* not considering every aspect of a situation; not willing to accept different ideas about sth: *a blinkered policy/attitude/approach* SYN **narrow-minded**

blinkers /ˈblɪŋkəz/ (*AmE also* **blinders**) *noun* [pl.] pieces of leather that are placed at the side of a horse's eyes to stop it from looking sideways

blip /blɪp/ *noun* [C] **1** a light flashing on the screen of a piece of equipment, sometimes with a short high sound **2** a small problem that does not last for long

bliss /blɪs/ *noun* [U] perfect happiness ▶ **blissful** /-fl/ *adj.* ▶ **blissfully** /-fəli/ *adv.*

blister[1] /ˈblɪstə(r)/ *noun* [C] (HEALTH) a small painful area of skin that looks like a bubble and contains clear liquid. **Blisters** are usually caused by rubbing or burning.

blister[2] /ˈblɪstə(r)/ *verb* [I,T] **1** (HEALTH) to get or cause BLISTERS **2** to swell and crack or to cause sth to do this: *The paint is starting to blister.*

blistering /ˈblɪstərɪŋ/ *adj.* very strong or extreme: *the blistering midday heat* ◇ *The runners set off at a blistering pace.*

blitz /blɪts/ *noun* **1** [C] **a** ~ **(on sth)** a sudden effort or attack on sb/sth **2 the Blitz** [sing.] (HISTORY) the German air attacks on Britain in 1940

blizzard /ˈblɪzəd/ *noun* [C] a very bad storm with strong winds and a lot of snow ➲ note at **storm**

bloated /ˈbləʊtɪd/ *adj.* unusually large and uncomfortable because of liquid, food or gas inside: *I felt a bit bloated after all that food.*

blob /blɒb/ *noun* [C] a small piece of a thick liquid: *a blob of paint/cream/ink*

bloc /blɒk/ *noun* [C, with sing. or pl. verb] (POLITICS) a group of countries that work closely together because they have the same political interests

block[1] ⊶ /blɒk/ *noun* [C] **1** a large, heavy piece of sth, usually with flat sides: *a block of wood* ◇ *huge concrete blocks* **2** a large building that is divided into separate flats or offices: *a block of flats* ➲ look at **apartment block**, **office block** ➲ note at **building** **3** a group of buildings in a town which has streets on all four sides: *The restaurant is three blocks away.* **4** a quantity of sth or an amount of time that is considered as a single unit: *The class is divided into two blocks of fifty minutes.* **5** [usually sing.] a thing that makes movement or progress difficult or impossible: *a block to further progress in the talks* ➲ look at **roadblock**

IDM **have a block (about sth)** to be unable to think or understand sth properly: *I had a complete* ***mental block.*** *I just couldn't remember his name.*

block[2] ⊶ /blɒk/ *verb* [T] **1** ~ **sth (up)** to make it difficult or impossible for sb/sth to pass: *Many roads are completely blocked by snow.* **2** to prevent sth from being done: *The management tried to block the deal.* **3** to prevent sth from being seen by sb: *Get out of the way, you're blocking the view!*

PHR V **block sth off** to separate one area from another with sth solid: *This section of the motorway has been blocked off by the police.*
block sth out to try not to think about sth unpleasant: *She tried to block out the memory of the crash.*

blockade /blɒˈkeɪd/ *noun* [C] a situation in which a place is surrounded by soldiers or ships in order to prevent goods or people from reaching it ▶ **blockade** *verb* [T]

blockage /ˈblɒkɪdʒ/ *noun* [C] a thing that is preventing sth from passing; the state of being blocked: *a blockage in the drainpipe* ◇ *There are blockages on some major roads.*

ˌblock and ˈtackle *noun* [sing.] a piece of equipment for lifting heavy objects, which works by a system of ropes and PULLEYS (= small wheels around which the ropes are stretched)

block and tackle

pulley

blockbuster /ˈblɒkbʌstə(r)/ *noun* [C] (LITERATURE, ARTS AND MEDIA) a book or film with an exciting story which is very successful and popular

ˌblock ˈcapitals *noun* [pl.] big letters such as 'A' (not 'a'): *Please write your name* ***in block capitals****.*

blog /blɒg/ *noun* [C] (COMPUTING) a personal record that sb puts on their website saying what they have been doing, giving their opinions, and discussing places on the Internet they have visited ▶ **blog** *verb* [I] (**blogging**; **blogged**) ▶ **blogger** *noun* [C]

blogosphere /ˈblɒgəʊsfɪə(r)/ *noun* [sing.] (*informal*) (COMPUTING) all the personal websites and messages (**blogs**) that exist on the Internet, seen as a network of people communicating with each other: *The story moved from the blogosphere to the mainstream press.*

bloke /bləʊk/ *noun* [C] (*BrE, slang*) a man: *He's a really nice bloke.*

blonde 🔑 (*also* **blond**) /blɒnd/ *noun* [C], *adj.* (a person) with fair or yellow hair: *Most of our family have blonde hair.* ◇ *a small, blond boy*

blood 🔑 /blʌd/ *noun* [U] the red liquid that flows through your body: *The heart pumps blood around the body.* ➲ look at **bleed**
IDM **in your blood** a strong part of your character: *A love of the countryside was in his blood.*
in cold blood → COLD[1]
shed blood → SHED[2]
your (own) flesh and blood → FLESH

bloodbath /ˈblʌdbɑːθ/ *noun* [sing.] an act of violently killing many people

ˈblood count *noun* [C] (HEALTH) the number of red and white cells in your blood; a medical test to count these: *to have a high/low/normal blood count*

ˈblood-curdling *adj.* very frightening: *a blood-curdling scream*

ˈblood donor *noun* [C] (HEALTH) a person who gives some of their blood for use in medical operations

ˈblood group (*also* **ˈblood type**) *noun* [C] (BIOLOGY) any of several different types of human blood: *'What blood group are you?' 'O.'*

bloodless /ˈblʌdləs/ *adj.* **1** without killing or violence: *a bloodless coup* **2** (used about a part of the body) very pale

ˈblood poisoning *noun* [U] (HEALTH) an illness in which the blood becomes infected with bacteria, especially because of a cut or an injury to the skin SYN **septicaemia**

ˈblood pressure *noun* [U] (BIOLOGY, HEALTH) the force with which the blood travels round the body: *to have* ***high/low blood pressure***

bloodshed /ˈblʌdʃed/ *noun* [U] the killing or harming of people: *Both sides in the war want to avoid further bloodshed.*

bloodshot /ˈblʌdʃɒt/ *adj.* (used about the white part of the eyes) full of red lines, for example when sb is tired

ˈblood sport *noun* [C] a sport in which animals or birds are killed

bloodstain /ˈblʌdsteɪn/ *noun* [C] a mark or spot of blood on sth ▶ **bloodstained** *adj.*

bloodstream /ˈblʌdstriːm/ *noun* [sing.] (BIOLOGY) the blood as it flows through the body: *drugs injected straight into the bloodstream*

ˈblood test *noun* [C] (HEALTH) an examination of a small amount of your blood by doctors in order to make judgements about your medical condition

bloodthirsty /ˈblʌdθɜːsti/ *adj.* wanting to use violence or to watch scenes of violence

ˈblood transfusion *noun* [C] (HEALTH) the process of putting new blood into a person's body

ˈblood type (BIOLOGY) = BLOOD GROUP

ˈblood vessel *noun* [C] (ANATOMY) any of the tubes in your body which blood flows through ➲ look at **vein**, **artery**, **capillary**

bloody /ˈblʌdi/ *adj.* (**bloodier**; **bloodiest**) **1** involving a lot of violence and killing: *a bloody war* **2** covered with blood: *a bloody knife*

ˌbloody-ˈminded *adj.* (*BrE, informal*) (used about a person) deliberately difficult; not helpful ▶ **ˌbloody-ˈmindedness** *noun* [U]

bloom[1] /bluːm/ *noun* [C] (*formal* or *technical*) a flower (usually one on a plant that people admire for its flowers)
IDM **in bloom** with its flowers open: *All the wild plants are in bloom.*

bloom[2] /bluːm/ *verb* [I] to produce flowers SYN **flower**: *This shrub blooms in May.*

blossom[1] /ˈblɒsəm/ *noun* [C,U] a flower or a mass of flowers, especially on a fruit tree in the spring: *The apple tree is* ***in blossom****.* ➲ picture at **tree**

blossom[2] /ˈblɒsəm/ *verb* [I] **1** (used especially about trees) to produce flowers **2** ~ **(into sth)** to become more healthy, confident or successful: *This young runner has blossomed into a top-class athlete.*

blot[1] /blɒt/ *noun* [C] **1** a spot of sth, especially one made by ink on paper; a STAIN **2 a** ~ **on sth** a thing that spoils your happiness or other people's opinion of you

blot[2] /blɒt/ *verb* [T] (**blotting**; **blotted**) **1** to make a spot or a mark on sth, especially ink on paper **2** to remove liquid from a surface by pressing soft paper or cloth on it
PHR V **blot sth out** to cover or hide sth: *Fog blotted out the view completely.* ◇ *She tried to blot out the memory of what happened.*

blotch /blɒtʃ/ ***noun*** [C] a temporary mark or an area of different colour on skin, plants, material, etc.: *The blotches on her face showed that she had been crying.* ▶ **blotchy** (*also* **blotched**) ***adj.***

'blotting paper ***noun*** [U] soft paper that you use for drying wet ink after you have written sth on paper

blouse /blaʊz/ ***noun*** [C] a piece of clothing like a shirt, worn by women

blow[1] 🔑 /bləʊ/ ***verb*** (*pt* **blew** /bluː/; *pp* **blown** /bləʊn/) **1** [I,T] (used about wind, air, etc.) to be moving or to cause sth to move: *A gentle breeze was blowing.* **2** [I] to move because of the wind or a current of air: *The balloons* ***blew away***. ◇ *My papers blew all over the garden.* **3** [I] to send air out of the mouth: *The policeman asked me to* ***blow into*** *the breathalyser.* **4** [T] to make or shape sth by blowing air out of your mouth: *to blow bubbles/smoke rings* ◇ *to* ***blow*** *(sb)* ***a kiss*** (= to kiss your hand and pretend to blow the kiss towards sb) **5** [I,T] to produce sound from a musical instrument, etc. by blowing air into it: *The referee's whistle blew for the end of the match.* ◇ *He blew a few notes on the trumpet.* **6** [T] (*informal*) to waste an opportunity: *I think I've blown my chances of promotion.* ◇ *You had your chance and you blew it.* **7** [T] (*informal*) ~ **sth (on sth)** to spend or waste a lot of money on sth: *She blew all her savings on a trip to China.* **8** [I,T] (PHYSICS) (used about a thin piece of wire (**a fuse**) in an electrical system) to stop working suddenly because the electric current is too strong; to make sth do this: *A fuse has blown.* ◇ *I think the kettle's blown a fuse.*

IDM **blow your nose** to clear your nose by blowing strongly through it into a piece of cloth (**handkerchief**)

PHR V **blow over** to disappear without having a serious effect: *The scandal will soon blow over.*

blow up 1 to explode or to be destroyed in an explosion: *The car blew up when the door was opened.* **2** to start suddenly and strongly: *A storm blew up in the night.* ◇ *A huge row blew up about money.* **3** (*informal*) to become very angry: *The teacher blew up when I said I'd forgotten my homework.*

blow sth up 1 to make sth explode or to destroy sth in an explosion: *The terrorists tried to blow up the plane.* **2** to fill sth with air or gas: *to blow up a balloon* **3** to make a photograph bigger

blow[2] 🔑 /bləʊ/ ***noun*** [C] **1** a hard hit from sb's hand, a weapon, etc.: *She aimed a blow at me.* **2** a ~ **(to sb/sth)** a sudden shock or disappointment: *It was a blow when I didn't get the job.* **3** an act of blowing: *Give your nose a blow!*

IDM **a blow-by-blow account, description, etc. (of sth)** an account, etc. of an event that gives all the exact details of it

come to blows (with sb) (over sth) to start fighting or arguing (about sth)

deal sb/sth a blow; deal a blow to sb/sth → DEAL[1]

'blow-dry ***verb*** [T] (*3rd person sing. pres.* **blow-dries**; *pt, pp* **blow-dried**) to dry and shape sb's hair using a machine that produces hot air (**a hairdryer**) and a brush

blowhole /ˈbləʊhəʊl/ ***noun*** [C] **1** (BIOLOGY) a hole in the top of the head of a WHALE (= a large sea creature) through which it breathes ➲ picture on **page 29** **2** (GEOGRAPHY) a hole in a large area of ice through which sea animals, for example SEALS, breathe

blowlamp /ˈbləʊlæmp/ (*AmE* **torch**; **blowtorch**) ***noun*** [C] a tool with a very hot flame that you can point at a surface, for example to remove paint

blown past participle of **blow[1]**

blowout /ˈbləʊaʊt/ ***noun*** [C] (*informal*) **1** a burst tyre: *We had a blowout on the motorway.* SYN **puncture** **2** a very large meal at which people eat too much; a large party or social event

blowtorch /ˈbləʊtɔːtʃ/ (*AmE*) = BLOWLAMP

blubber /ˈblʌbə(r)/ ***noun*** [U] the fat of WHALES and other sea animals

bludgeon /ˈblʌdʒən/ ***verb*** [T] **1** to hit sb several times with a heavy object: *He was bludgeoned to death with a hammer.* **2** ~ **sb (into sth/into doing sth)** to force sb to do sth, especially by arguing: *They tried to bludgeon me into joining their protest.*

blue[1] 🔑 /bluː/ ***adj.*** **1** having the colour of a clear sky when the sun shines: *His eyes were bright blue.* ◇ *light/dark blue* **2** (*informal*) (often used in songs) sad **3** films, jokes or stories that are blue are about sex: *a blue movie*

IDM **black and blue** → BLACK[1]

once in a blue moon → ONCE

blue[2] 🔑 /bluː/ ***noun*** [C,U] the colour of a clear sky when the sun shines: *a deep blue* ◇ *dressed* ***in blue*** (= blue clothes)

IDM **out of the blue** suddenly; unexpectedly: *I didn't hear from him for years and then this letter came out of the blue.*

ˌblue-'chip ***adj.*** (BUSINESS, ECONOMICS) a **blue-chip** investment is thought to be safe and likely to make a profit: *blue-chip companies*

ˌblue-'collar ***adj.*** doing or involving physical work with the hands rather than office work ➲ look at **white-collar**

blueprint /ˈbluːprɪnt/ ***noun*** [C] **1** a PHOTOGRAPHIC print of a plan for a building or a machine, with white lines on a blue background: *blueprints of a new aircraft* **2** ~ **(for sth)** a plan which shows what can be achieved and how it can be achieved: *a blueprint for the privatization of health care* **3** (BIOLOGY) the pattern in every living cell, which decides how the plant, animal or person will develop and what it will look like: *DNA carries the blueprint which tells any organism how to build itself.*

blues /bluːz/ ***noun*** **1** (often **the blues**) [U] (MUSIC) a type of slow sad music with strong rhythms, developed by African American musicians in the southern US: *a blues band/singer* **2** [C] (*pl.* **blues**) (MUSIC) a **blues** song **3 the blues** [pl.] feelings of sadness: *the Monday morning blues*

Bluetooth™ /ˈbluːtuːθ/ ***noun*** [U] (COMPUTING) a radio technology that makes it possible for mobile phones, computers and other electronic devices to be linked over short distances, without needing to be connected by wires: *Bluetooth-enabled devices*

bluff[1] /blʌf/ ***verb*** [I,T] to try to make people believe that sth is true when it is not, usually by appearing very confident

IDM **bluff your way in, out, through, etc. sth** to trick sb in order to get into, out of a place, etc.: *We managed to bluff our way into the stadium by saying we were journalists.*

bluff[2] /blʌf/ ***noun*** **1** [U, C] making sb believe that you will do sth when you really have no intention of doing it, or that you know sth when, in fact, you do not know it **2** [C] (GEOGRAPHY) a steep CLIFF, especially by the sea or a river ➲ picture at **flood plain**

IDM **call sb's bluff** → CALL[1]

bluish (*also* **blueish**) /ˈbluːɪʃ/ ***adj.*** (*informal*) slightly blue: *bluish green*

blunder¹ /ˈblʌndə(r)/ ***noun*** [C] a stupid mistake: *I'm afraid I've **made a** terrible **blunder**.*

blunder² /ˈblʌndə(r)/ ***verb*** [I] to make a stupid mistake

PHR V **blunder about, around, etc.** to move in an uncertain or careless way, as if you cannot see where you are going: *We blundered about in the dark, trying to find the light switch.*

blunt /blʌnt/ ***adj.*** **1** (used about a knife, pencil, tool, etc.) without a sharp edge or point OPP **sharp** **2** (used about a person, comment, etc.) very direct; saying what you think without trying to be polite: *I'm sorry to be so blunt, but I'm afraid you're just not good enough.* ▶ **blunt** ***verb*** [T] ▶ **bluntly** ***adv.*** ▶ **bluntness** ***noun*** [U]

blur¹ /blɜː(r)/ ***noun*** [C, usually sing.] something that you cannot see clearly or remember well: *Without my glasses, their faces were just a blur.*

blur² /blɜː(r)/ ***verb*** [I,T] (**blurring**; **blurred**) to become or to make sth less clear: *The words on the page blurred as tears filled her eyes.* ▶ **blurred** ***adj.***

blurt /blɜːt/ ***verb***

PHR V **blurt sth out** to say sth suddenly or without thinking: *We didn't want to tell Mum but Ann blurted the whole thing out.*

blush /blʌʃ/ ***verb*** [I] to become red in the face, especially because you are embarrassed or feel guilty: *She blushed with shame.* ▶ **blush** ***noun*** [C, usually sing.]

blusher /ˈblʌʃə(r)/ ***noun*** [U, C] a coloured cream or powder that some people put on their cheeks to give them more colour

blustery /ˈblʌstəri/ ***adj.*** (used to describe the weather) with strong winds: *The day was cold and blustery.*

BMI /ˌbiː em ˈaɪ/ ***abbr.*** (HEALTH) = BODY MASS INDEX

BMX /ˌbiː em ˈeks/ ***noun*** **1** [C] a strong bicycle which can be used for riding on rough ground **2** (*also* **BMXing**) [U] (SPORT) the sport of racing BMX bicycles on rough ground

BO /ˌbiː ˈəʊ/ ***abbr.*** = BODY ODOUR

boa /ˈbəʊə/ ***noun*** [C] a large snake, found in America, Africa and Asia, that kills animals for food by squeezing them

boa constrictor /ˈbəʊə kənstrɪktə(r)/ ***noun*** [C] a large South American snake that is a type of BOA

boar /bɔː(r)/ ***noun*** [C] (*pl.* **boar** or **boars**) **1** a male pig **2** a wild pig ➲ note at **pig**

board¹ 🔑 /bɔːd/ ***noun*** **1** [C] a long, thin, flat piece of wood used for making floors, walls, etc.: *The old house needed new **floorboards**.* **2** [C] a thin flat piece of wood, etc. used for a particular purpose: *an **ironing board** ◇ a **surfboard** ◇ a **noticeboard** ◇ **board games*** (= games you play on a board) **3** [C, with sing. or pl. verb] (BUSINESS) a group of people who control an organization, company, etc.: *The **board of directors** is/are meeting to discuss the firm's future. ◇ a **board meeting*** **4** [U] (TOURISM) the meals that are provided when you stay in a hotel, etc.: *The prices are for a double room and **full board*** (= all the meals).

IDM **above board** → ABOVE

across the board → ACROSS

on board on a ship or an aircraft: *All the passengers were safely on board.*

board² 🔑 /bɔːd/ ***verb*** [I,T] to get on a plane, ship, bus, etc.: *We said goodbye and boarded the train. ◇ Lufthansa flight LH120 to Hamburg is now boarding* (= ready to take passengers) *at Gate 27.*

PHR V **board sth up** to cover sth with boards¹(1): *Nobody lives there now – it's all boarded up.*

boarder /ˈbɔːdə(r)/ ***noun*** [C] (*BrE*) **1** (EDUCATION) a child who lives at school and goes home for the holidays. **2** a person who pays to live at sb's house ➲ look at **lodger**

ˈ**boarding card** (*also* ˈ**boarding pass**) ***noun*** [C] a card that you must show in order to get on a plane or ship

ˈ**boarding house** ***noun*** [C] a private house where you can pay to stay and have meals for a period of time

ˈ**boarding school** ***noun*** [C] (EDUCATION) a school that schoolchildren live at while they are studying, going home only in the holidays

boardroom /ˈbɔːdruːm; -rʊm/ ***noun*** [C] (BUSINESS) the room where the group of people in charge of a company or organization (**the board of directors**) meets

boast /bəʊst/ ***verb*** **1** [I] to talk with too much pride about sth that you have or can do: *I wish she wouldn't boast about her family so much.* **2** [T] (used about a place) to have sth that it can be proud of: *The town boasts over a dozen restaurants.* ▶ **boast** ***noun*** [C]

boastful /ˈbəʊstfl/ ***adj.*** (used about a person or the things that they say) showing too much pride

boat 🔑 /bəʊt/ ***noun*** [C] **1** a small vehicle that is used for travelling across water: *The cave can only be reached **by boat/in a boat**. ◇ a rowing/fishing/motor boat* **2** any ship: *When does the next boat to France sail?*

IDM **rock the boat** → ROCK²

boathouse /ˈbəʊthaʊs/ ***noun*** [C] a building beside a river or lake for keeping a boat in

bob /bɒb/ ***verb*** (**bobbing**; **bobbed**) [I,T] to move quickly up and down; to make sth do this: *The boats in the harbour were bobbing up and down in the water. ◇ She bobbed her head down below the top of the wall.*

PHR V **bob up** to appear suddenly from behind or under sth: *He disappeared and then bobbed up again on the other side of the pool.*

bobbin /ˈbɒbɪn/ ***noun*** [C] a small circular device which you put thread round and that is used, for example, in a sewing machine

bobby /ˈbɒbi/ ***noun*** [C] (*pl.* **bobbies**) (*BrE, old-fashioned, informal*) a POLICEMAN

bobsleigh /ˈbɒbsleɪ/ (*AmE* **bobsled** /ˈbɒbsled/) ***noun*** [C] (SPORT) a racing vehicle for two or more people that slides over snow along a track ➲ look at **sleigh**, **sledge**, **toboggan**

bode /bəʊd/ ***verb***

IDM **bode well/ill (for sb/sth)** to be a sign that sb/sth will have a good/bad future

bodice /ˈbɒdɪs/ ***noun*** [C] the top part of a woman's dress, above the waist

bodily¹ /ˈbɒdɪli/ ***adj.*** of the human body; physical: *First we must attend to their **bodily needs*** (= make sure that they have a home, enough to eat, etc.).

bodily² /ˈbɒdɪli/ ***adv.*** by taking hold of the body: *She picked up the child and carried him bodily from the room.*

body 🔑 /ˈbɒdi/ ***noun*** (*pl.* **bodies**) **1** [C] the whole physical form of a person or animal: *the human body* **2** [C] the part of a person that is not their legs, arms or head: *She had injuries to her head and body.*

body

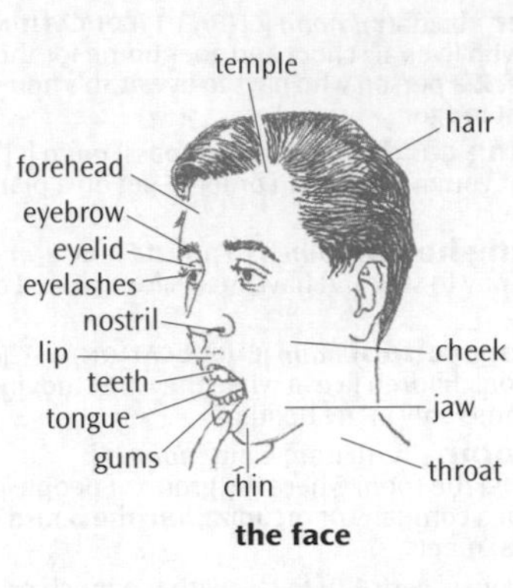

temple
hair
forehead
eyebrow
eyelid
eyelashes
nostril
lip
teeth
tongue
gums
chin
cheek
jaw
throat

the face

head
ear
neck
eye
nose
mouth
shoulder
fingernail
thumb
knuckle
armpit
chest
upper arm
hand
wrist
arm
forearm
elbow
finger
palm
stomach
waist
bottom
hip
leg
knee
thigh
calf
shin
ankle
big toe
foot
heel
toenail
toe
sole

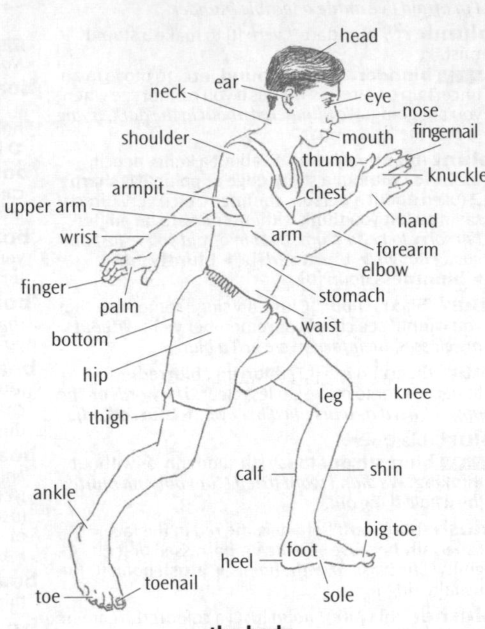

the body

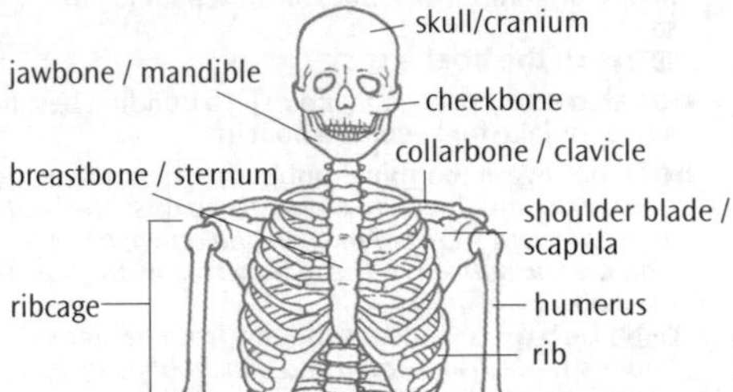

skull/cranium
jawbone / mandible
cheekbone
collarbone / clavicle
breastbone / sternum
shoulder blade / scapula
ribcage
humerus
rib
vertebra
backbone / spine
radius
hip bone
pelvis
ulna
tailbone/ coccyx
carpals
thigh bone / femur
metacarpals
kneecap / patella
shin bone / tibia
fibula
tarsals
metatarsals

the skeleton

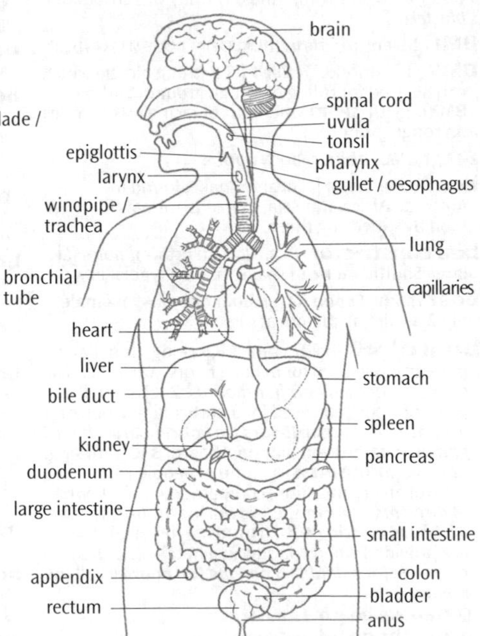

brain
spinal cord
uvula
tonsil
epiglottis
pharynx
larynx
gullet / oesophagus
windpipe / trachea
lung
bronchial tube
capillaries
heart
liver
stomach
bile duct
spleen
kidney
pancreas
duodenum
large intestine
small intestine
appendix
colon
bladder
rectum
anus

internal organs

3 [C] a dead person: *The police have found a body in the canal.* **4** [C, with sing. or pl. verb] a group of people who work or act together, especially in an official way: *The **governing body** of the college meets/meet once a month.* **5** [sing.] the main part of sth: *We agree with the body of the report, although not with certain details.* **6** [C] (*formal*) an object: ***heavenly bodies*** (= stars, planets, etc.) ◇ *The doctor removed a **foreign body*** (= sth that would not usually be there) *from the child's ear.*

IDM **in a body** all together

bodybuilding /ˈbɒdibɪldɪŋ/ ***noun*** [U] (SPORT) making the muscles of the body stronger and larger by exercise ▶ **bodybuilder** ***noun*** [C]

bodyguard /ˈbɒdigɑːd/ ***noun*** [C] a person or group of people whose job is to protect sb

ˈ**body language** ***noun*** [U] (SOCIAL STUDIES) showing how you feel by the way you move, stand, sit, etc., rather than by what you say: *I could tell by his body language that he was scared.*

ˈ**body mass index** ***noun*** [C] (*pl.* **body mass indices** /-ˈɪndɪsiːz/) (*abbr.* **BMI**) (HEALTH) a measure of body fat to show whether you are too heavy or too light, based on the relationship between your height and your weight: *Models continue to have a lower body mass index than the average woman.*

ˈ**body odour** ***noun*** [U] (*abbr.* **BO**) the unpleasant smell from a person's body, especially of sweat

bodywork /ˈbɒdiwɜːk/ ***noun*** [U] the main outside structure of a vehicle, usually made of painted metal

bog /bɒg/ ***noun*** [C,U] an area of ground that is very soft and wet: *a peat bog*

bogey /ˈbəʊgi/ ***noun*** [C] **1** something that causes fear, often without reason **2** (*informal*) a piece of the sticky substance (**mucus**) that forms inside your nose

ˌ**bogged ˈdown** ***adj.*** **1** (used about a vehicle) not able to move because it has sunk into soft ground **2** (used about a person) not able to make any progress

boggle /ˈbɒgl/ ***verb*** [I] ~ **(at sth)** to be unable to imagine sth; to be impossible to imagine or believe: *'What will happen if his plan doesn't work?' '**The mind boggles!**'* ➲ look at **mind-boggling**

boggy /ˈbɒgi/ ***adj.*** (used about land) soft and wet, so that your feet sink into it

bogus /ˈbəʊgəs/ ***adj.*** pretending to be real or genuine: *a bogus policeman*

boil[1] 🔑 /bɔɪl/ ***verb*** **1** [I] (SCIENCE) (used about a liquid) to reach a high temperature where bubbles rise to the surface and the liquid changes to a gas: *Water boils at 100°C.* ◇ *The kettle's boiling.* **2** [T] (SCIENCE) to heat a liquid until it boils and let it keep boiling: *Boil all drinking water for five minutes.* **3** [I,T] to cook (sth) in boiling water: *Put the potatoes on to boil, please.* ◇ *to boil an egg* **4** [I] (used about a person) to feel very angry: *She was boiling with rage.*

PHR V **boil down to sth** to have sth as the most important point: *What it all boils down to is that you don't want to spend too much money.*

boil over 1 (used about a liquid) to boil and flow over the sides of a pan: *You let the soup boil over.* **2** (used about an argument or sb's feelings) to become more serious or angry

boil[2] /bɔɪl/ ***noun*** **1** [sing.] (SCIENCE) a period of boiling; the point at which a liquid boils: *You'll have to give those shirts a boil to get them clean.* **2** [C] (HEALTH) a small, painful swelling under your skin, with a red or yellow top

boiler /ˈbɔɪlə(r)/ ***noun*** [C] a container in which water is heated to provide hot water or heating in a building or to produce steam in an engine ➲ picture at **generator**

ˈ**boiler suit** ***noun*** [C] (*AmE* **coveralls**) a piece of clothing that you wear over your normal clothes to protect them when you are doing dirty work

boiling /ˈbɔɪlɪŋ/ (*also* ˌ**boiling ˈhot**) ***adj.*** (*informal*) very hot: *Open a window – it's boiling hot in here.* ◇ *Can I open a window? I'm boiling.*

ˈ**boiling point** ***noun*** [C] (SCIENCE) the temperature at which a liquid starts to boil

boisterous /ˈbɔɪstərəs/ ***adj.*** (used about a person or behaviour) noisy and full of energy: *Their children are very nice but they can get a bit too boisterous.*

bold /bəʊld/ ***adj.*** **1** (used about a person or their behaviour) confident and not afraid: *Not many people are bold enough to say exactly what they think.* **2** that you can see clearly: *bold, bright colours* **3** (used about printed letters) in thick, dark type: *Make the important text **bold**.* ▶ **bold** ***noun*** [U]: *The important words are highlighted **in bold**.* ▶ **boldly** ***adv.*** ▶ **boldness** ***noun*** [U]

bole /bəʊl/ ***noun*** [C] (BIOLOGY) the main part of a tree that grows up from the ground SYN **trunk**

bollard /ˈbɒlɑːd/ ***noun*** [C] a short thick post that is used to stop motor vehicles from going into an area that they are not allowed to enter

bolshie (also **bolshy**) /ˈbɒlʃi/ ***adj.*** (*BrE, informal*) (used about a person) bad-tempered and often refusing to do what people ask them to do

bolster /ˈbəʊlstə(r)/ ***verb*** [T] ~ **sb/sth (up)** to support or encourage sb/sth; to make sth stronger: *His remarks did nothing to bolster my confidence.*

bolt

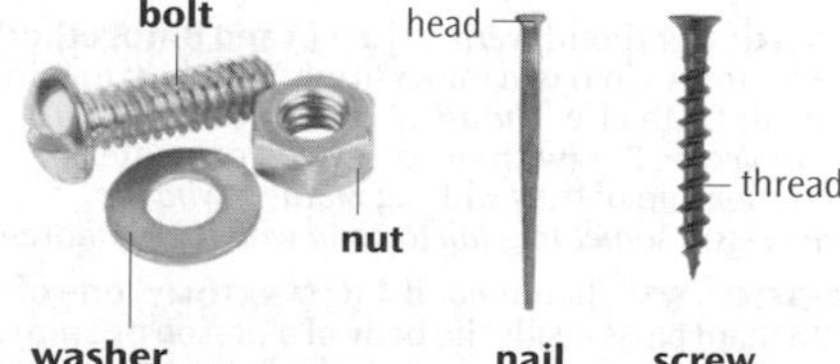

bolt[1] /bəʊlt/ ***noun*** [C] **1** a small piece of metal that is used with another piece of metal (**a nut**) for fastening things together **2** a bar of metal that you can slide across the inside of the door in order to fasten it

bolt[2] /bəʊlt/ ***verb*** **1** [I] (used especially about a horse) to run away very suddenly, usually in fear **2** [T] ~ **sth (down)** to eat sth very quickly **3** [T] to fasten one thing to another using a **bolt**[1](1): *All the tables have been bolted to the floor so that nobody can steal them.* **4** [T] to fasten a door, etc. with a **bolt**[1](2): *Make sure that the door is locked and bolted.*

bolt[3] /bəʊlt/ ***adv.***

IDM **bolt upright** sitting or standing very straight

bomb[1] 🔑 /bɒm/ ***noun*** **1** [C] a container that is filled with material that will explode when it is thrown or dropped, or when a device inside it makes it explode: *Fortunately, the car bomb failed to **go off**.* **2 the bomb** [sing.] nuclear weapons: *How many countries have the bomb now?* **3 a bomb** [sing.] (*BrE, informal*) a lot of money: *That car must have cost you a bomb!*

bomb² 🔑 /bɒm/ ***verb*** **1** [T] to attack a city, etc. with bombs: *Enemy forces have bombed the bridge.* **2** (*BrE, informal*) ~ **along, down, up, etc.** to move along very fast in the direction mentioned, especially in a vehicle: *He was bombing along at 100 miles an hour when the police stopped him.*

bombard /bɒmˈbɑːd/ ***verb*** [T] to attack a place with bombs or guns: *They bombarded the city until the enemy surrendered.* ◇ (*figurative*) *The reporters bombarded the minister with questions.* ▶ **bombardment** ***noun*** [C,U]: *The main radio station has* ***come under*** *enemy* ***bombardment***.

ˈbomb disposal ***noun*** [U] the removing or exploding of bombs in order to make an area safe: *a bomb disposal expert*

bomber /ˈbɒmə(r)/ ***noun*** [C] **1** a type of plane that drops bombs **2** a person who makes a bomb explode in a public place

bombing /ˈbɒmɪŋ/ ***noun*** [C, U] an occasion when a bomb is dropped or left somewhere; the act of doing this: *recent bombings in major cities* ◇ *enemy bombing*

bombshell /ˈbɒmʃel/ ***noun*** [C, usually sing.] an unexpected piece of news, usually about sth unpleasant: *The chairman* ***dropped a bombshell*** *when he said he was resigning.*

bona fide /ˌbəʊnə ˈfaɪdi/ ***adj.*** real or genuine: *This car park is for the use of bona fide customers only.*

bond¹ AW /bɒnd/ ***noun*** [C] **1** something that joins two or more people or groups of people together, such as a feeling of friendship **2** (FINANCE) an agreement by a government or a company to pay you interest on the money you have lent; a document containing this agreement: *government bonds* **3** (*especially AmE*) (LAW) a sum of money that is paid as BAIL: *He was released on $5 000 bond.* **4** (CHEMISTRY) the way in which atoms are held together in a chemical COMPOUND

bond² AW /bɒnd/ ***verb*** [I,T] **1** ~ **(A and B) (together)**; ~ **(A) to B** to join two things firmly together; to join firmly to sth else: *The atoms bond together to form a molecule.* **2** ~ **(with sb)** to develop or create a relationship of trust with sb: *Mothers who are depressed sometimes fail to bond with their children.*

bone¹ 🔑 /bəʊn/ ***noun*** **1** [C] (ANATOMY) one of the hard parts inside the body of a person or animal that are covered with muscle, skin, etc.: *He's broken a bone in his hand.* ◇ *This fish has got a lot of bones in it.* ➲ picture on **page 80** **2** [U] the substance that bones are made of

IDM **have a bone to pick with sb** to have sth that you want to complain to sb about

make no bones about (doing) sth to do sth in an open honest way without feeling nervous or worried about it: *She made no bones about telling him exactly what she thought about him.*

bone² /bəʊn/ ***verb*** [T] to take the bones out of sth: *to bone a fish*

ˌbone ˈdry ***adj.*** completely dry

ˈbone marrow (*also* **marrow**) ***noun*** [U] (ANATOMY) the soft substance that is inside the bones of a person or animal

bonemeal /ˈbəʊnmiːl/ ***noun*** [U] (AGRICULTURE) a substance made from animal bones which is used to make soil better for growing plants

bonfire /ˈbɒnfaɪə(r)/ ***noun*** [C] a large fire that you build outside to burn rubbish or as part of a festival, etc.

ˈBonfire Night ***noun*** [C] in Britain, the night of 5 November

> **CULTURE**
>
> On this day people in Britain light fireworks and sometimes burn a model of a man (called a **guy**) on top of a **bonfire**, to celebrate the failure of Guy Fawkes to blow up the Houses of Parliament in the seventeenth century.

bonkers /ˈbɒŋkəz/ ***adj.*** (*slang*) crazy; mad: *I'd go bonkers if I worked here full-time.*

bonnet /ˈbɒnɪt/ ***noun*** [C] **1** (*AmE* **hood**) the front part of a car that covers the engine **2** a type of hat which covers the sides of the face and is fastened with strings under the chin

bonus /ˈbəʊnəs/ ***noun*** [C] (*pl.* **bonuses**) **1** (FINANCE) a payment that is added to what is usual: *All our employees receive an annual bonus.* **2** something good that you get in addition to what you expect: *I enjoy my job, and having my own office is* ***an added bonus***.

bony /ˈbəʊni/ ***adj.*** so thin that you can see the shape of the bones: *long bony fingers*

boo /buː/ ***exclamation, noun*** [C] (*pl.* **boos**) **1** a sound you make to show that you do not like sb/sth: *The minister's speech was met with boos from the audience.* **2** a sound you make to frighten or surprise sb: *He jumped out from behind the door and said 'boo'.* ▶ **boo** ***verb*** [I,T]

boob /buːb/ ***noun*** [C] (*slang*) a silly mistake ▶ **boob** ***verb*** [I]: *I'm afraid I've boobed again.*

booby prize /ˈbuːbi praɪz/ ***noun*** [C] a prize that is given as a joke to the person or team that comes last in a competition

booby trap /ˈbuːbi træp/ ***noun*** [C] a device that will kill, injure or surprise sb when they touch the object that it is connected to ▶ **booby-trap** ***verb*** [T] (*pres. part.* **booby-trapping**; *pt, pp* **booby-trapped**)

boogie¹ /ˈbuːgi/ (*also* **ˌboogie-ˈwoogie** /ˌbuːgi ˈwuːgi/) ***noun*** [U] (MUSIC) a type of BLUES music played on the piano, with a fast strong rhythm

boogie² ***verb*** [I] (*informal*) to dance to fast pop music

book¹ 🔑 /bʊk/ ***noun*** **1** [C] a written work that is published as printed pages fastened together inside a cover, or in electronic form: *I'm reading a book on astrology.* ◇ *She's writing a book about her life abroad.* ◇ *Do you have any books by William Golding?* ◇ *hardback/paperback books* **2** [C] a number of pieces of paper, fastened together inside a cover, for people to write or draw on: *Please write down all the new vocabulary in your exercise books.* ◇ *a notebook* ◇ *a sketch book* **3** [C] a number of things fastened together in the form of a book: *a book of stamps* ◇ *a chequebook* **4** **books** [pl.] (FINANCE) the records that a company, etc., keeps of the amount of money it spends and receives: *We employ an accountant to* ***keep the books***.

IDM **be in sb's good/bad books** (*informal*) to have sb pleased/angry with you: *He's been in his girlfriend's bad books since he forgot her birthday.*

by the book exactly according to the rules: *A policeman must always do things by the book.*

(be) on sb's books (to be) on the list of an organization: *The employment agency has hundreds of qualified secretaries on its books.*

book² 🔑 /bʊk/ ***verb*** **1** [I,T] to arrange to have or do sth at a particular time: *Have you booked a table, sir?* ◇ *to book a seat on a plane/train/bus* ◇ *I've booked a hotel room for you/I've booked you a hotel room.* ◇ *I'm sorry, but this evening's performance is fully*

booked (= there are no seats left). **2** [T] (*informal*) to officially write down the name of a person who has done sth wrong: *The police booked her for* (= charged her with) *dangerous driving.* ◇ *The player was booked for a foul and then sent off for arguing.*
PHR V **book in** to say that you have arrived at a hotel, etc., and sign your name on a list
book sb in to arrange a room for sb at a hotel, etc. in advance: *I've booked you in at the George Hotel.*

bookcase /ˈbʊkkeɪs/ ***noun*** [C] a piece of furniture with shelves to keep books on

bookie /ˈbʊki/ (*informal*) = BOOKMAKER

booking /ˈbʊkɪŋ/ ***noun*** [C,U] the arrangement you make in advance to have a hotel room, a seat on a plane, etc.: *Did you manage to **make a booking**?* ◇ *No advance booking is necessary.*

ˈ**booking office** ***noun*** [C] an office where you buy tickets

bookkeeper /ˈbʊkkiːpə(r)/ ***noun*** [C] (BUSINESS, FINANCE) a person whose job is to keep an accurate record of the accounts of a business
▶ **bookkeeping** ***noun*** [U]

booklet /ˈbʊklət/ ***noun*** [C] a small thin book, usually with a soft cover, that gives information about sth

bookmaker /ˈbʊkmeɪkə(r)/ (also *informal* **bookie**) ***noun*** **1** [C] person whose job is to take bets on the result of horse races, etc. and pay out money to people who win **2 bookmaker's** [sing.] a shop, etc. where you can bet money on a race or an event ➲ look at **betting shop**

bookmark /ˈbʊkmɑːk/ ***noun*** [C] **1** a narrow piece of card, etc. that you put between the pages of a book so that you can find the same place again easily **2** (COMPUTING) a file from the Internet that you have stored on your computer ▶ **bookmark** ***verb*** [T] (COMPUTING): *Do you want to bookmark this site?*

bookseller /ˈbʊkselə(r)/ ***noun*** [C] a person whose job is selling books

bookshelf /ˈbʊkʃelf/ ***noun*** [C] (*pl.* **bookshelves** /ˈbʊkʃelvz/) a shelf that you keep books on

bookshop /ˈbʊkʃɒp/ (*AmE* **bookstore** /ˈbʊkstɔː(r)/) ***noun*** [C] a shop that sells books ➲ look at **library**

bookstall /ˈbʊkstɔːl/ (*AmE* ˈ**news-stand**) ***noun*** [C] a type of small shop, which is open at the front, selling newspapers, magazines and books, for example on a station

bookworm /ˈbʊkwɜːm/ ***noun*** [C] a person who likes reading books very much

Boolean /ˈbuːliən/ ***adj.*** (MATHEMATICS, COMPUTING) connected with a system, used especially in COMPUTING and ELECTRONICS, that uses only the numbers 1 (to show sth is true) and 0 (to show sth is false)

ˌ**Boolean** ˈ**operator** ***noun*** (COMPUTING) a symbol or word such as 'or' or 'and', used in computer programs and searches to show what is or is not included

boom¹ /buːm/ ***noun*** [C] **1** (ECONOMICS) a period in which sth increases or develops very quickly: *There was a boom in car sales in the 1980s.* **2** [usually sing.] a loud deep sound: *the boom of distant guns* **3** a long pole to which the sail of a boat is fixed. You move the **boom** to change the position of the sail.

boom² /buːm/ ***verb*** **1** [I,T] ~ **(sth) (out)** to make a loud deep sound: *The loudspeaker boomed out instructions to the crowd.* **2** [I] (ECONOMICS) to grow very quickly in size or value: *Business is booming in the computer industry.*

boomerang /ˈbuːməræŋ/ ***noun*** [C] a curved piece of wood that returns to you when you throw it in a particular way

boon /buːn/ ***noun*** [C] a thing that is very helpful and that you are grateful for

boorish /ˈbʊərɪʃ; ˈbɔːr-/ ***adj.*** (used about people and their behaviour) very unpleasant and rude

boost¹ /buːst/ ***verb*** [T] to increase sth in number, value or strength: *If we lower the price, that should boost sales.* ◇ *The good exam result boosted her confidence.*

boost² /buːst/ ***noun*** [C] something that encourages people; an increase: *The fall in the value of the pound has led to a boost in exports.* ◇ *The president's visit gave a **boost to** the soldiers' **morale**.*

boot¹ 🔑 /buːt/ ***noun*** [C] **1** a type of shoe that covers your foot completely and sometimes part of your leg: *ski boots* ◇ *walking/climbing boots* ◇ *football boots* **2** (*AmE* **trunk**) the part of a car where you put luggage, usually at the back

boot² /buːt/ ***verb*** (*informal*) **1** [T] to kick sth/sb hard: *He booted the ball over the fence.* **2** [I,T] (COMPUTING) to make a computer ready for use when it is first switched on
PHR V **boot sb/sth out** to force sb/sth to leave a place

booth /buːð/ ***noun*** [C] a small confined place where you can do sth privately, for example make a telephone call, or vote: *a phone booth*

booty /ˈbuːti/ ***noun*** [U] things that are taken by thieves or captured by soldiers in a war

booze¹ /buːz/ ***noun*** [U] (*informal*) alcohol

booze² /buːz/ ***verb*** [I] (*informal*) to drink a lot of alcohol

ˈ**booze-up** ***noun*** [C] (*BrE, informal*) an occasion when people drink a lot of alcohol

border¹ 🔑 /ˈbɔːdə(r)/ ***noun*** [C] **1** (GEOGRAPHY) a line that divides two countries, etc.; the land close to this line: *The refugees escaped **across /over the border**.* ◇ *the Moroccan border* ◇ *the border between France and Italy* ◇ *Italy's border with France* **2** a band or narrow line around the edge of sth, often for decoration: *a white tablecloth with a blue border*

border² /ˈbɔːdə(r)/ ***verb*** [T] to form a border to an area; to be on the border of an area: *The road was bordered with trees.*
PHR V **border on sth 1** to be almost the same as sth: *The dictator's ideas bordered on madness.* **2** to be next to sth: *Our garden borders on the railway line.*

borderline /ˈbɔːdəlaɪn/ ***noun*** [sing.] the line that marks a division between two different cases, conditions, etc.: *He's **a borderline case** – he may pass the exam or he may fail.*

bore¹ 🔑 /bɔː(r)/ ***verb*** **1** [T] to make sb feel bored, especially by talking too much: *I hope I'm not boring you.* **2** [I,T] to make a long deep hole with a tool or by digging: *This drill can bore (a hole) through solid rock.* **3** past tense of **bear²**

bore² /bɔː(r)/ ***noun*** **1** [C] a person who talks a lot in a way that is not interesting **2** [sing.] (*informal*) something that you have to do that you do not find interesting: *It's such a bore having to learn these lists of irregular verbs.* **3** [C] (*also* **borehole**) (GEOGRAPHY) a deep hole made in the ground, especially to find water or oil

bored ⊷ /bɔːd/ ***adj.*** ~ (with sth) feeling tired and perhaps slightly annoyed because sth is not interesting or because you do not have anything to do: *I'm bored with eating the same thing every day.* ◇ *The children* ***get bored*** *on long journeys.* ◇ *He gave a bored yawn.* ◇ *The play was awful – we were* ***bored stiff*** (= extremely bored).

boredom /ˈbɔːdəm/ ***noun*** [U] the state of being bored

borehole /ˈbɔːhəʊl/ ***noun*** [C] (GEOGRAPHY) = BORE² (3)

boring ⊷ /ˈbɔːrɪŋ/ ***adj.*** not at all interesting; dull: *a boring film/job/speech/man*

born¹ ⊷ /bɔːn/ ***verb*** **be born** to come into the world by birth; to start existing: *Where were you born?* ◇ *I was born in London, but I grew up in Leeds.* ◇ *I'm going to give up work after the baby is born.* ◇ *The idea of free education for all was born in the nineteenth century.* ◇ *His unhappiness was* ***born out of*** *a feeling of frustration.*

born² /bɔːn/ ***adj.*** **1** (only *before* a noun) having a natural ability to do sth: *She's a born leader.* **2 -born** (used to form compound adjectives) born in the place or state mentioned: *This Kenyan-born athlete now represents Denmark.*

ˌborn-aˈgain ***adj.*** (only *before* a noun) (RELIGION) having found new, strong religious belief: *a born-again Christian*

borne past participle of **bear²**

-borne /bɔːn/ ***adj.*** (used to form compound adjectives) carried by the thing mentioned: *water-borne diseases*

boron /ˈbɔːrɒn/ ***noun*** [U] (*symbol* **B**) (CHEMISTRY) a brown or black substance that is used for making steel harder ℹ For more information on the periodic table of elements, look at pages R34-5.

borough /ˈbʌrə/ ***noun*** [C] a town, or an area inside a large town, that has some form of local government

borrow ⊷ /ˈbɒrəʊ/ ***verb*** [I,T] ~ (sth) (from sb/sth) **1** to take or receive sth from sb/sth that you intend to give back, usually after a short time: *I had to borrow from the bank to pay for my car.* ◇ *We'll have to borrow a lot of money to buy a car.* ◇ *Could I borrow your pen for a minute?* ◇ *He's always borrowing from his mother.* ◇ *I borrowed a book from the library.* ➲ look at **lend 2** to take sth and use it as your own; to copy sth: *That idea is borrowed from another book.*

borrower /ˈbɒrəʊə(r)/ ***noun*** [C] a person who borrows sth

borrowing /ˈbɒrəʊɪŋ/ ***noun*** [C,U] (FINANCE) the money that a company, an organization or a person borrows; the act of borrowing money: *an attempt to reduce bank borrowings* ◇ *High interest rates help to keep borrowing down.*

bosom /ˈbʊzəm/ ***noun*** [C] a woman's chest or breasts: *She clutched the child to her bosom.*
IDM **in the bosom of sth** close to; with the protection of: *He was glad to be back in the bosom of his family.*

ˌbosom ˈfriend ***noun*** [C] a very close friend

boss¹ ⊷ /bɒs/ ***noun*** [C] (*informal*) a person whose job is to give orders to others at work; an employer; a manager: *I'm going to ask the boss for a day off work.* ◇ *OK. You're the boss* (= you make the decisions).

boss² /bɒs/ ***verb*** [T] ~ **sb (about/around)** to give orders to sb, especially in an annoying way: *I wish you'd stop bossing me around.*

bossy /ˈbɒsi/ ***adj.*** liking to give orders to other people, often in an annoying way: *Don't be so bossy!* ▶ **bossily** ***adv.*** ▶ **bossiness** ***noun*** [U]

bot /bɒt/ ***noun*** [C] (COMPUTING) a computer program that performs a particular task again and again many times

botanist /ˈbɒtənɪst/ ***noun*** [C] (BIOLOGY) a person who studies plants

botany /ˈbɒtəni/ ***noun*** [U] (BIOLOGY) the scientific study of plants ➲ look at **biology, zoology** ▶ **botanical** /bəˈtænɪkl/ ***adj.***: ***botanical gardens*** (= a type of park where plants are grown for scientific study)

botch /bɒtʃ/ ***verb*** [T] (*informal*) ~ **sth (up)** to do sth badly; to make a mess of sth: *I've completely botched up this typing, I'm afraid.*

both ⊷ /bəʊθ/ ***det., pronoun, adv.*** **1** the two; the one as well as the other: *Both women were French.* ◇ *Both the women were French.* ◇ *Both of the women were French.* ◇ *I liked them both.* ◇ *We were both very tired.* ◇ *Both of us were tired.* ◇ *I've got two sisters. They both live in London/Both of them live in London.* **2 both ... and ...** not only ...but also ...: *Both he and his wife are vegetarian.*

bother¹ ⊷ /ˈbɒðə(r)/ ***verb*** **1** [T] to disturb, annoy or worry sb: *I'm sorry to bother you, but could I speak to you for a moment?* ◇ *Don't bother Geeta with that now – she's busy.* SYN **trouble 2** [I] ~ **(to do sth/ doing sth)**; ~ **(about/with sth)** (usually negative) to make the effort to do sth: *'Shall I make you something to eat?' 'No, don't bother – I'm not hungry.'* ◇ *He didn't even bother to say thank you.* ◇ *Don't bother waiting for me – I'll catch you up later.* ◇ *Don't bother about the washing-up. I'll do it later.*
IDM **can't be bothered (to do sth)** used to say that you do not want to spend time or energy doing sth: *I can't be bothered to do my homework now. I'll do it tomorrow.*
not be bothered (about sth) (*especially BrE, informal*) to think that sth is not important: *'What would you like to do this evening?' 'I'm not bothered really.'*

bother² /ˈbɒðə(r)/ ***noun*** [U] trouble or difficulty: *Thanks for all your help. It's saved me a lot of bother.*

bothered /ˈbɒðəd/ ***adj.*** worried about sth: *Sam doesn't seem too bothered about losing his job.*

Botox™ /ˈbəʊtɒks/ ***noun*** [U] a substance that makes muscles relax. It is sometimes put under the skin around sb's eyes using a needle, in order to remove lines and make the skin look younger.
▶ **Botox** ***verb*** [T] (usually passive): *Do you think she's been Botoxed?*

bottle¹ ⊷ /ˈbɒtl/ ***noun*** [C] **1** a glass or plastic container with a narrow neck for keeping liquids in: *a beer bottle* ◇ *an empty bottle* **2** the amount of liquid that a bottle can hold: *a bottle of beer*

bottle² /ˈbɒtl/ ***verb*** [T] to put sth into bottles: *After three or four months the wine is bottled.* ◇ *bottled water* (= that you can buy in bottles)
PHRV **bottle sth up** to not allow yourself to express strong emotions: *You'll make yourself ill if you keep your feelings bottled up.*

ˈbottle bank ***noun*** [C] (ENVIRONMENT) a large container in a public place where people can leave their empty bottles so that the glass can be used again (**recycled**)

bottleneck /ˈbɒtlnek/ ***noun*** [C] **1** a narrow piece of road that causes traffic to slow down or stop **2** something that slows down progress, especially in business or industry

bottom¹ 🔑 /ˈbɒtəm/ ***noun*** **1** [C, usually sing.] the lowest part of sth: *The house is* ***at the bottom*** *of a hill.* ◇ *I think I've got a pen* ***in the bottom*** *of my bag.* ◇ *The sea is so clear that you can see the bottom.* **2** [C] the flat surface on the outside of an object, on which it stands: *There's a label* ***on the bottom*** *of the box.* **3** [sing.] the far end of sth: *The bus stop is* ***at the bottom*** *of the road.* **4** [sing.] the lowest position in relation to other people, teams, etc.: *She started* ***at the bottom*** *and now she's the Managing Director.* **5** [C] the part of your body that you sit on: *He fell over and landed on his bottom.* ➲ picture on **page 80** **6 bottoms** [pl.] the lower part of a piece of clothing that is in two parts: *pyjama bottoms* ◇ *track suit bottoms*

IDM **be at the bottom of sth** to be the cause of sth

from the (bottom of your) heart → HEART

get to the bottom of sth to find out the real cause of sth

bottom² 🔑 /ˈbɒtəm/ ***adj.*** (only *before* a noun) in the lowest position: *the bottom shelf* ◇ *I live on the bottom floor.*

bottomless /ˈbɒtəmləs/ ***adj.*** very deep; without limit

ˌbottom ˈline ***noun*** [sing.] **1 the bottom line** the most important thing to consider when you are discussing or deciding sth, etc.: *A musical instrument should look and feel good, but the bottom line is how it sounds.* **2** (BUSINESS) the final profit or loss that a company has made in a particular period of time: *The bottom line for 2005 was a pre-tax profit of £85 million* **3** the lowest price that sb will accept for sth

botulism /ˈbɒtjulɪzəm/ ***noun*** [U] (HEALTH) a serious illness caused by BACTERIA in food that is old and has gone bad

bougainvillea /ˌbuːɡənˈvɪliə/ ***noun*** [C] a tropical climbing plant with red, purple, white or pink flowers

bough /baʊ/ ***noun*** [C] (*formal*) one of the main branches of a tree

bought past tense, past participle of **buy¹**

boulder /ˈbəʊldə(r)/ ***noun*** [C] a very large rock

boulevard /ˈbuːləvɑːd/ ***noun*** [C] a wide street in a city, often with trees on each side

bounce /baʊns/ ***verb*** **1** [I,T] (used about a ball, etc.) to move away quickly after it has hit a hard surface; to make a ball do this: *The stone bounced off the wall and hit her on the head.* ◇ *A small boy came down the street, bouncing a ball.* **2** [I] to jump up and down continuously: *The children were bouncing on their beds.* **3** [I,T] (FINANCE) (used about a cheque) to be returned by a bank without payment because there is not enough money in the account **4** [I,T] ~ **(sth) (back)** (COMPUTING) if an email **bounces** or the system **bounces** it, it returns to the person who sent it because the system cannot deliver it ▶ **bounce** ***noun*** [C, U]

PHRV **bounce back** to become healthy, successful or happy again after an illness, a failure or a disappointment

bouncer /ˈbaʊnsə(r)/ ***noun*** [C] a person who is employed to stand at the entrance to a club, pub, etc. to stop people who are not wanted from going in, and to throw out people who are causing trouble inside

bouncy /ˈbaʊnsi/ ***adj.*** **1** that BOUNCES well or that can make things BOUNCE: *a bouncy ball/surface* **2** (used about a person) full of energy; lively: *She's a very bouncy person.*

bound¹ 🔑 /baʊnd/ ***adj.*** (not *before* a noun) **1** ~ **to do sth** certain to do sth: *You've done so much work that you're bound to pass the exam.* ➲ note at **certain** **2** having a legal or moral duty to do sth: *The company is bound by UK employment law.* ◇ *She felt bound to refuse the offer.* **3** ~ **(for...)** travelling to a particular place: *a ship bound for Australia*

IDM **bound up with sth** very closely connected with sth

bound² /baʊnd/ ***verb*** [I] to run quickly with long steps: *She bounded out of the house to meet us.* ▶ **bound** ***noun*** [C]: *With a couple of bounds he had crossed the room.*

bound³ past tense, past participle of **bind¹**

boundary /ˈbaʊndri/ ***noun*** [C] (*pl.* **boundaries**) a real or imagined line that marks the limits of sth and divides it from other places or things: *The main road is the boundary between the two districts.* ◇ *Scientists continue to push back the boundaries of human knowledge.*

boundless /ˈbaʊndləs/ ***adj.*** having no limit: *boundless energy*

bounds /baʊndz/ ***noun*** [pl.] limits that cannot or should not be passed: *Price rises must be kept within reasonable bounds.*

IDM **out of bounds** not to be entered by sb: *This area is out of bounds to all staff.*

bouquet /buˈkeɪ/ ***noun*** [C] a bunch of flowers that is arranged in an attractive way

bourbon /ˈbɜːbən/ ***noun*** [C,U] a type of WHISKY (= strong alcoholic drink) that is made mainly in the US

the bourgeoisie /ˌbʊəʒwɑːˈziː/ ***noun*** [sing., with sing. or pl. verb] (SOCIAL STUDIES) a class of people in society who are interested mainly in having more money and a higher social position ▶ **bourgeois** /ˈbʊəʒwɑː/ ***adj.***: *bourgeois attitudes/ideas/values*

bout /baʊt/ ***noun*** [C] **1** a short period of great activity: *a bout of hard work* **2** (HEALTH) a period of illness: *I'm just recovering from a bout of flu.*

boutique /buːˈtiːk/ ***noun*** [C] a small shop that sells fashionable clothes or expensive presents

bovine /ˈbəʊvaɪn/ ***adj.*** (AGRICULTURE) connected with cows: *bovine diseases*

bow¹ /baʊ/ ***verb*** **1** [I,T] ~ **(sth) (to sb)** to bend your head or the upper part of your body forward and down, as a sign of respect: *The speaker bowed to the guests and left the stage.* ◇ *He bowed his head respectfully.* **2** [I] ~ **to sth** to accept sth: *I do not think the unions should bow to pressure from the Government.*

PHRV **bow out (of sth/as sth)** to leave an important position or stop taking part in sth: *After a long and successful career, she has decided to bow out of politics.* ◇ *He finally bowed out as chairman after ten years.*

bow² /baʊ/ ***noun*** [C] **1** an act of **bowing¹**(1): *The director of the play came on stage to* ***take a bow.*** **2** the front part of a ship ➲ look at **stern**

bow³ /bəʊ/ ***noun*** [C] **1** a knot with two LOOPS and two loose ends which is used for decoration on clothes, in hair, etc. or for tying shoes: *He tied his laces* ***in a bow.*** **2** a weapon used for shooting arrows, consisting of a long curved piece of wood with a tight string joining its ends: *He was armed with a* ***bow and arrow.*** **3** a long thin piece of wood with string stretched across it that you use for playing some musical instruments: *a violin bow*

bowel /ˈbaʊəl/ ***noun*** [C, usually pl.] (**ANATOMY**) one of the tubes that carries waste food away from your stomach to the place where it leaves your body

ˈ**bowel movement** ***noun*** [C] (**HEALTH**) an act of emptying waste material from the **bowels**; the waste material that is emptied

bowl¹ /bəʊl/ ***noun*** [C] **1** a deep round dish without a lid that is used for holding food or liquid: *a soup bowl* **2** the amount of sth that is in a bowl: *I usually have a bowl of cereal for breakfast.* **3** a large plastic container that is used for washing dishes, washing clothes, etc.

bowl² /bəʊl/ ***verb*** [I,T] (**SPORT**) (in the game of CRICKET) to throw the ball in the direction of the person holding the BAT

PHR V **bowl sb over 1** to knock sb down when you are moving quickly **2** to surprise sb very much in a pleasant way

bow legs /ˌbəʊ ˈlegz/ ***noun*** [pl.] legs that curve out at the knees ▶ **bow-legged** /ˌbəʊ ˈlegɪd/ ***adj.***

bowler /ˈbəʊlə(r)/ ***noun*** [C] **1** (*also* ˌ**bowler ˈhat**, *AmE* **derby**) a round hard black hat, usually worn by men **2** (**SPORT**) (in the game of CRICKET) the player who BOWLS the ball in the direction of the person holding the BAT

bowling /ˈbəʊlɪŋ/ ***noun*** [U] (**SPORT**) a game in which you roll a heavy ball down a special track (**a lane**) towards a group of wooden objects (**pins**) and try to knock them all down: *to go bowling*

bowls /bəʊlz/ ***noun*** [U] (**SPORT**) a game in which you try to roll large wooden balls as near as possible to a smaller ball: *to play bowls*

bow tie /ˌbəʊ ˈtaɪ/ ***noun*** [C] a tie in the shape of a BOW³ (1), that is worn by men, especially on formal occasions

box¹ /bɒks/ ***noun*** **1** [C] a square or RECTANGULAR container for solid objects. A box often has a lid: *a cardboard box* ◇ *a shoebox* **2** [C] a box and the things inside it: *a box of chocolates/matches/tissues* **3** [C] an empty square or rectangular space on a form in which you have to write sth: *Write your name in the box below.* **4** [C] a small ENCLOSED area that is used for a particular purpose: ***a telephone box*** ◇ ***the witness box*** (= in a court of law) **5 the box** [sing.] (*BrE, informal*) television: *What's on the box tonight?*

box² /bɒks/ ***verb*** **1** (**SPORT**) [I,T] to fight in the sport of BOXING **2** [T] to put sth into a box: *a boxed set of DVDs*

PHR V **box sb/sth in** to prevent sb/sth from getting out of a small space: *Someone parked behind us and boxed us in.*

boxer /ˈbɒksə(r)/ ***noun*** [C] (**SPORT**) a person who does BOXING as a sport

ˈ**boxer shorts** (*also* **boxers**, *AmE also* **shorts**) ***noun*** [pl.] men's UNDERPANTS similar to the SHORTS worn by BOXERS

boxing /ˈbɒksɪŋ/ ***noun*** [U] (**SPORT**) a sport in which two people fight by hitting each other with their hands inside large gloves: *the world middleweight boxing champion* ◇ *boxing gloves* ➲ picture at **sport**

ˈ**Boxing Day** ***noun*** [C] (*BrE*) the day after Christmas Day; 26 December (a public holiday in England and Wales)

ˈ**box number** ***noun*** [C] a number used as an address, especially in newspaper advertisements

ˈ**box office** ***noun*** [C] the place in a cinema, theatre, etc. where the tickets are sold

boy /bɔɪ/ ***noun*** [C] a male child or a young man: *They've got three children – two boys and a girl.* ◇ *I used to play here when I was a boy.*

boycott /ˈbɔɪkɒt/ ***verb*** [T] to refuse to buy things from a particular company, take part in an event, etc. because you strongly disapprove of it: *Several countries boycotted the Olympic Games in protest.* ▶ **boycott** ***noun*** [C]: *a boycott of the local elections*

boyfriend /ˈbɔɪfrend/ ***noun*** [C] a man or boy with whom a person has a romantic and/or sexual relationship

boyhood /ˈbɔɪhʊd/ ***noun*** [U] the time of being a boy: *My father told me some of his boyhood memories.*

boyish /ˈbɔɪɪʃ/ ***adj.*** like a boy: *a boyish smile*

ˌ**Boy ˈScout** = SCOUT (1)

bps /ˌbiː piː ˈes/ ***abbr.*** (**COMPUTING**) **bits per second**; a measure of the speed at which data is sent or received

bra /brɑː/ ***noun*** [C] a piece of clothing that women wear under their other clothes to support their breasts

brace¹ /breɪs/ ***noun*** **1** [C] (*AmE* **braces** [pl.]) a metal frame that is fixed to a child's teeth in order to make them straight **2 braces** (*AmE* **suspenders**) [pl.] a pair of STRAPS that go over your shoulders to hold your trousers up

brace² /breɪs/ ***verb*** [T] **~ sth/yourself (for sth)** to prepare yourself for sth unpleasant: *You'd better brace yourself for some bad news.*

bracelet /ˈbreɪslət/ ***noun*** [C] a piece of jewellery, for example a metal chain or band, that you wear around your wrist or arm

bracing /ˈbreɪsɪŋ/ ***adj.*** making you feel healthy and full of energy: *bracing sea air*

bracken /ˈbrækən/ ***noun*** [U] a type of plant (**fern**) that grows thickly on hills and in woods ➲ look at **fern**

bracket¹ /ˈbrækɪt/ ***noun*** [C] **1** [usually pl.] (*especially AmE* **parenthesis**) one of two marks, ( ) or [ ], that you put round extra information in a piece of writing: *A translation of each word is given* ***in brackets***. **2 age, income, price, etc. ~** prices, ages, etc. which are between two limits: *to be in a high income bracket* **3** a piece of metal or wood that is fixed to a wall and used as a support for a shelf, lamp, etc.

bracket² /ˈbrækɪt/ ***verb*** [T] **1** to put BRACKETS¹ (1) round a word, number, etc. **2 ~ A and B (together)**; **~ A with B** to think of two or more people or things as similar in some way

brackish /ˈbrækɪʃ/ ***adj.*** (used about water) salty in an unpleasant way: *brackish lakes/lagoons/marshes*

brag /bræg/ ***verb*** [I] (**bragging**; **bragged**) **~ (to sb) (about/of sth)** to talk too proudly about sth: *She's always bragging to her friends about how clever she is.*

braid /breɪd/ ***noun*** **1** [U] thin coloured rope that is used to decorate military uniforms, etc. **2** [C] (*AmE*) = PLAIT

Braille /breɪl/ ***noun*** [U] a system of printing, using little round marks that are higher than the level of the paper they are on and which blind people can read by touching them: *The signs were written* ***in Braille***.

brain /breɪn/ ***noun*** **1** [C] (**ANATOMY**) the part of your body inside your head that controls your thoughts, feelings and movements: *He suffered serious brain damage in a road accident.* ◇ *a brain surgeon* ➲ picture on **page 80** **2** [C,U] the ability to think clearly; intelligence: *She has a very quick brain and learns fast.* ◇ *He hasn't got the brains to be a* *doctor.* **3** [C] (*informal*) a very clever person: *He's one of the best brains in the country.* **4 the brains** [sing.] the person who plans or organizes sth: *She's the real brains in the organization.*

IDM **have sth on the brain** (*informal*) to think about sth all the time

rack your brains → RACK²

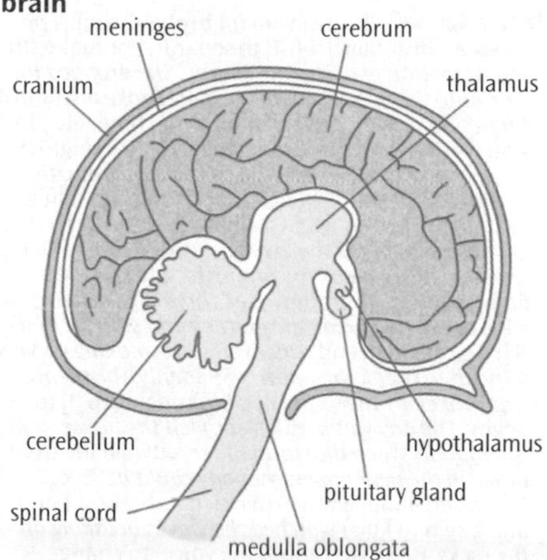

brainchild /'breɪntʃaɪld/ ***noun*** [sing.] the idea or invention of a particular person

'brain-dead ***adj.*** **1** (HEALTH) having serious brain damage and needing a machine to stay alive **2** (*informal*) unable to think clearly; stupid

'brain drain ***noun*** [sing.] (*informal*) (SOCIAL STUDIES) the movement of highly skilled and educated people to a country where they can work in better conditions and earn more money

brainless /'breɪnləs/ ***adj.*** (*informal*) very silly; stupid

brainstem /'breɪnstem/ ***noun*** [C] (ANATOMY) the part of the brain that joins the SPINAL CORD to the CEREBELLUM and the CEREBRUM

brainstorm¹ /'breɪnstɔːm/ ***noun*** [C] **1** a moment of sudden confusion: ***I had a brainstorm** in the exam and couldn't answer any questions.* **2** (*AmE*) = BRAINWAVE

brainstorm² /'breɪnstɔːm/ ***verb*** [I,T] to solve a problem or make a decision by thinking of as many ideas as possible in a short time: *We'll spend five minutes brainstorming ideas on how we can raise money.*

'brain-teaser ***noun*** [C] a problem that is difficult but fun to solve

brainwash /'breɪnwɒʃ/ ***verb*** [T] **~ sb (into doing sth)** to force sb to believe sth by using strong mental pressure: *Television advertisements try to brainwash people into buying things that they don't need.*
▶ **brainwashing** ***noun*** [U]

brainwave /'breɪnweɪv/ (*AmE*) (*also* **brainstorm**) ***noun*** [C] (*informal*) a sudden clever idea: *If I have a brainwave, I'll let you know.*

brainy /'breɪni/ ***adj.*** (*informal*) intelligent

braise /breɪz/ ***verb*** [T] to cook meat or vegetables slowly in a little liquid in a covered dish

brake¹ /breɪk/ ***noun*** [C] **1** the part of a vehicle that makes it go slower or stop: *She put her foot on the brake and just managed to stop in time.* **2** something that makes sth else slow down or stop: *The Government must try to **put a brake on** inflation.*

brake² /breɪk/ ***verb*** [I] to make a vehicle go slower or stop by using the BRAKES: *If the driver hadn't braked in time, the car would have hit me.*

'brake light (*AmE also* **'stop light**) ***noun*** [C] a red light on the back of a vehicle that comes on when the BRAKES are used

bramble /'bræmbl/ ***noun*** [C] (*especially BrE*) a wild bush on which BLACKBERRIES grow

bran /bræn/ ***noun*** [U] the brown outer covering of grains that is left when the grain is made into flour

branch¹ 🔑 /brɑːntʃ/ ***noun*** [C] **1** (BIOLOGY) one of the main parts of a tree that grows out of the thick central part (**trunk**) ➲ picture at **tree** **2** (BUSINESS) a local office or shop belonging to a large company or organization: *The company has branches in Paris and New York.* **3** a part of a government or other large organization that deals with one particular aspect of its work SYN **department**: *the anti-terrorist branch* **4** a division of an area of knowledge or a group of languages: *Psychiatry is a branch of medicine.* **5** a smaller or less important part of a river, road, railway, etc. that leads away from the main part: *a branch of the Rhine*

branch² /brɑːntʃ/ ***verb***

PHR V **branch off** (used about a road) to leave a larger road and go off in another direction: *A bit further on, the road branches off to the left.*

branch out (into sth) to start doing sth new and different from the things you usually do

brand¹ 🔑 /brænd/ ***noun*** [C] **1** (BUSINESS) the name of a product that is made by a particular company: *a well-known brand of coffee* **2** a particular type of sth: *a strange brand of humour*

brand² /brænd/ ***verb*** [T] **1** to mark a farm animal with a hot iron to show who it belongs to **2 ~ sb (as sth)** to say that sb has a bad character so that people have a bad opinion of them: *She was branded as a troublemaker after she complained about her long working hours.*

branding /'brændɪŋ/ ***noun*** [U] (BUSINESS) the activity of giving a particular name and image to goods and services so that people will be attracted to them and want to buy them

'branding iron ***noun*** [C] a metal tool that is heated and used for marking farm animals to show who they belong to

brandish /'brændɪʃ/ ***verb*** [T] to wave sth in the air in an aggressive or excited way: *The robber was brandishing a knife.*

,brand 'loyalty ***noun*** [U,C] (BUSINESS) the support that people give to a particular BRAND by continuing to buy it rather than changing to a product made by another company: *to build/develop brand loyalty* ◊ *powerful/strong brand loyalty*

'brand name (*also* **'trade name**) ***noun*** [C] (BUSINESS) the name given to a product by the company that produces it

,brand 'new ***adj.*** completely new

brandy /'brændi/ ***noun*** [C,U] (*pl.* **brandies**) a strong alcoholic drink that is made from wine

brash /bræʃ/ ***adj.*** too confident and direct: *Her brash manner makes her unpopular with strangers.*
▶ **brashness** ***noun*** [U]

brass /brɑːs/ ***noun*** **1** [U] a hard yellow metal that is a mixture of COPPER and ZINC: *brass buttons on a uniform* **2** [sing., with sing. or pl. verb] (MUSIC) the group of musical instruments that are made of brass

brat /bræt/ ***noun*** [C] a child who behaves badly and annoys you

bravado /brəˈvɑːdəʊ/ ***noun*** [U] a confident way of behaving that is intended to impress people, sometimes as a way of hiding a lack of confidence

brave[1] /breɪv/ ***adj.*** **1** ready to do things that are dangerous or difficult without showing fear: *the brave soldiers who fought in the war* ◇ *'This may hurt a little, so try and be brave,' said the dentist.* **2** needing or showing courage: *a brave decision* ▶ **bravely** ***adv.***: *The men bravely defended the town for three days.*

IDM **put on a brave face; put a brave face on sth** to pretend that you feel confident and happy when you do not

brave[2] /breɪv/ ***verb*** [T] to face sth unpleasant, dangerous or difficult without showing fear

bravery /ˈbreɪvəri/ ***noun*** [U] actions that are brave: *After the war he received a medal for bravery.*

bravo /ˌbrɑːˈvəʊ/ ***exclamation*** a word that people shout to show that they have enjoyed sth that sb has done, for example a play

brawl /brɔːl/ ***noun*** [C] a noisy fight among a group of people, usually in a public place ▶ **brawl** ***verb*** [I]: *We saw some football fans brawling in the street.*

brawn /brɔːn/ ***noun*** [U] physical strength: *To do this kind of job you need more brawn than brain* (= you need to be strong rather than clever). ▶ **brawny** ***adj.***

braze /breɪz/ ***verb*** [T] (CHEMISTRY) to join pieces of metal using a mixture of metals which is heated and melted

brazen /ˈbreɪzn/ ***adj.*** without embarrassment, especially in a way which shocks people: *Don't believe a word she says – she's a brazen liar!* ▶ **brazenly** ***adv.***

brazil /brəˈzɪl/ (*also* **braˈzil nut**) ***noun*** [C] a nut that we eat that has a very hard shell

breach[1] /briːtʃ/ ***noun*** **1** [C,U] ~ **(of sth)** (LAW) an act that breaks an agreement, a law, etc.: *Giving private information about clients is a breach of confidence.* ◇ *The company was found to be* ***in breach of*** *contract.* **2** [C] a break in friendly relations between people, groups, etc.: *The incident caused a breach between the two countries.* **3** [C] an opening in a wall, etc. that defends or protects sb/sth: *The waves made a breach in the sea wall.*

breach[2] /briːtʃ/ ***verb*** [T] **1** (LAW) to break an agreement, a law, etc.: *He accused the Government of breaching international law.* **2** to make an opening in a wall, etc. that defends or protects sb/sth

bread /bred/ ***noun*** [U] a type of food made from flour and water mixed together and baked in an oven. YEAST is usually added to make the bread rise: *a piece/slice of bread* ◇ *a loaf of bread* ◇ *white/brown/wholemeal bread*

breadcrumbs /ˈbredkrʌmz/ ***noun*** [pl.] very small bits of bread that are used in cooking

the breadline /ˈbredlaɪn/ ***noun*** [sing.] the level of INCOME (= the amount of money sb has to live on) of very poor people: *They are living* ***on the breadline*** (= are very poor).

breadth /bredθ/ ***noun*** **1** [C,U] the distance between the two sides of sth: *We measured the length and breadth of the garden.* SYN **width** **2** [U] the wide variety of things, subjects, etc. that sth includes: *I was amazed by the breadth of her knowledge.* ➲ adjective **broad**

IDM **the length and breadth of sth** → LENGTH

breadwinner /ˈbredwɪnə(r)/ ***noun*** [C, usually sing.] the person who earns most of the money that their family needs: *When his dad died, Steve became the breadwinner.*

break[1] /breɪk/ ***verb*** (*pt* **broke** /brəʊk/; *pp* **broken** /ˈbrəʊkən/) **1** [I,T] to separate, or make sth separate, into two or more pieces: *She dropped the vase onto the floor and it broke.* ◇ *He broke his leg in a car accident.* **2** [I,T] (used about a machine, etc.) to stop working; to stop a machine, etc. working: *The photocopier has broken.* ◇ *Be careful with my camera – I don't want you to break it.* **3** [T] to do sth that is against the law, or against what has been agreed or promised: *to break the law/rules/speed limit* ◇ *Don't worry – I never break my promises.* **4** [I,T] to stop doing sth for a short time: *Let's break for coffee now.* ◇ *We decided to break the journey and stop for lunch.* **5** [T] to make sth end: *Once you start smoking it's very difficult to* ***break the habit***. ◇ *Suddenly, the silence was broken by the sound of a bird singing.* **6** [I] to begin: *The day was breaking as I left the house.* ◇ *We ran indoors when the storm broke.* ◇ *When the story broke in the newspapers, nobody could believe it.* **7** [I] (used about a wave) to reach its highest point and begin to fall: *I watched the waves breaking on the rocks.* **8** [I] (used about the voice) to change suddenly: *Most boys' voices break when they are 13 or 14 years old.* ◇ *His voice was breaking with emotion as he spoke.*

PHR V **break away (from sb/sth)** **1** to escape suddenly from sb who is holding you **2** (POLITICS) to leave a political party, state, etc. in order to form a new one

break down **1** (used about a vehicle or machine) to stop working: *Akram's car broke down on the way to work this morning.* **2** (used about a system, discussion, etc.) to fail: *Talks between the two countries have completely broken down.* **3** to lose control of your feelings and start crying: *He broke down and cried when he heard the news.* **4** to divide into parts to be analysed: *Costs for the project break down as follows: wages $20m, plant $4m, raw materials $5m.* ➲ noun **breakdown**

break sth down **1** to destroy sth by using force: *The police had to break down the door to get into the house.* **2** (CHEMISTRY) to make a substance separate into parts or change into a different form in a chemical process: *Food is broken down in our bodies by the digestive system.* ➲ noun **breakdown**

3 to divide sth into parts in order to analyse it or make it easier to do: *Each lesson is broken down into several units.* ➲ noun **breakdown**

break in to enter a building by force, usually in order to steal sth

break in (on sth) to interrupt when sb else is speaking: *The waiter broke in on our conversation to tell me I had a phone call.*

break into sth **1** to enter a place that is closed: *Thieves broke into his car and stole the radio.* ◇ (*figurative*): *The company is trying to break into the Japanese market.* **2** to start doing sth suddenly: *to break into song/a run*

break off to suddenly stop doing or saying sth: *He started speaking and then broke off in the middle of a sentence.*

break (sth) off to remove a part of sth by force; to be removed in this way: *Could you break off another bit of chocolate for me?*

break sth off to end a relationship suddenly: *After*

a bad argument, they decided to ***break off*** *their* ***engagement****.*
break out (used about fighting, wars, fires, etc.) to start suddenly
break out in sth (HEALTH) to suddenly have a skin problem: *to break out in spots/a rash*
break out (of sth) to escape from a prison, etc.
break through (sth) to manage to get past sth that is stopping you
break up 1 to separate into smaller pieces: *The ship broke up on the rocks.* **2** (used about events that involve a group of people) to end or finish: *The meeting broke up just before lunch.* **3** (*BrE*) (EDUCATION) to start school holidays: *When do you break up for the summer holidays?*
break sth up 1 to make sth separate into parts **2** to make people leave sth or stop doing sth, especially by using force: *The police arrived and broke up the fight.*
break up (with sb) to end a relationship with a wife, husband, girlfriend or boyfriend
break with sth to end a relationship or connection with sb/sth: *to break with tradition/the past*

break² ⊶ /breɪk/ **noun** [C] **1** a place where sth has been broken: *a break in a pipe* **2** an opening or space in sth: *Wait for a break in the traffic before you cross the road.* **3** a short period of rest: *We worked all day without a break.* ◇ *to* ***take a break*** **4** (TOURISM) a short holiday: *We had a* ***weekend break*** *in New York.* ◇ *a well-earned break* **5** ~ **(in sth)**; ~ **(with sb/sth)** a change from what usually happens or an end to sth: *The incident led to a break in diplomatic relations.* ◇ *She wanted to make a complete break with the past.* **6** (*informal*) a piece of good luck: *to* ***give sb a break*** (= to help sb by giving them a chance to be successful)
IDM **break of day** the time when light first appears in the morning SYN **dawn**
give sb a break 1 used to tell sb to stop saying things that are annoying or not true: *Give me a break and stop nagging, OK!* **2** (*especially AmE*) to be fair to sb

breakage /ˈbreɪkɪdʒ/ **noun** [C, usually pl.] something that has been broken: *Customers must pay for any breakages.*

breakaway /ˈbreɪkəweɪ/ **adj.** (only *before* a noun) (POLITICS) (used about a political group, an organization, or a part of a country) that has separated from a larger group or country ▶ **breakaway noun** [C]

breakdown /ˈbreɪkdaʊn/ **noun** [C] **1** a time when a vehicle, machine, etc. stops working: *I hope we don't* ***have a breakdown*** *on the motorway.* **2** the failure or end of sth: *The breakdown of the talks means that a strike is likely.* **3** (HEALTH) = NERVOUS BREAKDOWN **4** a list of all the details of sth: *I would like a full breakdown of how the money was spent.*

ˈ**breakdown truck** (*AmE* ˈ**tow truck**) **noun** [C] a lorry that is used to take away cars that need to be repaired

breaker /ˈbreɪkə(r)/ **noun** [C] a large wave covered with white bubbles that is moving towards the beach

breakfast ⊶ /ˈbrekfəst/ **noun** [C,U] the meal which you have when you get up in the morning: *to* ***have breakfast*** ◇ *What do you usually have* ***for breakfast****?* ◇ *to eat a big breakfast*

CULTURE

In a hotel an **English** breakfast means cereal, fried eggs, bacon, sausages, tomatoes, toast, etc. A **continental** breakfast means bread and jam with coffee.

ˈ**break-in** **noun** [C] the act of entering a building by force, especially in order to steal sth

breakneck /ˈbreɪknek/ **adj.** (only *before* a noun) very fast and dangerous: *He drove her to the hospital* ***at breakneck speed****.*

breakthrough /ˈbreɪkθruː/ **noun** [C] **a ~ (in sth)** an important discovery or development: *Scientists are hoping to* ***make a breakthrough*** *in cancer research.*

ˈ**break-up** **noun** [C] **1** the end of a relationship between two people: *the break-up of a marriage* **2** the separation of a group or organization into smaller parts

breakwater /ˈbreɪkwɔːtə(r)/ **noun** [C] a wall built out into the sea to protect the land from the force of the waves

bream /briːm/ **noun** [C,U] (*pl.* **bream**) a type of fish that can live in fresh or salt water and that you can eat

breast ⊶ /brest/ **noun** [C] **1** either of the two round soft parts at the front of a woman's body that produce milk when she has had a baby **2** a word used especially in literature for the top part of the front of your body, below the neck **3** the front part of the body of a bird **4** meat from the front part of the body of a bird or an animal

breastbone /ˈbrestbəʊn/ **noun** [C] (ANATOMY) the long flat bone in the middle of your chest that the seven top pairs of curved bones (**ribs**) are connected to SYN **sternum** ➲ picture on **page 80**

breastfeed /ˈbrestfiːd/ **verb** [I,T] (*pt, pp* **breastfed**) to feed a baby with milk from the breast

breaststroke /ˈbreststrəʊk/ **noun** [U] (SPORT) a style of swimming on your front in which you start with your hands together, push both arms forward and then move them out and back through the water: *to do (the) breaststroke* ➲ look at **backstroke**, **butterfly**, **crawl** ➲ picture at **swim**

breath ⊶ /breθ/ **noun 1** [U] the air that you take into and blow out of your lungs: *to* ***have bad breath*** (= breath which smells unpleasant) **2** [C] an act of taking air into or blowing air out of your lungs: *Take a few deep breaths before you start running.*
IDM **a breath of fresh air** the clean air which you breathe outside, especially when compared to the air inside a room or building: *Let's go for a walk. I need a breath of fresh air.* ◇ (*figurative*): *James's happy face is like a breath of fresh air in that miserable place.*
catch your breath → CATCH¹
get your breath (again/back) to rest after physical exercise so that your breathing returns to normal
hold your breath to stop breathing for a short time, for example when you are swimming or because of fear or excitement
(be/get) out of/short of breath (to be/start) breathing very quickly, for example after physical exercise
say sth, speak, etc. under your breath to say sth very quietly, usually because you do not want people to hear you
take your breath away to surprise sb very much ➲ adjective **breathtaking**
take a deep breath → DEEP¹
with bated breath → BATED

breathalyse (*AmE* **breathalyze**) /ˈbreθəlaɪz/ **verb** [T] to check how much alcohol a driver has drunk by making him or her breathe into a BREATHALYSER (= a special machine): *Both drivers were breathalysed at the scene of the accident.*

breathe ⊶ /briːð/ *verb* [I,T] to take air, etc. into your lungs and blow it out again: ***Breathe out*** *as you lift the weight and* ***breathe in*** *as you lower it.* ◇ *I hate having to breathe (in) other people's cigarette smoke.*

IDM **not breathe a word (of/about sth) (to sb)** to not tell sb about sth that is secret

breather /ˈbriːðə(r)/ *noun* [C] (*informal*) a short rest: *to* ***have /take a breather***

breathing ⊶ /ˈbriːðɪŋ/ *noun* [U] the action of taking air into the lungs and sending it out again: *heavy/irregular breathing* ◇ *These deep breathing exercises will help you relax.* ◇ *Heavy* (= loud) *breathing was all I could hear.*

breathless /ˈbreθləs/ *adj.* **1** (HEALTH) having difficulty breathing: *I was hot and breathless when I got to the top of the hill.* **2** not able to breathe because you are so excited, frightened, etc.: *to be breathless with excitement* ▶ **breathlessly** *adv.*

breathtaking /ˈbreθteɪkɪŋ/ *adj.* extremely surprising, beautiful, etc.: *breathtaking scenery*

ˈbreath test *noun* [C] a test by the police on the breath of a driver to measure how much alcohol they have drunk

breed[1] ⊶ /briːd/ *verb* (*pt, pp* **bred** /bred/) **1** [I] (BIOLOGY) (used about animals) to have sex and produce young animals: *Many animals won't breed in zoos.* SYN **mate 2** [T] (AGRICULTURE) to keep animals or plants in order to produce young from them: *These cattle are bred to produce high yields of milk.* **3** [T] to cause sth: *This kind of thinking breeds intolerance.* ▶ **breeding** *noun* [U]: *the breeding of horses*

breed[2] ⊶ /briːd/ *noun* [C] a particular variety of an animal: *a breed of cattle/dog*

breeder /ˈbriːdə(r)/ *noun* [C] a person who breeds animals or plants: *a dog breeder*

ˈbreeding ground *noun* [C] **1** a place where wild animals go to breed **2** a place where sth can develop: *a breeding ground for crime*

breeze[1] /briːz/ *noun* [C] a light wind: *A warm breeze was blowing.*

breeze[2] /briːz/ *verb* [I] ~ **along, in, out, etc.** to move in a confident and relaxed way: *He just breezed in twenty minutes late without a word of apology.*

breezy /ˈbriːzi/ *adj.* **1** with a little wind **2** happy and relaxed: *You're bright and breezy this morning!*

breve /briːv/ *noun* [C] (MUSIC) a note that lasts as long as eight CROTCHETS, which is rarely used in modern music

brevity AW /ˈbrevəti/ *noun* [U] the state of being short or quick: *The report is a masterpiece of brevity.* ➲ adjective **brief**

brew /bruː/ *verb* **1** [T] to make beer **2** [T] to make a drink of tea or coffee by adding hot water: *to brew a pot of tea* **3** [I] (used about tea) to stand in hot water before it is ready to drink: *Leave it to brew for a few minutes.*

IDM **be brewing** (used about sth bad) to develop or grow: *There's* ***trouble brewing.***

brewery /ˈbruːəri/ *noun* [C] (*pl.* **breweries**) a place where beer is made

bribe /braɪb/ *noun* [C] money, etc. that is given to sb such as an official to persuade them to do sth to help you that is wrong or dishonest: *to* ***accept/take bribes*** ▶ **bribe** *verb* [T] ~ **sb (with sth)**: *They got a visa by bribing an official.* ▶ **bribery** /ˈbraɪbəri/ *noun* [U]

bric-a-brac /ˈbrɪk ə bræk/ *noun* [U] small items of little value, for decoration in a house

brick ⊶ /brɪk/ *noun* [C,U] a hard block of baked CLAY that is used for building houses, etc.: *a lorry carrying bricks* ◇ *a house built of red brick* ➲ picture at **building**

bricklayer /ˈbrɪkleɪə(r)/ *noun* [C] a person whose job is to build walls with bricks

brickwork /ˈbrɪkwɜːk/ *noun* [U] (ARCHITECTURE) the part of a building that is made of bricks

bridal /ˈbraɪdl/ *adj.* (only *before* a noun) connected with a BRIDE

bride /braɪd/ *noun* [C] a woman on or just before her wedding day: *a* ***bride-to-be*** (= a woman whose wedding is soon)

bridegroom /ˈbraɪdɡruːm/ (*also* **groom**) *noun* [C] a man on or just before his wedding day

bridesmaid /ˈbraɪdzmeɪd/ *noun* [C] a woman or girl who helps a woman on her wedding day (**the bride**)

bridge[1] ⊶ /brɪdʒ/ *noun* **1** [C] a structure that carries a road or railway across a river, valley, road or railway: *a bridge over the River Danube* **2** [sing.] the high part of a ship where the captain and the people who control the ship stand **3** [U] a card game for four people

bridge[2] /brɪdʒ/ *verb* [T] to build a bridge over sth

IDM **bridge a/the gap** to fill a space between two people, groups or things or to bring them closer together

bridle /ˈbraɪdl/ *noun* [C] the leather STRAPS that you put on a horse's head so that you can control it when you are riding it

brief[1] ⊶ AW /briːf/ *adj.* short or quick: *a brief description* ◇ *Please be brief. We don't have much time.* ➲ noun **brevity**

IDM **in brief** using only a few words: *In brief, the meeting was a disaster.*

brief[2] AW /briːf/ *noun* [C] **1** (*BrE*) the instructions that a person is given explaining what their job is and what their duties are: *He was* ***given the brief*** *of improving the image of the organization.* **2** (*BrE*) (LAW) a legal case that is given to a lawyer to argue in court; a piece of work for a BARRISTER **3** (*AmE*) (LAW) a written summary of the facts that support one side of a legal case, that will be presented to a court **4** (*BrE, informal*) (LAW) a SOLICITOR or a defence lawyer: *I want to see my brief.*

brief[3] AW /briːf/ *verb* [T] to give sb information about sth so that they are prepared to deal with it: *The minister has been fully briefed on what questions to expect.* ➲ look at **debrief**

briefcase /ˈbriːfkeɪs/ *noun* [C] a flat case that you use for carrying papers, etc., especially when you go to work

briefing /ˈbriːfɪŋ/ *noun* [C,U] instructions or information that you are given before sth happens: *a press/news briefing* (= where information is given to journalists)

briefly ⊶ AW /ˈbriːfli/ *adv.* **1** for a short time; quickly: *She glanced briefly at the letter.* **2** using only a few words: *I'd like to comment very briefly on that last statement.*

briefs /briːfs/ *noun* [pl.] pants for men or women

brigade /brɪˈɡeɪd/ ***noun*** [C] **1** a unit of soldiers in the army **2** a group of people who work together for a particular purpose: *the fire brigade*

brigadier /ˌbrɪɡəˈdɪə(r)/ ***noun*** [C] an important officer in the army

bright 🔑 /braɪt/ ***adj.*** **1** having a lot of light: *a bright, sunny day* ◇ *eyes bright with happiness* **2** (used about a colour) strong and easy to see: *a bright yellow jumper* **3** clever, or able to learn things quickly: *a bright child* ◇ *a* ***bright idea*** **4** likely to be pleasant or successful: *The future looks bright.* **5** happy; cheerful ▸ **brightness** ***noun*** [U] ▸ **brightly** ***adv.***: *brightly-coloured clothes*
IDM **look on the bright side** → LOOK[1]

brighten /ˈbraɪtn/ ***verb*** [I,T] ~ **(sth) (up)** to become brighter or happier; to make sth brighter: *His face brightened when he saw her.* ◇ *to brighten up sb's day* (= make it happier)

brilliant 🔑 /ˈbrɪliənt/ ***adj.*** **1** having a lot of light; very bright: *brilliant sunshine* **2** very clever, skilful or successful: *a brilliant young scientist* ◇ *That's a brilliant idea!* **3** (*informal*) very good: *That was a brilliant film!* ▸ **brilliance** ***noun*** [U] ▸ **brilliantly** ***adv.***

brim[1] /brɪm/ ***noun*** [C] **1** the top edge of a cup, glass, etc.: *The cup was full to the brim.* **2** the bottom part of a hat that is wider than the rest

brim[2] /brɪm/ ***verb*** [I] (**brimming**; **brimmed**) ~ **(with sth)** to be full of sth: *His eyes were brimming with tears.*
PHR V **brim over (with sth)** (used about a cup, glass, etc.) to have more liquid than it can hold: *The bowl was brimming over with water.* ◇ (*figurative*): *to be brimming over with health/happiness*

brine /braɪn/ ***noun*** [U] very salty water, used especially for keeping food fresh

bring 🔑 /brɪŋ/ ***verb*** [T] (*pt, pp* **brought** /brɔːt/) **1** to carry or take sb/sth to a place with you: *Is it all right if I bring a friend to the party?* ◇ *Could you bring us some water, please?* ◇ (*figurative*) *He will bring valuable skills and experience to the team.* ◇ *My sister went to Spain on holiday and brought me back a T-shirt.* **2** to move sth somewhere: *Louis brought a photo out of his wallet and showed it to us.* **3** to cause or result in sth: *The sight of her brought a smile to his face.* ◇ *Money doesn't always bring happiness.* **4** to cause sb/sth to be in a certain place or condition: *Their screams brought people running from all directions.* ◇ *Add water to the mixture and bring it to the boil.* ◇ *An injury can easily* ***bring*** *an athlete's career* ***to an end.*** **5** ~ **yourself to do sth** to force yourself to do sth: *The film was so horrible that I couldn't bring myself to watch it.*
PHR V **bring sth about** to cause sth to happen: *to bring about changes in people's lives*
bring sth back 1 to cause sth that existed before to be introduced again: *Nobody wants to bring back the days of child labour.* **2** to cause sb to remember sth: *The photographs brought back memories of his childhood.*
bring sb/sth down to defeat sb/sth; to make sb/sth lose a position of power: *to bring down the government*
bring sth down to make sth lower in level: *to bring down the price of sth*
bring sth forward 1 to move sth to an earlier time: *The date of the meeting has been brought forward by two weeks.* OPP **put sth back 2** to suggest sth for discussion
bring sb in to ask or employ sb to do a particular job: *A specialist was brought in to set up the new computer system.*
bring sth in to introduce sth: *The government have brought in a new law on dangerous dogs.*
bring sth off to manage to do sth difficult: *The team brought off an amazing victory.*
bring sth on to cause sth: *Her headaches are brought on by stress.*
bring sth out to produce sth or cause sth to appear: *When is the company bringing out its next new model?*
bring sb round to make sb become conscious again: *I splashed cold water on his face to try to bring him round.*
bring sb round (to sth) to persuade sb to agree with your opinion: *After a lot of discussion we finally brought them round to our point of view.*
bring sth round to sth to direct a conversation to a particular subject: *I finally brought the conversation round to the subject of money.*
bring sb up to look after a child until he/she is an adult and to teach him/her how to behave SYN **raise**: *After her parents were killed the child was brought up by her uncle.* ◇ *a well brought up child*
bring sth up 1 to be sick so that food that you have swallowed comes back out of your mouth; to VOMIT **2** to introduce sth into a discussion or conversation: *I intend to bring the matter up at the next meeting.*

brink /brɪŋk/ ***noun*** [sing.] **the ~ (of sth)** if you are on the **brink** of sth, you are almost in a very new, exciting or dangerous situation: *Just when the band were* ***on the brink*** *of becoming famous, they split up.*

brisk /brɪsk/ ***adj.*** **1** quick or using a lot of energy; busy: *They set off* ***at a brisk pace.*** ◇ *Trading has been brisk this morning.* **2** confident and practical; wanting to get things done quickly ▸ **briskly** ***adv.*** ▸ **briskness** ***noun*** [U]

bristle[1] /ˈbrɪsl/ ***noun*** [C] **1** a short thick hair: *The bristles on my chin hurt the baby's face.* **2** one of the short thick hairs of a brush

bristle[2] /ˈbrɪsl/ ***verb*** [I] **1** (used about hair or an animal's fur) to stand up straight because of fear, anger, cold, etc. **2** ~ **(with sth) (at sb/sth)** to show that you are angry
PHR V **bristle with sth** to be full of sth

Brit /brɪt/ ***noun*** [C] (*informal*) a British person

Britain /ˈbrɪtn/ (GEOGRAPHY) = GREAT BRITAIN ➲ note at **United Kingdom**

British /ˈbrɪtɪʃ/ ***adj.*** **1** of the United Kingdom (= Great Britain and Northern Ireland): *British industry* ◇ *to hold a British passport* **2 the British** ***noun*** [pl.] the people of the United Kingdom

Britisher /ˈbrɪtɪʃə(r)/ ***noun*** [C] (*old-fashioned*) (*AmE*) a person who comes from Great Britain

the ˌBritish ˈIsles ***noun*** [pl.] (GEOGRAPHY) Great Britain and Ireland with all the islands that are near their coasts ❶ The British Isles are only a geographical unit, not a political unit.

Briton /ˈbrɪtn/ ***noun*** [C] a person who comes from Great Britain

brittle /ˈbrɪtl/ ***adj.*** hard but easily broken: *The bones become brittle in old age.*

broach /brəʊtʃ/ ***verb*** [T] to start talking about a particular subject, especially one which is difficult or embarrassing: *How will you* ***broach the subject*** *of the money he owes us?*

ˈB-road ***noun*** [C] (in Britain) a road that is not as wide or important as a motorway or a main road (A-road)

broad ⊶ /brɔːd/ ***adj.*** **1** wide: *a broad street/river* ◇ *broad shoulders* ◇ *a broad smile* OPP **narrow** ➲ noun **breadth**
2 including many different people or things: *We sell a* ***broad range*** *of products.* **3** without a lot of detail; general: *I'll explain the new system* ***in broad terms.*** **4** if sb has a **broad accent**, you can hear very easily which area they come from SYN **strong**
IDM **(in) broad daylight** during the day, when it is easy to see

broadband /ˈbrɔːdbænd/ ***noun*** [U] **1** (**TECHNICAL**) signals that use a wide range of FREQUENCIES **2** (**COMPUTING**) a way of connecting a computer to the Internet, which allows you to receive information, including pictures, etc., very quickly: *We have broadband at home now.*

ˌbroad ˈbean ***noun*** [C] a type of large flat green BEAN that can be cooked and eaten

broadcast ⊶ /ˈbrɔːdkɑːst/ ***verb*** [I,T] (*pt, pp* **broadcast**) (**ARTS AND MEDIA**) to send out radio or television programmes: *The Olympics are* ***broadcast live*** *around the world.* ▶ **broadcast *noun*** [C]: *The next news broadcast is at 9 o'clock.* ▶ **broadcasting *noun*** [U]: *She works in broadcasting.*

broadcaster /ˈbrɔːdkɑːstə(r)/ ***noun*** [C] (**ARTS AND MEDIA**) a person who speaks on the radio or on television

broaden /ˈbrɔːdn/ ***verb*** [I,T] ~ **(sth) (out)** to become wider; to make sth wider: *The river broadens out beyond the bridge.* ◇ (*figurative*) *Travel* ***broadens the mind*** (= it makes you understand other people better).

broadly ⊶ /ˈbrɔːdli/ ***adv.*** **1** (used to describe a way of smiling) with a big, wide smile: *He smiled broadly as he shook everyone's hand.* **2** generally: ***Broadly speaking****, the scheme will work as follows...*

ˌbroad-ˈminded ***adj.*** happy to accept beliefs and ways of life that are different from your own OPP **narrow-minded**

broadsheet /ˈbrɔːdʃiːt/ ***noun*** [C] (**ARTS AND MEDIA**) a newspaper with long articles that is generally considered more serious than other newspapers ➲ look at **tabloid**

broccoli /ˈbrɒkəli/ ***noun*** [U] a vegetable with a thick STEM (= the main long part of a plant) and green or purple flower heads that can be cooked and eaten

brochure /ˈbrəʊʃə(r)/ ***noun*** [C] a small magazine or book containing pictures and information about sth or advertising sth: *a travel brochure*

broil /brɔɪl/ ***verb*** [T] (*especially AmE*) = GRILL[2] (1)

broke[1] past tense of **break[1]**

broke[2] /brəʊk/ ***adj.*** (not *before* a noun) (*informal*) having no money: *I can't come out tonight – I'm absolutely broke.*

broken[1] past participle of **break[1]**

broken[2] ⊶ /ˈbrəʊkən/ ***adj.*** **1** damaged or in pieces; not working: *The washing machine's broken.* ◇ *Watch out! There's broken glass on the floor.* ◇ *a broken leg* ◇ *How did the window* ***get broken****?* **2** (used about a promise or an agreement) not kept **3** not continuous; interrupted: *a broken line* ◇ *a broken night's sleep* **4** (used about a foreign language) spoken slowly with a lot of mistakes: *to speak in broken English*

ˌbroken-ˈdown ***adj.*** **1** in a very bad condition: *a broken-down old building* **2** (used about a vehicle) not working: *A broken-down bus was blocking the road.*

ˌbroken-ˈhearted = HEARTBROKEN

ˌbroken ˈhome ***noun*** [C] a family in which the parents do not live together, for example because they are divorced: *Many of the children came from broken homes.*

ˌbroken ˈmarriage ***noun*** [C] a marriage that has ended

broker[1] /ˈbrəʊkə(r)/ ***noun*** [C] (**BUSINESS, FINANCE**) a person who buys and sells things, for example shares in a business, for other people: *an insurance broker*

broker[2] /ˈbrəʊkə(r)/ ***verb*** [T] to arrange the details of an agreement, especially between different countries: *a peace plan brokered by the UN*

brolly /ˈbrɒli/ ***noun*** [C] (*pl.* **brollies**) (*BrE, informal*) = UMBRELLA

bromide /ˈbrəʊmaɪd/ ***noun*** [U] (**HEALTH**) a chemical which contains BROMINE, used in medicine, especially in the past, to make people feel calm

bromine /ˈbrəʊmiːn/ ***noun*** [U] (*symbol* **Br**) (**CHEMISTRY**) a dark red, poisonous gas with a strong smell ❶ For more information on the periodic table of elements, look at pages R34-5.

bronchial /ˈbrɒŋkiəl/ ***adj.*** (**ANATOMY**) connected with or affecting the two main branches of your WINDPIPE (**bronchial tubes**) leading to your lungs ➲ picture on **page 80**

bronchiole /ˈbrɒŋkiəʊl/ ***noun*** [C] (**ANATOMY**) one of many very small tubes connected to the BRONCHUS ➲ picture at **lung**

bronchitis /brɒŋˈkaɪtɪs/ ***noun*** [U] (**HEALTH**) an illness of the tubes leading to the lungs (**bronchial tubes**) that causes a very bad cough

bronchus /ˈbrɒŋkəs/ ***noun*** [C] (*pl.* **bronchi** /ˈbrɒŋkaɪ/) (**ANATOMY**) one of the two main tubes that carry air to the lungs ➲ picture at **lung**

bronze /brɒnz/ ***noun*** **1** [U] (**CHEMISTRY**) a reddish-brown metal that is made by mixing TIN with another metal (**copper**) **2** [U] the colour of **bronze** **3** [C] (**ART**) a work of art made of **bronze**, for example a statue **4** [C] = BRONZE MEDAL ▶ **bronze *adj.***

the ˈBronze Age ***noun*** [sing.] (**HISTORY**) the period in human history between the Stone Age and the Iron Age when people used tools and weapons made of bronze

bronzed /brɒnzd/ ***adj.*** having skin that has been turned brown, in an attractive way, by the sun SYN **tanned**

ˌbronze ˈmedal ***noun*** [C] a round piece of BRONZE that you get as a prize for coming third in a race or a competition ➲ look at **gold medal**, **silver medal**

brooch /brəʊtʃ/ ***noun*** [C] a piece of jewellery with a pin at the back that women wear on their clothes

brood[1] /bruːd/ ***verb*** [I] **1** ~ **(on/over/about sth)** to worry, or to think a lot about sth that makes you worried or sad: *to brood on a failure* **2** (used about a female bird) to sit on her eggs

brood[2] /bruːd/ ***noun*** [C] all the young birds that belong to one mother

broody /ˈbruːdi/ ***adj.*** **1** (used about a woman) wanting to have a baby **2** (used about a female bird) ready to have or sit on eggs: *a broody hen*

brook /brʊk/ ***noun*** [C] a small river SYN **stream**

broom /bru:m/ ***noun*** [C] a brush with a long handle that you use for removing (**sweeping**) dirt from the floor

broomstick /ˈbru:mstɪk/ ***noun*** [C] a BROOM with a long handle and small thin sticks at the end, or the handle of a BROOM. In stories WITCHES (= women with evil magic powers) ride through the air on **broomsticks**.

Bros (*especially AmE* **Bros.**) ***abbr.*** (BUSINESS) (used in the name of a company) Brothers: *Wentworth Bros Ltd*

broth /brɒθ/ ***noun*** [U] soup: *chicken broth*

brothel /ˈbrɒθl/ ***noun*** [C] a place where men can go and pay to have sex with a woman (**a prostitute**)

brother 🔑 /ˈbrʌðə(r)/ ***noun*** [C] **1** a man or boy who has the same parents as another person: *Michael and Jim are brothers.* ◇ *Michael is Jim's brother.* ◇ *a younger/older brother* ➲ look at **half-brother**, **stepbrother** **2** (RELIGION) a man who is a member of a Christian religious community **3** (*informal*) a man who you feel close to because he is a member of the same society, group, etc. as you

brotherhood /ˈbrʌðəhʊd/ ***noun*** **1** [U] a feeling of great friendship and understanding between people: *the **brotherhood of man*** (= a feeling of friendship between all the people in the world) **2** [C, with sing. or pl. verb] an organization which is formed for a particular, often religious, purpose

ˈbrother-in-law ***noun*** [C] (*pl.* **brothers-in-law**) **1** the brother of your husband or wife **2** the husband of your sister

brotherly /ˈbrʌðəli/ ***adj.*** showing feelings of love and kindness that you would expect a brother to show: *brotherly love/advice*

brought past tense, past participle of **bring**

brow /braʊ/ ***noun*** **1** [C, usually pl.] = EYEBROW **2** [C] = FOREHEAD **3** [sing.] the top part of a hill: *Suddenly a car came over the brow of the hill.*

browbeat /ˈbraʊbi:t/ ***verb*** [T] (*pt* **browbeat**; *pp* **browbeaten**) **~ sb (into doing sth)** to frighten or threaten sb in order to make them do sth: *They were browbeaten into accepting the deal.*

brown[1] 🔑 /braʊn/ ***adj.*** **1** having the colour of earth or coffee: *brown eyes/hair* ◇ *brown bread* ◇ *a package wrapped in brown paper* **2** having skin that is naturally brown or has been made brown by the sun: *Although I often sunbathe, I never seem to **go brown**.* ▶ **brown** ***noun*** [U,C]: *the yellows and browns of the trees in autumn* ◇ *Brown doesn't* (= brown clothes do not) *suit you.*

brown[2] 🔑 /braʊn/ ***verb*** [I,T] to become or make sth become brown: *Brown the meat in a frying pan.*

ˈbrown goods ***noun*** [pl.] small electrical items such as televisions, radios, music and video equipment ➲ look at **white goods**

brownie /ˈbraʊni/ ***noun*** [C] **1 Brownie** a young girl who is a member of the junior part of the Girl Guides organization **2** a type of heavy chocolate cake that often contains nuts

brownish /ˈbraʊnɪʃ/ ***adj.*** fairly brown: *She has brownish eyes.*

ˌbrown ˈpaper ***noun*** [U] strong, thick paper used for putting round packages, etc.

browse /braʊz/ ***verb*** **1** [I] to spend time pleasantly, looking round a shop, without a clear idea of what you are looking for: *I spent hours browsing in the local bookshop.* **2** [I] **~ through sth** to look through a book or magazine without reading every part or studying it carefully: *I enjoyed browsing through the catalogue but I didn't order anything.* **3** [I,T] (COMPUTING) to look for and read information on a computer: *I've just been browsing the Internet for information on Iceland.* ▶ **browse** ***noun*** [sing.]

browser /ˈbraʊzə(r)/ ***noun*** [C] (COMPUTING) a computer program that lets you look at words and pictures from other computer systems: *an Internet browser*

bruise /bru:z/ ***noun*** [C] a blue, brown or purple mark that appears on the skin after sb has fallen, been hit, etc. ⓘ A bruise on your eye is called a **black eye**. ▶ **bruise** ***verb*** [I,T]: *I fell over and bruised my arm.* ◇ *I've got the sort of skin that bruises easily.* ➲ note at **injure**

brunch /brʌntʃ/ ***noun*** [C,U] (*informal*) a meal that you eat in the late morning as a combination of breakfast and lunch

brunette /bru:ˈnet/ ***noun*** [C] a white woman with dark brown hair ➲ look at **blond**

brunt /brʌnt/ ***noun***

IDM **bear the brunt of sth** → BEAR[2]

brush[1] 🔑 /brʌʃ/ ***noun*** **1** [C] an object that is used for cleaning things, painting, tidying your hair, etc.: *I took a brush and swept the snow from the path.* ◇ *a toothbrush* ◇ *a paintbrush* ◇ *a hairbrush* **2** [sing.] an act of cleaning, tidying the hair, etc. with a brush: *Your hair needs a brush.*

IDM **(have) a brush with sb/sth** (to have or almost have) an unpleasant meeting with sb/sth

brush[2] 🔑 /brʌʃ/ ***verb*** **1** [T] to clean, tidy, etc. sth with a brush: *Make sure you **brush your teeth** twice a day.* ◇ ***Brush your hair** before you go out.* **2** [I,T] to touch sb/sth lightly when passing: *Her hand brushed his cheek.* ◇ *Leaves brushed against the car as we drove along the narrow road.*

PHR V **brush sb/sth aside** **1** to refuse to pay attention to sb/sth: *She brushed aside the protests and continued with the meeting.* **2** to push past sb/sth: *He hurried through the crowd, brushing aside the reporters who tried to stop him.*

brush sth off/away to remove sth with a brush or with the hand, as if using a brush: *I brushed the dust off my jacket.*

brush sth up/brush up on sth to study or practise sth in order to get back knowledge or skill that you had before and have lost: *She took a course to brush up her Spanish.*

ˈbrush-off ***noun***

IDM **give sb the brush-off** to refuse to be friendly to sb

brusque /bru:sk/ ***adj.*** using very few words and sounding rude: *He gave a brusque 'No comment!' and walked off.* ▶ **brusquely** ***adv.***

Brussels sprout /ˌbrʌslz ˈspraʊt/ (*also* **sprout**) ***noun*** [C, usually pl.] a small round green vegetable that looks like a CABBAGE, but is much smaller

brutal /ˈbru:tl/ ***adj.*** very cruel and/or violent: *a brutal murder* ◇ *a brutal dictatorship* ▶ **brutally** /-təli/ ***adv.***: *He was brutally honest and told her that he didn't love her any more.*

brutality /bru:ˈtæləti/ ***noun*** [C,U] (*pl.* **brutalities**) very cruel and violent behaviour

brute[1] /bru:t/ ***noun*** [C] **1** a cruel, violent man **2** a large strong animal

brute[2] /bru:t/ ***adj.*** (only *before* a noun) using strength to do sth rather than thinking about it: *I think you'll have to use **brute force** to get this window open.*

brutish /ˈbruːtɪʃ/ ***adj.*** cruel and unpleasant

BSc /ˌbiː es ˈsiː/ (*AmE* **B.S.**) ***abbr.*** (EDUCATION) **Bachelor of Science**; the degree that you receive when you complete a university or college course in a science subject ➲ look at **BA, MSc**

BSE /ˌbiː es ˈiː/ (also *informal* **mad 'cow disease**) ***noun*** [U] (AGRICULTURE, HEALTH) **bovine spongiform encephalopathy**; a disease of cows which affects their brains and usually kills them ➲ look at **CJD**

BST /ˌbiː es ˈtiː/ ***abbr.*** **British Summer Time**; the system used in Britain between March and October, when clocks are put one hour earlier than GREENWICH MEAN TIME

BTEC /ˈbiːtek/ ***noun*** [C] (EDUCATION) an exam for young people who have left secondary school and are training in commercial or technical subjects: *She's doing a BTEC in design.*

BTW ***abbr.*** used in emails and informal writing to mean 'by the way'

bubble[1] 🔑 /ˈbʌbl/ ***noun*** [C] a ball of air or gas, in liquid or floating in the air: *We knew where there were fish because of the bubbles on the surface.*

bubble[2] /ˈbʌbl/ ***verb*** [I] **1** to produce bubbles or to rise with bubbles: *Cook the pizza until the cheese starts to bubble.* ◇ *The clear water bubbled up out of the ground.* **2** ~ **(over) (with sth)** to be full of happy feelings

'bubble bath ***noun*** [U] a liquid that you can add to the water in a bath to produce a mass of white bubbles

bubblegum /ˈbʌblgʌm/ ***noun*** [U] a sticky sweet that you eat but do not swallow and that can be blown into bubbles out of the mouth ➲ look at **chewing gum**

bubbly /ˈbʌbli/ ***adj.*** **1** full of bubbles **2** (used about a person) happy and full of energy

buck[1] /bʌk/ ***noun*** [C] **1** (*AmE, informal*) a US dollar: *Could you lend me a few bucks?* **2** (*pl.* **buck** or **bucks**) a male DEER, HARE or RABBIT ➲ note at **deer**

IDM **pass the buck** → PASS[1]

buck[2] /bʌk/ ***verb*** [I] (used about a horse) to jump into the air or to kick the back legs in the air

PHR V **buck (sb/sth) up** (*informal*) to feel or to make sb feel better or happier: *Drink this – it'll buck you up.* ◇ *Unless you buck your ideas up* (= become more sensible and serious), *you'll never pass the exam.*

bucket /ˈbʌkɪt/ ***noun*** [C] **1** a round, open container, usually made of metal or plastic, with a handle, that is used for carrying sth **2** (*also* **bucketful** /-fʊl/) the amount that a **bucket** contains: *How many buckets of water do you think we'll need?*

IDM **a drop in the bucket** → DROP[2]

buckle[1] /ˈbʌkl/ ***noun*** [C] a piece of metal or plastic at the end of a belt or STRAP that is used for fastening it

buckle[2] /ˈbʌkl/ ***verb*** [I,T] **1** to fasten or be fastened with a BUCKLE **2** to become crushed or bent because of heat, force, weakness, etc.: *Some railway lines buckled in the heat.*

buckwheat /ˈbʌkwiːt/ ***noun*** [U] a type of grain that is small and dark and that is grown as food for animals and for making flour

bud /bʌd/ ***noun*** [C] (BIOLOGY) a small lump on a tree or plant that opens and develops into a flower or leaf: *rosebuds* ➲ picture at **tree**

IDM **nip sth in the bud** → NIP

Buddhism /ˈbʊdɪzəm/ ***noun*** [U] (RELIGION) an Asian religion based on the teaching of Siddhartha Gautama (or Buddha)

Buddhist /ˈbʊdɪst/ ***noun*** [C] (RELIGION) a person whose religion is Buddhism ▶ **Buddhist** ***adj.***: *a Buddhist temple*

budding /ˈbʌdɪŋ/ ***adj.*** (only *before* a noun) wanting or starting to develop and be successful: *Have you got any tips for budding young photographers?*

buddy /ˈbʌdi/ ***noun*** [C] (*pl.* **buddies**) (*informal*) a friend, especially a male friend of a man

budge /bʌdʒ/ ***verb*** [I,T] **1** to move or make sth move a little: *I tried as hard as I could to loosen the screw but it simply wouldn't budge.* ◇ *We just couldn't budge the car when it got stuck in the mud.* **2** to change or make sb change a firm opinion: *Neither side in the dispute is prepared to budge.*

budgerigar /ˈbʌdʒərigɑː(r)/ (also *informal* **budgie**) ***noun*** [C] a small, brightly-coloured bird that people often keep as a pet in a CAGE

budget[1] 🔑 /ˈbʌdʒɪt/ ***noun*** [C,U] **1** (FINANCE) a plan of how to spend an amount of money over a particular period of time; the amount of money that is mentioned: *What's your monthly budget for food?* ◇ *a country's defence budget* ◇ *The work was finished on time and* ***within budget***. ◇ *The builders are already 20%* ***over budget***. **2** (*also* **Budget**) (POLITICS, FINANCE) a statement by a government saying how much money it plans to spend on particular things in the next year and how it plans to collect money: *Do you think taxes will go up in this year's budget?*

budget[2] /ˈbʌdʒɪt/ ***verb*** [I,T] ~ **(sth) (for sth)** (FINANCE) to plan carefully how much money to spend on sth: *The government has budgeted £10 billion for education.*

budget[3] /ˈbʌdʒɪt/ ***adj.*** (*informal*) (used in advertisements) very cheap: *budget holidays*

budgetary /ˈbʌdʒɪtəri/ ***adj.*** (FINANCE) connected with plans for how to spend money during a particular period of time ➲ note at **economic**

budgie /ˈbʌdʒi/ (*informal*) = BUDGERIGAR

buff /bʌf/ ***noun*** [C] (*informal*) a person who knows a lot about a particular subject and is very interested in it: *a film/computer buff*

buffalo /ˈbʌfələʊ/ ***noun*** [C] (*pl.* **buffalo** or **buffaloes**) **1** a large wild animal that lives in Africa and Asia that looks like a cow with long curved horns: *a herd of buffalo* **2** = BISON ➲ look at **water buffalo**

buffer /ˈbʌfə(r)/ ***noun*** [C] **1** a thing or person that reduces a shock or protects sb/sth against difficulties: *UN forces are acting as a buffer between the two sides in the war.* ◇ *a* ***buffer state*** (= a small country between two powerful states that helps keep peace between them) **2** (*BrE*) one of two round metal devices on the front or end of a train, or at the end of a railway/railroad track, that reduce the shock if the train hits sth **3** (COMPUTING) an area in a computer's memory where data can be stored for a short time

buffet[1] /ˈbʊfeɪ/ ***noun*** [C] **1** a meal (usually at a party or a special occasion) at which food is placed on a long table and people serve themselves: *Lunch was a cold buffet.* ◇ *a buffet lunch* **2** part of a train where passengers can buy food and drinks; a CAFE at a station

buffet[2] /ˈbʌfɪt/ ***verb*** [T] to knock or push sth in a rough way from side to side: *The boat was buffeted by the rough sea.*

bug[1] /bʌg/ ***noun*** **1** [C] (*especially AmE*) any small insect **2** [C] (*informal*) (HEALTH) an illness that is not very serious and that people get from each other: *I* *don't feel very well – I think I've got the bug that's going round.* ➲ note at **disease** **3** [C] (COMPUTING) something wrong in a system or machine, especially a computer: *There's a bug in the software.* **4** (usually **the...bug**) [sing.] (*informal*) a sudden interest in sth: *They've been bitten by the golf bug.* **5** [C] a very small device (**microphone**) that is hidden and secretly records people's conversations

bug² /bʌg/ ***verb*** [T] (**bugging**; **bugged**) **1** to hide a MICROPHONE somewhere so that people's conversations can be recorded secretly: *Be careful what you say. This room is bugged.* **2** (*informal*) to annoy or worry sb

buggy /ˈbʌgi/ (*pl.* **buggies**) (*BrE*) = PUSHCHAIR

THESAURUS

build

construct • assemble • erect • put up • put together

These words all mean to make sth, especially by putting different parts together.

build: *to build a house*

construct: *When was the bridge constructed?*

assemble: *The cupboard is easy to assemble.*

erect: *Police erected barriers to keep the crowds back.*

put up : *They're putting up new hotels to boost tourism in the area.*

put together: *to put together a model plane*

build¹ ⊶ /bɪld/ ***verb*** (*pt, pp* **built** /bɪlt/) **1** [T] to make sth by putting pieces, materials, etc. together: *They've built a new bridge across the river.* ◇ *The house is built of stone.* **2** [I] to use land for building on: *There's plenty of land to build on around here.* **3** [T] to develop or increase sth: *The government is trying to build a more modern society.* ◇ *This book claims to help people to build their self-confidence.*

PHRV **build sth in/on**; **build sth into/onto sth** to make sth a part of sth else: *They've made sure that a large number of checks are built into the system.* ◇ *We're planning to build two more rooms onto the back of the house.*

build on sth to use sth as a base from which you can make further progress: *Now that we're beginning to make a profit, we must build on this success.*

build sth on sth to base sth on sth: *a society built on the principle of freedom and democracy*

build up (to sth) to become greater in amount or number; to increase: *The traffic starts to build up at this time of day.*

build sth up 1 to make sth seem more important or greater than it really is: *I don't think it's a very serious matter, it's just been built up in the newspapers.* **2** to increase or develop sth over a period: *You'll need to build up your strength again slowly after the operation.*

THESAURUS

building

property • premises • complex • structure • block • edifice

These are all words for a structure such as a house, office block or factory that has a roof and four walls.

building: *an industrial building*

property: *Several buyers viewed the property*

premises: *The company needs larger premises.*

complex: *a leisure complex*

structure: *a wooden structure*

block : *a block of flats*

edifice (*formal*): *an imposing edifice*

build² /bɪld/ ***noun*** [C,U] the shape and size of sb's body: *She **has a** very athletic **build**.*

builder /ˈbɪldə(r)/ ***noun*** [C] a person whose job is to build houses and other buildings

building materials

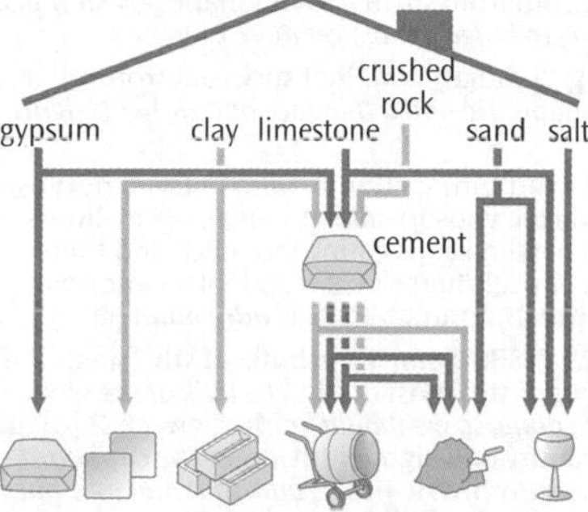

building ⊶ /ˈbɪldɪŋ/ ***noun*** **1** [C] a structure, such as a house, shop or school, that has a roof and walls: *There are a lot of very old buildings in this town.* **2** [U] the process or business of making buildings: *building materials* ◇ *the building industry*

ˈ**building site** ***noun*** [C] an area of land on which a building is being built

ˈ**building society** ***noun*** [C] (*BrE*) (FINANCE) an organization like a bank with which people can save money and which lends money to people who want to buy a house

ˈ**build-up** ***noun*** [C, usually sing.] **1 a build-up (of sth)** an increase of sth over a period: *The build-up of tension in the area has made war seem more likely.* **2 a build-up (to sth)** a period of preparation or excitement before an event: *The players started to get nervous in the build-up to the big game.*

-built /bɪlt/ (used to form compound adjectives) having a body with the shape and size mentioned: *a tall well-built man*

ˌ**built-ˈin** ***adj.*** that is a part of sth and cannot be removed: *built-in cupboards*

ˌ**built-ˈup** ***adj.*** covered with buildings: *a built-up area*

light bulb

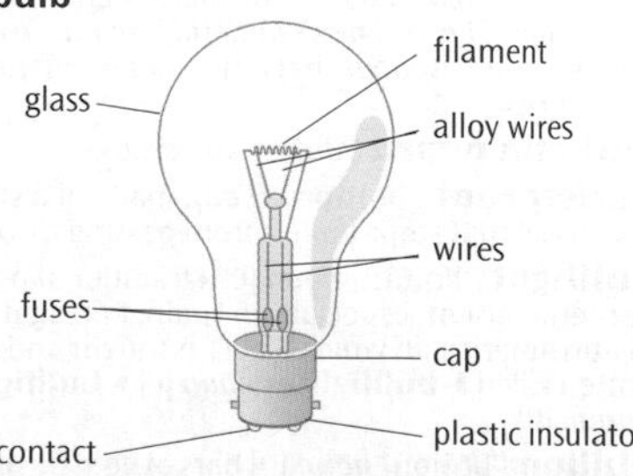

bulb /bʌlb/ ***noun*** [C] **1** (*also* ˈ**light bulb**) the glass part of an electric lamp that gives out light: *The **bulb's gone*** (= it no longer works) *in this lamp.*

2 (BIOLOGY) the round root of certain plants: *a tulip bulb* ➲ picture at **flower**

bulbous /ˈbʌlbəs/ ***adj.*** fat, round and ugly: *a bulbous red nose*

bulge¹ /bʌldʒ/ ***noun*** [C] a round lump that sticks out on sth

bulge² /bʌldʒ/ ***verb*** [I] **1** ~ **(with sth)** to be full of sth: *His bags were bulging with presents for the children.* **2** to stick out from sth in a round shape: *My stomach is starting to bulge. I must get more exercise.*

bulging /ˈbʌldʒɪŋ/ ***adj.*** that sticks out from sth in a round shape: *He had a thin face and rather bulging eyes.*

bulimia /buˈlɪmiə; -ˈliːmiə/ (*also* **bulimia nervosa** /buˌlɪmiə nɜːˈvəʊsə/) ***noun*** [U] (HEALTH) an illness in which a person keeps eating too much and then making himself/herself VOMIT ➲ look at **anorexia** ▶ **bulimic** /buˈlɪmɪk; -ˈliːmɪk/ ***adj.***, ***noun*** [C]

bulk AW /bʌlk/ ***noun*** **1 the bulk (of sth)** [sing.] the main part of sth; most of sth: *The bulk of the work has been done, so we should finish this week.* **2** [U] the size, quantity or weight of sth large: *The cupboard isn't especially heavy – it's its bulk that makes it hard to move.* ◇ *He slowly lifted his vast bulk out of the chair.*

IDM **in bulk** in large quantities: *If you buy in bulk, it's 10% cheaper.*

bulky AW /ˈbʌlki/ ***adj.*** large and heavy and therefore difficult to move or carry

bull /bʊl/ ***noun*** [C] **1** an adult male of the cow family ➲ note at **cow** **2** the male of the ELEPHANT, WHALE and some other large animals **3** (FINANCE) a person who buys shares in a company, hoping to sell them soon afterwards at a higher price: ***a bull market*** (= in which prices are rising) ➲ look at **bear**

bulldog /ˈbʊldɒg/ ***noun*** [C] a strong dog with short legs, a large head and a short, thick neck

ˈ**Bulldog clip™** ***noun*** [C] (*BrE*) a metal device for holding papers together

bulldoze /ˈbʊldəʊz/ ***verb*** [T] to make ground flat or knock down a building with a BULLDOZER: *The old buildings were bulldozed and new ones were built.*

bulldozer /ˈbʊldəʊzə(r)/ ***noun*** [C] a large, powerful vehicle with a broad piece of metal at the front, used for clearing ground or knocking down buildings

bullet ⊶ /ˈbʊlɪt/ ***noun*** [C] a small metal object that is fired from a gun: *The bullet hit her in the arm.* ◇ *a bullet wound*

bulletin /ˈbʊlətɪn/ ***noun*** [C] **1** a short news report on television or radio; an official statement about a situation: *The next **news bulletin** is at nine o'clock.* **2** a short newspaper that a club or an organization produces

ˈ**bulletin board** (*AmE*) = NOTICEBOARD

bulletproof /ˈbʊlɪtpruːf/ ***adj.*** made of a strong material that stops bullets from passing through it

bullfight /ˈbʊlfaɪt/ ***noun*** [C] a traditional public entertainment, especially in Spain, Portugal and Latin America, in which a BULL is fought and often killed ▶ **bullfighter** ***noun*** [C] ▶ **bullfighting** ***noun*** [U]

bullion /ˈbʊliən/ ***noun*** [U] bars of gold or silver

bullock /ˈbʊlək/ ***noun*** [C] a young BULL (= male cow) that has been CASTRATED (= had part of its sexual organs removed)

bullring /ˈbʊlrɪŋ/ ***noun*** [C] the large round area, like an outdoor theatre, where BULLFIGHTS take place

bullseye /ˈbʊlzaɪ/ ***noun*** [C] (SPORT) the centre of a round object (**target**) that you shoot or throw things at in certain sports, or a shot that hits this

bully¹ /ˈbʊli/ ***noun*** [C] (*pl.* **bullies**) a person who uses their strength or power to hurt or frighten people who are weaker: *the school bully*

bully² /ˈbʊli/ ***verb*** [T] (*pres. part.* **bullying**; *3rd person sing. pres.* **bullies**; *pt, pp* **bullied**) ~ **sb (into doing sth)** to use your strength or power to hurt or frighten sb who is weaker or to make them do sth: *Don't try to bully me into making a decision.* ▶ **bullying** ***noun*** [U]: *Bullying is a serious problem in many schools.*

bum /bʌm/ ***noun*** [C] (*informal*) **1** (*BrE*) the part of the body that you sit on SYN **backside, bottom** **2** (*especially AmE*) a person who has no home or job and who asks other people for money or food **3** a lazy or useless person: *a beach bum* (= sb who spends all their time on the beach)

bumbag /ˈbʌmbæg/ (*AmE* ˈ**fanny pack**) ***noun*** [C] (*informal*) a small bag worn around the waist to keep money, etc. in

bumblebee /ˈbʌmblbiː/ ***noun*** [C] a large BEE covered with small hairs that makes a loud noise as it flies ➲ picture on **page 29**

bump¹ /bʌmp/ ***verb*** **1** [I] ~ **against/into sb/sth** to hit sb/sth by accident when you are moving: *She bumped into a lamp post because she wasn't looking where she was going.* **2** [T] ~ **sth (against/on sth)** to hit sth against or on sth by accident: *I bumped my knee on the edge of the table.* **3** [I] to move along over a rough surface: *The car bumped along the track to the farm.*

PHR V **bump into sb** to meet sb by chance: *I bumped into an old friend on the bus today.*

bump sb off (*slang*) to murder sb

bump sth up (*informal*) to increase or make sth go up: *All this publicity will bump up sales of our new product.*

bump² /bʌmp/ ***noun*** [C] **1** the action or sound of sth hitting a hard surface: *She fell and hit the ground with a bump.* **2** a lump on the body, often caused by a hit **3** a part of a surface that is higher than the rest of it: *There are a lot of bumps in the road, so drive carefully.*

bumper¹ /ˈbʌmpə(r)/ ***noun*** [C] the bar fixed to the front and back of a motor vehicle to protect it if it hits sth

bumper² /ˈbʌmpə(r)/ ***adj.*** larger than usual: *The unusually fine weather has produced a **bumper harvest** this year.*

bumpy /ˈbʌmpi/ ***adj.*** not flat or smooth: *a bumpy road* ◇ *Because of the stormy weather, it was a very bumpy flight.* OPP **smooth**

bun /bʌn/ ***noun*** [C] **1** a small round sweet cake: *a currant bun* **2** a small soft bread roll: *a hamburger bun* **3** hair fastened tightly into a round shape at the back of the head: *She wears her hair **in a bun**.*

bunch¹ ⊶ /bʌntʃ/ ***noun*** **1** [C] a number of things, usually of the same type, fastened or growing together: *He bought her a bunch of flowers for her birthday.* ◇ *a bunch of bananas/grapes* ◇ *a bunch of keys* **2 bunches** [pl.] long hair that is tied on each side of the head **3** [C, with sing. or pl. verb] (*informal*) a group of people: *My colleagues are the best bunch of people I've ever worked with.*

bunch² /bʌntʃ/ ***verb*** [I,T] ~ **(sth/sb) (up/together)** to stay together in a group; to form sth into a group or bunch: *The runners bunched up as they came round the final bend.* ◇ *He kept his papers bunched together in his hand.*

bundle¹ /ˈbʌndl/ ***noun*** [C] a number of things tied or folded together: *a bundle of letters with an elastic band round them*

bundle² /ˈbʌndl/ ***verb*** [T] **1** ~ **sth (up)** to make or tie a number of things together: *I bundled up the old newspapers and threw them away.* **2** to put or push sb or sth quickly and in a rough way in a particular direction: *He was arrested and bundled into a police car.* **3** [T] ~ **sth (with sth)** (COMPUTING) to supply extra equipment, especially software when selling a new computer, at no extra cost: *A further nine applications are bundled with the system.*

bung¹ /bʌŋ/ ***verb*** [T] (*BrE, informal*) to put or throw sth somewhere, carelessly and quickly

PHR V **bung sth up (with sth)** to block sth: *My nose is all bunged up.*

bung² /bʌŋ/ ***noun*** [C] **1** a round piece of wood, rubber, etc. used for closing the hole in a container such as a BARREL or JAR **2** (*BrE, informal*) an amount of money that is given to sb to persuade them to do sth illegal

bungalow /ˈbʌŋgələʊ/ ***noun*** [C] a house that is all on one level, without stairs

bungee jumping /ˈbʌndʒi dʒʌmpɪŋ/ ***noun*** [U] (SPORT) a sport in which you jump from a high place, for example a bridge, with a thick ELASTIC rope tied round your feet

bungle /ˈbʌŋgl/ ***verb*** [I,T] to do sth badly or fail to do sth: *a bungled robbery*

bunk /bʌŋk/ ***noun*** [C] **1** a bed that is fixed to a wall, for example on a ship or train **2** (*also* **ˈbunk bed**) one of a pair of single beds built as a unit with one above the other

IDM **do a bunk** (*BrE, informal*) to run away or escape; to leave without telling anyone

bunker /ˈbʌŋkə(r)/ ***noun*** [C] **1** a strong underground building that gives protection in a war **2** a hole filled with sand on a GOLF COURSE

bunny /ˈbʌni/ ***noun*** [C] (*pl.* **bunnies**) a child's word for a RABBIT

Bunsen burner /ˌbʌnsn ˈbɜːnə(r)/ ***noun*** [C] (SCIENCE) an instrument used in scientific work that produces a hot gas flame ➲ picture at **laboratory**

buoy¹ /bɔɪ/ ***noun*** [C] a floating object, fastened to the bottom of the sea or a river, that shows the places where it is dangerous for boats to go

buoy² /bɔɪ/ ***verb*** [T] ~ **sb/sth (up) 1** to keep sb happy and confident: *His encouragement buoyed her up during that difficult period.* **2** to keep sth at a high level: *Share prices were buoyed by news of a takeover.*

buoyant /ˈbɔɪənt/ ***adj.*** **1** (ECONOMICS) (used about prices, business activity, etc.) staying at a high level or increasing, so that people make more money: *a* ***buoyant economy/market*** **2** happy and confident: *The team were in buoyant mood after their win.* **3** floating, able to float or able to keep things floating ▶ **buoyancy** /-ənsi/ ***noun*** [U]: *the buoyancy of the market*

burden¹ /ˈbɜːdn/ ***noun*** [C] **1** something that is heavy and difficult to carry **2** a responsibility or difficult task that causes a lot of work or worry

burden² /ˈbɜːdn/ ***verb*** [T] ~ **sb/yourself (with sth)** to give sb/yourself a responsibility or task that causes a lot of work or worry

ˌburden of ˈproof ***noun*** [sing.] (LAW) the task or responsibility of proving that sth is true

bureau /ˈbjʊərəʊ/ ***noun*** [C] (*pl.* **bureaux** or **bureaus** /-rəʊz/) **1** (*BrE*) a writing desk with drawers and a lid **2** an office or organization that provides information on a particular subject: *an employment bureau* **3** (POLITICS) (in the US) a government department or part of a government department: *the Federal Bureau of Investigation*

bureaucracy /bjʊəˈrɒkrəsi/ ***noun*** (*pl.* **bureaucracies**) **1** [U] (often used in a critical way) the system of official rules that an organization has for doing sth, that people often think is too complicated: *Getting a visa involves a lot of unnecessary bureaucracy.* **2** [C,U] (POLITICS) a system of government by a large number of officials who are not elected; a country with this system

bureaucrat /ˈbjʊərəkræt/ ***noun*** [C] an official working in an organization or a government department, especially one who follows the rules of the department too strictly

bureaucratic /ˌbjʊərəˈkrætɪk/ ***adj.*** connected with a BUREAUCRACY or BUREAUCRATS, and involving complicated official rules which may seem unnecessary: *You have to go through a complex bureaucratic procedure if you want to get your money back.*

bureau de change /ˌbjʊərəʊ də ˈʃɒndʒ/ ***noun*** [C] (*pl.* **bureaux de change**) (*BrE*) (TOURISM) an office at an airport, in a hotel, etc. where you can change the money of one country to the money of another country

burette (*AmE also* **buret**) /bjuˈret/ ***noun*** [C] (CHEMISTRY) a glass tube with measurements marked on it and a tap at one end, used in chemistry ➲ picture at **laboratory**

burger /ˈbɜːgə(r)/ = HAMBURGER (1)

-burger /bɜːgə(r)/ (in compounds) **1** a HAMBURGER with sth else on top: *a cheeseburger* **2** something that is cooked like and looks like a HAMBURGER, but is made of sth else: *a veggie burger*

burglar /ˈbɜːglə(r)/ ***noun*** [C] a person who enters a building illegally in order to steal ➲ note at **thief** ▶ **burgle** /ˈbɜːgl/ ***verb*** [T]: *Our flat was burgled while we were out.*

ˈburglar alarm ***noun*** [C] a piece of equipment, usually fixed on a wall, that makes a loud noise if a thief enters a building

burglary /ˈbɜːgləri/ ***noun*** [C,U] (*pl.* **burglaries**) the crime of entering a building illegally in order to steal: *There was a burglary next door last week.* ◇ *He is in prison for burglary.*

burgundy /ˈbɜːgəndi/ ***noun*** **1** **Burgundy** [U, C] (*pl.* **Burgundies**) a red or white wine from the Burgundy area of eastern France **2** [U] a dark red colour ▶ **burgundy** ***adj.***

burial /ˈberiəl/ ***noun*** [C,U] the ceremony when a dead body is put in the ground (**buried**)

burlap /ˈbɜːlæp/ (*AmE*) = HESSIAN

burly /ˈbɜːli/ ***adj.*** (used about a person or their body) strong and heavy

burn¹ ⊶ /bɜːn/ ***verb*** (*pt, pp* **burnt** /bɜːnt/ or **burned** /bɜːnd/) **1** [T] to destroy, damage or injure sb/sth with fire or heat: *We took all the rubbish outside and burned it.* ◇ *It was a terrible fire and the whole building was* ***burnt to the ground*** (= completely destroyed). ◇ *If you get too close to the fire you'll burn yourself.* ◇ *The people inside the building* *couldn't get out and they were all* ***burnt to death***. **2** [I] to be destroyed, damaged or injured by fire or heat: *If you leave the cake in the oven for much longer, it will burn.* ◇ *I can't spend too much time in the sun because I burn easily.* ◇ *They were trapped by the flames and they burned to death.* **3** [T] to produce a hole or mark in or on sth by burning: *He dropped his cigarette and it burned a hole in the carpet.* **4** [I] to be on fire: *Firemen raced to the burning building.* **5** [T] to use sth as fuel: *an oil-burning lamp* **6** [I] to produce light: *I don't think he went to bed at all – I could see his light burning all night.* **7** [I] to feel very hot and painful: *You have a temperature, your forehead's burning.* **8** [I] ~ **(with sth)** to be filled with a very strong feeling: *She was burning with indignation.*

IDM **sb's ears are burning** → EAR

PHR V **burn down** (used about a building) to be completely destroyed by fire

burn sth down to completely destroy a building by fire

burn (sth) off to remove sth or to be removed by burning

burn sth out (usually passive) to completely destroy sth by burning: *the burnt-out wreck of a car*

burn yourself out (usually passive) to work, etc., until you have no more energy or strength

burn (sth) up to destroy or to be destroyed by fire or strong heat: *The space capsule burnt up on its re-entry into the earth's atmosphere.*

burn[2] 🔑 /bɜːn/ ***noun*** [C] damage or an injury caused by fire or heat: ***minor/severe/third-degree burns*** ◇ *There's a cigarette burn on the carpet.*

burner /ˈbɜːnə(r)/ ***noun*** [C] (*especially AmE*) the part of a cooker, etc. that produces a flame ➲ look at **Bunsen burner**

IDM **on the back burner** → BACK[2]

burning /ˈbɜːnɪŋ/ ***adj.*** (only *before* a noun) **1** (used about a feeling) extremely strong: *a burning ambition/desire* **2** very important or urgent: *a burning issue/question* **3** feeling very hot: *the burning sun*

burp /bɜːp/ ***verb*** [I] to make a noise with the mouth when air rises from the stomach and is forced out SYN **belch**: *He sat back when he had finished his meal and burped loudly.* ▶ **burp *noun*** [C]

burr /bɜː(r)/ ***noun*** [C] **1** [usually sing.] a strong pronunciation of the 'r' sound, typical of some accents in English; an accent with this type of pronunciation **2** [usually sing.] the soft regular noise made by parts of machine moving quickly **3** (also **bur**) (TECHNICAL) a rough edge left on an object by the action of a tool or machine **4** (also **bur**) (TECHNICAL) a small tool for cutting that can be used with a DRILL (= a tool or machine that is used for making holes in wood, etc.) **5** (also **bur**) (BIOLOGY) the seed container of some plants which is covered in very small hooks that stick to clothes or fur

burrow[1] /ˈbʌrəʊ/ ***noun*** [C] a hole in the ground made by certain animals, for example RABBITS, in which they live

burrow[2] /ˈbʌrəʊ/ ***verb*** [I] to dig a hole in the ground, to make a tunnel or to look for sth: *These animals burrow for food.* ◇ (*figurative*) *She burrowed in her handbag for her keys.*

bursar /ˈbɜːsə(r)/ ***noun*** [C] (EDUCATION) the person who manages the financial matters of a school, college or university

bursary /ˈbɜːsəri/ ***noun*** [C] (*pl.* **bursaries**) (EDUCATION) a sum of money given to a specially chosen student to pay for his/her studies at a college or university

burst[1] 🔑 /bɜːst/ ***verb*** (*pt, pp* **burst**) **1** [I,T] to break open suddenly and violently, usually because there is too much pressure inside; to cause this to happen: *The ball burst when I kicked it.* ◇ *You'll burst that tyre if you blow it up any more.* ◇ (*figurative*) *If I eat any more I'll burst!* ◇ *If it rains much more, the river will burst its banks.* **2** [I] ~ **into, out of, through, etc.** to move suddenly in a particular direction, often using force: *She burst into the manager's office and demanded to speak to him.*

IDM **be bursting (with sth)** to be very full of sth: *I packed so many clothes that my suitcase was bursting.* ◇ *She was bursting with pride when she won the race.*

be bursting to do sth to want to do sth very much

burst (sth) open to open or make sth open suddenly or violently

PHR V **burst in on sb/sth** to interrupt sb/sth by arriving suddenly: *The police burst in on the gang as they were counting the money.*

burst into sth to start doing sth suddenly: *On hearing the news she* ***burst into tears*** (= started crying). ◇ *The lorry hit a wall and* ***burst into flames*** (= started burning).

burst out 1 to start doing sth suddenly: *He looked so ridiculous that I* ***burst out laughing***. **2** to say sth suddenly and with strong feeling: *Finally she burst out, 'I can't stand it any more!'*

burst[2] /bɜːst/ ***noun*** [C] **1** a short period of a particular activity, that often starts suddenly: *a burst of energy/enthusiasm/speed* ◇ *a burst of applause/gunfire* ◇ *He prefers to work* ***in short bursts***. **2** an occasion when sth bursts or explodes; a crack or hole caused by this: *a burst in a water pipe*

bury 🔑 /ˈberi/ ***verb*** [T] (*pres. part.* **burying**; *3rd person sing. pres.* **buries**; *pt, pp* **buried**) **1** to put a dead body in the ground: *She wants to be buried in the village graveyard.* **2** to put sth in a hole in the ground and cover it: *Our dog always buries its bones in the garden.* **3** (usually passive) to cover or hide sth/sb: *At last I found the photograph, buried at the bottom of a drawer.* ◇ (*figurative*) *Aisha was buried in a book and didn't hear us come in.*

bus 🔑 /bʌs/ ***noun*** [C] (*pl.* **buses**) a big public vehicle which takes passengers along a fixed route and stops regularly to let people get on and off: *Where do you usually get on/off the bus?* ◇ *We'll have to hurry up if we want to* ***catch the*** *9 o'clock* ***bus***. ◇ *We'd better run or we'll* ***miss the bus***.

bush 🔑 /bʊʃ/ ***noun*** **1** [C] (BIOLOGY) a plant like a small, thick tree with many low branches: *a rose bush* ◇ *The house was surrounded by thick bushes.* **2** (often **the bush**) [U] (GEOGRAPHY) wild land that has not been cleared, especially in Africa and Australia

IDM **beat about the bush** → BEAT[1]

bushwalking /ˈbʊʃwɔːkɪŋ/ ***noun*** [U] (TOURISM) the activity of going for long walks in the country for pleasure, especially in Australia or New Zealand SYN **hiking**: *They went bushwalking in Victoria Park Nature Reserve.*

bushy /bʊʃi/ ***adj.*** growing thickly: *bushy hair/eyebrows*

busier, busiest, busily → BUSY[1]

business 🔑 /ˈbɪznəs/ ***noun*** **1** [U] buying and selling as a way of earning money SYN **commerce**, **trade**: *She's planning to* ***set up in business*** *as a hairdresser.* ◇ *I'm going to* ***go into business*** *with my*

brother. ◇ *They are very easy to* ***do business with***.
2 [U] the work that you do as your job: *The manager will be away* ***on business*** *next week.* ◇ *a* ***business trip***
3 [U] the number of customers that a person or company has had: *Business has been good for the time of year.* **4** [C] a firm, a shop, a factory, etc. which produces or sells goods or provides a service: *She aims to* ***start a business*** *of her own.* ◇ *Small businesses are finding it hard to survive at the moment.*
5 [U] something that concerns a particular person: *The friends I choose are my business, not yours.* ◇ *Our business is to collect the information, not to comment on it.* ◇ *'How much did it cost?' 'It's* ***none of your business****!'* (= I don't want to tell you. It's private.)
6 [U] important matters that need to be dealt with or discussed: *First we have some unfinished business from the last meeting to deal with.* **7** [sing.] a situation or an event, especially one that is strange or unpleasant: *The divorce was an awful business.* ◇ *I found the whole business very depressing.*
IDM **get down to business** to start the work that has to be done
go out of business to have to close because there is no more money available: *The shop went out of business because it couldn't compete with the new supermarket.*
have no business to do sth/doing sth to have no right to do sth: *You have no business to read/reading my letters without asking me.*
mind your own business → MIND[2]
monkey business → MONKEY

'business card (*also* **card**) ***noun*** [C] (BUSINESS) a small card printed with sb's name and details of their job and company: *We exchanged business cards.*

businesslike /'bɪznəslaɪk/ ***adj.*** dealing with matters in a direct and practical way, without trying to be friendly: *She has a very businesslike manner.*

businessman ⊶ /'bɪznəsmæn; 'bɪznəsmən/ **businesswoman** /'bɪznəswʊmən/ ***noun*** [C] (*pl.* **-men** /-mən; -men/) (*pl.* **-women** /-wɪmɪn/) **1** a person who works in business, especially in a top position **2** a person who is skilful at dealing with money

'business person (*especially AmE*) (also **'businessperson**) ***noun*** [C] (*pl.* **business people**) **1** (BUSINESS) a person who works in business, especially in a top position HELP **Business people** is usually used to talk about a group of men and women, or to avoid having to say 'businessmen' or 'businesswomen'. **Business person/business people** is also used in more formal language.
2 a person who is skilful at dealing with money

'business school ***noun*** [C] (EDUCATION) a part of a college or university that teaches business, often to GRADUATES (= people who already have a first degree)

'business studies ***noun*** [U] (EDUCATION) the study of how to control and manage a company: *a course in business studies*

busk /bʌsk/ ***verb*** [I] to sing or play music in the street so that people will give you money

busker /'bʌskə(r)/ ***noun*** [C] a street musician

'bus lane ***noun*** [C] a part of a road that only buses are allowed to use

bust[1] /bʌst/ ***verb*** [T] (*pt, pp* **bust** or **busted**) (*informal*) **1** to break or damage sth so that it cannot be used **2** to arrest sb: *He was busted for possession of heroin.*

bust[2] /bʌst/ ***adj.*** (not before a noun) (*informal*) broken or not working: *The zip on these trousers is bust.*
IDM **go bust** (*informal*) (FINANCE) (used about a business) to close because it has lost so much money

bust[3] /bʌst/ ***noun*** [C] **1** (ART) a model in stone, etc. of a person's head, shoulders and chest **2** a woman's breasts; the measurement round a woman's chest: *This blouse is a bit too tight around the bust.* **3** (*informal*) an unexpected visit by the police in order to arrest people for doing sth illegal: *a drugs bust*

bustle[1] /'bʌsl/ ***verb*** **1** [I,T] to move in a busy, noisy or excited way; to make sb move somewhere quickly: *He bustled about the kitchen making tea.* ◇ *They bustled her out of the room before she could see the body.* **2** [I] ~ **(with sth)** to be full of people, noise or activity: *The streets were bustling with shoppers.*

bustle[2] /'bʌsl/ ***noun*** [U] excited and noisy activity: *She loved the bustle of city life.*

'bust-up ***noun*** [C] (*informal*) an argument: *He had a bust-up with his boss over working hours.*

busy[1] ⊶ /'bɪzi/ ***adj.*** (**busier**; **busiest**) **1** ~ **(at/with sth)**; ~ **(doing sth)** having a lot of work or tasks to do; not free; working on sth: *Mr Khan is busy until 4 o'clock but he could see you after that.* ◇ *Don't disturb him. He's busy.* ◇ *She's busy with her preparations for the party.* ◇ *We're busy decorating the spare room before our visitors arrive.* **2** (used about a period of time) full of activity and things to do: *I've had rather a busy week.* **3** (used about a place) full of people, movement and activity: *The town centre was so busy that you could hardly move.* **4** (*especially AmE*) (used about a telephone) being used SYN **engaged**: *The line's busy at the moment. I'll try again later.* ▸ **busily** ***adv.***: *When I came in she was busily writing something at her desk.*
IDM **get busy** to start working: *We'll have to get busy if we're going to be ready in time.*

busy[2] /'bɪzi/ ***verb*** [T] (*pres. part.* **busying**; *3rd person sing. pres.* **busies**; *pt, pp* **busied**) ~ **yourself with sth**; ~ **yourself doing sth** to keep yourself busy; to find sth to do

busybody /'bɪzibɒdi/ ***noun*** [C] (*pl.* **busybodies**) a person who is too interested in other people's private lives

but[1] ⊶ /bət strong form bʌt/ ***conj.*** **1** used for introducing an idea which contrasts with or is different from what has just been said: *The weather will be sunny but cold.* ◇ *Theirs is not the first but the second house on the left.* ◇ *James hasn't got a car but his sister has.* **2** however; and yet: *She's been learning Italian for five years but she doesn't speak it very well.* ◇ *I'd love to come but I can't make it till 8 o'clock.*
3 used when you are saying sorry for sth: *Excuse me, but is your name Cynthia Waters?* ◇ *I'm sorry, but I can't stay any longer.* **4** used for introducing a statement that shows that you are surprised or annoyed or that you disagree: *'Here's the book you lent me.' 'But it's all dirty and torn!'* ◇ *'But that's not possible!'*
IDM **but then** however; on the other hand: *We could go swimming. But then perhaps it's too cold.* ◇ *He's brilliant at the piano. But then so was his father* (= However, this is not surprising because...).

but[2] /bət strong form bʌt/ ***prep.*** except: *I've told no one but you about this.* ◇ *We've had nothing but trouble with this washing machine!*
IDM **but for sb/sth** except for or without sb/sth: *We wouldn't have managed but for your help.*

butane /'bju:teɪn/ ***noun*** [U] a gas produced from PETROLEUM, used in liquid form as a fuel for cooking etc.

butcher[1] /ˈbʊtʃə(r)/ *noun* **1** [C] a person who sells meat: *The butcher cut me four lamb chops.* **2 the butcher's** [sing.] a shop that sells meat: *She went to the butcher's for some sausages.* **3** [C] a person who kills a lot of people in a cruel way

butcher[2] /ˈbʊtʃə(r)/ *verb* [T] to kill a lot of people in a cruel way

butchery /ˈbʊtʃəri/ *noun* [U] cruel killing

butler /ˈbʌtlə(r)/ *noun* [C] the main male servant in a large house

butt[1] /bʌt/ *verb* [T] to hit sb/sth with the head
PHR V **butt in (on sb/sth)** to interrupt sb/sth or to join in sth without being asked: *I'm sorry to butt in but could I speak to you urgently for a minute?*

butt[2] /bʌt/ *noun* [C] **1** the thicker, heavier end of a weapon or tool: *the butt of a rifle* **2** a short piece of a cigarette which is left when it has been smoked **3** (*especially AmE, informal*) the part of your body that you sit on; your bottom: *Get up off your butt and do some work!* **4** a person who is often laughed at or talked about in an unkind way: *Fat children are often the butt of other children's jokes.* **5** the act of hitting sb with your head

butter[1] ⊶ /ˈbʌtə(r)/ *noun* [U] a soft yellow fat that is made from cream and used for spreading on bread, etc. or in cooking

butter[2] /ˈbʌtə(r)/ *verb* [T] to spread butter on bread, etc.: *I'll cut the bread and you butter it.* ◇ *hot buttered toast*

buttercup /ˈbʌtəkʌp/ *noun* [C] a wild plant with small shiny yellow flowers that look like cups

butterfly /ˈbʌtəflaɪ/ *noun* **1** [C] (*pl.* **butterflies**) an insect with a long, thin body and four brightly coloured wings: *Caterpillars develop into butterflies.* ➲ picture on **page 29** **2** [U] (SPORT) a style of swimming in which both arms are brought over the head at the same time, and the legs move up and down together
IDM **have butterflies (in your stomach)** (*informal*) to feel very nervous before doing sth

buttermilk /ˈbʌtəmɪlk/ *noun* [U] the liquid that is left when butter is separated from milk

buttock /ˈbʌtək/ *noun* [C, usually pl.] either of the two round soft parts at the top of your legs, which you sit on

button ⊶ /ˈbʌtn/ *noun* [C] **1** a small, often round, piece of plastic, wood or metal that you use for fastening your clothes: *One of the buttons on my jacket has come off.* ◇ *This blouse is too tight – I can't fasten the buttons.* **2** a small part of a machine, etc. that you press in order to operate sth: ***Press the button*** *to ring the bell.* ◇ *To dial the same number again,* ***push the*** *'redial' button.* ◇ *Which button turns the volume down?* ◇ *To print a file, simply click on the 'print' button.* ◇ *Double click the right mouse button.*

buttonhole /ˈbʌtnhəʊl/ *noun* [C] **1** a hole in a piece of clothing that you push a button through in order to fasten it **2** (*BrE*) a flower worn in the **buttonhole** of a coat or jacket

buttress /ˈbʌtrəs/ *noun* [C] (ARCHITECTURE) a stone or brick structure that supports a wall or makes it stronger: *Stone buttresses support the walls of the church.*

buy[1] ⊶ /baɪ/ *verb* [T] (*pt, pp* **bought** /bɔːt/) ~ **sth (for sb)**; ~ **sb sth** to get sth by paying money for it: *I'm going to buy a new dress for the party.* ◇ *We bought this book for you in London.* ◇ *Can I buy you a coffee?* ◇ *He bought the car from a friend.* ◇ *Did you buy your car new or second-hand?* ◇ *He bought the necklace as a present for his wife.*
IDM **buy time** to do sth in order to delay an event, a decision, etc.
PHR V **buy sb off** (*informal*) to pay sb money, especially dishonestly, to stop them from doing sth you do not want them to do
buy sb out to pay sb for their share in a house, business, etc. in order to get full control of it yourself

buy[2] /baɪ/ *noun* [C] an act of buying sth or a thing that you can buy: *I think your house was* ***a good buy*** (= worth the money you paid).

buyer ⊶ /ˈbaɪə(r)/ *noun* [C] **1** a person who buys sth, especially sth expensive SYN **purchaser**: *I think we've found a buyer for our house!* OPP **seller, vendor** **2** a person whose job is to choose and buy goods to be sold in a large shop

buyout /ˈbaɪaʊt/ *noun* [C] (BUSINESS) the act of buying enough or all of the shares in a company in order to get control of it

buzz[1] /bʌz/ *verb* **1** [I] to make the sound that BEES, etc. make when flying: *A large fly was buzzing against the windowpane.* **2** [I] ~ **(with sth)** to be full of excitement, activity, thoughts, etc.: *Her head was buzzing with questions that she wanted to ask.* ◇ *The room was buzzing with activity.* **3** [I,T] to call sb by using an electric bell, etc.: *The doctor will buzz for you when he's ready.*

buzz[2] /bʌz/ *noun* **1** [C] the sound that a BEE, etc. makes when flying: *the buzz of insects* **2** [sing.] the low sound made by many people talking at the same time: *I could hear the buzz of conversation in the next room.* **3** [sing.] (*informal*) a strong feeling of excitement or pleasure: *a buzz of expectation* ◇ *Flying first class* ***gave him a real buzz.*** ◇ *She* ***gets a buzz out of*** *shopping for expensive clothes.*

buzzard /ˈbʌzəd/ *noun* [C] a large European BIRD OF PREY (= a bird that kills other animals and birds for food)

buzzer /ˈbʌzə(r)/ *noun* [C] a piece of equipment that makes a BUZZING sound: *Press your buzzer if you know the answer to a question.*

buzzword /ˈbʌzwɜːd/ *noun* [C] (LANGUAGE) a word or phrase, especially one connected with a particular subject, that has become fashionable and popular

by ⊶ /baɪ/ *prep., adv.* **1** beside; very near: *Come and sit by me.* ◇ *We stayed in a cottage by the sea.* ◇ *The shops are close by.* **2** past: *He walked straight by me without speaking.* ◇ *We stopped to let the ambulance get by.* **3** not later than; before: *I'll be home by 7 o'clock.* ◇ *He should have telephoned by now/by this time.* **4** (usually without *the*) during a period of time; in a particular situation: *By day we covered about thirty miles and by night we rested.* ◇ *The electricity went off so we had to work by candlelight.* **5** used after a PASSIVE verb for showing who or what did or caused sth: *She was knocked down by a car.* ◇ *The event was organized by local people.* ◇ *I was deeply shocked by the news.* ◇ *Who was the book written by?/ Who is the book by?* **6** through doing or using sth; by means of sth: *You can get hold of me by phoning this number.* ◇ *Will you be paying by cheque?* ◇ *The house is heated by electricity.* ◇ *'How do you go to work?' 'By train, usually.'* ◇ *by bus/car/plane/bicycle* ◇ *We went in by the back door.* **7** as a result of sth; due to sth: *I got on the wrong bus by mistake/accident.* ◇ *I met an old friend by chance.* **8** according to sth; with regard to sth: *It's 8 o'clock by my watch.* ◇ *By law you have to attend school from the age of five.* ◇ *She's French by birth.* ◇ *He's a doctor by profession.* **9** (MATHEMATICS) used for multiplying or dividing: *4 multiplied by 5 is*

20. ◇ *6 divided by 2 is 3.* **10** used for showing the measurements of an area: *The table is six feet by three feet* (= six feet long and three feet wide). **11** (often used with *the*) in the quantity or period mentioned: *You can rent a car by the day, the week or the month.* ◇ *Copies of the book have sold by the million.* ◇ *They came in one by one.* ◇ *Day by day she was getting better.* **12** to the amount mentioned: *Prices have gone up by 10 per cent.* ◇ *I missed the bus by a few minutes.* **13** (used with a part of the body or an article of clothing) holding: *He grabbed me by the arm.*
IDM **by and large** → LARGE
by the way → WAY¹

by- (*also* **bye-**) /baɪ/ ***prefix*** (in nouns and verbs) **1** less important: *a by-product* **2** near: *a bystander*

bye ⊶ /baɪ/ (*also* ˌ**bye-ˈbye**; ˈ**bye-bye**) ***exclamation*** (*informal*) goodbye: *Bye! See you tomorrow.*

ˈ**bye-law** (LAW) = BY-LAW

ˈ**by-election** ***noun*** [C] (*BrE*) (POLITICS) an election to choose a new Member of Parliament for a particular town or area (**a constituency**). It is held when the former member has died or left suddenly. ➲ look at **general election**

bygone /ˈbaɪɡɒn/ ***adj.*** (only *before* a noun) that happened a long time ago: *a bygone era*

bygones /ˈbaɪɡɒnz/ ***noun*** [pl.]
IDM **let bygones be bygones** to decide to forget disagreements or arguments that happened in the past

ˈ**by-law** (also ˈ**bye-law**) ***noun*** [C] (*BrE*) (LAW) a law that is made by a local authority and that has to be obeyed only in that area

bypass¹ /ˈbaɪpɑːs/ ***noun*** [C] **1** a road which traffic can use to go round a town, instead of through it ➲ look at **ring road** **2** (HEALTH) an operation on the heart to send blood along a different route so that it does not go through a part which is damaged or blocked: *a triple bypass operation* ◇ *heart bypass surgery*

bypass² /ˈbaɪpɑːs/ ***verb*** [T] to go around or to avoid sth using a **bypass**: *Let's try to bypass the city centre.* ◇ (*figurative*) *It's no good trying to bypass the problem.*

ˈ**by-product** ***noun*** [C] **1** something that is formed during the making of sth else **2** something that happens as the result of sth else

bystander /ˈbaɪstændə(r)/ ***noun*** [C] a person who is standing near and sees sth that happens, without being involved in it: *Several* ***innocent bystanders*** *were hurt when the two gangs attacked each other.*

byte /baɪt/ ***noun*** [C] (COMPUTING) a unit of information that can represent one item, such as a letter or a number. A **byte** is usually made up of a series of eight smaller units (**bits**).

byword /ˈbaɪwɜːd/ ***noun*** [C, usually sing.] **1 a ~ for sth** a person or a thing that is a typical or well-known example of a particular quality: *A limousine is a byword for luxury.* **2** (*especially AmE*) a word or phrase that is often used

C c

C, c¹ /siː/ ***noun*** [C,U] (*pl.* **C's**; **c's** /siːz/) the third letter of the English alphabet: *'Car' begins with (a) 'C'.*

c² ⊶ /siː/ ***abbr.*** **1 C** (SCIENCE) CELSIUS; CENTIGRADE: *Water freezes at 0°C.* **2 C** (PHYSICS) coulomb(s) **3** (before dates) about; approximately: *c 1770*

C++ /ˌsiː plʌs ˈplʌs/ ***noun*** [U] (COMPUTING) a language that is used to write computer programs

cab /kæb/ ***noun*** [C] **1** (*especially AmE*) = TAXI¹: ***Let's take a cab /go by cab.*** **2** the part of a lorry, train, bus, etc. where the driver sits

cabaret /ˈkæbəreɪ/ ***noun*** [C,U] (ARTS AND MEDIA) entertainment with singing, dancing, etc. in a restaurant or club

cabbage /ˈkæbɪdʒ/ ***noun*** [C,U] a large round vegetable with thick green, dark red or white leaves: *Cabbages are easy to grow.* ◇ *Do you like cabbage?*

cabin /ˈkæbɪn/ ***noun*** [C] **1** a small room on a ship in which you live or sleep **2** one of the areas for passengers to sit in a plane ➲ picture at **plane** **3** a small house or shelter, usually made of wood: ***a log cabin***

ˈ**cabin boy** ***noun*** [C] a boy or young man who works as a servant on a ship

ˈ**cabin crew** ***noun*** [C] (TOURISM) the people whose job is to take care of passengers on a plane: *A member of the cabin crew demonstrated the safety procedures.*

ˈ**cabin cruiser** ***noun*** [C] = CRUISER (2)

cabinet ⊶ /ˈkæbɪnət/ ***noun*** [C] **1** (*also* the **Cabinet**) [with sing. or pl. verb] (POLITICS) a group of chosen members of a government, which is responsible for advising and deciding on government policy: *The Cabinet is/are meeting today to discuss the crisis.* ◇ *a cabinet meeting* ◇ (*BrE*) ***the shadow Cabinet*** (= the most important members of the opposition party) **2** a cupboard with shelves or drawers, used for storing things: *a medicine cabinet* ◇ *a filing cabinet*

cable

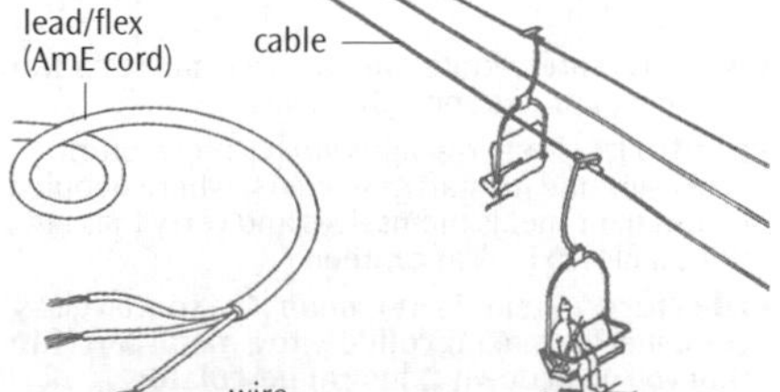

cable ⊶ /ˈkeɪbl/ ***noun*** **1** [C] a thick strong metal rope **2** [C,U] a set of wires covered with plastic, etc., for carrying electricity or signals: *underground/overhead cables* ◇ *a telephone cable* ◇ *two metres of cable* ➲ picture at **plug** **3** [U] = CABLE TELEVISION

ˈcable car *noun* [C] a vehicle like a box that hangs on a moving metal rope (**cable**) and carries passengers up and down a mountain

ˌcable ˈtelevision *noun* [U] (ARTS AND MEDIA) a system of sending out television programmes along wires instead of by radio signals

cache /kæʃ/ *noun* [C] **1** an amount of sth, especially drugs or weapons, that has been hidden **2** (COMPUTING) a part of a computer's memory that stores copies of data so that the data can be found very quickly

cackle /ˈkækl/ *verb* [I] to laugh in a loud, unpleasant way ▶ **cackle** *noun* [C]

cactus /ˈkæktəs/ *noun* [C] (*pl.* **cactuses** or **cacti** /ˈkæktaɪ/) a type of plant that grows in hot, dry areas, especially deserts. A **cactus** has a thick central part (**stem**) and sharp points (**prickles**) but no leaves.

CAD /kæd; ˌsiː eɪ ˈdiː/ *noun* [U] (COMPUTING) **computer aided design**; the use of computers to design machines, buildings, vehicles, etc.

cadaver /kəˈdævə(r)/ *noun* [C] (*formal*) the body of a dead person

cadence /ˈkeɪdns/ *noun* [C] **1** (*formal*) the rise and fall of the voice in speaking **2** (MUSIC) the end of a musical phrase

cadenza /kəˈdenzə/ *noun* [C] (MUSIC) (in CLASSICAL MUSIC) a short passage that is put into a piece of music to be played by one musician alone, and that shows the skill of that musician

cadet /kəˈdet/ *noun* [C] a young person who is training to be in the army, navy, air force or police

cadge /kædʒ/ *verb* [I,T] (*informal*) ~ **(sth) (from/off sb)** to try to persuade sb to give or lend you sth: *He's always trying to cadge money off me.*

cadmium /ˈkædmiəm/ *noun* [U] (*symbol* **Cd**) (CHEMISTRY) a soft poisonous bluish-white metal that is used in batteries and in some industries ❶ For more information on the periodic table of elements, look at pages R34-5.

Caesarean (also **-rian**; *AmE also* **cesarean**) /siˈzeəriən/ *noun* [C] (HEALTH) a medical operation in which an opening is cut in a mother's body in order to take out the baby when a normal birth would be impossible or dangerous: *to have a Caesarean* ❶ This operation is also called a **Caesarean section** or in American English a **C-section**.

caesium (*AmE* **cesium**) /ˈsiːziəm/ *noun* [U] (*symbol* **Cs**) (CHEMISTRY) a soft silver-white metal ❶ For more information on the periodic table of elements, look at pages R34-5.

cafe (also **café**) /ˈkæfeɪ/ *noun* [C] a small restaurant that serves drinks and light meals

cafeteria /ˌkæfəˈtɪəriə/ *noun* [C] a restaurant, especially one for staff or workers, where people collect their meals themselves and carry them to their tables ➲ look at **canteen**

cafetière /ˌkæfəˈtjeə(r)/ *noun* [C] a special glass container for making coffee with a metal part (**filter**) that you push down ➲ look at **percolator**

caffeine /ˈkæfiːn/ *noun* [U] the substance found in coffee and tea that makes you feel more awake and full of energy ➲ look at **decaffeinated**

cage /keɪdʒ/ *noun* [C] a box made of bars or wire, or a space surrounded by wire or metal bars, in which a bird or animal is kept so that it cannot escape: *a birdcage* ▶ **cage** *verb* [T] ▶ **caged** /keɪdʒd/ *adj.*: *He felt like a caged animal in the tiny office.*

cagey /ˈkeɪdʒi/ *adj.* (*informal*) ~ **(about sth)** not wanting to give information or to talk about sth

cagoule /kəˈguːl/ *noun* [C] a long jacket with a covering for the head (**hood**) that protects you from the rain or wind

cajole /kəˈdʒəʊl/ *verb* [T,I] ~ **(sb) (into sth/into doing sth)**; ~ **sth out of sb** to persuade a person to do sth or give sth by being very nice to them: *He cajoled me into agreeing to do the work.*

cake[1] 🔑 /keɪk/ *noun* **1** [C,U] a sweet food made by mixing flour, eggs, butter, sugar, etc. together and baking the mixture in the oven: *to make/bake a cake* ◇ *a wedding cake* ◇ *a piece/slice of birthday cake* ◇ *Would you like some more cake?* **2** [C] a mixture of other food, cooked in a round, flat shape: *fish/potato cakes*

IDM **have your cake and eat it** to enjoy the advantages of sth without its disadvantages; to have both things that are available

a piece of cake → PIECE[1]

cake[2] /keɪk/ *verb* [T] (usually passive) ~ **sth (in/with sth)** to cover sth thickly with a substance that becomes hard when it dries: *boots caked in mud*

calamity /kəˈlæməti/ *noun* [C,U] (*pl.* **calamities**) a terrible event that causes a lot of damage or harm SYN **disaster**

calcify /ˈkælsɪfaɪ/ *verb* [I,T] (*pres. part.* **calcifying**; *3rd person sing. pres.* **calcifies**; *pt, pp* **calcified**) to become hard or make sth hard by adding CALCIUM salts ▶ **calcification** /ˌkælsɪfɪˈkeɪʃn/ *noun* [U]

calcium /ˈkælsiəm/ *noun* [U] (*symbol* **Ca**) (CHEMISTRY) a chemical element that is found in foods such as milk and cheese. It helps to make bones and teeth strong. ❶ For more information on the periodic table of elements, look at pages R34-5.

ˌcalcium ˈcarbonate *noun* [U] (*symbol* $CaCO_3$) (CHEMISTRY) a white solid that exists naturally as CHALK, LIMESTONE (= a type of white stone used in building) and MARBLE (= a type of white stone that can be polished smooth and is used in building and for making statues)

calculate 🔑 /ˈkælkjuleɪt/ *verb* [T] **1** (MATHEMATICS) to find sth out by using mathematics; to work sth out: *It's difficult to calculate how long the project will take.* **2** to consider or expect sth: *We calculated that the advantages would be greater than the disadvantages.*

IDM **be calculated to do sth** to be intended or designed to do sth: *His remark was clearly calculated to annoy me.*

calculating /ˈkælkjuleɪtɪŋ/ *adj.* planning things in a very careful way in order to achieve what you want, without considering other people: *Her cold, calculating approach made her many enemies.*

calculation 🔑 /ˌkælkjuˈleɪʃn/ *noun* **1** [C,U] (MATHEMATICS) finding an answer by using mathematics: *I'll have to* ***do a few calculations*** *before telling you how much I can afford.* ◇ *Calculation of the exact cost is impossible.* **2** [U] (*formal*) careful planning in order to achieve what you want, without considering other people: *His actions were clearly the result of deliberate calculation.*

calculator /ˈkælkjuleɪtə(r)/ *noun* [C] a small electronic machine used for calculating figures: *a pocket calculator*

calculus /ˈkælkjələs/ *noun* [U] (MATHEMATICS) a type of mathematics that deals with rates of change, for example the speed of a falling object

caldron (*especially AmE*) = CAULDRON

calendar /ˈkælɪndə(r)/ ***noun*** [C] **1** a list that shows the days, weeks and months of a particular year **2** a system for dividing time into fixed periods and for marking the beginning and end of a year: *the Islamic calendar* **3** a list of dates and events in a year that are important in a particular area of activity: *Wimbledon is a major event in the sporting calendar.*

ˌcalendar ˈmonth = MONTH (1)

ˌcalendar ˈyear = YEAR (1)

calf /kɑːf/ ***noun*** [C] (*pl.* **calves** /kɑːvz/) **1** a young cow ➲ note at **meat 2** a young animal of some other type such as a young ELEPHANT or WHALE **3** the back of your leg, below your knee: *I've strained a calf muscle.* ➲ picture on **page 29**

calibrate /ˈkælɪbreɪt/ ***verb*** [T] (**TECHNICAL**) to mark units of measurement on an instrument such as a THERMOMETER so that it can be used for measuring sth accurately

calibration /ˌkælɪˈbreɪʃn/ ***noun*** (**TECHNICAL**) **1** [U] the act of CALIBRATING: *a calibration error* **2** [C] the units of measurement marked on a THERMOMETER or other instrument

calibre (*AmE* **caliber**) /ˈkælɪbə(r)/ ***noun*** **1** [U] the quality of sth, especially a person's ability: *He was impressed by the* ***high calibre*** *of applicants for the job.* **2** [C] the width of the inside of a tube or gun; the width of a bullet

calico /ˈkælɪkəʊ/ ***noun*** [U] (*especially BrE*) a type of heavy cotton cloth that is usually plain white

californium /ˌkælɪˈfɔːniəm/ ***noun*** [U] (*symbol* **Cf**) (**CHEMISTRY**) a chemical element. **Californium** is a RADIOACTIVE metal produced artificially with CURIUM or AMERICIUM. ❶ For more information on the periodic table of elements, look at pages R34-5.

caliper (*especially AmE*) = CALLIPER

CALL /kɔːl/ ***abbr.*** (**EDUCATION**) **computer-assisted language learning**; the use of computers to help people learn languages

call¹ 🔑 /kɔːl/ ***verb*** **1** [I,T] ~ **(out) to sb**; ~ **(sth) (out)** to say sth loudly or to shout in order to attract attention: *'Hello, is anybody there?' she called.* ◇ *He called out the names and the winners stepped forward.* ◇ *I could hear a man calling his dog.* **2** [I,T] to telephone sb: *Who's calling, please?* ◇ *I'll call you tomorrow.* ◇ *We're just in the middle of dinner. Can I call you back later?* **3** [T] ~ **sb sth** to name or describe a person or thing in a certain way: *They called the baby Evey.* ◇ *It was very rude to call her fat.* ◇ *Are you calling me a liar?* **4** [T] to order or ask sb to come to a certain place: *Can you call everybody in for lunch?* ◇ *I think we had better call the doctor.* **5** [T] to arrange for sth to take place at a certain time: ***to call a meeting/an election/a strike*** **6** [I] ~ **(in/round) (on sb/at...)** to make a short visit to a person or place: *I called in on Mike on my way home.* ◇ *We called at his house but there was nobody in.*

IDM **bring/call sb/sth to mind** → MIND¹

call it a day (*informal*) to decide to stop doing sth: *Let's call it a day. I'm exhausted.*

call sb's bluff to tell sb to actually do what they are threatening to do (believing that they will not risk doing it)

call sb names to use insulting words about sb

call the shots/tune (*informal*) to be in a position to control a situation and make decisions about what should be done

PHRV **call at...** (*BrE*) (used about a train, etc.) to stop at a place for a short time: *This train calls at Didcot and Reading.*

call by (*informal*) to make a short visit to a place or person as you pass: *I'll call by to pick up the book on my way to work.*

call for sb (*BrE*) to collect sb in order to go somewhere together: *I'll call for you when it's time to go.*

call for sth to demand or need sth: *The crisis calls for immediate action.* ◇ *This calls for a celebration!*

call sth off to cancel sth: *The football match was called off because of the bad weather.*

call sb out to ask sb to come, especially to an emergency: *We had to call out the doctor in the middle of the night.*

call sb up 1 (*especially AmE*) to telephone sb: *He called me up to tell me the good news.* **2** to order sb to join the army, navy or air force

call sth up to look at sth that is stored in a computer: *The bank clerk called up my account details on screen.*

call² 🔑 /kɔːl/ ***noun*** **1** (*also* ˈ**phone call**) [C] an act of telephoning or a conversation on the telephone: *Were there any calls for me while I was out?* ◇ *I'll* ***give*** *you* ***a call*** *at the weekend.* ◇ *to* ***make a*** *local* ***call*** ◇ *a long-distance call* **2** [C] a loud sound that is made to attract attention; a shout: *a call for help* ◇ *That bird's call is easy to recognize.* **3** [C] a short visit, especially to sb's house: *We could pay a call on Dave on our way home.* ◇ *The doctor has several calls to make this morning.* **4** [C] a request, demand for sth: *There have been calls for the President to resign.* **5** [C,U] ~ **for sth** a need for sth: *The doctor said there was no call for concern.*

IDM **at sb's beck and call** → BECK

(be) on call to be ready to work if necessary: *Dr Young will be on call this weekend.*

ˈcall box = TELEPHONE BOX

ˈcall centre (*BrE*) (*AmE* ˈ**call center**) ***noun*** [C] (**BUSINESS**) an office in which many people work using telephones, for example taking customers' orders or answering questions

called /kɔːld/ ***adj.*** (not *before* a noun) to have a particular name: *His wife is called Vanessa.* ◇ *I don't know anyone called Alex.*

caller /ˈkɔːlə(r)/ ***noun*** [C] a person who telephones or visits sb

calligraphy /kəˈlɪgrəfi/ ***noun*** [U] (**ART**) beautiful HANDWRITING that you do with a special pen or brush; the art of producing this

calliper (*especially AmE* **caliper**) /ˈkælɪpə(r)/ ***noun*** **1 callipers** [pl.] (**MATHEMATICS**) an instrument with two long thin parts joined at one end, used for measuring the DIAMETER of tubes and round objects (= the distance across them) **2** (*AmE* **brace**) [C, usually pl.] (**HEALTH**) a metal support for weak or injured legs

callous /ˈkæləs/ ***adj.*** not caring about the suffering of other people

callus /ˈkæləs/ ***noun*** [C] an area of thick hard skin on a hand or foot, usually caused by rubbing

calm¹ 🔑 /kɑːm/ ***adj.*** **1** not excited, worried or angry; quiet: *Try to* ***keep calm*** *– there's no need to panic.* ◇ *She spoke in a calm voice.* ◇ *The city is calm again after last night's riots.* **2** (used about the sea) without big waves: *a calm sea* OPP **rough 3** (used about the weather) without much wind: *a calm, cloudless day* ▶ **calmly** ***adv.***: *'I'll call the doctor,' he said calmly.* ▶ **calmness** ***noun*** [U]

calm² 🔑 /kɑːm/ ***verb*** [I,T] ~ **(sb/sth) (down)** to become or to make sb quiet or calm: *Calm down! Shouting at everybody won't help.* ◇ *I did some breathing exercises to calm my nerves.*

calm³ 🔑 /kɑːm/ ***noun*** [C,U] a period of time or a state when everything is peaceful: *After living in the city, I enjoyed the calm of country life.*

Calor gas™ /ˈkælə gæs/ (*AmE* **ˈcooking gas**) ***noun*** [U] a type of gas stored as a liquid under pressure in metal containers and used for heating and cooking in places where there is no gas supply

calorie /ˈkæləri/ ***noun*** [C] **1** a unit for measuring how much energy food will produce: *A fried egg contains about 100 calories.* ◇ *a* ***low-calorie*** *drink/yoghurt/diet* **2** (SCIENCE) a unit for measuring a quantity of heat; the amount of heat needed to increase the temperature of a gram of water by one degree Celsius

calorific /ˌkæləˈrɪfɪk/ ***adj.*** (SCIENCE) connected with or producing heat: *the calorific value of food* (=the amount of heat or energy produced by a particular amount of food)

calve /kɑːv/ ***verb*** **1** [I] (used about a cow) to give birth to a CALF (=a young cow) **2** [I,T] (**GEOGRAPHY**) (used about a large piece of ice) to break away from an ICEBERG or a GLACIER (=a mass of ice that moves slowly down a valley); to lose a piece of ice in this way ➲ picture at **glacial**

calves plural of **calf**

calypso /kəˈlɪpsəʊ/ ***noun*** [C,U] (*pl.* **-os**) (**MUSIC**) a Caribbean song about a subject of current interest; this type of music

calyx /ˈkeɪlɪks/ ***noun*** [C] (*pl.* **calyxes** or **calyces** /ˈkeɪlɪsiːz/) (**BIOLOGY**) the ring of small green leaves (**sepals**) that protect a flower before it opens

CAM /kæm/ ***abbr.*** computer aided manufacturing

camber /ˈkæmbə(r)/ ***noun*** [C] a slight downward curve from the middle of a road to each side

cambium /ˈkæmbiəm/ ***noun*** [U] (**BIOLOGY**) a layer of cells inside the STEM of a plant. **Cambium** cells grow into new XYLEM and PHLOEM tissue, which is needed to feed the plant. ➲ picture at **plant**

camcorder /ˈkæmkɔːdə(r)/ ***noun*** [C] a camera that you can carry around and use for recording pictures and sound on a VIDEO CASSETTE

came past tense of **come**

camel /ˈkæml/ ***noun*** [C] an animal that lives in the desert and has a long neck and either one or two large masses of fat (**humps**) on its back. It is used for carrying people and goods. ➲ look at **dromedary**

cameo /ˈkæmiəʊ/ ***noun*** [C] (*pl.* **cameos**) **1** (**ARTS AND MEDIA**) a small part in a film or play that is usually played by a famous actor: *Ian McKellen plays a cameo role as the dying king.* **2** a piece of jewellery that consists of a raised design, often of a head, on a background of a different colour

camera

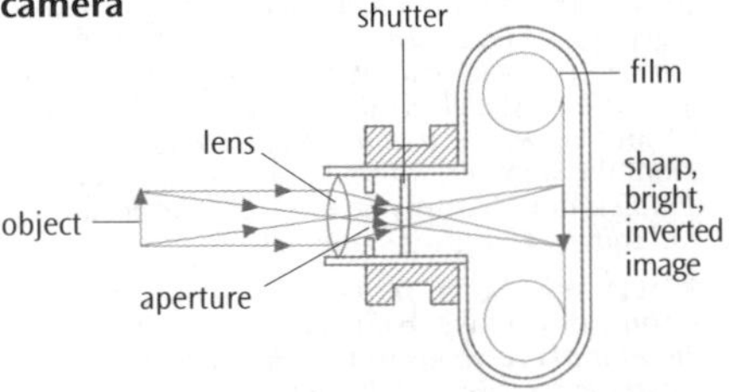

camera 🔑 /ˈkæmərə/ ***noun*** [C] a piece of equipment that you use for taking photographs or moving pictures: *I need a new film for my camera.* ◇ *a digital/video/television camera*

cameraman /ˈkæmrəmən/ ***noun*** [C] (*pl.* **-men** /-mən/) a person whose job is to operate a camera for a film or a television company ➲ look at **photographer**

camouflage /ˈkæməflɑːʒ/ ***noun*** [U] **1** materials or colours that soldiers use to make themselves and their equipment difficult to see **2** the way in which an animal's colour or shape matches its surroundings and makes it difficult to see: *The polar bear's white fur provides effective camouflage against the snow.* ▶ **camouflage** ***verb*** [T]

camp¹ 🔑 /kæmp/ ***noun*** [C,U] a place where people live in tents or simple buildings away from their usual home: *a refugee camp* ◇ *The climbers set up camp at the foot of the mountain.*

camp² 🔑 /kæmp/ ***verb*** [I] ~ **(out)** to sleep without a bed, especially outside in a tent: *We camped next to a river.* ◇ *They're* ***going camping*** *next week.*

THESAURUS

campaign

battle • struggle • drive • war • fight

These are all words for an effort made to achieve or prevent sth.

campaign: *the campaign for reform*

battle: *to win a legal battle*

struggle: *the struggle for independence*

drive: *a drive to reduce carbon emissions*

war: *the war against drugs*

fight: *a fight for justice*

campaign¹ 🔑 /kæmˈpeɪn/ ***noun*** [C] **1** a plan to do a number of things in order to achieve a special aim: *to launch an advertising/election campaign* **2** a planned series of attacks in a war

campaign² 🔑 /kæmˈpeɪn/ ***verb*** [I] ~ **(for/against sb/sth)** to take part in a planned series of activities in order to make sth happen or to prevent sth: *Local people are campaigning for lower speed limits in the town.* ▶ **campaigner** ***noun*** [C]: *an animal rights campaigner*

ˈcamp bed (*AmE* **cot**) ***noun*** [C] a light, narrow bed that you can fold up and carry easily

camper van (*AmE* **recreational vehicle,** *also* **RV**)

caravan (*AmE* **trailer**)

camper /ˈkæmpə(r)/ ***noun*** [C] **1** a person who stays in a tent on holiday **2** (*BrE also* **ˈcamper van**, *AmE* **RV**; **recreˌational ˈvehicle**, *BrE and AmE also* **motorhome**) a large vehicle designed for people to live and sleep in when they are travelling **3** (*AmE*) =CARAVAN

camping 🔑 /ˈkæmpɪŋ/ ***noun*** [U] (**TOURISM**) sleeping or spending a holiday in a tent: *Camping is cheaper than staying in hotels.* ◇ *to go on a camping holiday*

campsite /ˈkæmpsaɪt/ ***noun*** [C] (**TOURISM**) a place where people on holiday can put up their tents, park their CARAVAN, CAMPER, etc., often with toilets, water, etc.

campus /ˈkæmpəs/ ***noun*** [C,U] (*pl.* **campuses**) (**EDUCATION**) the area of land where the main buildings of a college or university are: *the college campus*

can[1] /kən; *strong form* kæn/ ***modal verb*** (*negative* **cannot** /ˈkænɒt/ *short form* **can't** /kɑːnt/; *pt* **could** /kəd/ *strong form* /kʊd/; *negative* **could not** *short form* **couldn't** /ˈkʊdnt/) **1** used for showing that it is possible for sb/sth to do sth or that sb/sth has the ability to do sth: *Can you ride a bike?* ◇ *He can't speak French.* **2** used to ask for or give permission: *Can I have a drink, please?* ◇ *He asked if he could have a drink.* **3** used to ask sb to do sth: *Can you help me carry these books?* **4** used for offering to do sth: *Can I help at all?* **5** used to talk about sb's typical behaviour or of a typical effect: *You can be very annoying.* ◇ *Wasp stings can be very painful.* **6** used in the negative for saying that you are sure sth is not true: *That can't be Maria – she's in London.* ◇ *Surely you can't be hungry. You've only just had lunch.* **7** used with the verbs 'feel', 'hear', 'see', 'smell', 'taste'

can[2] /kæn/ ***noun*** [C] **1** a metal or plastic container that is used for holding or carrying liquid: *an oil can* ◇ *a watering can* **2** a metal container in which food or drink is kept without air so that it stays fresh: *a can of sardines* ◇ *a can of beer*

can[3] /kæn/ ***verb*** [T] (**canning**; **canned**) to put food, drink, etc. into a can in order to keep it fresh for a long time: *canned fruit*

canal /kəˈnæl/ ***noun*** [C] **1** (**GEOGRAPHY**) a deep cut that is made through land so that boats or ships can travel along it or so that water can flow to an area where it is needed: *the Panama Canal* **2** (**ANATOMY**) a tube inside the body through which liquid, food or air can pass ➲ look at **alimentary canal**

caˈnal boat ***noun*** [C] a long narrow boat used on CANALS

canary /kəˈneəri/ ***noun*** [C] (*pl.* **canaries**) a small yellow bird that sings and is often kept in a CAGE as a pet

cancel /ˈkænsl/ ***verb*** [T] (**cancelling**; **cancelled**: *AmE* **canceling**; **canceled**) **1** to decide that sth that has been planned or arranged will not happen: *All flights have been cancelled because of the bad weather.* ➲ look at **postpone** **2** to stop sth that you asked for or agreed to: *to cancel a reservation* ◇ *I wish to cancel my order for these books.*

PHR V **cancel (sth) out** to be equal or have an equal effect: *What I owe you is the same as what you owe me, so our debts cancel each other out.*

cancellation /ˌkænsəˈleɪʃn/ ***noun*** [C,U] the act of cancelling sth: *We had to make a last-minute cancellation.*

cancer /ˈkænsə(r)/ ***noun*** **1** [U, C] (**HEALTH**) a very serious disease in which lumps grow in the body: *She has lung cancer.* ◇ *He died of cancer.* **2** [U] **Cancer** the fourth sign of the ZODIAC, the CRAB

cancerous /ˈkænsərəs/ ***adj.*** (**HEALTH**) (used especially about a part of the body or sth growing in the body) having cancer: *a cancerous growth* ◇ *cancerous cells*

candid /ˈkændɪd/ ***adj.*** saying exactly what you think SYN **frank** ➲ noun **candour** ▸ **candidly** ***adv.***

candidacy /ˈkændɪdəsi/ ***noun*** [U] (**POLITICS**) the fact of being a candidate in an election

candidate /ˈkændɪdət/ ***noun*** [C] **1** a person who is trying to be elected or is applying for a job: *We have some very good **candidates for** the post.* **2** (**EDUCATION**) a person who is taking an exam

candle /ˈkændl/ ***noun*** [C] a round stick of solid oil or fat (**wax**) with a piece of string (**a wick**) through the middle that you can burn to give light: *to light/blow out a candle*

candlelight /ˈkændllaɪt/ ***noun*** [U] light that comes from a CANDLE: *They had dinner **by candlelight**.*

candlestick /ˈkændlstɪk/ ***noun*** [C] an object for holding a CANDLE or CANDLES

candour (*AmE* **candor**) /ˈkændə(r)/ ***noun*** [U] the quality of being honest; saying exactly what you think ➲ adjective **candid**

candy /ˈkændi/ ***noun*** [C,U] (*pl.* **candies**) (*AmE*) = SWEET[2] (1): *You eat too much candy.*

cane /keɪn/ ***noun*** **1** [C,U] the long central part of some plants, for example BAMBOO or sugar, that is like a tube and is used as a material for making furniture, etc.: *sugar cane* ◇ *a cane chair* **2** [C] a stick that is used to help sb walk

canine[1] /ˈkeɪnaɪn/ ***adj.*** (**BIOLOGY**) connected with dogs

canine[2] /ˈkeɪnaɪn/ (*also* **ˈcanine tooth**) ***noun*** [C] (**ANATOMY**) one of the four pointed teeth in the front of a person's or an animal's mouth ➲ look at **incisor**, **molar**, **premolar** ➲ picture at **tooth**

canister /ˈkænɪstə(r)/ ***noun*** [C] a small round metal container: *a gas canister*

cannabis /ˈkænəbɪs/ ***noun*** [U] (**HEALTH**) a drug made from the HEMP plant that some people smoke for pleasure, but which is illegal in many countries

cannibal /ˈkænɪbl/ ***noun*** [C] a person who eats human flesh ▸ **cannibalism** /ˈkænɪbəlɪzəm/ ***noun*** [U]

cannon /ˈkænən/ ***noun*** [C] (*pl.* **cannon** or **cannons**) **1** a large gun on a ship, army vehicle, aircraft, etc. **2** a large, simple gun that was used in past times for firing large stone or metal balls (**cannon balls**)

cannot /ˈkænɒt/ → CAN[1]

canoes

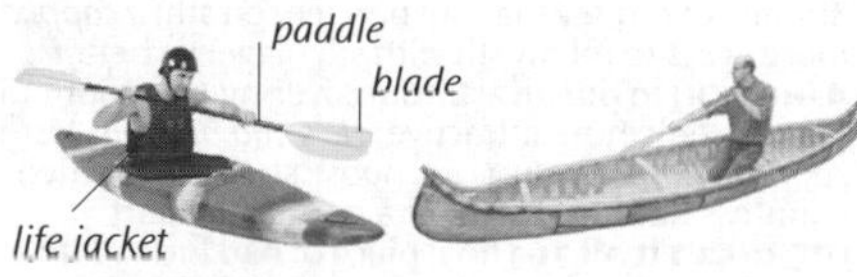

canoe /kəˈnuː/ ***noun*** [C] a light, narrow boat for one or two people that you can move through the water using a flat piece of wood (**a paddle**) ➲ look at **kayak** ▸ **canoe** ***verb*** [I] (*pres. part.* **canoeing**; *3rd person sing. pres.* **canoes**; *pt, pp* **canoed**): *They canoed down the river.* ◇ *We're **going canoeing** on the river tomorrow.*

canon /ˈkænən/ ***noun*** [C] **1** (**RELIGION**) a Christian priest with special duties in a CATHEDRAL (= the largest church in a district) **2** (*formal*) a generally accepted rule, standard or principle by which sth is judged: *the canons of good taste* **3** (**LITERATURE**) a list of books or other works that are generally accepted as the genuine work of a particular writer or as being important: *the Shakespeare canon* **4** (**MUSIC**) a piece of music in which singers or instruments take it in turns to repeat the tune

canopy /'kænəpi/ ***noun*** [C] (*pl.* **canopies**) a cover that hangs or spreads above sth: *The highest branches in the rainforest form a dense canopy.* ◊ *a parachute canopy*

can't short for CANNOT

canteen /kæn'tiːn/ ***noun*** [C] the place in a school, factory, office, etc. where the people who work there can get meals: *the staff canteen* ➲ look at **cafeteria**

canter /'kæntə(r)/ ***verb*** [I] (used about a horse and its rider) to run fairly fast but not very: *We cantered along the beach.* ➲ look at **gallop**, **trot**
▶ **canter *noun*** [sing.]

cantilever /'kæntɪliːvə(r)/ ***noun*** [C] (**ARCHITECTURE**) a long piece of metal or wood that sticks out from a wall to support the end of a bridge or other structure: *a cantilever bridge*

canvas /'kænvəs/ ***noun*** **1** [U] a type of strong cloth that is used for making sails, bags, tents, etc. **2** [C] (**ART**) a piece of strong cloth used by artists for painting a picture on

canvass /'kænvəs/ ***verb*** **1** [I,T] ~ **(sb) (for sth)** (**POLITICS**) to try to persuade people to vote for a particular person or party in an election or to support sb/sth: *to canvass for votes* ◊ *He's canvassing for the Conservative Party.* ◊ *The Prime Minister is trying to canvass support for the plan.* **2** [T] to find out what people's opinions are about sth

canyon /'kænjən/ ***noun*** [C] (**GEOGRAPHY**) a deep valley with very steep sides

canyoning /'kænjənɪŋ/ (*AmE also* **canyoneering** /'kænjə'nɪərɪŋ/) ***noun*** [U] (**SPORT**) a sport in which you climb down rocks or jump or swim down a WATERFALL into a CANYON

cap¹ 🔑 /kæp/ ***noun*** [C] **1** a soft hat that has a part sticking out at the front (**peak**): *a baseball cap* **2** a soft hat that is worn for a particular purpose: *a shower cap* **3** (*BrE*) (**SPORT**) a hat that is given to a player who is chosen to play for their country: *He won his first cap against France.* **4** a covering for the end or top of sth: *Please put the cap back on the bottle.*

cap² /kæp/ ***verb*** [T] (**capping**; **capped**) **1** to cover the top of sth: *mountains capped with snow* **2** to limit the amount of money that can be spent on sth: *a capped mortgage* **3** to follow sth with sth bigger or better **4** (**HEALTH**) to put an artificial covering on a tooth to make it look more attractive: *He's had his front teeth capped.* **5** (*BrE*) (**SPORT**) to choose sb to play in their country's national team for a particular sport
IDM **to cap it all** as a final piece of bad luck: *I had a row with my boss, my bike was stolen, and now to cap it all I've lost my keys!*

capability AW /ˌkeɪpə'bɪləti/ ***noun*** [C,U] (*pl.* **capabilities**) ~ **(to do sth/of doing sth)** the quality of being able to do sth: *Animals in the zoo have lost the capability to catch/of catching food for themselves.* ◊ *I tried to fix the computer, but it was* ***beyond*** *my* ***capabilities***.

capable 🔑 AW /'keɪpəbl/ ***adj.*** **1** ~ **of (doing) sth** having the ability or qualities necessary to do sth: *He's capable of passing the exam if he tries harder.* ◊ *That car is capable of 180 miles per hour.* ◊ *I do not believe that she's capable of stealing.* **2** having a lot of skill; good at doing sth: *She's a very capable teacher.* OPP **incapable** ▶ **capably *adv.***

capacitor /kə'pæsɪtə(r)/ ***noun*** [C] (**PHYSICS**) a device used to store an electric charge

capacity 🔑 AW /kə'pæsəti/ ***noun*** (*pl.* **capacities**) **1** [sing., U] the amount that a container or space can hold: *The tank has a capacity of 1000 litres.* ◊ *The stadium was* ***filled to capacity***. **2** [sing.] a ~ **(for sth/for doing sth)**; a ~ **(to do sth)** the ability to understand or do sth: *That book is beyond the capacity of young children.* ◊ *a capacity for hard work/for learning languages* **3** [C] the official position that sb has: ***In his capacity as*** *chairman of the council...* **4** [sing., U] the amount that a factory or machine can produce: *The power station is working* ***at full capacity***.

cape /keɪp/ ***noun*** [C] **1** a piece of clothing with no sleeves that hangs from your shoulders ➲ look at **cloak** **2** (**GEOGRAPHY**) a piece of high land that sticks out into the sea: *the Cape of Good Hope*

capillary /kə'pɪləri/ ***noun*** [C] (*pl.* **capillaries**) (**ANATOMY**) any of the smallest tubes in the body that carry blood ➲ picture at **skin**

capital¹ 🔑 /'kæpɪtl/ ***noun*** **1** (*also* **capital city**) [C] (**GEOGRAPHY, POLITICS**) the town or city where the government of a country is: *Madrid is the capital of Spain.* **2** [U] (**BUSINESS**) an amount of money that you use to start a business or to put in a bank, etc. so that you earn more money (**interest**) on it: *When she had enough capital, she bought a shop.* **3** (*also* **capital letter**) [C] the large form of a letter of the alphabet: *Write your name in capitals.* **4** [C] a place that is well known for a particular thing: *Niagara Falls is the honeymoon capital of the world.* **5** [C] (**ARCHITECTURE**) the top part of a column

capitals

Doric

Corinthian

Ionic

capital² 🔑 /'kæpɪtl/ ***adj.*** **1** (**LAW**) connected with punishment by death: *a* ***capital offence*** (= a crime for which sb can be sentenced to death) **2** (used about letters of the alphabet) written in the large form: *'David' begins with a capital 'D'.*

ˌcapital 'gain *noun* [U,C] (**FINANCE**) a profit that is made from the sale of property or an investment: *to generate/make/realize a capital gain*

ˌcapital 'gains tax *noun* [C,U] (*abbr.* **CGT**) (**FINANCE**) a tax that a person must pay when they have made a profit above a particular level by selling something of value such as a building, vehicle, shares in another company, etc.

ˌcapital in'vestment *noun* [U] (**BUSINESS**) money that a business spends on buildings, equipment, etc.

capitalism /'kæpɪtəlɪzəm/ ***noun*** [U] (**ECONOMICS**) the economic system in which businesses are owned and run for profit by individuals and not by the state ➲ look at **communism**, **Marxism**, **socialism**
▶ **capitalist *noun*** [C], ***adj.***

capitalize (also **-ise**) /'kæpɪtəlaɪz/ ***verb*** [T] **1** to write or print a letter of the alphabet as a CAPITAL; to begin a word with a capital letter **2** (**BUSINESS**) to sell possessions in order to change them into money **3** (usually passive) (**BUSINESS**) to provide a company etc. with the money it needs to function ▶ **capitalization** (also **-isation**) /ˌkæpɪtəlaɪ'zeɪʃn/ ***noun*** [U]
PHR V **capitalize on sth** to use sth to your

advantage: *We can capitalize on the mistakes that our rivals have made.*

ˌ**capital 'punishment** *noun* [U] (LAW) punishment by death for serious crimes ➲ look at **death penalty, corporal punishment**

capitulate /kə'pɪtʃuleɪt/ *verb* [I] (*formal*) to stop fighting and accept that you have lost; to give in to sb ▸ **capitulation** /kəˌpɪtʃu'leɪʃn/ *noun* [C,U]

capricious /kə'prɪʃəs/ *adj.* changing behaviour suddenly in a way that is difficult to predict

Capricorn /'kæprɪkɔːn/ *noun* [U] the tenth sign of the ZODIAC, the Goat

capsicum /'kæpsɪkəm/ *noun* [C] a type of plant which has hollow fruits. Some types of these are eaten as vegetables, either raw or cooked, for example RED PEPPERS or CHILLIES

capsize /kæp'saɪz/ *verb* [I,T] (used about boats) to turn over in the water: *The canoe capsized.* ◇ *A big wave capsized the yacht.*

capsule /'kæpsjuːl/ *noun* [C] **1** (**HEALTH**) a very small closed tube of medicine that you swallow ➲ picture at **health 2** a small plastic container with a substance or liquid inside **3** the part of a SPACECRAFT in which people travel and that often separates from the main ROCKET **4** (**BIOLOGY**) a shell or container for seeds or eggs in some plants and animals

Capt. *abbr.* = CAPTAIN[1]

captain[1] /'kæptɪn/ *noun* [C] **1** the person who is in command of a ship or an aircraft **2** (**SPORT**) a person who is the leader of a group or team: *Who's (the) captain of the French team?* **3** an officer at a middle level in the army or navy

captain[2] /'kæptɪn/ *verb* [T] to be the captain of a group or team

caption /'kæpʃn/ *noun* [C] the words that are written above or below a picture, photograph, etc. to explain what it is about

captivate /'kæptɪveɪt/ *verb* [T] to attract and hold sb's attention ▸ **captivating** *adj.*

captive[1] /'kæptɪv/ *adj.* **1** kept as a prisoner or in a confined space; unable to escape: *captive animals* **2** not free to leave a particular place or to choose what you want do to: *A salesman loves a **captive audience*** (= listening because they have no choice).
IDM **hold sb captive** to keep sb as a prisoner and not allow them to escape
take sb captive to catch sb and hold them as your prisoner

captive[2] /'kæptɪv/ *noun* [C] a person who is kept as a prisoner, especially in a war

captivity /kæp'tɪvəti/ *noun* [U] the state of being kept as a prisoner in a place that you cannot escape from: *Wild animals are often unhappy **in captivity**.*

captor /'kæptə(r)/ *noun* [C] (*formal*) a person who takes or keeps a person as a prisoner

capture[1] /'kæptʃə(r)/ *verb* [T] **1** to take a person or animal prisoner: *The lion was captured and taken back to the zoo.* **2** to take control of sth: *The town has been captured by the rebels.* ◇ *The company has captured 90% of the market.* **3** to make sb interested in sth: *The story captured the children's imagination.* **4** to succeed in representing or recording sth in words, pictures, etc.: *This poem captures the atmosphere of the carnival.* ◇ *The robbery was captured on video.* **5** (**COMPUTING**) to put sth into a computer in a form that it can use

capture[2] /'kæptʃə(r)/ *noun* [U] the act of capturing sth or being captured: *data capture*

car /kɑː(r)/ *noun* [C] **1** (*especially AmE* **automobile**) a road vehicle with four wheels that can carry a small number of people: *a new/second hand car* ◇ *Where can I park the car?* ◇ *They had a car crash.* ◇ *to get into/out of a car* **2** (*BrE*) a section of a train that is used for a particular purpose: *a dining/sleeping car* **3** (*AmE*) = CARRIAGE (1)

carafe /kə'ræf/ *noun* [C] a glass container like a bottle with a wide neck, in which wine or water is served

caramel /'kærəmel/ *noun* **1** [U] burnt sugar that is used to add flavour and colour to food **2** [C,U] a type of sticky sweet that is made from boiled sugar, butter and milk

carapace /'kærəpeɪs/ *noun* [C] (**BIOLOGY**) the hard shell on the back of some animals, for example CRABS, that protects them

carat (*AmE* **karat**) /'kærət/ *noun* [C] a unit for measuring how pure gold is or how heavy JEWELS are: *a 20-carat gold ring*

caravan /'kærəvæn/ *noun* [C] **1** (*AmE* **camper**) (**TOURISM**) a road vehicle without an engine that is pulled by a car, designed for people to live and sleep in, especially when they are on holiday: *a caravan site/park* ➲ picture at **camper 2** a group of people

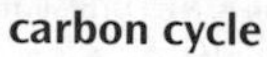

carbon cycle

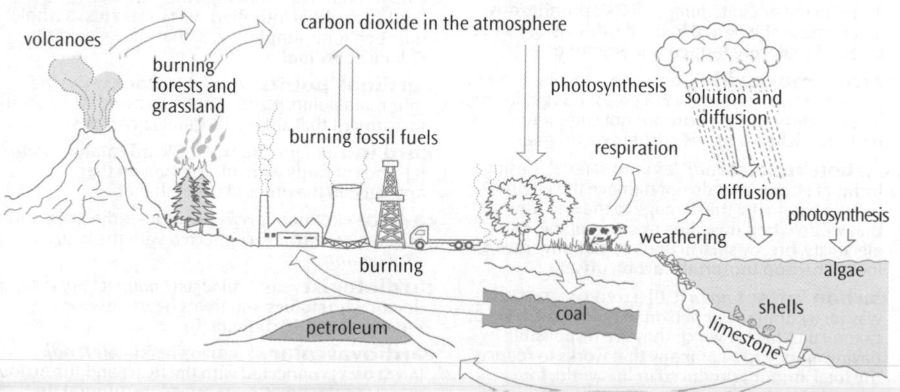

and animals that travel together, for example across a desert

caravanning /'kærəvænɪŋ/ ***noun*** [U] (*BrE*) (TOURISM) the activity of spending a holiday in a CARAVAN

caraway /'kærəweɪ/ ***noun*** [U] the dried seeds of the **caraway** plant, used to give flavour to food: *caraway seeds*

carbohydrate /ˌkɑːbəʊ'haɪdreɪt/ ***noun*** [C,U] (BIOLOGY) one of the substances in food, for example sugar, that gives your body energy: *Athletes need a diet that is high in carbohydrate.*

carbon /'kɑːbən/ ***noun*** [U] (*symbol* **C**) (CHEMISTRY) a chemical substance that is found in all living things, and also in diamonds, coal, petrol, etc. ❶ For more information on the periodic table of elements, look at pages R34-5.

carbonate /'kɑːbəneɪt/ ***noun*** [C] (*symbol* CO_3) (CHEMISTRY) a salt that contains CARBON and OXYGEN together with another chemical

carbonated /'kɑːbəneɪtɪd/ ***adj.*** (used about a drink) containing small bubbles of CARBON DIOXIDE **SYN** **fizzy**

ˌ**carbon 'copy** ***noun*** [C] **1** (BUSINESS) a copy of a document, letter, etc. made with CARBON PAPER ➲ look at **cc** **2** a person or thing that is very similar to sb/sth else

ˌ**carbon 'dating** ***noun*** [U] (SCIENCE) a method of calculating the age of very old objects by measuring the amounts of different forms of CARBON in them

ˌ**carbon di'oxide** ***noun*** [U] (*symbol* CO_2) (BIOLOGY, CHEMISTRY) a gas that has no colour or smell that people and animals breathe out of their lungs

ˌ**carbon 'footprint** ***noun*** [C] (ENVIRONMENT) a measure of the amount of CARBON DIOXIDE (= a gas that is harmful to the environment) that is produced by the daily activities of a person, company or an organization, such as driving a vehicle, using gas, electricity, etc.: *a carbon footprint calculator* ➲ look at **carbon neutral**, **carbon offset**

carbonic acid /kɑːˌbɒnɪk 'æsɪd/ ***noun*** [U] (CHEMISTRY) a very weak acid that is formed when CARBON DIOXIDE (= a gas that people and animals breathe out of their lungs) dissolves in water

carboniferous /ˌkɑːbə'nɪfərəs/ ***adj.*** (GEOLOGY) **1** producing or containing coal **2 Carboniferous** belonging to the period in the earth's history when layers of coal were formed underground

carbon monoxide /ˌkɑːbən mə'nɒksaɪd/ ***noun*** [U] (*symbol* **CO**) (CHEMISTRY) a poisonous gas formed when CARBON burns partly but not completely. It is produced when petrol is burnt in car engines.

ˌ**carbon 'neutral** ***adj.*** (ENVIRONMENT) **1** using forms of energy that do not damage the environment **2** balancing the damage to the environment that we do when travelling by car or plane, using electricity, etc. by such actions as planting trees ➲ look at **carbon footprint**, **carbon offset**

ˌ**carbon 'offset** ***noun*** [C,U] (ENVIRONMENT) a way for a company or person to reduce the level of CARBON DIOXIDE for which they are responsible by paying money to a company that works to reduce the total amount produced in the world, for example by planting trees: *carbon offset initiatives for air travellers*

'**carbon paper** ***noun*** [U] thin paper with a dark substance on one side that you put between two sheets of paper to make a copy of what you are writing

ˌ**car 'boot sale** ***noun*** [C] an outdoor sale where people sell things they do not want from the back of their cars

carburettor (*AmE* **carburetor**) /ˌkɑːbə'retə(r)/ ***noun*** [C] the piece of equipment in a car's engine that mixes petrol and air

carcass /'kɑːkəs/ ***noun*** [C] the dead body of an animal ➲ look at **corpse**

carcinogen /kɑː'sɪnədʒən/ ***noun*** [C] (HEALTH) a substance that can cause CANCER (= a very serious disease in which lumps grow in the body)

carcinogenic /ˌkɑːsɪnə'dʒenɪk/ ***adj.*** (HEALTH) likely to cause CANCER

card 🔑 /kɑːd/ ***noun*** **1** [U] (*BrE*) thick stiff paper: *a piece of card* **2** [C] a piece of card or plastic that has information on it: *Here is my **business card** in case you need to contact me.* ◇ *a **membership/identity/credit card*** **3** [C] a piece of card with a picture on it that you use for sending a special message to sb: *a **Christmas/birthday card*** ◇ *a **get-well card*** (= one that you send to sb who is ill) **4** (*also* **playing card**) [C] one of a set of 52 small pieces of card with shapes or pictures on them that are used for playing games: *a **pack of cards*** **5 cards** [pl.] games that are played with cards: *Let's **play cards**.* ◇ *Let's have a **game of cards**.* ◇ *I never win at cards!*

IDM **on the cards**; (*AmE*) **in the cards** (*informal*) likely to happen: *Their marriage break-up has been on the cards for some time now.*

cardamom /'kɑːdəməm/ ***noun*** [U] the dried seeds of a SE Asian plant, used in cooking as a spice

cardboard 🔑 /'kɑːdbɔːd/ ***noun*** [U] very thick paper that is used for making boxes, etc.: *The goods were packed in cardboard boxes.*

'**card catalog** (*AmE*) = CARD INDEX

cardholder /'kɑːdhəʊldə(r)/ ***noun*** [C] a person who uses a card from a bank, etc. to pay for things

cardiac /'kɑːdiæk/ ***adj.*** (*formal*) (HEALTH) connected with the heart: *cardiac surgery*

ˌ**cardiac ar'rest** ***noun*** [C] (HEALTH) a serious medical condition when the heart stops working

cardigan /'kɑːdɪgən/ ***noun*** [C] a knitted jacket made of wool, that fastens at the front

cardinal /'kɑːdɪnl/ ***noun*** [C] **1** (RELIGION) a priest at a high level in the Roman Catholic church **2** (*also* ˌ**cardinal 'number**) (MATHEMATICS) a whole number, for example 1, 2, 3, that shows quantity ➲ look at **ordinal**

ˌ**cardinal 'points** ***noun*** [pl.] (GEOGRAPHY) the four main points (North, South, East and West) on an instrument that shows direction (**a compass**)

'**card index** (*also* **index**, *AmE* '**card catalog**) ***noun*** [C] a box of cards with information on them, arranged in the order of the alphabet

cardio- /'kɑːdiəʊ/ ***prefix*** (in nouns, adjectives and adverbs) (ANATOMY) connected with the heart: *a cardiogram*

cardiologist /ˌkɑːdi'ɒlədʒɪst/ ***noun*** [C] (HEALTH) a doctor who studies and treats heart diseases ▶ **cardiology** /-dʒi/ ***noun*** [U]

cardiovascular /ˌkɑːdiəʊ'væskjələ(r)/ ***adj.*** (ANATOMY) connected with the heart and the BLOOD VESSELS (= the tubes that carry blood around the body)

THESAURUS

care

caution • prudence • discretion • wariness
These are all words for attention or thought that you give to sth in order to avoid mistakes or accidents.
care: *She chose her words with care.*
caution: *Proceed with the utmost caution.*
prudence: *We need to exercise financial prudence.*
discretion: *Can I rely on your complete discretion?*
wariness: *Her wariness soon turned to mistrust.*

care[1] ⊶ /keə(r)/ ***noun* 1** [U] ~ (**for sb**) the process of looking after sb/sth and providing what they need for their health or protection: *All the children in their care were healthy and happy.* ◊ *This hospital provides free medical care.* ◊ *She's in* ***intensive care*** (=the part of the hospital for people who are very seriously ill). ◊ *skin/hair care products* **2** [U] ~ (**over sth/in doing sth**) thinking about what you are doing so that you do it well or do not make a mistake: *You should* ***take*** *more* ***care*** *over your homework.* ◊ *This box contains glasses – please handle it* ***with care***. **3** [C,U] something that makes you feel worried or unhappy: *Since Charlie retired he* ***doesn't have a care in the world***. ◊ *It was a happy life, free from care.*
IDM **in care** (used about children) living in a home which is organized by the government or the local council, and not with their parents: *They were taken into care after their parents died.*
take care (that.../to do sth) to be careful: *Goodbye and take care!* ◊ *Take care that you don't spill your tea.* ◊ *He took care not to arrive too early.*
take care of sb/sth to deal with sb/sth; to organize or arrange sth: *I'll take care of the food for the party.*
take care of yourself/sb/sth to keep yourself/sb/sth safe from injury, illness, damage, etc.; to look after sb/sth: *My mother took care of me when I was ill.* ◊ *She always takes great care of her books.*

care[2] ⊶ /keə(r)/ ***verb*** [I,T] ~ (**about sb/sth**) to be worried about or interested in sb/sth: *Money is the thing that she cares about most.* ◊ *He really cares about his staff.* ◊ *I don't care what you do.*
IDM **I, etc. couldn't care less** (*informal*) it does not matter to me, etc. at all: *I couldn't care less what Barry thinks.*
who cares? (*informal*) nobody is interested; it is not important to anyone: *'I wonder who'll win the match.' 'Who cares?'*
would you care for.../to do sth (*formal*) a polite way to ask if sb would like sth or would like to do sth
PHR V **care for sb** to look after sb: *Who cared for her while she was ill?*
care for sb/sth to like or love sb/sth: *She still cares for Liam although he married someone else.* ◊ *I don't care for that colour very much.*

career[1] ⊶ /kəˈrɪə(r)/ ***noun*** [C] **1** the series of jobs that sb has in a particular area of work: *Sarah is considering a career in engineering.* ◊ *a successful career in politics* **2** the period of your life that you spend working: *She spent most of her career working in India.*

career[2] /kəˈrɪə(r)/ ***verb*** [I] to move quickly and in a dangerous way: *The car careered off the road and crashed into a wall.*

carefree /ˈkeəfriː/ ***adj.*** with no problems or worries

careful ⊶ /ˈkeəfl/ ***adj.* 1** ~ (**of/with sth**); ~ (**to do sth**) thinking about what you are doing so that you do not have an accident or make mistakes, etc.: ***Be careful!*** *There's a car coming.* ◊ *Please be very careful of the traffic.* ◊ *Be careful with that knife – it's very sharp.* ◊ *That ladder doesn't look very safe. Be careful you don't fall.* ◊ *I was careful not to say anything about the money.* ◊ *a careful driver* **2** giving a lot of attention to details to be sure sth is right: *I'll need to give this matter some careful thought.* ◊ *a careful worker* OPP **careless** ▶ **carefully** /ˈkeəfəli/ ***adv.***: *Please listen carefully. It's important that you remember all this.*

careless ⊶ /ˈkeələs/ ***adj.* 1** ~ (**about/with sth**) not thinking enough about what you are doing so that you make mistakes: *Jo's very careless.* ◊ *The accident was caused by careless driving.* **2** resulting from a lack of thought or attention to detail: *a careless mistake* ▶ **carelessly** ***adv.***: *She threw her coat carelessly on the chair.* ▶ **carelessness** ***noun*** [U]

carer /ˈkeərə(r)/ (*AmE* **caregiver** /ˈkeəgɪvə(r)/) ***noun*** [C] (HEALTH) a person who regularly looks after sb who is unable to look after himself/herself because of age, illness, etc.

caress /kəˈres/ ***verb*** [T] to touch sb/sth in a gentle and loving way ▶ **caress** ***noun*** [C]

caretaker /ˈkeəteɪkə(r)/ (*AmE* **janitor**) ***noun*** [C] a person whose job is to look after a large building, for example a school or a block of flats

cargo /ˈkɑːgəʊ/ ***noun*** [C,U] (*pl.* **cargoes**: *AmE also* **cargos**) the goods that are carried in a ship or an aircraft: *Luggage is carried in the cargo hold of the plane.* ◊ *a cargo ship*

ˈ**cargo pants** (*also* **cargoes**) ***noun*** [pl.] loose trousers that have pockets in various places, for example on the side of the leg above the knee

the Caribbean /ˌkærɪˈbiːən/ ***noun*** [sing.] (GEOGRAPHY) the area in the Caribbean Sea where the group of islands called the West Indies are situated ▶ **Caribbean** ***adj.***

caricature /ˈkærɪkətʃʊə(r)/ ***noun*** [C] a picture or description of sb that makes their appearance or behaviour funnier and more extreme than it really is: *Many of the people in the book are caricatures of the author's friends.*

caring /ˈkeərɪŋ/ ***adj.*** showing that you care about other people: *We must work towards a more caring society.*

carjacking /ˈkɑːdʒækɪŋ/ ***noun*** [U, C] the crime of forcing the driver of a car to take you somewhere or give you their car, using threats and violence ➲ look at **hijacking** ▶ **carjack** ***verb*** [T] ▶ **carjacker** ***noun*** [C]

carnage /ˈkɑːnɪdʒ/ ***noun*** [U] (*written*) the violent killing of a large number of people

carnation /kɑːˈneɪʃn/ ***noun*** [C] a white, pink or red flower with a pleasant smell

carnival /ˈkɑːnɪvl/ ***noun*** [C] a public festival that takes place in the streets with music and dancing: *the carnival in Rio*

carnivore /ˈkɑːnɪvɔː(r)/ ***noun*** [C] (BIOLOGY) any animal that eats meat ➲ look at **herbivore**, **insectivore**, **omnivore** ▶ **carnivorous** /kɑːˈnɪvərəs/ ***adj.***: *Lions are carnivorous animals.*

carol /ˈkærəl/ ***noun*** [C] (MUSIC) a Christian religious song that people sing at Christmas

carotid artery /kəˈrɒtɪd ɑːtəri/ ***noun*** [C] (ANATOMY) either of the ARTERIES (=two large tubes in your neck) that carry blood to your head

carousel /ˌkærəˈsel/ ***noun*** [C] **1** (*AmE*) =MERRY-GO-ROUND **2** (TOURISM) a moving belt at an airport that carries luggage for passengers to collect

carp /kɑːp/ ***noun*** [C,U] (*pl.* **carp**) a large fish that lives in lakes and rivers

carpal /ˈkɑːpl/ ***noun*** [C] (ANATOMY) any of the eight small bones in the wrist

ˈcar park (*AmE* **ˈparking lot**) ***noun*** [C] an area or a building where you can leave your car: *a multi-storey car park*

carpel /ˈkɑːpl/ ***noun*** [C] (BIOLOGY) the female REPRODUCTIVE organ of a flower ➲ picture at **flower**

carpenter /ˈkɑːpəntə(r)/ ***noun*** [C] a person whose job is to make things from wood ➲ look at **joiner**

carpentry /ˈkɑːpəntri/ ***noun*** [U] the skill or work of a CARPENTER

carpet 🔑 /ˈkɑːpɪt/ ***noun*** **1** [C,U] (a piece of) thick material that is used for covering floors and stairs: *a **fitted carpet*** (= one that is cut to the exact shape of a room) ◇ *a square metre of carpet* ➲ look at **rug 2** [C] a thick layer of sth that covers the ground: *The fields were under a carpet of snow.* ▶ **carpeted** ***adj.***: *All the rooms are carpeted.*

ˈcar phone ***noun*** [C] a telephone that you can use in a car

carpool /ˈkɑːpuːl/ ***verb*** [I] (ENVIRONMENT) if a group of people **carpool**, they travel to work together in one car and divide the cost between them

carriage /ˈkærɪdʒ/ ***noun*** [C] **1** (*also* **coach**, *AmE* **car**) one of the separate parts of a train where people sit: *a first-class carriage* **2** (*also* **coach**) a vehicle with wheels that is pulled by horses

carriageway /ˈkærɪdʒweɪ/ ***noun*** [C] (*BrE*) one of the two sides of a motorway or main road on which vehicles travel in one direction only: *the southbound carriageway of the motorway* ➲ look at **dual carriageway**

carrier /ˈkæriə(r)/ ***noun*** [C] **1** (BUSINESS) a company that transports people or goods: *the Dutch carrier, KLM* **2** a military vehicle or ship that is used for transporting soldiers, planes, weapons, etc.: *an aircraft carrier* **3** (HEALTH) a person or animal that can give an infectious disease to others but does not show the signs of the disease: *Some insects are carriers of tropical diseases.* **4** (*BrE*) = CARRIER BAG **5** (BUSINESS) a company that provides a telephone or Internet service: *a telecoms carrier*

ˈcarrier bag (*BrE also* **carrier**) ***noun*** [C] a plastic or paper bag for carrying shopping

carrion /ˈkæriən/ ***noun*** [U] the flesh of an animal that has been dead for some time ➲ picture on **page 29**

carrot 🔑 /ˈkærət/ ***noun*** **1** [C,U] a long thin orange vegetable that grows under the ground: *A pound of carrots, please.* ◇ *grated carrot* **2** [C] something attractive that is offered to sb in order to persuade them to do sth

carry 🔑 /ˈkæri/ ***verb*** (*pres. part.* **carrying**; *3rd person sing. pres.* **carries**; *pt, pp* **carried**) **1** [T] to hold sb/sth in your hand, arms or on your back while you are moving from one place to another: *Could you carry this bag for me? It's terribly heavy.* ◇ *She was carrying a rucksack on her back.* **2** [T] to have sth with you as you go somewhere: *I never carry much money with me when I go to London.* ◇ *Do the police carry guns in your country?* **3** [T] to transport sb/sth from one place to another: *A train carrying hundreds of passengers crashed yesterday.* ◇ *Strong winds carried the boat off course.* **4** [T] (HEALTH) to have an infectious disease that can be given to others, usually without showing any signs of the disease yourself **5** [T] (usually passive) (POLITICS) to officially approve of sth in a meeting, etc., because the largest number of people vote for it: *The motion was carried by 12 votes to 9.* **6** [I] (used about a sound) to reach a long distance: *You'll have to speak louder if you want your voice to carry to the back of the room.*

IDM **be/get carried away** to be so excited that you forget what you are doing

carry weight to have influence on the opinion of sb else: *Nick's views carry a lot of weight with the boss.*

PHR V **carry it/sth off** to succeed in doing sth difficult: *He felt nervous before he started his speech but he carried it off very well.*

carry on (with sth/doing sth) to continue: *They ignored me and carried on with their conversation.* ◇ *She intends to carry on studying after the course has finished.*

carry on sth to do an activity: *to carry on a conversation/a business*

carry out sth 1 to do sth that you have been ordered to do: *The soldiers carried out their orders without question.* **2** to do a task, repair, etc.: *to carry out tests/an investigation*

ˈcarry-all (*AmE*) = HOLDALL

carrycot /ˈkærikɒt/ ***noun*** [C] a small bed, like a box with handles, that you can carry a baby in

ˈcarry-on ***noun*** [C] (*AmE*) (TOURISM) a small bag or case that you carry onto a plane with you: *Only one carry-on is allowed* ◇ *carry-on baggage*

ˈcarry-out (*AmE*) = TAKEAWAY

carsick /ˈkɑːsɪk/ ***adj.*** feeling sick or VOMITING as a result of travelling in a car: *to get/feel/be carsick* ➲ look at **airsick**, **seasick**, **travel-sick**

cart[1] /kɑːt/ ***noun*** [C] **1** a vehicle with wheels that is used for transporting things: *a horse and cart* **2** (*AmE*) = TROLLEY: *a **shopping/baggage cart***

cart[2] /kɑːt/ ***verb*** [T] (*informal*) to take or carry sth/sb somewhere, often with difficulty: *We left our luggage at the station because we didn't want to cart it around all day.*

cartel /kɑːˈtel/ ***noun*** [C, with sing. or pl. verb] a group of separate companies that agree to increase profits by fixing prices and not competing with each other

cartilage /ˈkɑːtɪlɪdʒ/ ***noun*** [C,U] (ANATOMY) a strong substance in the places where your bones join ➲ picture at **synovial**

cartographer /kɑːˈtɒɡrəfə(r)/ ***noun*** [C] (GEOGRAPHY) a person who draws or makes maps

cartography /kɑːˈtɒɡrəfi/ ***noun*** [U] (GEOGRAPHY) the art or process of drawing or making maps ▶ **cartographic** /ˌkɑːtəˈɡræfɪk/ ***adj.***

carton /ˈkɑːtn/ ***noun*** [C] a small container made of cardboard or plastic: *a carton of milk/orange juice*

cartoon /kɑːˈtuːn/ ***noun*** [C] **1** (ART) a funny drawing, especially in a newspaper or magazine **2** (ARTS AND MEDIA) a film that tells a story by using moving drawings instead of real people and places **3** (ART) a drawing made by an artist as a preparation for a painting

cartoonist /kɑːˈtuːnɪst/ ***noun*** [C] a person who draws CARTOONS

cartridge /ˈkɑːtrɪdʒ/ ***noun*** [C] **1** a small tube that contains EXPLOSIVE powder and a bullet. You put a **cartridge** into a gun when you want to fire it. **2** a closed container that holds sth that is used in a machine, for example film for a camera, ink for printing, etc. **Cartridges** can be removed and replaced when they are finished or empty.

carve /kɑːv/ *verb* **1** [I,T] ~ (sth) (out of sth) (ART) to cut wood or stone in order to make an object or to put a pattern or writing on it: *The statue is carved out of marble.* ◇ *He carved his name on the desk.* **2** [T] to cut a piece of cooked meat into slices: *to carve a chicken*

carving /ˈkɑːvɪŋ/ *noun* [C,U] (ART) an object or design that has been CARVED: *There are ancient carvings on the walls of the cave.*

cascade[1] /kæˈskeɪd/ *noun* [C] **1** (GEOGRAPHY) a small WATERFALL, especially one of several falling down a steep slope with rocks **2** a large quantity of sth that falls or hangs down: *a cascade of blond hair*

cascade[2] /kæˈskeɪd/ *verb* [I] to fall or hang down, especially in large amounts or in stages: *Water cascaded from the roof.*

case 🔑 /keɪs/ *noun* **1** [C] a particular situation or example of sth: ***In some cases**, people have had to wait two weeks for a doctor's appointment.* ◇ *Most of us travel to work by tube – or,**in** Jim's **case**, by train and tube.* ◇ *Cases of the disease are very unusual in this country.* ➲ note at **example** **2 the case** [sing.] the true situation: *The man said he worked in publishing, but we discovered later that this was not the case.* **3** [C] (LAW) a crime or legal matter: *The police deal with hundreds of murder cases a year.* ◇ *The case will come to court in a few months.* **4** [C, usually sing.] the facts and reasons that support one side in a discussion or legal matter: *She tried to **make a case for** shorter working hours, but the others disagreed.* **5** [C] (especially in compounds) a container or cover for sth: *a pencil case* ◇ *a pillowcase* ◇ *a bookcase* ◇ *She put her glasses back in the case.* **6** [C] =SUITCASE: *Would you like me to carry your case?* **7** [C,U] (LANGUAGE) (in some languages) the form of a noun, an adjective or a pronoun that shows its relationship to another word: *The object of the verb is in the accusative case.* ➲ look at **accusative**, **dative**, **genitive**, **nominative**, **vocative**

IDM **(be) a case of sth/doing sth** a situation in which sth is needed: *There's no secret to success in this business. It's just a case of hard work.*

in any case whatever happens or has happened; anyway: *I don't know how much tickets for the match cost, but I'm going in any case.*

in case because sth might happen: *I think I'll take an umbrella in case it rains.* ◇ *I wasn't intending to buy anything but I took my credit card **just in case**.*

in case of sth (*formal*) if sth happens: *In case of fire, break this glass.*

in that case if that is the situation: *'I'm busy on Tuesday.' 'Oh well, in that case we'll have to meet another day.'*

prove your/the case/point → PROVE

ˌcase ˈhistory *noun* [C] (HEALTH) a record of a person's background, past illnesses, etc.

ˈcase law *noun* [U] (LAW) law based on decisions made by judges in earlier legal processes (**cases**) ➲ look at **common law**, **statute law**

ˈcase study *noun* [C] (SOCIAL STUDIES) a detailed study of a person, group, situation, etc. over a period of time

cash[1] 🔑 /kæʃ/ *noun* [U] **1** money in the form of coins or notes and not cheques, plastic cards, etc.: *Would you prefer me to pay **in cash** or by cheque?* ◇ *How much cash have you got with/on you?* **2** (*informal*) money in any form: *I'm a bit short of cash this month so I can't afford to go out much.*

cash[2] /kæʃ/ *verb* [T] to exchange a cheque for the amount of money that it is worth in coins and notes: *I'm just going to the bank to cash a cheque.*

PHR V **cash in (on sth)** to take advantage of a situation, especially in a way that other people think is wrong

cashback /ˈkæʃbæk/ *noun* [U] **1** if you ask for **cashback** when you are paying for goods in a shop with a DEBIT CARD (=a plastic card that takes money directly from your bank account), you get a sum of money in cash, that is added to your bill **2** an offer of money as a present that is made by some banks, companies selling cars, etc. in order to persuade customers to do business with them

ˈcash card (*AmE* **ATˈM card**) *noun* [C] a plastic card given by a bank to its customers so that they can get money from a CASH MACHINE in or outside a bank ➲ look at **cheque card**, **debit card**

ˈcash cow *noun* [C] (BUSINESS) the part of a business that always makes a profit and that provides money for the rest of the business

ˈcash crop *noun* [C] (AGRICULTURE) plants that people grow to sell, and not to eat or use themselves ➲ look at **subsistence crop**

ˈcash desk *noun* [C] the place in a large shop where you pay for things

cashew /ˈkæʃuː; kæˈʃuː/ (*also* **ˈcashew nut**) *noun* [C] a small curved nut that we eat

ˈcash flow *noun* [sing.] (BUSINESS) the movement of money into and out of a business as goods are bought and sold: *The company had cash-flow problems and could not pay its bills.*

cashier /kæˈʃɪə(r)/ *noun* [C] the person in a bank, shop, etc. that customers pay money to or get money from

ˈcash machine (*BrE also* **ˈcash dispenser**; **Cashpoint™** /ˈkæʃpɔɪnt/, *AmE also* **ATM** /ˌeɪ tiː ˈem/) *noun* [C] a machine inside or outside a bank that you can get money from at any time of day by putting in a CASH CARD

cashmere /ˈkæʃmɪə(r)/ *noun* [U] a type of wool that is very fine and soft

casing /ˈkeɪsɪŋ/ *noun* [C,U] a covering that protects sth: *The keyboard has a black plastic casing.* ➲ picture at **Thermos**

casino /kəˈsiːnəʊ/ *noun* [C] (*pl.* **casinos**) a place where people play games in which you can win or lose money, such as ROULETTE

cask /kɑːsk/ *noun* [C] a large wooden container in which alcoholic drinks, etc. are stored

casket /ˈkɑːskɪt/ *noun* [C] **1** a small decorated box for holding JEWELS or other valuable things, especially in the past **2** (*AmE*) =COFFIN

cassava /kəˈsɑːvə/ *noun* [U] a tropical plant that has thick roots; a type of flour that is made from these roots

casserole /ˈkæsərəʊl/ *noun* **1** [C,U] a type of food that you make by cooking meat and vegetables in liquid for a long time in the oven: *chicken casserole* **2** [C] a large dish with a lid for cooking **casseroles** in

cassette /kəˈset/ *noun* [C] a small flat plastic case containing tape for playing or recording music or sound: ***a cassette recorder/player*** SYN **tape**: *to put on/play/listen to a cassette* ◇ *a video cassette*

casˈsette recorder *noun* [C] a machine that you use for recording and playing CASSETTES

cast[1] 🔑 /kɑːst/ *verb* (*pt, pp* **cast**) **1** [T] (often passive) (ARTS AND MEDIA) to choose an actor for a particular role in a play, film, etc.: *She always seems to be cast in the same sort of role.* **2** [I,T] to throw a fishing line or net into the water **3** [T] to make an

object by pouring hot liquid metal into a shaped container (**a mould**): *a statue cast in bronze*
IDM **cast doubt on sth** to make people less sure about sth: *The newspaper report casts doubt on the truth of the President's statement.*
cast an eye/your eye(s) over sb/sth to look at sb/sth quickly
cast light on sth to help to explain sth: *Can you cast any light on the problem?*
cast your mind back to make yourself remember sth: *She cast her mind back to the day she met her husband.*
cast a shadow (across/over sth) to cause an area of shade to appear somewhere: (*figurative*): *The accident cast a shadow over the rest of the holiday* (=stopped people enjoying it fully).
cast a/your vote (POLITICS) to vote: *The MPs will cast their votes in the leadership election tomorrow.*
PHR V **cast around/about for sth** to try to find sth: *Jack cast around desperately for a solution to the problem.*

cast² /kɑːst/ ***noun*** [C, with sing. or pl. verb] (ARTS AND MEDIA) all the actors in a play, film, etc.: *The entire cast was/were excellent.*

castaway /ˈkɑːstəweɪ/ ***noun*** [C] a person who is left alone somewhere after their ship has sunk: *a castaway on a desert island*

caste /kɑːst/ ***noun*** [C,U] (SOCIAL STUDIES) a social class or group based on your position in society, how much money you have, family origin, etc.; the system of dividing people in this way: *Hindu society is based on a caste system.*

caster sugar (also **castor sugar**) /ˌkɑːstə ˈʃʊɡə(r)/ ***noun*** [U] (*BrE*) white sugar in the form of very small grains, used in cooking

ˌcast ˈiron ***noun*** [U] a hard type of iron that does not bend easily and is shaped by pouring the hot liquid metal into a shaped container (**a mould**)

ˌcast-ˈiron ***adj.*** **1** made of CAST IRON **2** very strong or certain; that cannot be broken or fail: ***a cast-iron alibi/excuse***

castle /ˈkɑːsl/ ***noun*** [C] **1** (HISTORY) a large building with high walls and towers that was built in the past to defend people against attack: *a medieval castle* ◇ *Edinburgh Castle* **2** (in the game of CHESS) any of the four pieces placed in the corner squares of the board at the start of the game, usually made to look like a **castle**

castle

ˈcast-off ***noun*** [C, usually pl.] a piece of clothing that you no longer want and that you give to sb else or throw away: *When I was little I had to wear my sister's cast-offs.*

ˌcastor ˈsugar = CASTER SUGAR

castrate /kæˈstreɪt/ ***verb*** [T] to remove part of the sexual organs of a male animal so that it cannot produce young ➲ look at **neuter²** ▶ **castration** /kæˈstreɪʃn/ ***noun*** [U]

casual /ˈkæʒuəl/ ***adj.*** **1** relaxed and not worried; not showing great effort or interest: *I'm not happy about your casual attitude to your work.* ◇ *It was only a casual remark so I don't know why he got so angry.* **2** (used about clothes) not formal: *I always change into casual clothes as soon as I get home from work.* **3** (used about work) done only for a short period; not regular or permanent: *Most of the building work was done by casual labourers.* ◇ *a casual job* ▶ **casually** /ˈkæʒuəli/ ***adv.***: *She walked in casually and said, 'I'm not late, am I?'* ◇ *Dress casually, it won't be a formal party.*

casualty /ˈkæʒuəlti/ ***noun*** (*pl.* **casualties**) **1** [C] a person who is killed or injured in a war or an accident: *After the accident the casualties were taken to hospital.* **2** [C] a person or thing that suffers as a result of sth else: *Many small companies became casualties of the economic crisis.* **3** (*also* **ˈcasualty department**; **ˌaccident and eˈmergency**, *AmE* **eˈmergency room**; **ER**) [U] (HEALTH) the part of a hospital where people who have been injured in accidents are taken for immediate treatment: *The victims were rushed to casualty.*

cat /kæt/ ***noun*** [C] **1** a small animal with soft fur that people often keep as a pet **2** a wild animal of the cat family: *the big cats* (=lions, tigers, etc.)

catabolism (also **katabolism**) /kəˈtæbəlɪzəm/ ***noun*** [U] (BIOLOGY) the process by which chemical structures are broken down and energy is released

catacombs /ˈkætəkuːmz/ ***noun*** [pl.] (HISTORY) a series of underground tunnels used for burying dead people, especially in ancient times

catalogue (*AmE* **catalog**) /ˈkætəlɒɡ/ ***noun*** [C] **1** a list of all the things that you can buy, see, etc. somewhere **2** a series, especially of bad things: *a catalogue of disasters/errors/injuries* ▶ **catalogue** ***verb*** [T]: *She started to catalogue all the new library books.*

catalyse (*AmE* **catalyze**) /ˈkætəlaɪz/ ***verb*** [T] (CHEMISTRY) to make a chemical reaction happen faster ▶ **catalysis** /kəˈtæləsɪs/ ***noun*** [U]

catalyst /ˈkætəlɪst/ ***noun*** [C] **1 a ~ (for sth)** a person or a thing that causes change: *The scandal was the catalyst for the President's election defeat.* **2** (CHEMISTRY) a substance that makes a chemical reaction happen faster ▶ **catalytic** /ˌkætəˈlɪtɪk/ ***adj.***

ˌcataˌlytic conˈverter ***noun*** [C] (ENVIRONMENT) a device used in motor vehicles to reduce the damage caused to the environment by poisonous gases

catamaran /ˌkætəməˈræn/ ***noun*** [C] a fast sailing boat with two HULLS (=with two main parts to its structure, like two boats joined together)

catapult¹ /ˈkætəpʌlt/ (*AmE* **slingshot**) ***noun*** [C] **1** a stick shaped like a Y with a rubber band attached to it, used by children for shooting stones **2** (HISTORY) a weapon used in the past to throw heavy stones

catapult² /ˈkætəpʌlt/ ***verb*** [T] to throw sb/sth suddenly and with great force: *When the car crashed the driver was catapulted through the windscreen.* ◇ (*figurative*) *The success of his first film catapulted him to fame.*

cataract /ˈkætərækt/ ***noun*** [C] **1** (HEALTH) a white area that grows over the eye as a result of disease **2** (*written*) a large WATERFALL (=a place where a river falls down a steep cliff or rock)

catarrh /kəˈtɑː(r)/ ***noun*** [U] (HEALTH) a thick liquid that forms in the nose and throat when you have a cold

catastrophe /kəˈtæstrəfi/ ***noun*** [C] **1** a sudden disaster that causes great suffering or damage: *major catastrophes such as floods and earthquakes* **2** an event that causes great difficulty, disappointment, etc.: *It'll be a catastrophe if I fail the exam* again. ▶ **catastrophic** /ˌkætəˈstrɒfɪk/ ***adj.***: *The war had a catastrophic effect on the whole country.*

catastrophism /kəˈtæstrəfɪzəm/ ***noun*** [U] (GEOLOGY) the theory that changes to the earth's CRUST (=surface) in the history of the planet were caused by sudden violent and unusual events

catch¹ 🔑 /kætʃ/ ***verb*** (*pt, pp* **caught** /kɔːt/) **1** [T] to take hold of sth that is moving, usually with your hand or hands: *The dog caught the ball in its mouth.* **2** [T] to capture sb/sth that you have been following or looking for: *Two policemen ran after the thief and caught him at the end of the street.* ◇ *to catch a fish* **3** [T] to notice or see sb doing sth bad: *I caught her taking money from my purse.* **4** [T] to get on a bus, train, plane, etc.: *I caught the bus into town.* OPP **miss** **5** [T] to be in time for sth; not to miss sb/sth: *We arrived just in time to catch the beginning of the film.* ◇ *I'll phone her now. I might just catch her before she leaves the office.* OPP **miss** **6** [I,T] to become or cause sth to become accidentally connected to or stuck in sth: *His jacket caught on a nail and ripped.* ◇ *If we leave early we won't get caught in the traffic.* **7** [T] to hit sb/sth: *The branch caught him on the head.* **8** [T] (HEALTH) to get an illness: *to **catch a cold/flu/measles*** **9** [T] to hear or understand sth that sb says: *I'm sorry, I didn't quite catch what you said. Could you repeat it?*

IDM **catch sb's attention/eye** to make sb notice sth: *I tried to catch the waiter's eye so that I could get the bill.*

catch your breath **1** to rest after physical exercise so that your breathing returns to normal **2** to breathe in suddenly because you are surprised

catch your death (of cold) to get very cold

catch fire to start burning, often accidentally: *Nobody knows how the building caught fire.*

catch sb red-handed to find sb just as they are doing sth wrong: *The police caught the burglars red-handed with the stolen jewellery.*

catch sight/a glimpse of sb/sth to see sb/sth for a moment: *We waited outside the theatre, hoping to catch a glimpse of the actress.*

catch the sun **1** to shine brightly in the SUNLIGHT: *The panes of glass flashed as they caught the sun.* **2** to become burned or brown in the sun: *Your face looks red. You've really caught the sun, haven't you?*

PHR V **catch on** (*informal*) **1** to become popular or fashionable: *The idea has never really caught on in this country.* **2** to understand or realize sth: *She's sometimes a bit slow to catch on.*

catch sb out to cause sb to make a mistake by asking a clever question: *Ask me anything you like – you won't catch me out.*

catch up (with sb); **catch sb up** to reach sb who is in front of you: *Sharon's missed so much school she'll have to work hard to catch up with the rest of the class.* ◇ *Go on ahead, I'll catch you up in a minute.*

catch up on sth to spend time doing sth that you have not been able to do for some time: *I'll have to go into the office at the weekend to catch up on my work.*

be/get caught up in sth to be or get involved in sth, usually without intending to: *I seem to have got caught up in a rather complicated situation.*

catch² /kætʃ/ ***noun*** [C] **1** (SPORT) an act of catching sth, for example a ball **2** the amount of fish that sb has caught: *The fishermen brought their catch to the harbour.* **3** a device for fastening sth and keeping it closed: *I can't close my suitcase – the catch is broken.* ◇ *a window catch* **4** a hidden disadvantage or difficulty in sth that seems attractive: *It looks like a good offer but I'm sure there must be a catch in it.*

catching /ˈkætʃɪŋ/ ***adj.*** (not *before* a noun) (*informal*) (HEALTH) (used about a disease) that can easily be passed from one person to another SYN **infectious**

catchment area /ˈkætʃmənt eəriə/ ***noun*** [C] **1** the area from which a school gets its students, a hospital gets its patients, etc. **2** (also **catchment**) (GEOGRAPHY) the area from which rain flows into a particular river or lake

catchphrase /ˈkætʃfreɪz/ ***noun*** [C] a phrase that becomes famous for a while because it is used by a famous person

catchy /ˈkætʃi/ ***adj.*** (used about a tune or song) easy to remember

catechism /ˈkætəkɪzəm/ ***noun*** [sing.] (RELIGION) a set of questions and answers that are used for teaching people about the beliefs of the Christian Church

categorical /ˌkætəˈɡɒrɪkl/ ***adj.*** very definite: *The answer was a categorical 'no'.* ▶ **categorically** /-kli/ ***adv.***: *The Minister categorically denied the rumour.*

categorize (also **-ise**) /ˈkætəɡəraɪz/ ***verb*** [T] to divide people or things into groups; to say that sb/sth belongs to a particular group

category 🔑 AW /ˈkætəɡəri/ ***noun*** [C] (*pl.* **categories**) a group of people or things that are similar to each other: *This painting won first prize in the junior category.* ◇ *These books are **divided into categories** according to subject.*

cater /ˈkeɪtə(r)/ ***verb*** [I] **1** ~ **for sb/sth**; ~ **to sth** to provide what sb/sth needs or wants: *We need a hotel that caters for small children.* ◇ *The menu caters to all tastes.* **2** to provide and serve food and drink at an event or in a place that a lot of people go to

caterer /ˈkeɪtərə(r)/ ***noun*** [C] a person or business that provides food and drink at events or in places that a lot of people go to

catering /ˈkeɪtərɪŋ/ ***noun*** [U] the activity or business of providing food and drink at events or in places that a lot of people go to: *the **hotel and catering industry*** ◇ *Who's going to **do the catering** at the wedding?*

caterpillar /ˈkætəpɪlə(r)/ ***noun*** [C] a small animal with a long body and a lot of legs, which eats the leaves of plants. A **caterpillar** later develops into a BUTTERFLY or MOTH (=flying insects with large, sometimes brightly coloured, wings) ➲ picture on **page 29**

catharsis /kəˈθɑːsɪs/ ***noun*** [U, C] (*pl.* **catharses** /kəˈθɑːsiːz/) (LITERATURE) the process of expressing strong feeling, for example through plays or other artistic activities, as a way of getting rid of anger, reducing suffering, etc. ▶ **cathartic** /kəˈθɑːtɪk/ ***adj.***: *It was a cathartic experience.*

cathedral /kəˈθiːdrəl/ ***noun*** [C] a large church that is the most important one in a district

catheter /ˈkæθɪtə(r)/ ***noun*** [C] (HEALTH) a thin tube that is put into the body in order to remove liquid such as URINE

cathode /ˈkæθəʊd/ ***noun*** [C] (PHYSICS, CHEMISTRY) an ELECTRODE in an electrical device; the negative ELECTRODE in an ELECTROLYTIC cell and the positive ELECTRODE in a battery ➲ look at **anode**

ˌcathode ˈray tube ***noun*** [C] (PHYSICS) a VACUUM tube inside a television or computer screen, etc. from which a stream of ELECTRONS produces images on the screen

Catholic /ˈkæθlɪk/ (RELIGION) = ROMAN CATHOLIC ▸ **Catholicism** /kəˈθɒləsɪzəm/ = ROMAN CATHOLICISM

cation /ˈkætaɪən/ ***noun*** [C] (CHEMISTRY, PHYSICS) an ION with a positive electrical charge ➲ look at anion

catkin /ˈkætkɪn/ ***noun*** [C] a group of very small soft flowers that grows on the branches of some trees. Some **catkins** are long and hang down like pieces of string; others are short and stand up.

CAT scan /ˈkæt skæn/ (*also* **CT scan** /ˌsiː ˈtiː skæn/) ***noun*** [C] (HEALTH) a medical examination that uses a computer to produce an image of the inside of sb's body from X-RAY or ULTRASOUND pictures

cattle /ˈkætl/ ***noun*** [pl.] male and female cows, for example on a farm: ***a herd of cattle*** (= a group of them) ➲ note at **cow**

catwalk /ˈkætwɔːk/ ***noun*** [C] (*AmE also* **runway**) (ARTS AND MEDIA) the long stage that models walk on during a fashion show

Caucasian /kɔːˈkeɪʒn/ ***noun*** [C], ***adj.*** (SOCIAL STUDIES) (of) a member of a race of people who have white or light-coloured skin

caucus /ˈkɔːkəs/ ***noun*** [C] **1** (*especially AmE*) (POLITICS) a meeting of the members or leaders of a political party to choose candidates or to decide policy; the members or leaders of a political party as a group **2** a group of people with similar interests, often within a larger organization or political party

caught past tense, past participle of **catch**[1]

cauldron (*especially AmE* **caldron**) /ˈkɔːldrən/ ***noun*** [C] a large, deep, metal pot that is used for cooking things over a fire

cauliflower /ˈkɒliflaʊə(r)/ ***noun*** [C,U] a large vegetable with green leaves and a round white centre that you eat when it is cooked

cause[1] 🗝 /kɔːz/ ***noun*** **1** [C] a thing or person that makes sth happen: *The police do not know the cause of the accident.* ◇ *Smoking is one of the causes of heart disease.* **2** [U] ~ **(for sth)** reason for feeling sth or behaving in a particular way: *The doctor assured us that there was no **cause for concern**.* ◇ *I don't think you have any real **cause for complaint**.* ➲ note at **reason**[1] **3** [C] an idea or organization that a group of people believe in and support: *We are all committed to the cause of racial equality.*

IDM **be for/in a good cause** to be worth doing because it will help other people

a lost cause → LOST[2]

cause[2] 🗝 /kɔːz/ ***verb*** [T] to make sth happen: *The fire was caused by an electrical fault.* ◇ *High winds caused many trees to fall during the night.* ◇ *Is your leg causing you any pain?*

causeway /ˈkɔːzweɪ/ ***noun*** [C] a road or path that is built higher than the area around it in order to cross water or wet ground: *The island is connected to the mainland by a causeway.*

caustic /ˈkɔːstɪk/ ***adj.*** **1** (CHEMISTRY) (used about a chemical substance) able to destroy or dissolve other substances SYN **corrosive** **2** critical in a cruel way: *a caustic remark*

ˌcaustic ˈsoda ***noun*** [U] (CHEMISTRY) a chemical used in making paper and soap

caution[1] /ˈkɔːʃn/ ***noun*** **1** [U] great care, because of possible danger: *Any advertisement that asks you to send money should be treated **with caution**.* ➲ note at **care**[1] **2** [C] (*BrE*) (LAW) a spoken warning that a judge or police officer gives to sb who has committed a small crime: *As a first offender, she got off with a caution.*

caution[2] /ˈkɔːʃn/ ***verb*** [I,T] **1** ~ **(sb) against sth** to warn sb not to do sth: *The President's advisers have cautioned against calling an election too early.* **2** to give sb an official warning: *Dixon was cautioned by the referee for wasting time.*

cautionary /ˈkɔːʃənəri/ ***adj.*** giving a warning: *The teacher told us a **cautionary tale** about a girl who cheated in her exams.*

cautious /ˈkɔːʃəs/ ***adj.*** taking great care to avoid possible danger or problems: *I'm very cautious about expressing my opinions in public.* ▸ **cautiously** ***adv.***

cavalry /ˈkævlri/ ***noun*** [sing., with sing. or pl. verb] the part of the army that fought on horses in the past; the part of the modern army that uses heavily protected vehicles

cave[1] /keɪv/ ***noun*** [C] (GEOGRAPHY) a large hole in the side of a hill or CLIFF, or under the ground

cave[2] /keɪv/ ***verb***

PHRV **cave in** **1** to fall in: *The roof of the tunnel had caved in and we could go no further.* **2** to suddenly stop arguing or being against sth: *He finally caved in and agreed to the plan.*

caveman /ˈkeɪvmæn/ ***noun*** [C] (*pl.* **-men** /-men/) **1** a person who lived many thousands of years ago in CAVES **2** (*informal*) a man who behaves in an aggressive way

cavern /ˈkævən/ ***noun*** [C] (GEOGRAPHY) a large, deep hole in the side of a hill or under the ground; a big CAVE ➲ picture at **limestone**

caviar (also **caviare**) /ˈkæviɑː(r)/ ***noun*** [U] the eggs of some types of fish, especially the STURGEON, that are preserved using salt and eaten as a very special and expensive type of food

cavity /ˈkævəti/ ***noun*** [C] (*pl.* **cavities**) **1** an empty space inside sth solid: *the abdominal cavity* ◇ *a wall cavity* **2** (HEALTH) a hole in a tooth

cayenne /keɪˈen/ (*also* **ˌcayenne ˈpepper**) ***noun*** [U] a type of red pepper used in cooking to give a hot flavour to food

CBI /ˌsiː biː ˈaɪ/ ***abbr.*** (BUSINESS) **the Confederation of British Industry**; an important organization to which businesses and industries belong

cc /ˌsiː ˈsiː/ ***abbr.*** **1** (BUSINESS) **carbon copy (to)**; used on business letters and emails to show that a copy is being sent to another person: *to Monika Davies, cc Penny Burgess* **2** **cubic centimetre(s)** : *a 1200cc engine*

CCTV /ˌsiː siː tiː ˈviː/ ***abbr.*** closed-circuit television

CD /ˌsiː ˈdiː/ (*also* **ˌcompact ˈdisc**) ***noun*** [C] a small, round piece of hard plastic on which sound is recorded or information stored. You play a CD on a special machine (**CD player**).

CD-ROM /ˌsiː diː ˈrɒm/ ***noun*** [C,U] **compact disc read-only memory**; a CD for use on a computer, which has a lot of information recorded on it. The information cannot be changed or removed. ➲ picture at **computer**

cease 🗝 AW /siːs/ ***verb*** [I,T] (*formal*) to stop or end: *Fighting in the area has now ceased.* ◇ *That organization has ceased to exist.*

ceasefire /ˈsiːsfaɪə(r)/ ***noun*** [C] an agreement between two groups to stop fighting each other ➲ look at **truce**

ceaseless /ˈsiːsləs/ ***adj.*** (*formal*) continuing for a long time without stopping ▸ **ceaselessly** ***adv.***

cedar /ˈsiːdə(r)/ *noun* **1** [C] a type of large tree that never loses its leaves and has wide spreading branches **2** (*also* **cedarwood** /ˈsiːdəwʊd/) [U] the hard red wood of the **cedar** tree

cede /siːd/ *verb* [T] (*written*) to give land or control of sth to another country or person

cedilla /sɪˈdɪlə/ *noun* [C] (LANGUAGE) the mark (¸) placed under the letter *c* in French, Portuguese, etc. to show that it is pronounced like an *s* rather than a *k*; a similar mark under *s* in Turkish and some other languages

ceiling /ˈsiːlɪŋ/ *noun* [C] **1** the top surface of the inside of a room: *a room with a high/low ceiling* **2** a top limit: *The Government has put a 10% ceiling on wage increases.*

celebrate /ˈselɪbreɪt/ *verb* [I,T] to do sth to show that you are happy about sth that has happened or because it is a special day: *When I got the job we celebrated by going out for a meal.* ◇ *Nora celebrated her 90th birthday yesterday.* ▶ **celebratory** /ˌseləˈbreɪtəri/ *adj.*: *We went out for a celebratory meal after the match.*

celebrated /ˈselɪbreɪtɪd/ *adj.* (*formal*) famous: *a celebrated poet*

celebration /ˌselɪˈbreɪʃn/ *noun* [C,U] the act or occasion of doing sth enjoyable because sth good has happened or because it is a special day: *Christmas celebrations* ◇ *I think this is an occasion for celebration!*

celebrity /səˈlebrəti/ *noun* [C] (*pl.* **celebrities**) (ARTS AND MEDIA) a famous person: *a TV celebrity*

celery /ˈseləri/ *noun* [U] a vegetable with long green and white sticks that can be eaten without being cooked: *a stick of celery*

celestial /səˈlestiəl/ *adj.* (*formal*) of the sky or of heaven: ***celestial bodies*** (=the sun, moon, stars, etc.) ➲ look at **terrestrial**

celibate /ˈselɪbət/ *adj.* (*formal*) (RELIGION) never having sexual relations, often because of religious beliefs ▶ **celibacy** /ˈselɪbəsi/ *noun* [U]

cell /sel/ *noun* [C] **1** a small room in a prison or police station in which a prisoner is locked **2** a small room without much furniture in which a MONK or NUN (=a member of a religious group) lives **3** (BIOLOGY) the smallest living part of an animal or a plant: *The human body consists of millions of cells.* ◇ *red **blood cells*** **4** (PHYSICS) a device for producing an electric current, for example by the action of chemicals or light: ***solar cells*** ◇ *a **photoelectric cell*** ➲ picture at **energy** **5** (POLITICS) a small group of people who work as part of a larger political organization, especially secretly: *a terrorist cell* **6** (COMPUTING) one of the small squares in a SPREADSHEET computer program in which you enter a single piece of data **7** (*informal*) (*especially AmE*) =CELLPHONE

cellar /ˈselə(r)/ *noun* [C] an underground room that is used for storing things ➲ look at **basement**

cellist /ˈtʃelɪst/ *noun* [C] a person who plays the CELLO

cello /ˈtʃeləʊ/ *noun* [C] (*pl.* **cellos**) a large musical instrument with strings. You sit down to play it and hold it between your knees. ➲ picture on **page 465**

Cellophane™ /ˈseləfeɪn/ *noun* [U] a transparent plastic material used for covering things

cellphone /ˈselfəʊn/ (*also* **cellular ˈphone**, (*informal* **cell**) (*especially AmE*) =MOBILE PHONE

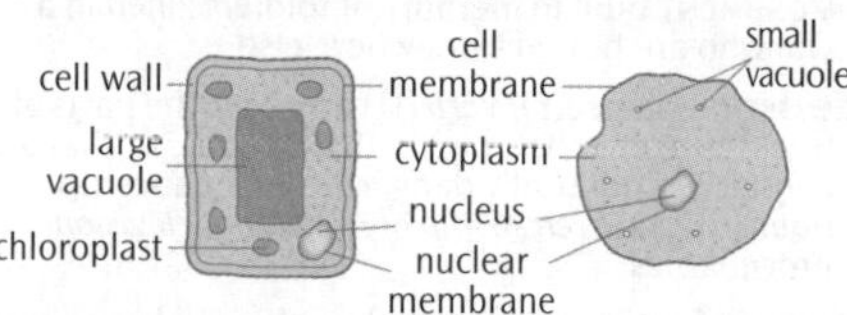

Plant cell
Cell walls made of cellulose Nucleus at the edge of the cell Chloroplasts present in many cells Thin lining of cytoplasm against wall Often one large central vacuole
Animal cell
Cell walls absent Nucleus anywhere but often at the centre Chloroplasts never present Cytoplasm throughout the cell Small vacuoles throughout the cytoplasm

cellular /ˈseljələ(r)/ *adj.* **1** (BIOLOGY) connected with or consisting of the cells of plants or animals: *cellular tissue* **2** (TECHNICAL) connected with a telephone system that works by radio instead of wires: *a cellular network*

cellulose /ˈseljuləʊs/ *noun* [U] (BIOLOGY) a natural substance that forms the cell walls of all plants and trees and is used in making plastics, paper, etc. ➲ picture at **cell**

Celsius /ˈselsiəs/ (*also* **centigrade**) *adj.* (*abbr.* **C**) (SCIENCE) the name of a scale for measuring temperatures, in which water freezes at 0° and boils at 100°: *The temperature tonight will fall to 7°C.* ➲ look at **Fahrenheit**, **kelvin**

Celtic /ˈkeltɪk/ *adj.* (HISTORY) connected with the race of people (**the Celts**) who lived in Wales, Scotland, Ireland and Brittany in ancient times, or with their culture

cement[1] /sɪˈment/ *noun* [U] **1** a grey powder, that becomes hard after it is mixed with water and left to dry. It is used in building for sticking bricks or stones together or for making very hard surfaces. ➲ picture at **building** **2** the hard substance that is formed when **cement** becomes dry and hard: *a floor of cement* ◇ *a cement floor* ➲ look at **concrete**, **mortar** **3** a soft substance that becomes hard when dry and is used for sticking things together or filling in holes: *dental cement* (=for filling holes in teeth) **4** (ANATOMY) a thin layer of material similar to bone that covers the root of a tooth and holds it in place ➲ picture at **tooth**

cement[2] /sɪˈment/ *verb* [T] **1** to join two things together using cement, or a strong sticky substance **2** to make a relationship, agreement, etc. very strong: *This agreement has cemented the relationship between our two countries.*

ceˈment mixer (*also* **ˈconcrete mixer**) *noun* [C] a machine with a large round container (**a drum**) that holds sand, water and CEMENT and turns to mix them all together

cemetery /ˈsemətri/ *noun* [C] (*pl.* **cemeteries**) a place where dead people are buried, especially a place that does not belong to a church ➲ look at **graveyard**, **churchyard**

cenotaph /'senətɑːf/ ***noun*** [C] (ARCHITECTURE) a MONUMENT built in memory of soldiers killed in a war who are buried somewhere else

censor[1] /'sensə(r)/ ***verb*** [T] to remove the parts of a book, film, etc. that might offend people or that are considered politically dangerous ▶ **censorship** ***noun*** [U]: *state censorship of radio and television programmes*

censor[2] /'sensə(r)/ ***noun*** [C] an official who CENSORS books, films, etc.

censure /'senʃə(r)/ ***verb*** [T] (*written*) to tell sb, in a strong and formal way, that they have done sth wrong: *The attorney was censured for not revealing the information earlier.* ▶ **censure *noun*** [U]

census /'sensəs/ ***noun*** [C] (*pl.* **censuses**) (SOCIAL STUDIES) an official count of the people who live in a country, including information about their ages, jobs, etc.

cent /sent/ ***noun*** [C] (*abbr.* c, ct) a unit of money that is worth 100th part of a US dollar or of the main unit of money in some other countries ➲ look at **per cent**

centenary /sen'tiːnəri/ ***noun*** [C] (*pl.* **centenaries**) (*AmE* **centennial** /sen'teniəl/) the year that comes exactly one hundred years after an important event or the beginning of sth: *The school will celebrate its centenary next year.*

center (*AmE*) = CENTRE

centi- /'sentɪ-/ ***prefix*** (in nouns) **1** one hundred: *centipede* **2** (often used in units of measurement) one HUNDREDTH: *centilitre*

centigrade /'sentɪgreɪd/ = CELSIUS: *a temperature of 40 degrees centigrade*

centimetre (*AmE* **centimeter**) /'sentɪmiːtə(r)/ ***noun*** [C] (*abbr.* cm) a measure of length. There are 100 centimetres in a metre.

centipede /'sentɪpiːd/ ***noun*** [C] a small animal like an insect, with a long thin body and very many legs

central /'sentrəl/ ***adj.*** **1** in the centre of sth: *a map of central Europe* ◇ *Our flat is very central* (= near the centre of the city and therefore very convenient). **2** most important; main: *The film's central character is a fifteen-year-old girl.* ➲ note at **main**[1] **3** (only *before* a noun) having control over all other parts: ***central government*** (= the government of a whole country, not local government) ◇ *the **central nervous system*** ▶ **centrally** /'sentrəli/ ***adv.***: *The hotel is centrally located for all major attractions.*

ˌcentral 'heating ***noun*** [U] a system for heating a building from one main point. Air or water is heated and carried by pipes to all parts of the building.

centralize (also **-ise**) /'sentrəlaɪz/ ***verb*** [T] (usually passive) (POLITICS) to give control of all the parts of a country or organization to a group of people in one place: *Our educational system is becoming increasingly centralized.* OPP **decentralize** ▶ **centralization** (also **-isation**) /ˌsentrəlaɪ'zeɪʃn/ ***noun*** [U]

ˌcentral 'processing unit ***noun*** [C] (*abbr.* **CPU**) (COMPUTING) the part of a computer that controls all the other parts of the system

ˌcentral reser'vation (*AmE* **median**; **'median strip**) ***noun*** [C] a narrow piece of land with a barrier that separates the two sides of a motorway

centre[1] (*AmE* **center**) /'sentə(r)/ ***noun*** **1** [C, usually sing.] the middle point or part of sth: *I work in the centre of Bangkok.* ◇ *Which way is the **town centre**, please?* ➲ picture at **circle** **2** [C] a building or place where a particular activity or service is based: *a sports/health/shopping centre* ◇ *This university is a centre of excellence for medical research.* **3** [C] a place where sb/sth is collected together; the point towards which sth is directed: *major urban/industrial centres* ◇ *She always likes to be **the centre of attention**.* ◇ *You should bend your legs to keep a low **centre of gravity**.* **4** [sing., with sing. or pl. verb] (POLITICS) a political position that is not extreme: *Her views are left of centre.*

centre[2] (*AmE* **center**) /'sentə(r)/ ***verb***

PHR V **centre on/around sb/sth** to have sb/sth as its centre: *The life of the village centres on the church, the school and the pub.*

-centric /'sentrɪk/ ***suffix*** (used in compounds) concerned with or interested in the thing mentioned: *Eurocentric policies* (= concerned with Europe)

centrifugal /ˌsentrɪ'fjuːgl/ ***adj.*** (TECHNICAL) moving or tending to move away from a centre

ˌcentriˌfugal 'force (*also* **cen'trifugal force**) ***noun*** [C] (PHYSICS) a force that appears to cause an object travelling around a centre to fly away from the centre and off its CIRCULAR path

centrifuge /'sentrɪfjuːdʒ/ ***noun*** [C] a machine with a part that turns round very quickly to separate substances, for example liquids from solids, by forcing the heavier substance to the outer edge

centriole /'sentrɪəʊl/ ***noun*** [C] (BIOLOGY) a structure in a cell that helps the cell to divide into two parts

centripetal /ˌsentrɪ'piːtl/ ***adj.*** (TECHNICAL) moving or tending to move towards a centre: *centripetal force*

century /'sentʃəri/ ***noun*** [C] (*pl.* **centuries**) **1** a particular period of 100 years that is used for giving dates: *We live in the 21st century* (= the period between the years 2000 and 2099). **2** any period of 100 years: *People have been making wine in this area for centuries.*

CEO /ˌsiː iː 'əʊ/ ***abbr.*** (BUSINESS) **chief executive officer**; the person with the most powerful position in a company or business

cereals

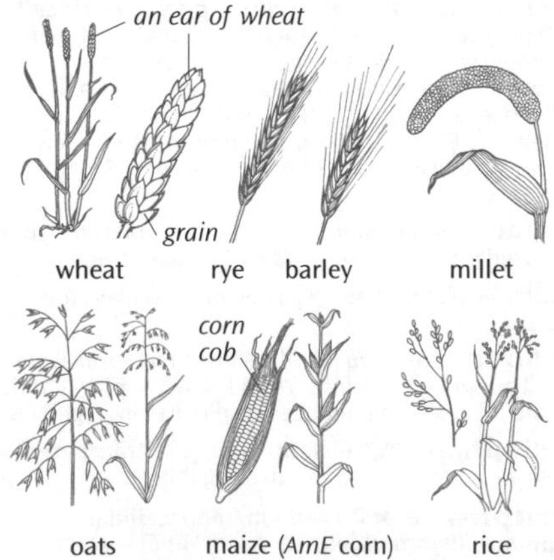

cephalopod /ˈsefləpɒd/ ***noun*** [C] (BIOLOGY) any of the class of sea animals that have a large soft head, large eyes and eight or ten long thin legs (**tentacles**): *Octopus and squid are cephalopods.* ➲ picture on **page 29**

ceramic /səˈræmɪk/ ***noun*** (ART) **1** [C, usually pl.] a pot or other object made of CLAY that has been made permanently hard by heat: *an exhibition of ceramics by Picasso* **2 ceramics** [U] the art of making and decorating **ceramics** ➲ look at **pottery** ▶ **ceramic *adj.***: *ceramic tiles*

cereal /ˈsɪəriəl/ ***noun*** [C,U] **1** (AGRICULTURE) any type of grain that can be eaten or made into flour, or the grass that the grain comes from: *Wheat, barley and rye are cereals.* **2** a food that is made from grain, often eaten for breakfast with milk: *a bowl of cereal*

cerebellum /ˌserɪˈbeləm/ ***noun*** [C] (*pl.* **cerebellums** or **cerebella** /-ˈbelə/) (ANATOMY) the part of the brain at the back of the head that controls the movement of the muscles ➲ picture at **brain**

cerebral /ˈserəbrəl/ ***adj.*** (ANATOMY) relating to the brain

ˌcerebral ˈpalsy ***noun*** [U] (HEALTH) a medical condition, usually caused by brain damage before or at birth, that causes the loss of control of the arms and legs

cerebrum /səˈriːbrəm/ ***noun*** [C] (*pl.* **cerebra** /-brə/) (ANATOMY) the front part of the brain, responsible for thoughts, emotions and personality ➲ picture at **brain**

ceremonial /ˌserɪˈməʊniəl/ ***adj.*** connected with a ceremony: *a ceremonial occasion* ▶ **ceremonially** /-niəli/ ***adv.***

ceremony 🔑 /ˈserəməni/ ***noun*** (*pl.* **ceremonies**) **1** [C] a formal public or religious event: *the opening ceremony of the Olympic Games* ◇ *a wedding ceremony* **2** [U] formal behaviour, speech, actions, etc. that are expected on special occasions: *The new hospital was opened **with great ceremony**.*

cerium /ˈsɪəriəm/ ***noun*** [U] (*symbol* **Ce**) (CHEMISTRY) a chemical element. **Cerium** is a silver-white metal used in the production of glass and CERAMICS. ℹ For more information on the periodic table of elements, look at pages R34-5.

THESAURUS

certain

bound • sure • definite • assured

These are all words describing sth that will definitely happen or is definitely true.

certain: *They are certain to agree.*

bound: *He's bound to pass the exam – he's worked so hard.*

sure: *She's sure to be picked for the team.*

definite: *Is it definite that he's leaving?*

assured (*formal*): *They were assured of victory.*

certain 🔑 /ˈsɜːtn/ ***adj.*** **1** (not before a noun) ~ **(that...)**; ~ **(of sth)** completely sure; without any doubts: *She's absolutely certain that there was somebody outside her window.* ◇ *We're not quite certain what time the train leaves.* ◇ *I'm certain of one thing – he didn't take the money.* ➲ note at **sure** **2** ~ **(that...)**; ~ **(to do sth)** sure to happen or to do sth; definite: *It is almost certain that unemployment will increase this year.* ◇ *The Director is certain to agree.* ◇ *We must rescue them today, or they will face certain death.* **3** (only *before* a noun) used for talking about a particular thing or person without naming it or them: *You can only contact me at certain times of the day.* ◇ *There are certain reasons why I'd prefer not to meet him again.* **4** (only *before* a noun) some, but not very much: *I suppose I have **a certain amount of** respect for Mr Nolan.* **5** noticeable but difficult to describe: *There was a certain feeling of autumn in the air.* **6** (*formal*) used before a person's name to show that you do not know them: *I received a letter from a certain Ms Groves.*

IDM **for certain** without doubt: *I don't know for certain what time we'll arrive.*

make certain (that...) **1** to do sth in order to be sure that sth else happens: *They're doing everything they can to make certain that they win.* **2** to do sth in order to be sure that sth is true: *We'd better phone Akram before we go to make certain he's expecting us.*

certainly 🔑 /ˈsɜːtnli/ ***adv.*** **1** without doubt; definitely: *The number of students will certainly increase after 2007.* **2** (used in answer to questions) of course: *'Do you think I could borrow your notes?' 'Certainly.'*

certainty /ˈsɜːtnti/ ***noun*** (*pl.* **certainties**) **1** [U] the state of being completely sure about sth: *We can't say with certainty that there is life on other planets.* OPP **uncertainty** **2** [C] something that is sure to happen: *It's now almost a certainty our team will win the league.*

certificate 🔑 /səˈtɪfɪkət/ ***noun*** [C] **1** (LAW) an official document that may be used to prove that the facts it states are true: *a **birth/marriage/medical certificate*** **2** (EDUCATION) an official document proving that you have completed a course of study or passed an exam; a qualification obtained after a course of study or an exam: *a Postgraduate Certificate in Education* (=a British qualification for teachers)

certify /ˈsɜːtɪfaɪ/ ***verb*** [T] (*pres. part.* **certifying**; *3rd person sing. pres.* **certifies**; *pt, pp* **certified**) **1** (LAW) to state officially, especially in writing, that sth is true: *We need someone to certify that this is her signature.* **2** (EDUCATION) to give sb a certificate to show that they have successfully completed a course of training for a particular profession: *a certified accountant* **3** (*BrE*) (LAW, HEALTH) to officially state that sb is mentally ill, so that they can be given medical treatment

certiorari /ˌsɜːtiəʊˈrɑːri/ ***noun*** [U] (LAW) an order by which a case tried in a lower court is tried again in a higher court: *an application for an order of certiorari*

certitude /ˈsɜːtɪtjuːd/ ***noun*** (*formal*) **1** [U] a feeling of being certain about sth **2** [C] a thing about which you are certain

cervix /ˈsɜːvɪks/ ***noun*** [C] (*pl.* **cervices** /-vɪsiːz/) (ANATOMY) the narrow passage at the opening of the UTERUS (=the place where a baby grows inside a woman's body) ▶ **cervical** /ˈsɜːvɪkl; səˈvaɪkl/ ***adj.***

cesarean (*AmE*) = CAESAREAN

cesium (*AmE*) = CAESIUM

cessation /seˈseɪʃn/ ***noun*** [U, C] (*formal*) the stopping of sth; a pause in sth: *The UN have demanded an immediate cessation of hostilities.*

cesspit /ˈsespɪt/ (*also* **cesspool** /ˈsespuːl/) ***noun*** [C] a covered hole or container in the ground for collecting waste from a building, especially from the toilets

cetacean /sɪˈteɪʃn/ ***noun*** [C] (BIOLOGY) a WHALE, DOLPHIN, or other sea creature that belongs to the same group ➲ picture on **page 29**

cf. ***abbr.*** (in writing) compare

CFC /ˌsiː ef ˈsiː/ ***noun*** [C,U] (**ENVIRONMENT**) **chlorofluorocarbon**; a type of gas found, for example, in cans of spray which is harmful to the earth's atmosphere ➲ look at **ozone layer**

CGI /ˌsiː dʒiː ˈaɪ/ ***abbr.*** computer-generated imagery: *The movie is full of stunts and has some amazing CGI special effects.*

CGT /ˌsiː dʒiː ˈtiː/ ***abbr.*** = CAPITAL GAINS TAX

ch. ***abbr.*** chapter

chain[1] ⊶ /tʃeɪn/ ***noun*** **1** [C,U] a line of metal rings that are joined together: *a **bicycle chain** ◇ She was wearing a **silver chain** round her neck. ◇ a length of chain* **2** [C] a series of connected things or people: *a chain of mountains/a mountain chain ◇ The book examines the complex **chain of events** that led to the Russian Revolution. ◇ The Managing Director is at the top of the **chain of command**.* **3** [C] a group of shops, hotels, etc. that are owned by the same company: *a chain of supermarkets ◇ a **fast-food chain***

chain[2] ⊶ /tʃeɪn/ ***verb*** [T] ~ **sb/sth (to sth)**; ~ **sb/sth (up)** to fasten sb/sth to sth else with a chain: *The dog is kept chained up outside.*

ˈ**chain mail** ***noun*** [U] (**HISTORY**) ARMOUR (= covering to protect the body when fighting) made of small metal rings linked together

ˌ**chain reˈaction** ***noun*** [C] **1** (**CHEMISTRY, PHYSICS**) a chemical change that forms products which themselves cause more changes and new products **2** a series of events, each of which causes the next

ˈ**chain-smoke** ***verb*** [I] to smoke continuously, lighting one cigarette after another
▶ **chain-smoker** ***noun*** [C]

ˈ**chain store** ***noun*** [C] one of a number of similar shops that are owned by the same company

chair[1] ⊶ /tʃeə(r)/ ***noun*** **1** [C] a piece of furniture for one person to sit on, with a seat, a back and four legs: *a kitchen chair ◇ an armchair* **2** [sing.] the person who is controlling a meeting: *Please address your questions to the chair.* **3** [C] (**EDUCATION**) the position of being in charge of a department in a university: *She holds the chair of economics at Cardiff University.*

chair[2] /tʃeə(r)/ ***verb*** [T] to be the chairman or chairwoman of a meeting: *Who's chairing the meeting this evening?*

chairman ⊶ /ˈtʃeəmən/ **chairwoman** /ˈtʃeəwʊmən/ ***noun*** [C] (*pl.* **-men** /-mən/) (*pl.* **-women** /-wɪmɪn/) **1** the person in charge of a meeting, who tells people when they can speak, etc. **2** (**BUSINESS**) the person in charge of a committee, a company, etc.: *The chairman of the company presented the annual report.* ▶ **chairmanship** ***noun*** [sing.]

chairperson /ˈtʃeəpɜːsn/ ***noun*** [C] (*pl.* **-persons**) a chairman or chairwoman

chalet /ˈʃæleɪ/ ***noun*** [C] (**TOURISM**) a wooden house, especially one built in a mountain area or used by people on holiday

chalk[1] /tʃɔːk/ ***noun*** **1** [U] (**GEOLOGY**) a type of soft white stone: *chalk cliffs* **2** [C,U] a substance similar to **chalk** that is made into white or coloured sticks for writing or drawing

chalk[2] /tʃɔːk/ ***verb*** [I,T] to write or draw sth with chalk: *Somebody had chalked a message on the wall.*
PHR V **chalk sth up** to succeed in getting sth: *The team has chalked up five wins this summer.*

chalkboard /ˈtʃɔːkbɔːd/ (*AmE*) = BLACKBOARD

challenge[1] ⊶ **AW** /ˈtʃælɪndʒ/ ***noun*** [C] **1** something new and difficult that forces you to make a lot of effort: *I'm finding my new job an exciting challenge. ◇ The company will have to **face** many **challenges** in the coming months. ◇ How will this government **meet the challenge** of rising unemployment?* **2** a ~ **(to sb) (to do sth)** an invitation from sb to fight, play, argue, etc. against them: *The Prime Minister should accept our challenge and call a new election now.*

challenge[2] ⊶ **AW** /ˈtʃælɪndʒ/ ***verb*** [T] **1** ~ **sb (to sth/to do sth)** to invite sb to fight, play, argue, etc. against you: *They've challenged us to a football match this Saturday.* **2** to question if sth is true, right, etc., or not: *She hates anyone challenging her authority.*

challenger /ˈtʃælɪndʒə(r)/ ***noun*** [C] a person who invites you to take part in a competition, because they want to win a title or position that you hold

challenging **AW** /ˈtʃælɪndʒɪŋ/ ***adj.*** forcing you to make a lot of effort: *a challenging job* ➲ note at **difficult**

chamber ⊶ /ˈtʃeɪmbə(r)/ ***noun*** [C] **1** a hall in a public building that is used for formal meetings: *The members left the council chamber. ◇ the **Senate/House chamber*** ➲ look at **Chamber of Commerce** **2** (**POLITICS**) one of the parts of a parliament: *the **Lower/Upper Chamber*** (= in Britain, the House of Commons/House of Lords) *◇ Under Senate rules, the chamber must vote on the bill by this Friday.* **3** a room used for the particular purpose that is mentioned: *a burial chamber* ➲ look at **gas chamber** **4** a space in the body, in a plant or in a machine, which is separated from the rest: *the four chambers of the heart* **5** (*old-fashioned*) a bedroom or private room

chambermaid /ˈtʃeɪmbəmeɪd/ ***noun*** [C] (**TOURISM**) a woman whose job is to clean and tidy hotel bedrooms

ˈ**chamber music** ***noun*** [U] (**MUSIC**) CLASSICAL music that is written for a small group of instruments

ˌ**Chamber of ˈCommerce** ***noun*** [C] (**BUSINESS**) a group of local business people who work together to help business and trade in a particular town

chameleon /kəˈmiːliən/ ***noun*** [C] a type of small REPTILE that can change the colour of its skin

chamfer /ˈtʃæmfə(r)/ ***noun*** [C] (**TECHNICAL**) a cut made along an edge or on a corner so that it slopes rather than being at 90°

champagne /ʃæmˈpeɪn/ ***noun*** [U, C] a French white wine which has a lot of bubbles in it and is often very expensive

champion[1] /ˈtʃæmpiən/ ***noun*** [C] **1** (**SPORT**) a person, team, etc. that has won a competition: *a world champion ◇ a champion swimmer* **2** (**POLITICS**) a person who speaks and fights for a particular group, idea, etc.: *a champion of free speech*

champion[2] /ˈtʃæmpiən/ ***verb*** [T] (**POLITICS**) to support or fight for a particular group or idea: *to champion the cause of human rights*

championship /ˈtʃæmpiənʃɪp/ ***noun*** [C] (often plural) (**SPORT**) a competition or series of competitions to find the best player or team in a sport or game: *the World Hockey Championships*

chance[1] ⊶ /tʃɑːns/ ***noun*** **1** [C] a ~ **of (doing) sth**; a ~ **(that...)** a possibility: *I think there's a good chance that she'll be the next Prime Minister. ◇ to have a slim/an outside chance of success ◇ I think we **stand a** good **chance** of winning the competition. ◇ Is there any chance of getting tickets for tonight's concert?* **2** [C] ~ **(of doing sth/to do sth)** an opportunity: *If* *somebody invited me to America, I'd* ***jump at the chance*** (=accept enthusiastically). ◇ *Be quiet and* ***give*** *her* ***a chance*** *to explain.* ◇ *I think you should tell him now. You may not* ***get*** *another* ***chance.*** **3** [C] a risk: *We may lose some money but we'll just have to take that chance.* ◇ *Fasten your seat belt – you shouldn't take (any) chances.* ◇ *I didn't want to* ***take a chance on*** *anyone seeing me, so I closed the curtains.* **4** [U] luck; the way that some things happen without any cause that you can see or understand: *We have to plan every detail – I don't want to* ***leave*** *anything* ***to chance.*** ◇ *We met* ***by chance*** (=we had not planned to meet) *as I was walking down the street.*

IDM **by any chance** (used for asking sth politely) perhaps or possibly: *Are you, by any chance, going into town this afternoon?*

the chances are (that)... (*informal*) it is probable that...: *The chances are that it will rain tomorrow.*

no chance (*informal*) there is no possibility of that happening: *'Perhaps your mother will give you the money.' 'No chance!'*

on the off chance in the hope that sth might happen, although it is not very likely: *I didn't think you'd be at home, but I just called in on the off chance.*

chance² /tʃɑːns/ ***verb*** **1** [T] (*informal*) **~ sth/doing sth** to risk sth: *'Take an umbrella.' 'No, I'll* ***chance it*** (=take the risk that it may rain). **2** [I] (*formal*) **~ to do sth** to happen or to do sth by chance: *They chanced to be staying at the same hotel.*

chance³ /tʃɑːns/ ***adj.*** (only *before* a noun) not planned: *a chance meeting*

chancel /ˈtʃɑːnsl/ ***noun*** [C] (ARCHITECTURE) the part of a church near the ALTAR, where the priests and the CHOIR (=singers) sit during services

chancellor /ˈtʃɑːnsələ(r)/ ***noun*** [C] (often **Chancellor**) (often used in a title) **1** (POLITICS) the head of government in Germany or Austria: *Chancellor Merkel* **2** (*BrE*) (POLITICS) = CHANCELLOR OF THE EXCHEQUER: *MPs waited for the chancellor's announcement.* **3** (EDUCATION) the official head of a university in Britain ➲ look at **vice chancellor** **4** (EDUCATION) the head of some American universities **5** used in the titles of some senior state officials in Britain: *the Lord Chancellor* (=a senior law official)

ˌChancellor of the Exˈchequer ***noun*** [C] (POLITICS, FINANCE) (in Britain) the government minister who is responsible for financial affairs

chandelier /ˌʃændəˈlɪə(r)/ ***noun*** [C] a large round frame with many branches for lights or CANDLES, that hangs from the ceiling and is decorated with small pieces of glass

change¹ ⊶ /tʃeɪndʒ/ ***verb*** **1** [I,T] to become different or to make sb/sth different: *This town has changed a lot since I was young.* ◇ *Our plans have changed – we leave in the morning.* ◇ *His lottery win has not changed him at all.* SYN **alter** **2** [I,T] **~ (sb/sth) to/into sth**; **~ (from A) (to/into B)** to become a different thing; to make sb/sth take a different form: *The traffic lights changed from green to red.* ◇ *They changed the spare bedroom into a study.* ◇ *The new job changed him into a more confident person.* **3** [T] **~ sth (for sth)** to take, have or use sth instead of sth else: *Could I change this blouse for a larger size?* ◇ *to change jobs* ◇ *to change a wheel on a car* ◇ *to change direction* ◇ *Can I change my appointment from Wednesday to Thursday?* **4** [T] **to ~ sth (with sb)** (used with a plural noun) to exchange sth with sb, so that you have what they had, and they have what you had: *The teams change ends at half-time.* ◇ *If you want to sit by the window I'll change seats with you.* SYN **swap** **5** [I,T] **~ (out of sth) (into sth)** to take off your clothes and put different ones on: *He's changed his shirt.* ◇ *I had a shower and changed before going out.* ◇ *She changed out of her work clothes and into a clean dress.* ◇ *You can* ***get changed*** *in the bedroom.* **6** [T] to put clean things onto sb/sth: *The baby's nappy needs changing.* ◇ *to* ***change the bed*** (=to put clean sheets on) **7** [T] **~ sth (for/into sth)** to give sb money and receive the same amount back in money of a different type: *Can you change a ten-pound note for two fives?* ◇ *I'd like to change fifty euros into US dollars.* **8** [I,T] to get out of one bus, train, etc. and get into another: *Can we get to Mumbai direct or do we have to change (trains)?*

IDM **change hands** to pass from one owner to another

change your mind to change your decision or opinion: *I'll have the green one. No, I've changed my mind – I want the red one.*

change/swap places (with sb) → PLACE¹

change the subject to start talking about sth different

change your tune (*informal*) to change your opinion or feelings about sth

change your ways to start to live or behave in a different and better way from before

chop and change → CHOP¹

PHR V **change over (from sth) (to sth)** to stop doing or using one thing and start doing or using sth else: *The theatre has changed over to a computerized booking system.*

change² ⊶ /tʃeɪndʒ/ ***noun*** **1** [C,U] **~ (in/to sth)** the process of becoming or making sth different: *There was little change in the patient's condition overnight.* ◇ *After two hot summers, people were talking about a change in the climate.* **2** [C] **a ~ (of sth)** something that you take, have or use instead of sth else: *We must notify the bank of our change of address.* ◇ *I packed my toothbrush and a change of clothes.* **3** [U] the money that you get back if you pay more than the amount sth costs: *If a paper costs 60p and you pay with a pound coin, you will get 40p change.* **4** [U] coins of low value: *He needs some change for the phone.* ◇ *Have you got* ***change for*** *a hundred dollar bill?* (=coins or notes of lower value that together make a hundred dollars)

IDM **a change for the better/worse** a person, thing or situation that is better/worse than the one before

a change of heart a change in your opinion or the way that you feel

for a change in order to do sth different from usual: *I usually cycle to work, but today I decided to walk for a change.*

make a change to be enjoyable or pleasant because it is different from what you usually do

changeable /ˈtʃeɪndʒəbl/ ***adj.*** likely to change; often changing

changeover /ˈtʃeɪndʒəʊvə(r)/ ***noun*** [C] a change from one system to another

ˈchanging room ***noun*** [C] a room for changing clothes in, for example before or after playing sport

channel¹ AW /ˈtʃænl/ ***noun*** [C] **1** (ARTS AND MEDIA) a television station: *Which channel is the film on?* ➲ look at **station¹** (4) **2** (ARTS AND MEDIA) a band of radio waves used for sending out radio or television programmes: *terrestrial/satellite channels* **3** a way or route along which news, information, etc. is sent: *a channel of communication* ◇ *You have to order new equipment through the official channels.* **4** a passage that water can flow along, especially in the ground, on the bottom of a river, etc.: *a drainage channel* **5** a deep passage of water in a river or near the coast that can be used as route for ships **6** (GEOGRAPHY) a passage of water that connects two areas of water, especially two seas **7 the Channel** (also **the ˌEnglish 'Channel**) (GEOGRAPHY) the area of sea between England and France: *the **Channel** Tunnel*

channel² AW /'tʃænl/ ***verb*** [T] (**channelling**; **channelled**: *AmE also* **channeling**; **channeled**) to make sth move along a particular path or route: *Water is channelled from the river to the fields.* ◇ (*figurative*) *You should channel your energies into something constructive.*

chant¹ /tʃɑːnt/ ***noun* 1** [C] a word or phrase that is sung or shouted many times: *A chant of 'we are the champions' went round the stadium.* **2** [C,U] (RELIGION) a religious song or prayer or a way of singing, using only a few notes that are repeated many times: *a Buddhist chant* ➲ look at **Gregorian chant**

chant² /tʃɑːnt/ ***verb*** [I,T] **1** to sing or shout a word or phrase many times: *The protesters marched by, chanting slogans.* **2** (RELIGION) to sing or say a religious song or prayer using only a few notes that are repeated many times

chanty, chantey (*AmE*) = SHANTY (2)

chaos /'keɪɒs/ ***noun*** [U] a state of complete confusion and lack of order: *The country was **in chaos** after the war.* ◇ *The heavy snow has **caused chaos** on the roads.*

chaotic /keɪ'ɒtɪk/ ***adj.*** in a state of CHAOS: *With no one in charge the situation became chaotic.*

chap /tʃæp/ ***noun*** [C] (*especially BrE, informal*) a man or boy

chap. ***abbr.*** (in writing) chapter

chapatti (also **chapati**) /tʃə'pæti; -'pɑːti/ ***noun*** [C] a type of flat round Indian bread

chapel /'tʃæpl/ ***noun*** [C,U] (RELIGION) a small building or room that is used by some Christians as a church or for prayer: *a Methodist chapel*

chaperone /'ʃæpərəʊn/ ***noun*** [C] (SOCIAL STUDIES) in the past, an older person, usually a woman, who went to public places with a young woman who was not married, to look after her and to make sure that she behaved correctly ▶ **chaperone *verb*** [T]

chaplain /'tʃæplɪn/ ***noun*** [C] (RELIGION) a priest who works in a hospital, school, prison, etc.: *an army chaplain*

chapped /tʃæpt/ ***adj.*** (HEALTH) (used about the lips or skin) rough, dry and sore, especially because of wind or cold weather

chapter ⊶ AW /'tʃæptə(r)/ ***noun*** [C] **1** (*abbr.* chap.) (LITERATURE) a separate section of a book, usually with a number or title: *Please read Chapter 2 for homework.* **2** a period of time in a person's life or in history: *The last few years have been a difficult chapter in the country's history.*

character ⊶ /'kærəktə(r)/ ***noun* 1** [C, usually sing., U] the qualities that make sb/sth different from other people or things; the nature of sb/sth: *Although they are twins, their characters are quite different.* ◇ *These two songs are very different **in character**.* **2** [U] strong personal qualities: *The match developed into a test of character rather than just physical strength.* **3** [U] qualities that make sb/sth interesting: *Modern houses often seem to lack character.* **4** [U] the good opinion that people have of you: *The article was a vicious attack on the President's character.* **5** [C] (*informal*) an interesting, amusing, strange or unpleasant person: *Neil's quite a character – he's always making us laugh.* ◇ *I saw a suspicious-looking character outside the bank, so I called the police.* **6** [C] (LITERATURE) a person in a book, story, etc.: *The main character in the film is a boy who meets an alien.* **7** [C] (LANGUAGE) a letter or sign that you use when you are writing or printing: *Chinese characters*

IDM **in/out of character** typical/not typical of sb/sth: *Emma's rude reply was completely out of character.*

characteristic¹ ⊶ /ˌkærəktə'rɪstɪk/ ***noun*** [C] a ~ of (sb/sth) a quality that is typical of sb/sth and that makes them or it different from other people or things

characteristic² ⊶ /ˌkærəktə'rɪstɪk/ ***adj.*** ~ (of sb/sth) very typical of sb/sth: *The flat landscape is characteristic of this part of the country.* OPP **uncharacteristic** ▶ **characteristically** /-kli/ ***adv.***: *'No' he said, in his characteristically direct manner.*

characterization (also **-isation**) /ˌkærəktəraɪ'zeɪʃn/ ***noun*** [U, C] **1** (LITERATURE) the way that a writer makes the characters in a book or play seem real **2** (*formal*) the way in which sb/sth is described

characterize (also **-ise**) /'kærəktəraɪz/ ***verb*** [T] (*formal*) **1** (often passive) to be typical of sb/sth: *the tastes that characterize Thai cooking* **2 ~ sb/sth (as sth)** to describe what sb/sth is like: *The President characterized the meeting as friendly and positive.*

charade /ʃə'rɑːd/ ***noun* 1** [C] a situation or event that is clearly false but in which people pretend to do or be sth: *They pretend to be friends but it's all a charade. Everyone knows they hate each other.* **2 charades** [U] a party game in which people try to guess the title of a book, film, etc. that one person must represent using actions but not words

charcoal /'tʃɑːkəʊl/ ***noun*** [U] a black substance that is produced from burned wood. It can be used for drawing or as a fuel.

charge¹ ⊶ /tʃɑːdʒ/ ***noun* 1** [C,U] the price that you must pay for sth: *The hotel makes a small **charge for** changing currency.* ◇ *We deliver **free of charge**.* ➲ note at **price 2** [C,U] a statement that says that sb has done sth illegal or bad: *He was arrested **on a charge of** murder.* ◇ *The writer dismissed the charge that his books were childish.* **3** [U] a position of control over sb/sth; responsibility for sb/sth: *Who is **in charge of** the office while Alan's away?* ◇ *The assistant manager had to **take charge of** the team when the manager resigned.* **4** [C] a sudden attack where sb/sth runs straight at sb/sth else **5** [C] (PHYSICS, CHEMISTRY) the amount of electricity that is put into a battery or carried by a substance: *a positive/negative charge*

IDM **bring/press charges (against sb)** (LAW) to formally accuse sb of a crime so that there can be a trial in a court of law

reverse the charges → REVERSE¹

charge² ⊶ /tʃɑːdʒ/ ***verb* 1** [I,T] **~ (sb/sth) for sth** to ask sb to pay a particular amount of money: *We charge £35 per night for a single room.* ◇ *They forgot to charge us for the drinks.* ➲ look at **overcharge 2** [T] **~ sb (with sth)** (LAW) to accuse sb officially of doing sth which is against the law: *Six men have been charged with attempted robbery.* **3** [I,T] to run straight at sb/sth, or in a particular direction, in an aggressive or noisy way: *The bull put its head down ready to charge (us).* ◇ *The children charged into the room.* **4** [T] to put electricity into sth: *to charge a battery* ➲ look at **recharge**

charger /ˈtʃɑːdʒə(r)/ ***noun*** [C] a piece of equipment for loading a battery with electricity: *a mobile phone charger*

chariot /ˈtʃæriət/ ***noun*** [C] (HISTORY) an open vehicle with two wheels that was pulled by a horse or horses in ancient times

charisma /kəˈrɪzmə/ ***noun*** [U] a powerful personal quality that some people have to attract and influence other people: *The president is not very clever, but he has great charisma.* ▶ **charismatic** /ˌkærɪzˈmætɪk/ ***adj.***

charitable /ˈtʃærətəbl/ ***adj.*** **1** kind; generous: *Some people accused him of lying, but a more charitable explanation was that he had made a mistake.* **2** connected with a charity

charity ⊶ /ˈtʃærəti/ ***noun*** (*pl.* **charities**) **1** [C,U] an organization that collects money to help people who are poor, sick, etc. or to do work that is useful to society: *We went on a sponsored walk to* ***raise money for charity***. **2** [U] kindness towards other people: *to act out of charity*

ˈ**charity shop** (*AmE* ˈ**thrift shop/store**) ***noun*** [C] a shop that sells clothes, books, etc. given by people to make money for charity

charlatan /ˈʃɑːlətən/ ***noun*** [C] a person who says that they have knowledge or skills that they do not really have

charm[1] /tʃɑːm/ ***noun*** **1** [C,U] a quality that pleases and attracts people: *The charm of the island lies in its unspoilt beauty.* ◇ *Barry found it hard to resist Linda's charms.* **2** [C] something that you wear because you believe it will bring you good luck: *a necklace with a* ***lucky charm*** *on it* ◇ *a* ***charm bracelet***

charm[2] /tʃɑːm/ ***verb*** [T] **1** to please and attract sb: *Her drawings have charmed children all over the world.* **2** to protect sb/sth as if by magic: *He has led a charmed life, surviving serious illness and a plane crash.*

charming /ˈtʃɑːmɪŋ/ ***adj.*** very pleasing or attractive ▶ **charmingly** ***adv.***

charred /tʃɑːd/ ***adj.*** burnt black by fire

chart[1] ⊶ AW /tʃɑːt/ ***noun*** **1** [C] a drawing which shows information in the form of a diagram, etc.: *a temperature chart* ◇ *This chart shows the company's sales for this year.* ➲ look at **bar chart**, **flow chart**, **pie chart** **2** [C] a map of the sea or the sky: *navigation charts* **3 the charts** [pl.] (MUSIC) an official list of the songs or CDs, etc., that have sold the most in a particular week

chart[2] ⊶ AW /tʃɑːt/ ***verb*** [T] **1** to follow or record sth carefully and in detail: *This television series* ***charts the history of*** *the country since independence.* **2** to make a map of one area of the sea or sky: *an uncharted coastline*

charter[1] /ˈtʃɑːtə(r)/ ***noun*** [C] **1** (POLITICS) a written statement describing the rights that a particular group of people should have: *the European Union's Social Charter of workers' rights* **2** [C] (POLITICS) a written statement of the principles and aims of an organization SYN **constitution**: *the United Nations Charter* **3** [C] (POLITICS) an official document stating that a ruler or government allows a new organization, town or university to be established and gives it particular rights: *Certain towns were allowed to hold weekly markets, by royal charter.* **4** [U] the hiring of a plane, boat, etc.: *a charter airline* ◇ *a yacht available for charter*

charter[2] /ˈtʃɑːtə(r)/ ***verb*** [T] to rent a ship, plane, etc. for a particular purpose or for a particular group of people: *As there was no regular service to the island we had to charter a boat.*

charts

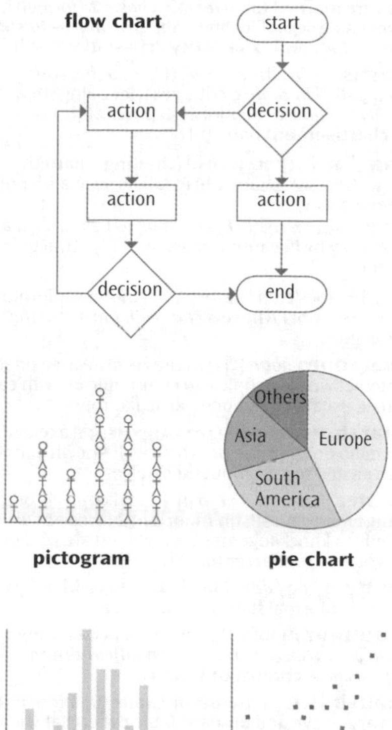

pictogram
pie chart

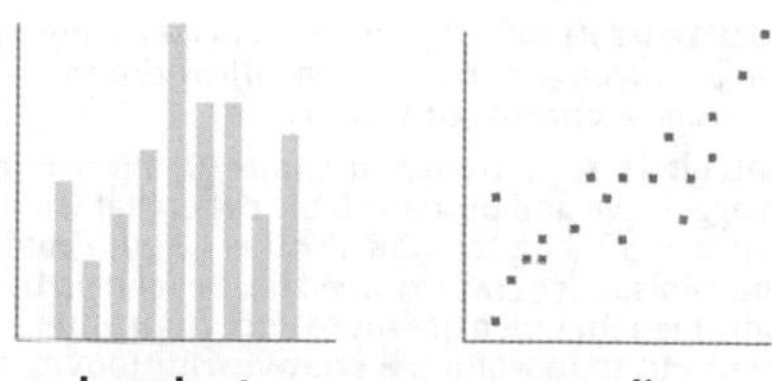
bar chart
scatter diagram

chartered /ˈtʃɑːtəd/ ***adj.*** (*BrE*) (only *before* a noun) (used about people in certain professions) fully trained; qualified according to the rules of a professional organization that has a royal CHARTER: ***a chartered accountant/surveyor/engineer**, etc.*

ˈ**charter flight** ***noun*** [C] (TOURISM) a flight in which all seats are paid for by a travel company and then sold to their customers, usually at a lower price than that of a SCHEDULED FLIGHT

chase[1] ⊶ /tʃeɪs/ ***verb*** **1** [I,T] ~ (**after**) **sb/sth** to run after sb/sth in order to catch them or it: *The dog chased the cat up a tree.* ◇ *The police car chased after the stolen van.* **2** [I] to run somewhere fast: *The kids were chasing around the park.*

chase[2] ⊶ /tʃeɪs/ ***noun*** [C] the act of following sb/sth in order to catch them or it: *an exciting car chase*

IDM **give chase** to begin to run after sb/sth in order to try to catch them or it: *The robber ran off and the policeman gave chase.*

chasm /ˈkæzəm/ ***noun*** [C] **1** (GEOGRAPHY) a very deep crack or hole in the ground **2** (*formal*) a wide difference of feelings, interests, etc. between two people or groups

chassis /ˈʃæsi/ ***noun*** [C] (*pl.* **chassis** /ˈʃæsi/) the metal frame of a vehicle onto which the other parts fit

chaste /tʃeɪst/ ***adj.*** **1** (*old-fashioned*) not having sex with anyone; only having sex with the person that you are married to: *to remain chaste* **2** (*formal*) not expressing sexual feelings: *She gave him a* ***chaste*** *kiss on the cheek.* ▸ **chastity** /ˈtʃæstəti/ ***noun*** [U]

chastise /tʃæˈstaɪz/ ***verb*** [T] **1** ~ **sb (for sth/for doing sth)** (*formal*) to criticize sb for doing sth wrong **2** (*old-fashioned*) to punish sb physically ▸ **chastisement** ***noun*** [U]

chat[1] ⊶ /tʃæt/ ***verb*** [I] (**chatting**; **chatted**) ~ **(with/to sb) (about sth)** to talk to sb in a friendly, informal way

PHR V **chat sb up** (*BrE, informal*) to talk to sb in a friendly way because you are sexually attracted to them

chat[2] ⊶ /tʃæt/ ***noun*** [C,U] a friendly informal conversation: *I'll* ***have a chat*** *with Jim about the arrangements.*

ˈ**chat room** ***noun*** [C] (COMPUTING) an area on the Internet where people can communicate with each other, usually about one particular topic

ˈ**chat show** ***noun*** [C] (ARTS AND MEDIA) a television or radio programme on which well-known people are invited to talk about themselves

chatter /ˈtʃætə(r)/ ***verb*** [I] **1** to talk quickly or for a long time about sth unimportant **2** (used about your teeth) to knock together because you are cold or frightened ▸ **chatter** ***noun*** [U]

chatty /ˈtʃæti/ ***adj.*** **1** talking a lot in a friendly way **2** in an informal style: *a chatty letter*

chauffeur /ˈʃəʊfə(r)/ ***noun*** [C] a person whose job is to drive a car for sb else: *a chauffeur-driven limousine* ▸ **chauffeur** ***verb*** [T]

chauvinism /ˈʃəʊvɪnɪzəm/ ***noun*** [U] **1** (POLITICS) an aggressive and unreasonable belief that your own country is better than all others **2** (*also* ˌ**male** ˈ**chauvinism**) (SOCIAL STUDIES) the belief held by some men that men are more important, intelligent, etc. than women ▸ **chauvinist** /ˈʃəʊvɪnɪst/ ***noun*** [C], ***adj.***

cheap[1] ⊶ /tʃiːp/ ***adj.*** **1** low in price, costing little money: *Oranges are cheap at the moment.* ◇ *Computers are getting cheaper all the time.* SYN **inexpensive** OPP **expensive** **2** charging low prices: *a cheap hotel/restaurant* **3** low in price and quality and therefore not attractive: *The clothes in that shop look cheap.*

IDM **dirt cheap** → DIRT

cheap[2] /tʃiːp/ ***adv.*** (*informal*) for a low price: *I got this coat cheap in the sale.*

IDM **be going cheap** (*informal*) to be on sale at a lower price than usual

cheapen /ˈtʃiːpən/ ***verb*** [T] **1** to make sb lose respect for himself or herself: *She felt cheapened by his treatment of her.* SYN **degrade** **2** to make sth lower in price **3** to make sth seem to have less value: *The movie was accused of cheapening human life.*

cheaply ⊶ /ˈtʃiːpli/ ***adv.*** without spending or costing much money: *I'm sure I could buy this more cheaply elsewhere.*

cheat[1] ⊶ /tʃiːt/ ***verb*** **1** [T] to trick sb or make them believe sth which is not true: *The shopkeeper cheated customers by giving them too little change.* **2** [I] ~ **(at sth)** to act in a dishonest way in order to gain an advantage, especially in a game, a competition, an exam, etc.: *Paul was caught cheating in the exam.* ◇ *to cheat at cards* **3** [I] ~ **(on sb)** to not be faithful to your husband, wife or regular partner by having a secret sexual relationship with sb else

PHR V **cheat sb (out) of sth** to take sth from sb in a dishonest or unfair way: *They cheated him out of his share of the profits.*

cheat[2] ⊶ /tʃiːt/ ***noun*** [C] a person who cheats

check[1] ⊶ /tʃek/ ***verb*** **1** [I,T] ~ **(sth) (for sth)** to examine or test sth in order to make sure that it is safe or correct, in good condition, etc.: *Check your work for mistakes before you hand it in.* ◇ *The doctor X-rayed me to check for broken bones.* **2** [I,T] ~ **(sth) (with sb)** to make sure that sth is how you think it is: *You'd better check with Tim that it's OK to borrow his bike.* ◇ *I'll phone and check what time the bus leaves.* **3** [T] to stop or make sb/sth stop or go more slowly: *She almost told her boss what she thought of him, but checked herself in time.* ◇ *Phil checked his pace as he didn't want to tire too early.* **4** [T] (*AmE*) = TICK[1] (2)

PHR V **check in (at...)**; **check into...** (TOURISM) to go to a desk in a hotel or an airport and tell the person there that you have arrived

check sth off to mark names or items on a list

check (up) on sb/sth to find out how sb/sth is: *We call my grandmother every evening to check up on her.*

check out (of...) (TOURISM) to pay your bill and leave a hotel

check sb/sth out **1** to find out more information about sb/sth, especially to find out if sth is true or not: *We need to check out these rumours of possible pay cuts.* **2** (*informal*) to look at or examine a person or thing that seems interesting or attractive: *Check out the prices at our new store!*

check up on sb/sth to make sure that sb/sth is working correctly, behaving well, etc., especially if you think they are not

check[2] ⊶ /tʃek/ ***noun*** **1** [C] **a** ~ **(on sth)** a close look at sth to make sure that it is safe, correct, in good condition, etc.: *We* ***carry out/do*** *regular* ***checks*** *on our products to make sure that they are of high quality.* ◇ *I don't go to games, but I like to* ***keep a check*** *on my team's results.* **2** [C,U] a pattern of squares, often of different colours: *a check jacket* ◇ *a pattern of blue and red checks* **3** [U] the situation in a game of CHESS, in which a player must move to protect their king ➲ look at **checkmate** **4** [C] (*AmE*) = CHEQUE **5** [C] (*AmE*) = BILL[1] (1) ➲ note at **bill**[1] **6** [C] (*AmE*) = TICK[2] (1)

IDM **hold/keep sth in check** to stop sth from advancing or increasing too quickly

checkbook (*AmE*) = CHEQUEBOOK

checkbox /ˈtʃekbɒks/ ***noun*** [C] (COMPUTING) a small square on a computer screen that you click on with the mouse in order to choose whether a particular function is switched on or off

checked /tʃekt/ ***adj.*** with a pattern of squares: *a red-and-white checked tablecloth*

checkers /ˈtʃekəz/ (*AmE*) = DRAUGHT[1] (2)

ˈ**check-in** ***noun*** (TOURISM) **1** [C,U] the place where you go first when you arrive at an airport, to show your ticket, etc. **2** [U] the act of showing your ticket, etc. when you arrive at an airport: *Our check-in time is 10.30 am.*

ˈ**checking account** (*AmE*) = CURRENT ACCOUNT

checklist /ˈtʃeklɪst/ ***noun*** [C] a list of things that you must do or have

checkmate /ˌtʃekˈmeɪt/ ***noun*** [U] the situation in a game of CHESS, in which you cannot protect your king and so have lost the game ➲ look at **check**[2] (3)

checkout /ˈtʃekaʊt/ ***noun*** [C] the place where you pay for the things that you are buying in a supermarket

checkpoint /ˈtʃekpɔɪnt/ ***noun*** [C] a place where all people and vehicles must stop and be checked: *an army checkpoint*

ˈcheck-up ***noun*** [C] (HEALTH) a general medical examination to make sure that you are healthy

Cheddar /ˈtʃedə(r)/ (*also* ˌ**Cheddar ˈcheese**) ***noun*** [U] a type of hard yellow cheese

cheek /tʃiːk/ ***noun*** **1** [C] either side of the face below your eyes ➲ picture on **page 80** **2** [C,U] (*BrE*) rude behaviour; lack of respect: *He's got a cheek, asking to borrow money again!*

IDM **(with) tongue in cheek** → TONGUE

cheekbone /ˈtʃiːkbəʊn/ ***noun*** [C] the bone below your eye ➲ picture on **page 80**

cheeky /ˈtʃiːki/ ***adj.*** (*BrE*) (**cheekier**; **cheekiest**) not showing respect; rude: *Don't be so cheeky! Of course I'm not fat!* ▸ **cheekily** ***adv.***

cheer[1] /tʃɪə(r)/ ***noun*** [C] a loud shout to show that you like sth or to encourage sb who is taking part in a competition, sport, etc.: *A great **cheer went up** from the crowd.*

cheer[2] /tʃɪə(r)/ ***verb*** **1** [I,T] to shout to show that you like sth or to encourage sb who is taking part in competition, sport, etc.: *Everyone cheered the winner as he crossed the finishing line.* **2** [T] to give hope, comfort or encouragement to sb: *They were all cheered by the good news.*

PHRV **cheer sb on** to shout in order to encourage sb in a race, competition, etc.: *As the runners started the last lap the crowd cheered them on.*

cheer (sb/sth) up to become or to make sb happier; to make sth look more attractive: *Cheer up! Things aren't that bad.* ◇ *A few pictures would cheer this room up a bit.*

cheerful /ˈtʃɪəfl/ ***adj.*** feeling happy; showing that you are happy: *Caroline is always very cheerful.* ◇ *a cheerful smile* ▸ **cheerfulness** ***noun*** [U] ▸ **cheerfully** /-fəli/ ***adv.***

cheerio /ˌtʃɪəriˈəʊ/ ***exclamation*** (*BrE, informal*) goodbye

cheerleader /ˈtʃɪəliːdə(r)/ ***noun*** [C] (especially in the US) one of a group of girls or women at a sports match who wear special uniforms and shout, dance, etc. in order to encourage people to support the players

cheers /tʃɪəz/ ***exclamation*** (*informal*) **1** used to express good wishes before you have an alcoholic drink: *'Cheers,' she said, raising her wine glass.* **2** (*BrE*) goodbye **3** (*BrE*) thank you

cheery /ˈtʃɪəri/ ***adj.*** happy and smiling: *a cheery remark/wave/smile* ▸ **cheerily** ***adv.***

cheese /tʃiːz/ ***noun*** **1** [U] a type of food made from milk. **Cheese** is usually white or yellow in colour and can be soft or hard: *a piece of cheese* ◇ *a cheese sandwich* **2** [C] a type of cheese: *a wide selection of cheeses*

cheesecake /ˈtʃiːzkeɪk/ ***noun*** [C,U] a type of cake that is made from soft cheese and sugar on a PASTRY or biscuit base, often with fruit on top

cheesy /ˈtʃiːzi/ ***adj.*** (**cheesier**; **cheesiest**) (*informal*) of low quality and without style: *an incredibly cheesy love song*

cheetah /ˈtʃiːtə/ ***noun*** [C] a large wild cat with black spots that can run very fast

chef /ʃef/ ***noun*** [C] a professional cook, especially the head cook in a hotel, restaurant, etc.

chemical[1] AW /ˈkemɪkl/ ***adj.*** (CHEMISTRY) **1** connected with chemistry: ***a chemical element*** **2** produced by or using processes which involve changes to atoms or MOLECULES: ***chemical reactions/ processes*** ▸ **chemically** /-kli/ ***adv.***: *The raw sewage is chemically treated.*

chemical[2] AW /ˈkemɪkl/ ***noun*** [C] (CHEMISTRY) a substance that is used or produced in a chemical process: *Sulphuric acid is a dangerous chemical.* ◇ *Farmers are being urged to reduce their use of chemicals and work with nature to combat pests.*

ˌ**chemical ˈwarfare** ***noun*** [U] the use of poisonous gases and chemicals as weapons in a war

ˌ**chemical ˈweapon** ***noun*** [C] a weapon that uses poisonous gases and chemicals to kill and injure people ➲ look at **biological weapon**

chemist /ˈkemɪst/ ***noun*** [C] **1** (*also* **pharmacist**, *AmE* **druggist**) a person who prepares and sells medicines **2** **the chemist's** (*AmE* **drugstore**) a shop that sells medicines, soap, camera film, etc.: *I got my tablets from the chemist's.* **3** a person who is a specialist in chemistry

chemistry /ˈkemɪstri/ ***noun*** [U] **1** the scientific study of the structure of substances and what happens to them in different conditions or when mixed with each other **2** the structure of a particular substance **3** the relationship between two people, usually a strong sexual attraction

chemotherapy /ˌkiːməʊˈθerəpi/ (also *informal* **chemo** /ˈkiːməʊ/) ***noun*** [U] (HEALTH) the treatment of disease, especially cancer, using chemical substances: *She was suffering from leukaemia and undergoing chemotherapy.* ➲ look at **radiation**, **radiotherapy**

cheque (*AmE* **check**) /tʃek/ ***noun*** [C,U] (FINANCE) a piece of paper printed by a bank that you sign and use to pay for things: *She **wrote out a cheque** for £1000.* ◇ *I went to the bank to **cash a cheque**.* ◇ *Can I **pay by cheque**?*

chequebook (*AmE* **checkbook**) /ˈtʃekbʊk/ ***noun*** [C] (FINANCE) a book of cheques

ˌ**chequebook ˈjournalism** ***noun*** [U] (*BrE*) (ARTS AND MEDIA) the practice of journalists paying people large amounts of money to give them personal or private information for a newspaper story

ˈ**cheque card** ***noun*** [C] (*BrE*) (FINANCE) a small plastic card that you show when you pay with a cheque as proof that your bank will pay the amount on the cheque ➲ look at **cash card**, **credit card**

cherish /ˈtʃerɪʃ/ ***verb*** [T] **1** to love sb/sth and look after them or it carefully **2** to keep a thought, feeling, etc. in your mind and think about it often: *a cherished memory*

cherry /ˈtʃeri/ ***noun*** [C] (*pl.* **cherries**) **1** a small soft round fruit with shiny red or black skin and a large seed inside **2** (*also* ˈ**cherry tree**) the tree that produces **cherries**

cherub /ˈtʃerəb/ ***noun*** [C] (RELIGION) a type of ANGEL (= a spirit who is believed to live in heaven with God), shown as a small fat, usually male, child with wings

chervil /ˈtʃɜːvɪl/ ***noun*** [U] a plant with leaves that are used in cooking as a HERB

chess /tʃes/ ***noun*** [U] a game for two people that is played on a board with 64 black and white squares (**a chessboard**). Each player has 16 pieces which can be moved according to fixed rules: ***Can you play chess?***

chest ⊶ /tʃest/ ***noun*** [C] **1** the top part of the front of the body between the neck and the stomach ➲ picture on **page 80** **2** a large strong box that is used for storing or carrying things
IDM **get sth off your chest** (*informal*) to talk about sth that you have been thinking or worrying about

chestnut /ˈtʃesnʌt/ ***noun*** [C] **1** (*also* ˈ**chestnut tree**) a tree with large leaves that produces smooth brown nuts in shells with sharp points on the outside **2** a smooth brown nut from the **chestnut** tree. You can eat some **chestnuts**: *roast chestnuts*
➲ look at **conker**

ˌ**chest of ˈdrawers** ***noun*** [C] a piece of furniture with drawers in it that is used for storing clothes, etc.

chevron /ˈʃevrən/ ***noun*** [C] a line or pattern in the shape of a V

chew ⊶ /tʃuː/ ***verb*** [I,T] **1** to break up food in your mouth with your teeth before you swallow it **2** ~ **(on) sth** to bite sth continuously with the back teeth: *The dog was chewing on a bone.*

ˈ**chewing gum** (*also* **gum**) ***noun*** [U] a sweet sticky substance that you chew in your mouth but do not swallow ➲ look at **bubblegum**

chewy /ˈtʃuːi/ ***adj.*** (used about food) difficult to break up with your teeth before it can be swallowed: *chewy meat/toffee*

chiaroscuro /kiˌɑːrəˈskʊərəʊ/ ***noun*** [U] (ART) the way light and shade are shown; the contrast between light and shade

chic /ʃiːk/ ***adj.*** fashionable and elegant
▶ **chic** ***noun*** [U]

chick /tʃɪk/ ***noun*** [C] a baby bird, especially a young chicken

chicken¹ ⊶ /ˈtʃɪkɪn/ ***noun*** **1** [C] a bird that people often keep for its eggs and its meat ➲ picture on **page 29** **2** [U] the meat of this bird: *chicken soup*

RELATED VOCABULARY

Notice that chicken is the general word for the bird and its meat. A male chicken is called a **cock** (*AmE* **rooster**), a female is called a **hen** and a young bird is called a **chick**.

IDM **Don't count your chickens (before they're hatched)** → COUNT¹

chicken² /ˈtʃɪkɪn/ ***verb***
PHR V **chicken out (of sth)** (*informal*) to decide not to do sth because you are afraid

chickenpox /ˈtʃɪkɪnpɒks/ ***noun*** [U] (HEALTH) a disease, especially of children. When you have **chickenpox** you feel very hot and get red spots on your skin that make you want to scratch.

chicory /ˈtʃɪkəri/ (*AmE* **endive**) ***noun*** [U] a small pale green plant with bitter leaves that can be eaten cooked or not cooked

chief¹ ⊶ /tʃiːf/ ***adj.*** (only *before* a noun) **1** most important; main: *One of the chief reasons for his decision was money.* ➲ note at **main¹** **2** (often **Chief**) of the highest level or position: *the chief executive of a company* ◇ *Detective Chief Inspector Garcia*

chief² ⊶ /tʃiːf/ ***noun*** [C] **1** the person who has command or control over an organization: *the chief of police* **2** (often as a title) the leader of a community or a TRIBE

ˌ**chief eˈxecutive officer** ***noun*** [C] (*abbr.* **CEO**) (BUSINESS) the person in a company who has the most power and authority

chiefly /ˈtʃiːfli/ ***adv.*** mainly; mostly: *His success was due chiefly to hard work.*

chieftain /ˈtʃiːftən/ ***noun*** [C] (SOCIAL STUDIES) the leader of a TRIBE

chiffon /ˈʃɪfɒn/ ***noun*** [U] a very thin, transparent type of cloth used for making clothes, etc.

chilblain /ˈtʃɪlbleɪn/ ***noun*** [C] (HEALTH) a painful red area on your foot, hand, etc. that is caused by cold weather

child ⊶ /tʃaɪld/ ***noun*** [C] (*pl.* **children** /ˈtʃɪldrən/) **1** a young boy or girl who is not yet an adult: *A group of children were playing in the park.* ◇ *a six-year-old child* ◇ *the children's room* **2** a son or daughter of any age: *She has two children but both are married and have moved away.*

ˌ**child ˈbenefit** ***noun*** [U] money that is paid every week by the British government to parents for each child that they have

childbirth /ˈtʃaɪldbɜːθ/ ***noun*** [U] the act of giving birth to a baby: *His wife died **in childbirth**.*

childcare /ˈtʃaɪldkeə(r)/ ***noun*** [U] the job of looking after children, especially while the parents are at work: *Some employers provide childcare facilities.*

childhood /ˈtʃaɪldhʊd/ ***noun*** [C,U] the time when you are a child: *Harriet had a very unhappy childhood.* ◇ *childhood memories*

childish /ˈtʃaɪldɪʃ/ ***adj.*** **1** connected with or typical of a child: *childish handwriting* **2** (used about an adult) behaving in a stupid or silly way
SYN **immature** ▶ **childishly** ***adv.***

childless /ˈtʃaɪldləs/ ***adj.*** having no children

childlike /ˈtʃaɪldlaɪk/ ***adj.*** having the qualities that children usually have, especially INNOCENCE: ***childlike enthusiasm/delight*** ➲ look at **childish**

childminder /ˈtʃaɪldmaɪndə(r)/ ***noun*** [C] (*BrE*) a person whose job is to look after children while their parents are at work ➲ look at **babysitter**

childproof /ˈtʃaɪldpruːf/ ***adj.*** designed so that young children cannot open, use or damage it: *childproof containers for medicine*

ˈ**children's home** ***noun*** [C] an institution where children live whose parents cannot look after them

chili (*AmE*) = CHILLI

chill¹ /tʃɪl/ ***noun*** **1** [sing.] an unpleasant cold feeling: *There's a chill in the air.* ◇ (*figurative*) *A chill of fear went down my spine.* **2** [C] (*informal*) (HEALTH) a common illness that affects your nose and throat; a cold: *to catch a chill*

chill² /tʃɪl/ ***verb*** [I,T] **1** to become or to make sb/sth colder **2** (*also* **chill out**) (*informal*) to relax and not feel angry or nervous about anything: *I work hard all week so on Sundays I just chill out.*

chilli (*AmE* **chili**) /ˈtʃɪli/ ***noun*** [C,U] (*pl.* **chillies**: *AmE* **chilies**) a small green or red vegetable that has a very strong hot taste: *chilli powder*

chilling /ˈtʃɪlɪŋ/ ***adj.*** frightening: *a chilling ghost story*

chilly /ˈtʃɪli/ ***adj.*** (**chillier**; **chilliest**) **1** (used about the weather but also about people) too cold to be comfortable: *It's a chilly morning. You need a coat on.* **2** unfriendly: *We got a very chilly reception.*

chime /tʃaɪm/ ***verb*** [I,T] (used about a bell or clock) to ring ▶ **chime** ***noun*** [C]
PHR V **chime in (with sth)** (*informal*) to interrupt a conversation and add your own comments

chimney /ˈtʃɪmni/ ***noun*** [C] a pipe through which smoke or steam is carried up and out through the roof of a building

'chimney sweep *noun* [C] a person whose job is to clean the inside of CHIMNEYS with long brushes

chimpanzee /ˌtʃɪmpæn'ziː/ (also *informal* **chimp** /tʃɪmp/) *noun* [C] a small intelligent African APE (=an animal like a large monkey without a tail) ➲ picture on **page 29**

chin ⊶ /tʃɪn/ *noun* [C] the part of your face below your mouth ➲ picture on **page 80**

china /'tʃaɪnə/ *noun* [U] **1** white CLAY of good quality that is used for making cups, plates, etc.: *a china vase* **2** cups, plates, etc. that are made from china

ˌchina 'clay =KAOLIN

chink /tʃɪŋk/ *noun* [C] a small narrow opening: *Daylight came in through a chink between the curtains.*

chintz /tʃɪnts/ *noun* [U] a shiny cotton cloth with a printed design, usually of flowers, which is used for making curtains, covering furniture, etc.

chip[1] ⊶ /tʃɪp/ *noun* [C] **1** the place where a small piece of stone, glass, wood, etc. has broken off sth: *This dish has a chip in it.* **2** a small piece of stone, glass, wood, etc. that has broken off sth **3** (*especially AmE* **ˌFrench 'fry; fry**) [usually pl.] a thin piece of potato that is fried in hot fat or oil **4** (*AmE*) =CRISP[2]: *potato chips* **5** (**COMPUTING**) =MICROCHIP: *chip technology* **6** a flat round piece of plastic that you use to represent a particular amount of money in some types of gambling

IDM **have a chip on your shoulder (about sth)** (*informal*) to feel angry about sth that happened a long time ago because you think it is unfair

chip[2] /tʃɪp/ *verb* [I,T] (**chipping**; **chipped**) **1** to break a small piece off the edge or surface of sth: *They chipped the paint trying to get the table through the door.* **2** (**SPORT**) to kick or hit a ball a short distance through the air

PHRV **chip in (with sth)** (*informal*) **1** to interrupt when sb else is talking **2** to give some money as part of the cost of sth: *We all chipped in and bought him a present when he left.*

chipmunk /'tʃɪpmʌŋk/ *noun* [C] a small North American animal with a long, thick tail and bands of dark and light colour on its back

'chip shop (*also* **chippy** /'tʃɪpi/) *noun* [C] (in Britain) a shop that cooks and sells fish and chips and other fried food to take away and eat

chiropodist /kɪ'rɒpədɪst/ (*AmE* **podiatrist**) *noun* [C] (**HEALTH**) a person whose job is the care and treatment of people's feet

chiropody /kɪ'rɒpədi/ (*AmE* **podiatry**) *noun* [U] (**HEALTH**) the care and treatment of people's feet

chiropractor /'kaɪrəʊpræktə(r)/ *noun* [C] (**HEALTH**) a person whose job involves treating some diseases and physical problems by pressing and moving the bones in a person's SPINE or joints ➲ look at **osteopath**

chirp /tʃɜːp/ *verb* [I] (used about small birds and some insects) to make short high sounds

chisel /'tʃɪzl/ *noun* [C] a tool with a sharp end that is used for cutting or shaping wood or stone ➲ picture at **tool**

chivalry /'ʃɪvlri/ *noun* [U] polite and kind behaviour by men which shows respect towards women ▶ **chivalrous** /'ʃɪvlrəs/ *adj.*

chive /tʃaɪv/ *noun* [C, usually pl.] a long thin green plant that tastes like onion and is used in cooking

chlamydia /klə'mɪdiə/ *noun* [U] (**HEALTH**) a disease caused by bacteria, which is caught by having sex with an infected person

chloride /'klɔːraɪd/ *noun* [U,C] a COMPOUND of CHLORINE and another chemical element

chlorinate /'klɔːrɪneɪt/ *verb* [T] to put CHLORINE in sth, especially water: *a chlorinated swimming pool* ▶ **chlorination** /ˌklɔːrɪ'neɪʃn/ *noun* [U] ➲ picture at **water**

chlorine /'klɔːriːn/ *noun* [U] (*symbol* **Cl**) (**CHEMISTRY**) a greenish-yellow gas with a strong smell, that is used for making water safe to drink or to swim in ❶ For more information on the periodic table of elements, look at pages R34-5.

chlorofluorocarbon /ˌklɔːrəʊˌflʊərəʊ'kɑːbən/ *noun* [C] (**CHEMISTRY, ENVIRONMENT**) a CFC; a COMPOUND (=a combination) of CARBON FLUORINE and CHLORINE that is harmful to the environment

chloroform /'klɒrəfɔːm/ *noun* [U] (*symbol* $CHCl_3$) (**CHEMISTRY**) a colourless liquid with a strong smell used by doctors in the past to make people unconscious, for example before an operation

chlorophyll /'klɒrəfɪl/ *noun* [U] (**BIOLOGY**) the green substance in plants that takes in light from the sun to help them grow ➲ look at **photosynthesis**

chloroplast /'klɒrəplɑːst/ *noun* [C] (**BIOLOGY**) the part of a green plant cell that contains CHLOROPHYLL and in which PHOTOSYNTHESIS (=the changing of light from the sun into energy) takes place ➲ picture at **cell**

chock-a-block /ˌtʃɒk ə 'blɒk/ *adj.* (not *before* a noun) completely full: *The High Street was chock-a-block with shoppers.*

chocoholic /ˌtʃɒkə'hɒlɪk/ *noun* [C] a person who loves chocolate and eats a lot of it

chocolate ⊶ /'tʃɒklət/ *noun* **1** [U] a sweet brown substance made from seeds (**cocoa beans**) that you can eat as a sweet or use to give flavour to food and drinks: *a bar of* ***milk/plain chocolate*** ◇ *a chocolate milkshake* **2** [C] a small sweet that is made from or covered with chocolate: *a box of chocolates* **3** [C,U] a drink made from powdered chocolate with hot milk or water: *a mug of* ***hot chocolate*** **4** [U] a dark brown colour

choice[1] ⊶ /tʃɔɪs/ *noun* **1** [C] a ~ (**between A and B**) an act of choosing between two or more people or things: *David was forced to* ***make a choice*** *between moving house and losing his job.* **2** [U] the right or chance to choose: *There is a rail strike so we* ***have no choice*** *but to cancel our trip.* ◇ *to have freedom of choice* SYN **option** **3** [C,U] two or more things from which you can or must choose: *This cinema offers a choice of six different films every night.* **4** [C] a person or thing that is chosen: *Colin would be my choice as team captain.* ➲ verb **choose**

IDM **by choice** because you have chosen: *I wouldn't go there by choice.*

choice[2] /tʃɔɪs/ *adj.* of very good quality: *choice beef*

choir /'kwaɪə(r)/ *noun* [C, with sing. or pl. verb] (**MUSIC**) a group of people who sing together in churches, schools, etc.

choke[1] /tʃəʊk/ *verb* **1** [I,T] ~ (**on sth**) to be or to make sb unable to breathe because sth is stopping air getting into the lungs: *She was choking on a fish bone.* ◇ *The smoke choked us.* ➲ look at **strangle** **2** [T] (usually passive) ~ **sth (up) (with sth)** to fill a passage, space, etc., so that nothing can pass through: *The roads to the coast were choked with traffic.*

PHRV **choke sth back** to hide or control a strong emotion: *to choke back tears/anger*

choke² /tʃəʊk/ ***noun*** [C] **1** the device in a car, etc. that controls the amount of air going into the engine. If you pull out the **choke** it makes it easier to start the car. **2** an act or the sound of sb CHOKING

cholera /ˈkɒlərə/ ***noun*** (**HEALTH**) [U] a serious disease that causes stomach pains and VOMITING and can cause death. **Cholera** is most common in hot countries and is carried by water.

cholesterol /kəˈlestərɒl/ ***noun*** [U] (**BIOLOGY**, **HEALTH**) a substance that is found in the blood, etc. of people and animals. Too much **cholesterol** is thought to be a cause of heart disease.

choose /tʃuːz/ ***verb*** [I,T] (*pt* **chose** /tʃəʊz/; *pp* **chosen** /ˈtʃəʊzn/) **1** ~ (**between A and/or B**); ~ (**A**) (**from B**); ~ **sb/sth as sth** to decide which thing or person you want out of the ones that are available: *Choose carefully before you make a final decision.* ◇ *Amy had to choose between getting a job or going to college.* ◇ *The viewers chose this programme as their favourite.* **2** ~ (**to do sth**) to decide or prefer to do sth: *You are free to leave whenever you choose.* ◇ *They chose to resign rather than work for the new manager.* ➲ noun **choice**
IDM **pick and choose** → PICK¹

choosy /ˈtʃuːzi/ ***adj.*** (*informal*) (used about a person) difficult to please

chop¹ /tʃɒp/ ***verb*** [T] (**chopping**; **chopped**) ~ **sth** (**up**) (**into sth**) to cut sth into pieces with a knife, etc.: *finely chopped herbs* ◇ *Chop the onions up into small pieces.*
IDM **chop and change** to change your plans or opinions several times
PHR V **chop sth down** to cut a tree, etc. at the bottom so that it falls down
chop sth off (**sth**) to remove sth from sth by cutting it with a knife or a sharp tool

chop² /tʃɒp/ ***noun*** [C] **1** a thick slice of meat with a piece of bone in it ➲ look at **steak** **2** an act of chopping sth: *a karate chop*

chopper /ˈtʃɒpə(r)/ ***noun*** [C] (*informal*) =HELICOPTER

ˈ**chopping board** ***noun*** [C] a piece of wood or plastic used for cutting meat or vegetables on

choppy /ˈtʃɒpi/ ***adj.*** (used about the sea) having a lot of small waves; slightly rough

chopstick /ˈtʃɒpstɪk/ ***noun*** [C, usually pl.] one of the two thin pieces of wood used for eating with, especially in Asian countries

choral /ˈkɔːrəl/ ***adj.*** (**MUSIC**) that is written for or involving a CHOIR (=a group of singers)

chord /kɔːd/ ***noun*** [C] **1** (**MUSIC**) two or more musical notes that are played at the same time ➲ look at **arpeggio** **2** (**MATHEMATICS**) a straight line that joins two points on a curve ➲ picture at **circle**

chore /tʃɔː(r)/ ***noun*** [C] a job that is not interesting but that you must do: *household chores*

choreograph /ˈkɒriəgrɑːf/ ***verb*** [T] (**ARTS AND MEDIA**) to design and arrange the movements of a dance ► **choreographer** /ˌkɒriˈɒgrəfə(r)/ ***noun*** [C]

choreography /ˌkɒriˈɒgrəfi/ ***noun*** [U] (**ARTS AND MEDIA**) the arrangement of movements for a dance performance

chorus¹ /ˈkɔːrəs/ ***noun*** **1** [C] (**MUSIC**) the part of a song that is repeated at the end of each VERSE SYN **refrain** **2** [C] (**MUSIC**) a piece of music, usually part of a larger work, that is written for a CHOIR (=a group of singers) **3** [C, with sing. or pl. verb] (**MUSIC**) a large group of people who sing together SYN **choir** **4** [C, with sing. or pl. verb] (**ARTS AND MEDIA**) a group of performers who sing and dance in a musical show: *the chorus line* (=a line of singers and dancers performing together) **5 a ~ of sth** [sing.] something that a lot of people say together: ***a chorus of cheers/criticism/disapproval***

chorus² /ˈkɔːrəs/ ***verb*** [T] (used about a group of people) to sing or say sth together: *'That's not fair!' the children chorused.*

chose past tense of **choose**

chosen past participle of **choose**

Christ /kraɪst/ (*also* **Jesus**; **Jesus Christ** /ˌdʒiːzəs ˈkraɪst/) ***noun*** (**RELIGION**) the man who Christians believe is the son of God and whose teachings the Christian religion is based on

christen /ˈkrɪsn/ ***verb*** [T] **1** (**RELIGION**) to give a person, usually a baby, a name during a Christian ceremony in which he or she is made a member of the Church: *The baby was christened James Harry.* ➲ look at **baptize** **2** to give sb/sth a name: *People drive so dangerously on this stretch of road that they've christened it 'The Mad Mile'.*

christening /ˈkrɪsnɪŋ/ ***noun*** [C] (**RELIGION**) the church ceremony in the Christian religion in which a baby is given a name ➲ look at **baptism**

Christian /ˈkrɪstʃən/ ***noun*** [C] (**RELIGION**) a person whose religion is Christianity ► **Christian** ***adj.***

Christianity /ˌkrɪstiˈænəti/ ***noun*** [U] (**RELIGION**) the religion that is based on the teachings of Jesus Christ

ˈ**Christian name** (*especially AmE* ˈ**given name**) ***noun*** [C] the name given to a child when he or she is born; first name

Christmas /ˈkrɪsməs/ ***noun*** **1** [C,U] the period of time before and after 25 December: *Where are you spending Christmas this year?* **2 Christmas Day** [C] a public holiday on 25 December. It is the day on which Christians celebrate the birth of Christ each year.

ˈ**Christmas card** ***noun*** [C] a card with a picture on the front and a message inside that people send to their friends and relatives at Christmas

ˌ**Christmas** ˈ**carol** (**MUSIC**) =CAROL

ˌ**Christmas** ˈ**cracker** =CRACKER (2)

ˌ**Christmas** ˈ**dinner** ***noun*** [C] the traditional meal eaten on Christmas Day: *We had a traditional Christmas dinner that year, with roast turkey, Christmas pudding and all the trimmings.*

ˌ**Christmas** ˈ**Eve** ***noun*** [C] 24 December, the day before Christmas Day

ˌ**Christmas** ˈ**pudding** ***noun*** [C,U] a sweet dish made from dried fruit and eaten hot with sauce at Christmas dinner

ˈ**Christmas tree** ***noun*** [C] a real or artificial tree, which people bring into their homes and cover with coloured lights and decorations at Christmas

chromatic /krəˈmætɪk/ ***adj.*** (**MUSIC**) used to describe a series of musical notes that rise and fall in SEMITONES (=notes that are next to each other on a piano): *the chromatic scale*

chromatography /ˌkrɒməˈtɒgrəfi/ ***noun*** [U] (**CHEMISTRY**) the separation of a liquid mixture by passing it through a material through which some parts of the mixture travel further than others

chrome /krəʊm/ (*also* **chromium** /ˈkrəʊmiəm/) ***noun*** [U] (*symbol* **Cr**) (**CHEMISTRY**) a hard shiny metal that is used for covering other metals ❶ For more information on the periodic table of elements, look at pages R34-5.

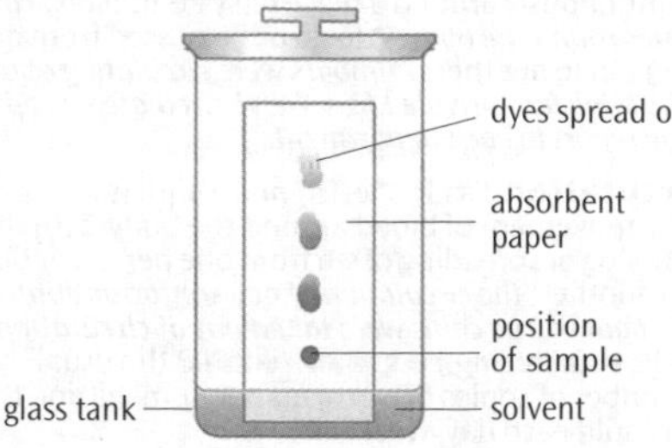

chromosome /ˈkrəʊməsəʊm/ ***noun*** [C] (BIOLOGY) a part of a cell in living things that decides the sex, character, shape, etc. that a person, an animal or a plant will have
➲ look at **X chromosome**, **Y chromosome**

chronic /ˈkrɒnɪk/ ***adj.*** (HEALTH) **1** (used especially about a disease) lasting for a long time; difficult to cure or get rid of: ***chronic bronchitis/arthritis/ asthma*** ◇ *the country's chronic unemployment problem* OPP **acute** **2** having had a disease for a long time: ***a chronic alcoholic/depressive*** ▸ **chronically** /-kli/ ***adv.***

chronicle /ˈkrɒnɪkl/ ***noun*** [C] (often plural) (HISTORY) a written record of historical events describing them in the order in which they happened: *the Anglo-Saxon Chronicle* ▸ **chronicle** ***verb*** [T] (*formal*): *Her achievements are chronicled in a new biography out this week.*

chronological /ˌkrɒnəˈlɒdʒɪkl/ ***adj.*** arranged in the order in which the events happened: *This book describes the main events in his life* ***in chronological order.*** ▸ **chronologically** /-kli/ ***adv.***

chronology /krəˈnɒlədʒi/ ***noun*** [U, C] (*pl.* **chronologies**) the order in which a series of events happened; a list of these events in order: *The exact chronology of these events is a subject for debate.* ◇ *a chronology of Kennedy's life*

chrysalis /ˈkrɪsəlɪs/ (*pl.* **chrysalises**) ***noun*** [C] (BIOLOGY) the form of an insect, especially a BUTTERFLY or a MOTH, while it is changing into an adult inside a hard case, also called a **chrysalis**
➲ look at **pupa** ➲ picture on **page 29**

chrysanthemum /krɪˈsænθəməm/ ***noun*** [C] a large garden flower which is brightly coloured and shaped like a ball

chubby /ˈtʃʌbi/ ***adj.*** slightly fat in a pleasant way: *a baby with chubby cheeks*

chuck /tʃʌk/ ***verb*** [T] (*informal*) to throw sth in a careless way: *You can chuck those old shoes in the bin.*
PHR V **chuck sth in** to give sth up: *He's chucked his job in because he was fed up.*
chuck sb out (of sth) to force sb to leave a place: *They were chucked out of the cinema for making too much noise.*

chuckle /ˈtʃʌkl/ ***verb*** [I] to laugh quietly: *Bruce chuckled to himself as he read the letter.* ▸ **chuckle** ***noun*** [C]

chug /tʃʌɡ/ ***verb*** [I] (**chugging**; **chugged**) **1** (used about a machine or engine) to make short repeated sounds while it is working or moving slowly
2 ~ **along, down, up, etc.** to move in a particular direction making this sound: *The train chugged out of the station.*

chunk /tʃʌŋk/ ***noun*** [C] a large or thick piece of sth: *chunks of bread and cheese*

chunky /ˈtʃʌŋki/ ***adj.*** **1** thick and heavy: *chunky jewellery* **2** (used about a person) short and strong **3** (used about food) containing thick pieces: *chunky banana milkshake*

church 🔑 /tʃɜːtʃ/ ***noun*** (RELIGION) **1** [C,U] a building where Christians go to pray, etc.: ***Do you go to church*** *regularly?* **2 Church** [C] a particular group of Christians: *the Anglican/Catholic/Methodist/ Church* **3 (the) Church** [sing.] the ministers or the institution of the Christian religion: *the conflict between Church and State*

churchgoer /ˈtʃɜːtʃɡəʊə(r)/ ***noun*** [C] (RELIGION) a person who goes to church regularly

the ˌChurch of ˈEngland ***noun*** [sing.] (*abbr.* **C. of E.**) (RELIGION) the Protestant Church, which is the official church in England, whose leader is the Queen or King ➲ look at **Anglican**

churchyard /ˈtʃɜːtʃjɑːd/ ***noun*** [C] the area of land that is around a church, often used for burying people in ➲ look at **cemetery**, **graveyard**

churn /tʃɜːn/ ***verb*** **1** [I,T] ~ **(sth) (up)** to move, or to make water, mud, etc. move around violently: *The dark water churned beneath the huge ship.* ◇ *Vast crowds had churned the field into a sea of mud.* **2** [I] if your stomach **churns** or sth makes it **churn**, you feel sick because you are disgusted or nervous: *Reading about the murder in the paper made my stomach churn.* **3** [T] to make butter from milk or cream
PHR V **churn sth out** (*informal*) to produce large numbers of sth very quickly: *Modern factories can churn out cars at an amazing speed.*

chute /ʃuːt/ ***noun*** [C] a passage down which you can drop or slide things, so that you do not have to carry them: ***a laundry/rubbish chute*** (=from the upper floors of a high building) ◇ *a water chute* (=at a swimming pool)

chutney /ˈtʃʌtni/ ***noun*** [U] a thick sweet sauce that is made from fruit or vegetables. You eat **chutney** cold with cheese or meat.

CIA /ˌsiː aɪ ˈeɪ/ ***abbr.*** (POLITICS) **the Central Intelligence Agency**; the US government organization that tries to discover secret information about other countries

ciabatta /tʃəˈbætə/ ***noun*** [U, C] a type of Italian bread made in a long flat shape; a SANDWICH made with this type of bread

cicada /sɪˈkɑːdə/ ***noun*** [C] a large insect that lives in many hot countries. It makes a continuous high sound by rubbing its legs together.

cider /ˈsaɪdə(r)/ ***noun*** [U, C] **1** (*BrE*) an alcoholic drink made from apples: *dry/sweet cider* **2** (*AmE*) a drink made from apples that does not contain alcohol

cigar /sɪˈɡɑː(r)/ ***noun*** [C] a roll of dried TOBACCO leaves that people smoke. **Cigars** are larger than cigarettes.

cigarette 🔑 /ˌsɪɡəˈret/ ***noun*** [C] TOBACCO in a tube of thin white paper that people smoke: *a packet of cigarettes*

cigaˈrette lighter (*also* **lighter**) ***noun*** [C] an object which produces a small flame for lighting cigarettes, etc.

ciliary muscle /ˈsɪliəri mʌsl/ ***noun*** [C] (ANATOMY) a muscle in the eye that controls how much the LENS (=the transparent part of the front of the eye that controls the direction of light that passes through it) curves ➲ picture at **eye**

cinder /ˈsɪndə(r)/ *noun* [C] a very small piece of burning coal, wood, etc.

cinema 🔑 /ˈsɪnəmə/ *noun* **1** [C] (*BrE*) a place where you go to see a film: *What's on at the cinema this week?* ❶ In American English, you use **movie theater** to talk about the building where films are shown but **the movies** when you are talking about going to see a film there: *There are five movie theaters in this town.* ◇ *Let's go to the movies this evening.* **2** [U] films in general; the film industry: *one of the great successes of British cinema*

cinnamon /ˈsɪnəmən/ *noun* [U] a sweet brown powder that is used for giving flavour to food

circa /ˈsɜːkə/ *prep.* (*abbr.* **c**) (*written*) (used with dates) about; approximately: *The vase was made circa 600 AD.*

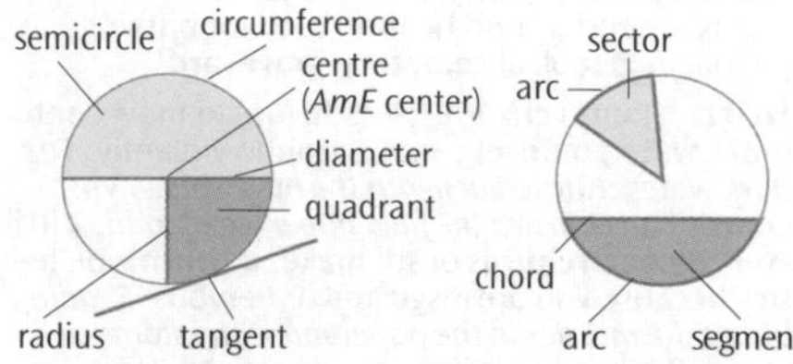

circle[1] 🔑 /ˈsɜːkl/ *noun* **1** [C] a round shape like a ring: *The children were drawing circles and squares on a piece of paper.* ◇ *We all stood in a circle and held hands.* **2** [C] a flat, round area: *She cut out a circle of paper.* **3** [C] a group of people who are friends, or who have the same interest or profession: *He has a large circle of friends.* ◇ *Her name was well known in artistic circles.* **4 the (dress) circle** (*AmE* **balcony**) [sing.] (**ARTS AND MEDIA**) an area of seats that is upstairs in a cinema, theatre, etc.
IDM **a vicious circle** → VICIOUS

circle[2] /ˈsɜːkl/ *verb* **1** [I,T] to move, or to move round sth, in a circle: *The plane circled the town several times before it landed.* **2** [T] to draw a circle round sth: *There are three possible answers to each question. Please circle the correct one.*

circuit /ˈsɜːkɪt/ *noun* **1** [C] a line, route, or journey around a place: *The cars have to complete ten circuits of the track.* ◇ *The earth takes a year to make a circuit of* (=go round) *the sun.* **2** [C] (**PHYSICS**) the complete path of wires and equipment along which an electric current flows: *an electrical circuit* ➲ picture at **switch** **3** [sing.] (**SPORT**) a series of sports competitions, meetings or other organized events that are regularly visited by the same people: *She's one of the best players on the tennis circuit.*

ˈcircuit board *noun* [C] (**PHYSICS**) a board inside a piece of electrical equipment that holds CIRCUITS around which electric currents can flow

ˈcircuit-breaker *noun* [C] (**PHYSICS**) a safety device that automatically stops the flow of electricity if there is danger

ˈcircuit training *noun* [U] (**SPORT**) a type of training in sport in which different exercises are each done for a short time

circular[1] /ˈsɜːkjələ(r)/ *adj.* **1** shaped like a circle; round: *a circular table* **2** moving around in a circle: *a circular tour of Oxford*

circular[2] /ˈsɜːkjələ(r)/ *noun* [C] a printed letter, notice or advertisement that is sent to a large number of people

circulate /ˈsɜːkjəleɪt/ *verb* [I,T] **1** (**SCIENCE**) when a liquid, gas, or air **circulates** or **is circulated**, it moves continuously around a place or system: *Blood circulates round the body.* **2** to go or be passed from one person to another: *Rumours were circulating about the Minister's private life.* ◇ *We've circulated a copy of the report to each department.*

circulation /ˌsɜːkjəˈleɪʃn/ *noun* **1** [U] (**BIOLOGY**) the movement of blood around the body **2** [U] the passing or spreading of sth from one person or place to another: *the circulation of news/information/rumours* ◇ *The coins were* ***taken out of circulation***. **3** [C, usually sing.] (**ARTS AND MEDIA**) the usual number of copies of a newspaper or magazine that are sold each day, week, etc.

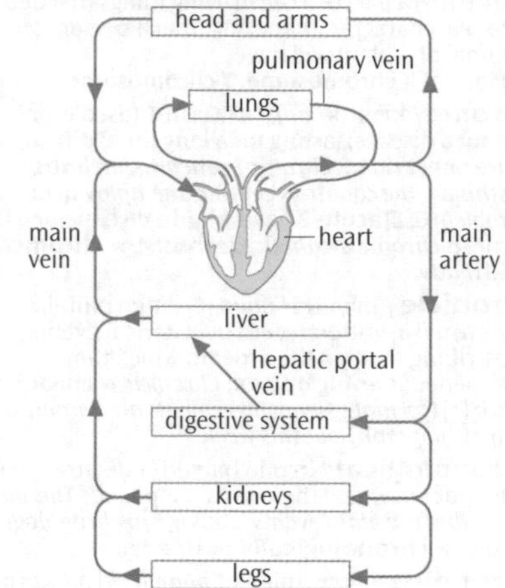

circulatory /ˌsɜːkjəˈleɪtəri/ *adj.* (**BIOLOGY**) connected with the movement of blood around the body

circum- /ˈsɜːkəm/ *prefix* (in adjectives, nouns and verbs) around: *to circumnavigate* (=sail around) *the world*

circumcise /ˈsɜːkəmsaɪz/ *verb* [T] to cut off the skin at the end of a man's sexual organ (**penis**) or to remove part of a woman's sexual organs, for religious or sometimes (in the case of a man) medical reasons ▸ **circumcision** /ˌsɜːkəmˈsɪʒn/ *noun* [C,U]

circumference /səˈkʌmfərəns/ *noun* [C,U] (**MATHEMATICS**) the distance round a circle or sth circular: *The Earth is about 40000 kilometres* ***in circumference***. ➲ look at **diameter**, **radius** ➲ picture at **circle**

circumflex /ˈsɜːkəmfleks/ (*also* ˌ**circumflex ˈaccent**) *noun* [C] (**LANGUAGE**) the mark placed over a vowel in some languages to show how it should be pronounced, as over the *o* in *rôle* ➲ look at **acute accent**, **grave**[3], **tilde**, **umlaut**

circumlocution /ˌsɜːkəmləˈkjuːʃn/ *noun* [U, C] (*formal*) using more words than are necessary, instead of speaking or writing in a clear, direct way ▸ **circumlocutory** /ˌsɜːkəmˈlɒkjʊtəri; ˌsɜːkəmləˈkjuːtəri/ *adj.*

circumnavigate /ˌsɜːkəmˈnævɪɡeɪt/ *verb* [T] (*formal*) to sail all the way around sth, especially all the way around the world ▸ **circumnavigation** /ˌsɜːkəmˌnævɪˈɡeɪʃn/ *noun* [U]

circumspect /ˈsɜːkəmspekt/ ***adj.*** (*formal*) thinking very carefully about sth before you do it because you think it may involve problems or dangers **SYN cautious**

circumstance ⊶ AW /ˈsɜːkəmstəns/ ***noun*** **1** [C, usually pl.] the facts and events that affect what happens in a particular situation: *Police said there were no **suspicious circumstances** surrounding the boy's death.* ◇ ***In normal circumstances*** *I would not have accepted the job, but at that time I had very little money.* ➲ note at **situation 2 circumstances** [pl.] (*formal*) the amount of money that you have: *The company has promised to repay the money when its financial circumstances improve.*

IDM **in/under no circumstances** never; not for any reason: *Under no circumstances should you lend Paul any money*

in/under the circumstances as the result of a particular situation: *It's not an ideal solution, but it's the best we can do in the circumstances.* ◇ *My father was ill at that time, so under the circumstances I decided not to go on holiday.*

circumstantial /ˌsɜːkəmˈstænʃl/ ***adj.*** (LAW) containing information and details that strongly suggest that sth is true but do not prove it: *circumstantial evidence* ◇ *The case against him was largely circumstantial.*

circumvent /ˌsɜːkəmˈvent/ ***verb*** [T] (*formal*) **1** to find a clever way of avoiding a difficulty or rule **2** to go round sth that is in your way

circus /ˈsɜːkəs/ ***noun*** [C] a show performed in a large tent by a company of people and animals

cirque /sɜːk/ = CORRIE ➲ picture at **glacial**

cirrhosis /səˈrəʊsɪs/ ***noun*** [U] (HEALTH) a serious disease of the LIVER (= the organ in the body that cleans the blood), caused especially by drinking too much alcohol

cirrostratus /ˌsɪrəʊˈstrɑːtəs; -ˈstreɪtəs/ ***noun*** [U] (GEOGRAPHY) a type of cloud that forms a thin layer at a very high level ➲ picture at **cloud**

cirrus /ˈsɪrəs/ ***noun*** [U] (GEOGRAPHY) a type of light cloud that forms high in the sky ➲ picture at **cloud**

CIS /ˌsiː aɪ ˈes/ ***abbr.*** (HISTORY, POLITICS) **Commonwealth of Independent States**; a group of independent countries that were part of the Soviet Union until 1991 ➲ look at **USSR**

cistern /ˈsɪstən/ ***noun*** [C] a container for storing water, especially one that is connected to a toilet

citadel /ˈsɪtədəl/ ***noun*** [C] (HISTORY) (in past times) a castle on high ground in or near a city where people could go when the city was being attacked: (*figurative*) *citadels of private economic power*

cite AW /saɪt/ ***verb*** [T] (*formal*) **1** ~ **sth (as sth)** to mention sth as a reason or an example, or in order to support what you are saying: *He cited his heavy workload as the reason for his breakdown.* ➲ note at **mention 2** to speak or write the exact words from a book, an author, etc.: *She cited a passage from the President's speech.* **SYN quote 3** (LAW) to order sb to appear in court; to name sb officially in a legal case: *She was cited in the divorce proceedings.* ▶ **citation** AW /saɪˈteɪʃn/ ***noun*** [C,U]

citizen ⊶ /ˈsɪtɪzn/ ***noun*** [C] **1** (SOCIAL STUDIES) a person who has the legal right to belong to a particular country: *She was born in Japan, but became an American citizen in 1991.* **2** a person who lives in a town or city: *the citizens of Rome* ➲ look at **senior citizen**

citizenship /ˈsɪtɪzənʃɪp/ ***noun*** [U] (SOCIAL STUDIES) **1** the legal right to belong to a particular country: *You can apply for citizenship after five years' residency.* **2** the state of being a citizen and accepting the responsibilities of it: *an education that prepares young people for citizenship*

citric acid /ˌsɪtrɪk ˈæsɪd/ ***noun*** [U] (CHEMISTRY) a weak acid that is found in the juice of oranges, lemons and other similar fruits

citrus /ˈsɪtrəs/ ***adj.*** used to describe fruit such as oranges and lemons

city ⊶ /ˈsɪti/ ***noun*** (*pl.* **cities**) **1** [C] a large and important town: *Venice is one of the most beautiful cities in the world.* ◇ *the **city centre*** ◇ *the country's **capital city*** ➲ look at **inner city 2 the City** [sing.] (*BrE*) (BUSINESS, FINANCE) Britain's financial and business centre, in the oldest part of London: *a City stockbroker*

civic /ˈsɪvɪk/ ***adj.*** **1** officially connected with a city or town: *civic buildings/leaders* **2** connected with the people who live in a town or city: ***civic pride*** (= feeling proud because you belong to a particular town or city) ◇ ***civic duties/responsibilities***

civil ⊶ AW /ˈsɪvl/ ***adj.*** **1** (POLITICS) (only *before* a noun) connected with the people who live in a country: ***civil disorder*** (= involving groups of people within the same country) = CIVIL WAR **2** (only *before* a noun) connected with the state, not with the army or the Church: ***a civil marriage ceremony*** (= not a religious one) **3** (LAW) (only *before* a noun) connected with the personal legal matters of ordinary people, and not criminal law: ***civil courts*** **4** polite, but not very friendly: *The less time I have to spend being civil to him the better!* ▶ **civility** /səˈvɪləti/ ***noun*** [U]: *Staff members are trained to treat customers with civility at all times.* ▶ **civilly** /ˈsɪvəli/ ***adv.***

ˌcivil engiˈneering ***noun*** [U] the design, building and repair of roads, bridges, etc.; the study of this as a subject

civilian /səˈvɪliən/ ***noun*** [C] a person who is not in the army, navy, air force or police force: *Two soldiers and one civilian were killed when the bomb exploded.*

civilization (also **-isation**) /ˌsɪvəlaɪˈzeɪʃn/ ***noun*** (SOCIAL STUDIES) **1** [C,U] a society which has its own highly developed culture and way of life: *the civilizations of ancient Greece and Rome* ◇ *Western civilization* **2** [U] an advanced state of social and cultural development, or the process of reaching this state: *the civilization of the human race* **3** [U] all the people in the world and the societies they live in considered as a whole: *Global warming poses a threat to the whole of civilization.*

civilize (also **-ise**) /ˈsɪvəlaɪz/ ***verb*** [T] (SOCIAL STUDIES) to make people or a society develop from a low social and cultural level to a more advanced one

civilized (also **-ised**) /ˈsɪvəlaɪzd/ ***adj.*** **1** (SOCIAL STUDIES) (used about a society) well organized; having a high level of social and cultural development **2** polite and reasonable: *a civilized conversation*

ˌcivil ˈlaw ***noun*** [U] (LAW) law that deals with the rights of private citizens rather than with crime

ˌcivil ˈliberty ***noun*** [C, usually pl., U] (SOCIAL STUDIES) the right of people to be free to say or do what they want while respecting others and staying within the law

ˌcivil ˈrights (*also* **ˌcivil ˈliberties**) ***noun*** [pl.] (SOCIAL STUDIES) a person's legal right to freedom and equal treatment in society, whatever their sex, race or religion: *the civil rights leader Martin Luther King*

ˌ**civil 'servant** *noun* [C] (*especially BrE*) a person who works in the CIVIL SERVICE

the ˌcivil 'service *noun* [sing.] (**POLITICS**) all the government departments (except for the armed forces) and all the people who work in them

ˌ**civil 'war** *noun* [C,U] (**POLITICS**) a war between groups of people who live in the same country

CJD /ˌsiː dʒeɪ 'diː/ *abbr.* (**HEALTH**) **Creutzfeldt-Jakob disease**; a disease of the brain caused by eating infected meat ➲ look at **BSE**

cl *abbr.* = CENTILITRE(S)

clad /klæd/ *adj.* (not *before* a noun) (*old-fashioned*) dressed (in); wearing a particular type of clothing: *The children were warmly clad in coats, hats and scarves.*

claim¹ ⊶ /kleɪm/ *verb* **1** [T] ~ (that); ~ (to be sth) to say that sth is true, without having any proof: *Mark claims the book belongs to him.* ◇ *The woman claims to be the oldest person in Britain.* **2** [T] to demand or ask for sth because you believe it is your legal right to own or to have it: *He claimed political asylum.* ◇ *A lot of lost property is never claimed.* ◇ (*figurative*) *No one has* ***claimed responsibility*** *for the bomb attack.* **3** [I,T] to ask for money from the government or a company because you have a right to it: *He's not entitled to claim unemployment benefit.* ◇ *You could have claimed the cost of the hotel room from your insurance.* **4** [T] (used about a disaster, an accident, etc.) to cause sb's death: *The earthquake claimed thousands of lives.*

THESAURUS

claim

allegation • assertion • contention

These are all words for a statement that sth is true, although it has not been proved.

claim: *A claim of corruption was made.*

allegation (*formal*): *Officials denied the allegations.*

assertion (*formal*): *He was correct in his assertion that she was lying.*

contention (*formal*): *The result was a matter of some contention.*

claim² ⊶ /kleɪm/ *noun* [C] **1** a ~ (that) a statement that sth is true although it has not been proved and other people may not agree with or believe it: *a report examining claims of corrupt links between politicians* **2** a ~ (to sth) a right that sb believes they have to sth, especially property, land, etc.: *You will have to prove your claim to the property in a court of law.* **3** a ~ (for sth) a demand for money that you think you have a right to, especially from the government, a company, etc.: *to make* ***an insurance claim*** ◇ *After the accident he decided* ***to put in a claim*** *for compensation.*
IDM **stake a/your claim** → STAKE²

claimant /'kleɪmənt/ *noun* [C] **1** a person who believes they have the right to have sth: *The insurance company refused to pay the claimant any money.* **2** (*BrE*) a person who is receiving money from the state because they are unemployed, etc.

clairvoyant /kleə'vɔɪənt/ *noun* [C] a person who some people believe has special mental powers and can see what will happen in the future

clam¹ /klæm/ *noun* [C] a type of SHELLFISH that can be eaten

clam² /klæm/ *verb* (**clamming**; **clammed**)
PHR V **clam up (on sb)** (*informal*) to stop talking and refuse to speak especially when sb asks you about sth

clamber /'klæmbə(r)/ *verb* [I] ~ **up, down, out etc.** to move or climb with difficulty, usually using both your hands and feet

clammy /'klæmi/ *adj.* cold, slightly wet and sticky in an unpleasant way: *clammy hands*

clamour (*AmE* **clamor**) /'klæmə(r)/ *verb* [I] ~ **for sth** to demand sth in a loud or angry way: *The public are clamouring for an answer to all these questions.* ▸ **clamour** (*AmE* **clamor**) *noun* [sing.]: *the clamour of angry voices*

clamp¹ /klæmp/ *noun* [C] **1** a tool that you use for holding two things together very tightly ➲ picture at **vice 2** (*also* **wheel clamp**) (*BrE*) a metal object that is fixed to the wheel of a car that has been parked illegally, so that it cannot drive away

clamp² /klæmp/ *verb* [T] **1** ~ **A and B (together)**; ~ **A to B** to fasten two things together with a CLAMP: *The metal rods were clamped together.* ◇ *Clamp the wood to the table so that it doesn't move.* **2** to hold sth very firmly in a particular position: *Her lips were clamped tightly together.* **3** (*BrE*) to fix a metal object to the wheel of a vehicle that has been parked illegally, so that it cannot move: *Oh no! My car's been clamped.*
PHR V **clamp down on sb/sth** (*informal*) to take strong action in order to stop or control sth

clampdown /'klæmpdaʊn/ *noun* [C] strong action to stop or control sth: *a clampdown on tax evasion*

clan /klæn/ *noun* [C, with sing. or pl. verb] (**SOCIAL STUDIES**) a group of families who are related to each other, especially in Scotland

clandestine /klæn'destɪn/ *adj.* (*formal*) secret and often not legal: *a clandestine meeting*

clang /klæŋ/ *verb* [I,T] to make or cause sth metal to make a loud ringing sound: *The iron gates clanged shut.* ▸ **clang** *noun* [C]

clank /klæŋk/ *verb* [I,T] to make or cause sth metal to make a loud unpleasant sound: *The lift clanked its way up to the seventh floor.* ▸ **clank** *noun* [C]

clap¹ ⊶ /klæp/ *verb* (**clapping**; **clapped**) **1** [I,T] to hit your hands together many times, usually to show that you like sth: *The audience clapped as soon as the singer walked onto the stage.* **2** [T] to put sth onto sth quickly and firmly: *'Oh no, I shouldn't have said that,' she said, clapping a hand over her mouth.*

clap² ⊶ /klæp/ *noun* [C] **1** a sudden loud noise: *a clap of thunder* **2** an act of clapping

claret /'klærət/ *noun* **1** [U, C] a dry red wine, especially from the Bordeaux area of France. There are several types of **claret**. **2** [U] a dark red colour ▸ **claret** *adj.*

clarification AW /ˌklærəfɪ'keɪʃn/ *noun* [U] an act of making sth clear and easier to understand: *We'd like some clarification of exactly what your company intends to do.* ➲ look at **clarity**

clarify AW /'klærəfaɪ/ *verb* [T] (*pres. part.* **clarifying**; *3rd person sing. pres.* **clarifies**; *pt, pp* **clarified**) to make sth become clear and easier to understand: *I hope that what I say will clarify the situation.* ➲ adjective **clear**

clarinet /ˌklærə'net/ *noun* [C] a musical instrument that is made of wood. You play a **clarinet** by blowing through it. ➲ picture on **page 465**

clarity AW /'klærəti/ *noun* [U] the quality of being clear and easy to understand: *clarity of expression* ➲ look at **clarification**

clash[1] /klæʃ/ ***verb*** **1** [I] ~ **(with sb) (over sth)** to fight or disagree seriously about sth: *A group of demonstrators clashed with police outside the Town Hall.* **2** [I] ~ **(with sth)** (used about two events) to happen at the same time: *It's a pity the two concerts clash. I wanted to go to both of them.* **3** [I] ~ **(with sth)** (used about colours, etc.) to not match or look nice together: *I don't think you should wear that tie – it clashes with your shirt.* **4** [I,T] (used about two metal objects) to hit together with a loud noise; to cause two metal objects to do this: *Their swords clashed.*

clash[2] /klæʃ/ ***noun*** [C] **1** a fight or serious disagreement: *a clash between police and demonstrators* **2** a big difference: *a clash of opinions* ◇ *There was **a personality clash** between the two men* (=they did not get well on together or like each other). **3** a loud noise, made by two metal objects hitting each other

clasp[1] /klɑːsp/ ***noun*** [C] an object, usually of metal, which fastens or holds sth together: *the clasp on a necklace/brooch/handbag*

clasp[2] /klɑːsp/ ***verb*** [T] to hold sb/sth tightly: *Kevin clasped the child in his arms.*

class[1] 🔑 /klɑːs/ ***noun*** **1** [C, with sing. or pl. verb] (EDUCATION) a group of students who are taught together: *Jane and I are in the same class at school.* ◇ *The whole class is/are going to the theatre tonight.* **2** [C,U] (EDUCATION) a lesson: *Classes begin at 9 o'clock in the morning.* ◇ *We watched an interesting video in class* (=during the lesson) *yesterday.* **3** [U, C] (SOCIAL STUDIES) the way people are divided into social groups; one of these groups: *The idea of class still divides British society.* ◇ *class differences* **4** [C] (BIOLOGY) a group into which animals, plants, etc. that have similar characteristics are divided, below a PHYLUM: *There are several different classes of insects.* ➲ picture on **page 29** **5** [U] (*informal*) high quality or style: *Pele was a football player of great class.* **6** [C] (especially in compounds) each of several different levels of service that are available to travellers on a plane, train, etc.: *a first-class carriage on a train* ◇ *He always travels business class.* **7** [C] (*BrE*) (used to form compound adjectives) (EDUCATION) a mark that you are given when you pass your final university exam: *a first-/second-/third-class degree*

class[2] /klɑːs/ ***verb*** [T] ~ **sb/sth (as sth)** to put sb/sth in a particular group or type: *Certain animals and plants are now classed as 'endangered species'.*

ˌclass ˈaction ***noun*** (*AmE*) (LAW) a type of LAWSUIT (=a legal argument in a court of law) that is started by a group of people who have the same problem

classic[1] 🔑 AW /ˈklæsɪk/ ***adj.*** (usually *before* a noun) **1** typical: *It was **a classic case** of bad management.* **2** (used about a book, play, etc.) important and having a value that will last: *the classic film 'Casablanca'*

classic[2] 🔑 AW /ˈklæsɪk/ ***noun*** **1** [C] (LITERATURE) a famous book, play, etc. which has a value that will last: *All of Charles Dickens' novels are classics.* **2 Classics** [U] (EDUCATION) the study of ancient Greek and Roman culture, especially their languages and literature

classical AW /ˈklæsɪkl/ ***adj.*** (usually *before* a noun) **1** widely accepted and used for a long time; traditional in style or idea: *the classical theory of unemployment* ◇ *classical and modern ballet* **2** connected with or influenced by the culture of ancient Greece and Rome: *classical studies* ◇ *classical architecture* **3** (MUSIC) written in a Western musical tradition, usually using an established form (for example a SYMPHONY) and not played on electronic instruments. **Classical** music is generally considered to be serious and to have a lasting value: *I prefer classical music to pop.* ◇ *a **classical composer/violinist*** ➲ look at **jazz**, **pop**, **rock** ▶ **classically** /-kli/ ***adv.***

classicism /ˈklæsɪsɪzəm/ ***noun*** [U] (ART, LITERATURE) a style of art and literature that is simple and elegant and is based on the styles of ancient Greece and Rome. **Classicism** was popular in Europe in the 18th century.

classified /ˈklæsɪfaɪd/ ***adj.*** officially secret: *classified information*

ˌclassified adˈvertisement (*BrE, informal* **ˌclassified ˈad**; **ˈsmall ad**) ***noun*** [usually pl.] a small advertisement that you put in a newspaper if you want to buy or sell sth, employ sb, find a flat, etc.

classify /ˈklæsɪfaɪ/ ***verb*** [T] (*pres. part.* **classifying**; *3rd person sing. pres.* **classifies**; *pt, pp* **classified**) ~ **sb/sth (as sth)** to put sb/sth into a group with other people or things of a similar type: *Would you classify it as an action film or a thriller?* ▶ **classification** /ˌklæsɪfɪˈkeɪʃn/ ***noun*** [C,U]: *the classification of the different species of butterfly*

classless /ˈklɑːsləs/ ***adj.*** (SOCIAL STUDIES) **1** with no division into social classes: *It is hard to imagine a truly classless society.* **2** not clearly belonging to any particular social class: *a classless accent*

classmate /ˈklɑːsmeɪt/ ***noun*** [C] a person who is in the same class as you at school or college

classroom 🔑 /ˈklɑːsruːm; -rʊm/ ***noun*** [C] a room in a school, college, etc. where lessons are taught

classy /ˈklɑːsi/ ***adj.*** (**classier**; **classiest**) (*informal*) of high quality or style; expensive and fashionable: *a classy restaurant*

clatter /ˈklætə(r)/ ***verb*** [I,T] to make or cause sth hard to make a series of short loud repeated sounds: *The horses clattered down the street.* ▶ **clatter** ***noun*** [C, usually sing.]

clause AW /klɔːz/ ***noun*** [C] **1** (LANGUAGE) a group of words that includes a subject and a verb, and forms a sentence or part of a sentence: *The sentence 'After we had finished eating, we watched a film on the video' contains two clauses.* ➲ look at **subordinate clause** **2** (LAW) an item in a legal document that says that a particular thing must or must not be done: *There is a clause in the contract forbidding tenants to sublet.*

claustrophobia /ˌklɔːstrəˈfəʊbiə/ ***noun*** [U] (HEALTH) an extreme fear of being in a small confined space

claustrophobic /ˌklɔːstrəˈfəʊbɪk/ ***adj.*** (HEALTH) **1** extremely afraid of small, confined spaces: *I always feel claustrophobic in lifts.* **2** used about sth that makes you feel afraid in this way: *a claustrophobic little room*

clavicle /ˈklævɪkl/ (ANATOMY) = COLLARBONE ➲ picture on **page 80**

claw[1] /klɔː/ ***noun*** [C] **1** one of the long curved nails on the end of an animal's or a bird's foot ➲ picture on **page 29** **2** a long, sharp curved part of the body that some types of SHELLFISH and some insects have. They use them for holding or picking things up: *the claws of a crab*

claw[2] /klɔː/ ***verb*** [I,T] ~ **(at) sb/sth** to scratch or tear sb/sth with CLAWS or with your nails: *The cat was clawing at the furniture.*

clay /kleɪ/ ***noun*** [U] heavy earth that is soft and sticky when it is wet and becomes hard when it is baked or dried: *clay pots*

clean[1] **⊶** /kliːn/ ***adj.*** **1** not dirty: *The whole house was beautifully clean.* ◇ *Cats are very clean animals.* OPP **dirty** **2** not offensive or referring to sex; not doing anything that is considered immoral or bad: *a clean joke* OPP **dirty** **3** having no record of offences or crimes: *a clean driving licence*

IDM **a clean sweep** a complete victory in a sports competition, election, etc. that you get by winning all the different parts of it ➲ noun **cleanliness**

clean[2] **⊶** /kliːn/ ***verb*** **1** [T] to remove dirt, dust and marks from sth: *to clean the windows* ◇ *Don't forget to clean your teeth!* **2** [I,T] to make the inside of a house, office, etc. free from dust and dirt: *Mr Burrows comes in to clean after office hours.* ◇ *I* ***do the cleaning*** *once a week.*

PHR V **clean sth out** to clean the inside of sth: *I'm going to clean out all the cupboards next week.*

clean (sth) up to remove all the dirt from a place that is particularly dirty: *I'm going to clean up the kitchen before Mum and Dad get back.* ◇ *Oh no, you've spilt coffee on the new carpet! Can you clean it up?* ➲ look at **dry-clean**, **spring-clean**

clean[3] /kliːn/ ***adv.*** (*informal*) used to emphasize that an action takes place completely: *I clean forgot it was your birthday.*

IDM **come clean (with sb) (about sth)** (*informal*) to tell the truth about sth that you have been keeping secret

go clean out of your mind to be completely forgotten

ˌ**clean-ˈcut** ***adj.*** (used especially about a young man) having a clean, tidy appearance that is attractive and socially acceptable: *The girls all go for James' clean-cut good looks.*

cleaner /ˈkliːnə(r)/ ***noun*** **1** [C] a person whose job is to clean the rooms and furniture inside a house or other building: *an office cleaner* **2** [C] a substance or a special machine that you use for cleaning sth: *liquid floor cleaners* ◇ *a carpet cleaner* ➲ look at **vacuum cleaner** **3 the cleaner's** = DRY-CLEANER'S

cleanliness /ˈklenlinəs/ ***noun*** [U] being clean or keeping things clean: *High standards of cleanliness are important in a hotel kitchen.*

cleanly /ˈkliːnli/ ***adv.*** easily or smoothly in one movement: *The knife cut cleanly through the rope.*

cleanse /klenz/ ***verb*** [T] to clean your skin or a wound ➲ look at **ethnic cleansing**

cleanser /ˈklenzə(r)/ ***noun*** [C] a substance that you use for cleaning your skin, especially your face

ˌ**clean-ˈshaven** ***adj.*** (used about men) having recently shaved

THESAURUS

clear

obvious • apparent • evident • plain

These words all describe sth that is easy to see or understand and leaves no doubts or confusion.

clear: *It was clear that she wasn't welcome.*

obvious: *It's obvious to me that something is wrong.*

apparent: *It was apparent from her face that she was upset.*

evident (*formal*): *The choir sang with evident enjoyment.*

plain: *He made it plain that he wanted us to leave.*

ˈ**clean-up** ***noun*** [C, usually sing.] the process of removing dirt or other bad things from a place: *The clean-up of the city centre means that tourists can now go there safely at night.*

WORD FAMILY
clear *adj.*
clarity *noun*
clarify *verb*

clear[1] **⊶** /klɪə(r)/ ***adj.*** **1** easy to see, hear or understand: *His voice wasn't very clear on the telephone.* ◇ *She gave me clear directions on how to get there.* **2** ~ **(about/on sth)** sure or definite; without any doubts or confusion: *I'm not quite clear about the arrangements for tomorrow.* ➲ verb **clarify**

3 ~ **(to sb)** obvious: *There are clear advantages to the second plan.* ◇ *It was clear to me that he was not telling the truth.* **4** easy to see through: *The water was so clear that we could see the bottom of the lake.* **5** ~ **(of sth)** free from things that are blocking the way: *The police say that most roads are now clear of snow.* **6** free from marks: *a clear sky* (=without clouds) ◇ *clear skin* (=without spots) **7** if you have a **clear** CONSCIENCE or your CONSCIENCE is **clear**, you do not feel guilty

IDM **make yourself clear**; **make sth clear/plain (to sb)** to speak so that there can be no doubt about what you mean: *'I do not want you to go to that concert,' said my mother. 'Do I make myself clear?'* ◇ *He made it quite clear that he was not happy with the decision.*

clear[2] /klɪə(r)/ ***adv.*** **1** = CLEARLY (1): *We can hear the telephone loud and clear from here.* **2** ~ **(of sth)** away from sth; not touching sth: *stand clear of the doors* (=on a train)

IDM **keep/stay/steer clear (of sb/sth)** to avoid sb/sth because they or it may cause problems

clear[3] **⊶** /klɪə(r)/ ***verb*** **1** [T] to remove sth that is not wanted or needed: *to clear the roads of snow/to clear snow from the roads* ◇ *It's your turn to clear the table* (=to take away the dirty plates, etc. after a meal). **2** [I] (used about smoke, etc.) to disappear: *The fog slowly cleared and the sun came out.* **3** [I] when the sky or the weather **clears**, it becomes brighter and free of cloud or rain: *After a cloudy start, the weather will clear during the afternoon.* **4** [T] ~ **sb (of sth)** (LAW) to provide proof that sb is innocent of sth: *The man has finally been cleared of murder.* **5** [T] to jump over or get past sth without touching it **6** [T] to give official permission for a plane, ship, etc. to enter or leave a place: *At last the plane was cleared for take-off.* **7** [T] ~ **sth (with sb)** to get official approval for sth to be done: *I'll have to clear it with the manager before I can refund your money.* **8** [I,T] if a cheque that you pay into your bank account **clears**, or a bank **clears** it, the money is available for you to use

IDM **clear the air** to improve a difficult or uncomfortable situation by talking honestly about worries, doubts, etc.

clear your throat to cough slightly in order to make it easier to speak

PHR V **clear off** (*informal*) used to tell sb to go away

clear sth out to tidy sth and throw away things that you do not want

clear up (used about the weather or an illness) to get better

clear (sth) up to make sth tidy: *Make sure you clear up properly before you leave.*

clear sth up to find the solution to a problem, cause of confusion, etc.: *There's been a slight misunderstanding but we've cleared it up now.*

clearance /ˈklɪərəns/ ***noun*** [U] **1** the removing of sth that is old or not wanted: *The shop is having a **clearance sale*** (=selling things cheaply in order to get rid of them). **2** the distance between an object and something that is passing under or beside it, for example a ship or vehicle: *There was not enough clearance for the bus to pass under the bridge safely.* **3** official permission for sb/sth to do sth: *All employees at the submarine base require security clearance.*

ˌclear-ˈcut ***adj.*** definite and easy to see or understand

ˌclear-ˈheaded ***adj.*** able to think clearly, especially if there is a problem

clearing /ˈklɪərɪŋ/ ***noun*** **1** [C] a small area without trees in the middle of a wood or forest **2** [U] (EDUCATION) (in Britain) the system used by universities to find students for the places on their courses that have not been filled shortly before the beginning of the academic year: *She got into university through clearing.*

clearly 🔑 /ˈklɪəli/ ***adv.*** **1** in a way that is easy to see, hear or understand: *It was so foggy that we couldn't see the road clearly.* **2** in a way that is not confused: *I'm so tired that I can't think clearly.* **3** without doubt; obviously: *She clearly doesn't want to speak to you any more.*

ˌclear-ˈsighted ***adj.*** able to understand situations well and to see what might happen in the future

cleavage /ˈkliːvɪdʒ/ ***noun*** [C,U] the space between a woman's breasts

clef /klef/ ***noun*** [C] (MUSIC) a sign (𝄞, 𝄢) at the beginning of a line of written music that shows the area of sound that the notes are in: *the bass/treble clef* ➲ picture at **music**

cleft /kleft/ ***noun*** [C] a natural opening or crack, especially in rock or in a person's chin

clemency /ˈklemənsi/ ***noun*** [U] (*formal*) (LAW) kindness shown to sb when they are being punished

clementine /ˈklemənti:n/ ***noun*** [C] a type of small orange

clench /klentʃ/ ***verb*** [T] to close or hold tightly: *She clenched her fists and looked as if she was going to hit him.*

clergy /ˈklɜ:dʒi/ ***noun*** [pl.] (RELIGION) the people who perform religious ceremonies in the Christian church: *a member of the clergy*

clergyman /ˈklɜ:dʒimən/ **clergywoman** /ˈklɜ:dʒiwʊmən/ ***noun*** [C] (*pl.* **-men** /-mən; -men/) (*pl.* **-women** /-wɪmɪn/) (RELIGION) a member of the CLERGY

cleric /ˈklerɪk/ ***noun*** [C] (RELIGION) **1** a priest in the Christian church SYN **clergyman** **2** a religious leader in any religion: *Muslim clerics*

clerical /ˈklerɪkl/ ***adj.*** **1** connected with the work of a clerk in an office: *clerical work* **2** (RELIGION) connected with the CLERGY

clerk 🔑 /klɑ:k/ ***noun*** [C] **1** a person whose job is to do written work or look after records or accounts in an office, bank, court of law, etc. **2** (*also* ˈsales clerk) (*AmE*) = SHOP ASSISTANT **3** (*AmE* ˈdesk clerk) (TOURISM) a person whose job is dealing with people arriving at or leaving a hotel SYN **receptionist**

clever 🔑 /ˈklevə(r)/ ***adj.*** **1** able to learn, understand or do sth quickly and easily; intelligent: *a clever student* ◇ *How clever of you to mend my watch!* **2** (used about things, ideas, etc.) showing skill or intelligence: *a clever device* ◇ *a clever plan* ▶ **cleverly** ***adv.*** ▶ **cleverness** ***noun*** [U]

cliché /ˈkli:ʃeɪ/ ***noun*** [C] (LANGUAGE) a phrase or idea that has been used so many times that it no longer has any real meaning or interest

click[1] 🔑 /klɪk/ ***verb*** **1** [I,T] to make a short sharp sound; to cause sth to do this: *The door clicked shut.* ◇ *He clicked his fingers at the waiter.* **2** [I,T] ~ (**on sth**) (COMPUTING) to press one of the buttons on a mouse: *To open a file, click on the menu.* ➲ look at **double-click** **3** [I] (*BrE, informal*) (used about two people) to become friendly immediately: *We met at a party and just clicked.* **4** [I] (*informal*) (used about a problem, etc.) to become suddenly clear or understood: *Once I'd found the missing letter, everything **clicked into place**.*

click[2] 🔑 /klɪk/ ***noun*** [C] **1** a short sharp sound: *the click of a switch* **2** (COMPUTING) the act of pressing the button on a computer mouse

client 🔑 /ˈklaɪənt/ ***noun*** [C] **1** somebody who receives a service from a professional person, for example a lawyer

> **RELATED VOCABULARY**
>
> Be careful. **Client** cannot be used for people in shops or restaurants. Those people are **customers**. **Clientele** is a general, formal word that includes both clients and customers.

2 (COMPUTING) a computer that is linked to a SERVER that stores shared information

clientele /ˌkli:ənˈtel/ ***noun*** [U] all the customers, guests or clients who regularly go to a particular shop, hotel, organization, etc.

cliff /klɪf/ ***noun*** [C] (GEOGRAPHY) a high, very steep area of rock, especially one next to the sea

cliffhanger /ˈklɪfhæŋə(r)/ ***noun*** [C] (ARTS AND MEDIA) an exciting situation in a story, film, etc. when you cannot guess what is going to happen next and you have to wait until the next part in order to find out

climactic /klaɪˈmæktɪk/ ***adj.*** (*written*) (used about an event or a point in time) very exciting, most important

climate 🔑 /ˈklaɪmət/ ***noun*** [C] **1** (GEOGRAPHY) the normal weather conditions of a particular region: *a **dry/humid/tropical climate*** **2** the general opinions, etc. that people have at a particular time: *What is the current **climate of opinion** regarding the death penalty?* ◇ *the political climate*

climatic /klaɪˈmætɪk/ ***adj.*** (GEOGRAPHY) connected with the climate (1): ***climatic changes/conditions*** ▶ **climatically** /-kli/ ***adv.***

climatology /ˌklaɪməˈtɒlədʒi/ ***noun*** [U] (GEOGRAPHY, SCIENCE) the scientific study of climate ▶ **climatological** /ˌklaɪmətəˈlɒdʒɪkl/ ***adj.*** ▶ **climatologist** /ˌklaɪməˈtɒlədʒist/ ***noun*** [C]

climax /ˈklaɪmæks/ ***noun*** [C] **1** the most exciting or important event or point in time: ***to come to a climax*** ◇ *the **climax of** his political career* **2** (ARTS AND MEDIA) the most important and exciting part of a book, play, piece of music, event, etc.: *The novel **reaches a dramatic climax** in the final chapter.* ▶ **climax** ***verb*** [I]

climb[1] 🔑 /klaɪm/ ***verb*** **1** [I,T] ~ (**up**) (**sth**) to move up towards the top of sth: *to climb a tree/mountain/rope* ◇ *She climbed the stairs to bed.* ◇ *to climb up a ladder* **2** [I] to move, with difficulty or effort, in the direction mentioned: *I managed to climb out of the window.* **3** **go climbing** [I] (SPORT) to go up mountains or climb rocks as a hobby or sport:

He likes to go climbing most weekends. **4** [I] to rise to a higher position: *The plane climbed steadily.* ◇ *The road climbed steeply up the side of the mountain.* ◇ (*figurative*) *The value of the dollar climbed against the pound.* ➲ note at **rise**[1]

IDM **climb/jump on the bandwagon** → BANDWAGON

PHR V **climb down (over sth)** (*informal*) to admit that you have made a mistake; to change your opinion about sth in an argument

climb[2] /klaɪm/ ***noun*** [C] an act of climbing or a journey made by climbing: *The monastery could only be reached by a three-hour climb.*

climbdown /'klaɪmdaʊn/ ***noun*** [C] an act of admitting you have been wrong; a change of opinion in an argument

climber /'klaɪmə(r)/ ***noun*** [C] **1** (SPORT) a person who climbs mountains as a sport **2** a climbing plant

climbing ⊶ /'klaɪmɪŋ/ ***noun*** [U] (SPORT) the sport or activity of climbing rocks or mountains: *to **go climbing*** ◇ *a climbing accident*

clinch /klɪntʃ/ ***verb*** [T] (*informal*) to finally manage to get what you want in an argument or business agreement: *to **clinch a deal***

cline /klaɪn/ ***noun*** [C] a continuous series of things, in which each one is only slightly different from the things next to it, but the last is very different from the first

cling /klɪŋ/ ***verb*** [I] (*pt, pp* **clung** /klʌŋ/) **1 ~ (on) to sb/sth; ~ together** to hold on tightly to sb/sth: *She clung to the rope with all her strength.* ◇ *They clung together for warmth.* **2 ~ (on) to sth** to continue to believe sth, often when it is not reasonable to do so: *They were still clinging to the hope that the girl would be found alive.* **3 ~ to sb/sth** to stick firmly to sth: *Her wet clothes clung to her.* ▶ **clingy** /klɪŋi/ ***adj.***: *a **clingy child*** (=that does not want to leave its parents) ◇ *a clingy sweater*

'cling film ***noun*** [U] thin transparent plastic used for covering food to keep it fresh

clinic /'klɪnɪk/ ***noun*** [C] (HEALTH) **1** a small hospital or a part of a hospital where you go to receive special medical treatment: *He's being treated at a private clinic.* **2** a time when a doctor sees patients and gives special treatment or advice: *The antenatal clinic is held on Thursdays.*

clinical /'klɪnɪkl/ ***adj.*** **1** (HEALTH) connected with the examination and treatment of patients at a CLINIC or hospital: ***Clinical trials** of the new drug have proved successful.* **2** (used about a person) cold and not emotional

clinically /'klɪnɪkli/ ***adv.*** **1** (HEALTH) according to medical examination: *to be **clinically dead*** (=judged to be dead from the condition of the body) ◇ *clinically depressed* **2** in a cold way; without showing any emotion

clink /klɪŋk/ ***noun*** [sing.] the short sharp ringing sound that objects made of glass, metal, etc. make when they touch each other: *the clink of glasses* ▶ **clink** ***verb*** [I,T]

clip[1] /klɪp/ ***noun*** [C] **1** a small object, usually made of metal or plastic, used for holding things together: *a paper clip* ◇ *a hairclip* **2** (ARTS AND MEDIA) a small section of a film that is shown so that people can see what the rest of the film is like ➲ look at **trailer** **3** (*informal*) a quick hit with the hand: *She gave the boy a clip round the ear.* **4** the act of cutting sth to make it shorter

clip[2] /klɪp/ ***verb*** (**clipping**; **clipped**) **1** [I,T] to be fastened with a CLIP; to fasten sth to sth else with a CLIP: *Clip the photo to the letter, please.* **2** [T] to cut sth, especially by cutting small parts off: *The hedge needs clipping.* **3** [T] to hit sb/sth quickly: *My wheel clipped the pavement and I fell off my bike.*

clipboard /'klɪpbɔːd/ ***noun*** [C] **1** a small board with a part that holds papers at the top, used by sb who wants to write while standing or moving around **2** (COMPUTING) a place where information from a computer file is stored for a short time until it is added to another file

clippers /'klɪpəz/ ***noun*** [pl.] a metal tool used for small pieces off things: *a pair of nail clippers*

clipping /'klɪpɪŋ/ (*AmE*) = CUTTING[1] (1)

clique /kliːk/ ***noun*** [C] a small group of people with the same interests who do not want others to join their group

clitoris /'klɪtərɪs/ ***noun*** [C] (ANATOMY) the small sensitive part of the female sex organs just above the entrance to the VAGINA

cloak /kləʊk/ ***noun*** **1** [C] a type of loose coat without sleeves that was more common in former times ➲ look at **cape** **2** [sing.] a thing that hides sth else: *a cloak of mist*

cloakroom /'kləʊkruːm/ ***noun*** [C] a room near the entrance to a building where you can leave your coat, bags, etc.

clobber /'klɒbə(r)/ ***verb*** [T] (*BrE, informal*) to hit sb hard

clock[1] ⊶ /klɒk/ ***noun*** [C] **1** an instrument that shows you what time it is: *an alarm clock* ◇ *a church clock* ➲ look at **watch** **2** an instrument in a car that measures how far it has travelled: *My car has only got 10000 miles on the clock.*

IDM **against the clock** if you do sth against the clock, you do it fast in order to finish before a certain time: *It was a race against the clock to get the building work finished on time.*

around/round the clock all day and all night: *They are working round the clock to repair the bridge.*

put the clock/clocks forward/back to change the time, usually by one hour, at the beginning/end of summer

clock[2] /klɒk/ ***verb***

PHR V **clock in/on**; **clock off** to record the time that you arrive at or leave work, especially by putting a card into a type of clock

clock sth up to achieve a certain number or total: *Our car clocked up over 2000 miles while we were on holiday.*

'clock tower ***noun*** [C] a tall tower, usually part of another building, with a clock at the top

clockwise /'klɒkwaɪz/ ***adv.***, ***adj.*** in the same direction as the hands of a clock: *Turn the handle clockwise.* ◇ *to move in a clockwise direction*
OPP **anticlockwise**

clockwork /'klɒkwɜːk/ ***noun*** [U] a type of machinery found in certain toys, etc. that you operate by turning a key: *a clockwork toy* ◇ *The plan went **like clockwork*** (=smoothly and without any problems).

clog[1] /klɒg/ ***noun*** [C] a type of shoe made completely of wood or with a thick wooden base

clog[2] /klɒg/ ***verb*** [I,T] (**clogging**; **clogged**) **~ (sth) (up) (with sth)** to block or become blocked: *The drain is always clogging up.* ◇ *The roads were clogged with traffic.*

cloister /'klɔɪstə(r)/ ***noun*** [C, usually pl.] (ARCHITECTURE) a covered passage with ARCHES around a square garden, usually forming part of a

CATHEDRAL, a MONASTERY or a CONVENT (=buildings where religious people live)

clone /kləʊn/ ***noun*** [C] (BIOLOGY) an exact copy of a plant or animal that is produced from one of its cells by scientific methods ▶ **clone** ***verb*** [T]: *A team from the UK were the first to successfully clone an animal.*

close[1] /kləʊz/ ***verb*** [I,T] **1** to shut: *The door closed quietly.* ◇ *to close a door/window* ◇ *Close your eyes – I've got a surprise.* **2** to be, or to make sth, not open to the public: *What time do the shops close?* ◇ *The police have closed the road to traffic.* **3** to end or to bring sth to an end: *The meeting closed at 10pm.* ◇ *Detectives have closed the case on the missing girl.* OPP **open**

PHR V **close (sth) down** (BUSINESS) to stop all business or work permanently at a shop or factory: *The factory has had to close down.* ◇ *Health inspectors have closed the restaurant down.*

close in (on sb/sth) to come nearer and gradually surround sb/sth, especially in order to attack

close sth off to prevent people from entering a place or an area: *The police closed off the city centre because of a bomb alert.*

close[2] /kləʊz/ ***noun*** [sing.] the end, especially of a period of time or an activity: *the close of trading on the stock market*

IDM **bring sth/come/draw to a close** to end: *The chairman brought the meeting to a close.* ◇ *The guests began to leave as the evening drew to a close.*

close[3] 🔑 /kləʊs/ ***adj., adv.*** **1** (not *before* a noun) ~ **(to sb/sth)**; ~ **(together)** near: *Is our hotel **close to** the beach?* ◇ *The tables are quite close together.* ◇ *to follow close behind someone* ◇ *I held her close* (=tightly). **2** (used about a friend, etc.) known very well and liked: *They invited only close friends to the wedding.* **3** near in a family relationship: *a close **relative*** **4** (used about a competition, etc.) only won by a small amount: *a close match* **5** careful; thorough: ***On close examination**, you could see that the banknote was a forgery.* **6** (used about the weather, etc.) heavy and with little movement of air: *It's so close today that there might be a storm.*
▶ **closeness** ***noun*** [U] ▶ **closely** ***adv.***: *to watch sb closely* ◇ *The insect closely resembles a stick.*

IDM **a close shave/thing** a bad thing that almost happened: *I wasn't injured, but it was a close shave.*

at close quarters at or from a position that is very near

close by (sb/sth) at a short distance from sb/sth: *She lives close by.*

close/near/dear to sb's heart → HEART

close on nearly; almost: *He was born close on a hundred years ago.*

close up (to sb/sth) at or from a very short distance to sb/sth

come close (to sth/to doing sth) to almost do sth: *We didn't win but we came close.*

close[4] /kləʊs/ ***noun*** [C] part of the name of a street: *5 Devon Close*

closed 🔑 /kləʊzd/ ***adj.*** not open; shut: *Keep your mouth closed.* ◇ *The supermarket is closed.* OPP **open**

ˌclosed-ˌcircuit ˈtelevision (*abbr.* CCTV) ***noun*** [U] a type of television system used inside a building, for example a shop, to protect it from crime

closet 🔑 /ˈklɒzɪt/ ***noun*** [C] (*especially AmE*) a large cupboard that is built into a room

close-up /ˈkləʊs ʌp/ ***noun*** [C] a photograph or film of sb/sth that you take from a very short distance away

closing[1] /ˈkləʊzɪŋ/ ***adj.*** (only *before* a noun) coming at the end of a speech, a period of time or an activity: *his closing remarks* ◇ *The football season is now in its closing stages.* OPP **opening**

closing[2] /ˈkləʊzɪŋ/ ***noun*** [U] the act of permanently shutting sth such as a factory, hospital, school, etc.: *the closing of the local school* OPP **opening**

ˈclosing time ***noun*** [C] the time when a shop, pub, etc. closes

closure /ˈkləʊʒə(r)/ ***noun*** [C,U] the permanent closing, for example of a business

clot[1] /klɒt/ ***noun*** [C] (BIOLOGY) a lump that is formed when blood dries or becomes thicker: *They removed a blood clot from his brain.*

clot[2] /klɒt/ ***verb*** [I,T] (**clotting**; **clotted**) if blood or another liquid **clots** or when sth **clots** it, it forms thick lumps or CLOTS: *a drug that stops blood from clotting during operations*

cloth 🔑 /klɒθ/ ***noun*** **1** [U] a material made of cotton, wool, etc. that you use for making clothes, curtains, etc.: *a metre of cloth* **2** [C] (*pl.* **cloths** /klɒθs/) a piece of material that you use for a particular purpose: *Wipe the table with a damp cloth.*
➲ look at **tablecloth**

clothe /kləʊð/ ***verb*** [T] (*formal*) to provide clothes for sb: *to feed and clothe a child*

clothed /kləʊðd/ ***adj.*** ~ **(in sth)** dressed; wearing sth: *He was clothed in leather from head to foot.*

clothes 🔑 /kləʊðz/ ***noun*** [pl.] the things that you wear, for example trousers, shirts, dresses, coats, etc.: *Take off those wet clothes.* ◇ *She was wearing new clothes.* ➲ look at **garment**

ˈclothes hanger = HANGER

ˈclothes line ***noun*** [C] a thin rope that you hang clothes on so that they can dry

ˈclothes peg (*AmE* **ˈclothes pin**) = PEG[1] (3)

clothing 🔑 /ˈkləʊðɪŋ/ ***noun*** [U] the clothes that you wear, especially for a particular activity: *waterproof/outdoor/winter clothing*

clouds

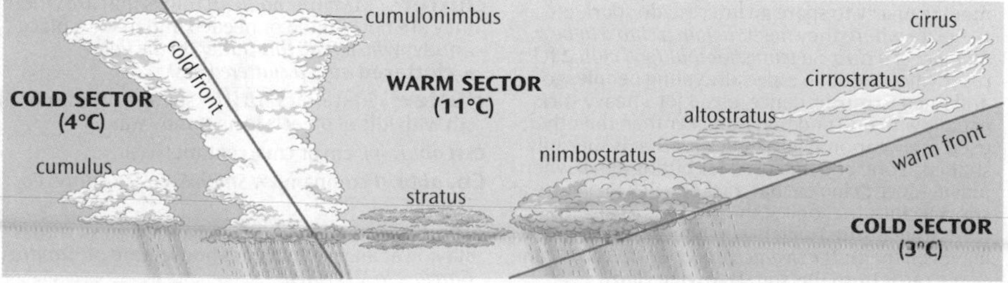

ˌclotted ˈcream *noun* [U] (*BrE*) a type of thick rich cream

cloud¹ ⊶ /klaʊd/ *noun* **1** [C,U] (GEOGRAPHY) a mass of very small drops of water that floats in the sky and is usually white or grey: *The sun disappeared behind a cloud.* ◇ *A band of thick cloud is spreading from the west.* **2** [C] a mass of smoke, dust, sand, etc.: *Clouds of smoke were pouring from the burning building.*
IDM **every cloud has a silver lining** every sad or difficult situation has a positive side
under a cloud with the disapproval of the people around you: *She left her job under a cloud because she'd been accused of stealing.*

cloud² /klaʊd/ *verb* **1** [I,T] to become or make sth difficult to see through: *His eyes clouded with tears.* **2** [T] to make sth less clear or easy to understand: *Her personal involvement in the case was beginning to **cloud her judgement**.* **3** [T] to make sth less enjoyable; to spoil: *Illness has clouded the last few years of his life.*
PHR V **cloud over** (used about the sky) to become full of clouds

cloudburst /ˈklaʊdbɜːst/ *noun* [C] a sudden heavy fall of rain

cloudless /ˈklaʊdləs/ *adj.* (used about the sky, etc.) clear; without any clouds

cloudy /ˈklaʊdi/ *adj.* **1** (used about the sky, etc.) full of clouds **2** (used about liquids, etc.) not clear: *cloudy water*

clout /klaʊt/ *noun* (*informal*) **1** [C] a hard hit, usually with the hand: *to give someone a clout* **2** [U] influence and power: *He's an important man – he has a lot of clout in the company.*

clove /kləʊv/ *noun* [C] **1** the small dried flower of a tropical tree, used to give a special flavour in cooking **2** one of the small separate sections into which the root of the GARLIC plant is divided

ˌcloven ˈhoof *noun* [C] the foot of an animal such as a cow or a sheep, that is divided into two parts

clover /ˈkləʊvə(r)/ *noun* [C] a small plant with pink or white flowers and leaves with three parts to them

clown¹ /klaʊn/ *noun* [C] a person who wears funny clothes and a big red nose and does silly things to make people laugh: (*figurative*) *At school, Bob was always the class clown.*

clown² /klaʊn/ *verb* [I] ~ **(about/around)** to behave in a silly way, especially in order to make other people laugh: *Stop clowning around and get some work done!*

cloying /ˈklɔɪɪŋ/ *adj.* (*formal*) **1** (used about food, a smell, etc.) so sweet that it is unpleasant **2** using emotion in a very obvious way, so that the result is unpleasant: *Her novels are full of cloying sentimentality.*

club¹ ⊶ /klʌb/ *noun* **1** [C] a group of people who meet regularly to share an interest, do sport, etc.; the place where they meet: *to join a club* ◇ *to be a member of a club* ◇ *a tennis/football/golf club* **2** [C] a place where people, especially young people, go and listen to music, dance, etc. **3** [C] a heavy stick, usually with one end that is thicker than the other, used as a weapon **4** [C] a long stick that is specially shaped at one end and used for hitting a ball when playing GOLF ➲ look at **bat**, **racket**, **stick** ➲ picture at **sport** **5** **clubs** [pl.] one of the four sets of playing cards (called **suits**) with black shapes with three leaves on them: *the two/ace/queen of clubs* **6** [C] one of the cards from this suit: *I played a club.*

club² /klʌb/ *verb* (**clubbing**; **clubbed**) **1** [T] to hit sb/sth hard with a heavy object **2** [I] **go clubbing** to go dancing and drinking in a club: *She goes clubbing every Saturday.*
PHR V **club together (to do sth)** to share the cost of sth, for example a present: *We clubbed together to buy him a leaving present.*

cluck /klʌk/ *noun* [C] the noise made by a chicken ▶ **cluck** *verb* [I]

clue /kluː/ *noun* [C] **a ~ (to sth)** a piece of information that helps you solve a problem or a crime, answer a question, etc.: *The police were looking for clues to his disappearance.* ◇ *the clues for solving a crossword puzzle*
IDM **not have a clue** (*informal*) to know nothing about sth

clued-up /ˌkluːd ˈʌp/ (*AmE also* **ˌclued-ˈin**) *adj.* ~ **(on sth)** knowing a lot about sth: *I'm not really clued-up on the technical details.*

clueless /ˈkluːləs/ *adj.* (*informal*) not able to understand; stupid: *I'm absolutely clueless about computers.*

clump¹ /klʌmp/ *noun* [C] a small group of things or people very close together, especially trees or plants; a bunch of sth such as grass or hair

clump² /klʌmp/ *verb* [I,T] ~ **(together)**; ~ **A and B (together)** to come together or be brought together to form a tight group: *Galaxies tend to clump together in clusters.*

clumsy /ˈklʌmzi/ *adj.* (**clumsier**; **clumsiest**) **1** (used about a person) careless and likely to knock into, drop or break things: *She undid the parcel with clumsy fingers.* **2** (used about a comment, etc.) likely to upset or offend people: *He made a clumsy apology.* **3** large, difficult to use, and not attractive in design: *a clumsy piece of furniture* ▶ **clumsily** *adv.* ▶ **clumsiness** *noun* [U]

clung past tense, past participle of **cling**

clunk /klʌŋk/ *noun* [C] a short low sound made when two hard objects hit each other: *The car door shut with a clunk.*

cluster¹ /ˈklʌstə(r)/ *noun* [C] a group of people, plants or things that stand or grow close together

cluster² /ˈklʌstə(r)/ *verb*
PHR V **cluster around sb/sth** to form a group around sb/sth: *The tourists clustered around their guide.*

clutch¹ /klʌtʃ/ *verb* [T] to hold sth tightly, especially because you are in pain, afraid or excited: *He clutched his mother's hand in fear.*
PHR V **clutch at sth** to try to take hold of sth: *She clutched at the money but the wind blew it away.*

clutch² /klʌtʃ/ *noun* **1** [C] the part of a vehicle, etc. that you press with your foot when you are driving in order to change the GEAR; the part of the engine that it is connected to: *to press/release the clutch* **2** **clutches** [pl.] power or control over sb: *He fell **into** the enemy's **clutches**.*

clutter¹ /ˈklʌtə(r)/ *noun* [U] things that are where they are not wanted or needed and make a place untidy: *Who left all this clutter on the floor?* ▶ **cluttered** *adj.*: *a cluttered desk*

clutter² /ˈklʌtə(r)/ *verb* [T] ~ **sth (up)** to cover or fill sth with lots of objects in an untidy way

cm *abbr.* (*pl.* **cm** or **cms**) centimetre(s)

Co. *abbr.* **1** company: *W Smith & Co.* **2** county: *Co. Down*

c/o *abbr.* (used for addressing a letter to sb who is staying at another person's house) care of: *Sandra Garcia, c/o Mrs Nolan*

co- /kəʊ/ ***prefix*** (in adjectives, adverbs, nouns and verbs) together with: *co-pilot* ◇ *coexist*

coach¹ 🔑 /kəʊtʃ/ ***noun*** [C] **1** (SPORT) a person who trains people to compete in certain sports: *a tennis coach* **2** (*BrE*) (TOURISM) a comfortable bus used for long journeys: *It's cheaper to travel* ***by coach*** *than by train.* **3** = CARRIAGE (1) **4** a large vehicle with four wheels pulled by horses, used in the past for carrying passengers ➲ look at **carriage, car**

coach² /kəʊtʃ/ ***verb*** [I,T] **~ sb (in/for sth)** to train or teach sb, especially to compete in a sport or pass an exam

coaching /ˈkəʊtʃɪŋ/ ***noun*** [U] **1** the process of training sb to play a sport, to do a job better or to improve a skill **2** (*especially BrE*) the process of giving a student extra teaching in a particular subject

coagulate /kəʊˈægjuleɪt/ ***verb*** [I] (used about a liquid) to become thick and partly solid: *The blood was starting to coagulate inside the cut.* ▶ **coagulation** /kəʊˌægjuˈleɪʃn/ ***noun*** [U]

coal 🔑 /kəʊl/ ***noun*** **1** [U] (GEOLOGY) a type of black mineral that is MINED (= dug) from the ground and burned to give heat: *a lump of coal* ◇ *a coal fire* **2 coals** [pl.] burning pieces of coal

coalesce /ˌkəʊəˈles/ ***verb*** [I] **~ (into/with sth)** (*formal*) to come together to form one larger group, substance, etc. ▶ **coalescence** ***noun*** [U]

coalface /ˈkəʊlfeɪs/ ***noun*** [C] the place deep inside a mine where the coal is cut out of the rock

coalition /ˌkəʊəˈlɪʃn/ ***noun*** [C, with sing. or pl. verb] (POLITICS) a government formed by two or more political parties working together: *a coalition between the socialists and the Green Party*

ˈcoal mine (*also* **pit**) ***noun*** [C] a place, usually underground, where coal is dug from the ground ➲ look at **colliery**

ˈcoal miner (*also* **miner**) ***noun*** [C] a person whose job is to dig coal from the ground

coarse /kɔːs/ ***adj.*** **1** consisting of large pieces; rough, not smooth: *coarse salt* ◇ *coarse cloth* **OPP** **fine 2** (used about a person or their behaviour) rude, likely to offend people; having bad manners ▶ **coarsely** ***adv.***: *Chop the onion coarsely* (= into pieces which are not too small). ◇ *He laughed coarsely.*

coarsen /ˈkɔːsn/ ***verb*** [I,T] to become or to make sth COARSE

coast¹ 🔑 /kəʊst/ ***noun*** [C] (GEOGRAPHY) the area of land that is next to or close to the sea: *After sailing for an hour we could finally see the coast.* ◇ *Scarborough is* ***on the east coast***.

coast² /kəʊst/ ***verb*** [I] **1** to travel in a car, on a bicycle, etc. (especially down a hill) without using power **2** to achieve sth without much effort: *They coasted to victory.*

coastal /ˈkəʊstl/ ***adj.*** (GEOGRAPHY) on or near a coast: *coastal areas* ➲ picture at **erode**

coastguard /ˈkəʊstgɑːd/ ***noun*** [C] a person or group of people whose job is to watch the sea near the coast in order to help people or ships that are in danger or to stop illegal activities

coastline /ˈkəʊstlaɪn/ ***noun*** [C] (GEOGRAPHY) the edge or shape of a coast: *a rocky coastline*

coat¹ 🔑 /kəʊt/ ***noun*** [C] **1** a piece of clothing that you wear over your other clothes to keep warm when you are outside: *Put your coat on – it's cold outside.* ➲ look at **overcoat, raincoat 2** the fur or hair covering an animal's body: *a dog with a smooth coat* **3** a layer of sth covering a surface: *The walls will probably need two* ***coats of paint***.

coat² /kəʊt/ ***verb*** [T] **~ sth (with/in sth)** to cover sth with a layer of sth: *biscuits coated with milk chocolate*

ˈcoat hanger = HANGER

coating /ˈkəʊtɪŋ/ ***noun*** [C] a thin layer of sth that covers sth else: *wire with a plastic coating*

ˌcoat of ˈarms (*pl.* **coats of arms**) (*also* **arms** [pl.]) ***noun*** [C] a design that is used as the symbol of a family, a town, a university, etc.

ˌco-ˈauthor ***noun*** [C] a person who writes a book or an article with sb else ▶ **ˌco-ˈauthor** ***verb*** [T]

coax /kəʊks/ ***verb*** [T] **~ sb (into/out of sth/doing sth); ~ sth out of/from sb** to persuade sb gently: *The child wasn't hungry, but his mother coaxed him into eating a little.* ◇ *At last he coaxed a smile out of her.*

coaxial /kəʊˈæksiəl/ ***adj.*** **1** (MATHEMATICS) sharing a common AXIS (= a line that divides a shape into two equal parts) **2** (used about a cable or line) sending signals using two wires inside one cable, one of which is wrapped around the other and both of which share the same AXIS. **Coaxial cable** is used by television and telephone companies and in computer connections.

cob /kɒb/ ***noun*** [C] **1** the long hard part of the MAIZE(corn) plant that the rows of yellow grains grow on ➲ look at **corn on the cob 2** a strong horse with short legs

cobalt /ˈkəʊbɔːlt/ ***noun*** [U] **1** (*symbol* **Co**) (CHEMISTRY) a hard silver-white metal that is often mixed with other metals and used to give a deep blue-green colour to glass ❶ For more information on the periodic table of elements, look at pages R34-5.
2 (*also* **ˌcobalt ˈblue**) a deep blue-green colour

cobble /ˈkɒbl/ ***verb***

PHR V **cobble sth together** to make sth or put sth together quickly and without much care

cobbler /ˈkɒblə(r)/ ***noun*** [C] (*old-fashioned*) a person who repairs shoes

cobbles /ˈkɒblz/ (*also* **cobblestones** /ˈkɒblstəʊnz/) ***noun*** [pl.] small rounded stones used (in the past) for covering the surface of streets ▶ **cobbled** ***adj.***: *cobbled streets*

cobra /ˈkəʊbrə/ ***noun*** [C] a poisonous snake that can spread out the skin at the back of its neck. **Cobras** live in India and Africa. ➲ picture on **page 29**

cobweb /ˈkɒbweb/ ***noun*** [C] a net of threads made by a spider in order to catch insects ➲ look at **web** (1)

cocaine /kəʊˈkeɪn/ (also *informal* **coke**) ***noun*** [U] (HEALTH) a dangerous drug that some people take for pleasure but which is ADDICTIVE (= difficult to stop using)

coccus /ˈkɒkəs/ ***noun*** [C] (*pl.* **-cocci** /-ˈkɒkaɪ; *AmE* "coccus-cocci"-ˈkɒkaɪ/) (BIOLOGY) any bacterium whose shape is SPHERICAL (= round). Some types of **cocci** can cause serious infections and illnesses. ➲ look at **streptococcus**

coccyx /ˈkɒksɪks/ ***noun*** [C] (ANATOMY) the small bone at the bottom of your SPINE ➲ picture on **page 80**

cochineal /ˌkɒtʃɪˈniːl/ ***noun*** [U] a bright red substance used to give colour to food

cochlea /ˈkɒkliə/ ***noun*** [C] (ANATOMY) the part of the INNER EAR (= the inside of your ear), which is shaped like a shell and is very important for hearing ➲ picture at **ear**

cock¹ /kɒk/ ***noun*** [C] **1** (*AmE* **rooster**) an adult male chicken ➲ note at **chicken 2** an adult male bird of any type

cock² /kɒk/ ***verb*** [T] to hold up a part of the body: *The horse cocked its ears on hearing the noise.*
PHR V cock sth up (*BrE, slang*) to do sth very badly and spoil sth ➲ **cock-up**

cock-a-doodle-doo /ˌkɒk ə ˌduːdl ˈduː/ ***noun*** [sing.] the noise made by COCK

cockatoo /ˌkɒkəˈtuː/ ***noun*** [C] (*pl.* **cockatoos**) a large brightly coloured bird with a lot of feathers standing up on top of its head

cockerel /ˈkɒkərəl/ ***noun*** [C] a young male chicken

cockle /ˈkɒkl/ ***noun*** [C] a small SHELLFISH (= a sea animal that lives inside a shell) that can be eaten

cockney /ˈkɒkni/ ***noun*** **1** [C] a person who was born and grew up in the East End of London **2** [U] (LANGUAGE) the way of speaking English that is typical of people living in this area: *a cockney accent*

cockpit /ˈkɒkpɪt/ ***noun*** [C] **1** the part of a plane where the pilot sits **2** the part of a racing car where the driver sits

cockroach /ˈkɒkrəʊtʃ/ (*AmE* **roach**) ***noun*** [C] a large brown insect with wings, that lives in houses, especially where there is dirt ➲ picture on **page 29**

cocktail /ˈkɒkteɪl/ ***noun*** [C] **1** a drink made from a mixture of alcoholic drinks and fruit juices: *a cocktail bar/party* **2** a mixture of small pieces of food that is served cold: *a prawn cocktail* **3** a mixture of different substances, usually ones that do not mix together well: *a lethal cocktail of drugs*

ˈcock-up ***noun*** [C] (*BrE, slang*) something that was badly done; a mistake that spoils sth ➲ look at **cock²**

cocoa /ˈkəʊkəʊ/ ***noun*** **1** [U] a dark brown powder made from the seeds of a tropical tree and used in making chocolate **2** [C,U] a hot drink made from this powder mixed with milk or water; a cup of this drink: *a cup of cocoa*

coconut /ˈkəʊkənʌt/ ***noun*** [C,U] the large nut of a tropical tree called a **coconut palm**. It grows inside a hard shell and contains a soft white substance that can be eaten and juice that can be drunk.

cocoon /kəˈkuːn/ ***noun*** [C] (BIOLOGY) a covering of thin threads that some insects make to protect themselves before becoming adults ➲ look at **chrysalis**

cod /kɒd/ ***noun*** [C,U] (*pl.* **cod**) a large sea fish that you can eat that lives in the North Atlantic

coda /ˈkəʊdə/ ***noun*** [C] (MUSIC) the final passage of a piece of music

code¹ ⊶ AW /kəʊd/ ***noun*** **1** [C,U] a system of words, letters, numbers, etc. that are used instead of the real letters or words to make a message or information secret: *They managed to* ***break/crack the enemy code*** (= find out what it means). ◇ *They wrote letters to each other* ***in code.*** ➲ look at **decode 2** [C] a group of numbers, letters, etc. that is used for identifying sth: *What's the code* (= the telephone number) *for Stockholm?* ➲ look at **bar code 3** [C] a set of rules for behaviour: ***a code of practice*** (= a set of standards agreed and accepted by a particular profession) ◇ *the* ***Highway Code*** (= the rules for driving on the roads) **4** [U] (COMPUTING) instructions used to form computer programs: *segments of code*

code² AW /kəʊd/ ***verb*** [T] **1** (*also* **encode**) to put or write sth in code¹(1): *coded messages* **OPP decode** **2** to use a particular system for identifying things: *The files are colour-coded: blue for Europe, green for Africa.* **3** (COMPUTING) to write a computer program by putting one system of numbers, words and symbols into another system

codec /ˈkəʊdek/ ***noun*** [C] (COMPUTING) a device that reduces the size of a file, etc. as it enters or leaves a computer, video, or other electronic device, so that it can be sent more quickly

codeine /ˈkəʊdiːn/ ***noun*** [U] (HEALTH) a drug that is used to reduce pain

codify /ˈkəʊdɪfaɪ/ ***verb*** [T] (*pres. part.* **codifying**; *3rd person sing. pres.* **codifies**; *pt, pp* **codified**) (TECHNICAL) to arrange laws, rules, etc. into a system ▶ **codification** /ˌkəʊdɪfɪˈkeɪʃn/ ***noun*** [U]

ˌco-eduˈcational (*abbr.* **coed**) ***adj.*** (EDUCATION) (used about a school) with both boys and girls together in the same classes **SYN mixed** ▶ **ˌco-eduˈcation** ***noun*** [U]

coefficient /ˌkəʊɪˈfɪʃnt/ ***noun*** [C] **1** (MATHEMATICS) a number which is placed before another quantity and which multiplies it, for example *3* in the quantity *3x* **2** (PHYSICS) a number that measures a particular property (= characteristic) of a substance: *the coefficient of friction/expansion*

coerce /kəʊˈɜːs/ ***verb*** [T] (*formal*) **~ sb (into sth/doing sth)** to force sb to do sth, for example by threatening them ▶ **coercion** /kəʊˈɜːʃn/ ***noun*** [U]

coexist /ˌkəʊɪɡˈzɪst/ ***verb*** [I] to live or be together at the same time or in the same place as sb/sth ▶ **coexistence** ***noun*** [U]

C. of E. /ˌsiː əv ˈiː/ ***abbr.*** (RELIGION) = CHURCH OF ENGLAND

coffee ⊶ /ˈkɒfi/ ***noun*** **1** [U] the cooked seeds (called **coffee beans**) of a tropical tree, made into powder and used for making a drink: *Coffee is the country's biggest export.* ◇ *decaffeinated/instant coffee* **2** [U] a drink made by adding hot water to this powder: *Would you prefer tea or coffee?* ◇ *a cup of coffee* **3** [C] a cup of this drink: *Two coffees please.*

ˈcoffee bar (*also* **ˈcoffee shop**) ***noun*** [C] (*BrE*) a place in a hotel, a large shop, etc., where simple food, coffee, tea and other drinks without alcohol are served

ˈcoffee pot ***noun*** [C] a container in which coffee is made and served

ˈcoffee table ***noun*** [C] a small low table for putting magazines, cups, etc., on

coffin /ˈkɒfɪn/ (*AmE* **casket**) ***noun*** [C] a box in which a dead body is buried or CREMATED (= burned)

cog /kɒɡ/ ***noun*** [C] (PHYSICS) one of a series of teeth on the edge of a wheel that fit into the teeth on the next wheel and cause it to move

cogent /ˈkəʊdʒənt/ ***adj.*** (*formal*) strongly and clearly expressed in a way that influences what people believe: *a cogent argument/reason*

cognac /ˈkɒnjæk/ ***noun*** **1** [U] a type of BRANDY (= a strong alcoholic drink) that is made in France **2** [C] a glass of this drink

cognition /kɒɡˈnɪʃn/ ***noun*** [U] (PSYCHOLOGY) the process by which knowledge and understanding is developed in the mind

cog

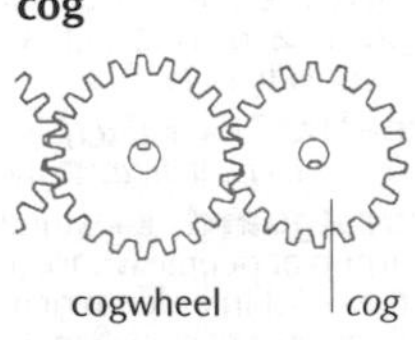

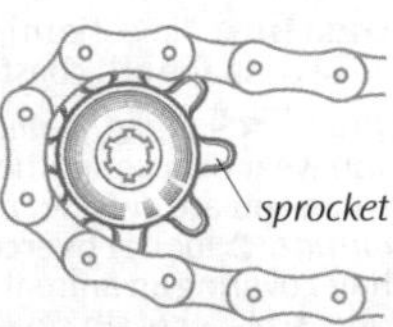

sprocket wheel

cognitive /ˈkɒɡnətɪv/ *adj.* (usually *before* a noun) (PSYCHOLOGY) connected with mental processes of understanding: *cognitive abilities* ◇ *the* ***cognitive process*** *of absorbing new information*

cohabit /kəʊˈhæbɪt/ *verb* [I] (*formal*) (used about a couple) to live together as if they are married

coherent AW /kəʊˈhɪərənt/ *adj.* **1** (of ideas, thoughts, arguments, etc.) logical and well organized; easy to understand and clear: ***a coherent narrative/explanation*** **2** (used about a person) able to talk and express yourself clearly: *She only became coherent again two hours after the attack.* OPP **incoherent** ▶ **coherence** AW *noun* [U] ▶ **coherently** *adv.*

cohesion /kəʊˈhiːʒn/ *noun* [U] **1** the act or state of keeping together SYN **unity**: *What the team lacks is cohesion – all the players play as individuals.* ◇ ***social/political/economic cohesion*** **2** (PHYSICS, CHEMISTRY) the force causing MOLECULES of the same substance to stick together

coil¹ /kɔɪl/ *verb* [I,T] to make sth into a round shape: *a snake coiled under a rock*

coil² /kɔɪl/ *noun* [C] a length of rope, wire, etc. that has been made into a round shape: *a coil of rope*

coin¹ 🔑 /kɔɪn/ *noun* [C] a piece of money made of metal: *a pound coin*

coin² /kɔɪn/ *verb* [T] (LANGUAGE) to invent a new word or phrase: *Who was it who coined the phrase 'a week is a long time in politics'?*

coinage /ˈkɔɪnɪdʒ/ *noun* [U] the system of coins used in a country: *decimal coinage*

coincide AW /ˌkəʊɪnˈsaɪd/ *verb* [I] **~ (with sth)** **1** (used about events) to happen at the same time as sth else: *The Queen's visit is timed to coincide with the country's centenary celebrations.* **2** to be exactly the same or very similar: *Our views coincide completely.*

coincidence AW /kəʊˈɪnsɪdəns/ *noun* [C,U] two or more similar things happening at the same time by chance, in a surprising way: *We hadn't planned to meet, it was just coincidence.*

coincident AW /kəʊˈɪnsɪdənt/ *adj.* **~ (with sth)** (*formal*) happening in the same place or at the same time

coincidental AW /kəʊˌɪnsɪˈdentl/ *adj.* resulting from two similar or related events happening at the same time by chance ▶ **coincidentally** *adv.*

coitus /ˈkɔɪtəs/ = SEX (3)

coke /kəʊk/ *noun* [U] **1** a solid black substance produced from coal and used as a fuel **2** = COCAINE

Col. *abbr.* (in writing) = COLONEL: *Col. Stewart*

col /kɒl/ *noun* [C] (GEOGRAPHY) a low point between two higher points in a line or group of mountains

cola /ˈkəʊlə/ *noun* [C,U] a brown, sweet cold drink that does not contain alcohol; a glass or can of this

colander /ˈkʌləndə(r)/ *noun* [C] a metal or plastic bowl with a lot of small holes in it that is used for removing water from food that has been boiled or washed

cold¹ 🔑 /kəʊld/ *adj.* **1** having a low temperature; not hot or warm: *I'm not going into the sea, the water's too cold.* ◇ *Shall I put the heating on? I'm cold.*
2 (used about food or drink) not heated or cooked; having become cold after being heated or cooked: *a cold drink* ◇ *Have your soup before it gets cold.* **3** (used about a person or sb's behaviour) very unfriendly; not showing kindness, understanding, etc.: *She gave him a cold, hard look.*

> **RELATED VOCABULARY**
>
> Compare **cold**, **hot**, **cool**, and **warm**.
> **Cold** indicates a lower temperature than **cool** and may describe a temperature that is unpleasantly low: *a terribly cold winter.*
> **Cool** means 'fairly cold' and may describe a pleasantly low temperature: *It's terribly hot outside but it's nice and cool in here.*
> **Hot** indicates a higher temperature than warm and may describe a temperature that is unpleasantly high: *I can't drink this yet, it's too hot.*
> **Warm** means 'fairly hot' and may describe a pleasantly high temperature: *Come and sit by the fire, you'll soon get warm again.*

IDM **cold turkey** suddenly and completely, without getting used to sth gradually: *I gave up smoking cold turkey.*
get/have cold feet (*informal*) to become/be afraid to do sth: *She started to get cold feet as her wedding day approached.*
in cold blood in a cruel way and without pity: *to kill sb in cold blood*

cold² 🔑 /kəʊld/ *noun* **1** [sing., U] lack of heat; low temperature; cold weather: *We walked home in the snow, shivering with cold.* ◇ *Come on, let's get out of the cold and go indoors.* **2** [C,U] (HEALTH) a common illness of the nose and throat. When you have a cold you have a sore throat and often cannot breathe through your nose: *I think I'm getting a cold.* ◇ *Wear some warm clothes when you go out or you'll* ***catch cold***.

ˌcold-ˈblooded *adj.* **1** (BIOLOGY) having a blood temperature that changes with the temperature of the surroundings: *Reptiles are cold-blooded.* OPP **warm-blooded** **2** cruel; having or showing no pity: *cold-blooded killers*

ˌcold-ˈcalling *noun* [U] (BUSINESS) the practice of telephoning or visiting sb you do not know in order to sell them sth: *One million people have said no to junk mail and cold-calling.* ▶ **ˌcold-ˈcall** *verb* [I,T]: *I cold-called 500 companies.* ▶ **ˌcold ˈcall** *noun* [C] ▶ **ˌcold-ˈcaller** *noun* [C]

ˌcold ˈcash (*AmE*) = HARD CASH

ˌcold-ˈhearted *adj.* unkind; showing no kindness, understanding, etc.

coldly 🔑 /ˈkəʊldli/ *adv.* in an unfriendly way; in a way that shows no kindness or understanding

coldness /ˈkəʊldnəs/ *noun* [U] the lack of warm feelings; unfriendly behaviour

ˈcold snap *noun* [C] a sudden short period of very cold weather

ˈcold sore *noun* [C] (HEALTH) a small painful area on the lips or inside the mouth that is caused by a VIRUS

ˌcold ˈstorage *noun* [U] a place where food, etc. can be kept fresh or frozen until it is needed; the keeping of sth in a place like this: *to keep meat* ***in cold storage***

ˌcold ˈwar *noun* [sing., U] (often **Cold War**) (POLITICS) a very unfriendly relationship between two countries who are not actually fighting each other, usually used about the situation between the US and the Soviet Union after the Second World War

colic /ˈkɒlɪk/ *noun* [U] (HEALTH) pain in the stomach area, which especially babies get

collaborate /kəˈlæbəreɪt/ *verb* [I] **1** **~ (with sb) (on sth)** to work together (with sb), especially to create or produce sth: *She collaborated with another* *author on the book.* **2** ~ **(with sb)** to help the enemy forces who have taken control of your country ▸ **collaboration** /kəˌlæbəˈreɪʃn/ ***noun*** [U, C] ▸ **collaborator** ***noun*** [C]

collaborative /kəˈlæbərətɪv/ ***adj.*** (*formal*) involving, or done by, several people or groups of people working together: *collaborative projects/ studies/research* ▸ **collaboratively** ***adv.***

collage /ˈkɒlɑːʒ/ ***noun*** [C,U] (ART) a picture made by fixing pieces of paper, cloth, photographs, etc. onto a surface; the art of making a picture like this

collagen /ˈkɒlədʒn/ ***noun*** [U] (BIOLOGY) a PROTEIN found in skin and bone, sometimes INJECTED into the body, especially the face, to improve its appearance

collapse¹ 🔑 AW /kəˈlæps/ ***verb*** **1** [I] to fall down or break into pieces suddenly: *A lot of buildings collapsed in the earthquake.* **2** [I] (used about a person) to fall down, usually because you are very ill, and perhaps become unconscious: *The winner collapsed at the end of the race.* **3** [I] (used about a business, plan, etc.) to fail suddenly or completely: *The company collapsed, leaving hundreds of people out of work.* **4** [I,T] to fold sth or be folded into a shape that uses less space

collapse² 🔑 AW /kəˈlæps/ ***noun*** **1** [C,U] the sudden or complete failure of sth, such as a business, plan, etc.: *The peace talks were on the brink/verge of collapse.* **2** [sing., U] (used about a building) a sudden fall: *the collapse of the motorway bridge* **3** [sing., U] (HEALTH) (used about a person) a medical condition when a person becomes very ill and suddenly falls down

collapsible /kəˈlæpsəbl/ ***adj.*** that can be folded into a shape that makes sth easy to store: *a collapsible bed*

collar¹ /ˈkɒlə(r)/ ***noun*** [C] **1** the part of a shirt, coat, dress, etc. that fits round the neck and is often folded over: *a coat with a fur collar* ➲ look at **dog collar**, **blue-collar**, **white-collar** **2** a band of leather that is put round an animal's neck (especially a dog or cat)

collar² /ˈkɒlə(r)/ ***verb*** [T] (*informal*) to catch hold of sb who does not want to be caught

collarbone /ˈkɒləbəʊn/ (also *formal* **clavicle**) ***noun*** [C] (ANATOMY) one of the two bones that connect your chest bones to your shoulder ➲ picture on **page 80**

collate /kəˈleɪt/ ***verb*** [T] **1** to collect information from different places in order to put it together, examine and compare it: *to collate data/information/figures* **2** to collect pieces of paper or pages from a book and arrange them in the correct order ▸ **collation** ***noun*** [U]: *the collation of data*

collateral¹ /kəˈlætərəl/ ***noun*** [U] (FINANCE) property or sth valuable that you promise to give to sb if you cannot pay back money that you borrow

collateral² /kəˈlætərəl/ ***adj.*** (*formal*) connected with sth else, but in addition to it and less important: *collateral benefits* ◇ *The government denied that there had been any* ***collateral damage*** (=injury to ordinary people or buildings) *during the bombing raid.*

colleague 🔑 AW /ˈkɒliːg/ ***noun*** [C] a person who works at the same place as you

collect¹ 🔑 /kəˈlekt/ ***verb*** **1** [T] to bring a number of things together: *All the exam papers will be collected at the end.* **2** [T] to get and keep together a number of objects of a particular type over a period of time as a hobby: *He used to collect stamps.* **3** [I,T] to ask for money from a number of people: *to collect for charity* ◇ *The landlord collects the rent at the end of each month.* **4** [I] to come together: *A crowd collected to see what was going on.* SYN **gather** **5** [T] (*especially BrE*) to go and get sb/sth from a particular place; to pick sb/sth up: *to collect the children from school* **6** [T] ~ **yourself/sth** to get control of yourself, your feelings, thoughts, etc.: *She collected herself and went back into the room as if nothing had happened.* ◇ *I tried to* ***collect my thoughts*** *before the exam.*

> **THESAURUS**
>
> **collect**
>
> **gather • accumulate • amass**
>
> These words all mean to get more of sth over a period of time, or to increase in quantity over a period of time.
>
> **collect**: *He collected data from various sources.*
>
> **gather**: *Detectives were gathering evidence.*
>
> **accumulate** (*formal*): *Debts began to accumulate.*
>
> **amass** (*formal*): *He amassed a large fortune.*

collect² /kəˈlekt/ ***adj.***, ***adv.*** (*AmE*) (used about a telephone call) to be paid for by the person who receives the call: *a* ***collect call*** ◇ *She called me collect.*

collected /kəˈlektɪd/ ***adj.*** calm and in control of yourself, your feelings, thoughts, etc.: *She felt cool, calm and collected before the interview.*

collection 🔑 /kəˈlekʃn/ ***noun*** **1** [C] a group of objects of a particular type that sb has collected as a hobby: *a stamp collection* **2** [C,U] the act of getting sth from a place or from people: *rubbish collections* **3** [C] a group of people or things: *a large collection of papers on the desk* **4** [C] (LITERATURE) a number of poems, stories, letters, etc. published together in one book: *a collection of modern poetry* **5** [C] the act of asking for money from a number of people (for charity, in church, etc.): *a collection for the poor* **6** [C] a variety of new clothes or items for the home that are specially designed and sold at a particular time: *Armani's stunning new autumn collection*

collective¹ /kəˈlektɪv/ ***adj.*** shared by a group of people together; not individual: *collective responsibility* ▸ **collectively** ***adv.***: *We took the decision collectively at a meeting.*

collective² /kəˈlektɪv/ ***noun*** [C, with sing. or pl. verb] (BUSINESS) an organization or business that is owned and controlled by the people who work in it

colˌlective ˈbargaining ***noun*** [U] (POLITICS) discussions between a TRADE UNION (=an organization that protects the rights of workers) and an employer about the pay and working conditions of the union members

colˌlective ˈnoun ***noun*** [C] (LANGUAGE) a singular noun, such as 'committee' or 'team', that refers to a group of people, animals or things and, in British English, can be used with either a singular or a plural verb

collectivism /kəˈlektɪvɪzəm/ ***noun*** [U] (POLITICS) the political system in which all farms, businesses and industries are owned by the government or by all the people ▸ **collectivist** ***adj.***

collectivize (also **-ise**) /kəˈlektɪvaɪz/ ***verb*** [T] (often passive) (POLITICS) to join several private farms, industries, etc. together so that they are controlled by the community or by the government ▸ **collectivization** (also **-isation**) /kəˌlektɪvaɪˈzeɪʃn/ ***noun*** [U]

collector /kəˈlektə(r)/ ***noun*** [C] (often in compounds) a person who collects things as a hobby or as part of their job: *a stamp collector ◇ a ticket/rent/tax collector*

college 🔑 /ˈkɒlɪdʒ/ ***noun*** (EDUCATION) **1** [C,U] an institution where you can study after you leave school (at the age of 16): *an **art college** ◇ a **sixth-form college*** (= an institution where pupils aged 16 to 18 can prepare for A Levels) ◇ *She's studying Spanish at the **college of further education*** (= a college that is not a university where people who have left school can study). **2** [C] (in Britain) one of the separate institutions into which certain universities are divided: *King's College, London* **3** [C] (in the US) a university, or part of one, where students can study for a degree

collide /kəˈlaɪd/ ***verb*** [I] ~ **(with sb/sth)** to crash; to hit sb/sth very hard while moving: *He ran along the corridor and collided with his teacher.*

colliery /ˈkɒliəri/ ***noun*** [C] (*pl.* **collieries**) (*especially BrE*) a coal mine and its buildings

collision /kəˈlɪʒn/ ***noun*** [C,U] a crash; an occasion when things or people COLLIDE: *It was a **head-on collision** and the driver was killed instantly.*

IDM **be on a collision course (with sb/sth) 1** to be in a situation which is certain to end in a disagreement or argument **2** to be moving in a direction which is certain to cause a crash: *The ship was **on a collision course** with an iceberg.*

collocate /ˈkɒləkeɪt/ ***verb*** [I] ~ **(with sth)** (LANGUAGE) (used about words) to be often used together in a language: *'Bitter' collocates with 'enemies' but 'sour' does not.* ▶ **collocate** /ˈkɒləkət/ ***noun*** [C]: *'Bitter' and 'enemies' are collocates.*

collocation /ˌkɒləˈkeɪʃn/ ***noun*** [C] (LANGUAGE) a combination of words in a language, that happens very often and more frequently than would happen by chance: *A 'resounding success' and a 'crying shame' are English collocations.*

colloquial /kəˈləʊkwiəl/ ***adj.*** (LANGUAGE) (used about words, phrases, etc.) used in spoken conversation, not in formal situations ▶ **colloquially** /-kwiəli/ ***adv.***

colloquialism /kəˈləʊkwiəlɪzəm/ ***noun*** [C] (LANGUAGE) a word or phrase that is used in conversation but not in formal speech or writing

collusion /kəˈluːʒn/ ***noun*** [U] (*formal*) secret agreement, especially in order to do sth dishonest: *The drugs were brought into the country with the collusion of customs officials.*

cologne /kəˈləʊn/ = EAU DE COLOGNE

colon /ˈkəʊlən/ ***noun*** [C] **1** (LANGUAGE) the mark (:) used before a list, an explanation, an example, etc. **2** (ANATOMY) the lower part of the large INTESTINE that carries food away from your stomach to the ANUS (= the place where it leaves the body) ➲ picture at **digestive system**

colonel /ˈkɜːnl/ ***noun*** [C] an officer of a high level in the army

colonial /kəˈləʊniəl/ ***adj.*** (POLITICS) connected with or belonging to a COLONY: *Spain used to be a major colonial power.*

colonialism /kəˈləʊniəlɪzəm/ ***noun*** [U] (POLITICS) the practice by which a powerful country controls another country or countries, in order to become richer

colonist /ˈkɒlənɪst/ ***noun*** [C] a person who goes to live in a country that has become a COLONY

colonize (also **-ise**) /ˈkɒlənaɪz/ ***verb*** [T] (POLITICS) to take control of another country or place and make it a COLONY ▶ **colonization** (also **-isation**) /ˌkɒlənaɪˈzeɪʃn/ ***noun*** [U]

colonnade /ˌkɒləˈneɪd/ ***noun*** [C] (ARCHITECTURE) a row of stone columns with equal spaces between them, usually supporting a roof

colony /ˈkɒləni/ ***noun*** [C] (*pl.* **colonies**) **1** (POLITICS) a country or an area that is ruled by another, more powerful country **2** [with sing. or pl. verb] (SOCIAL STUDIES) a group of people who go to live permanently in another country but keep their own habits and traditions **3** (BIOLOGY) a group of the same type of animals, insects or plants living or growing in the same place: *a colony of ants*

color 🔑 (*AmE*) = COLOUR

coloratura /ˌkɒlərəˈtʊərə/ ***noun*** [U] (MUSIC) complicated passages for a singer, for example in OPERA

colossal /kəˈlɒsl/ ***adj.*** extremely large: *a colossal building ◇ a colossal amount of money*

colour[1] 🔑 (*AmE* **color**) /ˈkʌlə(r)/ ***noun*** **1** [C,U] the fact that sth is red, green, yellow, blue, etc.: *'What colour is your car?' 'Red.' ◇ What colours do the Swedish team play in? ◇ a dark/deep colour ◇ a bright colour ◇ a light/pale colour ◇ Those flowers certainly give the room a bit of colour.* **2** [U] the use of all the colours, not just black and white: *All the pictures in the book are **in colour**. ◇ a colour television* **3** [U] a red or pink colour in your face, particularly when it shows how healthy you are or that you are embarrassed: *You look much better now, you've got a bit more colour. ◇ Colour flooded her face when she thought of what had happened.* **4** [U] interesting or exciting details: *It's a busy area, full of activity and colour.*

IDM **off colour** ill

with flying colours → FLYING

colour[2] 🔑 (*AmE* **color**) /ˈkʌlə(r)/ ***verb*** [T] **1** to put colour on sth, for example by painting it: *Colour the picture with your crayons. ◇ The area coloured yellow on the map is desert.* **2** to influence thoughts, opinions, etc.: *You shouldn't let one bad experience colour your attitude to everything.*

PHR V **colour sth in** to fill a shape, a picture, etc. with colour using pencils, paint, etc.: *The children were colouring in pictures of animals.*

ˈcolour-blind ***adj.*** (BIOLOGY) unable to see certain colours, especially red and green

coloured 🔑 (*AmE* **colored**) /ˈkʌləd/ ***adj.*** **1** having colour or a particular colour: *a coffee-coloured dress ◇ brightly-coloured lights* **2** (*old-fashioned*) (used about a person) belonging to a race that does not have white skin ❶ This word is considered offensive nowadays. To refer to a person belonging to a particular racial group, you should use black, Asian, etc. as appropriate.

colourful (*AmE* **colorful**) /ˈkʌləfl/ ***adj.*** **1** with bright colours; full of colour: *a colourful shirt* **2** full of interest or excitement: *a colourful story ◇ He has a rather colourful past.*

colouring (*AmE* **coloring**) /ˈkʌlərɪŋ/ ***noun*** **1** [U] the colour of a person's hair, skin, etc.: *to have fair/dark colouring* **2** [C,U] a substance that is used to give a particular colour to sth, especially food

colourless (*AmE* **colorless**) /ˈkʌlələs/ ***adj.*** **1** without any colour: *a colourless liquid, like water* **2** not interesting or exciting; dull

'colour scheme *noun* [C] the way in which colours are arranged, especially in a room

colt /kəʊlt/ *noun* [C] a young male horse ➲ look at **filly**

column ⊶ /ˈkɒləm/ *noun* [C] **1** (ARCHITECTURE) a tall solid vertical post made of stone, supporting or decorating a building or standing alone: *Nelson's Column is a monument in London.* ➲ picture at **arch** **2** something that has the shape of a column: *a column of smoke* (=smoke rising straight up) **3** one of the vertical sections into which a printed page, especially in a newspaper, is divided **4** a piece of writing in a newspaper or magazine that is part of a regular series or always written by the same writer: *the travel/gossip column* **5** a series of numbers written one under the other: *to add up a column of figures* **6** a long line of people, vehicles, etc., one following behind another: *a column of troops*

columnist /ˈkɒləmnɪst/ *noun* [C] (ARTS AND MEDIA) a journalist who writes regular articles in a newspaper or magazine: *a gossip columnist*

coma /ˈkəʊmə/ *noun* [C] (HEALTH) a deep unconscious state, often lasting for a long time and caused by serious illness or injury

comatose /ˈkəʊmətəʊs/ *adj.* **1** (*informal*) deeply asleep: *He had drunk a bottle of vodka and was comatose.* **2** (HEALTH) deeply unconscious; in a COMA

comb[1] /kəʊm/ *noun* **1** [C] a flat piece of metal or plastic with teeth that you use for making your hair tidy **2** [C, usually sing.] an act of **combing** the hair: *Give your hair a comb before you go out.*

comb[2] /kəʊm/ *verb* [T] **1** to make your hair tidy using a **comb** **2** ~ **sth (for sb/sth)** to search an area carefully: *Police are combing the woodland for the murder weapon.*

combat[1] /ˈkɒmbæt/ *noun* [C,U] a fight, especially in war: ***unarmed combat*** (=without weapons)

combat[2] /ˈkɒmbæt/ *verb* [T] to fight against sth; to try to stop or defeat sth: *to combat terrorism* ◇ *new medicines to combat heart disease*

combatant /ˈkɒmbətənt/ *noun* [C] a person who takes part in fighting, especially in war

combination ⊶ /ˌkɒmbɪˈneɪʃn/ *noun* [C,U] a number of people or things mixed or joined together; a mixture: *The team manager still hasn't found the right combination of players.* ◇ *On this course, you may study French in combination with Spanish or Italian.*

combine[1] ⊶ /kəmˈbaɪn/ *verb* **1** [I,T] ~ **(with sb/sth)** to join or mix two or more things together: *The two organizations combined to form one company.* ◇ *Bad planning, combined with bad luck, led to the company's collapse.* **2** [T] ~ **A and/with B** to do or have two or more things at the same time: *This car combines speed and reliability.*

combine[2] /ˈkɒmbaɪn/ (*BrE also* ˌ**combine 'harvester**) *noun* [C] (AGRICULTURE) a large farm machine that both cuts CORN and separates the grain from the rest of the plant ➲ look at **harvest**

combined /kəmˈbaɪnd/ *adj.* done by a number of people joining together, resulting from the joining of two or more things: *The **combined efforts** of the emergency services prevented a major disaster.*

combustible /kəmˈbʌstəbl/ *adj.* able to begin burning easily

combustion /kəmˈbʌstʃən/ *noun* [U] the process of burning

come ⊶ /kʌm/ *verb* [I] (*pt* **came** /keɪm/; *pp* **come**) **1** to move to or towards the person who is speaking or the place that sb is talking about: *Come here, please.* ◇ *Come and see what I've found.* ◇ *I hope you can come to my party.* ◇ *They're coming to stay for a week.* ◇ *The children came running into the room.* **2** ~ (to...) to arrive somewhere or reach a particular place or time: *What time are you coming home?* ◇ *Has the newspaper come yet?* ◇ *After a few hours in the jungle, we came to a river* ◇ *Her hair comes down to her waist.* ◇ *The water in the pool came up to our knees.* ◇ *The time has come to say goodbye.* **3** to be in a particular position in a series: *March comes after February.* ◇ *Charlie came second in the exam.* ◇ *I can't wait to find out what comes next in the story.* **4** ~ **in sth** to be available: *This blouse comes in a choice of four colours.* ◇ *Do these trousers come in a larger size?* **5** to be produced by or from sth: *Wool comes from sheep.* **6** to become open or loose: *Your blouse has come undone.* ◇ *Her hair has come untied.* **7** ~ **to do sth** used for talking about how, why or when sth happened: *How did you come to lose your passport?* **8** ~ **to/into sth** to reach a particular state: *We were all sorry when the holiday came to an end.* ◇ *The military government came to power in a coup d'état.*

IDM **come and go** to be present for a short time and then go away: *The pain in my ear comes and goes.*

come easily/naturally to sb to be easy for sb to do: *Apologizing does not come easily to her.*

come to nothing; not come to anything to fail; to not be successful: *Unfortunately, all his efforts came to nothing.*

how come...? (*informal*) why or how: *How come you're back so early?*

to come (used after a noun) in the future: *You'll regret it in years to come.*

when it comes to sth/to doing sth when it is a question of sth: *When it comes to value for money, these prices are hard to beat.*

PHR V **come about** to happen: *How did this situation come about?*

come across/over (as sth) to make an impression of a particular type: *Elizabeth comes across as being rather shy.*

come across sb/sth to meet or find sb/sth by chance: *I came across this book in a second-hand shop.*

come along **1** to arrive or appear: *When the right job comes along, I'll apply for it.* **2** =COME ON (2) **3** =COME ON (3)

come apart to break into pieces

come away (from sth) to become loose or separated from sth: *The wallpaper is coming away from the wall in the corner.*

come away with sth to leave a place with a particular opinion or feeling: *We came away with a very favourable impression of Cambridge.*

come back **1** to return: *I don't know what time I'll be coming back.* **2** to become popular or fashionable again: *Flared trousers are coming back again.*

come back (to sb) to be remembered: *When I went to Italy again, my Italian started to come back to me.*

come before sb/sth to be more important than sb/sth else: *Mark feels his family comes before his career.*

come between sb and sb to damage the relationship between two people: *Arguments over money came between the two brothers.*

come by sth to manage to get sth: *Fresh vegetables are hard to come by in the winter.*

come down **1** to fall down: *The power lines came down in the storm.* **2** (used about an aircraft or SPACECRAFT) to land: *The helicopter came down in a field.* **3** (used about prices) to become lower: *The price of land has come down in the past year.*

come down to sth/to doing sth (*informal*) to be

able to be explained by a single important point: *It all comes down to having the right qualifications.*
come down with sth (HEALTH) to become ill with sth: *I think I'm coming down with flu.*
come forward to offer help: *The police are asking witnesses to come forward.*
come from... to live in or have been born in a place: *Where do you come from originally?*
come from (doing) sth to be the result of sth: *'I'm tired.' 'That comes from all the late nights you've had.'*
come in 1 to enter a place: *Come in and sit down.* **2** (used about the TIDES of the sea) to move towards the land and cover the beach ➲ look at **tide**[1] **3** to become popular or fashionable: *Punk fashions came in in the seventies.* **4** (used about news or information) to be received: *Reports are coming in of fighting in Beirut.*
come in for sth to receive sth, especially sth unpleasant: *The government came in for a lot of criticism.*
come of sth/of doing sth to be the result of sth: *We've written to several companies asking for help but nothing has come of it yet.*
come off 1 to be able to be removed: *Does the hood come off?* **2** (*informal*) to be successful: *The deal seems unlikely to come off.* **3** (*informal*) (followed by an adverb) to be in a good, bad, etc. situation as a result of sth: *Unfortunately, Dennis came off worst in the fight.*
come off (sth) 1 to fall off sth: *Kim came off her bicycle and broke her leg.* **2** to become removed from sth: *One of the legs has come off this table.*
come off it (*spoken*) used to say that you do not believe sb/sth or that you strongly disagree with sb: *'I thought it was quite a good performance.' 'Oh, come off it – it was awful!'*
come on 1 to start to act, play in a game of sport, etc.: *The audience jeered every time the villain came on.* ◇ *The substitute came on in the second half.* **2** (*also* **come along**) to make progress or to improve: *Your English is coming on nicely.* **3** (*also* **Come along!**) used to tell sb to hurry up, try harder, etc.: *Come on or we'll be late!* **4** to begin: *I think I've got a cold coming on.*
come out 1 to appear; to be published: *The rain stopped and the sun came out.* ◇ *The report came out in 2000.* **2** to become known: *It was only after his death that the truth came out.* **3** (used about a photograph, etc.) to be produced successfully
come out (of sth) to be removed from sth: *Red wine stains don't come out easily.*
come out against sth to say in public that you do not like or agree with sth
come out in sth (HEALTH) to become covered in spots, etc.: *Heat makes him* ***come out in a rash.***
come out with sth to say sth unexpectedly: *The children came out with all kinds of stories.*
come over = COME ACROSS/OVER
come over (to...) (from...) to visit people or a place a long way away: *They've invited us to come over to Australia for a holiday.*
come over sb (used about a feeling) to affect sb: *A feeling of despair came over me.*
come round 1 (used about an event that happens regularly) to happen: *The end of the holidays always comes round very quickly.* **2** (*also* **come to**) (HEALTH) to become conscious again OPP **pass out**
come round (to...) to visit a person or place not far away
come round (to sth) to change your opinion so that you agree with sb/sth: *They finally came round to our way of thinking.*
come through (used about news, information, etc.) to arrive: *The football results are just coming through.*
come through (sth) to escape injury or death in a dangerous situation, illness, etc.: *to come through an enemy attack*
come to = COME ROUND (2)
come to sth 1 to equal or total a particular amount: *The bill for the meal came to £35.* **2** to result in a bad situation: *We will sell the house to pay our debts if we have to but we hope it won't come to that.*
come under to be included in a particular section, department, etc.: *Garages that sell cars come under 'car dealers' in the telephone book.*
come up 1 to happen or be going to happen in the future: *Something's come up at work so I won't be home until late tonight.* **2** to be discussed or mentioned: *The subject of religion came up.* **3** (used about the sun and moon) to rise **4** (used about a plant) to appear above the soil
come up against sb/sth to find a problem or difficulty that you have to deal with
come up to sth to be as good as usual or as necessary: *This piece of work does not come up to your usual standard.*
come up with sth to find an answer or solution to sth: *Engineers have come up with new ways of saving energy.*

comeback /ˈkʌmbæk/ ***noun*** [C] a return to a position of strength or importance that you had before: *The former world champion is hoping to* ***make a comeback.***

comedian /kəˈmiːdiən/ (*also* **comic**) ***noun*** [C] (ARTS AND MEDIA) a person whose job is to entertain people and make them laugh, for example by telling jokes

comedown /ˈkʌmdaʊn/ ***noun*** [C, usually sing.] (*informal*) a loss of importance or social position: *It's* ***a bit of a comedown*** *for her having to move to a smaller house.*

comedy ⊶ /ˈkɒmədi/ ***noun* 1** [C] (*pl.* **comedies**) (ARTS AND MEDIA) an amusing play, film, etc. that has a happy ending ➲ look at **tragedy 2** [U] the quality of being amusing or making people laugh

comet /ˈkɒmɪt/ ***noun*** [C] (ASTRONOMY) an object in space that looks like a bright star with a tail and that moves around the sun ➲ picture at **solar system**

comfort[1] ⊶ /ˈkʌmfət/ ***noun* 1** [U] the state of having everything your body needs, or of having a pleasant life: *Most people expect to live* ***in comfort*** *in their old age.* ◇ *to travel in comfort* **2** [U] the feeling of being physically relaxed and in no pain: *This car has been specially designed for extra comfort.* OPP **discomfort 3** [U] help or kindness to sb who is suffering: *I tried to offer a few words of comfort.* **4** a ~ (to sb) [sing.] a person or thing that helps you when you are very sad or worried: *You've been a real comfort to me.* **5** [C] something that makes your life easier or more pleasant: *the comforts of home*

comfort[2] ⊶ /ˈkʌmfət/ ***verb*** [T] to try to make sb feel less worried or unhappy: *to comfort a crying child*

comfortable ⊶ /ˈkʌmftəbl/ ***adj.* 1** (also *informal* **comfy**) that makes you feel physically relaxed and in no pain; that provides you with everything your body needs: *a comfortable temperature* (= not too hot or too cold) ◇ *Sit down and* ***make yourselves comfortable.*** ◇ *a comfortable pair of shoes* OPP **uncomfortable 2** not having or causing worry, difficulty, etc.: *He did not feel comfortable in the presence of so many women.* **3** having or providing enough money for all your needs: *They are not wealthy but they're quite comfortable.*

comfortably ⊶ /ˈkʌmftəbli/ *adv.* **1** in a comfortable way: *All the rooms were comfortably furnished.* ◇ *If you're all sitting comfortably, then I'll begin.* **2** with no problem SYN **easily**: *He can comfortably afford the extra expense.*
IDM **comfortably off** having enough money to buy what you want without worrying too much about the cost

comic¹ /ˈkɒmɪk/ *adj.* that makes you laugh; connected with comedy: *a comic scene in a play*

comic² /ˈkɒmɪk/ *noun* [C] **1** = COMEDIAN **2** (*especially AmE* **comic book**) a magazine for children that tells stories through pictures

comical /ˈkɒmɪkl/ *adj.* that makes you laugh; funny ▶ **comically** /-kli/ *adv.*

ˈ**comic strip** (*also* ˈ**strip cartoon**) *noun* [C] (ARTS AND MEDIA) a short series of pictures that tell a funny story, for example in a newspaper

coming /ˈkʌmɪŋ/ *noun* [C] the moment when sth new arrives or begins: *The coming of the computer meant the loss of many jobs.* ▶ **coming** *adj.*: *We've got a lot of plans for the coming year.*

comma /ˈkɒmə/ *noun* [C] (LANGUAGE) the mark (,) used for dividing parts of a sentence or items in a list

command¹ ⊶ /kəˈmɑːnd/ *noun* **1** [C] an order: *The captain's commands must be obeyed without question.* **2** [C] (COMPUTING) an instruction given to a computer **3** [U] control over sb/sth: *Who is **in command of** the expedition?* ◇ *to **take command of** a situation* **4** [sing.] the state of being able to do or use sth well: *She has a good command of French.*
IDM **at/by sb's command** (*formal*) because you were ordered by sb: *At the command of their officer the troops opened fire.*
be at sb's command to be ready to obey sb: *I'm completely at your command.*

command² ⊶ /kəˈmɑːnd/ *verb* **1** [I,T] (*formal*) ~ **(sb to do sth)** to tell or order sb to do sth: *I command you to leave now!* **2** ~ **sb/sth** [T] to control or be in charge of sb/sth: *to command a ship/regiment/army* **3** [T] to deserve and get sth: *The old man commanded great respect.*

commandant /ˈkɒməndænt/ *noun* [C] the officer in charge of a particular military group or institution

comˌmand eˈconomy = PLANNED ECONOMY

commandeer /ˌkɒmənˈdɪə(r)/ *verb* [T] to take control or possession of sth for military or police use

commander /kəˈmɑːndə(r)/ *noun* [C] **1** a person who controls or is in charge of a military organization or group **2** (*BrE*) an officer at a fairly high level in the navy

comˌmander-in-ˈchief *noun* [C] (*abbr.* **C-in-C**) (*pl.* **commanders-in-chief**) the officer who commands all the armed forces of a country or all its forces in a particular area

commanding /kəˈmɑːndɪŋ/ *adj.* **1** in charge or having control of sb/sth: *Who is your commanding officer?* **2** strong or powerful: *to speak in a commanding tone of voice*

commandment (*also* **Commandment**) /kəˈmɑːndmənt/ *noun* [C] (*formal*) (RELIGION) a law given by God, especially any of **the Ten Commandments** given to the Jews in the Bible

commando /kəˈmɑːndəʊ/ *noun* [C] (*pl.* **commandos**) one of a group of soldiers who is trained to make sudden attacks in enemy areas

commemorate /kəˈmeməreɪt/ *verb* [T] to exist or take place in order to make people remember a special event: *a statue commemorating all the soldiers who died in the last war* ▶ **commemoration** /kəˌmeməˈreɪʃn/ *noun* [C,U]: *The concerts were held **in commemoration of** the 200th anniversary of Mozart's death.*

commence AW /kəˈmens/ *verb* [I,T] (*formal*) ~ **sth/doing sth** to start or begin ▶ **commencement** AW *noun* [C,U]

commend /kəˈmend/ *verb* [T] (*formal*) to say officially that sb/sth is very good: *Dean was commended for his excellent work.*

commendable /kəˈmendəbl/ *adj.* (*formal*) that people think is good: *She acted with commendable honesty and fairness.* ▶ **commendably** /-əbli/ *adv.*

comment¹ ⊶ AW /ˈkɒment/ *noun* [C,U] ~ **(about/on sth)** something that you say or write that gives your opinion or feeling about sth: *The chancellor was not available for comment.* ◇ *I heard someone **make a** rude **comment** about my clothes.*
➲ note at **statement**
IDM **no comment** used in reply to a question when you do not want to say anything at all: *'Mr President, how do you feel about these latest developments?' 'No comment.'*

> **THESAURUS**
>
> **comment**
>
> **note • remark • observe**
>
> These words all mean to say or write a fact or opinion.
>
> **comment**: *He refused to comment.*
>
> **note** (*formal*): *He noted in passing that the company's record on safety issues was not good.*
>
> **remark**: *Critics remarked that the play was not original.*
>
> **observe** (*formal*): *She observed that it was getting late.*

comment² ⊶ AW /ˈkɒment/ *verb* [I] ~ **(on sth)** to say what you think or feel about sth: *Several people commented on how ill David looked.*

commentary AW /ˈkɒməntri/ *noun* (*pl.* **commentaries**) **1** [C,U] (ARTS AND MEDIA) a spoken description on the radio or television of sth as it is happening: *a **sports commentary*** **2** [C] (LITERATURE) a written explanation or discussion of sth such as a book or play **3** [C] something that shows what sth is like: *This drug scandal is a sad **commentary on** the state of the sport.*

commentate /ˈkɒmənteɪt/ *verb* [I] ~ **(on sth)** (ARTS AND MEDIA) to give a spoken description on the radio or television of sth as it is happening

commentator AW /ˈkɒmənteɪtə(r)/ *noun* [C] **1** a person who COMMENTATES on sth: *a sports commentator* **2** (ARTS AND MEDIA) a person who gives their opinion about sth on the radio, on television or in a newspaper: *a political commentator*

commerce /ˈkɒmɜːs/ *noun* [U] (BUSINESS) the business of buying and selling things

commercial¹ ⊶ /kəˈmɜːʃl/ *adj.* **1** (BUSINESS) connected with buying and selling goods and services: *commercial law* ➲ note at **economic** **2** (FINANCE) making or trying to make money: *Although it won a lot of awards, the film was not a commercial success.* ➲ note at **successful** **3** (BUSINESS) selling sth or sold in large quantities to the public: *commercial airlines* ◇ *commercial products* ▶ **commercially** /-ʃəli/ *adv.*: *The factory* *was closed down because it was no longer commercially viable.*

commercial² /kə'mɜːʃl/ ***noun*** [C] (ARTS AND MEDIA) an advertisement on television or the radio ➲ note at **ad**

commercialism /kə'mɜːʃəlɪzəm/ ***noun*** [U] the attitude that making money is more important than anything else

commercialize (also **-ise**) /kə'mɜːʃəlaɪz/ ***verb*** [T] to try to make money out of sth, even if it means spoiling it: *Christmas has become very commercialized over recent years.* ▶ **commercialization** (also **-isation**) /kəˌmɜːʃəlaɪ'zeɪʃn/ ***noun*** [U]

commis /'kɒmi/ (*pl.* **commis** /'kɒmi/) (*also* ˌ**commis 'chef**) ***noun*** [C] a junior cook who works in a kitchen ➲ look at **chef, sous-chef**

commiserate /kə'mɪzəreɪt/ ***verb*** [I] (*formal*) ~ **(with sb) (on/over/for sth)** to feel sorry for and show understanding towards sb who is unhappy or in difficulty: *I commiserated with Debbie over losing her job.*

commission¹ ⊶ AW /kə'mɪʃn/ ***noun*** **1** (often **Commission**) [C, with sing. or pl. verb] an official group of people who are asked to find out about sth: *A Commission was appointed to investigate the causes of the accident.* **2** [C,U] (FINANCE) money that you get for selling sth: *Agents get 10% commission on everything they sell.* **3** [C,U] (FINANCE) money that a bank, etc. charges for providing a particular service **4** [C] (ARTS AND MEDIA) a formal request to an artist, writer, etc. to produce a piece of work: *He received a commission to write a play for the festival.*

commission² ⊶ AW /kə'mɪʃn/ ***verb*** [T] ~ **sb (to do sth)**; ~ **sth (from sb)** to ask an artist, writer, etc. to do a piece of work: *to commission an architect to design a building*

commissionaire /kəˌmɪʃə'neə(r)/ ***noun*** [C] (*BrE, old-fashioned*) a person in uniform whose job is to stand at the entrance to a hotel, theatre, cinema, etc. and open the door for visitors SYN **doorman**

commissioner /kə'mɪʃənə(r)/ ***noun*** [C] the head of the police or of a government department in some countries ➲ look at **High Commissioner**

commit ⊶ AW /kə'mɪt/ ***verb*** [T] (**committing**; **committed**) **1** to do sth wrong or illegal: ***to commit a crime*** ◇ ***to commit suicide*** **2** ~ **sb/yourself (to sth/to doing sth)** to make a definite agreement or promise to do sth: *I can't commit myself to helping you tomorrow.* **3** ~ **yourself (on sth)** to make a decision or give an opinion publicly so that it is then difficult to change it: *I'm not going to commit myself on who will win the election.* ➲ look at **non-committal** **4** (*formal*) to decide to use money or time in a certain way: *The government has committed £2 billion to education.* **5** (*formal*) ~ **sb to sth** to send sb to a prison, mental hospital, etc.

commitment ⊶ AW /kə'mɪtmənt/ ***noun*** **1** [U] ~ **(to sth)** being prepared to give a lot of your time and attention to sth because you believe it is right or important: *I admire Gary's commitment to protecting the environment.* **2** [C,U] a promise or agreement to do sth; a responsibility: ***When I make a commitment*** *I always stick to it.* ◇ *Helen now works fewer hours because of* ***family commitments***.

committed AW /kə'mɪtɪd/ ***adj.*** ~ **(to sth)** prepared to give a lot of your time and attention to sth because you believe it is right or important: *The company is committed to providing quality products.*

committee ⊶ /kə'mɪti/ ***noun*** [C, with sing. or pl. verb] a group of people who have been chosen to discuss sth or decide sth: *to* ***be/sit on a committee*** ◇ *The planning committee meets/meet twice a week.*

commodity AW /kə'mɒdəti/ ***noun*** [C] (*pl.* **commodities**) (BUSINESS) a product or material that can be bought and sold: *Salt was once a very valuable commodity.* ➲ note at **product**

commodore /'kɒmədɔː(r)/ ***noun*** [C] an officer at a high level in the navy

common¹ ⊶ /'kɒmən/ ***adj.*** **1** happening or found often or in many places; usual: *Pilot error is the commonest/most common cause of plane crashes.* ◇ *The daisy is a common wild flower.* OPP **uncommon** **2** ~ **(to sb/sth)** shared by or belonging to two or more people or groups; shared by most or all people: *This type of behaviour is common to most children of that age.* ◇ *We have a common interest in gardening.* **3** (only *before* a noun) not special; ordinary: *The officers had much better living conditions than the common soldiers.* **4** (*BrE, informal*) having or showing a lack of education: *Don't speak like that. It's common!*

IDM **be common/public knowledge** → KNOWLEDGE

common² /'kɒmən/ ***noun*** [C] an area of open land that anyone can use

IDM **have sth in common (with sb/sth)** to share sth with sb/sth else: *to have a lot in common with sb*

in common with sb/sth (*formal*) in the same way as sb/sth else; like sb/sth: *This company, in common with many others, is losing a lot of money.*

ˌ**common de'nominator** ***noun*** [C] (MATHEMATICS) a number that can be divided exactly by all the numbers below the line in a set of FRACTIONS ➲ look at **denominator**

ˌ**common 'ground** ***noun*** [U] beliefs, interests, etc. that two or more people or groups share

ˌ**common 'law** ***noun*** [U] (LAW) laws in England that are based on customs and on decisions that judges have made, not laws that were made by Parliament ➲ look at **case law, statute law**

ˌ**common-law 'husband**ˌ**common-law 'wife** ***noun*** [C] a person that a woman or man has lived with for a long time and who is recognized as a husband or wife, without a formal marriage ceremony

commonly ⊶ /'kɒmənli/ ***adv.*** usually; very often; by most people: *This is one of the most commonly used methods.*

ˌ**common 'noun** ***noun*** [C] (LANGUAGE) a word, such as *book* or *town* that refers to an object or a thing but is not the name of a particular person, place or thing

commonplace /'kɒmənpleɪs/ ***adj.*** not exciting or unusual; ordinary

'**common room** ***noun*** [C] a room in a school, university, etc. where students or teachers can go to relax when they are not in class

the Commons /'kɒmənz/ (POLITICS) = THE HOUSE OF COMMONS ➲ note at **Parliament**

ˌ**common 'sense** ***noun*** [U] the ability to make good sensible decisions or to behave in a sensible way

the Commonwealth /'kɒmənwelθ/ ***noun*** [sing.] (POLITICS) the group of countries that once formed the British Empire and that work together in a friendly way

commotion /kə'məʊʃn/ *noun* [sing., U] great noise or excitement

communal /kə'mju:nl; 'kɒmjənl/ *adj.* shared by a group of people: *a communal kitchen*

commune /'kɒmju:n/ *noun* [C, with sing. or pl. verb] (SOCIAL STUDIES) a group of people, not from the same family, who live together and share their property and responsibilities

communicable AW /kə'mju:nɪkəbl/ *adj.* (*formal*) that sb can pass on to other people or communicate to sb else: *communicable diseases*

communicate ⊶ AW /kə'mju:nɪkeɪt/ *verb* **1** [I,T] to share and exchange information, ideas or feelings with sb: *Parents often have difficulty communicating with their teenage children.* ◇ *Our boss is good at communicating her ideas to the team.* **2** [T] (*formal*) (usually passive) (HEALTH) to pass a disease from one person or animal to another **3** [I] to lead from one place to another: *two rooms with a communicating door*

communication ⊶ AW /kə,mju:nɪ'keɪʃn/ *noun* **1** [U] the act of sharing or exchanging information, ideas or feelings: *Radio is the only means of communication in remote areas.* ◇ *We are in regular* ***communication with*** *our head office in New York.* **2 communications** [pl.] the methods that are used for travelling to and from a place or for sending messages between places: *The telephone lines are down so communications are very difficult.* **3** [C] (*formal*) a message: *a communication from head office*

communicative AW /kə'mju:nɪkətɪv/ *adj.* willing and able to talk and share ideas, etc.: *Paolo has excellent communicative skills.*

communion /kə'mju:niən/ *noun* [U] **1** (*formal*) the sharing of thoughts or feelings **2 Communion** (RELIGION) a Christian church ceremony in which people share bread and wine

communiqué /kə'mju:nɪkeɪ/ *noun* [C] (*written*) (POLITICS) an official statement, especially from a government, a political group, etc.

communism /'kɒmjunɪzəm/ *noun* [U] (POLITICS) the political system in which the state owns and controls all factories, farms, services etc. and aims to treat everyone equally ➲ look at **Marxism**, **socialism**, **capitalism**

communist (also **Communist**) /'kɒmjənɪst/ *noun* [C] (POLITICS) a person who believes in or supports COMMUNISM; a member of the Communist Party ▶ **communist** (also **Communist**) *adj.*: *communist sympathies*

community ⊶ AW /kə'mju:nəti/ *noun* (*pl.* **communities**) **1 the community** [sing.] (SOCIAL STUDIES) all the people who live in a particular place, area, etc. when considered as a group: *Recent increases in crime have disturbed the whole community.* **2** [C, with sing. or pl. verb] (SOCIAL STUDIES) a group of people who have sth in common: *the Asian community in Britain* ◇ *the business community* **3** [U] the feeling of belonging to a group in the place where you live: *There is a strong sense of community in the neighbourhood.*

com'munity centre *noun* [C] a building that local people can use for meetings, classes, sports, etc.

com,munity 'service *noun* [U] (LAW) work helping people in the local community that sb does without being paid, often because they have been ordered to do it by a court of law as a punishment

commutative /kə'mju:tətɪv/ *adj.* (MATHEMATICS) (used about a calculation) giving the same result whatever the order in which the quantities are shown

commutator /'kɒmjuteɪtə(r)/ *noun* [C] **1** (TECHNICAL) a device that connects a motor to the electricity supply **2** (PHYSICS) a device for changing the direction in which electricity flows

commute /kə'mju:t/ *verb* [I] to travel a long distance from home to work every day: *A lot of people commute to London from nearby towns.* ▶ **commuter** *noun* [C]

compact /kəm'pækt/ *adj.* small and easy to carry: *a compact camera*

,compact 'disc = CD

companion /kəm'pæniən/ *noun* [C] a person or animal with whom you spend a lot of time or go somewhere: *a travelling companion*

companionship /kəm'pæniənʃɪp/ *noun* [U] the pleasant feeling of having a friendly relationship with sb and not being alone

company ⊶ /'kʌmpəni/ *noun* (*pl.* **companies**) **1** [C, with sing. or pl. verb] (BUSINESS) a business organization selling goods or services: *The company is/are planning to build a new factory.* ⓘ In names company is written with a capital letter. The abbreviation is **Co.**: *the Walt Disney Company* ◇ *Milton & Co* **2** [C, with sing. or pl. verb] (ARTS AND MEDIA) a group of actors, singers, dancers, etc.: *a ballet company* ◇ *the Royal Shakespeare Company* **3** [U] being with a person: *I always enjoy Rachel's company.* ◇ *Jeff is very* ***good company*** (= pleasant to be with). **4** [U] a visitor or visitors: *Sorry, I wouldn't have called if I'd known you* ***had company***.

IDM **keep sb company** to go or be with sb so that they are not alone: *She was nervous so I went with her to keep her company.*

part company → PART[2]

comparable /'kɒmpərəbl/ *adj.* **~ (to/with sb/sth)** of a similar standard or size; that can be compared with sth: *The population of Britain is comparable to that of France.* ◇ *A comparable flat in my country would be a lot cheaper.*

comparably /'kɒmpərəbli/ *adv.* in a similar way or to a similar extent: *a comparably priced MP3 player*

comparative[1] /kəm'pærətɪv/ *adj.* **1** that compares things of the same kind: *a comparative study of systems of government* **2** compared with sth else or with what is usual or normal: *He had problems with the written exam but passed the practical exam with comparative ease.* **3** (LANGUAGE) (used about the form of an adjective or adverb) expressing a greater amount, quality, size, etc.: *'Hotter' and 'more quickly' are the comparative forms of 'hot' and 'quickly'.*

comparative[2] /kəm'pærətɪv/ *noun* [C] (LANGUAGE) the form of an adjective or adverb that expresses a greater amount, quality, size, etc.: *'Bigger' is the comparative of 'big'.*

comparatively /kəm'pærətɪvli/ *adv.* when compared with sth else or with what is usual; fairly: *The disease is comparatively rare nowadays.*

compare ⊶ /kəm'peə(r)/ *verb* **1** [T] **~ A and B; ~ A with/to B** to consider people or things in order to see how similar or how different they are: *I'm quite a patient person,* ***compared with*** *him.* ◇ ***Compared to*** *the place where I grew up, this town is exciting.* ◇ *When the police compared the two letters, they realized that they had been written by the same person.* **2** [T] **~ A to B** to say that sb/sth is similar to sb/sth else: *When it was built, people compared the*

stadium to a spaceship. **3** [I] ~ **(with/to sb/sth)** to be as good as sb/sth: *Her last film was brilliant but this one simply doesn't compare.* ◇ *There is nothing to compare with the taste of bread fresh from the oven.*
IDM **compare notes (with sb)** to discuss your opinions, ideas, experiences, etc. with sb else

comparison /kəm'pærɪsn/ *noun* [C,U] an act of comparing; a statement in which people or things are compared: *Put the new one and the old one side by side,* ***for comparison.*** ◇ *It's hard to* ***make comparisons*** *between two athletes from different sports.*
IDM **by/in comparison (with sb/sth)** when compared: *In comparison with many other people, they're quite well off.*

compartment /kəm'pɑːtmənt/ *noun* [C] **1** one of the separate sections into which some larger parts of a train (**carriages**) are divided: *a first-class compartment* **2** one of the separate sections into which certain containers are divided: *The drugs were discovered in a secret compartment in his suitcase.*

compasses

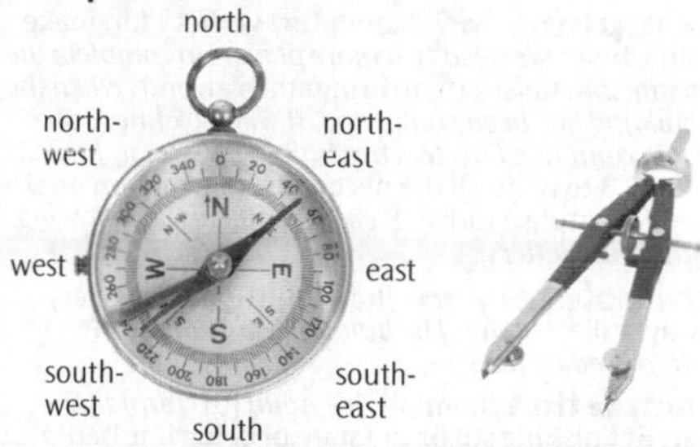

compass **compass / pair of compasses**

COLLOCATIONS AND PATTERNS

Points of the compass

A person or a place can **look** or **face** north, south, etc.
The garden faces south-east.
Looking north, she could see the mountains.

Somebody or something can **live in/come from/be to** the north/south, etc. **of** a place
I live in the south (of Poland).
The wind is coming from the east.
Oxford is to the north-west of London.

You can **drive, fly, go, run, travel, walk, continue** or **proceed** north, south, etc.
From Durham drive north for a couple of miles.
The road continues west for 3 kilometres.
Birds fly south in the winter.

compass /'kʌmpəs/ *noun* [C] **1** (GEOGRAPHY) an instrument for finding direction, with a needle that always points north: *They had to find their way back to the camp using a map and a compass.*
2 compasses [pl.] (MATHEMATICS) a V-shaped instrument that is used for drawing circles: ***a pair of compasses***

compassion /kəm'pæʃn/ *noun* [U] ~ **(for sb)** understanding or pity for sb who is suffering: *to have/feel/show compassion* ▸ **compassionate** /-ʃənət/ *adj.*

compatible AW /kəm'pætəbl/ *adj.* ~ **(with sb/sth)** suitable to be used together, or to live or exist together: *These two computer systems are not compatible.* ◇ *Lee's diet is not compatible with his active lifestyle.* OPP **incompatible** ▸ **compatibility** AW /kəm,pætə'bɪləti/ *noun* [U]

compatriot /kəm'pætriət/ *noun* [C] a person who comes from the same country as you

compel /kəm'pel/ *verb* [T] (**compelling**; **compelled**) (*formal*) ~ **sb to do sth** to force sb to do sth: *I felt compelled to tell her what I really thought of her.* ➲ noun **compulsion**

compelling /kəm'pelɪŋ/ *adj.* that forces or persuades you to do or to believe sth: *compelling evidence*

compensate AW /'kɒmpenseɪt/ *verb* **1** [I] ~ **(for sth)** to remove or reduce the bad effect of sth: *His willingness to work hard compensates for his lack of skill.* **2** [I,T] ~ **(sb) (for sth)** (LAW) to pay sb money because you have injured them or lost or damaged their property: *The airline sent me a cheque to compensate for losing my luggage.* ▸ **compensatory** AW /,kɒmpen'seɪtəri/ *adj.*: *He received a compensatory payment of $20000.*

compensation AW /,kɒmpen'seɪʃn/ *noun* **1** [U] ~ **(for sth)** (LAW) money that you pay to sb because you have injured them or lost or damaged their property: *I got £5000 (in) compensation for my injuries.* **2** [C,U] a fact or action that removes or reduces the bad effect of sth: *City life can be very tiring but there are compensations* (=good things about it).

compère /'kɒmpeə(r)/ *noun* [C] (*BrE*) (ARTS AND MEDIA) a person who entertains the audience and introduces the different performers in a show ▸ **compère** *verb* [T]: *Who compèred the show?*

compete /kəm'piːt/ *verb* [I] ~ **(in sth)** **(against/with sb)** **(for sth)** to try to win or achieve sth, or to try to be better than sb else: *The world's best athletes compete in the Olympic Games.* ◇ *We'll be competing against seven other teams for the trophy.* ◇ *As children, they always used to compete with each other.* ◇ *Supermarkets have such low prices that small shops just can't compete.*

competence /'kɒmpɪtəns/ *noun* [U] the fact of having the ability or skill that is needed for sth: *She quickly proved her competence in her new position.* OPP **incompetence**

competent /'kɒmpɪtənt/ *adj.* **1** having the ability or skill needed for sth: *a highly competent player* ◇ *She is competent at her job.* OPP **incompetent** **2** good enough, but not excellent: *The singer gave a competent, but not particularly exciting, performance.* ▸ **competently** *adv.*

competition /,kɒmpə'tɪʃn/ *noun* **1** [C] an organized event in which people try to win sth: *to* ***go in for/enter a competition*** ◇ *They* ***hold a competition*** *every year to find the best young artist.* ◇ *He came second in an international piano competition.* **2** [U] a situation where two or more people or organizations are trying to achieve, obtain, etc. the same thing or to be better than sb else: *He is* ***in competition with*** *three other people for promotion.* ◇ *There was* ***fierce competition*** *among the players for places in the team.* **3 the competition** [sing., with sing. or pl. verb] the other people, companies, etc. who are trying to achieve the same as you: *If we are going to succeed, we must offer a better product than the competition.*

competitive /kəm'petətɪv/ *adj.* **1** involving people or organizations competing against each other: *The travel industry is a highly competitive business.* ◇ *competitive sports* **2** able to be as successful as or more successful than others: *They are trying to make the company competitive in the international market.* ◇ *Our prices are **highly competitive*** (=as low as or lower than those of the others). **3** (used about people) wanting very much to win or to be more successful than others: *She's a very competitive player.* ▶ **competitively** ***adv.***: *Their products are competitively priced.* ▶ **competitiveness** ***noun*** [U]

competitor /kəm'petɪtə(r)/ ***noun*** [C] a person or organization that is competing against others: *There are ten competitors in the first race.* ◇ *Two local companies are our main competitors.*

compilation AW /ˌkɒmpɪ'leɪʃn/ ***noun*** **1** [C] a collection of pieces of music, writing, film, etc. that are taken from different places and put together: *A compilation CD of the band's greatest hits.* **2** [U] the act of COMPILING sth

compile AW /kəm'paɪl/ ***verb*** **1** [I] to collect information and arrange it in a list, book, etc.: *to compile a dictionary/a report/a list* **2** [I,T] (COMPUTING) to translate instructions from one computer language into another for a computer to understand

compiler /kəm'paɪlə(r)/ ***noun*** [C] **1** a person who COMPILES sth **2** (COMPUTING) a program that translates instructions from one computer language into another for a computer to understand

complacent /kəm'pleɪsnt/ ***adj.*** feeling too satisfied with yourself or with a situation, so that you think that there is no need to worry: *He had won his matches so easily that he was in danger of becoming complacent.* ▶ **complacency** /kəm'pleɪsnsi/ ***noun*** [U] ▶ **complacently** ***adv.***

complain 🔑 /kəm'pleɪn/ ***verb*** [I] **1** ~ **(to sb) (about sth/that...)** to say that you are not satisfied with or happy about sth: *People are always complaining about the weather.* ◇ *We complained to the hotel manager that the room was too noisy.* **2** (*formal*) ~ **of sth** (HEALTH) to say that you have a pain or illness: *He went to the doctor, complaining of chest pains.*

complaint 🔑 /kəm'pleɪnt/ ***noun*** ~ **(about sth);** ~ **(that...)** **1** [C] a statement that you are not satisfied with sth: *You should **make a complaint** to the company that made the machine.* **2** [U] the act of complaining: *I wrote a **letter of complaint** to the manager about the terrible service I had received.* ◇ *Jim's behaviour never gave the teachers **cause for complaint**.* **3** [C] (HEALTH) an illness or disease: *a heart complaint*

complement¹ AW /'kɒmplɪmənt/ ***noun*** [C] **1** (*formal*) a thing that goes together well with sth else: *Ice cream is the perfect complement to this dessert.* **2** the total number that makes a group complete: *Without **a full complement** of players, the team will not be able to take part in the match.* **3** (LANGUAGE) a word or words, especially a noun or adjective, used after a verb such as 'be' or 'become' and describing the subject of that verb: *In 'He's friendly' and 'He's a fool', 'friendly' and 'fool' are complements.*

complement² AW /'kɒmplɪment/ ***verb*** [T] to go together well with: *The colours of the furniture and the carpet complement each other.*

complementary AW /ˌkɒmplɪ'mentri/ ***adj.*** going together well with sb/sth; adding sth which the other person or thing does not have: *They work well together because their skills are complementary: he's practical and she's creative.*

ˌcomplementary 'angle ***noun*** [C] (GEOMETRY) either of two angles which together make 90° ➲ look at **supplementary angle** ➲ picture at **angle**

ˌcomplementary 'colour ***noun*** [C] (*written*) a colour that, when mixed with another colour, gives black or white

ˌcomplementary 'medicine ***noun*** [U] (*BrE*) (HEALTH) medical treatment that is not part of the usual scientific treatment used in Western countries, for example ACUPUNCTURE

complete¹ 🔑 /kəm'pli:t/ ***adj.*** **1** having or including all parts; with nothing missing: *I gave a complete list of the stolen items to the police.* ◇ *The book explains the complete history of the place.* OPP **incomplete** **2** (not *before* a noun) finished or ended: *The repair work should be complete by Wednesday.* OPP **incomplete** **3** ~ **(with sth)** including sth extra, in addition to what is expected: *The computer **comes complete with** instruction manual and printer.* **4** (only *before* a noun) as great as possible; total; in every way: *It was a complete waste of time.* ◇ *The room is a complete mess.* ▶ **completeness** ***noun*** [U]

complete² 🔑 /kəm'pli:t/ ***verb*** [T] **1** to make sth whole: *We need two more players to complete the team.* **2** to finish sth; to bring sth to an end: *When the building has been completed, it will look impressive.* ◇ *He completed his teacher training course in June 1997.* **3** to write all the necessary information on sth (for example a form): *Please complete the following in capital letters.*

completely 🔑 /kəm'pli:tli/ ***adv.*** in every way; fully; totally: *The building was completely destroyed by fire.*

completion /kəm'pli:ʃn/ ***noun*** [U] (*formal*) the act of finishing sth or the state of being finished: *You will be paid **on completion** of the work.* ◇ *The new motorway is due for completion within two years.*

complex¹ 🔑 AW /'kɒmpleks/ ***adj.*** made up of several connected parts and often difficult to understand; complicated: *a complex problem/subject*

complex² AW /'kɒmpleks/ ***noun*** [C] **1** a group of connected things, especially buildings: *a shopping/sports complex* ➲ note at **building** **2** **a** ~ **(about sth)** (HEALTH) a mental problem that makes sb worry a lot about sth: *He's got a complex about his height.* ◇ *an inferiority complex*

complexion /kəm'plekʃn/ ***noun*** [C] **1** the natural colour and quality of the skin on your face: *a dark/fair complexion* ◇ *a healthy complexion* **2** [usually sing.] the general nature or character of sth: *These announcements **put a different complexion on** our situation.*

complexity AW /kəm'pleksəti/ ***noun*** (*pl.* **complexities**) **1** [U] the state of being complex and difficult to understand: *an issue of great complexity* **2** [C] one of the many details that make sth complicated: *I haven't time to explain the complexities of the situation now.*

compliant /kəm'plaɪənt/ ***adj.*** (*formal*) ~ **(with sth)** working or done in agreement with particular rules, orders, etc.: *All new products must be compliant with EU specifications.* ▶ **compliance** ***noun*** [U]: *A hard hat must be worn at all times **in compliance with** safety regulations.*

complicate 🔑 /'kɒmplɪkeɪt/ ***verb*** [T] to make sth difficult to understand or deal with: *Let's not complicate things by adding too many details.*

complicated 🔑 /'kɒmplɪkeɪtɪd/ ***adj.*** made of many different things or parts that are connected; difficult to understand: *a novel with a very compli-*

cated plot ◇ The instructions look very complicated. ◇ It's all very complicated — but I'll try and explain.

complication /ˌkɒmplɪˈkeɪʃn/ ***noun*** [C] **1** something that makes a situation hard to understand or to deal with: *Unless there are any unexpected complications, I'll be arriving next month.* **2** (**HEALTH**) a new illness that you get when you are already ill: *Unless he develops complications, he'll be out of hospital in a week.*

complicity /kəmˈplɪsəti/ ***noun*** [U] (*formal*) (**LAW**) the fact of being involved with sb else in a crime

compliment[1] /ˈkɒmplɪmənt/ ***noun*** **1** [C] **a ~ (on sth)** a statement or action that shows admiration for sb: *People often* ***pay her compliments*** *on her piano playing.* **2 compliments** [pl.] (*formal*) used to say that you like sth or to thank sb for sth: *Tea and coffee are provided* ***with the compliments of*** *the hotel management* (=without charge).

compliment[2] /ˈkɒmplɪment/ ***verb*** [T] **~ sb (on sth)** to say that you think sb/sth is very good: *She complimented them on their smart appearance.*

complimentary /ˌkɒmplɪˈmentri/ ***adj.*** **1** showing that you think sb/sth is very good: *He made several complimentary remarks about her work.* **2** given free of charge: *a complimentary theatre ticket*

comply /kəmˈplaɪ/ ***verb*** [I] (*pres. part.* **complying**; *3rd person sing. pres.* **complies**; *pt, pp* **complied**) (*formal*) **~ (with sth)** to obey an order or request: *All office buildings must comply with the safety regulations.*

component AW /kəmˈpəʊnənt/ ***noun*** [C] one of several parts of which sth is made: *the components of a machine/system* ▶ **component** ***adj.***: *the component parts of an engine*

compose /kəmˈpəʊz/ ***verb*** **1** [T] to be the parts that together form sth: *the parties that compose the coalition government* **2** [I,T] (**MUSIC**) to write music: *Mozart composed forty-one symphonies.* **3** [T] to produce a piece of writing, using careful thought: *I sat down and composed a letter of reply.* **4** [T] to make yourself, your feelings, etc. become calm and under control: *The news came as such a shock that it took me a while to* ***compose myself***.

composed /kəmˈpəʊzd/ ***adj.*** **1 ~ of sth** made or formed from several different parts, people, etc.: *The committee is composed of politicians from all parties.* **2** calm, in control of your feelings: *Although he felt very nervous, he managed to appear composed.*

composer /kəmˈpəʊzə(r)/ ***noun*** [C] (**MUSIC**) a person who writes music

composite /ˈkɒmpəzɪt/ ***adj.*** consisting of different parts or materials ▶ **composite** ***noun*** [C]

composition /ˌkɒmpəˈzɪʃn/ ***noun*** **1** [U] the parts that form sth; the way in which the parts of sth are arranged: *the chemical composition of a substance ◇ the composition of the population* ➲ note at **structure[1]** **2** [C] (**ARTS AND MEDIA**) a piece of music or art, or a poem: *Chopin's best-known compositions* **3** [U] the act or skill of writing a piece of music or text: *She studied both musical theory and composition.* **4** [C] (**EDUCATION**) a short piece of writing done at school, in an exam, etc.: *Write a composition of about 300 words on one of the following subjects.*

compost /ˈkɒmpɒst/ ***noun*** [U] (**AGRICULTURE, BIOLOGY**) a mixture of dead plants, old food, etc. that is added to soil to help plants grow

composure /kəmˈpəʊʒə(r)/ ***noun*** [U] the state of being calm and having your feelings under control

compound[1] AW /ˈkɒmpaʊnd/ ***noun*** [C] **1** a thing consisting of two or more separate things combined together **2** (**CHEMISTRY**) a substance formed by a chemical reaction of two or more elements in fixed amounts relative to each other: *Common salt is a compound of sodium and chlorine.* ➲ look at **element, mixture** **3** (**LANGUAGE**) a noun, an adjective or a verb made of two or more words or parts of words, written as one or more words, or joined by a HYPHEN: *'Car park', 'bad-tempered' and 'bathroom' are all compounds.* **3** an area surrounded by a fence or wall in which a factory or other group of buildings stands: *a prison compound*

compound[2] AW /ˈkɒmpaʊnd/ ***adj.*** (only *before* a noun) (**TECHNICAL**) formed of two or more parts: *a* ***compound adjective****, such as fair-skinned ◇ A compound sentence contains two or more clauses.*

compound[3] AW /kəmˈpaʊnd/ ***verb*** [T] to make sth bad become even worse by causing further damage or problems: *The problems were compounded by severe food shortages.*

ˌcompound ˈeye ***noun*** [C] (**BIOLOGY**) an eye like that of most insects, made up of several parts that work separately: *the* ***compound eye*** *of a wasp*

ˌcompound ˈinterest ***noun*** [U] (**FINANCE**) interest that is paid both on the original amount of money saved and on the interest that has been added to it ➲ look at **simple interest**

comprehend /ˌkɒmprɪˈhend/ ***verb*** [T] (*formal*) to understand sth completely: *She's too young to comprehend what has happened.*

comprehensible /ˌkɒmprɪˈhensəbl/ ***adj.*** easy to understand: *The book is written in clear, comprehensible language.* OPP **incomprehensible**

comprehension /ˌkɒmprɪˈhenʃn/ ***noun*** **1** [U] (*formal*) the ability to understand: *The horror of war is* ***beyond comprehension***. OPP **incomprehension** **2** [C,U] (**EDUCATION**) an exercise that tests how well you understand spoken or written language: *a listening comprehension*

comprehensive[1] AW /ˌkɒmprɪˈhensɪv/ ***adj.*** **1** including everything or nearly everything that is connected with a particular subject: *a guide book giving comprehensive information on the area* **2** (*BrE*) (**EDUCATION**) educating children of all levels of ability in the same school: *a comprehensive education system*

comprehensive[2] AW /ˌkɒmprɪˈhensɪv/ (*also* **compreˈhensive school**) ***noun*** [C] (*BrE*) (**EDUCATION**) a secondary school in which children of all levels of ability are educated: *I went to the local comprehensive.*

comprehensively /ˌkɒmprɪˈhensɪvli/ ***adv.*** completely; thoroughly

compress /kəmˈpres/ ***verb*** [T] **1 ~ sth (into sth)** to make sth fill less space than usual: *Divers breathe compressed air from tanks. ◇ He found it hard to compress his ideas into a single page.* **2** (**COMPUTING**) to make computer files, etc. smaller so that they use less space on a disk, etc. OPP **decompress** ▶ **compression** /kəmˈpreʃn/ ***noun*** [U]: *Nurses used bandages to achieve compression at the ankle. ◇ data compression*

compressor /kəmˈpresə(r)/ ***noun*** [C] a machine that COMPRESSES air or other gases

comprise AW /kəmˈpraɪz/ ***verb*** [T] **1** to consist of; to have as parts or members: *a house comprising three bedrooms, kitchen, bathroom and a living room*

2 to form or be part of sth: *Women comprise 62% of the staff.*

compromise¹ /ˈkɒmprəmaɪz/ ***noun*** [C,U] **a ~ (on sth)** an agreement that is reached when each person gets part, but not all, of what they wanted: *to **reach a compromise** ◇ Both sides will have to be prepared to **make compromises**.*

compromise² /ˈkɒmprəmaɪz/ ***verb*** **1** [I] **~ (with sb) (on sth)** to accept less than you want or are aiming for, especially in order to reach an agreement: *Unless both sides are prepared to compromise, there will be no peace agreement. ◇ The company never compromises on the quality of its products.* **2** [T] **~ sb/sth/yourself** to put sb/sth/yourself in a bad or dangerous position, especially by doing sth that is not very sensible: *He compromised himself by accepting money from them.*

compulsion /kəmˈpʌlʃn/ ***noun*** **1** [U] the act of forcing sb to do sth or being forced to do sth: *There is no compulsion to take part. You can decide yourself.* ➲ verb **compel** **2** [C] a strong desire that you cannot control, often to do sth that you should not do **SYN** **urge**

compulsive /kəmˈpʌlsɪv/ ***adj.*** **1** (used about a bad or harmful habit) caused by a strong desire that you cannot control: *compulsive eating* **2** (used about a person) having a bad habit that they cannot control: *a compulsive gambler/shoplifter* **3** so interesting or exciting that you cannot take your attention away from it: *This book makes compulsive reading.* ▶ **compulsively** ***adv.***

compulsory /kəmˈpʌlsəri/ ***adj.*** that must be done, by law, rules, etc. **SYN** **obligatory**: *Maths and English are **compulsory subjects** at this level. ◇ **It is compulsory for** all motorcyclists to wear helmets.* **OPP** **voluntary, optional**

computation **AW** /ˌkɒmpjuˈteɪʃn/ ***noun*** [C,U] (*formal*) (**MATHEMATICS**) an act or the process of calculating sth: *All the statistical computations were performed by the new software system. ◇ an error in the computation*

compute **AW** /kəmˈpjuːt/ ***verb*** [T] (*formal*) to calculate sth

computer 🔑 **AW** /kəmˈpjuːtə(r)/ ***noun*** [C] an electronic machine that can store, find and arrange information, calculate amounts and control other machines: *The bills are all done **by computer**. ◇ a **computer program** ◇ a **personal computer** ◇ **computer software/games** ◇ First of all, the details are fed into a computer.*

comˌputer-ˈgenerated ***adj.*** (**COMPUTING**) produced by a computer after data or instructions are put into it: *a **computer-generated image** of a bridge* ➲ look at **CGI**

computerize (also **-ise**) /kəmˈpjuːtəraɪz/ ***verb*** [T] (**COMPUTING**) to use computers to do a job or to store information: *The whole factory has been computerized. ◇ We have now computerized the library catalogue.* ▶ **computerization** (also **-isation**) /kəmˌpjuːtəraɪˈzeɪʃn/ ***noun*** [U]

comˌputer-ˈliterate ***adj.*** (**COMPUTING**) able to use a computer

comˌputer ˈscience ***noun*** [U] (**COMPUTING**) the study of computers and how they can be used: *She has a degree in computer science.* ▶ **comˌputer ˈscientist** ***noun*** [C]

computing **AW** /kəmˈpjuːtɪŋ/ ***noun*** [U] (**COMPUTING**) the use of computers: *She did a course in computing.*

computer workstation

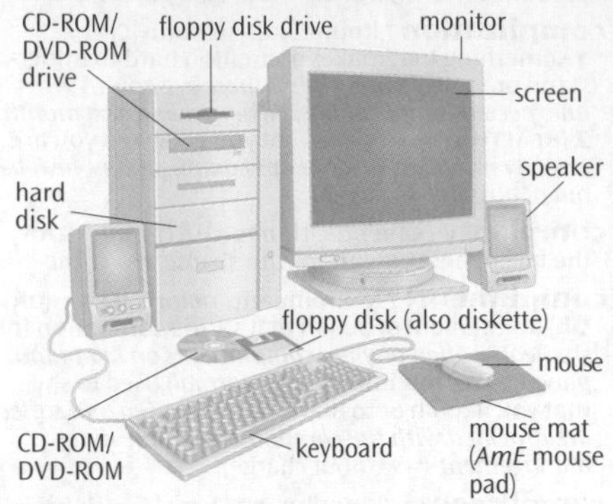

comrade /ˈkɒmreɪd/ ***noun*** [C] **1** (*formal*) a person who fights on the same side as you in a war: *He saw many of his comrades die in battle.* **2** (*old-fashioned*) (**POLITICS**) a person who is a member of the same SOCIALIST political party or group as the speaker: *Comrades, we will fight against injustice!* ▶ **comradeship** /ˈkɒmreɪdʃɪp/ ***noun*** [U]: *He enjoys the comradeship of the army.*

Con (*also* **Cons**) ***abbr.*** (in British politics) = CONSERVATIVE

con¹ /kɒn/ ***verb*** [T] (**conning**; **conned**) (*informal*) **~ sb (into doing sth/out of sth)** to cheat sb, especially in order to get money: *He conned her into investing in a company that didn't really exist. ◇ The old lady was conned out of her life savings.*

con² /kɒn/ ***noun*** [C] (*informal*) a trick, especially in order to cheat sb out of some money **IDM** **the pros and cons** → PRO

con- /kɒn/ ***prefix*** (used in adjectives, adverbs, nouns and verbs) with; together: *concurrent ◇ conurbation ◇ convene*

concave /kɒnˈkeɪv/ ***adj.*** having a surface that curves towards the inside of sth, like the inside of a bowl ➲ look at **convex** ➲ picture at **lens**

conceal /kənˈsiːl/ ***verb*** [T] (*formal*) **~ sth/sb (from sb/sth)** to hide sth/sb; to prevent sth/sb from being seen or discovered: *She tried to conceal her anger from her friend.* ▶ **concealment** ***noun*** [U]: *the concealment of the facts of the case*

concede /kənˈsiːd/ ***verb*** [T] (*formal*) **1** to admit that sth is true although you do not want to: *When it was clear that he would lose the election, he conceded defeat. ◇ She conceded that the problem was mostly her fault.* ➲ note at **admit** **2 ~ sth (to sb)** to allow sb to take sth although you do not want to: *They lost the war and had to concede territory to their enemy.* ➲ noun **concession**

conceit /kənˈsiːt/ ***noun*** [U] too much pride in yourself and your abilities and importance ▶ **conceited** ***adj.***: *He's so conceited – he thinks he's the best at everything!*

conceivable **AW** /kənˈsiːvəbl/ ***adj.*** possible to imagine or believe: *I made every conceivable effort to succeed.* **OPP** **inconceivable** ▶ **conceivably** /-əbli/ ***adv.***: *She might just conceivably be telling the truth.*

> **WORD FAMILY**
> **conceive** *verb*
> **concept** *noun*
> **conceivable** *adj.*
> (≠ **inconceivable**)
> **conceptual** *adj.*

conceive **AW** /kənˈsiːv/ ***verb*** **1** [T] (*formal*) to think of a new idea or plan: *He conceived the idea for the* novel during his journey through India. **2** [I,T] (*formal*) ~ **(of) sb/sth (as sth)** to think about sb/sth in a particular way; to imagine: *He started to conceive of the world as a dangerous place.* **3** [I,T] (BIOLOGY) to become pregnant ➲ noun **conception**

concentrate ⊶ AW /ˈkɒnsntreɪt/ *verb* [I,T] **1** ~ **(sth) (on sth/doing sth)** to give all your attention or effort to sth: *I need to concentrate on passing this exam.* ◇ *I tried to concentrate my thoughts on the problem.* **2** to come together or to bring people or things together in one place: *Most factories are concentrated in one small area of the town.*

concentrated /ˈkɒnsntreɪtɪd/ *adj.* **1** showing determination: *With one concentrated effort we can finish the work by tonight.* **2** made stronger by the removal of some liquid: *This is concentrated orange juice. You have to add water before you drink it.*

concentration ⊶ AW /ˌkɒnsnˈtreɪʃn/ *noun* **1** [U] ~ **(on sth)** the ability to give all your attention or effort to sth: *This type of work requires total concentration.* ◇ *Don't* ***lose your concentration*** *or you might make a mistake.* **2** [C] ~ **(of sth)** a large amount of people or things in one place: *There is a high concentration of chemicals in the drinking water here.*

ˌconcenˈtration camp *noun* [C] (POLITICS) a type of prison, often consisting of a number of buildings inside a fence, where political prisoners are kept in extremely bad conditions: *a Nazi concentration camp*

concentric /kənˈsentrɪk/ *adj.* (GEOMETRY) (used about circles of different sizes) having the same centre point

concentric circles

concept ⊶ AW /ˈkɒnsept/ *noun* [C] **the** ~ **(of sth/that...)** an idea; a basic principle: *It is difficult to* ***grasp the concept*** *of eternity.*

conception AW /kənˈsepʃn/ *noun* **1** [C,U] (a) ~ **(of sth)** an understanding of how or what sth is: *We have no real conception of what people suffered during the war.* **2** [U] the process of forming an idea or a plan **3** [U, C] (BIOLOGY) the moment when a woman or female animal becomes pregnant ➲ verb **conceive**

conceptual AW /kənˈseptʃuəl/ *adj.* (*formal*) related to or based on ideas

conˌceptual ˈart *noun* [U] (ART) art in which the idea which the work of art represents is considered to be the most important thing about it

concern[1] ⊶ /kənˈsɜːn/ *verb* [T] **1** to affect or involve sb/sth: *This does not concern you. Please go away.* ◇ *It is important that no risks are taken* ***where*** *safety* ***is concerned.*** **2** to be about sth: *The main problem concerns the huge cost of the project.* **3** to worry sb: *What concerns me is that we have no long-term plan.* **4** ~ **yourself with sth** to give your attention to sth: *You needn't concern yourself with the hotel booking. The travel agent will take care of it.*

IDM **be concerned in sth** to have a connection with or be involved in sth: *She was concerned in a drugs case some years ago.*

be concerned with sth to be about sth: *Tonight's programme is concerned with the effects of the law on ordinary people.*

concern[2] ⊶ /kənˈsɜːn/ *noun* **1** [C,U] ~ **(for/about/over sb/sth)**; ~ **(that...)** a feeling of worry; sth that causes worry: *The safety officer assured us that there was no* ***cause for concern.*** ◇ *My main concern is that we'll run out of money.* **2** [C] something that is important to you or that involves you: *Financial matters are not my concern.* **3** [C] (BUSINESS) a company or business: *a large industrial concern*

IDM **a going concern** → GOING[2]

concerned ⊶ /kənˈsɜːnd/ *adj.* ~ **(about/for sth)**; ~ **(that...)** worried and feeling concern about sth: *If you are concerned about your baby's health you should consult a doctor immediately.* OPP **unconcerned**

concerning ⊶ /kənˈsɜːnɪŋ/ *prep.* about; on the subject of: *She refused to answer questions concerning her private life.*

concert ⊶ /ˈkɒnsət/ *noun* [C] (MUSIC) a public performance of music: *The band is on tour doing concerts all over the country.* ➲ look at **recital**

IDM **in concert (with sb/sth)** (*formal*) working together with sb/sth

concerted /kənˈsɜːtɪd/ *adj.* done by a group of people working together: *We must all* ***make a concerted effort*** *to finish the work on time.*

concertina /ˌkɒnsəˈtiːnə/ *noun* [C] a musical instrument that you hold in your hands and play by pressing the ends together and pulling them apart

concerto /kənˈtʃɜːtəʊ/ *noun* [C] (*pl.* **concertos**) (MUSIC) a piece of music for one or more SOLO instruments playing with an ORCHESTRA (= a large group of musicians who play different musical instruments together): *a piano concerto*

concession /kənˈseʃn/ *noun* **1** [C,U] (a) ~ **(to sb/sth)** something that you agree to do in order to end an argument: *Employers have been forced to* ***make concessions*** *to the union.* ➲ verb **concede** **2** [C] a lower price for certain groups of people: *Concessions are available for students.*

concessionary /kənˈseʃənəri/ *adj.* having a lower price for certain groups of people: *a concessionary fare*

conciliation /kənˌsɪliˈeɪʃn/ *noun* [U] the process of ending an argument or a disagreement: *All attempts at conciliation have failed and civil war seems inevitable.*

conciliatory /kənˈsɪliətəri/ *adj.* that tries to end an argument or a disagreement: *a conciliatory speech/gesture*

concise /kənˈsaɪs/ *adj.* giving a lot of information in a few words; brief: *He gave a clear and concise summary of what had happened.* ▶ **concisely** *adv.* ▶ **conciseness** *noun* [U]

conclude ⊶ AW /kənˈkluːd/ *verb* **1** [T] ~ **sth from sth** to form an opinion as the result of thought or study: *From the man's strange behaviour I concluded that he was drunk.* **2** [I,T] (*formal*) to end or to bring sth to an end: *The Prince concluded his tour with a visit to a nursery school.* **3** [T] ~ **sth (with sb)** to formally arrange or agree to sth: *conclude a business deal/treaty*

conclusion ⊶ AW /kənˈkluːʒn/ *noun* **1** [C] **the** ~ **(that...)** an opinion that you reach after thinking about sth carefully: *After trying to phone Bob for days, I* ***came to the conclusion*** *that he was on holiday.* ◇ *Have you* ***reached*** *any* ***conclusions*** *from your studies?* **2** [C, usually sing.] (*formal*) an end to sth: *Let us hope the peace talks* ***reach a*** *successful* ***conclusion***. **3** [U] an act of arranging or agreeing to sth formally: *The summit ended with the conclusion of an arms-reduction treaty.*

IDM **a foregone conclusion** → FOREGONE
in conclusion finally; LASTLY
jump to conclusions → JUMP[1]

conclusive AW /kən'klu:sɪv/ ***adj.*** that shows sth is definitely true or real: *The blood tests gave **conclusive proof** of Robson's guilt.* OPP **inconclusive** ▶ **conclusively *adv.***

concoct /kən'kɒkt/ ***verb*** [T] **1** to make sth unusual by mixing different things together **2** to make up or invent sth (an excuse, a story, etc.) ▶ **concoction** /kən'kɒkʃn/ ***noun*** [C]

concord /'kɒŋkɔ:d/ ***noun*** [U] **1 ~ (with sth)** (*formal*) peace and agreement: *The two countries now live in concord.* SYN **harmony 2** (LANGUAGE) **~ (with sth)** (used about words in a phrase) the fact of having to have a particular form according to other words in the phrase

concordance /kən'kɔ:dəns/ ***noun*** **1** [C] a list in A to Z order of the words used in a book, etc. showing where and how often they are used **2** [C] (COMPUTING) a list produced by a computer that shows all the examples of an individual word in a book, etc. **3** [U] the state of being similar to or agreeing with sth: *There is reasonable concordance between the results.*

concourse /'kɒŋkɔ:s/ ***noun*** [C] (ARCHITECTURE) a large hall or space inside a building such as a station or an airport

concrete[1] 🔑 /'kɒŋkri:t/ ***adj.*** real or definite; not only existing in the imagination: *Can you give me a concrete example of what you mean?* OPP **abstract** ▶ **concretely *adv.***

concrete[2] 🔑 /'kɒŋkri:t/ ***noun*** [U] a hard substance made from CEMENT mixed with sand, water, GRAVEL (=small stones), etc., that is used in building: *a modern office building of glass and concrete* ◇ *a concrete floor/bridge* ➲ picture at **building**

concrete[3] /'kɒŋkri:t/ ***verb*** [T] **~ sth (over)** to cover sth with CONCRETE

'concrete mixer = CEMENT MIXER

concur /kən'kɜ:(r)/ ***verb*** [I] (**concurring**; **concurred**) (*formal*) to agree

concurrence /kən'kʌrəns/ ***noun*** (*formal*) **1** [U, sing.] agreement: *The doctor must seek the concurrence of a relative before carrying out the procedure.* **2** [sing.] an example of two or more things happening at the same time: *an unfortunate concurrence of events*

concurrent AW /kən'kʌrənt/ ***adj.*** existing or happening at the same time as sth else ▶ **concurrently *adv.***: *The semi-finals are played concurrently, so it is impossible to watch both.*

concuss /kən'kʌs/ ***verb*** [T] (usually passive) (HEALTH) to hit sb on the head, making them become unconscious or confused for a short time: *I was slightly concussed when I fell off my bicycle.*

concussion /kən'kʌʃn/ ***noun*** [U] (HEALTH) (this word is only [C] in *AmE*) a temporary injury to the brain that was caused by a blow to the head; the effects of a severe blow to the head such as confusion and temporary loss of physical and mental abilities (*BrE*): *He was rushed to hospital, but only suffered mild concussion.* (*AmE*): *He was taken to the hospital with a concussion.*

condemn /kən'dem/ ***verb*** [T] **1 ~ sb/sth (for/as sth)** to say strongly that you think sb/sth is very bad or wrong: *A government spokesman condemned the bombing as a cowardly act of terrorism.* **2 ~ sb (to sth/to do sth)** (LAW) to say what sb's punishment will be; to sentence sb: *The murderer was **condemned to death**.* ◇ (*figurative*) *Their poor education condemns them to a series of low-paid jobs.* **3 ~ sth (as sth)** to say officially that sth is not safe enough to use: *The building was condemned as unsafe and was demolished.*

condemnation /ˌkɒndem'neɪʃn/ ***noun*** [C,U] the act of CONDEMNING sth; a statement that CONDEMNS: *The bombing brought condemnation from all around the world.*

condensation /ˌkɒnden'seɪʃn/ ***noun*** [U] (SCIENCE) **1** small drops of liquid that are formed when warm air touches a cold surface **2** (CHEMISTRY) the process of changing a gas to a liquid ➲ picture at **water**

condense /kən'dens/ ***verb*** **1** [I,T] (CHEMISTRY) to change or make sth change from gas to liquid: *Steam condenses into water when it touches a cold surface.* ➲ look at **evaporate** ➲ picture at **water 2** [T] **~ sth (into sth)** to make smaller or shorter so that it fills less space: *We'll have to condense these three chapters into one.*

condenser /kən'densə(r)/ ***noun*** [C] **1** (CHEMISTRY, TECHNICAL) a piece of equipment that cools gas in order to turn it into liquid ➲ picture at **generator** **2** a device that stores electricity, especially in a car engine

condescend /ˌkɒndɪ'send/ ***verb*** [I] **1 ~ (to sb)** to behave towards sb in a way that shows that you think you are better or more important than them SYN **patronize 2 ~ (to do sth)** to do sth that you believe is below your level of importance: *Celia only condescends to speak to me when she wants me to do something for her.* ▶ **condescending *adj.***: *a condescending smile* ▶ **condescension** /ˌkɒndɪ'senʃn/ ***noun*** [U]

condiment /'kɒndɪmənt/ ***noun*** [C, usually pl.] **1** (*BrE*) a substance such as salt or pepper that is used to give flavour to food **2** (*especially AmE*) a sauce, etc. that is used to give flavour to food, or that is eaten with food

condition[1] 🔑 /kən'dɪʃn/ ***noun*** **1** [U, sing.] the state that sb/sth is in: *to be **in poor/good/excellent condition*** ◇ *He looks really ill. He is certainly not in a condition to drive home.* **2** [C] something that must happen so that sth else can happen or be possible: *One of the conditions of the job is that you agree to work on Sundays.* ◇ *He said I could borrow his bike **on one condition** – that I didn't let anyone else ride it.* **3 conditions** [pl.] the situation or surroundings in which people live, work or do things: *The prisoners were kept **in** terrible **conditions**.* ◇ *poor **living/housing/working conditions*** ➲ note at **situation** **4** [C] (HEALTH) a medical problem that you have for a long time: *to have a heart/lung condition* ➲ note at **disease**

IDM **on condition (that...)** only if: *I agreed to help on condition that I got half the profit.*
on no condition (*formal*) not for any reason: *On no condition must the press find out about this.*
out of condition not physically fit

condition[2] /kən'dɪʃn/ ***verb*** [T] to affect or control the way that sb/sth behaves: *Boys are conditioned to feel that they are stronger than girls.*

conditional /kən'dɪʃənl/ ***adj.*** **1 ~ (on/upon sth)** that only happens if sth else is done or happens first: *My university place is conditional on my getting good marks in the exams.* OPP **unconditional** **2** (LANGUAGE) describing a situation that must exist before sth else can happen. A conditional sentence often contains the word 'if': *'If you don't study, you*

won't pass the exam' is a conditional sentence.
▶ **conditionally** /-ʃənəli/ ***adv.***: *The offer was made conditionally.*

conditioner /kən'dɪʃənə(r)/ ***noun*** [C,U] a substance that keeps sth in a good condition: *Do you use conditioner on your hair?*

condolence /kən'dəʊləns/ ***noun*** [pl., U] an expression of how sorry you feel for sb whose relative or close friend has just died: *to **offer your condolences** ◇ a message of condolence*

condom /'kɒndɒm/ (also *informal* **rubber**) ***noun*** [C] (HEALTH) a thin rubber covering that a man wears over his PENIS (=sexual organ) during sex to prevent the woman from becoming pregnant or as protection against disease

condominium /ˌkɒndə'mɪniəm/ (also *informal* **condo** /'kɒndəʊ/) ***noun*** [C] (*AmE*) a flat or block of flats owned by the people who live in them

condone /kən'dəʊn/ ***verb*** [T] to accept or agree with sth that most people think is wrong: *I can never condone violence – no matter what the circumstances are.*

conducive /kən'dju:sɪv/ ***adj.*** (*formal*) ~ **(to sth)** helping or making sth happen: *This hot weather is not conducive to hard work.*

conduct¹ 🔑 AW /kən'dʌkt/ ***verb*** [T] **1** (*formal*) to organize and do sth, especially research: *to **conduct tests/a survey/an inquiry*** **2** (MUSIC) to direct a group of people who are singing or playing music: *a concert by the Philharmonic Orchestra, conducted by Sir Colin Davis* **3** (*formal*) ~ **yourself well, badly, etc.** to behave in a particular way **4** (PHYSICS, CHEMISTRY) to allow heat or electricity to pass along or through sth: *Rubber does not conduct electricity.*

conduct² 🔑 AW /'kɒndʌkt/ ***noun*** [U] **1** a person's behaviour: *His conduct has always been of the highest standard. ◇ **a code of conduct*** (=a set of rules for behaviour) ➲ look at **misconduct** **2** (*formal*) ~ **of sth** the act of controlling or organizing sth: *She was criticized for her conduct of the bank's affairs.*

conduction /kən'dʌkʃn/ ***noun*** [U] (PHYSICS, CHEMISTRY) the process by which heat or electricity passes through a material

conductive /kən'dʌktɪv/ ***adj.*** (PHYSICS, CHEMISTRY) able to conduct electricity, heat, etc.
▶ **conductivity** /ˌkɒndʌk'tɪvəti/ ***noun*** [U]

conductor /kən'dʌktə(r)/ ***noun*** [C] **1** (MUSIC) a person who stands in front of an ORCHESTRA, a group of singers etc., and directs their performance, especially sb who does this as a profession ➲ picture at **orchestra** **2** (*BrE*) a person whose job is to collect money from passengers on a bus or to check their tickets **3** (*AmE*) =GUARD¹ (5) **4** (PHYSICS, CHEMISTRY) a substance that allows heat or electricity to pass through or along it: *Wood is a poor conductor* ➲ look at **semiconductor**, **semiconductor**

cone /kəʊn/ ***noun*** [C] **1** (GEOMETRY) a shape or object that has a round base and a point at the top: *traffic cones ◇ an ice cream cone* ➲ adjective **conical** ➲ picture at **solid** **2** the hard fruit of PINE and FIR trees ➲ look at **conifer** ➲ picture at **tree**

confectionery /kən'fekʃənəri/ ***noun*** [U] sweets, cakes, chocolates, etc.

confederacy /kən'fedərəsi/ ***noun*** [sing.] (POLITICS) a union of states, groups of people or political parties with the same aim

confederate¹ /kən'fedərət/ ***noun*** [C] a person who helps sb, especially to do sth illegal or secret

confederate² /kən'fedərət/ ***adj.*** (POLITICS) belonging to a CONFEDERACY

confederation /kənˌfedə'reɪʃn/ ***noun*** [C,U] an organization of smaller groups which have joined together: *a confederation of independent republics*

confer AW /kən'fɜ:(r)/ ***verb*** (**conferring**; **conferred**) **1** [I] ~ **(with sb) (on/about sth)** to discuss sth with sb before making a decision: *The President is conferring with his advisers.* **2** [T] (*written*) ~ **sth (on sb)** to give sb a special right or advantage

conference 🔑 AW /'kɒnfərəns/ ***noun*** [C] a large official meeting, often lasting several days, at which members of an organization, profession, etc. meet to discuss important matters: *an international conference on global warming*

'conference call ***noun*** [C] a telephone call in which three or more people take part

confess /kən'fes/ ***verb*** [I,T] ~ **(to sth/to doing sth)**; ~ **(sth) (to sb)** to admit that you have done sth bad or wrong SYN **own up (to sth)**: *The young woman confessed to the murder of her boyfriend/to murdering her boyfriend. ◇ They confessed to their mother that they had spent all the money.* ➲ note at **admit**

confession /kən'feʃn/ ***noun*** [C,U] an act of admitting that you have done sth bad or wrong: *The police persuaded the man to make a full confession.*

confetti /kən'feti/ ***noun*** [U] small pieces of coloured paper that people throw over a man and woman who have just got married

confide /kən'faɪd/ ***verb*** [T] ~ **sth to sb** to tell sb sth that is secret: *She did not confide her love to anyone – not even to her best friend.*
PHR V **confide in sb** to talk to sb that you trust about sth secret or private

confidence 🔑 /'kɒnfɪdəns/ ***noun*** [U] **1** ~ **(in sb/sth)** trust or strong belief in sb/sth: *The public is **losing confidence** in the present government. ◇ I **have every confidence** in Emily's ability to do the job.* **2** the feeling that you are sure about your own abilities, opinion, etc.: *I didn't **have the confidence** to tell her I thought she was wrong. ◇ to be **full of confidence** ◇ 'Of course we will win,' the team captain said **with confidence**.* ➲ look at **self-confidence** **3** a feeling of trust in sb to keep sth a secret: *The information was given to me **in strict confidence**. ◇ It took a while to **win/gain her confidence**.*

'confidence trick ***noun*** [C] a way of getting money by cheating sb

confident 🔑 /'kɒnfɪdənt/ ***adj.*** ~ **(of sth/that...)**; ~ **(about sth)** feeling or showing that you are sure about your own abilities, opinions, etc.: *Kate feels confident of passing/that she can pass the exam. ◇ to be confident of success ◇ You should feel confident about your own abilities. ◇ Dillon has a very confident manner.* ➲ note at **sure** ➲ look at **self-confident**
▶ **confidently** ***adv.***: *She stepped confidently onto the stage and began to sing.*

confidential /ˌkɒnfɪ'denʃl/ ***adj.*** meant to be kept secret and not told to or shared with other people: ***confidential information/documents** ◇ Your medical records are **strictly confidential**.*
▶ **confidentiality** /ˌkɒnfɪˌdenʃi'æləti/ ***noun*** [U]
▶ **confidentially** /-ʃəli/ ***adv.***: *She told me confidentially that she is going to retire early.*

configuration /kənˌfɪgə'reɪʃn/ ***noun*** [C] **1** (*formal*) the way in which the parts of sth, or a group of things, are arranged **2** (COMPUTING) the equipment and programs that form a computer system and the particular way that these are arranged

configure /kən'fɪgə(r)/ ***verb*** [T] **1** (*formal*) to arrange parts of sth, or a group of things, in a particular way **2** (COMPUTING) to arrange computer equipment for a particular task

confine 🔑 AW /kən'faɪn/ ***verb*** [T] **1** ~ **sb/sth (in/to sth)** to keep a person or animal in a particular, usually small, place: *The prisoners are confined to their cells for long periods at a time.* **2** ~ **sb/sth/yourself to sth** to stay within the limits of sth: *Please confine your questions to the topic we are discussing.*

confined 🔑 AW /kən'faɪnd/ ***adj.*** (used about a space or an area) small and surrounded by walls or sides: *It is cruel to keep animals in confined spaces.*

confinement /kən'faɪnmənt/ ***noun*** [U] being kept in a small space: *to be kept **in solitary confinement*** (=in a prison)

confines /'kɒnfaɪnz/ ***noun*** [pl.] (*formal*) the limits of sth: *Patients are not allowed beyond the confines of the hospital grounds.*

confirm 🔑 AW /kən'fɜ:m/ ***verb*** [T] **1** to say or show that sth is true; to make sth definite: *Seeing the two of them together confirmed our suspicions.* ◇ *Can you confirm that you will be able to attend?* **2** (RELIGION) to accept sb as a full member of a Christian Church in a special ceremony: *He was confirmed at the age of thirteen.* ▶ **confirmation** AW /ˌkɒnfə'meɪʃn/ ***noun*** [C,U]: *We are waiting for confirmation of the report.*

confirmed /kən'fɜ:md/ ***adj.*** (only *before* a noun) fixed in a particular habit or way of life: *a **confirmed bachelor*** (=a man who is not likely to get married)

confiscate /'kɒnfɪskeɪt/ ***verb*** [T] to take sth away from sb as a punishment: *Any cigarettes found in school will be confiscated.* ▶ **confiscation** /ˌkɒnfɪ'skeɪʃn/ ***noun*** [C,U]

conflict[1] 🔑 AW /'kɒnflɪkt/ ***noun*** [C,U] **1** (a) ~ **with sb/sth (over sth)** a fight or an argument: *an armed conflict* ◇ *The new laws have brought the Government **into conflict** with the unions over pay increases.* **2** a difference between two or more ideas, wishes, etc.: *Many women have to cope with the conflict between their career and their family.* ◇ *a **conflict of interests*** (=a situation in which there are two jobs, aims, roles, etc. and it is not possible for both of them to be treated equally and fairly at the same time)

conflict[2] 🔑 AW /kən'flɪkt/ ***verb*** [I] **A and B ~; A conflicts with B** to disagree with or be different from sb/sth: *The statements of the two witnesses conflict.* ◇ *John's statement conflicts with yours.* ◇ *conflicting results*

confluence /'kɒnfluəns/ ***noun*** [C, usually sing.] (GEOGRAPHY) the place where two rivers flow together and become one

conform AW /kən'fɔ:m/ ***verb*** [I] ~ **(to sth) 1** to obey a rule or law: *This building does not conform to fire regulations.* **2** to behave in the way that other people and society expect you to behave: *Children are under a lot of pressure to conform when they first start school.*

conformation AW /ˌkɒnfɔ:'meɪʃn/ ***noun*** [U,C] (*formal*) the way in which sth is formed; the structure of sth, especially an animal

conformist AW /kən'fɔ:mɪst/ ***noun*** [C] (SOCIAL STUDIES) a person who behaves in the way that people are expected to behave by society OPP **nonconformist**

conformity AW /kən'fɔ:məti/ ***noun*** [U] (*formal*) (SOCIAL STUDIES) behaviour which CONFORMS to rules and customs

confront 🔑 /kən'frʌnt/ ***verb*** [T] **1** ~ **sth; ~ sb with sb/sth** to think about, or to make sb think about, sth that is difficult or unpleasant: *to confront a problem/difficulty/issue* ◇ *When the police confronted him with the evidence, he confessed.* **2** to stand in front of sb, for example because you want to fight them: *The unarmed demonstrators were confronted by a row of soldiers.*

confrontation /ˌkɒnfrʌn'teɪʃn/ ***noun*** [C,U] a fight or an argument

confuse 🔑 /kən'fju:z/ ***verb*** [T] **1** (usually passive) to make sb unable to think clearly or to know what to do: *He confused everybody with his pages of facts and figures.* **2** ~ **A and/with B** to mistake sb/sth for sb/sth else: *I often confuse Lee with his brother. They look very much alike.* **3** to make sth complicated: *The situation is confused by the fact that so many organizations are involved.*

confused 🔑 /kən'fju:zd/ ***adj.*** **1** not able to think clearly: *When he regained consciousness he was dazed and confused.* **2** difficult to understand: *The article is very confused – I don't know what the main point is.* ▶ **confusedly** /-ədli/ ***adv.***

confusing 🔑 /kən'fju:zɪŋ/ ***adj.*** difficult to understand: *Her instructions were contradictory and confusing.* ▶ **confusingly** ***adv.***

confusion 🔑 /kən'fju:ʒn/ ***noun*** [U] **1** the state of not being able to think clearly or not understanding sth: *He stared **in confusion** at the exam paper.* ◇ *There is still a great deal of confusion as to the true facts.* **2** a confused situation in which people do not know what action to take: *Their unexpected visit threw all our plans into confusion.* **3** the act of mistaking sb/sth for sb/sth else: *To avoid confusion, all luggage should be labelled with your name and destination.*

congeal /kən'dʒi:l/ ***verb*** [I,T] (used about a liquid) to become solid; to make a liquid solid: *congealed blood*

congenial /kən'dʒi:niəl/ ***adj.*** (*formal*) pleasant: *We spent an evening in congenial company.*

congenital /kən'dʒenɪtl/ ***adj.*** (HEALTH) (used about a disease) beginning at and continuing since birth

congested /kən'dʒestɪd/ ***adj.*** **1** crowded; full of traffic: *The streets are congested with traffic.* **2** (HEALTH) (used about a part of the body) blocked with blood or MUCUS (=a thick liquid that is produced in parts of the body such as the nose)

congestion /kən'dʒestʃən/ ***noun*** [U] the state of being very full of sth: *severe traffic congestion* ◇ *medicine to relieve nasal congestion*

con'gestion charge ***noun*** (*BrE*) an amount of money that people have to pay for driving their cars into the centre of some cities as a way of stopping the city centre from becoming too full of traffic ▶ **con'gestion charging** ***noun*** [U]

conglomerate /kən'glɒmərət/ ***noun*** [C] (BUSINESS) a large firm made up of several different companies

conglomeration /kənˌglɒmə'reɪʃn/ ***noun*** [C] (*formal*) a mixture of different things that are found all together

congratulate /kən'grætʃuleɪt/ ***verb*** [T] ~ **sb (on sth)** to tell sb that you are pleased about sth they have done; to praise sb: *I congratulated Sue on passing her driving test.*

congratulations /kən,grætʃu'leɪʃnz/ ***noun*** [pl.] used for telling sb that you are pleased about sth they have done: ***Congratulations on the birth of your baby boy!***

congregate /'kɒŋgrɪgeɪt/ ***verb*** [I] to come together in a crowd or group

congregation /,kɒŋgrɪ'geɪʃn/ ***noun*** [C, with sing. or pl. verb] (RELIGION) the group of people who attend a particular church

congress /'kɒŋgres/ ***noun*** [C, with sing. or pl. verb] **1** a large formal meeting or series of meetings: *a medical congress* **2 Congress** (POLITICS, LAW) the name in some countries (for example the US) for the group of people who are elected to make the laws ❶ The **US Congress** is made up of the **Senate** and the **House of Representatives**. ▶ **congressional** /kən'greʃənl/ ***adj.***: ***a congressional committee/bill*** ◇ *the midterm Congressional elections*

Congressman /'kɒŋgresmən/ **Congresswoman** /'kɒŋgreswʊmən/ ***noun*** [C] (*pl.* **-men** /-mən/) (*pl.* **-women** /-wɪmɪn/) (POLITICS) a member of Congress in the US, especially the House of Representatives

congruent /'kɒŋgruənt/ ***adj.*** **1** (GEOMETRY) having exactly the same size and shape: *congruent triangles* **2** (*formal*) ~ **(with sth)** suitable for sth ▶ **congruence** /'kɒŋgruəns/ ***noun*** [U]

conic /'kɒnɪk/ ***adj.*** (GEOMETRY) connected with CONES

conic sections

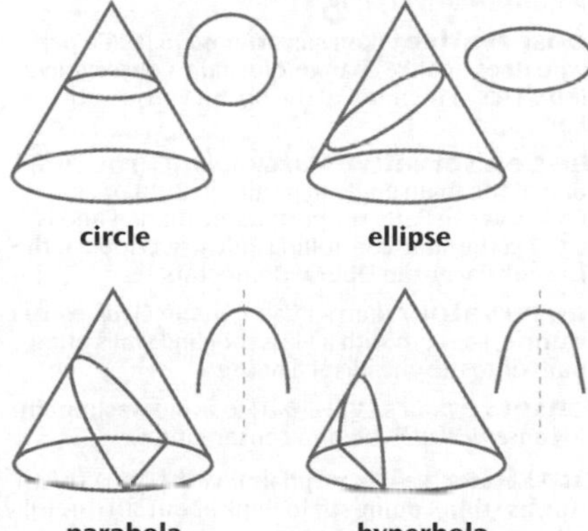

conical /'kɒnɪkl/ ***adj.*** (GEOMETRY) having a round base and getting narrower towards a point at the top ➲ noun **cone**

conifer /'kɒnɪfə(r); 'kəʊn-/ ***noun*** [C] (BIOLOGY) any tree that produces hard dry fruit called CONES. Most **conifers** are EVERGREEN (= have leaves that stay on the tree all year) ▶ **coniferous** /kə'nɪfərəs/ ***adj.***: *coniferous trees/forests*

conjecture /kən'dʒektʃə(r)/ ***verb*** [I,T] (*formal*) to guess about sth without real proof or evidence ▶ **conjecture** ***noun*** [C,U]

conjoin /kən'dʒɔɪn/ ***verb*** [I,T] (*formal*) to join together; to join two or more things together

con,joined 'twin (HEALTH) = SIAMESE TWIN

conjugal /'kɒndʒəgl/ ***adj.*** (*formal*) connected with marriage and the relationship between husband and wife

conjugate /'kɒndʒəgeɪt/ ***verb*** [T] (LANGUAGE) to give the different forms of a verb ▶ **conjugation** /,kɒndʒu'geɪʃn/ ***noun*** [C,U]

conjunction /kən'dʒʌŋkʃn/ ***noun*** [C] (LANGUAGE) a word that is used for joining other words, phrases or sentences: *'And', 'but' and 'or' are conjunctions.*
IDM **in conjunction with sb/sth** together with sb/sth

conjunctivitis /kən,dʒʌŋktɪ'vaɪtɪs/ ***noun*** [U] (HEALTH) an eye disease that causes pain and swelling in part of the eye, and that can be passed from one person to another

conjure /'kʌndʒə(r)/ ***verb*** [I] to do tricks by clever, quick hand movements, that appear to be magic ▶ **conjuring** ***noun*** [U]: ***a conjuring trick***
PHR V **conjure sth up 1** to cause an image to appear in your mind: *Hawaiian music conjures up images of sunshine, flowers and sandy beaches.* **2** to make sth appear quickly or suddenly: *Mum can conjure up a meal out of almost anything.*

conjuror (also **conjurer**) /'kʌndʒərə(r)/ ***noun*** [C] a person who does clever tricks that appear to be magic ➲ look at **magician**

conker /'kɒŋkə(r)/ (*especially BrE, informal*) ***noun*** [C] the smooth shiny brown nut of the HORSE CHESTNUT tree

connect /kə'nekt/ ***verb*** **1** [I,T] ~ **(sth) (up) (to/with sth)** to be joined to sth; to join sth to sth else: *The tunnels connect (up) ten metres further on.* ◇ *The printer is connected to the computer.* ◇ *This motorway connects Oxford with Birmingham.* ➲ look at **disconnect 2** [T] ~ **sb/sth (with sb/sth)** to have an association with sb/sth else; to realize or show that sb/sth is involved with sb/sth else: *There was no evidence that she was connected with the crime.* **3** [I] ~ **(with sth)** (used about a bus, train, plane, etc.) to arrive at a particular time so that passengers can change to another bus, train, plane, etc.: ***a connecting flight***

connection /kə'nekʃn/ ***noun*** [C] **1** a ~ **between A and B**; a ~ **with/to sth** an association or relationship between two or more people or things: *Is there any connection between the two organizations?* ◇ *What's your connection with Brazil? Have you worked there?* **2** a place where two wires, pipes, etc. join together: *The radio doesn't work. There must be a loose connection somewhere.* **3** a bus, train, plane, etc. that leaves soon after another arrives: *Our bus was late so we missed our connection.*
IDM **in connection with sb/sth** (*formal*) about or concerning: *I am writing to you in connection with your application.*
in this/that connection (*formal*) about or concerning this/that

connective tissue /kə,nektɪv 'tɪʃuː/ ***noun*** [U] (ANATOMY) any fat, CARTILAGE or other material that supports, connects or separates organs or other parts of the body

connive /kə'naɪv/ ***verb*** [I] ~ **at sth**; ~ **(with sb) (to do sth)** to work secretly with sb to do sth that is wrong; to do nothing to stop sb doing sth wrong: *The two parties connived to get rid of the president.*

connoisseur /,kɒnə'sɜː(r)/ ***noun*** [C] a person who knows a lot about art, good food, music, etc.

connotation /,kɒnə'teɪʃn/ ***noun*** [C] (LANGUAGE) an idea expressed by a word in addition to its main meaning: *'Spinster' means a single woman but it has negative connotations.*

conquer /'kɒŋkə(r)/ ***verb*** [T] **1** to take control of a country or city and its people by force, especially in a war: *Napoleon's ambition was to conquer Europe.* ◇ *(figurative) The young singer conquered the hearts of audiences all over the world.* **2** to succeed in controlling or dealing with a strong feeling, problem, etc.: *She's trying to conquer her fear of flying.*

conqueror /'kɒŋkərə(r)/ ***noun*** [C] a person who has CONQUERED sth: *William the Conqueror* (=King William I of England)

conquest /'kɒŋkwest/ ***noun*** **1** [C, U] an act of CONQUERING sth: *the **Norman conquest*** (=of England in 1066) ◇ *the conquest of Mount Everest* **2** [C] an area of land that has been taken in a war: *the Spanish conquests in South America*

conscience /'kɒnʃəns/ ***noun*** [C,U] the part of your mind that tells you if what you are doing is right or wrong: ***a clear/a guilty conscience***
IDM **have sth on your conscience** to feel guilty because you have done sth wrong

conscientious /ˌkɒnʃi'enʃəs/ ***adj.*** **1** (used about people) careful to do sth correctly and well: *He's a conscientious worker.* **2** (used about actions) done with great care and attention: *conscientious work*
▸ **conscientiously** ***adv.***

ˌ**conscientious ob'jector** ***noun*** [C] a person who refuses to join the army, etc. because they believe it is morally wrong to kill other people

conscious ⊶ /'kɒnʃəs/ ***adj.*** **1** able to see, hear, feel, etc. things; awake: *The injured driver was still conscious when the ambulance arrived.* OPP **unconscious** **2** ~ **(of sth/that...)** noticing or realizing that sth exists; aware of sth: *She didn't seem conscious of the danger.* ◇ *Bill suddenly became conscious that someone was following him.* **3** that you do on purpose or for a particular reason SYN **deliberate**: *We made **a conscious effort** to treat both children equally.* ▸ **consciously** ***adv.***

consciousness /'kɒnʃəsnəs/ ***noun*** **1** [U] the state of being able to see, hear, feel, etc.: *As he fell, he hit his head and **lost consciousness**.* ◇ *She **regained consciousness** after two weeks in a coma.* **2** [U, sing.] ~ **(of sth)** the state of realizing or noticing that sth exists: *There is (a) growing consciousness of the need to save energy.*

conscript[1] /kən'skrɪpt/ ***verb*** [T] to make sb join the army, navy or air force ▸ **conscription** ***noun*** [U]

conscript[2] /'kɒnskrɪpt/ ***noun*** [C] a person who has been CONSCRIPTED to join the armed forces: *conscript soldiers/armies* ➲ look at **volunteer[1]** (2)

consecrate /'kɒnsɪkreɪt/ ***verb*** [T] (RELIGION) to state formally in a special ceremony that a place or an object can be used for religious purposes
▸ **consecration** /ˌkɒnsɪ'kreɪʃn/ ***noun*** [C,U]

consecutive /kən'sekjətɪv/ ***adj.*** coming or happening one after the other: *This is the team's fourth consecutive win.* ▸ **consecutively** ***adv.***

consensus AW /kən'sensəs/ ***noun*** [sing., U] (a) ~ **(among/between sb) (on/about sth)** an opinion that all members of a group agree with: *to **reach a consensus*** ◇ *There is no consensus among experts about the causes of global warming.*

consent[1] AW /kən'sent/ ***verb*** [I] ~ **(to sth)** to agree to sth; to allow sth to happen ➲ note at **agree**

consent[2] AW /kən'sent/ ***noun*** [U] agreement; permission: *The child's parents had to give their consent to the operation.*
IDM **the age of consent** → AGE[1]

consequence ⊶ AW /'kɒnsɪkwəns/ ***noun*** **1** [C] something that happens or follows as a result of sth else: *Many people may lose their jobs **as a consequence of** recent poor sales.* ➲ note at **effect[1]** **2** [U] *(formal)* importance: *It is of no consequence.*

consequent AW /'kɒnsɪkwənt/ ***adj.*** *(formal)* (only *before* a noun) following as the result of sth else: *The lack of rain and consequent poor harvests have led to food shortages.* ▸ **consequently** AW ***adv.***: *She didn't work hard enough, and consequently failed the exam.*

conservation /ˌkɒnsə'veɪʃn/ ***noun*** [U] **1** (ENVIRONMENT) the protection of the natural world: *Conservation groups are protesting against the plan to build a road through the forest.* **2** not allowing sth to be wasted, damaged or destroyed: *the conservation of energy* ➲ verb **conserve**

conservationist /ˌkɒnsə'veɪʃənɪst/ ***noun*** [C] (ENVIRONMENT) a person who believes in protecting the natural world

conservatism /kən'sɜːvətɪzəm/ ***noun*** [U] **1** the disapproval of new ideas and change **2** (usually **Conservatism**) (POLITICS) the beliefs of the Conservative Party

conservative[1] ⊶ /kən'sɜːvətɪv/ ***adj.*** **1** not liking change; traditional **2 Conservative** (POLITICS) connected with the British Conservative Party: *Conservative voters* **3** (used when you are guessing how much sth costs) lower than the real figure or amount: *Even **a conservative estimate** would put the damage at about £4000 to repair.*
▸ **conservatively** ***adv.***

conservative[2] /kən'sɜːvətɪv/ ***noun*** [C] **1** a person who does not like change **2** (usually **Conservative**) (POLITICS) a member of the British Conservative Party

the Con'servative Party ***noun*** [C] (POLITICS) one of the main political parties in Britain. The Conservative Party supports a free market and is against the state controlling industry ➲ look at **the Labour Party**, **the Liberal Democrats**

conservatory /kən'sɜːvətri/ ***noun*** [C] (*pl.* **conservatories**) a room with a glass roof and walls often built onto the outside of a house

conserve /kən'sɜːv/ ***verb*** [T] to avoid wasting sth: *to conserve water* ➲ noun **conservation**

consider ⊶ /kən'sɪdə(r)/ ***verb*** [T] **1** ~ **sb/sth (for/as sth)**; ~ **doing sth** to think about sth carefully, often before making a decision: *She had never considered nursing as a career.* ◇ *We're considering going to Spain for our holidays.* **2** ~ **sb/sth (as/to be) sth**; ~ **that...** to think about sb/sth in a particular way: *He considered the risk (to be) too great.* ◇ *He considered that the risk was too great.* ◇ *Jane considers herself an expert on the subject.* ➲ note at **regard[1]** **3** to remember or pay attention to sth, especially sb's feelings: *I can't just move abroad. I have to consider my family.*

considerable ⊶ AW /kən'sɪdərəbl/ ***adj.*** great in amount or size: *A considerable number of people preferred the old building to the new one.*

considerably ⊶ AW /kən'sɪdərəbli/ ***adv.*** much; a lot: *This flat is considerably larger than our last one.* ◇ *The need for sleep varies considerably from person to person.*

considerate /kən'sɪdərət/ ***adj.*** **~ (towards sb); ~ (of sb) (to do sth)** careful not to upset people; thinking of others: *It was very considerate of you to offer to drive me home.* OPP **inconsiderate**

consideration /kən,sɪdə'reɪʃn/ ***noun*** **1** [U] (*formal*) an act of thinking about sth carefully or for a long time: *I have given some consideration to the idea but I don't think it would work.* **2** [C] something that you think about when you are making a decision: *If he changes his job, the salary will be an important consideration.* **3** [U] **~ (for sb/sth)** the quality of thinking about what other people need or feel: *Most drivers show little consideration for cyclists.*
IDM **take sth into consideration** to think about sth when you are forming an opinion or making a decision

considering /kən'sɪdərɪŋ/ ***prep., conj.*** (used for introducing a surprising fact) when you think about or remember sth: *Considering you've only been studying for a year, you speak English very well.*

consign /kən'saɪn/ ***verb*** [T] (*formal*) **~ sb/sth to sth** to put or send sb/sth somewhere, especially in order to get rid of them/it: *I think I can consign this junk mail straight to the bin.*

consignment /kən'saɪnmənt/ ***noun*** [C] goods that are being sent to sb/sth: *a new consignment of books*

consist /kən'sɪst/ ***verb*** (not used in the continuous tenses)
PHR V **consist in sth** (*formal*) to have sth as the main or only part or feature: *The beauty of the city consists in its magnificent buildings.*
consist of sth to be formed from the things or people mentioned: *The band consists of a singer, two guitarists and a drummer.*

consistency AW /kən'sɪstənsi/ ***noun*** (*pl.* **consistencies**) **1** [U] the quality of always having the same standard, opinions, behaviour, etc.: *Your work lacks consistency. Sometimes it's excellent but at other times it's full of mistakes.* OPP **inconsistency** **2** [C, U] how thick or smooth a liquid substance is: *The mixture should have a thick, sticky consistency.*

consistent AW /kən'sɪstənt/ ***adj.*** **1** always having the same opinions, standard, behaviour, etc.; not changing **2 ~ (with sth)** agreeing with or similar to sth: *I'm afraid your statement is not consistent with what the other witnesses said.* OPP **inconsistent** ▶ **consistently** ***adv.***: *We must try to maintain a consistently high standard.*

consolation /,kɒnsə'leɪʃn/ ***noun*** [C,U] a thing or person that makes you feel better when you are sad: *It was some consolation to me to know that I wasn't the only one who had failed the exam.* SYN **comfort**

console[1] /kən'səʊl/ ***verb*** [T] to make sb happier when they are very sad or disappointed SYN **comfort**

console[2] /'kɒnsəʊl/ ***noun*** [C] a flat surface which contains all the controls and switches for a machine, a piece of electronic equipment, etc.

consolidate /kən'sɒlɪdeɪt/ ***verb*** [I,T] to become or to make sth firmer or stronger: *We're going to consolidate what we've learnt so far by doing some revision exercises today.* ▶ **consolidation** /kən,sɒlɪ'deɪʃn/ ***noun*** [U]

consonant /'kɒnsənənt/ ***noun*** [C] (LANGUAGE) any of the letters of the English alphabet except a, e, i, o, and u ➲ look at **vowel**

consortium /kən'sɔːtiəm/ ***noun*** [C] (*pl.* **consortiums** or **consortia** /-tiə/) a group of people, countries, companies, etc. who are working together on a particular project: *Our company forms part of a consortium of local businesses working for environmental change.*

conspicuous /kən'spɪkjuəs/ ***adj.*** easily seen or noticed OPP **inconspicuous** ▶ **conspicuously** ***adv.***

conspiracy /kən'spɪrəsi/ ***noun*** [C,U] (*pl.* **conspiracies**) a secret plan by a group of people to do sth bad or illegal

conspirator /kən'spɪrətə(r)/ ***noun*** [C] a member of a group of people who are planning to do sth bad or illegal

conspire /kən'spaɪə(r)/ ***verb*** [I] **1 ~ (with sb) (to do sth)** to plan to do sth bad or illegal with a group of people: *A group of terrorists were conspiring to blow up the plane.* **2 ~ (against sb/sth)** (used about events) to seem to work together to make sth bad happen: *When we both lost our jobs in the same week, we felt that everything was conspiring against us.*

constable /'kʌnstəbl/ = POLICE CONSTABLE

constabulary /kən'stæbjələri/ ***noun*** [C] (*pl.* **constabularies**) the police force of a particular area: *the West Yorkshire Constabulary*

constancy AW /'kɒnstənsi/ ***noun*** [U] (*formal*) **1** the quality of staying the same and not changing **2** the quality of being faithful SYN **fidelity**

constant[1] AW /'kɒnstənt/ ***adj.*** **1** happening or existing all the time or again and again: *The constant noise gave me a headache.* **2** that does not change: *You use less petrol if you drive at a constant speed.*

constant[2] AW /'kɒnstənt/ ***noun*** [C] (MATHEMATICS) a number or quantity that does not vary OPP **variable**

constantly AW /'kɒnstəntli/ ***adv.*** always; again and again: *The situation is constantly changing.*

constellation /,kɒnstə'leɪʃn/ ***noun*** [C] (ASTRONOMY) a group of stars that forms a pattern and has a name

consternation /,kɒnstə'neɪʃn/ ***noun*** [U] a feeling of shock or worry: *We stared at each other in* ***consternation.***

constipated /'kɒnstɪpeɪtɪd/ ***adj.*** (HEALTH) not able to empty waste from your body ▶ **constipation** /,kɒnstɪ'peɪʃn/ ***noun*** [U]: *to suffer from/have constipation*

constituency AW /kən'stɪtjuənsi/ ***noun*** [C] (*pl.* **constituencies**) (POLITICS) a district and the people who live in it that a politician represents

constituent[1] AW /kən'stɪtjuənt/ ***noun*** [C] **1** one of the parts that form sth: *Hydrogen and oxygen are the constituents of water.* **2** (POLITICS) a person who lives in the district that a politician represents

constituent[2] AW /kən'stɪtjuənt/ ***adj.*** (only *before* a noun) (*formal*) forming or helping to make a whole: *to break something up into its* ***constituent parts/elements***

con,stituent as'sembly ***noun*** [C] (POLITICS) a group of elected representatives with the power to make or change a country's CONSTITUTION

constitute AW /'kɒnstɪtjuːt/ ***verb, linking verb*** (*formal*) (not used in the continuous tenses) **1** to be one of the parts that form sth: *Women constitute a high proportion of part-time workers.* **2** to be considered as sth; to be equal to sth: *The presence of the troops constitutes a threat to peace.*

constitution AW /ˌkɒnstɪˈtjuːʃn/ *noun* **1** [C] (POLITICS) the basic laws or rules of a country or an organization: *the United States Constitution* **2** [C] (HEALTH) the condition of a person's body and how healthy it is **3** [U, C] (*formal*) the way the parts of sth are put together SYN **structure**: *the constitution of DNA*

constitutional AW /ˌkɒnstɪˈtjuːʃənl/ *adj.* (POLITICS) connected with or allowed by the CONSTITUTION of a country, etc.: *It is not constitutional to imprison a person without trial.*

constrain AW /kənˈstreɪn/ *verb* [T] (*formal*) ~ **sb/sth (to do sth)** to limit sb/sth; to force sb/sth to do sth: *The company's growth has been constrained by high taxes.*

constrained AW /kənˈstreɪnd/ *adj.* (*formal*) not natural; forced or too controlled: *constrained emotions*

constraint AW /kənˈstreɪnt/ *noun* [C,U] something that limits you: *There are always some financial constraints on a project like this.* SYN **restriction** ➲ note at **limit**[1]

constrict /kənˈstrɪkt/ *verb* [I,T] **1** to become or make sth tighter, narrower or less: *She felt her throat constrict with fear.* ◇ *The valve constricts the flow of air.* **2** to limit a person's freedom to do sth ▶ **constriction** *noun* [C,U]

construct[1] 🔑 AW /kənˈstrʌkt/ *verb* [T] to build or make sth: *Early houses were constructed out of mud and sticks.* ➲ note at **build**[1]

construct[2] AW /ˈkɒnstrʌkt/ *noun* [C] **1** (*formal*) an idea or a belief that is based on various pieces of evidence which are not always true: *a contrast between lived reality and the construct held in the mind* **2** (LANGUAGE) a group of words that form a phrase **3** a thing that is built or made

construction 🔑 AW /kənˈstrʌkʃn/ *noun* **1** [U] the process or method of building or making sth, especially roads, buildings, bridges, etc.: *A new bridge is now* ***under construction***. ◇ *He works in the construction industry.* **2** [C] (*formal*) a thing that has been built or made: *The summer house was a simple wooden construction.* ➲ note at **structure**[1] **3** [C] (LANGUAGE) the way that words are used together in a phrase or sentence: *a grammatical construction*

constructive AW /kənˈstrʌktɪv/ *adj.* useful or helpful: *constructive suggestions/criticisms/advice* ▶ **constructively** *adv.*

construe /kənˈstruː/ *verb* [T] (*formal*) ~ **sth (as sth)** to understand the meaning of sth in a particular way: *Her confident manner is often construed as arrogance.* ➲ look at **misconstrue**

consul /ˈkɒnsl/ *noun* [C] (POLITICS) a government official who is the representative of his or her country in a foreign city: *the British consul in Miami* ➲ look at **ambassador** ▶ **consular** /ˈkɒnsjələ(r)/ *adj.*

consulate /ˈkɒnsjələt/ *noun* [C] (POLITICS) the government building where a CONSUL works ➲ look at **embassy**

consult 🔑 AW /kənˈsʌlt/ *verb* **1** [T] ~ **sb/sth (about sth)** to ask sb for some information or advice, or to look for it in a book, etc.: *If the symptoms continue, consult your doctor.* **2** [I] ~ **with sb** to discuss sth with sb: *Harry consulted with his brothers before selling the family business.*

consultancy AW /kənˈsʌltənsi/ *noun* (*pl.* **consultancies**) **1** [C] (BUSINESS) a company that gives expert advice on a particular subject **2** [U] expert advice that sb is paid to provide on a particular subject

consultant AW /kənˈsʌltənt/ *noun* [C] **1** a person who gives advice to people on business, law, etc.: *a firm of management consultants* **2** (*BrE*) (HEALTH) a hospital doctor who is a specialist in a particular area of medicine: *a consultant psychiatrist*

consultation AW /ˌkɒnslˈteɪʃn/ *noun* **1** [U,C] a discussion between people before a decision is taken: *Diplomats met for consultations on the hostage crisis.* ◇ *The measures were introduced without consultation.* **2** [C] a meeting with an expert, especially a doctor, to get advice or treatment

consultative AW /kənˈsʌltətɪv/ *adj.* giving advice or making suggestions SYN **advisory**: *a consultative committee/body/document*

con'sulting room *noun* [C] (HEALTH) a room where a doctor talks to and examines patients

consumable /kənˈsjuːməbl/ *adj.* (BUSINESS) intended to be bought, used and then replaced

consumables /kənˈsjuːməblz/ *noun* [pl.] (BUSINESS) goods that are intended to be used fairly quickly and then replaced

consume AW /kənˈsjuːm/ *verb* [T] (*formal*) **1** to use sth such as fuel, energy or time **2** to eat or drink sth: *Wrestlers can consume up to 10 000 calories in a day.* ➲ noun **consumption** **3** (used about fire) to destroy sth **4** (used about an emotion) to affect sb very strongly: *She was consumed by grief when her son was killed.*

consumer 🔑 AW /kənˈsjuːmə(r)/ *noun* [C] **1** (BUSINESS) a person who buys things or uses services **2** a person or an animal that eats or uses sth ➲ picture at **food chain**

consumerism /kənˈsjuːmərɪzəm/ *noun* [U] (ECONOMICS) the buying and using of goods and services; the belief that it is good for a society or an individual person to buy and use a large quantity of goods and services ▶ **consumerist** *adj.*: *consumerist values*

consuming /kənˈsjuːmɪŋ/ *adj.* (only *before* a noun) that takes up a lot of your time and attention: *Sport is her consuming passion.*

consummate[1] /ˈkɒnsəmət/ *adj.* (only *before* a noun) (*formal*) extremely skilled; a perfect example of sth: *a consummate performer/professional*

consummate[2] /ˈkɒnsəmeɪt/ *verb* [T] (*formal*) to make a marriage or relationship complete by having sex ▶ **consummation** /ˌkɒnsəˈmeɪʃn/ *noun* [C,U]

consumption AW /kənˈsʌmpʃn/ *noun* [U] **1** the amount of fuel, etc. that sth uses: *a car with low fuel consumption* **2** the act of using, eating, etc. sth: *The meat was declared* ***unfit for human consumption*** (=for people to eat). ➲ verb **consume** **3** (*old-fashioned*) (HEALTH) a serious infectious disease of the lungs SYN **tuberculosis**

cont. (*also* **contd**) *abbr.* continued: *cont. on p 91*

contact[1] 🔑 AW /ˈkɒntækt/ *noun* **1** [U] ~ **(with sb/sth)** meeting, talking to or writing to sb else: *They are trying to* ***make contact*** *with the kidnappers.* ◇ *We* ***keep in contact*** *with our office in New York.* ◇ *It's a pity to* ***lose contact*** *with old schoolfriends.* ◇ *Here's my* ***contact number*** (=temporary telephone number) *while I'm away.* **2** [U] ~ **(with sb/sth)** the state of touching sb/sth: *This product should not* ***come into contact*** *with food.* ➲ look at **contact sport** **3** [C] a person that you know who may be able to help you: *business contacts* **4** [C] (PHYSICS) an

electrical connection: *The switches close the contacts and complete the circuit.* ➲ picture at **switch**[1]
▸ **contact** ***adj.***: *contact dermatitis* (=caused by touching an infected person)

contact[2] ⊸ AW /ˈkɒntækt/ ***verb*** [T] to telephone or write to sb: *Is there a phone number where I can contact you?*

ˈcontact lens ***noun*** [C] a small piece of plastic that fits onto your eye to help you to see better

ˈcontact sport ***noun*** [C] (SPORT) a sport in which players have physical contact with each other OPP **non-contact sport**

contagious /kənˈteɪdʒəs/ ***adj.*** (HEALTH) (used about a disease) that you can get by touching sb/sth: *Smallpox is a highly contagious disease.* ◇ (*figurative*) *Her laugh is contagious.* ➲ note at **infectious**
▸ **contagion** /kənˈteɪdʒən/ ***noun*** [U]

contain ⊸ /kənˈteɪn/ ***verb*** [T] (not used in the continuous tenses) **1** to have sth inside or as part of itself: *Each box contains 24 tins.* **2** to keep sth within limits; to control sth: *efforts to contain inflation* ◇ *She found it hard to contain her anger.*

container ⊸ /kənˈteɪnə(r)/ ***noun*** [C] **1** a box, bottle, packet, etc. in which sth is kept: *a plastic container* **2** a large metal box that is used for transporting goods by sea, road or rail: *a container lorry/ship*

containment /kənˈteɪnmənt/ ***noun*** [U] (*formal*) **1** the act of keeping sth under control so that it cannot spread in a harmful way: *the containment of the epidemic* **2** (POLITICS) the act of keeping another country's power within limits so that it does not become too powerful: *a policy of containment*

contaminant /kənˈtæmɪnənt/ ***noun*** [C] any substance that makes sth dirty or not pure

contaminate /kənˈtæmɪneɪt/ ***verb*** [T] to add a substance which will make sth dirty or harmful: *The town's drinking water was contaminated with poisonous chemicals.* ▸ **contamination** /kənˌtæmɪˈneɪʃn/ ***noun*** [U]

contemplate /ˈkɒntəmpleɪt/ ***verb*** [T] **1** to think carefully about sth or the possibility of doing sth: *Before her illness she had never contemplated retiring.* **2** to look at sb/sth, often quietly or for a long time ▸ **contemplation** /ˌkɒntəmˈpleɪʃn/ ***noun*** [U]

contemporary[1] ⊸ AW /kənˈtemprəri/ ***adj.*** **1** belonging to the same time as sb/sth else: *The programme includes contemporary film footage of the First World War.* **2** of the present time; modern: *contemporary music/art/society*

contemporary[2] AW /kənˈtemprəri/ ***noun*** [C] (*pl.* **contemporaries**) a person who lives or does sth at the same time as sb else: *He was a contemporary of Freud and may have known him.*

contempt /kənˈtempt/ ***noun*** [U] **1** ~ **(for sb/sth)** the feeling that sb/sth does not deserve any respect or is without value: *The teacher treated my question* ***with contempt***. **2** (LAW) =CONTEMPT OF COURT: *She was held* ***in contempt*** *for refusing to testify.*
▸ **contemptuous** /kənˈtemptʃuəs/ ***adj.***: *The boy just gave a contemptuous laugh when I asked him to be quiet.*

contemptible /kənˈtemptəbl/ ***adj.*** (*formal*) not deserving any respect at all: *contemptible behaviour*

conˌtempt of ˈcourt (*also* **contempt**) ***noun*** [U] (LAW) the crime of refusing to obey an order made by a court; not showing respect for a court or judge: *Any person who disregards this order will be in contempt of court.*

contend /kənˈtend/ ***verb*** **1** [I] ~ **with/against sb/sth** to have to deal with a problem or a difficult situation: *She's had a lot of problems to contend with.* **2** [T] (*formal*) to say or argue that sth is true: *The young man contended that he was innocent.* **3** [I] ~ **(for sth)** to compete against sb to win or gain sth: *Two athletes are contending for first place.*

contender /kənˈtendə(r)/ ***noun*** [C] a person who may win a competition: *There are only two serious contenders for the leadership.*

content[1] /kənˈtent/ ***adj.*** (not before a noun) ~ **(with sth)**; ~ **to do sth** happy or satisfied with what you have or do: *I don't need a new car – I'm perfectly content with the one I've got.*

content[2] ⊸ /ˈkɒntent/ ***noun*** **1 contents** [pl.] the thing or things that are inside sth: *Add the contents of this packet to a pint of cold milk and mix well.* **2 contents** [pl.] the different sections that are contained in a book: *a table of contents* (=the list at the front of a book) **3** [sing.] (ARTS AND MEDIA) the main subject, ideas, etc. of a book, article, television programme, etc.: *The content of the essay is good, but there are too many grammatical mistakes.* **4** [sing.] the amount of a particular substance that sth contains: *Many processed foods have a high sugar content.*

content[3] /kənˈtent/ ***noun*** [sing.]
IDM **to your heart's content** → HEART

content[4] /kənˈtent/ ***verb*** [T] ~ **yourself with sth** to accept sth even though it was not exactly what you wanted: *The restaurant was closed, so we had to content ourselves with a sandwich.*

contented /kənˈtentɪd/ ***adj.*** happy or satisfied: *The baby gave a contented chuckle.* ▸ **contentedly** ***adv.***

contention /kənˈtenʃn/ ***noun*** (*formal*) **1** [U] arguing; disagreement **2** [C] your opinion; sth that you say is true: *The government's contention is that unemployment will start to fall next year.* ➲ note at **claim**[2]
IDM **in contention (for sth)** having a chance of winning a competition: *Four teams are still in contention for the cup.*

contentious /kənˈtenʃəs/ ***adj.*** likely to cause argument: *a contentious issue*

contentment /kənˈtentmənt/ ***noun*** [U] a feeling of happy satisfaction

contest[1] ⊸ /ˈkɒntest/ ***noun*** [C] a competition to find out who is the best, strongest, most beautiful, etc.: *I've decided to* ***enter*** *that writing* ***contest***. ◇ *The by-election will be a contest between the two main parties.*

contest[2] /kənˈtest/ ***verb*** [T] **1** to take part in a competition or try to win sth: *Twenty-four teams will contest next year's World Cup.* **2** to say that sth is wrong or that it was not done properly: *They contested the decision, saying that the judges had not been fair.*

contestant /kənˈtestənt/ ***noun*** [C] a person who takes part in a contest: *Four contestants appear on the quiz show each week.*

context ⊸ AW /ˈkɒntekst/ ***noun*** [C,U] **1** the situation in which sth happens or that caused sth to happen: *To* ***put*** *our company* ***in context***, *we are now the third largest in the country.* **2** (LANGUAGE) the words that come before or after a word, phrase or sentence that help you to understand its meaning: *You can often guess the meaning of a word from its* *context. ◇ Taken* ***out of context****, his comment made no sense.*

contextual AW /kən'tekstʃuəl/ ***adj.*** (*formal*) connected with a particular context: *contextual information ◇ contextual clues to the meaning*

contextualize (also -ise) AW /kən'tekstʃuəlaɪz/ ***verb*** [T] (*formal*) to consider sth in relation to the situation in which it happens or exists

continent 🔑 /'kɒntɪnənt/ ***noun*** (GEOGRAPHY) **1** [C] one of the seven main areas of land on the Earth: *Asia, Africa and Antarctica are continents.* **2 the Continent** [sing.] (*BrE*) the main part of Europe not including the British Isles

continental /ˌkɒntɪ'nentl/ ***adj.*** (GEOGRAPHY) **1** connected with or typical of a continent: *Moscow has a continental climate: hot summers and cold winters.* **2** (*BrE*) connected with the main part of Europe not including the British Isles: *continental holidays*

ˌcontinental 'breakfast ***noun*** [C] a light breakfast of bread and jam with coffee ➲ look at **English breakfast**

ˌcontinental 'drift ***noun*** [U] (GEOLOGY) the slow movement of the continents towards and away from each other during the history of the earth ➲ look at **plate tectonics**

ˌcontinental 'shelf ***noun*** [sing.] (GEOLOGY) the area of land under the sea on the edge of a continent

ˌcontinental 'slope ***noun*** [sing.] (GEOLOGY) the steep surface that goes down from the outer edge of the CONTINENTAL SHELF to the ocean floor

contingency /kən'tɪndʒənsi/ ***noun*** [C] (*pl.* **contingencies**) a possible future situation or event: *We'd better make* ***contingency plans*** *just in case something goes wrong. ◇ We've tried to prepare for every possible contingency.*

contingent /kən'tɪndʒənt/ ***noun*** [C, with sing. or pl. verb] **1** a group of people from the same country, organization, etc. who are attending an event: *the Irish contingent at the conference* **2** a group of armed forces forming part of a larger force

continual /kən'tɪnjuəl/ ***adj.*** happening again and again: *His continual phone calls started to annoy her.* ➲ look at **incessant** ▶ **continually** ***adv.***

continuation /kənˌtɪnju'eɪʃn/ ***noun*** [sing., U] something that continues or follows sth else; the act of making sth continue: *The team are hoping for a continuation of their recent good form. ◇ Continuation of the current system will be impossible.*

continue 🔑 /kən'tɪnjuː/ ***verb*** **1** [I] to keep happening or existing without stopping: *If the pain continues, see your doctor.* **2** [I,T] ~ **(doing/to do sth)**; ~ **(with sth)** to keep doing sth without stopping: *They ignored me and continued their conversation. ◇ He continued working/to work late into the night. ◇ Will you continue with the lessons after the exam?* **3** [I,T] to begin to do or say sth again after you had stopped: *The meeting will continue after lunch.* **4** [I,T] to go further in the same direction: *The next day we continued our journey.*

continued /kən'tɪnjuːd/ ***adj.*** going on without stopping: *There are reports of continued fighting near the border.*

continuity /ˌkɒntɪ'njuːəti/ ***noun*** [U] the fact of continuing without stopping or of staying the same: *The pupils will have the same teacher for two years to ensure continuity.*

continuo /kən'tɪnjuəʊ/ ***noun*** [U] (MUSIC) music that is played as a background to the main voice or instrument

continuous 🔑 /kən'tɪnjuəs/ ***adj.*** happening or existing without stopping: *There was a continuous line of cars stretching for miles.* ▶ **continuously** ***adv.***: *It has rained continuously here for three days.*

conˌtinuous as'sessment ***noun*** [U] (EDUCATION) a system of giving a student a final mark based on work done during a course of study rather than on one exam

the conˌtinuous 'tense (*also* **the proˌgressive 'tense**) ***noun*** [C] (LANGUAGE) the form of a verb such as '*I am waiting*', '*I was waiting*' or '*I have been waiting*' which is made from a part of '*be*' and a verb ending in '*-ing*' and is used to describe an action that continues for a period of time

continuum /kən'tɪnjuəm/ ***noun*** [C] (*pl.* **continua** /-juə/) a continuous series of things, in which each one is only slightly different from the things next to it, but the last is very different from the first

contort /kən'tɔːt/ ***verb*** [I,T] to move or to make sth move into a strange or unusual shape: *His face contorted/was contorted with pain.* ▶ **contortion** ***noun*** [C]

contour /'kɒntʊə(r)/ ***noun*** [C] **1** the shape of the outer surface of sth: *I could just make out the contours of the house in the dark.* **2** (*also* **'contour line**) (GEOGRAPHY) a line on a map joining places of equal height

contra- /'kɒntrə/ ***prefix*** (used in nouns, verbs and adjectives) against; opposite: *contradict* (=say the opposite)

contraband /'kɒntrəbænd/ ***noun*** [U] goods that are taken into or out of a country illegally: *contraband cigarettes*

contraception /ˌkɒntrə'sepʃn/ ***noun*** [U] (HEALTH) the ways of preventing a woman from becoming pregnant: *a reliable form of contraception* ➲ look at **birth control**, **family planning**

contraceptive /ˌkɒntrə'septɪv/ ***noun*** [C] (HEALTH) a drug or a device that prevents a woman from becoming pregnant ▶ **contraceptive** ***adj.***

contract[1] 🔑 AW /'kɒntrækt/ ***noun*** [C] (LAW) a written legal agreement: *They* ***signed a*** *three-year* ***contract with*** *a major record company. ◇ a temporary contract*

contract[2] 🔑 AW /kən'trækt/ ***verb*** **1** [I,T] to become or to make sth smaller or shorter: *Metals contract as they cool.* OPP **expand** **2** [T] (HEALTH) to get an illness or disease, especially a serious one: *to contract pneumonia* **3** [I,T] (LAW) to make a written legal agreement with sb to do sth: *His firm has been contracted to supply all the furniture for the new building.*

PHR V **contract sth out (to sb)** to arrange for work to be done by sb outside your own company

contraction /kən'trækʃn/ ***noun*** **1** [U] the process of becoming or of making sth become smaller or shorter: *the expansion and contraction of a muscle* **2** [C] (BIOLOGY) a strong movement of the muscles that happens to a woman as her baby is born **3** [C] (LANGUAGE) a shorter form of a word or words: *'Mustn't' is a contraction of 'must not'.*

contractor AW /kən'træktə(r)/ ***noun*** [C] a person or company that has a contract to do work or provide goods or services for another company

contractual /kən'træktʃuəl/ ***adj.*** (LAW) connected with the conditions of a legal written agreement; agreed in a contract

contradict AW /ˌkɒntrəˈdɪkt/ *verb* [T] to say that sth is wrong or not true; to say the opposite of sth: *These instructions seem to contradict previous ones.*

contradiction AW /ˌkɒntrəˈdɪkʃn/ *noun* [C,U] a statement, fact or action that is opposite to or different from another one: *There were a number of contradictions in what he told the police.* ◇ *This letter is **in complete contradiction to** their previous one.*

contradictory AW /ˌkɒntrəˈdɪktəri/ *adj.* being opposite to or not matching sth else: *Contradictory reports appeared in the newspapers.*

contraflow /ˈkɒntrəfləʊ/ *noun* [C] the system that is used when one half of a wide road is closed for repairs, and traffic going in both directions has to use the other side

contralto /kənˈtræltəʊ/ *noun* [C,U] (MUSIC) the lowest female singing voice; a woman with this voice

contraption /kənˈtræpʃn/ *noun* [C] a strange or complicated piece of equipment: *The first aeroplanes were dangerous contraptions.*

contrapuntal /ˌkɒntrəˈpʌntl/ *adj.* (MUSIC) having two or more tunes played together to form a whole ➲ noun **counterpoint**

contrary¹ AW /ˈkɒntrəri/ *adj.* **1** (only *before* a noun) completely different; opposite: *I thought it was possible, but she took the contrary view.* **2 contrary to** completely different from; opposite to; against: ***Contrary to popular belief*** (= to what many people think), *many cats dislike milk.*

contrary² /ˈkɒntrəri/ *noun*

IDM **on the contrary** the opposite is true; certainly not: *'You look as if you're not enjoying yourself.' 'On the contrary, I'm having a great time.'*

to the contrary (*formal*) saying the opposite: *Unless I hear anything to the contrary, I shall assume that the arrangements haven't changed.*

contrast¹ 🔑 AW /ˈkɒntrɑːst/ *noun* **1** [U] comparison between two people or things that shows the differences between them: ***In contrast to*** *previous years, we've had a very successful summer.* **2** [C,U] (a) ~ **(to/with sb/sth)**; (a) ~ **(between A and B)** a clear difference between two things or people that is seen when they are compared: *There is a tremendous contrast between the climate in the valley and the climate in the hills.* **3** [C] something that is clearly different from sth else when the two things are compared: *This house is quite a contrast to your old one!*

contrast² 🔑 AW /kənˈtrɑːst/ *verb* **1** [T] ~ **(A and/with B)** to compare people or things in order to show the differences between them: *The film contrasts his poor childhood with his later life as a millionaire.* **2** [I] ~ **with sb/sth** to be clearly different when compared: *This comment contrasts sharply with his previous remarks.*

contrasting 🔑 AW /kənˈtrɑːstɪŋ/ *adj.* very different in style, colour or attitude: *bright, contrasting colours* ◇ *The book explores contrasting views of the poet's early work.*

contravene /ˌkɒntrəˈviːn/ *verb* [T] (*formal*) (LAW) to break a law or a rule ► **contravention** /ˌkɒntrəˈvenʃn/ *noun* [C,U]

contribute 🔑 AW /ˈkɒntrɪbjuːt; kənˈtrɪbjuːt/ *verb* ~ **(sth) (to/towards sth) 1** [I,T] to give a part of the total, together with others: *Would you like to contribute towards our collection for famine relief?* ◇ *The research has contributed a great deal to our knowledge of cancer.* **2** [I] to be one of the causes of sth: *It is not known whether the bad weather contributed to the accident.* **3** [I,T] (ARTS AND MEDIA) to write articles for a magazine or newspaper

contribution 🔑 AW /ˌkɒntrɪˈbjuːʃn/ *noun* [C] a ~ **(to/toward sth)** something that you give, especially money or help, or do together with other people: *If we all **make a** small **contribution**, we'll be able to buy Ray a good present.*

contributor AW /kənˈtrɪbjətə(r)/ *noun* [C] a person who contributes to sth

contributory /kənˈtrɪbjətəri/ *adj.* helping to cause or produce sth: *Alcohol was a contributory factor in her death.*

contrive /kənˈtraɪv/ *verb* [T] **1** to manage to do sth, although there are difficulties: *If I can contrive to get off work early, I'll see you later.* **2** to plan or invent sth in a clever and/or dishonest way: *He contrived a scheme to cheat insurance companies.*

contrived /kənˈtraɪvd/ *adj.* hard to believe; not natural or realistic: *The ending of the film seemed rather contrived.*

control¹ 🔑 /kənˈtrəʊl/ *noun* **1** [U] ~ **(of/over sb/sth)** power and ability to make sb/sth do what you want: *Rebels managed to **take control** of the radio station.* ◇ *Some teachers find it difficult to **keep control** of their class.* ◇ *He **lost control** of the car and crashed.* ◇ *I was late because of circumstances **beyond my control**.* **2** [C,U] (a) ~ **(on/over sth)** a limit on sth; a way of keeping sb/sth within certain limits: *price controls* ◇ *The faults forced the company to review its **quality control** procedures.* ➲ note at **limit 3** [C] one of the parts of a machine that is used for operating it: *the controls of an aeroplane/a TV* ◇ *a control panel* **4** [sing.] the place from which sth is operated or where sth is checked: *We went through **passport control** and then got onto the plane.*

IDM **be in control (of sth)** to have the power or ability to deal with sth: *The police are again in control of the area following last night's violence.*

be/get out of control to be/become impossible to deal with: *The demonstration got out of control and fighting broke out.*

under control being dealt with successfully: *It took several hours to bring the fire under control.*

control² 🔑 /kənˈtrəʊl/ *verb* [T] (**controlling**; **controlled**) **1** to have power and ability to make sb/sth do what you want: *One family controls the company.* ◇ *Police struggled to control the crowd.* ◇ *I couldn't control myself any longer and burst out laughing.* **2** to keep sth within certain limits: *measures to control price rises* ► **controller** *noun* [C]: ***air traffic controllers***

con'trol freak *noun* [C] (*informal*) (used in a critical way) a person who always wants to be in control of their own and other people's lives, and to organize how things are done

con'trol tower *noun* [C] a building at an airport from which the movements of aircraft are controlled

controversial AW /ˌkɒntrəˈvɜːʃl/ *adj.* causing public discussion and disagreement: *a controversial issue/decision/plan*

controversy AW /ˈkɒntrəvɜːsi; kənˈtrɒvəsi/ *noun* [C,U] (*pl.* **controversies**) public discussion and disagreement about sth: *The plans for changing the city centre caused a great deal of controversy.*

conundrum /kəˈnʌndrəm/ *noun* [C] a confusing problem or question that is very difficult to solve

conurbation /ˌkɒnɜːˈbeɪʃn/ ***noun*** [C] (GEOGRAPHY) a very large area of houses and other buildings where towns have grown and joined together

convalesce /ˌkɒnvəˈles/ ***verb*** [I] (HEALTH) to rest and get better over a period of time after an illness ▶ **convalescence** /ˌkɒnvəˈlesns/ ***noun*** [sing., U] ▶ **convalescent** /ˌkɒnvəˈlesnt/ ***adj.***

convection currents

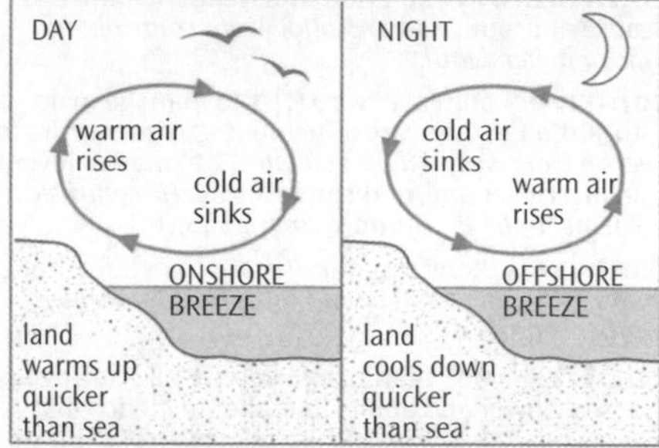

convection /kənˈvekʃn/ ***noun*** [U] (PHYSICS) the process in which heat moves through a gas or a liquid as the hotter part rises and the cooler, heavier part sinks: *convection currents*

convene AW /kənˈviːn/ ***verb*** [I,T] (*formal*) to come together or to bring people together for a meeting, etc.

convenience /kənˈviːniəns/ ***noun*** **1** [U] the quality of being easy, useful or suitable for sb: *a building designed* ***for the convenience of*** *disabled people* ◇ ***For convenience****, you can pay for everything at once.* **2** [C] something that makes things easier, quicker or more comfortable: *houses with all the modern conveniences* (= central heating, hot water, etc.) ➲ look at **public convenience**

conˈvenience food ***noun*** [C,U] food that you buy frozen or in a box or can, that you can prepare very quickly and easily

convenient 🔑 /kənˈviːniənt/ ***adj.*** **1** suitable or practical for a particular purpose; not causing difficulty: *I'm willing to meet you on any day that's convenient for you.* ◇ *It isn't convenient to talk at the moment, I'm in the middle of a meeting.* OPP **inconvenient** **2** close to sth; in a useful position: *Our house is convenient for the shops.* ▶ **conveniently** ***adv.***

convent /ˈkɒnvənt/ ***noun*** [C] (RELIGION) a place where NUNS (= members of a female religious community) live together ➲ look at **monastery**

convention 🔑 AW /kənˈvenʃn/ ***noun*** **1** [C,U] a traditional way of behaving or of doing sth: *A speech by the bride's father is one of the conventions of a wedding.* ◇ *The film shows no respect for convention.* **2** [C] a large meeting of the members of a profession, political party, etc.: *the Democratic Party Convention* SYN **conference** **3** [C] (LAW) a formal agreement, especially between different countries: *the Geneva Convention* ◇ *the United Nations convention on the rights of the child*

conventional 🔑 AW /kənˈvenʃənl/ ***adj.*** always behaving in a traditional or normal way: *conventional attitudes* ◇ *I quite like him but he's so conventional* (= boring, because of this). OPP **unconventional** ▶ **conventionally** /-ʃənəli/ ***adv.***

converge /kənˈvɜːdʒ/ ***verb*** [I] **1** ~ **(on...)** to move towards a place from different directions and meet: *Thousands of supporters converged on London for the rally.* **2** to move towards each other and meet at a point: *There was a signpost where the two paths converged.* ➲ picture at **short-sighted** ▶ **convergence** ***noun*** [U] ▶ **convergent** ***adj.*** ➲ picture at **plate tectonics**

conversant /kənˈvɜːsnt/ ***adj.*** (*formal*) ~ **with sth** knowing about sth; familiar with sth: *All employees should be conversant with basic accounting.*

conversation 🔑 /ˌkɒnvəˈseɪʃn/ ***noun*** [C,U] a talk between two or more people: *I* ***had a long conversation*** *with her about her plans for the future.* ◇ *His job is his only* ***topic of conversation****.*

IDM **deep in thought/conversation** → DEEP[1]

conversational /ˌkɒnvəˈseɪʃənl/ ***adj.*** **1** not formal; as used in conversation SYN **colloquial** **2** (only *before* a noun) connected with conversation ▶ **conversationally** /-nəli/ ***adv.***

converse[1] /kənˈvɜːs/ ***verb*** [I] (*formal*) to talk to sb; to have a conversation

converse[2] /ˈkɒnvɜːs/ ***noun*** [sing.] **the converse** (*formal*) the opposite or reverse of a fact or statement: *Building new roads increases traffic and the converse is equally true: reducing the number and size of roads means less traffic.* ▶ **converse** ***adj.***: *the converse effect*

conversely AW /ˈkɒnvɜːsli/ ***adv.*** (*formal*) in a way that is opposite to sth: *People who earn a lot of money have little time to spend it. Conversely, many people with limitless time do not have enough money to do what they want.*

conversion AW /kənˈvɜːʃn/ ***noun*** [C,U] (a) ~ **(from sth) (into/to sth)** **1** the act or process of changing from one form, system or use to another: *a conversion table for miles and kilometres* **2** (RELIGION) becoming a member of a different religion

convert[1] 🔑 AW /kənˈvɜːt/ ***verb*** [I,T] **1** ~ **(sth) (from sth) (into/to sth)** to change from one form, system or use to another: *a sofa that converts into a double bed* ◇ *How do you convert pounds into kilos?* **2** ~ **(sb) (from sth) (to sth)** (RELIGION) to change or to persuade sb to change to a different religion: *As a young man he converted to Islam.* ◇ *to convert people to Christianity*

convert[2] AW /ˈkɒnvɜːt/ ***noun*** [C] **a** ~ **(to sth)** (RELIGION) a person who has changed their religion

convertible[1] AW /kənˈvɜːtəbl/ ***adj.*** able to be changed into another form: *convertible currencies* (= those that can be exchanged for other currencies)

convertible[2] /kənˈvɜːtəbl/ ***noun*** [C] a car with a roof that can be folded down or taken off

convex /ˈkɒnveks/ ***adj.*** having a surface that curves towards the outside of sth, like an eye: *a convex lens* ➲ look at **concave** ➲ picture at **lens**

convey /kənˈveɪ/ ***verb*** [T] **1** ~ **sth (to sb)** to make ideas, thoughts, feelings, etc. known to sb: *The film conveys a lot of information but in an entertaining way.* ◇ *Please convey my sympathy to her at this sad time.* **2** (*formal*) to take sb/sth from one place to another, especially in a vehicle

conˈveyor belt ***noun*** [C] a moving belt that carries objects from one place to another, for example in a factory

convict[1] /kənˈvɪkt/ ***verb*** [T] ~ **sb (of sth)** (LAW) to say officially in a court of law that sb is guilty of a crime: *He was convicted of armed robbery and sent to prison.* OPP **acquit**

convict² /ˈkɒnvɪkt/ ***noun*** [C] (LAW) a person who has been found guilty of a crime and put in prison

conviction /kənˈvɪkʃn/ ***noun*** **1** [C,U] (LAW) the action of finding sb guilty of a crime in a court of law: *He has several* ***previous convictions for*** *burglary.* **2** [C] a very strong opinion or belief: *religious convictions* **3** [U] the feeling of being certain about what you are doing: *He played without conviction and lost easily.*

convince 🔑 AW /kənˈvɪns/ ***verb*** [T] **1 ~ sb (of sth/that...)** to succeed in making sb believe sth: *She convinced him of the need to go back.* ◇ *I couldn't convince her that I was right.* **2 ~ sb (to do sth)** to persuade sb to do sth: *The salesman convinced them to buy a new cooker.*

convinced AW /kənˈvɪnst/ ***adj.*** (not *before* a noun) completely sure about sth: *He's convinced of his ability to win.* ➲ note at **sure**

convincing AW /kənˈvɪnsɪŋ/ ***adj.*** **1** able to make sb believe sth: *Her explanation for her absence wasn't very convincing.* **2** (used about a victory) complete; clear: *a convincing win* ▶ **convincingly** ***adv.***

convivial /kənˈvɪviəl/ ***adj.*** (*formal*) happy and friendly in atmosphere or character ▶ **conviviality** /kənˌvɪviˈæləti/ ***noun*** [U]

convoy /ˈkɒnvɔɪ/ ***noun*** [C,U] a group of vehicles or ships travelling together: *a convoy of lorries* ◇ *warships travelling* ***in convoy***

convulse /kənˈvʌls/ ***verb*** [I,T] to make sudden violent movements that you cannot control; to cause sb to move in this way: *He was convulsed with pain.*

convulsion /kənˈvʌlʃn/ ***noun*** [C, usually pl.] (HEALTH) a sudden violent movement that you cannot control: *Children sometimes have convulsions when they are ill.*

convulsive /kənˈvʌlsɪv/ ***adj.*** (used about movements or actions) sudden and impossible to control

coo /kuː/ ***verb*** [I] **1** to make a soft low sound like a DOVE (= a type of bird) **2** to speak in a soft, gentle voice: *He went to the cot and cooed over the baby.*

cook¹ 🔑 /kʊk/ ***verb*** **1** [I,T] to prepare food for eating by heating it: *My mother taught me how to cook.* ◇ *The sauce should be cooked on a low heat for twenty minutes.* ◇ *He cooked us a meal.* **2** [I] (used about food) to be prepared for eating by being heated: *I could smell something cooking in the kitchen.*

RELATED VOCABULARY

Food can be cooked in various ways: by **boiling** in a saucepan of hot water; by **frying** in a frying pan with hot oil or fat; or by **grilling** under a grill, which heats the food from above. We can **toast** bread under a grill or in a toaster to make it crisp and brown. Cakes and bread are **baked** in the oven, but we use the word **roast** for cooking meat or potatoes in the oven.

PHR V **cook sth up** (*informal*) to invent sth that is not true: *She cooked up an excuse for not arriving on time.*

cook² 🔑 /kʊk/ ***noun*** [C] a person who cooks: *My sister is an excellent cook.*

cookbook /ˈkʊkbʊk/ (*BrE also* **ˈcookery book**) ***noun*** [C] a book that gives instructions on cooking and how to cook individual dishes

cooker 🔑 /ˈkʊkə(r)/ (*AmE* **range**, *BrE and AmE also* **stove**) ***noun*** [C] a large piece of kitchen equipment for cooking using gas or electricity. It consists of an oven, a flat top on which pans can be placed and often a GRILL (= a device which heats the food from above).

cookery /ˈkʊkəri/ ***noun*** [U] the skill or activity of preparing and cooking food: *Chinese/French/Italian cookery*

cookie 🔑 /ˈkʊki/ ***noun*** [C] **1** (*AmE*) = BISCUIT **2** (COMPUTING) a computer file with information in it that is sent to the central SERVER each time a particular person uses a NETWORK or the Internet

cooking 🔑 /ˈkʊkɪŋ/ ***noun*** [U] **1** the preparation of food for eating: *Cooking is one of her hobbies.* ◇ *I* ***do the cooking*** *in our house.* **2** food produced by cooking: *He missed his mother's cooking when he left home.*

ˈcooking gas ***noun*** [U] (*AmE*) = CALOR GAS

cool¹ 🔑 /kuːl/ ***adj.*** **1** fairly cold; not hot or warm: *It was a cool evening so I put on a pullover.* ◇ *What I'd like is a long cool drink.* ➲ note at **cold¹** **2** calm; not excited or angry: *She always manages to remain cool under pressure.* **3** unfriendly; not showing interest: *When we first met, she was rather cool towards me, but later she became friendlier.* **4** (*slang*) very good or fashionable: *Those are cool shoes you're wearing!*

cool² 🔑 /kuːl/ ***verb*** **1** [I,T] **~ (sth/sb) (down/off)** to lower the temperature of sth; to become cool: *Let the soup cool (down).* ◇ *After the game we needed to cool off.* ◇ *A nice cold drink will soon cool you down.* **2** [I] (used about feelings) to become less strong

PHR V **cool (sb) down/off** to become or make sb calmer

cool³ /kuːl/ ***noun*** [sing.] **the cool** a cool temperature or place; the quality of being cool: *We sat* ***in the cool*** *of a cafe, out of the sun.*

IDM **keep/lose your cool** (*informal*) to stay calm/to stop being calm and become angry, nervous, etc.

coolant /ˈkuːlənt/ ***noun*** [C,U] a liquid that is used for cooling an engine, a nuclear REACTOR, etc.

ˌcooling-ˈoff period ***noun*** [C] a period of time when sb can think again about a decision that they have made

coolly /ˈkuːlli/ ***adv.*** in a calm way; without showing much interest or excitement

coolness /ˈkuːlnəs/ ***noun*** [U] the quality or state of being cool: *the coolness of the water* ◇ *his coolness under stress* ◇ *their coolness towards strangers*

coop¹ /kuːp/ ***noun*** [C] a CAGE for chickens, etc.

coop² /kuːp/ ***verb***

PHR V **coop sb/sth up (in sth)** to keep sb/sth inside a small space: *The children were cooped up indoors all day because the weather was so bad.*

cooperate AW (*BrE also* **co-operate**) /kəʊˈɒpəreɪt/ ***verb*** [I] **~ (with sb/sth)** **1** to work with sb else to achieve sth: *Our company is cooperating with a Danish firm on this project.* **2** to be helpful by doing what sb asks you to do: *If everyone cooperates by following the instructions, there will be no problem.*

cooperation AW (*BrE also* **co-operation**) /kəʊˌɒpəˈreɪʃn/ ***noun*** [U] **1 ~ (with sb)** working together with sb else to achieve sth: *Schools are working in close cooperation with parents to improve standards.* **2** help that you give by doing what sb asks you to do: *The police asked the public for their cooperation in the investigation.*

cooperative¹ AW (*BrE also* **co-operative**) /kəʊˈɒpərətɪv/ ***adj.*** **1** (BUSINESS) owned and run by the people involved, with the profits shared by them: *a cooperative business venture ◇ a cooperative farm* **2** helpful; doing what sb asks you to do: *My firm were very cooperative and allowed me to have time off.* OPP **uncooperative**

cooperative² (*BrE also* **co-operative**) /kəʊˈɒpərətɪv/ ***noun*** [C] (BUSINESS) a business or organization that is owned and run by all of the people who work for it: *The factory is now a workers' cooperative.*

coordinate¹ AW (*BrE also* **co-ordinate**) /kəʊˈɔːdɪneɪt/ ***verb*** [T] to organize different things or people so that they work together: *It is her job to coordinate the various departments.*

coordinate² AW (*BrE* **co-ordinate**) /kəʊˈɔːdɪnət/ ***noun*** [C] (GEOGRAPHY) one of the two sets of numbers and/or letters that are used for finding the position of a point on a map

coordination AW (*BrE also* **co-ordination**) /kəʊˌɔːdɪˈneɪʃn/ ***noun*** [U] **1** the organization of different things or people so that they work together **2** the ability to control the movements of your body properly

coordinator AW (*BrE also* **co-ordinator**) /kəʊˈɔːdɪneɪtə(r)/ ***noun*** [C] a person who is responsible for organizing different things or people so that they work together

cop¹ /kɒp/ (*also* **copper**) ***noun*** [C] (*informal*) a police officer

cop² /kɒp/ ***verb*** (**copping**; **copped**) (*informal*)
PHR V **cop out (of sth)** (*informal*) to avoid sth that you should do, because you are afraid or lazy: *She was going to help me with the cooking but she copped out at the last minute.*

cope ⊶ /kəʊp/ ***verb*** [I] ~ **(with sb/sth)** to deal successfully with a difficult matter or situation: *She sometimes finds it difficult to cope with all the pressure at work.*

copier /ˈkɒpiə(r)/ (*especially AmE*) = PHOTOCOPIER

copious /ˈkəʊpiəs/ ***adj.*** in large amounts: *She made copious notes at the lecture.* SYN **plentiful** ▸ **copiously** ***adv.***

ˈ**cop-out** ***noun*** [C] (*informal*) a way of avoiding sth that you should do

copper /ˈkɒpə(r)/ ***noun*** **1** [U] (*symbol* **Cu**) (CHEMISTRY) a common reddish-brown metal: *water pipes made of copper* ❶ For more information on the periodic table of elements, look at pages R34-5. **2** [C] (*BrE*) a coin of low value made of brown metal: *I only had a few coppers left.* **3** [C] = COP¹

copra /ˈkɒprə/ ***noun*** [U] the dried white part of a COCONUT

copse /kɒps/ ***noun*** [C] a small area of trees or bushes

copulate /ˈkɒpjuleɪt/ ***verb*** [I] (BIOLOGY) to have sex ▸ **copulation** /ˌkɒpjuˈleɪʃn/ ***noun*** [U]

copy¹ ⊶ /ˈkɒpi/ ***noun*** [C] (*pl.* **copies**) **1** something that is made to look exactly like sth else: *I kept a copy of the letter I wrote. ◇ the **master copy*** (= the original piece of paper from which copies are made) ◇ *to **make a copy** of a computer file* ➲ look at **hard copy**, **photocopy** **2** one book, newspaper, record, etc. of which many have been printed or produced: *I managed to buy the last copy of the book left in the shop.*

copy² ⊶ /ˈkɒpi/ ***verb*** (*pres. part.* **copying**; *3rd person sing. pres.* **copies**; *pt, pp* **copied**) **1** [T] to make sth exactly the same as sth else: *The children copied pictures from a book. ◇ It is illegal to copy videos.* **2** [T] ~ **sth (down/out)** to write down sth exactly as it is written somewhere else: *I copied down the address on the brochure. ◇ I copied out the letter more neatly.* **3** [T] = PHOTOCOPY **4** [T] to do or try to do the same as sb else: *She copies everything her friends do.* SYN **imitate** **5** [I] ~ **(from sb)** to cheat in an exam or test by writing what sb else has written

copyright¹ /ˈkɒpiraɪt/ ***noun*** [C,U] (LAW) the legal right to be the only person who may print, copy, perform, etc. a piece of original work, such as a book, a song or a computer program ▸ **copyright** ***verb*** [T]

copyright² /ˈkɒpiraɪt/ ***adj.*** protected by COPYRIGHT; not allowed to be copied without permission: *copyright material*

copywriter /ˈkɒpiraɪtə(r)/ ***noun*** [C] a person whose job is to write the words for advertising material

coral /ˈkɒrəl/ ***noun*** [U] (BIOLOGY, GEOGRAPHY) a hard red, pink or white substance that forms in the sea from the bones of very small sea animals: ***a coral reef*** (= a line of rock in the sea formed by coral)

corbel /ˈkɔːbl/ ***noun*** [C] (ARCHITECTURE) a piece of stone or wood that sticks out from a wall to support sth, for example an ARCH

cord /kɔːd/ ***noun*** **1** [C,U] (a piece of) strong, thick string **2** [C,U] (*especially AmE*) (a piece of) wire covered with plastic ➲ picture at **cable** **3** **cords** [pl.] trousers made of a thick soft cotton cloth (**corduroy**) ➲ look at **vocal cords**

cordial /ˈkɔːdiəl/ ***adj.*** pleasant and friendly: *a cordial greeting/smile* ▸ **cordially** /-diəli/ ***adv.***

cordless /ˈkɔːdləs/ ***adj.*** (used about a telephone or an electrical tool) not connected to its power supply by wires: *a cordless phone/kettle/iron*

cordon¹ /ˈkɔːdn/ ***noun*** [C] a line or ring of police or soldiers that prevents people from entering an area

cordon² /ˈkɔːdn/ ***verb***
PHR V **cordon sth off** to stop people entering an area by surrounding it with a ring of police or soldiers: *The street where the bomb was discovered was quickly cordoned off.*

corduroy /ˈkɔːdərɔɪ/ ***noun*** [U] a thick soft cotton cloth with lines on it, used for making clothes: *a corduroy jacket*

core¹ ⊶ AW /kɔː(r)/ ***noun*** **1** [C] the hard central part of a fruit such as an apple, that contains the seeds **2** [C] the central part of an object: *the earth's core ◇ the core of a nuclear reactor* ➲ picture at **seismic** **3** [sing.] the central or most important part of sth: *Concern for the environment is **at the core** of our policies.*
IDM **to the core** completely; in every way: *The news shook him to the core* (= shocked him very much).

core² AW /kɔː(r)/ ***adj.*** **1** most important; main or essential: ***core subjects*** (= subjects that all the students have to study) *such as English and mathematics ◇ We need to concentrate on our **core business**.* **2** the most important or central beliefs, etc. of a person or group: *The party is losing touch with its **core values**.*

coriander /ˌkɒriˈændə(r)/ ***noun*** [U] a plant whose leaves and seeds are used in cooking to flavour food

Corinthian /kəˈrɪnθiən/ ***adj.*** (ARCHITECTURE) used to describe a style of ARCHITECTURE in ancient Greece that has thin columns with decorations of leaves at the top: ***Corinthian columns/capitals*** ➲ look at **Doric**, **Ionic** ➲ picture at **capital**

cork /kɔːk/ ***noun*** **1** [U] a light soft material which comes from the outside of a type of tree: *cork floor tiles* **2** [C] a round piece of **cork** that you push into the end of a bottle to close it, especially a bottle of wine

corkscrew /ˈkɔːkskruː/ ***noun*** [C] a tool that you use for pulling CORKS (2) out of bottles

corn /kɔːn/ ***noun*** **1** [U] (*especially BrE*) (**AGRICULTURE**) any plant that is grown for its grain, such as WHEAT; the seeds from these plants: *a field of corn* ◇ *a corn field* **2** [U] (*AmE*) (**AGRICULTURE**) = MAIZE ➲ picture at **cereal** **3** [U] (*AmE*) = SWEETCORN **4** [C] (**HEALTH**) a small, painful area of hard skin on the toe

cornea /ˈkɔːniə/ ***noun*** [C] (**ANATOMY**) the transparent part that covers and protects the outer part of your eye ➲ picture at **eye** ▶ **corneal** /ˈkɔːniəl/ ***adj.***

corner[1] 🔑 /ˈkɔːnə(r)/ ***noun*** [C] **1** a place where two lines, edges, surfaces or roads meet: *Put the lamp **in the corner** of the room* ◇ *Write your address in the top right-hand corner.* ◇ *The shop is **on the corner** of Wall Street and Long Road.* ◇ *He went **round the corner** at top speed.* **2** a quiet or secret place or area: *a remote corner of Scotland* **3** a difficult situation from which you cannot escape: *to get yourself into a corner* **4** (**SPORT**) (used in football) a free kick from the corner of the field

IDM **cut corners** to do sth quickly and not as well as you should

(just) round the corner very near: *There's a phone box just round the corner.*

corner[2] /ˈkɔːnə(r)/ ***verb*** [T] **1** to get a person or an animal into a position from which they/it cannot escape: *He cornered me at the party and started telling me all his problems.* **2** (**BUSINESS**) to get control in a particular area of business so that nobody else can have any success in it: *That company's really **cornered the market** in health foods.*

cornerstone /ˈkɔːnəstəʊn/ ***noun*** [C] **1** (**ARCHITECTURE**) a stone at the corner of the base of a building, often put there in a special ceremony **2** the most important part of sth that the rest depends on

cornflakes /ˈkɔːnfleɪks/ ***noun*** [pl.] food made of small pieces of dried CORN and eaten with milk for breakfast

cornflour /ˈkɔːnflaʊə(r)/ (*AmE* **cornstarch** /ˈkɔːnstɑːtʃ/) ***noun*** [U] very fine flour often used to make sauces, etc. thicker

cornice /ˈkɔːnɪs/ ***noun*** [C] (**ARCHITECTURE**) a decorative border around the top of the walls in a room or on the outside walls of a building

ˌcorn on the ˈcob ***noun*** [U] CORN that is cooked with all the yellow grains still on the inner part and eaten as a vegetable ➲ picture at **cereal**

cornucopia /ˌkɔːnjuˈkəʊpiə/ ***noun*** [C] **1** (**ART**) a decorative object shaped like an animal's horn, shown in art as full of fruit and flowers **2** (*formal*) something that is or contains a large supply of good things: *The book is a cornucopia of good ideas.*

corny /ˈkɔːni/ ***adj.*** (*informal*) too ordinary or familiar to be interesting or amusing: *a corny joke*

corollary /kəˈrɒləri/ ***noun*** [C] (*pl.* **corollaries**) a situation, a statement or a fact that is the natural and direct result of another one

corona /kəˈrəʊnə/ ***noun*** [C] (**ASTRONOMY**) a ring of light seen around the sun or moon, especially during an ECLIPSE

coronary[1] /ˈkɒrənri/ ***adj.*** (**HEALTH**) connected with the heart

coronary[2] /ˈkɒrənri/ ***noun*** [C] (*pl.* **coronaries**) (**HEALTH**) a type of heart attack

ˌcoronary ˈartery ***noun*** [C] (**ANATOMY**) either of the two ARTERIES that supply blood to the heart

coronation /ˌkɒrəˈneɪʃn/ ***noun*** [C] an official ceremony at which sb is made a king or queen

coroner /ˈkɒrənə(r)/ ***noun*** [C] (**LAW**) a person whose job is to find out the causes of death of people who have died in violent or unusual ways

Corp. ***abbr.*** (*AmE*) = CORPORATION: *West Coast Motor Corp.*

corporal /ˈkɔːpərəl/ ***noun*** [C] a person at a low level in the army or air force

ˌcorporal ˈpunishment ***noun*** [U] the punishment of people by hitting them, especially the punishment of children by parents or teachers ➲ look at **capital punishment**

corporate AW /ˈkɔːpərət/ ***adj.*** (**BUSINESS**) of or shared by all the members of a group or organization: *corporate responsibility* ◇ ***corporate identity*** (= the image of a company, that all its members share)

corporation AW /ˌkɔːpəˈreɪʃn/ ***noun*** [C, with sing. or pl. verb] **1** (**BUSINESS**) a large business company: *multinational corporations* ◇ *the British Broadcasting Corporation* **2** (*BrE*) (**POLITICS**) a group of people elected to govern a particular town or city

corps /kɔː(r)/ ***noun*** [C, with sing. or pl. verb] (*pl.* **corps** /kɔː(r)/) **1** a part of an army with special duties: *the medical corps* **2** a group of people involved in a special activity: *the diplomatic corps*

corpse /kɔːps/ ***noun*** [C] a dead body, especially of a person ➲ look at **carcass**

corpus /ˈkɔːpəs/ ***noun*** [C] (*pl.* **corpora** /ˈkɔːpərə/ or **corpuses** /-sɪz/) (**LANGUAGE**) a collection of written or spoken TEXTS

corpuscle /ˈkɔːpʌsl/ ***noun*** [C] (**ANATOMY**) any of the red or white cells found in blood: *red/white corpuscles*

correct[1] 🔑 /kəˈrekt/ ***adj.*** **1** with no mistakes; right or true: *Well done! All your answers were correct.* ◇ *Have you got the correct time, please?* ➲ note at **true** **2** (used about behaviour, manners, dress, etc.) suitable, proper or right: *What's the correct form of address for a vicar?* OPP **incorrect** ▶ **correctness** ***noun*** [U] ▶ **correctly** ***adv.***

correct[2] 🔑 /kəˈrekt/ ***verb*** [T] **1** to make a mistake, fault, etc. right or better: *to correct a spelling mistake* ◇ *to correct a test* (= mark the mistakes in it) **2** to tell sb what mistakes they are making or what faults they have: *He's always correcting me when I'm talking to people.* ▶ **correction** ***noun*** [C,U]: *Some parts of the report needed correction.*

corˈrection fluid ***noun*** [U] a white liquid that you use to cover mistakes that you make when you are writing or typing, and that you can write on top of ➲ look at **Tippex™**

corrective /kəˈrektɪv/ ***adj.*** intended to make sth right that is wrong: *to take corrective action*

correlate /ˈkɒrəleɪt/ ***verb*** [I,T] to have or to show a relationship or connection between two or more things ▶ **correlation** /ˌkɒrəˈleɪʃn/ ***noun*** [C,U]: *There is a correlation between a person's diet and height.*

correspond AW /ˌkɒrəˈspɒnd/ ***verb*** [I] **1** ~ **(to/with sth)** to be the same as or equal to sth; to match: *Does the name on the envelope correspond with the name inside the letter?* **2** (*formal*) ~ **(with sb)** to write letters to and receive them from sb: *They corresponded for a year before they met.*

correspondence AW /ˌkɒrəˈspɒndəns/ ***noun*** **1** [U] (*formal*) the act of writing letters; the letters themselves: *There hasn't been any correspondence between them for years.* **2** [C,U] a close connection or relationship between two or more things: *There is no correspondence between the two sets of figures.*

correˈspondence course *noun* [C] (EDUCATION) a course of study that you do at home, using books and exercises sent to you by post or by email

correspondent /ˌkɒrəˈspɒndənt/ ***noun*** [C] **1** (ARTS AND MEDIA) a person who provides news or writes articles for a newspaper, etc., especially from a foreign country: *our Middle East correspondent, Andy Jenkins* **2** a person who writes letters to sb

corresponding AW /ˌkɒrəˈspɒndɪŋ/ ***adj.*** (only *before* a noun) related or similar to sth: *Sales are up 10% compared with the corresponding period last year.* ▶ **correspondingly *adv.***

corresˈponding angles *noun* [C] (GEOMETRY) equal angles formed on the same side of a line that crosses two parallel lines ➲ look at **alternate angles** ➲ picture at **angle**

corridor /ˈkɒrɪdɔː(r)/ ***noun*** [C] a long narrow passage in a building or train, with doors that open into rooms, etc.

corrie /ˈkɒri/ (*also* **cirque**; **cwm**) ***noun*** [C] (GEOGRAPHY) a round area shaped like a bowl in the side of a mountain

corroborate /kəˈrɒbəreɪt/ ***verb*** [T] (*formal*) (LAW) to support a statement, idea, etc. by providing new evidence: *The witness corroborated Mr Patton's statement about the night of the murder.* ▶ **corroboration** /kəˌrɒbəˈreɪʃn/ ***noun*** [U]

corrode /kəˈrəʊd/ ***verb*** [I,T] (CHEMISTRY) (used about metals) to become weak or to be destroyed by chemical action; to cause a metal to do this: *Parts of the car were corroded by rust.* ▶ **corrosion** /kəˈrəʊʒn/ ***noun*** [U]

corrosive /kəˈrəʊsɪv/ ***adj.*** (CHEMISTRY) tending to destroy sth slowly by chemical action: *corrosive acid* ▶ **corrosive *noun*** [C]

corrugated /ˈkɒrəgeɪtɪd/ ***adj.*** (used about metal or cardboard) shaped into folds

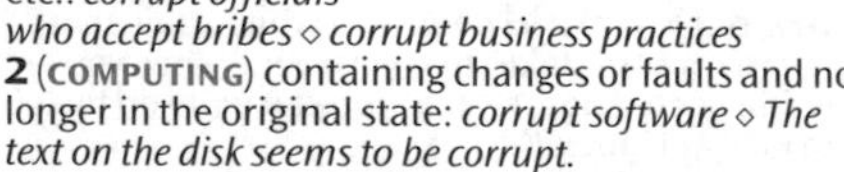

corrupt¹ /kəˈrʌpt/ ***adj.*** **1** doing or involving illegal or dishonest things in exchange for money, etc.: *corrupt officials who accept bribes* ◇ *corrupt business practices* **2** (COMPUTING) containing changes or faults and no longer in the original state: *corrupt software* ◇ *The text on the disk seems to be corrupt.*

corrupt² /kəˈrʌpt/ ***verb*** **1** [T] to cause sb/sth to start behaving in a dishonest or immoral way: *Too many people are corrupted by power.* **2** [I,T] (COMPUTING) to cause mistakes to appear in a computer file, etc. with the result that the information in it is no longer correct: *The program has somehow corrupted the system files.* ◇ *corrupted data* ◇ *The disk will corrupt if it is overloaded.*

corruption /kəˈrʌpʃn/ ***noun*** [U] **1** dishonest or immoral behaviour or activities: *There were accusations of corruption among senior police officers.* **2** the process of making sb/sth CORRUPT

corset /ˈkɔːsɪt/ ***noun*** [C] a piece of clothing that some women wear pulled tight around their middle to make them look thinner

cortex /ˈkɔːteks/ ***noun*** [C] (*pl.* **cortices** /ˈkɔːtɪsiːz/) (ANATOMY) the outer layer of an organ in the body, especially the brain: *the **cerebral cortex*** (= around the brain)

cortisol /ˈkɔːtɪsɒl/ ***noun*** [U] = HYDROCORTISONE

cortisone /ˈkɔːtɪzəʊn; -səʊn/ ***noun*** [U] (HEALTH) a HORMONE (= a natural substance produced by the body) that is used to reduce swelling caused by certain diseases and injuries

cosine /ˈkəʊsaɪn/ ***noun*** [C] (MATHEMATICS) (*abbr.* **cos**) the RATIO of the length of the side next to an ACUTE ANGLE (= one that is less than 90°) to the length of the HYPOTENUSE (= the longest side) in a RIGHT-ANGLED triangle ➲ look at **sine**, **tangent**

cosmetic¹ /kɒzˈmetɪk/ ***noun*** [C, usually pl.] a substance that you put on your face or hair to make yourself look more attractive ➲ look at **make-up**

cosmetic² /kɒzˈmetɪk/ ***adj.*** **1** used or done in order to make your face or body more attractive: *cosmetic products* ◇ ***cosmetic surgery*** **2** done in order to improve only the appearance of sth, without changing it in any other way: *changes in government policy which are purely cosmetic*

cosmic /ˈkɒzmɪk/ ***adj.*** (ASTRONOMY) connected with space or the universe

cosmology /kɒzˈmɒlədʒi/ ***noun*** [U] (ASTRONOMY) the scientific study of the universe and its origin and development ▶ **cosmological** /ˌkɒzməˈlɒdʒɪkl/ ***adj.*** ▶ **cosmologist** /kɒzˈmɒlədʒɪst/ ***noun*** [C]

cosmonaut /ˈkɒzmənɔːt/ ***noun*** [C] (ASTRONOMY) an ASTRONAUT (= a person who travels in space) from the former Soviet Union

cosmopolitan /ˌkɒzməˈpɒlɪtən/ ***adj.*** **1** containing people from all over the world: *a cosmopolitan city* **2** influenced by the culture of other countries: *a cosmopolitan and sophisticated young woman*

the cosmos /ˈkɒzmɒs/ ***noun*** [sing.] (ASTRONOMY) the universe

cost¹ ⊶ /kɒst/ ***noun*** **1** [C,U] the money that you have to pay for sth: *The cost of petrol has gone up again.* ◇ *The hospital was built **at a cost of** £10 million.* ◇ *The damage will have to be repaired regardless of cost.* ➲ note at **price** **2** [sing., U] what you have to give or lose in order to obtain sth else: *He achieved great success but only **at the cost of** a happy family life.* **3 costs** [pl.] (LAW) the amount of money that the losing side has to pay to the winning side in a court of law

IDM **at all costs/at any cost** using whatever means are necessary to achieve sth: *We must win at all costs.*

cover the cost (of sth) → COVER¹

to your cost in a way that is unpleasant or bad for you: *Life can be lonely at university, as I found out to my cost.*

cost² ⊶ /kɒst/ ***verb*** [T] (*pt, pp* **cost**) **1** to have the price of: *How much does a return ticket to London cost?* ◇ *We'll take the bus – it won't cost much.* ◇ (*informal*) *How much did your car cost you?* **2** to make you lose sth: *That one mistake cost him his job.*

IDM **cost the earth/a fortune** to be very expensive

ˈco-star *verb* (**co-starring**; **co-starred**) (ARTS AND MEDIA) **1** [I] (used about actors) to be one of two or more stars in a film, play, etc.: *a new movie in which Johnny Depp co-stars with Winona Ryder* **2** [T] (used about a film, play, etc.) to have two or more famous actors as its stars: *a new movie co-starring Johnny*

Depp and Winona Ryder ▸ **co-star** *noun* [C]: *His co-star was Marilyn Monroe.*

ˌcost-efˈfective *adj.* giving the best possible profit or results in comparison with the money that is spent: *This alarm system is the most cost-effective way of protecting your property.*

costly /ˈkɒstli/ *adj.* (**costlier**; **costliest**) **1** costing a lot of money; expensive: *a costly repair bill* **2** involving great loss of time, effort, etc.: *a costly mistake*

ˌcost ˈprice *noun* [U] (BUSINESS) the cost of producing sth or the price at which it is sold without profit ➲ look at **asking price**, **selling price**

costume /ˈkɒstjuːm/ *noun* **1** [C,U] a set or style of clothes worn by people in a particular country or in a particular historical period: *17th century costume* ◇ *Welsh* ***national costume*** **2** [C,U] clothes that an actor, etc. wears in order to look like sth else: *One of the children was dressed in a pirate's costume.* ◇ *The last rehearsal of the play will be done* ***in costume****.* **3** [C] (*BrE*) = SWIMSUIT

cosy /ˈkəʊzi/ *adj.* (**cosier**; **cosiest**) (*AmE* **cozy**) warm and comfortable: *The room looked cosy and inviting in the firelight.*

cot /kɒt/ (*AmE* **crib**) *noun* [C] **1** a bed with high sides for a baby **2** (*AmE*) = CAMP BED

cottage 🔑 /ˈkɒtɪdʒ/ *noun* [C] a small and usually old house, especially in the country

ˌcottage ˈcheese *noun* [U] a type of soft white cheese in small wet lumps

cotton 🔑 /ˈkɒtn/ *noun* [U] **1** a natural cloth or thread made from the thin white hairs of the cotton plant: *a cotton shirt* **2** (*AmE*) = COTTON WOOL

ˌcotton ˈwool (*AmE* **cotton**) *noun* [U] a soft mass of cotton, used for cleaning the skin, cuts, etc.

cotyledon /ˌkɒtɪˈliːdn/ *noun* [C] (BIOLOGY) a part inside a seed that looks like a small leaf, which the developing plant uses as a store of food. **Cotyledons** are the first parts of the seed to appear above the ground when it begins to grow.

couch[1] /kaʊtʃ/ *noun* [C] a long seat, often with a back and arms, for sitting or lying on: *They were sitting on the couch in the living room.*

couch[2] /kaʊtʃ/ *verb* [T] (usually passive) (*formal*) to express a thought, idea, etc. in the way mentioned: *His reply was couched in very polite terms.*

ˈcouch potato *noun* [C] (*informal*) a person who spends a lot of time sitting and watching television

cougar /ˈkuːɡə(r)/ (*AmE*) = PUMA

cough[1] 🔑 /kɒf/ *verb* **1** [I] to send air out of your throat and mouth with a sudden loud noise, especially when you have a cold, have sth in your throat, etc. **2** [T] ~ **(up) sth** to send sth out of your throat and mouth with a sudden loud noise: *When I started coughing (up) blood I called the doctor.*

PHR V **cough (sth) up** (*informal*) to give money when you do not want to: *Come on, cough up what you owe me!*

cough[2] 🔑 /kɒf/ *noun* [C] **1** an act or the sound of coughing: *He gave a nervous cough before he started to speak.* **2** (HEALTH) an illness or infection that makes you cough a lot: *Kevin's got a bad cough.*

could 🔑 /kəd; *strong form* kʊd/ *modal verb* (*negative* **could not**; *short form* **couldn't** /ˈkʊdnt/) **1** used for saying that sb had the ability or was allowed to do sth: *I could run three miles without stopping when I was younger.* ◇ *Elena said we could stay at her house.* **2** used for saying that sth may be or may have been possible: *I could do it now if you like.* ◇ *She could be famous one day.* ◇ *He could have gone to university but he didn't want to.* ◇ *You could have said you were going to be late!* (= I'm annoyed that you didn't) **3** used for asking permission politely: *Could I possibly borrow your car?* **4** used for asking sb politely to do sth for you: *Could you open the door? My hands are full.* **5** used for making a suggestion: *'What do you want to do tonight?' 'We could go to the cinema or we could just stay in.'* **6** used with the verbs 'feel', 'hear', 'see', 'smell', 'taste'

coulomb /ˈkuːlɒm/ *noun* [C] (*abbr.* **C**) (PHYSICS) a unit of electric charge, equal to the quantity of electricity carried in one second by one AMPERE (= one unit of current)

council 🔑 (*also* **Council**) /ˈkaʊnsl/ *noun* [C, with sing. or pl. verb] **1** (POLITICS) a group of people who are elected to govern an area such as a town or county: *The* ***city council*** *has/have decided to build a new road.* ◇ *a* ***council house*** (= one that a council owns and lets to people who do not have much money) ◇ *My dad's on the local council.* **2** a group of people chosen to give advice, manage affairs, etc. for a particular organization or activity: *the Arts Council*

councillor /ˈkaʊnsələ(r)/ *noun* [C] (POLITICS) a member of a council: *to elect new councillors*

counsel[1] /ˈkaʊnsl/ *verb* [T] (**counselling**; **counselled**: *AmE* **counseling**; **counseled**) **1** to give professional advice and help to sb with a problem **2** (*written*) to tell sb what you think they should do; to advise: *Mr Dean's lawyers counselled him against making public statements.*

counsel[2] /ˈkaʊnsl/ *noun* [U, C] **1** (*formal*) advice, especially given by older people or experts; a piece of advice **2** (LAW) a lawyer or group of lawyers representing sb in court: *the* ***counsel for the defence/ prosecution***

counselling (*AmE* **counseling**) /ˈkaʊnsəlɪŋ/ *noun* [U] professional advice and help given to people with problems: *Many students come to us for counselling.*

counsellor (*AmE* **counselor**) /ˈkaʊnsələ(r)/ *noun* [C] a person whose job is to give advice: *a marriage counsellor*

count[1] 🔑 /kaʊnt/ *verb* **1** [I] to say numbers one after another in order: *Close your eyes and count (up) to 20.* **2** [T] ~ **sth** to calculate the total number or amount of sth: *The teacher counted the children as they got on the bus.* **3** [T] to include sb/sth when you are calculating an amount or number: *There were thirty people on the bus, not counting the driver.* **4** [I] ~ **(for sth)** to be important or valuable: *I sometimes think my opinion counts for nothing at work.* **5** [I] ~ **(as sth)** to be valid or accepted: *The referee had already blown his whistle so the goal didn't count.* ◇ *Will my driving licence count as identification?* **6** [I,T] to consider sb/sth in a particular way: *You should count yourself lucky to have a good job.* ◇ *On this airline, children over 12 count/are counted as adults.*

IDM **Don't count your chickens (before they're hatched)** used to say that you should not be too confident that sth will be successful because sth might still go wrong

PHR V **count against sb** to be considered as a disadvantage: *Do you think my age will count against me?*

count on sb/sth to expect sth with confidence; to depend on sb/sth: *Can I count on you to help me?* ➲ note at **trust**[2]

count sb/sth out 1 to count things slowly, one by

one: *She carefully counted out the money into my hand.* **2** (*informal*) to not include sb/sth: *If you're going swimming, you can count me out!*

count[2] /kaʊnt/ ***noun*** [C] **1** [usually sing.] an act of counting or a number that you get after counting: ***On the count of** three, all lift together.* ◇ ***At the last count**, there were nearly 2 million unemployed.* **2** [usually pl.] a point that is made in a discussion, argument, etc.: *I proved her wrong* ***on all counts***.
IDM **keep/lose count (of sth)** to know/not know how many there are of sth: *I've lost count of the number of times he's told that joke!*

countable /ˈkaʊntəbl/ ***adj.*** (LANGUAGE) that can be counted: *'Chair' is a* ***countable noun***, *but 'sugar' isn't.* ◇ *Countable nouns are marked* [C] *in this dictionary.* OPP **uncountable**

countdown /ˈkaʊntdaʊn/ ***noun*** [C] the act of saying numbers backwards to zero just before sth important happens: *the countdown to the lift-off of a rocket* ◇ (*figurative*) *The countdown to this summer's Olympic Games has started.*

countenance /ˈkaʊntənəns/ ***noun*** [C] (*written*) a person's face or their expression

counter- /ˈkaʊntə(r)/ ***prefix*** (in nouns, verbs, adjectives and adverbs) against; opposite: *counter-terrorism* ◇ *a counter-argument* ◇ *counterproductive*

counter[1] 🔑 /ˈkaʊntə(r)/ ***noun*** [C] **1** a long, flat surface in a shop, bank, etc., where customers are served: *The man* ***behind the counter*** *in the bank was very helpful.* **2** a small object (usually round and made of plastic) that is used in some games to show where a player is on the board **3** an electronic device for counting sth: *The rev counter is next to the speedometer.* ➲ look at **Geiger counter**

counter[2] /ˈkaʊntə(r)/ ***verb*** **1** [I,T] to reply or react to criticism: *He countered our objections with a powerful defence of his plan.* **2** [T] to try to reduce or prevent the bad effects of sth: *The shop has installed security cameras to counter theft.*

counter[3] /ˈkaʊntə(r)/ ***adv.*** **~ to sth** in the opposite direction to sth: *The results of these experiments* ***run counter to*** *previous findings.*

counteract /ˌkaʊntərˈækt/ ***verb*** [T] to reduce the effect of sth by acting against it: *measures to counteract traffic congestion*

ˈcounter-attack ***noun*** [C] an attack made in reaction to an enemy or opponent's attack ▶ **counter-attack** ***verb*** [I,T]

counterclockwise /ˌkaʊntəˈklɒkwaɪz/ (*AmE*) = ANTICLOCKWISE

counterfeit /ˈkaʊntəfɪt/ ***adj.*** not genuine, but copied so that it looks like the real thing: *counterfeit money*

counterfoil /ˈkaʊntəfɔɪl/ ***noun*** [C] the part of a cheque, ticket, etc. that you keep when you give the other part to sb else

counterpart /ˈkaʊntəpɑːt/ ***noun*** [C] a person or thing that has a similar position or function in a different country or organization: *the French President and his Italian counterpart* (= the Italian President)

counterpoint /ˈkaʊntəpɔɪnt/ ***noun*** (MUSIC) **1** [U] the combination of two or more tunes to form a whole: *The two melodies are played in counterpoint.* ➲ adjective **contrapuntal**
2 [C] **a ~ (to sth)** a tune played in combination with another one

ˌcounterproˈductive ***adj.*** having the opposite effect to the one you want

countersign /ˈkaʊntəsaɪn/ ***verb*** [T] (LAW) to sign a document that has already been signed by another person, especially in order to show that it is valid

ˈcounter-tenor ***noun*** [C] (MUSIC) a man who is trained to sing with a very high voice

countless /ˈkaʊntləs/ ***adj.*** (only *before* a noun) very many: *I've tried to phone him countless times but he's not there.*

> **RELATED VOCABULARY**
>
> **Nation** is another word for country, or the people who live in a country: *The entire nation, it seemed, was watching TV.*
>
> **State** is used for talking about a country as an organized political community controlled by one government. It can also mean the government itself: *a politically independent state* ◇ *the member states of the EU* ◇ *You get a pension from the state when you retire.* ◇ *state education.*
>
> **Land** is more formal or literary: *Explorers who set out to discover new lands.*

country 🔑 /ˈkʌntri/ ***noun*** (*pl.* **countries**) **1** [C] (POLITICS, GEOGRAPHY) an area of land that has or used to have its own government and laws: *France, Spain and other European countries* ◇ *There was snow over much of the country during the night.* **2** [U] (GEOGRAPHY) an area of land, especially with particular physical features, suitable for a particular purpose or connected with a particular person or people: *We looked down over miles of open country.* ◇ *hilly country* **3 the country** [sing.] the people who live in a country: *a survey to find out what the country really thinks* **4 the country** [sing.] any area outside towns and cities, with fields, woods, farms, etc.: *Do you live in a town or* ***in the country***? **5** (MUSIC) = COUNTRY AND WESTERN

ˌcountry and ˈwestern ***noun*** [U] (MUSIC) a type of popular music based on traditional music from southern and western US

ˌcountry ˈhouse ***noun*** [C] a large house in the country, usually owned by an important family and often with a lot of land

countryman /ˈkʌntrimən/ **countrywoman** /ˈkʌntriwʊmən/ ***noun*** [C] (*pl.* **-men** /-mən/, **-women** /-wɪmɪn/) a person from your own country: *The Italian Castorri beat his* ***fellow countryman*** *Rossi in the final.*

countryside /ˈkʌntrisaɪd/ ***noun*** [U, sing.] land which is away from towns and cities, where there are fields, woods, etc.: *From the hill there is a magnificent view of the surrounding countryside.*

county 🔑 /ˈkaʊnti/ ***noun*** [C] (*pl.* **counties**) an area in Britain, Ireland or the US which has its own local government: *the county of Nottinghamshire* ◇ *Orange County, California* ➲ look at **province**, **state**[1] (5)

coup /kuː/ ***noun*** [C] **1** (*also* **coup d'état**) /ˌkuː deɪˈtɑː/ (POLITICS) a sudden, illegal and often violent change of government: *a coup to overthrow the President* ◇ ***an attempted coup*** (= one which did not succeed) **2** a clever and successful thing to do: *Getting that promotion was a real coup.*

couple[1] 🔑 AW /ˈkʌpl/ ***noun*** [C, with sing. or pl. verb] two people who are together because they are married or in a relationship: *a married couple* ◇ *Is/Are that couple over there part of our group?* ➲ look at **pair**
IDM **a couple of people/things 1** two people/

things: *I need a couple of glasses.* **2** a few: *I last saw her a couple of months ago.*

couple² AW /ˈkʌpl/ **verb** [T] (usually passive) to join or connect sb/sth to sb/sth else: *The fog, coupled with the amount of traffic on the roads, made driving very difficult.*

couplet /ˈkʌplət/ **noun** [C] (LITERATURE) two lines of poetry of equal length one after the other: *a poem written in rhyming couplets*

coupon /ˈkuːpɒn/ **noun** [C] **1** a small piece of paper which you can use to buy goods at a lower price, or which you can collect and then exchange for goods: *a coupon worth 10% off your next purchase* **2** a printed form in a newspaper or magazine which you use to order goods, enter a competition, etc.

courage 🔑 /ˈkʌrɪdʒ/ **noun** [U] the ability to control fear in a situation that may be dangerous or unpleasant: *It took real courage to go back into the burning building.* ◇ *She* ***showed*** *great* ***courage*** *all through her long illness.* SYN **bravery**
▶ **courageous** /kəˈreɪdʒəs/ **adj.**
IDM **pluck up courage** → PLUCK¹

courgette /kɔːˈʒet/ (*especially AmE* **zucchini**) **noun** [C] a long vegetable with dark green skin that is white inside

courier /ˈkʊriə(r)/ **noun** [C] **1** a person whose job is to carry letters, important papers, etc., especially when they are urgent: *The package was delivered by motorcycle courier.* **2** (*BrE*) (TOURISM) a person who is employed by a travel company to give advice and help to a group of tourists on holiday ▶ **courier verb** [T]: *Courier that letter — it needs to get there today* (=send it by courier).

course 🔑 /kɔːs/ **noun 1** [C] a ~ (in/on sth) (EDUCATION) a complete series of lessons or studies: *I've decided to* ***enrol on a*** *computer* ***course***. ◇ *I'm going to* ***take/do a course*** *in self-defence.* **2** [C,U] the route or direction that sth, especially an aircraft, ship or river, takes: *The hijackers forced the captain to* ***change course*** *and head for Cuba.* ◇ *to be* ***on/off course*** (=going in the right/wrong direction) ◇ (*figurative*) *I'm* ***on course*** (=making the right amount of progress) *to finish this work by the end of the week.* ◇ *The road follows the course of the river.* **3** (*also* **course of action**) [C] a way of dealing with a particular situation: *In that situation resignation was the only course open to him.* **4** [sing.] the development of sth over a period of time: *events that changed* ***the course of history*** ◇ ***In the normal course of events*** (=the way things normally happen) *such problems do not arise.* **5** [C] the first, second, third, etc. separate part of a meal: *a three-course lunch* ◇ *I had chicken for the* ***main course***. **6** [C] (SPORT) an area where the game of GOLF is played or where certain types of race take place: *a golf course* ◇ *a racecourse* **7** [C] a ~ (of sth) (HEALTH) a series of medical treatments: *The doctor put her on* ***a course of antibiotics***.
IDM **be on a collision course (with sb/sth)** → COLLISION
in the course of sth during sth: *He mentioned it in the course of conversation.*
in the course of time when enough time has passed; eventually
in due course → DUE¹
a matter of course → MATTER¹
of course naturally; certainly: *Of course, having children has changed their lives a lot.* ◇ *'Can I use your phone?' 'Of course (you can).'* ◇ *'You're not annoyed with me, are you?' 'Of course (I'm) not.'*

coursebook /ˈkɔːsbʊk/ **noun** [C] (EDUCATION) a book for studying from that is used regularly in class

coursework /ˈkɔːswɜːk/ **noun** [U] (EDUCATION) work that students do during a course of study, not in exams, that is included in their final mark: *Coursework accounts for 50% of the final marks.*

court¹ 🔑 /kɔːt/ **noun 1** [C,U] (LAW) a place where legal trials take place and crimes, etc. are judged: *A man has been charged and will* ***appear in court*** *tomorrow.* ◇ *Bill's company are refusing to pay him so he's decided to* ***take them to court***. ➲ look at **court of appeal** **2 the court** [sing.] (LAW) the people in a court, especially those taking part in the trial: *Please tell the court exactly what you saw.* **3** [C,U] (SPORT) an area where certain ball games are played: *a tennis/squash/badminton court* ➲ look at **pitch**

court² /kɔːt/ **verb** [T] **1** to try to gain sb's support by paying special attention to them: *Politicians from all parties will be courting voters this week.* **2** to do sth that might have a very bad effect: *Britain is* ***courting*** *ecological* ***disaster*** *if it continues to dump waste in the North Sea.*

courteous /ˈkɜːtiəs/ **adj.** polite and pleasant, showing respect for other people OPP **discourteous**
▶ **courteously adv.**

courtesy¹ /ˈkɜːtəsi/ **noun 1** [U] polite and pleasant behaviour that shows respect for other people: *She didn't even* ***have the courtesy*** *to say that she was sorry.* **2** [C] (*pl.* **courtesies**) (*formal*) a polite thing that you say or do when you meet people in formal situations: *The two presidents exchanged courtesies before their meeting.*
IDM **(by) courtesy of sb** (*formal*) with the permission or because of the kindness of sb: *These pictures are being shown by courtesy of BBC TV.*

courtesy² /ˈkɜːtəsi/ **adj.** provided free, at no cost to the person using it: *A* ***courtesy bus*** *operates between the hotel and the town centre.* ◇ *The dealer will provide you with a* ***courtesy car*** *while your vehicle is being repaired.*

ˌcourt ˈmartial noun [C] (LAW) a military court that deals with matters of military law; a trial that takes place in such a court: *His case will be heard by a court martial.* ▶ **court-martial verb** [T] (**court-martialling; court-martialled**: *AmE* **court-martialing; court-martialed**)

ˌcourt of apˈpeal noun (LAW) **1** [C] (*pl.* **courts of appeal**) a court that people can go to in order to try and change decisions that have been made by a lower court **2 Court of Appeal** [sing.] (*BrE*) the highest court in Britain (apart from the House of Lords), that can change decisions made by a lower court **3 Court of Appeals** [C] (*AmE*) one of the courts in the US that can change decisions made by a lower court

ˌcourt of ˈlaw = COURT¹ (1)

courtroom /ˈkɔːtruːm/ **noun** [C] (LAW) the place or room where a court of law meets

courtship /ˈkɔːtʃɪp/ **noun** [C,U] (*old-fashioned*) the relationship between a man and a woman before they get married

courtyard /ˈkɔːtjɑːd/ **noun** [C] an area of ground, without a roof, that has walls or buildings around it, for example in a castle or between houses or flats

couscous /ˈkuːskuːs/ **noun** [U] a type of North African food made from crushed WHEAT

cousin 🔑 /ˈkʌzn/ (*also* ˌ**first ˈcousin**) **noun** [C] the child of your aunt or uncle: *Paul and I are cousins.* ➲ look at **second cousin**

covalent /ˌkəʊˈveɪlənt/ ***adj.*** (CHEMISTRY) (used about a chemical BOND) (=the way atoms are joined together) sharing pair of ELECTRONS (=parts of an atom that have a negative electrical charge)

cove /kəʊv/ ***noun*** [C] (GEOGRAPHY) a small area of the coast where the land curves round so that it is protected from the wind, etc.: *a sandy cove*

covenant /ˈkʌvənənt/ ***noun*** [C] a promise to sb, or a legal agreement, especially one to pay a regular amount of money to sb/sth ▶ **covenant** ***verb*** [T]: *All profits are covenanted to local charities.*

cover[1] /ˈkʌvə(r)/ ***verb*** **1** [T] ~ **sb/sth (up/over) (with sth)** to put sth on or in front of sth to hide or protect it: *Could you cover the food and put it in the fridge?* ◇ *She couldn't look any more and covered her eyes.* ◇ *I covered the floor with newspaper before I started painting.* ◇ *(figurative) Paula laughed to cover (=hide) her embarrassment.* OPP **uncover** **2** [T] ~ **sb/sth in/with sth** to be on the surface of sth; to make sth do this: *A car went through the puddle and covered me with mud.* ◇ *Graffiti covered the walls.* ◇ *The eruption of the volcano covered the town in a layer of ash.* **3** [T] to fill or spread over a certain area: *The floods cover an area of about 15000 square kilometres.* **4** [T] to include or to deal with sth: *All the papers covered the election in depth.* ◇ *The course covered both British and European history.* **5** [T] to travel a certain distance: *We covered about 500 kilometres that day.* **6** [T] to be enough money for sth: *We'll give you some money to cover your expenses.* **7** [T] ~ **sb/sth against/for sth** to protect sb/sth by insurance: *The insurance policy covers us for any damage to our property.* **8** [I] ~ **(for sb)** to do sb's job while they are away from work: *Matt's phoned in sick so we'll have to find someone to cover (for him).*

IDM **cover the cost (of sth)** to have or make enough money to pay for sth

PHR V **cover sth up** to prevent people hearing about a mistake or sth bad: *The police have been accused of trying to cover up the facts of the case.*

cover up for sb to hide a person's mistakes or crimes in order to protect them

cover[2] /ˈkʌvə(r)/ ***noun*** **1** [C] something that is put on or over sth, especially in order to protect it: *a plastic cover for a computer* ◇ *a duvet cover* **2** [C] the outside part of a book or magazine: *I read the magazine* ***from cover to cover*** (=from beginning to end). **3** [U] ~ **(against sth)** insurance against sth, so that if sth bad happens you get money or help in return: *The policy* ***provides cover*** *against theft.* **4** [U] protection from the weather, damage, etc. SYN **shelter**: *When the storm started we had to* ***take cover*** *in a shop doorway.* ◇ *When the gunfire started everyone* ***ran for cover***. **5 the covers** [pl.] the sheets, etc. on a bed **6** [C,U] a ~ **(for sth)** something that hides what sb is really doing: *The whole company was just a cover for all kinds of criminal activities.* ◇ *police officers working* ***under cover*** **7** [U] doing sb's job for them while they are away from work: *Joanne's off next week so we'll have to arrange cover.*

IDM **under (the) cover of sth** hidden by sth: *They attacked* ***under cover of darkness.***

coverage /ˈkʌvərɪdʒ/ ***noun*** [U] **1** (ARTS AND MEDIA) the act or amount of reporting on an event in newspapers, on television, etc.: *TV coverage of the Olympic Games was excellent.* **2** the amount or quality of information included in a book, magazine, etc.: *The grammar section provides coverage of all the most problematic areas.*

coveralls /ˈkʌvərɔːlz/ (*AmE*) =OVERALL[2] (2)

covered /ˈkʌvəd/ ***adj.*** **1** ~ **in/with sth** having a layer or a large amount of sth on sb/sth: *She was covered in mud/sweat/dust.* ◇ *nuts covered with chocolate* **2** having a cover, especially a roof: *a covered shopping centre*

covering /ˈkʌvərɪŋ/ ***noun*** [C] something that covers the surface of sth: *There was a thick covering of dust over everything.*

ˌcovering ˈletter (*AmE* **ˈcover letter**) ***noun*** [C] a letter that you send with a package, etc. that gives more information about it

covert /ˈkʌvət/ ***adj.*** done secretly: *a covert police operation* ▶ **covertly** ***adv.***

ˈcover-up ***noun*** [C] an act of preventing sth bad or dishonest from becoming known: *Several newspapers claimed that there had been a government cover-up.*

covet /ˈkʌvət/ ***verb*** [T] (*formal*) to want to have sth very much (especially sth that belongs to sb else)

RELATED VOCABULARY

Cow is often used for both male and female animals.

The special word for a male is **bull**.

A male that cannot produce any young and which was used in past times for pulling heavy loads is an **ox**.

A young cow is a **calf**.

A number of cows together can be called **cattle**.

cow /kaʊ/ ***noun*** [C] **1** a large female animal that is kept on farms to produce milk: *to milk a cow* ◇ *a herd of cows* ➲ note at **meat** **2** the adult female of certain large animals, for example ELEPHANTS

coward /ˈkaʊəd/ ***noun*** [C] a person who has no courage and is afraid in dangerous or unpleasant situations ▶ **cowardly** ***adj.***

cowardice /ˈkaʊədɪs/ ***noun*** [U] a lack of courage; behaviour that shows that you are afraid

cowboy /ˈkaʊbɔɪ/ ***noun*** [C] **1** a man whose job is to look after cows (usually on a horse) in certain parts of the US **2** (*BrE, informal*) a person in business who is not honest or who does work badly

cower /ˈkaʊə(r)/ ***verb*** [I] to move back or into a low position because of fear: *The dog cowered under the table when the storm started.*

cowl /kaʊl/ ***noun*** [C] (RELIGION) a covering for the head that is worn especially by a MONK (=a man belonging to a religious group)

cowling /ˈkaʊlɪŋ/ ***noun*** [C] (TECHNICAL) a metal cover for an engine, especially on an aircraft ➲ picture at **plane**

ˈco-worker ***noun*** [C] a person that sb works with, doing the same kind of job SYN **colleague**

coy /kɔɪ/ ***adj.*** **1** pretending to be shy or innocent: *She lifted her head a little and gave him a coy smile.* **2** not wanting to give information about sth or to answer questions that tell people too much about you: *Don't be coy, tell me how much you earn.* ▶ **coyly** ***adv.***

cozy (*AmE*) =COSY

CPU /ˌsiː piː ˈjuː/ ***abbr.*** (COMPUTING) =CENTRAL PROCESSING UNIT

crab /kræb/ ***noun*** **1** [C] a sea animal with a flat shell and ten legs. The front two legs have PINCERS (=long curved points) on them. **Crabs** move sideways. **2** [U] the meat from a **crab** ➲ picture on **page 29**

crack¹ 🔑 /kræk/ ***verb*** **1** [I,T] to break or to make sth break so that a line appears on the surface, but without breaking into pieces: *Don't put boiling water into that glass – it'll crack.* ◇ *The stone cracked the window but didn't break it.* **2** [T] to break sth open: *Crack two eggs into a bowl.* **3** [I,T] to make a sudden loud, sharp sound; to cause sth to make this sound: *to crack a whip/your knuckles* **4** [T] to hit a part of your body against sth; to hit sb with sth: *She stood up and cracked her head on the cupboard door.* ◇ *She cracked the thief over the head with her umbrella.* **5** [I] to no longer be able to deal with pressure and so lose control: *He cracked under the strain of all his problems.* **6** [I] (used about sb's voice) to suddenly change in a way that is not controlled: *Her voice cracked as she spoke about her parents' death.* **7** [T] (*informal*) to solve a problem: *to crack a code* ◇ *The police have cracked an international drug-smuggling ring.* **8** [T] to tell or make a joke: *Stop **cracking jokes** and do some work!*

IDM **get cracking** (*BrE*, *informal*) to start doing sth immediately: *I have to finish this job today so I'd better get cracking.*

PHR V **crack down (on sb/sth)** (used about people in authority) to start dealing strictly with bad or illegal behaviour: *The police have started to crack down on drug dealers.*

crack up 1 (*informal*) (HEALTH) to be unable to deal with pressure and so lose control and become mentally ill: *He cracked up when his wife left him.* **2** (*slang*) to suddenly start laughing, especially when you should be serious

crack² 🔑 /kræk/ ***noun*** **1** [C] a line on the surface of sth where it has broken, but not into separate pieces: *a pane of glass with a crack in it* ◇ (*figurative*) *They had always seemed happy together, but then cracks began to appear in their relationship.* **2** [C] a narrow opening: *a crack in the curtains* **3** [C] a sudden loud, sharp sound: *There was a loud crack as the gun went off.* **4** [C] a hard hit on a part of the body: *Suddenly a golf ball gave him a nasty crack on the head.* **5** [C] (*informal*) an amusing, often critical, comment; a joke: *She **made a crack** about his bald head and he got angry.* **6** [U] (*also* ˌ**crack coˈcaine**) a dangerous and illegal drug that some people take for pleasure and cannot then stop taking: *a crack addict*

IDM **the crack of dawn** very early in the morning

have a crack (at sth/at doing sth) (*informal*) to try to do sth: *I'm not sure how to play but I'll have a crack at it.*

crack³ /kræk/ ***adj.*** (used about soldiers or sports players) very well trained and skilful: ***crack troops*** ◇ *He's **a crack shot*** (=very accurate at shooting) *with a rifle.*

crackdown /ˈkrækdaʊn/ ***noun*** [C] action to stop bad or illegal behaviour: *Fifty people have been arrested in a police crackdown on street crime.*

cracker /ˈkrækə(r)/ ***noun*** [C] **1** a thin dry biscuit that is often eaten with cheese **2** (*also* **Christmas cracker**) a cardboard tube covered in coloured paper and containing a small present. **Crackers** are pulled apart by two people, each holding one end, at Christmas parties. They make a loud noise as they break. **3** (*BrE*, *informal*) a very good example of sth: *That story he told was a real cracker.*

crackle /ˈkrækl/ ***verb*** [I] to make a series of short, sharp sounds: *The radio started to crackle and then it stopped working.* ► **crackle** ***noun*** [sing.]: *the crackle of dry wood burning*

cradle¹ /ˈkreɪdl/ ***noun*** [C] a small bed for a baby. **Cradles** can often be moved from side to side.

cradle² /ˈkreɪdl/ ***verb*** [T] to hold sb/sth carefully and gently in your arms

craft 🔑 /krɑːft/ ***noun*** **1** [C,U] a job or activity for which you need skill with your hands: *an **arts and crafts** exhibition* ◇ *I studied **craft and design** at school.* ➲ look at **handicraft** **2** [C] any job or activity for which you need skill: *He regards acting as a craft.* **3** [C] (*pl.* **craft**) a boat, aircraft or SPACECRAFT

craftsman /ˈkrɑːftsmən/ ***noun*** [C] (*pl.* **-men** /-mən/) a person who makes things skilfully, especially with their hands SYN **artisan**

craftsmanship /ˈkrɑːftsmənʃɪp/ ***noun*** [U] the skill used by sb to make sth of high quality with their hands

crafty /ˈkrɑːfti/ ***adj.*** clever at getting or achieving things by using unfair or dishonest methods ► **craftily** ***adv.***

crag /kræg/ ***noun*** [C] (GEOGRAPHY) a steep, rough rock on a hill or mountain

craggy /krægi/ ***adj.*** **1** (GEOGRAPHY) having a lot of steep rough rock **2** (used about a man's face) strong and with deep lines, especially in an attractive way

cram /kræm/ ***verb*** (**cramming**; **crammed**) **1** ~ **(sth) into/onto sth**; ~ **(sth) in** [T,I] to push people or things into a small space; to move into a small space with the result that it is full: *I managed to cram all my clothes into the bag but I couldn't close it.* ◇ (*figurative*) *We only spent two days in Rome but we managed to cram a lot of sightseeing in.* ◇ *He only had a small car but they all managed to cram in.* **2** [I] ~ **(for sth)** (*old-fashioned*) (EDUCATION) to study very hard and learn a lot in a short time before an exam SYN **swot**

crammed /kræmd/ ***adj.*** very or too full: *That book is crammed with useful information.*

cramp /kræmp/ ***noun*** [U] (HEALTH) a sudden pain that you get in a muscle, that makes it difficult to move

cramped /kræmpt/ ***adj.*** not having enough space: *The flat was terribly cramped with so many of us living there.*

cranberry /ˈkrænbəri/ ***noun*** [C] (*pl.* **cranberries**) a small red BERRY with a sour taste, that can be made into sauce or juice

crane¹ /kreɪn/ ***noun*** [C] a large machine with a long metal arm that is used for moving or lifting heavy objects

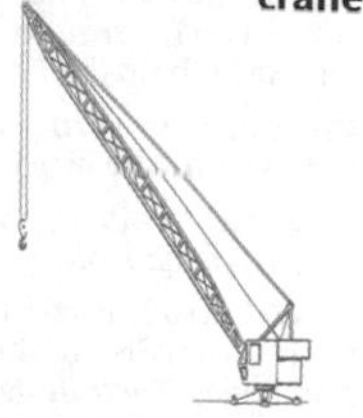
crane

crane² /kreɪn/ ***verb*** [I,T] to stretch your neck forward in order to see or hear sth: *We all craned forward to get a better view.*

ˈ**crane fly** ***noun*** [C] a small flying insect with very long legs

cranium /ˈkreɪniəm/ ***noun*** [C] (*formal*) (*pl.* **craniums** or **crania** /-niə/) (ANATOMY) the bone inside your head SYN **skull** ➲ picture at **brain** ► **cranial** ***adj.***

crank /kræŋk/ ***noun*** [C] **1** a person with strange ideas or who behaves in a strange way **2** a bar and handle in the shape of an L that you pull or turn to produce movement in a machine, etc.

crankshaft /ˈkræŋkʃɑːft/ *noun* [C] (TECHNICAL) a long straight piece of metal in a vehicle that connects the engine to the wheels and helps turn the engine's power into movement

cranny /ˈkræni/ *noun* [C] (*pl.* **crannies**) a small opening in a wall, rock, etc.
IDM **every nook and cranny** → NOOK

crash¹ /kræʃ/ *verb* **1** [I,T] to have an accident in a vehicle; to drive a vehicle into sth: *He braked too late and crashed into the car in front.* **2** [I] to hit sth hard, making a loud noise: *The tree crashed to the ground.* **3** [I] to make a loud noise: *I could hear thunder crashing outside.* **4** [I] (BUSINESS) (used about money or business) to suddenly lose value or fail **5** [I] (COMPUTING) (used about a computer) to suddenly stop working: *We lost the data when the computer crashed.*

crash² /kræʃ/ *noun* [C] **1** a sudden loud noise made by sth breaking, hitting sth, etc.: *I heard a crash and ran outside.* **2** an accident when a car or other vehicle hits sth and is damaged: *a car/plane crash* **3** (used about money or business) a sudden fall in the value or price of sth: *the Stock Market crash of 1987* **4** a sudden failure of a machine, especially a computer

crash³ /kræʃ/ *adj.* done in a very short period of time: *She did a **crash course** in Spanish before going to work in Madrid.*

ˈcrash barrier *noun* [C] a fence that keeps people or vehicles apart, for example when there are large crowds or between the two sides of the road

ˈcrash helmet *noun* [C] a hard hat worn by motorbike riders, racing drivers, etc.

ˌcrash-ˈland *verb* [I] to land a plane in a dangerous way in an emergency ▶ **crash-landing** *noun* [C]: *to make a crash-landing*

crass /kræs/ *adj.* stupid, showing that you do not understand sth: *It was a crass comment to make when he knew how upset she was.*

crate /kreɪt/ *noun* [C] a large box in which goods are carried or stored

crater /ˈkreɪtə(r)/ *noun* [C] **1** (GEOLOGY) the hole in the top of a VOLCANO ➲ picture at **volcano** **2** a large hole in the ground caused by the explosion of a bomb or by sth large hitting it: *The bomb left a large crater.* ◇ *a meteorite crater* ◇ *craters on the moon*

cravat /krəˈvæt/ *noun* [C] a wide piece of cloth that some men tie around their neck and wear inside the COLLAR of their shirt

crave /kreɪv/ *verb* [I,T] ~ **(for) sth** to want and need to have sth very much

craving /ˈkreɪvɪŋ/ *noun* [C] a strong desire for sth: *a craving for chocolate*

crawl¹ /krɔːl/ *verb* [I] **1** to move slowly with your body on or close to the ground, or on your hands and knees: *Their baby has just started to crawl.* ◇ *An insect crawled across the floor.* **2** (used about vehicles) to move very slowly: *The traffic crawls through the centre of town in the rush-hour.* **3** (*informal*) ~ **(to sb)** to be very polite or pleasant to sb in order to be liked or to gain sth
IDM **be crawling with sth** to be completely full of or covered with unpleasant animals: *The kitchen was crawling with insects.* ◇ (*figurative*): *The village is always crawling with tourists at this time of year.*

crawl² /krɔːl/ *noun* **1** [sing.] a very slow speed: *The traffic slowed to a crawl.* **2** (often **the crawl**) [sing., U] (SPORT) a style of swimming which you do on your front. When you do **the crawl**, you move first one arm and then the other over your head, turn your face to one side so that you can breathe and kick up and down with your legs. ➲ picture at **swim**

crayfish /ˈkreɪfɪʃ/ (*AmE also* **crawfish** /ˈkrɔːfɪʃ/) *noun* [C,U] (*pl.* **crayfish**; **crawfish**) a SHELLFISH that lives in rivers, lakes or the sea and can be eaten. A **crayfish** is similar to, but smaller than a LOBSTER.

crayon /ˈkreɪən/ *noun* [C,U] a soft, thick, coloured pencil that is used for drawing or writing, especially by children ▶ **crayon** *verb* [I,T]

craze /kreɪz/ *noun* [C] **a ~ (for sth)** **1** a strong interest in sth, that usually only lasts for a short time: *There was a craze for that kind of music last year.* **2** something that a lot of people are very interested in: *Pocket TVs are the latest craze among teenagers.*

crazy /ˈkreɪzi/ *adj.* (**crazier**; **craziest**) (*informal*) **1** (*especially AmE*) not sensible; stupid: *You must be crazy to turn down such a wonderful offer.* **2** very angry: *She **goes crazy** when people criticize her.* ◇ *That noise is **driving me crazy**.* **3** very enthusiastic or excited about sth: *The fans **went crazy** when their team scored the first goal.* ◇ *He's football-crazy.* **4** ~ **about sb/sth** liking sb very much; in love with sb: *I've been crazy about him since the first time I saw him.* **5** (*especially AmE*) mentally ill: *She's crazy — she ought to be locked up.* ▶ **crazily** *adv.* ▶ **craziness** *noun* [U]

creak /kriːk/ *verb* [I] to make the noise of wood bending or of sth not moving smoothly: *The floorboards creaked when I walked across the room.* ▶ **creak** *noun* [C] ▶ **creaky** *adj.*: *creaky stairs*

cream¹ /kriːm/ *noun* **1** [U] the thick yellowish-white liquid that rises to the top of milk: *coffee with cream* ◇ *whipped cream* (= cream that has been beaten) **2** [C,U] a substance that you rub into your skin to keep it soft or as a medical treatment: *(an) antiseptic cream* ➲ picture at **health** **3 the cream** [sing.] the best part of sth or the best people in a group

cream² /kriːm/ *adj.*, *noun* [U] (of) a yellowish-white colour

cream³ /kriːm/ *verb*
PHRV **cream sb/sth off** to take away the best people or part from sth for a particular purpose: *The big clubs cream off the country's best young players.*

creamy /ˈkriːmi/ *adj.* (**creamier**; **creamiest**) **1** containing cream; thick and smooth like cream: *a creamy sauce* **2** having a light colour like cream: *creamy skin*

crease¹ /kriːs/ *noun* [C] **1** an untidy line on paper, material, a piece of clothing, etc. that should not be there: *Your shirt needs ironing, it's full of creases.* ◇ *When I unrolled the poster, there was a crease in it.* **2** a tidy straight line that you make in sth, for example when you fold it: *He had a sharp crease in his trousers.*

crease² /kriːs/ *verb* [I,T] to get CREASES; to make sth get CREASES: *Hang up your jacket or it will crease.*

create AW /kriˈeɪt/ *verb* [T] to cause sth new to happen or exist: *a plan to create new jobs in the area* ◇ *He created a bad impression at the interview.* ➲ note at **make¹**

creation AW /kriˈeɪʃn/ *noun* **1** [U] the act of causing sth new to happen or exist: *the creation of new independent states* ➲ look at **job creation** **2** (usually **the Creation**) [sing.] (RELIGION) the act of making the whole universe, as described in the Bible **3** [C] something new that sb has made or produced

creative AW /kri'eɪtɪv/ ***adj.*** **1** using skill or imagination to make or do new things: *She's a fantastic designer – she's so creative.* **2** connected with producing new things: *His creative life went on until he was well over 80.* ▶ **creatively** ***adv.***

creativity AW /ˌkri:eɪ'tɪvəti/ ***noun*** [U] the ability to make or produce new things using skill or imagination: *We want teaching that encourages children's creativity.*

creator AW /kri'eɪtə(r)/ ***noun*** [C] a person who makes or produces sth new

creature ⊶ /'kri:tʃə(r)/ ***noun*** [C] a living thing such as an animal, a bird, a fish or an insect, but not a plant: *sea creatures*

crèche /kreʃ/ ***noun*** [C] a place where small children are looked after while their parents are working, shopping, etc.

credentials /krə'denʃlz/ ***noun*** [pl.] **1** the qualities, experience, etc. that make sb suitable for sth: *He has the perfect credentials for the job.* **2** a document that is proof that you have the training, education, etc. necessary to do sth, or proof that you are who you say you are

credibility /ˌkredə'bɪləti/ ***noun*** [U] the quality that sb has that makes people believe or trust them: *The Prime Minister had lost all credibility and had to resign.*

credible /'kredəbl/ ***adj.*** **1** that you can believe: *It's hardly credible that such a thing could happen without him knowing it.* OPP **incredible** **2** that seems possible: *We need to think of a credible alternative to nuclear energy.*

credit[1] ⊶ AW /'kredɪt/ ***noun*** **1** [U] (FINANCE) a way of buying goods or services and not paying for them until later: *I bought the television **on credit**.* **2** [C,U] (FINANCE) a sum of money that a bank, etc. lends to sb: *The company was not able to get any further credit and went bankrupt.* **3** [U] (FINANCE) having money in an account at a bank: *No bank charges are made if your account remains **in credit**.* **4** [C] (FINANCE) a payment made into an account at a bank: *There have been several **credits to** her account over the last month.* OPP **debit**[1] **5** [U] an act of saying that sb has done sth well: *He **got all the credit** for the success of the project.* ◇ *I can't **take** any **credit**; the others did all the work.* ◇ *She didn't do very well but at least **give** her **credit for** trying.* **6** [sing.] **a ~ to sb/sth** a person or thing that you should be proud of: *She is a credit to her school.* **7 the credits** [pl.] (ARTS AND MEDIA) the list of the names of the people who made a film or television programme, shown at the beginning or end of the film **8** [C] (*AmE*) (EDUCATION) a part of a course at a college or university, that a student has completed successfully

IDM **do sb credit** (used about sb's qualities or achievements) to be so good that people should be proud of them: *His courage and optimism do him credit.*

(be) to sb's credit used for showing that you approve of sth that sb has done, although you have criticized them for sth else: *The company, to its credit, apologized and refunded my money.*

have sth to your credit to have finished sth that is successful: *He has three best-selling novels to his credit.*

credit[2] AW /'kredɪt/ ***verb*** [T] **1** (FINANCE) to add money to a bank account: *Has the cheque been **credited to** my account yet?* **2 ~ sb/sth with sth; ~ sth to sb/sth** to believe or say that sb/sth has a particular quality or has done something well: *Of course I wouldn't do such a stupid thing – credit me with a bit more sense than that!* **3** (especially in negative sentences and questions) to believe sth: *I simply cannot credit that he has made the same mistake again!*

creditable /'kredɪtəbl/ ***adj.*** of a quite good standard that cannot be criticized, though not excellent

'credit card ***noun*** [C] (FINANCE) a small plastic card that allows sb to get goods or services without using money. You usually receive a bill once a month for what you have bought: *Can I pay by credit card?* ➲ look at **cash card**, **cheque card**, **debit card**

'credit note ***noun*** [C] a letter that a shop gives you when you have returned sth and that allows you to have goods of the same value in exchange

creditor AW /'kredɪtə(r)/ ***noun*** [C] (FINANCE) a person or company from whom you have borrowed money

'credit rating ***noun*** [C] (FINANCE) a judgement made by a bank, etc. about how likely sb is to pay back money that they borrow, and how safe it is to lend money to them

creed /kri:d/ ***noun*** [C] (RELIGION) a set of beliefs or principles (especially religious ones) that strongly influence sb's life

creek /kri:k/ ***noun*** [C] (GEOGRAPHY) **1** (*BrE*) a narrow piece of water where the sea flows into the land **2** (*AmE*) a small river; a stream

creep[1] /kri:p/ ***verb*** [I] (*pt, pp* **crept** /krept/) **1** to move very quietly and carefully so that nobody will notice you: *She crept into the room so as not to wake him up.* **2** to move forward slowly: *The traffic was only creeping along.*

IDM **make your flesh creep** → FLESH

PHR V **creep in** to begin to appear: *All sorts of changes are beginning to creep into the education system.*

creep[2] /kri:p/ ***noun*** [C] (*informal*) a person that you do not like because they try too hard to be liked by people in authority

IDM **give sb the creeps** (*informal*) to make sb feel frightened or nervous

creeper /'kri:pə(r)/ ***noun*** [C] a plant that grows up trees or walls or along the ground

creepy /'kri:pi/ ***adj.*** (*informal*) that makes you feel nervous or frightened

cremate /krə'meɪt/ ***verb*** [T] to burn the body of a dead person as part of a funeral service ▶ **cremation** /krə'meɪʃn/ ***noun*** [C,U]

crematorium /ˌkremə'tɔ:riəm/ ***noun*** [C] (*pl.* **crematoria** /-'tɔ:riə/ or **crematoriums**) a building in which the bodies of dead people are burned

creosote /'kri:əsəʊt/ ***noun*** [U] a thick brown liquid that is painted onto wood to protect it from rain, etc. ▶ **creosote** ***verb*** [T]

crêpe (also **crepe**) /'kreɪp/ ***noun*** **1** [U] a light thin material, made especially from cotton or another natural material (**silk**), with a surface that is covered in lines as if it has been folded: *a crêpe bandage* **2** [U] a type of strong rubber with a rough surface, used for making the bottoms of shoes: *crêpe-soled shoes* **3** [C] a very thin type of round cake (**pancake**)

crept past tense, past participle of **creep**[1]

crescendo /krə'ʃendəʊ/ ***noun*** [C,U] (*pl.* **crescendos**) (MUSIC) a noise or piece of music that gets louder and louder OPP **diminuendo**

crescent /'kresnt/ ***noun*** [C] **1** a curved shape that is pointed at both ends, like the moon in its first and last stages ➲ picture at **moon** **2** (often used in street names) a curved street with a row of houses on it

cress /kres/ ***noun*** [U] a small plant with very small green leaves that does not need to be cooked and is eaten in salads and SANDWICHES

crest /krest/ ***noun*** [C] **1** a group of feathers on the top of a bird's head ➲ picture on **page 28** **2** (**HISTORY**) a design used as the symbol of a particular family, organization, etc., especially one that has a long history: *the family/school crest* **3** the top part of a hill or wave: *surfers riding the crest of the wave* ➲ picture at **wave**

crestfallen /ˈkrestfɔːlən/ ***adj.*** sad or disappointed

crevasse /krəˈvæs/ ***noun*** [C] (**GEOGRAPHY**) a deep crack in a very thick layer of ice

crevice /ˈkrevɪs/ ***noun*** [C] a narrow crack in a rock, wall, etc.

crew /kruː/ ***noun*** [C, with sing. or pl. verb] **1** all the people who work on a ship, aircraft, etc. **2** a group of people who work together: *a **camera crew*** (=people who film things for television, etc.)

ˈcrew cut ***noun*** [C] a very short style of hair for men

crib¹ /krɪb/ (*especially AmE*) = COT

crib² /krɪb/ ***verb*** [I,T] (**cribbing**; **cribbed**) ~ (**sth**) (**from/off sb**) (*old-fashioned*) to copy sb else's work and pretend it is your own

crick /krɪk/ ***noun*** [sing.] a sudden painful stiff feeling in the muscles of your neck or back ▶ **crick** ***verb*** [T]: *I've cricked my neck.*

cricket /ˈkrɪkɪt/ ***noun*** **1** [U] (**SPORT**) a game played on grass by two teams of 11 players. Players score points (called **runs**) by hitting the ball with a wooden BAT and running between two sets of vertical wooden sticks, called **stumps**: *a **cricket match**/team/club/ball* **2** [C] an insect that makes a loud noise by rubbing its wings together

COLLOCATIONS AND PATTERNS

Crime

A crime is an act that is **illegal** or **against the law.** It is the job of the police to **investigate** a crime and try to **solve** it.
The public helped the police to solve the murder case.

When the police have enough **evidence** they can **arrest a suspect** and **charge him/her with** a crime.
A suspect was arrested this morning and charged with assault and robbery.

A **suspect** can **admit, confess to** or **deny the charge.**
All three men have denied assault.
He confessed to the murder.
She admitted 3 charges of theft.

The accused or **the defendant** (=the person the police have charged) must **stand trial** in **court** where he/she **pleads guilty or not guilty.**
The accused is charged with gross indecency and will stand trial on 3rd April.
Do you plead guilty or not guilty?

The defendant may be **acquitted** (=allowed to go free) or **found guilty** or **not guilty.**
The driver was acquitted of manslaughter.
She was found guilty of arson.

A defendant who is **found guilty** is **convicted** and then **sentenced to** a **term of imprisonment** or some other form of punishment.
He was convicted of fraud.
She was sentenced to life imprisonment.

COLLOCATIONS AND PATTERNS

Types of criminal

A person who **commits a crime** is a **criminal.** Different types of criminal have different names.
A **murderer** commits **murder** (=kills sb).
A **thief steals from** a person or a place and commits **theft.**
A thief broke into our car and stole the radio.

A **robber robs** sb and commits **robbery.**
A man was robbed of his wallet yesterday in Woodstock Road.

A **burglar breaks into a property,** committing **burglary.**
There was a burglary at the jewellery shop on Monday and the burglar escaped through a small window in a storeroom.
We were broken into while we were away on holiday.

A **terrorist** commits **acts of terrorism.**
Terrorists attempted to blow up the plane.

A **vandal** commits **acts of vandalism** (=damage to property for no reason).

A **kidnapper kidnaps** sb and **holds him/her to ransom.**
Three tourists were kidnapped and held to ransom for $30,000.

cricketer /ˈkrɪkɪtə(r)/ ***noun*** [C] (**SPORT**) a person who plays CRICKET

crime ⚷ /kraɪm/ ***noun*** **1** [C] something which is illegal and which people are punished for, for example by being sent to prison: *to **commit a crime*** ➲ note at **law court** **2** [U] illegal behaviour or activities: *There has been an increase in car crime recently.* ◇ *to fight crime* **3** (usually **a crime**) [sing.] something that is morally wrong: *It is a crime to waste food when people are starving.*

ˈcrime wave ***noun*** [sing.] a sudden increase in the number of crimes that are committed

criminal¹ ⚷ /ˈkrɪmɪnl/ ***noun*** [C] a person who has done something illegal

criminal² ⚷ /ˈkrɪmɪnl/ ***adj.*** **1** (only *before* a noun) connected with crime: *Deliberate damage to public property is a **criminal offence**.* ◇ ***criminal law*** **2** morally wrong: *a criminal waste of taxpayers' money*

criminality /ˌkrɪmɪˈnæləti/ ***noun*** [U] (**LAW**) the fact of people being involved in crime; criminal acts: *There is little evidence that juvenile criminality is increasing at a very much greater rate than crime in general.*

criminally /ˈkrɪmɪnəli/ ***adv.*** (**LAW**) according to the laws that deal with crime: ***criminally insane***

criminology /ˌkrɪmɪˈnɒlədʒi/ ***noun*** [U] the scientific study of crime and criminals ▶ **criminologist** /-dʒɪst/ ***noun*** [C] ▶ **criminological** /ˌkrɪmɪnəˈlɒdʒɪkl/ ***adj.***

crimson /ˈkrɪmzn/ ***adj.***, ***noun*** [U] (of) a dark red colour

cringe /krɪndʒ/ ***verb*** [I] **1** to feel embarrassed: *awful family photographs which **make you cringe*** **2** to move away from sb/sth because you are frightened: *The dog cringed in terror when the man raised his arm.*

crinkle /ˈkrɪŋkl/ ***verb*** [I,T] ~ (**sth**) (**up**) to have, or to make sth have, thin folds or lines in it: *He crinkled* *the silver paper up into a ball.* ▶ **crinkly** /ˈkrɪŋkli/ ***adj.***: *crinkly material*

cripple /ˈkrɪpl/ ***verb*** [T] (usually passive) **1** (HEALTH) to damage sb's body so that they are no longer able to walk or move normally: *to be **crippled with** arthritis* **2** to seriously damage or harm sb/sth: *The recession has crippled the motor industry.* ▶ **crippling** ***adj.***: *They had crippling debts and had to sell their house.*

crisis ⊶ /ˈkraɪsɪs/ ***noun*** [C,U] (*pl.* **crises** /-siːz/) a time of great danger or difficulty; the moment when things change and either improve or get worse: *the international crisis caused by the invasion* ◇ *a friend you can rely on in times of crisis*

crisp[1] ⊶ /krɪsp/ ***adj.*** **1** pleasantly hard and dry: *Store the biscuits in a tin to keep them crisp.* **2** firm and fresh or new: *a crisp salad/apple* ◇ *a crisp cotton dress* **3** (used about the air or weather) cold and dry: *a crisp winter morning* **4** (used about the way sb speaks) quick, clear but not very friendly: *a crisp reply* ▶ **crisply** ***adv.***: *'I disagree,' she said crisply.* ▶ **crispy** ***adj.*** (*informal*) = CRISP[1] (1,2)

crisp[2] /krɪsp/ (*AmE* **chip**; **poˈtato chip**) ***noun*** [C] a very thin piece of potato that is fried in oil, dried and then sold in packets. **Crisps** usually have salt or another flavouring on them: *a packet of crisps*

criss-cross /ˈkrɪs krɒs/ ***adj.*** (only *before* a noun) with many straight lines that cross over each other: *a criss-cross pattern* ▶ **criss-cross** ***verb*** [I,T]: *Many footpaths criss-cross the countryside.*

criterion ⊶ AW /kraɪˈtɪəriən/ ***noun*** [C] (*pl.* **criteria** /-riə/) the standard that you use when you make a decision or form an opinion about sb/sth: *The main criterion is value for money.* ◇ *What are the criteria for deciding who gets a place on the course?*

critic /ˈkrɪtɪk/ ***noun*** [C] **1** a person who says what is bad or wrong with sb/sth: *He is a long-standing critic of the council's transport policy.* **2** (ARTS AND MEDIA) a person whose job is to give their opinion about a play, film, book, work of art, etc.: *a film/restaurant/art critic*

critical ⊶ /ˈkrɪtɪkl/ ***adj.*** **1** ~ (of sb/sth) saying what is wrong with sb/sth: *The report was very critical of safety standards on the railways.* **2** (only *before* a noun) (ARTS AND MEDIA) describing the good and bad points of a play, film, book, work of art, etc.: *a critical guide to this month's new films* **3** dangerous or serious: *The patient is **in a critical condition**.* **4** very important; at a time when things can suddenly become better or worse: *The talks between the two leaders have **reached a critical stage**.* ➲ note at **essential** ▶ **critically** /-ɪkli/ ***adv.***: *a critically ill patient* ◇ *a critically important decision*

criticism ⊶ /ˈkrɪtɪsɪzəm/ ***noun*** **1** [C,U] (an expression of) what you think is bad about sb/sth: *The council has **come in for** severe **criticism** over the plans.* **2** [U] (ARTS AND MEDIA) the act of describing the good and bad points of a play, film, book, work of art, etc.: ***literary criticism***

criticize ⊶ (also -ise) /ˈkrɪtɪsaɪz/ ***verb*** [I,T] ~ (sb/sth) (for sth) to say what is bad or wrong with sb/sth: *The doctor was criticized for not sending the patient to hospital.*

critique /krɪˈtiːk/ ***noun*** [C] a piece of writing that describes the good and bad points of sb/sth

croak /krəʊk/ ***verb*** [I] to make a HARSH low noise like a FROG ▶ **croak** ***noun*** [C]

crochet /ˈkrəʊʃeɪ/ ***noun*** [U] a way of making clothes, cloth, etc. by using wool or cotton and a needle with a hook at one end ▶ **crochet** ***verb*** [I,T] (*pt, pp* **crocheted** /-ʃeɪd/) ➲ look at **knit**

crockery /ˈkrɒkəri/ ***noun*** [U] cups, plates and dishes

crocodile /ˈkrɒkədaɪl/ ***noun*** [C] a large REPTILE with a long tail and a big mouth with sharp teeth. **Crocodiles** live in rivers and lakes in hot countries. ➲ look at **alligator**

ˈcrocodile clip (*especially AmE* **ˈalligator clip**) ***noun*** [C] an object with sharp teeth used for holding things together, that is held closed by a spring and that you squeeze to open: *Use the crocodile clips to attach the cables to the battery.*

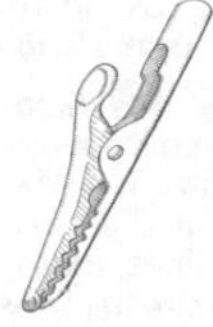

crocodile clip (*AmE* **alligator clip**)

crocus /ˈkrəʊkəs/ ***noun*** [C] a small yellow, purple or white flower that grows in early spring

croissant /ˈkrwæsɒ̃/ ***noun*** [C] a type of bread roll, shaped in a curve, that is often eaten with butter for breakfast

crony /ˈkrəʊni/ ***noun*** [C] (*pl.* **cronies**) (*informal*) (often used in a critical way) a friend

crook /krʊk/ ***noun*** [C] **1** (*informal*) a dishonest person; a criminal **2** a bend or curve in sth: *the **crook of your arm*** (= the inside of your elbow)

crooked /ˈkrʊkɪd/ ***adj.*** **1** not straight or even: *That picture is crooked.* ◇ *crooked teeth* **2** (*informal*) not honest: *a crooked accountant*

crop[1] ⊶ /krɒp/ ***noun*** **1** [C] (AGRICULTURE) all the grain, fruit, vegetables, etc. of one type that a farmer grows at one time: *a crop of apples* **2** [C, usually pl.] (AGRICULTURE) plants that are grown on farms for food: *Rice and soya beans are the main crops here.* **3** [sing.] a number of people or things which have appeared at the same time: *the recent crop of movies about aliens*

crop[2] /krɒp/ ***verb*** (**cropping**; **cropped**) **1** [T] to cut sth very short: *cropped hair* **2** (AGRICULTURE) [I] to produce a CROP[1] (1)

PHR V **crop up** to appear suddenly, when you are not expecting it: *We should have finished this work yesterday but some problems cropped up.*

ˈcrop dusting ***noun*** [U] (AGRICULTURE) the practice of spraying crops with chemicals such as PESTICIDES (= substances used for killing insects, etc. that eat food crops), especially from a plane

cropper /ˈkrɒpə(r)/ ***noun***

IDM **come a cropper** (*informal*) **1** to fall over or have an accident **2** to fail

ˈcrop rotation ***noun*** [U] (AGRICULTURE) the act of changing the type crop that is grown on an area of land in order to protect the soil and keep it healthy

croquet /ˈkrəʊkeɪ/ ***noun*** [U] a game that you play on grass. When you play **croquet** you use long wooden hammers (**mallets**) to hit balls through a series of metal HOOPS (= curved wires).

cross[1] ⊶ /krɒs/ ***noun*** [C] **1** a mark that you make by drawing one line across another (X). The sign is used for showing the position of sth, for showing that sth is not correct, etc.: *I drew a cross on the map to show where our house is.* ◇ *Incorrect answers were marked with a cross.* **2** (*also* **the Cross** [sing.]) (RELIGION) the two pieces of wood in the shape of a cross on which people were killed as a punishment in former times, or something in this shape (†) that is used as a symbol of the Christian

religion: *She wore a gold cross round her neck.* ➲ look at **crucifix** **3** [usually sing.] a ~ **(between A and B)** something (especially a plant or an animal) that is a mixture of two different types of thing: *a fruit which is a cross between a peach and an apple* **4** (SPORT) (in sports such as football) a kick or hit of the ball that goes across the front of the goal
IDM **noughts and crosses** → NOUGHT

cross² /krɒs/ *verb* **1** [I,T] ~ **(over) (from sth/to sth)** to go from one side of sth to the other: *to cross the road* ◇ *Where did you cross the border?* ◇ *Which of the runners crossed the finishing line first?* **2** [I] (used about lines, roads, etc.) to pass across each other: *The two roads cross just north of the village.* **3** [T] to put sth across or over sth else: *to **cross your arms*** **4** [T] to make sb angry by refusing to do what they want you to do: *He's an important man. It could be dangerous to cross him.* **5** [T] ~ **sth with sth** (BIOLOGY) to produce a new type of plant or animal by mixing two different types: *If you cross a horse with a donkey, you get a mule.* **6** [I,T] (SPORT) (in sports such as football and HOCKEY) to pass the ball across the front of the goal
IDM **cross my heart (and hope to die)** (*spoken*) used for emphasizing that what you are saying is true
cross your fingers; **keep your fingers crossed** → FINGER¹
cross your mind (used about a thought, idea, etc.) to come into your mind: *It never once crossed my mind that she was lying.*
PHR V **cross sth off (sth)** to remove sth from a list, etc. by drawing a line through it: *Cross Dave's name off the guest list – he can't come.*
cross sth out to draw a line through sth that you have written because you have made a mistake, etc.

cross³ /krɒs/ *adj.* (*informal*) ~ **(with sb) (about sth)** angry or annoyed: *I was really cross with her for leaving me with all the work.* ▶ **crossly** *adv.*: *'Be quiet,' Dad said crossly.*

crossbar /'krɒsbɑː(r)/ *noun* [C] **1** (SPORT) the piece of wood over the top of a goal in football, etc. **2** the metal bar that joins the front and back of a bicycle

'cross-breed¹ *verb* [I,T] (*pt, pp* **cross-bred**) (BIOLOGY) to make an animal or a plant breed with a different type of animal or plant; to breed with an animal or plant of a different type: *cross-bred sheep* ▶ ˌ**cross-'breeding** *noun* [U]

'cross-breed² *noun* [C] (BIOLOGY) an animal or a plant that has been produced by breeding two different types of animal or plant

ˌ**cross-'check** *verb* [T] **cross-check sth (against sth)** to make sure that information, figures, etc. are correct by using a different method or system to check them: *Cross-check your measurements against those suggested in the manual.*

ˌ**cross-'country** *adj., adv.* across fields and natural land; not using roads or tracks: *We walked about 10 miles cross-country before we saw a village.*

ˌ**cross-country 'skiing** *noun* [U] (SPORT) the sport of SKIING across the countryside, rather than down mountains

ˌ**cross-e'xamine** *verb* [T] (LAW) to ask sb questions in a court of law, etc. in order to find out the truth about sth ▶ ˌ**cross-eˌxami'nation** *noun* [C,U]

ˌ**cross-'eyed** *adj.* having one or both your eyes looking towards your nose

ˌ**cross-'fertilize** (also **-ise**) *verb* [T] (BIOLOGY) to make a plant develop and grow fruit or seeds using POLLEN from a different kind of plant ▶ ˌ**cross-ˌfertili'zation** (also **-isation**) *noun* [U, sing.]

crossfire /'krɒsfaɪə(r)/ *noun* [U] a situation in which guns are being fired from two or more different directions: *The journalist was killed in crossfire.* ◇ (*figurative*) *When my parents argued, I sometimes got **caught in the crossfire**.*

crossing /'krɒsɪŋ/ *noun* [C] **1** a place where you can cross over sth: *You should cross the road at the pedestrian crossing.* ◇ *a border crossing* **2** (*BrE* **level crossing**) a place where a road and a railway line cross each other **3** a journey from one side of a sea or river to the other: *We had a rough crossing.*

cross-legged /ˌkrɒs 'legd/ *adj., adv.* sitting on the floor with your legs pulled up in front of you and with one leg or foot over the other: *to sit cross-legged*

'cross link *noun* [C] (CHEMISTRY) the way in which different chains of atoms are held together in a particular type of MOLECULE (=the smallest unit into which a substance can be divided)

crossover /'krɒsəʊvə(r)/ *noun* [C] the process or result of changing from one area of activity or style of doing sth to another: *The album was an exciting jazz-pop crossover.*

ˌ**cross-'pollinate** *verb* [T] (BIOLOGY) to move POLLEN from a flower or plant onto another flower or plant so that it produces seeds ▶ ˌ**cross-'pollination** *noun* [U]

ˌ**cross 'purposes** *noun*
IDM **at cross purposes** if two people are **at cross purposes**, they do not understand each other because they are talking about different things, without realizing it

'cross reference *noun* [C] a note in a book that tells you to look in another place in the book for more information

crossroads /'krɒsrəʊdz/ *noun* [C] (*pl.* **crossroads**) a place where two or more roads cross each other: *When you come to the next crossroads turn right.*

'cross section *noun* [C] **1** a picture of what the inside of sth would look like if you cut through it: *a cross section of the human brain* ➲ picture at **flower** **2** a number of people, etc. that come from the different parts of a group, and so can be considered to represent the whole group: *The families we studied were chosen to represent a cross section of society.* ▶ ˌ**cross-'sectional** *adj.*

crosswalk /'krɒswɔːk/ (*AmE*) = PEDESTRIAN CROSSING

crosswind /'krɒswɪnd/ *noun* [C] a wind that is blowing across the direction that you are moving in

crossword /'krɒswɜːd/ (*also* **'crossword puzzle**) *noun* [C] a word game in which you have to write the answers to questions (**clues**) in square spaces, which are arranged in a pattern: *Every morning I try to **do the crossword** in the newspaper.*

crotch /krɒtʃ/ (*also* **crutch**) *noun* [C] the place where your legs, or a pair of trousers, join at the top

crotchet /'krɒtʃɪt/ (*AmE* **'quarter note**) *noun* [C] (MUSIC) a type of note

RELATED VOCABULARY

A **semibreve** is a musical note that lasts as long as 4 **crotchets**. A **minim** lasts twice as long as a **crotchet**, a **quaver** lasts half as long as a **crotchet** and a **semiquaver** lasts half as long as a **quaver**.

➲ picture at **music**

crouch /kraʊtʃ/ ***verb*** [I] ~ **(down)** to bend your legs and body so that you are close to the ground: *He crouched down behind the sofa.*

crow[1] /krəʊ/ ***noun*** [C] a large black bird that makes a loud noise

IDM **as the crow flies** (used for describing distances) in a straight line: *It's a kilometre as the crow flies but three kilometres by road.*

crow[2] /krəʊ/ ***verb*** [I] **1** to make a loud noise like a male chicken (**cock**) makes **2** (*informal*) to talk too proudly about sth you have achieved, especially when sb else has been unsuccessful SYN **boast**

crowbar /ˈkrəʊbɑː(r)/ ***noun*** [C] a long iron bar that is used for forcing sth open ➲ picture at **lever**

crowd[1] /kraʊd/ ***noun*** **1** [C, with sing. or pl. verb] a large number of people in one place: *The crowd was/were extremely noisy.* ◇ *He pushed his way through the crowd.* ◇ *I go shopping early in the morning to avoid the crowds.* **2 the crowd** [sing.] ordinary people: *He wears weird clothes because he wants to* ***stand out from the crowd.*** **3** [C, with sing. or pl. verb] (*informal*) a group of people who know each other: *Bob, Liz and Chris will be there – all the usual crowd.*

crowd[2] /kraʊd/ ***verb*** **1** [I] ~ **around/round (sb)** (used about a lot of people) to stand in a large group around sb/sth: *Fans crowded round the singer hoping to get his autograph.* **2** [T] (used about a lot of people) to fill an area: *Groups of tourists crowded the main streets.* ◇ *(figurative) Memories crowded her mind.*

PHR V **crowd into sth**; **crowd in** to go into a small place and make it very full: *Somehow we all crowded into their small living room.*

crowd sb/sth into sth; **crowd sb/sth in** to put a lot of people into a small place: *Ten prisoners were crowded into one small cell.*

crowd sth out; **crowd sb out (of sth)** to completely fill a place so that nobody else can enter: *Students crowd out the cafe at lunchtimes.* ◇ *Smaller companies are being crowded out of the market.*

crowded /ˈkraʊdɪd/ ***adj.*** full of people: *a crowded bus* ◇ *people living in poor and crowded conditions*

crown[1] /kraʊn/ ***noun*** **1** [C] an object in the shape of a circle, usually made of gold and PRECIOUS STONES, that a king or queen wears on his or her head on official occasions **2 the Crown** [sing.] (**POLITICS**) the government of a country, thought of as being represented by a king or queen: *an area of land belonging to the Crown* ◇ *Who's appearing for the Crown* (= bringing a criminal charge against sb on behalf of the state) *in this case?* **3** [sing.] the top of your head or of a hat **4** [sing.] the highest part of sth: *the crown of a hill* **5** [C] (**ANATOMY**) the part of a tooth that is above the GUM ➲ picture at **tooth** **6** [C] (**HEALTH**) an artificial cover for a damaged tooth

crown[2] /kraʊn/ ***verb*** [T] **1** (**POLITICS**) to put a crown on the head of a new king or queen as a sign of royal power: *Queen Elizabeth was crowned in 1953.* ◇ *(figurative) the newly crowned British champion* **2** (often passive) ~ **sth (with sth)** to have or put sth on the top of sth: *The mountain was crowned with snow.* ◇ *(figurative) Her years of hard work were finally crowned with success.*

crowning /ˈkraʊnɪŋ/ ***adj.*** (only *before* a noun) the best or most important: *Winning the World Championship was the crowning moment of her career.*

ˌCrown ˈprince, **ˌCrown prinˈcess** ***noun*** [C] (**POLITICS**) (in some countries), a prince or princess who will become king or queen when the present king or queen dies

crucial AW /ˈkruːʃl/ ***adj.*** ~ **(to/for sth)** extremely important: *Early diagnosis of the illness is crucial for successful treatment.* SYN **vital** ➲ note at **essential** ▸ **crucially** /-ʃəli/ ***adv.***

crucible /ˈkruːsɪbl/ ***noun*** [C] **1** (**SCIENCE**) a pot in which substances are heated to high temperatures, metals are melted, etc. ➲ picture at **laboratory** **2** (*formal*) a place or situation in which people or ideas are tested, often creating sth new or exciting in the process

crucifix /ˈkruːsəfɪks/ ***noun*** [C] (**RELIGION**) a small model of a cross with a figure of Jesus on it

crucifixion /ˌkruːsəˈfɪkʃn/ ***noun*** **1** [C,U] (**RELIGION**) (often **Crucifixion**) the act of killing sb by fastening them to a cross: *the Crucifixion* (= of Jesus) **2** [C] (**ART**) a painting or other work of art representing the **crucifixion** of Jesus Christ

cruciform /ˈkruːsɪfɔːm/ ***adj.*** (**ARCHITECTURE**) in the shape of a cross

crucify /ˈkruːsɪfaɪ/ ***verb*** [T] (*pres. part.* **crucifying**; *3rd person sing. pres.* **crucifies**; *pt, pp* **crucified**) to kill sb by fastening them to a cross

crude /kruːd/ ***adj.*** **1** simple and basic, without much detail, skill, etc.: *The method was crude but very effective.* ◇ *She explained how the system worked* ***in crude terms.*** **2** referring to sex or the body in a way that would offend many people: *He's always telling crude jokes.* **3** (used about oil and other natural substances) in its natural state, before it has been treated with chemicals: ***crude oil*** ▸ **crudely** ***adv.***: *a crudely drawn face*

cruel /kruːəl/ ***adj.*** (**crueller**; **cruellest**) causing physical or mental pain or suffering to sb/sth: *I think it's cruel to keep animals in cages.* ◇ *a cruel punishment* ▸ **cruelly** /ˈkruːəli/ ***adv.***

cruelty /ˈkruːəlti/ ***noun*** (*pl.* **cruelties**) **1** [U] ~ **(to sb/sth)** cruel behaviour: *cruelty to children* **2** [C, usually pl.] a cruel act: *the cruelties of war*

cruise[1] /kruːz/ ***verb*** [I] **1** (**TOURISM**) to travel by boat, visiting a number of places, as a holiday: *to cruise around the Caribbean* **2** to stay at the same speed in a car, plane, etc.: *cruising at 80 kilometres an hour*

cruise[2] /kruːz/ ***noun*** [C] (**TOURISM**) a holiday in which you travel on a ship and visit a number of different places: *They're planning to* ***go on a cruise.***

ˈcruise control ***noun*** [U] a device in a vehicle that allows it to stay at the speed that the driver has chosen

cruiser /ˈkruːzə(r)/ ***noun*** [C] **1** a large fast ship used in a war **2** a motor boat which has room for people to sleep in it = CABIN CRUISER

crumb /krʌm/ ***noun*** [C] a very small piece of bread, cake or biscuit

crumble /ˈkrʌmbl/ ***verb*** [I,T] ~ **(sth) (up)** to break or make sth break into very small pieces: *The walls of the church are beginning to crumble.* ◇ *We crumbled up the bread and threw it to the birds.* ◇ *(figurative) Support for the government is beginning to crumble.* ▸ **crumbly** /-bli/ ***adj.***: *This cheese has a crumbly texture.*

crumpet /ˈkrʌmpɪt/ ***noun*** [C] (*BrE*) a flat round type of bread roll with holes in the top that you eat hot with butter

crumple /ˈkrʌmpl/ ***verb*** [I,T] ~ **(sth) (into sth)**; ~ **(sth) (up)** to be pressed or to press sth into an untidy shape: *The front of the car crumpled when it hit the* wall. ◇ *She crumpled the letter into a ball and threw it away.*

crunch[1] /krʌntʃ/ ***verb*** **1** [T] ~ **sth (up)** to make a loud noise when you are eating sth hard: *to crunch an apple* **2** [I] to make a loud noise like the sound of sth being crushed: *We crunched through the snow.* ▸ **crunchy** /ˈkrʌntʃi/ ***adj.***: *a crunchy apple*

crunch[2] /krʌntʃ/ ***noun*** [sing.] an act or noise of CRUNCHING: *There was a loud crunch as he sat on the box of eggs.*

IDM **if/when it comes to the crunch** if/when you are in a difficult situation and must make a difficult decision: *If it comes to the crunch, I'll stay and fight.*

crusade /kruːˈseɪd/ ***noun*** [C] **1** a fight for sth that you believe to be good or against sth that you believe to be bad: *Mr Khan is leading a crusade against drugs in his neighbourhood.* **2 Crusade** (**HISTORY, RELIGION**) one of the wars fought in Palestine by European Christians against Muslims in the Middle Ages ▸ **crusader *noun*** [C]

crush[1] ⊶ /krʌʃ/ ***verb*** [T] **1** to press or squeeze sth so hard that it is damaged or injured, or loses its shape: *Most of the eggs got crushed when she sat on them.* ◇ *He was **crushed to death** in the accident.* **2** ~ **sth (up)** to break sth into very small pieces or a powder: *Crush the garlic and fry in oil.* **3** to defeat sb/sth completely: *The army was sent in to crush the rebellion.*

crush[2] /krʌʃ/ ***noun*** **1** [sing.] a large group of people in a small space: *There was such a crush that I couldn't get near the bar.* **2** [C] (*informal*) **a** ~ **(on sb)** a strong feeling of love for sb that only usually lasts for a short time: *Maria **had a huge crush** on her teacher.*

crushing /ˈkrʌʃɪŋ/ ***adj.*** (only *before* a noun) that defeats sb/sth completely; very bad: *a crushing defeat*

crust /krʌst/ ***noun*** [C,U] **1** the hard part on the outside of a piece of bread, a pie, etc. **2** a hard layer or surface, especially above or around sth soft or liquid: ***the earth's crust***

crustacean /krʌˈsteɪʃn/ ***noun*** [C] (**BIOLOGY**) any creature with a soft body in several sections and covered with a hard outer shell. **Crustaceans** usually live in water: *Crabs, lobsters, shrimps and prawns are crustaceans.* ➲ picture on **page 29**

crusty /ˈkrʌsti/ ***adj.*** **1** having a hard CRUST (1): *crusty bread* **2** (*informal*) bad-tempered and impatient: *a crusty old man*

crutch /krʌtʃ/ ***noun*** [C] **1** a type of stick that you put under your arm to help you walk when you have hurt your leg or foot: *She was **on crutches** for two months after she broke her ankle.* ➲ look at **walking stick** ➲ picture at **health** **2** = CROTCH

crux /krʌks/ ***noun*** [sing.] the most important or difficult part of a problem: *The **crux of the matter** is how to stop this from happening again.*

cry[1] ⊶ /kraɪ/ ***verb*** (*pres. part.* **crying**; *3rd person sing. pres.* **cries**; *pt, pp* **cried**) **1** [I] to make a noise and produce tears in your eyes, for example because you are unhappy or have hurt yourself: *The baby never stops crying.* ◇ *The child was **crying for*** (=because she wanted) *her mother.* **2** [I,T] ~ **(out)** to shout or make a loud noise: *We could hear someone **crying for help**.* ◇ *'Look!' he cried, 'There they are.'*

IDM **a shoulder to cry on** → SHOULDER[1]

cry your eyes out to cry a lot for a long time

PHRV **cry out for sth** to need sth very much: *The company is crying out for fresh new talent.*

cry[2] ⊶ /kraɪ/ ***noun*** (*pl.* **cries**) **1** [C] a shout or loud high noise: *the cries of the children in the playground* ◇ *We heard Adam give a **cry of** pain as the dog bit him.* ◇ (*figurative*) *Her suicide attempt was really **a cry for help**.* **2** [sing.] an action or a period of crying: *After a good cry I felt much better.*

IDM **a far cry from sth/from doing sth** → FAR[1]

crying /ˈkraɪɪŋ/ ***adj.*** (only *before* a noun) (used to talk about a bad situation) very great: *There's a crying need for more doctors.* ◇ *It's **a crying shame** that so many young people can't find jobs.*

cryogenics /ˌkraɪəˈdʒenɪks/ ***noun*** [U] (**PHYSICS**) the scientific study of the production and effects of very low temperatures

crypt /krɪpt/ ***noun*** [C] (**ARCHITECTURE**) a room that is under a church, where people were sometimes buried in the past

cryptic /ˈkrɪptɪk/ ***adj.*** having a hidden meaning that is not easy to understand; mysterious ▸ **cryptically** /-kli/ ***adv.***

crypto- /ˈkrɪptəʊ/ ***prefix*** (used in nouns) hidden; secret

crystal /ˈkrɪstl/ ***noun*** **1** [C] (**CHEMISTRY**) a regular shape that some mineral substances form when they become solid: *salt crystals* **2** (**GEOLOGY**) a clear mineral that can be used in making jewellery **3** [U] very good quality glass: *a crystal vase*

ˌcrystal ˈball ***noun*** [C] a glass ball in which some people say you can see what will happen in the future

ˌcrystal ˈclear ***adj.*** **1** (used about water, glass, etc.) completely clear and bright **2** very easy to understand: *The meaning is crystal clear.*

crystalline /ˈkrɪstəlaɪn/ ***adj.*** (**GEOLOGY**) made of or similar to CRYSTALS (=small pieces of a substance with many even sides)

crystallize (also **-ise**) /ˈkrɪstəlaɪz/ ***verb*** [I,T] **1** (used about thoughts, beliefs, plans, etc.) to become clear and fixed; to make thoughts, etc. become clear and fixed: *Our ideas gradually began to crystallize into a definite strategy.* **2** (**CHEMISTRY**) to change or make sth change into CRYSTALS: *The salt crystallizes as the water evaporates.* ▸ **crystallization** (also **-isation**) /ˌkrɪstəlaɪˈzeɪʃn/ ***noun*** [U]

CT scan /ˌsiː ˈtiː skæn/ ***noun*** [C] (**HEALTH**) = CAT SCAN

cu. ***abbr.*** CUBIC: *a volume of 2 cu. m* (=2 cubic metres)

cub /kʌb/ ***noun*** [C] **1** a young BEAR, LION, etc. ➲ picture at **lion** **2 the Cubs** [pl.] the part of the Scout organization that is for younger boys and girls **3 Cub** (*also* **Cub Scout**) [C] a member of the **Cubs**

cube[1] /kjuːb/ ***noun*** [C] **1** (**GEOMETRY**) a solid shape that has six equal square sides ➲ picture at **solid** **2** (**MATHEMATICS**) the number that you get if you multiply a number by itself twice: *the cube of 5* (=5^3) *is 125* (=5 x 5 x 5). ➲ look at **square[1]**

cube[2] /kjuːb/ ***verb*** [T] (**MATHEMATICS**) (usually passive) to multiply a number by itself twice: *Four cubed* (=4^3) *is 64* (=4 x 4 x 4). ➲ look at **square[1]**, **cube root**

ˌcube ˈroot ***noun*** [C] (**MATHEMATICS**) a number which, when multiplied by itself twice, produces a particular number: *The cube root of 64 ($\sqrt[3]{64}$) is 4.* ➲ look at **square root**

cubic /ˈkjuːbɪk/ ***adj.*** connected with a measurement of volume expressed as a CUBE[1] (2): *If a box is 4cm long, 4cm wide and 4cm high, its volume is 64 **cubic centimetres**.* ◇ *The lake holds more than a million **cubic metres** of water.*

cubicle /ˈkju:bɪkl/ ***noun*** [C] a small room that is made by separating off part of a larger room: *There are cubicles at the swimming pool for changing your clothes.*

cubism (also **Cubism**) /ˈkju:bɪzəm/ ***noun*** [U] (ART) a style and movement in early 20th century art in which objects and people are represented as GEOMETRIC shapes, often shown from many different angles at the same time ▶ **cubist** (also **Cubist**) ***noun*** [C]: *The exhibition includes works by the Cubists.* ▶ **cubist** (also **Cubist**) ***adj.***: *cubist paintings*

cuboid /ˈkju:bɔɪd/ ***noun*** [C] (**GEOMETRY**) a solid object which has six RECTANGULAR sides at RIGHT ANGLES to each other ▶ **cuboid** ***adj.***

cuckoo /ˈkʊku:/ ***noun*** [C] a bird which makes a sound like its name. **Cuckoos** put their eggs into the nests of other birds.

cucumber /ˈkju:kʌmbə(r)/ ***noun*** [C,U] a long, thin vegetable with a dark green skin that does not need to be cooked

cud /kʌd/ ***noun*** [U] the food that cows and similar animals bring back from the stomach into the mouth to eat again: *cows chewing the cud*

cuddle /ˈkʌdl/ ***verb*** [I,T] to hold sb/sth closely in your arms: *The little girl was cuddling her favourite doll.* ▶ **cuddle** ***noun*** [C]: *He gave the child **a cuddle** and kissed her goodnight.*

PHRV **cuddle up (to/against sb/sth)**; **cuddle up (together)** to move close to sb and sit or lie in a comfortable position: *They cuddled up together for warmth.*

cuddly /ˈkʌdli/ ***adj.*** soft and pleasant to hold close to you: *a cuddly toy*

cue /kju:/ ***noun*** [C] **1** a word or movement that is the signal for sb else to say or do sth, especially in a play: *When Julia puts the tray on the table, that's your cue to come on stage.* **2** an example of how to behave: *I'm not sure how to behave at a Japanese wedding, so I'll **take my cue from** the hosts.* **3** (**SPORT**) a long, thin wooden stick used to hit the ball in SNOOKER and BILLIARDS (=games that are played on a special table) ➲ picture at **sport**

IDM **(right) on cue** at exactly the moment expected: *Just as I was starting to worry about Stan, he phoned right on cue.*

cuff /kʌf/ ***noun*** [C] **1** the end part of a sleeve, which often fastens at the wrist **2 cuffs** [pl.] =HANDCUFFS **3** a light hit with the open hand

IDM **off the cuff** (used about sth you say) without thought or preparation before that moment: *I haven't got the figures here, but, off the cuff, I'd say the rise is about 10%.*

cufflink /ˈkʌflɪŋk/ ***noun*** [C, usually pl.] one of a pair of small objects used instead of a button to fasten a shirt sleeve together at the wrist

cuisine /kwɪˈzi:n/ ***noun*** [U] (*formal*) the style of cooking of a particular country, restaurant, etc.: *Italian cuisine*

cul-de-sac /ˈkʌl də sæk/ ***noun*** [C] (*pl.* **cul-de-sacs**) a street that is closed at one end

culinary /ˈkʌlɪnəri/ ***adj.*** (*formal*) connected with cooking

cull /kʌl/ ***verb*** [T] **1** to kill a number of animals in a group to prevent the group from becoming too large **2** to collect information, ideas, etc., from different places: *I managed to cull some useful addresses from the Internet.* ▶ **cull** ***noun*** [C]: *a deer cull*

culminate /ˈkʌlmɪneɪt/ ***verb*** [I] (*formal*) ~ **in sth** to reach a final result: *The team's efforts culminated in victory in the championships.* ▶ **culmination** /ˌkʌlmɪˈneɪʃn/ ***noun*** [sing.]: *The joint space mission was the culmination of years of research.*

culottes /kju:ˈlɒts/ ***noun*** [pl.] women's wide short trousers that are made to look like a skirt: *a pair of culottes*

culpable /ˈkʌlpəbl/ ***adj.*** (*formal*) responsible for sth bad that has happened

culprit /ˈkʌlprɪt/ ***noun*** [C] a person who has done sth wrong

cult /kʌlt/ ***noun*** [C] **1** (**RELIGION**) a type of religion or religious group, especially one that is considered unusual **2** a person or thing that has become popular with a particular group of people: *cult movies*

cultivar /ˈkʌltɪvɑ:(r)/ ***noun*** [C] (**AGRICULTURE**) a particular variety of a plant whose characteristics have been controlled by people in the way it has been bred

cultivate /ˈkʌltɪveɪt/ ***verb*** [T] **1** (**AGRICULTURE**) to prepare and use land for growing plants for food or to sell: *to cultivate the soil* **2** (**AGRICULTURE**) to grow plants for food or to sell: *Olives have been cultivated for centuries in Mediterranean countries.* **3** to try hard to develop a friendship with sb: *He cultivated links with colleagues abroad.* ▶ **cultivation** /ˌkʌltɪˈveɪʃn/ ***noun*** [U] ➲ look at **shifting cultivation**

cultivated /ˈkʌltɪveɪtɪd/ ***adj.*** **1** (used about people) well educated, with good manners **SYN** **cultured** **2** (**AGRICULTURE**) (used about land) used for growing plants for food or to sell **3** (**AGRICULTURE**) (used about plants) grown on a farm, not wild

cultural 🔑 **AW** /ˈkʌltʃərəl/ ***adj.*** **1** (**SOCIAL STUDIES**) connected with the customs, ideas, beliefs, etc. of a society or country: *The country's cultural diversity is a result of taking in immigrants from all over the world.* ➲ look at **multicultural** **2** (**ARTS AND MEDIA**) connected with art, music, literature, etc.: *The city has a rich cultural life, with many theatres, concert halls and art galleries.* ▶ **culturally** **AW** /-rəli/ ***adv.***

culture 🔑 **AW** /ˈkʌltʃə(r)/ ***noun*** **1** [C,U] (**SOCIAL STUDIES**) the customs, ideas, beliefs, etc. of a particular society, country, etc.: *the language and culture of the Aztecs ◇ people from many different cultures* **2** [U] (**ARTS AND MEDIA**) art, literature, music, etc.: *London has always been a centre of culture.* **3** [C] (**BIOLOGY**) a group of cells or bacteria, especially taken from a person or an animal and grown for medical or scientific study: *Yoghurt is made from active cultures.*

cultured /ˈkʌltʃəd/ ***adj.*** well educated, showing a good knowledge of art, music, literature, etc. **SYN** **cultivated**

ˈ**culture shock** ***noun*** [U] (**SOCIAL STUDIES**) a feeling of confusion, etc. that you may have when you go to live in or visit a country that is very different from your own

culvert /ˈkʌlvət/ ***noun*** [C] a pipe for water that goes under a road, etc.

cum /kʌm/ ***prep.*** (used for joining two nouns together) also used as; as well as: *a bedroom-cum-study*

cumbersome /ˈkʌmbəsəm/ ***adj.*** **1** heavy and difficult to carry, use, wear, etc. **2** (used about a system, etc.) slow and complicated: *cumbersome legal procedures*

cumin /'kʌmɪn/ *noun* [U] the dried seeds of the cumin plant, used in cooking as a spice

cumulative /'kju:mjələtɪv/ *adj.* increasing steadily in amount, degree, etc.: *a cumulative effect*

cumulonimbus /ˌkju:mjʊləʊ'nɪmbəs/ *noun* [U] (GEOGRAPHY) a type of cloud that forms a large very high mass, with a flat base at a fairly low level, and often a flat top. It is seen, for example, during THUNDERSTORMS ➲ picture at **cloud**

cumulus /'kju:mjələs/ *noun* [U] (GEOGRAPHY) a type of thick white cloud ➲ picture at **cloud**

cunning /'kʌnɪŋ/ *adj.* clever in a dishonest or bad way: *He was as cunning as a fox.* ◇ *a cunning trick* SYN sly, wily ▶ **cunning** *noun* [U] ▶ **cunningly** *adv.*

cup¹ 🔑 /kʌp/ *noun* [C] **1** a small container usually with a handle, used for drinking liquids: *a teacup* ◇ *a cup of coffee* **2** (SPORT) a large metal cup given as a prize; the competition for such a cup: *Our team won the cup in the basketball tournament.* ◇ *the World Cup* **3** an object shaped like a cup: *an eggcup*
IDM **not sb's cup of tea** not what sb likes or is interested in: *Horror films aren't my cup of tea.*

cup² /kʌp/ *verb* [T] (**cupping**; **cupped**) to form sth, especially your hands, into the shape of a cup; to hold sth with your hands shaped like a cup: *I cupped my hands to take a drink from the stream.*

cupboard 🔑 /'kʌbəd/ *noun* [C] a piece of furniture, usually with shelves inside and a door or doors at the front, used for storing food, clothes, etc.

'cup final *noun* [C] (*BrE*) (SPORT) (especially in football) the last match in a series of matches in a competition that gives a cup as a prize to the winner

cupful /'kʌpfʊl/ *noun* [C] the amount that a cup will hold: *two cupfuls of water*

Cupid /'kju:pɪd/ *noun* [C] (ART) **1** the Roman god of love who is shown as a beautiful baby boy with wings, carrying a BOW and arrow **2 cupid** a picture or statue of a baby boy who looks like **Cupid**: *little cupids painted in the clouds on the ceiling*

cupola /'kju:pələ/ *noun* [C] (ARCHITECTURE) a round part on top of a building (like a small DOME) ➲ picture at **dome**

'cup tie *noun* [C] (*BrE*) (SPORT) (especially in football) a match between two teams in a competition that gives a cup as a prize to the winner

curable /'kjʊərəbl/ *adj.* (HEALTH) (used about a disease) that can be made better OPP **incurable**

curate /'kjʊərət/ *noun* [C] (RELIGION) a priest at a low level in the Church of England, who helps the VICAR (=the priest in charge) of a church district

curator /kjʊə'reɪtə(r)/ *noun* [C] a person whose job is to look after the things that are kept in a museum

curb¹ 🔑 /kɜ:b/ *verb* [T] to limit or control sth, especially sth bad: *He needs to learn to curb his anger.*

curb² /kɜ:b/ *noun* [C] **1 a ~ (on sth)** a control or limit on sth: *a curb on local government spending* **2** (*especially AmE*) =KERB

curd /kɜ:d/ *noun* [U] (*also* **curds** [pl.]) a thick soft substance that forms when milk turns sour

curdle /'kɜ:dl/ *verb* [I,T] (used about liquids) to turn sour or to separate into different parts; to make something do this: *I've curdled the sauce.* ➲ look at **blood-curdling**

cure¹ 🔑 /kjʊə(r)/ *verb* [T] **1 ~ sb (of sth)** (HEALTH) to make sb healthy again after an illness: *The treatment cured him of cancer.* **2** (HEALTH) to make an illness, injury, etc. end or disappear: *It is still not possible to cure the common cold.* ◇ (*figurative*) *The plumber cured the problem with the central heating.* **3** to make certain types of food last longer by drying, smoking or SALTING them: *cured ham*

cure² 🔑 /kjʊə(r)/ *noun* [C] **a ~ (for sth)** (HEALTH) **1** a medicine or treatment that can cure an illness, etc.: *There is no cure for this illness.* **2** a return to good health; the process of being cured: *The new drug brought about a miraculous cure.*

curfew /'kɜ:fju:/ *noun* [C] **1** a time after which people are not allowed to go outside their homes, for example during a war: *The government imposed a dusk-to-dawn curfew.* **2** (*AmE*) a time when children must arrive home in the evening: *She has a ten o'clock curfew.*

curiosity /ˌkjʊəri'ɒsəti/ *noun* (*pl.* **curiosities**) **1** [U] a desire to know or learn: *I was full of curiosity about their plans.* ◇ ***Out of curiosity**, he opened her letter.* **2** [C] an unusual and interesting person or thing: *The museum was full of historical curiosities.*

curious 🔑 /'kjʊəriəs/ *adj.* **1 ~ (about sth)**; **~ (to do sth)** wanting to know or learn sth: *They were very curious about the people who lived upstairs.* ◇ *He was curious to know how the machine worked.* **2** unusual or strange: *It was curious that she didn't tell anyone about the incident.* ▶ **curiously** *adv.*

curium /'kjʊəriəm/ *noun* [U] (*symbol* **Cm**) (CHEMISTRY) a chemical element. **Curium** is a RADIOACTIVE metal produced artificially from PLUTONIUM ⓘ For more information on the periodic table of elements, look at pages R34-5.

curl¹ 🔑 /kɜ:l/ *verb* **1** [I,T] to form or to make sth form into a curved or round shape: *Does your hair curl naturally?* **2** [I] to move round in a curve: *The snake curled around his arm.* ◇ *Smoke curled up into the sky.*
PHR V **curl up** to pull your arms, legs and head close to your body: *The cat curled up in front of the fire.*

curl² 🔑 /kɜ:l/ *noun* [C] **1** a piece of hair that curves round: *Her hair fell in curls round her face.* **2** a thing that has a curved round shape: *a curl of blue smoke*

curler /'kɜ:lə(r)/ *noun* [C] a small plastic or metal tube that you roll your hair around in order to make it curly

COLLOCATIONS AND PATTERNS

Currency

In financial markets currencies can be **high/rising/strong** or **falling/low/weak.**
Business should benefit from a strong euro.
The yen gained 10 points against a weak dollar.

Currencies can **strengthen** and **weaken.**
The peso strengthened on the foreign exchanges.
The rand weakened by 5% to the euro.

One currency can **come under pressure against** another.
The pound came under pressure against the euro yesterday.

A currency may be **floated, devalued** or **revalued.**
The government allowed the peso to float freely.
The Fiji dollar may have to be devalued.
The yen is to be revalued.

The **exchange rate** is the relation in value of one currency against another.
The current exchange rate is 50 rupees to the euro.
A high/low/stable/strong/weak exchange rate.

curly 🔑 /ˈkɜːli/ ***adj.*** full of curls; shaped like a curl: *curly hair* OPP **straight**

currant /ˈkʌrənt/ ***noun*** [C] **1** a very small dried GRAPE used to make cakes, etc. **2** (often in compounds) one of several types of small soft fruit: *blackcurrants*

currency AW /ˈkʌrənsi/ ***noun*** (*pl.* **currencies**) **1** [C,U] (ECONOMICS, FINANCE) the system or type of money that a particular country uses: *a single European currency* ◇ *foreign currency* ◇ *a weak/strong/stable currency* **2** [U] the state of being believed, accepted or used by many people: *The new ideas soon* ***gained currency***.

current¹ 🔑 /ˈkʌrənt/ ***adj.*** **1** of the present time; happening now: *current fashions/events* **2** generally accepted; in common use: *Is this word still current?*

current² 🔑 /ˈkʌrənt/ ***noun*** **1** [C] a continuous flowing movement of water, air, etc.: *to swim* ***against/with the current*** ◇ (*figurative*) *a current of anti-government feeling* **2** [U] (PHYSICS) the flow of electricity through a wire, etc.

ˌcurrent acˈcount (*AmE* **ˈchecking account**) ***noun*** [C] (FINANCE) a bank account from which you can take out your money when you want, with a cheque book or cash card

ˌcurrent afˈfairs ***noun*** [pl.] (POLITICS, SOCIAL STUDIES) important political or social events that are happening at the present time

currently 🔑 /ˈkʌrəntli/ ***adv.*** at present; at the moment: *He is currently working in Spain.*

curriculum /kəˈrɪkjələm/ ***noun*** [C] (*pl.* **curriculums** or **curricula** /-lə/) (EDUCATION) all the subjects that are taught in a school, college or university; the contents of a particular course of study: *Latin is not* ***on the curriculum*** *at our school.* ➲ look at **syllabus**

curriculum vitae /kəˌrɪkjələm ˈviːtaɪ/ = CV

curry /ˈkʌri/ ***noun*** [C,U] (*pl.* **curries**) an Indian dish of meat, vegetables, etc. containing a lot of spices usually served with rice: *a hot/mild curry* ▶ **curried** ***adj.***: *curried chicken*

ˈcurry powder ***noun*** [U] a fine mixture of strongly flavoured spices that is used to make CURRY

curse¹ /kɜːs/ ***noun*** [C] **1** (LANGUAGE) a word used for expressing anger; a swear word **2** a word or words expressing a wish that sth terrible will happen to sb: *The family seemed to be* ***under a curse*** (= lots of bad things happened to them). **3** something that causes great harm: *the curse of drug addiction*

curse² /kɜːs/ ***verb*** **1** [I,T] ~ **(sb/sth) (for sth)** to swear at sb/sth; to use rude language to express your anger: *He dropped the box, cursing himself for his clumsiness.* **2** [T] to use a magic word or phrase against sb because you want sth bad to happen to them: *She cursed his family.*

cursor /ˈkɜːsə(r)/ ***noun*** [C] (COMPUTING) a small sign on a computer screen that shows the position you are at

cursory /ˈkɜːsəri/ ***adj.*** quick and short; done in a hurry: *a cursory glance*

curt /kɜːt/ ***adj.*** short and not polite: *She gave him a curt reply and slammed the phone down.* ▶ **curtly** ***adv.*** ▶ **curtness** ***noun*** [U]

curtail /kɜːˈteɪl/ ***verb*** [T] (*formal*) to make sth shorter or smaller; to reduce: *I had to curtail my answer as I was running out of time.* ▶ **curtailment** ***noun*** [C,U]

curtain 🔑 /ˈkɜːtn/ ***noun*** [C] **1** (*AmE also* **drape**) a piece of material that you can move to cover a window, etc.: *Could you* ***draw the curtains****, please?* (= Could you open/close the curtains) ◇ ***The curtain goes up*** *at 7pm* (= in a theatre, the play begins). **2** a thing that covers or hides sth: *a curtain of mist*

ˌcurtain ˈwall ***noun*** [C] (HISTORY) a thick, strong wall around a MEDIEVAL castle, especially one that connects one tower with another

curtsy (*also* **curtsey**) /ˈkɜːtsi/ ***noun*** [C] (*pl.* **curtsies** or **curtseys**) a movement made by a woman as a sign of respect, done by bending the knees, with one foot behind the other ▶ **curtsy** (*also* **curtsey**) ***verb*** [I]

curve¹ 🔑 /kɜːv/ ***noun*** [C] a line that bends round: *a curve on a graph* ➲ picture at **line**

ocean currents

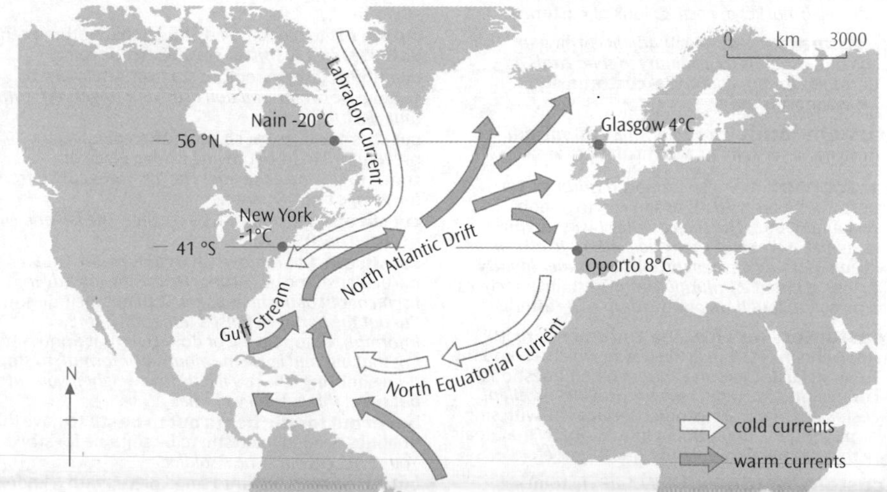

curve[2] **⊶** /kɜːv/ ***verb*** [I,T] to bend or to make sth bend in a curve: *The bay curved round to the south.* ◇ *a curved line* ➲ picture at **line**

cushion[1] /ˈkʊʃn/ ***noun*** [C] **1** a bag filled with soft material, for example feathers, which you put on a chair, etc. to make it more comfortable **2** something that acts or is shaped like a **cushion**: *A hovercraft rides on a cushion of air.*

cushion[2] /ˈkʊʃn/ ***verb*** [T] **1** to make a fall, hit, etc. less painful: *The snow cushioned his fall.* **2** to reduce the unpleasant effect of sth: *She spent her childhood on a farm, cushioned from the effects of the war.*

cushy /ˈkʊʃi/ ***adj.*** (*informal*) too easy, needing little effort (in a way that seems unfair to others): *a cushy job*

custard /ˈkʌstəd/ ***noun*** [U] a sweet yellow sauce made from milk, eggs and sugar. In Britain it is eaten hot or cold with sweet dishes

custodial /kʌˈstəʊdiəl/ ***adj.*** (LAW) **1** involving sending sb to prison: *The judge gave him a* ***custodial sentence*** (=sent him to prison). **2** connected with the right or duty of taking care of sb; having CUSTODY: *The mother is usually the custodial parent after a divorce.*

custodian /kʌˈstəʊdiən/ ***noun*** [C] **1** (*formal*) a person who looks after sth, especially a museum, library, etc. **2** (*AmE*) =CARETAKER

custody /ˈkʌstədi/ ***noun*** [U] (LAW) **1** the legal right or duty to take care of sb/sth: *After the divorce, the mother* ***had custody of*** *the children.* **2** the state of being guarded, or kept in prison temporarily, especially by the police: *The man was* ***kept in custody*** *until his trial.*

custom **⊶** /ˈkʌstəm/ ***noun*** **1** [C,U] (SOCIAL STUDIES) a way of behaving which a particular group or society has had for a long time: *It's the custom in Britain for a bride to throw her bouquet to the wedding guests.* ◇ *according to* ***local custom*** **2** [sing.] (*formal*) something that a person does regularly: *It's my custom to drink tea in the afternoon.* **3** [U] (*BrE*) (BUSINESS) commercial activity; the practice of people buying things regularly from a particular shop, etc.: *The local shop lost a lot of custom when the new supermarket opened.* ➲ look at **customs**

customary /ˈkʌstəməri/ ***adj.*** according to custom; usual: *Is it customary to send cards at Christmas in your country?* ▶ **customarily** /ˈkʌstəmərəli/ ***adv.***

ˌcustom-ˈbuilt (*especially AmE* **custom**) ***adj.*** designed and built for a particular person

customer **⊶** /ˈkʌstəmə(r)/ ***noun*** [C] **1** a person who buys goods or services in a shop, restaurant, etc.: *The shop assistant was serving a customer.* ◇ *We send 'thank-you letters' to all our clients as a way of strengthening* ***customer loyalty***. ➲ look at **client** **2** (*informal*) (after certain adjectives) a person: *a tough/an awkward/an odd customer*

ˌcustomer ˈservice (*also* **ˌcustomer ˈcare** [U]) ***noun*** (BUSINESS) **1** [U,C] the way in which a company treats its customers and answers their questions, complaints, etc.: *The company provides excellent customer service.* **2 customer services** [U, with sing. or pl. verb] the department in a company that deals with customers' complaints, questions, etc.

ˌcustom-ˈmade (*especially AmE* **custom**) ***adj.*** designed and made for a particular person

customs **⊶** (*also* **Customs**) /ˈkʌstəmz/ ***noun*** [pl.] the place at an airport, etc. where government officials check your luggage to make sure you are not bringing goods into the country illegally: *a customs officer* ➲ look at **excise**

cut[1] **⊶** /kʌt/ ***verb*** (*pres. part.* **cutting**; *pt, pp* **cut**) **1** [I,T] to make an opening, wound or mark in sth using a sharp tool, for example a pair of scissors or a knife: *Be careful not to cut yourself on that broken glass!* ◇ *This knife doesn't cut very well.* **2** [T] ~ **sth (from sth)** to remove sth or a part of sth, using a knife, etc.: *She cut two slices of bread (from the loaf).* **3** [T] ~ **sth (in/into sth)** to divide sth into pieces with a knife, etc.: *She cut the cake into eight (pieces).* ◇ *He cut the rope in two.* **4** [T] to make sth shorter by using scissors, etc.: *I cut my own hair.* ◇ *to* ***have your hair cut*** (=at the hairdresser's). ◇ *to cut the grass* **5** [T] to make or form sth by removing material with a sharp tool: *She cut a hole in the card and pushed the string through.* ◇ *They cut a path through the jungle.* **6** [T] to reduce sth or make it shorter; to remove sth: ***to cut taxes/costs/spending*** ◇ *Several violent scenes in the film were cut.* **7** [T] (COMPUTING) to remove a piece of text from the screen: *Use the* ***cut and paste*** *buttons to change the order of the paragraphs.* **8** [I] ~ **across, along, through, etc. (sth)** to go across, etc. sth, in order to make your route shorter: *It's much quicker if we cut across the field.* **9** [T] (*spoken*) to stop sth: *Cut the chat and get on with your work!* **10** [T] to deeply offend sb or hurt their feelings: *His cruel remarks cut her deeply.*

PHR V **cut across sth** to affect or be true for different groups that usually stay separate: *The question of aid for the earthquake victims cuts across national boundaries.*

cut sth back; cut back (on sth) to reduce sth: *to cut back on public spending*

cut sth down 1 to make sth fall down by cutting it: *to cut down a tree* **2** to make sth shorter: *I have to cut my essay down to 2000 words.*

cut sth down; cut down (on sth) to reduce the quantity or amount of sth; to do sth less often: *You should cut down on fatty foods.*

cut in (on sb/sth) to interrupt sb/sth: *She kept cutting in on our conversation.*

cut sb off (often passive) to stop or interrupt sb's telephone conversation: *We were cut off before I could give her my message.*

cut sb/sth off (often passive) to stop the supply of sth to sb

cut sth off to block a road, etc. so that nothing can pass: *We must cut off all possible escape routes.*

cut sth off (sth) to remove sth from sth larger by cutting: *Be careful you don't cut your fingers off using that electric saw.*

cut sb/sth off (from sb/sth) (often passive) to prevent sb/sth from moving from a place or contacting people outside: *The farm was cut off from the village by heavy snow.*

cut sth open to open sth by cutting: *She fell and cut her head open.*

cut sth out 1 to remove sth or to form sth into a particular shape by cutting: *He cut the job advertisement out of the newspaper.* **2** to not include sth: *Cut out the boring details!* **3** (*especially AmE, informal*) to stop saying or doing sth that annoys sb: *Cut that out and leave me alone!* **4** (*informal*) to stop doing or using sth: *You'll only lose weight if you cut out sweet things from your diet.*

be cut out for sth; be cut out to be sth to have the qualities needed to do sth; to be suitable for sth/sb: *You're not cut out to be a soldier.*

cut sth up to cut sth into small pieces with a knife, etc.

cut² /kʌt/ *noun* [C] **1** an injury or opening in the skin made with a knife, etc.: *He had a deep cut on his forehead.* **2** an act of cutting: *to have a cut and blow-dry* (=at a hairdresser's) **3** a ~ (in sth) a reduction in size, amount, etc.: *a cut in government spending* ◇ ***a power cut*** (=when the electric current is stopped temporarily) **4** a piece of meat from a particular part of an animal: *cheap cuts of lamb* **5** (*informal*) a share of the profits from sth, especially sth dishonest ➲ look at **short cut**

cutback /ˈkʌtbæk/ *noun* [C] a reduction in amount or number: *The management were forced to make cutbacks in staff.*

cute /kjuːt/ *adj.* attractive; pretty: *Your little girl is so cute!* ◇ *a cute smile*

cuticle /ˈkjuːtɪkl/ *noun* [C] **1** an area of hard skin at the base of the nails on your fingers and toes **2** (BIOLOGY) a hard outer layer that covers and protects parts of a plant

cutlery /ˈkʌtləri/ *noun* [U] the knives, forks and spoons that you use for eating food

cutlet /ˈkʌtlət/ *noun* [C] a small, thick piece of meat, often with bone in it, that is cooked

ˈcut-off *noun* [C] the level or time at which sth stops: *The cut-off date is 12 May. After that we'll end the offer.*

ˌcut-ˈprice (*AmE* ˌcut-ˈrate) *adj.* (BUSINESS) sold at a reduced price; selling goods at low prices: *cut-price offers* ◇ *a cut-price store*

cutters /ˈkʌtəz/ *noun* [pl.] a tool that you use for cutting through sth, for example metal: *a pair of wire cutters*

ˈcut-throat *adj.* caring only about success and not worried about hurting anyone: *cut-throat business practices*

cutting¹ /ˈkʌtɪŋ/ *noun* [C] **1** (*AmE* **clipping**) a piece cut out from a newspaper, etc.: *press cuttings* **2** (AGRICULTURE) a piece cut off from a plant that you use for growing a new plant

cutting² /ˈkʌtɪŋ/ *adj.* (used about sth you say) unkind; meant to hurt sb's feelings: *a cutting remark*

ˌcutting ˈedge *noun* [sing.] **1 the ~ (of sth)** the newest, most advanced stage in the development of sth: *working at the cutting edge of computer technology* **2** an aspect of sth that gives it an advantage: *We're relying on him to give the team a cutting edge.*

CV /ˌsiː ˈviː/ (*AmE* **résumé**) *noun* [C] **curriculum vitae**; a formal list of your education and work experience, often used when you are trying to get a new job

cwm /kʊm/ = CORRIE

cwt. *abbr.* (in writing) a HUNDREDWEIGHT; a measure of weight, about 50.8 kg

cyanide /ˈsaɪənaɪd/ *noun* [U] (CHEMISTRY) a poisonous chemical

cyber- /ˈsaɪbə(r)/ (in nouns and adjectives) (COMPUTING) connected with electronic communication networks, especially the Internet: *cybernetics* ◇ *cybercafe*

cybercafe /ˈsaɪbəkæfeɪ/ *noun* [C] a CAFE with computers where customers can pay to use the Internet

cybernetics /ˌsaɪbəˈnetɪks/ *noun* [U] the scientific study of communication and control, in which, for example, human and animal brains are compared with machines and electronic devices

cyberspace /ˈsaɪbəspeɪs/ *noun* [U] a place that is not real, where electronic messages exist while they are being sent from one computer to another

cycle¹ AW /ˈsaɪkl/ *noun* [C] **1** the fact of a series of events being repeated many times, always in the same order: *the carbon/nitrogen cycle* ➲ picture at **carbon**, **nitrogen**, **rock**, **water** **2** a bicycle or motor cycle: *a cycle shop* SYN **bike**

cycle² AW /ˈsaɪkl/ *verb* [I] to ride a bicycle: *He usually cycles to school.* ◇ *We **go cycling** most weekends.*

ˈcycle lane (*AmE* **ˈbicycle lane**; **ˈbike lane**) *noun* [C] a part of a road that only bicycles are allowed to use

cyclic AW /ˈsaɪklɪk; ˈsɪk-/ (*also* **cyclical** /ˈsaɪklɪkl; ˈsɪk-/) *adj.* repeated many times and always happening in the same order: *the cyclic processes of nature* ◇ *Economic activity often follows a cyclical pattern.* ▶ **cyclically** *adv.*: *events that occur cyclically*

cyclist /ˈsaɪklɪst/ *noun* [C] a person who rides a bicycle

cyclone /ˈsaɪkləʊn/ *noun* [C] (GEOGRAPHY) a violent tropical storm in which strong winds move in a circle ➲ note at **storm** ▶ **cyclonic** /saɪˈklɒnɪk/ *adj.*

cygnet /ˈsɪgnət/ *noun* [C] the young of a SWAN (=a large white bird)

cylinder /ˈsɪlɪndə(r)/ *noun* [C] **1** (GEOMETRY) a solid or hollow figure with round ends and long straight sides ➲ picture at **solid** **2** an object shaped like a **cylinder**, especially one used as a container: ***a gas/oxygen cylinder*** ◇ ***a measuring cylinder*** (=a container used in a laboratory) **3** a part of an engine that is shaped like a tube, for example in a car: *a six-cylinder engine* ▶ **cylindrical** /səˈlɪndrɪkl/ *adj.*

cymbal /ˈsɪmbl/ *noun* [C, usually pl.] (MUSIC) one of a pair of round metal plates used as a musical instrument. Cymbals make a loud ringing sound when you hit them together or with a stick. ➲ picture on **page 465**

cynic /ˈsɪnɪk/ *noun* [C] a person who believes that people only do things for themselves, rather than to help others: *Don't be such a cynic. He did it to help us, not for the money.* ▶ **cynical** /ˈsɪnɪkl/ *adj.*: *a cynical remark* ▶ **cynically** /-kli/ *adv.* ▶ **cynicism** /ˈsɪnɪsɪzəm/ *noun* [U]

cypress /ˈsaɪprəs/ *noun* [C] a tall straight EVERGREEN tree (=a tree of the kind that does not lose its leaves in winter)

Cyrillic /səˈrɪlɪk/ *noun* [U] (LANGUAGE) the alphabet that is used in languages such as Russian

cyst /sɪst/ *noun* [C] (HEALTH) a swelling or a lump filled with liquid in the body or under the skin

cystic fibrosis /ˌsɪstɪk faɪˈbrəʊsɪs/ *noun* [U] (HEALTH) a serious medical condition that some people are born with, in which some organs do not work correctly. It can cause death.

cystitis /sɪˈstaɪtɪs/ *noun* [U] (HEALTH) an infection, especially in women, of the BLADDER (=the organ in which liquid waste collects before leaving the body) that makes it painful to go to the toilet

cytology /saɪˈtɒlədʒi/ *noun* [U] (BIOLOGY) the scientific study of the structure and function of cells from living things

cytoplasm /ˈsaɪtəʊplæzəm/ *noun* [U] (BIOLOGY) all the living material in a cell, except for the NUCLEUS (=the central part) ➲ picture at **cell**

cytosine /ˈsaɪtəsiːn/ *noun* [U] (BIOLOGY) one of the four COMPOUNDS that make up DNA and RNA ➲ picture at **DNA**

czar, czarina = TSAR, TSARINA

D d

D, d /diː/ ***noun*** [C,U] (*pl.* **D's**; **d's** /diːz/) the fourth letter of the English alphabet: *'David' begins with (a) 'D'.*

d. *abbr.* died: *W A Mozart, d. 1791*

DA (*AmE* **D.A.**) /ˌdiː ˈeɪ/ (LAW) = DISTRICT ATTORNEY

dab[1] /dæb/ ***verb*** [I,T] (**dabbing**; **dabbed**) to touch sth lightly, usually several times: *He dabbed the cut with some cotton wool.*

PHR V **dab sth on/off (sth)** to put sth on or to remove sth lightly: *to dab some antiseptic on a wound*

dab[2] /dæb/ ***noun*** [C] **1** a light touch: *She gave her eyes a dab with a handkerchief.* **2** a small quantity of sth that is put on a surface: *a dab of paint/perfume*

dabble /ˈdæbl/ ***verb*** **1** [I] to become involved in sth in a way that is not very serious: *to dabble in politics* **2** [T] to put your hands, feet, etc. in water and move them around: *We sat on the bank and dabbled our toes in the river.*

dad 🔑 /dæd/ ***noun*** [C] (*informal*) father: *Is that your dad?* ◇ *Come on, Dad!*

Dada /ˈdɑːdɑː/ ***noun*** [U] (ART) an early 20th century movement in art, literature, music and film which made fun of social and artistic conventions ▶ **Dadaism** /ˈdɑːdɑːɪzəm/ ***noun*** [U] **Dadaist** /ˈdɑːdɑːɪst/ ***noun*** [C]

daddy /ˈdædi/ ***noun*** [C] (*pl.* **daddies**) (*informal*) (used by children) father: *I want my daddy!*

daffodil /ˈdæfədɪl/ ***noun*** [C] a tall yellow flower that grows in the spring

daft /dɑːft/ ***adj.*** (*informal*) silly, often in a way that is amusing: *Don't be daft.* ◇ *a daft idea*

dagger /ˈdæɡə(r)/ ***noun*** [C] a type of knife used as a weapon, especially in past times ➲ picture at **weapon**

daily[1] 🔑 /ˈdeɪli/ ***adj.***, ***adv.*** done, made or happening every day: *a daily routine/delivery/newspaper* ◇ *Our airline flies to Japan daily.*

daily[2] /ˈdeɪli/ ***noun*** [C] (*pl.* **dailies**) (*informal*) a newspaper that is published every day except Sunday

dainty /ˈdeɪnti/ ***adj.*** **1** small and pretty: *a dainty lace handkerchief* **2** (used about a person's movements) very careful in a way that tries to show good manners: *Veronica took a dainty bite of the giant hot dog.* ▶ **daintily** ***adv.***

dairy[1] /ˈdeəri/ ***noun*** [C] (*pl.* **dairies**) **1** a place on a farm where milk is kept and butter, cheese, etc. are made **2** a company which sells milk, butter, eggs, etc.

dairy[2] /ˈdeəri/ ***adj.*** (only *before* a noun) **1** made from milk: ***dairy products/produce*** (= milk, butter, cheese, etc.) **2** connected with the production of milk: *dairy cattle* ◇ *a dairy farm*

daisy /ˈdeɪzi/ ***noun*** [C] (*pl.* **daisies**) a small white flower with a yellow centre, which usually grows wild in grass

dam /dæm/ ***noun*** [C] a wall built across a river to hold back the water and form a lake (**reservoir**) behind it ▶ **dam** ***verb*** [T] (*pres. part.* **damming**; *pt*, *pp* **dammed**)

damage[1] 🔑 /ˈdæmɪdʒ/ ***noun*** **1** [U] ~ (to sth) harm or injury caused when sth is broken or spoiled: *Earthquakes can **cause** terrible **damage** in urban areas.* ◇ *It will take weeks to **repair the damage** done by the vandals.* **2** **damages** [pl.] (LAW) money that you can ask for if sb damages sth of yours or hurts you: *Mrs Rees, who lost a leg in the crash, was awarded damages of £100000.*

damage[2] 🔑 /ˈdæmɪdʒ/ ***verb*** [T] to spoil or harm sth, for example by breaking it: *The roof was damaged by the storm.* ▶ **damaging** ***adj.***: *These rumours could be damaging to her reputation.*

dame /deɪm/ ***noun*** **1** [C] **Dame** (*BrE*) a title given to a woman as an honour because of sth special that she has done: *Dame Agatha Christie* **2** (*old-fashioned*) (*AmE, informal*) a woman

damn[1] /dæm/ ***verb*** [I,T] (*slang*) a swear word that people use to show that they are angry: *Damn (it)! I've left my money behind.*

damn[2] /dæm/ (*also* **damned**) ***adj.***, ***adv.*** (*slang*) **1** (a swear word that people use for emphasizing what they are saying) very: *Read it! It's a damn good book.* **2** a swear word that people use to show that they are angry: *Some damn fool has parked too close to me.*

damn[3] /dæm/ ***noun***

IDM **not give a damn (about sb/sth)** (*slang*) not care at all: *I don't give a damn what he thinks about me.*

damning /ˈdæmɪŋ/ ***adj.*** that criticizes sth very much: *There was a damning article about the book in the newspaper.*

damp[1] 🔑 /dæmp/ ***adj.*** a little wet: *The house had been empty and felt rather damp.* ▶ **damp** ***noun*** [U]: *She hated the damp and the cold of the English climate.*

damp[2] /dæmp/ ***verb*** [T] ~ **sth (down)** **1** to make a fire burn less strongly or stop burning: *He tried to damp (down) the flames.* **2** to make sth less strong or urgent: *He tried to damp down their expectations in case they failed.*

dampen /ˈdæmpən/ ***verb*** [T] **1** to make sth less strong or urgent: *Even the awful weather did not dampen their enthusiasm for the trip.* **2** to make sth a little wet: *He dampened his hair to try to stop it sticking up.*

damson /ˈdæmzn/ ***noun*** [C] a type of small dark purple fruit (**plum**)

dance[1] 🔑 /dɑːns/ ***noun*** **1** [C] a series of steps and movements which you do to music **2** [U] dancing as a form of art or entertainment: *She's very interested in modern dance.* **3** [C] (*old-fashioned*) a social meeting at which people dance with each other: *My parents met at a dance.*

dance[2] 🔑 /dɑːns/ ***verb*** **1** [I,T] to move around to the rhythm of music by making a series of steps: *I can't dance very well.* ◇ *to dance the samba* **2** [I] to jump and move around with energy: *She was dancing up and down with excitement.*

dancer 🔑 /ˈdɑːnsə(r)/ ***noun*** [C] a person who dances, often as a job: *a ballet dancer* ◇ *She's a good dancer.*

dancing 🔑 /ˈdɑːnsɪŋ/ ***noun*** [U] moving your body to music: *I'm hopeless at dancing – I've got no sense of rhythm.* ◇ *Will there be dancing at the party?*

dandelion /ˈdændɪlaɪən/ ***noun*** [C] a small wild plant with a bright yellow flower

dandruff /ˈdændrʌf/ *noun* [U] small pieces of dead skin in the hair, that look like white powder

danger ⊶ /ˈdeɪndʒə(r)/ *noun* **1** [U, C] the chance that sb/sth may be hurt, killed or damaged or that sth bad may happen: *When he saw the men had knives, he realized his life was* ***in danger***. ◇ *The men kept on running until they thought they were* ***out of danger***. ◇ *If things carry on as they are,* ***there's a danger that*** *the factory may have to close.* **2** [C] a ~ **(to sb/sth)** a person or thing that can cause injury, pain or damage to sb: *Drunk drivers are* ***a danger to*** *everyone on the road.*

dangerous ⊶ /ˈdeɪndʒərəs/ *adj.* likely to cause injury or damage: *a dangerous animal/road/illness* ◇ *Police warn that the man is highly dangerous.* ▸ **dangerously** *adv.*: *He was standing dangerously close to the cliff edge.*

dangle /ˈdæŋɡl/ *verb* [I,T] to hang freely; to hold sth so that it hangs down in this way: *She sat on the fence with her legs dangling.* ◇ *The police dangled a rope from the bridge and the man grabbed it.*

dank /dæŋk/ *adj.* wet, cold and unpleasant

dare[1] ⊶ /deə(r)/ *verb* **1** [I] (usually in negative sentences) ~ **(to) do sth** to have enough courage to do sth: *Nobody dared (to) speak.* ◇ *I daren't ask her to lend me any more money.* ◇ *We were so frightened that we didn't dare (to) go into the room.* **2** [T] ~ **sb (to do sth)** to ask or tell sb to do sth in order to see if they have the courage to do it: *Can you jump off that wall? Go on, I dare you!* ◇ *He dared his friend to put a mouse in the teacher's bag.*

IDM **don't you dare** used for telling sb very strongly not to do sth: *Don't you dare tell my parents about this!*

how dare you used when you are angry about sth that sb has done: *How dare you speak to me like that!*

I dare say used when you are saying sth is probable: *'I think you should accept the offer.' 'I dare say you're right.'*

dare[2] /deə(r)/ *noun* [C, usually sing.] something dangerous that sb asks you to do, to see if you have the courage to do it: *'Why did you try to swim across the river?' '****For a dare****.'*

daredevil /ˈdeədevl/ *noun* [C] a person who likes to do dangerous things

daring /ˈdeərɪŋ/ *adj.* involving or taking risks; brave: *a daring attack* ▸ **daring** *noun* [U]: *The climb required skill and daring.*

dark[1] ⊶ /dɑːk/ *adj.* **1** with no light or very little light: *It was a dark night, with no moon.* ◇ *What time does it* ***get dark*** *in winter?* **2** (used about a colour) not light; nearer black than white: *dark blue* OPP **light**, **pale** **3** (*especially BrE*) (used about a person's hair, skin or eyes) brown or black; not fair: *She was small and dark with brown eyes.* **4** (only *before* a noun) hidden and frightening; mysterious: *He seemed friendly, but there was a dark side to his character.* **5** (only *before* a noun) sad; without hope: *the dark days of the recession*

dark[2] ⊶ /dɑːk/ *noun* [sing.] **the dark** the state of having no light: *He's afraid of the dark.* ◇ *Why are you sitting alone* ***in the dark****?*

IDM **before/after dark** before /after the sun goes down in the evening

(be/keep sb) in the dark (about sth) (be/keep sb) in a position of not knowing about sth: *Don't keep me in the dark. Tell me!*

the ˈdark ages *noun* [pl.] **1 the Dark Ages** (HISTORY) the period in western Europe between the end of the Roman Empire (about 500 AD) and the end of the 10th century AD **2** a period of history or a time when sth was not developed or modern: *Back in the dark ages of computing, in about 1980, they started a software company.*

darken /ˈdɑːkən/ *verb* [I,T] to become or to make sth darker: *The sky suddenly darkened and it started to rain.*

ˌdark ˈglasses = SUNGLASSES

darkly /ˈdɑːkli/ *adv.* (*written*) **1** in a frightening or unpleasant way: *He hinted darkly that someone would soon be going to hospital.* **2** showing a dark colour

darkness /ˈdɑːknəs/ *noun* [U] the state of being dark: *We sat* ***in total darkness****, waiting for the lights to come back on.*

darkroom /ˈdɑːkruːm; -rʊm/ *noun* [C] a room that can be made completely dark so that film can be taken out of a camera and photographs can be produced there

darling /ˈdɑːlɪŋ/ *noun* [C] a word that you say to sb you love

darmstadtium /ˌdɑːmˈʃtætiəm/ *noun* [U] (*symbol* **Ds**) (CHEMISTRY) a chemical element. **Darmstadtium** is a RADIOACTIVE element that is produced artificially. ❶ For more information on the periodic table of elements, look at pages R34-5.

darn /dɑːn/ *verb* [I,T] to repair a hole in clothes by sewing across it in one direction and then in the other: *I hate darning socks.*

dart[1] /dɑːt/ *noun* **1** [C] an object like a small arrow. It is thrown in a game or shot as a weapon: *The keeper fired a tranquillizer dart into the tiger to send it to sleep.* **2 darts** [U] a game in which you throw **darts** at a round board with numbers on it (**a dartboard**)

dart[2] /dɑːt/ *verb* [I,T] to move or make sth move suddenly and quickly in a certain direction: *A rabbit darted across the field.* ◇ *She darted an angry glance at me.*

dash[1] /dæʃ/ *noun* **1** [sing.] an act of going somewhere suddenly and quickly: *Suddenly the prisoner made a dash for the door.* **2** [C, usually sing.] a small amount of sth that you add to sth else: *a dash of lemon juice* **3** [C] (LANGUAGE) a small horizontal line (–) used in writing, especially for adding extra information ➲ look at **hyphen**

dash[2] /dæʃ/ *verb* **1** [I] to go somewhere suddenly and quickly: *We all dashed for shelter when it started to rain.* ◇ *I must dash – I'm late.* **2** [I,T] to hit sth with great force; to throw sth so that it hits sth else very hard: *She dashed her racket to the ground.*

IDM **dash sb's hopes (of sth/of doing sth)** to completely destroy sb's hopes of doing sth

PHR V **dash sth off** to write or draw sth very quickly: *I dashed off a note to my boss and left.*

dashboard /ˈdæʃbɔːd/ *noun* [C] the part in a car in front of the driver where most of the switches, etc. are

data ⊶ AW /ˈdeɪtə; ˈdɑːtə/ *noun* [U, pl.] (used as a plural noun in technical English, when the singular is *datum*) facts or information: *to gather/collect data* ◇ ***data capture/retrieval*** (=ways of storing and looking at information on a computer) ◇ ***data processing***

database /ˈdeɪtəbeɪs/ *noun* [C] (COMPUTING) a large amount of data that is stored in a computer and can easily be used, added to, etc.

date[1] ⊶ /deɪt/ *noun* **1** [C] a particular day of the month or year: *What's the date today?/What date is it today?/What's today's date?* ◇ *What's your* ***date of birth****?* ◇ *We'd better* ***fix a date*** *for the next meeting.*

2 [sing.] a particular time: *We can discuss this **at a later date**.* ➲ look at **sell-by date** **3** [C] an arrangement to meet sb, especially a boyfriend or girlfriend: *Shall we **make a date** to have lunch together?* ◇ *I've got a date with Roxanne on Friday night.* ➲ look at **blind date** **4** [C] a small, sweet, dark brown fruit that comes from a tree which grows in hot countries

IDM **out of date** **1** not fashionable; no longer useful: *out-of-date methods/machinery* **2** no longer able to be used: *I must renew my passport. It's out of date.*

to date (*formal*) until now: *We've had very few complaints to date.*

up to date **1** completely modern: *The new kitchen will be right up to date, with all the latest gadgets.* **2** with all the latest information; having done everything that you should: *In this report we'll bring you up to date with the latest news from the area.*

date² 🔑 /deɪt/ ***verb*** **1** [T] to discover or guess how old sth is: *The skeleton has been dated at about 3000 BC.* **2** [T] to write the day's date on sth: *The letter is dated 24 March, 2000.* **3** [I,T] to seem, or to make sb/sth seem, old-fashioned: *We chose a simple style so that it wouldn't date as quickly.*

PHR V **date back to…; date from…** to have existed since…: *The house dates back to the seventeenth century.* ◇ *photographs dating from before the war*

dated /ˈdeɪtɪd/ ***adj.*** old-fashioned; belonging to a time in the past: *This sort of jacket looks rather dated now.*

the ˈdate line (**GEOGRAPHY**) = THE INTERNATIONAL DATE LINE

dative /ˈdeɪtɪv/ ***noun*** [C] (**LANGUAGE**) the form of a noun, a pronoun, or an adjective in some languages when it is, or is connected with, the INDIRECT OBJECT of a verb: *In the sentence 'Give me the book', 'me' is in the dative.* ➲ look at **accusative**, **genitive**, **nominative**, **vocative**

datum /ˈdeɪtəm/ → DATA

daub /dɔːb/ ***verb*** [T] ~ **A on B**; ~ **B with A** to spread a substance such as paint, mud, etc. thickly and/or carelessly onto sth: *The walls had been daubed with graffiti.*

daughter 🔑 /ˈdɔːtə(r)/ ***noun*** [C] a female child: *I have two sons and one daughter.* ◇ *Janet's daughter is a doctor.*

ˈdaughter-in-law ***noun*** [C] (*pl.* **daughters-in-law**) the wife of your son

daunt /dɔːnt/ ***verb*** [T] (usually passive) to frighten or to worry sb by being too big or difficult: *Don't be daunted by all the controls – in fact it's a simple machine to use.* ▶ **daunting** ***adj.***: *a daunting task*

dawdle /ˈdɔːdl/ ***verb*** [I] to go somewhere very slowly: *Stop dawdling! We've got to be there by two.*

dawn¹ /dɔːn/ ***noun*** **1** [U, C] the early morning, when light first appears in the sky: *before/at dawn* ◇ ***Dawn was breaking*** (= it was starting to get light) *as I set off to work.* **2** [sing.] the beginning: *the dawn of civilization*

IDM **the crack of dawn** → CRACK²

dawn² /dɔːn/ ***verb*** [I] **1** (*formal*) to begin to grow light, after the night: *The day dawned bright and cold.* ◇ (*figurative*) *A new era of peace is dawning.* **2** ~ **(on sb)** to become clear (to sb): *Suddenly it dawned on her. 'Of course!' she said. 'You're Mike's brother!'*

day 🔑 /deɪ/ ***noun*** **1** [C] a period of 24 hours. Seven days make up a week: *'**What day is it** today?' 'Tuesday.'* ◇ *We went to Italy for ten days.* ◇ *We're meeting again **the day after tomorrow /in two days' time**.* ◇ *The next/following day I saw Mark again.* ◇ *I'd already spoken to him the day before/the previous day.* ◇ *I have to take these pills twice a day.* ◇ *I work six days a week. Sunday's my **day off*** (= when I do not work). **2** [C,U] the time when the sky is light; not night: *The days were warm but the nights were freezing.* ◇ *It's been raining all day (long).* ◇ *Owls sleep **by day*** (= during the day) *and hunt at night.* **3** [C] the hours of the day when you work: *She's expected to work a seven-hour day.* **4** [C] (*also* **days**) a particular period of time in the past: *in Shakespeare's day* ◇ *There weren't so many cars in those days.*

IDM **at the end of the day** → END¹

break of day → BREAK²

call it a day → CALL¹

day by day every day; as time passes: *Day by day, she was getting a little bit stronger.*

day in, day out every day, without any change: *He sits at his desk working, day in, day out.*

day-to-day happening as a normal part of each day; usual

from day to day; from one day to the next within a short period of time: *Things change so quickly that we never know what will happen from one day to the next.*

have a field day → FIELD DAY

it's early days (yet) → EARLY

make sb's day (*informal*) to make sb very happy

one day; some day at some time in the future: *Some day we'll go back and see all our old friends.*

the other day a few days ago; recently: *I bumped into him in town the other day.*

the present day → PRESENT¹

these days in the present age SYN **nowadays**

daybreak /ˈdeɪbreɪk/ ***noun*** [U] the time in the early morning when light first appears SYN **dawn**

daydream /ˈdeɪdriːm/ ***noun*** [C] thoughts that are not connected with what you are doing; often pleasant scenes in your imagination: *The child stared out of the window, lost in a daydream.* ▶ **daydream** ***verb*** [I]: *Don't just sit there daydreaming – do some work!*

daylight /ˈdeɪlaɪt/ ***noun*** [U] the light that there is during the day: *The colours look quite different **in daylight**.* ◇ *daylight hours*

IDM **broad daylight** → BROAD

ˌdaylight ˈsaving time (*also* **ˈdaylight time**) ***noun*** [U] (*AmE*) (*abbr.* **DST**) (**GEOGRAPHY**) = SUMMER TIME

ˌday reˈturn ***noun*** [C] (*BrE*) a train or bus ticket for going somewhere and coming back on the same day. It is cheaper than a normal return ticket.

daytime /ˈdeɪtaɪm/ ***noun*** [U] the time when it is light; not night: *These flowers open **in the daytime** and close again at night.* ◇ *daytime TV*

ˌday-to-ˈday ***adj.*** **1** planning for only one day at a time: *I have organized the cleaning **on a day-to-day basis**, until our usual cleaner returns.* **2** involving the usual events or tasks of each day: *She has been looking after the **day-to-day running** of the school.*

daze /deɪz/ ***noun***

IDM **in a daze** unable to think or react normally; confused

dazed /deɪzd/ ***adj.*** unable to think or react normally; confused: *He had a dazed expression on his face.*

dazzle /ˈdæzl/ ***verb*** [T] (usually passive) **1** (used about a bright light) to make sb unable to see for a short time: *She was dazzled by the other car's headlights.* **2** to impress sb very much: *He had been dazzled by her beauty.* ▶ **dazzling** ***adj.***: *a dazzling light*

DC /ˌdiː ˈsiː/ ***abbr.*** (PHYSICS) = DIRECT CURRENT

DDT /ˌdiː diː ˈtiː/ ***abbr., noun*** [U] (CHEMISTRY) a poisonous chemical substance that farmers use to kill insects

de- /diː/ ***prefix*** (in nouns, verbs, adjectives and adverbs) **1** the opposite of: *decompress* **2** taking sth away: *decaffeinated coffee*

deacon /ˈdiːkən/ ***noun*** [C] (*feminine* **deaconess**) (RELIGION) an official in some Christian churches

dead[1] /ded/ ***adj.*** **1** no longer alive: *My father's dead. He died two years ago.* ◇ *Police found a dead body under the bridge.* ◇ *The man was shot dead by a masked gunman.* ◇ *dead leaves* ➲ noun **death**, verb **die**
2 no longer used; finished: *Latin is a dead language.* OPP **living** **3** (not *before* a noun) (used about a part of the body) no longer able to feel anything: *Oh no, my foot's* ***gone dead****. I was sitting on it for too long.* **4** (not *before* a noun) (used about a piece of equipment) no longer working: *I picked up the telephone but the line was dead.* ◇ *This battery's dead.* **5** without movement, activity or interest: *This town is completely dead after 11 o'clock at night.* **6** (only *before* a noun) complete or exact: *a dead silence/calm* ◇ *The arrow hit the dead centre of the target.*
IDM **drop dead** → DROP[1]

dead[2] /ded/ **the dead** ***noun*** [pl.] people who have died: *A church service was held in memory of the dead.*
IDM **in the dead of night** in the middle of the night, when it is very dark and quiet

dead[3] /ded/ ***adv.*** completely, exactly or very: *The car made a strange noise and then stopped dead.* ◇ *He's dead keen to start work.*

deaden /ˈdedn/ ***verb*** [T] to make sth less strong, painful, etc.: *They gave her drugs to try and deaden the pain.*

ˌdead ˈend ***noun*** [C] **1** a road, passage, etc. that is closed at one end: *We came to a dead end and had to turn back.* **2** a point, situation, etc. from which you can make no further progress: *The police had reached a dead end in their investigations.* ◇ *He felt he was in* ***a dead-end job*** (= one with low wages and no hope of promotion), *so he left.*

ˌdead ˈheat ***noun*** [C] (SPORT) the result of a race when two people, etc. finish at exactly the same time

deadline /ˈdedlaɪn/ ***noun*** [C] a time or date before which sth must be done or finished: *I usually* ***set*** *myself* ***a deadline*** *when I have a project to do.* ◇ *A journalist is used to having to* ***meet deadlines****.*

deadlock /ˈdedlɒk/ ***noun*** [sing., U] a situation in which two sides cannot reach an agreement: *Talks have reached (a) deadlock.* ◇ *to try to break the deadlock*

ˌdead ˈloss ***noun*** [C, usually sing.] (*informal*) a person or thing that is not helpful or useful

deadly /ˈdedli/ ***adj., adv.*** (**deadlier**; **deadliest**) **1** causing or likely to cause death: *a deadly poison/weapon/disease* **2** very great; complete: *They're deadly enemies.* **3** completely; extremely: *I'm not joking. In fact I'm deadly serious.* **4** extremely accurate, so that no defence is possible: *That player is deadly when he gets in front of the goal.*

deadpan /ˈdedpæn/ ***adj.*** without any expression on your face or in your voice: *He told the joke with a completely deadpan face.*

deadweight /ˌdedˈweɪt/ ***noun*** [C, usually sing.] **1** a thing that is very heavy and difficult to lift or move **2** a person or thing that makes it difficult to make progress or succeed

ˌdead ˈwood ***noun*** [U] people or things that have become useless or unnecessary in an organization

deaf /def/ ***adj.*** **1** (HEALTH) unable to hear anything or unable to hear very well: *You'll have to speak louder. My father's a bit deaf.* ◇ *to* ***go deaf*** **2 the deaf** ***noun*** [pl.] people who cannot hear **3** ~ **to sth** not wanting to listen to sth: *I've told her what I think but she's deaf to my advice.* ▶ **deafness** ***noun*** [U]

deafen /ˈdefn/ ***verb*** [T] (usually passive) to make sb unable to hear by making a very loud noise: *We were deafened by the loud music.* ▶ **deafening** ***adj.***: *deafening music*

deal[1] /diːl/ ***verb*** (*pt, pp* **dealt** /delt/) **1** [I,T] ~ **(sth) (out)**; ~ **(sth) (to sb)** to give cards to players in a game of cards: *Start by dealing seven cards to each player.* **2** [I] ~ **(in sth)**; ~ **(with sb)** (BUSINESS) to do business, especially buying and selling goods: *He deals in second-hand cars.* ◇ *Our firm deals with customers all over the world.* **3** [I,T] (*informal*) to buy and sell illegal drugs
IDM **deal sb/sth a blow**; **deal a blow to sb/sth** **1** to hit sb/sth: *He was dealt a nasty blow to the head in the accident.* **2** to give sb a shock, etc.: *This news dealt a terrible blow to my father.*
PHR V **deal sth out** to give sth to a number of people: *The profits will be dealt out among us.*
deal with sb to treat sb in a particular way; to handle sb: *He's a difficult man. Nobody quite knows how to deal with him.*
deal with sth **1** to take suitable action in a particular situation in order to solve a problem, complete a task, etc.; to handle sth: *My secretary will deal with my correspondence while I'm away.* **2** to have sth as its subject: *This chapter deals with letter writing.*

deal[2] /diːl/ ***noun*** [C] **1** (BUSINESS) an agreement or arrangement, especially in business: *We're hoping to* ***do a deal*** *with an Italian company.* ◇ *Let's* ***make a deal*** *not to criticize each other's work.* ◇ *'I'll help you with your essay if you'll fix my bike.' 'OK,* ***it's a deal****!'* **2** the way that sb is treated: *With high fares and unreliable services, rail users are* ***getting a raw deal*** (= unfair treatment). ◇ *The new law aims to give pensioners* ***a fair deal****.* **3** the action of giving cards to players in a card game
IDM **a big deal/no big deal** → BIG
a good/great deal (of sth) a lot (of sth): *I've spent a great deal of time on this report.*

dealer /ˈdiːlə(r)/ ***noun*** [C] **1** a person whose business is buying and selling things: *a dealer in gold and silver* ◇ *a drug dealer* **2** the person who gives the cards to the players in a game of cards

dealing /ˈdiːlɪŋ/ ***noun*** (BUSINESS) **1 dealings** [pl.] relations, especially in business: *We had some dealings with that firm several years ago.* **2** [U] buying and selling: *share dealing*

dealt past tense, past participle of **deal**[1]

dean /diːn/ ***noun*** [C] **1** (RELIGION) a priest who is responsible for a large church or a number of small churches **2** (EDUCATION) a person in a university who is in charge of a department of studies
3 (EDUCATION) (in a college or university, especially at Oxford or Cambridge) a person who is responsible for the discipline of students

dear[1] /dɪə(r)/ ***adj.*** **1** used at the beginning of a letter before the name or title of the person you are writing to: *Dear Sarah, ...* ◇ *Dear Sir or Madam, ...* **2** ~ **(to sb)** loved by or important to sb: *It was a subject that was very dear to him.* ◇ *She's one of my dearest friends.* **3** (*BrE*) expensive: *How can people afford to smoke when cigarettes are so dear?*

IDM **close/dear/near to sb's heart** → HEART

dear² /dɪə(r)/ ***exclamation*** **1** used for expressing disappointment, sadness, surprise, etc.: *Dear me! Aren't you ready?* **2** (*old-fashioned*) used when speaking to sb you know well: *Would you like a cup of tea, dear?*

dearly /'dɪəli/ ***adv.*** **1** very much: *I'd dearly like to go there again.* **2** (*formal*) in a way that causes damage or suffering, or costs a lot of money: *I've already paid dearly for that mistake.*

dearth /dɜ:θ/ ***noun*** [sing.] **a ~ (of sb/sth)** a lack of sth; not enough of sth: *There's a dearth of young people in the village.*

death ⊶ /deθ/ ***noun*** **1** [C,U] the end of sb/sth's life; dying: *There were two deaths and many other people were injured in the accident.* ◇ *The police do not know the* ***cause of death****.* ◇ *There was no food and people were* ***starving to death****.* ➲ adjective **dead**, verb **die**
2 [U] the end (of sth): *the death of communism*
IDM **catch your death** → CATCH¹
a matter of life and/or death → MATTER¹
put sb to death (usually passive) (*formal*) to kill sb as a punishment, in past times
sick to death of sb/sth → SICK¹
sudden death → SUDDEN

deathbed /'deθbed/ ***noun*** [C] the bed in which sb is dying or dies

'**death certificate** ***noun*** [C] an official document signed by a doctor that states the time and cause of sb's death

deathly /'deθli/ ***adj.***, ***adv.*** like death: *There was a deathly silence.*

'**death penalty** ***noun*** [sing.] (LAW) the legal punishment of being killed for a crime ➲ look at **capital punishment**

'**death rate** ***noun*** [C] **1** (SOCIAL STUDIES) the number of deaths every year for every 1000 people in the population of a place: *a* ***high/low death rate*** **2** (HEALTH) the number of deaths every year from a particular disease or in a particular group: *Death rates from heart disease have risen considerably in recent years.*

ˌ**death 'row** ***noun*** [U] (especially in the US) the cells in a prison for prisoners who are waiting to be killed as punishment for a serious crime: *prisoners* ***on death row***

'**death toll** ***noun*** [C] the number of people killed in a disaster, war, accident, etc.

'**death trap** ***noun*** [C] a building, road, vehicle, etc. that is dangerous and could cause sb's death

debase /dɪ'beɪs/ ***verb*** [T] (usually passive) (*formal*) to reduce the quality or value of sth

debatable AW /dɪ'beɪtəbl/ ***adj.*** not certain; that you could argue about: *It's debatable whether people have a better lifestyle these days.*

debate¹ ⊶ AW /dɪ'beɪt/ ***noun*** **1** [C] a formal argument or discussion of a question at a public meeting or in Parliament **2** [U] general discussion about sth expressing different opinions: *There's been a lot of debate about the cause of acid rain.*

debate² ⊶ AW /dɪ'beɪt/ ***verb*** **1** [I,T] to discuss sth in a formal way or at a public meeting **2** [T] to think about or discuss sth before deciding what to do: *They debated whether to go or not.*

debauched /dɪ'bɔ:tʃt/ ***adj.*** behaving in a way that is immoral or unacceptable to most people: *debauched sexual practices*

debenture /dɪ'bentʃə(r)/ ***noun*** (*BrE*) (ECONOMICS) an official document that is given by a company, showing it has borrowed money from a person and stating the interest payments that it will make to them: *Payment of interest is made to the debenture holder at a specified rate and at clearly defined intervals.*

debilitate /dɪ'bɪlɪteɪt/ ***verb*** [T] (*formal*) **1** to make sb's body or mind weaker: *a debilitating disease* **2** to make a country, an organization, etc. weaker

debit¹ /'debɪt/ ***noun*** [C] (FINANCE) an amount of money paid out of a bank account OPP **credit¹** ➲ look at **direct debit**

debit² /'debɪt/ ***verb*** [T] (FINANCE) to take an amount of money out of a bank account, etc. usually as a payment; to record this

'**debit card** ***noun*** [C] (FINANCE) a plastic card that can be used to take money directly from your bank account when you pay for sth ➲ look at **credit card**

debrief /ˌdi:'bri:f/ ***verb*** [T] **~ sb (on sth)** to ask sb questions officially, in order to get information about the task that they have just completed: *He was taken to a US airbase to be debriefed on the mission.* ➲ look at **brief** ▸ **debriefing** ***noun*** [C]: *a debriefing session*

debris /'debri:/ ***noun*** [U] pieces from sth that has been destroyed, especially in an accident

debt ⊶ /det/ ***noun*** **1** [C] (FINANCE) an amount of money that you owe to sb: *She borrowed a lot of money and she's still paying off the debt.* **2** [U] (FINANCE) the state of owing money: *After he lost his job, he* ***got into debt****.* **3** [C, usually sing.] (*formal*) something that you owe sb, for example because they have helped or been kind to you: *In his speech he acknowledged his debt to his family and friends for their support.*
IDM **be in/out of debt** to owe/not owe money
be in sb's debt (*formal*) to feel grateful to sb for sth that they have done for you

debtor /'detə(r)/ ***noun*** [C] a person who owes money

debug /ˌdi:'bʌg/ ***verb*** [T] (**debugged**; **debugging**) (COMPUTING) to look for and remove the faults in a computer program

début (*also* **debut**) /'deɪbju:/ ***noun*** [C] (ARTS AND MEDIA) a first appearance in public of an actor, etc.: *She* ***made her début*** *in London in 1959.*

Dec. ***abbr.*** December: *5 Dec. 2006*

deca- /'dekə/ ***prefix*** (in nouns, verbs, adjectives and adverbs) ten; having ten: *decathlon* (= a competition in which people do ten different sports)

decade ⊶ AW /'dekeɪd; dɪ'keɪd/ ***noun*** [C] a period of ten years

decadence /'dekədəns/ ***noun*** [U] behaviour, attitudes, etc. that show low moral standards ▸ **decadent** /'dekədənt/ ***adj.***: *a decadent society*

decaffeinated /ˌdi:'kæfɪneɪtɪd/ ***adj.*** (used about coffee or tea) with most or all of the CAFFEINE (= the substance that makes you feel awake and gives you energy) removed

decant /dɪ'kænt/ ***verb*** [T] **~ sth (into sth)** to gradually pour a liquid from one container into another, for example to separate solid material from the liquid

decapitate /dɪ'kæpɪteɪt/ ***verb*** [T] (*formal*) to cut off a person's head

decathlon /dɪ'kæθlən/ ***noun*** [C] (SPORT) a sports event in which people compete in ten different sports

decay¹ 🔑 /dɪˈkeɪ/ ***verb*** [I] **1** to become bad or be slowly destroyed: *the decaying carcass of a dead sheep* SYN **rot 2** to become weaker or less powerful: *His business empire began to decay.* ▶ **decayed *adj.***: *a decayed tooth*

decay² 🔑 /dɪˈkeɪ/ ***noun*** [U] the process or state of being slowly destroyed: *tooth decay* ◇ *The old farm was in a terrible state of decay.*

the deceased /dɪˈsiːst/ ***noun*** [sing.] (*formal*) a person who has died, especially one who has died recently: *Many friends of the deceased were present at the funeral.* ▶ **deceased *adj.***

deceit /dɪˈsiːt/ ***noun*** [U] dishonest behaviour; trying to make sb believe sth that is not true: *Their marriage eventually broke up because she was tired of his lies and deceit.*

deceitful /dɪˈsiːtfl/ ***adj.*** dishonest; trying to make sb believe sth that is not true ▶ **deceitfully** /-fəli/ ***adv.*** ▶ **deceitfulness *noun*** [U]

deceive /dɪˈsiːv/ ***verb*** [T] **~ sb/yourself (into doing sth)** to try to make sb believe sth that is not true: *He deceived his mother into believing that he had earned the money, not stolen it.* ◇ *You're deceiving yourself if you think there's an easy solution to the problem.* ➲ noun **deception** or **deceit**

> WORD FAMILY
> **deceive** *verb*
> **deceit** *noun*
> **deceitful** *adj.*
> **deception** *noun*

December /dɪˈsembə(r)/ ***noun*** [U, C] (*abbr.* **Dec.**) the twelfth month of the year, coming after November

decency /ˈdiːsnsi/ ***noun*** [U] moral or correct behaviour: *She **had the decency to** admit that it was her fault.*

decent /ˈdiːsnt/ ***adj.*** **1** being of an acceptable standard; SATISFACTORY: *All she wants is a decent job with decent wages.* **2** (used about people or behaviour) honest and fair; treating people with respect **3** not likely to offend or shock sb: *I can't come to the door, I'm not decent* (=I'm not dressed). OPP **indecent** ▶ **decently *adv.***

decentralize (also **-ise**) /ˌdiːˈsentrəlaɪz/ ***verb*** [T,I] (**POLITICS**) to give some of the power of a central government, organization, etc. to smaller parts or organizations around the country: *decentralized authority/administration* OPP **centralize** ▶ **decentralization** (also **-isation**) /ˌdiːˌsentrəlaɪˈzeɪʃn/ ***noun*** [U, sing.]

deception /dɪˈsepʃn/ ***noun*** [C,U] making sb believe or being made to believe sth that is not true: *He had obtained the secret papers **by deception**.* ➲ verb **deceive**

deceptive /dɪˈseptɪv/ ***adj.*** likely to give a false impression or to make sb believe sth that is not true: *The water is deceptive. It's much deeper than it looks.* ▶ **deceptively *adv.***: *She made the task sound deceptively easy.*

deci- /ˈdesɪ-/ ***prefix*** (used in nouns) one tenth: *a decilitre*

decibel /ˈdesɪbel/ ***noun*** [C] (**PHYSICS**) a measurement of how loud a sound is

decide 🔑 /dɪˈsaɪd/ ***verb*** **1** [I,T] **~ (to do sth); ~ against (doing) sth; ~ about/on sth; ~ that...** to think about two or more possibilities and choose one of them: *There are so many to choose from – I can't decide!* ◇ *We've decided not to invite Isabel.* ◇ *She decided against borrowing the money.* ◇ *They decided on a name for the baby.* ◇ *He decided that it was too late to go.* ◇ *The date hasn't been decided yet.* **2** [T] to influence sth so that it produces a particular result: *Your votes will decide the winner.* **3** [T] to cause sb to make a decision: *What finally decided you to leave?* ➲ noun **decision**, adjective **decisive**

> WORD FAMILY
> **decide** *verb*
> **decision** *noun*
> (≠ **indecision**)
> **decisive** *adj.*
> (≠ **indecisive**)
> **undecided** *adj.*

decided /dɪˈsaɪdɪd/ ***adj.*** clear; definite: *There has been a decided improvement in his work.* ➲ look at **undecided** ▶ **decidedly *adv.***

deciduous /dɪˈsɪdʒuəs/ ***adj.*** (**BIOLOGY**) (used about a tree) of a type that loses its leaves every autumn ➲ look at **evergreen**

decimal¹ /ˈdesɪml/ (*also* **ˌdecimal ˈfraction**) ***noun*** [C] (**MATHEMATICS**) a FRACTION (=a number less than one) that is shown as a DECIMAL POINT followed by the number of TENTHS, HUNDREDTHS, etc.: *Three quarters expressed as a decimal is 0.75.* ➲ look at **vulgar fraction**

decimal² /ˈdesɪml/ ***adj.*** (**MATHEMATICS**) based on or counted in units of ten or TENTHS: *the decimal system*

ˌdecimal ˈplace *noun* [C] (**MATHEMATICS**) the position of a number after a DECIMAL POINT: *The figure is **accurate to two decimal places**.*

ˌdecimal ˈpoint *noun* [C] (**MATHEMATICS**) a mark like a full stop used to separate the whole number from the TENTHS, HUNDREDTHS, etc. of a decimal, for example in 0.61

decimate /ˈdesɪmeɪt/ ***verb*** [T] **1** (usually passive) to kill large numbers of animals, plants or people in a particular area: *The rabbit population was decimated by the disease.* **2** to badly damage sth or make sth weaker

decimetre (*AmE* **decimeter**) /ˈdesɪmiːtə(r)/ ***noun*** [C] a unit for measuring length. There are ten **decimetres** in a metre.

decipher /dɪˈsaɪfə(r)/ ***verb*** [T] to succeed in reading or understanding sth that is not clear: *It's impossible to decipher his handwriting.*

decision 🔑 /dɪˈsɪʒn/ ***noun*** **1** [C,U] **a ~ (to do sth); a ~ on/about sth; a ~ that...** a choice or judgement that you make after thinking about various possibilities: *Have you **made a decision** yet?* ◇ *I realize now that I made the wrong decision.* ◇ *There were good reasons for his decision to leave.* ◇ *I **took the decision** that I believed to be right.* **2** [U] being able to decide clearly and quickly: *We are looking for someone with decision for this job.* ➲ verb **decide**

deˈcision-making *noun* [U] the process of deciding about sth important, especially in a group of people or in an organization

decisive /dɪˈsaɪsɪv/ ***adj.*** **1** making sth certain or final: *the decisive battle of the war* ➲ note at **essential 2** having the ability to make clear decisions quickly: *It's no good hesitating. Be decisive.* OPP **indecisive** ➲ verb **decide** ▶ **decisively *adv.*** ▶ **decisiveness *noun*** [U]

deck /dek/ ***noun*** [C] **1** one of the floors of a ship or bus ➲ look at **flight deck** ➲ picture at **plane 2** (*AmE*) =PACK¹ (6): *a deck of cards*
IDM **on deck** on the part of a ship which you can walk on outside: *I'm going out on deck for some fresh air.*

deckchair /ˈdektʃeə(r)/ ***noun*** [C] a chair that you use outside, especially on the beach. You can fold it up and carry it.

declaration /ˌdekləˈreɪʃn/ ***noun*** **1** [C,U] an official statement about sth: *In his speech he made a strong declaration of support for the rebels.* ◇ *a declaration of war* ➲ note at **statement** **2** [C] (FINANCE) a written statement giving information on goods or money you have earned, on which you have to pay tax: *a customs declaration*

> **THESAURUS**
>
> **declare**
>
> **state • indicate • announce**
>
> These words all mean to say sth, usually firmly and clearly and often in public.
>
> **declare** (*formal*): *The picture was declared to be a forgery.*
>
> **state** (*formal*): *He stated his intention to run for election.*
>
> **indicate** (*formal*): *He indicated his interest in the project.*
>
> **announce**: *The winner will be announced next month.*

declare 🔑 /dɪˈkleə(r)/ ***verb*** [T] **1** to state sth publicly and officially or to make sth known in a firm, clear way: *to* ***declare war*** *on another country* ◇ *I declare that the winner of the award is Angels Conill.* **2** (FINANCE) to give information about goods or money you have earned, on which you have to pay tax: *You must declare all your income on this form.*

declension /dɪˈklenʃn/ ***noun*** [C] (LANGUAGE) **1** the forms of a word that change in some languages according to the number, CASE and GENDER of the word **2** the set of forms of a particular word in some languages: *Latin nouns of the second declension*

decline[1] 🔑 AW /dɪˈklaɪn/ ***verb*** **1** [I] to become weaker, smaller or less good: *declining profits* ◇ *The standard of education has declined in this country.* **2** [I,T] (*formal*) to refuse, usually politely: *Thank you for the invitation but I'm afraid I have to decline.* **3** [I,T] (LANGUAGE) if a noun, an adjective or a pronoun **declines**, it has different forms according to whether it is the subject or the object of a verb, whether it is in the SINGULAR or plural, etc. When you **decline** a noun, etc., you list these forms.

decline[2] 🔑 AW /dɪˈklaɪn/ ***noun*** [C,U] (a) ~ (in sth) a process or period of becoming weaker, smaller or less good: *a decline in sales* ◇ *As an industrial power, the country is* ***in decline***.

decode /ˌdiːˈkəʊd/ ***verb*** [T] **1** to find the meaning of sth, especially sth that has been written in code OPP **encode** **2** to receive an electronic signal and change it into pictures that can be shown on a television screen: *decoding equipment*

decoder /ˌdiːˈkəʊdə(r)/ ***noun*** [C] a device that changes electronic signals into a form that people can understand, such as sound and pictures: *a satellite/video decoder*

decolonization (also **decolonisation**) /diːˌkɒlənaɪˈzeɪʃn/ ***noun*** [U] (POLITICS) the process of a COLONY (=a country or an area that is ruled by another, more powerful country) or COLONIES becoming independent

decompose /ˌdiːkəmˈpəʊz/ ***verb*** [I,T] to slowly be destroyed by natural chemical processes: *The body was so badly decomposed that it couldn't be identified.* ▶ **decomposition** /ˌdiːkɒmpəˈzɪʃn/ ***noun*** [U]: *the decomposition of organic waste* ➲ picture at **food chain**

decompress /ˌdiːkəmˈpres/ ***verb*** **1** [I,T] to have the air pressure in sth reduced to a normal level or to reduce it to its normal level **2** [T] (COMPUTING) to give files their original size again after they have been made smaller to fit into less space on a disk, etc. SYN **unzip** OPP **compress**

decompression /ˌdiːkəmˈpreʃn/ ***noun*** [U] **1** a reduction in air pressure: ***decompression sickness*** (=the problems that people experience when they come up to the surface after swimming very deep in the sea) **2** the act of reducing the pressure of the air **3** the process of allowing sth that has been made smaller to fill the space that it originally needed

decor /ˈdeɪkɔː(r)/ ***noun*** [U, sing.] the style in which the inside of a building is decorated

decorate 🔑 /ˈdekəreɪt/ ***verb*** **1** [T] ~ sth (with sth) to add sth in order to make a thing more attractive to look at: *Decorate the cake with cherries and nuts.* **2** [I,T] (*especially BrE*) to put paint and/or WALLPAPER onto walls, ceilings and doors in a room or building

decoration 🔑 /ˌdekəˈreɪʃn/ ***noun*** **1** [C,U] something that is added to sth in order to make it look more attractive **2** [U] the process of decorating a room or building; the style in which sth is decorated: *The house is in need of decoration.*

decorative 🔑 /ˈdekərətɪv/ ***adj.*** attractive or pretty to look at: *The cloth had a decorative lace edge.*

ˌdecorative ˈarts ***noun*** [pl.] (ART) artistic activities which produce objects which are useful and beautiful at the same time

decorator /ˈdekəreɪtə(r)/ ***noun*** [C] a person whose job is to paint and decorate houses and buildings

decoy /ˈdiːkɔɪ/ ***noun*** [C] a person or object that is used in order to trick sb/sth into doing what you want, going where you want, etc. ▶ **decoy** ***verb*** [T]

decrease[1] 🔑 /dɪˈkriːs/ ***verb*** [I,T] to become or to make sth smaller or less: *Profits have decreased by 15%.* ◇ *Decrease speed when you are approaching a road junction.* OPP **increase** ➲ note at **fall**

decrease[2] 🔑 /ˈdiːkriːs/ ***noun*** [C,U] (a) ~ (in sth) the process of becoming or making sth smaller or less; the amount that sth is reduced by: *a 10% decrease in sales*

decree /dɪˈkriː/ ***noun*** [C] **1** (POLITICS, LAW) an official order from a ruler or a government that becomes the law **2** (LAW) a decision that is made in court ▶ **decree** ***verb*** [T]: *The government decreed a state of emergency.*

deˌcree ˈabsolute ***noun*** [sing.] (*BrE*) (LAW) an order from a court that finally ends a marriage, making the two people divorced: *The period between the decree nisi and the decree absolute was six weeks.*

decree nisi /dɪˌkriː ˈnaɪsaɪ/ ***noun*** [sing.] (*BrE*) (LAW) an order from a court that a marriage will end after a fixed amount of time unless there is a good reason why it should not

decrepit /dɪˈkrepɪt/ ***adj.*** (used about a thing or person) old and in very bad condition or poor health

dedicate /ˈdedɪkeɪt/ ***verb*** [T] **1** **~ sth to sth** to give all your energy, time, efforts, etc. to sth: *He dedicated his life to helping the poor.* **2** **~ sth to sb** to say that sth is specially for sb: *He dedicated the book he had written to his brother.*

dedicated /ˈdedɪkeɪtɪd/ ***adj.*** giving a lot of your energy, time, efforts, etc. to sth that you believe to be important: *dedicated nurses and doctors*

dedication /ˌdedɪˈkeɪʃn/ ***noun* 1** [U] wanting to give your time and energy to sth because you feel it is important: *I admire her dedication to her career.* **2** [C] a message at the beginning of a book or piece of music saying that it is for a particular person

deduce AW /dɪˈdjuːs/ ***verb*** [T] to form an opinion using the facts that you already know: *From his name I deduced that he was Polish.* ➲ noun **deduction**

deduct /dɪˈdʌkt/ ***verb*** [T] **~ sth (from sth)** to take sth such as money or points away from a total amount: *Marks will be deducted for untidy work.* ➲ noun **deduction**

deduction AW /dɪˈdʌkʃn/ ***noun*** [C,U] **1** something that you work out from facts that you already know; the ability to think in this way: *It was a brilliant piece of deduction by the detective.* ➲ verb **deduce** ➲ look at **induction** (2) **2 ~ (from sth)** taking away an amount or number from a total; the amount or number taken away from the total: *What is your total income after deductions?* (=when tax, insurance, etc. are taken away) ➲ verb **deduct**

deductive /dɪˈdʌktɪv/ ***adj.*** using knowledge about things that are generally true in order to think about and understand particular situations or problems ➲ look at **inductive**

deed /diːd/ ***noun*** [C] **1** (*formal*) something that you do; an action: *a brave/good/evil deed* ➲ note at **action**[1] **2** (**LAW**) (often plural in *BrE*) a legal document that shows that you own a house or building

deem /diːm/ ***verb*** [T] (*formal*) to have a particular opinion about sth: *He did not even deem it necessary to apologize.*

deep[1] 🔑 /diːp/ ***adj.* 1** going a long way down from the surface: *to dig a deep hole* ◇ *That's a deep cut.* ◇ *a coat with deep pockets* ➲ noun **depth** **2** going a long way from front to back: *deep shelves* **3** measuring a particular amount from top to bottom or from front to back: *The water is only a metre deep at this end of the pool.* ◇ *shelves 40 centimetres deep* **4** (used about sounds) low: *a deep voice* **5** (used about colours) dark; strong: *a deep red* **6** (used about an emotion) strongly felt: *He felt a very deep love for the child.* **7** (used about sleep) not easy to wake from: *I was in a **deep sleep** and didn't hear the phone ringing.* **8** dealing with difficult subjects or details; thorough: *His books show a deep understanding of human nature.* ▸ **the deep *noun*** [U]: *in the deep of the night* (=in the middle of the night) ◇ *the deep* (=a literary way of referring to the sea)

IDM **deep in thought/conversation** thinking very hard or giving sb/sth your full attention

take a deep breath to breathe in a lot of air, especially in preparation for doing something difficult: *He took a deep breath then walked on stage.*

deep[2] /diːp/ ***adv.*** a long way down or inside sth: *He gazed deep into her eyes.* ◇ *He dug his hands deep into his pockets.*

IDM **deep down** in what you really think or feel: *I tried to appear optimistic but deep down I knew there was no hope.*

dig deep → DIG[1]

deepen /ˈdiːpən/ ***verb*** [I,T] to become or to make sth deep or deeper: *The river deepens here.*

ˌdeep ˈfreeze = FREEZER

ˌdeep-ˈfried ***adj.*** cooked in oil that covers the food completely

deeply 🔑 /ˈdiːpli/ ***adv.* 1** very; very much: *a deeply unhappy person* ◇ *Opinion is **deeply divided** on this issue.* **2** used with some verbs to show that sth is done in a very complete way: *to breathe/sigh/exhale deeply* (=using all of the air in your lungs) ◇ *to sleep deeply* (=in a way that makes it difficult for you to wake up) **3** to a depth that is quite a long way from the surface of sth: *to drill deeply into the wood*

ˌdeep-ˈrooted (*also* **ˌdeep-ˈseated**) ***adj.*** strongly felt or believed and therefore difficult to change: *deep-rooted fears*

ˈdeep-sea ***adj.*** of or in the deeper parts of the sea: *deep-sea fishing/diving*

ˌdeep vein thromˈbosis ***noun*** [U,C] (*abbr.* **DVT**) (**HEALTH**) a serious condition caused by a blood CLOT (=a thick mass of blood) forming in a VEIN (=one of the tubes which carry blood from all parts of your body towards your heart): *Passengers on long-haul flights are being warned about the risks of deep vein thrombosis.*

deer /dɪə(r)/ ***noun*** [C] (*pl.* **deer**) an animal with long legs, that eats grass, leaves, etc. and can run fast. Most male **deer** have ANTLERS (=horns shaped like branches).

RELATED VOCABULARY

A male **deer** is called a **buck** or, especially if it has fully grown antlers, a **stag**.
The female is a **doe** and a young deer a **fawn**.
Venison is the meat from deer.

deface /dɪˈfeɪs/ ***verb*** [T] to spoil the way sth looks by writing on or marking its surface

de facto /ˌdeɪ ˈfæktəʊ/ ***adj.*** (*formal*) (**LAW**) a Latin expression used to say that sth exists as a fact although it may not be legally accepted as existing: *The general took de facto control of the country.* ▸ **de facto *adv.***: *He continued to rule the country de facto.*

defamatory /dɪˈfæmətri/ ***adj.*** (*formal*) (used about speech or writing) intended to harm sb by saying or writing bad or false things about them

defame /dɪˈfeɪm/ ***verb*** [T] (*formal*) to harm sb by saying or writing bad or false things about them ▸ **defamation** /ˌdefəˈmeɪʃn/ [U, C]: *The company sued the paper for defamation.*

default[1] /dɪˈfɔːlt/ ***noun*** [sing.] (**COMPUTING**) a course of action taken by a computer when it is not given any other instruction

IDM **by default** because nothing happened, not because of successful effort: *They won by default, because the other team didn't turn up.*

default[2] /dɪˈfɔːlt/ ***verb*** [I] **1 ~ (on sth)** (**LAW**) to not do sth that you should do by law: *If you default on the credit payments* (=you don't pay them)*, the car will be taken back.* **2** (**COMPUTING**) **~ (to sth)** to take a particular course of action when no other command is given

defeat[1] 🔑 /dɪˈfiːt/ ***verb*** [T] **1** to win a game, a fight, a vote, etc. against sb; to beat sb: *The army defeated the rebels after three days of fighting.* ◇ *In the last match France defeated Wales.* **2** to be too difficult for sb to do or understand: *I've tried to work out what's wrong with the car but it defeats me.* **3** to prevent sth from succeeding: *The local residents are determined to defeat the council's building plans.*

defeat[2] 🔑 /dɪˈfiːt/ ***noun* 1** [C] an occasion when sb fails to win or be successful against sb else: *This season they have had two victories and three defeats.* **2** [U] the act of losing or not being successful: *She refused to **admit defeat** and kept on trying.*

defeatism /dɪˈfiːtɪzəm/ ***noun*** [U] the attitude of expecting sth to end in failure

defeatist /dɪˈfiːtɪst/ *adj.* expecting not to succeed: *a defeatist attitude/view* ▶ **defeatist** *noun* [C]: *Don't be such a defeatist, we haven't lost yet!*

defecate /ˈdefəkeɪt/ *verb* [I] (*formal*) (BIOLOGY) to get rid of solid waste from the body; to go to the toilet

defect[1] /ˈdiːfekt/ *noun* [C] sth that is wrong with or missing from sb/sth: *a speech defect* ◇ *defects in the education system* ▶ **defective** /dɪˈfektɪv/ *adj.*

defect[2] /dɪˈfekt/ *verb* [I] (POLITICS) to leave your country, a political party, etc. and join one that is considered to be the enemy ▶ **defection** *noun* [C,U] ▶ **defector** *noun* [C]

defence ⚷ (*AmE* **defense**) /dɪˈfens/ *noun* **1** [U] something that you do or say to protect sb/sth from attack, bad treatment, criticism, etc.: *Would you fight* ***in defence of*** *your country?* ◇ *When her brother was criticized she* ***leapt to his defence***. ◇ *I must say* ***in*** *her* ***defence*** *that I have always found her very reliable.* ➲ look at **self-defence** **2** [C] a ~ (**against sth**) something that protects sb/sth from sth, or that is used to fight against attack: *the body's defences against disease* **3** [U] (POLITICS) the military equipment, forces, etc. for protecting a country: *Spending on defence needs to be reduced.* **4** [C] (LAW) an argument in support of the accused person in a court of law: *His defence was that he was only carrying out orders.* **5 the defence** [sing., with sing. or pl. verb] (LAW) the lawyer or lawyers who are acting for the accused person in a court of law: *The defence claims/claim that many of the witnesses were lying.* ➲ look at **the prosecution** **6** (usually **the defence**) [sing., U] (SPORT) action to prevent the other team scoring; the players who try to do this: *She plays in defence.*

defenceless /dɪˈfensləs/ *adj.* unable to defend yourself against attack

defend ⚷ /dɪˈfend/ *verb* **1** [T] ~ **sb/sth/ yourself** (**against/from sb/sth**) to protect sb/sth from harm or danger: *Would you be able to defend yourself if someone attacked you in the street?* **2** [T] ~ **sb/sth/yourself** (**against/from sb/sth**) to say or write sth to support sb/sth that has been criticized: *The minister went on television to defend the government's policy.* **3** [T] (LAW) to speak for sb who is accused of a crime in a court of law **4** [I,T] (SPORT) to try to stop the other team or player scoring: *They defended well and managed to hold onto their lead.* **5** [T] to take part in a competition that you won before and try to win it again: *She successfully defended her title.* ◇ *He is the defending champion.*

defendant /dɪˈfendənt/ *noun* [C] (LAW) a person who is accused of a crime in a court of law

defender /dɪˈfendə(r)/ *noun* [C] a person who defends sb/sth, especially in sport

defense ⚷ (*AmE*) = DEFENCE

defensible /dɪˈfensəbl/ *adj.* **1** that can be supported by reasons or arguments that show that it is right or should be allowed: *morally defensible* **2** (used about a place) that can be defended against an attack

defensive[1] /dɪˈfensɪv/ *adj.* **1** that protects sb/sth from attack: *The troops took up a defensive position.* OPP **offensive** **2** showing that you feel that sb is criticizing you: *When I asked him about his new job, he became very defensive and tried to change the subject.*

defensive[2] /dɪˈfensɪv/ *noun*
IDM **on the defensive** acting in a way that shows that you expect sb to attack or criticize you: *My questions about her past immediately put her on the defensive.*

defer /dɪˈfɜː(r)/ *verb* [T] (**deferring**; **deferred**) (*formal*) to leave sth until a later time: *She deferred her place at university for a year.*

deference /ˈdefərəns/ *noun* [U] polite behaviour that you show towards sb/sth, usually because you respect them
IDM **in deference to sb/sth** because you respect and do not wish to upset sb: *In deference to her father's wishes, she didn't mention the subject again.*

defiance /dɪˈfaɪəns/ *noun* [U] open refusal to obey sb/sth: *an* ***act of defiance*** ◇ *He continued smoking* ***in defiance of*** *the doctor's orders.*

defiant /dɪˈfaɪənt/ *adj.* showing open refusal to obey sb/sth ➲ verb **defy** ▶ **defiantly** *adv.*

defibrillator /diːˈfɪbrɪleɪtə(r)/ *noun* [C] (HEALTH) a piece of equipment used in hospitals to control the movements of the heart muscles by giving the heart a controlled electric shock

deficiency /dɪˈfɪʃnsi/ *noun* (*pl.* **deficiencies**) ~ (**in/ of sth**) **1** [C,U] the state of not having enough of sth; a lack: *a deficiency of vitamin C* **2** [C] a fault or a weakness in sb/sth: *The problems were caused by deficiencies in the design.*

deficient /dɪˈfɪʃnt/ *adj.* **1** ~ (**in sth**) not having enough of sth: *food that is deficient in minerals* **2** not good enough or not complete

deficit /ˈdefɪsɪt/ *noun* [C] (FINANCE) the amount by which the money you receive is less than the money you have spent: *a trade deficit*

define ⚷ AW /dɪˈfaɪn/ *verb* [T] **1** to say exactly what a word or idea means: *How would you define 'happiness'?* **2** to explain the exact nature of sth clearly: *We need to define the problem before we can attempt to solve it.*

definite ⚷ AW /ˈdefɪnət/ *adj.* **1** fixed and unlikely to change; certain: *I'll give you a definite decision in a couple of days.* ➲ note at **certain** OPP **indefinite** **2** clear; easy to see or notice: *There has been a definite change in her attitude recently.*

ˌdefinite ˈarticle *noun* [C] (LANGUAGE) the name used for the word 'the' ➲ look at **indefinite article**

definitely ⚷ AW /ˈdefɪnətli/ *adv.* certainly; without doubt: *I'll definitely consider your advice.*

definition ⚷ AW /ˌdefɪˈnɪʃn/ *noun* [C,U] a description of the exact meaning of a word or idea

definitive AW /dɪˈfɪnətɪv/ *adj.* in a form that cannot be changed or that cannot be improved: *This is the definitive version.* ◇ *the definitive performance of Hamlet* ▶ **definitively** *adv.*

deflate /dɪˈfleɪt; diː-/ *verb* **1** [I,T] to become or to make sth smaller by letting the air or gas out of it: *The balloon slowly deflated.* OPP **inflate** **2** [T] to make sb feel less confident, proud or excited: *I felt really deflated when I got my exam results.*

deflation /ˌdiːˈfleɪʃn/ *noun* [U] **1** (ECONOMICS) a reduction in the amount of money in a country's economy so that prices fall or remain the same **2** the action of air being removed from sth OPP **inflation**

deflect /dɪˈflekt/ *verb* **1** [I,T] to change direction after hitting sb/sth; to make sth change direction in this way: *The ball deflected off a defender and into the goal.* **2** [T] to turn sb's attention away from sth: *Nothing could deflect her from her aim.*

deflection /dɪˈflekʃn/ *noun* [C,U] a change of direction after hitting sb/sth

defoliate /ˌdiːˈfəʊlieɪt/ *verb* [T] to destroy the leaves of trees or plants, especially with chemicals ▶ **defoliation** /ˌdiːˌfəʊliˈeɪʃn/ *noun* [U]

deforestation /ˌdiːˌfɒrɪˈsteɪʃn/ *noun* [U] (ENVIRONMENT) cutting down trees over a large area OPP **afforestation**

deform /dɪˈfɔːm/ *verb* [T] to change or spoil the natural shape of sth

deformed /dɪˈfɔːmd/ *adj.* having a shape that is not normal because it has grown wrongly

deformity /dɪˈfɔːməti/ *noun* (*pl.* **deformities**) [C,U] the condition of having a part of the body that is an unusual shape because of disease, injury, etc.: *The drug caused women to give birth to babies with severe deformities.*

defraud /dɪˈfrɔːd/ *verb* [T] ~ **sb (of sth)** to get sth from sb in a dishonest way: *He defrauded the company of millions.*

defrost /ˌdiːˈfrɒst/ *verb* **1** [T] to remove the ice from sth: *to defrost a fridge* **2** [I,T] (used about frozen food) to return to a normal temperature; to make food do this: *Defrost the chicken thoroughly before cooking.* ➲ look at **de-ice**

deft /deft/ *adj.* (used especially about movements) skilful and quick ▶ **deftly** *adv.*

defunct /dɪˈfʌŋkt/ *adj.* no longer existing or in use

defuse /ˌdiːˈfjuːz/ *verb* [T] **1** to remove part of a bomb so that it cannot explode: *Army experts defused the bomb safely.* **2** to make a situation calmer or less dangerous: *She defused the tension by changing the subject.*

defy /dɪˈfaɪ/ *verb* [T] (*pres. part.* **defying**; *3rd person sing. pres.* **defies**; *pt, pp* **defied**) **1** to refuse to obey sb/sth: *She defied her parents and continued seeing him.* ➲ adjective **defiant**, noun **defiance** **2** ~ **sb to do sth** to ask sb to do sth that you believe to be impossible: *I defy you to prove me wrong.* **3** to make sth impossible or very difficult: *It's such a beautiful place that it defies description.*

> WORD FAMILY
> **defy** *verb*
> **defiance** *noun*
> **defiant** *adj.*

degenerate¹ /dɪˈdʒenəreɪt/ *verb* [I] to become worse, lower in quality, etc.: *The calm discussion degenerated into a nasty argument.* ▶ **degeneration** /dɪˌdʒenəˈreɪʃn/ *noun* [U]

degenerate² /dɪˈdʒenərət/ *adj.* having moral standards that have fallen to a very low level

degenerative /dɪˈdʒenərətɪv/ *adj.* (HEALTH) (used about an illness) getting or likely to get worse as time passes: *degenerative diseases such as arthritis*

degradation /ˌdegrəˈdeɪʃn/ *noun* [U] **1** the action of making sb be less respected; the state of being less respected: *the degradation of being in prison* **2** causing the condition of sth to become worse: *environmental degradation*

degrade /dɪˈgreɪd/ *verb* [T] to make people respect sb less: *It's the sort of film that really degrades women.* ▶ **degrading** *adj.*

degree 🔑 /dɪˈgriː/ *noun* **1** [C] (SCIENCE) a measurement of temperature: *Water boils at 100 degrees Celsius (100° C).* ◇ *three degrees below zero/minus three degrees (-3°)* **2** [C] (GEOMETRY) a measurement of angles: *a forty-five degree (45°) angle* ◇ *An angle of 90 degrees is called a right angle.* **3** [C,U] (used about feelings or qualities) a certain amount or level: *There is always* ***a degree of*** *risk involved in mountaineering.* ◇ *I sympathize with her* ***to some degree.*** **4** [C] (EDUCATION) an official document gained by successfully completing a course at university or college: *She's got* ***a degree in*** *Philosophy.* ◇ *to* ***do a*** *Chemistry* ***degree***

dehumanize (also **-ise**) /ˌdiːˈhjuːmənaɪz/ *verb* [T] to make sb lose their human qualities such as kindness, pity, etc. ▶ **dehumanization** (also **-isation**) /ˌdiːˌhjuːmənaɪˈzeɪʃn/ *noun* [U]

dehydrate /diːˈhaɪdreɪt/ *verb* **1** [T] (usually passive) to remove all the water from sth: *Dehydrated vegetables can be stored for months.* **2** [I,T] (HEALTH) to lose too much water from your body: *If you run for a long time in the heat, you start to dehydrate.* ▶ **dehydration** /ˌdiːhaɪˈdreɪʃn/ *noun* [U]: *Several of the runners were suffering from severe dehydration.*

de-ice /ˌdiː ˈaɪs/ *verb* [T] to remove the ice from sth: *The car windows need de-icing.* ➲ look at **defrost**

deign /deɪn/ *verb* [T] ~ **to do sth** to do sth although you think you are too important to do it: *He didn't even deign to look up when I entered the room.*

deity /ˈdeɪəti/ *noun* [C] (*pl.* **deities**) (*formal*) (RELIGION) a god

dejected /dɪˈdʒektɪd/ *adj.* very unhappy, especially because you are disappointed: *The fans went home dejected after watching their team lose.* ▶ **dejectedly** *adv.* ▶ **dejection** *noun* [U]

delay¹ 🔑 /dɪˈleɪ/ *verb* **1** [T] to make sb/sth slow or late: *The plane was delayed for several hours because of bad weather.* **2** [I,T] ~ **(sth/doing sth)** to decide not to do sth until a later time: *I was forced to delay the trip until the following week.*

delay² 🔑 /dɪˈleɪ/ *noun* [C,U] a situation or period of time where you have to wait: *Delays are likely on the roads because of heavy traffic.* ◇ *If you smell gas, report it* ***without delay*** (=immediately).

delegate¹ /ˈdelɪgət/ *noun* [C] a person who has been chosen to speak or take decisions for a group of people, especially at a meeting

delegate² /ˈdelɪgeɪt/ *verb* [I,T] to give sb with a lower job or position a particular task to do: *You can't do everything yourself. You must learn how to delegate.*

delegation /ˌdelɪˈgeɪʃn/ *noun* **1** [C, with sing. or pl. verb] a group of people who have been chosen to speak or take decisions for a larger group of people, especially at a meeting: *The British delegation walked out of the meeting in protest.* **2** [U] giving sb with a lower job or position a particular task to do

delete /dɪˈliːt/ *verb* [T] to remove sth that has been written or printed, or that has been stored on a computer: *Your name has been deleted from the list.* ◇ *This command deletes files from the directory.* ▶ **deletion** /dɪˈliːʃn/ *noun* [C,U]

deliberate¹ 🔑 /dɪˈlɪbərət/ *adj.* **1** done on purpose; planned: *Was it an accident or was it deliberate?* SYN **intentional** **2** done slowly and carefully, without hurrying: *She spoke in a calm, deliberate voice.*

deliberate² /dɪˈlɪbəreɪt/ *verb* [I,T] (*formal*) to think about or discuss sth fully before making a decision: *The judges deliberated for an hour before announcing the winner.*

deliberately 🔑 /dɪˈlɪbərətli/ *adv.* **1** on purpose: *I didn't break it deliberately, it was an accident.* SYN **intentionally**, **purposely** **2** slowly and carefully, without hurrying

deliberation /dɪˌlɪbəˈreɪʃn/ *noun* (*formal*) **1** [C,U] discussion or thinking about sth in detail: *After much deliberation I decided to reject the offer.* **2** [U] the quality of being very slow and careful in what you say and do: *He spoke with great deliberation.*

delicacy /ˈdelɪkəsi/ *noun* (*pl.* **delicacies**) **1** [U] the quality of being easy to damage or break **2** [U] the fact that a situation is difficult and sb may be easily offended: *Be tactful! It's a matter of some delicacy.* **3** [C] a type of food that is considered particularly good: *Try this dish, it's a local delicacy.*

delicate 🔑 /ˈdelɪkət/ *adj.* **1** easy to damage or break: *delicate skin ◇ the delicate mechanisms of a watch* **2** frequently ill or hurt: *He was a delicate child and often in hospital.* **3** (used about colours, flavours, etc.) light and pleasant; not strong: *a delicate shade of pale blue* **4** needing skilful treatment and care: *Repairing this is going to be a very delicate operation.* ▶ **delicately** *adv.*: *She stepped delicately over the broken glass.*

delicatessen /ˌdelɪkəˈtesn/ *noun* [C] a shop that sells special, unusual or foreign foods, especially cold cooked meat, cheeses, etc.

delicious /dɪˈlɪʃəs/ *adj.* having a very pleasant taste or smell: *This soup is absolutely delicious.*

delight¹ 🔑 /dɪˈlaɪt/ *noun* **1** [U] great pleasure; joy: *She laughed with delight as she opened the present.* **2** [C] something that gives sb great pleasure: *The story is a delight to read.* ▶ **delightful** /-fl/ *adj.*: *a delightful view* ▶ **delightfully** /-fəli/ *adv.*

delight² 🔑 /dɪˈlaɪt/ *verb* [T] to give sb great pleasure: *She delighted the audience by singing all her old songs.*

PHR V **delight in sth/in doing sth** to get great pleasure from sth: *He delights in playing tricks on people.*

delighted 🔑 /dɪˈlaɪtɪd/ *adj.* ~ **(at/with/about sth)**; ~ **to do sth/that...** extremely pleased: *She was delighted at getting the job/that she got the job. ◇ They're absolutely delighted with their baby.*

delinquency /dɪˈlɪŋkwənsi/ *noun* [U] (*formal*) bad or criminal behaviour, especially among young people

delinquent /dɪˈlɪŋkwənt/ *adj.* (*formal*) (usually used about a young person) behaving badly and often breaking the law ▶ **delinquent** *noun* [C]: *a juvenile delinquent*

delirious /dɪˈlɪriəs; -ˈlɪəriəs/ *adj.* **1** speaking or thinking in a crazy way, often because of illness **2** extremely happy ▶ **deliriously** *adv.*

deliver 🔑 /dɪˈlɪvə(r)/ *verb* **1** [I,T] to take sth (goods, letters, etc.) to the place requested or to the address on it: *Your order will be delivered within five days. ◇ We deliver free within the local area.* **2** [T] to help a mother to give birth to her baby: *to **deliver a baby*** **3** [T] (*formal*) to say sth formally: *to **deliver a speech/lecture/warning*** **4** [I] ~ **(on sth)** (*informal*) to do or give sth that you have promised: *The new leader has made a lot of promises, but can he deliver on them?*

IDM **come up with/deliver the goods** → GOODS

deliverable /dɪˈlɪvərəbl/ *noun* [usually pl.] (BUSINESS) a product that a company promises to have ready for a customer: *computer software deliverables*

delivery 🔑 /dɪˈlɪvəri/ *noun* (*pl.* **deliveries**) **1** [U] the act of taking sth (goods, letters, etc.) to the place or person who has ordered it or whose address is on it: *Please allow 28 days for delivery. ◇ a delivery van* **2** [C] an occasion when sth is delivered: *Is there a delivery here on Sundays?* **3** [C] something (goods, letters, etc.) that is delivered: *The shop is waiting for a new delivery of apples.* **4** [C] (HEALTH) the process of giving birth to a baby: *an easy delivery*

delta /ˈdeltə/ *noun* [C] (GEOGRAPHY) an area of flat land shaped like a triangle where a river divides into smaller rivers as it goes into the sea

delude /dɪˈluːd/ *verb* [T] to make sb believe sth that is not true: *If he thinks he's going to get rich quickly, he's deluding himself.* ➲ noun **delusion**

deluge¹ /ˈdeljuːdʒ/ *noun* [C] **1** a sudden very heavy fall of rain SYN **flood** **2** a ~ **(of sth)** a very large number of things that happen or arrive at the same time: *The programme was followed by **a deluge of complaints** from the public.*

deluge² /ˈdeljuːdʒ/ *verb* [T] (usually passive) to send or give sb/sth a very large quantity of sth, all at the same time: *They were deluged with applications for the job.*

delusion /dɪˈluːʒn/ *noun* [C,U] a false belief or opinion about yourself or your situation: *He seems to be **under the delusion** that he's popular. ◇ He was suffering from paranoid delusions and hallucinations.* ➲ verb **delude**

de luxe /ˌdə ˈlʌks/ *adj.* of extremely high quality and more expensive than usual: *a de luxe hotel*

delve /delv/ *verb* [I] ~ **into sth** to search inside sth: *She delved into the bag and brought out a tiny box. ◇ (figurative) We must delve into the past to find the origins of the custom.*

demand¹ 🔑 /dɪˈmɑːnd/ *noun* **1** [C] a ~ **(for sth/that...)** a strong request or order that must be obeyed: *a demand for changes in the law ◇ I was amazed by their demand that I should leave immediately.* ➲ note at **ask** **2 demands** [pl.] something that sb makes you do, especially sth that is difficult or tiring: *Running a marathon **makes** huge **demands** on the body.* **3** [U, sing.] ~ **(for sth/sb)** (BUSINESS) the desire or need for sth among a group of people: *We no longer sell that product because there is no demand for it.*

IDM **in demand** wanted by a lot of people: *I'm in demand this weekend – I've had three invitations!*
on demand whenever you ask for it: *This treatment is available from your doctor on demand.*

THESAURUS

demand

require • expect • insist • ask

These words all mean to say that sb should do or have sth.

demand: *She demanded an explanation.*
require: *All applicants are required to take a test.*
expect: *I expect to be paid promptly.*
insist: *Our teacher **insists on** punctuality.*
ask: *Total silence is asking too much of a child.*

demand² 🔑 /dɪˈmɑːnd/ *verb* [T] **1** ~ **to do sth/that...**; ~ **sth** to ask for sth in an extremely firm or aggressive way: *I walked into the office and demanded to see the manager. ◇ She demanded that I pay her immediately. ◇ Your behaviour was disgraceful and I demand an apology.* **2** to need sth: *a sport that demands skill as well as strength*

demanding /dɪˈmɑːndɪŋ/ *adj.* **1** (used about a job, task, etc.) needing a lot of effort, care, skill, etc.: *It will be a demanding schedule – I have to go to six cities in six days.* ➲ note at **difficult** **2** (used about a person) always wanting attention or expecting very high standards of people: *Young children are very demanding. ◇ a demanding boss*

demarcation /ˌdiːmɑːˈkeɪʃn/ ***noun*** [U, C] a border or line that separates two things, such as types of work, groups of people or areas of land

dementia /dɪˈmenʃə/ ***noun*** [U] (**HEALTH**) a serious mental problem caused by brain disease or injury, that affects the ability to think, remember and behave normally

demi- /ˈdemi/ ***prefix*** (in nouns) half; partly

demise /dɪˈmaɪz/ ***noun*** [sing.] **1** the end or failure of sth: *Poor business decisions led to the company's demise.* **2** (*written*) the death of a person

demo[1] /ˈdeməʊ/ ***noun*** [C] (*pl.* **demos**) = DEMONSTRATION (2),3)

demo[2] /ˈdeməʊ/ ***verb*** [T] (**BUSINESS**) to show or be shown how a piece of equipment or computer software works and what it does: *They will demo the phone at this year's technology fair.*

demo- ***prefix*** (in nouns, adjectives and verbs) connected with people or population: *democracy*

democracy /dɪˈmɒkrəsi/ ***noun*** (*pl.* **democracies**) (**POLITICS**) **1** [U] a system in which the government of a country is elected by the people **2** [C] a country that has this system **3** [U] the right of everyone in an organization, etc. to be treated equally and to vote on matters that affect them: *There is a need for more democracy in the company.*

democrat /ˈdeməkræt/ ***noun*** [C] (**POLITICS**) **1** a person who believes in and supports DEMOCRACY **2 Democrat** a member or supporter of the Democratic Party of the US ➲ look at **Republican**

democratic /ˌdeməˈkrætɪk/ ***adj.*** (**POLITICS**) **1** based on the system of DEMOCRACY: *democratic elections* ◇ *a democratic government* **2** having or supporting equal rights for all people: *a **democratic decision*** (= made by all the people involved) **OPP** **undemocratic** ▸ **democratically** /-kli/ ***adv.***: *a democratically elected government*

the ˌDemoˈcratic Party ***noun*** [sing.] (**POLITICS**) one of the two main political parties of the US ❶ The other main party is **the Republican Party**.

demographic /ˌdeməˈɡræfɪk/ ***noun*** **1 demographics** [pl.] (**SOCIAL STUDIES**) information about the members of a group of people, such as how old, rich, etc. they are, how many males and females there are, etc.: *the demographics of radio listeners* **2** [sing.] (**BUSINESS**) a group of customers who are of a similar age, sex, etc.: *The publication is popular within the 15 to 24-year-old male demographic.* ▸ **demographic** ***adj.***: *demographic changes/trends/factors*

demography /dɪˈmɒɡrəfi/ ***noun*** [U] (**SOCIAL STUDIES**) the changing number of births, deaths, diseases, etc. in a community over a period of time; the scientific study of these changes: *the social demography of Africa*

demolish /dɪˈmɒlɪʃ/ ***verb*** [T] to destroy sth, for example a building: *The old shops were demolished and a supermarket was built in their place.* ◇ (*figurative*) *She demolished his argument in one sentence.* ▸ **demolition** /ˌdeməˈlɪʃn/ ***noun*** [C,U]

demon /ˈdiːmən/ ***noun*** [C] an evil spirit

demonic /dɪˈmɒnɪk/ ***adj.*** connected with, or like, a DEMON

demonstrable **AW** /dɪˈmɒnstrəbl (*BrE also*) ˈdemənstrəbl/ ***adj.*** (*formal*) that can be shown or proved: *There is no demonstrable link between the two events.*

demonstrate 🔑 **AW** /ˈdemənstreɪt/ ***verb*** **1** [T] ~ **sth (to sb)** to show sth clearly by giving proof: *Using this chart, I'd like to demonstrate to you what has happened to our sales.* **2** [I,T] ~ **sth (to sb)** to show and explain to sb how to do sth or how sth works: *The crew demonstrated the use of life jackets just after take-off.* **3** [I] ~ **(against/for sb/sth)** (**POLITICS**) to take part in a public protest for or against sb/sth: *Enormous crowds have been demonstrating against the government.*

demonstration **AW** /ˌdemənˈstreɪʃn/ ***noun*** **1** [C,U] something that shows clearly that sth exists or is true: *This accident is a clear demonstration of the system's faults.* **2** [C,U] an act of showing or explaining to sb how to do sth or how sth works: *The salesman gave me a demonstration of what the computer could do.* **3** [C] **a ~ (against/for sb/sth)** (**POLITICS**) a public protest for or against sb/sth: *demonstrations against a new law*

demonstrative **AW** /dɪˈmɒnstrətɪv/ ***adj.*** **1** (used about a person) showing feelings, especially loving feelings, in front of other people **2** (**LANGUAGE**) used to identify the person or thing that is being referred to: *'This' and 'that' are demonstrative pronouns.*

demonstrator **AW** /ˈdemənstreɪtə(r)/ ***noun*** [C] (**POLITICS**) a person who takes part in a public protest

demoralize (also **-ise**) /dɪˈmɒrəlaɪz/ ***verb*** [T] to make sb lose confidence or the courage to continue doing sth: *Repeated defeats demoralized the team.* ▸ **demoralization** (also **-isation**) /dɪˌmɒrəlaɪˈzeɪʃn/ ***noun*** [U] ▸ **demoralizing** (also **-ising**) ***adj.***: *Constant criticism can be extremely demoralizing.*

demote /ˌdiːˈməʊt/ ***verb*** [T] (often passive) ~ **sb (from sth) (to sth)** to move sb to a lower position or level, often as a punishment **OPP** **promote** ▸ **demotion** /ˌdiːˈməʊʃn/ ***noun*** [C,U]

demure /dɪˈmjʊə(r)/ ***adj.*** (used especially about a girl or young woman) shy, quiet and polite

den /den/ ***noun*** [C] **1** the place where certain wild animals live, for example LIONS **2** a secret place, especially for illegal activities: *a gambling den*

denial **AW** /dɪˈnaɪəl/ ***noun*** **1** [C] a statement that sth is not true: *The minister issued a denial that he was involved in the scandal.* **2** [C,U] **(a)** ~ **(of sth)** refusing to allow sb to have or do sth: *a denial of personal freedom* **3** [U] a refusal to accept that sth unpleasant or painful has happened: *He's been **in denial** ever since the accident.* ➲ verb **deny**

denim /ˈdenɪm/ ***noun*** [U] a thick cotton material (often blue) that is used for making clothes, especially jeans: *a denim jacket*

denitrify /ˌdiːˈnaɪtrɪfaɪ/ ***verb*** [T] (*pres. part.* **denitrifying**; *3rd person sing. pres.* **denitrifies**; *pt, pp* **denitrified**) (**CHEMISTRY**) to remove NITRATES or NITRITES from sth, especially from soil, air or water ➲ picture at **nitrogen** ▸ **denitrification** /diːˌnaɪtrɪfɪˈkeɪʃn/ ***noun*** [U]

denomination /dɪˌnɒmɪˈneɪʃn/ ***noun*** [C] (**RELIGION**) one of the different religious groups that you can belong to

denominator /dɪˈnɒmɪneɪtə(r)/ ***noun*** [C] (**MATHEMATICS**) the number below the line in a FRACTION showing how many parts the whole is divided into, for example the 4 in ¾ ➲ look at **numerator, common denominator**

denote **AW** /dɪˈnəʊt/ ***verb*** [T] to mean or be a sign of sth: *In algebra the sign x always denotes an unknown quantity.*

denouement (also **dénouement**) /ˌdeɪˈnuːmɒ̃/ ***noun*** [C] (**LITERATURE**) the end of a play, book, etc., where everything is explained or settled; the end result of a situation: *an exciting/unexpected denouement*

denounce /dɪˈnaʊns/ ***verb*** [T] to say publicly that sth is wrong; to be very critical of a person in public: *The actor has been denounced as a bad influence on young people.* ➲ noun **denunciation**

dense /dens/ ***adj.*** **1** containing a lot of things or people close together: *dense forests* ◇ *areas of dense population* **2** difficult to see through: *dense fog* **3** (*informal*) not intelligent; stupid ▸ **densely** ***adv.***: *densely populated areas*

density /ˈdensəti/ ***noun*** (*pl.* **densities**) **1** [U] the number of things or people in a place in relation to its area: *There is a high density of wildlife in this area.* **2** [C,U] (**PHYSICS**) the thickness of a solid, liquid or gas measured by its mass per unit of volume: *Lead has a high density.*

dent¹ /dent/ ***noun*** [C] a place where a flat surface, especially metal, has been hit and damaged but not broken

dent² /dent/ ***verb*** [T] to damage a flat surface by hitting it but not breaking it: *I hit a wall and dented the front of the car.*

dental /ˈdentl/ ***adj.*** connected with teeth: *dental care/treatment*

ˈ**dental floss** ***noun*** [U] a type of thread that is used for cleaning between the teeth

dentine /ˈdentiːn/ ***noun*** [U] (**ANATOMY**) the hard substance that forms the main part of a tooth under the ENAMEL (the hard white outer covering of a tooth) ➲ picture at **tooth**

dentist 🔑 /ˈdentɪst/ ***noun*** **1** [C] (**HEALTH**) a person whose job is to look after people's teeth **2 the dentist's** [sing.] the place where a dentist works: *I have to go to the dentist's today.*

dentistry /ˈdentɪstri/ ***noun*** [U] **1** (**HEALTH**) the medical study of the teeth and mouth **2** the care and treatment of people's teeth

dentition /denˈtɪʃn/ ***noun*** [U] (**BIOLOGY**) the arrangement or condition of a person's or animal's teeth

dentures /ˈdentʃəz/ = FALSE TEETH

denunciation /dɪˌnʌnsiˈeɪʃn/ ***noun*** [C,U] an expression of strong disapproval of sb/sth in public ➲ verb **denounce**

deny 🔑 AW /dɪˈnaɪ/ ***verb*** [T] (*pres. part.* **denying**; *3rd person sing. pres.* **denies**; *pt, pp* **denied**) **1** ~ **sth/doing sth**; ~ **that...** to state that sth is not true; to refuse to admit or accept sth: *In court he denied all the charges.* ◇ *She denied telling lies/that she had told lies.* OPP **admit** **2** (*formal*) ~ **sb sth**; ~ **sth (to sb)** to refuse to allow sb to have sth: *She was denied permission to remain in the country.* ➲ noun **denial**

WORD FAMILY
deny *verb*
denial *noun*
undeniable *adj.*

deodorant /diˈəʊdərənt/ ***noun*** [C,U] a chemical substance that you put onto your body to prevent bad smells

deoxygenated /ˌdiːˈɒksɪdʒəneɪtɪd/ ***adj.*** (**CHEMISTRY**) having had OXYGEN removed

deoxyribonucleic acid /ˌdiːɒksɪˌraɪbəʊnjuːˌkleɪɪk ˈæsɪd/ = DNA

dep. ***abbr.*** DEPARTS: *dep. London 15.32*

depart /dɪˈpɑːt/ ***verb*** [I] (*formal*) to leave a place, usually at the beginning of a journey: *Ferries **depart for** Spain twice a day.* ◇ *The next train to the airport **departs from** platform 2.* ➲ noun **departure**

department 🔑 /dɪˈpɑːtmənt/ ***noun*** [C] (*abbr.* **Dept**) **1** one of the sections into which an organization, for example a school or a business, is divided: *the Modern Languages department* ◇ *She works in the accounts department.* **2** (**POLITICS**) a division of the government responsible for a particular subject; a ministry: *the Department of Health*

departmental /ˌdiːpɑːtˈmentl/ ***adj.*** concerning a department: *There is a departmental meeting once a month.*

deˈpartment store ***noun*** [C] a large shop that is divided into sections selling different types of goods

departure 🔑 /dɪˈpɑːtʃə(r)/ ***noun*** [C,U] **1** the act of leaving a place; an example of this: *Helen's sudden departure meant I had to do her job as well as mine.* ◇ *Passengers should check in at least one hour before departure.* ➲ verb **depart** OPP **arrival** **2** (**TOURISM**) a plane, train, etc. leaving a place at a particular time: *All departures are from London.* ◇ *the **departure lounge/time/gate*** OPP **arrival** **3** a ~ **(from sth)** an action which is different from what is usual or expected: *a departure from normal practice*

depend 🔑 /dɪˈpend/ ***verb***

IDM **that depends; it (all) depends** (used alone or at the beginning of a sentence) used to say that you are not certain of sth until other things have been considered: *'Can you lend me some money?' 'That depends. How much do you want?'* ◇ *I don't know whether I'll see him. It depends what time he gets here.*

PHR V **depend on sb/sth** to be able to trust sb/sth to do sth; to rely on sb/sth: *If you ever need any help, you know you can depend on me.* ◇ *You can't depend on the trains. They're always late.* ◇ *I was depending on getting the money today.* ➲ note at **trust²**

depend on sb/sth (for sth) to need sb/sth to provide sth: *Our organization depends on donations from the public.*

depend on sth to be decided or influenced by sb/sth: *His whole future depends on these exams.*

dependable /dɪˈpendəbl/ ***adj.*** that can be trusted: *The bus service is very dependable.* SYN **reliable** ▸ **dependably** /-əbli/ ***adv.***

dependant (*especially AmE* **dependent**) /dɪˈpendənt/ ***noun*** [C] a person who depends on sb else for money, a home, food, etc.: *insurance cover for you and all your dependants*

dependence /dɪˈpendəns/ ***noun*** [U] ~ **on sb/sth** the state of needing sb/sth: *The country wants to reduce its dependence on imported oil.*

dependency /dɪˈpendənsi/ ***noun*** [U] the state of being DEPENDENT on sb/sth; the state of being unable to live without sth, especially a drug

dependent /dɪˈpendənt/ ***adj.*** **1** ~ **(on sb/sth)** needing sb/sth to support you: *The industry is heavily dependent on government funding.* ◇ *Do you have any dependent children?* **2** ~ **on sb/sth** influenced or decided by sth: *The price you pay is dependent on the number in your group.* OPP **independent**

depict /dɪˈpɪkt/ ***verb*** [T] **1** to show sb/sth in a painting or drawing: *a painting depicting a country scene* **2** to describe sb/sth in words: *The novel depicts rural life a century ago.*

deplete /dɪˈpliːt/ ***verb*** [T] to reduce the amount of sth so that there is not much left: *We are depleting the world's natural resources.* ▸ **depletion** /dɪˈpliːʃn/ ***noun*** [U]

deplorable /dɪˈplɔːrəbl/ ***adj.*** (*formal*) very bad and deserving disapproval: *They are living in deplorable conditions.* ▶ **deplorably** /-əbli/ ***adv.***

deplore /dɪˈplɔː(r)/ ***verb*** [T] (*formal*) to feel or say that sth is morally bad: *I deplore such dishonest behaviour.*

deploy /dɪˈplɔɪ/ ***verb*** [T] **1** to put soldiers or weapons in a position where they are ready to fight **2** to use sth in a useful and successful way ▶ **deployment** ***noun*** [U]: *the deployment of troops*

depopulate /ˌdiːˈpɒpjuleɪt/ ***verb*** [T] (*formal*) (usually passive) (SOCIAL STUDIES) to reduce the number of people living in a place ▶ **depopulation** /ˌdiːˌpɒpjuˈleɪʃn/ ***noun*** [U]

deport /dɪˈpɔːt/ ***verb*** [T] (POLITICS) to force sb to leave a country because they have no legal right to be there: *A number of illegal immigrants have been deported.* ▶ **deportation** /ˌdiːpɔːˈteɪʃn/ ***noun*** [C,U]

depose /dɪˈpəʊz/ ***verb*** [T] (POLITICS) to remove a ruler or leader from power: *There was a revolution and the dictator was deposed.*

deposit¹ 🔑 /dɪˈpɒzɪt/ ***verb*** [T] **1** to put sth down somewhere: *He deposited his bags on the floor and sat down.* **2** (GEOGRAPHY) (used about liquid or a river) to leave sth lying on a surface, as the result of a natural or chemical process: *mud deposited by a flood* **3** (FINANCE) to put money into an account at a bank: *He deposited £20 a week into his savings account.* **4** ~ **sth (in sth)**; ~ **sth (with sb/sth)** to put sth valuable in an official place where it is safe until needed again: *Valuables can be deposited in the hotel safe.*

deposit² 🔑 /dɪˈpɒzɪt/ ***noun*** [C] **1** a ~ **(on sth)** (FINANCE) a sum of money which is the first payment for sth, with the rest of the money to be paid later: *Once you have paid a deposit, the booking will be confirmed.* **2** a ~ **(on sth)** [usually sing.] (FINANCE) a sum of money that you pay when you rent sth and get back when you return it without damage: *Boats can be hired for £5 an hour, plus £20 deposit.* **3** (FINANCE) a sum of money paid into a bank account **4** (GEOLOGY) a substance that has been left on a surface or in the ground as the result of a natural or chemical process: *mineral deposits*

deˈposit account ***noun*** [C] (*BrE*) (FINANCE) a type of bank account where your money earns interest. You cannot take money out of a deposit account without arranging it first with the bank.

deposition /ˌdepəˈzɪʃn/ ***noun*** **1** [U, C] (GEOLOGY) the natural process of leaving a layer of a substance on rocks or soil; a substance left in this way: *marine/river deposition* **2** [U, C] (POLITICS) the act of removing sb, especially a ruler, from power: *the deposition of the king* **3** [C] (LAW) a formal statement, taken from sb and used in a court of law

depot /ˈdepəʊ/ ***noun*** [C] **1** a place where large numbers of vehicles (buses, lorries, etc.) are kept when not in use **2** a place where large amounts of food, goods or equipment are stored **3** (*AmE*) a small bus or railway station

depraved /dɪˈpreɪvd/ ***adj.*** morally bad

depravity /dɪˈprævəti/ ***noun*** [U] (*formal*) the state of being morally bad: *a life of depravity*

depreciate /dɪˈpriːʃieɪt/ ***verb*** [I] to become less valuable over a period of time: *New cars start to depreciate the moment they are on the road.* ▶ **depreciation** /dɪˌpriːʃiˈeɪʃn/ ***noun*** [C,U]

depress 🔑 AW /dɪˈpres/ ***verb*** [T] **1** to make sb unhappy and without hope or enthusiasm: *The thought of going to work tomorrow really depresses me.* **2** (BUSINESS) to make trade, business, etc. less active: *The reduction in the number of tourists has depressed local trade.* **3** (*formal*) to press sth down on a machine, etc.: *To switch off the machine, depress the lever.* ▶ **depressingly** ***adv.***

depressed 🔑 /dɪˈprest/ ***adj.*** **1** very unhappy, often for a long period of time: *He's been very depressed since he lost his job.* **2** (ECONOMICS) (used about a place or an industry) without enough economic activity or jobs for people

depressing 🔑 /dɪˈpresɪŋ/ ***adj.*** making you feel very sad and without enthusiasm: ***a depressing sight/thought/experience*** ◇ *Looking for a job these days can be very depressing.* ▶ **de·press·ing·ly** ***adv.***: *a depressingly familiar experience*

depression AW /dɪˈpreʃn/ ***noun*** **1** [U] (HEALTH) a feeling of unhappiness that lasts for a long time. **Depression** can be a medical condition and may have physical signs, for example being unable to sleep, etc.: ***clinical/post-natal depression*** **2** [C,U] (ECONOMICS) a period when the economic situation is bad, with little business activity and many people without a job: *The country was in the grip of (an) economic depression.* **3** [C] a part of a surface that is lower than the parts around it: *Rainwater collects in shallow depressions in the ground.* **4** [C] (GEOGRAPHY) a weather condition in which the pressure of the air becomes lower, often causing rain ➲ look at **anticyclone**

deprive /dɪˈpraɪv/ ***verb*** [T] ~ **sb/sth of sth** to prevent sb/sth from having sth; to take away sth from sb: *The prisoners were deprived of food.* ▶ **deprivation** /ˌdeprɪˈveɪʃn/ ***noun*** [U]

deprived /dɪˈpraɪvd/ ***adj.*** not having enough of the basic things in life, such as food, money, etc.: *He came from a deprived background.*

Dept ***abbr.*** department: *the Sales Dept*

depth 🔑 /depθ/ ***noun*** **1** [C,U] the distance down from the top to the bottom of sth: *The hole should be 3cm in depth.* **2** [C,U] the distance from the front to the back of sth: *the depth of a shelf* ➲ picture at **dimension** **3** [U] the amount of emotion, knowledge, etc. that a person has: *He tried to convince her of the depth of his feelings for her.* **4** [C, usually pl.] the deepest, most extreme or serious part of sth: ***in the depths of*** *winter* (=when it is coldest) ➲ adjective **deep**

IDM **in depth** looking at all the details; in a thorough way: *to discuss a problem in depth*

out of your depth **1** (*BrE*) in water that is too deep for you to stand up in **2** in a situation that is too difficult for you

deputation /ˌdepjuˈteɪʃn/ ***noun*** [C, with sing. or pl. verb] a group of people sent to sb to act or speak for others

deputize (also **-ise**) /ˈdepjutaɪz/ ***verb*** [I] ~ **(for sb)** to act for sb in a higher position, who is away or unable to do sth

deputy /ˈdepjuti/ ***noun*** [C] (*pl.* **deputies**) the second most important person in a particular organization, who does the work of their manager if the manager is away: *the deputy head of a school*

derail /dɪˈreɪl/ ***verb*** [T] to cause a train to come off a railway track

derailment /dɪˈreɪlmənt/ ***noun*** [C,U] an occasion when sth causes a train to come off a railway track

deranged /dɪˈreɪndʒd/ ***adj.*** thinking and behaving in a way that is not normal, especially because of mental illness

derby /ˈdɑːbi/ ***noun*** [C] (*pl.* **derbies**) **1** (*BrE*) (**SPORT**) a race or sports competition: *a motorcycle derby* **2** (*BrE*) **the Derby** (**SPORT**) a horse race which takes place every year at Epsom **3** (*AmE*) = BOWLER (1)

deregulate /ˌdiːˈregjuleɪt/ ***verb*** [T] (often passive) (**BUSINESS**) to free a commercial or business activity from rules and controls: *deregulated financial markets* ▶ **deregulation** /ˌdiːˌregjuˈleɪʃn/ ***noun*** [U]

derelict /ˈderəlɪkt/ ***adj.*** no longer used and in bad condition: *a derelict house*

deride /dɪˈraɪd/ ***verb*** [T] to say that sb/sth is ridiculous; to laugh at sth in a cruel way ▶ **derision** /dɪˈrɪʒn/ ***noun*** [U]: *Her comments were met with derision.* ▶ **derisive** /dɪˈraɪsɪv/ ***adj.***: *'What rubbish!' he said with a derisive laugh.*

de rigueur /ˌdə rɪˈgɜː(r)/ ***adj.*** considered necessary if you wish to be accepted socially: *Evening dress is de rigueur at the casino.*

derisory /dɪˈraɪsəri/ ***adj.*** too small or of too little value to be considered seriously: *Union leaders rejected the derisory pay offer.*

derivation AW /ˌderɪˈveɪʃn/ ***noun*** [C,U] (**LANGUAGE**) the origin from which a word or phrase has developed

derivative[1] AW /dɪˈrɪvətɪv/ ***noun*** [C] **1** (**LANGUAGE**) a form of sth (especially a word) that has developed from the original form: *'Sadness' is a derivative of 'sad.'* **2** (**MATHEMATICS**) an expression representing the rate of change of a function with respect to an independent VARIABLE (= a quantity which varies in value)

derivative[2] AW /dɪˈrɪvətɪv/ ***adj.*** copied from sth else; not having new or original ideas: *a **derivative** design/style*

derive ⊶ AW /dɪˈraɪv/ ***verb*** **1** [T] (*formal*) **~ sth from sth** to get sth (especially a feeling or an advantage) from sth: *I derive great satisfaction from my work.* **2** [I,T] (**LANGUAGE**) (used about a name or word) to come from sth; to have sth as its origin: *The town derives its name from the river on which it was built.*

dermatitis /ˌdɜːməˈtaɪtɪs/ ***noun*** [U] (**HEALTH**) a skin condition in which the skin becomes red, swollen and sore

dermatologist /ˌdɜːməˈtɒlədʒɪst/ ***noun*** [C] (**HEALTH**) a doctor who studies and treats skin diseases

dermatology /ˌdɜːməˈtɒlədʒi/ ***noun*** [U] (**HEALTH**) the scientific study of skin diseases ▶ **dermatological** /ˌdɜːmətəˈlɒdʒɪkl/ ***adj.***

dermis /ˈdɜːmɪs/ ***noun*** [sing., U] (**ANATOMY**) the thick layer of skin just under the EPIDERMIS ➲ picture at **skin**

derogatory /dɪˈrɒgətri/ ***adj.*** expressing a lack of respect for, or a low opinion of sth: *derogatory comments about the standard of my work*

derrick /ˈderɪk/ ***noun*** [C] **1** a tall machine used for moving or lifting heavy weights, especially on a ship; a type of CRANE **2** a tall structure over an OIL WELL for holding the DRILL (= the machine that makes the hole in the ground for getting the oil out)

derring-do /ˌderɪŋ ˈduː/ ***noun*** [U] (*old-fashioned*) brave actions, like those in adventure stories: *tales of derring-do*

desalination /ˌdiːˌsælɪˈneɪʃn/ ***noun*** [U] the process of removing salt from sea water

descant /ˈdeskænt/ ***noun*** [C] (**MUSIC**) a tune that is sung or played at the same time as, and usually higher than, the main tune

descend /dɪˈsend/ ***verb*** [I,T] (*formal*) to go down to a lower place; to go down sth: *The plane started to descend and a few minutes later we landed.* ◇ *She descended the stairs slowly.* OPP **ascend**

IDM **be descended from sb** to have sb as a relative in past times: *He says he's descended from a Russian prince.*

descendant /dɪˈsendənt/ ***noun*** [C] a person who belongs to the same family as sb who lived a long time ago: *Her family are descendants of one of the first Englishmen to arrive in America.* ➲ look at **ancestor**

descent /dɪˈsent/ ***noun*** **1** [C] a movement down to a lower place: *The pilot informed us that we were about to begin our descent.* **2** [U] a person's family origins: *He is **of** Italian **descent**.*

describe ⊶ /dɪˈskraɪb/ ***verb*** [T] **~ sb/sth (to/for sb); ~ sb/sth (as sth)** to say what sb/sth is like, or what happened: *Can you describe the bag you lost?* ◇ *It's impossible to describe how I felt.* ◇ *The thief was described as tall, thin, and aged about twenty.*

description ⊶ /dɪˈskrɪpʃn/ ***noun*** **1** [C,U] a picture in words of sb/sth or of sth that happened: *The man gave the police a **detailed description** of the burglar.* **2** [C] a type or kind of sth: *It must be a tool **of some description**, but I don't know what it's for.*

descriptive /dɪˈskrɪptɪv/ ***adj.*** that describes sb/sth, especially in a skilful or interesting way: *a piece of descriptive writing* ◇ *She gave a highly descriptive account of the journey.*

desecrate /ˈdesɪkreɪt/ ***verb*** [T] (**RELIGION**) to damage a place of religious importance or treat it without respect: *desecrated graves* ▶ **desecration** /ˌdesɪˈkreɪʃn/ ***noun*** [U]: *the desecration of a cemetery*

desert[1] ⊶ /ˈdezət/ ***noun*** [C,U] (**GEOGRAPHY**) a large area of land, usually covered with sand, that is hot and has very little water and very few plants ➲ picture at **ecosystem**

desert[2] ⊶ /dɪˈzɜːt/ ***verb*** **1** [T] to leave sb/sth, usually for ever: *Many people have deserted the countryside and moved to the towns.* **2** [I,T] (used especially about sb in the armed forces) to leave without permission: *He deserted because he didn't want to fight.* ▶ **desertion** ***noun*** [C,U]

deserted ⊶ /dɪˈzɜːtɪd/ ***adj.*** empty, because all the people have left: *a deserted house*

deserter /dɪˈzɜːtə(r)/ ***noun*** [C] a person who leaves the armed forces without permission

desertification /dɪˌzɜːtɪfɪˈkeɪʃn/ ***noun*** [U] (**ENVIRONMENT**) the process of becoming a desert or of making an area of land into a desert

ˌdesert ˈisland ***noun*** [C] an island, especially a tropical one, where nobody lives

deserve ⊶ /dɪˈzɜːv/ ***verb*** [T] (not used in the continuous tenses) to earn sth, either good or bad, because of sth that you have done: *We've done a lot of work and we deserve a break.* ◇ *He deserves to be punished severely for such a crime.*

deservedly /dɪˈzɜːvɪdli/ ***adv.*** in a way that is right because of what sb has done: *He deservedly won the Best Actor award.*

deserving /dɪˈzɜːvɪŋ/ ***adj.*** **~ (of sth)** that you should give help, money, etc. to: *This charity is a most deserving cause.*

desiccated /ˈdesɪkeɪtɪd/ ***adj.*** **1** (used about food) dried in order to keep it for a long time: *desiccated coconut* **2** completely dry: *desiccated soil*

desiccation /ˌdesɪˈkeɪʃn/ ***noun*** [U] (**ENVIRONMENT**) the process of becoming completely dry: *the dramatic desiccation of North Africa*

design¹ 🔑 AW /dɪˈzaɪn/ ***noun*** **1** [U] the way in which sth is planned and made or arranged: *Design faults have been discovered in the car.* **2** [U] the process and skill of making drawings that show how sth should be made, how it will work, etc.: *to study industrial design* ◇ *graphic design* **3** [C] **a ~ (for sth)** a drawing or plan that shows how sth should be made, built, etc.: *The architect showed us her design for the new theatre.* **4** [C] a pattern of lines, shapes, etc. that decorate sth: *a T-shirt with a geometric design on it* SYN **pattern**

design² 🔑 AW /dɪˈzaɪn/ ***verb*** **1** [I,T] to plan and make a drawing of how sth will be made: *to design cars/dresses/houses* **2** [T] to invent, plan and develop sth for a particular purpose: *The bridge wasn't designed for such heavy traffic.*

designate /ˈdezɪgneɪt/ ***verb*** [T] (often passive) (*formal*) **1 ~ sth (as) sth** to give sth a name to show that it has a particular purpose: *This has been designated (as) a conservation area.* **2 ~ sb (as) sth** to choose sb to do a particular job or task: *Who has she designated (as) her deputy?* **3** to show or mark sth: *These arrows designate the emergency exits.*

ˌdesignated ˈdriver ***noun*** [C] (*informal*) the person who agrees to drive and not drink alcohol when people go to a party, a bar, etc.

designer AW /dɪˈzaɪnə(r)/ ***noun*** [C] a person whose job is to make drawings or plans showing how sth will be made: *a fashion/jewellery designer* ◇ ***designer jeans*** (= made by a famous designer)

desirable /dɪˈzaɪərəbl/ ***adj.*** **1** wanted, often by many people; worth having: *Experience is desirable but not essential for this job.* **2** sexually attractive OPP **undesirable**

desire¹ 🔑 /dɪˈzaɪə(r)/ ***noun*** [C,U] (a) **~ (for sth/ to do sth)** **1** the feeling of wanting sth very much; a strong wish: *the desire for a peaceful solution to the crisis* ◇ *I have no desire to visit that place again.* **2** the wish for a sexual relationship with sb

desire² 🔑 /dɪˈzaɪə(r)/ ***verb*** [T] **1** (*formal*) (not used in the continuous tenses) to want; to wish for: *They have everything they could possibly desire.* ◇ *The service in the restaurant **left a lot to be desired*** (= was very bad). **2** to find sb/sth sexually attractive

desk 🔑 /desk/ ***noun*** [C] **1** a type of table, often with drawers, that you sit at to write or work: *The pupils took their books out of their desks.* ◇ *He used to be a pilot but now he has **a desk job*** (= he works in an office). **2** a table or place in a building where a particular service is provided: *an information desk*

ˈdesk clerk ***noun*** [C] (*AmE*) = CLERK (3)

desktop /ˈdesktɒp/ ***noun*** [C] **1** the top of a desk **2** (**COMPUTING**) a computer screen on which you can see symbols (**icons**) showing the programs, etc. that are available to be used **3** (*also* **ˌdesktop comˈputer**) (**COMPUTING**) a computer that can fit on a desk ➲ look at **blackberry**, **laptop**, **palmtop**

ˌdesktop ˈpublishing (*abbr.* **DTP**) ***noun*** [U] (**ARTS AND MEDIA**) the use of a small computer and a machine for printing, to produce books, magazines and other printed material

desolate /ˈdesələt/ ***adj.*** **1** (used about a place) empty in a way that seems very sad: *desolate wasteland* **2** (used about a person) lonely, very unhappy and without hope ▸ **desolation** /ˌdesəˈleɪʃn/ ***noun*** [U]: *a scene of desolation.* ◇ *He felt utter desolation when his wife died.*

despair¹ /dɪˈspeə(r)/ ***noun*** [U] the state of having lost all hope: *I felt like giving up **in despair**.* ▸ **despairing** ***adj.***: *a despairing cry* ➲ look at **desperate**

despair² /dɪˈspeə(r)/ ***verb*** [I] **~ (of sb/sth)** to lose all hope that sth will happen: *We began to despair of ever finding somewhere to live.*

despatch /dɪˈspætʃ/ (*BrE*) = DISPATCH

desperate 🔑 /ˈdespərət/ ***adj.*** **1** out of control and ready to do anything to change the situation you are in because it is so terrible: *She became desperate when her money ran out.* **2** done with little hope of success, as a last thing to try when everything else has failed: *I made a desperate attempt to persuade her to change her mind.* **3 ~ (for sth/to do sth)** wanting or needing sth very much: *Let's go into a cafe. I'm desperate for a drink.* **4** terrible, very serious: *There is a desperate shortage of skilled workers.* ▸ **desperation** /ˌdespəˈreɪʃn/ ***noun*** [U] ▸ **desperately** ***adv.***: *She was desperately* (= extremely) *unlucky not to win.*

despicable /dɪˈspɪkəbl/ ***adj.*** very unpleasant or evil: *a despicable act of terrorism*

despise /dɪˈspaɪz/ ***verb*** [T] to hate sb/sth very much: *I despise him for lying to me.*

despite 🔑 AW /dɪˈspaɪt/ ***prep.*** without being affected by the thing mentioned: *Despite having very little money, they enjoy life.* ◇ *The scheme went ahead despite public opposition.* SYN **in spite of**

despondent /dɪˈspɒndənt/ ***adj.*** **~ (about/over sth)** without hope; expecting no improvement: *She was becoming increasingly despondent about finding a job.* ▸ **despondency** /dɪˈspɒndənsi/ ***noun*** [U]

despot /ˈdespɒt/ ***noun*** [C] (**POLITICS**) a ruler with great power, especially one who uses it in a cruel way ➲ look at **autocrat** ▸ **despotic** /dɪˈspɒtɪk/ ***adj.***: *despotic power/rule*

dessert /dɪˈzɜːt/ ***noun*** [C,U] something sweet that is eaten after the main part of a meal: *What would you like **for dessert** – ice cream or fresh fruit?* ➲ look at **pudding**, **sweet**

dessertspoon /dɪˈzɜːtspuːn/ ***noun*** [C] a spoon used for eating sweet food after the main part of a meal

destabilize (also **-ise**) /ˌdiːˈsteɪbəlaɪz/ ***verb*** [T] to make a system, government, country, etc. become less safe and successful: *Terrorist attacks were threatening to destabilize the government.* ➲ look at **stabilize**

destination /ˌdestɪˈneɪʃn/ ***noun*** [C] the place where sb/sth is going: *I finally reached my destination two hours late.* ◇ *popular holiday destinations like the Bahamas*

destiˈnation wedding ***noun*** [C] (**TOURISM**) a wedding held in an exciting or unusual place in a foreign country where all the people who travel to the wedding can also have a holiday

destined /ˈdestɪnd/ ***adj.*** **1 ~ for sth/to do sth** having a future that has been decided or planned at an earlier time: *I think she is destined for success.* ◇ *He was destined to become one of the country's leading politicians.* **2 ~ for...** travelling towards a particular place: *I boarded a bus destined for New York.*

destiny /ˈdestəni/ ***noun*** (*pl.* **destinies**) **1** [C] the things that happen to you in your life, especially things that you cannot control: *She felt that it was her destiny to be a great singer.* **2** [U] a power that people believe controls their lives SYN fate

destitute /ˈdestɪtjuːt/ ***adj.*** without any money, food or a home ▶ **destitution** /ˌdestɪˈtjuːʃn/ ***noun*** [U]

destroy /dɪˈstrɔɪ/ ***verb*** [T] **1** to damage sth so badly that it can no longer be used or no longer exists: *The building was destroyed by fire.* ◇ *The defeat destroyed his confidence.* **2** to kill an animal, especially because it is injured or dangerous: *The horse broke its leg and had to be destroyed.*

> WORD FAMILY
> **destroy** *verb*
> **destroyer** *noun*
> **destruction** *noun*
> **destructive** *adj.*
> **indestructible** *adj.*

destroyer /dɪˈstrɔɪə(r)/ ***noun*** [C] **1** a small ship that is used when there is a war **2** a person or thing that destroys sth

destruction /dɪˈstrʌkʃn/ ***noun*** [U] the action of destroying sth: *The war brought* ***death and destruction*** *to the city.* ◇ *the destruction of the rainforests* ◇ *weapons of mass destruction*

destructive /dɪˈstrʌktɪv/ ***adj.*** causing a lot of harm or damage

detach /dɪˈtætʃ/ ***verb*** [T] **~ sth (from sth)** to separate sth from sth it is connected to: *Detach the form at the bottom of the page and send it to this address...* OPP attach

detachable /dɪˈtætʃəbl/ ***adj.*** that can be separated from sth it is connected to: *a coat with a detachable hood*

detached /dɪˈtætʃt/ ***adj.*** **1** (used about a house) not joined to any other house **2** not being or not feeling personally involved in sth; without emotion

detachment /dɪˈtætʃmənt/ ***noun*** **1** [U] the fact or feeling of not being personally involved in sth **2** [C] a group of soldiers who have been given a particular task away from the main group

detail[1] /ˈdiːteɪl/ ***noun*** [C,U] one fact or piece of information: *Just give me the basic facts. Don't worry about the details.* ◇ *On the application form you should give details of your education and experience.* ◇ *The work involves close attention to detail.*

IDM **go into detail(s)** to talk or write about the details of sth; to explain sth fully: *I can't go into detail now because it would take too long.*

in detail including the details; thoroughly: *We haven't discussed the matter in detail yet.*

detail[2] /ˈdiːteɪl/ ***verb*** [T] to give a full list of sth; to describe sth completely: *He detailed all the equipment he needed for the job.*

detailed /ˈdiːteɪld/ ***adj.*** giving many details and a lot of information; paying great attention to details: *a* ***detailed description/analysis/study*** ◇ *He gave me* ***detailed instructions*** *on how to get there.*

detain /dɪˈteɪn/ ***verb*** [T] to stop sb from leaving a place; to delay sb: *A man has been detained by the police for questioning* (=kept at the police station). ◇ *Don't let me detain you if you're busy.* ➲ noun **detention**

detainee /ˌdiːteɪˈniː/ ***noun*** [C] (LAW, POLITICS) a person who is kept in prison, usually because of his or her political opinions

detect AW /dɪˈtekt/ ***verb*** [T] to notice or discover sth that is difficult to see, feel, etc.: *I detected a slight change in his attitude.* ◇ *Traces of blood were detected on his clothes.* ▶ **detectable** ***adj.*** ▶ **detection** AW ***noun*** [U]: *The crime escaped detection* (=was not discovered) *for many years.*

detective AW /dɪˈtektɪv/ ***noun*** [C] a person, especially a police officer, who tries to solve crimes

de'tective story ***noun*** [C] (LITERATURE) a story about a crime in which sb tries to find out who the guilty person is

detector AW /dɪˈtektə(r)/ ***noun*** [C] a machine that is used for finding or noticing sth: *a* ***smoke/metal/lie detector***

détente (*especially AmE* **detente**) /ˌdeɪˈtɑːnt/ ***noun*** [U] (*formal*) (POLITICS) an improvement in the relationship between two or more countries which have been unfriendly towards each other in the past

detention /dɪˈtenʃn/ ***noun*** [U, C] **1** (LAW) the act of stopping a person leaving a place, especially by keeping them in prison: *They were kept* ***in detention*** *for ten days.* **2** (EDUCATION) the punishment of being kept at school after the other schoolchildren have gone home ➲ verb **detain**

de'tention centre (*AmE* **de'tention center**) ***noun*** [C] (LAW) **1** a place like a prison where young people who have broken the law are kept **2** a place like a prison where people, especially people who have entered a country illegally, are kept for a short time

deter /dɪˈtɜː(r)/ ***verb*** [T] (**deterring**; **deterred**) **~ sb (from doing sth)** to make sb decide not to do sth, especially by telling them that it would have bad results ➲ noun **deterrent**

detergent /dɪˈtɜːdʒənt/ ***noun*** [C,U] a chemical liquid or powder that is used for cleaning things

deteriorate /dɪˈtɪəriəreɪt/ ***verb*** [I] to become worse: *The political tension is deteriorating into civil war.* ▶ **deterioration** /dɪˌtɪəriəˈreɪʃn/ ***noun*** [C,U]

determination /dɪˌtɜːmɪˈneɪʃn/ ***noun*** [U] **1 ~ (to do sth)** the quality of having firmly decided to do sth, even if it is very difficult: *her determination to win* ◇ *You need great determination to succeed in business.* **2** (*formal*) the process of deciding sth officially: *the determination of future government policy*

determine /dɪˈtɜːmɪn/ ***verb*** [T] **1** (*formal*) to discover the facts about sth: *We need to determine what happened immediately before the accident.* **2** to make sth happen in a particular way or be of a particular type: *The results of the tests will determine what treatment you need.* ◇ *Age and experience will be* ***determining factors*** *in our choice of candidate.* **3** (*formal*) to decide sth officially: *A date for the meeting has yet to be determined.*

determined /dɪˈtɜːmɪnd/ ***adj.*** **~ (to do sth)** having firmly decided to do sth or to succeed, even if it is difficult: *He is determined to leave school, even though his parents want him to stay.* ◇ *She's a very determined athlete.*

determiner /dɪˈtɜːmɪnə(r)/ ***noun*** [C] (LANGUAGE) a word that comes before a noun to show how the noun is being used: *'Her', 'most' and 'those' are all determiners.*

deterrent /dɪˈterənt/ ***noun*** [C] something that should stop you doing sth: *Their punishment will be a deterrent to others.* ➲ verb **deter** ▶ **deterrence** /dɪˈterəns/ ***noun*** [U] (*formal*) ▶ **deterrent** ***adj.***

detest /dɪˈtest/ ***verb*** [T] to hate or not like sb/sth at all: *They absolutely detest each other.*

detonate /ˈdetəneɪt/ ***verb*** [I,T] to explode or to make a bomb, etc. explode

detonator /ˈdetəneɪtə(r)/ ***noun*** [C] a device for making sth, especially a bomb, explode

detour /ˈdiːtʊə(r)/ ***noun*** [C] **1** a longer route from one place to another that you take in order to avoid sth/sb or in order to see or do sth: *Because of the accident we had to make a five-kilometre detour.* **2** (*AmE*) = DIVERSION (2)

detox /ˈdiːtɒks/ ***noun*** [U] (*informal*) (**HEALTH**) the process of removing harmful substances from your body by only eating and drinking particular things

detract /dɪˈtrækt/ ***verb*** [I] ~ **from sth** to make sth seem less good or important: *These criticisms in no way detract from the team's achievements.*

detriment /ˈdetrɪmənt/ ***noun*** [U,C, usually sing.] (*formal*) the act of causing harm or damage; sth that causes harm or damage

IDM **to the detriment of sb/sth** resulting in harm or damage to sb/sth: *Doctors claim that the changes will be to the detriment of patients.*

detrimental /ˌdetrɪˈmentl/ ***adj.*** ~ **(to sb/sth)** harmful: *Too much alcohol is **detrimental to** your health.*

detritus /dɪˈtraɪtəs/ ***noun*** [U] (**ENVIRONMENT**) natural waste material that is left after sth has been used or broken up

deuce /djuːs/ ***noun*** [U] (**SPORT**) a score of 40 points to each player in a game of TENNIS

deus ex machina /ˌdeɪʊs eks ˈmækɪnə/ ***noun*** [sing.] (**LITERATURE**) an unexpected power or event that saves a situation that seems without hope, especially in a play or novel

deuterium /djuˈtɪəriəm/ ***noun*** [U] (*symbol* **D**) (**CHEMISTRY**) a type of HYDROGEN that is twice as heavy as the usual type

devalue /ˌdiːˈvæljuː/ ***verb*** [T] **1** (**ECONOMICS**) to reduce the value of the money of one country in relation to the value of the money of other countries: *The pound has been devalued against the dollar.* **2** to reduce the value or importance of sth: *The refusal of the top players to take part devalues this competition.* ▶ **devaluation** /ˌdiːˌvæljuˈeɪʃn/ ***noun*** [U]

devastate /ˈdevəsteɪt/ ***verb*** [T] **1** to destroy sth or damage it badly: *a land devastated by war* **2** to make sb extremely upset and shocked: *This tragedy has devastated the community.* ▶ **devastation** /ˌdevəˈsteɪʃn/ ***noun*** [U]: *a scene of total devastation*

devastated /ˈdevəsteɪtɪd/ ***adj.*** extremely shocked and upset: *They were devastated when their baby died.*

devastating /ˈdevəsteɪtɪŋ/ ***adj.*** **1** that destroys sth completely: *a devastating explosion* **2** that shocks or upsets sb very much: *The closure of the factory was a devastating blow to the workers.*

develop 🔑 /dɪˈveləp/ ***verb*** **1** [I,T] to grow slowly, increase, or change into sth else; to make sb/sth do this: *to develop from a child into an adult* ◇ *a scheme to help pupils develop their natural talents* ◇ *Scientists have developed a drug against this disease.* ◇ *Over the years, she's developed her own unique singing style.* **2** [I,T] to begin to have a problem or disease; to start to affect sth: *to develop cancer/Aids* ◇ *Trouble is developing along the border.* **3** [T] to make an idea, a story, etc. clearer or more detailed by writing or talking about it more: *She went on to develop this theme later in the lecture.* **4** [T] to make pictures or negatives from a piece of film by using special chemicals: *to develop a film* **5** [T] to build houses, shops, factories, etc. on a piece of land: *This site is being developed for offices.* ➲ note at **make**[1]

developed /dɪˈveləpt/ ***adj.*** **1** (**ECONOMICS**) (used about a country, a society, etc.) having many industries and a complicated economic system: *financial aid to less developed countries* ➲ look at **developing**, **underdeveloped** **2** in an advanced state: *children with highly developed problem-solving skills*

developer /dɪˈveləpə(r)/ (*also* **ˈproperty developer**) ***noun*** [C] a person or company that builds houses, shops, etc. on a piece of land

developing /dɪˈveləpɪŋ/ ***adj.*** (**ECONOMICS**) (used about a poor country) that is trying to develop or improve its economy: ***a developing country*** ◇ *the developing world* ➲ look at **developed**, **underdeveloped**

development 🔑 /dɪˈveləpmənt/ ***noun*** **1** [U] the process of becoming bigger, stronger, better etc., or of making sb/sth do this: *the development of tourism in Cuba* ◇ *a child's intellectual development* **2** [U, C] the process of creating sth more advanced; a more advanced product: *She works in **research and development** for a drug company.* ◇ *the latest developments in space technology* **3** [C] a new event that changes a situation: *This week has seen a number of new developments in the crisis.* **4** [C,U] a piece of land with new buildings on it; the process of building on a piece of land: *a new housing development* ◇ *The land has been bought for development.*

developmental /dɪˌveləpˈmentl/ ***adj.*** **1** in a state of developing or being developed: *The product is still at a developmental stage.* **2** connected with the development of sb/sth: *developmental psychology*

deviant /ˈdiːviənt/ ***adj.*** different from what most people consider to be normal and acceptable: *deviant behaviour* ▶ **deviant** ***noun*** [C]: *sexual deviants* ▶ **deviance** /ˈdiːviəns/ **deviancy** /ˈdiːviənsi/ ***noun*** [U]: *a study of social deviance and crime*

deviate AW /ˈdiːvieɪt/ ***verb*** [I] ~ **(from sth)** to change or become different from what is normal or expected: *He never once deviated from his original plan.*

deviation AW /ˌdiːviˈeɪʃn/ ***noun*** [C,U] a difference from what is normal or expected, or from what is approved of by society: *sexual deviation* ◇ *a deviation from our usual way of doing things*

device 🔑 AW /dɪˈvaɪs/ ***noun*** [C] **1** a tool or piece of equipment made for a particular purpose: *a security device which detects any movement* ◇ *labour-saving devices such as washing machines and vacuum cleaners* ➲ note at **tool** **2** a clever method for getting the result you want: *Critics dismissed the speech as a political device for winning support.*

devil /ˈdevl/ ***noun*** [C] **1 the Devil** (**RELIGION**) the most powerful evil being, according to the Christian, Jewish and Muslim religions ➲ look at **Satan** **2** (**RELIGION**) an evil being; a spirit **3** (*spoken*) a word used to show pity, anger, etc. when you are talking about a person: *The poor devil died in hospital two days later.* ◇ *Those kids can be little devils sometimes.*

IDM **be a devil** used to encourage sb to do sth that they are not sure about doing: *Go on, be a devil – buy both of them.*

speak/talk of the devil used when the person who is being talked about appears unexpectedly

devious /ˈdiːviəs/ ***adj.*** clever but not honest or direct: *I wouldn't trust him – he can be very devious.* ◇ *a devious trick/plan* ▶ **deviously** ***adv.***

devise /dɪ'vaɪz/ ***verb*** [T] to invent a new way of doing sth: *They've devised a plan for keeping traffic out of the city centre.*

devoid /dɪ'vɔɪd/ ***adj.*** (*formal*) **~ of sth** not having a particular quality; without sth: *devoid of hope/ambition/imagination*

devolution /ˌdiːvə'luːʃn/ ***noun*** [U] (POLITICS) the act of giving political power from central to local government ➲ verb **devolve**

devolve /dɪ'vɒlv/ ***verb***

PHR V **devolve on/upon sb/sth** (*written*) **1** (LAW) if property, money, etc. **devolves** on/upon you, you receive it after sb dies **2** if a duty, responsibility, etc. **devolves** on/upon you, it is given to you by sb at a higher level of authority

devolve sth to/on/upon sb to give a duty, responsibility, power, etc. to sb who has less authority than you: *The central government devolved most tax-raising powers to the regional authorities.* ➲ noun **devolution**

devote 🔑 AW /dɪ'vəʊt/ ***verb*** [T] **~ yourself/sth to sb/sth** to give a lot of time, energy, etc. to sb/sth: *She gave up work to devote herself full-time to her music.* ◇ *Schools should devote more time to science subjects.*

devoted 🔑 AW /dɪ'vəʊtɪd/ ***adj.*** **~ (to sb/sth)** loving sb/sth very much; completely loyal to sb/sth: *Neil's absolutely devoted to his wife.*

devotee /ˌdevə'tiː/ ***noun*** [C] **a ~ (of sb/sth)** a person who likes sb/sth very much: *Devotees of science fiction will enjoy this new film.*

devotion AW /dɪ'vəʊʃn/ ***noun*** [U] **~ (to sb/sth)** **1** great love for sb/sth: *a mother's devotion to her children* **2** the act of giving a lot of your time, energy, etc. to sb/sth: *devotion to duty* **3** (RELIGION) very strong religious feeling

devour /dɪ'vaʊə(r)/ ***verb*** [T] **1** to eat sth quickly because you are very hungry **2** to do or use sth quickly and completely

devout /dɪ'vaʊt/ ***adj.*** (RELIGION) very religious: *a devout Muslim family* ▶ **devoutly** ***adv.***

dew /djuː/ ***noun*** [U] small drops of water that form on plants, leaves, etc. during the night

'**dew point** ***noun*** [U] (GEOGRAPHY) the temperature at which air can hold no more water. Below this temperature the water comes out of the air in the form of drops.

dexterity /dek'sterəti/ ***noun*** [U] skill at doing things, especially with your hands

dexterous (also **dextrous**) /'dekstrəs/ ***adj.*** (*formal*) skilful with your hands; skilfully done ▶ **dexterously** (also **dextrously**) ***adv.***

dextrose /'dekstrəʊz/ ***noun*** [U] (BIOLOGY) a form of GLUCOSE (= a natural type of sugar) ➲ look at **fructose**, **glucose**, **lactose**, **sucrose**

di- /daɪ/ ***prefix*** (in nouns) (CHEMISTRY) used to refer to substances that contain two atoms of the type mentioned: *dioxide*

diabetes /ˌdaɪə'biːtiːz/ ***noun*** [U] (HEALTH) a serious disease in which a person's body cannot control the level of sugar in the blood

diabetic[1] /ˌdaɪə'betɪk/ ***noun*** [C] (HEALTH) a person who suffers from DIABETES

diabetic[2] /ˌdaɪə'betɪk/ ***adj.*** (HEALTH) connected with diabetes or **diabetics**: *diabetic chocolate* (= safe for diabetics)

diacritic /ˌdaɪə'krɪtɪk/ ***noun*** [C] (LANGUAGE) a mark such as an accent, placed over, under or through a letter in some languages, to show that the letter should be pronounced in a different way from the same letter without a mark ▶ **diacritical** /-'krɪtɪkl/ ***adj.***: *diacritical marks*

diagnose /'daɪəgnəʊz/ ***verb*** [T] **~ sth (as sth); ~ sb as/with sth** (HEALTH) to find out and say exactly what illness a person has or what the cause of a problem is: *His illness was diagnosed as bronchitis.* ◇ *I've been diagnosed as (a) diabetic/with diabetes.*

diagnosis /ˌdaɪəg'nəʊsɪs/ ***noun*** [C,U] (*pl.* **diagnoses** /-siːz/) (HEALTH) the act of saying exactly what illness a person has or what the cause of a problem is: *to **make a diagnosis***

diagnostic /ˌdaɪəg'nɒstɪk/ ***adj.*** (HEALTH) connected with finding out exactly what a problem is and what caused it, especially an illness: *to carry out diagnostic tests*

diagonal /daɪ'ægənl/ ***adj.*** (MATHEMATICS) (used about a straight line) joining two sides of sth at an angle that is not 90° or vertical or horizontal: *Draw a diagonal line from one corner of the square to the opposite corner.* ➲ picture at **line** ▶ **diagonal** ***noun*** [C] ▶ **diagonally** /-nəli/ ***adv.***

diagram 🔑 /'daɪəgræm/ ***noun*** [C] a simple picture that is used to explain how sth works or what sth looks like: *a diagram of the body's digestive system* ▶ **diagrammatic** /ˌdaɪəgrə'mætɪk/ ***adj.***

dial[1] /'daɪəl/ ***noun*** [C] **1** the round part of a clock, watch, control on a machine, etc. that shows a measurement of time, amount, temperature, etc.: *a dial for showing air pressure* **2** the round control on a radio, cooker, etc. that you turn to change sth **3** the round part with holes in it on some older telephones that you turn to call a number

dial[2] /'daɪəl/ ***verb*** [I,T] (**dialling**; **dialled**: *AmE* **dialing**; **dialed**) to push the buttons or move the DIAL on a telephone in order to call a telephone number: *Dial 0033 for France.* ◇ *to dial the wrong number*

PHR V **dial up sb/sth** (also **dial into sth**) (COMPUTING) to make a connection between one computer and another using a telephone line: *I dial in from my PC at home to get the files I need.* ◇ *Every time I try to dial into the Internet I can't get a connection.*

dialect /'daɪəlekt/ ***noun*** [C,U] (LANGUAGE) a form of a language that is spoken in one part of a country: *a local dialect*

'**dialling code** ***noun*** [C] the numbers that you must DIAL on a telephone for a particular area or country: *international dialling codes*

'**dialling tone** ***noun*** [C,U] the sound that you hear when you pick up a telephone to make a call

dialogue (*AmE* **dialog**) /'daɪəlɒg/ ***noun*** [C,U] **1** (a) conversation between people in a book, play, etc.: *This movie is all action, with very little dialogue.* ◇ *On the tape you will hear a short dialogue between a shop assistant and a customer.* **2** (a) discussion between people who have different opinions: *(a) dialogue between the major political parties*

'**dialogue box** (*AmE* '**dialog box**) ***noun*** [C] (COMPUTING) a box that appears on a computer screen asking you to choose what you want to do next

'**dial-up** ***adj.*** (only *before* a noun) (COMPUTING) using a telephone line to connect your computer to the Internet

dialysis /ˌdaɪˈæləsɪs/ ***noun*** [U] (HEALTH) a process for separating substances from a liquid, especially for taking waste substances out of the blood of people with damaged KIDNEYS

diameter /daɪˈæmɪtə(r)/ ***noun*** [C] (MATHEMATICS) a straight line that goes from one side to the other of a circle, passing through the centre ➲ look at **radius**, **circumference** ➲ picture at **circle**

diamond /ˈdaɪəmənd/ ***noun*** **1** [C,U] a hard, bright, rare and valuable PRECIOUS STONE which is very expensive and is used for making jewellery. A diamond usually has no colour. **2** [C] (GEOMETRY) a flat shape that has four sides of equal length and points at two ends **3 diamonds** [pl.] the group (**suit**) of playing cards with red shapes like **diamonds** on them: *the seven of diamonds* **4** [C] one of the cards from this suit: *I haven't got any diamonds.*

ˌdiamond ˈwedding ***noun*** [C] the 60th anniversary of a wedding ➲ look at **golden wedding**, **ruby wedding**, **silver wedding**

diaper /ˈdaɪəpə(r)/ (*AmE*) = NAPPY

diaphragm /ˈdaɪəfræm/ ***noun*** [C] **1** (ANATOMY) the muscle between your lungs and your stomach that helps you to breathe ➲ picture at **lung** **2** (HEALTH) a thin piece of rubber that a woman puts inside her body before having sex to stop her having a baby

diarrhoea (*AmE* **diarrhea**) /ˌdaɪəˈrɪə/ ***noun*** [U] (HEALTH) an illness that causes you to get rid of waste material from your body very often and in a more liquid form than usual: *Symptoms include diarrhoea and vomiting.*

diary /ˈdaɪəri/ ***noun*** [C] (*pl.* **diaries**) **1** a book in which you write down things that you have to do, remember, etc.: *I'll just check in my diary to see if I'm free that weekend.* **2** a book in which you write down what happens to you each day: *Do you **keep a diary**?*

diastole /daɪˈæstəli/ ***noun*** [C] (HEALTH) the stage of the heart's rhythm when its muscles relax and the heart fills with blood ➲ look at **systole** ▶ **diastolic** /ˌdaɪəˈstɒlɪk/ ***adj.*** ➲ look at **systolic**: *diastolic blood pressure*

diatomic /ˌdaɪəˈtɒmɪk/ ***adj.*** (CHEMISTRY) consisting of two atoms

dice /daɪs/ (*especially AmE* **die**) ***noun*** [C] (*pl.* **dice**) a small square object with a different number of spots (from one to six) on each side, used in certain games: ***Throw the dice** to see who goes first.*

dichotomy /daɪˈkɒtəmi/ ***noun*** [C, usually sing.] (*pl.* **dichotomies**) **a ~ (between A and B)** (*formal*) the separation that exists between two groups or things that are completely opposite to and different from each other

dictate /dɪkˈteɪt/ ***verb*** **1** [I,T] **~ (sth) (to sb)** to say sth aloud so that sb else can write or type it: *to dictate a letter to a secretary* **2** [I,T] **~ (sth) (to sb)** to tell sb what to do in a way that seems unfair: *Parents can't dictate to their children how they should run their lives.* **3** [T] to control or influence sth: *The kind of house people live in is usually dictated by how much they earn.*

dictation /dɪkˈteɪʃn/ ***noun*** [C,U] (EDUCATION) spoken words that sb else must write or type: *We had a dictation in English today* (= a test in which we had to write down what the teacher said).

dictator /dɪkˈteɪtə(r)/ ***noun*** [C] (POLITICS) a ruler who has total power in a country, especially one who rules the country by force ▶ **dictatorship** ***noun*** [C,U]: *a military dictatorship*

dictatorial /ˌdɪktəˈtɔːriəl/ ***adj.*** **1** (POLITICS) connected with or controlled by a ruler who has total power, especially a DICTATOR: *a dictatorial regime* **2** using power in an unreasonable way by telling people what to do and not listening to their views or wishes

dictionary /ˈdɪkʃənri/ ***noun*** [C] (*pl.* **dictionaries**) **1** a book that contains a list of the words in a language in the order of the alphabet and that tells you what they mean, in the same or another language: *to look up a word in a dictionary* ◇ *a bilingual/monolingual dictionary* **2** a book that lists the words connected with a particular subject and tells you what they mean: *a dictionary of idioms* ◇ *a medical dictionary*

did past tense of **do**

didactic /daɪˈdæktɪk/ ***adj.*** (*formal*) **1** (EDUCATION) designed to teach people sth, especially a moral lesson: *didactic art/ poetry* **2** telling people things rather than letting them find out for themselves: *Her way of teaching literature is too didactic.* ▶ **didactically** /-kli/ ***adv.***

didn't short for DID NOT

die¹ /daɪ/ ***verb*** (*pres. part.* **dying**; *3rd person sing. pres.* **dies**; *pt, pp* **died**) **1** [I,T] **~ (from/of sth)** to stop living: *My father died when I was three.* ◇ *Thousands of people have died from this disease.* ◇ *to **die of hunger*** ◇ *to **die for** what you believe in* ◇ *to **die a natural/violent death*** ➲ adjective **dead**, noun **death** **2** [I] to stop existing; to disappear: *The old customs are dying.* ◇ *Our love will never die.*

IDM **be dying for sth/to do sth** (*spoken*) to want sth/to do sth very much: *I'm dying for a cup of coffee.*

die hard to change or disappear only slowly or with difficulty: *Old attitudes towards women die hard.*

to die for (*informal*) if you think that sth is to die for, you really want it and would do anything to get it: *They have a house in town that's to die for.*

die laughing to find sth very funny: *I thought I'd die laughing when he told that joke.*

PHR V **die away** to slowly become weaker before stopping or disappearing: *The sound of the engine died away as the car drove into the distance.*

die down to slowly become less strong: *Let's wait until the storm dies down before we go out.*

die off to die one by one until there are none left

die out to stop happening or disappear: *The use of horses on farms has almost died out in this country.*

die² /daɪ/ ***noun*** [C] **1** (ART) a block of metal with a special shape, or with a pattern cut into it, that is used for shaping other pieces of metal such as coins, or for making patterns on paper or leather **2** (*especially AmE*) = DICE

diesel /ˈdiːzl/ ***noun*** **1** [U] a type of heavy oil used in some engines instead of petrol: *a diesel engine* ◇ *a taxi that runs on diesel* ➲ picture at **fractional distillation** **2** [C] a vehicle that uses **diesel**: *My new car's a diesel.* ➲ look at **petrol**

diet¹ /ˈdaɪət/ ***noun*** **1** [C,U] (BIOLOGY) the food that a person or animal usually eats: *They **live on a diet of** rice and vegetables.* ◇ *I always try to have **a healthy, balanced diet*** (= including all the different types of food that our body needs). ◇ *Poor diet is a cause of ill health.* **2** [C] (HEALTH) certain foods that a person who is ill, or who wants to lose weight is allowed to eat: *a low-fat diet* ◇ *a sugar-free diet* ▶ **dietary** /ˈdaɪətəri/ ***adj.***: *dietary habits/requirements*

IDM **be/go on a diet** to eat only certain foods or a small amount of food because you want to lose weight

diet² /ˈdaɪət/ ***verb*** [I] to try to lose weight by eating less food or only certain kinds of food

dietetics /ˌdaɪə'tetɪks/ ***noun*** [U] (SCIENCE) the scientific study of the food we eat and its effect on our health

dietitian (also **dietician**) /ˌdaɪə'tɪʃn/ ***noun*** [C] a person whose job is to advise people on what kind of food they should eat to keep healthy

differ /'dɪfə(r)/ ***verb*** [I] **1** ~ **(from sb/sth)** to be different: *How does this car differ from the more expensive model?* **2** ~ **(with sb) (about/on sth)** to have a different opinion: *I'm afraid I differ with you on that question.*

difference 🔑 /'dɪfrəns/ ***noun*** **1** [C] a ~ **(between A and B)** the way that people or things are not the same or the way that sb/sth has changed: *What's the difference between this computer and that cheaper one?* ◇ *From a distance it's hard to* ***tell the difference*** *between the twins.* **2** [C,U] ~ **(in sth)** **(between A and B)** the amount by which people or things are not the same or by which sb/sth has changed: *There's* ***an age difference*** *of three years between the two children.* ◇ *There's very little difference in price since last year.* ◇ *We gave a 30% deposit and must* ***pay the difference*** *when the work is finished* (=the rest of the money). **3** [C] a disagreement that is not very serious: *All couples* ***have*** *their* ***differences*** *from time to time.* ◇ *There was* ***a difference of opinion*** *over how much we owed.*
IDM **make a, some, etc. difference (to sb/sth)** to have an effect (on sb/sth): *Marriage made a big difference to her life.*
make no difference (to sb/sth); not make any difference to not be important (to sb/sth); to have no effect
split the difference → SPLIT[1]

different 🔑 /'dɪfrənt/ ***adj.*** **1** ~ **(from/to sb/sth)** not the same: *The play was different from anything I had seen before.* ◇ *The two houses are very different in style.* ◇ *You'd look completely different with short hair.* ◇ *When Ulf started school in this country, the other kids were cruel to him because he was different.* ❶ In American English **different than** is also used. OPP **similar** **2** separate; individual: *This coat is available in three different colours.*
▶ **differently** ***adv.***: *I think you'll feel differently about it tomorrow.*

differential[1] /ˌdɪfə'renʃl/ ***noun*** [C] **1** a ~ **(between A and B)** a difference in the amount, value or size of sth, especially the difference in rates of pay for people doing different work in the same industry or profession **2** (*also* **ˌdifferential 'gear**) a GEAR that makes it possible for a vehicle's back wheels to turn around at different speeds when going around corners

differential[2] /ˌdɪfə'renʃl/ ***adj.*** (only *before* a noun) (*formal*) showing or depending on a difference; not equal

differentiate AW /ˌdɪfə'renʃieɪt/ ***verb*** **1** [I,T] ~ **between A and B**; ~ **A (from B)** to see or show how things are different: *It is hard to differentiate between these two types of seed.* **2** [T] ~ **sth (from sth)** to make one thing different from another: *The coloured feathers differentiate the male bird from the plain brown female.* SYN **distinguish** **3** [I] to treat one person or group differently from another: *We don't differentiate between the two groups – we treat everybody alike.* SYN **discriminate**
▶ **differentiation** /ˌdɪfəˌrenʃi'eɪʃn/ ***noun*** [U]

difficult 🔑 /'dɪfɪkəlt/ ***adj.*** **1** ~ **(for sb) (to do sth)** not easy to do or understand: *a difficult test/problem* ◇ *I* ***find it difficult to*** *get up early in the morning.* ◇ *It was difficult for us to hear the speaker.* ◇ *I'm in a difficult situation. Whatever I do, somebody will be upset.* **2** (used about a person) not friendly, reasonable or helpful: *a difficult customer*

THESAURUS

difficult

hard • challenging • demanding • taxing

These words all describe something that is not easy and requires a lot of effort or skill to do.
difficult: *a difficult exam*
hard: *hard work*
challenging: *a challenging task*
demanding: *a demanding job*
taxing: *a physically taxing role*

difficulty 🔑 /'dɪfɪkəlti/ ***noun*** (*pl.* **difficulties**) **1** [U, C] ~ **(in sth/in doing sth)** a problem; a situation that is hard to deal with: *I'm sure you won't* ***have*** *any* ***difficulty*** *getting a visa for America.* ◇ *We* ***had no difficulty*** *selling our car.* ◇ *We found a hotel* ***without difficulty.*** ◇ ***With difficulty,*** *I managed to persuade Alice to lend us the money.* ◇ *I could see someone* ***in difficulty*** *in the water so I went to help them.* ◇ *If you borrow too much money you may* ***get into*** *financial* ***difficulties.*** **2** [U] how hard sth is to do or to deal with: *The questions start easy and then increase in difficulty.*

diffident /'dɪfɪdənt/ ***adj.*** not having confidence in your own strengths or abilities ▶ **diffidence** ***noun*** [U]

diffraction

◆ wavelength
← path of wave

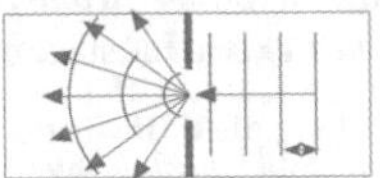

narrow opening similar in size to wavelength = greater diffraction

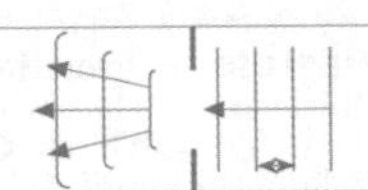

wide opening much larger than wavelength = less diffraction

diffract /dɪ'frækt/ ***verb*** [T] (PHYSICS) to break up a stream of light or a system of waves by passing them through a narrow opening or across an edge, causing INTERFERENCE (=patterns which form between the waves produced) ▶ **diffraction** /dɪ'frækʃn/ ***noun*** [U]

diffuse[1] /dɪ'fjuːz/ ***verb*** **1** [I,T] (*formal*) to spread sth or become spread widely in all directions **2** [I,T] (CHEMISTRY, PHYSICS) if a gas or liquid **diffuses** or is **diffused** in a substance, it becomes slowly mixed with that substance **3** [T] (*formal*) to make light shine less brightly by spreading it in many directions ▶ **diffusion** /dɪ'fjuːʒn/ ***noun*** [C]

diffusion

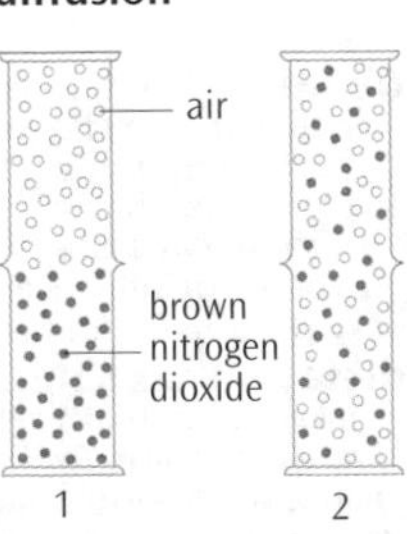

diffuse[2] /dɪ'fjuːs/ ***adj.*** spread over a wide area

dig[1] 🔑 /dɪɡ/ ***verb*** [I,T] (*pres. part.* **digging**; *pt, pp* **dug** /dʌɡ/) to move earth and make a hole in the ground: *The children are busy digging in the sand.* ◇ *to dig a hole*

IDM dig deep to try harder, give more, go further, etc. than is usually necessary: *Charities for the homeless are asking people to dig deep into their pockets in this cold weather.*
dig your heels in to refuse to do sth or to change your mind about sth
PHR V dig (sth) in; dig sth into sth to push or press (sth) into sb/sth: *My neck is all red where my collar is digging in.* ◇ *He dug his hands deep into his pockets.*
dig sb/sth out (of sth) 1 to get sb/sth out of sth by moving the earth, etc. that covers them or it: *Rescue workers dug the survivors out of the rubble.* **2** to get or find sb/sth by searching: *Bill went into the attic and dug out some old photos.*
dig sth up 1 to remove sth from the earth by digging: *to dig up potatoes* **2** to make a hole or take away soil by digging: *Workmen are digging up the road in front of our house.* **3** to find information by searching or studying: *Newspapers have dug up some embarrassing facts about his private life.*

dig[2] /dɪg/ ***noun*** [C] **1** a hard push: *to give sb **a dig in the ribs*** (=with your elbow) **2** something that you say to upset sb: *The others kept **making digs** at him because of the way he spoke.* **3** an occasion or place where a group of people try to find things of historical or scientific interest in the ground in order to study them: ***an archaeological dig***

digerati /ˌdɪdʒəˈrɑːti/ ***noun*** [pl.] (COMPUTING) people who are very good at using computers or who use computers a lot

digest /daɪˈdʒest/ ***verb*** [T] **1** (BIOLOGY) to change food in your stomach so that it can be used by the body **2** to think about new information so that you understand it fully: *The lecture was interesting, but too much to digest all at once.*

digestible /daɪˈdʒestəbl/ ***adj.*** (used about food) easy for your body to DIGEST

digestion /daɪˈdʒestʃən/ ***noun*** [U] (BIOLOGY) the process of changing food in your stomach so that it can be used by the body ▸ **digestive** /daɪˈdʒestɪv/ ***adj.***: *digestive problems*

diˈgestive system ***noun*** [C] (ANATOMY) the series of organs inside the body that DIGEST food

digger /ˈdɪgə(r)/ ***noun*** [C] **1** a large machine that is used for digging up the ground **2** a person or an animal that digs

digit /ˈdɪdʒɪt/ ***noun*** [C] **1** (MATHEMATICS) any of the numbers from 0 to 9: *a six-digit telephone number* **2** (ANATOMY) a finger, thumb or toe

digital /ˈdɪdʒɪtl/ ***adj.*** **1** (COMPUTING) using an

digestive system

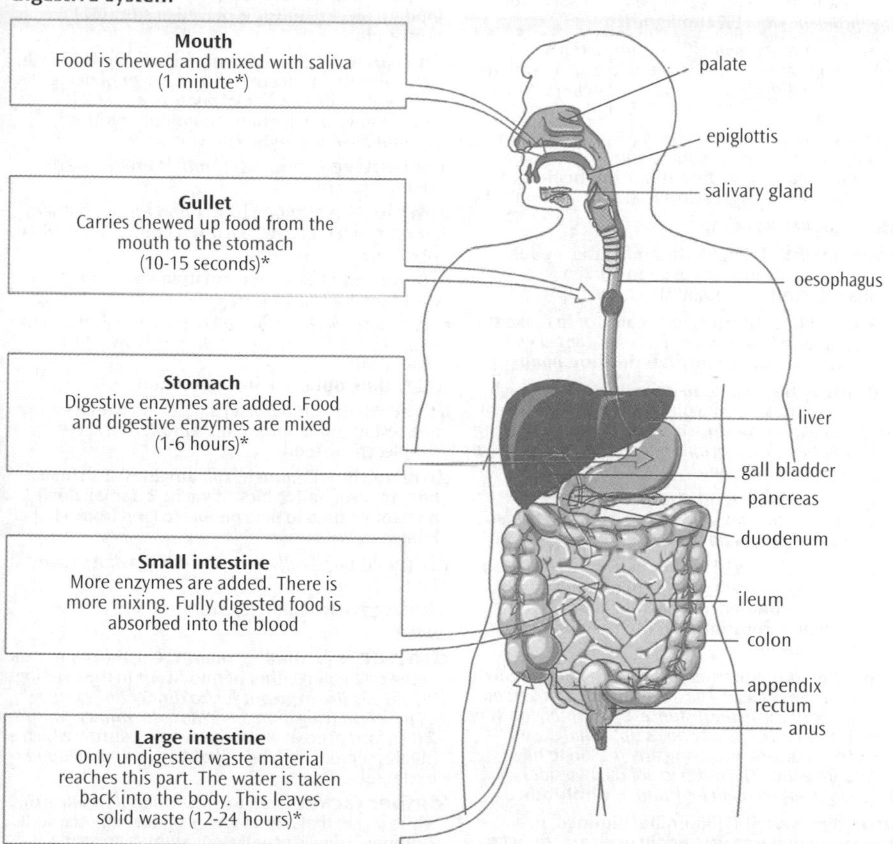

* = length of time food stays in this part of the digestive system

electronic system that uses the numbers 1 and 0 to record sound or store information, and that gives high-quality results: *a digital recording* ◇ *a digital camera* **2** showing information by using numbers: *a digital watch* ➲ look at **analogue** ▶ **digital** *noun* [U]: *How long have you had digital* (=digital television)? ▶ **digitally** /-təli/ *adv.*: *The photo has been digitally enhanced.*

digitalize (also **-ise**) /ˈdɪdʒɪtəlaɪz/ *verb* [T] =DIGITIZE

ˌ**digital ˈsignature** *noun* [C] (COMPUTING) a way of secretly adding sb's name to an electronic message or document to prove the identity of the person who is sending it and show that the data has not been changed at all

ˌ**digital ˈtelevision** *noun* **1** [U] (ARTS AND MEDIA) the system of broadcasting television using DIGITAL signals **2** [C] a television set that can receive DIGITAL signals

digitize (also **-ise**) /ˈdɪdʒɪtaɪz/ (also **digitalize**) *verb* [T] (COMPUTING) to change data into a DIGITAL form that can be easily read and processed by a computer: *a digitized map*

dignified /ˈdɪɡnɪfaɪd/ *adj.* behaving in a calm, serious way that makes other people respect you: *dignified behaviour* OPP **undignified**

dignity /ˈdɪɡnəti/ *noun* [U] **1** calm, serious behaviour that makes other people respect you: *to behave **with dignity*** **2** the quality of being serious and formal: *the quiet dignity of the funeral service*

digress /daɪˈɡres/ *verb* [I] (*formal*) to stop talking or writing about the main subject under discussion and start talking or writing about another less important one ▶ **digression** /daɪˈɡreʃn/ *noun* [C,U]

dike (GEOGRAPHY) → DYKE

dilapidated /dɪˈlæpɪdeɪtɪd/ *adj.* (used about buildings, furniture, etc.) old and broken ▶ **dilapidation** /dɪˌlæpɪˈdeɪʃn/ *noun* [U]

dilate /daɪˈleɪt/ *verb* [I,T] to become or to make sth larger, wider or more open: *Her eyes dilated with fear.* ◇ ***dilated pupils/nostrils*** ▶ **dilation** *noun* [U]

dilemma /dɪˈlemə/ *noun* [C] a situation in which you have to make a difficult choice between two or more things: *Doctors **face a moral dilemma** of when to keep patients alive artificially and when to let them die.* ◇ *to be **in a dilemma***

diligent /ˈdɪlɪdʒənt/ *adj.* (*formal*) showing care and effort in your work or duties: *a diligent student/worker* ▶ **diligently** *adv.*

dilute /daɪˈluːt/ *verb* [T] ~ **sth (with sth)** to make a liquid weaker by adding water or another liquid ▶ **dilute** (*also* **diluted**) (CHEMISTRY) *adj.*: *dilute acid/solution* ▶ **dilution** /daɪˈluːʃn/ *noun* [U]: *the dilution of sewage*

dim¹ /dɪm/ *adj.* (**dimmer**; **dimmest**) **1** not bright or easy to see; not clear: *The light was too dim to read by.* ◇ *a dim shape in the distance* **2** (*informal*) not very clever; stupid: *He's a bit dim.* **3** (*informal*) (used about a situation) not giving any reason to have hope; not good: *The prospects of the two sides reaching an agreement look dim.* ▶ **dimly** *adv.*

dim² /dɪm/ *verb* [I,T] (**dimming**; **dimmed**) to become or make sth less bright or clear: *The lights dimmed.* ◇ *to dim the lights*

dime /daɪm/ *noun* [C] a coin used in the US and Canada that is worth ten cents

dimensions

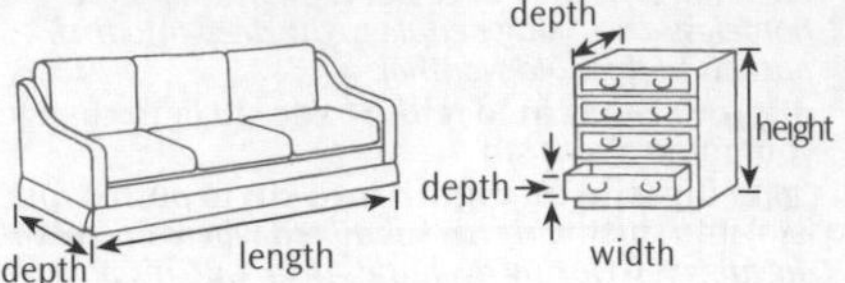

dimension AW /daɪˈmenʃn/ *noun* **1** [C,U] (MATHEMATICS) a measurement of the length, width or height of sth **2 dimensions** [pl.] the size of sth including its length, width and height: *to measure the dimensions of a room* ◇ (*figurative*) *The full dimensions of this problem are only now being recognized.* **3** [C] something that affects the way you think about a problem or situation: *to add a new dimension to a problem/situation* **4 -dimensional** /-ʃnəl/ (used to form compound adjectives) having the number of **dimensions** mentioned: *a three-dimensional object*

diminish AW /dɪˈmɪnɪʃ/ *verb* [I,T] (*formal*) to become or to make sth smaller or less important; decrease: *The world's rainforests are diminishing fast.* ◇ *The bad news did nothing to diminish her enthusiasm for the plan.* ➲ note at **fall¹**

diminuendo /dɪˌmɪnjuˈendəʊ/ *noun* [C,U] (*pl.* **diminuendos**) (MUSIC) a gradual decrease in how loudly a piece of music is played or sung OPP **crescendo**

diminution AW /ˌdɪmɪˈnjuːʃn/ *noun* ~ **(of/in sth)** (*formal*) **1** [U] the act of reducing sth or of being reduced: *the diminution of political power* **2** [C, usually sing.] a reduction; an amount reduced: *a diminution in population growth*

diminutive /dɪˈmɪnjətɪv/ *adj.* (*formal*) much smaller than usual

dimple /ˈdɪmpl/ *noun* [C] a round area in the skin on your cheek, etc., which often only appears when you smile

din /dɪn/ *noun* [sing.] a lot of unpleasant noise that continues for some time

dine /daɪn/ *verb* [I] (*formal*) to eat a meal, especially in the evening: *We dined at an exclusive French restaurant.*

PHR V **dine out** to eat in a restaurant

diner /ˈdaɪnə(r)/ *noun* [C] **1** a person who is eating at a restaurant **2** (*AmE*) a restaurant that serves simple, cheap food

dinghy /ˈdɪŋɡi/ *noun* [C] (*pl.* **dinghies**) **1** a small boat that you sail ➲ look at **yacht** **2** a small open boat, often used to take people to land from a larger boat

dingy /ˈdɪndʒi/ *adj.* dirty and dark: *a dingy room/hotel*

ˈ**dining room** *noun* [C] a room where you eat meals

dinner 🔑 /ˈdɪnə(r)/ *noun* **1** [C,U] the main meal of the day, eaten either at midday or in the evening: *Would you like to **go out for/to dinner** one evening?* ◇ *I never eat a big dinner.* ◇ *What's for dinner, Mum?* **2** [C] a formal occasion in the evening during which a meal is served: *The club is holding its annual dinner next week.*

ˈ**dinner jacket** (*AmE* **tuxedo**) *noun* [C] a black or white jacket that a man wears on formal occasions. A dinner jacket is usually worn with a BOW TIE.

dinosaur /ˈdaɪnəsɔː(r)/ *noun* [C] one of a number of very large animals that disappeared from the earth (**became extinct**) millions of years ago

diocese /ˈdaɪəsɪs/ ***noun*** [C] (RELIGION) an area containing a number of churches, for which a BISHOP is responsible

diode /ˈdaɪəʊd/ ***noun*** [C] (PHYSICS) an electronic device in which the electric current flows in one direction only

dioptre (*AmE* **diopter**) /daɪˈɒptə(r)/ ***noun*** [C] (PHYSICS) a unit for measuring the power of a LENS to REFRACT light (=make it change direction)

dioxide /daɪˈɒksaɪd/ ***noun*** [C,U] (CHEMISTRY) a COMPOUND formed by combining two atoms of OXYGEN and one atom of another chemical element: *carbon dioxide*

Dip. ***abbr.*** (EDUCATION) DIPLOMA

dip[1] /dɪp/ ***verb*** (**dipping**; **dipped**) **1** [T] **~ sth (into sth)**; **~ sth (in)** to put sth into liquid and immediately take it out again: *Julie dipped her toe into the pool to see how cold it was.* **2** [I,T] to go down or make sth go down to a lower level: *The road suddenly dipped down to the river.* ◇ *The company's sales have dipped disastrously this year.*

PHRV **dip into sth 1** to use part of an amount of sth that you have: *Tim had to dip into his savings to pay for his new suit.* **2** to read parts, but not all, of sth: *I've only dipped into the book. I haven't read it all the way through.*

dip[2] /dɪp/ ***noun*** **1** [C] a fall to a lower level, especially for a short time: *a dip in sales/temperature* **2** [C] an area of lower ground: *The cottage was in a dip in the hills.* **3** [C] (*informal*) a short swim: *We went for a dip before breakfast.* **4** [C,U] a thick sauce into which you DIP biscuits, vegetables, etc. before eating them: *a cheese/chilli dip*

diphtheria /dɪfˈθɪəriə/ ***noun*** [U] (HEALTH) a serious infectious disease of the throat that makes it difficult to breathe

diphthong /ˈdɪfθɒŋ/ ***noun*** [C] (LANGUAGE) two VOWEL sounds that are pronounced together to make one sound, for example the /aɪ/ sound in *'fine'*

diploid /ˈdɪplɔɪd/ ***adj.*** (BIOLOGY) (used about a cell) containing two complete sets of CHROMOSOMES (=the parts of the cell that decide the sex, character, shape, etc. that a living thing will have), one from each parent ➲ look at **haploid**

diploma /dɪˈpləʊmə/ ***noun*** [C] **a ~ (in sth)** (EDUCATION) a certificate that you receive when you complete a course of study, often at a college: *I'm studying for a diploma in hotel management.*

diplomacy /dɪˈpləʊməsi/ ***noun*** [U] **1** (POLITICS) the activity of managing relations between different countries: *If diplomacy fails, there is a danger of war.* **2** skill in dealing with people without upsetting or offending them: *He handled the tricky situation with tact and diplomacy.*

diplomat /ˈdɪpləmæt/ ***noun*** [C] (POLITICS) an official who represents his or her country in a foreign country: *a diplomat at the embassy in Rome*

diplomatic /ˌdɪpləˈmætɪk/ ***adj.*** **1** (POLITICS) connected with DIPLOMACY (1): *to break off diplomatic relations* **2** skilful at dealing with people: *He searched for a diplomatic reply so as not to offend her.* ▸ **diplomatically** /-kli/ ***adv.***

diptych /ˈdɪptɪk/ ***noun*** [C] (ART) a painting, especially a religious one, with two wooden panels that can be closed like a book

dire /ˈdaɪə(r)/ ***adj.*** (*formal*) very bad or serious; terrible: *dire consequences/poverty*

IDM **be in dire straits** to be in a very difficult situation: *The business is in dire straits financially.*

direct[1] ⊶ /dəˈrekt; dɪ-; daɪ-/ ***adj.***, ***adv.*** **1** with nobody/nothing in between; not involving anyone/anything else: *The British Prime Minister is* ***in direct contact with*** *the US President.* ◇ *a direct attack on the capital* ◇ *As a* ***direct result*** *of the new road, traffic jams in the centre have been reduced.* ◇ *You should protect your skin from* ***direct sunlight***. **2** going from one place to another without turning or stopping; straight: *a* ***direct flight*** *to Hong Kong* ◇ *This bus goes direct to London.* **3** saying what you mean; clear: *Politicians never give a* ***direct answer*** *to a* ***direct question***. ◇ *She sometimes offends people with her direct way of speaking.* OPP **indirect 4** (only *before* a noun) complete; exact: *What she did was in direct opposition to my orders.*

direct[2] ⊶ /dəˈrekt; dɪ-; daɪ-/ ***verb*** [T] **1 ~ sth to/towards sb/sth**; **~ sth at sb/sth** to point or send sth towards sb/sth or in a particular direction: *In recent weeks the media's attention has been directed towards events abroad.* ◇ *The advert is directed at young people.* ◇ *The actor directed some angry words at a photographer.* **2** to manage or control sb/sth: *A policeman was in the middle of the road,* ***directing the traffic***. ◇ ***to direct a play/film*** **3 ~ sb (to…)** to tell or show sb how to get somewhere: *I was directed to an office at the end of the corridor.* **4** (*formal*) to tell or order sb to do sth: *Take the tablets as directed by your doctor.*

diˌrect ˈaction ***noun*** [U, C] (POLITICS) the use of strikes, protests, etc. instead of discussion in order to get what you want

diˌrect ˈcost ***noun*** [C, usually pl.] (BUSINESS) the cost of basic materials and workers involved in making a particular product or providing a particular service: *The project manager's salary is a direct cost.* OPP **indirect cost**

diˌrect ˈcurrent ***noun*** [C,U] (*abbr.* **DC**) (PHYSICS) a flow of electricity that goes in one direction only ➲ look at **alternating current**

diˌrect ˈdebit ***noun*** [C,U] (FINANCE) an order to your bank that allows sb else to take a particular amount of money out of your account on certain dates

diˌrect ˈdialling (*BrE*) (*AmE* **diˌrect ˈdialing**) ***noun*** [U] the ability to make telephone calls without needing to be connected by the OPERATOR (=the person whose job is to connect telephone calls, for the public or in a particular building): *All our rooms have direct dialling telephones.*

direction ⊶ /dəˈrekʃn; dɪ-; daɪ-/ ***noun*** **1** [C,U] the path, line or way along which a person or thing is moving, looking, pointing, developing, etc.: *A woman was seen running* ***in the direction of*** *the station.* ◇ *We met him coming* ***in the opposite direction***. ◇ *I think the new speed limit is still too high, but at least it's* ***a step in the right direction***. ◇ *I think the wind has* ***changed direction***. ◇ *I've got such a hopeless* ***sense of direction*** *– I'm always getting lost.* ➲ note on next page **2** [C,U] a purpose; an aim: *I want a career that gives me a (sense of) direction in life.* **3** [C, usually pl.] information or instructions about how to do sth or how to get to a place: *I'll* ***give you directions*** *to my house.* **4** [U] the act of managing or controlling sth: *This department is* ***under the direction of*** *Mrs Walters.*

directive /dəˈrektɪv; dɪ-; daɪ-/ ***noun*** [C] an official order to do sth: *an EU directive on safety at work*

directly[1] ⊶ /dəˈrektli; dɪ-; daɪ-/ ***adv.*** **1** in a direct line or way: *The bank is directly opposite the supermarket.* ◇ *He refused to answer my question* *directly.* ◇ *Lung cancer is directly related to smoking.* OPP **indirectly 2** immediately; very soon: *Wait where you are. I'll be back directly.*

COLLOCATIONS AND PATTERNS

Asking for and giving directions

You can ask sb **the way.**
Can you tell me the way to the town centre?
Which way is the station?

A place can be **near, not far** or **a long way from** another place.
The station is near the centre of town.
The bus stop isn't far from the theatre.
Our hotel was a long way from the sea.

A place can be **nearby** or **a long way away.**
You can **turn right/left** or **go straight on.**
Turn right at the crossroads.
Go straight on along the high street.

You can **take** the **first/second**, etc. **road/turning/exit**, etc.
Take the second exit at the roundabout.
Take the next left.
Take the third turning on the right.

A place can be **on the right/left.**
You'll see the cinema on the left.

directly² /də'rektli; dɪ-; daɪ-/ ***conj.*** as soon as: *I phoned him directly I heard the news.*

diˌrect 'mail ***noun*** [U] (BUSINESS) advertisements that are sent to people through the post

diˌrect 'marketing ***noun*** [U] (BUSINESS) the business of selling products or services directly to customers who order by mail or by telephone instead of going to a shop

diˌrect 'object ***noun*** [C] (LANGUAGE) a noun or phrase that is affected by the action of a verb: *In the sentence 'Anna bought a record', 'a record' is the direct object.* ➲ look at **indirect object**

director 🔑 /də'rektə(r); dɪ-; daɪ-/ ***noun*** [C] **1** (BUSINESS) a person who manages or controls a company or organization: *the **managing director** of Rolls Royce* ◇ *She's on the **board of directors*** (=group of directors) *of a large computer company.* **2** a person who is responsible for a particular activity or department in a company, a college, etc.: *the director of studies of a language school* **3** (ARTS AND MEDIA) a person who tells the actors, etc. what to do in a film, play, etc.: ***a film/theatre director***

directory /də'rektəri; dɪ-; daɪ-/ ***noun*** [C] (*pl.* **directories**) **1** a list of names, addresses and telephone numbers in the order of the alphabet: *the **telephone directory*** ◇ *I tried to look up Joe's number but he's **ex-directory*** (=he has chosen not to be listed in the telephone directory). **2** (COMPUTING) a file containing a group of other files or programs in a computer

diˌrect 'speech ***noun*** [U] (LANGUAGE) the actual words that a person said ➲ look at **indirect speech**

dirt 🔑 /dɜːt/ ***noun*** [U] **1** a substance that is not clean, such as dust or mud: *His face and hands were covered in dirt.* **2** earth or soil: *a dirt track* **3** damaging information about sb: *The press are always trying to **dig up dirt** on the President's love life.*

IDM **dirt cheap** extremely cheap

dirty¹ 🔑 /'dɜːti/ ***adj.*** (**dirtier**; **dirtiest**) **1** not clean: *Your hands are dirty. Go and wash them!* ◇ *Gardening is dirty work* (=it makes you dirty). OPP **clean 2** referring to sex in a way that may upset or offend people: *to tell a dirty joke* **3** unpleasant or dishonest: *He's a dirty player.* ◇ *He doesn't sell the drugs himself – he gets kids to **do** his **dirty work** for him.*

IDM **a dirty word** an idea or thing that you do not like or agree with: *Work is a dirty word to Frank.*

dirty² /'dɜːti/ ***verb*** [I,T] (*pres. part.* **dirtying**; *3rd person sing. pres.* **dirties**; *pt, pp* **dirtied**) to become or to make sth dirty OPP **clean**

dirty³ /'dɜːti/ ***adv.***

IDM **dirty great/big** (*BrE, informal*) used to emphasize how large sth is: *When I turned around he was pointing a dirty great gun at me.*

play dirty (*informal*) to behave or play a game in an unfair way

dis- /dɪs/ ***prefix*** (in adjectives, adverbs, nouns and verbs) not; the opposite of: *discontinue* ◇ *disarmament*

disability /ˌdɪsə'bɪləti/ ***noun*** (*pl.* **disabilities**) **1** [U] the state of being unable to use a part of your body properly, usually because of injury or disease: *physical/mental disability* **2** [C] something that makes you unable to use a part of your body properly: *Because of his disability, he needs constant care.* ◇ *people with learning disabilities*

disable /dɪs'eɪbl/ ***verb*** [T] (often passive) to make sb unable to use part of their body properly, usually because of injury or disease: *Many soldiers were disabled in the war.*

disabled 🔑 /dɪs'eɪbld/ ***adj.*** **1** unable to use a part of your body properly: *A car accident left her permanently disabled.* **2 the disabled *noun*** [pl.] people who are disabled: *The hotel has improved facilities for the disabled.*

disadvantage 🔑 /ˌdɪsəd'vɑːntɪdʒ/ ***noun*** [C] **1** something that may make you less successful than other people: *Your qualifications are good. Your main disadvantage is your lack of experience.* **2** something that is not good or that causes problems: *The main disadvantage of the job is the long hours.* ◇ *What are the advantages and disadvantages of nuclear power?* OPP **advantage**

IDM **put sb/be at a disadvantage** to put sb/be in a situation where they or you may be less successful than other people: *The fact that you don't speak the language will put you at a disadvantage in France.*

to sb's disadvantage (*formal*) not good or helpful for sb: *The agreement will be to your disadvantage – don't accept it.*

disadvantaged /ˌdɪsəd'vɑːntɪdʒd/ ***adj.*** in a bad social or economic situation; poor: *extra help for the most disadvantaged members of society*

disadvantageous /ˌdɪsædvæn'teɪdʒəs/ ***adj.*** causing sb to be in a worse situation compared to other people

disagree 🔑 /ˌdɪsə'griː/ ***verb*** [I] **1** ~ **(with sb/sth) (about/on sth)** to have a different opinion from sb/sth; to not agree: *Noel often disagrees with his father about politics.* ◇ *They strongly disagreed with my idea.* ◇ *'We have to tell him.' 'No, I disagree. I don't think we should tell him at all.'* **2** to be different: *These two sets of statistics disagree.* OPP **agree**

PHR V **disagree with sb** (used about sth you have eaten or drunk) to make you feel ill; to have a bad effect on you

disagreeable /ˌdɪsə'griːəbl/ ***adj.*** (*formal*) unpleasant OPP **agreeable** ▸ **disagreeably** /-əbli/ ***adv.***

disagreement ⊶ /ˌdɪsəˈɡriːmənt/ ***noun*** [C,U] **~ (with sb) (about/on/over sth)** a situation in which people have a different opinion about sth and often also argue: *It's normal for couples to* ***have disagreements****.* ◇ *Mandy resigned after a disagreement with her boss.* ◇ *The conference ended in disagreement.* OPP **agreement**

disallow /ˌdɪsəˈlaʊ/ ***verb*** [I] to not allow or accept sth: *The goal was disallowed because the player was offside.*

disappear ⊶ /ˌdɪsəˈpɪə(r)/ ***verb*** [I] **1** to become impossible to see or to find: *He walked away and disappeared into a crowd of people.* ◇ *My purse was here a moment ago and now it's disappeared.* **2** to stop existing: *Plant and animal species are disappearing at an alarming rate.* SYN **vanish** OPP **appear** ▸ **disappearance** ***noun*** [C,U]: *The mystery of her disappearance was never solved.*

disappoint ⊶ /ˌdɪsəˈpɔɪnt/ ***verb*** [T] to make sb sad because what they had hoped for has not happened or is less good, interesting, etc. then they had hoped: *I'm sorry to disappoint you but I'm afraid you haven't won the prize.*

disappointed ⊶ /ˌdɪsəˈpɔɪntɪd/ ***adj.*** **~ (about/at sth); ~ (in/with sb/sth); ~ that...** sad because you/sb/sth did not succeed or because sth was not as good, interesting, etc. as you had hoped: *Lucy was deeply disappointed at not being chosen for the team.* ◇ *We were disappointed with our hotel.* ◇ *I'm disappointed in you. I thought you could do better.* ◇ *They are very disappointed that they can't stay longer.* ◇ *I was disappointed to hear that you can't come to the party.*

disappointing ⊶ /ˌdɪsəˈpɔɪntɪŋ/ ***adj.*** making you feel sad because sth was not as good, interesting, etc. as you had hoped: *It has been a disappointing year for the company.* ▸ **disappointingly** ***adv.***

disappointment ⊶ /ˌdɪsəˈpɔɪntmənt/ ***noun*** **1** [U] the state of being disappointed: ***To his*** *great* ***disappointment*** *he failed to get the job.* **2** [C] **a ~ (to sb)** a person or thing that disappoints you: *She has suffered many disappointments in her career.*

disapproval ⊶ /ˌdɪsəˈpruːvl/ ***noun*** [U] a feeling that sth is bad or that sb is behaving badly: *She shook her head* ***in disapproval****.*

disapprove ⊶ /ˌdɪsəˈpruːv/ ***verb*** [I] **~ (of sb/sth)** to think that sb/sth is not good or suitable; to not approve of sb/sth: *His parents* ***strongly disapproved*** *of him leaving college before he had finished his course.*

disapproving ⊶ /ˌdɪsəˈpruːvɪŋ/ ***adj.*** showing that you do not approve of sb/sth: *a* ***disapproving glance/tone/look*** ◇ *She sounded disapproving as we discussed my plans.* ▸ **disapprovingly** ***adv.***: *He looked disapprovingly at the row of empty wine bottles.*

disarm /dɪsˈɑːm/ ***verb*** **1** [T] to take weapons away from sb: *The police caught and disarmed the terrorists.* **2** [I] (used about a country) to reduce the number of weapons it has **3** [T] to make sb feel less angry: *Jenny could always disarm the teachers with a smile.*

disarmament /dɪsˈɑːməmənt/ ***noun*** [U] reducing the number of weapons that a country has: *nuclear disarmament*

disassociate = DISSOCIATE

disaster ⊶ /dɪˈzɑːstə(r)/ ***noun*** **1** [C] an event that causes a lot of harm or damage: *earthquakes, floods and other* ***natural disasters*** **2** [C,U] a terrible situation or event: *Losing your job is unpleasant, but it's not a disaster.* ◇ *This year's lack of rain could* ***spell disaster*** *for the region.* **3** [C,U] (*informal*) a complete failure: *The school play was an absolute disaster. Everything went wrong.*

COLLOCATIONS AND PATTERNS

Natural disasters

Disaster **strikes** in a number of forms, including **earthquakes, hurricanes, lightning** and **tsunamis/tidal waves.**
A massive earthquake struck on Monday.
As a result, a tsunami struck much of Indonesia.
The building was struck by lightning.

Forest fires rage and **volcanoes erupt** causing **devastation.**
Forest fires raged out of control for weeks, devastating parts of the country.
The volcano began erupting late last night.

After a tsunami or other disaster, areas may be **inundated with floods** or **flooding.**
Severe floods inundated dozens of villages.

Relief efforts (= money, food and other help from many organizations) begin in **the immediate aftermath of** (= the time straight after) a disaster.
A massive relief effort is under way to help victims of a tropical cyclone.
The president visited the village in the immediate aftermath of the hurricane.

disastrous /dɪˈzɑːstrəs/ ***adj.*** terrible, harmful or failing completely: *Our mistake had disastrous results.* ▸ **disastrously** ***adv.***: *The plan went disastrously wrong.*

disband /dɪsˈbænd/ ***verb*** [I,T] to stop existing as a group; to separate

disbelief /ˌdɪsbɪˈliːf/ ***noun*** [U] the feeling of not believing sb/sth: *'It can't be true!' he shouted* ***in disbelief****.*

disbelieve /ˌdɪsbɪˈliːv/ ***verb*** [T] to think that sth is not true or that sb is not telling the truth: *I have no reason to disbelieve her.* OPP **believe**

disc ⊶ (*especially AmE* **disk**) /dɪsk/ ***noun*** [C] **1** a round flat object **2** = DISK **3** (**ANATOMY**) one of the pieces of CARTILAGE (= thin strong material) between the bones in your back

discard /dɪsˈkɑːd/ ***verb*** [T] (*formal*) to throw sth away because it is not useful

discern /dɪˈsɜːn/ ***verb*** [T] to see or notice sth with difficulty: *I discerned a note of anger in his voice.* ▸ **discernible** ***adj.***: *The shape of a house was just discernible through the mist.*

discerning /dɪˈsɜːnɪŋ/ ***adj.*** able to recognize the quality of sb/sth: *The discerning music lover will appreciate the excellence of this recording.*

discharge[1] /dɪsˈtʃɑːdʒ/ ***verb*** **1** [T] to allow sb officially to leave; to send sb away: *to discharge sb from hospital* **2** (**LAW**) to allow sb to leave prison or court: *He was* ***conditionally discharged*** *after admitting the theft.* **3** [I,T] when a gas or a liquid **discharges** or **is discharged**, or sb **discharges** it, it flows somewhere: *The factory was fined for discharging chemicals into the river.* **4** [T] (*formal*) to do everything that is necessary to perform and complete a particular duty: *to discharge a duty/task*

discharge² /'dɪstʃɑːdʒ/ ***noun*** [C,U] **1** the action of sending sb/sth out or away: *The discharge of oil from the leaking tanker could not be prevented.* ◇ *The wounded soldier was given a medical discharge.* **2** a substance that has come out of somewhere: *yellowish discharge from a wound*

disciple /dɪ'saɪpl/ ***noun*** [C] (RELIGION) a person who follows a teacher, especially a religious one

disciplinary /ˌdɪsə'plɪnəri/ ***adj.*** connected with punishment for breaking rules

discipline¹ 🔑 /'dɪsəplɪn/ ***noun*** **1** [U] the practice of training people to obey rules and behave well: *A good teacher must be able to* ***maintain discipline*** *in the classroom.* **2** [U] the practice of training your mind and body so that you control your actions and obey rules; a way of doing this: *It takes a lot of* ***self-discipline*** *to study for three hours a day.* ◇ *Having to get up early every day is good discipline for a child.* **3** [C] (EDUCATION) a subject of study; a type of sporting event: *Barry's a good all-round athlete, but the long jump is his strongest discipline.*

discipline² /'dɪsəplɪn/ ***verb*** [T] **1** to train sb to obey and to behave in a controlled way: *You should discipline yourself to practise the piano every morning.* **2** to punish sb

'disc jockey = DJ

disclaim /dɪs'kleɪm/ ***verb*** [T] to say that you do not have sth: *to disclaim responsibility/knowledge* SYN **deny**

disclose /dɪs'kləʊz/ ***verb*** [T] *(formal)* to tell sth to sb or to make sth known publicly: *The newspapers did not disclose the victim's name.*

disclosure /dɪs'kləʊʒə(r)/ ***noun*** [C,U] making sth known; the facts that are made known: *the disclosure of secret information* ◇ *He resigned following disclosures about his private life.*

disco /'dɪskəʊ/ ***noun*** [C] (*pl.* **discos**) *(old-fashioned)* a place, party, etc. where people dance to pop music: *Are you going to the school disco?* ➲ look at **club¹** (2)

discolour (*AmE* **discolor**) /dɪs'kʌlə(r)/ ***verb*** [I,T] to change or to make sth change colour (often by the effect of light, age or dirt)

discomfort /dɪs'kʌmfət/ ***noun*** [U] **1** a slight feeling of pain: *There may be some discomfort after the operation.* OPP **comfort** **2** a feeling of embarrassment: *I could sense John's discomfort when I asked him about his job.*

disconcert /ˌdɪskən'sɜːt/ ***verb*** [T] (usually passive) to make sb feel confused or worried: *She was disconcerted when everyone stopped talking and looked at her.* ▶ **disconcerting** ***adj.*** ▶ **disconcertingly** ***adv.***

disconnect /ˌdɪskə'nekt/ ***verb*** [T] **1** to stop a supply of water, gas or electricity going to a piece of equipment or a building **2** to separate sth from sth: *The brake doesn't work because the cable has become disconnected from the lever.*

discontent /ˌdɪskən'tent/ (*also* **discontentment** /ˌdɪskən'tentmənt/) ***noun*** [U] the state of being unhappy with sth: *The management could sense growing discontent among the staff.* ▶ **discontented** ***adj.***: *to be/feel discontented*

discontinue /ˌdɪskən'tɪnjuː/ ***verb*** [T] *(formal)* to stop sth or stop producing sth

discord /'dɪskɔːd/ ***noun*** [U] *(formal)* disagreement or argument

discordant /dɪs'kɔːdənt/ ***adj.*** that spoils a general feeling of agreement: *Her criticism was the only discordant note in the discussion.*

discount¹ 🔑 /'dɪskaʊnt/ ***noun*** [C,U] a lower price than usual; reduction: *Staff get 20% discount on all goods.* ◇ *Do you give a discount for cash?*

discount² /dɪs'kaʊnt/ ***verb*** [T] to consider sth not true or not important: *I think we can discount that idea. It's just not practical.*

discourage /dɪs'kʌrɪdʒ/ ***verb*** [T] ~ **sb (from doing sth)** to stop sb doing sth, especially by making them realize that it would not be successful or a good idea: *I tried to discourage Jake from giving up his job.* ◇ *Don't let these little problems discourage you.* OPP **encourage** ▶ **discouraged** ***adj.***: *After failing the exam again Paul felt very discouraged.* ▶ **discouraging** ***adj.***: *Constant criticism can be very discouraging.*

discouragement /dɪs'kʌrɪdʒmənt/ ***noun*** [C,U] a thing that makes you not want to do sth; the action of trying to stop sb from doing sth

discourse /'dɪskɔːs/ ***noun*** [C,U] *(formal)* **1** a long and serious discussion of a subject in speech or writing **2** (LANGUAGE) the use of language in speech and writing in order to produce meaning; language that is studied, usually in order to see how the different parts of a text are connected: *discourse analysis*

discourteous /dɪs'kɜːtiəs/ ***adj.*** not polite or showing respect for people SYN **impolite** OPP **courteous**

discover 🔑 /dɪ'skʌvə(r)/ ***verb*** [T] **1** to find or learn sth that nobody had found or knew before: *Who discovered the lost city of Machu Picchu?* ◇ *Scientists are hoping to discover the cause of the epidemic.* **2** to find or learn sth without expecting to or that sb does not want you to find: *I think I've discovered why the computer won't print out.* ◇ *The police discovered drugs hidden under the floor.* ▶ **discoverer** ***noun*** [C]: *Parkinson's disease was named after its discoverer.*

discovery 🔑 /dɪ'skʌvəri/ ***noun*** (*pl.* **discoveries**) **1** [U] the act of finding sth: *The discovery of X-rays changed the history of medicine.* **2** [C] something that has been found: *scientific discoveries*

discredit /dɪs'kredɪt/ ***verb*** [T] to make people stop respecting or believing sb/sth: *Journalists are trying to discredit the President by inventing stories about his love life.* ▶ **discredit** ***noun*** [U]

discreet /dɪ'skriːt/ ***adj.*** careful in what you say and do so as not to cause embarrassment or difficulty for sb: *I don't want anyone to find out about our agreement, so please be discreet.* ▶ **discreetly** ***adv.*** ➲ noun **discretion** OPP **indiscreet**

> WORD FAMILY
> **discreet** *adj.* (≠ **indiscreet**)
> **discretion** *noun* (≠ **indiscretion**)

discrepancy /dɪs'krepənsi/ ***noun*** [C,U] (*pl.* **discrepancies**) a difference between two things that should be the same: *Something is wrong here. There is a discrepancy between these two sets of figures.*

discrete AW /dɪ'skriːt/ ***adj.*** *(formal)* independent of other things of the same type SYN **separate**: *The organisms can be divided into discrete categories.*

discretion AW /dɪ'skreʃn/ ***noun*** [U] **1** the freedom and power to make decisions by yourself: *You must decide what is best. Use your discretion.* **2** care in what you say and do so as not to cause embarrassment or difficulty for sb: *This is* *confidential but I know I can rely on your discretion.* ➲ note at **care**[1] ➲ adjective **discreet**

IDM **at sb's discretion** depending on what sb thinks or decides: *Pay increases are awarded at the discretion of the director.*

discretionary AW /dɪˈskreʃənəri/ *adj.* (*formal*) decided according to the judgement of a person in authority about what is necessary in each particular situation; not decided by rules: *You may be eligible for a discretionary grant for your university course.*

discriminate AW /dɪˈskrɪmɪneɪt/ *verb* **1** [I] ~ (**against sb**) (SOCIAL STUDIES) to treat one person or group worse than others: *It is illegal to discriminate against any ethnic or religious group.* **2** [I,T] ~ (**between A and B**) to see or make a difference between two people or things: *The immigration law discriminates between political and economic refugees.*

discriminating /dɪˈskrɪmɪneɪtɪŋ/ *adj.* able to judge that the quality of sth is good: *discriminating listeners*

discrimination AW /dɪˌskrɪmɪˈneɪʃn/ *noun* [U] **1** ~ (**against sb**) (SOCIAL STUDIES) treating one person or group worse than others: ***sexual/racial/religious discrimination*** ◇ *Discrimination against disabled people is illegal.* **2** (*formal*) the state of being able to see a difference between two people or things: *discrimination between right and wrong*

discriminatory /dɪˈskrɪmɪnətəri/ *adj.* (SOCIAL STUDIES) unfair; treating one person or a group of people worse than others: *discriminatory practices*

discursive /dɪsˈkɜːsɪv/ *adj.* (LANGUAGE) (used about a style of writing or speaking) moving from one point to another without any strict structure

discus /ˈdɪskəs/ *noun* (SPORT) **1** [C] a heavy round flat object that is thrown as a sport **2 the discus** [sing.] the sport or event of throwing a discus as far as possible

discuss 🔑 /dɪˈskʌs/ *verb* [T] ~ sth (with sb) to talk or write about sth seriously or formally: *I must discuss the matter with my parents before I make a decision.*

discussion 🔑 /dɪˈskʌʃn/ *noun* [C,U] the process of discussing sb/sth; a conversation about sb/sth: *After much discussion we all agreed to share the cost.* ◇ *We had a long discussion about art.*

IDM **under discussion** being talked about: *Plans to reform the Health Service are under discussion in Parliament.*

disdain /dɪsˈdeɪn/ *noun* [U] the feeling that sb/sth is not good enough to be respected: *Monica felt that her boss always **treated** her ideas **with disdain**.* ▶ **disdainful** /-fl/ *adj.* ▶ **disdainfully** /-fəli/ *adv.*

THESAURUS

disease

illness • disorder • infection • condition • ailment • bug

These are all words for a medical problem.

disease: *heart/liver/kidney disease*

illness: *a long/severe illness* ◇ *mental illness*

disorder (*formal*): *a personality disorder*

infection: *a throat infection*

condition: *a heart condition*

ailment: *childhood ailments*

bug (*informal*): *a nasty stomach bug*

disease 🔑 /dɪˈziːz/ *noun* [C,U] (HEALTH) an illness of the body in humans, animals or plants: *an infectious/contagious disease* ◇ *These children **suffer from** a rare **disease**.* ◇ *Rats and flies **spread disease**.* ◇ *Smoking causes heart disease.* ▶ **diseased** *adj.*: *His diseased kidney had to be removed.*

RELATED VOCABULARY

Illness and **disease** can be used in a similar way.

However, we use **disease** to describe a type of illness which has a name and is recognized by certain symptoms. Diseases may be caused by bacteria, viruses, etc., and you can often catch and pass them on to others.

Illness is used to describe the general state of being ill and the time during which you are not well.

disembark /ˌdɪsɪmˈbɑːk/ *verb* [I] (*formal*) to get off a ship or an aircraft OPP **embark** ▶ **disembarkation** /ˌdɪsˌembɑːˈkeɪʃn/ *noun* [U]

disembodied /ˌdɪsɪmˈbɒdid/ *adj.* coming from a person or place that cannot be seen or identified: *a disembodied voice*

disenchanted /ˌdɪsɪnˈtʃɑːntɪd/ *adj.* having lost your good opinion of sb/sth: *Fans are already becoming **disenchanted with** the new team manager.* ▶ **disenchantment** *noun* [U]

disenfranchise /ˌdɪsɪnˈfræntʃaɪz/ *verb* [T] (POLITICS) to take away sb's rights, especially their right to vote OPP **enfranchise**

disentangle /ˌdɪsɪnˈtæŋgl/ *verb* [T] to free sb/sth that had become connected to sb/sth else in a confused and complicated way: *My coat got caught up in some bushes and I couldn't disentangle it.* ◇ (*figurative*) *Listening to the woman's story, I found it hard to disentangle the truth from the lies.*

disestablish AW /ˌdɪsɪˈstæblɪʃ/ *verb* [T] (*formal*) (RELIGION) to end the official status of a national Church: *a campaign to disestablish the Church of England*

disfigure /dɪsˈfɪgə(r)/ *verb* [T] to spoil the appearance of sb/sth: *His face was permanently disfigured by the fire.*

disgrace[1] /dɪsˈgreɪs/ *noun* **1** [U] the state of not being respected by other people, usually because you have behaved badly: *She left the company **in disgrace** after admitting stealing from colleagues.* **2** [sing.] **a ~ (to sb/sth)** a person or thing that gives a very bad impression and makes you feel sorry and embarrassed: *The streets are covered in litter. It's a disgrace!* ◇ *Teachers who hit children are a disgrace to their profession.*

disgrace[2] /dɪsˈgreɪs/ *verb* [T] to behave badly in a way that makes you or other people feel sorry and embarrassed: *My brother disgraced himself by starting a fight at the wedding.*

disgraceful /dɪsˈgreɪsfl/ *adj.* very bad, making other people feel sorry and embarrassed: *The behaviour of the team's fans was absolutely disgraceful.* ▶ **disgracefully** /-fəli/ *adv.*

disgruntled /dɪsˈgrʌntld/ *adj.* disappointed and annoyed

disguise[1] /dɪsˈgaɪz/ *verb* [T] ~ **sb/sth (as sb/sth)** to change the appearance, sound, etc. of sb/sth so that people cannot recognize them or it: *They disguised themselves as fishermen and escaped in a boat.* ◇ (*figurative*) *His smile disguised his anger.*

disguise[2] /dɪsˈgaɪz/ *noun* [C,U] a thing that you wear or use to change your appearance so that nobody recognizes you: *She is so famous that she has to go shopping **in disguise**.* ◇ *The robbers were* *wearing heavy disguises so that they could not be identified.*

disgust¹ ⊶ /dɪsˈɡʌst/ ***noun*** [U] ~ **(at sth)** a strong feeling of not liking or approving of sth/sb that you feel is unacceptable, or sth/sb that looks, smells, etc. unpleasant: *The film was so bad that we walked out **in disgust**. ◇ **Much to my disgust**, I found a hair in my soup.*

disgust² ⊶ /dɪsˈɡʌst/ ***verb*** [T] **1** to cause a strong feeling of not liking or approving of sb/sth: *Cruelty towards animals absolutely disgusts me.* **2** to make sb feel sick: *The way he eats with his mouth open completely disgusts me.*

disgusted ⊶ /dɪsˈɡʌstɪd/ ***adj.*** ~ **(at/with sb/sth)** not liking or approving of sb/sth at all: *We were disgusted at the standard of service we received.*

disgusting ⊶ /dɪsˈɡʌstɪŋ/ ***adj.*** very unpleasant: *What a disgusting smell!*

disgustingly /dɪsˈɡʌstɪŋli/ ***adv.*** **1** (often used to show you are jealous of sb/sth) extremely: *Our neighbours are disgustingly rich.* **2** in a way that you do not like or approve of or that makes you feel sick: *The kitchen was disgustingly dirty.*

dish¹ ⊶ /dɪʃ/ ***noun*** **1** [C] a round container for food that is deeper than a plate **2** [C] a type of food prepared in a particular way: *The **main dish** was curry. It was served with a selection of **side dishes**. ◇ Paella is a typical Spanish dish, made with rice and shellfish.* **3 the dishes** [pl.] all the plates, cups, etc. that you use during a meal: *I'll cook and you can **wash the dishes**.* **4** = SATELLITE DISH

dish² /dɪʃ/ ***verb***

PHR V **dish sth out** (*informal*) to give away a lot of sth: *to dish out advice*

dish sth up (*informal*) to serve food

dishearten /dɪsˈhɑːtn/ ***verb*** [T] (usually passive) to make sb lose hope or confidence **OPP** **hearten**

disheartened /dɪsˈhɑːtnd/ ***adj.*** sad or disappointed

disheartening /dɪsˈhɑːtnɪŋ/ ***adj.*** making you lose hope and confidence; causing disappointment **OPP** **heartening**

dishevelled (*AmE* **disheveled**) /dɪˈʃevld/ ***adj.*** (used about a person's appearance) very untidy

dishonest ⊶ /dɪsˈɒnɪst/ ***adj.*** that you cannot trust; likely to lie, steal or cheat **OPP** **honest** ▶ **dishonesty** ***noun*** [U] ▶ **dishonestly** ***adv.***

dishonour¹ (*AmE* **dishonor**) /dɪsˈɒnə(r)/ ***noun*** [U, sing.] (*formal*) the state of no longer being respected, especially because you have done sth bad: *Her illegal trading has **brought dishonour on** the company.* **OPP** **honour** ▶ **dishonourable** /-nərəbl/ ***adj.*** **OPP** **honourable**

dishonour² (*AmE* **dishonor**) /dɪsˈɒnə(r)/ ***verb*** [T] (*formal*) to do sth bad that makes people stop respecting you or sb/sth close to you

dishwasher /ˈdɪʃwɒʃə(r)/ ***noun*** [C] a machine that washes plates, cups, knives, forks, etc.

disillusion /ˌdɪsɪˈluːʒn/ ***verb*** [T] to destroy sb's belief in or good opinion of sb/sth ▶ **disillusion** (*also* **disillusionment**) ***noun*** [U]: *I feel increasing disillusion with the government.*

disillusioned /ˌdɪsɪˈluːʒnd/ ***adj.*** disappointed because sb/sth is not as good as you first thought: *She's disillusioned with nursing.*

disinfect /ˌdɪsɪnˈfekt/ ***verb*** [T] to clean sth with a liquid that destroys bacteria: *to disinfect a wound* ▶ **disinfection** ***noun*** [U]

disinfectant /ˌdɪsɪnˈfektənt/ ***noun*** [C,U] a substance that destroys bacteria and is used for cleaning

disinherit /ˌdɪsɪnˈherɪt/ ***verb*** [T] (LAW) to prevent sb, especially your son or daughter, from receiving your money or property after your death ➲ look at **inherit**

disintegrate /dɪsˈɪntɪɡreɪt/ ***verb*** [I] to break into many small pieces: *The spacecraft exploded and disintegrated.* ▶ **disintegration** /dɪsˌɪntɪˈɡreɪʃn/ ***noun*** [U]: *the disintegration of the empire*

disinterest /dɪsˈɪntrəst/ ***noun*** [U] **1** lack of interest **2** the fact of not being involved in sth and therefore able to be fair

disinterested /dɪsˈɪntrəstɪd/ ***adj.*** fair, not influenced by personal feelings: *disinterested advice* ➲ look at **uninterested**

disjointed /dɪsˈdʒɔɪntɪd/ ***adj.*** (used especially about ideas, writing or speech) not clearly connected and therefore difficult to follow ▶ **disjointedly** ***adv.***

disk ⊶ /dɪsk/ ***noun*** [C] **1** (*AmE*) = DISC **2** (COMPUTING) a flat piece of plastic that stores information for use by a computer ➲ look at **floppy disk, hard disk**

ˈdisk drive ***noun*** [C] (COMPUTING) a piece of electrical equipment that passes information to or from a computer disk ➲ picture at **computer**

diskette /dɪsˈket/ = FLOPPY DISK ➲ picture at **computer**

dislike¹ ⊶ /dɪsˈlaɪk/ ***verb*** [T] ~ **(doing) sth** to think that sb/sth is unpleasant: *I really dislike flying. ◇ What is it that you dislike about living here?* **OPP** **like**

dislike² ⊶ /dɪsˈlaɪk/ ***noun*** [C,U, sing.] (a) ~ **(of/for sb/sth)** the feeling of not liking sb/sth: *She couldn't hide her dislike for him. ◇ He seems to have a strong dislike of hard work.*

IDM **take a dislike to sb/sth** to start disliking sb/sth: *He took an instant dislike to his boss.*

dislocate /ˈdɪsləkeɪt/ ***verb*** [T] (HEALTH) to put sth (usually a bone) out of its correct position: *He dislocated his shoulder during the game.* ▶ **dislocation** /ˌdɪsləˈkeɪʃn/ ***noun*** [C,U]

dislodge /dɪsˈlɒdʒ/ ***verb*** [T] ~ **sth (from sth)** to make sb/sth move from its correct fixed position: *The strong wind dislodged several tiles from the roof.*

disloyal /dɪsˈlɔɪəl/ ***adj.*** ~ **(to sb/sth)** not supporting your friends, family, country etc.; doing sth that will harm them: *It was disloyal to your friends to repeat their conversation to Peter.* **OPP** **loyal** ▶ **disloyalty** /-ˈlɔɪəlti/ ***noun*** [C,U] (*pl.* **disloyalties**)

dismal /ˈdɪzməl/ ***adj.*** **1** causing or showing sadness; depressing: *dismal surroundings* **SYN** **miserable** **2** (*informal*) of low quality; poor: *a dismal standard of work*

dismantle /dɪsˈmæntl/ ***verb*** [T] to take sth to pieces; to separate sth into the parts it is made from: *The photographer dismantled his equipment and packed it away.*

dismay /dɪsˈmeɪ/ ***noun*** [U] a strong feeling of disappointment and sadness: *I realized **to my dismay** that I was going to miss the plane.* ▶ **dismay** ***verb*** [T] (usually passive): *I was dismayed to hear that my old school had been knocked down.*

dismember /dɪsˈmembə(r)/ ***verb*** [T] to cut a dead body into pieces

dismiss ⊶ /dɪsˈmɪs/ ***verb*** [T] **1** ~ **sb/sth (as sth)** to decide not to think about sth/sb: *He dismissed the idea as nonsense.* **2** ~ **sb (from sth)** to officially remove sb from their job **SYN fire, sack**: *He was dismissed for refusing to obey orders.* **3** to send sb away: *The lesson ended and the teacher dismissed the class.* **4** (**LAW**) to say that a trial or court case should not continue, usually because there is not enough evidence: *The case was dismissed.*

dismissal /dɪsˈmɪsl/ ***noun*** **1** [U,C] the act of dismissing sb from their job; an example of this: *He still hopes to win his claim against **unfair dismissal**.* **2** [U] the failure to consider sth as important: *She was hurt at their dismissal of her offer of help.* **3** [C] (**LAW**) the act of not allowing a trial or legal case to continue, usually because there is not enough evidence: *the dismissal of the appeal*

dismissive /dɪsˈmɪsɪv/ ***adj.*** ~ **(of sb/sth)** saying or showing that you think that sb/sth is not worth considering seriously: *The boss was dismissive of all the efforts I had made.* ▶ **dismissively** ***adv.***

dismount /dɪsˈmaʊnt/ ***verb*** [I] to get off sth that you ride (a horse, a bicycle, etc.) **OPP mount**

disobedient /ˌdɪsəˈbiːdiənt/ ***adj.*** refusing or failing to obey **OPP obedient** ▶ **disobedience** ***noun*** [U]

disobey /ˌdɪsəˈbeɪ/ ***verb*** [I,T] to refuse to do what you are told to do: *He was punished for disobeying orders.* **OPP obey**

disorder /dɪsˈɔːdə(r)/ ***noun*** **1** [U] an untidy, confused or badly organized state: *His financial affairs are **in complete disorder**.* **OPP order** **2** [U] violent behaviour by a large number of people: *Disorder broke out on the streets of the capital.* **3** [C,U] (**HEALTH**) an illness in which the mind or part of the body is not working properly: *treatment for **eating disorders** such as anorexia* ◇ *a kind of **mental disorder*** ➲ note at **disease**

disordered /dɪsˈɔːdəd/ ***adj.*** untidy, confused or badly organized

disorderly /dɪsˈɔːdəli/ ***adj.*** **1** (used about people or behaviour) out of control and violent; causing trouble in public: *They were arrested for being **drunk and disorderly**.* **2** untidy **OPP orderly**

disorganization (also **-isation**) /dɪsˌɔːɡənaɪˈzeɪʃn/ ***noun*** [U] a lack of careful planning and order **OPP organization**

disorganized (also **-ised**) /dɪsˈɔːɡənaɪzd/ ***adj.*** badly planned; not able to plan well **OPP organized**

disorientate /dɪsˈɔːriənteɪt/ (*especially AmE* **disorient** /dɪsˈɔːrient/) ***verb*** [T] to make sb become confused about where they are: *The road signs were very confusing and I soon became disorientated.* ▶ **disorientation** /dɪsˌɔːriənˈteɪʃn/ ***noun*** [U]

disown /dɪsˈəʊn/ ***verb*** [T] to say that you no longer want to be connected with or responsible for sb/sth: *When he was arrested, his family disowned him.*

disparage /dɪˈspærɪdʒ/ ***verb*** [T] (*formal*) to talk about sb/sth in a critical way; to say that sb/sth is of little value or importance ▶ **disparaging** ***adj.***: *disparaging remarks*

disparate /ˈdɪspərət/ ***adj.*** (*formal*) **1** made up of parts or people that are very different from each other: *a disparate group of individuals* **2** (used about two or more things) so different from each other that they cannot be compared or cannot work together

disparity /dɪˈspærəti/ ***noun*** [U, C] (*pl.* **disparities**) (*formal*) a difference, especially one that is caused by unfair treatment

dispatch[1] (*BrE also* **despatch**) /dɪˈspætʃ/ ***verb*** [T] (*formal*) to send sb/sth somewhere, especially for a special purpose: *Troops have been dispatched to the area.* ◇ *Your order will be dispatched within 7 days.*

dispatch[2] (*BrE also* **despatch**) /dɪˈspætʃ/ ***noun*** **1** [U] (*formal*) the act of sending sb/sth somewhere **2** [C] (**POLITICS**) a message or report sent quickly from one military officer to another or between government officials **3** [C] (**ARTS AND MEDIA**) a report sent to a newspaper by a journalist who is working in a foreign country: *dispatches from the war zone*

dispel /dɪˈspel/ ***verb*** [T] (**dispelling**; **dispelled**) to make sth, especially a feeling or a belief, disappear: *His reassuring words dispelled all her fears.*

dispensable /dɪˈspensəbl/ ***adj.*** not necessary: *I suppose I'm dispensable. Anybody could do my job.* **OPP indispensable**

dispensary /dɪˈspensəri/ ***noun*** [C] (*pl.* **dispensaries**) (**HEALTH**) **1** a place in a hospital, shop, etc. where medicines are prepared for patients **2** (*old-fashioned*) a place where patients are treated, especially one run by a charity

dispense /dɪˈspens/ ***verb*** [T] (*formal*) to give or provide people with sth: *a machine that dispenses hot and cold drinks*

PHR V dispense with sb/sth to get rid of sb/sth that is not necessary: *They decided to dispense with luxuries and live a simple life.*

dispenser /dɪˈspensə(r)/ ***noun*** [C] a machine or container from which you can get sth: *a cash dispenser at a bank* ◇ *a soap dispenser*

dispersal /dɪˈspɜːsl/ ***noun*** [U, C] (*written*) the process of sending sb/sth in different directions; the process of spreading sth over a wide area: *police trained in crowd dispersal* ◇ *the dispersal of seeds*

disperse /dɪˈspɜːs/ ***verb*** [I,T] to separate and go in different directions; to make sb/sth do this: *When the meeting was over, the group dispersed.* ◇ *The police arrived and quickly dispersed the crowd.*

dispersion /dɪˈspɜːʃn/ ***noun*** [U] the process by which people or things are spread over a wide area: *population dispersion* ◇ *the dispersion of light*

dispirited /dɪˈspɪrɪtɪd/ ***adj.*** having lost confidence or hope; depressed

displace **AW** /dɪsˈpleɪs/ ***verb*** [T] **1** to remove and take the place of sb/sth: *Sampras was finally displaced as the top tennis player in the world.* **2** to force sb/sth to move from the usual or correct place: *refugees displaced by the war*

diˌsplaced ˈperson ***noun*** (*pl.* **diˌsplaced ˈpersons**) (**POLITICS**) a person who has been forced to leave his/her country for political or religious reasons, or because there is a war, not enough food, etc. **SYN refugee**

displacement **AW** /dɪsˈpleɪsmənt/ ***noun*** **1** [U] (*formal*) the act of DISPLACING sb/sth; the process of being DISPLACED: *the largest displacement of civilian population since World War Two* **2** [C] (**PHYSICS**) the amount of a liquid moved out of place by sth floating or put in it, especially a ship floating in water: *a ship with a displacement of 10000 tonnes*

display[1] ⊶ **AW** /dɪˈspleɪ/ ***verb*** [T] **1** to put sth in a place where people will see it or where it will attract attention: *Posters for the concert were displayed throughout the city.* **2** to show signs of sth (for example a feeling or a quality): *She displayed no interest in the discussion.*

display[2] 🔑 AW /dɪˈspleɪ/ ***noun*** [C] **1** an arrangement of things in a public place for people to see: *a window display in a shop* **2** a public event in which sth is shown in action: *a firework display* **3** behaviour that shows a particular feeling or quality: *a sudden display of aggression* **4** (COMPUTING) words, pictures, etc. that can be seen on a computer screen

IDM **on display** in a place where people will see it and where it will attract attention: *Treasures from the sunken ship were put on display at the museum.*

displease /dɪsˈpliːz/ ***verb*** [T] (*formal*) to annoy sb or to make sb angry or upset ▶ **displeased** ***adj.*** OPP **pleased**

displeasure /dɪsˈpleʒə(r)/ ***noun*** [U] (*formal*) the feeling of being annoyed or not satisfied: *I wrote to express my displeasure at not having been informed sooner.*

disposable AW /dɪˈspəʊzəbl/ ***adj.*** **1** made to be thrown away after being used once or for a short time: *a disposable razor* **2** (FINANCE) available for use: *disposable assets/capital/resources* ◇ *a person's* ***disposable income*** (= money they are free to spend after paying taxes, etc.)

disposal AW /dɪˈspəʊzl/ ***noun*** [U] the act of getting rid of sth or throwing sth away: *the disposal of dangerous chemical waste* ◇ *bomb disposal*

IDM **at sb's disposal** available for sb to use at any time

dispose AW /dɪˈspəʊz/ ***verb***

PHR V **dispose of sb/sth** to throw away or sell sth; to get rid of sb/sth that you do not want

disposition /ˌdɪspəˈzɪʃn/ ***noun*** **1** [C, usually sing.] the natural qualities of a person's character: *to have a cheerful disposition* ◇ *people of a nervous disposition* **2** [C, usually sing.] **a ~ to/towards sth; a ~ to do sth** (*formal*) a usual way of behaving: *to have/show a disposition towards acts of violence* **3** [C, usually sing.] (*formal*) the way sth is put or arranged in a place **4** [C,U] (LAW) a formal act of giving property or money to sb

disproportion AW /ˌdɪsprəˈpɔːʃn/ ***noun*** [U] **~ (between A and B)** (*formal*) the state of two things not being at an equally high or low level; an example of this: *a profession with a high disproportion of male to female employees*

disproportionate AW /ˌdɪsprəˈpɔːʃənət/ ***adj.*** **~ (to sth)** too large or too small when compared to sth else ▶ **disproportionately** ***adv.***

disprove /ˌdɪsˈpruːv/ ***verb*** [T] to show that sth is not true

dispute[1] /ˈdɪspjuːt; dɪˈspjuːt/ ***noun*** [C,U] **(a) ~ (between A and B) (over/about sth)** a disagreement or argument between two people, groups or countries: *There was some dispute between John and his boss about whose fault it was.* ◇ *a pay dispute*

IDM **in dispute** in a situation of arguing or being argued about: *He is in dispute with the tax office about how much he should pay.*

dispute[2] /dɪˈspjuːt/ ***verb*** [T] to argue about sth and to question if it is true or right: *The player disputed the referee's decision.*

disqualify /dɪsˈkwɒlɪfaɪ/ ***verb*** [T] (*pres. part.* **disqualifying**; *3rd person sing. pres.* **disqualifies**; *pt, pp* **disqualified**) **~ sb (from sth/doing sth); ~ sb (for sth)** to officially prevent sb from doing sth or taking part in sth, usually because they have broken a rule or law: *He was disqualified from driving for two years.* ◇ *The team were disqualified for cheating.* ▶ **disqualification** /dɪsˌkwɒlɪfɪˈkeɪʃn/ ***noun*** [C,U]

disregard /ˌdɪsrɪˈɡɑːd/ ***verb*** [T] to take no notice of sb/sth; to treat sth as unimportant: *These are the latest instructions. Please disregard any you received before.* ▶ **disregard** ***noun*** [U, sing.] **~ (for sb/sth)**: *He rushed into the burning building with complete disregard for his own safety.*

disrepair /ˌdɪsrɪˈpeə(r)/ ***noun*** [U] the state of being in bad condition because repairs have not been made: *Over the years the building* ***fell into disrepair***.

disreputable /dɪsˈrepjətəbl/ ***adj.*** not to be trusted; well known for being bad or dishonest: *disreputable business methods* OPP **reputable**

disrepute /ˌdɪsrɪˈpjuːt/ ***noun*** [U] the situation when people no longer respect sb/sth: *Such unfair decisions* ***bring*** *the legal system* ***into disrepute***.

disrespect /ˌdɪsrɪˈspekt/ ***noun*** [U] **~ (for/to sb/sth)** a lack of respect for sb/sth that is shown in what you do or say OPP **respect** ▶ **disrespectful** /-fl/ ***adj.*** OPP **respectful** ▶ **disrespectfully** /-fəli/ ***adv.***

disrupt /dɪsˈrʌpt/ ***verb*** [T] to stop sth happening as or when it should: *The strike severely disrupted flights to Spain.* ▶ **disruption** ***noun*** [C,U] ▶ **disruptive** /dɪsˈrʌptɪv/ ***adj.***

dissatisfaction /ˌdɪsˌsætɪsˈfækʃn/ ***noun*** [U] **~ (with/at sb/sth)** the feeling of not being satisfied or pleased: *There is some dissatisfaction among teachers with the plans for the new exam.* OPP **satisfaction**

dissatisfied /dɪsˈsætɪsfaɪd/ ***adj.*** **~ (with sb/sth)** not satisfied or pleased: *complaints from dissatisfied customers* OPP **satisfied**

dissect /dɪˈsekt/ ***verb*** [T] to cut up a dead body, a plant, etc. in order to study it ▶ **dissection** ***noun*** [C,U]

dissent[1] /dɪˈsent/ ***noun*** [U] (*formal*) disagreement with official or generally agreed ideas or opinions: *There is some dissent within the Labour Party on these policies.*

dissent[2] /dɪˈsent/ ***verb*** [I] (*formal*) **~ (from sth)** to have opinions that are different to those that are officially held ▶ **dissenting** ***adj.***

dissertation /ˌdɪsəˈteɪʃn/ ***noun*** [C] (EDUCATION) a long piece of writing on sth that you have studied, especially as part of a university degree ➲ look at **thesis**

disservice /dɪsˈsɜːvɪs/ ***noun*** [U, sing.]

IDM **do (a) disservice to sb/sth** to do sth that harms sb and the opinion other people have of them

dissident /ˈdɪsɪdənt/ ***noun*** [C] (POLITICS) a person who strongly disagrees with and criticizes their government, especially in a country where it is dangerous to do this ▶ **dissidence** ***noun*** [U]

dissimilar AW /dɪˈsɪmɪlə(r)/ ***adj.*** **~ (from/to sb/sth)** not the same; different: *The situation you're in is not dissimilar to mine.* OPP **similar**

dissociate /dɪˈsəʊʃieɪt; -ˈsəʊs-/ (*also* **disassociate** /ˌdɪsəˈsəʊʃieɪt; -ˈsəʊs-/) ***verb*** [T] **~ sb/sth/yourself (from sth)** to show that you are not connected with or do not support sb/sth; to show that two things are not connected with each other: *She dissociated herself from the views of the extremists in her party.* OPP **associate**

dissolve 🔑 /dɪˈzɒlv/ ***verb*** **1** [I,T] (used about a solid) to become or to make sth become liquid: *Sugar dissolves in water.* ◇ *Dissolve two tablets in cold water.* **2** [T] (LAW) to officially end a marriage, business agreement or parliament: *Their marriage was dissolved in 2006.* ◇ *The election was announced and parliament was dissolved.*

dissuade /dɪˈsweɪd/ ***verb*** [T] **~ sb (from doing sth)** to persuade sb not to do sth: *I tried to dissuade her from spending the money, but she insisted.* OPP **persuade**

distance¹ /ˈdɪstəns/ ***noun*** **1** [C,U] the amount of space between two places or things: *The map tells you the distances between the major cities.* ◇ *We can walk home from here, **it's no distance*** (= it isn't far). ◇ *The house is **within walking distance** of the shops.* **2** [sing.] a point that is a long way from sb/sth: ***At this distance** I can't read the number on the bus.* ◇ ***From a distance** the village looks quite attractive.*

IDM **in the distance** far away: *I could just see Paul in the distance.*

keep your distance to stay away from sb/sth

within striking distance → STRIKE²

distance² /ˈdɪstəns/ ***verb*** [T] **~ yourself from sb/sth** to become less involved or connected with sb/sth: *She was keen to distance herself from the views of her colleagues.*

ˈ**distance learning** ***noun*** [U] (**EDUCATION**) a system of education in which people study at home and send or email work to their teachers

distant /ˈdɪstənt/ ***adj.*** **1** a long way away in space or time: *travel to distant parts of the world* ◇ *in the not-too-distant future* (= quite soon) **2** (used about a relative) not closely related: *a distant cousin* **3** not very friendly: *He has a rather distant manner and it's hard to get to know him well.* **4** seeming to be thinking about sth else: *She had a distant look in her eyes and clearly wasn't listening to me.*

distaste /dɪsˈteɪst/ ***noun*** [U, sing.] not liking sth; the feeling that sb/sth is unpleasant or offends you: *She looked around the dirty kitchen with distaste.*

distasteful /dɪsˈteɪstfl/ ***adj.*** unpleasant or causing offence: *a distasteful remark*

distemper /dɪˈstempə(r)/ ***noun*** [U] **1** (**HEALTH**) an infectious disease of animals, especially cats and dogs, that causes fever and coughing **2** (*BrE*) a type of paint that is mixed with water and used on walls

distend /dɪˈstend/ ***verb*** [I,T] (*formal*) to swell or make sth swell because of pressure from inside: *starving children with distended bellies* ▶ **distension** /dɪˈstenʃn/ ***noun*** [U]

distillation

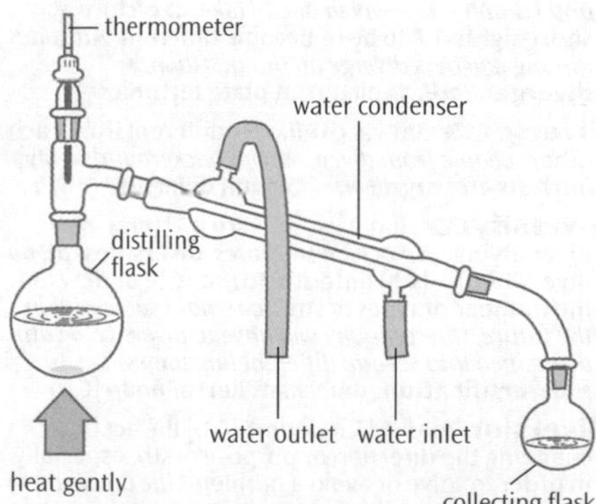

distil (*AmE* **distill**) /dɪˈstɪl/ ***verb*** [T] (**distilling; distilled**) (**CHEMISTRY**) to make a liquid pure by heating it until it becomes a gas and then collecting the liquid that forms when the gas cools ▶ **distillation** /ˌdɪstɪˈleɪʃn/ ***noun*** [C, U]

distillery /dɪˈstɪləri/ ***noun*** [C] (*pl.* **distilleries**) a factory where strong alcoholic drink is made by the process of DISTILLING

distinct AW /dɪˈstɪŋkt/ ***adj.*** **1** clear; easily seen, heard or understood: *There has been a distinct improvement in your work recently.* ◇ *I had **the distinct impression** that she was lying.* **2 ~ (from sth)** clearly different: *Her books fall into two distinct groups: the novels and the travel stories.* ◇ *This region, as distinct from other parts of the country, relies heavily on tourism.* OPP **indistinct**

distinction AW /dɪˈstɪŋkʃn/ ***noun*** **1** [C,U] (a) **~ (between A and B)** a clear or important difference between things or people: *We must **make a distinction** between classical and popular music here.* **2** [C,U] the quality of being excellent; fame for what you have achieved: *a violinist **of distinction*** **3** [C] (**EDUCATION**) the highest mark that is given to students in some exam for excellent work: *James got a distinction in maths.*

IDM **draw a distinction between sth and sth** → DRAW¹

distinctive AW /dɪˈstɪŋktɪv/ ***adj.*** clearly different from others and therefore easy to recognize: *The soldiers were wearing their distinctive red berets.* ▶ **distinctively** ***adv.***

distinctly AW /dɪˈstɪŋktli/ ***adv.*** **1** clearly: *I distinctly heard her say that she would be here on time.* **2** very; particularly: *His behaviour has been distinctly odd recently.*

distinguish /dɪˈstɪŋɡwɪʃ/ ***verb*** **1** [I,T] **~ between A and B; ~ A from B** to recognize the difference between two things or people: *He doesn't seem able to distinguish between what's important and what isn't.* ◇ *People who are colour-blind often can't distinguish red from green.* SYN **differentiate** **2** [T] **~ A (from B)** to make sb/sth different from others: *distinguishing features* (= things by which sb/sth can be recognized) ◇ *The power of speech distinguishes humans from animals.* **3** [T] to see, hear or recognize with effort: *I listened carefully but they were too far away for me to distinguish what they were saying.* **4** [T] **~ yourself** to do sth which causes you to be noticed and admired: *She distinguished herself in the exams.*

distinguishable /dɪˈstɪŋɡwɪʃəbl/ ***adj.*** **1** possible to recognize as different from sb/sth else: *The male bird is distinguishable from the female by the colour of its beak.* **2** possible to see, hear or recognize with effort: *The letter is so old that the signature is barely distinguishable.* OPP **indistinguishable**

distinguished /dɪˈstɪŋɡwɪʃt/ ***adj.*** important, successful and respected by other people

distort AW /dɪˈstɔːt/ ***verb*** [T] **1** to change the shape or sound of sth so that it seems strange or is not clear: *Her face was distorted with grief.* **2** to change sth and show it FALSELY: *Foreigners are often given a distorted view of this country.* ▶ **distortion** ***noun*** [C,U]

distract /dɪˈstrækt/ ***verb*** [T] **~ sb (from sth)** to take sb's attention away from sth

distracted /dɪˈstræktɪd/ ***adj.*** unable to give your full attention to sth because you are worried or thinking about sth else

distraction /dɪˈstrækʃn/ ***noun*** [C,U] something that takes your attention away from what you were doing or thinking about

IDM **to distraction** with the result that you become upset, excited, or angry and unable to think clearly:

The noise of the traffic outside at night is driving me to distraction.

distraught /dɪ'strɔːt/ ***adj.*** extremely upset and anxious so that you cannot think clearly

distress[1] /dɪ'stres/ ***noun*** [U] **1** the state of being very upset or of suffering great pain or difficulty: *She was **in such distress** that I didn't want to leave her on her own.* **2** the state of being in great danger and needing immediate help: *The ship's captain radioed that it was **in distress**.*

distress[2] /dɪ'stres/ ***verb*** [T] to make sb very upset or unhappy: *Try not to say anything to distress the patient further.* ▶ **distressed** ***adj.***: *She was too distressed to talk.* ▶ **distressing** ***adj.***: *a distressing experience/illness*

distribute ⊶ AW /dɪ'strɪbjuːt; 'dɪstrɪbjuːt/ ***verb*** [T] **1** ~ **sth (to/among sb/sth)** to give things to a number of people: *Tickets will be distributed to all club members.* ◇ *They distributed emergency food supplies to the areas that were most in need.* **2** (BUSINESS) to transport and supply goods to shops, companies, etc.: *Which company distributes this product in your country?* **3** to spread sth equally over an area: *Make sure that the weight is **evenly distributed**.*

distribution ⊶ AW /ˌdɪstrɪ'bjuːʃn/ ***noun*** **1** [U, C] the act of giving or transporting sth to a number of people or places: *the distribution of food parcels to the refugees* **2** [U] the way sth is shared out; the pattern in which sth is found: *a map to show the distribution of rainfall in Africa*

distributive AW /dɪ'strɪbjətɪv/ ***adj.*** (BUSINESS) connected with distribution of goods

distributor /dɪ'strɪbjətə(r)/ ***noun*** [C] (BUSINESS) a person or company that transports and supplies goods to a number of shops and companies

district ⊶ /'dɪstrɪkt/ ***noun*** [C] **1** a part of a town or country that is special for a particular reason or is of a particular type: *rural districts* ◇ *the financial district of the city* **2** an official division of a town or country: *the district council* ◇ *postal districts*

ˌ**district at'torney** ***noun*** [C] (*abbr.* **DA**) (LAW) (in the US) a lawyer who is responsible for bringing criminal charges against sb in a particular area or state

distrust /dɪs'trʌst/ ***noun*** [U, sing.] (a) ~ **(of sb/sth)** the feeling that you cannot believe sb/sth; a lack of trust ▶ **distrust** ***verb*** [T]: *She distrusts him because he lied to her once before.* ➲ look at **mistrust** ▶ **distrustful** ***adj.***

disturb ⊶ /dɪ'stɜːb/ ***verb*** [T] **1** to interrupt sb while they are doing sth or sleeping; to spoil a peaceful situation: *I'm sorry to disturb you but there's a phone call for you.* ◇ *Their sleep was disturbed by a loud crash.* **2** to cause sb to worry: *It disturbed her to think that he might be unhappy.* **3** to move sth or change its position: *I noticed a number of things had been disturbed and realized that there had been a burglary.*

disturbance /dɪ'stɜːbəns/ ***noun*** [C,U] something that makes you stop what you are doing, or that upsets the normal condition of sth: *They were arrested for causing a disturbance* (= fighting) *in the town centre.* ◇ *emotional disturbance*

disturbed /dɪ'stɜːbd/ ***adj.*** (HEALTH) having mental or emotional problems

disturbing ⊶ /dɪ'stɜːbɪŋ/ ***adj.*** making you worried or upset

disuse /dɪs'juːs/ ***noun*** [U] the state of not being used any more: *The farm buildings had been allowed to **fall into disuse**.*

disused /ˌdɪs'juːzd/ ***adj.*** not used any more: *a disused railway line*

ditch[1] /dɪtʃ/ ***noun*** [C] a long narrow hole that has been dug into the ground, especially along the side of a road or field for water to flow along
IDM **a last-ditch attempt** → LAST[1]

ditch[2] /dɪtʃ/ ***verb*** [T] (*informal*) to get rid of or leave sb/sth: *She ditched her old friends when she became famous.*

dither /'dɪðə(r)/ ***verb*** [I] to be unable to decide sth; to hesitate: *Stop dithering and make up your mind!*

ditto /'dɪtəʊ/ ***noun*** [C] (represented by the mark (″) and used instead of repeating the thing written above it) the same ▶ **ditto** ***adv.***: *'I'm starving.' 'Ditto* (= me too).*'*

diurnal /daɪ'ɜːnl/ ***adj.*** **1** (BIOLOGY) (used about animals and birds) active during the day OPP **nocturnal** **2** (ASTRONOMY) taking one day: *the diurnal rotation of the earth*

divan /dɪ'væn/ ***noun*** [C] (*BrE*) a type of bed with only a thick base to lie on but no frame at either end

dive[1] /daɪv/ ***verb*** [I] (*pt* **dived**: *AmE also* **dove** /dəʊv/; *pp* **dived**) **1** ~ **(off/from sth) (into sth)**; ~ **in** to jump into water with your arms and head first: *In Acapulco, men dive off the cliffs into the sea.* ◇ *A passer-by dived in and saved the drowning man.* ➲ picture at **swim** **2** to swim under the surface of the sea, a lake, etc.: *people diving for pearls* ◇ *I'm hoping to **go diving** on holiday.* **3** to move quickly and suddenly downwards: *He dived under the table and hid there.* ◇ *The goalkeeper dived to save the penalty.*
PHRV **dive into sth** to put your hand quickly into a pocket or bag in order to find or get sth

dive[2] /daɪv/ ***noun*** [C] **1** the act of **diving** into water **2** a quick and sudden downwards movement

diver /'daɪvə(r)/ ***noun*** [C] **1** a person who swims under the surface of water using special equipment **2** a person who jumps into water with their arms and head first

diverge /daɪ'vɜːdʒ/ ***verb*** [I] ~ **(from sth)** **1** (used about roads, lines, etc.) to separate and go in different directions: *The paths suddenly diverged and I didn't know which one to take.* ➲ picture at **short-sighted** **2** to be or become different: *Attitudes among teachers diverge on this question.* ▶ **divergent** ***adj.*** ➲ picture at **plate tectonics**

diverse AW /daɪ'vɜːs/ ***adj.*** very different from each other: *people from diverse social backgrounds* ◇ *My interests are very diverse.* ➲ noun **diversity**

diversify AW /daɪ'vɜːsɪfaɪ/ ***verb*** [I,T] (*pres. part.* **diversifying**; *3rd person sing. pres.* **diversifies**; *pt, pp* **diversified**) ~ **(sth) (into sth)** to increase or develop the number or types of sth: *To remain successful in the future, the company will have to diversify.* ◇ *Latin diversified into several different languages.*
▶ **diversification** /daɪˌvɜːsɪfɪ'keɪʃn/ ***noun*** [C,U]

diversion /daɪ'vɜːʃn/ ***noun*** **1** [C,U] the act of changing the direction or purpose of sth, especially in order to solve or avoid a problem: *the diversion of a river to prevent flooding* ◇ *the diversion of government funds to areas of greatest need* **2** [C] (*AmE* **detour**) a different route which traffic can take when a road is closed: *For London, follow the diversion.* **3** [C] something that takes your attention away from sth: *Some prisoners created a diversion while others escaped.*

diversity AW /daɪˈvɜːsəti/ *noun* [U] (SOCIAL STUDIES) the wide variety of sth: *cultural and ethnic diversity* ➲ adjective **diverse**

divert /daɪˈvɜːt/ *verb* [T] **~ sb/sth (from sth) (to sth)**; **~ sth (away from sth)** to change the direction or purpose of sb/sth, especially to avoid a problem: *During the road repairs, all traffic is being diverted.* ◇ *Government money was diverted from defence to education.* ◇ *Politicians often criticize each other to divert attention away from their own mistakes.*

divide¹ 🔑 /dɪˈvaɪd/ *verb* **1** [I,T] **~ (sth) (up) (into sth)** to separate into different parts: *The egg divides into two cells.* ◇ *The house was divided up into flats.* **2** [T] **~ sth (out/up) (between/among sb)** to separate sth into parts and give a part to each of a number of people: *The robbers divided the money out between themselves.* ◇ *When he died, his property was divided up among his children.* **3** [T] **~ sth (between A and B)** to use different parts or amounts of sth for different purposes: *They divide their time between their two homes.* **4** [T] to separate two places or things: *The river divides the old part of the city from the new.* **5** [T] to cause people to disagree: *The question of immigration has divided the country.* **6** [T] **~ sth by sth** to calculate how many times a number will go into another number: *10 divided by 5 is 2.* OPP **multiply**

> WORD FAMILY
> **divide** *verb, noun*
> **division** *noun*
> **divisive** *adj.*

divide² /dɪˈvaɪd/ *noun* [C] **a ~ (between A and B)** a difference between two groups of people that separates them from each other: *a divide between the rich and the poor*

di,vided 'highway (*AmE*) = DUAL CARRIAGEWAY

dividend /ˈdɪvɪdend/ *noun* [C] (ECONOMICS) a part of a company's profits that is paid to the people who own shares in it (**shareholders**)

divine /dɪˈvaɪn/ *adj.* (RELIGION) connected with God or a god

diving /ˈdaɪvɪŋ/ *noun* [U] the activity or sport of jumping into water or swimming under the surface of the sea, a lake, etc.

'diving board *noun* [C] a board at the side of a swimming pool from which people can jump into the water

divisible /dɪˈvɪzəbl/ *adj.* (MATHEMATICS) that can be divided: *12 is divisible by 3.*

division 🔑 /dɪˈvɪʒn/ *noun* **1** [U, sing.] **~ (of sth) (into sth)**; **~ (of sth) (between A and B)** the separation of sth into different parts; the sharing of sth between different people, groups, places, etc.: *There is a growing economic division between the north and south of the country.* ◇ *an unfair division of the profits* **2** [U] (MATHEMATICS) dividing one number by another: *the teaching of multiplication and division* **3** [C] **a ~ (in/within sth)**; **a ~ (between A and B)** a disagreement or difference of opinion between sb/sth: *deep divisions within the Labour Party* **4** [C] a part or section of an organization: *the company's sales division* ◇ *the First Division* (= of the football league) **5** [C] a line that separates sth; a border: *The river marks the division between the two counties.*

divisive /dɪˈvaɪsɪv/ *adj.* (*formal*) likely to cause disagreements or arguments between people: *a divisive policy*

divorce¹ 🔑 /dɪˈvɔːs/ *noun* [C,U] the legal end of a marriage: *to get a divorce*

divorce² 🔑 /dɪˈvɔːs/ *verb* [T] **1** to legally end your marriage to sb: *My parents **got divorced** when I was three.* ◇ *She divorced him a year after their marriage.* **2 ~ sb/sth from sth** to separate sb/sth from sth: *Sometimes these modern novels seem completely divorced from everyday life.*

divorced 🔑 /dɪˈvɔːst/ *adj.* **1** no longer married: *Many divorced men remarry and have second families.* ◇ *My parents are divorced.* ◇ *Are they going to **get divorced**?* **2 ~ from sth** (*formal*) appearing not to be affected by sth; separate from sth: *He seems completely divorced from reality.*

divorcee /dɪ,vɔːˈsiː/ *noun* [C] a person who is divorced

divulge /daɪˈvʌldʒ/ *verb* [T] (*formal*) to tell sth that is secret: *The phone companies refused to divulge details of their costs.*

Diwali /diːˈwɑːli/ *noun* [sing.] (RELIGION) a festival in several Indian religions that takes place in October or November, in which people decorate their homes with lights

DIY /,diː aɪ ˈwaɪ/ ***abbr.*** **do-it-yourself**; the activity of making and repairing things yourself around your home: *a DIY expert*

dizzy /ˈdɪzi/ *adj.* **1** feeling as if everything is turning round and that you might fall: *I **feel/get dizzy** in high places.* **2** very great; extreme: *the dizzy pace of life in London* ◇ *The following year, the band's popularity reached **dizzy heights**.* ▶ **dizziness** *noun* [U]

DJ /,diː ˈdʒeɪ/ (*also* **'disc jockey**) *noun* [C] (MUSIC) a person who plays records and talks about music on the radio or in a club

DNA

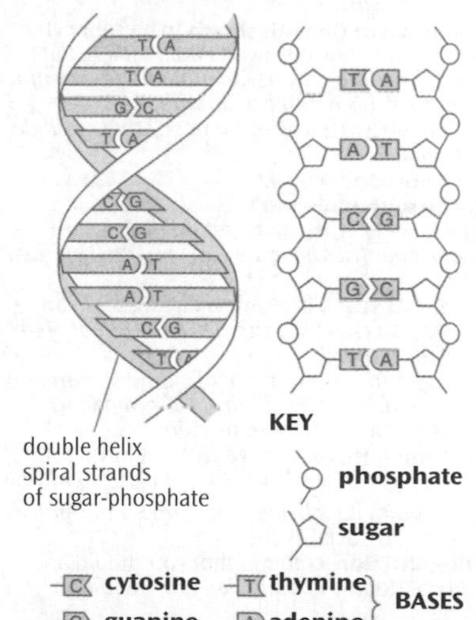

DNA /,diː en ˈeɪ/ *noun* [U] (BIOLOGY) **deoxyribonucleic acid**; the chemical in the cells of an animal or a plant that controls what characteristics that animal or plant will have: *a DNA test* ◇ *Police produced a **DNA profile** of the wanted man.*

,DNA 'fingerprinting (*also* **ge,netic 'fingerprinting**) *noun* [U] the method of finding the particular pattern of GENES in an individual person, particularly to identify sb or find out if sb has committed a crime

do¹ /də; *strong form* duː/ ***aux. verb*** (*pt* **did** /dɪd/; *pp* **done** /dʌn/) **1** used with other verbs to form questions and negative sentences, also in short answers and QUESTION TAGS (=short questions at the end of a sentence): *You don't like milk in your coffee, do you?* ◇ *She lives in New York, doesn't she?* **2** used for emphasizing the main verb: *I can't find the receipt now but I'm sure I did pay the phone bill.* **3** used to avoid repeating the main verb: *He earns a lot more than I do.* ◇ *She's feeling much better than she did last week.*

do² /duː/ ***verb*** (*pt* **did** /dɪd/; *pp* **done** /dʌn/) **1** [T] to perform an action, activity or job: *What are you doing?* ◇ *What is the government doing about pollution* (=what action are they taking)? ◇ *What do you do* (=what is your job)? ◇ *Have you done your homework?* ◇ *I do twenty minutes exercise every morning.* ◇ *to do the cooking/cleaning/ironing* ◇ *to do judo/aerobics/windsurfing* ◇ *What did you* ***do with*** *the keys* (=where did you put them)? **2** [I] to make progress or develop; to improve sth: *'How's your daughter doing at school?' 'She's doing well.'* ◇ *Last week's win has* ***done wonders for*** *the team's confidence.* ◇ *This latest scandal will* ***do nothing for*** (=will harm) *this government's reputation.* **3** [T] to make or produce sth: *The photocopier does 60 copies a minute.* ◇ *to do a painting/drawing* **4** [T] to provide a service: *Do you do eye tests here?* **5** [T] to study sth or find the answer to sth: *to do French/a course/a degree* ◇ *I can't do question three.* **6** [T] to travel a certain distance or at a certain speed: *This car does 120 miles per hour.* ◇ *I normally do about five miles when I go running.* **7** [T] to have a particular effect: *A holiday will do you good.* ◇ *The storm did a lot of damage.* **8** [I,T] to be enough or suitable: *If you haven't got a pen, a pencil will do.*

IDM **be/have to do with sb/sth** to be connected with sb/sth: *I'm not sure what Paola's job is, but I think it's something to do with animals.* ◇ *'How much do you earn?' 'It's nothing to do with you!'*

could do with sth to want or need sth: *I could do with a holiday.*

how do you do? → HOW

make do with sth → MAKE¹

PHR V **do away with sth** to get rid of sth: *Most European countries have done away with their royal families.*

do sb out of sth to prevent sb having sth in an unfair way; to cheat sb: *They've done me out of my share of the money!*

do sth up 1 to fasten a piece of clothing: *Hurry up. Do up your jacket and we can go!* **2** to repair a building and make it more modern

do without (sth) to manage without having sth: *If there isn't any coffee left, we'll just have to do without.*

do³ /duː/ ***noun*** [C] (*pl.* **dos** /duːz/) (*BrE, informal*) a party or other social event

IDM **dos and don'ts** things that you should and should not do: *the dos and don'ts of mountain climbing*

docile /ˈdəʊsaɪl/ ***adj.*** (used about a person or animal) quiet and easy to control

dock¹ /dɒk/ ***noun*** **1** [C,U] an area of a port where ships stop to be loaded, repaired, etc. **2 docks** [pl.] a group of **docks** with all the buildings, offices, etc. that are around them: *He works down at the docks.* **3** [C, usually sing.] the place in a court of law where the person who is accused sits or stands **4** (*AmE*) =LANDING STAGE

dock² /dɒk/ ***verb*** **1** [I,T] if a ship **docks** or you **dock** a ship, it sails into a port and stops at the **dock**: *The ship had docked/was docked at Lisbon.* **2** [T] to take away part of the money sb earns, especially as a punishment: *They've docked £20 off my wages because I was late.*

docker /ˈdɒkə(r)/ ***noun*** [C] a person whose job is moving goods on and off ships

doctor¹ /ˈdɒktə(r)/ ***noun*** (*abbr.* **Dr**) **1** [C] a person who has been trained in medicine and who treats people who are ill: *Our family doctor is Dr Young.* ◇ *I've got a doctor's appointment at 10 o'clock.*

RELATED VOCABULARY

A doctor **sees** or **treats** his/her **patients**. He/she may **prescribe** treatment or **medicine**. This is written on a **prescription**.

2 the doctor's [sing.] the place where a doctor sees their patients; a doctor's SURGERY: *I'm going to the doctor's today.* **3** [C] (**EDUCATION**) a person who has got a DOCTORATE: *a Doctor of Philosophy*

doctor² /ˈdɒktə(r)/ ***verb*** [T] **1** to change sth that should not be changed in order to gain an advantage: *The results of the survey had been doctored.* **2** to add sth harmful to food or drink

doctorate /ˈdɒktərət/ ***noun*** [C] (**EDUCATION**) the highest university degree

doctrine /ˈdɒktrɪn/ ***noun*** [C,U] (**RELIGION, POLITICS**) a set of beliefs that is taught by a church, political party, etc.

docudrama /ˈdɒkjudrɑːmə/ ***noun*** [C] (**ARTS AND MEDIA**) a film, usually made for television, in which real events are shown in the form of a story

document¹ AW /ˈdɒkjumənt/ ***noun*** [C] **1** an official piece of writing which gives information, proof or evidence: *Her solicitor asked her to read and sign a number of documents.* **2** (**COMPUTING**) a computer file that contains text that has a name that identifies it: *Save the document before closing.*

document² AW /ˈdɒkjumənt/ ***verb*** [T] **1** to record the details of sth: *Causes of the disease have been well documented.* **2** to prove or support sth with documents: *documented evidence*

documentary /ˌdɒkjuˈmentri/ ***noun*** [C] (**ARTS AND MEDIA**) (*pl.* **documentaries**) a film, television or radio programme that gives facts or information about a particular subject

documentation AW /ˌdɒkjumenˈteɪʃn/ ***noun*** [U] the documents that are required for sth, or that give evidence or proof of st: *I couldn't enter the country because I didn't have all the necessary documentation.*

docusoap /ˈdɒkjusəʊp/ ***noun*** [C] (**ARTS AND MEDIA**) a television programme about the lives of real people, presented as entertainment ➲ look at **soap opera**

doddle /ˈdɒdl/ ***noun*** [sing.] (*BrE, informal*) something that is very easy to do: *The exam was an absolute doddle!*

dodecagon /dəʊˈdekəgən/ ***noun*** [C] (**MATHEMATICS**) a flat shape with twelve straight sides and twelve angles

dodecahedron /ˌdəʊdekəˈhiːdrən; -ˈhed-/ ***noun*** [C] (**MATHEMATICS**) a solid

dodecahedron

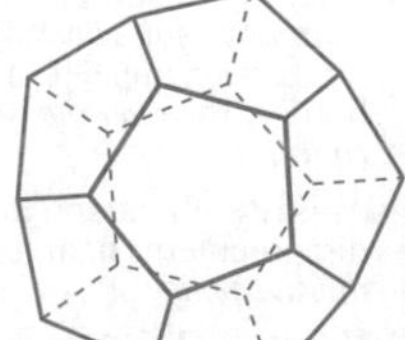

figure with twelve flat sides

dodge[1] /dɒdʒ/ ***verb*** **1** [I,T] to move quickly in order to avoid sb/sth: *I had to dodge between the cars to cross the road.* **2** [T] to avoid doing sth that you should do: *Don't try to dodge your responsibilities!*

dodge[2] /dɒdʒ/ ***noun*** [C] (*informal*) a clever way of avoiding sth: *The man had been involved in a massive tax dodge.*

dodgy /ˈdɒdʒi/ ***adj.*** (**dodgier**; **dodgiest**) (*BrE, informal*) involving risk; not honest or not to be trusted: *a dodgy business deal*

doe /dəʊ/ ***noun*** [C] a female RABBIT, DEER OR HARE ➲ note at **deer**

does /dʌz/ → DO

doesn't /ˈdʌznt/ short for DOES NOT

dog[1] ⊶ /dɒg/ ***noun*** [C] **1** an animal that many people keep as a pet, or for working on farms, hunting, etc. **2** a male dog or FOX

dog[2] /dɒg/ ***verb*** [T] (**dogging**; **dogged**) to follow sb closely: *A shadowy figure was dogging their every move.* ◇ *(figurative) Bad luck and illness have dogged her career from the start.*

ˈdog collar ***noun*** [C] (*informal*) (**RELIGION**) a white COLLAR that is worn by priests in the Christian church

ˈdog-eared ***adj.*** (used about a book or piece of paper) in bad condition with untidy corners and edges because it has been used a lot

dogged /ˈdɒgɪd/ ***adj.*** refusing to give up even when sth is difficult: *I was impressed by his* ***dogged determination*** *to succeed.* ▸ **doggedly** ***adv.***: *She doggedly refused all offers of help.*

dogma /ˈdɒgmə/ ***noun*** [C,U] (**RELIGION**) a belief or set of beliefs that people are expected to accept as true without questioning

dogmatic /dɒgˈmætɪk/ ***adj.*** being certain that your beliefs are right and that others should accept them, without considering other opinions or evidence ▸ **dogmatically** /-kli/ ***adv.***

dogsbody /ˈdɒgzbɒdi/ ***noun*** [C] (*pl.* **dogsbodies**) (*BrE, informal*) a person who has to do the boring or unpleasant jobs that no one else wants to do and who is considered less important than other people

ˌdo-it-yourˈself (*especially BrE*) = DIY

the doldrums /ˈdɒldrəmz/ ***noun*** [pl.] (**GEOGRAPHY**) an area of the Atlantic Ocean near the EQUATOR (= the imagined line around the middle of the earth) where the weather can be calm for long periods of time or there can be sudden storms
IDM **in the doldrums 1** sad or unhappy: *He's been in the doldrums ever since she left him.* **2** not active or busy: *Business has been in the doldrums recently.*

dole[1] /dəʊl/ ***verb*** (*informal*)
PHR V **dole sth out** to give sth, especially food, money, etc. in small amounts to a number of people

the dole[2] /dəʊl/ ***noun*** [sing.] (*BrE, informal*) money that the State gives every week to people who are unemployed: *I lost my job and had to go* ***on the dole***.

doleful /ˈdəʊlfl/ ***adj.*** sad or unhappy: *She looked at him with doleful eyes.* ▸ **dolefully** /-fəli/ ***adv.***

doll /dɒl/ ***noun*** [C] a child's toy that looks like a small person or a baby

dollar ⊶ /ˈdɒlə(r)/ ***noun*** (**ECONOMICS**) **1** [C] (*symbol* $) a unit of money in some countries, for example the US, Canada and Australia **2** [C] a note or coin that is worth one dollar **3 the dollar** [sing.] the value of the US dollar on international money markets

dollop /ˈdɒləp/ ***noun*** [C] (*informal*) a lump of sth soft, especially food: *a dollop of ice cream*

dolphin /ˈdɒlfɪn/ ***noun*** [C] an intelligent animal that lives in the sea and looks like a large fish. **Dolphins** usually swim in large groups (**schools**).

domain AW /dəˈmeɪn; dəʊ-/ ***noun*** [C] **1** an area of knowledge or activity: *I don't know – that's outside my domain.* ◇ *This issue is now* ***in the public domain*** (= the public knows about it). **2** (**COMPUTING**) a set of websites on the Internet which end with the same group of letters, for example *.com* or *.org* **3** (**MATHEMATICS**) the range of possible values of a particular VARIABLE (= a quantity which can vary)

doˈmain name ***noun*** [C] (**COMPUTING**) a name which identifies a website or group of websites on the Internet

dome /dəʊm/ ***noun*** [C] (**ARCHITECTURE**) a round roof on a building: *the dome of St Paul's in London* ▸ **domed** ***adj.***: *a domed roof*

dome

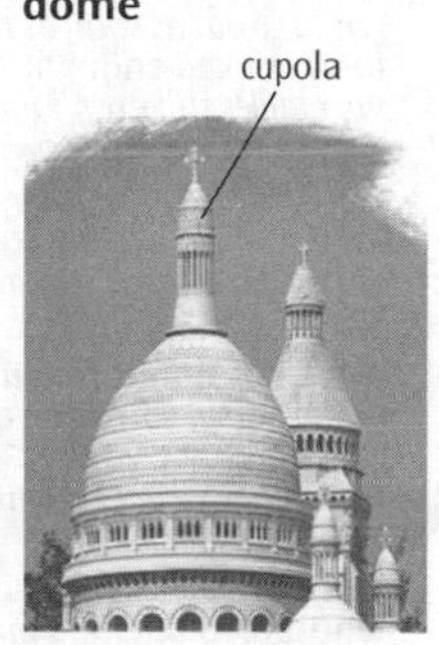

domestic ⊶ AW /dəˈmestɪk/ ***adj.*** **1** not international; only within one country: *domestic flights* ◇ *domestic affairs/politics* **2** (only *before* a noun) connected with the home or family: *domestic chores/tasks* ◇ *the growing problem of* ***domestic violence*** (= violence between members of the same family) ◇ *domestic water/gas/electricity supplies* **3** (used about animals) kept as pets or on farms; not wild: *domestic animals such as cats, dogs and horses* **4** (used about a person) enjoying doing things in the home, such as cooking and cleaning

domesticate AW /dəˈmestɪkeɪt/ ***verb*** [T] **1** to make a wild animal used to living with or working for humans SYN **tame 2** (**AGRICULTURE**) to grow plants or crops for human use SYN **cultivate** ▸ **domesticated** AW ***adj.***: *domesticated animals*

dominance AW /ˈdɒmɪnəns/ ***noun*** [U] control or power: *Japan's dominance of the car industry*

dominant AW /ˈdɒmɪnənt/ ***adj.*** **1** more powerful, important or noticeable than others: *His mother was the dominant influence in his life.* **2** (**BIOLOGY**) a **dominant** physical characteristic, for example brown eyes, appears in a child even if it has only one GENE (= the unit inside the cells that control the characteristics that will be passed on from parents) for this characteristic ➲ look at **recessive**

dominate ⊶ AW /ˈdɒmɪneɪt/ ***verb*** **1** [I,T] to be more powerful, important or noticeable than others: *The Italian team dominated throughout the second half of the game.* ◇ *She always tends to dominate the conversation.* **2** [T] (used about a building or place) to be much higher than everything else: *The cathedral dominates the area for miles around.* ▸ **domination** /ˌdɒmɪˈneɪʃn/ ***noun*** [U]

domineering /ˌdɒmɪˈnɪərɪŋ/ ***adj.*** having a very strong character and wanting to control other people

dominion /dəˈmɪniən/ ***noun*** (*formal*) **1** [U] the power to rule and control: *to have dominion over an area* **2** [C] (**POLITICS**) an area controlled by one government or ruler: *the dominions of the Roman empire*

domino /ˈdɒmɪnəʊ/ ***noun*** [C] (*pl.* **dominoes**) one of a set of small flat pieces of wood or plastic, marked on one side with two groups of spots representing numbers, that are used for playing a game (**dominoes**)

donate /dəʊˈneɪt/ ***verb*** [T] ~ **sth (to sb/sth)** to give money or goods to an organization, especially one for people or animals who need help: *She donated a large sum of money to Cancer Research.*

donation /dəʊˈneɪʃn/ ***noun*** [C] money, etc. that is given to a person or an organization such as a charity, in order to help people or animals in need

done[1] past participle of **do**[2]

done[2] /dʌn/ ***adj.*** (not *before* a noun) **1** finished: *I've got to go out as soon as this job is done.* **2** (used about food) cooked enough: *The meat's ready but the vegetables still aren't done.*

IDM **over and done with** completely finished; in the past

done[3] /dʌn/ ***exclamation*** used for saying that you accept an offer: *'I'll give you twenty pounds for it.' 'Done!'*

donkey /ˈdɒŋki/ ***noun*** [C] (*also* **ass**) an animal like a small horse, with long ears

IDM **donkey's years** (*BrE, informal*) a very long time: *They've been going out together for donkey's years.*

donor /ˈdəʊnə(r)/ ***noun*** [C] **1** (HEALTH) a person who gives blood or a part of their own body for medical use: *a blood/kidney donor* **2** somebody who gives money or goods to a CHARITY (=an organization that helps people or animals)

don't → DO

donut (*AmE*) = DOUGHNUT

doodle /ˈduːdl/ ***verb*** [I] to draw lines, patterns, etc. without thinking, especially when you are bored ▶ **doodle *noun*** [C]

doom /duːm/ ***noun*** [U] death or a terrible event in the future which you cannot avoid: *a sense of impending doom* (=that something bad is going to happen) ◇ *Don't listen to her. She's always full of **doom and gloom*** (=expecting bad things to happen). ▶ **doomed *adj.***: *The plan was doomed from the start.*

door 🔑 /dɔː(r)/ ***noun*** [C] **1** a piece of wood, glass, etc. that you open and close to get in or out of a room, building, car, etc.: *to open/shut/close the door* ◇ *to answer the door* (=to open the door when sb knocks or rings the bell) ◇ *Have you bolted/locked the door?* ◇ *I could hear someone knocking on the door.* ◇ *the front/back door* ◇ *the fridge door* **2** the entrance to a building, room, car, etc.: *I looked through the door and saw her sitting there.*

IDM **(from) door to door** (from) house to house: *The journey takes about five hours, door to door.* ◇ *a door-to-door salesman* (=a person who visits people in their homes to try and sell them things)

next door (to sb/sth) in the next house, room, etc.: *Do you know the people who live next door?*

out of doors outside: *Shall we eat out of doors today?* SYN **outdoors** OPP **indoors**

doorbell /ˈdɔːbel/ ***noun*** [C] a bell on the outside of a house which you ring when you want to go in

doorman /ˈdɔːmən/ ***noun*** [C] (*pl.* **-men** /-mən/) a man, often in uniform, whose job is to stand at the entrance to a large building such as a hotel or a theatre, and open the door for visitors, find them taxis, etc.

doormat /ˈdɔːmæt/ ***noun*** [C] **1** a piece of material on the floor in front of a door which you can clean your shoes on before going inside **2** (*informal*) a person who allows other people to treat them badly without complaining

doorstep /ˈdɔːstep/ ***noun*** [C] a step in front of a door outside a building

IDM **on your/the doorstep** very near to you: *The sea was right on our doorstep.*

doorway /ˈdɔːweɪ/ ***noun*** [C] (ARCHITECTURE) an opening filled by a door leading into a building, room, etc.: *She was standing in the doorway.*

dope[1] /dəʊp/ ***noun*** (*informal*) **1** [U] (HEALTH) an illegal drug, especially CANNABIS or MARIJUANA **2** [U] (SPORT) a drug that is taken by a person or given to an animal to affect their performance in a race or sport: *The athlete failed a **dope test*** (=a medical test showed that he had taken such drugs). **3** [C] a stupid person: *What a dope!*

dope[2] /dəʊp/ ***verb*** [T] to give a drug secretly to a person or an animal, especially to make them sleep

dopey /ˈdəʊpi/ ***adj.*** **1** tired and not able to think clearly, especially because of drugs, alcohol or lack of sleep **2** (*informal*) stupid; not intelligent

Doric /ˈdɒrɪk/ ***adj.*** (ARCHITECTURE) used to describe the oldest style of ARCHITECTURE in ancient Greece that has thick plain columns and no decoration at the top: *a Doric column/temple* ➲ picture at **capital**

dormant /ˈdɔːmənt/ ***adj.*** not active for some time: *a dormant volcano*

ˌdormer ˈwindow (*also* **dormer**) ***noun*** [C] (ARCHITECTURE) a vertical window in a room that is built into a sloping roof

dormitory /ˈdɔːmətri/ ***noun*** [C] (*pl.* **dormitories**) (*also* **dorm**) **1** a large bedroom with a number of beds in it, especially in a school, etc. **2** (*AmE*) a building at a college or university where students live

dormouse /ˈdɔːmaʊs/ ***noun*** [C] (*pl.* **dormice** /-maɪs/) a small animal like a mouse, with a tail covered in fur

dorsal /ˈdɔːsl/ ***adj.*** (only *before* a noun) (BIOLOGY) on or connected with the back of a fish or an animal: *a shark's dorsal fin* ➲ look at **pectoral**, **ventral** ➲ picture on **page 29**

dosage /ˈdəʊsɪdʒ/ ***noun*** [C, usually sing.] (HEALTH) the amount of a medicine you should take over a period of time: *The recommended dosage is one tablet every four hours.*

dose[1] /dəʊs/ ***noun*** [C] **1** (HEALTH) an amount of medicine that you take at one time ➲ look at **overdose** **2** an amount of sth, especially sth unpleasant: *a dose of the flu* ◇ *I can only stand him in small doses.*

dose[2] /dəʊs/ ***verb*** [T] (HEALTH) to give sb/yourself a medicine or drug: *She dosed herself with aspirin and went to work.*

doss /dɒs/ ***verb*** (*BrE, slang*)

PHR V **doss about/around** to waste time not doing very much

doss down to lie down to sleep, without a proper bed: *Do you mind if I doss down on your floor tonight?*

dot[1] 🔑 /dɒt/ ***noun*** [C] **1** a small, round mark, like a full stop: *a white dress with black dots* ◇ *The letters i and j have dots above them.*

SPEAKING

We use **dot** when we say a person's email address. For the address written as **ann@smithuni.co.uk** we would say 'Ann **at** smithuni **dot** co **dot** uk'.

2 something that looks like a dot: *He watched until the aeroplane was just a dot in the sky.*
IDM **on the dot** (*informal*) at exactly the right time or at exactly the time mentioned

dot² /dɒt/ *verb* [T] (**dotting**; **dotted**) (usually passive) to mark with a dot
IDM **be dotted about/around** to be spread over an area: *There are restaurants dotted about all over the centre of town.*
be dotted with to have several things or people in or on it: *a hillside dotted with sheep*

dot-com /dɒt'kɒm/ *noun* [C] (BUSINESS) a company that sells goods and services on the Internet, especially one whose address ends '.com': *The weaker dot-coms have collapsed.* ◇ *a dot-com millionaire*

dote /dəʊt/ *verb* [I] ~ **on sb/sth** to have or show a lot of love for sb/sth and think they or it are perfect: *He's always doted on his eldest son.* ▶ **doting** *adj.*: *doting parents*

ˌ**dotted 'line** *noun* [C] a line of small round marks (**dots**) which show where sth is to be written on a form, etc.: *Sign on the dotted line.* ➲ picture at **line**

double¹ ⊶ /'dʌbl/ *adj., det.* **1** twice as much or as many (as usual): *His income is double hers.* ◇ *We'll need double the amount of wine.* **2** having two equal or similar parts: *double doors* ◇ *Does 'necessary' have (a) double 's'?* ◇ *My phone number is two four double three four* (=24334). **3** made for or used by two people or things: *a double garage*

double² ⊶ /'dʌbl/ *adv.* in twos or two parts: *When I saw her with her twin sister I thought I was* ***seeing double***.

double³ ⊶ /'dʌbl/ *noun* **1** [U] twice the (usual) number or amount: *When you work overtime, you get paid double.* **2** [C] a glass of strong alcoholic drink containing twice the usual amount **3** [C] a person who looks very much like another: *I thought it was you I saw in the supermarket. You must have a double.* **4** [C] an actor who replaces another actor in a film to do dangerous or other special things **5** [C] a bedroom for two people in a hotel, etc. ➲ look at **single²** (3) **6 doubles** [pl.] (in some sports, for example TENNIS) with two pairs playing: *the Men's Doubles final* ➲ look at **single²** (4)

double⁴ ⊶ /'dʌbl/ *verb* **1** [I,T] to become or to make sth twice as much or as many; to multiply by two: *The price of houses has almost doubled.* ◇ *Think of a number and double it.* **2** [I] ~ **(up) as sth** to have a second use or function: *The small room doubles (up) as a study.*
PHR V **double (sb) up/over** (to cause sb) to bend the body: *to be doubled up with pain/laughter*

ˌ**double-'barrelled** (*AmE* ˌ**double-'barreled**) *adj.* **1** (used about a gun) having two BARRELS (=long metal tubes through which bullets are fired) **2** (used about a family name) having two parts, sometimes joined by the mark (-) (**a hyphen**): *Mr Day-Lewis*

ˌ**double 'bass** (*also* **bass**) *noun* [C] (MUSIC) the largest musical instrument with strings, that you can play either standing up or sitting down ➲ picture on **page 465**

ˌ**double-'breasted** *adj.* (used about a coat or jacket) having two rows of buttons down the front ➲ look at **single-breasted**

ˌ**double-'check** *verb* [I,T] to check sth again, or with great care

ˌ**double 'chin** *noun* [C] fat under a person's chin that looks like another chin

ˌ**double-'click** *verb* [I,T] ~ **(on sth)** (COMPUTING) to press one of the buttons on a computer mouse twice quickly: *To run an application, just double-click on the icon.*

ˌ**double-'cross** *verb* [T] to cheat sb who believes that they can trust you after you have agreed to do sth dishonest together

ˌ**double-'decker** *noun* [C] a bus with two floors

ˌ**double 'Dutch** *noun* [U] conversation or writing that you cannot understand at all

ˌ**double 'figures** *noun* [U] a number that is more than nine: *Inflation is now* ***in double figures***.

ˌ**double 'glazing** *noun* [U] two layers of glass in a window to keep a building warm or quiet ▶ ˌ**double-'glazed** *adj.*

ˌ**double 'helix** *noun* (BIOLOGY) the structure of DNA, consisting of two connected long thin pieces that form a SPIRAL shape ➲ picture at **DNA**

doubly /'dʌbli/ *adv.* **1** in two ways: *He was doubly blessed with both good looks and talent.* **2** more than usually: *I made doubly sure that the door was locked.*

doubt¹ ⊶ /daʊt/ *noun* [C,U] ~ **(about sth)**; ~ **that ...**; ~ **as to sth** (a feeling of) UNCERTAINTY: *If you have any doubts about the job, feel free to ring me and discuss them.* ◇ *There's some doubt that Jan will pass the exam.*
IDM **cast doubt on sth** → CAST¹
give sb the benefit of the doubt → BENEFIT¹
in doubt not sure or definite
no doubt (used when you expect sth to happen but you are not sure that it will) probably: *No doubt she'll write when she has time.*
without (a) doubt definitely: *It was, without doubt, the coldest winter for many years.*

doubt² ⊶ /daʊt/ *verb* [T] to think sth is unlikely or to feel uncertain (about sth): *She never doubted that he was telling the truth.* ◇ *He had never doubted her support.*

doubtful /'daʊtfl/ *adj.* **1** unlikely or uncertain: *It's doubtful whether/if we'll finish in time.* ◇ *It was doubtful that he was still alive.* **2** ~ **(about sth/about doing sth)** (used about a person) not sure: *He still felt doubtful about his decision.* ▶ **doubtfully** /-fəli/ *adv.*: *'I suppose it'll be all right,' she said doubtfully.*

doubtless /'daʊtləs/ *adv.* almost certainly: *Doubtless she'll have a good excuse for being late!*

dough /dəʊ/ *noun* [U] **1** a mixture of flour, water, etc. used for baking into bread, etc. **2** (*informal*) money

doughnut (*AmE* **donut**) /'dəʊnʌt/ *noun* [C] a small cake in the shape of a ball or a ring, made from a sweet DOUGH cooked in very hot oil

dour /dʊə(r)/ *adj.* (used about a person's manner or expression) cold and unfriendly

douse (*also* **dowse**) /daʊs/ *verb* [T] **1** ~ **sth (with sth)** to stop a fire from burning by pouring liquid over it: *The firefighters managed to douse the flames.* **2** ~ **sb/sth (in/with sth)** to cover sb/sth with liquid: *to douse yourself in perfume* (=wear too much of it)

dove¹ /dʌv/ *noun* [C] a type of white bird, often used as a sign of peace

dove² /dəʊv/ (*AmE*) past tense of **dive¹**

dovetail¹ /'dʌvteɪl/ *verb* [I,T] (*formal*) ~ **(sth) (with/into sth)** if two things **dovetail** or if one thing **dovetails** with another, they fit together well

dovetail

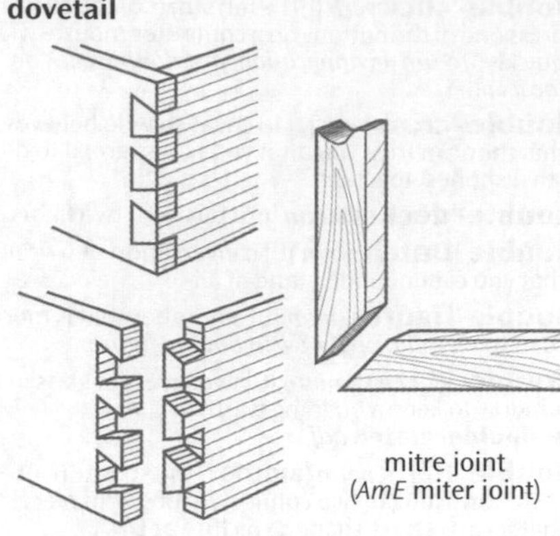

dovetail² /ˈdʌvteɪl/ ***noun*** [C] (*also* ˌ**dovetail ˈjoint**) a joint for fixing two pieces of wood together

dowdy /ˈdaʊdi/ ***adj.*** (used about a person or the clothes they wear) not attractive or fashionable

Dow Jones Index /ˌdaʊ ˈdʒəʊnz ɪndeks/ (*also* ˌ**Dow ˈJones average**; **the ˈDow**) ***noun*** [sing.] (BUSINESS) a list of the share prices of 30 US industrial companies that can be used to compare the prices to previous levels

down¹ /daʊn/ ***adv., prep.*** **1** to or at a lower level or place; from the top towards the bottom of sth: *Can you get that book down from the top shelf?* ◇ *'Where's Mary?' 'She's down in the basement.'* ◇ *Her hair hung down her back.* ◇ *The rain was running down the window.* **2** along: *We sailed down the river towards the sea.* ◇ *'Where's the nearest garage?' 'Go down this road and take the first turning on the right.'* **3** from a standing or vertical position to a sitting or horizontal one: *I think I'll sit/lie down.* **4** to or in the south: *We went down to Devon for our holiday.* **5** used for showing that the level, amount, strength, etc. of sth is less or lower: *Do you mind if I turn the heating down a bit?* **6** (written) on paper: *Put these dates down in your diary.* **7** ~ **to sb/sth** even including: *We had everything planned down to the last detail.*

IDM **be down to sb** to be sb's responsibility: *When my father died it was down to me to look after the family's affairs.*

be down to sth to have only the amount mentioned left: *I need to do some washing – I'm down to my last shirt.*

down and out having no money, job or home

down under (*informal*) (in) Australia

down² /daʊn/ ***verb*** [T] (*informal*) to finish a drink quickly: *She* ***downed*** *her drink* ***in one*** (=she drank the whole glass without stopping).

down³ /daʊn/ ***adj.*** **1** sad: *You're looking a bit down today.* **2** lower than before: *Unemployment figures are down again this month.* **3** (used about computers) not working: *I can't access the file as our computers have been down all morning.*

down⁴ /daʊn/ ***noun*** [U] very soft feathers: *a duvet filled with duck down*

IDM **ups and downs** → UP²

ˈ**down-and-out** ***noun*** [C] a person who has got no money, job or home

downcast /ˈdaʊnkɑːst/ ***adj.*** **1** (used about a person) sad and without hope **2** (used about eyes) looking down

downfall /ˈdaʊnfɔːl/ ***noun*** [sing.] a loss of a person's money, power, social position, etc.; the thing that causes this: *The government's downfall seemed inevitable.* ◇ *Greed was her downfall.*

downgrade /ˌdaʊnˈgreɪd/ ***verb*** [T] ~ **sb/sth (from sth) (to sth)** to reduce sb/sth to a lower level or position of importance: *Tom's been downgraded from manager to assistant manager.*

downhearted /ˌdaʊnˈhɑːtɪd/ ***adj.*** sad

downhill /ˌdaʊnˈhɪl/ ***adj., adv.*** (going) in a downward direction; towards the bottom of a hill: *It's an easy walk. The road runs downhill most of the way.* OPP **uphill**

IDM **go downhill** to get worse: *Their relationship has been going downhill for some time now.*

download¹ /ˌdaʊnˈləʊd/ ***verb*** [T] (COMPUTING) to copy a computer file, etc. from a large computer system to a smaller one OPP **upload¹** ▶ **downloadable** /-əbl/ ***adj.***

download² /ˈdaʊnləʊd/ ***noun*** (COMPUTING) **1** [U] the act or process of copying data from a large computer system to a smaller one **2** [C] a computer file that is copied from a large computer system to a smaller one: *It's one of the most popular free software downloads.* ➲ look at **upload²**

downmarket /ˌdaʊnˈmɑːkɪt/ ***adj., adv.*** cheap and of low quality

downpour /ˈdaʊnpɔː(r)/ ***noun*** [C] a heavy, sudden fall of rain

downright /ˈdaʊnraɪt/ ***adj.*** (only *before* a noun) (used about sth bad or unpleasant) complete: *The holiday was a downright disaster.* ▶ **downright** ***adv.***: *The way he spoke to me was downright rude!*

downside /ˈdaʊnsaɪd/ ***noun*** [C, usually sing.] the disadvantages or negative aspects of sth: *All good ideas have a downside.*

downsize /ˈdaʊnsaɪz/ ***verb*** [I,T] (BUSINESS) to reduce the number of people who work in a company, business, etc. in order to reduce costs ▶ **downsizing** ***noun*** [U]

Down's syndrome /ˈdaʊnz sɪndrəʊm/ ***noun*** [U] (HEALTH) a condition that some people are born with. People with this condition have a flat, wide face and lower than average intelligence.

downstairs /ˌdaʊnˈsteəz/ ***adv., adj.*** towards or on a lower floor of a house or building: *He fell downstairs and broke his arm.* ◇ *Dad's downstairs, in the kitchen.* ◇ *a downstairs toilet* OPP **upstairs**

downstream /ˌdaʊnˈstriːm/ ***adv., adj.*** in the direction in which a river flows: *We were rowing downstream.* OPP **upstream**

ˌ**down-to-ˈearth** ***adj.*** (used about a person) sensible, realistic and practical

downtown /ˌdaʊnˈtaʊn/ ***adv., adj.*** (*especially AmE*) in or towards the centre of a city, especially its main business area: *to go/work downtown*

downtrodden /ˈdaʊntrɒdn/ ***adj.*** (used about a person) made to suffer bad treatment or living conditions by people in power, but being too tired, poor, ill, etc. to change this

downturn /ˈdaʊntɜːn/ ***noun*** [C, usually sing.] **a ~ (in sth)** (ECONOMICS) a drop in the amount of business that is done; a time when the economy becomes weaker: *a downturn in sales/trade/business* OPP **upturn**

downward ⚿ /ˈdaʊnwəd/ ***adj.*** (only *before* a noun) towards the ground or a lower level: *a downward movement*

downwards ⚿ /ˈdaʊnwədz/ (*also especially AmE* **downward**) ***adv.*** towards the ground or towards a lower level: *She was lying* ***face downwards*** *on the grass.* ◇ *The garden sloped gently downwards to the river.* ◇ *It was a policy welcomed by world leaders from the US president downwards.* OPP **upward(s)**

dowry /ˈdaʊri/ ***noun*** [C] (*pl.* **dowries**) an amount of money or property which, in some countries, a woman's family gives to the man she is marrying

dowse = DOUSE

doz. ***abbr.*** dozen

doze /dəʊz/ ***verb*** [I] to sleep lightly and/or for a short time: *He was dozing in front of the television.* ▶ **doze** ***noun*** [sing.]

PHR V **doze off** to go to sleep, especially during the day: *I'm sorry – I must have dozed off for a minute.*

dozen ⚿ /ˈdʌzn/ (*abbr.* **doz.**) ***noun*** [C] (*pl.* **dozen**) twelve or a group of twelve: *A dozen eggs, please.* ◇ *half a dozen* (=six) ◇ *two dozen sheep*

IDM **dozens (of sth)** (*informal*) very many: *I've tried phoning her dozens of times.*

dozy /ˈdəʊzi/ ***adj.*** **1** wanting to sleep; not feeling awake **2** (*BrE, informal*) stupid: not intelligent: *You dozy thing – look what you've done!*

DPhil /ˌdiː ˈfɪl/ ***abbr.*** (*BrE*) (EDUCATION) Doctor of Philosophy; an advanced university degree that you receive when you complete a piece of research into a special subject SYN **PhD**

Dr ***abbr.*** doctor: *Dr John Waters*

drab /dræb/ ***adj.*** not interesting or attractive: *a drab grey office building*

draft[1] ⚿ AW /drɑːft/ ***noun*** [C] **1** a piece of writing, etc. which will probably be changed and improved; not the final version: *the first draft of a speech/essay* **2** a written order to a bank to pay money to sb: *Payment must be made* ***by bank draft***. **3** (*AmE*) = DRAUGHT[1] (1)

draft[2] ⚿ AW /drɑːft/ ***verb*** [T] **1** to make a first or early copy of a piece of writing: *I'll draft a letter and show it to you before I type it.* **2** (*AmE*) (usually passive) to force sb to join the armed forces: *He was drafted into the army.*

draftsman (*AmE*) = DRAUGHTSMAN

drafty (*AmE*) = DRAUGHTY

drag[1] ⚿ /dræg/ ***verb*** (**dragging**; **dragged**) **1** [T] to pull sb/sth along with difficulty: *The box was so heavy we had to drag it along the floor.* **2** [T] to make sb come or go somewhere: *She's always trying to drag me along to museums and galleries, but I'm not interested.* **3** [I] ~ (**on**) to be boring or to seem to last a long time: *The speeches dragged on for hours.* **4** [T] (COMPUTING) to move sth across the screen of the computer using the mouse: *Click on the file and drag it into the new folder.*

PHR V **drag sth out** to make sth last longer than necessary: *Let's not drag this decision out – shall we go or not?*

drag sth out (of sb) to force or persuade sb to give you information

drag[2] /dræg/ ***noun*** **1** [sing.] (*informal*) a person or thing that is boring or annoying: *'The car's broken down.' 'Oh no! What a drag!'* **2** [U] women's clothes worn by a man, especially as part of a show, etc.: *men in drag* **3** [C] an act of breathing in cigarette smoke: *He took a long drag on his cigarette.* **4** [U] (PHYSICS) the force of the air that acts against the movement of an aircraft or other vehicle

ˌdrag-and-ˈdrop ***adj.*** (COMPUTING) relating to the moving of items across a computer screen using the mouse

dragon /ˈdrægən/ ***noun*** [C] (in stories) a large animal with wings, which can breathe fire

dragonfly /ˈdrægənflaɪ/ ***noun*** [C] (*pl.* **dragonflies**) an insect with a long thin body, often brightly coloured, and two pairs of large wings. **Dragonflies** often live near water. ➲ picture on **page 29**

drain[1] /dreɪn/ ***noun*** [C] a pipe or hole in the ground that dirty water, etc. goes down to be carried away

IDM **a drain on sb/sth** something that uses up time, money, strength, etc.: *The cost of travelling is a great drain on our budget.*

(go) down the drain (*informal*) (to be) wasted: *All that hard work has gone down the drain.*

drain[2] /dreɪn/ ***verb*** **1** [I,T] to become empty or dry as liquid flows away and disappears; to make sth dry or empty in this way: *The whole area will have to be drained before it can be used for farming.* ◇ *Drain the pasta and add the sauce.* **2** [I,T] ~ **(sth) (from/out of sth)**; ~ **(sth) (away/off)** to flow away; to make a liquid flow away: *The sink's blocked – the water won't drain away at all.* ◇ *The plumber had to drain the water from the heating system.* ◇ (*figurative*) *He felt all his anger begin to drain away.* **3** [T] to drink all the liquid in a glass, cup, etc.: *He drained his glass in one gulp.* **4** [T] ~ **sb/sth (of sth)** to make sb/sth weaker, poorer, etc. by slowly using all the strength, money, etc. available: *My mother's hospital expenses were slowly draining my funds.* ◇ *The experience left her* ***emotionally drained***.

drainage /ˈdreɪnɪdʒ/ ***noun*** [U] a system used for making water, etc. flow away from a place

ˈdraining board ***noun*** [C] the place in the kitchen where you put plates, cups, knives, etc. to dry after washing them

drainpipe /ˈdreɪnpaɪp/ ***noun*** [C] a pipe which goes down the side of a building and carries water from the roof into a hole in the ground (**drain**)

drama ⚿ AW /ˈdrɑːmə/ ***noun*** **1** [C] a play for the theatre, radio or television **2** [U] (LITERATURE) plays as a form of writing; the performance of plays: *He wrote some drama, as well as poetry.* **3** [C,U] an exciting event; exciting things that happen: *a real-life courtroom drama*

dramatic ⚿ AW /drəˈmætɪk/ ***adj.***

1 noticeable or sudden and often surprising: *a dramatic change/increase/fall/improvement*

2 exciting or impressive: *The film's dramatic opening scene* **3** (ARTS AND MEDIA) connected with plays or the theatre: *Shakespeare's dramatic works* **4** (used about a person, a person's behaviour, etc.) showing feelings, etc. in a very obvious way because you want other people to notice you: *Calm down. There's no need to be so dramatic about everything!* ▶ **dramatically** /-kli/ ***adv.***

dramatist AW /ˈdræmətɪst/ ***noun*** [C] (ARTS AND MEDIA) a person who writes plays for the theatre, radio or television

dramatize (also -ise) AW /ˈdræmətaɪz/ ***verb*** **1** [T] (ARTS AND MEDIA) to make a book, an event, etc. into a play: *The novel has been dramatized for television.* **2** [I,T] to make sth seem more exciting or important than it really is: *The newspaper was accused of dramatizing the situation.* ▶ **dramatization** (also **-isation**) /ˌdræmətaɪˈzeɪʃn/ ***noun*** [C,U]

drank past tense of **drink**[1]

drape /dreɪp/ ***verb*** [T] **1 ~ sth round/over sth** to put a piece of material, clothing, etc. loosely on sth: *He draped his coat over the back of his chair.* **2 ~ sb/sth (in/with sth)** (usually passive) to cover sb/sth (with cloth, etc.): *The furniture was draped in dust sheets.* ▶ **drape *noun*** [C] (*AmE*) = CURTAIN

drastic /ˈdræstɪk/ ***adj.*** extreme, and having a sudden very strong effect: *There has been a drastic rise in crime in the area.* ▶ **drastically** /-kli/ ***adv.***

draught[1] /drɑːft/ ***noun*** **1** (*AmE* **draft**) [C] a flow of cold air that comes into a room: *Can you shut the door? There's a draught in here.* **2 draughts** (*AmE* **checkers**) [U] a game for two players that you play on a black and white board using round black and white pieces ▶ **draughty *adj.***

draught[2] (*AmE* **draft**) /drɑːft/ ***adj.*** (used about beer, etc.) served from a BARREL (= a large container) rather than in a bottle: *draught beer*

draughtsman (*AmE* **draftsman** /ˈdrɑːftsmən/) ***noun*** [C] (*pl.* **-men** /-mən/) a person whose job is to do technical drawings

draw[1] ⊶ /drɔː/ ***verb*** (*pt* **drew** /druː/; *pp* **drawn** /drɔːn/) **1** [I,T] to do a picture or diagram of sth with a pencil, pen, etc. but not paint: *Shall I draw you a map of how to get there?* ◇ *I'm good at painting but I can't draw.* **2** [I] to move in the direction mentioned: *The train drew into the station* ◇ (*figurative*) *I became more anxious as my exams drew nearer.* **3** [T] to pull sth/sb into a new position or in the direction mentioned: *She drew the letter out of her pocket and handed it to me.* ◇ *to draw* (= open or close) *the curtains* ◇ *He drew me by the hand into the room.* **4** [T] **~ sth (from sth)** to learn or decide sth as a result of study, research or experience: *Can we **draw** any **conclusions** from this survey?* ◇ *There are important **lessons to be drawn** from this tragedy.* **5** [T] **~ sth (from sb/sth)** to get or take sth from sb/sth: *He draws the inspiration for his stories from his family.* **6** [T] **~ sth (from sb); ~ sb (to sb/sth)** to make sb react to or be interested in sb/sth: *The advertisement has drawn criticism from people all over the country.* ◇ *The musicians drew quite a large crowd.* **7** [I,T] to finish a game, competition, etc. with equal scores so that neither person or team wins: *The two teams drew.* ◇ *The match was drawn.*

IDM **bring sth/come/draw to an end** → END[1]

draw (sb's) attention to sth to make sb notice sth: *The article draws attention to the problem of homelessness.*

draw a blank to get no result or response: *Detectives investigating the case have drawn a blank so far.*

draw a distinction between sth and sth to show how two things are different

draw the line at sth to say 'no' to sth even though you are happy to help in other ways: *I do most of the cooking but I draw the line at washing up as well!*

draw lots to decide sth by chance: *They drew lots to see who should stay behind.*

PHR V **draw in** to become dark earlier in the evening as winter gets nearer: *The **days/nights** are drawing in.*

draw out to become lighter in the evening as summer gets nearer: *The **days/evenings** are drawing out.*

draw sth out to take money out of a bank account

draw up (used about a car, etc.) to drive up and stop in front of or near sth: *A police car drew up outside the building.*

draw sth up to prepare and write a document, list, etc.: *Our solicitor is going to draw up the contract.*

draw[2] /drɔː/ ***noun*** [C] **1** a result of a game or competition in which both players or teams get the same score so that neither of them wins: *The match **ended in a draw**.* **2** an act of deciding sth by chance by pulling out names or numbers from a bag, etc.: *She won her bike in a prize draw.*

drawback /ˈdrɔːbæk/ ***noun*** [C] a disadvantage or problem: *His lack of experience is a major drawback.*

drawbridge /ˈdrɔːbrɪdʒ/ ***noun*** [C] a bridge that can be pulled up, for example to stop people from entering a castle or to allow ships to pass under it: *to raise/lower a drawbridge*

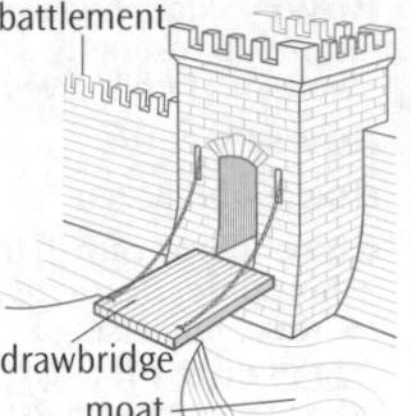

drawer ⊶ /drɔː(r)/ ***noun*** [C] a container which forms part of a piece of furniture such as a desk, that you can pull out to put things in: *There's some paper in the top drawer of my desk.*

drawing ⊶ /ˈdrɔːɪŋ/ ***noun*** (ART) **1** [C] a picture made with a pencil, pen, etc. but not paint ➲ note at **painting 2** [U] the art of drawing pictures: *She's good at drawing and painting.*

ˈdrawing pin (*AmE* **thumbtack**) ***noun*** [C] a short pin with a flat top, used for fastening paper, etc. to a board or wall

ˈdrawing room *noun* [C] (*old-fashioned*) a living room, especially in a large house

drawl /drɔːl/ ***verb*** [I,T] to speak slowly, making the VOWEL sounds very long ▶ **drawl *noun*** [sing.]: *to speak with a drawl*

drawn[1] past participle of **draw**[1]

drawn[2] /drɔːn/ ***adj.*** (used about a person or their face) looking tired, worried or ill

ˌdrawn-ˈout *adj.* lasting longer than necessary: *long drawn-out negotiations*

drawstring /ˈdrɔːstrɪŋ/ ***noun*** [C] a piece of string that is sewn inside the material at the top of a bag, pair of trousers, etc. that can be pulled tighter in order to make the opening smaller: *The trousers fasten with a drawstring.*

dread[1] /dred/ ***verb*** [T] to be very afraid of or worried about sth: *I'm dreading the exams.* ◇ *She dreaded having to tell him what had happened.* ◇ *I **dread to think** what my father will say.* ▶ **dreaded *adj.***

dread[2] /dred/ ***noun*** [U, sing.] great fear: *He lived **in dread of** the same thing happening to him one day.*

dreadful /ˈdredfl/ ***adj.*** very bad or unpleasant: *We had a dreadful journey – traffic jams all the way!* ◇ *I'm afraid there's been a dreadful* (= very serious) *mistake.*

dreadfully /ˈdredfəli/ ***adv.*** **1** very; extremely: *I'm dreadfully sorry, I didn't mean to upset you.* **2** very badly: *The party went dreadfully and everyone left early.*

dreadlocks /ˈdredlɒks/ ***noun*** [pl.] hair worn in long thick pieces, especially by some black people

dream[1] ⊶ /driːm/ ***noun*** **1** [C] a series of events or pictures which happen in your mind while you are asleep: *I **had** a strange **dream** last night.* ◇ *That horror film has given me **bad dreams**.* ➲ look at **nightmare 2** [C] something that you want very much to happen, although it is not likely: *His dream was to give up his job and live in the country.* ◇ *My dream* *house would have a huge garden and a swimming pool.* ◇ *Becoming a professional dancer was* ***a dream come true*** *for Nicola.* **3** [sing.] a state of mind in which you are not thinking about what you are doing: *You've been in a dream all morning!*

dream² ⊶ /dri:m/ ***verb*** (*pt, pp* **dreamed** /dri:md/ or **dreamt** /dremt/) **1** [I,T] ~ **(about sb/sth)** to see or experience pictures and events in your mind while you are asleep: *I dreamt about the house that I lived in as a child.* ◇ *I dreamed that I was running but I couldn't get away.* ➲ look at **daydream** **2** [I] ~ **(about/of sth/doing sth)** to imagine sth that you would like to happen: *I've always dreamt about winning lots of money.* **3** [I] ~ **(of doing sth/that...)** to imagine that sth might happen: ***I wouldn't dream of*** *telling Stuart that I don't like his music.* ◇ *When I watched the Olympics on TV, I* ***never dreamt*** *that one day I'd be here competing!*

PHR V **dream sth up** (*informal*) to think of a plan, an idea, etc., especially sth strange

dreamer /'dri:mə(r)/ ***noun*** [C] a person who thinks a lot about ideas, plans, etc. which may never happen instead of thinking about real life

dreamlike /'dri:mlaɪk/ ***adj.*** as if existing or happening in a dream

dreamy /'dri:mi/ ***adj.*** looking as though you are not paying attention to what you are doing because you are thinking about sth else: *a dreamy look/expression* ▸ **dreamily *adv.***

dreary /'drɪəri/ ***adj.*** (**drearier**; **dreariest**) not at all interesting or attractive; boring

dredge /dredʒ/ ***verb*** [T] to clear the mud, etc. from the bottom of a river, CANAL, etc. using a special machine

PHR V **dredge sth up** to mention sth unpleasant from the past that sb would like to forget: *The newspaper had dredged up all sorts of embarrassing details about her private life.*

dredger /'dredʒə(r)/ ***noun*** [C] a boat or machine that is used to clear mud, etc. from the bottom of a river, or to make the river wider

dregs /dregz/ ***noun*** [pl.] **1** the last drops in a container of liquid, containing small pieces of solid waste **2** the worst and most useless part of sth: *These people were regarded as the dregs of society.*

drench /drentʃ/ ***verb*** [T] (usually passive) to make sb/sth completely wet: *Don't go out while it's raining so hard or you'll* ***get drenched****.*

dress¹ ⊶ /dres/ ***noun*** **1** [C] a piece of clothing worn by a girl or a woman. It covers the body from the shoulders to the knees or below. **2** [U] clothes for either men or women: *formal/casual dress* ◇ *He was wearing Bulgarian national dress.*

dress² ⊶ /dres/ ***verb*** **1** [I,T] to put clothes on sb or yourself: *He dressed quickly and left the house.* ◇ *Get up and* ***get dressed****!* ◇ *My husband dressed the children while I got breakfast ready.* ◇ *Hurry up, Simon! Aren't you dressed yet?* OPP **undress** **2** [I] to put or have clothes on, in the way or style mentioned: *to dress well/badly/casually* ◇ *to be well dressed/badly dressed/casually dressed* **3** [T] to put a clean covering on the place on sb's body where they have been hurt: *to dress a wound*

IDM **(be) dressed in sth** wearing sth: *The people at the funeral were all dressed in black.*

PHR V **dress up** **1** to put on special clothes, especially in order to look like sb/sth else: *The children decided to dress up* ***as*** *pirates.* **2** to put on formal clothes, usually for a special occasion: *You don't need to dress up for the party.*

ˌdress 'circle (*AmE* **ˌfirst 'balcony**) ***noun*** [C] (ARTS AND MEDIA) the first level of seats above the ground floor in a theatre

dresser /'dresə(r)/ ***noun*** [C] (*especially BrE*) a piece of furniture with cupboards at the bottom and shelves above. It is used for holding dishes, cups, etc.

dressing /'dresɪŋ/ ***noun*** **1** [C] a covering that you put on a part of sb's body that has been hurt to protect it and keep it clean **2** [C,U] a sauce for food, especially for salads

'dressing gown (*also* **bathrobe** *AmE* **robe**) ***noun*** [C] a piece of clothing like a loose coat with a belt, which you wear before or after a bath, before you get dressed in the morning, etc.

'dressing room ***noun*** [C] a room for changing your clothes in, especially one for actors or, in British English, for sports players

'dressing table ***noun*** [C] a piece of furniture in a bedroom, which has drawers and a mirror

drew past tense of **draw¹**

dribble /'drɪbl/ ***verb*** **1** [I,T] (used about a liquid) to move downwards in a thin flow; to make a liquid move in this way: *The paint dribbled down the side of the pot.* **2** [I] to allow liquid (**saliva**) to run out of the mouth: *Small children often dribble.* **3** [I] (used in ball games) to make a ball move forward by using many short kicks or hits: *He dribbled round the goalkeeper and scored.*

dried¹ past tense, past participle of **dry²**

dried² /draɪd/ ***adj.*** (used about food) with all the liquid removed from it: *dried milk* ◇ *dried fruit*

drier¹ ***adj.*** → DRY¹

drier² (also **dryer**) /'draɪə(r)/ ***noun*** [C] a machine that you use for drying sth: *a hairdrier*

drift¹ /drɪft/ ***verb*** [I] **1** to be carried or moved along by wind or water: *The boat drifted out to sea.* **2** to move slowly or without any particular purpose: *He drifted from room to room.* ◇ *She drifted into acting almost by accident.* **3** (used about snow or sand) to be moved into piles by wind or water: *The snow drifted up to two metres deep in some places.*

PHR V **drift apart** to slowly become less close or friendly with sb

drift² /drɪft/ ***noun*** **1** [C] a slow movement towards sth: *the country's drift into economic decline* **2** [sing.] the general meaning of sth: *I don't understand all the details of the plan but I* ***get the drift****.* **3** [C] a pile of snow or sand that was made by wind or water

drill¹ /drɪl/ ***noun*** **1** [C] a tool or machine that is used for making holes in things: *a dentist's drill* ➲ picture at **tool** **2** [U] exercise in marching, etc. that soldiers do **3** [C] (EDUCATION) something that you repeat many times in order to learn sth **4** [C,U] practice for what you should do in an emergency: *a fire drill*

drill² /drɪl/ ***verb*** **1** [I,T] to make a hole in sth with a **drill**: *to drill a hole in sth* ◇ *to drill for oil* **2** [T] (EDUCATION) to teach sb by making them repeat sth many times

drily (also **dryly**) /'draɪli/ ***adv.*** (used about the way sb says sth) in an amusing way that sounds serious: *'I can hardly contain my excitement,' Peter said drily* (= he was not excited at all).

drink¹ ⊶ /drɪŋk/ ***verb*** (*pt* **drank** /dræŋk/; *pp* **drunk** /drʌŋk/) **1** [I,T] to take liquid into your body through your mouth: *Would you like anything to drink?* ◇ *We sat drinking coffee and chatting for hours.* **2** [I,T] to drink alcohol: *I never* ***drink and drive*** *so I'll have an orange juice.* ◇ *What do you drink – beer or*

wine? ◇ *Her father used to* ***drink heavily*** *but he's teetotal now.*
PHR V **drink to sb/sth** to wish sb/sth good luck by holding your glass up in the air before you drink: *We all drank to the future of the bride and groom.* ➲ look at **toast**[2]
drink (sth) up to finish drinking sth: *Drink up your tea – it's getting cold.*

drink[2] 🗝 /drɪŋk/ ***noun*** [C,U] **1** liquid for drinking: *Can I* ***have a drink*** *please?* ◇ *a drink of milk* ◇ *soft drinks* (=cold drinks without alcohol) **2** alcoholic drink: *He's got a drink problem.* ◇ *Shall we* ***go for a drink****?*

ˌ**drink-'driver** (*especially AmE* ˌ**drunk-'driver**) ***noun*** [C] a person who drives after drinking too much alcohol ▸ ˌ**drink-'driving *noun*** [U]: *He was convicted of drink-driving and was banned for two years.*

ˌ**drink-'driving** (*BrE also* ˌ**drunken 'driving**, *AmE* **'drunk driving**) ***noun*** [U] driving a vehicle after drinking too much alcohol

drinker /'drɪŋkə(r)/ ***noun*** [C] a person who drinks a lot of sth, especially alcohol: *a heavy drinker* ◇ *I'm not a big coffee drinker.*

drinking /'drɪŋkɪŋ/ ***noun*** [U] drinking alcohol: *Her drinking became a problem.*

'**drinking water *noun*** [U] water that is safe to drink

drip[1] /drɪp/ ***verb*** (**dripping**; **dripped**) **1** [I] (used about a liquid) to fall in small drops: *Water was dripping down through the roof.* **2** [I,T] to produce drops of liquid: *The tap is dripping.* ◇ *Her finger was dripping blood.*

drip[2] /drɪp/ ***noun*** **1** [sing.] the act or sound of water dripping **2** [C] a drop of water that falls down from sb/sth: *We put a bucket under the hole in the roof to catch the drips.* **3** (*AmE* **IV**) [C] (HEALTH) a piece of medical equipment, like a tube, that is used for putting liquid food or medicine straight into a person's blood: *She's* ***on a drip****.*

drive[1] 🗝 /draɪv/ ***verb*** (*pt* **drove** /drəʊv/; *pp* **driven** /'drɪvn/) **1** [I,T] to control or operate a car, train, bus, etc.: *Can you drive?* ◇ *to drive a car/train/bus/lorry* **2** [I,T] to go or take sb somewhere in a car, etc.: *I usually drive to work.* ◇ *We drove Aisha to the airport.* **3** [T] to force people or animals to move in a particular direction: *The dogs drove the sheep into the field.* **4** [T] to force sth into a particular position by hitting it: *to drive a post into the ground* **5** [T] to cause sb to be in a particular state or to do sth: *His constant stupid questions* ***drive me mad****.* ◇ *to drive sb to despair* **6** [T] to make sb/sth work very hard: *You shouldn't drive yourself so hard.* **7** [T] to make a machine work, by giving it power: *What drives the wheels in this engine?*
IDM **be driving at** (*informal*) to want to say sth; to mean: *I'm afraid I don't understand what you are driving at.*
drive sth home (to sb) to make sth clear so that people understand it
PHR V **drive off** (used about a car, driver, etc.) to leave
drive sb/sth off to make sb/sth go away

drive[2] 🗝 /draɪv/ ***noun*** **1** [C] a journey in a car: *The supermarket is only a five-minute drive away.* ◇ *Let's* ***go for a drive****.* **2** [C] a wide path or short road that leads to the door of a house: *We keep our car on the drive.* **3** [C] a street, usually where people live: *They live at 23 Woodlands Drive.* **4** [C] a big effort by a group of people in order to achieve sth: *The company is launching a big sales drive.* ➲ note at **campaign**[1] **5** [U] the energy and determination you need to succeed in doing sth: *You need lots of drive to run your own company.* **6** [C,U] a strong natural need or desire: *a strong sex drive* **7** [C] (SPORT) a long hard hit: *This player has the longest drive in golf.* **8** [C] (COMPUTING) the part of a computer that reads and stores information: *a 224 MB hard drive* ◇ *a CD drive* ➲ look at **disk drive** **9** [U] the equipment in a vehicle that takes power from the engine to the wheels: *a car with four-wheel drive*

'**drive-by** ***adj.*** (*AmE*) (only *before* a noun) (used about a shooting) done from a moving car: *drive-by killings*

'**drive-in** ***noun*** [C] (*AmE*) a place where you can eat, watch a film, etc. in your car

driven[1] past participle of **drive**[1]

driven[2] /'drɪvn/ ***adj.*** **1** determined to succeed, and working very hard to do so **2 -driven** (in compounds) influenced or caused by a particular thing: *a market-driven economy*

driver 🗝 /'draɪvə(r)/ ***noun*** [C] a person who drives a vehicle: *a bus/train driver*

'**drive-through** ***noun*** [C] (*especially AmE*) a restaurant, bank, etc. where you can be served without getting out of your car

driving[1] 🗝 /'draɪvɪŋ/ ***noun*** [U] the action or skill of controlling a car, etc.: *She was arrested for dangerous driving.* ◇ *Joe's having* ***driving lessons****.* ◇ *She works as a* ***driving instructor****.* ◇ *a* ***driving school***
IDM **be in the driving seat** → SEAT[1]

driving[2] /'draɪvɪŋ/ ***adj.*** very strong: *driving rain* ◇ *driving ambition* ◇ *Who's the driving force behind this plan?*

'**driving licence** (*AmE* **'driver's license**) ***noun*** [C] an official document that shows that you are qualified to drive

'**driving test** (*AmE also* **'driver's test**) ***noun*** [C] a test that you must pass before you are qualified to drive a car, etc.: *Did you pass your driving test first time?*

ˌ**driving under the 'influence *noun*** [U] (*abbr.* **DUI**) (*AmE*) (LAW) (in some states in the US) the crime of driving a vehicle after drinking too much alcohol. It is a less serious crime than DRIVING WHILE INTOXICATED.

ˌ**driving while in'toxicated *noun*** [U] (*abbr.* **DWI**) (*AmE*) (LAW) the crime of driving a vehicle after drinking too much alcohol

drizzle /'drɪzl/ ***noun*** [U] light rain with very small drops ▸ **drizzle *verb*** [I] ➲ note at **weather**

dromedary /'drɒmədəri/ ***noun*** [C] (*pl.* **dromedaries**) an animal that lives in the desert and has a long neck and a large mass of fat (**hump**) on its back. A **dromedary** is a type of CAMEL.

drone[1] /drəʊn/ ***verb*** [I] to make a continuous low sound: *the sound of the tractors droning away in the fields*
PHR V **drone on** to talk in a flat or boring voice: *We had to listen to the chairman drone on about sales for hours.*

drone[2] /drəʊn/ ***noun*** [C, usually sing.] **1** a continuous low noise: *the distant drone of traffic* **2** (MUSIC) a continuous low sound made by some musical instruments, for example the BAGPIPES, over which other notes are played or sung; the part of the instrument that makes this noise

drool /druːl/ *verb* [I] **1** to let liquid (**saliva**) come out from the mouth, usually at the sight or smell of sth good to eat **2** ~ **(over sb/sth)** to show in a silly or exaggerated way that you want or admire sb/sth very much: *teenagers drooling over photographs of their favourite pop stars*

droop /druːp/ *verb* [I] to bend or hang downwards, especially because of weakness or because you are tired: *The flowers were drooping without water.*
▶ **drooping** *adj.*: *a drooping moustache*

drop[1] /drɒp/ *verb* (**dropping**; **dropped**) **1** [T] to let sth fall: *That vase was very expensive. Whatever you do, don't drop it!* **2** [I] to fall: *The parachutist dropped safely to the ground.* ◇ *At the end of the race she dropped to her knees exhausted.* **3** [I,T] to become lower; to make sth lower: *The temperature will drop to minus 3 overnight.* ◇ *They ought to drop their prices.* ◇ *to drop your voice* (=speak more quietly) ➲ note at **fall[1]** **4** [T] ~ **sb/sth (off)** to stop your car, etc. so that sb can get out, or in order to take sth out: *Drop me off at the traffic lights, please.* ◇ *I'll drop the parcel at your house.* **5** [T] ~ **sb/sth (from sth)** to no longer include sb/sth in sth: *Joe has been dropped from the team.* **6** [T] to stop doing sth: *I'm going to drop geography next term* (=stop studying it).
IDM **drop dead** (*informal*) to die suddenly
drop sb a line (*informal*) to write a letter to sb
PHR V **drop back; drop behind (sb)** to move into a position behind sb else, because you are moving more slowly: *Towards the end of the race she dropped behind the other runners.*
drop by; drop in (on sb) to go to sb's house on an informal visit or without having told them you were coming
drop off (*informal*) to fall into a light sleep: *I dropped off in front of the television.*
drop out (of sth) to leave or stop doing sth before you have finished: *His injury forced him to drop out of the competition.*

drop[2] /drɒp/ *noun* **1** [C] a very small amount of liquid that forms a round shape: *a drop of blood/rain* **2** [C, usually sing.] a small amount of liquid: *I just have a drop of milk in my coffee.* **3** [sing.] a fall to a smaller amount or level: *The job is much more interesting but it will mean a drop in salary.* ◇ *a drop in prices/temperature* **4** [sing.] a distance down from a high point to a lower point: *a sheer drop of 40 metres to the sea* **5 drops** [pl.] (HEALTH) liquid medicine that you put into your eyes, ears or nose: *The doctor prescribed me drops to take twice a day.*
IDM **a drop in the ocean**; (*AmE*) **a drop in the bucket** an amount of sth that is too small or unimportant to make any real difference to a situation
at the drop of a hat immediately; without having to stop and think about it

ˈdrop-dead *adv.* (*informal*) used before an adjective to emphasize how attractive sb/sth is: *She's drop-dead gorgeous.*

ˌdrop-down ˈmenu *noun* [C] (*also* **ˌpull-down ˈmenu**) (COMPUTING) a list of choices which appears on a computer screen and stays there until you choose one of the functions on it

droplet /ˈdrɒplət/ *noun* [C] a small amount of a liquid that forms a round shape

ˈdrop-off *noun* [C] (TOURISM) a place where vehicles can stop for people to get out, or where sth can be left; the action of doing this: *It is easier to get a taxi at passenger* ***drop-off points*** *than at flight arrival stands.*

dropout /ˈdrɒpaʊt/ *noun* [C] **1** (EDUCATION) a person who leaves school, university, etc. before finishing their studies **2** (SOCIAL STUDIES) a person who does not accept the ideas and ways of behaving of the rest of society

dropper /ˈdrɒpə(r)/ *noun* [C] (CHEMISTRY) a short glass tube that has a rubber end with air in it. A dropper is used for measuring drops of liquids, especially medicines. ➲ picture at **laboratory**

droppings /ˈdrɒpɪŋz/ *noun* [pl.] waste material from the bodies of small animals or birds

drought /draʊt/ *noun* [C,U] a long period without rain

drove past tense of **drive[1]**

drown /draʊn/ *verb* **1** [I,T] to die in water because it is not possible to breathe; to make sb die in this way: *The girl fell into the river and drowned.* ◇ *Twenty people were drowned in the floods.* **2** [T] ~ **sb/sth (out)** (used about a sound) to be so loud that you cannot hear sb/sth else: *His answer was drowned out by the music.*

drowse /draʊz/ *verb* [I] to be in a light sleep or to be almost asleep

drowsy /ˈdraʊzi/ *adj.* not completely awake SYN **sleepy** ▶ **drowsily** *adv.* ▶ **drowsiness** *noun* [U]

drudgery /ˈdrʌdʒəri/ *noun* [U] hard and boring work

drug[1] /drʌg/ *noun* [C] (HEALTH) **1** a chemical which people use to give them pleasant or exciting feelings. It is illegal in many countries to use drugs: *He doesn't drink or* ***take drugs****.* ◇ *She suspected her son was* ***on drugs****.* ◇ *hard drugs such as heroin and cocaine* ◇ *soft drugs* **2** a chemical which is used as a medicine: *drug companies* ◇ *Some drugs can only be obtained with a prescription from a doctor.*

drug[2] /drʌg/ *verb* [T] (**drugging**; **drugged**) **1** to give a person or animal a chemical to make them or it fall asleep or unconscious: *The lion was drugged before the start of the journey.* **2** to put a drug into food or drink: *I think his drink was drugged.*

ˈdrug addict *noun* [C] (HEALTH) a person who cannot stop taking drugs ▶ **ˈdrug addiction** *noun* [U]

druggist /ˈdrʌgɪst/ (*AmE*) =CHEMIST (1)

drugstore /ˈdrʌgstɔː(r)/ (*AmE*) =CHEMIST (2)

drum[1] /drʌm/ *noun* [C] **1** (MUSIC) a musical instrument like an empty container with plastic or skin stretched across the ends. You play a drum by hitting it with your hands or with sticks: *She plays the drums in a band.* ➲ picture on **page 465** **2** a round container: *an oil drum*

drum[2] /drʌm/ *verb* (**drumming**; **drummed**) **1** [I] (MUSIC) to play a drum **2** [I,T] to make a noise like a drum by hitting sth many times: *to drum your fingers on the table* (=because you are annoyed, impatient, etc.)
PHR V **drum sth into sb** to make sb remember sth by repeating it many times
drum sth up to try to get support or business: *to drum up more custom*

drumlin /ˈdrʌmlɪn/ *noun* [C] (GEOGRAPHY) a very small hill formed by the movement of a large mass of ice (**a glacier**)

drummer /ˈdrʌmə(r)/ *noun* [C] (MUSIC) a person who plays a drum or drums

drumstick /ˈdrʌmstɪk/ *noun* [C] **1** (MUSIC) a stick used for playing the drums **2** the lower leg of a chicken or similar bird that we cook and eat

drunk¹ /drʌŋk/ ***adj.*** (not *before* a noun) having drunk too much alcohol: *to get drunk* ▶ **drunk** (also *old-fashioned* **drunkard**) ***noun*** [C]: *There were two drunks asleep under the bridge.*

drunk² past participle of **drink¹**

ˌdrunk ˈdriver (*especially AmE*) = DRINK-DRIVER

ˈdrunk driving (*especially AmE*) = DRINK-DRIVING

drunken /ˈdrʌŋkən/ ***adj.*** (only *before* a noun) **1** having drunk too much alcohol **2** showing the effects of too much alcohol: *drunken singing* ▶ **drunkenly** ***adv.*** ▶ **drunkenness** ***noun*** [U]

ˌdrunken ˈdriving ***noun*** [U] = DRINK DRIVING

dry¹ /draɪ/ ***adj.*** (**drier**; **driest**) **1** without liquid in it or on it; not wet: *The washing isn't dry yet.* ◇ *The paint is dry now.* ◇ *Rub your hair dry with a towel.* OPP **wet** **2** having little or no rain: *a hot, dry summer* ◇ *a dry climate* OPP **wet** **3** (used about hair or skin) not having enough natural oil **4** (used about wine) not sweet **5** (used about what sb says, or sb's way of speaking) amusing, although it sounds serious: *a dry sense of humour* **6** boring: *dry legal documents* **7** without alcohol; where no alcohol is allowed: *Saudi Arabia is a dry country.* ▶ **dryness** ***noun*** [U]

IDM **be left high and dry** → HIGH¹

dry² /draɪ/ ***verb*** [I,T] (*pres. part.* **drying**; *3rd person sing. pres.* **dries**; *pt, pp* **dried**) to become dry; to make sth dry: *I hung my shirt in the sun to dry.* ◇ *to dry your hands on a towel*

PHR V **dry (sth) out** to become or make sth become completely dry: *Don't allow the soil to dry out.*

dry up 1 (used about a river, etc.) to have no more water in it **2** to stop being available: *Because of the recession a lot of building work has dried up.* **3** to forget what you were going to say, for example because you are very nervous

dry (sth) up to dry plates, knives, forks, etc. with a towel after they have been washed

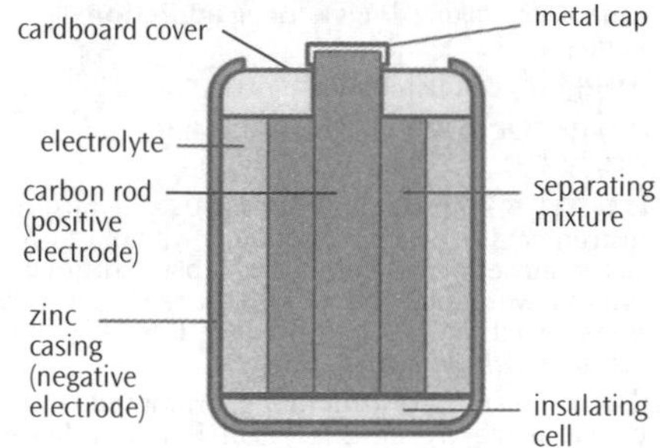

cross section of a simple dry cell

ˌdry ˈcell ***noun*** [C] (PHYSICS) an electric cell in which the ELECTROLYTE (= a liquid that an electric current can pass through) is absorbed in a thick or solid substance inside its container

ˌdry-ˈclean ***verb*** [T] to clean clothes using special chemicals, without using water

ˌdry-ˈcleaner's (*also* **cleaner's**) ***noun*** [C] the shop where you take your clothes to be cleaned

ˌdry ˈland ***noun*** [U] land, not the sea: *I was glad to be back* ***on dry land*** *again.*

DTP /ˌdiː tiː ˈpiː/ ***abbr.*** (ARTS AND MEDIA) = DESKTOP PUBLISHING

dual /ˈdjuːəl/ ***adj.*** (only *before* a noun) having two parts; double: *to have dual nationality*

ˌdual ˈcarriageway (*AmE* **diˌvided ˈhighway**) ***noun*** [C] a wide road that has an area of grass or a fence in the middle to separate the traffic going in one direction from the traffic going in the other direction

duality /djuːˈæləti/ ***noun*** [U,C] (*pl.* **-ies**) (*formal*) the state of having two parts or aspects

dub /dʌb/ ***verb*** [T] (**dubbing**; **dubbed**) **1** to give sb/sth a new or amusing name (**a nickname**): *Bill Clinton was dubbed 'Slick Willy'.* **2** ~ **sth (into sth)** to change the sound in a film so that what the actors said originally is spoken by actors using a different language: *I don't like foreign films when they're dubbed into English. I prefer subtitles.* ➲ look at **subtitle** **3** (MUSIC) to make a piece of music by mixing different pieces of recorded music together

dubious /ˈdjuːbiəs/ ***adj.*** **1** ~ **(about sth/about doing sth)** not sure or certain: *I'm very dubious about whether we're doing the right thing.* **2** that may not be honest or safe: *dubious financial dealings* ▶ **dubiously** ***adv.***

duchess /ˈdʌtʃəs/ (*also* **Duchess**) ***noun*** [C] a woman who has the same position as a DUKE, or who is the wife of a DUKE

duck¹ /dʌk/ ***noun*** (*pl.* **ducks** or **duck**) **1** [C] a common bird that lives on or near water. **Ducks** have short legs, special (**webbed**) feet for swimming and a wide beak. ➲ picture on **page 29** **2** [C] a female duck ❶ A male duck is called a **drake** and a young duck is a **duckling**. The sound a duck makes is a **quack**. **3** [U] the meat of a **duck**: *roast duck with orange sauce*

duck² /dʌk/ ***verb*** **1** [I,T] to move your head down quickly so that you are not seen or hit by sb/sth: *The boys ducked out of sight behind a hedge.* ◇ *I had to duck my head down to avoid the low doorway.* **2** [I,T] (*informal*) ~ **(out of) sth** to try to avoid sth difficult or unpleasant: *She tried to duck out of apologizing.* ◇ *The President is trying to duck responsibility for the crisis.* **3** [T] to push sb's head under water for a short time, especially when playing: *The kids were ducking each other in the pool.*

duct /dʌkt/ ***noun*** [C] a tube that carries liquid, gas, etc.: *They got into the building through the air duct.* ◇ *tear ducts* (= in the eye) ◇ *sweat ducts* ➲ picture at **skin**

ductile /ˈdʌktaɪl/ ***adj.*** (PHYSICS) (used about a metal) that can be made into a thin wire

dud /dʌd/ ***noun*** [C] (*informal*) a thing that cannot be used because it is not real or does not work properly

dude /duːd/ ***noun*** [C] (*especially AmE, slang*) a man

due¹ /djuː/ ***adj.*** **1** (not *before* a noun) expected or planned to happen or arrive: *The conference is due to start in four weeks' time.* ◇ *What time is the next train due (in)?* ◇ *The baby is due in May.* **2** (not *before* a noun) having to be paid: *The rent is due on the fifteenth of each month.* **3** ~ **(to sb)** that is owed to you because it is your right to have it: *Make sure you claim all the benefits that are due to you.* **4** ~ **to sb/sth** caused by or because of sb/sth: *His illness is probably due to stress.* **5** ~ **for sth** expecting sth or having the right to sth: *I think that I'm due for a pay rise.*

IDM **in due course** at some time in the future, quite soon: *All applicants will be informed of our decision in due course.*

due² /djuː/ ***adv.*** (used before 'north', 'south', 'east' and 'west') exactly: *The aeroplane was flying due east.*

due³ /dju:/ ***noun***
IDM **give sb his/her due** to be fair to a person: *She doesn't work very quickly, but to give Sarah her due, she is very accurate.*

duel /ˈdju:əl/ ***noun*** [C] (HISTORY) a formal type of fight with guns or other weapons which was used in the past to decide an argument between two men

duet /djuˈet/ (*also* **duo**) ***noun*** [C] (MUSIC) a piece of music for two people to sing or play ➲ look at **solo**

duffel coat (*also* **duffle coat**) /ˈdʌfl kəʊt/ ***noun*** [C] a coat made of heavy WOOLLEN cloth with a covering for the head (**a hood**). A **duffel coat** has special long buttons (**toggles**).

dug past tense, past participle of **dig**[1]

dugout /ˈdʌɡaʊt/ ***noun*** [C] **1** a rough shelter made by digging a hole in the ground and covering it, used by soldiers **2** (SPORT) a shelter by the side of a football or BASEBALL field where a team's manager, etc. can sit and watch the game

DUI /ˌdi: ju: ˈaɪ/ ***abbr.*** (*AmE*) = DRIVING UNDER THE INFLUENCE

duke /dju:k/ (*also* **Duke**) ***noun*** [C] a man of a very high social position ➲ look at **duchess**

dull[1] ⊶ /dʌl/ ***adj.*** **1** not interesting or exciting; boring: *Miss Potter's lessons are always so dull.* **2** not bright: *a dull and cloudy day* **3** not loud, sharp or strong: *Her head hit the floor with a dull thud.* ◇ *a dull pain* OPP **sharp** ▶ **dullness** ***noun*** [U] ▶ **dully** ***adv.***

dull[2] /dʌl/ ***verb*** [I,T] (used about pain or an emotion) to become or be made weaker or less strong: *The tablets they gave him dulled the pain for a while.*

duly /ˈdju:li/ ***adv.*** (*formal*) in the correct or expected way: *We all duly assembled at 7.30 as agreed.*

dumb /dʌm/ ***adj.*** **1** not able to speak: *to be deaf and dumb* ◇ (*figurative*) *They were* ***struck dumb*** *with amazement.* **2** (*informal*) stupid: *What a dumb thing to do!* ▶ **dumbly** ***adv.***: *Ken did all the talking, and I just nodded dumbly.*

dumbfounded /dʌmˈfaʊndɪd/ ***adj.*** very surprised

dummy /ˈdʌmi/ ***noun*** [C] (*pl.* **dummies**) **1** a model of the human body used for putting clothes on in a shop window or while you are making clothes: *a tailor's dummy* **2** (*informal*) a stupid person **3** (*AmE* **pacifier**) a rubber object that you put in a baby's mouth to keep them quiet and happy **4** something that is made to look like sth else but that is not the real thing: *The robbers used dummy handguns in the raid.*

dump[1] ⊶ /dʌmp/ ***verb*** [T] **1** to get rid of sth that you do not want, especially in a place which is not suitable: *Nuclear waste should not be dumped in the sea.* ◇ (*figurative*) *I wish you wouldn't keep dumping the extra work on me.* **2** to put sth down quickly or in a careless way: *The children dumped their bags in the hall and ran off to play.* **3** (*informal*) to get rid of sb, especially a boyfriend or girlfriend: *Did you hear that Laura dumped Chris last night?*

dump[2] ⊶ /dʌmp/ ***noun*** [C] **1** a place where rubbish or waste material from factories, etc. is left: *a rubbish dump* **2** (*informal*) a place that is very dirty, untidy or unpleasant: *The flat is cheap but it's a real dump.* SYN **tip**
IDM **down in the dumps** unhappy or sad

ˈdumper truck (*BrE*) (*AmE* **ˈdump truck**) ***noun*** [C] a lorry that carries material such as stones or earth in a special container which can be lifted up so that the load can fall out

dumpling /ˈdʌmplɪŋ/ ***noun*** [C] a small ball of flour and fat (**dough**) that is cooked and usually eaten with meat

dune /dju:n/ (*also* **ˈsand dune**) ***noun*** [C] (GEOGRAPHY) a low hill of sand by the sea or in the desert

dung /dʌŋ/ ***noun*** [U] waste material from the bodies of large animals: *cow dung*

dungarees /ˌdʌŋɡəˈri:z/ (*AmE* **overalls**) ***noun*** [pl.] a piece of clothing, similar to trousers, but covering your chest as well as your legs and with STRAPS that go over the shoulders: *a pair of dungarees*

dungeon /ˈdʌndʒən/ ***noun*** [C] an old underground prison, especially in a castle

duo /ˈdju:əʊ/ ***noun*** [C] (*pl.* **duos**) **1** (MUSIC) two people playing music or singing together **2** = DUET

duodenum /ˌdju:əˈdi:nəm/ ***noun*** [C] (ANATOMY) the first part of the small INTESTINE (= the tube that carries food from your stomach), next to the stomach ➲ picture at **digestive system**

dupe /dju:p/ ***verb*** [T] to lie to sb in order to make them believe sth or do sth: *The woman was duped into carrying the drugs.*

duplicate[1] /ˈdju:plɪkeɪt/ ***verb*** [T] **1** to make an exact copy of sth **2** to do sth that has already been done: *We don't want to duplicate the work of other departments.* ▶ **duplication** /ˌdju:plɪˈkeɪʃn/ ***noun*** [U]

duplicate[2] /ˈdju:plɪkət/ ***noun*** [C] something that is exactly the same as sth else ▶ **duplicate** ***adj.*** (only *before* a noun): *a duplicate key*
IDM **in duplicate** with two copies (for example of an official piece of paper) that are exactly the same: *The contract must be in duplicate.* ➲ look at **triplicate**

durable /ˈdjʊərəbl/ ***adj.*** likely to last for a long time without breaking or getting weaker: *a durable fabric* ▶ **durability** /ˌdjʊərəˈbɪləti/ ***noun*** [U]

duration AW /djuˈreɪʃn/ ***noun*** [U] the time that sth lasts: *Please remain seated for the duration of the flight.*

duress /djuˈres/ ***noun*** [U] threats or force that are used to make sb do sth: *He signed the confession under duress.*

during ⊶ /ˈdjʊərɪŋ/ ***prep.*** within the period of time mentioned: *During the summer holidays we went swimming every day.* ◇ *Grandpa was taken very ill during the night.*

dusk /dʌsk/ ***noun*** [U] the time in the evening when the sun has already gone down and it is nearly dark ➲ look at **dawn**, **twilight**

dust[1] ⊶ /dʌst/ ***noun*** [U] very small pieces of dry dirt, sand, etc. in the form of a powder: *a thick layer of dust* ◇ *chalk/coal dust* ◇ *The tractor came up the track in a cloud of dust.* ◇ *a speck* (= small piece) *of dust* ▶ **dusty** ***adj.***: *This shelf has got very dusty.*

dust[2] ⊶ /dʌst/ ***verb*** [I,T] to clean a room, furniture, etc. by removing dust with a cloth: *Let me dust those shelves before you put the books on them.*

dustbin /ˈdʌstbɪn/ (*AmE* **garbage can**; **trash can**) ***noun*** [C] a large container for rubbish that you keep outside your house

ˈdust bowl ***noun*** [C] (GEOGRAPHY) an area of land that has become desert because there has been too little rain or too much farming

duster /ˈdʌstə(r)/ ***noun*** [C] a soft dry cloth that you use for cleaning furniture, etc.

dustman /ˈdʌstmən/ ***noun*** [C] (*pl.* **-men** /-mən/) a person whose job is to take away the rubbish that people put in DUSTBINS

dustpan /ˈdʌstpæn/ ***noun*** [C] a flat container with a handle into which you brush dirt from the floor: *Where do you keep your* ***dustpan and brush****?*

Dutch /dʌtʃ/ ***adj.*** from the Netherlands

ˌDutch ˈcourage ***noun*** [U] (*BrE*) a feeling of courage or confidence that a person gets from drinking alcohol

dutiful /ˈdjuːtɪfl/ ***adj.*** happy to respect and obey sb: *a dutiful son* ▶ **dutifully** /-fəli/ ***adv.***

duty 🔑 /ˈdjuːti/ ***noun*** [C,U] (*pl.* **duties**) **1** something that you have to do because people expect you to do it or because you think it is right: *A soldier must* ***do his duty****.* ◇ *a sense of moral duty* **2** the tasks that you do when you are at work: *the duties of a policeman* ◇ *Which nurses are on night duty this week?* **3** ~ **(on sth)** (ECONOMICS) a tax that you pay, especially on goods that you bring into a country
IDM **on/off duty** (used about doctors, nurses, police officers, etc.) to be working/not working: *The porter's on duty from 8 till 4.* ◇ *What time does she go off duty?*

ˌduty-ˈfree ***adj.***, ***adv.*** (used about goods) that you can bring into a country without paying tax: *an airport duty-free shop* ◇ *How much wine can you bring into Britain duty-free?* ➲ look at **tax-free**

ˌduty ˈmanager ***noun*** [C] (TOURISM) the manager, for example in a hotel, an airport, etc., who is on duty at a particular time

ˈduty officer ***noun*** [C] the officer, for example in the police, army, etc., who is on duty at a particular time in a particular place

duvet /ˈduːveɪ/ ***noun*** [C] a thick cover filled with feathers or another soft material that you sleep under to keep warm in bed ➲ look at **eiderdown**, **quilt**

DVD /ˌdiː viː ˈdiː/ ***noun*** [C] (COMPUTING) a disc with different types of information on it, especially photographs and video, that can be used on a computer (short for 'digital videodisc' or 'digital versatile disc'): *a DVD-ROM drive* ➲ picture at **computer**

DVT /ˌdiː viː ˈtiː/ ***abbr.*** = DEEP VEIN THROMBOSIS

dwarf[1] /dwɔːf/ ***noun*** [C] (*pl.* **dwarfs** or **dwarves** /dwɔːvz/) **1** (BIOLOGY) a person, animal or plant that is much smaller than the usual size **2** (in children's stories) a very small person

dwarf[2] /dwɔːf/ ***verb*** [T] (used about a large object) to make sth seem very small in comparison: *The skyscraper dwarfs all the other buildings around.*

dwell /dwel/ ***verb*** [I] (*pt, pp* **dwelt** /dwelt/ or **dwelled**) (*old-fashioned, formal*) to live or stay in a place
PHRV **dwell on/upon sth** to think or talk a lot about sth that it would be better to forget: *I don't want to dwell on the past. Let's think about the future.*

dweller /ˈdwelə(r)/ ***noun*** [C] (often in compounds) a person or animal that lives in the place mentioned: *city-dwellers*

dwelling /ˈdwelɪŋ/ ***noun*** [C] (*formal*) the place where a person lives; a house

DWI /ˌdiː dʌbljuː ˈaɪ/ ***abbr.*** (*AmE*) = DRIVING WHILE INTOXICATED

dwindle /ˈdwɪndl/ ***verb*** [I] ~ **(away)** to become smaller or weaker: *Their savings dwindled away to nothing.*

dye[1] /daɪ/ ***verb*** [T] (*pres. part.* **dyeing**; *3rd person sing. pres.* **dyes**; *pt, pp* **dyed**) to make sth a different colour: *Does she dye her hair?* ◇ *I'm going to dye this blouse black.*

dye[2] /daɪ/ ***noun*** [C,U] a substance that is used to change the colour of sth

dying 🔑 present participle of **die**

dyke (*also* **dike**) /daɪk/ ***noun*** [C] **1** a long thick wall that is built to prevent the sea or a river from flooding low land **2** (*especially BrE*) a long narrow space dug in the ground and used for taking water away from land

dynamic[1] AW /daɪˈnæmɪk/ ***adj.*** **1** (used about a person) full of energy and ideas; active **2** (PHYSICS) (used about a force or power) that causes movement OPP **static** ▶ **dynamism** /ˈdaɪnəmɪzəm/ ***noun*** [U]

dynamic[2] AW /daɪˈnæmɪk/ ***noun*** **1** **dynamics** [pl.] the way in which people or things behave and react to each other in a particular situation **2** **dynamics** [U] (PHYSICS) the scientific study of the forces involved in movement: *fluid dynamics* **3** [sing.] (*formal*) a force that produces change, action or effects **4** **dynamics** [pl.] (MUSIC) changes in volume in music

dynamite /ˈdaɪnəmaɪt/ ***noun*** [U] **1** a powerful EXPLOSIVE substance **2** a thing or person that causes great excitement, shock, etc.: *His news was dynamite.*

dynamo /ˈdaɪnəməʊ/ ***noun*** [C] (*pl.* **dynamos**) (PHYSICS) a device that changes energy from the movement of sth such as wind or water into electricity

dynasty /ˈdɪnəsti/ ***noun*** [C] (*pl.* **dynasties**) a series of rulers who are from the same family: *the Ming dynasty in China*

dysentery /ˈdɪsəntri/ ***noun*** [U] (HEALTH) a serious disease which causes you to have DIARRHOEA (= an illness which causes your body to get rid of waste material very often in liquid form), and to lose blood

dyslexia /dɪsˈleksiə/ ***noun*** [U] (HEALTH) a difficulty that some people have with reading and spelling ▶ **dyslexic** ***noun*** [C], ***adj.***

dysprosium /dɪsˈprəʊziəm/ ***noun*** [U] (*symbol* **Dy**) (CHEMISTRY) a chemical element. **Dysprosium** is a soft silver-white metal used in nuclear research. ℹ For more information on the periodic table of elements, look at pages R34-5.

E e

E, e[1] /iː/ ***noun*** [C,U] (*pl.* **E's**; **e's** /iːz/) the fifth letter of the English alphabet: *'Egg' begins with (an) 'E'.*

E[2] ***abbr.*** east(ern): *E Asia*

e- /iː/ ***prefix*** (COMPUTING) (used in nouns and verbs) connected with the use of electronic communication, especially the Internet, for sending information, doing business, etc.: *e-business/e-commerce* ➲ look at **email**

ea. ***abbr.*** each

each 🔑 /iːtʃ/ ***det.***, ***pronoun*** every individual person or thing: *Each lesson lasts an hour.* ◇ *Each of the lessons lasts an hour.* ◇ *The lessons each last an hour.* ◇ *These T-shirts are £5 each.*

ˌeach ˈother ***pronoun*** used for saying that A does the same thing to B as B does to A: *Emma and Dave love each other very much* (= Emma loves Dave and Dave loves Emma). ◇ *We looked at each other.*

eager /ˈiːɡə(r)/ ***adj.*** **~ (to do sth); ~ (for sth)** full of desire or interest: *We're all eager to start work on the new project.* ◇ *eager for success* **SYN keen** ▶ **eagerly** ***adv.*** ▶ **eagerness** ***noun*** [U]

eagle /ˈiːɡl/ ***noun*** [C] a very large bird that can see very well. It eats small birds and animals. ➲ picture on **page 29**

EAP /ˌiː eɪ ˈpiː/ ***abbr.*** (EDUCATION) English for Academic Purposes

ear 🔑 /ɪə(r)/ ***noun*** **1** [C] one of the two parts of the body of a person or animal that are used for hearing **2** [sing.] **an ~ (for sth)** an ability to recognize and repeat sounds, especially in music or language: *Yuka has a good ear for languages.* **3** [C] (AGRICULTURE) the top part of a plant that produces grain: *an ear of corn* ➲ picture at **cereal**

IDM sb's ears are burning used when a person thinks that other people are talking about them, especially in an unkind way

go in one ear and out the other (used about information, etc.) to be forgotten quickly: *Everything I tell him seems to go in one ear and out the other.*

play (sth) by ear (MUSIC) to play a piece of music that you have heard without using written notes

play it by ear to decide what to do as things happen, instead of planning in advance: *We don't know what Alan's reaction will be, so we'll just have to play it by ear.*

prick up your ears → PRICK[1]

earache /ˈɪəreɪk/ ***noun*** [U] a pain in your ear: *I've got earache.* ➲ note at **ache**

eardrum /ˈɪədrʌm/ ***noun*** [C] (ANATOMY) a thin piece of skin inside the ear that is tightly stretched and that allows you to hear sound ➲ picture at **ear**

earl /ɜːl/ ***noun*** [C] a British man of a high social position

ˈear lobe ***noun*** [C] the round soft part at the bottom of your ear

early 🔑 /ˈɜːli/ ***adj., adv.*** **(earlier; earliest)** **1** near the beginning of a period of time, a piece of work, a series, etc.: *I have to get up early on weekday mornings.* ◇ *I think John's in his early twenties.* ◇ *The project is still in its early stages.* **2** before the usual or expected time: *She arrived five minutes early for her interview.*

IDM at the earliest not before the date or time mentioned: *I can repair it by Friday at the earliest.*

it's early days (yet) used to say that it is too soon to know how a situation will develop

the early hours very early in the morning in the hours after midnight

an early/a late night → NIGHT

early on soon after the beginning: *He achieved fame early on in his career.*

an early riser a person who usually gets up early in the morning

earmark /ˈɪəmɑːk/ ***verb*** [T] **~ sb/sth (for sth/sb)** to choose sb/sth to do sth in the future: *Everybody says Elena has been earmarked as the next manager.*

earn 🔑 /ɜːn/ ***verb*** [T] **1** to get money by working: *How much does a dentist earn?* ◇ *I earn £20000 a year.* ◇ *It's hard to* **earn a living** *as an artist.* **2** to win the right to sth, for example by working hard: *The team's victory today has earned them a place in the final.* **3** to get money as profit or interest on money you have in a bank, lent to sb, etc.: *How much interest will my savings earn in this account?*

earnest /ˈɜːnɪst/ ***adj.*** serious or determined: *He's such an earnest young man – he never makes a joke.* ◇ *They were having a very earnest discussion.* ▶ **earnestly** ***adv.***

IDM in earnest 1 serious and sincere about what you are going to do: *He was in earnest about wanting to leave university.* **2** happening more seriously or with more force than before: *After two weeks work began in earnest on the project.*

earnings /ˈɜːnɪŋz/ ***noun*** [pl.] the money that a person earns by working: *Average earnings have increased by 5%.* ➲ note at **income**

earphones /ˈɪəfəʊnz/ ***noun*** [pl.] a piece of equipment that fits over or in the ears and is used for listening to music, the radio, etc.

earring /ˈɪərɪŋ/ ***noun*** [C] a piece of jewellery that is worn in or on the lower part of the ear: *Do these earrings clip on or are they for pierced ears?*

earshot /ˈɪəʃɒt/ ***noun*** [U]

IDM (be) out of/within earshot where a person cannot/can hear: *Wait until he's out of earshot before you say anything about him.*

earth[1] 🔑 /ɜːθ/ ***noun*** **1** (*also* **the earth; the Earth**) [sing.] (ASTRONOMY) the world; the planet on which we live: *life on earth* ◇ *The earth goes round the*

human ear

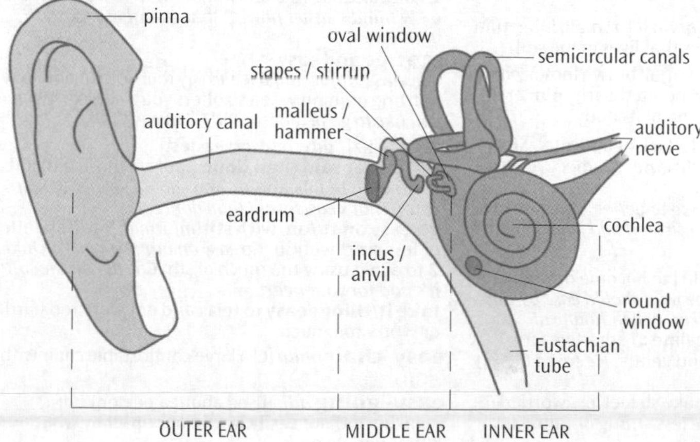

the earth

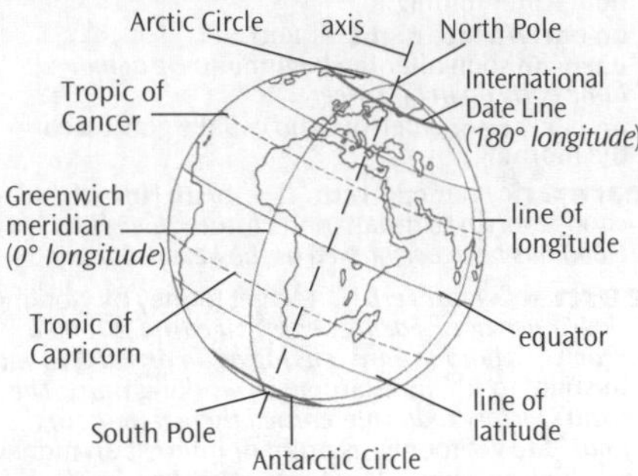

sun. ➲ look at **the solar system 2** [sing.] the surface of the world; land: *The spaceship fell towards earth.* ◇ *I could feel the earth shake when the earthquake started.* **3** [U] the substance that plants grow in; soil: *The earth around here is very fertile.* ➲ note at **ground 4** [C, usually sing.] (*AmE* **ground**) (PHYSICS) a wire that makes a piece of electrical equipment safer by connecting it to the ground ➲ picture at **plug**

IDM **charge/pay the earth** (*informal*) to charge/pay a very large amount of money

cost the earth/a fortune → COST²

how/why/where/who etc. on earth (*informal*) used for emphasizing sth or expressing surprise: *Where on earth have you been?*

earth² /ɜːθ/ (*AmE* **ground**) *verb* [T] (PHYSICS) to make a piece of electrical equipment safer by connecting it to the ground with a wire

earthenware /ˈɜːθnweə(r)/ *adj.* made of very hard baked CLAY: *an earthenware bowl*
▸ **earthenware** *noun* [U]

earthly /ˈɜːθli/ *adj.* (often in questions or negatives) possible: *What earthly use is a gardening book to me? I haven't got a garden!*

earthquake /ˈɜːθkweɪk/ (also *informal* **quake**) *noun* [C] (GEOLOGY) violent movement of the earth's surface

earthworm /ˈɜːθwɜːm/ *noun* [C] a small, long, thin animal with no legs or eyes that lives in the soil

earwig /ˈɪəwɪɡ/ *noun* [C] a small brown insect with a long body and two curved pointed parts (**pincers**) that stick out at the back end of its body

ease¹ ⊷ /iːz/ *noun* [U] a lack of difficulty: *She answered the questions* ***with ease***. ➲ adjective easy OPP **unease**

IDM **(be/feel) at (your) ease** to be/feel comfortable, relaxed, etc.: *They were all so kind and friendly that I felt completely at ease.*

ease² ⊷ /iːz/ *verb* **1** [I,T] to become or make sth less painful or serious: *The pain should ease by this evening.* ◇ *This money will ease their financial problems a little.* SYN **alleviate** ➲ adjective easy **2** [T] to move sth slowly and gently: *He eased the key into the lock.*

IDM **ease sb's mind** to make sb feel less worried

PHR V **ease off** to become less strong or unpleasant

ease up to work less hard

easel /ˈiːzl/ *noun* [C] (ART) a wooden frame that holds a picture while it is being painted

easily ⊷ /ˈiːzəli/ *adv.* **1** without difficulty: *I can easily ring up and check the time.* **2** ~ **the best, worst, nicest, etc.** without doubt: *It's easily his best novel.*

east¹ ⊷ /iːst/ *noun* [sing.] (*abbr.* **E**) **1** (*also* **the east**) the direction you look towards in order to see the sun rise; one of THE POINTS OF THE COMPASS (= the four main directions that we give names to) ➲ picture at **compass**: *Which way is east?* ◇ *a cold wind from the east* ◇ *Which county is* ***to the east of*** *Oxfordshire?* **2 the east** the part of any country, city, etc. that is further to the east than the other parts: *Norwich is in the east of England.* **3 the East** the countries of Asia, for example China and Japan ➲ look at **the Far East, the Middle East** ➲ look at **north, south, west**

east² ⊷ (also **East**) /iːst/ *adj., adv.* in or towards the east or from the east: *They headed east.* ◇ *the East Coast of America* ◇ *We live east of the city.* ◇ *an east wind*

eastbound /ˈiːstbaʊnd/ *adj.* travelling or leading towards the east: *The eastbound carriageway of the motorway is blocked.*

Easter /ˈiːstə(r)/ *noun* [U] (RELIGION) a festival on a Sunday in March or April when Christians celebrate Christ's return to life; the time before and after Easter Sunday: *the Easter holidays* ◇ *Are you going away* ***at Easter***?

ˈEaster egg *noun* [C] an egg, usually made of chocolate, that you give as a present at Easter

easterly /ˈiːstəli/ *adj.* **1** towards or in the east: *They travelled in an easterly direction.* **2** (used about winds) coming from the east: *cold easterly winds*

eastern ⊷ (also **Eastern**) /ˈiːstən/ *adj.* **1** of, in or from the east of a place: *Eastern Scotland* ◇ *the eastern shore of the lake* **2** from or connected with the countries of the East: *Eastern cookery* (= that comes from Asia)

ˌeast-north-ˈeast *noun* [sing.] (*abbr.* **ENE**) the direction halfway between east and north-east

ˌeast-south-ˈeast *noun* [sing.] (*abbr.* **ESE**) the direction halfway between east and south-east

eastward /ˈiːstwəd/ *adj.* (*also* **eastwards**) *adj., adv.* towards the east: *to travel in an eastward direction* ◇ *The Amazon flows eastwards.*

easy¹ ⊷ /ˈiːzi/ *adj.* (**easier**; **easiest**) **1** not difficult: *an easy question* ◇ *It isn't easy to explain the system.* ◇ *The system isn't easy to explain.* OPP **hard 2** comfortable, relaxed and not worried: *an easy life* ◇ *My mind's easier now.* ➲ look at **uneasy** ➲ noun, verb ease

IDM **free and easy** → FREE¹

I'm easy (*informal*) used to say that you do not have a strong opinion when sb offers you a choice: *'Would you like to go first or second?' 'I'm easy.'*

easy² /ˈiːzi/ *adv.* (**easier**; **easiest**)

IDM **easier said than done** (*spoken*) more difficult to do than to talk about: *'You should get her to help you.' 'That's easier said than done.'*

go easy on sb/on/with sth (*informal*) **1** to be gentle or less strict with sb: *Go easy on him; he's just a child.* **2** to avoid using too much of sth: *Go easy on the salt; it's bad for your heart.*

take it/things easy to relax and not work too hard or worry too much

ˌeasy ˈchair *noun* [C] a large comfortable chair with arms

ˌeasy-ˈgoing *adj.* (used about a person) calm, relaxed and not easily worried or upset by what other people do

eat ⊶ /iːt/ ***verb*** (*pt* **ate** /et/; *pp* **eaten** /ˈiːtn/) **1** [I,T] to put food into your mouth, then bite and swallow it: *Who ate all the biscuits?* ◇ *Eat your dinner up, Joe* (=finish it all). ◇ *She doesn't eat properly. No wonder she's so thin.* **2** [I] to have a meal: *What time shall we eat?*
IDM **have sb eating out of your hand** to have control and power over sb
have your cake and eat it → CAKE[1]
PHR V **eat sth away/eat away at sth** to damage or destroy sth slowly over a period of time: *The sea had eaten away at the cliff.*
eat out to have a meal in a restaurant

eater /ˈiːtə(r)/ ***noun*** [C] a person who eats in a particular way: *My uncle's a big eater* (=he eats a lot). ◇ *We're not great meat eaters in our family.*

eau de cologne /ˌəʊ də kəˈləʊn/ (*also* **cologne**) ***noun*** [U] a type of pleasant smelling liquid (**perfume**) that is not very strong

eaves /iːvz/ ***noun*** [pl.] the edges of a roof that stick out over the walls

eavesdrop /ˈiːvzdrɒp/ ***verb*** [I] (**eavesdropping**; **eavesdropped**) ~ **(on sb/sth)** to listen secretly to other people talking: *They caught her eavesdropping on their conversation.*

ebb[1] /eb/ ***verb*** [I] **1** (used about sea water) to flow away from the land, which happens twice a day SYN **go out 2** ~ **(away)** (used about a feeling, etc.) to become weaker: *The crowd's enthusiasm began to ebb.*

ebb[2] /eb/ ***noun*** [sing.] **the ebb** the time when sea water flows away from the land ❶ The movement of sea water twice a day is called the **tide**. ➲ look at **high tide**
IDM **the ebb and flow (of sth)** (used about a situation, noise, feeling, etc.) a regular increase and decrease in the progress or strength of sth

ebony /ˈebəni/ ***noun*** [U] a hard black wood

eccentric /ɪkˈsentrɪk/ ***adj.*** (used about people or their behaviour) strange or unusual: *People said he was mad but I think he was just slightly eccentric.* ▶ **eccentric** ***noun*** [C]: *She's just an old eccentric.* ▶ **eccentricity** /ˌeksenˈtrɪsəti/ ***noun*** [C,U] (*pl.* **eccentricities**)

ecclesiastical /ɪˌkliːziˈæstɪkl/ ***adj.*** (RELIGION) connected with or belonging to the Christian Church: *ecclesiastical law*

ECDL /ˌiː siː diː ˈel/ ***abbr.*** (COMPUTING) **European Computer Driving Licence**; a test you can take to show your ability in computer skills

echo[1] /ˈekəʊ/ ***noun*** [C] (*pl.* **echoes**) a sound that is repeated as it is sent back off a surface such as the wall of a tunnel: *I could hear the echo of footsteps somewhere in the distance.*

echo[2] /ˈekəʊ/ ***verb*** **1** [I] (used about a sound) to be repeated; to come back as an **echo**: *Their footsteps echoed in the empty church.* **2** [I,T] ~ **sth (back)**; ~ **(with/to sth)** to repeat or send back a sound; to be full of a particular sound: *The tunnel echoed back their calls.* ◇ *The hall echoed with their laughter.* **3** [T] to repeat what sb has said, done or thought: *The child echoed everything his mother said.* ◇ *The newspaper article echoed my views completely.*

ˈecho sounder ***noun*** [C] (SCIENCE) a device for finding how deep the sea is or where objects are in the water by measuring the time it takes for sound to return to the person listening ▶ **ˈecho-sounding** ***noun*** [C, U] ➲ picture at **sonar**

eclair /ɪˈkleə(r)/ ***noun*** [C] a type of long thin cake, usually filled with cream and covered with chocolate

eclipse[1] /ɪˈklɪps/ ***noun*** [C] an occasion when the moon passes between the earth and the sun so that you cannot see all or part of the sun for a time; an occasion when the earth passes between the moon and the sun so that you cannot see all or part of the moon for a time: *a total/partial eclipse of the sun* ➲ picture at **shadow**

eclipse[2] /ɪˈklɪps/ ***verb*** [T] (ASTRONOMY) (used about the moon, etc.) to cause an **eclipse** of the sun, etc.

eco- /ˈiːkəʊ/ (ENVIRONMENT) (in nouns, adjectives and adverbs) connected with the environment: *eco-friendly* ◇ *eco-warriors* (=people who protest about damage to the environment) ◇ *eco-terrorism* (=the use of force or violent action in order to protest about damage to the environment)

eco-friendly /ˌiːkəʊ ˈfrendli/ ***adj.*** (ENVIRONMENT) not harmful to the environment: *eco-friendly products/fuel*

ecologist /iˈkɒlədʒɪst/ ***noun*** [C] (BIOLOGY, ENVIRONMENT) a person who studies or is an expert in ECOLOGY

ecology /iˈkɒlədʒi/ ***noun*** [U] (BIOLOGY, ENVIRONMENT) the relationship between living things and their surroundings; the study of this subject ▶ **ecological** /ˌiːkəˈlɒdʒɪkl/ ***adj.***: *an ecological disaster* ▶ **ecologically** /-kli/ ***adv.***

ˈe-commerce ***noun*** [U] (BUSINESS) the business of buying and selling things using the Internet: ***to be involved in/move into e-commerce*** ◇ *an e-commerce business/company*

THESAURUS

economic

financial • commercial • monetary • budgetary
These words all describe activities or situations that are connected with the use of money, especially by a business or country.
economic: *the current economic situation*
financial: *in financial difficulties*
commercial: *the commercial heart of the city*
monetary (*formal*): *closer European monetary union*
budgetary: *budgetary control/reform*

economic ⊶ AW /ˌiːkəˈnɒmɪk; ˌekə-/ ***adj.*** **1** (ECONOMICS) (only *before* a noun) connected with the supply of money, business, industry, etc.: *The country faces growing economic problems.*
2 producing a profit: *The mine was closed because it was not economic.* ❶ note at **successful** ➲ look at **economical** OPP **uneconomic** ▶ **economically** /ˌiːkəˈnɒmɪkli; ˌekə-/ ***adv.***: *The country was economically very underdeveloped.*

economical AW /ˌiːkəˈnɒmɪkl; ˌekə-/ ***adj.*** that costs or uses less time, money, fuel, etc. than usual: *an economical car to run* OPP **uneconomical** ➲ look at **economic** ▶ **economically** AW /-kli/ ***adv.***: *The train service could be run more economically.*

economics AW /ˌiːkəˈnɒmɪks; ˌekə-/ ***noun*** [U] (ECONOMICS) the study or principles of the way money, business and industry are organized: *a degree in economics* ◇ *the economics of a company*

economist AW /ɪˈkɒnəmɪst/ ***noun*** [C] (ECONOMICS) a person who studies or is an expert in economics

economize (also **-ise**) /ɪˈkɒnəmaɪz/ ***verb*** [I] ~ **(on sth)** to save money, time, fuel, etc.; to use less of sth

economy 🔑 AW /ɪ'kɒnəmi/ *noun* (*pl.* **economies**) **1** (*also* **the economy**) [C] (ECONOMICS) the operation of a country's money supply, commercial activities and industry: *There are signs of improvement in the economy.* ◇ *the economies of America and Japan* **2** [C,U] careful spending of money, time, fuel, etc.; trying to save, not waste sth: *Our department is **making economies** in the amount of paper it uses.* ◇ *economy class* (= the cheapest class of air travel)

e'conomy class syndrome *noun* [U] (*BrE*) (HEALTH) the fact of a person suffering from DEEP VEIN THROMBOSIS after they have travelled on a plane. This condition is thought to be more common among people who travel in the cheapest seats because they do not have space to move their legs much.

ecosystem /'iːkəʊsɪstəm/ *noun* [C] (BIOLOGY, ENVIRONMENT) all the plants and animals in a particular area considered together with their surroundings

ecotourism /'iːkəʊtʊərɪzəm/ *noun* [U] (TOURISM) organized holidays that are designed so that the tourists damage the environment as little as possible, especially when some of the money they pay is used to protect the local environment and animals: *Ecotourism is financing rainforest preservation.* ▶ **ecotourist** /'iːkəʊtʊərɪst/ *noun* [C]

ecstasy /'ekstəsi/ *noun* [C,U] (*pl.* **ecstasies**) a feeling or state of great happiness: *to be in ecstasy* ◇ *She **went into ecstasies** about the ring he had bought her.*

ecstatic /ɪk'stætɪk/ *adj.* extremely happy

ecu (*also* **ECU**) /'ekjuː/ (*pl.* **ecus**; **ecu**) *noun* [C] (ECONOMICS) (until 1999) money used for business and commercial activities between member countries of the European Union. **Ecu** is short for (**European Currency Unit**) ➲ look at **euro**

ecumenical /ˌiːkjuː'menɪkl; ˌekjuː-/ *adj.* (RELIGION) connected with the idea of uniting all the different parts of the Christian Church

eczema /'eksɪmə/ *noun* [U] (HEALTH) a disease which makes your skin red and dry so that you want to scratch it

ed. *abbr.* EDITED by; edition; editor

eddy /'edi/ *noun* [C] (*pl.* **eddies**) a circular movement of water, wind, dust, etc.

edema (*AmE*) = OEDEMA

edge[1] 🔑 /edʒ/ *noun* [C] **1** the place where sth, especially a surface, ends: *the edge of a table* ◇ *The leaves were brown and curling at the edges.* ◇ *I stood at the water's edge.* **2** the sharp cutting part of a knife, etc.

IDM **an/the edge on/over sb/sth** a small advantage over sb/sth: *She knew she had the edge over the other candidates.*

(be) on edge to be nervous, worried or quick to become upset or angry: *I'm a bit on edge because I get my exam results today.*

edge[2] /edʒ/ *verb* **1** [T] (usually passive) ~ **sth (with sth)** to put sth along the edge of sth else: *The cloth was edged with lace.* **2** [I,T] ~ **(your way/sth) across, along, away, back, etc.** to move yourself/sth somewhere slowly and carefully: *We edged closer to get a better view.* ◇ *She edged her chair up to the window.*

edgeways /'edʒweɪz/ (*also* **edgewise** /-waɪz/) *adv.*

IDM **not get a word in edgeways** → WORD[1]

ecosystems

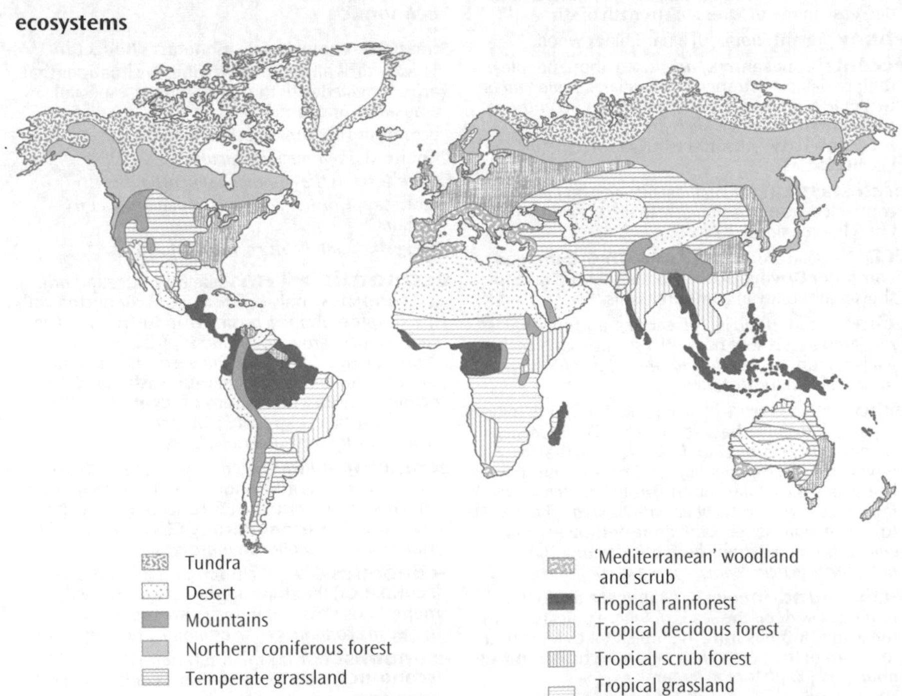

edgy /'edʒi/ ***adj.*** (*informal*) nervous, worried or quick to become upset or angry

edible /'edəbl/ ***adj.*** good or safe to eat: *Are these mushrooms edible?* OPP **inedible**

edifice /'edɪfɪs/ ***noun*** [C] (*formal*) a large impressive building ➲ note at **building**

edit AW /'edɪt/ ***verb*** [T] **1** to prepare a piece of writing to be published, making sure that it is correct, the right length, etc. **2** to prepare a film, television or radio programme by cutting and arranging filmed material in a particular order **3** to be in charge of a newspaper, magazine, etc.

edition ⊶ AW /ɪ'dɪʃn/ ***noun*** [C] **1** the form in which a book is published; all the books, newspapers, etc. published in the same form at the same time: *a paperback/hardback edition* ◇ *the morning edition of a newspaper* **2** one of a series of newspapers, magazines, television or radio programmes: *And now for this week's edition of 'Panorama'...*

editor ⊶ AW /'edɪtə(r)/ ***noun*** [C] **1** the person who is in charge of all or part of a newspaper, magazine, etc. and who decides what should be included: *the financial editor* ◇ *Who is the editor of 'The Times'?* **2** a person whose job is to prepare a book to be published by checking for mistakes and correcting the text **3** a person whose job is to prepare a film, television programme, etc. for showing to the public by cutting and putting the filmed material in the correct order

editorial[1] AW /ˌedɪ'tɔːriəl/ ***adj.*** (ARTS AND MEDIA) connected with the task of preparing sth such as a newspaper, a book or a television or radio programme, to be published or broadcast: *the magazine's editorial staff*

editorial[2] AW /ˌedɪ'tɔːriəl/ ***noun*** [C] (ARTS AND MEDIA) an important article in a newspaper that expresses the EDITOR'S opinion about an item of news or an issue; in the US also a comment on radio or television that expresses the opinion of the STATION or network

educate ⊶ /'edʒukeɪt/ ***verb*** [T] to teach or train sb, especially in school: *Young people should be educated to care for their environment.* ◇ *All their children were educated at private schools.*

educated ⊶ /'edʒukeɪtɪd/ ***adj.*** having studied and learnt a lot of things to a high standard: *a highly educated woman*

education ⊶ /ˌedʒu'keɪʃn/ ***noun*** [C, usually sing., U] the teaching or training of people, especially in schools: ***primary/secondary/higher/adult*** *education* ◇ *She received an excellent education.* ▶ **educational** /-ʃənl/ ***adj.***: *an educational toy/visit/experience*

Edwardian /ed'wɔːdiən/ ***adj.*** (HISTORY) from the time of the British king Edward VII (1901–1910): *an Edwardian terraced house* ▶ **Edwardian** ***noun*** [C]

eel /iːl/ ***noun*** [C] a long fish that looks like a snake

eerie /'ɪəri/ ***adj.*** strange and frightening: *an eerie noise* ▶ **eerily** ***adv.*** ▶ **eeriness** ***noun*** [U]

efface /ɪ'feɪs/ ***verb*** [T] (*formal*) to make sth disappear; to remove sth

effect[1] ⊶ /ɪ'fekt/ ***noun*** **1** [C,U] **(an) ~ (on sb/sth)** a change that is caused by sth; a result: *the effects of acid rain on the lakes and forests* ◇ *Her shouting* ***had little or no effect*** *on him.* ◇ *Despite her terrible experience, she seems to have suffered no* ***ill effects.*** ➲ look at **after-effect, the greenhouse effect, side effect** **2** [C,U] a particular look, sound or impression that an artist, writer, etc. wants to create: *How does the artist* ***create the effect of*** *moonlight?* ◇ *He likes to say things just for effect* (=to impress people). ➲ look at **special effects, sound effect** **3 effects** [pl.] (*formal*) your personal possessions

IDM **come into effect** (used especially about laws or rules) to begin to be used

in effect **1** in fact; for all practical purposes: *Though they haven't made an official announcement, she is, in effect, the new director.* **2** (used about a rule, a law, etc.) in operation; in use: *The new rules will be in effect from next month.*

take effect **1** (used about a drug, etc.) to begin to work; to produce the result you want: *The anaesthetic took effect immediately.* **2** (used about a law, etc.) to come into operation: *The ceasefire takes effect from midnight.*

to this/that effect with this/that meaning: *I told him to leave her alone, or words to that effect.*

> **THESAURUS**
>
> **effect**
>
> **result • consequence • outcome • repercussion**
>
> These are all words for a thing that is caused because of sth else.
>
> **effect**: *His criticism had the effect of discouraging her.*
>
> **result**: *She died as a result of her injuries.*
>
> **consequence**: *This decision could have serious consequences for everyone.*
>
> **outcome**: *We're waiting to hear the final outcome.*
>
> **repercussion**: *His dismissal will have serious repercussions.*

effect[2] ***verb*** [T] (*formal*) to make sth happen: *to effect a cure/change/recovery*

effective ⊶ /ɪ'fektɪv/ ***adj.*** **1** successfully producing the result that you want: *a medicine that is effective against the common cold* ◇ *That picture would look more effective on a dark background.* OPP **ineffective** **2** real or actual, although perhaps not official: *The soldiers gained effective control of the town.* ▶ **effectiveness** ***noun*** [U]

effectively ⊶ /ɪ'fektɪvli/ ***adv.*** **1** in a way that successfully produces the result you wanted: *She dealt with the situation effectively.* **2** in fact; in reality: *It meant that, effectively, they had lost.*

effector /ɪ'fektə(r)/ ***noun*** [C] (BIOLOGY) an organ or a cell in the body that is made to react by sth outside the body

effeminate /ɪ'femɪnət/ ***adj.*** (used about a man or his behaviour) like a woman

effervescent /ˌefə'vesnt/ ***adj.*** **1** (used about people and their behaviour) excited, enthusiastic and full of energy **2** (used about a liquid) having or producing small bubbles of gas ▶ **effervescence** /ˌefə'vesns/ ***noun*** [U]

efficient ⊶ /ɪ'fɪʃnt/ ***adj.*** able to work well without making mistakes or wasting time and energy: *Our secretary is very efficient.* ◇ *You must find a more efficient way of organizing your time.* OPP **inefficient** ▶ **efficiency** /ɪ'fɪʃnsi/ ***noun*** [U] ▶ **efficiently** ***adv.***

effigy /'efɪdʒi/ ***noun*** [C] (*pl.* **effigies**) **1** (RELIGION) a statue of a famous or religious person or a god **2** a model of a person that makes them look ugly: *The demonstrators burned a crude effigy of the president.*

effluent /'efluənt/ ***noun*** [U] (ENVIRONMENT) liquid waste, especially chemicals produced by factories

effort 🔑 /ˈefət/ *noun* **1** [U] the physical or mental strength or energy that you need to do sth; sth that takes a lot of energy: *They have* ***put a lot of effort into*** *their studies this year.* ◇ *He* ***made no effort*** *to contact his parents.* **2** [C] **an ~ (to do sth)** something that is done with difficulty or that takes a lot of energy: *It was a real effort to stay awake in the lecture.*

effortless /ˈefətləs/ *adj.* needing little or no effort so that sth seems easy ▶ **effortlessly** *adv.*

EFL /ˌiː ef ˈel/ *abbr.* (EDUCATION) English as a Foreign Language

e.g. 🔑 /ˌiː ˈdʒiː/ *abbr.* for example: *popular sports, e.g. football, tennis, swimming*

egalitarian /iˌgælɪˈteəriən/ *adj.* (POLITICS) (used about a person, system, society, etc.) following the principle that everyone should have equal rights

egg[1] 🔑 /eg/ *noun* **1** [C] an almost round object with a hard shell that contains a young bird, REPTILE or insect ➲ picture on **page 29** ❶ A female bird **lays** her eggs and then **sits on** them until they **hatch**. **2** [C,U] a bird's egg, especially one from a chicken, etc. that we eat **3** [C] (in women and female animals) the small cell that can join with a male seed (**sperm**) to make a baby

IDM **put all your eggs in one basket** to risk everything by depending completely on one thing, plan, etc. instead of giving yourself several possibilities

egg[2] /eg/ *verb*

PHR V **egg sb on (to do sth)** to encourage sb to do sth that they should not do

ˈ**egg cup** *noun* [C] a small cup for holding a boiled egg

eggplant /ˈegplɑːnt/ (*especially AmE*) = AUBERGINE

eggshell /ˈegʃel/ *noun* [C,U] the hard outside part of an egg

ego /ˈegəʊ/ *noun* [C] (*pl.* **egos**) the (good) opinion that you have of yourself: *It was a blow to her ego when she lost her job.*

egocentric /ˌegəʊˈsentrɪk/ *adj.* thinking only about yourself and not what other people need or want SYN **selfish**

egoism /ˈegəʊɪzəm; ˈiːg-/ (*also* **egotism** /ˈegətɪzəm; ˈiːg-/) *noun* [U] thinking about yourself too much; thinking that you are better or more important than anyone else ▶ **egoist** /ˈegəʊɪst; ˈiːg-/ (*also* **egotist** /ˈegətɪst; ˈiːgə-/) *noun* [C]: *I hate people who are egoists.* ▶ **egoistic** /ˌegəʊˈɪstɪk/ (*also* **egotistical** /ˌegəˈtɪstɪkl; ˌiːgə-/) *adj.*

eh /eɪ/ *exclamation* (*BrE, informal*) **1** used for asking sb to agree with you: *'Good party, eh?'* **2** used for asking sb to repeat sth: *'Did you like the film?' 'Eh?' 'I asked if you liked the film!'*

Eid (also **Id**) /iːd/ *noun* [C] (RELIGION) any of several Muslim festivals, especially one that celebrates the end of a month when people do not eat during the day (**Ramadan**)

eiderdown /ˈaɪdədaʊn/ *noun* [C] a covering for a bed filled with soft feathers (**down**), usually used on top of other COVERINGS for the bed ➲ look at **duvet**

eight /eɪt/ *number* **1** 8 ➲ note at **six** **2** **eight-** (used to form compounds) having eight of sth: *an eight-sided shape*

eighteen /ˌeɪˈtiːn/ *number* 18 ➲ note at **six**

eighteenth /ˌeɪˈtiːnθ/ *ordinal number, noun* [C] 18th ➲ note at **sixth**[1]

eighth[1] /eɪtθ/ *noun* [C] the FRACTION ⅛; one of eight equal parts of sth

eighth[2] /eɪtθ/ *ordinal number* 8th ➲ note at **sixth**[1]

ˈ**eighth note** (*AmE*) = QUAVER

eightieth /ˈeɪtiəθ/ *ordinal number, noun* [C] 80th ➲ note at **sixth**[1]

eighty /ˈeɪti/ *number* **1** 80 **2 the eighties** [pl.] numbers, years or temperatures from 80 to 89

einsteinium /aɪnˈstaɪniəm/ *noun* [U] (*symbol* **Es**) (CHEMISTRY) a chemical element. **Einsteinium** is a RADIOACTIVE element produced artificially from PLUTONIUM and other elements. ❶ For more information on the periodic table of elements, look at pages R34-5.

either[1] 🔑 /ˈaɪðə(r); ˈiːðə(r)/ *det., pronoun* **1** one or the other of two; it does not matter which: *You can choose either soup or salad, but not both.* ◇ *You can ask either of us for advice.* ◇ *Either of us is willing to help.* **2** both: *It is a pleasant road, with trees on either side.*

either[2] 🔑 /ˈaɪðə(r); ˈiːðə(r)/ *adv.* **1** (used after two negative statements) also: *I don't like Pat and I don't like Nick much either.* ◇ *'I can't remember his name.' 'I can't either.'* **2** used for emphasizing a negative statement: *The restaurant is quite good. And it's not expensive either.*

either[3] 🔑 /ˈaɪðə(r); ˈiːðə(r)/ *conj.* **either ... or ...** used when you are giving a choice, usually of two things: *I can meet you either Thursday or Friday.* ◇ *Either you leave or I do.* ◇ *You can either write or phone.*

ejaculate /iˈdʒækjuleɪt/ *verb* **1** [I] (BIOLOGY) to send out liquid (**semen**) from the male sexual organ (**penis**) **2** [I,T] (*old-fashioned*) to say sth suddenly ▶ **ejaculation** /iˌdʒækjuˈleɪʃn/ *noun* [C,U]

eject /iˈdʒekt/ *verb* **1** [T] (*formal*) (often passive) **~ sb (from sth)** to push or send sb/sth out of a place (usually with force): *The protesters were ejected from the building.* **2** [I,T] to remove a tape, disk, etc. from a machine, usually by pressing a button: *To eject the CD, press this button.* ◇ *After recording for three hours the video will eject automatically.* **3** [I] to escape from an aircraft that is going to crash

eke /iːk/ *verb*

PHR V **eke sth out** to make a small amount of sth last a long time

elaborate[1] /ɪˈlæbərət/ *adj.* very complicated; done or made very carefully: *an elaborate pattern* ◇ *elaborate plans*

elaborate[2] /ɪˈlæbəreɪt/ *verb* [I] (*formal*) **~ (on sth)** to give more details about sth: *Could you elaborate on that idea?*

elapse /ɪˈlæps/ *verb* [I] (*formal*) (used about time) to pass

elastic[1] /ɪˈlæstɪk/ *noun* [U] material with rubber in it which can stretch

elastic[2] /ɪˈlæstɪk/ *adj.* **1** (used about material, etc.) that returns to its original size and shape after being stretched **2** that can be changed; not fixed: *Our rules are quite elastic.*

eˌlastic ˈband = RUBBER BAND

elasticity /ˌiːlæˈstɪsəti; ˌelæ-; ɪˌlæ-/ *noun* [U] the quality that sth has of being able to stretch and return to its original size and shape

elated /iˈleɪtɪd/ *adj.* very happy and excited ▶ **elation** /iˈleɪʃn/ *noun* [U]

elbow[1] ⊶ /'elbəʊ/ ***noun*** [C] **1** the place where the bones of your arm join and your arm bends ➲ picture on **page 80** **2** the part of the sleeve of a coat, jacket, etc. that covers the elbow

elbow[2] /'elbəʊ/ ***verb*** [T] to push sb with your elbow: *She elbowed me out of the way.*

'elbow room ***noun*** [U] enough space to move freely

elder[1] /'eldə(r)/ ***adj.*** (only *before* a noun) older (of two members of a family): *My elder daughter is at university now but the other one is still at school.* ◇ *an elder brother/sister*

elder[2] /'eldə(r)/ ***noun*** **1** [sing.] **the elder** the older of two people: *Who is the elder of the two?* **2 my, etc. elder** [sing.] a person who is older than me, etc.: *He is her elder by several years.* **3 elders** [pl.] older people: *Do children still respect the opinions of their elders?*

elderly ⊶ /'eldəli/ ***adj.*** **1** (used about a person) old **2 the elderly** ***noun*** [pl.] old people in general: *The elderly need special care in winter.* ➲ look at **old**

eldest /'eldɪst/ ***adj.***, ***noun*** [C] (the) oldest (of three or more members of a family): *Their eldest child is a boy.* ◇ *John's got four boys. The eldest has just gone to university.*

elect[1] ⊶ /ɪ'lekt/ ***verb*** [T] **1** ~ **sb (to sth)**; ~ **sb (as sth)** (POLITICS) to choose sb to have a particular job or position by voting for them: *He was elected to Parliament in 1970.* ◇ *The committee elected her as their representative.* **2** (*formal*) ~ **to do sth** to decide to do sth

elect[2] /ɪ'lekt/ ***adj.*** used after nouns to show that sb has been chosen for a job, but is not yet doing that job: *the president elect*

election ⊶ /ɪ'lekʃn/ ***noun*** [C,U] (POLITICS) (the time of) choosing a Member of Parliament, President, etc. by voting: *In America, presidential elections are held every four years.* ◇ *If you're interested in politics why not* ***stand for election*** *yourself?*

CULTURE

In Britain, **general elections** are held about every five years. Sometimes **by-elections** are held at other times. In each region (**constituency**) voters must choose one person from a list of **candidates**.

elective /ɪ'lektɪv/ ***adj.*** (usually *before* a noun) (*formal*) **1** (POLITICS) using or chosen by election: *an elective democracy* ◇ *an elective member* **2** having the power to elect: *an elective body* **3** (used about medical treatment) that you choose to have; that is not urgent: *elective surgery* **4** (used about a course or subject) that a student can choose

elector /ɪ'lektə(r)/ ***noun*** [C] (POLITICS) a person who has the right to vote in an election ▶ **electoral** /ɪ'lektərəl/ ***adj.***: *the electoral register/roll* (=the list of electors in an area)

electorate /ɪ'lektərət/ ***noun*** [C, with sing. or pl. verb] (POLITICS) all the people who can vote in a region, country, etc.

electric ⊶ /ɪ'lektrɪk/ ***adj.*** **1** producing or using electricity: *an electric current* ◇ *an electric kettle* **2** very exciting: *The atmosphere in the room was electric.*

electrical ⊶ /ɪ'lektrɪkl/ ***adj.*** of or about electricity: *an electrical appliance* (=a machine that uses electricity) ◇ *an electrical engineer* (=a person who produces electrical systems and equipment)

the e,lectric 'chair ***noun*** [sing.] a chair used in some countries for killing criminals with a very strong electric current

electrician /ɪ,lek'trɪʃn/ ***noun*** [C] a person whose job is to make and repair electrical systems and equipment

electricity ⊶ /ɪ,lek'trɪsəti/ ***noun*** [U] (PHYSICS) a type of energy that we use to make heat, light and power to work machines, etc.: *Turn that light off. We don't want to waste electricity.*

RELATED VOCABULARY

Electricity is usually **generated** in **power stations**. It may also be produced by **generators** or by **batteries**.

e,lectric 'razor = SHAVER

e,lectric 'shock (*also* **shock**) ***noun*** [C] (HEALTH) a sudden painful feeling that you get if electricity goes through your body

electrify /ɪ'lektrɪfaɪ/ ***verb*** [T] (*pres. part.* **electrifying**; *3rd person sing. pres.* **electrifies**; *pt, pp* **electrified**) **1** (PHYSICS) to supply sth with electricity: *The railways are being electrified.* **2** to make sb very excited: *Ronaldo electrified the crowd with his pace and skill.*

electro- /ɪ'lektrəʊ/ ***prefix*** (PHYSICS) (in nouns, adjectives, verbs and adverbs) connected with electricity: *electromagnetism*

electrocute /ɪ'lektrəkju:t/ ***verb*** [T] to kill sb with electricity that goes through the body ▶ **electrocution** /ɪ,lektrə'kju:ʃn/ ***noun*** [U]

electrode /ɪ'lektrəʊd/ ***noun*** [C] (PHYSICS) one of two points (**terminals**) where an electric current enters or leaves a battery, etc.

electrolysis /ɪ,lek'trɒləsɪs/ ***noun*** [U] **1** a way of permanently getting rid of hairs on the body by using an electric current **2** (CHEMISTRY, PHYSICS) a way of separating a liquid into its different chemical parts by passing an electric current through it

electrolyte /ɪ'lektrəlaɪt/ ***noun*** [C] (PHYSICS, CHEMISTRY) a liquid that an electric current can pass through, especially in an electric cell or battery ➲ picture at **cell**

electrolytic cell /ɪ,lektrə,lɪtɪk 'sel/ ***noun*** [C] (CHEMISTRY, PHYSICS) a device that produces an electric current caused by the chemical reaction between an ELECTROLYTE and two ELECTRODES inside a container

electromagnet /ɪ'lektrəʊmægnət/ ***noun*** [C] (PHYSICS) a piece of metal which becomes MAGNETIC (=having the ability to attract metal objects) when electricity is passed through it

electromagnetic /ɪ,lektrəʊmæg'netɪk/ ***adj.*** (PHYSICS) having both electrical characteristics and the ability to attract metal objects: *an* ***electromagnetic wave/field*** ▶ **electromagnetism** /ɪ,lektrəʊ'mægnətɪzəm/ ***noun*** [U]

electron /ɪ'lektrɒn/ ***noun*** [C] (CHEMISTRY, PHYSICS) one of the three types of PARTICLES that form all atoms. **Electrons** have a negative electric charge. ➲ look at **neutron**, **proton**

electronic ⊶ /ɪ,lek'trɒnɪk/ ***adj.*** **1** (PHYSICS, COMPUTING) using **electronics**: *electronic equipment* ◇ *This dictionary is available in electronic form* (=on a computer disk). **2** (COMPUTING) done using a computer: *electronic banking/shopping* ▶ **electronically** /-kli/ ***adv.***

electronics /ɪ,lek'trɒnɪks/ ***noun*** [U] (PHYSICS, COMPUTING) the technology used to produce computers, radios, etc.: *the electronics industry*

electrostatic /ɪˌlektrəʊˈstætɪk/ *adj.* (PHYSICS) used to talk about electric charges that are not moving, rather than electric currents

elegant /ˈelɪɡənt/ *adj.* having a good or attractive style: *She looked very elegant in her new dress.* ◇ *an elegant coat* ▸ **elegance** /ˈelɪɡəns/ *noun* [U] ▸ **elegantly** *adv.*

elegy /ˈelədʒi/ *noun* [C] (*pl.* **elegies**) (LITERATURE, MUSIC) a poem or song that expresses sadness, especially for sb who has died

element AW /ˈelɪmənt/ *noun* **1** [C] one important part of sth: *Cost is an important element when we're thinking about holidays.* **2** [C, usually sing.] **an ~ of sth** a small amount of sth: *There was an element of truth in what he said.* **3** [C] people of a certain type: *The criminal element at football matches causes a lot of trouble.* **4** [C] (CHEMISTRY) a simple chemical substance that consists of atoms of only one type and cannot be split by chemical means into a simpler substance. Gold, OXYGEN and CARBON are all **elements**. ➲ look at **compound**[1] (2) **5** [C] the metal part of a piece of electrical equipment that produces heat **6 the elements** [pl.] (bad) weather: *to be exposed to the elements*
IDM **in/out of your element** in a situation where you feel comfortable/uncomfortable: *Bill's in his element speaking to a large group of people, but I hate it.*

elementary /ˌelɪˈmentri/ *adj.* **1** (EDUCATION) connected with the first stages of learning sth: *an elementary course in English* ◇ *a book for elementary students* **2** basic; not difficult: *elementary physics*

ˌelementary ˈparticle *noun* [C] (PHYSICS) any of the different types of very small pieces of matter (= a substance) smaller than an atom

ˌeleˈmentary school *noun* [C] (*AmE*) (EDUCATION) a school for children aged six to eleven

elephant /ˈelɪfənt/ *noun* [C] a very large grey animal with big ears, two long curved teeth (**tusks**) and a long nose (**trunk**)

elevate /ˈelɪveɪt/ *verb* [T] (*formal*) to move sb/sth to a higher place or more important position: *an elevated platform* ◇ *He was elevated to the Board of Directors.*

elevation /ˌelɪˈveɪʃn/ *noun* **1** [C,U] (*formal*) the process of moving to a higher place or more important position: *his elevation to the presidency* **2** [C] (GEOGRAPHY) the height of a place, especially its height above sea level: *The city is **at an elevation of** 2000 metres.* **3** [C] (*formal*) a piece of ground that is higher than the area around **4** [C] (ARCHITECTURE) one side of a building, or a drawing of this by an ARCHITECT: *the **front/rear/side elevation** of a house* **5** [U, sing.] (TECHNICAL) an increase in the level or amount of sth: *elevation of blood sugar levels*

elevator /ˈelɪveɪtə(r)/ *noun* [C] **1** (*AmE*) = LIFT[2] (1) **2** a part in the tail of an aircraft that is moved to make it go up or down ➲ picture at **plane**

eleven /ɪˈlevn/ *number* 11

eleventh /ɪˈlevnθ/ *pronoun, det., adv.* 11th

elf /elf/ *noun* [C] (*pl.* **elves** /elvz/) (in stories) a small creature with pointed ears who has magic powers

elicit /iˈlɪsɪt/ *verb* [T] (*formal*) **~ sth (from sb)** to manage to get information, facts, a reaction, etc. from sb

eligible /ˈelɪdʒəbl/ *adj.* **~ (for sth/to do sth)** having the right to do or have sth: *In Britain, you are eligible to vote when you are eighteen.* OPP **ineligible** ▸ **eligibility** /ˌelɪdʒəˈbɪləti/ *noun* [U]: *Marriage to a national gave automatic eligibility for citizenship.*

eliminate AW /ɪˈlɪmɪneɪt/ *verb* [T] **1** to remove sb/sth that is not wanted or needed: *We must try and eliminate the problem.* **2** (often passive) to stop sb going further in a competition, etc.: *The school team was eliminated in the first round of the competition.* ▸ **elimination** AW /ɪˌlɪmɪˈneɪʃn/ *noun* [U]

elite /eɪˈliːt/ *noun* [C, with sing. or pl. verb] a social group that is thought to be the best or most important because of its power, money, intelligence, etc.: *an intellectual elite* ◇ *an elite group of artists*

elitism /eɪˈliːtɪzəm/ *noun* [U] the belief that some people should be treated in a special way ▸ **elitist** /-tɪst/ *noun* [C], *adj.*

Elizabethan /ɪˌlɪzəˈbiːθn/ *adj.* (HISTORY) connected with the time when Queen Elizabeth I was queen of England (1558–1603): *Elizabethan drama/music* ◇ *The Elizabethan age was a time of exploration and discovery.* ▸ **Elizabethan** *noun* [C]: *Shakespeare was an Elizabethan.*

elk /elk/ (*AmE* **moose**) *noun* [C] a very large wild animal (**deer**) with large flat horns (**antlers**)

ellipse /ɪˈlɪps/ *noun* [C] (GEOMETRY) a regular OVAL, like a circle that has been pressed in from two sides ➲ picture at **conic**

ellipsis /ɪˈlɪpsɪs/ *noun* [C, U] (*pl.* **ellipses** /-siːz/) **1** (LANGUAGE) the act of leaving out a word or words from a sentence deliberately, when the meaning can be understood without them **2** (LANGUAGE) three dots (...) used to show that a word or words have been left out

elliptical /ɪˈlɪptɪkl/ *adj.* **1** having a word or words left out of a sentence deliberately: *an elliptical remark* (= one that suggests more than is actually said) **2** (*also* **elliptic** /ɪˈlɪptɪk/) (GEOMETRY) connected with or in the form of an ELLIPSE ▸ **elliptically** /-kli/ *adj.*: *to speak/write elliptically*

elm /elm/ (*also* **ˈelm tree**) *noun* [C] a tall tree with broad leaves

El Niño /el ˈniːnjəʊ/ *noun* [C, usually sing.] (GEOGRAPHY) a series of changes in the climate affecting parts of the Pacific region every few years

elocution /ˌeləˈkjuːʃn/ *noun* [U] the ability to speak clearly, correctly and without a strong ACCENT (= a particular way of pronouncing words that is connected with the country, area or social class that you come from)

elongate /ˈiːlɒŋɡeɪt/ *verb* [I,T] to become longer; to make sth longer: *The seal pup's body elongates as it gets older.* ▸ **elongation** /ˌiːlɒŋˈɡeɪʃn/ *noun* [U]: *the elongation of vowel sounds*

elongated /ˈiːlɒŋɡeɪtɪd/ *adj.* long and thin

elope /ɪˈləʊp/ *verb* [I] **~ (with sb)** to run away secretly to get married

eloquent /ˈeləkwənt/ *adj.* (*formal*) able to use language and express your opinions well, especially when you speak in public ▸ **eloquence** *noun* [U] ▸ **eloquently** *adv.*

else /els/ *adv.* (used after words formed with *any-, no-, some-* and after question words) another, different person, thing or place: *This isn't mine. It must be **someone else's**.* ◇ *Was it you who phoned me, or **somebody else**?* ◇ ***Everybody else** is allowed to stay up late.* ◇ *You'll have to pay. **Nobody else** will.* ◇ ***What else** would you like?* ◇ *I'm tired of that cafe – shall we go **somewhere else** for a change?*
IDM **or else** otherwise; if not: *You'd better go to bed now or else you'll be tired in the morning.* ◇ *He's either forgotten or else he's decided not to come.*

elsewhere 🔑 /ˌelsˈweə(r)/ ***adv.*** in or to another place: *He's travelled a lot – in Europe and elsewhere.*

ELT /ˌiː el ˈtiː/ ***abbr.*** (**EDUCATION**) English Language Teaching

elude /iˈluːd/ ***verb*** [T] (*formal*) **1** to manage to avoid being caught: *The escaped prisoner eluded the police for three days.* **2** to be difficult or impossible to remember: *I remember his face but his name eludes me.*

elusive /iˈluːsɪv/ ***adj.*** not easy to catch, find or remember

elves plural of **elf**

'em /əm/ ***pronoun*** (*informal*) = THEM

emaciated /ɪˈmeɪʃieɪtɪd/ ***adj.*** (**HEALTH**) extremely thin and weak because of illness, lack of food, etc. ▶ **emaciation** /ɪˌmeɪsiˈeɪʃn/ ***noun*** [U]

email 🔑 /ˈiːmeɪl/ ***noun*** **1** [U] (**COMPUTING**) a way of sending electronic messages or data from one computer to another: *to send a message* ***by email*** **2** [C,U] a message or messages sent by email: ***I'll send you an email*** *tomorrow.* ▶ **email** ***verb*** [T]: *I'll email the information to you*

emanate /ˈeməneɪt/ ***verb*** [T] (*formal*) to produce or show sth: *He emanates power and confidence.*
PHR V **emanate from sth** to come from sth or somewhere: *The sound of loud music emanated from the building.*

emancipate /ɪˈmænsɪpeɪt/ ***verb*** [T] (*formal*) (**SOCIAL STUDIES**) to give sb the same legal, social and political rights as other people ▶ **emancipation** /ɪˌmænsɪˈpeɪʃn/ ***noun*** [U]

embalm /ɪmˈbɑːm/ ***verb*** [T] to treat a dead body with special substances in order to keep it in good condition

embankment /ɪmˈbæŋkmənt/ ***noun*** [C] a wall of stone or earth that is built to stop a river from flooding or to carry a road or railway

embargo /ɪmˈbɑːɡəʊ/ ***noun*** [C] (*pl.* **embargoes**) (**POLITICS**) an official order to stop doing business with another country: *to impose an embargo on sth* ◇ *to lift/remove an embargo*

embark /ɪmˈbɑːk/ ***verb*** [I] to get on a ship: *Passengers with cars must embark first.* OPP **disembark** ▶ **embarkation** /ˌembɑːˈkeɪʃn/ ***noun*** [C,U]
PHR V **embark on sth** (*formal*) to start sth (new): *I'm embarking on a completely new career.*

embarrass 🔑 /ɪmˈbærəs/ ***verb*** [T] to make sb feel uncomfortable or shy: *Don't ever embarrass me in front of my friends again!* ◇ *The Minister's mistake embarrassed the government.*

embarrassed 🔑 /ɪmˈbærəst/ ***adj.*** feeling uncomfortable or shy because of sth silly you have done, because people are looking at you, etc.: *I felt so embarrassed when I dropped my glass.*

embarrassing 🔑 /ɪmˈbærəsɪŋ/ ***adj.*** making you feel uncomfortable or shy: *an embarrassing question/mistake/situation* ▶ **embarrassingly** ***adv.***

embarrassment 🔑 /ɪmˈbærəsmənt/ ***noun*** **1** [U] the feeling you have when you are embarrassed **2** [C] a person or thing that makes you embarrassed

embassy /ˈembəsi/ ***noun*** [C] (*pl.* **embassies**) (**POLITICS**) (the official building of) a group of officials (**diplomats**) and their head (**ambassador**), who represent their government in a foreign country ➲ look at **consulate**

embed /ɪmˈbed/ ***verb*** [T] (**embedding**; **embedded**) (usually passive) to fix sth firmly and deeply (in sth else): *The axe was embedded in the piece of wood.*

embellish /ɪmˈbelɪʃ/ ***verb*** [T] (*written*) **1** to make sth more beautiful by adding decoration to it **2** to make a story more interesting by adding details that are not always true ▶ **embellishment** ***noun*** [U, C]: *Good meat needs very little embellishment.*

ember /ˈembə(r)/ ***noun*** [C, usually pl.] a piece of wood or coal that is not burning, but is still red and hot after a fire has died

embezzle /ɪmˈbezl/ ***verb*** [T] (**LAW**) to steal money that you are responsible for or that belongs to your employer ▶ **embezzlement** ***noun*** [U]

embitter /ɪmˈbɪtə(r)/ ***verb*** [T] to make sb feel angry or disappointed about sth over a long period of time ▶ **embittered** ***adj.***: *a sick and embittered old man*

emblem /ˈembləm/ ***noun*** [C] an object or symbol that represents sth: *The dove is the emblem of peace.*

embody /ɪmˈbɒdi/ ***verb*** [T] (*pres. part.* **embodying**; *3rd person sing. pres.* **embodies**; *pp, pt* **embodied**) (*formal*) **1** to be a very good example of sth: *To me she embodies all the best qualities of a teacher.* **2** to include or contain sth: *This latest model embodies many new features.* ▶ **embodiment** ***noun*** [C]: *She is the embodiment of a caring mother.*

emboss /ɪmˈbɒs/ ***verb*** [T] ~ **A with B**; ~ **B on A** (**ART**) to put a raised design or piece of writing on paper, leather, etc.: *stationery embossed with the hotel's name* ◇ *The hotel's name was embossed on the stationery.* ▶ **embossed** ***adj.***: *embossed stationery*

embrace /ɪmˈbreɪs/ ***verb*** **1** [I,T] to put your arms around sb as a sign of love, happiness, etc. **2** [T] (*formal*) to include: *His report embraced all the main points.* **3** [T] (*formal*) to accept sth with enthusiasm: *She embraced Christianity in her later years.* ▶ **embrace** ***noun*** [C]: *He held her in a warm embrace.*

embroider /ɪmˈbrɔɪdə(r)/ ***verb*** **1** [I,T] to decorate cloth by sewing a pattern or picture on it **2** [T] to add details that are not true to a story to make it more interesting ▶ **embroidery** /-dəri/ ***noun*** [U]

embryo /ˈembriəʊ/ ***noun*** [C] (*pl.* **embryos** /-əʊz/) (**BIOLOGY**) a baby, an animal or a plant in the early stages of development before birth ➲ look at **foetus** ➲ picture at **fertilize** ▶ **embryonic** /ˌembriˈɒnɪk/ ***adj.***

emcee /emˈsiː/ ***noun*** [C] **1** (*AmE*, *informal*) a person who introduces guests or entertainers at a formal occasion SYN **master of ceremonies** **2** an MC at a club or a party

emerald /ˈemərəld/ ***noun*** [C] a bright green PRECIOUS STONE ▶ **emerald** (*also* ˌ**emerald** ˈ**green**) ***adj.***: *an emerald green dress*

emerge 🔑 AW /iˈmɜːdʒ/ ***verb*** [I] ~ (**from sth**) **1** to appear or come out from somewhere: *A man emerged from the shadows.* ◇ (*figurative*) *The country emerged from the war in ruins.* **2** to become known: *During investigations* ***it emerged that*** *she was lying about her age.* ▶ **emergence** AW /-dʒəns/ ***noun*** [U]: *the emergence of Aids in the 1980s*

emergency 🔑 /iˈmɜːdʒənsi/ ***noun*** [C,U] (*pl.* **emergencies**) a serious event that needs immediate action: *In an emergency phone 999 for help.* ◇ *The government has declared* ***a state of emergency.*** ◇ *an emergency exit*

e'mergency room (*AmE*) = ACCIDENT AND EMERGENCY

emergent AW /iˈmɜːdʒənt/ *adj.* new and still developing: *emergent nations/states*

emigrant /ˈemɪɡrənt/ *noun* [C] (SOCIAL STUDIES) a person who has gone to live in another country ➲ look at **immigrant**

emigrate /ˈemɪɡreɪt/ *verb* [I] ~ **(from…) (to…)** (SOCIAL STUDIES) to leave your own country to go and live in another: *They emigrated from Ireland to Australia twenty years ago.* ➲ look at **immigrate**, **migrate** ▶ **emigration** /ˌemɪˈɡreɪʃn/ *noun* [C,U] ➲ look at **immigration**

eminent /ˈemɪnənt/ *adj.* (*formal*) (used about a person) famous and important: *an eminent scientist*

eminently /ˈemɪnəntli/ *adv.* (*formal*) very; extremely: *She is eminently suitable for the job.*

emir (also **amir**) /eˈmɪə(r); ˈemɪə(r)/ *noun* [C] (POLITICS) the title given to some Muslim rulers: *the Emir of Kuwait*

emirate /ˈemɪərət; ˈemɪrət/ *noun* [C] **1** (POLITICS) the position held by an emir; the period of time that he is in power **2** an area of land that is ruled over by an emir: *the United Arab Emirates*

emissary /ˈemɪsəri/ *noun* [C] (*pl.* **emissaries**) (*formal*) (POLITICS) a person who is sent somewhere, especially to another country, in order to give sb an official message or to perform a special task

emit /iˈmɪt/ *verb* [T] (**emitting**; **emitted**) (*formal*) to send out sth, for example a smell, a sound, smoke, heat or light: *The animal emits a powerful smell when scared.* ▶ **emission** /iˈmɪʃn/ (ENVIRONMENT) *noun* [C,U]: *sulphur dioxide emissions from power stations*

emoticon /ɪˈməʊtɪkɒn/ *noun* [C] (COMPUTING) a symbol that shows your feelings when you send an email or text message. For example:-) represents a smiling face.

emotion ⊶ /ɪˈməʊʃn/ *noun* [C,U] a strong feeling such as love, anger, fear, etc.: *to control/express your emotions* ◇ *His voice was filled with emotion.* ◇ *He showed no emotion as the police took him away.*

emotional ⊶ /ɪˈməʊʃənl/ *adj.* **1** connected with people's feelings: *emotional problems* **2** causing strong feelings: *He gave an emotional speech.* **3** having strong emotions and showing them in front of people: *She always **gets** very **emotional** when I leave.* ▶ **emotionally** /-ʃənəli/ *adv.*: *She felt physically and emotionally drained after giving birth.*

emotive /iˈməʊtɪv/ *adj.* causing strong feelings: *emotive language* ◇ *an emotive issue*

empathy /ˈempəθi/ *noun* [C,U] ~ **(with/for sb/sth)**; ~ **(between A and B)** the ability to imagine how another person is feeling and so understand their mood: *Some adults **have** (a) great **empathy** with children.* ▶ **empathize** (also **-ise**) /ˈempəθaɪz/ *verb* [I] ~ **(with sb/sth)**: *He's a popular teacher because he empathizes with his students.*

emperor /ˈempərə(r)/ *noun* [C] (POLITICS, HISTORY) the ruler of an empire

emphasis ⊶ AW /ˈemfəsɪs/ *noun* [C,U] (*pl.* **emphases** /-siːz/) **1** ~ **(on sth)** (giving) special importance or attention (to sth): *There's a lot of emphasis on science at our school.* ◇ *You should **put** a greater **emphasis** on quality rather than quantity when you write.* **2** the force that you give to a word or phrase when you are speaking; a way of writing a word to show that it is important: *In the word 'photographer' the emphasis is on the second syllable.* ◇ *I underlined the key phrases of my letter for emphasis.* SYN **stress**[1]

emphasize (also **-ise**) ⊶ AW /ˈemfəsaɪz/ *verb* [T] ~ **(that…)** to put emphasis on sth: *They emphasized that healthy eating is important.* ◇ *They emphasized the importance of healthy eating.* SYN **stress**[2]

emphatic AW /ɪmˈfætɪk/ *adj.* said or expressed in a strong way: *an emphatic refusal* ▶ **emphatically** /-kli/ *adv.*

emphysema /ˌemfɪˈsiːmə/ *noun* [U] (HEALTH, HEALTH) a condition that affects the lungs, making it difficult to breathe

empire ⊶ /ˈempaɪə(r)/ *noun* [C] **1** (POLITICS, HISTORY) a group of countries that is governed by one country: *the Roman Empire* ➲ look at **emperor**, **empress** **2** a very large company or group of companies

empirical AW /ɪmˈpɪrɪkl/ *adj.* (*formal*) based on experiments and practical experience, not on ideas: *empirical evidence* ▶ **empirically** /-kli/ *adv.*

empiricism AW /ɪmˈpɪrɪsɪzəm/ *noun* [U] (*formal*) the use of experiments or experience as the basis for your ideas; the belief in these methods ▶ **empiricist** *noun* [C]: *the English empiricist, John Locke*

employ ⊶ /ɪmˈplɔɪ/ *verb* [T] **1** ~ **sb (in/on sth)**; ~ **sb (as sth)** (ECONOMICS, SOCIAL STUDIES) to pay sb to work for you: *He is employed as a lorry driver.* ◇ *They employ 600 workers.* ◇ *Three people are employed on the task of designing a new computer system.* ➲ look at **unemployed** **2** (*formal*) ~ **sth (as sth)** to use: *In an emergency, an umbrella can be employed as a weapon.*

employee ⊶ /ɪmˈplɔɪiː/ *noun* [C] (ECONOMICS, SOCIAL STUDIES) a person who works for sb: *The factory has 500 employees.*

employer ⊶ /ɪmˈplɔɪə(r)/ *noun* [C] (ECONOMICS, SOCIAL STUDIES) a person or company that employs other people

employment ⊶ /ɪmˈplɔɪmənt/ *noun* [U] **1** (ECONOMICS, SOCIAL STUDIES) the state of having a paid job: *to be in/out of employment* ◇ *This bank can **give employment to** ten extra staff.* ◇ *It is difficult to **find employment** in the north of the country.* ➲ look at **unemployment** ➲ note at **work**[1] **2** (*formal*) the use of sth: *the employment of force*

em'ployment agency *noun* [C] a company that helps people to find work and other companies to find workers

empower /ɪmˈpaʊə(r)/ *verb* [T] (*formal*) (usually passive) to give sb power or authority (to do sth) ▶ **empowerment** *noun* [U]

empress /ˈemprəs/ *noun* [C] **1** (POLITICS, HISTORY) a woman who rules an empire **2** the wife of a man who rules an empire (**emperor**)

empty[1] ⊶ /ˈempti/ *adj.* (**emptier**; **emptiest**) **1** having nothing or nobody inside it: *an empty box* ◇ *The bus was half empty.* **2** without meaning or value: *It was an empty threat* (=it was not meant seriously). ◇ *My life feels empty now the children have left home.* ▶ **emptiness** /ˈemptinəs/ *noun* [U]

empty[2] ⊶ /ˈempti/ *verb* (*pres. part.* **emptying**; *3rd person sing. pres.* **empties**; *pt, pp* **emptied**) **1** [T] ~ **sth (out/out of sth)** to remove everything that is inside a container, etc.: *I've emptied a wardrobe for you to use.* ◇ *Luke emptied everything out of his desk and left.* **2** [I] to become empty: *The cinema emptied very quickly once the film was finished.*

ˌ**empty-ˈhanded** *adj.* without getting what you wanted; without taking sth to sb: *The robbers fled empty-handed.*

EMU /ˌiː em ˈjuː/ *abbr.* (ECONOMICS) **Economic and Monetary Union** (of the countries of the European Union)

emulate /ˈemjuleɪt/ *verb* [T] (*formal*) to try to do sth as well as sb else because you admire them

emulsifier /ɪˈmʌlsɪfaɪə(r)/ *noun* [C] a substance that is added to mixtures of food to make the different liquids or substances in them combine to form a smooth mixture

emulsify /ɪˈmʌlsɪfaɪ/ *verb* [I,T] (*pres. part.* **emulsifying**; *3rd person sing. pres.* **emulsifies**; *pt, pp* **emulsified**) (CHEMISTRY) if two liquids of different thicknesses **emulsify** or are **emulsified**, they combine to form a smooth mixture

emulsion /ɪˈmʌlʃn/ *noun* [C,U] **1** (CHEMISTRY) any mixture of liquids that do not normally mix together, such as oil and water **2** (*also* **eˈmulsion paint**) a type of paint used on walls and ceilings that dries without leaving a shiny surface **3** a substance on the surface of film used for photographs that makes it sensitive to light

en- /ɪn/ (also **em-** /ɪm/ before b, m or p) *prefix* (in verbs) **1** to put into the thing or condition mentioned: *encase* ◇ *endanger* ◇ *empower* **2** to cause to be: *enlarge* ◇ *embolden*

enable 🔑 AW /ɪˈneɪbl/ *verb* [T] **~ sb/sth to do sth** to make it possible for sb/sth to do sth: *The new law has enabled more women to return to work.*

enact /ɪˈnækt/ *verb* [T] **1** (LAW) to pass a law: *legislation enacted by parliament* **2** (*formal*) to perform a play or act a part in a play: *scenes from history enacted by local residents* **3 be enacted** (*formal*) to take place: *They were unaware of the drama being enacted a few feet away from them.*

enamel /ɪˈnæml/ *noun* [U] **1** (ART) a hard, shiny substance used for protecting or decorating metal, etc.: *enamel paint* **2** (BIOLOGY) the hard white outer covering of a tooth ➲ picture at **tooth**

enc. = ENCL.

encephalitis /enˌsefəˈlaɪtəs; -ˌkefə-/ *noun* [U] (HEALTH) a condition in which the brain becomes swollen, caused by an infection or ALLERGIC reaction

encephalopathy /enˌsefəˈlɒpəθi; -ˌkefə-/ *noun* [U] (HEALTH) a disease in which the functioning of the brain is affected by infection, BLOOD POISONING, etc. ➲ look at **BSE**

enchanted /ɪnˈtʃɑːntɪd/ *adj.* **1** (in stories) affected by magic powers **2** (*formal*) pleased or very interested: *The audience was enchanted by her singing.*

enchanting /ɪnˈtʃɑːntɪŋ/ *adj.* very nice or pleasant; attractive

encircle /ɪnˈsɜːkl/ *verb* [T] (*formal*) to make a circle round sth; to surround: *London is encircled by the M25 motorway.*

encl. (also **enc.**) *abbr.* **enclosed**; used on business letters to show that another document is being sent in the same envelope

enclose /ɪnˈkləʊz/ *verb* [T] **1 ~ sth (in sth)** (usually passive) to surround sth with a wall, fence, etc.; to put one thing inside another: *The jewels were enclosed in a strong box.* ◇ *He gets very nervous in enclosed spaces.* **2** to put sth in an envelope, package, etc. with sth else: *Can I enclose a letter with this parcel?* ◇ ***Please find enclosed** a cheque for £100.*

enclosure /ɪnˈkləʊʒə(r)/ *noun* [C] **1** a piece of land inside a wall, fence, etc. that is used for a particular purpose: *a wildlife enclosure* **2** something that is placed inside an envelope together with the letter

encode /ɪnˈkəʊd/ *verb* [T] **1** to change ordinary language into letters, symbols, etc. in order to send secret messages **2** (COMPUTING) to change information into a form that a computer can deal with ▶ **encoder** *noun* [C]

encompass /ɪnˈkʌmpəs/ *verb* [T] (*formal*) **1** to include a large number or range of things: *The job encompasses a wide range of responsibilities.* **2** to surround or cover sth completely: *The fog soon encompassed the whole valley.*

encore[1] /ˈɒŋkɔː(r)/ *exclamation* called out by an audience that wants the performers in a concert, etc. to sing or play sth extra

encore[2] /ˈɒŋkɔː(r)/ *noun* [C] a short, extra performance at the end of a concert, etc.

encounter[1] 🔑 AW /ɪnˈkaʊntə(r)/ *verb* [T] **1** to experience sth (a danger, difficulty, etc.): *I've never encountered any discrimination at work.* SYN **meet with 2** (*formal*) to meet sb unexpectedly; to experience or find sth unusual or new SYN **come across**

encounter[2] 🔑 AW /ɪnˈkaʊntə(r)/ *noun* [C] **an ~ (with sb/sth); an ~ (between A and B)** an unexpected (often unpleasant) meeting or event: *I've had a number of **close encounters*** (=situations which could have been dangerous) *with bad drivers.*

encourage 🔑 /ɪnˈkʌrɪdʒ/ *verb* [T] **1 ~ sb/sth (in sth/to do sth)** to give hope, support or confidence to sb: *The teacher encouraged her students to ask questions.* **2** to make sth happen more easily: *The government wants to encourage new businesses.* OPP **discourage** ▶ **encouraging** *adj.*

encouragement 🔑 /ɪnˈkʌrɪdʒmənt/ *noun* [C,U] **~ (to sb) (to do sth)** the act of encouraging sb to do sth; something that encourages sb: *a few words of encouragement* ◇ *He needs all the support and encouragement he can get.*

encroach /ɪnˈkrəʊtʃ/ *verb* [I] (*formal*) **~ (on/upon sth)** to use more of sth than you should: *I do hope that I am not encroaching too much upon your free time.*

encrypt /ɪnˈkrɪpt/ *verb* [T] (COMPUTING) to put information into a special form (**code**) especially in order to stop people being able to look at or understand it ▶ **encryption** /ɪnˈkrɪpʃn/ *noun* [U]

encyclopedia (also **encyclopaedia**) /ɪnˌsaɪkləˈpiːdiə/ *noun* [C] (*pl.* **encyclopedias**) a book or set of books that gives information about very many subjects, arranged in the order of the alphabet (=from A to Z)

end[1] 🔑 /end/ *noun* [C] **1** the furthest or last part of sth; the place or time where sth stops: *My house is **at the end of** the street.* ◇ *There are some seats **at the far end of** the room.* ◇ *I'm going on holiday **at the end of** October.* ◇ *He promised to give me an answer by the end of the week.* ◇ *She couldn't wait to hear the end of the story.* HELP The noun **finish** is used to mean **end** only in connection with races and competitions. **2** (*formal*) an aim or purpose: *They were prepared to do anything to achieve their ends.* ➲ note at **target**[1] **3** a little piece of sth that is left after the rest has been used: *a cigarette end*

IDM **at an end** (*formal*) finished or used up: *Her career is at an end.*

at the end of your tether having no more patience or strength
at the end of the day (*spoken*) used to say the most important fact in a situation: *At the end of the day, you have to make the decision yourself.*
at a loose end → LOOSE[1]
at your wits' end → WIT
bring sth/come/draw to an end (to cause sth) to finish: *His stay in England was coming to an end.*
a dead end → DEAD[1]
end to end in a line with the ends touching: *They put the tables end to end.*
in the end finally; after a long period of time or series of events: *He wanted to get home early but in the end it was midnight before he left.*
make ends meet to have enough money for your needs: *It's hard for us to make ends meet.*
make sb's hair stand on end → HAIR
a means to an end → MEANS
no end of sth (*spoken*) too many or much; a lot of sth: *She has given us no end of trouble.*
odds and ends → ODDS
on end (used about time) continuously: *He sits and reads for hours on end.*
put an end to sth to stop sth from happening any more

end[2] 🔑 /end/ ***verb*** [I,T] ~ (**in/with sth**) (to cause sth) to finish: *The road ends here.* ◇ *How does this story end?* ◇ *The match ended in a draw.* ◇ *I think we'd better end this conversation now.*
PHR V **end up (as sth); end up (doing sth)** to find yourself in a place/situation that you did not plan or expect: *We got lost and ended up in the centre of town.* ◇ *She had always wanted to be a writer but ended up as a teacher.* ◇ *There was nothing to eat at home so we ended up getting a takeaway.*

endanger /ɪn'deɪndʒə(r)/ ***verb*** [T] to cause danger to sb/sth: *Smoking endangers your health.*

endangered /ɪn'deɪndʒəd/ ***adj.*** (used about animals, plants, etc.) in danger of disappearing from the world (**becoming extinct**): *The giant panda is **an endangered species**.*

endear /ɪn'dɪə(r)/ ***verb*** [T] (*formal*) ~ **sb/yourself to sb** to make sb/yourself liked by sb: *She managed to endear herself to everybody by her kindness.* ▶ **endearing** ***adj.*** ▶ **endearingly** ***adv.***

endeavour (*AmE* **endeavor**) /ɪn'devə(r)/ ***verb*** [I] (*formal*) ~ (**to do sth**) to try hard: *She endeavoured to finish her work on time.* ▶ **endeavour** ***noun*** [C,U]

endemic /en'demɪk/ ***adj.*** (often used about a disease or problem) (HEALTH) regularly found in a particular place or among a particular group of people and difficult to get rid of: *Malaria is endemic in many hot countries.* ➲ look at **epidemic**, **pandemic**

ending 🔑 /'endɪŋ/ ***noun*** [C] **1** (ARTS AND MEDIA) the end (of a story, play, film, etc.): *That film made me cry but I was pleased that it had **a happy ending**.* **2** (LANGUAGE) the last part of a word, which can change: *When nouns end in -ch or -sh or -x, the plural ending is -es not -s.*

endive /'endaɪv/ (*AmE*) = CHICORY

endless /'endləs/ ***adj.*** **1** very large in size or amount and seeming to have no end: *The possibilities are endless.* **2** lasting for a long time and seeming to have no end: *Our plane was delayed for hours and the wait seemed endless.* SYN **interminable** ▶ **endlessly** ***adv.***

endorse /ɪn'dɔːs/ ***verb*** [T] **1** to say publicly that you give official support or agreement to a plan, statement, decision, etc.: *Members of all parties endorsed a ban on firearms.* **2** (ARTS AND MEDIA) to say in an advertisement that you use and like a particular product so that other people will want to buy it: *I wonder how many celebrities actually use the products they endorse.* **3** (*BrE*) (usually passive) (LAW) to add a note to a DRIVING LICENCE (= the document which allows you to drive a vehicle) to say that the driver has broken the law ▶ **endorsement** ***noun*** [C,U]

endoscope /'endəskəʊp/ ***noun*** [C] (HEALTH) an instrument used in medical operations which consists of a very small camera on a long thin tube which can be put into a person's body so that the parts inside can be seen

endoscopy /en'dɒskəpi/ ***noun*** [C, U] (*pl.* **-ies**) (HEALTH) a medical operation in which a very small camera (**endoscope**) is put into a person's body so that the parts inside can be seen

endoskeleton /'endəʊskelɪtn/ ***noun*** [C] the bones inside the body of animals that give it shape and support ➲ look at **exoskeleton**

endosperm /'endəʊspɜːm/ ***noun*** [U] (BIOLOGY) the part of a seed that stores food for the development of a plant

endothermic /ˌendəʊ'θɜːmɪk/ ***adj.*** (CHEMISTRY, PHYSICS) (used about a chemical reaction or process) needing heat in order to take place ➲ picture at **water**

endow /ɪn'daʊ/ ***verb*** [T] to give a large sum of money to a school, a college or another institution
PHR V **be endowed with sth** to naturally have a particular characteristic, quality, etc.: *She was endowed with courage and common sense.*
endow sb/sth with sth 1 to believe or imagine that sb/sth has a particular quality: *He had endowed the girl with the personality he wanted her to have.* **2** (*formal*) to give sth to sb/sth

endowment /ɪn'daʊmənt/ ***noun*** [C,U] money that sb gives to a school, a college or another institution; the act of giving this money

'end product ***noun*** [C] something that is produced by a particular process or activity

endurance /ɪn'djʊərəns/ ***noun*** [U] the ability to continue doing sth painful or difficult for a long period of time without complaining

endure /ɪn'djʊə(r)/ ***verb*** (*formal*) **1** [T] to suffer sth painful or uncomfortable, usually without complaining: *She endured ten years of loneliness.* SYN **bear 2** [I] to continue SYN **last** ▶ **enduring** ***adj.***

ˌend-'user ***noun*** [C] (BUSINESS) a person who actually uses a product rather than one who makes or sells it, especially a person who uses a product connected with computers

ENE ***abbr.*** (GEOGRAPHY) east-north-east

enemy 🔑 /'enəmi/ ***noun*** (*pl.* **enemies**) **1** [C] a person who hates and tries to harm you: *They used to be friends but became **bitter enemies**.* ◇ *He has **made** several **enemies** during his career.* ➲ noun **enmity**
2 the enemy [with sing. or pl. verb] the army or country that your country is fighting against: *The enemy is/are approaching.* ◇ *enemy forces*

energetic AW /ˌenə'dʒetɪk/ ***adj.*** full of or needing energy and enthusiasm: *Jogging is a very energetic form of exercise.* ▶ **energetically** /-kli/ ***adv.***

energy 🔑 AW /'enədʒi/ ***noun*** (*pl.* **energies**) **1** [U] the ability to be very active or do a lot of work without getting tired: *Children are usually **full of***

energy. **2** [U] (PHYSICS) the power that comes from coal, electricity, gas, etc. that is used for producing heat, driving machines, etc.: *nuclear energy* **3 energies** [pl.] the effort and attention that you give to doing sth: *She devoted all her energies to helping the blind.* **4** [U] (PHYSICS) the ability of a substance or system to produce movement: *kinetic/potential energy*

enforce AW /ɪn'fɔːs/ ***verb*** [T] to make people obey a law or rule or do sth that they do not want to: *How will they enforce the new law?* ▶ **enforced** AW ***adj.***: *enforced redundancies* ▶ **enforcement** AW ***noun*** [U]

enfranchise /ɪn'fræntʃaɪz/ ***verb*** [T] (*formal*) (usually passive) (POLITICS) to give sb the right to vote in an election OPP **disenfranchise** ▶ **enfranchisement** /ɪn'fræntʃɪzmənt/ ***noun*** [U]

engage /ɪn'geɪdʒ/ ***verb*** (*formal*) **1** [T] to interest or attract sb: *You need to engage the students' attention right from the start.* **2** [T] ~ **sb (as sth)** to give work to sb: *They engaged him as a cook.* **3** [I,T] ~ **(sth) (with sth)** to make parts of a machine fit together: *Engage the clutch before selecting a gear.*
PHR V **engage in sth** to take part in sth: *I don't engage in that kind of gossip!*

engaged /ɪn'geɪdʒd/ ***adj.*** **1** (*formal*) ~ **(in/on sth)** (used about a person) busy doing sth: *They are engaged in talks with the Irish government.* **2** ~ **(to sb)** having agreed to get married: *We've just **got engaged**.* ◇ *Susan is engaged to Jim.* **3** (*AmE* **busy**) (used about a telephone) in use: *I can't get through – the line is engaged.* **4** (used about a toilet) in use OPP **vacant**

engagement /ɪn'geɪdʒmənt/ ***noun*** [C] **1** an agreement to get married; the time when you are engaged: *He broke off their engagement.* **2** (*formal*) an arrangement to go somewhere or do sth at a fixed time; an appointment: *I can't come on Tuesday as I have a **prior engagement**.*

en'gagement ring ***noun*** [C] a ring, usually with PRECIOUS STONES in it, that a man gives to a woman when they agree to get married

engine /'endʒɪn/ ***noun*** [C] **1** (PHYSICS) the part of a vehicle that produces power to make the vehicle move: *This engine runs on diesel.* ◇ *a car/jet engine* **2** (*also* **locomotive**) a vehicle that pulls a railway train

'engine driver (*also* **'train driver**, *AmE* **engineer**) ***noun*** [C] a person whose job is to drive a railway engine

engineer[1] /ˌendʒɪ'nɪə(r)/ ***noun*** [C] **1** a person whose job is to design, build or repair engines, machines, etc.: *a civil/chemical/electrical/mechanical engineer* **2** (*AmE*) = ENGINE DRIVER

engineer[2] /ˌendʒɪ'nɪə(r)/ ***verb*** [T] **1** (*formal*) to arrange for sth to happen by careful secret planning: *Her promotion was engineered by her father.* **2** (BIOLOGY) to change the GENETIC structure of sth SYN **genetically modify**: *genetically engineered crops*

engineering /ˌendʒɪ'nɪərɪŋ/ ***noun*** [U] (the study of) the work that is done by an engineer: *mechanical/civil/chemical engineering*

energy resources

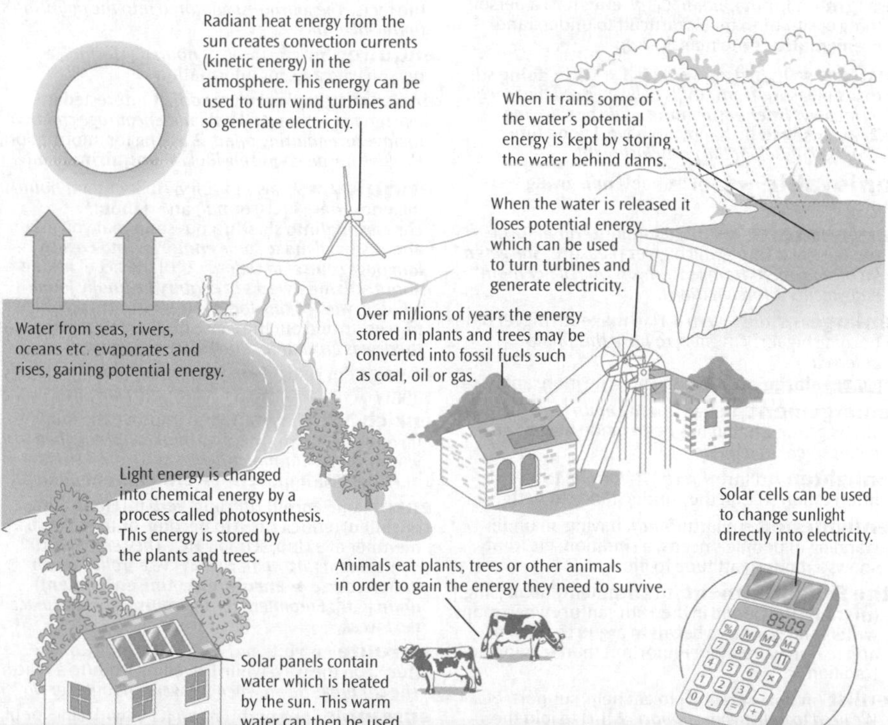

English¹ /ˈɪŋɡlɪʃ/ ***noun*** **1** [U] (LANGUAGE) the language that is spoken in Britain, the US, Australia, etc.: *Do you speak English?* ◇ *I've been learning English for 5 years.* **2 the English** [pl.] the people of England

English² /ˈɪŋɡlɪʃ/ ***adj.*** belonging to England, the English people, the English language, etc.: *English history* ◇ *the English countryside*

ˌEnglish ˈbreakfast ***noun*** [C] a meal that is eaten in the morning and consists of a lot of fried food, TOAST, tea, coffee, etc. ➲ look at **continental breakfast**

engrave /ɪnˈɡreɪv/ ***verb*** [T] **~ B on A; ~ A with B** (ART) to cut words or designs on metal, stone, etc.: *His name is engraved on the cup.* ◇ *The cup is engraved with his name.*

engraving /ɪnˈɡreɪvɪŋ/ ***noun*** [C,U] (ART) a design that is cut into a piece of metal or stone; a picture made from this

engrossed /ɪnˈɡrəʊst/ ***adj.*** **~ (in/with sth)** so interested in sth that you give it all your attention: *She was completely engrossed in her book.*

engulf /ɪnˈɡʌlf/ ***verb*** [T] (*formal*) **1** to surround or to cover sb/sth completely: *He was engulfed by a crowd of reporters.* **2** to affect sb/sth very strongly

enhance AW /ɪnˈhɑːns/ ***verb*** [T] to make the quality of sth even better or to make sb/sth more attractive: *This is an opportunity to enhance the reputation of the company.* ◇ *the skilled use of make-up to enhance your best features* ▶ **enhanced** AW ***adj.***: *enhanced efficiency*

enigma /ɪˈnɪɡmə/ ***noun*** [C] (*pl.* **enigmas**) a person, thing or situation that is difficult to understand ▶ **enigmatic** /ˌenɪɡˈmætɪk/ ***adj.***

enjoy 🔑 /ɪnˈdʒɔɪ/ ***verb*** [T] **1 ~ sth/~ doing sth** to get pleasure from sth: *I really enjoyed that meal.* ◇ *He enjoys listening to music while he's driving.* **2 ~ yourself** to be happy; to have a good time: *I enjoyed myself at the party last night.*

enjoyable 🔑 /ɪnˈdʒɔɪəbl/ ***adj.*** giving pleasure

enjoyment 🔑 /ɪnˈdʒɔɪmənt/ ***noun*** [U, C] pleasure or a thing which gives pleasure: *She gets a lot of enjoyment from teaching.* ◇ *One of her main enjoyments is foreign travel.*

enlarge /ɪnˈlɑːdʒ/ ***verb*** [I,T] to make sth bigger or to become bigger: *I'm going to have this photo enlarged.*
PHR V **enlarge on sth** to say or write more about sth

enlargement /ɪnˈlɑːdʒmənt/ ***noun*** [C,U] making sth bigger or sth that has been made bigger: *an enlargement of a photo*

enlighten /ɪnˈlaɪtn/ ***verb*** [T] (*formal*) to give sb information so that they understand sth better

enlightened /ɪnˈlaɪtnd/ ***adj.*** having an understanding of people's needs, a situation, etc. that shows a modern attitude to life

the Enlightenment /ɪnˈlaɪtnmənt/ ***noun*** [sing.] (HISTORY) the period in the 18th century when many writers and scientists began to argue that science and reason were more important than religion and tradition

enlist /ɪnˈlɪst/ ***verb*** **1** [T] to get help, support, etc.: *We need to enlist your support.* **2** [I,T] to join the army, navy or air force; to make sb a member of the army, etc.: *They enlisted as soon as war was declared.*

enmity /ˈenməti/ ***noun*** [U] the feeling of hatred towards an enemy

enormity AW /ɪˈnɔːməti/ ***noun*** [sing.] (*formal*) the very great size, effect, etc. of sth; the fact that sth is very serious: *the enormity of a task/decision/problem*

enormous 🔑 AW /ɪˈnɔːməs/ ***adj.*** very big or very great: *an enormous building* ◇ *enormous pleasure* ▶ **enormously** AW ***adv.***

enough¹ 🔑 /ɪˈnʌf/ ***det., pronoun*** **1** as much or as many of sth as necessary: *We've saved enough money to buy a computer.* ◇ *Not everybody can have a book – there aren't enough.* ◇ *If enough of you are interested, we'll arrange a trip to the theatre.* **2** as much or as many as you want: *I've had enough of living in a city* (=I don't want to live in a city any more). ◇ *Don't give me any more work. I've got quite enough already.*

enough² 🔑 /ɪˈnʌf/ ***adv.*** (used *after* verbs, adjectives and adverbs) **1** to the necessary amount or degree; sufficiently: *You don't practise enough.* ◇ *He's not old enough to travel alone.* ◇ *Does she speak Italian well enough to get the job?* **2** quite, but not very: *She plays well enough, for a beginner.*
IDM **fair enough** → FAIR¹
funnily, strangely, etc. enough it is funny, etc. that...: *Funnily enough, I thought exactly the same myself.*
sure enough → SURE

enquire (also **inquire**) /ɪnˈkwaɪə(r)/ ***verb*** (*formal*) [I,T] **~ (about sb/sth)** to ask for information about sth: *Could you enquire when the trains to Cork leave?* ◇ *We need to enquire about hotels in Vienna.* ➲ note at **ask**
PHR V **enquire after sb** to ask about sb's health
enquire into sth to study sth in order to find out all the facts: *The journalist enquired into the politician's financial affairs.*

enquirer /ɪnˈkwaɪərə(r)/ ***noun*** [C] (*formal*) a person who asks for information

enquiring /ɪnˈkwaɪərɪŋ/ ***adj.*** **1** interested in learning new things: *We should encourage children to have an enquiring mind.* **2** asking for information: *He gave me an enquiring look.* ▶ **enquiringly** ***adv.***

enquiry 🔑 (also **inquiry**) /ɪnˈkwaɪəri/ ***noun*** (*pl.* **enquiries**) **1** [C] (*formal*) **an ~ (about/concerning/into sb/sth)** a question that you ask about sth: *I'll **make** some **enquiries** into English language courses in Oxford.* **2** [U] the act of asking about sth: *After weeks of enquiry he finally found what he was looking for.* **3** [C] **~ (into sth)** an official process to find out the cause of sth: *After the accident there was an enquiry into safety procedures.*

enrage /ɪnˈreɪdʒ/ ***verb*** [T] (*formal*) to make sb very angry

enrich /ɪnˈrɪtʃ/ ***verb*** [T] **1** to improve the quality, flavour, etc. of sth: *These cornflakes are enriched with vitamins/are vitamin-enriched.* **2** to make sb/sth rich or richer OPP **impoverish** ▶ **enrichment** ***noun*** [U]

enrol (*AmE* **enroll**) /ɪnˈrəʊl/ ***verb*** [I,T] (**enrolling; enrolled**) (EDUCATION) to become or to make sb a member of a club, school, etc.: *They enrolled 100 new students last year.* ◇ (*BrE*) *I've enrolled on an Italian course.* ▶ **enrolment** (*AmE* **enrollment**) ***noun*** [C,U]: *Enrolment for the course will take place next week.*

en route /ˌɒ̃ ˈruːt; ˌɒn/ ***adv.*** **~ (from...) (to...); ~ (for...)** on the way; while travelling from/to a place: *The car broke down when we were en route for Dover.*

ensemble /ɒnˈsɒmbl/ ***noun*** [C] **1** [with sing. or pl. verb] (MUSIC) a small group of musicians, dancers or actors who perform together: *a brass/wind/string* ensemble ◇ *The ensemble is/are based in Leeds.* **2** [usually sing.] (*formal*) a number of things considered as a group **3** [usually sing.] a set of clothes that are worn together

ensue /ɪn'sjuː/ ***verb*** [I] (*formal*) to happen after (and often as a result of) sth else

en suite /ˌɒ̃ 'swiːt; ˌɒn/ ***adj., adv.*** (used about a bedroom and bathroom) forming one unit: *The bedroom has a bathroom en suite.*

ensure 🔑 (AW) (*AmE* also **insure**) /ɪn'ʃɔː(r)/ ***verb*** [T] to make sure that sth happens or is definite: *Please ensure that the door is locked before you leave.*

entail /ɪn'teɪl/ ***verb*** [T] (*formal*) to make sth necessary; to involve sth: *The job sounds interesting but I'm not sure what it entails.*

entangled /ɪn'tæŋgld/ ***adj.*** caught in sth else: *The bird was entangled in the net.* ◇ (*figurative*) *I've got myself entangled in some financial problems.*

entente /ɒn'tɒnt/ ***noun*** [U, sing.] (POLITICS) a friendly relationship between two countries: *the Franco-Russian entente*

enter 🔑 /'entə(r)/ ***verb*** **1** [I,T] (*formal*) to come or go into a place: *Don't enter without knocking.* ◇ *They all stood up when he entered the room.* ➲ nouns **entrance** and **entry**
2 [I] to become a member of sth, especially a profession or an institution: *She entered the legal profession in 2000.* ◇ *to enter school/college/university* ➲ noun **entrant**
3 [T] to begin or become involved in an activity, a situation, etc.: *When she entered the relationship, she had no idea he was already married.* ◇ *We have just entered a new phase in international relations.* **4** [I,T] ~ **(for) sth**; ~ **sb (in/for sth)** to put your name or sb's name on the list for an exam, race, competition, etc.: *I entered a competition in the Sunday paper and I won £20!* **5** [T] ~ **sth (in/into/on/onto sth)** to put names, numbers, details, etc. in a list, book, computer, etc.: *I've entered all the data onto the computer.* ◇ *Enter your password and press return.*
PHR V **enter into sth 1** to start to think or talk about sth: *I don't want to enter into details now.* **2** to be part of sth; to be involved in sth: *This is a business matter. Friendship doesn't enter into it.*
enter into sth (with sb) to begin sth: *The government has entered into negotiations with the unions.*

enterprise /'entəpraɪz/ ***noun*** **1** [C] a new plan, project, business, etc.: *It's a very exciting new enterprise.* ◇ *a new industrial enterprise* **2** [U] the ability to think of new projects or create new businesses and make them successful: *We need men and women of enterprise and energy.*

enterprising /'entəpraɪzɪŋ/ ***adj.*** having or showing the ability to think of new projects or new ways of doing things and make them successful: *One enterprising farmer opened up his field as a car park and charged people to park there.*

entertain 🔑 /ˌentə'teɪn/ ***verb*** **1** [T] ~ **(sb) (with sth)** to interest and amuse sb in order to please them: *I find it very hard to keep my class entertained on a Friday afternoon.* **2** [I,T] to welcome sb as a guest, especially to your home; to give sb food and drink: *They entertain a lot./They do a lot of entertaining.*

entertainer 🔑 /ˌentə'teɪnə(r)/ ***noun*** [C] (ARTS AND MEDIA) a person whose job is to amuse people, for example by singing, dancing or telling jokes

entertaining 🔑 /ˌentə'teɪnɪŋ/ ***adj.*** interesting and amusing

entertainment 🔑 /ˌentə'teɪnmənt/ ***noun*** [U, C] (ARTS AND MEDIA) film, music, etc. used to interest and amuse people: *There isn't much entertainment for young people in this town.* ◇ *There's a full programme of entertainments every evening.*

enthral (*AmE* **enthrall**) /ɪn'θrɔːl/ ***verb*** [T] (**enthralling**; **enthralled**) to hold sb's interest and attention completely: *He was enthralled by her story.* ▶ **enthralling** ***adj.***

enthusiasm 🔑 /ɪn'θjuːziæzəm/ ***noun*** [U] ~ **(for/about sth/doing sth)** a strong feeling of excitement or interest in sth and a desire to become involved in it: *Jan showed great enthusiasm for the new project.*

enthusiast /ɪn'θjuːziæst/ ***noun*** [C] a person who is very interested in an activity or subject

enthusiastic 🔑 /ɪnˌθjuːzi'æstɪk/ ***adj.*** ~ **(about sth/doing sth)** full of excitement and interest in sth ▶ **enthusiastically** /-kli/ ***adv.***

entice /ɪn'taɪs/ ***verb*** [T] ~ **sb (into sth/doing sth)** to persuade sb to do sth or to go somewhere by offering them something nice: *Advertisements try to entice people into buying more things than they need.* ▶ **enticement** ***noun*** [C,U]

enticing /ɪn'taɪsɪŋ/ ***adj.*** attractive and interesting

entire 🔑 /ɪn'taɪə(r)/ ***adj.*** (only *before* a noun) (used when you are emphasizing that the whole of sth is involved) including everything, everyone or every part SYN **whole**: *He managed to read the entire book in two days.* ▶ **entirety** /ɪn'taɪərəti/ ***noun*** [U]: *We must consider the problem in its entirety* (=as a whole).

entirely 🔑 /ɪn'taɪəli/ ***adv.*** in every way possible; completely: *I entirely agree with you.* ◇ *That's an **entirely different** matter.* ◇ *The audience was almost entirely female.*

entitle 🔑 /ɪn'taɪtl/ ***verb*** [T] ~ **sb (to sth)** (usually passive) to give sb the right to have or do sth: *I think I'm entitled to a day's holiday – I've worked hard enough.*

entitled /ɪn'taɪtld/ ***adj.*** (used about books, plays, etc.) with the title: *Duncan's first book was entitled 'Aquarium'.*

entitlement /ɪn'taɪtlmənt/ ***noun*** (*formal*) **1** [U] ~ **(to sth)** the official right to have or do sth: *This may affect your entitlement to compensation.* **2** [C] something that you have the official right to; the amount that you have the right to receive: *The contributions will affect your pension entitlements.*

entity (AW) /'entəti/ ***noun*** [C] (*pl.* **entities**) something that exists separately from sth else and has its own identity: *The kindergarten and the school are in the same building but they're really **separate entities**.*

entomology /ˌentə'mɒlədʒi/ ***noun*** [U] (BIOLOGY) the scientific study of insects

entrails /'entreɪlz/ ***noun*** [pl.] (ANATOMY) the organs inside the body of a person or an animal, especially the INTESTINES (=the tubes that carry food away from the stomach)

entrance 🔑 /'entrəns/ ***noun*** **1** [C] **the** ~ **(to/of sth)** the door, gate or opening where you go into a place: *I'll meet you at the entrance to the theatre.* OPP **exit** **2** [C] ~ **(into/onto sth)** the act of coming or going into a place, especially in a way that attracts attention: *He made a dramatic entrance onto the stage.* OPP **exit** **3** [U] ~ **(to sth)** the right to enter a place: *They were refused entrance to the club because* *they were wearing shorts.* ◇ *an entrance fee* ➲ look at **admission** **4** [U] ~ **(into/to sth)** permission to join a club, society, university, etc.: *You don't need to take an entrance exam to get into university.* ➲ look at **admission**

entrant /ˈentrənt/ ***noun*** [C] a person who enters a profession, competition, exam, university, etc.

entreat /ɪnˈtriːt/ ***verb*** [T] (*formal*) to ask sb to do sth, often in an emotional way **SYN** **beg**

entrepreneur /ˌɒntrəprəˈnɜː(r)/ ***noun*** [C] (**BUSINESS**) a person who makes money by starting or running businesses, especially when this involves taking financial risks ▶ **entrepreneurial** /-ˈnɜːriəl/ ***adj.*** ▶ **entrepreneurship** ***noun*** [U]

entrust /ɪnˈtrʌst/ ***verb*** [T] (*formal*) ~ **A with B/ ~ B to A** to make sb responsible for sth: *I entrusted Rachel with the arrangements for the party./I entrusted the arrangements for the party to Rachel.*

entry 🔑 /ˈentri/ ***noun*** (*pl.* **entries**) **1** [C] the act of coming or going into a place: *The thieves forced an entry into the building.* **SYN** **entrance** **2** [U] ~ **(to/into sth)** the right to enter a place: *The immigrants were refused entry at the airport.* ◇ *The sign says 'No Entry'.* ◇ *an entry visa* ➲ look at **admission**, **admittance** **3** [U] the right to take part in sth or become a member of a group: *countries seeking entry into the European Union* **4** [C] a person or thing that is entered for a competition, etc.: *There were fifty entries for the Eurovision song contest.* ◇ *The winning entry is number 45!* **5** [C] one item that is written down in a list, account book, dictionary, etc.: *an entry in a diary* ◇ *You'll find 'ice-skate' after the entry for 'ice'.* **6** [C] (*AmE*) a door, gate, passage, etc. where you enter a building, etc. **SYN** **entrance**

ˈ**E-number** ***noun*** [C] (*BrE*) a number beginning with the letter E that is printed on packets and containers to show what artificial flavours and colours have been added to food and drink; an artificial flavour, colour, etc. added to food and drink

envelop /ɪnˈveləp/ ***verb*** [T] (*formal*) to cover or surround sb/sth completely (in sth): *The hills were enveloped in mist.*

envelope 🔑 /ˈenvələʊp; ˈɒn-/ ***noun*** [C] the paper cover for a letter ➲ look at **stamped/self-addressed envelope**

enviable /ˈenviəbl/ ***adj.*** (used about sth that sb else has and that you would like) attractive **OPP** **unenviable** ➲ verb and noun **envy**

envious /ˈenviəs/ ***adj.*** ~ **(of sb/sth)** wanting sth that sb else has: *She was envious of her sister's success.* **SYN** **jealous** ➲ verb and noun **envy** ▶ **enviously** ***adv.***

environment 🔑 **AW** /ɪnˈvaɪrənmənt/ ***noun*** **1** [C,U] the conditions in which you live, work, etc.: *a pleasant working environment* **2 the environment** [sing.] (**ENVIRONMENT**) the natural world, for example the land, air and water, in which people, animals and plants live: *We need stronger laws to protect the environment.* ➲ look at **surroundings**

environmental 🔑 **AW** /ɪnˌvaɪrənˈmentl/ ***adj.*** **1** (**ENVIRONMENT**) connected with the natural conditions in which people, animals and plants live; connected with the environment: *the environmental impact of pollution* ◇ ***environmental issues/problems*** ◇ *an* ***environmental group/movement*** (=that aims to improve or protect the natural environment) **2** connected with the conditions that affect the behaviour and development of sb/sth: *environmental influences* ◇ *an environmental health officer* ▶ **environmentally** /-təli/ ***adv.***: *an* ***environmentally sensitive area*** (=one that is easily damaged or that contains rare animals, plants, etc.)

environmentalist **AW** /ɪnˌvaɪrənˈmentəlɪst/ ***noun*** [C] (**ENVIRONMENT**) a person who wants to protect the environment ▶ **environmentalism** ***noun*** [U]

envisage /ɪnˈvɪzɪdʒ/ ***verb*** [T] (*formal*) to think of sth as being possible in the future; to imagine: *I don't envisage any problems with this.*

envoy /ˈenvɔɪ/ ***noun*** [C] (**POLITICS**) a person who is sent by a government with a message to another country

envy¹ /ˈenvi/ ***noun*** [U] ~ **(of sb)**; ~ **(at/of sth)** the feeling that you have when sb else has sth that you want: *It was difficult for her to hide her envy of her friend's success.*

IDM **be the envy of sb** to be the thing that causes sb to feel **envy**: *The city's transport system is the envy of many of its European neighbours.* ➲ Look at **enviable** and **envious**.

envy² /ˈenvi/ ***verb*** [T] (*pres. part.* **envying**; *3rd person sing. pres.* **envies**; *pt, pp* **envied**) ~ **(sb) (sth)** to want sth that sb else has; to feel **envy**: *I've always envied your good luck.* ◇ *I don't envy you that job* (=I'm glad that I don't have it).

enzyme /ˈenzaɪm/ ***noun*** [C] (**BIOLOGY**) a substance, produced by all living things, which helps a chemical change to happen more quickly, without being changed itself

eolian (*AmE*) =AEOLIAN

eon =AEON

epaulette (*AmE usually* **epaulet**) /ˈepəlet/ ***noun*** [C] a decoration on the shoulder of a coat, jacket, etc., especially when part of a military uniform

ephemeral /ɪˈfemərəl/ ***adj.*** (*formal*) lasting or used for only a short period of time: *ephemeral pleasures*

epic¹ /ˈepɪk/ ***noun*** **1** [C,U] (**LITERATURE**) a long poem about the actions of great men and women or about a nation's history; this style of poetry: *one of the great Hindu epics* ➲ look at **lyric** **2** [C] (**ARTS AND MEDIA**) a long film/movie or book that contains a lot of action, usually about a historical subject **3** [C] a long and difficult job or activity that you think people should admire: *Their four-hour match on Centre Court was an epic.*

epic² /ˈepɪk/ ***adj.*** very long and exciting: *an epic struggle/journey*

epicentre (*AmE* **epicenter**) /ˈepɪsentə(r)/ ***noun*** [C] (**GEOLOGY**) the point on the earth's surface where the effects of an EARTHQUAKE (=a sudden, violent movement) are felt most strongly ➲ picture at **seismic**

epicurean /ˌepɪkjʊəˈriːən/ ***adj.*** (*formal*) devoted to pleasure and enjoying yourself ▶ **epicureanism** /ˌepɪkjʊəˈriːənɪzəm/ ***noun*** [U]

epidemic /ˌepɪˈdemɪk/ ***noun*** [C] (**HEALTH**) a large number of people or animals suffering from the same disease at the same time ➲ look at **endemic**, **pandemic**

epidemiology /ˌepɪˌdiːmiˈɒlədʒi/ ***noun*** [U] (**HEALTH**) the scientific study of the spread and control of diseases ▶ **epidemiological** /ˌepɪˌdiːmiəˈlɒdʒɪkl/ ***adj.*** ▶ **epidemiologist** /ˌepɪˌdiːmiˈɒlədʒɪst/ ***noun*** [C]

epidermis /ˌepɪˈdɜːmɪs/ ***noun*** [sing., U] the outer layer of the skin ➲ pictures at **flower**, **skin** ▶ **epidermal** ***adj.***

epidural /ˌepɪˈdjʊərəl/ ***noun*** (HEALTH) an ANAESTHETIC (=a drug that stops you feeling pain) that is put into the lower part of the back so that no pain is felt below the waist: *Some mothers choose to have an epidural when giving birth.*

epiglottis /ˌepɪˈglɒtɪs/ ***noun*** [C] (ANATOMY) a small thin thing at the back of your tongue that moves to prevent food or drink from entering your lungs when you swallow ➲ picture at **digestive system**

epigram /ˈepɪgræm/ ***noun*** [C] (LITERATURE) a short poem or phrase that expresses an idea in a clever or amusing way ▶ **epigrammatic** /ˌepɪgrəˈmætɪk/ ***adj.***

epilepsy /ˈepɪlepsi/ ***noun*** [U] (HEALTH) a disease of the brain that can cause a person to become unconscious (sometimes with violent movements that they cannot control)

epileptic /ˌepɪˈleptɪk/ ***noun*** [C] (HEALTH) a person who suffers from EPILEPSY ▶ **epileptic** ***adj.***: *an epileptic fit*

epilogue /ˈepɪlɒg/ ***noun*** [C] (LITERATURE) a short piece that is added at the end of a book, play, etc. and that comments on what has gone before ➲ look at **prologue**

episode /ˈepɪsəʊd/ ***noun*** [C] **1** one separate event in sb's life, a novel, etc.: *That's an episode in my life I'd rather forget.* **2** one part of a television or radio story that is shown in several parts (**a serial**)

epistolary /ɪˈpɪstələri/ ***adj.*** (*formal*) (LITERATURE) written or expressed in the form of letters: *an epistolary novel*

epitaph /ˈepɪtɑːf/ ***noun*** [C] (LITERATURE) words that are written or said about a dead person, especially words written on a stone where they are buried

epithet /ˈepɪθet/ ***noun*** [C] **1** an adjective or phrase that is used to describe sb/sth's character or most important quality, especially in order to say sth good or bad about sb/sth: *The novel is neither old enough nor good enough to deserve the epithet 'classic'.* **2** (*especially AmE*) an insulting word or phrase that is used about a person or group of people: *Racial epithets were written all over the wall.*

epitome /ɪˈpɪtəmi/ ***noun*** [sing.] **the ~ (of sth)** a perfect example of sth: *Her clothes are the epitome of good taste.*

epitomize (also **-ise**) /ɪˈpɪtəmaɪz/ ***verb*** [T] to be typical of sth: *This building epitomizes modern trends in architecture.*

epoch /ˈiːpɒk/ ***noun*** [C] a period of time in history (that is important because of special events, characteristics, etc.)

EPOS /ˈiːpɒs/ ***abbr.*** (BUSINESS) **electronic point of sale**; the electronic machines and computer systems used in shops to record information about the goods sold

equal¹ 🔑 /ˈiːkwəl/ ***adj.*** **1 ~ (to sb/sth)** the same in size, amount, value, number, level, etc.: *This animal is equal in weight to a small car.* ◇ *They are equal in weight.* ◇ *They are of equal weight.* ◇ *Divide it into two equal parts.* OPP **unequal** **2** having the same rights or being treated the same as other people: *This company has an equal opportunities policy* (=gives the same chance of employment to everyone). **3** (*formal*) **~ to sth** having the strength, ability etc. to do sth: *I'm afraid Bob just isn't equal to the job.*
IDM **be on equal terms (with sb)** to have the same advantages and disadvantages as sb else

equal² 🔑 /ˈiːkwəl/ ***verb*** (**equalling**; **equalled**: *AmE* **equaling**; **equaled**) **1** *linking verb* (MATHEMATICS) (used about numbers, etc.) to be the same as sth: *44 plus 17 equals 61 is written: 44 + 17 =61.* **2** [T] to be as good as sb/sth: *He ran an excellent race, equalling the world record.*

equal³ 🔑 /ˈiːkwəl/ ***noun*** [C] a person who has the same ability, rights, etc. as you do: *to treat sb as an equal*

equality /iˈkwɒləti/ ***noun*** [U] the situation in which everyone has the same rights and advantages: *racial equality* (=between people of different races) OPP **inequality**

equalize (also **-ise**) /ˈiːkwəlaɪz/ ***verb*** [I] (SPORT) to reach the same number of points as your opponent

equally 🔑 /ˈiːkwəli/ ***adv.*** **1** to the same degree or amount: *They both worked equally hard.* **2** in equal parts: *His money was divided equally between his children.* **3** (*formal*) (used when you are comparing two ideas or commenting on what you have just said) at the same time; but/and also: *I do not think what he did was right. Equally, I can understand why he did it.*

ˈequals sign (also **ˈequal sign**) ***noun*** [C] (MATHEMATICS) the symbol (=), used in mathematics

equate AW /iˈkweɪt/ ***verb*** [T] **~ sth (with sth)** to consider one thing as being the same as sth else: *You can't always equate money with happiness.*

equation /ɪˈkweɪʒn/ ***noun*** [C] (MATHEMATICS) a statement that two quantities are equal: *2x + 5 =11 is an equation.*

the equator (*also* **the Equator**) /ɪˈkweɪtə(r)/ ***noun*** [sing.] (GEOGRAPHY) the imagined line around the earth at an equal distance from the North and South Poles: *north/south of the Equator* ◇ *The island is on the equator.* ➲ picture at **earth**

equatorial /ˌekwəˈtɔːriəl/ ***adj.*** (GEOGRAPHY) near THE EQUATOR: *equatorial rainforests*

equestrian /ɪˈkwestriən/ ***adj.*** (*formal*) connected with horse riding

equidistant /ˌiːkwɪˈdɪstənt; ˌek-/ ***adj.*** **~ (from sth)** (*formal*) equally far from two or more places

equilateral triangle /ˌiːkwɪˌlætərəl ˈtraɪæŋgl/ ***noun*** [C] (GEOMETRY) a triangle whose three sides are all the same length ➲ picture at **triangle**

equilibrium /ˌiːkwɪˈlɪbriəm; ˌek-/ ***noun*** [U, sing.] **1** (PHYSICS, CHEMISTRY) a state of balance, especially between forces or influences that are working in opposite ways: *The point at which the solid and the liquid are **in equilibrium** is called the freezing point.* **2** a calm state of mind and a balance of emotions

equine /ˈekwaɪn/ ***adj.*** connected with horses; like a horse

equinox /ˈiːkwɪnɒks; ˈek-/ ***noun*** [C] (ASTRONOMY) one of the two times in the year (around 20 March and 22 September) when the sun is above THE EQUATOR (=the imagined line round the centre of the earth) and day and night are of equal length: *the spring/autumn equinox* ➲ look at **solstice** ➲ picture at **season**

equip AW /ɪˈkwɪp/ ***verb*** [T] (**equipping**; **equipped**) **~ sb/sth (with sth)** **1** (usually passive) to supply sb/sth with what is needed for a particular purpose: *We shall equip all schools with new computers over the next year.* ◇ *The flat has a **fully-equipped** kitchen.* **2** to prepare sb for a particular task: *The course equips students with all the skills necessary to become a chef.*

equipment ⊶ AW /ɪˈkwɪpmənt/ ***noun*** [U] the things that are needed to do a particular activity: *office/sports/computer equipment*

equitable /ˈekwɪtəbl/ ***adj.*** (*formal*) fair and reasonable; treating everyone in an equal way: *an equitable distribution of resources* OPP **inequitable**

equity /ˈekwəti/ ***noun*** **1** [U] (BUSINESS) the value of a company's shares; the value of a property after all charges and debts have been paid ➲ look at **negative equity** **2 equities** [pl.] (BUSINESS) shares in a company which do not pay a fixed amount of interest

equivalent ⊶ AW /ɪˈkwɪvələnt/ ***adj.*** ~ (to sth) equal in value, amount, meaning, importance, etc.: *The British House of Commons is roughly equivalent to the American House of Representatives.* ▶ **equivalent** ***noun*** [C]: *There is no English equivalent to the French 'bon appétit'.*

er /ɜː(r)/ ***exclamation*** used in writing to show the sound that sb makes when they cannot decide what to say next

era /ˈɪərə/ ***noun*** [C] (HISTORY) a period of time in history (that is special for some reason): *We are living in the era of the computer.*

eradicate /ɪˈrædɪkeɪt/ ***verb*** [T] (*formal*) to destroy or get rid of sth completely: *Scientists have completely eradicated some diseases, such as smallpox.* ▶ **eradication** /ɪˌrædɪˈkeɪʃn/ ***noun*** [U]

erase /ɪˈreɪz/ ***verb*** [T] (*formal*) to remove sth completely (a pencil mark, a recording on tape, a computer file, etc.): (*figurative*) *He tried to erase the memory of those terrible years from his mind.* ▶ **eraser** ***noun*** [C] (*especially AmE*) = RUBBER (2)

erbium /ˈɜːbiəm/ ***noun*** [U] (*symbol* **Er**) (CHEMISTRY) a chemical element. **Erbium** is a soft silver-white metal. ℹ For more information on the periodic table of elements, look at pages R34-5.

erect[1] /ɪˈrekt/ ***adj.*** **1** standing straight up: *He stood with his head erect.* SYN **upright** **2** (used about the male sexual organ) hard and standing up because of sexual excitement

erect[2] /ɪˈrekt/ ***verb*** [T] (*formal*) to build sth or to stand sth straight up: *to erect a statue* ◇ *Huge TV screens were erected above the stage.* ➲ note at **build**[1]

erection /ɪˈrekʃn/ ***noun*** **1** [C] if a man has an **erection**, his sexual organ (**penis**) becomes hard and stands up because he is sexually excited: *to get/have an erection* **2** [U] (*formal*) the act of building sth or standing sth straight up

ergonomic /ˌɜːɡəˈnɒmɪk/ ***adj.*** designed to improve people's working conditions and to help them work more efficiently: *ergonomic design* ▶ **ergonomically** ***adv.***: *The layout is hard to fault ergonomically.*

ergonomics /ˌɜːɡəˈnɒmɪks/ ***noun*** [U] the study of working conditions, especially the design of equipment and furniture, in order to help people work more efficiently

erode AW /ɪˈrəʊd/ ***verb*** [T] (usually passive) (GEOLOGY) (used about the sea, the weather, etc.) to destroy sth slowly: *The cliff has been eroded by the sea.* ▶ **erosion** AW /ɪˈrəʊʒn/ ***noun*** [U]: *the erosion of rocks by the sea*

erotic /ɪˈrɒtɪk/ ***adj.*** causing sexual excitement: *an erotic film/poem/dream*

err /ɜː(r)/ ***verb*** [I] (*formal*) to be or do wrong; to make mistakes

IDM **err on the side of sth** to do more of sth than is necessary in order to avoid the opposite happening: *It is better to err on the side of caution* (= it is better to be too careful rather than not careful enough).

coastal erosion

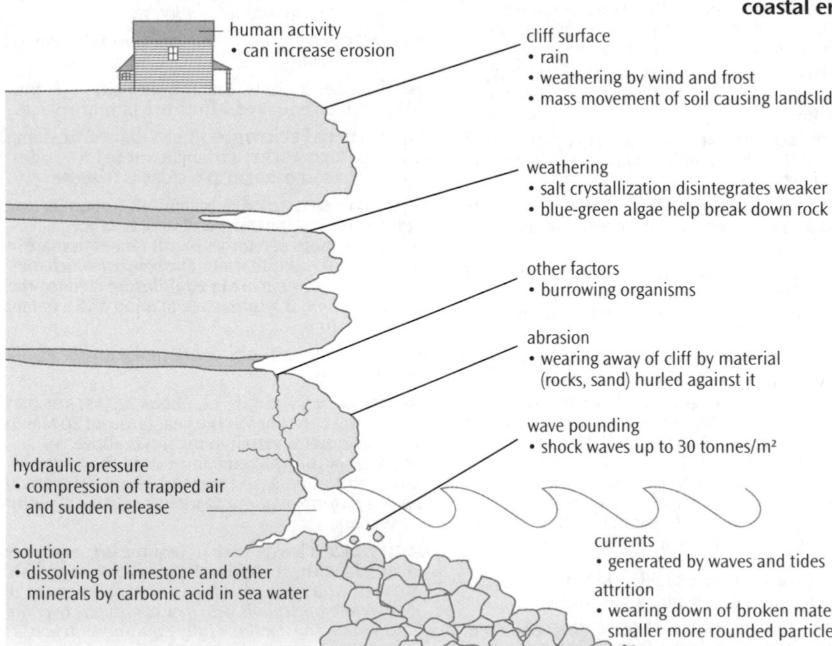

features of coastal erosion

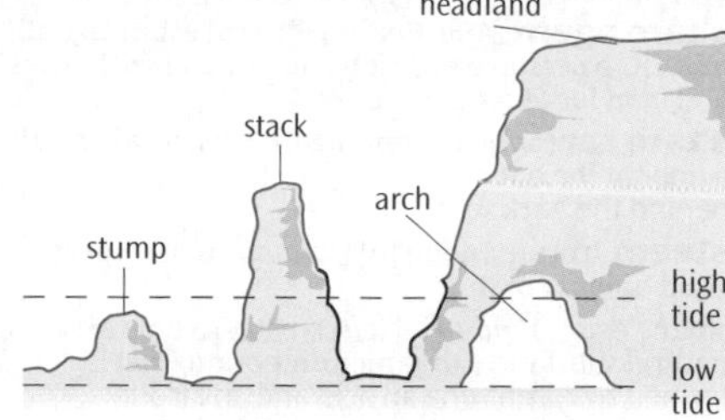

errand /ˈerənd/ ***noun*** [C] (*old-fashioned*) a short journey to take or get sth for sb, for example to buy sth from a shop

erratic[1] /ɪˈrætɪk/ ***adj.*** (used about a person's behaviour, or about the quality of sth) changing without reason; that you can never be sure of: *Jones is a talented player but he's very erratic* (= sometimes he plays well, sometimes badly). ▶ **erratically** /-kli/ ***adv.***

erratic[2] /ɪˈrætɪk/ ***noun*** [C] (GEOLOGY) a large rock than has been carried by a moving mass of ice (**a glacier**) and left far away from where it was formed when the ice melted

erroneous AW /ɪˈrəʊniəs/ ***adj.*** (*formal*) not correct; based on wrong information: *erroneous conclusions/assumptions* ▶ **erroneously** ***adv.***

error ⊶ AW /ˈerə(r)/ ***noun*** **1** [C] (*formal*) a mistake: *The telephone bill was far too high due to a* ***computer error.*** ◊ *an* ***error of judgement*** ◊ *to* ***make an error***

COLLOCATIONS AND PATTERNS

Error is more formal than **mistake**. There are some expressions such as *error of judgement, human error* where only **error** can be used.

2 [U] the state of being wrong: *The letter was sent to you* ***in error.*** ◊ *The accident was the result of* ***human error.***

IDM **trial and error** → TRIAL

erupt /ɪˈrʌpt/ ***verb*** [I] **1** (GEOLOGY) (used about a VOLCANO) to explode and throw out fire, rock that has melted (**lava**), smoke, etc. **2** (used about violence, shouting, etc.) to start suddenly: *The demonstration erupted into violence.* **3** (used about a person) to suddenly become very angry ▶ **eruption** ***noun*** [C,U]: *a volcanic eruption*

erythrocyte /ɪˈrɪθrəsaɪt/ ***noun*** [C] (BIOLOGY) a red blood cell

escalate /ˈeskəleɪt/ ***verb*** [I,T] **1** ~ **(sth) (into sth)** (to cause sth) to become stronger or more serious: *The demonstrations are escalating into violent protest in all the major cities.* ◊ *The terrorist attacks escalated tension in the capital.* **2** (to cause sth) to become greater or higher; to increase: *The cost of housing has escalated in recent years.* ➲ note at **rise**[1] ▶ **escalation** /ˌeskəˈleɪʃn/ ***noun*** [C,U]

escalator /ˈeskəleɪtə(r)/ ***noun*** [C] a moving STAIRCASE in a shop, etc.

escapade /ˌeskəˈpeɪd/ ***noun*** [C] an exciting experience that may be dangerous

escape[1] ⊶ /ɪˈskeɪp/ ***verb*** **1** [I] ~ **(from sb/sth)** to manage to get away from a place where you do not want to be; to get free: *Two prisoners have escaped.* ◊ *They managed to escape from the burning building.* **2** [I,T] to manage to avoid sth dangerous or unpleasant: *The two men in the other car escaped unhurt in the accident.* ◊ *Ben Hales escaped injury when his car skidded off the road.* ◊ *to escape criticism/punishment* **3** [T] to be forgotten or not noticed by sb: *His name escapes me.* ◊ *to escape sb's notice* **4** [I] (used about gases or liquids) to come or get out of a container, etc.: *There's gas escaping somewhere.* ▶ **escaped** ***adj.***: *an escaped prisoner*

escape[2] ⊶ /ɪˈskeɪp/ ***noun*** **1** [C,U] ~ **(from sth)** the act of escaping (1,2): *There have been twelve escapes from the prison this year.* ◊ *She had* ***a narrow/lucky escape*** *when a lorry crashed into her car.* ◊ *When the guard fell asleep they were able to* ***make their escape.*** ➲ look at **fire escape** **2** [U, sing.] something that helps you forget your normal life: *For him, listening to music is a means of escape.* ◊ *an escape from reality*

escapism /ɪˈskeɪpɪzəm/ ***noun*** [U] an activity, a form of entertainment, etc. that helps you to avoid or forget unpleasant or boring things: *For John, reading is a* ***form of escapism.*** ▶ **escapist** /-pɪst/ ***adj.***

escarpment /ɪˈskɑːpmənt/ ***noun*** [C] (GEOGRAPHY, GEOLOGY) a very steep piece of ground that separates an area of high ground from an area of lower ground

escort[1] /ˈeskɔːt/ ***noun*** [C] **1** [with sing. or pl. verb] one or more people or vehicles that go with and protect sb/sth, or that go with sb/sth as an honour: *an armed escort* ◊ *He arrived* ***under police escort.*** **2** (*formal*) a person who takes sb to a social event **3** a person, especially a woman, who is paid to go out socially with sb: *an escort agency*

escort[2] /ɪsˈkɔːt/ ***verb*** [T] **1** to go with sb as an **escort** (1): *The President's car was escorted by several police cars.* **2** to take sb somewhere: *Philip escorted her to the door.*

ESE ***abbr.*** (GEOGRAPHY) east-south-east

esker /ˈeskə(r)/ ***noun*** [C] (GEOLOGY) a long line of small stones and earth that has been left by a large mass of ice that has melted

Eskimo /ˈeskɪməʊ/ (*old-fashioned*) = INUIT

ESL /ˌiː es ˈel/ ***abbr.*** (EDUCATION) English as a Second Language

esophagus (*AmE*) = OESOPHAGUS

esp. ***abbr.*** **1** especially **2** **ESP** /ˌiː es ˈpiː/ (EDUCATION) English for Specific/Special Purposes; the teaching of English to people who need it for a special reason, such as scientific study, engineering, etc.

especial /ɪˈspeʃl/ ***adj.*** (only *before* a noun) (*formal*) not usual; special: *This will be of especial interest to you.*

especially ⊶ /ɪˈspeʃəli/ ***adv.*** **1** more than other things, people, situations, etc. SYN **particularly**: *She loves animals, especially dogs.* ◊ *Teenage boys especially can be very competitive.* ◊ *He was very disappointed with his mark in the exam, especially as he had worked so hard for it.* **2** for a particular purpose or person: *I made this especially for you.* **3** very (much): *It's not an especially difficult exam.* ◊ *'Do you like jazz?' 'Not especially.'*

espionage /ˈespiənɑːʒ/ ***noun*** [U] the act of finding out secret information about another country or organization ➲ verb **spy**

Esq. ***abbr.*** (*especially BrE, formal*) **Esquire**; used when you are writing a man's name on an envelope: *Edward Hales, Esq.*

essay ⊶ /ˈeseɪ/ ***noun*** [C] an ~ (on/about sth) (EDUCATION) a short piece of writing on one subject: *We have to write a 1000-word essay on tourism for homework.*

essence /ˈesns/ ***noun*** **1** [U] the basic or most important quality of sth: *The essence of the problem is that there is not enough money available.* ◇ *Although both parties agree **in essence**, some minor differences remain.* **2** [C,U] a substance (usually a liquid) that is taken from a plant or food and that has a strong smell or taste of that plant or food: *coffee/vanilla essence*

THESAURUS

essential

vital • crucial • critical • decisive • indispensable

These words all describe sb/sth that is extremely important and completely necessary because a particular situation or activity depends on them.

essential: *Experience is essential for this job.*

vital: *The police play a vital role in society.*

crucial: *It is crucial that we get this right.*

critical: *Your decision is critical to our future.*

decisive: *She played a decisive role in the investigations.*

indispensable: *Cars have become an indispensable part of our lives.*

essential ⊶ /ɪˈsenʃl/ ***adj.*** completely necessary; that you must have or do: *essential medical supplies* ◇ *Maths is essential for a career in computers.* ◇ *It is essential that all school-leavers should have a qualification.* ▶ **essential *noun*** [C, usually pl.]: *food, and other essentials such as clothing and heating*

essentially ⊶ /ɪˈsenʃəli/ ***adv.*** when you consider the basic or most important part of sth: *The problem is essentially one of money.* SYN **basically**

establish ⊶ AW /ɪˈstæblɪʃ/ ***verb*** [T] **1** to start or create an organization, a system, etc.: *The school was established in 1875.* ◇ *Before we start on the project we should establish some rules.* **2** to start a formal relationship with sb/sth: *The government is trying to establish closer links between the two countries.* **3** ~ sb/sth (as sth) to become accepted and recognized as sth: *She has been trying to establish herself as a novelist for years.* **4** to discover or find proof of the facts of a situation: *The police have not been able to establish the cause of the crash.*

established AW /ɪˈstæblɪʃt/ ***adj.*** respected or given official status because it has existed or been used for a long time: *They are an established company with a good reputation.*

establishment AW /ɪˈstæblɪʃmənt/ ***noun*** **1** [C] (*formal*) an organization, a large institution or a hotel: *an educational establishment* **2 the Establishment** [sing.] the people in positions of power in a country, who usually do not support change **3** [U] the act of creating or starting a new organization, system, etc.: *the establishment of new laws on taxes*

estate ⊶ AW /ɪˈsteɪt/ ***noun*** [C] **1** a large area of land in the countryside that is owned by one person or family: *He owns a large estate in Scotland.* ◇ *She receives rent from all the people whose cottages are on estate land.* **2** (*BrE*) an area of land that has a lot of houses or factories of the same type on it: *an industrial estate* (= where there are a lot of factories) ◇ *a housing estate* **3** all the money and property that a person owns, especially everything that is left when they die: *Her estate was left to her daughter.*

esˈtate agent (*AmE* **Realtor™**; **ˈreal estate agent**) ***noun*** [C] a person whose job is to buy and sell houses and land for other people

esˈtate car (*AmE* **station wagon**) ***noun*** [C] a car with a door at the back and a long area for luggage behind the back seat

esteem /ɪˈstiːm/ ***noun*** [U] (*formal*) great respect; a good opinion of sb

ester /ˈestə(r)/ ***noun*** [C] (CHEMISTRY) a type of natural substance (**organic compound**) that is formed by combining an acid and an alcohol

esthetic (*AmE*) = AESTHETIC

estimate¹ ⊶ AW /ˈestɪmət/ ***noun*** [C] **1** an ~ (of sth) a guess or judgement about the size, cost, etc. of sth, before you have all the facts and figures: *Can you give me **a rough estimate** of how many people will be at the meeting?* ◇ ***At a conservative estimate*** (= the real figure will probably be higher), *the job will take six months to complete.* **2** an ~ (for sth/doing sth) a written statement from a person who is going to do a job for you, for example a BUILDER or a painter, telling you how much it will cost: *They gave me an estimate for repairing the roof.* ➲ look at **quotation**

IDM **a ballpark figure/estimate** → BALLPARK

estimate² ⊶ AW /ˈestɪmeɪt/ ***verb*** [T] ~ sth (at sth); ~ that... to calculate the size, cost, etc. of sth approximately, before you have all the facts and figures: *The police estimated the crowd at 10 000.* ◇ *She estimated that the work would take three months.*

estimation AW /ˌestɪˈmeɪʃn/ ***noun*** [U] (*formal*) opinion or judgement: *Who is to blame, **in** your **estimation**?*

estranged /ɪˈstreɪndʒd/ ***adj.*** **1** no longer living with your husband/wife: *her estranged husband* **2** ~ (from sb) no longer friendly or in contact with sb who was close to you: *He became estranged from his family following an argument.*

estrogen (*AmE*) = OESTROGEN

estuary /ˈestʃuəri/ ***noun*** [C] (*pl.* **estuaries**) (GEOGRAPHY) the wide part of a river where it flows into the sea

ETA /ˌiː tiː ˈeɪ/ ***abbr.*** estimated time of arrival; the time at which an aircraft, ship, etc. is expected to arrive

et al. /ˌet ˈæl/ ***abbr.*** used especially after names to mean 'and other people or things' (from Latin **et alii/alia**): *research by West et al., 1996*

etc. /ˌet ˈsetərə/ ***abbr.*** et cetera; and so on, and other things of a similar kind: *sandwiches, biscuits, cakes, etc.*

etch /etʃ/ ***verb*** [T] (ART) to cut lines into a piece of glass, metal, etc. in order to make words or a picture: *a beer glass with his initials etched on it*

etching /ˈetʃɪŋ/ ***noun*** [C,U] (ART) a picture that is printed from an ETCHED piece of metal; the art of making these pictures

eternal /ɪˈtɜːnl/ ***adj.*** **1** without beginning or end; existing or continuing for ever: *Some people believe in eternal life* (= after death). **2** happening too often; seeming to last for ever: *I'm tired of these eternal arguments!* ▶ **eternally** /-əli/ ***adv.***: *I'll be **eternally grateful** if you could help me.*

eternity /ɪˈtɜːnəti/ ***noun*** **1** [U] time that has no end; the state or time after death **2 an eternity** [sing.] a period of time that never seems to end: *It seemed like an eternity before the ambulance arrived.*

ethane /'i:θeɪn/ ***noun*** [U] (*symbol* C_2H_6) (**CHEMISTRY**) a gas that has no colour or smell and that can burn. Ethane is found in natural gas and in PETROLEUM (=oil that can be made into fuel).

ethanol /'eθənɒl/ (*also* **ethyl alcohol**) ***noun*** [U] (**CHEMISTRY**) the type of alcohol in alcoholic drinks, also used as a fuel or as a SOLVENT (=for dissolving other substances)

ether /'i:θə(r)/ ***noun*** [U] **1** a clear liquid made from alcohol, used in industry as a SOLVENT (=a liquid that can dissolve another substance) and, in the past, in medicine to make people unconscious before an operation **2 the ether** the air, when it is thought of as the place in which radio or electronic communication takes place

ethereal /ɪ'θɪəriəl/ ***adj.*** (*formal*) extremely delicate and light; seeming to belong to another, more spiritual, world: *her ethereal beauty*

Ethernet /'i:θənet/ ***noun*** [U] (**COMPUTING**) a system for connecting a number of computer systems to form a network

ethic AW /'eθɪk/ ***noun*** **1 ethics** [pl.] moral principles that control or influence a person's behaviour: *business/professional/medical ◇ to draw up a **code of ethics*** **2** [sing.] a system of moral principles or rules of behaviour: *a strongly defined work ethic* **3 ethics** [U] the branch of philosophy that deals with moral principles

ethical AW /'eθɪkl/ ***adj.*** **1** connected with beliefs of what is right or wrong: *That is an ethical problem.* **2** morally correct: *Although she didn't break the law, her behaviour was certainly not ethical.* ▶ **ethically** /-kli/ ***adv.***

ethics /'eθɪks/ ***noun*** **1** [U] the study of what is right and wrong in human behaviour **2** [pl.] beliefs about what is morally correct or acceptable: *The medical profession has its own **code of ethics**.*

ethnic[1] AW /'eθnɪk/ ***adj.*** (**SOCIAL STUDIES**) connected with or typical of a particular race or religion: *ethnic food/music/clothes*

ethnic[2] AW /'eθnɪk/ ***noun*** [C] (*especially AmE*) (**SOCIAL STUDIES**) a person from an ETHNIC MINORITY

ˌethnic 'cleansing ***noun*** [U] (**SOCIAL STUDIES**) the policy of forcing people of a certain race or religion to leave an area or country

ˌethnic mi'nority ***noun*** [C] (**SOCIAL STUDIES**) a group of people from a particular culture or of a particular race living in a country where the main group is of a different culture or race

ethnography /eθ'nɒgrəfi/ ***noun*** [U] (**SOCIAL STUDIES**) the scientific description of different races and cultures ▶ **ethnographic** /ˌeθnə'græfɪk/ ***adj.***: *ethnographic research/studies*

ethnology /eθ'nɒlədʒi/ ***noun*** [U] (**SOCIAL STUDIES**) the scientific study and comparison of human races ▶ **ethnological** /ˌeθnə'lɒdʒɪkl/ ***adj.*** **ethnologist** /eθ'nɒlədʒɪst/ ***noun*** [C]

ethyl alcohol /ˌeθɪl 'ælkəhɒl; ˌi:θaɪl/ =ETHANOL

etiology (*AmE*) =AETIOLOGY

etiquette /'etɪket/ ***noun*** [U] the rules of polite and correct behaviour: *social/professional etiquette*

etymology /ˌetɪ'mɒlədʒi/ ***noun*** (*pl.* **etymologies**) **1** [U] (**LANGUAGE**) the study of the origins and history of words and their meanings **2** [C] an explanation of the origin and history of a particular word

EU /ˌi: 'ju:/ ***abbr.*** (**POLITICS**) European Union

eucalyptus /ˌju:kə'lɪptəs/ ***noun*** [C] (*pl.* **eucalyptuses** or **eucalypti** /-taɪ/) a tall straight tree that grows especially in Australia and Asia. Its leaves produce an oil with a strong smell, that is used in medicine.

eukaryote (also **eucaryote**) /ju:'kæriəʊt/ ***noun*** [C] (**BIOLOGY**) an ORGANISM (=a very small living thing) consisting of one or more cells in which DNA (=the chemical that controls what characteristics that animal or plant will have) is contained inside a clear NUCLEUS (=central part). **Eukaryotes** include most living things except for some bacteria. ➲ look at **prokaryote** ▶ **eukaryotic** /ju:ˌkæri'ɒtɪk/ ***adj.***

eulogy /'ju:lədʒi/ ***noun*** (*pl.* **eulogies**) **1** [C,U] **(a) ~ (of/to sb/sth)** (**LITERATURE**) a speech or piece of writing that says good things about sb/sth: *a eulogy to marriage* **2** [C] **a ~ (for/to sb)** (*especially AmE*) a speech given at a funeral saying good things about the person who has died

euphemism /'ju:fəmɪzəm/ ***noun*** [C,U] an indirect word or expression that you use instead of a more direct one when you are talking about sth that is unpleasant or embarrassing; the use of such expressions: *'Pass away' is a euphemism for 'die'.* ▶ **euphemistic** /ˌju:fə'mɪstɪk/ ***adj.***: *euphemistic language* ▶ **euphemistically** /-kli/ ***adv.***

euphoria /ju:'fɔ:riə/ ***noun*** [U] (*formal*) an extremely strong feeling of happiness ▶ **euphoric** /ju:'fɒrɪk/ ***adj.***: *My euphoric mood could not last.*

Eurasian /ju'reɪʒn; -'reɪʃn/ ***adj.*** (**SOCIAL STUDIES**) **1** of or connected with both Europe and Asia **2** having one Asian parent and one parent who is white or from Europe ▶ **Eurasian** ***noun*** [C]: *Singapore Eurasians*

euro 🔑 /'jʊərəʊ/ ***noun*** [C] (*symbol* €) (**ECONOMICS**) the unit of money of some countries of the European Union: *The price is given in dollars or euros.*

Euro- /'jʊərəʊ/ ***prefix*** (used in nouns and adjectives) connected with Europe or the European Union: *a Euro-MP ◇ Euro-elections*

European[1] /ˌjʊərə'pi:ən/ ***adj.*** of or from Europe: *European languages*

European[2] /ˌjʊərə'pi:ən/ ***noun*** [C] a person from a European country

the Euroˌpean 'Union ***noun*** [sing.] (*abbr.* **EU**) (**POLITICS**) an economic and political association of certain European countries

europium /jʊər'əʊpiəm/ ***noun*** [U] (*symbol* **Eu**) (**CHEMISTRY**) a chemical element. **Europium** is a silver-white metal used in colour television screens. ❶ For more information on the periodic table of elements, look at pages R34-5.

Eustachian tube /ju:'steɪʃn tju:b/ ***noun*** [C] (**ANATOMY**) a narrow tube that joins the throat to the middle ear ➲ picture at **ear**

euthanasia /ˌju:θə'neɪziə/ ***noun*** [U] (**SOCIAL STUDIES**) the practice (illegal in most countries) of killing without pain sb who wants to die because they are suffering from a disease that cannot be cured

eutrophication /ˌju:trəfɪ'keɪʃn/ ***noun*** [U] (**BIOLOGY, ENVIRONMENT**) the process of too many plants growing on the surface of a river, lake, etc., often because chemicals that are used to help crops grow have been carried there by rain

evacuate /ɪ'vækjueɪt/ ***verb*** [T] to move people from a dangerous place to somewhere safer; to leave a place because it is dangerous: *Thousands of people were evacuated from the war zone. ◇ The* *village had to be evacuated when the river burst its banks.* ▶ **evacuation** /ɪˌvækju'eɪʃn/ ***noun*** [C,U]

evacuee /ɪˌvækju'iː/ ***noun*** [C] (POLITICS) a person who is sent away from a place because it is dangerous, especially during a war

evade /ɪ'veɪd/ ***verb*** [T] **1** to manage to escape from or to avoid meeting sb/sth: *They managed to evade capture and escaped to France.* **2** to avoid dealing with or doing sth: *to evade responsibility* ◇ *I asked her directly, but she evaded the question.* ➲ noun **evasion**

evaluate AW /ɪ'væljueɪt/ ***verb*** [T] (*formal*) to form an opinion of the amount, value or quality of sth after thinking about it carefully: *We evaluated the situation very carefully before we made our decision.* ▶ **evaluation** AW /ɪˌvælju'eɪʃn/ ***noun*** [C,U]

evangelical /ˌiːvæn'dʒelɪkl/ ***adj.*** (RELIGION) (of certain Protestant churches) believing that religious ceremony is not as important as belief in Jesus Christ and study of the Bible

evaporate /ɪ'væpəreɪt/ ***verb*** [I] **1** (SCIENCE) (used about a liquid) to change into steam or gas and disappear: *The water evaporated in the sunshine.* ➲ look at **condense** ➲ picture at **water** **2** to disappear completely: *All her confidence evaporated when she saw the exam paper.* ▶ **evaporation** /ɪˌvæpə'reɪʃn/ ***noun*** [U]

evasion /ɪ'veɪʒn/ ***noun*** [C,U] **1** the act of avoiding sth that you should do: *He has been sentenced to two years' imprisonment for **tax evasion**.* ◇ *an evasion of responsibility* **2** a statement that avoids dealing with a question or subject in a direct way: *The President's reply was full of evasions.* ➲ verb **evade**

evasive /ɪ'veɪsɪv/ ***adj.*** trying to avoid sth; not direct: *Ann gave an evasive answer.*

eve /iːv/ ***noun*** [C] the day or evening before a religious festival, important event, etc.: *Christmas Eve* ◇ *He injured himself on the eve of the final.*

even[1] ⊶ /'iːvn/ ***adj.*** **1** flat, level or smooth: *The game must be played on an even surface.* OPP **uneven** **2** not changing; regular: *He's very **even-tempered** – in fact I've never seen him angry.* OPP **uneven** **3** (used about a competition, etc.) equal, with one side being as good as the other: *The contest was very even until the last few minutes of the game.* OPP **uneven** **4** (MATHEMATICS) (used about numbers) that can be divided by two: *2, 4, 6, 8, 10, etc. are even numbers.* OPP **odd**

IDM **be/get even (with sb)** (*informal*) to hurt or harm sb who has hurt or harmed you

break even to make neither a loss nor a profit

even[2] ⊶ /'iːvn/ ***adv.*** **1** used for emphasizing sth that is surprising: *It isn't very warm here even in summer.* ◇ *He didn't even open the letter.* **2** ~ **more, less, bigger, nicer, etc.** used when you are comparing things, to make the comparison stronger: *You know even less about it than I do.* ◇ *It is even more difficult than I expected.* ◇ *We are even busier than yesterday.*

IDM **even if** used for saying that what follows 'if' makes no difference: *I wouldn't ride a horse, even if you paid me.*

even so (used for introducing a new idea, fact, etc. that is surprising) in spite of that; nevertheless: *There are a lot of spelling mistakes; even so it's quite a good essay.*

even though although: *I like her very much even though she can be very annoying.*

evening ⊶ /'iːvnɪŋ/ ***noun*** [C,U] the part of the day between the afternoon and the time that you go to bed: *What are you doing this evening?* ◇ *We were out yesterday evening.* ◇ *I went to the cinema on Saturday evening.* ◇ *Tom usually goes swimming on Wednesday evenings.* ◇ *Most people watch television **in the evening**.* ◇ *an evening class* (=a course of lessons for adults that takes place in the evening)

IDM **good evening** used when you see sb for the first time in the evening

'**evening dress** ***noun*** **1** [U] elegant clothes worn for formal occasions in the evening: *Everyone was in evening dress.* **2** [C] a woman's long formal dress

evenly /'iːvnli/ ***adv.*** in a smooth, regular or equal way: *The match was very evenly balanced.* ◇ *Spread the cake mixture evenly in the tin.*

event ⊶ /ɪ'vent/ ***noun*** [C] **1** something that happens, especially sth important or unusual: *a historic event* ◇ *The events of the past few days have made things very difficult for the Government.* **2** a planned public or social occasion: *a fund-raising event* **3** one of the races, competitions, etc. in a sports programme: *The next event is the 800 metres.*

IDM **at all events/in any event** whatever happens: *I hope to see you soon, but in any event I'll phone you on Sunday.*

in the event of sth (*formal*) if sth happens: *In the event of fire, leave the building as quickly as possible.*

eventful /ɪ'ventfl/ ***adj.*** full of important, dangerous or exciting things happening

eventual AW /ɪ'ventʃuəl/ ***adj.*** (only *before* a noun) happening as a result at the end of a period of time or of a process: *It is impossible to say what the eventual cost will be.*

eventuality AW /ɪˌventʃu'æləti/ ***noun*** [C] (*pl.* **-ies**) (*formal*) something that may possibly happen, especially sth unpleasant: *We were prepared for **every eventuality**.*

eventually ⊶ AW /ɪ'ventʃuəli/ ***adv.*** in the end; finally: *He eventually managed to persuade his parents to let him buy a motor bike.* SYN **finally**

ever[1] ⊶ /'evə(r)/ ***adv.*** **1** (used in questions and negative sentences, when you are comparing things, and in sentences with 'if') at any time: *Do you ever wish you were famous?* ◇ *Nobody ever comes to see me.* ◇ *She **hardly ever*** (=almost never) *goes out.* ◇ *Today is hotter **than ever**.* ◇ *This is the best meal I have ever had.* ◇ *If you ever visit England, you must come and stay with us.* **2** (used in questions with verbs in the PERFECT TENSES) at any time up to now: *Have you ever been to Spain?* **3** used with a question that begins with 'when', 'where', 'who', 'how', etc., to show that you are surprised or shocked: ***How ever** did he get back so quickly?* ◇ ***What ever** were you thinking about when you wrote this?* ➲ look at **whatever**, **whenever**, **however**

IDM **(as) bad, good, etc. as ever** (as) bad, good, etc. as usual or as always: *In spite of his problems, Andrew is as cheerful as ever.*

ever after (used especially at the end of stories) from that moment on for always: *The prince married the princess and they lived happily ever after.*

ever since... all the time from...until now: *She has had a car ever since she was at university.*

ever so/ever such (a) (*BrE, informal*) very: *He's ever so kind.* ◇ *He's ever such a kind man.*

for ever → FOREVER (1)

ever-[2] /'evə(r)/ (in compounds) always; continuously: *the ever-growing problem of pollution*

evergreen /'evəgriːn/ ***noun*** [C], ***adj.*** (BIOLOGY) (a tree or bush) with green leaves all through the year ➲ look at **deciduous**

everlasting /ˌevəˈlɑːstɪŋ/ ***adj.*** (*formal*) continuing for ever; never changing: *everlasting life/love*

every ⊶ /ˈevri/ ***det.*** **1** (used with singular nouns) all of the people or things in a group of three or more: *She knows every student in the school.* ◇ *There are 200 students in the school, and she knows every one of them.* ◇ *I've read every book in this house.* ◇ *You were out every time I phoned.* **2** all that is possible: *You have every chance of success.* ◇ *She had every reason to be angry.* **3** used for saying how often sth happens: *We see each other* ***every day****.* ◇ *Take the medicine every four hours* (=at 8, 12, 4 o'clock, etc.). ◇ *I work* ***every other day*** (=on Monday, Wednesday, Friday, etc.). ◇ ***One in every*** *three marriages ends in divorce.*

everybody ⊶ /ˈevribɒdi/ (*also* **everyone** /ˈevriwʌn/) ***pronoun*** [with sing. verb] every person; all people: *Is everybody here?* ◇ *The police questioned everyone who was at the party.* ◇ *I'm sure everybody else* (=all the other people) *will agree with me.*

everyday /ˈevrideɪ/ ***adj.*** (only *before* a noun) normal or usual: *The computer is now part of everyday life.*

everyplace /ˈevripleɪs/ (*AmE*) =EVERYWHERE

everything ⊶ /ˈevriθɪŋ/ ***pronoun*** [with sing verb] **1** each thing; all things: *Sam lost everything in the fire.* ◇ *Everything is very expensive in this shop.* ◇ *We can leave* ***everything else*** (=all the other things) *until tomorrow.* **2** the most important thing: *Money isn't everything.*

everywhere ⊶ /ˈevriweə(r)/ ***adv.*** in or to every place: *I've looked everywhere, but I still can't find it.*

evict /ɪˈvɪkt/ ***verb*** [T] to force sb (officially) to leave the house or land which they are renting: *They were evicted for not paying the rent.* ▶ **eviction** ***noun*** [C,U]

evidence ⊶ AW /ˈevɪdəns/ ***noun*** [U] ~ **(of/for sth)**; ~ **that...** the facts, signs, etc. that make you believe that sth is true: *There was no evidence of a struggle in the room.* ◇ *There was not enough evidence to prove him guilty.* ◇ *Her statement to the police was* ***used in evidence*** *against him.* ◇ *The witnesses to the accident will be asked to* ***give evidence*** *in court.* ◇ *You have absolutely no evidence for what you're saying!*
IDM **(to be) in evidence** that you can see; present in a place: *When we arrived there was no ambulance in evidence.*

evident AW /ˈevɪdənt/ ***adj.*** clear (to the eye or mind); obvious: *It was evident that the damage was very serious.* ➲ note at **clear**[1]

evidently AW /ˈevɪdəntli/ ***adv.*** **1** clearly; that can be easily seen or understood: *She was evidently extremely shocked at the news.* **2** according to what people say: *Evidently he has decided to leave.*

evil[1] ⊶ /ˈiːvl/ ***adj.*** morally bad; causing trouble or harming people: *In the play Richard is portrayed as an evil king.*

evil[2] ⊶ /ˈiːvl/ ***noun*** [C,U] a force that causes bad or harmful things to happen: *The play is about the good and evil in all of us.* ◇ *Drugs and alcohol are two of the evils of modern society.*
IDM **the lesser of two evils** → LESSER

evocative /ɪˈvɒkətɪv/ ***adj.*** ~ **(of sth)** making you think of or remember a strong image or feeling, in a pleasant way: *evocative smells/sounds/music* ◇ *Her book is wonderfully evocative of village life.*

evoke /ɪˈvəʊk/ ***verb*** [T] (*formal*) to produce a memory, feeling, etc. in sb: *For me, that music always evokes hot summer evenings.* ◇ *Her novel evoked a lot of interest.*

evolution AW /ˌiːvəˈluːʃn; ˌev-/ ***noun*** [U] **1** (BIOLOGY) the development of plants, animals, etc. over many thousands of years from simple early forms to more advanced ones: *Darwin's theory of evolution* **2** the gradual process of change and development of sth: *Political evolution is a slow process.* ▶ **evolutionary** AW /ˌiːvəˈluːʃənri; ˌev-/ ***adj.***: *evolutionary theory*

evolve AW /iˈvɒlv/ ***verb*** **1** [I,T] (*formal*) to develop or to make sth develop gradually, from a simple to a more advanced form: *His style of painting has evolved gradually over the past 20 years.* **2** [I] ~ **(from sth)** (BIOLOGY) (used about plants, animals, etc.) to develop over many thousands of years from simple forms to more advanced ones

ewe /juː/ ***noun*** [C] a female sheep ➲ note at **sheep** ➲ picture at **sheep**

ex- /eks/ ***prefix*** (in nouns) former: *ex-wife* ◇ *ex-president*

exacerbate /ɪɡˈzæsəbeɪt/ ***verb*** [T] (*formal*) to make sth worse, especially a disease or problem SYN **aggravate** ▶ **exacerbation** /ɪɡˌzæsəˈbeɪʃn/ ***noun*** [U, C]

exact[1] ⊶ /ɪɡˈzækt/ ***adj.*** **1** (completely) correct; accurate: *He's in his mid fifties. Well, fifty-six* ***to be exact****.* ◇ *I can't tell you the exact number of people who are coming.* ◇ *She's* ***the exact opposite*** *of her sister.* ➲ note at **true** **2** able to work in a way that is completely accurate: *You need to be very exact when you calculate the costs.* ▶ **exactness** ***noun*** [U]

exact[2] ⊶ /ɪɡˈzækt/ ***verb*** [T] (*formal*) ~ **sth (from sb)** to demand and get sth from sb

exacting /ɪɡˈzæktɪŋ/ ***adj.*** needing a lot of care and attention; difficult: *exacting work*

exactly ⊶ /ɪɡˈzæktli/ ***adv.*** **1** (used to emphasize that sth is correct in every way) just: *You've arrived at exactly the right moment.* ◇ *I found exactly what I wanted.* **2** used to ask for, or give, completely correct information: *He took exactly one hour to finish.* SYN **precisely** **3** (*spoken*) (used for agreeing with a statement) yes; you are right: *'I don't think she's old enough to travel on her own.' 'Exactly.'*
IDM **not exactly** (*spoken*) **1** (used when you are saying the opposite of what you really mean) not really; not at all: *He's not exactly the most careful driver I know.* **2** (used as an answer to say that sth is almost true): *'So you think I'm wrong?' 'No, not exactly, but ...'*

exaggerate ⊶ /ɪɡˈzædʒəreɪt/ ***verb*** [I,T] to make sth seem larger, better, worse, etc. than it really is: *Don't exaggerate. I was only two minutes late, not twenty.* ◇ *The problems have been greatly exaggerated.* ▶ **exaggeration** /ɪɡˌzædʒəˈreɪʃn/ ***noun*** [C,U]: *It's rather an exaggeration to say that all the students are lazy.*

exam ⊶ /ɪɡˈzæm/ (also *formal* **examination**) ***noun*** [C] (EDUCATION) a written, spoken or practical test of what you know or can do: *an English exam* ◇ *the exam results* ◇ *to* ***do/take/sit an exam*** ◇ *to* ***pass/fail an exam***

examination ⊶ /ɪɡˌzæmɪˈneɪʃn/ ***noun*** **1** [C,U] the act of looking at sth carefully, especially to see if there is anything wrong or to find the cause of a problem: *On close examination, it was found that the passport was false.* ◇ *a medical examination* **2** [C] (*formal*) =EXAM

examine ⊶ /ɪɡˈzæmɪn/ ***verb*** [T] **1** to consider or study an idea, a subject, etc. very carefully: *These theories will be examined in more detail later on in*

THESAURUS

examine

review • study • take stock • survey

These words all mean to think about, study or describe sb/sth carefully, especially in order to understand them, form an opinion of them or make a decision about them.

examine: *He examined the letter in detail.*

review: *Let us review the situation.*

study: *Study the report carefully.*

take stock: *It was time to stand back and take stock of his career.*

survey: *This chapter surveys the current state of Finnish politics.*

the lecture. **2** ~ **sb/sth (for sth)** to look at sb/sth carefully in order to find out sth: *The detective examined the room for clues.* **3** (*formal*) ~ **sb (in/on sth)** (EDUCATION) to test what sb knows or can do: *You will be examined on everything that has been studied in the course.*

examiner /ɪɡ'zæmɪnə(r)/ ***noun*** [C] (EDUCATION) a person who tests sb in an exam

THESAURUS

example

case • instance • specimen • illustration

These are all words for a thing or situation that is typical of a particular group or set, and is sometimes used to support an argument.

example: *Give an example of what you mean.*

case: *In some cases people have had to wait several weeks for an appointment.*

instance (*formal*): *It was an instance of terrible injustice.*

specimen: *The aquarium has some interesting specimens of unusual fish.*

illustration (*formal*): *The statistics are a clear illustration of the point I am trying to make.*

example 🔑 /ɪɡ'zɑːmpl/ ***noun*** [C] **1** an ~ **(of sth)** something such as an object, a fact or a situation which shows, explains or supports what you say: *I don't quite understand you. Can you* ***give me an example of*** *what you mean? ◇ This is* ***a typical example of*** *a Victorian house.* **2** an ~ **(to sb)** a person or thing or a type of behaviour that is good and should be copied: *Joe's bravery should be an example to us all.*

IDM **follow sb's example/lead** → FOLLOW

for example; **e.g.** used for giving a fact, situation, etc., which explains or supports what you are talking about: *In many countries, Italy, for example, family life is much more important than here.*

set a(n) (good/bad) example (to sb) to behave in a way that should/should not be copied: *Parents should always take care when crossing roads in order to set a good example to their children.*

exasperate /ɪɡ'zæspəreɪt/ ***verb*** [T] to make sb angry; to annoy sb very much: *She was exasperated by the lack of progress.* ▶ **exasperating** ***adj.***: *an exasperating problem* ▶ **exasperation** /ɪɡˌzæspə'reɪʃn/ ***noun*** [U]: *She finally threw the book across the room* ***in exasperation.***

excavate /'ekskəveɪt/ ***verb*** [I,T] (HISTORY) to dig in the ground to look for old objects or buildings that have been buried for a long time; to find sth by digging in this way: *A Roman villa has been excavated in a valley near the village.* ▶ **excavation** /ˌekskə'veɪʃn/ ***noun*** [C,U]: *Excavations on the site have revealed Saxon objects.*

excavator /'ekskəveɪtə(r)/ ***noun*** [C] **1** a large machine that is used for digging and moving earth **2** a person who digs in the ground to look for old buildings and objects

exceed AW /ɪk'siːd/ ***verb*** [T] **1** to be more than a particular number or amount: *The weight should not exceed 20 kilos.* **2** to do more than the law, a rule, an order, etc. allows you to do: *He was stopped by the police for exceeding the speed limit* (= driving faster than is allowed). ➲ Look at **excess** and **excessive**.

exceedingly /ɪk'siːdɪŋli/ ***adv.*** (*formal*) very: *an exceedingly difficult problem*

excel /ɪk'sel/ ***verb*** (**excelling**; **excelled**) (*formal*) **1** [I] ~ **(in/at sth/doing sth)** to be very good at doing sth: *Anne excels at sports.* **2** [T] ~ **yourself** (*BrE*) to do sth even better than you usually do: *Rick's cooking is always good but this time he really excelled himself.*

excellence /'eksələns/ ***noun*** [U] the quality of being very good: *The head teacher said that she wanted the school to be a centre of academic excellence.*

Excellency /'eksələnsi/ ***noun*** [C] (*pl.* **Excellencies**) **(His/Her/Your) Excellency** a title used when talking to or about an AMBASSADOR (= sb who has a very important official position as the representative of his or her own country in another country)

excellent 🔑 /'eksələnt/ ***adj.*** very good; of high quality: *He speaks excellent French.* ▶ **excellently** ***adv.***

except[1] 🔑 /ɪk'sept/ ***prep.*** ~ **(for) sb/sth**; ~ **that...** not including sb/sth; apart from the fact that: *The museum is open every day except Mondays. ◇ I can answer all of the questions except for the last one. ◇ It was a good hotel except that it was rather noisy.*

except[2] 🔑 /ɪk'sept/ ***verb*** [T] (*formal*) ~ **sb/sth (from sth)** (often passive) to leave sb/sth out; to not include sb/sth: *Nobody is excepted from helping with the housework.* ▶ **excepting** ***prep.***: *I swim every day excepting Sundays.*

exception 🔑 /ɪk'sepʃn/ ***noun*** [C] a person or thing that is not included in a general statement: *Most of his songs are awful but this one is an exception. ◇ Everybody was poor as a student and I was* ***no exception.***

IDM **make an exception (of sb/sth)** to treat sb/sth differently: *We don't usually allow children under 14 but we'll make an exception in your case.*

with the exception of except for; apart from: *He has won every major tennis championship with the exception of Wimbledon.*

without exception in every case; including everyone/everything: *Everybody without exception must take the test.*

exceptional /ɪk'sepʃənl/ ***adj.*** very unusual; unusually good: *You will only be allowed to leave early in exceptional circumstances.* ➲ look at **unexceptional** ▶ **exceptionally** /-ʃənəli/ ***adv.***: *The past year has been exceptionally difficult for us.*

excerpt /'eksɜːpt/ ***noun*** [C] (LITERATURE) a short piece taken from a book, film, piece of music, etc.

excess[1] /ɪk'ses/ ***noun*** [sing.] **an ~ (of sth)** more of sth than is necessary or usual; too much of sth: *An excess of fat in your diet can lead to heart disease.*

IDM **in excess of** more than: *Her debts are in excess of £1000.* ➲ verb **exceed**

excess² /'ekses/ ***adj.*** (only *before* a noun) more than is usual or allowed; extra: *Cut any excess fat off the meat.* ➲ verb **exceed**

ˌ**excess 'baggage** ***noun*** [U] (TOURISM) bags, cases, etc. taken on to a plane that weigh more than the amount each passenger is allowed to carry without paying extra: *The baggage allowance is 20kg, after which excess baggage charges apply.*

excessive /ɪk'sesɪv/ ***adj.*** too much; too great or extreme: *He was driving at excessive speed when he crashed.* ▶ **excessively** ***adv.***

exchange¹ 🔑 /ɪks'tʃeɪndʒ/ ***noun*** **1** [C,U] giving or receiving sth in return for sth else: *a useful exchange of information* ◇ *We can offer free accommodation **in exchange for** some help in the house.* **2** [U] (FINANCE) the relation in value between kinds of money used in different countries: *What's the **exchange rate/rate of exchange** for dollars?* ◇ *Most of the country's **foreign exchange** comes from oil.* ➲ look at **Stock Exchange** **3** [C] (EDUCATION) a visit by a group of students or teachers to another country and a return visit by a similar group from that country: *She went on an exchange to Germany when she was sixteen.* **4** (often **Exchange**) [C] (often in compounds) a building where business people met in the past to buy and sell a particular type of goods: *the old Corn Exchange* ➲ look at **stock exchange** **5** = TELEPHONE EXCHANGE **6** [C] an angry conversation or argument: *She ended up having a **heated exchange** with her neighbours about the noise the night before.*

exchange² 🔑 /ɪks'tʃeɪndʒ/ ***verb*** [T] ~ **A for B**; ~ **sth (with sb)** to give or receive sth in return for sth else: *I would like to exchange this skirt for a bigger size.* ◇ *Claire and Molly exchanged addresses with the boys.* ◇ *They exchanged glances* (= they looked at each other).

exchequer /ɪks'tʃekə(r)/ ***noun*** [sing.] (often **the Exchequer**) (POLITICS) (in Britain) the government department that controls public money SYN **the Treasury** ➲ look at **Chancellor of the Exchequer**

excise /'eksaɪz/ ***noun*** [U] (ECONOMICS) a government tax on certain goods that are produced or sold inside a country, for example TOBACCO, alcohol, etc. ➲ look at **customs**

excitable /ɪk'saɪtəbl/ ***adj.*** easily excited

excite 🔑 /ɪk'saɪt/ ***verb*** [T] **1** to make sb feel happy and enthusiastic or nervous: *Don't excite the baby too much or we'll never get him off to sleep.* **2** to make sb react in a particular way: *The programme excited great interest.*

excited 🔑 /ɪk'saɪtɪd/ ***adj.*** ~ **(about/at/by sth)** feeling or showing happiness and enthusiasm; not calm: *Are you getting excited about your holiday?* ◇ *We're all very excited at the thought of moving house.* ▶ **excitedly** ***adv.***

excitement 🔑 /ɪk'saɪtmənt/ ***noun*** [U] the state of being excited, especially because sth interesting is happening or will happen: *There was **great excitement** as the winner's name was announced.* ◇ *The match was **full of excitement** until the very last minute.*

exciting 🔑 /ɪk'saɪtɪŋ/ ***adj.*** causing strong feelings of pleasure and interest: *That's very exciting news.* ◇ *Berlin is one of the most exciting cities in Europe.*

exclaim /ɪk'skleɪm/ ***verb*** [I,T] to say sth suddenly and loudly because you are surprised, angry, etc.: *'I just don't believe it!' he exclaimed.*

exclamation /ˌekskləˈmeɪʃn/ ***noun*** [C] a short sound, word or phrase that you say suddenly because of a strong emotion, pain, etc.: *'Ouch!' is an exclamation.* SYN **interjection**

ˌ**excla'mation mark** (*AmE* ˌ**excla'mation point**) ***noun*** [C] (LANGUAGE) a mark (!) that is written after an EXCLAMATION

exclude 🔑 AW /ɪk'sklu:d/ ***verb*** [T] (not used in the continuous tenses) **1** to leave out; not include: *The price excludes all extras such as drinks or excursions.* **2** ~ **sb/sth (from sth)** to prevent sb/sth from entering a place or taking part in sth: *Women are excluded from the temple.* ◇ *Jake was excluded from the game for cheating.* OPP **include** **3** to decide that sth is not possible: *The police had **excluded the possibility** that the child had run away.*

excluding 🔑 AW /ɪk'sklu:dɪŋ/ ***prep.*** leaving out; without: *Lunch costs £10 per person excluding drinks.* OPP **including**

exclusion AW /ɪk'sklu:ʒn/ ***noun*** [U] keeping or leaving sb/sth out

exclusive¹ AW /ɪk'sklu:sɪv/ ***adj.*** **1** (only *before* a noun) only to be used by or given to one person, group, etc.; not to be shared: *This car is for the Director's exclusive use.* ◇ *Tonight we are showing an exclusive interview with the new leader of the Labour Party* (= on only one television station). **2** expensive and not welcoming people who are thought to be of a lower social class: *an exclusive restaurant* ◇ *a flat in an exclusive part of the city* **3** ~ **of sb/sth** not including sb/sth; without: *Lunch costs £7 per person exclusive of drinks.*

exclusive² /ɪk'sklu:sɪv/ ***noun*** [C] (ARTS AND MEDIA) a newspaper story that is given to and published by only one newspaper

exclusively AW /ɪk'sklu:sɪvli/ ***adv.*** only; not involving anyone/anything else: *The swimming pool is reserved exclusively for members of the club.*

excrement /'ekskrɪmənt/ ***noun*** [U] (*formal*) (BIOLOGY) the solid waste material that you get rid of when you go to the toilet SYN **faeces**

excrete /ɪk'skri:t/ ***verb*** [T] (*formal*) (BIOLOGY) to get rid of solid waste material from the body ▶ **excretion** /ɪk'skri:ʃn/ ***noun*** [U]

excruciating /ɪk'skru:ʃieɪtɪŋ/ ***adj.*** extremely painful

excursion /ɪk'skɜ:ʃn/ ***noun*** [C] a short journey or trip that a group of people make for pleasure: *to go **on an excursion** to the seaside* ➲ note at **travel**

excusable /ɪk'skju:zəbl/ ***adj.*** that you can forgive: *an excusable mistake* OPP **inexcusable**

excuse¹ 🔑 /ɪk'skju:s/ ***noun*** [C] an ~ **(for sth/doing sth)** a reason (that may or may not be true) that you give in order to explain your behaviour: *There's **no excuse for** rudeness.* ◇ *He always **finds an excuse** for not helping with the housework.* ◇ *to **make an excuse*** ➲ note at **reason¹**

excuse² 🔑 /ɪk'skju:z/ ***verb*** [T] **1** ~ **sb/sth (for sth/for doing sth)** to forgive sb for sth they have done wrong that is not very serious: *Please excuse the interruption but I need to talk to you.* **2** to explain sb's bad behaviour and make it seem less bad: *Nothing can excuse such behaviour.* **3** ~ **sb (from sth)** to free sb from a duty, responsibility, etc.: *She excused herself* (= asked if she could leave) *and left the meeting early.*

execute /ˈeksɪkjuːt/ ***verb*** [T] **1** ~ **sb (for sth)** (usually passive) (LAW) to kill sb as an official punishment: *He was executed for murder.* **2** (*formal*) to perform a task, etc. or to put a plan into action ▸ **execution** /ˌeksɪˈkjuːʃn/ ***noun*** [C,U]

executioner /ˌeksɪˈkjuːʃənə(r)/ ***noun*** [C] a person whose job is to EXECUTE criminals

executive[1] 🔑 /ɪɡˈzekjətɪv/ ***adj.*** **1** (used in connection with people in business, government, etc.) concerned with managing, making plans, decisions, etc.: *an executive director of the company* ◇ *executive decisions/jobs/duties* **2** (BUSINESS) (used about goods, buildings, etc.) designed to be used by important business people: *an executive briefcase*

executive[2] 🔑 /ɪɡˈzekjətɪv/ ***noun*** **1** [C] (BUSINESS) a person who has an important position as a manager of a business or organization: *She's a senior executive in a computer company.* **2** [sing.] the group of people who are in charge of an organization or a company

exemplary /ɪɡˈzempləri/ ***adj.*** very good; that can be an example to other people: *exemplary behaviour*

exemplify /ɪɡˈzemplɪfaɪ/ ***verb*** [T] (*pres. part.* **exemplifying**; *3rd person sing. pres.* **exemplifies**; *pt, pp* **exemplified**) to be a typical example of sth

exempt[1] /ɪɡˈzempt/ ***adj.*** (not before a noun) ~ **(from sth)** free from having to do sth or pay for sth: *Children under 16 are exempt from dental charges.* ▸ **exemption** /ɪɡˈzempʃn/ ***noun*** [C,U]

exempt[2] /ɪɡˈzempt/ ***verb*** [T] (*formal*) ~ **sb/sth (from sth)** to say officially that sb does not have to do sth or pay for sth

exercise[1] 🔑 /ˈeksəsaɪz/ ***noun*** **1** [U] physical or mental activity that keeps you healthy and strong: *The doctor advised him to* ***take regular exercise****.* ◇ *Swimming is a good form of exercise.* **2** [C] (often plural) a movement or activity that you do in order to stay healthy or to become skilled at sth: *I* ***do*** *keep-fit* ***exercises*** *every morning.* ◇ *breathing/stretching/relaxation exercises* **3** [C] (EDUCATION) a piece of work that is intended to help you learn or practise sth: *an exercise on phrasal verbs* **4** [C] **an** ~ **in sth** an activity or a series of actions that has a particular aim: *The project is an exercise in getting the best results at a low cost.* **5** [U] (*formal*) ~ **of sth** the use of sth, for example a power, right, etc.: *the exercise of patience/judgement/discretion* **6** [C, usually pl.] a series of activities by soldiers to practise fighting: *military exercises*

exercise[2] 🔑 /ˈeksəsaɪz/ ***verb*** **1** [I] to do some form of physical activity in order to stay fit and healthy: *It is important to exercise regularly.* **2** [T] to make use of sth, for example a power, right, etc.: *You should exercise your right to vote.*

ˈ**exercise book** ***noun*** [C] (*AmE* **notebook**) a small book for students to write their work in

exert /ɪɡˈzɜːt/ ***verb*** [T] **1** to make use of sth, for example influence, strength, etc., to affect sb/sth: *Parents exert a powerful influence on their children's opinions.* **2** ~ **yourself** to make a big effort: *You won't make any progress if you don't exert yourself a bit more.*

exertion /ɪɡˈzɜːʃn/ ***noun*** [U, C] using your body in a way that takes a lot of effort; sth that you do that makes you tired: *At his age physical exertion was dangerous.* ◇ *I'm tired after the exertions of the past few days.*

ex gratia /ˌeks ˈɡreɪʃə/ ***adj.*** (LAW) given or done as a gift or favour, not because there is a legal duty to do it: *ex gratia payments* ▸ **ex gratia** ***adv.***: *The sum was paid ex gratia.*

exhale /eksˈheɪl/ ***verb*** [I,T] (*formal*) (BIOLOGY) to breathe out the air, smoke, etc. in your lungs OPP **inhale** ▸ **exhalation** /ˌekshəˈleɪʃn/ ***noun*** [U]

exhaust[1] /ɪɡˈzɔːst/ ***noun*** **1** [U] the waste gas that comes out of a vehicle, an engine or a machine: *car exhaust fumes/emissions* **2** [C] (*also* **exhaust pipe**, *AmE* **tailpipe**) a pipe (particularly at the back of a car) through which waste gas escapes from an engine or machine

exhaust[2] /ɪɡˈzɔːst/ ***verb*** [T] **1** to make sb very tired: *The long journey to work every morning exhausted him.* **2** to use sth up completely; to finish sth: *All the supplies of food have been exhausted.* **3** to say everything you can about a subject, etc.: *Well, I think we've exhausted that topic.*

exhausted /ɪɡˈzɔːstɪd/ ***adj.*** very tired

exhausting /ɪɡˈzɔːstɪŋ/ ***adj.*** making sb very tired: *Teaching young children is exhausting work.*

exhaustion /ɪɡˈzɔːstʃən/ ***noun*** [U] the state of being extremely tired

exhaustive /ɪɡˈzɔːstɪv/ ***adj.*** including everything possible: *This list is certainly not exhaustive.*

exhibit[1] 🔑 AW /ɪɡˈzɪbɪt/ ***noun*** [C] an object that is shown in a museum, etc. or as a piece of evidence in a court of law

exhibit[2] 🔑 AW /ɪɡˈzɪbɪt/ ***verb*** [T] **1** (ART) to show sth in a public place for people to enjoy or to give them information: *His paintings have been exhibited in the local art gallery.* **2** (*formal*) to show clearly that you have a particular quality, feeling, etc.: *The refugees are exhibiting signs of exhaustion and stress.*

exhibition 🔑 AW /ˌeksɪˈbɪʃn/ ***noun*** **1** [C] (ART) a collection of objects, for example works of art, that are shown to the public: *an exhibition of photographs* ◇ *Her paintings will be* ***on exhibition*** *in London for the whole of April.* **2** [C] an occasion when a particular skill is shown to the public: *We saw an exhibition of Scottish dancing last night.* **3** [sing.] (*formal*) the act of showing a quality, feeling, etc.: *The game was a superb exhibition of football at its best.*

exhibitor /ɪɡˈzɪbɪtə(r)/ ***noun*** [C] (ART) a person, for example an artist, a photographer, etc., who shows their work to the public

exhilarate /ɪɡˈzɪləreɪt/ ***verb*** [T] (usually passive) to make sb feel very excited and happy: *We felt exhilarated by our walk along the beach.* ▸ **exhilarating** ***adj.*** ▸ **exhilaration** /ɪɡˌzɪləˈreɪʃn/ ***noun*** [U]

exhume /eksˈhjuːm/ ***verb*** [T] (usually passive) (*formal*) to remove a dead body from the ground especially in order to examine how the person died ▸ **exhumation** /ˌekshjuːˈmeɪʃn/ ***noun*** [U]

exile /ˈeksaɪl/ ***noun*** **1** [U] (POLITICS) the state of being forced to live outside your own country (especially for political reasons): *He went into exile after the revolution of 1968.* ◇ *They lived* ***in exile*** *in London for many years.* **2** [C] (POLITICS) a person who is forced to live outside their own country (especially for political reasons) ➲ look at **refugee** ▸ **exile** ***verb*** [T] (usually passive): *After the revolution the king was exiled.*

exist 🔑 /ɪɡˈzɪst/ ***verb*** [I] **1** (not used in the continuous tenses) to be real; to be found in the real world; to live: *Dreams only exist in our imagination.* ◇ *Fish cannot exist out of water.* **2** ~ **(on sth)** to manage to live: *I don't know how she exists on the wage she earns.*

existence /ɪɡˈzɪstəns/ ***noun* 1** [U] the state of existing: *This is the oldest human skeleton **in existence**.* ◇ *How did the universe **come into existence**?* **2** [sing.] a way of living, especially when it is difficult: *They lead a miserable existence in a tiny flat in London.*

existing /ɪɡˈzɪstɪŋ/ ***adj.*** (only *before* a noun) that is already there or being used; present: *Under the existing law you are not allowed to work in this country.*

exit[1] /ˈeksɪt; ˈeɡzɪt/ ***noun*** [C] **1** a door or way out of a public building or vehicle: *The emergency exit is at the back of the bus.* OPP **entrance 2** the act of leaving sth: *If I see her coming I'll make a quick exit.* ◇ *an exit visa* (=one that allows you to leave a country) OPP **entrance 3** a place where traffic can leave a road or a motorway to join another road: *At the roundabout take the third exit.*

exit[2] /ˈeksɪt; ˈeɡzɪt/ ***verb*** [I,T] (*formal*) to leave a place: *He exited through the back door.* ◇ *I exited the database and switched off the computer.*

exodus /ˈeksədəs/ ***noun*** [sing.] (*formal*) a situation in which many people leave a place at the same time

exonerate /ɪɡˈzɒnəreɪt/ ***verb*** [T] (*formal*) (often passive) to say officially that sb was not responsible for sth bad that happened

exorbitant /ɪɡˈzɔːbɪtənt/ ***adj.*** (*formal*) (used about the cost of sth) much more expensive than it should be

exoskeleton /ˈeksəʊskelɪtn/ ***noun*** [C] (BIOLOGY) a hard outer covering that protects the bodies of certain animals, such as insects ➲ look at **endoskeleton**

exosphere /ˈeksəʊsfɪə(r)/ ***noun*** [sing.] **the exosphere** (ENVIRONMENT) the region near the edge of a planet's atmosphere

exothermic /ˌeksəʊˈθɜːmɪk/ ***adj.*** (CHEMISTRY, PHYSICS) (used about a chemical reaction or process) producing heat ➲ picture at **water**

exotic /ɪɡˈzɒtɪk/ ***adj.*** unusual or interesting because it comes from a different country or culture: *exotic plants/animals/fruits*

expand AW /ɪkˈspænd/ ***verb*** [I,T] to become or to make sth bigger: *Metals expand when they are heated.* ◇ *We hope to expand our business this year.* OPP **contract**

PHR V **expand on sth** to give more details of a story, plan, idea, etc.

expanse /ɪkˈspæns/ ***noun*** [C] a large open area (of land, sea, sky, etc.)

expansion AW /ɪkˈspænʃn/ ***noun*** [U] the action of becoming bigger or the state of being bigger than before: *The rapid expansion of the university has caused a lot of problems.*

expansionism AW /ɪkˈspænʃənɪzəm/ ***noun*** [U] (POLITICS) the belief in and process of increasing the size and importance of sth, especially in a country or a business: ***military/territorial expansion***
▸ **expansionist** /-ʃənɪst/ ***adj.***: *expansionist policies*
▸ **expansionist** ***noun*** [C]: *He was a ruthless expansionist.*

expansive AW /ɪkˈspænsɪv/ ***adj.*** (*formal*) (used about a person) talking a lot in an interesting way; friendly

expatriate /ˌeksˈpætriət/ (also *informal* **expat** /ˌeksˈpæt/) ***noun*** [C] (POLITICS) a person who lives outside their own country: *American expatriates in London*

expect /ɪkˈspekt/ ***verb*** [T] **1** to think or believe that sb/sth will come or that sth will happen: *She was expecting a letter from the bank this morning but it didn't come.* ◇ *I expect that it will rain this afternoon.* ◇ *I know the food's not so good, but what did you expect from such a cheap restaurant?* (=it's not surprising) ◇ *She's expecting a baby in the spring* (=she's pregnant). ➲ note at **demand**[2] **2** ~ **sth (from sb)**; ~ **sb to do sth** to feel confident that you will get sth from sb or that they will do what you want: *He expects a high standard of work from everyone.* ◇ *Factory workers are often expected to work at nights.* **3** (*BrE*) (not used in the continuous tenses) to think that sth is true or correct; to suppose: *'Whose is this suitcase?' 'Oh it's Maureen's, I expect.'* ◇ *'Will you be able to help me later on?' '**I expect so**.'*

expectancy /ɪkˈspektənsi/ ***noun*** [U] the state of expecting sth to happen; hope: *a look/feeling of expectancy* ➲ look at **life expectancy**

expectant /ɪkˈspektənt/ ***adj.* 1** thinking that sth good will happen; HOPEFUL: *an expectant audience* ◇ *expectant faces* **2** (HEALTH) pregnant: *Expectant mothers need a lot of rest.* ▸ **expectantly** ***adv.***

expectation /ˌekspekˈteɪʃn/ ***noun*** (*formal*) **1** [U] ~ **(of sth)** the belief that sth will happen or come: *The dog was sitting under the table **in expectation** of food.* **2** [C, usually pl.] hope for the future: *They had great expectations for their daughter, but she didn't really live up to them.*

IDM **against/contrary to (all) expectation(s)** very different to what was expected

not come up to (sb's) expectations to not be as good as expected

expedient /ɪkˈspiːdiənt/ ***adj.*** (*formal*) (used about an action) convenient or helpful for a purpose, but possibly not completely honest or moral: *The government decided that it was expedient not to increase taxes until after the election.* ▸ **expediency** /-ənsi/ ***noun*** [U]

expedition /ˌekspəˈdɪʃn/ ***noun*** [C] **1** a long journey for a special purpose: *a scientific expedition to Antarctica* **2** a short journey that you make for pleasure: *a fishing expedition*

expel /ɪkˈspel/ ***verb*** [T] (**expelling**; **expelled**) **1** to force sb to leave a country, school, club, etc.: *The government has expelled all foreign journalists.* ◇ *The boy was expelled from school for smoking.* **2** to send sth out by force: *to expel air from the lungs* ➲ noun **expulsion**

expend /ɪkˈspend/ ***verb*** [T] (*formal*) ~ **sth (on sth)** to spend or use money, time, care, etc. in doing sth

expendable /ɪkˈspendəbl/ ***adj.*** (*formal*) not considered important enough to be saved: *In a war human life is expendable.*

expenditure /ɪkˈspendɪtʃə(r)/ ***noun*** [U, sing.] (*formal*) (FINANCE) the act of spending money; the amount of money that is spent: *Government expenditure on education is very low.*

expense /ɪkˈspens/ ***noun* 1** [C,U] (FINANCE) the cost of sth in time or money: *Running a car is a great expense.* ◇ *The movie was filmed in Tahiti **at great expense**.* **2 expenses** [pl.] (FINANCE) money that is spent for a particular purpose: *You can claim back your travelling expenses.*

IDM **at sb's expense 1** (FINANCE) with sb paying; at sb's cost: *My trip is at the company's expense.* **2** against sb, so that they look silly: *They were always making jokes at Paul's expense.*

at the expense of sth harming or damaging sth: *He*

was a successful businessman, but it was at the expense of his family life.

expensive 🔑 /ɪk'spensɪv/ ***adj.*** costing a lot of money **OPP** **inexpensive**, **cheap** ▶ **expensively** ***adv.***

experience¹ 🔑 /ɪk'spɪəriəns/ ***noun*** **1** [U] the things that you have done in your life; the knowledge or skill that you get from seeing or doing sth: *We all learn* ***by experience****. ◇ She has five years' teaching experience. ◇ I know* ***from experience*** *what will happen.* **2** [C] something that has happened to you (often something unusual or exciting): *She wrote a book about her experiences in Africa.*

experience² 🔑 /ɪk'spɪəriəns/ ***verb*** [T] to have sth happen to you; to feel: *It was the first time I'd ever experienced failure. ◇ to experience pleasure/pain/difficulty*

experienced 🔑 /ɪk'spɪəriənst/ ***adj.*** having the knowledge or skill that is necessary for sth: *He's an experienced diver.* **OPP** **inexperienced**

experiment¹ 🔑 /ɪk'sperɪmənt/ ***noun*** [C,U] (**SCIENCE**) a scientific test that is done in order to get proof of sth or new knowledge: *to carry out/perform/conduct/do an experiment ◇ We need to prove this theory* ***by experiment****.* ▶ **experimentally** /-təli/ ***adv.***

experiment² 🔑 /ɪk'sperɪmənt/ ***verb*** [I] ~ (**on/with sth**) to do tests to see if sth works or to try to improve it: *Is it really necessary to experiment on animals? ◇ We're experimenting with a new timetable this month.*

experimental /ɪkˌsperɪ'mentl/ ***adj.*** connected with experiments or trying new ideas: *We're still at the experimental stage with the new product. ◇ experimental schools*

experimentation /ɪkˌsperɪmen'teɪʃn/ ***noun*** [U] (*formal*) the activity or process of experimenting: *experimentation with new teaching methods ◇ Many people object to experimentation on embryos.*

expert 🔑 **AW** /'ekspɜːt/ ***noun*** [C] **an ~ (at/in/on sth)** a person who has a lot of special knowledge or skill: *She's a leading expert in the field of genetics. ◇ a computer expert ◇ Let me try – I'm an expert at parking cars in small spaces.* ▶ **expert** ***adj.***: *He's an expert cook. ◇ I think we should get expert advice on the problem.* ▶ **expertly** **AW** ***adv.***

expertise **AW** /ˌekspɜː'tiːz/ ***noun*** [U] a high level of special knowledge or skill

ˌexpert 'system ***noun*** [C] (**COMPUTING**) a computer system that can provide information and expert advice on a particular subject. The program asks the people who use it a series of questions about their problem and gives them advice based on its store of knowledge: *expert systems to aid medical diagnosis*

expire /ɪk'spaɪə(r)/ ***verb*** [I] (*formal*) (used about an official document, agreement, etc.) to come to the end of the time when you can use it or in which it has effect **SYN** **run out**: *My passport's expired. I'll have to renew it.*

expiry /ɪk'spaɪəri/ ***noun*** [U] the end of a period when you can use sth: *The expiry date on this yoghurt was 20 November.*

ex'piry date (*AmE* **expi'ration date**) ***noun*** [C] the date after which an official document, agreement, etc. is no longer valid, or after which sth should not be used

explain 🔑 /ɪk'spleɪn/ ***verb*** [I,T] ~ (**sth**) (**to sb**) **1** to make sth clear or easy to understand: *She explained how I should fill in the form. ◇ I don't understand this. Can you explain it to me?* **2** to give a reason for sth: *'This work isn't very good.' 'I wasn't feeling very well.' 'Oh, that explains it then.' ◇ The manager explained to the customers why the goods were late.*

> **WORD FAMILY**
> **explain** *verb*
> **explanation** *noun*
> **explanatory** *adj.*
> **explicable** *adj.*
> (≠ **inexplicable**)

IDM **explain yourself** **1** to give reasons for your behaviour, especially when it has upset sb **2** to say what you mean in a clear way

PHR V **explain sth away** to give reasons why sth is not your fault or is not important

explanation 🔑 /ˌeksplə'neɪʃn/ ***noun*** **1** [C,U] **an ~ (for sth)** a statement, fact or situation that gives a reason for sth: *He could not* ***give an explanation*** *for his behaviour.* **2** [C] a statement or a piece of writing that makes sth easier to understand: *That idea needs some explanation.*

explanatory /ɪk'splænətri/ ***adj.*** giving an explanation: *There are some explanatory notes at the back of the book. ◇ Those instructions are self-explanatory* (=they don't need explaining).

expletive /ɪk'spliːtɪv/ ***noun*** [C] (*formal*) a word, especially a rude word, that you use when you are angry or in pain **SYN** **swear word**

explicable /ɪk'splɪkəbl; 'eksplɪkəbl/ ***adj.*** that can be explained: *Barry's strange behaviour is only explicable in terms of the stress he is under.* **OPP** **inexplicable**

explicit **AW** /ɪk'splɪsɪt/ ***adj.*** **1** clear, making sth easy to understand: *I gave you explicit instructions not to touch anything. ◇ She was quite explicit about her feelings on the subject.* ➲ look at **implicit** **2** not hiding anything: *Some of the sex scenes in that TV play were very explicit.* ▶ **explicitly** ***adv.***: *He was explicitly forbidden to stay out later than midnight.*

explode 🔑 /ɪk'spləʊd/ ***verb*** [I,T] to burst with a loud noise: *The bomb exploded without warning. ◇ The army exploded the bomb at a safe distance from the houses. ◇* (*figurative*) *My father exploded* (=became very angry) *when I told him how much the car would cost to repair.* ➲ noun **explosion**

> **WORD FAMILY**
> **explode** *verb*
> **explosion** *noun*
> **explosive** *adj., noun*
> **unexploded** *adj.*

exploit¹ **AW** /ɪk'splɔɪt/ ***verb*** [T] **1** to use sth or to treat sb unfairly for your own advantage: *Some employers exploit foreign workers, making them work long hours for low pay.* **2** to develop sth or make the best use of sth: *This region has been exploited for oil for fifty years. ◇ Solar energy is a source of power that needs to be exploited more fully.* ▶ **exploitation** **AW** /ˌeksplɔɪ'teɪʃn/ ***noun*** [U]: *They're making you work 80 hours a week? That's exploitation!*

exploit² **AW** /'eksplɔɪt/ ***noun*** [C] something exciting or interesting that sb has done

exploration /ˌeksplə'reɪʃn/ ***noun*** [C,U] the act of travelling around a place in order to learn about it: *space exploration*

exploratory /ɪk'splɒrətri/ ***adj.*** done in order to find sth out: *The doctors are doing some exploratory tests to try and find out what's wrong.*

explore 🔑 /ɪk'splɔː(r)/ ***verb*** [I,T] to travel around a place, etc. in order to learn about it: *They went on an expedition to explore the River Amazon. ◇ I've never been to Paris before – I'm going out to* *explore.* ◇ (*figurative*) *We need to explore* (= look carefully at) *all the possibilities before we decide.*

explorer /ɪk'splɔːrə(r)/ ***noun*** [C] a person who travels around a place in order to learn about it

explosion 🔑 /ɪk'spləʊʒn/ ***noun*** [C] **1** a sudden, loud and extremely violent bursting: *Two people were killed in the explosion.* **2** a sudden dramatic increase in sth: *the population explosion* ➲ verb **explode**

explosive¹ /ɪk'spləʊsɪv/ ***adj.*** **1** (SCIENCE) capable of exploding and therefore dangerous: *Hydrogen is highly explosive.* **2** causing strong feelings or having dangerous effects

explosive² /ɪk'spləʊsɪv/ ***noun*** [C] a substance that is used for causing explosions

exponent /ɪk'spəʊnənt/ ***noun*** [C] **1** a person who supports an idea, a THEORY, etc. and persuades others that it is good: *She was* ***a leading exponent*** *of free trade during her political career.* **2** a person who is able to perform a particular activity with skill: *the most famous exponent of the jazz harmonica* **3** (MATHEMATICS) a small number or symbol that shows how many times a quantity must be multiplied by itself

exponential /ˌekspə'nenʃl/ ***adj.*** **1** (MATHEMATICS) of or shown by an EXPONENT: *an* ***exponential curve/function*** ◇ *22^4 is an exponential expression.* **2** (*formal*) (used about a rate of increase) becoming faster and faster: *exponential growth/increase* ▶ **exponentially** /-ʃəli/ ***adv.***: *to increase exponentially*

export¹ 🔑 AW /ɪk'spɔːt/ ***verb*** [I,T] **1** (ECONOMICS) to send goods, etc. to another country, usually for sale: *India exports tea and cotton.* OPP **import 2** (COMPUTING) to move information from one program to another

export² 🔑 AW /'ekspɔːt/ ***noun*** **1** [U] (ECONOMICS) sending goods to another country for sale: *Most of our goods are produced for export.* ◇ *the export trade* **2** [C, usually pl.] (ECONOMICS) something that is sent to another country for sale: *What are Brazil's main exports?* OPP **import** ▶ **exporter** AW ***noun*** [C]: *Japan is the largest exporter of electronic goods.* OPP **importer**

expose 🔑 AW /ɪk'spəʊz/ ***verb*** [T] **1** ~ **sth (to sb)**; ~ **sb/sth (as sth)** to show sth that is usually hidden; to tell sth that has been kept secret: *She didn't want to expose her true feelings to her family.* ◇ *The politician was exposed as a liar on TV.* **2** ~ **sb/sth to sth** to put sb/sth or yourself in a situation that could be difficult or dangerous: *to be exposed to radiation/danger* **3** ~ **sb to sth** to give sb the chance to experience sth: *I like jazz because I was exposed to it as a child.* **4** (ARTS AND MEDIA) (in photography) to allow light onto the film inside a camera when taking a photograph

exposed /ɪk'spəʊzd/ ***adj.*** (used about a place) not protected from the wind and bad weather

exposition /ˌekspə'zɪʃn/ ***noun*** [C] (*formal*) a full explanation of a theory, plan, etc.

exposure AW /ɪk'spəʊʒə(r)/ ***noun*** **1** [U, C] the act of making sth public; the thing that is made public: *The new movie has been given a lot of exposure in the media.* ◇ *The politician resigned because of the exposures about his private life.* **2** [U] being allowed or forced to experience sth: *Exposure to radiation is almost always harmful.* ◇ *Television can give children exposure to other cultures from an early age.* **3** [U] (HEALTH) a harmful condition when a person becomes very cold because they have been outside in very bad weather: *The climbers all died of exposure.* **4** [C] (ARTS AND MEDIA) the amount of film that is used when you take one photograph: *How many exposures are there on this film?*

express¹ 🔑 /ɪk'spres/ ***verb*** [T] **1** to show sth such as a feeling or an opinion by words or actions: *I found it very hard to express what I felt about her.* ◇ *to express fears/concern about sth* **2** ~ **yourself** to say or write your feelings, opinions, etc.: *I don't think she expresses herself very well in that article.*

express² 🔑 /ɪk'spres/ ***adj.***, ***adv.*** **1** going or sent quickly: *an express coach* ◇ *We'd better send the parcel express if we want it to get there on time.* **2** (used about a wish, command, etc.) clearly and definitely stated: *It was her express wish that he should have the picture after her death.*

express³ /ɪk'spres/ (*also* **exˌpress 'train**) ***noun*** [C] a fast train that does not stop at all stations

expression 🔑 /ɪk'spreʃn/ ***noun*** **1** [C,U] something that you say that shows your opinions or feelings: *Freedom of expression is a basic human right.* ◇ *an expression of gratitude/sympathy/anger* **2** [C] the look on a person's face that shows what they are thinking or feeling: *He had a puzzled expression on his face.* **3** [C] a word or phrase with a particular meaning: *'I'm starving' is an expression meaning 'I'm very hungry'.* ◇ *a slang/an idiomatic expression*

expressionism (also **Expressionism**) /ɪk'spreʃənɪzəm/ ***noun*** [U] (ART) a style and movement in early 20th century art, theatre, cinema and music that tries to express people's feelings and emotions rather than showing events or objects in a realistic way ▶ **expressionist** (also **Expressionist**) /-ʃənɪst/ ***noun***, ***adj.***

expressive /ɪk'spresɪv/ ***adj.*** showing feelings or thoughts: *That is a very expressive piece of music.* ◇ *Dave has a very expressive face.* ▶ **expressively** ***adv.***

expressly /ɪk'spresli/ ***adv.*** **1** clearly; definitely: *I expressly told you not to do that.* **2** for a special purpose; specially: *These scissors are expressly designed for left-handed people.*

expressway /ɪk'spresweɪ/ (*AmE*) = MOTORWAY

expulsion /ɪk'spʌlʃn/ ***noun*** [C,U] the act of making sb leave a place or an institution: *There have been three expulsions from school this year.* ➲ verb **expel**

exquisite /'ekskwɪzɪt; ɪk'skwɪzɪt/ ***adj.*** extremely beautiful and pleasing: *She has an exquisite face.* ◇ *I think that ring is exquisite.* ▶ **exquisitely** ***adv.***

ext. ***abbr.*** extension number of a telephone: *ext. 3492*

extend 🔑 /ɪk'stend/ ***verb*** **1** [T] to make sth longer or larger (in space or time): *Could you extend your visit for a few days?* ◇ *We're planning to extend the back of the house to give us more space.* ◇ *Since my injury I can't extend this leg fully* (= make it completely straight). **2** [I,T] to cover the area or period of time mentioned: *The desert extends over a huge area of the country.* ◇ *The company is planning to extend its operations into Asia.* **3** [T] (*formal*) to offer sth to sb: *to extend hospitality/a warm welcome/an invitation to sb*

exˌtended 'family ***noun*** [C] (SOCIAL STUDIES) a family group with a close relationship among the members that includes not only parents and children but also uncles, aunts, grandparents, etc. ➲ look at **nuclear family**

extension 🔑 /ɪk'stenʃn/ *noun* [C] **1** an extra period of time that you are allowed for sth: *I've applied for an extension to my work permit.* **2** (ARCHITECTURE) a part that is added to a building: *They're building an extension on the hospital.* **3** a telephone that is connected to a central telephone in a house or to a central point (**switchboard**) in a large office building: *What's your extension number?* ◇ *Can I have extension 4342, please?*

extensive 🔑 /ɪk'stensɪv/ *adj.* **1** large in area or amount: *The house has extensive grounds.* ◇ *Most of the buildings suffered extensive damage.* **2** (AGRICULTURE) (used about methods of farming) producing a small amount of food from a large area of land with a small amount of money and effort: *extensive agriculture* ➲ look at **intensive** ▸ **extensively** *adv.*

extent 🔑 /ɪk'stent/ *noun* [U] the ~ of sth the length, area, size or importance of sth: *I was amazed at the extent of his knowledge.* ◇ *The* ***full extent of*** *the damage is not yet known.*
IDM **to a certain/to some extent** used to show that sth is only partly true: *I agree with you to a certain extent but there are still a lot of points I disagree with.* **to what extent** how far; how much: *I'm not sure to what extent I believe her.*

exterior[1] /ɪk'stɪəriə(r)/ *adj.* on the outside: *the exterior walls of a house* OPP **interior**

exterior[2] /ɪk'stɪəriə(r)/ *noun* [C] the outside of sth; the appearance of sb/sth: *The exterior of the house is fine but inside it isn't in very good condition.* ◇ *Despite his calm exterior, Steve suffers badly from stress.*

ex'terior angle *noun* [C] (GEOMETRY) an angle formed between the side of a shape and the side next to it, when this side is made longer ➲ look at **interior angle** ➲ picture at **angle**

exterminate /ɪk'stɜːmɪneɪt/ *verb* [T] to kill a large group of people or animals ▸ **extermination** /ɪkˌstɜːmɪ'neɪʃn/ *noun* [U]

external AW /ɪk'stɜːnl/ *adj.* **1** connected with the outside of sth: *The cream is for external use only* (=to be used on the skin). **2** coming from another place: *You will be tested by an external examiner.* OPP **internal** ▸ **externally** /-nəli/ *adv.*

externalize (also **-ise**) AW /ɪk'stɜːnəlaɪz/ *verb* [T] (*formal*) (PSYCHOLOGY) to show what you are thinking and feeling by what you say or do ➲ look at **internalize**

extinct /ɪk'stɪŋkt/ *adj.* **1** (used about a type of animal, plant, etc.) no longer existing: *Tigers are nearly extinct in the wild.* **2** (GEOLOGY) (used about a VOLCANO) no longer active ▸ **extinction** /ɪk'stɪŋkʃn/ *noun* [U]: *The giant panda is in danger of extinction.*

extinguish /ɪk'stɪŋgwɪʃ/ *verb* [T] (*formal*) to cause sth to stop burning SYN **put out**: *The fire was extinguished very quickly.* ▸ **extinguisher** = FIRE EXTINGUISHER

extort /ɪk'stɔːt/ *verb* [T] (*formal*) ~ **sth** (**from sb**) to get sth by using threats or violence: *The gang were found guilty of extorting money from small businesses.* ▸ **extortion** *noun* [U]

extortionate /ɪk'stɔːʃənət/ *adj.* (used especially about prices) much too high

extra[1] 🔑 /'ekstrə/ *adj., adv.* more than is usual, expected, or than exists already: *I'll need some extra money for the holidays.* ◇ *'What size is this sweater?' 'Extra large.'* ◇ *Is wine included in the price of the meal or is it extra?* ◇ *I tried to be extra nice to him yesterday because it was his birthday.*

extra[2] 🔑 /'ekstrə/ *noun* [C] **1** something that costs more, or that is not normally included: *Optional extras such as colour printer, scanner and modem are available on top of the basic package.* **2** (ARTS AND MEDIA) a person in a film, etc. who has a small unimportant part, for example in a crowd

extra- /'ekstrə/ *prefix* (in adjectives) **1** outside; beyond: *extramarital sex* ◇ *extraterrestrial beings* **2** very; more than usual: *extra-thin* ◇ *extra-special*

extract[1] AW /ɪk'strækt/ *verb* [T] (*formal*) to take sth out, especially with difficulty: *I think this tooth will have to be extracted.* ◇ *I wasn't able to extract an apology from her.*

extract[2] AW /'ekstrækt/ *noun* [C] (ARTS AND MEDIA) a part of a book, piece of music, etc., that has often been specially chosen to show sth: *The newspaper published extracts from the controversial novel.*

extraction AW /ɪk'strækʃn/ *noun* (*formal*) **1** [C,U] the act of taking sth out: *extraction of salt from the sea* ◇ *Dentists report that children are requiring fewer extractions.* **2** [U] family origin: *He's an American but he's of Italian extraction.*

extra-curricular /ˌekstrə kə'rɪkjələ(r)/ *adj.* (EDUCATION) not part of the usual course of work or studies at a school or college: *The school offers many extra-curricular activities such as yoga and chess.*

extradite /'ekstrədaɪt/ *verb* [T] (LAW, POLITICS) to send a person who may be guilty of a crime from the country in which they are living to the country which wants to put them on trial for the crime: *The suspected terrorists were captured in Spain and extradited to France.* ▸ **extradition** /ˌekstrə'dɪʃn/ *noun* [C,U]

extraordinary 🔑 /ɪk'strɔːdnri/ *adj.* **1** very unusual: *She has an extraordinary ability to whistle and sing at the same time.* **2** not what you would expect in a particular situation; very strange: *That was extraordinary behaviour for a teacher!* OPP **ordinary** ▸ **extraordinarily** /ɪk'strɔːdnrəli/ *adv.*: *He was an extraordinarily talented musician.*

extrapolate /ɪk'stræpəleɪt/ *verb* [I,T] ~ (**sth**) (**from/to sth**) (*formal*) to form an opinion or make a judgement about a situation by using facts that you know from a different situation: *The figures were obtained by extrapolating from past trends.* ◇ *We have extrapolated the results from research done in other countries.* ▸ **extrapolation** /ɪkˌstræpə'leɪʃn/ *noun* [U, C]: *Their age can be determined by extrapolation from their growth rate.*

extraterrestrial /ˌekstrətə'restriəl/ *noun* [C] (in stories) a creature that comes from another planet; a creature that may exist on another planet ▸ **extraterrestrial** *adj.*

extravagant /ɪk'strævəgənt/ *adj.* **1** spending or costing too much money: *He's terribly extravagant – he travels everywhere by taxi.* ◇ *an extravagant present* **2** exaggerated; more than is usual, true or necessary: *The advertisements made extravagant claims for the new medicine.* ▸ **extravagance** *noun* [C,U] ▸ **extravagantly** *adv.*

ˌextra-'virgin *adj.* used to describe the good quality oil obtained the first time that OLIVES (=small green or black fruit with a bitter taste) are pressed

extreme 🔑 /ɪk'striːm/ *adj.* **1** (only *before* a noun) the greatest or strongest possible: *You must take extreme care when driving at night.* ◇ *extreme heat/difficulty/poverty* **2** much stronger than is considered usual, acceptable, etc.: *Her extreme* *views on immigration are shocking to most people.* **3** (only *before* a noun) as far away as possible from the centre in the direction mentioned: *There could be snow in the extreme north of the country.* ◇ *politicians on the extreme left of the party* ➲ look at **moderate, radical** ▶ **extreme** ***noun*** [C]: *Alex used to be very shy but now she's gone to the opposite extreme.*

extremely 🔑 /ɪk'stri:mli/ ***adv.*** very: *Listen carefully because this is extremely important.*

ex'treme sports ***noun*** [pl.] (SPORT) sports that are extremely exciting to do and often dangerous, for example SKYDIVING and BUNGEE JUMPING

extremist /ɪk'stri:mɪst/ ***noun*** [C] (**POLITICS**) a person who has extreme political opinions ➲ look at **moderate, radical** ▶ **extremism** ***noun*** [U]

extremity /ɪk'streməti/ ***noun*** [C] (*pl.* **extremities**) the part of sth that is furthest from the centre

extricate /'ekstrɪkeɪt/ ***verb*** [T] to manage to free sb/sth from a difficult situation or position

extrovert /'ekstrəvɜ:t/ ***noun*** [C] a person who is confident and full of life and who prefers being with other people to being alone OPP **introvert**

extrusive /ɪk'stru:sɪv/ ***adj.*** (**GEOLOGY**) (used about rock) that has been pushed out of the earth by a VOLCANO

exuberant /ɪg'zju:bərənt/ ***adj.*** (used about a person or their behaviour) full of energy and excitement ▶ **exuberance** ***noun*** [U]

eye

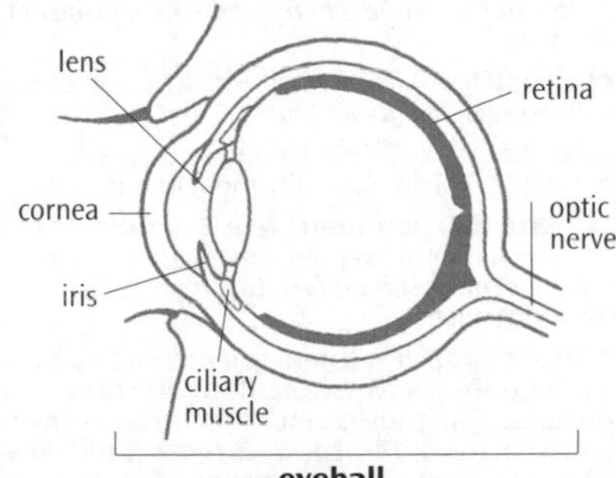

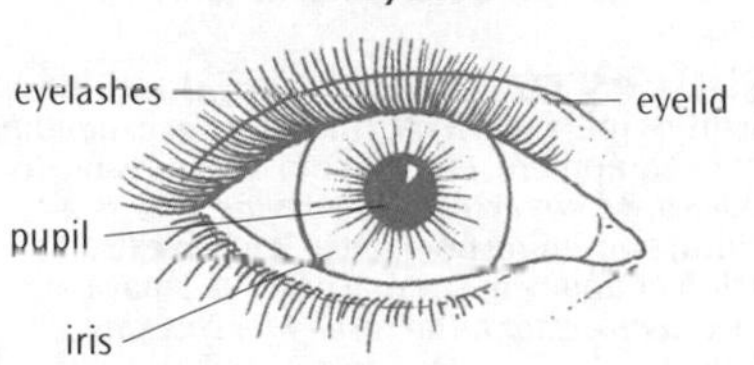

eye¹ 🔑 /aɪ/ ***noun*** [C] **1** one of the two organs of your body that you use to see with: *She opened/closed her eyes.* ◇ *He's got blue eyes.* ➲ look at **black eye 2** the ability to see sth: *He has **sharp eyes*** (= he can see very well). ◇ *She has **an eye for detail*** (= she notices small details). **3** the hole at one end of a needle that the thread goes through

IDM **an eye for an eye** used to say that you should punish sb by doing to them what they have done to sb else

as far as the eye can see → FAR²

be up to your eyes in sth (*informal*) to have more of sth than you can easily do or manage

before sb's very eyes in front of sb so that they can clearly see what is happening

cast an eye/your eye(s) over sb/sth → CAST¹

catch sb's attention/eye → CATCH¹

cry your eyes out → CRY¹

have (got) your eye on sb to watch sb carefully to make sure that they do nothing wrong

have (got) your eye on sth to be thinking about buying sth

in the eyes of sb/in sb's eyes in the opinion of sb: *She was still a child in her mother's eyes.*

in the public eye → PUBLIC¹

keep an eye on sb/sth to make sure that sb/sth is safe; to look after sb/sth: *Please could you keep an eye on the house while we're away?*

keep an eye open/out (for sb/sth) to watch or look out for sb/sth

keep your eyes peeled/skinned (for sb/sth) to watch carefully for sb/sth

look sb in the eye → LOOK¹

the naked eye → NAKED

not bat an eye → BAT²

see eye to eye (with sb) → SEE

set eyes on sb/sth → SET¹

turn a blind eye → BLIND¹

with your eyes open knowing what you are doing: *You went into the new job with your eyes open, so you can't complain now.*

eye² /aɪ/ ***verb*** [T] (*pres. part.* **eyeing** or **eying**; *pt, pp* **eyed**) to look at sb/sth closely: *She eyed him with suspicion.*

eyeball /'aɪbɔ:l/ ***noun*** [C] the whole of your eye (including the part which is hidden inside the head)

eyebrow /'aɪbraʊ/ ***noun*** [C] the line of hair that is above your eye ➲ picture on **page 80**

IDM **raise your eyebrows** → RAISE

'eye-catching ***adj.*** (used about a thing) attracting your attention immediately because it is interesting, bright or pretty

eyeglasses /'aɪglɑ:sɪz/ (*AmE*) = GLASSES

eyelash /'aɪlæʃ/ (also **lash**) ***noun*** [C] one of the hairs that grow on the edges of your EYELIDS

'eye level ***adj.*** at the same height as sb's eyes when they are standing up: *an eye-level grill*

eyelid /'aɪlɪd/ (also **lid**) ***noun*** [C] the piece of skin that can move to cover your eye

IDM **not bat an eyelid** → BAT²

eyeliner /'aɪlaɪnə(r)/ ***noun*** [U] colour that is put around the edge of sb's eyes with a type of pencil to make them look more attractive

'eye-opener ***noun*** [C] something that makes you realize the truth about sth

eyepiece /'aɪpi:s/ ***noun*** [C] (**SCIENCE**) the piece of glass (**lens**) at the end of a TELESCOPE or MICROSCOPE that you look through ➲ picture at **binoculars, microscope**

eyeshadow /'aɪʃædəʊ/ ***noun*** [U] colour that is put on the skin above the eyes to make them look more attractive

eyesight /'aɪsaɪt/ ***noun*** [U] the ability to see: *good/poor eyesight*

eyesore /'aɪsɔ:(r)/ ***noun*** [C] something that is ugly and unpleasant to look at: *All this litter in the streets is a real eyesore.*

eyewitness /'aɪwɪtnəs/ = WITNESS¹ (1)

e-zine /'i:zi:n/ ***noun*** [C] a magazine that you can pay to read in electronic form on your computer

F f

F, f¹ /ef/ ***noun*** [C,U] (*pl.* **F's**; **f's** /efs/) the sixth letter of the English alphabet: *'Father' begins with (an) 'F'.*

F² ***abbr.*** **1** Fahrenheit: *Water freezes at 32°F* **2** (*also* **fem**) female; feminine

FA /ˌef ˈeɪ/ ***abbr.*** (*BrE*) the Football Association: *the FA Cup*

fable /ˈfeɪbl/ ***noun*** [C] (LITERATURE) a short story that teaches a lesson (**a moral**) and that often has animals as the main characters: *Aesop's fables*

fabric /ˈfæbrɪk/ ***noun*** **1** [C,U] (a type of) cloth or soft material that is used for making clothes, curtains, etc.: *cotton fabrics* **2** [sing.] the basic structure of a building or system: *The Industrial Revolution changed the fabric of society.* ➲ note at **structure¹**

fabulous /ˈfæbjələs/ ***adj.*** **1** very good; excellent: *It was a fabulous concert.* **2** very great: *fabulous wealth/riches/beauty*

façade (also **facade**) /fəˈsɑːd/ ***noun*** [C] **1** the front wall of a large building that you see from the outside **2** the way sb/sth appears to be, which is not the way he/she/it really is: *His good humour was just a façade.*

face¹ 🔑 /feɪs/ ***noun*** [C] **1** the front part of your head; the expression that is shown on it: *Go and wash your face.* ◇ *She has a very pretty face.* ◇ *He came in with a smile on his face.* ◇ *Her face lit up* (=showed happiness) *when John came into the room.* ➲ picture on **page 80** **2** the front or one side of sth: *the north face of the mountain* ◇ *He put the cards* ***face up / down*** *on the table.* ◇ *a clock face* **3 -faced** (used to form compound adjectives) having the type of face or expression mentioned: *red/round/sour-faced*

IDM **face to face (with sb/sth)** close to and looking at sb/sth

keep a straight face → STRAIGHT¹

lose face → LOSE

make/pull faces/a face (at sb/sth) to make an expression that shows that you do not like sb/sth

make/pull faces to make rude expressions with your face: *The children made faces behind the teacher's back.*

put on a brave face; **put a brave face on sth** → BRAVE¹

save face → SAVE¹

to sb's face if you say sth to sb's face, you do it when that person is with you OPP **behind sb's back**

face² 🔑 /feɪs/ ***verb*** [T] **1** to have your face or front pointing towards sb/sth or in a particular direction: *The garden faces south.* ◇ *Can you all face the front, please?* **2** to have to deal with sth unpleasant; to deal with sb in a difficult situation: *I can't face another argument.* ◇ *He couldn't face going to work yesterday – he felt too ill.* **3** to need attention or action from sb: *There are several problems facing the government.* ◇ *We are faced with a difficult decision.*

IDM **let's face it** (*informal*) we must accept it as true: *Let's face it, we can't afford a holiday this year.*

PHR V **face up to sth** to accept a difficult or unpleasant situation and do sth about it

facecloth /ˈfeɪsklɒθ/ (*also* **flannel**) ***noun*** [C] a small square towel that is used for washing the face, hands, etc.

faceless /ˈfeɪsləs/ ***adj.*** without individual character or identity: *faceless civil servants*

facelift /ˈfeɪslɪft/ ***noun*** [C] (HEALTH) a medical operation that makes your face look younger ➲ look at **plastic surgery**

ˈface-off ***noun*** [C] (*informal*) **1** (*especially AmE*) an argument or a fight: *a face-off between the presidential candidates* **2** (SPORT) the way of starting play in a game of ICE HOCKEY ➲ note at **hockey**

ˈface-saving ***adj.*** (only *before* a noun) said or done in order to avoid looking silly or losing other people's respect: *In his interview, the captain made face-saving excuses for his team's defeat.*

facet /ˈfæsɪt/ ***noun*** [C] **1** one part or particular aspect of sth **2** one side of a PRECIOUS STONE

ˈface time ***noun*** [U] (*AmE, informal*) (BUSINESS) time that you spend talking in person to people you work with, rather than speaking on the phone or sending emails

facetious /fəˈsiːʃəs/ ***adj.*** trying to be amusing about a subject at a time that is not appropriate so that other people become annoyed: *He kept making facetious remarks during the lecture.* ▶ **facetiously** ***adv.***

ˌface ˈvalue ***noun*** [U, sing.] the cost or value that is shown on the front of stamps, coins, etc.

IDM **take sb/sth at (its, his, etc.) face value** to accept sb/sth as it, he, etc. appears to be: *Don't take his story at face value. There's something he hasn't told us yet.*

facial /ˈfeɪʃl/ ***adj.*** connected with a person's face: *a facial expression* ◇ *facial hair*

facile /ˈfæsaɪl/ ***adj.*** (used about a comment, argument, etc.) not carefully thought out

facilitate AW /fəˈsɪlɪteɪt/ ***verb*** [T] (*formal*) to make an action or a process possible or easier: *The new trade agreement should facilitate more rapid economic growth.*

facilitator AW /fəˈsɪlɪteɪtə(r)/ ***noun*** [C] **1** a person who helps sb do sth more easily by discussing problems, giving advice, etc. rather than telling them what to do: *The teacher acts as a facilitator of learning.* **2** (*formal*) a thing that helps a process take place

facility 🔑 AW /fəˈsɪləti/ ***noun*** (*pl.* **facilities**) **1 facilities** [pl.] (ARCHITECTURE) a service, building, piece of equipment, etc. that makes it possible to do sth: *Our town has excellent sports facilities* (=a stadium, swimming pool, etc.). **2** [C] an extra function or ability that a machine, etc. may have: *This word processor has a facility for checking spelling.*

facsimile /fækˈsɪməli/ ***noun*** [C,U] an exact copy of a picture, piece of writing, etc. ➲ look at **fax**

fact 🔑 /fækt/ ***noun*** **1** [C] something that you know has happened or is true: *It is a scientific fact that light travels faster than sound.* ◇ *We need to know all the facts before we can decide.* ◇ *I know* ***for a fact*** *that Peter wasn't ill yesterday.* ◇ ***The fact that*** *I am older than you makes no difference at all.* ◇ *You must* ***face facts*** *and accept that he has gone.* **2** [U] true things; reality: *The film is based on fact.* OPP **fiction**

IDM **as a matter of fact** → MATTER¹

the fact (of the matter) is (that)... the truth is that...: *I would love a car, but the fact is that I just can't afford one.*

facts and figures detailed information: *Before we*

make a decision, we need some more facts and figures.

a fact of life something unpleasant that you must accept because you cannot change it

the facts of life the details of sexual behaviour and how babies are born

hard facts → HARD[1]

in (actual) fact 1 (used for emphasizing that sth is true) really; actually: *I thought the lecture would be boring but in actual fact it was rather interesting.* **2** used for introducing more detailed information: *It was cold. In fact it was freezing.*

faction /ˈfækʃn/ ***noun*** [C] (**POLITICS**) a small group of people within a larger one whose members have some different aims and beliefs to those of the larger group: *rival factions within the organization* ▸ **factional** ***adj.***: *factional rivalries/disputes*

factor[1] ⊶ AW /ˈfæktə(r)/ ***noun*** [C] **1** one of the things that influences a decision, situation, etc.: *His unhappiness at home was a major factor in his decision to go abroad.* **2** (**MATHEMATICS**) a whole number (except 1) by which a larger number can be divided: *2, 3, 4 and 6 are factors of 12.*

factor[2] AW /ˈfæktə(r)/ ***verb***

PHR V **factor sth in; factor sth into sth** (*technical*) to include a particular fact or situation when you are thinking about or planning sth: *Remember to factor in staffing costs when you are planning the project.*

factorize /ˈfæktəraɪz/ ***verb*** [T] (**MATHEMATICS**) to express a number in terms of its FACTORS[1] (2)

> **THESAURUS**
>
> **factory**
>
> **plant • mill • works • yard • workshop • foundry**
>
> These are all words for buildings or places where things are made or where industrial processes take place.
>
> **factory**: *a chocolate/clothing factory*
> **plant**: *a nuclear processing plant*
> **mill**: *a cotton/paper/textile mill*
> **works**: *a brickworks ◇ a steelworks*
> **yard**: *a shipyard*
> **workshop**: *a car repair workshop*
> **foundry**: *an iron foundry*

factory ⊶ /ˈfæktri; -təri/ ***noun*** [C] (*pl.* **factories**) a building or group of buildings where goods are made in large quantities by machine

factual /ˈfæktʃuəl/ ***adj.*** based on or containing things that are true or real: *a factual account of the events* ➲ look at **fictional** ▸ **factually** /-tʃuəli/ ***adv.***: *factually correct*

faculty /ˈfæklti/ ***noun*** [C] (*pl.* **faculties**) **1** one of the natural abilities of a person's body or mind: *the faculty of hearing/sight/speech* **2** (*also* **Faculty**) (**EDUCATION**) one department in a university, college, etc.: *the Faculty of Law/Arts*

fad /fæd/ ***noun*** [C] (*informal*) a fashion, interest, etc. that will probably not last long

fade /feɪd/ ***verb*** **1** [I,T] to become or make sth become lighter in colour or less strong or fresh: *Jeans fade when you wash them. ◇ Look how the sunlight has faded these curtains.* **2** [I] ~ **(away)** to disappear slowly (from sight, hearing, memory, etc.): *The cheering of the crowd faded away. ◇ The smile faded from his face.*

faeces (*AmE* **feces**) /ˈfiːsiːz/ ***noun*** [pl.] (**BIOLOGY**) the solid waste material that you get rid of when you go to the toilet

fag /fæɡ/ ***noun*** (*BrE*) **1** [C] (*slang*) a cigarette **2** [sing.] (*informal*) a piece of work that you do not want to do

Fahrenheit /ˈfærənhaɪt/ ***noun*** [U] (*abbr.* **F**) the name of a scale which measures temperatures: *Water freezes at 32° Fahrenheit (32°F).* ➲ look at **Celsius**

fail[1] ⊶ /feɪl/ ***verb*** **1** [I,T] to not be successful in sth: *She failed her driving test. ◇ I feel that I've failed – I'm 25 and I still haven't got a steady job.* ➲ look at **pass, succeed 2** [T] (**EDUCATION**) to decide that sb is not successful in a test, exam, etc.: *The examiners failed half of the candidates.* OPP **pass 3** [I] ~ **to do sth** to not do sth: *She never fails to do her homework.* **4** [I,T] to not be enough or not do what people are expecting or wanting: *If the crops fail, people will starve. ◇ I think the government has failed us.* **5** [I] (**HEALTH**) (used about health, EYESIGHT, etc.) to become weak: *His health is failing.* **6** [I] to stop working: *My brakes failed on the hill but I managed to stop the car.*

fail[2] /feɪl/ ***noun*** [C] (**EDUCATION**) the act of not being successful in an exam OPP **pass**

IDM **without fail** always, even if there are difficulties: *The postman always comes at 8 o'clock without fail.*

failing[1] /ˈfeɪlɪŋ/ ***noun*** [C] a weakness or fault: *She's not very patient – that's her only failing.*

failing[2] /ˈfeɪlɪŋ/ ***prep.*** if sth is not possible: *Ask Jackie to go with you, or failing that, try Anne.*

failure ⊶ /ˈfeɪljə(r)/ ***noun*** **1** [U] lack of success: *All my efforts ended in failure.* OPP **success 2** [C] a person or thing that is not successful: *His first attempt at skating was a miserable failure.* OPP **success 3** [C,U] ~ **to do sth** not doing sth that people expect you to do: *I was very disappointed at his failure to come to the meeting.* **4** [C,U] an example of sth not working properly: *She died of heart failure. ◇ There's been a failure in the power supply.*

faint[1] ⊶ /feɪnt/ ***adj.*** **1** (used about things that you can see, hear, feel, etc.) not strong or clear: *a faint light/sound ◇ There is still a faint hope that they will find more people alive.* **2** (used about people) almost losing CONSCIOUSNESS; very weak: *I feel faint – I'd better sit down.* **3** (used about actions, etc.) done without much effort: *He made a faint protest.* ▸ **faintly** ***adv.***

IDM **not have the faintest/foggiest (idea)** to not know at all: *I haven't the faintest idea where they've gone.*

faint[2] /feɪnt/ ***verb*** [I] to lose consciousness

fair[1] ⊶ /feə(r)/ ***adj., adv.*** **1** appropriate and acceptable in a particular situation: *That's a fair price for that house. ◇ I think **it's fair to say that** the number of homeless people is increasing.* OPP **unfair 2** ~ **(to/on sb)** treating each person or side equally, according to the law, the rules, etc.: *That's not fair – he got the same number of mistakes as I did and he's got a better mark. ◇ It wasn't fair on her to ask her to stay so late. ◇ a fair trial* OPP **unfair 3** quite good, large, etc.: *They have a fair chance of success.* **4** (used about the skin or hair) light in colour: *Chloe has fair hair and blue eyes.* **5** (used about the weather) good, without rain

IDM **fair enough** (*spoken*) used to show that you agree with what sb has suggested

fair play (**SPORT**) equal treatment of both/all sides according to the rules: *The referee is there to ensure fair play during the match.*

(more than) your fair share of sth (more than) the usual or expected amount of sth

fair² /feə(r)/ ***noun*** [C] **1** (*also* **funfair**) a type of entertainment in a field or park. At a fair you can ride on machines or try and win prizes at games. Fairs usually travel from town to town. **2** (BUSINESS) a large event where people, businesses, etc. show and sell their goods: *a trade fair ◊ the Frankfurt book fair*

fairground /'feəgraʊnd/ ***noun*** [C] a large outdoor area where a FAIR is held

ˌfair-'haired ***adj.*** with light-coloured hair SYN **blond**

fairly ⊶ /'feəli/ ***adv.*** **1** in an acceptable way; in a way that treats people equally or according to the law, rules, etc.: *I felt that the teacher didn't treat us fairly.* OPP **unfairly** **2** quite, not very: *He is fairly tall.* ➲ note at **rather**

fairness /'feənəs/ ***noun*** [U] treating people equally or according to the law, rules, etc.

ˌfair-'trade ***adj.*** (BUSINESS) involving trade which supports producers in developing countries by paying fair prices and making sure that workers have good working conditions and fair pay

fairway /'feəweɪ/ ***noun*** [C] (SPORT) the long strip of short grass that you must hit the ball along in GOLF before you get to the GREEN and the hole

fairy /'feəri/ ***noun*** [C] (*pl.* **fairies**) (in stories) a small creature with wings and magic powers

'fairy tale (also **'fairy story**) ***noun*** [C] (LITERATURE) a story that is about fairies, magic, etc.

faith ⊶ /feɪθ/ ***noun*** **1** [U] **~ (in sb/sth)** strong belief (in sb/sth); trust: *I've got great/little faith in his ability to do the job. ◊ I have **lost faith** in him.* **2** [U] (RELIGION) strong religious belief: *I've lost my faith.* **3** [C] (RELIGION) a particular religion: *the Jewish faith* IDM **in good faith** with honest reasons for doing sth: *I bought the car in good faith. I didn't know it was stolen.*

faithful ⊶ /'feɪθfl/ ***adj.*** **~ (to sb/sth)** **1** always staying with and supporting a person, organization or belief: *Peter has been a faithful friend. ◊ He was always **faithful to** his wife* (= he didn't have sexual relations with anyone else). SYN **loyal** OPP **unfaithful** **2** true to the facts; accurate: *a faithful description* ▶ **faithfulness** ***noun*** [U] ➲ look at **fidelity**

faithfully ⊶ /'feɪθfəli/ ***adv.*** **1** accurately; carefully: *to **follow instructions faithfully** ◊ The events were faithfully recorded in her diary.* **2** in a loyal way; in a way that you can rely on: *He had supported the local team faithfully for 30 years. ◊ She **promised faithfully** not to tell anyone my secret.* ℹ **Yours faithfully** is used to end formal letters.

fake¹ /feɪk/ ***noun*** [C] **1** a work of art, etc. that seems to be real or genuine but is not **2** a person who is not really what they appear to be ▶ **fake** ***adj.***: *a fake passport* ➲ note at **artificial**

fake² /feɪk/ ***verb*** [T] **1** to copy sth and try to make people believe it is the real thing: *He faked his father's signature.* **2** to make people believe that you are feeling sth that you are not: *I faked surprise when he told me the news.*

falcon /'fɔːlkən/ ***noun*** [C] a bird with long pointed wings that kills and eats other animals, a type of BIRD OF PREY. **Falcons** can be trained to hunt.

fall¹ ⊶ /fɔːl/ ***verb*** [I] (*pt* **fell** /fel/; *pp* **fallen** /'fɔːlən/) **1** to drop down towards the ground: *He fell off the ladder onto the grass. ◊ The rain was falling steadily.* **2 ~ (down/over)** to suddenly stop standing and drop to the ground: *She slipped on the ice and fell. ◊ The little boy fell over and hurt his knee.* **3** to hang down: *Her hair fell down over her shoulders.* **4** to become lower or less: *The temperature is falling. ◊ The price of coffee has fallen again.* OPP **rise** **5** to be defeated: *The Government fell because of the scandal.* **6** (*written*) to be killed (in battle): *Millions of soldiers fell in the war.* **7** to change into a different state; to become: *He **fell asleep** on the sofa. ◊ They **fell in love** with each other in Spain. ◊ I must get some new shoes – these ones are **falling to pieces**.* **8** (*formal*) to come or happen: *My birthday falls on a Sunday this year.* **9** to belong to a particular group, type, etc.: *Animals fall into two groups, those with backbones and those without.*

IDM **fall flat** → FLAT¹
fall/slot into place → PLACE¹
fall short (of sth) → SHORT¹

PHR V **fall apart** to break (into pieces): *My car is falling apart.*
fall back on sb/sth to use sb/sth when you are in difficulty: *When the electricity was cut off we fell back on candles.*
fall for sb (*informal*) to be strongly attracted to sb; to fall in love with sb
fall for sth (*informal*) to be tricked into believing sth that is not true: *He makes excuses and she falls for them every time.*
fall out (with sb) to argue and stop being friendly (with sb)
fall through to fail or not happen: *Our trip to Japan has fallen through.*

> **THESAURUS**
>
> **fall**
>
> **decline • drop • diminish • slump • decrease**
>
> These are all words that can be used when the amount, level or number of sth goes down.
>
> **fall**: *Profits have fallen by 30 per cent.*
>
> **decline**: *The market for these products has slowly declined.*
>
> **drop**: *The Dutch team dropped to fifth place.*
>
> **diminish**: *The world's resources are rapidly diminishing.*
>
> **slump**: *Oil prices have slumped badly in recent months.*
>
> **decrease**: *The number of students decreased significantly last year.*

fall² ⊶ /fɔːl/ ***noun*** **1** [C] an act of falling down or off sth: *She **had a** nasty **fall** from her horse.* **2** [C] **a ~ (of sth)** the amount of sth that has fallen or the distance that sth has fallen: *We have had a heavy fall of snow. ◊ a fall of four metres* **3** [C] **a ~ (in sth)** a decrease (in value, quantity, etc.): *There has been a sharp fall in the price of oil.* SYN **drop** OPP **rise** **4** [sing.] **the ~ of sth** a (political) defeat; a failure: *the fall of the Roman Empire* **5 falls** [pl.] a large amount of water that falls from a height down the side of a mountain, etc.: *Niagara Falls* SYN **waterfall** **6** [C] (*AmE*) = AUTUMN

fallacy /'fæləsi/ ***noun*** (*pl.* **fallacies**) [C,U] (*formal*) a false belief or a wrong idea: *It's a fallacy to believe that money brings happiness* (= it's not true).

fallen past participle of **fall¹**

fallible /'fæləbl/ ***adj.*** able or likely to make mistakes: *Even our new computerized system is fallible.* OPP **infallible**

Fallopian tube /fə'ləʊpiən tjuːb/ ***noun*** [C] (ANATOMY) one of the two tubes in the body of a woman or a female animal along which eggs travel from the OVARIES (= the place where they are produced) to the UTERUS (=the place where a baby is formed) ➲ picture at **fertilize**

fallout /ˈfɔːlaʊt/ ***noun*** [U] (**PHYSICS**) dangerous waste that is carried in the air after a nuclear explosion

fallow /ˈfæləʊ/ ***adj.*** (used about land) (**AGRICULTURE**) not used for growing plants, especially so that the quality of the land will improve: *The farmer let the field **lie fallow** for two years.*

false 🔑 /fɔːls/ ***adj.*** **1** not true; not correct: *I think the information you have been given is false.* ◇ *I got a completely false impression of him from our first meeting.* OPP **true** **2** not real; artificial: *false hair/eyelashes/teeth* ➲ note at **artificial** OPP **real**, **natural** **3** not genuine, but made to look real in order to trick people: *This suitcase has a false bottom.* ◇ *a false name/passport* **4** (used about sb's behaviour or expression) not sincere or honest: *a false smile* ◇ *false modesty* ▶ **falsely** ***adv.***: *She was falsely accused of stealing a wallet.*
IDM **a false alarm** a warning about a danger that does not happen
a false friend (**LANGUAGE**) a word in another language that looks similar to a word in your own but has a different meaning
under false pretences pretending to be or to have sth in order to trick people: *She got into the club under false pretences – she isn't a member at all!*

ˌfalse ˈteeth (also **dentures**) ***noun*** [pl.] artificial teeth that are worn by sb who has lost their natural teeth

falsify /ˈfɔːlsɪfaɪ/ ***verb*** [T] (*pres. part.* **falsifying**; *3rd person sing. pres.* **falsifies**; *pt, pp* **falsified**) (*formal*) to change a document, information, etc. so that it is no longer true in order to trick sb

falter /ˈfɔːltə(r)/ ***verb*** [I] **1** to become weak or move in a way that is not steady: *The engine faltered and stopped.* **2** to lose confidence and determination: *Sampras faltered and missed the ball.*

fame 🔑 /feɪm/ ***noun*** [U] being known or talked about by many people because of what you have achieved: *Pop stars achieve fame at a young age.* ◇ *The town's only **claim to fame** is that there was a riot there.*

famed /feɪmd/ ***adj.*** ~ **(for sth)** well known (for sth) SYN **famous**: *Welsh people are famed for their singing.*

familiar 🔑 /fəˈmɪliə(r)/ ***adj.*** **1** ~ **(to sb)** well known to you; often seen or heard and therefore easy to recognize: *to look/sound familiar* ◇ *Chinese music isn't very familiar to people in Europe.* ◇ *It was a relief to see a familiar face in the crowd.* OPP **unfamiliar** **2** ~ **with sth** having a good knowledge of sth: *People in Europe aren't very familiar with Chinese music.* OPP **unfamiliar** **3** ~ **(with sb)** (used about a person's behaviour) too friendly and informal: *I was annoyed by the waiter's familiar behaviour.*

familiarity /fəˌmɪliˈærəti/ ***noun*** [U] **1** ~ **(with sth)** having a good knowledge of sth: *His familiarity with the area was an advantage.* **2** being too friendly and informal

faˌmiliariˈzation trip (also *informal* **ˈfam trip**) ***noun*** [C] (**TOURISM**) a trip made by a TRAVEL AGENT (=a person whose job is to make travel arrangements for people) in order to find out more about a place, its hotels and services, so that they can sell holidays there

familiarize (also **-ise**) /fəˈmɪliəraɪz/ ***verb*** [T] ~ **sb/yourself (with sth)** to teach sb about sth or learn about sth until you know it well: *I want to familiarize myself with the plans before the meeting.*
▶ **familiarization** /fəˌmɪliəraɪˈzeɪʃn/ ***noun*** [U]

family 🔑 /ˈfæməli/ ***noun*** (*pl.* **families**) **1** [C, with sing. or pl. verb] a group of people who are related to each other: *I have quite a large family.* **2** [C,U] children: *Do you have any family?* ◇ *We are planning to **start a family** next year* (=to have our first baby). ◇ *to bring up/raise a family* **3** [C] a group of animals, plants, etc. that are of a similar type: *Lions belong to the cat family.* ➲ picture on **page 29**
IDM **run in the family** to be found very often in a family: *Red hair runs in the family.*

ˌfamily ˈdoctor (*especially BrE*) = GP

ˈfamily name ***noun*** [C] the name that is shared by members of a family SYN **surname**

ˌfamily ˈplanning ***noun*** [U] (**HEALTH**) controlling the number of children you have by using birth control ➲ look at **contraception**

ˈfamily room ***noun*** [C] **1** (*AmE*) a room in a house where the family can relax, watch television, etc. **2** (**TOURISM**) a room in a hotel for three or four people to sleep in, especially parents and children

ˌfamily ˈtree ***noun*** [C] (**SOCIAL STUDIES**) a diagram that shows the relationship between different members of a family over a long period of time

famine /ˈfæmɪn/ ***noun*** [C,U] a lack of food over a long period of time in a large area that can cause the death of many people: *There is a severe famine in many parts of Africa.* ◇ *The long drought* (=a lack of rain or water) *was followed by famine.*

famished /ˈfæmɪʃt/ ***adj.*** (*informal*) (not before a noun) very hungry

famous 🔑 /ˈfeɪməs/ ***adj.*** ~ **(for sth)** well known to many people: *a famous singer* ◇ *Glasgow is famous for its museums and art galleries.*

famously /ˈfeɪməsli/ ***adv.*** in a way that is famous: *the words he famously uttered just before he died*
IDM **get on/along famously** to have a very good relationship with sb

fan¹ 🔑 /fæn/ ***noun*** [C] **1** somebody who admires and is very enthusiastic about a sport, a film star, a singer, etc.: *football fans* ◇ *He's a Van Morrison fan.* ◇ *fan mail* (=letters from fans to the person they admire) **2** a machine with parts that turn around very quickly to create a current of cool or warm air: *an electric fan* ◇ *a fan heater* **3** an object in the shape of a HALF-CIRCLE made of paper, feathers, etc. that you wave in your hand to create a current of cool air

fan² /fæn/ ***verb*** [T] (**fanning**; **fanned**) **1** to make air blow on sb/sth by waving a fan¹(3), your hand, etc. in the air: *She used a newspaper to fan her face.* **2** to make a fire burn more strongly by blowing on it: *The strong wind really fanned the flames.*
PHR V **fan out** to spread out: *The police fanned out across the field.*

fanatic /fəˈnætɪk/ ***noun*** [C] (**RELIGION**, **POLITICS**) a person who is very enthusiastic about sth and may have extreme or dangerous opinions (especially about religion or politics): *a religious fanatic* ◇ *She's a health-food fanatic.* SYN **fiend**, **freak** ▶ **fanatical** /-kl/ ***adj.***: *He's fanatical about keeping things tidy.* ▶ **fanatically** /-kli/ ***adv.*** ▶ **fanaticism** /-tɪsɪzəm/ ***noun*** [U]

ˈfan belt ***noun*** [C] the belt that operates the machinery that cools a car engine

fancy¹ 🔑 /ˈfænsi/ ***verb*** [T] (*pres. part.* **fancying**; *3rd person sing. pres.* **fancies**; *pt, pp* **fancied**) **1** (*BrE, informal*) to like the idea of having or doing sth; to want sth or to want to do sth: *What do you fancy to eat?* ◇ *I don't fancy going out in this rain.* **2** (*BrE, informal*) to be sexually attracted to sb: *Jack keeps looking at you. I think he fancies you.* **3 ~ yourself** (as) sth to think that you would be good at sth; to think that you are sth (although this may not be true): *He fancied himself (as) a poet.*

fancy² 🔑 /ˈfænsi/ ***adj.*** (**fancier**; **fanciest**) not simple or ordinary: *My father doesn't like fancy food.* ◇ *I just want a pair of black shoes – nothing fancy.*

fancy³ /ˈfænsi/ ***noun***
IDM take sb's fancy to attract or please sb: *If you see something that takes your fancy I'll buy it for you.*
take a fancy to sb/sth to start liking sb/sth: *I think that Laura's really taken a fancy to you.*

ˌfancy ˈdress ***noun*** [U] special clothes that you wear to a party at which people dress up to look like a different person (for example from history or a story): *It was a Hallowe'en party and everyone went **in fancy dress**.*

fanfare /ˈfænfeə(r)/ ***noun*** [C] (**MUSIC**) a short loud piece of music that is used for introducing sb important, for example a king or queen

fang /fæŋ/ ***noun*** [C] (**BIOLOGY**) a long sharp tooth of a dog, snake, etc. ➲ picture on **page 29**

fanlight /ˈfænlaɪt/ ***noun*** [C] (**ARCHITECTURE**) a small window above a door or another window

fanny pack /ˈfæni pæk/ (*AmE*) = BUMBAG

fantasize (also **-ise**) /ˈfæntəsaɪz/ ***verb*** [I,T] to imagine sth that you would like to happen: *He liked to fantasize that he had won a gold medal at the Olympics.*

fantastic /fænˈtæstɪk/ ***adj.*** **1** (*informal*) very good; excellent: *She's a fantastic swimmer.* **2** strange and difficult to believe: *a story full of fantastic creatures from other worlds* **3** (*informal*) very large or great: *A Rolls Royce costs a fantastic amount of money.*
▸ **fantastically** /-kli/ ***adv.***

fantasy /ˈfæntəsi/ ***noun*** [C,U] (*pl.* **fantasies**) a situation that is not true, that you just imagine: *I have a fantasy about going to live in the Bahamas.* ◇ *They live in a world of fantasy.*

fanzine /ˈfænziːn/ ***noun*** [C] (**ARTS AND MEDIA**) a magazine that is written by and for FANS (= people who like a particular sports team, singer, etc.)

FAQ /ˌef eɪ ˈkjuː/ ***noun*** [C] (**COMPUTING**) a document on the Internet that contains the most *frequently asked questions* about a subject and the answers to these questions

far¹ 🔑 /fɑː(r)/ ***adj.*** (**farther** /ˈfɑːðə(r)/ or **further** /ˈfɜːðə(r)/, **farthest** /ˈfɑːðɪst/ or **furthest** /ˈfɜːðɪst/)
1 a long way away; DISTANT: *Let's walk – it's not far.* **2** (only *before* a noun) the largest distance away of two or more things: *the far side of the river* **3** (only *before* a noun) a long way from the centre in the direction mentioned: *politicians from the far left of the party*
IDM a far cry from sth/from doing sth an experience that is very different from sth/doing sth

far² 🔑 /fɑː(r)/ ***adv.*** (**farther** /ˈfɑːðə(r)/ or **further** /ˈfɜːðə(r)/, **farthest** /ˈfɑːðɪst/ or **furthest** /ˈfɜːðɪst/)
1 (at) a distance: *London's not far from here.* ◇ *How far did we walk yesterday?* ◇ *If we sit too far away from the screen I won't be able to see the film.* ◇ *I can't swim as far as you.* ◇ *How much further is it?* **2** very much: *She's far more intelligent than I thought.* ◇ *There's far too much salt in this soup.* **3** (to) a certain degree: *How far have you got with your homework?* ◇ *The company employs local people as far as possible.* **4** a long time: *We danced far into the night.*
IDM as far as to the place mentioned but not further: *We walked as far as the river and then turned back.*
as/so far as used for giving your opinion or judgement of a situation: ***As far as I know**, she's not coming, but I may be wrong.* ◇ ***So far as** school work **is concerned**, he's hopeless.* ◇ ***As far as I'm concerned**, this is the most important point.* ◇ ***As far as I can see**, the accident was John's fault, not Ann's.*
as far as the eye can see to the furthest place you can see
by far (used for emphasizing COMPARATIVE or SUPERLATIVE words) by a large amount: *Carmen is by far the best student in the class.*
far afield far away, especially from where you live or from where you are staying
far from doing sth instead of doing sth: *Far from enjoying the film, he fell asleep in the middle.*
far from sth almost the opposite of sth; not at all: *He's far from happy* (= he's very sad or angry).
far from it (*informal*) certainly not; just the opposite: *'Did you enjoy your holiday?' 'No, far from it. It was awful.'*
few and far between → FEW
go far 1 to be enough: *This food won't go very far between three of us.* **2** to be successful in life: *Dan is very talented and should go far.*
go too far to behave in a way that causes trouble or upsets other people: *He's always been naughty but this time he's gone too far.*
so far until now: *So far the weather has been good but it might change.*
so far so good (*spoken*) everything has gone well until now

faraway /ˈfɑːrəweɪ/ ***adj.*** (only *before* a noun)
1 (*written*) a great distance away: *He told us stories of faraway countries.* **2** (used about a look in a person's eyes) as if you are thinking of sth else: *She stared out of the window with a faraway look in her eyes.*

farce /fɑːs/ ***noun*** [C] **1** something important or serious that is not organized well or treated with respect: *The meeting was a farce – everyone was shouting at the same time.* **2** (**ARTS AND MEDIA**) a funny play for the theatre full of ridiculous situations ▸ **farcical** /ˈfɑːsɪkl/ ***adj.***

fare¹ /feə(r)/ ***noun*** [C] the amount of money you pay to travel by bus, train, taxi, etc.: *What's the fare to Birmingham?* ◇ *Adults pay **full fare**, children pay **half fare**.*

fare² /feə(r)/ ***verb*** [I] (*formal*) to be successful or not successful in a particular situation: *How did you fare in your examination* (= did you do well or badly)?

the ˌFar ˈEast ***noun*** [sing.] (**GEOGRAPHY**) China, Japan and other countries in E and SE Asia ➲ look at **the Middle East**

farewell /ˌfeəˈwel/ ***noun*** [C,U] the act of saying goodbye to sb: *He said his farewells and left.* ◇ *a farewell party/drink* ▸ **farewell** *exclamation* (*old-fashioned*)

ˌfar-ˈfetched ***adj.*** not easy to believe: *It's a good book but the story's too far-fetched.*

farm¹ 🔑 /fɑːm/ ***noun*** [C] (**AGRICULTURE**) an area of land with fields and buildings that is used for growing crops and keeping animals: *to work **on a farm*** ◇ *farm buildings/workers/animals*

farm² /fɑːm/ ***verb*** [I,T] (**AGRICULTURE**) to use land for growing crops or keeping animals: *She farms 200 acres.*

farmer 🔑 /ˈfɑːmə(r)/ ***noun*** [C] (**AGRICULTURE**) a person who owns or manages a farm

farmhouse /ˈfɑːmhaʊs/ *noun* [C] (AGRICULTURE) the house on a farm where the farmer lives

farming ⊶ /ˈfɑːmɪŋ/ *noun* [U] (AGRICULTURE) managing a farm or working on it: *farming methods/areas*

farmland /ˈfɑːmlænd/ *noun* [U, pl.] (AGRICULTURE) land that is used for farming: *250 acres of farmland*

farmyard /ˈfɑːmjɑːd/ *noun* [C] (AGRICULTURE) an outside area near a FARMHOUSE surrounded by buildings or walls

ˌfar-ˈreaching *adj.* having a great influence on a lot of other things: *far-reaching changes*

ˌfar-ˈsighted *adj.* **1** being able to see what will be necessary in the future and making plans for it **2** (*AmE*) = LONG-SIGHTED

fart /fɑːt/ *verb* [I] (*informal*) to suddenly let gas from the stomach escape from your bottom ▶ **fart** *noun* [C]

farther ⊶ /ˈfɑːðə(r)/ comparative of **far**

farthest ⊶ /ˈfɑːðɪst/ superlative of **far**

fascinate /ˈfæsɪneɪt/ *verb* [T] to attract or interest sb very much: *Chinese culture has always fascinated me.* ▶ **fascinating** *adj.* ▶ **fascination** /ˌfæsɪˈneɪʃn/ *noun* [C,U]

fascism (also **Fascism**) /ˈfæʃɪzəm/ *noun* [U] (POLITICS) an extreme (**right-wing**) political system ▶ **fascist** (also **Fascist**) /ˈfæʃɪst/ *noun* [C], *adj.*

fashion ⊶ /ˈfæʃn/ *noun* **1** [C,U] the style of dressing or behaving that is the most popular at a particular time: *What is **the latest fashion** in hairstyles?* ◇ *a fashion show/model/magazine* ◇ *Jeans are always **in fashion**.* ◇ *I think hats will **come back into fashion**.* ◇ *That colour is **out of fashion** this year.* **2** [sing.] the way you do sth: *Watch him. He's been behaving **in a** very strange **fashion**.*

fashionable ⊶ /ˈfæʃnəbl/ *adj.* **1** popular or in a popular style at the time: *a fashionable area/dress/opinion* **2** considering fashion to be important: *fashionable society* OPP **unfashionable**, **old-fashioned** ▶ **fashionably** /-əbli/ *adv.*

ˈfashion designer *noun* [C] a person who designs fashionable clothes

fast¹ ⊶ /fɑːst/ *adj.* **1** able to move or act at great speed: *a fast car/worker/runner/reader* **2** (used about a clock or watch) showing a time that is later than the real time: *The clock is five minutes fast.* OPP **slow** **3** (used about camera film) very sensitive to light, and therefore good for taking photographs in poor light or of things that are moving quickly **4** (not before a noun) firmly fixed: *He made the boat fast* (= he tied it to something) *before he got out.* ◇ *Do you think the colour in this T-shirt is fast* (= will not come out when washed)?

IDM **fast and furious** very fast and exciting

hard and fast → HARD¹

fast² ⊶ /fɑːst/ *adv.* **1** quickly: *She ran very fast.* **2** firmly or deeply: *Sam was **fast asleep** by ten o'clock.* ◇ *Our car was stuck fast in the mud.*

fast³ /fɑːst/ *verb* [I] to eat no food for a certain time, usually for religious reasons: *Muslims fast during Ramadan.* ▶ **fast** *noun* [C]

fasten ⊶ /ˈfɑːsn/ *verb* **1** [I,T] ~ (sth) (up) to close or join the two parts of sth; to become closed or joined: *Please fasten your seat belts.* ◇ *Fasten your coat up – it's cold outside.* ◇ *My dress fastens at the back.* **2** [T] ~ sth (on/to sth); ~ A and B (together) to fix or tie sth to sth, or two things together: *Fasten this badge on your jacket.* ◇ *How can I fasten these pieces of wood together?* **3** [T] to close or lock sth firmly so that it will not open: *Close the window and fasten it securely.*

fastener /ˈfɑːsnə(r)/ (*also* **fastening** /ˈfɑːsnɪŋ/) *noun* [C] something that fastens things together

ˌfast ˈfood *noun* [U] food that can be served very quickly in special restaurants and is often taken away to be eaten in the street: *a fast food restaurant*

ˌfast ˈforward *verb* [T] to make a VIDEOTAPE or a CASSETTE go forward quickly without playing it ▶ **fast forward** *noun* [U]: *Press fast forward to advance the tape.* ◇ *the fast-forward button* ➲ look at **rewind**

fastidious /fæˈstɪdiəs/ *adj.* difficult to please; wanting everything to be perfect

fat¹ ⊶ /fæt/ *adj.* (**fatter**; **fattest**) **1** (used about people's or animal's bodies) weighing too much; covered with too much flesh: *You'll **get fat** if you eat too much.* OPP **thin** **2** (used about a thing) thick or full: *a fat wallet/book*

fat² ⊶ /fæt/ *noun* **1** [U] (BIOLOGY) the soft white substance under the skins of animals and people: *I don't like meat with fat on it.* ➲ adjective **fatty** **2** [C,U] the substance containing oil that we obtain from animals, plants or seeds and use for cooking: *Cook the onions in a little fat.*

fatal /ˈfeɪtl/ *adj.* **1** causing or ending in death: *a fatal accident/disease* ➲ look at **mortal** **2** causing trouble or a bad result: *She made the fatal mistake of trusting him.* ▶ **fatally** /-əli/ *adv.*: *fatally injured*

fatality /fəˈtæləti/ *noun* [C] (*pl.* **fatalities**) a person's death caused by an accident, in war, etc.: *There were no fatalities in the fire.*

ˈfat cat *noun* [C] (*informal*) (BUSINESS) a person who earns, or who has, a lot of money (especially when compared to people who do not earn so much)

fate /feɪt/ *noun* **1** [U] the power that some people believe controls everything that happens: *It was fate that brought them together again after twenty years.* **2** [C] your future; something that happens to you: *Both men suffered the same fate – they both lost their jobs.* SYN **fortune**

fateful /ˈfeɪtfl/ *adj.* having an important effect on the future: *a fateful decision*

father¹ ⊶ /ˈfɑːðə(r)/ *noun* [C] **1** a person's male parent: *John looks exactly like his father.* **2** **Father** (RELIGION) the title of certain priests: *Father O'Reilly*

father² /ˈfɑːðə(r)/ *verb* [T] to become a father: *to father a child*

ˌFather ˈChristmas (*also* **ˈSanta Claus**) *noun* [C] an old man with a red coat and a long white beard who, children believe, brings presents at Christmas

fatherhood /ˈfɑːðəhʊd/ *noun* [U] the state of being a father

ˈfather-in-law *noun* [C] (*pl.* **fathers-in-law**) the father of your husband or wife

fatherly /ˈfɑːðəli/ *adj.* like or typical of a father: *Would you like a piece of fatherly advice?*

fathom¹ /ˈfæðəm/ *verb* [T] (usually in the negative) to understand sth: *I can't fathom what he means.*

fathom² /ˈfæðəm/ *noun* [C] a measure of the depth of water; 6 feet (1.8 metres)

fatigue /fəˈtiːɡ/ *noun* [U] **1** the feeling of being extremely tired: *He was suffering from mental and physical fatigue.* **2** (CHEMISTRY, PHYSICS) weakness in metals caused by a lot of use: *The plane crash was caused by metal fatigue in a wing.*

fatten /ˈfætn/ *verb* [T] ~ **sb/sth (up)** to make sb/sth fatter: *He's fattening the pigs up for market.*

fattening /ˈfætnɪŋ/ ***adj.*** (used about food) that makes people fat: *Chocolate is very fattening.*

fatty /ˈfæti/ ***adj.*** (**fattier**; **fattiest**) (used about food) having a lot of fat in or on it

ˌfatty ˈacid ***noun*** [C] (BIOLOGY, CHEMISTRY) an acid that is found in fats and oils

faucet /ˈfɔːsɪt/ (*AmE*) = TAP² (1)

fault¹ /fɔːlt/ ***noun*** **1** [C] something wrong or not perfect in a person's character or in a thing: *One of my faults is that I'm always late.* ➲ note at **mistake** **2** [U] responsibility for a mistake: *It will be your* ***own fault*** *if you don't pass your exams.* **3** [C] (GEOLOGY) a place where there is a break in the layers of rock in the earth's surface and the rocks on either side have moved in opposite directions: *the San Andreas fault* ◇ *a fault line* ➲ picture at **plate tectonics**

IDM **be at fault** to be wrong or responsible for a mistake: *The other driver was at fault – he didn't stop at the traffic lights.*

find fault (with sb/sth) → FIND¹

fault² /fɔːlt/ ***verb*** [T] to find sth wrong with sb/sth: *It was impossible to fault her English.*

faultless /ˈfɔːltləs/ ***adj.*** without any mistakes; perfect: *The pianist gave a faultless performance.*

faulty /ˈfɔːlti/ ***adj.*** (used especially about electricity or machinery) not working properly: *a faulty switch*

fauna /ˈfɔːnə/ ***noun*** [U] (BIOLOGY) all the animals of an area or a period of time: *the flora and fauna of South America* ➲ look at **flora**

Fauvism /ˈfəʊvɪzəm/ ***noun*** [U] (ART) a style of painting that uses bright colours and in which objects and people are represented in a non-realistic way. It was popular in Paris for a short period from 1905.

faux pas /ˌfəʊ ˈpɑː/ ***noun*** [C] (*pl.* **faux pas** /ˌfəʊ ˈpɑːz/) something you say or do that is embarrassing or offends people: *to* ***make a faux pas***

favour¹ (*AmE* **favor**) /ˈfeɪvə(r)/ ***noun*** **1** [C] something that helps sb: *Would you* ***do me a favour*** *and post this letter for me?* ◇ *Could I* ***ask*** *you* ***a favour****?* ◇ *Are they paying you for the work, or are you doing it* ***as a favour****?* **2** [U] ~ **(with sb)** liking or approval: *I'm afraid I'm* ***out of favour*** *with my neighbour since our last argument.* ◇ *The new boss's methods didn't* ***find favour*** *with the staff.*

IDM **in favour of sb/sth** in agreement with: *Are you in favour of private education?*

in sb's favour to the advantage of sb: *The committee decided in their favour.*

favour² (*AmE* **favor**) /ˈfeɪvə(r)/ ***verb*** [T] **1** to support sb/sth; to prefer: *Which suggestion do you favour?* **2** to treat one person very well and so be unfair to others: *Parents must try not to favour one of their children.*

favourable (*AmE* **favorable**) /ˈfeɪvərəbl/ ***adj.*** **1** showing liking or approval: *He made a favourable impression on the interviewers.* **2** (often used about the weather) suitable or helpful: *Conditions are favourable for skiing today.* OPP **unfavourable**, **adverse** ▶ **favourably** (*AmE* **favorably**) /-əbli/ ***adv.***

favourite¹ (*AmE* **favorite**) /ˈfeɪvərɪt/ ***adj.*** liked more than any other: *What is your favourite colour?* ◇ *Who is your favourite singer?*

favourite² (*AmE* **favorite**) /ˈfeɪvərɪt/ ***noun*** [C] **1** a person or thing that you like more than any others: *The other kids were jealous of Rose because she was the teacher's favourite.* **2** ~ **(for sth/to do sth)** the horse, team, COMPETITOR, etc. who is expected to win: *Mimms is the hot favourite for the leadership of the party.* OPP **outsider**

favouritism (*AmE* **favoritism**) /ˈfeɪvərɪtɪzəm/ ***noun*** [U] giving unfair advantages to the person or people that you like best: *The referee was accused of* ***showing favouritism*** *to the home side.*

fawn¹ /fɔːn/ ***adj.***, ***noun*** [U] (of) a light yellowish-brown colour

fawn² /fɔːn/ ***noun*** [C] a young DEER ➲ note at **deer**

fax¹ /fæks/ ***noun*** **1** [C,U] a copy of a letter, etc. that you can send by telephone lines using a special machine: *They need an answer today so I'll* ***send a fax****.* ◇ *They contacted us* ***by fax****.* **2** [C] (*also* **ˈfax machine**) the machine that you use for sending faxes: *Have you got a fax?* ◇ *What's your fax number?*

fax² /fæks/ ***verb*** [T] ~ **sth (to sb)**; ~ **sb (sth)** to send sb a **fax**: *We will fax our order to you tomorrow.* ◇ *I've faxed her a copy of the letter.*

faze /feɪz/ ***verb*** [T] (*informal*) to make sb worried or nervous

FBI /ˌef biː ˈaɪ/ ***abbr.*** (*AmE*) Federal Bureau of Investigation; the section of the US Justice Department which tries to catch people who have committed crimes that are against the laws of the US as a whole, such as bank ROBBERY and TERRORISM

FC /ˌef ˈsiː/ ***abbr.*** (*BrE*) Football Club: *Everton FC*

FCO /ˌef siː ˈəʊ/ ***abbr.*** Foreign and Commonwealth Office

fear¹ /fɪə(r)/ ***noun*** [C,U] the feeling that you have when sth dangerous, painful or frightening might happen: *He was shaking* ***with fear*** *after the accident.* ◇ *People in this area live* ***in constant fear*** *of crime.* ◇ *This book helped me overcome my fear of dogs.* ◇ *She showed no fear.* ◇ *My fears for his safety were unnecessary.*

IDM **no fear** (*spoken*) (used when answering a suggestion) certainly not

fear² /fɪə(r)/ ***verb*** [T] **1** to be afraid of sb/sth or of doing sth: *We all fear illness and death.* **2** to feel that sth bad might happen or might have happened: *The government fears that it will lose the next election.* ◇ *Thousands of people are feared dead in the earthquake.*

PHR V **fear for sb/sth** to be worried about sb/sth: *Parents often fear for the safety of their children.*

fearful /ˈfɪəfl/ ***adj.*** (*formal*) **1** ~ **(of sth/doing sth)**; ~ **that...** afraid or worried about sth: *You should never be fearful of starting something new.* ◇ *They were fearful that they would miss the plane.* **2** terrible: *the fearful consequences of war* ▶ **fearfully** /-fəli/ ***adv.*** ▶ **fearfulness** ***noun*** [U]

fearless /ˈfɪələs/ ***adj.*** never afraid ▶ **fearlessly** ***adv.*** ▶ **fearlessness** ***noun*** [U]

feasible /ˈfiːzəbl/ ***adj.*** possible to do: *a feasible plan* ▶ **feasibility** /ˌfiːzəˈbɪləti/ ***noun*** [U]

feast /fiːst/ ***noun*** [C] a large, special meal, especially to celebrate sth ▶ **feast** ***verb*** [I] ~ **(on sth)**: *They feasted on exotic dishes.*

feat /fiːt/ ***noun*** [C] something you do that shows great strength, skill or courage: *That new bridge is a remarkable feat of engineering.* ◇ *Persuading Helen to give you a pay rise was* ***no mean feat*** (= difficult to do). ➲ note at **action¹**

feather /ˈfeðə(r)/ ***noun*** [C] (BIOLOGY) one of the light, soft things that grow in a bird's skin and cover its body ➲ picture on **page 29**

feature¹ AW /ˈfiːtʃə(r)/ ***noun*** [C] **1** an important or noticeable part of sth: *Mountains and lakes are the main features of the landscape of Wales.* ◇ *Noise is a feature of city life.* **2** a part of the face: *Her* *eyes are her best feature.* **3** a ~ (on sth) (ARTS AND MEDIA) a newspaper or magazine article or television programme about sth: *There's a feature on kangaroos in this magazine.* ▶ **featureless** *adj.*: *dull, featureless landscape*

feature² 🔑 AW /ˈfiːtʃə(r)/ *verb* **1** [T] to include sb/sth as an important part: *The film features many well-known actors.* **2** [I] ~ in sth to have a part in sth: *Does marriage feature in your future plans?* SYN **figure**

ˈfeature film *noun* [C] (ARTS AND MEDIA) a main film with a story, rather than a DOCUMENTARY, etc.

Feb. *abbr.* February: *18 Feb. 1993*

February /ˈfebruəri/ *noun* [U, C] (*abbr.* **Feb.**) the second month of the year, coming after January

feces (*AmE*) = FAECES

fed past tense, past participle of **feed¹**

federal 🔑 AW /ˈfedərəl/ *adj.* **1** (POLITICS) organized as a FEDERATION: *a federal system of rule* **2** connected with the central government of a federation: *That is a federal not a state law.*

federalist /ˈfedərəlɪst/ *noun* [C] (POLITICS) a supporter of a system of government in which the individual states of a country have control of their own affairs, but are controlled by a central government for national decisions ▶ **federalist** *adj.*: *a federalist future for Europe* ▶ **federalism** /ˈfedərəlɪzəm/ *noun* [U]: *European federalism*

federate /ˈfedəreɪt/ *verb* [I] (used about states, organizations, etc.) (POLITICS) to unite under a central government or organization while keeping some local control

federation AW /ˌfedəˈreɪʃn/ *noun* [C] (POLITICS) a group of states, etc. that have joined together to form a single group

ˌfed ˈup *adj.* (*informal*) (not before a noun) **fed up (with/of sb/sth/doing sth)** bored or unhappy; tired of sth: *What's the matter? You look really fed up.* ◇ *I'm fed up with waiting for the phone to ring.*

fee 🔑 AW /fiː/ *noun* [C] **1** (usually plural) the money you pay for professional advice or service from doctors, lawyers, schools, universities, etc.: *We can't afford private school fees.* ◇ *Most ticket agencies will **charge a small fee**.* **2** the cost of an exam, the cost of becoming a member of a club, the amount you pay to go into certain buildings, etc.: *How much is the entrance fee?* ➲ note at **pay²**

feeble /ˈfiːbl/ *adj.* **1** with no energy or power; weak: *a feeble old man* ◇ *a feeble cry* **2** not able to make sb believe sth: *a feeble argument/excuse* ▶ **feebly** *adv.*: *He shook his head feebly.*

feed¹ 🔑 /fiːd/ *verb* (*pt, pp* **fed** /fed/) **1** [T] ~ sb/sth (on) (sth) to give food to a person or an animal: *Don't forget to feed the dog.* ◇ *I can't come yet. I haven't fed the baby.* ◇ *Some of the snakes in the zoo are fed (on) rats.* **2** [I] ~ (on sth) (used about animals or babies) to eat: *What do horses feed on in the winter?* ◇ *Bats feed at night.* **3** [T] ~ A (with B); ~ B into/to/through A to supply sb/sth with sth; to put sth into sth else: *This channel feeds us with news and information 24 hours a day.* ◇ *Metal sheets are fed through the machine one at a time.*

feed² /fiːd/ *noun* **1** [C] a meal for an animal or a baby: *When's the baby's next feed due?* **2** [U] (AGRICULTURE) food for animals: *cattle feed*

feedback /ˈfiːdbæk/ *noun* [U] information or comments about sth that you have done which tells you how good or bad it is: *The teacher spent five minutes with each of us to **give us feedback on** our homework.*

feedstock /ˈfiːdstɒk/ *noun* [U] (CHEMISTRY) basic material that is supplied to a machine or used in an industrial process which changes it to make another product

feel¹ 🔑 /fiːl/ *verb* (*pt, pp* **felt** /felt/) **1** *linking verb* (usually with an adjective) to be in the state that is mentioned: *to feel cold/sick/tired/happy* ◇ *How are you feeling today?* ◇ *You'll feel better in the morning.* **2** *linking verb* used to say how sth seems to you when you touch, see, smell, experience, etc. it: *My new coat feels like leather but it's not.* ◇ *He **felt as if** he had been there before.* ◇ *My head **feels as though** it will burst.* ◇ *I felt (that) it was a mistake not to ask her advice.* **3** [T] to notice or experience sth physical or emotional: *I damaged the nerves and now I can't feel anything in this hand.* ◇ *I felt something crawling up my back.* ◇ *I don't feel any sympathy for Matt at all.* ◇ *You could feel the tension in the courtroom.* **4** [T] to touch sth in order to find out what it is like: *Feel this material. Is it cotton or silk?* ◇ *I felt her forehead to see if she had a temperature.* **5** [I] ~ (about) (for sb/sth) to try to find sth with your hands instead of your eyes: *She felt about in the dark for the light switch.* **6** [T] to be affected by sth: *Do you feel the cold in winter?* ◇ *She felt it badly when her mother died.*

IDM **feel free (to do sth)** (*informal*) used to tell sb they are allowed to do sth: *Feel free to use the phone.*

feel like sth/doing sth to want sth or to want to do sth: *Do you feel like going out?*

feel your age to realize that you are getting old, especially compared to other younger people around you

not feel yourself to not feel healthy or well

PHR V **feel for sb** to understand sb's feelings and situation and feel sorry for them: *I really felt for him when his wife died.*

feel up to sth/to doing sth to have the strength and the energy to do or deal with sth: *I really don't feel up to eating a huge meal.*

feel² /fiːl/ *noun* [sing.] **1** the impression sth gives you when you touch it; the impression that a place or situation gives you: *You can tell it's wool by the feel.* ◇ *The town has a friendly feel.* ➲ note at **think** **2** an act of touching sth in order to learn about it: *Let me have a feel of that material.*

feeler /ˈfiːlə(r)/ *noun* [C, usually pl.] (BIOLOGY) either of the two long thin parts on the heads of some insects and of some animals that live in shells that they use to feel and touch things with SYN **antenna**

feeling 🔑 /ˈfiːlɪŋ/ *noun* **1** [C] a ~ (of sth) something that you feel in your mind or body: *a feeling of hunger/happiness/fear/helplessness* ◇ *I've got a funny feeling in my leg.* **2** [sing.] a belief or idea that sth is true or is likely to happen: *I **get the feeling** that Ian doesn't like me much.* ◇ *I **have a** nasty **feeling** that Jan didn't get our message.* **3** [C,U] feeling(s) (about/on sth) an attitude or opinion about sth: *What are your feelings on this matter?* ◇ *My own feeling is that we should postpone the meeting.* ◇ *Public feeling seems to be against the new road.* **4** [U, C, usually pl.] a person's emotions; strong emotion: *I have to tell Jeff his work's not good enough but I don't want to **hurt** his **feelings**.* ◇ *Let's practise that song again, this time **with feeling**.* **5** [C,U] (a) ~feeling/feelings (for sb/sth) love or understanding for sb/sth: *She doesn't have much (of a) feeling for music.* ◇ *He still has feelings for his ex-wife.* **6** [U] the ability to feel in your body: *After the accident he lost all feeling in his legs.*

IDM **bad/ill feeling** unhappy relations between

people: *The decision caused a lot of bad feeling at the factory.*
no hard feelings → HARD[1]

feet plural of **foot**[1]

feisty /ˈfaɪsti/ ***adj.*** (**feistier**; **feistiest**) (*informal*) (used about people) strong, determined and not afraid to argue

feldspar /ˈfeldspɑː(r)/ ***noun*** [U, C] (GEOLOGY) a type of white or red rock

feline /ˈfiːlaɪn/ ***adj.*** (BIOLOGY) connected with an animal of the cat family; like a cat

fell[1] past tense of **fall**[1]

fell[2] /fel/ ***verb*** [T] to cut down a tree

fellow[1] ⊶ /ˈfeləʊ/ ***noun*** [C] **1** (EDUCATION) a member of an academic or professional organization, or of certain universities: *a fellow of the Royal College of Surgeons* **2** (EDUCATION) a person who is paid to study a particular thing at a university: *Jill is a research fellow in the biology department.* **3** (*old-fashioned*) a man

fellow[2] ⊶ /ˈfeləʊ/ ***adj.*** (only *before* a noun) another or others like yourself in the same situation: *Her fellow students were all older than her.* ◊ *fellow workers/passengers/citizens*

fellowship /ˈfeləʊʃɪp/ ***noun*** **1** [U] a feeling of friendship between people who share an interest **2** [C] a group or society of people who share the same interest or belief **3** [C] (EDUCATION) the position of a college or university fellow

felon /ˈfelən/ ***noun*** [C] (*especially AmE*) (LAW) a person who commits a serious crime such as murder

felony /ˈfeləni/ ***noun*** [C,U] (*pl.* **felonies**) (*especially AmE*) (LAW) the act of committing a serious crime such as murder; a crime of this type ➲ look at **misdemeanour**

felt[1] past tense, past participle of **feel**[1]

felt[2] /felt/ ***noun*** [U] a type of soft cloth made from wool, etc. which has been pressed tightly together: *a felt hat*

ˌfelt-tip ˈpen (also **ˈfelt tip**) ***noun*** [C] a type of pen with a point made of felt

female[1] ⊶ /ˈfiːmeɪl/ ***adj.*** (BIOLOGY) **1** being a woman or a girl: *a female artist/employer/student* **2** being of the sex that produces eggs or gives birth to babies: *a female cat* **3** (used about plants and flowers) that can produce fruit

female[2] ⊶ /ˈfiːmeɪl/ ***noun*** (BIOLOGY) [C] **1** an animal that can produce eggs or give birth to babies; a plant that can produce fruit **2** a woman or a girl

feminine /ˈfemənɪn/ ***adj.*** **1** typical of or looking like a woman; connected with women: *My daughter always dresses like a boy. She hates looking feminine.* **2** (*abbr.* **fem**) (LANGUAGE) (in English) of the forms of words used to describe females: *'Lioness' is the feminine form of 'lion'.* **3** (*abbr.* **fem**) (LANGUAGE) (in the grammar of some languages) belonging to a certain class of nouns, adjectives or pronouns: *The German word for a flower is feminine.* ➲ look at **masculine**, **neuter** ▶ **femininity** /ˌfeməˈnɪnəti/ ***noun*** [U]

feminism /ˈfemənɪzəm/ ***noun*** [U] (SOCIAL STUDIES) the belief that women should have the same rights and opportunities as men ▶ **feminist** /ˈfemənɪst/ ***noun*** [C], ***adj.***

femur /ˈfiːmə(r)/ ***noun*** [C] (ANATOMY) the large thick bone in the top part of your leg above the knee SYN **thigh bone** ➲ picture on **page 80**

fence[1] ⊶ /fens/ ***noun*** [C] a line of wooden or metal posts joined by wood, wire, metal, etc. to divide land or to keep in animals
IDM **sit on the fence** → SIT

fence[2] ⊶ /fens/ ***verb*** **1** [T] (ARCHITECTURE) to surround land with a fence **2** [I] to fight with a long thin pointed weapon (**a foil**) as a sport
PHR V **fence sb/sth in 1** to surround sb/sth with a fence: *They fenced in their garden to make it more private.* **2** to limit sb's freedom: *She felt fenced in by so many responsibilities.*
fence sth off to separate one area from another with a fence

fencing /ˈfensɪŋ/ ***noun*** [U] the sport of fighting with long thin pointed weapons (**foils**)

fend /fend/ ***verb***
PHR V **fend for yourself** to look after yourself without help from anyone else: *It's time Ben left home and learned to fend for himself.*
fend sb/sth off to defend yourself from sb/sth that is attacking you: *Politicians usually manage to fend off awkward questions.*

fender /ˈfendə(r)/ ***noun*** [C] **1** (*AmE*) = WING (4) **2** a low metal frame in front of an open fire that stops coal or wood falling out

feng shui /ˌfeŋ ˈʃuːi; ˌfʌŋ ˈʃweɪ/ ***noun*** [U] a Chinese system for deciding the right position for a building and for placing objects inside a building in order to make people feel comfortable and happy

fennel /ˈfenl/ ***noun*** [U] a plant that has a thick round part at the base of the leaves with a strong taste. The base is used as a vegetable and the seeds and leaves are also used in cooking.

feral /ˈferəl/ ***noun*** [C] (used about animals) living wild, especially after escaping from life as a pet or on a farm

ferment[1] /fəˈment/ ***verb*** [I,T] (BIOLOGY, CHEMISTRY) to change or make the chemistry of sth change, especially sugar changing to alcohol: *The wine is starting to ferment.* ▶ **fermentation** /ˌfɜːmenˈteɪʃn/ ***noun*** [U]

ferment[2] /ˈfɜːment/ ***noun*** [U] a state of political or social excitement and change: *The country is in ferment and nobody's sure what will happen next.*

fermium /ˈfɜːmiəm/ ***noun*** [U] (*symbol* **Fm**) (CHEMISTRY) a chemical element. **Fermium** is a very rare RADIOACTIVE metal. ℹ For more information on the periodic table of elements, look at pages R34-5.

fern /fɜːn/ ***noun*** [C] a green plant with no flowers and a lot of long thin leaves ➲ picture at **plant**

ferocious /fəˈrəʊʃəs/ ***adj.*** very aggressive and violent: *a ferocious beast/attack/storm/war*
▶ **ferociously** ***adv.***

ferocity /fəˈrɒsəti/ ***noun*** [U] violence; cruel and aggressive behaviour ➲ adjective **fierce**

ferret /ˈferɪt/ ***noun*** [C] a small aggressive animal used for hunting RATS and RABBITS

ferrite /ˈferaɪt/ ***noun*** [U] **1** (PHYSICS) a chemical containing iron, used in electrical devices such as radio and television AERIALS **2** (CHEMISTRY) a form of pure iron that is found in steel which contains low amounts of CARBON

ferrous /ˈferəs/ ***adj.*** (CHEMISTRY) containing iron

ferry[1] /ˈferi/ ***noun*** [C] (*pl.* **ferries**) a boat that carries people, vehicles or goods across a river or across a narrow part of the sea: *a car ferry*

ferry[2] /ˈferi/ ***verb*** [T] (*pres. part.* **ferrying**; *3rd person sing. pres.* **ferries**; *pt, pp* **ferried**) to carry people or goods in a boat or other vehicle from one place to another, usually for a short distance: *Could you ferry* *us across to the island? ◇ We share the job of ferrying the children to school.*

fertile /ˈfɜːtaɪl/ ***adj.*** **1** (AGRICULTURE) (used about land or soil) that plants grow well in **2** (BIOLOGY) (used about people, animals or plants) that can produce babies, fruit or new plants **3** (used about a person's mind) full of ideas: *a fertile imagination* OPP **infertile** ➲ look at **sterile**. ▶ **fertility** /fəˈtɪləti/ ***noun*** [U]: *Nowadays women can take drugs to increase their fertility* (=their chances of having a child). OPP **infertility**

fertilize (also **-ise**) /ˈfɜːtəlaɪz/ ***verb*** [T] **1** (BIOLOGY) to put a male seed into an egg, a plant or a female animal so that a baby, fruit or a young animal starts to develop **2** (AGRICULTURE) to put natural or artificial substances on soil in order to make plants grow better ▶ **fertilization** (also **-isation**) /ˌfɜːtəlaɪˈzeɪʃn/ ***noun*** [U]

fertilizer (also **-iser**) /ˈfɜːtɪlaɪzə(r)/ ***noun*** [C,U] (AGRICULTURE) a natural or chemical substance that is put on land or soil to make plants grow better ➲ look at **manure**

fervent /ˈfɜːvənt/ ***adj.*** having or showing very strong feelings about sth: *She's a fervent believer in women's rights.* ◇ *a fervent belief/hope/desire* ▶ **fervently** ***adv.***

fervour (*AmE* **fervor**) /ˈfɜːvə(r)/ ***noun*** [U] very strong feelings about sth; enthusiasm

fester /ˈfestə(r)/ ***verb*** [I] **1** (used about a cut or an injury) to become infected: *a festering sore/wound* **2** (used about an unpleasant situation, feeling or thought) to become more unpleasant because you do not deal with it successfully

festival 🔑 /ˈfestɪvl/ ***noun*** [C] **1** a series of plays, films, musical performances, etc. often held regularly in one place: *the Cannes Film Festival* ◇ *a jazz festival* **2** a day or time when people celebrate sth (especially a religious event): *Christmas is an important Christian festival.*

festive /ˈfestɪv/ ***adj.*** happy, because people are enjoying themselves celebrating sth: *the festive season* (=Christmas)

festivity /feˈstɪvəti/ ***noun*** **1** **festivities** [pl.] happy events when people celebrate sth: *The festivities went on until dawn.* **2** [U] being happy and

fertilization

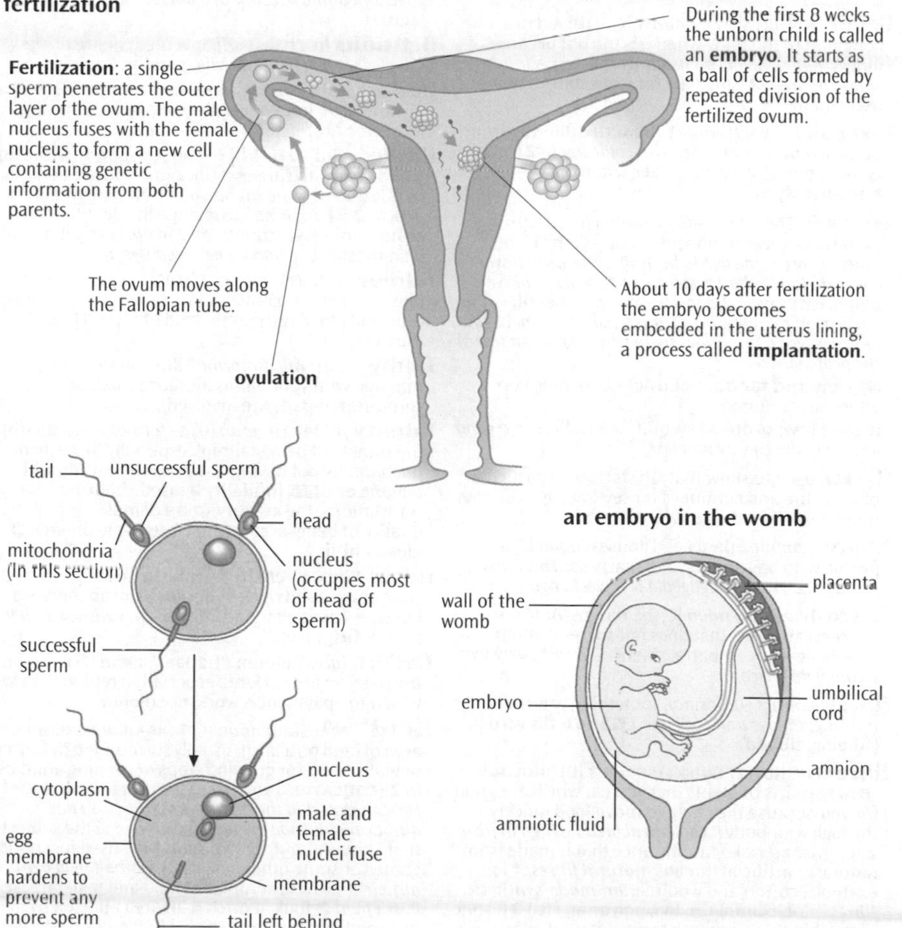

celebrating sth: *The wedding was followed by three days of festivity.*

fetal (*AmE*) = FOETAL

fetch 🔑 /fetʃ/ ***verb*** [T] **1** (*especially BrE*) to go to a place and bring back sb/sth: *Shall I fetch you your coat?/Shall I fetch your coat for you?* **2** (used about goods) to be sold for the price mentioned: *'How much will your car fetch?' 'It should fetch about £900.'*

fetus (*AmE*) = FOETUS

feud /fjuːd/ ***noun*** [C] **a ~ (between A and B); a ~ (with sb) (over sb/sth)** an angry and serious argument between two people or groups that continues over a long period of time: *a family feud* (= within a family or between two families) ▶ **feud** ***verb*** [I]

feudal /ˈfjuːdl/ ***adj.*** (**POLITICS**, **HISTORY**) connected with the system of FEUDALISM: *the feudal system*

feudalism /ˈfjuːdəlɪzəm/ ***noun*** [U] (**POLITICS**, **HISTORY**) the social system which existed in the Middle Ages in Europe, in which people worked and fought for a person who owned land and received land and protection from him in return

fever 🔑 /ˈfiːvə(r)/ ***noun*** **1** [C,U] (**HEALTH**) a condition of the body when it is too hot because of illness: *A high fever can be dangerous, especially in small children.* **2** [sing.] **a ~ (of sth)** a state of nervous excitement

feverish /ˈfiːvərɪʃ/ ***adj.*** **1** (**HEALTH**) suffering from or caused by a fever: *a feverish cold/dream* **2** (usually *before* a noun) showing great excitement ▶ **feverishly** ***adv.***

few 🔑 /fjuː/ ***det., adj., pronoun*** (used with a plural countable noun and a plural verb) **1** not many: *Few people live to be 100.* ◇ *There are fewer cars here today than yesterday.* ◇ *Few of the players played really well.* **2** **a few** a small number of; some: *a few people* ◇ *a few hours/days/years* ◇ *I'll meet you later. I've got a few things to do first.* ◇ *I knew a few of the people there.*

IDM **few and far between** not happening very often; not common

a good few; quite a few quite a lot: *It's been a good few years since I saw him last.*

ff. ***abbr.*** used to show that sth starts on a particular page or line and continues for several pages or lines more: *British Politics, p10ff.*

fiancé (*feminine* **fiancée**) /fiˈɒnseɪ/ ***noun*** [C] a person who has promised to marry sb: *This is my fiancée Liz. We got engaged a few weeks ago.*

fiasco /fiˈæskəʊ/ ***noun*** [C] (*pl.* **fiascos**, *AmE also* **fiascoes**) an event that does not succeed, often in a way that causes embarrassment: *Our last party was a complete fiasco.*

fib /fɪb/ ***noun*** [C] (*informal*) something you say that is not true: *Please don't tell fibs.* SYN **lie** ▶ **fib** ***verb*** [I] (**fibbing**; **fibbed**)

fibre (*AmE* **fiber**) /ˈfaɪbə(r)/ ***noun*** **1** [U] (**BIOLOGY**, **HEALTH**) parts of plants that you eat which are good for you because they help to move food quickly through your body: *Wholemeal bread is **high in fibre**.* **2** [C,U] a material or a substance that is made from natural or artificial threads: ***natural fibres*** (= for example, cotton and wool) ◇ ***man-made/synthetic fibres*** (= for example, nylon, polyester, etc.) **3** [C] one of the thin threads which form a natural or artificial substance: *cotton/wood/nerve/muscle fibres*

fibreglass (*AmE* **fiberglass**) /ˈfaɪbəglɑːs/ (*also* **glass ˈfibre**) ***noun*** [U] a material made from small threads of plastic or glass, used for making small boats, parts of cars, etc.

ˌfibre ˈoptics (*AmE* **ˌfiber ˈoptics**) ***noun*** [U] (**PHYSICS**) the use of thin FIBRES of glass, etc. for sending information in the form of light signals ▶ **ˌfibre-ˈoptic** ***adj.***: *fibre-optic cables*

fibrin /ˈfaɪbrɪn; ˈfɪb-/ ***noun*** [U] a substance that forms in the blood to help stop the blood from flowing, for example when there is a cut

fibrinogen /faɪˈbrɪnədʒən/ ***noun*** [U] (**BIOLOGY**) a substance in the blood from which FIBRIN is made

fibula /ˈfɪbjələ/ ***noun*** [C] (**ANATOMY**) the outer bone of the two bones in the lower part of your leg, between your knee and your foot ➲ look at **tibia** ➲ picture on **page 80**

fickle /ˈfɪkl/ ***adj.*** always changing your mind or your feelings so you cannot be trusted: *a fickle friend*

fiction /ˈfɪkʃn/ ***noun*** [U] (**LITERATURE**) stories, novels, etc. which describe events and people that are not real: *I don't read much fiction.* OPP **non-fiction** ➲ look at **fact**

fictional /ˈfɪkʃənl/ ***adj.*** (**LITERATURE**) not real or true; only existing in stories, novels, etc.: *The book gave a fictional account of a doctor's life.* ➲ look at **factual**

fictitious /fɪkˈtɪʃəs/ ***adj.*** invented; not real: *The novel is set in a fictitious village called Paradise.*

fiddle¹ /ˈfɪdl/ ***noun*** [C] (*informal*) **1** = VIOLIN **2** (*BrE*) a dishonest action, especially one connected with money: *a tax fiddle*

fiddle² /ˈfɪdl/ ***verb*** **1** [I] **~ (about/around) (with sth)** to play with sth carelessly, because you are nervous or not thinking: *He sat nervously, fiddling with a pencil.* **2** [T] (*informal*) to change the details or facts of sth (business accounts, etc.) in order to get money dishonestly: *She fiddled her expenses form.*

fiddler /ˈfɪdlə(r)/ ***noun*** [C] (**MUSIC**) a person who plays a VIOLIN (= a musical instrument with strings), especially to play a certain kind of music (**folk music**)

fiddly /ˈfɪdli/ ***adj.*** (*informal*) difficult to do or manage with your hands (because small or complicated parts are involved)

fidelity /fɪˈdeləti/ ***noun*** [U] **1** (*formal*) **~ (to sb/sth)** the quality of being faithful, especially to a wife or husband by not having a sexual relationship with anyone else OPP **infidelity** **2** (used about translations, the REPRODUCTION of music, etc.) the quality of being accurate or close to the original ➲ look at **hi-fi**

fidget /ˈfɪdʒɪt/ ***verb*** [I] **~ (with sth)** to keep moving your body, hands or feet because you are nervous, bored, excited, etc.: *She fidgeted nervously with her keys.* ▶ **fidgety** ***adj.***

fief /fiːf/ (*also* **fiefdom** /ˈfiːfdəm/) ***noun*** [C] (**LAW**) (in the past) an area of land, especially a rented area for which the payment is work, not money

field¹ 🔑 /fiːld/ ***noun*** [C] **1** (**AGRICULTURE**) an area of land on a farm, usually surrounded by fences or walls, used for growing crops or keeping animals in **2** (**EDUCATION**) an area of study or knowledge: *He's an expert in the field of economics.* ◇ *That question is outside my field* (= not one of the subjects that I know about). **3** an area of land used for sports, games or some other activity: *a football field* ◇ *an airfield* (= where aeroplanes land and take off) ◇ *a battlefield* ➲ look at **pitch** **4** an area affected by or included in sth: *a magnetic field* ◇ *It's outside my field of vision* (= I can't see it). ➲ picture at **magnet**

5 (GEOLOGY) an area of land where oil, coal or other minerals are found: *a coalfield ◇ a North Sea oilfield*

field² /fi:ld/ *verb* (SPORT) **1** [I,T] (in CRICKET, BASEBALL, etc.) to (be ready to) catch and throw back the ball after sb has hit it ❶ When one team is **fielding**, the other is **batting**.
2 [T] to choose a team for a game of football, CRICKET, etc.: *New Zealand is fielding an excellent team for the next match.*

'field day *noun*
IDM **have a field day** to get the opportunity to do sth you enjoy, especially sth other people disapprove of: *The newspapers always have a field day when there's a political scandal.*

fielder /'fi:ldə(r)/ *noun* [C] (SPORT) (in CRICKET, BASEBALL etc.) a member of the team that is trying to catch the ball rather than hit it

'field event *noun* [C] (SPORT) a sport, such as jumping and throwing, that is not a race and does not involve running ➲ look at **track event**

'field sports *noun* [pl.] (*BrE*) outdoor sports such as hunting, fishing and shooting

'field trip *noun* [C] (EDUCATION) a journey made to study sth in its natural environment: *We went on a geography field trip.*

fieldwork /'fi:ldwɜ:k/ *noun* [U] (EDUCATION) practical research work done outside school, college, etc.

fiend /fi:nd/ *noun* [C] **1** a very cruel person
2 (*informal*) a person who is very interested in one particular thing: *a health fiend* SYN **fanatic**

fiendish /'fi:ndɪʃ/ *adj.* **1** very unpleasant or cruel **2** (*informal*) clever and complicated: *a fiendish plan* ▸ **fiendishly** *adv.*

fierce /fɪəs/ *adj.* **1** angry, aggressive and frightening: *The house was guarded by fierce dogs.* **2** very strong; violent: *fierce competition for jobs ◇ a fierce attack* ➲ noun **ferocity** ▸ **fiercely** *adv.*

fiery /'faɪəri/ *adj.* **1** looking like fire: *She has fiery red hair.* **2** quick to become angry: *a fiery temper*

FIFA /'fi:fə/ *abbr.* (SPORT) the organization that is in charge of international football

fifteen /ˌfɪf'ti:n/ *number* 15 ➲ note at **six**

fifteenth /ˌfɪf'ti:nθ/ *ordinal number*, *noun* [C] 15th ➲ note at **sixth¹**

fifth¹ /fɪfθ/ *ordinal number* 5th ➲ note at **sixth¹**

fifth² /fɪfθ/ *noun* [C] the FRACTION ⅕; one of five equal parts of sth

fiftieth /'fɪftiəθ/ *ordinal number*, *noun* [C] 50th ➲ note at **sixth¹**

fifty /'fɪfti/ *number* **1** 50 **2 the fifties** [pl.] numbers, years or temperatures from 50 to 59: *She was born in the fifties.* ➲ note at **six**

ˌfifty-'fifty *adj.*, *adv.* equal or equally (between two people, groups, etc.): *You've got **a fifty-fifty chance** of winning. ◇ We'll divide the money fifty-fifty.*

fig /fɪg/ *noun* [C] (a type of tree with) a soft sweet fruit full of small seeds that grows in warm countries and is often eaten dried

fig. *abbr.* **1** figure, ILLUSTRATION: *See diagram at fig. 2.* **2** FIGURATIVE(LY)

fight¹ 🔑 /faɪt/ *verb* (*pt*, *pp* **fought** /fɔ:t/) **1** [I,T] ~ (**against sb**) to use physical strength, guns, weapons, etc. against sb/sth: *They gathered soldiers to fight the invading army. ◇ My younger brothers were always fighting.* **2** [I,T] ~ (**against sth**) to try very hard to stop or prevent sth: *to fight a fire/a decision/prejudice ◇ to fight against crime/disease* **3** [I] ~ (**for sth/to do sth**) to try very hard to get or keep sth: *to fight for your rights* ➲ note at **campaign¹** **4** [I] ~ (**with sb**) (**about/over sth**) to argue: *It's not worth fighting about money.* ➲ look at **argue**, **quarrel²**
PHR V **fight back** to protect yourself with actions or words by attacking sb who has attacked you: *If he hits you again, fight back!*

fight² 🔑 /faɪt/ *noun* **1** [C] **a** ~ (**with sb/sth**); **a** ~ (**between A and B**) the act of using physical force against sb/sth: *Don't **get into a fight** at school, will you? ◇ Fights broke out between rival groups of fans.* **2** [sing.] **a** ~ (**against/for sth**) (**to do sth**) the work done trying to destroy, prevent or achieve sth: *Workers won their fight against the management to stop the factory from closing down.* **3** [C] (*especially AmE*) **a** ~ (**with sb/sth**) (**about/over sth**) an argument about sth: *I **had a fight** with my mum over what time I had to be home.* **4** [U] the desire to continue trying or fighting: *I've had some bad luck but I've still got plenty of fight in me.*
IDM **pick a fight** → PICK¹

fighter /'faɪtə(r)/ *noun* [C] **1** (*also* **fighter plane**) a small fast military aircraft used for attacking enemy aircraft: *a fighter pilot ◇ a jet fighter* **2** a BOXER (= a person who fights in sport) or a person who fights in a war

fighting 🔑 /'faɪtɪŋ/ *noun* [U] an occasion when people fight: *There has been street fighting in many parts of the city today.*

figurative /'fɪgərətɪv/ *adj.* **1** (*abbr.* **fig.**) (LANGUAGE) (used about a word or an expression) not used with its exact meaning but used for giving an IMAGINATIVE description or a special effect: *'He exploded with rage' is a figurative use of the verb 'to explode'.* ➲ look at **literal**, **metaphor** **2** (ART) showing people, animals and objects as they really look: *a figurative artist* ➲ look at **abstract**
▸ **figuratively** *adv.*

figure¹ 🔑 /'fɪgə(r)/ *noun* [C] **1** an amount (in numbers) or a price: *The unemployment figures are lower this month. ◇ What sort of figure are you thinking of for your house?* **2** (MATHEMATICS) a written sign for a number (0 to 9): *Write the numbers in figures, not words. ◇ He has a six-figure income/an income in six figures* (= £100000 or more). *◇ Interest rates are now down to single figures* (= less than 10%). *◇ double figures* (= 10 to 99) **3 figures** [pl.] (*informal*) (MATHEMATICS) mathematics: *I don't **have a head for figures*** (= I'm not very good with numbers). **4** a well-known or important person: *an important political figure* **5** the shape of the human body, especially a woman's body that is attractive: *She's got a beautiful slim figure.* **6** a person that you cannot see very clearly or do not know: *Two figures were coming towards us in the dark. ◇ There were two figures on the right of the photo that I didn't recognize.* **7** (*abbr.* **fig.**) a diagram or picture used in a book to explain sth: *Figure 3 shows the major cities of Italy.*
IDM **a ballpark figure/estimate** → BALLPARK
facts and figures → FACT
in round figures/numbers → ROUND¹

figure² 🔑 /'fɪgə(r)/ *verb* **1** [I] ~ (**as sth**) (**in/among sth**) to be included in sth; to be an important part of sth: *Women don't figure much in his novels.* SYN **feature** **2** [T] ~ (**that**) (*especially AmE*) to think or guess sth: *I figured he was here because I saw his car outside.*
IDM **it/that figures** (*informal*) that is what I expected
PHR V **figure on sth/on doing sth** (*especially AmE*)

to include sth in your plans: *I figure on arriving in New York on Wednesday.*
figure sb/sth out to find an answer to sth or to understand sb: *I can't figure out why she married him in the first place.*

ˌfigure of ˈeight (*AmE* ˌ**figure ˈeight**) **noun** [C] (*pl.* **figures of eight**) something in the shape of an 8

ˌfigure of ˈspeech **noun** [C] (*pl.* **figures of speech**) (LANGUAGE) a word or expression used not with its original meaning but in an IMAGINATIVE way to make a special effect

filament /ˈfɪləmənt/ **noun** [C] **1** (PHYSICS) a thin wire in a LIGHT BULB (= the glass part of an electric lamp) that produces light when electricity is passed through it ➲ picture at **bulb** **2** a long thin piece of sth that looks like a thread: *glass/metal filaments* **3** (BIOLOGY) a long thin part of the STAMEN (= the male part of a flower) that supports the part where POLLEN is produced (**anther**) ➲ picture at **flower**

file[1] 🔑 AW /faɪl/ **noun** [C] **1** a box or a cover that is used for keeping papers together **2** (COMPUTING) a collection of information or material on one subject that is stored together in a computer or on a disk, with a particular name: *to open/close a file* ◇ *to create/delete/save/copy a file* **3** a ~ (**on sb/sth**) a collection of papers or information about sb/sth kept inside a file: *The police are now keeping a file on all known football hooligans.* **4** a metal tool with a rough surface used for shaping hard substances or for making surfaces smooth: *a nail file* ➲ picture at **tool**
IDM **on file** kept in a file: *We have all the information you need on file.*
in single file in a line, one behind the other
the rank and file → RANK[1]

file[2] AW /faɪl/ **verb** **1** [T] ~ **sth** (**away**) to put and keep documents, etc. in a particular place so that you can find them easily; to put sth into a file: *I filed the letters away in a drawer.* **2** [I,T] ~ (**for sth**) (LAW) to present sth so that it can be officially recorded and dealt with: *to file for divorce* ◇ *to* ***file a claim/complaint/lawsuit*** **3** [I] ~ **in, out, past, etc.** to walk or march in a line: *The children filed out of the classroom.* **4** [T] ~ **sth** (**away, down, etc.**) to shape sth hard or make sth smooth with a file: *to file your nails*

filibuster /ˈfɪlɪbʌstə(r)/ **noun** [C] (*especially AmE*) (POLITICS) a long speech made in a parliament in order to delay a vote ▶ **filibuster** **verb** [I]

filing AW /ˈfaɪlɪŋ/ **noun** **1** [U] the act of putting documents, letters, etc. into a file **2** [C] (*especially AmE*) something that is placed in an official record: *a bankruptcy filing* **3 filings** [pl.] very small pieces of metal, made when a larger piece of metal is filed: *iron filings*

fill 🔑 /fɪl/ **verb** **1** [I,T] ~ (**sth/sb**) (**with sth**) to make sth full or to become full: *Can you fill the kettle for me?* ◇ *The news filled him with excitement.* ◇ *The room filled with smoke within minutes.* **2** [T] to take a position or to use up your time doing sth: *I'm afraid that teaching post has just been filled* (= somebody has got the job). ◇ *How do you fill your day now you're not working?*
PHR V **fill sth in** (*AmE also* **fill sth out**) **1** to complete a form, etc. by writing information on it: *Could you fill in the application form, please?* **2** to fill a hole or space completely to make a surface flat: *You had better fill in the cracks in the wall before you paint it.*
fill (sth) up to become or to make sth completely full: *There weren't many people at first but then the room filled up.*

ˈfiller cap **noun** [C] a lid for covering the end of the pipe through which petrol is put into a motor vehicle

fillet (*AmE* **filet**) /ˈfɪlɪt/ **noun** [C,U] a piece of meat or fish with the bones taken out

filling[1] /ˈfɪlɪŋ/ **noun** **1** [C] the material that a dentist uses to fill a hole in a tooth: *a gold filling* **2** [C,U] the food inside a SANDWICH, pie, cake, etc.

filling[2] /ˈfɪlɪŋ/ **adj.** (used about food) that makes you feel full: *Pasta is very filling.*

filly /ˈfɪli/ **noun** [C] (*pl.* **fillies**) a young female horse ➲ look at **colt**

film[1] 🔑 /fɪlm/ **noun** **1** (*AmE also* **movie**) [C] (ARTS AND MEDIA) a story, play, etc. shown in moving pictures at the cinema or on television: *Let's go to the cinema – there's a good film on this week.* ◇ *to* ***watch a film*** *on TV* ◇ *to* ***see a film*** *at the cinema* ◇ *a horror/documentary/feature film* ◇ *a film director/producer/critic* **2** [U] (ARTS AND MEDIA) the art or business of making films: *She's studying film and theatre.* ◇ *the film industry* **3** [U] (ARTS AND MEDIA) moving pictures of real events: *The programme included film of the town one hundred years ago.* **4** [C,U] a roll of thin plastic that you use in a camera to take photographs: *to have a film developed* ◇ *Fast film is better if there's not much light.* ➲ picture at **camera** **5** [C, usually sing.] a thin layer of a substance or material: *The oil forms a film on the surface of the water.*

film[2] 🔑 /fɪlm/ **verb** [I,T] (ARTS AND MEDIA) to record moving pictures of an event, story, etc. with a camera: *A lot of westerns are filmed in Spain.* ◇ *The man was filmed stealing from the shop.*

ˈfilm star **noun** [C] (ARTS AND MEDIA) a person who is a well-known actor in films

filter[1] /ˈfɪltə(r)/ **noun** [C] **1** (SCIENCE) a device for holding back solid substances from a liquid or gas that passes through it: *a coffee filter* ◇ *an oil filter* **2** a piece of coloured glass used with a camera to hold back some types of light **3** (COMPUTING) a program that stops certain types of electronic information, email, etc. being sent to a computer

filter[2] /ˈfɪltə(r)/ **verb** **1** [T] to pass a liquid through a filter: *Do you filter your water?* **2** [T] (COMPUTING) to use a special program to check the content of emails or websites before they are sent to your computer **3** [I] ~ **in, out, through, etc.** to move slowly and/or in small amounts: *Sunlight filtered into the room through the curtains.* ◇ (*figurative*) *News of her illness filtered through to her friends.*
PHR V **filter sth out (of sth)** to remove sth that you do not want from a liquid, light, etc. using a special device or substance: *This chemical filters impurities out of the water.* ◇ (*figurative*) *This test is designed to filter out weaker candidates before the interview stage.*

ˈfilter paper **noun** [U, C] (SCIENCE) a type of paper used in chemistry for separating solids from liquids; a piece of this paper used, for example, in making coffee ➲ picture at **filtration**

filth /fɪlθ/ **noun** [U] **1** unpleasant dirt: *The room was covered in filth.* **2** sexual words or pictures that cause offence

filthy /ˈfɪlθi/ **adj.** (**filthier**; **filthiest**) **1** very dirty **2** (used about language, books, films, etc.) connected with sex, and causing offence

filtrate /ˈfɪltreɪt/ ***noun*** [C] (CHEMISTRY) a liquid that has passed through a FILTER (=a device containing paper, sand, chemicals, etc. to remove material that is not wanted from the liquid that is passed through it) ➲ picture at **filtration**

filtration

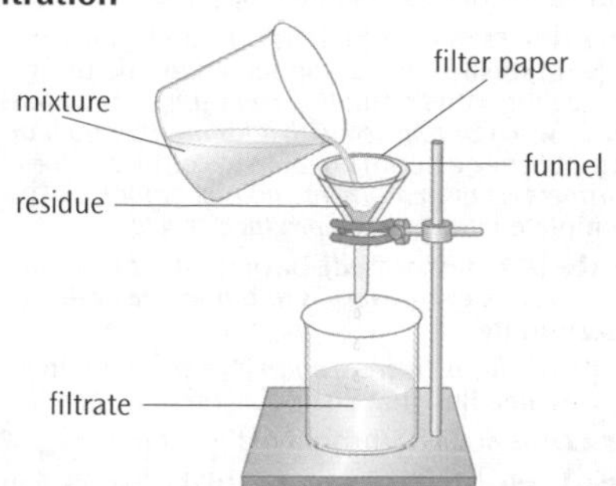

filtration /fɪlˈtreɪʃn/ ***noun*** [U] (CHEMISTRY) the process of passing a liquid or gas through a FILTER (=a device containing paper, sand, chemicals, etc. that remove material that is not wanted from the liquid or gas that is passed through it)

fin /fɪn/ ***noun*** [C] **1** (BIOLOGY) one of the parts of a fish that it uses for swimming ➲ picture on **page 29** **2** a flat, thin part that sticks out of an aircraft, a vehicle, etc. to improve its balance and movement through the air or water ➲ picture at **plane**

final[1] 🔑 AW /ˈfaɪnl/ ***adj.*** **1** (only *before* a noun) last (in a series): *This will be the final lesson of our course.* ◇ *I don't want to miss the final episode of that serial.* **2** not to be changed: *The judge's decision is always final.* ◇ *I'm not lending you the money, and that's final!*

IDM **the last/final straw** → STRAW

final[2] 🔑 AW /ˈfaɪnl/ ***noun*** **1** [C] (SPORT) the last game or match in a series of competitions or sporting events: *The first two runners in this race go through to the final.* ➲ look at **semi-final** **2 finals** [pl.] (EDUCATION) the exams you take in your last year at university

finale /fɪˈnɑːli/ ***noun*** [C] (ARTS AND MEDIA, MUSIC) the last part of a piece of music, an OPERA, a show, etc.

finalist /ˈfaɪnəlɪst/ ***noun*** [C] a person who is in the final[2](1) of a competition ➲ look at **semi-finalist**

finality AW /faɪˈnæləti/ ***noun*** [U] the quality of being final and impossible to change: *the finality of death*

finalize (also **-ise**) AW /ˈfaɪnəlaɪz/ ***verb*** [T] to make firm decisions about plans, dates, etc.: *Have you finalized your holiday arrangements yet?*

finally 🔑 AW /ˈfaɪnəli/ ***adv.*** **1** after a long time or delay: *It was getting dark when the plane finally took off.* SYN **eventually** **2** used to introduce the last in a list of things: *Finally, I would like to say how much we have all enjoyed this evening.* SYN **lastly** **3** in a definite way so that sth will not be changed: *We haven't decided finally who will get the job yet.*

finance[1] 🔑 AW /ˈfaɪnæns/ ***noun*** (FINANCE) **1** [U] the money you need to start or support a business, etc.: *How will you raise the finance to start the project?* **2** [U] the activity of managing money: *Who is the new Minister of Finance?* ◇ *an expert in finance* **3 finances** [pl.] the money a person, company, country, etc. has to spend: *What are our finances like at the moment* (=how much money have we got)?

finance[2] 🔑 AW /ˈfaɪnæns; fəˈnæns/ ***verb*** [T] (FINANCE) to provide the money to pay for sth: *Your trip will be financed by the company.*

financial 🔑 /faɪˈnænʃl; fəˈnæ-/ ***adj.*** (FINANCE) connected with money: *The business got into financial difficulties.* ➲ note at **economic**
▸ **financially** ***adv.*** /-ʃəli/

fiˌnancial ˈyear (*AmE* **ˌfiscal ˈyear**) ***noun*** [C, usually sing.] (FINANCE) a period of twelve months over which the accounts and taxes of a company or a person are calculated

financier AW /faɪˈnænsiə(r); fə-/ ***noun*** [C] (FINANCE) a person who lends large amounts of money to businesses

finch /fɪntʃ/ ***noun*** [C] a small bird with a short strong beak ➲ picture on **page 29**

find[1] 🔑 /faɪnd/ ***verb*** [T] (*pt, pp* **found** /faʊnd/) **1** to discover sth that you want or that you have lost after searching for it: *Did you find the pen you lost?* ◇ *After six months she finally found a job.* ◇ *Scientists haven't yet found a cure for colds.* ◇ *I hope you find an answer to your problem.* **2** to discover sth by chance: *I've found a piece of glass in this milk.* ◇ *We went into the house and found her lying on the floor.* ◇ *This animal can be found* (=exists) *all over the world.* **3** to have an opinion about sth because of your own experience: *I find that book very difficult to understand.* ◇ *We didn't find the film at all funny.* ◇ *How are you finding life as a student?* **4** to suddenly realize or see sth: *I got home to find that I'd left the tap on all day.* ◇ *Ben turned a corner and suddenly found himself in the port.* **5** to arrive at sth naturally; to reach sth: *Water always finds its own level.* ◇ *These birds* ***find their way*** *to Africa every winter.*

IDM **find fault (with sb/sth)** to look for things that are wrong with sb/sth and complain about them

find your feet to become confident and independent in a new situation

PHR V **find (sth) out** to get some information; to discover a fact: *Have you found out how much the tickets cost?* ◇ *I later found out that Will had been lying to me.*

find sb out to discover that sb has done sth wrong: *He had used a false name for years before they found him out.*

find[2] /faɪnd/ ***noun*** [C] a thing or a person that has been found, especially one that is valuable or useful: *Archaeologists made some interesting finds when they dug up the field.* ◇ *This new young player is quite a find!*

finder /ˈfaɪndə(r)/ ***noun*** [C] a person or thing that finds sth

finding /ˈfaɪndɪŋ/ ***noun*** [C, usually pl.] information that is discovered as a result of research into sth: *the findings of a survey/report/committee*

fine[1] 🔑 /faɪn/ ***adj.*** **1** in good health, or happy and comfortable: *'How are you?' '****Fine thanks****.'* ◇ *'Do you want to change places?' 'No I'm fine here, thanks.'* **2** all right; acceptable: *'Do you want some more milk in your coffee?' 'No* ***that's fine****, thanks.'* ◇ *Don't cook anything special – a sandwich will be fine.* ◇ *The hotel rooms were fine but the food was awful.* **3** (used about weather) bright with SUNLIGHT; not raining: *Let's hope it stays fine for the match tomorrow.* **4** (only *before* a noun) of very good quality, beautiful, well made: *a fine piece of work* ◇ *fine detail/carving/china* **5** very thin or narrow: *That hairstyle's no good for me*

– *my hair's too fine.* ◇ *You must use a fine pencil for the diagrams.* OPP **thick** **6** made of very small pieces, grains, etc.: *Salt is finer than sugar.* OPP **coarse** **7** difficult to notice or understand: *I couldn't understand **the finer points** of his argument.* ◇ *There's **a fine line between** being reserved and being unfriendly.*

fine² 🔑 /faɪn/ ***noun*** [C] (LAW) a sum of money that you have to pay for breaking a law or rule: *a parking fine* ◇ *You'll **get a fine** if you park your car there.* ▶ **fine** ***verb*** [T] ~ **sb (for sth/doing sth)**: *He was fined £50 for driving without lights.*

fine 'art ***noun*** [U] (also **fine 'arts** [pl.]) (ART) forms of art, especially painting, drawing and SCULPTURE, that are created to be beautiful rather than useful

finely 🔑 /'faɪnli/ ***adv.*** **1** into small pieces: *The onions must be finely chopped for this recipe.* **2** very accurately: *a finely tuned instrument*

finger¹ 🔑 /'fɪŋgə(r)/ ***noun*** [C] one of the five parts at the end of each hand: *little finger, ring finger, middle finger, forefinger (or index finger), thumb* ➲ picture on **page 80**

IDM **cross your fingers; keep your fingers crossed** to hope that sb/sth will be successful or lucky: *I'll keep my fingers crossed for you in your exams.* ◇ *There's nothing more we can do now – just cross our fingers and hope for the best.*

have green fingers → GREEN¹

snap your fingers → SNAP¹

finger² /'fɪŋgə(r)/ ***verb*** [T] to touch or feel sth with your fingers

fingering /'fɪŋgərɪŋ/ ***noun*** [U,C] (MUSIC) the positions in which you put your fingers when playing a musical instrument

fingermark /'fɪŋgəmɑːk/ ***noun*** [C] a mark on sth made by a dirty finger

fingernail /'fɪŋgəneɪl/ (*also* **nail**) ***noun*** [C] the thin hard layer that covers the outer end of each finger ➲ picture on **page 80**

fingerprint /'fɪŋgəprɪnt/ ***noun*** [C] (LAW) the mark made by the skin of a finger, used for identifying people: *The burglar left his fingerprints all over the house.*

fingertip /'fɪŋgətɪp/ ***noun*** [C] the end of a finger

IDM **have sth at your fingertips** to have sth ready for quick and easy use: *They asked some difficult questions but luckily I had all the facts at my fingertips.*

finish¹ 🔑 /'fɪnɪʃ/ ***verb*** **1** [I,T] ~ **(sth/doing sth)** to complete sth or reach the end of sth: *What time does the film finish?* ◇ *Haven't you finished yet? You've taken ages!* ◇ *The Ethiopian runner won and the Kenyans finished second and third.* ◇ *Finish your work quickly!* ◇ *Have you finished typing that letter?* **2** [T] ~ **sth (off/up)** to eat, drink or use the last part of sth: *Finish up your milk, Tony!* ◇ *Who finished off all the bread?* **3** [T] ~ **sth (off)** to complete the last details of sth or make sth perfect: *He stayed up all night to finish off the article he was writing.* ◇ *He's just **putting the finishing touches to** his painting.*

PHR V **finish sb/sth off** (*informal*) to kill sb/sth; to be the thing that makes sb unable to continue: *The cat played with the mouse before finishing it off.* ◇ *I was very tired towards the end of the race, and that last hill finished me off.*

finish with sb (*informal*) to end a relationship with sb: *Sally's not going out with David any more – she finished with him last week.*

finish with sth to stop needing or using sth: *I'll borrow that book when you've finished with it.*

finish² 🔑 /'fɪnɪʃ/ ***noun*** [C] **1** the last part or end of sth: *There was a dramatic finish to the race when two runners fell.* ◇ *I enjoyed the film **from start to finish**.* **2** the last covering of paint, polish, etc. that is put on a surface to make it look good

finished 🔑 /'fɪnɪʃt/ ***adj.*** **1** (not *before* a noun) ~ **(with sb/sth)** having stopped doing sth, using sth or dealing with sb/sth: *'Are you using the computer?' 'Yes, I won't be finished with it for another hour or so.'* **2** (not *before* a noun) not able to continue: *The business is finished – there's no more money.* **3** made; completed: *the finished product/article*

finite AW /'faɪnaɪt/ ***adj.*** having a definite limit or a fixed size: *The world's resources are finite.* OPP **infinite**

fir /fɜː(r)/ (*also* **'fir tree**) ***noun*** [C] a tree with thin leaves (**needles**) that do not fall off in winter

'fir cone ***noun*** [C] the fruit of the FIR tree

fire¹ 🔑 /'faɪə(r)/ ***noun*** **1** [C,U] the flames, light and heat and often smoke that are produced when sth burns, especially flames that are out of control and destroy buildings, trees, etc.: *Firemen struggled for three hours to **put out the fire**.* ◇ *It had been a dry summer so there were many forest fires.* ◇ *In very hot weather, dry grass can **catch fire*** (=start burning). ◇ *Did someone **set fire to** that pile of wood?* ◇ *Help! The frying pan's **on fire**!* **2** [C] burning wood or coal used for warming people or cooking food: *They tried to **light a fire** to keep warm.* ◇ *It's cold – don't let the fire go out!* **3** [C] a machine for heating a room, etc.: *a gas/an electric fire* **4** [U] shooting from guns: *The soldiers came **under fire** from all sides.* ◇ *I could hear gunfire in the distance.*

IDM **get on/along like a house on fire** → HOUSE¹

open fire → OPEN²

come/be under fire be strongly criticized: *The government has come under fire from all sides for its foreign policy.*

fire² 🔑 /'faɪə(r)/ ***verb*** **1** [I,T] ~ **(sth) (at sb/sth)**; ~ **(sth) (on/into sb/sth)** to shoot bullets, etc. from a gun or other weapon: *Can you hear the guns firing?* ◇ *The soldiers fired on the crowd, killing twenty people.* ◇ *She fired an arrow at the target.* ◇ *(figurative) If you stop firing questions at me I might be able to answer!* **2** [T] (*informal*) to remove an employee from a job: *He was fired for always being late.* **3** [T] ~ **sb with sth** to produce a strong feeling in sb: *Her speech fired me with determination.* **4** [T] (ART) to heat a CLAY object to make it hard and strong: *to fire pottery* ◇ *to fire bricks in a kiln*

'fire alarm ***noun*** [C] a bell or other signal to warn people that there is a fire

firearm /'faɪərɑːm/ ***noun*** [C] a gun that you can carry

'fire brigade (*AmE* **'fire department**) ***noun*** [C, with sing. or pl. verb] an organization of people trained to deal with fires

-fired /'faɪəd/ (in compounds) using the fuel mentioned: *gas-fired central heating*

'fire engine ***noun*** [C] a special vehicle that carries equipment for dealing with large fires

'fire escape ***noun*** [C] a special STAIRCASE on the outside of a building that people can go down if there is a fire

'fire extinguisher (*also* **extinguisher**) ***noun*** [C] a metal container with water or chemicals inside that you use for stopping small fires

firefighter /'faɪəfaɪtə(r)/ ***noun*** [C] a person whose job is to stop fires

firelight /ˈfaɪəlaɪt/ ***noun*** [U] the light that comes from a fire

fireman /ˈfaɪəmən/ (*pl.* **-men** /-mən/) = FIREFIGHTER

fireplace /ˈfaɪəpleɪs/ ***noun*** [C] the open place in a room where you light a fire

fireproof /ˈfaɪəpruːf/ ***adj.*** able to take great heat without burning or being badly damaged: *a fireproof door*

fireside /ˈfaɪəsaɪd/ ***noun*** [sing.] the part of a room beside the fire: *Come and sit by the fireside.*

ˈfire station ***noun*** [C] a building where FIREFIGHTERS wait to be called, and where the vehicles that they use are kept

firewall /ˈfaɪəwɔːl/ ***noun*** [C] (COMPUTING) a part of a computer system that is designed to prevent people from getting information without authority but still allows them to receive information that is sent to them

firewood /ˈfaɪəwʊd/ ***noun*** [U] wood used for burning on fires

firework /ˈfaɪəwɜːk/ ***noun*** [C] a small object that burns or explodes with coloured lights and loud sounds, used for entertainment

ˈfiring line ***noun***

IDM **be in the firing line 1** to be in a position where you can be shot at **2** to be in a position where people can criticize you or say that sth is your fault

ˈfiring squad ***noun*** [C] a group of soldiers who have been ordered to shoot and kill a prisoner

firm[1] **O—** /fɜːm/ ***noun*** [C, with sing. or pl. verb] (**BUSINESS**) a business or company: *Which firm do you work for?*

firm[2] **O—** /fɜːm/ ***adj.*** **1** able to stay the same shape when pressed; quite hard: *a firm mattress* ◇ *firm muscles* **2** strong and steady or not likely to change: *She kept a firm grip on her mother's hand.* ◇ *a firm commitment/decision/offer* **3** ~ **(with sb)** strong and in control: *He's very firm with his children.* ◇ *You have to show the examiner that you have a firm grasp* (= good knowledge) *of grammar.* ▶ **firmness** ***noun*** [U]

IDM **a firm hand** strong control or discipline

firm[3] /fɜːm/ ***verb*** **1** [T] to make sth become stronger or harder: *Firm the soil around the plant.* ◇ *This product claims to firm your body in six weeks.* **2** [I] ~ **(to/at...)** (**BUSINESS**) to become steady or rise steadily: *Rank's shares firmed 3p to 696p.*

PHR V **firm up sth 1** to make arrangements more final and fixed: *The company has not yet firmed up its plans for expansion.* ◇ *The precise details still have to be firmed up.* **2** to make sth harder or more solid: *A few weeks of aerobics will firm up that flabby stomach.*

firmly **O—** /ˈfɜːmli/ ***adv.*** in a strong or definite way: *'I can manage,' she said firmly.* ◇ *It is now **firmly established** as one of the leading brands in the country.* ◇ *Keep your eyes **firmly fixed** on the road ahead.*

first[1] **O—** /fɜːst/ ***det., ordinal number*** coming before all others; that has not happened before: *She's expecting her first baby.* ◇ *the first half of the game* ◇ *You've won first prize!* ◇ *What were your first impressions of this country when you arrived?* ◇ *King Charles I* (= King Charles the First) ➲ look at **one**

IDM **at first glance/sight** when first seen or examined: *The task seemed impossible at first glance, but it turned out to be quite easy.*

first/last thing → THING

first[2] **O—** /fɜːst/ ***adv.*** **1** before any others: *Sue arrived first at the party.* ◇ *Mike's very competitive – he always wants to **come first** when he plays a game.* ◇ *Do you want to **go first** or second?* **2** before doing anything else: *I'll come out later. I've got to finish my homework first.* **3** the time before all the other times; for the first time: *Where did you first meet your husband?* **4** at the beginning: *When I first started my job I hated it.* **5** used for introducing the first thing in a list: *There are several people I would like to thank: First, my mother.* SYN **firstly**

IDM **at first** at the beginning: *At first I thought he was joking, but then I realized he was serious.*

come first to be more important to sb than anything else

first and foremost more than anything else; most importantly

first come, first served (*informal*) people will be dealt with, served, seen, etc. strictly in the order in which they arrive: *Tickets can be bought here on a first come, first served basis.*

first of all as the first thing (to be done or said): *In a moment I'll introduce our guest speaker, but first of all, let me thank you all for coming.*

first off (*informal*) before anything else: *First off, let's decide who does what.*

head first → HEAD[1]

first[3] **O—** /fɜːst/ ***noun, pronoun*** **1 the first** [C] (*pl.* **the first**) the first person or thing, people or things: *Are we the first to arrive?* ◇ *I'd be **the first to admit*** (= I will most willingly admit) *I might be wrong.* **2 a first** [sing.] an important event that is happening for the first time: *This operation is a first in medical history.* **3** [C] (*BrE*) (**EDUCATION**) the highest mark given for a university degree: *He **got a first** in History.*

IDM **from the (very) first** from the beginning

ˌfirst ˈaid ***noun*** [U] (**HEALTH**) medical help that you give to sb who is hurt or ill before the doctor arrives: *a first aid kit/course* ◇ *to give sb first aid*

the ˌFirst Aˈmendment ***noun*** [sing.] (**LAW**) the statement in the US Constitution that protects freedom of speech and religion and the right to meet in peaceful groups

ˌfirst ˈbalcony (*AmE*) = DRESS CIRCLE

firstborn /ˈfɜːstbɔːn/ ***noun*** [C] (*old-fashioned*) a person's first child ▶ **firstborn** ***adj.*** (only *before* a noun)

ˌfirst ˈclass ***noun*** [U] **1** the best and most expensive seats or accommodation on a train, ship, etc. **2** the quickest form of mail: *First class costs more.* **3** (**EDUCATION**) the highest standard of degree given by a British university ▶ **first class** ***adv.***: *to travel first class* ◇ *I sent the letter first class on Tuesday.*

ˌfirst-ˈclass ***adj.*** **1** in the best group; of the highest standard: *a first-class player* SYN **excellent** **2** giving or using the best and most expensive type of service: *Ten first-class stamps, please.* ◇ *first-class rail travel* **3** (only *before* a noun) (**EDUCATION**) used to describe a university degree of the highest class from a British university: *She was awarded a first-class degree in French.*

ˈfirst degree ***noun*** (*especially BrE*) (**EDUCATION**) an academic qualification given by a university or college, for example a BA or BSc, that is given to sb who does not already have a degree in that subject: *What was your first degree in?* ◇ *to study geography at first-degree level*

ˌfirst-deˈgree ***adj.*** (only *before* a noun) **1** (*especially AmE*) (**LAW**) (used about murder) of the most serious kind **2** (**HEALTH**) (used about burns) of the least serious of three kinds, affecting only the surface of the skin ➲ look at **second-degree**, **third-degree**

ˌfirst ˈfloor *noun* [C] (usually **the first floor**) **1** (*BrE*) the floor of a building above the one on street level (**the ground floor**): *I live in a flat **on the first floor**.* ◇ *a first-floor flat* **2** (*AmE*) the floor of a building on street level

ˌfirst ˈgear *noun* [C] the lowest GEAR (=the machinery that turns power into movement) on a car, bicycle, etc.: *To move off, **put the car into first gear** and slowly release the clutch.*

ˌfirst geneˈration *noun* [sing.] people who have left their country to go and live in a new country ▶ **first-generation** *adj.*: *first-generation Caribbeans in the UK*

ˌfirst-ˈhand *adj.*, *adv.* (used about information, experience, a story, etc.) heard, seen or learnt by yourself, not from other people: *He gave me a first-hand account of the accident* (=he had seen it). ◇ *I've experienced the problem first-hand, so I know how you feel.*

ˌfirst ˈlady *noun* [C, usually sing.] **the First Lady** (POLITICS) (in the US) the wife of the President or the leader of a state

firstly /ˈfɜːstli/ *adv.* used to introduce the first point in a list: *They were angry, firstly because they had to pay extra, and secondly because no one had told them about it.* SYN **first**

ˈfirst name *noun* [C] the first of your names that come before your family name: *'What's Mr Munn's first name?' 'Robert, I think.'*

the ˌfirst ˈperson *noun* [sing.] **1** (LANGUAGE) the set of pronouns and verb forms used by a speaker to refer to himself or herself, or to a group including himself or herself: *'I am' is the first person singular of the verb 'to be'.* ◇ *'I', 'me', 'we' and 'us' are first-person pronouns.* **2** (LITERATURE) the style of writing a novel, telling a story, etc. as if it happened to you: *The author writes in the first person.* ➲ look at **the second person**, **the third person**

ˌfirst-ˈrate *adj.* excellent; of the best quality

ˌFirst ˈWorld *noun* [sing.] the rich industrial countries of the world ➲ look at **Third World**

fiscal /ˈfɪskl/ *adj.* (FINANCE) connected with government or public money, especially taxes

ˌfiscal ˈyear *noun* (*AmE*) (FINANCE) = FINANCIAL YEAR

fish¹ 🔑 /fɪʃ/ *noun* (*pl.* **fish** or **fishes**) **1** [C] an animal that lives and breathes in water and swims: *How many fish have you caught?* ◇ *The list of endangered species includes nearly 600 fishes.* ➲ picture on **page 29** **2** [U] fish as food: *We're having fish for dinner.*

fish² 🔑 /fɪʃ/ *verb* [I] **1** ~ (**for sth**) to try to catch fish: *He's fishing for trout.* ◇ *They often **go fishing** at weekends.* **2** ~ (**around**) (**in sth**) (**for sth**) to search for sth in water or in a deep or hidden place: *She fished (around) for her keys in the bottom of her bag.*

PHR V **fish for sth** to try to get sth you want in an indirect way: *to fish for an invitation*

fish sth out (**of sth**) to take or pull sth out (of sth) especially after searching for it: *After the accident they fished the car out of the canal.*

fishcake /ˈfɪʃkeɪk/ *noun* [C] (*especially BrE*) pieces of fish mixed with potato that are made into a flat round shape, covered with BREADCRUMBS (=very small pieces of bread) and fried

fisherman /ˈfɪʃəmən/ *noun* [C] (*pl.* **-men** /-men/) a person who catches fish either as a job or as a sport ➲ look at **angler**

fishing 🔑 /ˈfɪʃɪŋ/ *noun* [U] catching fish as a job, sport or hobby: *Fishing is a major industry in Iceland.* ➲ look at **angling**

ˈfishing line *noun* [C,U] a long thread with a sharp hook attached, that is used for catching fish

ˈfishing rod *noun* [C] a long thin stick with a FISHING LINE and a hook on it, that is used for catching fish

fishmeal /ˈfɪʃmiːl/ *noun* [U] dried fish made into powder and used as animal food or used by farmers to make plants grow well

fishmonger /ˈfɪʃmʌŋɡə(r)/ *noun* (*BrE*) **1** [C] a person whose job is to sell fish **2 the fishmonger's** [sing.] a shop that sells fish

fishy /ˈfɪʃi/ *adj.* **1** tasting or smelling like a fish: *a fishy smell* **2** (*informal*) seeming suspicious or dishonest: *The police thought the man's story sounded extremely fishy.*

fission /ˈfɪʃn/ *noun* [U] **1** (*also* **ˌnuclear ˈfission**) (PHYSICS) the action or process of dividing the central part (**nucleus**) of an atom, when a large amount of energy is created ➲ look at **fusion** **2** (BIOLOGY) the division of cells into new cells as a method of creating more cells

fissure /ˈfɪʃə(r)/ *noun* [C] (GEOLOGY) a long deep crack in sth, especially in rock or in the earth

fist /fɪst/ *noun* [C] a hand with the fingers closed together tightly: *She **clenched her fists** in anger.*

fit¹ 🔑 /fɪt/ *verb* (**fitting**; **fitted**; *AmE pt, pp* usually **fit**) **1** [I,T] to be the right size or shape for sb/sth: *These jeans fit very well.* ◇ *This dress doesn't fit me any more.* ◇ *This key doesn't fit in the lock.* **2** [T] ~ (**sb/sth**) **in/into/on/onto sth** to find or have enough space for sb/sth: *I can't fit into these trousers any more.* ◇ *Can you fit one more person in the car?* ◇ *I can't fit all these books onto the shelf.* **3** [T] to put or fix sth in the right place: *The builders are fitting new windows today.* ◇ *I can't fit these pieces of the model together.* **4** [T] to be or make sb/sth right or suitable: *I don't think Ruth's fitted for such a demanding job.* ◇ *That description fits Jim perfectly.*

PHR V **fit sb/sth in**; **fit sb/sth in/into sth** to find time to see sb or to do sth: *The doctor managed to fit me in this morning.*

fit in (**with sb/sth**) to be able to live, work, etc. in an easy and natural way (with sb/sth): *The new girl found it difficult to fit in (with the other children) at school.*

fit² 🔑 /fɪt/ *adj.* (**fitter**; **fittest**) **1** ~ (**for sth/to do sth**) (HEALTH) strong and in good physical health (especially because of exercise): *Swimming is a good way to **keep fit**.* ◇ *My dad's almost recovered from his illness, but he's still not fit enough for work.* ◇ *She goes to keep-fit classes.* OPP **unfit** **2** ~ (**for sb/sth**); ~ **to do sth** good enough; suitable: *Do you think she is fit for the job?* ◇ *These houses are not fit (for people) to live in.*

fit³ /fɪt/ *noun* **1** [C] (HEALTH) a sudden attack of an illness, in which sb loses CONSCIOUSNESS and their body may make violent movements: *to have fits* **2** [C] a sudden short period of coughing, laughing, etc. that you cannot control: *a fit of laughter/anger* **3** [sing.] (usually after an adjective) the way in which sth (for example a piece of clothing) fits: *a good/bad/tight/loose fit*

fitness /ˈfɪtnəs/ *noun* [U] **1** the condition of being strong and healthy: *Fitness is important in most sports.* **2** ~ **for sth/to do sth** the quality of being suitable: *The directors were not sure about his fitness for the job.*

'fitness centre (*AmE* **'fitness center**) ***noun*** [C] (SPORT) a place where people go to do physical exercise in order to stay or become healthy and fit

fitted /'fɪtɪd/ ***adj.*** made or cut to fit a particular space and fixed there: *a fitted carpet* ◇ *a fitted kitchen* (=one with fitted cupboards)

fitting[1] /'fɪtɪŋ/ ***adj.*** **1** (*formal*) right; suitable: *It would be fitting for the Olympics to be held in Greece, as that is where they originated.* **2 -fitting** used in compounds to describe how clothes, etc. fit: *a tight-fitting dress* ◇ *loose-fitting trousers*

fitting[2] /'fɪtɪŋ/ ***noun*** [C, usually pl.] (ARCHITECTURE) the things that are fixed in a building or on a piece of furniture but that can be changed or moved if necessary ➲ look at **fixture**

'fitting room ***noun*** [C] a room in a shop where you can put on clothes to see how they look ➲ look at **changing room**

five /faɪv/ ***number*** **1** 5 ➲ Look at **fifth** (=5th). **2 five-** (used in compounds) having five of the thing mentioned: *a five-day week* ◇ *a five-hour flight*

fiver /'faɪvə(r)/ ***noun*** [C] (*BrE, informal*) a FIVE-POUND note; £5

'five-star ***adj.*** (TOURISM) having five stars in a system that measures quality. Five stars usually represents the highest quality: *a five-star hotel*

fix[1] ⊶ /fɪks/ ***verb*** [T] **1** to put sth firmly in place so that it will not move: *Can you fix this new handle to the door?* ◇ (*figurative*) *I found it difficult to keep my mind fixed on my work.* **2** to repair sth: *The electrician's coming to fix the cooker.* SYN **repair** **3 ~ sth (up)** to decide or arrange sth: *We need to fix the price.* ◇ *Have you fixed (up) a date for the party?* **4 ~ sth (up)** to get sth ready: *They're fixing up their spare room for the new baby.* **5** (usually passive) (*informal*) (SPORT) to arrange the result of sth in a way that is not honest or fair: *Fans of the losing team suspected that the match had been fixed.* **6 ~ sth (for sb)** (*especially AmE*) to prepare sth (especially food or drink): *Can I fix you a drink/a drink for you?*
PHR V **fix sb up (with sth)** (*informal*) to arrange for sb to have sth: *I can fix you up with a place to stay.*

fix[2] /fɪks/ ***noun*** [C] **1** a solution to a problem, especially one that is easy or temporary: *There's no* ***quick fix*** *to this problem.* **2** [usually sing.] (*informal*) a difficult situation: *I was* ***in a real fix*** *– I'd locked the car keys inside the car.* **3** [usually sing.] (*informal*) a result that is dishonestly arranged

fixation /fɪk'seɪʃn/ ***noun*** [C] **a ~ (with sth)** an interest in sth that is too strong and not normal

fixative /'fɪksətɪv/ ***noun*** [C, U] **1** (ART) a substance that is used to prevent colours or smells from changing or becoming weaker, for example in photography, art or the making of PERFUME **2** a substance that is used to stick things together or keep things in position

fixed ⊶ /fɪkst/ ***adj.*** **1** already decided: *a fixed date/price/rent* **2** not changing: *He has such fixed ideas that you can't discuss anything with him.*
IDM **(of) no fixed abode/address** (*formal*) (with) no permanent place to live: *Daniel Stephens, of no fixed abode, was found guilty of robbery.*

fixed 'assets ***noun*** [pl.] (BUSINESS) land, buildings and equipment that are owned and used by a company

fixed 'costs ***noun*** [pl.] (BUSINESS) the costs that a business must pay that do not change even if the amount of work produced changes

fixture /'fɪkstʃə(r)/ ***noun*** [C] **1** (SPORT) a sporting event arranged for a particular day: *to arrange/cancel/play a fixture* **2** [usually pl.] (ARCHITECTURE) a piece of furniture or equipment that is fixed in a house or building and sold with it: *Does the price of the house include fixtures and fittings?* ➲ look at **fitting**

fizz /fɪz/ ***noun*** [U] the bubbles in a liquid and the sound they make: *This lemonade's lost its fizz.* ▶ **fizz** ***verb*** [I]

fizzle /'fɪzl/ ***verb***
PHR V **fizzle out** to end in a weak or disappointing way: *The game started well but it fizzled out in the second half.*

fizzy /'fɪzi/ ***adj.*** (used about a drink) containing many small bubbles of gas ➲ look at **still**

,fizzy 'drink (*AmE* **soda**) ***noun*** [C] a sweet drink without alcohol that contains many small bubbles

fjord /'fjɔːd/ ***noun*** [C] (GEOGRAPHY) a long narrow piece of sea between CLIFFS, especially in Norway

flabbergasted /'flæbəgɑːstɪd/ ***adj.*** (*informal*) extremely surprised and/or shocked

flabby /'flæbi/ ***adj.*** having too much soft fat instead of muscle: *a flabby stomach*

flaccid /'flæsɪd/ ***adj.*** **1** (*formal*) soft and weak: *flaccid muscles* **2** (used about parts of plants) not containing enough water

flag[1] ⊶ /flæg/ ***noun*** [C] a piece of cloth with a pattern or picture on it, often tied to a pole (**flagpole**) or rope and used as a symbol of a country, club, etc. or as a signal

flag[2] /flæg/ ***verb*** [I] (**flagging**; **flagged**) to become tired or less strong
PHR V **flag sb/sth down** to wave to sb in a car to make them stop

flagrant /'fleɪgrənt/ ***adj.*** (only *before* a noun) (used about an action) shocking because it is done in a very obvious way and shows no respect for people, laws, etc.

flail /fleɪl/ ***verb*** [I,T] to wave or move about without control: *The insect's legs were flailing in the air.* ◇ *Don't flail your arms about like that – you might hurt someone.*

flair /fleə(r)/ ***noun*** **1 (a) ~ for sth** [sing.] a natural ability to do sth well: *She has a flair for languages.* **2** [U] the quality of being interesting or having style: *That poster is designed with her usual flair.*

flak /flæk/ ***noun*** [U] (*informal*) criticism: *He'll get some flak for missing that goal.*

flake[1] /fleɪk/ ***noun*** [C] a small thin piece of sth: *snowflakes* ◇ *flakes of paint*

flake[2] /fleɪk/ ***verb*** [I] **~ (off)** to come off in FLAKES: *This paint is very old – it's beginning to flake (off).*

flamboyant /flæm'bɔɪənt/ ***adj.*** **1** (used about a person) acting in a loud, confident way that attracts attention: *a flamboyant gesture/style/personality* **2** bright and easily noticed: *flamboyant colours* ▶ **flamboyance** ***noun*** [U] ▶ **flamboyantly** ***adv.***

flame[1] ⊶ /fleɪm/ ***noun*** **1** [C,U] an area of bright burning gas that comes from sth that is on fire: *The flame of the candle flickered by the open window.* ◇ *The house was* ***in flames*** *when the fire engine arrived.* ◇ *The piece of paper* ***burst into flames*** *in the fire* (=suddenly began to burn strongly). **4** [C] (*informal*) (COMPUTING) an angry or insulting message sent to sb by email or on the Internet

flame[2] *verb* **1** [I] (*written*) to burn with a bright flame: *The logs flamed on the hearth.* ◇ (*figurative*) *Hope flamed in her.* **2** [I,T] (*written*) to become red as a result of a strong emotion; to make sth become red: *Her cheeks flamed with rage.* **3** [T] (*informal*) (COMPUTING) to send sb an angry or insulting message by email or on the Internet

flamenco /flə'meŋkəʊ/ *noun* [U] (MUSIC) a traditional kind of dancing and music from Spain

flaming /'fleɪmɪŋ/ *adj.* (only *before* a noun) **1** (used about anger, an argument, etc.) violent: *We had a flaming argument over the bills.* **2** burning brightly **3** (*slang*) used as a mild swear word: *I can't get in – I've lost the flaming key.* **4** (used about colours, especially red) very bright: *flaming red hair* ◇ *a flaming sunset*

flamingo /flə'mɪŋgəʊ/ *noun* [C] (*pl.* **flamingoes** or **flamingos**) a large pink and red bird that has long legs and stands in water

flammable /'flæməbl/ (*especially BrE* **inflammable**) *adj.* (CHEMISTRY) able to burn easily: ***highly flammable*** *liquids* OPP **non-flammable**

flan /flæn/ *noun* [C,U] a round open pie that is filled with fruit, cheese, vegetables, etc.

flank[1] /flæŋk/ *noun* [C] **1** the side of an animal's body **2** the parts of an army at the sides in a battle

flank[2] /flæŋk/ *verb* [T] (usually passive) to be placed at the side or sides of: *The road was flanked by trees.*

flannel /'flænl/ *noun* **1** a type of soft WOOLLEN cloth **2** = FACECLOTH

flap[1] /flæp/ *noun* [C] a piece of material, paper, etc. that is fixed to sth at one side only, often covering an opening: *the flap of an envelope* ➲ picture at **plane**
IDM **be in/get into a flap** (*informal*) to be in/get into a state of worry or excitement

flap[2] /flæp/ *verb* (**flapping**; **flapped**) **1** [I,T] to move (sth) up and down or from side to side, especially in the wind: *The sails were flapping in the wind.* ◇ *The bird flapped its wings and flew away.* **2** [I] (*informal*) to become worried or excited: *Stop flapping – it's all organized!*

flare[1] /fleə(r)/ *verb* [I] to burn for a short time with a sudden bright flame
PHR V **flare up 1** (used about a fire) to suddenly burn more strongly **2** (used about violence, anger, etc.) to start suddenly or to become suddenly worse

flare[2] /fleə(r)/ *noun* **1** [sing.] a sudden bright light or flame **2** [C] a thing that produces a bright light or flame, used especially as a signal

flared /fleəd/ *adj.* (used about trousers and skirts) becoming wider towards the bottom

flash[1] 🔑 /flæʃ/ *verb* **1** [I,T] to produce or make sth produce a sudden bright light for a short time: *The neon sign above the door flashed on and off all night.* ◇ *That lorry driver's flashing his lights at us* (= in order to tell us sth). **2** [I] to move very fast: *I saw something flash past the window.* ◇ *Thoughts kept flashing through my mind and I couldn't sleep.* **3** [T] to show sth quickly: *The detective flashed his card and went straight in.* **4** [T] to send sth by radio, television, etc.: *The news of the disaster was flashed across the world.*
PHR V **flash back** (used about a person's thoughts) to return suddenly to a time in the past: *Something he said made my mind flash back to my childhood.*

flash[2] 🔑 /flæʃ/ *noun* **1** [C] a sudden bright light that comes and goes quickly: *a flash of lightning* **2** [C] **a ~ (of sth)** a sudden strong feeling or idea: *a flash of inspiration* ◇ *The idea came to me in a flash.* **3** [C,U] a bright light that you use with a camera for taking photographs when it is dark; the device for producing this light
IDM **in/like a flash** very quickly
(as) quick as a flash → QUICK[1]

flashback /'flæʃbæk/ *noun* [C,U] a part of a film, play, etc. that shows sth that happened before the main story

'flash flood *noun* [C] a sudden flood of water caused by heavy rain

flashlight /'flæʃlaɪt/ (*AmE*) = TORCH (1)

'flash memory *noun* [U] (COMPUTING) computer memory that does not lose data when the power supply is lost

flashy /'flæʃi/ *adj.* (**flashier**; **flashiest**) attracting attention by being very big, bright and expensive: *a flashy sports car*

flask /flɑːsk/ *noun* [C] **1** (*BrE also* **Thermos™**) a type of container for keeping a liquid hot or cold **2** (SCIENCE) a bottle with a narrow neck that is used for storing and mixing chemicals in scientific work ➲ picture at **laboratory**

flat[1] 🔑 /flæt/ *adj., adv.* (**flatter**; **flattest**) **1** smooth and level, with no parts that are higher than the rest: *The countryside in Essex is quite flat* (= there are not many hills). ◇ *I need a flat surface to write this letter on.* ◇ *a flat roof* ◇ *She lay flat on her back in the sunshine.* ◇ *He* ***fell flat on his face*** *in the mud.* **2** not high or deep: *You need flat shoes for walking.* ◇ *a flat dish* **3** without much interest or energy: *Things have been a bit flat since Alex left.* **4** (only *before* a noun) (used about sth that you say or decide) that will not change; firm: *He answered our request with a flat 'No!'* **5** (MUSIC) half a note lower than the stated note ➲ look at **sharp 6** (MUSIC) lower than the correct note: *That last note was flat. Can you sing it again?* ◇ *You're singing flat.* ➲ look at **sharp 7** (used about a drink) not fresh because it has lost its bubbles: *Open a new bottle. That lemonade has* ***gone flat.*** **8** (*BrE*) (used about a battery) no longer producing electricity; not working: *We couldn't start the car because the battery was completely flat.* **9** (used about a tyre) without enough air in it: *This tyre looks flat – has it got a puncture?* **10** (used about the cost of sth) that is the same for everyone; that is fixed: *We charge a flat fee of £20, however long you stay.* **11** (used for emphasizing how quickly sth is done) in exactly the time mentioned and no longer: *She can get up and out of the house in ten minutes flat.*
IDM **fall flat** (used about a joke, a story, an event, etc.) to fail to produce the effect that you wanted
flat out as fast as possible; without stopping: *He's been working flat out for two weeks and he needs a break.*

flat[2] 🔑 /flæt/ *noun* **1** [C] (*especially AmE* **apartment**) a set of rooms that is used as a home (usually in a large building): *Do you rent your flat or have you bought it?* ❶ **Apartment** is the normal word in American English. In British English we say **apartment** when talking about a flat we are renting for a holiday, etc. rather than to live in: *We're renting an apartment in the South of France.* **2** [C] (*symbol* ♭) (MUSIC) a note which is half a note lower than the note with the same letter ➲ look at **sharp** ➲ picture at **music 3** [sing.] **the ~ (of sth)** the flat part or side of sth: *the flat of your hand* **4** [C] (*especially AmE*) a tyre on a vehicle that has no air in it

flatfish /'flætfɪʃ/ *noun* [C] (*pl.* **flatfish**) any sea fish with a flat body: *Plaice and turbot are flatfish.*

flatly /ˈflætli/ ***adv.*** **1** in a direct way; absolutely: *He flatly denied the allegations.* **2** in a way that shows no interest or emotion

flatten /ˈflætn/ ***verb*** [I,T] ~ **(sth) (out)** to become or make sth flat: *The countryside flattens out as you get nearer the sea.* ◇ *The storms have flattened crops all over the country.*

flatter /ˈflætə(r)/ ***verb*** [T] **1** to say nice things to sb, often in a way that is not sincere, because you want to please them or because you want to get an advantage for yourself **2** ~ **yourself (that)** to choose to believe sth good about yourself although other people may not think the same: *He flatters himself that he speaks fluent French.* **3** (usually passive) to give pleasure or honour to sb: *I felt very flattered when they gave me the job.*

flattering /ˈflætərɪŋ/ ***adj.*** making sb look or sound more attractive or important than they really are

flattery /ˈflætəri/ ***noun*** [U] saying good things about sb/sth that you do not really mean

flatworm /ˈflætwɜːm/ ***noun*** [C] (**BIOLOGY**) a very simple WORM (=a long thin creature with no bones or legs) with a flat body

flaunt /flɔːnt/ ***verb*** [T] to show sth that you are proud of so that other people will admire it

flautist /ˈflɔːtɪst/ (*AmE* **flutist**) ***noun*** [C] (**MUSIC**) a person who plays a FLUTE (=a musical instrument that you blow into)

flavour[1] ⊶ (*AmE* **flavor**) /ˈfleɪvə(r)/ ***noun*** [C,U] **1** the taste (of food): *Do you think a little salt would improve the flavour?* ◇ *ten different flavours of yoghurt* ◇ *yoghurt in ten different flavours* **2** [sing.] an idea of the particular quality or character of sth: *This video will give you a flavour of what the city is like.*

flavour[2] ⊶ (*AmE* **flavor**) /ˈfleɪvə(r)/ ***verb*** [T] to give flavour to sth: *Add a little nutmeg to flavour the sauce.* ◇ *strawberry-flavoured milkshake*

flavouring (*AmE* **flavoring**) /ˈfleɪvərɪŋ/ ***noun*** [C,U] something that you add to food or drink to give it a particular taste: *no artificial flavourings*

flaw /flɔː/ ***noun*** [C] **1 a** ~ **(in sth)** a mistake in sth that makes it not good enough, or means that it does not function as it should: *There are some flaws in her argument.* **2** a mark or crack in an object that means that it is not perfect **3 a** ~ **(in sb/sth)** a bad quality in sb's character ▸ **flawed** ***adj.***: *I think your plan is flawed.*

flawless /ˈflɔːləs/ ***adj.*** perfect; with no faults or mistakes: *a flawless diamond*

flax /flæks/ ***noun*** [U] a plant with blue flowers, grown for its STEM (=the main long thin part of a plant) that is used to make thread and its seeds that are used to make LINSEED OIL

flea /fliː/ ***noun*** [C] a very small jumping insect without wings that lives on animals, for example cats and dogs. **Fleas** bite people and animals and make them scratch. ➲ picture on **page 29**

ˈflea market ***noun*** [C] (**BUSINESS**) a market, often in a street, that sells old and used goods

fleck /flek/ ***noun*** [C, usually pl.] a very small mark on sth; a very small piece of sth: *After painting the ceiling, her hair was covered with flecks of blue paint.*

fledgling (*BrE also* **fledgeling**) /ˈfledʒlɪŋ/ ***noun*** [C] **1** (**BIOLOGY**) a young bird that has just learnt to fly **2** (usually before another noun) a person, an organization or a system that is new and without experience: *fledgling democracies*

flee /fliː/ ***verb*** [I,T] (*pt, pp* **fled** /fled/) ~ **(to.../into...)**; ~ **(from) sb/sth** to run away or escape from sth: *The robbers fled the country with £100000.*

fleece /fliːs/ ***noun*** [C] **1** the wool coat of a sheep ➲ picture at **sheep** **2** a piece of clothing like a jacket, made of warm artificial material

fleet /fliːt/ ***noun*** [C, with sing. or pl. verb] **1** a group of ships or boats that sail together: *a fishing fleet* **2 a** ~ **(of sth)** a group of vehicles (especially taxis, buses or aircraft) that are travelling together or owned by one person

flesh ⊶ /fleʃ/ ***noun*** [U] **1** the soft part of a human or animal body (between the bones and under the skin) **2** the part of a fruit or vegetable that is soft and can be eaten

IDM **your (own) flesh and blood** a member of your family

in the flesh in person, not on television, in a photograph, etc.

make your flesh creep to make you feel disgusted and/or nervous: *The way he smiled made her flesh creep.*

flew past tense of **fly[1]**

flex[1] /fleks/ (*especially AmE* **cord**) ***noun*** [C,U] (a piece of) wire inside a plastic tube, used for carrying electricity to electrical equipment ➲ picture at **cable**
ℹ At the end of a flex there is a **plug** which you fit into a **socket** or a **power point** (*AmE* **outlet**).

flex[2] /fleks/ ***verb*** [T] to bend or move a leg, arm, muscle, etc. in order to exercise it

flexible AW /ˈfleksəbl/ ***adj.*** **1** able to bend or move easily without breaking **2** that can be changed easily: *flexible working hours* OPP **inflexible**
▸ **flexibility** AW /ˌfleksəˈbɪləti/ ***noun*** [U]

flexitime /ˈfleksitaɪm/ (*AmE usually* **flextime** /ˈflekstaɪm/) ***noun*** [U] a system in which employees work a particular number of hours each week or month but can choose when they start and finish work each day: *She works flexitime.*

flick /flɪk/ ***verb*** **1** [T] ~ **sth (away, off, onto, etc.)** to hit sth lightly and quickly with your finger or hand in order to move it: *She flicked the dust off her jacket.* ◇ *Please don't flick ash on the carpet.* **2** [I,T] ~ **(sth) (away, off, out, etc.)** to move, or to make sth move, with a quick sudden movement: *She flicked the switch and the light came on.* ▸ **flick** ***noun*** [C]

PHR V **flick/flip through sth** to turn over the pages of a book, magazine, etc. quickly without reading everything

flicker[1] /ˈflɪkə(r)/ ***verb*** [I] **1** (used about a light or a flame) to keep going on and off as it burns or shines: *The candle flickered and went out.* **2** (used about a feeling, thought, etc.) to appear for a short time: *A smile flickered across her face.* **3** to move lightly and quickly up and down: *His eyelids flickered for a second and then he lay still.*

flicker[2] /ˈflɪkə(r)/ ***noun*** [C, usually sing.] **1** a light that shines on and off quickly **2** a small, sudden movement of part of the body **3** a feeling of sth that only lasts for a short time: *a flicker of hope/interest/doubt*

flier = FLYER

flies /flaɪz/ ***noun*** [pl.] **1** plural of **fly[2]** (1) **2** (*BrE*) = FLY[2] (2) **3 the flies** (**ARTS AND MEDIA**) the space above the stage in a theatre, used for lights and for storing SCENERY (=the furniture, painted cloth, boards, etc. that are used on the stage)

flight ⊶ /flaɪt/ ***noun*** **1** [C] a journey by air: *to book a flight* ◇ *a direct/scheduled/charter flight* ◇ *They met **on a flight** to Australia.* ◇ *a manned space flight to Mars* **2** [C] an aircraft that takes you on a particular journey: *Flight number 340 from London* to New York is boarding now (=is ready for passengers to get on it). **3** [U] the action of flying: *It's unusual to see swans **in flight*** (=when they are flying). **4** [C] (ARCHITECTURE) a number of stairs or steps going up or down: *a flight of stairs* **5** [C,U] the action of running away or escaping from a dangerous or difficult situation: *the refugees' flight from the war zone*

'flight attendant ***noun*** [C] (TOURISM) a person whose job is to serve and take care of passengers on an aircraft SYN **air hostess, steward, stewardess**

'flight crew ***noun*** [C] (TOURISM) the people who work on a plane during a flight

'flight deck ***noun*** [C] **1** an area at the front of a large plane where the pilot sits to use the controls and fly the plane ➲ picture at **plane 2** a long flat surface on top of an AIRCRAFT CARRIER (=a ship that carries aircraft) where they take off and land

flightless /'flaɪtləs/ ***adj.*** (used about birds and insects) not able to fly

'flight path ***noun*** [C] the route taken by an aircraft through the air

flimsy /'flɪmzi/ ***adj.*** **1** not strong; easily broken or torn: *a flimsy bookcase* ◇ *a flimsy blouse* **2** weak; not making you believe that sth is true: *He gave a **flimsy excuse** for his absence.*

flinch /flɪntʃ/ ***verb*** [I] **1** ~ **(at sth)**; ~ **(away)** to make a sudden movement backwards because of sth painful or frightening **2** ~ **from sth/doing sth** to avoid doing sth because it is unpleasant: *She didn't flinch from telling him the whole truth.*

fling[1] /flɪŋ/ ***verb*** [T] (*pt, pp* **flung** /flʌŋ/) to throw sb/sth suddenly and carelessly or with great force: *He flung his coat on the floor.*

fling[2] /flɪŋ/ ***noun*** [C, usually sing.] a short period of fun and pleasure

flint /flɪnt/ ***noun*** **1** [U] (GEOLOGY) very hard grey stone that produces SPARKS (=small flames) when you hit it against steel **2** [C] a small piece of FLINT or metal that is used to produce SPARKS (for example in a CIGARETTE LIGHTER)

flip /flɪp/ ***verb*** (**flipping**; **flipped**) **1** [I,T] to turn (sth) over with a quick movement: *She flipped the book open and started to read.* **2** [T] to throw sth into the air and make it turn over: *Let's flip a coin to see who starts.* **3** [I] ~ **(out)** (*spoken*) to become very angry or excited: *When his father saw the damage to the car he flipped.*

PHR V **flick/flip through sth** → FLICK

'flip chart ***noun*** [C] (BUSINESS) large sheets of paper fixed at the top to a stand so that they can be turned over, used for presenting information at a talk or meeting

'flip-flop (*AmE* **thong**) ***noun*** [C, usually pl.] a simple open shoe with a thin STRAP that goes between your big toe and the toe next to it

flippant /'flɪpənt/ (also *informal* **flip**) ***adj.*** not serious enough about things that are important

flipper /'flɪpə(r)/ ***noun*** [C, usually pl.] **1** (BIOLOGY) a flat arm that is part of the body of some sea animals which they use for swimming: *Seals have flippers.* ➲ picture on **page 29 2** a rubber shoe shaped like an animal's **flipper** that people wear so that they can swim better, especially under water: *a pair of flippers*

'flip phone ***noun*** [C] a small mobile phone with a cover that opens upwards

flipping /'flɪpɪŋ/ ***adj.***, ***adv.*** (*slang*) used as a mild way of swearing: *When's the flipping bus coming?*

flirt[1] /flɜːt/ ***verb*** [I] ~ **(with sb)** to behave in a way that suggests you find sb attractive and are trying to attract them: *Who was that boy Irene was flirting with at the party?*

PHR V **flirt with sth 1** to think about doing sth (but not very seriously): *She had flirted with the idea of becoming a teacher for a while.* **2** to take risks or not worry about danger: *to flirt with death/danger/disaster*

flirt[2] /flɜːt/ ***noun*** [C] a person who often FLIRTS with people

flirtatious /flɜː'teɪʃəs/ ***adj.*** behaving in a way that shows a sexual attraction to sb that is not serious: *a flirtatious smile* ▶ **flirtatiously** ***adv.***

flit /flɪt/ ***verb*** [I] (**flitting**; **flitted**) ~ **(from A to B)**; ~ **(between A and B)** to fly or move quickly from one place to another without staying anywhere for long

float[1] 🔑 /fləʊt/ ***verb*** **1** [I] to move slowly through air or water: *The boats were floating gently down the river.* ◇ *The smell of freshly-baked bread floated in through the window.* **2** [I] ~ **(in/on sth)** to stay on the surface of a liquid and not sink: *Wood floats in water.* **3** [T] (BUSINESS) to sell shares in a company or business for the first time: *The company was floated on the stock market in 2001.* **4** [I,T] (ECONOMICS) if a government **floats** its country's money, or allows it to **float**, it allows its value to change freely according to the value of the money of other countries

float[2] /fləʊt/ ***noun*** [C] **1** a lorry or other vehicle that is decorated and used in a celebration that travels through the streets: *a carnival float* **2** a light object used in fishing that moves on the water when a fish has been caught **3** a light object used for helping people to learn to swim

floating /'fləʊtɪŋ/ ***adj.*** not fixed; not living permanently in one place: *London's floating population*

flock[1] /flɒk/ ***noun*** [C] **1** a group of sheep or birds ➲ look at **herd 2** a large number of people: *Flocks of tourists visit London every summer.*

flock[2] /flɒk/ ***verb*** [I] (used about people) to go or meet somewhere in large numbers: *People are flocking to her latest exhibition.*

floe /fləʊ/ = ICE FLOE

flog /flɒg/ ***verb*** [T] (**flogging**; **flogged**) **1** (usually passive) to hit sb hard several times with a stick or a long thin piece of leather (**whip**) as a punishment **2** (*BrE, informal*) to sell sth

flogging /'flɒgɪŋ/ ***noun*** [C,U] the act of hitting sb several times with a long thin piece of leather (**whip**) or a stick as a punishment

flood[1] 🔑 /flʌd/ ***verb*** **1** [I,T] to fill a place with water; to be filled or covered with water: *I left the taps on and flooded the bathroom.* ◇ *The River Trent floods almost every year.* **2** [I] ~ **in/into/out of sth** to go somewhere in large numbers: *Since the television programme was shown, phone calls have been flooding into the studio.* **3** [I,T] (used about a thought, feeling, etc.) to fill sb's mind suddenly: *At the end of the day all his worries came flooding back.*

flood[2] 🔑 /flʌd/ ***noun*** [C] **1** a large amount of water that has spread from a river, the sea, etc. that covers an area which should be dry: *Many people have been forced to leave their homes because of the floods.* ➲ look at **flash flood 2** a ~ **(of sth)** a large number or amount: *She received a flood of letters after the accident.*

floodlight /ˈflʌdlaɪt/ ***noun*** [C] a powerful light that is used for lighting places where sports are played, the outside of public buildings, etc.

floodlit /ˈflʌdlɪt/ ***adj.*** lit by FLOODLIGHTS: *a floodlit hockey match*

flood plain

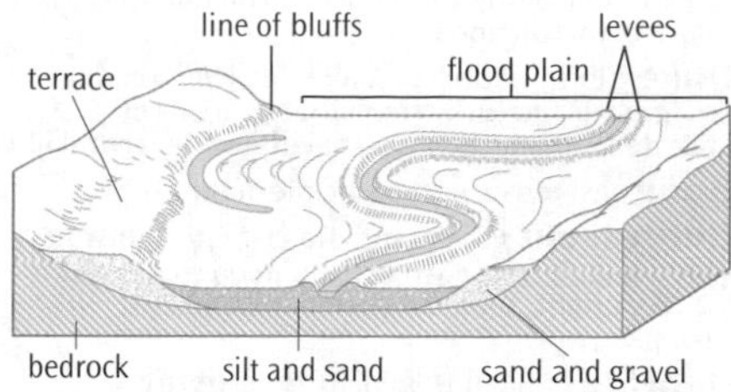

ˈflood plain ***noun*** [C] (**GEOGRAPHY**) an area of flat land beside a river that regularly becomes flooded when there is too much water in the river

floor¹ ⊶ /flɔː(r)/ ***noun*** **1** [C, usually sing.] the flat surface that you walk on indoors: *Don't come in – there's broken glass **on the floor**! ◇ a wooden/concrete/marble floor* ➲ note at **ground 2** [C] all the rooms that are on the same level of a building: *My office is **on the second floor**.* **3** [C, usually sing.] (**GEOGRAPHY**) the ground or surface at the bottom of the sea, a forest, etc.: *the ocean/valley/cave/forest floor*

floor² /flɔː(r)/ ***verb*** [T] (*informal*) to surprise or confuse sb completely with a question or a problem: *Some of the questions I was asked in the interview completely floored me.*

floorboard /ˈflɔːbɔːd/ ***noun*** [C] one of the long wooden boards used to make a floor ➲ picture at **joist**

ˈfloor plan ***noun*** [C] (**ARCHITECTURE**) a drawing of the shape of a room or building, as seen from above, showing the position of the furniture, etc.

ˈfloor show ***noun*** [C] (**ARTS AND MEDIA**) a series of performances by singers, dancers, etc. at a restaurant or club

flop¹ /flɒp/ ***verb*** [I] (**flopping**; **flopped**) **1 ~ into/onto sth**; **~ (down/back)** to sit or lie down in a sudden and careless way because you are very tired: *I was so tired that all I could do was flop onto the sofa and watch TV.* **2 ~ around, back, down, etc.** to move, hang or fall in a careless way without control: *I can't bear my hair flopping in my eyes.* **3** (**ARTS AND MEDIA**) (used about a book, film, record, etc.) to be a complete failure with the public

flop² /flɒp/ ***noun*** [C] (**ARTS AND MEDIA**) (used about a film, play, party, etc.) something that is not a success; a failure: *a box-office flop*

floppy /ˈflɒpi/ ***adj.*** soft and hanging downwards; not RIGID: *a floppy hat*

ˌfloppy ˈdisk (*also* **floppy**) (*pl.* **floppies**), *also* (**diskette**) ***noun*** [C] (**COMPUTING**) a square piece of plastic that can store information from a computer: *Don't forget to back up your files onto a floppy disk.* ➲ look at **hard disk** ➲ picture at **computer**

flora /ˈflɔːrə/ ***noun*** [pl.] (**BIOLOGY**) all the plants growing in a particular area: *He's studying the **flora and fauna** (=the plants and animals) of South America.* ➲ look at **fauna**

floral /ˈflɔːrəl/ ***adj.*** decorated with a pattern of flowers, or made with flowers

florist /ˈflɒrɪst/ ***noun*** **1** [C] a person who has a shop that sells flowers **2 the florist's** [sing.] a shop that sells flowers

floss¹ /flɒs/ ***noun*** [U] =DENTAL FLOSS

floss² /flɒs/ ***verb*** [I,T] to clean between your teeth with DENTAL FLOSS (=a type of thin thread for cleaning between the teeth): *You should floss every day to avoid gum disease.*

flotation /fləʊˈteɪʃn/ ***noun*** **1** (*also* **float**) [C,U] (**BUSINESS**) the process of selling shares in a company to the public for the first time in order to obtain money: *plans for (a) flotation on the stock exchange* **2** [U] the act of floating on or in water

flounder¹ /ˈflaʊndə(r)/ ***verb*** [I] **1** to find it difficult to speak or act (usually in a difficult or embarrassing situation): *The questions they asked her at the interview had her floundering helplessly.* **2** to have a lot of problems and be in danger of failing completely: *By the late nineties, the business was floundering.* **3** to move with difficulty, for example when trying to get out of some water, wet earth, etc.

flounder² /ˈflaʊndə(r)/ ***noun*** [C] a small flat sea fish that is used for food

flour ⊶ /ˈflaʊə(r)/ ***noun*** [U] a very thin powder made from WHEAT or other grain and used for making bread, cakes, biscuits, etc.

flourish¹ /ˈflʌrɪʃ/ ***verb*** **1** [I] to be strong and healthy; to develop in a successful way: *a flourishing business* **2** [T] to wave sth in the air so that people will notice it: *He proudly flourished two tickets for the concert.*

flourish² /ˈflʌrɪʃ/ ***noun*** [C] an exaggerated movement: *He opened the door for her with a flourish.*

flout /flaʊt/ ***verb*** [T] to refuse to obey or accept sth: *to flout the rules of the organization ◇ to flout sb's advice*

flow¹ ⊶ /fləʊ/ ***noun*** [sing.] a ~ (**of sth/sb**) **1** a steady, continuous movement of sth/sb: *Press hard on the wound to stop the flow of blood.* **2** a supply of sth: *the flow of information between the school and the parents* **3** the way in which words, ideas, etc. are joined together smoothly: *Once Charlie's **in full flow**, it's hard to stop him talking.*

IDM **the ebb and flow (of sth)** → EBB²

flow² ⊶ /fləʊ/ ***verb*** [I] **1** to move in a smooth and continuous way (like water): *This river flows south into the English Channel. ◇ a fast-flowing stream ◇ Traffic began to flow normally again after the accident.* **2** (used about words, ideas, actions, etc.) to be joined together smoothly: *As soon as we sat down at the table, the conversation began to flow.* **3** (used about hair and clothes) to hang down in a loose way: *a long flowing dress.*

ˈflow chart (*also* **ˈflow diagram**) ***noun*** [C] a diagram that shows the connections between different stages of a process or parts of a system ➲ picture at **chart**

flower¹ ⊶ /ˈflaʊə(r)/ ***noun*** [C] **1** (**BIOLOGY**) the coloured part of a plant or tree from which seeds or fruit grow **2** a plant that is grown for its flowers: *to grow flowers*

flower² /ˈflaʊə(r)/ ***verb*** [I] (**BIOLOGY**) to produce flowers: *This plant flowers in late summer.*

ˈflower bed ***noun*** [C] a piece of ground in a garden or park where flowers are grown

flowerpot /ˈflaʊəpɒt/ ***noun*** [C] a pot in which a plant can be grown

flowery /ˈflaʊəri/ *adj.* **1** covered or decorated with flowers: *a flowery dress/hat/pattern* **2** (LITERATURE) (used about a style of speaking or writing) using long, difficult words when they are not necessary

flown past participle of **fly**[1]

fl oz *abbr.* fluid ounce(s)

flu /fluː/ (also *formal* **influenza**) *noun* [U] an illness that is like a bad cold but more serious. You usually feel very hot and your arms and legs hurt.

fluctuate AW /ˈflʌktʃueɪt/ *verb* [I] ~ **(between A and B)** (used about prices and numbers, or people's feelings) to change frequently from one thing to another: *The number of students fluctuates between 100 and 150.* ▶ **fluctuation** AW /ˌflʌktʃuˈeɪʃn/ *noun* [C,U]

flue /fluː/ *noun* [C] a pipe or tube that takes smoke, gas or hot air away from a fire or an oven

fluent /ˈfluːənt/ *adj.* **1** ~ **(in sth)** able to speak or write a foreign language easily and accurately: *After a year in France she was fluent in French.* **2** (used about speaking, reading or writing) expressed in a smooth and accurate way: *He speaks fluent German.* ▶ **fluency** /ˈfluːənsi/ *noun* [U]: *My knowledge of Japanese grammar is good but I need to work on my fluency.* ▶ **fluently** *adv.*

fluff /flʌf/ *noun* [U] **1** very small pieces of wool, cotton, etc. that form into balls and collect on clothes and other surfaces **2** the soft new fur on young animals or birds

fluffy /ˈflʌfi/ *adj.* **1** covered in soft fur: *a fluffy kitten* **2** that looks or feels very soft and light: *fluffy clouds/towels*

fluid[1] /ˈfluːɪd/ *noun* [C,U] a substance that can flow; a liquid: *The doctor told her to drink plenty of fluids.* ◇ *cleaning fluid*

fluid[2] /ˈfluːɪd/ *adj.* **1** able to flow smoothly like a liquid: (*figurative*) *I like her fluid style of dancing.* **2** (used about plans, etc.) able to change or likely to be changed

fluidize (also **-ise**) /ˈfluːɪdaɪz/ *verb* [T] (CHEMISTRY) to make a solid substance more like a liquid by passing a gas upwards through it ▶ **fluidization** (also **-isation**) *noun* [U]

ˌfluid ˈounce *noun* [C] (*abbr.* **fl oz**) a measure of liquid; in Britain, 0.0284 of a litre; in the US, 0.0295 of a litre. ❶ For more information about measurements look at the special section on numbers at the back of this dictionary.

fluke /fluːk/ *noun* [C, usually sing.] (*informal*) a surprising and lucky result that happens by accident, not because you have been clever or skilful

flung past tense, past participle of **fling**[1]

fluorescent /ˌflɔːˈresnt; ˌflʊəˈr-/ *adj.* **1** (PHYSICS) producing a bright white light: *fluorescent lighting* **2** very bright; seeming to shine: *fluorescent pink paint*

fluoride /ˈflɔːraɪd/ *noun* [U] (CHEMISTRY) a chemical substance that can be added to water or TOOTHPASTE to help prevent bad teeth

fluorine /ˈflɔːriːn/ *noun* [U] (*symbol* **F**) (CHEMISTRY) a poisonous pale yellow gas ❶ For more information on the periodic table of elements, look at pages R34-5.

fluorocarbon /ˈflɔːrəʊkɑːbən; ˈflʊərəʊkɑːbən/ *noun* [C] (CHEMISTRY) a COMPOUND (= a combination) of FLUORINE and CARBON. **Fluorocarbons** are used in things such as cleaning products, fridges and AEROSOLS and are harmful to the environment. ➲ look at **chlorofluorocarbon**

flurry /ˈflʌri/ *noun* [C] (*pl.* **flurries**) **1** a short time in which there is suddenly a lot of activity: *a flurry of excitement/activity* **2** a sudden short fall of snow or rain

flush[1] /flʌʃ/ *verb* **1** [I] (used about a person or their face) to go red SYN **blush**: *Susan flushed and could not hide her embarrassment.* **2** [T] to clean a toilet by pressing or pulling a handle that sends water into the toilet **3** [I] (used about a toilet) to be cleaned with a short flow of water: *The toilet won't flush.* **4** [T] ~ **sth away, down, etc.** to get rid of sth in a flow of water: *You can't flush tea leaves down the sink – they'll block it.*

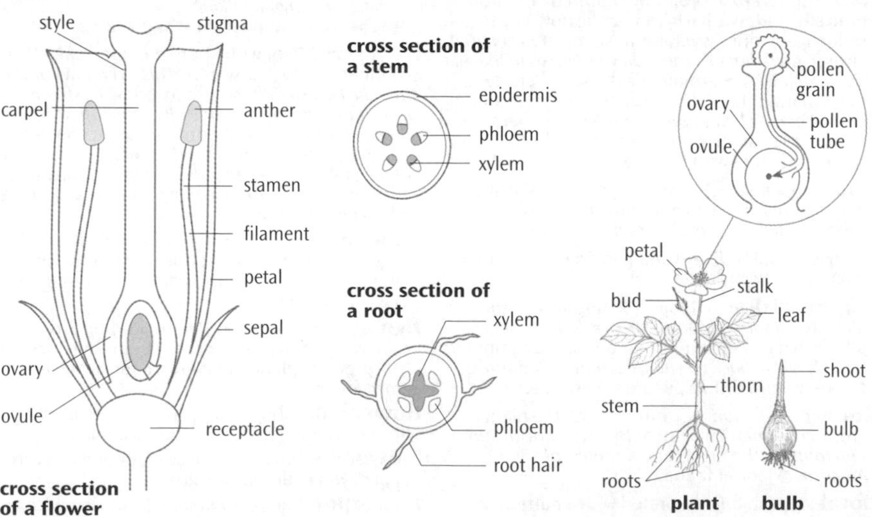

flush² /flʌʃ/ ***noun*** [C, usually sing.] **1** a hot feeling or red colour that you have in your face when you are embarrassed, excited, angry, etc.: *The cold wind brought a flush to our cheeks.* ◇ *a flush of anger* **2** the act of cleaning a toilet with a quick flow of water; the system for doing this

flushed /flʌʃt/ ***adj.*** with a hot red face: *You look very flushed. Are you sure you're all right?*

fluster /ˈflʌstə(r)/ ***verb*** [T] (usually passive) to make sb feel nervous and confused (because there is too much to do or not enough time): *Don't get flustered – there's plenty of time.* ▶ **fluster** ***noun*** [sing.]: *I always get **in a fluster** before exams.*

flute /fluːt/ ***noun*** [C] (MUSIC) a musical instrument like a pipe that you hold sideways and play by blowing over a hole at one side ➲ picture on **page 465** ▶ **flutist** /ˈfluːtɪst/ (*AmE*) = FLAUTIST

flutter¹ /ˈflʌtə(r)/ ***verb*** **1** [I,T] to move or make sth move quickly and lightly, especially through the air: *The flags were fluttering in the wind.* ◇ *The bird fluttered its wings and tried to fly.* **2** [I] your heart or stomach flutters when you feel nervous and excited

flutter² /ˈflʌtə(r)/ ***noun*** [C, usually sing.] **1** a quick, light movement: *the flutter of wings/eyelids* **2** (*BrE, slang*) a bet on a race, etc.: *I sometimes **have a flutter** on the horses.*

fluvial /ˈfluːviəl/ ***adj.*** (GEOGRAPHY) connected with rivers

flux /flʌks/ ***noun*** [C, usually sing., U] a continuous movement: *a flux of neutrons* ◇ *magnetic flux*

fly¹ 🔑 /flaɪ/ ***verb*** (*pres. part.* **flying**; *3rd person sing. pres.* **flies**; *pt* **flew** /fluː/; *pp* **flown** /fləʊn/) **1** [I] (used about a bird, insect, aircraft, etc.) to move through the air: *This bird has a broken wing and can't fly.* ◇ *I can hear a plane flying overhead.* **2** [I,T] to travel or carry sth in an aircraft, etc.: *My daughter is flying (out) to Singapore next week.* ◇ *Supplies of food were flown (in) to the starving people.* **3** [I,T] (used about a pilot) to control an aircraft: *You have to have special training to fly a jumbo jet.* **4** [I] to move quickly or suddenly, especially through the air: *A large stone **came flying** through the window.* ◇ *I slipped and my shopping **went flying** everywhere.* ◇ *Suddenly the door **flew open** and Mark came running in.* ◇ (*figurative*) *The weekend has just **flown by** and now it's Monday again.* **5** [I,T] to move about in the air; to make sth move about in the air: *The flags are flying.* ◇ *to fly a flag/kite* ➲ noun **flight**

IDM **as the crow flies** → CROW¹

fly off the handle (*informal*) to become very angry in an unreasonable way

let fly (at sb/sth) 1 to shout angrily at sb **2** to hit sb in anger: *She let fly at him with her fists.*

fly² 🔑 /flaɪ/ ***noun*** [C] **1** (*pl.* **flies**) a small insect with two wings: *Flies buzzed round the dead cow.* ➲ picture on **page 29** **2** [sing.] (*BrE also* **flies** [pl.]) an opening down the front of a pair of trousers that fastens with buttons or a ZIP and is covered with a narrow piece of material

ˈfly-by ***noun*** [C] (*pl.* **fly-bys**) (SCIENCE) the flight of a SPACECRAFT near a planet to record data

ˈfly-drive ***adj.*** (*BrE*) (TOURISM) organized by a travel company at a fixed price that includes your flight to a place, a car to drive while you are there and somewhere to stay: *a fly-drive break* ▶ **ˈfly-drive** ***noun*** [C]: *a 14-night fly-drive to New Zealand*

flyer (also **flier**) /ˈflaɪə(r)/ ***noun*** [C] **1** (*informal*) a person who flies a plane (usually a small one, not a passenger plane) **2** a person who travels in a plane as a passenger: *frequent flyers* **3** a thing, especially a bird or an insect, that flies in a particular way: *Ducks are strong flyers.* **4** a small sheet of paper that advertises a product or an event and is given to a large number of people **5** (*informal*) a person, an animal or a vehicle that moves very quickly

flying 🔑 /ˈflaɪɪŋ/ ***adj.*** able to fly: *flying insects*

IDM **with flying colours** with great success; very well: *Martin passed the exam with flying colours.*

get off to a flying start to begin sth well; to make a good start

ˌflying ˈsaucer ***noun*** [C] a round SPACECRAFT that some people say they have seen and that they believe comes from another planet

ˌflying ˈvisit ***noun*** [C] a very quick visit: *I can't stop. This is just a flying visit.*

flyover /ˈflaɪəʊvə(r)/ (*AmE* **overpass**) ***noun*** [C] a type of bridge that carries a road over another road

flywheel /ˈflaɪwiːl/ ***noun*** [C] a heavy wheel in a machine or an engine that helps to keep it working smoothly and at a steady speed

FM /ˌef ˈem/ ***abbr.*** (PHYSICS) frequency modulation; one of the systems of sending out radio signals

foal /fəʊl/ ***noun*** [C] a young horse ➲ note at **horse**

foam¹ /fəʊm/ ***noun*** [U] **1** (*also* **ˌfoam ˈrubber**) a soft light rubber material that is used inside seats, CUSHIONS, etc.: *a foam mattress* **2** a mass of small air bubbles that form on the surface of a liquid: *white foam on the tops of the waves* **3** an artificial substance that is between a solid and a liquid and is made from very small bubbles: *shaving foam*

foam² /fəʊm/ ***verb*** [I] to produce foam: *We watched the foaming river below.*

fob /fɒb/ ***verb*** (**fob<u>b</u>ing**; **fob<u>b</u>ed**)

PHR V **fob sb off (with sth) 1** to try to stop sb asking questions or complaining by telling them sth that is not true: *Don't let them fob you off with any more excuses.* **2** to try to give sb sth that they do not want: *Don't try to fob me off with that old car – I want a new one.*

focal /ˈfəʊkl/ ***adj.*** (only *before* a noun) central; very important; connected with or providing a focus

ˌfocal ˈlength ***noun*** [C] (PHYSICS) the distance between the centre of a mirror or a LENS and its FOCUS ➲ picture at **lens**

ˌfocal ˈpoint ***noun*** **1** [sing.] the centre of interest or activity **2** [C] = FOCUS² (2) ➲ picture at **lens**

focus¹ 🔑 AW /ˈfəʊkəs/ ***verb*** [I,T] (**focusing** or **focussing**; **focused** or **focussed**) ~ (sth) (on sth) **1** to give all your attention to sth: *to focus on a problem* **2** (used about your eyes or a camera) to change or be changed so that things can be seen clearly: *Gradually his eyes focused.* ◇ *I focussed (the camera) on the person in the middle of the group.*

focus² 🔑 AW /ˈfəʊkəs/ ***noun*** [C] (*pl.* **focuses** or **foci** /ˈfəʊsaɪ/) **1** [usually sing.] the centre of interest or attention; special attention that is given to sb/sth: *The school used to be the focus of village life.* **2** (*also* **focal point**) (PHYSICS) a point at which RAYS or waves of light, sound, etc. meet after REFLECTION or REFRACTION; the point from which RAYS or waves of light, sound, etc. seem to come

IDM **in focus/out of focus** (used about a photograph or sth in a photograph) clear/not clear: *This picture is so badly out of focus that I can't recognize anyone.*

focused (also **focussed**) AW /ˈfəʊkəst/ ***adj.*** with your attention directed to what you want to do, with very clear aims

KIDNEYS. We must eat this substance so that our bodies can produce red blood cells.

ˈ**focus group** *noun* [C] (BUSINESS, POLITICS) a small group of people, specially chosen to represent different social classes, etc., who are asked to discuss and give their opinions about a particular subject. The information obtained is used by people doing MARKET RESEARCH, for example about new products or for a political party.

fodder /ˈfɒdə(r)/ *noun* [U] (AGRICULTURE) food that is given to farm animals

foe /fəʊ/ *noun* [C] (*written*) an enemy

foetal (*AmE* **fetal**) /ˈfiːtl/ *adj.* (BIOLOGY) connected with or typical of a baby that is still developing in its mother's body

foetus (*AmE* **fetus**) /ˈfiːtəs/ *noun* [C] (*pl.* **foetuses**; **fetuses**) (BIOLOGY) a young human or animal that is still developing in its mother's body ❶ An **embryo** is at an earlier stage of development.

fog /fɒg/ *noun* [U, C] thick white cloud that forms close to the land or sea. **Fog** makes it difficult for us to see: *Patches of dense fog are making driving dangerous.* ◇ *Bad fogs are common in November.* ➲ note at **weather**

foggy /ˈfɒgi/ *adj.* (**foggier**; **foggiest**) used to describe the weather when there is FOG
IDM **not have the faintest/foggiest (idea)** → FAINT[1]

foil[1] /fɔɪl/ *noun* **1** [U] (*also* **tinfoil**) metal that has been made into very thin sheets, used for putting around food: *aluminium foil* **2** [C] a long, thin, pointed weapon used in FENCING (=a type of sport)

foil[2] /fɔɪl/ *verb* [T] to prevent sb from succeeding, especially with a plan; to prevent a plan from succeeding: *The prisoners were foiled in their attempt to escape.*

foist /fɔɪst/ *verb*
PHR V **foist sth on/upon sb** to force sb to accept sth that they do not want

fold[1] 🔑 /fəʊld/ *verb* **1** [T] ~ **sth** (**up**) to bend one part of sth over another part in order to make it smaller, tidier, etc.: *He folded the letter into three before putting it into the envelope.* ◇ *Fold up your clothes neatly, please.* OPP **unfold** **2** [I] ~ (**up**) to be able to be made smaller in order to be carried or stored more easily: *This table folds up flat.* ◇ *a folding bed* **3** [T] ~ **A in B**; ~ **B round/over A** to put sth around sth else: *I folded the photos in a sheet of paper and put them away.* **4** [I] (used about a business, a play in the theatre, etc.) to close because it is a failure
IDM **cross/fold your arms** → ARM[1]

fold[2] 🔑 /fəʊld/ *noun* [C] **1** the mark or line where sth has been folded **2** a curved shape that is made when there is more material, etc. than is necessary to cover sth: *the folds of a dress/curtain*
3 (AGRICULTURE) a small area inside a fence where sheep are kept together in a field

-fold *suffix* (in adjectives and adverbs) multiplied by; having the number of parts mentioned: *to increase tenfold*

folder /ˈfəʊldə(r)/ *noun* [C] **1** a cardboard or plastic cover that is used for holding papers, etc.
2 (COMPUTING) a collection of information or files on one subject that is stored in a computer or on a disk

foliage /ˈfəʊliɪdʒ/ *noun* [U] (*formal*) (BIOLOGY) all the leaves of a tree or plant

folic acid /ˌfɒlɪk ˈæsɪd/ *noun* [U] (HEALTH) a natural substance that is found in green vegetables, and certain types of meat, for example LIVER and KIDNEYS. We must eat this substance so that our bodies can produce red blood cells.

folio /ˈfəʊliəʊ/ *noun* [C] (*pl.* **folios**) **1** (ARTS AND MEDIA) a book made with large sheets of paper, especially as used in early printing **2** a single sheet of paper from a book

folk[1] /fəʊk/ *noun* **1** (*AmE* **folks**) [pl.] (*informal*) people in general: *Some folk are never satisfied.*
2 [pl.] a particular type of people: *Old folk often don't like change.* ◇ *country folk* **3 folks** [pl.] (*informal*) used as a friendly way of addressing more than one person: *What shall we do today, folks?* **4 folks** [pl.] (*informal*) your parents or close relatives: *How are your folks?* **5** [U] (*also* ˈ**folk music**) (MUSIC) music in the traditional style of a country or community: *Do you like Irish folk?*

folk[2] /fəʊk/ *adj.* traditional in a community; of a traditional style: *Robin Hood is an English folk hero.* ◇ *folk music* ◇ *a folk song*

ˈ**folk dance** *noun* [C, U] a traditional dance of a particular area or country; a piece of music for such a dance

folklore /ˈfəʊklɔː(r)/ *noun* [U] (SOCIAL STUDIES) traditional stories and beliefs

follicle /ˈfɒlɪkl/ *noun* [C] (ANATOMY) one of the very small holes in the skin which hairs grow from ➲ picture at **skin**

follow 🔑 /ˈfɒləʊ/ *verb* **1** [I,T] to come, go or happen after sb/sth: *You go first and I'll follow (on) later.* ◇ *The dog followed her (around) wherever she went.* ◇ *I'll have soup followed by spaghetti.* **2** [T] to go along a road, etc.; to go in the same direction as sth: *Follow this road for a mile and then turn right at the pub.* ◇ *The road follows the river for a few miles.* **3** [T] to do sth or to happen according to instructions, an example, what is usual, etc.: *When lighting fireworks, it is important to* ***follow the instructions*** *carefully.* ◇ *The day's events followed the usual pattern.* **4** [I,T] to understand the meaning of sth: *The children couldn't follow the plot of that film.* **5** [T] to keep watching or listening to sth as it happens or develops: *The film follows the career of a young dancer.* ◇ *Have you been following the tennis championships?* **6** [I] ~ (**on**) (**from sth**) to be the logical result of sth; to be the next logical step after sth: *It doesn't follow that old people can't lead active lives.* ◇ *Intermediate Book One follows on from Elementary Book Two.*
IDM **a hard act to follow** → HARD[1]
as follows used for introducing a list: *The names of the successful candidates are as follows...*
follow in sb's footsteps to do the same job as sb else who did it before you: *He followed in his father's footsteps and joined the army.*
follow sb's example/lead to do what sb else has done or decided to do
follow suit to do the same thing that sb else has just done
follow your nose to go straight forward
PHR V **follow sth through** to continue doing sth until it is finished
follow sth up 1 to take further action about sth: *You should follow up your letter with a phone call.*
2 to find out more about sth: *We need to follow up the story about the school.*

follower /ˈfɒləʊə(r)/ *noun* [C] a person who follows or supports a person, belief, etc.

following[1] 🔑 /ˈfɒləʊɪŋ/ *adj.* **1** next (in time): *He became ill on Sunday and died the following day.* **2** that are going to be mentioned next: *Please could you bring the following items to the meeting...*

following² ⊶ /ˈfɒləʊɪŋ/ ***noun*** **1** [sing.] a group of people who support or admire sth: *The Brazilian team has a large following all over the world.* **2 the following** [pl.] the people or things that are going to be mentioned next: *The following are the winners of the competition...*

following³ ⊶ /ˈfɒləʊɪŋ/ ***prep.*** after; as a result of: *Following the riots many students have been arrested.*

ˈfollow-up ***noun*** [C] something that is done as a second stage to continue or develop sth: *As a follow-up to the television series, the BBC is publishing a book.*

folly /ˈfɒli/ ***noun*** [C,U] (*pl.* **follies**) (*formal*) an act that is not sensible and may have a bad result: *It would be folly to ignore their warnings.*

fond /fɒnd/ ***adj.*** **1** (not before a noun) ~ **of sb/sth**; ~ **of doing sth** liking a person or thing, or liking doing sth: *Elephants are very fond of bananas.* ◇ *I'm not very fond of getting up early.* ◇ *Teachers often* ***grow fond*** *of their students.* **2** (only *before* a noun) kind and loving: *I have* ***fond memories*** *of my grandmother.*

fondle /ˈfɒndl/ ***verb*** [T] to touch sb/sth gently in a loving or sexual way

fondly /ˈfɒndli/ ***adv.*** in a loving way: *Miss Murphy will be fondly remembered by all her former students.*

fondness /ˈfɒndnəs/ ***noun*** [U, sing.] **(a)** ~ **(for sb/sth)** a liking for sb/sth: *I've always had a fondness for cats.* ◇ *My grandmother talks about her schooldays* ***with fondness***.

font /fɒnt/ ***noun*** [C] **1** (RELIGION) a large stone bowl in a church that holds water for the ceremony of BAPTISM (= in which a person becomes a member of the Christian Church by being held under water for a short time or having drops of water put onto their head) **2** (TECHNICAL) the particular size and style of a set of letters that are used in printing, on a computer screen, etc.

food ⊶ /fuːd/ ***noun*** **1** [U] something that people or animals eat: *Food and drink will be provided after the meeting.* ◇ *There is a shortage of food in some areas.* **2** [C,U] a particular type of food that you eat: *My favourite food is pasta.* ◇ *Have you ever had Japanese food?* ◇ *baby food* ◇ *dog food* ◇ *health foods*

ˈfood chain ***noun*** [C] (BIOLOGY) a series of living creatures in which each creature eats the one below it in the series

foodie /ˈfuːdi/ ***noun*** [C] (*informal*) a person who is very interested in cooking and eating different kinds of food

ˈfood mile ***noun*** [C] (ENVIRONMENT) a measurement of the distance food has to be transported from the producer to the consumer and the fuel that this uses: *Keep food miles to a minimum by buying local produce.*

ˈfood poisoning ***noun*** [U] (HEALTH) an illness that is caused by eating food that is bad

ˈfood processor ***noun*** [C] an electric machine that can mix food and also cut food into small pieces

foodstuff /ˈfuːdstʌf/ ***noun*** [C, usually pl.] a substance that is used as food: *There has been a sharp rise in the cost of basic foodstuffs.*

food web

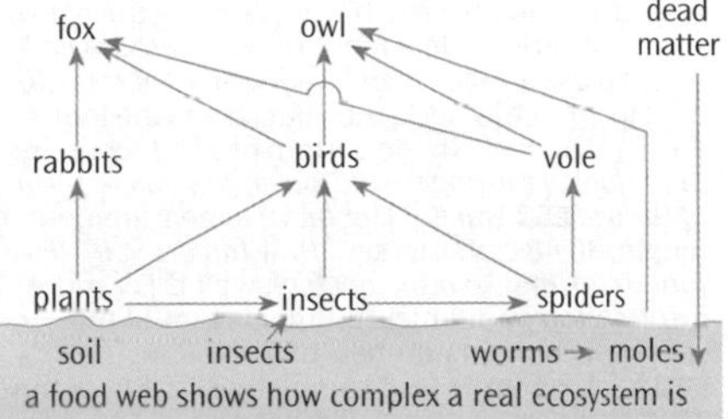

a food web shows how complex a real ecosystem is

ˈfood web ***noun*** [C] (BIOLOGY, ENVIRONMENT) a system of FOOD CHAINS that are connected and that depend on each other

fool¹ /fuːl/ ***noun*** [C] a person who is silly or who acts in a silly way: *I felt such a fool when I realized my mistake.* ➲ look at **April Fool**

IDM **make a fool of sb/yourself** to make sb/yourself look FOOLISH or silly: *Barry got drunk and made a complete fool of himself.*

fool² /fuːl/ ***verb*** **1** [T] ~ **sb (into doing sth)** to trick sb: *Don't be fooled into believing everything that the salesman says.* **2** [I] to speak without being serious: *You didn't really believe me when I said I was going to America, did you? I was only fooling.*

PHR V **fool about/around** to behave in a silly way: *Stop fooling around with that knife or someone will get hurt!*

foolhardy /ˈfuːlhɑːdi/ ***adj.*** taking unnecessary risks

foolish /ˈfuːlɪʃ/ ***adj.*** **1** silly; not sensible: *I was foolish enough to trust him.* **2** looking silly or feeling embarrassed: *I felt a bit foolish when I couldn't remember the man's name.* ▸ **foolishly** ***adv.***: *I*

food chain

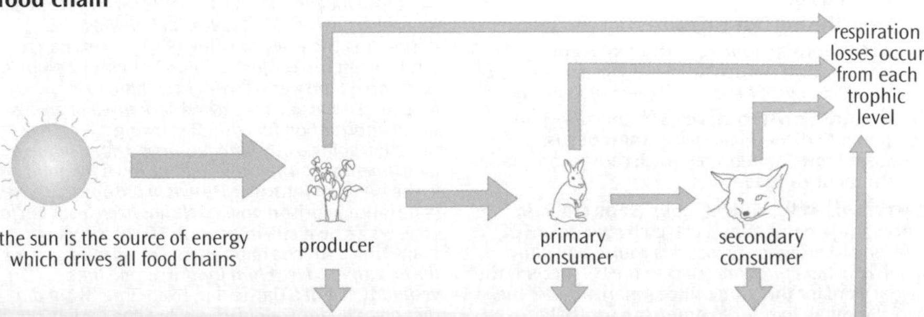

foolishly agreed to lend him money. ▸ **foolishness** *noun* [U]

foolproof /ˈfuːlpruːf/ ***adj.*** not capable of going wrong or being wrongly used: *Our security system is absolutely foolproof.*

foot[1] ⊶ /fʊt/ ***noun*** (*pl.* **feet** /fiːt/) **1** [C] the lowest part of the body, at the end of the leg, on which a person or animal stands: *to get/rise **to your feet*** (=stand up) ◇ *I usually go to school **on foot*** (=walking). ◇ *I need to sit down – I've been **on my feet** all day.* ◇ *There's broken glass on the floor, so don't walk around **in bare feet*** (=without shoes and socks). ◇ *She sat by the fire and the dog sat at her feet.* ◇ *a foot brake/pedal/pump* (=one that is operated by your foot) **2 -footed** (used to form compound adjectives and adverbs) having or using the type of foot or number of feet mentioned: *There are no left-footed players in the team.* ◇ *a four-footed creature* **3** [C] the part of a sock, etc. that covers the foot **4** [sing.] **the ~ of sth** the bottom of sth: *There's a note at the foot of the page.* ◇ *the foot of the stairs* ◇ *the foot of the bed* OPP **top 5** [C] (*abbr.* ft) a measurement of length; 30.48 CENTIMETRES: *'How tall are you?' 'Five foot six (inches).'* ◇ *a six-foot high wall* ❶ For more information about measurements look at the special section on numbers on page R36.

IDM **back on your feet** completely healthy again after an illness or a time of difficulty

be rushed/run off your feet to be extremely busy; to have too many things to do: *Over Christmas we were rushed off our feet at work.*

fall/land on your feet to be lucky in finding yourself in a good situation, or in getting out of a difficult situation

find your feet → FIND[1]

get/have cold feet → COLD[1]

get/start off on the right/wrong foot (with sb) (*informal*) to start a relationship well/badly

have one foot in the grave (*informal*) to be so old or ill that you are not likely to live much longer

put your foot down (*informal*) to say firmly that sth must (not) happen: *I put my foot down and told Andy he couldn't use our car any more.*

put your foot in it (*informal*) to say or do sth that makes sb embarrassed or upset

put your feet up to sit down and relax, especially with your feet off the floor and supported: *I'm so tired that I just want to go home and put my feet up.*

set foot in/on sth → SET[1]

stand on your own (two) feet to take care of yourself without help; to be independent

under your feet in the way; stopping you from working, etc.: *Would somebody get these children out from under my feet and take them to the park?*

foot[2] /fʊt/ ***verb***

IDM **foot the bill (for sth)** to pay (for sth)

footage /ˈfʊtɪdʒ/ ***noun*** [U] (ARTS AND MEDIA) part of a film showing a particular event: *The documentary included footage of the assassination of Kennedy.*

ˌfoot-and-ˈmouth disease (*AmE also* **ˌhoof-and-ˈmouth disease**) ***noun*** [U] (AGRICULTURE) a disease of cows, sheep, etc. which causes sore places on the mouth and feet

football ⊶ /ˈfʊtbɔːl/ ***noun*** (SPORT) **1** (*also* **soccer**) [U] a game that is played by two teams of eleven players who try to kick a round ball into a goal: *a football pitch/match* ❶ In the US **soccer** is the usual word for this game since Americans use the word **football** to refer to **American football**. **2** [C] the large round ball that is used in this game ➲ picture at **sport**

footballer /ˈfʊtbɔːlə(r)/ ***noun*** [C] (SPORT) a person who plays football: *a talented footballer*

ˈfootball pools (*also* **the pools**) ***noun*** [pl.] a game in which people bet money on the results of football matches and can win large amounts of money

footbridge /ˈfʊtbrɪdʒ/ ***noun*** [C] a narrow bridge used only by people who are walking

footer /ˈfʊtə(r)/ ***noun*** [C] (COMPUTING) a line or block of text that is automatically added to the bottom of every page that is printed from a computer ➲ look at **header**

foothills /ˈfʊthɪlz/ ***noun*** [pl.] (GEOGRAPHY) hills or low mountains at the base of a higher mountain or line of mountains

foothold /ˈfʊthəʊld/ ***noun*** [C] a place where you can safely put your foot when you are climbing: (*figurative*) *We need to get a foothold in the European market.*

footing /ˈfʊtɪŋ/ ***noun*** [sing.] **1** the position of your feet when they are safely on the ground or some other surface: *Climbers usually attach themselves to a rope in case they **lose their footing*** (=slip or lose their balance). ◇ (*figurative*) *The company is now **on a firm footing** and should soon show a profit.* **2** the level or position of sb/sth (in relation to sb/sth else): *to be **on an equal footing** with sb*

footnote /ˈfʊtnəʊt/ ***noun*** [C] an extra piece of information that is added at the bottom of a page in a book

footpath /ˈfʊtpɑːθ/ ***noun*** [C] a path for people to walk on: *a public footpath*

footprint /ˈfʊtprɪnt/ ***noun*** [C] a mark that is left on the ground by a foot or a shoe ➲ look at **track**

footstep /ˈfʊtstep/ ***noun*** [C] the sound of sb walking: *I heard his footsteps in the hall.*

IDM **follow in sb's footsteps** → FOLLOW

footwear /ˈfʊtweə(r)/ ***noun*** [U] boots or shoes

for[1] ⊶ /fə(r); *strong form* fɔː(r)/ ***prep.*** **1** showing the person that will use or have sth: *Here is a letter for you.* ◇ *He made lunch for them.* ◇ *It's a book for children.* **2** in order to do, have or get sth: *What's this gadget for?* ◇ *What did you do that for* (=why did you do that)? ◇ *Do you learn English for your job or for fun?* ◇ *She asked me for help.* ◇ *Phone now for information.* ◇ *to go for a walk/swim/drink* **3** in order to help sb/sth: *What can I do for you?* ◇ *You should take some medicine for your cold.* ◇ *Doctors are fighting for his life.* ◇ *shampoo for dry hair* **4** in support of (sb/sth): *Are you for or against shops opening on Sundays?* **5** meaning sth or representing sb/sth: *What's the 'C' for in 'BBC'?* ◇ *What's the Russian for 'window'?* **6** showing the place that sb/sth will go to: *Is this the train for Glasgow?* ◇ *They set off for the shops.* **7** (showing a reason) as a result of: *Ben didn't want to come for some reason.* ◇ *He was sent to prison for robbery.* ◇ *I couldn't speak for laughing.* **8** (showing the price or value of sth); in exchange for: *I bought this car for £2000.* ◇ *You get one point for each correct answer.* ◇ *I want to exchange this sweater for a larger one.* ◇ *The officer was accused of giving secret information for cash.* **9** showing a length of time: *I'm going away for a few days.* ◇ *for a while/a long time/ages* ◇ *They have left the town **for good*** (=they will not return). ◇ *He was in prison for 20 years* (=he is not in prison now). ◇ *He has been in prison for 20 years* (=he is still in prison). **10** showing how many times sth has happened: *I'm warning you for the last time.* ◇ *I met him for the second time yesterday.* **11** at a particular, fixed time: *What did they give you for your birthday?* ◇ *Shall we have eggs for breakfast?* ◇ *I'm going to my parents' for Christmas.* ◇ *The appointment is for 10.30.*

12 showing a distance: *He walked for ten miles.* **13** (after an adjective) showing how usual, suitable, difficult, etc. sb/sth is in relation to sb/sth else: *She's tall for her age.* ◇ *It's quite warm for January.* ◇ *It's unusual for Alex to be late.* ◇ *I think Sandra is perfect for this job.*

IDM **be (in) for it** (*BrE, informal*) to be going to get into trouble or be punished: *If you arrive late again you'll be in for it.*

for all in spite of: *For all his money, he's a very lonely man.*

for ever → FOREVER (1)

for² /fə(r) *strong form* fɔː(r)/ ***conj.*** (*formal*) because: *The children soon lost their way, for they had never been in the forest alone before.*

forage¹ /ˈfɒrɪdʒ/ ***verb*** [I] ~ **(for sth)** (used about animals) to search for food

forage² /ˈfɒrɪdʒ/ ***noun*** [U] (AGRICULTURE) plants that are grown as food for horses and cows

forbear /fɔːˈbeə(r)/ ***verb*** [I] (*pt* **forbore** /-ˈbɔː(r)/; *pp* **forborne** /-ˈbɔːn/) (*formal*) **forbear (from sth/ from doing sth)** to stop yourself from saying or doing sth that you could or would like to say or do: *He wanted to answer back, but he forbore from doing so.* ◇ *She forbore to ask any further questions.*

forbid /fəˈbɪd/ ***verb*** [T] (*pres. part.* **forbidding**; *pt* **forbade** /fəˈbæd/; *pp* **forbidden** /fəˈbɪdn/) **1** (usually passive) to not allow sth: *Smoking is forbidden inside the building.* **2** ~ **sb to do sth** to order sb not to do sth: *My parents forbade me to see Tim again.*

forbidding /fəˈbɪdɪŋ/ ***adj.*** looking unfriendly or frightening

force¹ ⊶ /fɔːs/ ***noun*** **1** [U] physical strength or power: *The force of the explosion knocked them to the ground.* ◇ *The police **used force** to break up the demonstration.* ➲ picture at **vectors** **2** [U] power and influence: *the force of public opinion* **3** [C] a person or thing that has power or influence: *Britain is no longer a major force in international affairs.* ◇ *Julia has been **the driving force** behind the company's success.* **4** [C] a group of people who are trained for a particular purpose: *a highly trained workforce* ◇ *the police force* **5** (usually plural) the soldiers and weapons that an army, etc. has: *the armed forces* **6** [C,U] (PHYSICS) a power that can cause change or movement: *the force of gravity* ◇ *magnetic/centrifugal force* ➲ picture at **hydraulic** **7** [C, usually sing.] (GEOGRAPHY) a measure of wind strength: *a force 9 gale*

IDM **bring sth/come into force** to start using a new law, etc.; to start being used: *The government want to bring new anti-pollution legislation into force next year.*

force of habit if you do sth from or out of force of habit, you do it in a particular way because you have always done it that way in the past

in force 1 (used about people) in large numbers: *The police were present in force at the football match.* **2** (used about a law, rule, etc.) being used: *The new speed limit is now in force.*

join forces (with sb) to work together in order to achieve a shared goal

force² ⊶ /fɔːs/ ***verb*** [T] **1** ~ **sb (to do sth)**; ~ **sb (into sth/doing sth)** to make sb do sth that they do not want to do: *She forced herself to speak to him.* ◇ *The President was forced into resigning.* **2** to use physical strength to do sth or to move sth: *The window had been forced (open).* ◇ *We had to force our way through the crowd.* **3** to make sth happen when it will not happen naturally: *to force a smile/laugh* ◇ *To force the issue, I gave him until midday to decide.*

IDM **force sb's hand** to make sb do sth that they do not want to do, or make them do it sooner than intended

ˌforced ˈlabour (*AmE* **ˌforced ˈlabor**) ***noun*** [U] (LAW) hard physical work that sb, often a prisoner or a SLAVE, is forced to do

forceful /ˈfɔːsfl/ ***adj.*** having the power to persuade people: *He has a very forceful personality.* ◇ *a forceful speech*

forceps /ˈfɔːseps/ ***noun*** [pl.] (HEALTH) a special instrument that looks like a pair of scissors but is not sharp. Forceps are used by doctors for holding things firmly: *a pair of forceps*

forcible /ˈfɔːsəbl/ ***adj.*** (only *before* a noun) done using (physical) force: *The police made a forcible entry into the building.* ▶ **forcibly** /ˈfɔːsəbli/ ***adv.***: *The squatters were forcibly removed by the police.*

ford /fɔːd/ ***noun*** [C] (GEOGRAPHY) a place in a river where you can walk or drive across because the water is not deep

fore¹ /fɔː(r)/ ***noun***

IDM **be/come to the fore** to be in or get into an important position so that you are noticed by people

fore² /fɔː(r)/ ***adj.*** (only *before* a noun) ***adv.*** at, near or towards the front of a ship or an aircraft ➲ look at **aft**

fore- /fɔː/ ***prefix*** (in nouns and verbs) **1** before; in advance: *foreword* ◇ *foretell* **2** in front of: *the foreground of the picture*

forearm /ˈfɔːrɑːm/ ***noun*** [C] the lower part of your arm ➲ picture on **page 80**

forebear (also **forbear**) /ˈfɔːbeə(r)/ ***noun*** [C, usually pl.] (*formal*) a person in your family who lived a long time before you SYN **ancestor**

foreboding /fɔːˈbəʊdɪŋ/ ***noun*** [U, sing.] a strong feeling that danger or trouble is coming: *She was suddenly filled with **a sense of foreboding**.*

forecast ⊶ /ˈfɔːkɑːst/ ***verb*** [T] (*pt, pp* **forecast**) to say (with the help of information) what will probably happen in the future: *The Chancellor did not forecast the sudden rise in inflation.* ◇ *Rain has been forecast for tomorrow.* ▶ **forecast** ***noun*** [C]: *a sales forecast for the coming year* ➲ look at **weather forecast**

forecourt /ˈfɔːkɔːt/ ***noun*** [C] a large open area in front of a building such as a hotel or petrol station

forefinger /ˈfɔːfɪŋgə(r)/ (*also* **index finger**) ***noun*** [C] the finger next to the thumb

forefront /ˈfɔːfrʌnt/ ***noun*** [sing.] the leading position; the position at the front: *Our department is right **at the forefront of** scientific research.*

forego = FORGO

foregone /ˈfɔːgɒn/ ***adj.***

IDM **a foregone conclusion** a result that is or was certain to happen

foreground /ˈfɔːgraʊnd/ ***noun*** [sing.] **1** (ART) the part of a view, picture, photograph, etc. that appears closest to the person looking at it: *Notice the artist's use of colour **in the foreground** of the picture.* **2** a position where you will be noticed most: *He likes to be in the foreground at every meeting.*
OPP **background**

forehand /ˈfɔːhænd/ ***noun*** [C] (SPORT) a way of hitting the ball in TENNIS, etc. that is made with the inside of your hand facing forward OPP **backhand**

forehead /ˈfɔːhed; ˈfɒrɪd/ (*also* **brow**) ***noun*** [C] the part of a person's face above the eyes and below the hair ➲ picture on **page 80**

foreign ⊶ /ˈfɒrən/ ***adj.*** **1** belonging to or connected with a country that is not your own: *a foreign country/coin/accent* ◇ *to learn a foreign language* **2** (only *before* a noun) dealing with or involving other countries: *foreign policy* (=government decisions concerning other countries) ◇ *foreign affairs/news/trade* **3** (used about an object or a substance) not being where it should be: *The X-ray showed up a foreign body* (=object) *in her stomach.*

the ˌForeign and ˈCommonwealth Office (*abbr.* **FCO**) ***noun*** [sing., with sing. or pl. verb] (POLITICS) the British government department that deals with relations with other countries ⓘ Many people still refer to this department by its old name **the Foreign Office**.

foreigner /ˈfɒrənə(r)/ ***noun*** [C] a person who belongs to a country that is not your own

ˌforeign exˈchange ***noun*** [C,U] (FINANCE, ECONOMICS) the system of buying and selling money from a different country; the place where it is bought and sold

ˌforeign ˈminister ***noun*** [C] (POLITICS) a member of the government who is in charge of his or her country's relations with other countries: *the French foreign minister*

the ˌForeign ˈSecretary ***noun*** [C] (POLITICS) the person in the British government who is responsible for dealing with foreign countries ➲ look at **the Home Secretary**

foreleg /ˈfɔːleg/ (*also* **ˈfront leg**) ***noun*** [C] either of the two legs at the front of an animal that has four legs ➲ look at **hind**

foremost /ˈfɔːməʊst/ ***adj.*** most famous or important; best: *Laurence Olivier was among the foremost actors of the last century.*
IDM **first and foremost** → FIRST²

forename /ˈfɔːneɪm/ ***noun*** [C] (*formal*) your first name, that is given to you when you are born

forensic /fəˈrensɪk; -ˈrenzɪk/ ***adj.*** (only *before* a noun) (LAW) using scientific tests to find out about a crime: *The police are carrying out forensic tests to try and find out the cause of death.*

forensics /fəˈrensɪks; -ˈrenzɪks/ ***noun*** [pl.] (LAW) scientific tests and techniques that are used to investigate a crime

forerunner /ˈfɔːrʌnə(r)/ ***noun*** [pl.] **a ~ (of sb/sth)** a person or thing that is an early example or a sign of sth that appears or develops later: *Country music was undoubtedly one of the forerunners of rock and roll.*

foresee /fɔːˈsiː/ ***verb*** [T] (*pt* **foresaw** /fɔːˈsɔː/; *pp* **foreseen** /fɔːˈsiːn/) to know or guess that sth is going to happen in the future: *Nobody could have foreseen the result of the election.* ➲ Look at **unforeseen**.

foreseeable /fɔːˈsiːəbl/ ***adj.*** that can be expected; that you can guess will happen: *These problems were foreseeable.* ◇ *The weather won't change* ***in the foreseeable future*** (=as far ahead as we can see).

foreshore /ˈfɔːʃɔː(r)/ ***noun*** [C, usually sing., U] (GEOGRAPHY) **1** (on a beach or by a river) the part of the SHORE (=the land at the edge of the water) between the highest and lowest levels reached by the water **2** the part of the SHORE (=the land at the edge of the water) between the highest level reached by the water and the area of land that has buildings, plants, etc. on it

foresight /ˈfɔːsaɪt/ ***noun*** [U] the ability to see what will probably happen in the future and to use this knowledge to make careful plans: *My neighbour had the foresight to move house before the new motorway was built.* ➲ look at **hindsight**

foreskin /ˈfɔːskɪn/ ***noun*** [C] (ANATOMY) the piece of skin that covers the end of the male sexual organ

forest ⊶ /ˈfɒrɪst/ ***noun*** [C,U] a large area of land covered with trees: *the* ***tropical rainforests*** *of South America* ◇ *a forest fire* ⓘ A **forest** is larger than a **wood**. A **jungle** is a forest in a tropical part of the world.

forestall /fɔːˈstɔːl/ ***verb*** [T] (*written*) to take action to prevent sb from doing sth or sth from happening

forestry /ˈfɒrɪstri/ ***noun*** [U] (ENVIRONMENT) the science of planting and taking care of trees in forests

foretaste /ˈfɔːteɪst/ ***noun*** [sing.] **a ~ (of sth)** a small amount of a particular experience or situation that shows you what it will be like when the same thing happens on a larger scale in the future

forethought /ˈfɔːθɔːt/ ***noun*** [U] careful thought about, or preparation for, the future

forever ⊶ /fərˈevə(r)/ ***adv.*** **1** (*also* **for ever**) for all time; permanently: *I wish the holidays would last forever!* ◇ *I realized that our relationship had finished forever.* **2** (only used with continuous tenses) very often; in a way which is annoying: *Our neighbours are forever having noisy parties.*

foreword /ˈfɔːwɜːd/ ***noun*** [C] (LITERATURE) a piece of writing at the beginning of a book that introduces the book and/or its author

forfeit /ˈfɔːfɪt/ ***verb*** [T] to lose sth or have sth taken away from you, usually because you have done sth wrong: *Because of his violent behaviour he forfeited the right to visit his children.* ▶ **forfeit** ***noun*** [C]

forgave past tense of **forgive**

forge¹ /fɔːdʒ/ ***verb*** [T] **1** to make an illegal copy of sth: *to forge a signature/banknote/passport/cheque* ➲ look at **counterfeit** **2** to put a lot of effort into making sth strong and successful: *Our school has forged links with a school in Romania.*
PHRV **forge ahead** to go forward or make progress quickly

forge² /fɔːdʒ/ ***noun*** [C] a place where objects are made by heating and shaping metal

forgery /ˈfɔːdʒəri/ ***noun*** (*pl.* **forgeries**) **1** [U] the crime of illegally copying a document, signature, painting, etc. **2** [C] a document, signature, picture, etc. that is a copy of the real one

forget ⊶ /fəˈget/ ***verb*** (*pt* **forgot** /fəˈgɒt/; *pp* **forgotten** /fəˈgɒtn/) **1** [T] **~ (doing) sth** to not be able to remember sth: *I've forgotten what I was going to say.* ◇ *I've forgotten her telephone number.* ◇ *He forgot that he had invited her to the party.* ◇ *I'll never forget meeting my husband for the first time.* **2** [I,T] **~ (about) sth; ~ to do sth** to fail to remember to do sth that you ought to have done: *'Why didn't you come to the party?' 'Oh dear! I completely forgot about it!'* ◇ *'Did you feed the cat?' 'Sorry, I forgot.'* ◇ *Don't forget to do your homework!* **3** [T] to fail to bring sth with you: *When my father got to the airport he realized he'd forgotten his passport.* **4** [I,T] **~ (about) sb/sth; ~ about doing sth** to make an effort to stop thinking about sb/sth; to stop thinking that sth is possible: *Forget about your work and enjoy yourself!* ◇ *'I'm sorry I shouted at you.' 'Forget it* (=don't worry about it).'

forgetful /fəˈgetfl/ ***adj.*** often forgetting things: *My mother's nearly 80 and she's starting to get a bit forgetful.* SYN **absent-minded**

forgivable /fəˈgɪvəbl/ ***adj.*** that can be forgiven

forgive 🔑 /fəˈɡɪv/ ***verb*** [T] (*pt* **forgave** /fəˈɡeɪv/; *pp* **forgiven** /fəˈɡɪvn/) **1** ~ **sb/yourself (for sth/for doing sth)** to stop being angry towards sb for sth that they have done wrong: *I can't forgive his behaviour last night.* ◇ *I can't forgive him for his behaviour last night.* ◇ *I can't forgive him for behaving like that last night.* **2** ~ **me (for doing sth)** used for politely saying sorry: *Forgive me for asking, but where did you get that dress?* ▶ **forgiveness** ***noun*** [U]: *He* ***begged for forgiveness*** *for what he had done.*

forgiving /fəˈɡɪvɪŋ/ ***adj.*** ready and able to forgive

forgo (*also* **forego**) /fɔːˈɡəʊ/ ***verb*** [T] (*pt* **forwent** /fɔːˈwent/; *pp* **forgone** /fɔːˈɡɒn/) (*formal*) to decide not to have or do sth that you want

forgot past tense of **forget**

forgotten past participle of **forget**

fork[1] 🔑 /fɔːk/ ***noun*** [C] **1** a small metal object with a handle and two or more points (**prongs**) that you use for lifting food to your mouth when eating: *a knife and fork* **2** a large tool with a handle and three or more points (**prongs**) that you use for digging the ground: *a garden fork* ➲ picture at **agriculture** **3** a place where a road, river, etc. divides into two parts; one of these parts: *After about two miles you'll come to a fork in the road.*

fork[2] /fɔːk/ ***verb*** [I] **1** (used about a road, river, etc.) to divide into two parts: *Bear right where the road forks at the top of the hill.* **2** to go along the left or right fork of a road: *Fork right up the hill.*
PHR V **fork out (for sth)** (*informal*) to pay for sth when you do not want to: *I forked out over £20 for that book.*

forked /fɔːkt/ ***adj.*** with one end divided into two parts, like the shape of the letter Y: *a bird with a forked tail* ◇ *the forked tongue of the snake*

ˌ**forked** ˈ**lightning** ***noun*** [U] the type of LIGHTNING (=flashes of light in the sky when there is a storm) that is like a line that divides into smaller lines near the ground ➲ look at **sheet lightning**

ˌ**fork-lift** ˈ**truck** (*also* ˈ**fork-lift**) ***noun*** [C] a vehicle with special equipment on the front for moving and lifting heavy objects ➲ picture at **truck**

forlorn /fəˈlɔːn/ ***adj.*** lonely and unhappy; not cared for

form[1] 🔑 /fɔːm/ ***noun*** **1** [C] a particular type or variety of sth or a way of doing sth: *Swimming is an excellent form of exercise.* ◇ *We never eat meat* ***in any form***. **2** [C,U] the shape of sb/sth: *The articles will be published* ***in book form***. **3** [C] an official document with questions on it and spaces where you give answers and personal information: *an* ***entry form*** *for a competition* ◇ *to fill in an* ***application form*** **4** [C] (EDUCATION) a class in a school

CULTURE

In Britain, the years at secondary school used to be called **first/second/third**, etc. **form** but now they are called **Year 7** to **Year 11**. However, the last two years of school (for pupils aged between 16 and 18) are still referred to as **the sixth form**.
In the US, the years at elementary and high schools are called **grades**, from **first grade** to **twelfth grade**.

5 [C] (LANGUAGE) a way of spelling or changing a word in a sentence: *the irregular forms of the verbs* ◇ *The plural form of mouse is mice.* **6** [U] (SPORT) the state of being fit and strong for a sports player, team, etc.: *to be* ***in/out of form*** **7** [U] how well sb/sth is performing at a particular time, for example in sport or business: *to be* ***on/off form*** ◇ *On present form the Italian team should win easily.*
IDM **true to form** → TRUE

form[2] 🔑 /fɔːm/ ***verb*** **1** [I,T] to begin to exist or to make sth exist: *A pattern was beginning to form in the monthly sales figures.* ◇ *These tracks were formed by rabbits.* ➲ note at **make**[1] **2** [T] to make or organize sth: *to form a government* ◇ *In English we usually form the past tense by adding '-ed'.* **3** [T] to become or make a particular shape: *The police formed a circle around the house.* ◇ *to form a line/queue* **4** ***linking verb*** to be the thing mentioned: *Seminars form the main part of the course.* ◇ *The survey* ***formed part of*** *a larger programme of market research.* **5** [T] to begin to have or think sth: *I haven't formed an opinion about the new boss yet.* ◇ *to form a friendship*

formal 🔑 /ˈfɔːml/ ***adj.*** **1** (used about language or behaviour) used when you want to appear serious or official and in situations in which you do not know the other people very well: *'Yours faithfully' is a formal way of ending a letter.* ◇ *She has a very formal manner – she doesn't seem to be able to relax.* ◇ *a formal occasion* (=one where you must behave politely and wear the clothes that people think are suitable) **2** official: *I shall make* ***a formal complaint*** *to the hospital about the way I was treated.*
OPP **informal** ▶ **formally** /-məli/ ***adv.***

formaldehyde /fɔːˈmældɪhaɪd/ ***noun*** [U] **1** (*symbol* CH_2O) (CHEMISTRY) a colourless gas with a strong smell **2** (*also* **formalin** /ˈfɔːməlɪn/) (BIOLOGY) a liquid made by mixing **formaldehyde** and water, used especially for keeping examples of animals, plants, etc. (**specimens**) in a good condition for a long time so that they can be studied by experts or scientists

formality /fɔːˈmæləti/ ***noun*** (*pl.* **formalities**) **1** [C] an action that is necessary according to custom or law: *There are certain formalities to attend to before we can give you a visa.* **2** [U] careful attention to rules of language and behaviour

format[1] AW /ˈfɔːmæt/ ***noun*** [C] the shape of sth or the way it is arranged or produced: *It's the same book but in a different format.*

format[2] AW /ˈfɔːmæt/ ***verb*** [T] (**formatting**; **formatted**) **1** (COMPUTING) to prepare a computer disk so that data can be recorded on it **2** to arrange text on a page or a screen: *to format a letter*

formation /fɔːˈmeɪʃn/ ***noun*** **1** [U] the act of making or developing sth: *the formation of a new government* **2** [C,U] a number of people or things in a particular shape or pattern: *rock formations* ◇ *A number of planes flew over* ***in formation***. ◇ *formation dancing*

formative /ˈfɔːmətɪv/ ***adj.*** having an important and lasting influence (on sb's character and opinions): *A child's early years are thought to be the most formative ones.*

former 🔑 /ˈfɔːmə(r)/ ***adj.*** (only *before* a noun) of an earlier time; belonging to the past: *Ronald Reagan, the former American President* ◇ *In former times people often had larger families.*

the former /ˈfɔːmə(r)/ ***noun*** [sing.] the first (of two people or things just mentioned): *Of the two hospitals in the town – the General and the Royal – the former* (=the General) *has the better reputation.*
➲ look at **the latter**

formerly 🔑 /ˈfɔːməli/ ***adv.*** in the past; before now SYN **previously**: *the country of Myanmar (formerly Burma)* ◇ *The hotel was formerly a castle.*

formidable /ˈfɔːmɪdəbl/ ***adj.*** **1** causing you to be quite frightened: *His mother is a rather formidable lady.* **2** difficult to deal with; needing a lot of effort

formula 🔑 AW /ˈfɔːmjələ/ ***noun*** [C] (*pl.* **formulas** or **formulae** /-liː/) **1** (MATHEMATICS, SCIENCE) a group of signs, letters or numbers used in science or mathematics to express a general law or fact: *What is the formula for converting miles to kilometres?* **2** a list of (often chemical) substances used for making sth; the instructions for making sth **3** a ~ **for (doing) sth** a plan of how to get or do sth: *What is her formula for success?* ◇ *Unfortunately, there's no* ***magic formula*** *for a perfect marriage.*

formulate AW /ˈfɔːmjuleɪt/ ***verb*** [T] **1** to prepare and organize a plan or ideas for doing sth: *to formulate a plan* **2** to express sth (clearly and exactly): *She struggled to formulate a simple answer to his question.*

forsake /fəˈseɪk/ ***verb*** [T] (*pt* **forsook** /fəˈsʊk/; *pp* **forsaken** /fəˈseɪkən/) (*old-fashioned*) to leave a person or a place for ever (especially when you should stay)

fort /fɔːt/ ***noun*** [C] a strong building that is used for military defence

forth /fɔːθ/ ***adv.***

IDM **and so forth** and other things like those just mentioned: *The sort of job that you'll be doing is taking messages, making tea and so forth.*
back and forth → BACK³

forthcoming AW /ˌfɔːθˈkʌmɪŋ/ ***adj.*** **1** that will happen or appear in the near future: *Look in the local paper for a list of* ***forthcoming events.*** **2** (not before a noun) offered or given: *If no money is forthcoming, we shall not be able to continue the project.* **3** (not before a noun) (used about a person) ready to be helpful, give information, etc.

forthright /ˈfɔːθraɪt/ ***adj.*** saying exactly what you think in a clear and direct way

forthwith /ˌfɔːθˈwɪθ/ ***adv.*** (*old-fashioned*) immediately

fortieth /ˈfɔːtiəθ/ ***ordinal number, noun*** [C] 40th ➲ note at **sixth¹**

fortification /ˌfɔːtɪfɪˈkeɪʃn/ ***noun*** [C, usually pl.] walls, towers, etc., built especially in the past to protect a place against attack

fortify /ˈfɔːtɪfaɪ/ ***verb*** [T] (*pres. part.* **fortifying**; *3rd person sing. pres.* **fortifies**; *pt, pp* **fortified**) to make a place stronger and ready for an attack: *to fortify a city*

fortnight /ˈfɔːtnaɪt/ ***noun*** [C, usually sing.] (*BrE*) two weeks: *We're going on holiday for a fortnight.* ◇ *School finishes in a fortnight/in a fortnight's time* (=two weeks from now).

fortnightly /ˈfɔːtnaɪtli/ ***adj., adv.*** (happening or appearing) once every two weeks: *This magazine is published fortnightly.*

fortress /ˈfɔːtrəs/ ***noun*** [C] a castle or other large strong building that it is not easy to attack

fortunate /ˈfɔːtʃənət/ ***adj.*** lucky: *It was fortunate that he was at home when you phoned.*
OPP **unfortunate**

fortunately /ˈfɔːtʃənətli/ ***adv.*** by good luck: *Fortunately the traffic wasn't too bad so I managed to get to the meeting on time.* SYN **luckily**

fortune 🔑 /ˈfɔːtʃuːn/ ***noun*** **1** [C,U] a very large amount of money: *I always* ***spend a fortune*** *on presents at Christmas.* ◇ *She went to Hollywood in search of* ***fame and fortune****.* **2** [U] chance or the power that affects what happens in a person's life; luck: *Fortune was not on our side that day* (=we were unlucky). SYN **fate** **3** [C, usually pl.] the things (both good and bad) that happen to a person, family, country, etc.: *The country's fortunes depend on its industry being successful.* **4** [C] what is going to happen to a person in the future: *Show me your hand and I'll try to* ***tell your fortune.*** SYN **fate, destiny**

IDM **cost the earth/a fortune** → COST²

ˈ**fortune-teller** ***noun*** [C] a person who tells people what will happen to them in the future

forty /ˈfɔːti/ ***number*** **1** 40 **2 the forties** [pl.] numbers, years or temperatures from 40 to 49 ➲ note at **six**

IDM **forty winks** (*informal*) a short sleep, especially during the day

forum /ˈfɔːrəm/ ***noun*** [C] **1** a ~ **(for sth)** a place or meeting where people can exchange and discuss ideas: *Television is now an important forum for political debate.* ◇ *an Internet forum* ◇ *to hold an international forum on drug abuse* **2** (HISTORY) (in ancient Rome) a public place where meetings were held

forward¹ 🔑 /ˈfɔːwəd/ ***adv.*** **1** (*also* **forwards**) in the direction that is in front of you; towards the front, end or future: *Keep going forward and try not to look back.* OPP **back, backward(s)** **2** in the direction of progress; ahead: *The new form of treatment is a big step forward in the fight against Aids.*

IDM **backward(s) and forward(s)** → BACKWARDS
put the clock/clocks forward/back → CLOCK¹

forward² /ˈfɔːwəd/ ***adj.*** **1** (only *before* a noun) towards the front or future: *forward planning* **2** having developed earlier than is normal or expected; advanced OPP **backward** **3** behaving towards sb in a way that is too confident or too informal: *I hope you don't think I'm being too forward, asking you so many questions.*

forward³ /ˈfɔːwəd/ ***verb*** [T] **1** to send a letter, etc. received at one address to a new address **2** to help to improve sth or to make sth progress

forward⁴ /ˈfɔːwəd/ ***noun*** [C] (SPORT) an attacking player in a sport such as football

ˈ**forwarding address** ***noun*** [C] a new address to which letters, etc. should be sent: *The previous owners didn't leave a forwarding address.*

ˈ**forward-looking** ***adj.*** thinking about or planning for the future; having modern ideas

ˈ**forward slash** ***noun*** [C] (COMPUTING) the symbol (/) used in computer commands and in Internet addresses to separate the different parts ➲ look at **backslash**

forwent past tense of **forgo**

fossil /ˈfɒsl/ ***noun*** [C] (GEOLOGY, BIOLOGY) (part of) an animal or plant that lived thousands of years ago which has turned into rock

ˈ**fossil fuel** ***noun*** [C,U] (SCIENCE, ENVIRONMENT) a natural fuel such as coal or oil, that was formed MILLIONS of years ago from dead animals or plants in the ground

fossilize (also -ise) /ˈfɒsəlaɪz/ ***verb*** [I,T] (usually passive) (GEOLOGY) to turn into rock or to make (part of) an animal or plant turn into rock over thousands of years: *fossilized bones*

foster /ˈfɒstə(r)/ ***verb*** [T] **1** (*especially BrE*) to take a child who needs a home into your family and to care for them without becoming the legal parent: *to foster a homeless child* **2** to help or encourage the development of sth (especially feelings or ideas)

fought past tense, past participle of **fight¹**

foul[1] /faʊl/ ***adj.*** **1** that smells or tastes disgusting: *a foul-smelling cigar* ◇ *This coffee tastes foul!* **2** (*especially BrE*) very bad or unpleasant: *Careful what you say – he's* ***in a foul temper/mood.*** ◇ *The* ***foul weather*** *prevented our plane from taking off.* **3** (used about language) very rude; full of swearing: *foul language*

IDM **fall foul of sb/sth** to get in trouble with sb/sth because you have done sth wrong: *At sixteen she fell foul of the law for the first time.*

foul[2] /faʊl/ ***verb*** **1** [I,T] (SPORT) to attack another player in a way that is not allowed **2** [T] to make sth dirty (with rubbish, waste, etc.): *Dogs must not foul the pavement.*

PHR V **foul sth up** (*informal*) to spoil sth: *The delay on the train fouled up my plans for the evening.*

foul[3] /faʊl/ ***noun*** [C] (SPORT) an action that is against the rules: *He was sent off for a foul on the goalkeeper.*

ˌfoul ˈplay ***noun*** [U] **1** (LAW) violence or crime that causes sb's death: *The police suspect foul play.* **2** (SPORT) action that is against the rules of a sport

found[1] AW past tense, past participle of **find**[1]

found[2] 🔑 AW /faʊnd/ ***verb*** [T] **1** to start an organization, institution, etc.: *This museum was founded in 1683.* **2** (HISTORY) to be the first to start building and living in a town or country: *Liberia was founded by freed American slaves.* **3** ~ sth (on sth) (usually passive) to base sth on sth: *The book was founded on real life.*

foundation 🔑 AW /faʊnˈdeɪʃn/ ***noun*** **1 foundations** [pl.] (ARCHITECTURE) a layer of bricks, etc. under the surface of the ground that forms the solid base of a building **2** [C,U] the idea, principle or fact on which sth is based: *This coursebook aims to give students a solid foundation in grammar.* ◇ *That rumour is completely without foundation* (=it is not true). ➲ note at **basis** **3** [C] an organization that provides money for a special purpose: *The British Heart Foundation* **4** [U] the act of starting a new institution or organization

founˈdation course ***noun*** [C] (*BrE*) (EDUCATION) a general course at a college that prepares students for longer or more difficult courses: *an art foundation course*

founˈdation stone ***noun*** [C] (ARCHITECTURE) a large block of stone that is put at the base of an important new public building in a special ceremony

founder[1] AW /ˈfaʊndə(r)/ ***noun*** [C] a person who starts a new institution or organization

founder[2] /ˈfaʊndə(r)/ ***verb*** [I] ~ **(on sth)** (*formal*) **1** to fail because of a particular problem or difficulty: *The project foundered after problems with funding.* **2** to fill with water and sink: *Our boat foundered on a reef.*

ˌfounder ˈmember ***noun*** [C] one of the original members of a club, organization, etc.

foundry /ˈfaʊndri/ ***noun*** [C] (*pl.* **foundries**) a place where metal or glass is melted and shaped into objects ➲ note at **factory**

fountain /ˈfaʊntən/ ***noun*** [C] **1** (ARCHITECTURE) a decoration (in a garden or in a square in a town) that sends a flow of water into the air; the water that comes out of a **fountain** **2** a strong flow of liquid or another substance that is forced into the air: *a fountain of blood/sparks*

ˈfountain pen ***noun*** [C] a type of pen that you fill with ink

four /fɔː(r)/ ***number*** **1** 4 **2 four-** (in compounds) having four of the thing mentioned: *four-legged animals*

IDM **on all fours** with your hands and knees on the ground; CRAWLING: *The children went through the tunnel on all fours.*

ˌfour-letter ˈword ***noun*** [C] a swear word that shocks or offends people (often with four letters)

ˈfour-star ***adj.*** (TOURISM) having four stars in a system that measures quality. The highest quality is shown by either four or five stars: *a four-star hotel*

fourteen /ˌfɔːˈtiːn/ ***number*** 14 ➲ note at **sixth**[1]

fourteenth /ˌfɔːˈtiːnθ/ ***ordinal number, noun*** [C] 14th ➲ note at **sixth**[1]

the ˌFourteenth Aˈmendment ***noun*** [sing.] (HISTORY) a change made to the US Constitution in 1866 that gave all Americans equal rights and allowed former SLAVES (=people in past times who were owned by other people and had to work for them without being paid) to become citizens

fourth /fɔːθ/ ***ordinal number*** 4th ➲ note at **sixth**[1]

ˌfour-wheel ˈdrive ***noun*** [C,U] a system which provides power to all four wheels of a vehicle, making it easier to control; a vehicle with this system: *a car with four-wheel drive* ◇ *We rented a four-wheel drive to get around the island.* ➲ look at **ATV**

fowl /faʊl/ ***noun*** [C] (*pl.* **fowl** or **fowls**) (AGRICULTURE) a bird, especially a chicken, that is kept on a farm

fox /fɒks/ ***noun*** [C] a wild animal like a small dog with reddish fur, a pointed nose and a thick tail

foyer /ˈfɔɪeɪ/ ***noun*** [C] an entrance hall in a cinema, theatre, hotel, etc. where people can meet or wait

fraction /ˈfrækʃn/ ***noun*** [C] **1** a small part or amount: *For a fraction of a second I thought the car was going to crash.* **2** (MATHEMATICS) a division of a number: *½ and ¼ are fractions.* ➲ look at **vulgar fraction, integer**

fractional distillation /ˌfrækʃənl dɪstɪˈleɪʃn/ ***noun*** [U] (CHEMISTRY) the process of separating the parts of a liquid mixture by heating it. As the temperature goes up, each part in turn becomes a gas, which then cools as it moves up a tube and can be collected as a liquid. ➲ picture on next page

fractionally /ˈfrækʃənəli/ ***adv.*** to a very small degree; slightly: *fractionally faster/taller/heavier*

fracture /ˈfræktʃə(r)/ ***noun*** [C,U] a break in a bone or other hard material ▸ **fracture** ***verb*** [I,T]: *She fell and fractured her ankle.* ◇ *A water pipe fractured and flooded the bathroom.*

fragile /ˈfrædʒaɪl/ ***adj.*** easily damaged or broken

fragment[1] /ˈfrægmənt/ ***noun*** [C] a small piece that has broken off or that comes from sth larger: *The builders found fragments of Roman pottery on the site.* ◇ *I heard only a fragment of their conversation.*

fragment[2] /frægˈment/ ***verb*** [I,T] (*formal*) to break (sth) into small pieces: *The country is becoming increasingly fragmented by civil war.*

fragrance /ˈfreɪgrəns/ ***noun*** [C,U] a pleasant smell

fragrant /ˈfreɪgrənt/ ***adj.*** having a pleasant smell

frail /freɪl/ ***adj.*** weak or not healthy: *My aunt is still very frail after her accident.*

frailty /ˈfreɪlti/ ***noun*** [C,U] (*pl.* **frailties**) weakness of a person's body or character

frame[1] 🔑 /freɪm/ ***noun*** [C] **1** a border of wood or metal that goes around the outside of a door, picture, window, etc.: *a window frame* **2** the basic strong structure of a piece of furniture, building, vehicle, etc. which gives it its shape: *the frame of a* *bicycle/an aircraft* **3** [usually pl.] a structure made of plastic or metal that holds the LENSES in a pair of glasses **4** [usually sing.] the basic shape of a human or animal body: *He has a large frame but he's not fat.* **5** [C] (COMPUTING) one of the separate areas on an Internet page that you can SCROLL through (=read by using the mouse to move the text up or down)

IDM **frame of mind** a particular state or condition of your feelings; your mood: *I'm not in the right frame of mind for a party. I'd prefer to be on my own.*

frame² /freɪm/ ***verb*** [T] **1** to put a border around sth (especially a picture or photograph): *Let's have this photograph framed.* **2** (usually passive) (LAW) to give false evidence against sb in order to make them seem guilty of a crime: *The man claimed that he had been framed by the police.* **3** (*formal*) to express sth in a particular way: *The question was very carefully framed.*

framework AW /ˈfreɪmwɜːk/ ***noun*** [C] **1** the basic structure of sth that gives it shape and strength: *A greenhouse is made of glass panels fixed in a metal framework.* ◇ *(figurative) the basic framework of society* ➲ note at **structure¹** **2** a system of rules or ideas which help you decide what to do: *The plan may be changed but it will provide a framework on which we can build.*

franc /fræŋk/ ***noun*** [C] (ECONOMICS) the unit of money in Switzerland and several other countries (replaced in 2002 in France, Belgium and Luxembourg by the euro)

franchise¹ /ˈfræntʃaɪz/ ***noun*** **1** [C,U] (BUSINESS) official permission to sell a company's goods or services in a particular area: *They have the franchise to sell this product in Cyprus.* ◇ *Most fast-food restaurants are operated **under franchise**.* **2** [U] (*formal*) (POLITICS) the right to vote in elections

franchise² /ˈfræntʃaɪz/ ***verb*** [T] (BUSINESS) (usually passive) to give or sell a FRANCHISE¹ (1) to sb: *Catering has been franchised (out) to a private company.* ◇ *franchised restaurants* ▶ **franchising** ***noun*** [U]

francium /ˈfrænsiəm/ ***noun*** [U] (*symbol* **Fr**) (CHEMISTRY) a chemical element. **Francium** is a RADIOACTIVE metal. ❶ For more information on the periodic table of elements, look at pages R34-5.

frank /fræŋk/ ***adj.*** showing your thoughts and feelings clearly; saying what you mean: *To be perfectly frank with you, I don't think you'll pass your driving test.* ▶ **frankly** ***adv.***: *Please tell me frankly what you think about my idea.* ▶ **frankness** ***noun*** [U]

frankfurter /ˈfræŋkfɜːtə(r)/ (*AmE also* **wiener**) ***noun*** [C] a type of small smoked SAUSAGE

frantic /ˈfræntɪk/ ***adj.*** **1** extremely worried or frightened: *The mother went frantic when she couldn't find her child.* ◇ *frantic cries for help* **2** very busy or done in a hurry: *a frantic search for the keys* ◇ *We're not busy at work now, but things get frantic at Christmas.* ▶ **frantically** /-kli/ ***adv.***

fraternal /frəˈtɜːnl/ ***adj.*** (*formal*) connected with the relationship that exists between brothers; like a brother: *fraternal love/rivalry*

fraternity /frəˈtɜːnəti/ ***noun*** (*pl.* **fraternities**) **1** [C] a group of people who share the same work or interests: *the medical fraternity* **2** [C] (EDUCATION) (*AmE also informal* **frat**) /fræt/ a club for a group of male students at an American college or university ➲ look at **sorority** **3** [U] (*formal*) the feeling of friendship and support between people in the same group

fraud /frɔːd/ ***noun*** **1** [C,U] (LAW) (an act of) cheating sb in order to get money, etc. illegally: *The accountant was sent to prison for fraud.* ◇ *Massive amounts of money are lost every year in credit card frauds.* **2** [C] a person who tricks sb by pretending to be sb else

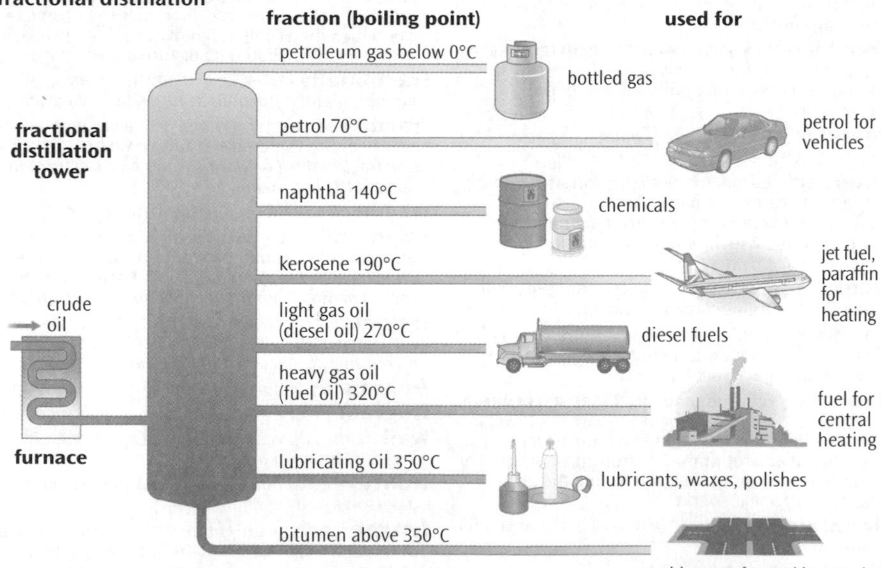

fraudulent /ˈfrɔːdjələnt/ ***adj.*** (*formal*) done in order to cheat sb; dishonest: *the fraudulent use of stolen cheques*

fraught /frɔːt/ ***adj.*** **1** **~ with sth** filled with sth unpleasant: *a situation fraught with danger/difficulty* **2** (used about people) worried and nervous; (used about a situation) very busy so that people become nervous: *Things are usually fraught at work on Mondays.*

fray /freɪ/ ***verb*** [I,T] **1** if cloth, etc. **frays** or becomes **frayed**, some of the threads at the end start to come apart: *This shirt is beginning to fray at the cuffs.* ◇ *a frayed rope* **2** if a person's nerves, etc. **fray** or become **frayed**, they start to get annoyed: *Tempers began to fray towards the end of the match.*

freak¹ /friːk/ ***noun*** [C] **1** (*informal*) a person who has a very strong interest in sth: *a fitness/computer freak* **SYN** **fanatic** **2** a very unusual and strange event, person, animal, etc.: *a freak accident/storm/result* ◇ *The other kids think Ally's a freak because she doesn't watch TV.*

freak² /friːk/ ***verb*** [I,T] (*informal*) **~ (sb) (out)** to react very strongly to sth that makes you feel shocked, frightened, upset, etc.; to make sb react strongly: *She freaked out when she heard the news.* ◇ *The film 'Psycho' really freaked me out.*

freckle /ˈfrekl/ ***noun*** [C, usually pl.] a small brown spot on your skin: *A lot of people with red hair have got freckles.* ➲ look at **mole** ▸ **freckled** ***adj.***

free¹ ⊶ /friː/ ***adj.*** **1** not in prison, in a CAGE, etc.; not held or controlled: *The government* ***set*** *Mandela* ***free*** *in 1989.* ◇ *There is nowhere around here where dogs can run free.* **2** **~ (to do sth)** not controlled by the government, rules, etc.: *There is free movement of people across the border.* ◇ *free speech/press* **3** costing nothing: *Admission to the museum is free/free of charge.* ◇ *Children under five usually travel free on trains.* **4** not busy or being used: *I'm afraid Mr Spencer is not free this afternoon.* ◇ *I don't get much* ***free time***. ◇ *Is this seat free?* **5** **~ from/of sth** not having sth dangerous, unpleasant, etc.: *free of worries/responsibility* ◇ *free from pain*

IDM **feel free** → FEEL¹

free and easy informal or relaxed: *The atmosphere in our office is very free and easy.*

get, have, etc. a free hand to get, have, etc. permission to make your own decisions about sth

of your own free will because you want to, not because sb forces you

free² ⊶ /friː/ ***verb*** [T] **1** **~ sb/sth (from sth)** to let sb/sth leave or escape from a place where he/she/it is held: *to free a prisoner* ◇ *The protesters freed the animals from their cages.* **2** **~ sb/sth of/from sth** to take away sth that is unpleasant from sb: *The medicine freed her from pain for a few hours.* **3** **~ sb/sth (up) for sth; ~ sb/sth (up) to do sth** to make sth available so that it can be used; to put sb in a position in which they can do sth

free³ ⊶ ***adv.*** **1** (*also* ˌfree of ˈcharge) without payment: *Children under five travel free.* **2** away from or out of a position in which sb/sth is stuck or trapped: *The wagon broke free from the train.*

-free ***suffix*** (in adjectives) without the thing mentioned: *fat-free yoghurt* ◇ *tax-free earnings*

ˌ**free ˈagent** ***noun*** [C] a person who can do what they want because nobody else has the right to tell them what to do

freebie /ˈfriːbi/ ***noun*** [C] (*informal*) (BUSINESS) something that is given to sb without payment, usually by a company: *He took all the freebies that were on offer.* ◇ *a freebie holiday*

freedom ⊶ /ˈfriːdəm/ ***noun*** **1** [U] the state of not being held prisoner or controlled by sb else: *The opposition leader was given his freedom after 25 years.* **2** [C,U] the right or ability to do or say what you want: *You have the freedom to come and go as you please.* ◇ *freedom of speech* ◇ *the rights and freedoms of the individual* ➲ look at **liberty** **3** [U] **~ from sth** the state of not being affected by sth unpleasant: *freedom from fear/hunger/pain* **4** [U] **the ~ of sth** the right to use sth with nothing to limit you: *You can have the freedom of the whole house while we're away.*

ˈ**freedom fighter** ***noun*** [C] (POLITICS) a person who belongs to a group that uses violence to try to remove a government from power

ˌ**free ˈenterprise** ***noun*** [U] (BUSINESS) the operation of private business without government control

freehand /ˈfriːhænd/ ***adj.***, ***adv.*** (ART) (used about a drawing) done by hand, without the help of any instruments: *a freehand sketch* ◇ *to draw freehand*

freehold /ˈfriːhəʊld/ ***noun*** [C,U] (LAW) the fact of owning a building or piece of land for a period of time that is not limited: *Do you own the freehold of this house?* ▸ **freehold** ***adj.***, ***adv.***: *a freehold property* ◇ *to buy a house freehold* ➲ look at **leasehold**

ˌ**free ˈkick** ***noun*** [C] (SPORT) (in football or RUGBY) a situation in which a player of one team is allowed to kick the ball because a member of the other team has broken a rule

freelance /ˈfriːlɑːns/ ***adj.***, ***adv.*** (BUSINESS) earning money by selling your services or work to different organizations rather than being employed by a single company: *a freelance journalist* ◇ *She works freelance.* ▸ **freelance** (*also* **freelancer**) ***noun*** [C] ▸ **freelance** ***verb*** [I]

freely ⊶ /ˈfriːli/ ***adv.*** **1** in a way that is not controlled or limited: *He is the country's first freely elected president for 40 years.* **2** without trying to avoid the truth even though it might be embarrassing; in an honest way: *I freely admit that I made a mistake.*

freeman /ˈfriːmən/ ***noun*** [C] (*pl.* **freemen** /-mən/) (HISTORY) (in past times) a person who is not a SLAVE (= a person who is legally owned by another person and is forced to work for them)

ˌ**free ˈmarket** ***noun*** [C] (ECONOMICS) an economic system in which the price of goods and services is affected by supply and demand rather than controlled by the government

Freemason /ˈfriːmeɪsn/ (*also* **mason**) ***noun*** [C] a man who belongs to an international secret society whose members help each other and who recognize each other by secret signs

ˌ**free ˈport** ***noun*** [C] (ECONOMICS) a port at which tax is not paid on goods that have been brought there for a short time before being sent to a different country

ˌ**free ˈradical** ***noun*** [C] (CHEMISTRY, HEALTH) an atom or group of atoms that has an ELECTRON that is not part of a pair, causing it to take part easily in chemical reactions. **Free radicals** in the body are thought to be one of the causes of diseases such as cancer.

ˌ**free-ˈrange** ***adj.*** (AGRICULTURE) (used about farm birds or their eggs) kept or produced in a place where birds can move around freely: *free-range hens/eggs* ➲ look at **battery**

ˌfree ˈspeech *noun* [U] the right to express any opinion in public

ˌfree-ˈstanding *adj.* not supported by or attached to anything: *a free-standing sculpture*

freestyle /ˈfriːstaɪl/ *noun* [U] (**SPORT**) **1** a swimming race in which people taking part can use any swimming style they want (usually CRAWL[2] (2)): *the men's 400m freestyle* **2** (often used as an adjective) a sports competition in which people taking part can use any style that they want: *freestyle skiing*

ˌfree ˈtrade *noun* [U] (**ECONOMICS**) a system of international commercial activity in which there are no limits or taxes on imports and exports: *a free-trade agreement/area*

ˌfree ˈverse *noun* [U] (**LITERATURE**) poetry without a regular rhythm or RHYME (=words that have the same sound) ➲ look at **blank verse**

freeware /ˈfriːweə(r)/ *noun* [U] (**COMPUTING**) computer software that is offered free for anyone to use ➲ look at **shareware**

freeway /ˈfriːweɪ/ (*AmE*) =MOTORWAY

freeze[1] ⊶ /friːz/ *verb* (*pt* **froze** /frəʊz/; *pp* **frozen** /ˈfrəʊzn/) **1** [I,T] to become hard (and often change into ice) because of extreme cold; to make sth do this: *Water freezes at 0° Celsius.* ◇ *The ground was* ***frozen solid*** *for most of the winter.* ◇ *frozen peas/fish/food* **2** [I] used with 'it' to describe extremely cold weather when water turns into ice: *I think it's going to freeze tonight.* **3** [I,T] to be very cold or to die from cold: *It was so cold on the mountain that we thought we would* ***freeze to death****.* ◇ *Turn the heater up a bit – I'm* ***frozen stiff****.* **4** [I] to stop moving suddenly and completely because you are frightened or in danger: *The terrible scream made her freeze with terror.* ◇ *Suddenly the man pulled out a gun and shouted 'Freeze!'* **5** [T] (**ECONOMICS**) to keep the money you earn, prices, etc. at a fixed level for a certain period of time: *Spending on defence has been frozen for one year.*

freeze[2] /friːz/ *noun* [C] **1** a period of weather when the temperature stays below 0° Celsius (**freezing point**) **2** (**ECONOMICS**) the fixing of the money you earn, prices, etc. at one level for a certain period of time: *a wage/pay/price freeze*

ˈfreeze-dried *adj.* (used about food or drink) frozen and then dried very quickly, so that it can be kept for a long time

freezer /ˈfriːzə(r)/ (*also* **ˌdeep ˈfreeze**) *noun* [C] a large box or cupboard in which you can store food for a long time at a temperature below FREEZING POINT so that it stays frozen ➲ look at **fridge**

freezing[1] /ˈfriːzɪŋ/ *adj.* (*informal*) very cold: *Can we turn the central heating on? I'm freezing.* ◇ *Put a coat on, it's absolutely freezing outside.*

freezing[2] /ˈfriːzɪŋ/ (*also* **ˈfreezing point**) *noun* [U] (**SCIENCE**) the temperature at which water freezes: *Last night the temperature fell to six degrees below freezing.*

ˈfreezing point *noun* (**SCIENCE**) **1** (*also* **freezing**) [U] 0° Celsius, the temperature at which water freezes: *Tonight temperatures will fall well below freezing (point).* **2** [C, usually sing.] the temperature at which a particular liquid freezes: *the freezing point of polar sea water*

freight /freɪt/ *noun* [U] goods that are carried from one place to another by ship, lorry, etc.; the system for carrying goods in this way: *Your order will be sent by air freight.* ◇ *a freight train* ▸ **freight** *verb* [T]: *Donated goods are then freighted to the islands.*

ˈfreight car (*AmE*) =WAGON

freighter /ˈfreɪtə(r)/ *noun* [C] a ship or an aircraft that carries only goods and not passengers

ˌFrench ˈfry *noun* [usually pl.] (*especially AmE*) =CHIP[1] (3)

ˌFrench ˈhorn *noun* [C] (**MUSIC**) a BRASS musical instrument that consists of a long tube curved around in a circle with a wide opening at the end ➲ picture on **page 465**

ˌFrench ˈloaf *noun* [C] =BAGUETTE

ˌFrench ˈwindow (*AmE* **ˌFrench ˈdoor**) *noun* [C] one of a pair of glass doors that open onto a garden or BALCONY

frenetic /frəˈnetɪk/ *adj.* involving a lot of energy and activity in a way that is not organized: *a scene of frenetic activity* ▸ **frenetically** /-kli/ *adv.*

frenzied /ˈfrenzid/ *adj.* that is wild and out of control: *a frenzied attack* ◇ *frenzied activity*

frenzy /ˈfrenzi/ *noun* [sing., U] a state of great emotion or activity that is not under control

frequency /ˈfriːkwənsi/ *noun* (*pl.* **frequencies**) **1** [U] the number of times sth happens in a particular period: *Fatal accidents have decreased in frequency in recent years.* **2** [U] the fact that sth happens often: *The frequency of child deaths from cancer near the nuclear power station is being investigated.* **3** [C,U] (**PHYSICS**) the rate at which a sound wave or radio wave moves up and down (**vibrates**): *high-frequency/low-frequency sounds* ➲ picture at **wavelength**

frequent[1] ⊶ /ˈfriːkwənt/ *adj.* happening often: *His visits became less frequent.* OPP **infrequent**

frequent[2] /friˈkwent/ *verb* [T] (*formal*) to go to a place often: *He spent most of his evenings in Paris frequenting bars and clubs.*

frequently ⊶ /ˈfriːkwəntli/ *adv.* often: *Buses run frequently between the city and the airport.* ◇ *some of the most* ***frequently asked questions*** *about the Internet*

fresco /ˈfreskəʊ/ *noun* [C,U] (*pl.* **-oes** or **-os**) (**ART**) a picture that is painted on a wall while the PLASTER (=a mixture of powder and water that becomes hard when it is dry) is still wet; the method of painting in this way: *The church is famous for its frescoes.*

fresh ⊶ /freʃ/ *adj.* **1** (used especially about food) produced or picked very recently; not frozen or in a tin: *fresh bread/fruit/flowers* ➲ look at **stale** **2** left somewhere or experienced recently: *fresh blood/footprints* ◇ *Write a few notes while the lecture is still* ***fresh in your mind****.* **3** new and different: *They have decided to* ***make a fresh start*** *in a different town.* ◇ *I'm sure he'll have some fresh ideas on the subject.* **4** (used about water) without salt; not sea water **5** pleasantly clean or bright: *Open the window and let some* ***fresh air*** *in.* **6** not tired: *I'll think about the problem again in the morning when I'm fresh.* **7** ~ **from/out of sth** having just finished sth: *Life isn't easy for a young teacher fresh from university.* ▸ **freshness** *noun* [U]

IDM **break fresh/new ground** → GROUND[1]

freshen /ˈfreʃn/ *verb* [T] ~ **sth (up)** to make sth cleaner or brighter

PHR V **freshen up** to wash and make yourself clean and tidy

fresher /ˈfreʃə(r)/ *noun* [C] (*BrE*) (**EDUCATION**) a student who is in their first year at university, college, etc.

freshly ⊶ /ˈfreʃli/ ***adv.*** usually followed by a past participle showing that sth has been made, prepared, etc. recently: ***freshly baked*** *bread*

freshman /ˈfreʃmən/ ***noun*** [C] (*pl.* **-men** /-mən/) (*AmE*) (**EDUCATION**) a student who is in their first year at college, high school, university, etc.

freshwater /ˈfreʃwɔːtə(r)/ ***adj.*** (only *before* a noun) **1** (**BIOLOGY**) living in water that is not the sea and is not salty: *freshwater fish* **2** (**GEOGRAPHY**) having water that is not salty: *freshwater lakes/pools* ➲ look at **saltwater**

fret[1] /fret/ ***verb*** [I] (**fretting**; **fretted**) ~ (**about/at/over sth**) to be worried and unhappy about sth

fret[2] /fret/ ***noun*** [C] (**MUSIC**) one of the bars across the long thin part of a GUITAR, etc. that show you where to put your fingers to produce a particular sound ➲ picture at **music**

fretsaw /ˈfretsɔː/ ***noun*** [C] a tool with a narrow cutting edge in a frame, used for cutting patterns into wood for decoration

fretwork /ˈfretwɜːk/ ***noun*** [U] (**ART**) patterns cut into wood, metal, etc. to decorate it; the process of making these patterns

Fri. ***abbr.*** Friday: *Fri. 27 May*

friar /ˈfraɪə(r)/ ***noun*** [C] (**RELIGION**) a member of one of several Roman Catholic religious communities of men who in the past travelled around teaching people about Christianity and lived by asking other people for food (= by BEGGING)

friction /ˈfrɪkʃn/ ***noun*** [U] **1** (**PHYSICS**) the rubbing of one surface or thing against another: *You have to put oil in the engine to reduce friction between the moving parts.* **2** ~ (**between A and B**) disagreement between people or groups: *There is a lot of friction between the older and younger members of staff.*

Friday /ˈfraɪdeɪ; -di/ ***noun*** [C,U] (*abbr.* **Fri.**) the day of the week after Thursday

fridge ⊶ /frɪdʒ/ (also *formal* **refrigerator**, *AmE* **icebox**) ***noun*** [C] a metal container with a door in which food, etc. is kept cold (but not frozen) so that it stays fresh ➲ look at **freezer**

fried[1] past tense, past participle of **fry**[1]

fried[2] /fraɪd/ ***adj.*** (used about food) cooked in hot fat or oil: *a fried egg*

friend ⊶ /frend/ ***noun*** [C] **1** a person that you know and like (not a member of your family), and who likes you: *Trevor and I are* ***old friends****. We were at school together.* ◇ *We're only inviting* ***close friends*** *and relatives to the wedding.* ◇ *Helen's my* ***best friend****.* ◇ *A friend of mine told me about this restaurant.* ◇ *One of my friends told me about this restaurant.* ➲ look at **boyfriend**, **girlfriend**, **penfriend** **2** a ~ **of/to sth** a person who supports an organization, a charity, etc., especially by giving money; a person who supports a particular idea, etc.: *the Friends of the Churchill Hospital*

IDM **be/make friends (with sb)** to be/become a friend (of sb): *Tony is rather shy and finds it hard to make friends.*

a false friend → FALSE

friendly[1] ⊶ /ˈfrendli/ ***adj.*** (**friendlier**; **friendliest**) **1** ~ (**to/toward(s) sb**) behaving in a kind and open way: *Everyone here has been very friendly towards us.* OPP **unfriendly** **2** showing kindness in a way that makes people feel happy and relaxed: *a friendly smile/atmosphere* OPP **unfriendly** **3** ~ **with sb** treating sb as a friend: *Nick's* ***become quite friendly*** *with the boy next door.* ◇ *Are you* ***on friendly terms*** *with your neighbours?* **4** (in compounds) helpful to sb/sth; not harmful to sth: *Our computer is extremely* ***user-friendly****.* ◇ *ozone-friendly sprays* **5** in which the people, teams, etc. taking part are not competing seriously: *a friendly argument* ◇ *I've organized a friendly match against my brother's team.* ▶ **friendliness** ***noun*** [U]

friendly[2] /ˈfrendli/ ***noun*** [C] (*pl.* **friendlies**) (**SPORT**) a sports match that is not part of a serious competition

friendship ⊶ /ˈfrendʃɪp/ ***noun*** **1** [C] a ~ (**with sb**); a ~ (**between A and B**) a relationship between people who are friends: *a close/lasting/lifelong friendship* **2** [U] the state of being friends: *Our relationship is based on friendship, not love.*

frieze /friːz/ ***noun*** [C] (**ARCHITECTURE**) a border that goes around the top of a room or building with pictures or CARVINGS (= designs that have been cut in wood or stone) on it

frigate /ˈfrɪgət/ ***noun*** [C] a small fast ship in the navy that travels with other ships in order to protect them

fright /fraɪt/ ***noun*** [C,U] a sudden feeling of fear or shock: *I hope I didn't* ***give you a fright*** *when I shouted.* ◇ *The child cried out* ***in fright****.*

frighten ⊶ /ˈfraɪtn/ ***verb*** [T] to make sb/sth afraid or shocked: *That programme about crime really frightened me.*

PHR V **frighten sb/sth away/off** to cause a person or animal to go away by frightening them or it: *Walk quietly so that you don't frighten the birds away.*

frightened ⊶ /ˈfraɪtnd/ ***adj.*** **1** full of fear or worry: *Frightened children were calling for their mothers.* ◇ *I was frightened that they would think that I was rude.* **2** ~ **of sb/sth** afraid of a particular person, thing or situation: *When I was young I was frightened of spiders.*

frightening ⊶ /ˈfraɪtnɪŋ/ ***adj.*** making you feel afraid or shocked: *a frightening experience* ◇ *It's frightening that time passes so quickly.*

frightful /ˈfraɪtfl/ ***adj.*** (*old-fashioned*) **1** very bad or unpleasant: *The weather this summer has been frightful.* **2** (used for emphasizing sth) very bad or great: *We're in a frightful rush.*

frightfully /ˈfraɪtfəli/ ***adv.*** (*old-fashioned*) very: *I'm frightfully sorry.*

frigid /ˈfrɪdʒɪd/ ***adj.*** **1** (usually used about a woman) unable to enjoy sex **2** not showing any emotion

frill /frɪl/ ***noun*** [C] **1** a decoration for the edge of a dress, shirt, etc. which is made by forming many folds in a narrow piece of cloth **2** [usually pl.] something that is added for decoration that you feel is not necessary: *We just want a plain simple meal – no frills.* ▶ **frilly** ***adj.***: *a frilly dress*

fringe[1] /frɪndʒ/ ***noun*** [C] **1** (*AmE* **bangs** [pl.]) the part of your hair that is cut so that it hangs over your FOREHEAD: *Your hair looks better with a fringe.* **2** a border for decoration on a piece of clothing, etc. that is made of lots of hanging threads **3** (*BrE*) the outer edge of an area or a group that is a long way from the centre or from what is usual: *Some people* ***on the fringes of*** *the socialist party are opposed to the policy on Europe.*

fringe[2] /frɪndʒ/ ***verb***

IDM **be fringed with sth** to have sth as a border or around the edge: *The lake was fringed with pine trees.*

ˌ**fringe ˈbenefit** ***noun*** [C, usually pl.] an extra thing that is given to an employee in addition to the money they earn

Frisbee /ˈfrɪzbi/ ***noun*** [C] a light plastic object, shaped like a plate, that is thrown from one player to another in a game

frisk /frɪsk/ ***verb* 1** [T] to pass your hands over sb's body in order to search for hidden weapons, drugs, etc. **2** [I] (used about an animal or child) to play and jump about happily and with a lot of energy

frisky /ˈfrɪski/ ***adj.*** full of life and wanting to play

fritter /ˈfrɪtə(r)/ ***verb***
PHR V **fritter sth away (on sth)** to waste time or money on things that are not important

frivolity /frɪˈvɒləti/ ***noun*** [U] silly behaviour (especially when you should be serious)

frivolous /ˈfrɪvələs/ ***adj.*** not serious; silly

frizzy /ˈfrɪzi/ ***adj.*** (used about hair) very curly

fro /frəʊ/ ***adv.***
IDM **to and fro** → TO

frock /frɒk/ ***noun*** [C] (*especially BrE*) (*old-fashioned*) a dress: *a party frock*

frog /frɒg/ ***noun*** [C] a small animal with smooth skin and long back legs that it uses for jumping. **Frogs** live in or near water. ➲ picture on **page 29**

frogman /ˈfrɒgmən/ ***noun*** [C] (*pl.* **-men** /-mən/) a person whose job is to work under the surface of water wearing special rubber clothes and using breathing equipment: *Police frogmen searched the river.*

frogspawn /ˈfrɒgspɔːn/ ***noun*** [U] (**BIOLOGY**) an almost transparent substance that is between a liquid and a solid and contains the eggs of a FROG ➲ picture on **page 29**

from ⊶ /frəm *strong form* frɒm/ ***prep.***
1 showing the place, direction or time that sb/sth starts or started: *She comes home from work at 7 o'clock.* ◇ *a cold wind from the east* ◇ *Water was dripping from the tap.* ◇ *Peter's on holiday from next Friday.* ◇ *The supermarket is open* ***from*** *8 a.m.* ***till*** *8 p.m. every day.* **2** showing the person who sent or gave sth: *I borrowed this jacket from my sister.* ◇ *a phone call from my father* **3** showing the origin of sb/sth: *'Where do you come from?' 'I'm from Australia.'* ◇ *cheeses from France and Italy* ◇ *quotations from Shakespeare* **4** showing the material which is used to make sth: *Paper is* ***made from*** *wood.* ◇ *This sauce is made from cream and wine.* **5** showing the distance between two places: *The house is five miles from the town centre.* ◇ *I work not far from here.* **6** showing the point at which a series of prices, figures, etc., start: *Our prices start from £2.50 a bottle.* ◇ *Tickets cost from £3 to £11.* **7** showing the state of sb/sth before a change: *The time of the meeting has been changed* ***from*** *7* ***to*** *8 o'clock.* ◇ *The article was translated* ***from*** *Russian* ***into*** *English.* ◇ *Things have gone* ***from bad to worse.*** **8** showing that sb/sth is taken away, removed or separated from sb/sth else: *Children don't like being separated from their parents for a long period.* ◇ *(in mathematics) 8 from 12 leaves 4.* **9** showing sth that you want to avoid: *There was no shelter from the wind.* ◇ *This game will stop you from getting bored.* **10** showing the cause of sth: *People in the camps are suffering from hunger and cold.* **11** showing the reason for making a judgement or forming an opinion: *You can tell quite a lot from a person's handwriting.* **12** showing the difference between two people, places or things: *Can you tell margarine from butter?* ◇ *Is Portuguese very different from Spanish?*
IDM **from...on** starting at a particular time and continuing for ever: *She never spoke to him again* ***from that day on.*** ◇ ***From now on*** *you must earn your own living.*

frond /frɒnd/ ***noun*** [C] (**BIOLOGY**) **1** a long leaf, often divided into parts along the edge, of some plants or trees: *the fronds of a palm tree* **2** a long piece of SEAWEED (= a plant that grows in the sea) that looks like one of these leaves

front¹ ⊶ /frʌnt/ ***noun* 1 the front** [C, usually sing.] the side or surface of sth/sb that faces forward: *a dress with buttons down the front* ◇ *the front of a building* (= the front wall) ◇ *a card with flowers* ***on the front*** ◇ *She slipped on the stairs and spilt coffee all down her front.* **2 the front** [C, usually sing.] the most forward part of sth; the area that is just outside of or before sb/sth: *Young children should not travel* ***in the front of*** *the car.* ◇ *There is a small garden* ***at the front of*** *the house.* **3** [C] a particular area of activity: *Things are difficult* ***on the*** *domestic/political/economic* ***front*** *at the moment.* ◇ *Progress has been made* ***on all fronts.*** **4 the front** [sing.] the line or area where fighting takes place in a war: *to be sent to the front* **5** [sing.] a way of behaving that hides your true feelings: *His brave words were just a front. He was really feeling very nervous.* **6** [C] (**GEOGRAPHY**) a line or area where warm air and cold air meet: *A* ***cold front*** *is moving in from the north.* ➲ picture at **cloud**
IDM **back to front** → BACK¹
in front further forward than sb/sth; ahead: *Some of the children ran on in front.* ◇ *After three laps the Kenyan runner was in front.*
in front of sb/sth 1 in a position further forward than but close to sb/sth: *The bus stops right in front of our house.* ◇ *Don't stand in front of the television.* ◇ *The book was open in front of her on the desk.* **2** if you do sth in front of sb, you do it when that person is there in the same room or place as you: *I couldn't talk about that in front of my parents.*
up front (*informal*) as payment before sth is done: *I want half the money up front and half when the job is finished.*

front² ⊶ /frʌnt/ ***adj.*** (only *before* a noun) of or at the front (1,2): *the front door/garden/room* ◇ *sit in the front row* ◇ *front teeth*

frontage /ˈfrʌntɪdʒ/ ***noun*** [C,U] (**ARCHITECTURE**) the front of a building, especially when this faces a road or river

frontal /ˈfrʌntl/ ***adj.*** (only *before* a noun) from the front: *a frontal attack*

ˌfront ˈdesk ***noun*** [C] the desk inside the entrance of a hotel, an office building, etc. where guests or visitors go when they first arrive ➲ look at **reception**

frontier /ˈfrʌntɪə(r)/ ***noun* 1** [C] **the ~ (between A and B)** the line where one country joins another; border: *the end of frontier controls in Europe* **2 the frontiers** [pl.] the limit between what we do and do not know: *Scientific research is constantly* ***pushing back the frontiers of*** *our knowledge about the world.*

ˌfront ˈline ***noun*** [C] **1** [sing.] an area where the enemies are facing each other during a war and where fighting takes place: *Tanks have been deployed all along the front line.* **2** [usually sing.] (**BUSINESS**) the group of employees in a company who deal directly with customers or who physically produce sth; the work that they do: *Managers weren't giving feedback to the people* ***on the front line.*** ▶ **front-line** ***adj.***: *Front-line staff should know all the products on sale.*

ˌfront-of-ˈhouse ***noun*** [U] (**TOURISM**) the part of a hotel, restaurant or other business that involves dealing directly with customers: *I cooked and my wife did front-of-house* ◇ *a front-of-house manager/worker*

ˌ**front-ˈpage** *adj.* interesting or important enough to appear on the front page of a newspaper: *front-page news/headlines*

frost[1] /frɒst/ ***noun*** [C,U] the weather condition when the temperature falls below 0° Celsius (**freezing point**) and a thin layer of ice forms on the ground and other surfaces, especially at night: *There was a* ***hard frost*** *last night.* ◇ *It will be a chilly night with some* ***ground frost***.

frost[2] /frɒst/ ***verb*** [T] (*especially AmE*) = ICE[2]
PHRV **frost over/up** to become covered with a thin layer of ice: *The window has frosted over/up.* ➲ look at **defrost**

frostbite /ˈfrɒstbaɪt/ ***noun*** [U] (HEALTH) a serious medical condition of the fingers, toes, etc. that is caused by very low temperatures

frosted /ˈfrɒstɪd/ ***adj.*** (used about glass or a window) with a special surface so you cannot see through it

frosting /ˈfrɒstɪŋ/ (*especially AmE*) = ICING

frosty /ˈfrɒsti/ ***adj.*** **1** very cold, with FROST: *a cold and frosty morning* **2** cold and unfriendly: *a frosty welcome*

froth[1] /frɒθ/ ***noun*** [U] a mass of small white bubbles on the top of a liquid, etc. ▶ **frothy** ***adj.***: *frothy beer* ◇ *a frothy cappuccino*

froth[2] /frɒθ/ ***verb*** [I] to have or produce a mass of white bubbles: *The mad dog was frothing at the mouth.*

frown /fraʊn/ ***verb*** [I] to show you are angry, serious, etc. by making lines appear on your FOREHEAD above your nose ▶ **frown** ***noun*** [C]
PHRV **frown on/upon sth** to disapprove of sth: *Smoking is very much frowned upon these days.*

froze past tense of **freeze[1]**

frozen[1] past participle of **freeze[1]**

frozen[2] 🔑 /ˈfrəʊzn/ ***adj.*** **1** (used about food) stored at a low temperature in order to keep it for a long time: *frozen meat/vegetables* **2** (*informal*) (used about people and parts of the body) very cold: *My feet are frozen!* ◇ *I was* ***frozen stiff***. SYN **freezing** **3** (used about water) with a layer of ice on the surface: *The pond is frozen. Let's go skating.*

fructose /ˈfrʌktəʊs; -təʊz/ ***noun*** [U] (BIOLOGY) a type of natural sugar that is found in fruit juice ➲ look at **dextrose**, **glucose**, **lactose**, **sucrose**

frugal /ˈfruːɡl/ ***adj.*** **1** using only as much money or food as is necessary: *a frugal existence/life* **2** (used about meals) small, simple and not costing very much ▶ **frugality** /fruˈɡæləti/ ***noun*** [U] ▶ **frugally** /ˈfruːɡəli/ ***adv.***: *to live/eat frugally*

fruit 🔑 /fruːt/ ***noun*** **1** [C,U] (BIOLOGY) the part of a plant or tree that contains seeds and that we eat: *Try and eat more* ***fresh fruit*** *and vegetables.* ◇ *Marmalade is made with* ***citrus fruit*** (= oranges, lemons, grapefruit, etc.). ◇ *fruit juice* **2** [C] (BIOLOGY) the part of any plant in which the seed is formed **3** [pl.] **the fruits (of sth)** a good result or success from work that you have done
IDM **bear fruit** → BEAR[2]

ˈ**fruit fly** ***noun*** [C] (*pl.* **fruit flies**) a small flying insect that eats plants that have died, especially fruit

fruitful /ˈfruːtfl/ ***adj.*** producing good results; useful: *fruitful discussions*

fruition /fruˈɪʃn/ ***noun*** [U] (*formal*) the time when a plan, etc. starts to be successful: *After months of hard work, our efforts were* ***coming to fruition***.

fruitless /ˈfruːtləs/ ***adj.*** producing poor or no results; not successful: *a fruitless search*

frustrate /frʌˈstreɪt/ ***verb*** [T] **1** to cause a person to feel annoyed or impatient because they cannot do or achieve what they want: *It's the lack of money that really frustrates him.* **2** (*formal*) to prevent sb from doing sth or sth from happening: *The rescue work has been frustrated by bad weather conditions.* ▶ **frustrated** ***adj.***: *He felt very frustrated at his lack of progress in learning Chinese.* ▶ **frustrating** ***adj.***

frustration /frʌˈstreɪʃn/ ***noun*** [C,U] a feeling of anger because you cannot get what you want; sth that causes you to feel like this: *He felt anger and frustration at no longer being able to see very well.* ◇ *Every job has its frustrations.*

fry[1] 🔑 /fraɪ/ ***verb*** [I,T] (*pres. part.* **frying**; *3rd person sing. pres.* **fries**; *pt, pp* **fried** /fraɪd/) to cook sth or to be cooked in hot fat or oil: *to fry an egg* ◇ *I could smell bacon frying in the kitchen.* ➲ note at **cook**

fry[2] 🔑 /fraɪ/ ***noun*** [C] (*pl.* **fries**) (*especially AmE*) = CHIP[1] (3): *Would you like ketchup with your fries?*

ˈ**frying pan** (*AmE also* **frypan, skillet**) ***noun*** [C] a flat pan with a long handle that is used for frying food

ft ***abbr.*** foot, feet; a measure of length, about 30.5 cm: *a room 10 ft by 6 ft*

fête /feɪt/ ***noun*** [C] an outdoor event with competitions, entertainment and things to buy, often organized to make money for a particular purpose: *the school/village/church fête*

FTP /ˌef tiː ˈpiː/ ***abbr.*** (COMPUTING) **file transfer protocol**; a set of rules for sending files from one computer to another on the Internet

FTSE index /ˈfʊtsi ɪndeks/ (*also* **the FT index** /ˌef ˈtiː/; **the Fiˌnancial Times ˈindex; the Footsie** /ˈfʊtsiː/) ***noun*** [sing.] (FINANCE) a figure that shows the relative price of shares on the London Stock Exchange

fudge /fʌdʒ/ ***noun*** [U] a type of soft brown sweet made from sugar, butter and milk

fuel[1] 🔑 /ˈfjuːəl/ ***noun*** **1** [U] material that is burned to produce heat or power **2** [C] a type of fuel: *I think gas is the best fuel for central heating.*

fuel[2] /ˈfjuːəl/ ***verb*** [T] (**fuelling**; **fuelled**: *AmE* **fueling**; **fueled**) to make sb feel an emotion more strongly: *Her interest in the Spanish language was fuelled by a visit to Spain.*

fugitive /ˈfjuːdʒətɪv/ ***noun*** [C] a person who is running away or escaping (for example from the police) ➲ look at **refugee**

fugue /fjuːɡ/ ***noun*** [C] (MUSIC) a piece of music in which one or more tunes are introduced and then repeated in a complicated pattern

fulcrum /ˈfʊlkrəm/ ***noun*** [C, usually sing.] (PHYSICS) the point on which sth turns or is supported SYN **pivot** ➲ picture at **lever**

fulfil (*AmE* **fulfill**) /fʊlˈfɪl/ ***verb*** [T] (**fulfilling**; **fulfilled**) **1** to make sth that you wish for happen; to achieve a goal: *He finally fulfilled his childhood dream of becoming a doctor.* ◇ *to fulfil your ambition/potential* **2** to do or have everything that you should or that is necessary: *to fulfil a duty/obligation/promise/need* ◇ *The conditions of entry to university in this country are quite difficult to fulfil.* **3** to have a particular role or purpose: *Italy fulfils a very important role within the European Union.* **4** to make sb feel completely happy and satisfied: *I need a job that really fulfils me.* ▶ **fulfilled** ***adj.***: *When I had my baby I felt totally fulfilled.* ▶ **fulfilling** ***adj.***: *I found working abroad a very fulfilling experience.*

fulfilment /fʊlˈfɪlmənt/ (*AmE* **fulfillment**) *noun* [U] the act of achieving a goal; the feeling of satisfaction that you have when you have done sth: *the fulfilment of your dreams/hopes/ambitions* ◇ *to find personal/emotional fulfilment*

full¹ ⊷ /fʊl/ *adj.* **1** holding or containing as much or as many as possible: *The bin needs emptying. It's* ***full up*** (=completely full). ◇ *a full bottle* ◇ *The bus was full so we had to wait for the next one.* ◇ (*figurative*) *We need a good night's sleep because we've got a full* (=busy) *day tomorrow.* **2** ~ **of sb/sth** containing a lot of sb/sth: *The room was full of people.* ◇ *His work was full of mistakes.* ◇ *The children are full of energy.* **3** ~ **(up)** having had enough to eat and drink: *No more, thank you. I'm full (up).* **4** (only *before* a noun) complete; not leaving anything out: *I should like* ***a full report*** *on the accident, please.* ◇ ***Full details*** *of today's TV programmes are on page 20.* ◇ *He took* ***full responsibility*** *for what had happened.* ◇ *Please give your* ***full name and address***. **5** (only *before* a noun) the highest or greatest possible: *She got* ***full marks*** *in her French exam.* ◇ *The train was travelling* ***at full speed***. **6** ~ **of sb/sth/yourself** thinking or talking a lot about sb/sth/yourself: *When she got back from holiday she was full of everything they had seen.* ◇ *He's* ***full of himself*** (=thinks that he is very important) *since he got that new job.* **7** round in shape: *She's got quite* ***a full figure***. ◇ *He's quite* ***full in the face***. **8** (used about clothes) made with plenty of material: *a full skirt*

IDM **at full stretch** working as hard as possible

full of beans/life with a lot of energy and enthusiasm

have your hands full → HAND¹

in full with nothing missing; completely: *Your money will be refunded in full* (=you will get all your money back). ◇ *Please write your name in full.*

in full swing at the stage when there is the most activity: *When we arrived the party was already in full swing.*

in full view (of sb/sth) in a place where you can easily be seen: *In full view of the guards, he tried to escape over the prison wall.*

to the full as much as possible: *to enjoy life to the full*

full² /fʊl/ *adv.* ~ **in/on (sth)** straight; directly: *John hit him full in the face.* ◇ *The two cars crashed full on.*

ˌfull-ˈblown *adj.* fully developed: *to have full-blown Aids*

ˌfull ˈboard *noun* [U] (TOURISM) (in a hotel, etc.) including all meals ➲ look at **half board**, **bed and breakfast**

ˌfull-ˈfledged (*especially AmE and BrE*) = FULLY FLEDGED

ˌfull-ˈlength *adj.* **1** (used about a picture, mirror, etc.) showing a person from head to foot **2** not made shorter: *a full-length film* **3** (used about a dress, skirt, etc.) reaching the feet

ˌfull ˈmoon *noun* [sing.] the moon when it appears as a complete circle ➲ look at **new moon**

ˌfull-ˈscale *adj.* (only *before* a noun) **1** using every thing or person that is available: *The police have started a full-scale murder investigation.* **2** (used about a plan, drawing, etc.) of the same size as the original object: *a full-scale plan/model*

ˌfull ˈstop (*especially AmE* **period**) *noun* [C] (LANGUAGE) a mark (.) that is used in writing to show the end of a sentence

ˌfull-ˈtime *adj., adv.* (BUSINESS) for a whole of the normal period of work: *He has a full-time job.* ◇ *He works full-time.* ◇ *We employ 800 full-time staff.* ➲ look at **part-time**

fully ⊷ /ˈfʊli/ *adv.* completely; to the highest possible degree: *I'm fully aware of the problem.* ◇ *All our engineers are fully trained.*

fully fledged /ˌfʊli fledʒd/ (*AmE and BrE also* **ˌfull-ˈfledged**) *adj.* completely developed; with all the qualifications necessary for sth: *the emergence of a fully fledged market economy*

fumble /ˈfʌmbl/ *verb* [I] to try to find or take hold of sth with your hands in a nervous or careless way: *'It must be here somewhere', she said, fumbling in her pocket for her key.*

fume /fjuːm/ *verb* [I] to be very angry about sth

fumes /fjuːmz/ *noun* [pl.] smoke or gases that smell unpleasant and that can be dangerous to breathe in: *diesel/petrol/exhaust fumes*

fumigate /ˈfjuːmɪgeɪt/ *verb* [T] to use special chemicals, smoke or gas to destroy the harmful insects or bacteria in a place: *to fumigate a room* ▶ **fumigation** /ˌfjuːmɪˈgeɪʃn/ *noun* [U]

fun¹ ⊷ /fʌn/ *noun* [U] pleasure and enjoyment; an activity or a person that gives you pleasure and enjoyment: *We* ***had a lot of fun*** *at the party last night.* ◇ *The party was* ***great fun***. ◇ *Have fun* (=enjoy yourself)*!* ◇ ***It's no fun*** *having to get up at 4 o'clock every day.*

IDM **(just) for fun/for the fun of it** (just) for AMUSEMENT or pleasure; not seriously: *I don't need English for my work. I'm just learning it for fun.*

in fun as a joke: *It was said in fun. They didn't mean to upset you.*

make fun of sb/sth to laugh at sb/sth in an unkind way; to make other people do this: *The older children are always making fun of him because of his accent.*

poke fun at sb/sth → POKE

fun² ⊷ /fʌn/ *adj.* amusing or enjoyable: *to have a fun time/day out* ◇ *Brett's a fun guy.*

function¹ ⊷ AW /ˈfʌŋkʃn/ *noun* [C] **1** the purpose or special duty of a person or thing: *The function of the heart is to pump blood through the body.* ◇ *to perform/fulfil a function* **2** an important social event, ceremony, etc.: *The princess attends hundreds of official functions every year.* **3** (MATHEMATICS) a quantity whose value depends on the varying values of others. In the statement $2x = y$, y is a function of x.

function² ⊷ AW /ˈfʌŋkʃn/ *verb* [I] to work correctly; to be in action: *Only one engine was still functioning.* SYN **operate**

functional AW /ˈfʌŋkʃənl/ *adj.* **1** practical and useful rather than attractive: *cheap functional furniture* **2** working; being used: *The system is now fully functional.*

functionality /ˌfʌŋkʃəˈnæləti/ *noun* [C,U] (*pl.* **functionalities**) (COMPUTING) the set of functions that a computer or other electronic system can perform: *new software with additional functionality*

ˈfunction key *noun* [C] (COMPUTING) one of the KEYS on a computer which are used to perform a particular operation

fund¹ ⊷ AW /fʌnd/ *noun* **1** [C] a sum of money that is collected for a particular purpose: *They contributed £30 to the disaster relief fund.* **2 funds** [pl.] (FINANCE) money that is available and can be spent: *The hospital is trying to* ***raise funds*** *for a new kidney machine.*

fund[2] **AW** /fʌnd/ *verb* [T] to provide a project, school, charity etc. with money: *The Channel Tunnel is not funded by government money.*

fundamental **AW** /ˌfʌndəˈmentl/ *adj.* basic and important; from which everything else develops: *There will be fundamental changes in the way the school is run.* ◊ *There is a fundamental difference between your opinion and mine.* ▶ **fundamentally** **AW** /-təli/ *adv.*: *The government's policy has changed fundamentally.*

fundamentals /ˌfʌndəˈmentlz/ *noun* [pl.] basic facts or principles

funding **AW** /ˈfʌndɪŋ/ *noun* [U] (FINANCE) money for a particular purpose; the act of providing money for such a purpose: *There have been large cuts in government funding for scientific research.*

ˈ**fund-raiser** *noun* [C] a person whose job is to find ways of collecting money for a charity or an organization ▶ **fund-raising** *noun* [U]: *fund-raising events*

funeral /ˈfjuːnərəl/ *noun* [C] a ceremony (usually religious) for burying or burning a dead person

ˈ**funeral director** = UNDERTAKER

funfair /ˈfʌnfeə(r)/ = FAIR[2] (1)

fungicide /ˈfʌŋgɪsaɪd/ *noun* [C,U] (AGRICULTURE) a substance that kills FUNGUS

fungus /ˈfʌŋgəs/ *noun* [C,U] (*pl.* **fungi** /ˈfʌŋgiː; -gaɪ/ or **funguses**) (BIOLOGY) a plant that is not green and does not have leaves or flowers (for example a MUSHROOM), or that is like a wet powder and grows on old wood or food, walls, etc. Some **fungi** can be harmful. ➲ look at **mould**, **toadstool** ▶ **fungal** *adj.*: *a fungal disease/infection/growth*

ˈ**fun-loving** *adj.* liking to enjoy themselves

funnel /ˈfʌnl/ *noun* [C] **1** an object that is wide at the top and narrow at the bottom, used for pouring liquid, powder, etc. into a small opening ➲ pictures at **filtration**, **laboratory** **2** the metal CHIMNEY of a ship, engine, etc.

funnily /ˈfʌnɪli; -əli/ *adv.* in a strange or unusual way: *She's walking very funnily.*
IDM **funnily enough** used for expressing surprise at sth strange that has happened: *Funnily enough, my parents weren't at all cross about it.*

funny /ˈfʌni/ *adj.* (**funnier**; **funniest**) **1** that makes you smile or laugh: *a funny story* ◊ *He's an extremely funny person.* ◊ *That's the funniest thing I've heard in ages!* **2** strange or unusual; difficult to explain or understand: *Oh dear, the engine is making a funny noise.* ◊ *It's funny that they didn't phone to let us know they couldn't come.* ◊ ***That's funny*** *– he was here a moment ago and now he's gone.* ◊ *Can I sit down for a minute? I* ***feel a bit funny*** (= a bit ill).

ˈ**funny bone** *noun* [C, usually sing.] (*informal*) the bone at your elbow

fur /fɜː(r)/ *noun* **1** [U] the soft thick hair that covers the bodies of some animals **2** [C,U] the skin and hair of an animal that is used for making clothes, etc.; a piece of clothing that is made from this: *a fur coat*

furious /ˈfjʊəriəs/ *adj.* **1** ~ **(with sb)**; ~ **(at sth)** very angry: *He was furious with her for losing the car keys.* ◊ *He was furious at having to catch the train home.* ➲ noun **fury**
2 very strong; violent: *A furious row has broken out over the closure of the school.* ▶ **furiously** *adv.*
IDM **fast and furious** → FAST[1]

furnace /ˈfɜːnɪs/ *noun* [C] a large, very hot, ENCLOSED fire that is used for melting metal, burning rubbish, etc.

furnish /ˈfɜːnɪʃ/ *verb* [T] to put furniture in a room, house, etc.: *The room was comfortably furnished.* ▶ **furnished** *adj.*: *She's renting a furnished room in Birmingham.*

furnishings /ˈfɜːnɪʃɪŋz/ *noun* [pl.] the furniture, carpets, curtains, etc. in a room, house, etc.

furniture /ˈfɜːnɪtʃə(r)/ *noun* [U] the things that can be moved, for example tables, chairs, beds, etc. in a room, house or office: *modern/antique/second-hand furniture* ◊ *garden/office furniture*

furrow /ˈfʌrəʊ/ *noun* [C] **1** (AGRICULTURE) a line in a field that is made for planting seeds in by a PLOUGH (= a farming machine that turns the earth) **2** a deep line in the skin on a person's face, especially on the FOREHEAD ➲ look at **wrinkle**

furry /ˈfɜːri/ *adj.* having fur: *a small furry animal*

further[1] /ˈfɜːðə(r)/ *adj.*, *adv.* **1** more; to a greater degree: *Are there* ***any further questions****?* ◊ *Please let us know if you require any* ***further information****.* ◊ *I have* ***nothing further to say*** *on the subject.* ◊ *The museum is closed* ***until further notice*** (= until another announcement is made). ◊ *Can I have time to consider the matter further?* **2** (*also* **farther**) (the comparative of *far*) at or to a greater distance in time or space: *It's not safe to go any further.* ◊ *I can't remember any further back than 1970.*
IDM **further afield** → FAR[2]

further[2] /ˈfɜːðə(r)/ *verb* [T] (*formal*) to help sth to develop or be successful: *to further the cause of peace*

ˌ**further eduˈcation** *noun* [U] (*abbr.* **FE**) (*BrE*) (EDUCATION) education for people who have left school (but not at a university) ➲ look at **higher education**

furthermore **AW** /ˌfɜːðəˈmɔː(r)/ *adv.* also; in addition

furthest superlative of **far**

furtive /ˈfɜːtɪv/ *adj.* secret, acting as though you are trying to hide sth because you feel guilty ▶ **furtively** *adv.*

fury /ˈfjʊəri/ *noun* [U] very great anger: *She was speechless with fury.* ➲ adjective **furious**

fuse[1] /fjuːz/ *noun* [C] **1** a small piece of wire in an electrical system, machine, etc. that melts and breaks if there is too much power. This stops the flow of electricity and prevents fire or damage: *A fuse has blown – that's why the house is in darkness.* ◊ *That plug needs a 15 amp fuse.* ➲ picture at **plug** **2** a piece of rope, string, etc. or a device that is used to make a bomb, etc. explode at a particular time

fuse[2] /fjuːz/ *verb* [I,T] **1** (used about two things) to join together to become one; to make two things do this: *As they heal, the bones will fuse together.* ◊ *The two companies have been fused into one large organization.* **2** to stop working because a FUSE[1](1) has melted; to make a piece of electrical equipment do this: *The lights have fused.* ◊ *I've fused the lights.*

fuselage /ˈfjuːzəlɑːʒ/ *noun* [C] the main part of a plane (not the engines, wings or tail) ➲ picture at **plane**

fusion /ˈfjuːʒn/ *noun* **1** [U, sing.] the process or the result of joining different things together to form one: *the fusion of two political systems* **2** (*also* ˌ**nuclear ˈfusion**) [U] (PHYSICS) the action or process of combining the NUCLEI (= central parts) of atoms to form a heavier NUCLEUS, with energy being created ➲ look at **fission**

fuss[1] /fʌs/ ***noun*** [sing., U] a time when people behave in an excited, a nervous or an angry way, especially about sth unimportant: *The waiter didn't **make a fuss** when I spilt my drink.* ◇ *What's all the fuss about?*

IDM **make/kick up a fuss (about/over sth)** to complain strongly

make a fuss of/over sb/sth to pay a lot of attention to sb/sth: *My grandmother used to make a big fuss of me when she visited.*

fuss[2] /fʌs/ ***verb*** [I] **1** to be worried or excited about small things: *Stop fussing. We're not going to be late.* **2 ~ (over sb/sth)** to pay too much attention to sb/sth: *Stop fussing over all the details.*

IDM **not be fussed (about sb/sth)** (*BrE, spoken*) to not care very much: *'Where do you want to go for lunch?' 'I'm not fussed.'*

fussy /'fʌsi/ ***adj.*** (**fussier**; **fussiest**) **1 ~ (about sth)** (used about people) giving too much attention to small details and therefore difficult to please: *He is very fussy about food* (=there are many things which he does not eat). ➲ look at **particular**, **picky** **2** having too much detail or decoration: *I don't like that pattern. It's too fussy.*

futile /'fju:taɪl/ ***adj.*** (used about an action) having no success; useless: *They made a last futile attempt to make him change his mind.* ▶ **futility** ***noun*** [U]

futon /'fu:tɒn/ ***noun*** [C] a Japanese MATTRESS (=the soft part of a bed), often on a wooden frame, that can be used for sitting on or rolled out to make a bed

future ⊶ /'fju:tʃə(r)/ ***noun*** **1 the future** [sing.] the time that will come after the present: *Who knows what will happen **in the future**?* ◇ *in the near/distant future* (=soon/not soon) **2** [C] what will happen to sb/sth in the time after the present: *Our children's futures depend on a good education.* ◇ *The company's future does not look very hopeful.* **3** [U] the possibility of being successful: *I could see no future in this country so I left to work abroad.* **4 futures** [pl.] (BUSINESS) goods or shares that are bought at agreed prices but that will be delivered and paid for at a later time: *oil futures* ◇ *the futures market* **5 the future** [sing.] =THE FUTURE TENSE ▶ **future** ***adj.*** (only *before* a noun): *She met her future husband when she was still at school.* ◇ *You can keep that book **for future reference*** (=to look at again later).

IDM **in future** from now on: *Please try to be more careful in future.*

the ˌfuture 'perfect ***noun*** [sing.] (LANGUAGE) the form of a verb which expresses an action in the future that will be finished before the time mentioned. The future perfect is formed with the future tense of *have* and the past participle of the verb: *'We'll have been married for ten years next month' is **in the future perfect**.*

the ˌfuture 'tense (*also* **the future**) ***noun*** [sing.] (LANGUAGE) the form of a verb that expresses what will happen after the present

futurism /'fju:tʃərɪzəm/ ***noun*** [U] (ARTS AND MEDIA) a movement in art and literature in the 1920s and 30s that did not try to show realistic figures and scenes but aimed to express confidence in the modern world, particularly in modern machines ▶ **futurist** ***noun*** [C], ***adj.***: *futurist poets*

fuzzy /'fʌzi/ ***adj.*** not clear: *The photo was a bit fuzzy but I could just make out my mother on it.*

FYI ***abbr.*** used in writing to mean 'for your information'

G g

G, g[1] /dʒi:/ ***noun*** [C,U] (*pl.* **G's**; **g's** /dʒi:z/) the seventh letter of the English alphabet: *'Girl' begins with (a) 'G'.*

g[2] ⊶ ***abbr.*** gram(s)

gable /'geɪbl/ ***noun*** [C] (ARCHITECTURE) the pointed part at the top of an outside wall of a house between two parts of the roof

gadget /'gædʒɪt/ ***noun*** [C] (*informal*) a small device, tool or machine that has a particular but usually unimportant purpose

gadolinium /ˌgædə'lɪniəm/ ***noun*** [U] (*symbol* **Gd**) (CHEMISTRY) a chemical element. **Gadolinium** is a soft silver-white metal. ❶ For more information on the periodic table of elements, look at pages R34-5.

Gaelic ***adj.***, ***noun*** [U] (LANGUAGE) **1** /'gælɪk; 'geɪlɪk/ (of) the Celtic language of Scotland **2** /'geɪlɪk/ (*also* **ˌIrish 'Gaelic**) (of) the Celtic language of Ireland

gaffer /'gæfə(r)/ ***noun*** [C] (ARTS AND MEDIA) the person who is in charge of the electrical work and the lights when a film or television programme is being made

gag[1] /gæg/ ***noun*** [C] **1** a piece of cloth, etc. that is put in or over sb's mouth in order to stop them from talking **2** a joke

gag[2] /gæg/ ***verb*** [T] (**gagging**; **gagged**) to put a GAG in or over sb's mouth

gage (*AmE*) =GAUGE[1]

gaiety /'geɪəti/ ***noun*** [U] a feeling of happiness and fun

gaily /'geɪli/ ***adv.*** happily; cheerfully

gain[1] ⊶ /geɪn/ ***verb*** **1** [T] to obtain or win sth, especially sth that you need or want: *They managed to gain access to secret information.* ◇ *The country gained its independence ten years ago.* **2** [T] to gradually get more of sth: *The train was gaining speed.* ◇ *to gain weight/confidence* OPP **lose** **3** [I,T] ~ **(sth) (by/from sth/doing sth)** to get an advantage: *I've got **nothing to gain** by staying in this job.* OPP **lose**

IDM **gain ground** to make progress; to become stronger or more popular

PHR V **gain in sth** to gradually get more of sth: *He's gained in confidence in the past year.*

gain on sb/sth to get closer to sb/sth that you are trying to catch: *I saw the other runners were gaining on me so I increased my pace.*

gain[2] ⊶ /geɪn/ ***noun*** [C,U] an increase, improvement or advantage in sth: *We hope to make a gain* (=more money) *when we sell our house.* ◇ *a **gain in weight** of one kilo*

gait /geɪt/ ***noun*** [sing.] the way that sb/sth walks

gala /'gɑ:lə/ ***noun*** [C] a special social or sporting occasion: *a swimming gala*

galactic /gə'læktɪk/ ***adj.*** (ASTRONOMY) relating to a GALAXY: *A galactic year is the time the galaxy takes to rotate once completely.*

galaxy /'gæləksi/ ***noun*** (*pl.* **galaxies**) (ASTRONOMY) **1** [C] any of the large systems of stars, etc. in outer space **2 the Galaxy** (*also* **the Milky Way**) [sing.] the system of stars that contains our sun and its planets, seen as a bright band in the night sky

gale /geɪl/ ***noun*** [C] a very strong wind: *Several trees blew down in the gale.* ➲ note at **storm**

gall[1] /gɔːl/ ***noun*** **1** [U] rude behaviour showing a lack of respect that is surprising because the person doing it is not embarrassed: *He arrived two hours late then* ***had the gall*** *complain about the food.* **2** [U] (*formal*) a bitter feeling full of hatred **SYN** **resentment** **3** [C] (**BIOLOGY**) a swelling on plants and trees caused by insects, disease, etc. **4** (*old-fashioned*) = BILE

gall[2] /gɔːl/ ***verb*** [T] to make sb feel upset and angry, especially because sth is unfair: *It galls me to have to apologize to her.*

gall. ***abbr.*** gallon(s)

gallant /ˈgælənt/ ***adj.*** (*formal*) **1** showing courage in a difficult situation: *gallant men/soldiers/heroes* **SYN** **brave** **2** (used about men) polite to and showing respect for women

gallantry /ˈgæləntri/ ***noun*** [C,U] (*pl.* **gallantries**) **1** courage, especially in battle **2** polite behaviour towards women by men

ˈ**gall bladder** ***noun*** [C] (**ANATOMY**) an organ that is connected to your LIVER (= the organ that cleans your blood) where BILE (= a greenish brown liquid) is stored, which helps your body to deal with fats ➲ picture at **digestive system**

gallery /ˈgæləri/ ***noun*** [C] (*pl.* **galleries**) **1** a building or room where works of art are shown to the public: *an art gallery* **2** a small private shop where you can see and buy works of art **3** an upstairs area at the back or sides of a large hall or theatre where people can sit **4** the highest level in a theatre where the cheapest seats are

galley /ˈgæli/ ***noun*** [C] **1** (**HISTORY**) a long flat ship with sails, especially one used by the ancient Greeks or Romans in war, which was usually rowed by criminals or SLAVES (= people who were owned by other people and had to work for them without being paid) **2** the kitchen on a ship or plane

gallium /ˈgæliəm/ ***noun*** [U] (*symbol* **Ga**) (**CHEMISTRY**) a chemical element. **Gallium** is a soft silver-white metal. ❶ For more information on the periodic table of elements, look at pages R34-5.

gallon 🗝 /ˈgælən/ ***noun*** [C] (*abbr.* **gall.**) a measure of liquid; 4.5 litres (or 3.8 litres in an American gallon)

gallop /ˈgæləp/ ***verb*** [I] (used about a horse or a rider) to go at the fastest speed ➲ look at **canter**, **trot** ▶ **gallop** ***noun*** [sing.]

gallows /ˈgæləʊz/ ***noun*** [C] (*pl.* **gallows**) (**HISTORY**) a wooden frame used in the past for killing people by hanging

gallstone /ˈgɔːlstəʊn/ ***noun*** [C] (**HEALTH**) a hard painful mass that can form in the GALL BLADDER

galore /gəˈlɔː(r)/ ***adv.*** (only *after* a noun) in large numbers or amounts

galvanize (also **-ise**) /ˈgælvənaɪz/ ***verb*** [T] (**CHEMISTRY**) to cover iron or steel in ZINC to protect it from being damaged by water (**rusting**)

gamble[1] 🗝 /ˈgæmbl/ ***verb*** [I,T] ~ **(sth) (on sth)** to bet money on the result of a card game, horse race, etc.: *She gambled all her money on the last race.* **SYN** **bet** ▶ **gambler** ***noun*** [C]: *He's a compulsive gambler.*

PHR V **gamble on sth/on doing sth** to act in the hope that sth will happen although it may not: *I wouldn't gamble on the weather staying fine.*

gamble[2] 🗝 /ˈgæmbl/ ***noun*** [C] something you do that is a risk: *Setting up this business was a bit of a gamble, but it paid off (= was successful) in the end.*

gambling 🗝 /ˈgæmblɪŋ/ ***noun*** [U] the activity of playing games of chance for money and of betting on horses, etc.: *heavy gambling debts*

game[1] 🗝 /geɪm/ ***noun*** **1** [C] a ~ **(of sth)** a form of play or sport with rules; a time when you play it: *Shall we* ***play a game****?* ◇ *Let's* ***have a game*** *of chess.* ◇ *a game of football/rugby/tennis* ◇ *'Monopoly' is a very popular* ***board game****.* ◇ *Tonight's game is between Holland and Italy.* ◇ *The game ended in a draw.* **2** [C] an activity that you do to have fun: *Some children were playing a game of cowboys and Indians.* **3** [C] (**SPORT**) how well sb plays a sport: *My new racket has really improved my game.* **4 games** [pl.] (**SPORT**) an important sports competition: *Where were the last Olympic Games held?* **5** [C] (*informal*) a secret plan or trick: *Stop* ***playing games*** *with me and tell me where you've hidden my bag.* **6** [U] wild animals or birds that are killed for sport or food: *big game* (= lions, tigers, etc.)

IDM **give the game away** to tell a person sth that you are trying to keep secret: *It was the expression on her face that gave the game away.*

game[2] /geɪm/ ***adj.*** (used about a person) ready to try sth new, unusual, difficult, etc.: *I've never been sailing before but I'm game to try.*

gamekeeper /ˈgeɪmkiːpə(r)/ ***noun*** [C] a person who is responsible for private land where people hunt animals and birds

gamelan /ˈgæməlæn/ ***noun*** [C] (**MUSIC**) a traditional group of Indonesian musicians, playing instruments such as XYLOPHONES and GONGS

ˈ**game show** ***noun*** [C] (**ARTS AND MEDIA**) a television programme in which people play games or answer questions to win prizes

gamete /ˈgæmiːt/ ***noun*** [C] (**BIOLOGY**) a male or female cell that joins with a cell of the opposite sex to form a ZYGOTE (= a single cell that develops into a person, animal or plant) ➲ picture at **fertilize**

gamma /ˈgæmə/ ***noun*** [C] (**LANGUAGE**) the third letter of the Greek alphabet (Γ, γ)

ˌ**gamma radiˈation** ***noun*** [U] (*also* ˌ**gamma** ˈ**rays** [pl.]) (**PHYSICS**) RAYS that are sent out by some RADIOACTIVE substances ➲ picture at **wavelength**

gammon /ˈgæmən/ ***noun*** [U] (*BrE*) meat from the back leg or side of a pig that has been CURED (= treated with salt or smoke to make it last for a long time). **Gammon** is usually served in thick slices.

gander /ˈgændə(r)/ ***noun*** [C] a male GOOSE

gang[1] /gæŋ/ ***noun*** [C, with sing. or pl. verb] **1** an organized group of criminals **2** a group of young people who cause trouble, fight other groups, etc.: *The woman was robbed by a gang of youths.* ◇ *gang warfare/violence* **3** (*informal*) a group of friends who meet regularly

gang[2] /gæŋ/ ***verb***

PHR V **gang up on sb** (*informal*) to join together with other people in order to act against sb: *She's upset because she says the other kids are ganging up on her.*

gangrene /ˈgæŋgriːn/ ***noun*** [U] (**HEALTH**) the death of a part of the body because the blood supply to it has been stopped as a result of disease or injury ▶ **gangrenous** /ˈgæŋgrɪnəs/ ***adj.***

gangster /ˈgæŋstə(r)/ ***noun*** [C] a member of a group of criminals

gangway /ˈgæŋweɪ/ ***noun*** [C] **1** a passage between rows of seats in a cinema, an aircraft, etc. **2** a bridge that people use for getting on or off a ship

gantry /ˈgæntri/ ***noun*** [C] (*pl.* **gantries**) a tall metal frame like a bridge that is used to support signs over a road, lights over a stage, etc.

gaol, gaoler (*BrE*) = JAIL, JAILER

gap ⊶ /gæp/ ***noun*** [C] **1** a ~ **(in/between sth)** an empty space in sth or between two things: *The sheep got out through a gap in the fence.* **2** a period of time when sth stops, or between two events: *I returned to teaching after a gap of about five years.* ◇ *a gap in the conversation* **3** a difference between people or their ideas: *The gap between the rich and the poor is getting wider.* **4** a part of sth that is missing: *In this exercise you have to fill (in) the gaps in the sentences.* ◇ *I think our new product should fill **a gap in the market**.*

IDM **bridge a/the gap** → BRIDGE[2]

gape /geɪp/ ***verb*** [I] **1** ~ **(at sb/sth)** to stare at sb/sth with your mouth open: *We gaped in astonishment when we saw what Amy was wearing.* **2** ~ **(open)** to be or become wide open: *a gaping hole/wound*

ˈ**gap year** ***noun*** (*BrE*) (EDUCATION) a year that a young person spends working and/or travelling, often between leaving school and starting university: *I'm planning to take a gap year and go backpacking in India.*

garage ⊶ /ˈgærɑːʒ; ˈgærɪdʒ/ ***noun*** [C] **1** a small building where a car, etc. is kept: *The house has a double garage* (= with space for two cars). **2** a place where vehicles are repaired and/or petrol is sold: *a garage mechanic* ➲ look at **petrol station**

garbage ⊶ /ˈgɑːbɪdʒ/ (*especially AmE*) = RUBBISH

ˈ**garbage can** (*AmE*) = DUSTBIN

garbled /ˈgɑːbld/ ***adj.*** (used about a message, story, etc.) difficult to understand because it is not clear

garden[1] ⊶ /ˈgɑːdn/ ***noun*** [C] **1** (*AmE* **yard**) a piece of land next to a house where flowers and vegetables can be grown, usually with a piece of grass (**lawn**): *the back/front garden* ◇ *garden flowers* ◇ *garden chairs* (= for using in the garden) **2 gardens** [pl.] a public park

garden[2] /ˈgɑːdn/ ***verb*** [I] to work in a garden: *She's been gardening all afternoon.*

ˈ**garden centre** ***noun*** [C] a place where plants, seeds, garden equipment, etc. are sold

gardener /ˈgɑːdnə(r)/ ***noun*** [C] a person who works in a garden as a job or for pleasure

gardening /ˈgɑːdnɪŋ/ ***noun*** [U] looking after a garden: *I'm going to **do** some **gardening** this afternoon.* ◇ *gardening tools/gloves*

ˈ**garden party** ***noun*** [C] a formal social event that takes place outside, usually in a large garden in summer

gargle /ˈgɑːgl/ ***verb*** [I] to wash your throat with a liquid (which you do not swallow)

gargoyle /ˈgɑːgɔɪl/ ***noun*** [C] (ARCHITECTURE) an ugly figure of a person or an animal that is made of stone and through which water is carried away from the roof of a building, especially a church

garish /ˈgeərɪʃ/ ***adj.*** very bright or decorated and therefore unpleasant SYN **gaudy**

garlic /ˈgɑːlɪk/ ***noun*** [U] a plant with a strong taste and smell that looks like a small onion and is used in cooking: *Chop two **cloves of garlic** and fry in oil.*

garment /ˈgɑːmənt/ ***noun*** [C] (*formal*) one piece of clothing ➲ look at **clothes**

garnish /ˈgɑːnɪʃ/ ***verb*** [T] to decorate a dish of food with a small amount of another food ▶ **garnish** ***noun*** [U, C]

garrison /ˈgærɪsn/ ***noun*** [C] a group of soldiers who are living in and guarding a town or building

gas[1] ⊶ /gæs/ ***noun*** (*pl.* **gases**: *AmE also* **gasses**) **1** [C,U] (SCIENCE) a substance like air that is not a solid or a liquid: *Hydrogen and oxygen are gases.* ➲ picture at **state[1]** **2** [U] a particular type of gas or mixture of gases that is used for heating or cooking: *a gas cooker* **3** [U] (*AmE*) = PETROL

gas[2] /gæs/ ***verb*** [T] (**gassing**; **gassed**) to poison or kill sb with gas

ˈ**gas chamber** ***noun*** [C] a room that can be filled with poisonous gas in order to kill animals or people

gaseous /ˈgæsiəs; ˈgeɪsiəs/ ***adj.*** like gas or containing gas

gash /gæʃ/ ***noun*** [C] a long deep cut or wound: *He had a nasty gash in his arm.* ▶ **gash** ***verb*** [T]

gasket /ˈgæskɪt/ ***noun*** [C] a flat piece of rubber, etc. placed between two metal surfaces in a pipe or an engine to prevent steam, gas or oil from escaping: *The engine had **blown a gasket*** (= had allowed steam, etc. to escape). ◇ (*figurative*) *He **blew a gasket*** (= became very angry) *at the news.*

ˈ**gas mask** ***noun*** [C] a piece of equipment that is worn over the face to protect against poisonous gas

ˈ**gas meter** ***noun*** [C] an instrument that measures the amount of gas that you use in your home

gasoline ⊶ /ˈgæsəliːn/ (*also* **gas**) (*AmE*) = PETROL

gasp /gɑːsp/ ***verb*** [I] **1** ~ **(at sth)** to take a sudden loud breath with your mouth open, usually because you are surprised or in pain **2** to have difficulty breathing: *I pulled the boy out of the pool and he lay there **gasping for breath**.* ▶ **gasp** ***noun*** [C]: *to give a gasp of surprise/pain/horror*

ˈ**gas station** (*AmE*) = PETROL STATION

gastric /ˈgæstrɪk/ ***adj.*** (ANATOMY) (only *before* a noun) connected with the stomach: *a gastric ulcer* ◇ *gastric juices* (= the acids in your stomach that deal with the food you eat)

gastritis /gæˈstraɪtɪs/ ***noun*** [U] (HEALTH) an illness in which the inside of the stomach becomes swollen and painful

gastro-enteritis /ˌgæstrəʊ ˌentəˈraɪtɪs/ ***noun*** [U] (HEALTH) an illness in which the inside of the stomach and the INTESTINE (= the tube that carries food out of the stomach) become swollen and painful

gastroenterology /ˌgæstrəʊentəˈrɒlədʒi/ ***noun*** [U] (HEALTH) the study and treatment of diseases of the stomach and INTESTINES

gastronomic /ˌgæstrəˈnɒmɪk/ ***adj.*** connected with good food

gastropod /ˈgæstrəpɒd/ ***noun*** [C] (BIOLOGY) any of a CLASS of animals with a soft body and usually a shell, that can live either on land or in water: *Snails and slugs are gastropods.* ➲ picture on **page 29**

gate ⊶ /geɪt/ ***noun*** [C] **1** the part of a fence, wall, etc. like a door that can be opened to let people or vehicles through: *Please keep the garden gate closed.* **2** (*also* **gateway**) the space in a wall, fence, etc. where the gate is: *Drive through the gates and you'll find the car park on the right.* **3** the place at an airport where you get on or off a plane: *Swissair Flight 139 to Geneva is now boarding at gate 16.*

gateau /ˈgætəʊ/ ***noun*** [C] (*pl.* **gateaux**) a large cake that is usually decorated with cream, fruit, etc.

gatecrash /ˈgeɪtkræʃ/ *verb* [I,T] to go to a private party without being invited ▶ **gatecrasher** *noun* [C]

gatehouse /ˈgeɪthaʊs/ *noun* [C] (ARCHITECTURE) a house built at or over a gate, for example at the entrance to a park or castle

gatepost /ˈgeɪtpəʊst/ *noun* [C] either of the posts at the end of a gate which it is supported by or fastened to when it is closed

gateway /ˈgeɪtweɪ/ *noun* [C] **1** = GATE (2) **2** [sing.] **the ~ to sth** the place which you must go through in order to get to somewhere else

gather ⊶ /ˈgæðə(r)/ *verb* **1** [I,T] ~ **(round) (sb/sth)**; ~ **sb/sth (round) (sb/sth)** (used about people) to come or be brought together in a group: *A crowd soon gathered at the scene of the accident.* ◇ *We all gathered round and listened to what the guide was saying.* **2** [T] ~ **sth (together/up)** to bring many things together: *He gathered up all his papers and put them away.* ◇ *They have gathered together a lot of information on the subject.* ➲ note at **collect**[1] **3** [T] (*formal*) to pick wild flowers, fruit, etc. from a wide area: *to gather mushrooms* **4** [T] to understand or find out sth (from sb/sth): *I gather from your letter that you have several years' experience of this kind of work.* ◇ *'She's been very ill recently.' 'So I gather.'* **5** [I,T] to gradually become greater; to increase: *I gathered speed as I cycled down the hill.*

gathering /ˈgæðərɪŋ/ *noun* [C] a time when people come together; a meeting: *a family gathering*

gaudy /ˈgɔːdi/ *adj.* very bright or decorated and therefore unpleasant **SYN** **garish**

gauge[1] (*AmE also* **gage**) /geɪdʒ/ *noun* [C] **1** an instrument for measuring the amount of sth: *a fuel/temperature/pressure gauge* **2** a measurement of the width of sth or of the distance between two things: *a narrow-gauge railway* **3 a ~ (of sth)** a fact that you can use to judge a situation, sb's feelings, etc.

gauge[2] /geɪdʒ/ *verb* [T] **1** to make a judgement or to calculate sth by guessing: *It was difficult to gauge the mood of the audience.* **2** to measure sth accurately using a special instrument

gaunt /gɔːnt/ *adj.* (used about a person) very thin because of HUNGER, illness, etc.

gauze /gɔːz/ *noun* **1** [U] light transparent material, usually made of cotton or SILK **2** [U] a thin material like a net, that is used for covering an area of skin that you have hurt or cut **3** [U, C] material made from a NETWORK of wire; a piece of this: *a wire gauze* ➲ picture at **laboratory**

gave past tense of **give**[1]

gawp /gɔːp/ *verb* [I] (*informal*) ~ **(at sb/sth)** to look or stare in a stupid way: *Lots of drivers slowed down to gawp at the accident.*

gay[1] /geɪ/ *adj.* **1** sexually attracted to people of the same sex **SYN** **homosexual**: *the gay community of New York* ◇ *a gay bar/club* (= for gay people) ➲ noun **gayness** ➲ look at **lesbian** **2** (*old-fashioned*) happy and full of fun ➲ noun **gaiety**

gay[2] /geɪ/ *noun* [C] a person, especially a man, who is sexually attracted to people of the same sex **SYN** **homosexual** ➲ look at **lesbian**

gaze /geɪz/ *verb* [I] to look steadily for a long time: *She sat at the window gazing dreamily into space.* ▶ **gaze** *noun* [sing.]

gazebo /gəˈziːbəʊ/ *noun* [C] (*pl.* **gazebos**) (ARCHITECTURE) a small building with open sides in a garden, especially one with a view

GB *abbr.* Great Britain

GCSE /ˌdʒiː siː es ˈiː/ *abbr.* (EDUCATION) **General Certificate of Secondary Education;** an examination that schoolchildren in England, Wales and Northern Ireland take when they are about 16. They often take **GCSEs** in five or more subjects. For Scottish examinations, look at SCE. ➲ look at **A level**

GDP /ˌdʒiː diː ˈpiː/ *abbr.* (ECONOMICS) gross domestic product; the total value of all the goods and services produced in a country in one year ➲ look at **GNP**

gear[1] ⊶ /gɪə(r)/ *noun* **1** [C] the machinery in a vehicle that turns engine power into a movement forwards or backwards: *Most cars have four or five forward gears and a reverse.* **2** [U] a particular position of the gears in a vehicle: *first/second/top/reverse gear* ◇ *to change gear* **3** [U] equipment or clothing that you need for a particular activity, etc.: *camping/fishing/sports gear* **4** [sing.] an instrument or part of a machine that is used for a particular purpose: *the landing gear of an aeroplane*

gear[2] /gɪə(r)/ *verb*

PHR V **gear sth to/towards sb/sth** (often passive) to make sth suitable for a particular purpose or person: *There is a special course geared towards the older learner.*

gear up (for sb/sth); gear sb/sth up (for sb/sth) to get ready or to make sb/sth ready

gearbox /ˈgɪəbɒks/ *noun* [C] the metal case that contains the gears[1](1) of a car, etc.

gearing /ˈgɪərɪŋ/ *noun* [U] (*BrE and AmE also* **leverage**) (BUSINESS) the relationship between the amount of money that a company owes and the value of its shares

ˈgear lever (*AmE* **ˈgear shift**) *noun* [C] a stick that is used for changing gear[1](2) in a car, etc.

gecko /ˈgekəʊ/ *noun* [C] (*pl.* **-os** or **-oes**) a small LIZARD (= a type of reptile) that lives in warm countries

gee /dʒiː/ *exclamation* (*AmE*) used for expressing surprise, pleasure, etc.

geek /giːk/ *noun* [C] (*informal*) a person who is not popular or fashionable: *a computer geek* **SYN** **nerd** ▶ **geeky** *adj.*

geese plural of **goose**

Geiger counter /ˈgaɪgə kaʊntə(r)/ *noun* [C] (PHYSICS) a machine used for finding and measuring the RAYS that are sent out by RADIOACTIVE substances

gel /dʒel/ *noun* [C,U] (often in compounds) a thick substance that is between a liquid and a solid: *hair gel* ◇ *shower gel*

gelatin /ˈdʒelətɪn/ (also **gelatine** /ˈdʒelətiːn/) *noun* [U] (CHEMISTRY) a clear substance without any taste that is made from boiling animal bones and is used to make liquid food SET (= become firm or hard)

gelignite /ˈdʒelɪgnaɪt/ *noun* [U] (CHEMISTRY) a substance that is used for making explosions

gem /dʒem/ *noun* [C] **1** a JEWEL or PRECIOUS STONE **2** a person or thing that is especially good

Gemini /ˈdʒemɪnaɪ/ *noun* [U] the third sign of the ZODIAC, the Twins

Gen. *abbr.* General; an officer in the British and US armies

gender **AW** /ˈdʒendə(r)/ *noun* [C,U] **1** (*formal*) the fact of being male or female **SYN** **sex** **2** (LANGUAGE) (in some languages) the division of nouns, pronouns, etc. into MASCULINE, FEMININE and NEUTER; one of these three types

gene /dʒiːn/ ***noun*** [C] (BIOLOGY) a unit of information inside a cell which controls what a living thing will be like. **Genes** are passed from parents to children. ➲ look at **genetics**

general¹ ⊶ /ˈdʒenrəl/ ***adj.*** **1** affecting all or most people, places, things, etc.: *Fridges were once a luxury, but now they are in general use.* ◇ *That is a matter of general interest.* ◇ *the general public* (=most ordinary people) **2** (only *before* a noun) referring to or describing the main part of sth, not the details: *Your general health is very good.* ◇ *The introduction gives you a general idea of what the book is about.* ◇ ***As a general rule****, the most common verbs in English tend to be irregular.* **3** not limited to one subject or area of study; not SPECIALIZED: *Children need a good general education.* ◇ *The quiz tests your* ***general knowledge****.* ◇ *a general hospital* **4** (often in compounds) with responsibility for the whole of an organization: *a general manager*
IDM **in general 1** in most cases; usually: *In general, standards of hygiene are good.* **2** as a whole: *I'm interested in Spanish history in general, and the civil war in particular.*

general² /ˈdʒenrəl/ ***noun*** [C] (*abbr.* **Gen.**) an army officer in a very high position

ˌGeneral Cerˌtificate of ˌSecondary Eduˈcation ***noun*** [C,U] = GCSE

ˌgeneral eˈlection ***noun*** [C] (POLITICS) an election in which all the people of a country vote to choose a government ➲ look at **by-election**

generalization (also **-isation**) /ˌdʒenrəlaɪˈzeɪʃn/ ***noun*** [C,U] a general statement that is based on only a few facts or examples; the act of making such a statement: *You can't* ***make*** *sweeping* ***generalizations about*** *French people if you've only been there for a day!*

generalize (also **-ise**) /ˈdʒenrəlaɪz/ ***verb*** [I] ~ **(about sth)** to form an opinion or make a statement using only a small amount of information instead of looking at the details

generally ⊶ /ˈdʒenrəli/ ***adv.*** **1** by or to most people: *He is generally considered to be a good doctor.* **2** usually: *She generally cycles to work.* **3** without discussing the details of sth: *Generally speaking, houses in America are bigger than houses in this country.*

ˌgeneral pracˈtitioner (*especially BrE*) = GP

generate ⊶ AW /ˈdʒenəreɪt/ ***verb*** [T] to produce or create sth: *to generate heat/power/electricity* ➲ note at **make¹**

generation ⊶ AW /ˌdʒenəˈreɪʃn/ ***noun*** **1** [C] all the people in a family, group or country who were born at about the same time: *We should look after the planet for future generations.* ◇ *This photograph shows three generations of my family* (=children, parents and grandparents). ➲ look at **first generation 2** [C] the average time that children take to grow up and have children of their own, usually considered to be about 25-30 years: *A generation ago foreign travel was still only possible for a few people.* **3** [U] the production of sth, especially heat, power, etc.

the ˌgeneˈration gap ***noun*** [sing.] (SOCIAL STUDIES) the difference in behaviour, and the lack of understanding, between young people and older people

generator /ˈdʒenəreɪtə(r)/ ***noun*** [C] (PHYSICS) a machine that produces electricity

generic /dʒəˈnerɪk/ ***adj.*** **1** shared by, including or typical of a whole group of things; not specific **2** (used about a product, especially a drug) not using the name of the company that made it ▶ **generically** /dʒəˈnerɪkli/ ***adv.***

generosity /ˌdʒenəˈrɒsəti/ ***noun*** [U] the quality of being generous

generous ⊶ /ˈdʒenərəs/ ***adj.*** **1** happy to give more money, help, etc. than is usual or expected: *It was very generous of your parents to lend us all that money.* **2** larger than usual: *a generous helping of pasta* ▶ **generously** ***adv.***: *People gave very generously to our appeal for the homeless.*

generator

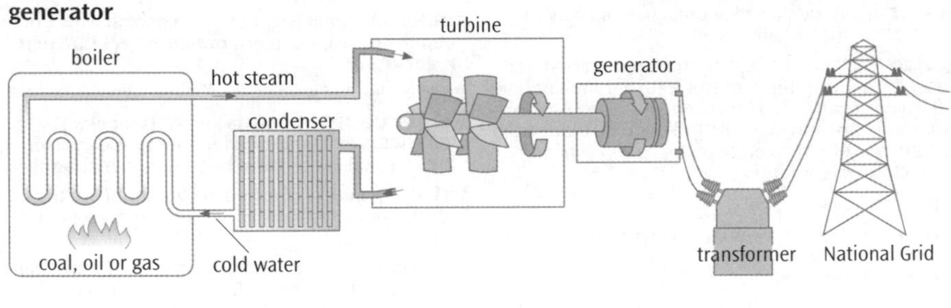

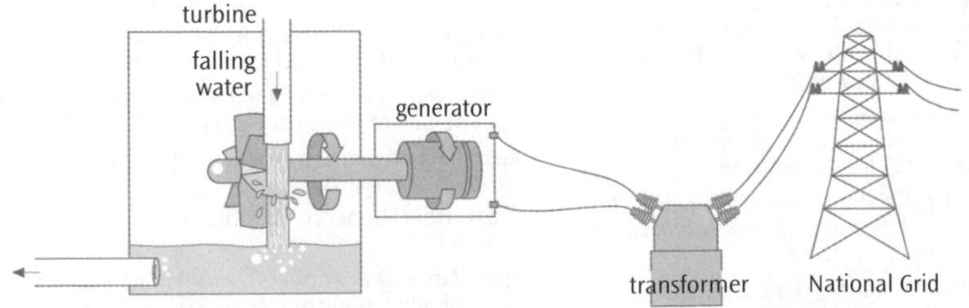

genesis /ˈdʒenəsɪs/ ***noun*** [sing.] (*formal*) the beginning or origin of sth

ˈgene therapy ***noun*** [U] (**HEALTH**) a treatment in which normal GENES (=units of information inside a cell) are put into cells to replace ones that are missing or not normal

genetic /dʒəˈnetɪk/ ***adj.*** (**BIOLOGY**) connected with GENES (=the units in the cells of living things that control what a person or plant is like), or with GENETICS (=the study of genes): *The disease is caused by a genetic defect.* ▶ **genetically** /-kli/ ***adv.***

geˌnetically ˈmodified ***adj.*** (*abbr.* **GM**) (**BIOLOGY, AGRICULTURE**) (used about food, plants, etc.) that has been grown from cells whose GENES have been changed artificially

geˌnetic ˈcode ***noun*** [C] (**BIOLOGY**) the arrangement of GENES that controls how each living thing will develop

geˌnetic engiˈneering ***noun*** [U] (**BIOLOGY**) the science of changing the way a human, an animal or a plant develops by changing the information in its GENES

geˌnetic ˈfingerprinting ***noun*** [U] = DNA FINGERPRINTING

geneticist /dʒəˈnetɪsɪst/ ***noun*** [C] (**BIOLOGY**) a scientist who studies GENETICS

genetics /dʒəˈnetɪks/ ***noun*** [U] (**BIOLOGY**) the scientific study of the way that the development of living things is controlled by qualities that have been passed on from parents to children ➲ look at **gene**

genial /ˈdʒiːniəl/ ***adj.*** (used about a person) pleasant and friendly

genie /ˈdʒiːni/ ***noun*** [C] a spirit with magic powers, especially one that lives in a bottle or a lamp

genitals /ˈdʒenɪtlz/ (*also* **genitalia** /ˌdʒenɪˈteɪliə/) ***noun*** [pl.] (*formal*) (**ANATOMY**) the parts of a person's sex organs that are outside the body ▶ **genital** /ˈdʒenɪtl/ ***adj.***

genitive /ˈdʒenətɪv/ ***noun*** [C] (**LANGUAGE**) (in some languages) the special form of a noun, a pronoun or an adjective that is used to show possession or close connection between two things ➲ look at **accusative, dative, nominative, vocative** ▶ **genitive** ***adj.***

genius /ˈdʒiːniəs/ ***noun*** **1** [U] very great and unusual ability: *Her idea was **a stroke of genius**.* **2** [C] a person who has very great and unusual ability, especially in a particular subject: *Einstein was a mathematical genius.* ➲ look at **prodigy 3** [sing.] **a ~ for (doing) sth** a very good natural skill or ability

genocide /ˈdʒenəsaɪd/ ***noun*** [U] the murder of all the people of a particular race, religion, etc.

genome /ˈdʒiːnəʊm/ ***noun*** [C] (**BIOLOGY**) the complete set of GENES (=units of information that control what a living thing will be like) in a cell or living thing: *the decoding of the human genome*

genre /ˈʒɑːnrə/ ***noun*** [C] (*formal*) (**ARTS AND MEDIA**) a particular type or style of literature, art, film or music that you can recognize because of its special characteristics

gent /dʒent/ (*informal*) = GENTLEMAN

genteel /dʒenˈtiːl/ ***adj.*** behaving in a very polite way, often in order to make people think that you are from a high social class ▶ **gentility** /dʒenˈtɪləti/ ***noun*** [U]

gentle 🔑 /ˈdʒentl/ ***adj.*** **1** (used about people) kind and calm; touching or treating people or things in a careful way so that they are not hurt: *'I'll try and be as gentle as I can,' said the dentist.* **2** not strong, violent or extreme: *gentle exercise* ◇ *a gentle slope/curve* ▶ **gentleness** /ˈdʒentlnəs/ ***noun*** [U]

gentleman 🔑 /ˈdʒentlmən/ ***noun*** [C] (*pl.* **-men** /-mən/) **1** a man who is polite and who behaves well towards other people **2** (*formal*) used when speaking to or about a man or men in a polite way: ***Ladies and gentlemen*** (=at the beginning of a speech) ◇ *Mrs Flinn, there is a gentleman here to see you.* **3** (*old-fashioned*) a rich man with a high social position

gently 🔑 /ˈdʒentli/ ***adv.*** **1** in a gentle way: *She held the baby gently.* ◇ *Simmer the soup gently for 30 minutes.* ◇ *Massage the area **gently but firmly**.* **2 Gently!** used to tell sb to be careful: *Gently! You'll hurt the poor thing!* ◇ *Don't go too fast — **gently does it!***

the gents /dʒents/ ***noun*** [sing.] (*BrE, informal*) a public toilet for men

genuine 🔑 /ˈdʒenjuɪn/ ***adj.*** **1** real; true: *He thought that he had bought a genuine Rolex watch but it was a cheap fake.* ➲ look at **imitation 2** sincere and honest; that can be trusted ▶ **genuinely** ***adv.***

genus /ˈdʒiːnəs/ ***noun*** [C] (*pl.* **genera** /ˈdʒenərə/) (**BIOLOGY**) a group into which animals, plants, etc. that have similar characteristics are divided, smaller than a FAMILY and larger than a SPECIES ➲ picture on **page 29**

geo- ***prefix*** (in nouns, adjectives and adverbs) of the earth: *geophysical* ◇ *geoscience*

geocentric /ˌdʒiːəʊˈsentrɪk/ ***adj.*** (**ASTRONOMY**) with the earth as the centre ➲ look at **heliocentric**

geodesic /ˌdʒiːəʊˈdesɪk; -ˈdiːsɪk/ ***adj.*** (**TECHNICAL**) relating to the shortest possible line between two points on a curved surface

ˌgeoˌdesic ˈdome ***noun*** [C] (**ARCHITECTURE**) a DOME (=a round roof on a building) which is built from square or RECTANGULAR pieces of glass, metal, etc. whose edges form GEODESIC lines

geodesic dome

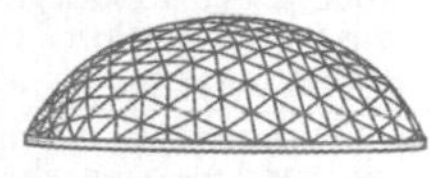

geographer /dʒiˈɒɡrəfə(r)/ ***noun*** [C] (**GEOGRAPHY**) an expert in geography or a student of geography

geography 🔑 /dʒiˈɒɡrəfi/ ***noun*** [U] (**GEOGRAPHY**) **1** the study of the world's surface, physical qualities, climate, population, products, etc.: *human/physical/economic geography* **2** the physical arrangement of a place: *We're studying the geography of Asia.* ▶ **geographical** /ˌdʒiːəˈɡræfɪkl/ (also **geographic** /ˌdʒiːəˈɡræfɪk/) ***adj.*** ▶ **geographically** /-kli/ ***adv.***

geologist /dʒiˈɒlədʒɪst/ ***noun*** [C] (**GEOLOGY**) an expert in GEOLOGY or a student of GEOLOGY

geology /dʒiˈɒlədʒi/ ***noun*** [U] (**GEOLOGY**) the study of rocks, and of the way they are formed ▶ **geological** /ˌdʒiːəˈlɒdʒɪkl/ ***adj.***

geometric /ˌdʒiːəˈmetrɪk/ (*also* **geometrical** /-ɪkl/) ***adj.*** **1** (**GEOMETRY**) of GEOMETRY **2** consisting of regular shapes and lines: *a geometric design/pattern* ▶ **geometrically** /-kli/ ***adv.***

geoˈmetric mean ***noun*** [C] = MEAN³ (2)

geoˌmetric proˈgression ***noun*** [C] (**MATHEMATICS**) a series of numbers in which each is multiplied or divided by a fixed number to produce the next, for example 1, 3, 9, 27, 81 ➲ look at **arithmetic progression**

geometry /dʒiˈɒmətri/ ***noun*** [U] (GEOMETRY) the study in mathematics of lines, shapes, curves, etc.

geopolitics /ˌdʒiːəʊˈpɒlətɪks/ ***noun*** [U, with sing. or pl. verb] (POLITICS) the political relations between countries and groups of countries in the world; the study of these relations ▶ **geopolitical** /ˌdʒiːəʊpəˈlɪtɪkl/ ***adj.***

Georgian /ˈdʒɔːdʒən/ ***adj.*** (used especially about ARCHITECTURE and furniture) from the time of the British kings George I–IV (1714–1830): *a beautiful Georgian house*

geothermal /ˌdʒiːəʊˈθɜːml/ ***adj.*** (GEOLOGY) connected with the natural heat of rock deep in the ground: *geothermal energy*

geriatrics /ˌdʒeriˈætrɪks/ ***noun*** [U] (HEALTH) the medical care of old people ▶ **geriatric** ***adj.***

germ /dʒɜːm/ ***noun*** **1** [C] (BIOLOGY) a very small living thing that causes disease ➲ look at **bacteria**, **virus 2** [sing.] **the ~ of sth** the beginning of sth that may develop: *the germ of an idea*

Germanic /dʒɜːˈmænɪk/ ***adj.*** **1** connected with or considered typical of Germany or its people: *She had an almost Germanic regard for order.* **2** (LANGUAGE) connected with the language family that includes German, English, Dutch and Swedish among others

germanium /dʒɜːˈmeɪniəm/ ***noun*** [U] (*symbol* **Ge**) (CHEMISTRY) a chemical element. **Germanium** is a shiny grey element that is similar to a metal. ❶ For more information on the periodic table of elements, look at pages R34-5.

German measles /ˌdʒɜːmən ˈmiːzlz/ (*also* **rubella**) ***noun*** [U] (HEALTH) a mild disease that causes red spots all over the body. It may damage a baby if the mother catches it when she is pregnant.

ˌGerman ˈshepherd = ALSATIAN

germinate /ˈdʒɜːmɪneɪt/ ***verb*** [I,T] (BIOLOGY) (used about a seed) to start growing; to cause a seed to do this ▶ **germination** /ˌdʒɜːmɪˈneɪʃn/ ***noun*** [U]

ˌgerm ˈwarfare ***noun*** [U] = BIOLOGICAL WARFARE

gerrymander /ˈdʒerimændə(r)/ ***verb*** [I,T] (POLITICS) to change the size and borders of an area for voting in order to give an unfair advantage to one party in an election ▶ **gerrymandering** ***noun*** [U]

gerund /ˈdʒerənd/ ***noun*** [C] (LANGUAGE) a noun, ending in -ing, that has been made from a verb: *In the sentence 'His hobby is collecting stamps', 'collecting' is a gerund.*

gestation /dʒeˈsteɪʃn/ ***noun*** [U, sing.] (BIOLOGY) the period of time that a baby human or animal develops inside its mother's body; the process of developing inside the mother's body: *The **gestation period** of a horse is about eleven months.*

gesticulate /dʒeˈstɪkjuleɪt/ ***verb*** [I] to make movements with your hands and arms in order to express sth

gesture[1] /ˈdʒestʃə(r)/ ***noun*** [C] **1** a movement of the hand, head, etc. that expresses sth: *I saw the boy **make a** rude **gesture** at the policeman before running off.* **2** something that you do that shows other people what you think or feel ➲ note at **action**[1]

gesture[2] /ˈdʒestʃə(r)/ ***verb*** [I,T] to point at sth, to make a sign to sb: *She asked them to leave and gestured towards the door.*

get 🔑 /get/ ***verb*** (*pres. part.* **getting**; *pt* **got** /gɒt/; *pp* **got**: *AmE* **gotten** /ˈgɒtn/) **1** [T] (no passive) to receive, obtain or buy sth: *I got a letter from my sister.* ◇ *Did you get a present for your mother?* ◇ *Did you get your mother a present?* ◇ *She got a job in a travel agency.* ◇ *Louise got 75% in the maths exam.* ◇ *I'll come if I can get time off work.* ◇ *How much did you get for your old car* (=when you sold it)? ◇ *to get a shock/surprise* **2** [T] **have/has got sth** to have sth: *I've got a lot to do today.* ◇ *Lee's got blond hair.* ◇ *Have you got a spare pen?* **3** [T] (no passive) to go to a place and bring sth back; fetch: ***Go and get** me a pen, please.* ◇ *Sam's gone to get his mother from the station.* **4** [I] to become; to reach a particular state or condition; to make sb/sth be in a particular state or condition: *It's getting dark.* ◇ *to get angry/bored/hungry/fat* ◇ *I can't **get used to** my new bed.* ◇ *to **get dressed*** ◇ *When did you **get married**?* ◇ *to get pregnant* ◇ *Just give me five minutes to **get ready**.* ◇ *He's always **getting into trouble** with the police.* ◇ *She's shy, but she's great fun once you **get to know** her.* **5** [I] to arrive at or reach a place: *We should get to London at about ten.* ◇ *Can you tell me how to get to the hospital?* ◇ *What time do you usually **get home**?* ◇ *I got half way up the mountain then gave up.* ◇ *How far have you got with your book?* ➲ look at **get in**, **on**, **etc.** **6** [I,T] to move or go somewhere; to move or put sth somewhere: *I can't swim so I couldn't get across the river.* ◇ *My grandmother's 92 and she doesn't get out of the house much.* ◇ *We couldn't get the piano upstairs.* ◇ *My foot was swollen and I couldn't get my shoe off.* **7** [I] used instead of 'be' in the PASSIVE: *She got bitten by a dog.* ◇ *Don't leave your wallet on the table or it'll get stolen.* **8** [T] **~ sth done, mended, etc.** to cause sth to be done, MENDED, etc.: *Let's get this work done, then we can go out.* ◇ *I'm going to **get my hair cut**.* **9** [T] **~ sb/sth to do sth** to make or persuade sb/sth to do sth: *I got him to agree to the plan.* ◇ *I can't get the television to work.* **10** [T] to catch or have an illness, pain, etc.: *I think I'm getting a cold.* ◇ *He gets really bad headaches.* **11** [T] to use a form of transport: *Shall we walk or get the bus?* **12** [I] to hit, hold or catch sb/sth: *He got me by the throat and threatened to kill me.* ◇ *A boy threw a stone at me but he didn't get me.* **13** [T] to hear or understand sth: *I'm sorry, I didn't get that. Could you repeat it?* ◇ *Did you **get** that **joke** that Karen told?* **14** [T] **~ (sb) sth; ~ sth (for sb)** to prepare food: *Can I get you anything to eat?* ◇ *Joe's in the kitchen getting breakfast for everyone.* **15** [I] **~ to do sth** to have the chance to do sth: *Did you get to try the new computer?* **16** [I] (used with verbs in the -ing form) to start doing sth: *We don't have much time so we'd better get working.* ◇ *I got talking to a woman on the bus.* ◇ *We'd better **get going** if we don't want to be late.*

IDM **get somewhere/nowhere (with sb/sth)** to make/not make progress: *I'm getting nowhere with my research.*

PHR V **get about/around** to move or travel from place to place: *My grandmother needs a stick to get around these days.*

get about/around/round (used about news, a story, etc.) to become known by many people

get sth across (to sb) to succeed in making people understand sth: *The party failed to get its policies across to the voters.*

get ahead to progress and be successful in sth, especially a career

get along 1 (*spoken*) (usually used in the continuous tenses) to leave a place: *I'd love to stay, but I should be getting along now.* **2** → GET ON

get around 1 → GET ABOUT/AROUND **2** → GET ABOUT/AROUND/ROUND

get around sb → GET ROUND/AROUND SB

get around sth → GET ROUND/AROUND STH

get around to sth/doing sth → GET ROUND/AROUND TO STH/DOING STH

get at sb to criticize sb a lot: *The teacher's always getting at me about my spelling.*

get at sb/sth to be able to reach sth; to have sth

available for immediate use: *The files are locked away and I can't get at them.*
get at sth (only used in the continuous tenses) to try to say sth without saying it in a direct way; to suggest: *I'm not quite sure what you're getting at – am I doing something wrong?*
get away (from...) to succeed in leaving or escaping from sb or a place: *He kept talking to me and I couldn't get away from him.* ◇ *The thieves got away in a stolen car.*
get away with sth/doing sth to do sth bad and not be punished for it: *He lied but he got away with it.*
get back to return to the place where you live or work
get sth back to be given sth that you had lost or lent: *Can I borrow this book? You'll get it back next week, I promise.*
get back to sb to speak to, write to or telephone sb later, especially in order to give an answer: *I'll get back to you on prices when I've got some more information.*
get back to sth to return to doing sth or talking about sth: *I woke up early and couldn't get back to sleep.* ◇ *Let's get back to the point you raised earlier.*
get behind (with sth) to fail to do, pay sth, etc. on time, and so have more to do, pay, etc. the next time: *to get behind with your work/rent*
get by (on/in/with sth) to manage to live or do sth with difficulty: *It's very hard to get by on such a low income.* ◇ *My Italian is good and I can get by in Spanish.*
get sb down to make sb unhappy
get down to sth/doing sth to start working on sth: *We'd better stop chatting and get down to work.* ◇ *I must get down to answering these letters.*
get in to reach a place: *What time does your train get in?*
get in; get into sth 1 to climb into a car: *We all got in and Tim drove off.* **2** to be elected to a political position: *She got into Parliament in 1999.*
get sb in to call sb to your house to do a job
get sth in 1 to collect or bring sth inside; to buy a supply of sth: *It's going to rain – I'd better get the washing in from outside.* **2** to manage to find an opportunity to say or do sth: *He talked all the time and I couldn't get a word in.*
get in on sth to become involved in an activity
get into sb (*informal*) (used about a feeling or attitude) to start affecting sb strongly, causing them to behave in an unusual way: *I wonder what's got into him – he isn't usually unfriendly.*
get into sth 1 to put on a piece of clothing with difficulty: *I've put on so much weight I can't get into my trousers.* **2** to start a particular activity; to become involved in sth: *How did you first get into the music business?* ◇ *She has got into the habit of turning up late.* ◇ *We got into an argument about politics.* **3** to become more interested in or familiar with sth: *I've been getting into yoga recently.*
get off (sb/sth) used especially to tell sb to stop touching you/sb/sth: *Get off (me) or I'll call the police!* ◇ *Get off that money, it's mine!*
get off (sth) 1 to leave a bus, train, etc.; to climb down from a bicycle, horse, etc. **2** to leave work with permission at a particular time: *I might be able to get off early today.*
get off (with sth) to be lucky to receive no serious injuries or punishment: *to get off with just a warning*
get on 1 to progress or become successful in life, in a career, etc. **2** (only used in the continuous tenses) to be getting old: *He's getting on – he's over 70, I'm sure.* **3** (only used in the continuous tenses) to be getting late: *Time's getting on – we don't want to be late.*
get on/along to have a particular amount of success: *How are you getting on in your course?* ◇ *'How did you get on at your interview?' 'I got the job!'*
get on/along with sb; get on/along (together) to have a friendly relationship with sb: *Do you get on well with your colleagues?*
get on/along with sth to make progress with sth that you are doing: *How are you getting on with that essay?*
get on/onto sth to climb onto a bus, train, bicycle, horse, etc.: *I got on just as the train was about to leave.*
get on for (only used in the continuous tenses) to be getting near to a certain time or age: *I'm not sure how old he is but he must be getting on for 50.*
get on to sb (about sth) to speak or write to sb about a particular matter
get on with sth to continue doing sth, especially after an interruption: *Stop talking and get on with your work!*
get out (used about a piece of information) to become known, after being secret until now
get sth out (of sth) to take sth from its container: *I got my keys out of my bag.*
get out of sth/doing sth to avoid a duty or doing sth that you have said you will do
get sth out of sb to persuade or force sb to give you sth
get sth out of sb/sth to gain sth from sb/sth: *I get a lot of pleasure out of music.*
get over sth 1 to deal with a problem successfully: *We'll have to get over the problem of finding somewhere to live first.* **2** to feel normal again after being ill or having an unpleasant experience: *He still hasn't got over his wife's death.*
get sth over with (*informal*) to do and complete sth unpleasant that has to be done: *I'll be glad to get my visit to the dentist's over with.*
get round → GET ABOUT/AROUND/ROUND
get round/around sb (*informal*) to persuade sb to do sth or agree with sth: *My father says he won't lend me the money but I think I can get round him.*
get round/around sth to find a way of avoiding or dealing with a problem
get round/around to sth/doing sth to find the time to do sth, after a delay: *I've been meaning to reply to that letter for ages but I haven't got round to it yet.*
get through sth to use or complete a certain amount or number of sth: *I got through a lot of money at the weekend.* ◇ *I got through an enormous amount of work today.*
get (sb) through (sth) to manage to complete sth difficult or unpleasant; to help sb to do this: *She got through her final exams easily.*
get through (to sb) 1 to succeed in making sb understand sth: *They couldn't get through to him that he was completely wrong.* **2** to succeed in speaking to sb on the telephone: *I couldn't get through to them because their phone was engaged all day.*
get to sb (*informal*) to affect sb in a bad way: *Public criticism is beginning to get to the team manager.*
get sb/sth together to collect people or things in one place: *I'll just get my things together and then we'll go.*
get together (with sb) to meet socially or in order to discuss or do sth: *Let's get together and talk about it.*
get up to stand up: *He got up to let an elderly woman sit down.*
get (sb) up to get out of bed or make sb get out of bed: *What time do you have to get up in the morning?* ◇ *Could you get me up at 6 tomorrow?*
get up to sth 1 to reach a particular point or stage in

sth: *We've got up to the last section of our grammar book.* **2** to be busy with sth, especially sth secret or bad: *I wonder what the children are getting up to?*

getaway /ˈgetəweɪ/ ***noun*** [C] an escape (after a crime): *to **make a getaway** ◊ a getaway car/driver*

ˈget-together ***noun*** [C] (*informal*) an informal social meeting or party

geyser /ˈgiːzə(r)/ ***noun*** [C] (**GEOGRAPHY**) a place where naturally hot water comes out of the ground. Sometimes hot water or steam goes up into the air. ➲ picture at **volcano**

ghastly /ˈgɑːstli/ ***adj.*** extremely unpleasant or bad: *a ghastly accident*

gherkin /ˈgɜːkɪn/ (*AmE* **pickle**) ***noun*** [C] a small CUCUMBER that is stored in salt water or VINEGAR before being eaten

ghetto /ˈgetəʊ/ ***noun*** [C] (*pl.* **ghettoes**) (**SOCIAL STUDIES**) a part of a town where many people of the same race, religion, etc. live in poor conditions

ghost /gəʊst/ ***noun*** [C] the spirit of a dead person that is seen or heard by sb who is still living: *I don't believe in ghosts. ◊ a ghost story* ➲ look at **spectre**

ghostly /ˈgəʊstli/ ***adj.*** looking or sounding like a GHOST; full of GHOSTS: *ghostly noises*

ˈghost town ***noun*** [C] a town where a lot of people used to live but that is now empty

ghostwriter /ˈgəʊstraɪtə(r)/ ***noun*** [C] (**LITERATURE**) a person who writes a book, etc. for a famous person (whose name appears as the author)

giant 🔑 /ˈdʒaɪənt/ ***noun*** [C] **1** (in stories) an extremely large, strong person **2** something that is very large: *the multinational oil giants* (=very large companies) ▶ **giant** ***adj.***: *a giant new shopping centre*

gibberish /ˈdʒɪbərɪʃ/ ***noun*** [U] words that have no meaning or that are impossible to understand

gibbon /ˈgɪbən/ ***noun*** [C] a small APE (=an animal like a monkey but without a tail) with long arms, which is found in South East Asia

giblets /ˈdʒɪbləts/ ***noun*** [pl.] the inside parts of a chicken or other bird, including the heart and LIVER, that are usually removed before it is cooked

giddy /ˈgɪdi/ ***adj.*** having the feeling that everything is going round and that you are going to fall: *I feel giddy. I must sit down.* **SYN** **dizzy**

gift 🔑 /gɪft/ ***noun*** [C] **1** something that you give to sb; a present: *This watch was a gift from my mother. ◊ This week's magazine contains a **free gift** of some make-up. ◊ The company **made a gift of** a computer to a local school.* **2 a ~ (for sth/doing sth)** natural ability

gifted /ˈgɪftɪd/ ***adj.*** having natural ability or great intelligence

gig /gɪg/ ***noun*** [C] (*informal*) **1** (**ARTS AND MEDIA**) an event where a musician, band or COMEDIAN is paid to perform **2** =GIGABYTE

gigabyte /ˈgɪgəbaɪt/ (also *informal* **gig**) (*abbr.* **Gb**) ***noun*** [C] (**COMPUTING**) a unit of computer memory, equal to 2^{30} (or about a billion) BYTES (=small units of information)

gigantic /dʒaɪˈgæntɪk/ ***adj.*** extremely big

giggle /ˈgɪgl/ ***verb*** [I] to laugh in a silly way that you cannot control, because you are amused or nervous ▶ **giggle** ***noun*** [C]: *I've got the giggles* (=I can't stop laughing).

gild /gɪld/ ***verb*** [T] to cover sth with a thin layer of gold or gold paint

gill /gɪl/ ***noun*** [C, usually pl.] (**BIOLOGY**) one of the parts on the side of a fish's head that it breathes through ➲ picture on **page 29**

gilt /gɪlt/ ***noun*** [U] a thin covering of gold

gimmick /ˈgɪmɪk/ ***noun*** [C] an idea for attracting customers or persuading people to buy sth: *New magazines often use free gifts or other gimmicks to get people to buy them.*

gin /dʒɪn/ ***noun*** [C,U] a strong, colourless alcoholic drink

ginger /ˈdʒɪndʒə(r)/ ***noun*** [U], ***adj.*** **1** a root that tastes hot and is used in cooking: *ground ginger ◊ ginger biscuits* **2** (of) a light brownish-orange colour: *ginger hair*

ˌginger ˈale (*also* **ˌginger ˈbeer**) ***noun*** [U] a drink that does not contain alcohol and is flavoured with GINGER

gingerly /ˈdʒɪndʒəli/ ***adv.*** very slowly and carefully so as not to cause harm, make a noise, etc.

gipsy =GYPSY

giraffe /dʒəˈrɑːf/ ***noun*** [C] (*pl.* **giraffe** or **giraffes**) a large African animal with a very long neck and legs and big dark spots on its skin

girder /ˈgɜːdə(r)/ ***noun*** [C] a long, heavy piece of iron or steel that is used in the building of bridges, large buildings, etc.

girl 🔑 /gɜːl/ ***noun*** [C] **1** a female child: *Is the baby a boy or a girl? ◊ There are more boys than girls in the class.* **2** a daughter: *They have two boys and a girl.* **3** a young woman: *He was eighteen before he became interested in girls. ◊ The girl at the cash desk was very helpful.* **4 girls** [pl.] a woman's female friends of any age: *a night out with the girls*

girlfriend 🔑 /ˈgɜːlfrend/ ***noun*** [C] **1** a girl or woman with whom sb has a romantic and/or sexual relationship: *Have you got a girlfriend?* **2** (*especially AmE*) a girl or woman's female friend

Girl ˈGuide (*BrE, old-fashioned*) =GUIDE[1] (5)

girlhood /ˈgɜːlhʊd/ ***noun*** [U] the time when sb is a girl (1)

girlish /ˈgɜːlɪʃ/ ***adj.*** looking, sounding or behaving like a girl: *a girlish figure/giggle*

giro /ˈdʒaɪrəʊ/ ***noun*** (*pl.* **giros**) (*BrE*) **1** [U] (**FINANCE**) a system for moving money from one bank, etc. to another **2** [C] a cheque that the government pays to people who are unemployed or cannot work

girth /gɜːθ/ ***noun*** **1** [U, C] the measurement around sth, especially a person's waist **2** [C] a leather or cloth STRAP that is fastened around the middle of a horse to keep the seat (**saddle**) or a load in place

gist /dʒɪst/ ***noun*** **the ~ (of sth)** [sing.] the general meaning of sth rather than all the details: *I know a little Spanish so I was able to **get the gist** of what he said.*

give[1] 🔑 /gɪv/ ***verb*** (*pt* **gave** /geɪv/; *pp* **given** /ˈgɪvn/) **1** [T] **~ sb sth; ~ sth to sb** to let sb have sth, especially sth that they want or need: *I gave Jackie a book for her birthday. ◊ Give me that book a minute – I just want to check something. ◊ I gave my bag to my friend to look after. ◊ I'll give you my telephone number. ◊ The doctor gave me this cream for my skin. ◊ He was thirsty so I gave him a drink. ◊ Just phone and I'll give you all the help you need.* **2** [T] **~ sb sth; ~ sth to sb** to make sb have sth, especially sth he/she does not want: *Mr Johns gives us too much homework. ◊ Playing chess gives me a headache.* **3** [T] to make sb have a particular feeling, idea, etc.: *Swimming always gives me a good appetite. ◊ to give* sb a surprise/shock/fright ◇ *What gives you the idea that he was lying?* **4** [T] ~ **(sb) sth**; ~ **sth to sb** to let sb have your opinion, decision, judgement, etc.: *Can you give me some advice?* ◇ *My boss has given me permission to leave early.* ◇ *The judge gave him five years in prison.* **5** [T] ~ **sb sth**; ~ **sth to sb** to speak to people in a formal situation: *to give a speech/talk/lecture* ◇ *The officer was called to give evidence in court.* ◇ *Sarah's going to give me a cooking lesson.* **6** [T] ~ **(sb) sth for sth**; ~ **(sb) sth (to do sth)** to pay in order to have sth: *How much did you give him for fixing the car?* ◇ (*figurative*) *I'd give anything* (=I would love) *to be able to sing like that.* **7** [T] to spend time dealing with sb/sth: *We need to give some thought to this matter urgently.* **8** [T] ~ **(sb/sth) sth** to do sth to sb/sth; to make a particular sound or movement: *to give sb a kiss/push/hug* ◇ *to give sth a clean/wash/polish* ◇ ***Give me a call*** *when you get home.* ◇ *She opened the door and gave a shout of horror.* **9** [T] to perform or organize sth for people: *The company gave a party to celebrate its 50th anniversary.* **10** [I] to bend or stretch under pressure: *The branch began to give under my weight.*

IDM **not care/give a damn (about sb/sth)** → DAMN³

give or take more or less the number mentioned: *It took us two hours to get here, give or take five minutes.*

PHR V **give sth away** to give sth to sb without wanting money in return: *When she got older she gave all her toys away.* ◇ *We are giving away a free CD with this month's issue.*

give sth/sb away to show or tell the truth about sth/sb which was secret: *He smiled politely and didn't give away his real feelings.*

give (sth) back to return sth to the person that you took or borrowed it from: *I lent him some books months ago and he still hasn't given them back to me.*

give sth in to give sth to the person who is collecting it: *I've got to give this essay in to my teacher by Friday.*

give in (to sb/sth) to stop fighting against sb/sth; to accept that you have been defeated

give sth off to send sth (for example smoke, a smell, heat, etc.) out into the air: *Cars give off poisonous fumes.*

give out (used about a machine, a part of the body, etc.) to stop working: *His heart gave out and he died.*

give sth out to give one of sth to each person: *Could you give out these books to the class, please?*

give up to stop trying to do sth; to accept that you cannot do sth: *They gave up once the other team had scored their third goal.* ◇ *I give up. What's the answer?*

give sb up; **give up on sb** to stop expecting sb to arrive, succeed, improve, etc.: *Her work was so poor that all her teachers gave up on her.*

give sth up; **give up doing sth** to stop doing or having sth that you did or had regularly before: *I've tried many times to give up smoking.* ◇ *Don't give up hope. Things are bound to improve.*

give yourself/sb up (to sb) to go to the police when they are trying to catch you; to tell the police where sb is

give sth up (to sb) to give sth to sb who needs or asks for it: *He gave up his seat on the bus to an elderly woman.*

give² /ɡɪv/ ***noun*** [U] the quality of being able to bend or stretch a little

IDM **give and take** a situation in which two people, groups, etc. respect each others' rights and needs: *There has to be some give and take for a marriage to succeed.*

giveaway /ˈɡɪvəweɪ/ ***noun*** [C] (*informal*) **1** a thing that is included free when you buy sth **2** something that makes you guess the truth about sb/sth: *She said she didn't know about the money but her face was **a dead giveaway**.*

given¹ /ˈɡɪvn/ ***adj.*** (only *before* a noun) already stated or decided: *At any given time, up to 200 people are using the library.*

given² /ˈɡɪvn/ ***prep.*** considering sth: *Given that you had very little help, I think you did very well.*

ˈgiven name (*especially AmE*) = FIRST NAME

gizzard /ˈɡɪzəd/ ***noun*** [C] (**BIOLOGY**) the part of a bird's stomach in which food is changed into smaller pieces before it can be DIGESTED

glacial /ˈɡleɪʃl; ˈɡleɪsiəl/ ***adj.*** **1** (**GEOGRAPHY**) caused by ice or a GLACIER: *a glacial valley* **2** extremely cold: *glacial winds*

glaciation /ˌɡleɪsiˈeɪʃn/ ***noun*** [U] (**GEOGRAPHY**) the movement of a mass of ice over an area of land, and the things that are caused or created by this

glacier /ˈɡlæsiə(r); ˈɡleɪs-/ ***noun*** [C] (**GEOGRAPHY**) a mass of ice that moves slowly down a valley

glad 🔑 /ɡlæd/ ***adj.*** **1** (not before a noun) ~ **(about sth)**; ~ **to do sth/that…** happy; pleased: *Are you glad about your new job?* ◇ *I'm glad to hear he's feeling better.* ◇ *I'm glad (that) he's feeling better.* ◇ *I'll be glad when these exams are over.* **2** ~ **(of sth)**; ~ **(if…)** grateful for sth: *If you are free, I'd be glad of*

glacial features

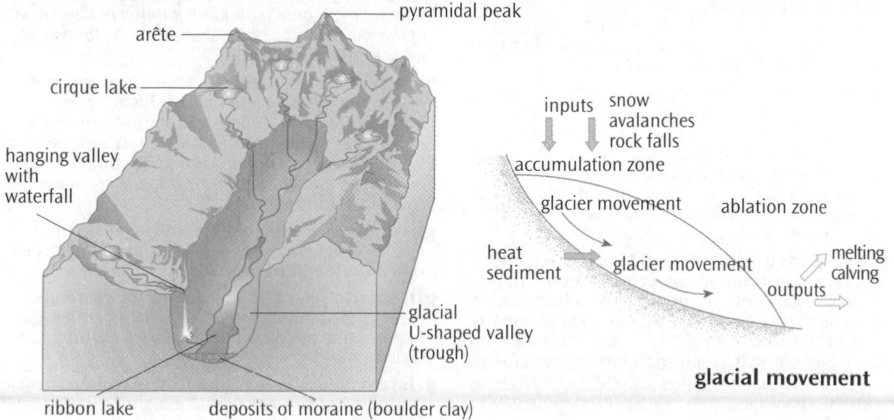

glacial movement

some help. ◇ *I'd be glad if you could help me.* **3** (only *before* a noun) (*old-fashioned*) bringing happiness: *I want to be the first to tell her the glad news.* ▶ **gladness** ***noun*** [U]

gladden /'glædn/ ***verb*** [T] to make sb glad or happy

glade /gleɪd/ ***noun*** [C] (*written*) (**GEOGRAPHY**) an open space in a forest or wood where there are no trees **SYN** **clearing**

gladiator /'glædieɪtə(r)/ ***noun*** [C] (**HISTORY**) (in ancient Rome) a man who fought against another man or a wild animal in a public show ▶ **gladiatorial** /ˌglædiə'tɔːriəl/ ***adj.***: *gladiatorial combat*

gladly /'glædli/ ***adv.*** used for politely agreeing to a request or accepting an invitation: *'Could you help me carry these bags?' 'Gladly.'* ◇ *She gladly accepted the invitation to stay the night.*

glamorize (also **-ise**) /'glæməraɪz/ ***verb*** [T] to make sth appear more attractive or exciting than it really is: *Television tends to glamorize violence.*

glamour (*AmE also* **glamor**) /'glæmə(r)/ ***noun*** [U] the quality of seeming to be more exciting or attractive than ordinary things or people: *Young people are attracted by the glamour of city life.* ▶ **glamorous** /-mərəs/ ***adj.***: *the glamorous world of show business* ▶ **glamorously** ***adv.***

glance¹ /glɑːns/ ***verb*** [I] to look quickly at sb/sth: *She glanced round the room to see if they were there.* ◇ *He glanced at her and smiled.* ◇ *The receptionist glanced down the list of names.*
PHR V **glance off (sth)** to hit sth at an angle and move off again in another direction: *The ball glanced off his knee and into the net.*

glance² /glɑːns/ ***noun*** [C] a quick look: *to take/have a glance at the newspaper headlines*
IDM **at a (single) glance** with one look: *I could tell at a glance that something was wrong.*
at first glance/sight → FIRST¹

gland /glænd/ ***noun*** [C] (**ANATOMY**) any of the small parts (**organs**) inside your body that produce chemical substances for your body to use: *sweat glands* ▶ **glandular** /'glændjʊlə(r)/ ***adj.***

glare¹ /gleə(r)/ ***verb*** [I] **1** ~ **(at sb/sth)** to look at sb in a very angry way **2** to shine with strong light that hurts your eyes

glare² /gleə(r)/ ***noun*** **1** [U] strong light that hurts your eyes: *the glare of the sun/a car's headlights* **2** [C] a very angry look

glaring /'gleərɪŋ/ ***adj.*** **1** very easy to see; shocking: *a glaring mistake/injustice* **2** (used about a light) too strong and bright **3** angry: *glaring eyes* ▶ **glaringly** ***adv.***: *a* ***glaringly obvious*** *mistake*

glass ⊶ /glɑːs/ ***noun*** **1** [U] a hard substance that you can usually see through that is used for making windows, bottles, etc.: *He cut himself on broken glass.* ◇ *a sheet/pane of glass* ◇ *a glass jar/dish/vase* ➲ *picture at* **building** **2** [C] a drinking container made of glass; the amount of liquid it contains: *a wine glass* ◇ *Could I have a glass of water?* ◇ *He drank three glasses of milk.*

glasses ⊶ /'glɑːsɪz/ (also *formal* **spectacles**, *informal* **specs**, *AmE also* **eyeglasses**) ***noun*** [pl.] two LENSES (= pieces of glass or plastic) in a frame that rests on the nose and ears. People wear **glasses** in order to be able to see better or to protect their eyes from bright SUNLIGHT: *My sister has to* ***wear glasses.*** ◇ *I need* ***a*** *new* ***pair of glasses.*** ◇ *I need some new glasses.* ◇ *reading glasses* ◇ *dark glasses/sunglasses*

glass 'fibre = FIBREGLASS

glassful /'glɑːsfʊl/ ***noun*** [C] the amount of liquid that one glass holds

glasshouse /'glɑːshaʊs/ = GREENHOUSE

glassy /'glɑːsi/ ***adj.*** **1** looking like glass **2** (used about the eyes) showing no interest or expression

glaucoma /glɔː'kəʊmə/ ***noun*** [U] (**HEALTH**) an eye disease that causes gradual loss of sight

glaze¹ /gleɪz/ ***verb*** [T] **1** to fit a sheet of glass into a window, etc. ➲ look at **double-glazing** **2** ~ **sth (with sth)** to cover a pot, brick, pie, etc. with a shiny transparent substance (before it is put into an oven)
PHR V **glaze over** (used about the eyes) to show no interest or expression

glaze² /gleɪz/ ***noun*** [C,U] (a substance that gives) a shiny transparent surface on a pot, brick, pie, etc.

glazed /gleɪzd/ ***adj.*** (used about the eyes, etc.) showing no interest or expression

glazier /'gleɪziə(r)/ ***noun*** [C] a person whose job is to fit glass into windows, etc.

gleam /gliːm/ ***noun*** [C, usually sing.] **1** a soft light that shines for a short time: *the gleam of moonlight on the water* **2** a sudden expression of an emotion in sb's eyes: *I saw a gleam of amusement in his eyes.* **3** a small amount of sth: *a faint gleam of hope* ▶ **gleam** ***verb*** [I]: *gleaming white teeth* ◇ *Their eyes gleamed with enthusiasm.*

glean /gliːn/ ***verb*** [T] ~ **sth (from sb/sth)** to obtain information, knowledge, etc., sometimes with difficulty and often from various different places: *These figures have been gleaned from a number of studies.*

glee /gliː/ ***noun*** [U] a feeling of happiness, usually because sth good has happened to you or sth bad has happened to sb else: *She couldn't hide her glee when her rival came last in the race.* ▶ **gleeful** /-fl/ ***adj.*** ▶ **gleefully** /-fəli/ ***adv.***

glen /glen/ ***noun*** [C] (**GEOGRAPHY**) a deep, narrow valley, especially in Scotland or Ireland

glib /glɪb/ ***adj.*** using words in a way that is clever and quick, but not sincere: *a glib salesman/politician* ◇ *a glib answer/excuse* ▶ **glibly** ***adv.*** ▶ **glibness** ***noun*** [U]

glide /glaɪd/ ***verb*** [I] **1** to move smoothly without noise or effort: *The dancers glided across the floor.* **2** to fly in a GLIDER: *I've always wanted to* ***go gliding.***

glider /'glaɪdə(r)/ ***noun*** [C] a light aircraft without an engine that flies using air currents ➲ look at **hang-glider** ▶ **gliding** ***noun*** [U]

glimmer /'glɪmə(r)/ ***noun*** [C] **1** a weak light that is not steady: *I could see a faint glimmer of light in one of the windows.* **2** a small sign of sth: *a glimmer of hope* ▶ **glimmer** ***verb*** [I]

glimpse /glɪmps/ ***noun*** [C] **1** **a** ~ **(at/of sth)** a very quick and not complete view of sb/sth: *I just managed to* ***catch a glimpse*** *of the fox's tail as it ran down a hole.* **2** **a** ~ **(into/of sth)** a short experience of sth that helps you understand it: *The programme gives us an interesting glimpse into the life of the cheetah.* ▶ **glimpse** ***verb*** [T]

glint /glɪnt/ ***verb*** [I] to shine with small bright flashes of light: *His eyes glinted at the thought of all that money.* ▶ **glint** ***noun*** [C]

glissando /glɪ'sændəʊ/ ***noun*** [C] (*pl.* **glissandi** /-diː/ or **glissandos**) (**MUSIC**) a falling or rising series of notes that are played so as to give a continuous sliding sound

glisten /'glɪsn/ ***verb*** [I] (used about wet surfaces) to shine: *Her eyes glistened with tears.* ◇ *Tears glistened in her eyes.*

glitter /ˈɡlɪtə(r)/ ***noun*** [U] **1** a shiny appearance consisting of many small flashes of light: *the glitter of jewellery* **2** the exciting quality that sth appears to have: *the glitter of a career in show business* **3** very small, shiny pieces of thin metal or paper, used as a decoration: *The children decorated their pictures with glitter.* ▶ **glitter** ***verb*** [I]

glittering /ˈɡlɪtərɪŋ/ ***adj.*** **1** very impressive or successful: *a glittering career/performance* **2** shining brightly with many small flashes of light

gloat /ɡləʊt/ ***verb*** [I] ~ **(about/over sth)** to feel or express happiness in an unpleasant way because sth good has happened to you or sth bad has happened to sb else

global 🔑 /ˈɡləʊbl/ ***adj.*** **1** affecting the whole world: *the global effects of pollution* **2** considering or including all parts: *We must take a global view of the problem.* ▶ **globally** /-bəli/ ***adv.***

globalization (also **-isation**) AW /ˌɡləʊbəlaɪˈzeɪʃn/ ***noun*** [U] (ECONOMICS, SOCIAL STUDIES) the fact that different cultures and economic systems around the world are becoming connected and similar to each other because of the influence of large MULTINATIONAL companies and of improved communication: *the globalization of world trade*

globalize (also **-ise**) /ˈɡləʊbəlaɪz/ ***verb*** [I,T] (ECONOMICS) if sth, for example a business company, **globalizes** or is **globalized**, it operates all around the world

the ˌglobal ˈvillage ***noun*** [sing.] the world considered as a single community connected by computers, telephones, etc.

ˌglobal ˈwarming ***noun*** [sing.] (ENVIRONMENT) the increase in the temperature of the earth's atmosphere, caused by the increase of certain gases ➲ look at **greenhouse effect**

globe AW /ɡləʊb/ ***noun*** **1 the globe** [sing.] the earth: *to travel all over the globe* **2** [C] a round object with a map of the world on it **3** [C] any object shaped like a ball

ˌglobe ˈartichoke = ARTICHOKE

globetrotter /ˈɡləʊbtrɒtə(r)/ ***noun*** [C] (*informal*) a person who travels to many countries

globule /ˈɡlɒbjuːl/ ***noun*** [C] a small drop or ball of a liquid: *There were globules of fat in the soup.*

gloom /ɡluːm/ ***noun*** [U] **1** a feeling of being sad and without hope: *The news brought deep gloom to the village.* **2** a state when it is almost completely dark

gloomy /ˈɡluːmi/ ***adj.*** (**gloomier**; **gloomiest**) **1** dark in way that makes you feel sad: *This dark paint makes the room very gloomy.* **2** sad and without much hope: *Don't be so gloomy – cheer up!* ▶ **gloomily** ***adv.***

glorified /ˈɡlɔːrɪfaɪd/ ***adj.*** (only *before* a noun) described in a way that makes sb/sth seem better, bigger, more important, etc. than they or it really are

glorify /ˈɡlɔːrɪfaɪ/ ***verb*** [T] (*pres. part.* **glorifying**; *3rd person sing. pres.* **glorifies**; *pt, pp* **glorified**) to make sb/sth appear better or more important than they or it really are: *His biography does not attempt to glorify his early career.*

glorious /ˈɡlɔːriəs/ ***adj.*** **1** having or deserving fame or success: *a glorious victory* **2** wonderful; SPLENDID: *a glorious day/view* ▶ **gloriously** ***adv.***

glory[1] /ˈɡlɔːri/ ***noun*** [U] **1** fame or honour that you get for achieving sth: *The winning team was welcomed home* ***in a blaze of glory***. **2** great beauty

glory[2] /ˈɡlɔːri/ ***verb*** (*pres. part.* **glorying**; *3rd person sing. pres.* **glories**; *pt, pp* **gloried**)

PHR V **glory in sth** to take (too much) pleasure or pride in sth: *He gloried in his sporting successes.*

gloss[1] /ɡlɒs/ ***noun*** [U, sing.] (a substance that gives sth) a smooth, shiny surface: *gloss paint* ◇ *gloss photographs* ➲ look at **matt**

gloss[2] /ɡlɒs/ ***verb***

PHR V **gloss over sth** to avoid talking about a problem, mistake, etc. in detail

glossary /ˈɡlɒsəri/ ***noun*** [C] (*pl.* **glossaries**) a list of special or unusual words and their meanings, usually at the end of a text or book

glossy /ˈɡlɒsi/ ***adj.*** (**glossier**; **glossiest**) smooth and shiny: *glossy hair* ◇ *a glossy magazine* (= printed on shiny paper)

glottal stop /ˌɡlɒtl ˈstɒp/ ***noun*** [C] (LANGUAGE) a speech sound made by closing and opening the GLOTTIS, which in English sometimes takes the place of a /t/, for example in *butter*

glottis /ˈɡlɒtɪs/ ***noun*** [C] (ANATOMY) the part of the LARYNX in the throat that contains the VOCAL CORDS (= muscles that move to produce the voice) and the narrow opening between them

glove 🔑 /ɡlʌv/ ***noun*** [C] a piece of clothing that covers your hand and has five separate parts for the fingers: *I need a new pair of gloves for the winter.* ◇ *leather/woollen/rubber gloves* ➲ look at **mitten**

ˈglove compartment (*also* **ˈglove box**) ***noun*** [C] a small ENCLOSED space or shelf facing the front seats of a car, used for keeping small things in

glow /ɡləʊ/ ***verb*** [I] **1** to produce light and/or heat without smoke or flames: *A cigarette glowed in the dark.* **2** ~ **(with sth)** to be warm or red because of excitement, exercise, etc.: *to glow with health/enthusiasm/pride* ▶ **glow** ***noun*** [sing.]: *the glow of the sky at sunset*

glower /ˈɡlaʊə(r)/ ***verb*** [I] ~ **(at sb/sth)** to look angrily (at sb/sth)

glowing /ˈɡləʊɪŋ/ ***adj.*** saying that sb/sth is very good: *His teacher wrote a glowing report about his work.* ▶ **glowingly** ***adv.***

ˈglow-worm ***noun*** [C] a type of insect. The female has no wings and produces a green light at the end of her tail.

glucose /ˈɡluːkəʊs/ ***noun*** [U] (BIOLOGY) a type of sugar that is found in fruit ➲ look at **dextrose**, **fructose**, **lactose**, **sucrose**

glue[1] 🔑 /ɡluː/ ***noun*** [U] a thick sticky liquid that is used for joining things together: *Stick the photo in with glue.*

glue[2] 🔑 /ɡluː/ ***verb*** [T] (*pres. part.* **gluing**) ~ **A (to/onto B)**; ~ **A and B (together)** to join a thing or things together with glue: *Do you think you can glue the handle back onto the teapot?*

IDM **glued to sth** (*informal*) giving all your attention to sth and not wanting to leave it: *He just sits there every evening glued to the television.*

glum /ɡlʌm/ ***adj.*** sad and quiet ▶ **glumly** ***adv.***

glut /ɡlʌt/ ***noun*** [C, usually sing.] more of sth than is needed: *The glut of coffee has forced down the price.*

gluten /ˈɡluːtn/ ***noun*** [U] a sticky substance that is found in plants that we make into flour, for example WHEAT

glutton /ˈɡlʌtn/ ***noun*** [C] **1** a person who eats too much **2** (*informal*) **a ~ for sth** a person who enjoys having or doing sth difficult, unpleasant, etc.: *She's a glutton for hard work – she never stops.*

gluttony /ˈglʌtəni/ ***noun*** [U] the habit of eating and drinking too much

glycerine (*AmE usually* **glycerin**) /ˈglɪsəriːn/ ***noun*** [U] (CHEMISTRY) a thick sweet colourless liquid made from fats and oils and used in medicines, beauty products and EXPLOSIVE substances

GM /ˌdʒiː ˈem/ ***abbr.*** genetically modified

GMT /ˌdʒiː em ˈtiː/ ***abbr.*** Greenwich Mean Time; the time system that is used in Britain during the winter and for calculating the time in other parts of the world

gnarled /nɑːld/ ***adj.*** rough and having grown into a strange shape, because of old age or hard work: *The old man had gnarled fingers.* ◇ *a gnarled oak tree*

gnash /næʃ/ ***verb***
IDM **gnash your teeth** to feel very angry and upset about sth

gnat /næt/ ***noun*** [C] a type of very small fly that bites SYN **midge**

gnaw /nɔː/ ***verb*** **1** [I,T] ~ **(away) (at/on) sth** to bite a bone, etc. many times with your back teeth **2** [I] ~ **(away) at sb** to make sb feel worried or frightened over a long period of time: *Fear of the future gnawed away at her all the time.*

gneiss /naɪs/ ***noun*** [U] (GEOLOGY) a type of METAMORPHIC rock formed at high pressure and temperature deep in the ground

gnome /nəʊm/ ***noun*** [C] (in children's stories, etc.) a little old man with a beard and a pointed hat who lives under the ground

GNP /ˌdʒiː en ˈpiː/ ***abbr.*** (ECONOMICS) **gross national product**; the total value of all the goods and services produced by a country in one year, including the total amount of money that comes from foreign countries ❶ **GNP** = **GDP** + net foreign income ➲ look at **GDP**

GNVQ /ˌdʒiː en viː ˈkjuː/ ***noun*** [C] (EDUCATION) **General National Vocational Qualification**; a qualification taken in British schools by students aged 15-18 to prepare them for university or work: *She's doing a GNVQ in Business Studies at the local college.*

go¹ ⊶ /gəʊ/ ***verb*** [I] (*pres. part.* **going**; *3rd person sing. pres.* **goes** /gəʊz/; *pt* **went** /went/; *pp* **gone** /gɒn/) **1** to move or travel from one place to another: *She always goes home by bus.* ◇ *We're going to London tomorrow.* ◇ *He went to the cinema yesterday.* ◇ *We've still got fifty miles to go.* ◇ *How fast does this car go?* ◇ *I threw the ball and the dog went running after it.* **2** to travel to a place to take part in an activity or do sth: *Are you going to Dave's party?* ◇ *Shall we go swimming this afternoon?* ◇ *to go for a swim/drive/drink/walk/meal* ◇ *We went on a school trip to a museum.* ◇ *They've gone on holiday.* ◇ *We went to watch the match.* ◇ *I'll go and make the tea.* **3** to belong to or stay in an institution: *Which school do you go to?* ◇ *to go to hospital/prison/college/university* **4** to leave a place: *I have to go now. It's nearly 4 o'clock.* ◇ *What time does the train go?* **5** to lead to or reach a place or time: *Where does this road go to?* **6** to be put or to fit in a particular place: *Where does this vase go?* ◇ *My clothes won't all go in one suitcase.* **7** to happen in a particular way; to develop: *How's the new job going?* **8** ***linking verb*** to become; to reach a particular state: *Her hair is going grey.* ◇ *to go blind/deaf/bald/senile/mad* ◇ *The baby has gone to sleep.* **9** to stay in the state mentioned: *Many mistakes go unnoticed.* **10** to be removed, lost, used, etc.; to disappear: *Has your headache gone yet?* ◇ *I like the furniture, but that carpet will have to go.* ◇ *About half my salary goes on rent.* ◇ *Jeans will never go out of fashion.* **11** to work correctly: *This clock doesn't go.* ◇ *Is your car going at the moment?* **12** to become worse or stop working correctly: *The brakes on the car have gone.* ◇ *His sight/voice/mind has gone.* **13** ~ **(with sth)**; ~ **(together)** to look or taste good with sth else: *This sauce goes well with rice or pasta.* ◇ *These two colours don't really go.* **14** to have certain words or a certain tune: *How does that song go?* **15** (used about time) to pass: *The last hour went very slowly.* **16** to start an activity: *Everybody ready to sing? Let's go!* **17** to make a sound: *The bell went early today.* ◇ *Cats go 'miaow'.* **18** (*spoken, informal*) used in the present tense for saying what a person said: *I said, 'How are you, Jim?' and he goes, 'It's none of your business!'* **19** (*informal*) (only used in the continuous tenses) to be available: *Are there any jobs going in your department?* **20** (*informal*) used for saying that you do not want sb to do sth bad or stupid: *You can borrow my bike again, but don't go breaking it this time!* ◇ *I hope John doesn't go and tell everyone about our plan.*

IDM **as people, things, etc. go** compared to the average person or thing: *As Chinese restaurants go, it wasn't bad.*

be going to do sth 1 used for showing what you plan to do in the future: *We're going to sell our car.* **2** used for saying that you think sth will happen: *It's going to rain soon.* ◇ *Oh no! He's going to fall!*

go all out for sth; **go all out to do sth** to make a great effort to do sth

go for it (*informal*) to do sth after not being sure about it: *'Do you think we should buy it?' 'Yeah, let's go for it!'*

have a lot going for you to have many advantages

Here goes! said just before you start to do sth difficult or exciting

to go that is/are left before sth ends: *How long (is there) to go before the end of the lesson?*

PHR V **go about** → GO ROUND/AROUND/ABOUT

go about sth/doing sth to start trying to do sth difficult: *I wouldn't have any idea how to go about building a house.*

go about with sb → GO ROUND/AROUND/ABOUT WITH SB

go after sb/sth to try to catch or get sb/sth

go against sb to not be in sb's favour or not be to sb's advantage: *The referee's decision went against him.*

go against sb/sth to do sth that sb/sth says you should not do: *She went against her parents' wishes and married him.*

go ahead 1 to take place after being delayed or in doubt: *Although several members were missing, the meeting went ahead without them.* **2** to travel in front of other people in your group and arrive before them

go ahead (with sth) to do sth after not being sure that it was possible: *We decided to go ahead with the match in spite of the heavy rain.* ◇ *'Can I take this chair?' 'Sure, go ahead.'*

go along to continue; to progress: *The course gets more difficult as you go along.*

go along with sb/sth to agree with sb/sth; to do what sb else has decided: *I'm happy to go along with whatever you suggest.*

go around → GO ROUND/AROUND/ABOUT

go around with sb → GO ROUND/AROUND/ABOUT WITH SB

go away 1 to disappear or leave: *I've got a headache that just won't go away.* ◇ *Just go away and leave me alone!* **2** to leave the place where you live for at least one night: *We're going away to the coast this weekend.*

go back (to sth) 1 to return to a place: *It's a wonderful city and I'd like to go back there one day.* **2** to return to an earlier matter or situation: *Let's go back to the subject we were discussing a few minutes ago.* **3** to have its origins in an earlier period of time: *A lot of the buildings in the village go back to the fifteenth century.*
go back on sth to break a promise, an agreement, etc.: *I promised to help them and I can't go back on my word.*
go back to sth/doing sth to start doing again sth that you had stopped doing: *When the children got a bit older she went back to full-time work.*
go by 1 (used about time) to pass: *As time went by, her confidence grew.* **2** to pass a place: *She stood at the window watching people go by.*
go by sth to use particular information, rules, etc. to help you decide your actions or opinions
go down 1 (used about a ship, etc.) to sink **2** (used about the sun) to disappear from the sky **3** to become lower in price, level, etc.; to fall: *The number of people out of work went down last month.*
go down (with sb) (used with adverbs, especially 'well' or 'badly' or in questions beginning with 'how') to be received in a particular way by sb: *The film went down well with the critics.*
go down with sth to catch an illness; to become ill with sth
go for sb to attack sb
go for sb/sth 1 to be true for a particular person or thing: *We've got financial problems but I suppose the same goes for a great many people.* **2** to choose sb/ sth: *I think I'll go for the roast chicken.*
go in (used about the sun) to disappear behind a cloud
go in for sth to enter or take part in an exam or competition
go in for sth/doing sth to do or have sth as a hobby or interest
go into sth 1 to hit sth while travelling in/on a vehicle: *I couldn't stop in time and went into the back of the car in front.* **2** to start working in a certain type of job: *When she left school she went into nursing.* **3** to look at or describe sth in detail: *I haven't got time to go into all the details now.*
go off 1 to explode: *A bomb has gone off in the city centre.* **2** to make a sudden loud noise: *I woke up when my alarm clock went off.* **3** (used about lights, heating, etc.) to stop working: *There was a power cut and all the lights went off.* **4** (used about food and drink) to become too old to eat or drink; to go bad **5** to become worse in quality: *I used to like that band but they've gone off recently.*
go off sb/sth to stop liking or being interested in sb/ sth: *I went off spicy food after I was ill last year.*
go off (with sb) to leave with sb: *I don't know where Sid is – he went off with some girls an hour ago.*
go off with sth to take sth that belongs to sb else
go on 1 (used about lights, heating, etc.) to start working: *I saw the lights go on in the house opposite.* **2** (used about time) to pass: *As time went on, she became more and more successful.* **3** (used especially in the continuous tenses) to happen or take place: *Can anybody tell me what's going on here?* **4** (used about a situation) to continue without changing: *This is a difficult period but it won't go on forever.* **5** to continue speaking after stopping for a moment: *Go on. What happened next?* **6** used for encouraging sb to do sth: *Oh go on, let me borrow your car. I'll bring it back in an hour.*
go on sth to use sth as information so that you can understand a situation: *There were no witnesses to the crime, so the police had very little to go on.*
go on (about sb/sth) to talk about sb/sth for a long time in a boring or annoying way: *She went on and on about work.*
go/be on (at sb) (about sth) to keep complaining about sth: *She's always (going) on at me to mend the roof.*
go on (doing sth) to continue doing sth without stopping or changing: *We don't want to go on living here for the rest of our lives.*
go on (with sth) to continue doing sth, perhaps after a pause or break: *She ignored me and went on with her meal.*
go on to do sth to do sth after completing sth else
go out 1 to leave the place where you live or work for a short time, returning on the same day: *Let's go out for a meal tonight* (=to a restaurant). ◇ *I'm just going out for a walk, I won't be long.* **2** to stop shining or burning: *Suddenly all the lights went out.* **3** to stop being fashionable or in use: *That kind of music went out in the seventies.* **4** (used about the sea) to move away from the land: *Is the tide coming in or going out?* **SYN** **ebb** ➲ look at **tide**[1]
go out (with sb); go out (together) to spend time regularly with sb, having a romantic and/or sexual relationship: *Is Fiona going out with anyone?* ◇ *They went out together for five years before they got married.*
go over sth to look at, think about or discuss sth carefully from beginning to end: *Go over your work before you hand it in.*
go over to sth to change to a different side, system, habit, etc.
go round (used especially after 'enough') to be shared among all the people: *In this area, there aren't enough jobs to go round.*
go round/around/about (used about a story, an illness, etc.) to pass from person to person: *There's a rumour going round that he's going to resign.* ◇ *There's a virus going round at work.*
go round (to...) to visit sb's home, usually a short distance away: *I'm going round to Jo's for dinner tonight.*
go round/around/about with sb to spend time and go to places regularly with sb: *Her parents don't like the people she has started going round with.*
go through to be completed successfully: *The deal went through as agreed.*
go through sth 1 to look in or at sth carefully, especially in order to find sth: *I went through all my pockets but I couldn't find my wallet.* **2** to look at, think about or discuss sth carefully from beginning to end: *We'll start the lesson by going through your homework.* **3** to have an unpleasant experience: *I'd hate to go through such a terrible ordeal again.*
go through with sth to do sth unpleasant or difficult that you have decided, agreed or threatened to do: *Do you think she'll go through with her threat to leave him?*
go together (used about two or more things) **1** to belong to the same set or group **2** to look or taste good together
go towards sth to be used as part of the payment for sth: *The money I was given for my birthday went towards my new bike.*
go under 1 to sink below the surface of some water **2** (*informal*) (used about a company) to fail and close: *A lot of firms are going under in the recession.*
go up 1 to become higher in price, level, amount, etc.; to rise: *The birth rate has gone up by 10%.* ➲ note at **rise**[1] **2** to start burning suddenly and strongly: *The car crashed into a wall and went up in flames.* **3** to be built
go with sth 1 to be included with sth; to happen as a result of sth: *Pressure goes with the job.* **2** to look or

taste good with sth else: *What colour carpet would go with the walls?*
go without (sth) to choose or be forced to not have sth: *They went without sleep night after night while the baby was ill.*

go² /gəʊ/ ***noun*** (*pl.* **goes** /gəʊz/) [C] **1** a turn to play in a game, etc.: *Whose go is it?* ◇ *Hurry up – it's your go.* **SYN turn 2** (*informal*) **a ~ (at sth/doing sth)** an occasion when you try to do sth; an attempt: *Shall I **have a go** at fixing it for you?* ◇ *I've never played this game before, but I'll **give it a go**.* ◇ *Andrew passed his driving test **first go**.*
IDM be on the go (*informal*) to be very active or busy: *I'm exhausted. I've been on the go all day.*
have a go at sb (*informal*) to criticize sb/sth
make a go of sth (*informal*) to be successful at sth

goad /gəʊd/ ***verb*** [T] **~ sb/sth (into sth/doing sth)** to cause sb to do sth by making them angry

'go-ahead¹ ***noun*** [sing.] **the go-ahead (for sth)** permission to do sth: *It looks like the council are going to **give us the go-ahead** for the new building.*

'go-ahead² ***adj.*** enthusiastic to try new ways of doing things

goal 🔑 AW /gəʊl/ ***noun*** [C] **1** (SPORT) (in football, RUGBY, HOCKEY, etc.) the area between two posts into which the ball must be kicked, hit, etc. for a point or points to be scored: *He crossed the ball in front of the goal.* **2** (SPORT) a point that is scored when the ball goes into the goal: *Everton won by three goals to two.* ◇ *to score a goal* **3** your purpose or aim: *This year I should **achieve** my **goal** of visiting all the capital cities of Europe.* ➲ note at **target¹**

goalkeeper /'gəʊlki:pə(r)/ (also *informal* **goalie** /'gəʊli/ or **keeper**) ***noun*** [C] (SPORT) (in football, HOCKEY, etc.) the player who stands in front of the goal(1) and tries to stop the other team from scoring: *The goalkeeper made a magnificent save.*

goalless /'gəʊlləs/ ***adj.*** (SPORT) with no goals scored: *a goalless draw* ◇ *The match finished goalless.*

'goal line ***noun*** [C] (SPORT) (in football, HOCKEY, etc.) the line at either end of a sports field on which the goal stands or which the ball must cross to score a goal or TOUCHDOWN

goalpost /'gəʊlpəʊst/ ***noun*** [C] (SPORT) (in football, HOCKEY, etc.) one of the two posts that form the sides of a goal. They are joined together by the CROSSBAR.

goat /gəʊt/ ***noun*** [C] a small animal with horns which lives in mountain areas or is kept on farms for its milk and meat ℹ A male goat is called a **billy goat** and a female goat is called a **nanny goat**. A young goat is called a **kid**.

goat

goatee /gəʊ'ti:/ ***noun*** [C] a small pointed beard on a man's chin

gobble /'gɒbl/ ***verb*** [I,T] (*informal*) **~ sth (up/down)** to eat quickly and noisily

gobbledegook (also **gobbledygook**) /'gɒbldigu:k/ ***noun*** [U] (*informal*) complicated language that is hard to understand

'go-between ***noun*** [C] a person who takes messages between two people or groups

goblin /'gɒblɪn/ ***noun*** [C] (in stories) a small ugly creature who tricks people

gobsmacked /'gɒbsmækt/ ***adj.*** (*informal*) so surprised that you cannot speak **SYN speechless**

god 🔑 /gɒd/ ***noun*** **1** [sing.] **God** (not used with *the*) the being or spirit in Christianity, Islam and Judaism who people pray to and who people believe created the universe: *Do you believe in God?* ◇ *Muslims worship God in a mosque.* **2** (*feminine* **goddess**) [sing.] a being or spirit that people believe has power over a particular part of nature or that represents a particular quality: *Mars was the Roman god of war and Venus was the goddess of love.*

godchild /'gɒdtʃaɪld/ (*also* **'god-daughter**; **'godson**) ***noun*** [C] (*pl.* **god·chil·dren** /'gɒdtʃɪldrən/) (RELIGION) a child that a GODPARENT promises to help and to make sure is educated as a Christian

goddess /'gɒdes/ ***noun*** [C] (RELIGION) a female god

godforsaken /'gɒdfəseɪkən/ ***adj.*** (used about a place) not interesting or attractive in any way

godparent /'gɒdpeərənt/ (*also* **'godfather**; **'godmother**) ***noun*** [C] (RELIGION) a person chosen by a child's family who promises to help the child and to make sure they are educated as a Christian

godsend /'gɒdsend/ ***noun*** [C] something unexpected that is very useful because it comes just when it is needed

goggles /'gɒglz/ ***noun*** [pl.] special glasses that you wear to protect your eyes from water, wind, dust, etc. ➲ look at **mask**

going¹ /'gəʊɪŋ/ ***noun*** **1** [sing.] (*formal*) the act of leaving a place: *We were all saddened by his going.* **SYN departure 2** [U] the rate or speed of travel, progress, etc.: *Three children in four years? That's **not bad going**!* **3** [U] how difficult it is to make progress: *The path up the mountain was **rough going**.* ◇ *It'll be **hard going** if we need to finish this by Friday!*
IDM get out, go, leave, etc. while the going is good to leave a place or stop doing sth while it is still easy to do so

going² /'gəʊɪŋ/ ***adj.***
IDM a going concern (BUSINESS) a successful business
the going rate (for sth) the usual cost (of sth): *What's the going rate for an office cleaner?*

,going-'over ***noun*** [sing.] (*informal*) **1** a very careful examination of sth: ***Give the car a good going-over** before deciding whether to buy it.* **2** a serious physical attack on sb

,goings-'on ***noun*** [pl.] (*informal*) unusual things that are happening

go-kart /'gəʊ kɑ:t/ ***noun*** [C] a vehicle like a very small car with no roof or doors, used for racing

gold 🔑 /gəʊld/ ***noun*** **1** [U] (*symbol* **Au**) a PRECIOUS yellow metal that is used for making coins, jewellery, etc.: *Is your bracelet made of solid gold?* ◇ *22 carat gold* ◇ *a gold chain/ring/watch* ℹ For more information on the periodic table of elements, look at pages R34-5.
2 [C] = GOLD MEDAL ▶ **gold *adj.***: *The invitation was written in gold letters.* ➲ look at **golden**
IDM (as) good as gold → GOOD¹
have a heart of gold → HEART

golden /'gəʊldən/ ***adj.*** **1** made of gold or bright yellow in colour like gold: *a golden crown* ◇ *golden hair/sand* **2** best, most important, favourite, etc.: *The golden rule is 'Keep your eye on the ball'.* ◇ *a golden opportunity*
IDM the golden rule (of sth) → RULE¹ (2)

,golden 'wedding ***noun*** [C] the 50th anniversary of a wedding: *The couple celebrated their golden wedding in August.* ➲ look at **diamond wedding**, **ruby wedding**, **silver wedding**

goldfish /ˈgəʊldfɪʃ/ ***noun*** [C] (*pl.* **goldfish**) a small orange fish, often kept as a pet in a bowl or a small pool in the garden (**pond**)

ˌ**gold ˈmedal** (*also* **gold**) ***noun*** [C] (SPORT) the prize for first place in a sports competition ➲ look at **bronze medal**, **silver medal**

ˈ**gold mine** ***noun*** [C] **1** a place where gold is taken from the ground **2 a gold mine (of sth)** a place, person or thing that provides a lot of sth: *This website is a gold mine of information.*

golf /gɒlf/ ***noun*** [U] (SPORT) a game that is played outdoors on a large area of grass (**golf course**) and in which you use a stick (**golf club**) to hit a small hard ball (**golf ball**) into a series of holes (usually 18): *to play a round of golf* ➲ picture at **sport**

golfer /ˈgɒlfə(r)/ ***noun*** [C] (SPORT) a person who plays GOLF

golly /ˈgɒli/ ***exclamation*** (*informal*) used for expressing surprise

gondola /ˈgɒndələ/ ***noun*** [C] **1** a long boat with a flat bottom and high parts at each end, used on CANALS in Venice, Italy **2** the part on a CABLE CAR or SKI LIFT where the passengers sit **3** (*especially AmE*) the part of a hot air BALLOON or an AIRSHIP where the passengers sit

gone[1] past participle of **go**[1]

gone[2] /gɒn/ ***adj.*** (not before a noun) not present any longer; completely used or finished: *He stood at the door for a moment, and then he was gone.* ◇ *Can I have some more ice cream, please, or is it all gone?*

gone[3] /gɒn/ ***prep.*** later than: *Hurry up! It's gone six already!*

gonna /ˈgɒnə/ (*informal*) a way of writing 'going to' to show that sb is speaking in an informal way

gonorrhoea (*AmE* **gonorrhea**) /ˌgɒnəˈrɪə/ ***noun*** [U] (HEALTH) a disease of the sexual organs, caught by having sex with a person who has it

goo /guː/ ***noun*** [U] (*informal*) a sticky wet substance ➲ adjective **gooey**

good[1] ⊶ /gʊd/ ***adj.*** (**better** /ˈbetə(r)/, **best** /best/) **1** of a high quality or standard: *a good book/film/actor* ◇ *That's a really good idea!* ◇ *The hotel was quite/pretty good, but not fantastic.* **2** ~ **at sth**; ~ **with sb/sth** able to do sth or deal with sb/sth well: *Jane's really good at science subjects but she's* ***no good at*** *languages.* ◇ *He's very good with children.* ◇ *Are you any good at drawing?* **3** pleasant or enjoyable: *It's good to be home again.* ◇ *good news/weather* ◇ ***Have a good time*** *at the party!* **4** morally right or well behaved: *She was a very good person – she spent her whole life trying to help other people.* ◇ *Were the children good while we were out?* **5** ~ **(to sb)**; ~ **of sb (to do sth)** kind; helpful: *They were good to me when I was ill.* ◇ *It was good of you to come.* **6** ~ **(for sb/sth)** having a positive effect on sb/sth's health or condition: *Green vegetables are very good for you.* ◇ *This cream is good for burns.* **7** ~ **(for sb/sth)** suitable or convenient: *This beach is very good for surfing.* ◇ *I think Paul would be a good person for the job.* ◇ *'When shall we meet?' 'Thursday would be a good day for me.'* **8** (used about a reason, etc.) acceptable and easy to understand: *a good excuse/explanation/reason* ◇ *She has good reason to be pleased – she's just been promoted.* **9** ~ **(for sth)** that can be used or can provide sth: *I've only got one good pair of shoes.* ◇ *This ticket's good for another three days.* **10 a good...** more, larger, etc. than is usual or expected: ***a good many/a good few*** *people* (= a lot of people) ◇ *a good distance* (= a long way) ◇ *a good* (= at least) *ten minutes/a good three miles* ◇ *Take a good* (= long and careful) *look at this photograph.* ◇ *What you need is a good rest.* ◇ *Give the fruit a good wash before you eat it.* **11** used when you are pleased about sth: *'Lisa's invited us to dinner next week.' 'Oh, good!'*

IDM **a good/great many** → MANY

as good as almost; virtually: *The project is as good as finished.*

(as) good as gold very well behaved

be in/for a good cause → CAUSE[1]

in good faith → FAITH

good for you, him, her, etc. (*informal*) used to show that you are pleased that sb has done sth clever: *'I passed my driving test!' 'Well done! Good for you!'*

for good measure → MEASURE[2]

so far so good → FAR[2]

good[2] ⊶ /gʊd/ ***noun*** [U] **1** behaviour that is morally right or acceptable: *the difference between good and evil* ◇ *I'm sure there's some good in everybody.* **2** something that will help sb/sth; advantage: *She did it* ***for the good of*** *her country.* ◇ *I know you don't want to go into hospital, but it's* ***for your own good.*** ◇ ***What's the good of*** *learning French if you have no chance of using it?* ➲ look at **goods**

IDM **be no good (doing sth)** to be of no use or value: *It's no good standing here in the cold. Let's go home.* ◇ *This sweater isn't any good. It's too small.*

do you good to help or be useful to you: *It'll do you good to meet some new people.*

for good for ever: *I hope they've gone for good this time!*

not much good (*informal*) bad or not useful: *'How was the party?' 'Not much good.'*

a/the world of good → WORLD

goodbye ⊶ /ˌgʊdˈbaɪ/ ***exclamation*** said when sb goes or you go: *We said goodbye to Steven at the airport.* ▶ **goodbye** ***noun*** [C]: *We said our goodbyes and left.*

ˌ**Good ˈFriday** ***noun*** [C] (RELIGION) the Friday before Easter when Christians remember the death of Christ

ˌ**good-ˈhumoured** ***adj.*** pleasant and friendly

goodies /ˈgʊdiz/ ***noun*** [pl.] (*informal*) exciting things that are provided or given: *There were lots of cakes and other goodies on the table.*

ˌ**good-ˈlooking** ***adj.*** (usually used about a person) attractive

ˌ**good ˈlooks** ***noun*** [pl.] the physical beauty of a person: *an actor famous for his rugged good looks*

ˌ**good-ˈnatured** ***adj.*** friendly or kind

goodness /ˈgʊdnəs/ ***noun*** [U] **1** the quality of being good SYN **virtue 2** the part of sth that has a good effect, especially on sb/sth's health: *Wholemeal bread has more goodness in it than white.*

goods ⊶ /gʊdz/ ***noun*** [pl.] **1** things that are for sale: *a wide range of consumer goods* ◇ *electrical goods* ◇ *stolen goods* ➲ note at **product 2** (*especially AmE* **freight**) things that are carried by train or lorry: *a goods train* ◇ *a heavy goods vehicle* (= HGV)

IDM **come up with/deliver the goods** (*informal*) to do what you have promised to do

ˌ**good ˈsense** ***noun*** [U] good judgement or intelligence: *He had the good sense to refuse the offer.*

goodwill /ˌgʊdˈwɪl/ ***noun*** [U] friendly, helpful feelings towards other people: *The visit was designed to promote friendship and goodwill.*

goody (also **goodie**) /ˈgʊdi/ ***noun*** [C] (*pl.* **goodies**) (*informal*) a good person in a film, book, etc. OPP **baddy**

'goody-goody ***noun*** [C] a person who always behaves very well in order to please people in authority

gooey /'guːi/ ***adj.*** (*informal*) soft and sticky: *gooey cakes*

goof /guːf/ ***verb*** [I] (*especially AmE, informal*) to make a silly mistake

goose /guːs/ ***noun*** [C] (*pl.* **geese** /giːs/) a large white bird that is like a DUCK, but bigger. **Geese** are kept on farms for their meat and eggs. ❶ A male goose is called a **gander** and a young goose is a **gosling**.

gooseberry /'gʊzbəri/ ***noun*** [C] (*pl.* **gooseberries**) a small green fruit that is covered in small hairs and has a sour taste

IDM **play gooseberry** to be present when two lovers want to be alone

'goose pimples (*also* **'goose bumps**) ***noun*** [pl.] small points or lumps which appear on your skin because you are cold or frightened

gore¹ /gɔː(r)/ ***noun*** [U] thick blood that comes from a wound ➲ adjective **gory**

gore² /gɔː(r)/ ***verb*** [T] (used about an animal) to wound sb with a horn, etc.: *She was gored to death by a bull.*

gorge¹ /gɔːdʒ/ ***noun*** [C] (**GEOGRAPHY**) a narrow valley with steep sides and a river running through it ➲ picture at **limestone**

gorge² /gɔːdʒ/ ***verb*** [I,T] ~ **(yourself) (on/with sth)** to eat a lot of food

gorgeous /'gɔːdʒəs/ ***adj.*** (*informal*) extremely pleasant or attractive: *What gorgeous weather!* ◇ *You look gorgeous in that dress.* ▶ **gorgeously** ***adv.***

gorilla /gə'rɪlə/ ***noun*** [C] a large very powerful African APE (=an animal like a large monkey but without a tail) with a black or brown hairy body

gory /'gɔːri/ ***adj.*** full of violence and blood: *a gory film*

gosh /gɒʃ/ ***exclamation*** (*informal*) used for expressing surprise, shock, etc.

gosling /'gɒzlɪŋ/ ***noun*** [C] a young GOOSE (=a bird like a large duck)

gospel /'gɒspl/ ***noun*** **1** **Gospel** [sing.] (**RELIGION**) one of the four books in the Bible that describe the life and teachings of Jesus Christ: *St Matthew's/ Mark's/Luke's/John's Gospel* **2** (*also* ˌ**gospel 'truth**) [U] the truth: *You can't take what he says as gospel.* **3** (*also* **'gospel music**) [U] (**MUSIC**) a style of religious music that is especially popular among African American Christians

gossip /'gɒsɪp/ ***noun*** **1** [U] informal talk about other people and their private lives, that is often unkind or not true: *Matt phoned me up to tell me the latest gossip.* **2** [C] an informal conversation about other people and their private lives: *The two neighbours were having a good gossip over the fence.* **3** [C] a person who enjoys talking about other people's private lives ▶ **gossip** ***verb*** [I]

'gossip column ***noun*** [C] (**ARTS AND MEDIA**) a part of a newspaper or magazine where you can read about the private lives of famous people

got past tense, past participle of **get**

Gothic /'gɒθɪk/ ***adj.*** **1** (**HISTORY**) connected with the Goths (=a Germanic people who fought against the Roman Empire) **2** (**ARCHITECTURE**) built in the style that was popular in western Europe from the 12th to the 16th centuries, and which has pointed ARCHES and windows and tall thin PILLARS: *a Gothic church* **3** (**LITERATURE**) written in the style popular in the 18th and 19th centuries, which described romantic adventures in mysterious or frightening surroundings

gotta /'gɒtə/ (*AmE, informal*) a way of writing 'got to' or 'got a' to show that sb is speaking in an informal way

gotten (*AmE*) past participle of **get**

gouache /gu'ɑːʃ; gwɑːʃ/ ***noun*** [C] (**ART**) **1** [U] a method of painting using colours that are mixed with water and made thick with a type of glue; the paints used in this method **2** [C] a picture painted using this method

gouge /gaʊdʒ/ ***verb*** [T] to make a hole in a surface using a sharp object in a rough way

PHRV **gouge sth out** to remove or form sth by digging into a surface

goulash /'guːlæʃ/ ***noun*** [C,U] a hot Hungarian dish of meat that is cooked slowly in liquid with PAPRIKA (=a strong spice)

gourd /gʊəd; gɔːd/ ***noun*** [C] a type of large fruit, not normally eaten, with hard skin and a soft inside. **Gourds** are often dried and used as containers.

gourmand /'gʊəmənd/ ***noun*** [C] a person who enjoys eating and eats large amounts of food

gourmet /'gʊəmeɪ/ ***noun*** [C] a person who enjoys food and knows a lot about it

gout /gaʊt/ ***noun*** [U] (**HEALTH**) a disease that causes painful swelling in the JOINTS (=the places where two bones fit together), especially of the toes, knees and fingers

govern 🔑 /'gʌvn/ ***verb*** **1** [I,T] (**POLITICS**) to rule or control the public affairs of a country, city, etc.: *Britain is governed by the Prime Minister and the Cabinet.* **2** [T] (often passive) to influence or control sb/sth: *Our decision will be governed by the amount of money we have to spend.*

government 🔑 /'gʌvənmənt/ ***noun*** (**POLITICS**) **1** [C] (often **the Government**) (*abbr.* **govt**) the group of people who rule or control a country: *He has resigned from the Government.* ◇ *The foreign governments involved are meeting in Geneva.* ◇ *government policy/money/ministers*
2 [U] the activity or method of controlling a country: *weak/strong/corrupt government* ◇ *Which party is* ***in government***? ▶ **governmental** /ˌgʌvn'mentl/ ***adj.***: *a governmental department* ◇ *different governmental systems*

governor 🔑 /'gʌvənə(r)/ ***noun*** [C] **1** (**POLITICS**) a person who rules or controls a region or state (especially in the US): *the Governor of New York State* **2** the leader or member of a group of people who control an organization: *the governor of the Bank of England* ◇ *school governors*

govt ***abbr.*** (*written*) = GOVERNMENT

gown /gaʊn/ ***noun*** [C] **1** a long formal dress for a special occasion: *a ball gown* **2** a long loose piece of clothing that is worn over clothes by judges, doctors performing operations, etc.

GP /ˌdʒiː 'piː/ ***abbr.*** (**HEALTH**) general practitioner; a doctor who treats all types of illnesses and works in the local community in a PRACTICE, not in a hospital. In Britain a **GP** is also called a **family doctor**.

GPS /ˌdʒiː piː 'es/ ***abbr.*** (**TECHNICAL**) **global positioning system**;a system by which signals are sent from SATELLITES to a special device, used to show the position of a person or thing on the surface of the earth very accurately

grab ⊶ /græb/ ***verb*** (**grabbing**; **grabbed**) **1** [I,T] ~ **sth (from sb)** to take sth with a sudden movement: *Helen grabbed the toy car from her little brother.* ◇ ***Grab hold of*** *his arm in case he tries to run!* ◇ *Someone had arrived before us and grabbed all the seats.* ◇ (*figurative*) *He grabbed the opportunity of a free trip to America.* ◇ (*figurative*) *I'll try to grab the waitress's attention.* ➲ look at **snatch 2** [I] ~ **at/for sth** to try to get or catch sb/sth: *Jonathan grabbed at the ball but missed.* **3** [T] to do sth quickly because you are in a hurry: *I'll just grab something to eat and then we'll go.* ▶ **grab** /græb/ ***noun*** [C]: *She made a grab for the boy but she couldn't stop him falling.*

grace /greɪs/ ***noun*** [U] **1** the ability to move in a smooth and controlled way **2** extra time that is allowed for sth **3** (RELIGION) a short prayer of thanks to God before or after a meal

IDM **sb's fall from grace** a situation in which sb loses the respect that people had for them by doing sth wrong or immoral

have the grace to do sth to be polite enough to do sth

with good grace in a pleasant and reasonable way, without complaining: *He accepted the refusal with good grace.*

graceful /'greɪsfl/ ***adj.*** having a smooth, attractive movement or form: *a graceful dancer* ◇ *graceful curves* ➲ look at **gracious** ▶ **gracefully** /-fəli/ ***adv.***: *The goalkeeper rose gracefully to catch the ball.* ◇ *She accepted the decision gracefully* (=without showing her disappointment). ▶ **gracefulness** ***noun*** [U]

graceless /'greɪsləs/ ***adj.*** **1** not knowing how to be polite to people **2** (used about a movement or a shape) ugly and not elegant ▶ **gracelessly** ***adv.***

gracious /'greɪʃəs/ ***adj.*** **1** (used about a person or their behaviour) kind, polite and generous: *a gracious smile* **2** (only *before* a noun) showing the easy comfortable way of life that rich people can have: *gracious living* ➲ look at **graceful** ▶ **graciously** ***adv.*** ▶ **graciousness** ***noun*** [U]

IDM **good gracious!** used for expressing surprise: *Good gracious! Is that the time?*

grade[1] ⊶ AW /greɪd/ ***noun*** [C] **1** the quality or the level of ability, importance, etc. that sb/sth has: *Which grade of petrol do you need?* ◇ *We need to use high-grade materials for this job.* **2** (EDUCATION) a mark that is given for school work, etc. or in an exam: *He got good/poor grades this term.* ◇ *Very few students pass the exam with a grade A.* **3** (*AmE*) (EDUCATION) a class or classes in a school in which all the children are the same age: *My daughter is in the third grade.* ➲ note at **form**[1] (4)

IDM **make the grade** (*informal*) to reach the expected standard; to succeed

grade[2] ⊶ AW /greɪd/ ***verb*** [T] (often passive) to put things or people into groups according to their quality, ability, size, etc.: *I've graded their work from 1 to 10.* ◇ *Eggs are graded by size.* ▶ **graded** AW ***adj.***: *graded tests for language students*

'grade school ***noun*** [C] (*AmE*) = ELEMENTARY SCHOOL

gradient /'greɪdiənt/ ***noun*** [C] the degree at which a road, etc. goes up or down: *The hill has a gradient of 1 in 4 (=25%).* ◇ *a steep gradient*

gradual ⊶ /'grædʒuəl/ ***adj.*** happening slowly or over a long period of time; not sudden: *a gradual increase*

gradually ⊶ /'grædʒuəli/ ***adv.*** slowly, over a long period of time: *After the war life gradually got back to normal.* ◇ *The weather gradually improved.*

graduate[1] /'grædʒuət/ ***noun*** [C] (EDUCATION) **1 a** ~ **(in sth)** a person who has a first degree from a university, etc.: *a law graduate/a graduate in law* ◇ *a graduate of London University/a London University graduate* ➲ look at **postgraduate**, **undergraduate**, **bachelor**, **student** **2** (*AmE*) a person who has completed a course at a school, college, etc.: *a high-school graduate*

graduate[2] /'grædʒueɪt/ ***verb*** [I] **1** ~ **(in sth)** **(from sth)** (EDUCATION) to get a (first) degree from a university, etc.: *She graduated in History from Cambridge University.* **2** (*AmE*) ~ **(from sth)** (EDUCATION) to complete a course at a school, college, etc. **3** ~ **(from sth) to sth** to change (from sth) to sth more difficult, important, expensive, etc.

'graduate school (also *informal* **'grad school**) (*AmE*) ***noun*** [C] (EDUCATION) a part of a college or university where you can study for a second or further degree

graduation /ˌgrædʒu'eɪʃn/ ***noun*** (EDUCATION) **1** [U] the act of successfully completing a university degree or (in the US) studies at a high school **2** [sing.] a ceremony in which certificates are given to people who have GRADUATED

graffiti /grə'fi:ti/ ***noun*** [U, pl.] pictures or writing on a wall, etc. in a public place: *Vandals had covered the walls in graffiti.*

graft /grɑ:ft/ ***noun*** [C] **1** (AGRICULTURE) a piece of a living plant that is fixed onto another plant so that it will grow **2** (HEALTH) a piece of living skin, bone, etc. that is fixed onto a damaged part of a body in an operation: *a skin graft* ▶ **graft** ***verb*** [T] ~ **sth onto sth**: *Skin from his leg was grafted onto the burnt area of his face.* ➲ look at **transplant**

grain ⊶ /greɪn/ ***noun*** **1** [U, C] (AGRICULTURE) the seeds of WHEAT, rice, etc.: *The US is a major producer of grain.* ◇ *grain exports* ◇ *a few grains of rice* ➲ picture at **cereal** **2** [C] a ~ **of sth** a very small piece of sth: *a grain of sand/salt/sugar* ◇ (*figurative*) *There isn't* ***a grain of truth*** *in the rumour.* **3** [U] the natural pattern of lines that can be seen or felt in wood, rock, stone, etc.

IDM **(be/go) against the grain** to be different from what is usual or natural

gram ⊶ (also **gramme**) /græm/ ***noun*** [C] (*abbr.* g) a measure of weight. There are 1000 **grams** in a kilogram.

grammar ⊶ /'græmə(r)/ ***noun*** (LANGUAGE) **1** [U]the rules of a language, for example for forming words or joining words together in sentences: *Russian grammar can be difficult for foreign learners.* **2** [U] the way in which sb uses the rules of a language: *You have a good vocabulary, but your grammar needs improvement.* **3** [C] a book that describes and explains the rules of a language: *a French grammar*

'grammar school ***noun*** [C] (EDUCATION) (in Britain, especially in the past) a type of secondary school for children from 11-18 who are good at academic subjects

grammatical /grə'mætɪkl/ ***adj.*** (LANGUAGE) **1** connected with grammar: *the grammatical rules for forming plurals* **2** following the rules of a language: *The sentence is not grammatical.* ▶ **grammatically** /-kli/ ***adv.***

gramme ⊶ = GRAM

gramophone /'græməfəʊn/ (*BrE, old-fashioned*) = RECORD PLAYER

gran /græn/ (*BrE, informal*) = GRANDMOTHER

granary bread /'grænəri bred/ ***noun*** [U] a type of brown bread containing whole grains of WHEAT

grand[1] /grænd/ ***adj.*** **1** impressive and large or important (also used in names): *Our house isn't very grand, but it has a big garden.* ◇ *She thinks she's very grand because she drives a Porsche.* ◇ *the Grand Canyon* ◇ *the Grand Hotel* ➲ noun **grandeur** **2** used in compounds before a noun to show a family relationship: *grandson* **3** (*informal*) very good or pleasant: *You've done a grand job!* ▶ **grandly** ***adv.*** ▶ **grandness** ***noun*** [U]

grand[2] /grænd/ ***noun*** [C] (*pl.* **grand**) (*slang*) 1000 pounds or dollars

grandad /'grændæd/ (*BrE, informal*) = GRANDFATHER

grandchild /'græntʃaɪld/ (*pl.* **grandchildren**) (*also* **granddaughter**; **grandson**) ***noun*** [C] the daughter or son of your child

grandeur /'grændʒə(r)/ ***noun*** [U] (*formal*) **1** the quality of being large and impressive: *the grandeur of the Swiss Alps* **2** the feeling of being important

ˌgrandfather 'clock ***noun*** [C] a clock that stands on the floor in a tall wooden case

grandiose /'grændiəʊs/ ***adj.*** bigger or more complicated than necessary

grandma /'grænmɑː/ (*informal*) = GRANDMOTHER

grandpa /'grænpɑː/ (*informal*) = GRANDFATHER

grandparent /'grænpeərənt/ (*also* **grandmother**; **grandfather**) ***noun*** [C] the mother or father of one of your parents: *This is a picture of two of my great-grandparents* (= the parents of one of my grandparents).

ˌgrand pi'ano ***noun*** [C] (**MUSIC**) a large flat piano (with horizontal strings)

Grand Prix /ˌgrɑ̃ː 'priː/ ***noun*** [C] (*pl.* **Grands Prix** /ˌgrɑ̃ː 'priː/) (**SPORT**) one of a series of important international races for racing cars or motorbikes

ˌgrand 'slam ***noun*** [C] (**SPORT**) winning all the important matches or competitions in a particular sport, for example TENNIS or RUGBY

grandstand /'grænstænd/ ***noun*** [C] (**SPORT**) rows of seats, usually covered by a roof, from which you get a good view of a sports competition, etc.

ˌgrand 'total ***noun*** [C] the amount that you get when you add several totals together

granite /'grænɪt/ ***noun*** [U] (**GEOLOGY**) a hard grey rock

granny /'græni/ (*pl.* **grannies**) (*informal*) = GRANDMOTHER

grant[1] AW /grɑːnt/ ***verb*** [T] **1** (*formal*) to (officially) give sb what they have asked for: *He was granted permission to leave early.* **2** to agree (that sth is true): *I grant you that New York is an interesting place but I still wouldn't want to live there.* ➲ note at **admit**

IDM **take sb/sth for granted** to be so used to sb/sth that you forget their or its true value and are not grateful: *In developed countries we take running water for granted.*

take sth for granted to accept sth as being true: *We can take it for granted that the new students will have at least an elementary knowledge of English.*

grant[2] AW /grɑːnt/ ***noun*** [C] money that is given by the government, etc. for a particular purpose: *a student grant* (= to help pay for university education) ◇ *to apply for/be awarded a grant*

granted /'grɑːntɪd/ ***adv.*** used for saying that sth is true, before you make a comment about it: *'We've never had any problems before.' 'Granted, but this year there are 200 more people coming.'*

granular /'grænjələ(r)/ ***adj.*** made of a mass of small hard pieces; looking or feeling like a mass of small hard pieces

granulated sugar /ˌgrænjuleɪtɪd 'ʃʊgə(r)/ ***noun*** [U] white sugar in the form of small grains

granule /'grænjuːl/ ***noun*** [C] a small hard piece of sth; a small grain: *instant coffee granules*

grape /greɪp/ ***noun*** [C] a green or purple BERRY that grows in bunches on a climbing plant (**a vine**) and that is used for making wine: *a bunch of grapes*

IDM **sour grapes** → SOUR

grapefruit /'greɪpfruːt/ ***noun*** [C] (*pl.* **grapefruit** or **grapefruits**) a large round yellow fruit with a thick skin and a sour taste

the grapevine /'greɪpvaɪn/ ***noun*** [sing.] the way that news is passed from one person to another: *I heard* ***on/through the grapevine*** *that you're moving.*

graph

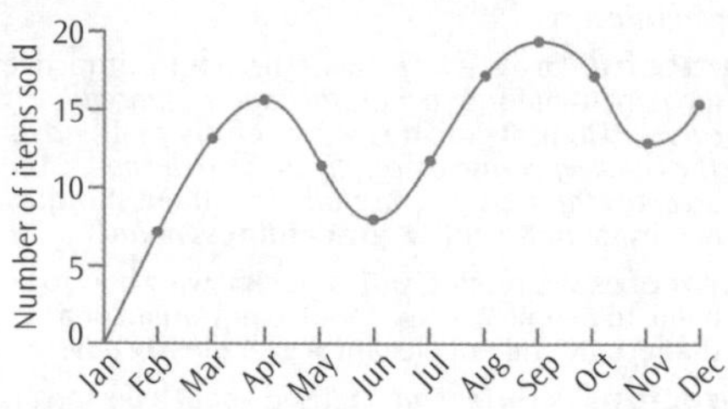

graph /grɑːf/ ***noun*** [C] (**MATHEMATICS**) a diagram in which a line or a curve shows the relationship between two quantities, measurements, etc.: *a graph showing/to show the number of cars sold each month* ➲ look at **bar graph**

graphic /'græfɪk/ ***adj.*** **1** (only *before* a noun) connected with drawings, diagrams, etc.: *graphic design* ◇ *a graphic artist* **2** (used about descriptions) clear and giving a lot of detail, especially about sth unpleasant: *She described the accident in graphic detail.* ▶ **graphically** /-kli/ ***adv.***

graphics /'græfɪks/ ***noun*** [pl.] (**ART, COMPUTING**) the production of drawings, diagrams, etc.: *computer graphics*

graphite /'græfaɪt/ ***noun*** [U] (**CHEMISTRY**) a soft black substance (a form of CARBON) that is used in pencils

'graph paper ***noun*** [U] (**MATHEMATICS**) paper with small squares of equal size printed on it, used for drawing GRAPHS and other diagrams

grapple /'græpl/ ***verb*** [I] ~ **(with sb)** to get hold of sb/sth and fight with or try to control them or it

grasp[1] /grɑːsp/ ***verb*** [T] **1** to take hold of sb/sth suddenly and firmly: *Lisa grasped the child firmly by the hand before crossing the road.* ◇ (*figurative*) *to grasp an opportunity/a chance* **2** to understand sth completely: *I don't think you've grasped how serious the situation is.*

PHR V **grasp at sth** to try to take hold of sth

grasp[2] /grɑːsp/ ***noun*** [sing., U] **1** a firm hold of sb/sth: *Get a good grasp on the rope before pulling yourself up.* ◇ *I grabbed the boy, but he slipped from my grasp.* **2** a person's understanding of a subject or of difficult facts: *He has* ***a good grasp of*** *English grammar.* **3** the ability to get or achieve sth: *Finally their dream was* ***within their grasp***.

grasping /ˈgrɑːspɪŋ/ ***adj.*** wanting very much to have a lot more money, power, etc.

grass ⊶ /grɑːs/ ***noun*** **1** [U] the common green plant with thin leaves which covers fields and parts of gardens. Cows, sheep, horses, etc. eat grass: *Don't walk on the grass.* ◇ *I must cut the grass at the weekend.* ◇ *a blade* (=one leaf) *of grass* **2** [C] one type of grass: *an arrangement of dried flowers and grasses*

grasshopper /ˈgrɑːshɒpə(r)/ ***noun*** [C] an insect that lives in long grass or trees and that can jump high in the air. **Grasshoppers** make loud noises. ➲ picture on **page 29**

grassland /ˈgrɑːslænd/ ***noun*** [U] (*also* **grasslands** [pl.]) (GEOGRAPHY) a large area of open land covered with wild grass

ˌgrass ˈroots ***noun*** [pl.] the ordinary people in an organization, not those who make decisions

grassy /ˈgrɑːsi/ ***adj.*** covered with grass

grate¹ /greɪt/ ***verb*** **1** [T] to rub food into small pieces using a GRATER: *grated cheese/carrot* **2** [I] ~ **(on sb)** to annoy or irritate **3** [I] ~ **(against/on sth)** to make a sharp unpleasant sound (when two metal surfaces rub against each other)

grate² /greɪt/ ***noun*** [C] the metal frame that holds the wood, coal, etc. in a FIREPLACE (=the space at the bottom of the chimney where you make a fire)

grateful ⊶ /ˈgreɪtfl/ ***adj.*** ~ **(to sb)** **(for sth)**; ~ **(that...)** feeling or showing thanks (to sb): *We are very grateful to you for all the help you have given us.* ◇ *He was very grateful that you did as he asked.* ▸ **gratefully** /-fəli/ ***adv.***

> WORD FAMILY
> **grateful** *adj.* (≠ **ungrateful**)
> **gratitude** *noun* (≠ **ingratitude**)

grater /ˈgreɪtə(r)/ ***noun*** [C] a kitchen tool that is used for cutting food (for example cheese) into small pieces by rubbing it across its rough surface

gratify /ˈgrætɪfaɪ/ ***verb*** [T] (*pres. part.* **gratifying**; *3rd person sing. pres.* **gratifies**; *pt, pp* **gratified**) (usually passive) (*formal*) to give sb pleasure and satisfaction ▸ **gratifying** ***adj.***

grating /ˈgreɪtɪŋ/ ***noun*** [C] a flat frame made of metal bars that is fixed over a hole in the road, a window, etc.

gratitude /ˈgrætɪtjuːd/ ***noun*** [U] ~ **(to sb) (for sth)** the feeling of being grateful or of wanting to give your thanks to sb OPP **ingratitude**

gratuity /grəˈtjuːəti/ ***noun*** [C] (*pl.* **gratuities**) (*formal*) a small amount of extra money that you give to sb who serves you, for example in a restaurant SYN **tip**

grave¹ ⊶ /greɪv/ ***noun*** [C] the place where a dead body is buried: *I put some flowers on my grandmother's grave.* ➲ look at **tomb**

IDM **have one foot in the grave** → FOOT¹

grave² ⊶ /greɪv/ ***adj.*** (*formal*) **1** bad or serious: *These events could have* ***grave consequences*** *for us all.* ◇ *The children were* ***in grave danger***. **2** (used about people) sad or serious ➲ noun **gravity** ▸ **gravely** ***adv.***: *gravely ill*

grave³ /grɑːv/ (*also* **ˌgrave ˈaccent**) ***noun*** [C] (LANGUAGE) a mark placed over a vowel in some languages to show how it should be pronounced, as over the *e* in the French word *père* ➲ look at **acute accent**, **circumflex**, **tilde**, **umlaut**

gravel /ˈgrævl/ ***noun*** [U] very small stones that are used for making roads, paths, etc.

gravelly /ˈgrævəli/ ***adj.*** **1** full of or containing many small stones: *Silt and gravelly deposits had been left by the tide.* **2** (used about a voice) deep and with a rough sound: *His gravelly voice is perfect for radio.*

gravestone /ˈgreɪvstəʊn/ ***noun*** [C] a stone in the ground that shows the name, dates, etc. of the dead person who is buried there ➲ look at **headstone**, **tombstone**

graveyard /ˈgreɪvjɑːd/ ***noun*** [C] an area of land next to a church where dead people are buried ➲ look at **cemetery**, **churchyard**

gravitational /ˌgrævɪˈteɪʃənl/ ***adj.*** (PHYSICS) connected with or caused by the force of GRAVITY: *a gravitational field* ◇ *the gravitational pull of the moon* ▸ **gravitationally** /-ʃənəli/ ***adv.***

gravity /ˈgrævəti/ ***noun*** [U] **1** (*abbr.* **g**) (PHYSICS) the natural force that makes things fall to the ground when you drop them: *the force of gravity* **2** (*formal*) importance ➲ adjective **grave**

gravy /ˈgreɪvi/ ***noun*** [U] a thin sauce that is made from the juices that come out of meat while it is cooking ➲ look at **sauce**

gray ⊶ (*especially AmE*) =GREY

graze¹ /greɪz/ ***verb*** [I] **1** (AGRICULTURE) (used about cows, sheep, etc.) to eat grass (that is growing in a field): *There were cows grazing by the river.* **2** [T] to break the surface of your skin by rubbing it against sth rough: *The child fell and grazed her knee.* **3** [T] to pass sth and touch it lightly: *The bullet grazed his shoulder.*

graze² /greɪz/ ***noun*** [C] a slight injury where the surface of the skin has been broken by rubbing it against sth rough

grease¹ /griːs/ ***noun*** [U] **1** a thick substance containing oil and used, for example, to make engines run smoothly: *engine grease* **2** animal fat that has been made soft by cooking: *You'll need very hot water to get all the grease off those pans.*

grease² /griːs/ ***verb*** [T] to rub GREASE or fat on or in sth: *Grease the tin thoroughly to stop the cake from sticking.*

greaseproof paper /ˌgriːspruːf ˈpeɪpə(r)/ (*AmE* **ˈwax paper**) ***noun*** [U] paper that does not let fat, oil etc. pass through it, used in cooking and for putting round food

greasy /ˈgriːsi/ ***adj.*** (**greasier**; **greasiest**) covered with or containing a lot of GREASE: *greasy skin/hair* ◇ *greasy food*

great¹ ⊶ /greɪt/ ***adj.*** **1** large in amount, degree, size, etc.; a lot of: *The party was a great success.* ◇ *We had great difficulty in solving the problem.* **2** particularly important; of unusually high quality: *Einstein was perhaps the greatest scientist of the century.* **3** (*informal*) good; wonderful: *We had* ***a great time*** *in Paris.* ◇ ***It's great*** *to see you again.* **4** (*informal*) (used to emphasize adjectives of size, quantity, etc.) very; very good: *There was a* ***great big*** *dog in the garden.* ◇ *They were great friends.* **5 great-** used before a noun to show a family relationship ▸ **greatness** ***noun*** [U]

IDM **go to great lengths** → LENGTH
a good/great deal → DEAL²
a good/great many → MANY

great² /greɪt/ ***noun*** [C, usually pl.] (*informal*) a person or thing of special ability or importance: *That film is one of the all-time greats.*

ˌ**Great ˈBritain** (*also* **Britain**) *noun* [sing.] (*abbr.* **GB**) England, Wales and Scotland ➲ note at **United Kingdom**

greatly ⊶ /ˈgreɪtli/ *adv.* very much: *Your help would be greatly appreciated.*

greed /griːd/ *noun* [U] ~ **(for sth)** a desire for more food, money, power, etc. than you really need

greedy /ˈgriːdi/ *adj.* (**greedier**; **greediest**) ~ **(for sth)** wanting more food, money, power, etc. than you really need: *Don't be so greedy – you've had three pieces of cake already.* ▶ **greedily** *adv.* ▶ **greediness** *noun* [U]

Greek /griːk/ *noun* **1** [C] a person from modern or ancient Greece **2** [U] (LANGUAGE) the language of modern or ancient Greece

green¹ ⊶ /griːn/ *adj.* **1** having the colour of grass or leaves: *dark/light/pale green* **2** connected with protecting the environment or the natural world: *the Green Party* ◇ *green products* (=that do not damage the environment) **3** (*informal*) (used about a person) with little experience of life or a particular job **4** jealous (wanting to have what sb else has got): *He was* ***green with envy*** *when he saw his neighbour's new car.* **5** (used about the skin) a strange, pale colour (because you feel sick): *At the sight of all the blood he* ***turned green*** *and fainted.*
IDM **give sb/get the green light** (*informal*) to give sb/get permission to do sth
have green fingers; (*AmE*) **have a green thumb** (*informal*) to have the ability to make plants grow well

green² ⊶ /griːn/ *noun* **1** [C,U] the colour of grass or leaves: *They were dressed in green.* ◇ *The room was decorated in greens and blues.* **2 greens** [pl.] green vegetables that are usually eaten cooked: *To have a healthy complexion you should eat more greens.* **3** [C] (*BrE*) an area of grass in the centre of a village **4** [C] (SPORT) a flat area of very short grass used in games such as GOLF **5 the Greens** [pl.] (POLITICS, ENVIRONMENT) the Green Party (=the party whose main aim is the protection of the environment)

ˌ**green ˈbelt** *noun* [C,U] (*BrE*) an area of open land around a city where building is not allowed

ˈ**green card** *noun* [C] a document that allows sb from another country to live and work in the US

greenery /ˈgriːnəri/ *noun* [U] attractive green leaves and plants

greenfield /ˈgriːnfiːld/ *adj.* (only *before* a noun) used to describe an area of land that has not yet had buildings on it, but for which building development may be planned: *a greenfield site*

greenfly /ˈgriːnflaɪ/ *noun* [C] (*pl.* **greenflies** or **greenfly**) a small flying insect that is harmful to plants

greengage /ˈgriːngeɪdʒ/ *noun* [C] a small round yellowish-green fruit like a PLUM

greengrocer /ˈgriːngrəʊsə(r)/ *noun* (*BrE*) **1** [C] a person who has a shop that sells fruit and vegetables ➲ look at **grocer 2 the greengrocer's** [sing.] a shop that sells fruit and vegetables

greenhouse /ˈgriːnhaʊs/ (*also* **glasshouse**) *noun* [C] a building made of glass in which plants are grown ➲ look at **hothouse**

the ˈgreenhouse effect *noun* [sing.] (ENVIRONMENT) the warming of the earth's atmosphere as a result of harmful gases, etc. in the air: *The destruction of forests is contributing to the greenhouse effect.* ➲ look at **global warming**

ˌ**greenhouse ˈgas** *noun* [C] (ENVIRONMENT) any of the gases that are thought to cause THE GREENHOUSE EFFECT, especially CARBON DIOXIDE

greenish /ˈgriːnɪʃ/ *adj.* slightly green

ˌ**green ˈpepper** *noun* [C] → PEPPER¹ (2)

ˌ**green ˈtea** *noun* [U] a pale tea made from leaves that have been dried but that have not gone through a chemical process (**fermentation**)

Greenwich Mean Time /ˌgrenɪtʃ ˈmiːn taɪm/ =GMT

greet /griːt/ *verb* [T] **1** ~ **sb (with sth)** to welcome sb when you meet them; to say hello to sb: *He greeted me with a friendly smile.* ◇ (*figurative*) *As we entered the house we were greeted by the smell of cooking.* **2** ~ **sb/sth (as/with) sth** (usually passive) to react to sb or receive sth in a particular way: *The news was greeted with a loud cheer.*

greeting /ˈgriːtɪŋ/ *noun* [C] the first words you say when you meet sb or write to them: *'Hello' and 'Hi' are informal greetings.*

gregarious /grɪˈgeəriəs/ *adj.* liking to be with other people SYN **sociable**

Gregorian calendar /grɪˌgɔːriən ˈkælɪndə(r)/ *noun* [sing.] the system used since 1582 in Western countries of arranging the months in the year and the days in the months and of counting the years from the birth of Christ ➲ look at **Julian calendar**

Gregorian chant /grɪˌgɔːriən ˈtʃɑːnt/ *noun* [U, C] (MUSIC) a type of church music for voices alone, used since the Middle Ages

grenade /grəˈneɪd/ *noun* [C] a small bomb that is thrown by hand or fired from a gun

grew past tense of **grow**

grey¹ ⊶ (*especially AmE* **gray**) /greɪ/ *adj.* **1** having the colour between black and white: *dark/light/pale grey* ◇ *He was wearing a grey suit.* **2** having grey hair: *He's* ***going grey.*** **3** (used about the weather) full of cloud; not bright: *grey skies* ◇ *a grey day* **4** boring and sad; without interest or variety

grey² ⊶ /greɪ/ (*especially AmE* **gray**) *noun* [C,U] the colour between black and white: *dressed in grey*

greyhound /ˈgreɪhaʊnd/ *noun* [C] a large thin dog that can run very fast and that is used for racing: *greyhound racing*

greyish /ˈgreɪɪʃ/ (*especially AmE* **grayish**) *adj.* slightly grey

ˌ**grey ˈmarket** (*AmE* ˌ**gray ˈmarket**) *noun* [C, usually sing.] (BUSINESS) **1** a system in which products are imported into a country and sold without the permission of the company that produced them **2** (*BrE*) old people, when they are thought of as customers for goods

grid /grɪd/ *noun* [C] **1** a pattern of straight lines that cross each other to form squares: *She drew a grid to show how the students had scored in each part of the test.* **2** a frame of parallel metal or wooden bars, usually covering a hole in sth **3** (GEOGRAPHY) a system of squares that are drawn on a map so that the position of any place can be described or found: *a grid reference* **4** the system of electricity wires, etc. taking power to all parts of a country: *the National Grid* ➲ picture at **generator**

griddle /ˈgrɪdl/ *noun* [C] a circular iron plate that is heated on a cooker or over a fire and used for cooking

gridlock /ˈgrɪdlɒk/ *noun* [U, C] a situation in which there are so many cars in the streets of a town that the traffic cannot move at all ▶ **gridlocked** *adj.*

grief /griːf/ ***noun*** [U] great sadness (especially because of the death of sb you love)
IDM **good grief** (*spoken*) used for expressing surprise or shock: *Good grief! Whatever happened to you?*

grievance /ˈgriːvəns/ ***noun*** [C] **a ~ (against sb)** something that you think is unfair and that you want to complain or protest about

grieve /griːv/ ***verb*** **1** [I] **~ (for sb)** to feel great sadness (especially about the death of sb you love) **2** [T] (*formal*) to cause unhappiness

grill¹ /grɪl/ ***noun*** [C] **1** a part of a cooker where the food is cooked by heat from above **2** a metal frame that you put food on to cook over an open fire **3** = GRILLE

grill² /grɪl/ ***verb*** **1** (*especially AmE* **broil**) [I,T] to cook under a **grill**: *grilled steak/chicken/fish* **2** [T] (*informal*) **~ sb (about sth)** to question sb for a long time

grille (also **grill**) /grɪl/ ***noun*** [C] a metal frame that is placed over a window, a piece of machinery, etc.

grim /grɪm/ ***adj.*** (**grimmer**; **grimmest**) **1** (used about a person) very serious; not smiling **2** (used about a situation, news, etc.) unpleasant or worrying: *The news is grim, I'm afraid.* **3** (used about a place) unpleasant to look at; not attractive: *a grim block of flats* **4** (*BrE, informal*) feeling ill: *I was feeling grim yesterday but I managed to get to work.* ▸ **grimly** ***adv.***

grimace /ˈgrɪməs; grɪˈmeɪs/ ***noun*** [C] an ugly expression on your face that shows that you are angry, disgusted or that sth is hurting you: *a grimace of pain* ▸ **grimace** ***verb*** [I]: *She grimaced with pain.*

grime /graɪm/ ***noun*** [U] a thick layer of dirt

grimy /ˈgraɪmi/ ***adj.*** very dirty

grin /grɪn/ ***verb*** [I] (**grinning**; **grinned**) **~ (at sb)** to give a broad smile (so that you show your teeth): *She grinned at me as she came into the room.* ▸ **grin** ***noun*** [C]

grind¹ /graɪnd/ ***verb*** [T] (*pt, pp* **ground** /graʊnd/) **1 ~ sth (down/up); ~ sth (to/into sth)** to press and break sth into very small pieces or into a powder between two hard surfaces or in a special machine: *Wheat is ground into flour.* ◇ *ground pepper/coffee* **2** to make sth sharp or smooth by rubbing it on a rough hard surface: *to grind a knife on a stone* **3 ~ sth in/into sth** to press or rub sth into a surface: *He ground his cigarette into the ashtray.* **4** to rub sth together or make sth rub together, often producing an unpleasant noise: *Some people* ***grind*** *their* ***teeth*** *while they're asleep.*
IDM **grind to a halt/standstill** to stop slowly

grind² /graɪnd/ ***noun*** [sing.] (*informal*) an activity that is tiring and boring and that takes a lot of time: *the* ***daily grind*** *of working life*

grinder /ˈgraɪndə(r)/ ***noun*** [C] a machine for GRINDING: *a coffee grinder*

grip¹ /grɪp/ ***verb*** [I,T] (**gripping**; **gripped**) **1** to hold sb/sth tightly: *She gripped my arm in fear.* **2** to interest sb very much; to hold sb's attention: *The book grips you from start to finish.* ➲ adjective **gripping**

grip² /grɪp/ ***noun*** **1** [sing.] **a ~ (on sb/sth)** a firm hold (on sb/sth): *I relaxed my grip and he ran away.* ◇ *The climber slipped and lost her grip.* ◇ (*figurative*) *The teacher kept a firm grip on the class.* **2** [sing.] **a ~ (on sth)** an understanding of sth **3** [C] (ARTS AND MEDIA) the person whose job it is to move the cameras while a film is being made
IDM **come/get to grips with sth** to start to understand and deal with a problem
get/keep/take a grip/hold (on yourself) (*informal*) to try to behave in a calmer or more sensible way; to control yourself
in the grip of sth experiencing sth unpleasant that cannot be stopped: *a country in the grip of recession*

gripe /graɪp/ ***noun*** [C] (*informal*) a complaint about sb/sth ▸ **gripe** ***verb*** [I]

gripping /ˈgrɪpɪŋ/ ***adj.*** exciting; holding your attention: *a gripping film/book*

grisly /ˈgrɪzli/ ***adj.*** (used for describing sth that is concerned with death or violence) terrible; HORRIBLE: *a grisly crime/death/murder* ➲ look at **gruesome**

gristle /ˈgrɪsl/ ***noun*** [U] a hard substance in a piece of meat that is unpleasant to eat ▸ **gristly** ***adv.***

grit¹ /grɪt/ ***noun*** [U] **1** small pieces of stone or sand: *I've got some grit/a piece of grit in my shoe.* **2** (*informal*) courage; determination that makes it possible for sb to continue doing sth difficult or unpleasant

grit² /grɪt/ ***verb*** [T] (**gritting**; **gritted**) to spread small pieces of stone and sand on a road that is covered with ice
IDM **grit your teeth 1** to bite your teeth tightly together: *She gritted her teeth against the pain as the doctor examined her injured foot.* **2** to use your courage or determination in a difficult situation

groan /grəʊn/ ***verb*** [I] **~ (at/with sth)** to make a deep sad sound because you are in pain, or to show that you are unhappy about sth: *He groaned with pain.* ◇ *All the students were* ***moaning and groaning*** (= complaining) *about the amount of work they had to do.* ▸ **groan** ***noun*** [C]

grocer /ˈgrəʊsə(r)/ ***noun*** **1** [C] a person who has a shop that sells food and other things for the home ➲ look at **greengrocer** **2 the grocer's** [sing.] a shop that sells food and other things for the home

groceries ⚷ /ˈgrəʊsəriz/ ***noun*** [pl.] food, etc. that is sold by a GROCER or in a larger food shop (**supermarket**)

groggy /ˈgrɒgi/ ***adj.*** (*informal*) weak and unable to walk steadily because you feel ill, have not had enough sleep, etc.

groin /grɔɪn/ ***noun*** [C] **1** the front part of your body where it joins your legs **2** (*AmE*) = GROYNE

groom¹ /gruːm/ ***noun*** [C] **1** = BRIDEGROOM **2** a person who looks after horses, especially by cleaning and brushing them

groom² /gruːm/ ***verb*** [T] **1** to clean or look after an animal by brushing, etc.: *to groom a horse/dog/cat* **2 ~ sb (for/as sth)** (usually passive) to choose and prepare sb for a particular career or job

groove /gruːv/ ***noun*** [C] a long deep line that is cut in the surface of sth

grope /grəʊp/ ***verb*** **1** [I] **~ (about/around) (for sth)** to search for sth or find your way using your hands because you cannot see: *He groped around for the light switch.* **2** [T] (*informal*) to touch sb sexually, especially when they do not want you to

gross¹ /grəʊs/ ***adj.*** **1** (only *before* a noun) (FINANCE) being the total amount before anything is taken away: *gross income* (= before tax, etc. is taken away) OPP **net** **2** (*formal*) (only *before* a noun) very great or serious: *gross indecency/negligence/misconduct* **3** very rude and unpleasant **4** very fat and ugly

gross² /grəʊs/ ***adv.*** (FINANCE) in total, before anything is taken away: *She earns £25000 a year gross.* ➲ look at **net**

gross³ /grəʊs/ ***verb*** [T] (**FINANCE**) to earn a particular amount of money before tax has been taken off it: *It is one of the biggest grossing movies of all time.*

ˌgross doˌmestic ˈproduct ***noun*** [sing., U] =GDP

grossly /ˈgrəʊsli/ ***adv.*** very: *That is grossly unfair.*

ˌgross ˌnational ˈproduct ***noun*** [sing., U] =GNP

grotesque /grəʊˈtesk/ ***adj.*** strange or ugly in a way that is not natural

grotto /ˈgrɒtəʊ/ ***noun*** (*pl.* **-oes** or **-os**) (**ARCHITECTURE**) a small CAVE (=a hole in the side of a hill or under the ground), especially one that has been made artificially, for example in a garden

grotty /ˈgrɒti/ ***adj.*** (*BrE, informal*) (**grottier**; **grottiest**) unpleasant; of poor quality: *She lives in a grotty flat.*

ground¹ 🗝 /graʊnd/ ***noun*** **1 the ground** [sing.] the solid surface of the earth: *We sat on the ground to eat our picnic.* ◇ *He slipped off the ladder and fell to the ground.* ◇ *waste ground* (=that is not being used) **2** [U] an area or type of soil: *solid/marshy/stony ground* ❶ The **Earth** is the name of the planet where we live. **Land** is the opposite of sea: *The sailors sighted land.* ◇ *The astronauts returned to Earth.* **Land** is also something that you can buy or sell: *The price of land in Tokyo is extremely high.* When you are outside, the surface under your feet is called **the ground**. When you are inside it is called **the floor**: *Don't sit on the ground. You'll get wet.* ◇ *Don't sit on the floor. I'll get another chair.* Plants grow in **earth** or **soil**. **3** [C] a piece of land that is used for a particular purpose: *a sports ground* ◇ *a playground* **4 grounds** [pl.] land or gardens surrounding a large building: *the grounds of the palace* **5** [U] an area of interest, study, discussion, etc.: *The lecture went over* ***the same old ground*** / *covered a lot of* ***new ground***. ◇ *to be on dangerous ground* (=saying sth likely to cause anger) **6** [C, usually pl.] **grounds (for sth/doing sth)** a reason for sth: *She retired* ***on medical grounds***. ◇ *grounds for divorce* ➲ note at **reason¹** **7** (*AmE*) =EARTH¹ (4)

IDM **above/below ground** above/below the surface of the earth

break fresh/new ground to make a discovery or introduce a new method or activity

gain ground → GAIN¹

get off the ground (used about a business, project, etc.) to make a successful start

give/lose ground (to sb/sth) to allow sb to have an advantage; to lose an advantage for yourself: *Labour lost a lot of ground to the Liberal Democrats at the election.*

hold/keep/stand your ground to refuse to change your opinion or to be influenced by pressure from other people

thin on the ground difficult to find; not common

ground² /graʊnd/ ***verb*** [T] **1** (usually passive) to force an aircraft, etc. to stay on the ground: *to be grounded by fog* **2** (usually passive) to punish a child by not allowing them to go out with their friends for a period of time **3** (*especially AmE*) =EARTH²

ground³ past tense, past participle of **grind¹**: *ground almonds*

ˌground ˈbeef (*AmE*) =MINCE

ˈground crew (*also* **ˈground staff**) ***noun*** [C,U] the people in an airport whose job it is to look after an aircraft while it is on the ground

ˌground ˈfloor (*AmE* **ˌfirst ˈfloor**) ***noun*** [C] the floor of a building that is at ground level: *a ground-floor flat*

grounding /ˈgraʊndɪŋ/ ***noun*** [sing.] **a ~ (in sth)** the teaching of the basic facts or principles of a subject

groundless /ˈgraʊndləs/ ***adj.*** having no reason or cause: *Our fears were groundless.*

groundnut /ˈgraʊndnʌt/ =PEANUT

groundsheet /ˈgraʊndʃiːt/ ***noun*** [C] a large piece of material that does not let water through, that is placed on the ground inside a tent

groundwater /ˈgraʊndwɔːtə(r)/ ***noun*** [U] (**GEOLOGY**) water that is found under the ground in soil, rocks, etc.

groundwork /ˈgraʊndwɜːk/ ***noun*** [U] work that is done in preparation for further work or study

ˌground ˈzero ***noun*** [U] **1** the point on the earth's surface where a nuclear bomb explodes **2 Ground Zero** the site of the World Trade Center in New York, destroyed on 11 September 2001 **3** the beginning; a starting point for an activity

group¹ 🗝 /gruːp/ ***noun*** [C] **1** [with sing. or pl. verb] a number of people or things that are together in the same place or that are connected in some way: *Our discussion group is/are meeting this week.* ◇ *A group of us are planning to meet for lunch.* ◇ *Students were standing* ***in groups*** *waiting for their exam results.* ◇ *He is in the 40-50* ***age group***. ◇ *people of many different social groups* ◇ *a* ***pressure group*** (=a political group that tries to influence the government) ◇ *Which* ***blood group*** (=for example A, O, etc.) *are you?* ◇ *Divide the class into groups.* **2** (**BUSINESS**) a number of companies that are owned by the same person or organization **3** (*old-fashioned*) (**MUSIC**) a number of people who play music together: *a pop group* ➲ look at **band**

group² /gruːp/ ***verb*** [I,T] **~ (sb/sth) (around/round sb/sth)**; **~ (sb/sth) (together)** to put sb/sth or to form into one or more groups: *Group these words according to their meaning.*

grouping /ˈgruːpɪŋ/ ***noun*** **1** [C] (**SOCIAL STUDIES**) a number of people or organizations that have the same interests, aims or characteristics and are often part of a larger group: *These small nations constitute an important grouping within the EU.* **2** [U] the act of forming sth into a group

grouse /graʊs/ ***noun*** [C] (*pl.* **grouse**) a fat brown bird with feathers on its legs that is shot for sport

grove /grəʊv/ ***noun*** [C] (**GEOGRAPHY**) a small group of trees, especially of one particular type: *an olive grove*

grovel /ˈgrɒvl/ ***verb*** [I] (**grovelling**; **grovelled**: *AmE* **groveling**; **groveled**) **1 ~ (to sb) (for sth)** to try too hard to please sb who is more important than you or who can give you sth that you want: *to grovel for forgiveness* **2 ~ (around/about) (for sth)** to move around on your hands and knees (usually when you are looking for sth) ▸ **grovelling** ***adj.***: *I wrote a grovelling letter to my bank manager.*

grow 🗝 /grəʊ/ ***verb*** (*pt* **grew** /gruː/; *pp* **grown** /grəʊn/) **1** [I] **~ (in sth)** to increase in size or number; to develop into an adult form: *a growing child* ◇ *She's growing in confidence all the time.* ◇ *You must invest if you want your business to grow.* ◇ *Plants grow from seeds.* ◇ *Kittens soon grow into cats.* ➲ note at **rise¹** **2** [I,T] (used about plants) to exist and develop in a particular place; to make plants grow by giving them water, etc.: *Palm trees don't grow in cold climates.* ◇ *We grow vegetables in our garden.* **3** [T] to allow your hair or nails to grow: *Claire's growing her* hair long. ◇ to grow a beard/moustache **4** ***linking verb*** to gradually change from one state to another; to become SYN **get**: *It began to grow dark.* ◇ *to grow older/wiser/taller/bigger* ◇ *The teacher was growing more and more impatient.*

PHR V **grow into sth 1** to gradually develop into a particular type of person: *She has grown into a very attractive young woman.* **2** to become big enough to fit into clothes, etc.: *The coat is too big for him, but he will soon grow into it.*

grow on sb to become more pleasing: *I didn't like ginger at first, but it's a taste that grows on you.*

grow out of sth to become too big or too old for sth: *She's grown out of that dress I made her last year.*

grow (sth) out (used about HAIRSTYLES, etc.) to disappear gradually as your hair grows; to allow your hair to grow in order to change the style

grow up 1 to develop into an adult; to MATURE: *What do you want to be when you grow up?* (=what job do you want to do later?) ◇ *She grew up* (=spent her childhood) *in Spain.* **2** (used about a feeling, etc.) to develop or become strong: *A close friendship has grown up between them.*

grower /ˈɡrəʊə(r)/ ***noun*** [C] (**AGRICULTURE**) a person or company that grows plants, fruit or vegetables to sell: *a tobacco grower* ◇ *All our vegetables are supplied by local growers.*

growing /ˈɡrəʊɪŋ/ ***adj.*** increasing: *A growing number of people are becoming vegetarian these days.*

growl /ɡraʊl/ ***verb*** [I] **~ (at sb/sth)** (used about dogs and other animals) to make a low noise in the throat to show anger or to give a warning ▶ **growl** ***noun*** [C]

grown /ɡrəʊn/ ***adj.*** physically an adult: *a fully-grown elephant*

ˌ**grown-ˈup**[1] ***adj.*** physically or mentally adult: *She's very grown-up for her age.* SYN **mature**

ˈ**grown-up**[2] ***noun*** [C] an adult person

growth ⊶ /ɡrəʊθ/ ***noun* 1** [U] the process of growing and developing: *A good diet is very important for children's growth.* ◇ *a growth industry* (=one that is growing) **2** [U, sing.] an increase (in sth): *population growth* **3** [U] (**ECONOMICS**) an increase in economic activity: *policies aimed at sustaining economic growth* ◇ *an annual growth rate of 10%* ◇ *a* ***growth area/industry*** (=one that is growing) **4** [C] (**HEALTH**) a lump caused by a disease that grows in a person's or an animal's body: *a cancerous growth* **5** [U] something that has grown: *several days' growth of beard*

groyne (*AmE* **groin**) /ɡrɔɪn/ ***noun*** [C] (**ENVIRONMENT**) a low wall built out into the sea to prevent it from washing away sand and stones from the beach

grub /ɡrʌb/ ***noun* 1** [C] (**BIOLOGY**) the first form that an insect takes when it comes out of the egg. **Grubs** are short, fat and white. **2** [U] (*informal*) food

grubby /ˈɡrʌbi/ ***adj.*** (**grubbier**; **grubbiest**) (*informal*) dirty after being used and not washed

grudge[1] /ɡrʌdʒ/ ***noun*** [C] **a ~ (against sb)** unfriendly feelings towards sb, because you are angry about what has happened in the past: *to* ***bear a grudge*** *against sb*

grudge[2] /ɡrʌdʒ/ ***verb*** [T] **~ sb sth**; **~ doing sth** to be unhappy that sb has sth or that you have to do sth: *I don't grudge him his success – he deserves it.* ◇ *I grudge having to pay so much tax.* ➲ look at **begrudge**

grudging /ˈɡrʌdʒɪŋ/ ***adj.*** given or done although you do not want to: *grudging thanks* ▶ **grudgingly** ***adv.***

gruelling (*AmE* **grueling**) /ˈɡruːəlɪŋ/ ***adj.*** very tiring and long: *a gruelling nine-hour march*

gruesome /ˈɡruːsəm/ ***adj.*** (used about sth concerned with death or injury) very unpleasant or shocking ➲ look at **grisly**

gruff /ɡrʌf/ ***adj.*** (used about a person or a voice) rough and unfriendly ▶ **gruffly** ***adv.***

grumble /ˈɡrʌmbl/ ***verb*** [I] to complain in a bad-tempered way; to keep saying that you do not like sth: *The students were always grumbling about the standard of the food.* ▶ **grumble** ***noun*** [C]

grumpy /ˈɡrʌmpi/ ***adj.*** (*informal*) bad-tempered ▶ **grumpily** ***adv.***

grunge /ɡrʌndʒ/ ***noun*** [U] (**MUSIC**) (*also* ˈ**grunge rock**) a type of loud rock music, which was popular in the early 1990s

grunt /ɡrʌnt/ ***verb*** [I,T] to make a short low sound in the throat. People **grunt** when they do not like sth or are not interested and do not want to talk: *I tried to find out her opinion but she just grunted when I asked her.* ▶ **grunt** ***noun*** [C]

guanine /ɡwaːniːn/ ***noun*** [U] (**BIOLOGY**) one of the four COMPOUNDS that make up DNA and RNA ➲ picture at **DNA**

guano /ˈɡwɑːnəʊ/ ***noun*** [U] (**AGRICULTURE**) the waste substance passed from the bodies of SEABIRDS, that is used by farmers to make plants grow well

guarantee[1] ⊶ AW /ˌɡærənˈtiː/ ***noun*** [C,U] **1** a firm promise that sth will be done or that sth will happen: *The refugees are demanding guarantees about their safety before they return home.* **2** (**BUSINESS**) a written promise by a company that it will repair or replace a product if it breaks in a certain period of time: *The watch comes with a year's guarantee.* ◇ *Is the computer still* ***under guarantee****?* ➲ look at **warranty 3** something that makes sth else certain to happen: *Without a reservation there's no guarantee that you'll get a seat on the train.*

guarantee[2] ⊶ AW /ˌɡærənˈtiː/ ***verb*** [T] **1** to promise that sth will be done or will happen: *They have guaranteed delivery within one week.* **2** (**BUSINESS**) to give a written promise to repair or replace a product if anything is wrong with it: *This washing machine is guaranteed for three years.* **3** to make sth certain to happen: *Tonight's win guarantees the team a place in the final.*

guarantor /ˌɡærənˈtɔː(r)/ ***noun*** [C] (*formal* or **LAW**) a person who agrees to be responsible for sb or for making sure that sth happens or is done

guard[1] ⊶ /ɡɑːd/ ***noun* 1** [C] a person who protects a place or people, or who stops prisoners from escaping: *a security guard* ➲ look at **warder**, **bodyguard 2** [U] the state of being ready to prevent attack or danger: *Soldiers* ***keep guard*** *at the gate.* ◇ *Who is* ***on guard****?* ◇ *The prisoner arrived* ***under armed guard****.* ◇ *a guard dog* **3** [sing., with sing. or pl. verb] a group of soldiers, police officers, etc. who protect sb/sth: *The president always travels with an armed guard.* **4** [C] (often in compounds) something that covers sth dangerous or protects sth: *a fireguard* ◇ *a mudguard* (=over the wheel of a bicycle) **5** (*AmE* **conductor**) [C] a person who is in charge of a train but does not drive it **6** [U] a position that you take to defend yourself, especially in sports such as BOXING

IDM **off/on (your) guard** not ready/ready for an attack, surprise, mistake, etc.: *The question caught me off (my) guard and I didn't know what to say.*

guard² 🔑 /ɡɑːd/ ***verb*** [T] **1** to keep sb/sth safe from other people; protect: *The building was guarded by men with dogs.* ◇ *(figurative) a closely guarded secret* **2** to be ready to stop prisoners from escaping
PHR V **guard against sth** to try to prevent sth or stop sth happening

guarded /ˈɡɑːdɪd/ ***adj.*** (used about an answer, statement, etc.) careful; not giving much information or showing what you feel OPP **unguarded** ▶ **guardedly** ***adv.***

guardian /ˈɡɑːdiən/ ***noun*** [C] **1** a person or institution that guards or protects sth: *The police are the guardians of law and order.* **2** (LAW) a person who is legally responsible for the care of another person, especially of a child whose parents are dead

guava /ˈɡwɑːvə/ ***noun*** [C] the fruit of a tropical American tree, with yellow skin and a pink inside

guerrilla (also **guerilla**) /ɡəˈrɪlə/ ***noun*** [C] a member of a small military group who are not part of an official army and who make surprise attacks on the enemy

guess¹ 🔑 /ɡes/ ***verb*** **1** [I,T] ~ (**at sth**) to try to give an answer or make a judgement about sth without being sure of all the facts: *I'd guess that he's about 45.* ◇ *If you're not sure of an answer, guess.* ◇ *We can only guess at her reasons for leaving.* **2** [I,T] to give the correct answer when you are not sure about it; to guess correctly: *Can you guess my age?* ◇ *You'll never guess what Adam just told me!* ◇ *Did I guess right?* **3** [T] (*especially AmE, informal*) to imagine that sth is probably true or likely: *I guess you're tired after your long journey.* SYN **suppose** **4** [T] used to show that you are going to say sth surprising or exciting: *Guess what! I'm getting married!*

guess² 🔑 /ɡes/ ***noun*** [C] an effort you make to imagine a possible answer or give an opinion when you cannot be sure if you are right: *If you don't know the answer, then* ***have a guess****!* ◇ *I don't know how far it is, but* ***at a guess*** *I'd say about 50 miles.* ◇ *I'd say it'll take about four hours, but that's just* ***a rough guess****.*
IDM **anybody's/anyone's guess** something that nobody can be certain about: *What's going to happen next is anybody's guess.*
your guess is as good as mine I do not know: *'Where's Ron?' 'Your guess is as good as mine.'*

guesswork /ˈɡeswɜːk/ ***noun*** [U] an act of guessing: *I arrived at the answer* ***by pure guesswork****.*

guest 🔑 /ɡest/ ***noun*** [C] **1** a person who is invited to a place or to a special event: *wedding guests* ◇ *Who is the guest speaker at the conference?* **2** (TOURISM) a person who is staying at a hotel, etc.: *This hotel has accommodation for 500 guests.*
IDM **be my guest** (*informal*) used to give sb permission to do sth that they have asked to do: *'Do you mind if I have a look at your newspaper?' 'Be my guest!'*

ˈguest house ***noun*** [C] (TOURISM) a small hotel, sometimes in a private house

GUI /ˌdʒiː juː ˈaɪ/ ***abbr.*** (COMPUTING) **graphical user interface**; a way of giving instructions to a computer using things that can be seen on the screen such as symbols and menus

guidance /ˈɡaɪdns/ ***noun*** [U] ~ (**on sth**) help or advice: *The centre offers guidance for unemployed people on how to find work.*

guide¹ 🔑 /ɡaɪd/ ***noun*** [C] **1** a book, magazine, etc. that gives information or help on a subject: *Your Guide to Using the Internet* **2** (*also* ˈ**guidebook**) (TOURISM) a book that gives information about a place for travellers and tourists **3** (TOURISM) a person who shows tourists or travellers where to go: *She works as a* ***tour guide*** *in Venice.* **4** something that helps you to judge or plan sth: ***As a rough guide****, use twice as much water as rice.* **5 Guide** a member of THE GUIDES (= an organization that teaches girls practical skills and organizes activities such as camping)

guide² 🔑 /ɡaɪd/ ***verb*** [T] **1** to help a person or a group of people to find the way to a place; to show sb a place that you know well: *He guided us through the busy streets to our hotel.* **2** to have an influence on sb/sth: *I was guided by your advice.* **3** to help sb deal with sth difficult or complicated: *The manual will guide you through every step of the procedure.* **4** to carefully move sb/sth or to help sb/sth to move in a particular direction: *A crane lifted the piano and two men carefully guided it through the window.*

guidebook /ˈɡaɪdbʊk/ ***noun*** [C] = GUIDE¹ (2)

guided /ˈɡaɪdɪd/ ***adj.*** (TOURISM) led by a guide: *a guided tour/walk*

ˈguide dog (*AmE also* ˌ**Seeing ˈEye dog™**) ***noun*** [C] a dog trained to guide a person who is unable to see

guideline AW /ˈɡaɪdlaɪn/ ***noun*** **1 guidelines** [pl.] rules or instructions that are given by an official organization telling you how to do sth, especially sth difficult **2** [C] something that can be used to help you make a decision or form an opinion: *These figures are a useful guideline when buying a house.*

guild /ɡɪld/ ***noun*** [C, with sing. or pl. verb] **1** an organization of people who do the same job or who have the same interests or aims: *the Screen Actors' Guild* **2** (HISTORY) an association of skilled workers in the Middle Ages

guillotine /ˈɡɪlətiːn/ ***noun*** [C] **1** a machine used for cutting paper **2** (HISTORY) a machine that was used in France in the past for cutting people's heads off ▶ **guillotine** ***verb*** [T]

guilt /ɡɪlt/ ***noun*** [U] **1** ~ (**about/at sth**) the bad feeling that you have when you know that you have done sth wrong: *He sometimes had a sense of guilt about not spending more time with his children.* **2** (LAW) the fact of having broken a law: *We took his refusal to answer questions as an admission of guilt.* OPP **innocence** **3** the responsibility for doing sth wrong or for sth bad that has happened; the blame for sth: *It's difficult to say whether the guilt lies with the parents or the children.*

guilty 🔑 /ˈɡɪlti/ ***adj.*** (**guiltier**; **guiltiest**) **1** ~ (**of sth**) having broken a law; being responsible for doing sth wrong: *She* ***pleaded guilty/not guilty*** *to the crime.* ◇ *to be guilty of murder* ◇ *The jury* ***found*** *him* ***guilty*** *of fraud.* OPP **innocent** **2** ~ (**about sth**) having an unpleasant feeling because you have done sth bad: *I* ***feel*** *really* ***guilty*** *about lying to Sam.* ◇ *It's hard to sleep with* ***a guilty conscience****.* ▶ **guiltily** ***adv.***

guinea pig /ˈɡɪni pɪɡ/ ***noun*** [C] **1** a small animal with no tail that is often kept as a pet **2** (SCIENCE) a person who is used in an experiment: *I volunteered to act as a guinea pig in their research into dreams.*

guise /ɡaɪz/ ***noun*** [C] a way in which sb/sth appears, which is often different from usual or hides the truth: *The President was at the meeting* ***in*** *his* ***guise as*** *chairman of the charity.* ◇ *His speech presented racist ideas* ***under the guise of*** *nationalism.*

guitar /ɡɪˈtɑː(r)/ ***noun*** [C] (MUSIC) a type of musical instrument with strings that you play with your fingers or with a piece of plastic (**a plectrum**) ➲ picture on **page 465**

guitarist /ɡɪˈtɑːrɪst/ ***noun*** [C] (MUSIC) a person who plays the GUITAR

gulf /gʌlf/ ***noun*** **1** [C] (GEOGRAPHY) a part of the sea that is almost surrounded by land: *the Gulf of Mexico* **2 the Gulf** [sing.] (*informal*) (GEOGRAPHY) a way of referring to the Persian Gulf **3** [C] an important or serious difference between people in the way they live, think or feel: *the gulf between rich and poor*

the 'Gulf Stream ***noun*** [sing.] (GEOGRAPHY) a warm current of water flowing across the Atlantic Ocean from the Gulf of Mexico towards Europe ➲ picture at **current**

gull /gʌl/ (*also* **seagull**) ***noun*** [C] a white or grey SEABIRD that makes a loud noise ➲ picture on **page 29**

gullet /'gʌlɪt/ ***noun*** [C] (ANATOMY) the tube through which food passes from your mouth to your stomach SYN **oesophagus** ➲ picture on **page 80** ➲ picture at **digestive system**

gullible /'gʌləbl/ ***adj.*** (used about a person) believing and trusting people too easily, and therefore easily tricked

gully /'gʌli/ ***noun*** [C] (*pl.* **gullies**) (GEOGRAPHY) a small, narrow passage or valley, usually formed by a STREAM or by rain

gulp[1] /gʌlp/ ***verb*** **1** [I,T] **~ sth (down); ~ (for) sth** to swallow large amounts of food, drink, etc. quickly: *He gulped down his breakfast and went out.* ◇ *She finally came to the surface, desperately gulping (for) air.* **2** [I] to make a swallowing movement because you are afraid, surprised, etc.

gulp[2] /gʌlp/ ***noun*** [C] **1** the action of breathing in or swallowing sth: *I drank my coffee **in one gulp** and ran out of the door.* **2 a ~ (of sth)** the amount that you swallow when you **gulp**

gum /gʌm/ ***noun*** **1** [C] either of the firm pink parts of your mouth that hold your teeth ➲ picture on **page 80** ➲ picture at **tooth** **2** [U] a substance that you use to stick things together (especially pieces of paper) **3** =CHEWING GUM ➲ look at **bubblegum**

gun[1] 🔑 /gʌn/ ***noun*** [C] **1** a weapon that is used for shooting: *The robber held a gun to the bank manager's head.*

RELATED VOCABULARY

Verbs often used with 'gun' are **load**, **unload**, **point**, **aim** and **fire**. Different types of gun include a **machine gun**, **pistol**, **revolver**, **rifle** and **shotgun**.

2 a tool that uses pressure to send out a substance or an object: *a grease gun* ◇ *a staple gun*
IDM **jump the gun** → JUMP[1]

gun[2] 🔑 /gʌn/ ***verb*** [T] (**gunning**; **gunned**)
PHR V **gun sb down** (*informal*) to shoot and kill or seriously injure sb

gunboat /'gʌnbəʊt/ ***noun*** [C] a small ship used in war that carries heavy guns

gunfire /'gʌnfaɪə(r)/ ***noun*** [U] the repeated firing of guns: *We could hear gunfire.*

gunman /'gʌnmən/ ***noun*** [C] (*pl.* **-men** /-mən/) a man who uses a gun to rob or kill people

gunpoint /'gʌnpɔɪnt/ ***noun***
IDM **at gunpoint** threatening to shoot sb: *He held the hostages at gunpoint.*

gunpowder /'gʌnpaʊdə(r)/ ***noun*** [U] an EXPLOSIVE powder that is used in guns, etc.

gunshot /'gʌnʃɒt/ ***noun*** [C] the firing of a gun or the sound that it makes

gurgle /'gɜːgl/ ***verb*** [I] **1** to make a sound like water flowing quickly through a narrow space: *a gurgling stream* **2** if a baby **gurgles**, it makes a noise in its throat because it is happy ▶ **gurgle** ***noun*** [C]

guru /'gʊruː/ ***noun*** [C] **1** (RELIGION) a spiritual leader or teacher in the Hindu religion **2** somebody whose opinions you admire and respect, and whose ideas you follow: *a management/fashion guru*

gush /gʌʃ/ ***verb*** **1** [I] **~ (out of/from/into sth); ~ out/in** (used about a liquid) to flow out suddenly and in great quantities: *Blood gushed from the wound.* ◇ *I turned the tap on and water gushed out.* **2** [T] (used about a container, vehicle, etc.) to produce large amounts of a liquid: *The broken pipe was gushing water all over the road.* **3** [I,T] to express pleasure or admiration too much so that it does not sound sincere ▶ **gush** ***noun*** [C]: *a sudden gush of water*

gust /gʌst/ ***noun*** [C] a sudden strong wind ▶ **gust** ***verb*** [I]

gusto /'gʌstəʊ/ ***noun***
IDM **with gusto** with great enthusiasm

gut[1] /gʌt/ ***noun*** **1** [C] (ANATOMY) the tube in your body that food passes through when it leaves your stomach SYN **intestine** **2 guts** [pl.] (ANATOMY) the organs in and around the stomach, especially of an animal **3 guts** [pl.] (*informal*) courage and determination: *It **takes guts** to admit that you are wrong.* ◇ *I don't **have the guts** to tell my boss what he's doing wrong.* **4** [C] a person's fat stomach: *a beer gut* (=caused by drinking beer)
IDM **work/sweat your guts out** to work extremely hard

gut[2] /gʌt/ ***verb*** [T] (**gutting**; **gutted**) **1** to remove the organs from inside an animal, fish, etc. **2** to destroy the inside of a building: *The warehouse was gutted by fire.*

gut[3] /gʌt/ ***adj.*** (only *before* a noun) based on emotion or feeling rather than on reason: *a gut feeling/reaction*

gutter /'gʌtə(r)/ ***noun*** [C] **1** a long piece of metal or plastic with a curved bottom that is fixed to the edge of a roof to carry away the water when it rains **2** a lower part at the edge of a road along which the water flows away when it rains **3** the very lowest level of society: *She rose from the gutter to become a great star.*

,gutter 'press ***noun*** [sing.] (ARTS AND MEDIA) newspapers that print a lot of shocking stories about people's private lives rather than serious news

guy 🔑 /gaɪ/ ***noun*** **1** [C] (*informal*) a man or a boy: *He's a nice guy.* **2 guys** [pl.] (*informal*) used when speaking to a group of men and women: *What do you guys want to eat?* **3** [sing.] (*BrE*) a model of a man that is burned on 5 November in memory of Guy Fawkes ➲ look at **Bonfire Night**

guzzle /'gʌzl/ ***verb*** [I,T] (*informal*) to eat or drink too fast and too much

gym /dʒɪm/ ***noun*** **1** (also *formal* **gymnasium**) [C] a large room or a building with equipment for doing physical exercise: *I work out at the gym twice a week.* **2** [U] =GYMNASTICS: *gym shoes*

gymnasium /dʒɪm'neɪziəm/ ***noun*** [C] (*pl.* **gymnasiums** or **gymnasia** /-zɪə/) =GYM (1)

gymnast /'dʒɪmnæst/ ***noun*** [C] (SPORT) a person who does GYMNASTICS

gymnastics /dʒɪm'næstɪks/ (*also* **gym**) ***noun*** [U] (SPORT) physical exercises that are done indoors, often using special equipment such as bars and ropes

gynaecology (*AmE* **gynecology**) /,gaɪnə'kɒlədʒi/ ***noun*** [U] (HEALTH) the study and treatment of the diseases and medical problems of women

▶ **gynaecological** (*AmE* **gyne-**) /ˌɡaɪnəkəˈlɒdʒɪkl/ ***adj.*** ▶ **gynaecologist** (*AmE* **gyne-**) /ˌɡaɪnəˈkɒlədʒɪst/ ***noun*** [C]

gypsum /ˈdʒɪpsəm/ ***noun*** [U] a soft white rock like CHALK that is used in the building industry ➲ picture at **building**

Gypsy (also **Gipsy**) /ˈdʒɪpsi/ ***noun*** [C] (*pl.* **Gypsies**) a member of a race of people who traditionally spend their lives travelling around from place to place, living in CARAVANS (= homes with wheels) ➲ look at **traveller**

gyroscope /ˈdʒaɪrəskəʊp/ (also *informal* **gyro** /ˈdʒaɪrəʊ/) ***noun*** [C] a device consisting of a wheel that turns very quickly inside a frame and does not change position when the frame is moved

H h

H, h /eɪtʃ/ ***noun*** [C,U] (*pl.* **H's**; **h's** /ˈeɪtʃɪz/) the eighth letter of the English alphabet: *'Hat' begins with (an) 'H'.*

ha[1] /hɑː/ ***exclamation*** **1** used for showing that you are surprised or pleased: *Ha! I knew he was hiding something!* **2 ha! ha!** used in written language to show that sb is laughing

ha[2] ***abbr.*** hectare(s)

habit 🔑 /ˈhæbɪt/ ***noun*** **1** [C] **a/the ~ (of doing sth)** something that you do often and almost without thinking, especially sth that is hard to stop doing: *I'm trying to* ***get into the habit*** *of hanging up my clothes every night.* ◇ *Once you start smoking it's hard to* ***break the habit****.* ➲ adjective **habitual**
2 [U] usual behaviour: *I think I only smoke* ***out of habit*** *now – I don't really enjoy it.*
IDM **force of habit** → FORCE[1]
kick the habit → KICK[1]

habitable /ˈhæbɪtəbl/ ***adj.*** (used about buildings) suitable to be lived in OPP **uninhabitable**

habitat /ˈhæbɪtæt/ ***noun*** [C] (**BIOLOGY**) the natural home of a plant or an animal: *I've seen wolves in the zoo, but not in their natural habitat.*

habitation /ˌhæbɪˈteɪʃn/ ***noun*** [U] (*formal*) living in a place

habitual /həˈbɪtʃuəl/ ***adj.*** **1** doing sth very often: *a habitual liar* **2** which you always have or do; usual: *He had his habitual cigarette after lunch.*
▶ **habitually** /-tʃuəli/ ***adv.***

hack /hæk/ ***verb*** [I,T] **1 ~ (away) (at) sth** to cut sth in a rough way with a tool such as a large knife: *He hacked at the branch of the tree until it fell.*
2 (*informal*) **~ (into) (sth)** (**COMPUTING**) to use a computer to look at and/or change information that is stored on another computer without permission

hacker /ˈhækə(r)/ ***noun*** [C] (*informal*) (**COMPUTING**) a person who uses a computer to look at and/or change information on another computer without permission

hacksaw /ˈhæksɔː/ ***noun*** [C] a tool with a narrow cutting edge in a frame, used for cutting metal

had[1] /hæd; həd/ past tense, past participle of **have**

had[2] /hæd/ ***adj.***
IDM **be had** (*informal*) to be tricked: *I've been had. This watch I bought doesn't work.*

haddock /ˈhædək/ ***noun*** [C,U] (*pl.* **haddock**) a sea fish that you can eat and that lives in the North Atlantic

hadn't short for HAD NOT

haematite (*AmE* **hematite**) /ˈhiːmətaɪt/ ***noun*** [U] (**GEOLOGY**) a dark red rock from which we get iron

haematology (*AmE* **hematology**) /ˌhiːməˈtɒlədʒi/ ***noun*** [U] (**HEALTH**) the scientific study of the blood and its diseases ▶ **haematologist** (*AmE* **hematologist**) /ˌhiːməˈtɒlədʒɪst/ ***noun*** [C]

haemo- (*AmE* **hemo-**) /ˈhiːməʊ/ ***prefix*** (**BIOLOGY**) (in nouns and adjectives) connected with blood: *haemophilia*

haemoglobin (*AmE* **hemoglobin**) /ˌhiːməˈɡləʊbɪn/ ***noun*** [U] (**BIOLOGY**) a red substance in the blood that carries OXYGEN (= the gas we need to live) and contains iron

haemophilia (*AmE* **hemophilia**) /ˌhiːməˈfɪliə/ ***noun*** [U] (**HEALTH**) a disease that causes a person to BLEED a lot even from very small injuries because the blood does not CLOT (= stop flowing)

haemophiliac (*AmE* **hemophiliac**) /ˌhiːməˈfɪliæk/ ***noun*** [C] (**HEALTH**) a person who suffers from HAEMOPHILIA

haemorrhage (*AmE* **hemorrhage**) /ˈhemərɪdʒ/ ***noun*** [C,U] (**HEALTH**) a lot of BLEEDING inside the body ▶ **haemorrhage** ***verb*** [I]

haemorrhoids (*especially AmE* **hemorrhoids**) /ˈhemərɔɪdz/ (*also* **piles**) ***noun*** [pl.] (**HEALTH**) a medical condition in which the VEINS (= the tubes that carry blood) at or near the ANUS (= the opening where waste food leaves the body) swell and become painful

hafnium /ˈhæfniəm/ ***noun*** [U] (*symbol* **Hf**) (**CHEMISTRY**) a RADIOACTIVE chemical element. **Hafnium** is a hard silver-grey metal. ❶ For more information on the periodic table of elements, look at pages R34-5.

haggard /ˈhæɡəd/ ***adj.*** (used about a person) looking tired or worried

haggle /ˈhæɡl/ ***verb*** [I] **~ (with sb) (over/about sth)** to argue with sb until you reach an agreement, especially about the price of sth: *In the market, some tourists were haggling over the price of a carpet.*

haiku /ˈhaɪkuː/ (*pl.* **haiku** or **haikus**) ***noun*** [C] (**LITERATURE**) a Japanese poem with three lines and usually 17 SYLLABLES

hail[1] /heɪl/ ***verb*** **1** [T] **~ sb/sth as sth** to say in public that sb/sth is very good or very special: *The book was hailed as a masterpiece.* **2** [T] to call or wave to sb/sth: *to hail a taxi* **3** [I] when it **hails**, small balls of ice fall from the sky like rain ➲ note at **weather**

hail[2] /heɪl/ ***noun*** **1** [U] (*also* **hailstones** [pl.]) small balls of ice that fall from the sky like rain **2** [sing.] **a ~ of sth** a large amount of sth that is aimed at sb in order to harm them: *a hail of bullets/stones/abuse*

hair 🔑 /heə(r)/ ***noun*** **1** [U, C] the mass of long thin things that grow on the head and body of people and animals; one of these things: *He has got short black hair.* ◇ *Dave's losing his hair* (= going bald). ◇ *The dog left hairs all over the furniture.* ➲ picture on **page 80** **2 -haired** ***adj.*** (used in compounds) having the type of hair mentioned: *a dark-haired woman* ◇ *a long-haired dog* **3** (**BIOLOGY**) a thing that looks like a very thin thread that grows on the surface of some plants: *The leaves and stem are covered in fine hairs.*
IDM **keep your hair on** (*spoken*) (used to tell sb to stop shouting and become less angry) calm down

let your hair down (*informal*) to relax and enjoy yourself after being formal
make sb's hair stand on end to frighten or shock sb
not turn a hair to not show any reaction to sth that many people would find surprising or shocking
split hairs → SPLIT[1]

hairbrush /'heəbrʌʃ/ ***noun*** [C] a brush that you use on your hair

haircut /'heəkʌt/ ***noun*** [C] **1** the act of sb cutting your hair: *You need (to have) a haircut.* **2** the style in which your hair has been cut: *That haircut really suits you.*

hairdo /'heədu:/ (*informal*) = HAIRSTYLE

hairdresser ⊶ /'heədresə(r)/ ***noun*** **1** [C] a person whose job is to cut, shape, colour, etc. hair **2 the hairdresser's** [sing.] the place where you go to have your hair cut

hairdryer (also **hairdrier**) /'heədraɪə(r)/ ***noun*** [C] a machine that dries hair by blowing hot air through it

hairgrip /'heəgrɪp/ ***noun*** [C] a U-SHAPED pin that is used for holding the hair in place

hairless /'heələs/ ***adj.*** without hair ➲ look at **bald**

hairline[1] /'heəlaɪn/ ***noun*** [C] the place on a person's FOREHEAD where their hair starts growing

hairline[2] /'heəlaɪn/ ***adj.*** (used about a crack in sth) very thin: *a hairline fracture of the leg*

hairpin bend /ˌheəpɪn 'bend/ ***noun*** [C] (*BrE*) a very sharp bend in a road, especially a mountain road

'hair-raising ***adj.*** that makes you very frightened: *a hair-raising experience*

hairspray /'heəspreɪ/ ***noun*** [U, C] a substance you spray onto your hair to hold it in place SYN **lacquer**

hairstyle /'heəstaɪl/ (also *informal* **hairdo**) ***noun*** [C] the style in which your hair has been cut or arranged

hairstylist /'heəstaɪlɪst/ (*also* **stylist**) ***noun*** [C] a person whose job is to cut and shape sb's hair

hairy /'heəri/ ***adj.*** (**hairier**; **hairiest**) **1** having a lot of hair **2** (*slang*) dangerous or worrying

hajj (also **haj**) /hædʒ/ ***noun*** [sing.] (**RELIGION**) the religious journey (**pilgrimage**) to Mecca that many Muslims make

hake /heɪk/ ***noun*** [C,U] (*pl.* **hake**) a large sea fish that is used for food

halal /'hælæl/ ***adj.*** (only *before* a noun) (**RELIGION**) (used about meat) from an animal that has been killed according to Muslim law

half[1] ⊶ /hɑ:f/ ***det.***, ***noun*** [C] (*pl.* **halves** /hɑ:vz/) one of two equal parts of sth: *three and a half kilos of potatoes* ◇ *Two halves make a whole.* ◇ *half an hour* ◇ *an hour and a half* ◇ *The second half of the book is more exciting.* ◇ *Giggs scored in the first half* (= of a match). ◇ *Half of this money is yours.* ◇ *Half the people in the office leave at 5.* ➲ verb **halve**
IDM **break, cut, etc. sth in half** to break, etc. sth into two parts
do nothing/not do anything by halves to do whatever you do completely and properly
go half and half/go halves with sb (*BrE*) to share the cost of sth with sb

half[2] ⊶ /hɑ:f/ ***adv.*** not completely; to the amount of half: ***half full*** ◇ *The hotel was only* ***half finished***. ◇ *He's half German* (= one of his parents is German).
IDM **half past...** (in time) 30 minutes past an hour: *half past six* (= 6.30)
not half as much, many, good, bad, etc. much less: *This episode wasn't half as good as the last.*

ˌhalf-'baked ***adj.*** (*informal*) not well planned or considered: *a half-baked idea/scheme*

ˌhalf 'board ***noun*** [U] (*BrE*) (**TOURISM**) a price for a room in a hotel, etc., which includes breakfast and an evening meal ➲ look at **full board**, **bed and breakfast**

'half-brother ***noun*** [C] a brother with whom you share one parent ➲ look at **stepbrother**

ˌhalf-'hearted ***adj.*** without interest or enthusiasm ► **ˌhalf-'heartedly** ***adv.***

'half-life ***noun*** [C] (**PHYSICS**) the time taken for the RADIOACTIVITY (= the amount of harmful RAYS sent out when an atom breaks up) of a substance to fall to half its original value

'half note (*AmE*) = MINIM

ˌhalf-'price ***adj.*** costing half the usual price: *a half-price ticket* ► **ˌhalf-'price** ***adv.***: *Children aged under four go half-price.*

'half-sister ***noun*** [C] a sister with whom you share one parent ➲ look at **stepsister**

ˌhalf-'term ***noun*** [C] (*BrE*) (**EDUCATION**) a short holiday in the middle of TERM (= a three-month period of school)

ˌhalf-'time ***noun*** [U] (**SPORT**) the period of time between the two halves of a match

halfway /ˌhɑ:f'weɪ/ ***adj.***, ***adv.*** at an equal distance between two places; in the middle of a period of time: *They have a break halfway through the morning.* SYN **midway**

halibut /'hælɪbət/ ***noun*** [C,U] (*pl.* **halibut**) a large flat sea fish that is used for food

halitosis /ˌhælɪ'təʊsi/ ***noun*** [U] (**HEALTH**) a condition in which the breath smells unpleasant

hall ⊶ /hɔ:l/ ***noun*** [C] **1** (*also* **hallway**) a room or passage that is just inside the front entrance of a house or public building: *There is a public telephone in the* ***entrance hall*** *of this building.* **2** a building or large room in which meetings, concerts, dances, etc. can be held: *a concert hall* ➲ look at **town hall**

hallmark /'hɔ:lmɑ:k/ ***noun*** [C] **1** a characteristic that is typical of sb: *The ability to motivate students is the hallmark of a good teacher.* **2** a mark that is put on objects made of valuable metals, giving information about the quality of the metal and when and where the object was made

hallo = HELLO

ˌhall of 'residence ***noun*** [C] (*pl.* **halls of residence**) (*AmE* **dormitory**) (**EDUCATION**) (in colleges, universities, etc.) a building where students live

Halloween /ˌhæləʊ'i:n/ ***noun*** [sing.] (*also* **Hallowe'en**) the night of October 31st (before All Saints' Day)

CULTURE

Halloween is the time when people say that witches and ghosts appear. Children now dress up as witches, etc. and play tricks on people. They go to people's houses and say '**trick or treat**' and the people give them sweets.

hallucination /həˌlu:sɪ'neɪʃn/ ***noun*** [C,U] seeing or hearing sth that is not really there (because you are ill or have taken a drug)

hallucinogen /ˌhæ'lu:sɪnədʒən/ ***noun*** [C] (**HEALTH**) a drug that affects people's minds and makes them see and hear things that are not really there ▶ **hallucinogenic** /həˌluːsɪnəˈdʒenɪk/ ***adj.***: *hallucinogenic drugs*

hallway /ˈhɔːlweɪ/ = HALL

halo /ˈheɪləʊ/ ***noun*** [C] (*pl.* **halos** or **haloes**) (**RELIGION**) the circle of light that is drawn around the head of an important religious person in a painting

halogen /ˈhælədʒən/ ***noun*** [C] (**CHEMISTRY**) any of five chemical substances that are not metals and that combine with HYDROGEN to form strong acid COMPOUNDS from which simple salts can be made: *the halogens fluorine, chlorine, bromine, iodine and astatine*

halt /hɔːlt/ ***noun*** [sing.] a stop (that does not last very long): *Work **came to a halt** when the machine broke down.* ▶ **halt** ***verb*** [I,T] (*formal*): *An accident halted the traffic in the town centre for half an hour.*
IDM **grind to a halt/standstill** → GRIND[1]

halter /ˈhɔːltə(r)/ ***noun*** [C] **1** a rope or leather STRAP put around the head of a horse for leading it with **2** (usually used as an adjective) a STRAP around the neck that holds a woman's dress or shirt in position without the back and shoulders being covered

halve /hɑːv/ ***verb*** **1** [I,T] to reduce by a half; to make sth reduce by a half: *Shares in the company have halved in value.* ◇ *We aim to halve the number of people on our waiting list in the next six months.* **2** [T] to divide sth into two equal parts: *First halve the peach and then remove the stone.*

ham /hæm/ ***noun*** [U] meat from a pig's back leg that has been CURED (= dried, smoked or treated with salt) to keep it fresh ➲ note at **meat** ➲ look at **bacon**, **pork**

hamburger /ˈhæmbɜːgə(r)/ ***noun*** **1** (*also* **burger**) [C] meat that has been cut up small and pressed into a flat round shape. **Hamburgers** are often eaten in a bread roll. ➲ look at **beefburger** **2** [U] (*AmE*) = MINCE

hamlet /ˈhæmlət/ ***noun*** [C] a very small village

hammer[1] 🔑 /ˈhæmə(r)/ ***noun*** [C] **1** a tool with a heavy metal head that is used for hitting nails, etc. ➲ picture at **tool** **2** (also *technical* **malleus**) (**ANATOMY**) the first of three small bones in the middle ear which carry sound to the inner ear

hammer[2] /ˈhæmə(r)/ ***verb*** **1** [I,T] **~ sth (in/into/onto sth)** to hit with a hammer: *She hammered the nail into the wall.* **2** [I] to hit sth several times, making a loud noise
IDM **hammer sth into sb** to force sb to remember sth by repeating it many times
hammer sth out to succeed in making a plan or agreement after a lot of discussion

hammering /ˈhæmərɪŋ/ ***noun*** **1** [U] the noise that is made by sb using a hammer or by sb hitting sth many times **2** [C] (*BrE, informal*) (**SPORT**) a very bad defeat

hammock /ˈhæmək/ ***noun*** [C] a bed, made of strong cloth (**canvas**) or rope, which is hung up between two trees or poles

hamper[1] /ˈhæmpə(r)/ ***verb*** [T] (usually passive) to make sth difficult: *The building work was hampered by bad weather.*

hamper[2] /ˈhæmpə(r)/ ***noun*** [C] a large BASKET with a lid that is used for carrying food

hamster /ˈhæmstə(r)/ ***noun*** [C] a small animal that is kept as a pet. **Hamsters** are like small RATS but are fatter and do not have a tail. They store food in the sides of their mouths.

hamstring /ˈhæmstrɪŋ/ ***noun*** [C] (**ANATOMY**) one of the five strong thin parts (**tendons**) behind your knee that connect the muscles of your upper leg to the bones of your lower leg

hand[1] 🔑 /hænd/ ***noun*** **1** [C] the part of your body at the end of your arm which has five fingers: *He **took** the child **by the hand**.* ◇ *She was on her hands and knees* (= crawling on the floor) *looking for an earring.* ➲ picture on **page 80** **2 a hand** [sing.] (*informal*) some help: *I'll give you a hand with the washing up.* ◇ *Do you want/need a hand?* **3** [C] the part of a clock or watch that points to the numbers: *the hour/minute/second hand* **4** [C] a person who does physical work on a farm, in a factory etc.: *farmhands* **5** [C] the set of playing cards that sb has been given in a game of cards: *have a good/bad hand* **6 -handed *adj.*** (used in compounds) having, using or made for the type of hand(s) mentioned: *heavy-handed* (= clumsy and careless) ◇ *right-handed/left-handed*
IDM **(close/near) at hand** (*formal*) near in space or time: *Help is close at hand.*
be an old hand (at sth) → OLD
by hand **1** done by a person and not by machine: *I had to do all the sewing by hand.* **2** not by post: *The letter was delivered by hand.*
catch sb red-handed → CATCH[1]
change hands → CHANGE[1]
a firm hand → FIRM[1]
(at) first hand (used about information that you have received) from sb who was closely involved: *Did you get this information first hand?* ➲ look at **second-hand**
force sb's hand → FORCE[2]
get, have, etc. a free hand → FREE[1]
get, etc. the upper hand → UPPER
get/lay your hands on sb/sth **1** to find or obtain sth: *I need to get my hands on a good computer.* **2** (*informal*) to catch sb: *Just wait till I get my hands on that boy!*
give sb a big hand to hit your hands together to show approval, enthusiasm, etc.: *The audience gave the girl a big hand when she finished her song.*
hand in hand **1** holding each other's hands: *The couple walked hand in hand along the beach.* **2** usually happening together; closely connected: *Drought and famine usually go hand in hand.*
your hands are tied to not be in a position to do as you would like because of rules, promises, etc.
hands off (sb/sth) (*informal*) used for ordering sb not to touch sth
hands up **1** used in a school, etc. for asking people to lift one hand and give an answer: *Hands up, who'd like to go on the trip this afternoon?* **2** used by a person with a gun to tell other people to put their hands in the air
have a hand in sth to take part in or share sth
have sb eating out of your hand → EAT
have your hands full to be very busy so that you cannot do anything else
a helping hand → HELP[1]
hold sb's hand to give sb support in a difficult situation: *I'll come to the dentist's with you to hold your hand.*
hold hands (with sb) (used about two people) to hold each other's hands
in hand **1** being dealt with at the moment; under control: *The situation is in hand.* OPP **out of hand** **2** (used about money, etc.) not yet used: *If you have time in hand at the end of the exam, check what you have written.*
in safe hands → SAFE[1]
in your hands in your possession, control or care: *The matter is in the hands of a solicitor.*
keep your hand in to do an activity from time to

time so that you do not forget how to do it or lose the skill
lend (sb) a hand/lend a hand (to sb) → LEND
off your hands not your responsibility any more
on hand available to help or to be used: *There is always an adult on hand to help when the children are playing outside.*
on your hands being your responsibility: *We seem to have a problem on our hands.*
on the one hand...on the other (hand) used for showing opposite points of view: *On the one hand, of course, cars are very useful. On the other hand, they cause a huge amount of pollution.*
(get/be) out of hand not under control: *Violence at football matches is getting out of hand.* OPP **in hand**
out of your hands not in your control; not your responsibility: *I can't help you, I'm afraid. The matter is out of my hands.*
shake sb's hand/shake hands (with sb)/shake sb by the hand → SHAKE[1]
to hand near or close to you: *I'm afraid I haven't got my diary to hand.*
try your hand at sth → TRY[1]
turn your hand to sth to have the ability to do sth: *She can turn her hand to all sorts of jobs.*
wash your hands of sb/sth → WASH[1]
with your bare hands → BARE

hand² /hænd/ *verb* [T] ~ sb sth; ~ sth to sb to give or pass sth to sb
IDM **have (got) to hand it to sb** used to show admiration and approval of sb's work or efforts: *You've got to hand it to Rita – she's a great cook.*
PHR V **hand sth back (to sb)** to give or return sth to the person who owns it or to where it belongs
hand sth down (to sb) 1 to pass customs, traditions, etc. from older people to younger ones **2** to pass clothes, toys, etc. from older children to younger ones in the family
hand sth in (to sb) to give sth to sb in authority: *I found a wallet and handed it in to the police.*
hand sth on (to sb) to send or give sth to another person: *When you have read the article, please hand it on to another student.*
hand sth out (to sb) to give sth to many people in a group: *Food was handed out to the starving people.*
hand (sth) over (to sb) to give sb else your position of power or the responsibility for sth
hand (sb) over to sb (used at a meeting or on the television, radio, telephone, etc.) to let sb speak or listen to another person
hand sb/sth over (to sb) to give sb/sth (to sb): *People were tricked into handing over large sums of money.*
hand sth round to offer to pass sth, especially food and drinks, to all the people in a group

handbag /ˈhændbæg/ (*AmE* **purse**) *noun* [C] a small bag in which women carry money, keys, etc.

handbook /ˈhændbʊk/ *noun* [C] a small book that gives instructions on how to use sth or advice and information about a particular subject

handbrake /ˈhændbreɪk/ (*AmE* **eˈmergency brake**, **ˈparking brake**) *noun* [C] a device that is operated by hand to stop a car from moving when it is parked

handcuffs /ˈhændkʌfs/ (*also* **cuffs**) *noun* [pl.] a pair of metal rings that are joined together by a chain and put around the wrists of prisoners

handful /ˈhændfʊl/ *noun* **1** [C] **a ~ (of sth)** as much or as many of sth as you can hold in one hand: *a handful of sand* **2** [sing.] a small number (of sb/sth): *Only a handful of people came to the meeting.* **3 a handful** [sing.] (*informal*) a person or an animal that is difficult to control

handgun /ˈhændgʌn/ *noun* [C] a small gun that you can hold and fire with one hand

ˌhand-ˈheld¹ *adj.* small enough to be held in the hand while being used: *hand-held electronic devices*

ˈhand-held² *noun* [C] (COMPUTING) a small computer or electronic device that can be held in the hand

handicap¹ /ˈhændikæp/ *noun* [C] **1** something that makes doing sth more difficult; a disadvantage: *Not speaking French is going to be a bit of a handicap in my new job.* **2** (SPORT) a disadvantage that is given to a strong COMPETITOR in a sports event, etc. so that the other COMPETITORS have more chance **3** (*old-fashioned*) = DISABILITY ❶ Many people now find this word offensive.

handicap² /ˈhændikæp/ *verb* [T] (**handicapping**; **handicapped**) (usually passive) to give or be a disadvantage to sb: *They were handicapped by their lack of education.*

handicapped /ˈhændikæpt/ *adj.* (*old-fashioned*) = DISABLED ❶ Many people now find this word offensive.

handicraft /ˈhændikrɑːft/ *noun* **1** [C] (ART) an activity that needs skill with the hands as well as artistic ability, for example sewing **2 handicrafts** [pl.] the objects that are produced by this activity

handiwork /ˈhændiwɜːk/ *noun* [U] **1** a thing that you have made or done, especially using your artistic skill: *She put the dress on and stood back to admire her handiwork.* **2** a thing done by a particular person or group, especially sth bad

handkerchief /ˈhæŋkətʃɪf; -tʃiːf/ *noun* [C] (*pl.* **handkerchiefs** or **handkerchieves** /-tʃiːvz/) a square piece of cloth or soft thin paper that you use for clearing your nose

handle¹ /ˈhændl/ *verb* [T] **1** to touch or hold sth with your hand(s): *Wash your hands before you handle food.* **2** to deal with or to control sb/sth: *This port handles 100 million tons of cargo each year.* ◇ *I have a problem at work and I don't really know how to handle it.* ▶ **handler** *noun* [C]: *baggage/dog/food handlers*

handle² /ˈhændl/ *noun* [C] a part of sth that is used for holding or opening it: *She turned the handle and opened the door.* ➲ picture at **agriculture**
IDM **fly off the handle** → FLY[1]

handlebar /ˈhændlbɑː(r)/ *noun* [C, usually pl.] the metal bar at the front of a bicycle that you hold when you are riding it

ˈhand luggage (*AmE* **ˈcarry-on baggage**) *noun* [U] (TOURISM) a small bag, etc. that you can keep with you on a plane

handmade /ˌhændˈmeɪd/ *adj.* made by hand and of very good quality, not by machine

handout /ˈhændaʊt/ *noun* [C] **1** food, money, etc. given to people who need it badly **2** a free document that is given to a lot of people, to advertise sth or explain sth, for example in a class

ˌhand-ˈpicked *adj.* chosen carefully or personally

handrail /ˈhændreɪl/ *noun* [C] a long narrow wooden or metal bar at the side of some steps, a bath, etc. that you hold for support or balance

handset = RECEIVER (1)

ˈhands-free *adj.* if a telephone, etc. is **hands-free**, you can use it without needing to hold it in your hand: *hands-free mobile phones*

handshake /ˈhændʃeɪk/ ***noun*** [C] the action of shaking sb's right hand with your own when you meet them

ˌ**hands-ˈoff** ***adj.*** dealing with people or a situation by not becoming involved and by allowing people to do what they want to: *a hands-off approach to staff management* ➲ look at **hands-on**

handsome /ˈhænsəm/ ***adj.*** **1** (used about a man) attractive **2** (used about money, an offer, etc.) large or generous: *a handsome profit* ▸ **handsomely** ***adv.***: *Her efforts were handsomely rewarded.*

ˌ**hands-ˈon** ***adj.*** learnt by doing sth yourself, not watching sb else do it; practical: *She needs some hands-on computer experience.* ➲ look at **hands-off**

handstand /ˈhændstænd/ ***noun*** [C] a movement in which you put your hands on the ground and lift your legs straight up in the air

handwriting /ˈhændraɪtɪŋ/ ***noun*** [U] a person's style of writing by hand

handwritten /ˌhændˈrɪtn/ ***adj.*** written by hand, not typed or printed

handy /ˈhændi/ ***adj.*** (**handier**; **handiest**) **1** useful; easy to use: *a handy tip* ◇ *a handy gadget* **2** ~ (**for sth/doing sth**) within easy reach of sth; nearby: *Always keep a first-aid kit handy for emergencies.* **3** skilful in using your hands or tools to make or repair things: *James is very handy around the house.*
IDM **come in handy** to be useful at some time: *Don't throw that box away. It may come in handy.*

handyman /ˈhændimæn/ ***noun*** [sing.] a person who is clever at making or repairing things, especially around the house

hang¹ 🔑 /hæŋ/ ***verb*** (*pt*, *pp* **hung** /hʌŋ/) ⓘ The past tense and past participle **hanged** is only used in sense 2. **1** [I,T] to fasten sth or be fastened at the top so that the lower part is free or loose: *Hang your coat on the hook.* ◇ *I left the washing hanging on the line all day.* ◇ *A cigarette hung from his lips.* **2** [T] to kill sb/yourself by putting a rope around the neck and allowing the body to drop downwards: *He was hanged for murder.* **3** [I] ~ (**above/over sb/sth**) to stay in the air in a way that is unpleasant or threatening: *Smog hung in the air over the city.*
IDM **be/get hung up (about/on sb/sth)** to think about sb/sth all the time in a way that is not healthy or good: *She's really hung up about her parents' divorce.*
hang (on) in there (*spoken*) to have courage and keep trying, even though a situation is difficult: *The worst part is over now. Just hang on in there and be patient.*
PHR V **hang about/around** (*informal*) to stay in or near a place not doing very much
hang back 1 to not want to do or say sth, often because you are shy or not sure of yourself **2** to stay in a place after other people have left it
hang on 1 to wait for a short time: *Hang on a minute. I'm nearly ready.* **2** to hold sth tightly: *Hang on, don't let go!*
hang on sth to depend on sth
hang on to sth 1 (*informal*) to keep sth: *Let's hang on to the car for another year.* **2** to hold sth tightly: *He hung on to the child's hand as they crossed the street.*
hang sth out to put washing, etc. on a clothes line so that it can dry
hang over sb to be present or about to happen in a way which is unpleasant or threatening: *This essay has been hanging over me for days.*
hang sth up to put sth on a nail, hook, etc.: *Hang your coat up over there.*
hang up to end a telephone conversation and put the telephone down
hang up on sb (*informal*) to end a telephone conversation without saying goodbye because you are angry

hang² /hæŋ/ ***noun***
IDM **get the hang of (doing) sth** (*informal*) to learn how to use or do sth: *It took me a long time to get the hang of my new computer.*

hangar /ˈhæŋə(r)/ ***noun*** [C] a big building where planes are kept

hanger /ˈhæŋə(r)/ (*also* ˈ**coat hanger**, ˈ**clothes-hanger**) ***noun*** [C] a metal, plastic or wooden object with a hook that is used for hanging up clothes in a cupboard

hanger-on /ˌhæŋər ˈɒn/ ***noun*** [C] (*pl.* **hangers-on**) a person who tries to be friendly with sb who is rich or important

ˈ**hang-glider** ***noun*** [C] (SPORT) a type of frame covered with cloth, which a person holds and flies through the air with as a sport ➲ look at **glider**
▸ **hang-gliding** ***noun*** [U]

hanging /ˈhæŋɪŋ/ ***noun*** **1** [U, C] (LAW) the practice of killing sb as a punishment by putting a rope around their neck and hanging them from a high place; an occasion when this happens: *to sentence sb to death by hanging* ◇ *public hangings* **2** [C, usually pl.] (ART) a large piece of material that is hung on a wall for decoration: *wall hangings*

ˌ**hanging ˈvalley** ***noun*** [C] (GEOGRAPHY) a valley which has been cut across by a deeper valley or CLIFF ➲ picture at **glacial**

hangman /ˈhæŋmən/ ***noun*** [sing.] **1** (LAW) a person whose job is to kill criminals as a form of punishment by hanging them with a rope **2** a word game where the aim is to guess all the letters of a word before a picture of a person hanging is completed

hangover /ˈhæŋəʊvə(r)/ ***noun*** [C] pain in your head and a sick feeling that you have if you have drunk too much alcohol the night before

ˈ**hang-up** ***noun*** [C] (*slang*) **a hang-up (about sb/sth)** an emotional problem about sth that makes you embarrassed or worried: *He has a real hang-up about his height.*

hanker /ˈhæŋkə(r)/ ***verb*** [I] ~ **after/for sth** to want sth very much (often sth that you cannot easily have)

hanky (also **hankie**) /ˈhæŋki/ ***noun*** [C] (*pl.* **hankies**) (*informal*) = HANDKERCHIEF

Hanukkah /ˈhænʊkə/ ***noun*** [U] (RELIGION) an eight-day Jewish festival and holiday in November or December

haphazard /hæpˈhæzəd/ ***adj.*** with no particular order or plan; badly organized ▸ **haphazardly** ***adv.***

haploid /ˈhæplɔɪd/ ***adj.*** (BIOLOGY) (used about a cell) containing only the set of CHROMOSOMES (= the parts of the cell that decide the sex, character, shape, etc. that a living thing will have) from one parent ➲ look at **diploid**

happen 🔑 /ˈhæpən/ ***verb*** [I] **1** (of an event or situation) to take place, usually without being planned first: *Can you describe to the police what happened after you left the party?* ◇ *How did the accident happen?* **2** ~ **to sb/sth** to be what sb/sth experiences: *What do you think has happened to Julie? She should have been here an hour ago.* ◇ *What will happen to the business when your father retires?* **3** ~ **to do sth** to do sth by chance: *I happened to meet him in London yesterday.*
IDM **as it happens/happened** (used when you are adding to what you have said) actually: *As it*

happens, I did remember to bring the book you wanted.
it (just) so happens → SO[1]

happening /ˈhæpənɪŋ/ ***noun*** [C] **1** [usually pl.] an event; something that happens, often sth unusual: *Strange happenings have been reported in that old hotel.* **2** (ARTS AND MEDIA) an artistic performance or event that is not planned

happily ⊷ /ˈhæpɪli/ ***adv.*** **1** in a happy way: *I would happily give up my job if I didn't need the money.* **2** it is lucky that; FORTUNATELY: *The police found my handbag and, happily, nothing had been stolen.*

happy ⊷ /ˈhæpi/ ***adj.*** (**happier**; **happiest**) **1** ~ (**to do sth**); ~ **for sb**; ~ **that...** feeling or showing pleasure; pleased: *I was really happy to see Mark again yesterday.* ◇ *You look very happy today.* ◇ *Congratulations! I'm very happy for you.* OPP **unhappy**, **sad 2** giving or causing pleasure: *a happy marriage/memory/childhood* ◇ *The film is sad but it has **a happy ending**.* **3** ~ (**with/about sb/sth**) satisfied that sth is good and right; not worried: *I'm not very happy with what you've done.* ◇ *She doesn't feel happy about the salary she's been offered.* **3** (not before a noun) ~ **to do sth** ready to do sth; pleased: *I'll be happy to see you any day next week.* **4 Happy** used to wish sb an enjoyable time: *Happy Birthday!* **5** (only *before* a noun) lucky; FORTUNATE: *a happy coincidence.* OPP **unhappy** ▶ **happiness** ***noun*** [U]

ˌ**happy-go-ˈlucky** ***adj.*** not caring or worried about life and the future

ˈ**happy hour** ***noun*** [C, usually sing.] a time, usually in the evening, when a pub or bar sells alcoholic drinks at lower prices than usual

harass /ˈhærəs; həˈræs/ ***verb*** [T] to annoy or worry sb by doing unpleasant things to them, especially over a long time: *The court ordered him to stop harassing his ex-wife.* ▶ **harassment** ***noun*** [U]: *She accused her boss of **sexual harassment**.*

harassed /ˈhærəst; həˈræst/ ***adj.*** tired and worried because you have too much to do

harbinger /ˈhɑːbɪndʒə(r)/ ***noun*** [C] ~ (**of sth**) (*written*) a sign that shows that sth is going to happen soon, often sth bad

harbour[1] (*AmE* **harbor**) /ˈhɑːbə(r)/ ***noun*** [C,U] a place on the coast where ships can be tied up (**moored**) and protected from the sea and bad weather

harbour[2] (*AmE* **harbor**) /ˈhɑːbə(r)/ ***verb*** [T] **1** to keep feelings or thoughts secret in your mind for a long time: *She began to **harbour doubts** about the decision.* **2** to hide or protect sb/sth that is bad: *They were accused of harbouring terrorists.*

hard[1] ⊷ /hɑːd/ ***adj.*** **1** not soft to touch; not easy to break or bend: *The bed was so hard that I couldn't sleep.* ◇ *Diamonds are the hardest known mineral.* OPP **soft 2** ~ (**for sb**) (**to do sth**) difficult to do or understand; not easy: *The first question in the exam was very hard.* ◇ *This book is hard to understand./It is a hard book to understand.* ◇ *It's hard for young people to find good jobs nowadays.* ◇ *I find his attitude very hard to take* (= difficult to accept). ➲ note at **difficult** OPP **easy 3** needing or using a lot of physical strength or mental effort: *It's a hard climb to the top of the hill.* ◇ ***Hard work** is said to be good for you.* ◇ *He's a hard worker.* **4** (used about a person) not feeling or showing kindness or pity; not gentle: *You have to be hard to succeed in business.* OPP **soft**, **lenient 5** (used about conditions) unpleasant or unhappy; full of difficulty: *He had a hard time when his parents died.* ◇ *to have a hard day/life/childhood* **6** (used about the weather) very cold: *The forecast is for a hard winter/frost.* OPP **mild 7** (used about water) containing particular minerals so that soap does not make many bubbles: *We live in a **hard water** area.* OPP **soft** ▶ **hardness** ***noun*** [U]

IDM **a hard act to follow** a person or a thing that it is difficult to do better than

be hard at it to be working very hard doing sth

be hard on sb/sth 1 to treat sb/sth in a HARSH way or to make things difficult: *Don't be too hard on her – she's only a child.* **2** to be unfair to sb: *Moving the office to the country is a bit hard on the people who haven't got a car.*

give sb a hard time (*informal*) to make a situation unpleasant, embarrassing or difficult for sb

hard and fast (used about rules, etc.) that cannot be changed: *There are no hard and fast rules about this.*

hard facts information that is true, not just people's opinions

hard luck → LUCK

hard of hearing unable to hear well

hard to swallow difficult to believe

have a hard job doing/to do sth; **have a hard time doing sth** to do sth with great difficulty

no hard feelings (*spoken*) used to tell sb you do not feel angry after an argument, etc.: *'No hard feelings, I hope,' he said, offering me his hand.*

the hard way through having unpleasant or difficult experiences, rather than learning from what you are told: *She won't listen to my advice so she'll just have to **learn the hard way**.*

take a hard line (on sth) to deal with sth in a very serious way that you will not allow anyone to change: *The government has taken a hard line on people who drink and drive.*

hard[2] ⊷ /hɑːd/ ***adv.*** **1** with great effort, energy or attention: *He worked hard all his life.* ◇ *You'll have to try a bit harder than that.* **2** with great force; heavily: *It was raining/snowing hard.* ◇ *He hit her hard across the face.*

IDM **be hard up (for sth)** to have too few or too little of sth, especially money

be hard pressed/pushed/put to do sth to find sth very difficult to do: *He was hard pressed to explain his wife's sudden disappearance.*

die hard → DIE

hard done by (*BrE*) not fairly treated: *He felt very hard done by when he wasn't chosen for the team.*

hardback /ˈhɑːdbæk/ ***noun*** [C] a book that has a hard RIGID cover: *This book is only available **in hardback**.* ➲ look at **paperback**

hardboard /ˈhɑːdbɔːd/ ***noun*** [U] a type of wooden board made by pressing very small pieces of wood together into thin sheets

ˌ**hard-ˈboiled** ***adj.*** (used about an egg) boiled until it is solid inside

ˌ**hard ˈcash** (*AmE* ˌ**cold ˈcash**) ***noun*** [U] money, especially in the form of coins and notes, that you can spend

ˌ**hard ˈcopy** ***noun*** [U] (COMPUTING) information from a computer that has been printed on paper

ˌ**hard ˈcore** ***noun*** [sing., with sing. or pl. verb] the members of a group who are the most active

ˌ**hard ˈcurrency** ***noun*** [U] (ECONOMICS) money belonging to a particular country that is easy to exchange and not likely to fall in value

ˌ**hard ˈdisk** ***noun*** [C] (COMPUTING) a piece of hard plastic that is fixed inside a computer and is used for storing data and programs permanently ➲ look at **floppy disk** ➲ picture at **computer**

ˈ**hard drive** ***noun*** [C] (COMPUTING) a part of a computer that reads data on a HARD DISK ➲ picture at **computer**

ˌ**hard ˈdrug** ***noun*** [C, usually pl.] (LAW) a powerful and illegal drug that some people take for pleasure and may become ADDICTED TO (= unable to stop taking): *Heroin and cocaine are hard drugs.* ➲ look at **soft** (6)

harden /ˈhɑːdn/ ***verb*** **1** [I,T] to become or to make sth hard or less likely to change: *The concrete will harden in 24 hours.* ◇ *The firm has hardened its attitude on this question.* **2** [T] (usually passive) ~ **sb (to sth/doing sth)** to make sb less kind or less easily shocked: *a hardened reporter/criminal* ◇ *Police officers get hardened to seeing dead bodies.* **3** [I] (used about a person's face, voice, etc.) to become serious and unfriendly

ˌ**hard-ˈheaded** ***adj.*** determined and not allowing yourself to be influenced by emotions: *a hard-headed businessman*

ˌ**hard-ˈhearted** ***adj.*** not kind to other people and not considering their feelings OPP **soft-hearted**

ˌ**hard-ˈhitting** ***adj.*** that talks about or criticizes sb/sth in an honest and very direct way: *a hard-hitting campaign/speech/report*

hardly 🔑 /ˈhɑːdli/ ***adv.*** **1** almost no; almost not; almost none: *There's **hardly any** coffee left.* ◇ *We **hardly ever** go out nowadays.* ◇ *I hardly spoke any English when I first came here.* ➲ look at **almost** **2** used especially after 'can' and 'could' and before the main verb to emphasize that sth is difficult to do: *Speak up – I can hardly hear you.* **3** (used to say that sth has just begun, happened, etc.) only just: *She'd **hardly** gone to sleep **than** it was time to get up again.* **4** (used to suggest that sth is unlikely or unreasonable) not really: *You can hardly expect me to believe that excuse!* ➲ look at **barely**, **scarcely**

ˌ**hard-ˈnosed** ***adj.*** not affected by feelings or emotions when trying to get what you want

hardship /ˈhɑːdʃɪp/ ***noun*** [C,U] the fact of not having enough money, food, etc.: *This new tax is going to cause a lot of hardship.*

ˌ**hard ˈshoulder** (*AmE* **shoulder**) ***noun*** [C] a narrow section of road at the side of a motorway where cars are allowed to stop in an emergency

hardware /ˈhɑːdweə(r)/ ***noun*** [U] **1** (COMPUTING) the machinery of a computer, not the programmes written for it ➲ look at **software** **2** tools and equipment that are used in the house and garden: *a hardware shop*

ˌ**hard-ˈwearing** ***adj.*** (*BrE*) (used about materials, clothes, etc.) strong and able to last for a long time

ˌ**hard-ˈwired** ***adj.*** **1** if a computer or a machine is **hard-wired**, it works in a particular way because that was built into the permanent system and cannot be changed **2** if a person or an animal's behaviour is **hard-wired**, they were born to behave that way and they cannot change what they do

hardwood /ˈhɑːdwʊd/ ***noun*** [U, C] hard heavy wood from trees that lose their leaves in winter (**deciduous trees**): *tropical hardwoods* ➲ look at **softwood**

ˌ**hard-ˈworking** ***adj.*** working with effort and energy: *a hard-working man*

hardy /ˈhɑːdi/ ***adj.*** (**hardier**; **hardiest**) strong and able to survive difficult conditions and bad weather: *a hardy plant* ▶ **hardiness** ***noun*** [U]

hare /heə(r)/ ***noun*** [C] an animal like a RABBIT but bigger with longer ears and legs

harem /ˈhɑːriːm/ ***noun*** [C] a number of women living with one man, especially in Muslim societies. The part of the building the women live in is also called a **harem**.

harm[1] 🔑 /hɑːm/ ***noun*** [U] damage or injury: *Peter ate some of those berries but they didn't **do** him **any harm**.* ◇ *Experienced staff watch over the children to make sure they don't **come to any harm**.*

IDM **no harm done** (*informal*) used to tell sb that they have not caused any damage or injury: *'Sorry about what I said to you last night.' 'That's all right, Jack, no harm done!'*

out of harm's way in a safe place: *Put the medicine out of harm's way where the children can't reach it.*

there is no harm in doing sth; **it does no harm (for sb) to do sth** there's nothing wrong in doing sth (and sth good may result): *I'm sure he'll say no, but there's no harm in asking.*

harm[2] 🔑 /hɑːm/ ***verb*** [T] to cause injury or damage; hurt: *Too much sunshine can harm your skin.*

harmful 🔑 /ˈhɑːmfl/ ***adj.*** ~ (to sb/sth) causing harm: *Traffic fumes are harmful to the environment.*

harmless 🔑 /ˈhɑːmləs/ ***adj.*** **1** not able or not likely to cause damage or injury; safe: *You needn't be frightened – these insects are completely harmless.* **2** not likely to upset people: *The children can watch that film – it's quite harmless.* ▶ **harmlessly** ***adv.***

harmonic[1] /hɑːˈmɒnɪk/ ***adj.*** (MUSIC) (usually *before* a noun) used to describe the way notes are played or sung together to make a pleasing sound

harmonic[2] /hɑːˈmɒnɪk/ ***noun*** [C, usually pl.] (MUSIC) **1** a note that can be played on some musical instruments, that is higher and quieter than the main note being played **2** a high quiet note that can be played on some instruments like the VIOLIN by touching the string very lightly

harmonica /hɑːˈmɒnɪkə/ (*BrE also* ˈ**mouth organ**) ***noun*** [C] (MUSIC) a small musical instrument that you play by moving it across your lips while you are blowing

harmonious /hɑːˈməʊniəs/ ***adj.*** **1** friendly, peaceful and without disagreement **2** (used about musical notes, colours, etc.) producing a pleasant effect when heard or seen together ▶ **harmoniously** ***adv.***

harmonize (also **-ise**) /ˈhɑːmənaɪz/ ***verb*** [I] **1** ~ **(with sth)** (used about two or more things) to produce a pleasant effect when seen, heard, etc. together **2** ~ **(with sb/sth)** (MUSIC) to sing or play music that sounds good combined with the main tune ▶ **harmonization** (also **-isation**) /ˌhɑːmənaɪˈzeɪʃn/ ***noun*** [U]

harmony /ˈhɑːməni/ ***noun*** (*pl.* **harmonies**) **1** [U] a state of agreement or of peaceful existence together: *We need to live more **in harmony with** our environment.* **2** [C,U] (MUSIC) a pleasing combination of musical notes, colours, etc.: *There are some beautiful harmonies in that music.*

harness[1] /ˈhɑːnɪs/ ***noun*** [C] **1** a set of leather STRAPS that is put around a horse's neck and body so that it can pull sth **2** a set of STRAPS for fastening sth to a person's body or for stopping sb from moving around, falling, etc.: *a safety harness*

harness[2] /ˈhɑːnɪs/ ***verb*** [T] **1** ~ **sth (to sth)** to put a **harness** on a horse, etc. or to tie a horse, etc. to sth using a **harness**: *Two ponies were harnessed to the cart.* **2** to control the energy of sth in order to produce power or to achieve sth: *to harness the sun's rays as a source of energy*

harp /hɑːp/ ***noun*** [C] (MUSIC) a large musical instrument which has many strings stretching from the top to the bottom of a frame. You play the **harp** with your fingers. ➲ picture on **page 465** ▶ **harpist** ***noun*** [C]

harpoon /hɑːˈpuːn/ ***noun*** [C] a long thin weapon with a sharp pointed end and a rope tied to it that is used to catch large sea animals such as WHALES ▶ **harpoon** ***verb*** [T]

harrow /ˈhærəʊ/ ***noun*** [C] (AGRICULTURE) a piece of farming equipment that is pulled over land that has been PLOUGHED to break up the earth before planting

harrowing /ˈhærəʊɪŋ/ ***adj.*** making people feel very sad or upset: *The programme showed harrowing scenes of the victims of the war.*

harsh /hɑːʃ/ ***adj.*** **1** very strict and unkind: *a harsh punishment/criticism* ◇ *The judge had some* ***harsh words*** *for the journalist's behaviour.* **2** unpleasant and difficult to live in, look at, listen to, etc.: *She grew up in the harsh environment of New York City.* ◇ *a harsh light/voice* **3** too strong or rough and likely to damage sth: *This soap is too harsh for a baby's skin.* ▶ **harshly** ***adv.*** ▶ **harshness** ***noun*** [U]

harvest /ˈhɑːvɪst/ ***noun*** (AGRICULTURE) **1** [C,U] the time of year when the grain, fruit, etc. is collected on a farm; the act of collecting the grain, fruit, etc.: *Farmers always need extra help with the harvest.* **2** [C] the amount of grain, fruit, etc. that is collected: *This year's wheat harvest was very poor.* ▶ **harvest** ***verb*** [I,T] ➲ look at **combine harvester**

has /həz *strong form* hæz/ → HAVE

ˈ**has-been** ***noun*** [C] (*informal*) a person or thing that is no longer as famous, successful or important as before

hash /hæʃ/ ***noun*** **1** [U] a hot dish of meat mixed together with potato and fried **2** [U] = HASHISH **3** (*also* ˈ**hash sign**) (*BrE*) [C] the symbol (#), especially one on the telephone

IDM **make a hash of sth** (*informal*) to do sth badly

hashish /ˈhæʃiːʃ/ (*also* **hash**) ***noun*** [U] a drug made from a plant (**hemp**) that some people smoke for pleasure and which is illegal in many countries

hasn't short for HAS NOT

hassle¹ /ˈhæsl/ ***noun*** (*informal*) **1** [C,U] a thing or situation that is annoying because it is complicated or involves a lot of effort: *It's going to be a hassle having to change trains with all this luggage.* **2** [U] disagreeing or arguing: *I've decided what to do – please don't give me any hassle about it.*

hassle² /ˈhæsl/ ***verb*** [T] to annoy sb, especially by asking them to do sth many times

haste /heɪst/ ***noun*** [U] speed in doing sth, especially because you do not have enough time: *It was obvious that the letter had been written* ***in haste***.

hasten /ˈheɪsn/ ***verb*** (*formal*) **1** [I] ~ **to do sth** to be quick to do or say sth: *She hastened to apologize.* **2** [T] to make sth happen or be done earlier or more quickly

hasty /ˈheɪsti/ ***adj.*** **1** said or done too quickly: *He said a hasty 'goodbye' and left.* **2** ~ **(in doing sth/to do sth)** (used about a person) acting or deciding sth too quickly or without enough thought: *Maybe I was too hasty in rejecting her for the job.* ▶ **hastily** ***adv.***

hat ⊶ /hæt/ ***noun*** [C] a covering that you wear on your head, usually when you are outside: *to wear a hat*

IDM **at the drop of a hat** → DROP²

hatch¹ /hætʃ/ ***verb*** **1** [I] ~ **(out)** (BIOLOGY) (used about a baby bird, insect, fish, etc.) to come out of an egg: *Ten chicks hatched (out) this morning.* **2** [T] (BIOLOGY) to make a baby bird, etc. come out of an egg **3** [T] ~ **sth (up)** to think of a plan (usually to do sth bad): *He hatched a plan to avoid paying any income tax.*

hatch² /hætʃ/ ***noun*** [C] **1** an opening in the DECK (= the floor) of a ship through which CARGO is passed down into the ship **2** (ARCHITECTURE) an opening in the wall between a kitchen and another room that is used for passing food through **3** the door in a plane or SPACECRAFT

hatchback /ˈhætʃbæk/ ***noun*** [C] a car with a large door at the back that opens upwards

hatchet /ˈhætʃɪt/ ***noun*** [C] a tool with a short handle and a heavy metal head with a sharp edge used for cutting wood ➲ picture at **axe**

hate¹ ⊶ /heɪt/ ***verb*** [T] **1** to have a very strong feeling of not liking sb/sth at all: *I hate grapefruit.* ◇ *I hate it when it's raining like this.* ◇ *I hate to see the countryside spoilt.* ◇ *He hates driving at night.* **2** used as a polite way of saying sorry for sth you would prefer not to have to say: *I hate to bother you, but did you pick up my keys by mistake?*

hate² ⊶ /heɪt/ ***noun*** **1** [U] a very strong feeling of not liking sb/sth at all; hatred: *Do you feel any hate towards the kidnappers?* **2** [C] a thing that you do not like at all: *Plastic flowers are one of my pet hates* (= the things that I particularly dislike).

hateful /ˈheɪtfl/ ***adj.*** ~ **(to sb)** extremely unpleasant: *It was a hateful thing to say.* SYN **horrible**

hatred ⊶ /ˈheɪtrɪd/ ***noun*** [U] ~ **(for/of sb/sth)** a very strong feeling of not liking sb/sth; hate

ˈ**hat-trick** ***noun*** [C] (SPORT) three points, goals, etc. scored by one player in the same game; three successes achieved by one person: *to score a hat-trick*

haughty /ˈhɔːti/ ***adj.*** proud, and thinking that you are better than other people ▶ **haughtily** ***adv.***

haul¹ /hɔːl/ ***verb*** [T] to pull sth with a lot of effort or difficulty: *A lorry hauled the car out of the mud.*

haul² /hɔːl/ ***noun*** **1** [C, usually sing.] **a** ~ **(of sth)** a large amount of sth that has been stolen, caught, collected, etc.: *The fishermen came back with a good haul of fish.* **2** [sing.] a distance to be travelled: *It seemed* ***a long haul*** *back home at night.*

haulage /ˈhɔːlɪdʒ/ ***noun*** [U] (*BrE*) the transport of goods by road, rail, etc.; the money charged for this

haunches /ˈhɔːntʃɪz/ ***noun*** [pl.] the back end of an animal, including the tops of its back legs; a person's bottom and the tops of his or her legs: *The lion rested on its haunches.*

haunt¹ /hɔːnt/ ***verb*** [T] **1** (often passive) (used about a GHOST of a dead person) to appear in a place regularly: *The house is said to be haunted.* **2** (used about sth unpleasant or sad) to be always in your mind: *His unhappy face has haunted me for years.*

haunt² /hɔːnt/ ***noun*** [C] a place that you visit regularly: *This cafe has always been a favourite haunt of mine.*

haunting /ˈhɔːntɪŋ/ ***adj.*** having a quality that stays in your mind: *a haunting song*

have¹ ⊶ /həv *strong form* hæv/ ***aux. verb*** used for forming the PERFECT TENSES

have² 🔑 /hæv/ ***verb*** [T] **1** (*BrE also* **have got**) (not used in the continuous tenses) to own or to hold sth; to possess: *I've got a new camera.* ◇ *The flat has two bedrooms.* ◇ *He's got short dark hair.* ◇ *to have patience/enthusiasm/skill* ◇ *Have you got any brothers or sisters?* ◇ *Do you have time to check my work?* **2** used with many nouns to talk about doing sth: *What time do you have breakfast?* ◇ *to have a drink/something to eat* ◇ *I'll just have a shower then we'll go.* ◇ *to have an argument/talk/chat* **3** to experience sth: *to have fun* ◇ *to have problems/difficulties* ◇ *to have an idea/an impression/a feeling* ◇ *to have an accident* ◇ *She had her bag stolen on the underground.* **4** (*also* **have got**) (not used in the continuous tenses) to be ill with sth: *She's got a bad cold.* ◇ *to have flu/a headache/cancer/Aids* **5 have sth done** to arrange for sb to do sth: *I have my hair cut every six weeks.* ◇ *You should have your eyes tested.* **6** (*also* **have got**) to have a particular duty or plan: *Do you have any homework tonight?* ◇ *I've got a few things to do this morning, but I'm free later.* **7** (*also* **have got**) (not used in the continuous tenses) to hold sb/sth; to keep sth in a particular place: *The dog had me by the leg.* ◇ *We've got our TV up on a shelf.* **8** to cause sb/sth to do sth or to be in a particular state: *The music soon had everyone dancing.* ◇ *I'll have dinner ready when you get home.* **9** to look after or entertain sb: *We're having some people to dinner tomorrow.*

IDM **have had it** used about things that are completely broken, or dead: *This television has had it. We'll have to buy a new one.*

PHR V **have sb on** to trick sb as a joke: *Don't listen to what Jimmy says – he's only having you on.*

have (got) sth on 1 to be wearing sth: *She's got a green jumper on.* **2** (*informal*) to have an arrangement to do sth: *I've got a lot on this week* (=I'm very busy).

have sth out to allow part of your body to be removed: *to have a tooth/your appendix out*

haven /ˈheɪvn/ ***noun*** [C] **a ~ (of sth)**; **a ~ (for sb/sth)** a place where people or animals can be safe and rest: *The lake is a haven for water birds.* ➲ look at **tax haven**

have to /ˈhæv tə; ˈhæf tə strong form and before vowels ˈhæv tuː; ˈhæf tuː/ (*also* **have got to**) ***modal verb*** used for saying that sb must do sth or that sth must happen: *I usually have to work on Saturday mornings.* ◇ *Do you have to have a visa to go to America?* ◇ *She's got to go to the bank this afternoon.* ◇ *We don't have to* (=it's not necessary to) *go to the party if you don't want to* ◇ *We had to do lots of boring exercises.*

havoc /ˈhævək/ ***noun*** [U] a situation in which there is a lot of damage or confusion: *The rail strikes will* ***cause havoc*** *all over the country.*

hawk¹ /hɔːk/ ***noun*** [C] a type of large bird that catches and eats small animals and birds. **Hawks** can see very well. ❶ Hawks are a type of **bird of prey**.

hawk² /hɔːk/ ***verb*** [T] to try to sell things by going from place to place asking people to buy them ▶ **hawker** ***noun*** [C]

hay /heɪ/ ***noun*** [U] (AGRICULTURE) grass that has been cut and dried for use as animal food

ˈ**hay fever** ***noun*** [U] (HEALTH) an illness that affects the eyes, nose and throat and is caused by breathing in the powder (**pollen**) produced by some plants

haywire /ˈheɪwaɪə(r)/ ***adj.***

IDM **be/go haywire** (*informal*) to be or become out of control

hazard¹ /ˈhæzəd/ ***noun*** [C] a danger or risk: *Smoking is a serious health hazard.* ◇ ***hazard lights*** (=flashing lights on a car that warn other drivers of possible danger)

hazard² /ˈhæzəd/ ***verb*** [T] to make a guess or to suggest sth even though you know it may be wrong: *I don't know what he paid for the house but I could* ***hazard a guess.***

hazardous /ˈhæzədəs/ ***adj.*** dangerous SYN **risky**

haze /heɪz/ ***noun*** **1** [C,U] air that is difficult to see through because it contains very small drops of water, especially caused by hot weather: *a heat haze* ➲ note at **weather 2** [sing.] air containing sth that makes it difficult to see through it: *a haze of smoke/dust/steam* **3** [sing.] a mental state in which you cannot think clearly

hazel¹ /ˈheɪzl/ ***noun*** [C] a small tree or bush that produces nuts

hazel² /ˈheɪzl/ ***adj.*** (used especially about eyes) light brown in colour

hazelnut /ˈheɪzlnʌt/ ***noun*** [C] a small nut that we eat

hazy /ˈheɪzi/ ***adj.*** **1** not clear, especially because of heat: *The fields were hazy in the early morning sun.* **2** difficult to remember or understand clearly: *a hazy memory* **3** (used about a person) uncertain, not expressing things clearly: *She's a bit hazy about the details of the trip.*

ˈ**H-bomb** = HYDROGEN BOMB

HCF /ˌeɪtʃ siː ˈef/ ***abbr.*** (MATHEMATICS) **highest common factor**

HDI ***abbr.*** = HUMAN DEVELOPMENT INDEX

he¹ 🔑 /hiː/ ***pronoun*** (the subject of a verb) the male person mentioned earlier: *I spoke to John before he left.* ◇ *Look at that little boy – he's going to fall in!*

he² /hiː/ ***noun*** [sing.] a male animal: *Is your cat a he or a she?*

head¹ 🔑 /hed/ ***noun*** [C] **1** the part of your body above your neck: *She turned her head to look at him.* ➲ picture on **page 80** **2 -headed** (used to form compound adjectives) having the type of head mentioned: *a bald-headed man* **3** a person's mind, brain or mental ability: *Use your head!* (=think!) ◇ *A horrible thought entered my head.* **4** the top, front or most important part: *to sit at the head of the table* ◇ *the head of a nail* ◇ *the head of the queue* **5** the person in charge of a group of people: *the head of the family* ◇ *the head waiter* **6** (*also* **head teacher**) (EDUCATION) the teacher in charge of a school: *Who is going to be the new head?* **7 heads** the side of a coin with the head of a person on it: *Heads or tails? Heads I go first, tails you do.* **8** the white mass of small bubbles on the top of a glass of beer **9 a head** [sing.] the height or length of one head: *She's a head taller than her sister.* **10** the part of a TAPE/VIDEO RECORDER that touches the tape and changes the electronic signal into sounds and/or pictures

IDM **a/per head** for each person: *How much will the meal cost a head?*

bite sb's head off → BITE¹

come to a head; **bring sth to a head** if a situation comes to a head or if you bring it to a head, it suddenly becomes very bad and you have to deal with it immediately

do sb's head in (*BrE, informal*) to make sb upset and confused

get sth into your head; **put sth into sb's head** to start or to make sb start believing or thinking sth

go to sb's head 1 to make sb too proud: *If you keep telling him how clever he is, it will go to his head!* **2** to

make sb drunk: *Wine always goes straight to my head.*
have a head for sth to be able to deal with sth easily: *You need a good head for heights if you live on the top floor!* ◇ *to have a head for business/figures*
head first 1 with your head before the rest of your body: *Don't go down the slide head first.* **2** too quickly or suddenly: *Don't rush head first into a decision.*
head over heels (in love) loving sb very much; MADLY: *Jane's fallen head over heels in love with her new boss.*
hit the nail on the head → HIT[1]
keep your head to stay calm
keep your head above water to just manage to survive in a difficult situation, especially one in which you do not have enough money
keep your head down to try not to be noticed
laugh, scream, etc. your head off to laugh, shout, etc. very loudly and for a long time
lose your head → LOSE
make head or tail of sth to understand sth: *I can't make head or tail of this exercise.*
off the top of your head → TOP[1]
out of/off your head (*informal*) crazy, often because of the effects of drugs or alcohol
put/get your heads together to make a plan with sb
a roof over your head → ROOF
shake your head → SHAKE[1]
take it into your head to do sth to suddenly decide to do sth that other people consider strange: *I don't know why Kevin took it into his head to enter that marathon!*

head² 🔑 /hed/ ***verb*** **1** [I] to move in the direction mentioned: *The ship headed towards the harbour.* ◇ *Where are you heading?* **2** [T] to be in charge of or to lead sth **3** [T] to be at the front of a line, top of a list, etc. **4** [T] (often passive) to give a title at the top of a piece of writing: *The report was headed 'The State of the Market'.* **5** [T] (**SPORT**) (in football) to hit the ball with your head
PHR V **head for** to move towards a place: *It's getting late – I think it's time to head for home.*

headache 🔑 /'hedeɪk/ ***noun*** [C] **1** a pain in your head: *I've got a splitting* (=very bad) *headache.* ➲ note at **ache 2** a person or thing that causes worry or difficulty: *Paying the bills is a constant headache.*

header /'hedə(r)/ ***noun*** [C] **1** (**SPORT**) an act of hitting the ball with your head **2** (**COMPUTING**) a line or block of text that is automatically added to the top of every page that is printed from a computer ➲ look at **footer**

headhunter /'hedhʌntə(r)/ ***noun*** [C] a person whose job is to find people to work for a particular company and to persuade them to join it

heading /'hedɪŋ/ ***noun*** [C] the words written as a title at the top of a page or a piece of writing: *I've grouped our ideas under three main headings.*

headland /'hedlənd; -lænd/ ***noun*** [C] (**GEOGRAPHY**) a narrow piece of land that sticks out into the sea ➲ picture at **erode**

headlight /'hedlaɪt/ (*also* **headlamp** /'hedlæmp/) ***noun*** [C] one of the two large bright lights at the front of a vehicle

headline /'hedlaɪn/ ***noun*** (**ARTS AND MEDIA**) **1** [C] the title of a newspaper article printed in large letters above the story **2 the headlines** [pl.] the main items of news read on television or radio

headlong /'hedlɒŋ/ ***adv.***, ***adj.*** **1** with your head before the rest of your body: *I tripped and fell headlong into the road.* **2** too quickly; without enough thought: *He rushed headlong into buying the business.*

'head louse ***noun*** [C, usually pl.] (*pl.* **head lice**) (**HEALTH**) a small insect which lives in the hair on people's heads and is especially common among schoolchildren

headmaster /ˌhed'mɑːstə(r)/ ***noun*** [C] (*old-fashioned*) (**EDUCATION**) the man who is in charge of a school

headmistress /ˌhed'mɪstrəs/ ***noun*** [C] (*old-fashioned*) (**EDUCATION**) the woman who is in charge of a school

ˌhead 'office ***noun*** [C] (**BUSINESS**) the main office of a company; the managers who work there: *Their head office is in New York.*

ˌhead of 'state ***noun*** [C] (*pl.* **heads of state**) (**POLITICS**) the official leader of a country who is sometimes also the leader of the government

ˌhead-'on ***adj.***, ***adv.*** with the front of one car, etc. hitting the front of another: *a head-on crash*

headphones /'hedfəʊnz/ ***noun*** [pl.] a piece of equipment worn over the ears that makes it possible to listen to music, the radio, etc. without other people hearing it

headquarters /ˌhed'kwɔːtəz/ ***noun*** [pl., with sing. or pl. verb] (*abbr.* **HQ**) the place from where an organization is controlled; the people who work there: *Where is/are the firm's headquarters?*

headrest /'hedrest/ ***noun*** [C] the part of a seat or chair that supports a person's head, especially on the front seat of a car

headroom /'hedruːm/ ***noun*** [U] **1** the amount of space between the top of a vehicle and an object, for example a bridge, that it drives under **2** the amount of space between the top of your head and the inside roof of a vehicle

headset /'hedset/ ***noun*** [C] a piece of equipment that you wear on your head that includes HEADPHONES (=a device for listening) and/or a MICROPHONE (=a device for speaking into): *The pilot was talking into his headset.*

ˌhead 'start ***noun*** [sing.] an advantage that you have from the beginning of a race or competition ➲ look at **start²** (4)

headstone /'hedstəʊn/ ***noun*** [C] a large stone with writing on, used to mark where a dead person is buried ➲ look at **gravestone**, **tombstone**

headstrong /'hedstrɒŋ/ ***adj.*** doing what you want, without listening to advice from other people

ˌhead 'teacher = HEAD[1] (6)

headway /'hedweɪ/ ***noun***
IDM **make headway** to go forward or make progress in a difficult situation

headwind /'hedwɪnd/ ***noun*** [C] a wind that is blowing towards a person or vehicle, so that it is blowing from the direction in which the person or vehicle is moving ➲ look at **tailwind**

headword /'hedwɜːd/ ***noun*** [C] the first word of an entry in a dictionary, which is followed by an explanation of its meaning

heal 🔑 /hiːl/ ***verb*** [I,T] ~ **(over/up)** to become healthy again; to make sth healthy again: *The cut will heal up in a few days.* ◇ (*figurative*) *Nothing he said could heal the damage done to their relationship.*

healer /'hiːlə(r)/ ***noun*** [C] a person who cures people of illnesses and disease using natural powers rather than medicine

health ⊶ /helθ/ *noun* [U] (HEALTH) **1** the condition of a person's body or mind: *Fresh fruit and vegetables are good for your health.* ◇ *in good /poor health* ◇ (*figurative*) *the health of your marriage/ finances* **2** the state of being well and free from illness: *As long as you have your health, nothing else matters.* **3** the work of providing medical care: *health and safety regulations*

health

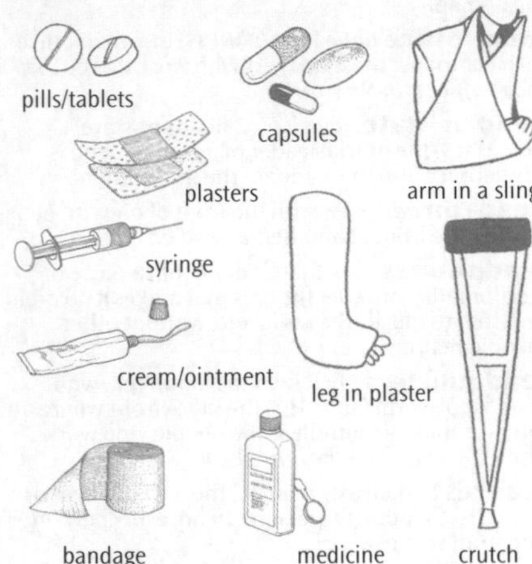

ˈ**health care** *noun* [U] (HEALTH) the service of providing medical care: *the costs of health care for the elderly* ◇ ***health-care workers/professionals***

ˈ**health centre** *noun* [C] (HEALTH) a building where a group of doctors see their patients

ˈ**health club** *noun* [C] (SPORT) a private club where people go to do physical exercise in order to stay or become healthy and fit SYN **gym**

ˈ**health farm** *noun* [C] (*especially BrE*) = HEALTH SPA

ˈ**health food** *noun* [C,U] natural food that many people think is especially good for your health because it has been made or grown without adding chemicals

ˈ**health service** *noun* [C] (HEALTH) the organization of the medical services of a country ➲ look at **the National Health Service**

ˈ**health spa** *noun* [C] (*especially BrE*) (*also* ˈ**health farm**) (HEALTH) a place where people can stay for short periods of time in order to try to improve their health by eating special food, doing physical exercise, etc.

ˈ**health visitor** *noun* [C] (HEALTH) (in Britain) a trained nurse whose job is to visit people in their homes, for example new parents, and give them advice on some areas of medical care

healthy ⊶ /ˈhelθi/ *adj.* (**healthier**; **healthiest**) **1** (HEALTH) not often ill; strong and well: *a healthy child/animal/plant* **2** (HEALTH) showing good health (of body or mind): *healthy skin and hair* **3** (HEALTH) helping to produce good health: *a healthy climate/ diet/lifestyle* **4** normal and sensible: *There was plenty of healthy competition between the brothers.* OPP **unfriendly** ▶ **healthily** *adv.*

heap¹ /hiːp/ *noun* [C] **1 a ~ (of sth)** an untidy pile of sth: *a heap of books/papers* ◇ *All his clothes are* ***in a heap*** *on the floor!* **2** (*informal*) **a ~ (of sth)**; **heaps (of sth)** a large number or amount; plenty: *I've got a heap of work to do.* ◇ *There's heaps of time before the train leaves.*

IDM **heaps better, more, older, etc.** (*informal*) much better, etc.

heap² /hiːp/ *verb* [T] **1 ~ sth (up)** to put things in a pile: *I'm going to heap all the leaves up over there.* ◇ *Add six heaped tablespoons of flour* (= in a recipe). **2 ~ A on/onto B**; **~ B with A** to put a large amount of sth on sth/sb: *He heaped food onto his plate.* ◇ *The press heaped the team with praise.*

hear ⊶ /hɪə(r)/ *verb* (*pt, pp* **heard** /hɜːd/) **1** [I,T] (not used in the continuous tenses) to receive sounds with your ears: *Can you speak a little louder – I can't hear very well.* ◇ *I didn't hear you go out this morning.* ◇ *Did you hear what I said?* **2** [T] (not used in the continuous tenses) to be told or informed about sth: *I hear that you've been offered a job in Canada.* ◇ *'I passed my test!'* ***'So I've heard*** *– well done!'* ◇ *I was sorry to hear about your mum's illness.* **3** [T] (LAW) (used about a judge, a court, etc.) to listen to the evidence in a trial in order to make a decision about it: *Your case will be heard this afternoon.*

IDM **hear! hear!** used for showing that you agree with what sb has just said, especially in a meeting

won't/wouldn't hear of sth to refuse to allow sth: *I wanted to go to art school but my parents wouldn't hear of it.*

PHR V **hear from sb** to receive a letter, telephone call, etc. from sb

hear of sb/sth to know that sb/sth exists because you have heard them or it mentioned: *Have you heard of the Bermuda Triangle?*

hearing ⊶ /ˈhɪərɪŋ/ *noun* **1** [U] the ability to hear: *Her hearing isn't very good so you need to speak louder.* **2** [sing.] (LAW) a time when evidence is given to a judge in a court of law: *a court/disciplinary hearing* **3** [sing.] a chance to give your opinion or explain your position: *to get/give sb a fair hearing*

IDM **hard of hearing** → HARD¹

in/within sb's hearing near enough to sb so that they can hear what is being said

ˈ**hearing aid** *noun* [C] a small device for people who cannot hear well that fits inside the ear and makes sounds louder

hearsay /ˈhɪəseɪ/ *noun* [U] things you have heard another person or other people say, which may or may not be true

hearse /hɜːs/ *noun* [C] a large, black car used for carrying a dead person to their funeral

heart ⊶ /hɑːt/ *noun* **1** [C] (ANATOMY) the organ inside your chest that sends blood round your body: *When you exercise your heart beats faster.* ◇ *heart disease/failure* ➲ picture at **circulation** **2** [C] the centre of a person's feelings and emotions: *She has a kind heart* (= she is kind and gentle). ◇ *They say he died of a broken heart* (= unhappiness caused by sb he loved). **3 -hearted** (used to form compound adjectives) having the type of feelings or character mentioned: *kind-hearted* ◇ *cold-hearted* **4** [sing.] **the ~ (of sth)** the most central or important part of sth; the middle: *Rare plants can be found* ***in the heart of*** *the forest.* ◇ *Let's get straight to* ***the heart of the matter***. **5** [C] a symbol ♡ that is shaped like a heart, often red or pink and used to show love: *He sent her a card with a big red heart on it.* **6 hearts** [pl.] the group (**suit**) of playing cards with red shapes like hearts (5) on them: *the queen of hearts* **7** [C] one of the cards from this suit: *Play a heart, if you've got one.*

IDM **after your own heart** (used about people) similar to yourself or of the type you like best

heart

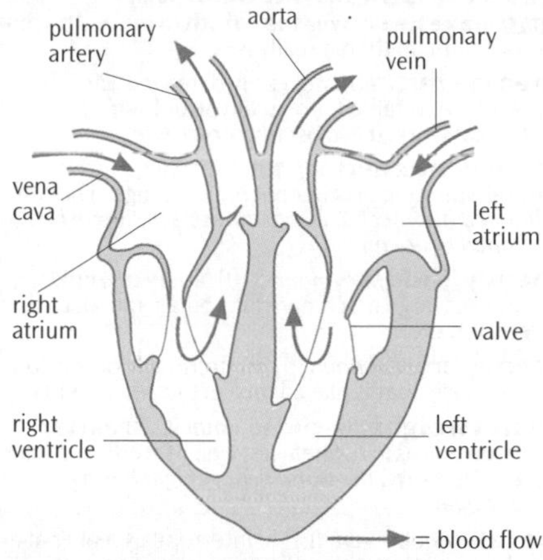

at heart really; in fact: *My father seems strict but he's a very kind man at heart.*
break sb's heart to make sb very sad
by heart by remembering exactly; from memory: *Learning lists of words off by heart isn't a good way to increase your vocabulary.*
a change of heart → CHANGE²
close/dear/near to sb's heart having a lot of importance and interest for sb
cross my heart → CROSS²
from the (bottom of your) heart in a way that is true and sincere: *I mean what I said from the bottom of my heart.*
have a heart of gold to be a very kind person
have/with sb's (best) interests at heart → INTEREST¹
heart and soul with a lot of energy and enthusiasm
your heart is not in sth used to say that you are not very interested in or enthusiastic about sth
in your heart (of hearts) used to say that you know that sth is true although you do not want to admit or believe it: *She knew in her heart of hearts that she was making the wrong decision.*
lose heart → LOSE
not have the heart (to do sth) to be unable to do sth unkind: *I didn't have the heart to say no.*
pour your heart out (to sb) → POUR
sb's heart sinks used to say that sb suddenly feels sad or depressed about sth: *My heart sank when I saw how much work there was left.*
set your heart on sth; have your heart set on sth to decide you want sth very much; to be determined to do or have sth
take heart (from sth) to begin to feel positive and HOPEFUL about sth
take sth to heart to be deeply affected or upset by sth
to your heart's content as much as you want
with all your heart; with your whole heart completely: *I hope with all my heart that things work out for you.*
young at heart → YOUNG¹

heartache /ˈhɑːteɪk/ ***noun*** [U] great sadness or worry

ˈheart attack ***noun*** [C] (**HEALTH**) a sudden serious illness when the heart stops working correctly, sometimes causing death: *She's had a heart attack.*

heartbeat /ˈhɑːtbiːt/ ***noun*** [C] (**BIOLOGY**) the regular movement or sound of the heart as it sends blood round the body

heartbreak /ˈhɑːtbreɪk/ ***noun*** [U] very great sadness

heartbreaking /ˈhɑːtbreɪkɪŋ/ ***adj.*** making you feel very sad

heartbroken /ˈhɑːtbrəʊkən/ (also ˌ**broken-ˈhearted**) ***adj.*** extremely sad because of sth that has happened: *Mary was heartbroken when John left her.*

heartburn /ˈhɑːtbɜːn/ ***noun*** [U] (**HEALTH**) a pain that feels like sth burning in your chest and that you get when your stomach cannot deal with a particular food

hearten /ˈhɑːtn/ ***verb*** [T] (usually passive) to encourage sb; to make sb feel happier **OPP dishearten**

heartening /ˈhɑːtnɪŋ/ ***adj.*** making you feel more HOPEFUL; encouraging **OPP disheartening**

heartfelt /ˈhɑːtfelt/ ***adj.*** deeply felt; sincere: *a heartfelt apology*

hearth /hɑːθ/ ***noun*** [C] (**ARCHITECTURE**) the place where you have an open fire in the house or the area in front of it

heartily /ˈhɑːtɪli/ ***adv.*** **1** with obvious enthusiasm and enjoyment: *He joined in heartily with the singing.* **2** very much; completely

heartland /ˈhɑːtlænd/ ***noun*** [C] the most central or important part of a country, area, etc.: *Germany's industrial heartland*

heartless /ˈhɑːtləs/ ***adj.*** unkind; cruel ▸ **heartlessly** ***adv.*** ▸ **heartlessness** ***noun*** [U]

ˈheart-rending ***adj.*** making you feel very sad

ˌ**heart-to-ˈheart** ***noun*** [C] a conversation in which you say exactly what you really feel or think

hearty /ˈhɑːti/ ***adj.*** **1** showing warm and friendly feelings: *a hearty welcome* **2** loud, happy and full of energy: *a hearty laugh* **3** large; making you feel full: *a hearty appetite* **4** showing that you feel strongly about sth: *He nodded his head in hearty agreement.*

heat¹ 🔑 /hiːt/ ***noun*** **1** [U] the feeling of sth hot: *This fire doesn't **give out** much **heat**.* **2** [sing.] (often with *the*) hot weather: *I like the English climate because I can't stand the heat.* **3** [sing.] a thing that produces heat: *Remove the pan from the heat* (= the hot part of the cooker). **4** [U] a state or time of anger or excitement: ***In the heat of the moment**, she threatened to resign.* **5** [C] (**SPORT**) one of the first parts of a race or competition. The winners of the heats compete against other winners until the final result is decided.
IDM be on heat (**BIOLOGY**) (used about some female animals) to be ready to have sex because it is the right time of the year

heat² 🔑 /hiːt/ ***verb*** [I,T] ~ (sth) (up) to become or to make sth hot or warm: *Wait for the oven to heat up before you put the pie in.* ◇ *The meal is already cooked but it will need heating up.*

heated /ˈhiːtɪd/ ***adj.*** (used about a person or discussion) angry or excited: *a heated argument/debate* ▸ **heatedly** ***adv.***

heater /ˈhiːtə(r)/ ***noun*** [C] a machine used for making water or the air in a room, car, etc. hotter: *an electric/gas heater* ◇ *a water heater*

heath /hiːθ/ ***noun*** [C] (**GEOGRAPHY**) an area of open land that is not used for farming and that is often covered with rough grass and other wild plants

heathen /ˈhiːðn/ ***noun*** [C] (*old-fashioned*) (RELIGION, HISTORY) a person who does not belong to one of the main world religions

heather /ˈheðə(r)/ ***noun*** [U] a low wild plant that grows especially on hills and land that is not farmed and has small purple, pink or white flowers

heating /ˈhiːtɪŋ/ ***noun*** [U] a system for making rooms and buildings warm: *Our heating goes off at 10 p.m. and comes on again in the morning.* ➲ look at **central heating**

heatstroke /ˈhiːtstrəʊk/ ***noun*** [C] (HEALTH) a medical condition that you can get if you are in a hot place for too long

heatwave /ˈhiːtweɪv/ ***noun*** [C] a period of unusually hot weather

heave¹ /hiːv/ ***verb*** **1** [I,T] to lift, pull or throw sb/sth heavy with one big effort: *Take hold of this rope and heave!* ◇ *We heaved the cupboard up the stairs.* **2** [I] ~ **(with sth)** to move up and down or in and out in a heavy but regular way: *His chest was heaving with the effort of carrying the cooker.* **3** [I] to experience the tight feeling you get in your stomach when you are just about to VOMIT: *The sight of all that blood made her stomach heave.*

IDM **heave a sigh** to breathe out slowly and loudly: *He heaved a sigh of relief when he heard the good news.*

heave² /hiːv/ ***noun*** [C,U] a strong pull, push, throw, etc.

heaven /ˈhevn/ ***noun*** **1** [sing.] the place where, in some religions, it is believed that God lives and where good people go when they die: *to go to/be in heaven* ➲ look at **hell** **2** [U, C] a place or a situation in which you are very happy: *It was heaven being away from work for a week.* **3 the heavens** [pl.] (used in poetry and literature) the sky

heavenly /ˈhevnli/ ***adj.*** **1** (only *before* a noun) connected with heaven or the sky: *heavenly bodies* (=the sun, moon, stars, etc.) **2** (*informal*) very pleasant; wonderful

heavily /ˈhevɪli/ ***adv.*** **1** to a great degree; in large amounts: *It was raining heavily.* ◇ *to **drink/smoke** heavily.* ◇ ***heavily armed** police* (=carrying a lot of weapons) ◇ *a **heavily pregnant** woman* (=one whose baby is nearly ready to be born) **2** with a lot of force or effort: *She fell heavily to the ground.* **3** ~ **built** (used about a person) with a large, solid and strong body **4** slowly and loudly: *She was now breathing heavily.* **5** in a slow way that sounds as though you are worried or sad: *He sighed heavily.* **6** in a way that makes you feel uncomfortable or anxious: *The burden of guilt weighed heavily on his mind.* **7** ~ **loaded/laden** full of or loaded with heavy things: *a heavily loaded van*

heavy /ˈhevi/ ***adj.*** (**heavier**; **heaviest**) **1** weighing a lot; difficult to lift or move: *This box is too heavy for me to carry.* **2** used when asking or stating how much sb/sth weighs: ***How heavy** is your suitcase?* **3** larger, stronger or more than usual: ***heavy rain*** ◇ ***heavy traffic*** ◇ *a **heavy smoker/drinker*** (=a person who smokes/drinks a lot) ◇ *The sound of his **heavy*** (=loud and deep) ***breathing** told her that he was asleep.* ◇ *a **heavy sleeper*** (=sb who is difficult to wake) ◇ *a **heavy meal*** **4** serious, difficult or boring: *His latest novel makes **heavy reading**.* ◇ *Things got a bit heavy when she started talking about her failed marriage.* **5** full of hard work; (too) busy: *a heavy day/schedule/timetable* **6** (used about a material or substance) solid or thick: *heavy soil* ◇ *a heavy coat* OPP **light** ▸ **heaviness** ***noun*** [U]

IDM **make heavy weather of sth** to make sth seem more difficult than it really is

ˌheavy-ˈduty ***adj.*** not easily damaged and therefore suitable for regular use or for hard physical work: *a heavy-duty carpet/tyre*

ˌheavy-ˈhanded ***adj.*** **1** not showing much understanding of other people's feelings: *a heavy-handed approach* **2** using unnecessary force: *heavy-handed police methods*

ˌheavy ˈindustry ***noun*** [C,U] (BUSINESS) industry that uses large machinery to produce metal, coal, vehicles, etc.

ˌheavy ˈmetal ***noun*** [U] (MUSIC) a style of very loud rock music that is played on electric instruments

heavyweight /ˈheviweɪt/ ***noun*** [C] (SPORT) a person who is in the heaviest weight group in certain fighting sports: *the world heavyweight boxing champion*

heckle /ˈhekl/ ***verb*** [I,T] to interrupt a speaker at a public meeting with difficult questions or rude comments ▸ **heckler** ***noun*** [C]

hectare /ˈhekteə(r)/ ***noun*** [C] (*abbr.* **ha**) a measurement of land; 10000 square metres

hectic /ˈhektɪk/ ***adj.*** very busy with a lot of things that you have to do quickly ▸ **hectically** /-kli/ ***adv.***

he'd /hiːd/ short for HE HAD; HE WOULD

hedge¹ /hedʒ/ ***noun*** [C] a row of bushes or trees planted close together at the edge of a garden or field to separate one piece of land from another

hedge² /hedʒ/ ***verb*** [I] to avoid giving a direct answer to a question

IDM **hedge your bets** to protect yourself against losing or making a mistake by supporting more than one person or opinion

hedgehog /ˈhedʒhɒg/ ***noun*** [C] a small brown animal covered with SPINES (=sharp parts like needles)

hedgerow /ˈhedʒrəʊ/ ***noun*** [C] a row of bushes, etc. especially at the side of a country road or around a field

heed¹ /hiːd/ ***verb*** [T] (*formal*) to pay attention to advice, a warning, etc.

heed² /hiːd/ ***noun*** (*formal*)

IDM **take heed (of sb/sth)**; **pay heed (to sb/sth)** to pay careful attention to what sb says: *You should take heed of your doctor's advice.*

heel¹ /hiːl/ ***noun*** [C] **1** the back part of your foot ➲ picture on **page 80** **2** the part of a sock, etc. that covers your heel **3** the higher part of a shoe under the heel of your foot: *High heels* (=shoes with high heels) *are not practical for long walks.* **4 -heeled** having the type of heel mentioned: *high-heeled/low-heeled shoes*

IDM **dig your heels in** → DIG¹

head over heels → HEAD¹

heel² /hiːl/ ***verb*** [T] to repair the heel of a shoe

hefty /ˈhefti/ ***adj.*** (*informal*) big and strong or heavy: *a hefty young man*

hegemony /hɪˈdʒeməni; -ˈge-/ ***noun*** [U, C] (*pl.* **hegemonies**) (*formal*) control by one country, organization, etc. over other countries, etc. within a particular group ▸ **hegemonic** /ˌhedʒɪˈmɒnɪk; ˌhegɪ-/ ***adj.***

heifer /ˈhefə(r)/ ***noun*** [C] a young female cow, especially one that has not yet had a baby (**calf**)

height /haɪt/ ***noun*** **1** [C,U] the measurement from the bottom to the top of a person or thing: *The nurse is going to check your height and weight.* ◇ *We need a fence that's about two metres* ***in height.*** ➲ adjective **high** ➲ picture at **dimension** **2** [U] the fact that sb/sth is tall or high: *He looks older than he is because of his height.* **3** [C,U] the distance that sth is above the ground: *We are now flying at a height of 10000 metres.* ⓘ An aeroplane **gains** or **loses** height. When talking about aeroplanes a more formal word for height is **altitude**. **4** [C, usually pl.] a high place or area: *I can't go up there. I'm afraid of heights.* **5** [U] the strongest or most important part of sth: *the height of summer*

heighten /ˈhaɪtn/ ***verb*** [I,T] to become or to make sth greater or stronger

heir /eə(r)/ ***noun*** [C] ~ **(to sth)** (LAW) the person with the legal right to receive (**inherit**) money, property or a title when the owner dies: *He's the heir to a large fortune.*

heirloom /ˈeəluːm/ ***noun*** [C] something valuable that has belonged to the same family for many years

held past tense, past participle of **hold**[1]

helicopter /ˈhelɪkɒptə(r)/ (also *informal* **chopper**) ***noun*** [C] a small aircraft that can go straight up into the air. **Helicopters** have long thin metal parts on top that go round

heliocentric /ˌhiːliəˈsentrɪk/ ***adj.*** (ASTRONOMY) with the sun as the centre: *the heliocentric model of the solar system* ➲ look at **geocentric**

helium /ˈhiːliəm/ ***noun*** [U] (*symbol* **He**) (CHEMISTRY) a very light colourless gas that does not burn, often used to fill BALLOONS (=objects that float in the air) ⓘ **Helium** is a **noble gas**. ⓘ For more information on the periodic table of elements, look at pages R34-5.

helix /ˈhiːlɪks/ ***noun*** [C] (*pl.* **helices** /ˈhiːlɪsiːz/) a shape like a SPIRAL (=a long curved line that moves round and round away from a central point) or a line curved round a CYLINDER or CONE ➲ look at **double helix**

helix

he'll /hiːl/ short for HE WILL

hell ***noun*** /hel/ ***noun*** **1** [sing.] (RELIGION) the place where, in some religions, it is believed that the DEVIL lives and where bad people go to when they die: *to go to/be in hell* ➲ look at **heaven** **2** [C,U] (*informal*) a situation or place that is very unpleasant or painful: *He went through hell when his wife left him.* **3** [U] (*slang*) used as a swear word to show anger: *Oh hell, I've forgotten my money!* **4** **the hell** (*slang*) used as a swear word in questions to show anger or surprise: *Why the hell didn't you tell me this before?*

IDM **a/one hell of a...** (*informal*) used to make an expression stronger or to mean 'very': *He got into a hell of a fight* (=a terrible fight).

all hell broke loose (*informal*) there was suddenly a lot of noise and confusion

(just) for the hell of it (*informal*) for fun

give sb hell (*informal*) to speak to sb very angrily or to be very strict with sb

like hell (*informal*) very much; with a lot of effort: *I'm working like hell at the moment.*

hellish /ˈhelɪʃ/ ***adj.*** terrible; awful: *a hellish experience*

hello (*BrE also* **hallo**) /həˈləʊ/ ***exclamation*** used when you meet sb, for attracting sb's attention or when you are using the telephone

helm /helm/ ***noun*** [C] the part of a boat or ship that is used to guide it. The **helm** can be a handle or a wheel.

IDM **at the helm** in charge of an organization, group of people, etc.

helmet /ˈhelmɪt/ ***noun*** [C] a type of hard hat that you wear to protect your head: *a crash helmet* ➲ picture at **sport**

help[1] /help/ ***verb*** **1** [I,T] ~ **(sb) (with sth)**; ~ **(sb) (to) do sth**; ~ **sb (across, over, out of, into, etc.)** to do sth for sb in order to be useful or to make sth easier for them: *Can I help?* ◇ *Could you help me with the cooking?* ◇ *I helped her to organize the day.* ◇ *My son's helping in our shop at the moment.* ◇ *She helped her grandmother up the stairs* (=supported her as she climbed the stairs). **2** [I,T] to make sth better or easier: *If you apologize to him it might help.* ◇ *This medicine should help your headache.* **3** [T] ~ **yourself (to sth)** to take sth (especially food and drink) that is offered to you: *'Can I borrow your pen?' 'Yes, help yourself.'* **4** [T] ~ **yourself to sth** to take sth without asking permission; to steal **5** [I] (*spoken*) used to get sb's attention when you are in danger or difficulty: *Help! I'm going to fall!*

IDM **can/can't/couldn't help sth** be able/not be able to stop or avoid doing sth: *It was so funny I couldn't help laughing.* ◇ *I just couldn't help myself – I had to laugh.*

a helping hand some help: *My neighbour is always ready to give me a helping hand.*

PHR V **help (sb) out** to help sb in a difficult situation; to give money to help sb

help[2] /help/ ***noun*** **1** [U] ~ **(with sth)** the act of helping: *Do you need any help with that?* ◇ *This map isn't much help.* ◇ *She stopped smoking* ***with the help of*** *her family and friends.* ◇ *'Run and* ***get help*** *– my son's fallen in the river!'* **2** [sing.] **a** ~ **(to sb)** a person or thing that helps: *Your directions were a great help – we found the place easily.*

ˈhelp desk ***noun*** [C] (COMPUTING) a service, usually in a business company, that gives people information and help, especially if they are having problems with a computer

helper /ˈhelpə(r)/ ***noun*** [C] a person who helps (especially with work)

helpful /ˈhelpfl/ ***adj.*** giving help: *helpful advice* ▶ **helpfully** /-fəli/ ***adv.*** ▶ **helpfulness** ***noun*** [U]

helping /ˈhelpɪŋ/ ***noun*** [C] the amount of food that is put on a plate at one time: *After two helpings of pasta, I couldn't eat any more.* ➲ look at **portion**

helpless /ˈhelpləs/ ***adj.*** unable to take care of yourself or do things without the help of other people: *a helpless baby* ▶ **helplessly** ***adv.***: *They watched helplessly as their house went up in flames.* ▶ **helplessness** ***noun*** [U]

helpline /ˈhelplaɪn/ ***noun*** [C] (*BrE*) a telephone service that provides advice and information about particular problems

hem[1] /hem/ ***noun*** [C] the edge at the bottom of a piece of cloth (especially on a skirt, dress or trousers) that has been turned up and sewn

hem[2] /hem/ ***verb*** [T] (**hemming**; **hemmed**) to turn up and sew the bottom of a piece of clothing or cloth

PHR V **hem sb in** to surround sb and prevent them from moving away: *We were hemmed in by the crowd and could not leave.*

hematite (*AmE*) =HAEMATITE

hemisphere /ˈhemɪsfɪə(r)/ ***noun*** [C] **1** (GEOGRAPHY) one half of the earth: *the northern/ southern/eastern/western hemisphere* ➲ picture at **earth** **2** (ANATOMY) either half of the brain: *the left/ right cerebral hemisphere* **3** (GEOMETRY) one half of a SPHERE (=a round solid object)

hemoglobin (*AmE*) =HAEMOGLOBIN

hemophilia, hemophiliac (*AmE*) =HAEMO-PHILIA, HAEMOPHILIAC

hemorrhage (*AmE*) =HAEMORRHAGE

hemorrhoids (*AmE*) =HAEMORRHOIDS

hemp /hemp/ ***noun*** [U] a plant that is used for making rope and rough cloth and for producing an illegal drug (**cannabis**)

hen /hen/ ***noun*** [C] **1** (AGRICULTURE) a female bird that is kept for its eggs or its meat ➲ note at **chicken** **2** the female of any type of bird: *a hen pheasant*

hence AW /hens/ ***adv.*** (*formal*) for this reason: *I've got some news to tell you – hence the letter.*

henceforth /ˌhensˈfɔːθ/ (*also* **henceforward** /ˌhensˈfɔːwəd/) ***adv.*** (*written*) from now on; in future

henchman /ˈhentʃmən/ ***noun*** [C] (*pl.* **-men** /-mən/) a person who is employed by sb to protect them and who may do things that are illegal or violent

hendecagon /henˈdekəgən/ ***noun*** [C] (GEOMETRY) a flat shape with eleven straight sides and eleven angles

henna /ˈhenə/ ***noun*** [U] a reddish-brown colour (**dye**) that is obtained from a type of plant. **Henna** is used to colour and decorate the hair, FINGERNAILS, etc.

ˈ**hen party** (*also* ˈ**hen night**) ***noun*** [sing.] a party that a woman who is getting married soon has with her female friends ➲ look at **stag night**

henpecked /ˈhenpekt/ ***adj.*** used to describe a husband who always does what his wife tells him to do

hepatic /hɪˈpætɪk/ ***adj.*** (ANATOMY) connected with the LIVER (=the large organ in your body that cleans your blood)

heˌpatic ˌportal ˈvein =PORTAL VEIN ➲ picture at **circulation**

hepatitis /ˌhepəˈtaɪtɪs/ ***noun*** [U] (HEALTH) a serious disease of the LIVER (=one of the body's main organs)

hepta- /ˈheptə/ ***prefix*** (used in nouns, adjectives and adverbs) seven; having seven: *heptathlon* (=an athletics competition, usually one for women, that consists of seven different events)

heptagon /ˈheptəgən/ ***noun*** [C] (GEOMETRY) a flat shape with seven straight sides ▶ **heptagonal** /hepˈtægənl/ ***adj.***

her¹ /hɜː(r)/ ***pronoun*** (the object of a verb or preposition) the female person that was mentioned earlier: *He told Sue that he loved her.* ◇ *I've got a letter for your mother. Could you give it to her, please?* ➲ look at **she**

her² /hɜː(r)/ ***det.*** of or belonging to the female person mentioned earlier: *That's her book. She left it there this morning.* ◇ *Fiona has broken her leg.* ➲ look at **hers**

herald /ˈherəld/ ***verb*** [T] (*written*) to be a sign that sth is going to happen soon: *The minister's speech heralded a change of policy.*

heraldry /ˈherəldri/ ***noun*** [U] the study of the history of old and important families and their special family symbols (**coats of arms**)

herb /hɜːb/ ***noun*** [C] a plant whose leaves, seeds, etc. are used in medicine or in cooking: *Add some herbs, such as rosemary and thyme.* ➲ look at **spice**

herbaceous /hɜːˈbeɪʃəs/ ***noun*** [C] (BIOLOGY) connected with plants that have soft STEMS (=long central parts): *a herbaceous plant*

herbal /ˈhɜːbl/ ***adj.*** made of or using HERBS: *herbal medicine/remedies*

herbicide /ˈhɜːbɪsaɪd/ ***noun*** [C,U] (AGRICULTURE) a chemical substance that farmers use to kill plants that are growing where they are not wanted

herbivore /ˈhɜːbɪvɔː(r)/ ***noun*** [C] (BIOLOGY) an animal that only eats grass and plants ➲ look at **carnivore, insectivore, omnivore** ▶ **herbivorous** /hɜːˈbɪvərəs/ ***adj.***: *herbivorous dinosaurs*

herd¹ /hɜːd/ ***noun*** [C] a large number of animals that live and feed together: *a herd of cattle/deer/ elephants* ➲ look at **flock**

herd² /hɜːd/ ***verb*** [T] to move people or animals somewhere together in a group: *The prisoners were herded onto the train.*

herdsman /ˈhɜːdzmən/ (*pl.* **-men** /-mən/) ***noun*** [C] (AGRICULTURE) a man who looks after a group of animals

here¹ /hɪə(r)/ ***adv.*** **1** (after a verb or a preposition) in, at or to the place where you are or which you are pointing to: *Come (over) here.* ◇ *The school is a mile from here.* ◇ *Please sign here.* **2** used at the beginning of a sentence to introduce or draw attention to sb/sth: *Here is the nine o'clock news.* ◇ *Here comes the bus.* ◇ *Here we are* (=we've arrived). **3** (used for emphasizing a noun): *I think you'll find this book here very useful.* **4** at this point in a discussion or a piece of writing: *Here the speaker stopped and looked around the room.*

IDM **here and there** in various places

here goes (*informal*) used to say that you are about to do sth exciting, dangerous, etc.: *I've never done a backward dive before, but here goes!*

here's to sb/sth used for wishing for the health, success, etc. of sb/sth while holding a drink: *Here's to a great holiday!*

neither here nor there not important: *My opinion is neither here nor there. If you like the dress then buy it.*

here² /hɪə(r)/ ***exclamation*** used for attracting sb's attention, when offering help or when giving sth to sb: *Here, let me help!*

hereabouts /ˌhɪərəˈbaʊts/ (*AmE* **hereabout**) ***adv.*** around or near here

hereafter /ˌhɪərˈɑːftə(r)/ ***adv.*** (*written*) (used in legal documents, etc.) from now on

hereditary /həˈredɪtri/ ***adj.*** passed on from parent to child: *a hereditary disease*

heredity /həˈredəti/ ***noun*** [U] the process by which physical or mental qualities pass from parent to child

heresy /ˈherəsi/ ***noun*** [C,U] (*pl.* **heresies**) (RELIGION) a (religious) opinion or belief that is different from what is generally accepted to be true

heretic /ˈherətɪk/ ***noun*** [C] (RELIGION) a person whose religious beliefs are believed to be wrong or evil ▶ **heretical** /həˈretɪkl/ ***adj.***

herewith /ˌhɪəˈwɪð/ ***adv.*** (*formal*) with this letter, etc.: *Please fill in the form enclosed herewith.*

heritage /ˈherɪtɪdʒ/ ***noun*** [C, usually sing.] the traditions, qualities and culture of a country that have existed for a long time and that have great importance for the country

hermaphrodite /hɜːˈmæfrədaɪt/ ***noun*** [C] (**BIOLOGY**) a person, an animal or a flower that has both male and female sexual organs or characteristics

hermit /ˈhɜːmɪt/ ***noun*** [C] a person who prefers to live alone, without contact with other people

hernia /ˈhɜːniə/ (*also* **rupture**) ***noun*** [C,U] (**HEALTH**) the medical condition in which an organ inside the body, for example the stomach, pushes through the wall of muscle which surrounds it

hero ⊶ /ˈhɪərəʊ/ ***noun*** [C] (*pl.* **heroes**) **1** a person who is admired, especially for having done sth difficult or good: *The team were given a **hero's welcome** on their return home.* **2** (**LITERATURE, ARTS AND MEDIA**) the most important male character in a book, play, film, etc.: *The hero of the film is a little boy.* ➲ look at **anti-hero, heroine, villain**

heroic /həˈrəʊɪk/ ***adj.*** (used about people or their actions) having a lot of courage: *a heroic effort* ▸ **heroically** /-kli/ ***adv.***

heroin /ˈherəʊɪn/ ***noun*** [U] (**HEALTH**) a powerful illegal drug that some people take for pleasure and then cannot stop taking

heroine /ˈherəʊɪn/ ***noun*** [C] **1** a woman who is admired, especially for having done sth difficult or good **2** (**LITERATURE, ARTS AND MEDIA**) the most important female character in a book, play, film, etc. ➲ look at **hero**

heroism /ˈherəʊɪzəm/ ***noun*** [U] great courage

heron /ˈherən/ ***noun*** [C] a large bird with a long neck and long legs, that lives near water

herpes /ˈhɜːpiːz/ ***noun*** [U] (**HEALTH**) a disease that is passed from one person to another and that causes painful spots on the skin, especially on the face and sexual organs

herring /ˈherɪŋ/ ***noun*** [C,U] (*pl.* **herring** or **herrings**) a fish that swims in large groups (**shoals**) in cold seas and is used for food

IDM **a red herring** → RED

herringbone /ˈherɪŋbəʊn/ ***noun*** [U] a pattern used in cloth consisting of lines of V shapes that are parallel to each other

hers ⊶ /hɜːz/ ***pronoun*** of or belonging to her: *I didn't have a pen but Helen lent me hers.*

herself ⊶ /hɜːˈself/ ***pronoun*** **1** used when the female who does an action is also affected by it: *She hurt herself quite badly when she fell downstairs.* ◇ *Irene looked at herself in the mirror.* **2** used to emphasize the female who did the action: *She told me the news herself.* ◇ *Has Rosy done this herself?* (=or did sb else do it for her?)

IDM **(all) by herself 1** alone: *She lives by herself.* **2** without help: *I don't think she needs any help – she can change a tyre by herself.*

(all) to herself without having to share: *Julie has the bedroom to herself now her sister's left home.*

hertz /hɜːts/ ***noun*** [C] (*pl.* **hertz**) (*abbr.* **Hz**) (**PHYSICS**) a unit for measuring the FREQUENCY of sound waves

he's short for HE IS, HE HAS

hesitant /ˈhezɪtənt/ ***adj.*** ~ **(to do/about doing sth)** slow to speak or act because you are not sure if you should or not: *I'm very hesitant about criticizing him too much.* ▸ **hesitancy** /-ənsi/ ***noun*** [U] ▸ **hesitantly** ***adv.***

hesitate ⊶ /ˈhezɪteɪt/ ***verb*** [I] **1** ~ **(about/over sth)** to pause before you do sth or before you take a decision, usually because you are uncertain or worried: *He hesitated before going into the room.* ◇ *She's still hesitating about whether to accept the job or not.* **2** ~ **(to do sth)** to not want to do sth because you are not sure that it is right: *Don't hesitate to phone if you have any problems.* ▸ **hesitation** /ˌhezɪˈteɪʃn/ ***noun*** [C,U]: *She agreed without a moment's hesitation.*

hessian /ˈhesiən/ (*AmE usually* **burlap**) ***noun*** [U] a strong rough brown cloth, used especially for making large bags (**sacks**)

hetero- /ˈhetərəʊ/ ***prefix*** (in nouns, adjectives and adverbs) other; different: *heterogeneous* ◇ *heterosexual* ➲ look at **homo-**

heterogeneous /ˌhetərəˈdʒiːniəs/ ***adj.*** (*formal*) consisting of different kinds of people or things ➲ look at **homogeneous**

heterosexual /ˌhetərəˈsekʃuəl/ ***adj.*** sexually attracted to a person of the opposite sex ➲ look at **bisexual, homosexual** ▸ **heterosexual** ***noun*** [C]

heterozygote /ˌhetərəˈzaɪgəʊt; ˌhetərəʊ-/ ***noun*** [C] (**BIOLOGY**) a living thing that has two varying forms of a particular GENE (=one of the units of information that control what a living thing will be like), and whose young may therefore vary in a particular characteristic ▸ **heterozygous** /ˌhetərəˈzaɪgəs/ ***adj.***

het up /ˌhet ˈʌp/ ***adj.*** (*informal*) (not before a noun) ~ **(about/over sth)** worried or excited about sth

hexa- /ˈheksə/ (*also* **hex-**) ***prefix*** (in nouns, adjectives and adverbs) six; having six: *hexagonal*

hexagon /ˈheksəgən/ ***noun*** [C] (**GEOMETRY**) a flat shape with six sides ▸ **hexagonal** /heksˈægənl/ ***adj.***

hey /heɪ/ ***exclamation*** (*informal*) used to attract sb's attention or to show that you are surprised or interested: *Hey, what are you doing?*

IDM **hey presto** people sometimes say 'hey presto' when they have done sth so quickly that it seems like magic

heyday /ˈheɪdeɪ/ ***noun*** [sing.] the period when sb/sth was most powerful, successful, rich, etc.

HGV /ˌeɪtʃ dʒiː ˈviː/ ***abbr.*** (*BrE*) heavy goods vehicle, such as a lorry

hi ⊶ /haɪ/ ***exclamation*** (*informal*) an informal word used when you meet sb you know well; hello

hibernate /ˈhaɪbəneɪt/ ***verb*** [I] (**BIOLOGY**) (used about animals) to spend the winter in a state like deep sleep ▸ **hibernation** /ˌhaɪbəˈneɪʃn/ ***noun*** [U]

hiccup (also **hiccough**) /ˈhɪkʌp/ ***noun*** **1** [C] a sudden, usually repeated sound that is made in the throat and that you cannot control **2 (the) hiccups** [pl.] a series of **hiccups**: *Don't eat so fast or you'll **get hiccups**!* ◇ *If you **have the hiccups**, try holding your breath.* **3** [C] a small problem or difficulty ▸ **hiccup** (also **hiccough**) ***verb*** [I]

hide[1] ⊶ /haɪd/ ***verb*** (*pt* **hid** /hɪd/; *pp* **hidden** /ˈhɪdn/) **1** [T] to put or keep sb/sth in a place where they or it cannot be seen; to cover sth so that it cannot be seen: *Where shall I hide the money?* ◇ *You couldn't see Bill in the photo – he was hidden behind John.* **2** [I] to be or go in a place where you cannot be seen or found: *Quick, run and hide!* ◇ *The child was hiding under the bed.* **3** [T] ~ **sth (from sb)** to keep sth secret, especially your feelings: *She tried to hide her disappointment from them.*

hide² /haɪd/ ***noun*** **1** [C,U] the skin of an animal that will be used for making leather, etc. ➲ picture at **pachyderm** **2** [C] a place from which people can watch wild animals, birds, etc. without being seen

ˌhide-and-ˈseek ***noun*** [U] a children's game in which one person hides and the others try to find them

hideous /ˈhɪdiəs/ ***adj.*** very ugly or unpleasant: *a hideous sight ◇ a hideous crime* ▶ **hideously** ***adv.***

hiding /ˈhaɪdɪŋ/ ***noun*** **1** [U] the state of being hidden: *The escaped prisoners are believed to be* ***in hiding*** *somewhere in London. ◇ to go into hiding* **2** [C, usually sing.] (*informal*) a punishment involving being hit hard many times: *You deserve a good hiding for what you've done.*

hierarchy AW /ˈhaɪərɑːki/ ***noun*** [C] (*pl.* **hierarchies**) a system or organization that has many levels from the lowest to the highest ▶ **hierarchical** AW /ˌhaɪəˈrɑːkɪkl/ ***adj.***

hieroglyph /ˈhaɪərəglɪf/ ***noun*** [C] (LANGUAGE) a picture or symbol of an object, representing a word, syllable or sound, especially as used in ancient Egyptian and other writing systems ▶ **hieroglyphic** /ˌhaɪərəˈglɪfɪk/ ***noun*** [C], ***adj.***: *pages filled with illegible hieroglyphics*

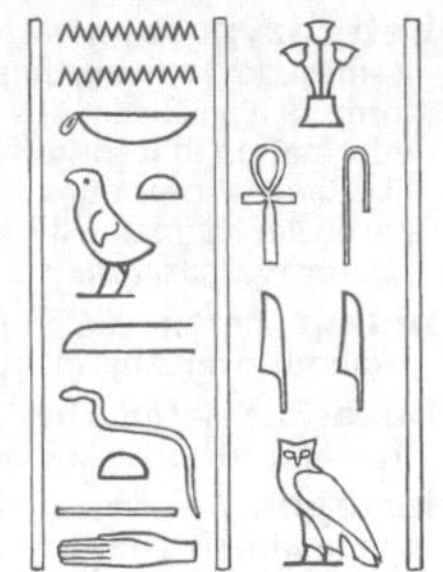
hieroglyphics

hieroglyphics /ˌhaɪərəˈglɪfɪks/ ***noun*** [pl.] (LANGUAGE) the system of writing that was used in ancient Egypt in which a small picture represents a word or sound

hi-fi /ˈhaɪ faɪ/ ***noun*** [C] equipment for playing recorded music that produces high quality sound ▶ **hi-fi** ***adj.***: *a hi-fi system*

higgledy-piggledy /ˌhɪgldi ˈpɪgldi/ ***adv.***, ***adj.*** (*informal*) not in any order; mixed up together

high¹ ⊶ /haɪ/ ***adj.*** **1** (used about things) having a large distance between the bottom and the top: *high cliffs ◇ What's the highest mountain in the world? ◇ high heels* (=on shoes) *◇ The garden wall was so high that we couldn't see over it.* OPP **low** ➲ noun **height** **2** having a particular height: *The hedge is one metre high. ◇ knee-high boots* **3** at a level which is a long way from the ground, or from sea level: *a high shelf ◇ The castle was built on high ground.* OPP **low** **4** above the usual or normal level or amount: *high prices ◇ at high speed ◇ a high level of unemployment ◇ He's got a high temperature. ◇ Oranges are high in vitamin C.* OPP **low** **5** better than what is usual: *high-quality goods ◇ Her work is of a very high standard. ◇ He has a high opinion of you.* OPP **low** **6** having an important position: *Sam only joined the company three years ago, but she's already quite high up.* **7** morally good: *high ideals* **8** (used about a sound or voice) not deep or low: *Dogs can hear very high sounds. ◇ Women usually have higher voices than men.* OPP **low** **9** (*informal*) ~ **(on sth)** under the influence of drugs, alcohol, etc. **10** (used about a gear in a car) that allows a faster speed OPP **low**

IDM **be left high and dry** to be left without help in a difficult situation

high² ⊶ /haɪ/ ***adv.*** **1** at or to a high position or level: *The sun was high in the sky. ◇ I can't jump any higher. ◇ The plane flew high overhead.* ➲ noun **height** **2** (used about a sound) at a high level: *How high can you sing?* OPP **low**

IDM **high and low** everywhere: *We've searched high and low for the keys.*

run high (used about the feelings of a group of people) to be especially strong: *Emotions are running high in the neighbourhood where the murders took place.*

high³ /haɪ/ ***noun*** [C] **1** a high level or point: *Profits reached an all-time high last year.* **2** an area of high air pressure **3** (*informal*) a feeling of great pleasure or happiness that sb gets from doing sth exciting or being successful: *He was* ***on a high*** *after passing all his exams. ◇ She talked about the* ***highs and lows*** *of her career.* **4** (*informal*) a feeling of great pleasure or happiness that may be caused by a drug, alcohol, etc. OPP **low**

IDM **on high** (*formal*) (in) a high place, the sky or heaven: *The order came from on high.*

highbrow /ˈhaɪbraʊ/ ***adj.*** interested in or concerned with matters that many people would find too serious to be interesting: *highbrow newspapers/television programmes*

ˈhigh-class ***adj.*** of especially good quality: *a high-class restaurant*

ˌHigh Comˈmissioner ***noun*** [C] **1** a person who is sent by one Commonwealth country to live in another, to protect the interests of their own country **2** a person who is head of an important international project: *the United Nations High Commissioner for Refugees*

ˌHigh ˈCourt ***noun*** [C] =SUPREME COURT

ˌhigher eduˈcation ***noun*** [U] (EDUCATION) education and training at a college or university, especially to degree level ➲ look at **further education**

ˌhighest common ˈfactor ***noun*** [C] (*abbr.* **HCF**) (MATHEMATICS) the highest number that can be divided exactly into two or more numbers

ˈhigh jump ***noun*** [sing.] (SPORT) the sport in which people try to jump over a bar in order to find out who can jump the highest ➲ look at **long jump**

highland /ˈhaɪlənd/ ***adj.*** (GEOGRAPHY) **1** in or connected with an area of land that has mountains: *highland streams* ➲ look at **lowland** **2 Highland** connected with the HIGHLANDS (=the high mountain region of Scotland)

highlander /ˈhaɪləndə(r)/ ***noun*** [C] (SOCIAL STUDIES) **1** a person who comes from an area where there are a lot of mountains ➲ look at **lowlander** **2 Highlander** a person who comes from the Scottish Highlands

ˌhigh-ˈlevel ***adj.*** **1** involving important people: *high-level talks* **2** (COMPUTING) (of a computer language) similar to an existing language such as English, making it fairly simple to use OPP **low-level**

highlight¹ ⊶ AW /ˈhaɪlaɪt/ ***verb*** [T] **1** to emphasize sth so that people give it special attention: *The report highlighted the need for improved safety at football grounds.* **2** to mark part of a text with a different colour, etc. so that people give it more attention **3** to make some parts of a person's hair a lighter colour: *Have you had your hair highlighted?*

highlight² ⊶ AW /ˈhaɪlaɪt/ ***noun*** **1** [C] the best or most interesting part of sth: *The highlights of the match will be shown on TV tonight.* **2 highlights**

[pl.] areas of lighter colour that are put in a person's hair

highlighter /'haɪlaɪtə(r)/ (*also* **'highlighter pen**) ***noun*** [C] a special pen used for marking words in a text in a bright colour

highly ⊶ /'haɪli/ ***adv.*** **1** to a high degree; very: *highly trained/educated/developed* ◇ *a highly paid job* ◇ *It's highly unlikely that anyone will complain.* **2** with admiration: *I think very highly of your work.*

ˌhighly 'strung ***adj.*** nervous and easily upset

Highness /'haməs/ ***noun*** [C] **your/his/her Highness** a title used when speaking about or to a member of a royal family

high-pitched

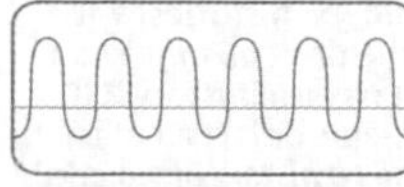
high-pitched sound

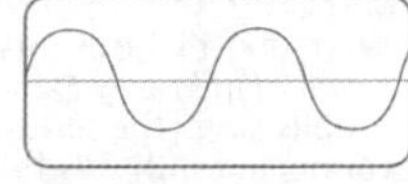
low-pitched sound

ˌhigh-'pitched ***adj.*** (used about sounds) very high: *a high-pitched voice/whistle* OPP **low-pitched**

ˌhigh-'powered ***adj.*** **1** (used about things) having great power: *a high-powered engine* **2** (used about people) important and successful: *high-powered executives*

'high-rise ***adj.*** (only *before* a noun) (used about a building) very tall and having a lot of floors

'high school ***noun*** [C,U] (EDUCATION) **1** (in the US and some other countries) a school for young people between the ages of 14 and 18 **2** often used in Britain in the names of schools for young people between the ages of 11 and 18: *Edgbaston High School* ➲ look at **secondary school**

ˌhigh 'season ***noun*** [C] (*especially BrE*) (TOURISM) the time of year when a hotel or tourist area receives most visitors ➲ look at **low season**

'high street ***noun*** [C] (*BrE*) (often used in names) the main street of a town: *The Post Office is in the High Street.*

high-tech (also **hi-tech**) /ˌhaɪ 'tek/ ***adj.*** **1** using the most modern methods and machines, especially electronic ones: *high-tech industries/hospitals* **2** very modern in appearance; using modern materials: *a high-tech table made of glass and steel* ➲ look at **low-tech**

ˌhigh 'tide ***noun*** [U] (GEOGRAPHY) the time when the sea comes furthest onto the land OPP **low tide**

highway ⊶ /'haɪweɪ/ ***noun*** [C] (*especially AmE*) a main road (between towns)

hijack /'haɪdʒæk/ ***verb*** [T] **1** to take control of a plane, etc. by force, usually for political reasons: *The plane was hijacked on its flight to Sydney.* ➲ look at **kidnap** **2** to take control of a meeting, an event, etc. in order to force people to pay attention to sth: *The peace rally was hijacked by right-wing extremists.* ▸ **hijack** ***noun*** [C]: *The hijack was ended by armed police.* ▸ **hijacker** ***noun*** [C] ▸ **hijacking** ***noun*** [C,U]

hike /haɪk/ ***noun*** [C] a long walk in the country: *We went on a ten-mile hike at the weekend.* ▸ **hike** ***verb*** [I] ▸ **hiker** ***noun*** [C]

hilarious /hɪ'leəriəs/ ***adj.*** extremely funny ▸ **hilariously** ***adv.***

hilarity /hɪ'lærəti/ ***noun*** [U] great AMUSEMENT or loud LAUGHTER

hill ⊶ /hɪl/ ***noun*** [C] (GEOGRAPHY) a high area of land that is not as high as a mountain: *There was a wonderful view from the top of the hill.* ➲ look at **downhill**, **uphill**

hillock /'hɪlək/ ***noun*** [C] (GEOGRAPHY) a small hill

hillside /'hɪlsaɪd/ ***noun*** [C] (GEOGRAPHY) the side of a hill

hilltop /'hɪltɒp/ ***noun*** [C] (GEOGRAPHY) the top of a hill

hilly /'hɪli/ ***adj.*** (GEOGRAPHY) having a lot of hills: *The country's very hilly around here.*

hilt /hɪlt/ ***noun*** [C] the handle of a knife or SWORD ➲ picture at **weapon**

IDM **to the hilt** to a high degree; completely: *I'll defend you to the hilt.*

him ⊶ /hɪm/ ***pronoun*** (the object of a verb or preposition) the male person who was mentioned earlier: *Helen told Ian that she loved him.* ◇ *I've got a letter for your father – can you give it to him, please?*

himself ⊶ /hɪm'self/ ***pronoun*** **1** used when the male who does an action is also affected by it: *He cut himself when he was shaving.* ◇ *John looked at himself in the mirror.* **2** used to emphasize the male who did the action: *He told me the news himself.* ◇ *Did he write this himself?* (= or did sb else do it for him?)

IDM **(all) by himself** **1** alone: *He lives by himself.* **2** without help: *He should be able to cook a meal by himself.*

(all) to himself without having to share: *Charlie has the bedroom to himself now his brother's left home.*

hind /haɪnd/ ***adj.*** (used about an animal's legs, etc.) at the back

hinder /'hɪndə(r)/ ***verb*** [T] to make it more difficult for sb/sth to do sth: *A lot of scientific work is hindered by lack of money.*

Hindi /'hɪndi/ ***noun*** [U] (LANGUAGE) one of the official languages of India, spoken especially in North India ▸ **Hindi** ***adj.***

hindquarters /ˌhaɪnd'kwɔːtəz/ ***noun*** [pl.] the back part of an animal that has four legs, including its two back legs

hindrance /'hɪndrəns/ ***noun*** [C] a person or thing that makes it difficult for you to do sth

hindsight /'haɪndsaɪt/ ***noun*** [U] the understanding that you have of a situation only after it has happened: ***With hindsight****, I wouldn't have lent him the money.* ➲ look at **foresight**

Hindu /'hɪnduː; ˌhɪn'duː/ ***noun*** [C] (RELIGION) a person whose religion is Hinduism ▸ **Hindu** ***adj.***: *Hindu beliefs*

Hinduism /'hɪnduːɪzəm/ ***noun*** [U] (RELIGION) the main religion of India. Hindus believe in many gods and that, after death, people will return to life in a different form.

hinge[1] /hɪndʒ/ ***noun*** [C] a piece of metal that joins two sides of a box, door, etc. together and allows it to be opened or closed

hinge

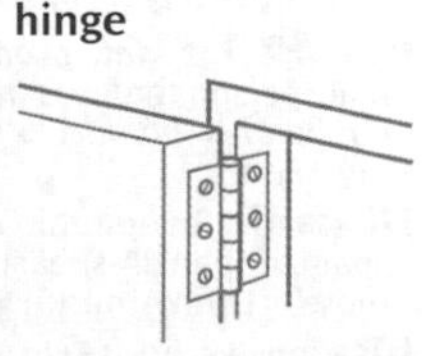

hinge[2] /hɪndʒ/ ***verb***

PHRV **hinge on sth** to depend on sth: *The future of the project hinges on the meeting today.*

hint[1] /hɪnt/ ***noun*** [C] **1** something that you suggest in an indirect way: *If you keep mentioning parties, maybe they'll **take the hint** and invite you.* **2** sth that suggests what will happen in the future: *The first half of the match **gave** no **hint** of the excitement to come.* **3** a small amount of sth: *There was a hint of sadness in his voice.* **4** a piece of advice or information: *helpful hints*

hint[2] /hɪnt/ ***verb*** [I,T] ~ **(at sth)**; ~ **that...** to suggest sth in an indirect way: *They only hinted at their great disappointment.* ◇ *He hinted that he might be moving to Greece.*

hinterland /ˈhɪntəlænd/ ***noun*** [C, usually sing.] (GEOGRAPHY) the areas of a country that are away from the coast, from the banks of a large river or from the main cities: *the rural/agricultural hinterland*

hip[1] 🔑 /hɪp/ ***noun*** [C] the part of the side of your body above your legs and below your waist: *He stood there angrily with his hands on his hips.* ◇ *the hip bone* ➲ picture on **page 80**

hip[2] 🔑 /hɪp/ ***exclamation***

IDM **hip, hip, hurray/hurrah** shouted three times when a group wants to show that it is pleased with sb or with sth that has happened

ˈ**hip hop** ***noun*** [U] (MUSIC) a type of dance music with spoken words and a steady beat played on electronic instruments

hippie (also **hippy**) /ˈhɪpi/ ***noun*** [C] (*pl.* **hippies**) a person who rejects the usual values and way of life of western society. Especially in the 1960s, **hippies** showed that they were different by wearing colourful clothes, having long hair and taking drugs.

the Hippocratic oath /ˌhɪpəkrætɪk ˈəʊθ/ ***noun*** [sing.] (HEALTH) the promise that doctors make to keep to the principles of the medical profession

hippopotamus /ˌhɪpəˈpɒtəməs/ ***noun*** [C] (*pl.* **hippopotamuses** /-sɪz/ or **hippopotami** /-maɪ/) (also *informal* **hippo** /ˈhɪpəʊ/) a large African animal with a large head and short legs that lives in or near rivers ➲ picture at **pachyderm**

hire[1] 🔑 /ˈhaɪə(r)/ ***verb*** [T] **1** (*AmE* **rent**) ~ **sth (from sb)** to have the use of sth for a short time by paying for it **2** to give sb a job for a short time: *We'll have to hire somebody to mend the roof.* ❶ In American English **hire** is also used for talking about permanent jobs: *We just hired a new secretary.* **3** (*AmE* **rent**) ~ **sth (out) (to sb)** to allow sb to use sth for a short fixed period in exchange for money: *We hire (out) our vans by the day.*

hire[2] 🔑 /ˈhaɪə(r)/ ***noun*** [U] the act of paying to use sth for a short time: *Car hire is expensive in this country.* ◇ *Do you have bicycles **for hire**?*

ˌ**hire ˈpurchase** ***noun*** [U] (*BrE*) (*abbr.* **HP**) (FINANCE) a way of buying goods. You do not pay the full price immediately, but pay by INSTALMENTS (=regular small payments) until the full amount is paid: *We're buying the video on hire purchase.*

his 🔑 /hɪz/ ***det.***, ***pronoun*** of or belonging to the male person that was mentioned earlier: *Matthew has hurt his shoulder.* ◇ *This is my book so that one must be his.*

Hispanic /hɪˈspænɪk/ ***adj.*** of or connected with Spain or Spanish-speaking countries, especially those of Latin America ▸ **Hispanic** ***noun*** [C]

hiss /hɪs/ ***verb*** **1** [I,T] to make a sound like a very long 's' to show that you are angry or do not like sth: *The cat hissed at me.* ◇ *The speech was hissed and booed.* **2** [T] to say sth in an angry **hissing** voice: *'Stay away from me!' she hissed.* ▸ **hiss** ***noun*** [C]

histamine /ˈhɪstəmiːn/ ***noun*** [U] (BIOLOGY) a chemical substance that is produced by the body if you are injured or have a bad reaction to sth that you touch, eat or breathe ➲ look at **antihistamine**

historian /hɪˈstɔːriən/ ***noun*** [C] (HISTORY) a person who studies or who is an expert in history

historic /hɪˈstɒrɪk/ ***adj.*** (HISTORY) famous or important in history: *The ending of apartheid was a historic event.*

historical 🔑 /hɪˈstɒrɪkl/ ***adj.*** (HISTORY) that really lived or happened; connected with real people or events in the past: *historical events/records* ◇ *This house has great historical interest.* ▸ **historically** /-kli/ ***adv.***

history 🔑 /ˈhɪstri/ ***noun*** (*pl.* **histories**) **1** [U] (HISTORY) all the events of the past: *an important moment in history* ➲ look at **natural history** **2** [C, usually sing.] the series of events or facts that is connected with sb/sth: *He has a history of violence.* ◇ *a patient's medical history* **3** [U] (HISTORY) the study of past events: *She has a degree in history.* ◇ *History was my favourite subject at school.* **4** [C] (HISTORY) a written description of past events: *a new history of Europe*

IDM **go down in/make history** to be or do sth so important that it will be recorded in history

the rest is history used when you are telling a story to say that you are not going to tell the end of the story, because everyone knows it already

hit[1] 🔑 /hɪt/ ***verb*** [T] (*pres. part.* **hitting**; *pt, pp* **hit**) **1** to make sudden, violent contact with sb/sth: *The bus left the road and hit a tree.* ◇ *to hit somebody in the eye/across the face/on the nose* **2** ~ **sth (on/against sth)** to knock a part of your body, etc. against sth: *Peter hit his head on the low beam.* **3** to have a bad or unpleasant effect on sb/sth: *Inner city areas have been badly hit by unemployment.* ◇ *Her father's death has hit her very hard.* **4** to experience sth unpleasant or difficult: *Things were going really well until we hit this problem.* **5** to reach a place or a level: *If you follow this road you should hit the motorway in about ten minutes.* ◇ *The price of oil hit a new high yesterday.* **6** to suddenly come into sb's mind; to make sb realize or understand sth: *I thought I recognized the man's face and then it hit me – he was my old maths teacher!*

IDM **hit it off (with sb)** (*informal*) to like sb when you first meet them: *When I first met Tony's parents, we didn't really hit it off.*

hit the nail on the head to say sth that is exactly right

hit the jackpot to win a lot of money or have a big success

hit the roof (*informal*) to become very angry

PHR V **hit back (at sb/sth)** to attack (with words) sb who has attacked you

hit on sth to suddenly find sth by chance: *I finally hit on a solution to the problem.*

hit out (at sb/sth) to attack sb/sth: *The man hit out at the policeman.*

hit[2] 🔑 /hɪt/ ***noun*** [C] **1** the act of hitting sth: *The ship took a **direct hit** and sank.* ◇ *She gave her brother a hard hit on the head.* ➲ look at **miss** **2** a person or thing that is very popular or successful: *The record was a big hit.* **3** (COMPUTING) a result of a search on a computer, especially on the Internet

IDM **make a hit (with sb)** (*informal*) to make a good impression on sb

ˌ**hit-and-ˈmiss** (*also* ˌ**hit-or-ˈmiss**) ***adj.*** not done in a careful or planned way and therefore not likely to be successful

ˌhit-and-ˈrun *adj.* (used about a road accident) caused by a driver who does not stop to help

hitch[1] /hɪtʃ/ *verb* **1** [I,T] (*informal*) to travel by waiting by the side of a road and holding out your hand or a sign until a driver stops and takes you in the direction you want to go: *I managed to hitch to Paris in just six hours.* ◇ *We missed the bus so we had to* ***hitch a lift***. ➲ look at **hitchhike** **2** [T] to fasten sth to sth else: *to hitch a trailer to the back of a car*

hitch[2] /hɪtʃ/ *noun* [C] a small problem or difficulty: *a technical hitch*

hitchhike /ˈhɪtʃhaɪk/ (also *informal* **hitch**) *verb* [I] to travel by waiting by the side of a road and holding out your hand or a sign until a driver stops and takes you in the direction you want to go: *He hitchhiked across Europe.* ▶ **hitchhiker** *noun* [C]

hi-tech /ˌhaɪ ˈtek/ *adj.* =HIGH-TECH

hitherto /ˌhɪðəˈtuː/ *adv.* (*formal*) until now

HIV /ˌeɪtʃ aɪ ˈviː/ *abbr.* (HEALTH) human immunodeficiency virus; the VIRUS that is believed to cause the illness AIDS

hive /haɪv/ =BEEHIVE

hiya /ˈhaɪjə/ *exclamation* (*informal*) an informal word used when you meet sb you know well; hello

HM *abbr.* His/Her Majesty's: *HMS* (=Her Majesty's Ship) *Invincible*

hm *exclamation* used when you are not sure or when you are thinking about sth

hoard[1] /hɔːd/ *noun* [C] a store (often secret) of money, food, etc.

hoard[2] /hɔːd/ *verb* [I,T] ~ **(sth) (up)** to collect and store large quantities of sth (often secretly)

hoarding /ˈhɔːdɪŋ/ (*BrE*) =BILLBOARD

hoarse /hɔːs/ *adj.* (used about a person or their voice) sounding rough and quiet, especially because of a sore throat: *a hoarse whisper* ▶ **hoarsely** *adv.*

hoax /həʊks/ *noun* [C] a trick to make people believe sth that is not true, especially sth unpleasant: *The fire brigade answered the call, but found that it was a hoax.*

hob /hɒb/ *noun* [C] (*BrE*) the surface on the top of a cooker that is used for boiling, frying, etc.

hobble /ˈhɒbl/ *verb* [I] to walk with difficulty because your feet or legs are hurt: *He hobbled home on his twisted ankle.*

hobby ⊶ /ˈhɒbi/ *noun* [C] (*pl.* **hobbies**) something that you do regularly for pleasure in your free time: *Barry's hobbies are stamp collecting and surfing the net.* SYN **pastime**

hockey /ˈhɒki/ *noun* [U] **1** (SPORT) a game that is played on a field (**pitch**) by two teams of eleven players who try to hit a small hard ball into a goal with a curved wooden stick (**hockey stick**) ❶ In the US hockey is usually called **field hockey** to show that it is not **ice hockey**. ➲ picture at **sport** **2** (*AmE*) =ICE HOCKEY

hoe /həʊ/ *noun* [C] a garden tool with a long handle that is used for turning the soil and for removing plants that you do not want ➲ picture at **agriculture**

hog[1] /hɒg/ *noun* [C] a male pig that is kept for its meat

IDM **go the whole hog** (*informal*) to do sth as completely as possible

hog[2] /hɒg/ *verb* [T] (**hogging**; **hogged**) (*informal*) to take or keep too much or all of sth for yourself: *The red car was hogging the middle of the road so no one could overtake.*

Hogmanay /ˈhɒgməneɪ/ *noun* [C] the Scottish name for New Year's Eve (31 December) and the celebrations that take place then

hoist /hɔɪst/ *verb* [T] to lift or pull sth up, often by using ropes, etc.: *to hoist a flag/sail*

hold[1] ⊶ /həʊld/ *verb* (*pt, pp* **held** /held/) **1** [T] to take sb/sth and keep them or it in your hand, etc.: *He held a gun in his hand.* ◇ *The woman was holding a baby in her arms.* ◇ *Hold my hand. This is a busy road.* **2** [T] to keep sth in a certain position: *Hold your head up straight.* ◇ *Hold the camera still or you'll spoil the picture.* ◇ *These two screws hold the shelf in place.* **3** [T] to take the weight of sb/sth: *Are you sure that branch is strong enough to hold you?* **4** [T] to organize an event; to have a meeting, an election, a concert, etc.: *They're holding a party for his fortieth birthday.* ◇ *The Olympic Games are held every four years.* **5** [I] to stay the same: *I hope this weather holds till the weekend.* ◇ *What I said still holds – nothing has changed.* **6** [T] to contain or have space for a particular amount: *The car holds five people.* ◇ *How much does this bottle hold?* **7** [T] to keep a person in a position or place by force: *The terrorists are* ***holding*** *three men* ***hostage***. ◇ *A man is being held at the police station.* **8** [T] to have sth, usually in an official way: *Does she* ***hold a*** *British* ***passport***? ◇ *She holds the world record in the 100 metres.* **9** [T] to have an opinion, etc.: *They* ***hold the view that*** *we shouldn't spend any more money.* **10** [T] to believe that sth is true about a person: *I* ***hold*** *the parents* ***responsible*** *for the child's behaviour.* **11** [I,T] (used when you are telephoning) to wait until the person you are calling is ready: *I'm afraid his phone is engaged. Will you* ***hold the line***? **12** [T] to have a conversation: *It's impossible to* ***hold a conversation*** *with all this noise.*

IDM **Hold it!** (*spoken*) Stop! Don't move!

PHR V **hold sth against sb** to not forgive sb because of sth they have done

hold sb/sth back **1** to prevent sb from making progress **2** to prevent sb/sth from moving forward

hold sth back **1** to refuse to give some of the information that you have **2** to control an emotion and stop yourself from showing what you really feel

hold off (sth/doing sth) to delay sth

hold on **1** to wait or stop for a moment: *Hold on. I'll be with you in a minute.* **2** to manage in a difficult or dangerous situation: *They managed to hold on until a rescue party arrived.*

hold onto sb/sth to hold sb/sth tightly: *The child held on to his mother; he didn't want her to go.*

hold onto sth to keep sth; to not give or sell sth: *They've offered me a lot of money for this painting, but I'm going to hold onto it.*

hold out to last (in a difficult situation): *How long will our supply of water hold out?*

hold sth out to offer sth by moving it towards sb in your hand: *He held out a carrot to the horse.*

hold out for sth (*informal*) to cause a delay while you continue to ask for sth: *Union members are holding out for a better pay offer.*

hold sb/sth up to make sb/sth late; to cause a delay: *We were held up by the traffic.*

hold up sth to rob a bank, shop, vehicle, etc. using a gun

hold[2] ⊶ /həʊld/ *noun* **1** [C] the act or manner of having sb/sth in your hand(s): *to have a firm hold on the rope* ◇ *judo/wrestling holds* **2** [sing.] a ~ **(on/over sb/sth)** influence or control: *The new government has strengthened its hold on the country.* **3** [C] the part of a ship or an aircraft where CARGO is carried ➲ picture at **plane**

IDM catch, get, grab, take, etc. hold (of sb/sth) **1** to take sb/sth in your hands: *I managed to catch hold of the dog before it ran out into the road.* **2** to take control of sb/sth; to start to have an effect on sb/sth: *Mass hysteria seemed to have taken hold of the crowd.*
get hold of sb to find sb or make contact with sb: *I've been trying to get hold of the complaints department all morning.*
get hold of sth to find sth that will be useful: *I must try and get hold of a good second-hand bicycle.*

holdall /ˈhəʊldɔːl/ ***noun*** [C] a large bag that is used for carrying clothes, etc. when you are travelling ➲ picture at **luggage**

holder /ˈhəʊldə(r)/ ***noun*** [C] (often in compound nouns) **1** a person who has or holds sth: *a season ticket holder* ◇ *the world record holder in the 100 metres* ◇ *holders of European passports* **2** something that contains or holds sth: *a toothbrush holder*

holding /ˈhəʊldɪŋ/ ***noun*** [C] **1** ~ **(in sth)** (BUSINESS) a number of shares that sb has in a company: *She has a 40% holding in the company.* **2** an amount of property that is owned by a person, museum, library, etc.: *one of the most important private holdings of Indian art* **3** (AGRICULTURE) a piece of land that is rented by sb and used for farming ➲ look at **smallholding**

ˈ**holding company** ***noun*** [C] (BUSINESS) a company that is formed to buy shares in other companies which it then controls

ˈ**hold-up** ***noun*** [C] **1** a delay: *'What's the hold-up?' 'There's been an accident ahead of us.'* **2** (LAW) the act of robbing a bank, etc. using a gun: *The gang have carried out three hold-ups of high street banks.*

hole 🔑 /həʊl/ ***noun*** **1** [C] an opening; an empty space in sth solid: *The pavement is full of holes.* ◇ *There are holes in my socks.* ◇ *I've got a hole in my tooth.* **2** [C] the place where an animal lives in the ground or in a tree: *a mouse hole* **3** [C] (SPORT) (in GOLF) the hole in the ground that you must hit the ball into. Each section of a GOLF COURSE (=the land where you play) is also called a hole: *an eighteen-hole golf course* **4** [sing.] (*informal*) a small dark and unpleasant room, flat, etc.: *This place is a hole – you can't live here!*

holiday 🔑 /ˈhɒlədeɪ/ ***noun*** **1** (*AmE* **vacation**) [C,U] a period of rest from work or school (often when you go and stay away from home): *We're going to Italy* ***for our*** *summer* ***holidays*** *this year.* ◇ *How much holiday do you get a year in your new job?* ◇ *Mr Philips isn't here this week. He's away* ***on holiday.*** ◇ *I'm going to* ***take a*** *week's* ***holiday*** *in May and spend it at home.* ◇ *the school/Christmas/Easter/summer holidays* **2** [C] a day of rest when people do not go to work, school, etc. often for religious or national celebrations: *Next Monday is a holiday.* ◇ *New Year's Day is a* ***bank/public holiday*** *in Britain.*

ˈ**holiday camp** ***noun*** [C] (*BrE*) (TOURISM) a place that provides a place to stay and organized entertainment for people on holiday

holidaymaker /ˈhɒlədeɪmeɪkə(r); -dimeɪ-/ ***noun*** [C] (*BrE*) (TOURISM) a person who is away from home on holiday

holistic /həʊˈlɪstɪk; hɒˈl-/ ***adj.*** **1** (*informal*) considering a whole thing or being to be more than a collection of parts: *a holistic approach to life* **2** (HEALTH) treating the whole person rather than just the SYMPTOMS (=effects) of a disease: *holistic medicine* ▸ **holistically** /-kli/ ***adv.***

hollow[1] 🔑 /ˈhɒləʊ/ ***adj.*** **1** with a hole or empty space inside: *a hollow tree* **2** (used about parts of the face) sinking deep into the face: *hollow cheeks* ◇ *hollow-eyed* **3** not sincere: *a hollow laugh/voice* ◇ *hollow promises/threats* **4** (used about a sound) seeming to come from a hollow place: *hollow footsteps*

hollow[2] /ˈhɒləʊ/ ***verb***
PHR V hollow sth out to take out the inside part of sth

hollow[3] /ˈhɒləʊ/ ***noun*** [C] (GEOGRAPHY) an area that is lower than the land around it

holly /ˈhɒli/ ***noun*** [U] a plant that has shiny dark green leaves with sharp points and red BERRIES in the winter. It is often used as a Christmas decoration.

holmium /ˈhəʊlmiəm/ ***noun*** [U] (*symbol* **Ho**) (CHEMISTRY) a chemical element. **Holmium** is a soft silver-white metal. ❶ For more information on the periodic table of elements, look at pages R34-5.

holocaust /ˈhɒləkɔːst/ ***noun*** [C] a situation where a great many things are destroyed and a great many people die: *a nuclear holocaust*

hologram /ˈhɒləgræm/ ***noun*** [C] an image or picture which appears to stand out from the flat surface it is on when light falls on it

holster /ˈhəʊlstə(r)/ ***noun*** [C] a leather case for a gun that is fixed to a belt or worn under the arm

holy 🔑 /ˈhəʊli/ ***adj.*** (**holier**; **holiest**) (RELIGION) **1** connected with God or with religion and therefore very special or important: *the Holy Bible* ◇ *holy water* ◇ *The Koran is the holy book of Islam.* **2** (used about a person) serving God; pure ▸ **holiness** ***noun*** [U]

homage /ˈhɒmɪdʒ/ ***noun*** [U, C, usually sing.] (*formal*) ~ **(to sb/sth)** something that is said or done to show respect publicly for sb: *Thousands came to* ***pay /do homage*** *to the dead leader.*

home[1] 🔑 /həʊm/ ***noun*** **1** [C,U] the place where you live or where you feel that you belong: *She* ***left home*** (=left her parents' house and began an independent life) *at the age of 21.* ◇ *Children from* ***broken homes*** (=whose parents are divorced) *sometimes have learning difficulties.* ◇ *That old house would make an ideal* ***family home.*** **2** [C] a place that provides care for a particular type of person or for animals: *a children's home* (=for children who have no parents to look after them) ◇ *an* ***old people's home*** **3** [sing.] **the ~ of sth** the place where sth began: *Greece is said to be the home of democracy.*
IDM at home 1 in your house, flat, etc.: *Is anybody at home?* ◇ *Tomorrow we're staying at home all day.* **2** comfortable, as if you were in your own home: *Please make yourself at home.* **3** (SPORT) played in the town to which the team belongs: *Manchester City are playing at home on Saturday.*
romp home/to victory → ROMP

home[2] /həʊm/ ***adj.*** (only *before* a noun) **1** connected with home: *home cooking* ◇ *your home address/town* ◇ *a happy home life* (=with your family) **2** (*especially BrE*) connected with your own country, not with a foreign country: *The* ***Home Secretary*** *is responsible for* ***home affairs.*** **3** (SPORT) connected with a team's own sports ground: *The home team has a lot of support.* ◇ *a home game*
OPP away

home[3] 🔑 /həʊm/ ***adv.*** at, in or to your home or home country: *We must be getting home soon.* ◇ *She'll be flying home for New Year.*
IDM bring sth home to sb to make sb understand sth fully
drive sth home (to sb) → DRIVE[1]

home[4] /həʊm/ ***verb***

PHR V home in on sb/sth to move towards sb/sth: *The police homed in on the house where the thieves were hiding.*

homecoming /'həʊmkʌmɪŋ/ ***noun*** [C,U] the act of returning home, especially when you have been away for a long time

ˌhome-'grown ***adj.*** (used about fruit and vegetables) grown in your own garden

homeland /'həʊmlænd/ ***noun*** [C] the country where you were born or that your parents came from, or to which you feel you belong

homeless /'həʊmləs/ ***adj.*** **1** having no home **2 the homeless** ***noun*** [pl.] people who have no home ▸ **homelessness** ***noun*** [U]

homely /'həʊmli/ ***adj.*** (*BrE*) (used about a place) simple but also pleasant or welcoming

ˌhome-'made ***adj.*** made at home; not bought in a shop: *home-made cakes*

the 'Home Office ***noun*** [sing.] (**POLITICS**) the British government department that deals with the law, the police and prisons, and with decisions about who can enter the country

homeopath (also **homoeopath**) /'həʊmiəpæθ/ ***noun*** [C] (**HEALTH**) a person who treats sick people using HOMOEOPATHY

homeopathy (also **homoeopathy**) /ˌhəʊmi'ɒpəθi/ ***noun*** [U] (**HEALTH**) the treatment of a disease by giving very small amounts of a drug that would cause the disease if given in large amounts ▸ **homeopathic** (also **homoeopathic**) /ˌhəʊmiə'pæθɪk/ ***adj.***: *homeopathic medicine*

homeostasis /ˌhəʊmiəʊ'steɪsɪs; ˌhɒm-/ ***noun*** [U] (**BIOLOGY**) the process by which the body reacts to changes in order to keep conditions inside the body, for example temperature, the same

'home page ***noun*** [C] (**COMPUTING**) the first of a number of pages of information on the Internet that belongs to a person or an organization. A home page contains connections to other pages of information.

ˌhome 'rule ***noun*** [U] (**POLITICS**) the right of a country or region to govern itself, especially after another country or region has governed it

ˌHome 'Secretary ***noun*** [C] (**POLITICS**) the British government minister in charge of the Home Office ➲ look at **the Foreign Secretary**

homesick /'həʊmsɪk/ ***adj.*** ~ **(for sb/sth)** sad because you are away from home and you miss it ▸ **homesickness** ***noun*** [U]

hometown /'həʊmtaʊn/ ***noun*** [C] the place where you were born or lived as a child

homeward /'hoʊmwəd/ ***adj.***, ***adv.*** going towards home: *the homeward journey ◇ to travel homeward*

homework 🔑 /'həʊmwɜːk/ ***noun*** [U] (**EDUCATION**) the written work that teachers give to students to do away from school: *Have we got any homework? ◇ We've got a translation to do for homework.*

homicidal /ˌhɒmɪ'saɪdl/ ***adj.*** likely to murder sb: *a homicidal maniac*

homicide /'hɒmɪsaɪd/ ***noun*** [C,U] (*especially AmE*) (**LAW**) the illegal killing of one person by another; murder

homo- /'hɒməʊ; 'həʊməʊ/ ***prefix*** (in nouns, adjectives and adverbs) the same: *homogeneous ◇ homosexual* ➲ look at **hetero-**

homogeneous /ˌhɒmə'dʒiːniəs/ ***adj.*** made up of parts that are all of the same type ➲ look at **heterogeneous**

homograph /'hɒməgrɑːf/ ***noun*** [C] (**LANGUAGE**) a word that is spelled like another word but has a different meaning and may have a different pronunciation, for example 'bow' /baʊ/ and 'bow' /bəʊ/

homologous /hə'mɒləgəs/ ***adj.*** ~ **(with sth)** similar in position, structure, etc. to sth else: *The seal's flipper is homologous with the human arm.*

homonym /'hɒmənɪm/ ***noun*** [C] (**LANGUAGE**) a word that is spelt and pronounced like another word but that has a different meaning

homophobia /ˌhɒmə'fəʊbiə/ ***noun*** [U] a strong dislike and fear of HOMOSEXUAL people ▸ **homophobic** ***adj.***

homophone /'hɒməfəʊn/ ***noun*** [C] (**LANGUAGE**) a word that is pronounced the same as another word but that has a different spelling and meaning: *'Flower' and 'flour' are homophones.*

Homo sapiens /ˌhəʊməʊ 'sæpienz/ ***noun*** [U] (**BIOLOGY**) the kind or SPECIES of human being that exists now

homosexual /ˌhəʊmə'sekʃuəl; ˌhɒm-/ ***adj.*** sexually attracted to people of the same sex ➲ look at **bisexual**, **gay**, **heterosexual**, **lesbian** ▸ **homosexual** ***noun*** [C] ▸ **homosexuality** /ˌhəʊməˌsekʃu'æləti; ˌhɒm-/ ***noun*** [U]

homozygote /ˌhɒmə'zaɪgəʊt; ˌhɒməʊ-/ ***noun*** [C] (**BIOLOGY**) a living thing that has only one form of a particular GENE (=one of the units of information that control what a living thing will be like), and so whose young are more likely to share a particular characteristic ▸ **homozygous** /ˌhɒmə'zaɪgəs/ ***adj.***

Hon ***abbr.*** **1** Honorary; used to show that sb holds a position without being paid for it: *Hon President* **2** (**POLITICS**) Honourable: a title for Members of Parliament and some high officials

honest 🔑 /'ɒnɪst/ ***adj.*** **1** (used about a person) telling the truth; not lying to people or stealing: *Just be honest – do you like this skirt or not? ◇* ***To be honest****, I don't think that's a very good idea.* **2** showing honest qualities: *an honest face ◇ I'd like your honest opinion, please.* **OPP dishonest** ▸ **honesty** ***noun*** [U] **OPP dishonesty**

honestly 🔑 /'ɒnɪstli/ ***adv.*** **1** in an honest way: *He tried to answer the lawyer's questions honestly.* **2** used for emphasizing that what you are saying is true: *I honestly don't know where she has gone.* **3** used for expressing disapproval: *Honestly! What a mess!*

honey /'hʌni/ ***noun*** [U] **1** the sweet sticky substance that is made by BEES and that people eat **2** a word for 'DARLING', used especially in American English

honeycomb /'hʌnikəʊm/ ***noun*** [C,U] a structure of holes (**cells**) with six sides, in which BEES keep their eggs and the substance they produce (**honey**)

honeymoon /'hʌnimuːn/ ***noun*** [C] a holiday that is taken by a man and a woman who have just got married: *We had our first argument while we were* ***on our honeymoon****.* ▸ **honeymooner** ***noun*** [C]: *The Seychelles is the perfect place for honeymooners.*

honk /hɒŋk/ ***verb*** [I,T] to sound the horn of a car; to make this sound

honorary /'ɒnərəri/ ***adj.*** **1** given as an honour (without the person needing the usual certificates, etc.): *to be awarded an honorary degree* **2** (often **Honorary**) (*abbr.* **Hon**) not paid: *He is the Honorary President.*

honour¹ ⊶ (*AmE* **honor**) /ˈɒnə(r)/ ***noun*** **1** [U] the respect from other people that a person, country, etc. gets because of high standards of behaviour and moral character: *the guest of honour* (=the most important one) ➲ look at **dishonour** **2** [sing.] (*formal*) something that gives pride or pleasure: *It was a great honour to be asked to speak at the conference.* **3** [U] the quality of doing what is morally right: *I give you my word of honour.* **4 Honours** [pl.] (EDUCATION) the four highest marks you can be given in Bachelor degrees **5** [C] something that is given to a person officially, to show great respect: *He was buried with full military honours* (=with a military ceremony as a sign of respect).

IDM **in honour of sb/sth; in sb/sth's honour** out of respect for sb/sth: *A party was given in honour of the guests from Bonn.*

honour² ⊶ (*AmE* **honor**) /ˈɒnə(r)/ ***verb*** [T] **1** ~ **sb/sth (with sth)** to show great (public) respect for sb/sth or to give sb pride or pleasure: *I am very honoured by the confidence you have shown in me.* **2** to do what you have agreed or promised

honourable (*AmE* **honorable**) /ˈɒnərəbl/ ***adj.*** **1** acting in a way that makes people respect you; having or showing honour OPP **dishonourable** **2 the Honourable** (*abbr.* **the Hon**) a title that is given to some high officials and to Members of Parliament when they are speaking to each other
▸ **honourably** /-əbli/ ***adv.***

Hons /ɒnz/ ***abbr.*** (EDUCATION) Honours (in Bachelor degrees): *John North BSc (Hons)*

hood /hʊd/ ***noun*** [C] **1** the part of a coat, etc. that you pull up to cover your head and neck in bad weather **2** (*especially BrE*) a soft cover for a car that has no roof, or a folding cover on a baby's PRAM, which can be folded down in good weather **3** (*AmE*) =BONNET (1)

hoody (also **hoodie**) /ˈhʊdi/ ***noun*** [C] (*pl.* **hoodies**) (*BrE, informal*) a jacket or SWEATSHIRT (=a warm piece of clothing with long sleeves) with a HOOD

hoof /huːf/ ***noun*** [C] (*pl.* **hoofs** or **hooves** /huːvz/) (BIOLOGY) the hard part of the foot of horses and some other animals ➲ look at **paw** ➲ picture at **goat**

ˌhoof-and-ˈmouth disease ***noun*** [U] (*AmE*) =FOOT-AND-MOUTH DISEASE

hook¹ ⊶ /hʊk/ ***noun*** [C] **1** a curved piece of metal, plastic, etc. that is used for hanging sth on or for catching fish: *Put your coat on the hook over there.* ◇ *a fish-hook* **2** (SPORT) (used in BOXING) a way of hitting sb that is done with the arm bent: *a right hook* (=with the right arm)

IDM **off the hook** (used about the top part of a telephone) not in position, so that telephone calls cannot be received

get/let sb off the hook (*informal*) to free yourself or sb else from a difficult situation or punishment: *My father paid the money I owed and got me off the hook.*

hook² /hʊk/ ***verb*** **1** [I,T] to fasten or catch sth with a hook or sth in the shape of a hook; to be fastened in this way: *We hooked the trailer to the back of the car.* ◇ *The curtain simply hooks onto the rail.* **2** [T] to put sth through a hole in sth else: *Hook the rope through your belt.*

PHRV **hook (sth) up (to sth)** to connect sb/sth to a piece of electronic equipment or to a power supply

ˌhook and ˈeye ***noun*** [C] a thing that is used for fastening clothes

hooked /hʊkt/ ***adj.*** **1** shaped like a hook: *a hooked nose* **2** (not before a noun) (*informal*) ~ **(on sth)** DEPENDENT on sth bad, especially drugs: *to be hooked on gambling* SYN **addicted** **3** (not before a noun) (*informal*) ~ **(on sth)** enjoying sth very much, so that you want to do it, see it, etc. as much as possible: *Suzi is hooked on computer games.*

hooligan /ˈhuːlɪgən/ ***noun*** [C] a person who behaves in a violent and aggressive way in public places: *football hooligans* ➲ look at **lout**, **yob**
▸ **hooliganism** /-ɪzəm/ ***noun*** [U]

hoop /huːp/ ***noun*** [C] a large metal or plastic ring

hooray =HURRAY

hoot¹ /huːt/ ***noun*** **1** [C] (*especially BrE*) a short loud laugh or shout: *hoots of laughter* **2** [sing.] (*spoken*) a situation or a person that is very funny: *Bob is a real hoot!* **3** [C] the loud sound that is made by the horn of a vehicle **4** [C] the cry of an OWL (=a bird that hunts at night)

hoot² /huːt/ ***verb*** [I,T] to sound the horn of a car or to make a loud noise: *The driver hooted (his horn) at the dog but it wouldn't move.* ◇ *They hooted with laughter at the suggestion.*

hoover /ˈhuːvə(r)/ ***verb*** [I,T] (*BrE*) to clean a carpet, etc. with a machine that sucks up the dirt: *This carpet needs hoovering.* SYN **vacuum**
▸ **Hoover™** ***noun*** [C] SYN **vacuum cleaner**

hooves /huːvz/ plural of **hoof**

hop¹ /hɒp/ ***verb*** [I] (**hopping**; **hopped**) **1** (used about a person) to jump on one leg **2** (used about an animal or bird) to jump with both or all feet together **3** ~ **(from sth to sth)** to change quickly from one activity or subject to another

IDM **hop it!** (*slang*) Go away!

PHRV **hop in/into sth**; **hop out/out of sth** (*informal*) to get in or out of a car, etc. (quickly)
hop on/onto sth; **hop off sth** (*informal*) to get onto/off a bus, etc. (quickly)

hop² /hɒp/ ***noun*** **1** [C] a short jump by a person on one leg or by a bird or animal with its feet together **2** [C] a tall climbing plant with flowers **3 hops** [pl.] the flowers of this plant that are used in making beer

hope¹ ⊶ /həʊp/ ***verb*** [I,T] ~ **that...**; ~ **to do sth**; ~ **(for sth)** to want sth to happen or be true: *'Is it raining?' '**I hope not**. I haven't got a coat with me.'* ◇ *'Are you coming to London with us?' 'I'm not sure yet but **I hope so**.'* ◇ *I hope that you feel better soon.* ◇ *Hoping to hear from you soon* (=at the end of a letter).

hope² ⊶ /həʊp/ ***noun*** **1** [C,U] (a) ~ **(of/for sth)**; (a) ~ **of doing sth**; (a) ~ **that...** the feeling of wanting sth to happen and thinking that it will: *What hope is there for the future?* ◇ *There is no hope of finding anybody else alive.* ◇ *David has **high hopes** of becoming a jockey* (=is very confident about it). ◇ *She never **gave up hope** that a cure for the disease would be found.* **2** [sing.] a person, a thing or a situation that will help you get what you want: *Please can you help me? You're my **last hope**.*

IDM **dash sb's hopes (of sth/of doing sth)** → DASH²
in the hope of sth/that... because you want sth to happen: *I came here in the hope that we could talk privately.*
pin (all) your hopes on sb/sth → PIN²
a ray of hope → RAY

hopeful /ˈhəʊpfl/ ***adj.*** **1** ~ **(about sth)**; ~ **that...** believing that sth that you want will happen: *He's very hopeful about the success of the business.* ◇ *The ministers seem hopeful that an agreement will be reached.* **2** making you think that sth good will happen: *a hopeful sign*

hopefully /ˈhəʊpfəli/ *adv.* **1** (*informal*) I/We hope; if everything happens as planned: *Hopefully, we'll be finished by six o'clock.* **2** hoping that what you want will happen: *She smiled hopefully at me, waiting for my answer.*

hopeless /ˈhəʊpləs/ *adj.* **1** giving no hope that sth/sb will be successful or get better: *It's hopeless. There is nothing we can do.* **2** (*informal*) ~ **(at sth)** (*especially BrE*) (used about a person) often doing things wrong; very bad at doing sth: *I'm absolutely hopeless at tennis.* ▶ **hopelessly** *adv.*: *They were hopelessly lost.* ▶ **hopelessness** *noun* [U]

horde /hɔːd/ *noun* [C] a very large number of people

horizon /həˈraɪzn/ *noun* **1** [sing.] the line where the earth and sky appear to meet: *The ship appeared on/disappeared over the horizon.* **2 horizons** [pl.] the limits of your knowledge or experience: *Foreign travel is a good way of expanding your horizons.*

IDM **on the horizon** likely to happen soon: *There are further job cuts on the horizon.*

horizontal 🔑 /ˌhɒrɪˈzɒntl/ *adj.* going from side to side, not up and down; flat or level: *horizontal lines* ➲ look at **perpendicular**, **vertical** ➲ picture at **line** ▶ **horizontally** /-təli/ *adv.*

ˌ**horizontal ˈbar** *noun* [C] (SPORT) a steel bar that stands on the ground and that sb uses to show actions and movements in GYMNASTICS (= physical exercises that are done indoors): *The gymnasts were exercising on the horizontal bars.*

hormone /ˈhɔːməʊn/ *noun* [C] (BIOLOGY) a substance in your body that influences growth and development ▶ **hormonal** /hɔːˈməʊnl/ *adj.*: *the hormonal changes occurring during pregnancy*

horn 🔑 /hɔːn/ *noun* [C] **1** (BIOLOGY) one of the hard pointed things that some animals have on their heads ➲ picture on **page 29** **2** the thing in a car, etc. that gives a loud warning sound: *Don't sound your horn late at night.* **3** (MUSIC) one of the family of metal musical instruments that you play by blowing into them: *the French horn* ➲ picture on **page 465**

hornet /ˈhɔːnɪt/ *noun* [C] a black and yellow flying insect that has a very powerful sting ℹ A **hornet** is bigger than a **wasp**.

horoscope /ˈhɒrəskəʊp/ *noun* [C] (*also* **stars** [pl.]) a statement about what is going to happen to a person in the future, based on the position of the stars and planets when they were born: *What does my horoscope for next week say?* ➲ look at **astrology**, **zodiac**

horrendous /hɒˈrendəs/ *adj.* (*informal*) very bad or unpleasant ▶ **horrendously** *adv.*

horrible /ˈhɒrəbl/ *adj.* **1** (*informal*) bad or unpleasant: *This coffee tastes horrible!* ◇ *Don't be so horrible!* (= unkind) ◇ *I've got* ***a horrible feeling*** *that I've forgotten something.* SYN **horrid** **2** shocking and/or frightening: *a horrible murder/death/nightmare* ▶ **horribly** /-əbli/ *adv.*

horrid /ˈhɒrɪd/ *adj.* (*informal*) very unpleasant or unkind: *horrid weather* ◇ *I'm sorry that I was so horrid last night.* SYN **horrible**

horrific /həˈrɪfɪk/ *adj.* **1** extremely bad and shocking or frightening: *a horrific murder/accident/attack* **2** (*informal*) very bad or unpleasant ▶ **horrifically** /-kli/ *adv.*: *horrifically expensive*

horrify /ˈhɒrɪfaɪ/ *verb* [T] (*pres. part.* **horrifying**; *3rd person sing. pres.* **horrifies**; *pt, pp* **horrified**) to make sb feel extremely shocked, disgusted or frightened ▶ **horrifying** *adj.*

horror 🔑 /ˈhɒrə(r)/ *noun* **1** [U, sing.] a feeling of great fear or shock: *They watched* ***in horror*** *as the building collapsed.* **2** [C] something that makes you feel frightened or shocked: ***a horror film/story***

horse 🔑 /hɔːs/ *noun* **1** [C] a large animal that is used for riding on or for pulling or carrying heavy loads

> **RELATED VOCABULARY**
>
> A male horse is a **stallion**, a female horse is a **mare** and a young horse is a **foal**.

2 the horses [pl.] (*informal*) horse racing

IDM **on horseback** sitting on a horse

ˌ**horse ˈchestnut** *noun* [C] **1** a large tree that has leaves divided into seven sections and pink or white flowers **2** (also *informal* **conker**) the nut from this tree

horseman /ˈhɔːsmən/ **horsewoman** /ˈhɔːswʊmən/ *noun* [C] (*pl.* **-men** /-mən/) (*pl.* **-women** /-wɪmɪn/) a person who rides a horse well: *an experienced horseman*

horsepower /ˈhɔːspaʊə(r)/ *noun* [C] (*pl.* **horsepower**) (*abbr.* **h.p.**) a measurement of the power of an engine

ˈ**horse racing** (*also* **racing**) *noun* [U] (SPORT) the sport in which a JOCKEY rides a horse in a race to win money

horseshoe /ˈhɔːsʃuː/ (*also* **shoe**) *noun* [C] a U-shaped piece of metal that is fixed to the bottom of a horse's foot (**hoof**). Some people believe that **horseshoes** bring good luck.

horticulture /ˈhɔːtɪkʌltʃə(r)/ *noun* [U] (AGRICULTURE) the study or practice of growing flowers, fruit and vegetables ▶ **horticultural** /ˌhɔːtɪˈkʌltʃərəl/ *adj.*

hose /həʊz/ (*also* **hosepipe** /ˈhəʊzpaɪp/) *noun* [C,U] a long rubber or plastic tube that water can flow through ➲ picture at **agriculture**

hospice /ˈhɒspɪs/ *noun* [C] (HEALTH) a special hospital where people who are dying are cared for

hospitable /hɒˈspɪtəbl; ˈhɒspɪtəbl/ *adj.* (used about a person) friendly and kind to visitors OPP **inhospitable**

hospital 🔑 /ˈhɒspɪtl/ *noun* [C] (HEALTH) a place where ill or injured people are treated: *He was rushed* ***to hospital*** *in an ambulance.* ◇ *to be admitted to/discharged from hospital* ◇ *a psychiatric/mental hospital*

hospitality /ˌhɒspɪˈtæləti/ *noun* [U] **1** looking after guests and being friendly and welcoming towards them: *Thank you for your kind hospitality.* **2** (BUSINESS) food, drink or services that are provided by an organization for guests, customers, etc.: *We were entertained in the company's* ***hospitality suite***. ◇ *the hospitality industry* (= hotels, restaurants, etc.)

host 🔑 /həʊst/ *noun* [C] **1** a person who invites guests to their house, etc. and provides them with food, drink, etc. ➲ look at **hostess** **2** (ARTS AND MEDIA) a person who introduces a television or radio show and talks to the guests **3 a ~ of sth** a large number of people or things **4** (BIOLOGY) an animal or a plant on which another animal or plant lives and feeds ▶ **host** *verb* [T]: *The city is aiming to host the Olympic Games in ten years' time.*

hostage /ˈhɒstɪdʒ/ *noun* [C] a person who is caught and kept prisoner. A **hostage** may be killed or injured if the person who is holding them does not get what they are asking for: *The robbers tried to* ***take*** *the staff* ***hostage****.* ◇ *The hijackers say they will* ***hold*** *the passengers* ***hostage*** *until their demands are met.* ➲ look at **ransom**

hostel /ˈhɒstl/ ***noun*** [C] **1** (TOURISM) a place like a cheap hotel where people can stay when they are living away from home: *a youth hostel* ◇ *a student hostel* **2** a building where people who have no home can stay for a short time

hostess /ˈhəʊstəs; -es/ ***noun*** [C] **1** a woman who invites guests to her house, etc. and provides them with food, drink, etc. ➲ look at **host 2** (ARTS AND MEDIA) a woman who introduces a television or radio show and talks to the guests **3** = AIR HOSTESS

hostile /ˈhɒstaɪl/ ***adj.*** ~ **(to/towards sb/sth)** having very strong feelings against sb/sth: *a hostile crowd* ◇ *They are very hostile to any change.*

hostility /hɒˈstɪləti/ ***noun*** **1** [U] ~ **(to/towards sth)** very strong feelings against sb/sth: *She didn't say anything but I could sense her hostility.* SYN **animosity** **2 hostilities** [pl.] fighting in a war

hot[1] ⊶ /hɒt/ ***adj.*** (**hotter**; **hottest**) **1** having a high temperature: *Can I open the window? I'm really hot.* ◇ *It was* ***boiling hot*** *on the beach.* ◇ *a hot meal* ◇ *Don't touch the plates – they're* ***red hot****!*

RELATED VOCABULARY

You can describe the temperature of sth as **freezing (cold), cold, cool, tepid** (used about water), **warm, hot** or **boiling (hot).**

➲ note at **cold**[1] **2** (used about food) causing a burning feeling in your mouth: *hot curry* SYN **spicy** **3** (*informal*) difficult or dangerous to deal with: *The defenders found the Italian strikers* ***too hot to handle****.* **4** (*informal*) exciting and popular: *This band is* ***hot stuff****!*

IDM **in hot pursuit** following sb who is moving fast

hot[2] /hɒt/ ***verb*** (**hotting**; **hotted**)

PHR V **hot up** (*BrE, informal*) to become more exciting: *The election campaign has really hotted up in the past few days.*

ˌ**hot-ˈair balloon** = BALLOON (2)

ˈ**hot dog** ***noun*** [C] a hot SAUSAGE in a soft bread roll

hotel ⊶ /həʊˈtel/ ***noun*** [C] (TOURISM) a place where you pay to stay when you are on holiday or travelling: *to stay in/at a hotel* ◇ *I've booked a double room at the Grand Hotel.* ◇ *a two-star hotel*

RELATED VOCABULARY

You book a **double**, **single** or **twin-bedded** room at a hotel. When you arrive you **check in** or **register** and when you leave you **check out**.

hotelier /həʊˈteliə(r); -lieɪ/ ***noun*** [C] (TOURISM) a person who owns or manages a hotel

hothouse /ˈhɒthaʊs/ ***noun*** [C] a heated glass building where plants are grown ➲ look at **greenhouse**

hotline /ˈhɒtlaɪn/ ***noun*** [C] a direct telephone line to a business or organization

hotly /ˈhɒtli/ ***adv.*** **1** in an angry or excited way: *They hotly denied the newspaper reports.* **2** closely and with determination: *The dog ran off, hotly pursued by its owner.*

ˈ**hot spot** ***noun*** [C] (*informal*) **1** a place where there is a lot of activity or entertainment: *a tourist hot spot* **2** (COMPUTING) an area on a computer screen that you can click on to start an operation such as loading a file

ˌ**hot-ˈwater bottle** ***noun*** [C] a rubber container that is filled with hot water and put in a bed to warm it

hound[1] /haʊnd/ ***noun*** [C] a type of dog that is used for hunting or racing: *a foxhound*

hound[2] /haʊnd/ ***verb*** [T] to follow and disturb sb: *Many famous people complain of being hounded by the press.*

hour ⊶ /ˈaʊə(r)/ ***noun*** **1** [C] a period of 60 minutes: *He studies* ***for*** *three* ***hours*** *most evenings.* ◇ *The programme lasts about half an hour.* ◇ *I'm going shopping now. I'll be back in about an hour.* ◇ ***In*** *two* ***hours' time*** *I'll be having lunch.* ◇ *a four-hour journey* ◇ *Japan is eight hours ahead of the UK.* ◇ *I get paid* ***by the hour****.* ◇ *How much do you get paid* ***per/an hour****?* **2** [C] the distance that you can travel in about 60 minutes: *London is only two hours away.* **3 hours** [pl.] the period of time when sb is working or a shop, etc. is open: *Employees are demanding shorter* ***working hours****.* **4** [C] a period of about an hour when sth particular happens: *I'm going shopping in my* ***lunch hour****.* ◇ *The traffic is very bad in* ***the rush hour****.* **5 the hour** [sing.] the time when a new hour starts (= 1 o'clock, 2 o'clock, etc.): *Buses are* ***on the hour*** *and at twenty past the hour.* **6 hours** [pl.] a long time: *He went on speaking* ***for hours*** *and hours.*

IDM **at/till all hours** at/until any time: *She stays out till all hours* (= very late).

the early hours → EARLY

hourly /ˈaʊəli/ ***adj., adv.*** **1** done, happening, etc. every hour: *an hourly news bulletin* ◇ *Trains are hourly.* **2** for one hour: *What is your hourly rate of pay?*

house[1] ⊶ /haʊs/ ***noun*** [C] (*pl.* **houses** /ˈhaʊzɪz/) **1** a building that is made for people to live in: *Is yours a four-bedroomed or a three-bedroomed house?* ➲ look at **bungalow, cottage, flat** **2** [usually sing.] all the people who live in one house: *Don't shout. You'll wake the whole house up.* **3** a building that is used for a particular purpose: *a warehouse* **4** [C] (in compounds) (BUSINESS) a company involved in a particular kind of business: *a fashion/publishing house* ◇ *I work* ***in house*** (= in the offices of the company that I work for, not at home) **5** [C] (in compounds) a restaurant, usually that sells one particular type of food: *a curry/spaghetti house* ◇ *house wine* (= the cheapest wine on a restaurant's menu) **6 House** [sing.] (POLITICS) a group of people who meet to make a country's laws: *the House of Commons* ◇ *the Houses of Parliament* ➲ note at **Parliament** **7** [usually sing.] (ARTS AND MEDIA) the audience at a theatre or cinema, or the area where they sit: *There was a full house for the play this evening.* **8** [U] = HOUSE MUSIC

IDM **move house** → MOVE[1]

on the house paid for by the pub, restaurant, etc. that you are visiting; free: *Your first drink is on the house.*

get on/along like a house on fire to immediately become good friends with sb

house[2] /haʊz/ ***verb*** [T] **1** to provide sb with a place to live: *The Council must house homeless families.* **2** to contain or keep sth: *Her office is housed in a separate building.*

ˈ**house arrest** ***noun*** [U] (LAW) the state of being a prisoner in your own house rather than in a prison: *to be kept/held/placed* ***under house arrest***

houseboat /ˈhaʊsbəʊt/ ***noun*** [C] a boat on a river, etc. where sb lives and which usually stays in one place

housebound /'haʊsbaʊnd/ ***adj.*** unable to leave your house because you are old or ill

household /'haʊshəʊld/ ***noun*** [C] all the people who live in one house and the work, money, organization, etc. that is needed to look after them: *household expenses*

householder /'haʊshəʊldə(r)/ ***noun*** [C] a person who rents or owns a house

housekeeper /'haʊski:pə(r)/ ***noun*** [C] **1** a person, usually a woman, whose job is to manage the shopping, cooking, cleaning, etc. in a house or an institution **2** (TOURISM) a person whose job is to manage the cleaning of rooms in a hotel

housekeeping /'haʊski:pɪŋ/ ***noun*** [U] **1** the work involved in taking care of a house, especially shopping and managing money **2** the department in a hotel, a hospital, an office building, etc. that is responsible for cleaning the rooms, etc.: *Call housekeeping and ask them to bring us some clean towels.* **3** (*especially BrE* **'housekeeping money**) the money used to buy food, cleaning materials and other things needed for taking care of a house

'house music (*also* **house**) ***noun*** [U] (MUSIC) a type of popular dance music with a fast beat, played on electronic instruments

the ˌHouse of 'Commons ***noun*** [sing.] (POLITICS) the group of people (**Members of Parliament**) who are elected to make new laws in Britain ➲ note at **parliament**

'house officer ***noun*** [C] (HEALTH) (in Britain) a doctor who has finished medical school and who is working at a hospital to get further practical experience ➲ look at **intern**

the ˌHouse of 'Lords ***noun*** [sing.] (POLITICS) the group of people (who are not elected) who meet to discuss the laws that have been suggested by the House of Commons ➲ note at **parliament**

the ˌHouse of ˌRepre'sentatives ***noun*** [sing.] (POLITICS) the group of people who are elected to make new laws in the US ➲ look at **Congress, the Senate**

'house-proud ***adj.*** paying great attention to the care, cleaning, etc. of your house

ˌhouse-to-'house ***adj.*** going to each house: *The police are making house-to-house enquiries.*

'house-warming ***noun*** [C] a party that you have when you have just moved into a new home

housewife /'haʊswaɪf/ ***noun*** [C] (*pl.* **housewives**) a woman who does not have a job outside the home and who spends her time cleaning the house, cooking, looking after her family, etc.

housework /'haʊswɜ:k/ ***noun*** [U] the work that is needed to keep a house clean and tidy

housing /'haʊzɪŋ/ ***noun*** [U] houses, flats, etc. for people to live in

'housing estate ***noun*** [C] an area where there are a large number of similar houses that were built at the same time

hovel /'hɒvl/ ***noun*** [C] a house or room that is not fit to live in because it is dirty or in very bad condition

hover /'hɒvə(r)/ ***verb*** [I] **1** (used about a bird, etc.) to stay in the air in one place **2** (used about a person) to wait near sb/sth: *He hovered nervously outside the office.*

hovercraft /'hɒvəkrɑ:ft/ ***noun*** [C] (*pl.* **hovercraft**) a type of boat that moves over land or water on a CUSHION of air

how /haʊ/ ***adv., conj.*** **1** (often used in questions) in what way: *How do you spell your name?* ◇ *Can you show me how to use this machine?* ◇ *I can't remember how to get there.* **2** used when you are asking about sb's health or feelings: *'How is your mother?' 'She's much better, thank you.'* ◇ *How are you feeling today?* ◇ *How do you feel about your son joining the army?* **3** used when you are asking about sb's opinion of a thing or a situation: *How was the weather?* ◇ *How is your meal?* ◇ ***How** did the interview go?* **4** used in questions when you are asking about the degree, amount, age, etc. of sb/sth: *How old are you?* ◇ *How much is that?* **5** used for expressing surprise, pleasure, etc.: *She's gone. How strange!* ◇ *I can't believe how expensive it is!*

IDM **how/what about...?** → ABOUT[2]

how come? → COME

how do you do? (*formal*) used when meeting sb for the first time

however /haʊ'evə(r)/ ***adv., conj.*** **1** (*formal*) (used for adding a comment to what you have just said) although sth is true: *Sales are poor this month. There may, however, be an increase before Christmas.* **2** (used in questions for expressing surprise) in what way; how: *However did you manage to find me here?* **3** in whatever way: *However I sat I couldn't get comfortable.* ◇ *You can dress however you like.* **4** (before an adjective or adverb) to whatever degree: *He won't wear a hat however cold it is.* ◇ *You can't catch her however fast you run.*

howl /haʊl/ ***verb*** [I] to make a long loud sound: *I couldn't sleep because there was a dog howling all night.* ◇ *The wind howled around the house.* ▶ **howl** ***noun*** [C]

h.p. /ˌeɪtʃ 'pi:/ ***abbr.*** **1** (used about an engine) horsepower **2 HP** (*BrE*) hire purchase

HQ /ˌeɪtʃ 'kju:/ ***abbr.*** headquarters

HR /ˌeɪtʃ 'ɑ:(r)/ ***abbr.*** = HUMAN RESOURCES

hr (*pl.* **hrs**) ***abbr.*** hour: *3 hrs 15 min*

HRH /ˌeɪtʃ ɑ:r 'eɪtʃ/ ***abbr.*** His/Her Royal Highness

HTML /ˌeɪtʃ ti: em 'el/ ***abbr.*** (COMPUTING) Hypertext Mark-up Language (a system used to mark text for WORLD WIDE WEB pages in order to obtain colours, style, pictures, etc.)

HTTP (also **http**) /ˌeɪtʃ ti: ti: 'pi:/ ***abbr.*** (COMPUTING) **Hypertext Transfer Protocol**; the set of rules that control the way data is sent and received over the Internet

hub /hʌb/ ***noun*** [usually sing.] **1 the ~ (of sth)** the central and most important part of a place or an activity: *the commercial hub of the city* **2** the central part of a wheel

hubbub /'hʌbʌb/ ***noun*** [sing., U] **1** the noise made by a lot of people talking at the same time **2** a situation in which there is a lot of noise, excitement and activity

hubcap /'hʌbkæp/ ***noun*** [C] a round metal cover that fits over the HUB of a vehicle's wheel

hubris /'hju:brɪs/ ***noun*** [U] (LITERATURE) the fact of sb being too proud. A character with this pride usually dies because they ignore warnings.

huddle[1] /'hʌdl/ ***verb*** [I] ~ **(up) (together) 1** to get close to other people because you are cold or frightened: *The campers huddled together around the fire.* **2** to make your body as small as possible because you are cold or frightened: *She huddled up in her sleeping bag and tried to get some sleep.* ▶ **huddled** ***adj.***: *We found the children lying huddled together on the ground.*

huddle² /ˈhʌdl/ ***noun*** [C] a small group of people or things that are close together: *They all stood **in a huddle**, laughing and chatting.*

hue /hjuː/ ***noun*** [C] **1** (*written*) a colour; a particular shade of a colour **2** (*formal*) a type of belief or opinion

IDM **hue and cry** strong public protest about sth

huff /hʌf/ ***noun*** [C]

IDM **in a huff** (*informal*) in a bad mood because sb has annoyed or upset you: *Did you see Stan **go off in a huff** when he wasn't chosen for the team?*

hug /hʌg/ ***verb*** [T] (**hugging**; **hugged**) **1** to put your arms around sb, especially to show that you love them **2** to hold sth close to your body: *She hugged the parcel to her chest as she ran.* **3** (used about a ship, car, road, etc.) to stay close to sth: *to hug the coast* ▸ **hug** ***noun*** [C]: *Noel's crying – I'll go and **give him a hug**.*

huge 🔑 /hjuːdʒ/ ***adj.*** very big: *a huge amount/quantity/sum/number* ◇ *a huge building* ◇ *The film was a huge success.* ▸ **hugely** ***adv.***: *hugely successful/popular/expensive*

huh /hʌ/ ***exclamation*** (*informal*) used for expressing anger, surprise, etc. or for asking a question: *They've gone away, huh? They didn't tell me.*

hull /hʌl/ ***noun*** [C] the body of a ship

hullabaloo /ˌhʌləbəˈluː/ ***noun*** [sing.] a lot of loud noise, for example made by people shouting

hum /hʌm/ ***verb*** (**humming**; **hummed**) **1** [I] to make a continuous low noise: *The machine began to hum as I switched it on.* **2** [I,T] (MUSIC) to sing with your lips closed: *You can hum the tune if you don't know the words.* ▸ **hum** ***noun*** [sing.]: *the hum of machinery/distant traffic*

human¹ 🔑 /ˈhjuːmən/ ***adj.*** connected with people, not with animals, machines or gods; typical of people: *the human body* ◇ *The disaster was caused by **human error**.* ▸ **humanly** ***adv.***: *They did all that was humanly possible to rescue him* (=everything that a human being could possibly do).

human² 🔑 /ˈhjuːmən/ (*also* ˌ**human ˈbeing**) ***noun*** [C] a person

ˌ**Human De'velopment Index** ***noun*** [C] (*abbr.* **HDI**) (GEOGRAPHY) a measure that compares education, health and standards of living, etc. in different countries every year

RELATED VOCABULARY

HDI is measured by comparing **life expectancy** (=the number of years an average person can expect to live for) and **literacy** (=the ability to read) and number of years of **education** and **standard of living** (GDP per capita). **HDI** is used to determine whether a country is **developed**, **developing** or **underdeveloped**.

humane /hjuːˈmeɪn/ ***adj.*** having or showing kindness or understanding, especially to a person or animal that is suffering: *Zoo animals must be kept in humane conditions.* **OPP** **inhumane** ▸ **humanely** ***adv.***

humanism /ˈhjuːmənɪzəm/ ***noun*** [U] a system of thought that considers that solving human problems with the help of reason is more important than religious beliefs. It emphasizes the fact that the basic nature of humans is good. ▸ **humanistic** /ˌhjuːməˈnɪstɪk/ ***adj.***: *humanistic ideals*

humanitarian /hjuːˌmænɪˈteəriən/ ***adj.*** concerned with trying to make people's lives better and reduce suffering: *Many countries have sent humanitarian aid to the earthquake victims.*

humanity /hjuːˈmænəti/ ***noun*** **1** [U] all the people in the world, thought of as a group: *crimes against humanity* **SYN** **the human race** **2** [U] the quality of being kind and understanding: *The prisoners were treated with humanity.* **OPP** **inhumanity** **3** **(the) humanities** [pl.] (EDUCATION) the subjects of study that are connected with the way people think and behave, for example literature, language, history and PHILOSOPHY

ˌ**human ˈnature** ***noun*** [U] feelings, behaviour, etc. that all people have in common

the ˌ**human ˈrace** ***noun*** [sing.] all the people in the world, thought of as a group **SYN** **humanity**

ˌ**human reˈsources** ***noun*** [U, with sing. or pl. verb] (*abbr.* **HR**) (BUSINESS) the department in a company that deals with employing and training people **SYN** **personnel**: *the human resources director*

ˌ**human ˈrights** ***noun*** [pl.] (SOCIAL STUDIES) the basic freedoms that all people should have, for example the right to say what you think, to travel freely, etc.

humble¹ /ˈhʌmbl/ ***adj.*** **1** not thinking that you are better or more important than other people; not proud: *He became very rich and famous but he always remained a very humble man.* ➲ noun **humility** ➲ look at **modest** **2** not special or important: *She comes from a humble background.* ▸ **humbly** /ˈhʌmbli/ ***adv.***: *He apologized very humbly for his behaviour.*

humble² /ˈhʌmbl/ ***verb*** [T] to make sb feel that they are not as good or important as they thought

humerus /ˈhjuːmərəs/ ***noun*** [C] (ANATOMY) the large bone in the top part of the arm between your shoulder and your elbow ➲ picture on **page 80**

humid /ˈhjuːmɪd/ ***adj.*** (used about the air or climate) containing a lot of water; damp: *Hong Kong is hot and humid in summer.* ▸ **humidity** /hjuːˈmɪdəti/ ***noun*** [U]

humiliate /hjuːˈmɪlieɪt/ ***verb*** [T] to make sb feel very embarrassed: *I felt humiliated when the teacher laughed at my work.* ▸ **humiliating** ***adj.***: *a humiliating defeat* ▸ **humiliation** /hjuːˌmɪliˈeɪʃn/ ***noun*** [C,U]

humility /hjuːˈmɪləti/ ***noun*** [U] the quality of not thinking that you are better than other people ➲ adjective **humble**

humorous 🔑 /ˈhjuːmərəs/ ***adj.*** amusing or funny ▸ **humorously** ***adv.***

humour¹ 🔑 (*AmE* **humor**) /ˈhjuːmə(r)/ ***noun*** [U] **1** the funny or amusing qualities of sb/sth: *It is sometimes hard to understand the humour* (=the jokes) *of another country.* **2** being able to see when sth is funny and to laugh at things: *Rose has a good **sense of humour**.* **3** **-humoured** (*AmE* **-humored**) (used to form compound adjectives) having or showing a particular mood: *good-humoured*

humour² (*AmE* **humor**) /ˈhjuːmə(r)/ ***verb*** [T] to keep sb happy by doing what they want

humourless /ˈhjuːmələs/ (*AmE* **humorless**) ***adj.*** having no sense of fun; serious

hump /hʌmp/ ***noun*** [C] a large round lump, for example on the back of a CAMEL (=an animal that lives in the desert)

humus /ˈhjuːməs/ ***noun*** [U] (AGRICULTURE) a substance made from dead leaves and plants, that you put into the ground to help plants grow

hunch¹ /hʌntʃ/ ***noun*** [C] (*informal*) a thought or an idea that is based on a feeling rather than on facts or information: *I'm not sure, but I've got a hunch that she's got a new job.*

hunch² /hʌntʃ/ ***verb*** [I,T] to bend your back and shoulders forward into a round shape

hunchback /ˈhʌntʃbæk/ ***noun*** [C] a person with a back that has a round lump on it

hundred /ˈhʌndrəd/ ***number*** **1** (*pl.* **hundred**) 100: *two hundred* ◇ *There were a/one hundred people in the room.* ◇ *She's a hundred today.* **2 hundreds** (*informal*) a lot; a large amount: *I've got hundreds of things to do today.* ❶ For more information about numbers look at the special section on numbers at the back of this dictionary.

hundredth¹ /ˈhʌndrədθ/ ***noun*** [C] the FRACTION ¹⁄₁₀₀; one of a hundred equal parts of sth

hundredth² /ˈhʌndrədθ/ ***pronoun, det., adv.*** 100th

hundredweight /ˈhʌndrədweɪt/ ***noun*** [C] (*pl.* **hundredweight**) (*abbr.* **cwt.**) a unit for measuring weight equal to 112 pounds in the UK and 100 pounds in the US. There are 20 **hundredweight** in a ton. ❶ For more information about weights look at the special section on numbers on page R36.

hung past tense, past participle of **hang¹**

hunger¹ /ˈhʌŋɡə(r)/ ***noun*** **1** [U] the state of not having enough food to eat, especially when this causes illness or death SYN **starvation**: *In some parts of the world many people die of hunger each year.* ➲ look at **thirst** **2** [U] the feeling caused by a need to eat: *Hunger is one reason why babies cry.* **3** [sing.] **a ~ (for sth)** a strong desire for sth: *a hunger for knowledge/fame/success*

hunger² /ˈhʌŋɡə(r)/ ***verb*** (*formal*)
PHR V **hunger for/after sth** to have a strong desire for sth

ˈhunger strike ***noun*** [C,U] a time when sb (especially a prisoner) refuses to eat because they are protesting about sth: *to be/go* ***on hunger strike***

hungry 🔑 /ˈhʌŋɡri/ ***adj.*** (**hungrier**; **hungriest**) **1** wanting to eat: *I'm hungry. Let's eat soon.* ◇ *There were hungry children begging for food in the streets.* ➲ look at **thirsty** **2 ~ for sth** wanting sth very much: *I'm hungry for some excitement tonight.* ▶ **hungrily** ***adv.***
IDM **go hungry** to not have any food

hunk /hʌŋk/ ***noun*** [C] **1** a large piece of sth: *a hunk of bread/cheese/meat* **2** (*informal*) a man who is big, strong and attractive

hunt¹ 🔑 /hʌnt/ ***verb*** [I,T] **1** to run after wild animals, etc. in order to catch or kill them either for sport or for food: *Owls hunt at night.* ◇ *Are tigers still hunted in India?* **2 ~ (for) (sb/sth)** to try to find sb/sth: *The police are still hunting the murderer.*

hunt² /hʌnt/ ***noun*** [C] **1** the act of hunting wild animals, etc.: *a fox-hunt* **2** [usually sing.] **a ~ (for sb/sth)** the act of looking for sb/sth that is difficult to find: *The police have launched a hunt for the missing child.*

hunter /ˈhʌntə(r)/ ***noun*** [C] a person that hunts wild animals for food or sport; an animal that hunts its food

hunter-gatherer /ˌhʌntə ˈɡæðərə(r)/ ***noun*** [C] (SOCIAL STUDIES) a member of a group of people who do not live in one place but move around and live by hunting and fishing

hunting 🔑 /ˈhʌntɪŋ/ ***noun*** [U] the act of following and killing wild animals or birds as a sport or for food ➲ look at **shoot**

hurdle¹ /ˈhɜːdl/ ***noun*** **1** [C] (SPORT) a type of light fence that a person or a horse jumps over in a race: *to clear a hurdle* (= to jump over it successfully) **2 hurdles** [pl.] (SPORT) a race in which runners or horses have to jump over **hurdles**: *the 200 metres hurdles* **3** [C] a problem or difficulty that you must solve or deal with before you can achieve sth

hurdle² /ˈhɜːdl/ ***verb*** [I,T] **~ (over sth)** to jump over sth while you are running

hurl /hɜːl/ ***verb*** [T] to throw sth with great force

hurray /həˈreɪ/ (*also* **hooray** /huˈreɪ/, **hurrah** /həˈrɑː/) ***exclamation*** used for expressing great pleasure, approval, etc.: *Hurray! We've won!*
IDM **hip, hip, hurray/hurrah** → HIP²

hurricane /ˈhʌrɪken/ ***noun*** [C] (GEOGRAPHY) a violent storm with very strong winds ➲ note at **storm**

hurried /ˈhʌrid/ ***adj.*** done (too) quickly: *a hurried meal* ▶ **hurriedly** ***adv.***

hurry¹ 🔑 /ˈhʌri/ ***noun*** [U] the need or wish to do sth quickly: *Take your time. There's* ***no hurry***.
IDM **in a hurry** quickly: *She got up late and left in a hurry.*
in a hurry (to do sth) wanting to do sth soon; impatient: *They are in a hurry to get the job done before the winter.*
in no hurry (to do sth); not in any hurry (to do sth) **1** not needing or wishing to do sth quickly: *We weren't in any hurry so we stopped to admire the view.* **2** not wanting to do sth: *I am in no hurry to repeat that experience.*

hurry² 🔑 /ˈhʌri/ ***verb*** (*pres. part.* **hurrying**; *3rd person sing. pres.* **hurries**; *pt, pp* **hurried**) **1** [I] to move or do sth quickly because there is not much time: *Don't hurry. There's plenty of time.* ◇ *They hurried back home after school.* ◇ *Several people hurried to help.* **2 ~ sb (into sth/doing sth)** [T] to cause sb/sth to do sth, or sth to happen more quickly: *Don't hurry me. I'm going as fast as I can.* ◇ *He was hurried into a decision.* **3** [T] (usually passive) to do sth too quickly
PHR V **hurry up (with sth)** (*informal*) to move or do sth more quickly: *Hurry up or we'll miss the train.*

hurt¹ 🔑 /hɜːt/ ***verb*** (*pt, pp* **hurt**) **1** [T,I] to cause sb/yourself physical pain or injury: *Did he hurt himself?* ◇ *I fell and hurt my arm.* ◇ *No one was seriously hurt in the accident.* ◇ *These shoes hurt; they're too tight.* ➲ note at **injure**

> **WHICH WORD?**
>
> Compare **hurt**, **injure** and **wound**. A person may be **wounded** by a knife, sword, gun, etc., usually as a result of fighting: *a wounded soldier.* People are usually **injured** in an accident: *Five people were killed in the crash and twelve others were injured.* **Hurt** and **injured** are similar in meaning but **hurt** is more often used when the damage is not very great: *I hurt my leg when I fell off my bike.*

2 [I] to feel painful: *My leg hurts.* ◇ ***It hurts*** *when I lift my leg.* ◇ *Where exactly does it hurt?* **3** [T] to make sb unhappy; to upset sb: *His unkind remarks hurt her deeply.* ◇ *I didn't want to* ***hurt*** *his* ***feelings***.
IDM **it won't/wouldn't hurt (sb/sth) (to do sth)** (*informal*) used to say that sb should do sth: *It wouldn't hurt you to help with the housework occasionally.*

hurt² 🔑 /hɜːt/ ***adj.*** **1** injured physically: *None of the passengers were* ***badly/seriously hurt***. **2** upset and offended by sth that sb has said or done: *She* *was **deeply hurt** that she had not been invited to the party.*

hurt³ /hɜːt/ ***noun*** [U] a feeling of unhappiness because sb has been unkind or unfair to you

hurtful /ˈhɜːtfl/ ***adj.*** ~ **(to sb)** unkind; making sb feel upset and offended

hurtle /ˈhɜːtl/ ***verb*** [I] to move with great speed, perhaps causing danger: *The lorry **came hurtling** towards us.*

husband 🔑 /ˈhʌzbənd/ ***noun*** [C] a man that a woman is married to: *Her ex-husband sees the children once a month.*

husbandry /ˈhʌzbəndri/ ***noun*** [U] (**AGRICULTURE**) farming; looking after animals and food crops

hush¹ /hʌʃ/ ***verb*** [I] (*spoken*) used to tell sb to be quiet, to stop talking or crying: *Hush now and try to sleep.*

PHR V **hush sth up** to hide information to stop people knowing about sth; to keep sth secret

hush² /hʌʃ/ ***noun*** [sing.] silence

ˌhush-ˈhush ***adj.*** (*informal*) very secret

husk /hʌsk/ ***noun*** [C] (**BIOLOGY**) the dry outside layer of nuts, fruits and seeds, especially of grain

husky¹ /ˈhʌski/ ***adj.*** (used about a person's voice) sounding rough and quiet as if your throat were dry

husky² /ˈhʌski/ ***noun*** [C] (*pl.* **huskies**) a strong dog with thick fur that is used in teams for pulling heavy loads over snow

hustle /ˈhʌsl/ ***verb*** [T] to push or move sb in a way that is not gentle

hut /hʌt/ ***noun*** [C] a small building with one room, usually made of wood or metal: *a wooden/mud hut*

hutch /hʌtʃ/ ***noun*** [C] a wooden box with a front made of wire, that is used for keeping RABBITS or other small animals

hybrid /ˈhaɪbrɪd/ ***noun*** [C] (**BIOLOGY**) an animal or a plant that has parents of two different types (**species**): *A mule is a hybrid of a male donkey and a female horse.* ▶ **hybrid** ***adj.***: *a hybrid flower*

hydrant /ˈhaɪdrənt/ ***noun*** [C] a pipe in a street from which water can be taken for stopping fires, cleaning the streets, etc.

hydrate /ˈhaɪdreɪt; haɪˈdreɪt/ ***verb*** [T] to make sth take in water ▶ **hydration** /haɪˈdreɪʃn/ ***noun*** [U] ➲ look at **dehydrate**

hydraulic /haɪˈdrɔːlɪk/ ***adj.*** operated by water or another liquid moving through pipes, etc. under pressure: *hydraulic brakes* ◇ *hydraulic jack* (= a device for lifting heavy objects)

hydraulic jack

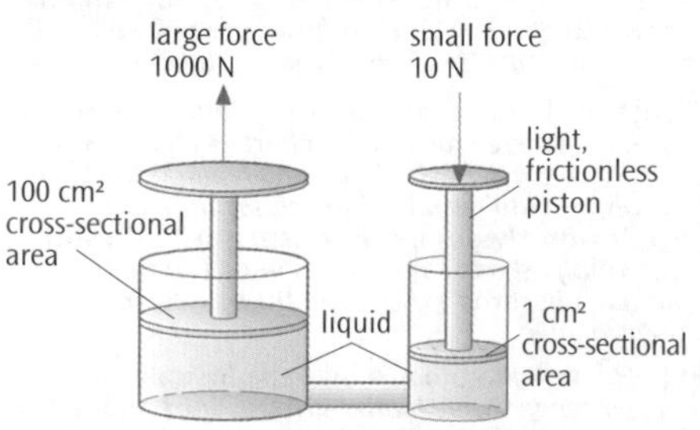

hydraulics /haɪˈdrɔːlɪks; -ˈdrɒl-/ ***noun*** **1** [pl.] machinery that works by the use of liquid moving under pressure **2** [U] the science of the use of liquids moving under pressure

hydr(o)- /ˈhaɪdr(əʊ)/ ***prefix*** (in nouns, adjectives and adverbs) **1** connected with water: *hydroelectricity* **2** (**SCIENCE**) connected with or mixed with HYDROGEN

hydrocarbon /ˌhaɪdrəˈkɑːbən/ ***noun*** [C] (**CHEMISTRY**) a combination of HYDROGEN (= a very light gas) and CARBON (= a substance that is found in all living things). **Hydrocarbons** are found in petrol, coal and natural gas.

hydrochloric acid /ˌhaɪdrəˌklɒrɪk ˈæsɪd/ ***noun*** [U] (*symbol* **HCl**) (**CHEMISTRY**) a type of acid containing HYDROGEN (= a very light gas) and CHLORINE (= a greenish-yellow gas with a strong smell)

hydrocortisone /ˌhaɪdrəˈkɔːtɪzəʊn/ (*also* **cortisol**) ***noun*** [U] (**HEALTH**) a HORMONE produced in the body that is used in drugs to help with diseases of the skin and muscles

hydroelectric /ˌhaɪdrəʊɪˈlektrɪk/ ***adj.*** (**PHYSICS**) using the power of water to produce electricity; produced by the power of water: *a hydroelectric dam* ◇ *hydroelectric power*

hydrofoil /ˈhaɪdrəfɔɪl/ ***noun*** [C] a boat which rises above the surface of the water when it is travelling fast

hydrogen /ˈhaɪdrədʒən/ ***noun*** [U] (*symbol* **H**) (**CHEMISTRY**) a light colourless gas. **Hydrogen** and OXYGEN form water. ❶ For more information on the periodic table of elements, look at pages R34-5.

ˈhydrogen bomb (*also* **ˈH-bomb**) ***noun*** [C] (**SCIENCE**) a very powerful nuclear bomb

ˌhydrogen peˈroxide = PEROXIDE

hydrology /haɪˈdrɒlədʒi/ ***noun*** [U] (**SCIENCE**) the scientific study of the earth's water, especially its movement in relation to land

hydroplane /ˈhaɪdrəpleɪn/ ***noun*** [C] **1** a light boat with an engine and a flat bottom, designed to travel fast over the surface of water **2** (*AmE*) = SEAPLANE

hydroponics /ˌhaɪdrəˈpɒnɪks/ ***noun*** [U] (**AGRICULTURE**) the process of growing plants in water or sand, rather than in soil

hydrosphere /ˈhaɪdrəʊsfɪə(r)/ ***noun*** [usually sing.] (**GEOGRAPHY**) all of the water on or over the earth's surface

hydroxide /haɪˈdrɒksaɪd/ ***noun*** [C] (**CHEMISTRY**) a chemical COMPOUND consisting of a metal and a combination of OXYGEN and HYDROGEN

hyena (also **hyaena**) /haɪˈiːnə/ ***noun*** [C] a wild animal like a dog that lives in Africa and Asia. **Hyenas** eat the meat of animals that are already dead and can make a sound like a human laugh.

hygiene /ˈhaɪdʒiːn/ ***noun*** [U] (the rules of) keeping yourself and things around you clean, in order to prevent disease: *High standards of hygiene are essential when you are preparing food.* ◇ *personal hygiene*

hygienic /haɪˈdʒiːnɪk/ ***adj.*** clean, without the bacteria that cause disease: *hygienic conditions* ▶ **hygienically** /-kli/ ***adv.***

hymn /hɪm/ ***noun*** [C] (**MUSIC**) a religious song that Christians sing together in church, etc.

hype¹ /haɪp/ ***noun*** [U] (**ARTS AND MEDIA**) advertisements that tell you how good and important a new product, film, etc. is: *Don't believe all the hype – the book is rubbish!*

hype[2] /haɪp/ ***verb*** [T] **~ sth (up)** to exaggerate how good or important sth is

hyper- /ˈhaɪpə(r)/ ***prefix*** (in adjectives and nouns) more than normal; too much: *hypercritical* ◇ *hypersensitive* ➲ look at **hypo-**

hyperactive /ˌhaɪpərˈæktɪv/ ***adj.*** (used especially about children and their behaviour) too active and only able to keep quiet and still for short periods ▶ **hyperactivity** /ˌhaɪpərækˈtɪvəti/ ***noun*** [U]

hyperbole /haɪˈpɜːbəli/ ***noun*** [U, C, usually sing.] a way of speaking or writing that makes sth sound better, more exciting, dangerous, etc. than it really is **SYN** **exaggeration**: *His latest movie is accompanied by the usual hyperbole.*

hyperlink /ˈhaɪpəlɪŋk/ ***noun*** [C] (**COMPUTING**) a place in an electronic document on a computer that is connected to another electronic document: *Click on the hyperlink.*

hypermarket /ˈhaɪpəmɑːkɪt/ ***noun*** [C] (*BrE*) (**BUSINESS**) a very large shop that is usually built outside a town and sells a wide variety of goods

hypertension /ˌhaɪpəˈtenʃn/ ***noun*** [U] (**HEALTH**) blood pressure that is higher than is normal

hypertext /ˈhaɪpətekst/ ***noun*** [U] (**COMPUTING**) text stored in a computer system that contains links that allow the user to move from one piece of text or document to another: *a hypertext link on the Internet* ➲ look at **HTML**

hyphen /ˈhaɪfn/ ***noun*** [C] (**LANGUAGE**) the mark (-) used for joining two words together (for example *left-handed*, *red-hot*) or to show that a word has been divided and continues on the next line ➲ look at **dash**

hyphenate /ˈhaɪfəneɪt/ ***verb*** [T] (**LANGUAGE**) to join two words together with a HYPHEN ▶ **hyphenation** /ˌhaɪfəˈneɪʃn/ ***noun*** [U]

hypnosis /hɪpˈnəʊsɪs/ ***noun*** [U] (**PSYCHOLOGY**) (the producing of) an unconscious state where sb's mind and actions can be controlled by another person: *She was questioned **under hypnosis**.*

hypnotize (also **-ise**) /ˈhɪpnətaɪz/ ***verb*** [T] (**PSYCHOLOGY**) to put sb into an unconscious state where the person's mind and actions can be controlled ▶ **hypnotic** /hɪpˈnɒtɪk/ ***adj.*** ▶ **hypnotism** /ˈhɪpnətɪzəm/ ***noun*** [U] ▶ **hypnotist** /ˈhɪpnətɪst/ ***noun*** [C]

hypo- /ˈhaɪpəʊ/ (*also* **hyp-**) ***prefix*** (in adjectives and nouns) under; below normal: *hypodermic* ◇ *hypothermia* ➲ look at **hyper-**

hypochondria /ˌhaɪpəˈkɒndriə/ ***noun*** [U] (**HEALTH**) a mental condition in which sb believes that they are ill, even when there is nothing wrong

hypochondriac /ˌhaɪpəˈkɒndriæk/ ***noun*** [C] (**HEALTH**) a person who is always worried about their health and believes they are ill, even when there is nothing wrong

hypocrisy /hɪˈpɒkrəsi/ ***noun*** [U] behaviour in which sb pretends to have moral standards or opinions that they do not really have

hypocrite /ˈhɪpəkrɪt/ ***noun*** [C] a person who pretends to have moral standards or opinions which they do not really have. **Hypocrites** say one thing and do another: *What a hypocrite! She says she's against the hunting of animals but she's wearing a fur coat.* ▶ **hypocritical** /ˌhɪpəˈkrɪtɪkl/ ***adj.*** ▶ **hypocritically** /-kli/ ***adv.***

hypodermic /ˌhaɪpəˈdɜːmɪk/ (*also* **ˌhypodermic ˈneedle**, **ˌhypodermic syˈringe**) ***noun*** [C] (**HEALTH**) a medical instrument with a long needle that is used to give an INJECTION (= put drugs under the skin)

hypotenuse /haɪˈpɒtənjuːz/ ***noun*** [C] (**MATHEMATICS**) the side opposite the RIGHT ANGLE of a RIGHT-ANGLED triangle (= a triangle with one angle of 90°) ➲ picture at **triangle**

hypothalamus /ˌhaɪpəˈθæləməs/ ***noun*** [C] (*pl.* **hypothalami** /-maɪ/) (**ANATOMY**) the part of the brain that controls body temperature, HUNGER and THIRST ➲ picture at **brain**

hypothermia /ˌhaɪpəˈθɜːmiə/ ***noun*** [U] (**HEALTH**) a medical condition in which the body temperature is much lower than normal

hypothesis **AW** /haɪˈpɒθəsɪs/ ***noun*** [C] (*pl.* **hypotheses** /-siːz/) an idea that is suggested as the possible explanation for sth but has not yet been found to be true or correct

hypothesize (also **-ise**) **AW** /haɪˈpɒθəsaɪz/ ***verb*** [I,T] (*formal*) to suggest a way of explaining sth when you do not definitely know about it; to form a HYPOTHESIS

hypothetical **AW** /ˌhaɪpəˈθetɪkl/ ***adj.*** based on situations that have not yet happened, not on facts: *That's a hypothetical question because we don't know what the situation will be next year.* ▶ **hypothetically** /-kli/ ***adv.***

hypoxia /haɪˈpɒksiə/ ***noun*** [U] (**HEALTH**) a condition in which not enough OXYGEN reaches the body's TISSUES (= groups of cells that form the different parts of the body)

hysteria /hɪˈstɪəriə/ ***noun*** [U] a state in which a person or a group of people cannot control their emotions, for example cannot stop laughing, crying, shouting, etc.: *mass hysteria*

hysterical /hɪˈsterɪkl/ ***adj.*** **1** very excited and unable to control your emotions: *hysterical laughter* ◇ *She was hysterical with grief.* **2** (*informal*) very funny ▶ **hysterically** /-kli/ ***adv.***

hysterics /hɪˈsterɪks/ ***noun*** [pl.] **1** an expression of extreme fear, excitement or anger that makes sb lose control of their emotions: *She **went into hysterics** when they told her the news.* ◇ (*informal*) *My father would **have hysterics*** (= be furious) *if he knew I was going out with you.* **2** (*informal*) LAUGHTER that you cannot control: *The comedian had the audience in hysterics.*

Hz ***abbr.*** hertz; (used in radio) a measure of FREQUENCY

I, i[1] /aɪ/ ***noun*** [C,U] (*pl.* **I's**; **i's** /aɪz/) the ninth letter of the English alphabet: *'Island' begins with (an) 'I'.*

I[2] /aɪ/ ***pronoun*** (the subject of a verb) the person who is speaking or writing: *I phoned and said that I was busy.* ◇ *I'm not going to fall, am I?*

iambic /aɪˈæmbɪk/ ***adj.*** (**LITERATURE**) (used about rhythm in poetry) having one short or weak SYLLABLE followed by one long or strong SYLLABLE: *a poem written in iambic pentameters* (= in lines of ten syllables, five short and five long)

IATA /aɪˈɑːtə/ ***abbr.*** (**TOURISM**) **International Air Transport Association**; the organization that most of the world's airlines belong to, which helps them to operate efficiently and sets standards for how tickets are sold, the safety of aircraft, etc.: *an IATA approved travel agency*

ice¹ /aɪs/ ***noun*** [U] water that has frozen and become solid: *Do you want ice in your orange juice?* ◇ *I slipped on a patch of ice.* ◇ *black ice* (=ice on roads, that cannot be seen easily)
IDM **break the ice** to say or do sth that makes people feel more relaxed, especially at the beginning of a party or meeting
cut no ice (with sb) to have no influence or effect on sb
on ice 1 (used about wine, etc.) kept cold by being surrounded by ice **2** (used about a plan, etc.) waiting to be dealt with later; delayed: *We've had to put our plans to go to Australia on ice for the time being.*

ice² /aɪs/ (*especially AmE* **frost**) ***verb*** [T] to decorate a cake by covering it with a mixture of sugar, butter, chocolate, etc. ➲ look at **icing**
PHR V **ice (sth) over/up** to cover sth or become covered with ice: *The windscreen of the car had iced over in the night.*

iceberg /ˈaɪsbɜːg/ ***noun*** [C] (GEOGRAPHY) a very large block of ice that floats in the sea
IDM **the tip of the iceberg** → TIP¹

icebox /ˈaɪsbɒks/ (*AmE*) = FRIDGE

ˈice cap ***noun*** [C] (GEOGRAPHY) a layer of ice permanently covering parts of the earth, especially around the North and South Poles: *the polar ice caps*

ˌice-ˈcold ***adj.*** very cold: *ice-cold beer* ◇ *Your hands are ice-cold.*

ˌice ˈcream ***noun* 1** [U] a frozen sweet food that is made from cream **2** [C] an amount of ice cream that is served to sb, often in a special container (**a cone**): *a strawberry ice cream*

ˈice cube ***noun*** [C] a small block of ice that you put in a drink to make it cold

iced /aɪst/ ***adj.*** (used about drinks) very cold: *iced tea*

ˈice floe ***noun*** [C] (GEOGRAPHY) a large area of ice, floating in the sea

ˈice hockey (*AmE* **hockey**) ***noun*** [U] (SPORT) a game that is played on ice by two teams who try to hit a PUCK (=a small flat rubber object) into a goal with long wooden sticks ➲ note at **hockey**

ˌice ˈlolly ***noun*** [C] (*pl.* **ice lollies**) (*AmE* **Popsicle**) a piece of flavoured ice on a stick ➲ look at **lollipop**

ˈice rink = SKATING RINK

ˈice-skate = SKATE²

ˈice skating = SKATING (1)

icicle /ˈaɪsɪkl/ ***noun*** [C] a pointed piece of ice that is formed by water freezing as it falls or runs down from sth

icing /ˈaɪsɪŋ/ (*AmE* **frosting**) ***noun*** [U] a sweet mixture of sugar and water, milk, butter, etc. that is used for decorating cakes

icon /ˈaɪkɒn/ ***noun*** [C] **1** (COMPUTING) a small picture or symbol on a computer screen that represents a program: *Click on the printer icon with the mouse.* **2** a person or thing that is considered to be a symbol of sth: *Madonna and other pop icons of the 1980s* **3** (also **ikon**) (RELIGION) a picture or figure of an important religious person, used by some types of Christians

iconography /ˌaɪkəˈnɒgrəfi/ ***noun*** [U] (ART) the use or study of images or symbols in art

icy /ˈaɪsi/ ***adj.* 1** very cold: *icy winds/water/weather* **2** covered with ice: *icy roads*

ID /ˌaɪ ˈdiː/ ***abbr.*** (*informal*) identification; identity: *an ID card*

Id = EID

I'd /aɪd/ short for I HAD, I WOULD

idea /aɪˈdɪə/ ***noun* 1** [C] **an ~ (for sth); an ~ (of sth/of doing sth)** a plan, thought or suggestion, especially about what to do in a particular situation: *That's a good idea!* ◇ *He's **got an idea** for a new play.* ◇ *I had the **bright idea** of getting Jane to help me with my homework.* ◇ *Has anyone got any ideas of how to tackle this problem?* ◇ *It was your idea to invite so many people to the party.* **2** [sing.] **an ~ (of sth)** a picture or impression in your mind: *You have no idea* (=you can't imagine) *how difficult it was to find a time that suited everybody.* ◇ *The programme **gave a good idea** of what life was like before the war.* ◇ *Staying in to watch the football on TV is not my idea of a good time.* **3** [C] **an ~ (about sth)** an opinion or belief: *She has her own ideas about how to bring up children.* **4 the idea** [sing.] **the ~ (of sth/of doing sth)** the aim or purpose of sth: *The idea of the course is to teach the basics of car maintenance.* ➲ note at **purpose**
IDM **get the idea** to understand the aim or purpose of sth: *Right! I think I've got the idea now.*
get the idea that... to get the feeling or impression that...: *Where did you get the idea that I was paying for this meal?*
have an idea that... to have a feeling or think that...: *I'm not sure but I have an idea that they've gone on holiday.*
not have the faintest/foggiest (idea) → FAINT¹

ideal¹ /aɪˈdiːəl/ ***adj.*** **~ (for sb/sth)** the best possible; perfect: *She's the ideal candidate for the job.* ◇ ***In an ideal world** there would be no poverty.* ◇ *It would be an **ideal opportunity** for you to practise your Spanish.*

ideal² /aɪˈdiːəl/ ***noun*** [C] **1** an idea or principle that seems perfect to you and that you want to achieve: *She finds it hard to live up to her parents' high ideals.* ◇ *political/moral/social ideals* **2** [usually sing.] **an ~ (of sth)** a perfect example of a person or thing: *It's my ideal of what a family home should be.*

idealism /aɪˈdiːəlɪzəm/ ***noun*** [U] the belief that a perfect life, situation, etc. can be achieved, even when this is not very likely: *Young people are usually full of idealism.* ➲ look at **realism** ▸ **idealist** ***noun*** [C] ▸ **idealistic** /ˌaɪdiəˈlɪstɪk/ ***adj.***

idealize (also **-ise**) /aɪˈdiːəlaɪz/ ***verb*** [T] to imagine or show sb/sth as being better than they or it really are: *Old people often idealize the past.*

ideally /aɪˈdiːəli/ ***adv.* 1** perfectly: *They are ideally suited to each other.* **2** in an ideal situation: *Ideally, no class should be larger than 25.*

identical AW /aɪˈdentɪkl/ ***adj.* 1 ~ (to/with sb/sth)** exactly the same as; similar in every detail: *I can't see any difference between these two pens – they look identical to me.* ◇ *That watch is identical to the one I lost yesterday.* **2 the identical** (only *before* a noun) the same: *This is the identical room we stayed in last year.* ▸ **identically** /-kli/ ***adv.***

iˌdentical ˈtwin ***noun*** [C] (BIOLOGY) one of two children born at the same time from the same mother, and who are of the same sex and look very similar

identifiable AW /aɪˌdentɪˈfaɪəbl/ ***adj.*** that can be recognized: *identifiable characteristics*

identification AW /aɪˌdentɪfɪˈkeɪʃn/ ***noun*** [U, C] **1** the process of showing, recognizing or giving proof of who or what sb/sth is: *The identification of the bodies of those killed in the explosion was very difficult.* **2** (*abbr.* **ID**) [U] an official paper, document, etc. that is proof of who you are: *Do you have any* *identification?* **3** ~ **(with sb/sth)** a strong feeling of understanding or sharing the same feelings as sb/sth: *children's identification with TV heroes*

identify 🔑 AW /aɪ'dentɪfaɪ/ ***verb*** [T] (*pres. part.* **identifying**; *3rd person sing. pres.* **identifies**; *pt, pp* **identified**) ~ **sb/sth (as sb/sth)** to recognize or be able to say who or what sb/sth is: *The police need someone to identify the body.* ◇ *We must identify the cause of the problem before we look for solutions.*
PHR V **identify sth with sth** to think or say that sth is the same as sth else: *You can't identify nationalism with fascism.*
identify with sb to feel that you understand and share what sb else is feeling: *I found it hard to identify with the woman in the film.*
identify (yourself) with sb/sth to support or be closely connected with sb/sth: *She became identified with the new political party.*

identity 🔑 AW /aɪ'dentəti/ ***noun*** [C,U] (*pl.* **identities**) who or what a person or a thing is: *There are few clues to the identity of the killer.* ◇ *The region has its own* ***cultural identity****.* ◇ *The arrest was a case of mistaken identity* (= the wrong person was arrested).

i'dentity card (*also* **I'D card**) ***noun*** [C] a card with your name, photograph, etc. that is proof of who you are

ideogram /'ɪdiəgræm/ (*also* **ideograph** /'ɪdiəgrɑːf/) ***noun*** [C] **1** (LANGUAGE) a symbol that is used in a writing system, for example Chinese, to represent the idea of a thing, rather than the sounds of a word **2** (TECHNICAL) a sign or a symbol for sth

ideology AW /ˌaɪdi'ɒlədʒi/ ***noun*** [C,U] (*pl.* **ideologies**) a set of ideas which form the basis for a political or economic system: *Marxist ideology* ▶ **ideological** AW /ˌaɪdiə'lɒdʒɪkl/ ***adj.***

idiom /'ɪdiəm/ ***noun*** [C] (LANGUAGE) an expression whose meaning is different from the meanings of the individual words in it: *The idiom 'bring sth home to sb' means 'make sb understand sth'.*

idiomatic /ˌɪdiə'mætɪk/ ***adj.*** (LANGUAGE) **1** using language that contains expressions that are natural to sb who learned the language as a child: *He speaks good idiomatic English.* **2** containing an IDIOM: *an idiomatic expression*

idiosyncrasy /ˌɪdiə'sɪŋkrəsi/ ***noun*** [C,U] (*pl.* **idiosyncrasies**) a person's particular way of behaving, thinking, etc., especially when it is unusual; an unusual characteristic
SYN **eccentricity**: *Eating garlic every morning is one of his idiosyncrasies.* ◇ *The car has its little idiosyncrasies.* ▶ **idiosyncratic** /ˌɪdiəsɪŋ'krætɪk/: *His teaching methods are idiosyncratic but successful.*

idiot /'ɪdiət/ ***noun*** [C] (*informal*) a very stupid person: *I was an idiot to forget my passport.* ▶ **idiotic** /ˌɪdi'ɒtɪk/ ***adj.*** ▶ **idiotically** /-kli/ ***adv.***

idle /'aɪdl/ ***adj.*** **1** not wanting to work hard; lazy: *He has the ability to succeed but he is just* ***bone*** (= very) *idle.* **2** not doing anything; not being used: *She can't bear to be idle.* ◇ *The factory* ***stood idle*** *while the machines were being repaired.* **3** (only *before* a noun) not to be taken seriously because it will not have any result: *an idle promise/threat* ◇ *idle chatter/curiosity* ▶ **idleness** ***noun*** [U] ▶ **idly** /'aɪdli/ ***adv.***

idol /'aɪdl/ ***noun*** [C] **1** a person (such as a film star or pop musician) who is admired or loved: *a pop/football/teen/screen idol* **2** (RELIGION) a statue that people treat as a god

idolatry /aɪ'dɒlətri/ ***noun*** [U] (RELIGION) the practice of worshipping statues as gods

idolize (also -ise) /'aɪdəlaɪz/ ***verb*** [T] to love or admire sb very much or too much: *He is an only child and his parents idolize him.*

idyllic /ɪ'dɪlɪk/ ***adj.*** very pleasant and peaceful; perfect: *an idyllic holiday*

i.e. 🔑 /ˌaɪ 'iː/ ***abbr.*** that is; in other words: *deciduous trees, i.e. those which lose their leaves in autumn*

IELTS /'aɪelts/ ***abbr.*** (EDUCATION) **International English Language Testing System**; a British test, set by the University of Cambridge, that measures a person's ability to speak and write English at the level that is necessary to go to university in Britain, Australia, Canada and New Zealand

if 🔑 /ɪf/ ***conj.*** **1** used in sentences in which one thing only happens or is true when another thing happens or is true: *If you see him, give him this letter.* ◇ *We won't go to the beach if it rains.* ◇ *If I had more time, I would learn another language.* ◇ *I might see her tomorrow. If not, I'll see her at the weekend.* **2** when; every time: *If I try to phone her she just hangs up.* ◇ *If metal gets hot it expands.* **3** used after verbs such as 'ask', 'know', 'remember': *They asked if we would like to go too.* ◇ *I can't remember if I posted the letter or not.* **4** used when you are asking sb to do sth or suggesting sth politely: *If you could just come this way, sir.* ◇ *If I might suggest something...*
IDM **as if** → AS
even if → EVEN²
if I were you used when you are giving sb advice: *If I were you, I'd leave now.*
if it wasn't/weren't for sb/sth if a particular person or situation did not exist or was not there; without sb/sth: *If it wasn't for him, I wouldn't stay in this country.*
if only used for expressing a strong wish: *If only I could drive.* ◇ *If only he'd write.*

IGCSE /ˌaɪ dʒiː siː es 'iː/ ***abbr.*** (EDUCATION) **International General Certificate of Secondary Education**; an international examination in different subjects that students can take when they are between 14 and 16 ➲ look at **GCSE, International Baccalaureate**

igloo /'ɪgluː/ ***noun*** [C] (*pl.* **igloos**) a small house that is built from blocks of hard snow

igneous /'ɪgniəs/ ***adj.*** (GEOLOGY) (used about rocks) formed when MAGMA (= melted or liquid material from below the earth's surface) comes out of a VOLCANO and becomes solid ➲ look at **metamorphic, sedimentary** ➲ picture at **rock**

ignite /ɪg'naɪt/ ***verb*** [I,T] (*formal*) to start burning or to make sth start burning: *A spark from the engine ignited the petrol.*

ignition /ɪg'nɪʃn/ ***noun*** **1** [C] the electrical system that starts the engine of a car: *to turn the ignition on/off* ◇ *First of all, put the key in the ignition.* **2** [U] the action of starting to burn or making sth start to burn

ignominious /ˌɪgnə'mɪniəs/ ***adj.*** (*formal*) making you feel embarrassed: *The team suffered an ignominious defeat.* ▶ **ignominiously** ***adv.***

ignorance AW /'ɪgnərəns/ ***noun*** [U] ~ **(of/about sth)** a lack of information or knowledge: *The workers were* ***in complete ignorance*** *of the management's plans.*

ignorant AW /'ɪgnərənt/ ***adj.*** **1** ~ **(of/about sth)** not knowing about sth: *Many people are ignorant of their rights.* **2** (*informal*) having or showing bad manners: *an ignorant person/remark*

ignore 🔑 AW /ɪɡˈnɔː(r)/ ***verb*** [T] to pay no attention to sb/sth: *I said hello to Debbie but she totally ignored me* (=acted as though she hadn't seen me). ◇ *Sue ignored her doctor's advice about drinking and smoking less.*

ikon = ICON (3)

il- ***prefix*** → IN

ileum /ˈɪliəm/ ***noun*** [C] (*pl.* **ilea** /ˈɪliə/) (ANATOMY) one part of the INTESTINE (=the tube that carries food away from the stomach) ➲ picture at **digestive system**

I'll /aɪl/ short for I WILL, I SHALL

ill[1] 🔑 /ɪl/ ***adj.*** **1** (*AmE* sick) (not before a noun) (HEALTH) not in good health; not well: *I can't drink milk because it makes me **feel ill**.* ◇ *My mother was **taken ill** suddenly last week.* ◇ *My grandfather is **seriously ill** in hospital.* **2** (only *before* a noun) bad or harmful: *He resigned because of **ill health**.* ◇ *I'm glad to say I suffered no **ill effects** from all that rich food.* ➲ noun **illness**

ill[2] /ɪl/ ***adv.*** **1** (often in compounds) badly or wrongly: *You would be **ill-advised** to drive until you have fully recovered.* **2** only with difficulty; not easily: *They could ill afford the extra money for better heating.*

IDM **augur well/ill for sb/sth** → AUGUR
bode well/ill (for sb/sth) → BODE

illegal 🔑 AW /ɪˈliːɡl/ ***adj.*** (LAW) not allowed by the law: *It is illegal to own a gun without a special licence.* ◇ *illegal drugs/immigrants/activities* OPP **legal** ▶ **illegally** /-ɡəli/ ***adv.***

illegality /ˌɪliˈɡæləti/ ***noun*** (*pl.* **illegalities**) (LAW) **1** [U] the state of being illegal: *No illegality is suspected.* **2** [C] an illegal act ➲ look at **legality**

illegible /ɪˈledʒəbl/ ***adj.*** difficult or impossible to read: *Your handwriting is quite illegible.* OPP **legible** ▶ **illegibly** /-əbli/ ***adv.***

illegitimate /ˌɪləˈdʒɪtəmət/ ***adj.*** **1** (*old-fashioned*) (used about a child) born to parents who are not married to each other **2** not allowed by law; against the rules: *the illegitimate use of company money* OPP **legitimate** ▶ **illegitimacy** /ˌɪləˈdʒɪtəməsi/ ***noun*** [U]

ˌill-ˈfated ***adj.*** not lucky: *the ill-fated ship, the Titanic*

illicit /ɪˈlɪsɪt/ ***adj.*** (used about an activity or substance) not allowed by law or by the rules of society: *the illicit trade in ivory* ◇ *They were having an illicit affair.*

illiterate /ɪˈlɪtərət/ ***adj.*** **1** not able to read or write OPP **literate** **2** (used about a piece of writing) very badly written **3** not knowing much about a particular subject: *computer illiterate* ▶ **illiteracy** /ɪˈlɪtərəsi/ ***noun*** [U]: *adult illiteracy* OPP **literacy**

illness 🔑 /ˈɪlnəs/ ***noun*** (HEALTH) **1** [U] the state of being physically or mentally ill: *He's missed a lot of school through illness.* ◇ *There is a history of mental illness in the family.* ➲ note at **disease** **2** [C] a type or period of physical or mental ill health: *minor/serious/childhood illnesses* ◇ *My dad is just getting over his illness.* ➲ adjective **ill** ➲ note at **disease**

illogical AW /ɪˈlɒdʒɪkl/ ***adj.*** not sensible or reasonable: *It seems illogical to me to pay somebody to do work that you could do yourself.* OPP **logical** ▶ **illogicality** /ɪˌlɒdʒɪˈkæləti/ ***noun*** [C,U] (*pl.* **illogicalities**) ▶ **illogically** /-kli/ ***adv.***

ˌill-ˈtreat ***verb*** [T] to treat sb/sth badly or in an unkind way ▶ **ˌill-ˈtreatment** ***noun*** [U]

illuminate /ɪˈluːmɪneɪt/ ***verb*** [T] (*formal*) **1** to shine light on sth or to decorate sth with lights: *Floodlights illuminated the stadium.* **2** to explain sth or make sth clear

illuminated /ɪˈluːmɪneɪtɪd/ ***adj.*** **1** lit with bright lights: *the illuminated city at night* **2** (ART) decorated with gold, silver and bright colours in a way that was done in the past, by hand: *illuminated manuscripts*

illuminating /ɪˈluːmɪneɪtɪŋ/ ***adj.*** helping to explain sth or make sth clear: *an illuminating discussion*

illumination /ɪˌluːmɪˈneɪʃn/ ***noun*** **1** [U, C] light or the place where a light comes from **2 illuminations** [pl.] (*BrE*) bright colourful lights that are used for decorating a street, town, etc.

illusion /ɪˈluːʒn/ ***noun*** **1** [C,U] a false idea, belief or impression: *I **have no illusions** about the situation – I know it's serious.* ◇ *I think Peter's **under the illusion** that he will be the new director.* **2** [C] something that your eyes tell you is there or is true but in fact is not: *That line looks longer, but in fact they're the same length. It's an **optical illusion**.*

illusory /ɪˈluːsəri/ ***adj.*** (*formal*) not real, although seeming to be: *The profits they had hoped for proved to be illusory.*

illustrate 🔑 AW /ˈɪləstreɪt/ ***verb*** [T] **1** to explain or make sth clear by using examples, pictures or diagrams: *These statistics **illustrate the point** that I was making very well.* **2** to add pictures, diagrams, etc. to a book or magazine: *Most cookery books are illustrated.*

illustration AW /ˌɪləˈstreɪʃn/ ***noun*** **1** [C] a drawing, diagram or picture in a book or magazine: *colour illustrations* **2** [U] (ART) the activity or art of illustrating **3** [C] an example that makes a point or an idea clear: *Can you give me an illustration of what you mean?* ➲ note at **example**

illustrative AW /ˈɪləstrətɪv/ ***adj.*** (*formal*) helping to explain sth or show it more clearly SYN **explanatory**

illustrator /ˈɪləstreɪtə(r)/ ***noun*** [C] (ART) a person who draws or paints pictures for books, etc.

illustrious /ɪˈlʌstriəs/ ***adj.*** (*formal*) famous and successful

ILO /ˌaɪ el ˈəʊ/ ***abbr.*** (POLITICS) **International Labour Organization**; an organization within the United Nations concerned with work and working conditions

I'm /aɪm/ short for I AM

im- ***prefix*** → IN

image 🔑 AW /ˈɪmɪdʒ/ ***noun*** [C] **1** the general impression that a person or organization gives to the public: *When you meet him, he's very different from his public image.* **2** a mental picture or idea of sb/sth: *I have an image of my childhood as always sunny and happy.* **3** a picture or description that appears in a book, film or painting: *horrific images of war* **4** a copy or picture of sb/sth seen in a mirror, through a camera, on television, computer, etc.: *A perfect image of the building was reflected in the lake.* ◇ (*figurative*) *He's **the (spitting) image of** his father* (=he looks exactly like him).

imagery AW /ˈɪmɪdʒəri/ ***noun*** [U] (LITERATURE) language that produces pictures in the minds of the people reading or listening: *poetic imagery*

imaginable /ɪˈmædʒɪnəbl/ ***adj.*** that you can imagine: *Sophie made all the excuses imaginable when she was caught stealing.* ◇ *His house was equipped with every imaginable luxury.*

imaginary ⊶ /ɪˈmædʒɪnəri/ ***adj.*** existing only in the mind; not real: *Many children have imaginary friends.*

imagination ⊶ /ɪˌmædʒɪˈneɪʃn/ ***noun*** **1** [U, C] the ability to create mental pictures or new ideas: *He has a lively imagination.* ◇ *She's very clever but she doesn't* ***have*** *much* ***imagination***. **2** [C] the part of the mind that uses this ability: *If you* ***use*** *your* ***imagination***, *you should be able to guess the answer.* ▸ **imaginatively** ***adv.***

imaginative /ɪˈmædʒɪnətɪv/ ***adj.*** having or showing imagination: *She's always full of imaginative ideas.*

imagine ⊶ /ɪˈmædʒɪn/ ***verb*** [T] **1** ~ **that...**; ~ **sb/sth (doing/as sth)** to form a picture or idea in your mind of what sth/sb might be like: *Imagine that you're lying on a beach.* ◇ *It's not easy to imagine your brother as a doctor.* ◇ *I can't imagine myself cycling 20 miles a day.* **2** to see, hear or think sth that is not true or does not exist: *She's always imagining that she's ill but she's fine really.* ◇ *I thought I heard someone downstairs, but I must have been* ***imagining things***. **3** to think that sth is probably true; to suppose: *I imagine he'll be coming by car.*

imbalance /ɪmˈbæləns/ ***noun*** [C] **an** ~ **(between A and B)**; **an** ~ **(in/of sth)** a difference; not being equal: *an imbalance in the numbers of men and women teachers*

imbecile /ˈɪmbəsiːl/ ***noun*** [C] a stupid person **SYN** **idiot**

IMF /ˌaɪ em ˈef/ ***abbr.*** (**ECONOMICS**) the International Monetary Fund

imitate /ˈɪmɪteɪt/ ***verb*** [T] **1** to copy the behaviour of sb/sth: *Small children learn by imitating their parents.* **2** to copy the speech or actions of sb/sth, often in order to make people laugh: *She could imitate her mother perfectly.*

imitation /ˌɪmɪˈteɪʃn/ ***noun*** **1** [C] a copy of sth real: *Some artificial flowers are good imitations of real ones.* ➲ note at **artificial** ➲ look at **genuine** **2** [U] the act of copying sb/sth: *Good pronunciation of a language is best learnt* ***by imitation***. **3** [C] the act of copying the way sb talks and behaves, especially in order to make people laugh: *Can you* ***do*** *any* ***imitations*** *of politicians?*

immaculate /ɪˈmækjələt/ ***adj.*** **1** perfectly clean and tidy: *immaculate white shirts* **2** without any mistakes; perfect: *His performance of 'Romeo' was immaculate.* ▸ **immaculately** ***adv.***

immaterial /ˌɪməˈtɪəriəl/ ***adj.*** ~ **(to sb/sth)** not important: *It's immaterial to me whether we go today or tomorrow.*

immature **AW** /ˌɪməˈtjʊə(r)/ ***adj.*** **1** not fully grown or developed: *an immature body* **2** (used about a person) behaving in a way that is not sensible and is typical of people who are much younger: *I think he's too immature to take his work seriously.* **OPP** **mature**

immeasurable /ɪˈmeʒərəbl/ ***adj.*** (*formal*) too large, great, etc. to be measured: *to cause immeasurable harm* ◇ *Her contribution was of immeasurable importance.* ▸ **immeasurably** /-əbli/ ***adv.***: *Housing standards have improved immeasurably since the war.*

immediacy /ɪˈmiːdiəsi/ ***noun*** [U] the quality of being available or seeming to happen close to you and without delay: *Letters do not have the same immediacy as email.*

immediate ⊶ /ɪˈmiːdiət/ ***adj.*** **1** happening or done without delay: *I'd like an immediate answer to my proposal.* ◇ *The government responded with immediate action.* **2** (only *before* a noun) existing now and needing urgent attention: *Tell me what your immediate needs are.* **3** (only *before* a noun) nearest in time, position or relationship: *They won't make any changes in* ***the immediate future***. ◇ *He has left most of his money to his immediate family* (= parents, children, brothers and sisters).

immediately ⊶ /ɪˈmiːdiətli/ ***adv., conj.*** **1** at once; without delay: *Can you come home immediately after work?* ◇ *I couldn't immediately see what he meant.* **2** very closely; directly: *He wasn't immediately involved in the crime.* **3** nearest in time or position: *Who's the girl immediately in front of Simon?* ◇ *What did you do immediately after the war?* **4** (*BrE*) as soon as: *I opened the letter immediately I got home.*

immense /ɪˈmens/ ***adj.*** very big or great: *immense difficulties/importance/power* ◇ *She gets immense pleasure from her garden.*

immensely /ɪˈmensli/ ***adv.*** extremely; very much: *immensely enjoyable*

immensity /ɪˈmensəti/ ***noun*** [U] an extremely large size: *the immensity of the universe*

immerse /ɪˈmɜːs/ ***verb*** [T] **1** ~ **sth (in sth)** to put sth into a liquid so that it is covered: *Make sure the spaghetti is fully immersed in the boiling water.* **2** ~ **yourself (in sth)** to involve yourself completely in sth so that you give it all your attention: *Rachel's usually immersed in a book.*

immersion /ɪˈmɜːʃn/ ***noun*** [U] **1** ~ **(in sth)** the act of putting sb/sth into a liquid so that they or it are completely covered; the state of being completely covered by a liquid: *Immersion in cold water resulted in rapid loss of heat.* **2** ~ **(in sth)** the state of being completely involved in sth: *a two-week immersion course in French* (= in which the student hears and uses only French)

immigrant **AW** /ˈɪmɪɡrənt/ ***noun*** [C] (**SOCIAL STUDIES**) a person who has come into a foreign country to live there permanently: *The government plans to tighten controls to prevent* ***illegal immigrants***. ◇ *London has a high immigrant population.*

immigrate **AW** /ˈɪmɪɡreɪt/ ***verb*** [T] ~ **(to...)** **(from...)** (*especially AmE*) (**SOCIAL STUDIES**) to come and live permanently in a country after leaving your own country ➲ look at **emigrate**

immigration **AW** /ˌɪmɪˈɡreɪʃn/ ***noun*** [U] **1** (**SOCIAL STUDIES**) the process of coming to live permanently in a country that is not your own; the number of people who do this: *There are greater controls on immigration than there used to be.* **2** (*also* **immiˈgration control**) the control point at an airport, port, etc. where the official documents of people who want to come into a country are checked: *When you leave the plane you have to go through customs and immigration.* ➲ look at **emigrant**, **emigrate**, **emigration**

imminent /ˈɪmɪnənt/ ***adj.*** (usually used about sth unpleasant) almost certain to happen very soon: *Heavy rainfall means that flooding is imminent.* ▸ **imminently** ***adv.***

immiscible /ɪˈmɪsəbl/ ***adj.*** (**CHEMISTRY**) (used about liquids) that cannot be mixed together **OPP** **miscible**

immobile /ɪˈməʊbaɪl/ ***adj.*** not moving or not able to move **OPP** **mobile** ▸ **immobility** /ˌɪməˈbɪləti/ ***noun*** [U]

immobilize (also -ise) /ɪˈməʊbəlaɪz/ ***verb*** [T] to prevent sb/sth from moving or working normally: *This device immobilizes the car to prevent it being stolen.* OPP **mobilize**

immobilizer (also -iser) /ɪˈməʊbəlaɪzə(r)/ ***noun*** [C] a device in a vehicle that prevents thieves from starting the engine when the vehicle is parked

immoral ⊶ /ɪˈmɒrəl/ (used about people or their behaviour) considered wrong or not honest by most people: *It's immoral to steal.* OPP **moral** ➲ look at **amoral** ▶ **immorality** /ˌɪməˈræləti/ ***noun*** [U] OPP **morality** ▶ **immorally** /-rəli/ ***adv.***

immortal /ɪˈmɔːtl/ ***adj.*** living or lasting for ever: *Nobody is immortal – we all have to die some time.* OPP **mortal** ▶ **immortality** /ˌɪmɔːˈtæləti/ ***noun*** [U]

immortalize (also -ise) /ɪˈmɔːtəlaɪz/ ***verb*** [T] to give lasting fame to sb/sth: *He immortalized their relationship in a poem.*

immovable /ɪˈmuːvəbl/ ***adj.*** that cannot be moved: *an immovable object* ◇ *immovable property* (=houses, land, etc.)

immune /ɪˈmjuːn/ ***adj.*** **1** ~ **(to sth)** (HEALTH) having natural protection against a certain disease or illness: *You should be immune to measles if you've had it already.* **2** ~ **(to sth)** not affected by sth: *You can say what you like – I'm immune to criticism!* **3** ~ **(from sth)** (LAW) protected from a danger or punishment: *Young children are immune from prosecution.*

imˌmune resˈponse ***noun*** [C] (HEALTH) the reaction of the body to the presence of an ANTIGEN (=a substance that can cause disease)

imˈmune system ***noun*** [C] (HEALTH) the system in your body that produces substances to help it fight against infection and disease

immunity /ɪˈmjuːnəti/ ***noun*** [U] the ability to avoid or not be affected by disease, criticism, punishment by law, etc.: *In many countries people have no immunity to diseases like measles.* ◇ *Ambassadors to other countries receive diplomatic immunity* (=protection from prosecution, etc.).

immunize (also -ise) /ˈɪmjʊnaɪz/ ***verb*** [T] (HEALTH) to make sb IMMUNE to a disease, usually by putting a substance (**vaccine**) into their body: *Before visiting certain countries you will need to be immunized against cholera.* ➲ look at **inoculate**, **vaccinate** ▶ **immunization** (also -isation) /ˌɪmjʊnaɪˈzeɪʃn/ ***noun*** [C,U]

imp /ɪmp/ ***noun*** [C] (in stories) a small creature like a little DEVIL

impact[1] ⊶ AW /ˈɪmpækt/ ***noun*** **1** [C, usually sing.] **an** ~ **(on/upon sb/sth)** an effect or impression: *I hope this anti-smoking campaign will **make/have an impact** on young people.* **2** [U] the action or force of one object hitting another: *The impact of the crash threw the passengers out of their seats.* ◇ *The bomb exploded **on impact**.*

impact[2] AW /ɪmˈpækt/ ***verb*** [I,T] ~ **(on/upon) sth** to have an effect on sth SYN **affect**: *Her father's death impacted greatly on her childhood years.*

impair /ɪmˈpeə(r)/ ***verb*** [T] to damage sth or make it weaker: *Ear infections can result in impaired hearing.*

impairment /ɪmˈpeəmənt/ ***noun*** [U, C] (HEALTH) the state of having a physical or mental condition which means that part of your body or brain does not work properly; a particular condition of this sort

impale /ɪmˈpeɪl/ ***verb*** [T] ~ **sb/sth (on sth)** to push a sharp pointed object through sb/sth: *The boy fell out of the tree and impaled his leg on some railings.*

impart /ɪmˈpɑːt/ ***verb*** [T] (*formal*) **1** ~ **sth (to sb)** to pass information, knowledge, etc. to other people **2** ~ **sth (to sth)** to give a certain quality to sth: *The low lighting imparted a romantic atmosphere to the room.*

impartial /ɪmˈpɑːʃl/ ***adj.*** not supporting one person or group more than another; fair SYN **neutral** ▶ **impartiality** /ˌɪmˌpɑːʃiˈæləti/ ***noun*** [U] ▶ **impartially** /-ʃəli/ ***adv.***

impassable /ɪmˈpɑːsəbl/ ***adj.*** (used about a road, etc.) impossible to travel on because it is blocked OPP **passable**

impasse /ˈæmpɑːs/ ***noun*** [C, usually sing.] a difficult situation in which no progress can be made because the people involved cannot agree what to do SYN **deadlock**: *to break/end the impasse* ◇ *Negotiations have reached an impasse.*

impassioned /ɪmˈpæʃnd/ ***adj.*** (usually *before* a noun) (usually used about speech) showing strong feelings about sth: *an impassioned defence/plea/speech*

impassive /ɪmˈpæsɪv/ ***adj.*** (used about a person) showing no emotion or reaction ▶ **impassively** ***adv.***

impatient ⊶ /ɪmˈpeɪʃnt/ ***adj.*** **1** ~ **(at sth/with sb)** not able to stay calm and wait for sb/sth; easily annoyed by sb/sth that seems slow: *The passengers are getting impatient at the delay.* ◇ *It's no good being impatient with small children.* OPP **patient** **2** ~ **for/to do sth** wanting sth to happen soon: *By the time they are sixteen many young people are impatient to leave school.* ▶ **impatience** ***noun*** [U]: *He began to explain for the third time with growing impatience.* ▶ **impatiently** ***adv.***

impeach /ɪmˈpiːtʃ/ ***verb*** [T] ~ **sb (for sth)** (LAW) to officially accuse a public official of committing a serious crime while they are still in office ▶ **impeachment** ***noun*** [U, C]

impeccable /ɪmˈpekəbl/ ***adj.*** without any mistakes or faults; perfect ▶ **impeccably** /-bli/ ***adv.***

impede /ɪmˈpiːd/ ***verb*** [T] (*formal*) to make it difficult for sb/sth to move or go forward

impediment /ɪmˈpedɪmənt/ ***noun*** [C] (*formal*) **1 an** ~ **(to sth)** something that makes it difficult for a person or thing to move or progress **2** (HEALTH) something that makes speaking difficult: *a speech impediment*

impel /ɪmˈpel/ ***verb*** [T] (**impelling**; **impelled**) ~ **sb (to do sth)** if an idea or a feeling **impels** you to do sth, you feel as if you are forced to do it: *He felt impelled to investigate further.* ◇ *There are various reasons that impel me to that conclusion.*

impending /ɪmˈpendɪŋ/ ***adj.*** (only *before* a noun) (usually used about sth bad) that will happen soon: *There was a feeling of impending disaster in the air.*

impenetrable /ɪmˈpenɪtrəbl/ ***adj.*** **1** impossible to enter or go through: *The jungle was impenetrable.* **2** impossible to understand: *an impenetrable mystery*

imperative[1] /ɪmˈperətɪv/ ***adj.*** very important or urgent: *It's imperative that you see a doctor immediately.*

the imperative[2] /ɪmˈperətɪv/ ***noun*** [C] (LANGUAGE) the form of the verb that is used for giving orders: *In 'Shut the door!' the verb is in the imperative.*

imperceptible /ˌɪmpəˈseptəbl/ ***adj.*** too small to be seen or noticed: *The difference between the original painting and the copy was almost imperceptible.* OPP **perceptible** ▶ **imperceptibly** /-əbli/ ***adv.***: *Almost imperceptibly winter was turning into spring.*

imperfect[1] /ɪmˈpɜːfɪkt/ ***adj.*** with mistakes or faults: *This is a very imperfect system.* OPP **perfect** ▶ **imperfection** /ˌɪmpəˈfekʃn/ ***noun*** [C,U]: *They learned to live with each other's imperfections.* ▶ **imperfectly** ***adv.***

the imperfect[2] /ɪmˈpɜːfɪkt/ ***noun*** [U] (LANGUAGE) used for expressing action in the past that is not completed: *In 'I was having a bath', the verb is in the imperfect.*

imperial /ɪmˈpɪəriəl/ ***adj.*** **1** connected with an empire or its ruler: *the imperial palace* **2** belonging to a system of weighing and measuring that, in the past, was used for all goods in the United Kingdom and is still used for some ➲ look at **foot**, **gallon**, **inch**, **metric**, **ounce**, **pint**, **pound**, **yard**

imperialism /ɪmˈpɪəriəlɪzəm/ ***noun*** [U] (POLITICS) a political system in which a rich and powerful country controls other countries (**colonies**) which are not as rich and powerful as itself ▶ **imperialist** ***noun*** [C]

impermeable /ɪmˈpɜːmiəbl/ ***adj.*** ~ **(to sth)** not allowing a liquid or gas to pass through: *impermeable rock* ◇ *The container is impermeable to water vapour.* OPP **permeable**

impersonal /ɪmˈpɜːsənl/ ***adj.*** **1** not showing friendly human feelings; cold in feeling or atmosphere: *The hotel room was very impersonal.* **2** not referring to any particular person: *Can we try to keep the discussion as impersonal as possible, please?*

impersonate /ɪmˈpɜːsəneɪt/ ***verb*** [T] to copy the behaviour and way of speaking of a person or to pretend to be a different person: *a comedian who impersonates politicians* ▶ **impersonation** /ɪmˌpɜːsəˈneɪʃn/ ***noun*** [C,U] ▶ **impersonator** ***noun*** [C]

impertinent /ɪmˈpɜːtɪnənt/ ***adj.*** (*formal*) not showing respect to sb who is older and more important; rude OPP **polite**, **respectful** ▶ **impertinence** ***noun*** [U] ▶ **impertinently** ***adv.***

imperturbable /ˌɪmpəˈtɜːbəbl/ ***adj.*** (*formal*) not easily worried by a difficult situation

impervious /ɪmˈpɜːviəs/ ***adj.*** ~ **(to sth)** **1** not affected or influenced by sth: *She was impervious to criticism.* **2** not allowing water, etc. to pass through

impetigo /ˌɪmpɪˈtaɪɡəʊ/ ***noun*** [U] (HEALTH) an infectious disease that causes sore areas on the skin

impetuous /ɪmˈpetʃuəs/ ***adj.*** acting or done quickly and without thinking SYN **impulsive**: *Her impetuous behaviour often got her into trouble.* ▶ **impetuously** ***adv.***

impetus /ˈɪmpɪtəs/ ***noun*** [U, sing.] **(an)** ~ **(for sth)**; **(an)** ~ **(to do sth)** something that encourages sth else to happen: *This scandal provided the main impetus for changes in the rules.* ◇ *I need fresh impetus to start working on this essay again.*

impinge /ɪmˈpɪndʒ/ ***verb*** [I] (*formal*) ~ **on/upon sth** to have a noticeable effect on sth, especially a bad one: *I'm not going to let my job impinge on my home life.*

implant[1] /ɪmˈplɑːnt/ ***verb*** [T] ~ **(sth) (in/into sth)** (HEALTH) to put sth (usually sth artificial) into a part of the body for medical purposes, usually by means of an operation: *an electrode implanted into the brain* ➲ look at **transplant** ▶ **implantation** /ˌɪmplɑːnˈteɪʃn/ ***noun*** [U]: *the implantation of the fertilized ovum* ➲ picture at **fertilize**

implant[2] /ˈɪmplɑːnt/ ***noun*** [C] (HEALTH) something that is put into a part of the body in a medical operation, often in order to make it bigger or a different shape

implausible /ɪmˈplɔːzəbl/ ***adj.*** not easy to believe: *an implausible excuse* OPP **plausible**

implement[1] AW /ˈɪmplɪmənt/ ***noun*** [C] a tool or instrument (especially for work outdoors): *farm implements* ➲ note at **tool**

implement[2] AW /ˈɪmplɪment/ ***verb*** [T] to start using a plan, system, etc.: *Some teachers are finding it difficult to implement the government's educational reforms.* ▶ **implementation** /ˌɪmplɪmenˈteɪʃn/ ***noun*** [U]

implicate AW /ˈɪmplɪkeɪt/ ***verb*** [T] ~ **sb (in sth)** to show that sb is involved in sth unpleasant, especially a crime: *A well-known politician was implicated in the scandal.*

implication 🔑 AW /ˌɪmplɪˈkeɪʃn/ ***noun*** **1** [C, usually pl.] **implications (for/of sth)** the effect that sth will have on sth else in the future: *The new law will **have** serious **implications** for our work.* **2** [C,U] something that is suggested or said indirectly: *The implication of what she said was that we had made a bad mistake.* ➲ verb **imply** **3** [U] ~ **(in sth)** the fact of being involved, or of involving sb, in sth unpleasant, especially a crime ➲ verb **implicate**

implicit AW /ɪmˈplɪsɪt/ ***adj.*** **1** not expressed in a direct way but understood by the people involved: *We had an implicit agreement that we would support each other.* ➲ look at **explicit** **2** complete; total: *I have implicit faith in your ability to do the job.* ▶ **implicitly** ***adv.***

implore /ɪmˈplɔː(r)/ ***verb*** [T] (*formal*) to ask sb with great emotion to do sth, because you are in a very serious situation: *She implored him not to leave her alone.* SYN **beg**

imply 🔑 AW /ɪmˈplaɪ/ ***verb*** [T] (*pres. part.* **implying**; *3rd person sing. pres.* **implies**; *pt, pp* **implied**) to suggest sth in an indirect way or without actually saying it: *He didn't say so – but he implied that I was lying.* ➲ noun **implication**

impolite /ˌɪmpəˈlaɪt/ ***adj.*** rude: *I think it was impolite of him to ask you to leave.* OPP **polite** ▶ **impolitely** ***adv.***

import[1] 🔑 /ˈɪmpɔːt/ ***noun*** (ECONOMICS) **1** [C, usually pl.] a product or service that is brought into one country from another: *What are your country's major imports?* OPP **export** **2** [U] (*also* **importation**) the act of bringing goods or services into a country: *new controls on the import of certain goods from abroad*

import[2] 🔑 /ɪmˈpɔːt/ ***verb*** [I,T] **1** ~ **sth (from...)** (ECONOMICS) to buy goods, etc. from a foreign country and bring them into your own country: *imported goods* ◇ *Britain imports wine from Spain.* ◇ (*figurative*) *We need to import some extra help from somewhere.* OPP **export** **2** (COMPUTING) to move information onto a program from another program ▶ **importer** ***noun*** [C] OPP **exporter**

importance 🔑 /ɪmˈpɔːtns/ ***noun*** [U] the quality of being important: *The decision was **of** great **importance** to the future of the business.*

important 🔑 /ɪmˈpɔːtnt/ ***adj.*** **1** ~ **(to sb)**; ~ **(for sb/sth) (to do sth)**; ~ **that...** having great value or influence; very necessary: *an important meeting/decision/factor* ◇ *This job is very important to me.* ◇ *It's important not to be late.* ◇ *It's important for*

people to see the results of what they do. ◇ It was important to me that you were there. **2** (used about a person) having great influence or authority: *He was one of the most important writers of his time.*
▶ **importantly** *adv.*

importation /ˌɪmpɔːˈteɪʃn/ = IMPORT¹ (2)

impose ⊶ AW /ɪmˈpəʊz/ *verb* **1** [T] ~ **sth (on/upon sb/sth)** to make a law, rule, opinion, etc. be accepted by using your power or authority **2** [I] ~ **(on/upon sb/sth)** to ask or expect sb to do sth that may cause extra work or trouble: *I hate to impose on you, but can you lend me some money?*
▶ **imposition** AW /ˌɪmpəˈzɪʃn/ *noun* [U, C]: *the imposition of military rule*

imposing /ɪmˈpəʊzɪŋ/ *adj.* big and important; impressive: *They lived in a large, imposing house near the park.*

impossible ⊶ /ɪmˈpɒsəbl/ *adj.* **1** not able to be done or to happen: *It's impossible for me to be there before 12.* ◇ *I find it almost impossible to get up in the morning!* ◇ *That's impossible!* (= I don't believe it!) **2** very difficult to deal with or control: *This is an impossible situation!* ◇ *He's always been an impossible child.* OPP **possible** ▶ **the impossible** *noun* [sing.]: *Don't attempt the impossible!*
▶ **impossibility** /ɪmˌpɒsəˈbɪləti/ *noun* [C,U] (*pl.* **impossibilities**): *What you are suggesting is a complete impossibility!*

impossibly /ɪmˈpɒsəbli/ *adv.* extremely: *impossibly complicated*

impostor /ɪmˈpɒstə(r)/ *noun* [C] a person who pretends to be sb else in order to trick other people

impotent /ˈɪmpətənt/ *adj.* **1** without enough power to influence a situation or to change things **2** (HEALTH) (used about men) not capable of having sex ▶ **impotence** *noun* [U]

impound /ɪmˈpaʊnd/ *verb* [T] (LAW) **1** to take sth away from sb, so that they cannot use it: *The car was impounded by the police after the accident.* **2** to shut up dogs, cats, etc. found on the streets in a POUND, until their owners collect them

impoverish /ɪmˈpɒvərɪʃ/ *verb* [T] (*formal*) to make sb/sth poor or lower in quality OPP **enrich**

impractical /ɪmˈpræktɪkl/ *adj.* **1** not sensible or realistic: *It would be impractical to take our bikes on the train.* **2** (used about a person) not good at doing ordinary things that involve using your hands; not good at organizing or planning things OPP **practical**

imprecise AW /ˌɪmprɪˈsaɪs/ *adj.* not clear or exact: *imprecise instructions* OPP **precise**

impregnable /ɪmˈpregnəbl/ *adj.* **1** an **impregnable** building is so strongly built that it cannot be entered by force **2** strong and impossible to defeat or change SYN **invincible**

impregnate /ˈɪmpregneɪt/ *verb* [T] **1** to make a substance spread through an area so that the area is full of the substance: *The pad is impregnated with insecticide.* **2** (*formal*) (BIOLOGY) to make a woman or female animal pregnant

impress ⊶ /ɪmˈpres/ *verb* [T] **1** ~ **sb (with sth)**; ~ **sb that...** to make sb feel admiration and respect: *She's always trying to impress people with her new clothes.* ◇ *It impressed me that he understood immediately what I meant.* **2** (*formal*) ~ **sth on/upon sb** to make the importance of sth very clear to sb: *I wish you could impress on John that he must pass these exams.*

impression ⊶ /ɪmˈpreʃn/ *noun* [C] **1** an idea, a feeling or an opinion that you get about sb/sth: *What's your **first impression** of the new director?* ◇ *I'm not sure but I **have/get the impression** that Jane's rather unhappy.* ◇ *I was **under the impression*** (= I believed, but I was wrong) *that you were married.* ➲ note at **think 2** the effect that a person or thing produces on sb else: *She **gives the impression** of being older than she really is.* ◇ *Do you think I **made a good impression on** your parents?* **3** an amusing copy of the way a person acts or speaks: *My brother can do a good impression of the Prime Minister.* SYN **imitation 4** a mark that is left when an object has been pressed hard into a surface

impressionable /ɪmˈpreʃənəbl/ *adj.* easy to influence: *Sixteen is a very impressionable age.*

Impressionism /ɪmˈpreʃənɪzəm/ *noun* [U] (ART) a style in painting developed in France in the late 19th century that uses colour to show the effects of light on things and to suggest atmosphere rather than showing exact details

impressionist /ɪmˈpreʃənɪst/ *noun* [C] **1 Impressionist** (ART) an artist who paints in the style of Impressionism: *Impressionists such as Monet and Pissarro* **2** a person who makes people laugh by copying the way a famous person speaks or behaves ▶ **Impressionist** *adj.*: *Impressionist landscapes*

impressive ⊶ /ɪmˈpresɪv/ *adj.* causing a feeling of admiration and respect because of the importance, size, quality, etc. of sth: *an impressive building/speech* ◇ *The way he handled the situation was most impressive.*

imprint /ˈɪmprɪnt/ *noun* [C] a mark made by pressing an object on a surface: *the imprint of a foot in the sand*

imprison /ɪmˈprɪzn/ *verb* [T] (often passive) (LAW) to put or keep in prison SYN **jail**: *He was imprisoned for armed robbery.* ▶ **imprisonment** *noun* [U]: *She was sentenced to **life imprisonment** for murder.*

improbable /ɪmˈprɒbəbl/ *adj.* not likely to be true or to happen: *an improbable explanation* ◇ *It is **highly improbable** that she will arrive tonight.* SYN **unlikely** OPP **probable** ▶ **improbability** /ɪmˌprɒbəˈbɪləti/ *noun* [U] ▶ **improbably** /-əbli/ *adv.*

impromptu /ɪmˈprɒmptjuː/ *adj.* (done) without being prepared or organized: *an impromptu party*

improper /ɪmˈprɒpə(r)/ *adj.* **1** illegal or dishonest: *It seems that she had been involved in improper business deals.* **2** not suitable for the situation; rude in a sexual way: *It would be improper to say anything else at this stage.* ◇ *He lost his job for making improper suggestions to several of the women.* OPP **proper** ▶ **improperly** *adv.* OPP **properly**

imˌproper ˈfraction *noun* [C] (MATHEMATICS) a FRACTION in which the top number is greater than the bottom number, for example $^7/_6$ ➲ look at **proper fraction**

impropriety /ˌɪmprəˈpraɪəti/ *noun* [U, C] (*pl.* **improprieties**) (*formal*) behaviour or actions that are morally wrong or not appropriate: *She was unaware of the impropriety of her remark.*

improve ⊶ /ɪmˈpruːv/ *verb* [I,T] to become or to make sth better: *Your work has greatly improved.* ◇ *I hope the weather will improve later on.* ◇ *Your vocabulary is excellent but you could improve your pronunciation.*
PHR V **improve on/upon sth** to produce sth that is better than sth else: *Nobody will be able to improve on that score* (= nobody will be able to make a higher score).

improvement ⊶ /ɪm'pru:vmənt/ ***noun*** [C,U] (an) ~ (on/in sth) (a) change which makes the quality or condition of sb/sth better: *Your written work is in need of some improvement.*

improvise /'ɪmprəvaɪz/ ***verb*** [I,T] **1** to make, do or manage sth without preparation, using what you have: *If you're short of teachers today you'll just have to improvise* (=manage somehow with the people that you've got). **2** to play music, speak or act using your imagination instead of written or remembered material: *It was obvious that the actor had forgotten his lines and was trying to improvise.* ▶ **improvisation** /ˌɪmprəvaɪ'zeɪʃn/ ***noun*** [C,U]

impudent /'ɪmpjədənt/ ***adj.*** (*formal*) very rude; lacking respect and not polite SYN **cheeky** ▶ **impudently** ***adv.*** ▶ **impudence** ***noun*** [U]

impulse /'ɪmpʌls/ ***noun*** [C] **1** [usually sing.] an ~ (to do sth) a sudden desire to do sth without thinking about the results: *She felt a terrible impulse to rush out of the house and never come back.* **2** (SCIENCE) a force or movement of energy that causes a reaction: *nerve/electrical impulses*
IDM **on (an) impulse** without thinking or planning and not considering the results

impulsive /ɪm'pʌlsɪv/ ***adj.*** likely to act suddenly and without thinking; done without careful thought: *an impulsive character* ▶ **impulsively** ***adv.*** ▶ **impulsiveness** ***noun*** [U]

impure /ɪm'pjʊə(r)/ ***adj.*** **1** not pure or clean; consisting of more than one substance mixed together (and therefore not of good quality): *impure metals* **2** (*old-fashioned*) (used about thoughts and actions connected with sex) not moral; bad OPP **pure**

impurity /ɪm'pjʊərəti/ ***noun*** (*pl.* **impurities**) **1** [C, usually pl.] a substance that is present in small amounts in another substance, making it dirty or of poor quality **2** [U] (*old-fashioned*) the state of being morally bad ➲ look at **purity**

in¹ ⊶ /ɪn/ ***adv.***, ***prep.*** **1** (used to show place) inside or to a position inside a particular area or object: *a country in Africa* ◇ *an island in the Pacific* ◇ *in a box* ◇ *I read about it in the newspaper.* ◇ *He lay **in bed**.* ◇ *She put the keys in her pocket.* ◇ *His wife's **in hospital**.* ◇ *She opened the door and went in.* ◇ *My suitcase is full. I can't get any more in.* ◇ *When does the train get in* (=to the station)? **2** at home or at work: *I phoned him last night but he wasn't in.* ◇ *She won't **be in** till late today.* **3** (showing time) during a period of time: *My birthday is in August.* ◇ *in spring/summer/autumn/winter* ◇ *He was born in 1980.* ◇ *You could walk there in about an hour* (=it would take that long to walk there). **4** (showing time) after a period of time: *I'll be finished in ten minutes.* **5** wearing sth: *They were all dressed in black for the funeral.* ◇ *I've never seen you in a suit before.* ◇ *a woman in a yellow dress* **6** showing the condition or state of sb/sth: *My father is in poor health.* ◇ *This room is **in a mess**!* ◇ *Richard's **in love**.* ◇ *He's in his mid-thirties.* **7** showing sb's job or the activity sb is involved in: *He's got a good job in advertising.* ◇ *All her family are in politics* (=they are politicians). ◇ *He's in the army.* **8** contained in; forming the whole or part of sth: *There are 31 days in January.* ◇ *What's in this casserole?* **9** used for saying how things are arranged: *We sat in a circle.* ◇ *She had her hair in plaits.* **10** used for saying how sth is written or expressed: *Please write in pen.* ◇ *They were talking **in Italian/French/Polish**.* ◇ *to work in groups/teams* **11** used with feelings: *I watched **in horror** as the plane crashed to the ground.* ◇ *He was **in such a rage** I didn't dare to go near him.* **12** used for giving the rate of sth and for talking about numbers: ***One family in ten** owns a dishwasher.* **13** received by sb official: *Entries should **be in** by 20 March.* ◇ *All applications must be in by Friday.* **14** (used about the sea) at the highest point, when the water is closest to the land: *The tide's coming in.*
IDM **be in for it/sth** to be going to experience sth unpleasant: *He'll be in for a shock when he gets the bill.* ◇ *You'll be in for it when Mum sees what you've done.*
be/get in on sth to be included or involved in sth: *I'd like to be in on the new project.*
have (got) it in for sb (*informal*) to be unpleasant to sb because they have done sth to upset you: *The boss has had it in for me ever since I asked to be considered for the new post.*

in² /ɪn/ ***noun***
IDM **the ins and outs (of sth)** the details and difficulties (involved in sth): *Will somebody explain the ins and outs of the situation to me?*

in³ /ɪn/ ***adj.*** (*informal*) fashionable at the moment: *the in place to go* ◇ *The colour grey is very in this season.*

in. ***abbr.*** inch(es)

in- /ɪn/ ***prefix*** **1** (*also* **il-** /ɪl/; **im-** /ɪm/; **ir-** /ɪr/) (in adjectives, adverbs and nouns) not; the opposite of: *infinite* ◇ *illogical* ◇ *immorally* ◇ *irrelevance* **2** (*also* **im-** /ɪm/) (in verbs) to put into the condition mentioned: *inflame* ◇ *imperil*

inability ⊶ /ˌɪnə'bɪləti/ ***noun*** [sing.] ~ (to do sth) lack of ability, power or skill: *He has a complete inability to listen to other people's opinions.* ➲ adjective **unable**

inaccessible AW /ˌɪnæk'sesəbl/ ***adj.*** very difficult or impossible to reach or contact: *That beach is inaccessible by car.* OPP **accessible** ▶ **inaccessibility** /ˌɪnækˌsesə'bɪləti/ ***noun*** [U]

inaccurate AW /ɪn'ækjərət/ ***adj.*** not correct or accurate; with mistakes: *an inaccurate report/description/statement* OPP **accurate** ▶ **inaccuracy** AW /ɪn'ækjərəsi/ ***noun*** [C,U] (*pl.* **inaccuracies**): *There are always some inaccuracies in newspaper reports.* OPP **accuracy** ▶ **inaccurately** ***adv.***

inaction /ɪn'ækʃn/ ***noun*** [U] doing nothing; lack of action: *The crisis was blamed on the government's earlier inaction.* OPP **action**

inactive /ɪn'æktɪv/ ***adj.*** doing nothing; not active: *The virus remains inactive in the body.* OPP **active** ▶ **inactivity** /ˌɪnæk'tɪvəti/ ***noun*** [U] OPP **activity**

inadequate AW /ɪn'ædɪkwət/ ***adj.*** **1** ~ (for sth/to do sth) not enough; not good enough: *the problem of inadequate housing* **2** (used about a person) not able to deal with a problem or situation; not confident: *There was so much to learn in the new job that for a while I felt totally inadequate.* OPP **adequate** ▶ **inadequately** ***adv.*** ▶ **inadequacy** AW /ɪn'ædɪkwəsi/ ***noun*** [C,U] (*pl.* **inadequacies**): *his inadequacy as a parent*

inadmissible /ˌɪnəd'mɪsəbl/ ***adj.*** (*formal*) that cannot be allowed or accepted, especially in a court of law: *inadmissible evidence*

inadvertent /ˌɪnəd'vɜ:tənt/ ***adj.*** (used about actions) done without thinking, not on purpose OPP **deliberate**, **intentional** ▶ **inadvertently** ***adv.***: *She had inadvertently left the letter where he could find it.*

inadvisable /ˌɪnəd'vaɪzəbl/ ***adj.*** not sensible; not showing good judgement: *It is inadvisable to go swimming when you have a cold.* OPP **advisable**

inalienable /ɪn'eɪliənəbl/ ***adj.*** (*formal*) that cannot be taken away from you

inane /ɪˈneɪn/ ***adj.*** without any meaning; silly: *an inane remark* ▶ **inanely *adv.***

inanimate /ɪnˈænɪmət/ ***adj.*** not alive in the way that people, animals and plants are: *A rock is an inanimate object.* OPP **animate²**

inappropriate AW /ˌɪnəˈprəʊpriət/ ***adj.*** not suitable: *Isn't that dress rather inappropriate for the occasion?* OPP **appropriate**

inarticulate /ˌɪnɑːˈtɪkjələt/ ***adj.*** **1** (used about a person) not able to express ideas and feelings clearly **2** (used about speech) not clear or well expressed OPP **articulate** ▶ **inarticulately *adv.***

inasmuch as /ˌɪnəzˈmʌtʃ əz/ ***conj.*** (*formal*) because of the fact that: *We felt sorry for the boys inasmuch as they had not realized that what they were doing was wrong.*

inattention /ˌɪnəˈtenʃn/ ***noun*** [U] lack of attention: *a moment of inattention* OPP **attention**

inattentive /ˌɪnəˈtentɪv/ ***adj.*** not paying attention: *One inattentive student can disturb the whole class.* OPP **attentive**

inaudible /ɪnˈɔːdəbl/ ***adj.*** not loud enough to be heard OPP **audible** ▶ **inaudibly** /-bli/ ***adv.***

inaugurate /ɪˈnɔːgjəreɪt/ ***verb*** [T] **1** to introduce a new official, leader, etc. at a special formal ceremony: *He will be inaugurated as President next month.* **2** to start, introduce or open sth new (often at a special formal ceremony) ▶ **inaugural** /ɪˈnɔːgjərəl/ ***adj.*** (only *before* a noun): *the President's inaugural speech* ▶ **inauguration** /ɪˌnɔːgjəˈreɪʃn/ ***noun*** [C,U]

inauspicious /ˌɪnɔːˈspɪʃəs/ ***adj.*** (*formal*) showing signs that the future will not be good or successful: *an inauspicious start* OPP **auspicious**

inborn /ˌɪnˈbɔːn/ ***adj.*** an **inborn** quality is one that you are born with SYN **innate**

inbound /ˈɪnbaʊnd/ ***adj.*** (*formal*) (TOURISM) travelling towards a place rather than leaving it: ***inbound flights/passengers*** OPP **outbound**

ˈin box ***noun*** [C] (*AmE*) = IN TRAY

inbox /ˈɪnbɒks/ ***noun*** [C] (COMPUTING) the place on a computer where new email messages are shown: *I have a stack of emails in my inbox.*

inbred /ˌɪnˈbred/ ***adj.*** produced by breeding among closely related members of a group of animals, people or plants

inbreeding /ˈɪnbriːdɪŋ/ ***noun*** [U] breeding between closely related people or animals

Inc. (*also* **inc**) /ɪŋk/ ***abbr.*** (*AmE*) (BUSINESS) Incorporated: *Manhattan Drugstores Inc.*

incalculable /ɪnˈkælkjələbl/ ***adj.*** very great; too great to calculate: *an incalculable risk*

incapable AW /ɪnˈkeɪpəbl/ ***adj.*** **1** ~ **of sth/doing sth** not able to do sth: *She is incapable of hard work/working hard.* ◇ *He's quite incapable of unkindness* (= too nice to be unkind). **2** not able to do, manage or organize anything well: *As a doctor, she's totally incapable.* OPP **capable**

incapacitate AW /ˌɪnkəˈpæsɪteɪt/ ***verb*** [T] to make sb unable to do sth

ˌin-ˈcar ***adj.*** (only *before* a noun) relating to sth that you have or use inside a car, for example a radio or CD player: *in-car entertainment*

incarcerate /ɪnˈkɑːsəreɪt/ ***verb*** [T] (*formal*) (usually passive) (LAW) to put sb in prison or in another place from which they cannot escape SYN imprison ▶ **incarceration** /ɪnˌkɑːsəˈreɪʃn/ ***noun*** [U]

incarnation /ˌɪnkɑːˈneɪʃn/ ***noun*** [C] **1** a period of life on earth in a particular form: *He believed he was a prince in a previous incarnation.* **2 the ~ of sth** (a person that is) a perfect example of a particular quality: *She is the incarnation of goodness.* ➲ look at **reincarnation**

incendiary /ɪnˈsendiəri/ ***adj.*** that causes a fire: *an incendiary bomb/device*

incense /ˈɪnsens/ ***noun*** [U] a substance that produces a sweet smell when burnt, used especially in religious ceremonies

incensed /ɪnˈsenst/ ***adj.*** ~ **(by/at sth)** very angry SYN **furious**

incentive AW /ɪnˈsentɪv/ ***noun*** [C,U] **(an) ~ (for/to sb/sth) (to do sth)** something that encourages you (to do sth): *There's no incentive for young people to do well at school because there aren't any jobs when they leave.*

incessant /ɪnˈsesnt/ ***adj.*** never stopping (and usually annoying): *incessant rain/noise/chatter* ➲ look at **continual** ▶ **incessantly *adv.***

incest /ˈɪnsest/ ***noun*** [U] (LAW) illegal sex between members of the same family, for example brother and sister

incestuous /ɪnˈsestjuəs/ ***adj.*** **1** involving illegal sex between members of the same family: *an incestuous relationship* **2** (used about a group of people and their relationships with each other) too close; not open to anyone outside the group: *Life in a small community can be very incestuous.*

inch¹ ⊶ /ɪntʃ/ ***noun*** [C] (*abbr.* **in.**) a measure of length; 2.54 CENTIMETRES. There are 12 inches in a foot: *He's 5 foot 10 inches tall.* ◇ *Three inches of rain fell last night.*

inch² /ɪntʃ/ ***verb*** [I,T] ~ **forward, past, through, etc.** to move slowly and carefully in the direction mentioned: *He inched (his way) forward along the cliff edge.*

incidence AW /ˈɪnsɪdəns/ ***noun*** **1** [sing.] (*formal*) **an ~ of sth** the number of times sth (usually sth unpleasant) happens; the rate of sth: *a high incidence of crime/disease/unemployment* **2** [U] (PHYSICS) the way in which a RAY of light meets a surface: *the angle of incidence* ▶ **incident *adj.***: *the incident ray* (= the one that meets a surface) ◇ *the incident angle* (= at which a ray of light meets a surface) ➲ picture at **reflection**

incident ⊶ AW /ˈɪnsɪdənt/ ***noun*** [C] (*formal*) something that happens (especially sth unusual or unpleasant): *There were a number of incidents after the football match.* ◇ *a diplomatic incident* (= a dangerous or unpleasant situation between countries)

incidental /ˌɪnsɪˈdentl/ ***adj.*** ~ **(to sth)** happening as part of sth more important: *The book contains various themes that are incidental to the main plot.*

incidentally AW /ˌɪnsɪˈdentli/ ***adv.*** used to introduce extra news, information, etc. that the speaker has just thought of SYN **by the way**: *Incidentally, that new restaurant you told me about is excellent.*

incinerate /ɪnˈsɪnəreɪt/ ***verb*** [T] (*formal*) to destroy sth completely by burning ▶ **incineration** /ɪnˌsɪnəˈreɪʃn/ ***noun*** [U]: *high-temperature incineration plants*

incinerator /ɪnˈsɪnəreɪtə(r)/ ***noun*** [C] a container or machine for burning rubbish, etc.

incipient /ɪnˈsɪpiənt/ ***adj.*** (*formal*) just beginning: *signs of incipient unrest*

incision /ɪnˈsɪʒn/ ***noun*** [C] (*formal*) a cut carefully made into sth (especially into a person's body as part of a medical operation)

incisive /ɪnˈsaɪsɪv/ ***adj.*** **1** showing clear thought and good understanding of what is important, and the ability to express this: *incisive comments/ criticism/analysis* ◇ *an incisive mind* **2** showing sb's ability to take decisions and act firmly: *an incisive performance*

incisor /ɪnˈsaɪzə(r)/ ***noun*** [C] (ANATOMY) one of the eight sharp teeth at the front of the mouth that are used for biting ➲ look at **canine**, **molar**, **premolar** ➲ picture at **tooth**

incite /ɪnˈsaɪt/ ***verb*** [T] **~ sb (to sth)** to encourage sb to do sth by making them very angry or excited: *He was accused of inciting the crowd to violence.* ▸ **incitement** ***noun*** [C,U]: *He was guilty of incitement to violence.*

incl. ***abbr.*** including; inclusive: *total £59.00 incl. tax*

inclination AW /ˌɪnklɪˈneɪʃn/ ***noun*** [C,U] **~ (to do sth)**; **~ (towards/for sth)** a feeling that makes sb want to behave in a particular way: *He did not show* ***the slightest inclination*** *to help.* ◇ *She had no inclination for a career in teaching.*

incline[1] AW /ɪnˈklaɪn/ ***verb*** **1** [I] (*formal*) **~ to/ towards sth** to want to behave in a particular way or make a particular choice **2** [T] (*formal*) to bend (your head) forward: *They sat round the table, heads inclined, deep in discussion.* **3** [I] **~ towards sth** to be at an angle in a particular direction: *The land inclines towards the shore.*

incline[2] AW /ˈɪnklaɪn/ ***noun*** [C] (*formal*) (GEOGRAPHY) a slight hill: *a steep/slight incline* SYN **slope**

inclined /ɪnˈklaɪnd/ ***adj.*** **1 ~ (to do sth)** (not before a noun) wanting to behave in a particular way: *I know Amir well so I'm* ***inclined to believe*** *what he says.* **2 ~ to do sth** likely to do sth: *She's inclined to change her mind very easily.* **3** having a natural ability in the subject mentioned: *to be musically inclined*

include ⊶ /ɪnˈkluːd/ ***verb*** [T] (not used in the continuous tenses) **1** to have as one part; to contain (among other things): *The price of the holiday includes the flight, the hotel and car hire.* ◇ *The crew included one woman.* OPP **exclude** **2 ~ sb/sth (as/in/ on sth)** to make sb/sth part (of another group, etc.): *The children immediately included the new girl in their games.* ◇ *Everyone was disappointed, myself included.* ▸ **inclusion** /ɪnˈkluːʒn/ ***noun*** [U]: *The inclusion of all that violence in the film was unnecessary.*

including ⊶ /ɪnˈkluːdɪŋ/ ***prep.*** having as a part: *It costs $17.99, including postage and packing.* OPP **excluding**

inclusive /ɪnˈkluːsɪv/ ***adj.*** **1 ~ (of sth)** (used about a price, etc.) including or containing everything; including the thing mentioned: *Is that an inclusive price or are there some extras?* ◇ *The rent is inclusive of electricity.* **2** (only *after* a noun) including the dates, numbers, etc. mentioned: *You are booked at the hotel from Monday to Friday inclusive* (=including Monday and Friday). ❶ When talking about time **through** is often used in American English instead of **inclusive**: *We'll be away from Friday through Sunday.*

incognito /ˌɪnkɒɡˈniːtəʊ/ ***adv.*** hiding your real name and identity (especially if you are famous and do not want to be recognized): *to travel incognito*

incoherent AW /ˌɪnkəʊˈhɪərənt/ ***adj.*** not clear or easy to understand; not saying sth clearly OPP **coherent** ▸ **incoherence** ***noun*** [U] ▸ **incoherently** ***adv.***

THESAURUS

income

wage/wages • pay • salary • earnings

These are all words for money that a person earns or receives for their work.

income: *people on low incomes*

wage/wages: *a weekly wage of £280*

pay: *good rates of pay*

salary: *a small monthly salary*

earnings: *a rise in average earnings*

income ⊶ AW /ˈɪnkʌm; -kəm/ ***noun*** [C,U] (FINANCE) the money you receive regularly as payment for your work or as interest on money you have saved, etc.: *It's often difficult for a family to live on one income.*

RELATED VOCABULARY

We talk about a **monthly** or an **annual** income. An income may be **high** or **low**. Your **gross** income is the amount you earn before paying tax. Your **net** income is your income after tax. Look at the note at **pay**[2].

ˈ**income tax** ***noun*** [U] (FINANCE) the amount of money you pay to the government according to how much you earn

incoming /ˈɪnkʌmɪŋ/ ***adj.*** (only *before* a noun) **1** arriving or being received: *incoming flights/ passengers* ◇ *incoming telephone calls* **2** new; recently elected: *the incoming government*

incomparable /ɪnˈkɒmprəbl/ ***adj.*** so good or great that it does not have an equal: *incomparable beauty* ➲ verb **compare**

incompatible AW /ˌɪnkəmˈpætəbl/ ***adj.*** **~ with sb/sth** very different and therefore not able to live or work happily with sb or exist with sth: *The working hours of the job are incompatible with family life.* OPP **compatible** ▸ **incompatibility** /ˌɪnkəmˌpætəˈbɪləti/ ***noun*** [C,U] (*pl.* **incompatibilities**)

incompetent /ɪnˈkɒmpɪtənt/ ***adj.*** lacking the necessary skill to do sth well: *He is completely incompetent at his job.* ◇ *an incompetent teacher/ manager* OPP **competent** ▸ **incompetent** ***noun*** [C]: *She's a total incompetent at basketball.* ▸ **incompetence** ***noun*** [U] ▸ **incompetently** ***adv.***

incomplete /ˌɪnkəmˈpliːt/ ***adj.*** having a part or parts missing OPP **complete** ▸ **incompletely** ***adv.***

incomprehensible /ɪnˌkɒmprɪˈhensəbl/ ***adj.*** impossible to understand: *an incomprehensible explanation* ◇ *Her attitude is incomprehensible to the rest of the committee.* OPP **comprehensible**, **understandable** ▸ **incomprehension** /ɪnˌkɒmprɪˈhenʃn/ ***noun*** [U]

inconceivable AW /ˌɪnkənˈsiːvəbl/ ***adj.*** impossible or very difficult to believe or imagine: *It's inconceivable that he would have stolen anything.* OPP **conceivable**

inconclusive AW /ˌɪnkənˈkluːsɪv/ ***adj.*** not leading to a definite decision or result: *an inconclusive discussion* ◇ *inconclusive evidence* (=that doesn't prove anything) OPP **conclusive** ▸ **inconclusively** ***adv.***

incongruous /ɪnˈkɒŋɡruəs/ ***adj.*** strange and out of place; not suitable in a particular situation: *That huge table looks rather incongruous in such a small room.* ▶ **incongruously** ***adv.*** ▶ **incongruity** /ˌɪnkɒnˈɡruːəti/ ***noun*** [U]

inconsiderate /ˌɪnkənˈsɪdərət/ ***adj.*** (used about a person) not thinking or caring about the feelings or needs of other people **SYN** **thoughtless** **OPP** **considerate** ▶ **inconsiderately** ***adv.*** ▶ **inconsiderateness** ***noun*** [U]

inconsistent AW /ˌɪnkənˈsɪstənt/ ***adj.*** **1** ~ **(with sth)** (used about statements, facts, etc.) not the same as sth else; not matching, so that one thing must be wrong or not true: *The witnesses' accounts of the event are inconsistent.* ◇ *These new facts are inconsistent with the earlier information.* **2** (used about a person) likely to change (in attitude, behaviour, etc.) so that you cannot depend on them **OPP** **consistent** ▶ **inconsistency** AW /-ənsi/ ***noun*** [C, U] (*pl.* **inconsistencies**): *There were a few inconsistencies in her argument.* **OPP** **consistency** ▶ **inconsistently** ***adv.***

inconspicuous /ˌɪnkənˈspɪkjuəs/ ***adv.*** not easily noticed: *I tried to **make myself as inconspicuous** as possible so that no one would ask me a question.* **OPP** **conspicuous** ▶ **inconspicuously** ***adv.***

incontinent /ɪnˈkɒntɪnənt/ ***adj.*** (HEALTH) unable to control the passing of waste (**urine** and **faeces**) from the body ▶ **incontinence** ***noun*** [U]

inconvenience /ˌɪnkənˈviːniəns/ ***noun*** [U, C] trouble or difficulty, especially when it affects sth that you need to do; a person or thing that causes this: *We apologize for any inconvenience caused by the delays.* ▶ **inconvenience** ***verb*** [T]

inconvenient /ˌɪnkənˈviːniənt/ ***adj.*** causing trouble or difficulty, especially when it affects sth that you need to do: *It's a bit inconvenient at the moment – could you phone again later?* **OPP** **convenient** ▶ **inconveniently** ***adv.***

incorporate AW /ɪnˈkɔːpəreɪt/ ***verb*** [T] ~ **sth (in/into/within sth)** to make sth a part of sth else; to have sth as a part: *I'd like you to incorporate this information into your report.* **SYN** **include** ▶ **incorporation** /ɪnˌkɔːpəˈreɪʃn/ ***noun*** [U]

incorporated AW /ɪnˈkɔːpəreɪtɪd/ ***adj.*** (*abbr.* **Inc.**) (BUSINESS) (following the name of a company) formed into a legal organization (**corporation**)

incorrect /ˌɪnkəˈrekt/ ***adj.*** not right or true: *Incorrect answers should be marked with a cross.* **OPP** **correct** ▶ **incorrectly** ***adv.***

incorrigible /ɪnˈkɒrɪdʒəbl/ ***adj.*** (used about a person or their behaviour) very bad; too bad to be corrected or improved: *an incorrigible liar*

increase[1] ⊶ /ɪnˈkriːs/ ***verb*** [I,T] ~ **(sth) (from A) (to B)**; ~ **(sth) (by sth)** to become or to make sth larger in number or amount: *The rate of inflation has increased by 1% to 7%.* ◇ *My employer would like me to increase my hours of work from 25 to 30.* ◇ *She increased her speed to overtake the lorry.* ➲ note at **rise[1]** **OPP** **decrease**, **reduce**

increase[2] ⊶ /ˈɪŋkriːs/ ***noun*** [C,U] **(an)** ~ **(in sth)** a rise in the number, amount or level of sth: *There has been a **sharp increase** of nearly 50% on last year's figures.* ◇ *Doctors expect some further increase in the spread of the disease.* ◇ *They are demanding a large wage increase.* **OPP** **decrease**, **reduction**

IDM **on the increase** becoming larger or more frequent; increasing: *Attacks by dogs on children are on the increase.*

increasingly ⊶ /ɪnˈkriːsɪŋli/ ***adv.*** more and more: *It's becoming increasingly difficult/important/dangerous to stay here.*

incredible /ɪnˈkredəbl/ ***adj.*** **1** impossible or very difficult to believe: *I found his account of the event incredible.* **OPP** **credible** ➲ look at **unbelievable** **2** (*informal*) extremely good or big: *He earns an incredible salary.* ▶ **incredibly** /-əbli/ ***adv.***: *We have had some incredibly strong winds recently.*

increment /ˈɪŋkrəmənt/ ***noun*** [C] **1** (FINANCE) a regular increase in the amount of money that sb is paid for their job: *a salary with annual increments* **2** (*formal*) an increase in a number or an amount ▶ **incremental** /ˌɪŋkrəˈmentl/ ***adj.***: *incremental costs* ▶ **incrementally** /-təli/ ***adv.***

incriminate /ɪnˈkrɪmɪneɪt/ ***verb*** [T] (LAW) to provide evidence that sb is guilty of a crime: *The police searched the house but found nothing to incriminate the man.*

incubate /ˈɪŋkjubeɪt/ ***verb*** **1** [T] (BIOLOGY) to keep an egg at the right temperature so that it can develop and produce a bird (**hatch**) **2** [I,T] (HEALTH) (used about a disease) to develop without showing signs; (used about a person or an animal) to carry a disease without showing signs: *Some viruses take weeks to incubate.*

incubation /ˌɪŋkjuˈbeɪʃn/ ***noun*** **1** [U] (BIOLOGY) the process of INCUBATING eggs **2** [C] (*also* **ˌincuˈbation period**) (HEALTH) the period between catching a disease and the time when signs of it (**symptoms**) appear

incubator /ˈɪŋkjubeɪtə(r)/ ***noun*** [C] **1** (HEALTH) a heated machine used in hospitals for keeping small or weak babies alive **2** a heated machine for keeping eggs warm until they break open (**hatch**)

inculcate /ˈɪnkʌlkeɪt/ ***verb*** [T] ~ **sth (in/into sb)**; ~ **sb with sth** (*formal*) to cause sb to learn and remember ideas, moral principles, etc., especially by repeating them often: *to inculcate a sense of responsibility in sb*

incumbent /ɪnˈkʌmbənt/ ***noun*** [C] a person who has an official position: *the **present incumbent** of the White House* ▶ **incumbent** ***adj.***: *the incumbent president*

incur /ɪnˈkɜː(r)/ ***verb*** [T] (**incurred**; **incurring**) (*formal*) to suffer the unpleasant results of a situation that you have caused: *to incur debts/sb's anger*

incurable /ɪnˈkjʊərəbl/ ***adj.*** that cannot be cured or made better: *an incurable disease* **OPP** **curable** ▶ **incurably** /-əbli/ ***adv.***: *incurably ill*

incus /ˈɪŋkəs/ ***noun*** [sing.] (*also* **anvil**) (ANATOMY) a small bone in the middle ear, between the MALLEUS and the STAPES ➲ picture at **ear**

Ind. ***abbr.*** (*BrE*) (POLITICS) = INDEPENDENT[2]: *G. Green (Ind.)*

indebted /ɪnˈdetɪd/ ***adj.*** ~ **(to sb) (for sth)** very grateful to sb: *I am deeply indebted to my family and friends for all their help.*

indecent /ɪnˈdiːsnt/ ***adj.*** shocking to many people in society, especially because sth involves sex or the body: *indecent photos/behaviour/language* ◇ *You can't wear those tiny swimming trunks – they're indecent!* **OPP** **decent** ▶ **indecency** /-nsi/ ***noun*** [U, sing.] ▶ **indecently** ***adv.***

indecision /ˌɪndɪˈsɪʒn/ (*also* **indecisiveness**) ***noun*** [U] the state of being unable to decide: *His indecision about the future is really worrying me.*

indecisive /ˌɪndɪˈsaɪsɪv/ ***adj.*** not able to make decisions easily **OPP** **decisive** ▶ **indecisively** ***adv.*** ▶ **indecisiveness** ***noun*** [U]

indeed ⊶ /ɪn'diːd/ ***adv.*** **1** (used for emphasizing a positive statement or answer) really; certainly: *'Have you had a good holiday?' 'We have indeed.'* **2** used after 'very' with an adjective or adverb to emphasize the quality mentioned: *Thank you very much indeed.* ◇ *She's very happy indeed.* **3** (used for adding information to a statement) in fact: *It's important that you come at once. Indeed, it's essential.* **4** used for showing interest, surprise, anger, etc.: *'They were talking about you last night.' 'Were they indeed!'*

indefensible /ˌɪndɪ'fensəbl/ ***adj.*** (used about behaviour, etc.) completely wrong; that cannot be defended or excused

indefinable /ˌɪndɪ'faɪnəbl/ ***adj.*** difficult or impossible to describe: *There was an indefinable atmosphere of hostility.* ▶ **indefinably** /-əbli/ ***adv.***

indefinite AW /ɪn'defɪnət/ ***adj.*** not fixed or clear: *Our plans are still rather indefinite.* OPP **definite**

inˌdefinite 'article ***noun*** [C] (LANGUAGE) the name used for the words *a* and *an* ➲ look at **definite article**

indefinitely AW /ɪn'defɪnətli/ ***adv.*** for a period of time that has no fixed end: *The meeting was postponed indefinitely.*

indelible /ɪn'deləbl/ ***adj.*** that cannot be removed or washed out: *indelible ink* ◇ (*figurative*) *The experience made an indelible impression on me.* ▶ **indelibly** /-əbli/ ***adv.***

indemnify /ɪn'demnɪfaɪ/ ***verb*** [T] (*pres. part.* **indemnifying**; *3rd person sing. pres.* **indemnifies**; *pt, pp* **indemnified**) (LAW) **1** ~ **sb (against sth)** to promise to pay sb an amount of money if they suffer any damage or loss **2** ~ **sb (for sth)** to pay sb an amount of money because of the damage or loss that they have suffered ▶ **indemnification** /ɪnˌdemnɪfɪ'keɪʃn/ ***noun*** [U]

indemnity /ɪn'demnəti/ ***noun*** (*formal*) **1** [U] protection against damage or loss, especially in the form of a promise to pay for any that happens **2** [C] (*pl.* **indemnities**) an amount of money that is given as payment for damage or loss

indent[1] /ɪn'dent/ ***verb*** [I,T] to start a line of writing further from the left-hand side of the page than the other lines

indent[2] /'ɪndent/ ***noun*** [C] **1** (*especially BrE*) ~ **(for sth)** (BUSINESS) an official order for goods or equipment **2** = INDENTATION (2)

indentation /ˌɪnden'teɪʃn/ ***noun*** [C] **1** a cut or mark on the edge or surface of sth **2** (*also* **indent**) a cut or mark on the edge or surface of sth

independence ⊶ /ˌɪndɪ'pendəns/ ***noun*** [U] ~ **(from sb/sth)** (used about a person, country, etc.) the state of being free and not controlled by another person, country, etc.: *In 1947 India achieved independence from Britain.* ◇ *financial independence*

> **CULTURE**
>
> On **Independence Day** (4 July) Americans celebrate the day in 1776 when America declared itself independent from Britain.

independent[1] ⊶ /ˌɪndɪ'pendənt/ ***adj.*** **1** ~ **(of/from sb/sth)** free from and not controlled by another person, country, etc.: *Many former colonies are now independent nations.* ◇ *independent schools/television* (= not supported by government money) **2** ~ **(of/from sb/sth)** not needing or wanting help: *I got a part-time job because I wanted to be financially independent from my parents.* OPP **dependent 3** not influenced by or connected with sb/sth: *Complaints against the police should be investigated by an independent body.* ◇ *Two independent opinion polls have obtained similar results.* **4** (POLITICS) not representing or belonging to a particular political party: *an independent candidate* ▶ **independently** ***adv.*** ~ **(of sb/sth)**: *Scientists working independently of each other have had very similar results in their experiments.*

independent[2] /ˌɪndɪ'pendənt/ ***noun*** [C] (*abbr.* **Ind.**) (POLITICS) a member of parliament, candidate, etc. who does not belong to a particular political party: *She's standing as an independent at the next election.*

indeˌpendent 'school ***noun*** [C] = PRIVATE SCHOOL

ˌin-'depth ***adj.*** very thorough and full of detail: *an in-depth discussion/study*

indescribable /ˌɪndɪ'skraɪbəbl/ ***adj.*** too good or bad to be described: *indescribable poverty/luxury/noise* ▶ **indescribably** /-əbli/ ***adv.***

indestructible /ˌɪndɪ'strʌktəbl/ ***adj.*** that cannot be easily damaged or destroyed

index ⊶ AW /'ɪndeks/ ***noun*** [C] (*pl.* **indexes**) **1** a list in order from A to Z, usually at the end of a book, of the names or subjects that are referred to in the book: *If you want to find all the references to London, look it up in the index.* **2** (*BrE*) = CARD INDEX **3** (*pl.* **indexes** or **indices** /'ɪndɪsiːz/) (ECONOMICS) a way of showing how the price, value, rate, etc. of sth has changed: *the cost-of-living index* ▶ **index** ***verb*** [T]: *The books in the library are indexed by subject and title.*

'index card ***noun*** [C] a small card that you can write information on and keep with other cards in a box or file

'index finger ***noun*** [C] the finger next to your thumb that you use for pointing SYN **forefinger**

Indian /'ɪndiən/ ***noun*** [C], ***adj.*** **1** (a person) from the Republic of India: *Indian food is hot and spicy.* **2** = NATIVE AMERICAN: *The Sioux were a famous Indian tribe.* ➲ look at **West Indian**

indicate ⊶ AW /'ɪndɪkeɪt/ ***verb*** **1** [T] to show that sth is probably true or exists: *Recent research indicates that children are getting too little exercise.* **2** [T] to say sth in an indirect way: *The spokesman indicated that an agreement was likely soon.* ➲ note at **declare 3** [T] to make sb notice sth, especially by pointing to it: *The receptionist indicated where I should sign.* ◇ *The boy seemed to be indicating that I should follow him.* **4** [I,T] to signal that your car, etc. is going to turn: *The lorry indicated left but turned right.*

indication ⊶ AW /ˌɪndɪ'keɪʃn/ ***noun*** [C,U] an ~ **(of sth/doing sth)**; an ~ **that...** something that shows sth; a sign: *There was no indication of a struggle.* ◇ *There is every indication that he will make a full recovery.* ➲ note at **sign**[1]

indicative[1] AW /ɪn'dɪkətɪv/ ***adj.*** **1** ~ **(of sth)** (*formal*) showing or suggesting sth: *Is the unusual weather indicative of climatic changes?* **2** (LANGUAGE) stating a fact

the indicative[2] AW /ɪn'dɪkətɪv/ ***noun*** [sing.] (LANGUAGE) the form of a verb that states a fact: *In 'Ben likes school', the verb 'like' is* ***in the indicative.***

indicator AW /'ɪndɪkeɪtə(r)/ ***noun*** [C] **1** something that gives information or shows sth; a sign: *The indicator showed that we had plenty of petrol.* ◇ *The unemployment rate is a reliable indicator of economic health.* ➲ note at **sign**[1]

2 (*AmE* **turn signal**) the flashing light on a car, etc. that shows that it is going to turn right or left

indices /ˈɪndɪsiːz/ plural of **index** (3)

indict /ɪnˈdaɪt/ ***verb*** [T] (usually passive) (*especially AmE*) **~ sb (for sb)** (LAW) to officially charge sb with a crime: *The senator was indicted for murder.*

indictment /ɪnˈdaɪtmənt/ ***noun*** [C] **1** (LAW) a written paper that officially accuses sb of a crime **2 an ~ (of sth)** something that shows how bad sth is: *The fact that many children leave school with no qualifications is an indictment of our education system.*

indie /ˈɪndi/ ***adj.*** (only *before* a noun) (used about a company, person or product) not part of a large organization; independent: *an indie publisher* ◇ *indie music*

indifference /ɪnˈdɪfrəns/ ***noun*** [U] **~ (to sb/sth)** a lack of interest or feeling towards sb/sth: *He has always shown indifference to the needs of others.*

indifferent /ɪnˈdɪfrənt/ ***adj.*** **1 ~ (to sb/sth)** not interested in or caring about sb/sth: *The manager of the shop seemed indifferent to our complaints.* **2** not very good: *The standard of football in the World Cup was rather indifferent.* ▶ **indifferently *adv.***

indigenous /ɪnˈdɪdʒənəs/ ***adj.*** (used about people, animals or plants) living or growing in the place where they are from originally

indigestible /ˌɪndɪˈdʒestəbl/ ***adj.*** (used about food) difficult or impossible for the stomach to deal with OPP **digestible**

indigestion /ˌɪndɪˈdʒestʃən/ ***noun*** [U] (HEALTH) pain in the stomach that is caused by difficulty in dealing with food

indignant /ɪnˈdɪɡnənt/ ***adj.*** **~ (with sb) (about/at sth); ~ that...** shocked or angry because sb has said or done sth that you do not like and do not agree with: *They were indignant that they had to pay more for worse services.* ▶ **indignantly *adv.***

indignation /ˌɪndɪɡˈneɪʃn/ ***noun*** [U] **~ (at/about sth); ~ that...** shock and anger: *commuters' indignation at the rise in fares*

indignity /ɪnˈdɪɡnəti/ ***noun*** [U, C] (*pl.* **indignities**) ~ (of sth/of doing sth) a situation that makes you feel embarrassed because you are not treated with respect; an act that causes these feelings SYN **humiliation**: *The chairman* ***suffered the indignity*** *of being refused admission to the meeting.* ◇ *the daily indignities of imprisonment*

indigo /ˈɪndɪɡəʊ/ ***adj.*** very dark blue in colour ▶ **indigo *noun*** [U]

indirect 🔑 /ˌɪndəˈrekt; -daɪˈr-/ ***adj.*** **1** not being the direct cause of sth; not having a direct connection with sth: *an indirect result* **2** that avoids saying sth in an obvious way: *She gave only an indirect answer to my question.* **3** not going in a straight line or using the shortest route: *We came the indirect route to avoid driving through London.* OPP **direct** ▶ **indirectly *adv.*** OPP **directly** ▶ **indirectness *noun*** [U]

ˌindirect ˈcost ***noun*** [C, usually pl.] (FINANCE) costs that are not directly connected with making a particular product or providing a particular service, for example training, heating, rent, etc. OPP **direct cost**

ˌindirect ˈobject ***noun*** [C] (LANGUAGE) a person or thing that an action is done to or for: *In the sentence, 'I wrote him a letter', 'him' is the indirect object.* ➲ look at **direct object**

ˌindirect ˈspeech (also **reˈported speech**) ***noun*** [U] (LANGUAGE) reporting what sb has said, not using the actual words ➲ look at **direct speech**

indiscreet /ˌɪndɪˈskriːt/ ***adj.*** not careful or polite in what you say or do OPP **discreet** ▶ **indiscreetly *adv.***

indiscretion AW /ˌɪndɪˈskreʃn/ ***noun*** [C,U] behaviour that is not careful or polite, and that might cause embarrassment or offence

indiscriminate /ˌɪndɪˈskrɪmɪnət/ ***adj.*** done or acting without making sensible judgement or caring about the possible harmful effects: *He's indiscriminate in his choice of friends.* ▶ **indiscriminately *adv.***

indispensable /ˌɪndɪˈspensəbl/ ***adj.*** very important, so that it is not possible to be without it: *A car is indispensable nowadays if you live in the country.* SYN **essential** ➲ note at **essential** OPP **dispensable**

indisputable /ˌɪndɪˈspjuːtəbl/ ***adj.*** definitely true; that cannot be shown to be wrong

indistinct AW /ˌɪndɪˈstɪŋkt/ ***adj.*** not clear: *indistinct figures/sounds/memories* OPP **distinct** ▶ **indistinctly *adv.***

indistinguishable /ˌɪndɪˈstɪŋɡwɪʃəbl/ ***adj.*** **~ (from sth)** appearing to be the same: *From a distance the two colours are indistinguishable.* OPP **distinguishable**

indium /ˈɪndiəm/ ***noun*** [U] (*symbol* **In**) (CHEMISTRY) a chemical element. **Indium** is a soft silver-white metal. ❶ For more information on the periodic table of elements, look at pages R34-5.

individual[1] 🔑 AW /ˌɪndɪˈvɪdʒuəl/ ***adj.*** **1** (only *before* a noun) considered separately rather than as part of a group: *Each individual animal is weighed and measured before being set free.* **2** for or from one person: *an individual portion of butter* ◇ *Children need individual attention when they are learning to read.* **3** typical of one person in a way that is different from other people: *I like her individual style of dressing.*

individual[2] 🔑 AW /ˌɪndɪˈvɪdʒuəl/ ***noun*** [C] **1** one person, considered separately from others or a group: *Are the needs of society more important than the rights of the individual?* **2** (*informal*) a person of the type that is mentioned: *She's a strange individual.*

individualism AW /ˌɪndɪˈvɪdʒuəlɪzəm/ ***noun*** [U] **1** the quality of being different from other people and doing things in your own way: *She owes her success to her individualism and flair.* **2** the belief that individual people in society should have the right to make their own decisions, etc., rather than being controlled by the government ▶ **individualist** AW /-əlɪst/ ***noun*** [C]: *He's a complete individualist in the way he paints.* ▶ **individualistic** /ˌɪndɪˌvɪdʒuəˈlɪstɪk/ (*also* **individualist**) ***adj.***: *an individualistic culture* ◇ *Her music is highly individualistic and may not appeal to everyone.*

individuality AW /ˌɪndɪˌvɪdʒuˈæləti/ ***noun*** [U] the qualities that make sb/sth different from other people or things: *Young people often try to express their individuality by the way they dress.*

individually AW /ˌɪndɪˈvɪdʒuəli/ ***adv.*** separately; one by one: *The teacher talked to each member of the class individually.*

indivisible /ˌɪndɪˈvɪzəbl/ ***adj.*** that cannot be divided or split into smaller pieces

indoctrinate /ɪnˈdɒktrɪneɪt/ ***verb*** [T] to force sb to accept particular beliefs without considering others: *For 20 years the people have been* *indoctrinated by the government.* ▶ **indoctrination** /ɪnˌdɒktrɪˈneɪʃn/ ***noun*** [U]

ˌIndo-ˌEuroˈpean ***adj.*** (LANGUAGE) of or connected with the family of languages spoken in most of Europe and parts of western Asia (including English, French, Latin, Greek, Swedish, Russian and Hindi)

indoor /ˈɪndɔː(r)/ ***adj.*** (only *before* a noun) done or used inside a building: *indoor games* ◇ *an indoor swimming pool* OPP **outdoor**

indoors /ˌɪnˈdɔːz/ ***adv.*** in or into a building: *Let's go indoors.* ◇ *Oh dear! I've left my sunglasses indoors.* OPP **outdoors, out of doors**

induce AW /ɪnˈdjuːs/ ***verb*** [T] (*formal*) **1** to make or persuade sb to do sth: *Nothing could induce him to change his mind.* **2** to cause or produce: *drugs that induce sleep* ◇ *a drug-induced coma* **3** (HEALTH) to make a woman start giving birth to her baby by giving her special drugs

inducement /ɪnˈdjuːsmənt/ ***noun*** [C,U] something that is offered to sb to make them do sth: *The player was offered a car as an inducement to join the club.*

induction AW /ɪnˈdʌkʃn/ ***noun*** **1** [U,C] the process of introducing sb to a new job, skill, organization, etc.; an event at which this takes place: *an induction day for new students* **2** [U,C] (HEALTH) the act of making a pregnant woman start to give birth, using artificial means such as a special drug **3** [U] (TECHNICAL) a method of discovering general rules and principles from particular facts and examples ➲ look at **deduction** **4** [U] (PHYSICS) the process by which electricity or MAGNETISM passes from one object to another without them touching

inductive /ɪnˈdʌktɪv/ ***adj.*** **1** using particular facts and examples to form general rules and principles: *an inductive argument* ◇ *inductive reasoning* ➲ look at **deductive** **2** connected with the INDUCTION of electricity

indulge /ɪnˈdʌldʒ/ ***verb*** **1** [I,T] ~ **(yourself) (in sth)** to allow yourself to have or do sth for pleasure: *I'm going to indulge myself and go shopping for some new clothes.* ◇ *Maria never indulges in gossip.* **2** [T] to give sb/sth what they or it want or need: *You shouldn't indulge that child. It will make him very selfish.* ◇ *At the weekends he indulges his passion for fishing.*

indulgence /ɪnˈdʌldʒəns/ ***noun*** **1** [U] the state of having or doing whatever you want: *to lead a life of indulgence* ◇ *Over-indulgence in chocolate makes you fat.* **2** [C] something that you have or do because it gives you pleasure: *A cigar after dinner is my only indulgence.*

indulgent /ɪnˈdʌldʒənt/ ***adj.*** allowing sb to have or do whatever they want: *indulgent parents* ▶ **indulgently** ***adv.***

industrial /ɪnˈdʌstriəl/ ***adj.*** **1** (only *before* a noun) connected with industry: *industrial development* ◇ *industrial workers* **2** having a lot of factories, etc.: *an industrial region/country/town*

inˌdustrial ˈaction ***noun*** [U] (SOCIAL STUDIES) action that workers take, especially stopping work, in order to protest about sth to their employers; a strike: *to threaten (to take) industrial action*

industrialist /ɪnˈdʌstriəlɪst/ ***noun*** [C] (BUSINESS) a person who owns or manages a large industrial company

industrialize (also **-ise**) /ɪnˈdʌstriəlaɪz/ ***verb*** [I,T] (ECONOMICS) to develop industries in a country: *Japan industrialized rapidly in the late nineteenth century.* ▶ **industrialization** (also **-isation**) /-eɪʃn/ ***noun*** [U]

Inˌdustrial Revoˈlution ***noun*** [sing.] (HISTORY) the period in the 18th and 19th centuries in Europe and the US when machines began to be used to do work, and industry grew rapidly

inˌdustrial triˈbunal ***noun*** [C] (*BrE*) (LAW) a type of court that can decide on disagreements between employees and employers

industrious /ɪnˈdʌstriəs/ ***adj.*** always working hard

industry /ˈɪndəstri/ ***noun*** (*pl.* **industries**) **1** [U] (ECONOMICS) the production of goods in factories: *Is British industry being threatened by foreign imports?* ◇ *heavy/light industry* **2** [C] (BUSINESS) the people and activities involved in producing sth, providing a service, etc.: *the tourist/catering/entertainment industry*

inedible /ɪnˈedəbl/ ***adj.*** (*formal*) not suitable to be eaten OPP **edible**

ineffable /ɪnˈefəbl/ ***adj.*** (*formal*) too great or beautiful to describe in words ▶ **ineffably** /-əbli/ ***adv.***

ineffective /ˌɪnɪˈfektɪv/ ***adj.*** not producing the effect or result that you want OPP **effective**

inefficient /ˌɪnɪˈfɪʃnt/ ***adj.*** not working or producing results in the best way, so that time or money is wasted: *Our heating system is very old and extremely inefficient.* ◇ *an inefficient secretary* OPP **efficient** ▶ **inefficiency** /-ənsi/ ***noun*** [U] ▶ **inefficiently** ***adv.***

ineligible /ɪnˈelɪdʒəbl/ ***adj.*** ~ **(for/to do sth)** without the necessary certificates, etc. to do or get sth: *She was ineligible for the job because she wasn't a German citizen.* OPP **eligible** ▶ **ineligibility** /ɪnˌelɪdʒəˈbɪləti/ ***noun*** [U]

inept /ɪˈnept/ ***adj.*** ~ **(at sth)** not able to do sth well: *She is totally inept at dealing with people.* OPP **adept**

inequality /ˌɪnɪˈkwɒləti/ ***noun*** [C,U] (*pl.* **inequalities**) **1** (SOCIAL STUDIES) (a) difference between groups in society because one has more money, advantages, etc. than the other: *There will be problems as long as inequality between the races exists.* OPP **equality** **2** (MATHEMATICS) the relation between two expressions that are not equal, using a sign such as ≠ 'not equal to', > 'greater than' or < 'less than' **3** (MATHEMATICS) a symbol which shows that two quantities are not equal

inert /ɪˈnɜːt/ ***adj.*** **1** not able to move or act **2** (CHEMISTRY) (used about chemical elements) that do not react with other chemicals

> **RELATED VOCABULARY**
>
> **Inert gases** are also called **noble gases. Helium, argon, krypton** and **neon** are inert gases.

inertia /ɪˈnɜːʃə/ ***noun*** [U] **1** a lack of energy; an inability to move or change **2** (PHYSICS) the physical force that keeps things where they are or keeps them moving in the direction they are travelling

inescapable /ˌɪnɪˈskeɪpəbl/ ***adj.*** (*formal*) that cannot be avoided: *an inescapable conclusion*

inevitable AW /ɪnˈevɪtəbl/ ***adj.*** that cannot be avoided or prevented from happening: *With more cars on the road, traffic jams are inevitable.* ▶ **the inevitable** ***noun*** [sing.]: *They fought to save the firm from closure, but eventually had to accept the inevitable.* ▶ **inevitability** AW /ɪnˌevɪtəˈbɪləti/ ***noun*** [U]

inevitably 🔑 AW /ɪn'evɪtəbli/ ***adv.*** **1** as is certain to happen: *Inevitably, the press exaggerated the story.* **2** as you would expect: *Inevitably, it rained on the day of the wedding.*

inexcusable /ˌɪnɪk'skjuːzəbl/ ***adj.*** that cannot be allowed or FORGIVEN: *Their behaviour was quite inexcusable.* SYN **unforgivable** OPP **excusable**

inexhaustible /ˌɪnɪg'zɔːstəbl/ ***adj.*** that cannot be finished or used up completely: *Our energy supplies are not inexhaustible.*

inexpensive /ˌɪnɪk'spensɪv/ ***adj.*** low in price SYN **cheap** OPP **expensive** ▶ **inexpensively** ***adv.***

inexperience /ˌɪnɪk'spɪəriəns/ ***noun*** [U] not knowing how to do sth because you have not done it before: *The mistakes were all due to inexperience.* OPP **experience** ▶ **inexperienced** ***adj.***: *He's too young and inexperienced to be given such responsibility.*

inexplicable /ˌɪnɪk'splɪkəbl/ ***adj.*** that cannot be explained: *Her sudden disappearance is quite inexplicable.* OPP **explicable** ▶ **inexplicably** /-əbli/ ***adv.***

infallible /ɪn'fæləbl/ ***adj.*** **1** (used about a person) never making mistakes or being wrong **2** always doing what you want it to do; never failing: *No computer is infallible.* OPP **fallible** ▶ **infallibility** /ɪnˌfælə'bɪləti/ ***noun*** [U]

infamous /'ɪnfəməs/ ***adj.*** ~ **(for sth)** famous for being bad: *The area is infamous for drugs and crime.* SYN **notorious** ➲ look at **famous**

infancy /'ɪnfənsi/ ***noun*** [U] the time when you are a baby or young child: (*figurative*) *Research in this field is still in its infancy.*

infant /'ɪnfənt/ ***noun*** [C] a baby or very young child: *There is a high rate of* ***infant mortality*** (= many children die when they are still babies). ◇ (*BrE*) ***infant school*** (= a school for children aged between four and seven)

infanticide /ɪn'fæntɪsaɪd/ ***noun*** (*formal*) [U, C] (LAW) the crime of killing a baby, especially when a parent kills their own child

infantile /'ɪnfəntaɪl/ ***adj.*** (of behaviour) typical of, or connected with, a baby or very young child and therefore not appropriate for adults or older children: *infantile jokes*

infantry /'ɪnfəntri/ ***noun*** [U, with sing. or pl. verb] soldiers who fight on foot: *The infantry was/were supported by heavy gunfire.*

infatuated /ɪn'fætʃueɪtɪd/ ***adj.*** ~ **(with sb/sth)** having a very strong feeling of love or attraction for sb/sth that usually does not last long and makes you unable to think about anything else ▶ **infatuation** /ɪnˌfætʃu'eɪʃn/ ***noun*** [C,U]

infect 🔑 /ɪn'fekt/ ***verb*** [T] **1** ~ **sb/sth (with sth)** (usually passive) (HEALTH) to cause sb/sth to have a disease or illness: *We must clean the wound before it becomes infected.* ◇ *Many thousands of people have been infected with the virus.* **2** to make people share a particular feeling or emotion: *Paul's happiness infected the whole family.*

infection 🔑 /ɪn'fekʃn/ ***noun*** (HEALTH) **1** [U] the act of becoming or making sb ill: *A dirty water supply can be a source of infection.* ➲ note at **disease** **2** [C] a disease or illness that is caused by harmful bacteria, etc. and affects one part of your body: *She is suffering from a chest infection.* ◇ *an ear infection*

> **RELATED VOCABULARY**
>
> Infections can be caused by **bacteria** or **viruses**. An informal word for these is **germs**.

infectious 🔑 /ɪn'fekʃəs/ ***adj.*** (HEALTH) (used about a disease, illness, etc.) that can be easily passed on to another person: *Flu is very infectious.* ◇ (*figurative*) *infectious laughter*

> **RELATED VOCABULARY**
>
> **Infectious** diseases are usually passed on by the air that we breathe. **Contagious** diseases are passed from one person to another by touch.

infer AW /ɪn'fɜː(r)/ ***verb*** [T] (**inferring**; **inferred**) ~ **sth (from sth)** to form an opinion or decide that sth is true from the information you have: *I inferred from our conversation that he was unhappy with his job.* ▶ **inference** AW /'ɪnfərəns/ ***noun*** [C]

inferior /ɪn'fɪəriə(r)/ ***adj.*** ~ **(to sb/sth)** low or lower in social position, importance, quality, etc.: *This material is obviously inferior to that one.* ◇ *Don't let people make you* ***feel inferior****.* OPP **superior** ▶ **inferior** ***noun*** [C]: *She always treats me as her intellectual inferior.* ▶ **inferiority** /ɪnˌfɪəri'ɒrəti/ ***noun*** [U]

inferi'ority complex ***noun*** [C] the state of feeling less important, clever, successful, etc. than other people

infertile /ɪn'fɜːtaɪl/ ***adj.*** **1** (BIOLOGY) (used about a person or animal) not able to have babies or produce young **2** (AGRICULTURE) (used about land) not able to grow strong healthy plants OPP **fertile** ▶ **infertility** /ˌɪnfɜː'tɪləti/ ***noun*** [U]: *infertility treatment* OPP **fertility**

infested /ɪn'festɪd/ ***adj.*** ~ **(with sth)** (used about a place) with large numbers of unpleasant animals or insects in it: *The warehouse was infested with rats.* ▶ **infestation** /ˌɪnfe'steɪʃn/ ***noun*** [C,U]: *an infestation of lice*

infidelity /ˌɪnfɪ'deləti/ ***noun*** [U, C] (*pl.* **infidelities**) the act of not being faithful to your wife or husband by having a sexual relationship with sb else SYN **unfaithfulness**

infiltrate /'ɪnfɪltreɪt/ ***verb*** [T] to enter an organization, etc. secretly so that you can find out what it is doing: *The police managed to infiltrate the gang of terrorists.* ▶ **infiltration** /-eɪʃn/ ***noun*** [C,U] ▶ **infiltrator** ***noun*** [C]

infinite AW /'ɪnfɪnət/ ***adj.*** **1** very great: *You need infinite patience for this job.* **2** without limits; that never ends: *Supplies of oil are not infinite.* OPP **finite**

infinitely AW /'ɪnfɪnətli/ ***adv.*** very much: *Compact discs sound infinitely better than audio cassettes.*

infinitesimal /ˌɪnfɪnɪ'tesɪml/ ***adj.*** (*formal*) extremely small: *infinitesimal traces of poison* ◇ *an infinitesimal risk* ▶ **infinitesimally** /-məli/ ***adv.***

infinitive /ɪn'fɪnətɪv/ ***noun*** [C] (LANGUAGE) the basic form of a verb

infinity /ɪn'fɪnəti/ ***noun*** **1** [U] space or time without end: (*figurative*) *The ocean seemed to stretch over the horizon into infinity.* **2** [U, C] (*symbol* ∞) (MATHEMATICS) the number that is larger than any other that you can think of

infirmary /ɪn'fɜːməri/ ***noun*** [C] (*pl.* **infirmaries**) (HEALTH) (used mainly in names) a hospital: *The Manchester Royal Infirmary*

inflamed /ɪn'fleɪmd/ ***adj.*** (HEALTH) (used about a part of the body) red and swollen or painful because of an infection or injury

inflammable /ɪnˈflæməbl/ (*especially BrE* **flammable**) ***adj.*** that burns easily: *Petrol is highly inflammable.* OPP **non-flammable**

inflammation /ˌɪnfləˈmeɪʃn/ ***noun*** [C,U] (HEALTH) a condition in which a part of the body becomes red, sore and swollen because of infection or injury

inflatable /ɪnˈfleɪtəbl/ ***adj.*** that can or must be filled with air: *an inflatable dinghy/mattress*

inflate /ɪnˈfleɪt/ ***verb*** [I,T] (*formal*) to fill sth with air; to become filled with air SYN **blow (sth) up** OPP **deflate**

inflation /ɪnˈfleɪʃn/ ***noun*** [U] (ECONOMICS) a general rise in prices; the rate at which prices rise: *the inflation rate/rate of inflation ◇ Inflation now stands at 3%.*

inflect /ɪnˈflekt/ ***verb*** [I] (LANGUAGE) if a word **inflects**, its ending or spelling changes according to its function in the grammar of the sentence; if a language **inflects**, it has words that do this ▸ **inflected** ***adj.***: *an inflected language/form/verb*

inflection (also **inflexion**) /ɪnˈflekʃn/ ***noun*** [C,U] **1** (LANGUAGE) a change in the form of a word, especially its ending, that changes its function in the grammar of the language, for example *-ed, -est* **2** the rise and fall of your voice when you are talking SYN **intonation**

inflexible AW /ɪnˈfleksəbl/ ***adj.*** **1** that cannot be changed or made more suitable for a particular situation; RIGID: *He has a very inflexible attitude to change.* **2** (used about a material) not able to bend or be bent easily OPP **flexible** ▸ **inflexibly** /-əbli/ ***adv.*** ▸ **inflexibility** /ɪnˌfleksəˈbɪləti/ ***noun*** [U]

inflict /ɪnˈflɪkt/ ***verb*** [T] ~ **sth (on sb)** to force sb to have sth unpleasant or sth that they do not want: *Don't inflict your problems on me – I've got enough of my own.*

ˈin-flight ***adj.*** (only *before* a noun) (TOURISM) happening or provided during a journey in a plane: *in-flight entertainment*

inflow /ˈɪnfləʊ/ ***noun*** **1** [C,U] the movement of a lot of money, people or things into a place from somewhere else SYN **influx**: *inflows of capital from abroad* **2** [sing., U] the movement of a liquid or of air into a place from somewhere else: *an inflow pipe*

influence[1] 🔑 /ˈɪnfluəns/ ***noun*** **1** [U, C] **(an) ~ (on/upon sb/sth)** the power to affect, change or control sb/sth: *Television can have a strong influence on children. ◇ Nobody should drive while they are* ***under the influence of*** *alcohol.* **2** [C] **an ~ (on sb/sth)** a person or thing that affects or changes sb/sth: *His new girlfriend has been a good influence on him. ◇ cultural/environmental influences*

influence[2] 🔑 /ˈɪnfluəns/ ***verb*** [T] to have an effect on or power over sb/sth so that they or it changes: *You must decide for yourself. Don't let anyone else influence you. ◇ Her style of painting has been influenced by Japanese art.*

influential /ˌɪnfluˈenʃl/ ***adj.*** ~ **(in sth/in doing sth)** having power or influence: *an influential politician ◇ He was influential in getting the hostages set free.*

influenza /ˌɪnfluˈenzə/ (*formal*) = FLU

influx /ˈɪnflʌks/ ***noun*** [C, usually sing.] **an ~ (of sb/sth) (into...)** large numbers of people or things arriving suddenly: *the summer influx of visitors from abroad*

info /ˈɪnfəʊ/ ***noun*** **1** [U] (*informal*) information: *Have you had any more info about the job yet?* **2 info-** ***prefix*** (used in nouns) connected with information: *an infosheet ◇ Phone now for a free infopack.*

inform 🔑 /ɪnˈfɔːm/ ***verb*** [T] ~ **sb (of/about sth)** to give sb information (about sth), especially in an official way: *You should inform the police of the accident. ◇ Do* ***keep me informed*** *of any changes.* PHR V **inform on sb** to give information to the police, etc. about what sb has done wrong: *The wife of the killer informed on her husband.*

informal 🔑 /ɪnˈfɔːml/ ***adj.*** relaxed and friendly or suitable for a relaxed occasion: *Don't get dressed up for the party – it'll be very informal. ◇ The two leaders had informal discussions before the conference began.* OPP **formal** ▸ **informality** /ˌɪnfɔːˈmæləti/ ***noun*** [U]: *an atmosphere of informality* ▸ **informally** /-məli/ ***adv.***: *I was told informally* (=unofficially) *that our plans had been accepted.*

informant /ɪnˈfɔːmənt/ ***noun*** [C] a person who gives secret knowledge or information about sb/sth to the police or a newspaper ➲ look at **informer**

information 🔑 /ˌɪnfəˈmeɪʃn/ (also *informal* **info**) ***noun*** [U] ~ **(on/about sb/sth)** knowledge or facts: *For further information please send for our fact sheet. ◇ Can you give me some information about evening classes in Italian, please?*

inforˌmation superˈhighway ***noun*** [C] (COMPUTING) a name for a large electronic system such as the Internet that used for sending information to people

inforˌmation techˈnology ***noun*** [U] (*abbr.* **IT**) (COMPUTING) the study or use of electronic equipment, especially computers, for collecting, storing and sending out information

informative /ɪnˈfɔːmətɪv/ ***adj.*** giving useful knowledge or information

informed /ɪnˈfɔːmd/ ***adj.*** having knowledge or information about sth: *Consumers cannot make informed choices unless they are told all the facts.*

informer /ɪnˈfɔːmə(r)/ ***noun*** [C] (LAW) a criminal who gives the police information about other criminals ➲ look at **informant**

infra- ***prefix*** (in adjectives) below a particular limit: *infrared* ➲ look at **ultra-**

infrared /ˌɪnfrəˈred/ ***adj.*** (PHYSICS) (used about light) that is produced by hot objects but cannot be seen ➲ look at **ultraviolet** ➲ picture at **wavelength**

infrasonic /ˌɪnfrəˈsɒnɪk/ ***adj.*** (PHYSICS) (used about sounds) lower than humans are able to hear

infrastructure AW /ˈɪnfrəstrʌktʃə(r)/ ***noun*** [C,U] (ECONOMICS) the basic systems and services that are necessary for a country or an organization, for example buildings, transport and water and power supplies: *economic/social/transport infrastructure* ▸ **infrastructural** /ˌɪnfrəˈstrʌktʃərəl/ ***adj.***

infrequent /ɪnˈfriːkwənt/ ***adj.*** not happening often OPP **frequent** ▸ **infrequently** ***adv.***

infringe /ɪnˈfrɪndʒ/ ***verb*** (*formal*) **1** [T] (LAW) to break a rule, law, agreement, etc.: *The material can be copied without infringing copyright.* **2** [I] ~ **on/upon sth** to reduce or limit sb's rights, freedom, etc.: *She refused to answer questions that infringed on her private affairs.* ▸ **infringement** ***noun*** [C,U]

infuriate /ɪnˈfjʊərieɪt/ ***verb*** [T] to make sb very angry ▸ **infuriating** ***adj.***: *an infuriating habit* ▸ **infuriatingly** ***adv.***

infuse /ɪnˈfjuːz/ ***verb*** **1** [T] ~ **A into B**; ~ **B with A** (*formal*) to make sb/sth have a particular quality: *Her novels are infused with sadness.* **2** [T] (*formal*) to have an effect on all parts of sth: *Politics infuses all aspects of our lives.* **3** [I,T] if you **infuse** HERBS (=plants whose leaves are used to give flavour to sth or as medicine) or they **infuse**, you put them in hot water until the flavour has passed into the water

infusion /ɪn'fjuːʒn/ ***noun*** **1** [C,U] **~ of sth (into sth)** (*formal*) the act of adding sth to sth else in order to make it stronger or more successful: *an infusion of new talent into teaching* ◇ *The company needs an infusion of new blood* (=new employees with new ideas). **2** [C] a drink or medicine made by putting HERBS (=plants whose leaves are used to give flavour to sth or as medicine) in hot water **3** [C,U] (**HEALTH**) the act of introducing a liquid substance into the body, especially into a VEIN

ingenious /ɪn'dʒiːniəs/ ***adj.*** **1** (used about a thing or an idea) made or planned in a clever way: *an ingenious plan for making lots of money* ◇ *an ingenious device/experiment/invention* **2** (used about a person) full of new ideas and clever at finding solutions to problems or at inventing things ▶ **ingeniously** ***adv.*** ▶ **ingenuity** /ˌɪndʒə'njuːəti/ ***noun*** [U]

ingest /ɪn'dʒest/ ***verb*** [T] (**BIOLOGY**) to take food, drugs, etc. into your body, usually by swallowing ▶ **ingestion** ***noun*** [U]

ingot /'ɪŋgət/ ***noun*** [C] a solid piece of metal, especially gold or silver, usually shaped like a brick

ingrained /ɪn'greɪnd/ ***adj.*** **~ (in sb/sth)** (used about a habit, an attitude, etc.) that has existed for a long time and is therefore difficult to change: *ingrained prejudices/beliefs*

ingratiate /ɪn'greɪʃieɪt/ ***verb*** [T] (*formal*) **~ yourself (with sb)** to make yourself liked by doing or saying things that will please people, especially people who might be useful to you: *He was always trying to ingratiate himself with his teachers.* ▶ **ingratiating** ***adj.***: *an ingratiating smile* ▶ **ingratiatingly** ***adv.***

ingratitude /ɪn'grætɪtjuːd/ ***noun*** [U] (*formal*) the state of not showing or feeling thanks for sth that has been done for you; not being grateful OPP **gratitude**

ingredient ⊶ /ɪn'griːdiənt/ ***noun*** [C] **1** one of the items of food you need to make sth to eat: *Mix all the ingredients together in a bowl.* **2** one of the qualities necessary to make sth successful: *The film has all the ingredients of success.*

inhabit /ɪn'hæbɪt/ ***verb*** [T] to live in a place: *Are the Aran Islands still inhabited* (=do people live there)?

> **WORD FAMILY**
> **inhabit** *verb*
> **habitable** *adj.*
> (≠ **uninhabitable**)
> **uninhabited** *adj.*
> **inhabitant** *noun*
> **habitation** *noun*

inhabitable /ɪn'hæbɪtəbl/ ***adj.*** that can be lived in: *The house was no longer inhabitable after the fire.* OPP **uninhabitable**

inhabitant /ɪn'hæbɪtənt/ ***noun*** [C, usually pl.] a person or animal that lives in a place: *The local inhabitants protested at the plans for a new motorway.*

inhalant /ɪn'heɪlənt/ ***noun*** [C] (**HEALTH**) a drug or medicine that you breathe in

inhale /ɪn'heɪl/ ***verb*** [I,T] (**BIOLOGY**) to breathe in: *Be careful not to inhale the fumes from the paint.* OPP **exhale** ▶ **inhalation** /ˌɪnhə'leɪʃn/ ***noun*** [U]: *They were treated for the effects of smoke inhalation.*

inhaler /ɪn'heɪlə(r)/ ***noun*** [C] (**HEALTH**) a small device containing medicine that you breathe in through your mouth, used by people who have problems with breathing

inherent AW /ɪn'hɪərənt/ ***adj.*** **~ (in sb/sth)** that is a basic or permanent part of sb/sth and that cannot be removed: *The risk of collapse is inherent in any business.* ▶ **inherently** ***adv.***: *No matter how safe we make them, cars are inherently dangerous.*

inherit /ɪn'herɪt/ ***verb*** [T] **~ sth (from sb)** **1** to receive property, money, etc. from sb who has died: *I inherited quite a lot of money from my mother. She left me $12000 when she died.* ➲ look at **disinherit**, **heir** **2** (**HEALTH**, **BIOLOGY**) to receive a quality, characteristic, etc. from your parents or family: *She has inherited her father's gift for languages.*

inheritance /ɪn'herɪtəns/ ***noun*** [C,U] the act of INHERITING; the money, property, etc. that you INHERIT: *inheritance tax*

inhibit AW /ɪn'hɪbɪt/ ***verb*** [T] **1** to prevent sth or make sth happen more slowly: *a drug to inhibit the growth of tumours* **2** **~ sb (from sth/from doing sth)** to make sb nervous and embarrassed so that he/she is unable to do sth: *The fact that her boss was there inhibited her from saying what she really felt.* ▶ **inhibited** ***adj.***: *The young man felt shy and inhibited in the roomful of women.* OPP **uninhibited**

inhibition AW /ˌɪnhɪ'bɪʃn; ˌɪnɪ'b-/ ***noun*** [C,U] a shy or nervous feeling that stops you from saying or doing what you really want: *After the first day of the course, people started to **lose** their **inhibitions**.*

inhospitable /ˌɪnhɒ'spɪtəbl/ ***adj.*** **1** (used about a place) not pleasant to live in, especially because of the weather: *the inhospitable Arctic regions* **2** (used about a person) not friendly or welcoming to guests OPP **hospitable**

ˌ**in-'house** ***adj.*** (**BUSINESS**) existing or happening within a company or an organization: *an in-house magazine* ◇ *in-house language training*

inhuman /ɪn'hjuːmən/ ***adj.*** **1** very cruel and without pity: *inhuman treatment/conditions* **2** not seeming to be human and therefore frightening: *an inhuman noise*

inhumane /ˌɪnhjuː'meɪn/ ***adj.*** very cruel; not caring if people or animals suffer: *the inhumane conditions in which animals are kept on some large farms* OPP **humane**

inhumanity /ˌɪnhjuː'mænəti/ ***noun*** [U] very cruel behaviour: *The twentieth century is full of examples of man's inhumanity to man.* OPP **humanity**

initial[1] ⊶ AW /ɪ'nɪʃl/ ***adj.*** (only *before* a noun) happening at the beginning; first: *My initial reaction was to refuse, but I later changed my mind.* ◇ *the initial stages of our survey*

initial[2] ⊶ AW /ɪ'nɪʃl/ ***noun*** [C, usually pl.] the first letter of a name: *Alison Elizabeth Waters' initials are A.E.W.*

initial[3] AW /ɪ'nɪʃl/ ***verb*** [T] (**initialling**; **initialled**: *AmE* **initialing**; **initialed**) to mark or sign sth with your initials: *Any changes made when writing a cheque should be initialled by you.*

initialize (also **-ise**) /ɪ'nɪʃəlaɪz/ ***verb*** [T] (**COMPUTING**) to make a computer program or system ready for use or to FORMAT a disk ▶ **initialization** (also **-isation**) /ɪˌnɪʃəlaɪ'zeɪʃn/ ***noun*** [U]

initially ⊶ AW /ɪ'nɪʃəli/ ***adv.*** at the beginning; at first: *I liked the job initially but it soon got quite boring.*

initiate AW /ɪ'nɪʃieɪt/ ***verb*** [T] **1** (*formal*) to start sth: *to initiate peace talks* **2** **~ sb (into sth)** to explain sth to sb or make them experience sth for the first time: *I wasn't initiated into the joys of skiing until I was 30.* **3 ~ sb (into sth)** to bring sb into a group by means of a special ceremony: *to initiate sb into a secret society* ▶ **initiation** AW /-eɪʃn/ **noun** [U]: *All the new students had to go through a strange* ***initiation ceremony.***

initiative 🔑 AW /ɪ'nɪʃətɪv/ **noun** **1** [C] official action that is taken to solve a problem or improve a situation: *a new government initiative to help people start small businesses* **2** [U] the ability to see and do what is necessary without waiting for sb to tell you: *Don't keep asking me how to do it. Use your initiative.* **3 the initiative** [sing.] the stronger position because you have done sth first; the advantage: *The enemy forces have* ***lost the initiative.***

IDM **on your own initiative** without being told by sb else what to do

take the initiative to be first to act to influence a situation

initiator AW /ɪ'nɪʃieɪtə(r)/ **noun** [C] (*formal*) the person who starts sth

inject /ɪn'dʒekt/ **verb** [T] **1** (HEALTH) to put a drug under the skin of a person's or an animal's body with a needle (**syringe**) **2 ~ sth (into sth)** to add sth: *They injected a lot of money into the business.*

injection /ɪn'dʒekʃn/ **noun** **1** [C,U] **(an) ~ (of sth) (into sb/sth)** (HEALTH) the act of putting a drug or substance under the skin of a person's or an animal's body with a needle (**syringe**): *to give sb an injection* ◇ *a tetanus injection* ◇ *An anaesthetic was administered* ***by injection.*** SYN **jab** **2** [C] a large amount of sth that is added to sth to help it: *The theatre needs a huge* ***cash injection*** *if it is to stay open.* **3** [U, C] the act of forcing liquid into sth: *fuel injection*

injunction /ɪn'dʒʌŋkʃn/ **noun** [C] **an ~ (against sb)** an official order from a court of law to do/not do sth: *A court injunction prevented the programme from being shown on TV.*

THESAURUS

injure

wound • hurt • bruise • maim • sprain • pull • twist • strain

These words all mean to harm yourself or sb else physically, especially in an accident.

injure: *He was badly injured in a car crash.*

wound: *Five people were seriously wounded in the attack.*

hurt: *Did you hurt yourself?*

bruise: *She had slipped and badly bruised her back.*

maim (*formal*): *She was maimed in the accident.*

sprain: *He fell and sprained his wrist/ankle/knee.*

pull: *He pulled a muscle playing hockey.*

twist: *She twisted her ankle/wrist/knee.*

strain: *Using a computer can strain your eyes.*

injure 🔑 AW /'ɪndʒə(r)/ **verb** [T] to harm or hurt yourself or sb else physically, especially in an accident: *The goalkeeper seriously injured himself when he hit the goalpost.* ◇ *She fell and injured her back.* ➲ note at **hurt**

injured 🔑 AW /'ɪndʒəd/ **adj.** **1** physically or mentally hurt: *an injured arm/leg* ◇ *injured pride* **2 the injured noun** [pl.] people who have been hurt: *The injured were rushed to hospital.*

injury 🔑 AW /'ɪndʒəri/ **noun** [C,U] (*pl.* **injuries**) **~ (to sb/sth)** harm done to a person's or an animal's body, especially in an accident: *They escaped from the accident with only* ***minor injuries.*** ◇ *Injury to the head can be extremely dangerous.*

'injury time **noun** [U] (*BrE*) (SPORT) time that is added to the end of a RUGBY, football, etc. match when there has been time lost because of injuries to players

injustice /ɪn'dʒʌstɪs/ **noun** [U, C] the fact of a situation being unfair; an unfair act: *racial/social injustice* ◇ *People are protesting about the injustice of the new tax.*

IDM **do sb an injustice** to judge sb unfairly: *I'm afraid I've done you both an injustice.*

ink 🔑 /ɪŋk/ **noun** [U, C] coloured liquid that is used for writing, drawing, etc.: *Please write* ***in ink,*** *not pencil.*

inkling /'ɪŋklɪŋ/ **noun** [C, usually sing.] **an ~ (of sth/ that...)** a slight feeling (about sth): *I had an inkling that something was wrong.*

inky /'ɪŋki/ **adj.** made black with ink; very dark: *inky fingers* ◇ *an inky night sky*

inlaid /ˌɪn'leɪd/ **adj.** **~ (with sth)** (ART) (used about furniture, floors, etc.) decorated with designs of wood, metal, etc. that are put into the surface: *a box inlaid with gold*

inland /'ɪnlænd/ **adj.** /ˌɪn'lænd/ **adv.** away from the coast or borders of a country: *The village lies twenty miles inland.* ◇ *Goods are carried inland along narrow mountain roads.*

ˌInland 'Revenue **noun** [sing.] (*BrE*) (FINANCE) the government department that collects taxes

'in-laws **noun** [pl.] (*informal*) your husband's or wife's mother and father or other relations

inlay /ˌɪn'leɪ/ **verb** (*pres. part.* **inlaying**; *pt, pp* **inlaid** /ˌɪn'leɪd/) [T] **~ A (with B)**; **~ B (in/into A)** (ART) to decorate the surface of sth by putting pieces of wood or metal into it in such a way that the surface remains smooth: *The lid of the box had been inlaid with silver.* ▶ **inlay** /'ɪnleɪ/ [C,U]: *The table was decorated with gold inlay.*

inlet /'ɪnlet/ **noun** [C] **1** (GEOGRAPHY) a narrow area of water that stretches into the land from the sea or a lake **2** (TECHNICAL) an opening through which liquid, air or gas can enter a machine: *a fuel inlet* OPP **outlet**

inmate /'ɪnmeɪt/ **noun** [C] one of the people living in an institution such as a prison

inn /ɪn/ **noun** [C] (*BrE*) a small hotel or old pub, usually in the country

innate /ɪ'neɪt/ **adj.** (used about an ability or quality) that you have when you are born: *the innate ability to learn*

inner 🔑 /'ɪnə(r)/ **adj.** (only *before* a noun) **1** (of the) inside; towards or close to the centre of a place: *The inner ear is very delicate.* ◇ *an inner courtyard* OPP **outer** **2** (used about a feeling, etc.) that you do not express or show to other people; private: *Everyone has inner doubts.*

ˌinner 'city **noun** [C] (SOCIAL STUDIES) the poor parts of a large city, near the centre, that often have a lot of social problems ▶ **'inner-city** **adj.** (only *before* a noun): *Inner-city schools often have difficulty in attracting good teachers.*

ˌinner 'ear **noun** [C] (ANATOMY) the part of your ear that is inside your head and that consists of the organs that control your balance and hearing ➲ look at **middle ear**

innermost /ˈɪnəməʊst/ *adj.* (only *before* a noun) **1** (used about a feeling or thought) most secret or private: *She never told anyone her innermost thoughts.* **2** nearest to the centre or inside of sth: *the innermost shrine of the temple*

ˈ**inner tube** *noun* [C] a rubber tube filled with air inside a tyre

innings /ˈɪnɪŋz/ *noun* [C] (*pl.* **innings**) (SPORT) a period of time in a game of CRICKET when it is the turn of one player or team to hit the ball (**to bat**)

innocence /ˈɪnəsns/ *noun* [U] **1** the fact of not being guilty of a crime, etc.: *The accused man **protested** his **innocence** throughout his trial.* OPP **guilt 2** lack of knowledge and experience of the world, especially of bad things: *the innocence of childhood*

innocent ⊶ /ˈɪnəsnt/ *adj.* **1** ~ (of sth) not having done wrong: *An innocent man was arrested by mistake.* ◇ *to be innocent of a crime* SYN **blameless** OPP **guilty 2** (only *before* a noun) being hurt or killed in a crime, war, etc. although not involved in it in any way: ***innocent victims** of a bomb blast* ◇ *an innocent bystander* **3** not wanting to cause harm or upset sb, although it does: *He got very aggressive when I asked an **innocent question** about his past life.* **4** not knowing the bad things in life; believing everything you are told: *She was so innocent as to believe that politicians never lie.* SYN **naive** ▶ **innocently** *adv.*: *'What are you doing here?' she asked innocently* (=pretending she did not know the answer).

innocuous /ɪˈnɒkjuəs/ *adj.* (*formal*) not meant to cause harm or upset sb: *I made an **innocuous remark** about teachers and she got really angry.* SYN **harmless** ▶ **innocuously** *adv.*

innovate AW /ˈɪnəveɪt/ *verb* [I] to create new things, ideas or ways of doing sth ▶ **innovation** AW /ˌɪnəˈveɪʃn/ *noun* [C,U] (an) ~ (in sth) [C]: *technological innovations in industry* ▶ **innovative** AW /ˈɪnəvətɪv; ˈɪnəveɪtɪv/ *adj.*: *innovative methods/designs/products* ▶ **innovator** AW *noun* [C]

innuendo /ˌɪnjuˈendəʊ/ *noun* [C,U] (*pl.* **innuendoes** or **innuendos**) an indirect way of talking about sb/sth, usually suggesting sth bad or rude: *His speech was full of sexual innuendo.*

innumerable /ɪˈnjuːmərəbl/ *adj.* too many to be counted

inoculate /ɪˈnɒkjuleɪt/ *verb* [T] ~ **sb (against sth)** (HEALTH) to protect a person or animal from a disease by giving them or it a mild form of the disease with a needle which is put under the skin (**an injection**): *The children have been inoculated against tetanus.* ➲ look at **immunize**, **vaccinate** ▶ **inoculation** /-eɪʃn/ *noun* [C,U]

inoffensive /ˌɪnəˈfensɪv/ *adj.* not likely to offend or upset sb; harmless OPP **offensive**

inoperable /ɪnˈɒpərəbl/ *adj.* (HEALTH) (used about a disease) that cannot be cured by a medical operation OPP **operable**

inopportune /ɪnˈɒpətjuːn/ *adj.* (*formal*) happening at a bad time SYN **inappropriate**, **inconvenient** OPP **opportune**

inordinate /ɪnˈɔːdɪnət/ *adj.* (*formal*) much greater than usual or expected: *They spent an **inordinate amount** of time and money on the production.* ▶ **inordinately** *adv.*

inorganic /ˌɪnɔːˈɡænɪk/ *adj.* (SCIENCE) not made of or coming from living things: *Rocks and metals are inorganic substances.* OPP **organic**

ˌ**inorganic** ˈ**chemistry** *noun* [U] (CHEMISTRY) the branch of chemistry that deals with substances that do not contain CARBON ➲ look at **organic chemistry**

input[1] AW /ˈɪnpʊt/ *noun* **1** [C,U] ~ **(of sth) (into/to sth)** what you put into sth to make it successful; the act of putting sth in: *Growing anything in this soil will require heavy inputs of nutrients.* ◇ *We need some input from teachers into this book.* **2** [U] (COMPUTING) the act of putting information into a computer: *The computer breakdown means we have lost the whole day's input.* **3** [C] (TECHNICAL) a place or means for electricity, data, etc. to enter a machine or system: *an input lead* ➲ look at **output**

input[2] AW /ˈɪnpʊt/ *verb* [T] (*pres. part.* **inputting**; *pt, pp* **input** or **inputted**) to put information into a computer

inquest /ˈɪŋkwest/ *noun* [C] (LAW) an official process that tries to find out how sb died: *to hold an inquest*

inquire, inquirer, inquiring, inquiry =ENQUIRE, ENQUIRER, ENQUIRING, ENQUIRY

inquisition /ˌɪnkwɪˈzɪʃn/ *noun* **1 the Inquisition** [sing.] (HISTORY) the organization formed by the Roman Catholic Church to find and punish people who did not agree with its beliefs, especially from the 15th to the 17th century **2** [C] (*formal*) a series of questions that sb asks you, especially when they ask them in an unpleasant way

inquisitive /ɪnˈkwɪzətɪv/ *adj.* **1** too interested in finding out about what other people are doing: *Don't be so inquisitive. It's none of your business.* **2** interested in finding out about many different things: *You need an inquisitive mind to be a scientist.* ▶ **inquisitively** *adv.* ▶ **inquisitiveness** *noun* [U]

insane /ɪnˈseɪn/ *adj.* **1** crazy or mentally ill **2** not showing sensible judgement: *You must be insane to leave your job before you've found another one.* ▶ **insanely** *adv.*: *insanely jealous* ▶ **insanity** /ɪnˈsænəti/ *noun* [U]

insanitary /ɪnˈsænətri/ *adj.* (*formal*) dirty and likely to cause disease: *The restaurant was closed because of the insanitary conditions of the kitchen.* ➲ look at **sanitary**

insatiable /ɪnˈseɪʃəbl/ *adj.* that cannot be satisfied; very great: *an insatiable desire for knowledge* ◇ *an insatiable appetite*

inscribe /ɪnˈskraɪb/ *verb* [T] (*formal*) ~ **A (on/in B)**; ~ **B (with A)** to write or cut words on sth: *The names of all the previous champions are inscribed on the cup.* ◇ *The book was inscribed with the author's name.*

inscription /ɪnˈskrɪpʃn/ *noun* [C] words that are written or cut on sth: *There was a Latin inscription on the tombstone.*

insect ⊶ /ˈɪnsekt/ *noun* [C] (BIOLOGY) a small animal with six legs, two pairs of wings and a body which is divided into three parts: *Ants, flies, beetles, butterflies and mosquitoes are all insects.* ◇ *an insect bite/sting* ➲ picture on **page 29**

insecticide /ɪnˈsektɪsaɪd/ *noun* [C,U] (AGRICULTURE) a substance that is used for killing insects ➲ look at **pesticide**

insectivore /ɪnˈsektɪvɔː(r)/ *noun* [C] (BIOLOGY) any animal that eats insects ➲ look at **carnivore**, **herbivore**, **omnivore**

insecure AW /ˌɪnsɪˈkjʊə(r)/ *adj.* **1** ~ **(about sb/sth)** not confident about yourself or your relationships with other people: *Many teenagers are insecure about their appearance.* **2** not safe or protected: *This ladder feels a bit insecure.* ◇ *The future of the company looks very insecure.* OPP **secure**

▸ **insecurely** *adv.* ▸ **insecurity** /-rəti/ *noun* [U, C] (*pl.* **insecurities**): *Their aggressive behaviour is really a sign of insecurity.* OPP **security**

insensitive /ɪnˈsensətɪv/ *adj.* ~ **(to sth) 1** not knowing or caring how another person feels and therefore likely to hurt or upset them: *Some insensitive reporters tried to interview the families of the accident victims.* ◇ *an insensitive remark* **2** not able to feel or react to sth: *insensitive to pain/cold/criticism* OPP **sensitive** ▸ **insensitively** *adv.* ▸ **insensitivity** /ɪnˌsensəˈtɪvəti/ *noun* [U]

inseparable /ɪnˈseprəbl/ *adj.* that cannot be separated from sb/sth: *inseparable friends* OPP **separable**

insert ⊶ AW /ɪnˈsɜːt/ *verb* [T] (*formal*) to put sth into sth or between two things: *I decided to insert an extra paragraph in the text.* ▸ **insertion** AW /ɪnˈsɜːʃn/ *noun* [C,U]

inshore /ˈɪnʃɔː(r)/ *adj.* /ˌɪnˈʃɔː(r)/ *adv.* (GEOGRAPHY) in or towards the part of the sea that is close to the land: *inshore fishermen* ◇ *Sharks don't often come inshore.*

inside[1] ⊶ /ˌɪnˈsaɪd/ *prep., adj., adv.* **1** in, on or to the inner part or surface of sth: *Is there anything inside the box?* ◇ *It's safer to be inside the house in a thunderstorm.* ◇ *We'd better stay inside until the rain stops.* ◇ *It's getting cold. Let's go inside.* ◇ *the inside pages of a newspaper* **2** (*formal*) (used about time) in less than; within: *Your photos will be ready inside an hour.* **3** (used about information, etc.) told secretly by sb who belongs to a group, organization, etc.: *The robbers seemed to have had some inside information about the bank's security system.* **4** (*slang*) in prison

inside[2] ⊶ /ˌɪnˈsaɪd/ *noun* **1** [C] the inner part or surface of sth: *The door was locked from the inside.* ◇ *There's a label somewhere* ***on the inside***. **2 insides** [pl.] (*informal*) the organs inside the body: *The coffee warmed his insides.*

IDM **inside out 1** with the inner surface on the outside: *You've got your jumper on inside out.* **2** very well, in great detail: *She knows these streets inside out.*

insider /ɪnˈsaɪdə(r)/ *noun* [C] a person who knows a lot about a group or an organization because they are a part of it: *The book gives us an insider's view of how government works.*

insidious /ɪnˈsɪdiəs/ *adj.* (*formal*) spreading gradually or without being noticed, but causing serious harm: *the insidious effects of polluted water supplies* ▸ **insidiously** *adv.*

insight AW /ˈɪnsaɪt/ *noun* [C,U] **(an)** ~ **(into sth)** an understanding of what sb/sth is like: *The book gives a good insight into the lives of the poor.*

insightful AW /ɪnˈsaɪtfʊl/ *adj.* showing a clear understanding of a person or situation

insignia /ɪnˈsɪgniə/ *noun* [U, with sing. or pl. verb] the symbol, sign, etc. that shows that sb is a member of, or has a particular position in, a group or an organization: *His uniform bore the insignia of a captain.*

insignificant AW /ˌɪnsɪgˈnɪfɪkənt/ *adj.* of little value or importance: *an insignificant detail* ◇ *Working in such a big company made her feel insignificant.* ▸ **insignificance** *noun* [U] ▸ **insignificantly** *adv.*

insincere /ˌɪnsɪnˈsɪə(r)/ *adj.* saying or doing sth that you do not really believe: *His apology sounded insincere.* ◇ *an insincere smile* OPP **sincere** ▸ **insincerely** *adv.* ▸ **insincerity** /ˌɪnsɪnˈserəti/ *noun* [U] OPP **sincerity**

insinuate /ɪnˈsɪnjueɪt/ *verb* [T] to suggest sth unpleasant in an indirect way: *She seemed to be insinuating that our work was below standard.* ▸ **insinuation** /ɪnˌsɪnjuˈeɪʃn/ *noun* [C,U]: *to* ***make insinuations*** *about sb's honesty*

insipid /ɪnˈsɪpɪd/ *adj.* having too little taste, flavour or colour

insist ⊶ /ɪnˈsɪst/ *verb* [I] **1** ~ **(on sth/doing sth)**; ~ **that...** to say strongly that you must have or do sth, or that sb else must do sth: *He always insists on the best.* ◇ *Dan insisted on coming too.* ◇ *My parents insist that I come home by taxi.* ◇ *'Have another drink.' 'Oh all right, if you insist.'* ➲ note at **demand**[2] **2** ~ **(on sth)**; ~ **that...** to say firmly that sth is true (when sb does not believe you): *She insisted on her innocence.* ◇ *James insisted that the accident wasn't his fault.* ▸ **insistence** *noun* [U]

insistent /ɪnˈsɪstənt/ *adj.* **1** ~ **(on sth/doing sth)**; ~ **that...** saying strongly that you must have or do sth, or that sb else must do sth: *Doctors are insistent on the need to do more exercise.* ◇ *She was most insistent that we should all be there.* **2** continuing for a long time in a way that cannot be ignored: *the insistent ringing of the telephone* ▸ **insistently** *adv.*

insolent /ˈɪnsələnt/ *adj.* (*formal*) lacking respect; rude: *insolent behaviour* ▸ **insolence** *noun* [U] ▸ **insolently** *adv.*

insoluble /ɪnˈsɒljəbl/ *adj.* **1** that cannot be explained or solved: *We faced almost insoluble problems.* **2** (CHEMISTRY) that cannot be dissolved in a liquid OPP **soluble**

insolvent /ɪnˈsɒlvənt/ *adj.* (*formal*) (FINANCE) not having enough money to pay what you owe SYN **bankrupt**: *The company has been declared insolvent.* ▸ **insolvency** /-ənsi/ *noun* [U, C] (*pl.* **insolvencies**)

insomnia /ɪnˈsɒmniə/ *noun* [U] (HEALTH) inability to sleep: *Do you ever suffer from insomnia?* ➲ look at **sleepless**

insomniac /ɪnˈsɒmniæk/ *noun* [C] (HEALTH) a person who cannot sleep

inspect AW /ɪnˈspekt/ *verb* [T] **1** ~ **sb/sth (for sth)** to look at sth closely or in great detail: *The detective inspected the room for fingerprints.* **2** to make an official visit to make sure that rules are being obeyed, work is being done properly, etc.: *All food shops should be inspected regularly.* ▸ **inspection** AW *noun* [C,U]: *The fire prevention service will* ***carry out an inspection*** *of the building next week.* ◇ ***On inspection****, the passport turned out to be false.*

inspector AW /ɪnˈspektə(r)/ *noun* [C] **1** an official who visits schools, factories, etc. to make sure that rules are being obeyed, work is being done properly, etc.: *a health and safety inspector* **2** (*BrE*) (LAW) a police officer with quite an important position **3** a person whose job is to check passengers' tickets on buses or trains

inspiration /ˌɪnspəˈreɪʃn/ *noun* **1** [C,U] **an** ~ **(to/for sb)**; ~ **(to do/for sth)** a feeling, person or thing that makes you want to do sth or gives you exciting new ideas: *The beauty of the mountains was a great* ***source of inspiration*** *to the writer.* ◇ *What gave you the inspiration to become a dancer?* **2** [C] (*informal*) a sudden good idea: *I've had an inspiration – why don't we go to that new club?*

inspire /ɪnˈspaɪə(r)/ *verb* [T] **1** ~ **sth**; ~ **sb (to do sth)** to make sb want to do or create sth: *Nelson Mandela's autobiography inspired her to go into politics.* ◇ *The attack was inspired by racial hatred.* **2** ~ **sb (with sth)**; ~ **sth (in sb)** to make sb feel, think, etc. sth: *to be inspired with enthusiasm* ◇ *The guide's nervous manner did not **inspire** much **confidence** in us.* ▸ **inspiring** *adj.*: *an inspiring speech.*

inspired /ɪn'spaɪəd/ ***adj.*** influenced or helped by a particular feeling, thing or person: *The pianist gave an inspired performance.* ◇ *a politically inspired killing*

instability AW /ˌɪnstə'bɪləti/ ***noun*** [U] the state of being likely to change: *There are growing signs of political instability.* ➲ adjective **unstable** OPP **stability**

install 🔑 (*AmE also* **instal**) /ɪn'stɔːl/ ***verb*** [T] **1** to put a piece of equipment, etc. in place so that it is ready to be used: *We are waiting to have our new washing machine installed.* ◇ *to install a computer system* SYN **put in 2** ~ **sb (as sth)** to put sb/sth or yourself in a position or place: *He was installed as President yesterday.*

installation /ˌɪnstə'leɪʃn/ ***noun*** **1** [U,C] the act of fixing equipment or furniture in position so that it can be used: *installation costs* **2** [C] a piece of equipment or machinery that has been fixed in position so that it can be used: *a heating installation* **3** [C] a place where specialist equipment is kept and used: *a military installation* **4** [C] (**ART**) a piece of modern SCULPTURE that is made using sound, light, etc. as well as objects

instalment (*AmE* **installment**) /ɪn'stɔːlmənt/ ***noun*** [C] **1** (**FINANCE**) one of the regular payments that you make for sth until you have paid the full amount: *to pay for sth **in instalments*** **2** one part of a story that is shown or published as a series: *Don't miss next week's exciting instalment.*

instance¹ 🔑 AW /'ɪnstəns/ ***noun*** [C] **an** ~ **(of sth)** an example or case (of sth): *There have been several instances of racial attacks in the area.* ◇ *In most instances the drug has no side effects.* ➲ note at **example**

IDM **for instance** for example: *There are several interesting places to visit around here – Warwick, for instance.*

instance² AW /'ɪnstəns/ ***verb*** [T] (*formal*) to give sth as an example: *I refer to the situation instanced above.*

instant¹ /'ɪnstənt/ ***adj.*** **1** happening suddenly or immediately: *The film was an instant success.* **2** (used about food) that can be prepared quickly and easily, usually by adding hot water: *instant coffee*

instant² /'ɪnstənt/ ***noun*** [usually sing.] **1** a very short period of time: *Alex thought **for an instant** and then agreed.* **2** a particular point in time: ***At that instant** I realized I had been tricked.* ◇ *Stop doing that this instant!* (=now)

instantaneous /ˌɪnstən'teɪniəs/ ***adj.*** happening immediately or extremely quickly ▸ **instantaneously** ***adv.***

instantly /'ɪnstəntli/ ***adv.*** without delay; immediately: *I asked him a question and he replied instantly.*

ˌinstant 'messaging ***noun*** [U] (**COMPUTING**) a system on the Internet that allows people to exchange written messages with each other very quickly

ˌinstant 'replay ***noun*** (*AmE*) =ACTION REPLAY

instead 🔑 /ɪn'sted/ ***adv.***, ***prep.*** ~ **(of sb/sth/doing sth)** in the place of sb/sth: *I couldn't go so my husband went instead.* ◇ *You should play football instead of just watching it on TV.* ◇ *Instead of 7.30 could I come at 8.00?*

instigate /'ɪnstɪgeɪt/ ***verb*** [T] (*formal*) to make sth start to happen ▸ **instigation** /ˌɪnstɪ'geɪʃn/ ***noun*** [U]

instil (*AmE* **instill**) /ɪn'stɪl/ ***verb*** [T] (**instilling**; **instilled**) ~ **sth (in/into sb)** to make sb think or feel sth: *Parents should try to instil a sense of responsibility into their children.*

instinct /'ɪnstɪŋkt/ ***noun*** [C,U] (**BIOLOGY**) the natural force that causes a person or animal to behave in a particular way without thinking or learning about it: *Birds learn to fly **by instinct**.* ◇ *In a situation like that you don't have time to think – you just **act on instinct**.* ▸ **instinctive** /ɪn'stɪŋktɪv/ ***adj.***: *Your instinctive reaction is to run from danger.* ▸ **instinctively** ***adv.***

institute¹ 🔑 AW /'ɪnstɪtjuːt/ ***noun*** [C] an organization that has a particular purpose; the building used by this organization: *the Institute of Science and Technology* ◇ *institutes of higher education*

institute² AW /'ɪnstɪtjuːt/ ***verb*** [T] (*formal*) to introduce a system, policy, etc., or start a process: *The government has instituted a new scheme for youth training.*

institution 🔑 AW /ˌɪnstɪ'tjuːʃn/ ***noun*** **1** [C] a large, important organization that has a particular purpose, such as a bank, a university, etc.: *the financial institutions in the City of London* **2** [C] (**HEALTH**) a building where certain people with special needs live and are looked after: *a mental institution* (=a hospital for the mentally ill) ◇ *She's been in institutions all her life.* **3** [C] (**SOCIAL STUDIES**) a social custom or habit that has existed for a long time: *the institution of marriage* **4** [U] the act of introducing a system, policy, etc., or of starting a process: *the institution of new safety procedures*

institutional AW /ˌɪnstɪ'tjuːʃənl/ ***adj.*** connected with an institution: *The old lady is in need of institutional care.*

institutionalized (also **-ised**) AW /ˌɪnstɪ'tjuːʃənəlaɪzd/ ***adj.*** **1** that has happened or been done for so long that it is considered normal **2** (used about people) lacking the ability to live and think independently because they have spent so long in an institution: *institutionalized patients*

instruct AW /ɪn'strʌkt/ ***verb*** [T] **1** ~ **sb (to do sth)** to give an order to sb; to tell sb to do sth: *The soldiers were instructed to shoot above the heads of the crowd.* **2** (*formal*) ~ **sb (in sth)** to teach sb sth: *Children must be instructed in road safety before they are allowed to ride a bike on the road.*

instruction 🔑 AW /ɪn'strʌkʃn/ ***noun*** **1 instructions** [pl.] detailed information on how you should use sth, do sth, etc.: *Read the instructions on the back of the packet carefully.* ◇ *You should always **follow the instructions**.* **2** [C] **an** ~ **(to do sth)** an order that tells you what to do or how to do sth: *The guard was **under** strict **instructions** not to let anyone in or out.* **3** [U] ~ **(in sth)** the act of teaching sth to sb: *The staff need instruction in the use of computers.*

instructive AW /ɪn'strʌktɪv/ ***adj.*** giving useful information ▸ **instructively** ***adv.***

instructor AW /ɪn'strʌktə(r)/ ***noun*** [C] a person whose job is to teach a practical skill or sport: *a driving/fitness/golf instructor*

instrument 🔑 /'ɪnstrəmənt/ ***noun*** [C] **1** a tool that is used for doing a particular job or task: *surgical/optical/precision instruments* ➲ note at **tool** **2** (**MUSIC**) something that is used for playing music: *'What instrument do you play?' 'The violin.'* ➲ picture on **page 465**

RELATED VOCABULARY

Musical instruments may be **stringed** (*violins, guitars, etc.*), **brass** (*horns, trumpets, etc.*), **woodwind** (*flutes, clarinets, etc.*) or **keyboard** (*piano, organ, synthesizer, etc.*). **Percussion** instruments include *drums* and *cymbals*.

3 something that is used for measuring speed, distance, temperature, etc. in a car, plane or ship: *the instrument panel of a plane* **4** something that sb uses in order to achieve sth: *The press should be more than an instrument of the government.*

instrumental /ˌɪnstrəˈmentl/ ***adj.*** **1** ~ **in doing sth** helping to make sth happen: *She was instrumental in getting him the job.* **2** (MUSIC) for musical instruments without voices: *instrumental music*

insubordinate /ˌɪnsəˈbɔːdɪnət/ ***adj.*** (*formal*) (used about a person or behaviour) not obeying rules or orders ▶ **insubordination** /ˌɪnsəˌbɔːdɪˈneɪʃn/ ***noun*** [C,U]: *He was dismissed from the army for insubordination.*

insubstantial /ˌɪnsəbˈstænʃl/ ***adj.*** not large, solid or strong: *a hut built of insubstantial materials* OPP **substantial**

insufferable /ɪnˈsʌfrəbl/ ***adj.*** (*formal*) (used about a person or behaviour) extremely unpleasant or annoying

insufficient AW /ˌɪnsəˈfɪʃnt/ ***adj.*** ~ **(for sth/to do sth)** not enough: *The students complained that they were given insufficient time for the test.* OPP **sufficient** ▶ **insufficiently** ***adv.***

insular /ˈɪnsjələ(r)/ ***adj.*** not interested in or able to accept new people or different ideas SYN **narrow-minded** ▶ **insularity** /ˌɪnsjuˈlærəti/ ***noun*** [U]

insulate /ˈɪnsjuleɪt/ ***verb*** [T] ~ **sth (against/from sth)** (PHYSICS) to protect sth with a material that prevents electricity, heat or sound from passing through: *The walls are insulated against noise.* ◇ (*figurative*) *This industry has been insulated from the effects of competition.* ▶ **insulation** /ˌɪnsjuˈleɪʃn/ ***noun*** [U]

ˈinsulating tape ***noun*** [U] a thin band of sticky material used for covering electrical wires to prevent the possibility of an electric shock

insulator /ˈɪnsjuleɪtə(r)/ ***noun*** [C] (PHYSICS) a material or device used to prevent heat, electricity or sound from escaping from sth ➲ picture at **bulb**

insulin /ˈɪnsjəlɪn/ ***noun*** [U] (BIOLOGY, HEALTH) a substance, normally produced by the body itself, which controls the amount of sugar in the blood: *a diabetic relies on insulin injections*

insult[1] 🔑 /ɪnˈsʌlt/ ***verb*** [T] to speak or act rudely to sb: *I felt very insulted when I didn't even get an answer to my letter.* ◇ *He was thrown out of the hotel for insulting the manager.*

insult[2] 🔑 /ˈɪnsʌlt/ ***noun*** [C] a rude comment or action: *The drivers were standing in the road yelling insults at each other.*

insulting 🔑 /ɪnˈsʌltɪŋ/ ***adj.*** ~ (to sb/sth) making sb feel offended: *insulting behaviour/remarks* ◇ *That poster is insulting to women.*

insuperable /ɪnˈsuːpərəbl/ ***adj.*** (*formal*) (used about a problem, etc.) impossible to solve

insurance 🔑 /ɪnˈʃɔːrəns/ ***noun*** **1** [U] ~ **(against sth)** (FINANCE) an arrangement with a company in which you pay them regular amounts of money and they agree to pay the costs if, for example, you die or are ill, or if you lose or damage sth: *Builders should always have insurance against personal injury.*

RELATED VOCABULARY

We **take out** an **insurance policy**. An **insurance premium** is the regular amount you pay to the insurance company. We can take out **life, health, car, travel** and **household insurance**.

2 [U] the business of providing insurance: *He works in insurance.* **3** [U, sing.] **(an)** ~ **(against sth)** something you do to protect yourself (against sth unpleasant): *Many people take vitamin pills as an insurance against illness.*

insure /ɪnˈʃɔː(r)/ ***verb*** [T] **1** ~ **yourself/sth (against/for sth)** (FINANCE) to buy or to provide insurance: *They insured the painting for £10000 against damage or theft.* **2** (*AmE*) = ENSURE

insurer /ɪnˈʃʊərə(r); -ˈʃɔːr-/ ***noun*** [C] (FINANCE) a person or company that provides people with insurance

insurgency /ɪnˈsɜːdʒənsi/ ***noun*** [U,C] (*pl.* **insurgencies**) (POLITICS) an attempt to take control of a country by force SYN **rebellion**

insurgent /ɪnˈsɜːdʒənt/ ***noun*** [C, usually pl.] (*formal*) (POLITICS) a person fighting against the government or armed forces of their own country SYN **rebel** ▶ **insurgent** ***adj.*** SYN **rebellious**

insurmountable /ˌɪnsəˈmaʊntəbl/ ***adj.*** (*formal*) (used about a problem, etc.) impossible to solve ➲ look at **surmountable**

insurrection /ˌɪnsəˈrekʃn/ ***noun*** [C,U] (*formal*) (POLITICS) violent action against the rulers of a country or the government

intact /ɪnˈtækt/ ***adj.*** (not before a noun) complete; not damaged: *Very few of the buildings **remain intact** following the earthquake.*

intake /ˈɪnteɪk/ ***noun*** [C, usually sing.] **1** the amount of food, drink, etc. that you take into your body: *The doctor told me to cut down my alcohol intake.* **2** the (number of) people who enter an organization or institution during a certain period: *This year's intake of students is down 10%.* **3** the act of taking sth into your body, especially breath **4** a place where liquid, air, etc. enters a machine

intangible /ɪnˈtændʒəbl/ ***adj.*** difficult to describe, understand or measure: *The benefits of good customer relations are intangible.* OPP **tangible**

integer /ˈɪntɪdʒə(r)/ ***noun*** [C] (MATHEMATICS) a whole number, such as 3 or 4 but not 3.5 ➲ look at **fraction**

integral AW /ˈɪntɪɡrəl/ ***adj.*** **1** ~ **(to sth)** necessary in order to make sth complete: *Spending a year in France is **an integral part of** the university course.* **2** including sth as a part: *The car has an integral CD player.*

integrate AW /ˈɪntɪɡreɪt/ ***verb*** **1** [T] ~ **sth (into sth)**; ~ **A and B/**~ **A with B** to join things so that they become one thing or work together: *The two small schools were integrated into one large one.* ◇ *These programs can be integrated with your existing software.* **2** [I,T] ~ **(sb) (into/with sth)** (SOCIAL STUDIES) to join in and become part of a group or community, or to make sb do this: *It took Amir a while to integrate into his new school.* ➲ look at **segregate** ▶ **integration** AW /ˌɪntɪˈɡreɪʃn/ ***noun*** [U]: *racial integration* ➲ look at **segregation**

integrated AW /ˈɪntɪɡreɪtɪd/ ***adj.*** in which many different parts are closely connected and work successfully together: *an integrated school* (=attended by students of all races and religions)

integrity AW /ɪnˈtegrəti/ ***noun*** [U] the quality of being honest and having strong moral principles: *He's a person **of great integrity** who can be relied on to tell the truth.*

intellect /ˈɪntəlekt/ ***noun*** **1** [U] the power of the mind to think and to learn: *a woman of considerable intellect* **2** [C] an extremely intelligent person: *He was one of the most brilliant intellects of his time.*

intellectual[1] /ˌɪntəˈlektʃuəl/ ***adj.*** **1** (only *before* a noun) connected with a person's ability to think in a logical way and to understand things: *The boy's intellectual development was very advanced for his age.* **2** (used about a person) enjoying activities in which you have to think deeply about sth ▶ **intellectually** ***adv.***

intellectual[2] /ˌɪntəˈlektʃuəl/ ***noun*** [C] a person who enjoys thinking deeply about things

ˌintelˌlectual ˈproperty ***noun*** [U] (LAW) an idea, a design, etc. that sb has created and that the law prevents other people from copying: *intellectual property rights*

intelligence ⊶ AW /ɪnˈtelɪdʒəns/ ***noun*** [U] **1** the ability to understand, learn and think: *a person of normal intelligence* ◇ *an intelligence test* **2** important information about an enemy country

intelligent ⊶ AW /ɪnˈtelɪdʒənt/ ***adj.*** having or showing the ability to understand, learn and think; clever: *All their children are very intelligent.* ◇ *an intelligent question* ▶ **intelligently** ***adv.***

intelligible /ɪnˈtelɪdʒəbl/ ***adj.*** (used especially about speech or writing) possible or easy to understand OPP **unintelligible** ▶ **intelligibility** /ɪnˌtelɪdʒəˈbɪləti/ ***noun*** [U]

intend ⊶ /ɪnˈtend/ ***verb*** [T] **1** ~ **to do sth/doing sth** to plan or mean to do sth: *I'm afraid I spent more money than I had intended.* ◇ *I certainly don't intend to wait here all day!* ◇ *They had intended staying in Wales for two weeks but the weather was so bad that they left after one.* ➲ noun **intention** **2** ~ **sth for sb/sth**; ~ **sb to do sth** to plan, mean or make sth for a particular person or purpose: *You shouldn't have read that letter – it wasn't intended for you.* ◇ *I didn't intend you to have all the work.*

> WORD FAMILY
> **intend** *verb*
> **intended** *adj.* (≠ **unintended**)
> **intention** *noun*
> **intentional** *adj.* (≠ **unintentional**)

intense AW /ɪnˈtens/ ***adj.*** very great, strong or serious: *intense heat/cold/pressure* ◇ *intense anger/interest/desire* ▶ **intensely** ***adv.***: *They obviously dislike each other intensely.* ▶ **intensity** AW /-səti/ ***noun*** [U]: *I wasn't prepared for the intensity of his reaction to the news.*

intensifier /ɪnˈtensɪfaɪə(r)/ ***noun*** [C] (LANGUAGE) a word, especially an adjective or an adverb, for example 'so' or 'very', that makes the meaning of another word stronger ➲ look at **modifier**

intensify AW /ɪnˈtensɪfaɪ/ ***verb*** [I,T] (*pres. part.* **intensifying**; *3rd person sing. pres.* **intensifies**; *pt, pp* **intensified**) to become or to make sth greater or stronger: *Fighting in the region has intensified.* ◇ *The government has intensified its anti-smoking campaign.* ▶ **intensification** /ɪnˌtensɪfɪˈkeɪʃn/ ***noun*** [U]

intensive AW /ɪnˈtensɪv/ ***adj.*** **1** involving a lot of work or care in a short period of time: *an intensive investigation/course* **2** (AGRICULTURE) (used about methods of farming) aimed at producing as much food as possible from the land or money available: *intensive agriculture* ➲ look at **extensive** ▶ **intensively** ***adv.***

inˌtensive ˈcare ***noun*** [U] (HEALTH) special care in hospital for patients who are very seriously ill or injured; the department that gives this care: *She was in intensive care for a week after the crash.*

intent[1] /ɪnˈtent/ ***adj.*** **1** ~ **(on/upon sth)** showing great attention: *She was so intent upon her work that she didn't hear me come in.* **2** ~ **on/upon sth/doing sth** determined to do sth: *He's always been intent on making a lot of money.* ▶ **intently** ***adv.***

intent[2] /ɪnˈtent/ ***noun*** [U] (*formal*) what sb intends to do; intention: *He was charged with possession of a gun **with intent to** commit a robbery.* ◇ *to do sth with evil/good intent*

IDM **to/for all intents and purposes** in effect, even if not completely true: *When they scored their fourth goal the match was, to all intents and purposes, over.*

intention ⊶ /ɪnˈtenʃn/ ***noun*** [C,U] **(an) ~ (of doing sth/to do sth)** what sb intends or means to do; a plan or purpose: *Our intention was to leave early in the morning.* ◇ *I **have no intention of** staying indoors on a nice sunny day like this.* ◇ *I borrowed the money **with the intention of** paying it back the next day.* ➲ note at **purpose**

intentional /ɪnˈtenʃənl/ ***adj.*** done on purpose, not by chance: *I'm sorry I took your jacket – it wasn't intentional!* SYN **deliberate** OPP **unintentional**, **inadvertent** ▶ **intentionally** /-ʃənəli/ ***adv.***: *I can't believe the boys broke the window intentionally.*

inter- /ˈɪntə(r)/ ***prefix*** (in verbs, nouns, adjectives and adverbs) between; from one to another: *interface* ◇ *interaction* ◇ *international* ➲ look at **intra-**

interact AW /ˌɪntərˈækt/ ***verb*** [I] **1** ~ **(with sb)** (used about people) to communicate or mix with sb, especially while you work, play or spend time together: *He is studying the way children interact with each other at different ages.* **2** (of two things) to have an effect on each other ▶ **interaction** AW ***noun*** [U, C] ~ **(between/with sb/sth)** [U]: *There is a need for greater interaction between the two departments.*

interactive AW /ˌɪntərˈæktɪv/ ***adj.*** **1** that involves people working together and having an influence on each other: *interactive language learning techniques* **2** (COMPUTING) involving direct communication both ways, between the computer and the person using it: *interactive computer games*

ˌinteractive ˈwhiteboard ***noun*** [C] (EDUCATION) a piece of classroom equipment using a computer connected to a large screen that you can write on or use to control the computer by touching it or pointing at it with a pen

intercept /ˌɪntəˈsept/ ***verb*** [T] to stop or catch sb/sth that is moving from one place to another: *Detectives intercepted him at the airport.* ▶ **interception** ***noun*** [U, C]

interchangeable /ˌɪntəˈtʃeɪndʒəbl/ ***adj.*** ~ **(with sth)** able to be used in place of each other without making any difference to the way sth works: *Are these two words interchangeable* (= do they have the same meaning)? ▶ **interchangeably** /-əbli/ ***adv.***

intercom /ˈɪntəkɒm/ ***noun*** [C] a system of communication by radio or telephone inside an office, plane, etc.; the device you press or switch on to start using this system

interconnect /ˌɪntəkəˈnekt/ ***verb*** [I,T] ~ **(A) (with B)**; ~ **A and B** to connect similar things; to be connected to similar things: *electronic networks* *which interconnect thousands of computers around the world*

intercontinental /ˌɪntəˌkɒntɪˈnentl/ *adj.* between continents: *intercontinental flights*

intercostal /ˌɪntəˈkɒstl/ *adj.* (ANATOMY) between the RIBS (= the curved bones that go around the chest): *intercostal muscles* ➲ picture at **lung**

intercourse /ˈɪntəkɔːs/ = SEX (3)

interdependent /ˌɪntədɪˈpendənt/ *adj.* depending on each other: *Exercise and good health are generally interdependent.* ◇ *interdependent economies/organizations* ▶ **interdependence** *noun* [U]

interest¹ 🔑 /ˈɪntrəst/ *noun* **1** [U, sing.] **an ~ (in sb/sth)** a desire to learn or hear more about sb/sth or to be involved with sb/sth: *She's begun to **show** a great **interest** in politics.* ◇ *I wish he'd **take** more **interest in** his children.* ◇ *Don't **lose interest** now!* **2** [U] the quality that makes sth interesting: *I thought this article might **be of interest to** you.* ◇ *Computers **hold no interest for** me.* ◇ *places of historical interest* **3** [C, usually pl.] something that you enjoy doing or learning about: *What are your interests and hobbies?* **4** [U] **~ (on sth)** (FINANCE) the money that you pay for borrowing money from a bank, etc. or the money that you earn when you keep money in a bank, etc.: *We pay 6% interest on our mortgage at the moment.* ◇ *The **interest rate** has never been so high/low.* ➲ look at **interest-free**

IDM **have/with sb's interests at heart** to want sb to be happy and successful, even though your actions may not show it

in sb's interest(s) to sb's advantage: *Using lead-free petrol is in the public interest.*

in the interest(s) of sth in order to achieve or protect sth: *In the interest(s) of safety, please fasten your seat belts.*

interest² 🔑 /ˈɪntrəst/ *verb* [T] to make sb want to learn or hear more about sth or to become involved in sth: *It might interest you to know that I didn't accept the job.* ◇ *The subject of the talk was one that interests me greatly.*

PHR V **interest sb in sth** to persuade sb to buy, have, do sth: *Can I interest you in our new brochure?*

interested 🔑 /ˈɪntrəstɪd/ *adj.* **1** (not before a noun) **~ (in sth/sb); ~ in doing sth; ~ to do sth** wanting to know or hear more about sth/sb; enjoying or liking sth/sb: *They weren't interested in my news at all!* ◇ *I'm really not interested in going to university.* ◇ *I was interested to hear that you've got a new job. Where is it?* OPP **uninterested 2** (only *before* a noun) involved in or affected by sth; in a position to gain from sth: *As an interested party* (= a person directly involved), *I was not allowed to vote.* OPP **disinterested**

ˌ**interest-ˈfree** *adj.* (FINANCE) with no interest charged on money borrowed: *an interest-free loan* ◇ *interest-free credit*

interesting 🔑 /ˈɪntrəstɪŋ; -trest-/ *adj.* **~ (to do sth); ~ that...** enjoyable and entertaining; holding your attention: *an interesting person/book/idea/job* ◇ *It's always interesting to hear about the customs of other societies.* ◇ *It's interesting that Luisa chose Peru for a holiday.* ▶ **interestingly** *adv.*

interface¹ /ˈɪntəfeɪs/ *noun* [C] **1** (COMPUTING) the way a computer program presents information to or receives information from the person who is using it, in particular the LAYOUT of the screen and the MENUS: *the user interface* **2** (COMPUTING) an electrical CIRCUIT, connection or program that joins one device or system to another: *the interface between computer and printer* **3 an ~ (between A and B)** (*written*) the point where two subjects, systems, etc. meet and affect each other: *the interface between manufacturing and sales*

interface² /ˈɪntəfeɪs/ *verb* [I,T] **~ (sth) (with sth); ~ A and B** (COMPUTING) to be connected with sth using an **interface**; to connect sth in this way: *The new system interfaces with existing telephone equipment.*

interfere /ˌɪntəˈfɪə(r)/ *verb* [I] **1 ~ (in sth)** to get involved in a situation which does not involve you and where you are not wanted: *You shouldn't interfere in your children's lives – let them make their own decisions.* **2 ~ (with sb/sth)** to prevent sth from succeeding or to slow down the progress that sb/sth makes: *Every time the telephone rings it interferes with my work.* ◇ *She never lets her private life interfere with her career.* **3 ~ (with sth)** to touch or change sth without permission: *Many people feel that scientists shouldn't interfere with nature.* ▶ **interfering** *adj.*

interference /ˌɪntəˈfɪərəns/ *noun* [U] **1 ~ (in sth)** the act of getting involved in a situation that does not involve you and where you are not wanted: *I left home because I couldn't stand my parents' interference in my affairs.* **2** extra noise (because of other signals or bad weather) that prevents you from receiving radio, television or telephone signals clearly **3** (PHYSICS) the combination of two or more wave movements to form a new wave, which may be bigger or smaller than the first

interim¹ /ˈɪntərɪm/ *adj.* (only *before* a noun) not final or lasting; temporary until sb/sth more permanent is found: *an interim arrangement* ◇ *The deputy head teacher took over in **the interim period** until a replacement could be found.*

interim² /ˈɪntərɪm/ *noun*

IDM **in the interim** in the time between two things happening; until a particular event happens

interior 🔑 /ɪnˈtɪəriə(r)/ *noun* **1** [C, usually sing.] the inside part of sth: *I'd love to see the interior of the castle.* ◇ *interior walls* OPP **exterior 2 the interior** [sing.] (GEOGRAPHY) the central part of a country or continent that is a long way from the coast **3 the Interior** [sing.] (POLITICS) a country's own news and affairs that do not involve other countries: *the Department of the Interior*

inˈterior angle *noun* (GEOMETRY) an angle formed inside a shape where two sides of the shape meet ➲ look at **exterior angle** ➲ picture at **angle**

inˌterior deˈsign *noun* [U] the art or job of choosing colours, furniture, carpets, etc. to decorate the inside of a house ▶ **inˌterior deˈsigner** *noun* [C]

interjection /ˌɪntəˈdʒekʃn/ *noun* [C] (LANGUAGE) a word or phrase that is used to express surprise, pain, pleasure, etc. (for example Oh!, Hurray! or Wow!) SYN **exclamation**

interlude /ˈɪntəluːd/ *noun* [C] a period of time between two events or activities

intermarry /ˌɪntəˈmæri/ *verb* (*pres. part.* **intermarrying**; *3rd person sing. pres.* **intermarries**; *pt, pp* **intermarried**) [I] to marry sb from a different religion, culture, country, etc. ▶ **intermarriage** /ˌɪntəˈmærɪdʒ/ *noun* [U]

intermediary /ˌɪntəˈmiːdiəri/ *noun* [C] (*pl.* **intermediaries**) **an ~ (between A and B)** a person or an organization that helps two people or groups to reach an agreement, by being a means of communication between them

intermediate AW /ˌɪntəˈmiːdiət/ *adj.* **1** SITUATED between two things in position, level, etc.: *an intermediate step/stage in a process* **2** having more than a basic knowledge of sth but not yet advanced; suitable for sb who is at this level: *an intermediate student/book/level*

interminable /ɪn'tɜːmɪnəbl/ ***adj.*** lasting for a very long time and therefore boring or annoying: *an interminable delay/wait/speech* SYN **endless** ▶ **interminably** /-əbli/ ***adv.***

intermission /ˌɪntə'mɪʃn/ ***noun*** [C] (*especially AmE*) (ARTS AND MEDIA) a short period of time separating the parts of a film, play, etc.

intermittent /ˌɪntə'mɪtənt/ ***adj.*** stopping for a short time and then starting again several times: *There will be intermittent showers.* ▶ **intermittently** ***adv.***

intern[1] /ɪn'tɜːn/ ***verb*** [T] (*formal*) ~ **sb (in sth)** (usually passive) (LAW) to keep sb in prison for political reasons, especially during a war ▶ **internment** ***noun*** [U]

intern[2] (also **interne**) /'ɪntɜːn/ ***noun*** [C] (*AmE*) **1** (HEALTH) an advanced student of medicine, whose training is nearly finished and who is working in a hospital to get further practical experience: *Interns and residents at the hospital are working 12-hour shifts.* ➲ look at **house officer** **2** (EDUCATION) a student or new GRADUATE (=a person who has a first degree from a university) who is getting practical experience in a job, for example during the summer holiday: *a summer intern at a law firm* ➲ look at **internship**

internal 🔑 AW /ɪn'tɜːnl/ ***adj.*** **1** (only *before* a noun) of or on the inside (of a place, person or object): *He was rushed to hospital with internal injuries.* **2** happening or existing inside a particular organization: *an internal exam* (=one arranged and marked inside a particular school or college) ◇ *an internal police inquiry* **3** (POLITICS, ECONOMICS) inside a country; not abroad: *a country's internal affairs/trade/markets* ◇ *an internal flight* OPP **external** ▶ **internally** /-nəli/ ***adv.***: *This medicine is not to be taken internally* (=not swallowed).

inˌternal-com'bustion engine ***noun*** [C] (PHYSICS) a type of engine used in cars that produces power by burning petrol/gas inside

internalize (also **-ise**) AW /ɪn'tɜːnəlaɪz/ ***verb*** [I,T] (PSYCHOLOGY) to make a feeling, an attitude, or a belief part of the way you think and behave ➲ look at **externalize**

international 🔑 /ˌɪntə'næʃnəl/ ***adj.*** involving two or more countries: *an international agreement/flight/football match* ◇ *international trade/law/sport* ➲ look at **local**, **national**, **regional** ▶ **internationally** /-nəli/ ***adv.***

the ˌInterˌnational Bacca'laureate™ ***noun*** [sing.] (*abbr.* **IB**) (EDUCATION) an exam which is taken by students in many different countries in the world around the age of 18 or 19, and which includes up to six subjects

the Interˌnational 'Dateline (*also* **'date line**) ***noun*** [sing.] (GEOGRAPHY) the imagined line that goes from north to south through the Pacific Ocean. The date on the east side is one day earlier than that on the west side. ➲ picture at **earth**

internationalism /ˌɪntə'næʃnəlɪzəm/ ***noun*** [U] (POLITICS) the belief that countries should work together in a friendly way

the Internet /'ɪntənet/ (also *informal* **the Net**) ***noun*** [sing.] (COMPUTING) the international system of computers that makes it possible for you to see information from all around the world on your computer and to send information to other computers: *I read about it* ***on the Internet.*** ➲ look at **Intranet**, **World Wide Web**

internship /'ɪntɜːnʃɪp/ ***noun*** [C] **1** (EDUCATION) a period of time during which a student or new GRADUATE (=a person who has a first degree from a university) gets practical experience in a job, for example during the summer holiday: *an internship at a television station* **2** (HEALTH) a job that an advanced student of medicine, whose training is nearly finished, does in a hospital to get further practical experience

Interpol /'ɪntəpɒl/ ***noun*** [sing., with sing. or pl. verb] (LAW) an international organization that makes it possible for the police forces of different countries to help each other to solve crimes

interpret 🔑 AW /ɪn'tɜːprɪt/ ***verb*** **1** [T] ~ **sth (as sth)** to explain or understand the meaning of sth: *Your silence could be interpreted as arrogance.* ◇ *How would you interpret this part of the poem?* OPP **misinterpret** **2** [I] ~ **(for sb)** to translate what sb is saying into another language as you hear it: *He can't speak much English so he'll need somebody to interpret for him.*

interpretation 🔑 AW /ɪnˌtɜːprɪ'teɪʃn/ ***noun*** [C,U] **1** an explanation or understanding of sth: *What's your interpretation of these statistics?* ◇ *What he meant by that remark is* ***open to interpretation*** (=it can be explained in different ways). **2** (ARTS AND MEDIA) the way an actor or musician chooses to perform or understand a character or piece of music: *a modern interpretation of 'Hamlet'*

interpretative AW /ɪn'tɜːprɪtətɪv/ (*especially AmE* **interpretive** /ɪn'tɜːprɪtɪv/) ***adj.*** connected with the particular way in which sth is understood, explained or performed; providing an interpretation: *an interpretative problem* ◇ *an interpretative exhibition*

interpreter /ɪn'tɜːprɪtə(r)/ ***noun*** [C] a person whose job is to translate what sb is saying immediately into another language: *The president spoke through an interpreter.* ➲ look at **translator**

interracial /ˌɪntə'reɪʃl/ ***adj.*** (only *before* a noun) involving people of different races: *interracial marriage*

interrelate /ˌɪntərɪ'leɪt/ ***verb*** [I,T] (usually passive) (*formal*) (used about two or more things) to connect or be connected very closely so that each has an effect on the other ▶ **interrelated** ***adj.***

interrogate /ɪn'terəgeɪt/ ***verb*** [T] ~ **sb (about sth)** to ask sb a lot of questions over a long period of time, especially in an aggressive way: *The prisoner was interrogated for six hours.* ▶ **interrogator** ***noun*** [C] ▶ **interrogation** /ɪnˌterə'geɪʃn/ ***noun*** [C,U]: *The prisoner broke down* ***under interrogation*** *and confessed.*

interrogative[1] /ˌɪntə'rɒgətɪv/ ***adj.*** **1** (*formal*) asking a question; having the form of a question: *an interrogative tone/gesture/remark* **2** (LANGUAGE) used in questions: *an interrogative sentence/pronoun/determiner/adverb*

interrogative[2] /ˌɪntə'rɒgətɪv/ ***noun*** [C] (LANGUAGE) a question word: *'Who', 'what' and 'where' are interrogatives.*

interrupt 🔑 /ˌɪntə'rʌpt/ ***verb*** **1** [I,T] ~ **(sb/sth) (with sth)** to say or do sth that makes sb stop what they are saying or doing: *He kept interrupting me with silly questions.* **2** [T] to stop the progress of sth for a short time: *The programme was interrupted by an important news flash.*

interruption ⊷ /ˌɪntəˈrʌpʃn/ ***noun*** [U, C] the act of interrupting sb/sth; the person or thing that interrupts sb/sth: *I need to work for a few hours without interruption.* ◇ *I've had so many interruptions this morning that I've done nothing!*

intersect /ˌɪntəˈsekt/ ***verb*** [I,T] (used about roads, lines, etc.) to meet or cross each other: *The lines intersect at right angles.*

intersection /ˌɪntəˈsekʃn/ ***noun*** [C] the place where two or more roads, lines, etc. meet or cross each other

intersperse /ˌɪntəˈspɜːs/ ***verb*** [T] (usually passive) to put things at various points in sth: *He interspersed his speech with jokes.*

interstate /ˈɪntəsteɪt/ ***noun*** [C] (*also* ˌ**interstate ˈhighway**) (in the US) a wide road, with at least two lanes in each direction, where traffic can travel fast for long distances across many states. You can only enter and leave **interstates** at special RAMPS. ➲ look at **motorway**

intertwine /ˌɪntəˈtwaɪn/ ***verb*** [I,T] if two things **intertwine** or if you **intertwine** them, they become very closely connected and difficult to separate

interval ⊷ AW /ˈɪntəvl/ ***noun*** [C] **1** a period of time between two events: *There was a long interval between sending the letter and getting a reply.* **2** (**ARTS AND MEDIA**) a short break separating the different parts of a play, film, concert, etc. **3** [usually pl.] a short period during which sth different happens from what is happening for the rest of the time: *There'll be a few* ***sunny intervals*** *between the showers today.*
IDM **at intervals** with time or spaces between: *I write home* ***at regular intervals.*** ◇ *Plant the trees at two-metre intervals.*

intervene AW /ˌɪntəˈviːn/ ***verb*** [I] **1** ~ **(in sth)** to act in a way that prevents sth happening or influences the result of sth: *She would have died if the neighbours hadn't intervened.* ◇ *to intervene in a dispute* **2** to interrupt sb who is speaking in order to say sth **3** (used about events, etc.) to happen in a way that delays sth or stops it from happening: *If no further problems intervene we should be able to finish in time.* ▶ **intervention** AW /ˌɪntəˈvenʃn/ ***noun*** [U, C] ~ **(in sth)**: *military intervention in the crisis*

intervening AW /ˌɪntəˈviːnɪŋ/ ***adj.*** (only *before* a noun) coming or existing between two events, dates, objects, etc.: *the intervening years/days/months*

interventionism /ˌɪntəˈvenʃənɪzəm/ ***noun*** [U] (**POLITICS**) the policy or practice of a government influencing the economy of its own country, or of becoming involved in the affairs of other countries ▶ **interventionist** /-ʃənɪst/ ***adj.***, ***noun*** [C]: *interventionist policies*

interview[1] ⊷ /ˈɪntəvjuː/ ***noun*** [C] **1** an ~ **(for sth)** a meeting at which sb is asked questions to find out if they are suitable for a job, course of study, etc.: *to attend an interview* **2** an ~ **(with sb)** (**ARTS AND MEDIA**) a meeting at which a journalist asks sb questions in order to find out their opinion, etc.: *There was an interview with the Prime Minister on television last night.* ◇ *The actress refused to* ***give an interview*** (=answer questions).

interview[2] ⊷ /ˈɪntəvjuː/ ***verb*** [T] **1** ~ **sb (for sth)** to ask sb questions to find out if they are suitable for a job, course of study, etc.: *How many applicants did you interview for the job?* **2** ~ **sb (about sth)** (**ARTS AND MEDIA**) to ask sb questions about their opinions, private life, etc., especially on the radio or television or for a newspaper, magazine, etc. **3** ~ **sb (about sth)** to ask sb questions at a private meeting: *The police are waiting to interview the injured girl.*

interviewee /ˌɪntəvjuːˈiː/ ***noun*** [C] a person who is questioned in an interview

interviewer /ˈɪntəvjuːə(r)/ ***noun*** [C] a person who asks the questions in an interview

intestine /ɪnˈtestɪn/ ***noun*** [C, usually pl.] (**ANATOMY**) a long tube in the body between the stomach and the ANUS (=the place where solid waste leaves the body). Food passes from the stomach to the **small intestine** and from there to the **large intestine** SYN **gut** ➲ picture on **page 80** ➲ picture at **digestive system** ▶ **intestinal** /ɪnˈtestɪnl; ˌɪnteˈstaɪnl/ ***adj.***

intimacy /ˈɪntɪməsi/ ***noun*** [U] the state of having a close personal relationship with sb: *Their intimacy grew over the years.*

intimate /ˈɪntɪmət/ ***adj.*** **1** (used about people) having a very close relationship: *They're intimate friends.* **2** very private and personal: *They told each other their most intimate thoughts and secrets.* **3** (used about a place, an atmosphere, etc.) quiet and friendly: *I know an intimate little restaurant we could go to.* **4** very detailed: *He's lived here all his life and has an* ***intimate knowledge*** *of the area.* ▶ **intimately** ***adv.***

intimation /ˌɪntɪˈmeɪʃn/ ***noun*** [C,U] (*formal*) the act of stating sth or of making it known, especially in an indirect way: *There was no intimation from his doctor that his condition was serious.*

intimidate /ɪnˈtɪmɪdeɪt/ ***verb*** [T] ~ **sb (into sth/doing sth)** to frighten or threaten sb, often in order to make them do sth: *She refused to be intimidated by their threats.* ▶ **intimidating** ***adj.***: *The teacher had rather an intimidating manner.* ▶ **intimidation** /ɪnˌtɪmɪˈdeɪʃn/ ***noun*** [U]: *The rebel troops controlled the area by intimidation.*

into ⊷ /ˈɪntə before vowels ˈɪntə; ˈɪntuː/ ***prep.*** **1** moving to a position inside or in sth: *Come into the house.* ◇ *I'm going into town.* OPP **out of** (1) **2** in the direction of sth: *Please speak into the microphone.* ◇ *At this point we were driving into the sun and had to shade our eyes.* **3** to a point at which you hit sth: *I backed the car into a wall.* ◇ *She walked into a glass door.* **4** showing a change from one thing to another: *We're turning the spare room into a study.* ◇ *She changed into her jeans.* ◇ *Translate the passage into German.* **5** concerning or involving sth: *an inquiry into safety procedures* **6** (**MATHEMATICS**) used when you are talking about dividing numbers: *7 into 28 goes 4 times.*
IDM **be into sth** (*spoken*) to be very interested in sth, for example as a hobby: *I'm really into canoeing.*

intolerable /ɪnˈtɒlərəbl/ ***adj.*** too bad, unpleasant or difficult to bear or accept: *The living conditions were intolerable.* ◇ *intolerable pain* SYN **unbearable** OPP **tolerable** ➲ verb **tolerate** ▶ **intolerably** /-əbli/ ***adv.***

intolerant /ɪnˈtɒlərənt/ ***adj.*** ~ **(of sb/sth)** not able to accept behaviour or opinions that are different from your own; finding sb/sth too unpleasant to bear: *She's very intolerant of young children.* OPP **tolerant** ▶ **intolerance** ***noun*** [U]: *religious intolerance* OPP **tolerance** ▶ **intolerantly** ***adv.***

intonation /ˌɪntəˈneɪʃn/ ***noun*** [C,U] (**LANGUAGE**) the rise and fall of your voice while you are speaking SYN **inflection**

intoxicated /ɪn'tɒksɪkeɪtɪd/ ***adj.*** (*formal*) **1** having had too much alcohol to drink; drunk **2** very excited and happy: *She was intoxicated by her success.* ▶ **intoxication** /ɪnˌtɒksɪ'keɪʃn/ ***noun*** [U]

intra- *prefix* (in adjectives and adverbs) inside; within: *intravenous* ◇ *intra-departmental* ➲ look at **inter-**

intranet /'ɪntrənet/ ***noun*** [C] (COMPUTING) a system of computers inside an organization that makes it possible for people who work there to look at the same information and to send information to each other ➲ look at **the Internet**

intransitive /ɪn'trænsətɪv/ ***adj.*** (LANGUAGE) (used about a verb) used without an object OPP **transitive** ▶ **intransitively** ***adv.***

intrauterine /ˌɪntrə'juːtəraɪn/ ***adj.*** (ANATOMY) inside the UTERUS (=the part of a woman's body where a baby grows) ➲ look at **IUD**

intravenous /ˌɪntrə'viːnəs/ ***adj.*** (*abbr.* **IV**) (used about drugs or food) (HEALTH) going into a VEIN (=a tube in your body that carries blood): *an intravenous injection* ▶ **intravenously** ***adv.***: *The patient had to be fed intravenously.*

'in tray (*AmE also* **'in box**) ***noun*** [C] (in an office) a container on your desk for letters that are waiting to be read or answered ➲ look at **out tray**

intrepid /ɪn'trepɪd/ ***adj.*** without any fear of danger: *an intrepid climber*

intricacy /'ɪntrɪkəsi/ ***noun*** **1 intricacies** [pl.] **the intricacies of sth** the complicated parts or details of sth: *It's difficult to understand all the intricacies of the situation.* **2** [U] the quality of having complicated parts, details or patterns

intricate /'ɪntrɪkət/ ***adj.*** having many small parts or details put together in a complicated way: *an intricate pattern* ◇ *The story has an intricate plot.* ▶ **intricately** ***adv.***

intrigue[1] /ɪn'triːg/ ***verb*** [T] to make sb very interested and wanting to know more: *I was intrigued by the way he seemed to know all about us already.*

intrigue[2] /'ɪntriːg/ ***noun*** [C,U] secret plans to do sth, especially sth bad: *The film is about political intrigues against the government.* ◇ *His new novel is full of intrigue and suspense.*

intriguing /ɪn'triːgɪŋ/ ***adj.*** very interesting because of being unusual or not having an obvious answer: *These discoveries raise intriguing questions.* ▶ **intriguingly** ***adv.***: *The book is intriguingly titled, 'The Revenge of the Goldfish'.*

intrinsic AW /ɪn'trɪnsɪk; -zɪk/ ***adj.*** (only *before* a noun) belonging to sth as part of its nature; basic: *The object is of no intrinsic value* (=the material it is made of is not worth anything). ▶ **intrinsically** /-kli/ ***adv.***

introduce 🔑 /ˌɪntrə'djuːs/ ***verb*** [T] **1** ~ **sth (in/into sth)** to bring in sth new, use sth, or take sth to a place for the first time: *The new law was introduced in 1999.* ◇ *The company is introducing a new range of cars this summer.* ◇ *Goats were first introduced to the island in the 17th century.* **2** ~ **sb (to sb)** to tell two or more people who have not met before what each others' names are: *'Who's that girl over there?' 'Come with me and I'll introduce you to her.'* **3** ~ **yourself (to sb)** to tell sb you have met for the first time what your name is: *He just walked over and introduced himself to me.* **4** ~ **sb to sth** to make sb begin to learn about sth or do sth for the first time: *This pamphlet will introduce you to the basic aims of our society.* **5** (ARTS AND MEDIA) to be the first or main speaker on a radio or television programme telling the audience who is going to speak, perform, etc.: *May I introduce my first guest on the show tonight...*

introduction 🔑 /ˌɪntrə'dʌkʃn/ ***noun*** **1** [U] ~ **of sth (into sth)** the action of bringing in sth new; using sth or taking sth to a place for the first time: *the introduction of computers into the classroom* **2** [C, usually pl.] the act of telling two or more people each others' names for the first time: *I think I'll get my husband to* ***make/do the introductions*** *– he's better at remembering names!* **3** [C] the first part of a book, a piece of written work or a talk which gives a general idea of what is going to follow **4** [C] **an ~ (to sth)** (EDUCATION) a book for people who are beginning to study a subject: *'An Introduction to English Grammar'* **5** [sing.] **an ~ to sth** first experience of sth: *My first job – in a factory – was not a pleasant introduction to work.*

introductory /ˌɪntrə'dʌktəri/ ***adj.*** **1** happening or said at the beginning in order to give a general idea of what will follow: *an introductory speech/chapter/remark* **2** intended as an introduction to a subject or activity: *introductory courses*

introvert /'ɪntrəvɜːt/ ***noun*** [C] a quiet, shy person who prefers to be alone than with other people OPP **extrovert** ▶ **introverted** ***adj.***

intrude /ɪn'truːd/ ***verb*** [I] ~ **on/upon sb/sth** to enter a place or situation without permission or when you are not wanted: *I'm sorry to intrude on your Sunday lunch but...*

intruder /ɪn'truːdə(r)/ ***noun*** [C] a person who enters a place without permission and often secretly

intrusion /ɪn'truːʒn/ ***noun*** **1** [C,U] **(an) ~ (on/upon/into sth)** something that disturbs you or your life when you want to be private: *This was another example of press intrusion into the affairs of the royals.* **2** [C] (GEOLOGY) a mass of hot liquid rock that has been forced up from below the earth's surface and cooled in between other layers of rock ▶ **intrusive** /ɪn'truːsɪv/ ***adj.***

intuition /ˌɪntju'ɪʃn/ ***noun*** [C,U] the feeling or understanding that makes you believe or know that sth is true without being able to explain why: *She knew, by intuition, about his illness, although he never mentioned it.* ▶ **intuitive** /ɪn'tjuːɪtɪv/ ***adj.*** ▶ **intuitively** ***adv.***: *Intuitively, she knew that he was lying.*

Inuit /'ɪnuɪt/ ***noun*** [C] (*pl.* **Inuit** or **Inuits**) (a member of) the race of people from northern Canada and parts of Alaska, Greenland, and eastern Siberia ▶ **Inuit** ***adj.***

inundate /'ɪnʌndeɪt/ ***verb*** [T] (usually passive) **1** ~ **sb (with sth)** to give or send sb so many things that they cannot deal with them all: *We were inundated with applications for the job.* SYN **swamp** **2** (*formal*) to cover an area of land with water SYN **flood**: *After the heavy rains the fields were inundated.*

invade /ɪn'veɪd/ ***verb*** **1** [I,T] to enter a country with an army in order to attack and take control of it: *When did the Romans invade Britain?* **2** [T] to enter in large numbers, often where sb/sth is not wanted: *The whole area has been invaded by tourists.* ➲ noun **invasion** ▶ **invader** ***noun*** [C]

invalid[1] /ɪn'vælɪd/ ***adj.*** **1** not legally or officially acceptable: *I'm afraid your passport is invalid.* **2** not correct according to reason; not based on all the facts: *an invalid argument* **3** (COMPUTING) (used about an instruction, etc.) of a type that the computer cannot recognize: *an invalid command* OPP **valid**

invalid² /ˈɪnvəlɪd/ ***noun*** [C] (HEALTH) a person who has been very ill for a long time and needs to be looked after

invalidate AW /ɪnˈvælɪdeɪt/ ***verb*** [T] **1** to show that an idea, a story, an argument, etc. is wrong: *This new piece of evidence invalidates his version of events.* **2** if you **invalidate** a document, contract, election, etc., you make it no longer legally or officially valid or acceptable OPP **validate** ▸ **invalidation** /ɪnˌvælɪˈdeɪʃn/ ***noun*** [U]

invalidity AW /ˌɪnvəˈlɪdəti/ ***noun*** [U] **1** (*BrE*) (HEALTH) the state of being unable to take care of yourself because of illness or injury **2** (*formal*) the state of not being legally or officially acceptable ➲ look at **validity**

invaluable /ɪnˈvæljuəbl/ ***adj.*** ~ **(to/for sb/sth)** extremely useful: *invaluable help/information/support*

invariable AW /ɪnˈveəriəbl/ ***adj.*** not changing

invariably AW /ɪnˈveəriəbli/ ***adv.*** almost always: *She invariably arrives late.*

invasion /ɪnˈveɪʒn/ ***noun*** **1** [C,U] the action of entering another country with an army in order to take control of it: *the threat of invasion* **2** [C] the action of entering a place where you are not wanted and disturbing sb: *Such questions are an* ***invasion of privacy***. ➲ verb **invade**

invent ⊶ /ɪnˈvent/ ***verb*** [T] **1** to think of or make sth for the first time: *When was the camera invented?* **2** to say or describe sth that is not true: *I realized that he had invented the whole story.* ▸ **inventor** ***noun*** [C]

invention ⊶ /ɪnˈvenʃn/ ***noun*** **1** [C] a thing that has been made or designed by sb for the first time: *The microwave oven is a very useful invention.* **2** [U] the action or process of making or designing sth for the first time: *Books had to be written by hand before the invention of printing.* **3** [C,U] telling a story or giving an excuse that is not true: *It was obvious that his story about being robbed was (an) invention.*

inventive /ɪnˈventɪv/ ***adj.*** having clever and original ideas ▸ **inventiveness** ***noun*** [U]

inventory /ˈɪnvəntri/ ***noun*** [C] (*pl.* **inventories**) a detailed list, for example of all the furniture in a house: *The landlord is coming to* ***make an inventory*** *of the contents of the flat.*

inverse¹ /ˌɪnˈvɜːs/ ***adj.*** (only *before* a noun) opposite in amount or position to sth else: *A person's wealth is often* ***in inverse proportion to*** *their happiness* (= the more money a person has, the less happy he/she is). ▸ **inversely** ***adv.***

inverse² /ˈɪnvɜːs/ **the inverse** ***noun*** [sing.] the exact opposite of sth

inversion /ɪnˈvɜːʃn/ ***noun*** [U, C] (TECHNICAL) the act of changing the position or order of sth to its opposite, or of turning sth upside down: *the inversion of normal word order* ◇ *an inversion of the truth*

invert /ɪnˈvɜːt/ ***verb*** [T] (*formal*) to put sth in the opposite order or position to the way it usually is

invertebrate /ɪnˈvɜːtɪbrət/ ***noun*** [C] (BIOLOGY) an animal without a solid line of bones (**backbone**) going along its body: *slugs, worms and other small invertebrates* OPP **vertebrate**

inˌverted ˈcommas (*BrE*) = QUOTATION MARKS: *to* ***put sth in inverted commas***

invest ⊶ AW /ɪnˈvest/ ***verb*** [I,T] ~ **(sth) (in sth)** **1** (FINANCE) to put money into a bank, business, property, etc. in the hope that you will make a profit: *Many firms have invested heavily in this project.* ◇ *I've invested all my money in the company.* **2** to spend money, time or energy on sth that you think is good or useful: *I'm thinking of investing in a computer.* ◇ *You have to invest a lot of time if you really want to learn a language well.* ▸ **investor** AW ***noun*** [C]: *small investors* (= private people)

investigate ⊶ AW /ɪnˈvestɪɡeɪt/ ***verb*** [I,T] to try to find out all the facts about sth: *A murder was reported and the police were sent to investigate.* ◇ *A group of experts are investigating the cause of the crash.* ▸ **investigator** AW ***noun*** [C]

investigation ⊶ AW /ɪnˌvestɪˈɡeɪʃn/ ***noun*** [C,U] **(an)** ~ **(into sth)** an official examination of the facts about a situation, crime, etc.: *The airlines are going to* ***carry out an investigation*** *into security procedures at airports.* ◇ *The matter is still* ***under investigation***.

investigative AW /ɪnˈvestɪɡətɪv/ ***adj.*** trying to find out all the facts about sb/sth: *investigative journalism*

investment ⊶ AW /ɪnˈvestmənt/ ***noun*** **1** [U, C] **(an)** ~ **(in sth)** (ECONOMICS) the act of putting money in a bank, business, property, etc.; the amount of money that you put in: *investment in local industry* ◇ *The company will have to* ***make an*** *enormous* ***investment*** *to computerize production.* **2** [C] (*informal*) a thing that you have bought: *This coat has been a good investment – I've worn it for three years.*

invigilate /ɪnˈvɪdʒɪleɪt/ ***verb*** [I,T] (*BrE*) (EDUCATION) to watch the people taking an exam to make sure that nobody is cheating ▸ **invigilator** ***noun*** [C]

invigorate /ɪnˈvɪɡəreɪt/ ***verb*** [I,T] to make sb feel healthy, fresh and full of energy: *I felt invigorated after my run.* ▸ **invigorating** ***adj.***

invincible /ɪnˈvɪnsəbl/ ***adj.*** too strong or powerful to be defeated

invisible AW /ɪnˈvɪzəbl/ ***adj.*** ~ **(to sb/sth)** that cannot be seen: *bacteria that are invisible to the naked eye* OPP **visible** ▸ **invisibility** /ɪnˌvɪzəˈbɪləti/ ***noun*** [U] ▸ **invisibly** /-bli/ ***adv.***

invitation ⊶ /ˌɪnvɪˈteɪʃn/ ***noun*** **1** [U] the act of inviting sb or being invited: *Entry is by invitation only.* ◇ *a letter of invitation* **2** [C] **an** ~ **to sb/sth (to sth/to do sth)** a written or spoken request to go somewhere or do sth: *Did you get an invitation to the conference?* ◇ *a wedding invitation*

invite ⊶ /ɪnˈvaɪt/ ***verb*** [T] **1** ~ **sb (to/for sth)** to ask sb to come somewhere or to do sth: *We invited all the family to the wedding.* ◇ *Successful applicants will be invited for interview next week.* **2** to make sth unpleasant likely to happen: *You're inviting trouble if you carry so much money around.*

PHR V **invite sb back** **1** to ask sb to return with you to your home **2** to ask sb to come to your home a second time, or after you have been a guest at their home

invite sb in to ask sb to come into your home

invite sb out to ask sb to go out somewhere with you: *We've been invited out to lunch by the neighbours.*

invite sb over/round (*informal*) to ask sb to come to your home ❶ **Ask** can be used instead of **invite** in all senses.

inviting /ɪnˈvaɪtɪŋ/ ***adj.*** attractive and pleasant: *The smell of cooking was very inviting.*

in vitro /ˌɪn ˈviːtrəʊ/ *adj., adv.* (BIOLOGY) (used about a process or a reaction) taking place in a glass tube or dish, not inside a living body: *in vitro experiments* ◇ *the development of* ***in vitro*** *fertilization* ◇ *an egg fertilized in vitro*

invoice[1] /ˈɪnvɔɪs/ *noun* [C] (FINANCE) an official paper that lists goods or services that you have received and says how much you have to pay for them ➲ note at **bill[1]**

invoice[2] /ˈɪnvɔɪs/ *verb* [T] ~ **sb (for sth)**; ~ **sth (to sb/sth)** (FINANCE) to write or send sb a bill for work you have done or goods you have provided: *You will be invoiced for these items at the end of the month.* ◇ *Invoice the goods to my account.*

invoke AW /ɪnˈvəʊk/ *verb* [T] (*formal*) **1** ~ **sth (against sb)** to mention or use a law, rule, etc. as a reason for doing sth: *It is unlikely that libel laws will be invoked.* **2** to mention a person, a theory, an example, etc. to support your opinions or ideas, or as a reason for sth: *She invoked several eminent scholars to back up her argument.*

involuntary /ɪnˈvɒləntri/ *adj.* done without wanting or meaning to: *She gave an involuntary gasp of pain as the doctor inserted the needle.* OPP **voluntary, deliberate** ▸ **involuntarily** /ɪnˈvɒləntrəli/ *adv.*

involve 🔑 AW /ɪnˈvɒlv/ *verb* [T] **1** (not used in the continuous tenses) to make sth necessary: *The job involves a lot of travelling.* **2** (not used in the continuous tenses) if a situation, an event or an activity **involves** sb/sth, they take part in it: *The story involves a woman who went on holiday with her child.* ◇ *More than 100 people were involved in the project.* **3** ~ **sb/sth in (doing) sth** to cause sb/sth to take part in or be concerned with sth: *Please don't involve me in your family arguments.*

involved 🔑 /ɪnˈvɒlvd/ *adj.* **1** difficult to understand; complicated: *The book has a very involved plot.* **2** (not *before* a noun) ~ **(in sth)** closely connected with sth; taking an active part in sth: *I'm very involved in local politics.* **3** (not *before* a noun) ~ **(with sb)** having a sexual relationship with sb: *She is involved with an older man.*

involvement 🔑 AW /ɪnˈvɒlvmənt/ *noun* [C,U] **1** ~ **(in/with sth)** the act of taking part in sth: *US involvement in European wars* ◇ *The men deny any involvement in the robbery.* **2** [C,U] ~ **(in/with sth)** the act of giving a lot of time and attention to sth you care about: *her growing involvement with contemporary music* **3** [C,U] ~ **(with sb)** a romantic or sexual relationship with sb that you are not married to: *He spoke openly about his involvement with the actress.*

invulnerable /ɪnˈvʌlnərəbl/ *adj.* ~ **(to sth)** that cannot be harmed or defeated; safe: *The submarine is invulnerable to attack while at sea.* ▸ **invulnerability** /ɪnˌvʌlnərəˈbɪləti/ *noun* [U]

inward /ˈɪnwəd/ *adv., adj.* **1** (also **inwards**) towards the inside or centre: *Stand in a circle facing inwards.* **2** inside your mind, not shown to other people: *my inward feelings* OPP **outward**

inwardly /ˈɪnwədli/ *adv.* in your mind; secretly: *He was inwardly relieved that they could not come.*

iodide /ˈaɪədaɪd/ *noun* [C] (CHEMISTRY) a chemical COMPOUND consisting of IODINE and another chemical element

iodine /ˈaɪədiːn/ *noun* [U] (*symbol* **I**) (CHEMISTRY) a dark-coloured substance that is found in sea water. A purple liquid containing **iodine** is sometimes used to clean cuts in your skin. ❶ For more information on the periodic table of elements, look at pages R34-5.

ion /ˈaɪən/ *noun* [C] (CHEMISTRY) an atom or a MOLECULE (=a group of atoms) that has gained or lost one or more of its parts (**electrons**) and so has a positive or negative electric charge

ionic /aɪˈɒnɪk/ *adj.* **1** (CHEMISTRY) of or related to ions **2** (CHEMISTRY) (used about the way chemicals join together) using the electrical pull between positive and negative IONS: *ionic bonds/compounds* **3 Ionic** (ARCHITECTURE) used to describe a style of ARCHITECTURE in ancient Greece that uses a curved decoration in the shape of a SCROLL (=a shape like a roll of paper) ➲ look at **Doric**, **Corinthian** ➲ picture at **capital**

ionize (also **-ise**) /ˈaɪənaɪz/ *verb* [I,T] (CHEMISTRY) (used about atoms and molecules) to gain a positive or negative electric charge by losing or gaining one part (**an electron**)

ionosphere /aɪˈɒnəsfɪə(r)/ *noun* [sing.] **the ionosphere** (GEOGRAPHY) the layer of the earth's atmosphere between about 80 and 1 000 kilometres above the surface of the earth, that sends radio waves back around the earth ➲ look at **atmosphere**

IOU /ˌaɪ əʊ ˈjuː/ *abbr.* I owe you; a piece of paper that you sign showing that you owe sb some money

IPA /ˌaɪ piː ˈeɪ/ *abbr.* the International Phonetic Alphabet

IP address /ˌaɪ ˈpiː ədres/ *noun* [C] (COMPUTING) a series of numbers separated by dots that identifies a particular computer connected to the Internet

IPO /ˌaɪ piː ˈəʊ/ *abbr.* (BUSINESS) **initial public offering**; the act of selling shares in a company for the first time

IQ /ˌaɪ ˈkjuː/ *abbr.* (EDUCATION) intelligence quotient; a measure of how intelligent sb is: *have a high/low IQ* ◇ *an IQ of 120*

IRA /ˌaɪ ɑːr ˈeɪ/ *abbr.* (POLITICS) **the Irish Republican Army**; the **IRA** is an illegal organization which has fought for Northern Ireland to be united with the Republic of Ireland.

irate /aɪˈreɪt/ *adj.* (*formal*) very angry

iridescent /ˌɪrɪˈdesnt/ *adj.* (*formal*) showing many bright colours that seem to change in different lights ▸ **iridescence** *noun* [U]

iridium /ɪˈrɪdiəm/ *noun* [U] (*symbol* **Ir**) (CHEMISTRY) a very hard yellow-white metal, used especially to mix with other metals to form another metal (**an alloy**) ❶ For more information on the periodic table of elements, look at pages R34-5.

iris /ˈaɪrɪs/ *noun* [C] the coloured part of your eye ➲ picture at **eye**

Irish /ˈaɪrɪʃ/ *adj.* from Ireland

iron[1] 🔑 /ˈaɪən/ *noun* **1** [U] (*symbol* **Fe**) (CHEMISTRY) a hard strong metal that is used for making steel and is found in small quantities in food and in blood: *an iron bar* ◇ *iron ore* ◇ *The doctor gave me iron tablets.* ◇ (*figurative*) *The general has an iron* (=very strong) *will.* ➲ look at **pig iron** ❶ For more information on the periodic table of elements, look at pages R34-5.
2 [C] an electrical instrument with a flat bottom that is heated and used to smooth clothes after you have washed and dried them: *a steam iron*

iron[2] 🔑 /ˈaɪən/ *verb* [I,T] to use an iron to make clothes, etc. smooth: *Could you iron this dress for me?*

PHR V **iron sth out** to get rid of any problems or difficulties that are affecting sth

the 'Iron Age *noun* [sing.] (HISTORY) the period in human history after the Bronze Age, about 3000 years ago when people first used iron tools and weapons

the ˌIron 'Curtain *noun* [U] (HISTORY, POLITICS) the name that people used for the border that used to exist between Western Europe and the COMMUNIST countries of Eastern Europe

ironic /aɪ'rɒnɪk/ (*also* **ironical** /aɪ'rɒnɪkl/) *adj.* **1** meaning the opposite of what you say: *Jeff sometimes offends people with his ironic sense of humour.* ➲ look at **sarcastic** **2** (used about a situation) strange or amusing because it is unusual or unexpected: *It is ironic that the busiest people are often the most willing to help.* ▸ **ironically** /-kli/ *adv.*

ironing /'aɪənɪŋ/ *noun* [U] clothes, etc. that need ironing or that have just been ironed: *a large pile of ironing*

'ironing board *noun* [C] a special table that is used for putting clothes on when we are making them smooth with an iron

irony /'aɪrəni/ *noun* (*pl.* **ironies**) **1** [C,U] an unusual or unexpected part of a situation, etc. that seems strange or amusing: *The irony was that he was killed in a car accident soon after the end of the war.* **2** [U] a way of speaking that shows you are joking or that you mean the opposite of what you say: *'The English are such good cooks', he said with heavy irony.*

irradiate /ɪ'reɪdieɪt/ *verb* [T] to treat food with RADIOACTIVE RAYS in order to be able to keep it for a long time: *Irradiated food lasts longer, but some people think it is not safe.*

irrational AW /ɪ'ræʃənl/ *adj.* not based on reason or clear thought: *an irrational fear of spiders* ▸ **irrationality** /ɪˌræʃə'næləti/ *noun* [U] ▸ **irrationally** /-nəli/ *adv.*

irreconcilable /ɪˌrekən'saɪləbl/ *adj.* (*formal*) (used about people or their ideas and beliefs) so different that they cannot be made to agree ▸ **irreconcilably** /-əbli/ *adv.*

irregular /ɪ'regjələ(r)/ *adj.* **1** not having a shape or pattern that we recognize or can predict: *an irregular shape* OPP **regular** **2** happening at times that you cannot predict: *His visits became more and more irregular.* OPP **regular** **3** not allowed according to the rules or social customs: *It is highly irregular for a doctor to give information about patients without their permission.* **4** (LANGUAGE) not following the usual rules of grammar: *irregular verbs* ◇ *'Caught' is an irregular past tense form.* OPP **regular** ▸ **irregularity** /ɪˌregjə'lærəti/ *noun* [C,U] (*pl.* **irregularities**) ▸ **irregularly** *adv.*

irrelevancy /ɪ'reləvənsi/ *noun* [C] (*pl.* **irrelevancies**) something that is not important because it is not connected with sth else

irrelevant AW /ɪ'reləvənt/ *adj.* not connected with sth or important to it: *That's completely irrelevant to the subject under discussion.* OPP **relevant** ▸ **irrelevance** AW *noun* [U, C] ▸ **irrelevantly** *adv.*

irreparable /ɪ'repərəbl/ *adj.* that cannot be repaired: *Irreparable damage has been done to the forests of Eastern Europe.* ▸ **irreparably** /-əbli/ *adv.*

irreplaceable /ˌɪrɪ'pleɪsəbl/ *adj.* (used about sth very valuable or special) that cannot be replaced OPP **replaceable**

irrepressible /ˌɪrɪ'presəbl/ *adj.* full of life and energy: *young people full of irrepressible good humour* ▸ **irrepressibly** /-əbli/ *adv.*

irresistible /ˌɪrɪ'zɪstəbl/ *adj.* **1** so strong that it cannot be stopped or prevented: *an irresistible urge to laugh* **2** ~ **(to sb)** very attractive: *He seems to think he's irresistible to women.* ➲ verb **resist** ▸ **irresistibly** /-əbli/ *adv.*

irrespective of /ɪrɪ'spektɪv əv/ *prep.* not affected by: *Anybody can take part in the competition, irrespective of age.*

irresponsible /ˌɪrɪ'spɒnsəbl/ *adj.* not thinking about the effect your actions will have; not sensible: *It is irresponsible to let small children go out alone.* OPP **responsible** ▸ **irresponsibility** /ˌɪrɪˌspɒnsə'bɪləti/ *noun* [U] ▸ **irresponsibly** /-əbli/ *adv.*

irreverent /ɪ'revərənt/ *adj.* not feeling or showing respect: *This comedy takes an irreverent look at the world of politics.* ▸ **irreverence** *noun* [U] ▸ **irreverently** *adv.*

irreversible AW /ˌɪrɪ'vɜːsəbl/ *adj.* that cannot be stopped or changed: *The disease can do irreversible damage to the body.* ▸ **irreversibly** /-əbli/ *adv.*

irrigate /'ɪrɪgeɪt/ *verb* [T] (AGRICULTURE) to supply water to land and crops using pipes, small CANALS, etc. ▸ **irrigation** /ˌɪrɪ'geɪʃn/ *noun* [U]

irritable /'ɪrɪtəbl/ *adj.* becoming angry easily: *to be/feel/get irritable* ▸ **irritability** /ˌɪrɪtə'bɪləti/ *noun* [U] ▸ **irritably** /-əbli/ *adv.*

irritant /'ɪrɪtənt/ *noun* [C] (HEALTH) a substance that makes part of your body painful or sore ▸ **irritant** *adj.*

irritate 🔑 /'ɪrɪteɪt/ *verb* [T] **1** to make sb angry; to annoy: *It really irritates me the way he keeps repeating himself.* **2** (HEALTH) to cause a part of the body to be painful or sore: *I don't use soap because it irritates my skin.* ▸ **irritation** /ˌɪrɪ'teɪʃn/ *noun* [C,U]

is → BE

ISDN /ˌaɪ es diː 'en/ *abbr.* (COMPUTING) **integrated services digital network**; a system for carrying sound signals, images, etc. along wires at high speed: *an ISDN Internet connection*

-ish *suffix* (in adjectives) **1** from the country mentioned: *Turkish* ◇ *Irish* **2** having the nature of; like: *childish* **3** fairly; approximately: *reddish* ◇ *thirtyish* ▸ **-ishly** *suffix* (in adverbs): *foolishly*

Islam /ɪz'lɑːm/ *noun* [U] (RELIGION) the religion of Muslim people. Islam teaches that there is only one God and that Muhammad is His Prophet. ▸ **Islamic** *adj.*: *Islamic law*

island 🔑 /'aɪlənd/ *noun* [C] **1** (GEOGRAPHY) a piece of land that is surrounded by water: *the Greek islands* **2** = TRAFFIC ISLAND

islander /'aɪləndə(r)/ *noun* [C] a person who lives on a small island

isle /aɪl/ *noun* [C] (GEOGRAPHY) an island: *the Isle of Wight* ◇ *the British Isles*

isn't short for IS NOT

ISO /ˌaɪ es 'əʊ/ *abbr.* **International Organization for Standardization**; an organization established in 1946 to make the measurements used in science, industry and business standard throughout the world

iso- /'aɪsəʊ/ *prefix* (in nouns, adjectives and adverbs) equal: *isotope* ◇ *isometric*

isobar /'aɪsəbɑː(r)/ *noun* [C] (GEOGRAPHY) a line on a weather map that joins places that have the same air pressure at a particular time

isolate AW /'aɪsəleɪt/ ***verb*** [T] ~ **sb/sth (from sb/sth)** to put or keep sb/sth separate from other people or things: *Some farms were isolated by the heavy snowfalls.* ◇ *We need to isolate all the animals with the disease so that the others don't catch it.*

isolated AW /'aɪsəleɪtɪd/ ***adj.*** **1** ~ **(from sb/sth)** alone or apart from other people or things: *an isolated village deep in the countryside* ◇ *I was kept isolated from the other patients.* **2** not connected with others; happening once: *Is this an isolated case or part of a general pattern?*

isolation AW /ˌaɪsə'leɪʃn/ ***noun*** [U] ~ **(from sb/sth)** the state of being separate and alone; the act of separating sb/sth: *He lived **in complete isolation** from the outside world.* ◇ ***In isolation** each problem does not seem bad, but together they are quite daunting.* ➲ look at **loneliness**, **solitude**

isolationism AW /ˌaɪsə'leɪʃənɪzəm/ ***noun*** [U] (POLITICS) the policy of not becoming involved in the affairs of other countries or groups ▸ **isolationist** /-ʃənɪst/ ***adj.***, ***noun*** [C]: *an isolationist foreign policy*

isosceles triangle /aɪˌsɒsəliːz 'traɪæŋgl/ ***noun*** [C] (GEOMETRY) a triangle with two of its three sides the same length ➲ picture at **triangle**

isotherm /'aɪsəθɜːm/ ***noun*** [C] (GEOGRAPHY) a line on a weather map that joins places that have the same temperature at a particular time

isotope /'aɪsətəʊp/ ***noun*** [C] (CHEMISTRY) one of two or more forms of a chemical element that have different physical characteristics but the same chemical characteristics

RELATED VOCABULARY

Isotopes of the same element have the same number of **protons** in the **nucleus**, but a different number of **neutrons**.

ISP /ˌaɪ es 'piː/ ***abbr.*** (COMPUTING) Internet service provider; a company that provides you with an Internet connection and services such as email, etc.

issue[1] AW /'ɪʃuː; 'ɪsjuː/ ***noun*** **1** [C] a problem or subject for discussion: *I want to **raise the issue** of overtime pay at the meeting.* ◇ *The government cannot avoid the issue of homelessness any longer.* **2** [C] (ARTS AND MEDIA) one in a series of things that are published or produced: *Do you have last week's issue of this magazine?* **3** [U] the act of publishing or giving sth to people: *the issue of blankets to the refugees*

IDM **make an issue (out) of sth** to give too much importance to a small problem

issue[2] AW /'ɪʃuː; 'ɪsjuː/ ***verb*** **1** [T] to print and supply sth: *to issue a magazine/newsletter* **2** [T] to give or say sth to sb officially: *The new employees were issued with uniforms.* ◇ *to issue a visa* ◇ *The police will issue a statement later today.* **3** [I] (*formal*) to come or go out: *An angry voice issued from the loudspeaker.*

isthmus /'ɪsməs/ ***noun*** [C] (GEOGRAPHY) a narrow piece of land, with water on each side, that joins two larger pieces of land

IT /ˌaɪ 'tiː/ ***abbr.*** (COMPUTING) Information Technology

it /ɪt/ ***pronoun*** **1** (used as the subject or object of a verb, or after a preposition) the animal or thing mentioned earlier: *Look at that car. It's going much too fast.* ◇ *The children went up to the dog and patted it.* **2** used for identifying a person: *It's your Mum on the phone.* ◇ *'Who's that?' 'It's the postman.'* ◇ *It's me!* ◇ *It's him!* **3** used in the position of the subject or object of a verb when the real subject or object is at the end of the sentence: *It's hard for them to talk about their problems.* ◇ *I think it doesn't really matter what time we arrive.* **4** used in the position of the subject of a verb when you are talking about time, the date, distance, the weather, etc.: *It's nearly half past eight.* ◇ *It's Tuesday today.* ◇ *It's about 100 kilometres from London.* ◇ *It was very cold at the weekend.* ◇ *It's raining.* **5** used when you are talking about a situation: *It gets very crowded here in the summer.* ◇ *I'll come at 7 o'clock if it's convenient.* ◇ *It's a pity they can't come to the party.* **6** used for emphasizing a part of a sentence: *It was Jerry who said it, not me.* ◇ *It's your health I'm worried about, not the cost.*

IDM **that/this is it** **1** that/this is the answer: *That's it! You've solved the puzzle!* **2** that/this is the end: *That's it, I've had enough! I'm going home!*

italics /ɪ'tælɪks/ ***noun*** [pl.] (also **italic** [sing.]) printed letters that lean to the right: *All the example sentences in the dictionary are printed **in italics**.* ➲ look at **roman** ▸ **italic** ***adj.***: *Use an italic font.*

itch /ɪtʃ/ ***noun*** [C] the feeling on your skin that makes you want to rub or scratch it ▸ **itch** ***verb*** [I]: *My nose is itching.*

itchy /'ɪtʃi/ ***adj.*** having or producing an ITCH: *This shirt is itchy.* ◇ *I feel itchy all over.* ▸ **itchiness** ***noun*** [U]

it'd /'ɪtəd/ short for IT HAD, IT WOULD

item AW /'aɪtəm/ ***noun*** [C] **1** one single thing on a list or in a collection: *Some items arrived too late to be included in the catalogue.* ◇ *What is the first item on the agenda?* **2** one single article or object: *Can I pay for each item separately?* ◇ *an item of clothing* **3** (ARTS AND MEDIA) a single piece of news: *There was an interesting item about Spain in yesterday's news.*

itemize (also -ise) /'aɪtəmaɪz/ ***verb*** [T] to make a list of all the separate items in sth: *an itemized telephone bill*

itinerant /aɪ'tɪnərənt/ ***adj.*** (only *before* a noun) travelling from place to place: *an itinerant circus family*

itinerary /aɪ'tɪnərəri/ ***noun*** [C] (*pl.* **itineraries**) a plan of a journey, including the route and the places that you will visit

it'll /'ɪtl/ short for IT WILL

its /ɪts/ ***det.*** of or belonging to a thing: *The club held its Annual General Meeting last night.*

it's /ɪts/ short for IT IS; IT HAS

itself /ɪt'self/ ***pronoun*** **1** used when the animal or thing that does an action is also affected by it: *The cat was washing itself.* ◇ *The company has got itself into financial difficulties.* **2** used to emphasize sth: *The building itself is beautiful, but it's in a very ugly part of town.*

IDM **(all) by itself** **1** without being controlled by a person; automatically: *The central heating comes on by itself before we get up.* **2** alone: *The house stood all by itself on the hillside.*

ITV /ˌaɪ tiː 'viː/ ***abbr.*** (*BrE*) (ARTS AND MEDIA) Independent Television; a group of television companies that are paid for by advertising

IUD /ˌaɪ juː 'diː/ ***noun*** [C] (HEALTH) intrauterine device; a small metal or plastic object that is placed inside the UTERUS (=the part of a woman's body where a baby grows) to stop her becoming pregnant

IV[1] /ˌaɪ 'viː/ ***abbr.*** intravenous

IV[2] /ˌaɪ 'viː/ (*AmE*) = DRIP[2] (3)

I've /aɪv/ short for I HAVE

ivory /ˈaɪvəri/ ***noun*** [U] the hard white substance that the TUSKS (=long teeth) of an ELEPHANT are made of

ivy /ˈaɪvi/ ***noun*** [U] a climbing plant that has dark leaves with three or five points ➲ picture at **plant**

J j

J, j /dʒeɪ/ ***noun*** [C,U] (*pl.* **J's; j's** /dʒeɪz/) the tenth letter of the English alphabet: *'Jam' begins with (a) 'J'.*

jab[1] /dʒæb/ ***verb*** [I,T] **~ sb/sth (with sth); ~ sth into sb/sth** to push at sb/sth with a sudden, rough movement, usually with sth sharp: *She jabbed me in the ribs with her elbow. ◇ The robber jabbed a gun into my back and ordered me to move.*

jab[2] /dʒæb/ ***noun*** [C] **1** a sudden rough push with sth sharp: *He **gave me a jab** in the ribs with the stick.* **2** (*informal*) the action of putting a drug, etc. under sb's skin with a needle: *I'm going to the doctor's to **have a flu jab** today.* **SYN** **injection**

jack[1] /dʒæk/ ***noun*** [C] **1** a piece of equipment for lifting a car, etc. off the ground, for example in order to change its wheel ➲ picture at **hydraulic 2** the card between the ten and the queen in a pack of cards
IDM **a jack of all trades** a person who can do many different types of work, but who perhaps does not do them very well

jack[2] /dʒæk/ ***verb***
PHR V **jack sth in** (*slang*) to stop doing sth: *Jerry got fed up with his job and jacked it in.*
jack sth up to lift a car, etc. using a **jack**: *We jacked the car up to change the wheel.*

jackal /ˈdʒækl/ ***noun*** [C] a wild animal like a dog that lives in Africa and Asia. **Jackals** eat the meat of animals that are already dead.

jacket 🔑 /ˈdʒækɪt/ ***noun*** [C] **1** a short coat with sleeves: *Do you have to wear a jacket and tie to work?* ➲ look at **life jacket 2** a cover for a HOT-WATER, TANK (=container), etc. that stops heat from being lost

ˌjacket poˈtato ***noun*** [C] a potato that is cooked in the oven in its skin

jackhammer /ˈdʒækhæmə(r)/ (*AmE*) =PNEUMATIC DRILL

jackknife /ˈdʒæknaɪf/ ***verb*** [I] (used about a lorry that is in two parts) to go out of control and bend suddenly in a dangerous way

jackpot /ˈdʒækpɒt/ ***noun*** [C] the largest money prize that you can win in a game
IDM **hit the jackpot** → HIT[1]

Jacuzzi™ /dʒəˈkuːzi/ ***noun*** [C] a special bath in which powerful movements of air make bubbles in the water

jade /dʒeɪd/ ***noun*** [U] **1** a hard stone that is usually green and is used in making jewellery **2** a bright green colour ▶ **jade** ***adj.***

jaded /ˈdʒeɪdɪd/ ***adj.*** tired and bored after doing the same thing for a long time without a break

jagged /ˈdʒægɪd/ ***adj.*** rough with sharp points: *jagged rocks*

jaguar /ˈdʒægjuə(r)/ ***noun*** [C] a large wild cat with black spots that comes from Central and South America

jail[1] /dʒeɪl/ ***noun*** [C,U] (**LAW**) (a) prison: *She was **sent to jail** for ten years.*

jail[2] /dʒeɪl/ ***verb*** [T] (**LAW**) to put sb in prison: *She was jailed for ten years.*

jailer /ˈdʒeɪlə(r)/ ***noun*** [C] (*old-fashioned*) (**LAW**) a person whose job is to guard prisoners

jam[1] 🔑 /dʒæm/ ***noun*** **1** [U] (*especially AmE* **jelly**) a sweet substance that you spread on bread, made by boiling fruit and sugar together: *a jar of raspberry jam* **2** [C] a situation in which you cannot move because there are too many people or vehicles: *a traffic jam* **3** [C] (*informal*) a difficult situation: *We're in a bit of a jam without our passports or travel documents.* **4** [C] (*informal*) (**MUSIC**) the act of playing music together with other musicians in a way which has not been planned or prepared first: *a jam session*

jam[2] /dʒæm/ ***verb*** (**jamming; jammed**) **1** [T] **~ sb/sth in, under, between, etc. sth** to push or force sb/sth into a place where there is not much room: *She managed to jam everything into her suitcase.* **2** [I,T] **~ (sth) (up)** to become or to make sth unable to move or work: *Something is jamming (up) the machine. ◇ The paper keeps jamming in the photocopier. ◇ I can't open the door. The lock has jammed.* **3** [T] **~ sth (up) (with sb/sth)** (usually passive) to fill sth with too many people or things: *The cupboard was **jammed full** of old newspapers and magazines. ◇ The suitcase was **jam-packed with*** (=completely full of) *designer clothes. ◇ The switchboard was jammed with calls from unhappy customers.* **4** [T] to send out signals in order to stop radio programmes, etc. from being received or heard clearly **5** [I] (*informal*) (**MUSIC**) to play music with other musicians in an informal way without preparing or practising first: *They continued to jam together and write music and eventually they made their first record.*
PHR V **jam on the brakes/jam the brakes on** to stop a car suddenly by pushing hard on the controls (**brakes**) with your feet

Jan. ***abbr.*** January: *1 Jan. 1993*

jangle /ˈdʒæŋgl/ ***verb*** [I,T] to make a noise like metal hitting against metal; to move sth so that it makes this noise: *The baby smiles if you jangle your keys.* ▶ **jangle** ***noun*** [U]

janitor /ˈdʒænɪtə(r)/ (*AmE*) =CARETAKER

January /ˈdʒænjuəri/ ***noun*** [U, C] (*abbr.* **Jan.**) the first month of the year, coming after December: *We're going skiing **in January**. ◇ last/next January ◇ We first met **on January 31st**, 1989. ◇ Christine's birthday is (on) January 17. ◇ Our wedding anniversary is at the end of January. ◇ January mornings can be very dark in Britain.*

jar[1] /dʒɑː(r)/ ***noun*** [C] **1** a container with a lid, usually made of glass and used for keeping food, etc. in: *a jam jar ◇ a large storage jar for flour* **2** the food that a **jar** contains: *a jar of honey/jam/coffee*

jar[2] /dʒɑː(r)/ ***verb*** (**jarring; jarred**) **1** [T] to hurt or damage sth as a result of a sharp knock: *He fell and jarred his back.* **2** [I] **~ (on sb/sth)** to have an unpleasant or annoying effect: *The dripping tap jarred on my nerves.*

jargon /ˈdʒɑːgən/ ***noun*** [U] (**LANGUAGE**) special or technical words that are used by a particular group of people in a particular profession and that other people do not understand: *medical/scientific/legal/computer jargon*

jaundice /ˈdʒɔːndɪs/ ***noun*** [U] (**HEALTH**) a medical condition in which the skin and white parts of the eyes become yellow ▶ **jaundiced** ***adj.***

Java™ /ˈdʒɑːvə/ ***noun*** [U] (COMPUTING) a computer language that can be used to create programs that will run on any computer

javelin /ˈdʒævlɪn/ ***noun*** (SPORT) **1** [C] a long stick with a pointed end that is thrown in sports competitions **2 the javelin** [sing.] the event or sport of throwing the **javelin** as far as possible

jaw /dʒɔː/ ***noun*** **1** [C] (ANATOMY) either of the two bones in your face that contain your teeth: *the lower/upper jaw* ➲ picture on **page 80** **2 jaws** [pl.] the mouth (especially of a wild animal): *The lion came towards him with its jaws open.* **3 jaws** [pl.] the parts of a tool or machine that are used to hold things tightly: *the jaws of a vice* ➲ picture at **vice**

jawbone /ˈdʒɔːbəʊn/ ***noun*** [C] (ANATOMY) the bone that forms the lower JAW **SYN** **mandible** ➲ picture on **page 80**

jazz[1] /dʒæz/ ***noun*** [U] (MUSIC) a style of music with a strong rhythm, originally of African American origin: *modern/traditional jazz* ➲ look at **classical**, **pop**, **rock**

jazz[2] /dʒæz/ ***verb***
PHRV **jazz sth up** (*informal*) to make sth brighter, more interesting or exciting

JCB™ /ˌdʒeɪ siː ˈbiː/ ***noun*** [C] (*BrE*) a powerful motor vehicle with a long arm for digging and moving earth

jealous 🔑 /ˈdʒeləs/ ***adj.*** **1** feeling upset or angry because you think that sb you like or love is showing interest in sb else: *Tim seems to get jealous whenever Sue speaks to another boy!* **2** ~ **(of sb/sth)** feeling angry or sad because you want to be like sb else or because you want what sb else has: *He's always been jealous of his older brother.* ◇ *I'm very jealous of your new car – how much did it cost?* **SYN** **envious** ▶ **jealously** ***adv.*** ▶ **jealousy** ***noun*** [C,U] (*pl.* **jealousies**)

jeans 🔑 /dʒiːnz/ ***noun*** [pl.] trousers made of DENIM (= strong cotton cloth that is usually blue): *These jeans are a bit too tight.* ◇ *a pair of jeans*

Jeep™ /dʒiːp/ ***noun*** [C] a small strong vehicle suitable for travelling over rough ground ➲ picture at **truck**

jeer /dʒɪə(r)/ ***verb*** [I,T] ~ **(at) sb/sth** to laugh or shout rude comments at sb/sth to show your lack of respect for them or it: *The spectators booed and jeered at the losing team.* ▶ **jeer** ***noun*** [C, usually pl.]: *The Prime Minister was greeted with jeers in the House of Commons today.*

jelly 🔑 /ˈdʒeli/ ***noun*** (*pl.* **jellies**) **1** (*AmE* **Jell-O™**) [C,U] a soft, solid brightly-coloured food that shakes when it is moved. Jelly is made from sugar and fruit juice and is eaten cold at the end of a meal, especially by children. **2** [U] (*especially AmE*) a type of jam that does not contain any solid pieces of fruit
IDM **be/feel like jelly** (used especially about the legs or knees) to feel weak because you are nervous, afraid, etc.
turn to jelly (used about the legs and knees) to suddenly become weak because of fear

jellyfish /ˈdʒelifɪʃ/ ***noun*** [C] (*pl.* **jellyfish**) a sea animal with a soft colourless body and long thin parts called TENTACLES that can sting you.

jellyfish

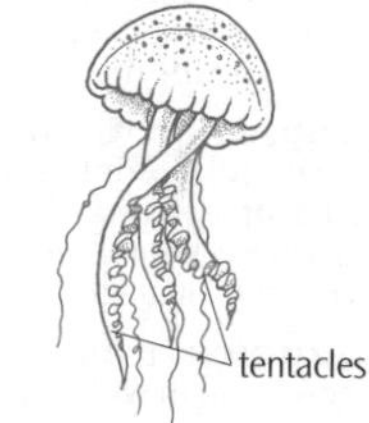

jeopardize (also **-ise**) /ˈdʒepədaɪz/ ***verb*** [T] to do sth that may damage sth or put it at risk: *He would never do anything to jeopardize his career.*

jeopardy /ˈdʒepədi/ ***noun***
IDM **in jeopardy** in a dangerous position and likely to be lost or harmed: *The future of the factory and 15,000 jobs are in jeopardy.*

jerk[1] /dʒɜːk/ ***verb*** [I,T] to move or make sb/sth move with a sudden sharp movement: *She jerked the door open.* ◇ *His head jerked back as the car suddenly set off.* ▶ **jerky** ***adj.*** ▶ **jerkily** ***adv.***

jerk[2] /dʒɜːk/ ***noun*** [C] **1** a sudden sharp movement **2** (*especially AmE, slang*) a stupid or annoying person

jersey /ˈdʒɜːzi/ ***noun*** **1** [C] a piece of clothing made of wool that you wear over a shirt **2** [U] a soft thin material made of cotton or wool that is used for making clothes

Jesus /ˈdʒiːzəs/ = CHRIST

jet[1] /dʒet/ ***noun*** [C] **1** a fast modern plane: *a jet plane/aircraft* **2** a fast, thin current of water, gas, etc. coming out of a small hole

jet[2] /dʒet/ (**jetting**; **jetted**) ***verb*** [I] (*informal*) **jet off** to fly somewhere in a plane

ˌjet ˈblack ***adj.*** very dark black in colour

ˈjet engine ***noun*** [C] a powerful engine that makes planes fly by pushing out a current of hot air and gases at the back ➲ picture at **plane**

ˈjet lag ***noun*** [U] (TOURISM) the tired feeling that people often have after a long journey in a plane to a place where the local time is different ▶ **ˈjet-lagged** ***adj.***

the ˈjet set ***noun*** [sing.] the group of rich, successful and fashionable people (especially those who travel around the world a lot)

ˈJet Ski ***noun*** [C] a vehicle with an engine, like a motorbike, for riding across water ▶ **ˈjet-skiing** ***noun*** [U]

jetty /ˈdʒeti/ ***noun*** [C] (*pl.* **jetties**) (*AmE* **dock**) a stone wall or wooden platform built out into the sea or a river where boats are tied and where people can get on and off them **SYN** **landing stage**

Jew /dʒuː/ ***noun*** [C] a person whose family was originally from the ancient land of Israel or whose religion is Judaism ▶ **Jewish** ***adj.***

jewel /ˈdʒuːəl/ ***noun*** **1** [C] a valuable stone (for example a diamond) **2** [usually pl.] pieces of jewellery or decorative objects that contain PRECIOUS STONES

jeweller (*AmE* **jeweler**) /ˈdʒuːələ(r)/ ***noun*** **1** [C] a person whose job is to buy, sell, make or repair jewellery and watches **2 the jeweller's** [sing.] a shop where jewellery and watches are made, sold and repaired

jewellery 🔑 (*AmE* **jewelry**) /ˈdʒuːəlri/ ***noun*** [U] objects such as rings, etc. that are worn as personal decoration: *a piece of jewellery*

jib[1] /dʒɪb/ ***noun*** [C] **1** a small sail in front of the large sail on a boat **2** the arm of a CRANE (= a large machine that lifts or moves heavy objects)

jib[2] /dʒɪb/ (**jibbing**; **jibbed**) ***verb*** [I] ~ **(at sth/at doing sth)** (*old-fashioned*) to refuse to do or accept sth: *She agreed to attend but jibbed at making a speech.*

jig[1] /dʒɪg/ ***noun*** [C] (MUSIC) a type of quick dance with jumping movements; the music for this dance

jig[2] /dʒɪg/ ***verb*** [I] (**jigging**; **jigged**) ~ **about/around** to move about in an excited or impatient way

COLLOCATIONS AND PATTERNS

Jobs

While you are learning, you **study/train to be** or **train as** a doctor, teacher, etc.
She trained as a painter and sculptor.

A **trainee** is someone who **starts work** while they are still **training.**
He started work as a trainee chef.

Somebody who has **completed their training** or passed their exams is **qualified.**
She qualified as a vet last year.

We say sb **is** or **works as** a writer, teacher, etc.
Tim worked as a bus driver for many years.
Gerry is a cello teacher.

You **look for, apply for** or **find** a job.
He applied for 16 jobs before he found one.

A job can be **full-time** or **part-time, permanent** or **temporary.**
Many students find temporary jobs in hotels during the summer.
I only worked part-time while Gloria was a baby.

Job-sharing can suit two people who want to work part-time.
Job-sharing allows employees to be parents as well as business people.

A company **engages (sb as)/hires (sb as)/recruits/takes on** a new employee.
They have taken on a new designer.

When an organization chooses sb for a high level position they **appoint sb (as)** or **make sb** president, chairman, head, etc.
She was appointed Professor of Law at Yale.
At 35 he was made chairman of the board.

If you want to leave your job, you **resign** or **hand in** your **resignation.**
He resigned from his post as finance director in April.

If a company no longer needs an employee, it will **make** him/her **redundant.**
Hundreds of car workers were made redundant when the factory closed down.

jiggle /ˈdʒɪɡl/ ***verb*** [T] (*informal*) to move sth quickly from side to side: *She jiggled her car keys to try to distract the baby.*

jigsaw /ˈdʒɪɡsɔː/ (*also* **ˈjigsaw puzzle**) ***noun*** [C] **1** a picture on cardboard or wood that is cut into small pieces and has to be fitted together again **2** a SAW (=a type of tool) with a fine blade for cutting designs in thin pieces of wood or metal

jihad /dʒɪˈhɑːd/ ***noun*** [C] (**RELIGION**) a religious war that is fought by Muslims against those who reject Islam

jingle[1] /ˈdʒɪŋɡl/ ***noun*** **1** [sing.] a ringing sound like small bells, made by metal objects gently hitting each other: *the jingle of coins* **2** [C] (**ARTS AND MEDIA**) a short simple tune or song that is easy to remember and is used in advertising on television or radio

jingle[2] /ˈdʒɪŋɡl/ ***verb*** [I,T] to make or cause sth to make a pleasant gentle sound like small bells ringing: *She jingled the coins in her pocket.*

jinx /dʒɪŋks/ ***noun*** [C, usually sing.] (*informal*) bad luck; a person or thing that people believe brings bad luck to sb/sth ▶ **jinx** ***verb*** [T] ▶ **jinxed** ***adj.***: *After my third accident in a month, I began to think I was jinxed.*

the jitters /ˈdʒɪtəz/ ***noun*** [pl.] (*informal*) feelings of fear or worry, especially before an important event or before having to do sth difficult: *Just thinking about the exam **gives me the jitters!***

jittery /ˈdʒɪtəri/ ***adj.*** (*informal*) nervous or worried

Jnr (also **Jr.**) ***abbr.*** (*especially AmE*) Junior: *Samuel P Carson, Jnr*

job 🔑 AW /dʒɒb/ ***noun*** [C] **1** the work that you do regularly to earn money: *She **took/got a job** as a waitress.* ◇ *A lot of people will **lose** their **jobs** if the factory closes.*
➲ note at **work 2** a task or a piece of work: *I always have a lot of jobs to do in the house at weekends.* ◇ *The garage has **done a good/bad job on** our car.*
3 [usually sing.] a duty or responsibility: *It's not his job to tell us what we can and can't do.*
IDM **do the job/trick** (*informal*) to get the result that is wanted
have a hard job to do sth/doing sth → HARD[1]
it's a good job (*spoken*) it is a good or lucky thing: *It's a good job you reminded me – I had completely forgotten!*
just the job/ticket (*informal*) exactly what is needed in a particular situation
make a bad, good, etc. job of sth to do sth badly, well, etc.
make the best of a bad job → BEST[3]
out of a job without paid work SYN **unemployed**

ˈjob-hunt ***verb*** [I] (usually used in the progressive tenses) to try to find a job: *At that time I had been job-hunting for six months.*

jobless /ˈdʒɒbləs/ ***adj.*** **1** (usually used about large numbers of people) without paid work SYN **unemployed 2 the jobless** ***noun*** [pl.] people without paid work ▶ **joblessness** ***noun*** [U] SYN **unemployment**

ˈjob-sharing ***noun*** [U] an arrangement for two people to share the hours of work and the pay of one job ▶ **ˈjob-share** ***noun*** [C]: *The company encourages job-shares and part-time working.* ▶ **ˈjob-share** ***verb*** [I]: *She's looking for someone to job-share with.*

jockey /ˈdʒɒki/ ***noun*** [C] (**SPORT**) a person who rides horses in races, especially as a profession ➲ look at **DJ**

jocular /ˈdʒɒkjələ(r)/ ***adj.*** (*formal*) **1** funny; humorous: *a jocular comment* **2** (used about a person) enjoying making people laugh SYN **jolly** ▶ **jocularity** /ˌdʒɒkjuˈlærəti/ ***noun*** [U]

jodhpurs /ˈdʒɒdpəz/ ***noun*** [pl.] special trousers that you wear for riding a horse

joey /ˈdʒəʊi/ ***noun*** [C] a young KANGAROO or WALLABY
➊ picture on page 29

jog[1] /dʒɒɡ/ ***verb*** (**jogging; jogged**) **1** [I] to run slowly, especially as a form of exercise **2** [T] to push or knock sb/sth slightly: *He jogged my arm and I spilled the milk.*
IDM **jog sb's memory** to say or do sth that makes sb remember sth

jog[2] /dʒɒɡ/ ***noun*** [sing.] **1** a slow run as a form of exercise: *She **goes for a jog** before breakfast.* **2** a slight push or knock

jogger /ˈdʒɒɡə(r)/ ***noun*** [C] a person who goes JOGGING for exercise

join[1] 🔑 /dʒɔɪn/ ***verb*** **1** [T] ~ **A to B**; ~ **A and B (together)** to fasten or connect one thing to another: *The Channel Tunnel joins Britain to Europe.* ◇ *The two pieces of wood had been carefully joined together.* ◇ *We've knocked down the wall and joined the two rooms into one.* **2** [I,T] ~ **(up) (with sb/sth)** to meet or unite (with sb/sth) to form one thing or group: *Do the two rivers join (up) at any point?* ◇ *Where does this road join the motorway?* ◇ *Would you like to join us for a drink?* **3** [T] to become a member of a club or organization: *I've joined an aerobics class.* ◇ *He joined the company three months ago.* **4** [T] to take your place in sth or to take part in sth: *We'd better go and join the queue if we want to see the film.* ◇ *Come downstairs and join the party.* **5** [I,T] ~ (with) sb in sth/in doing sth/to do sth; ~ together in doing sth/to do sth to take part with sb (often in doing sth for sb else): *Everybody here joins me in wishing you the best of luck in your new job.* ◇ *The whole school joined together to sing the school song.*

IDM **join forces (with sb)** → FORCE[1]

PHR V **join in (sth/doing sth)** to take part in an activity: *Everyone started singing but Frank refused to join in.*

join up to become a member of the army, navy or air force

join² /dʒɔɪn/ ***noun*** [C] a place where two things are fixed or connected: *He glued the handle back on so cleverly that you couldn't see the join.*

joiner /ˈdʒɔɪnə(r)/ ***noun*** [C] a person who makes the wooden parts of a building ➲ look at **carpenter**

joinery /ˈdʒɔɪnəri/ ***noun*** [U] the work of a JOINER or the things made by them

joint¹ ⊶ /dʒɔɪnt/ ***noun*** [C] **1** (ANATOMY) a part of the body where two bones fit together and are able to bend **2** the place where two or more things are fastened or connected together, especially to form a corner **3** a large piece of meat that you cook whole in the oven: *a joint of lamb*

joint² ⊶ /dʒɔɪnt/ ***adj.*** (only *before* a noun) shared or owned by two or more people: *Have you and your husband got a **joint account**?* (=a shared bank account) ◇ *a joint decision* ▶ **jointly** ***adv.***

ˌjoint ˈventure ***noun*** [C] (BUSINESS) a business project or activity that is begun by two or more companies, etc., which remain separate organizations

joist /dʒɔɪst/ ***noun*** [C] a long thick piece of wood or metal that is used to support a floor or ceiling in a building

joist

floorboard

joist

joke¹ ⊶ /dʒəʊk/ ***noun*** **1** [C] something said or done to make you laugh, especially a funny story: *to tell/crack jokes* ◇ *a dirty joke* (=about sex) ◇ *I'm sorry, I didn't **get the joke*** (=understand it). ➲ look at **practical joke** **2** [sing.] a ridiculous person, thing or situation: *The salary he was offered was a joke!*

IDM **play a joke/trick on sb** to trick sb in order to amuse yourself or other people

see the joke to understand what is funny about a joke or trick

take a joke to be able to laugh at a joke against yourself: *The trouble with Pete is he can't take a joke.*

joke² ⊶ /dʒəʊk/ ***verb*** [I] **1** ~ (with sb) (about sth) to say sth to make people laugh; to tell a funny story: *She spent the evening laughing and joking with her old friends.* **2** to say sth that is not true because you think it is funny: *I never joke about religion.* ◇ *Don't get upset. I was **only joking**!*

IDM **you must be joking**; **you're joking** (*spoken*) (used to express great surprise) you cannot be serious

joker /ˈdʒəʊkə(r)/ ***noun*** [C] **1** a person who likes to tell jokes or play tricks **2** an extra card which can be used instead of any other one in some card games

jolly /ˈdʒɒli/ ***adj.*** **1** happy and cheerful: *a jolly crowd/face/mood* **2** (*old-fashioned*) enjoyable: *a jolly evening/party/time*

jolt¹ /dʒəʊlt/ ***verb*** [I,T] to move or make sb/sth move in a sudden rough way: *The lorry jolted along the bumpy track.* ◇ *The crash jolted all the passengers forward.*

jolt² /dʒəʊlt/ ***noun*** [C, usually sing.] **1** a sudden movement: *The train stopped with a jolt.* **2** a sudden surprise or shock: *His sudden anger gave her quite a jolt.*

jostle /ˈdʒɒsl/ ***verb*** [I,T] to push hard against sb in a crowd

jot /dʒɒt/ ***verb*** (**jotting**; **jotted**)

PHR V **jot sth down** to make a quick short note of sth: *Let me jot down your address.*

joule /dʒuːl/ ***noun*** [C] (PHYSICS) a measurement of energy or work²(7) ➲ look at **kilojoule**

journal AW /ˈdʒɜːnl/ ***noun*** [C] **1** (ARTS AND MEDIA) a newspaper or a magazine, especially one in which all the articles are about a particular subject or profession: *a medical/scientific/trade journal* **2** a written account of what you have done each day: *Have you read his journal of the years he spent in India?* ➲ look at **diary**

journalism /ˈdʒɜːnəlɪzəm/ ***noun*** [U] (ARTS AND MEDIA) the profession of collecting and writing about news in newspapers and magazines or talking about it on the television or radio

journalist ⊶ /ˈdʒɜːnəlɪst/ ***noun*** [C] (ARTS AND MEDIA) a person whose job is to collect and write about news in newspapers and magazines or to talk about it on the television or radio ➲ look at **reporter**

journey ⊶ /ˈdʒɜːni/ ***noun*** [C] the act of travelling from one place to another, usually on land: *Did you have a good journey?* ◇ *a two-hour journey* ◇ *The journey to work takes me forty-five minutes.* ◇ *We'll have to break the journey* (=stop for a rest). ➲ note at **travel**

joust /dʒaʊst/ ***verb*** [I] (HISTORY) to fight on horses using a long stick (**a lance**) to try to knock the other person off their horse, especially as part of a formal contest in the past ▶ **joust** ***noun*** [C] ▶ **jousting** ***noun*** [U]

jovial /ˈdʒəʊviəl/ ***adj.*** (used about a person) happy and friendly

joy ⊶ /dʒɔɪ/ ***noun*** **1** [U] a feeling of great happiness: *We'd like to wish you joy and success in your life together.* **2** [C] a person or thing that gives you great pleasure: *the joys of fatherhood* ◇ *That class is a joy to teach.* **3** [U] (*BrE, informal*) (used in questions and negative sentences) success or satisfaction: *'I asked again if we could have seats with more legroom but **got no joy** from the check-in clerk.'*

IDM **jump for joy** → JUMP[1]

sb's pride and joy → PRIDE[1]

joyful /ˈdʒɔɪfl/ ***adj.*** very happy; causing people to be happy: *a joyful occasion* ▶ **joyfully** /-fəli/ ***adv.*** ▶ **joyfulness** ***noun*** [U]

joyless /ˈdʒɔɪləs/ ***adj.*** unhappy: *a joyless marriage*

joyous /ˈdʒɔɪəs/ ***adj.*** (*written*) very happy; causing people to be happy SYN **joyful**

joyriding /ˈdʒɔɪraɪdɪŋ/ ***noun*** [U] (LAW) the crime of stealing a car and driving it for pleasure, usually in a fast and dangerous way ▶ **joyrider** ***noun*** [C] ▶ **joyride** ***noun*** [C]

joystick /ˈdʒɔɪstɪk/ ***noun*** [C] a handle used for controlling movement on a computer, aircraft, etc.

JP /ˌdʒeɪ ˈpiː/ ***abbr.*** (LAW) Justice of the Peace

JPEG /ˈdʒeɪpeg/ ***noun*** (COMPUTING) **1** [U] **Joint Photographic Experts Group**; technology which reduces the size of files that contain images: *JPEG files* **2** [C] an image created using this technology: *You can download the pictures as JPEGs.*

Jr. ***abbr.*** =JNR

jubilant /ˈdʒuːbɪlənt/ ***adj.*** (*formal*) extremely happy, especially because of a success: *The football fans were jubilant at their team's victory in the cup.*

jubilation /ˌdʒuːbɪˈleɪʃn/ ***noun*** [U] (*formal*) great happiness because of a success

jubilee /ˈdʒuːbɪliː/ ***noun*** [C] a special anniversary of an event that took place a certain number of years ago, and the celebrations that go with it: *It's the company's* ***golden jubilee*** *this year* (=it is fifty years since it was started).

Judaism /ˈdʒuːdeɪɪzəm/ ***noun*** [U] (RELIGION) the religion of the Jewish people

judge[1] 🔑 /dʒʌdʒ/ ***noun*** [C] **1** (LAW) a person in a court of law whose job is to decide how criminals should be punished and to make legal decisions: *The judge sentenced the man to three years in prison.* **2** (SPORT) a person who decides who has won a competition: *a panel of judges* **3** [usually sing.] **a ~ of sth** a person who has the ability or knowledge to give an opinion about sth: *You're a good judge of character – what do you think of him?*

judge[2] 🔑 /dʒʌdʒ/ ***verb*** **1** [I,T] to form or give an opinion about sb/sth based on the information you have: ***Judging by/from*** *what he said, his work is going well.* ◇ *It's difficult to judge how long the project will take.* ◇ *The party was judged a great success by everybody.* **2** [T] to decide the result or winner of a competition: *The head teacher will judge the competition.* **3** [T] to form an opinion about sb/sth, especially when you disapprove of them or it: *Don't judge him too harshly – he's had a difficult time.* **4** [T] (LAW) to decide if sb is guilty or innocent in a court of law

judgement 🔑 (also **judgment**) /ˈdʒʌdʒmənt/ ***noun*** **1** [U] the ability to form opinions or to make sensible decisions: *He always shows excellent judgement in his choice of staff.* ◇ *to have good/poor/sound judgement* **2** [C,U] an opinion formed after carefully considering the information you have: *What,* ***in your judgement****, would be the best course of action?* **3 judgment** [C] (LAW) an official decision made by a judge or a court of law: *The man collapsed when the judgment was read out in court.*

ˈJudgement Day (*also* **the ˌDay of ˈJudgement**; **the ˌLast ˈJudgement**) ***noun*** [sing.] (RELIGION) the day at the end of the world when, according to some religions, God will judge everyone who has ever lived

judicial /dʒuˈdɪʃl/ ***adj.*** (LAW) connected with a court of law, a judge or a legal judgment: *the judicial system*

judiciary /dʒuˈdɪʃəri/ ***noun*** [C, with sing. or pl. verb] (*pl.* **judiciaries**) (LAW) the judges of a country or a state, when they are considered as a group: *an independent judiciary*

judicious /dʒuˈdɪʃəs/ ***adj.*** (used about a decision or an action) sensible and carefully considered; showing good judgement ▶ **judiciously** ***adv.***

judo /ˈdʒuːdəʊ/ ***noun*** [U] (SPORT) a sport from Asia in which two people fight and try to throw each other to the ground ➲ look at **martial arts**

jug /dʒʌg/ (*AmE* **pitcher**) ***noun*** [C] a container with a handle used for holding or pouring liquids: *a milk jug* ◇ *a jug of water*

juggle /ˈdʒʌgl/ ***verb*** [I,T] **1 ~ (with sth)** to keep three or more objects such as balls in the air at the same time by throwing them one at a time and catching them quickly **2 ~ sth (with sth)** to try to deal with two or more important jobs or activities at the same time

juggler /ˈdʒʌglə(r)/ ***noun*** [C] a person who JUGGLES to entertain people

jugular /ˈdʒʌgjələ(r)/ (*also* **ˌjugular ˈvein**) ***noun*** [C] (ANATOMY) any of the three large tubes (**veins**) in your neck that carry blood away from your head to your heart

juice 🔑 /dʒuːs/ ***noun*** [C,U] **1** the liquid that comes from fruit and vegetables: *carrot/grapefruit/lemon juice* ◇ *I'll have an orange juice, please.* **2** the liquid that comes from a piece of meat when it is cooked: *You can use the juices of the meat to make gravy.* **3** (BIOLOGY) the liquid in your stomach or another part of your body that deals with the food you eat: *gastric/digestive juices*

juicy /ˈdʒuːsi/ ***adj.*** (**juicier**; **juiciest**) **1** containing a lot of juice: *juicy oranges* **2** (*informal*) (used about information) interesting because it is shocking: *juicy gossip*

jukebox /ˈdʒuːkbɒks/ ***noun*** [C] (MUSIC) a machine in a CAFE or bar, that plays music when money is put in

Jul. ***abbr.*** July: *4 Jul. 2001*

Julian calendar /ˌdʒuːliən ˈkælɪndə(r)/ ***noun*** [sing.] (HISTORY) the system of arranging days and months in the year introduced by Julius Caesar, and used in Western countries until the GREGORIAN CALENDAR replaced it

July /dʒuˈlaɪ/ ***noun*** [U, C] (*abbr.* **Jul.**) the seventh month of the year, coming after June

jumble[1] /ˈdʒʌmbl/ ***verb*** [T] (usually passive) **~ sth (up/together)** to mix things together in a confused and untidy way

jumble[2] /ˈdʒʌmbl/ ***noun*** **1** [sing.] an untidy group of things: *a jumble of papers/ideas* **2** [U] (*BrE*) a collection of old things for a JUMBLE SALE: *Have you got any jumble you don't want?*

ˈjumble sale (*AmE* **ˈrummage sale**) ***noun*** [C] a sale of old things that people do not want any more. Clubs, churches, schools and other organizations hold **jumble sales** to get money.

jumbo[1] /ˈdʒʌmbəʊ/ ***adj.*** (*informal*) (only *before* a noun) very large

jumbo[2] /ˈdʒʌmbəʊ/ ***noun*** [C] (*pl.* **jumbos**) (*also* **ˌjumbo ˈjet**) a very large aircraft that can carry several hundred passengers

jump[1] 🔑 /dʒʌmp/ ***verb*** **1** [I] to move quickly into the air by pushing yourself up with your legs and feet, or by stepping off a high place: *to jump into the air/off a bridge/onto a chair* ◇ *How high can you jump?* ◇ *Jump up and down to keep warm.* **2** [I] to move quickly and suddenly: *The telephone rang and she jumped up to answer it.* ◇ *A taxi stopped and we jumped in.* **3** [T] to get over sth by jumping: *The dog jumped the fence and ran off down the road.* **4** [I] to make a sudden movement because of surprise or fear: *'Oh, it's only you – you made me jump,' he said.*

5 [I] ~ **(from sth) to sth**; ~ **(by) (sth)** to increase suddenly by a very large amount: *His salary jumped from £20000 to £28000 last year.* ◇ *Prices jumped (by) 50% in the summer.* **6** [I] ~ **(from sth) to sth** to go suddenly from one point in a series, a story, etc. to another: *The book kept jumping from the present to the past.*

IDM climb/jump on the bandwagon → BANDWAGON
jump for joy to be extremely happy about sth
jump the gun to do sth too soon, before the proper time
jump the queue to go to the front of a line of people (**queue**) without waiting for your turn
jump to conclusions to decide that sth is true without thinking about it carefully enough

PHR V jump at sth to accept an opportunity, offer, etc. with enthusiasm: *Of course I jumped at the chance to work in New York for a year.*

jump[2] ⊶ /dʒʌmp/ ***noun*** [C] **1** an act of jumping: *With a huge jump the horse cleared the hedge.* ◇ *to do a parachute jump* ➲ look at **high jump**, **long jump** **2** a ~ **(in sth)** a sudden increase in amount, price or value **3** a thing to be jumped over: *The horse fell at the first jump.*

jumper /ˈdʒʌmpə(r)/ ***noun*** [C] **1** (*BrE*) a piece of clothing with sleeves, usually made of wool, that you wear on the top part of your body **2** a person or animal that jumps

jumpy /ˈdʒʌmpi/ ***adj.*** (*informal*) nervous or worried

Jun. ***abbr.*** June: *10 Jun. 2001*

junction /ˈdʒʌŋkʃn/ ***noun*** [C] a place where roads, railway lines, etc. meet

June /dʒuːn/ ***noun*** [U, C] (*abbr.* **Jun.**) the sixth month of the year, coming after May

jungle /ˈdʒʌŋɡl/ ***noun*** [C,U] (**GEOGRAPHY**) a thick forest in a hot tropical country: *the jungles of Africa and South America* ➲ note at **forest**

junior[1] ⊶ /ˈdʒuːniə(r)/ ***adj.*** **1** ~ **(to sb)** having a low or lower position (than sb) in an organization, etc.: *a junior officer/doctor/employee* ◇ *A lieutenant is junior to a captain in the army.* **2 Junior** (*abbr.* **Jnr**, **Jr.**) (*especially AmE*) used after the name of a son who has the same first name as his father: *Sammy Davis, Junior* **3** (*BrE*) of or for children below a particular age: *the junior athletics championships* ➲ look at **senior**[1] **4** (*AmE*) (**EDUCATION**) connected with the year before the last year in a HIGH SCHOOL or college

junior[2] ⊶ /ˈdʒuːniə(r)/ ***noun*** **1** [C] a person who has a low position in an organization, etc. **2** [sing.] (with *his*, *her*, *your*, etc.) a person who is younger than sb else by the number of years mentioned: *She's two years his junior/his junior by two years.* **3** [C] (*BrE*) (**EDUCATION**) a child who goes to junior school: *The juniors are having an outing to a museum today.* **4** [C] (*AmE*) (**EDUCATION**) a student in the year before the last year in a HIGH SCHOOL or college ➲ look at **senior**[2], **sophomore**

ˌjunior ˈcollege ***noun*** [C] (**EDUCATION**) (in the US) a college that offers programmes that are two years long. Some students go to a university or a college offering four-year programmes after they have finished studying at a **junior college**.

ˌjunior ˈhigh school (*also* **ˌjunior ˈhigh**) ***noun*** [C,U] (**EDUCATION**) (in the US) a school for young people between the ages of 12 and 14 ➲ look at **senior high school**

ˈjunior school ***noun*** [C] a school for children aged between seven and eleven

junk /dʒʌŋk/ ***noun*** **1** [U] (*informal*) things that are old or useless or do not have much value: *There's an awful lot of junk up in the attic.* **2** [U] = JUNK FOOD **3** [C] a Chinese boat with a square sail and a flat bottom

ˈjunk food ***noun*** [U] (*informal*) food that is not very good for you but that is ready to eat or quick to prepare

junkie /ˈdʒʌŋki/ ***noun*** [C] (*informal*) a person who is unable to stop taking dangerous drugs **SYN addict**

ˈjunk mail ***noun*** [U] (**BUSINESS**) advertising material that is sent to people who have not asked for it ➲ look at **spam**

junta /ˈdʒʌntə/ ***noun*** [C, with sing. or pl. verb] a group, especially of military officers, who rule a country by force

Jupiter /ˈdʒuːpɪtə(r)/ ***noun*** [sing.] (**ASTRONOMY**) the planet that is fifth in order from the sun ➲ picture at **solar system**

jurisdiction /ˌdʒʊərɪsˈdɪkʃn/ ***noun*** [U] (**LAW**) legal power or authority; the area in which this power can be used: *That question is outside the jurisdiction of this council.*

jurisprudence /ˌdʒʊərɪsˈpruːdns/ ***noun*** [U] (**LAW**) the scientific study of law: *a professor of jurisprudence*

juror /ˈdʒʊərə(r)/ ***noun*** [C] (**LAW**) a member of a JURY

jury /ˈdʒʊəri/ ***noun*** [C, with sing. or pl. verb] (*pl.* **juries**) **1** (**LAW**) a group of members of the public in a court of law who listen to the facts about a crime and decide if sb is guilty or not guilty: *Has/have the jury reached a verdict?* **2** (**SPORT**) a group of people who decide who is the winner in a competition: *The jury is/are about to announce the winners.*

just[1] ⊶ /dʒʌst/ ***adv.*** **1** a very short time before: *She's just been to the shops.* ◇ *He'd just returned from France when I saw him.* ◇ *They came here just before Easter.* **2** at exactly this/that moment, or immediately after: *He was* ***just about to*** *break the window when he noticed a policeman.* ◇ *I was* ***just going to*** *phone my mother when she arrived.* ◇ ***Just as*** *I was beginning to enjoy myself, John said it was time to go.* ◇ ***Just then*** *the door opened.* **3** exactly: *It's just eight o'clock.* ◇ *That's just what I meant.* ◇ *You're* ***just as*** *clever* ***as*** *he is.* ◇ *The room was too hot before, but now it's* ***just right***. ◇ *He looks* ***just like*** *his father.* ◇ *My arm hurts just here.* **4** only: *She's just a child.* ◇ *Just a minute! I'm nearly ready.* **5** almost not; hardly: *I could* ***only just*** *hear what she was saying.* ◇ *We got to the station* ***just in time***. **6** (often with the imperative) used for getting attention or to emphasize what you are saying: *Just let me speak for a moment, will you?* ◇ *I just don't want to go to the party.* **7** used with *might*, *may* or *could* to express a slight possibility: *This might just/just might be the most important decision of your life.* **8** really; absolutely: *The whole day was just fantastic!*

IDM all/just the same → SAME
it is just as well (that...) it is a good thing: *It's just as well you remembered to bring your umbrella!*
just about almost or approximately: *I've just about finished.* ◇ *Karen's plane should be taking off just about now.*
just in case in order to be completely prepared or safe: *It might be hot in France – take your shorts just in case.*
just now **1** at this exact moment or during this exact period: *I can't come with you just now – can you wait 20 minutes?* **2** a very short time ago: *I saw Tony just now.*
just so exactly right
not just yet not now, but probably quite soon

just² /dʒʌst/ ***adj.*** fair and right; reasonable: *I don't think that was a very just decision.* ▶ ***justly adv.***

justice 🔑 /ˈdʒʌstɪs/ ***noun*** **1** [U] the fair treatment of people: *a struggle for justice* **2** [U] the quality of being fair or reasonable: *Everybody realized the justice of what he was saying.* **3** [U] (LAW) the law and the way it is used: *the criminal justice system* **4** [C] (*AmE*) (LAW) a judge in a court of law
IDM **do justice to sb/sth; do sb/sth justice** to treat sb/sth fairly or to show the real quality of sb/sth: *I don't like him, but to do him justice, he's a very clever man.* ◇ *The photograph doesn't do her justice – she's actually very pretty.*
a miscarriage of justice → MISCARRIAGE

ˌJustice of the ˈPeace (*abbr.* **JP**) ***noun*** [C] (LAW) a person who judges less serious cases in a court of law in Britain

justifiable AW /ˌdʒʌstɪˈfaɪəbl/ ***adj.*** that you can accept because there is a good reason for it: *His action was entirely justifiable.* ▶ **justifiably** /ˈdʒʌstɪfaɪəbli; ˌdʒʌstɪˈfaɪəbli/ ***adv.***

justification AW /ˌdʒʌstɪfɪˈkeɪʃn/ ***noun*** [C,U] (a) ~ **(for sth/doing sth)** (a) good reason: *I can't see any justification for cutting his salary.* ➲ note at **reason¹**

justified AW /ˈdʒʌstɪfaɪd/ ***adj.*** **1** ~ **(in doing sth)** having a good reason for doing sth: *She felt fully justified in asking for her money back.* **2** existing or done for a good reason: *His fears proved justified.* OPP **unjustified**

justify 🔑 AW /ˈdʒʌstɪfaɪ/ ***verb*** [T] (*pres. part.* **justifying**; *3rd person sing. pres.* **justifies**; *pt, pp* **justified**) to give or be a good reason for sth: *Can you justify your decision?*

jut /dʒʌt/ ***verb*** [I] (**jutting**; **jutted**) ~ **(out) (from/into/over sth)** to stick out further than the surrounding surface, objects, etc.: *rocks that jut out into the sea*

jute /dʒuːt/ ***noun*** [U] thin threads from a plant that are used for making rope and rough cloth (**sackcloth**)

juvenile /ˈdʒuːvənaɪl/ ***adj.*** **1** (*formal*) of, for or involving young people who are not yet adults: *juvenile crime* **2** behaving like sb of a younger age; childish: *He's twenty but he is still quite juvenile.*
▶ ***juvenile noun*** [C]

ˌjuvenile deˈlinquent ***noun*** [C] (LAW) a young person who is guilty of committing a crime

juxtapose /ˌdʒʌkstəˈpəʊz/ ***verb*** [T] (*formal*) to put two people, things, etc. very close together, especially in order to show how they are different: *The artist achieves a special effect by juxtaposing light and dark.* ▶ **juxtaposition** /ˌdʒʌkstəpəˈzɪʃn/ ***noun*** [U]

K k

K, k¹ /keɪ/ ***noun*** [C,U] (*pl.* **K's**; **k's** /keɪz/) the eleventh letter of the English alphabet: *'Kate' begins with (a) 'K'.*

K² /keɪ/ ***abbr.*** **1** (*informal*) one thousand: *She earns 22K (=£22000) a year.* **2** kelvin

kaleidoscope /kəˈlaɪdəskəʊp/ ***noun*** [C] **1** a large number of different things **2** a toy that consists of a tube containing mirrors and small pieces of coloured glass. When you look into one end of the tube and turn it, you see changing patterns of colours.

kangaroo /ˌkæŋɡəˈruː/ ***noun*** [C] (*pl.* **kangaroos**) an Australian animal that moves by jumping on its strong back legs and that carries its young in a pocket of skin (**a pouch**) on its stomach ➲ picture on **page 29**

kaolin /ˈkeɪəlɪn/ (*also* **ˌchina ˈclay**) ***noun*** [U] (GEOLOGY, HEALTH) a type of fine white CLAY that is used in some medicines and in making cups, plates, etc.

karaoke /ˌkæriˈəʊki/ ***noun*** [U] (MUSIC) a type of entertainment in which a machine plays only the music of popular songs so that people can sing the words themselves: *a karaoke machine/night/bar*

karat (*AmE*) = CARAT

karate /kəˈrɑːti/ ***noun*** [U] (SPORT) a style of fighting originally from Japan in which the hands and feet are used as weapons ➲ look at **martial arts**

karma /ˈkɑːmə/ ***noun*** [U] (RELIGION) (in Buddhism and Hinduism) all of sb's good and bad actions in one of their lives, that are believed to decide what will happen to them in the next life

kart /kɑːt/ = GO-KART

katabolism ***noun*** [U] = CATABOLISM

kayak /ˈkaɪæk/ ***noun*** [C] a light narrow boat (**canoe**) for one person, that you move using a PADDLE (= a stick with a flat part at each end) ➲ picture at **canoe**

KC /ˌkeɪ ˈsiː/ ***noun*** [C] (LAW) the highest level of BARRISTER (= a type of lawyer) who can speak for the government in a court of law in Britain. **KC** is an abbreviation for 'King's Counsel' and is used when there is a king in Britain. ➲ look at **QC** ➲ note at **lawyer**

kebab /kɪˈbæb/ ***noun*** [C] small pieces of meat, vegetables, etc. that are cooked on a stick (**a skewer**)

keel¹ /kiːl/ ***noun*** [C] a long piece of wood or metal on the bottom of a boat that stops it falling over sideways in the water

keel² /kiːl/ ***verb***
PHR V **keel over** to fall over

keen 🔑 /kiːn/ ***adj.*** **1** ~ **(to do sth/that...)** very interested in sth; wanting to do sth: *They are both keen gardeners.* ◇ *I failed the first time but I'm keen to try again.* ◇ *She was keen that we should all be there.* **2** (used about one of the senses, a feeling, etc.) good or strong: *Foxes have a keen sense of smell.*
▶ ***keenly adv.*** ▶ ***keenness noun*** [U]
IDM **keen on sb/sth** very interested in or having a strong desire for sb/sth: *He's very keen on jazz.*

keep¹ 🔑 /kiːp/ ***verb*** (*pt, pp* **kept** /kept/) **1** [I] to continue to be in a particular state or position: *You must keep warm.* ◇ *That child can't keep still.* ◇ *I still keep in touch with my old school friends.* **2** [T] to make sb/sth stay in a particular state, place or condition: *Please keep this door closed.* ◇ *He kept his hands in his pockets.* ◇ *I'm sorry to keep you waiting.* **3** [T] to continue to have sth; to save sth for sb: *You can keep that book – I don't need it any more.* ◇ *Can I keep the car until next week?* ◇ *Can you keep my seat for me till I get back?* **4** [T] to have sth in a particular place: *Where do you keep the matches?* ◇ *Keep your passport in a safe place.* **5** [T] ~ **doing sth** to continue doing sth or to repeat an action many times: *Keep going until you get to the church and then turn left.* ◇ *She keeps asking me silly questions.* **6** [T] to do what you promised or arranged: *Can you keep a promise?* ◇ *She didn't keep her appointment at the dentist's.* ◇ *to keep a secret* (= not tell it to anyone) **7** [T] to write down sth that you want to remember: *Keep a record of how much you spend.* ◇ *to keep a diary* **8** [I] (used about food) to stay fresh: *Drink up all the milk – it won't keep in this weather.* **9** [T] to support sb with your money: *You can't keep a family on the money I earn.* **10** [T] to have and look after animals: *They keep ducks on their farm.* **11** [T] to delay sb/sth; to prevent sb from leaving: *Where's the doctor? What's keeping him?*

IDM **keep it up** to continue doing sth as well as you are doing it now

PHR V **keep at it/sth** to continue to work on/at sth: *Keep at it – we should be finished soon.*

keep away from sb/sth to not go near sb/sth: *Keep away from the town centre this weekend.*

keep sb/sth back to prevent sb/sth from moving forwards: *The police tried to keep the crowd back.*

keep sth back (from sb) to refuse to tell sb sth: *I know he's keeping something back; he knows much more than he says.*

keep sth down to make sth stay at a low level, to stop sth increasing: *Keep your voice down.*

keep sb from sth/from doing sth to prevent sb from doing sth

keep sth from sb to refuse to tell sb sth

keep your mouth shut → MOUTH[1]

keep off sth to not go near or on sth: *Keep off the grass!*

keep sth off (sb/sth) to stop sth touching or going on sb/sth: *I'm trying to keep the flies off the food.*

keep on (doing sth) to continue doing sth or to repeat an action many times, especially in an annoying way: *He keeps on interrupting me.*

keep on (at sb) (about sb/sth) to continue talking to sb in an annoying or complaining way: *She kept on at me about my homework until I did it.*

keep (sb/sth) out (of sth) to not enter sth; to stop sb/sth entering sth: *They put up a fence to keep people out of their garden.*

keep to sth to not leave sth; to do sth in the usual, agreed or expected way: *Keep to the path!* ◇ *He didn't keep to our agreement.*

keep sth to/at sth to not allow sth to rise above a particular level: *We're trying to keep costs to a minimum.*

keep sth up 1 to prevent sth from falling down **2** to make sth stay at a high level: *We want to keep up standards of education.* **3** to continue doing sth

keep up (with sb) to move at the same speed as sb: *Can't you walk a bit slower? I can't keep up.*

keep up (with sth) to know about what is happening: *You have to read the latest magazines if you want to keep up.*

keep² /kiːp/ ***noun* 1** [U] food, clothes and the other things that you need to live; the cost of these things **2** [C] (HISTORY) a large strong tower, built as part of an old castle

IDM **for keeps** (*informal*) for always: *Take it. It's yours for keeps.*

keeper /ˈkiːpə(r)/ ***noun*** [C] **1** a person who guards or looks after sth: *a zookeeper* **2** (*informal*) = GOALKEEPER

keeping /ˈkiːpɪŋ/ ***noun***

IDM **in/out of keeping (with sth) 1** that does/does not look good with sth: *That modern table is out of keeping with the style of the room.* **2** in/not in agreement with a rule, belief, etc.: *The Council's decision is in keeping with government policy.*

keg /keg/ ***noun*** [C] a round metal or wooden container, used especially for storing beer

kelvin /ˈkelvɪn/ ***noun*** [C,U] (*abbr.* **K**) (SCIENCE) a unit for measuring temperature ℹ One degree **kelvin** is equal to one degree **Celsius**. Zero kelvin is **absolute zero**.

kennel /ˈkenl/ ***noun*** [C] a small house for a dog

kept past tense, past participle of **keep¹**

keratin /ˈkerətɪn/ ***noun*** [U] (BIOLOGY) a PROTEIN that forms hair, feathers, horns, HOOFS, etc.

kerb (*especially AmE* **curb**) /kɜːb/ ***noun*** [C] the edge of the PAVEMENT (= the path along the sides of a road): *They stood on the kerb waiting to cross the road.*

kernel /ˈkɜːnl/ ***noun*** [C] the inner part of a nut or seed

kerosene /ˈkerəsiːn/ (*AmE*) = PARAFFIN ➲ picture at **fractional distillation**

ketchup /ˈketʃəp/ ***noun*** [U] a cold sauce made from TOMATOES that is eaten with hot or cold food

kettle /ˈketl/ ***noun*** [C] a container with a lid, used for boiling water: *an electric kettle*

kettledrum /ˈketldrʌm/ ***noun*** [C] (MUSIC) a large metal drum with a round bottom and a thin plastic top that can be made looser or tighter to produce different musical notes. A set of kettledrums is usually called TIMPANI. ➲ picture on **page 465**

key¹ 🔑 /kiː/ ***noun*** [C] **1** a metal object that is used for locking a door, starting a car, etc.: *Have you seen my car keys anywhere?* ◇ *We need a spare key to the front door.* ◇ *a bunch of keys* ➲ picture at **padlock** **2** [usually sing.] **the ~ (to sth)** something that helps you achieve or understand sth: *A good education is the key to success.* **3** (MUSIC) one of the parts of a piano, computer, etc. that you press with your fingers to make it work **4** (MUSIC) a set of musical notes that is based on one particular note: *The concerto is in the key of A minor.* ➲ picture at **music** **5** (EDUCATION) a set of answers to exercises or problems: *an answer key* **6** a list of the symbols and signs used in a map or book, showing what they mean

IDM **under lock and key** → LOCK²

key² /kiː/ ***verb*** [T] **~ sth (in)** to put information into a computer or give it an instruction by typing: *Have you keyed that report yet?* ◇ *First, key in your password.*

key³ 🔑 /kiː/ ***adj.*** (only *before* a noun) very important: *Tourism is a key industry in Spain.* ➲ note at **main¹**

keyboard 🔑 /ˈkiːbɔːd/ ***noun*** [C] **1** (MUSIC, COMPUTING) the set of keys on a piano, computer, etc. ➲ picture at **piano**, **computer** **2** (MUSIC) an electrical musical instrument like a small piano ➲ picture on **page 465**

keyhole /ˈkiːhəʊl/ ***noun*** [C] the hole in a lock where you put the key

ˌkeyhole ˈsurgery ***noun*** [U] (*especially BrE*) (HEALTH) medical operations which involve only a very small cut being made in the patient's body

keypal /ˈkiːpæl/ ***noun*** [C] (*informal*) a person that you regularly send emails to, often sb you have never met

ˈkey ring ***noun*** [C] a ring on which you keep keys

ˈkey signature ***noun*** [C] (MUSIC) the set of marks at the beginning of a piece of music which are used to show what KEY the piece is in (= the particular set of notes that it uses) ➲ picture at **music**

keyword /ˈkiːwɜːd/ ***noun*** [C] **1** a word that tells you about the main idea or subject of sth: *When you're studying a language, the keyword is patience.*

2 (COMPUTING) a word or phrase that is used to give an instruction to a computer

kg ⊶ *abbr.* kilogram(s): *weight 10kg*

khaki /ˈkɑːki/ *adj., noun* [U] (of) a pale brownish-yellow or brownish-green colour: *The khaki uniforms of the desert soldiers.*

kHz *abbr.* (PHYSICS) kilohertz; (used in radio) a measure of FREQUENCY

kibbutz /kɪˈbʊts/ *noun* [C] (*pl.* **kibbutzim** /ˌkɪbʊtˈsiːm/) (SOCIAL STUDIES) (in Israel) a type of farm or factory where a group of people live together and share all the work, decisions and income

kick¹ ⊶ /kɪk/ *verb* **1** [T] to hit or move sb/sth with your foot: *He kicked the ball wide of the net.* ◇ *The police kicked the door down.* **2** [I,T] to move your foot or feet: *You must kick harder if you want to swim faster.*
IDM **kick the habit** to stop doing sth harmful that you have done for a long time
kick yourself to be annoyed with yourself because you have done sth stupid, missed an opportunity, etc.
make, kick up, etc. a fuss → FUSS¹
PHR V **kick off** (SPORT) to start a game of football
kick sb out (of sth) (*informal*) to force sb to leave a place: *to be kicked out of university*

kick² ⊶ /kɪk/ *noun* [C] **1** an act of kicking: *She gave the door a kick and it closed.* **2** (*informal*) a feeling of great pleasure, excitement, etc.: *He seems to get a real* ***kick out of*** *driving fast.*

ˈ**kick-off** *noun* [C] (SPORT) the start of a game of football: *The kick-off is at 2.30.*

ˈ**kick-start¹** *verb* [T] **1** to start a motorbike by pushing down on one of the controls with your foot **2** to do sth to help a process or project start more quickly

ˈ**kick-start²** *noun* [C] **1** (*also* ˈ**kick-starter**) the part of a motorbike that you push down with your foot in order to start it **2** a quick start that you give to sth by taking some action

kid¹ ⊶ /kɪd/ *noun* **1** [C] (*informal*) a child or young person: *How are your kids?* **2** [C] **kid brother/sister** (*especially AmE, informal*) younger brother/sister **3** [C] a young GOAT ➲ picture at **goat** **4** [U] soft leather made from the skin of a young GOAT

kid² /kɪd/ *verb* [I,T] (**kidding**; **kidded**) (*informal*) to trick sb/yourself by saying sth that is not true; to make a joke about sth: *I didn't mean it. I was only kidding.*

kiddy (also **kiddie**) /ˈkɪdi/ *noun* [C] (*pl.* **kiddies**) (*informal*) a child

kidnap /ˈkɪdnæp/ *verb* [T] (**kidnapping**; **kidnapped**) (LAW) to take sb away by force and demand money for their safe return: *The child was kidnapped and a ransom of £50000 was demanded for her release.* ➲ look at **hijack** ▶ **kidnapper** *noun* [C]: *The kidnappers demanded £50000.*
▶ **kidnapping** *noun* [C, U]

kidney /ˈkɪdni/ *noun* **1** [C] (ANATOMY) one of the two parts of your body that separate waste liquid from your blood ➲ picture on **page 80** **2** [U, C] the kidneys of an animal when they are cooked and eaten as food: *steak and kidney pie* ➲ adjective **renal**

ˈ**kidney bean** *noun* [C] a type of reddish-brown BEAN shaped like a KIDNEY

kilim /kɪˈliːm; ˈkiːlɪm/ (*also* **kelim**) *noun* [C] a type of Turkish carpet or RUG

kill¹ ⊶ /kɪl/ *verb* **1** [I,T] to make sb/sth die: *Smoking kills.* ◇ *She was killed instantly in the crash.*

> **WHICH WORD?**
>
> **Murder** means to kill a person on purpose: *This was no accident. The old lady was murdered.* **Assassinate** means to kill for political reasons: *President Kennedy was assassinated.* **Slaughter** and **massacre** mean to kill a large number of people: *Hundreds of people were massacred when the army opened fire on the crowd.* **Slaughter** is also used of killing an animal for food.

2 [T] (*informal*) to cause sb pain; to hurt: *My feet are killing me.* **3** [T] to cause sth to end or fail: *The minister's opposition killed the idea stone dead.* **4** [T] (*spoken*) to be very angry with sb: *My mum will kill me when she sees this mess.* **5** [T] (*informal*) **~ yourself/sb** to make yourself/sb laugh a lot: *We were* ***killing ourselves laughing.***
IDM **kill time, an hour, etc.** to spend time doing sth that is not interesting or important while you are waiting for sth else to happen
kill two birds with one stone to do one thing which will achieve two results
PHR V **kill sth off** to cause sth to die or to not exist any more

kill² /kɪl/ *noun* [sing.] **1** the act of killing: *Lions often make a kill in the evening.* **2** an animal or animals that have been killed: *The eagle took the kill back to its young.*

killer /ˈkɪlə(r)/ *noun* [C] a person, animal or thing that kills: *a killer disease* ◇ *He's a dangerous killer who may strike again.*

killing ⊶ /ˈkɪlɪŋ/ *noun* [C] act of killing a person on purpose; a murder: *There have been a number of brutal killings in the area recently.*
IDM **make a killing** to make a large profit quickly

kiln /kɪln/ *noun* [C] a large oven for baking CLAY and bricks, drying wood and grain etc.

kilo ⊶ /ˈkiːləʊ/ (*also* **kilogram**; **kilogramme** /ˈkɪləɡræm/) *noun* [C] (*pl.* **kilos**) (*abbr.* **kg**) a measure of weight; 1000 grams

kilo- /ˈkɪləʊ/ *prefix* (used in nouns, often in units of measurement) one thousand: *kilometre* ◇ *kilogram*

kilobyte /ˈkɪləbaɪt/ *noun* [C] (*abbr.* **KB**; **Kb**) (COMPUTING) a unit of computer memory, equal to 1024 BYTES (=small units of information)

kilogram /ˈkɪləɡræm/ (*also* **kilogramme**; **kilo**) *noun* [C] (*abbr.* **kg**) a measure of weight; 1000 grams
ⓘ For more information about weights, look at the section on using numbers at the back of this dictionary.

kilohertz /ˈkɪləhɜːts/ *noun* [C] (*pl.* **kilohertz**) (*abbr.* **kHz**) (PHYSICS) (used in radio) a measure of FREQUENCY

kilojoule /ˈkɪlədʒuːl/ *noun* [C] (*abbr.* **kJ**) (SCIENCE) a measurement of the energy that you get from food; 1000 JOULES

kilometre ⊶ (*AmE* **kilometer**) /ˈkɪləmiːtə(r); kɪˈlɒmɪtə(r)/ *noun* [C] (*abbr.* **km**) a measure of length; 1000 metres

kilowatt /ˈkɪləwɒt/ *noun* [C] (*abbr.* **kW**) (PHYSICS) a unit for measuring electrical power; 1000 WATTS

kilt /kɪlt/ *noun* [C] a skirt with many folds (**pleats**) that is worn by men as part of the national dress of Scotland

kimono /kɪˈməʊnəʊ/ *noun* [C] (*pl.* **kimonos**) a traditional Japanese piece of clothing like a long dress with wide sleeves, worn on formal occasions

kin /kɪn/ → NEXT OF KIN

kind[1] /kaɪnd/ ***noun*** [C] a group whose members all have the same qualities: *The concert attracted people* ***of all kinds****. ◇ The concert attracted* ***all kinds of*** *people. ◇* ***What kind of*** *car have you got? ◇ Many kinds of plant and animal are being lost every year. ◇ In the evenings I listen to music, write letters, that* ***kind of thing****.* SYN **sort, type**

IDM **a kind of** (*informal*) used for describing sth in a way that is not very clear: *I had a kind of feeling that something would go wrong. ◇ There's a funny kind of smell in here.*

kind of (*informal*) slightly; a little bit: *I'm kind of worried about the interview.*

of a kind 1 the same: *The friends were two of a kind – very similar in so many ways.* **2** not as good as it could be: *You're making progress of a kind.*

kind[2] /kaɪnd/ ***adj.*** ~ **(to sb)**; ~ **(of sb) (to do sth)** caring about others; friendly and generous: *Everyone's been so kind to us since we came here! ◇ It was kind of you to offer, but I don't need any help.* OPP **unkind**

kindergarten /ˈkɪndəɡɑːtn/ ***noun*** [C] (EDUCATION) a school for very young children, aged from about 3 to 5 ➲ look at **nursery school**

ˌ**kind-ˈhearted** ***adj.*** kind and generous

kindly /ˈkaɪndli/ ***adv.***, ***adj.*** **1** in a kind way: *The nurse smiled kindly.* **2** (used for asking sb to do sth) please: *Would you kindly wait a moment?* **3** kind and friendly

kindness /ˈkaɪndnəs/ ***noun*** [C,U] the quality of being kind; a kind act: *Thank you very much for all your kindness.*

kinetic /kɪˈnetɪk/ ***adj.*** (PHYSICS) of or produced by movement: *kinetic energy* ➲ picture at **energy**

king /kɪŋ/ ***noun*** [C] **1** (POLITICS) (the title of) a man who rules a country. A king is usually the son or close relative of the former ruler: *The new king was crowned yesterday in Westminster Abbey. ◇ King Edward VII* (=the seventh) ◇ (*figurative*) *The lion is the king of the jungle.* ➲ look at **queen**, **prince**, **princess 2** one of the four playing cards in a pack with a picture of a king: *the king of spades* **3** the most important piece in the game of CHESS that can move one square in any direction

kingdom /ˈkɪŋdəm/ ***noun*** [C] **1** (POLITICS) a country that is ruled by a king or queen: *the United Kingdom* **2** (BIOLOGY) one of the five major groups into which all living things are organized, larger than a CLASS or a PHYLUM: *the animal kingdom* ➲ picture on **page 29**

kingfisher /ˈkɪŋfɪʃə(r)/ ***noun*** [C] a small bright blue bird with a long beak, that catches fish in rivers

ˈ**king-size** (also ˈ**king-sized**) ***adj.*** bigger than usual: *a king-size bed*

kink /kɪŋk/ ***noun*** [C] a turn or bend in sth that should be straight

kiosk /ˈkiːɒsk/ ***noun*** [C] a very small building in the street where newspapers, sweets, cigarettes, etc. are sold

kip /kɪp/ ***verb*** [I] (**kipping**; **kipped**) (*BrE, slang*) to sleep: *You could kip on the sofa if you like.*
▶ **kip** ***noun*** [sing., U]: *I'm going to have a kip. ◇ I didn't get much kip last night.*

kipper /ˈkɪpə(r)/ ***noun*** [C] a type of fish that has been kept for a long time in salt, and then smoked

kiss /kɪs/ ***verb*** [I,T] to touch sb with your lips to show love or friendship: *He kissed her on the cheek. ◇ They kissed each other goodbye.* ▶ **kiss** ***noun*** [C]: *a kiss on the lips/cheek*

kit[1] /kɪt/ ***noun*** **1** [C,U] a set of tools, equipment or clothes that you need for a particular purpose, sport or activity: *a tool kit ◇ a drum kit ◇ football/gym kit* **2** [C] a set of parts that you buy and put together in order to make sth: *a kit for a model aeroplane*

kit[2] /kɪt/ ***verb*** (**kitting**; **kitted**)

PHR V **kit sb/yourself out/up (in/with sth)** to give sb all the necessary clothes, equipment, tools, etc. for sth

kitchen /ˈkɪtʃɪn/ ***noun*** [C] a room where food is prepared and cooked: *We usually eat in the kitchen.*

kite /kaɪt/ ***noun*** [C] a toy which consists of a light frame covered with paper or cloth. **Kites** are flown in the wind on the end of a long piece of string: *to fly a kite*

kitsch /kɪtʃ/ ***noun*** [U] works of art or objects that are popular but that are considered to have no real artistic value and to be lacking in good taste, for example because they are SENTIMENTAL

kitten /ˈkɪtn/ ***noun*** [C] a young cat

kitty /ˈkɪti/ ***noun*** [C] (*pl.* **kitties**) **1** a sum of money that is collected from a group of people and used for a particular purpose: *All the students in the flat put £5 a week into the kitty.* **2** (*spoken*) a way of calling or referring to a cat

kiwi /ˈkiːwiː/ ***noun*** [C] (*pl.* **kiwis**) **1** a New Zealand bird with a long beak and short wings that cannot fly **2** (*also* ˈ**kiwi fruit**) a fruit with brown skin that is green inside with black seeds

kJ ***abbr.*** kilojoule(s)

km ***abbr.*** kilometre(s)

knack /næk/ ***noun*** [sing.] (*informal*) ~ **(of/for doing sth)** skill or ability to do sth (difficult) that you have naturally or you can learn: *Knitting isn't difficult once you've got the knack of it.*

knead /niːd/ ***verb*** [T] to press and squeeze a mixture of flour and water (**dough**) with your hands in order to make bread, etc.

knee /niː/ ***noun*** [C] **1** the place where your leg bends in the middle: *Angie fell and grazed her knee. ◇ She was* ***on her hands and knees*** *on the floor looking for her earrings. ◇ Come and sit on my knee.* ➲ picture on **page 80 2** the part of a pair of trousers, etc. that covers the knee: *There's a hole in the knee of those jeans.*

IDM **bring sth to its knees** to badly affect an organization, etc. so that it can no longer function: *The strikes brought the industry to its knees.*

kneecap /ˈniːkæp/ ***noun*** [C] (ANATOMY) the bone that covers the front of the knee SYN **patella** ➲ picture on **page 80**

ˈ**knee-deep** ***adj.***, ***adv.*** up to your knees: *The water was knee-deep in places.*

kneel /niːl/ ***verb*** [I] (*pt, pp* **knelt** /nelt/ or **kneeled**) ~ **(down)** to rest on one or both knees: *She knelt down to talk to the child.*

knew past tense of **know[1]**

knickers /ˈnɪkəz/ (*especially AmE* **panties**) ***noun*** [pl.] a piece of underwear for women that covers the area between the waist and the top of the legs: *a pair of knickers*

knife[1] /naɪf/ ***noun*** [C] (*pl.* **knives** /naɪvz/) a sharp flat piece of metal (**a blade**) with a handle. A knife is used for cutting things or as a weapon: *The* *carving knife is very blunt/sharp.* ◇ *a knife and fork* ◇ *a penknife/pocket knife/flick knife*

knife² /naɪf/ ***verb*** [T] to deliberately injure sb with a knife **SYN** **stab**

knight /naɪt/ ***noun*** [C] **1** a man who has been given a title of honour by a king or queen for good work he has done and who can use *Sir* in front of his name **2** (HISTORY) a soldier of a high level who fought on a horse in the Middle Ages **3** a piece used in the game of CHESS that is shaped like a horse's head
▶ **knighthood** /ˈnaɪthʊd/ ***noun*** [C,U]

knit /nɪt/ ***verb*** [I,T] (**knitting**; **knitted** or (*AmE*) *pt, pp* **knit**) **1** to make sth (for example an article of clothing) with wool using two long needles or a special machine: *I'm knitting a sweater for my nephew.* ➲ look at **crochet 2 knit** (only used in this form) joined closely together: *a **closely/tightly knit** village community*

knitting /ˈnɪtɪŋ/ ***noun*** [U] **1** an item that is being knitted: *Where's my knitting?* **2** the activity of knitting: *I usually do some knitting while I'm watching TV.*

ˈ**knitting needle** = NEEDLE (2)

knitwear /ˈnɪtweə(r)/ ***noun*** [U] articles of clothing that have been knitted: *the knitwear department*

knob /nɒb/ ***noun*** [C] **1** a round switch on a machine (for example a television) that you press or turn: *the volume control knob* **2** a round handle on a door, drawer, etc.

knock¹ /nɒk/ ***verb*** **1** [I] ~ **(at/on sth)** to make a noise by hitting sth firmly with your hand: *Someone is knocking at the door.* ◇ *I knocked on the window but she didn't hear me.* **2** [T] ~ **sth (on/against sth)** to hit sb/sth hard, often by accident: *He knocked the vase onto the floor.* ◇ *Be careful not to knock your head on the shelf when you get up.* ◇ *to knock sb unconscious* **3** [T] (*informal*) to say bad things about sb/sth; to criticize sb/sth

IDM **knock on wood** → WOOD

PHR V **knock about/around** (*informal*) to be in a place; to travel and live in various places: *Is last week's newspaper still knocking about?*
knock sb down to hit sb causing them to fall to the ground: *The old lady was knocked down by a cyclist.*
knock sth down to destroy a building, etc.: *They knocked down the old factory because it was unsafe.*
knock off (sth) (*spoken*) to stop working: *What time do you knock off?*
knock sth off 1 (*informal*) to reduce a price by a certain amount: *He agreed to knock £10 off the price.* **2** (*slang*) to steal sth
knock sb out 1 to hit sb so that they become unconscious or cannot get up again for a while **2** (used about a drug, alcohol, etc.) to cause sb to sleep
knock sb out (of sth) (SPORT) to beat a person or team in a competition so that they do not play any more games in it: *Belgium was knocked out of the European Cup by France.*
knock sb/sth over to cause sb/sth to fall over: *Be careful not to knock over the drinks.*

knock² /nɒk/ ***noun*** [C] a sharp hit from sth hard or the sound it makes: *a nasty knock on the head* ◇ *I thought I heard a knock at the door.* ◇ (*figurative*) *She has suffered some hard knocks* (= bad experiences) *in her life.*

knocker /ˈnɒkə(r)/ ***noun*** [C] a piece of metal fixed to the outside of a door that you hit against the door to attract attention

ˈ**knock-on** ***adj.*** (*especially BrE*) causing other events to happen one after the other: *An increase in the price of oil has **a knock-on effect** on other fuels.*

knockout /ˈnɒkaʊt/ ***noun*** [C] **1** a hard hit that causes sb to become unconscious or to be unable to get up again for a while **2** (*especially BrE*) (SPORT) a competition in which the winner of each game goes on to the next part but the person who loses plays no more games

knot¹ /nɒt/ ***noun*** [C] **1** a place where two ends or pieces of rope, string, etc. have been tied together: *to tie/untie a knot* **2** a measure of the speed of a ship; approximately 1.8 kilometres per hour **3** a hard round spot in a piece of wood where there was once a branch

knot² /nɒt/ ***verb*** [T] (**knotting**; **knotted**) to fasten sth together with a knot

know¹ /nəʊ/ ***verb*** (*pt* **knew** /njuː/; *pp* **known** /nəʊn/) (not used in the continuous tenses) **1** [I,T] ~ **(about sth)**; ~ **that...** to have knowledge or information in your mind: *I don't know much about sport.* ◇ *Do you know where this bus stops?* ◇ *Do you know their telephone number?* ◇ *'You've got a flat tyre.' 'I know.'* ◇ *Do you **know the way** to the restaurant?* ◇ *Knowing Katie, she'll be out with her friends.* **2** [T] to be familiar with a person or a place; to have met sb or been somewhere before: *We've known each other for years.* ◇ *I don't know this part of London well.* **3** [T,I] to feel certain; to be sure of sth: *I just know you'll pass the exam!* ◇ ***As far as I know*** (= I think it is true but I am not absolutely sure), *the meeting is next Monday afternoon.* **4** [T] (only in the past and perfect tenses) to have seen, heard, or experienced sth: *I've known him go a whole day without eating.* ◇ *It's been known to snow in June.* **5** [T] (often passive) ~ **sb/sth as sth** to give sth a particular name; to recognize sb/sth as sth: *Istanbul was previously known as Constantinople.* **6** [T] ~ **how to do sth** to have learned sth and be able to do it: *Do you know how to use a computer?* **7** [T] to have personal experience of sth: *Many people in western countries don't know what it's like to be hungry.*

IDM **God/goodness/Heaven knows 1** I do not know: *They've ordered a new car but goodness knows how they're going to pay for it.* **2** used for emphasizing sth: *I hope I get an answer soon. Goodness knows, I've waited long enough.*
know better (than that/than to do sth) to have enough sense to realize that you should not do sth
know sth inside out/like the back of your hand (*informal*) to be very familiar with sth
know what you are talking about (*informal*) to have knowledge of sth from your own experience
know what's what (*informal*) to have all the important information about sth; to fully understand sth
let sb know to tell sb; to inform sb about sth: *Could you let me know what time you're arriving?*
you know used when the speaker is thinking of what to say next, or to remind sb of sth: *Well, you know, it's rather difficult to explain.* ◇ *I've just met Marta. You know – Jim's ex-wife.*
you never know (*spoken*) you cannot be certain: *Keep those empty boxes. You never know, they might come in handy one day.*

PHR V **know of sb/sth** to have information about or experience of sb/sth: *Do you know of any pubs around here that serve food?*

know² /nəʊ/ ***noun***

IDM **in the know** (*informal*) having information that other people do not

ˈ**know-all** (*AmE* ˈ**know-it-all**) ***noun*** [C] an annoying person who behaves as if they know everything

'know-how *noun* [U] (*informal*) practical knowledge of or skill in sth

knowing /'nəʊɪŋ/ *adj.* showing that you know about sth that is thought to be secret: *a knowing look*

knowingly /'nəʊɪŋli/ *adv.* **1** on purpose; deliberately: *I've never knowingly lied to you.* **2** in a way that shows that you know about sth that is thought to be secret: *He smiled knowingly at her.*

knowledge /'nɒlɪdʒ/ *noun* **1** [U, sing.] ~ (of/about sth) information, understanding and skills that you have gained through learning or experience: *I have **a working knowledge** of French* (=enough to be able to make myself understood). **2** [U] the state of knowing about a particular fact or situation: ***To my knowledge*** (=from the information I have, although I may not know everything) *they are still living there.* ◇ *She did it **without my knowledge*** (=I did not know about it).

IDM **be common/public knowledge** to be sth that everyone knows

knowledgeable /'nɒlɪdʒəbl/ *adj.* having a lot of knowledge: *She's very knowledgeable about history.* ▶ **knowledgeably** /-əbli/ *adv.*

knuckle /'nʌkl/ *noun* [C] (ANATOMY) any of the joints in the fingers, especially those connecting the fingers to the rest of the hand ➲ picture on **page 80**

koala /kəʊ'ɑːlə/ *noun* [C] an Australian animal with thick grey fur that lives in trees and looks like a small bear ➲ picture on **page 29**

the Koran (also **Quran, Qur'an**) /kə'rɑːn/ *noun* [sing.] (RELIGION) the most important book in the Islamic religion

kosher /'kəʊʃə(r)/ *adj.* (used about food) prepared according to the rules of Jewish law

kph /ˌkeɪ piː 'eɪtʃ/ *abbr.* kilometres per hour

krill /krɪl/ *noun* [pl.] very small SHELLFISH that live in the sea around the Antarctic and are eaten by WHALES

krypton /'krɪptɒn/ *noun* [U] (*symbol* **Kr**) (CHEMISTRY) a colourless gas that does not react with chemicals, used in FLUORESCENT lights ❶ **Krypton** is a **noble gas.** ❶ For more information on the periodic table of elements, look at page R34.

kung fu /ˌkʌŋ 'fuː/ *noun* [U] (SPORT) a Chinese style of fighting using the feet and hands as weapons ➲ look at **martial arts**

kW (*also* **kw**) *abbr.* (PHYSICS) kilowatt(s): *a 2kw electric heater*

L l

L, l¹ /el/ *noun* [C,U] (*pl.* **L's; l's** /elz/) the twelfth letter of the English alphabet: *'Lake' begins with (an) 'L'.*

l² *abbr.* **1 l** litre(s) **2** (*BrE*) **L** (on a sign on a car) learner driver **3 L** large (size)

Lab *abbr.* (POLITICS) (in British politics) Labour

lab /læb/ *noun* [C] (*informal*) = LABORATORY: *science labs* ◇ *a lab technician* ◇ *a lab coat* (=a white coat worn by scientists, etc. working in a laboratory)

label¹ AW /'leɪbl/ *noun* [C] **1** a piece of paper, etc. that is fixed to sth and which gives information about it: *There is a list of all the ingredients on the label.* **2 record label** (MUSIC) a company that produces and sells records, CDs, etc.

laboratory apparatus

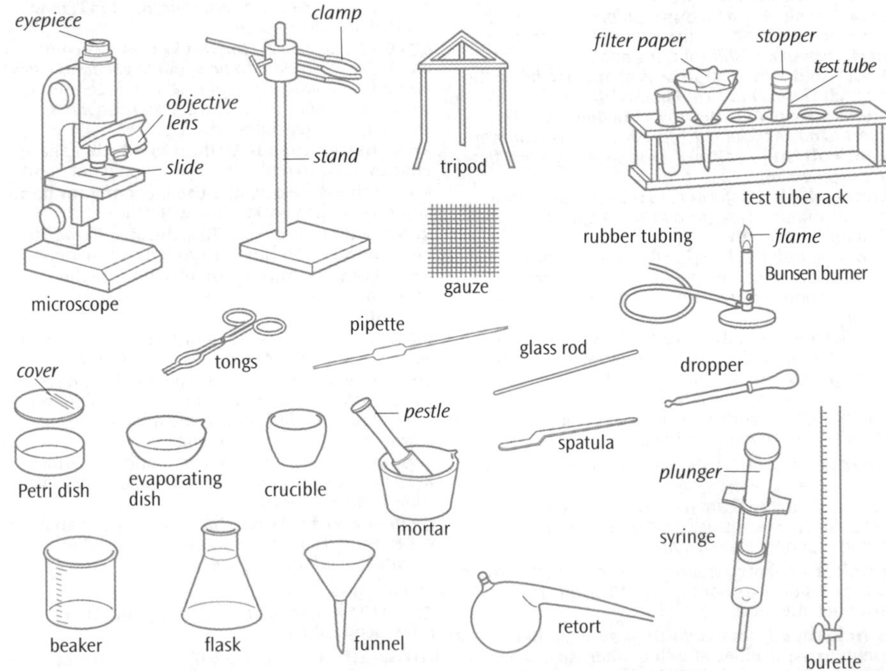

label² ⊷ AW /ˈleɪbl/ *verb* [T] (**labelling**; **labelled**: *AmE* **labeling**; **labeled**) **1** (usually passive) to fix a label or write information on sth **2** ~ **sb/sth (as) sth** to describe sb/sth in a particular way, especially unfairly

laboratory ⊷ /ləˈbɒrətri/ *noun* [C] (*pl.* **laboratories**) (also *informal* **lab**) (SCIENCE, EDUCATION) a room or building that is used for scientific research, testing, experiments, etc. or for teaching about science: *The blood samples were sent to the laboratory for analysis.* ◇ *a physics laboratory* ➲ look at **language laboratory**

laborious /ləˈbɔːriəs/ *adj.* needing a lot of time and effort: *a laborious task/process/job* ▶ **laboriously** *adv.*

labour¹ ⊷ AW (*AmE* **labor**) /ˈleɪbə(r)/ *noun* **1** [U] work, usually of a hard, physical kind: *manual labour* (=work using your hands) **2** [U] (ECONOMICS) workers, when thought of as a group: *There is a shortage of skilled labour.* **3** [U, C, usually sing.] (HEALTH) the process of giving birth to a baby: *She **went into labour** in the early hours of this morning.* ◇ *She was **in labour** for ten hours.*

labour² AW (*AmE* **labor**) /ˈleɪbə(r)/ *verb* [I] **1** ~ **(away)** to work hard at sth: *She laboured on her book for two years.* **2** to move or do sth with difficulty and effort

laboured AW (*AmE* **labored**) /ˈleɪbəd/ *adj.* done slowly or with difficulty: *laboured breathing*

labourer (*AmE* **laborer**) /ˈleɪbərə(r)/ *noun* [C] a person whose job involves hard physical work: *unskilled/farm labourers*

ˌlabour-inˈtensive (*AmE* **labor-intensive**) *adj.* (BUSINESS) (used about work) needing a lot of people to do it: *labour-intensive methods*

the ˈLabour Party (*also* **Labour**) *noun* [sing., with sing. or pl. verb] (POLITICS) one of the main political parties in Britain. The Labour Party supports the interests of working people: *He has always voted Labour.* ◇ *a Labour MP* ➲ look at **the Conservative Party**, **the Liberal Democrats**

ˈlabour-saving *adj.* reducing the amount of work needed to do sth: *labour-saving devices such as washing machines and dishwashers*

labyrinth /ˈlæbərɪnθ/ *noun* [C] a complicated set of paths and passages, through which it is difficult to find your way: *a labyrinth of corridors* SYN **maze**

lace¹ /leɪs/ *noun* **1** [U] a delicate material that is made from very thin threads that make a pattern of small holes: *lace curtains* ◇ *a collar made of lace* ➲ adjective **lacy** **2** [C] a string that is used for tying a shoe: *Your shoelace is undone.* ◇ *Do up your laces or you'll trip over them.*

lace² /leɪs/ *verb* [I,T] ~ **(sth) (up)** to tie or fasten sth with a **lace¹**(2): *She was sitting on the end of the bed lacing up her boots.* ▶ **lace-up** *adj.*, *noun* [C]: *lace-up boots/shoes*

lack¹ ⊷ /læk/ *noun* [U, sing.] (a) ~ **(of sth)** the state of not having sth or not having enough of sth: *A lack of food forced many people to leave their homes.*

lack² ⊷ /læk/ *verb* [T] to have none or not enough of sth: *She seems to lack the will to succeed.*

lacking ⊷ /ˈlækɪŋ/ *adj.* (not *before* a noun) **1** ~ **in sth** not having enough of sth: *He's certainly not lacking in intelligence.* **2** not present or available: *I feel there is something lacking in my life.*

lacklustre (*AmE* **lackluster**) /ˈlæklʌstə(r)/ *adj.* not interesting or exciting; dull: *a lacklustre performance*

laconic /ləˈkɒnɪk/ *adj.* (*formal*) using only a few words to say sth ▶ **laconically** /-kli/ *adv.*

lacquer /ˈlækə(r)/ *noun* [U] **1** a type of transparent paint that is put on wood, metal, etc. to give it a hard, shiny surface **2** (*old fashioned*) a liquid that you put on your hair to keep it in place SYN **hairspray**

lactate /lækˈteɪt/ *verb* [I] (BIOLOGY) (of a woman or female animal) to produce milk from the body to feed a baby or young animal ▶ **lactation** /lækˈteɪʃn/ *noun* [U]: *the period of lactation*

lactic acid /ˌlæktɪk ˈæsɪd/ *noun* [U] (BIOLOGY) a substance that forms in old milk and is also produced in your muscles when you do hard physical exercise

lactose /ˈlæktəʊs/ *noun* [U] (BIOLOGY) a type of sugar found in milk and used in some baby foods ➲ look at **dextrose**, **fructose**, **glucose**, **sucrose**

lacy /ˈleɪsi/ *adj.* made of or looking like LACE (=material made of thin threads with small holes to form a pattern)

lad /læd/ *noun* [C] (*informal*) a boy or young man: *School has changed since I was a lad.*

ladder /ˈlædə(r)/ *noun* [C] **1** a piece of equipment that is used for climbing up sth. A **ladder** consists of two long pieces of metal, wood or rope with steps fixed between them: (*figurative*) *to climb the ladder of success* ➲ look at **stepladder** **2** (*AmE* **run**) a long hole in TIGHTS or STOCKINGS (=the thin pieces of clothing that women wear to cover their legs), where the threads have broken: *Oh no! I've got a ladder in my tights.* ▶ **ladder** *verb* [I,T]

laden /ˈleɪdn/ *adj.* ~ **(with sth)** (not *before* a noun) having or carrying a lot of sth: *The travellers were laden down with luggage.* ◇ *The orange trees were laden with fruit.*

the ˈLadies *noun* [sing.] (*BrE*, *informal*) a public toilet for women

ladle¹ /ˈleɪdl/ *noun* [C] a large deep spoon with a long handle, used especially for serving soup

ladle² /ˈleɪdl/ *verb* [T] to serve food with a **ladle**

lady ⊷ /ˈleɪdi/ *noun* [C] (*pl.* **ladies**) **1** a polite way of saying 'woman', especially when you are referring to an older woman: *The old lady next door lives alone.* **2** (*formal*) used when speaking to or about a woman or women in a polite way: ***Ladies and gentlemen!*** (=at the beginning of a speech) ◇ *Mrs Flinn, there's a lady here to see you.* **3** a title that is used before the name of a woman who has a high social position: *Lady Elizabeth Groves* ➲ look at **Lord**

ladybird /ˈleɪdibɜːd/ (*AmE* **ladybug** /ˈleɪdibʌg/) *noun* [C] a small insect that is red or yellow with black spots ➲ picture on **page 29**

lag¹ /læg/ *verb* [I] (**lagging**; **lagged**) ~ **(behind) (sb/sth)** to move or develop more slowly than sb/sth

lag² /læg/ (also **ˈtime lag**) *noun* [C] a period of time between two events; a delay ➲ look at **jet lag**

lager /ˈlɑːgə(r)/ *noun* [C,U] (*BrE*) a type of light beer that is a gold colour: *Three pints of lager, please.*

lagoon /ləˈguːn/ *noun* [C] (GEOGRAPHY) a lake of salt water that is separated from the sea by sand or rock

laid past tense, past participle of **lay¹**

laid-back /ˌleɪd ˈbæk/ *adj.* (*informal*) calm and relaxed; seeming not to worry about anything

lain past participle of **lie²**

laissez-faire /ˌleseɪ ˈfeə(r)/ ***noun*** [U] (POLITICS) the policy of allowing private businesses to develop without government control ▶ **laissez-faire** ***adj.***: *a laissez-faire economy* ◇ *They have a laissez-faire approach to bringing up their children* (=they give them a lot of freedom).

lake 🔑 /leɪk/ ***noun*** [C] (GEOGRAPHY) a large area of water that is surrounded by land: *They've gone sailing **on the lake**.* ◇ *We all swam **in the lake**.* ◇ *Lake Constance* ➲ picture at **oxbow**

lamb /læm/ ***noun*** **1** [C] a young sheep ➲ note at **sheep** ➲ picture at **sheep** **2** [U] the meat of a young sheep: *lamb chops* ➲ note at **meat**

lame /leɪm/ ***adj.*** **1** (used mainly about animals) not able to walk properly because of an injury to the leg or foot: *The horse is lame and cannot work.* **2** (used about an excuse, argument, etc.) not easily believed; weak

lament /ləˈment/ ***noun*** [C] (*formal*) (LITERATURE, MUSIC) a song, poem or other expression of sadness for sb who has died or for sth that has ended ▶ **lament** ***verb*** [T]

laminate /ˈlæmɪnət/ ***noun*** [U,C] a material that is LAMINATED

laminated /ˈlæmɪneɪtɪd/ ***adj.*** **1** (used about wood, plastic, etc.) made by sticking several thin layers together: *laminated glass* **2** covered with thin transparent plastic for protection

lamp 🔑 /læmp/ ***noun*** [C] a device that uses electricity, gas or oil to produce light: *a street lamp* ◇ *a table/desk/bicycle lamp* ◇ *a sunlamp*

ˈ**lamp post** ***noun*** [C] a tall pole at the side of the road with a light on the top

lampshade /ˈlæmpʃeɪd/ ***noun*** [C] a cover for a lamp that makes it look more attractive and makes the light softer

LAN /læn/ ***abbr.*** (COMPUTING) local area network (a system for communicating by computer within a large building) ➲ look at **WAN**

lance¹ /lɑːns/ ***noun*** [C] (HISTORY) a weapon with a long wooden handle and a pointed metal end that was used by people fighting on horses in the past

lance² /lɑːns/ ***verb*** [T] (HEALTH) to cut open an infected place on sb's body with a sharp knife in order to let out the PUS (=a yellow substance produced by infection): *to lance an abscess*

land¹ 🔑 /lænd/ ***noun*** **1** [U] the solid part of the surface of the earth (=not sea): *Penguins can't move very fast **on land**.* ➲ note at **ground** OPP **sea** **2** [U] (GEOGRAPHY) an area of ground: *The land rose to the east.* ◇ *She owns 500 acres of land in Scotland.* **3** [U] (AGRICULTURE) ground, soil or earth of a particular kind: *The land is rich and fertile.* ◇ *arid/barren land* ◇ *arable/agricultural/industrial land* **4** [C] (*written*) a country or region: *She died far from her native land.* ◇ *to travel to distant lands* ➲ note at **country**

land² 🔑 /lænd/ ***verb*** **1** [I,T] to come down from the air or to bring sth down to the ground: *The bird landed on the roof.* ◇ *He fell off the ladder and landed on his back.* ◇ *The pilot landed the aeroplane safely.* ◇ *His flight is due to land at 3 o'clock.* **2** [I,T] to go onto land or put sth onto land from a ship **3** [T] to succeed in getting sth, especially sth that a lot of people want: *The company has just landed a million-dollar contract.*

IDM **fall/land on your feet** → FOOT¹

PHR V **land up (in...)** (*BrE, informal*) to finish in a certain position or situation: *He landed up in a prison cell for the night.*

land sb with sb/sth (*informal*) to give sb sth unpleasant to do, especially because no one else wants to do it

landfill /ˈlændfɪl/ ***noun*** (ENVIRONMENT) **1** [C,U] an area of land where large amounts of waste material are buried **2** [U] waste material that will be buried; the burying of waste material

landform /ˈlændfɔːm/ ***noun*** [C] (GEOGRAPHY) a natural feature of the earth's surface

landholding /ˈlændhəʊldɪŋ/ ***noun*** [C,U] (TECHNICAL) a piece of land that sb owns or rents; the fact of owning or renting land: *a map of tribal landholdings* ▶ **landholder** ***noun*** [C]: *farmers and landholders*

landing /ˈlændɪŋ/ ***noun*** [C] **1** the action of coming down onto the ground (in an aircraft): *The plane made an **emergency landing** in a field.* ◇ *a crash landing* ◇ *a safe landing* OPP **take-off** **2** the area at the top of a STAIRCASE in a house, or between one STAIRCASE and another in a large building

ˈ**landing card** ***noun*** [C] (TOURISM) a form on which you have to write details about yourself when flying to a foreign country

ˈ**landing gear** ***noun*** [U] =UNDERCARRIAGE ➲ picture at **plane**

ˈ**landing stage** (*AmE* **dock**) ***noun*** [C] a wooden platform built out into the sea or a river where boats are tied and where people can get on or off them SYN **jetty**

ˈ**landing strip** =AIRSTRIP

landlady /ˈlændleɪdi/ ***noun*** [C] (*pl.* **landladies**) **1** a woman who rents a house or room to people for money **2** a woman who owns or manages a pub, small hotel, etc.

landless /ˈlændləs/ ***adj.*** (AGRICULTURE) not owning land for farming; not allowed to own land

landline /ˈlændlaɪn/ ***noun*** [C] a telephone connection that uses wires carried on poles or under the ground, in contrast to a mobile phone: *I'll call you later on your landline.* ➲ note at **telephone**

landlocked /ˈlændlɒkt/ ***adj.*** (GEOGRAPHY) completely surrounded by land

landlord /ˈlændlɔːd/ ***noun*** [C] **1** a person who rents a house or room to people for money **2** a person who owns or manages a pub, small hotel, etc.

landmark /ˈlændmɑːk/ ***noun*** [C] **1** an object (often a building) that can be seen easily from a distance and will help you to recognize where you are: *Big Ben is one of the landmarks on London's skyline.* **2** **a ~ (in sth)** an important stage or change in the development of sth

ˈ**land mass** ***noun*** [C] (GEOGRAPHY) a large area of land, for example a continent

landmine /ˈlændmaɪn/ ***noun*** [C] a bomb placed on or under the ground, which explodes when vehicles or people move over it

landowner /ˈlændəʊnə(r)/ ***noun*** [C] (SOCIAL STUDIES) a person who owns land, especially a large area of land

landscape¹ 🔑 /ˈlændskeɪp/ ***noun*** **1** [C, usually sing.] everything you can see when you look across a large area of land: *an urban/industrial landscape* **2** [C,U] (ART) a picture or a painting that shows a view of the countryside; this style of painting

landscape² /ˈlændskeɪp/ ***verb*** [T] to improve the appearance of an area of land by changing its design and planting trees, flowers, etc.

REFERENCE PAGES

Contents

Using your dictionary for Content and Language Integrated Learning
(= using English to study other subjects)

EXERCISE 1

Mind Maps

A Spidergrams (= a diagram in the shape of a spider)
Find the word **bulb**. Look at the illustration and make a spidergram of eight words belonging to the bulb family. Do it like this:

i Draw two or three more spidergrams for any of these words, using the illustrations in the dictionary to help you:

ecosystems	**lights**	**clouds**	**erosion**
ear	**limestone landscape**	**cereal**	**digestive system**
heart	**brain**	**earth**	**flower**
plane	**atmosphere**	**cell**	**building materials**

ii Always make a spidergram for a new word/concept in your text book, whatever subject you are studying.

B Concept Maps
Look up the word **body** and make a concept map like the one below, putting the information into four categories. Now do the same for **plate tectonics**.

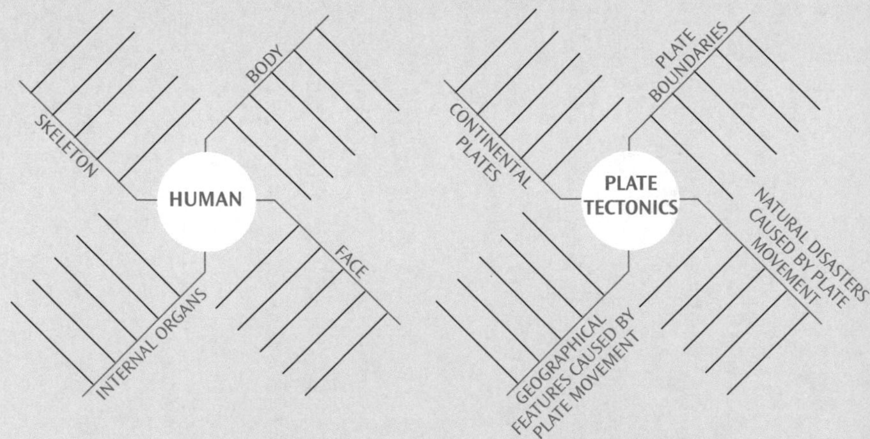

i Do the same with any complex concepts you are studying in your text book.

EXERCISE 2

Categorization

i Look up **laboratory** and find the illustration **laboratory apparatus**. Make a diagram and divide the list of items into two categories.

LABORATORY APPARATUS	
Containers	*Non-containers*

ii Do the same with the following words:

agricultural tools (divide into *for cutting, for digging, other*)
building materials (divide into *natural* and *man-made*)
health (divide into *on the body* and *in the body*)
musical instruments (divide into *stringed, woodwind, brass* and *percussion*)
insects (divide into *winged* and *non-winged*)
sports equipment (divide into *team sports* and *other*)

EXERCISE 3

Explaining a process

Look up these words and find the accompanying illustration. Use the picture to write a paragraph explaining in detail the process associated with each of these words or phrases. Use complete sentences. The **Collocations and Patterns** note at **water cycle** will also help you.

generator	**energy resources**	**water cycle**	**circulation**
rock cycle	**carbon cycle**	**reflection**	**digestive system**

EXERCISE 4

Extending your vocabulary

Go to the note at **law court** and find examples of
a vocabulary specific to the subject **b** collocations

Subject	*Vocabulary*	*Collocations*
Law courts	case	is tried
	judge	passes sentence
	trial	await trial
		trial by jury
	jury	trial by jury
		returns a verdict
	evidence	comes to light
		to give evidence
	the accused	is guilty/not guilty
	verdict	to overturn /quash the verdict
		to return a verdict
	sentence	pass sentence
		carry a sentence
		be sentenced to

Now do the same exercise with the **Collocations and Patterns** notes at the following entries:

art (works of art)	**crime**	**medical** (medical practitioners)
jobs	**currency**	**religion**
study (studying and exams)	**measure**	**disasters**

EXERCISE 5

Parts of Speech

Look at a text you have studied recently, and choose six or seven important verbs from the text. List them in the box below and use your dictionary to find out if they have adjectives and nouns which are similar in form. You may find some words do not have both forms.

Text: Add Title here

	Verb (v)	Adjective (adj)	Noun (n)
1	pollute	polluted	pollution
2	______	______	______
3	______	______	______
4	______	______	______
5	______	______	______
6	______	______	______
7	______	______	______

EXERCISE 6

Acronyms and abbreviations

What do the following acronyms/abbreviations stand for and into which subject area do they go? Find more acronyms for your subject. Write them down with their meanings.

GNP	BBC	WAP
BC	CD	VDU
FAQ	UFO	WHO
CIA	MD	NASA
DIY	VIP	HGV
ISP	EU	CCTV

Acronyms and abbreviations

Short form	Full form	Subject
GNP	Gross National Product	economics
BC	______	______
______	______	______
______	______	______
______	______	______
______	______	______
______	______	______

EXERCISE 7

Abbreviations

Find these words and write them out with their abbreviation next to them:

Celsius	gigabyte	litre	senior
centimetre	gramme	milligram	sergeant
Fahrenheit	hertz	Newton	third
February	inches	pound	tuberculosis
for example	kilo	road	yard

EXERCISE 8

Animal Information

Look at the list of animals below and fill in the boxes with as much information as you can find. The first one has been done for you.

ANIMAL	MALE	FEMALE	YOUNG	SOUND	GROUP NAME	MEAT
cow	*bull*	*cow*	*heifer*	*moo*	*cattle/herd*	*beef*
sheep						
goat						
chicken						
pig						
horse						

EXERCISE 9

Understanding comparisons from diagrams

Look up the following words/phrases and find the diagram or illustration to go with it. Draw the illustration in your notebook and explain the differences between the concepts in your own words:

1 **Capital** (ARCHITECTURE)
What's the difference between Doric, Corinthian and Ionic?

2 **Diffract** and **diffuse**
What's the difference between diffraction and diffusion?

3 **Cell**
What's the difference between an animal cell and a plant cell?

4 **Short-sighted** and **long-sighted**
What's the difference?

5 **Shadow**
What's the difference between eclipse, partial eclipse and no eclipse?

Reading test 1

The coral reefs of Agatti Island

A Agatti is one of the Lakshadweep Islands off the south- west coast of India. These islands are surrounded by lagoons and coral reefs which are in turn surrounded by the open ocean. Coral reefs, which are formed from the skeletons of minute sea creatures, give shelter to a variety of plants and animals, and therefore have the potential to provide a stream of diverse benefits to the inhabitants of Agatti Island.

B In the first place, reefs provide food and other products for consumption by islanders themselves. Foods include different types of fish, octopus and molluscs, and in the case of poorer families these constitute as much as 90% of the protein they consume. Reef resources are also used for medicinal purposes. For example, the money cowrie, a shell known locally as *Vallakavadi*, is commonly made into a paste and used as a home remedy to treat cysts in the eye.

C In addition, the reef contributes to income generation. According to a recent survey, 20% of the households on Agatti report lagoon fishing, or shingle, mollusc, octopus and cowrie collection as their main occupation (Hoon et al, 2002). For poor households, the direct contribution of the reef to their financial resources is significant: 12% of poor households are completely dependent on the reef for their household income, while 59% of poor households rely on the reef for 70% of their household income, and the remaining 29% for 50% of their household income.

D Bartering of reef resources also commonly takes place, both between islanders and between islands. For example, Agatti Island is known for its abundance of octopus, and this is often used to obtain products from nearby Androth Island. Locally, reef products may be given to islanders in return for favours, such as help in constructing a house or net mending, or for other products such as rice, coconuts or fish.

E The investment required to exploit the reefs is minimal. It involves simple, locally available tools and equipment, some of which can be used without a boat, such as the fishing practice known as *Kat moodsal.* This is carried out in the shallow eastern lagoon of Agatti by children and adults, close to shore at low tide, throughout the year. A small cast net, a leaf bag and plastic slippers are all that are required and the activity can yield 10–12 small fish (approximately 1kg) for household consumption. Cast nets are not expensive and all the households in Agatti own at least one. Even the boats, which operate in the lagoon and near-shore reef, are constructed locally and have low running costs. They are either small, non-mechanized, traditional wooden rowing boats, known as *Thonis*, or rafts, known as *Tharappam.*

F During more than 400 years of occupation and survival, the Agatti islanders have developed an intimate knowledge of the reefs. They have knowledge of numerous different types of fish and where they can be found according to the tide or lunar cycle. They have also developed a local naming system or folk taxonomy, naming fish according to their shape. Sometimes the same species is given different names depending on its size and age. For example, a full grown Emperor fish is called *Metti* and a juvenile is called *Killokam.* The abundance of each species at different fishing grounds is also well known. Along with this knowledge of reef resources, the islanders have developed a wide range of skills and techniques for exploiting them. A multitude of different fishing techniques are still used by the islanders, each targeting different areas of the reef and particular species.

G The reef plays an important role in the social lives of the islanders too, being an integral part of traditions and rituals. Most of the island's folklore revolves around the reef and sea. There is hardly any tale or song which does not mention the traditional sailing crafts, known as *Odams*, the journeys of enterprising 'heroes', the adventures of sea fishing and encounters with sea creatures. Songs that women sing recollect women looking for returning *Odams*, and requesting the waves to be gentler and the breeze just right for the sails. There are stories of the benevolent sea ghost *baluvam*, whose coming to shore is considered a harbinger of prosperity for that year, bringing more coconuts, more fish and general well-being.

H The reef is regarded by the islanders as common property, and all the islanders are entitled to use the lagoon and reef resources. In the past, fishing groups would obtain permission from the *Amin* (island head person) and go fishing in the grounds allotted by him. On their return, the *Amin* would be given a share of the catch, normally one of the best or biggest fish. This practice no longer exists, but there is still a code of conduct or etiquette for exploiting the reef, and common respect for this is an effective way of avoiding conflict or disputes.

I Exploitation of such vast and diverse resources as the reefs and lagoon surrounding the island has encouraged collaborative efforts, mainly for purposes of safety, but also as a necessity in the operation of many fishing techniques. For example, the practice of fishing using an indigenous drag net known as *Bala fadal* involves 25–30 men. Reef gleaning for cowrie collection by groups of 6–10 women is also a common activity, and even today, although its economic significance is marginal, it continues as a recreational activity.

Reading Passage 1 has nine paragraphs **A–I**. Choose the correct heading for each paragraph from the list of headings below.

- i Island legends
- ii Resources for exchange
- iii Competition for fishing rights
- iv The low cost of equipment
- v Agatti's favourable location
- vi Rising income levels
- vii The social nature of reef occupations
- viii Resources for islanders' own use
- ix High levels of expertise
- x Alternative sources of employment
- xi Resources for earning money
- xii Social rights and obligations

1 Paragraph **A** ____________

2 Paragraph **B** ____________

3 Paragraph **C** ____________

4 Paragraph **D** ____________

5 Paragraph **E** ____________

6 Paragraph **F** ____________

7 Paragraph **G** ____________

8 Paragraph **H** ____________

9 Paragraph **I** ____________

Questions 10–13 Choose the correct letter, A, B, C or D

10 What proportion of poor households get all their income from reef products?

A 12% B 20% C 29% D 59%

11 *Kat moodsal* fishing

A is a seasonal activity.
B is a commercial activity.
C requires little investment.
D requires use of a rowing boat.

12 Which characteristic of present-day islanders does the writer describe?

A physical strength
B fishing expertise
C courage
D imagination

13 What does the writer say about the system for using the reef on Agatti?

A Fish catches are shared equally.
B The reef owner issues permits.
C There are frequent disputes.
D There is open access.

Reading test 2

Urban planning in Singapore

British merchants established a trading post in Singapore in the early nineteenth century, and for more than a century trading interests dominated. However, in 1965 the newly independent island state was cut off from its hinterland, and so it set about pursuing a survival strategy. The good international communications it already enjoyed provided a useful base, but it was decided that if Singapore was to secure its economic future, it must develop its industry. To this end, new institutional structures were needed to facilitate, develop, and control foreign investment. One of the most important of these was the Economic Development Board (EDB), an arm of government that developed strategies for attracting investment. Thus from the outset, the Singaporean government was involved in city promotion.

Towards the end of the twentieth century, the government realised that, due to limits on both the size of the country's workforce and its land area, its labour-intensive industries were becoming increasingly uncompetitive. So an economic committee was established which concluded that Singapore should focus on developing as a service centre, and seek to attract company headquarters to serve South East Asia, and develop tourism, banking, and offshore activities. The land required for this service-sector orientation had been acquired in the early 1970s, when the government realized that it lacked the banking infrastructure for a modern economy. So a new banking and corporate district, known as the 'Golden Shoe', was planned, incorporating the historic commercial area. This district now houses all the major companies and various government financial agencies.

Singapore's current economic strategy is closely linked to land use and development planning. Although it is already a major city, the current development plan seeks to ensure Singapore's continued economic growth through restructuring, to ensure that the facilities needed by future business are planned now. These include transport and telecommunication infrastructure, land, and environmental quality. A major concern is to avoid congestion in the central area, and so the latest plan deviates from previous plans by having a strong decentralization policy. The plan makes provision for four major regional centres, each serving 800,000 people, but this does not mean that the existing central business district will not also grow. A major extension planned around Marina Bay draws on examples of other 'world cities', especially those with waterside central areas such as Sydney and San Francisco. The project involves major land reclamation of 667 hectares in total. Part of this has already been developed as a conference and exhibition zone, and the rest will be used for other facilities. However the need for vitality has been recognised and a mixed zoning approach has been adopted, to include housing and entertainment.

One of the new features of the current plan is a broader conception of what contributes to economic success. It encompasses high quality residential provision, a good environment, leisure facilities and exciting city life. Thus there is more provision for low-density housing, often in waterfront communities linked to beaches and recreational facilities. However, the lower housing densities will put considerable pressure on the very limited land available for development, and this creates problems for another of the plan's aims, which is to stress environmental quality. More and more of the remaining open area will be developed, and the only natural landscape surviving will be a small zone in the centre of the island which serves as a water catchment area. Environmental policy is therefore very much concerned with making the built environment greener by introducing more plants – what is referred to as the 'beautification' of Singapore. The plan focuses on green zones defining the boundaries of settlements, and running along transport corridors. The incidental green provision within housing areas is also given considerable attention.

Much of the environmental provision, for example golf courses, recreation areas, and beaches, is linked to the prime objective of attracting business. The plan places much emphasis on good leisure provision and the need to exploit Singapore's island setting. One way of doing this is through further land reclamation, to create a whole new island devoted to leisure and luxury housing which will stretch from the central area to the airport. A current concern also appears to be how to use the planning system to create opportunities for greater spontaneity: planners have recently given much attention to the concept of the 24-hour city and the cafe society. For example, a promotion has taken place along the Singapore river to create a cafe zone. This has included the realization, rather late in the day, of the value of retaining older buildings, and the creation of a continuous riverside promenade. Since the relaxation in 1996 of strict guidelines on outdoor eating areas, this has become an extremely popular area in the evenings. Also, in 1998 the Urban Redevelopment Authority created a new entertainment area in the centre of the city which they are promoting as 'the city's one-stop, dynamic entertainment scene'.

In conclusion, the economic development of Singapore has been very consciously centrally planned, and the latest strategy is very clearly oriented to establishing Singapore as a leading 'world city'. It is well placed to succeed, for a variety of reasons. It can draw upon its historic roots as a world trading centre; it has invested heavily in telecommunications and air transport infrastructure; it is well located in relation to other Asian economies; it has developed a safe and clean environment; and it has utilized the international language of English.

Complete the summary below using words from the box.

Singapore

When Singapore became an independent, self-sufficient state it decided to build up its **14** ________________, and government organizations were created to support this policy. However, this initial plan met with limited success due to a shortage of **15** ________________ and land. It was therefore decided to develop the **16** ________________ sector of the economy instead. Singapore is now a leading city, but planners are working to ensure that its economy continues to grow. In contrast to previous policies, there is emphasis on **17** ________________. In addition, land will be recovered to extend the financial district, and provide **18** ________________ as well as housing. The government also plans to improve the quality of Singapore's environment, but due to the shortage of natural landscapes it will concentrate instead on what it calls **19** ________________ .

decentralization	labour	loans	industry	hygiene	recycling
hospitals	agriculture	transport	deregulation	transport	beautification
trade	fuel	tourism	entertainment	service	

Do the following statements agree with the information given in Reading Passage 2?

Write **True** if the statement agrees with the information
False if the statement contradicts the information
Not Given if there is no information on this.

20 After 1965, the Singaporean government switched the focus of the island's economy. __________

21 The creation of Singapore's financial centre was delayed while a suitable site was found. __________

22 Singapore's four regional centres will eventually be the same size as its central business district. __________

23 Planners have modelled new urban developments on other coastal cities. __________

24 Plants and trees are amongst the current priorities for Singapore's city planners. __________

25 The government has enacted new laws to protect Singapore's old buildings. __________

26 Singapore will find it difficult to compete with leading cities in other parts of the world. __________

Five practical tips to improve academic writing skills using the Academic Word List

Averil Coxhead, Massey University, New Zealand

Learning new words in another language is essential to all language learners and it's very important to know which words are the most useful. Usefulness relates to the context of your learning and the tasks you need to complete in the language, such as taking language exams, studying for university entrance exams, or writing academic essays at university.

For learners with such goals in mind, the Academic Word List (AWL) gives good support. The 570 word families in the AWL account for around 10% of the words in an academic text, such as an article or a text book. They occur across a wide range of academic subject areas, such as Biology, History, Marketing, and Commercial Law, but do not occur in the most frequent 2,000 words of English. The first 2,000 words account for around 75%–80% of a textbook, depending on the level of technical vocabulary in the book. This means that together the first 2,000 words and the AWL are the key to successful study.

Because 570 word families are a lot to learn at once, the AWL is divided into ten sublists, arranged by frequency. Sublist One contains the sixty most frequent words in the AWL, Sublist Two contains the next sixty most frequent words, and so on. In this dictionary, the words in the AWL are marked AW, as in the example below:

ˌso-ˈcalled AW *adj.* **1** used to show that the words you describe sb/sth with are not correct: *Her so-called friends only wanted her money.* **2** used to show that a special name has been given to sb/sth

1 Second language learners tend to use words they know well. It isn't often you would consider using unknown words in your writing. So what can you do with unknown words in the AWL?

Start with the list of headwords on pages R12–R14 because it contains the parent words in the families. Decide which words are unknown, and start by learning the main meanings of these words with word cards. You might meet a word that is being used with a different meaning from the one you know. Perhaps you know the meaning of *volume* in connection with 'sound volume'. Do you know any other meanings? Have a look at the entry for *volume* in this dictionary. Which meanings do you think you would find most often in academic texts? Look up the new meaning in this dictionary and use your judgment as to whether it is worth your time and energy to learn the new meaning or not.

TIP 1

Develop your knowledge of the meaning of words in the AWL, starting with the meaning of the words you do not know. The more words you know well, the more likely it is you will use them in your academic writing.

2 Words often occur with other words in patterns called 'collocations', using two or more words that go together frequently. Native speakers use collocations naturally in their writing, but non-native speakers do not find this easy. You can use the dictionary to help you find common collocations of AWL words.

Below is an entry from this dictionary for the word *trend*. Look at the example sentences (in *italics*) and find two collocations of *trend*.

trend 🔑 AW /trend/ ***noun*** [C] a ~ (towards sth) a general change or development: *The current trend is towards smaller families.* ◇ *He always followed the latest trends in fashion.*
IDM **set a/the trend** to start a new style or fashion

One is *current*, as in *current trend*, and another is *latest*, as in *latest trends*. You can use such examples as models of collocations in your writing. For example, in an essay on housing, you could write, '*The current trend in housing is towards smaller houses.*'

Another useful feature of this dictionary is the **Collocations and Patterns** boxes, like the one on *Describing economic trends* opposite:

TIP 2

Focus on the collocations of words in the AWL, as well as the words themselves. Check the dictionary for new patterns of words you know well to increase your knowledge of these words. Find patterns for the AWL words you are learning.

COLLOCATIONS AND PATTERNS

Describing economic trends

An amount can **be down/up (at)** or **be/remain unchanged (at).**
The share price is down at 234p.
The FT index was up 18.84 points.
The 100 Share Index remained unchanged at 5297.

Something can **stand at** or **reach** a figure or amount.
Second quarter sales stood at £18 billion.
Customer confidence reached a 30-year high.

A share can **gain** or **lose** an amount.
The share gained 19 cents to close at $4.38.

Markets, shares, profits, etc. **suffer** when there are economic problems.
Profit margins suffered when prices were lowered.

When amounts are **going up** they **climb, increase or rise.** When they go up suddenly, they **jump, rocket, shoot up** or **soar.**
Earnings per share climbed from 3.5p to 5.1p.
The pound increased in value relative to the euro.
Profits shot up by a staggering 25%.
Oil prices have rocketed.

When amounts are **going down** they **decline, drop or fall.** When they go down suddenly, they **crash, plummet, plunge** or **slump.**
Banana exports crashed nearly 50%.
The pound fell to a 14-year low against the dollar.
Net income plummeted to USD 3.7 million.
Sales have slumped by over 50%.

3 Academic writing is different from everyday writing because academic words are used to describe complex ideas, and these words occur mostly in textbooks.

Think about an email you might write in English to a friend. Would your message include words from the AWL such as *ongoing, specific* and *percentage*? It is unlikely that it would. However, in an academic essay you are expected to use words such as these correctly and fluently.

The AWL covers around 10% of an academic text. Do your academic essays and reports contain around 10% of words from the AWL? Academic textbooks are the one of the best places to encounter AWL words while reading. Ensure you have plenty of academic reading in your language development programme. Mark words you look up in your dictionary so that when you see that mark, you know this word needs your attention.

TIP 3

If you are focused on learning words in the AWL, ensure you are reading and writing about academic topics such as in the IELTS exam, so that you encounter these words in context.

4 The AWL has 570 word families. Below is an example from this dictionary of the word family *conceive*.

WORD FAMILY
conceive *verb*
concept *noun*
conceivable *adj.* (≠ **inconceivable**)
conceptual *adj.*

Word families are usually made up of regular patterns. For example, *conceivable* can have *in-* added to the front of it to become the word that means the opposite; *inconceivable*. You can see this at the dictionary entry for *conceivable*.

conceivable AW /kən'siːvəbl/ ***adj.*** possible to imagine or believe: *I made every conceivable effort to succeed.* OPP **inconceivable** ▶ **conceivably** /-əbli/ ***adv.***: *She might just conceivably be telling the truth.*

conceive AW /kən'siːv/ ***verb*** **1** [T] (*formal*) to think of a new idea or plan: *He conceived the idea for the novel during his journey through India.* **2** [I,T] (*formal*) ~ **(of) sb/sth (as sth)** to think about sb/sth in a particular way; to imagine: *He started to conceive of the world as a dangerous place.* **3** [I,T] (BIOLOGY) to become pregnant ➲ noun **conception**

TIP 4

Focus on learning word family members for AWL words to increase your ability to use the words in grammatically different ways.

5 Finally, practice makes perfect. Make sure you take opportunities to use these words and to get feedback when you use them, to check that you are using them correctly. Use your dictionary for practice. For example, if you want to practise your spelling, try looking up a word, then covering it with your hand, and writing the word from memory. You can look for collocations in the example sentences and practise word formation using the word family boxes.

TIP 5

Practise the words from the AWL by using them in your writing. Practising little and often makes it easier to remember what you have learnt.

Being an active, organized learner will help you improve your writing skills with the Academic Word List.

The **Academic Word List** was developed by Averil Coxhead, Massey University, New Zealand. The list is available at **language.massey.ac.nz/staff/awl**

ACADEMIC WORD LIST

This list contains the head words of the families in the Academic Word List. The numbers indicate the sublist of the Academic Word List, with Sublist 1 containing the most frequent words, Sublist 2 the next most frequent and so on. For example, abandon and its family members are in Sublist 8 of the Academic Word List.

abandon 8
abstract 6
academy 5
access 4
accommodate 9
accompany 8
accumulate 8
accurate 6
achieve 2
acknowledge 6
acquire 2
adapt 7
adequate 4
adjacent 10
adjust 5
administrate 2
adult 7
advocate 7
affect 2
aggregate 6
aid 7
albeit 10
allocate 6
alter 5
alternative 3
ambiguous 8
amend 5
analogy 9
analyse 1
annual 4
anticipate 9
apparent 4
append 8
appreciate 8
approach 1
appropriate 2
approximate 4
arbitrary 8
area 1
aspect 2
assemble 10
assess 1
assign 6
assist 2
assume 1
assure 9
attach 6

attain 9
attitude 4
attribute 4
author 6
authority 1
automate 8
available 1
aware 5
behalf 9
benefit 1
bias 8
bond 6
brief 6
bulk 9
capable 6
capacity 5
category 2
cease 9
challenge 5
channel 7
chapter 2
chart 8
chemical 7
circumstance 3
cite 6
civil 4
clarify 8
classic 7
clause 5
code 4
coherent 9
coincide 9
collapse 10
colleague 10
commence 9
comment 3
commission 2
commit 4
commodity 8
communicate 4
community 2
compatible 9
compensate 3
compile 10
complement 8
complex 2
component 3

compound 5
comprehensive 7
comprise 7
compute 2
conceive 10
concentrate 4
concept 1
conclude 2
concurrent 9
conduct 2
confer 4
confine 9
confirm 7
conflict 5
conform 8
consent 3
consequent 2
considerable 3
consist 1
constant 3
constitute 1
constrain 3
construct 2
consult 5
consume 2
contact 5
contemporary 8
context 1
contract 1
contradict 8
contrary 7
contrast 4
contribute 3
controversy 9
convene 3
converse 9
convert 7
convince 10
cooperate 6
coordinate 3
core 3
corporate 3
correspond 3
couple 7
create 1
credit 2
criteria 3

crucial 8
culture 2
currency 8
cycle 4
data 1
debate 4
decade 7
decline 5
deduce 3
define 1
definite 7
demonstrate 3
denote 8
deny 7
depress 10
derive 1
design 2
despite 4
detect 8
deviate 8
device 9
devote 9
differentiate 7
dimension 4
diminish 9
discrete 5
discriminate 6
displace 8
display 6
dispose 7
distinct 2
distort 9
distribute 1
diverse 6
document 3
domain 6
domestic 4
dominate 3
draft 5
drama 8
duration 9
dynamic 7
economy 1
edit 6
element 2
eliminate 7
emerge 4

emphasis 3
empirical 7
enable 5
encounter 10
energy 5
enforce 5
enhance 6
enormous 10
ensure 3
entity 5
environment 1
equate 2
equip 7
equivalent 5
erode 9
error 4
establish 1
estate 6
estimate 1
ethic 9
ethnic 4
evaluate 2
eventual 8
evident 1
evolve 5
exceed 6
exclude 3
exhibit 8
expand 5
expert 6
explicit 6
exploit 8
export 1
expose 5
external 5
extract 7
facilitate 5
factor 1
feature 2
federal 6
fee 6
file 7
final 2
finance 1
finite 7
flexible 6
fluctuate 8
focus 2
format 9
formula 1
forthcoming 10
foundation 7
found 9
framework 3
function 1
fund 3
fundamental 5
furthermore 6
gender 6
generate 5
generation 5
globe 7
goal 4
grade 7
grant 4
guarantee 7
guideline 8
hence 4
hierarchy 7
highlight 8
hypothesis 4
identical 7
identify 1
ideology 7
ignorance 6
illustrate 3
image 5
immigrate 3
impact 2
implement 4
implicate 4
implicit 8
imply 3
impose 4
incentive 6
incidence 6
incline 10
income 1
incorporate 6
index 6
indicate 1
individual 1
induce 8
inevitable 8
infer 7
infrastructure 8
inherent 9
inhibit 6
initial 3
initiate 6
injure 2
innovate 7
input 6
insert 7
insight 9
inspect 8
instance 3
institute 2
instruct 6
integral 9
integrate 4
integrity 10
intelligence 6
intense 8
interact 3
intermediate 9
internal 4
interpret 1
interval 6
intervene 7
intrinsic 10
invest 2
investigate 4
invoke 10
involve 1
isolate 7
issue 1
item 2
job 4
journal 2
justify 3
label 4
labour 1
layer 3
lecture 6
legal 1
legislate 1
levy 10
liberal 5
licence 5
likewise 10
link 3
locate 3
logic 5
maintain 2
major 1
manipulate 8
manual 9
margin 5
mature 9
maximise 3
mechanism 4
media 7
mediate 9
medical 5
medium 9
mental 5
method 1
migrate 6
military 9
minimal 9
minimise 8
minimum 6
ministry 6
minor 3
mode 7
modify 5
monitor 5
motive 6
mutual 9
negate 3
network 5
neutral 6
nevertheless 6
nonetheless 10
norm 9
normal 2
notion 5
notwithstanding 10
nuclear 8
objective 5
obtain 2
obvious 4
occupy 4
occur 1
odd 10
offset 8
ongoing 10
option 4
orient 5
outcome 3
output 4
overall 4
overlap 9
overseas 6
panel 10
paradigm 7
paragraph 8
parallel 4
parameter 4
participate 2
partner 3
passive 9
perceive 2
percent 1
period 1
persist 10
perspective 5
phase 4
phenomenon 7
philosophy 3
physical 3
plus 8
policy 1
portion 9
pose 10
positive 2
potential 2
practitioner 8
precede 6

precise 5
predict 4
predominant 8
preliminary 9
presume 6
previous 2
primary 2
prime 5
principal 4
principle 1
prior 4
priority 7
proceed 1
process 1
professional 4
prohibit 7
project 4
promote 4
proportion 3
prospect 8
protocol 9
psychology 5
publication 7
publish 3
purchase 2
pursue 5
qualitative 9
quote 7
radical 8
random 8
range 2
ratio 5
rational 6
react 3
recover 6
refine 9
regime 4
region 2
register 3
regulate 2
reinforce 8
reject 5
relax 9
release 7
relevant 2
reluctance 10
rely 3
remove 3
require 1
research 1
reside 2
resolve 4
resource 2
respond 1
restore 8
restrain 9
restrict 2
retain 4
reveal 6
revenue 5
reverse 7
revise 8
revolution 9
rigid 9
role 1
route 9
scenario 9
schedule 8
scheme 3
scope 6
section 1
sector 1
secure 2
seek 2
select 2
sequence 3
series 4
sex 3
shift 3
significant 1
similar 1
simulate 7
site 2
so-called 10
sole 7
somewhat 7
source 1
specific 1
specify 3
sphere 9
stable 5
statistic 4
status 4
straightforward 10
strategy 2
stress 4
structure 1
style 5
submit 7
subordinate 9
subsequent 4
subsidy 6
substitute 5
successor 7
sufficient 3
sum 4
summary 4
supplement 9
survey 2
survive 7
suspend 9
sustain 5
symbol 5
tape 6
target 5
task 3
team 9
technical 3
technique 3
technology 3
temporary 9
tense 8
terminate 8
text 2
theme 8
theory 1
thereby 8
thesis 7
topic 7
trace 6
tradition 2
transfer 2
transform 6
transit 5
transmit 7
transport 6
trend 5
trigger 9
ultimate 7
undergo 10
underlie 6
undertake 4
uniform 8
unify 9
unique 7
utilise 6
valid 3
vary 1
vehicle 8
version 5
via 8
violate 9
virtual 8
visible 7
vision 9
visual 8
volume 3
voluntary 7
welfare 5
whereas 5
whereby 10
widespread 8

ESSAY WRITING

Using links and markers

When you are writing an essay that asks you to discuss a topic or give your opinion on a question, it is important to organize your thoughts and present your arguments clearly and to work out the structure of your essay before you start to write.

1 *Introducing the topic (saying why it is important now)*
2 *Giving one point of view, in support of the argument, with reasons*
3 *Giving more information or arguments*
4 *Giving a contrasting or different view*
5 *Concluding (giving your own opinion or interpretation of the facts)*

EXERCISE 1

In the box opposite are phrases that you can use to guide your readers through your essay. Which phrases could be used for each type of paragraph? Put a number 1–5 against each of the expressions.

in conclusion (**5**)	therefore	moreover
furthermore	on the other hand	consequently
recently	nevertheless	finally
in addition	to sum up	while
as a result	however	nowadays (**1**)

EXERCISE 2

Don't repeat yourself – say it another way.

In the lists on the right, you will find expressions that can be used to give your essay structure. Using these phrases will improve the style of your writing and your language will be more varied as a result. Match up an expression on the left with one on the right, so that you have pairs of phrases with similar meanings. The first one has been done for you as an example.

compared with	serious problems
obviously	in comparison with
affect sth drastically	furthermore
in particular	plays an important role
appreciate	especially
moreover	have a devastating impact on sth
whereas	consequently
is a significant factor	while
in contrast	clearly
a cross section	on the other hand
as a result	a representative group
grave difficulties	value

Planning and writing an essay

- **Read the question or essay title carefully** to make sure that you understand what exactly is required.
- For many longer essays, you are given a topic to discuss. Here, you should present more than one point of view on the subject, and support each point with arguments or examples.

  Now look at the following essay title: '*Genetic engineering brings with it more dangers than benefits and should be banned worldwide.*' Discuss.

Brainstorming

Quickly note down some ideas on the topic as you think of them. Then, write down some vocabulary that you know you will need to write about this subject. If you are allowed to use a dictionary, check the spellings and grammar patterns now so that you can refer to your list quickly when you have begun to write your essay. Look at the next page for an example of brainstorming.

IDEAS

- recent advances in science – new possibilities
- unknown dangers
- 'designer' babies
- new cures for illnesses
- cloning humans – political purposes
- religious concerns
- interfering with nature
- banning impractical – impossible to regulate
- can't go back

VOCABULARY

genes	genetics
clone	scientific
modify	scientists
incurable	conduct research
therapy	hereditary diseases
possibility of doing sth	interfere with sth

EXERCISE 3

Now think about the structure of your essay. Look at the structure suggested in Exercise 1 and put the paragraph number against each of the arguments in the example above, according to where you think it fits into the plan suggested:

▶ *recent advances in science – new possibilities*
paragraph 1

▶ *unknown dangers*
paragraph 2

EXERCISE 4

Look at the final version of the essay. Using the expressions from **EXERCISES 1** and **2**, fill in the gaps with suitable links.

'Genetic engineering brings with it more dangers than benefits and should be banned worldwide.' DISCUSS.

__________ , advances in science have demonstrated to us that things that once seemed possible only in science fiction could become a reality. The cloning of a sheep brought the possibility of using genetic engineering to create new organs, or even whole human beings, one step closer.

Some people consider this to be a dangerous development, and believe that all such research should be banned. Interfering with nature in this way could bring with it dangers that none of us can imagine. We have no idea how an artificially-created person might behave, or indeed how he or she might suffer. __________ , we may find ourselves in a position which we do not like, but which we are unable to reverse.

__________ , many people would say that it is not for human beings to decide what other human beings should be like. It is not only people with deep religious beliefs who feel that it is wrong, for example, for parents to choose whether their baby will be a boy or a girl, or have blue eyes or musical talent. The idea of a political regime cloning its citizens until it has the right sort of population for its purposes is even more horrific.

__________ , the latest research in genetics has also opened up the possibility of new treatment for many diseases which up to now have been incurable. If it were possible to prevent a baby from developing a hereditary disease by modifying its genes, should we stop the scientists? If doctors could replace a diseased organ with a new one grown from cells, should it not be allowed?

__________ , I would say that genetic engineering has the potential to be both a huge benefit and a terrible curse for humankind. To make sure that we benefit from it, it will be necessary to control it very strictly. The real challenge will be to find ways of monitoring the research that is conducted in laboratories all over the world and to make sure that it is only used for the good of everyone.

WRITING A REPORT

If you are asked to write a report, for example, analysing the results of some research, summarizing articles, or interpreting statistics, your aim should be to present facts clearly so that the reader will understand the main points quickly.

- Look at the report below and notice how the information is divided up using headings.
- The style of a report is impersonal: it is not important who the writer is or what his or her opinion is. Often the writer will use verbs in the passive to describe how the research was done. Look at the section headed '**Method**' and find two verbs that are in the passive.
- Notice whether you are told who the reader is. This will help you to decide how much you need to explain.
- In many reports, the important information involves numbers. Read the report again and find out what these expressions refer to:

50+50	two thirds
eight out of ten	four
75%	the majority
a large majority	5%
a half	twice
three	

Your style of writing will not be personal, but it need not be boring. Vary your language so that you do not overuse the same expressions. Think of other ways of saying the words and phrases that are written in **bold** in the report below. Look at '*Don't repeat yourself*' on page **R15** if you need help.

AIM

The objective of our survey was to find out whether shopping habits have changed since the building of the new out-of-town mall at Lakewater, and to identify trends for the future.

METHOD

Four groups of people were targeted: (A) town-centre residents, (B) residents of the suburbs up to three miles around the town centre, (C) shopkeepers in the central area of town, and (D) traders in the new mall.

The research was conducted using two questionnaires, one for shoppers and one for traders. Researchers visited 50 homes in the central area and 50 in the suburbs as well as **a cross section** of shops in both locations.

RESULTS

Shoppers

75% of all residents said that they had been to the new mall at least twice during the last month. Of these, the majority were from group B. Among the most popular reasons cited for visiting Lakewater in preference to the town centre were the ample free parking there **compared with** the difficulties of parking in the town centre and the convenience of having a large number of stores in one location in the mall. Families, **in particular**, mentioned the Lakewater children's play area as an important advantage.

In contrast, two thirds of those questioned in group A reported that they **valued** the convenience of being able to walk to the shops. Eight out of ten of the older shoppers surveyed said that their daily shopping trip was their only contact with other people. **Moreover**, they preferred the personal attention of the smaller shops compared with the anonymous atmosphere of the larger outlets. They were, **however**, concerned that prices were increasing.

Traders

The town-centre traders have seen business drop off by up to a half, **whereas** Lakewater traders have recorded a steady increase in sales over the year. When asked whether they viewed the future with optimism, a large majority of group D replied positively, while only 5% of group C said that they expected to see a growth in their business in the coming year.

CONCLUSIONS

The opening of the Lakewater shopping centre has **clearly had a devastating effect on** the town centre, and this trend seems set to continue. Parking problems in the town centre **have been a significant factor** in changing people's habits. Mobile, better-off consumers are deserting the high street for the new mall, leaving the town-centre traders relying on the custom of local residents, particularly the elderly and those without cars. **As a result**, many long-established businesses now face **grave difficulties**.

INTERPRETING GRAPHS

Line graphs

The verbs in the box on the right can all be used to describe changes commonly represented on line graphs. Use your dictionary to look up the meanings of the verbs and then answer the following questions:

1 Which 5 verbs mean go up?

2 Of these, which 3 mean go up suddenly/a lot?

3 Which 5 verbs mean go down?

4 Which verb means reach its highest level?

5 Which verb means stay the same?

6 Which verb means go up and down?

plummet	**decrease**	**fluctuate**
peak	**rise**	**drop**
rocket	**increase**	**decline**
level out	**soar**	**fall**

Now decide which parts of the graphs below, showing the sales of a book between 1997 and 2006, can be described using the verbs given.

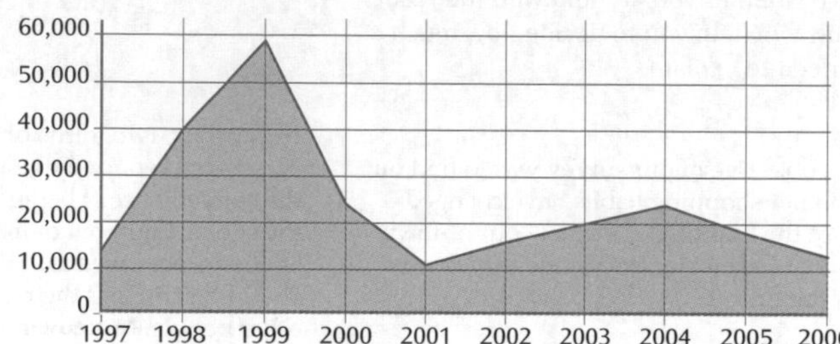

Book Sales Jan–Dec 2006

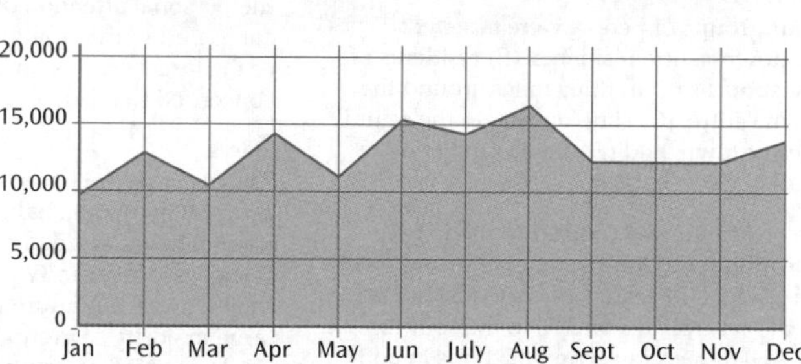

EXERCISE 1

Now, using the verbs above, complete these sentences using the information shown on the graphs:

1 In the year 2006 sales ______________ in August.

2 Sales rocketed between ______________ and ______________.

3 From 1999 to 2000 sales of the book ______________.

4 Book sales fluctuated between ______________ in 2006.

5 Sales ______________ between Sep. and Nov. 2006.

6 Sales started to fall for the first time in ______________.

7 Book sales ______________ from 2001 to 2004.

8 However, from 2004 to 2006, sales ______________.

EXERCISE 2

Changes can also be described in more detail by modifying a verb with an adverb. Using a verb from the box at the top, and an adverb from the box below, make sentences describing the changes represented on the line graphs on the previous page for the years or months shown. The first one has been done for you as an example.

1 1997–1999
Sales increased/rose dramatically/sharply.

2 1999–2001

3 2001–2004

4 2004–2006

5 July–August 2006

6 November–December 2006

increase	**decrease**	**decline**
fall	**rise**	**drop**

dramatically	**sharply**	**gradually**
slightly	**rapidly**	**moderately**
slowly	**steadily**	

Look at the following two ways of expressing the same idea:

– *Sales* ***increased dramatically*** *from 1997 to 1999.*
subj + verb + adverb

– *There was a* ***dramatic increase*** *in sales from 1997 to 1999.*
There was/were + adjective + noun + in + sth

Now turn the rest of the sentences you made in **EXERCISE 2** into similar sentences with an adjective + noun

---

EXERCISE 3

Check your prepositions. Choose a preposition from the box on the right to go into each of the gaps in the sentences below, which describe the graphs on page R18.

1 There was an increase ______ 50,000 between 1997 and 1999.

2 ______ 2001 ______ 2004, sales rose steadily ______ over 20,000.

3 Overall sales peaked ______ nearly 60,000 ______ 1999, but then plummeted ______ about 10,000 over the next two years.

4 In the year 2006, sales started ______ around 10,000. In the first month, there was a rise ______ around 5,000.

5 After some fluctuations, sales in 2006 reached their peak ______ just over 15,000, a rise ______ 5,000 since the beginning of the year.

6 Sales increased ______ over 10,000 between 2001 to 2004, but then dropped ______ more than 10,000 between 2004 and 2006.

at
in
of
from
by
to

EXERCISE 4

The following paragraph summarizes the information in the two graphs on page R18. Notice the expressions in **bold** that refer to time and amount.

Just over 10,000 copies of the book were sold in 1997. Sales increased dramatically **over the next two years**, to peak at **almost** 60,000 in 1999. However, sales then fell sharply to **well under** 30,000 in the following year, and they went down by a further 12,000 **or so** between 2000 and 2001. There was a steady increase in sales **over the next three years**, and by 2004 there had been a rise of **slightly more than** 10,000. However, after this sales began to drop once more to **approximately** 10,000 in 2006.

In the first six months of the year 2006, sales fluctuated, although there was a moderate increase in July-August, reaching a peak at **well over** 15,000. A sharp decrease followed, with sales falling to around 12,000 in September. They remained steady until November, when there was a slight increase.

Now put the expressions from the box on the left into the table on the right, from the greatest amount to the smallest. The first one has been done for you as an example.

~~well over~~	*well over*	↑
just under	________	
almost/nearly	________	10000
well under	________	half
exactly	________	
just over	________	↓

Look at the two tables below for other ways to express amounts:

APPROXIMATIONS

approximately	
around	10,000
about	half
roughly	3 times
more or less	

COMPARISONS

a little	
slightly	more
far	less [+ uncountable noun]
a lot	fewer [+ countable noun]
much	
considerably	
significantly	

Pie charts

EXERCISE 5

The two pie charts below illustrate two families' average monthly expenditure. In the summary there are **ten** factual errors. Using the information on the pie charts, <u>underline</u> the mistakes and then rewrite the text, making the corrections necessary. The first one has been done for you as an example.

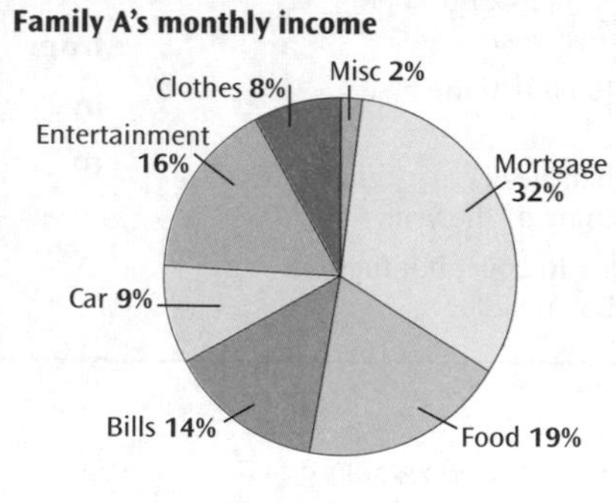

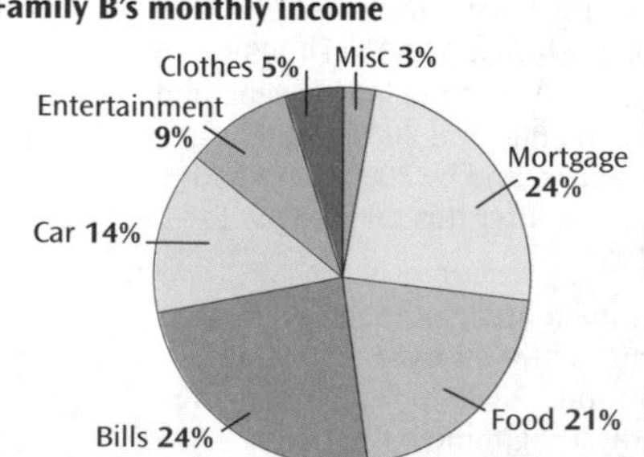

<u>Both families'</u> biggest expenditure each month is the mortgage. Family A spends far more on their mortgage than they do on anything else (32%). This is exactly half what they spend on entertainment each month. Their food budget (19%) is significantly higher than their entertainment budget, while they spend well under 10% each month on clothes. Family B's clothes budget is far less (5%). Family B's entertainment budget is similar to Family A's, at just 9%. In contrast, Family B spends much more on bills each month, over a quarter of the whole monthly budget. This is compensated by their mortgage, which is slightly less than Family A's, at only 24%. Just over 15% of their monthly budget goes on the car, significantly more than the 9% that Family A spends each month. In general, Family B spends more on necessary items such as bills, food and car, while Family A allows slightly more money for entertainment and clothes.

– *Family A's biggest expenditure each month is the mortgage …*

WRITING A CV OR RÉSUMÉ

British style

Curriculum Vitae

Name	Mark Slater
Address	40 Walton Crescent, London E14 9PD
Telephone	020 8726 4562
Nationality	British
Date of birth	29 October 1983
Education/qualifications	
2002–05	Oxford Brookes University: BA in Computing (2:i)
1994–2002	Compton School, 3 A levels: Mathematics (B), Physics (B), Chemistry (C); 10 GCSEs
Employment to date	
2005-present	Web designer, Docklands Technology, 30 Jamaica Road, London SE1 2PF
Skills	Familiar with a number of Web design and DTP packages; clean driving licence
Interests	Football, karate, reading
References	
Dr J Brown	Department of Computing and Mathematical Sciences, Oxford Brookes University, Gipsy Lane, Oxford
Anna Dean	Project manager, Docklands Technology

- On a British CV it is usual to put your date of birth. On an American résumé you may choose whether or not to include your birth date, marital status, children, etc.
- One or more references may be included on the CV/résumé or they may be included in the letter of application instead.

Some useful phrases

- Near-native command of English
- Adequate spoken Dutch and German
- Native French speaker
- Baccalauréat, série C (equivalent of A levels in Maths and Physics)
- The qualifications described do not have exact equivalents in the American system.

American style

Résumé

Jenny Woo	1450 Diamond St Noe Valley San Francisco, CA65952 tel: (650) 498-785 email: jenny_woo@usaemail.com
Objective	To obtain a trainee position within a major consultancy firm
Education	
2005–06	Masters in Financial Engineering, UCB
2001–05	Major: Economics; Minor: Politics, UCLA
Work experience	
Summer 2005	Vacation work at JPNG, San Francisco
Skills	Computing, working knowledge of German
Personal	Interests include swimming, cooking and going to the theater
References	Dr M Goldberg, Haas School of Business, University of California, Berkeley, CA 94720

LETTER WRITING

Formal letters

A covering letter to enclose with a job application

Never write your name at the **top** of a letter.

Write your own address here and the date in full underneath it.

3 Brook Road
Edinburgh
EH2 3EB

2 May 2007

Write the address and name or position of the person you are writing to here.

Mr Chris Summit
Human Resources
BLC Computers
12 Wharf Way
London NW3 7AD

Use **Sir** or **Madam**, if you do not know the name of the person you are writing to, and use the person's title (Mr, Ms, etc.) and his/her family name if you do.

Dear Mr Summit

Avoid contractions.

I am writing to apply for the position of software technician advertised in The Echo of 29 April. I have enclosed a copy of my CV. ❶

Use formal linking words and phrases.

Since graduating from Cardiff University, I have been working in software design and have gained considerable experience in developing personalized packages. I am proficient at programming in five different languages, including C++ and Java. My job has also given me some insight into systems analysis. ❷

I am now seeking employment with a firm where I can gain more experience and where there are more opportunities for promotion. I am sure I could make a significant contribution and would be happy to demonstrate some of my programs to you. ❸

I am available for interview next week and look forward to hearing from you. ❹

Yours sincerely

End your letter '**Yours sincerely**' if you have begun it with a person's title and family name. If you have begun '**Dear Sir or Madam**', then end your letter '**Yours faithfully**'.

Andrew Mason

Andrew Mason

Sign your name in full and print it afterwards.

paragraph ❶
explain which job you are applying for and how/where you heard about it

paragraph ❷
briefly describe your most relevant qualifications and/or experience

paragraph ❸
explain why you want the job and why you think you would be good at it

paragraph ❹
say how you can be contacted and/or when you are available for interview

Here are some other useful expressions that you might include in a covering letter of this type:

paragraph ❶

- I noted with interest your advertisement for a … in today's edition of …
- I am writing in response to your advertisement in … for the position of …
- I am writing to apply for the post of … advertised in …
- With reference to your advertisement in …, I am interested in applying for the post of …
- As you will see from my CV …
- I have enclosed a copy of my CV, from which you will see …
- Please find enclosed a copy of my CV

paragraph ❷

- After graduating from … , I …
- Since leaving university, I have …
- On leaving school, I …
- Having gained a degree, I …
- While I was working at …
- During my employment at …

paragraph ❸

- I would welcome the chance to …
- I would be grateful for the opportunity to ...

paragraph ❹

- If you consider that my experience and qualifications are suitable …
- I am available for interview any afternoon and would be pleased to discuss the post available in person …
- I can arrange to attend an interview whenever convenient for you …

EXERCISE 1

Choosing the correct register

Knowing how formal or informal to be is very important when communicating in writing. To practise this, match the formal phrase on the left with its informal equivalent on the right. The first one has been done for you as an example.

	Formal letter		Informal letter
a	I regret to inform you that …	1	Let us know when you get …
b	I would like to inform you that …	2	I'm happy to tell you …
c	It appears that …	3	I'm sorry …
d	Please accept our apologies for …	4	I'm writing to let you know that …
e	I would be grateful if you could …	5	We're waiting for …
f	We would appreciate it if …	6	I'm sorry to tell you that …
g	I can assure you that …	7	I'm writing to ask …
h	We are pleased to confirm …	8	We'd be really happy if …
i	We have pleasure in enclosing …	9	I want to tell you that …
j	We look forward to receiving …	10	I'm writing back to you …
k	We are writing to advise you that …	11	I'm sending it with this letter.
l	In reply to your enquiry of 10 May …	12	Please could you …
m	Please confirm receipt of …	13	I promise …
n	I am writing to enquire …	14	It seems …

A letter of complaint

Most letters of complaint use formal language and have a standard organization.

Paragraphing

paragraph 1 explain why you are writing
paragraph 2 explain what the problem is
paragraph 3 say what inconvenience it has caused you
paragraph 4 state what you want done about the problem

EXERCISE 2

Below is a memo written in an informal style because it is from one colleague to another. Read the memo and the formal letter of complaint underneath. Change the underlined expressions in the memo into formal language using the expressions listed a–f and then fill in the gaps 1–6 in the formal letter.

MEMO

To: Alice Porter
From: Brian Adams
Date: 16 January 2007
Subject: Faulty Video Recorders

Can you write to Lassiters and tell them we are really unhappy with their last order? Say we're sorry but we simply can't accept the goods in their current condition. Remind them how long we've been customers of theirs! Say we want the goods replaced at once or we will have to cancel the order. Ask them to let us know what they're going to do about it.

Brian

a We will be obliged to …
b We must insist that …
c Could you please confirm …
d We are writing to express our dissatisfaction …
e I am afraid we are unable …
f We would like to remind you …

Dear Mr Waldron

Order 5600: 20 Video Recorders

1 ____________________ with the last order you sent us on 2nd January. Most of the videos have faulty wiring and are unusable. **2** ____________________ to accept these goods in their current condition. **3** ____________________ that we have been good customers of yours for several years and expect better service than this. **4** ____________________ these goods are replaced immediately or **5** ____________________ cancel our order. **6** ____________________ when you will be able to replace the goods?

Yours sincerely

Alice Porter

Alice Porter
PA to Mr Adams

Writing emails and faxes

Business emails between colleagues can be very informal but emails to clients, etc. may be either semi-formal or formal depending on the individual relationship and what the email contains. However, all emails should follow certain basic rules:

- Be consistent in style. Don't vary between formal and informal.
- Appearance is still important – remember to use paragraphs and proper sentences.
- Keep it short and to the point.
- Use the subject line to summarize the point of the message so the reader is clear about the content
  — *Enquiry re delivery dates.*
- Refer to any original message in your email.
- Paraphrase relevant parts of the original email rather than quoting whole chunks.
- In a more formal email it is better to write *Dear* ... but you do not have to use a particular formula at the end; you can just write your name.

EXERCISE 3

Here are three different emails requesting something. The relationship between the sender and receiver is different and what is being asked for varies in difficulty. Use appropriate phrases from the box below to complete the blank spaces in the three emails.

- **a** I am writing to ask you
- **b** I need to know
- **c** Should we also
- **d** We need to
- **e** We would like you to
- **f** Could you please
- **g** I would be grateful if you
- **h** Can you arrange this
- **i** Can you also let me know

Informal request to a colleague:

Andrew
1 _______ re-order 20 packs of the high-grade photocopying paper. 2 _______ and let me know the delivery date? 3 _______ get some packs of staples at the same time?
Sarah

Semi-formal request to a known business contact:

Dear Alan
4 _______ send details of this year's April conference? 5 _______ by next week to arrange numbers. 6 _______ if accommodation is available?
Thanks
David

Formal request to someone in business if you have not met him/her before:

Dear Mr Webb
7 _______ if you would be able to give a presentation at our Board meeting on Thursday 7 February. 8 _______ talk about your current projects and how your consultants could help our company. 9 _______ could let me know as soon as possible.
Regards
Elaine Jackson

Faxes

Normal business letters can be sent as faxes. You can also send a fax which is a note but if this is to business clients, etc. you should use the language of a formal letter.

Bute Electronics

FAX from: Sandra Corker, Production Dept
F.A.O: Alan Wheeler, Operations Manager
Date: 23 February 2007
Subject: Car components: Order No. 6133

Our suppliers have only just delivered the parts we need to complete your order above. We will therefore not be able to deliver until Friday. I apologize for any inconvenience caused.

Sandra Corker

TAKING NOTES

When you are studying you will often want to write notes to help you remember what you have heard or read. These pages will show you how to take notes efficiently by using symbols and abbreviations, and by organizing your notes.

Symbols

Using symbols can save you a lot of time. The symbols in this section are widely used and understood.

EXERCISE 1

Look at the symbols in the box and match them to their meanings below:

1 this is an important point
2 is approximately equal to
3 is not, does not equal
4 and, plus
5 is, equals
6 because
7 at
8 is more than
9 is less than
10 male
11 female
12 therefore, so
13 and
14 the same word as above

You can use these symbols in place of a range of words. For example, + can mean *also, in addition, as well as*. Try to think of some other words or phrases that the other symbols could stand for.

Arrows are also useful symbols:

↗ or ↑ an increase/a rise/an improvement in something.

↘ or ↓ a decrease/a fall/a reduction/ a deterioration in something

→ causes/results in/becomes/makes
Certain chemicals used in industry have caused a hole to develop in the ozone layer.
This could be written in note form as:
Chemicals used in industry → hole in ozone layer.

← is caused by/is the result of/ is made from
We can help reduce pollution by using environmentally-friendly forms of transport.
This could be written in note form as:
Reduce pollution ← using environmentally-friendly transport.

Abbreviations

You have probably come across some abbreviations in your textbooks or in a dictionary:

esp. = especially
p. = page
sb = somebody
ch. = chapter
etc. = and so on

NOTE: A full stop is often used at the end of an abbreviation to show that this is not the full form of the word.

EXERCISE 2

The following abbreviations are very common. Try to guess what the full forms are.

vol. usu. sing. incl.
ex. diffs. approx.

EXERCISE 3

Do you know what these common abbreviations mean? If not, look them up in the dictionary.

i.e. e.g. cf. c no. pp

You should try to develop your own system of abbreviations, especially for words that you use frequently. These are some widely-used methods:

- write only the first few letters of the word:
  pop. = population
  prog. = programme/program
  elec. = electricity
- write the first few letters of the word, and the last letter:
  govt. = government
  dept. = department
  probs = problems
  environt. = environment

- write only the consonants, omitting the vowels:
  mrkt. = market
  mngr. = manager
  wld. = would

EXERCISE 4

Now, suggest some abbreviations of your own for the following words:

industry	industrialization
chemicals	technology
global warming	underdevelopment
temperature	international

However you abbreviate words, remember that you will need to understand your abbreviations when you look at your notes later.

Omitting words

Another way of keeping your notes short is by omitting words. Many words in a sentence do not carry much meaning, but just show the grammar of the sentence. Look at this sentence. The underlined words are the **content words** that give the meaning; the others are the **grammar words**:

It is useful to be able to take notes from lessons and textbooks quickly and efficiently.

You could note this:

Useful: take notes – lessons, textbooks quickly, efficiently.

Notice how the colon (:), the dash (–) and the comma (,) are used instead of words here.

You can omit:

- **articles** (a, an, the):
  The Internet is an enormous network that covers the world.
  Internet = enormous network that covers world.
- **most forms of the verb 'be'**:
  The euro was introduced on January 1 1999.
  Euro introduced 1/1/99.
- **pronouns** (I, me, my, he, his, we, us, our, etc.):
  We pollute water by dumping waste.
  Pollute water ← dumping waste.
- that, which, who:
  We are producing too much carbon dioxide, which is causing temperatures to rise.
  Producing too much carbon dioxide → temperatures ↑.

Always try to look for the shortest, simplest way to write things. For example, *The government of the United Kingdom* could be written: *UK govt.*

Organizing notes

Your notes will be much easier to understand later if you use headings and underlining for the main points, and numbers, letters, etc. for the subordinate points. Start new points on a new line. Underline important points or anything you especially wish to remember. Think carefully about the layout of your notes. It should be clear and reflect the structure of the lecture or text.

EXERCISE 5

Now read the sample text below and take notes, using the abbreviations, symbols and headings suggested on this page. When you have finished, compare your notes with the sample notes in the key at the back of the Study page section.

Energy

Most of the energy we use to heat and light buildings, run machines, etc. is made by burning fossil fuels. These will eventually run out, so we need to use more alternative sources of energy, such as wind and solar power, that are renewable and do not pollute the air. We should also avoid wasting energy by using less electricity and water and insulating our houses.

Further practice

You can continue to practise taking notes by reading newspaper articles or passages from a textbook, or by asking a friend to read a text to you.

PUNCTUATION

Full stop (.)

A **full stop** (*AmE* **period**) is used at the end of a sentence, unless the sentence is a question or an exclamation:

We're leaving now. *That's all.*

It is also often used after an abbreviation:

Acacia Ave. *a.m.*

Question mark (?)

A **question mark** is written at the end of a direct question:

'Who's that man?' Jenny asked.

but not after an indirect question:

Jenny asked who the man was.

Comma (,)

A **comma** shows a slight pause in a sentence:

I ran all the way to the station, but I still missed the train.

Although it was cold, the sun was shining.

He did, nevertheless, leave his phone number.

However, we may be wrong.

It is also used before a quotation or direct speech:

Fiona said, 'I'll help you.'

'I'll help you', said Fiona, 'but you'll have to wait till Monday.'

Commas are also used between the items in a list, although they may be omitted before 'and':

It was a cold, rainy day.

This shop sells clothing, shoes, and household goods.

potatoes, beans and carrots

In relative clauses, commas are used around a phrase which adds some new, but not essential, information:

The Pennine Hills, which are very popular with walkers, are situated between Lancashire and Yorkshire.

Do not use commas before and after a clause that defines the noun it follows:

The hills which separate Lancashire from Yorkshire are called the Pennines.

Exclamation mark (!)

An **exclamation mark** (*AmE* **exclamation point**) is used at the end of a sentence which expresses surprise, enthusiasm, or shock:

What an amazing story!

You look well!

Oh no! I've broken it!

or after an exclamation or a word describing a loud sound:

Bye! *Ow!* *Crash!*

Colon (:)

A **colon** is used to introduce something, such as a long quotation or a list:

There is a choice of main course: roast beef, turkey or omelette.

Semicolon (;)

A **semicolon** is used to separate two contrasting parts of a sentence:

John wanted to go; I did not.

or to separate items in a list where commas have already been used:

The school uniform consists of navy skirt or trousers; grey, white or pale blue shirt; navy jumper or cardigan; grey, blue or white socks.

Apostrophe (')

An **apostrophe** shows either that a letter is missing, in short forms such as

hasn't, don't, I'm, he's

or that a person or thing belongs to somebody:

Peter's scarf *Jane's mother*

my friend's car

With some names that end in 's', another 's' is not always added:

James's/James' name

Notice the position of the apostrophe with singular and plural nouns:

the girl's keys
(= the keys belonging to the girl)
the girls' keys
(= the keys belonging to the girls)

Quotation marks (“ ”or ‘ ’)

Quotation marks or **inverted commas** are used to show the words that somebody said:

‘Come and see,’ said Martin.

‘Oh, no!’ said Martin. ‘Come and see what’s happened.’

Angela shouted, ‘Over here!’

or what somebody thought, when the thoughts are presented like speech:

‘Will they get here on time?’ she wondered.

They are also used around a title, for example of a book, play, film, etc.:

‘Bambi’ was the first film I ever saw.

‘Have you read “Emma”?’ he asked.

This quotation is from ‘The geology of Great Britain’.

Hyphen (-)

A **hyphen** is used to join two words which together form one idea:

a tin-opener

a ten-ton truck

or sometimes to link a prefix to a word:

non-violent

anti-British

and in compound numbers:

thirty-four

seventy-nine.

You also write a hyphen at the end of a line if you have to divide a word and write part of it on the next line.

Dots/ellipsis (...)

Dots/ellipsis are used to show that words have been left out, especially from a quotation or at the end of a conversation:

‘Please help me, I can’t ...’ She burst into tears.

Dash (—)

A **dash** can be used to separate a phrase from the rest of a sentence.

It can be used near the end of the sentence before a phrase which sums up the rest of the sentence:

The burglars had taken the furniture, the TV and the stereo – absolutely everything.

You can also put a dash at the beginning and the end of a phrase which adds extra information:

A few people – not more than ten – had already arrived.

A dash can also show that the speaker has been interrupted in the middle of a sentence:

‘Have you seen –’ ‘Look out!’ she screamed as the ball flew towards them.

Brackets ( )

Brackets (*or especially in AmE* **parentheses**) are also used to keep extra information separate from the rest of a sentence:

Two of the runners (Johns and Smith) finished the race in under an hour.

Numbers or letters used in sentences may also have a bracket after them or brackets around them:

The camera has three main advantages: 1) its compact size 2) its low price and 3) the quality of the photographs.

What would you do if you won a lot of money? (a) save it (b) travel round the world (c) buy a new house (d) buy presents for your friends

THE LANGUAGE OF LITERARY CRITICISM

Figurative language

Imagery is language that produces pictures in the mind. The term can be used to discuss the various stylistic devices listed below, especially **figures of speech** (= ways of using language to convey or suggest a meaning beyond the literal meaning of the words).

Metaphor is the imaginative use of a word or phrase to describe something else, to show that the two have the same qualities:

All the world's a stage
And all the men and women merely players.
(WILLIAM SHAKESPEARE, *As You Like It*)

In a **simile** the comparison between the two things is made explicit by the use of the words 'as' or 'like':

I wandered lonely as a cloud
(WILLIAM WORDSWORTH, *Daffodils*)

Like as the waves make towards the pebbled shore,
So do our minutes hasten to their end.
(SHAKESPEARE, *Sonnet 60*)

Metonymy is the fact of referring to something by the name of something else closely connected with it, used especially as a form of shorthand for something familiar or obvious, as in 'I've been reading Shakespeare' instead of 'I've been reading the plays of Shakespeare'.

Allegory is a style of writing in which each character or event is a symbol representing a particular quality. In John Bunyan's *Pilgrim's Progress,* Christian escapes from the City of Destruction, travels through the Slough of Despond, visits Vanity Fair and finally arrives at the Celestial City. He meets characters such as the Giant Despair and Mr Worldly Wiseman and is accompanied by Faithful and Hopeful.

Personification is the act of representing objects or qualities as human beings:

Love bade me welcome: yet my soul drew back,
Guilty of dust and sin.
(GEORGE HERBERT, *Love*)

Pathetic fallacy is the effect produced when animals and things are shown as having human feeling. For example, in John Milton's poem, *Lycidas*, the flowers are shown as weeping for the dead shepherd, Lycidas.

Patterns of sound

Alliteration is the use of the same letter or sound at the beginning of words that are close together. It was used systematically in Anglo-Saxon (= Old English) poetry but in modern English poetry is generally only used for a particular effect:

*On the **b**ald street **b**reaks the **b**lank day.*
(ALFRED, LORD TENNYSON, *In Memoriam*)

Assonance is the effect created when two syllables in words that are close together have the same vowel sound but different consonants, or the same consonants but different vowels:

*It seemed that out of battle I e**scaped***
*Down some profound dull tunnel long since **scooped**...*
(WILFRED OWEN, *Strange Meeting*)

Onomatopoeia is the effect produced when the words used contain similar sounds to the noises they describe:

murmuring of innumerable bees
(TENNYSON, *The Princess*)

Other stylistic effects

Irony is the use of words that say the opposite of what you really mean, often in order to make a critical comment.

Hyperbole is the use of exaggeration:

An hundred years should go to praise
Thine eyes and on thy forehead gaze
(ANDREW MARVELL, *To His Coy Mistress*)

An **oxymoron** is a phrase that combines two words that seem to be the opposite of each other:

*Parting is such **sweet sorrow***
(SHAKESPEARE, *Romeo and Juliet*)

A **paradox** is a statement that contains two opposite ideas or seems to be impossible:

The Child is father of the Man.
(WORDSWORTH, *'My heart leaps up...'*)

Poetry

Lyric poetry is usually fairly short and expresses thoughts and feelings. Examples are Wordsworth's *Daffodils* and Dylan Thomas's *Fern Hill*.

Epic poetry can be much longer and deals with the actions of great men and women or the history of nations. Examples are Homer's *Iliad* and Virgil's *Aeneid*.

Narrative poetry tells a story, like Chaucer's *Canterbury Tales*, or Coleridge's *Rime of the Ancient Mariner*.

Dramatic poetry takes the form of a play, and includes the plays of Shakespeare (which also contain scenes in **prose**).

A **ballad** is a traditional type of narrative poem with short **verses** or **stanzas** and a simple **rhyme scheme** (= pattern of rhymes).

An **elegy** is a type of lyric poem that expresses sadness for someone who has died. Thomas Gray's *Elegy Written in a Country Churchyard* mourns all who lived and died quietly and never had the chance to be great.

An **ode** is a lyric poem that addresses a person or thing or celebrates an event. John Keats wrote five great odes, including *Ode to a Nightingale*, *Ode to a Grecian Urn* and *To Autumn*.

Metre is the rhythm of poetry determined by the arrangement of stressed and unstressed, or long and short, syllables in each line of the poem.

Prosody is the theory and study of metre.

Iambic pentameter is the most common metre in English poetry. Each line consists of five **feet** (pentameter), each containing an unstressed syllable followed by a stressed syllable (iambic):

/ / / / /
The curfew tolls the knell of parting day
(GRAY, *Elegy)*

Most lines of iambic pentameter, however, are not absolutely regular in their pattern of stresses:

/ / / /
Shall I compare thee to a summer's day?
(shakespeare, Sonnet 18)

A **couplet** is a pair of lines of poetry with the same metre, especially ones that rhyme:

For never was a story of more woe
Than this of Juliet and her Romeo.
(SHAKESPEARE, *Romeo and Juliet)*

A **sonnet** is a poem of 14 lines, in English written in iambic pentameter, and with a fixed pattern of rhyme, often ending with a rhyming couplet.

Blank verse is poetry written in iambic pentameters that do not rhyme. A lot of Shakespeare's dramatic verse is in blank verse, as is Milton's epic *Paradise Lost*.

Free verse is poetry without a regular metre or rhyme scheme. Much twentieth-century poetry is written in free verse, for example T.S. Eliot's *The Waste Land*.

Drama

The different **genres** of drama include **comedy**, **tragedy** and **farce**.

Catharsis is the process of releasing and providing relief from strong emotions such as pity and fear by watching the same emotions being played out on stage.

A **deus ex machina** is an unexpected power or event that suddenly appears to resolve a situation that seems hopeless. It is often used to talk about a character in a play or story who only appears at the end.

Dramatic irony is when a character's words carry an extra meaning, especially because of what is going to happen that the character does not know about. For example, King Duncan in Shakespeare's *Macbeth* is pleased to accept Macbeth's hospitality, not knowing that Macbeth is going to murder him that night.

Hubris is too much pride or self-confidence, especially when shown by a tragic hero or heroine who tries to defy the gods or fate.

Nemesis is what happens when the hero or heroine's past mistakes or sins finally cause his or her downfall and death.

A **soliloquy** is a speech in a play for one character who is alone on the stage and speaks his or her thoughts aloud. The most famous soliloquy in English drama is Hamlet's beginning 'To be or not to be...'

Narrative

A **novel** is a **narrative** (= a story) long enough to fill a complete book. The story may be told by a **first-person narrator**, who is a character in the story and relates what happens to himself or herself, or there may be an **omniscient narrator** who relates what happens to all the characters in the third person.

A **short story** is a story that is short enough to be read from beginning to end without stopping.

The **denouement** is the end of a book or play in which everything is explained or settled. It is often used to talk about mystery or detective stories.

Stream of consciousness is a style of writing used in novels that shows the continuous flow of a character's thoughts and feelings without using the usual methods of description or conversation. It was used particularly in the twentieth century by writers such as James Joyce and Virginia Woolf.

COLLOCATIONS

Health

You can **have** any illness or disease:

I'm warning you—I've got a bad cold.

Have the kids had chickenpox yet?

Get can be used with diseases or illnesses that you often have:

He gets really bad hay fever every summer.

Suffer from is used in more formal contexts and with more serious diseases:

This medicine is often recommended for patients who suffer from arthritis.

a heavy cold

You can also:

catch	develop	come/go down with	contract	suffer
chickenpox	Aids	appendicitis	Aids	a breakdown
a cold	an allergy (to sth)	bronchitis	cancer	a heart attack
a cough	arthritis	chickenpox	conjunctivitis	a stroke
flu	cancer	diarrhoea	hepatitis	
German measles	cataracts	flu	HIV	
glandular fever	epilepsy	food poisoning	meningitis	
measles	heart/liver trouble	measles	pneumonia	
mumps	high blood pressure	mumps		
a stomach bug	an infection			
whooping cough	pneumonia			
	rheumatism			

- ▶ an **attack of** flu, nerves, shingles; an asthma **attack**
- ▶ a **bout of** bronchitis, coughing, flu, pneumonia, sickness
- ▶ a coughing, an epileptic **fit**

Is it serious?

no	yes
a bit of a cold, a cough, an infection	a bad/heavy/nasty cold
mild depression	a bad/nasty/severe attack of sth, bout of sth
a mild attack of sth, bout of sth	a bad/hacking/racking cough
a mild heart attack, infection	a bad/splitting headache
a slight cold, headache	a massive/serious heart attack, stroke

What's the treatment?

take	be given/ be on/take	have/ undergo	have/ be given	have/be given/ undergo
medicine	antibiotics	an operation	acupuncture	hypnosis
pills	drugs	surgery	an anaesthetic	therapy
tablets	medication	a transplant	a blood transfusion	treatment
	painkillers		an injection	
			a scan	
			an X-ray	

Computers

installing software

- **boot up/start up** the **computer**
- **insert** the program **disk/CD-ROM**
- **follow** the set up **instructions**
- **reboot/restart** the **computer**

creating a document

- **select** the new document **option** from the **pull-down menus** or **click on** the new document **icon**
- **type**, **edit** and **format** the **document**
- **print out** the **document**
- **save** and **close** the **document**

cutting and pasting text

- **scroll down** the **text** to find the **block** of **text** you want to **move**
- **position** the **cursor** at the beginning of the block of text
- **hold down** the **left mouse button** and **drag** the **mouse** to **highlight** the block of **text**
- **release** the **left mouse button**
- **click on** the **right mouse button** and **select** the cut text **option from** the **pop-up menu**
- **move** the **cursor** to where you want the text to go
- **select** the paste text **option**

looking up something on the Internet

- **connect to** the **Internet**
- **type in** the **website address** or **click (on)/ follow** a **link**
- **access** the **website**
- **browse/search** the **website** to find the information
- if necessary, **download** the **information**

running several applications at the same time

- **double click on** the different program **icons**
- **move** and **resize** the program **windows** as required
- **click on** a program's **window** to use that program
- when finished, **close** the **windows**

resizing a window

backing-up a file on to a USB stick

- **insert** a **USB stick**
- **compress/zip** the **file** if it is too large
- **copy/save** the **file** onto a **USB stick**
- if necessary, **rename** the backed-up **file**
- **remove/take out** the **USB stick**

THE PERIODIC TABLE OF ELEMENTS

The periodic table arranges all known elements according to their atomic numbers.

Periods →

- The horizontal rows of elements are called **periods**.
- A period contains elements with different properties.
- Each period (apart from the first) shows a trend from metallic to non-metallic properties.

Groups ↓

- The long vertical rows of elements are called **groups**.
- The groups are numbered 0 to 7.
- A group contains elements with similar chemical properties.
- Going down a group, the properties of the elements show trends.
- Hydrogen is unlike any other element – it is not part of a group.

Metals and non-metals

The black zigzag line divides the periodic table into metallic and non-metallic elements. The metals appear on the left and the non-metals appear on the right. There are many more metals than non-metals.

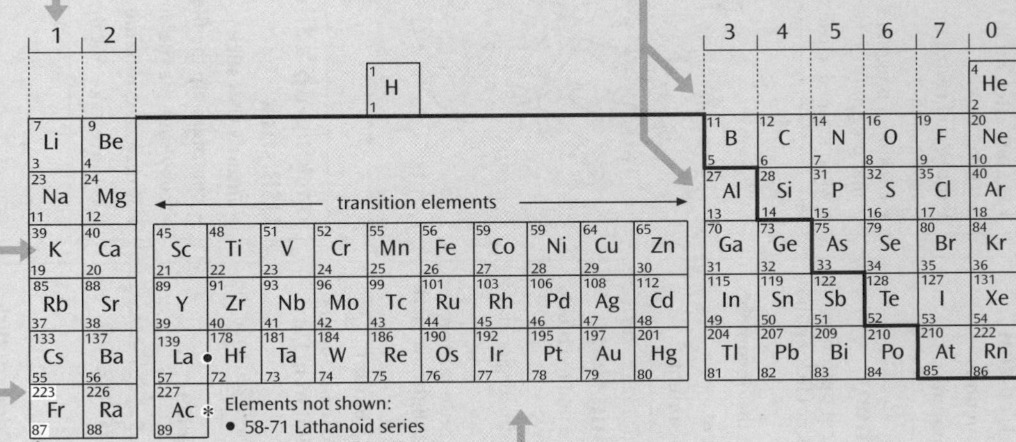

1	2	←				transition elements					→	3	4	5	6	7	0
						1 H 1											4 He 2
7 Li 3	9 Be 4											11 B 5	12 C 6	14 N 7	16 O 8	19 F 9	20 Ne 10
23 Na 11	24 Mg 12											27 Al 13	28 Si 14	31 P 15	32 S 16	35 Cl 17	40 Ar 18
39 K 19	40 Ca 20	45 Sc 21	48 Ti 22	51 V 23	52 Cr 24	55 Mn 25	56 Fe 26	59 Co 27	59 Ni 28	64 Cu 29	65 Zn 30	70 Ga 31	73 Ge 32	75 As 33	79 Se 34	80 Br 35	84 Kr 36
85 Rb 37	88 Sr 38	89 Y 39	91 Zr 40	93 Nb 41	96 Mo 42	99 Tc 43	101 Ru 44	103 Rh 45	106 Pd 46	108 Ag 47	112 Cd 48	115 In 49	119 Sn 50	122 Sb 51	128 Te 52	127 I 53	131 Xe 54
133 Cs 55	137 Ba 56	139 La ● 57	178 Hf 72	181 Ta 73	184 W 74	186 Re 75	190 Os 76	192 Ir 77	195 Pt 78	197 Au 79	201 Hg 80	204 Tl 81	207 Pb 82	209 Bi 83	210 Po 84	210 At 85	222 Rn 86
223 Fr 87	226 Ra 88	227 Ac * 89															

Elements not shown:
- ● 58-71 Lathanoid series
- * 90-103 Actinoid series

Atomic number

The elements in the periodic table are arranged in order of increasing atomic number. This tells us the number of protons in the nucleus of the element. It also tells us the number of electrons in an atom.

Atomic mass

The mass number of an atom is the sum of the protons and neutrons in the nucleus of the atom.

223 Fr 87	223 = atomic number 87 = relative atomic mass **Fr** = chemical symbol

Transition metals

- These metals come between Group 2 and Group 3. They are generally hard metals with high boiling points.
- Many form coloured salts, e.g. copper(II) sulphate is blue, potassium manganate(VII) is purple and iron(II) sulphate is green.
- They form ions with different charges e.g. Cu+ and Cu2+, Fe2+ and Fe3+. This means they can form different compounds with the same elements e.g. copper(I) oxide Cu2O and copper(II) oxide CuO.
- Some transition metals are useful catalysts for important reactions, e.g. vanadium(V) oxide in making sulphuric acid, iron for making ammonia, nickel for making margarine.

Names and symbols of the elements

name	symbol	atomic number	atomic mass
actinium	**Ac**	89	227
aluminium	**Al**	13	27
americium	**Am**	95	243
antimony	**Sb**	51	122
argon	**Ar**	18	40
arsenic	**As**	33	75
astatine	**At**	85	210
barium	**Ba**	56	137
berkelium	**Bk**	97	247
beryllium	**Be**	4	9
bismuth	**Bi**	83	209
boron	**B**	5	11
bromine	**Br**	35	80
cadmium	**Cd**	48	112
caesium	**Cs**	55	133
calcium	**Ca**	20	40
californium	**Cf**	98	251
carbon	**C**	6	12
cerium	**Ce**	58	140
chlorine	**Cl**	17	35
chromium	**Cr**	24	52
cobalt	**Co**	27	59
copper	**Cu**	29	64
curium	**Cm**	96	247
darmstadtium	**Ds**	110	282
dysprosium	**Dy**	66	162
einsteinium	**Es**	99	252
erbium	**Er**	68	167
europium	**Eu**	63	152
fermium	**Fm**	100	257
fluorine	**F**	9	19
francium	**Fr**	87	223
gadolinium	**Gd**	64	157
gallium	**Ga**	31	70
germanium	**Ge**	32	73
gold	**Au**	79	197
hafnium	**Hf**	72	178
helium	**He**	2	4
holmium	**Ho**	67	165
hydrogen	**H**	1	1
indium	**In**	49	115
iodine	**I**	53	127
iridium	**Ir**	77	192
iron	**Fe**	26	56
krypton	**Kr**	36	84
lanthanum	**La**	57	139
lawrencium	**Lr**	103	260
lead	**Pb**	82	207
lithium	**Li**	3	7
lutetium	**Lu**	71	175
magnesium	**Mg**	12	24
manganese	**Mn**	25	55
mendelevium	**Md**	101	258

name	symbol	atomic number	atomic mass
mercury	**Hg**	80	201
molybdenum	**Mo**	42	96
neodymium	**Nd**	60	144
neon	**Ne**	10	20
neptunium	**Np**	93	237
nickel	**Ni**	28	59
niobium	**Nb**	41	93
nitrogen	**N**	7	14
nobelium	**No**	102	259
osmium	**Os**	76	190
oxygen	**O**	8	16
palladium	**Pd**	46	106
phosphorus	**P**	15	31
platinum	**Pt**	78	195
plutonium	**Pu**	94	244
polonium	**Po**	84	210
potassium	**K**	19	39
praseodymium	**Pr**	59	141
promethium	**Pm**	61	145
protactinium	**Pa**	91	231
radium	**Ra**	88	226
radon	**Rn**	86	222
rhenium	**Re**	75	186
rhodium	**Rh**	45	103
rubidium	**Rb**	37	85
ruthenium	**Ru**	44	101
samarium	**Sm**	62	150
scandium	**Sc**	21	45
selenium	**Se**	34	79
silicon	**Si**	14	28
silver	**Ag**	47	108
sodium	**Na**	11	23
strontium	**Sr**	38	88
sulphur	**S**	16	32
tantalum	**Ta**	73	181
technetium	**Tc**	43	99
tellurium	**Te**	52	128
terbium	**Tb**	65	159
thallium	**Tl**	81	204
thorium	**Th**	90	232
thulium	**Tm**	69	169
tin	**Sn**	50	119
titanium	**Ti**	22	48
tungsten	**W**	74	184
uranium	**U**	92	238
vanadium	**V**	23	51
xenon	**Xe**	54	131
ytterbium	**Yb**	70	173
yttrium	**Y**	39	89
zinc	**Zn**	30	65
zirconium	**Zr**	40	91

EXPRESSIONS USING NUMBERS

Cardinal numbers

1	one
2	two
3	three
4	four
5	five
6	six
7	seven
8	eight
9	nine
10	ten
11	eleven
12	twelve
13	thirteen
14	fourteen
15	fifteen
16	sixteen
17	seventeen
18	eighteen
19	nineteen
20	twenty
21	twenty-one
22	twenty-two
30	thirty
40	forty
50	fifty
60	sixty
70	seventy
80	eighty
90	ninety
100	a/one hundred*
101	a/one hundred and one*
200	two hundred
1 000	a/one thousand*
10 000	ten thousand
100 000	a/one hundred thousand*
1 000 000	a/one million*

Ordinal numbers

1st	first
2nd	second
3rd	third
4th	fourth
5th	fifth
6th	sixth
7th	seventh
8th	eighth
9th	ninth
10th	tenth
11th	eleventh
12th	twelfth
13th	thirteenth
14th	fourteenth
15th	fifteenth
16th	sixteenth
17th	seventeenth
18th	eighteenth
19th	nineteenth
20th	twentieth
21st	twenty-first
22nd	twenty-second
30th	thirtieth
40th	fortieth
50th	fiftieth
60th	sixtieth
70th	seventieth
80th	eightieth
90th	ninetieth
100th	hundredth
101st	hundred and first
200th	two hundredth
1 000th	thousandth
10 000th	ten thousandth
100 000th	hundred thousandth
1 000 000th	millionth

EXAMPLES:
697 *six hundred and ninety-seven*
3402 *three thousand, four hundred and two*
80534 *eighty thousand, five hundred and thirty-four*

* You use **one hundred**, **one thousand**, etc. instead of **a hundred**, **a thousand** when it is important to stress that you mean one (not two, for example). In numbers over a thousand, you use a comma or a small space: 1,200 or 1 200.

Roman numerals

I	one	V	five	IX	nine	L	fifty
II	two	VI	six	X	ten	C	a hundred
III	three	VII	seven	XV	fifteen	D	five hundred
IV	four	VIII	eight	XX	twenty	M	a thousand

Telephone numbers

In telephone numbers, you say each number separately, often with a pause after two or three numbers:
— *509236 **five o nine – two three six***

You can say **six six** or **double six** for 66:
— *02166 **o two one – double six*** or ***o two one – six six**.*

If you are calling a number in a different town, you have to use the **area code** before the number:
— *01865 is the code for Oxford.*

If you are phoning somebody in a large firm, you can ask for their **extension number**.
— *(01865) 556767 x 4840 (extension 4840)*

Fractions and decimals

$\frac{1}{2}$	a half	$\frac{1}{3}$	a/one third
$\frac{1}{4}$	a quarter	$\frac{2}{5}$	two fifths
$\frac{1}{8}$	an/one eighth	$\frac{7}{12}$	seven twelfths
$\frac{1}{10}$	a/one tenth	$1\frac{1}{2}$	one and a half
$\frac{1}{16}$	a/one sixteenth	$2\frac{3}{8}$	two and three eighths
0.1	(nought) point one	1.75	one point seven five
0.25	(nought) point two five	3.976	three point nine seven six
0.33	(nought) point three three		

Percentages and proportions

90% of the land is cultivated.
Nine out of ten households have a television.
Nine tenths of all households have a television.
The ratio of households with a television to those without is **9:1** (nine to one).

Mathematical expressions

$+$	plus	$\approx$	is approximately equal to
$-$	minus	$>$	is greater than
$\times$	times/multiplied by	$\geq$	is greater than or equal to
$\div$	divided by	$<$	is less than
$=$	equals	$\leq$	is less than or equal to
$\neq$	is not equal to	%	per cent
3^2	three squared	$\sqrt{\ }$	square root
5^3	five cubed	$\sqrt[3]{\ }$	cube root
6^{10}	six to the power of ten		

EXAMPLES: $7 + 6 = 13$ *seven plus six equals* (or *is*) *thirteen*
$5 \times 8 = 40$ *five times eight equals forty*
OR *five eights are forty*
OR *five multiplied by eight is forty*
$\sqrt{9} = 3$ *the square root of nine is three*
$\sqrt[3]{125} = 5$ *the cube root of one hundred and twenty-five is five*

Temperature

In Britain, temperatures are now usually given in **degrees Celsius**, (although many people are still more familiar with **Fahrenheit**). In the United States, **Fahrenheit** is used, except in science.

To convert **Fahrenheit** to **Celsius**,	**68°F –**
subtract 32 from the number,	32
then	= 36 ×
multiply by 5	5
and divide by 9:	= 180 ÷ 9
	= **20°C**

EXAMPLES: — *Water freezes at 32°F and boils at 212°F.*
— *The maximum temperature this afternoon will be 15°C, and the minimum tonight may reach -5 (minus five).*
— *She was running a temperature of 102°C last night, and it's still above normal.*

Weight

	Imperial	Metric
	1 ounce (oz)	= 28.35 grams (g)
16 ounces	= 1 pound (lb)	= 0.454 kilogram (kg)
14 pounds	= 1 stone (st)	= 6.356 kilograms
112 pounds	= 1 hundredweight (cwt)	= 50.8 kilograms
20 hundredweight	= 1 ton (t)	= 1.016 tonnes

EXAMPLES: *The baby weighed 8 lb 2oz (eight pounds two ounces).*
For this recipe you need 750g (seven hundred and fifty grams) of flour.

NOTE: In the United States, one hundredweight is equal to 100 pounds and one ton is 2 000 lb or 0.907 tonne. Americans do not use stones, so they talk about their weight in pounds: *He weighs 180 pounds.*

Length

	Imperial	Metric
	1 inch (in.)	= 25.4 millimetres (mm)
12 inches	= 1 foot (ft)	= 30.48 centimetres (cm)
3 feet	= 1 yard (yd)	= 0.914 metre (m)
1 760 yards	= 1 mile	= 1.609 kilometres (km)

EXAMPLES: — *300 dots per inch*
— *flying at 7 000 feet*
— *The speed limit is 30 mph (thirty miles per hour).*
— *The room is 11' × 9'6" (eleven feet by nine feet and six inches*
OR
eleven foot by nine foot six).

Area

	Imperial	Metric
	1 square inch (sq in.)	= 6.452 square centimetres
144 square inches	= 1 square foot (sq ft)	= 929.03 square centimetres
9 square feet	= 1 square yard (sq yd)	= 0.836 square metre
4 840 square yards	= 1 acre	= 0.405 hectare
640 acres	= 1 square mile	= 2.59 square kilometres or 259 hectares

EXAMPLES: — *an 80-acre country park*
— *160 000 square miles of the jungle have been destroyed.*

Cubic Measure

	1 cubic inch (cu. in.)	= 16.39 cubic centimetres (cc)
1 728 cubic inches	= 1 cubic foot (cu. ft)	= 0.028 cubic metre
27 cubic feet	= 1 cubic yard	= 0.765 cubic metre

EXAMPLE: — *a car with a 1500 cc engine*

Capacity

	UK	US	Metric
20 fluid ounces (fl oz)	= 1 pint (pt)	= 1.201 pints	= 0.568 litre (l)
2 pints	= 1 quart (qt)	= 1.201 quarts	= 1.136 litres
4 quarts	= 1 gallon (gal.)	= 1.201 gallons	= 4.546 litres

EXAMPLES: — *I drink a litre of water a day.*
— *a quart of orange juice*

NOTE: Quart is not often used in British English.

Times

	In conversation	In official language
06.00	six o'clock	(o) six hundred (hours)
06.05	five past six	(o) six o five
06.10	ten past six	(o) six ten
06.15	(a) quarter past six	(o) six fifteen
06.20	twenty past six	(o) six twenty
06.30	half past six	(o) six thirty
06.35	twenty-five to seven	(o) six thirty-five
06.40	twenty to seven	(o) six forty
06.45	(a) quarter to seven	(o) six forty-five
06.50	ten to seven	(o) six fifty
06.55	five to seven	(o) six fifty-five
10.12	twelve minutes past ten	ten twelve
13.10	ten past one	thirteen ten
19.56	four minutes to eight	nineteen fifty-six

NOTE: In American English, **after** is sometimes used instead of 'past' and **of** instead of 'to'.

NOTE: The 24-hour clock is used in official language:
— *The next train is the 07.02 to Marlow. (o seven o two)*

In conversation, you can say:
— *I left at seven in the morning/two in the afternoon/eight in the evening/eleven at night.*

a.m. (for times before midday) and **p.m.** (for times after midday) are used in slightly more formal language:
— *School starts at 9 a.m.*

Dates

You can write dates in numbers or in numbers and words:
— *15/4/07 (AmE 4/15/07)*
15 April 2007
April 15th, 2007 (especially AmE)

You can say:
— *April the fifteenth, two thousand and seven*
OR *the fifteenth of April, two thousand and seven*
(In American English, *April fifteenth, two thousand and seven*)

EXAMPLES: *She was born on 4 May (May the fourth/the fourth of May).*
My passport expires in 2012 (two thousand and twelve).

SI Units

UNITS

	Physical Quantity	Name	Symbol
Base units	length	metre	m
	mass	kilogram	kg
	time	second	s
	electric current	ampere	A
	thermodynamic temperature	kelvin	K
	luminous intensity	candela	cd
	amount of substance	mole	mol

Supplementary units	**Physical Quantity**	**Name**	**Symbol**
	plane angle	radian	rad
	solid angle	steradian	sr

AFFIXES

Multiple	Affix	Symbol	Sub-multiple	Affix	Symbol
10	deca-	da	**10^{-1}**	deci-	d
10^{2}	hecto-	h	**10^{-2}**	centi-	c
10^{3}	kilo-	k	**10^{-3}**	milli-	m
10^{6}	mega-	M	**10^{-6}**	micro-	*m*
10^{9}	giga-	G	**10^{-9}**	nano-	n
10^{12}	tera-	T	**10^{-12}**	pico-	p
10^{15}	peta-	P	**10^{-15}**	femto-	f
10^{18}	exa-	E	**10^{-18}**	atto-	a

PREFIXES AND SUFFIXES

What do you do when you find a new word in English? Before you reach for your dictionary, do you try to work out what it means? Often long words are made from shorter words that you know, combined with a few letters at the beginning (a **prefix**), or a few letters at the end (a **suffix**).

Prefixes generally alter the meaning of a word and suffixes change its **part of speech** (whether it is a noun, a verb, an adjective or an adverb). Below you can find a full list of prefixes and suffixes with their meanings and use.

Prefixes

a- not; without: *atypical, amoral*

aero- connected with air or aircraft:*aerodynamic*

agro-, **agri-** connected with farming: *agro-industry*

all- **1** completely: *an all-inclusive price* **2** in the highest degree: *all-important, all-powerful*

ambi- referring to both of two: *ambivalent*

Anglo- connected with England or Britain (and another country or countries): *Anglo-American relations*

ante- before; in front of: *antenatal, ante-room*

anthropo- connected with human beings: *anthropology*

anti- against: *anti-war*

arch- main; most important or most extreme: *archbishop*

astro- connected with the stars or outer space: *astrophysics*

audio- connected with hearing or sound: *audio-visual*

auto- **1** about or by yourself: *autobiography* (= the story of the writer's own life) **2** by itself, without a person to operate it: *automatic*

be- **1** to make or treat sb/sth as: *They befriended him.* **2** wearing or covered with: *bejewelled*

bi- two; twice; double: *bilingual, bicentenary*

biblio- connected with books: *bibliography*

bio- connected with living things or human life: *biodegradable*

by- **1** less important: a by-product **2** near: *a bystander*

cardio- connected with the heart: *cardiology*

centi- hundred; hundredth: *centipede*, *centimetre* (= one hundredth of a metre)
chrono- connected with time: *chronology*
circum- around: *circumnavigate* (= sail around)
co- together with: *co-pilot*, *coexist*
con- with; together: *concurrent*
contra- against; opposite: *contradict* (= say the opposite)
counter- against; opposite: *counter-terrorism*, *counterproductive* (= producing the opposite of the desired effect)
cross- involving movement or action from one thing to another or between two things: *cross-fertilize*
crypto- hidden; secret: *a crypto-communist*
cyber- connected with electronic communication, especially the Internet: *cybercafe*
de- 1 the opposite of: *decompress* **2** taking sth away: *decaffeinated coffee*
deca- ten; having ten: *decathlon*
deci- one tenth: *decilitre*
demi- half; partly: *demigod*
demo- connected with people or population: *democracy*
di- used in chemistry to refer to substances that contain two atoms of the type mentioned: *dioxide*
dis- not; the opposite of: *discontinue*, *disarmament*
e- connected with the use of electronic communication, especially the Internet, for sending information, doing business, etc.: *e-commerce*
eco- connected with the environment: *eco-friendly*
electro- connected with electricity: *electromagnetism*
en- (**em-**) **1** to put into the thing or condition mentioned: *endanger*, *empower* **2** to cause to be: *enlarge*, *embolden*
equi- equal; equally: *equidistant*
Euro- connected with Europe or the European Union: *Euro-elections*
ever- always; continuously: *the ever-growing problem of pollution*
ex- former: *ex-wife*
extra- 1 outside; beyond: *extraterrestrial* (= coming from somewhere beyond the earth) **2** very; more than usual: *extra-thin*
fore- 1 before; in advance: *foreword* (= at the beginning of a book) **2** in front of: *foreground* (= the front part of a picture)
geo- of the earth: *geoscience*
haemo-, hemo- connected with blood: *haemophilia*
hepta- seven; having seven: *heptathlon* (= an athletics competition, usually one for women, that consists of seven different events)
hetero- other; different: *heterogeneous*
hexa- six; having six: *hexagonal*
homo- the same: *homogeneous*
hydr(o)- 1 connected with water: *hydroelectricity* **2** connected with or mixed with hydrogen: *hydroxide*
hyper- more than normal; too much: *hypersensitive*
hypo- under; below normal: *hypodermic*
ill- badly or wrongly: *You would be ill-advised to drive until you have fully recovered.*
in- (**il-**, **im-**, **ir-**) not; the opposite of: *incorrect*, *illegal*, *immoral*, *impatient*, *irregular*
info- connected with information: *an infosheet*
infra- below a particular limit: *infrared*
inter- between; from one to another: *interaction*
intra- inside; within: *intravenous*
iso- equal: *isotope*
kilo- thousand: *kilogram*
macro- large; on a large scale: *macroeconomics*
mal- bad or badly; not correct or correctly: *malnutrition*
many- having a lot of the thing mentioned: *a many-sided shape*
mega- 1 very large or great: a *megastore*, **2** one million: *a megawatt*
meta- 1 connected with a change of position or state: *metamorphosis* **2** higher; beyond: *metaphysics*
micro- small; on a small scale: *microchip*
mid- in the middle of: *mid-afternoon*
milli- thousandth: *millisecond*
mini- very small: *miniskirt*
mis- bad or wrong; badly or wrongly: *misbehaviour*, *misunderstand*
mono- one; single: *monolingual* (= using one language), *monorail*
multi- many; more than one: *multicoloured*, *a multimillionaire*
nano- (especially in units of measurement) one billionth (= one of one thousand million equal parts of sth): *nanosecond*
near- almost: *a near-perfect performance*
neo- new; in a later form: *neo-fascist*
neuro- connected with the nerves: *neuroscience*
non- not: *non-biodegradable*
nona- nine; having nine: *nonagenarian* (= a person who is between 90 and 99 years old)
octa-, octo- eight; having eight: *octagon* (= a shape with eight sides), *octogenarian*
off- not on; away from: *offstage*
omni- of all things; in all ways or places: *omnivore*
ortho- correct; standard: *orthography*
osteo- connected with bones: *osteopath*
out- 1 greater, better, further, longer, etc.: *outdo*, *outrun* **2** outside; away from: *outpatient*
over- 1 more than normal; too much: *overeat* **2** completely: *overjoyed* **3** upper; outer; extra: *overcoat*, *overtime* **4** over; above: *overhang*

paed-, **ped-** connected with children: *paediatrics*
palaeo-, **paleo-** connected with ancient times: *palaeontology*
pan- including all of sth; connected with the whole of sth: *pan-African*
para- 1 beyond: *paranormal* **2** similar to but not official or not fully qualified: *a paramedic*
patho- connected with disease: *pathology*
penta- five; having five: *pentagon, pentathlon* (= a competition involving five different sports)
petro- 1 connected with rocks: *petrology* **2** connected with petrol: *petrochemical*
philo- liking: *philanthropist*
phono- connected with sound or sounds: *phonetic, phonology*
photo- 1 connected with light: *photosynthesis* **2** connected with photography: *photocopier*
physio- 1 connected with nature **2** connected with physiology (= the way in which living things function, and the scientific study of this)
poly- many: *polygamy*
post- after: *post-war*
pre- before: *prepay, preview*
pro- in favour of; supporting: *pro-democracy*
proto- original; from which others develop: *prototype*
pseudo- not genuine; false or pretended: *pseudonym*
psycho- connected with the mind: *psychology*
quad-, **quadri-** four; having four: *quadruple* (= multiply by four), *quadrilateral*
quasi- 1 that appears to be sth but is not really so: *a quasi-scientific explanation* **2** partly; almost: *a quasi-official body*
radio- 1 connected with radio waves or the activity of sending out radio or television programmes (= broadcasting): *a radio-controlled car* **2** connected with radioactivity (= powerful and very dangerous rays that are produced when atoms are broken up): *radiographer*
re- again: *rewrite, reappearance*
retro- back or backwards: *retrospective*
self- of, to or by yourself or itself: *self-control*
semi- half: *semicircle, semi-final*
septa- seven; having seven
socio- connected with society or the study of society: *socio-economic*
step- related as a result of one parent marrying again: *stepmother*
sub- 1 below; less than: *sub-zero* **2** under: *subway* **3** making a smaller part of sth: *subdivide*
super- 1 extremely; more or better than normal: *superhuman* **2** above; over: *superstructure, superimpose*
techno- connected with technology: *technophobe* (= a person who is afraid of technology)
tele- 1 over a long distance; far: *telepathy, telescopic* **2** connected with television: *teletext* **3** done using a telephone: *telesales*
theo- connected with God or a god: *theology*
thermo- connected with heat: *thermonuclear*
trans- 1 across; beyond: *transatlantic* **2** into another place or state: *transplant*
tri- three; having three: *triangle*
ultra- extremely; beyond a certain limit: *ultra-modern*
un- not; the opposite of: *unable, unlock*
under- 1 below: *underground* **2** lower in age, level or position: *the under-fives* **3** not enough: *undercooked food*
uni- one; having one: *uniform, unilaterally*
up- higher; upwards; towards the top of sth: *upturned*

Suffixes

-able, **-ible**, **-ble** (to make adjectives) possible to: *acceptable, noticeable, divisible* (= possible to divide), *irresistible* (= that you cannot resist)
-age (to make nouns) a process or state: *storage, shortage*
-al (to make adjectives) connected with: *experimental, environmental*
-ance, **-ence**, **-ancy**, **-ency** (to make nouns) an action, process or state: *appearance, existence, pregnancy, efficiency*
-ant, **-ent** (to make nouns) a person who does sth: *assistant, student*
-ation (to make nouns) a state or an action: *examination, organization*
-ble → -ABLE
-centric (to make adjectives) concerned with or interested in the thing mentioned: *Eurocentric*
-cracy (to make nouns) the government or rule of: *democracy*
-ectomy (to make nouns) a medical operation in which part of the body is removed: *appendectomy* (= removal of the appendix)
-ed (to make adjectives) having a particular state or quality: *bored, patterned*
-ee (to make nouns) a person to whom sth is done: *employee* (= sb who is employed), *trainee* (= sb who is being trained)
-en (to make verbs) to give sth a particular quality: *shorten, blacken, loosen,* (but note: *lengthen*)

-ence, **-ency**, **-ance**
-ent → -ANT
-er (to make nouns) a person who does sth: *rider, painter, banker, driver, teacher*
-ese (to make adjectives) from a place: *Japanese, Chinese, Viennese*
-ess (to make nouns) a woman who does sth as a job: *waitress, actress*
-fold (to make adjectives and adverbs) multiplied by; having the number of parts mentioned: *to increase tenfold*
-free (to make adjectives) without the thing mentioned: *fat-free, tax-free*
-ful (to make adjectives) having a particular quality: *helpful, useful, beautiful*
-graphy (to make nouns) **1** a type of art or science: *geography* **2** a method of producing images: *radiography* **3** a form of writing or drawing: *biography*
-hood (to make nouns) **1** a state, often during a particular period of time: *childhood, motherhood* **2** a group with sth in common: *sisterhood, neighbourhood*
-ial (to make adjectives) typical of: *dictatorial*
-ian (to make nouns) a person who does sth as a job or hobby: *historian, comedian*
-ible → -ABLE
-ic 1 (to make adjectives and nouns) connected with: *economic, Arabic* **2** (to make adjectives) that performs the action mentioned: *horrific*
-ics (to make nouns) the science, art or activity of: *physics, dramatics, athletics*
-ical (to make adjectives from nouns ending in -y or -ics) connected with: *economical, mathematical, physical*
-ide (to make nouns) (in chemistry) a compound of: *chloride*
-ify (to make verbs) to produce a state or quality: *beautify, simplify, purify*
-ing (to make adjectives) producing a particular state or effect: *interesting*
-ion (to make nouns) a state or process: *action, connection, exhibition*
-ish (to make adjectives) **1** describing nationality or language: *English, Polish* **2** like sth: *babyish* **3** fairly, sort of: *longish, brownish*
-ist (to make nouns) **1** a person who has studied sth or does sth as a job: *artist, scientist* **2** a person who believes in sth or belongs to a particular group: *capitalist, pacifist*
-ite (to make nouns and adjectives) a person who follows or supports; following: *Blairite*
-ity (to make nouns) the quality or state of: *purity*
-ive (to make adjectives) having a particular quality: *attractive, effective*
-ize, **-ise** (to make verbs) producing a particular state: *magnetize, standardize*
-legged (to make adjectives) having the number or type of legs mentioned: *three-legged, long-legged*
-less (to make adjectives) not having sth: *hopeless*
-like (to make adjectives) similar to: *childlike*
-looking (to make adjectives) having the appearance mentioned: *odd-looking, good-looking*
-ly (to make adverbs) in a particular way: *badly, beautifully*
-ment (to make nouns) a state, action or quality: *development, arrangement, excitement*
-most (to make adjectives) the furthest: *southernmost, topmost* (= the furthest up/the nearest to the top)
-ness (to make nouns) a state or quality: *kindness, happiness*
-oid (to make adjectives and nouns) similar to: *humanoid*
-ology (to make nouns) the study of a subject: *biology, zoology*
-or (to make nouns) a person who does sth, often as a job: *actor, conductor*
-ory 1 (to make adjectives) that does: *explanatory* **2** (to make nouns) a place for: *observatory*
-ous (to make adjectives) having a particular quality: *dangerous, religious*
-phile 1 (to make adjectives) liking a particular thing: *Anglophile* **2** (to make nouns) a person who likes a particular thing: *bibliophile*
-philia (to make nouns) love of sth
-phobe (to make nouns) a person who dislikes a particular thing or particular people: *Anglophobe*
-phobia (to make nouns) a fear of the thing mentioned: *claustrophobia*
-proof (to make adjectives) able to protect against the thing mentioned: *soundproof*
-ship (to make nouns) showing status: *friendship, membership, citizenship*
-ward, **-wards** (to make adverbs) in a particular direction: *backward, upwards*
-ways (to make adjectives and adverbs) in the direction of: *lengthways*
-wise (to make adjectives and adverbs) 1 in the manner or direction of: clockwise 2 concerning: Things aren't too good businesswise.
-y (to make adjectives) having the quality of the thing mentioned: rainy, fatty, thirsty

GEOGRAPHICAL NAMES

This list shows the English spelling and pronunciation of geographical names and the adjectives that go with them.

To talk in general about the people from a country, you can use the word **people**

Moroccan people, French people, Israeli people, Japanese people

You can also add an **-s** to the adjective

Moroccans, Israelis

If the adjective ends in an /s/, /z/ or /ʃ/ sound, use **the** and no **-s**

the Swiss, the Chinese, the French

To talk about a number of people from one country, add an **-s** to the adjective, unless it ends in an /s/, /z/ or /ʃ/ sound

two Germans, some Pakistanis, a group of Japanese, a few Swiss

Sometimes there is a special word for a person from a country, in which case this is shown after the adjective, for example **Denmark: Danish, a Dane**

two Danes, several Turks

COUNTRY OR CONTINENT	ADJECTIVE/NOUN
Afghanistan /æf'gænɪstɑːn/	**Afghan** /'æfgæn/
Africa /'æfrɪkə/	**African** /'æfrɪkən/
Albania /æl'beɪniə/	**Albanian** /æl'beɪniən/
Algeria /æl'dʒɪəriə/	**Algerian** /æl'dʒɪəriən/
America /ə'merɪkə/	→**(the) United States of America**
Andorra /æn'dɔːrə/	**Andorran** /æn'dɔːrən/
Angola /æŋ'gəʊlə/	**Angolan** /æŋ'gəʊlən/
Antarctica /æn'tɑːktɪkə/	**Antarctic** /æn'tɑːktɪk/
Antigua and Barbuda /ænˌtiːgə ən bɑː'bjuːdə/	**Antiguan** /æn'tiːgən/, **Barbudan** /bɑː'bjuːdən/
(the) Arctic /'ɑːktɪk/	**Arctic** /'ɑːktɪk/
Argentina /ˌɑːdʒən'tiːnə/	**Argentine** /'ɑːdʒəntaɪn/, **Argentinian** /ˌɑːdʒən'tɪniən/
Armenia /ɑː'miːniə/	**Armenian** /ɑː'miːniən/
Asia /'eɪʃə, 'eɪʒə/	**Asian** /'eɪʃn, 'eɪʒn/
Australia /ɒ'streɪliə/	**Australian** /ɒ'streɪliən/
Austria /'ɒstriə/	**Austrian** /'ɒstriən/
Azerbaijan /ˌæzəbaɪ'dʒɑːn/	**Azerbaijani** /ˌæzəbaɪ'dʒɑːni/, an **Azeri** /ə'zeəri/
(the) Bahamas /bə'hɑːməz/	**Bahamian** /bə'heɪmiən/
Bahrain /bɑː'reɪn/	**Bahraini** /bɑː'reɪni/
Bangladesh /ˌbæŋglə'deʃ/	**Bangladeshi** /ˌbæŋglə'deʃi/
Barbados /bɑː'beɪdɒs/	**Barbadian** /bɑː'beɪdiən/
Belarus /ˌbelə'ruːs/	**Belarusian** /ˌbelə'ruːsiən/
Belgium /'beldʒəm/	**Belgian** /'beldʒən/
Benin /be'niːn/	**Beninese** /ˌbenɪ'niːz/
Bhutan /buː'tɑːn/	**Bhutanese** /ˌbuːtə'niːz/
Bolivia /bə'lɪviə/	**Bolivian** /bə'lɪviən/
Bosnia and Herzegovina /ˌbɒzniə ən ˌhɜːtsəgə'viːnə/	**Bosnian and Herzegovinian** /'bɒzniən ən ˌhɜːtsəgə'vɪniən/
Botswana /bɒt'swɑːnə/	**Botswanan** /bɒt'swɑːnən/, **person: Motswana** /mɒt'swɑːnə/, **people: Batswana** /bæt'swɑːnə/
Brazil /brə'zɪl/	**Brazilian** /brə'zɪliən/
Brunei /ˌbruː'naɪ/	**Bruneian** /bruː'naɪən/
Bulgaria /bʌl'geəriə/	**Bulgarian** /bʌl'geəriən/
Burkina /bɜː'kiːnə/	**Burkinan** /ˌbɜː'kiːnən/

COUNTRY OR CONTINENT	ADJECTIVE/NOUN
Burma /ˈbɜːmə/ (now officially **Myanmar**)	**Burmese** /bɜːˈmiːz/
Burundi /bʊˈrʊndi/	**Burundian** /bʊˈrʊndiən/
Cambodia /kæmˈbəʊdiə/	**Cambodian** /kæmˈbəʊdiən/
Cameroon /ˌkæməˈruːn/	**Cameroonian** /ˌkæməˈruːniən/
Canada /ˈkænədə/	**Canadian** /kəˈneɪdiən/
Cape Verde /ˌkeɪp ˈvɜːd/	**Cape Verdean** /ˌkeɪp ˈvɜːdiən/
(the) **Central African Republic** /ˌsentrəl ˌæfrɪkən rɪˈpʌblɪk/	**Central African** /ˌsentrəl ˈæfrɪkən/
Chad /tʃæd/	**Chadian** /ˈtʃædiən/
Chile /ˈtʃɪli/	**Chilean** /ˈtʃɪliən/
China /ˈtʃaɪnə/	**Chinese** /tʃaɪˈniːz/
Colombia /kəˈlɒmbiə/	**Colombian** /kəˈlɒmbiən/
Comoros /ˈkɒmərəʊz/	**Comoran** /kəˈmɔːrən/
Congo /ˈkɒŋgəʊ/	**Congolese** /ˌkɒŋgəˈliːz/
Costa Rica /ˌkɒstəˈriːkə/	**Costa Rican** /ˌkɒstə ˈriːkən/
Côte d'Ivoire /ˌkəʊt diːˈvwɑː/	**Ivorian** /aɪˈvɔːrɪən/
Croatia /krəʊˈeɪʃə/	**Croatian** /krəʊˈeɪʃn/
Cuba /ˈkjuːbə/	**Cuban** /ˈkjuːbən/
Cyprus /ˈsaɪprəs/	**Cypriot** /ˈsɪpriət/
(the) **Czech Republic** /ˌtʃek rɪˈpʌblɪk/	**Czech** /tʃek/
(the) **Democratic Republic of the Congo** /deməˌkrætɪk rɪˌpʌblɪk əv ðə ˈkɒŋgəʊ/	**Congolese** /ˌkɒŋgəˈliːz/
Denmark /ˈdenmɑːk/	**Danish** /ˈdeɪnɪʃ/, **a Dane** /deɪn/
Djibouti /dʒɪˈbuːti/	**Djiboutian** /dʒɪˈbuːtiən/
Dominica /ˌdɒmɪˈniːkə/	**Dominican** /ˌdɒmɪˈniːkən/
(the) **Dominican Republic** /dəˈmɪnɪkən rɪˈpʌblɪk/	**Dominican** /dəˈmɪnɪkən/
East Timor /ˌiːst ˈtiːmɔː(r)/	**East Timorese** /ˌiːst tɪməˈriːz/
Ecuador /ˈekwədɔː(r)/	**Ecuadorian, Ecuadorean** /ˌekwəˈdɔːriən/
Egypt /ˈiːdʒɪpt/	**Egyptian** /iˈdʒɪpʃn/
El Salvador /el ˈsælvədɔː(r)/	**Salvadorean** /ˌsælvəˈdɔːriən/
England /ˈɪŋglənd/	**English** /ˈɪŋglɪʃ/, **an Englishman** /ˈɪŋglɪʃmən/, **an Englishwoman** /ˈɪŋglɪʃwʊmən/
Equatorial Guinea /ˌekwəˌtɔːriəl ˈgɪni/	**Equatorial Guinean** /ˌekwəˌtɔːriəl ˈgɪniən/
Eritrea /ˌerɪˈtreɪə/	**Eritrean** /ˌerɪˈtreɪən/
Estonia /eˈstəʊniə/	**Estonian** /eˈstəʊniən/
Ethiopia /ˌiːθiˈəʊpiə/	**Ethiopian** /ˌiːθiˈəʊpiən/
Europe /ˈjʊərəp/	**European** /ˌjʊərəˈpiːən/
Fiji /ˈfiːdʒiː/	**Fijian** /fɪˈdʒiːən/
Finland /ˈfɪnlənd/	**Finnish** /ˈfɪnɪʃ/, **a Finn** /fɪn/
France /frɑːns/	**French** /frentʃ/, **a Frenchman** /ˈfrentʃmən/, **a Frenchwoman** /ˈfrentʃwʊmən/
(the) **FYROM** /ˌfɔːmə ˌjuːgəʊslɑːv rɪˈpʌblɪk əv ˌmæsəˈdəʊniə/	**Macedonian** /ˌmæsəˈdəʊniən/
Gabon /gæˈbɒn/	**Gabonese** /ˌgæbəˈniːz/
(the) **Gambia** /ˈgæmbiə/	**Gambian** /ˈgæmbiən/
Georgia /ˈdʒɔːdʒə/	**Georgian** /ˈdʒɔːdʒən/
Germany /ˈdʒɜːməni/	**German** /ˈdʒɜːmən/
Ghana /ˈgɑːnə/	**Ghanaian** /gɑːˈneɪən/
Great Britain /ˌgreɪt ˈbrɪtn/	**British** /ˈbrɪtɪʃ/, **a Briton** /ˈbrɪtn/

COUNTRY OR CONTINENT	ADJECTIVE/NOUN
Greece /gri:s/	**Greek** /gri:k/
Grenada /grə'neɪdə/	**Grenadian** /grə'neɪdiən/
Guatemala /ˌgwɑ:tə'mɑ:lə/	**Guatemalan** /ˌgwɑ:tə'mɑ:lən/
Guinea /'gɪni/	**Guinean** /'gɪniən/
Guinea-Bissau /ˌgɪni bɪ'saʊ/	**Guinean** /'gɪniən/
Guyana /gaɪ'ænə/	**Guyanese** /ˌgaɪə'ni:z/
Haiti /'heɪti/	**Haitian** /'heɪʃn/
Holland /'hɒlənd/	→**(the) Netherlands**
Honduras /hɒn'djʊərəs/	**Honduran** /hɒn'djʊərən/
Hungary /'hʌŋgəri/	**Hungarian** /hʌŋ'geəriən/
Iceland /'aɪslənd/	**Icelandic** /aɪs'lændɪk/, an **Icelander** /'aɪsləndə(r)/
India /'ɪndiə/	**Indian** /'ɪndiən/
Indonesia /ˌɪndə'ni:ʒə/	**Indonesian** /ˌɪndə'ni:ʒn/
Iran /ɪ'rɑ:n/	**Iranian** /ɪ'reɪniən/
Iraq /ɪ'rɑ:k/	**Iraqi** /ɪ'rɑ:ki/
Ireland /'aɪələnd/	**Irish** /'aɪrɪʃ/, an **Irishman**, /'aɪrɪʃmən/, an **Irishwoman** /'aɪrɪʃwʊmən/
Israel /'ɪzreɪl/	**Israeli** /ɪz'reɪli/
Italy /'ɪtəli/	**Italian** /ɪ'tæliən/
(the) Ivory Coast /ˌaɪvəri 'kəʊst/	→**Côte d'Ivoire**
Jamaica /dʒə'meɪkə/	**Jamaican** /dʒə'meɪkən/
Japan /dʒə'pæn/	**Japanese** /ˌdʒæpə'ni:z/
Jordan /'dʒɔ:dn/	**Jordanian** /dʒɔ:'deɪniən/
Kazakhstan /ˌkæzæk'stɑ:n/	**Kazakh** /kə'zæk/
Kenya /'kenjə/	**Kenyan** /'kenjən/
Kiribati /'kɪrɪbæs/	**Kiribati** /'kɪrɪbæs/
Korea, North /ˌnɔ:θ kə'rɪə/	**North Korean** /ˌnɔ:θ kə'rɪən/
Korea, South /ˌsaʊθ kə'rɪə/	**South Korean** /ˌsaʊθ kə'rɪən/
Kuwait /kʊ'weɪt/	**Kuwaiti** /kʊ'weɪti/
Kyrgyzstan /ˌkɪəgɪ'stɑ:n/	**Kyrgyz** /'kɪəgɪz/
Laos /laʊs/	**Laotian** /'laʊʃn/
Latvia /'lætviə/	**Latvian** /'lætviən/
Lebanon /'lebənən/	**Lebanese** /ˌlebə'ni:z/
Lesotho /lə'su:tu:/	**Sotho** /'su:tu:/, person: **Mosotho** /mə'su:tu:/, people: **Basotho** /bə'su:tu:/
Liberia /laɪ'bɪəriə/	**Liberian** /laɪ'bɪəriən/
Libya /'lɪbiə/	**Libyan** /'lɪbiən/
Liechtenstein /'lɪktənstaɪn/	**Liechtenstein, a Liechtensteiner** /'lɪktənstaɪnə(r)/
Lithuania /ˌlɪθju'eɪniə/	**Lithuanian** /ˌlɪθju'eɪniən/
Luxembourg /'lʌksəmbɜ:g/	**Luxembourg, a Luxembourger** /'lʌksəmbɜ:gə(r)/
Madagascar /ˌmædə'gæskə(r)/	**Madagascan** /ˌmædə'gæskən/, a **Malagasy** /ˌmælə'gæsi/
Malawi /mə'lɑ:wi/	**Malawian** /mə'lɑ:wiən/
Malaysia /mə'leɪʒə/	**Malaysian** /mə'leɪʒn/
(the) Maldives /'mɔ:ldi:vz/	**Maldivian** /mɔ:l'dɪviən/
Mali /'mɑ:li/	**Malian** /'mɑ:liən/
Malta /'mɔ:ltə/	**Maltese** /mɔ:l'ti:z/
Mauritania /ˌmɒrɪ'teɪniə/	**Mauritanian** /ˌmɒrɪ'teɪniən/

COUNTRY OR CONTINENT	ADJECTIVE/NOUN
Mauritania /ˌmɒrɪˈteɪniə/	**Mauritanian** /ˌmɒrɪˈteɪniən/
Mauritius /məˈrɪʃəs/	**Mauritian** /məˈrɪʃn/
Mexico /ˈmeksɪkəʊ/	**Mexican** /ˈmeksɪkən/
Micronesia /ˌmaɪkrəˈniːziə/	**Micronesian** /ˌmaɪkrəˈniːziən/
Moldova /mɒlˈdəʊvə/	**Moldovan** /mɒlˈdəʊvən/
Monaco /ˈmɒnəkəʊ/	**Monacan** /ˈmɒnəkən/
Mongolia /mɒŋˈgəʊliə/	**Mongolian** /mɒŋˈgəʊliən/, a **Mongol** /ˈmɒŋgl/
Montenegro /ˌmɒntɪˈniːgrəʊ/	**Montenegrin** /ˌmɒntɪˈniːgrɪn/
Morocco /məˈrɒkəʊ/	**Moroccan** /məˈrɒkən/
Mozambique /ˌməʊzæmˈbiːk/	**Mozambican** /ˌməʊzæmˈbiːkən/
Myanmar /miˌænˈmɑː(r)/	→**Burma**
Namibia /nəˈmɪbiə/	**Namibian** /nəˈmɪbiən/
Nauru /ˈnaʊruː/	**Nauruan** /ˌnaʊˈruːən/
Nepal /nɪˈpɔːl/	**Nepalese** /ˌnepəˈliːz/
(the) **Netherlands** /ˈneðələndz/	**Dutch** /dʌtʃ/, a **Dutchman/Dutchwoman**
New Zealand /ˌnjuː ˈziːlənd/	**New Zealand**, a **New Zealander** /ˌnjuː ˈziːləndə(r)/
Nicaragua /ˌnɪkəˈrægjuə/	**Nicaraguan** /ˌnɪkəˈrægjuən/
Niger /niːˈʒeə(r)/	**Nigerien** /niːˈʒeəriən/
Nigeria /naɪˈdʒɪəriə/	**Nigerian** /naɪˈdʒɪəriən/
Northern Ireland /ˌnɔːðən ˈaɪələnd/	**Northern Irish** /ˌnɔːðən ˈaɪrɪʃ/, a **Northern Irishman/Irishwoman**
Norway /ˈnɔːweɪ/	**Norwegian** /nɔːˈwiːdʒən/
Oceania /ˌəʊsɪˈɑːniə/	**Oceanian** /ˌəʊsɪˈɑːniən/
Oman /əʊˈmɑːn/	**Omani** /əʊˈmɑːni/
Pakistan /ˌpɑːkɪˈstɑːn/	**Pakistani** /ˌpɑːkɪˈstɑːni/
Palau /pəˈlaʊ/	**Palauan** /pəˈlaʊən/
Panama /ˈpænəmɑː/	**Panamanian** /ˌpænəˈmeɪniən/
Papua New Guinea /ˌpæpuə ˌnjuː ˈgɪni/	**Papua New Guinean** /ˌpæpjuə ˌnjuː ˈgɪniən/
Paraguay /ˈpærəgwaɪ/	**Paraguayan** /ˌpærəˈgwaɪən/
Peru /pəˈruː/	**Peruvian** /pəˈruːviən/
(the) **Philippines** /ˈfɪlɪpiːnz/	**Philippine** /ˈfɪlɪpiːn/, a **Filipino** /ˌfɪlɪˈpiːnəʊ/, a **Filipina** /ˌfɪlɪˈpiːnə/
Poland /ˈpəʊlənd/	**Polish** /ˈpəʊlɪʃ/, a **Pole** /pəʊl/
Portugal /ˈpɔːtʃʊgl/	**Portuguese** /ˌpɔːtʃʊˈgiːz/
Qatar /ˈkæˈtɑː(r), ˈkʌtə(r)/	**Qatari** /kæˈtɑːri/
Romania /ruˈmeɪniə/	**Romanian** /ruˈmeɪniən/
Russia /ˈrʌʃə/	**Russian** /ˈrʌʃn/
Rwanda /ruˈændə/	**Rwandan** /ruˈændən/
Samoa /səˈməʊə/	**Samoan** /səˈməʊən/
San Marino /ˌsæn məˈriːnəʊ/	
São Tomé and Principe /ˌsaʊ təˌmeɪ ən ˈprɪnsɪpeɪ/	
Saudi Arabia /ˌsaʊdi əˈreɪbiə/	**Saudi** /ˈsaʊdi/, **Saudi Arabian** /ˌsaʊdi əˈreɪbiən/
Scandinavia /ˌskændɪˈneɪviə/	**Scandinavian** /ˌskændɪˈneɪviən/
Scotland /ˈskɒtlənd/	**Scottish** /ˈskɒtɪʃ/, **Scots** /skɒts/, a **Scot** /skɒt/, a **Scotsman/Scotswoman**
Senegal /ˌsenɪˈgɔːl/	**Senegalese** /ˌsenɪgəˈliːz/
Serbia /ˈsɜːbiə/	**Serbian** /ˈsɜːbiən/, a **Serb** /sɜːb/

COUNTRY OR CONTINENT	ADJECTIVE/NOUN
(the) Seychelles /seɪ'ʃelz/	**Seychellois** /ˌseɪʃel'wɑː/
Sierra Leone /siˌerə li'əʊn/	**Sierra Leonean** /siˌerə li'əʊniən/
Singapore /ˌsɪŋə'pɔː(r)/	**Singaporean** /ˌsiŋə'pɔːriən/
Slovakia /sləʊ'vækiə/	**Slovak** /'sləʊvæk/
Slovenia /sləʊ'viːniə/	**Slovene** /'sləʊviːn/, **Slovenian** /sləʊ'viːniən/
(the) Solomon Islands /'sɒləmən aɪləndz/	**Solomon Islander** /'sɒləmən aɪləndə(r)/
Somalia /sə'mɑːliə/	**Somali** /sə'mɑːli/
South Africa /ˌsaʊθ 'æfrɪkə/	**South African** /ˌsaʊθ 'æfrɪkən/
Spain /speɪn/	**Spanish** /'spænɪʃ/, **a Spaniard** /'spænɪəd/
Sri Lanka /sri 'læŋkə/	**Sri Lankan** /sri 'læŋkən/
St Kitts and Nevis /snt ˌkɪts ən 'niːvɪs/	**Kittitian** /kɪ'tɪʃn/, **Nevisian** /nə'vɪʒn/
St Lucia /snt 'luːʃə/	**St Lucian** /snt 'luːʃən/
St Vincent and the Grenadines /snt ˌvɪnsnt ən ðə 'grenədiːnz/	**Vincentian** /vɪn'senʃn/
Sudan /su'dɑːn/	**Sudanese** /ˌsuːdə'niːz/
Suriname /ˌsʊərɪ'næm/	**Surinamese** /ˌsʊərɪnə'miːz/
Swaziland /'swɑːzilænd/	**Swazi** /'swɑːzi/
Sweden /'swiːdn/	**Swedish** /'swiːdɪʃ/, **a Swede** /swiːd/
Switzerland /'swɪtsələnd/	**Swiss** /swɪs/
Syria /'sɪriə/	**Syrian** /'sɪriən/
Tajikistan /tæˌdʒiːkɪ'stɑːn/	**Tajik** /tæ'dʒiːk/
Tanzania /ˌtænzə'niːə/	**Tanzanian** /ˌtænzə'niːən/
Thailand /'taɪlænd/	**Thai** /taɪ/
Togo /'təʊgəʊ/	**Togolese** /ˌtəʊgə'liːz/
Tonga /'tɒŋə, 'tɒŋgə/	**Tongan** /'tɒŋən, 'tɒŋgən/
Trinidad and Tobago /ˌtrɪnɪdæd ən tə'beɪgəʊ/	**Trinidadian** /ˌtrɪnɪ'dædiən/, **Tobagonian** /ˌtəʊbə'gəʊniən/
Tunisia /tju'nɪziə/	**Tunisian** /tju'nɪziən/
Turkey /'tɜːki/	**Turkish** /'tɜːkɪʃ/, **a Turk** /tɜːk/
Turkmenistan /tɜːkˌmenɪ'stɑːn/	**Turkmen** /'tɜːkmen/
Tuvalu /tu'vɑːluː/	**Tuvaluan** /ˌtuːvɑː'luːən/
Uganda /ju'gændə/	**Ugandan** /ju'gændən/
Ukraine /ju'kreɪn/	**Ukrainian** /ju'kreɪniən/
(the) United Arab Emirates /juˌnaɪtɪd ˌærəb 'emɪrəts/	**Emirati** /emɪ'rɑːti/
(the) United Kingdom /juˌnaɪtɪd 'kɪŋdəm/	**British** /'brɪtɪʃ/, **a Briton** /'brɪtn/
(the) United States of America /juˌnaɪtɪd ˌsteɪts əv ə'merɪkə/	**American** /ə'merɪkən/
Uruguay /'jʊərəgwaɪ/	**Uruguayan** /ˌjʊərə'gwaɪən/
Uzbekistan /ʊzˌbekɪ'stɑːn/	**Uzbek** /'ʊzbek/
Vanuatu /ˌvænu'ɑːtuː/	**Vanuatan** /ˌvænuɑː'tuːən/
Venezuela /ˌvenə'zweɪlə/	**Venezuelan** /ˌvenə'zweɪlən/
Vietnam /ˌvjet'næm/	**Vietnamese** /ˌvjetnə'miːz/
Wales /weɪlz/	**Welsh** /welʃ/, **a Welshman** /'welʃmən/, **a Welshwoman** /'welʃwʊmən/
(the) West Indies /ˌwest 'ɪndiz/	**West Indian** /ˌwest 'ɪndiən/
Yemen /ˌjemən/	**Yemeni** /'jeməni/
Zambia /'zæmbiə/	**Zambian** /'zæmbiən/
Zimbabwe /zɪm'bɑːbwi/	**Zimbabwean** /zɪm'bɑːbwiən/

landslide /ˈlændslaɪd/ *noun* [C] **1** (GEOGRAPHY) the sudden fall of a mass of earth, rocks, etc. down the side of a mountain **2** (POLITICS) a great victory for one person or one political party in an election

lane /leɪn/ *noun* [C] **1** a narrow road in the country: *We found a route through country lanes to avoid the traffic jam on the main road.* **2** used in the names of roads: *Crossley Lane* **3** a section of a wide road that is marked by painted white lines to keep lines of traffic separate: *a four-lane motorway* ◇ *the inside/middle/fast/outside lane* **4** (SPORT) a section of a sports track, swimming pool, etc. for one person to go along **5** a route or path that is regularly used by ships or aircraft

THESAURUS

language

vocabulary • terms • wording • terminology

These are all terms for the words and expressions people use when they speak or write, or for a particular style of speaking and writing.

language: *Give your instructions in everyday language.*

vocabulary: *to have a wide/limited vocabulary*

terms: *I'll explain it in simple terms.*

wording: *It was the standard form of wording for a letter of consent.*

terminology (*formal*): *medical terminology*

language /ˈlæŋgwɪdʒ/ *noun* **1** [C] (LANGUAGE) the system of communication in speech and writing that is used by people of a particular country: *How many languages can you speak?* ◇ *They fell in love in spite of the language barrier* (=being unable to speak or understand each other's native language). ◇ *What is your first language* (=your mother tongue)? **2** [U] (LANGUAGE) the system of sounds and writing that humans use to express their thoughts, ideas and feelings: *written/spoken language* **3** [U] (LANGUAGE) words of a particular type or words that are used by a particular person or group: *bad* (=rude) *language* ◇ *legal language* ◇ *the language of Shakespeare* **4** [U] (LANGUAGE) any system of signs, symbols, movements, etc. that is used to express sth: *sign language* (=using your hands, not speaking) ➲ look at **body language** **5** [C,U] (COMPUTING) a system of symbols and rules that is used to operate a computer

COLLOCATIONS AND PATTERNS

Speaking a foreign language

Someone who **is fluent in** a language speaks it without making any mistakes.
She was fluent in German, Urdu and Swahili.
He speaks fluent Japanese.

Someone who **masters** a language **has a good command** of that language (=can speak and understand it well).
I never really mastered Latin.
She has a good command of Arabic.

Someone who makes many mistakes speaks **bad/broken/poor** English, Spanish, Turkish, etc.
I got by with broken Chinese and sign language.

People often compare their use of **spoken** and **written** language.
My spoken Polish is better than my written Polish.

A **translator** is sb who **translates sth into** another language.
He translated her book into Korean.

An **interpreter** is sb who **translates** for sb else, usually when they are speaking.
The health service needs Gujarati interpreters.

ˈ**language laboratory** *noun* [C] (EDUCATION) a room in a school or college that contains special equipment to help students to learn foreign languages by listening to tapes, watching videos, recording themselves, etc.

lanky /ˈlæŋki/ *adj.* (used about a person) very tall and thin

lantern /ˈlæntən/ *noun* [C] a type of light that can be carried with a metal frame, glass sides and a light or CANDLE inside

lanthanum /ˈlænθənəm/ *noun* [U] (*symbol* **La**) (CHEMISTRY) a chemical element. **Lanthanum** is a silver-white metal. ❶ For more information on the periodic table of elements, look at pages R34-5.

lap¹ /læp/ *noun* [C] **1** the flat area that is formed by the upper part of your legs when you are sitting down: *The child sat quietly on his mother's lap.* **2** (SPORT) one journey around a running track, etc.: *There are three more laps to go in the race.* **3** one part of a long journey

lap² /læp/ *verb* (**lapping**; **lapped**) **1** [I] (used about water) to make gentle sounds as it moves against sth: *The waves lapped against the side of the boat.* **2** [T] ~ **sth (up)** (usually used about an animal) to drink sth using the tongue: *The cat lapped up the cream.* **3** [T] (SPORT) to pass another COMPETITOR in a race who has been round the track fewer times than you

PHR V **lap sth up** (*informal*) to accept sth with great enjoyment without stopping to think if it is good, true, etc.

laparotomy /ˌlæpəˈrɒtəmi/ *noun* [C] (*pl.* **laparotomies**) (HEALTH) a cut in the ABDOMEN (=the part of the body below your chest) in order to perform an operation or an examination

lapel /ləˈpel/ *noun* [C] one of the two parts of the front of a coat or jacket that are folded back

lapse¹ /læps/ *noun* [C] **1** a short time when you cannot remember sth or you are not thinking about what you are doing: *a lapse of memory* ◇ *The crash was the result of a temporary lapse in concentration.* **2** a period of time between two things that happen: *She returned to work after a lapse of ten years bringing up her family.* ➲ Look at the verb **elapse**. **3** a piece of bad behaviour from sb who usually behaves well

lapse² /læps/ *verb* [I] **1** (used about a contract, an agreement, etc.) to finish or stop, often by accident: *My membership has lapsed because I forgot to renew it.* **2** to become weaker or stop for a short time: *My concentration lapsed during the last part of the exam.*

PHR V **lapse into sth** to gradually pass into a worse or less active state or condition; to start speaking or behaving in a less acceptable way: *to lapse into silence/a coma*

laptop /ˈlæptɒp/ *noun* [C] (COMPUTING) a small computer that is easy to carry and that can use batteries for power ➲ look at **blackberry**, **desktop**, **palmtop**

lard /lɑːd/ *noun* [U] a firm white substance made from melted fat that is used in cooking

larder /ˈlɑːdə(r)/ *noun* [C] a large cupboard or small room that is used for storing food **SYN** **pantry**

large ⊶ /lɑːdʒ/ ***adj.*** greater in size, amount, etc. than usual; big: *a large area/house/family/appetite* ◇ *a large number of people* ◇ *I'd like a large coffee, please.* ◇ *We have this shirt in small, medium or large.*
IDM **at large 1** as a whole; in general: *He is well known to scientists but not to the public at large.* **2** (used about a criminal, animal, etc.) not caught; free
by and large mostly; in general: *By and large the school is very efficient.*

largely ⊶ /ˈlɑːdʒli/ ***adv.*** mostly: *His success was largely due to hard work.*

ˈlarge-scale ***adj.*** happening over a large area or affecting a lot of people: *large-scale production/unemployment*

lark /lɑːk/ ***noun*** [C] a small brown bird that makes a pleasant sound

larva /ˈlɑːvə/ ***noun*** [C] (*pl.* **larvae** /ˈlɑːviː/) (BIOLOGY) an insect at the stage when it has just come out of an egg and has a short fat soft body with no legs ➲ look at **pupa** ➲ picture on **page 29**

laryngitis /ˌlærɪnˈdʒaɪtɪs/ ***noun*** [U] (HEALTH) a mild illness of the throat that makes it difficult to speak

larynx /ˈlærɪŋks/ ***noun*** [C] (ANATOMY) the area at the top of your throat that contains your VOCAL CORDS (=the muscles that move to produce the voice) SYN **voice box** ➲ picture on **page 80**

laser /ˈleɪzə(r)/ ***noun*** [C] (PHYSICS) a device that produces a controlled RAY of very powerful light that can be used as a tool

ˈlaser printer ***noun*** [C] (COMPUTING) a machine that produces very good quality printed material from a computer by using a controlled LASER BEAM

lash[1] /læʃ/ ***verb* 1** [I,T] (used especially about wind, rain and storms) to hit sth with great force: *The rain lashed against the windows.* **2** [T] to hit sb with a piece of rope, leather, etc.; to move sth like a piece of rope, leather, etc. violently **3** [T] **~ A to B**; **~ A and B together** to tie two things together firmly with rope, etc.: *The two boats were lashed together.*
PHR V **lash out (at/against sb/sth)** to suddenly attack sb/sth (with words or by hitting them or it): *The actor lashed out at a photographer outside his house.*

lash[2] /læʃ/ ***noun*** [C] **1** =EYELASH **2** a hit with a long piece of rope, leather, etc. (**a whip**)

lass /læs/ (*also* **lassie** /ˈlæsi/) ***noun*** [C] (*informal*) a girl or young woman

lasso /læˈsuː/ ***noun*** [C] (*pl.* **lassos** or **lassoes**) a long rope tied in a circle at one end that is used for catching cows and horses ▶ **lasso *verb*** [T]

last[1] ⊶ /lɑːst/ ***det.***, ***adj.***, ***adv.* 1** at the end; after all the others: *December is the last month of the year.* ◇ *Would the last person to leave please turn off the lights?* ◇ *Our house is the last one on the left.* ◇ *She lived alone for the last years of her life.* ◇ *The British athlete came in last.* ◇ *Her name is last on the list.* **2** used about a time, period, event, etc. in the past that is nearest to the present: *last night/week/Saturday/summer* ◇ *We have been working on the book for the last six months.* ◇ ***The last time*** *I saw her was in London.* ◇ *We'll win this time, because they beat us* ***last time***. ◇ *When did you last have your eyes checked?* ◇ *When I saw her last she seemed very happy.* **3** final: *This is my last chance to take the exam.* ◇ *Alison's retiring – tomorrow is her last day at work.* **4** (only *before* a noun) not expected or not suitable: *He's the last person I thought would get the job.*
▶ **lastly *adv.***: *Lastly, I would like to thank the band who played this evening.* SYN **finally**
IDM **the last/next but one, two, etc.** one, two, etc. away from the last/next: *I live in the next house but one on the right.* ◇ *X is the last letter but two of the alphabet* (=the third letter from the end).
first/last thing → THING
have the last laugh to be the person, team, etc. who is successful in the end
have, etc. the last word to be the person who makes the final decision or the final comment
in the last resort; **(as) a last resort** when everything else has failed; the person or thing that helps when everything else has failed
last but not least (used before the final item in a list) just as important as all the other items
a last-ditch attempt a final effort to avoid sth unpleasant or dangerous
the last/final straw → STRAW
the last minute/moment the final minute/moment before sth happens: *We arrived at the last minute to catch the train.* ◇ *a last-minute change of plan*

last[2] ⊶ /lɑːst/ ***noun***, ***pronoun* 1 the last** (*pl.* **the last**) the person or thing that comes or happens after all other similar people or things: *Alex was the last to arrive.* **2 the ~ of sth** [sing.] the only remaining part or items of sth: *We finished the last of the bread at breakfast so we'd better get some more.*
IDM **at (long) last** in the end; finally: *After months of separation they were together at last.*

last[3] ⊶ /lɑːst/ ***verb*** (not used in the continuous tenses) **1 *linking verb*** to continue for a period of time: *The exam lasts three hours.* ◇ *How long does a cricket match last?* ◇ *The flight seemed to last forever.* **2** [I,T] to continue to be good or to function: *Do you think this weather will last till the weekend?* ◇ *It's only a cheap radio but it'll probably last a year or so.* **3** [I,T] to be enough for what sb needs: *This money won't last me till the end of the month.*

lasting /ˈlɑːstɪŋ/ ***adj.*** continuing for a long time: *The museum left a lasting impression on me.*

ˌlast-ˈminute ***adj.*** done, decided or organized just before sth happens or before it is too late: *a last-minute holiday*

ˈlast name =SURNAME

latch[1] /lætʃ/ ***noun*** [C] **1** a small metal bar that is used for fastening a door or a gate. You have to lift the **latch** in order to open the door. **2** a type of lock for a door that you open with a key from the outside

latch[2] /lætʃ/ ***verb***
PHR V **latch on (to sth)** (*informal*) to understand sth: *It took them a while to latch on to what she was talking about.*

late ⊶ /leɪt/ ***adj.***, ***adv.* 1** near the end of a period of time: *in the late afternoon/summer/twentieth century* ◇ *in the late morning* ◇ *His mother's in her late fifties* (=between 55 and 60). ◇ *in late May/late in May* ◇ *We got back home late in the evening.* **2** after the usual or expected time: *I'm sorry I'm late.* ◇ *She was ten minutes late for school.* ◇ *The ambulance arrived too late to save him.* ◇ *to be late with the rent* ◇ *The buses are running late today.* ◇ *to stay up late* **3** near the end of the day: *It's getting late – let's go home.* **4** (only *before* a noun) no longer alive; dead: *his late wife*
IDM **an early/a late night** → NIGHT
later on at a later time: *Later on you'll probably wish that you'd worked harder at school.* ◇ *Bye – I'll see you a bit later on.*
sooner or later → SOON

latecomer /ˈleɪtkʌmə(r)/ ***noun*** [C] a person who arrives or starts sth late

lately /ˈleɪtli/ *adv.* in the period of time up until now; recently: *What have you been doing lately?* ◇ *Hasn't the weather been dreadful lately?*

latent /ˈleɪtnt/ *adj.* (usually *before* a noun) existing, but not yet very noticeable, active or well developed: *latent defects/disease* ◇ *latent talent* ▶ **latency** *noun* [U]

lateral /ˈlætərəl/ *adj.* (usually *before* a noun) connected with the side of sth or with movement to the side: *the lateral branches of a tree* ◇ *lateral eye movements* ▶ **laterally** *adv.*

latest ⊶ /ˈleɪtɪst/ *adj.* very recent or new: *the latest fashions/news* ◇ *the terrorists' latest attack on the town*

the latest *noun* [sing.] (*informal*) the most recent or the newest thing or piece of news: *This is the very latest in computer technology.* ◇ *This is the latest in a series of attacks by this terrorist group.*
IDM **at the latest** no later than the time or the date mentioned: *You need to hand your projects in by Friday at the latest.*

latex /ˈleɪteks/ *noun* [U] **1** (BIOLOGY) a thick white liquid that is produced by some plants and trees, especially rubber trees **2** (CHEMISTRY) an artificial substance that is used to make paints, GLUES and materials

lathe /leɪð/ *noun* [C] a machine that shapes pieces of wood or metal by holding and turning them against a fixed cutting tool

lather /ˈlɑːðə(r)/ *noun* [U] a white mass of bubbles that are produced when you mix soap with water

Latin /ˈlætɪn/ *noun* [U] (LANGUAGE) the language that was used in ancient Rome ▶ **Latin** *adj.*: *Latin poetry* ◇ *Spanish, Italian and other Latin languages* (=that developed from Latin)

ˌ**Latin Aˈmerican** *noun* [C], *adj.* (a person who comes) from Latin America (ie Mexico or the parts of Central and South America where Spanish or Portuguese is spoken): *Latin American music*

latitude /ˈlætɪtjuːd/ *noun* [U] (GEOGRAPHY) the distance of a place north or south of the EQUATOR (=the imaginary line around the middle of the earth) ⓘ Latitude is measured in **degrees**.
➲ look at **longitude** ➲ picture at **earth**

latrine /ləˈtriːn/ *noun* [C] a type of toilet made by digging a hole in the ground

latter ⊶ /ˈlætə(r)/ *adj.* (*formal*) (only *before* a noun) nearer to the end of a period of time; later: *Interest rates should fall in the latter half of the year.* ▶ **latterly** *adv.*

the ˈlatter *noun* [sing.], *pronoun* the second (of two people or things that are mentioned): *The options were History and Geography. I chose the latter.*

lattice /ˈlætɪs/ *noun* [C,U] **1** (*also* ˈ**latticework** [U]) a structure that is made of long thin pieces of wood or metal that cross over each other with spaces shaped like a diamond between them, used as a fence or a support for climbing plants; any structure or pattern like this: *a lattice of branches* **2** (SCIENCE) a regular repeated arrangement of points or objects over an area or in space, for example atoms in a CRYSTAL (=a regular shape that some minerals form when they become solid).

laugh[1] ⊶ /lɑːf/ *verb* [I] to make the sounds that show you are happy or amused: *His jokes always make me laugh.* ◇ *to laugh out loud*
IDM **die laughing** → DIE
PHR V **laugh at sb/sth 1** to show, by laughing, that you think sb/sth is funny: *The children laughed at the clown.* **2** to show that you think sb is ridiculous: *Don't laugh at him. He can't help the way he speaks.*

laugh[2] ⊶ /lɑːf/ *noun* [C] **1** the sound or act of laughing: *Her jokes got a lot of laughs.* ◇ *We all had a good laugh at what he'd written.* **2** (*informal*) a person or thing that is amusing
IDM **for a laugh** as a joke
have the last laugh → LAST[1]

laughable /ˈlɑːfəbl/ *adj.* deserving to be laughed at; of very poor quality; ridiculous

ˈ**laughing gas** *noun* [U] (*informal*) = NITROUS OXIDE

ˈ**laughing stock** *noun* [C] a person or thing that other people laugh at or make fun of (in an unpleasant way)

laughter /ˈlɑːftə(r)/ *noun* [U] the sound or act of laughing: *Everyone roared with laughter.*

launch[1] ⊶ /lɔːntʃ/ *verb* [T] **1** to send a ship into the water or a SPACECRAFT into the sky **2** to start sth new or to show sth for the first time: *to launch a new product onto the market*

launch[2] ⊶ /lɔːntʃ/ *noun* [C] **1** [usually sing.] the act of launching a ship, SPACECRAFT, new product, etc. **2** a large motor boat

launder /ˈlɔːndə(r)/ *verb* [T] **1** (*formal*) to wash and dry clothes, etc.: *freshly laundered sheets* **2** (LAW) to move money that sb has got illegally into foreign bank accounts or legal businesses so that it is difficult for people to know where the money came from: *Most of the money was laundered through Swiss bank accounts.*

launderette /lɔːnˈdret/ (*AmE* **Laundromat** /ˈlɔːndrəmæt/) *noun* [C] a type of shop where you pay to wash and dry your clothes in machines

laundry /ˈlɔːndri/ *noun* (*pl.* **laundries**) **1** [U] clothes, etc. that need washing or that are being washed: *dirty laundry* **2** [C] a business where you send sheets, clothes, etc. to be washed and dried

lava /ˈlɑːvə/ *noun* [U] (GEOLOGY) hot liquid rock that comes out of a VOLCANO (=a mountain with an opening in the top) ➲ picture at **volcano**

lavatory /ˈlævətri/ *noun* [C] (*pl.* **lavatories**) (*formal*) **1** a toilet **2** a room that contains a toilet, a place to wash your hands, etc.: *Where's the ladies' lavatory, please?*

lavender /ˈlævəndə(r)/ *noun* [U] a garden plant with purple flowers that smells very pleasant

lavish[1] /ˈlævɪʃ/ *adj.* **1** giving or spending a large amount of money: *She was always very lavish with her presents.* **2** large in amount or number: *a lavish meal*

lavish[2] /ˈlævɪʃ/ *verb*
PHR V **lavish sth on sb/sth** to give sth generously or in large quantities to sb

law ⊶ /lɔː/ *noun* **1** [C] (LAW) an official rule of a country or state that says what people may or may not do: *There's a new law about wearing seat belts in the back of cars.* **2 the law** [U] (LAW) all the laws in a country or state: *Stealing is* ***against the law***. ◇ *to break the law* ◇ *to obey the law* ➲ Look at legal.
3 [U] (LAW, EDUCATION) the law as a subject of study or as a profession: *She is studying law.* ◇ *My brother works for* ***a law firm*** *in Brighton.* ➲ Look at legal.
4 [C] (SCIENCE) a statement of what always happens in certain situations or conditions: *the laws of mathematics/gravity*
IDM **law and order** a situation in which the law is obeyed

'law-abiding *adj.* (LAW) (used about a person) obeying the law: *law-abiding citizens*

lawbreaker /'lɔːbreɪkə(r)/ *noun* [C] (LAW) a person who does not obey the law; a criminal

COLLOCATIONS AND PATTERNS

Law courts

A **case** is **tried** in a law court.
A judge (=the official in charge of the court) says what will happen and makes the final decisions in the **trial.**
The defendant has the right to trial by jury.
She is awaiting trial on corruption charges.

A **jury** (=a group of members of the public) listens to the **evidence** to decide whether **the accused** is **guilty** or **not guilty** (=innocent).
New evidence came to light.
An expert witness gave evidence.

After hearing all the evidence, the jury **returns** (=gives) its **verdict.** Sometimes the verdict is changed later if there is an **appeal.**
The jury returned a verdict of guilty.
The verdict was overturned/quashed on appeal.

The judge then **passes sentence** (=decides how sb is to be punished).
The offence carries a sentence of up to six years in jail.
He was sentenced to four months in prison.

'law court (*also* ˌ**court of 'law**) *noun* [C] (LAW) a place where legal cases are decided by a judge and often by twelve members of the public (**a jury**) ➲ look at **defence**, **prosecution**, **witness**

lawful /'lɔːfl/ *adj.* (LAW) allowed or recognized by law: *We shall use all lawful means to obtain our demands.* ➲ look at **legal**, **legitimate**

lawless /'lɔːləs/ *adj.* (LAW) (used about a person or their actions) breaking the law ▶ **lawlessness** *noun* [U]

'law lord *noun* [C] (*BrE*) (LAW) a member of the British House of Lords who is qualified to perform its legal work

lawn /lɔːn/ *noun* [C,U] an area of grass in a garden or park that is regularly cut

lawnmower /'lɔːnməʊə(r)/ *noun* [C] a machine that is used for cutting the grass in a garden

lawrencium /lɒ'rensiəm/ *noun* [U] (*symbol* **Lr**) (CHEMISTRY) a chemical element. **Lawrencium** is a RADIOACTIVE metal. ❶ For more information on the periodic table of elements, look at pages R34-5.

lawsuit /'lɔːsuːt/ *noun* [C] (LAW) a legal argument in a court of law that is between two people or groups and not between the police and a criminal

lawyer ⊶ /'lɔːjə(r)/ *noun* [C] (LAW) a person who has a certificate in law: *to consult a lawyer*

lax /læks/ *adj.* not having high standards; not strict: *Their security checks are rather lax.*

laxative /'læksətɪv/ *noun* [C] (HEALTH) a medicine, food or drink that sb can take to make them get rid of solid waste from their body more easily ▶ **laxative** *adj.*

lay[1] ⊶ /leɪ/ *verb* [T] (*pt, pp* **laid** /leɪd/) **1** to put sb/sth carefully in a particular position or on a surface: *She laid a sheet over the dead body.* ◇ *He laid the child gently down on her bed.* ◇ *'Don't worry,' she said, laying her hand on my shoulder.* **2** to put sth in the correct position for a particular purpose: *They're laying new electricity cables in our street.* **3** to prepare sth for use: *The police have laid a trap for him and I think they'll catch him this time.* ◇ *Can you lay the table please* (=put the knives, forks, plates, etc. on it)? **4** (BIOLOGY) to produce eggs: *Hens lay eggs.* **5** (used with some nouns to give a similar meaning to a verb) to put: *They laid all the blame on him* (=they blamed him). ◇ *to lay emphasis on sth* (=emphasize it)

PHR V **lay sth down** to give sth as a rule: *It's all laid down in the rules of the club.*

lay off (sb) (*informal*) to stop annoying sb: *Can't you lay off me for a bit?*

lay sb off to stop giving work to sb: *They've laid off 500 workers at the car factory.*

lay sth on (*informal*) to provide sth: *They're laying on a trip to London for everybody.*

lay sth out 1 to spread out a number of things so that you can see them easily or so that they look nice: *All the food was laid out on a table in the garden.* **2** to arrange sth in a planned way

RELATED VOCABULARY

Lawyers

Lawyer is a general term for a person who is qualified to advise people about the law, to prepare legal documents for them and/or to represent them in a court of law.

In *BrE*, a **lawyer** who is qualified to speak in the higher courts of law is called a **barrister**. The highest level of **barrister** in Britain is called a **QC** or a **KC**.

In *AmE* **attorney** is a more formal word used for a lawyer and is used especially in job titles: *district attorney*.

Counsel is the formal legal word used for a lawyer who is representing someone in court: *counsel for the prosecution/defence*.

Solicitor is the *BrE* term for a lawyer who gives legal advice and prepares documents, for example when you are buying a house, and sometimes has the right to speak in court.

lay[2] /leɪ/ *adj.* (only *before* a noun) **1** (RELIGION) (used about a religious teacher) who has not been officially trained as a priest: *a lay preacher* **2** without special training in or knowledge of a particular subject

lay[3] past tense of **lie**[2]

layabout /'leɪəbaʊt/ *noun* [C] (*BrE, informal*) a person who is lazy and does not do much work

'lay-by (*AmE* **'rest stop**) *noun* [C] (*pl.* **lay-bys**) an area at the side of a road where vehicles can stop for a short time

layer ⊶ AW /'leɪə(r)/ *noun* [C] a quantity or thickness of sth that lies over a surface or between surfaces: *A thin layer of dust covered everything in the room.* ◇ *It's very cold. You'll need several layers of clothing.* ◇ *the top/bottom layer* ◇ *the inner/outer layer* ➲ look at **ozone layer** ▶ **layer** *verb* [T]: *Layer the potatoes and onions in a dish.*

layman /'leɪmən/ *noun* [C] (*pl.* **-men** /-mən/) a person who does not have special training in or knowledge of a particular subject: *a medical reference book for the layman*

layout /'leɪaʊt/ *noun* [usually sing.] the way in which the parts of sth such as the page of a book, a garden or a building are arranged: *the layout of streets* ◇ *the magazine's attractive new page layout*

laze /leɪz/ ***verb*** [I] ~ **(about/around)** to do very little; to rest or relax

lazy ⊶ /ˈleɪzi/ ***adj.*** **(lazier; laziest) 1** (used about a person) not wanting to work: *Don't be lazy. Come and give me a hand.* **2** moving slowly or without much energy: *a lazy smile* **3** making you feel that you do not want to do very much: *a lazy summer's afternoon* ▸ **lazily** ***adv.*** ▸ **laziness** ***noun*** [U]

lb ***abbr.*** pound(s); a measurement of weight equal to about 454 grams

LCD /ˌel siː ˈdiː/ ***abbr.*** **1** liquid crystal display; a way of showing information in electronic equipment. An electric current is passed through a special liquid and numbers and letters can be seen on a small screen: *a pocket calculator with LCD*
2 (**MATHEMATICS**) = LOWEST COMMON DENOMINATOR

LEA /ˌel iː ˈeɪ/ ***abbr.*** (*BrE*) (**EDUCATION**) Local Education Authority; a department responsible for education in British local government

leach /liːtʃ/ ***verb*** (**GEOLOGY**) **1** [I] (used about chemicals, etc.) to be removed from soil by liquids passing through it **2** [T] (used about liquids) to remove chemicals, etc. from soil by passing through it

lead¹ ⊶ /liːd/ ***verb*** (*pt, pp* **led** /led/) **1** [T] to go with or in front of a person or animal to show the way or to make them or it go in the right direction: *The teacher led the children out of the hall and back to the classroom.* ◇ *She led the horse into its stable.* ◇ *The receptionist* ***led the way*** *to the boardroom.* ◇ *to lead sb by the hand* **2** [I] (used about a road or path) to go to a place: *I don't think this path leads anywhere.* **3** [I] ~ **to sth** to have sth as a result: *Eating too much sugar can lead to all sorts of health problems.* **4** [T] ~ **sb to do sth** to influence what sb does or thinks: *He led me to believe he really meant what he said.* **5** [T] to have a particular type of life: *They lead a very busy life.* ◇ *to lead a life of crime* **6** [I,T] to be winning or in first place in front of sb: *Hingis is leading by two games to love.* ◇ *Hingis is leading Williams by two games to love.* **7** [I,T] to be in control or the leader of sth: *Who is going to lead the discussion?*

IDM **lead sb astray** to make sb start behaving or thinking in the wrong way

PHR V **lead up to sth** to be an introduction to or cause of sth

lead² ⊶ /liːd/ ***noun*** **1 the lead** [sing.] the first place or position in front of other people or organizations: *The French athlete has gone* ***into the lead.*** ◇ *Who is* ***in the lead?*** ◇ *Britain has* ***taken the lead*** *in developing computer software for that market.*
2 [sing.] the distance or amount by which sb/sth is in front of another person or thing: *The company has a lead of several years in the development of the new technology.* **3** [C] (**ARTS AND MEDIA**) the main part in a play, show or other situation: *Who's playing the lead in the new film?* **4** [C] (**LAW**) a piece of information that may help to give the answer to a problem: *The police are* ***following*** *all possible* ***leads*** *to track down the killer.* **5** [C] a long chain or piece of leather that is connected to the COLLAR around a dog's neck and used for keeping the dog under control: *All dogs must be* ***kept on a lead.*** **6** [C] a piece of wire that carries electricity to a piece of equipment ➲ picture at **cable**

IDM **follow sb's example/lead** → FOLLOW

lead³ /led/ ***noun*** **1** [U] (*symbol* **Pb**) (**CHEMISTRY**) a soft heavy grey metal. Lead is used in pipes, roofs, etc. ❶ For more information on the periodic table of elements, look at pages R34-5. ➲ picture at **acid**
2 [C,U] the black substance inside a pencil that makes a mark when you write

leader ⊶ /ˈliːdə(r)/ ***noun*** [C] **1** a person who is a manager or in charge of sth: *a weak/strong leader* ◇ *She is a natural leader* (= she knows how to tell other people what to do). **2** the person or thing that is best or in first place: *The leader has just finished the third lap.* ◇ *The new shampoo soon became a market leader.*

leadership /ˈliːdəʃɪp/ ***noun*** **1** [U] the state or position of being a manager or the person in charge: *Who will take over the leadership of the party?* **2** [U] the qualities that a leader should have: *She's got good leadership skills.* **3** [C, with sing. or pl. verb] the people who are in charge of a country, organization, etc.

leading ⊶ /ˈliːdɪŋ/ ***adj.*** **1** best or most important: *He's one of the leading experts in this field.* ◇ *She played a leading role in getting the business started.* **2** that tries to make sb give a particular answer: *The lawyer was warned not to ask the witness* ***leading questions.***

ˈlead story ***noun*** [C] (**ARTS AND MEDIA**) the most important piece of news in a newspaper or on a news programme

leaf¹ ⊶ /liːf/ ***noun*** [C] (*pl.* **leaves** /liːvz/) (**BIOLOGY**) one of the thin, flat, usually green parts of a plant or tree: *The trees lose their leaves in autumn.* ➲ picture at **tree**

leaf² /liːf/ ***verb***

PHR V **leaf through sth** to turn the pages of a book, etc. quickly and without looking at them carefully

leaflet /ˈliːflət/ ***noun*** [C] a printed piece of paper that gives information about sth. **Leaflets** are usually given free of charge: *I picked up a leaflet advertising a new club.*

leafy /ˈliːfi/ ***adj.*** **1** having many leaves: *a leafy bush* **2** (used about a place) with many trees

league ⊶ /liːg/ ***noun*** [C] **1** (**SPORT**) a group of sports clubs that compete with each other for a prize: *the football league* ◇ *Which team is top of the league at the moment?* **2** a group of people, countries, etc. that join together for a particular purpose: *the League of Nations* **3** a level of quality, ability, etc.: *He is so much better than the others. They're just not in the same league.*

IDM **in league (with sb)** having a secret agreement (with sb)

ˈleague table ***noun*** [C] (*BrE*) **1** (**SPORT**) a table that shows the position of sports teams and how successfully they are performing in a competition **2** a table that shows how well institutions such as schools or hospitals are performing in comparison with each other

leak¹ /liːk/ ***verb*** **1** [I,T] to allow liquid or gas to get through a hole or crack: *The boat was leaking badly.* **2** [I] (used about liquid or gas) to get out through a hole or crack: *Water is leaking in through the roof.* **3** [T] ~ **sth (to sb)** to give secret information to sb: *The committee's findings were leaked to the press before the report was published.*

PHR V **leak out** (used about secret information) to become known

leak² /liːk/ ***noun*** [C] **1** a small hole or crack which liquid or gas can get through: *There's a leak in the pipe.* ◇ *The roof has sprung a leak.* **2** the liquid or gas that gets through a hole: *a gas leak* **3** the act of giving away information that should be kept secret ▸ **leaky** ***adj.***

leakage /ˈliːkɪdʒ/ ***noun*** [C,U] the action of coming out of a hole or crack; the liquid or gas that comes out: *a leakage of dangerous chemicals*

lean[1] /liːn/ ***verb*** (*pt, pp* **leant** /lent/ or **leaned** /liːnd/) **1** [I] to move the top part of your body and head forwards, backwards or to the side: *He leaned across the table to pick up the phone.* ◇ *She leaned out of the window and waved.* ◇ *Just lean back and relax.* **2** [I] to be in a position that is not straight or UPRIGHT: *That wardrobe leans to the right.* **3** [I,T] ~ (**sth**) **against/on sth** to rest against sth so that it gives support; to put sth in this position: *She had to stop and lean on the gate.* ◇ *Please don't lean bicycles against this window.*

lean[2] /liːn/ ***adj.*** **1** (used about a person or animal) thin and in good health **2** (used about meat) having little or no fat **3** not producing much: *a lean harvest*

leap[1] /liːp/ ***verb*** [I] (*pt, pp* **leapt** /lept/ or **leaped** /liːpt/) **1** to jump high or a long way: *The horse leapt over the wall.* ◇ *A fish suddenly leapt out of the water.* ◇ *We all leapt into the air when they scored the goal.* ◇ (*figurative*) *Share prices leapt to a record high yesterday.* **2** to move quickly: *I looked at the clock and leapt out of bed.* ◇ *She leapt back when the pan caught fire.*

PHR V **leap at sth** to accept a chance or offer with enthusiasm: *She leapt at the chance to work in television.*

leap[2] /liːp/ ***noun*** [C] **1** a big jump: *He took **a flying leap** at the wall but didn't get over it.* ◇ (*figurative*) *My heart gave a leap when I heard the news.* **2** a sudden large change or increase in sth: *The development of penicillin was a great **leap forward** in the field of medicine.*

leapfrog /ˈliːpfrɒg/ ***noun*** [U] a children's game in which one person bends over and another person jumps over their back

ˈ**leap year** ***noun*** [C] one year in every four, in which February has 29 days instead of 28

learn /lɜːn/ ***verb*** (*pt, pp* **learnt** /lɜːnt/ or **learned** /lɜːnd/) **1** [I,T] ~ (**sth**) (**from sb/sth**) to get knowledge, a skill, etc. (from sb/sth): *I'm not very good at driving yet – I'm still learning.* ◇ *We're learning about China at school.* ◇ *Debbie is learning to play the piano.* ◇ *to learn a foreign language/a musical instrument* ◇ *Where did you learn how to swim?* **2** [I] ~ (**of/about**) **sth** to get some information about sth; to find out: *I was sorry to learn about your father's death.* **3** [T] (EDUCATION) to study sth so that you can repeat it from memory **4** [I] to understand or realize: *We should have learned by now that we can't rely on her.* ◇ *It's important to learn from your mistakes.*

IDM **learn your lesson** to understand what you must do/not do in the future because you have had an unpleasant experience

learned /ˈlɜːnɪd/ ***adj.*** having a lot of knowledge from studying; for people who have a lot of knowledge

learner /ˈlɜːnə(r)/ ***noun*** [C] a person who is learning: *a learner driver* ◇ *books for young learners*

learning /ˈlɜːnɪŋ/ ***noun*** [U] (EDUCATION) **1** the process of learning sth: *new methods of language learning* **2** knowledge that you get from studying

lease /liːs/ ***noun*** [C] (LAW) a legal agreement that allows you to use a building or land for a fixed period of time in return for rent: *The lease on the flat runs out/expires next year.* ▶ **lease** ***verb*** [T]: *They lease the land from a local farmer.* ◇ *Part of the building is leased out to tenants.* ▶ **leasing** ***noun*** [U]: *car leasing* ◇ *a leasing company*

leasehold /ˈliːshəʊld/ ***adj.*** (used about property or land) that you can pay to use for a limited period of time: *a leasehold property* ▶ **leasehold** ***noun*** [U] ➲ look at **freehold**

least /liːst/ ***det., pronoun, adv.*** **1** (used as the superlative of *little*) smallest in size, amount, degree, etc.: *He's got the least experience of all of us.* ◇ *You've done the most work, and I'm afraid John has done the least.* **2** less than anyone/anything else; less than at any other time: *He's the person who needs help least.* ◇ *I bought the least expensive tickets.* ◇ *My uncle always appears when we're least expecting him.* OPP **most**

IDM **at least 1** not less than, and probably more: *It'll take us at least two hours to get there.* ◇ *You could at least say you're sorry!* **2** even if other things are wrong: *It may not be beautiful but at least it's cheap.* **3** used for correcting sth that you have just said: *I saw him – at least I think I saw him.*

at the (**very**) **least** not less and probably much more: *It'll take six months to build at the very least.*

least of all especially not: *Nobody should be worried, least of all you.*

not in the least (**bit**) not at all: *It doesn't matter in the least.* ◇ *I'm not in the least bit worried.*

last but not least → LAST[1]

to say the least used to say that sth is in fact much worse, more serious, etc. than you are saying: *Adam's going to be annoyed, to say the least, when he sees his car.*

leather /ˈleðə(r)/ ***noun*** [U] the skin of animals which has been specially treated. Leather is used to make shoes, bags, coats, etc.: *a leather jacket*

leave[1] /liːv/ ***verb*** (*pt, pp* **left** /left/) **1** [I,T] to go away from sb/sth: *We should leave now if we're going to get there by eight o'clock.* ◇ *I felt sick in class so I left the room.* ◇ *At what age do most people leave school in your country?* ◇ *Barry left his wife for another woman.* **2** [T] to cause or allow sb/sth to stay in a particular place or condition; to not deal with sth: *Leave the door open, please.* ◇ *Don't leave the iron on when you are not using it.* ◇ *Why do you always leave your homework till the last minute?* **3** [T] ~ **sth** (**behind**) to forget to bring sth with you: *I'm afraid I've left my homework at home. Can I give it to you tomorrow?* ◇ *I can't find my glasses. Maybe I left them behind at work.* **4** [T] to make sth happen or stay as a result: *Don't put that cup on the table. It'll leave a mark.* **5** [T] to not use sth: *Leave some milk for me, please.* **6** [T] to put sth somewhere: *Val left a message on her answerphone.* ◇ *I left him a note.* **7** [T] to give sth to sb when you die: *In his will he left everything to his three sons.* **8** [T] to give the care of or responsibility for sb/sth to another person: *I'll **leave it to** you to organize all the food.*

IDM **leave sb/sth alone** to not touch, annoy or speak to sb/sth

leave go (**of sth**) to stop touching or holding sth: *Will you please leave go of my arm.*

leave sb in the lurch to leave sb without help in a difficult situation

leave sth on one side → SIDE[1]

be left high and dry → HIGH[1]

PHR V **leave sb/sth out** (**of sth**) to not include sb/sth: *This doesn't make sense. I think the typist has left out a line.*

leave[2] /liːv/ ***noun*** [U] a period of time when you do not go to work: *Diplomats working abroad usually get a month's home leave each year.* ◇ *annual leave* ◇ *sick leave* ◇ *Molly's not working – she's **on** maternity **leave**.*

leaves plural of **leaf**[1]

lectern /ˈlektən/ ***noun*** a stand for holding a book, notes, etc. when you are reading in church, giving a talk, etc.

lecture 🔑 AW /ˈlektʃə(r)/ ***noun*** [C] **1** a ~ (on/about sth) (EDUCATION) a talk that is given to a group of people to teach them about a particular subject, especially as part of a university course: *The college has asked a journalist to come and* ***give a lecture*** *on the media.* ◇ *a course of lectures* **2** a serious talk to sb that explains what they have done wrong or how they should behave: *We got a lecture from a policeman about playing near the railway.* ▶ **lecture** ***verb*** [I,T]: *Alex lectures in European Studies at London University.* ◇ *The policeman lectured the boys about playing ball games in the road.*

lecturer AW /ˈlektʃərə(r)/ ***noun*** [C] (EDUCATION) a person who gives talks to teach people about a subject, especially as a job in a university

ˈlecture theatre (*AmE* **ˈlecture theater**) ***noun*** [C] (EDUCATION) a large room with rows of seats on a slope, where lectures are given

LED /ˌel iː ˈdiː/ ***abbr.*** (PHYSICS) light emitting diode (a device that produces a light on electrical and electronic equipment)

led past tense, past participle of **lead**[1]

ledge /ledʒ/ ***noun*** [C] a narrow shelf underneath a window, or a narrow piece of rock that sticks out on the side of a CLIFF or mountain

lee /liː/ ***noun*** [sing.] the side or part of a hill, building, etc. that provides protection from the wind: *We built the house* ***in the lee of*** *the hill.* ➲ look at **leeward**, **windward**

leech /liːtʃ/ ***noun*** [C] a small creature with a soft body and no legs that usually lives in water. **Leeches** fasten themselves to other creatures and drink their blood.

leek /liːk/ ***noun*** [C] a long thin vegetable that is white at one end with thin green leaves

leeward /ˈliːwəd/ ***adj.*** on the side of a hill, building, etc. that is protected from the wind ➲ look at **lee**, **windward**

left[1] past tense, past participle of **leave**[1]

left[2] 🔑 /left/ ***adj.*** **1** on the side where your heart is in the body: *I've broken my left arm.* OPP **right** **2** still available after everything else has been taken or used: ***Is*** *there any bread* ***left****?* ◇ *How much time do we* ***have left****?* ◇ *If there's any money* ***left over****, we'll have a cup of coffee.*

left[3] 🔑 /left/ ***adv.*** to or towards the left: *Turn left just past the Post Office.* OPP **right**

left[4] 🔑 /left/ ***noun*** **1** [U] the left side: *In Britain we drive* ***on the left****.* ◇ *Our house is just* ***to/on the left of*** *that tall building.* ◇ *If you look* ***to*** *your* ***left*** *you'll see one of the city's most famous landmarks.* OPP **right** **2 the Left** [with sing. or pl. verb] (POLITICS) political groups who support the ideas and beliefs of SOCIALISM

ˈleft-hand ***adj.*** (only *before* a noun) of or on the left: *the left-hand side of the road* ◇ *a left-hand drive car*

ˌleft-ˈhanded ***adj.***, ***adv.*** **1** using the left hand rather than the right hand: *Are you left-handed?* ◇ *I write left-handed.* **2** made for **left-handed** people to use: *left-handed scissors* ▶ **ˌleft-ˈhandedness** ***noun*** [U]

ˌleft-ˈluggage office (*BrE*) (*AmE* **ˈbaggage room**) ***noun*** [C] the place at a railway station, etc. where you can leave your luggage for a short time

leftovers /ˈleftəʊvəz/ ***noun*** [pl.] food that has not been eaten when a meal has finished

ˌleft ˈwing ***noun*** [sing.] **1** [with sing. or pl. verb] (POLITICS) the members of a political party, group, etc. that want more social change than the others in their party: *the left wing of the Labour Party* **2** (SPORT) the left side of the field in some team sports: *He plays on the left wing for Ajax.* ▶ **left-wing** ***adj.*** OPP **right-wing**

leg 🔑 /leg/ ***noun*** [C] **1** one of the parts of the body on which a person or animal stands or walks: *A spider has eight legs.* ◇ *She sat down and crossed her legs.* ➲ picture on **page 80** **2** one of the parts of a chair, table etc. on which it stands: *the leg of a chair/table* ◇ *a chair/table leg* **3** the part of a pair of trousers, SHORTS, etc. that covers the leg: *There's a hole in the leg of my trousers/my trouser leg.* **4** one part or section of a journey, competition, etc.: *The band are in Germany on the first leg of their world tour.*

IDM **pull sb's leg** → PULL[1]
stretch your legs → STRETCH[1]

legacy /ˈlegəsi/ ***noun*** [C] (*pl.* **legacies**) money or property that is given to you after sb dies, because they wanted you to have it

legal 🔑 AW /ˈliːgl/ ***adj.*** (LAW) **1** (only *before* a noun) using or connected with the law: *legal advice* ◇ *to take legal action against sb* ◇ *the legal profession* **2** allowed by law: *It is not legal to own a gun without a licence.* OPP **illegal** ➲ look at **lawful**, **legitimate** ▶ **legally** AW /ˈliːgəli/ ***adv.***: *Schools are legally responsible for the safety of their pupils.*

legality AW /liːˈgæləti/ ***noun*** [U] (LAW) the state of being legal ➲ look at **illegality**

legalize (also **-ise**) /ˈliːgəlaɪz/ ***verb*** [T] (LAW) to make sth legal ▶ **legalization** (also **-isation**) /ˌliːgəlaɪˈzeɪʃn/ ***noun*** [U]

ˌlegal ˈtender ***noun*** [U] (ECONOMICS) money that can be legally used to pay for things in a particular country: *These coins are no longer legal tender.*

legato /lɪˈgɑːtəʊ/ ***adj.***, ***adv.*** (MUSIC) to be played or sung in a smooth manner ▶ **legato** OPP **staccato**

legend /ˈledʒənd/ ***noun*** **1** [C] an old story that may or may not be true: *the legend of Robin Hood* **2** [U] such stories when they are grouped together: *According to legend, Robin Hood lived in Sherwood Forest.* **3** [C] a famous person or event: *a movie/jazz/baseball legend* ▶ **legendary** /ˈledʒəndri/ ***adj.***: *the legendary heroes of Greek myths* ◇ *Michael Jordan, the legendary basketball star*

-legged /ˈlegɪd; legd/ ***suffix*** (in adjectives) having the number or type of **legs** mentioned: *a three-legged stool* ◇ *a long-legged insect*

leggings /ˈlegɪŋz/ ***noun*** [pl.] a piece of women's clothing that fits tightly over both legs from the waist to the feet, like a very thin pair of trousers

legible /ˈledʒəbl/ ***adj.*** that is clear enough to be read easily: *His writing is so small that it's barely legible.* OPP **illegible** ➲ look at **readable** ▶ **legibility** /ˌledʒəˈbɪləti/ ***noun*** [U] ▶ **legibly** /-əbli/ ***adv.***

legion /ˈliːdʒən/ ***noun*** [C] **1** a large group of soldiers that forms part of an army, especially the one that existed in ancient Rome: *Caesar's legions* ◇ *the French Foreign Legion* **2** (*formal*) a large number of people of one particular type: *legions of photographers*

legislate AW /ˈledʒɪsleɪt/ ***verb*** [I] ~ **(for/against sth)** (LAW) to make a law or laws

legislation AW /ˌledʒɪsˈleɪʃn/ *noun* [U] (LAW) **1** a group of laws: *The government is introducing new legislation to help small businesses.* **2** the process of making laws

legislative AW /ˈledʒɪslətɪv/ *adj.* (only *before* a noun) (*formal*) (LAW) connected with the act of making laws: *a legislative assembly/body/council*

legislator AW /ˈledʒɪsleɪtə(r)/ *noun* [C] (*formal*) (LAW) a member of a group of people that has the power to make laws

legislature AW /ˈledʒɪsleɪtʃə(r)/ *noun* [C] (*formal*) (LAW) a group of people who have the power to make and change laws

legitimate /lɪˈdʒɪtɪmət/ *adj.* **1** reasonable or acceptable: *a legitimate excuse/question/concern* **2** (LAW) allowed by law: *Could he earn so much from legitimate business activities?* ➲ look at **lawful**, **legal** **3** (*old-fashioned*) (used about a child) having parents who are married to each other OPP **illegitimate** ▶ **legitimacy** /lɪˈdʒɪtɪməsi/ *noun* [U]: *I intend to challenge the legitimacy of his claim.* ▶ **legitimately** *adv.*

legume /ˈlegjuːm; lɪˈgjuːm/ *noun* [C] any plant that has seeds in long PODS (= seed containers). PEAS and BEANS are **legumes**.

leisure /ˈleʒə(r)/ *noun* [U] the time when you do not have to work; free time: *Shorter working hours mean that people have more leisure.* ◇ *leisure activities*

IDM **at your leisure** (*formal*) when you have free time: *Look through the catalogue at your leisure and then order by telephone.*

ˈ**leisure centre** *noun* [C] a public building where you can do sports and other activities in your free time

leisurely /ˈleʒəli/ *adj.* without hurry: *a leisurely Sunday breakfast* ◇ *I always cycle at a leisurely pace.*

lemon ⊶ /ˈlemən/ *noun* [C,U] a yellow fruit with sour juice that is used for giving flavour to food and drink: *a slice of lemon* ◇ *Add the juice of 2 lemons.*

lemonade /ˌleməˈneɪd/ *noun* [C,U] **1** (*BrE*) a colourless sweet drink with a lot of bubbles in it **2** a drink that is made from fresh lemon juice, sugar and water

lemur /ˈliːmə(r)/ *noun* [C] an animal like a MONKEY, with thick fur and a long tail, that lives in trees in Madagascar. There are many different types of **lemur**.

lend ⊶ /lend/ *verb* [T] (*pt, pp* **lent** /lent/) **1** ~ **sb sth**; ~ **sth to sb** to allow sb to use sth for a short time or to give sb money that must be paid back after a certain period of time: *Could you lend me £10 until Friday?* ◇ *He lent me his bicycle.* ◇ *He lent his bicycle to me.* OPP **borrow**

> **RELATED VOCABULARY**
>
> If a bank, etc. lends you money you must **pay it back**/**repay** it over a fixed period of time with extra payments (called **interest**).

2 (*formal*) ~ **sth (to sth)** to give or add sth: *to lend advice/support* ◇ *This evidence lends weight to our theory.*

IDM **lend (sb) a hand/lend a hand (to sb)** (*informal*) to help sb

PHR V **lend itself to sth** to be suitable for sth

lender /ˈlendə(r)/ *noun* [C] a person or organization that lends sth, especially money

lending /ˈlendɪŋ/ *noun* [U] (FINANCE) the act of lending money: *Lending by banks rose to $10 billion last year.*

length ⊶ /leŋθ/ *noun* **1** [U, C] the size of sth from one end to the other; how long sth is: *to measure the length of a room* ◇ *It took an hour to walk the length of Oxford Street.* ◇ *The tiny insect is only one millimetre **in length**.* ◇ *This snake can grow to a length of two metres.* ➲ adjective **long** ➲ look at **breadth**, **width** ➲ picture at **dimension** **2** [U] the amount of time that sth lasts: *Many people complained about the **length of time** they had to wait.* ◇ *the length of a class/speech/film* **3** [U] the number of pages in a book, a letter, etc. **4** [C] (SPORT) the distance from one end of a swimming pool to the other: *I can swim a length in thirty seconds.* **5** [C] a piece of sth long and thin: *a length of material/rope/string*

IDM **at length** for a long time or in great detail: *We discussed the matter at great length.*

go to great lengths to make more effort than usual in order to achieve sth

the length and breadth of sth to or in all parts of sth: *They travelled the length and breadth of India.*

lengthen /ˈleŋθən/ *verb* [I,T] to become longer or to make sth longer

lengthways /ˈleŋθweɪz/ (also **lengthwise** /ˈleŋθwaɪz/) *adv.* in a direction from one end to the other of sth: *Fold the paper lengthwise.*

lengthy /ˈleŋθi/ *adj.* very long

lenient /ˈliːniənt/ *adj.* (used about a punishment or person who punishes) not as strict as expected ▶ **lenience** (*also* **leniency** /-ənsi/) *noun* [U] ▶ **leniently** *adv.*

lenses

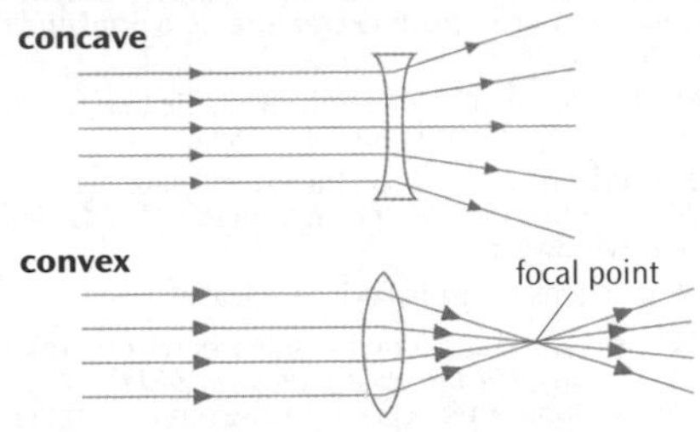

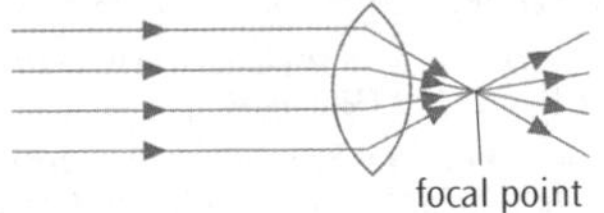

main parts of a lens

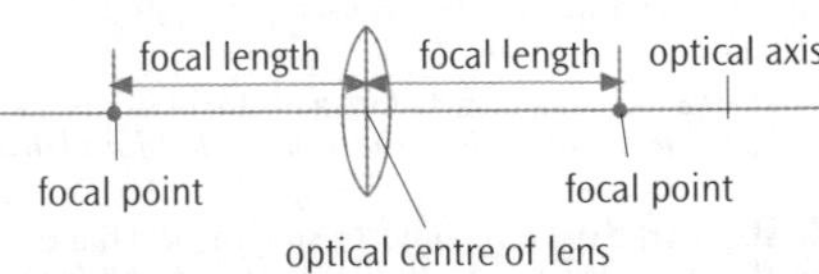

lens /lenz/ *noun* [C] (*pl.* **lenses**) **1** (SCIENCE) a curved piece of glass that makes things look bigger, clearer, etc. when you look through it: *a camera with a **zoom lens*** ➲ picture at **binoculars** **2** = CONTACT LENS **3** (ANATOMY) the transparent part of the eye, behind the PUPIL (= the round hole in the middle of the eye), that changes shape in order to direct light so that you can see clearly ➲ picture at **eye**

Lent /lent/ ***noun*** [U] (RELIGION) a period of 40 days starting in February or March, when some Christians stop doing or eating certain things for religious reasons: *I'm giving up smoking for Lent.*

lent past tense, past participle of **lend**

lentil /ˈlentl/ ***noun*** [C] a small brown, orange or green seed that can be dried and used in cooking: *lentil soup/stew*

Leo /ˈliːəʊ/ ***noun*** [U] the fifth sign of the ZODIAC, the Lion

leopard /ˈlepəd/ ***noun*** [C] a large wild animal of the cat family that has yellow fur with dark spots. **Leopards** live in Africa and Southern Asia. ❶ A female leopard is called a **leopardess** and a baby is called a **cub**. ➲ picture at **lion**

leotard /ˈliːətɑːd/ ***noun*** [C] a piece of clothing that fits the body tightly from the neck down to the tops of the legs. **Leotards** are worn by dancers or women doing certain sports.

leper /ˈlepə(r)/ ***noun*** [C] (HEALTH) a person who has LEPROSY

leprosy /ˈleprəsi/ ***noun*** [U] (HEALTH) a serious infectious disease that affects the skin, nerves, etc. and can cause parts of the body to fall off

lesbian /ˈlezbiən/ ***noun*** [C] a woman who is sexually attracted to other women ▶ **lesbian** ***adj.***: *a lesbian relationship* ▶ **lesbianism** ***noun*** [U] ➲ look at **gay**, **homosexual**

less[1] 🔑 /les/ ***det.***, ***pronoun***, ***adv.*** **1** (used with uncountable nouns) a smaller amount (of): *It took less time than I thought.* ◇ *I'm too fat – I must try to eat less.* ◇ *It's not far – it'll take less than an hour to get there.* **2** not so much (as): *He's less intelligent than his brother.* ◇ *It rains less in London than in Manchester.* ◇ *People work less well when they're tired.* OPP **more**

IDM **less and less** becoming smaller and smaller in amount or degree

more or less → MORE[2]

less[2] 🔑 /les/ ***prep.*** taking a certain number or amount away; MINUS: *You'll earn £10 an hour, less tax.*

lessee /leˈsiː/ ***noun*** [C] (LAW) a person who has a legal agreement (**a lease**) allowing them use of a building, an area of land, etc.

lessen /ˈlesn/ ***verb*** [I,T] to become less; to make sth less

lesser /ˈlesə(r)/ ***adj.***, ***adv.*** (only *before* a noun) not as great/much as: *He is guilty and so, **to a lesser extent**, is his wife.* ◇ *a lesser-known artist*

IDM **the lesser of two evils** the better of two bad things

lesson 🔑 /ˈlesn/ ***noun*** [C] **1** (EDUCATION) a period of time when you learn or teach sth: *She gives piano lessons.* ◇ *I want to take extra lessons in English conversation.* ◇ *a driving lesson* **2** something that is intended to be or should be learnt: *I hope we can learn some lessons from this disaster.*

IDM **learn your lesson** → LEARN

teach sb a lesson → TEACH

lessor /leˈsɔː(r)/ ***noun*** [C] (LAW) a person who gives sb the use of a building, an area of land, etc., having made a legal agreement (**a lease**)

let 🔑 /let/ ***verb*** [T] (*pres. part.* **letting**; *pt*, *pp* **let**) **1** ~ **sb/sth do sth** to allow sb/sth to do sth; to make sb/sth able to do sth: *My parents let me stay out till 11 o'clock.* ◇ *I wanted to borrow Dave's bike but he wouldn't let me.* ◇ *This ticket lets you travel anywhere in the city for a day.* **2** to allow sth to happen: *He's let the dinner burn again!* ◇ *Don't let the fire go out.* **3** used for offering help to sb: *Let me help you carry your bags.* **4** to allow sb/sth to go somewhere: *Open the windows and let some fresh air in.* ◇ *She was let out of prison yesterday.* **5** used for making suggestions about what you and other people can do: *'Let's go to the cinema tonight.' 'Yes, let's.'* **6** ~ **sth (out) (to sb)** to allow sb to use a building, room, etc. in return for rent: *They let out two rooms to students.* ◇ *There's a flat to let in our block.*

IDM **let alone** and certainly not: *We haven't decided where we're going yet, let alone booked the tickets.*

let sb/sth go; let go of sb/sth to stop holding sb/sth: *Let me go. You're hurting me!* ◇ *Hold the rope and don't let go of it.*

let sb know → KNOW[1]

let me see; let's see used when you are thinking or trying to remember sth: *Where did I put the car keys? Let's see. I think I left them by the telephone.*

let sth slip to accidentally say sth that you should keep secret

let's say for example: *You could work two mornings a week, let's say Tuesday and Friday.*

let yourself go 1 to relax without worrying what other people think **2** to allow yourself to become untidy, dirty, etc.

PHRV **let sb down** to not do sth that you promised to do for sb; to disappoint sb

let on (about sth) (to sb) to tell sb a secret: *He didn't let on how much he'd paid for the vase.*

let sb off to not punish sb, or to give sb a less serious punishment than expected: *He expected to go to prison but they let him off with a fine.*

let sth out to make a sound with your voice: *to let out a scream/sigh/groan/yell*

lethal /ˈliːθl/ ***adj.*** that can cause death or great damage: *a lethal weapon/drug* ▶ **lethally** /ˈliːθəli/ ***adv.***

lethargy /ˈleθədʒi/ ***noun*** [U] the feeling of being very tired and not having any energy ▶ **lethargic** /ləˈθɑːdʒɪk/ ***adj.***

letter 🔑 /ˈletə(r)/ ***noun*** [C] **1** a written or printed message that you send to sb: *I got a letter from Matthew this morning.* ◇ *I'm writing **a thank-you letter** to my uncle for the flowers he sent.* **2** (LANGUAGE) a written or printed sign that represents a sound in a language: *'Z' is the last letter of the English alphabet.*

ˈletter bomb ***noun*** [C] a small bomb that is sent to sb hidden in a letter that explodes when the envelope is opened

ˈletter box ***noun*** [C] **1** a hole in a door or wall for putting letters, etc. through **2** (*AmE* **ˈmailbox**) a small box near the main door of a building or by the road in which letters are left for the owner to collect **3** = POSTBOX

letterhead /ˈletəhed/ ***noun*** [C] the name and address of a person, a company or an organization printed at the top of their writing paper

lettuce /ˈletɪs/ ***noun*** [C,U] a plant with large green leaves which are eaten cold in salads: *a lettuce leaf*

leucocyte /ˈluːkəsaɪt/ ***noun*** [C] (BIOLOGY) a white blood cell

leukaemia (*AmE* **leukemia**) /luːˈkiːmɪə/ ***noun*** [U] (HEALTH) a serious disease of the blood which often results in death

levee /ˈlevi/ ***noun*** [C] (GEOGRAPHY) a low wall built at the side of a river to prevent it from flooding ➲ picture at **flood plain**

level¹ 🔑 /ˈlevl/ ***noun*** [C] **1** the amount, size or number of sth (compared to sth else): *a low level of unemployment* ◇ *high stress/pollution levels* **2** the height, position, standard, etc. of sth: *He used to play tennis at a high level.* ◇ *an intermediate-level student* ◇ *top-level discussions* **3** a way of considering sth: ***on a** spiritual/personal/professional **level*** **4** a flat surface or layer: *a multi-level shopping centre* **5** = SPIRIT LEVEL

level² 🔑 /ˈlevl/ ***adj.*** **1** with no part higher than any other; flat: *Make sure the shelves are level before you fix them in position.* ◇ *Put the tent up on level ground.* ◇ *a level teaspoon of sugar* **2** ~ **(with sb/sth)** at the same height, standard or position: *The boy's head was level with his father's shoulder.* ◇ *The teams are level on 34 points.*

IDM **a level playing field** a situation in which everyone has an equal chance of success

level³ /ˈlevl/ ***verb*** [T] (**levelling**; **levelled**: *AmE* **leveling**; **leveled**) to make sth flat, equal or level: *The ground needs levelling before we lay the patio.* ◇ *Juventus levelled the score with a late goal.* ◇ *Many buildings were levelled* (= destroyed) *in the earthquake.*

PHR V **level sth at sb/sth** to aim sth at sb/sth: *They levelled serious criticisms at the standard of teaching.*

level off/out to become flat, equal or level

ˌlevel ˈcrossing (*AmE* **ˈrailroad crossing**) ***noun*** [C] a place where a railway crosses the surface of a road

ˌlevel-ˈheaded ***adj.*** calm and sensible; able to make good decisions in a difficult situation

lever /ˈliːvə(r)/ ***noun*** [C] **1** a handle that you pull or push in order to make a machine, etc. work: *Pull the lever towards you.* ◇ *the gear lever in a car* **2** (PHYSICS) a bar or tool that is used to lift or open sth when you put pressure or force on one end: *You need to get the tyre off with a lever.* ▶ **lever *verb*** [T]: *The police had to lever the door open.*

leverage /ˈliːvərɪdʒ/ ***noun*** [U] **1** (*formal*) the ability to influence what people do: *diplomatic leverage* **2** (PHYSICS) the act of using a LEVER to lift or open sth; the force needed to do this **3** (*AmE*) (BUSINESS) = GEARING

levitate /ˈlevɪteɪt/ ***verb*** [I,T] to rise and float in the air with no physical support, especially by means of magic or by using special mental powers; to make sth rise in this way ▶ **levitation *noun*** [U]

levy¹ AW /ˈlevi/ ***noun*** [C] (*pl.* **-ies**) (POLITICS) an extra amount of money that has to be paid, especially as a tax to the government: *to **put/impose a levy on** oil imports*

levy² AW /ˈlevi/ ***verb*** [T] (*pres. part.* **levying**; *3rd person sing. pres.* **levies**; *pt, pp* **levied**) (*written*) ~ **sth (on sb)** to officially demand and collect money, etc.: *to levy a tax/fine*

lexical /ˈleksɪkl/ ***adj.*** (only before a noun) (LANGUAGE) connected with the words of a language: *lexical items* (= words and phrases) ▶ **lexically** /-kli/ ***adv.***

lexicographer /ˌleksɪˈkɒɡrəfə(r)/ ***noun*** [C] a person who writes and EDITS (= prepares a piece of writing to be published) dictionaries

lexicography /ˌleksɪˈkɒɡrəfi/ ***noun*** [U] the theory and practice of writing dictionaries

lexicon /ˈleksɪkən/ ***noun*** **1** (also **the lexicon**) [sing.] (LANGUAGE) all the words and phrases used in a particular language or subject; all the words and phrases used and known by a particular person or group of people **2** [C] a list of words from A to Z on a particular subject or in a language: *a lexicon of technical scientific terms*

lexis /ˈleksɪs/ ***noun*** [U] (LANGUAGE) all the words and phrases of a particular language
SYN **vocabulary**

liability /ˌlaɪəˈbɪləti/ ***noun*** (*pl.* **liabilities**) **1** [U] ~ **(for sth)** (LAW) the state of being legally responsible for sth: *The company cannot accept liability for damage to cars in this car park.* **2** [C] (*informal*) a person or thing that can cause a lot of problems, cost a lot of money, etc. **3** [C, usually pl.] (FINANCE) the amount of money that a person or company owes: *The company is reported to have liabilities of nearly $90000.* ➲ look at **asset**

liable /ˈlaɪəbl/ ***adj.*** (not before a noun) **1** ~ **to do sth** likely to do sth: *We're all liable to have accidents when we are very tired.* **2** ~ **to sth** likely to have or suffer from sth: *The area is liable to floods.* **3** ~ **(for sth)** (LAW) responsible for sth

liaise /liˈeɪz/ ***verb*** [I] ~ **(with sb/sth)** to work closely with a person, group, etc. and give them or it regular information about what you are doing

liaison /liˈeɪzn/ ***noun*** **1** [U, sing.] ~ **(between A and B)** communication between two or more people or groups that work together **2** [C] a secret sexual relationship

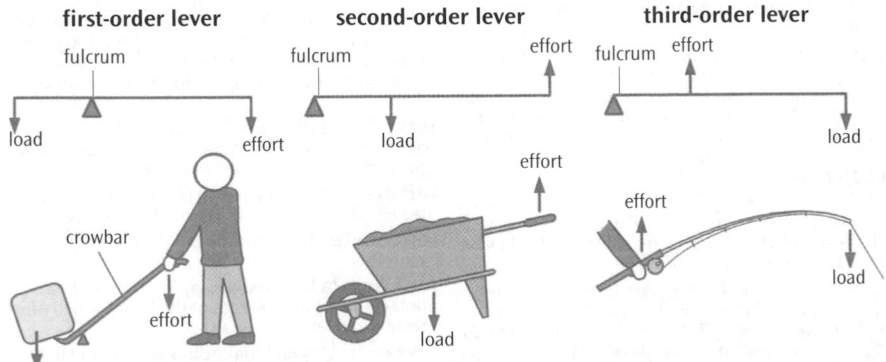

liar /ˈlaɪə(r)/ ***noun*** [C] a person who does not tell the truth: *She called me a liar.* ➲ Look at the verb and noun **lie**.

Lib Dem /ˌlɪb ˈdem/ ***abbr.*** (POLITICS) (in British politics) Liberal Democrat

libel /ˈlaɪbl/ ***noun*** [C,U] (LAW) the act of printing a statement about sb that is not true and would give people a bad opinion of them: *The singer is suing the newspaper for libel.* ▶ **libel** ***verb*** [T] (**libelling**; **libelled**: *AmE* **libeling**; **libeled**): *The actor claims he was libelled in the magazine article.*

liberal AW /ˈlɪbərəl/ ***adj.*** **1** accepting different opinions or kinds of behaviour; TOLERANT: *He has very liberal parents.* **2** (POLITICS) believing in or based on principles of commercial freedom, freedom of choice, and avoiding extreme social and political change: *liberal policies/politicians* **3** not strictly limited in amount or variety
▶ **liberal** ***noun*** [C]: *He's always considered himself a liberal.* ▶ **liberalism** AW /-ɪzəm/ ***noun*** [U]

the ˌLiberal ˈDemocrats ***noun*** [pl.] (POLITICS) a political party in Britain that represents views that are not extreme

liberalize AW (also **-ise**) /ˈlɪbrəlaɪz/ ***verb*** [T] to make sth such as a law or a political or religious system less strict ▶ **liberalization** (also **-isation**) /ˌlɪbrəlaɪˈzeɪʃn/ ***noun*** [U]

liberally AW /ˈlɪbərəli/ ***adv.*** freely or in large amounts

liberate AW /ˈlɪbəreɪt/ ***verb*** [T] **~ sb/sth (from sth)** to allow sb/sth to be free: *France was liberated in 1945.* ▶ **liberation** /ˌlɪbəˈreɪʃn/ ***noun*** [U]

liberated AW /ˈlɪbəreɪtɪd/ ***adj.*** free from traditional opinions or ways of behaving that might limit you in what you think or do

liberty /ˈlɪbəti/ ***noun*** [C,U] (*pl.* **liberties**) the freedom to go where you want, do what you want, etc.: *We must defend our civil liberties at all costs.* ➲ look at **freedom**
IDM **at liberty (to do sth)** free or allowed to do sth: *You are at liberty to leave when you wish.*

Libra /ˈliːbrə/ ***noun*** [U] the seventh sign of the ZODIAC, the Scales

librarian /laɪˈbreəriən/ ***noun*** [C] a person who works in or is in charge of a library

library 🔑 /ˈlaɪbrəri; ˈlaɪbri/ ***noun*** [C] (*pl.* **libraries**) **1** a room or building that contains a collection of books, etc. that can be looked at or borrowed: *My library books are due back tomorrow.* ➲ look at **bookshop** **2** a private collection of books, etc.

libretto /lɪˈbretəʊ/ ***noun*** [C] (*pl.* **librettos** or **libretti** /-tiː/) (MUSIC) the words that are sung or spoken in an OPERA or a musical play

lice plural of **louse**

licence 🔑 AW (*AmE* **license**) /ˈlaɪsns/ ***noun*** **1** [C] **a ~ (for sth/to do sth)** (LAW) an official paper that shows you are allowed to do or have sth: *Do you have a licence for this gun?* ◇ *The shop has applied for a licence to sell alcoholic drinks.* ➲ look at **driving licence** **2** [U] (*formal*) **~ (to do sth)** permission or freedom to do sth: *The soldiers were given licence to kill if they were attacked.*

ˈlicence plate (*AmE* **license plate**) = NUMBER PLATE

license¹ 🔑 AW /ˈlaɪsns/ ***verb*** [T] to give sb official permission to do, own, or use sth: *The new drug has not yet been licensed in the US.*

license² 🔑 (*AmE*) = LICENCE: *a driver's license*

licensed AW /ˈlaɪsnst/ ***adj.*** **1** (*BrE*) having official permission to sell alcoholic drinks: *a licensed restaurant* **2** that you have official permission to own: *Is that gun licensed?* **3** having official permission to do sth: *She is licensed to fly solo.*

licensee /ˌlaɪsənˈsiː/ ***noun*** [C] a person who has a licence to sell alcoholic drinks

ˈlicensing laws ***noun*** [pl.] (*BrE*) (LAW) the laws that control when and where alcoholic drinks can be sold

lichen /ˈlaɪkən; ˈlɪtʃən/ ***noun*** [U, C] (BIOLOGY) a very small grey or yellow plant that spreads over the surface of rocks, walls and trees and does not have any flowers

lick /lɪk/ ***verb*** [T] to move your tongue across sth: *The child licked the spoon clean.* ◇ *I licked the envelope and stuck it down.* ▶ **lick** ***noun*** [C]

licorice = LIQUORICE

lid 🔑 /lɪd/ ***noun*** [C] **1** the top part of a box, pot, etc. that can be lifted up or taken off ➲ picture at **piano** **2** = EYELID

lie¹ 🔑 /laɪ/ ***verb*** [I] (*pres. part.* **lying**; *pt, pp* **lied**) **~ (to sb) (about sth)** to say or write sth that you know is not true: *He lied about his age in order to join the army.* ◇ *How could you lie to me?!* ▶ **lie** ***noun*** [C]: *to tell a lie* ◇ *That story about his mother being ill was just **a pack of lies**.*

lie² 🔑 /laɪ/ ***verb*** [I] (*pres. part.* **lying**; *pt* **lay** /leɪ/; *pp* **lain** /leɪn/) **1** to be in or move into a flat or horizontal position (so that you are not standing or sitting): *He lay on the sofa and went to sleep.* ◇ *to lie on your back/side/front* ◇ *The book lay open in front of her.* **2** to be or stay in a certain state or position: *Snow lay thick on the ground.* ◇ *The hills lie to the north of the town.* ◇ *They are young and their whole lives **lie ahead** of them.* **3 ~ (in sth)** to exist or to be found somewhere: *The problem lies in deciding when to stop.*
IDM **lie in wait (for sb)** to hide somewhere waiting to attack, surprise or catch sb
lie low to try not to attract attention to yourself
PHR V **lie about/around** to relax and do nothing
lie back to relax and do nothing while sb else works, etc.
lie behind sth to be the real hidden reason for sth: *We may never know what lay behind his decision to resign.*
lie down (used about a person) to be in or move into a flat or horizontal position so that you can rest
lie in (*informal*) to stay in bed later than usual because you do not have to get up ➲ look at **oversleep**
lie with sb (to do sth) (*informal*) to be sb's responsibility to do sth

ˈlie detector ***noun*** [C] a piece of equipment that can show if a person is telling the truth or not

Lieut. (*also* **Lt**) ***abbr.*** Lieutenant

lieutenant /lefˈtenənt/ ***noun*** [C] an officer at a middle level in the army, navy or air force: *Lieutenant Paul Fisher* ◇ *flight lieutenant*

life 🔑 /laɪf/ ***noun*** (*pl.* **lives** /laɪvz/) **1** [U] the quality that people, animals or plants have when they are not dead: *Do you believe in life after death?* ◇ *to bring sb/come back to life* **2** [U] (BIOLOGY) living things: *Life on earth began in a very simple form.* ◇ *No life was found on the moon.* ◇ *There was no sign of life in the deserted house.* ◇ *plant life* **3** [C,U] the state of being alive as a human being: *Would you **risk your life** to protect your property?* ◇ *Doctors fought all night to **save her life**.* **4** [C,U] the period during which sb/sth is alive or exists: *I've lived in this town **all** my **life**.* ◇ *I spent my early life in London.* ◇ *to have a short/long/exciting life* **5** [U] the things that you may experience while you are alive: *Life can be hard for a single parent.* ◇ *I'm not happy with the situation, but I suppose **that's life**.* **6** [C,U] a way of living: *They went to America to **start a new life**.* ◇ *They **lead a** busy **life**.* ◇ *married life* **7** [U] energy; activity: *Young children are **full of life**.* ◇ *These streets **come to life** in the evenings.* **8** [U] something that really exists and is not just a story, a picture, etc.: *I wonder what that actor's like **in real life**.* ◇ *Do you draw people **from life** or from photographs?*

IDM **a fact of life** → FACT
the facts of life → FACT
full of beans/life → FULL[1]
get a life (*spoken*) used to tell sb to stop being boring and do sth more interesting
have the time of your life → TIME[1]
lose your life → LOSE
a matter of life and/or death → MATTER[1]
take your (own) life to kill yourself
a walk of life → WALK[2]
a/sb's way of life → WAY[1]

ˌlife-and-ˈdeath (*also* **ˌlife-or-ˈdeath**) ***adj.*** (only *before* a noun) very serious or dangerous: *a life-and-death struggle/matter/decision*

lifebelt /ˈlaɪfbelt/ (*also* **lifebuoy** /ˈlaɪfbɔɪ/) ***noun*** [C] (*BrE*) a ring that is made from light material which will float. A **lifebelt** is thrown to a person who has fallen into water to stop them from sinking.

lifeboat /ˈlaɪfbəʊt/ ***noun*** [C] **1** a small boat that is carried on a large ship and that is used to escape from the ship if it is in danger of sinking **2** a special boat that is used for rescuing people who are in danger at sea

ˈlife coach ***noun*** [C] a person who is employed by sb to give them advice about how to achieve the things they want in their life and work

ˈlife cycle ***noun*** [C] (BIOLOGY) the series of forms into which a living thing changes as it develops: *the life cycle of a frog*

ˈlife expectancy ***noun*** [C,U] (*pl.* **life expectancies**) (SOCIAL STUDIES) the number of years that a person is likely to live

lifeguard /ˈlaɪfɡɑːd/ ***noun*** [C] a person at a beach or swimming pool whose job is to rescue people who are in difficulty in the water

ˈlife jacket (*AmE also* **ˈlife vest**) ***noun*** [C] a plastic or rubber jacket without sleeves that can be filled with air. A **life jacket** is used to make sb float if they fall into water. ➲ picture at **canoe**

lifeless /ˈlaɪfləs/ ***adj.*** **1** dead or appearing to be dead **2** without energy or interest; dull

lifelike /ˈlaɪflaɪk/ ***adj.*** looking like a real person or thing: *The flowers are made of silk but they are very lifelike.*

lifeline /ˈlaɪflaɪn/ ***noun*** [C] something that is very important for sb and that they depend on: *For many old people their telephone is a lifeline.*

lifelong /ˈlaɪflɒŋ/ ***adj.*** (only *before* a noun) for all of your life: *a lifelong friend*

ˌlife ˈpeer ***noun*** [C] (POLITICS) (in Britain) a person who is given the title of PEER (='Lord' or 'Lady') but who cannot pass it on to their son or daughter

ˈlife-size(d) ***adj.*** of the same size as the real person or thing: *a life-sized statue*

lifespan /ˈlaɪfspæn/ ***noun*** [C] the length of time that sth is likely to live, work, last, etc.: *A mosquito has a lifespan of only a few days.*

ˈlife story ***noun*** [C] (*pl.* **life stories**) the story of sb's life

lifestyle /ˈlaɪfstaɪl/ ***noun*** [C] (SOCIAL STUDIES) the way that you live

ˌlife supˈport ***noun*** [U] (HEALTH) the fact of being kept alive by a special machine: *After the accident he was **on life support** for a week.*

ˌlife-supˈport machine ***noun*** [C] (HEALTH) a piece of equipment in a hospital that keeps sb alive when they cannot breathe without help

lifetime /ˈlaɪftaɪm/ ***noun*** [C] the period of time that sb is alive

ˈlife vest ***noun*** (*AmE*) = LIFE JACKET

lift[1] 🔑 /lɪft/ ***verb*** **1** [T] ~ **sb/sth (up)** to move sb/sth to a higher level or position: *He lifted the child up onto his shoulders.* ◇ *Lift your arm very gently and see if it hurts.* ◇ *It took two men to lift the piano.* **2** [T] to move sb/sth from one place or position to another: *She lifted the suitcase down from the rack.* **3** [T] to end or remove a rule, law, etc.: *The ban on public meetings has been lifted.* **4** [I,T] to become or make sb happier: *The news lifted our spirits.* **5** [I] (used about clouds, FOG, etc.) to rise up or disappear: *The mist lifted towards the end of the morning.* **6** [T] (*informal*) ~ **sth (from sb/sth)** to steal or copy sth: *Most of his essay was lifted straight from the textbook.* ➲ look at **shoplifting**

PHR V **lift off** (used about a SPACECRAFT) to rise straight up from the ground

lift[2] 🔑 /lɪft/ ***noun*** **1** (*AmE* **elevator**) [C] a machine in a large building that is used for carrying people or goods from one floor to another: *It's on the third floor so we'd better **take the lift**.* **2** [C] a free ride in a car, etc.: *Can you **give me a lift** to the station, please?* ◇ *I got a lift from a passing car.* **3** [sing.] (*informal*) a feeling of being happier or more confident than before: *Her words of encouragement **gave** the whole team **a lift**.* **4** [sing.] the action of moving or being moved to a higher position

IDM **thumb a lift** → THUMB[2]

ˈlift-off ***noun*** [C] the start of the flight of a SPACECRAFT when it leaves the ground

ligament /ˈlɪɡəmənt/ ***noun*** [C] (ANATOMY) a strong band in a person's or animal's body that holds the bones, etc. together ➲ picture at **synovial**

light[1] 🔑 /laɪt/ ***noun*** **1** [U, C] the energy from the sun, a lamp, etc. that allows you to see things: *a beam/ray of light* ◇ *The light was too dim for us to read by.* ◇ *Strong light is bad for the eyes.* ◇ *We could see strange lights in the sky.* **2** [C] something that produces light, for example an electric lamp: *Suddenly all the lights went out/came on.* ◇ *the lights of the city in the distance* ◇ *If the lights* (=traffic lights) *are red, stop!* ◇ *That car hasn't got its lights on.* **3** [C] something, for example a match, that can be used to light a cigarette, start a fire, etc.: *Have you got a light?*

IDM **bring sth/come to light** to make sth known or to become known
cast light on sth → CAST[1]
give sb/get the green light → GREEN[1]
in a good, bad, etc. light (used about the way that sth is seen or described by other people) well, badly, etc.: *The newspapers often portray his behaviour in a bad light.*
in the light of because of; considering
set light to sth to cause sth to start burning
shed light on sth → SHED[2]

light² 🔑 /laɪt/ ***adj.*** **1** not of great weight: *Carry this bag – it's the lightest.* ◇ *I've lost weight – I'm five kilos lighter than I used to be.* ◇ *light clothes* (=for summer) OPP **heavy** **2** having a lot of light: *In summer it's still light at 10 o'clock.* ◇ *a light room* OPP **dark** **3** (used about a colour) pale: *a light-blue sweater* OPP **dark** **4** not great in amount, degree, etc.: *Traffic in London is light on a Sunday.* ◇ *a light prison sentence* ◇ *a light wind* ◇ *a light breakfast* **5** not using much force; gentle: *a light touch on the shoulder* **6** not hard or tiring: *light exercise* ◇ *light entertainment/reading* **7** (used about sleep) not deep: *I'm a light sleeper, so the slightest noise wakes me.* ▶ **lightness** ***noun*** [U]

light³ 🔑 /laɪt/ ***verb*** (*pt, pp* **lit** or **lighted**) **1** [I,T] to begin or to make sth begin to burn: *The gas cooker won't light.* ◇ *to light a fire* **2** [T] to give light to sth: *The street is well/badly lit at night.* ◇ *We only had a small torch to light our way.*

PHR V **light (sth) up** **1** to make sth bright with light: *The fireworks lit up the whole sky.* **2** (used about sb's face, eyes, etc.) to become bright with happiness or excitement **3** to start smoking a cigarette

light⁴ /laɪt/ ***adv.*** (TOURISM) without much luggage: *I always travel light.*

ˈlight bulb = BULB (1)

lighten /ˈlaɪtn/ ***verb*** [I,T] **1** to become lighter in weight or to make sth lighter **2** to become or to make sth brighter

lighter /ˈlaɪtə(r)/ = CIGARETTE LIGHTER

ˌlight-ˈheaded ***adj.*** feeling slightly ill and not in control of your thoughts and movements

ˌlight-ˈhearted ***adj.*** **1** intended to be funny and enjoyable **2** happy and without problems

lighthouse /ˈlaɪthaʊs/ ***noun*** [C] a tall building with a light at the top to warn and guide ships near the coast

lighting /ˈlaɪtɪŋ/ ***noun*** [U] the quality or type of lights used in a room, building, etc.

lightly 🔑 /ˈlaɪtli/ ***adv.*** **1** gently; with very little force: *He touched her lightly on the arm.* **2** only a little; not much: *lightly cooked/spiced/whisked* **3** not seriously; without serious thought: *We do not take our customers' complaints lightly.*

IDM **get off/be let off lightly** to avoid serious punishment or trouble

lightning¹ /ˈlaɪtnɪŋ/ ***noun*** [U] a bright flash of light that appears in the sky during a storm, and is usually followed by THUNDER (=a loud noise): *The tree was **struck by lightning** and burst into flames.* ◇ *a flash of lightning*

lightning² /ˈlaɪtnɪŋ/ ***adj.*** (only *before* a noun) very quick or sudden: *a lightning attack*

lightweight /ˈlaɪtweɪt/ ***noun*** [C], ***adj.*** **1** (SPORT) a person who is in one of the lightest weight groups in certain fighting sports: *a lightweight boxing champion* **2** (a thing) weighing less than usual: *a lightweight suit for the summer*

ˈlight year ***noun*** [C] (PHYSICS) the distance that light travels in one year, 9.4607×10^{12} kilometres

lignite /ˈlɪɡnaɪt/ ***noun*** [U] (GEOLOGY) a soft brown type of coal

likable = LIKEABLE

like¹ 🔑 /laɪk/ ***verb*** [T] **1** ~ **sb/sth**; ~ **doing sth**; ~ **to do sth**; ~ **sth about sb/sth** to find sb/sth pleasant; to enjoy sth: *He's nice. I like him a lot.* ◇ *Do you like their new flat?* ◇ *How do you like John's new girlfriend?* ◇ *I like my coffee strong.* ◇ *I like playing tennis.* ◇ *I like to go to the cinema on Thursdays.* ◇ *What is it you like about Sarah so much?* ◇ *She didn't like it when I shouted at her.* ◇ *I don't like him borrowing my things without asking.* ◇ *The job seems strange at first, but you'll **get to like it**.* OPP **dislike** **2** to want: *Do what you like. I don't care.* ◇ *We can go whenever you like.* ◇ *I didn't like to disturb you while you were eating.*

IDM **if you like** used for agreeing with sb or suggesting sth in a polite way: *'Shall we stop for a rest?' 'Yes, if you like.'*

I like that! (*BrE, informal*) used for saying that sth is not true or not fair

like the look/sound of sb/sth to have a good impression of sb/sth after seeing or hearing about them or it

like² 🔑 /laɪk/ ***prep., conj.*** **1** similar to sb/sth: *You **look** very/just/exactly **like** your father.* ◇ *Those two singers **sound like** cats!* ◇ *Your house is **nothing like** how I imagined it.* **2** (in compounds) in the manner of; similar to: *childlike innocence/simplicity* ◇ *a very lifelike statue* **3** in the same way as sb/sth: *Stop behaving like children.* ◇ *That's not right. Do it like this.* ◇ *She can't draw like her sister can.* **4** for example; such as: *They enjoy most team games, like football and rugby.* **5** typical of a particular person: *It was just like Maria to be late.* **6** (*informal*) as if: *She behaves like she owns the place.* **7** (*slang*) (used before saying what sb said, how sb felt, etc.): *When I saw the colour of my hair I was like 'Wow, I can't believe it!'*

IDM **like anything** (*spoken*) very much, fast, hard, etc.: *We had to pedal like anything to get up the hill.*

nothing like → NOTHING

something like about; approximately: *The cathedral took something like 200 years to build.*

that's more like it (used to say that sth is better than before): *The sun's coming out now – that's more like it!*

like³ /laɪk/ ***noun*** **1** [sing.] a person or thing that is similar to sb/sth else: *I enjoy going round castles, old churches **and the like**.* ◇ *She was a great singer, and we may never see her like/the like of her again.* **2 likes** [pl.] things that you like: *Tell me about some of your **likes and dislikes**.* ▶ **like** ***adj.*** (*formal*)

-like ***suffix*** (in adjectives) similar to; typical of: *childlike* ◇ *shell-like*

likeable (also **likable**) /ˈlaɪkəbl/ ***adj.*** (used about a person) easy to like; pleasant

likelihood /ˈlaɪklihʊd/ ***noun*** [U] the chance of sth happening; how likely sth is to happen: *There seems very little likelihood of success.*

likely 🔑 /ˈlaɪkli/ ***adj., adv.*** (**likelier**; **likeliest**) **1** ~ (**to do sth**) probable or expected: *Do you think it's likely to rain?* ◇ *The boss is not likely to agree.* ◇ *It's not likely that the boss will agree.* **2** probably suitable: *a likely candidate for the job* OPP **unlikely**

IDM **not likely!** (*informal*) certainly not

liken /ˈlaɪkən/ ***verb*** [T] (*formal*) ~ **sb/sth to sb/sth** to compare one person or thing with another: *This young artist has been likened to Picasso.*

likeness /ˈlaɪknəs/ ***noun*** [C,U] the fact of being similar in appearance; an example of this: *The witness's drawing turned out to be **a good likeness of** the attacker.*

likewise AW /ˈlaɪkwaɪz/ ***adv.*** (*formal*) the same; in a similar way: *I intend to send a letter of apology and suggest that you do likewise.*

liking /ˈlaɪkɪŋ/ ***noun*** [sing.] **a** ~ (**for sb/sth**) the feeling that you like sb/sth: *I have a liking for spicy food.*

IDM **too...for your liking** that you do not like

because he/she/it has too much of a particular quality: *The music was a bit too loud for my liking.*

lilac /ˈlaɪlək/ ***noun*** [C,U], ***adj.*** **1** a tree or large bush that has large purple or white flowers in spring **2** (of) a pale purple colour

lilo (also **Li-lo™**) /ˈlaɪləʊ/ ***noun*** [C] (*pl.* **lilos**) (*BrE*) a plastic or rubber bed that you fill with air when you want to use it. It is used on the beach or for camping.

lily /ˈlɪli/ ***noun*** [C] (*pl.* **lilies**) a type of plant that has large white or coloured flowers in the shape of a bell ➲ look at **water lily**

limb /lɪm/ ***noun*** [C] **1** a leg or an arm of a person **2** one of the main branches of a tree
IDM **out on a limb** without the support of other people

lime /laɪm/ ***noun*** **1** [C] a fruit that looks like a small green lemon **2** [U] (*also* ˌ**lime ˈgreen**) a yellowish-green colour **3** [U] (**AGRICULTURE, CHEMISTRY**) a white substance that is used for making CEMENT and also for adding to soil to improve its quality

the limelight /ˈlaɪmlaɪt/ ***noun*** [U] the centre of public attention: *to be in/out of the limelight*

limerick /ˈlɪmərɪk/ ***noun*** [C] (**LITERATURE**) a humorous short poem, with two long lines that RHYME (=end with the same sound) with each other, followed by two short lines that RHYME with each other and ending with a long line that RHYMES with the first two

limestone /ˈlaɪmstəʊn/ ***noun*** [U] (**GEOLOGY**) a type of hard white SEDIMENTARY rock that is used for building or for making CEMENT

limit¹ 🔑 /ˈlɪmɪt/ ***noun*** [C] **1** the greatest or smallest amount of sth that is allowed or possible: *a speed/age/time limit* ◇ *He was fined for exceeding the speed limit.* ◇ *There's a limit to the amount of time I'm prepared to spend on this.* **2** the outside edge of a place or area: *the city limits* ◇ *Lorries are not allowed within a two-mile limit of the town centre.*
3 (**MATHEMATICS**) a point or value which you aim for with a number or series of numbers, until they are as close to it as you want
IDM **off limits** (*AmE*) =OUT OF BOUNDS

THESAURUS

limit

restriction • control • constraint • restraint • limitation

These are all words for sth that limits what you can do or what can happen.

limit: *The EU has set strict limits on pollution levels.*
restriction: *Speed restrictions are in place.*
control: *international talks on arms control*
constraint (*formal*): *We have to work within severe time constraints.*
restraint (*formal*): *Wage restraints were imposed.*
limitation: *He recognized the limitations of the medium.*

within limits only up to a reasonable point or amount

limit² 🔑 /ˈlɪmɪt/ ***verb*** [T] ~ **sb/sth (to sth)** to keep sb/sth within or below a certain amount, size, degree or area: *In China families are limited to just one child.*

limitation /ˌlɪmɪˈteɪʃn/ ***noun*** **1** [C,U] (a) ~ **(on sth)** the act of limiting or controlling sth; a condition that puts a limit on sth: *There are no limitations on what we can do.* **2** [pl.] **limitations** things that you cannot do: *It is important to know your own limitations.*
➲ note at **limit**

limited 🔑 /ˈlɪmɪtɪd/ ***adj.*** small or controlled in number, amount, etc.: *Book early because there are only a limited number of seats available.*
OPP **unlimited**

ˌ**limited ˈcompany** ***noun*** [C] (*abbr.* **Ltd**) (**BUSINESS**) a company whose owners only have to pay a limited amount of its debts if it fails

limousine /ˈlɪməziːn; ˌlɪməˈziːn/ (also *informal* **limo** /ˈlɪməʊ/) ***noun*** [C] a large expensive car that usually has a sheet of glass between the driver and the passengers in the back

limp¹ /lɪmp/ ***verb*** [I] to walk with difficulty because you have hurt your leg or foot ▶ **limp** ***noun*** [sing.]: *to walk with a limp*

limp² /lɪmp/ ***adj.*** not firm or strong: *You should put those flowers in water before they go limp.*

limestone landscape

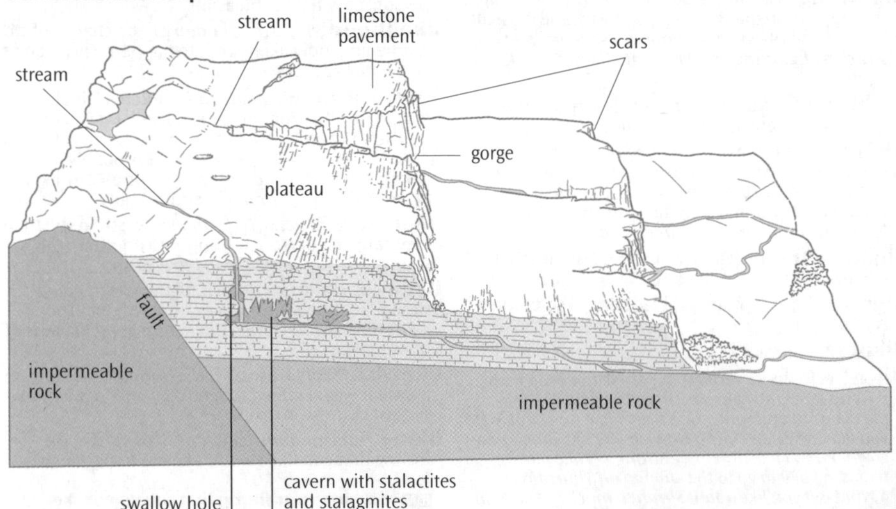

line¹ ⊶ /laɪn/ ***noun*** [C] **1** a long thin mark on the surface of sth or on the ground: *to draw a line* ◇ *a straight/wiggly/dotted line* ◇ *The old lady had lines on her forehead.* ◇ *The ball was definitely over the line.* ◇ *the finishing line of a race* **2** a row of people, things, words on a page, etc.: *There was a long line of people waiting at the Post Office.* ◇ *a five-line poem* ◇ *Start each paragraph on a new line.* **3** a border or limit between one place or thing and another: *to cross state lines* ◇ *There's a thin line between showing interest and being nosy.* **4** a direction or course of movement, thought or action: *He was so drunk he couldn't walk* ***in a straight line.*** ◇ *The answer's not quite correct, but you're* ***on the right lines.*** ◇ *The two countries' economies are developing* ***along*** *similar* ***lines.*** **5** a piece of rope or string: *Hang out the clothes on the (washing) line, please.* ◇ *a fishing line* **6** a telephone or electricity wire or connection: *I'm sorry – the line is engaged. Can you try again later?* ◇ *I'll just check for you. Can you* ***hold the line*** (=wait)? **7** a section of railway track **8 lines** [pl.] (**ARTS AND MEDIA**) the words that are spoken by an actor in a play, etc. **9** a company that provides transport by air, ship, etc.: *an airline* **10** [sing.] (**BUSINESS**) one type of goods in a shop, etc. **11** the place where an army is fighting: *There's renewed fighting on* ***the front line.*** **12** a series of people in a family, things or events that follow one another in time: *He comes from* ***a long line of*** *musicians.* **13** something that you do as a job, do well, or enjoy doing: *What* ***line of business/work*** *are you in?*

IDM **draw the line at sth/doing sth** → DRAW¹
drop sb a line → DROP¹
in line for sth likely to get sth: *You could be in line for promotion if you keep working like this.*
in line with sth similar to sth; in agreement with sth: *These changes will bring the industry in line with the new laws.*
somewhere along/down the line at some time; sooner or later
take a hard line (on sth) → HARD¹
toe the (party) line → TOE²

lines

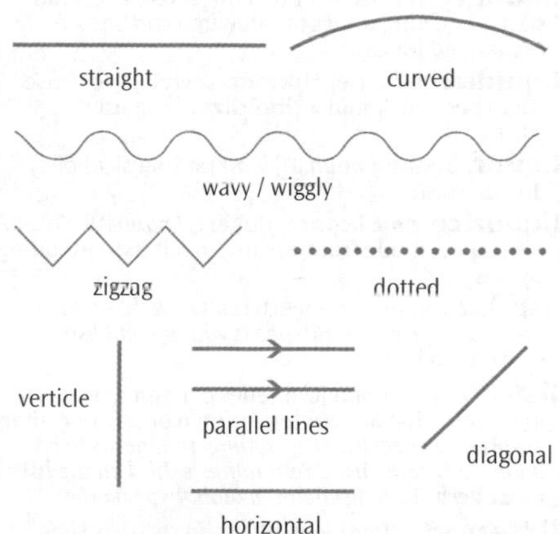

line² /laɪn/ ***verb*** [T] **1** (often passive) to cover the inside surface of sth with a different material **2** to form lines or rows along sth: *Crowds lined the streets to watch the race.*

PHR V **line up (for sth)** to form a line of people; to QUEUE
line sth up (*informal*) to arrange or organize sth: *She lined the bottles up on the shelf.*

linear /ˈlɪniə(r)/ ***adj.*** **1** of or in lines: *In his art he broke the laws of scientific linear perspective.* **2** going from one thing to another in a single series of stages: *Students do not always progress in a linear fashion.* **3** of length: *linear measurement* (=for example metres, feet, etc.) **4** (**MATHEMATICS**) able to be represented by a straight line on a GRAPH: *linear equations*

lined /laɪnd/ ***adj.*** **1** covered in lines: *a face lined with age* ◇ *lined paper* **2 -lined** (used in compounds) having the object mentioned all along the side(s); having the inside surface covered with the material mentioned: *a tree-lined avenue* ◇ *fur-lined boots*

linen /ˈlɪnɪn/ ***noun*** [U] **1** a type of strong cloth that is made from a natural substance (**flax**) **2** sheets and other cloth COVERINGS used in the house on a bed, table, etc.: *bedlinen*

liner /ˈlaɪnə(r)/ ***noun*** [C] **1** a large ship that carries people, etc. long distances **2** something that is put inside sth else to keep it clean or protect it. A **liner** is usually thrown away after it has been used: *a dustbin liner*

linesman /ˈlaɪnzmən/ ***noun*** [C] (*pl.* **-men** /-mən/) (**SPORT**) an official who helps the REFEREE in some games that are played on a field or court, especially in deciding whether or where a ball crosses one of the lines. **Linesmen** are now officially called (**referee's assistants**) in football.

linger /ˈlɪŋɡə(r)/ ***verb*** [I] ~ **(on)** to stay somewhere or do sth for longer than usual: *His eyes lingered on the money in her bag.*

lingerie /ˈlænʒəri/ ***noun*** [U] (used in shops, etc.) women's underwear

lingua franca /ˌlɪŋɡwə ˈfræŋkə/ ***noun*** [usually sing.] (**LANGUAGE**) a shared language of communication used between people whose main languages are different: *English has become a lingua franca in many parts of the world.*

linguist /ˈlɪŋɡwɪst/ ***noun*** [C] (**LANGUAGE**) **1** a person who knows several foreign languages well **2** a person who studies languages or LINGUISTICS

linguistic /lɪŋˈɡwɪstɪk/ ***adj.*** (**LANGUAGE**) connected with language or the study of language

linguistics /lɪŋˈɡwɪstɪks/ ***noun*** [U] (**LANGUAGE**) the scientific study of language

lining /ˈlaɪnɪŋ/ ***noun*** [C,U] material that covers the inside surface of sth: *I've torn the lining of my coat.*

IDM **every cloud has a silver lining** → CLOUD¹

link¹ ⊶ AW /lɪŋk/ ***noun*** [C] **1** a ~ **(between A and B)**; a ~ **(with sb/sth)** a connection or relationship between two or more people or things: *There is a strong link between smoking and heart disease.* **2** one ring of a chain **3** a means of travelling or communicating between two places: *To visit similar websites to this one, click on the links at the bottom of the page.*

link² ⊶ AW /lɪŋk/ ***verb*** [T] ~ **A to/with B**; ~ **A and B (together)** to make a connection between two or more people or things: *The new bridge will link the island to the mainland.* ◇ *The computers are linked together in a network.*

PHR V **link up (with sb/sth)** to join together (with sb/sth): *All our branches are linked up by computer.*

linkage AW /ˈlɪŋkɪdʒ/ ***noun*** **1** [U,C] ~ **(between A and B)** the act of linking things; a link or system of links SYN **connection** **2** [C] a device that links two or more things

'linking verb *noun* [C] (LANGUAGE) a verb such as *be* or *become* that connects a subject with the adjective or noun that describes it: *In 'She became angry', the verb 'became' is a linking verb.*

'link-up *noun* [C] the joining together or connection of two or more things

linocut /'laɪnəʊkʌt/ *noun* [C] (ART) a design or shape cut in a piece of LINOLEUM, used to make a print; a print made in this way

linoleum /lɪ'nəʊliəm/ (*BrE, informal* **lino** /'laɪnəʊ/) *noun* [U] strong, shiny material used for covering floors

linseed oil /ˌlɪnsiːd 'ɔɪl/ *noun* [U] an oil made from FLAX seeds, used in paint or to protect wood, etc.

lint /lɪnt/ *noun* [U] **1** soft cotton cloth used for covering and protecting injuries **2** small soft pieces of wool, cotton, etc. that stick on the surface of clothes, etc.

lintel /'lɪntl/ *noun* [C] (ARCHITECTURE) a piece of wood or stone over a door or window

LINUX /'laɪnəks/ *noun* [U] (COMPUTING) a computer OPERATING SYSTEM that you do not have to pay to use

lion

lion /'laɪən/ *noun* [C] a large animal of the cat family that lives in Africa and parts of southern Asia. A male **lion** has a MANE (=a large amount of hair around his head and neck). ❶ A female lion is called a **lioness** and a young lion is called a **cub**. The noise a lion makes is a **roar**.
IDM **the lion's share (of sth)** (*BrE*) the largest or best part of sth when it is divided

lioness /'laɪənes/ *noun* [C] a female LION ➲ picture at **lion**

lip ⊶ /lɪp/ *noun* [C] **1** either of the two soft edges at the opening of your mouth: *to kiss sb on the lips ◇ top/upper lip ◇ bottom/lower lip* ➲ picture on **page 80** **2 -lipped** (used to form compound adjectives) having the type of lips mentioned: *thin-lipped* **3** the edge of a cup or sth that is shaped like a cup
IDM **purse your lips** → PURSE[2]

lipase /'laɪpeɪz/ *noun* [U] (BIOLOGY) an ENZYME (=a chemical substance in the body) that makes fats change into acids and alcohol

lipid /'lɪpɪd/ *noun* [C] (BIOLOGY) any of a group of natural substances which do not dissolve in water, including plant oils and STEROIDS (=chemical substances produced naturally in the body)

'lip-read *verb* [I,T] (*pt, pp* **lip-read** /-red/) to understand what sb is saying by looking at the movements of their lips

'lip service *noun* [U] if sb pays **lip service** to sth, they say that they approve of it or support it, without proving their support by what they actually do: *All the political parties pay lip service to environmental issues.*

lipstick /'lɪpstɪk/ *noun* [C,U] a substance that is used for giving colour to your lips: *to put on some lipstick ◇ a new lipstick*

liquefy /'lɪkwɪfaɪ/ *verb* [I,T] (*pres. part.* **liquefying**; *3rd person sing. pres.* **liquefies**; *pt, pp* **liquefied**) (*formal*) to become liquid; to make sth liquid

liqueur /lɪ'kjʊə(r)/ *noun* [U, C] a strong sweet alcoholic drink that is often drunk in small quantities after a meal

liquid[1] ⊶ /'lɪkwɪd/ *noun* [C,U] (PHYSICS) a substance, for example water, that is not solid or a gas and that can flow or be poured: *the transition from liquid to vapour* ➲ picture at **state[1]**

liquid[2] ⊶ /'lɪkwɪd/ *adj.* **1** in the form of a liquid; not a solid or a gas: *liquid soap ◇ liquid nitrogen* **2** (BUSINESS) that can easily be changed into cash: ***liquid assets***

liquidate /'lɪkwɪdeɪt/ *verb* **1** [I,T] (BUSINESS) to close a business because it has no money left **2** [T] (FINANCE) to sell sth in order to get money: *to liquidate assets* **3** [T] (FINANCE) to pay a debt **4** [T] to destroy or remove sb/sth that causes problems ▶ **liquidation** /ˌlɪkwɪ'deɪʃn/ *noun* [U]: *If the company doesn't receive a big order soon, it will have to* ***go into liquidation***.

ˌliquid ˌcrystal 'display *noun* [C] = LCD

liquidity /lɪ'kwɪdəti/ *noun* [U] (ECONOMICS) the state of owning things of value that can be exchanged for cash

liquidize (also **-ise**) /'lɪkwɪdaɪz/ *verb* [T] to cause sth to become liquid ▶ **liquidizer** (also **-iser**) = BLENDER

liquor /'lɪkə(r)/ *noun* [U] (*AmE*) strong alcoholic drinks; spirits

liquorice (*AmE* **licorice**) /'lɪkərɪʃ/ *noun* [U] a black substance, made from a plant, that is used in some sweets

lisp /lɪsp/ *noun* [C] a speech fault in which 's' is pronounced as 'th': *He speaks with a slight lisp.* ▶ **lisp** *verb* [I,T]

list ⊶ /lɪst/ *noun* [C] a series of names, figures, items, etc. that are written, printed or said one after another: *a checklist of everything that needs to be done ◇ a waiting list ◇ Your name is third* ***on the list***. ▶ **list** *verb* [T]: *to list items in alphabetical order*

listen ⊶ /'lɪsn/ *verb* [I] **1** ~ (**to sb/sth**) to pay attention to sb/sth in order to hear them or it: *Now please listen carefully to what I have to say. ◇ to listen to music/the radio* **2** ~ **to sb/sth** to take notice of or believe what sb says: *You should listen to your parents' advice.* ▶ **listen** *noun* [sing.] (*informal*): ***Have a listen*** *and see if you can hear anything.*
PHR V **listen (out) for sth** to wait to hear sth: *to listen (out) for a knock on the door*
listen in (on/to sth) to listen to sb else's private

conversation: *Have you been listening in on my phone calls?*

listener /ˈlɪsənə(r)/ ***noun*** [C] a person who listens: *When I'm unhappy I always phone Charlie – he's such a good listener.* ◇ *The new radio show has attracted a record number of listeners.*

ˈlistening post ***noun*** [C] a place where people who are part of an army listen to enemy communications to try to get information that will give them an advantage

listeria /lɪˈstɪəriə/ ***noun*** [U] (BIOLOGY, HEALTH) a type of bacteria that makes people sick if they eat infected food

listless /ˈlɪstləs/ ***adj.*** tired and without energy ▸ **listlessly** ***adv.***

lit past tense, past participle of **light**³

liter (*AmE*) = LITRE

literacy /ˈlɪtərəsi/ ***noun*** [U] (EDUCATION) the ability to read and write OPP **illiteracy**

literal /ˈlɪtərəl/ ***adj.*** (LANGUAGE) **1** (used about the meaning of a word or phrase) original or basic: *The adjective 'big-headed' is hardly ever used in its literal sense.* ➲ look at **figurative**, **metaphor** **2** (used when translating, etc.) dealing with each word separately without looking at the general meaning

literally /ˈlɪtərəli/ ***adv.*** **1** according to the basic or original meaning of the word, etc.: *You can't translate these idioms literally.* **2** (*informal*) used for emphasizing sth: *We were literally frozen to death* (= we were very cold).

literary /ˈlɪtərəri/ ***adj.*** (LITERATURE) of or concerned with literature: *literary criticism* ◇ *a literary journal*

literate /ˈlɪtərət/ ***adj.*** **1** (EDUCATION) able to read and write OPP **illiterate** ➲ noun **literacy** ➲ look at **numerate** **2** well educated

literati /ˌlɪtəˈrɑːti/ **the literati** ***noun*** [pl.] (*formal*) educated and intelligent people who enjoy literature: *He was underrated as a writer by the literati.*

literature /ˈlɪtrətʃə(r)/ ***noun*** [U] **1** (LITERATURE) writing that is considered to be a work of art. **Literature** includes novels, plays and poetry: *French literature* **2** ~ **(on sth)** printed material about a particular subject

lithium /ˈlɪθiəm/ ***noun*** [U] (*symbol* **Li**) (CHEMISTRY) a soft, very light, silver-white metal that is used in batteries ℹ For more information on the periodic table of elements, look at pages R34-5.

lithograph /ˈlɪθəɡrɑːf/ ***noun*** [C] (ART) a picture printed by LITHOGRAPHY

lithography /lɪˈθɒɡrəfi/ ***noun*** [U] (also *informal* **litho** /ˈlaɪθəʊ/) (ART) the process of printing from a smooth surface, for example a metal plate, that has been specially prepared so that ink only sticks to the design to be printed

lithosphere /ˈlɪθəsfɪə(r)/ ***noun*** [sing.] (GEOLOGY) the layer of rock that forms the outer part of the earth

litigant /ˈlɪtɪɡənt/ ***noun*** [C] (LAW) a person who is taking legal action in a court of law

litigate /ˈlɪtɪɡeɪt/ ***verb*** [I,T] (LAW) to take legal action in a court of law ▸ **litigator** ***noun*** [C]

litigation /ˌlɪtɪˈɡeɪʃn/ ***noun*** [U] (LAW) the process of taking legal action in a court of law

litmus /ˈlɪtməs/ ***noun*** [U] (CHEMISTRY) a substance that turns red when it touches an acid and blue when it touches an ALKALI ➲ picture at **pH**

litotes /laɪˈtəʊtiːz/ ***noun*** [U] (LANGUAGE) the use of a negative or weak statement to emphasize a positive meaning, for example *He wasn't slow to accept the offer* (= he was quick to accept the offer). ➲ look at **understatement**

litre (*AmE* **liter**) /ˈliːtə(r)/ ***noun*** [C] (*abbr.* **l**) a measure of liquid: *ten litres of petrol* ◇ *a litre bottle of wine*

litter /ˈlɪtə(r)/ ***noun*** **1** [U] pieces of paper, rubbish, etc. that are left in a public place **2** [C] all the young animals that are born to one mother at the same time: *a litter of six puppies* ▸ **litter** ***verb*** [T]: *The streets were littered with rubbish.*

ˈlitter bin ***noun*** [C] a container to put rubbish in, in the street or a public building

little¹ /ˈlɪtl/ ***adj.*** **1** not big; small: *a little bag of sweets* ◇ *Do you want the big one or the little one?* ◇ *a little mistake/problem* **2** (used about distance or time) short: *Do you mind waiting **a little while**?* ◇ *We only live **a little way** from here.* ◇ *It's only a little further.* **3** young: *a little girl/boy* ◇ *my little brother* ◇ *I was very naughty when I was little.*

little² /ˈlɪtl/ ***adv.***, ***pronoun***, ***det.*** (**less**; **least**) **1** (also as a noun after *the*) not much or not enough: *I slept very little last night.* ◇ *a little-known author* ◇ *They have very little money.* ◇ *There is little hope that she will recover.* **2** **a little** a small amount of sth: *I like a little sugar in my tea.* ◇ *Could I have a little help, please?* **3** rather; to a small degree: *This skirt is a little too tight.*

IDM **little by little** slowly: *After the accident her strength returned little by little.*

littoral /ˈlɪtərəl/ ***noun*** [C] (GEOGRAPHY) the part of a country that is near the coast: *the Hawaiian littoral* ▸ **littoral** ***adj.***

live¹ /lɪv/ ***verb*** **1** [I] to have your home in a particular place: *Where do you live?* ◇ *He still lives with his parents.* **2** [I] to be or stay alive: *She hasn't got long to live.* ◇ *to live to a great age* **3** [I,T] to pass or spend your life in a certain way: *to live a quiet life* ◇ *to live in comfort/poverty* **4** [I] to enjoy all the opportunities of life fully: *I want to live a bit before settling down and getting married.*

IDM **live/sleep rough** → ROUGH³

PHR V **live by sth** to follow a particular belief or set of principles

live by doing sth to get the money, food, etc. you need by doing a particular activity: *They live by hunting and fishing.*

live for sb/sth to consider sb/sth to be the most important thing in your life: *He felt he had nothing to live for after his wife died*

not live sth down to be unable to make people forget sth bad or embarrassing that you have done

live it up to enjoy yourself in an exciting way, usually spending a lot of money

live off sb/sth to depend on sb/sth in order to live: *Barry lives off tinned food.* ◇ *She could easily get a job but she still lives off her parents.*

live on to continue to live or exist: *Mozart is dead but his music lives on.*

live on sth **1** to have sth as your only food: *to live on bread and water* **2** to manage to buy what you need to live: *I don't know how they live on so little money!*

live out sth **1** to actually do sth that you only imagined doing before: *to live out your dreams/fantasies* **2** to spend the rest of your life in a particular way

live through sth to survive an unpleasant experience: *She lived through two wars.*

live together (*also* **live with sb**) **1** to live in the same house, flat, etc.: *Rhoda and I lived together when we were students.* **2** to share a home and have a sexual relationship, but without being married

live up to sth to be as good as expected: *Children sometimes find it hard to live up to their parents' expectations.*

live with sb = LIVE TOGETHER

live with sth to accept sth unpleasant that you cannot change: *It can be hard to live with the fact that you are getting older.*

live² 🔑 /laɪv/ ***adj., adv.*** **1** having life; not dead: *Have you ever touched a **real live** snake?* **2** (ARTS AND MEDIA) (used about a radio or television programme) seen or heard as it is happening: *live coverage of the Olympic Games* ◇ *This programme is coming live from Wembley Stadium.* ◇ *to go out live on TV* **3** (ARTS AND MEDIA) performed or performing for an audience: *That pub has live music on Saturdays.* **4** (used about a bomb, bullet, etc.) that has not yet exploded **5** (PHYSICS) (used about a wire, etc.) carrying electricity ➲ picture at **plug**

livelihood /ˈlaɪvlihʊd/ ***noun*** [C, usually sing.] the way that you earn money: *to lose your livelihood*

lively 🔑 /ˈlaɪvli/ ***adj.*** (**livelier**; **liveliest**) full of energy, interest, excitement, etc.: *lively children* ◇ *The town is quite lively at night.*

liven /ˈlaɪvn/ ***verb***

PHR V **liven (sb/sth) up** to become or make sb/sth become more interesting and exciting: *Once the band began to play the party livened up.*

liver /ˈlɪvə(r)/ ***noun*** **1** [C] (ANATOMY) the part of your body that cleans your blood ➲ picture on **page 80** ➲ picture at **digestive system** **2** [U] the **liver** of an animal when it is cooked and eaten as food: *fried liver and onions*

lives plural of **life**

livestock /ˈlaɪvstɒk/ ***noun*** [U] (AGRICULTURE) animals that are kept on a farm, such as cows, pigs, sheep, etc.

livid /ˈlɪvɪd/ ***adj.*** extremely angry SYN **furious**

living¹ 🔑 /ˈlɪvɪŋ/ ***adj.*** **1** alive now: *He has no living relatives.* **2** still used or practised now: *living languages/traditions* OPP **dead**

living² /ˈlɪvɪŋ/ ***noun*** **1** [C, usually sing.] money to buy things that you need in life: *What do you do **for a living**?* **2** [U] your way or quality of life: *The **cost of living** has risen in recent years.* ◇ *The **standard of living** is very high in that country.*

ˈliving room (*especially BrE* **ˈsitting room**) ***noun*** [C] the room in a house where people sit, relax, watch television, etc. together

lizard /ˈlɪzəd/ ***noun*** [C] a small REPTILE with four legs, dry skin and a long tail

lizard

load¹ 🔑 /ləʊd/ ***noun*** **1** [C] something (heavy) that is being or is waiting to be carried: *a truck carrying a load of sand* **2** [C] (often in compounds) the quantity of sth that can be carried: *bus loads of tourists* **3** **loads (of sth)** [pl.] (*informal*) a lot (of sth): *There are loads of things to do in London in the evenings.*

IDM **a load of rubbish, etc.** (*informal*) nonsense

load² 🔑 /ləʊd/ ***verb*** **1** [I,T] ~ **(sth/sb) (up) (with sth)**; ~ **(sth/sb) (into/onto sth)** to put a large quantity of sth into or onto sb/sth: *They loaded the plane (up) with supplies.* ◇ *Load the washing into the machine.* **2** [I] to receive a load: *The ship is still loading.* **3** [I,T] (COMPUTING) to put a program or disk into a computer: *First, switch on the machine and load the disk.* ◇ *The program is now loading.* **4** [T] to put sth into a machine, a weapon, etc. so that it can be used: *to load film into a camera* ◇ *to load a gun* OPP **unload**

loaded /ˈləʊdɪd/ ***adj.*** **1** **loaded (with sth)** carrying a load; full and heavy **2** (used especially about a gun or a camera) containing a bullet, a film, etc. **3** giving an advantage: *The system is loaded in their favour.* **4** (*informal*) (not *before* a noun) having a lot of money; rich

loaf /ləʊf/ ***noun*** [C] (*pl.* **loaves** /ləʊvz/) bread baked in one piece: *a loaf of bread*

loam /ləʊm/ ***noun*** [U] (AGRICULTURE) good quality soil containing sand, CLAY and dead plants

loan 🔑 /ləʊn/ ***noun*** **1** [C] (FINANCE) money, etc. that sb/sth lends you: *to **take out a** bank **loan*** ◇ *to pay off a loan* **2** [U] the act of lending sth or the state of being lent: *The books are **on loan** from the library.* ▸ **loan** ***verb*** [T] (*formal*) ~ **sth (to sb)** ℹ In American English **loan** is less formal and more common.

loath /ləʊθ/ ***adj.*** ~ **to do sth** (*formal*) not willing to do sth

loathe /ləʊð/ ***verb*** [T] (not used in the continuous tenses) to hate sb/sth ▸ **loathsome** /ˈləʊðsəm/ ***adj.*** ▸ **loathing** ***noun*** [U]

loaves plural of **loaf**

lob /lɒb/ ***verb*** [I,T] (**lobbing**; **lobbed**) (SPORT) to hit, kick or throw a ball high into the air, so that it lands behind your opponent ▸ **lob** ***noun*** [C]

lobby¹ /ˈlɒbi/ ***noun*** [C] (*pl.* **lobbies**)

1 (ARCHITECTURE) the area that is just inside a large building, where people can meet and wait: *a hotel lobby* **2** [with sing. or pl. verb] (POLITICS) a group of people who try to influence politicians to do or not do sth: *the anti-smoking lobby*

lobby² /ˈlɒbi/ ***verb*** [I,T] (*pres. part.* **lobbying**; *3rd person sing. pres.* **lobbies**; *pt, pp* **lobbied**) (POLITICS) to try to influence a politician or the government to do or not do sth: *Farmers will lobby Congress for higher subsidies.* ▸ **lobbyist** /ˈlɒbiɪst/ ***noun*** [C]: *political lobbyists*

lobe /ləʊb/ ***noun*** [C] **1** = EAR LOBE **2** (ANATOMY) one part of an organ of the body, especially the brain or lungs

lobster /ˈlɒbstə(r)/ ***noun*** **1** [C] a large SHELLFISH that has eight legs. A **lobster** is bluish-black but it turns red when it is cooked. **2** [U] a cooked **lobster** eaten as food

local¹ 🔑 /ˈləʊkl/ ***adj.*** of a particular place (near you): *local newspapers/radio* ◇ *the local doctor/policeman/butcher* ➲ look at **international, national, regional** ▸ **locally** ***adv.***: *I do most of my shopping locally.*

local² /ˈləʊkl/ ***noun*** [C] **1** [usually pl.] a person who lives in a particular place: *The locals seem very friendly.* **2** (*BrE, informal*) a pub that is near your home where you often go to drink

ˌlocal ˈgovernment ***noun*** [U] (*especially BrE*) (POLITICS) the system of government of a town or an area by elected representatives of the people who live there

localize (also **-ise**) /ˈləʊkəlaɪz/ ***verb*** [T] to limit sth to a particular place or area

ˈlocal time ***noun*** [U] the time at a particular place in the world: *We arrive in Singapore at 2 o'clock in the afternoon, local time.*

locate ⊶ AW /ləʊˈkeɪt/ *verb* [T] **1** to find the exact position of sb/sth: *The damaged ship has been located two miles off the coast.* **2** to put or build sth in a particular place

located ⊶ /ləʊˈkeɪtɪd/ *adj.* if sth is **located** in a particular place, it exists there or has been put there: *a small town located 30 miles south of Chicago* ◇ *The offices are conveniently located just a few minutes from the main station.*

location ⊶ AW /ləʊˈkeɪʃn/ *noun* **1** [C] a place or position: *Several locations have been suggested for the new office block.* **2** [U] the action of finding where sb/sth is

IDM **on location** (ARTS AND MEDIA) (used about a film, television programme, etc.) made in a suitable place outside a STUDIO (= the place where films, etc. are usually made): *The series was filmed on location in Thailand.*

loch /lɒk/ *noun* [C] (GEOGRAPHY) the Scottish word for a lake: *the Loch Ness monster*

lock[1] ⊶ /lɒk/ *verb* **1** [I,T] to close or fasten (sth) so that it can only be opened with a key: *Have you locked the car?* ◇ *The door won't lock.* OPP **unlock** **2** [T] to put sb/sth in a safe place and lock it: *Lock your passport in a safe place.* **3** [T] **be locked in sth** to be involved in an angry argument, etc. with sth, or to be holding sb very tightly: *The two sides were locked in a bitter dispute.* ◇ *They were locked in a passionate embrace.*

PHR V **lock sth away** to keep sth in a safe or secret place that is locked

lock sb in/out to lock a door so that a person cannot get in/out: *I locked myself out of the house and had to climb in through the window.*

lock (sth) up to lock all the doors, windows, etc. of a building: *Make sure that you lock up before you leave.*

lock sb up to put sb in prison

lock[2] ⊶ /lɒk/ *noun* [C] **1** something that is used for fastening a door, lid, etc. so that you need a key to open it again: *to turn the key in the lock* ➲ look at **padlock** **2** a part of a river or a CANAL where the level of water changes. Locks have gates at each end and are used to allow boats to move to a higher or lower part of the canal or river.

IDM **pick a lock** → PICK[1]

under lock and key in a locked place

locker /ˈlɒkə(r)/ *noun* [C] a small cupboard that can be locked in a school or sports centre, where you can leave your clothes, books, etc.

locket /ˈlɒkɪt/ *noun* [C] a piece of jewellery that you wear on a chain around your neck and which opens so that you can put a picture, etc. inside

locksmith /ˈlɒksmɪθ/ *noun* [C] a person who makes and repairs locks

locomotion /ˌləʊkəˈməʊʃn/ *noun* [U] (*formal*) movement or the ability to move

locomotive /ˌləʊkəˈməʊtɪv/ = ENGINE (2)

locus /ˈləʊkəs/ *noun* [C] (*pl.* **loci** /ˈləʊsaɪ/)*formal* or *technical*) the exact place where sth happens or which is thought to be the centre of sth

locust /ˈləʊkəst/ *noun* [C] a flying insect from Africa and Asia that moves in very large groups, eating and destroying large quantities of plants ➲ picture on **page 29**

lodge[1] /lɒdʒ/ *verb* **1** [I] to pay to live in sb's house with them: *He lodged with a family for his first term at university.* **2** [I,T] to become firmly fixed or to make sth do this **3** [T] (*formal*) to make an official statement complaining about sth

lodge[2] /lɒdʒ/ *noun* [C] **1** (ARCHITECTURE) a room at the entrance to a large building such as a college or factory **2** a small house in the country

lodger /ˈlɒdʒə(r)/ *noun* [C] a person who pays rent to live in a house as a member of the family ➲ look at **boarder**

lodging /ˈlɒdʒɪŋ/ *noun* **1** [C,U] a place where you can stay: *The family offered full board and lodging* (= a room and all meals) *in exchange for English lessons.* **2** (*old-fashioned*) **lodgings** [pl.] a room or rooms in sb's house where you can pay to stay

loft /lɒft/ *noun* [C] the room or space under the roof of a house or other building ➲ look at **attic**

log[1] /lɒg/ *noun* [C] **1** a thick piece of wood that has fallen or been cut from a tree ➲ picture at **tree** **2** (*also* **ˈlogbook**) the official written record of a ship's or an aircraft's journey: *to keep a log*

log[2] /lɒg/ *verb* [T] (**logging**; **logged**) to keep an official written record of sth

PHR V **log in/on** (COMPUTING) to perform the actions that allow you to start using a computer system: *You need to key in your password to log on.*

log off/out (COMPUTING) to perform the actions that allow you to finish using a computer system

logarithm /ˈlɒgərɪðəm/ (also *informal* **log**) *noun* [C] (MATHEMATICS) one of a series of TABLES (= numbers arranged in lists) that allow you to solve problems in mathematics by adding or SUBTRACTING numbers instead of MULTIPLYING or dividing
▶ **logarithmic** /ˌlɒgəˈrɪðmɪk/ *adj.*

ˌlog ˈcabin *noun* (ARCHITECTURE) a small house built of LOGS (a thick piece of wood that has been cut from a tree)

loggerheads /ˈlɒgəhedz/ *noun*

IDM **at loggerheads (with sb)** strongly disagreeing (with sb)

logging /ˈlɒgɪŋ/ *noun* [U] (AGRICULTURE) the work of cutting down trees for their wood

logic ⊶ AW /ˈlɒdʒɪk/ *noun* [U] **1** a sensible reason or way of thinking: *There is no logic in your argument.* **2** the science of using reason

logical ⊶ AW /ˈlɒdʒɪkl/ *adj.* **1** seeming natural, reasonable or sensible: *As I see it, there is only one logical conclusion.* OPP **illogical** **2** thinking in a sensible way: *a logical mind*
▶ **logically** /-kli/ *adv.*

logician AW /ləˈdʒɪʃn/ *noun* [C] a person who studies or is skilled in logic

logjam /ˈlɒgdʒæm/ *noun* [C] **1** a mass of LOGS (= large pieces of wood cut from trees) that are floating on a river and blocking it **2** a difficult situation in which you cannot make progress easily because there are too many things to do

logo /ˈləʊgəʊ/ *noun* [C] (*pl.* **logos**) (BUSINESS) a printed symbol or design that a company or an organization uses as its special sign

loiter /ˈlɔɪtə(r)/ *verb* [I] to stand or walk around somewhere for no obvious reason

lollipop /ˈlɒlipɒp/ (*also* **lolly**) *noun* [C] a sweet on a stick ➲ look at **ice lolly**

lone /ləʊn/ *adj.* (only *before* a noun) **1** without any other people; alone: *a lone swimmer* SYN **solitary** **2** (used about a parent) single; without a partner: *a support group for lone parents*

lonely ⊶ /ˈləʊnli/ *adj.* (**lonelier**; **loneliest**) **1** unhappy because you are not with other people: *to feel sad and lonely* **2** (used about a situation or a period of time) sad and spent alone **3** (only *before* a noun) far from other people and places where people live ▶ **loneliness** ***noun*** [U] ➲ look at **solitude, isolation**

loner /ˈləʊnə(r)/ ***noun*** [C] (*informal*) a person who prefers being alone to being with other people

lonesome /ˈləʊnsəm/ ***adj.*** (*AmE*) lonely or making you feel lonely

long[1] 🔑 /lɒŋ/ ***adj.*** (**longer** /ˈlɒŋɡə(r)/, **longest** /ˈlɒŋɡɪst/) **1** measuring or covering a large amount in distance or time: *She has lovely long hair.* ◇ *We had to wait **a long time**.* ◇ *a very long journey/book/corridor* ◇ *I walked **a long way** today.* ◇ *Nurses work very long hours.* **2** used for asking or talking about how much something measures in length, distance or time: ***How long** is the film?* ◇ *The insect was only 2 millimetres long.* ◇ *a five-mile-long traffic jam*
➲ noun **length** OPP **short**

IDM **a long shot** a person or thing that probably will not succeed, win, etc.

at (long) last → LAST[2]

at the longest not longer than the stated time: *It will take a week at the longest.*

go a long way (used about money, food, etc.) to be used for buying a lot of things, feeding a lot of people, etc.

have a long way to go to need to make a lot more progress before sth can be achieved

in the long run after a long time; in the end

in the long/short term → TERM[1]

long[2] 🔑 /lɒŋ/ ***adv.*** (**longer** /-ŋɡə(r)/, **longest** /-ŋɡɪst/) **1** for a long time: *She didn't stay long.* ◇ *You shouldn't have to wait long.* ◇ *This shouldn't **take long**.* ◇ *I hope we don't have to wait much longer.* ◇ *They won't be gone **for long**.* ◇ *Just wait here – I won't be long.* ◇ *'How long will it take to get there?' 'Not long.'* **2** a long time before or after a particular time or event: *We got married **long before** we moved here.* ◇ *Don't worry – they'll be here **before long**.* ◇ *All that happened long ago.* **3** for the whole of the time that is mentioned: *The baby cried **all night long**.*

IDM **as/so long as** on condition that; provided (that): *As long as no problems arise we should get the job finished by Friday.*

no/not any longer not any more: *They no longer live here.* ◇ *They don't live here any longer.*

long[3] /lɒŋ/ ***verb*** [I] **~ for sth; ~ (for sb) to do sth** to want sth very much, especially sth that is not likely: *She longed to return to Greece.* ▶ **longing** ***noun*** [C,U]: *a longing for peace* ▶ **longingly** ***adv.***

ˌ**long-ˈdistance** ***adj., adv.*** (used about travel or communication) between places that are far from each other: *to phone long-distance*

longevity /lɒnˈdʒevəti/ ***noun*** [U] (*formal*) long life; the fact of lasting a long time: *Elephants are known for their longevity.* ◇ *He prides himself on the longevity of the company.*

longhand /ˈlɒŋhænd/ ***noun*** [U] ordinary writing that is not typed and does not use any special signs or short forms ➲ look at **shorthand**

ˈ**long-haul** ***adj.*** (only *before* a noun) connected with the transport of people or goods over long distances: *a long-haul flight*

longitude /ˈlɒndʒɪtjuːd; ˈlɒŋɡɪ-/ ***noun*** [U] (GEOGRAPHY) the distance of a place east or west of a line from the North Pole to the South Pole that passes through Greenwich in London. **Longitude** is measured in degrees. ➲ look at **latitude** ➲ picture at **earth**

ˌ**longiˌtudinal ˈwave** ***noun*** [C] (PHYSICS) a wave that VIBRATES (= makes very small, fast movements from side to side) in the direction that it is moving ➲ look at **transverse wave**

ˈ**long jump** ***noun*** [sing.] (SPORT) the sport in which people try to jump as far as possible ➲ look at **high jump**

ˌ**long-ˈlife** ***adj.*** made to last for a long time: *a long-life battery* ◇ *long-life milk*

ˌ**long-ˈlived** ***adj.*** that has lived or lasted for a long time: *a long-lived dispute*

ˈ**long-range** ***adj.*** **1** of or for a long period of time starting from the present: *the long-range weather forecast* **2** that can go or be sent over long distances: *long-range nuclear missiles*

longshore drift /ˌlɒŋʃɔː ˈdrɪft/ ***noun*** [U] (GEOGRAPHY) the movement of sand, etc. along a beach caused by waves hitting the beach at an angle and going back in a straight line

longshore drift

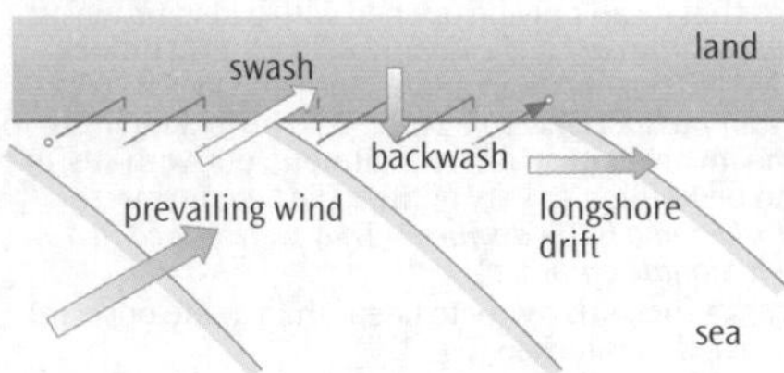

ˌ**long-ˈsighted** (*AmE* ˌ**far-ˈsighted**) ***adj.*** able to see things clearly only when they are quite far away OPP **short-sighted** ➲ picture at **short-sighted**

ˌ**long-ˈstanding** ***adj.*** that has lasted for a long time: *a long-standing arrangement*

ˌ**long-ˈsuffering** ***adj.*** (used about a person) having a lot of troubles but not complaining

ˌ**long-ˈterm** ***adj.*** of or for a long period of time: *long-term planning*

ˈ**long wave** ***noun*** [U] (*abbr.* **LW**) (PHYSICS) the system of sending radio signals using sound waves of 1 000 metres or more ➲ look at **short wave, medium wave**

ˌ**long-ˈwinded** ***adj.*** (used about sth that is written or spoken) boring because it is too long

loo /luː/ ***noun*** [C] (*pl.* **loos**) (*BrE, informal*) a toilet

look[1] 🔑 /lʊk/ ***verb*** **1** [I,T] **~ (at sth)** to turn your eyes in a particular direction (in order to pay attention to sb/sth): *Sorry, I wasn't looking. Can you show me again?* ◇ *Look carefully at this picture.* ◇ *to look out of the window* ◇ *She blushed and looked away.* ◇ *Look who's come to see us.* ◇ *Look where you're going!* **2** [I] **~ (for sb/sth)** to try to find (sb/sth): *We've been looking for you everywhere. Where have you been?* ◇ *to look for work* ◇ *'I can't find my shoes.' 'Have you looked under the bed?'* **3** ***linking verb*** **~ (like sb/sth) (to sb); ~ (to sb) as if.../as though...** to seem or appear: *You look very smart in that shirt.* ◇ *to look tired/ill/sad/well/happy* ◇ *The boy looks like his father.* ◇ *That film looks good – I might go and see it.* ◇ *You look (to me) as if/as though you need some sleep.* **4** [I] used for asking sb to listen to what you are saying: *Look, Will, I know you are busy but could you give me a hand?* **5** [I] to face a particular direction: *This room looks south so it gets the sun.* **6** [I] **~ to do sth** to aim to do sth: *We are looking to double our profits over the next five years.*

IDM **look bad**; **not look good** to be considered bad manners: *It'll look bad if we get there an hour late.*

look good to seem to be encouraging: *This year's sales figures are looking good.*
look sb in the eye to look straight at sb without feeling embarrassed or afraid
(not) look yourself to (not) look as well or healthy as usual
look on the bright side (of sth) to think only about the good side of a bad situation and be happy and HOPEFUL
never/not look back to become and continue being successful
PHR V **look after sb/sth/yourself** to be responsible for or take care of sb/sth/yourself: *I want to go back to work if I can find somebody to look after the children.* ◇ *The old lady's son looked after all her financial affairs.*
look ahead to think about or plan for the future
look at sth 1 to examine or study sth: *My tooth aches. I think a dentist should look at it.* ◇ *The government is looking at ways of reducing unemployment.* **2** to read sth: *Could I look at the newspaper when you've finished with it?* **3** to consider sth: *Different races and nationalities look at life differently.*
look back (on sth) to think about sth in your past
look down on sb/sth to think that you are better than sb/sth
look forward to sth/doing sth to wait with pleasure for sth to happen: *I'm really looking forward to the weekend.*
look into sth to study or try to find out sth: *A committee was set up to look into the causes of the accident.*
look on to watch sth happening without taking any action: *All we could do was look on as the house burned.*
look on sb/sth as sth; look on sb with sth to think of sb/sth in a particular way: *They seem to look on me as someone who can advise them.*
look out to be careful or to pay attention to sth dangerous: *Look out! There's a bike coming.*
look out (for sb/sth) to pay attention in order to see, find or avoid sb/sth: *Look out for thieves!*
look round 1 to turn your head in order to see sb/sth **2** to look at many things (before buying sth): *She looked round but couldn't find anything she liked.*
look round sth to walk around a place looking at things: *to look round a town/shop/museum*
look through sth to read sth quickly
look to sb for sth; look to sb to do sth to expect sb to do or to provide sth: *He always looked to his father for advice.*
look up 1 to move your eyes upwards to look at sb/sth: *She looked up and smiled.* **2** (*informal*) to improve: *Business is looking up.*
look sth up to search for information in a book: *to look up a word in a dictionary*
look up to sb to respect and admire sb

look² ⊶ /lʊk/ ***noun* 1** [C] the act of looking: ***Have a look*** *at this article.* ◇ ***Take a*** *close* ***look*** *at the contract before you sign it.* **2** [C, usually sing.] **a ~ (for sb/sth)** a search: *I'll* ***have a*** *good* ***look*** *for that book later.* **3** [C] the expression on sb's face: *He had a worried look on his face.* **4 looks** [pl.] a person's appearance: *He's lucky – he's got good looks and intelligence.* **5** [C] a fashion or style: *The shop has a new look to appeal to younger customers.*
IDM **by/from the look of sb/sth** judging by the appearance of sb/sth: *It's going to be a fine day by the look of it.*
like the look/sound of sb/sth → LIKE¹

ˈlook-in ***noun***
IDM **(not) give sb a look-in; (not) get/have a look-in** (*informal*) to (not) give sb, or to (not) have a chance to do sth

-looking /ˈlʊkɪŋ/ ***suffix*** (used to form compound adjectives) having the appearance mentioned: *an odd-looking building* ◇ *He's very good-looking.*

lookout /ˈlʊkaʊt/ ***noun*** [C] (a person who has) the responsibility of watching to see if danger is coming; the place this person watches from: *One of the gang acted as lookout.*
IDM **be on the lookout for sb/sth; keep a lookout for sb/sth** to pay attention in order to see, find or avoid sb/sth

loom

loom¹ /luːm/ ***noun*** [C] a machine that is used for making cloth (**weaving**) by passing pieces of thread across and under other pieces

loom² /luːm/ ***verb*** [I] ~ **(up)** to appear as a shape that is not clear and in a way that seems frightening: *The mountain loomed (up) in the distance.*

loony /ˈluːni/ ***noun*** [C] (*pl.* **loonies**) (*slang*) a person who is crazy ▶ **loony** ***adj.***

loop /luːp/ ***noun*** [C] a curved or round shape made by a line curving round and joining or crossing itself: *a loop in a rope* ◇ *The road goes around the lake in a loop.* ▶ **loop** ***verb*** [I,T]: *He was trying to loop a rope over the horse's head.*
IDM **in the loop/out of the loop** (*informal*) part of a group of people that is dealing with sth important/not part of this group

loophole /ˈluːphəʊl/ ***noun*** [C] a way of avoiding sth because the words of a rule or law are badly chosen

loose¹ ⊶ /luːs/ ***adj.* 1** not tied up or shut in sth; free: *The horse managed to* ***get loose*** *and escape.* ◇ *I take the dog to the woods and* ***let him loose****.* ◇ *She wore her long hair loose.* **2** not firmly fixed: *a loose tooth* **3** not contained in sth or joined together: *loose change* (=coins) ◇ *some loose sheets of paper* **4** not fitting closely; not tight: *These trousers don't fit. They're much too loose round the waist.* OPP **tight** **5** not completely accurate or the same as sth: *a loose translation*
IDM **all hell broke loose** → HELL
at a loose end having nothing to do and feeling bored

loose² /luːs/ ***noun***
IDM **on the loose** escaped and dangerous: *a lion on the loose from a zoo*

ˌloose ˈcannon ***noun*** [C] a person, usually a public figure, who often behaves in a way that nobody can predict

ˌloose-ˈleaf ***adj.*** (used about a book, file, etc.) with pages that can be removed or added separately

loosely 🔑 /ˈluːsli/ ***adv.*** **1** in a way that is not firm or tight: *She fastened the belt loosely around her waist.* **2** in a way that is not exact: *to use a term loosely* ◇ *The play is loosely based on his childhood in Russia.*

loosen /ˈluːsn/ ***verb*** [I,T] to become or make sth less tight: *to loosen your tie/belt* ◇ *Don't loosen your grip on the rope or you'll fall.*
PHR V **loosen (sb/sth) up** to relax or move more easily: *These exercises will help you to loosen up.*

loot[1] /luːt/ ***verb*** [I,T] (LAW) to steal things from shops or buildings during a war, a RIOT (=a period of fighting), a fire, etc. ▶ **looting** ***noun*** [U]

loot[2] /luːt/ ***noun*** [U] **1** money and valuable objects taken by soldiers from the enemy after winning a battle **2** (*informal*) money and valuable objects that have been stolen by thieves

lop /lɒp/ ***verb*** [T] (**lopping**; **lopped**) to cut branches off a tree
PHR V **lop sth off/away** to cut sth off/away

lopsided /ˌlɒpˈsaɪdɪd/ ***adj.*** with one side lower or smaller than the other: *a lopsided smile*

lord 🔑 /lɔːd/ ***noun*** [C] **1** a man with a very high position in society: *the Lord Mayor of London* ◇ *Lord and Lady Derby* **2 the Lord** [sing.] (RELIGION) God; Christ **3 the Lords** [with sing. or pl. verb] (*BrE*) (POLITICS) (members of) the House of Lords: *The Lords has/have voted against the bill.*

lorry 🔑 /ˈlɒri/ (*BrE*) ***noun*** [C] (*pl.* **lorries**) (*especially AmE* **truck**) a large strong motor vehicle that is used for carrying goods by road ➲ picture at **truck**

lose 🔑 /luːz/ ***verb*** (*pt, pp* **lost** /lɒst/) **1** [T] to become unable to find sth: *I've lost my purse. I can't find it anywhere.* **2** [T] to no longer have sb/sth: *She lost a leg in the accident.* ◇ *He lost his wife last year* (=she died). ◇ *to lose your job* **3** [T] to have less of sth: *to lose weight/interest/patience* ◇ *The company is losing money all the time.* OPP **gain** **4** [I,T] to not win; to be defeated: *We played well but we lost 2–1.* ◇ *to lose a court case/an argument* ◇ *Parma lost to Milan in the final.* **5** [T] to waste time, a chance, etc.: *Hurry up! There's* ***no time to lose.*** **6** [I,T] to become poorer (as a result of sth): *The company lost on the deal.* **7** [T] (*informal*) to cause sb not to understand sth: *You've totally lost me! Please explain again.*
IDM **give/lose ground (to sb/sth)** → GROUND[1]
keep/lose your cool → COOL[3]
keep/lose count (of sth) → COUNT[2]
keep/lose your temper → TEMPER
keep/lose track of sb/sth → TRACK[1]
lose your bearings to become confused about where you are
lose face to lose the respect of other people
lose your head to become confused or very excited
lose heart to stop believing that you will be successful in sth you are trying to do
lose it (*spoken*) to go crazy or suddenly become unable to control your emotions
lose your life to be killed
lose sight of sb/sth to no longer be able to see sb/sth: *We eventually lost sight of the animal in some trees.* ◇ (*figurative*) *We mustn't lose sight of our original aim.*
lose your touch to lose a special skill or ability
lose touch (with sb/sth) to no longer have contact (with sb/sth): *I've lost touch with a lot of my old school friends.*
a losing battle a competition, fight, etc. in which it seems that you will not be successful
win/lose the toss → TOSS
PHR V **lose out (on sth/to sb)** (*informal*) to be at a disadvantage: *If a teacher pays too much attention to the bright students, the others lose out.*

loser /ˈluːzə(r)/ ***noun*** [C] **1** a person who is defeated: *He is a bad loser. He always gets angry if I beat him.* **2** a person who is never successful **3** a person who suffers because of a particular situation, decision, etc.

loss 🔑 /lɒs/ ***noun*** **1** [C,U] (a) ~ (of sth) the state of no longer having sth or not having as much as before; the act of losing sth: *loss of blood/sleep* ◇ *weight/hair loss* ◇ *Have you reported the loss of your wallet?* ◇ *The plane crashed with great* ***loss of life.*** **2** [C] a ~ (of sth) (FINANCE) the amount of money which is lost by a business: *The firm* ***made a loss*** *of £5 million.* ➲ look at **profit** **3** [C] a ~ (to sb) the disadvantage that is caused when sb/sth leaves or is taken away; the person or thing that causes this disadvantage: *If she leaves, it/she will be a big loss to the school.*
IDM **at a loss** not knowing what to do or say
cut your losses to stop wasting time or money on sth that is not successful

ˈloss-leader ***noun*** [C] (BUSINESS) an item that a shop sells at a very low price to attract customers

lost[1] past tense, past participle of **lose**

lost[2] 🔑 /lɒst/ ***adj.*** **1** unable to find your way; not knowing where you are: *This isn't the right road – we're completely lost!* ◇ *If you* ***get lost,*** *stop and ask someone the way.* **2** that cannot be found or that no longer exists: *The letter must have* ***got lost*** *in the post.* **3** unable to deal with a situation or to understand sth: *Sorry, I'm lost. Could you explain the last part again?* **4** ~ **on sb** not noticed or understood by sb: *The humour of the situation was completely lost on Joe.*
IDM **get lost** (*slang*) used to rudely tell sb to go away
a lost cause a goal or an aim that cannot be achieved
lost for words not knowing what to say

ˌlost ˈproperty ***noun*** [U] things that people have lost or left in a public place and that are kept in a special office for the owners to collect

lot[1] 🔑 /lɒt/ ***noun*** **1** [C] a ~ (of sth); **lots (of sth)** a large amount or number of things or people: *Sit here – there's lots of room.* ◇ *There seem to be* ***quite a lot*** *of new shops opening.* ◇ ***An awful lot*** *of* (=very many) *people will be disappointed if the concert is cancelled.* ◇ *I've got a lot to do today.* **2** [sing., with sing. or pl. verb] (*informal*) all of sth; the whole of a group of things or people: *When we opened the bag of potatoes* ***the whole lot*** *was/were bad.* ◇ *The manager has just sacked* ***the lot of them!*** ◇ *Just one more suitcase and* ***that's the lot!*** ◇ *'How many of these books shall we take?'* ***'The lot.'*** ◇ *You count those kids and I'll count* ***this lot.*** **3** [C] an object or group of objects that are being sold at a public sale (**an auction**): *Lot 27 is six chairs.* **4** [sing.] the quality or state of your life; your FATE: *I'm quite happy with my lot in life.* **5** [C] (*AmE*) an area of land used for a particular purpose: *a parking lot*
IDM **draw lots** → DRAW[1]

lot[2] 🔑 /lɒt/ ***adv.*** (*informal*) **1 a lot**; **lots** (before adjectives and adverbs) very much: *a lot bigger/better/faster* ◇ *They see lots more of each other than before.* **2 a lot** very much or often: ***Thanks a lot*** *– that's very kind.* ◇ *It generally rains a lot at this time of year.*

a lot of[1] 🔑 /ə ˈlɒt əv/ (also *informal* **lots of** /ˈlɒts əv/) ***det.*** a large amount or number of (sb/sth): *There's been a lot of rain this year.* ◇ *Lots of love, Billy*

(=an informal ending for a letter). ◇ *There were a lot of people at the meeting.*

lo-tech /ˌləʊ ˈtek/ ***adj.*** =LOW TECH

lotion /ˈləʊʃn/ ***noun*** [C,U] liquid that you use on your hair or skin: *suntan lotion*

lottery /ˈlɒtəri/ ***noun*** [C] (*pl.* **lotteries**) a way of making money for the government, for charity, etc. by selling tickets with numbers on them and giving prizes to the people who have bought certain numbers which are chosen by chance

loud ⊶ /laʊd/ ***adj.***, ***adv.*** **1** making a lot of noise; not quiet: *Can you turn the television down, it's too loud.* ◇ *Could you speak a bit louder – the people at the back can't hear.* OPP **quiet**, **soft** **2** (used about clothes or colours) too bright: *a loud shirt* ▸ **loudness** ***noun*** [U] ▸ **loudly** ***adv.***

IDM **out loud** so that people can hear it: *Shall I read this bit out loud to you?*

loudspeaker /ˌlaʊdˈspiːkə(r)/ ***noun*** [C] **1** (*also* **speaker**) the part of a radio, CD player, etc. which the sound comes out of **2** a piece of electrical equipment for speaking, playing music, etc. to a lot of people

lounge[1] /laʊndʒ/ ***noun*** [C] **1** a comfortable room in a house or hotel where you can sit and relax **2** (TOURISM) the part of an airport where passengers wait: *the departure lounge*

lounge[2] /laʊndʒ/ ***verb*** [I] ~ (**about/around**) to sit, stand or lie in a lazy way

louse /laʊs/ ***noun*** [C] (*pl.* **lice** /laɪs/) a small insect that lives on the bodies of animals and people ➲ look at **head louse**

lousy /ˈlaʊzi/ ***adj.*** (*informal*) very bad: *We had lousy weather on holiday.*

lout /laʊt/ ***noun*** [C] a young man who behaves in a rude, rough or stupid way ➲ look at **hooligan**, **yob**

lovable (also **loveable**) /ˈlʌvəbl/ ***adj.*** having a personality or appearance that is easy to love: *a lovable little boy*

love[1] ⊶ /lʌv/ ***noun*** **1** [U] a strong feeling that you have when you like sb/sth very much: *a mother's love for her children* ◇ *to* ***fall in love*** *with sb* ◇ *It was* ***love at first sight****. They got married two months after they met!* ◇ *He's* ***madly in love*** *with her.* ◇ *a love song/story* **2** [U, sing.] a strong feeling of interest in or enjoyment of sth: *a love of adventure/nature/sport* **3** [C] a person, a thing or an activity that you like very much: *His great love was always music.* ◇ *Who was your first love?* **4** [C] (*BrE, informal*) used as a friendly way of speaking to sb, often sb you do not know: *'Hello, love. What can I do for you?'* **5** [U] (SPORT) (used in TENNIS) a score of zero: *The score is forty-love.*

IDM **give/send sb your love** to give/send sb a friendly message: *Give Maria my love when you next see her.*

(lots of) love (from) used at the end of a letter to a friend or a member of your family: *See you soon. Love, Richard.*

make love (to sb) to have sex

love[2] ⊶ /lʌv/ ***verb*** [T] **1** to like sb/sth in the strongest possible way: *I split up with my girlfriend last year, but I still love her.* ◇ *She loves her children.* **2** to like or enjoy sth very much: *I love the summer!* ◇ *I really love swimming in the sea.* ◇ *'What do you think of this music?' 'I love it!'* **3 would ~ sth/to do sth** used to say that you would very much like sth/to do sth: *'Would you like to come?' 'I'd love to.'* ◇ *'What about a drink?' 'I'd love one.'* ◇ *We'd love you to come and stay with us.*

ˈ**love affair** ***noun*** [C] **1** a usually sexual relationship between two people who love each other but are not married: *She had a love affair with her tennis coach.* **2** a great enthusiasm for sth

ˈ**love life** ***noun*** [C] the part of your life that involves your romantic and sexual relationships

lovely ⊶ /ˈlʌvli/ ***adj.*** (**lovelier**; **loveliest**) **1** beautiful or attractive: *a lovely room/voice/expression* ◇ *You look lovely with your hair short.* **2** enjoyable or pleasant; very nice: *We had a lovely holiday.* ▸ **loveliness** ***noun*** [U]

IDM **lovely and warm, peaceful, fresh, etc.** used for emphasizing how good sth is because of the quality mentioned: *These blankets are lovely and soft.*

lover ⊶ /ˈlʌvə(r)/ ***noun*** [C] **1** a partner in a sexual relationship with sb who they are not married to: *He discovered that his wife had a lover.* ◇ *The park was full of young lovers holding hands.* **2** a person who likes or enjoys the thing mentioned: *a music lover* ◇ *an animal lover*

loving /ˈlʌvɪŋ/ ***adj.*** **1** feeling or showing love or care: *She's very loving towards her brother.* **2** (used to form compound adjectives) **-loving** loving the thing or activity mentioned: *a fun-loving girl* ▸ **lovingly** ***adv.***

low[1] ⊶ /ləʊ/ ***adj.***, ***adv.*** **1** close to the ground or to the bottom of sth: *Hang that picture a bit higher, it's much too low!* ◇ *That plane is flying very low.* **2** below the usual or normal level or amount: *Temperatures were very low last winter.* ◇ *The price of fruit is lower in the summer.* ◇ *low wages* ◇ *low-fat yoghurt* **3** below what is normal or acceptable in quality, importance or development: *a low standard of living* ◇ *low status* **4** (used about a sound or voice) deep or quiet: *His voice is already lower than his father's.* ◇ *A group of people in the library were speaking in low voices.* **5** not happy and lacking energy: *He's been* ***feeling*** *a bit* ***low*** *since his illness.* **6** (used about a light, an oven, etc.) made to produce only a little light or heat: *Cook the rice on a low heat for 20 minutes.* ◇ *The low lighting adds to the restaurant's atmosphere.* **7** (used about a gear in a car) that allows a slower speed OPP **high**

IDM **high and low** → HIGH[2]

lie low → LIE[2]

run low (on sth) to start to have less of sth than you need; to start to be less than is needed: *We're running low on coffee – shall I go and buy some?*

low[2] /ləʊ/ ***noun*** [C] a low point, level, figure, etc.: *Unemployment has fallen to a new low.* OPP **high**

ˈ**low-down** ***noun*** [sing.] (*informal*)

IDM **give sb/get the low-down (on sb/sth)** to tell sb/be told the true facts or secret information (about sb/sth)

lower[1] /ˈləʊə(r)/ ***adj.*** (only *before* a noun) below sth or at the bottom of sth: *She bit her lower lip.* ◇ *the lower deck of a ship* OPP **upper**

lower[2] /ˈləʊə(r)/ ***verb*** [T] **1** to make or let sb/sth go down: *They lowered the boat into the water.* ◇ *to lower your head/eyes* **2** to make sth less in amount, quality, etc.: *The virus lowers resistance to other diseases.* ◇ *Could you* ***lower*** *your* ***voice*** *slightly? I'm trying to sleep.* OPP **raise**

ˌ**lower** ˈ**case** ***noun*** [U] (LANGUAGE) letters that are written or printed in their small form; not in capital letters: *The text is all in lower case.* ◇ *lower-case letters* OPP **upper case**

ˌlower ˈhouse (*also* ˌ**lower ˈchamber**) ***noun*** [sing.] (POLITICS) the larger group of people who make laws in a country, usually consisting of elected representatives, such as the House of Commons in Britain or the House of Representatives in the US ➲ look at **upper house**

ˌlowest ˌcommon deˈnominator ***noun*** [C] (*abbr.* **LCD**) (MATHEMATICS) the smallest number that the bottom numbers of a group of FRACTIONS can be divided into exactly

ˌlowest ˌcommon ˈmultiple ***noun*** [C] (MATHEMATICS) the smallest number that a group of numbers can be divided into exactly

ˌlow-ˈkey ***adj.*** quiet and not wanting to attract a lot of attention: *The wedding will be very low-key. We're only inviting ten people.*

lowland /ˈləʊlənd/ ***noun*** [C, usually pl.] (GEOGRAPHY) a flat area of land at about sea level: *the lowlands near the coast* ◇ *lowland areas*

lowlander /ˈləʊləndə(r)/ ***noun*** [C] a person who comes from an area which is flat and low ➲ look at **highlander**

ˌlow-ˈlevel ***adj.*** (COMPUTING) (used about a computer language) not like an existing language, but using a system of numbers that a computer can understand and act on; similar to MACHINE CODE OPP **high-level**

ˌlow-ˈlying ***adj.*** (GEOGRAPHY) (used about land) near to sea level; not high

ˌlow-ˈpitched ***adj.*** (used about sounds) deep; low: *a low-pitched voice* OPP **high-pitched** ➲ picture at **high-pitched**

ˈlow season ***noun*** [U, sing.] (*especially BrE*) (TOURISM) the time of year when a hotel or tourist area receives fewest visitors SYN **off season** ➲ look at **high season**

low-tech (also **lo-tech**) /ˌləʊ ˈtek/ ***adj.*** (*informal*) not using the most modern technology or methods OPP **high-tech**

ˌlow ˈtide ***noun*** [U] (GEOGRAPHY) the time when the sea is at its lowest level: *At low tide you can walk out to the island.* OPP **high tide**

loyal ⊶ /ˈlɔɪəl/ ***adj.*** (used about a person) not changing in your friendship or beliefs: *a loyal friend/supporter* SYN **faithful** OPP **disloyal** ▶ **loyally** ***adv.*** ▶ **loyalty** /ˈlɔɪəlti/ ***noun*** [C,U] (*pl.* **loyalties**)

ˈloyalty card ***noun*** (*BrE*) (BUSINESS) a card given to customers by a shop/store to encourage them to shop there regularly. Each time they buy sth they collect points which will allow them to have an amount of money taken off goods they buy in the future.

lozenge /ˈlɒzɪndʒ/ ***noun*** [C] **1** (MATHEMATICS) a figure with four sides in the shape of a diamond that has two opposite angles more than 90° and the other two less than 90° **2** (HEALTH) a sweet that you suck if you have a cough or a sore throat

ˈL-plate ***noun*** [C] a sign with a large red letter L (for 'learner') on it, that you fix to a car to show that the driver is learning to drive

Lt ***abbr.*** (*written*) Lieutenant

Ltd ***abbr.*** (*BrE*) (BUSINESS) (used about private companies) Limited: *Pierce and Co. Ltd*

lubricant /ˈluːbrɪkənt/ ***noun*** [C,U] a substance, for example oil, that makes the parts of a machine work easily and smoothly

lubricate /ˈluːbrɪkeɪt/ ***verb*** [T] to put oil, etc. onto or into sth so that it works smoothly ▶ **lubrication** /ˌluːbrɪˈkeɪʃn/ ***noun*** [U]

lucid /ˈluːsɪd/ ***adj.*** (*formal*) **1** (used about sth that is said or written) clear and easy to understand: *a lucid style/description* **2** (HEALTH) (used about a person's mind) not confused; clear and normal ▶ **lucidly** ***adv.*** ▶ **lucidity** /luːˈsɪdəti/ ***noun*** [U]

luck ⊶ /lʌk/ ***noun*** [U] **1** success or good things that happen by chance: *We'd like to **wish** you lots of **luck** in your new career.* ◇ *He says this necklace will **bring you luck**.* ◇ *I could hardly believe my luck when they offered me the job.* ◇ ***With a bit of luck**, we'll finish this job today.* **2** chance; the force that people believe makes things happen: *There's no skill in this game – it's all luck.* ◇ *to have good/bad luck*

IDM **bad luck!**; **hard luck!** used to show pity for sb: *'Bad luck. Maybe you'll win next time.'*

be in/out of luck to be lucky/to not be lucky: *I was in luck – they had one ticket left!*

good luck (to sb) used to wish that sb is successful: *Good luck! I'm sure you'll get the job.*

worse luck → WORSE

lucky ⊶ /ˈlʌki/ ***adj.*** (**luckier**; **luckiest**) **1** (used about a person) having good luck: *He's lucky to be alive after an accident like that.* ◇ *With so much unemployment, I **count myself lucky** that I've got a job.* ◇ *'I'm off on holiday next week.' 'Lucky you!'* **2** (used about a situation, event, etc.) having a good result: *It's lucky I got here before the rain started.* ◇ *a lucky escape* **3** (used about a thing) bringing success or good luck: *a lucky number* ◇ *It was not my lucky day.* OPP **unlucky** ▶ **luckily** ***adv.***: *Luckily, I remembered to bring some money.*

IDM **you'll be lucky** used to tell sb that sth that they are expecting will probably not happen: *You're looking for a good English restaurant? You'll be lucky!*

lucrative /ˈluːkrətɪv/ ***adj.*** (*formal*) allowing sb to earn a lot of money: *a lucrative contract/business* ➲ note at **successful**

ludicrous /ˈluːdɪkrəs/ ***adj.*** very silly; ridiculous: *What a ludicrous idea!* ▶ **ludicrously** ***adv.***

lug /lʌg/ ***verb*** [T] (**lugging**; **lugged**) (*informal*) to carry or pull sth very heavy with great difficulty

luge /luːʒ; luːdʒ/ ***noun*** **1** [C] a type of SLEDGE(=a vehicle for sliding over ice) for racing, used by one person lying on their back with their feet pointing forwards **2 the luge** [sing.] (SPORT) the event or sport of racing down a track of ice on a **luge**

luggage

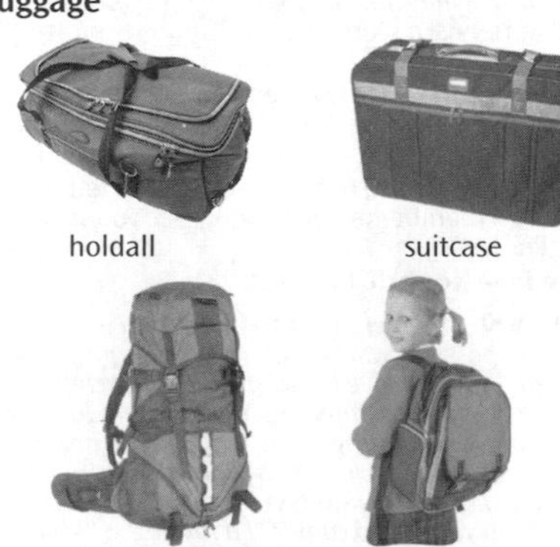

backpacks (*BrE also* rucksacks)

luggage /ˈlʌɡɪdʒ/ ***noun*** [U] (TOURISM) bags, suitcases, etc. used for carrying a person's clothes and things on a journey: *'How much luggage are you taking with you?' 'Only one suitcase.'* ◇ *You're only allowed one piece of* ***hand luggage*** (= a bag that you carry with you on the plane). SYN **baggage**

ˈluggage rack ***noun*** [C] (TOURISM) a shelf above the seats in a train or bus for putting your bags, etc. on

lukewarm /ˌluːkˈwɔːm/ ***adj.*** **1** (used about liquids) only slightly warm **2 ~ (about sb/sth)** not showing much interest; not keen

lull¹ /lʌl/ ***noun*** [C, usually sing.] **a ~ (in sth)** a short period of quiet between times of activity

lull² /lʌl/ ***verb*** [T] **1** to make sb relaxed and calm: *She sang a song to* ***lull*** *the children* ***to sleep***. **2 ~ sb into sth** to make sb feel safe, and not expecting anything bad to happen: *Our first success* ***lulled us into a false sense of security***.

lullaby /ˈlʌləbaɪ/ ***noun*** [C] (*pl.* **lullabies**) (MUSIC) a gentle song that you sing to help a child to go to sleep

lumber¹ /ˈlʌmbə(r)/ (*especially AmE*) = TIMBER (1)

lumber² /ˈlʌmbə(r)/ ***verb*** **1** [I] to move in a slow, heavy way: *A family of elephants lumbered past.* **2** [T] (*informal*) **~ sb (with sb/sth)** (usually passive) to give sb a responsibility or job that they do not want

luminous /ˈluːmɪnəs/ ***adj.*** that shines in the dark: *a luminous watch*

lump¹ /lʌmp/ ***noun*** [C] **1** a piece of sth solid of any size or shape: *a lump of coal/cheese/wood* ◇ *The sauce was full of lumps.* **2** (HEALTH) a swelling under the skin: *You'll have a bit of a lump on your head where you banged it.*

IDM **have/feel a lump in your throat** to feel pressure in your throat because you are about to cry

lump² /lʌmp/ ***verb*** [T] **~ A and B together; ~ A (in) with B** to put or consider different people or things together in the same group

IDM **lump it** (*informal*) to accept sth unpleasant because you have no choice: *That's the deal – like it or lump it.*

ˌlump ˈsum ***noun*** [C] (FINANCE) an amount of money paid all at once rather than in several smaller amounts

lumpy /ˈlʌmpi/ ***adj.*** full of or covered with lumps: *This bed is very lumpy.* OPP **smooth**

lunacy /ˈluːnəsi/ ***noun*** [U] very stupid behaviour: *It was lunacy to drive so fast in that terrible weather.* SYN **madness**

lunar /ˈluːnə(r)/ ***adj.*** (usually *before* a noun) (ASTRONOMY) connected with the moon: *a lunar spacecraft/eclipse/landscape*

lungs and respiratory system

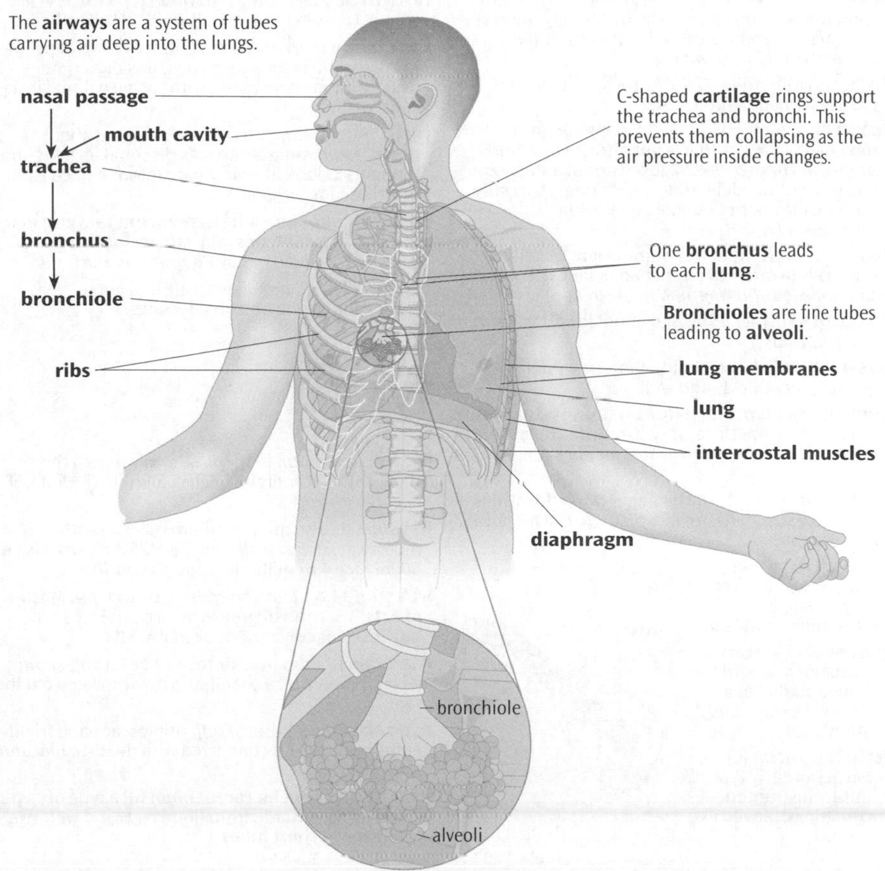

lunatic[1] /ˈluːnətɪk/ ***noun*** [C] (*informal*) a person who behaves in a stupid way doing crazy and often dangerous things **SYN** **madman**

lunatic[2] /ˈluːnətɪk/ ***adj.*** stupid; crazy: *a lunatic idea*

lunch /lʌntʃ/ ***noun*** [C,U] a meal that you have in the middle of the day: *Hot and cold lunches are served between 12 and 2.* ◇ *What would you like for lunch?* ▸ **lunch** ***verb*** [I] (*formal*)

ˈlunch hour ***noun*** [C, usually sing.] the time around the middle of the day when you stop work or school to have lunch: *I went to the shops in my lunch hour.*

lunchtime /ˈlʌntʃtaɪm/ ***noun*** [C,U] the time around the middle of the day when lunch is eaten: *I'll meet you at lunchtime.*

lung /lʌŋ/ ***noun*** [C] (ANATOMY) one of the two organs of your body that are inside your chest and are used for breathing ➲ picture on previous page

lunge /lʌndʒ/ ***noun*** [C, usually sing.] **a ~ (at sb)**; **a ~ (for sb/sth)** a sudden powerful forward movement of the body, especially when trying to attack sb/sth: *She made a lunge for the ball.* ▸ **lunge** ***verb*** [I]: *He lunged towards me with a knife.*

lurch /lɜːtʃ/ ***noun*** [C, usually sing.] a sudden movement forward or to one side ▸ **lurch** ***verb*** [I]
IDM **leave sb in the lurch** → LEAVE[1]

lure[1] /lʊə(r)/ ***verb*** [T] to persuade or trick sb to go somewhere or do sth, usually by offering them sth nice: *Young people are lured to the city by the prospect of a job and money.*

lure[2] /lʊə(r)/ ***noun*** [C] the attractive qualities of sth: *the lure of money/fame/adventure*

lurid /ˈlʊərɪd; ˈljʊər-/ ***adj.*** **1** having colours that are too bright, in a way that is not attractive: *a lurid purple and orange dress* **2** (used about a story or a piece of writing) deliberately shocking, especially because of violent or unpleasant detail
▸ **luridly** ***adv.***

lurk /lɜːk/ ***verb*** [I] to wait somewhere secretly especially in order to do sth bad or illegal: *I thought I saw somebody lurking among the trees.*

luscious /ˈlʌʃəs/ ***adj.*** (used about food) tasting very good: *luscious fruit*

lush /lʌʃ/ ***adj.*** (used about plants or gardens) growing very thickly and well

lust[1] /lʌst/ ***noun*** **1** [U] **~ (for sb)** strong sexual desire **2** [C,U] **(a) ~ (for sth)** (a) very strong desire to have or get sth: *a lust for power* ◇ *(a) lust for life* (=enjoyment of life)

lust[2] /lʌst/ ***verb*** [I] **~ (after sb)**; **~ (after/for sth)** to feel a very strong desire for sb/sth: *to lust for power/success/fame*

lustful /ˈlʌstfl/ ***adj.*** full of sexual desire: *lustful thoughts*
▸ **lustfully** /-fəli/ ***adv.***

lustre (*AmE* **luster**) /ˈlʌstə(r)/ ***noun*** [U] the shining quality of a surface: *Her hair had lost its lustre.*

lute /luːt/ ***noun*** [C] (MUSIC) an early type of musical instrument with strings, played like a GUITAR

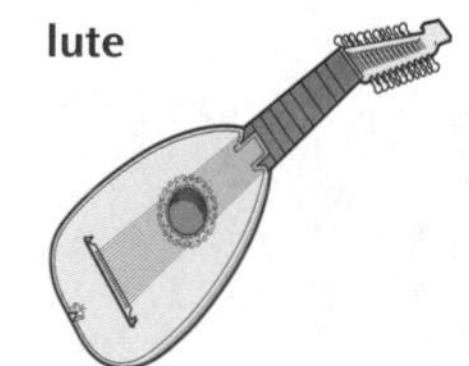
lute

lutetium /luːˈtiːʃiəm (*BrE also*)-siəm/ ***noun*** [U] (*symbol* **Lu**) (CHEMISTRY) a chemical element. **Lutetium** is a rare silver-white metal used in the nuclear industry. ❶ For more information on the periodic table of elements, look at pages R34-5.

luxurious /lʌgˈʒʊəriəs/ ***adj.*** very comfortable; full of expensive and beautiful things: *a luxurious hotel* ▸ **luxuriously** ***adv.***

luxury /ˈlʌkʃəri/ ***noun*** (*pl.* **luxuries**) **1** [U] the enjoyment of expensive and beautiful things; a very comfortable and enjoyable situation: *They are said to be* ***living in luxury*** *in Barbados.* ◇ *to lead* ***a life of luxury*** ◇ *a luxury hotel/car/yacht* **2** [C] something that is enjoyable and expensive that you do not really need: *luxury goods, such as wine and chocolates* **3** [U, sing.] a pleasure which you do not often have: *It was (an) absolute luxury to do nothing all weekend.*

LW ***abbr.*** =LONG WAVE ➲ picture at **wavelength**

lychee /ˌlaɪˈtʃiː; ˈlaɪtʃiː/ ***noun*** [C] a small Chinese fruit with thick rough red skin, that is white inside and has a large stone

lymph /lɪmf/ ***noun*** [U] (BIOLOGY) a colourless liquid containing white blood cells that cleans the inside of your body and helps to prevent infections from spreading ▸ **lymphatic** /lɪmˈfætɪk/ ***adj.*** (only *before* a noun): *the lymphatic system*

ˈlymph node (*also* **ˈlymph gland**) ***noun*** [C] (ANATOMY) a small hard mass in your body through which LYMPH passes

lymphocyte /ˈlɪmfəsaɪt/ ***noun*** [C] (BIOLOGY) a type of LEUCOCYTE (=a small white blood cell)

lynch /lɪntʃ/ ***verb*** [T] (used about a crowd of people) to kill sb who is thought to be guilty of a crime, usually by hanging them, without a legal trial in a court of law

lyric[1] /ˈlɪrɪk/ ***adj.*** **1** (LITERATURE) (used about poetry) expressing a person's personal feelings and thoughts ➲ look at **epic 2** (MUSIC) connected with, or written for, singing

lyric[2] /ˈlɪrɪk/ ***noun*** **1** [C] (LITERATURE) a LYRIC poem ➲ look at **epic 2** **lyrics** [pl.] (MUSIC) the words of a song: *music and lyrics by Rodgers and Hart*

lyrical /ˈlɪrɪkl/ ***adj.*** like a song or a poem, expressing strong personal feelings

M m

M, m[1] /em/ ***noun*** [C,U] (*pl.* **M's**; **m's** /emz/) the thirteenth letter of the English alphabet: *'Miranda' begins with (an) 'M'.*

M[2] ***abbr.*** **1** (*also* **med**) medium (size) **2** /em/ (*BrE*) motorway: *heavy traffic on the M25* **3 m** metre(s): *a 500m race* **4 m** million(s): *population 10m*

MA (*AmE* **M.A.**) /ˌem ˈeɪ/ ***abbr.*** (EDUCATION) **Master of Arts**; a second degree in an arts subject at university or college ➲ look at **BA**, **MSc**

mac /mæk/ (*also* **mackintosh** /ˈmækɪntɒʃ/) ***noun*** [C] (*especially BrE*) a coat that is made to keep out the rain

macabre /məˈkɑːbrə/ ***adj.*** unpleasant and frightening because it is connected with death: *a macabre tale/joke/ritual*

macaroni /ˌmækəˈrəʊni/ ***noun*** [U] a type of PASTA (=Italian food made from flour, eggs and water) in the shape of short tubes

Mace™ /meɪs/ ***noun*** [U] a chemical that hurts your eyes and skin, that some people, including police officers, carry in spray cans so that they can defend themselves against people attacking them

mace /meɪs/ ***noun*** **1** [C] a special stick, carried as a sign of authority by an official such as a MAYOR (=the person who manages the affairs of a town or city) **2** [C] a large heavy stick that has a head with metal points on it, used in the past as a weapon **3** [U] the dried outer covering of NUTMEGS (=the hard nuts of an East Indian tree), used in cooking as a spice

Mach /mɑːk; mæk/ ***noun*** [U] (often followed by a number) (**SCIENCE**) a measurement of speed, used especially for aircraft. **Mach 1** is the speed of sound.

machete /mə'ʃeti/ ***noun*** [C] a broad heavy knife used as a cutting tool and as a weapon

machine 🔑 /mə'ʃiːn/ ***noun*** [C] (often in compounds) a piece of equipment with moving parts that is designed to do a particular job. A machine usually needs electricity, gas, steam, etc. in order to work: *a washing/sewing/knitting machine* ◇ *a machine for making pasta* ➲ note at **tool**

ma'chine code ***noun*** [U] (**COMPUTING**) a language used for computer programs in which instructions are written in the form of numbers so that a computer can understand and act on them

ma'chine-gun ***noun*** [C] a gun that fires bullets very quickly and continuously

ma,chine-'readable ***adj.*** (**COMPUTING**) (of data) in a form that a computer can understand

machinery 🔑 /mə'ʃiːnəri/ ***noun*** [U] machines in general, especially large ones; the moving parts of a machine: *farm/agricultural/industrial machinery*

ma'chine tool ***noun*** [C] a tool for cutting or shaping metal, wood, etc., driven by a machine

machinist /mə'ʃiːnɪst/ ***noun*** [C] **1** a person whose job is operating a machine, especially machines used in industry for cutting and shaping things, or a sewing machine **2** a person whose job is to make or repair machines

macho /'mætʃəʊ/ ***adj.*** (*informal*) (used about a man or his behaviour) having typically male qualities like strength and courage, but using them in an aggressive way: *He's too macho to ever admit he was wrong and apologize.*

mackerel /'mækrəl/ ***noun*** [C,U] (*pl.* **mackerel**) a sea fish that you can eat, with greenish-blue bands on its body

mackintosh =MAC

macramé /mə'krɑːmi/ ***noun*** [U] (**ART**) the art of tying knots in string in a decorative way, to make things

macro /'mækrəʊ/ ***noun*** [C] (*pl.* **macros**) (**COMPUTING**) a single instruction that a computer automatically reads as a set of instructions necessary to do a particular task

macro- /'mækrəʊ/ ***prefix*** (used in nouns, adjectives and adverbs) large; on a large scale: *macroeconomics* **OPP** **micro-**

macrobiotic /,mækrəʊbaɪ'ɒtɪk/ ***adj.*** (used about food) that is grown without using chemicals and is thought to make us live longer

macrocosm /'mækrəʊkɒzəm/ ***noun*** [C] any large complete structure that contains smaller structures, for example the universe ➲ look at **microcosm**

mad 🔑 /mæd/ ***adj.*** **1** (**HEALTH**) having a mind that does not work normally; mentally ill **2** (*BrE*) not at all sensible; crazy: *You must be mad to drive in this weather.* **3** (not before a noun) ~ **(at/with sb) (about sth)** very angry: *His laziness **drives me mad**!* ◇ (*especially AmE*) *Don't **get/go mad** at him. He didn't mean to do it.* **4** (*informal*) ~ **about/on sb/sth** liking sb/sth very much: *He's mad on computer games at the moment.* ◇ *Steve's mad about Jane.* **5** not controlled; wild or very excited: *The audience was cheering and clapping like mad* (=very hard). ◇ *When DiCaprio appeared on the hotel balcony his fans **went mad**.*

madam /'mædəm/ ***noun*** [sing.] **1** (*formal*) used as a polite way of speaking to a woman, especially to a customer in a shop or restaurant: *Can I help you, madam?* ➲ look at **sir 2 Madam** used for beginning a formal letter to a woman when you do not know her name: *Dear Madam, I am writing in reply...*

,mad 'cow disease =BSE

maddening /'mædnɪŋ/ ***adj.*** that makes you very angry or annoyed: *She has some really maddening habits.* ▶ **maddeningly** ***adv.***

made past tense, past participle of **make**[1]

IDM **made to measure** → MEASURE[2]

madly /'mædli/ ***adv.*** **1** in a wild or crazy way: *They were rushing about madly.* **2** (*informal*) very; extremely: *They're madly in love.*

madman /'mædmən/ ***noun*** [C] (*pl.* **madmen** /-mən/) a person who behaves in a wild or crazy way **SYN** **lunatic**

madness /'mædnəs/ ***noun*** [U] crazy or stupid behaviour that could be dangerous: *It would be madness to take a boat out in such rough weather.*

madonna /mə'dɒnə/ ***noun*** **1 the Madonna** [sing.] (**RELIGION**) the Virgin Mary, mother of Jesus Christ **2** [C] (**ART**) a statue or picture of the Virgin Mary: *a madonna and child*

madrigal /'mædrɪgl/ ***noun*** [C] (**MUSIC**) a song for several singers, usually without musical instruments, popular in the 16th century

magazine 🔑 /,mægə'ziːn/ (also *informal* **mag** /mæg/) ***noun*** [C] (**ARTS AND MEDIA**) a type of large thin book with a paper cover that you can buy every week or month containing articles, photographs, etc. often on a particular topic: *a woman's/computer/gardening magazine*

magenta /mə'dʒentə/ ***adj.*** reddish-purple in colour ▶ **magenta** ***noun*** [U]

maggot /'mægət/ ***noun*** [C] a young insect before it grows wings and legs and becomes a fly

magic[1] 🔑 /'mædʒɪk/ ***noun*** [U] **1** the secret power that some people believe can make strange or impossible things happen if you say special words or do special things ➲ look at **black magic 2** the art of doing tricks that seem impossible in order to entertain people **3** a special quality that makes sth seem wonderful: *I'll never forget the magic of that moment.*

magic[2] 🔑 /'mædʒɪk/ ***adj.*** **1** used in or using magic: *a magic spell/potion/charm/trick* ◇ *There is no magic formula for passing exams – just hard work.* **2** having a special quality that makes sth seem wonderful: *Respect is the magic ingredient in our relationship.* ▶ **magically** /-kli/ ***adv.***

magical /'mædʒɪkl/ ***adj.*** **1** that seems to use magic: *a herb with magical powers to heal* **2** wonderful and exciting: *Our holiday was absolutely magical.*

magician /məˈdʒɪʃn/ ***noun*** [C] **1** a person who performs magic tricks to entertain people ➲ look at **conjuror 2** (in stories) a man who has magic powers ➲ look at **wizard**

magistrate /ˈmædʒɪstreɪt/ ***noun*** [C] (LAW) an official who acts as a judge in cases involving less serious crimes

maglev /ˈmæglev/ ***noun*** [U] a transport system in which trains travel very fast just above a track, supported by MAGNETIC REPULSION (=the force by which objects push away from each other)

magma /ˈmægmə/ ***noun*** [U] (GEOLOGY) very hot liquid rock found below the earth's surface ➲ picture at **volcano**

magnanimous /mægˈnænɪməs/ ***adj.*** kind, generous and forgiving (especially towards an enemy or a COMPETITOR that you have beaten)

magnate /ˈmægneɪt/ ***noun*** [C] a person who is rich, powerful and successful, especially in business: *a media/property/shipping magnate*

magnesium /mægˈniːziəm/ ***noun*** [U] (*symbol* **Mg**) (CHEMISTRY) a light, silver-white metal that burns with a bright white flame ❶ For more information on the periodic table of elements, look at pages R34-5.

magnet

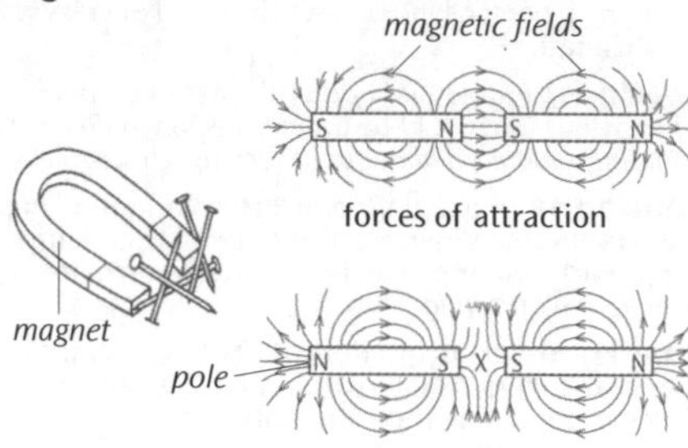

magnet /ˈmægnət/ ***noun*** [C] (PHYSICS) a piece of iron, steel, etc. that can attract and pick up other metal objects

magnetic /mægˈnetɪk/ ***adj.*** **1** (PHYSICS) having the ability to attract metal objects: *a magnetic tape/disk* (=containing electronic information which can be read by a computer or other machine) **2** having a quality that strongly attracts people: *a magnetic personality*

magˌnetic ˈfield ***noun*** [C] (PHYSICS) an area around a MAGNET or materials that behave like a magnet, where there is a force that will attract some metals towards it

magˌnetic ˈnorth ***noun*** [U] (GEOGRAPHY) the direction that is approximately north as it is shown on a COMPASS (=an instrument that shows direction) ➲ look at **true north**

magnetism /ˈmægnətɪzəm/ ***noun*** [U] **1** (PHYSICS) a characteristic of some metals such as iron, produced by electric currents, that causes forces between objects, either pulling them towards each other or pushing them apart **2** qualities that strongly attract people: *Nobody could resist his magnetism.*

magnetize (also **-ise**) /ˈmægnətaɪz/ ***verb*** [T] **1** (PHYSICS) to make sth metal behave like a MAGNET **2** (*written*) to strongly attract sb

magnificent /mægˈnɪfɪsnt/ ***adj.*** extremely impressive and attractive ► **magnificence** /-sns/ ***noun*** [U] ► **magnificently** ***adv.***

magnify /ˈmægnɪfaɪ/ ***verb*** [T] (*pres. part.* **magnifying**; *3rd person sing. pres.* **magnifies**; *pt, pp* **magnified**) **1** to make sth look bigger than it is, usually using a special piece of equipment: *to magnify sth under a microscope* **2** to make sth seem more important than it really is: *to magnify a problem* ► **magnification** /ˌmægnɪfɪˈkeɪʃn/ ***noun*** [U]

magnify

magnifying glass

ˈmagnifying glass ***noun*** [C] a round piece of glass, usually with a handle, that is used for making things look bigger than they are ➲ picture at **magnify**

magnitude /ˈmægnɪtjuːd/ ***noun*** [U] the great size or importance of sth

mahogany /məˈhɒgəni/ ***noun*** [U] hard dark reddish-brown wood (from a tropical tree) that is used for making furniture

maid /meɪd/ ***noun*** [C] a woman whose job is to clean in a hotel or large house ➲ look at **chambermaid**

maiden name /ˈmeɪdn neɪm/ ***noun*** [C] a woman's family name before marriage ➲ look at **née**

maiden voyage /ˌmeɪdn ˈvɔɪɪdʒ/ ***noun*** [C] the first journey of a new ship

mail¹ ⊶ /meɪl/ (*BrE also* **post**) ***noun*** [U] **1** the system for collecting and sending letters and packages: *to send a parcel by airmail/surface mail* **2** the letters, etc. that you receive: *junk mail* (=letters, usually advertising sth, that are sent to people although they have not asked for them) **3** (*especially AmE*) =EMAIL

mail² ⊶ /meɪl/ (*BrE also* **post**) ***verb*** [T] **1** ~ **sth (to sb/sth)**; ~ **(sb) sth** (*especially AmE*) to send sth to sb using the POSTAL system: *Don't forget to mail that letter to your mother.* ◇ *Don't forget to mail your mother that letter.* **2** ~ **sb**; ~ **sth (to sb/sth)**; ~ **(sb) sth** (*BrE*) to send a message to sb by email: *The virus mails itself forward to everyone in your address book.*

ˈmail bomb ***noun*** [C] **1** (*AmE*) =LETTER BOMB **2** (COMPUTING) an extremely large number of email messages that are sent to sb

ˈmail-bomb ***verb*** [T] (COMPUTING) to send sb an extremely large number of email messages: *The newspaper was mail-bombed by angry readers after the article was published.*

mailbox /ˈmeɪlbɒks/ ***noun*** [C] **1** (*AmE*) =LETTER BOX (2) **2** (*AmE*) =POSTBOX **3** (COMPUTING) a computer program that receives and stores electronic messages (**email**)

ˈmailing list ***noun*** [C] a list of the names and addresses of people to whom advertising material or information is regularly sent by a business or an organization

mailman /ˈmeɪlmæn/ (*pl.* **-men** /-mən/) (*AmE*) =POSTMAN

ˈmail order ***noun*** [U] a method of shopping. You choose what you want from a special book (**a catalogue**) and the goods are then sent to you by post.

mailshot /ˈmeɪlʃɒt/ ***noun*** [C] (BUSINESS) advertising or information that is sent to a large number of people at the same time by mail

maim /meɪm/ ***verb*** [T] to hurt sb so badly that part of their body can no longer be used

THESAURUS

main

major • key • central • principal • chief • prime
These words all describe sb/sth that is the largest or most important of its kind.
main: *The main thing is to keep calm.*
major: *He played a major role in the organization.*
key: *She was a key figure in the campaign*
central: *The environment is a central issue.*
principal: *The principal reason for this omission is lack of time.*
chief: *Smoking is the chief cause of lung disease.*
prime: *Our prime concern is for your safety.*

main[1] /meɪn/ ***adj.*** (only *before* a noun) most important: *My main reason for wanting to learn English is to get a better job.* ◇ *a busy main road* ◇ *He doesn't earn very much but he's happy, and that's* ***the main thing.*** SYN **chief**
IDM **in the main** (*formal*) generally; mostly: *We found English people very friendly in the main.*

main[2] /meɪn/ ***noun*** **1** [C] a large pipe or wire that carries water, gas or electricity between buildings: *The water main has burst.* **2 the mains** [pl.] (*BrE*) the place where the supply of gas, water or electricity to a building starts; the system of providing these services to a building: *Turn the water off at the mains.* ◇ *mains gas/water/electricity*

mainframe /ˈmeɪnfreɪm/ (*also* **ˌmainframe comˈputer**) ***noun*** [C] (COMPUTING) a large powerful computer, usually the centre of a system (**network**) that is shared by many people (**users**)

mainland /ˈmeɪnlænd/ ***noun*** [sing.] (GEOGRAPHY) the main part of a country or continent, not including the islands around it: *mainland Greece*

mainline /ˈmeɪnlaɪn/ ***adj.*** (*especially AmE*) belonging to the system, or connected with the ideas that most people accept or believe in SYN **mainstream**

mainly /ˈmeɪnli/ ***adv.*** mostly: *The students here are mainly from Japan.*

mainsail /ˈmeɪnseɪl; ˈmeɪnsl/ ***noun*** [C] the largest and most important sail on a boat or ship

mainstay /ˈmeɪnsteɪ/ ***noun*** [C] a person or thing that is the most important part of sth, which makes it possible for it to exist or to be successful: *Cocoa is the mainstay of the country's economy.*

mainstream /ˈmeɪnstriːm/ ***noun*** [sing.] **the mainstream** the ideas and opinions that are considered normal because they are shared by most people; the people who hold these opinions and beliefs: *The Green Party is not* ***in the mainstream*** *of British politics.* ► **mainstream** ***adj.***

maintain AW /meɪnˈteɪn/ ***verb*** [T] **1** to make sth continue at the same level, standard, etc.: *We need to maintain the quality of our goods but not increase the price.* ◇ *to maintain law and order* **2** to keep sth in good condition by checking and repairing it regularly: *to maintain a road/building/machine* ◇ *The house is large and expensive to maintain.* **3** to keep saying that sth is true even when others disagree or do not believe it: *I still maintain that I was right to sack him.* ◇ *She has always maintained her innocence.* **4** to support sb with your own money: *He has to maintain two children from his previous marriage.*

maintenance AW /ˈmeɪntənəns/ ***noun*** [U] **1** keeping sth in good condition: *This house needs a lot of maintenance.* ◇ *car maintenance* **2** (*BrE*) (LAW) money that sb must pay regularly to a former wife, husband or partner especially when they have had children together: *He has to pay maintenance to his ex-wife.*

maisonette /ˌmeɪzəˈnet/ ***noun*** [C] (*BrE*) a flat on two floors that is part of a larger building

maître d' /ˌmeɪtrə ˈdiː/ ***noun*** (*pl.* **maître d's** /ˌmeɪtrə ˈdiːz/) (also *formal* **maître d'hôtel** /ˌmeɪtrə dəʊˈtel/ (*pl.* **maîtres d'hôtel** /ˌmeɪtrə dəʊˈtel/) (*formal*) **1** a head waiter **2** a man who manages a hotel

maize /meɪz/ (*AmE* **corn**) ***noun*** [U] a tall plant that produces yellow grains in a large mass (**a cob**) ⓘ The yellow grains from **maize** that we eat as a vegetable are called **corn** or **sweetcorn**. ➲ picture at **cereal**

Maj. ***abbr.*** (*written*) Major; an officer of a middle level in the army or the US air force

majestic /məˈdʒestɪk/ ***adj.*** impressive because of its size or beauty: *a majestic mountain landscape* ► **majestically** /-kli/ ***adv.***

majesty /ˈmædʒəsti/ ***noun*** (*pl.* **majesties**) **1** [U] the impressive and attractive quality that sth has: *the splendour and majesty of the palace and its gardens* **2 His/Her/Your Majesty** [C] (*formal*) used when speaking to or about a king or queen: *Her Majesty the Queen*

major[1] AW /ˈmeɪdʒə(r)/ ***adj.*** **1** (only *before* a noun) very large, important or serious: *The patient needs major heart surgery.* ◇ *There haven't been any major problems.* OPP **minor** **2** (MUSIC) of one of the two types of key[1](4) in which music is usually written: *the key of D major* ➲ look at **minor**

major[2] AW /ˈmeɪdʒə(r)/ ***noun*** **1** (*abbr.* **Maj.**) [C] an officer of a middle level in the army or the US air force **2** [C] (*AmE*) (EDUCATION) the main subject or course of a student at college or university; the student who studies it: *Her major is French.* **3** [U] (MUSIC) a type of key[1](4) or scale: *a change from major to minor*

major[3] AW /ˈmeɪdʒə(r)/ ***verb***
PHRV **major in sth** (*AmE*) (EDUCATION) to study sth as your main subject at college or university

ˌmajor ˈgeneral ***noun*** [C] an officer of a high level in the army

majority AW /məˈdʒɒrəti/ ***noun*** (*pl.* **majorities**) **1** [sing., with sing. or pl. verb] ~ (**of sb/sth**) the largest number or part of a group of people or things: *The majority of students in the class come/comes from Japan.* ◇ *This treatment is not available in* ***the vast majority*** *of hospitals.* OPP **minority** **2** [C, usually sing.] ~ (**over sb**) (POLITICS) (in an election) the difference in the number of votes for the person/party who came first and the person/party who came second: *He was elected by/with a majority of almost 5000 votes.* ⓘ If you have an **overall majority** you got more votes than all the other people/parties added together. ➲ look at **absolute majority**
IDM **be in the/a majority** to form the largest number or part of sth: *Women are in the majority in the teaching profession.*

make[1] /meɪk/ ***verb*** (*pt, pp* **made** /meɪd/) **1** [T] to produce or create sth: *to make bread* ◇ *This model is* ***made of*** *steel, and that one is* ***made out of*** *used matches.* ◇ *Cheese is* ***made from*** *milk.* ◇ *Those cars are* ***made in*** *Slovakia.* ◇ *Shall I make you a sandwich/make a sandwich for you?* ◇ *to make a hole*

THESAURUS

make

create • develop • produce • generate • form
These words all mean to make sth from parts or materials, or to cause sth to exist or happen.
make: *She makes her own clothes.*
create: *How was the universe created?*
develop: *to develop new software*
produce: *a factory that produces microchips*
generate: *to generate electricity ◇ Brainstorming is a good way of generating new ideas.*
form: *Rearrange the letters to form a new word.*

in sth ◇ to make a law/rule ◇ to make a movie **2** [T] (used with nouns) to perform a certain action: *to make a mistake ◇ to make a guess/comment/statement/suggestion ◇ to make progress ◇ I've made an appointment to see the doctor.* **3** [T] to cause a particular effect, feeling, situation, etc.: *The film made me cry. ◇ Flying makes him nervous. ◇ Her remarks made the situation worse. ◇ I'll* ***make it clear*** *to him that we won't pay. ◇* ***Make sure*** *you lock the car. ◇ You don't need to know much of a language to* ***make yourself understood****. ◇ to make trouble/a mess/a noise* **4** [T] to force sb/sth to do sth: *You can't make her come with us if she doesn't want to. ◇ They made him wait at the police station all day.* **5** [T] used with money, numbers and time: *How much do you think he makes* (=earns) *a month? ◇ to make a lot of money ◇ 5 and 7 make 12. ◇ 'What's the time?' 'I make it 6.45.'* **6** ***linking verb*** to make sb/sth become sth; to have the right qualities to become sth: *She was made* (=given the job of) *President. ◇ You can borrow some money this time, but don't* ***make a habit of*** *it. ◇ Karen explains things very clearly – she'd make a good teacher.* **7** ***linking verb*** to become sth; to achieve sth: *I'm hoping to make head of department by the time I'm thirty.* **8** to manage to reach a place or go somewhere: *We should make Bristol by about 10. ◇ I can't make the meeting next week.*

IDM **make do with sth** to use sth that is not good enough because nothing better is available: *If we can't get limes, we'll have to make do with lemons.*
make it to manage to do sth; to succeed: *She'll never make it as an actress. ◇ He's badly injured – it looks like he might not make it* (=survive).
make the most of sth to get as much pleasure, profit, etc. as possible from sth: *You won't get another chance – make the most of it!*

PHR V **be made for sb/each other** to be well suited to sb/each other: *Jim and Alice seem made for each other.*
make for sb/sth to move towards sb/sth
make for sth to help or allow sth to happen: *Arguing all the time doesn't make for a happy marriage.*
make sb/sth into sb/sth to change sb/sth into sb/sth: *She made her spare room into an office.*
make sth of sb/sth to understand the meaning or nature of sb/sth: *What do you make of Colin's letter?*
make off (with sth) (*informal*) to leave or escape in a hurry, for example after stealing sth: *Someone's made off with my wallet!*
make sb/sth out 1 to understand sb/sth: *I just can't make him out.* **2** to be able to see or hear sb/sth; to manage to read sth: *I could just make out her signature.*
make out that...; make yourself out to be sth to say that sth is true and try to make people believe it: *He made out that he was a millionaire. ◇ She's not as clever as she makes herself out to be.*
make (yourself/sb) up to put powder, colour, etc. on your/sb's face to make it look attractive
make sth up 1 to form sth: *the different groups that make up our society* **2** to invent sth, often sth that is not true: *to make up an excuse* **3** to make a number or an amount complete; to replace sth that has been lost: *We need one more person to make up our team.*
make up for sth to do sth that corrects a bad situation: *Her enthusiasm makes up for her lack of experience.*
make it up to sb (*informal*) to do sth that shows that you are sorry for what you have done to sb or that you are grateful for what they have done for you: *You've done me a big favour. How can I make it up to you?*
make (it) up (with sb) to become friends again after an argument: *Has she made it up with him yet?*

make² 🔑 /meɪk/ ***noun*** [C] (BUSINESS) the name of the company that produces sth: *'What make is your television?' 'It's a Sony.'*
IDM **on the make** always trying to make money for yourself, especially in a dishonest way: *The country is being ruined by politicians on the make.*

'make-believe ***noun*** [U] things that sb imagines or invents that are not real

makeover /'meɪkəʊvə(r)/ ***noun*** [C,U] the process of improving the appearance of a person or a place, or of changing the impression that sth gives

maker /'meɪkə(r)/ ***noun*** [C] a person, company or machine that makes sth: *a film-maker ◇ If it doesn't work, send it back to the maker. ◇ an ice cream maker*

makeshift /'meɪkʃɪft/ ***adj.*** made to be used for only a short time until there is sth better: *makeshift shelters of old cardboard boxes*

'make-up 🔑 ***noun*** **1** [U] powder, cream, etc. that you put on your face to make yourself more attractive. Actors use make-up to change their appearance when they are acting: *to put on/take off make-up* ➲ look at **cosmetic¹** ➲ verb **make (yourself/sb) up** **2** [sing.] a person's character: *He can't help his temper. It's part of his make-up.*

making /'meɪkɪŋ/ ***noun*** [sing.] the act of doing or producing sth; the process of being made: *breadmaking ◇ This movie has been three years in the making.*
IDM **be the making of sb** to be the reason that sb is successful: *University was the making of Gina.*
have the makings of sth to have the necessary qualities for sth: *The book has the makings of a good film.*

mal- /mæl/ ***prefix*** (used in nouns, verbs and adjectives) bad or badly; not correct or correctly: *malnutrition ◇ maltreat*

maladjusted /ˌmælə'dʒʌstɪd/ ***adj.*** (used about a person) not able to behave well with other people

malaria /mə'leəriə/ ***noun*** [U] (HEALTH) a serious disease in hot countries that you get from the bite of a small flying insect (**a mosquito**) ▶ **malarial** ***adj.***: *a malarial mosquito*

male 🔑 /meɪl/ ***adj.*** (BIOLOGY) belonging to the sex that does not give birth to babies or produce eggs: *a male goat ◇ a male model/nurse* ➲ look at **masculine** ▶ **male** ***noun*** [C]: *The male of the species has a white tail.*

malformation /ˌmælfɔː'meɪʃn/ ***noun*** **1** [C] (HEALTH) a part of the body that is not formed correctly: *foetal malformations* **2** [U] the state of not being correctly formed

malice /ˈmælɪs/ ***noun*** [U] a wish to hurt other people ▸ **malicious** /məˈlɪʃəs/ ***adj.*** ▸ **maliciously** ***adv.***

IDM **with malice aforethought** with the deliberate intention of committing a crime or harming sb

malignant /məˈlɪɡnənt/ ***adj.*** (HEALTH) (used about a serious disease (**cancer**) or a growing mass caused by disease (**a tumour**)) likely to cause death if not controlled: *He has a malignant brain tumour.* OPP **benign**

mall ⊶ /mæl; mɔːl/ = SHOPPING CENTRE

malleable /ˈmæliəbl/ ***adj.*** **1** (used about metals, etc.) that can be hit or pressed into shape easily without breaking or cracking **2** (used about people, ideas, etc.) easily influenced or changed ▸ **malleability** /ˌmæliəˈbɪləti/ ***noun*** [U]

mallet /ˈmælɪt/ ***noun*** [C] a heavy wooden hammer ➲ picture at **tool**

malleus /ˈmæliəs/ (*pl.* **mallei** /ˈmæl/) ***noun*** [sing.] (ANATOMY) (*also* **hammer**) the first of three small bones in the middle ear which carry sound VIBRATIONS from the EARDRUM to the inner ear ➲ picture at **ear**

malnutrition /ˌmælnjuːˈtrɪʃn/ ***noun*** [U] (HEALTH) bad health that is the result of not having enough food or enough of the right kind of food ▸ **malnourished** /ˌmælˈnʌrɪʃt/ ***adj.***: *The children were badly malnourished.*

malpractice /ˌmælˈpræktɪs/ ***noun*** [U, C] (LAW) careless, wrong or illegal behaviour while in a professional job: *medical malpractice* ◇ *He is standing trial for alleged malpractices.*

malt /mɔːlt/ ***noun*** [U] (AGRICULTURE) grain that is used for making beer and WHISKY (= a strong alcoholic drink)

maltose /ˈmɔːltəʊz/ ***noun*** [U] (BIOLOGY) a sugar that chemicals in the body make from STARCH (= a food substance found in flour, rice, potatoes, etc.)

maltreat /ˌmælˈtriːt/ ***verb*** [T] (*formal*) to treat a person or animal in a cruel or unkind way ▸ **maltreatment** ***noun*** [U]

mammal /ˈmæml/ ***noun*** [C] (BIOLOGY) an animal of the type that gives birth to live babies, not eggs, and feeds its young on milk from its own body: *Whales, dogs and humans are mammals.* ➲ picture on **page 29**

mammary /ˈmæməri/ ***adj.*** (only *before* a noun) (ANATOMY) connected with the breasts: *mammary glands* (= parts of the breast that produce milk)

mammogram /ˈmæməɡræm/ ***noun*** [C] (HEALTH) an examination of a breast using X-RAYS to check for cancer

mammoth /ˈmæməθ/ ***adj.*** very big

man[1] ⊶ /mæn/ ***noun*** (*pl.* **men** /men/) **1** [C] an adult male person **2** [C] a person of either sex, male or female: *All men are equal.* ◇ *No man could survive long in such conditions.* **3** [U] the human race; humans: *Early man lived by hunting.* ◇ *the damage man has caused to the environment* **4** [C] (often in compounds) a man who comes from a particular place; a man who has a particular job or interest: *a Frenchman* ◇ *a businessman* ◇ *sportsmen and women*

IDM **the man in the street** (*BrE*) an ordinary man or woman

the odd man/one out → ODD

man[2] /mæn/ ***verb*** [T] (**manning**; **manned**) to operate sth or to provide people to operate sth: *The telephones are manned 24 hours a day.*

manage ⊶ /ˈmænɪdʒ/ ***verb*** **1** [I,T] (often with *can* or *could*) to succeed in doing or dealing with sth difficult; to be able to do sth: *However did you manage to find us here?* ◇ *I can't manage this suitcase. It's too heavy.* ◇ *Paula can't manage next Tuesday* (= she can't come then) *so we'll meet another day.* **2** [T] to be in charge or control of sth: *She manages a small advertising business.* ◇ *You need to manage your time more efficiently.* **3** [I] ~ (**without/with sb/sth**); ~ (**on sth**) to deal with a difficult situation; to continue in spite of difficulties: *My grandmother couldn't manage without her neighbours.* ◇ *Can you manage with just one assistant?* ◇ *It's hard for a family to manage on just one income.*

manageable /ˈmænɪdʒəbl/ ***adj.*** not too big or too difficult to deal with

management ⊶ /ˈmænɪdʒmənt/ ***noun*** **1** [U] the control or organization of sth: *Good classroom management is vital with large groups of children.* **2** [C,U] (BUSINESS) the people who control a business or company: *The hotel is now* ***under new management****.*

manager ⊶ /ˈmænɪdʒə(r)/ ***noun*** [C] **1** (BUSINESS) a man or woman who controls an organization or part of an organization: *a bank manager* **2** (ARTS AND MEDIA) a person who looks after the business affairs of a singer, actor, etc. **3** (SPORT) a person who is in charge of a sports team: *the England manager*

manageress /ˌmænɪdʒəˈres/ ***noun*** [C] (BUSINESS) the woman who is in charge of a shop or restaurant

managerial /ˌmænəˈdʒɪəriəl/ ***adj.*** (BUSINESS) connected with the work of a manager: *Do you have any managerial experience?*

ˌmanaging diˈrector ***noun*** [C] (BUSINESS) a person who controls a business or company

mandarin /ˈmændərɪn/ ***noun*** **1** [C] (HISTORY) a government official of high rank in China in the past **2** **Mandarin** [U] (LANGUAGE) the standard form of Chinese, which is the official language of China **3** (*also* **ˌmandarin ˈorange**) [C] a type of small orange with loose skin that comes off easily

mandate /ˈmændeɪt/ ***noun*** [C, usually sing.] (POLITICS) the power that is officially given to a group of people to do sth, especially after they have won an election: *The union leaders had a clear mandate from their members to call a strike.*

mandatory /ˈmændətəri; mænˈdeɪtəri/ ***adj.*** (*formal*) that you must do, have, obey, etc.: *The crime carries a mandatory life sentence.* SYN **obligatory** OPP **optional**

mandible /ˈmændɪbl/ ***noun*** [C] **1** (ANATOMY) the lower of the two bones in your face that contain your teeth SYN **jawbone** ➲ picture on **page 80** **2** (BIOLOGY) either of the two parts that are at the front and on either side of an insect's mouth, used especially for biting and crushing food ➲ picture on **page 29**

mane /meɪn/ ***noun*** [C] the long hair on the neck of a horse or male LION ➲ picture at **lion**

maneuver (*AmE*) = MANOEUVRE

manganese /ˈmæŋɡəniːz/ ***noun*** [U] (*symbol* **Mn**) (CHEMISTRY) a type of hard grey metal ❶ For more information on the periodic table of elements, look at pages R34-5.

mangle /ˈmæŋɡl/ ***verb*** [T] (usually passive) to damage sth so badly that it is difficult to see what it looked like originally: *The motorway was covered with the mangled wreckage of cars.*

mango /ˈmæŋɡəʊ/ ***noun*** [C] (*pl.* **mangoes**) a tropical fruit that has a yellow and red skin and is yellow inside

mangrove /ˈmæŋɡrəʊv/ ***noun*** [C] a tropical tree that grows in wet ground or at the edge of rivers and has some roots that are above ground

manhole /ˈmænhəʊl/ ***noun*** [C] a hole in the street with a lid over it through which sb can go to look at the pipes, wires, etc. that are underground

manhood /ˈmænhʊd/ ***noun*** [U] the state of being a man rather than a boy

mania /ˈmeɪniə/ ***noun*** **1** [C] (*informal*) a great enthusiasm for sth: *World Cup mania is sweeping the country.* **2** [U] (HEALTH) a serious mental illness that may cause sb to be very excited or violent

maniac /ˈmeɪniæk/ ***noun*** [C] **1** a person who behaves in a wild and stupid way: *to drive like a maniac* **2** a person who has a stronger love of sth than is normal: *a football/sex maniac*

manic /ˈmænɪk/ ***adj.*** **1** full of nervous energy or excited activity: *His behaviour became more manic as he began to feel stressed.* **2** (HEALTH) connected with MANIA(2)

ˌmanic deˈpression = BIPOLAR DISORDER

ˌmanic deˈpressive = BIPOLAR

manicure /ˈmænɪkjʊə(r)/ ***noun*** [C,U] treatment to make your hands and FINGERNAILS look attractive

manifest /ˈmænɪfest/ ***verb*** [I,T] (*formal*) **manifest (sth/itself) (in/as sth)** to show sth or to be shown clearly: *Mental illness can manifest itself in many forms.* ▶ **manifest** ***adj.***: *manifest failure/anger* ▶ **manifestly** ***adv.***

manifestation /ˌmænɪfeˈsteɪʃn/ ***noun*** [C,U] (*formal*) a sign that sth is happening

manifesto /ˌmænɪˈfestəʊ/ ***noun*** [C] (*pl.* **manifestos**) (POLITICS) a written statement by a political party that explains what it hopes to do if it becomes the government in the future

manifold[1] /ˈmænɪfəʊld/ ***adj.*** (*formal*) many; of many different types

manifold[2] /ˈmænɪfəʊld/ ***noun*** [C] a pipe or an ENCLOSED space with several openings for taking gases in and out of a car engine

manipulate AW /məˈnɪpjuleɪt/ ***verb*** [T] **1** to influence sb so that they do or think what you want: *Clever politicians know how to manipulate public opinion.* **2** to use, move or control sth with skill: *The doctor manipulated the bone back into place.* ▶ **manipulation** /məˌnɪpjuˈleɪʃn/ ***noun*** [C,U]

manipulative AW /məˈnɪpjələtɪv/ ***adj.*** **1** skilful at influencing sb or forcing sb to do what you want, often in an unfair way **2** (*formal*) connected with the ability to move things with your hands skilfully: *manipulative skills such as typing and knitting*

mankind /mænˈkaɪnd/ ***noun*** [U] all the people in the world: *A nuclear war would be a threat to all mankind.*

manly /ˈmænli/ ***adj.*** typical of or suitable for a man: *a deep manly voice* ▶ **manliness** ***noun*** [U]

ˌman-ˈmade ***adj.*** made by people, not formed in a natural way; artificial: *man-made fabrics such as nylon and polyester*

manner 🔑 /ˈmænə(r)/ ***noun*** **1** [sing.] the way that you do sth or that sth happens: *Stop arguing! Let's try to act* ***in a*** *civilized* ***manner***. **2** [sing.] the way that sb behaves towards other people: *to have an aggressive/a relaxed/a professional manner* **3 manners** [pl.] a way of behaving that is considered acceptable in your country or culture: *In some countries it is bad manners to show the soles of your feet.* ◇ *Their children have no manners.*
IDM **all manner of...** every kind of...: *You meet all manner of people in my job.*

mannerism /ˈmænərɪzəm/ ***noun*** **1** [C] sb's particular way of speaking or a particular movement they often do **2 Mannerism** [U] (ART) a style in 16th century Italian art that did not show things in a natural way but made them look strange or out of their usual shape

manoeuvre[1] (*AmE* **maneuver**) /məˈnuːvə(r)/ ***noun*** **1** [C] a movement that needs care or skill: *Parking the car in such a small space would be a tricky manoeuvre.* **2** [C,U] something clever that you do in order to win sth, trick sb, etc.: *political manoeuvre(s)* **3 manoeuvres** [pl.] a way of training soldiers when large numbers of them practise fighting in battles

manoeuvre[2] (*AmE* **maneuver**) /məˈnuːvə(r)/ ***verb*** [I,T] to move (sth) to a different position using skill: *The driver was manoeuvring his lorry into a narrow gateway.*

manor /ˈmænə(r)/ (*also* **ˈmanor house**) ***noun*** [C] a large house in the country that has land around it

manpower /ˈmænpaʊə(r)/ ***noun*** [U] the people that you need to do a particular job: *There is a shortage of skilled manpower in the computer industry.*

mansion /ˈmænʃn/ ***noun*** [C] a very large house

manslaughter /ˈmænslɔːtə(r)/ ***noun*** [U] (LAW) the crime of killing sb without intending to do so ➲ look at **murder**

mantelpiece /ˈmæntlpiːs/ ***noun*** [C] a narrow shelf above the space in a room where a fire goes

mantle /ˈmæntl/ ***noun*** [sing.] (GEOLOGY) the part of the earth between the surface (**crust**) and the centre (**core**) ➲ picture at **rock**

manual[1] AW /ˈmænjuəl/ ***adj.*** using your hands; operated by hand: *Office work can sometimes be more tiring than* ***manual work***. ◇ *a skilled* ***manual worker*** ◇ *Does your car have a manual or an automatic gearbox?* ▶ **manually** ***adv.***

manual[2] AW /ˈmænjuəl/ ***noun*** [C] a book that explains how to do or operate sth: *a training manual* ◇ *a car manual*

manufacture 🔑 /ˌmænjuˈfæktʃə(r)/ ***verb*** [T] to make sth in large quantities using machines: *a local factory that manufactures furniture* ◇ *manufacturing industries* SYN **produce** ▶ **manufacture** ***noun*** [U]: *The manufacture of chemical weapons should be illegal.*

manufacturer 🔑 /ˌmænjuˈfæktʃərə(r)/ ***noun*** [C] a person or company that makes sth: *a car manufacturer*

manure /məˈnjʊə(r)/ ***noun*** [U] (AGRICULTURE) the waste matter from animals that is put on the ground in order to make plants grow better ➲ look at **fertilizer**

manuscript /ˈmænjuskrɪpt/ ***noun*** [C] (LITERATURE) **1** a copy of a book, piece of music, etc. before it has been printed **2** a very old book or document that was written by hand

many 🔑 /ˈmeni/ ***det.***, ***pronoun*** (used with plural nouns or verbs) **1** a large number of people or things: *Have you made many friends at school yet?* ◇ *Not many of my friends smoke.* ◇ *Many of the mistakes were just careless.* ◇ *There are* ***too many*** *mistakes in this essay.* **2** used to ask about the number of people or things, or to refer to a known number: ***How many*** *children have you got?* ◇ *How* *many came to the meeting?* ◇ *I don't work* ***as many*** *hours* ***as*** *you.* ◇ *There are* ***half/twice as many*** *boys as girls in the class.* **3** (used to form compound adjectives) having a lot of the thing mentioned: *a many-sided shape* **4 many a** (*formal*) (used with a singular noun and verb) a large number of: *I've heard him say that many a time.*

IDM **a good/great many** very many

Maori /'maʊri/ ***noun*** [C] (*pl.* **Maori** or **Maoris**) a member of the race of people who were the original INHABITANTS of New Zealand ▶ **Maori** ***adj.***

map ⊶ /mæp/ ***noun*** [C] a drawing or plan of (part of) the surface of the earth that shows countries, rivers, mountains, roads, etc.: *a map of the world* ◇ *a road/street map* ◇ *I can't find Cambridge* ***on the map***. ◇ *to read a map* ▶ **map** ***verb*** [T] (**mapping**; **mapped**): *The region is so remote it has not yet been mapped.*

maple /'meɪpl/ ***noun*** [C] a tree that has leaves with five points

ˌ**maple 'syrup** ***noun*** [U] a sweet, sticky sauce made with liquid obtained from some types of MAPLE tree, often eaten with PANCAKES

mapping /'mæpɪŋ/ ***noun*** [C] (**MATHEMATICS**) an operation that associates each element of the DOMAIN (=a given set) with one or more elements of the RANGE (=a second set)

Mar. ***abbr.*** March: *17 Mar. 1956*

marathon /'mærəθən/ ***noun*** [C] **1** (**SPORT**) a LONG-DISTANCE running race, in which people run about 42 kilometres or 26 miles **2** an activity that lasts much longer than expected: *The interview was a real marathon.*

marauding /mə'rɔːdɪŋ/ ***adj.*** (used about people or animals) going around a place in search of things to steal or people to attack: *marauding wolves*

marble /'mɑːbl/ ***noun*** **1** [U] (**GEOLOGY**) a hard attractive stone that is used to make statues and parts of buildings: *a marble statue* **2** [C] a small ball of coloured glass that children play with **3 marbles** [U] the children's game that you play by rolling **marbles** along the ground trying to hit other **marbles**

March /mɑːtʃ/ ***noun*** [U, C] (*abbr.* **Mar.**) the third month of the year, coming after February

march[1] ⊶ /mɑːtʃ/ ***verb*** **1** [I] to walk with regular steps (like a soldier): *The President saluted as the troops marched past.* **2** [I] to walk in a determined way: *She marched up to the manager and demanded an apology.* **3** [T] to make sb walk or march somewhere: *The prisoner was marched away.* **4** [I] (**SOCIAL STUDIES**) to walk in a large group to protest about sth: *The demonstrators marched through the centre of town.*

march[2] ⊶ /mɑːtʃ/ ***noun*** [C] **1** (**SOCIAL STUDIES**) an organized walk by a large group of people who are protesting about sth: *a peace march* ➲ look at **demonstration** **2** a journey made by marching: *The soldiers were tired after their long march.*

mare /meə(r)/ ***noun*** [C] a female horse ➲ note at **horse**

margarine /ˌmɑːdʒə'riːn/ ***noun*** [U] a food that is similar to butter, made of animal or vegetable fats

margin AW /'mɑːdʒɪn/ ***noun*** [C] **1** the empty space at the side of a page in a book, etc. **2** [usually sing.] the amount of space, time, votes, etc. by which you win sth: *He won by a wide/narrow/comfortable margin.* **3** (*also* '**profit margin**) (**BUSINESS**) the amount of profit that a company makes on sth: *a gross margin of 45%* **4** the area around the edge of sth: *the margins of the Pacific Ocean* **5** [usually sing.] an amount of space, time, etc. that is more than you need: *It is a complex operation with little* ***margin for error***.

marginal AW /'mɑːdʒɪnl/ ***adj.*** small in size or importance: *The differences are marginal.* ▶ **marginally** AW ***adv.***: *In most cases costs will increase only marginally.*

marijuana /ˌmærə'wɑːnə/ ***noun*** [U] a drug that is smoked and is illegal in many countries

marina /mə'riːnə/ ***noun*** [C] a small area of water (**a harbour**) designed for pleasure boats

marinade /ˌmærɪ'neɪd/ ***noun*** [C,U] a mixture of oil, spices, etc. which you leave meat or fish in for a long time before it is cooked in order to make it softer or give it a particular flavour

marinate /'mærɪneɪt/ (also **marinade**) ***verb*** [I,T] if you **marinate** food or it **marinates**, you leave it in a MARINADE for a long time before it is cooked in order to make it softer or give it a particular flavour

marine[1] /mə'riːn/ ***adj.*** **1** connected with the sea: *the study of marine life* **2** connected with ships or sailing: *marine insurance*

marine[2] /mə'riːn/ ***noun*** [C] a soldier who has been trained to fight on land or at sea

marital /'mærɪtl/ ***adj.*** (only *before* a noun) connected with marriage: *marital problems*

ˌ**marital 'status** ***noun*** [U] (*written*) (used on official documents) if you are married, single, divorced, etc.

maritime /'mærɪtaɪm/ ***adj.*** connected with the sea or ships

mark[1] ⊶ /mɑːk/ ***noun*** [C] **1** a spot or line that spoils the appearance of sth: *There's a dirty mark on the front of your shirt.* ◇ *If you put a hot cup down on the table it will* ***leave a mark***. ➲ look at **birthmark** **2** something that shows who or what sb/sth is, especially by making them or it different from others: *My horse is the one with the white mark on its face.* **3** (**LANGUAGE**) a written or printed symbol that is a sign of sth: *a question/punctuation/exclamation mark* **4** a sign of a quality or feeling: *They stood in silence for two minutes as* ***a mark of respect***. **5** (**EDUCATION**) a number or letter you get for school work that tells you how good your work was: *She got very good marks in the exam.* ◇ *The* ***pass mark*** *is 60 out of 100.* ◇ *to get* ***full marks*** (=everything correct) **6** the level or point that sth/sb has reached: *The race is almost at the half-way mark.* **7** an effect that people notice and will remember: *The time he spent in prison* ***left*** *its* ***mark on*** *him.* ◇ *He was only eighteen when he first* ***made*** *his* ***mark*** *in politics.* **8** a particular model or type of sth: *the new SL 53 Mark III* **9** (*formal*) a person or an object towards which sth is directed; a target: *the arrow hit/missed its mark* ◇ *His judgement of the situation is* ***wide of the mark*** (=wrong).

IDM **on your marks, get set, go!** (**SPORT**) used at the start of a sports race

quick, slow, etc. off the mark quick, slow, etc. in reacting to a situation

mark[2] ⊶ /mɑːk/ ***verb*** [T] **1** to put a sign on sth: *We marked the price on all items in the sale.* ◇ *I'll mark all the boxes I want you to move.* **2** to spoil the appearance of sth by making a mark on it: *The white walls were dirty and marked.* **3** to show where sth is or where sth happened: *The route is marked in red.* ◇ *Flowers mark the spot where he died.* **4** to celebrate or officially remember an important event: *The ceremony marked the fiftieth anniversary of the* *opening of the school.* **5** to be a sign that sth new is going to happen: *This decision marks a change in government policy.* **6** (EDUCATION) to look at sb's school, etc. work, show where there are mistakes and give it a number or letter to show how good it is: *Why did you mark that answer wrong?* ◇ *He has 100 exam papers to mark.* **7** (SPORT) to stay close to a player of the opposite team so that they cannot play easily

PHR V **mark sb/sth down as/for sth** to decide that sb/sth is of a particular type or suitable for a particular use: *From the first day of school, the teachers marked Fred down as a troublemaker.*

mark sth out to draw lines to show the position of sth: *Spaces for each car were marked out in the car park.*

mark sth up/down (BUSINESS) to increase/ decrease the price of sth that you are selling: *All goods have been marked down by 15%.*

marked /mɑːkt/ ***adj.*** clear; noticeable: *There has been a marked increase in vandalism in recent years.* ▶ **markedly** /ˈmɑːkɪdli/ ***adv.***: *This year's sales have risen markedly.*

marker /ˈmɑːkə(r)/ ***noun*** [C] something that shows the position of sth: *I've highlighted the important sentences with a marker pen.*

market[1] ⊶ /ˈmɑːkɪt/ ***noun*** (BUSINESS) **1** [C] a place where people go to buy and sell things: *a market stall/trader/town* ◇ *a cattle/fish/meat market* ➲ look at **flea market**, **hypermarket**, **supermarket** **2** [C] business or commercial activity; the amount of buying or selling of a particular type of goods: *The company currently has a 10% share of the market.* ◇ *the property/job market* **3** [C,U] a country, an area or a group of people that buys sth; the number of people who buy sth: *The company is hoping to expand into the European market.* ◇ *There's no market for very large cars when petrol is so expensive.* ➲ look at **black market**, **stock market**

IDM **on the market** available to buy: *This is one of the best cameras on the market.*

market[2] /ˈmɑːkɪt/ ***verb*** [T] (BUSINESS) to sell sth with the help of advertising

marketable /ˈmɑːkɪtəbl/ ***adj.*** (BUSINESS) that can be sold easily because people want it

ˈmarket day ***noun*** [C,U] the day of the week when a town usually has a market: *All the farmers come to town* ***on market day****.*

ˌmarket ˈgarden ***noun*** [C] (AGRICULTURE) a type of farm where vegetables and fruit are grown for sale

marketing ⊶ /ˈmɑːkɪtɪŋ/ ***noun*** [U] (BUSINESS) the activity of showing and advertising a company's products in the best possible way: *Effective marketing will lead to increased sales.* ◇ *the marketing department*

ˈmarketing mix ***noun*** [C] (BUSINESS) the combination of things that a company decides to try in order to persuade people to buy a product

ˌmarket ˈleader ***noun*** [C] (BUSINESS) **1** the company that sells the largest quantity of a particular kind of product **2** a product that is the most successful of its kind

marketplace /ˈmɑːkɪtpleɪs/ ***noun*** **1 the marketplace** [sing.] (BUSINESS) the activity of competing with other companies to buy and sell goods, services, etc. **2** [C] the place in a town where a market is held

ˌmarket ˈprice ***noun*** [C] (BUSINESS) the price that people in general will pay for sth at a particular time

ˌmarket reˈsearch ***noun*** [U] (BUSINESS) the study of what people want to buy and why: *to carry out/do market research*

ˌmarket ˌsegmenˈtation ***noun*** [U,C] (BUSINESS) the act of dividing possible customers into groups according to their age, sex, class, INCOME (= how much money they earn), etc.; one of these parts

ˌmarket ˈshare ***noun*** [U, sing.] (BUSINESS) the amount that a company sells of its products or services compared with other companies selling the same things: *They claim to have a 40% worldwide market share.*

ˈmarket town ***noun*** [C] a town that has a regular market, or that had one in the past

marking /ˈmɑːkɪŋ/ ***noun*** [C, usually pl.] shapes, lines and patterns of colour on an animal or a bird, or painted on a road, vehicle, etc.

marksman /ˈmɑːksmən/ ***noun*** [C] (*pl.* **-men** /-mən/) a person who can shoot very well with a gun

markup /ˈmɑːkʌp/ ***noun*** [C, usually sing.] (BUSINESS) the difference between the cost of producing sth and the price it is sold at

marmalade /ˈmɑːməleɪd/ ***noun*** [U] a type of jam that is made from oranges or lemons

marmoset /ˈmɑːməzet/ ***noun*** [C] a small MONKEY with a long thick tail, that lives in Central and S America

maroon /məˈruːn/ ***adj.***, ***noun*** [U] (of) a dark brownish-red colour

marooned /məˈruːnd/ ***adj.*** in a place that you cannot leave: *The sailors were marooned on a desert island.*

marquee /mɑːˈkiː/ ***noun*** [C] a very large tent that is used for parties, shows, etc.

marriage ⊶ /ˈmærɪdʒ/ ***noun*** **1** [C,U] the state of being husband and wife: *They are getting divorced after five years of marriage.* ◇ *a happy marriage* **2** [C] a wedding ceremony: *The marriage took place at a registry office in Birmingham.* ➲ verb **get married (to sb)** or **marry (sb)**

married ⊶ /ˈmærid/ ***adj.*** **1** ~ (to sb) having a husband or wife: *a married man/woman/couple* ◇ *Sasha's married to Mark.* ◇ *They're planning to* ***get married*** *in the summer.* OPP **unmarried**, **single** **2** (only *before* a noun) connected with marriage: *How do you like married life?*

marrow /ˈmærəʊ/ ***noun*** **1** [C,U] a large vegetable with green skin that is white inside **2** = BONE MARROW

marry ⊶ /ˈmæri/ ***verb*** (*pres. part.* **marrying**; *3rd person sing. pres.* **marries**; *pt, pp* **married**) **1** [I,T] to take sb as your husband or wife: *They married when they were very young.* ◇ *When did Rick ask you to marry him?* **2** [T] to join two people together as husband and wife: *We asked the local vicar to marry us.* ➲ noun **marriage**

> WORD FAMILY
> **marry** *verb*
> **marriage** *noun*
> **married** *adj.*
> (≠ **unmarried**)

Mars /mɑːz/ ***noun*** [sing.] (ASTRONOMY) the red planet, that is fourth in order from the sun ➲ Look at **Martian**. ➲ picture at **solar system**

marsh /mɑːʃ/ ***noun*** [C,U] (GEOGRAPHY) an area of soft wet land ▶ **marshy** ***adj.***

marshal /ˈmɑːʃl/ ***noun*** [C] **1** a person who helps to organize or control a large public event: *Marshals are directing traffic in the car park.* **2** (*AmE*) an officer of a high level in the police or fire department or in a court of law

marsupial /mɑːˈsuːpiəl/ ***noun*** [C] (BIOLOGY) any Australian animal that carries its baby in a pocket of skin (**pouch**) on the mother's stomach: *Kangaroos are marsupials.* ▶ **marsupial** ***adj.*** ➲ picture on **page 29**

martial /ˈmɑːʃl/ ***adj.*** (*formal*) connected with fighting or war

ˌ**martial ˈart** ***noun*** [C, usually pl.] (SPORT) any of the fighting sports that include KARATE and JUDO, in which you use your hands and feet as weapons

ˌ**martial ˈlaw** ***noun*** [U] (POLITICS) a situation in which the army of a country instead of the police controls an area during a time of trouble: *The city remains **under martial law**.*

Martian /ˈmɑːʃn/ ***noun*** [C] (in stories) a creature that comes from the planet Mars

martyr /ˈmɑːtə(r)/ ***noun*** [C] **1** a person who is killed because of what they believe **2** a person who tries to make people feel sorry for them: *Don't be such a martyr! You don't have to do all the housework.* ▶ **martyrdom** /ˈmɑːtədəm/ ***noun*** [U]

marvel /ˈmɑːvl/ ***noun*** [C] a person or thing that is wonderful or that surprises you: *the marvels of modern technology* ▶ **marvel** ***verb*** [I] (**marvelling**; **marvelled**: *AmE* **marveling**; **marveled**) (*formal*) ~ **(at sth)**: *We marvelled at how much they had managed to do.*

marvellous (*AmE* **marvelous**) /ˈmɑːvələs/ ***adj.*** very good; wonderful: *a marvellous opportunity* ▶ **marvellously** (*AmE* **marvelously**) ***adv.***

Marxism /ˈmɑːksɪzəm/ ***noun*** [U] (POLITICS) the political and economic thought of Karl Marx ➲ look at **communism**, **socialism**, **capitalism** ▶ **Marxist** ***noun*** [C], ***adj.***: *Marxist ideology*

marzipan /ˈmɑːzɪpæn/ ***noun*** [U] a food that is made of sugar, egg and ALMONDS (= a type of nut). Marzipan is used to make sweets or to put on cakes.

masc ***abbr.*** masculine

mascara /mæˈskɑːrə/ ***noun*** [U] a substance that you put on your EYELASHES (= the hairs around your eyes) to make them look dark and attractive

mascot /ˈmæskət; -skɒt/ ***noun*** [C] a person, animal or thing that is thought to bring good luck

masculine /ˈmæskjəlɪn/ ***adj.*** **1** typical of or looking like a man; connected with men: *a deep, masculine voice* ◇ *Her short hair makes her look quite masculine.* ➲ look at **feminine 2** (*abbr.* **masc**) (LANGUAGE) belonging to a class of words that refer to male people or animals and often have a special form: *'He' is a masculine pronoun.* **3** (*abbr.* **masc**) (LANGUAGE) (in the grammar of some languages) belonging to a certain class of nouns, pronouns or adjectives: *The French word for 'sun' is masculine.* ➲ look at **feminine**, **neuter** ▶ **masculinity** /ˌmæskjuˈlɪnəti/ ***noun*** [U]

mash /mæʃ/ ***verb*** [T] to mix or crush sth until it is soft: *mashed potatoes*

ˌ**mashed poˈtato** (*especially BrE* ˌ**mashed poˈtatoes**; **mash**) ***noun*** [U] potatoes that have been boiled and crushed into a soft mass, often with butter and milk

mask¹ /mɑːsk/ ***noun*** [C] something that you wear that covers your face or part of your face. People wear **masks** in order to hide or protect their faces or to make themselves look different. ➲ look at **gas mask**, **goggles**

mask² /mɑːsk/ ***verb*** [T] **1** to cover or hide your face with a **mask**: *a masked gunman* **2** to hide a feeling, smell, fact, etc.: *He masked his anger with a smile.*

masochism /ˈmæsəkɪzəm/ ***noun*** [U] the enjoyment of pain, or of what most people would find unpleasant: *He swims in the sea even in winter – that's sheer masochism!* ➲ look at **sadism** ▶ **masochist** /-kɪst/ ***noun*** [C] ▶ **masochistic** /ˌmæsəˈkɪstɪk/ ***adj.***

mason /ˈmeɪsn/ ***noun*** [C] **1** a person who makes things from stone **2** = FREEMASON

masonry /ˈmeɪsənri/ ***noun*** [U] (ARCHITECTURE) the parts of a building that are made of stone

masquerade /ˌmæskəˈreɪd; ˌmɑːsk-/ ***noun*** [C] a way of behaving that hides the truth or sb's true feelings ▶ **masquerade** ***verb*** [I] ~ **as sth**: *Two people, masquerading as doctors, knocked at the door and asked to see the child.*

mass¹ 🔑 /mæs/ ***noun*** **1** [C] a ~ (**of sth**) a large amount or number of sth: *a dense mass of smoke* ◇ (*informal*) *There were masses of people at the market today.* **2 the masses** [pl.] (SOCIAL STUDIES) ordinary people when considered as a political group **3** [U] (PHYSICS) the quantity of material that sth contains **4 Mass** [C,U] (RELIGION) the ceremony in some Christian churches when people eat bread and drink wine in order to remember the last meal that Christ had before he died: *to go to Mass*

mass² 🔑 /mæs/ ***adj.*** (only *before* a noun) involving a large number of people or things: *a mass murderer*

mass³ /mæs/ ***verb*** [I,T] to come together or bring people or things together in large numbers: *The students massed in the square.*

massacre /ˈmæsəkə(r)/ ***noun*** [C] the killing of a large number of people or animals ▶ **massacre** ***verb*** [T] ➲ note at **kill**

massage /ˈmæsɑːʒ/ ***noun*** [C,U] the act of rubbing and pressing sb's body in order to reduce pain or to help them relax: *to give sb a massage* ▶ **massage** ***verb*** [T]

massive 🔑 /ˈmæsɪv/ ***adj.*** very big: *a massive increase in prices* SYN **huge** ▶ **massively** ***adv.***

ˌ**mass-ˈmarket** ***adj.*** (BUSINESS) produced for very large numbers of people

ˌ**mass ˈmedia** ***noun*** [pl.] (ARTS AND MEDIA) newspapers, television and radio that reach a large number of people

ˈ**mass number** ***noun*** [C] (CHEMISTRY, PHYSICS) the total number of PROTONS and NEUTRONS in an atom

ˌ**mass-proˈduce** ***verb*** [T] (BUSINESS) to make large numbers of similar things by machine in a factory: *mass-produced goods* ▶ **mass production** ***noun*** [U]

mast /mɑːst/ ***noun*** [C] **1** a tall wooden or metal pole for a flag, a ship's sails, etc. **2** a tall pole that is used for sending out radio or television signals

master¹ 🔑 /ˈmɑːstə(r)/ ***noun*** [C] **1** (*old-fashioned*) a man who has people working for him, often as servants in his home: *They lived in fear of their master.* **2** a person who has great skill at doing sth: *a master builder* **3** (*BrE, old-fashioned*) (EDUCATION) a male teacher (usually in a private school): *the chemistry master* **4 Master** (EDUCATION) a person who has a MASTER'S degree: *a Master of Arts/Science* ➲ look at **MA 5** (ART) a famous painter who lived in the past: *an exhibition of work by the French master, Monet* ➲ look at **old master 6** a version of a record, tape, CD, film, etc. from which copies are made: *the master copy*

master² /ˈmɑːstə(r)/ ***verb*** [T] **1** to learn how to do sth well: *It takes a long time to master a foreign language.* **2** to control sth: *to master a situation*

mastermind /ˈmɑːstəmaɪnd/ ***noun*** [C] a very clever person who has planned or organized sth: *The mastermind behind the robbery was never caught.* ▶ **mastermind** ***verb*** [T]: *The police failed to catch the man who masterminded the robbery.*

ˌmaster of ˈceremonies ***noun*** [C] (*abbr.* **MC**) a person who introduces guests or entertainers at a formal occasion

masterpiece /ˈmɑːstəpiːs/ ***noun*** [C] a work of art, music, literature, etc. that is of the highest quality

Master's /ˈmɑːstəz/ (*also* **ˈMaster's degree**) ***noun*** [C] (EDUCATION) a second or higher university degree. You usually get a master's degree by studying for one or two years after your first degree: *He has a Master's in Business Administration.* ➲ look at **Bachelor's degree**

mastery /ˈmɑːstəri/ ***noun*** [U] **1 ~ (of sth)** great skill at doing sth: *His mastery of the violin was quite exceptional for a child.* **2 ~ (of/over sb/sth)** control over sb/sth: *The battle was fought for mastery of the seas.*

masthead /ˈmɑːsthed/ ***noun*** [C] **1** the top of a MAST on a ship **2** (ARTS AND MEDIA) the name of a newspaper at the top of the front page

masturbate /ˈmæstəbeɪt/ ***verb*** [I,T] to make yourself or sb else feel sexually excited by touching and rubbing the sex organs ▶ **masturbation** /ˌmæstəˈbeɪʃn/ ***noun*** [U]

mat /mæt/ ***noun*** [C] **1** a piece of carpet or other thick material that you put on the floor: *a doormat* ➲ look at **rug 2** a small piece of material that you put under sth on a table: *a table mat* ◇ *a beer mat* ◇ *a mouse mat* ➲ picture at **computer**

match¹ 🔑 /mætʃ/ ***noun*** **1** [C] a small stick of wood, cardboard, etc. that you use for starting a fire, lighting a cigarette, etc.: *to light/strike a match* ◇ *a box of matches* **2** [C] (SPORT) an organized game or sports event: *a tennis/football match* **3** [sing.] **a ~ for sb; sb's ~** a person or thing that is as good as or better than sb/sth else: *Charo is no match for her mother when it comes to cooking* (=she doesn't cook as well as her mother). ◇ *I think you've **met** your **match** in Dave – you won't beat him.* **4** [sing.] a person or thing that combines well with sb/sth else: *Richard and Vanessa are a **perfect match** for each other.*

match² 🔑 /mætʃ/ ***verb*** **1** [I,T] to have the same colour or pattern as sth else; to look good with sth else: *That shirt doesn't match your jacket.* ◇ *Your shirt and jacket don't match.* **2** [T] to find sb/sth that is like or suitable for sb/sth else: *The agency tries to match single people with suitable partners.* **3** [T] to be as good as or better than sb/sth else: *The two teams are very evenly matched.* ◇ *Taiwan produces the goods at a price that Europe cannot match.*

PHR V **match up** to be the same: *The statements of the two witnesses don't match up.*

match sth up (with sth) to fit or put sth together (with sth else): *What you have to do is match up each star with his or her pet.*

match up to sb/sth to be as good as sb/sth: *The film didn't match up to my expectations*

matchbox /ˈmætʃbɒks/ ***noun*** [C] a small box for matches

matchstick /ˈmætʃstɪk/ ***noun*** [C] the thin wooden part of a match

mate¹ 🔑 /meɪt/ ***noun*** [C] **1** (*informal*) a friend or sb you live, work or do an activity with: *He's an old mate of mine.* ◇ *a flatmate/classmate/team-mate/playmate* **2** (*BrE, slang*) used when speaking to a man: *Can you give me a hand, mate?* **3** (BIOLOGY) one of a male and female pair of animals, birds, etc.: *The female sits on the eggs while her mate hunts for food.* **4** an officer on a ship

mate² 🔑 /meɪt/ ***verb*** **1** [I] (BIOLOGY) (used about animals and birds) to have sex and produce young: *Pandas rarely mate in zoos.* **2** [T] to bring two animals together so that they can mate SYN **breed**

material¹ 🔑 /məˈtɪəriəl/ ***noun*** **1** [C,U] a substance that can be used for making or doing sth: *raw materials* ◇ *writing/teaching/building materials* ◇ *This new material is strong but it is also very light.* **2** [C,U] cloth (for making clothes, etc.): *Is there enough material for a dress?* **3** [U] (ARTS AND MEDIA) facts or information that you collect before you write a book, article, etc.

material² 🔑 /məˈtɪəriəl/ ***adj.*** **1** connected with real or physical things rather than the spirit or emotions: *We should not value material comforts too highly.* ➲ look at **spiritual 2** important and needing to be considered: *material evidence* ▶ **materially** ***adv.***

materialism /məˈtɪəriəlɪzəm/ ***noun*** [U] the belief that money and possessions are the most important things in life ▶ **materialist** /-lɪst/ ***noun*** [C] ▶ **materialistic** /məˌtɪəriəˈlɪstɪk/ ***adj.***

materialize (also -ise) /məˈtɪəriəlaɪz/ ***verb*** [I] to become real; to happen: *The pay rise that they had promised never materialized.*

maternal /məˈtɜːnl/ ***adj.*** **1** behaving as a mother would behave; connected with being a mother: *maternal love/instincts* **2** (only *before* a noun) related through your mother's side of the family: *your maternal grandfather* ➲ look at **paternal**

maternity /məˈtɜːnəti/ ***adj.*** connected with women who are going to have or have just had a baby: *maternity clothes* ◇ *the hospital's maternity ward* ➲ look at **paternity**

maˈternity leave ***noun*** [U] a period of time when a woman temporarily leaves her job to have a baby

mathematician /ˌmæθəməˈtɪʃn/ ***noun*** [C] (MATHEMATICS) a person who studies or is an expert in mathematics

mathematics 🔑 /ˌmæθəˈmætɪks/ ***noun*** [U] (MATHEMATICS) the science or study of numbers, quantities or shapes ➲ look at **arithmetic**, **algebra**, **geometry** ▶ **mathematical** /ˌmæθəˈmætɪkl/ ***adj.***: *mathematical calculations* ▶ **mathematically** /-kli/ ***adv.***

matinée /ˈmætɪneɪ/ ***noun*** [C] (ARTS AND MEDIA) an afternoon performance of a play, film, etc.

matriarch /ˈmeɪtriɑːk/ ***noun*** [C] (SOCIAL STUDIES) a woman who is the head of a family or social group ➲ look at **patriarch**

matriarchal /ˌmeɪtriˈɑːkl/ ***adj.*** (SOCIAL STUDIES) (used about a society or system) controlled by women rather than men; passing power, property, etc. from mother to daughter rather than from father to son ➲ look at **patriarchal**

matriarchy /ˈmeɪtriɑːki/ ***noun*** [C,U] (*pl.* **matriarchies**) (SOCIAL STUDIES) a social system that gives power and control to women rather than men ➲ look at **patriarchy**

matricide /ˈmætrɪsaɪd/ ***noun*** [U] (*formal*) (LAW) the crime of killing your mother ➲ look at **patricide**

matrimony /ˈmætrɪməni/ ***noun*** [U] (*formal*) the state of being married ▶ **matrimonial** /ˌmætrɪˈməʊniəl/ ***adj.***

matrix /ˈmeɪtrɪks/ ***noun*** [C] (*pl.* **matrices** /ˈmeɪtrɪsiːz/) **1** (MATHEMATICS) an arrangement of numbers, symbols, etc. in rows and columns, treated as a single quantity **2** (*formal*) (SOCIAL STUDIES) the social, political, etc. situation from which a society or person grows and develops: *the European cultural matrix* **3** (*formal*) a system of lines, roads, etc. that cross each other, forming a series of squares or shapes in between SYN **network**: *a matrix of paths* **4** a MOULD (=container into which a liquid is poured) in which sth is shaped **5** (GEOLOGY) a mass of rock in which minerals, precious stones, etc. are found in the ground

matron /ˈmeɪtrən/ ***noun*** [C] (HEALTH) **1** (*old-fashioned*) a nurse who is in charge of the other nurses in a hospital ❶ **Senior nursing officer** is now used instead.
2 a woman who works as a nurse in a school

matt (*AmE also* **matte**) /mæt/ ***adj.*** not shiny: *This paint gives a matt finish.* ➲ look at **gloss**

matted /ˈmætɪd/ ***adj.*** (used especially about hair) forming a thick mass, especially because it is wet and/or dirty

matter¹ 🔑 /ˈmætə(r)/ ***noun*** **1** [C] a subject or situation that you must think about and give your attention to: *It's a personal matter and I don't want to discuss it with you.* ◇ *Finding a job will be **no easy matter**.* ◇ *to simplify/complicate matters* **2** [sing.] **the ~ (with sb/sth)** the reason sb/sth has a problem or is not good: *She looks sad. **What's the matter** with her?* ◇ *There seems to be **something the matter** with the car.* ◇ *Eat that food! There's **nothing the matter** with it.* **3** [U] all physical substances; a substance of a particular kind: *reading matter* **4** [U] the contents of a book, film, etc.: *I don't think the **subject matter** of this programme is suitable for children.*

IDM **a matter of hours, miles, etc.** used to say that sth is not very long, far, expensive, etc.: *The fight lasted a matter of seconds.*
a matter of life and/or death extremely urgent and important
another/a different matter something much more serious, difficult, etc.: *I can speak a little Japanese, but reading it is quite another matter.*
as a matter of fact to tell the truth; in reality: *I like him very much, as a matter of fact.*
for that matter in addition; now that I think about it: *Mick is really fed up with his course. I am too, for that matter.*
to make matters/things worse → WORSE
a matter of course something that you always do; the usual thing to do: *Goods leaving the factory are checked as a matter of course.*
a matter of opinion a subject on which people do not agree: *'I think the government is doing a good job.' 'That's a matter of opinion.'*
(be) a matter of sth/doing sth a situation in which sth is needed: *Learning a language is largely a matter of practice.*
no matter who, what, where, etc. whoever, whatever, wherever, etc.: *They never listen no matter what you say.*

matter² 🔑 /ˈmætə(r)/ ***verb*** [I] **~ (to sb)** (not used in the continuous tenses) to be important: ***It doesn't** really **matter** how much it costs.* ◇ *Nobody's hurt, and **that's all that matters**.* ◇ *Some things matter more than others.* ◇ *It doesn't matter to me what he does in his free time.*

ˌmatter-of-ˈfact ***adj.*** said or done without showing any emotion, especially when it would seem more normal to express your feelings: *He was very matter-of-fact about his illness.*

mattress /ˈmætrəs/ ***noun*** [C] a large soft thing that you lie on to sleep, usually put on a bed

maturation AW /ˌmætʃuˈreɪʃn/ ***noun*** [U] (*formal*) **1** the process of becoming or being made MATURE (=ready to eat or drink after being left for a period of time) **2** (BIOLOGY) the process of becoming adult

mature¹ AW /məˈtʃʊə(r)/ ***adj.*** **1** fully grown or fully developed: *a mature tree/bird/animal*
2 behaving in a sensible adult way: *Is she mature enough for such responsibility?* OPP **immature**
▶ **maturity** AW /məˈtʃʊərəti/ ***noun*** [U]

mature² AW /məˈtʃʊə(r)/ ***verb*** [I] **1** to become fully grown or developed: *This particular breed of cattle matures early.* ◇ *Technology in this field has matured considerably over the last decade.* **2** to develop emotionally and start to behave like a sensible adult: *He has matured a great deal over the past year.* **3** (BUSINESS) to reach the date when it must be paid: *She has a number of investments that mature at the end of the year.*

maul /mɔːl/ ***verb*** [T] (usually used about a wild animal) to attack and injure sb

mausoleum /ˌmɔːsəˈliːəm/ ***noun*** [C] (ARCHITECTURE) a special building made to hold the dead body of an important person or the dead bodies of a family: *the royal mausoleum*

mauve /məʊv/ ***adj.***, ***noun*** [U] (of) a pale purple colour

maverick /ˈmævərɪk/ ***noun*** [C] a person who does not behave or think like everyone else, but who has independent, unusual opinions ▶ **maverick** ***adj.***

max /mæks/ ***abbr.*** maximum: *max temp 21°C*

maxim /ˈmæksɪm/ ***noun*** [C] a few words that express a rule for good or sensible behaviour: *Our maxim is: 'If a job's worth doing, it's worth doing well.'*

maximize (also **-ise**) AW /ˈmæksɪmaɪz/ ***verb*** [T] to increase sth as much as possible: *to maximize profits* OPP **minimize**

maximum 🔑 AW /ˈmæksɪməm/ ***noun*** [sing.] (*abbr.* **max**) the greatest amount or level of sth that is possible, allowed, etc.: *The bus can carry a maximum of 40 people.* ◇ *That is the maximum we can afford.* OPP **minimum** ▶ **maximum** ***adj.*** (only *before* a noun): *a maximum speed of 120 miles per hour*

May /meɪ/ ***noun*** [U, C] the fifth month of the year, coming after April

may 🔑 /meɪ/ ***modal verb*** (*negative* **may not**) **1** used for saying that sth is possible: *'Where's Sue?' 'She may be in the garden.'* ◇ *You may be right.* ◇ *I may be going to China next year.* ◇ *They may have forgotten the meeting.* **2** used as a polite way of asking for and giving permission: *May I use your phone?* ◇ *You may not take photographs in the museum.* **3** used for contrasting two facts: *He may be very clever but he can't do anything practical.*
4 (*formal*) used for expressing wishes and hopes: *May you both be very happy.*

IDM **may/might as well (do sth)** → WELL¹

maybe 🔑 /ˈmeɪbi/ ***adv.*** perhaps; possibly: *'Are you going to come?' 'Maybe.'* ◇ *There were three, maybe four armed men.* ◇ *Maybe I'll accept the invitation and maybe I won't.* ➲ note at **perhaps**

'May Day *noun* [C] 1st May

CULTURE

May Day is traditionally celebrated as a spring festival and in some countries as a holiday in honour of working people

mayfly /'meɪflaɪ/ *noun* [C] (*pl.* **-ies**) a small insect that lives near water and only lives for a very short time

mayonnaise /ˌmeɪə'neɪz/ *noun* [U] a cold thick pale yellow sauce made with eggs and oil

mayor /meə(r)/ *noun* [C] (POLITICS) a person who is elected to be the leader of a COUNCIL (=the group of people who manage the affairs of a town or city)

mayoress /meə'res/ *noun* [C] (POLITICS) a woman mayor, or a woman who is married to or helps a mayor

maze /meɪz/ *noun* [C] a system of paths which is designed to confuse you so that it is difficult to find your way out: (*figurative*) *a maze of winding streets* SYN **labyrinth**

MBA /ˌem bi: 'eɪ/ *abbr.* (BUSINESS, EDUCATION) **Master of Business Administration**; an advanced university degree in business

MBE /ˌem bi: 'i:/ *noun* [C] **Member of the Order of the British Empire**; an honour given to some people in Britain because they have achieved something special: *She was made an MBE in 2001.*

MC /ˌem 'si:/ *noun* [C] **1** the abbreviation for 'master of ceremonies' **2** (*abbr.* **M.C.**) (POLITICS) the abbreviation for 'Member of Congress' **3** (MUSIC) a person who speaks the words of a RAP song

MD /ˌem 'di:/ *abbr.* (HEALTH) Doctor of Medicine

me /mi:/ *pronoun* (used as an object) the person who is speaking or writing: *He telephoned me yesterday.* ◇ *She wrote to me last week.* ◇ *Hello, is that Frank? It's me, Sadiq.*

meadow /'medəʊ/ *noun* [C] a field of grass

meagre (*AmE* **meager**) /'mi:gə(r)/ *adj.* too small in amount: *a meagre salary*

meal /mi:l/ *noun* [C] the time when you eat or the food that is eaten at that time: *Shall we **go out for a meal** on Friday?* ◇ *a heavy/light meal*

IDM **a square meal** → SQUARE²

mealtime /'mi:ltaɪm/ *noun* [C] the time at which a meal is usually eaten

mean¹ /mi:n/ *verb* [T] (*pt, pp* **meant** /ment/) **1** (not used in the continuous tenses) to express, show or have as a meaning: ***What does** this word **mean**?* ◇ *The bell means that the lesson has ended.* ◇ *Does the name 'Michael Potter' mean anything to you?* **2** to want or intend to say sth; to refer to sb/sth: *Well, she said 'yes' but I think she really meant 'no'.* ◇ *What do you mean by 'a lot of money'?* ◇ *I only meant that I couldn't come tomorrow – any other day would be fine.* ◇ ***I see what you mean**, but I'm afraid it's not possible.* **3** (often passive) ~ **(sb) to do sth**; ~ **sth (as/for sth/sb)**; ~ **sb/sth to be sth** to intend sth; to be supposed to be/do sth: *I'm sure she didn't mean to upset you.* ◇ *She meant the present to be for both of us.* ◇ *I didn't mean you to cook the whole meal!* ◇ *It was only meant as a joke.* ◇ *What's this picture meant to be?* **4** to make sth likely; to cause: *The shortage of teachers means that classes are larger.* **5** ~ **sth (to sb)** to be important to sb: *This job means a lot to me.* ◇ *Money means nothing to her.* **6** to be serious or sincere about sth: *He said he loved me but I don't think he meant it!*

IDM **be meant to be sth** to be considered or said to be sth: *That restaurant is meant to be excellent.*

mean well to want to be kind and helpful but usually without success: *My mother means well but I wish she'd stop treating me like a child.*

mean² /mi:n/ *adj.* **1** ~ **(with sth)** wanting to keep money, etc. for yourself rather than let other people have it: *It's no good asking him for any money – he's much too mean.* ◇ *They're mean with the food in the canteen.* **2** ~ **(to sb)** (used about people or their behaviour) unkind: *It was mean of him not to invite you too.* **3** (only *before* a noun) (MATHEMATICS) average: *What is the mean annual temperature in California?* ▶ **meanness** *noun* [U]

mean³ *noun* [C] (MATHEMATICS) **1** (*also* **arithˌmetic 'mean**) the value found by adding together all the numbers in a group, and dividing the total by the number of numbers **2** (*also* **geo'metric mean**) a value which can be calculated by multiplying a series of numbers together and then finding the ROOT of the number of numbers that have been multiplied, for example the CUBE ROOT of three numbers

meander /mi'ændə(r)/ *verb* [I] **1** (used about a river, road, etc.) to have a lot of curves and bends **2** (used about a person or animal) to walk or travel slowly or without any definite direction ▶ **meander** *noun* [C] (GEOGRAPHY): *the meanders of a river* ➲ picture at **oxbow**

meaning /'mi:nɪŋ/ *noun* **1** [C,U] the thing or idea that sth represents; what sb is trying to communicate: *This word has two different meanings in English.* ◇ *What's the meaning of the last line of the poem?* **2** [U] the purpose or importance of an experience: *With his child dead there seemed to be no meaning in life.*

meaningful /'mi:nɪŋfl/ *adj.* **1** useful, important or interesting: *Most people need a meaningful relationship with another person.* **2** (used about a look, expression, etc.) trying to express a certain feeling or idea: *They kept giving each other meaningful glances across the table.* ▶ **meaningfully** /-fəli/ *adv.*

meaningless /'mi:nɪŋləs/ *adj.* without meaning, reason or sense: *The figures are meaningless if we have nothing to compare them with.*

means /mi:nz/ *noun* (*pl.* **means**) **1** [C] a ~ **(of doing sth)** a method of doing sth: *Do you have any means of transport (=a car, bicycle, etc.)?* ◇ *Is there any means of contacting your husband?* **2** [pl.] (*formal*) all the money that sb has: *This car is **beyond the means of** most people.*

IDM **by all means** used to say that you are happy for sb to have or do sth: *'Can I borrow your newspaper?' 'By all means.'*

by means of by using: *We got out of the hotel by means of the fire escape.*

by no means; not by any means (used to emphasize sth) not at all: *I'm by no means sure that this is the right thing to do.*

a means to an end an action or thing that is not important in itself but is a way of achieving sth else: *I don't enjoy my job, but it's a means to an end.*

meant past tense, past participle of **mean¹**

meantime /'mi:ntaɪm/ *noun*

IDM **in the meantime** in the time between two things happening: *Our house isn't finished so in the meantime we're living with my mother.*

meanwhile 🔑 /'mi:nwaɪl/ ***adv.*** during the same time or during the time between two things happening: *Peter was at home studying. Omar, meanwhile, was out with his friends.*

measles /'mi:zlz/ ***noun*** [U] (**HEALTH**) a common infectious disease, especially among children, in which your body feels hot and your skin is covered in small red spots

measly /'mi:zli/ ***adj.*** (*informal*) much too small in size, amount or value: *All that work for this measly amount of money!*

measurable /'meʒərəbl/ ***adj.*** **1** that can be measured **2** (usually *before* a noun) large enough to be noticed or to have a clear and noticeable effect: *measurable improvements* ▶ **measurably** /-əbli/ ***adv.***: *Working conditions have changed measurably in the last ten years.*

measure[1] 🔑 /'meʒə(r)/ ***verb*** **1** [I,T] to find the size, weight, quantity, etc. of sb/sth in standard units by using an instrument: *to measure the height/ width/length/depth of sth* ◇ *Could you measure the table to see if it will fit into our room?* **2** ***linking verb*** to be a certain height, width, length, etc.: *The room measures five metres across.* **3** [T] ~ **sth (against sth)** to judge the value or effect of sth: *Our sales do not look good when measured against those of our competitors.*

PHR V **measure up (to sth)** to be as good as you need to be or as sb expects you to be: *Did the holiday measure up to your expectations?*

COLLOCATIONS AND PATTERNS

Weights and measures

Liquids are measured in **litres/liters** in most countries.
a litre of milk
half a litre of beer
a quarter of a litre of water
How many centilitres are there in a litre?
One litre is equivalent to 1000 cubic centimetres.

In the past, people in Britain used **pints** and **gallons** to measure liquids, rather than **litres/liters.** Nowadays, most people use and understand both.
My grandfather liked a pint of beer with his lunch.
Our old car used gallons of petrol.

People in the US still use **pints** and **gallons** (but note than an American **pint** =0.47 litres).
You can use **about/approximately/around** to convert measurements roughly.
A pint is about half a litre.
1 foot is approximately 0.3 metres

You can say how **long/wide/high/tall/deep sth is** when you measure in just one direction.
The garden was 10 metres long and 6 wide.
The fence is 2 metres high to keep out the animals.
He's 1.89 m tall.
The snow was 25 cms deep in places.

Area (=the size of a surface) is calculated by multiplying the **length** by the **width** and is expressed as a **square** measurement.
The floor is about 15 square metres (=3 x 5 metres).

We use **be** or **weigh** with measures of weight
I'm just under 10 stone.
Jo's baby weighed just over 3 kilos.

measure[2] 🔑 /'meʒə(r)/ ***noun*** **1** [C, usually pl.] an action that is done for a special reason: *The government is to **take** new **measures** to reduce inflation.* ◇ *As a temporary measure, the road will have to be closed.* **2** [sing.] (*formal*) a/some ~ **of sth** a certain amount of sth; some: *The play achieved a measure of success.* **3** [sing.] a way of understanding or judging sth: *The school's popularity is a measure of the teachers' success.* **4** [C] a way of describing the size, amount, etc. of sth: *A metre is a measure of length.* ➲ look at **tape measure** **5** (**MUSIC**) (*AmE*) = BAR[1] (6) **6** [C] (**POLITICS**) (*AmE*) a written suggestion for a new law that people can vote for or against in an election

IDM **for good measure** in addition to sth, especially to make sure that there is enough: *He made a few extra sandwiches for good measure.*

made to measure specially made or perfectly suitable for a particular person, use, etc.: *I'm getting a suit made to measure for the wedding.*

measurement 🔑 /'meʒəmənt/ ***noun*** **1** [C] a size, amount, etc. that is found by measuring: *What are the exact measurements of the room?* (=how wide, long, etc. is it?) **2** [U] the act or process of measuring sth

meat 🔑 /mi:t/ ***noun*** [U] the parts of animals or birds that people eat: *She doesn't eat meat – she's a vegetarian.* ◇ *meat-eating animals*

RELATED VOCABULARY

Some types of meat have different names from the animals they come from. **Pork**, **ham** or **bacon** comes from a pig, **beef** from a cow and **veal** from a calf. **Mutton** comes from a sheep, but you get **lamb** from a lamb. For birds and fish there is not a different word.

Meat from beef, mutton, lamb and pork is called **red meat**. The meat from birds is called **white meat**.

You can **fry**, **grill**, **roast** or **stew** meat. You **carve** a **joint** of meat.

Meat can be described as **tough** or **tender**, **lean** or **fatty**. Uncooked meat is **raw**.

meatball /'mi:tbɔ:l/ ***noun*** [C] a small round ball of meat, usually eaten hot with a sauce

meaty /'mi:ti/ ***adj.*** **1** like meat, or containing a lot of meat: *meaty sausages* **2** large and fat: *meaty tomatoes* **3** containing a lot of important or good ideas: *a meaty topic for discussion*

Mecca /'mekə/ ***noun*** **1** [sing.] (**RELIGION**) the city in Saudi Arabia where Muhammad was born, which is the centre of Islam **2 mecca** [C, usually sing.] a place that many people wish to visit because of a particular interest: *Italy is a mecca for art lovers.*

mechanic /mə'kænɪk/ ***noun*** **1** [C] a person whose job is to repair and work with machines: *a car mechanic* **2 mechanics** [U] (**SCIENCE**) the science of how machines work **3 the mechanics** [pl.] the way in which sth works or is done: *Don't ask me – I don't understand the mechanics of the legal system.*

mechanical /mə'kænɪkl/ ***adj.*** **1** connected with or produced by machines: *a mechanical pump* ◇ *mechanical engineering* ◇ *mechanical problems* **2** (used about a person's behaviour) done like a machine, as if you are not thinking about what you are doing: *He played the piano in a dull and mechanical way.* ▶ **mechanically** /-kli/ ***adv.***

mechanism **AW** /'mekənɪzəm/ ***noun*** [C] **1** a set of moving parts in a machine that does a certain task: *Our car has an automatic locking mechanism.* **2** the way in which sth works or is done: *I'm afraid there is no mechanism for dealing with your complaint.*

mechanize (also -ise) /ˈmekənaɪz/ ***verb*** [T] to use machines instead of people to do work: *We have mechanized the entire production process.* ▶ **mechanization** (also **-isation**) /ˌmekənaɪˈzeɪʃn/ ***noun*** [U]

the Med (*informal*) = THE MEDITERRANEAN

medal /ˈmedl/ ***noun*** [C] a small flat piece of metal, usually with a design and words on it, which is given to sb who has shown courage or as a prize in a sporting event: *to win a gold/silver/bronze medal in the Olympics*

medallion /məˈdæliən/ ***noun*** [C] a small round piece of metal on a chain which is worn as jewellery around the neck

medallist (*AmE* **medalist**) /ˈmedəlɪst/ ***noun*** [C] (**SPORT**) a person who has won a MEDAL, especially in sport: *an Olympic gold medallist*

meddle /ˈmedl/ ***verb*** [I] ~ **(in/with sth)** to take too much interest in sb's private affairs or to touch sth that does not belong to you: *She criticized her mother for meddling in her private life.*

media ⊷ AW /ˈmiːdiə/ ***noun*** [pl.] (**ARTS AND MEDIA**) television, radio and newspapers used as a means of communication: *The reports **in the media** have been greatly exaggerated.* ➲ look at **mass media**, **the press**

mediaeval = MEDIEVAL

median[1] /ˈmiːdiən/ ***adj.*** (only *before* a noun) **1** (**MATHEMATICS**) having a value in the middle of a series of values: *the median age/price* **2** located in or passing through the middle: *a median point/line* **3** (*also* ˈ**median strip** *AmE*) = CENTRAL RESERVATION

median[2] /ˈmiːdiən/ ***noun*** [C] (**MATHEMATICS**) **1** the middle value of a series of numbers arranged in order of size **2** a straight line passing from a point of a triangle to the centre of the opposite side.

ˈ**media studies** ***noun*** [U, pl.] (**ARTS AND MEDIA**) the study of newspapers, television, radio, etc., especially as an academic subject

mediate AW /ˈmiːdieɪt/ ***verb*** [I,T] ~ **(in sth) (between A and B)** to try to end a disagreement between two or more people or groups: *As a supervisor she had to mediate between her colleagues and the management.* ▶ **mediation** /ˌmiːdiˈeɪʃn/ ***noun*** [U] ▶ **mediator** ***noun*** [C]

Medicaid /ˈmedɪkeɪd/ ***noun*** [U] (**HEALTH**) (in the US) the insurance system that provides medical care for poor people

medical[1] ⊷ AW /ˈmedɪkl/ ***adj.*** (**HEALTH**) connected with medicine and the treatment of illness: *medical treatment/care* ◇ *the medical profession* ▶ **medically** /-kli/ ***adv.***

medical[2] AW /ˈmedɪkl/ ***noun*** [C] (**HEALTH**) an examination of your body by a doctor to check your state of health: *to have a medical*

Medicare /ˈmedɪkeə(r)/ ***noun*** [U] (**HEALTH**) **1** (in the US) the federal insurance system that provides medical care for people over 65 **2** (in Australia and Canada) the national medical care system for all people that is paid for by taxes (spelt 'medicare' in Canada)

medication /ˌmedɪˈkeɪʃn/ ***noun*** [C,U] (*especially AmE*) (**HEALTH**) medicine that a doctor has given to you: *Are you **on** any **medication**?*

medicinal /məˈdɪsɪnl/ ***adj.*** (**HEALTH**) useful for curing illness or infection: *medicinal plants*

COLLOCATIONS AND PATTERNS

Medical practitioners

Medical practitioners **practise as** (=work as) dentists, doctors, opticians, etc.
She practises as a clinical psychologist.
Not many doctors practise from home these days.

If you are ill, you **consult** or **see a doctor.**
She ought to see a doctor with that rash.

A doctor **prescribes treatment** or gives **the patient** (=the person consulting him/her) a **prescription.**
The psychiatrist prescribed antidepressants.
The doctor gave her patient a prescription for antibiotics.

You can **be treated by** sb or **be treated for /have treatment for** sth.
He is being treated by a physiotherapist.
She was treated for malaria at St James' Hospital.

Sometimes one doctor **refers sb to** a specialist or another type of doctor.
The clinic referred her to a cardiologist.

medicine ⊷ /ˈmedsn/ ***noun*** (**HEALTH**) **1** [U] the science of preventing and treating illness: *to study medicine* **2** [C,U] a substance, especially a liquid, that you take in order to cure an illness: ***Take** this **medicine** three times a day.* ◇ *cough medicine* ➲ picture at **health**

medieval (also **mediaeval**) /ˌmediˈiːvl/ ***adj.*** (**HISTORY**) connected with the period in history between about 1100 and 1500 AD (**the Middle Ages**)

mediocre /ˌmiːdiˈəʊkə(r)/ ***adj.*** of not very high quality: *a mediocre performance* ▶ **mediocrity** /ˌmiːdiˈɒkrəti/ ***noun*** [U]

meditate /ˈmedɪteɪt/ ***verb*** [I] ~ **(on/upon sth)** to think carefully and deeply, especially for religious reasons or to make your mind calm: *I've been meditating on what you said last week.* ▶ **meditation** /ˌmedɪˈteɪʃn/ ***noun*** [U]

the Mediterranean /ˌmedɪtəˈreɪniən/ (also *informal* **the Med**) ***noun*** [sing.] (**GEOGRAPHY**) the Mediterranean Sea or the countries around it ▶ **Mediterranean** ***adj.***: *Mediterranean cookery*

medium[1] ⊷ AW /ˈmiːdiəm/ ***adj.*** **1** in the middle between two sizes, lengths, temperatures, etc.; average: *She was of medium height.* ◇ *Would you like the small, medium or large packet?* ◇ *a medium-sized car/town/dog* **2** (used about meat) cooked until it is brown all the way through ➲ look at **rare**, **well done**

medium[2] ⊷ AW /ˈmiːdiəm/ ***noun*** (*pl.* **media** or **mediums**) **1** [C] a means you can use to express or communicate sth: *the **medium of radio/television*** ◇ *English is the **medium of instruction** in the school.* ➲ look at **media**, **mass media** **2** [C,U] medium size: *Have you got this shirt in (a) medium?* **3** (**ARTS AND MEDIA**) the material or the form that an artist, a writer or a musician uses: *the **medium of paint/poetry/drama*** ◇ *Watercolour is his favourite medium.* **4** [C] (*pl.* **mediums**) a person who says that they can speak to the spirits of dead people **5** (**BIOLOGY**) a substance that sth exists or grows in or that it travels through: *The bacteria were growing in a sugar medium.*

ˈ**medium wave** ***noun*** [U] (*abbr.* **MW**) (**PHYSICS**) the system of sending out radio signals using sound waves between 100 and 1000 metres ➲ look at **long wave**, **short wave**

medley /ˈmedli/ ***noun*** [C] **1** (MUSIC) a piece of music consisting of several tunes or songs played one after the other without a break **2** a mixture of different things: *a medley of styles/flavours*

medulla oblongata /meˌdʌlə ɒblɒŋˈɡɑːtə/ ***noun*** [C] (ANATOMY) the part of the brain that controls the way the heart and lungs work ➲ picture at **brain**

meek /miːk/ ***adj.*** (used about people) quiet, and doing what other people say without asking questions ▶ **meekly** ***adv.*** ▶ **meekness** ***noun*** [U]

meet 🔑 /miːt/ ***verb*** (*pt, pp* **met** /met/) **1** [I,T] to come together by chance or because you have arranged it: *I just met Kareem on the train.* ◇ *What time shall we meet for lunch?* **2** [I,T] to see and know sb for the first time: *Where did you first meet your husband?* ◇ *Have you two met before?* **3** [T] to go to a place and wait for sb/sth to arrive: *I'll come and meet you at the station.* **4** [I,T] (SPORT) to play, fight, etc. together as opponents in a sports competition: *These two teams met in last year's final.* ◇ *Yamaha will meet Suzuki in the second round.* **5** [T] to experience sth, often sth unpleasant: *We will never know how he met his death.* **6** [I,T] to touch, join or make contact with: *The two roads meet not far from here.* ◇ *His eyes met hers.* **7** [T] to be enough for sth; to be able to deal with sth: *The money that I earn is enough to meet our basic needs.* ◇ *to meet a challenge*

IDM **make ends meet** → END[1]

there is more to sb/sth than meets the eye sb/sth is more interesting or complicated than they or it seem: *Do you think there's more to their relationship than meets the eye?*

PHR V **meet up (with sb)** to meet sb, especially after a period of being apart: *I have a few things I need to do now, but let's meet up later.*

meet with sb (*especially AmE*) to meet sb, especially for discussion: *The President met with his advisers early this morning.*

meet with sth to get a particular answer, reaction or result: *to meet with success/failure/opposition*

ˌmeet-and-ˈgreet ***adj.*** (BUSINESS) arranged so that sb, especially a famous person, can meet and talk to people: *His publishers had arranged a signing and meet-and-greet session.* ▶ **ˌmeet and ˈgreet** ***noun*** [C]

COLLOCATIONS AND PATTERNS

Formal meetings

Somebody can **call/convene, arrange** or **organize a meeting**
She convened a meeting for the following morning.

Before a meeting, that person will **draw up** and **circulate the agenda** (=a list of items to be discussed).
The manager drew up and then circulated the agenda.

It is sometimes necessary to **cancel/call off** or **postpone** a meeting.
The meeting has been postponed until next week.
The committee meeting had to be cancelled due to illness.

A **chairperson opens/closes** a meeting
Mrs Green opened the meeting on Friday.
The chairperson thanked everybody for coming, and closed the meeting.

A **secretary keeps/takes the minutes** (=a summary of what is said or decided at a formal meeting).
Sam offered to take the minutes.

At the beginning of a meeting, the **minutes** of the last meeting are **approved** and **an agenda** is **agreed on.**
Can we approve the minutes of the last meeting?
The agenda was agreed on.

At the end of the meeting the chairperson asks if there is **any other business.**
If there is no other business then I declare this meeting closed.

meeting 🔑 /ˈmiːtɪŋ/ ***noun*** **1** [C] an organized occasion when a number of people come together in order to discuss or decide sth: *The group* ***hold*** *regular* ***meetings*** *all year.* ◇ *We need to* ***have a meeting*** *to discuss these matters.* **2** [sing.] the people at a meeting: *The meeting was in favour of the new proposals.* **3** [C] the coming together of two or more people: *Christmas is a time of family meetings and reunions.*

mega- /ˈmeɡə/ ***prefix*** (used in nouns) **1** (*informal*) very large or great: *a megastore* **2** (used in units of measurement) one million: *a megawatt* **3** (COMPUTING) 1048576 (=2^{20}): *megabyte*

megabyte /ˈmeɡəbaɪt/ ***noun*** [C] (*abbr.* **MB**) (COMPUTING) a unit of computer memory, equal to 2^{20} BYTES (=small units of information): *a 40-megabyte hard disk*

megahertz /ˈmeɡəhɜːts/ ***noun*** [C] (*pl.* **megahertz**) (*abbr.* **MHz**) (COMPUTING) a unit for measuring radio waves and the speed at which a computer operates; 1000000 HERTZ

megaphone /ˈmeɡəfəʊn/ ***noun*** [C] a piece of equipment that you speak through to make your voice sound louder when speaking to a crowd

megathermal /ˌmeɡəˈθɜːml/ ***adj.*** (GEOGRAPHY) (used about a climate) hot and wet ➲ look at **mesothermal, microthermal**

meiosis /maɪˈəʊsɪs/ ***noun*** [U] (BIOLOGY) the division of a cell in two stages that results in four cells, each with half the number of CHROMOSOMES (=the parts of a cell that carry information about what characteristics a living thing will have) of the original cell ➲ look at **mitosis**

melancholy /ˈmelənkəli; -kɒli/ ***noun*** [U] (*formal*) a feeling of sadness which lasts for a long time ▶ **melancholy** ***adj.***

melanin /ˈmelənɪn/ ***noun*** [U] (BIOLOGY) a dark substance in the skin and hair that causes the skin to change colour in the sun's light

melee /ˈmeleɪ/ ***noun*** [C, sing.] a situation in which a crowd of people are in a hurry or pushing each other in a confused way

melisma /məˈlɪzmə/ ***noun*** [C] (*pl.* **melismas**; **melismata** /-mətə/) (MUSIC) a group of notes sung to one syllable of text

mellow /ˈmeləʊ/ ***adj.*** **1** (used about colours or sounds) soft and pleasant **2** (used about people) calm and relaxed: *My dad's grown mellower as he's got older.* ▶ **mellow** ***verb*** [I,T]: *Experience had mellowed her views about many things.*

melodic /məˈlɒdɪk/ ***adj.*** **1** (only *before* a noun) (MUSIC) connected with the main tune in a piece of music: *The melodic line is carried by the two clarinets.* **2** =MELODIOUS

melodious /məˈləʊdiəs/ (*also* **melodic**) ***adj.*** pleasant to listen to, like music: *a rich melodious voice*

melodrama /ˈmelədrɑːmə/ ***noun*** [C,U] (ARTS AND MEDIA, LITERATURE) a story, play or film in which a lot of exciting things happen and in which people's emotions are stronger than in real life

melodramatic /ˌmelədrəˈmætɪk/ ***adj.*** (used about a person's behaviour) making things seem more exciting or serious than they really are: *Don't be so melodramatic, Simon – of course you're not going to die!*

melody /ˈmelədi/ ***noun*** [C] (*pl.* **melodies**) (MUSIC) a song or tune; the main tune of a piece of music

melon /ˈmelən/ ***noun*** [C,U] a large ROUNDISH fruit with a thick yellow or green skin and a lot of seeds

melt ⊶ /melt/ ***verb*** **1** [I,T] **1** (SCIENCE) to change or make sth change from a solid to a liquid by means of heat: *Ice melts as the temperature rises.* ◇ *First melt the butter in a saucepan.* ➲ look at **thaw** **2** [I] (used about sb's feelings, etc.) to become softer or less strong: *My heart melted when I saw the baby.*

PHR V **melt away** to disappear: *The crowd slowly melted away when the speaker had finished.*

melt sth down to heat a metal or glass object until it becomes liquid

ˈmelting point ***noun*** [U, C] (PHYSICS) the temperature at which a substance will melt

ˈmelting pot ***noun*** [C] a place where a lot of different cultures, ideas, etc. come together

meltwater /ˈmeltwɔːtə(r)/ ***noun*** [U] (*also* **meltwaters**) (GEOGRAPHY) water formed by the melting of snow and ice, especially from a GLACIER (=a large mass of ice, formed by snow on mountains, that moves very slowly down a valley)

member ⊶ /ˈmembə(r)/ ***noun*** [C] a person, an animal or a thing that belongs to a group, club, organization, etc.: *All the members of the family were there.* ◇ *to become a member of a club* ◇ *a member of staff*

ˌMember of ˈParliament ***noun*** [C] (*abbr.* **MP**) (POLITICS) a person who has been elected to represent people from a particular area in Parliament: *the MP for Oxford East*

membership ⊶ /ˈmembəʃɪp/ ***noun*** **1** [U] the state of being a member of a group, organization, etc.: *To* ***apply for membership****, please fill in the enclosed form.* ◇ *a membership card/fee* **2** [C,U] the people who belong to a group, organization, etc.: *Membership has fallen in the past year* (=the number of members).

membrane /ˈmembreɪn/ ***noun*** [C] **1** (ANATOMY) a thin layer of skin or TISSUE that connects or covers parts inside the body ➲ look at **mucous membrane** **2** (BIOLOGY) a very thin layer found in the structure of cells in plants ➲ picture at **cell** **3** a thin layer of material used to prevent air, liquid, etc. from entering a particular part of sth: *a waterproof membrane*

memento /məˈmentəʊ/ ***noun*** [C] (*pl.* **mementoes**; **mementos**) something that you keep to remind you of sb/sth

memo /ˈmeməʊ/ ***noun*** [C] (*pl.* **memos**) (also *formal* **memorandum**) (BUSINESS) a note sent from one person or office to another within an organization

memoirs /ˈmemwɑːz/ ***noun*** [pl.] (LITERATURE) a person's written account of their own life and experiences SYN **autobiography**

memorabilia /ˌmemərəˈbɪliə/ ***noun*** [U] things that people buy because they are connected with a famous person, event, etc.: *Beatles/Titanic/war memorabilia*

memorable /ˈmemərəbl/ ***adj.*** worth remembering or easy to remember ▸ **memorably** ***adv.***

memorandum /ˌmeməˈrændəm/ (*pl.* **memoranda** /-də/) (*formal*) =MEMO

memorial /məˈmɔːriəl/ ***noun*** [C] **a ~ (to sb/sth)** something that is built or done to remind people of an event or a person: *a memorial to the victims of the bombing* ◇ *a war memorial* ◇ *a memorial service*

memorize (also **-ise**) /ˈmeməraɪz/ ***verb*** [T] to learn sth so that you can remember it exactly: *Actors have to memorize their lines.*

memory ⊶ /ˈmeməri/ ***noun*** (*pl.* **memories**) **1** [C] a person's ability to remember things: *to have a good/bad memory* ◇ *The drug can affect your short-term memory.* **2** [C,U] the part of your mind in which you store things that you remember: *That day remained firmly* ***in*** *my* ***memory*** *for the rest of my life.* ◇ *Are you going to do your speech* ***from memory****, or are you going to use notes?* **3** [C] something that you remember: *That is one of my happiest memories.* ◇ *childhood memories* **4** [C,U] (COMPUTING) the part of a computer where information is stored: *This computer has a 640k memory/640k of memory.*

IDM **in memory of sb** in order to remind people of sb who has died: *A service was held in memory of the dead.*

jog sb's memory → JOG[1]

refresh your memory → REFRESH

ˈMemory Stick™ ***noun*** [C] (COMPUTING) a small device that you can carry around with you which is used for storing and moving data onto a computer SYN **Pen drive™**, **USB drive**

men plural of **man**[1]

menace /ˈmenəs/ ***noun*** **1** [C] **a ~ (to sb/sth)** a danger or threat: *The new road is a menace to everyone's safety.* **2** [U] a quality, feeling, etc. that is threatening or frightening: *He spoke with menace in his voice.* **3** [C] a person or thing that causes trouble ▸ **menace** ***verb*** [T] ▸ **menacing** ***adj.***

mend[1] /mend/ ***verb*** [T] to repair sth that is damaged or broken: *Can you mend the hole in this jumper for me?* SYN **repair**

mend[2] /mend/ ***noun***

IDM **be on the mend** (*informal*) to be getting better after an illness or injury

mendelevium /ˌmendəˈliːviəm; -ˈleɪv-/ ***noun*** [U] (*symbol* **Md**) (CHEMISTRY) a chemical element. **Mendelevium** is a RADIOACTIVE element that does not exist naturally. ❶ For more information on the periodic table of elements, look at pages R34-5.

menial /ˈmiːniəl/ ***adj.*** (used about work) not skilled or important: *a menial job*

meninges /məˈnɪndʒiːz/ ***noun*** [U] (BIOLOGY) the three thin layers of material (**membranes**) that surround the brain and the inside of the bones in your back (**the spinal cord**) ➲ picture at **brain**

meningitis /ˌmenɪnˈdʒaɪtɪs/ ***noun*** [U] (HEALTH) a dangerous illness which affects the brain and the SPINAL CORD (=the inside of the bones in your back)

the menopause /ˈmenəpɔːz/ ***noun*** [sing.] (HEALTH) the time when a woman stops losing blood once a month (**menstruating**) and can no longer have children. This usually happens around the age of 50.

menstrual /ˈmenstruəl/ ***adj.*** (HEALTH) connected with the time when a woman MENSTRUATES: *The average length of a woman's* ***menstrual cycle*** *is 28 days.*

menstruate /ˈmenstrueɪt/ ***verb*** [I] (*formal*) (HEALTH) (used about women) to lose blood once a month from the WOMB (= the part of the body where a baby can develop) ⓘ A less formal way of saying this is to **have a period**. ▶ **menstruation** /ˌmenstruˈeɪʃn/ ***noun*** [U]

mental 🔑 AW /ˈmentl/ ***adj.*** (only *before* a noun) **1** connected with or happening in the mind; involving the process of thinking: *It's fascinating to watch a child's mental development.* **2** (HEALTH) connected with illness of the mind: *a mental disorder/illness*

ˌmental aˈrithmetic ***noun*** [U] (MATHEMATICS) adding, multiplying, etc. numbers in your mind without writing anything down or using a CALCULATOR

mentality AW /menˈtæləti/ ***noun*** [C] (*pl.* **mentalities**) a type of mind or way of thinking: *I just can't understand his mentality!* ◇ *the criminal mentality*

mentally 🔑 /ˈmentəli/ ***adv.*** connected with or happening in the mind: *She's mentally ill.* ◇ *Mentally, I began making a list of things I had to do.*

> **THESAURUS** ⓘ
>
> **mention**
>
> **refer to • cite • quote • allude to**
>
> These words all mean to write or speak about sb/sth, often in order to give an example or prove sth.
>
> **mention**: *I didn't like to mention it.*
>
> **refer to**: *He referred to an earlier matter.*
>
> **cite** (*formal*): *She cited her heavy workload as the reason for her breakdown.*
>
> **quote** (*formal*): *He quoted two instances of violence suffered.*
>
> **allude to** (*formal*): *She alluded briefly to the problem.*

mention 🔑 /ˈmenʃn/ ***verb*** [T] to say or write sth about sb/sth without giving much information: *He mentioned (to me) that he might be late.* ◇ *Did she mention what time the film starts?* ▶ **mention** ***noun*** [C,U]: *It was odd that there wasn't even a mention of the riots in the newspaper.*

IDM **don't mention it** used as a polite reply when sb thanks you for sth: *'Thank you for all your help.' 'Don't mention it.'*

not to mention (used to emphasize sth) and also; as well as: *This is a great habitat for birds, not to mention other wildlife.*

mentor /ˈmentɔː(r)/ ***noun*** [C] an experienced person who advises and helps sb with less experience over a period of time ▶ **mentoring** ***noun*** [U]: *a mentoring programme*

menu 🔑 /ˈmenjuː/ ***noun*** [C] **1** a list of the food that you can choose at a restaurant: *I hope there's soup on the menu.* ◇ *They do a special lunchtime menu here.* **2** (COMPUTING) a list of choices in a computer program which is shown on the screen: *a pull-down menu*

MEP /ˌem iː ˈpiː/ ***abbr.*** (POLITICS) Member of the European parliament

mercantile /ˈmɜːkəntaɪl/ ***adj.*** (*formal*) (BUSINESS) connected with trade and commercial affairs

mercantilism /mɜːˈkæntɪlɪzəm/ ***noun*** [U] (BUSINESS) the economic theory that trade increases wealth

mercenary¹ /ˈmɜːsənəri/ ***adj.*** interested only in making money: *His motives are entirely mercenary.*

mercenary² /ˈmɜːsənəri/ ***noun*** [C] (*pl.* **mercenaries**) a soldier who fights for any group or country that will pay them

merchandise /ˈmɜːtʃəndaɪs; -daɪz/ ***noun*** [U] (*formal*) (BUSINESS) goods that are for sale ➲ note at **product** ▶ **merchandise** /ˈmɜːtʃəndaɪz/ ***verb*** [T]: *The movie is being merchandised like any big blockbuster release.*

merchandising /ˈmɜːtʃəndaɪzɪŋ/ ***noun*** [U] **1** (*especially AmE*) (BUSINESS) the activity of selling goods, or of trying to sell them, by advertising or showing them **2** products connected with a popular film, person or event; the process of selling these goods: *millions of dollars' worth of Batman merchandising*

merchant /ˈmɜːtʃənt/ ***noun*** [C] (BUSINESS) a person whose job is to buy and sell goods, usually of one particular type, in large amounts

ˌmerchant ˈnavy ***noun*** [C, with sing. or pl. verb] a country's commercial ships and the people who work on them

merciful /ˈmɜːsɪfl/ ***adj.*** feeling or showing MERCY: *His death was a merciful release from pain.* ▶ **mercifully** /-fəli/ ***adv.***

merciless /ˈmɜːsɪləs/ ***adj.*** showing no MERCY ▶ **mercilessly** ***adv.***

Mercury¹ /ˈmɜːkjəri/ ***noun*** [sing.] (ASTRONOMY) the planet that is nearest to the sun ➲ picture at **solar system**

mercury² /ˈmɜːkjəri/ ***noun*** [U] (*symbol* **Hg**) (CHEMISTRY) a heavy silver-coloured metal that is usually in liquid form. **Mercury** is used in instruments that measure temperature (**thermometers**). ⓘ For more information on the periodic table of elements, look at pages R34-5.

mercy /ˈmɜːsi/ ***noun*** [U] kindness shown by sb/sth who has the power to make sb suffer: *The rebels were shown no mercy. They were taken out and shot.*

IDM **at the mercy of sb/sth** having no power against sb/sth that is strong: *The climbers spent the night on the mountain at the mercy of the wind and rain.*

mere 🔑 /mɪə(r)/ ***adj.*** (only *before* a noun) **1** (used for emphasizing how small or unimportant sth is) nothing more than: *90% of the country's land is owned by a mere 2% of the population.* **2** used to say that just the fact that sb/sth is present in a situation is enough to have an influence: *The mere thought of giving a speech in public makes me feel sick.*

IDM **the merest** even a very small amount of sth: *The merest smell of the fish market made her feel ill.*

merely 🔑 /ˈmɪəli/ ***adv.*** (*formal*) only; just: *I don't want to place an order. I am merely making an enquiry.*

merge /mɜːdʒ/ ***verb*** **1** [I] **~ (with/into sth); ~ (together)** to become part of sth larger: *Three small companies merged into one large one.* ◇ *This stream merges with the river a few miles downstream.* **2** [T] to join things together so that they become one: *We have merged the two classes into one.*

merger /ˈmɜːdʒə(r)/ ***noun*** [C,U] **a ~ (with sb/sth); a ~ (between/of A and B)** (BUSINESS) the act of joining two or more companies together

meridian /məˈrɪdiən/ ***noun*** [C] (**GEOGRAPHY**) a line that we imagine on the surface of the earth that joins the North Pole to the South Pole and passes through a particular place: *the Greenwich meridian* ➲ look at **longitude** ➲ picture at **earth**

meringue /məˈræŋ/ ***noun*** [C,U] a mixture of sugar and egg whites that is cooked in the oven; a cake made from this

merit¹ /ˈmerɪt/ ***noun*** **1** [U] the quality of being good: *There is a lot of merit in her ideas.* ◇ *He got the job* ***on merit****, not because he's the manager's son.* **2** [C, usually pl.] an advantage or a good quality of sb/sth: *Each case must be judged separately on its own merits* (=not according to general principles).

merit² /ˈmerɪt/ ***verb*** [T] (*formal*) to be good enough for sth; to deserve: *This suggestion merits further discussion.*

meritocracy /ˌmerɪˈtɒkrəsi/ ***noun*** [C] (*pl.* **meritocracies**) (**SOCIAL STUDIES**) **1** [C,U] a country or social system where people get power or money on the basis of their ability **2 the meritocracy** [sing.] the group of people with power in this kind of social system

mermaid /ˈmɜːmeɪd/ ***noun*** [C] (in stories) a woman who has the tail of a fish instead of legs and who lives in the sea

merriment /ˈmerimənt/ ***noun*** [U] LAUGHTER and enjoyment

merry /ˈmeri/ ***adj.*** (**merrier**; **merriest**) **1** happy: *merry laughter* ◇ ***Merry Christmas*** (=used to say you hope sb has a happy holiday) **2** (*informal*) slightly drunk ▶ **merrily** ***adv.***

ˈ**merry-go-round** (*BrE* **roundabout** *AmE* **carousel**) ***noun*** [C] a big round platform that turns round and round and has model animals, etc. on it for children to ride on

mesh /meʃ/ ***noun*** [C,U] material that is like a net (=made of plastic, wire or rope threads with holes in between): *a fence made of wire mesh*

mesmerize (also **-ise**) /ˈmezməraɪz/ ***verb*** [T] to hold sb's attention completely: *The audience seemed to be mesmerized by the speaker's voice.*

mesopause /ˈmezəʊpɔːz; ˈmiːzəpɔːz/ ***noun*** [sing.] (**GEOGRAPHY**) the part of the earth's atmosphere where the MESOSPHERE meets the THERMOSPHERE, and where the temperature stops decreasing and begins to increase with height ➲ picture at **atmosphere**

mesophyll /ˈmesəʊfɪl/ ***noun*** [U] (**BIOLOGY**) the material that the inside of a leaf is made of

mesosphere /ˈmesəsfɪə(r); ˈmez-/ ***noun*** [sing.] **the mesosphere** (**GEOGRAPHY**) the region of the earth's atmosphere between about 50 and 80 kilometres above the surface of the earth, above the STRATOSPHERE and below the THERMOSPHERE ➲ picture at **atmosphere**

mesothermal /ˌmezəʊˈθɜːml; ˈmiːzəʊˈθɜːml/ ***adj.*** (**GEOGRAPHY**) (used about a climate) not very hot and not very cold ➲ look at **megathermal**, **microthermal**

mess¹ 🔑 /mes/ ***noun*** **1** [C, usually sing.] the state of being dirty or untidy; a person or thing that is dirty or untidy: *The kitchen's* ***in a*** *terrible* ***mess****!* ◇ *My hair is a mess.* ◇ *You can paint the door, but don't* ***make a mess!*** **2** [sing.] the state of having problems or troubles: *The company is* ***in a*** *financial* ***mess****.* ◇ *to* ***make a mess of*** *your life*

mess² /mes/ ***verb*** [T] (*AmE, informal*) to make sth dirty or untidy: *Don't mess your hands.*

PHR V **mess about/around 1** to behave in a silly and annoying way **2** to spend your time in a relaxed way without any real purpose: *We spent Sunday just messing around at home.*

mess sb about/around to treat sb in a way that is not fair or reasonable, for example by changing your plans without telling them

mess about/around with sth to touch or use sth in a careless way: *It is dangerous to mess about with fireworks.*

mess sth up 1 to make sth dirty or untidy **2** to do sth badly or spoil sth: *I really messed up the last question in the exam.*

mess with sb/sth to deal or behave with sb/sth in a way that you should not: *You shouldn't mess with people's feelings.*

message 🔑 /ˈmesɪdʒ/ ***noun*** **1** [C] a written or spoken piece of information that you send to or leave for a person when you cannot speak to them: *Mr Khan is not here at the moment. Can I* ***take a message****?* ◇ *Could you* ***give a message*** *to Jake, please?* ◇ *If he's not in I'll* ***leave a message*** *on his answering machine.* **2** [sing.] an important idea that a book, speech, etc. is trying to communicate: *It was a funny film but it also had a serious message.* ◇ *The advertising campaign is trying to* ***get the message across*** *that smoking kills.*

IDM **get the message** (*informal*) to understand what sb means even if it is not clearly stated: *He finally got the message and went home.*

ˈ**message board** ***noun*** [C] (**COMPUTING**) a place on a website where a user can write or read messages: *I posted a question on the message board.*

messenger /ˈmesɪndʒə(r)/ ***noun*** [C] a person who carries a message

Messiah (also **messiah**) /məˈsaɪə/ ***noun*** [C] (**RELIGION**) a person, for example Jesus Christ, who is expected to come and save the world

Messrs ***abbr.*** (used as the plural of *Mr* before a list of men's names and before names of business firms): *Messrs Smith, Brown and Robinson* ◇ *Messrs T Brown and Co.*

messy /ˈmesi/ ***adj.*** (**messier**; **messiest**) **1** dirty or untidy: *a messy room* **2** that makes sb/sth dirty: *Painting the ceiling is a messy job.* **3** having or causing problems or trouble: *a messy divorce*

met past tense of **meet**

meta- /ˈmetə/ ***prefix*** (used in nouns, adjectives and verbs) **1** connected with a change of position or state: *metamorphosis* ◇ *metabolism* **2** higher; beyond: *metaphysics*

metabolism /məˈtæbəlɪzəm/ ***noun*** [U, sing.] (**BIOLOGY**) the chemical processes in plants or animals that change food into energy and help them grow: *An athlete has a faster metabolism than most ordinary people.* ▶ **metabolic** /ˌmetəˈbɒlɪk/ ***adj.***: *a high/low metabolic rate*

metacarpal /ˌmetəˈkɑːpl/ ***noun*** [C] (**ANATOMY**) any of the five bones in the hand between the wrist and the fingers

metal 🔑 /ˈmetl/ ***noun*** [C,U] (**CHEMISTRY**) a type of solid substance that is usually hard and shiny and that heat and electricity can travel through: *metals such as tin, iron, gold and steel* ◇ *to recycle scrap metal* ◇ *a metal bar/pipe*

metallic /məˈtælɪk/ ***adj.*** **1** connected with metal or metals: *metallic alloys* **2** looking like metal or making a noise like one piece of metal hitting another: *a metallic blue car* ◇ *harsh metallic sounds*

metalloid /ˈmetlɔɪd/ *noun* [C] (CHEMISTRY) a chemical element which has properties both of metals and of other solid substances

metallurgist /məˈtælədʒɪst/ *noun* [C] (CHEMISTRY) a scientist who studies metals and their uses

metallurgy /məˈtælədʒi/ *noun* [U] (CHEMISTRY) the scientific study of metals and their uses

metamorphic /ˌmetəˈmɔːfɪk/ *adj.* (GEOLOGY) (used about rocks) that have been changed by heat or pressure ➲ look at **igneous**, **sedimentary** ➲ picture at **rock**

metamorphosis /ˌmetəˈmɔːfəsɪs/ *noun* [C] (*pl.* **metamorphoses** /-əsiːz/) (*formal*) (BIOLOGY) a complete change of form (as part of natural development): *the metamorphosis of a tadpole into a frog*

metaphor /ˈmetəfə(r)/ *noun* [C,U] (LITERATURE) a word or phrase that is used in an IMAGINATIVE way to show that sb/sth has the same qualities as another thing. 'Her words were a knife in his heart' is a **metaphor**. ➲ look at **figurative**, **literal**, **simile** ▶ **metaphorical** /ˌmetəˈfɒrɪkl/ *adj.* ▶ **metaphorically** /-kli/ *adv.*

metaˌphysical ˈpoets *noun* [pl.] (LITERATURE) a group of 17th century English POETS who explored the nature of the world and human life, and who used images that were surprising at that time

metaphysics /ˌmetəˈfɪzɪks/ *noun* [U] (SOCIAL STUDIES) the area of PHILOSOPHY that deals with the nature of existence, truth and knowledge ▶ **metaphysical** /ˌmetəˈfɪzɪkl/ *adj.*: *metaphysical problems/speculation*

metatarsal /ˌmetəˈtɑːsl/ *noun* [C] (ANATOMY) any of the bones in the part of the foot between the ankle and the toes

mete /miːt/ *verb*
PHR V **mete sth out (to sb)** (*formal*) to give sb a punishment or HARSH treatment

meteor /ˈmiːtiə(r); -iɔː(r)/ *noun* [C] (ASTRONOMY) a small piece of rock, etc. from space that enters the earth's atmosphere and makes a bright line in the night sky.

meteoric /ˌmiːtiˈɒrɪk/ *adj.* very fast or successful: *a meteoric rise to fame*

meteorite /ˈmiːtiəraɪt/ *noun* [C] (ASTRONOMY) a piece of rock from space that hits the earth's surface

meteoroid /ˈmiːtiərɔɪd/ *noun* [C] (ASTRONOMY) a piece of rock in space that would become a METEOR if it entered the earth's atmosphere

meteorologist /ˌmiːtiəˈrɒlədʒɪst/ *noun* [C] a person who studies the weather

meteorology /ˌmiːtiəˈrɒlədʒi/ *noun* [U] the study of the weather and climate ▶ **meteorological** /ˌmiːtiərəˈlɒdʒɪkl/ *adj.*

meter ⊷ /ˈmiːtə(r)/ *noun* [C] **1** a piece of equipment that measures the amount of gas, water, electricity, etc. you have used: *a parking meter* **2** (*AmE*) = METRE ▶ **meter** *verb* [T]: *Is your water metered?*

methane /ˈmiːθeɪn/ *noun* [U] (*symbol* CH_4) (CHEMISTRY) a gas without colour or smell, that burns easily and that we can use to produce heat

methanol /ˈmeθənɒl/ *noun* [U] (*symbol* CH_3OH) (CHEMISTRY) a poisonous form of alcohol that is colourless, has no smell and changes easily into a gas

method ⊷ AW /ˈmeθəd/ *noun* [C] a way of doing sth: *What method of payment do you prefer? Cash, cheque or credit card?* ◇ *modern teaching methods*

methodical AW /məˈθɒdɪkl/ *adj.* having or using a WELL-ORGANIZED and careful way of doing sth: *Paul is a very methodical worker.* ▶ **methodically** /-kli/ *adv.*

methodology AW /ˌmeθəˈdɒlədʒi/ (*pl.* **methodologies**) *noun* [C,U] a way of doing sth based on particular principles and methods: *language teaching methodologies* ▶ **methodological** /ˌmeθədəˈlɒdʒɪkl/ *adj.*

methylated spirits /ˌmeθəleɪtɪd ˈspɪrɪts/ (also *informal* **meths** /meθs/) *noun* [U] a type of alcohol that you cannot drink, used as a fuel for lighting and heating and for cleaning off dirty marks

meticulous /məˈtɪkjələs/ *adj.* giving or showing great attention to detail; very careful ▶ **meticulously** *adv.*

metonymy /məˈtɒnəmi/ *noun* [U] (LANGUAGE) the act of referring to sth by the name of sth else that is closely connected with it, for example using *the White House* for the US President

metre ⊷ (*AmE* **meter**) /ˈmiːtə(r)/ *noun* **1** [C] (*abbr.* **m**) a measure of length; 100 CENTIMETRES: *a two-metre high wall* ◇ *Who won the 100 metres?* **2 metres** (SPORT) used in the name of races: *She came second in the 100 metres.* **3** [U, C] (LITERATURE) the arrangement of strong and weak STRESSES (= the force that you put on a particular word or part of a word when you speak) in lines of poetry that produces the rhythm; a particular example of this

metric /ˈmetrɪk/ *adj.* using THE METRIC SYSTEM ➲ look at **imperial**

metrication /ˌmetrɪˈkeɪʃn/ *noun* [U] the process of changing to using THE METRIC SYSTEM

the ˈmetric system *noun* [sing.] the system of measurement that uses the metre, the kilogram and the litre as basic units

ˌmetric ˈton (*also* **tonne**) *noun* [C] a unit for measuring weight, equal to 1000 kilograms

metronome /ˈmetrənəʊm/ *noun* [C] (MUSIC) a device that makes a regular sound like a clock and is used by musicians to help them keep the correct rhythm when playing a piece of music

metronome

metropolis /məˈtrɒpəlɪs/ *noun* [C] a very large city ▶ **metropolitan** /ˌmetrəˈpɒlɪtən/ *adj.*

mezzanine /ˈmezəniːn; ˈmetsə-/ *noun* [C] **1** (ARCHITECTURE) a floor that is built between two floors of a building and is smaller than the other floors: *a bedroom on the mezzanine* ◇ *a mezzanine floor* **2** (*AmE*) (ARTS AND MEDIA) the first area of seats above the ground floor in a theatre; the first few rows of these seats ➲ look at **dress circle**

mg ⊷ *abbr.* milligram(s)

MHz *abbr.* (in writing) **megahertz**

miaow /miˈaʊ/ *noun* [C] the sound that a cat makes ▶ **miaow** *verb* [I] ➲ look at **purr**

mice plural of **mouse**

micro- /ˈmaɪkrəʊ/ *prefix* (used in nouns, adjectives and adverbs) small, on a small scale: *microchip* ◇ *micro-organism* OPP **macro-**

microbe /ˈmaɪkrəʊb/ ***noun*** [C] (**BIOLOGY**) an extremely small living thing that you can only see with a special piece of equipment (**a microscope**) and that can cause disease
▶ **microbial** /maɪˈkrəʊbiəl/ ***adj.***: *Cool soil temperatures slow down microbial activity.*

microbiologist /ˌmaɪkrəʊbaɪˈɒlədʒɪst/ ***noun*** [C] (**BIOLOGY**) a scientist who studies very small living things

microbiology /ˌmaɪkrəʊbaɪˈɒlədʒi/ ***noun*** [U] (**BIOLOGY**) the scientific study of very small living things

microchip /ˈmaɪkrəʊtʃɪp/ (*also* **chip**) ***noun*** [C] (**COMPUTING**) a very small piece of a special material (**silicon**) that is used inside a computer, etc. to make it work

microcomputer /ˈmaɪkrəʊkəmpjuːtə(r)/ ***noun*** [C] (**COMPUTING**) a small computer that contains a MICROPROCESSOR

microcosm /ˈmaɪkrəʊkɒzəm/ ***noun*** [C] **a ~ (of sth)** something that is a small example of sth larger: *Our little village is a microcosm of society as a whole.*
➲ look at **macrocosm**

microelectronics /ˌmaɪkrəʊɪˌlekˈtrɒnɪks/ ***noun*** [U] (**PHYSICS**) the design, production and use of very small electronic CIRCUITS (= circular paths that electric currents can flow around)

microfiche /ˈmaɪkrəʊfiːʃ/ ***noun*** [C,U] a piece of film on which information is stored in very small print

microfilm /ˈmaɪkrəʊfɪlm/ ***noun*** [U,C] film used for storing written information on in print of very small size

microgram /ˈmaɪkrəʊɡræm/ ***noun*** [C] (*symbol* µg) a unit for measuring weight. There are one million **micrograms** in one gram.

micrometre /ˈmaɪkrəʊmiːtə(r)/ ***noun*** [C] (*symbol* **µm**) a unit for measuring length. There are one million **micrometres** in one metre.

micron /ˈmaɪkrɒn/ ***noun*** [C] = MICROMETRE

ˌmicro-ˈorganism ***noun*** [C] (**BIOLOGY**) a very small living thing that you can only see with a special piece of equipment (**a microscope**)

microphone /ˈmaɪkrəfəʊn/ (also *informal* **mike**) ***noun*** [C] a piece of electrical equipment that is used for making sounds louder or for recording them

microprocessor /ˌmaɪkrəʊˈprəʊsesə(r)/ ***noun*** [C] (**COMPUTING**) a small unit of a computer that contains all the functions of the CENTRAL PROCESSING UNIT (= the part of the computer that controls all the other parts of the system)

microscope /ˈmaɪkrəskəʊp/ ***noun*** [C] (**SCIENCE**) a piece of equipment that makes very small objects look big enough for you to be able to see them: *to examine sth* ***under a microscope***

microscopic /ˌmaɪkrəˈskɒpɪk/ ***adj.*** too small to be seen without a MICROSCOPE

microsurgery /ˈmaɪkrəʊsɜːdʒəri/ ***noun*** [U] (**HEALTH**) the use of extremely small instruments and MICROSCOPES in order to perform very detailed and complicated medical operations

microthermal /ˌmaɪkrəʊˈθɜːml/ ***adj.*** (**GEOGRAPHY**) (used about a climate) having hot summers and cold winters ➲ look at **megathermal**, **mesothermal**

microscope

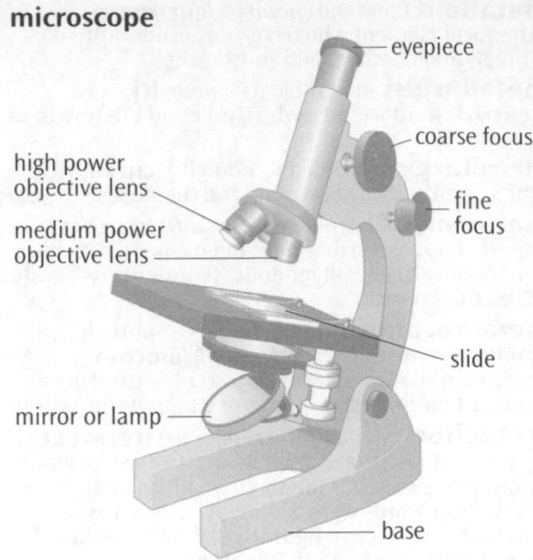

microwave /ˈmaɪkrəweɪv/ ***noun*** [C] **1** (**PHYSICS**) a short electric wave that is used for sending radio messages and for cooking food **2** (*also* **ˌmicrowave ˈoven**) a type of oven that cooks or heats food very quickly using **microwaves** ➲ picture at **wavelength**

mid /mɪd/ ***adj.*** (only *before* a noun) the middle of: *I'm away from mid June.* ◇ *the mid 1990s*

mid- /mɪd/ ***prefix*** (used in nouns and adjectives) in the middle of: *mid-afternoon* ◇ *a mid-air collision*

midday 🔑 /ˌmɪdˈdeɪ/ ***noun*** [U] at or around twelve o'clock in the middle of the day: *We arranged to meet* ***at midday***. ◇ *the heat of the midday sun*
SYN **noon** ➲ look at **midnight**

middle[1] 🔑 /ˈmɪdl/ ***noun*** **1** [sing.] **the ~ (of sth)** the part, point or position that is at about the same distance from the two ends or sides of sth: *the white line* ***in the middle of*** *the road* ◇ *Here's a photo of me with my two brothers. I'm the one* ***in the middle***. **2** [C] (*informal*) your waist: *I want to lose weight around my middle.*
IDM **be in the middle of sth/doing sth** to be busy doing sth: *Can you call back in five minutes – I'm in the middle of feeding the baby.*
in the middle of nowhere a long way from any town

middle[2] 🔑 /ˈmɪdl/ ***adj.*** (only *before* a noun) in the middle: *I wear my ring on my middle finger.*

ˌmiddle ˈage ***noun*** [U] the time when you are about 40 to 60 years old: *a woman in early middle age* ▶ **ˌmiddle-ˈaged** ***adj.***: *a middle-aged man*

the ˌMiddle ˈAges ***noun*** [pl.] (**HISTORY**) the period of European history from about 1100 to 1500 AD

the ˌmiddle ˈclass ***noun*** [sing.] (*also* **the ˌmiddle ˈclasses** [pl.]) (**SOCIAL STUDIES**) the group of people in a society who are neither very rich nor very poor and that includes professional and business people
▶ **ˌmiddle ˈclass** ***adj.***: *They're middle class.* ◇ *a middle-class background* ➲ look at **the upper class**, **the working class**

ˌmiddle ˈear ***noun*** [sing.] (**ANATOMY**) the central part of your ear behind your EARDRUM (= the thin piece of skin that allows you to hear sound) ➲ look at **inner ear**

the ˌMiddle ˈEast ***noun*** [sing.] (**GEOGRAPHY**) an area that covers SW Asia and NE Africa ➲ look at **the Far East** ▶ **ˌMiddle ˈEastern** ***adj.***

middleman /'mɪdlmæn/ ***noun*** [C] (*pl.* **-men** /-men/) **1** (BUSINESS) a person or company who buys goods from the company that makes them and then sells them to sb else **2** a person who helps to arrange things between two people who do not want to meet each other

ˌmiddle 'name ***noun*** [C] a name that comes after your first name and before your family name

ˌmiddle-of-the-'road ***adj.*** (used about people, policies, etc.) not extreme; acceptable to most people

'middle school ***noun*** [C] (*BrE*) (EDUCATION) a school for children aged between 9 and 13

midfield /'mɪdfiːld; ˌmɪd'fiːld/ ***noun*** [U, C, sing.] (SPORT) the central part of a sports field; the group of players in this position: *He plays (in) midfield.* ◇ *a midfield player* ▶ **midfielder** /'mɪdfiːldə(r)/ ***noun*** [C]

midge /mɪdʒ/ ***noun*** [C] a very small flying insect that can bite people SYN **gnat**

midget /'mɪdʒɪt/ ***noun*** [C] a very small person

MIDI /'mɪdi/ ***noun*** [U] (MUSIC) **Musical Instrument Digital Interface**; a connection or program that connects electronic musical instruments and computers

the Midlands /'mɪdləndz/ ***noun*** [sing., with sing. or pl. verb] (GEOGRAPHY) the central part of England around Birmingham and Nottingham

midnight 🔑 /'mɪdnaɪt/ ***noun*** [U] twelve o'clock at night: *They left the party* ***at midnight.*** ◇ *The clock struck midnight.* ➲ look at **midday**

'mid-point ***noun*** [C, usually sing.] (MATHEMATICS) the point that is at an equal distance between the beginning and the end of sth; the point that is at an equal distance between two things: *the mid-point between the first number and the last*

midriff /'mɪdrɪf/ ***noun*** [C] the part of your body between your chest and your waist

midst /mɪdst/ ***noun*** [U] the middle of sth; among a group of people or things: *The country is* ***in the midst of*** *a recession.* ◇ *They realized with a shock that there was an enemy* ***in their midst.***

midsummer /ˌmɪd'sʌmə(r)/ ***noun*** [U] the time around the middle of summer: *a beautiful midsummer's evening*

midway /ˌmɪd'weɪ/ ***adj., adv.*** in the middle of a period of time or between two places: *The village lies midway between two large towns.* SYN **halfway**

midweek /ˌmɪd'wiːk/ ***noun*** [U] the middle of the week (=Tuesday, Wednesday and Thursday) ▶ **midweek** ***adv.***: *If you travel midweek it will be less crowded.*

the Midwest /ˌmɪd'west/ ***noun*** [sing.] (GEOGRAPHY) the northern central part of the US

midwife /'mɪdwaɪf/ ***noun*** [C] (*pl.* **midwives** /-waɪvz/) (HEALTH) a person who has been trained to help women give birth to babies

midwifery /ˌmɪd'wɪfəri/ ***noun*** [U] (HEALTH) the work of a MIDWIFE

midwinter /ˌmɪd'wɪntə(r)/ ***noun*** [U] the time around the middle of winter

might[1] 🔑 /maɪt/ ***modal verb*** (*negative* **might not**; *short form* **mightn't** /'maɪtnt/) **1** used for saying that sth is possible: *'Where's Vinay?' 'He might be upstairs.'* ◇ *I think I might have forgotten the tickets.* ◇ *She might not come if she's very busy.* **2** (*BrE, formal*) used to ask for sth or suggest sth very politely: *I wonder if I might go home half an hour early today?* **3** used as the form of 'may' when you report what sb has said: *He said he might be late* (=his words were, 'I may be late').

IDM **may/might as well (do sth)** → WELL[1]

you, etc. might do sth used when you are angry to say what sb could or should have done: *They might at least have phoned if they're not coming.*

I might have known used for saying that you are not surprised that sth has happened: *I might have known he wouldn't help.*

might[2] /maɪt/ ***noun*** [U] (*formal*) great strength or power: *I pushed* ***with all*** *my* ***might,*** *but the rock did not move.*

mighty[1] /'maɪti/ ***adj.*** (**mightier**; **mightiest**) very strong or powerful

mighty[2] /'maɪti/ ***adv.*** (*AmE, informal*) very: *That's mighty kind of you.*

migraine /'miːgreɪn/ ***noun*** [C,U] (HEALTH) very bad pain in your head that makes you feel sick; a severe headache

migrant AW /'maɪgrənt/ ***noun*** [C] **1** (SOCIAL STUDIES) a person who moves from place to place, especially looking for work: *migrant workers* **2** (BIOLOGY) a bird or an animal that moves from one place to another according to the season

migrate AW /maɪ'greɪt/ ***verb*** [I] **1** (BIOLOGY) (used about animals and birds) to travel from one part of the world to another at the same time every year **2** (SOCIAL STUDIES) (used about a large number of people) to go and live and work in another place: *Many country people were forced to migrate to the cities to look for work.* ➲ look at **emigrate** ▶ **migration** AW /maɪ'greɪʃn/ ***noun*** [C,U]: *the migration routes of birds*

migratory AW /'maɪgrətri; maɪ'greɪtəri/ ***adj.*** (BIOLOGY) (used about animals and birds) travelling from one part of the world to another at the same time every year

mike /maɪk/ (*informal*) = MICROPHONE

milage = MILEAGE

mild 🔑 /maɪld/ ***adj.*** **1** not strong; not very bad: *a mild soap* ◇ *a mild winter* ◇ *a mild punishment* **2** (used about food) not having a strong taste: *mild cheese* **3** kind and gentle: *He's a very mild man – you never see him get angry.* ▶ **mildness** ***noun*** [U]

mildew /'mɪldjuː/ ***noun*** [U] (BIOLOGY) a living white substance (**fungus**) that grows on walls, plants, food, etc. in warm wet conditions

mildly /'maɪldli/ ***adv.*** **1** not very; slightly: *mildly surprised* **2** in a gentle way

mile 🔑 /maɪl/ ***noun*** **1** [C] a measure of length; 1.6 kilometres. There are 1760 yards in a mile: *The nearest beach is seven miles away.* ◇ *It's a seven-mile drive to the beach.* **2** [C] a lot: *He missed the target by a mile.* ◇ *I'm feeling miles better this morning.* **3 miles** [pl.] a long way: *How much further is it? We've walked miles already.* ◇ *From the top of the hill you can see* ***for miles.***

IDM **see, hear, tell, spot, etc. sb/sth a mile off** (*informal*) used to say that sb/sth is very obvious: *He's lying – you can tell that a mile off.*

mileage (also **milage**) /'maɪlɪdʒ/ ***noun*** **1** [C,U] the distance that has been travelled, measured in miles: *The car is five years old but it has a low mileage.* **2** [U] (*informal*) the amount of use that you get from sth: *The newspapers got a lot of mileage out of the scandal.*

mileometer ***noun*** [C] = MILOMETER

milestone /ˈmaɪlstəʊn/ ***noun*** [C] a very important event: *The concert was a milestone in the band's history.*

militant /ˈmɪlɪtənt/ ***adj.*** ready to use force or strong pressure to get what you want: *The workers were in a very militant mood.* ▶ **militant** ***noun*** [C] ▶ **militancy** /-ənsi/ ***noun*** [U]

militarism /ˈmɪlɪtərɪzəm/ ***noun*** [U] (**POLITICS**) the belief that a country should have great military strength in order to be powerful

military[1] 🔑 AW /ˈmɪlətri/ ***adj.*** (only *before* a noun) connected with soldiers or the army, navy, etc.: *All men in that country have to do two years' military service.* ◇ *to take military action*

military[2] AW /ˈmɪlətri/ ***noun*** [sing., with sing. or pl. verb] **the military** soldiers; the armed forces: *The military was/were called in to deal with the riot.*

militia /məˈlɪʃə/ ***noun*** [C, with sing. or pl. verb] a group of people who are not professional soldiers but who have had military training

milk[1] 🔑 /mɪlk/ ***noun*** [U](**BIOLOGY**) **1** a white liquid that is produced by women and female animals to feed their babies. People drink the milk of some animals and use it to make butter and cheese: *skimmed/long-life/low-fat milk* ◇ *a bottle/carton of milk* **2** the juice of some plants or trees that looks like milk: *coconut milk*

milk[2] /mɪlk/ ***verb*** [T] **1** (**AGRICULTURE**) to take milk from a cow, GOAT, etc. **2** to get as much money, advantage, etc. for yourself from sb/sth as you can, without caring about others

milkman /ˈmɪlkmən/ ***noun*** [C] (*pl.* **-men** /-mən; -men/) a person who takes milk to people's houses every day

ˈmilkshake /ˈmɪlkʃeɪk/ ***noun*** [C,U] a drink made of milk with an added flavour of fruit or chocolate

ˈmilk tooth ***noun*** [C] any of the first set of teeth in young children that fall out and are replaced by others

milky /ˈmɪlki/ ***adj.*** like milk, or made with milk: *milky white skin* ◇ *milky coffee*

the ˌMilky ˈWay ***noun*** [sing.] = THE GALAXY

mill[1] /mɪl/ ***noun*** [C] **1** (**BUSINESS**) a factory that is used for making certain kinds of material: *a cotton/paper/steel mill* ➲ note at **factory** **2** a building that contains a large machine that was used in the past for making grain into flour: *a windmill* **3** a kitchen tool that is used for making sth into powder: *a pepper mill*

mill[2] /mɪl/ ***verb*** [T] to produce sth in a **mill**
PHR V **mill about/around** (*informal*) (used about a large number of people or animals) to move around in a place with no real purpose

millennium /mɪˈleniəm/ ***noun*** [C] (*pl.* **millennia** /-niə/ or **millenniums**) a period of 1000 years: *We are at the start of the new millennium.*

miller /ˈmɪlə(r)/ ***noun*** a person who owns or works in a MILL for making flour

millet /ˈmɪlɪt/ ***noun*** [U] (**AGRICULTURE**) a plant with a lot of small seeds that are used as food for people and birds ➲ picture at **cereal**

milli- /ˈmɪli/ ***prefix*** (used in nouns, often in units of measurement) one THOUSANDTH: *millisecond* ◇ *millimetre*

millibar /ˈmɪlibɑː(r)/ ***noun*** [C] (**PHYSICS**) a unit for measuring the pressure of the atmosphere. One thousand **millibars** are equal to one BAR

milligram 🔑 (*also* **milligramme**) /ˈmɪligræm/ ***noun*** [C] (*abbr.* **mg**) a measure of weight. There are 1000 milligrams in a gram.

millilitre (*AmE* **milliliter**) /ˈmɪliliːtə(r)/ ***noun*** [C] (*abbr.* **ml**) a measure of liquid. There are 1000 **millilitres** in a litre.

millimetre 🔑 (*AmE* **millimeter**) /ˈmɪlimiːtə(r)/ ***noun*** [C] (*abbr.* **mm**) a measure of length. There are 1000 millimetres in a metre.

millinery /ˈmɪlɪnəri/ ***noun*** [U] (**BUSINESS**) the business of making or selling women's hats

million /ˈmɪljən/ ***number*** **1** 1000000: *Nearly 60 million people live in Britain.* ◇ *Millions of people are at risk from the disease.*
HELP Notice that you use **million** without **s** when talking about more than one **million**: *six million people.*
2 a million; **millions (of)** (*informal*) a very large amount: *I still have a million things to do.* ◇ *There are millions of reasons why you shouldn't go.*
HELP For more information about numbers look at the special section on numbers on page R36.

millionaire /ˌmɪljəˈneə(r)/ ***noun*** [C] a person who has a million pounds, dollars, etc.; a very rich person

millionth[1] /ˈmɪljənθ/ ***pronoun, det.*** 1000000th

millionth[2] /ˈmɪljənθ/ ***noun*** [C] one of a million equal parts of sth: *a millionth of a second*

millipede /ˈmɪlɪpiːd/ ***noun*** [C] a small animal like an insect with a long thin body divided into many sections, each with two pairs of legs

milometer (also **mileometer**) /maɪˈlɒmɪtə(r)/ (*AmE* **odometer**) ***noun*** [C] a piece of equipment in a vehicle that measures the number of miles you have travelled

mime /maɪm/ (*AmE* **pantomime**) ***noun*** [U, C] (**ARTS AND MEDIA**) the use of movements of your hands and body and the expression on your face to tell a story or to act sth without speaking; a performance using this method of acting: *The performance consisted of dance, music and mime.* ▶ **mime** ***verb*** [I,T]

mimic[1] /ˈmɪmɪk/ ***verb*** [T] (*pres. part.* **mimicking**; *pt, pp* **mimicked**) to copy sb's behaviour, movements, voice, etc. in an amusing way

mimic[2] /ˈmɪmɪk/ ***noun*** [C] a person who can copy sb's behaviour, movements, voice, etc. in an amusing way ▶ **mimicry** /ˈmɪmɪkri/ ***noun*** [U]

min. ***abbr.*** **1** minimum: *min. temp tomorrow 2°* **2** minute(s): *fastest time: 6 min.*

minaret /ˌmɪnəˈret/ ***noun*** [C] (**RELIGION**) a tall thin tower, usually forming part of a building where Muslims meet and pray (**a mosque**)

minaret

mince /mɪns/ (*BrE*) (*AmE* **ground ˈbeef**; **hamburger**) ***noun*** [U] meat that has been cut into very small pieces with a special machine ▶ **mince** ***verb*** [T]

mincemeat /ˈmɪnsmiːt/ ***noun*** [U] a mixture of dried fruit, nuts, sugar, etc. (but no meat) that is used as a filling for sweet dishes, especially MINCE PIES

ˌ**mince ˈpie** *noun* [C] a small round cake with a MINCEMEAT inside, traditionally eaten in Britain at Christmas time

mind¹ ⊶ /maɪnd/ *noun* [C,U] the part of your brain that thinks and remembers; your thoughts, feelings and intelligence: *He has a brilliant mind.* ◇ *Not everybody has the right sort of mind for this work.*
IDM **at/in the back of your mind** → BACK¹
be in two minds (about sth/doing sth) to not feel sure of sth: *I'm in two minds about leaving Will alone in the house while we're away.*
be/go out of your mind (*informal*) to be or become crazy or very worried: *I was going out of my mind when Tina didn't come home on time.*
bear in mind (that); bear/keep sb/sth in mind to remember or consider (that); to remember sb/sth: *We'll bear/keep your suggestion in mind for the future.*
bring/call sb/sth to mind to be reminded of sb/sth; to remember sb/sth
cast your mind back → CAST¹
change your mind → CHANGE¹
come/spring to mind if sth comes/springs to mind, you suddenly remember or think of it
cross your mind → CROSS²
ease sb's mind → EASE²
frame of mind → FRAME¹
give sb a piece of your mind → PIECE¹
go clean out of your mind → CLEAN³
have/keep an open mind → OPEN¹
have sb/sth in mind (for sth) to be considering sb/sth as suitable for sth; to have a plan: *Who do you have in mind for the job?*
keep your mind on sth to continue to pay attention to sth: *Keep your mind on the road while you're driving!*
make up your mind to decide: *I can't make up my mind which sweater to buy.*
on your mind worrying you: *Don't bother her with that. She's got enough on her mind already.*
prey on sb's mind → PREY²
put/set sb's mind at rest to make sb stop worrying: *The results of the blood test set his mind at rest.*
slip your mind → SLIP¹
speak your mind → SPEAK
state of mind → STATE¹
take sb's mind off sth to help sb not to think or worry about sth
to my mind in my opinion: *To my mind, this is a complete waste of time!*

mind² ⊶ /maɪnd/ *verb* **1** [I,T] (especially in questions, answers, and negative sentences) to feel annoyed, upset or uncomfortable about sth/sb: *I'm sure Simon won't mind if you don't invite him.* ◇ *I don't mind what you do – it's your decision.* ◇ *Do you mind having to travel so far to work every day?* ◇ *Are you sure your parents won't mind me coming?* ◇ *'Would you like tea or coffee?' 'I don't mind.'* (=I'm happy to have either) ◇ *I wouldn't mind a break right now* (=I would like one). **2** [T] (used in a question as a polite way of asking sb to do sth or for permission to do sth) could you...?; may I...?: *Would you mind closing the window for me?* ◇ *Do you mind driving? I'm feeling rather tired.* **3** [T] used to tell sb to be careful of sth or to pay attention to sb/sth: *It's a very low doorway so mind your head.* ◇ *Mind that step!* ◇ *Don't mind me! I won't disturb you.* **4** [T] (*especially BrE*) to look after or watch sb/sth for a short time: *Could you mind my bag while I go and get us some drinks?*
IDM **mind you** used for attracting attention to a point you are making or for giving more information: *Paul seems very tired. Mind you, he has been working very hard recently.*
mind your own business to pay attention to your own affairs, not other people's: *Stop asking me personal questions and mind your own business!*
never mind don't worry; it doesn't matter: *'I forgot to post your letter.' 'Never mind, I'll do it later.'*
PHR V **mind out** (*informal*) 'Get out of the way!': *Mind out! There's a car coming.*

ˈ**mind-boggling** *adj.* (*informal*) difficult to imagine, understand or believe: *Mind-boggling amounts of money were being discussed.*

-minded /maɪndɪd/ *adj.* (used to form compound adjectives) **1** having the type of mind mentioned: *a strong-minded/open-minded/narrow-minded person* **2** interested in the thing mentioned: *money-minded*

minder /ˈmaɪndə(r)/ *noun* [C] a person whose job is to look after and protect sb/sth: *My son goes to a childminder so that I can work part-time.*

mindful /ˈmaɪndfl/ *adj.* **~ of sb/sth; ~ that...** (*formal*) remembering sb/sth and considering them or it when you do sth: *mindful of our responsibilities* ◇ *Mindful of the danger of tropical storms, I decided not to go out.* SYN **conscious**

mindless /ˈmaɪndləs/ *adj.* **1** done or acting without thought and for no particular reason: *mindless violence* **2** not needing thought or intelligence: *a mindless and repetitive task*

mine¹ ⊶ /maɪn/ *pronoun* of or belonging to me: *'Whose is this jacket?' 'It's mine.'* ◇ *Don't take your car – you can come in mine.* ◇ *May I introduce a friend of mine* (=one of my friends)? ➲ look at **my**

mine² ⊶ /maɪn/ *noun* [C] **1** (GEOLOGY) a deep hole, or a system of passages under the ground where minerals such as coal, tin, gold, etc. are dug: *a coal/salt/gold mine* ➲ look at **quarry 2** a bomb that is hidden under the ground or under water and explodes when sb/sth touches it: *The car went over a mine and blew up.*

mine³ /maɪn/ *verb* **1** [I,T] (GEOLOGY) to dig in the ground for minerals such as coal, tin, gold, etc.: *Diamonds are mined in South Africa.* ➲ look at **mining 2** [T] to put mines²(2) in an area of land or sea

minefield /ˈmaɪnfiːld/ *noun* [C] **1** an area of land or sea where mines²(2) have been hidden **2** a situation that is full of hidden dangers or difficulties: *a political minefield*

miner /ˈmaɪnə(r)/ *noun* [C] (GEOLOGY) a person whose job is to work in a mine²(1) to get coal, salt, tin, etc.

mineral ⊶ /ˈmɪnərəl/ *noun* [C] (GEOLOGY, HEALTH) a natural substance such as coal, salt, oil, etc., especially one that is found in the ground. Some minerals are also present in food and drink and are very important for good health: *a country rich in minerals* ◇ *the recommended daily intake of vitamins and minerals*

ˈ**mineral water** *noun* [U] water that comes straight from a place in the ground (**a spring**), which contains minerals or gases and is thought to be good for your health

mingle /ˈmɪŋgl/ *verb* [I,T] **~ A and B (together); ~ (A) (with B)** to mix with other things or people: *The colours slowly mingled together to make a muddy brown.* ◇ *His excitement was mingled with fear.* ◇ *to mingle with the rich and famous*

mini- /ˈmɪni/ (used to form compound nouns) very small: *a miniskirt* ◇ *minigolf*

miniature /ˈmɪnətʃə(r)/ ***noun*** [C] a small copy of sth which is much larger: *a miniature camera*
IDM **in miniature** exactly the same as sb/sth else but in a very small form

minibar /ˈmɪnibɑː(r)/ ***noun*** [C] a small fridge in a hotel room, with drinks in it for guests to use

ˈ**mini-break** ***noun*** [C] (TOURISM) a short holiday, usually of only two or three days

minibus /ˈmɪnibʌs/ ***noun*** [C] (*especially BrE*) a small bus, usually for no more than 12 people

minidisc /ˈmɪnɪdɪsk/ ***noun*** [C] a disc like a small CD that can record and play sound or data

minim /ˈmɪnɪm/ (*AmE* ˈ**half note**) ***noun*** [C] (MUSIC) a type of note ➲ note at **crotchet** ➲ picture at **music**

minimal AW /ˈmɪnɪməl/ ***adj.*** very small in amount, size or level; as little as possible: *The project must be carried out at minimal cost.*

minimalist /ˈmɪnɪməlɪst/ ***noun*** [C] (ARTS AND MEDIA) an artist, a musician, etc. who uses very simple ideas or a very small number of simple things in their work ▶ **minimalism** ***noun*** [U]

minimize (also -ise) AW /ˈmɪnɪmaɪz/ ***verb*** [T] **1** to make sth as small as possible (in amount or level): *We shall try to minimize the risks to the public.* **2** to try to make sth seem less important than it really is **3** (COMPUTING) to make sth small on a computer screen OPP **maximize**

minimum[1] ⊶ AW /ˈmɪnɪməm/ ***noun*** [sing.] the smallest amount or level that is possible or allowed: *I need a minimum of seven hours' sleep.* ◇ *We will try and* ***keep*** *the cost of the tickets* ***to a minimum***. OPP **maximum**

minimum[2] ⊶ AW /ˈmɪnɪməm/ ***adj.*** (only *before* a noun) the smallest possible or allowed; extremely small: *to introduce a national* ***minimum wage*** (=the lowest wage that an employer is legally allowed to pay) OPP **maximum** ▶ **minimum *adv.***: *We'll need £200 minimum for expenses.*

mining /ˈmaɪnɪŋ/ ***noun*** [U] (often used to form compound nouns) (GEOLOGY) the process or industry of getting minerals, metals, etc. out of the ground by digging: *coal/tin/gold mining*

minister ⊶ /ˈmɪnɪstə(r)/ ***noun*** [C] **1 Minister** (*AmE* **Secretary**) (POLITICS) a member of the government, often the head of a government department: *the Minister for Trade and Industry* ➲ look at **Prime Minister**, **Cabinet Minister** **2** (RELIGION) a priest in some Protestant churches ➲ look at **vicar**

ministerial AW /ˌmɪnɪˈstɪəriəl/ ***adj.*** (POLITICS) connected with a government minister or department

ministry ⊶ AW /ˈmɪnɪstri/ ***noun*** [C] (*pl.* **ministries**) (*also* **department**) (POLITICS) a government department that has a particular area of responsibility: *the Ministry of Defence*
ℹ **Department** is the only word used in American English.

minivan /ˈmɪnivæn/ (*AmE*) = PEOPLE CARRIER

mink /mɪŋk/ ***noun*** [C] a small wild animal that is kept for its thick brown fur which is used to make expensive coats

minor[1] ⊶ AW /ˈmaɪnə(r)/ ***adj.*** **1** not very big, serious or important (when compared with others): *It's only a minor problem. Don't worry.* ◇ *She's gone into hospital for a minor operation.* OPP **major** **2** (MUSIC) of one of the two types of key[1](4) in which music is usually written: *a symphony in F minor* ➲ look at **major**

minor[2] AW /ˈmaɪnə(r)/ ***noun*** [C] (LAW) a person who is under the age at which you legally become an adult and are responsible for your actions: *It is an offence to serve alcohol to minors.*

minority ⊶ AW /maɪˈnɒrəti/ ***noun*** [C] (*pl.* **minorities**) **1** [usually sing., with sing. or pl. verb] the smaller number or part of a group; less than half: *Only a minority of teenagers become/becomes involved in crime.* OPP **majority** **2** (SOCIAL STUDIES) a small group of people who are of a different race or religion to most of the people in the community or country where they live: *Schools in Britain need to do more to help children of* ***ethnic/racial minorities***.
IDM **be in a/the minority** to be the smaller of two groups: *Men are in the minority in the teaching profession.* ➲ look at **in a/the majority**

minster /ˈmɪnstə(r)/ ***noun*** [C] (*BrE*) (RELIGION) a large or important church: *York Minster*

mint /mɪnt/ ***noun*** **1** [U] a plant whose leaves are used to give flavour to food, drinks, TOOTHPASTE and are used in cooking as a HERB: *lamb with mint sauce* **2** [C] a type of sweet with a strong fresh flavour **3** [sing.] the place where money in the form of coins and notes is made by the government ▶ **mint *verb*** [T]: *freshly minted coins*

minuet /ˌmɪnjuˈet/ ***noun*** [C] (MUSIC) a slow elegant dance that was popular in the 17th and 18th centuries; a piece of music for this dance, that has a rhythm of three beats

minus[1] /ˈmaɪnəs/ ***prep.*** **1** (MATHEMATICS) (used in sums) less; SUBTRACT; take away: *Six minus two is four (6 – 2 = 4).* OPP **plus** **2** (MATHEMATICS) (used about a number) below zero: *The temperature will fall to minus 10.* **3** (*informal*) without sth that was there before: *We're going to be minus a car for a while.*

minus[2] /ˈmaɪnəs/ ***noun*** [C] **1** (*also* ˈ**minus sign**) (*symbol* **–**) (MATHEMATICS) the symbol which is used in mathematics to show that a number is below zero or that you should subtract the second number from the first **2** (*also* ˈ**minus point**) (*informal*) a negative quality; a disadvantage: *Let's consider the pluses and minuses of moving out of the city.* OPP **plus**

minus[3] /ˈmaɪnəs/ ***adj.*** **1** (MATHEMATICS) lower than zero: *a minus figure* **2** (not *before* a noun) (EDUCATION) (used in a system of marks given for school work) slightly lower than: *I got A minus (A–) for my essay.* OPP **plus**

minuscule /ˈmɪnəskjuːl/ ***adj.*** extremely small

minute[1] ⊶ /ˈmɪnɪt/ ***noun*** **1** [C] (*abbr.* **min.**) one of the 60 parts that make up one hour; 60 seconds: *It's twelve minutes to nine.* ◇ *He telephoned ten minutes ago.* ◇ *The programme lasts for about fifty minutes.* **2** [sing.] (*spoken*) a very short time; a moment: ***Just/Wait a minute*** (=wait)*! You've forgotten your notes.* ◇ *Have you got a minute? – I'd like to talk to you.* **3 the minutes** [pl.] (BUSINESS) a written record of what is said and decided at a meeting **4** each of the 60 equal parts of a degree, used in measuring angles: *37 degrees 30 minutes (37° 30')*
IDM **(at) any minute/moment (now)** (*informal*) very soon: *The plane should be landing any minute now.*
in a minute very soon: *I'll be with you in a minute.*
the last minute/moment → LAST[1] (1)
the minute/moment (that) as soon as: *I'll tell him you rang the minute (that) he gets here.*
this minute immediately; now: *I don't know what I'm going to do yet – I've just this minute found out.*

up to the minute (*informal*) having the most recent information: *For up-to-the-minute information on flight times, phone this number...*

minute² /'mɪnɪt/ ***verb*** [T] (**BUSINESS**) to write THE MINUTES: *I'd like that last remark to be minuted.*

minute³ /maɪ'nju:t/ ***adj.*** (*superlative* **minutest**) (no comparative) **1** very small: *I couldn't read his writing. It was minute!* **2** very exact or accurate: *She was able to describe the man* ***in minute detail/the minutest detail.***

miracle /'mɪrəkl/ ***noun*** **1** [C] (**RELIGION**) a wonderful event that seems impossible and that is believed to be caused by God or a god **2** [sing.] a lucky thing that happens that you did not expect or think was possible: *It's a miracle (that) nobody was killed in the crash.*

IDM work/perform miracles to achieve very good results: *The new diet and exercise programme have worked miracles for her.*

miraculous /mɪ'rækjələs/ ***adj.*** completely unexpected and very lucky: *She's made a miraculous recovery.* ▶ **miraculously** ***adv.***

mirage /'mɪrɑ:ʒ; mɪ'rɑ:ʒ/ ***noun*** [C] something that you think you see in very hot weather, for example water in a desert, but which does not really exist

mirror 🔑 /'mɪrə(r)/ ***noun*** [C] a piece of special flat glass that you can look into in order to see yourself or what is behind you: *to look* ***in the mirror*** ◇ *a* ***rear-view mirror*** (=in a car, so that the driver can see what is behind) ◇ *a* ***mirror image*** ❶ A mirror **reflects** images. What you see in a mirror is a **reflection**. ▶ **mirror** ***verb*** [T]: *The trees were mirrored in the lake.*

'mirror site ***noun*** [C] (**COMPUTING**) a copy of a busy website that is created to reduce the number of people visiting the main website

mirth /mɜ:θ/ ***noun*** [U] (*written*) AMUSEMENT or LAUGHTER

mis- /mɪs/ ***prefix*** (used in verbs and nouns) bad or wrong; badly or wrongly: *misbehaviour* ◇ *misunderstand*

misapprehension /ˌmɪsæprɪ'henʃn/ ***noun*** [U, C] (*formal*) a wrong idea about sth, or sth you believe to be true that is not true: *I was* ***under the misapprehension*** *that this course was for beginners.*

misbehave /ˌmɪsbɪ'heɪv/ ***verb*** [I] to behave badly **OPP behave** ▶ **misbehaviour** (*AmE* **misbehavior**) /ˌmɪsbɪ'heɪvjə(r)/ ***noun*** [U]

misc. ***abbr.*** miscellaneous

miscalculate /ˌmɪs'kælkjuleɪt/ ***verb*** [I,T] to make a mistake in calculating or judging a situation, an amount, etc. ▶ **miscalculation** /ˌmɪskælkju'leɪʃn/ ***noun*** [C,U]

miscarriage /'mɪskærɪdʒ/ ***noun*** [C,U] (**HEALTH**) giving birth to a baby a long time before it is ready to be born, with the result that it cannot live ➲ look at **abortion**

IDM a miscarriage of justice an occasion when sb is punished for a crime that they did not do

miscarry /ˌmɪs'kæri/ ***verb*** [I] (*pres. part.* **miscarrying**; *3rd person sing. pres.* **miscarries**; *pt, pp* **miscarried**) (**HEALTH**) to give birth to a baby before it is ready to be born, with the result that it cannot live

miscellaneous /ˌmɪsə'leɪniəs/ ***adj.*** (*abbr.* **misc.**) consisting of many different types or things: *a box of miscellaneous items for sale*

mischief /'mɪstʃɪf/ ***noun*** [U] bad behaviour (usually of children) that is not very serious: *The children in Class 9 are always* ***getting into mischief.***

mischievous /'mɪstʃɪvəs/ ***adj.*** (usually used about children) liking to behave badly and embarrassing or annoying people ▶ **mischievously** ***adv.***

miscible /'mɪsəbl/ ***adj.*** (**CHEMISTRY**) (used about liquids) that can be mixed together **OPP immiscible**

misconception /ˌmɪskən'sepʃn/ ***noun*** [C] a wrong idea or understanding of sth: *It is a popular misconception* (=many people wrongly believe) *that people need meat to be healthy.*

misconduct /ˌmɪs'kɒndʌkt/ ***noun*** [U] (*formal*) unacceptable behaviour, especially by a professional person: *The doctor was dismissed for* ***gross*** (=very serious) ***misconduct.***

misconstrue /ˌmɪskən'stru:/ ***verb*** [T] (*formal*) **~ sth (as sth)** to understand sb's words or actions wrongly ➲ look at **construe**

misdemeanour (*AmE* **misdemeanor**) /ˌmɪsdɪ'mi:nə(r)/ ***noun*** [C] something slightly bad or wrong that a person does; a crime that is not very serious ➲ look at **felony**

miser /'maɪzə(r)/ ***noun*** [C] a person who loves having a lot of money but hates spending it ▶ **miserly** ***adj.***

miserable /'mɪzrəbl/ ***adj.*** **1** very unhappy: *Oh dear, you look miserable. What's wrong?* **2** unpleasant; making you feel unhappy: *What miserable weather!* (=grey, cold and wet) **SYN dismal** **3** too small or of bad quality: *I was offered a miserable salary so I didn't take the job.* ▶ **miserably** /-əbli/ ***adv.***: *I stared miserably out of the window.* ◇ *He* ***failed miserably*** *as an actor.*

misery /'mɪzəri/ ***noun*** [U, C] (*pl.* **miseries**) great unhappiness or suffering: *I couldn't bear to see him in such misery.* ◇ *the miseries of war*

IDM put sb out of his/her misery (*informal*) to stop sb worrying about sth by telling the person what they want to know: *Put me put of my misery – did I pass or not?*

put sth out of its misery to kill an animal because it has an illness or injury that cannot be treated

misfire /ˌmɪs'faɪə(r)/ ***verb*** [I] to fail to have the intended result or effect: *The plan misfired.*

misfit /'mɪsfɪt/ ***noun*** [C] a person who not is accepted by other people, especially because their behaviour or ideas are very different

misfortune /ˌmɪs'fɔ:tʃu:n/ ***noun*** [C,U] (*formal*) (an event, accident, etc. that brings) bad luck or disaster: *I hope I don't ever* ***have the misfortune to*** *meet him again.*

misgiving /ˌmɪs'gɪvɪŋ/ ***noun*** [C, U] a feeling of doubt, worry or suspicion: *I* ***had serious misgivings*** *about leaving him on his own.*

misguided /ˌmɪs'gaɪdɪd/ ***adj.*** wrong because you have understood or judged a situation badly

mishap /'mɪshæp/ ***noun*** [C,U] a small accident or piece of bad luck that does not have serious results: *to have a slight mishap*

misinform /ˌmɪsɪn'fɔ:m/ ***verb*** [T] (*formal*) to give sb the wrong information: *I think you've been misinformed – no one is going to lose their job.*

misinterpret **AW** /ˌmɪsɪn'tɜ:prɪt/ ***verb*** [T] **~ sth (as sth)** to understand sth wrongly: *His comments were misinterpreted as a criticism of the project.* **OPP interpret** ▶ **misinterpretation** /ˌmɪsɪntɜ:prɪ'teɪʃn/ ***noun*** [C,U]: *Parts of the speech were* ***open to misinterpretation*** (=easy to understand wrongly).

misjudge /ˌmɪsˈdʒʌdʒ/ *verb* [T] **1** to form a wrong opinion of sb/sth, usually in a way which is unfair to them or it **2** to guess time, distance, etc. wrongly: *He completely misjudged the speed of the other car and almost crashed.* ▶ **misjudgement** (also **misjudgment**) *noun* [C,U]

mislay /ˌmɪsˈleɪ/ *verb* [T] (*pres. part.* **mislaying**; *3rd person sing. pres.* **mislays**; *pt, pp* **mislaid** /-ˈleɪd/) to lose sth, usually for a short time, because you cannot remember where you put it

mislead /ˌmɪsˈliːd/ *verb* [T] (*pt, pp* **misled** /-ˈled/) to make sb have the wrong idea or opinion about sb/sth ▶ **misleading** *adj.*: *a misleading advertisement*

mismanage /ˌmɪsˈmænɪdʒ/ *verb* [T] to manage or organize sth badly ▶ **mismanagement** *noun* [U]

misogynist /mɪˈsɒdʒɪnɪst/ *noun* [C] (*formal*) a man who hates women ▶ **misogynistic** /mɪˌsɒdʒɪˈnɪstɪk/ (*also* **misogynist**) *adj.* ▶ **misogyny** /mɪˈsɒdʒɪni/ *noun* [U]

misplaced /ˌmɪsˈpleɪst/ *adj.* given to sb/sth that is not suitable or good enough to have it: *misplaced loyalty*

misprint /ˈmɪsprɪnt/ *noun* [C] a mistake in printing or typing

mispronounce /ˌmɪsprəˈnaʊns/ *verb* [T] to say a word or letter wrongly: *People always mispronounce my surname.* ▶ **mispronunciation** /ˌmɪsprənʌnsiˈeɪʃn/ *noun* [C,U]

misread /ˌmɪsˈriːd/ *verb* [T] (*pt, pp* **misread** /-ˈred/) ~ **sth (as sth)** to read or understand sth wrongly: *He misread my silence as a refusal.*

misrepresent /ˌmɪsˌreprɪˈzent/ *verb* [T] (usually passive) to give a wrong description of sb/sth: *In the newspaper article they were misrepresented as uncaring parents.* ▶ **misrepresentation** /ˌmɪsˌreprɪzenˈteɪʃn/ *noun* [C,U]

Miss[1] /mɪs/ used as a title before the family name of a young woman or a woman who is not married

miss[2] 🔑 /mɪs/ *verb* **1** [I,T] to fail to hit, catch, etc. sth: *She tried to catch the ball but she missed.* ◇ *The bullet narrowly missed his heart.* **2** [T] to not see, hear, understand, etc. sb/sth: *The house is on the corner so* ***you can't miss it.*** ◇ *They completely* ***missed the point*** *of what I was saying.* ◇ *My Mum will know there's something wrong. She* ***doesn't miss much.*** **3** [T] to arrive too late for sth or to fail to go to or do sth: *Hurry up or you'll miss the plane!* ◇ *Of course I'm coming to your wedding. I* ***wouldn't miss it for the world*** (= used to emphasize that you really want to do sth). **4** [T] to feel sad because sb is not with you any more, or because you have not got or cannot do sth that you once had or did: *I'll miss you terribly when you go away.* ◇ *What did you miss most when you lived abroad?* **5** [T] to notice that sb/sth is not where they or it should be: *When did you first miss your handbag?* **6** [T] to avoid sth unpleasant: *If we leave now, we'll miss the rush-hour traffic.*

PHR V **miss sb/sth out** to not include sb/sth: *You've missed out several important points in your report.*

miss out (on sth) to not have a chance to have or do sth: *You'll miss out on all the fun if you stay at home.*

miss[3] 🔑 /mɪs/ *noun* [C] a failure to hit, catch or reach sth: *After several misses he finally managed to hit the target.*

IDM **give sth a miss** (*especially BrE, informal*) to decide not to do or have sth: *I think I'll give aerobics a miss tonight.*

a near miss → NEAR[1]

missile /ˈmɪsaɪl/ *noun* [C] **1** a powerful exploding weapon that can be sent long distances through the air: *nuclear missiles* **2** an object or weapon that is fired from a gun or thrown in order to hurt sb or damage sth: *The rioters threw missiles such as bottles and stones.*

missing 🔑 /ˈmɪsɪŋ/ *adj.* **1** lost, or not in the right or usual place: *a missing person* ◇ *Two files have* ***gone missing*** *from my office.* **2** (used about a person) not present after a battle, an accident, etc. but not known to have been killed: *Many soldiers were listed as* ***missing in action.*** **3** not included, often when it should have been: *Fill in the missing words in the text.*

mission /ˈmɪʃn/ *noun* [C] **1** an important official job that sb is sent somewhere to do, especially to another country: *Your mission is to send back information about the enemy's movements.* **2** a group of people who are sent to a foreign country to perform a special task: *a British trade mission to China* **3** a special journey made by a SPACECRAFT or military aircraft: *a mission to the moon* **4** (**RELIGION**) a place where people are taught about the Christian religion, given medical help, etc. by MISSIONARIES **5** a particular task which you feel it is your duty to do: *Her work with the poor was more than just a job – it was her* ***mission in life.***

missionary /ˈmɪʃənri/ *noun* [C] (*pl.* **missionaries**) (**RELIGION**) a person who is sent to a foreign country to teach about the Christian religion

ˈmission statement *noun* [C] (**BUSINESS**) an official statement of the aims of a company or an organization

misspell /ˌmɪsˈspel/ *verb* [T] (*pt, pp* **misspelled** or **misspelt** /ˌmɪsˈspelt/) to spell sth wrongly

mist[1] /mɪst/ *noun* [C,U] a cloud made of very small drops of water in the air just above the ground, that makes it difficult to see: *The fields were covered in mist.* ➲ note at **weather** ▶ **misty** *adj.*: *a misty morning* ➲ look at **foggy**

mist[2] /mɪst/ *verb*

PHR V **mist (sth) up/over** to cover or be covered with very small drops of water that make it difficult to see: *My glasses keep misting up.*

mistake[1] 🔑 /mɪˈsteɪk/ *noun* [C] something that you think or do that is wrong: *Try not to* ***make*** *any* ***mistakes*** *in your essays.* ◇ *a spelling mistake* ◇ *It was a big mistake to trust her.* ◇ *I made the mistake of giving him my address.*

IDM **by mistake** as a result of being careless: *The terrorists shot the wrong man by mistake.*

WHICH WORD?

Error is more formal than **mistake**: *a computing error.* **Fault** indicates who is responsible for sth bad: *The accident wasn't my fault. The other driver pulled out in front of me.* **Fault** is also used to describe a problem or weakness that sb/sth has: *a technical fault*

mistake[2] 🔑 /mɪˈsteɪk/ *verb* [T] (*pt* **mistook** /mɪˈstʊk/; *pp* **mistaken** /mɪˈsteɪkən/) **1** ~ **A for B** to think wrongly that sb/sth is sb/sth else: *I'm sorry, I mistook you for a friend of mine.* **2** to be wrong about sth: *I think you've mistaken my meaning.*

mistaken 🔑 /mɪˈsteɪkən/ *adj.* wrong; not correct: *a case of mistaken identity* ◇ *a mistaken belief/idea* ▶ **mistakenly** *adv.*

mister → MR

mistletoe /ˈmɪsltəʊ/ ***noun*** [U] a plant with white BERRIES that grows on other trees and is often used as a decoration at Christmas: *the tradition of kissing under the mistletoe*

mistook past tense of **mistake**[2]

mistreat /ˌmɪsˈtriːt/ ***verb*** [T] to be cruel to a person or animal: *The owner of the zoo was accused of mistreating the animals.* ▶ **mistreatment** ***noun*** [U]

mistress /ˈmɪstrəs/ ***noun*** [C] a man's (usually a married man's) **mistress** is a woman that he is having a regular sexual relationship with and who is not his wife

mistrust /ˌmɪsˈtrʌst/ ***verb*** [T] to have no confidence in sb/sth because you think they or it may be harmful: *I always mistrust politicians who smile too much.* ▶ **mistrust** ***noun*** [U, sing.]: *She has a deep mistrust of strangers.* ➲ look at **distrust**

misty /ˈmɪsti/ → MIST[1]

misunderstand /ˌmɪsʌndəˈstænd/ ***verb*** [I,T] (*pt, pp* **misunderstood** /-ˈstʊd/) to understand sb/sth wrongly: *I misunderstood the instructions and answered too many questions.*

misunderstanding /ˌmɪsʌndəˈstændɪŋ/ ***noun*** **1** [C,U] a situation in which sb/sth is not understood correctly: *The contract is written in both languages to avoid any misunderstanding.* **2** [C] a disagreement or an argument

misuse /ˌmɪsˈjuːz/ ***verb*** [T] to use sth in the wrong way or for the wrong purpose: *These chemicals can be dangerous if misused.* ▶ **misuse** /ˌmɪsˈjuːs/ ***noun*** [C,U]

mite /maɪt/ ***noun*** [C] a very small creature like a spider that lives on plants and animals and in carpets, etc.

mitigate /ˈmɪtɪɡeɪt/ ***verb*** [T] (*formal*) to make sth less serious, painful, unpleasant, etc.

mitigating /ˈmɪtɪɡeɪtɪŋ/ ***adj.*** (*formal*) (only *before* a noun) providing a reason that explains sb's actions or why they committed a crime, which makes it easier to understand so that the punishment may be less HARSH: *mitigating circumstances/factors*

mitochondria

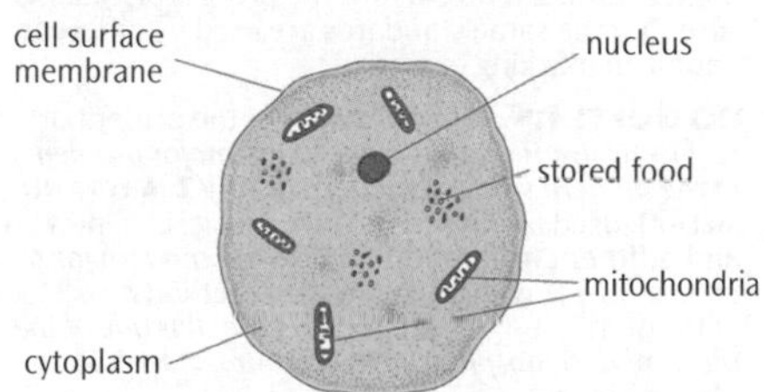

mitochondrion /ˌmaɪtəʊˈkɒndriən/ ***noun*** [pl.] (*pl.* **mitochondria** /ˌmaɪtəʊˈkɒndriə/) (**BIOLOGY**) a small part found in most cells, in which the energy in food is released ➲ picture at **gamete**

mitosis /maɪˈtəʊsɪs/ ***noun*** [U] (**BIOLOGY**) the division of a cell of the body that results in two cells, each with the same number of CHROMOSOMES (=the parts of a cell that carry information about what characteristics a living thing will have) as the original cell ➲ look at **meiosis**

mitre (*AmE* **miter**) /ˈmaɪtə(r)/ ***noun*** [C] **1** (**RELIGION**) a tall pointed hat worn by BISHOPS (=Christian priests with a high position in the church) at special ceremonies as a symbol of their position and authority **2** (*also* **ˈmitre joint**) a corner joint, formed by two pieces of wood each cut at an angle, as in a picture frame ➲ picture at **dovetail**[2]

mitten /ˈmɪtn/ ***noun*** [C] a type of glove that has one part for the thumb and another part for all four fingers ➲ look at **glove**

mix[1] 🔑 /mɪks/ ***verb*** **1** [I,T] ~ (A) (with B); ~ (A and B) (together) if two or more substances mix or if you mix them, they combine to form a new substance: *Oil and water don't mix.* ◇ *Mix all the ingredients together in a bowl.* ◇ *to mix cement* (=to make cement by mixing other substances) **2** [I] ~ (with sb) to be with and talk to other people: *He mixes with all types of people at work.*

IDM **be/get mixed up in sth** (*informal*) to be/become involved in sth bad or unpleasant

PHR V **mix sth up** to put something in the wrong order: *He was so nervous that he dropped his speech and got the pages all mixed up.*

mix sb/sth up (with sb/sth) to confuse sb/sth with sb/sth else: *I always get him mixed up with his brother.*

mix[2] 🔑 /mɪks/ ***noun*** **1** [C, usually sing.] a group of different types of people or things: *We need a good racial mix in the police force.* **2** [C,U] a special powder that contains all the substances needed to make sth. You add water or another liquid to this powder: *cake mix*

mixed 🔑 /mɪkst/ ***adj.*** **1** being both good and bad: *I have* ***mixed feelings*** *about leaving my job.* **2** made or consisting of different types of person or thing: *Was your school mixed or single-sex?* ◇ *a mixed salad*

ˌmixed ˈmarriage ***noun*** [C] a marriage between people of different races or religions

ˌmixed ˈnumber ***noun*** [C] (**MATHEMATICS**) a number consisting of a whole number and a PROPER FRACTION, for example 3 ¼

ˌmixed-ˈup ***adj.*** (*informal*) confused because of emotional problems: *He has been very mixed-up since his parents' divorce.*

mixer /ˈmɪksə(r)/ ***noun*** [C] a machine that is used for mixing sth: *a food/cement mixer*

mixture 🔑 /ˈmɪkstʃə(r)/ ***noun*** **1** [sing.] a combination of different things: *Monkeys eat a mixture of leaves and fruit.* **2** [C,U] a substance that is made by mixing other substances together: *cake mixture* ◇ *a mixture of eggs, flour and milk* **3** (**CHEMISTRY**) a combination of two or more substances that mix together without any chemical reaction taking place ➲ look at **compound**[1] (2)

ˈmix-up ***noun*** [C] (*informal*) a mistake in the planning or organization of sth: *There was a mix-up and we were given the wrong ticket.*

ml ***abbr.*** millilitre(s): *contents 75ml*

mm 🔑 ***abbr.*** millimetre(s): *a 35mm camera*

moan /məʊn/ ***verb*** [I] **1** to make a low sound because you are in pain, very sad, etc.: *to moan with pain* **2** (*informal*) to keep saying what is wrong about sth; to complain: *The English are always moaning about the weather.* ▶ **moan** ***noun*** [C]

moat /məʊt/ ***noun*** [C] (**HISTORY**) a hole that was dug around a castle and filled with water to make it difficult for enemies to attack ➲ picture at **castle**, **drawbridge**

mob[1] /mɒb/ ***noun*** [C, with sing. or pl. verb] a large crowd of people that may become violent or cause trouble

mob[2] /mɒb/ ***verb*** [T] (**mobbing**; **mobbed**) to form a large crowd around sb, for example in order to see or touch them: *The band was mobbed by fans as they left the hotel.*

mobile[1] /ˈməʊbaɪl/ ***adj.*** able to move or be moved easily: *My daughter is much more mobile now she has her own car.* OPP **immobile** ▶ **mobility** /məʊˈbɪləti/ ***noun*** [U]

mobile[2] /ˈməʊbaɪl/ ***noun*** [C] **1** a decoration that you hang from the ceiling and that moves when the air around it moves **2** = MOBILE PHONE

ˌmobile ˈhome ***noun*** [C] **1** (*especially AmE*) (*AmE also* **trailer**) a small building for people to live in that is made in a factory and moved to a permanent place **2** (*AmE* **trailer**) a large CARAVAN that can be moved, sometimes with wheels, that is usually parked in one place and used for living in

ˌmobile ˈphone (*BrE, informal* **mobile**; *especially AmE* **cellphone**; **ˌcellular ˈphone**; **cell**) ***noun*** [C] a telephone that you can carry around with you ➲ note at **telephone**

mobilize (also **-ise**) /ˈməʊbɪlaɪz/ ***verb*** **1** [T] to organize people or things to do sth: *They mobilized the local residents to oppose the new development.* **2** [I,T] (used about the army, navy, etc.) to get ready for war OPP **immobilize**

Möbius strip (also **Moebius strip**) /ˈmɜːbiəs strɪp/ ***noun*** [C] (MATHEMATICS) a surface with one continuous side, formed by joining the ends of a strip of material after twisting one end through 180 degrees

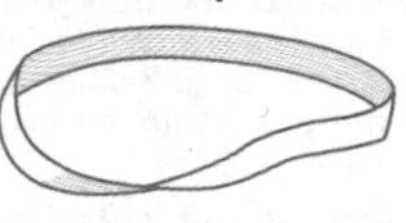
Möbius strip

moccasin /ˈmɒkəsɪn/ ***noun*** [C] a flat shoe that is made from soft leather and has large STITCHES around the front, of a type originally worn by Native Americans

mock[1] /mɒk/ ***verb*** [I,T] (*formal*) to laugh at sb/sth in an unkind way or to make other people laugh at them or it

mock[2] /mɒk/ ***adj.*** (only *before* a noun) not real or genuine: *He held up his hands in mock surprise.* ◇ *a mock* (= practice) *exam*

mock[3] /mɒk/ ***noun*** [C, usually pl.] (EDUCATION) (in Britain) a practice exam that you do before the official one

mockery /ˈmɒkəri/ ***noun*** **1** [U] comments or actions that are intended to make sb/sth seem ridiculous: *She couldn't face any more of their mockery.* **2** [sing.] an action, a decision, etc. that is a failure and that is not as it is should be: *It was a mockery of a trial.*

IDM **make a mockery of sth** to make sth seem ridiculous or useless

ˈmock-up ***noun*** [C] a model of sth that shows what it will look like or how it will work

modal /ˈməʊdl/ (*also* **ˈmodal verb**) ***noun*** [C] (LANGUAGE) a verb, for example 'might', 'can' or 'must' that is used with another verb for expressing possibility, permission, intention, etc.

mode AW /məʊd/ ***noun*** [C] **1** a type of sth or way of doing sth: *a mode of transport/life* **2** one of the ways in which a machine can work: *Switch the camera to automatic mode.* **3** (MUSIC) a particular arrangement of notes in music for example the musical SCALE system: *major/minor mode* **4** (MATHEMATICS) the most frequent number or value in a group of numbers

model[1] /ˈmɒdl/ ***noun*** [C] **1** a copy of sth that is usually smaller than the real thing: *a model aeroplane* **2** one of the machines, vehicles, etc. that is made by a particular company: *The latest models are on display at the show.* **3** a person or thing that is a good example to copy: *a model student* ◇ *Children often use older brothers or sisters as **role models*** (= copy the way they behave). **4** a person who is employed to wear clothes at a fashion show or for magazine photographs **5** (ART) a person who is painted, drawn or photographed by an artist

model[2] /ˈmɒdl/ ***verb*** (**modelling**; **modelled**: *AmE* **modeling**; **modeled**) **1** [T] ~ **sth/yourself on sb/sth** to make sth/yourself similar to sth/sb else: *The house is modelled on a Roman villa.* **2** [I,T] to wear and show clothes at a fashion show or for photographs: *to model swimsuits* **3** [I,T] to make a model of sth: *This clay is difficult to model.*

modelling (*AmE* **modeling**) /ˈmɒdəlɪŋ/ ***noun*** [U] the work of a fashion model

modem /ˈməʊdem/ ***noun*** [C] (COMPUTING) a piece of equipment that connects two or more computers together by means of a telephone line so that information can go from one to the other

moderate[1] /ˈmɒdərət/ ***adj.*** **1** being, having, using, etc. neither too much nor too little of sth: *a moderate speed* ◇ *We've had a moderate amount of success.* **2** having or showing opinions, especially about politics, that are not extreme: *moderate policies/views* ➲ look at **extreme**, **radical** ▶ **moderately** ***adv.***: *His career has been moderately successful.*

moderate[2] /ˈmɒdəreɪt/ ***verb*** [I,T] to become or to make sth less strong or extreme: *The union moderated its original demands.*

moderate[3] /ˈmɒdərət/ ***noun*** [C] (POLITICS) a person whose opinions, especially about politics, are not extreme ➲ look at **extremist**

moderation /ˌmɒdəˈreɪʃn/ ***noun*** [U] **1** the quality of being reasonable and not being extreme: *Alcohol can harm unborn babies even if it's taken **in moderation**.* **2** (EDUCATION) the process of making sure that the same standards are used by different people in marking exams, etc.

modern /ˈmɒdn/ ***adj.*** **1** of the present or recent times: *Pollution is one of the major problems in the modern world.* ◇ *modern history* **2** (ARTS AND MEDIA) (used about styles of art, music, etc.) new and different from traditional styles: *modern jazz/architecture* **3** with all the newest methods, equipment, designs, etc.; up to date: *It is one of the most modern hospitals in the country.* ➲ look at **old-fashioned**

ˌmodern-ˈday ***adj.*** (only *before* a noun) **1** of the present time SYN **contemporary**: *modern-day America* **2** used to describe a modern form of sb/sth, usually sb/sth bad or unpleasant, that existed in the past: *It has been called modern-day slavery.*

modernism /ˈmɒdənɪzəm/ ***noun*** [U] **1** modern ideas or methods **2** (ARTS AND MEDIA) a style and movement in art, ARCHITECTURE and literature popular in the middle of the 20th century in which modern ideas, methods and materials were used rather than traditional ones ➲ look at **postmodernism** ▶ **modernist** /ˈmɒdənɪst/ ***adj.***, ***noun*** [C]: *modernist art*

modernity /məˈdɜːnəti/ ***noun*** [U] (*written*) the condition of being new and modern

modernize (also **-ise**) /ˈmɒdənaɪz/ ***verb*** [T] to make sth suitable for use today using new methods, styles, etc. ▶ **modernization** (also -**isation**) /ˌmɒdənaɪˈzeɪʃn/ ***noun*** [U]: *The house is large but is in need of modernization.*

ˌmodern ˈlanguages ***noun*** [pl.] (LANGUAGE) languages that are spoken now

modest /ˈmɒdɪst/ ***adj.*** **1** not talking too much about your own abilities, good qualities, etc.: *She got the best results in the exam but she was too modest to tell anyone.* ➲ look at **humble**, **proud** **2** not very large: *a modest pay increase* **3** (used about a woman's clothes) not showing much of the body ▶ **modesty** ***noun*** [U] ▶ **modestly** ***adv.***

modifier /ˈmɒdɪfaɪə(r)/ ***noun*** [C] (LANGUAGE) a word, such as an adjective or adverb, that describes another word, or changes its meaning in some way ➲ look at **intensifier**

modify AW /ˈmɒdɪfaɪ/ ***verb*** [T] (*pres. part.* **modifying**; *3rd person sing. pres.* **modifies**; *pt, pp* **modified**) to change sth slightly ▶ **modification** AW /ˌmɒdɪfɪˈkeɪʃn/ ***noun*** [C,U]

modular /ˈmɒdjələ(r)/ ***adj.*** **1** (EDUCATION) (used about a course of study, especially at a British university or college) consisting of separate units from which students may choose several: *a modular course* **2** (used about machines, buildings, etc.) consisting of separate parts or units that can be joined together

module /ˈmɒdjuːl/ ***noun*** [C] **1** (EDUCATION) a unit that can form part of a course of study, especially at a college or university in Britain: *You must complete three modules* (=courses that you study) *in your first year.* **2** (COMPUTING) a unit of a computer system or program that has a particular function **3** one of a set of separate parts or units that can be joined together to make a machine, a piece of furniture, a building, etc. **4** a unit of a SPACECRAFT that can function independently of the main part: *the lunar module*

mohair /ˈməʊheə(r)/ ***noun*** [U] very soft wool that comes from a GOAT

Mohammed =MUHAMMAD

moist /mɔɪst/ ***adj.*** slightly wet; damp: *Her eyes were moist with tears.* ◇ *Keep the soil moist or the plant will die.* ▶ **moisten** /ˈmɔɪsn/ ***verb*** [I,T]

moisture /ˈmɔɪstʃə(r)/ ***noun*** [U] water in small drops on a surface, in the air, etc.

moisturize (also **-ise**) /ˈmɔɪstʃəraɪz/ ***verb*** [I,T] to put special cream on your skin to make it less dry

moisturizer (also **-iser**) /ˈmɔɪstʃəraɪzə(r)/ ***noun*** [C,U] a special cream that you put on your skin to make it less dry

molar /ˈməʊlə(r)/ ***noun*** [C] (ANATOMY) one of the large teeth at the back of your mouth ➲ look at **canine**, **incisor**, **premolar** ➲ picture at **tooth**

molasses /məˈlæsɪz/ (*AmE*) =TREACLE

mold (*AmE*) =MOULD

moldy (*AmE*) =MOULDY

mole /məʊl/ ***noun*** [C] **1** a small dark spot on a person's skin that never goes away ➲ look at **freckle** **2** a small animal with dark fur that lives underground and is almost blind **3** (*informal*) a person who works in one organization and gives secret information to another organization SYN **spy** **4** (CHEMISTRY) a unit for measuring the amount of a substance

molecule /ˈmɒlɪkjuːl/ ***noun*** [C] (CHEMISTRY) the smallest unit into which a substance can be divided without changing its chemical nature ➲ look at **atom** ▶ **molecular** /məˈlekjələ(r)/ ***adj.***

molest /məˈlest/ ***verb*** [T] (LAW) to attack sb, especially a child, in a sexual way

mollify /ˈmɒlɪfaɪ/ ***verb*** [T] (*pres. part.* **mollifying**; *3rd person sing. pres.* **mollifies**; *pt, pp* **mollified**) (*formal*) to make sb feel less angry or upset: *His explanation failed to mollify her.*

mollusc (*AmE* **mollusk**) /ˈmɒləsk/ ***noun*** [C] (BIOLOGY) any creature with a soft body that is not divided into different sections, and usually a hard outer shell. **Molluscs** can live either on land or in water: *Snails and mussels are molluscs.*

molt (*AmE*) =MOULT

molten /ˈməʊltən/ ***adj.*** (used about metal or rock) made liquid by very great heat

molybdenum /məˈlɪbdənəm/ ***noun*** [U] (*symbol* **Mo**) (CHEMISTRY) a chemical element. **Molybdenum** is a silver-grey metal that breaks easily and is used in some ALLOY steels. ❶ For more information on the periodic table of elements, look at pages R34-5.

mom 🔑 (*AmE*) =MUM

moment 🔑 /ˈməʊmənt/ ***noun*** **1** [C] a very short period of time: *One moment, please* (=please wait). ◇ *Joe left just a few moments ago.* **2** [sing.] a particular point in time: *Just at that moment my mother arrived.* ◇ *the moment of birth/death*

IDM **(at) any minute/moment (now)** → MINUTE[1]

at the moment now: *I'm afraid she's busy at the moment. Can I take a message?*

for the moment/present for a short time; for now: *I'm not very happy at work but I'll stay there for the moment.*

in a moment very soon: *Just wait here. I'll be back in a moment.*

the last minute/moment → LAST[1]

the minute/moment (that) → MINUTE[1]

on the spur of the moment → SPUR[1]

momentary /ˈməʊməntri/ ***adj.*** lasting for a very short time ▶ **momentarily** /ˈməʊməntrəli/ ***adv.***

momentous /məˈmentəs/ ***adj.*** very important: *a momentous decision/event/change*

momentum /məˈmentəm/ ***noun*** [U] the ability to keep increasing or developing; the force that makes sth move faster and faster: *The environmental movement is* ***gathering momentum****.*

mommy (*AmE*) =MUMMY (1)

Mon. ***abbr.*** Monday: *Mon. 6 June*

monarch /ˈmɒnək/ ***noun*** [C] (POLITICS) a king or queen

monarchy /ˈmɒnəki/ ***noun*** (*pl.* **monarchies**) (POLITICS) **1** [sing., U] the system of government or rule by a king or queen **2** [C] a country that is governed by a king or queen ➲ look at **republic**

monastery /ˈmɒnəstri/ ***noun*** [C] (*pl.* **monasteries**) (RELIGION) a place where MONKS (=members of a male religious community) live together ➲ look at **convent**

Monday /ˈmʌndeɪ; -di/ ***noun*** [C,U] (*abbr.* **Mon.**) the day of the week after Sunday: *I'm going to see her* ***on Monday****.* ◇ (*informal*) *I'll see you Monday.* ◇ *I finish work a bit later* ***on Mondays*** */* ***on a Monday****.* ◇ *Monday morning/afternoon/evening/night* ◇ *last/next Monday* ◇ *a week on Monday/Monday week* (=not next Monday, but the Monday after that) ◇ *The museum is open Monday to Friday, 10 till 4.30.* ◇ *Did you see that article about Italy in Monday's paper?*

monetarism /ˈmʌnɪtərɪzəm/ *noun* [U] (ECONOMICS) the policy of controlling the amount of money available in a country as a way of keeping the economy strong

monetary /ˈmʌnɪtri/ *adj.* connected with money: *the government's monetary policy* ➲ note at **economic**

money ⊶ /ˈmʌni/ *noun* [U] the means of paying for sth or buying sth (=coins or notes): *Will you **earn** more **money** in your new job?* ◇ *The new road will **cost** a lot of **money**.* ◇ *If we do the work ourselves we will **save money**.* ◇ *The government **make** a huge amount of **money** out of tobacco tax.* ➲ look at **pocket money**

IDM **be rolling in money/in it** → ROLL[2]

get your money's worth to get full value for the money you have spent

mongoose /ˈmɒŋɡuːs/ *noun* [C] (*pl.* **mongooses**) a small animal with fur that lives in hot countries and kills snakes, RATS, etc.

mongrel /ˈmʌŋɡrəl/ *noun* [C] a dog that has parents of different types (**breeds**) ➲ look at **pedigree**

monitor[1] ⊶ AW /ˈmɒnɪtə(r)/ *noun* [C] **1** (COMPUTING) a machine that shows information or pictures on a screen like a television; a screen that shows information from a computer ➲ picture at **computer 2** a machine that records or checks sth: *A monitor checks the baby's heartbeat.*

monitor[2] ⊶ AW /ˈmɒnɪtə(r)/ *verb* [T] to check, record or test sth regularly for a period of time: *Pollution levels in the lake are closely monitored.*

monk /mʌŋk/ *noun* [C] (RELIGION) a member of a religious group of men who live in a special building (**monastery**) and do not get married or have possessions ➲ look at **nun**

monkey /ˈmʌŋki/ *noun* [C] an animal with a long tail that lives in hot countries and can climb trees ➲ look at **ape** ❶ **Chimpanzees** and **gorillas** are **apes**, although people sometimes call them **monkeys**. ➲ picture on **page 29**

IDM **monkey business** (*informal*) silly or dishonest behaviour

ˈ**monkey wrench** =ADJUSTABLE SPANNER ➲ picture at **tool**

monkfish /ˈmʌŋkfɪʃ/ *noun* [C,U] (*pl.* **monkfish** or **monkfishes**) a large European fish that lives on the bottom of the sea and can be eaten

mono /ˈmɒnəʊ/ *adj.* (used about recorded music or a system for playing it) having the sound coming from one direction only ➲ look at **stereo**

mono- /ˈmɒnəʊ/ *prefix* (used in nouns and adjectives) one; single: *monorail* ◇ *monolingual*

monochrome /ˈmɒnəkrəʊm/ *adj.* (used about a photograph or picture) using only black, white and shades of grey

monoculture /ˈmɒnəʊkʌltʃə(r)/ *noun* [U] (AGRICULTURE) the growing of a single crop in a particular area

monogamy /məˈnɒɡəmi/ *noun* [U] (SOCIAL STUDIES) the fact or custom of being married to only one person at a particular time ➲ look at **bigamy**, **polygamy** ▶ **monogamous** /məˈnɒɡəməs/ *adj.*: *a monogamous society*

monolingual /ˌmɒnəˈlɪŋɡwəl/ *adj.* (LANGUAGE) speaking or using only one language: *This is a monolingual dictionary.* ➲ look at **bilingual**, **multilingual**

monolith /ˈmɒnəlɪθ/ *noun* [C] (HISTORY) a large single standing block of stone, especially one that was put there by people living in ancient times ▶ **monolithic** /ˌmɒnəˈlɪθɪk/ *adj.*

monologue (*AmE also* **monolog**) /ˈmɒnəlɒɡ/ *noun* [C] (ARTS AND MEDIA) a long speech by one person, for example in a play ➲ look at **soliloquy**

monopolize (also **-ise**) /məˈnɒpəlaɪz/ *verb* [T] to control sth so that other people cannot share it: *She completely monopolized the conversation. I couldn't get a word in.*

monopoly /məˈnɒpəli/ *noun* [C] (*pl.* **monopolies**) **a ~ (on/in sth) 1** (BUSINESS) the control of an industry or service by only one company; a type of goods or a service that is controlled in this way: *The company has a monopoly on broadcasting international football.* **2** the complete control, possession or use of sth; something that belongs to only one person or group and is not shared

monorail /ˈmɒnəʊreɪl/ *noun* [C] a railway in which the train runs on a single track, usually high above the ground

monosodium glutamate /ˌmɒnəˌsəʊdiəm ˈɡluːtəmeɪt/ *noun* [U] (*abbr.* **MSG**) a chemical mixture (**compound**) that is sometimes added to food to improve its flavour

monosyllabic /ˌmɒnəsɪˈlæbɪk/ *adj.* **1** (LANGUAGE) having only one SYLLABLE **2** (used about a person or his/her way of speaking) saying very little, in a way that appears rude to other people: *He gave monosyllabic replies to everything I asked him.*

monosyllable /ˈmɒnəsɪləbl/ *noun* [C] (LANGUAGE) a short word, such as 'leg', that has only one SYLLABLE

monotheism /ˈmɒnəʊθiɪzəm/ *noun* [U] (RELIGION) the belief that there is only one God ➲ look at **polytheism**

monotonous /məˈnɒtənəs/ *adj.* never changing and therefore boring: *monotonous work* ◇ *a monotonous voice* ▶ **monotonously** *adv.*

monotony /məˈnɒtəni/ *noun* [U] the state of being always the same and therefore boring: *the monotony of working on a production line*

monozygotic /ˌmɒnəʊzaɪˈɡɒtɪk/ *adj.* (BIOLOGY) (used about TWINS) from the same egg and therefore IDENTICAL (=looking the same)

monsoon /ˌmɒnˈsuːn/ *noun* [C] (GEOGRAPHY) the season when it rains a lot in Southern Asia; the rain that falls during this period

monster /ˈmɒnstə(r)/ *noun* [C] (in stories) a creature that is large, ugly and frightening: (*figurative*) *The murderer was described as a dangerous monster.*

monstrosity /mɒnˈstrɒsəti/ *noun* [C] (*pl.* **monstrosities**) something that is very large and ugly, especially a building

monstrous /ˈmɒnstrəs/ *adj.* **1** that people think is shocking and unacceptable because it is morally wrong or unfair: *It's monstrous that she earns less than he does for the same job!* **2** very large (and often ugly or frightening): *a monstrous spider/wave*

montage /ˌmɒnˈtɑːʒ; ˈmɒn-/ *noun* [C] (ARTS AND MEDIA) a picture, film or piece of music or writing that consists of many separate items put together, especially in an interesting or unusual combination: *a photographic montage*

month 🔑 /mʌnθ/ ***noun*** [C] **1** one of the twelve periods of time into which the year is divided: *They are starting work next month.* ◇ *Have you seen this month's 'Vogue'?* **2** the period of about four weeks from a certain date in one month to the same date in the next, for example 13 May to 13 June; a CALENDAR MONTH: *'How long will you be away?' 'For about a month.'* ◇ *a six-month course*

monthly¹ /ˈmʌnθli/ ***adj., adv.*** (happening or produced) once every month: *a monthly meeting/magazine/visit* ◇ *Are you paid weekly or monthly?*

monthly² /ˈmʌnθli/ ***noun*** [C] (*pl.* **monthlies**) (**ARTS AND MEDIA**) a magazine that is published once a month

monument /ˈmɒnjumənt/ ***noun*** [C] **a ~ (to sb/sth)** **1** (**ARCHITECTURE**) a building or statue that is built to remind people of a famous person or event **2** an old building or other place that is of historical importance

monumental /ˌmɒnjuˈmentl/ ***adj.*** (only *before* a noun) very great, large or important: *a monumental success/task/achievement*

moo /muː/ ***noun*** [C] the sound that a cow makes ▶ **moo** ***verb*** [I]

mood 🔑 /muːd/ ***noun*** **1** [C,U] the way that you are feeling at a particular time: *to be in a bad/good mood* (=to feel angry/happy) ◇ *Turn that music down a bit – I'm not **in the mood for** it.* **2** [C] a time when you are angry or bad-tempered: *Debby's in one of her moods again.* **SYN** **temper** **3** [sing.] the way that a group of people feel about sth: *The mood of the crowd suddenly changed and violence broke out.*

moody /ˈmuːdi/ ***adj.*** **1** often changing moods in a way that people cannot predict: *You never know where you are with Andy because he's so moody.* **2** bad-tempered or unhappy, often for no particular reason ▶ **moodily** ***adv.*** ▶ **moodiness** ***noun*** [U]

phases of the moon

half moon (anticlockwise rotation) G H F light from sun EARTH A E new moon full moon B D C half moon

moon 🔑 /muːn/ ***noun*** **1 the moon** [sing.] the object that shines in the sky at night and that moves around the earth once every 28 days ❶ The moon as it appears at its different stages can be called a **new moon**, a **full moon**, a **half-moon** or a **crescent moon.** ➲ adjective **lunar** **2** [C] an object like the moon that moves around another planet: *How many moons does Neptune have?*

IDM **once in a blue moon** → ONCE

over the moon (*especially BrE, informal*) extremely happy and excited about sth

moonlight /ˈmuːnlaɪt/ ***noun*** [U] light that comes from the moon: *The lake looked beautiful in the moonlight.*

moonlit /ˈmuːnlɪt/ ***adj.*** lit by the moon

Moor /mɔː(r); mʊə(r)/ ***noun*** [C] (**HISTORY**) a member of a race of Muslim people living in NW Africa who entered and took control of part of Spain in the 8th century ▶ **Moorish** ***adj.***: *the Moorish architecture of Cordoba*

moor¹ /mɔː(r)/ (*also* **moorland** /ˈmɔːlənd/) ***noun*** [C,U] (**GEOGRAPHY**) a wild open area of high land that is covered with grass and HEATHER: *We walked across **the moors**.* ➲ look at **heath**

moor² /mɔː(r)/ ***verb*** [I,T] **~ (sth to sth)** to fasten a boat to the land or to an object in the water with a rope or chain

mooring /ˈmɔːrɪŋ/ ***noun*** [C, usually pl.] a place where a boat is tied; the ropes, chains, etc. used to fasten a boat

moose /muːs/ (*especially AmE*) = ELK

mop¹ /mɒp/ ***noun*** [C] a tool for washing floors that consists of a long stick with thick strings, pieces of cloth or a SPONGE on the end

mop² /mɒp/ ***verb*** [T] (**mopping**; **mopped**) **1** to clean a floor with water and a **mop** **2** to remove liquid from sth using a dry cloth: *to mop your forehead with a handkerchief*

PHR V **mop sth up** to get rid of liquid from a surface with a **mop** or dry cloth

mope /məʊp/ ***verb*** [I] **~ (about/around)** to spend your time doing nothing and feeling sorry for yourself because you are unhappy

moped /ˈməʊped/ ***noun*** [C] a type of small, not very powerful motorbike

moraine /məˈreɪn/ ***noun*** [U] (**GEOGRAPHY**) earth, stones, etc., that have been carried along by a mass of ice (**a glacier**) and left when it melted ➲ picture at **glacial**

moral¹ 🔑 /ˈmɒrəl/ ***adj.*** **1** (only *before* a noun) concerned with what is right and wrong: *Some people refuse to eat meat **on moral grounds*** (=because they believe it to be wrong). ◇ *a moral dilemma/issue/question* **2** having a high standard of behaviour that is considered good and right by most people: *She has always led a very moral life.* **OPP** **immoral** ➲ look at **amoral**

IDM **moral support** help or encouragement that you give to sb who is nervous or worried: *I went to the dentist's with him just to give him some moral support.*

moral² /ˈmɒrəl/ ***noun*** **1 morals** [pl.] standards of good behaviour: *These people appear to have no morals.* **2** [C] a lesson in the right way to behave that can be learnt from a story or an experience: *The moral of the play is that friendship is more important than money.*

morale /məˈrɑːl/ ***noun*** [U] how happy, sad, confident, etc. a group of people feels at a particular time: *The team's morale was low/high before the match* (=they felt worried/confident). ◇ *to boost/raise/improve morale*

moralistic /ˌmɒrəˈlɪstɪk/ ***adj.*** (*formal*) having or showing very fixed ideas about what is right and wrong, especially when this causes you to judge other people's behaviour

morality /məˈræləti/ ***noun*** [U] principles concerning what is good and bad or right and wrong behaviour: *a debate about the morality of abortion* **OPP** **immorality**

moralize (also -ise) /ˈmɒrəlaɪz/ ***verb*** [I] **~ (about/on sth)** to tell other people what the right or wrong way to behave is

morally 🔑 /'mɒrəli/ ***adv.*** connected with standards of what is right or wrong

moratorium /,mɒrə'tɔ:riəm/ ***noun*** [C] **a ~ (on sth)** a temporary stopping of an activity, especially by official agreement: *The convention called for a two-year moratorium on commercial whaling.*

morbid /'mɔ:bɪd/ ***adj.*** showing interest in unpleasant things, for example disease and death

more[1] 🔑 /mɔ:(r)/ ***det., pronoun*** a larger number or amount of people or things; sth extra as well as what you have: *There were* ***more*** *people* ***than*** *I expected.* ◇ *We had more time than we thought.* ◇ *There's room for three more people.* ◇ *I couldn't eat any more.* ◇ *I can't stand much more of this.* ◇ *Tell me more about your job.* OPP **less, fewer**

IDM **more and more** an increasing amount or number: *There are more and more cars on the road.*

what's more (used for adding another fact) also; in addition: *The hotel was awful and what's more it was miles from the beach.*

more[2] 🔑 /mɔ:(r)/ ***adv.*** **1** (used to form the comparative of many adjectives and adverbs): *She was* ***far/much more*** *intelligent* ***than*** *her sister.* ◇ *a course for more advanced students* ◇ *Please write more carefully.* OPP **less 2** to a greater degree than usual or than sth else: *I like him* ***far/much more*** *than his wife.* OPP **less**

IDM **more or less** approximately; almost: *We are more or less the same age.*

not any more not any longer: *She doesn't live here any more.*

moreover 🔑 /mɔ:r'əʊvə(r)/ ***adv.*** (*written*) (used for adding another fact) also; in addition: *This firm did the work very well. Moreover, the cost was not too high.*

morgue /mɔ:g/ ***noun*** [C] a building where dead bodies are kept until they are buried or CREMATED (= burned as part of a funeral service) ➲ look at **mortuary**

morning 🔑 /'mɔ:nɪŋ/ ***noun*** [C,U] **1** the early part of the day between the time when the sun rises and midday: *Pat's going to London* ***tomorrow morning.*** ◇ *Bye, see you* ***in the morning*** (= tomorrow morning). ◇ *I've been studying hard* ***all morning.*** ◇ *Dave makes breakfast* ***every morning.*** ◇ *She only works* ***in the mornings.*** **2** the part of the night that is after midnight: *I was woken by a strange noise in* ***the early hours of the morning.*** ◇ *He didn't come home until three* ***in the morning.***

IDM **Good morning** (*formal*) used when you see sb for the first time in the morning

moron /'mɔ:rɒn/ ***noun*** [C] (*informal*) a rude way of referring to sb who you think is very stupid: *Stop treating me like a moron!* ▶ **moronic** /mə'rɒnɪk/ ***adj.***

morose /mə'rəʊs/ ***adj.*** bad-tempered, and not saying much to other people ▶ **morosely** ***adv.***

morphine /'mɔ:fi:n/ ***noun*** [U] (**HEALTH**) a powerful drug that is used for reducing pain

morphology /mɔ:'fɒlədʒi/ ***noun*** [U] **1** (**BIOLOGY**) the form and structure of animals and plants, studied as a science **2** (**LANGUAGE**) the form of words, studied as a branch of LINGUISTICS ➲ look at **grammar** ▶ **morphological** /,mɔ:fə'lɒdʒɪkl/ ***adj.***

morsel /'mɔ:sl/ ***noun*** [C] a very small piece of sth, usually food

mortal[1] /'mɔ:tl/ ***adj.*** **1** that cannot live for ever and must die: *We are all mortal.* OPP **immortal 2** (*written*) that will result in death: *a mortal wound/blow* ◇ *to be in mortal danger* ➲ look at **fatal 3** very great or extreme: *They were in mortal fear of the enemy* ▶ **mortally** /-təli/ ***adv.***

mortal[2] /'mɔ:tl/ ***noun*** [C] (*formal*) a human being

mortality /mɔ:'tæləti/ ***noun*** [U] (**SOCIAL STUDIES**) **1** the number of deaths in one period of time or in one place: *the infant* ***mortality rate*** (= the number of babies that die at or just after birth) **2** the fact that nobody can live for ever: *He didn't like to think about his own mortality.*

mortar /'mɔ:tə(r)/ ***noun*** **1** [U] a mixture of CEMENT, sand and water used in building for holding bricks and stones together ➲ picture at **building 2** [C] a type of heavy gun that fires a type of bomb high into the air **3** [C] a small heavy bowl used when crushing food or other substances into powder with a PESTLE ➲ picture at **laboratory**

mortgage[1] /'mɔ:gɪdʒ/ ***noun*** [C] (**FINANCE**) money that you borrow in order to buy a house or flat: *We took out a £40000 mortgage.*

> **RELATED VOCABULARY**
>
> You usually borrow money from a **bank** or a **building society**, who decide what **rate of interest** you must pay on the **loan**.

mortgage[2] /'mɔ:gɪdʒ/ ***verb*** [T] (**FINANCE**) to give a bank, etc. the legal right to own your house, land, etc. if you do not pay the money back that you have borrowed from the bank to buy the house or land: *He had to mortgage his house to pay his legal costs.*

mortician /mɔ:'tɪʃn/ (*AmE*) = UNDERTAKER

mortify /'mɔ:tɪfaɪ/ ***verb*** [T] (usually passive) (*pres. part.* **mortifying**; *3rd person sing. pres.* **mortifies**; *pt, pp* **mortified**) (*formal*) to make sb feel very embarrassed: *She* ***was mortified to*** *realize he had heard every word she said.* ▶ **mortification** /,mɔ:tɪfɪ'keɪʃn/ ***noun*** [U] ▶ **mortifying** ***adj.***: *How mortifying to have to apologize to him!*

mortise (also **mortice**) /'mɔ:tɪs/ ***noun*** [C] a hole cut in a piece of wood, etc. to receive the end of another piece of wood, so that the two are held together

mortuary /'mɔ:tʃəri/ ***noun*** [C] (*pl.* **mortuaries**) a room, usually in a hospital, where dead bodies are kept before they are buried or CREMATED (= burned as part of a funeral service) ➲ look at **morgue**

mosaic /məʊ'zeɪɪk/ ***noun*** [C,U] (**ART**) a picture or pattern that is made by placing together small coloured stones, pieces of glass, etc.

Moslem = MUSLIM

mosque /mɒsk/ ***noun*** [C] (**RELIGION**) a building where Muslims meet and pray

mosquito /mə'ski:təʊ; mɒs-/ ***noun*** [C] (*pl.* **mosquitoes**) a small flying insect that lives in hot countries and bites people or animals to drink their blood. Some types of **mosquito** spread a very serious disease (**malaria**). ➲ picture on **page 29**

moss /mɒs/ ***noun*** [C,U] (**BIOLOGY**) a small soft green plant, with no flowers, that grows in wet places, especially on rocks or trees ▶ **mossy** ***adj.***

most[1] 🔑 /məʊst/ ***det., pronoun*** **1** (used as the superlative of *many* and *much*) greatest in number or amount: *Who got the most points?* ◇ *The children had the most fun.* ◇ *We all worked hard but I did the most.* OPP **least, fewest 2** nearly all of a group of people or things: *Most people in this country have a television.* ◇ *I like most Italian food.*

IDM **at (the) most** not more than a certain number, and probably less: *There were 20 people there, at the most.*

make the most of sth → MAKE[1]

most[2] /məʊst/ ***adv.*** **1** (used to form the superlative of many adjectives and adverbs): *It's the most beautiful house I've ever seen.* ◇ *I work most efficiently in the morning.* OPP **least 2** more than anyone/anything else: *What do you miss most when you're abroad?* OPP **least 3** (*formal*) very: *We heard a most interesting talk about Japan.*

mostly /ˈməʊstli/ ***adv.*** in almost every case; almost all the time: *Our students come mostly from Japan.*

MOT /ˌem əʊ ˈtiː/ ***abbr.*** (*also* **MO'T test**) a test to make sure that vehicles over a certain age are safe to drive: *My car failed its MOT.*

motel /məʊˈtel/ ***noun*** [C] (**TOURISM**) a hotel near a main road for people who are travelling by car

moth /mɒθ/ ***noun*** [C] an insect with a hairy body and large wings that usually flies at night. Some **moths** eat cloth and leave small holes in your clothes. ➲ picture on **page 29**

mothball /ˈmɒθbɔːl/ ***noun*** [C] a small ball made of a chemical substance that protects clothes in cupboards from MOTHS

mother[1] /ˈmʌðə(r)/ ***noun*** [C] the female parent of a person or an animal ➲ look at **mum, mummy, stepmother**

mother[2] /ˈmʌðə(r)/ ***verb*** [T] to look after sb as a mother does: *Stop mothering me – I can look after myself!*

motherhood /ˈmʌðəhʊd/ ***noun*** [U] the state of being a mother

ˈmother-in-law ***noun*** [C] (*pl.* **mothers-in-law**) the mother of your husband or wife

motherland /ˈmʌðəlænd/ ***noun*** [C] (*formal*) the country where you or your family were born and which you feel a strong emotional connection with

motherly /ˈmʌðəli/ ***adj.*** having the qualities of a good mother: *motherly love*

ˈmother tongue ***noun*** [C] (**LANGUAGE**) the first language that you learned to speak as a child

motif /məʊˈtiːf/ ***noun*** [C] a picture or pattern on sth

motion[1] /ˈməʊʃn/ ***noun*** **1** [U] movement or a way of moving: *The motion of the ship made us all feel sick.* ◇ *Pull the lever to* ***set*** *the machine* ***in motion*** (= make it start moving). ➲ look at **slow motion 2** [C] a formal suggestion at a meeting that you discuss and vote on: *The motion was carried/rejected by a majority of eight votes.*

motion[2] /ˈməʊʃn/ ***verb*** [I,T] **~ to sb (to do sth)**; **~ (for) sb (to do sth)** to make a movement, usually with your hand, that tells sb what to do: *I motioned to the waiter.* ◇ *The manager motioned for me to sit down.*

motionless /ˈməʊʃnləs/ ***adj.*** not moving

motivate /ˈməʊtɪveɪt/ ***verb*** [T] **1** (usually passive) to cause sb to act in a particular way: *Her reaction was motivated by fear.* **2** to make sb want to do sth, especially sth that involves hard work and effort: *Our new teacher certainly knows how to motivate his classes.* ▶ **motivated** AW ***adj.***: *highly motivated students* ▶ **motivation** AW /ˌməʊtɪˈveɪʃn/ ***noun*** [C,U]: *He's clever enough, but he lacks motivation.*

motive[1] AW /ˈməʊtɪv/ ***noun*** [C,U] **(a) ~ (for sth/doing sth)** a reason for doing sth, often sth bad: *The police couldn't discover a motive for the murder.* ➲ note at **reason**[1]

motive[2] AW /ˈməʊtɪv/ ***adj.*** (only *before* a noun) (**PHYSICS**) causing movement or action: *motive power/force* (= for example, electricity, to operate machinery)

motor[1] /ˈməʊtə(r)/ ***noun*** [C] (**PHYSICS**) a device that uses petrol, gas, electricity, etc. to produce movement and makes a machine, etc. work: *The washing machine doesn't work. I think something is wrong with the motor.*

motor[2] /ˈməʊtə(r)/ ***adj.*** (only *before* a noun) **1** having or using the power of an engine or a motor: *a motor vehicle* **2** (*especially BrE*) connected with vehicles that have engines, especially cars: *the motor industry* ◇ *motor racing* **3** (**ANATOMY**) connected with movement of the body that is produced by muscles; connected with the nerves that control movement: *uncoordinated motor activity* ◇ *Both motor and sensory functions are affected.*

motorbike /ˈməʊtəbaɪk/ (*also formal* **motorcycle**) ***noun*** [C] a vehicle that has two wheels and an engine

motorboat /ˈməʊtəbəʊt/ ***noun*** [C] a small fast boat that has a motor

ˈmotor car (*BrE, formal*) = CAR (1)

motorcycle /ˈməʊtəsaɪkl/ (*formal*) = MOTORBIKE

motorcyclist /ˈməʊtəsaɪklɪst/ ***noun*** [C] a person who rides a motorbike

motorhome /ˈməʊtəhəʊm/ ***noun*** [C] = CAMPER (2)

motoring /ˈməʊtərɪŋ/ ***noun*** [U] driving in a car: *a motoring holiday*

motorist /ˈməʊtərɪst/ ***noun*** [C] a person who drives a car ➲ look at **pedestrian**

motorized (*also* **-ised**) /ˈməʊtəraɪzd/ ***adj.*** (only *before* a noun) that has an engine: *a motorized wheelchair*

ˌmotor ˈneuron ***noun*** [C] (**ANATOMY**) a nerve cell which sends signals to a muscle or GLAND

ˌmotor ˈneuron disease ***noun*** [U] (**HEALTH**) a disease in which the nerves and muscles become gradually weaker until the person dies

motorway /ˈməʊtəweɪ/ (*AmE* **expressway; freeway**) ***noun*** [C] a wide road connecting cities that is specially built for fast traffic

motte /mɒt/ ***noun*** [C] (**HISTORY**) the small hill on which the FORT (= a strong building used for military defence) is built in a MOTTE-AND-BAILEY CASTLE

ˌmotte-and-ˌbailey ˈcastle ***noun*** [C] (**HISTORY**) an old type of castle that consists of a FORT (= a strong building used for military defence) on a small hill surrounded by an outer wall

mottled /ˈmɒtld/ ***adj.*** marked with shapes of different colours without a regular pattern: *the mottled skin of a snake*

motto /ˈmɒtəʊ/ ***noun*** [C] (*pl.* **mottoes** or **mottos**) a short sentence or phrase that expresses the aims and beliefs of a person, a group, an organization, etc.: *'Live and let live' – that's my motto.*

mould[1] (*AmE* **mold**) /məʊld/ ***noun*** **1** [C] a container that you pour a liquid or substance into. The liquid then SETS (= becomes solid) in the same shape as the container, for example after it has cooled or cooked. **2** [C, usually sing.] a particular type: *She doesn't fit into the usual mould of sales directors.* **3** [U] (**BIOLOGY**) a soft green or black substance like fur (**fungus**) that grows in wet places or on old food ▶ **mouldy** (*AmE* **moldy**) ***adj.***: *The cheese had gone mouldy.*

mould[2] (*AmE* **mold**) /məʊld/ ***verb*** [T] **~ A (into B)**; **~ B (from/out of A)** to make sth into a particular shape or form by pressing it, or by putting it into a mould[1](1): *First mould the dough into a ball.* ◇ *a bowl moulded from clay*

moulder (*AmE* **molder**) /ˈməʊldə(r)/ ***verb*** [I] to decay slowly and steadily: *The room smelt of disuse and mouldering books.*

moulding (*AmE* **molding**) /ˈməʊldɪŋ/ ***noun*** [C] (ARCHITECTURE) a decorative strip of plastic, stone, wood, etc. around the top edge of a wall, on a door, etc.: *There were elaborate plaster mouldings around the ceiling.*

moult (*AmE* **molt**) /məʊlt/ ***verb*** [I] (BIOLOGY) (used about an animal or a bird) to lose hairs or feathers before growing new ones

mound /maʊnd/ ***noun*** [C] **1** a large pile of earth or stones; a small hill **2** (*spoken*) **a ~ (of sth)** a pile or a large amount of sth: *I've got a mound of work to do.*

mount[1] 🔑 /maʊnt/ ***verb*** **1** [T] to organize sth: *to mount a protest/a campaign/an exhibition/an attack* **2** [I] to increase gradually in level or amount: *The tension mounted as the end of the match approached.* **3** [T] (*written*) to go up sth or up on to sth: *He mounted the platform and began to speak.* **4** [I,T] to get on a horse or bicycle OPP **dismount** **5** [T] **~ sth (on/onto/in sth)** to fix sth firmly on sth else: *The gas boiler was mounted on the wall.*

PHR V **mount up** to increase (often more than you want): *When you're buying food for six people the cost soon mounts up.*

mount[2] 🔑 /maʊnt/ ***noun*** [C] (*abbr.* **Mt**) (used in names) a mountain: *Mt Everest*

mountain 🔑 /ˈmaʊntən/ ***noun*** [C] **1** (GEOGRAPHY) a very high hill: *Which is the highest mountain in the world?* ◇ *mountain roads/scenery/villages* ◇ *a mountain range* **2** **a ~ (of sth)** a large amount of sth: *I've got a mountain of work to do.* ◇ *We made mountains of sandwiches.*

ˈmountain bike ***noun*** [C] a bicycle with a strong frame, wide tyres and many different GEARS, designed for riding on rough ground

mountaineering /ˌmaʊntəˈnɪərɪŋ/ ***noun*** [U] (SPORT) the sport of climbing mountains ▸ **mountaineer** /-ˈnɪə(r)/ ***noun*** [C]

ˈmountain lion (*AmE*) = PUMA

mountainous /ˈmaʊntənəs/ ***adj.*** **1** (GEOGRAPHY) having many mountains: *a mountainous region* **2** very large in size or amount: *The mountainous waves made sailing impossible.*

mountainside /ˈmaʊntənsaɪd/ ***noun*** [C] (GEOGRAPHY) the land on the side of a mountain

mounted /ˈmaʊntɪd/ ***adj.*** riding a horse: *mounted police*

mounting /ˈmaʊntɪŋ/ ***adj.*** (only *before* a noun) increasing: *mounting unemployment/tension*

mourn /mɔːn/ ***verb*** [I,T] **~ (for/over) sb/sth** to feel and show great sadness, especially because sb has died: *She is still mourning (for) her child.* ▸ **mourning** ***noun*** [U]: *He wore a black armband to show he was **in mourning**.*

mourner /ˈmɔːnə(r)/ ***noun*** [C] a person who goes to a funeral as a friend or relative of the person who has died

mournful /ˈmɔːnfl/ ***adj.*** (*written*) very sad: *a mournful song* ▸ **mournfully** /-fəli/ ***adv.***

mouse 🔑 /maʊs/ ***noun*** [C] (*pl.* **mice** /maɪs/) **1** a very small animal with fur and a long thin tail **2** (COMPUTING) a piece of equipment, connected to a computer, for moving around the screen and entering commands without touching the keys: *Use the mouse to drag the icon to a new position.* ➲ picture at **computer**

ˈmouse mat (*AmE* **ˈmouse pad**) ***noun*** [C] (COMPUTING) a small piece of material that is the best kind of surface on which to use a computer mouse ➲ picture at **computer**

ˈmouse potato ***noun*** [C] (*informal*) (COMPUTING) a person who spends too much time using a computer

mousse /muːs/ ***noun*** [C,U] **1** a type of light food that is made by mixing together cream and egg whites and adding another food for flavour: *(a) chocolate/salmon mousse* **2** a light substance containing a lot of bubbles that you use to make your hair stay in a particular style

moustache /məˈstɑːʃ; ˈmʌstæʃ/ (*AmE* **mustache**) ***noun*** [C] hair that grows on a man's top lip, between the mouth and nose

mouth[1] 🔑 /maʊθ/ ***noun*** [C] (*pl.* **mouths** /maʊðz/) **1** the part of your face that you use for eating and speaking: *to open/close your mouth* ➲ picture on **page 80** **2** **-mouthed** /maʊðd/ (used to form compound adjectives) having a particular type of mouth or a particular way of speaking: *We stared open-mouthed in surprise.* ◇ *He's a loud-mouthed bully.* **3** (GEOGRAPHY) the place where a river enters the sea

IDM **keep your mouth shut** (*informal*) to not say sth to sb because it is a secret or because it will upset or annoy them

mouth[2] /maʊð/ ***verb*** [I,T] to move your mouth as if you were speaking but without making any sound: *Vinay was outside the window, mouthing something to us.*

mouthful /ˈmaʊθfʊl/ ***noun*** **1** [C] the amount of food or drink that you can put in your mouth at one time **2** [sing.] a word or phrase that is long or difficult to say: *Her name is a bit of a mouthful.*

ˈmouth organ = HARMONICA

mouthpiece /ˈmaʊθpiːs/ ***noun*** [C] **1** the part of a telephone, musical instrument, etc. that you put in or near your mouth **2** a person, newspaper, etc. that a particular group uses to express its opinions

mouthwash /ˈmaʊθwɒʃ/ ***noun*** [C, U] (HEALTH) a liquid used to make the mouth fresh and healthy

ˈmouth-watering ***adj.*** (used about food) that looks or smells very good

movable (also **moveable**) /ˈmuːvəbl/ ***adj.*** **1** that can be moved from one place or position to another: *a doll with a movable head* **2** (LAW) (used about property) able to be taken from one house, etc. to another

move[1] 🔑 /muːv/ ***verb*** **1** [I,T] to change position or to put sth in a different position: *Please move your car. It's blocking the road.* ◇ *The station is so crowded you **can hardly move**.* ◇ *The meeting has been moved to Thursday.* **2** [I,T] **~ along, down, over, up, etc.** to move (sth) further in a particular direction in order to make space for sb/sth else: *If we move up a bit, Rob can sit here too.* ◇ *Move your head down – I can't see the screen.* **3** [I,T] to change the place where you live, work, study, etc.: *Our neighbours are moving to York next week.* ◇ *They're going to **move house**.* ◇ *Yuka's moved down to the beginners' class.* **4** [I] **~ (on/ahead)** to make progress: *When the new team of builders arrived things started moving very quickly.* **5** [I] to take action: *Unless we move quickly lives will be lost.* **6** [T] to cause sb to have strong feelings, especially of sadness: *Many people were **moved to tears** by reports of the massacre.*

IDM **get moving** to go, leave or do sth quickly

get sth moving to cause sth to make progress

PHR V **move in (with sb)** to start living in a house (with sb)
move on (to sth) to start doing or discussing sth new
move off (used about a vehicle) to start a journey; to leave
move out to leave your old home

move² /muːv/ ***noun*** [C] **1** a change of place or position: *She was watching every move I made.* ➲ note at **action¹** **2** a change in the place where you live or work: *a move to a bigger house* **3** action that you take because you want to achieve a particular result: *Both sides want to negotiate but neither is prepared to* ***make the first move.*** ◇ *Asking him to help me was* ***a good move.*** **4** (in CHESS and other games) a change in the position of a piece: *It's your move.*
IDM **be on the move** to be going somewhere
get a move on (*informal*) to hurry: *I'm late. I'll have to get a move on.*
make a move to start to go somewhere: *It's time to go home. Let's make a move.*

moveable ***adj.*** = MOVABLE

movement /ˈmuːvmənt/ ***noun*** **1** [C,U] an act of moving: *The dancer's movements were smooth and controlled.* ◇ *The seat belt doesn't allow much freedom of movement.* ◇ *I could see some movement* (= sb/sth moving) *in the trees.* **2** [C,U] an act of moving or being moved from one place to another: *the slow movement of the clouds across the sky* **3** [C, usually sing.] **a ~ (away from/towards sth)** a general change in the way people think or behave: *There's been a movement away from the materialism of the 1980s.* **4 movements** [pl.] a person's actions or plans during a period of time: *Detectives have been watching the man's movements for several weeks.* **5** [C] a group of people who have the same aims or ideas: *I support the Animal Rights movement.* **6** [C] (**MUSIC**) one of the main parts of a long piece of music

movie /ˈmuːvi/ ***noun*** (*especially AmE*) **1** = FILM¹ (1): *Shall we go and* ***see a movie?*** ◇ *a science fiction/horror movie* ◇ *a movie director/star* ◇ *a movie theater* (= cinema) **2 the movies** [pl.] = CINEMA: *Let's go to the movies.*

moving /ˈmuːvɪŋ/ ***adj.*** **1** causing strong feelings, especially of sadness: *a deeply moving speech/story* **2** that moves: *It's a computerized machine with few moving parts.*

mow /məʊ/ ***verb*** [I,T] (*pt* **mowed**; *pp* **mown** /məʊn/ or **mowed**) to cut grass using a MOWER: *to mow the lawn*
PHR V **mow sb down** to kill sb with a gun or a car

mower /ˈməʊə(r)/ ***noun*** [C] a machine for cutting grass: *a lawnmower* ◇ *an electric mower*

MP /ˌem ˈpiː/ ***abbr.*** (*especially BrE*) (**POLITICS**) Member of Parliament

MP3 /ˌem piː ˈθriː/ ***noun*** [C,U] (**COMPUTING**) a method of reducing the size of a computer file containing sound, or a file that is reduced in size in this way

MP'3 player ***noun*** [C] (**COMPUTING**) a small piece of equipment that can open and play MP3 FILES (= files containing sound, that have been reduced in size)

mpg /ˌem piː ˈdʒiː/ ***abbr.*** miles per gallon: *This car does 40 mpg* (= you can drive 40 miles on one gallon of petrol).

mph /ˌem piː ˈeɪtʃ/ ***abbr.*** miles per hour: *a 70 mph speed limit*

MPV /ˌem piː ˈviː/ ***noun*** [C] **multi-purpose vehicle**; a large car like a van SYN **people carrier**

Mr /ˈmɪstə(r)/ used as a title before the name of a man: *Mr (Matthew) Botham*

MRI /ˌem ɑːr ˈaɪ/ ***abbr.*** (**HEALTH**) **magnetic resonance imaging**; a method of producing an image of the inside of a person's body using a strong MAGNETIC FIELD: *an MRI scan*

Mrs /ˈmɪsɪz/ used as a title before the name of a married woman: *Mrs (Sylvia) Allen*

MRSA /ˌem ɑːr es ˈeɪ/ ***noun*** [U] **methicillin-resistant Staphylococcus aureus** (**HEALTH**); a type of bacteria that cannot be killed by ANTIBIOTICS (= medicines which are used for destroying bacteria and curing infections): *rising rates of MRSA infections in hospitals* ➲ look at **superbug**

MS /ˌem ˈes/ ***abbr.*** multiple sclerosis

Ms /mɪz; məz/ used as a title before the family name of a woman who may or may not be married: *Ms (Donna) Hackett*

MSc /ˌem es ˈsiː/ (*AmE* **M.S.**) ***abbr.*** (**EDUCATION**) **Master of Science**; a second degree that you receive when you complete a more advanced course or piece of research in a science subject at university or college ➲ look at **BSc**, **MA**

MSG /ˌem es ˈdʒiː/ ***abbr.*** = MONOSODIUM GLUTAMATE

Mt ***abbr.*** Mount: *Mt Everest*

much /mʌtʃ/ ***det.***, ***pronoun***, ***adv.*** **1** (used with uncountable nouns, mainly in negative sentences and questions, or after *as, how, so, too*) a large amount of sth: *I haven't got much money.* ◇ *Did she say much?* ◇ *You've given me* ***too much*** *food.* ◇ ***How much*** *time have you got?* ◇ *I can't carry* ***that much!*** ◇ *Eat* ***as much as*** *you can.* **2** to a great degree: *I don't like her very much.* ◇ *Do you see Sashi much?* (= very often) ◇ *Do you see much of Sashi?* ◇ *much taller/prettier/harder* ◇ *much more interesting/unusual* ◇ *much more quickly/happily* ◇ *You ate* ***much more*** *than me.* **3** (with past participles used as adjectives) very: *She was much loved by all her friends.* ◇ *a much-needed rest*
IDM **much the same** very similar: *Softball is much the same as baseball.*
nothing much → NOTHING
not much good (at sth) not skilled (at sth): *I'm not much good at singing.*
not much of a... not a good...: *She's not much of a cook.*
not up to much → UP

muck¹ /mʌk/ ***noun*** [U] **1** (**AGRICULTURE**) the waste from farm animals, used to make plants grow better SYN **manure** **2** (*informal*) dirt or mud

muck² /mʌk/ ***verb*** (*informal*)
PHR V **muck about/around** to behave in a silly way or to waste time: *Stop mucking around and come and help me!*
muck sth up to do sth badly; to spoil sth: *I was so nervous that I completely mucked up my interview.*

mucky /ˈmʌki/ ***adj.*** (*informal*) (*especially BrE*) dirty: *mucky hands*

mucous membrane /ˌmjuːkəs ˈmembreɪn/ ***noun*** [C] (**ANATOMY**) a thin layer of skin that covers the inside of the nose and mouth and the outside of other organs in the body, producing MUCUS to stop these parts from becoming dry

mucus /ˈmjuːkəs/ ***noun*** [U] (*formal*) (**BIOLOGY**) a sticky substance that is produced in some parts of the body, especially the nose ► **mucous** /ˈmjuːkəs/ ***adj.***: *mucous glands*

mud ⊶ /mʌd/ *noun* [U] soft, wet earth: *He came home from the football match* ***covered in mud***.

muddle /ˈmʌdl/ *verb* [T] **1** ~ **sth (up)** to put things in the wrong place or order or to make them untidy: *Try not to* ***get*** *those papers* ***muddled up***. **2** ~ **sb (up)** to confuse sb: *I do my homework and schoolwork in separate books so that I don't* ***get muddled up***. ▶ **muddle** *noun* [C,U]: *If you* ***get in a muddle****, I'll help you.* ▶ **muddled** *adj.*

muddy /ˈmʌdi/ *adj.* full of or covered in mud: *muddy boots* ◇ *It's very muddy down by the river.*

mudflat /ˈmʌdflæt/ *noun* [C] (*also* **mudflats** [pl.]) (**GEOGRAPHY**) an area of flat wet land that is covered by the sea when it is at its highest level (**high tide**)

mudguard /ˈmʌdgɑːd/ *noun* [C] a curved cover over the wheel of a bicycle or motorbike

mudslide /ˈmʌdslaɪd/ *noun* [C] (**GEOGRAPHY**) a large amount of mud sliding down a mountain, often destroying buildings and injuring or killing people below

muesli /ˈmjuːzli/ *noun* [U] food made of grains, nuts, dried fruit, etc. that you eat with milk for breakfast

muezzin /muːˈezɪn/ *noun* [C] (**RELIGION**) a man who calls Muslims to come to a special building (**a mosque**) to pray

muffin /ˈmʌfɪn/ *noun* [C] **1** (*AmE* ˌ**English ˈmuffin**) a type of bread roll often eaten hot with butter **2** a type of small cake

muffle /ˈmʌfl/ *verb* [T] to make a sound quieter and more difficult to hear: *He put his hand over his mouth to muffle his laughter.* ▶ **muffled** *adj.*: *I heard muffled voices outside.*

muffler /ˈmʌflə(r)/ (*AmE*) = SILENCER

mug[1] /mʌg/ *noun* [C] **1** a large cup with straight sides and a handle: *a coffee mug* ◇ *a mug of tea* **2** (*informal*) a person who seems stupid

mug[2] /mʌg/ *verb* [T] (**mugging**; **mugged**) (**LAW**) to attack and rob sb in the street: *Keep your wallet out of sight or you'll* ***get mugged***. ▶ **mugger** *noun* [C] ➲ note at **thief** ▶ **mugging** *noun* [C,U]: *The mugging took place around midnight.*

muggy /ˈmʌgi/ *adj.* (used about the weather) warm and slightly wet in an unpleasant way **SYN** **humid**

Muhammad (also **Mohammed**) /məˈhæmɪd/ *noun* [sing.] (**RELIGION**) the PROPHET (= a person who is sent by God to teach and give people messages from God) who started the religion of Islam

mulch /mʌltʃ/ *noun* [C,U] (**AGRICULTURE**) material, for example dead leaves, that you put around a plant to protect its base and its roots, to improve the soil or to stop WEEDS (= wild plants) from growing ▶ **mulch** *verb* [I,T]

mule /mjuːl/ *noun* [C] **1** an animal that is used for carrying heavy loads and whose parents are a horse and a DONKEY **2** (*slang*) a person who is paid to take drugs illegally from one country to another

mull /mʌl/ *verb*

PHR V **mull sth over** to think about sth carefully and for a long time: *Don't ask me for a decision right now. I'll have to mull it over.*

multi- /ˈmʌlti/ *prefix* (used in nouns and adjectives) more than one; many: *multicoloured* ◇ *a multimillionaire*

multicultural /ˌmʌltiˈkʌltʃərəl/ *adj.* (**SOCIAL STUDIES**) for or including people of many different races, languages, religions and traditions: *a multicultural society*

multilateral /ˌmʌltiˈlætərəl/ *adj.* involving more than two groups of people, countries, etc. ➲ look at **unilateral**

multilingual /ˌmʌltiˈlɪŋgwəl/ *adj.* (**LANGUAGE**) speaking or using several different languages: ◇ *a multilingual classroom* ➲ look at **bilingual**, **monolingual**

multimedia /ˌmʌltiˈmiːdiə/ *adj.* (only *before* a noun) (**COMPUTING**) using sound, pictures and film in addition to text on a screen: *multimedia systems/products*

multinational /ˌmʌltiˈnæʃnəl/ *adj.* existing in or involving many countries: *multinational companies* ▶ **multinational** *noun* [C]: *The company is owned by Ford, the US multinational.*

multiple[1] /ˈmʌltɪpl/ *adj.* involving many people or things or having many parts: *Three drivers died in a multiple pile-up on the motorway.*

multiple[2] /ˈmʌltɪpl/ *noun* [C] (**MATHEMATICS**) a number that contains another number an exact number of times: *12, 18 and 24 are multiples of 6.*

ˌ**multiple-ˈchoice** *adj.* (**EDUCATION**) (used about exam questions) showing several different answers from which you have to choose the right one

multiple sclerosis /ˌmʌltɪpl skləˈrəʊsɪs/ *noun* [U] (*abbr.* **MS**) (**HEALTH**) a serious disease which causes you to slowly lose control of your body and become less able to move

multiplex /ˈmʌltɪpleks/ (*BrE also* ˌ**multiplex ˈcinema**) *noun* [C] (**ARTS AND MEDIA**) a large cinema with several separate rooms with screens

ˌ**multipliˈcation table** (*also* **table**) *noun* [C] (**MATHEMATICS**) a list showing the results when a number is multiplied by a set of other numbers, especially 1 to 12, in turn

multiply ⊶ /ˈmʌltɪplaɪ/ *verb* (*pres. part.* **multiplying**; *3rd person sing. pres.* **multiplies**; *pt, pp* **multiplied**) **1** [I,T] ~ **A by B** (**MATHEMATICS**) to increase a number by the number of times mentioned: *2 multiplied by 4 makes 8* (= 2 x 4 = 8) **OPP** **divide** **2** [I,T] to increase or make sth increase by a very large amount: *We've multiplied our profits over the last two years.*
▶ **multiplication** /ˌmʌltɪplɪˈkeɪʃn/ *noun* [U] ➲ look at **division**, **addition**, **subtraction**

ˌ**multi-ˈpurpose** *adj.* that can be used for several different purposes: *a multi-purpose tool/machine*

ˌ**multi-storey ˈcar park** (also ˌ**multi ˈstorey**, *AmE* ˈ**parking garage**) *noun* [C] a large building with several floors for parking cars in

multitasking /ˌmʌltiˈtɑːskɪŋ/ *noun* [U] **1** (**COMPUTING**) the ability of a computer to operate several programs at the same time **2** the ability to do several things at the same time

multitude /ˈmʌltɪtjuːd/ *noun* [C] (*formal*) a very large number of people or things

ˌ**multi-ˈuser** *adj.* (**COMPUTING**) able to be used by more than one person at the same time: *a multi-user software licence*

mum ⊶ /mʌm/ (*AmE* **mom** /mɒm/) *noun* [C] (*informal*) mother: *Is that your mum?* ◇ *Can I have a drink, Mum?* ➲ look at **mummy**

mumble /ˈmʌmbl/ *verb* [I,T] to speak quietly without opening your mouth properly, so that people cannot hear the words: *I can't hear if you mumble.* ➲ look at **mutter**

musical instruments

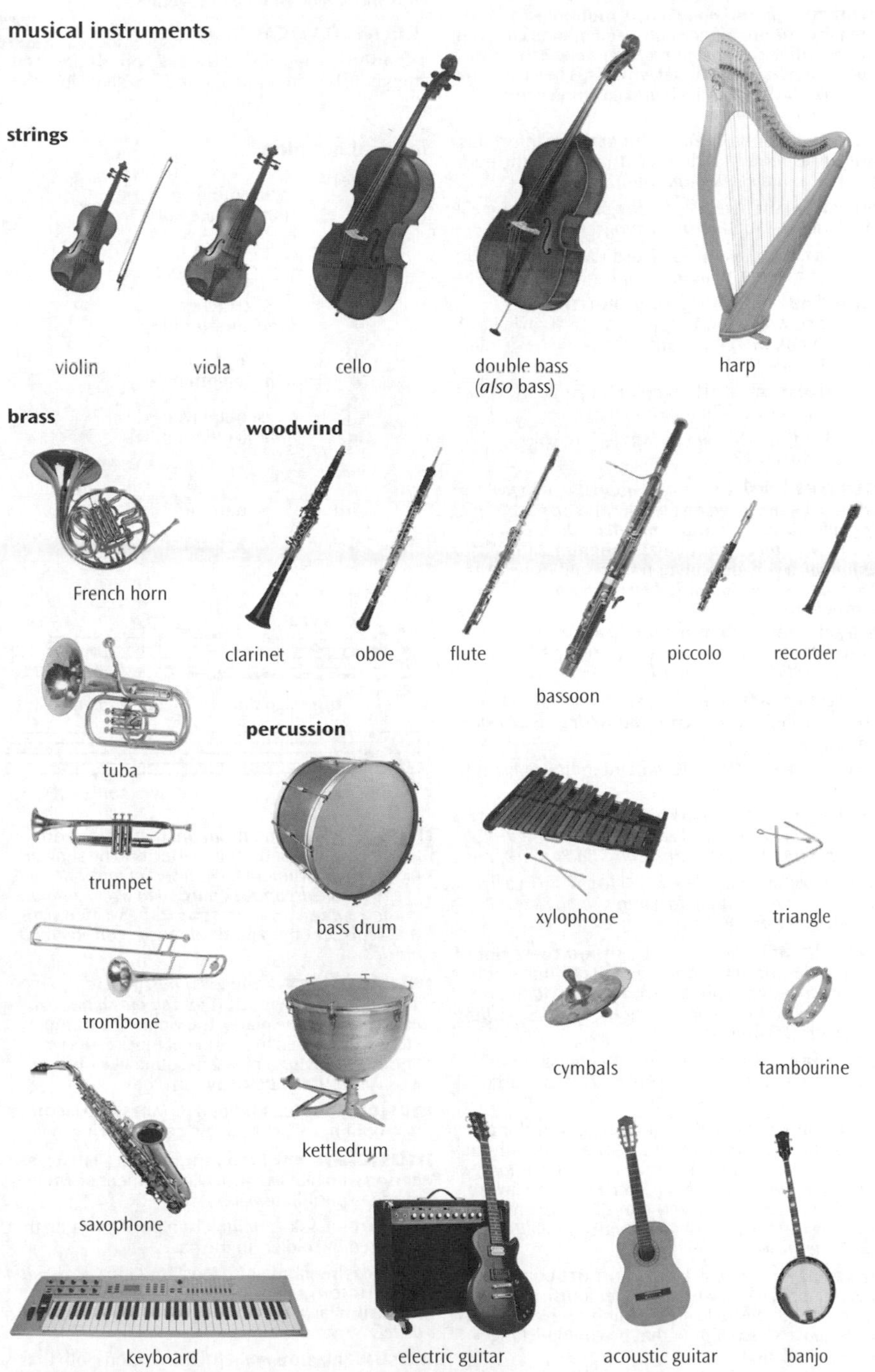

mummy /ˈmʌmi/ ***noun*** [C] (*pl.* **mummies**) **1** (*AmE* **mommy** /ˈmɒmi/) (*informal*) (used by or to children) mother: *Here comes your mummy now.* **2** the dead body of a person or animal which has been kept by rubbing it with special oils and covering it in cloth: *an Egyptian mummy*

mumps /mʌmps/ ***noun*** [U] (**HEALTH**) an infectious disease, especially of children, that causes the neck to swell: *to have/catch (the) mumps*

munch /mʌntʃ/ ***verb*** [I,T] ~ **(on sth)** to bite and eat sth noisily: *He sat there munching (on) an apple.*

mundane /mʌnˈdeɪn/ ***adj.*** ordinary; not interesting or exciting: *a mundane job*

municipal /mjuːˈnɪsɪpl/ ***adj.*** (**POLITICS**) connected with a town or city that has its own local government: *municipal buildings* (=the town hall, public library, etc.)

munitions /mjuːˈnɪʃnz/ ***noun*** [pl.] military supplies, especially bombs and guns

mural /ˈmjʊərəl/ ***noun*** [C] (**ART**) a large picture painted on a wall

murder[1] /ˈmɜːdə(r)/ ***noun*** **1** [C,U] (**LAW**) the crime of killing a person illegally and on purpose: *to **commit murder** ◇ a vicious murder ◇ the murder victim/weapon* ➲ look at **manslaughter** **2** [U] (*informal*) a very difficult or unpleasant experience: *It's murder trying to work when it's as hot as this.*
▶ ***murderer noun*** [C]
IDM **get away with murder** to do whatever you want without being stopped or punished: *He lets his students get away with murder.*

murder[2] ***verb*** [I,T] (**LAW**) to kill sb deliberately and illegally: *He denies murdering his ex-wife's lover.* ➲ note at **kill**

murderous /ˈmɜːdərəs/ ***adj.*** intending or likely to murder

murky /ˈmɜːki/ ***adj.*** dark and unpleasant or dirty: *The water in the river looked very murky.* ◇ (*figurative*) *According to rumours, the new boss had a murky past.*

murmur /ˈmɜːmə(r)/ ***verb*** [I,T] to say sth in a low quiet voice: *He murmured a name in his sleep.*
▶ **murmur *noun*** [C]

muscle /ˈmʌsl/ ***noun*** [C,U] (**ANATOMY**) one of the parts inside your body that you can make tight or relax in order to produce movement: *Riding a bicycle is good for developing the leg muscles.* ◇ *Lifting weights builds muscle.*

muscular /ˈmʌskjələ(r)/ ***adj.*** **1** connected with the muscles: *muscular pain/tissue* **2** having large strong muscles: *a muscular body*

muse[1] /mjuːz/ ***verb*** [I] **1** ~ **(about/on/over/upon sth)** to think carefully about sth for a time, without noticing what is happening around you: *She looked out to sea, musing on what he had said.* **2** to say sth, usually to yourself, in a way that shows you are thinking carefully about it: *'I wonder if I should tell him?' she mused.*

muse[2] /mjuːz/ ***noun*** [C] (**ARTS AND MEDIA**) a person or spirit that gives a writer, painter, musician, etc. ideas and the desire to create things: *He felt that his muse had deserted him* (=that he could no longer write, paint, etc.).

museum /mjuˈziːəm/ ***noun*** [C] a building where collections of valuable and interesting objects are kept and shown to the public: *Have you been to the Science Museum in London?*

mushroom /ˈmʌʃrʊm; -ruːm/ ***noun*** [C] a type of plant which grows very quickly, has a flat or rounded top and can be eaten as a vegetable

RELATED VOCABULARY

A mushroom is a type of **fungus**. Some, but not all, **fungi** can be eaten. **Toadstool** is the name for some types of poisonous fungi.

musical notation

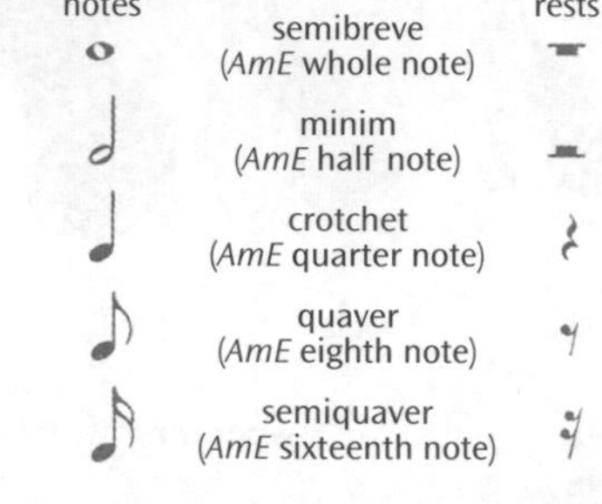

sharp ♯ natural ♮ flat ♭

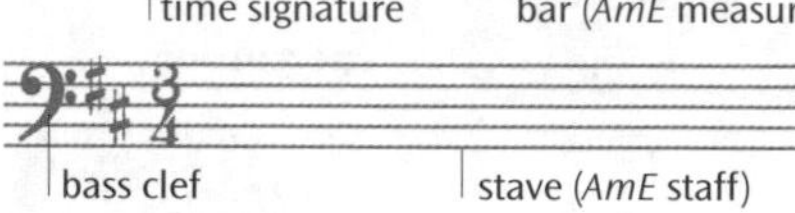

music /ˈmjuːzɪk/ ***noun*** [U] (**MUSIC**) **1** an arrangement of sounds in patterns to be sung or played on instruments: *What sort of music do you like?* ◇ *classical/pop/rock music* ◇ *to write/compose music* ◇ *a music lesson/teacher* **2** the written signs that represent the sounds of music: *Can you **read music**?*

musical[1] /ˈmjuːzɪkl/ ***adj.*** (**MUSIC**) **1** connected with music: *Can you play a **musical instrument*** (=the piano, the violin, the trumpet, etc.)? **2** interested in or good at music: *He's very musical.* **3** having a pleasant sound like music: *a musical voice* ▶ **musically** /-kli/ ***adv.***

musical[2] /ˈmjuːzɪkl/ ***noun*** [C] (**ARTS AND MEDIA**) a play or film which has singing and dancing in it

musician /mjuˈzɪʃn/ ***noun*** [C] (**MUSIC**) a person who plays a musical instrument or writes music, especially as a job

musket /ˈmʌskɪt/ ***noun*** [C] a type of long gun that was used by soldiers in the past

Muslim /ˈmʊzlɪm/ (*also* **Moslem** /ˈmɒzləm/) ***noun*** [C] (**RELIGION**) a person whose religion is Islam
▶ **Muslim** (also **Moslem**) ***adj.***: *Muslim traditions/beliefs*

muslin /ˈmʌzlɪn/ ***noun*** [U] thin cotton cloth that is almost transparent, used, especially in the past, for making clothes and curtains

mussel /ˈmʌsl/ ***noun*** [C] a type of SHELLFISH that you can eat, with a black shell in two parts

must¹ /məst *strong form* mʌst/ ***modal verb*** (*negative* **must not**; *short form* **mustn't** /ˈmʌsnt/) **1** used for saying that it is necessary that sth happens: *I must remember to go to the bank today.* ◇ *You mustn't take photographs in here. It's forbidden.* **2** used for saying that you feel sure that sth is true: *Have something to eat. You must be hungry.* ◇ *I can't find my cheque book. I must have left it at home.* **3** used for giving sb advice: *You really must see that film. It's wonderful.*

must² /mʌst/ ***noun*** [C] a thing that you strongly recommend: *This book is a must for all science fiction fans.*

mustache /ˈmʌstæʃ/ (*AmE*) = MOUSTACHE

mustard /ˈmʌstəd/ ***noun*** [U] a cold yellow or brown sauce that tastes hot and is eaten in small amounts with meat

muster /ˈmʌstə(r)/ ***verb*** **1** [T] to find as much support, courage, etc. as you can: *We mustered all the support we could for the project.* SYN **summon** **2** [I,T] to come together, or bring people, especially soldiers, together, for example for military action: *The troops mustered.* ◇ *to muster an army*

musty /ˈmʌsti/ ***adj.*** having an unpleasant old or wet smell because of a lack of fresh air: *The rooms in the old house were dark and musty.*

mutant /ˈmjuːtənt/ ***noun*** [C] (**BIOLOGY**) a living thing that is different from other living things of the same type because of a change in its GENETIC structure

mutate /mjuːˈteɪt/ ***verb*** ~ **(into sth) 1** [I,T] (**BIOLOGY**) to develop or make sth develop a new form or structure, because of a GENETIC change: *the ability of the virus to mutate into new forms* ◇ *mutated genes* **2** [I] (*formal*) to change into a new form: *Rhythm and blues mutated into rock and roll.*

mutation /mjuːˈteɪʃn/ ***noun*** [C,U] (**BIOLOGY**) a change in the GENETIC structure of a living or developing thing; an example of such a change: *mutations caused by radiation*

mute /mjuːt/ ***adj.*** **1** not speaking SYN **silent**: *a look of mute appeal* ◇ *The child sat mute in the corner of the room.* **2** (*old-fashioned*) not able to speak

muted /ˈmjuːtɪd/ ***adj.*** **1** (used about colours or sounds) not bright or loud; soft **2** (used about a feeling or reaction) not strongly expressed: *muted criticism* ◇ *a muted response*

mutilate /ˈmjuːtɪleɪt/ ***verb*** [T] (usually passive) to damage sb's body very badly, often by cutting off parts ▶ **mutilation** /ˌmjuːtɪˈleɪʃn/ ***noun*** [C,U]

mutiny /ˈmjuːtəni/ ***noun*** [C,U] (*pl.* **mutinies**) an act of a group of people, especially sailors or soldiers, refusing to obey the person who is in command ▶ **mutiny** ***verb*** [I]

mutter /ˈmʌtə(r)/ ***verb*** [I,T] to speak in a low, quiet and often angry voice that is difficult to hear: *He muttered something about being late and left the room.* ➲ look at **mumble**

mutton /ˈmʌtn/ ***noun*** [U] the meat from an adult sheep ➲ note at **meat**

mutual AW /ˈmjuːtʃuəl/ ***adj.*** **1** (used about a feeling or an action) felt or done equally by both people involved: *We have **a mutual agreement*** (= we both agree) *to help each other out when necessary.* ◇ *I just can't stand her and I'm sure **the feeling is mutual*** (= she doesn't like me either). **2** shared by two or more people: *mutual interests* ◇ *It seems that Jane is **a mutual friend** of ours.* ▶ **mutually** AW /-uəli/ ***adv.***

Muzak™ /ˈmjuːzæk/ ***noun*** [U] (**MUSIC**) continuous recorded music that is played in shops, restaurants, airports, etc.

muzzle /ˈmʌzl/ ***noun*** [C] **1** the nose and mouth of an animal, such as a dog or FOX ➲ picture on **page 29** **2** a cover made of leather or wire that is put over an animal's nose and mouth so that it cannot bite **3** the open end of a gun where the bullets come out ▶ **muzzle** ***verb*** [T] (usually passive): *Dogs must be kept muzzled.*

MW ***abbr.*** = MEDIUM WAVE ➲ picture at **wavelength**

my /maɪ/ ***det.*** of or belonging to me: *This is my husband, Jim.* ◇ *My favourite colour is blue.* ➲ look at **mine¹**

myelin /ˈmaɪəlɪn/ ***noun*** [U] (**BIOLOGY**) a substance that forms a covering over many of the NERVES in the body, increasing the speed at which messages travel

myopia /maɪˈəʊpiə/ ***noun*** [U] (**HEALTH**) the inability to see things clearly when they are far away SYN **short-sightedness** ▶ **myopic** /maɪˈɒpɪk/ ***adj.*** SYN **short-sighted**

myriad /ˈmɪriəd/ ***noun*** [C] (*written*) an extremely large number of sth ▶ **myriad** ***adj.***

myself /maɪˈself/ ***pronoun*** **1** used when the person who does an action is also affected by it: *I saw myself in the mirror.* ◇ *I felt rather pleased with myself.* **2** used to emphasize the person who does the action: *I'll speak to her myself.* ◇ *I'll do it myself* (= if you don't want to do it for me).

IDM **(all) by myself 1** alone: *I live by myself.* **2** without help: *I painted the house all by myself.*

mysterious /mɪˈstɪəriəs/ ***adj.*** **1** that you do not understand or cannot explain; strange: *Several people reported seeing mysterious lights in the sky.* **2** (used about a person) keeping sth secret or refusing to explain sth: *They're being very mysterious about where they're going this evening.* ▶ **mysteriously** ***adv.***

mystery /ˈmɪstri/ ***noun*** (*pl.* **mysteries**) **1** [C] a thing that you cannot understand or explain: *The cause of the accident is a complete mystery.* ◇ ***It's a mystery to me** what my daughter sees in her boyfriend.* **2** [U] the quality of being strange and secret and full of things that are difficult to explain: *There's a lot of mystery surrounding this case.* **3** [C] (**ARTS AND MEDIA**) a story, film or play in which crimes or strange events are only explained at the end

ˌmystery ˈshopper ***noun*** [C] (**BUSINESS**) a person whose job is to visit or telephone a shop or other business pretending to be a customer, in order to get information on the quality of the service, the facilities, etc. ▶ **ˌmystery ˈshopping** ***noun*** [U]

mystic /ˈmɪstɪk/ ***noun*** [C] (**RELIGION**) a person who spends their life developing their spirit and communicating with God or a god

mystical /ˈmɪstɪkl/ (*also* **mystic** /ˈmɪstɪk/) ***adj.*** connected with the spirit; strange and wonderful: *Watching the sun set over the island was an almost mystical experience.*

mysticism /ˈmɪstɪsɪzəm/ ***noun*** [U] (**RELIGION**) the belief that you can reach complete truth and knowledge of God or gods by prayer, thought and development of the spirit

mystify /ˈmɪstɪfaɪ/ ***verb*** [T] (*pres. part.* **mystifying**; *3rd person sing. pres.* **mystifies**, *pt, pp* **mystified**) to make sb confused because they cannot understand sth: *I was mystified by the strange note he'd left behind.*

mystique /mɪ'stiːk/ ***noun*** [U, sing.] the quality of having hidden or secret characteristics that makes sb/sth seem interesting or attractive

myth /mɪθ/ ***noun*** [C] **1** (LITERATURE) a story from past times, especially one about gods and men of courage. **Myths** often explain natural or historical events. **2** an idea or story which many people believe but which does not exist or is false: *The idea that money makes you happy is a myth.*

mythical /'mɪθɪkl/ ***adj.*** **1** existing only in MYTHS(1): *mythical beasts/heroes* **2** not real or true; existing only in the imagination

mythology /mɪ'θɒlədʒi/ ***noun*** [U] very old stories and the beliefs contained in them: *Greek and Roman mythology* ▶ **mythological** /ˌmɪθə'lɒdʒɪkl/ ***adj.***: *mythological beasts/figures/stories*

N n

N, n[1] /en/ ***noun*** [C,U] (*pl.* **N's** or **n's** /enz/) the fourteenth letter of the English alphabet: *'Nicholas' begins with (an) 'N'.*

N[2] ***abbr.*** **1** (*AmE* **No**) (GEOGRAPHY) north(ern): *N Yorkshire* **2 newton** (PHYSICS) ; a unit of force

nadir /'neɪdiə(r)/ ***noun*** [sing.] (*written*) the worst moment of a particular situation: *the nadir of her career* OPP **zenith**

naff /næf/ ***adj.*** (*BrE, informal*) lacking style, taste or quality: *There was a naff band playing.*

nag /næg/ ***verb*** (**nagging**; **nagged**) **1** [I,T] ~ **(at) sb** to continuously complain to sb about their behaviour or to ask them to do sth many times: *My parents are always nagging (at) me to work harder.* **2** [T] to worry or irritate sb continuously: *a nagging doubt/headache*

nail ⊶ /neɪl/ ***noun*** [C] **1** the thin hard layer that covers the ends of your fingers and toes: *fingernails/toenails* **2** a small thin piece of metal that is used for holding pieces of wood together, hanging pictures on, etc.: *to hammer in a nail* ➲ picture at **bolt**
▶ **nail** ***verb*** [T]
IDM **hit the nail on the head** → HIT[1]
PHR V **nail sb down (to sth)** to make a person say clearly what they want or intend to do: *She says she'll visit us in the summer but I can't nail her down to a definite date.*

'nail brush ***noun*** [C] a small brush for cleaning your FINGERNAILS

'nail file ***noun*** [C] a small metal tool with a rough surface that you use for shaping your nails

'nail polish (*BrE also* **'nail varnish**) ***noun*** [U] a liquid that people paint on their nails to give them colour

naive (*also* **naïve**) /naɪ'iːv/ ***adj.*** **1** without enough experience of life and too ready to believe or trust other people: *I was too naive to realize what was happening.* ◇ *a naive remark/question/view* SYN **innocent** **2** (ART) in a style which is deliberately very simple, often uses bright colours and is similar to that produced by a child ▶ **naively** (also **naïvely**) ***adv.***: *She naively accepted the first price he offered.*
▶ **naivety** (*also* **naïvety** /naɪ'iːvəti/) ***noun*** [U]

naked ⊶ /'neɪkɪd/ ***adj.*** **1** not wearing any clothes: *He came to the door naked except for a towel.* ◇ *naked shoulders/arms* ➲ look at **bare**, **nude** **2** (only *before* a noun) (used about sth that is usually covered) not covered: *a naked flame/bulb/light* **3** (only *before* a noun) clearly shown or expressed in a way that is often shocking: *naked aggression/ambition/fear*
IDM **the naked eye** the normal power of your eyes without the help of glasses, a machine, etc.: *Bacteria are too small to be seen with the naked eye.*

name[1] ⊶ /neɪm/ ***noun*** **1** [C] a word or words by which sb/sth is known: *What's your name, please?* ◇ *Do you know the name of this flower?* **2** [sing.] an opinion that people have of a person or thing: *That area of London has rather a bad name.* SYN **reputation** **3** [C] a famous person: *All the big names in show business were invited to the party.*
IDM **by name** using the name of sb/sth: *It's a big school but the head teacher knows all the children by name.*
call sb names → CALL[1]
in the name of sb; **in sb's name** for sb/sth; officially belonging to sb: *The contract is in my name.*
in the name of sth used to give a reason or excuse for an action, even when what you are doing might be wrong: *They acted in the name of democracy.*
make a name for yourself; **make your name** to become well known and respected: *She made a name for herself as a journalist.*

name[2] ⊶ /neɪm/ ***verb*** [T] **1** ~ **sb/sth (after sb)** to give sb/sth a name: *Columbia was named after Christopher Columbus.* **2** to say what the name of sb/sth is: *The journalist refused to name the person who had given her the information.* ◇ *Can you name all the planets?* **3** to state sth exactly: *Name your price – we'll pay it!*

nameless /'neɪmləs/ ***adj.*** **1** without a name or with a name that you do not know **2** whose name is kept a secret: *a well-known public figure who shall remain nameless*

namely /'neɪmli/ ***adv.*** (used for giving more detail about what you are saying) that is to say: *There is only one person who can overrule the death sentence, namely the President.*

namesake /'neɪmseɪk/ ***noun*** [C] a person who has the same name as another person

nan (also **naan**) /nɑːn/ ***noun*** [C,U] a type of flat Indian bread

nanny /'næni/ ***noun*** [C] (*pl.* **nannies**) a woman whose job is to look after a family's children and who usually lives in the family home

'nanny goat ***noun*** [C] a female GOAT(=an animal like a sheep that has a hairy coat and often lives in mountain areas) ➲ look at **billy goat**

nano- /'nænəʊ/ ***prefix*** (used in nouns and adjectives, especially in units of measurement) one BILLIONTH (=one of one thousand million equal parts of sth): *nanosecond*

nanometre (*AmE* **nanometer**) /'nænəʊmiːtə(r)/ ***noun*** [C] (*abbr.* **nm**) one thousand millionth of a metre

nanotechnology /ˌnænəʊtek'nɒlədʒi/ ***noun*** [U] (SCIENCE) the branch of technology that deals with structures that are less than 100 NANOMETRES long. Scientists often build these structures using individual MOLECULES of substances.

nap /næp/ ***noun*** [C] a short sleep that you have during the day ➲ look at **snooze** ▶ **nap** ***verb*** [I] (**napping**; **napped**)

nape /neɪp/ ***noun*** [sing.] the back part of your neck

naphtha /ˈnæfθə/ ***noun*** [U] (CHEMISTRY) a type of oil that starts burning very easily, used as fuel or in making chemicals ➲ picture at **fractional distillation**

napkin /ˈnæpkɪn/ ***noun*** [C] a piece of cloth or paper that you use when you are eating to protect your clothes or for cleaning your hands and mouth: *a paper napkin* SYN **serviette**

nappy /ˈnæpi/ ***noun*** [C] (*pl.* **nappies**) (*AmE* **diaper**) a piece of soft thick cloth or paper that a baby or very young child wears around its bottom and between its legs: *Does his nappy need changing?* ◇ *disposable nappies* (=that you throw away when they have been used)

narcotic /nɑːˈkɒtɪk/ ***noun*** [C] **1** (LAW) a powerful illegal drug that affects your mind in a harmful way **2** (HEALTH) a substance or drug that relaxes you, stops pain, or makes you sleep ▶ **narcotic** ***adj.***

narrate /nəˈreɪt/ ***verb*** [T] (*formal*) to tell a story ▶ **narration** /nəˈreɪʃn/ ***noun*** [C,U]

narrative /ˈnærətɪv/ ***noun*** (*formal*) **1** [C] (LITERATURE) the description of events in a story **2** [U] the process or skill of telling a story

narrator /nəˈreɪtə(r)/ ***noun*** [C] (LITERATURE) the person who tells a story or explains what is happening in a play, film, etc.

narrow 🔑 /ˈnærəʊ/ ***adj.*** **1** having only a short distance from side to side: *The bridge is too narrow for two cars to pass.* OPP **wide, broad 2** not large: *a narrow circle of friends* **3** by a small amount: *That was a very narrow escape. You were lucky.* ◇ *a narrow defeat/victory* ▶ **narrow** ***verb*** [I,T]: *The road narrows in 50 metres.* ▶ **narrowness** ***noun*** [U]

PHR V **narrow sth down** to make a list of things smaller: *The police have narrowed down their list of suspects to three.*

narrowboat /ˈnærəʊbəʊt/ ***noun*** [C] (*BrE*) a long narrow boat, used on CANALS (=artificial rivers)

narrowly /ˈnærəʊli/ ***adv.*** only by a small amount

ˌnarrow-ˈminded ***adj.*** not wanting to accept new ideas or the opinions of other people if they are not the same as your own SYN **insular** OPP **broad-minded**

narthex /ˈnɑːθeks/ ***noun*** [C] (ARCHITECTURE) a small room at the western entrance of some Christian churches

NASA /ˈnæsə/ ***abbr.*** **National Aeronautics and Space Administration**; a US government organization that does research into space and organizes space travel

nasal /ˈneɪzl/ ***adj.*** **1** of or for the nose **2** produced partly through the nose: *a nasal voice*

nasty /ˈnɑːsti/ ***adj.*** (**nastier**; **nastiest**) very bad or unpleasant: *a nasty accident* ◇ *I had a nasty feeling he would follow me.* ◇ *When she was asked to leave she* ***got/turned nasty***. ◇ *a nasty bend in the road* ◇ *What's that nasty smell in this cupboard?* ▶ **nastily** ***adv.*** ▶ **nastiness** ***noun*** [U]

nation 🔑 /ˈneɪʃn/ ***noun*** [C] (POLITICS) a country or all the people in a country: *a summit of the leaders of seven nations* ➲ note at **country**

national[1] 🔑 /ˈnæʃnəl/ ***adj.*** connected with all of a country; typical of a particular country: *Here is today's national and international news.* ◇ *a national newspaper* ➲ look at **international**, **regional**, **local** ▶ **nationally** ***adv.***

national[2] /ˈnæʃnəl/ ***noun*** [C] (*technical*) (POLITICS) a citizen of a particular country

ˌnational ˈanthem ***noun*** [C] (MUSIC) the official song of a country that is played at public events

ˌnational curˈriculum ***noun*** [sing.] (EDUCATION) (in Britain) a programme of study in all the main subjects that children aged 5 to 16 in state schools must follow

ˌnational ˈdebt ***noun*** [usually sing.] (FINANCE) the total amount of money that the government of a country owes

the ˌNational ˈHealth Service ***noun*** [sing.] (*abbr.* **NHS**) (*BrE*) (HEALTH) the system that provides free or cheap medical care for everyone in Britain and that is paid for by taxes ➲ look at **health service**

ˌNational Inˈsurance ***noun*** [U] (*abbr.* **NI**) (*BrE*) the system of payments that have to be made by employers and employees to the government to help people who are ill, unemployed, old, etc.: *to pay National Insurance contributions*

nationalism /ˈnæʃnəlɪzəm/ ***noun*** [U] **1** (POLITICS) the desire of a group of people who share the same race, culture, language, etc. to form an independent country **2** a feeling of love or pride for your own country; a feeling that your country is better than any other country

nationalist /ˈnæʃnəlɪst/ ***noun*** [C] (POLITICS) a person who wants their country or region to become independent: *a Welsh nationalist*

nationalistic /ˌnæʃnəˈlɪstɪk/ ***adj.*** having strong feelings of love for or pride in your own country, so that you think it is better than any other country

nationality /ˌnæʃəˈnæləti/ ***noun*** [C,U] (*pl.* **nationalities**) (POLITICS) the state of being legally a citizen of a particular nation or country: *to have French nationality* ◇ *students of many nationalities* ◇ *to have* ***dual nationality*** (=of two countries)

nationalize (also **-ise**) /ˈnæʃnəlaɪz/ ***verb*** [T] (POLITICS) to put a company or organization under the control of the government OPP **privatize** ▶ **nationalization** (also **-isation**) /ˌnæʃnəlaɪˈzeɪʃn/ ***noun*** [U]

ˌnational ˈpark ***noun*** [C] a large area of beautiful land that is protected by the government so that the public can enjoy it

nationwide /ˌneɪʃnˈwaɪd/ ***adj.***, ***adv.*** over the whole of a country: *The police launched a nationwide hunt for the killer.*

native[1] /ˈneɪtɪv/ ***adj.*** **1** (only *before* a noun) connected with the place where you were born or where you have always lived: *your native language/country/city* ◇ *native Londoners* **2** (only *before* a noun) connected with the people who originally lived in a country before other people, especially white people, came to live there: *native art/dance* **3** ~ (**to...**) (used about an animal or plant) living or growing naturally in a particular place: *This plant is native to South America.* ◇ *a native species/habitat*

native[2] /ˈneɪtɪv/ ***noun*** [C] **1** a person who was born in a particular place: *a native of New York* **2** [usually pl.] (*old-fashioned*) the people who were living in Africa, America, etc. originally, before the Europeans arrived there

ˌNative Aˈmerican (*also* **AˌmericanˈIndian**) ***adj.***, ***noun*** [C] (of) a member of the race of people who were the original INHABITANTS of America

ˌnative ˈspeaker ***noun*** [C] (LANGUAGE) a person who speaks a language as their first language and has not learned it as a foreign language: *All our Spanish teachers are native speakers.*

NATO (*also* **Nato**) /'neɪtəʊ/ ***abbr.*** (POLITICS) North Atlantic Treaty Organization; a group of European countries, Canada and the US, who agree to give each other military help if necessary

natter /'nætə(r)/ ***verb*** [I] (*BrE, informal*) to talk a lot about things that are not important SYN **chat** ▶ **natter** ***noun*** [sing.]: *to have a natter*

natural[1] ⊶ /'nætʃrəl/ ***adj.*** **1** (only *before* a noun) existing in nature; not made or caused by humans: *I prefer to see animals in their **natural habitat** rather than in zoos.* ◇ *Britain's **natural resources** include coal, oil and gas.* ◇ *She died of **natural causes*** (= of old age or illness). **2** usual or normal: *It's natural to feel nervous before an interview.* OPP **unnatural** **3** that you had from birth or that was easy for you to learn: *a natural gift for languages* **4** (only *before* a noun) (used about parents or their children) related by blood: *She's his stepmother, not his natural mother.* **5** (MUSIC) used after the name of a note to show that the note is neither SHARP, (= half a note higher), nor FLAT, (= half a note lower). The written symbol is (♮): *B natural*

natural[2] /'nætʃrəl/ ***noun*** [C] (MUSIC) a normal musical note, not its SHARP or FLAT form. The written symbol is (♮). ➲ picture at **music**

ˌnatural 'gas ***noun*** [U] (CHEMISTRY) gas that is found under the ground or the sea, and that we burn for light and heat

ˌnatural 'history ***noun*** [U] the study of plants and animals

naturalist /'nætʃrəlɪst/ ***noun*** [C] a person who studies plants and animals

naturalize (also **-ise**) /'nætʃrəlaɪz/ ***verb*** [T] (usually passive) (POLITICS) to make sb a citizen of a country where they were not born ▶ **naturalization** (also **-isation**) /ˌnætʃrəlaɪ'zeɪʃn/ ***noun*** [U]

ˌnatural 'language ***noun*** [C, U] (LANGUAGE) a language that has developed in a natural way and is not designed by humans

naturally ⊶ /'nætʃrəli/ ***adv.*** **1** of course; as you would expect: *The team was naturally upset about its defeat.* **2** in a natural way; not forced or made artificially: *naturally wavy hair* ◇ *Vera is naturally a very cheerful person.* **3** in a way that is relaxed and normal: *Don't try and impress people. Just **act naturally**.*

ˌnatural se'lection ***noun*** [U] (BIOLOGY) the process by which plants, animals, etc. that can adapt to their environment survive and reproduce, while the others disappear

nature ⊶ /'neɪtʃə(r)/ ***noun*** **1** [U] all the plants, animals, etc. in the universe and all the things that happen in it that are not made or caused by people: *the forces of nature* (= for example volcanoes, hurricanes, etc.) ◇ *the wonders/beauties of nature* **2** [C,U] the qualities or character of a person or thing: *He's basically honest **by nature**.* ◇ *It's **not in his nature** to be unkind.* ◇ *It's **human nature** never to be completely satisfied.* **3** [sing.] a type or sort of sth: *I'm not very interested in things of that nature.* ◇ *books of a scientific nature* **4 -natured** (used to form compound adjectives) having a particular quality or type of character: *a kind-natured man*
IDM **second nature** → SECOND[1]

naughty /'nɔːti/ ***adj.*** (*especially BrE*) (used when you are talking to or about a child) badly behaved; not obeying: *It was very naughty of you to wander off on your own.* ▶ **naughtily** ***adv.*** ▶ **naughtiness** ***noun*** [U]

nausea /'nɔːziə/ ***noun*** [U] (HEALTH) the feeling that you are going to VOMIT (= bring up food from your stomach) ➲ look at **sick** (2)

nauseate /'nɔːzieɪt/ ***verb*** [T] to cause sb to feel sick or disgusted ▶ **nauseating** ***adj.***

nautical /'nɔːtɪkl/ ***adj.*** connected with ships, sailors or sailing

ˌnautical 'mile (*also* **'sea mile**) ***noun*** [C] a unit for measuring distance at sea; 1852 metres

naval /'neɪvl/ ***adj.*** connected with the navy: *a naval base/officer/battle*

nave /neɪv/ ***noun*** [C] (ARCHITECTURE) the long central part of a church where most of the seats are ➲ look at **transept**

navel /'neɪvl/ (also *informal* **'belly button**) ***noun*** [C] the small hole or lump in the middle of your stomach

navigable /'nævɪgəbl/ ***adj.*** (used about a river or narrow area of sea) that boats can sail along

navigate /'nævɪgeɪt/ ***verb*** **1** [I] to use a map, etc. to find your way to somewhere: *If you drive, I'll navigate.* **2** [T] (*written*) to sail a boat along a river or across a sea ▶ **navigator** ***noun*** [C] ▶ **navigation** /ˌnævɪ'geɪʃn/ ***noun*** [U]

navy ⊶ /'neɪvi/ ***noun*** [C] (*pl.* **navies**) the part of a country's armed forces that fights at sea in times of war: *to join the navy* ◇ *Their son is **in the Navy**.* ➲ adjective **naval**

ˌnavy 'blue (*also* **navy**) ***adj.***, ***noun*** [U] (of) a very dark blue colour

Nazi /'nɑːtsi/ ***noun*** [C] **1** (HISTORY, POLITICS) a member of the National Socialist party which controlled Germany from 1933 to 1945 **2** a person who uses their power in a cruel way; a person with extreme and unreasonable views about race ▶ **Nazi** ***adj.*** ▶ **Nazism** /'nɑːtsɪzəm/ ***noun*** [U]

NB (*AmE and BrE also* **N.B., nb**) /ˌen 'biː/ ***abbr.*** (used before a written note) take special notice of: *NB There is an extra charge for reservations*

NCT /ˌen siː 'tiː/ ***noun*** [C] (EDUCATION) **National Curriculum Test** (previously called SAT); a test taken by children at the ages of 7, 11 and 14

NE ***abbr.*** north-east: *NE Scotland*

near[1] ⊶ /nɪə(r)/ ***adj.***, ***adv.***, ***prep.*** **1** not far away in time or distance; close: *Let's walk to the library. It's quite near.* ◇ *We're hoping to move to Wales **in the near future*** (= very soon). ◇ *Where's the nearest Post Office?* ◇ *The day of the interview was getting nearer.* **2 near-** (used to form compound adjectives) almost: *a near-perfect performance*
IDM **close/dear/near to sb's heart** → HEART
or near(est) offer; ono (used when you are selling sth) or an amount that is less than but near the amount that you have asked for: *Motorbike for sale. £750 ono.*
a near miss a situation where sth nearly hits you or where sth bad nearly happens
nowhere near far from; not at all: *We've sold nowhere near enough tickets to make a profit.*

near[2] ⊶ /nɪə(r)/ ***verb*** [T,I] to get closer to sth in time or distance: *At last we were nearing the end of the project.*

nearby ⊶ /ˌnɪə'baɪ/ ***adj.***, ***adv.*** not far away in distance: *A new restaurant has opened nearby.* ◇ *We went out to a nearby restaurant.*

nearly ⊶ /'nɪəli/ ***adv.*** almost; not completely or exactly: *It's nearly five years since I've seen him.* ◇ *Linda was so badly hurt she very nearly died.* ◇ *It's not far now. We're nearly there.*

IDM **not nearly** much less than; not at all: *It's not nearly as warm as it was yesterday.*

nearsighted /ˌnɪəˈsaɪtɪd/ (*AmE*) = SHORT-SIGHTED (1)

neat /niːt/ ***adj.*** **1** arranged or done carefully; tidy and in order: *Please keep your room **neat and tidy**.* ◇ *neat rows of figures* **2** (used about a person) liking to keep things tidy and in order: *The new secretary was very neat and efficient.* **3** simple but clever: *a neat solution/explanation/idea/trick* **4** (*AmE, spoken*) good; nice: *That's a really neat car!* **5** (*AmE* **straight**) (used about an alcoholic drink) on its own, without ice, water or any other liquid: *a neat whisky* ▶ **neatness** ***noun*** [U] ▶ **neatly** ***adv.***: *neatly folded clothes*

nebula /ˈnebjələ/ ***noun*** [C] (*pl.* **nebulae** /-liː/) (ASTRONOMY) a bright area in the night sky that is caused by a mass of dust or gas or by a large cloud of stars that are far away

necessarily /ˈnesəsərəli; ˌnesəˈserəli/ ***adv.*** used to say that sth cannot be avoided or has to happen: *The number of tickets available is necessarily limited.*

IDM **not necessarily** used to say that sth might be true but is not definitely or always true

necessary /ˈnesəsəri/ ***adj.*** ~ **(for sb/sth) (to do sth)** that is needed for a purpose or a reason: *A good diet is necessary for a healthy life.* ◇ *It's not necessary for you all to come.* ◇ *If necessary I can take you to work that day.* OPP **unnecessary**

necessitate /nəˈsesɪteɪt/ ***verb*** [T] (*formal*) to make sth necessary

necessity /nəˈsesəti/ ***noun*** (*pl.* **necessities**) **1** [U] ~ **(for sth/to do sth)** the need for sth; the fact that sth must be done or must happen: *Is there any necessity for change?* ◇ *There's no necessity to write every single name down.* ◇ *They sold the car **out of necessity*** (= because they had to). **2** [C] something that you must have: *Clean water is an absolute necessity.*

neck /nek/ ***noun*** **1** [C] the part of your body that joins your head to your shoulders: *She wrapped a scarf around her neck.* ◇ *Giraffes have long necks.* ➲ picture on **page 80** **2** [C] the part of a piece of clothing that goes round your neck: *a polo-neck/V-neck sweater* ◇ *The neck on this shirt is too tight.* **3** [C] the long narrow part of sth: *the neck of a bottle* **4 -necked** (used to form compound adjectives) having the type of neck mentioned: *a round-necked sweater*

IDM **by the scruff (of the/your neck)** → SCRUFF

neck and neck (with sb/sth) equal or level with sb in a race or competition

up to your neck in sth having a lot of sth to deal with: *We're up to our necks in work at the moment.*

necklace /ˈnekləs/ ***noun*** [C] a piece of jewellery that you wear around your neck

neckline /ˈneklaɪn/ ***noun*** [C] the edge of a piece of clothing, especially a woman's, which fits around or below the neck: *a dress with a low/round neckline*

necktie /ˈnektaɪ/ (*AmE*) = TIE[1] (1)

nectar /ˈnektə(r)/ ***noun*** [U] **1** the sweet liquid that BEES collect from flowers to make HONEY **2** the thick juice of some fruit, used as a drink: *apricot nectar*

nectarine /ˈnektəriːn/ ***noun*** [C] a soft round red and yellow fruit that looks like a PEACH with smooth skin

née /neɪ/ ***adj.*** used in front of the family name that a woman had before she got married: *Cynthia Waters, née Marsden* ➲ look at **maiden name**

need[1] /niːd/ ***verb*** [T] (not usually used in the continuous tenses) **1** ~ **sb/sth (for sth/to do sth)** if you need sth, you want it or must have it: *All living things need water.* ◇ *I need a new film for my camera.* ◇ *Does Roshni need any help?* ◇ *I need to find a doctor.* ◇ *I need you to go to the shop for me.* **2** to have to; to be OBLIGED to: *Do we need to buy the tickets in advance?* ◇ *You didn't need to bring any food but it was very kind of you.* **3** ~ **(sth) doing** if sth needs doing, it is necessary or must be done: *This jumper needs washing.* ◇ *He needed his eyes testing.*

need[2] /niːd/ ***modal verb*** (not used in the continuous tenses; used mainly in questions or negative sentences after *if* and *whether*, or with words like *hardly, only, never*) to have to; to be obliged to: *Need we pay the whole amount now?* ◇ *You needn't come to the meeting if you're too busy.* ◇ *I **hardly need** remind you* (= you already know) *that this is very serious.*

need[3] /niːd/ ***noun*** **1** [U, sing.] ~ **(for sth)**; ~ **(for sb/sth) to do sth** a situation in which you must have or do sth: *We are all **in need of** a rest.* ◇ *There is a growing need for new books in schools.* ◇ *There's **no need for** you to come if you don't want to.* ◇ *Do phone me if you **feel the need** to talk to someone.* ➲ note at **reason[1]** **2** [C, usually pl.] the things that you must have: *He doesn't earn enough to pay for his basic needs.* ◇ *Parents must consider their children's emotional as well as their physical needs.* **3** [U] the state of not having enough food, money or support: *a campaign to help families **in need***

needle /ˈniːdl/ ***noun*** [C] **1** a small thin piece of metal with a point at one end and a hole (**an eye**) at the other that is used for sewing: *to thread a needle with cotton* ➲ look at **pins and needles** **2** (*also* **knitting needle**) one of two long thin pieces of metal or plastic with a point at one end that are used for knitting **3** the sharp metal part of a SYRINGE (= a device that is used for putting drugs into sb's body and for taking blood out) **4** a thin metal part on a scientific instrument that moves to point to the correct measurement or direction **5** the thin, hard pointed leaf of certain trees that stay green all year: *pine needles* ➲ picture at **tree**

needlepoint /ˈniːdlpɔɪnt/ ***noun*** [U] (ART) a type of decorative sewing in which you use very small STITCHES to make a picture on strong cloth

needless /ˈniːdləs/ ***adj.*** that is not necessary and that you can easily avoid: *Banning smoking would save needless deaths.* SYN **unnecessary** ▶ **needlessly** ***adv.***: *Many soldiers died needlessly.*

needlework /ˈniːdlwɜːk/ ***noun*** [U] sth that you sew by hand, especially for decoration

needy /ˈniːdi/ ***adj.*** **1** not having enough money, food, clothes, etc. **2 the needy** ***noun*** [pl.] people who do not have enough money, food, clothes, etc.

neg. ***abbr.*** negative

negate AW /nɪˈɡeɪt/ ***verb*** [T] (*formal*) **1** to stop sth from having any effect: *Alcohol negates the effects of the drug.* **2** to state that sth does not exist

negative[1] AW /ˈneɡətɪv/ ***adj.*** **1** bad or harmful: *The effects of the new rule have been rather negative.* OPP **positive** **2** only thinking about the bad qualities of sb/sth: *I'm feeling very negative about my job – in fact I'm thinking about leaving.* ◇ *If you go into the match with a negative attitude, you'll never win.* OPP **positive** **3** (used about a word, phrase or sentence) meaning 'no' or 'not': *a negative sentence* ◇ *His reply was negative/He gave a negative reply*

(=he said 'no'). OPP **affirmative 4** (used about a medical or scientific test) showing that sth has not happened or has not been found: *The results of the pregnancy test were negative.* OPP **positive 5** (used about a number) less than zero OPP **positive**
▶ **negatively** ***adv.***

negative² AW /'negətɪv/ ***noun*** [C] **1** a word, phrase or sentence that says or means 'no' or 'not': *Aisha answered* ***in the negative*** (=she said no). ◇ *'Never', 'neither' and 'nobody' are all negatives.* OPP **affirmative 2** a piece of film from which we can make a photograph. The light areas of a negative are dark on the final photograph and the dark areas are light.

ˌnegative 'equity ***noun*** [U] (FINANCE) the situation in which the value of sb's house is less than the amount of money that is still owed to a MORTGAGE company, such as a bank

neglect /nɪ'glekt/ ***verb*** [T] **1** to give too little or no attention or care to sb/sth: *Don't neglect your health.* ◇ *The old house had stood neglected for years.* **2 ~ to do sth** to fail or forget to do sth: *He neglected to mention that he had spent time in prison.* ▶ **neglect** ***noun*** [U]: *The garden was like a jungle after years of neglect.* ▶ **neglected** ***adj.***: *neglected children*

negligence /'neglɪdʒəns/ ***noun*** [U] (*formal* or LAW) the failure to give sb/sth enough care or attention: *The accident was a result of negligence.*
▶ **negligent** /'neglɪdʒənt/ ***adj.*** ▶ **negligently** ***adv.***

negligible /'neglɪdʒəbl/ ***adj.*** very small and therefore not important

negotiable /nɪ'gəʊʃiəbl/ ***adj.*** that can be decided or changed by discussion: *The price is not negotiable/non-negotiable.*

negotiate /nɪ'gəʊʃieɪt/ ***verb*** **1** [I] ~ **(with sb) (for/about sth)** to talk to sb in order to decide or agree about sth: *The unions are still negotiating with management about this year's pay claim.* **2** [T] to decide or agree sth by talking about it: *to negotiate an agreement/a deal/a settlement* **3** [T] to get over, past or through sth difficult: *To escape, prisoners would have to negotiate a five-metre wall.*
▶ **negotiator** ***noun*** [C]

negotiation /nɪˌgəʊʃi'eɪʃn/ ***noun*** [pl., U] discussions at which people try to decide or agree sth: *to enter into/break off negotiations* ◇ *The pay rise is still* ***under negotiation***.

Negro /'niːgrəʊ/ ***noun*** [C] (*pl.* **Negroes**) (*old-fashioned*) a member of a race of people with dark skin who originally came from Africa ❶ Be careful. This word is now considered offensive.

ˌNegro 'spiritual ***noun*** [C] =SPIRITUAL²

neigh /neɪ/ ***noun*** [C] the long high sound that a horse makes ▶ **neigh** ***verb*** [I]

neighbour 🔑 (*AmE* **neighbor**) /'neɪbə(r)/ ***noun*** [C] **1** a person who lives near you: *My neighbours are very friendly.* ◇ *our* ***next-door neighbours*** **2** a person or thing that is near or next to another: *Britain's nearest neighbour is France.* ◇ *Try not to look at what your neighbour is writing.*

neighbourhood 🔑 (*AmE* **neighborhood**) /'neɪbəhʊd/ ***noun*** [C] a particular part of a town and the people who live there

neighbouring (*AmE* **neighboring**) /'neɪbərɪŋ/ ***adj.*** (only *before* a noun) near or next to: *Farmers from neighbouring villages come into town each week for the market.*

neighbourly (*AmE* **neighborly**) /'neɪbəli/ ***adj.*** friendly and helpful

neither 🔑 /'naɪðə(r); 'niːðə(r)/ ***det.***, ***pronoun***, ***adv.*** **1** (used about two people or things) not one and not the other: *Neither team played very well.* ◇ *Neither of the teams played very well.* ◇ *'Would you like tea or juice?' 'Neither, thank you. I'm not thirsty.'* **2** also not; not either: *I don't eat meat and neither does Carlos.* ◇ *'I don't like fish.' 'Neither do I.'* ◇ (*informal*) *'I don't like fish.' 'Me neither.'* **3 neither...nor** not...and not: *Neither Carlos nor I eat meat.*

nemesis /'neməsɪs/ ***noun*** [U, sing.] (*formal*) a punishment or defeat that sb deserves and cannot avoid

neo- /'niːəʊ/ ***prefix*** (used in adjectives and nouns) new; in a later form: *neo-Georgian* ◇ *neo-fascist*

neoclassical /ˌniːəʊ'klæsɪkl/ ***adj.*** (ART, ARCHITECTURE) used to describe art and ARCHITECTURE that is based on the style of ancient Greece or Rome, or music, literature, etc. that uses traditional ideas or styles

neoconservative /ˌniːəʊkən'sɜːvətɪv/ ***adj.*** (POLITICS) relating to political, economic, religious, etc. beliefs that return to traditional conservative views in a slightly changed form
▶ **neoconservative** (*also* **neocon**) ***noun*** [C]

neodymium /ˌniːəʊ'dɪmiəm/ ***noun*** [U] (*symbol* **Nd**) (CHEMISTRY) a chemical element. **Neodymium** is a silver-white metal. ❶ For more information on the periodic table of elements, look at pages R34-5.

Neolithic /ˌniːə'lɪθɪk/ ***adj.*** (HISTORY) from or connected with the later part of the STONE AGE (=the very early period of human history): *Neolithic stone axes* ➲ look at **Palaeolithic**

neon /'niːɒn/ ***noun*** [U] (*symbol* **Ne**) (CHEMISTRY) a type of gas that does not react with anything and is used for making bright lights and signs ❶ **Neon** is a **noble gas**. ❶ For more information on the periodic table of elements, look at pages R34-5.

nephew 🔑 /'nefjuː; 'nevjuː/ ***noun*** [C] the son of your brother or sister, or the son of your husband's or wife's brother or sister ➲ look at **niece**

nephron /'nefrɒn/ ***noun*** [C] (ANATOMY) one of the tiny tubes in the KIDNEYS that FILTER your blood

nepotism /'nepətɪzəm/ ***noun*** [U] using your power or influence to give unfair advantage to your family, especially by giving them jobs

Neptune /'neptjuːn/ ***noun*** [sing.] (ASTRONOMY) the planet that is eighth in order from the sun ➲ picture at **solar system**

neptunium /nep'tjuːniəm (*AmE also*)-'tuːn-/ ***noun*** [U] (*symbol* **Np**) (CHEMISTRY) a chemical element. **Neptunium** is a RADIOACTIVE metal. ❶ For more information on the periodic table of elements, look at pages R34-5.

nerd /nɜːd/ ***noun*** [C] a person who is not fashionable and has a boring hobby ▶ **nerdy** ***adj.***

nerve 🔑 /nɜːv/ ***noun*** **1** [C] (ANATOMY, BIOLOGY) one of the long thin threads in your body that carry feelings or other messages to and from your brain **2 nerves** [pl.] worried, nervous feelings: *Breathing deeply should help to* ***calm /steady your nerves***. ◇ *I was* ***a bag of nerves*** *before my interview.* **3** [U] the courage that you need to do sth difficult or dangerous: *Racing drivers need a lot of nerve.* ◇ *He didn't* ***have the nerve*** *to ask Maria to go out with him.* ◇ *Some pilots* ***lose*** *their* ***nerve*** *and can't fly any more.* **4** [sing.] a way of behaving that people think is not acceptable: *You've got a nerve, calling me lazy!*
IDM **get on sb's nerves** (*informal*) to annoy sb or make sb angry

'nerve cell *noun* [C] (**ANATOMY, BIOLOGY**) a cell that carries information between the brain and the other parts of the body **SYN** **neuron**

'nerve ending *noun* [C] (**ANATOMY, BIOLOGY**) the end of a nerve

'nerve-racking *adj.* making you very nervous or worried

nervous ⊶ /'nɜːvəs/ *adj.* **1** ~ (**about/of sth/ doing sth**) worried or afraid: *I'm a bit nervous about travelling on my own.* ◇ *I always* ***get nervous*** *just before a match.* ◇ *a nervous laugh/smile/voice* ◇ *She was nervous of giving the wrong answer.* **2** (**ANATOMY**) connected with the nerves of the body: *a nervous disorder* ▸ **nervousness** *noun* [U] ▸ **nervously** *adv.*

,nervous 'breakdown (*also* **breakdown**) *noun* [C] (**HEALTH**) a time when sb suddenly becomes so unhappy that they cannot continue living and working normally: *to have a nervous breakdown*

'nervous system *noun* [C] (**ANATOMY, BIOLOGY**) your brain and all the nerves in your body

nest ⊶ /nest/ *noun* [C] (**BIOLOGY**) **1** a structure that a bird builds to keep its eggs and babies in ➲ picture on **page 28** **2** the home of certain animals or insects: *a wasps' nest* ▸ **nest** *verb* [I]

'nest egg *noun* [C] (*informal*) an amount of money that you save to use in the future

nestle /'nesl/ *verb* [I,T] to be or go into a position where you are comfortable, protected or hidden: *The baby nestled her head on her mother's shoulder.*

net[1] ⊶ /net/ *noun* **1** [U] material that has large, often square, spaces between the threads **2** [C] a piece of net that is used for a particular purpose: *a tennis/fishing/mosquito net* ➲ look at **safety net** ➲ picture at **sport** **3** **the net** [sing.] = THE INTERNET **IDM** **surf the net** → SURF[2]

net[2] (*BrE also* **nett**) /net/ *adj.* **1** (**FINANCE**) a **net** amount of money is the amount that remains when nothing more is to be taken away: ***a net profit*** *of £500* ◇ ***net income/earnings*** ➲ look at **gross** **2** the **net** weight of sth is the weight without its container or the material it is wrapped in: *450gms net weight* ➲ look at **gross** **3** final, after all the important facts have been included: *The* ***net result*** *is that small shopkeepers are being forced out of business.* ▸ **net** *adv.*: *a salary of $50000 net*

net[3] /net/ *verb* [T] (**netting**; **netted**) **1** (**FINANCE**) to earn an amount of money as a profit after you have paid tax on it: *The sale of paintings netted £17000.* **2** (**SPORT**) (*especially BrE*) to kick or hit a ball into the goal **SYN** **score**

netball /'netbɔːl/ *noun* [U] (**SPORT**) a game that is played by two teams of seven players, usually women. Players score by throwing the ball through a high net hanging from a ring.

netiquette /'netɪket/ *noun* [U] (*informal*) (**COMPUTING**) the rules of correct or polite behaviour among people using the Internet

netizen /'netɪzn/ *noun* [C] (*informal*) (**COMPUTING**) a person who uses the Internet a lot

netting /'netɪŋ/ *noun* [U] material that is made of long pieces of string, thread, wire, etc. that are tied together with spaces between them

nettle /'netl/ *noun* [C] a wild plant with hairy leaves. Some **nettles** make your skin red and painful if you touch them.

network[1] ⊶ **AW** /'netwɜːk/ *noun* [C] **1** a system of roads, railway lines, nerves, etc. that are connected to each other: *an underground railway network* **2** (**BUSINESS**) a group of people or companies that work closely together: *We have a network of agents who sell our goods all over the country.* **3** (**COMPUTING**) a number of computers that are connected together so that information can be shared **4** (**ARTS AND MEDIA**) a group of television or radio companies that are connected and that send out the same programmes at the same time in different parts of a country

network[2] **AW** *verb* [T] **1** (**COMPUTING**) to connect a number of computers and other devices together so that equipment and information can be shared: *networked computer systems* **2** [I] (**BUSINESS**) to try to meet and talk to people who may be useful to you in your work: *Conferences are a good place to network.*

networking **AW** /'netwɜːkɪŋ/ *noun* [U] (**BUSINESS**) a system of trying to meet and talk to other people who may be useful to you in your work

neuro- /'njʊərəʊ/ *prefix* (used in nouns, adjectives and adverbs) (**BIOLOGY**) connected with the nerves: *neuroscience* ◇ *a neurosurgeon*

neurologist /njʊə'rɒlədʒɪst/ *noun* [C] (**HEALTH**) a scientist who studies nerves and treats their diseases

neurology /njʊə'rɒlədʒi/ *noun* [U] (**HEALTH**) the scientific study of nerves and their diseases ▸ **neurological** /,njʊərə'lɒdʒɪkl/ *adj.*: *neurological damage/diseases*

neuron /'njʊərɒn/ (*also* **neurone** /'njʊərəʊn/) *noun* [C] (**ANATOMY, BIOLOGY**) a cell that carries information between the brain and the other parts of the body ❶ A less technical term is **nerve cell**.

neurosis /njʊə'rəʊsɪs/ *noun* [C] (*pl.* **neuroses** /-əʊsiːz/) (**HEALTH**) a mental illness that causes strong feelings of fear and worry

neurotic /njʊə'rɒtɪk/ *adj.* **1** worried about things in a way that is not normal **2** (**HEALTH**) suffering from a NEUROSIS

neuter[1] /'njuːtə(r)/ *adj.* (**LANGUAGE**) (used about a word in some languages) not MASCULINE or FEMININE according to the rules of grammar

neuter[2] /'njuːtə(r)/ *verb* [T] to remove the sexual parts of an animal ➲ look at **castrate**

neutral[1] **AW** /'njuːtrəl/ *adj.* **1** not supporting or belonging to either side in an argument, war, etc.: *I don't take sides when my brothers argue – I* ***remain neutral.*** ◇ *The two sides agreed to meet on neutral ground.* **2** having or showing no strong qualities, emotions or colour: *neutral colours* ◇ *a neutral tone of voice* **3** (**CHEMISTRY**) neither acid nor ALKALINE ➲ picture at **pH** **4** (**PHYSICS**) having neither a positive nor a negative charge ➲ picture at **plug**

neutral[2] **AW** /'njuːtrəl/ *noun* [U] the position of the GEARS in a vehicle when no power is sent from the engine to the wheels

neutrality **AW** /njuː'træləti/ *noun* [U] the state of not supporting either side in an argument, war, etc.

neutralize (also **-ise**) **AW** /'njuːtrəlaɪz/ *verb* [T] **1** to take away the effect of sth: *to neutralize a threat* **2** (**CHEMISTRY**) to have an effect on a substance so that it becomes neither an acid nor an ALKALI **3** to make a country or area NEUTRAL (= not belonging to or supporting any of the countries in a war) ▸ **neutralization** (also **-isation**) /,njuːtrəlaɪ'zeɪʃn/ *noun* [U]

neutron /'njuːtrɒn/ *noun* [C] (**CHEMISTRY, PHYSICS**) one of the three types of PARTICLES that form all atoms. **Neutrons** have no electric charge. ➲ look at **electron**, **proton**

never /ˈnevə(r)/ ***adv.*** **1** at no time; not ever: *I've never been to Portugal.* ◇ *He never ever eats meat.* ◇ (*formal*) *Never before has such a high standard been achieved.* **2** used for emphasizing a negative statement: *I never realized she was so unhappy.* ◇ *Roy never so much as looked at us* (=he didn't even look at us). ◇ *'I got the job!' 'Never!'* (=expressing surprise)

IDM **never mind** → MIND²
you never know → KNOW¹

nevertheless AW /ˌnevəðəˈles/ ***adv., conj.*** (*formal*) in spite of that: *It was a cold, rainy day. Nevertheless, more people came than we had expected.* SYN **nonetheless**

new /njuː/ ***adj.*** **1** that has recently been built, made, discovered, etc.: *a new design/film/hospital* ◇ *a new method of treating mental illness* ◇ *new evidence* OPP **old 2** different or changed from what was before: *I've just started reading a new book.* ◇ *to make new friends* OPP **old 3** ~ **(to sb)** that you have not seen, learnt, etc. before: *This type of machine is new to me.* ◇ *to learn a new language* **4** ~ **(to sth)** having just started being or doing sth: *a new parent* ◇ *She's new to the job and needs a lot of help.* ◇ *a new member of the club* ▶ **newness** ***noun*** [U]

IDM **break fresh/new ground** → GROUND¹

ˈ**New Age** ***adj.*** connected with a way of life that rejects modern Western values and is based on spiritual ideas and beliefs: *a New Age festival* ◇ ***New Age travellers*** (=people in Britain who reject the values of modern society and travel from place to place living in their vehicles)

newbie /ˈnjuːbi/ ***noun*** [C] (*informal*) (**COMPUTING**) a person who is new and has little experience in doing sth, especially in using computers

newborn /ˈnjuːbɔːn/ ***adj.*** (only *before* a noun) (**HEALTH**) (used about a baby) that has been born very recently

newcomer /ˈnjuːkʌmə(r)/ ***noun*** [C] a person who has just arrived in a place

newfangled /ˌnjuːˈfæŋgld/ ***adj.*** new or modern in a way that the speaker does not like

newly /ˈnjuːli/ ***adv.*** (usually before a past participle) recently: *the newly appointed Minister of Health*

ˈ**newly-wed** ***noun*** [C, usually pl.] a person who has recently got married: *The newly-weds went to Venice for their honeymoon.*

ˌ**new ˈmoon** ***noun*** [sing.] (**ASTRONOMY**) the moon when it appears as a thin curved line ➲ look at **full moon**

news /njuːz/ ***noun*** **1** [U] information about sth that has happened recently: *Write and tell me all your news.* ◇ *Have you had any news from Nadia recently?* ◇ *That's news to me* (=I didn't know that). ◇ *News is coming in of a plane crash in Thailand.* **2 the news** [sing.] (**ARTS AND MEDIA**) a regular programme giving the latest news on the radio or television: *We always watch the ten o'clock news on television.* ◇ *I heard about the accident* ***on the news***.

IDM **break the news (to sb)** to be the first to tell sb about sth important that has happened

newsagent /ˈnjuːzeɪdʒənt/ (*AmE* **newsdealer** /ˈnjuːzdiːlə(r)/) ***noun*** **1** [C] a person who owns or works in a shop that sells newspapers and magazines, etc. **2 the newsagent's** [sing.] a shop that sells newspapers, magazines, etc.

ˈ**news conference** ***noun*** [C] (*especially AmE*) =PRESS CONFERENCE

newsflash /ˈnjuːzflæʃ/ ***noun*** [C] (**ARTS AND MEDIA**) a short report on television or radio, which interrupts the normal programme to give information about an important event that has just happened

newsgroup /ˈnjuːzgruːp/ ***noun*** [C] (**COMPUTING**) a place in a computer network, especially the Internet, where people can discuss a particular subject and exchange information about it

newsletter /ˈnjuːzletə(r)/ ***noun*** [C] a report about a club or an organization that is sent regularly to members and other people who may be interested

newspaper /ˈnjuːzpeɪpə(r)/ ***noun*** **1** (*also* **paper**) [C] (**ARTS AND MEDIA**) large folded pieces of paper printed with news, advertisements and articles on various subjects. Newspapers are printed and sold either every day or every week: *a daily/weekly/Sunday newspaper* ◇ *a newspaper article* ◇ *I read about it* ***in the newspaper***. **2** (*also* **paper**) [C] (**ARTS AND MEDIA**) an organization that produces a newspaper: *Which newspaper does he work for?* **3** [U] the paper on which newspapers are printed: *We wrapped the plates in newspaper so they would not get damaged.*

RELATED VOCABULARY

newspapers

Newspapers and the **journalists/reporters** who write articles for them are called **the press**.

The **editor** decides what is printed.

Quality newspapers deal with the news in a serious way. **Tabloids** are smaller in size and some of them have **sensational** (=shocking) stories and **gossip columns** (=unkind reports about famous people).

Photographers who follow famous people in order to take photographs of them are called **paparazzi**.

newspaper /ˈnjuːzpeɪpə(r)/ ***noun*** **1** (*also* **paper**) [C] (**ARTS AND MEDIA**) large folded pieces of paper printed with news, advertisements and articles on various subjects. Newspapers are printed and sold either every day or every week: *a daily/weekly/Sunday newspaper* ◇ *a newspaper article* ◇ *I read about it* ***in the newspaper***. **2** (*also* **paper**) [C] (**ARTS AND MEDIA**) an organization that produces a newspaper: *Which newspaper does he work for?* **3** [U] the paper on which newspapers are printed: *We wrapped the plates in newspaper so they would not get damaged.*

newspaper /ˈnjuːzpeɪpə(r)/ ***noun*** **1** (*also* **paper**) [C] (**ARTS AND MEDIA**) large folded pieces of paper printed with news, advertisements and articles on various subjects. Newspapers are printed and sold either every day or every week: *a daily/weekly/Sunday newspaper* ◇ *a newspaper article* ◇ *I read about it* ***in the newspaper***. **2** (*also* **paper**) [C] (**ARTS AND MEDIA**) an organization that produces a newspaper: *Which newspaper does he work for?* **3** [U] the paper on which newspapers are printed: *We wrapped the plates in newspaper so they would not get damaged.*

newsreader /ˈnjuːzriːdə(r)/ (*also* **newscaster** /ˈnjuːzkɑːstə(r)/) ***noun*** [C] (**ARTS AND MEDIA**) a person who reads the news on the radio or television

ˈ**news-stand** (*AmE*) =BOOKSTALL

the ˌNew ˈTestament ***noun*** [sing.] (**RELIGION**) the second part of the Bible, that describes the life and teachings of Jesus Christ ➲ look at **the Old Testament**

newton /'nju:tən/ ***noun*** [C] (*abbr.* **N**) (**PHYSICS**) a unit of force. One newton is equal to the force that would give a mass of one kilogram an ACCELERATION (=an increase in speed) of one metre per second.

'new town ***noun*** [C] one of the towns that were planned by the government as complete units and built in Britain after 1946

,new 'year (also ,**New 'Year**) ***noun*** [sing.] the first few days of January: *Happy New Year!* ◇ *We will get in touch in the new year.* ◇ *New Year's Eve* (=31 December) ◇ *New Year's Day* (=1 January)

next 🔑 /nekst/ ***adj., adv.*** **1** (usually with *the*) coming immediately after sth in order, space or time; closest: *The next bus leaves in twenty minutes.* ◇ *The next name on the list is Paulo.* **2** (used without *the* before days of the week, months, seasons, years, etc.) the one immediately following the present one: *See you again next Monday.* ◇ *Let's go camping next weekend.* ◇ *next summer/next year/next Christmas* **3** after this or after that; then: *I wonder what will happen next.* ◇ *I know Joe arrived first, but who came next?* ◇ *It was ten years until I next saw her.* **4 the next *noun*** [sing.] the person or thing that is next: *If we miss this train we'll have to wait two hours for the next.*

IDM **last/next but one, two etc.** → LAST[1]

,next 'door ***adj., adv.*** in or into the next house or building: *our **next-door neighbours*** ◇ *Who lives next door?* ◇ *The school is **next door to** an old people's home.* ◇ *He's gone next door.*

,next of 'kin ***noun*** [C] (*pl.* **next of kin**) your closest living relative or relatives: *My husband is my next of kin.*

'next to ***prep.*** **1** at the side of sb/sth; beside: *He sat down next to Gita.* ◇ *There's a public telephone next to the bus stop.* **2** in a position after sth: *Next to English my favourite subject is Maths.*

IDM **next to nothing** almost nothing: *We took plenty of money but we've got next to nothing left.*

NGO /,en dʒi: 'əʊ/ ***abbr.*** **non-governmental organization**; a charity, an association, etc. that is independent of government and business

NHS /,en eɪtʃ 'es/ ***abbr.*** (*BrE*) (**HEALTH**) National Health Service

nib /nɪb/ ***noun*** [C] the metal point of a pen

nibble /'nɪbl/ ***verb*** [I,T] to eat sth by taking small bites: *The bread had been nibbled by mice.* ▶ **nibble *noun*** [C]

nice 🔑 /naɪs/ ***adj.*** **1** pleasant, enjoyable or attractive: *a nice place/feeling/smile* ◇ *I'm not eating this – it doesn't taste very nice.* ◇ *It would be nice to spend more time at home.* ◇ *'Hi, I'm Tony.' 'I'm Ray -**nice to meet you**.'* **2** ~ **(to sb)**; ~ **(of sb) (to do sth)**; ~ **(about sth)** kind; friendly: *What a nice girl!* ◇ *Everyone was very nice to me when I felt ill.* ◇ *It was really nice of Donna to help us.* **3** (*informal*) used before adjectives and adverbs to emphasize how pleasant or suitable sth is: *It's nice and warm by the fire.* ◇ *a nice long chat* ◇ *Everyone arrived nice and early.* ▶ **niceness *noun*** [U]

nicely 🔑 /'naɪsli/ ***adv.*** **1** in an attractive or acceptable way; well: *The room was nicely furnished.* ◇ *The plants are **coming along nicely*** (=growing well). **2** in a kind, friendly or polite way: *If you ask her nicely she might say yes.* **3** carefully; exactly: *His novels nicely describe life in Britain between the wars.*

IDM **do nicely 1** to be making good progress: *Her new business is doing very nicely.* **2** to be acceptable: *Tomorrow at ten will do nicely* (=will be a good time).

niche /nɪtʃ; ni:ʃ/ ***noun*** [C] **1** a job, position, etc. that is suitable for you: *to find your niche in life* **2** (**BUSINESS**) an opportunity to sell a particular product to a particular group of people: *the development of **niche marketing*** (=aiming products at particular groups) **3** (**ARCHITECTURE**) a place in a wall that is further back, where a statue, etc. can be put **4** (**BIOLOGY**) the conditions of its environment within which a particular type of living thing can live successfully: *Within each niche, similar animals avoid competing with each other.*

nick[1] /nɪk/ ***noun*** [C] a small cut in sth

IDM **in good/bad nick** (*BrE, slang*) in a good/bad state or condition

in the nick of time only just in time

nick[2] /nɪk/ ***verb*** [T] **1** to make a very small cut in sb/sth **2** (*BrE, slang*) to arrest sb **3** (*BrE, slang*) to steal sth

nickel /'nɪkl/ ***noun*** **1** [U] (*symbol* **Ni**) (**CHEMISTRY**) a hard silver-white metal that is often mixed with other metals ❶ For more information on the periodic table of elements, look at pages R34-5. **2** [C] an American or Canadian coin that is worth five cents

nickname /'nɪkneɪm/ ***noun*** [C] an informal name that is used instead of your real name, usually by your family or friends ▶ **nickname *verb*** [T]

nicotine /'nɪkəti:n/ ***noun*** [U] (**HEALTH**) the poisonous chemical substance in TOBACCO

niece 🔑 /ni:s/ ***noun*** [C] the daughter of your brother or sister; the daughter of your husband's or wife's brother or sister ➲ look at **nephew**

nifty /'nɪfti/ ***adj.*** (*informal*) **1** skilful and accurate: *There's some nifty guitar work on his latest CD.* **2** practical; working well SYN **handy**

niggle /'nɪgl/ ***verb*** **1** [I,T] ~ **(at) sb** to annoy or worry sb: *His untidy habits really niggled her.* **2** [I] ~ **(about/over sth)** to complain or argue about things that are not important

niggling /'nɪglɪŋ/ ***adj.*** not very serious (but that does not go away): *niggling doubts* ◇ *a niggling injury*

night 🔑 /naɪt/ ***noun*** [C,U] **1** the part of the day when it is dark and when most people sleep: *I had a strange dream **last night**.* ◇ *The baby cried **all night**.* ◇ *It's a long way home. Why don't you **stay the night**?* ◇ *We will be away for a few nights.* **2** the time between late afternoon and when you go to bed: *Let's go out on Saturday night.* ◇ *He doesn't get home until 8 o'clock **at night**.* ◇ *I went out with Kate **the other night*** (=a few nights ago).

IDM **an early/a late night** an evening when you go to bed earlier/later than usual

a night out an evening that you spend out of the house enjoying yourself

in the/at dead of night → DEAD[2]

good night said in the evening, before you go home or before you go to sleep

nightclub /'naɪtklʌb/ ***noun*** [C] a place that is open late in the evening where people can go to dance, drink, etc.

nightdress /'naɪtdres/ (also *informal* **nightie** /'naɪti/) ***noun*** [C] a loose dress that a girl or woman wears in bed

nightingale /'naɪtɪŋgeɪl/ ***noun*** [C] a small brown bird that has a beautiful song

nightlife /'naɪtlaɪf/ ***noun*** [U] the entertainment that is available in the evenings in a particular place: *It's a small town with very little nightlife.*

nightly /ˈnaɪtli/ ***adj., adv.*** happening every night: *a nightly news bulletin*

nightmare /ˈnaɪtmeə(r)/ ***noun*** [C] **1** a frightening or unpleasant dream: *I had a terrible nightmare about being stuck in a lift last night.* **2** (*informal*) an experience that is very unpleasant or frightening: *Travelling in the rush hour can be a real nightmare.*

ˈnight-time ***noun*** [U] the time when it is dark

nightwatchman /naɪtˈwɒtʃmən/ ***noun*** [C] (*pl.* **nightwatchmen** /-mən/) a person who guards a building at night

nil /nɪl/ ***noun*** [U] the number 0 (especially as the score in some games): *We won by two goals to nil.* ◇ *They lost two-nil.* ➲ note at **zero**

nimble /ˈnɪmbl/ ***adj.*** able to move quickly and lightly ▸ **nimbly** /ˈnɪmbli/ ***adv.***

nimbostratus /ˌnɪmbəʊˈstrɑːtəs; -ˈstreɪtəs/ ***noun*** [U] (GEOGRAPHY) a type of cloud that forms a thick grey layer at a low level, from which rain or snow often falls ➲ picture at **cloud**

nimbus /ˈnɪmbəs/ ***noun*** [C, usually sing.] (GEOGRAPHY) a large grey rain cloud

nine /naɪn/ ***number*** 9 ➲ note at **six**
IDM **nine to five** the hours that you work in most offices: *a nine-to-five job*

nineteen /ˌnaɪnˈtiːn/ ***number*** 19 ➲ note at **six**

nineteenth /ˌnaɪnˈtiːnθ/ **1** ***ordinal number*** 19th ➲ note at **sixth**[1] **2** ***noun*** [C] one of 19 equal parts of sth

ninetieth /ˈnaɪntiəθ/ **1** ***ordinal number*** 90th ➲ note at **sixth**[1] **2** ***noun*** [C] one of 90 equal parts of sth

ninety /ˈnaɪnti/ ***number*** **1** 90 **2 the nineties** [pl.] numbers, years or temperatures from 90 to 99 ➲ note at **sixty**

ninth[1] /naɪnθ/ ***noun*** [C] the FRACTION ⅑; one of nine equal parts of sth

ninth[2] /naɪnθ/ ***ordinal number*** 9th ➲ note at **sixth**[1]

niobium /naɪˈəʊbiəm/ ***noun*** [U] (*symbol* **Nb**) (CHEMISTRY) a chemical element. **Niobium** is a silver-grey metal used in steel ALLOYS. ❶ For more information on the periodic table of elements, look at pages R34-5.

nip /nɪp/ ***verb*** (**nipping**; **nipped**) **1** [I,T] to give sb/sth a quick bite or to quickly squeeze a piece of sb's skin between your thumb and finger: *She nipped him on the arm.* **2** [I] (*BrE, spoken*) to go somewhere quickly and/or for a short time ▸ **nip** ***noun*** [C]
IDM **nip sth in the bud** to stop sth bad before it develops or gets worse

nipple /ˈnɪpl/ ***noun*** [C] either of the two small dark circles on either side of your chest. A baby can suck milk from its mother's breasts through the **nipples**.

nit /nɪt/ ***noun*** [C] the egg of a small insect that lives in the hair of people or animals

ˈnit-picking ***adj., noun*** [U] (the habit of) finding small mistakes in sb's work or paying too much attention to small, unimportant details

nitrate /ˈnaɪtreɪt/ ***noun*** [C, U] (CHEMISTRY, BIOLOGY) a COMPOUND containing NITROGEN. **Nitrates** are often used to improve the quality of soil.

nitric acid /ˌnaɪtrɪk ˈæsɪd/ ***noun*** [U] (*symbol* **HNO_3**) (CHEMISTRY) a powerful acid that can destroy most substances and is used to make EXPLOSIVE substances and other chemical products

nitrify /ˈnaɪtrɪfaɪ/ ***verb*** [T] (*pres. part.* **nitrifying**; *3rd person sing. pres.* **nitrifies**; *pt, pp* **nitrified**) (CHEMISTRY) to change a substance into a COMPOUND that contains NITROGEN ➲ look at **nitrates** ➲ picture at **nitrogen**

nitrite /ˈnaɪtraɪt/ ***noun*** [C,U] (CHEMISTRY) a chemical COMPOUND containing NITROGEN and OXYGEN. There are several different **nitrites**.

the nitrogen cycle

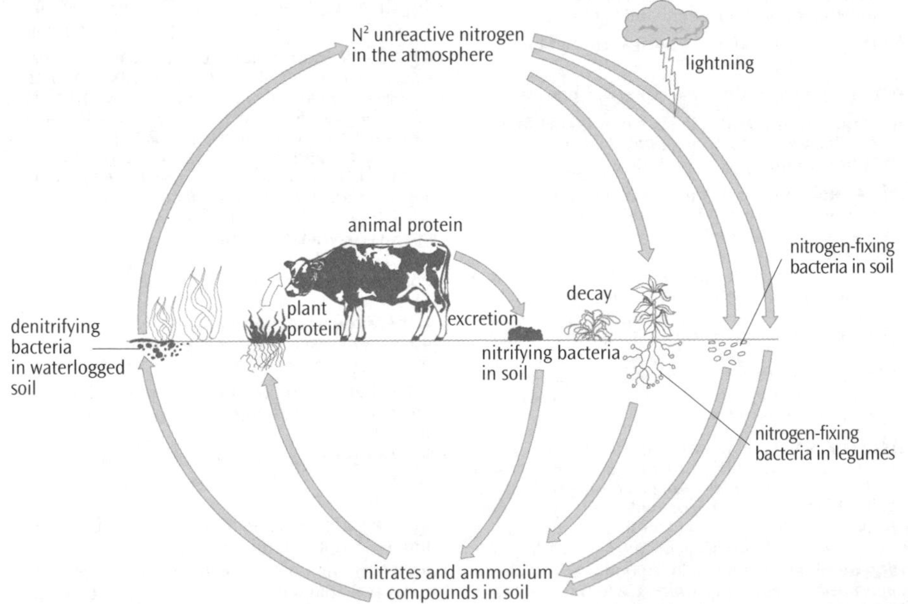

nitrogen /ˈnaɪtrədʒən/ *noun* [U] (*symbol* **N**) (CHEMISTRY) a gas that has no colour, taste or smell. Nitrogen forms about 80% of the air around the earth. ❶ For more information on the periodic table of elements, look at pages R34-5. ▶ **nitrogenous** /naɪˈtrɒdʒənəs/ *adj.*: *nitrogenous fertilizers*

ˈnitrogen cycle *noun* [C,U] (BIOLOGY, AGRICULTURE) the processes by which NITROGEN in the atmosphere is changed into NITRATES in the soil which are then absorbed by plants. Animals eat the plants and their waste goes back into the soil, together with decaying plant matter and this is then changed back into NITROGEN and released into the atmosphere.

ˌnitrogen diˈoxide *noun* [U] (CHEMISTRY) a reddish-brown poisonous gas. **Nitrogen dioxide** is formed when some metals dissolve in NITRIC ACID.

ˈnitrogen fixation *noun* [U] (BIOLOGY, CHEMISTRY) the chemical process by which NITROGEN from the atmosphere is changed by bacteria into COMPOUNDS in the soil that plants and other organisms can use, especially as part of the NITROGEN CYCLE ➲ picture at **nitrogen** ▶ **ˈnitrogen-fixing** *adj.*: *nitrogen-fixing bacteria*

nitrous oxide /ˌnaɪtrəs ˈɒksaɪd/ (also *informal* **ˈlaughing gas**) *noun* [U] (HEALTH) a gas used especially by dentists to prevent you from feeling pain

the nitty-gritty /ˌnɪti ˈɡrɪti/ *noun* [sing.] (*spoken*) the most important facts, not the small or unimportant details

nm *abbr.* (*pl.* **nm** or **nms**) **nanometre**

NNE *abbr.* (GEOGRAPHY) north-north-east

NNW *abbr.* (GEOGRAPHY) north-north-west

No. (*also* **no.**) (*pl.* **Nos**; **nos**) *abbr.* number: *No. 10 Downing Street* ◇ *tel. no. 512364*

no[1] /nəʊ/ *det., adv.* **1** not any; not a: *I have no time to talk now.* ◇ *No visitors may enter without a ticket.* ◇ *He's no friend of mine.* ◇ *Alice is feeling no better this morning.* **2** used for saying that sth is not allowed: *No smoking.* ◇ *No flash photography.* ◇ *No parking.*

no[2] /nəʊ/ *exclamation* **1** used for giving a negative reply: *'Are you ready?' 'No, I'm not.'* ◇ *'Would you like something to eat?' **'No, thank you.'*** OPP **Yes, please** ◇ *'Can I borrow the car?' 'No, you can't.'* OPP **yes** **2** used for expressing surprise or shock: *'Mike's had an accident.' 'Oh, no!'*

nobelium /nəʊˈbiːliəm; -ˈbel-/ *noun* [U] (*symbol* **No**) (CHEMISTRY) a chemical element. **Nobelium** is a RADIOACTIVE metal that does not exist naturally and is produced from CURIUM. ❶ For more information on the periodic table of elements, look at pages R34-5.

Nobel Prize /nəʊˌbel ˈpraɪz/ *noun* [C] an international prize given each year for achievements in physics, chemistry, PHYSIOLOGY, ECONOMICS, medicine, literature and peace

nobility /nəʊˈbɪləti/ *noun* **1 the nobility** [sing., with sing. or pl. verb] the group of people who belong to the highest social class and have special titles such as DUKE or DUCHESS SYN **aristocracy** **2** [U] (*formal*) the quality of having courage and honour

noble[1] /ˈnəʊbl/ *adj.* **1** honest; full of courage and care for others: *a noble leader* ◇ *noble ideas/actions* **2** belonging to the highest social class: *a man of noble birth* ▶ **nobly** /ˈnəʊbli/ *adv.*

noble[2] /ˈnəʊbl/ *noun* [C] a person who comes from a family of high social rank; a member of the NOBILITY

ˌnoble ˈgas *noun* [C] (CHEMISTRY) any of a group of gases that do not react with other chemicals ❶ **Noble gases** are also called **inert gases** and include **argon**, **helium**, **krypton** and **neon**.

nobleman /ˈnəʊblmən/ **noblewoman** /ˈnəʊblwʊmən/ (*pl.* **-men** /-mən/, **-women** /-wɪmɪn/) *noun* [C] a person from a family of high social rank; a member of the NOBILITY (=the group of people who belong to the highest social class) SYN **aristocrat**

ˌnoble ˈmetal *noun* [C] (CHEMISTRY) a metal, such as gold or silver, which does not react easily with air or acid

nobody[1] 🔑 /ˈnəʊbədi/ (*also* **no one** /ˈnəʊ wʌn/) *pronoun* no person; not anyone: *He screamed but nobody came to help him.* ◇ *No one else was around.* ◇ *There was nobody at home.*

nobody[2] /ˈnəʊbədi/ *noun* [C] (*pl.* **nobodies**) a person who is not important or famous: *She rose from being a nobody to a superstar.*

nocturnal /nɒkˈtɜːnl/ *adj.* **1** (used about animals and birds) awake and active at night and asleep during the day: *Owls are nocturnal birds.* OPP **diurnal** **2** (*written*) happening in the night: *a nocturnal adventure*

nod /nɒd/ *verb* [I,T] (**nodding**; **nodded**) to move your head up and down as a way of saying 'yes' or as a sign to sb to do sth: *Everybody at the meeting nodded in agreement.* ◇ *Nod your head if you understand what I'm saying and shake it if you don't.* ▶ **nod** *noun* [C]

PHR V **nod off** (*informal*) to fall asleep for a short time

node /nəʊd/ *noun* [C] **1** (BIOLOGY) a place on the long thin part (**stem**) of a plant from which a branch or leaf grows **2** (MATHEMATICS) a point at which two lines or systems meet or cross **3** (BIOLOGY) a small hard mass, especially near a JOINT (=the place where two bones meet) in the human body ➲ look at **lymph node**

nodule /ˈnɒdjuːl/ *noun* [C] (BIOLOGY) a small round lump, especially on a plant

ˌno-ˈfrills *adj.* including only the basic features, without anything that is unnecessary, especially things added to make sth more attractive or comfortable: *a no-frills airline*

ˌno-ˈgo area *noun* [sing.] a place, especially part of a city, where it is very dangerous to go because there is a lot of violence or crime

Noh (*also* **No**) /nəʊ/ *noun* [U] (ARTS AND MEDIA) traditional Japanese theatre in which songs, dance, and MIME are performed by people wearing MASKS

noise 🔑 /nɔɪz/ *noun* [C,U] a sound, especially one that is loud or unpleasant: *Did you hear a noise downstairs?* ◇ *Try not to **make a noise** if you come home late.* ◇ *What an awful noise!* ◇ *Why is the engine making so much noise?*

noiseless /ˈnɔɪzləs/ *adj.* making no sound ▶ **noiselessly** *adv.*

noisy 🔑 /ˈnɔɪzi/ *adj.* (**noisier**; **noisiest**) making a lot of or too much noise; full of noise: *The clock was so noisy that it kept me awake.* ◇ *noisy children/traffic/crowds* ◇ *The classroom was very noisy.* ▶ **noisily** *adv.*

nomad /ˈnəʊmæd/ *noun* [C] a member of a TRIBE (=a group of people) that moves with its animals from place to place ▶ **nomadic** /nəʊˈmædɪk/ *adj.*: *nomadic tribes*

'no-man's-land *noun* [U, sing.] an area of land between the borders of two countries or between two armies during a war and which is not controlled by either

nomenclature /nə'menklətʃə(r)/ *noun* [U, C] (*formal*) a system of naming things, especially in science: *zoological nomenclature*

nominal /'nɒmɪnl/ *adj.* **1** being sth in name only but not in reality: *the nominal leader of the country* (=sb else is really in control) **2** (used about a price, sum of money, etc.) very small; much less than normal: *Because we are friends he only charges me a **nominal rent**.* ▸ **nominally** /-nəli/ *adv.*

nominate /'nɒmɪneɪt/ *verb* [T] ~ **sb/sth (for/as sth)** to formally suggest that sb/sth should be given a job, role, prize, etc.: *I would like to nominate Bob Turner as chairman.* ◇ *The novel has been nominated for the Booker prize.* ◇ *You may nominate a representative to speak for you.* ▸ **nomination** /ˌnɒmɪ'neɪʃn/ *noun* [C,U]

nominative /'nɒmɪnətɪv/ *noun* [C] (LANGUAGE) (in some languages) the form of a noun, a pronoun or an adjective when it is the subject of a verb ▸ **nominative** *adj.*: *nominative pronouns* ➲ look at **accusative, dative, genitive, vocative**

nominee /ˌnɒmɪ'ni:/ *noun* [C] a person who is suggested for an important job, prize, etc.

non- /nɒn/ (used to form compounds) not: *non-biodegradable* ◇ *non-flammable*

nona- /'nɒnə; 'nəʊnə/ (used in nouns and adjectives) nine; having nine: *nonagenarian* (=a person who is between 90 and 99 years old)

ˌnon-aca'demic *adj.* connected with technical or practical subjects rather than subjects of interest to the mind

nonagon /'nɒnəgən/ *noun* [C] (GEOMETRY) a flat shape with nine straight sides and nine angles

ˌnon-alco'holic *adj.* (used about drinks) not containing any alcohol: *non-alcoholic drinks*

ˌnon-a'ligned *adj.* (POLITICS) (used about a country) not providing support for or receiving support from any of the powerful countries in the world OPP **aligned**

nonchalant /'nɒnʃələnt/ *adj.* not feeling or showing interest or excitement about sth ▸ **nonchalance** /-ləns/ *noun* [U] ▸ **nonchalantly** *adv.*

ˌnon-co'mmittal *adj.* not saying or showing exactly what your opinion is or which side of an argument you agree with

nonconformist AW /ˌnɒnkən'fɔ:mɪst/ *noun* [C] a person who behaves or thinks differently from most other people in society OPP **conformist** ▸ **nonconformist** *adj.*

ˌnon-'contact sport *noun* [C] (SPORT) a sport in which players do not have physical contact with each other OPP **contact sport**

nondescript /'nɒndɪskrɪpt/ *adj.* not having any interesting or unusual qualities

none[1] 🔑 /nʌn/ *pronoun* ~ **(of sb/sth)** not any, not one (of a group of three or more): *They gave me a lot of information but none of it was very helpful.* ◇ *I've got four brothers but none of them live/lives nearby.* ◇ *'Have you brought any books to read?' 'No, none.'* ◇ *I went to several shops but none had what I wanted.*

none[2] /nʌn/ *adv.*

IDM **none the wiser/worse** knowing no more than before; no worse than before: *We talked for a long time but I'm still **none the wiser**.*

none too happy, clean, pleased, etc. (*informal*) not very happy, clean, pleased, etc.

nonetheless AW /ˌnʌnðə'les/ *adv.* (*written*) in spite of this fact: *It won't be easy but they're going to try nonetheless.* SYN **nevertheless**

ˌnon-e'xistent *adj.* not existing or not available

ˌnon-'fiction *noun* [U] (LITERATURE) writing that is about real people, events and facts: *You'll find biographies in the non-fiction section of the library.* OPP **fiction**

ˌnon-'flammable *adj.* not likely to burn easily

nonplussed /ˌnɒn'plʌst/ *adj.* confused; not able to understand

ˌnon-re'newable *adj.* (ENVIRONMENT) (used about natural sources of energy such as gas or oil) that cannot be replaced after use

nonsense 🔑 /'nɒnsns/ *noun* [U] **1** ideas, statements or beliefs that you think are ridiculous or not true: *Don't **talk nonsense**!* **2** silly or unacceptable behaviour: *The head teacher won't stand for any nonsense.*

nonsensical /nɒn'sensɪkl/ *adj.* ridiculous; without meaning

ˌnon-'smoker *noun* [C] a person who does not smoke cigarettes or CIGARS OPP **smoker** ▸ **ˌnon-'smoking** *adj.*: *Would you like a table in the smoking or the non-smoking section?*

ˌnon-'starter *noun* [C] a person, plan or idea that has no chance of success

ˌnon-'stick *adj.* (used about a pan, etc.) covered with a substance that prevents food from sticking to it

ˌnon-'stop *adj.*, *adv.* without a stop or a rest: *a non-stop flight to Delhi* ◇ *He talked non-stop for two hours about his holiday.*

ˌnon-'violence *noun* [U] fighting for political or social change without using force, for example by not obeying laws ▸ **ˌnon-'violent** *adj.*

noodle /'nu:dl/ *noun* [C, usually pl.] long thin pieces of food made of flour, egg and water that are cooked in boiling water or used in soups

nook /nʊk/ *noun* [C] a small quiet place or corner (in a house, garden, etc.)

IDM **every nook and cranny** (*informal*) every part of a place

noon /nu:n/ *noun* [U] 12 o'clock in the middle of the day; midday: ***At noon** the sun is at its highest point in the sky.* ➲ look at **midnight**

'no one = NOBODY[1]

noose /nu:s/ *noun* [C] a circle that is tied in the end of a rope and that gets smaller as one end of the rope is pulled

nor 🔑 /nɔ:(r)/ *conj.*, *adv.* **1 neither…nor…** and not: *I have neither the time nor the inclination to listen to his complaints again.* **2** (used before a positive verb to agree with sth negative that has just been said) also not; neither: *'I don't like football.' 'Nor do I.'* ◇ *'We haven't been to America.' 'Nor have we.'* ℹ In this sense **neither** can be used in the same way: *'I won't be here tomorrow.' 'Nor/Neither will I.'* **3** (used after a negative statement to add some more information) also not: *Michael never forgot her birthday. Nor their wedding anniversary for that matter.*

Nordic /'nɔ:dɪk/ *adj.* **1** connected with Scandinavia, Finland and Iceland **2** typical of a member of a European race of people who are tall and have blue eyes and fair hair: *Nordic features*

ˌ**Nordic ˈskiing** *noun* [U] (SPORT) the sport of SKIING across the countryside ➲ look at **Alpine skiing**

norm AW /nɔːm/ *noun* [C] (often with *the*) a situation or way of behaving that is usual or expected

normal¹ ⊶ AW /ˈnɔːml/ *adj.* typical, usual or ordinary; what you expect: *I'll meet you at the normal time.* ◇ *It's quite normal to feel angry in a situation like this.* OPP **abnormal**

normal² ⊶ AW /ˈnɔːml/ *noun* [U] the usual or average state, level or standard: *temperatures above/below normal* ◇ *Things are* ***back to normal*** *at work now.*

normality AW /nɔːˈmæləti/ (*AmE* **normalcy** /ˈnɔːmlsi/) *noun* [U] the state of being normal

normalize (also -**ise**) AW /ˈnɔːməlaɪz/ *verb* [I,T] (*written*) to become or make sth become normal again or return to how it was before: *The two countries agreed to normalize relations* (=return to a normal, friendly relationship, for example after a disagreement or a war).

normally ⊶ AW /ˈnɔːməli/ *adv.* **1** usually: *I normally leave the house at 8 o'clock.* ◇ *Normally he takes the bus.* **2** in the usual or ordinary way: *His heart is beating normally.*

Norman /ˈnɔːmən/ *adj.* **1** (ARCHITECTURE) used to describe the style of ARCHITECTURE in Britain in the 11th and 12th centuries that developed from the ROMANESQUE style: *a Norman church/castle* **2** (HISTORY) connected with the Normans (=the people from northern Europe who defeated the English in 1066 and then ruled the country): *the Norman Conquest*

Norse¹ /nɔːs/ *noun* [U] (LANGUAGE) the Norwegian language, especially in an ancient form, or the Scandinavian language group

Norse² /nɔːs/ *adj.* (HISTORY) relating to Norway or Scandinavia in the ancient past

north¹ ⊶ /nɔːθ/ *noun* [sing.] (*abbr.* **N**) (*also* **the north**) **1** (GEOGRAPHY) the direction that is on your left when you watch the sun rise; one of THE POINTS OF THE COMPASS (=the four main directions that we give names to): *cold winds from the north* ◇ *Which way is north?* ◇ *I live* ***to the north of*** (=further north than) *Belfast.* ➲ picture at **compass 2** (*also* **the North**) the northern part of any country, city, region or the world: *Houses are less expensive in the North of England than in the South.* ◇ *I live in the north of Athens.* ➲ look at **south, east, west, magnetic north, true north**

north² ⊶ /nɔːθ/ *adj., adv.* (GEOGRAPHY) **1** (*also* **North**) (only *before* a noun) in the north: *The new offices will be in North London.* ◇ *The north wing of the hospital was destroyed in a fire.* **2** to or towards the north: *We got onto the motorway going north instead of south.* ◇ *The house faces north.* ◇ *Is Leeds north of Manchester?* **3** (used about a wind) coming from the north

ˌ**North Atlantic ˈDrift** *noun* [sing.] (GEOGRAPHY) a current of warm water in the Atlantic Ocean, that has the effect of making the climate of NW Europe warmer ➲ picture at **current²**

northbound /ˈnɔːθbaʊnd/ *adj.* travelling or leading towards the north: *northbound traffic*

ˌ**north-ˈeast¹** *noun* [sing.] (*abbr.* **NE**) (*also* **the North-East**) (GEOGRAPHY) the direction or a region halfway between north and east

ˌ**north-ˈeast²** *adj., adv.* (GEOGRAPHY) in, from or to the north-east of a place or country: *the north-east coast of Australia* ◇ *If you look north-east you can see the sea.* ➲ picture at **compass**

ˌ**north-ˈeasterly** *adj.* **1** towards the north-east: *in a north-easterly direction* **2** (used about a wind) coming from the north-east

ˌ**north-ˈeastern** *adj.* (only *before* a noun) (GEOGRAPHY) connected with the north-east of a place or country

ˌ**north-ˈeastward(s)** *adv.* (GEOGRAPHY) towards the north-east: *Follow the A619 north-eastward.*

northerly /ˈnɔːðəli/ *adj.* (GEOGRAPHY) **1** to, towards or in the north: *Keep going in a northerly direction.* **2** (used about a wind) coming from the north

northern ⊶ (*also* **Northern**) /ˈnɔːðən/ *adj.* (GEOGRAPHY) of, in or from the north of a place: *She has a northern accent.* ◇ *in northern Australia*

northerner (*also* **Northerner**) /ˈnɔːðənə(r)/ *noun* [C] a person who was born in or who lives in the northern part of a country OPP **southerner**

the ˌNorthern ˈLights *noun* [pl.] (*also* **aurora borealis**) (ASTRONOMY) bands of coloured light, mainly green and red, that are sometimes seen in the sky at night in the most northern countries of the world

northernmost /ˈnɔːðənməʊst/ *adj.* (GEOGRAPHY) furthest north: *the northernmost island of Japan*

ˌ**north-north-ˈeast** *noun* [sing.] (*abbr.* **NNE**) (GEOGRAPHY) the direction halfway between north and north-east

ˌ**north-north-ˈwest** *noun* [sing.] (*abbr.* **NNW**) (GEOGRAPHY) the direction halfway between north and north-west

the ˌNorth ˈPole *noun* [sing.] (GEOGRAPHY) the point on the Earth's surface which is furthest north ➲ picture at **earth**

northward /ˈnɔːθwəd/ (*also* **northwards**) *adv., adj.* (GEOGRAPHY) towards the north: *Continue northwards out of the city for about five miles.* ◇ *in a northward direction*

ˌ**north-ˈwest¹** *adj., adv.* (GEOGRAPHY) in, from or to the north-west of a place or country: *the north-west coast of Scotland* ◇ *Our house faces north-west.* ➲ picture at **compass**

ˌ**north-ˈwest²** *noun* [sing.] (*abbr.* **NW**) (*also* **the North-West**) (GEOGRAPHY) the direction or region halfway between north and west

ˌ**north-ˈwesterly** *adj.* (GEOGRAPHY) **1** towards the north-west: *in a north-westerly direction* **2** (used about a wind) coming from the north-west

ˌ**north-ˈwestern** *adj.* (only *before* a noun) (GEOGRAPHY) connected with the north-west of a place or country

ˌ**north-ˈwestward(s)** *adv.* (GEOGRAPHY) towards the north-west: *Follow the A40 north-westward for ten miles.*

nose¹ ⊶ /nəʊz/ *noun* [C] **1** the part of your face, above your mouth, that is used for breathing and smelling ➲ picture on **page 80 2 -nosed** (used to form compound adjectives) having the type of nose mentioned: *red-nosed* ◇ *big-nosed* **3** the front part of a plane, SPACECRAFT, etc. ➲ picture at **plane**

IDM **blow your nose** → BLOW¹

follow your nose → FOLLOW

look down your nose at sb/sth (*especially BrE, informal*) to think that you are better than sb else; to think that sth is not good enough for you

poke/stick your nose into sth (*spoken*) to be

interested in or try to become involved in sth which does not concern you
turn your nose up at sth (*informal*) to refuse sth because you do not think it is good enough for you

nose² /nəʊz/ ***verb*** [I] (used about a vehicle) to move forward slowly and carefully
PHR V **nose about/around** (*informal*) to look for sth, especially private information about sb

nosebleed /ˈnəʊzbliːd/ ***noun*** [C] (HEALTH) a sudden flow of blood that comes from your nose

nosedive /ˈnəʊzdaɪv/ ***noun*** [C] a sudden sharp fall or drop: *Oil prices* ***took a nosedive*** *in the crisis.*
▶ **nosedive** ***verb*** [I]

nostalgia /nɒˈstældʒə/ ***noun*** [U] a feeling of pleasure, mixed with sadness, when you think of happy times in the past: *She was suddenly filled with* ***nostalgia for*** *her university days.* ▶ **nostalgic** /-dʒɪk/ ***adj.*** ▶ **nostalgically** /-dʒɪkli/ ***adv.***

nostril /ˈnɒstrəl/ ***noun*** [C] one of the two openings at the end of your nose that you breathe through ➲ picture on **page 80**

nosy (also **nosey**) /ˈnəʊzi/ ***adj.*** too interested in other people's personal affairs: *a nosy neighbour*

not ⊶ /nɒt/ ***adv.*** **1** used to form the negative with the verbs *be*, *do* and *have* (**auxiliary verbs**) and with verbs such as *can*, *must*, *will*, etc. (**modal verbs**). *Not* is often pronounced or written *n't* in informal situations: *It's not/it isn't raining now.* ◇ *I cannot/can't see from here.* ◇ *He didn't invite me.* ◇ *Don't you like spaghetti?* ◇ *I hope she will not/won't be late.* ◇ *You're German, aren't you?* **2** used to give the following word or phrase a negative meaning: *He told me not to telephone.* ◇ *She accused me of not telling the truth.* ◇ *Not one person replied to my advertisement.* ◇ *It's not easy.* ◇ *He's not very tall.* **3** used to give a short negative reply: *'Do you think they'll get divorced?' 'I hope not.'* (= I hope that they will not.) ◇ *'Can I borrow £20?'* ***'Certainly not!'*** ◇ *'Whose turn is it to do the shopping?' 'Not mine.'* **4** used with the word *or* to give a negative possibility: *Shall we tell her* ***or not****?*
IDM **not at all 1** used as a way of replying when sb has thanked you: *'Thanks for the present.' 'Not at all, don't mention it.'* **2** used as a way of saying 'no' or 'definitely not': *'Do you mind if I come too?' 'Not at all.'* ◇ *The instructions are not at all clear.*
not only... (but) also used for emphasizing the fact that there is something more to add: *They not only have two houses in London, they also have one in France.*

notable /ˈnəʊtəbl/ ***adj.*** ~ (**for sth**) interesting or important enough to receive attention: *The area is notable for its wildlife.*

notably /ˈnəʊtəbli/ ***adv.*** used for giving an especially important example of what you are talking about: *Several politicians, most notably the Prime Minister and the Home Secretary, have given the proposal their full support.*

notary /ˈnəʊtəri/ (*pl.* **-ies**) (*also* ˌ**notary ˈpublic** *pl.* ˌ**notaries ˈpublic**) ***noun*** [C] (LAW) a person, especially a lawyer, with official authority to be a witness when sb signs a document and to make this document valid in law

notation /nəʊˈteɪʃn/ ***noun*** [U, C] a system of symbols that represent information, especially in mathematics, science and music ➲ picture at **music**

notch¹ /nɒtʃ/ ***noun*** [C] **1** a level on a scale of quality: *This meal is certainly* ***a notch above*** *the last one we had here.* **2** a cut in an edge or surface in the shape of a V or a circle, sometimes used to help you count sth

notch² /nɒtʃ/ ***verb***
PHR V **notch sth up** to score or achieve sth: *Lewis notched up his best ever time in the 100 metres.*

note¹ ⊶ /nəʊt/ ***noun*** **1** [C] some words that you write down quickly to help you remember sth: *I'd better* ***make a note of*** *your name and address.* ◇ ***Keep a note of*** *who has paid and who hasn't.* ◇ *The lecturer advised the students to* ***take notes*** *while he was speaking.* **2** [C] a short letter: *This is just a note to thank you for having us to dinner.* ◇ *If Mark's not at home we'll leave a note for him.* ◇ *a sick note from your doctor* **3** [C] a short explanation or extra piece of information that is given at the back of a book, etc. or at the bottom or side of a page: *See note 5, page 340.* ➲ look at **footnote 4** [C] (*also* **banknote** *AmE* **bill**) a piece of paper money: *I'd like the money in £10 notes, please.* **5** [C] (MUSIC) a single musical sound made by a voice or an instrument; a written sign that represents a musical sound: *I can only remember the first few notes of the song.* ➲ picture at **music 6** [sing.] something that shows a certain quality or feeling: *The meeting ended on a rather unpleasant note.*
IDM **compare notes (with sb)** → COMPARE
take note (of sth) to pay attention to sth and be sure to remember it

note² ⊶ /nəʊt/ ***verb*** [T] **1** to notice or pay careful attention to sth: *He noted a slight change in her attitude towards him.* ◇ *Please note that this office is closed on Tuesdays.* ➲ note at **comment² 2** to mention sth: *I'd like to note that the project has so far been extremely successful.*
PHR V **note sth down** to write sth down so that you remember it

notebook /ˈnəʊtbʊk/ ***noun*** [C] **1** a small book in which you write things that you want to remember **2** (*AmE*) = EXERCISE BOOK **3** (*also* ˌ**notebook comˈputer**) (COMPUTING) a very small computer that you can carry with you and use anywhere ➲ look at **desktop computer, laptop**

noted /ˈnəʊtɪd/ ***adj.*** (*formal*) ~ (**for/as sth**) well known; famous: *The hotel is noted for its food.*

notepad /ˈnəʊtpæd/ ***noun*** [C] some sheets of paper in a block that are used for writing things on

notepaper /ˈnəʊtpeɪpə(r)/ ***noun*** [U] paper that you write letters on

noteworthy /ˈnəʊtwɜːði/ ***adj.*** interesting or important; that is worth noticing

nothing ⊶ /ˈnʌθɪŋ/ ***pronoun*** not anything; no thing: *There's nothing in this suitcase.* ◇ *I'm bored – there's* ***nothing to do*** *here.* ◇ *There was* ***nothing else*** *to say.* ◇ *'What's the matter?' 'Oh, nothing.'* ◇ *'Thank you so much for all your help.' 'It was nothing.'* ◇ *The doctor said there's nothing wrong with me.* ➲ note at **zero**
IDM **be/have nothing to do with sb/sth** to have no connection with sb/sth: *That question has nothing to do with what we're discussing.* ◇ *Put my diary down – it's nothing to do with you.*
come to nothing → COME
for nothing 1 for no good reason or with no good result: *His hard work was all for nothing.* **2** for no payment; free: *Children under four are allowed in for nothing.*
nothing but only: *He does nothing but sit around watching TV all day.*
nothing like 1 not at all like: *She looks nothing like either of her parents.* **2** not at all; not nearly: *There's nothing like enough food for all of us.*
nothing much not a lot of sth; nothing of importance: *It's a nice town but there's nothing much to do*

in the evenings. ◇ *'What did you do at the weekend?' 'Nothing much.'*
(there's) nothing to it (it's) very easy: *You'll soon learn – there's nothing to it really.*
there is/was nothing (else) for it (but to do sth) there is/was no other action possible: *There was nothing for it but to resign.*

notice¹ 🔑 /'nəʊtɪs/ ***noun*** **1** [U] the act of paying attention to sth or knowing about sth: *The protests are finally making the government* ***take notice.*** ◇ ***Take no notice of*** *what he said – he was just being silly.* ◇ *Some people don't take any notice of* (=choose to ignore) *speed limits.* ◇ *It has* ***come to my notice*** *that you have missed a lot of classes.* **2** [C] a piece of paper or a sign giving information, a warning, etc. that is put where everyone can read it: *There's a notice on the board saying that the meeting has been cancelled.* ◇ *The notice said 'No dogs allowed'.* **3** [U] a warning that sth is going to happen: *I can't produce a meal* ***at*** *such* ***short notice!*** ◇ *I wish you'd* ***give*** *me more* ***notice*** *when you're going to be off work.* ◇ *The swimming pool is closed* ***until further notice*** (=until we are told that it will open again).

notice² 🔑 /'nəʊtɪs/ ***verb*** [I,T] (not usually used in the continuous tenses) to see and become conscious of sth: *'What kind of car was the man driving?' 'I'm afraid I didn't notice.'* ◇ *I noticed (that) he was carrying a black briefcase.* ◇ *Did you notice which direction she went in?* ◇ *We didn't notice him leave/him leaving.*

noticeable 🔑 /'nəʊtɪsəbl/ ***adj.*** easy to see or notice: *The scar from the accident was hardly noticeable.* ▶ **noticeably** /-əbli/ ***adv.***

noticeboard /'nəʊtɪsbɔːd/ (*AmE* **'bulletin board**) ***noun*** [C] a board on a wall for putting written information where everyone can read it

notify /'nəʊtɪfaɪ/ ***verb*** [T] (*pres. part.* **notifying**; *3rd person sing. pres.* **notifies**; *pt, pp* **notified**) **~ sb (of sth)** to inform sb about sth officially ▶ **notification** /ˌnəʊtɪfɪ'keɪʃn/ ***noun*** [C,U]

notion AW /'nəʊʃn/ ***noun*** [C] **a ~ (that.../of sth)** something that you have in your mind; an idea: *I had a vague notion that I had seen her before.*

notional /'nəʊʃənl/ ***adj.*** existing only in the mind; not based on facts or reality

notoriety /ˌnəʊtə'raɪəti/ ***noun*** [U] the state of being well known for sth bad

notorious /nəʊ'tɔːriəs/ ***adj.*** **~ (for/as sth)** well known for sth bad: *a notorious drug dealer* ◇ *This road is notorious for the number of accidents on it.*
SYN infamous ▶ **notoriously** ***adv.***

notwithstanding AW /ˌnɒtwɪθ'stændɪŋ/ ***prep., adv.*** (*written*) in spite of sth

nougat /'nuːɡɑː/ ***noun*** [U] a hard pink or white sweet containing nuts

nought /nɔːt/ (*especially AmE* **zero**) ***noun*** [C] (**MATHEMATICS**) the figure 0: *A million is written with six noughts.* ◇ *We say 0.1 'nought point one'.*
IDM noughts and crosses a game for two players in which each person tries to win by writing three 0s or three Xs in a line.

noun /naʊn/ ***noun*** [C] (**LANGUAGE**) a word that is the name of a thing, an idea, a place or a person: *'Water', 'happiness', 'James' and 'France' are all nouns.* ➲ look at **countable**, **uncountable**

nourish /'nʌrɪʃ/ ***verb*** [T] **1** to give sb/sth the right kind of food so that they can grow and be healthy **2** (*formal*) to allow a feeling, an idea, etc. to grow stronger ▶ **nourishment** ***noun*** [U]

Nov. ***abbr.*** November: *17 Nov. 2001*

nova /'nəʊvə/ ***noun*** [C] (*pl.* **novae** /-viː/ or **novas**) (**ASTRONOMY**) a star that suddenly becomes much brighter for a short period ➲ look at **supernova**

novel¹ 🔑 /'nɒvl/ ***noun*** [C] (**LITERATURE**) a book that tells a story about people and events that are not real: *a romantic/historical/detective novel*

novel² /'nɒvl/ ***adj.*** new and different: *That's a novel idea! Let's try it.*

novelist /'nɒvəlɪst/ ***noun*** [C] (**LITERATURE**) a person who writes novels

novella /nə'velə/ ***noun*** [C] (**LITERATURE**) a short novel

novelty /'nɒvlti/ ***noun*** (*pl.* **novelties**) **1** [U] the quality of being new and different: *The novelty of her new job soon wore off.* **2** [C] something new and unusual: *It was quite a novelty not to have to get up early.* **3** [C] a small, cheap object that is sold as a toy or decoration

November /nəʊ'vembə(r)/ ***noun*** [U, C] (*abbr.* **Nov.**) the eleventh month of the year, coming after October

novice /'nɒvɪs/ ***noun*** [C] a person who is new and without experience in a job, situation, etc
SYN beginner

now 🔑 /naʊ/ ***adv., conj.*** **1** (at) the present time: *We can't go for a walk now – it's raining.* ◇ *Where are you living now?* ◇ ***From now on*** *I'm going to work harder.* ◇ ***Up till now*** *we haven't been able to afford a house of our own.* ◇ *He will be on his way home* ***by now.*** ◇ *I can manage* ***for now*** *but I might need some help later.* **2** immediately: *Go now before anyone sees you.* ◇ *You must go to the doctor* ***right now.*** **3** used to introduce or to emphasize what you are saying, or while pausing to think: *Now listen to what he's saying.* ◇ *What does he want now?* ◇ *Now, let me think.* **4 ~ (that)...** because of the fact that: *Now (that) the children have left home we can move to a smaller house.*
IDM any moment/second/minute/day (now) → ANY
(every) now and again/then from time to time; occasionally: *We see each other now and then, but not very often.*
just now → JUST¹
right now → RIGHT²

nowadays /'naʊədeɪz/ ***adv.*** at the present time (when compared with the past): *I don't go to London much nowadays* (=but I did in the past). **SYN today**

nowhere 🔑 /'nəʊweə(r)/ ***adv.*** not in or to any place; not anywhere: *I'm afraid there's nowhere to stay in this village.* ◇ *I don't like it here, but there's* ***nowhere else*** *for us to sit.*
IDM get nowhere (with sth) to not make any progress with sth
in the middle of nowhere → MIDDLE¹
nowhere near → NEAR¹

noxious /'nɒkʃəs/ ***adj.*** (*formal*) harmful or poisonous: *noxious gases*

nozzle /'nɒzl/ ***noun*** [C] a narrow tube that is put on the end of a pipe to control the liquid or gas coming out

nr ***abbr.*** (used in addresses) near: *Masham, nr Ripon*

nuance /'njuːɑːns/ ***noun*** [C] a very small difference in meaning, feeling, sound, etc.

nuclear 🔑 AW /'njuːkliə(r)/ ***adj.*** **1** (**PHYSICS, CHEMISTRY**) using, producing or resulting from the energy that is produced when the central part (**nucleus**) of an atom is split: *nuclear energy* ◇ *a* *nuclear power station* ◇ *nuclear war/weapons* ➲ look at **atomic 2** (**PHYSICS**) connected with the NUCLEUS of an atom: *nuclear physics* **3** (**BIOLOGY**) connected with the NUCLEUS of a cell

ˌnuclear 'energy (*also* **ˌnuclear 'power**) ***noun*** [U] (**PHYSICS**) a powerful form of energy produced by splitting the central parts of atoms (**nuclei**). It is used to produce electricity.

ˌnuclear 'family ***noun*** [C] (**SOCIAL STUDIES**) a family that consists of father, mother and children, when it is thought of as a unit in society: *Not everybody nowadays lives in the conventional nuclear family.* ➲ look at **extended family**

ˌnuclear 'fission = FISSION

ˌnuclear 'fusion = FUSION

ˌnuclear 'physics ***noun*** [U] (**PHYSICS**) the scientific study of the centres (**nuclei**) of atoms, especially of how energy can be produced from them

ˌnuclear re'actor (*also* **reactor**) ***noun*** [C] (**PHYSICS**) a very large machine that produces nuclear energy

nucleic acid /nju:ˌkli:ɪk 'æsɪd/ ***noun*** [U] (**BIOLOGY**) either of two acids (**DNA** and **RNA**), that are present in all living cells

nucleus /'nju:kliəs/ ***noun*** [C] (*pl.* **nuclei** /-kliaɪ/) **1** (**SCIENCE**) the central part of an atom or of some cells ➲ picture at **amoeba**, **cell 2** the central or most important part of sth

nude[1] /nju:d/ ***adj.*** not wearing any clothes ➲ look at **bare**, **naked** ▶ **nudity** /'nju:dəti/ ***noun*** [U]: *This film contains scenes of nudity.*

nude[2] /nju:d/ ***noun*** [C] (**ART**) a picture or photograph of a person who is not wearing any clothes
IDM in the nude not wearing any clothes

nudge /nʌdʒ/ ***verb*** [T] to touch or push sb/sth with your elbow ▶ **nudge *noun*** [C]: *to give sb a nudge*

nudist /'nju:dɪst/ ***noun*** [C] a person who likes wearing no clothes, often in groups with other people: *a nudist beach*

nugget /'nʌgɪt/ ***noun*** [C] a small lump of a valuable metal or mineral, especially gold, that is found in the earth

nuisance /'nju:sns/ ***noun*** [C] a person, thing or situation that annoys you or causes you trouble: *It's a nuisance having to queue for everything.*

null /nʌl/ ***adj.***
IDM null and void (*written*) (**LAW**) not valid

numb /nʌm/ ***adj.*** not able to feel anything; not able to move: *My fingers were numb with cold.* ◇ *I'll give you an injection and the tooth will **go numb**.*
▶ **numb *verb*** [T]: *We were numbed by the dreadful news.* ▶ **numbness *noun*** [U]

number[1] **🔑** /'nʌmbə(r)/ ***noun*** **1** [C] (**MATHEMATICS**) a word or symbol that indicates a quantity: *Choose a number between ten and twenty.* ◇ *2, 4, 6, etc. are **even numbers** and 1, 3, 5, etc. are **odd numbers**.* ◇ *a three-figure number* (=from 100 to 999) **2** [C] a group of numbers that is used to identify sb/sth: *a telephone number* ◇ *a code number* **3** [C,U] a ~ (**of sth**) a quantity of people or things: *a large number of visitors* ◇ *We must reduce the number of accidents on the roads.* ◇ *Pupils in the school have doubled **in number** in recent years.* ◇ *There are **a number of*** (=several) *things I don't understand.* **4** [C] (*abbr.* **No.**) (*symbol* ♯) used before a number to show the position of sth in a series: *We live in Hazel Road, at number 21.* ◇ *room No. 347* **5** [C] (**ARTS AND MEDIA**) a copy of a magazine, newspaper, etc.: *Back numbers of 'New Scientist' are available from the publishers.* **6** [C] (*informal*) a song or dance
IDM any number of very many: *There could be any number of reasons why she hasn't arrived yet.*
in round figures/numbers → ROUND[1]
opposite number → OPPOSITE

number[2] /'nʌmbə(r)/ ***verb*** [T] **1** to give a number to sth: *The houses are numbered from 1 to 52.* **2** used for saying how many people or things there are: *Our forces number 40000.*

'number plate (*AmE* **license plate**) ***noun*** [C] the sign on the front and back of a vehicle that shows a particular combination of numbers and letters (**the registration number**)

numeracy /'nju:mərəsi/ ***noun*** [U] (**MATHEMATICS**) a good basic knowledge of mathematics; the ability to work with and understand numbers: *standards of literacy and numeracy*

numeral /'nju:mərəl/ ***noun*** [C] (**MATHEMATICS**) a sign or symbol that represents a quantity: *Roman numerals* (=I, II, III, IV, etc.)

numerate /'nju:mərət/ ***adj.*** (**EDUCATION**) having a good basic knowledge of mathematics ➲ look at **literate**

numerator /'nju:məreɪtə(r)/ ***noun*** [C] (**MATHEMATICS**) the number above the line in a FRACTION, for example the 3 in ¾
➲ look at **denominator**

numerical /nju:'merɪkl/ ***adj.*** of or shown by numbers: *to put sth **in numerical order***

numerous /'nju:mərəs/ ***adj.*** (*formal*) existing in large numbers; many

nun /nʌn/ ***noun*** [C] (**RELIGION**) a member of a religious group of women who live together in a special building (**a convent**) away from other people ➲ look at **monk**

nurse[1] **🔑** /nɜ:s/ ***noun*** [C] (**HEALTH**) a person who is trained to look after sick or injured people: *a male nurse* ◇ *a psychiatric nurse* (=one who works in a hospital for people with mental illnesses) ◇ *a qualified/registered nurse*

nurse[2] /nɜ:s/ ***verb*** **1** [T] (**HEALTH**) to take care of sb who is sick or injured: *She nursed her mother back to health.* **2** [T] (**HEALTH**) to have an injury: *Ahmed is still nursing a back injury.* **3** [T] to hold sb/sth in a loving way: *He nursed the child in his arms.* **4** [T] (*formal*) to have a strong feeling or idea in your mind for a long time: *Tim had long nursed the hope that Sharon would marry him.* **5** [I,T] to feed a baby or young animal with milk from the breast; to drink milk from the mother's breast

nursery /'nɜ:səri/ ***noun*** [C] (*pl.* **nurseries**) **1** a place where small children and babies are looked after so that their parents can go to work ➲ look at **crèche**
2 (**AGRICULTURE**) a place where young plants are grown and sold

'nursery rhyme ***noun*** [C] a traditional poem or song for young children

'nursery school (*also* **playgroup**; **playschool**) ***noun*** [C] (**EDUCATION**) a school for children aged from three to five ➲ look at **kindergarten**

nursing /'nɜ:sɪŋ/ ***noun*** [U] (**HEALTH**) the job of being a nurse

'nursing home ***noun*** [C] (**HEALTH**) a small private hospital, often for old people

nurture[1] /'nɜ:tʃə(r)/ ***verb*** [T] **1** to look after and protect sb/sth while they or it are growing and developing **2** to encourage sth to develop and to help it succeed: *This is a talent which should be nurtured.*

nurture² /'nɜːtʃə(r)/ ***noun*** [U] care, encouragement and support for sb/sth while they or it are growing and developing

nut ⊶ /nʌt/ ***noun*** [C] **1** a dry fruit that consists of a hard shell with a seed inside. Many types of nut can be eaten **2** a small piece of metal with a round hole in the middle through which you screw a BOLT (= a long round piece of metal) to fasten things together ➲ picture at **bolt**

nutcrackers /'nʌtkrækəz/ ***noun*** [pl.] a tool that you use for breaking open the shell of a nut

nutmeg /'nʌtmeg/ ***noun*** [C,U] a type of hard seed that is often made into powder and used as a spice in cooking

nutrient /'njuːtriənt/ ***noun*** [C] (BIOLOGY) a substance that is needed to keep a living thing alive and to help it grow: *Plants get minerals and other nutrients from the soil.*

nutrition /nju'trɪʃn/ ***noun*** [U] (HEALTH) the food that you eat and the way that it affects your health ▶ **nutritional** /-ʃənl/ ***adj.***

nutritionist /nju'trɪʃənɪst/ ***noun*** [C] a person who is an expert on the relationship between food and health ➲ look at **dietitian**

nutritious /nju'trɪʃəs/ ***adj.*** (used about food) very good for you

nuts /nʌts/ ***adj.*** (*informal*) (not *before* a noun) crazy: *She's driving me nuts with her stupid questions.*

nutshell /'nʌtʃel/ ***noun***
IDM **in a nutshell** using few words

nutty /'nʌti/ ***adj.*** containing or tasting of nuts

nuzzle /'nʌzl/ ***verb*** [I,T] to press or rub sb/sth gently with the nose

NVQ /ˌen viː 'kjuː/ ***noun*** [C] (EDUCATION) **National Vocational Qualification**; a British qualification that shows that you have reached a particular standard in the work that you do

NW ***abbr.*** (GEOGRAPHY) north-west(ern): *NW Australia*

nylon /'naɪlɒn/ ***noun*** [U] a very strong MAN-MADE material that is used for making clothes, rope, BRUSHES, etc.

nymph /nɪmf/ ***noun*** [C] (LITERATURE) (in Greek and Roman stories) a spirit in the form of a young woman that lives in rivers, woods, etc.

O o

O, o /əʊ/ ***noun*** [C,U] (*pl.* **O's**; **o's** /əʊz/) **1** the fifteenth letter of the English alphabet: *'Orange' begins with (an) 'O'.* **2** (spoken) zero: *My number is five O nine double four* (= 50944). ➲ note at **zero**

oak /əʊk/ ***noun*** **1** (*also* **'oak tree**) [C] a type of large tree with hard wood that is common in many northern parts of the world ❶ The fruit of the **oak** is an **acorn**. **2** [U] the wood from the **oak** tree: *a solid oak table*

OAP /ˌəʊ eɪ 'piː/ ***abbr.*** (*BrE*) old-age pensioner

oar /ɔː(r)/ ***noun*** [C] a long pole with a flat end that you use for ROWING (= moving a small boat through water) ➲ look at **paddle**

oasis /əʊ'eɪsɪs/ ***noun*** [C] (*pl.* **oases** /-siːz/) (GEOGRAPHY) a place in the desert where there is water and where plants grow

oath /əʊθ/ ***noun*** [C] **1** a formal promise: *They have to **swear**/**take an oath** of loyalty.* **2** (*old-fashioned*) = SWEAR WORD
IDM **be on/under oath** to have made a formal promise to tell the truth in a court of law

oatmeal /'əʊtmiːl/ ***noun*** [U] **1** flour made from OATS that is used to make biscuits, cakes, etc. **2** a pale brown colour

oats /əʊts/ ***noun*** [pl.] a type of grain that is used as food for people and animals ➲ picture at **cereal**

obbligato /ˌɒblɪ'gɑːtəʊ/ ***noun*** [C] (*pl.* **-os**) (MUSIC) an important part for an instrument in a piece of music which cannot be left out

OBE /ˌəʊ biː 'iː/ ***noun*** [C] **Officer of the Order of the British Empire**; an honour given to some people in Britain because they have achieved something special

obedient /ə'biːdiənt/ ***adj.*** ~ **(to sb/sth)** doing what you are told to do: *As a child he was always obedient to his parents.* OPP **disobedient** ▶ **obedience** ***noun*** [U] ▶ **obediently** ***adv.***

obelisk /'ɒbəlɪsk/ ***noun*** [C] a tall pointed stone column with four sides, put up in memory of a person or an event

obelisk

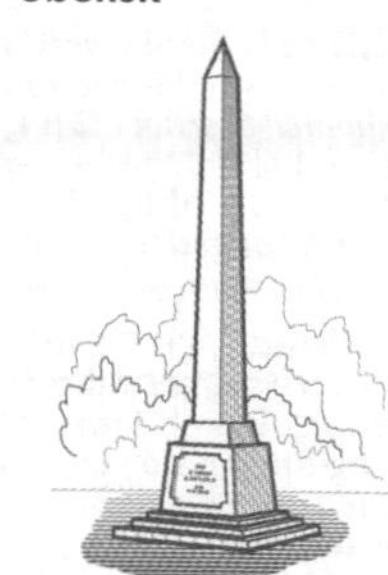

obese /əʊ'biːs/ ***adj.*** (HEALTH) (used about people) very fat, in a way that is not healthy ▶ **obesity** /əʊ'biːsəti/ ***noun*** [U]

obey ⊶ /ə'beɪ/ ***verb*** [I,T] to do what you are told to do: *Soldiers are trained to obey orders.* OPP **disobey**

obituary /ə'bɪtʃuəri/ ***noun*** [C] (*pl.* **obituaries**) a piece of writing about a person's life that is printed in a newspaper soon after they have died

object¹ ⊶ /'ɒbdʒɪkt/ ***noun*** [C] **1** a thing that can be seen and touched, but is not alive: *The shelves were filled with objects of all shapes and sizes.* ◇ *everyday/household objects* **2** an aim or a purpose: *Making money is his sole object in life.* ➲ note at **target¹** **3 the ~ of sth** (*written*) a person or thing that causes a feeling, interest, thought, etc.: *the object of his desire/affections/interest* **4** (LANGUAGE) the noun or phrase describing the person or thing that is affected by the action of a verb ➲ look at **subject**
IDM **money, etc. is no object** money, etc. is not important or is no problem: *They always want the best. Expense is no object.*

object² /əb'dʒekt/ ***verb*** **1** [I] ~ **(to sb/sth)**; ~ **(to doing sth/to sb doing sth)** to not like or to be against sb/sth: *Many people object to the new tax.* ◇ *I object to companies trying to sell me things over the phone.* **2** [T] to say a reason why you think sth is wrong: *'I think that's unfair,' he objected.* ▶ **objector** ***noun*** [C]

objection /əb'dʒekʃn/ ***noun*** [C] **an ~ (to sb/sth)**; **an ~ (to doing sth/to sb doing sth)** a reason why you do not like or are against sb/sth: *We listed our objections to the proposed new road.* ◇ *I **have no objection** to you using my desk while I'm away.*

objectionable /əb'dʒekʃənəbl/ ***adj.*** very unpleasant

objective¹ 🔑 AW /əb'dʒektɪv/ ***noun*** [C] **1** something that you are trying to achieve; an aim: *Our objective is to finish by the end of the year.* ◇ *to achieve your objective* ➲ note at **target¹** **2** (*also* **ob,jective 'lens**) (SCIENCE) the LENS (=curved piece of glass) that is nearest to the object being looked at in a MICROSCOPE (=an instrument that makes very small objects look bigger) ➲ picture at **microscope**

objective² 🔑 AW /əb'dʒektɪv/ ***adj.*** not influenced by your own personal feelings; considering only facts: *Please try and give an objective report of what happened.* ◇ *It's hard to be objective about your own family.* OPP **subjective** ▶ **objectively** AW ***adv.*** ▶ **objectivity** /,ɒbdʒek'tɪvəti/ ***noun*** [U]

obligation /,ɒblɪ'geɪʃn/ ***noun*** [C,U] **(an) ~ (to sb) (to do sth)** the state of having to do sth because it is a law or duty, or because you have promised: *The shop is* ***under*** *no* ***obligation*** *to give you your money back.* ◇ *We* ***have an obligation*** *to help people who are in need.*

obligatory /ə'blɪgətri/ ***adj.*** (*formal*) that you must do: *It is obligatory to get insurance before you drive a car.* OPP **optional**

oblige /ə'blaɪdʒ/ ***verb*** **1** [T] (usually passive) to force sb to do sth: *Parents are obliged by law to send their children to school.* **2** [I,T] (*formal*) to do what sb asks; to be helpful: *If you ever need any help, I'd be happy to oblige.* ▶ **obliged** ***adj.***: *Thanks for your help. I'm* ***much obliged*** *to you.* ▶ **obliging** ***adj.***: *I asked my neighbour for advice and he was very obliging.*

oblique¹ /ə'bli:k/ ***adj.*** **1** not expressed or done in a direct way SYN **indirect** **2** (used about a line) at an angle; sloping **3** (GEOMETRY) used to describe an angle that is not an angle of 90°: *The extension was built at an oblique angle to the house.*
▶ **obliquely** ***adv.***

oblique² /ə'bli:k/ ***noun*** [C] (*BrE*) =SLASH² (3)

obliterate /ə'blɪtəreɪt/ ***verb*** [T] (*formal*) (often passive) to remove all signs of sth by destroying or covering it completely

oblivion /ə'blɪviən/ ***noun*** [U] **1** a state in which you do not realize what is happening around you, usually because you are unconscious or asleep: *I was in a state of complete oblivion.* **2** the state in which sb/sth has been forgotten and is no longer famous or important: *His work* ***faded into oblivion*** *after his death.*

oblivious /ə'blɪviəs/ ***adj.*** **~ (to/of sb/sth)** not noticing or realizing what is happening around you: *She was completely oblivious of all the trouble she had caused.*

oblong /'ɒblɒŋ/ ***adj.***, ***noun*** [C] (GEOMETRY) (of) a shape with two long sides and two short sides and four angles of 90 degrees (**right angles**) ➲ look at **rectangle**

obnoxious /əb'nɒkʃəs/ ***adj.*** extremely unpleasant, especially in a way that offends people

oboe /'əʊbəʊ/ ***noun*** [C] (MUSIC) a musical instrument made of wood that you play by blowing through it ➲ picture on **page 465**

obscene /əb'si:n/ ***adj.*** **1** connected with sex in a way that most people find disgusting and which causes offence: *obscene books/gestures/language* **2** very large in size or amount in a way that some people find unacceptable: *He earns an obscene amount of money.*

obscenity /əb'senəti/ ***noun*** [C,U] (*pl.* **obscenities**) sexual language or behaviour which shocks people and causes offence: *He shouted a string of obscenities out of the car window.*

obscure¹ /əb'skjʊə(r)/ ***adj.*** **1** not well known: *an obscure Spanish poet* **2** not easy to see or understand: ***For some obscure reason****, he decided to give up his well-paid job, to become a writer.*
▶ **obscurity** /əb'skjʊərəti/ ***noun*** [U]

obscure² /əb'skjʊə(r)/ ***verb*** [T] to make sth difficult to see or understand

observance /əb'zɜ:vəns/ ***noun*** [U, sing.] **~ (of sth)** the practice of obeying or following a law, custom, etc.

observant /əb'zɜ:vənt/ ***adj.*** good at noticing things around you: *An observant passer-by gave the police a full description of the men.*

observation 🔑 /,ɒbzə'veɪʃn/ ***noun*** **1** [U] the act of watching sb/sth carefully, especially to learn sth: *My research involves the observation of animals in their natural surroundings.* ◇ *The patient is being kept* ***under observation****.* **2** [U] the ability to notice things: *Scientists need good* ***powers of observation****.* **3** [C] **an ~ (about/on sth)** something that you say or write about sth: *He began by making a few general observations about the sales figures.* ➲ note at **statement** ▶ **observational** /,ɒbzə'veɪʃənl/ ***adj.***: *observational skills*

observatory /əb'zɜ:vətri/ ***noun*** [C] (*pl.* **observatories**) a building from which scientists can watch the stars, the weather, etc.

observe 🔑 /əb'zɜ:v/ ***verb*** [T] **1** to watch sb/sth carefully, especially to learn more about them or it: *We observed the birds throughout the breeding season.* **2** (*formal*) to see or notice sb/sth: *A man and a woman were observed leaving by the back door.* **3** (*formal*) to make a comment: *'We're late,' she observed.* ➲ note at **comment²** **4** (*formal*) to obey a law, rule, etc.: *to observe the speed limit*

observer /əb'zɜ:və(r)/ ***noun*** [C] **1** a person who watches sb/sth: *According to observers, the plane exploded shortly after take-off.* **2** a person who attends a meeting, lesson, etc. to watch and listen but who does not take part

obsess /əb'ses/ ***verb*** [T] (usually passive) **be obsessed (about/with sb/sth)** to completely fill your mind so that you cannot think of anything else: *He became obsessed with getting his revenge.*

obsession /əb'seʃn/ ***noun*** **~ (with sb/sth)** **1** [U] the state in which you can only think about one person or thing so that you cannot think of anything else: *the tabloid press's obsession with the sordid details of the affair* **2** [C] a person or thing that you think about too much

obsessive /əb'sesɪv/ ***adj.*** thinking too much about one particular person or thing; behaving in a way that shows this: *He's obsessive about not being late.* ◇ *obsessive cleanliness*

obsolescence /,ɒbsə'lesns/ ***noun*** [U] (*formal*) the state of becoming OBSOLETE

obsolete /'ɒbsəli:t/ ***adj.*** no longer used because sth new has been invented

obstacle /'ɒbstəkl/ ***noun*** [C] **an ~ (to sth/doing sth)** something that makes it difficult for you to do sth or go somewhere: *Not speaking a foreign language was a major obstacle to her career.*

'obstacle course ***noun*** [C] **1** a series of objects that COMPETITORS in a race have to climb over, under, through, etc. **2** a series of difficulties that people have to deal with in order to achieve a particular aim **3** (*AmE*) =ASSAULT COURSE

obstetrician /ˌɒbstəˈtrɪʃn/ ***noun*** [C] (HEALTH) a hospital doctor who looks after women who are pregnant

obstetrics /əbˈstetrɪks/ ***noun*** [U] (HEALTH) the area of medicine connected with the birth of children

obstinate /ˈɒbstɪnət/ ***adj.*** refusing to change your opinions, way of behaving, etc. when other people try to persuade you to change: *an obstinate refusal to apologize* SYN **stubborn** ▸ **obstinacy** /ˈɒbstɪnəsi/ ***noun*** [U] ▸ **obstinately** ***adv.***

obstruct /əbˈstrʌkt/ ***verb*** [T] to stop sth from happening or sb/sth from moving either by accident or deliberately: *Could you move on, please? You're obstructing the traffic if you park there.*

obstruction /əbˈstrʌkʃn/ ***noun*** **1** [U] the act of stopping sth from happening or moving **2** [C] a thing that stops sb/sth from moving or doing sth: *This car is **causing an obstruction**.*

obstructive /əbˈstrʌktɪv/ ***adj.*** trying to stop sb/sth from moving or doing sth

obtain 🔑 AW /əbˈteɪn/ ***verb*** [T] (*formal*) to get sth: *to obtain advice/information/permission*

obtainable AW /əbˈteɪnəbl/ ***adj.*** that you can get: *That make of vacuum cleaner is no longer obtainable.*

obtuse /əbˈtjuːs/ ***adj.*** (*formal*) slow to or not wanting to understand sth ▸ **obtuseness** ***noun*** [U]

obˌtuse ˈangle ***noun*** [C] (GEOMETRY) an angle between 90° and 180° ➲ look at **acute angle**, **reflex angle**, **right angle** ➲ picture at **angle**

obvious 🔑 AW /ˈɒbviəs/ ***adj.*** ~ (to sb) easily seen or understood; clear: ***For obvious reasons**, I'd prefer not to give my name.* ◇ *His disappointment was obvious to everyone.* ➲ note at **clear**[1]

obviously 🔑 AW /ˈɒbviəsli/ ***adv.*** **1** used when giving information that you expect other people to know already or agree with: *Obviously, we don't want to spend too much money.* **2** used to say that a particular situation or fact is easy to see or understand: *They're obviously not coming.*

occasion 🔑 /əˈkeɪʒn/ ***noun*** **1** [C] a particular time when sth happens: *I have met Bill on two occasions.* **2** [C] a special event, ceremony, etc.: *Their wedding was a memorable occasion.* **3** [sing.] the suitable or right time (for sth): *I shall tell her what I think if the occasion arises* (= if I get the chance).
IDM **on occasion(s)** sometimes, but not often

occasional /əˈkeɪʒənl/ ***adj.*** done or happening from time to time but not very often: *We have the occasional argument but most of the time we get on.*

occasionally 🔑 /əˈkeɪʒnəli/ ***adv.*** sometimes but not often: *We see each other occasionally.* ◇ *We occasionally meet for a drink after work.*

occlusion /əˈkluːʒn/ ***noun*** **1** [U] (HEALTH) the closing or blocking of a BLOOD VESSEL (= a narrow tube through which blood passes) or an organ of the body **2** [C] (GEOGRAPHY) a process by which, when a band of cold air meets and passes a band of warm air in the atmosphere, the warm air is pushed upwards off the earth's surface

occult /ˈɒkʌlt/ ***adj.*** **1** (only *before* a noun) connected with magic powers and things that cannot be explained by reason or science **2 the occult** /əˈkʌlt/ ***noun*** [sing.] magic powers, ceremonies, etc.

occupancy AW /ˈɒkjəpənsi/ ***noun*** [C] (*formal*) the act of living in or using a building, room, piece of land, etc.: *Prices are based on full occupancy of an apartment.*

occupant AW /ˈɒkjəpənt/ ***noun*** [C] a person who is in a building, car, etc. at a particular time

occupation AW /ˌɒkjuˈpeɪʃn/ ***noun*** **1** [C] (*written*) a job or profession; the way in which you spend your time: *Please state your occupation on the form.* ➲ note at **work**[1] **2** [U] the act of the army of one country taking control of another country; the period of time that this situation lasts: *the Roman occupation of Britain* **3** [U] the act of living in or using a room, building, etc.

occupational AW /ˌɒkjuˈpeɪʃənl/ ***adj.*** (only *before* a noun) connected with your work: *Accidents are an **occupational hazard** (= a risk connected with a particular job) on building sites.*

occupied 🔑 /ˈɒkjupaɪd/ ***adj.*** **1** (not *before* a noun) being used by sb: *Is this seat occupied?* **2** busy doing sth: *Looking after the children keeps me fully occupied.* ➲ look at **preoccupied** **3** (used about a country or a piece of land) under the control of another country

occupier AW /ˈɒkjupaɪə(r)/ ***noun*** [C] (*written*) a person who owns, lives in or uses a house, piece of land, etc.

occupy 🔑 AW /ˈɒkjupaɪ/ ***verb*** [T] (*pres. part.* **occupying**; *3rd person sing. pres.* **occupies**; *pt, pp* **occupied**) **1** to fill a space or period of time: *The large table occupied most of the room.* SYN **take up** **2** (*formal*) to live in or use a house, piece of land, etc. **3** to enter a place in a large group and take control of it, especially by military force: *The capital has been occupied by the rebel army.* **4** ~ **sb/yourself** to keep sb/yourself busy

occur 🔑 AW /əˈkɜː(r)/ ***verb*** [I] (**occurring**; **occurred**) **1** (*formal*) to happen, especially in a way that has not been planned: *The accident occurred late last night.* **2** to exist or be found somewhere: *The virus occurs more frequently in children.* **3** ~ **to sb** (used about an idea or a thought) to come into sb's mind: *It never occurred to John that his wife might be unhappy.*

occurrence AW /əˈkʌrəns/ ***noun*** [C] something that happens or exists

ocean 🔑 /ˈəʊʃn/ ***noun*** (GEOGRAPHY) **1** [U] (*especially AmE*) the mass of salt water that covers most of the surface of the earth: *Two thirds of the earth's surface is covered by ocean.* **2** [C] (also **Ocean**) one of the five main areas into which the water is divided: *the Atlantic/Indian/Pacific Ocean* ➲ look at **sea** ➲ picture at **current**
IDM **a drop in the ocean** → DROP[2]

oceanic /ˌəʊʃiˈænɪk/ ***adj.*** connected with the oceans

oceanography /ˌəʊʃəˈnɒɡrəfi/ ***noun*** [U] the scientific study of the oceans

ˌocean ˈtrench ***noun*** [C] = TRENCH (3)

ochre (*AmE also* **ocher**) /ˈəʊkə(r)/ ***noun*** [U] a pale brownish-yellow colour ▸ **ochre** ***adj.***

o'clock /əˈklɒk/ ***adv.*** used after the numbers one to twelve for saying what the time is: *Lunch is at twelve o'clock.*

Oct. ***abbr.*** October: *13 Oct. 2001*

octa- /ˈɒktə/ ***prefix*** (used in nouns, adjectives and adverbs) eight; having eight: *octagon* ◇ *octagonal*

octagon /ˈɒktəɡən/ ***noun*** [C] (GEOMETRY) a shape that has eight straight sides
▸ **octagonal** /ɒkˈtæɡənl/ ***adj.***

octahedron /ˌɒktəˈhiːdrən; -ˈhed-/ ***noun*** [C] (GEOMETRY) a solid figure with eight flat sides, especially one whose sides are eight equal triangles ➲ picture at **solid**

octane /ˈɒkteɪn/ ***noun*** [U] (CHEMISTRY) a substance in petrol that is used for measuring its quality: *high-octane fuel*

octave /ˈɒktɪv/ ***noun*** [C] (MUSIC) the set of eight musical notes that western music is based on

octet /ɒkˈtet/ ***noun*** [C] (MUSIC) **1** a group of eight singers or musicians **2** [C] a piece of music for eight singers or musicians

octo- /ˈɒktəʊ/ ***prefix*** (used in nouns, adjectives and adverbs) eight; having eight: *octogenarian*

October /ɒkˈtəʊbə(r)/ ***noun*** [U, C] (*abbr.* **Oct.**) the tenth month of the year, coming after September

octopus /ˈɒktəpəs/ ***noun*** [C] (*pl.* **octopuses**) a sea animal with a soft body and eight long arms (**tentacles**) ➲ picture on **page 28**

odd ⊶ AW /ɒd/ ***adj.*** **1** strange; unusual: *There's something odd about him.* ◇ *It's a bit odd that she didn't phone to say she couldn't come.* SYN **peculiar** **2 odd-** (used to form compound adjectives) strange or unusual in the way mentioned: *an odd-sounding name* **3** (only *before* a noun) not regular or fixed; happening sometimes: *He makes the odd mistake, but nothing very serious.* **4** (only *before* a noun) that is left after other similar things have been used: *He made the bookshelves out of a few odd bits of wood.* **5** not with the pair or set it belongs to; not matching: *You're wearing odd socks.* **6** (MATHEMATICS) (used about a number) that cannot be divided by two: *One, three, five and seven are all odd numbers.* OPP **even** **7** (used after a number) a little more than: *'How old do you think he is?' 'Well, he must be thirty-odd, I suppose.'* ▶ **oddness** ***noun*** [U]

IDM **the odd man/one out** one that is different from all the others in a group: *Her brothers and sisters were much older than she was. She was always the odd one out.*

oddity /ˈɒdəti/ ***noun*** (*pl.* **oddities**) [C] a person or thing that is unusual

ˌ**odd ˈjobs** ***noun*** [pl.] small jobs or tasks of various types

oddly ⊶ /ˈɒdli/ ***adv.*** **1** in a strange or unusual way: *She's been behaving very oddly lately.* **2** used to show that sth is surprising: ***Oddly enough****, the most expensive tickets sold fastest.*

oddment /ˈɒdmənt/ ***noun*** [C, usually pl.] (*especially BrE*) a small piece of material, wood, etc. that is left after the rest has been used

odds AW /ɒdz/ ***noun*** [pl.] **the ~ (on/against sth/sb)** the degree to which sth is likely to happen; the PROBABILITY of sth happening: *The odds on him surviving are very slim* (=he will probably die). ◇ *The odds are against you* (=you are not likely to succeed). ◇ *The odds are in your favour* (=you are likely to succeed).

IDM **against (all) the odds** happening although it seemed impossible

be at odds (with sb) (over sth) to disagree with sb about sth

be at odds (with sth) to be different from sth, when the two things should be the same

odds and ends (*BrE, informal*) small things of little value or importance

ode /əʊd/ ***noun*** [C] (LITERATURE) a poem that is written for a special occasion or that speaks to a particular person or thing: *Keats's 'Ode to a Nightingale'*

odious /ˈəʊdiəs/ ***adj.*** (*formal*) extremely unpleasant

odometer /əʊˈdɒmɪtə(r)/ (*AmE*) = MILOMETER

odour (*AmE* **odor**) /ˈəʊdə(r)/ ***noun*** [C] (*formal*) a smell (often an unpleasant one)

odourless (*AmE* **odorless**) /ˈəʊdələs/ ***adj.*** without a smell

odyssey /ˈɒdəsi/ ***noun*** [C, sing.] (*written*) a long journey full of experiences

oedema (*AmE* **edema**) /ɪˈdiːmə/ ***noun*** [U] (HEALTH) a condition in which liquid collects in the spaces inside the body and makes it swell

oesophagus (*AmE* **esophagus**) /iˈsɒfəgəs/ ***noun*** [C, usually sing.] (*formal*) (ANATOMY) the tube through which food passes from your mouth to your stomach SYN **gullet** ➲ picture at **digestive system**

oestrogen (*AmE* **estrogen**) /ˈiːstrədʒən/ ***noun*** [U] (BIOLOGY) the chemical (**hormone**) produced in a woman's body that makes her develop female physical and sexual characteristics and that causes the body to prepare to become pregnant ➲ look at **progesterone**, **testosterone**

of ⊶ /əv *strong form* ɒv/ ***prep.*** **1** belonging to, connected with, or part of sth/sb: *the roof of the house* ◇ *the result of the exam* ◇ *the back of the book* ◇ *the leader of the party* ◇ *a friend of mine* (=one of my friends) **2** made, done or produced by sb: *the poems of Milton* **3** used for saying what sb/sth is or what a thing contains or is made of: *a woman of intelligence* ◇ *the city of Paris* ◇ *a glass of milk* ◇ *a crowd of people* ◇ *It's made of silver.* ◇ *a feeling of anger* **4** showing sb/sth: *a map of York* ◇ *a photograph of my parents* **5** used for showing that sb/sth is part of a larger group: *some of the people* ◇ *three of the houses* **6** used with measurements, directions and expressions of time and age: *a litre of milk* ◇ *the fourth of July* ◇ *a girl of 12* ◇ *an increase of 2.5%* ◇ *five miles north of Leeds* **7** used for indicating the reason for or cause of sth: *He died of pneumonia.* **8** used with some adjectives: *I'm proud of you.* ◇ *She's jealous of her.* **9** used with some verbs: *This perfume smells of roses.* ◇ *Think of a number.* ◇ *It reminds me of you.* **10** used after a noun describing an action to show either who did the action or who it happened to: *the arrival of the president* (=he arrives) ◇ *the murder of the president* (=he is murdered)

off[1] ⊶ /ɒf/ ***adv.***, ***prep.*** **1** down or away from a place or a position on sth: *to fall off a ladder/motorbike/wall* ◇ *We got off the bus.* ◇ *I shouted to him but he just walked off.* ◇ *I **must be off*** (=I must leave here). *It's getting late.* ◇ *When are you off to Spain?* ◇ (*figurative*) *We've got off the subject.* **2** used to say that something has been removed: *She took her coat off.* ◇ *He shook the rain off his umbrella.* **3** joined to and leading away from: *My road is off the Cowley Road.* **4** at some distance from sth: *The Isle of Wight is just off the south coast of England.* ◇ *Christmas is still a long way off* (=it is a long time till then). **5** (used about a machine, a light, etc.) not connected, working or being used: *Please make sure the TV/light/heating is off.* OPP **on** **6** not present at work, school, etc.: *She's **off work/off sick** with a cold.* ◇ *I'm having **a day off*** (=a day's holiday) *next week.* **7** (used about a plan or arrangement) not going to happen; cancelled: *The meeting/wedding/trip is off.* OPP **on** **8** cheaper; less by a certain amount: *cars with £400 off* ◇ *£400 off the price of a car* **9** not eating or using sth: *The baby's off his food.*

IDM **off and on; on and off** sometimes; starting and stopping: *It rained on and off all day.*
off limits that you are not allowed to do; where you are not allowed to go
off the top of your head → TOP[1]
well/badly off having/not having a lot of money

off² /ɒf/ ***adj.*** (not *before* a noun) **1** (used about food or drink) no longer fresh enough to eat or drink: *The milk's off.* **2** (*spoken*) unfriendly: *My neighbour was rather off with me today.*

off- /ɒf/ ***prefix*** (used in nouns, adjectives, verbs and adverbs) not on; away from: *offstage* ◇ *offload*

offal /ˈɒfl/ ***noun*** [U] the heart and other organs of an animal, used as food

ˈoff chance ***noun*** [sing.] a slight possibility: *She popped round **on the off chance** of finding him at home.*

ˈoff day ***noun*** [C] (*informal*) a day when things go badly or you do not work well: *Even the best players have off days occasionally.*

offence (*AmE* offense) /əˈfens/ ***noun*** **1** [C] (*formal*) an ~ **(against sth)** (LAW) a crime; an illegal action: *to commit an offence* ◇ *a criminal/minor/serious/sexual offence* **2** [U] ~ **(to sb/sth)** the act of upsetting or insulting sb: *I didn't mean to **cause** you any **offence**.*
IDM **take offence (at sth)** to feel upset or hurt by sb/sth

offend /əˈfend/ ***verb*** **1** [T] (often passive) to hurt sb's feelings; to upset sb: *I hope they won't be offended if I don't come.* ◇ *He felt offended that she hadn't written for so long.* **2** [I] (LAW) to do sth illegal; to commit a crime

offender /əˈfendə(r)/ ***noun*** [C] **1** (LAW) a person who breaks the law or commits a crime: ***Young offenders** should not be sent to adult prisons.* ◇ *a first offender* (= sb who has committed a crime for the first time) **2** a person or thing that does sth wrong

offensive¹ /əˈfensɪv/ ***adj.*** **1** ~ **(to sb)** unpleasant; insulting: *offensive behaviour/language/remarks* OPP **inoffensive** **2** (*formal*) (only *before* a noun) used for or connected with attacking: *offensive weapons* OPP **defensive** ▸ **offensively** ***adv.***

offensive² /əˈfensɪv/ ***noun*** [C] a military attack
IDM **be on the offensive** to be the first to attack, rather than waiting for others to attack you

offer¹ /ˈɒfə(r)/ ***verb*** **1** [T] ~ **sth (to sb) (for sth)**; ~ **(sb) sth** to ask if sb would like sth or to give sb the chance to have sth: *He offered his seat on the bus to an old lady.* ◇ *I've been offered a job in London.* ◇ *He offered (me) £2000 for the car and I accepted.* **2** [I] ~ **(to do sth)** to say or show that you will do sth for sb if they want: *I don't want to do it but I suppose I'll have to offer.* ◇ *My brother's offered to help me paint the house.* **3** [T] to make sth available or to provide the opportunity for sth: *The job offers plenty of opportunity for travel.*

offer² /ˈɒfə(r)/ ***noun*** [C] **1** an ~ **(of sth)**; an ~ **(to do sth)** a statement offering to do sth or give sth to sb: *She accepted my offer of help.* ◇ *Thank you for your kind offer to help.* ◇ *to **accept/refuse/decline an offer*** **2** an ~ **(of sth) (for sth)** an amount of money that you say you will give for sth: *They've **made an offer** for the house.* ◇ *We've **turned down*** (= refused) ***an offer** of £90 000.* ◇ *The offer has been withdrawn.* **3** a low price for sth in a shop, usually for a short time: *See below for details of our special holiday offer.*
IDM **on offer 1** for sale or available: *The college has a wide range of courses on offer.* **2** (*especially BrE*) for sale at a lower price than usual: *This cheese is on offer until next week.*
or nearest offer; ono → NEAR[1]

offering /ˈɒfərɪŋ/ ***noun*** [C] something that is given or produced for other people to watch, enjoy, etc.

offhand¹ /ˌɒfˈhænd/ ***adj.*** (used about behaviour) not showing any interest in sb/sth in a way that seems rude: *an offhand manner/voice*

offhand² /ˌɒfˈhænd/ ***adv.*** without having time to think; immediately: *I can't tell you what it's worth offhand.*

office /ˈɒfɪs/ ***noun*** **1** [C] a room, set of rooms or a building where people work, usually sitting at desks: *I usually get to the office at about 9 o'clock.* ◇ *The firm's **head office*** (= the main branch of the company) *is in Glasgow.* ◇ *Please phone again during **office hours**.* ❶ In the US doctors and dentists have **offices**. In Britain they have **surgeries**.
2 [C] (often used to form compound nouns) a room or building that is used for a particular purpose, especially for providing a service: *the tax/ticket/tourist office* ➲ look at **booking office**, **box office**, **post office** **3 Office** [sing.] (POLITICS) a government department, including the people who work there and the work they do: *the Foreign/Home Office* **4** [U] (POLITICS) an official position, often as part of a government or other organization: *The Labour party has been **in office** since 1997.*

ˈoffice block ***noun*** [C] (ARCHITECTURE) a large building that contains offices, usually belonging to more than one company

officer /ˈɒfɪsə(r)/ ***noun*** [C] **1** a person who is in a position of authority in the armed forces: *an army/air-force officer* **2** a person who is in a position of authority in the government or a large organization: *a prison/customs/welfare officer* **3** = POLICE OFFICER

official¹ /əˈfɪʃl/ ***adj.*** **1** (only *before* a noun) connected with the position of sb in authority: *official duties/responsibilities* **2** accepted and approved by the government or some other authority: *The scheme has not yet received official approval.* ◇ *The country's official language is Spanish.* **3** that is told to the public, but which may or may not be true: *The official reason for his resignation was that he wanted to spend more time with his family.* OPP **unofficial**

official² /əˈfɪʃl/ ***noun*** [C] a person who has a position of authority: *The reception was attended by MPs and high ranking officials.*

officialdom /əˈfɪʃldəm/ ***noun*** [U] people in authority, especially in government, who seem more interested in following the rules than in being helpful

officially /əˈfɪʃəli/ ***adv.*** **1** done publicly and by sb in a position of authority: *The new school was officially opened last week.* **2** according to a particular set of laws, rules, etc.: *Officially we don't accept children under six, but we'll make an exception in this case.*

officious /əˈfɪʃəs/ ***adj.*** too ready to tell other people what to do and use the power you have to give orders

offing /ˈɒfɪŋ/ ***noun***
IDM **in the offing** (*informal*) likely to appear or happen soon

ˈoff-licence (*AmE* **ˈliquor store**) ***noun*** [C] a shop which sells alcoholic drinks in bottles and cans

offline /ˌɒfˈlaɪn/ ***adj.***, ***adv.*** (COMPUTING) not directly controlled by or connected to a computer or to the Internet

offload /ˌɒfˈləʊd/ ***verb*** [T] (*informal*) **~ sth (on/onto sb)** to give away sth that you do not want to sb else: *It's nice to have someone you can offload your problems onto.*

ˌoff-ˈpeak ***adj.*** (only *before* a noun) ***adv.*** available, used or done at a less popular or busy time: *an off-peak train ticket/bus pass/phone call ◇ It's cheaper to travel off-peak.* ➲ look at **peak**

ˌoff-ˈputting ***adj.*** (*especially BrE*) unpleasant in a way that stops you from liking sb/sth

ˈoff season ***noun*** [U, sing.] (TOURISM) the time of the year that is less busy in business and travel SYN **low season**: *We don't get many tourists in the off season.* OPP **high season** ▶ **ˌoff-ˈseason** ***adj.***, ***adv.***: *off-season prices ◇ We prefer to travel off-season.*

offset[1] AW /ˈɒfset/ ***verb*** [T] (**offsetting**; *pt*, *pp* **offset**) to make the effect of sth less strong or noticeable: *The disadvantages of the scheme are more than offset by the advantages.*

offset[2] /ˈɒfset/ ***adj.*** (only *before* a noun) (TECHNICAL) used to describe a method of printing in which ink is put onto a metal plate, then onto a rubber surface and only then onto the paper

offshoot /ˈɒfʃuːt/ ***noun*** [C] a thing that develops from sth else, especially a small organization that develops from a larger one

offshore /ˌɒfˈʃɔː(r)/ ***adj.*** in the sea but not very far from the land: *an offshore oil rig*

offside ***adj.*** **1** /ˌɒfˈsaɪd/ (SPORT) (used about a player in football) in a position that is not allowed by the rules of the game **2** /ˈɒfsaid/ (*BrE*) (used about a part of a vehicle) on the side that is furthest away from the edge of the road

offspring /ˈɒfsprɪŋ/ ***noun*** [C] (*pl.* **offspring**) (*formal*) a child or children; the young of an animal: *to produce/raise offspring*

ˌoff-ˈwhite ***adj.*** not pure white

OFSTED /ˈɒfsted/ ***abbr.*** (EDUCATION) **the Office for Standards in Education**; the British government department that is responsible for checking that standards in schools are acceptable

often ⊶ /ˈɒfn; ˈɒftən/ ***adv.*** **1** many times; frequently: *We often go swimming at the weekend. ◇ I'm sorry I didn't write very often. ◇* ***How often*** *should you go to the dentist?* **2** in many cases; commonly: *Old houses are often damp.*

IDM **every so often** sometimes; from time to time
more often than not usually

ogre /ˈəʊɡə(r)/ ***noun*** [C] **1** (in children's stories) a very large, cruel and frightening creature that eats people **2** a person who is unpleasant and frightening

oh (*also* **O**) /əʊ/ ***exclamation*** used for reacting to sth that sb has said, for emphasizing what you are saying, or when you are thinking of what to say next: *'I'm a teacher.' 'Oh? Where?' ◇ 'Oh no!' she cried as she began to read the letter.*

ohm /əʊm/ ***noun*** [C] (*symbol* Ω) (PHYSICS) a unit for measuring electrical RESISTANCE (=the fact of not allowing heat or electricity to pass through) ➲ picture at **resistor**

oil ⊶ /ɔɪl/ ***noun*** [U] **1** (CHEMISTRY, GEOLOGY) a thick dark liquid that comes from under the ground and is used as a fuel or to make machines work smoothly **2** (BIOLOGY) a thick liquid that comes from animals or plants and is used in cooking: *cooking/vegetable/sunflower/olive oil* ▶ **oil** ***verb*** [T]

oilfield /ˈɔɪlfiːld/ ***noun*** [C] (GEOLOGY) an area where there is oil under the ground or under the sea

ˈoil painting ***noun*** [C] (ART) a picture that has been painted using paint made with oil

ˈoil rig (*also* **rig**) ***noun*** [C] a large platform in the sea with equipment for getting oil out from under the sea

oilseed rape /ˌɔɪlsiːd ˈreɪp/ =RAPE (3)

ˈoil slick (*also* **slick**) ***noun*** [C] (ENVIRONMENT) an area of oil that floats on the sea, usually after a ship carrying oil has crashed

ˈoil well (*also* **well**) ***noun*** [C] a hole that is made deep in the ground or under the sea in order to obtain oil

oily /ˈɔɪli/ ***adj.*** covered with or containing oil: *oily food ◇ Mechanics always have oily hands.*

ointment /ˈɔɪntmənt/ ***noun*** [C,U] (HEALTH) a smooth substance that you put on sore skin or on an injury to help it get better ➲ picture at **health**

OK[1] (also **okay**) /əʊˈkeɪ/ ***adj.***, ***adv.***, ***exclamation*** (*informal*) **1** all right; good or well enough: *'Did you have a nice day?' 'Well, it was OK, I suppose.' ◇ Is it okay if I come at about 7?* **2** yes; all right: *'Do you want to come with us?' 'OK.'*

OK[2] (also **okay**) /ˌəʊˈkeɪ/ ***noun*** [sing.] agreement or permission: *As soon as my parents* ***give me the OK****, I'll come and stay with you.*

OK[3] (also **okay**) /ˌəʊˈkeɪ/ (*3rd person sing. pres.* **OK's**; *pres. part.* **OK'ing**; *pt*, *pp* **OK'd**) ***verb*** [T] (*informal*) **~ sth (with sb)** to officially agree to something or allow it to happen: *If you need time off, you have to OK it with your boss.*

okra /ˈəʊkrə; ˈɒkrə/ ***noun*** [U] the green seed cases of the **okra** plant, eaten as a vegetable

old ⊶ /əʊld/ ***adj.*** **1** that has existed for a long time; connected with past times: *This house is quite old. ◇ old ideas/traditions ◇ In the old days, people generally had larger families than nowadays.* OPP **new**, **modern** **2** (used about people and animals) having lived a long time: *My mother wasn't very old when she died. ◇ He's only 50 but he looks older. ◇ to* ***get /grow old*** OPP **young** **3** (used with a period of time or with *how*) of a particular age: *That building is 500 years old. ◇ The book is aimed at eight- to ten-year-olds. ◇ How old are you?* **4 the old** ***noun*** [pl.] old people ➲ look at **the elderly**, **the aged** **5** having been used a lot: *I got rid of all my old clothes.* OPP **new** ➲ look at **second-hand** **6** (only *before* a noun) former; previous: *I earn more now than I did in my old job.* **7** (only *before* a noun) known for a long time: *She's a very old friend of mine. We knew each other at school.* **8** (only *before* a noun) (*informal*) used for emphasizing that sth has little importance or value: *I write any old rubbish in my diary.*

IDM **be an old hand (at sth)** to be good at sth because you have done it often before

ˌold ˈage ***noun*** [U] the part of your life when you are old: *He's enjoying life* ***in his old age****.* ➲ look at **youth**

ˌold-age ˈpension ***noun*** [U] money paid by the state to people above a certain age ▶ **ˌold-age ˈpensioner** (*also* **pensioner**) ***noun*** [C] (*abbr.* **OAP**)

ˌold-ˈfashioned ⊶ ***adj.*** **1** usual in the past but not now: *old-fashioned clothes/ideas* **2** (used about people) believing in old ideas, customs, etc.:

My parents are quite old-fashioned about some things. ➲ look at **modern**, **unfashionable**

ˌold ˈmaster ***noun*** [C] (ART) **1** a famous painter, especially of the 13th–17th centuries in Europe **2** a picture painted by an **old master**

ˌOld ˈNorse ***noun*** [U] (LANGUAGE) the language of Norway, Iceland, Denmark and Sweden until the 14th century

the ˌOld ˈTestament ***noun*** [sing.] (RELIGION) the first part of the Bible, which tells the history of the Jewish people. ➲ look at **the New Testament**

ˈO level (*also* **ˈordinary level**) ***noun*** [C,U] (EDUCATION) an exam in a particular subject, at a lower level than A LEVEL, usually taken at the age of 16. In 1988, it was replaced in England and Wales by the GCSE, but it is still taken in some other countries.

olive /ˈɒlɪv/ ***noun*** **1** [C] a small green or black fruit with a bitter taste, used for food and oil: *Fry the onions in a little olive oil.* ➲ look at **virgin olive oil** **2** (*also* **ˌolive ˈgreen**) [U], ***adj.*** (of) a colour between yellow and green

ˌolive ˈoil ***noun*** [U] oil produced from OLIVES, used in cooking and on salad ➲ look at **extra-virgin**

the OˌIympic ˈGames (*also* **the Olympics** /əˈlɪmpɪks/) ***noun*** [pl.] (SPORT) an international sports competition which is organized every four years in a different country: *to win a medal at/in the Olympics* ▶ **Olympic** ***adj.*** (only *before* a noun): *Who holds the Olympic record for the 1500 metres?*

ombudsman /ˈɒmbʊdzmən; -mæn/ ***noun*** [C] (*pl.* **-men** /-mən/) (POLITICS) a government official who deals with complaints made by ordinary people against public organizations

omega /ˈəʊmɪɡə/ ***noun*** [C] the last letter of the Greek alphabet (Ω, ω)

omega-3 fatty-acid /ˌəʊmɪɡə ˌθriː ˌfæti ˈæsɪd/ ***noun*** [C] (SCIENCE, HEALTH) a kind of fat that is found mainly in fish oils and is good for your health

omelette (also **omelet**) /ˈɒmlət/ ***noun*** [C] a dish made of eggs that have been mixed together very fast (**beaten**) and fried

omen /ˈəʊmən/ ***noun*** [C] a sign of sth that will happen in the future: *a good/bad omen for the future*

ominous /ˈɒmɪnəs/ ***adj.*** suggesting that sth bad is going to happen: *Those black clouds look ominous.*

omission /əˈmɪʃn/ ***noun*** [C,U] something that has not been included; the act of not including sb/sth: *There were several omissions on the list of names.*

omit /əˈmɪt/ ***verb*** [T] (**omitting**; **omitted**) **1** to not include sth; to leave sth out: *Several verses of the song can be omitted.* **2** (*formal*) ~ **to do sth** to forget or choose not to do sth

omni- /ˈɒmni/ ***prefix*** (used in nouns, adjectives and adverbs) of all things; in all ways or places: *omnivore*

omniscient /ɒmˈnɪsiənt/ ***adj.*** (*formal*) knowing everything: *The novel has an omniscient narrator.* ▶ **omniscience** /-siəns/ ***noun*** [U]

omnivore /ˈɒmnɪvɔː(r)/ ***noun*** [C] (BIOLOGY) an animal that eats both plants and meat ➲ look at **carnivore**, **herbivore**, **insectivore** ▶ **omnivorous** /ɒmˈnɪvərəs/ ***adj.***: *an omnivorous diet*

on 🔑 /ɒn/ ***adv.***, ***prep.*** **1** (also *formal* **upon**) supported by, fixed to or touching sth, especially a surface: *on the table/ceiling/wall* ◇ *We sat on the beach/grass/floor.* ◇ *She was carrying the baby on her back.* ◇ *Write it down on a piece of paper.* ◇ *The ball hit me on the head.* **2** in a place or position: *on a farm/housing estate/campsite* ◇ *a house on the river/seafront/border* ◇ *I live on the other side of town.* **3** showing direction: *on the right/left* ◇ *on the way to school* **4** used with ways of travelling and types of travel: *on the bus/train/plane* ◇ *We came **on foot*** (=we walked). ◇ *Eddie went past on his bike.* ◇ *to go on a trip/journey/excursion* **5** with expressions of time: *on August 19th* ◇ *on Monday* ◇ *on Christmas Day* ◇ *on your birthday* **6** working; being used: *All the lights were on.* ◇ ***Switch** the television **on**.* OPP **off** **7** wearing sth; carrying sth in your pocket or bag: *What did she **have on**?* ◇ *to **put** your shoes/coat/hat/make-up **on*** ◇ *I've got no money on me.* ◇ *You should carry ID on you at all times.* **8** about sth: *We've got a test on irregular verbs tomorrow.* ◇ *a talk/a book/an article on Japan* **9** happening or arranged to happen: *What's on at the cinema?* ◇ *Is the meeting still on, or has it been cancelled?* **10** using sth; by means of sth: *I was (talking) **on the phone** to Laura.* ◇ *I saw it **on television**.* ◇ *I cut my hand on some glass.* ◇ *Dave spends most evenings **on the Internet**.* **11** showing the thing or person that is affected by an action or is the object of an action: *Divorce can have a bad effect on children.* ◇ *He spends a lot on clothes.* ◇ *Don't waste your time on that.* **12** using drugs or medicine; using a particular kind of food or fuel: *to be on medication/antibiotics/heroin* ◇ *Gorillas live on leaves and fruit.* ◇ *Does this car run on petrol or diesel?* **13** receiving a certain amount of money: *What will you be on* (=how much will you earn) *in your new job?* ◇ *He's been (living) on unemployment benefit since he lost his job.* **14** showing that sth continues: *The man shouted at us but we walked on.* ◇ *The speeches went **on and on** until everyone was bored.* **15** showing the reason for or basis for sth: *She doesn't eat meat **on principle**.* ◇ *The film is **based on** a true story.* **16** compared to: *Sales are up 10% on last year.* **17** immediately; soon after: *He telephoned her on his return from New York.* **18** paid for by sb: *The drinks are on me!*

IDM **from now/then on** starting from this/that time and continuing: *From then on she never smoked another cigarette.*

not on (*informal*) not acceptable: *No, you can't stay out that late. It's just not on.*

off and on; **on and off** → OFF[1]

be/go on at sb → GO[1]

ˌon-ˈboard ***adj.*** (only *before* a noun) on a ship, an aircraft or a vehicle: *an on-board motor*

once 🔑 /wʌns/ ***adv.***, ***conj.*** **1** one time only; on one occasion: *I've only been to France once.* ◇ *once a week/month/year* ◇ *I visit them about once every six months.* **2** at some time in the past; formerly: *This house was once the village school.* **3** as soon as; when: *Once you've practised a bit you'll find that it's quite easy.*

IDM **all at once** all at the same time or suddenly: *People began talking all at once.* ◇ *All at once she got up and left the room.*

at once 1 immediately; now: *Come here at once!* **2** at the same time: *I can't hear if you all speak at once.*

just this once; **(just) for once** on this occasion only: *Just this once, I'll help you with your homework.*

once again; **once more** one more time; another time: *Once again the train was late.* ◇ *Let's listen to that track once more.*

once and for all now and for the last time: *You've got to make a decision once and for all.*

once in a blue moon (*informal*) very rarely; almost never

once in a while sometimes but not often

once upon a time (used at the beginning of a children's story) a long time ago; in the past: *Once upon a time there was a beautiful princess...*

oncology /ɒŋˈkɒlədʒi/ ***noun*** [U] (HEALTH) the scientific study of and treatment of TUMOURS (=cells caused by disease) in the body ▶ **oncologist** /ɒŋˈkɒlədʒɪst/ ***noun*** [C]

oncoming /ˈɒnkʌmɪŋ/ ***adj.*** (only *before* a noun) coming towards you: *oncoming traffic*

one[1] /wʌn/ ***pronoun, det., noun*** [C] **1** 1: *There's only one biscuit left.* ◇ *The journey takes one hour.* ◇ *If you take one from ten it leaves nine.* ➲ look at **first 2** used when you are talking about a time in the past or the future, without actually saying which one: *He came to see me one evening last week.* ◇ *We must go and visit them one day.* **3** used with *the other, another* or *other(s)* to make a contrast: *The twins are so alike that it's hard to tell one from the other.* **4 the one** used for emphasizing that there is only one of sth: *She's the one person I trust.* ◇ *We can't all get in the one car.*

IDM **(all) in one** all together or combined: *It's a phone and fax machine all in one.*

one after another/the other first one, then the next, etc.: *One after another the winners went up to get their prizes.*

one at a time separately; INDIVIDUALLY: *I'll deal with the problems one at a time.*

one by one separately; individually: *One by one, people began to arrive at the meeting.*

one or two a few: *I've borrowed one or two new books from the library.*

one[2] /wʌn/ ***pronoun, noun*** [C] **1** used instead of repeating a noun: *I think I'll have an apple. Would you like one?* **2 ~ of** a member of a group: *He's staying with one of his friends.* ◇ *One of the children is crying.* **3** used after *this, that, which* or after an adjective instead of a noun: *'Which dress do you like?' 'This one.'* ◇ *'Can I borrow some books of yours?' 'Yes. Which ones?'* ◇ *'This coat's a bit small. You need a bigger one.'* ◇ *That idea is a very good one.* **4 the one/the ones** used before a group of words that show which person or thing you are talking about: *My house is the one after the post office.* ◇ *If you find some questions difficult, leave out the ones you don't understand.* **5** (*formal*) used for referring to people in general, including the speaker or writer: *One must be sure of one's facts before criticizing other people.*

ˌone aˈnother ***pronoun*** each other: *We exchanged news with one another.*

ˌone-ˈoff ***noun*** [C], ***adj.*** made or happening only once and not regularly: *a one-off payment/opportunity*

onerous /ˈəʊnərəs/ ***adj.*** (*formal*) difficult and needing a lot of effort

oneself /wʌnˈself/ ***pronoun*** (*formal*) **1** used when the person who does an action is also affected by it: *One can teach oneself to play the piano but it is easier to have lessons.* **2** used to emphasize sth: *One could easily arrange it all oneself.*

IDM **(all) by oneself 1** alone **2** without help

ˌone-ˈsided ***adj.*** **1** (used about an opinion, an argument, etc.) showing only one point of view; not balanced: *Some newspapers give a very one-sided view of politics.* **2** (used about a relationship or a competition) not equal: *The match was very one-sided – we lost 12-1.*

ˌone-ˈstar ***adj.*** (TOURISM) having one star in a system that measures quality. The highest standard is usually represented by four or five stars: *a one-star hotel*

ˌone-to-ˈone ***adj., adv.*** **1** (*also* **ˌone-on-ˈone**) between only two people: *one-to-one English lessons* (=one teacher to one student) **2** (MATHEMATICS) in which each member of one set is associated with one member of another

ˌone-ˈway ***adj.*** (usually before a noun) **1** (used about roads) that you can only drive along in one direction: *a one-way street* **2** (*especially AmE*) (TOURISM) (used about a ticket) that you can use to travel somewhere but not back again: *a one-way ticket* SYN **single** OPP **return**

ongoing AW /ˈɒngəʊɪŋ/ ***adj.*** (only *before* a noun) continuing to exist now: *It's an ongoing problem.*

onion /ˈʌnjən/ ***noun*** [C,U] a white or red vegetable with many layers. **Onions** are often used in cooking and have a strong smell that makes some people cry: *a kilo of onions* ◇ *onion soup*

online /ˌɒnˈlaɪn/ ***adj., adv.*** (COMPUTING) controlled by or connected to a computer or to the Internet: *an online ticket booking system* ◇ *I'm studying French online.*

onlooker /ˈɒnlʊkə(r)/ ***noun*** [C] a person who watches sth happening without taking part in it

only /ˈəʊnli/ ***adj.*** (only *before* a noun) ***adv., conj.*** **1** with no others existing or present: *I was the only woman in the room.* ◇ *This is the only dress we have in your size.* **2** and no one or nothing else; no more than: *She only likes pop music.* ◇ *I've only asked a few friends to the party.* ◇ *It's only one o'clock.* **3** the most suitable or the best: *It's so cold that the only thing to do is to sit by the fire.* **4** (*informal*) except that; but: *The film was very good, only it was a bit too long.*

IDM **if only** → IF

not only...but also both...and: *He not only did the shopping but he also cooked the meal.*

only just 1 not long ago: *I've only just started this job.* **2** almost not; hardly: *We only just had enough money to pay for the meal.*

ˌonly ˈchild ***noun*** [C] a child who has no brothers or sisters

onomatopoeia /ˌɒnəˌmætəˈpiːə/ ***noun*** [U] (LITERATURE) the fact of words containing sounds similar to the noises they describe, for example 'hiss' or 'thud'; the use of words like this in a piece of writing ▶ **onomatopoeic** /-ˈpiːɪk/ ***adj.***

onset /ˈɒnset/ ***noun*** [sing.] **the ~ (of sth)** the beginning (often of sth unpleasant): *the onset of winter/a headache*

onslaught /ˈɒnslɔːt/ ***noun*** [C] **an ~ (on/against sb/sth)** a violent or strong attack: *an onslaught on government policy*

onto (*also* **on to**) /ˈɒntə; *before vowels* ˈɒntu/ ***prep.*** to a position on sth: *The cat jumped onto the sofa.* ◇ *The bottle fell off the table onto the floor.* ◇ *The crowd ran onto the pitch.*

IDM **be onto sb** (*informal*) to have found out about sth illegal that sb is doing: *The police were onto the car thieves.*

be onto sth to have some information, etc. that could lead to an important discovery

onwards /ˈɒnwədz/ (*also* **onward** /ˈɒnwəd/) ***adv.*** **1 from...onwards** continuing from a particular time: *From September onwards it usually begins to get colder.* **2** (*formal*) forward: *The road stretched onwards into the distance.*

ooze /uːz/ ***verb*** [I,T] **~ from/out of sth; ~ (with) sth** to flow slowly out or to allow sth to flow slowly out: *Blood oozed from the cut on his head.* ◇ *The fruit was oozing with juice.* ◇ *The wound was oozing blood.*

op /ɒp/ (*spoken*) =OPERATION (1)

opaque /əʊ'peɪk/ ***adj.*** **1** that you cannot see through: *opaque glass in the door* **2** (*formal*) difficult to understand; not clear **OPP** **transparent**

'op art ***noun*** [U] (ART) a style of modern art that uses patterns and colours in a way that makes the images seem to move as you look at them

OPEC /'əʊpek/ ***abbr.*** Organization of Petroleum Exporting Countries

open[1] /'əʊpən/ ***adj.*** **1** not closed or covered: *Don't leave the door open.* ◇ *an open window* ◇ *I can't get this bottle of wine open.* ◇ *She stared at me with her eyes wide open.* ◇ *The diary was lying open on her desk.* ◇ *The curtains were open so that we could see into the room.* ◇ *His shirt was open at the neck.* **2** ~ (to sb/sth); ~ (for sth) available for people to enter, visit, use, etc.; not closed to the public: *The bank isn't open till 9.30.* ◇ *The new shopping centre will soon be open.* ◇ *The hotel damaged by the bomb is now* ***open for business*** *again.* ◇ *The competition is open to everyone.* ◇ *The gardens are* ***open to the public*** *in the summer.* **OPP** **closed**, **shut** **3** not keeping feelings and thoughts hidden: *Elena doesn't mind talking about her feelings – she's a very open person.* ◇ *He looked at him with open dislike.* **4** (only *before* a noun) (used about an area of land) away from towns and buildings; (used about an area of sea) at a distance from the land: *open country* ◇ *open sea* **5** (not *before* a noun) not finally decided; still being considered: *Let's leave the details open.*

IDM **have/keep an open mind (about/on sth)** to be ready to listen to or consider new ideas and suggestions

in the open air outside: *Somehow, food eaten in the open air tastes much better.*

keep an eye open/out (for sb/sth) → EYE[1]

open to sth willing to receive sth: *I'm always open to suggestions.*

with your eyes open → EYE[1]

with open arms in a friendly way that shows that you are pleased to see sb or have sth: *The unions welcomed the government's decision with open arms.*

open[2] /'əʊpən/ ***verb*** **1** [I,T] to move sth or part of sth so that it is no longer closed; to move so as to be no longer closed: *This window won't open – it's stuck.* ◇ *The parachute failed to open and he was killed.* ◇ *The book opened at the very page I needed.* ◇ *Open the curtains, will you?* ◇ *to open your eyes/hand/mouth* ◇ *to open a bag/letter/box* **OPP** **close**, **shut** **2** [I,T] to make it possible for people to enter a place: *Does that shop open on Sundays?* ◇ *The museum opens at 10.* ◇ *The company are opening two new branches soon.* ◇ *Police finally opened the road six hours after the accident.* **OPP** **close**, **shut** **3** [I,T] to start: *The chairman opened the meeting by welcoming everybody.* ◇ *I'd like to open a bank account.* **OPP** **close** **4** [T] (COMPUTING) to start a program or file so that you can use it on the screen **OPP** close

IDM **open fire (at/on sb/sth)** to start shooting: *He ordered his men to open fire.*

PHR V **open into/onto sth** to lead to another room, area or place: *This door opens onto the garden.*

open out to become wider

open up 1 to talk about what you feel and think **2** to open a door

open (sth) up 1 [T] to become available or to make sth available: *When I left school all sorts of opportunities opened up for me.* **2** (BUSINESS) to start business: *The restaurant opened up last year.*

the open[3] /'əʊpən/ ***noun*** [sing.] outside or in the countryside: *After working in an office I like to be* ***out in the open*** *at weekends.*

IDM **bring sth out into the open; come out into the open** to make sth known publicly; to be known publicly: *I'm glad our secret has come out into the open at last.*

,open-'air ***adj.*** not inside a building: *an open-air swimming pool*

opencast /'əʊpənkɑːst/ ***adj.*** in **opencast** mines, coal is taken out of the ground near the surface

'open day ***noun*** [C] a day when the public can visit a place that they cannot usually go into: *The college is having an open day next month.*

opener /'əʊpnə(r)/ ***noun*** [C] (in compound nouns) a thing that takes the lid, etc. off sth: *a tin-opener* ◇ *a bottle-opener*

opening /'əʊpnɪŋ/ ***noun*** [C] **1** a space or hole that sb/sth can go through: *We were able to get through an opening in the hedge.* **2** the beginning or first part of sth: *The film is famous for its dramatic opening.* **3** a ceremony to celebrate the first time a public building, road, etc. is used: *the opening of the new hospital* **4** a job which is available: *We have an opening for a sales manager at the moment.* **5** a good opportunity: *I'm sure she'll be a great journalist – all she needs is an opening.* ▶ **opening** ***adj.*** (only *before* a noun): *the opening chapter of a book* ◇ *the opening ceremony of the Olympic Games*

,open-'jaw ***adj.*** (TOURISM) allowing sb to fly to one place and fly back from another place

openly /'əʊpənli/ ***adv.*** honestly; not keeping anything secret: *I think you should discuss your feelings openly with each other.*

,open-'minded ***adj.*** ready to consider new ideas and opinions

openness /'əʊpənnəs/ ***noun*** [U] the quality of being honest and ready to talk about your feelings

,open-'plan ***adj.*** (used about a large area indoors) not divided into separate rooms: *an open-plan office*

,open-'source ***adj.*** (COMPUTING) used to describe software for which the original SOURCE CODE is made available to anyone

the ,Open Uni'versity ***noun*** [sing.] (*BrE*) (EDUCATION) a university whose students study mainly at home. Their work is sent to them by post or email and there are special television and radio programmes for them.

opera /'ɒprə/ ***noun*** [C, U] (ARTS AND MEDIA) a dramatic work in which all or most of the words are sung to music; works of this kind performed as entertainment: *an opera by Wagner* ◇ *Do you like opera?* ◇ *a comic opera* ➲ look at **soap opera**

operable /'ɒpərəbl/ ***adj.*** (HEALTH) (used about a disease) that can be cured by a medical operation **OPP** **inoperable**

'opera house ***noun*** [C] (ARCHITECTURE) a theatre where OPERAS are performed

operate /'ɒpəreɪt/ ***verb*** **1** [I,T] to work, or to make sth work: *I don't understand how this machine operates.* ◇ *These switches here operate the central heating.* **2** [I,T] (BUSINESS) to do business; to manage sth: *The firm operates from its central office in Bristol.* **3** [I] to act or to have an effect: *Several factors were operating to our advantage.* **4** [I] ~ (on sb/sth) (for sth) (HEALTH) to cut open a person's body in hospital in order to deal with a part that is damaged, infected, etc.: *The surgeon is going to operate on her in the morning.* ◇ *He was operated on for appendicitis.*

operatic /,ɒpə'rætɪk/ ***adj.*** (ARTS AND MEDIA) connected with OPERA: *operatic music*

'operating system *noun* [C] (COMPUTING) a set of programs that controls the way a computer works and runs other programs

'operating theatre (*also* **theatre**) (*AmE* **'operating room**) *noun* [C] (HEALTH) a room in a hospital where operations are performed

operation ⊶ /ˌɒpəˈreɪʃn/ *noun* **1** [C] (also *spoken* **op**) (HEALTH) the process of cutting open a patient's body in order to deal with a part inside: *He **had an operation** to remove his appendix.* **2** [C] an organized activity that involves many people doing different things: *A rescue operation was mounted to find the missing children.* **3** [C] (BUSINESS) a business or company involving many parts **4** [C] an act performed by a machine, especially a computer **5** [U] the way in which you make sth work: *The operation of these machines is extremely simple.* **6** [C] (MATHEMATICS) a process in which a number or quantity is changed by adding, multiplying, etc.
IDM **be in operation**; **come into operation** to be/start working or having an effect: *The new tax system will come into operation in the spring.*

operational /ˌɒpəˈreɪʃənl/ *adj.* **1** (usually *before* a noun) connected with the way a business, machine, system, etc. works **2** (not usually *before* a noun) ready for use: *The new factory is now fully operational.* **3** (only *before* a noun) connected with military operations

operative /ˈɒpərətɪv/ *adj.* (*formal*) **1** working, able to be used; in use: *The new law will be operative from 1 May.* **2** (HEALTH) connected with a medical operation

operator /ˈɒpəreɪtə(r)/ *noun* [C] **1** a person whose job is to work a particular machine or piece of equipment: *a computer operator* **2** a person whose job is to connect telephone calls, for the public or in a particular building: *Dial 100 for the operator.* ◇ *a switchboard operator* **3** (BUSINESS) a person or company that does certain types of business: *a tour operator*

ophthalmology /ˌɒfθælˈmɒlədʒi/ *noun* [U] (HEALTH) the scientific study of the eye and its diseases

opiate /ˈəʊpiət/ *noun* [C] (HEALTH) a drug containing OPIUM

COLLOCATIONS AND PATTERNS

Giving your opinion

You can **give/state a view/an opinion.**
You will have an opportunity to state your view.
He invited the committee members to give their opinion.

You can **make a suggestion, proposal** or **point.**
I'd like to make a suggestion to the chairman.
He made an interesting point.
Could I make a proposal?

You can **raise an objection, an issue** or **a point.**
The workers raised an objection to longer working hours.
I'm glad you've raised that issue/point.

opinion ⊶ /əˈpɪnjən/ *noun* **1** [C] **an ~ (of sb/sth)**; **an ~ (on/about sth)** what you think about sb/sth: *She asked me for my opinion of her new hairstyle and I told her.* ◇ *He has very strong opinions on almost everything.* ◇ ***In my opinion**, you're making a terrible mistake.* **2** [U] what people in general think about sth: *Public opinion is in favour of a change in the law.*
IDM **be of the opinion that...** (*formal*) to think or believe that... ➲ note at **think**
have a good/high opinion of sb/sth; **have a bad/low/poor opinion of sb/sth** to think that sb/sth is good/bad
a matter of opinion → MATTER[1]

o'pinion poll = POLL[1] (1)

opium /ˈəʊpiəm/ *noun* [U] (HEALTH) a powerful drug that is made from the seeds of a POPPY (= a type of flower)

opp. *abbr.* opposite

opponent ⊶ /əˈpəʊnənt/ *noun* [C] **1** (SPORT) (in sport or competitions) a person who plays against sb: *They are the toughest opponents we've played against.* **2 an ~ (of sth)** a person who disagrees with sb's actions, plans or beliefs and tries to stop or change them: *the President's political opponents*

opportune /ˈɒpətjuːn/ *adj.* (*formal*) **1** (used about a time) suitable for doing sth or for sth to happen: *I waited for an opportune moment to ask him.* **2** done or happening at the right time to be successful: *the opportune visit of the managing director* OPP **inopportune**

opportunism /ˌɒpəˈtjuːnɪzəm/ *noun* [U] the practice of using situations unfairly to get an advantage for yourself without thinking about how your actions will affect other people: *political opportunism*

opportunist /ˌɒpəˈtjuːnɪst/ (*also* **opportunistic**) *adj.* (usually *before* a noun) making use of an opportunity, especially to get an advantage for yourself; not done in a planned way: *an opportunist crime* ▸ **opportunist** *noun* [C]: *80% of burglaries are committed by casual opportunists.*

opportunistic /ˌɒpətjuːˈnɪstɪk/ *adj.* **1** = OPPORTUNIST **2** (only *before* a noun) (HEALTH) harmful to people whose IMMUNE SYSTEM (= the system in your body that produces substances to fight infection) has been made weak by disease or drugs: *an opportunistic infection*

opportunity ⊶ /ˌɒpəˈtjuːnəti/ *noun* [C,U] (*pl.* **opportunities**) **an ~ (for sth/to do sth)** a chance to do sth that you would like to do; a situation or a time in which it is possible to do sth: *There will be plenty of opportunity for asking questions later.* ◇ *I have a **golden opportunity** to go to America now that my sister lives there.* ◇ *When we're finally alone, I'll **take the opportunity** to ask him a few personal questions.* ◇ *I'll give Steve your message if I **get the opportunity**.*

oppose ⊶ /əˈpəʊz/ *verb* [T] to disagree with sb's beliefs, actions or plans and to try to change or stop them: *They opposed the plan to build a new road.*

opposed ⊶ /əˈpəʊzd/ *adj.* **~ to sth** disagreeing with a plan, action, etc.; believing that sth is wrong: *She has always been strongly opposed to experiments on animals.*
IDM **as opposed to** (used to emphasize the difference between two things) rather than; and not: *Your work will be judged by quality, as opposed to quantity.*

opposing ⊶ /əˈpəʊzɪŋ/ *adj.* **1** playing, fighting, working, etc. against each other: *a player from the opposing side* ◇ *It is time for opposing factions to unite and work towards a common goal.* **2** very different from each other

opposite ⊶ /ˈɒpəzɪt/ *adj.*, *adv.*, *prep.* **1** in a position on the other side of sb/sth; facing: *The old town and the new town are on opposite sides of the* river. ◇ *You sit there and I'll sit opposite.* **2** completely different: *I can't walk with you because I'm going in the opposite direction.* ◇ *the opposite sex* (=the other sex) ▶ **opposite** *noun* [C]: *'Hot' is* ***the opposite of*** *'cold'.*

IDM **your opposite number** a person who does the same job or has the same position as you in a different company, organization, team, etc.: *The Prime Minister met his Italian opposite number.*

opposition 🔑 /ˌɒpəˈzɪʃn/ *noun* [U] **1** ~ **(to sb/sth)** the feeling of disagreeing with sth and the action of trying to change it: *He expressed strong opposition to the plan.* **2 the opposition** [sing.] the person or team who you compete against in sport, business, etc.: *We need to find out what the opposition is doing.* **3 the Opposition** [sing.] (POLITICS) the politicians or the political parties that are in Parliament but not in the government: *the leader of the Opposition* ◇ *Opposition MPs* ℹ In numbers **2** and **3**, **opposition** can be used with either a singular or a plural verb.

oppress /əˈpres/ *verb* [T] (usually passive) to treat a group of people in a cruel and unfair way by not allowing them the same freedom and rights as others ▶ **oppressed** *adj.*: *an oppressed minority* ▶ **oppression** *noun* [U]: *a struggle against oppression*

oppressive /əˈpresɪv/ *adj.* **1** allowing no freedom; controlling by force **2** (used especially about heat or the atmosphere) causing you to feel very uncomfortable

opt /ɒpt/ *verb* [I] ~ **to do sth/for sth** to choose or decide to do or have sth after thinking about it

PHRV **opt out (of sth)** to choose not to take part in sth; to decide to stop being involved in sth

optic /ˈɒptɪk/ *adj.* (ANATOMY) connected with the eye or the sense of sight: *the* ***optic nerve*** (=from the eye to the brain) ➲ picture at **eye**

optical /ˈɒptɪkl/ *adj.* (BIOLOGY) connected with the sense of sight: *optical effects*

ˌ**optical ilˈlusion** *noun* [C] an image that tricks the eye and makes you think you can see sth that you cannot see

optician /ɒpˈtɪʃn/ *noun* [C] a person whose job is to test eyes, sell glasses, etc.: *I have to go to the optician's* (=the shop) *for an eye test.*

optics /ˈɒptɪks/ *noun* [U] (SCIENCE) the scientific study of sight and light

optimal /ˈɒptɪməl/ = OPTIMUM (1)

optimism /ˈɒptɪmɪzəm/ *noun* [U] the feeling that the future will be good or successful: *There is considerable optimism that the economy will improve.* OPP **pessimism** ▶ **optimist** *noun* [C] OPP **pessimist**

optimistic /ˌɒptɪˈmɪstɪk/ *adj.* ~ **(about sth/that...)** expecting good things to happen or sth to be successful; showing this feeling: *I've applied for the job but I'm not very optimistic that I'll get it.* OPP **pessimistic** ▶ **optimistically** /-kli/ *adv.* OPP **pessimistically**

optimum /ˈɒptɪməm/ *adj.* (only *before* a noun) **1** (*also* **optimal**) the best possible; giving the best possible results **2 the optimum** *noun* [sing.] the best possible result or the best set of conditions to get good results

option 🔑 AW /ˈɒpʃn/ *noun* **1** [U, C] something that you can choose to do; the freedom to choose: *She looked carefully at all the options before deciding on a career.* ◇ *Students* ***have the option*** *of studying part-time or full-time.* ◇ *If you're late again, you will give us* ***no option but to*** *dismiss you.* SYN **choice 2** [C] (EDUCATION) a subject that a student can choose to study, but that they do not have to do: *The course offers options in design and computing.* **3** [C] ~ **(on sth)**; ~ **(to do sth)** (BUSINESS) the right to buy or sell sth at some time in the future: *We have an option on the house.* ◇ *share options* (=the right to buy shares in a company) **4** [C] (COMPUTING) one of the choices you can make when using a computer program: *Choose the 'Cut' option from the Edit menu.*

optional AW /ˈɒpʃənl/ *adj.* that you can choose or not choose: *an optional subject at school* OPP **compulsory, obligatory**

or 🔑 /ɔː(r)/ *conj.* **1** used in a list of possibilities or choices: *Would you like to sit here or next to the window?* ◇ *Are you interested or not?* ◇ *For the main course, you can have lamb, beef or fish.* ➲ look at **either...or 2** if not; otherwise: *Don't drive so fast or you'll have an accident!* **3** (after a negative) and neither; and not: *She hasn't phoned or written to me for weeks.* ◇ *I've never been either to Italy or Spain.* ➲ look at **neither...nor 4** used between two numbers to show approximately how many: *I've been there five or six times.* **5** used before a word or phrase that explains or comments on what has been said before: *20% of the population, or one in five*

IDM **or else** → ELSE

or so about: *You should feel better in three days or so.*

or something/somewhere (*spoken*) used for showing that you are not sure, cannot remember or do not know which thing or place: *She's a computer programmer or something.*

oracle /ˈɒrəkl/ *noun* [C] **1** (HISTORY) (in ancient Greece) a place where people could go to ask the gods for advice and information about the future; the priest through whom the gods were thought to give their message: *They consulted the oracle at Delphi.* **2** (HISTORY) (in ancient Greece) the advice or information that the gods gave, which often had a hidden meaning **3** [usually sing.] a person or book that gives valuable advice or information: *My sister's the oracle on financial matters.*

oral[1] /ˈɔːrəl/ *adj.* **1** spoken, not written: *an oral test* **2** concerning or using the mouth: *oral hygiene* ➲ look at **aural** ▶ **orally** *adv.*: *You can ask the questions orally or in writing.* ◇ *This medicine is taken orally* (=is swallowed).

oral[2] /ˈɔːrəl/ *noun* [C] (EDUCATION) a spoken exam: *I've got my German oral next week.*

orange[1] 🔑 /ˈɒrɪndʒ/ *noun* **1** [C,U] (*BrE*) a round fruit with a thick skin that is divided into sections (**segments**) inside and is a colour between red and yellow: *orange juice/peel* ◇ *an orange tree* **2** [U, C] a drink made from oranges or with the taste of oranges; a glass of this drink **3** [U, C] the colour of this fruit, between red and yellow

orange[2] 🔑 /ˈɒrɪndʒ/ *adj.* of the colour orange: *orange paint*

ˌ**orange ˈsquash** *noun* [C,U] (*BrE*) a drink made by adding water to an orange-flavoured liquid

orang-utan /ɔːˌræŋuːˈtæn/ *noun* [C] a large APE (=an animal like a large monkey with no tail) with long arms and reddish hair, that lives in Borneo and Sumatra

orator /ˈɒrətə(r)/ *noun* [C] (*formal*) a person who is good at making public speeches

oratorio /ˌɒrəˈtɔːriəʊ/ *noun* [C] (*pl.* **oratorios**) (MUSIC) a long piece of music for singers and an ORCHESTRA, usually based on a religious story

orbit /ˈɔːbɪt/ ***noun*** [C,U] (**ASTRONOMY**) a curved path taken by a planet or another object as it moves around another planet, star, moon, etc. ➲ picture at **season** ▶ **orbit** *verb* [I,T]

orbital /ˈɔːbɪtl/ ***adj.*** **1** (used about a road) built around the outside of a city or town to reduce the amount of traffic travelling through the centre **2** (**ASTRONOMY**) connected with the ORBIT of a planet or another object in space ▶ **orbital** ***noun*** [C, usually sing.]

orbiter /ˈɔːbɪtə(r)/ ***noun*** [C] (**ASTRONOMY**) a SPACECRAFT designed to move around a planet or moon rather than to land on it

orchard /ˈɔːtʃəd/ ***noun*** [C] (**AGRICULTURE**) a piece of land on which fruit trees are grown: *a cherry orchard*

orchestra /ˈɔːkɪstrə/ ***noun*** [C] (**MUSIC**) a large group of musicians who play different musical instruments together, led by a CONDUCTOR: *a symphony orchestra* ▶ **orchestral** /ɔːˈkestrəl/ ***adj.***

ˈ**orchestra pit** (*also* **pit**) ***noun*** [C] (**ARTS AND MEDIA**) the place in a theatre just in front of the stage where the ORCHESTRA sits and plays for an OPERA, a BALLET, etc.

orchestration /ˌɔːkrˈstreɪʃn/ ***noun*** [U] **1** (**MUSIC**) the way that a piece of music is written so that an ORCHESTRA can play it **2** (*written*) the careful organization of a complicated plan or event, done secretly

orchid /ˈɔːkɪd/ ***noun*** [C] a plant with brightly coloured flowers of unusual shapes. There are many different types of **orchid** and some of them are very rare.

ordain /ɔːˈdeɪn/ ***verb*** [T] (usually passive) **~ sb (as) (sth)** (**RELIGION**) to make sb a priest of the Church: *He was ordained (as) a priest last year.* ➲ noun **ordination**

ordeal /ɔːˈdiːl; ˈɔːdiːl/ ***noun*** [C, usually sing.] a very unpleasant or difficult experience

order[1] 🔑 /ˈɔːdə(r)/ ***noun*** **1** [U, C] the way in which people or things are arranged in relation to each other: *a list of names in* ***alphabetical order*** ◇ *Try to put the things you have to do* ***in order of importance.*** ◇ *What's the order of events today?* **2** [U] an organized state, where everything is in its right place: *I really must* ***put*** *my notes* ***in order***, *because I can never find what I'm looking for.* OPP **disorder** **3** [C] **an ~ (for sb) (to do sth)** sth that you are told to do by sb in a position of authority: *In the army, you have to* ***obey orders*** *at all times.* ◇ *She* ***gave the order*** *for the work to be started.* **4** [U] the situation in which laws, rules, authority, etc. are obeyed: *Following last week's riots, order has now been restored.* ➲ look at **disorder** **5** [C,U] **an ~ (for sth)** a request asking for sth to be made, supplied or sent: *The company has just received a major export order.* ◇ *The book I need is* ***on order*** (= they are waiting for it to arrive). **6** [C] a request for food or drinks in a hotel, restaurant, etc.; the food or drinks you asked for: *Can I* ***take your order*** *now, sir?* **7** [C] (**BIOLOGY**) a group into which animals, plants, etc. that have similar characteristics are divided, smaller than a CLASS and larger than a FAMILY: *the order of primates* ➲ picture on **page 29**

IDM **in order to do sth** with the purpose or intention of doing sth; so that sth can be done: *We left early in order to avoid the traffic.*

in/into reverse order → REVERSE[3]

in working order (used about machines, etc.) working properly, not broken

law and order → LAW

out of order 1 (used about a machine, etc.) not working properly or not working at all: *I had to walk up to the tenth floor because the lift was out of order.* **2** (*informal*) (used about a person's behaviour) unacceptable, because it is rude, etc.: *That comment was completely out of order!*

order[2] 🔑 /ˈɔːdə(r)/ ***verb*** **1** [T] **~ sb (to do sth)** to use your position of authority to tell sb to do sth or to say that sth must happen: *I'm not asking you to do your homework, I'm ordering you!* ◇ *The company was ordered to pay compensation to its former employees.* **2** [T] to ask for sth to be made, supplied or sent somewhere: *The shop didn't have the book I wanted so I ordered it.* **3** [I,T] **~ (sb) (sth); ~ (sth) (for sb)** (**TOURISM**) to ask for food or drinks in a restaurant, hotel, etc.: *Are you ready to order yet,*

orchestra

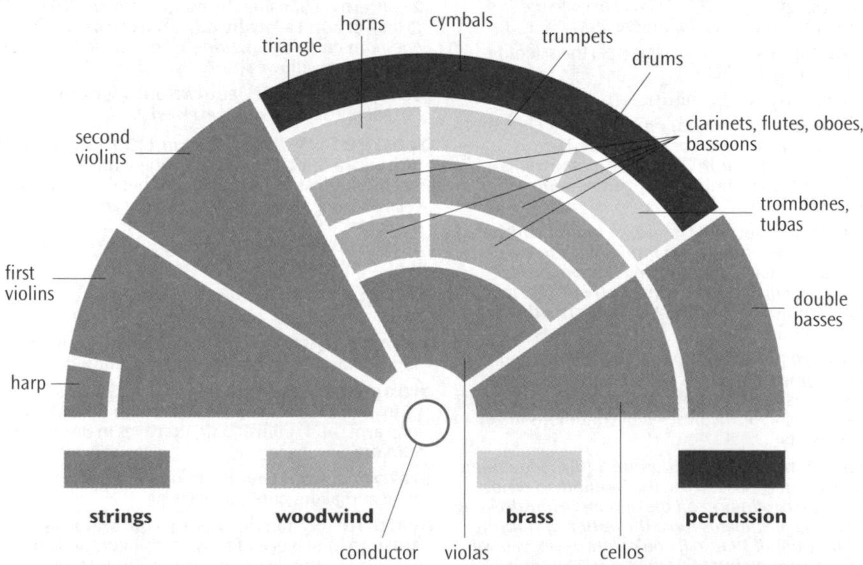

madam? ◇ *Can you order me a sandwich while I make a phone call?* ◇ *Could you order a sandwich for me?*
PHR V **order sb about/around** to keep telling sb what to do and how to do it: *Stop ordering me about! You're not my father.*

orderly[1] /'ɔːdəli/ ***adj.*** **1** arranged or organized in a tidy way: *an orderly office/desk* **2** well behaved; peaceful OPP **disorderly**

orderly[2] /'ɔːdəli/ ***noun*** [C] (*pl.* **orderlies**) (HEALTH) a worker in a hospital, usually doing jobs that do not need special training

ordinal /'ɔːdɪnl/ (*also* **ˌordinal 'number**) ***noun*** [C] (MATHEMATICS) a number that shows the order or position of sth in a series: *'First', 'second', and 'third' are ordinals.* ➲ look at **cardinal**

ordinarily /'ɔːdnrəli/ ***adv.*** usually; generally: *Ordinarily, I don't work as late as this.*

ordinary 🔑 /'ɔːdnri/ ***adj.*** normal; not unusual or different from others: *It's interesting to see how ordinary people live in other countries.*
IDM **out of the ordinary** unusual; different from normal

ordination /ˌɔːdɪ'neɪʃn/ ***noun*** [U, C] (RELIGION) the act or ceremony of making sb a priest of the Church ➲ verb **ordain**

ore /ɔː(r)/ ***noun*** [C,U] (GEOLOGY) rock or earth from which metal can be taken: *iron ore*

oregano /ˌɒrɪ'gɑːnəʊ/ ***noun*** [U] a plant with leaves that have a sweet smell and are used in cooking as a HERB

organ 🔑 /'ɔːgən/ ***noun*** [C] **1** (BIOLOGY, ANATOMY) one of the parts inside your body that have a particular function: ***vital organs*** (=those such as the heart and liver which help to keep you alive) ◇ *sexual/reproductive organs* ➲ picture on **page 465** **2** (MUSIC) a large musical instrument like a piano with pipes through which air is forced. Organs are often found in churches: *organ music*
▸ **organist** ***noun*** [C]

organic /ɔː'gænɪk/ ***adj.*** **1** (AGRICULTURE) (used about food or farming methods) produced by or using natural materials, without artificial chemicals: *organic vegetables* ◇ *organic farming* **2** (BIOLOGY) produced by or existing in living things: *organic compounds/molecules* OPP **inorganic** ▸ **organically** /-kli/ ***adv.***: *organically grown/produced*

orˌganic 'chemistry ***noun*** [U] (CHEMISTRY) the branch of chemistry that deals with substances that contain CARBON ➲ look at **inorganic chemistry**

organism /'ɔːgənɪzəm/ ***noun*** [C] (BIOLOGY) a living thing, especially one that is so small that you can only see it with a special instrument (**microscope**)

COLLOCATIONS AND PATTERNS

Organizations

You can **create, establish, form, found, set up** or **start** an organization.
an association created to promote local industry
The company was founded in 1991.

You can **dissolve a company** or **partnership.**
a court order to have the partnership dissolved

You can **run/manage a firm, company, etc.**
He runs an accountancy firm.
The executive committee manages the group on a day-to-day basis.

You can **join** or **be/become a member of** a society or an organization.
She became a member of the Society of Arts.
She joined Greenpeace in 2006.

organization 🔑 (also -isation) /ˌɔːgənaɪ'zeɪʃn/ ***noun*** **1** [C] a group of people who form a business, club, etc. together in order to achieve a particular aim: *She works for a voluntary organization helping homeless people.* **2** [U] the activity of making preparations or arrangements for sth: *An enormous amount of organization went into the festival.* **3** [U] the way in which sth is organized, arranged or prepared OPP **disorganization**
▸ **organizational** (also -isational) /-ʃənl/ ***adj.***: *The job requires a high level of organizational ability.*

organize 🔑 (also -ise) /'ɔːgənaɪz/ ***verb*** **1** [T] to plan or arrange an event, activity, etc.: *The school organizes trips to various places of interest.* **2** [I,T] to put or arrange things into a system or logical order: *Can you decide what needs doing? I'm hopeless at organizing.* ◇ *You need to organize your work more carefully.* ▸ **organizer** (also -iser) ***noun*** [C]: *The organizers of the concert said that it had been a great success.*

organized 🔑 (also -ised) /'ɔːgənaɪzd/ ***adj.*** **1** arranged or planned in the way mentioned: *a carefully/badly/well organized trip* OPP **disorganized** **2** (used about a person) able to plan your work, life, etc. well: *I wish I were as organized as you!* OPP **disorganized** **3** (only *before* a noun) involving a large number of people working together to do sth in a way that has been carefully planned: *an organized campaign against cruelty to animals* ◇ *organized crime* (=done by a large group of professional criminals)

orgasm /'ɔːgæzəm/ ***noun*** [U, C] the point of greatest sexual pleasure: *to have an orgasm*

orgy /'ɔːdʒi/ ***noun*** [C] (*pl.* **orgies**) **1** a party involving a lot of eating, drinking and sexual activity **2 an ~ (of sth)** a period of doing sth in a wild way, without control: *an orgy of destruction*

the Orient /'ɔːrɪənt/ ***noun*** [sing.] (*formal*) (GEOGRAPHY) the eastern part of the world, especially China and Japan

orient AW /'ɔːrient/ (*BrE also* **orientate** /'ɔːriənteɪt/) ***verb*** [T] **~ yourself** to find out where you are; to become familiar with a place ➲ look at **disorientate**

oriental (*also* **Oriental**) /ˌɔːri'entl/ ***adj.*** (*old-fashioned*) coming from or belonging to the East or Far East: *oriental languages*

orientation AW /ˌɔːriən'teɪʃn/ ***noun*** **1** [U, C] **~ (to/towards sth)** the type of aims or interests that a person or an organization has; the act of directing your aims towards a particular thing **2** [U,C] a person's basic beliefs or feelings about a particular subject: *religious/political orientation* **3** [C] (TECHNICAL) the direction in which an object faces: *The orientation of the planet's orbit is changing continuously.*

oriented AW /'ɔːrientɪd/ (*BrE also* **orientated** /'ɔːrɪənteɪtɪd/) ***adj.*** (only *after* a noun) for or interested in a particular type of person or thing: *Our products are male-oriented.* ◇ *She's very career orientated.*

orienteering /ˌɔːriən'tɪərɪŋ/ ***noun*** [U] (SPORT) a sport in which you find your way across country on foot, using a map and an instrument that shows direction (**a compass**)

orifice /'ɒrɪfɪs/ ***noun*** [C] (*formal*) a hole or opening, especially in the body

origin 🔑 /ˈɒrɪdʒɪn/ ***noun*** [C,U] **1** (often used in the plural) the point from which sth starts; the cause of sth: *This particular tradition* ***has its origins in*** *Wales.* ◇ *Many English words are* ***of*** *Latin* ***origin***. **2** a person's social and family background: *people of African origin* ◇ *children of various ethnic origins*

original¹ 🔑 /əˈrɪdʒənl/ ***adj.*** **1** (only *before* a noun) first; earliest (before any changes or developments): *The original meaning of this word is different from the meaning it has nowadays.* **2** new and interesting; different from others of its type: *There are no original ideas in his work.* **3** made or created first, before copies: *'Is that the original painting?' 'No, it's a copy.'*

original² 🔑 /əˈrɪdʒənl/ ***noun*** [C] the first document, painting, etc. that was made; not a copy: *Could you make a photocopy of my birth certificate and give the original back to me?*

originality /əˌrɪdʒəˈnæləti/ ***noun*** [U] the quality of being new and interesting

originally 🔑 /əˈrɪdʒənəli/ ***adv.*** **1** in the beginning, before any changes or developments: *I'm from London originally, but I left there when I was very young.* **2** in a way or style that is new and different from any others: *She has a talent for expressing simple ideas originally.*

originate /əˈrɪdʒɪneɪt/ ***verb*** [I] (*formal*) to happen or appear for the first time in a particular place or situation

ornament /ˈɔːnəmənt/ ***noun*** [C] an object that you have because it is attractive, not because it is useful. **Ornaments** are used to decorate rooms, etc.

ornamental /ˌɔːnəˈmentl/ ***adj.*** made or put somewhere in order to look attractive, not for any practical use

ornate /ɔːˈneɪt/ ***adj.*** covered with a lot of small complicated designs as decoration

ornithology /ˌɔːnɪˈθɒlədʒi/ ***noun*** [U] (**BIOLOGY**) the study of birds ▸ **ornithologist** /-ɪst/ ***noun*** [C]

orographic /ɒrəˈɡræfɪk/ ***adj.*** (**GEOGRAPHY**) connected with mountains, especially with their position and shape

orphan /ˈɔːfn/ ***noun*** [C] a child whose parents are dead ▸ **orphan** ***verb*** [T] (usually passive): *She was orphaned when she was three and went to live with her grandparents.*

orphanage /ˈɔːfənɪdʒ/ ***noun*** [C] a home for children whose parents are dead

ortho- /ˈɔːθəʊ/ ***prefix*** (used in nouns, adjectives and adverbs) correct; standard: *orthography*

orthodontics /ˌɔːθəˈdɒntɪks/ ***noun*** [U] (**HEALTH**) the treatment of problems concerning the position of the teeth and JAWS (=the two bones in your face that contain your teeth) ▸ **orthodontic** ***adj.***: *orthodontic treatment*

orthodontist /ˌɔːθəˈdɒntɪst/ ***noun*** [C] (**HEALTH**) a dentist who treats problems concerning the position of the teeth and JAWS (=the two bones in your face that contain your teeth)

orthodox /ˈɔːθədɒks/ ***adj.*** **1** that most people believe, do or accept; usual: *orthodox opinions/methods* **OPP** **unorthodox** **2** (**RELIGION**) closely following the old, traditional beliefs, ceremonies, etc.: *an orthodox Jew* ◇ *the Greek Orthodox Church*

orthography /ɔːˈθɒɡrəfi/ ***noun*** [U] (*formal*) (**LANGUAGE**) the system of spelling in a language ▸ **orthographic** /ˌɔːθəˈɡræfɪk/ ***adj.***

orthopaedics (*AmE* **orthopedics**) /ˌɔːθəˈpiːdɪks/ ***noun*** [U] (**HEALTH**) the area of medicine connected with injuries and diseases of the bones or muscles ▸ **orthopaedic** (*AmE* **orthopedic**) ***adj.***

oscillate /ˈɒsɪleɪt/ ***verb*** [I] (*formal*) **(between A and B)** **1** to keep changing from one extreme of feeling or behaviour to another, and back again: *Her moods oscillated between joy and depression.* **2** to keep moving from one position to another and back again: *Watch how the needle oscillates as the current changes.* **3** (**PHYSICS**) (used about electric current, radio waves, etc.) to change in strength or direction at regular times ▸ **oscillation** /ˌɒsɪˈleɪʃn/ ***noun*** [C,U]

oscillator /ˈɒsɪleɪtə(r)/ ***noun*** [C] (**PHYSICS**) a piece of equipment for producing OSCILLATING electric currents

oscilloscope

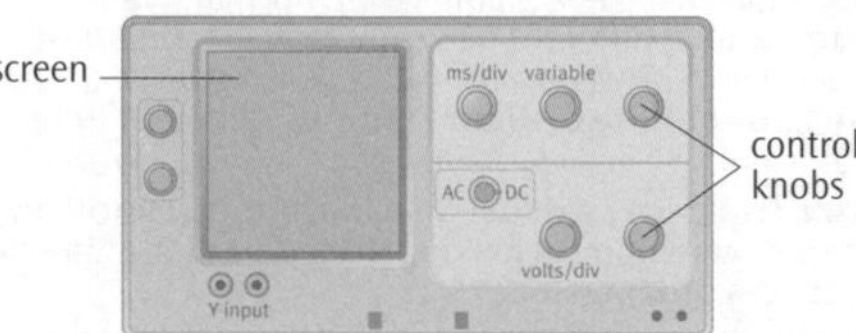

the front of an oscilloscope

oscilloscope /əˈsɪləskəʊp/ ***noun*** [C] (**PHYSICS**) a piece of equipment that shows changes in electrical current as waves in a line on a screen

osmium /ˈɒzmiəm/ ***noun*** [U] (*symbol* **Os**) (**CHEMISTRY**) a chemical element. **Osmium** is a hard silver-white metal. ❶ For more information on the periodic table of elements, look at pages R34-5.

osmosis /ɒzˈməʊsɪs/ ***noun*** [U] (**BIOLOGY, CHEMISTRY**) the gradual passing of a liquid through a thin layer of material (**membrane**): *Water passes into the roots of a plant* ***by osmosis***.

ossicle /ˈɒsɪkl/ ***noun*** [C] (**ANATOMY**) a very small bone in the MIDDLE EAR

ostentatious /ˌɒstenˈteɪʃəs/ ***adj.*** **1** expensive or noticeable in a way that is intended to impress other people: *ostentatious gold jewellery* **2** behaving in a way that is intended to impress people with how rich or important you are ▸ **ostentatiously** ***adv.***

osteo- /ˈɒstiəʊ/ ***prefix*** (used in nouns and adjectives) (**ANATOMY**) connected with bones: *osteopathy*

osteopath /ˈɒstiəpæθ/ ***noun*** [C] (**HEALTH**) a person whose job involves treating some diseases and physical problems by pressing and moving the bones and muscles ➲ look at **chiropractor**

osteoporosis /ˌɒstiəʊpəˈrəʊsɪs/ ***noun*** [U] (**HEALTH**) a medical condition in which the bones become weak and are easily broken

ostracize (also **-ise**) /ˈɒstrəsaɪz/ ***verb*** [T] (*formal*) to refuse to allow sb to be a member of a social group; to refuse to meet or talk to sb

ostrich /ˈɒstrɪtʃ/ ***noun*** [C] a very large African bird with a long neck and long legs, which can run very fast but which cannot fly

other 🔑 /ˈʌðə(r)/ ***det., pronoun*** **1** in addition to or different from the one or ones that have already been mentioned: *I hadn't got any other plans that evening so I accepted their invitation.* ◇ *If you're busy now, I'll come back some other time.* ◇ *I like this jumper but not the colour. Have you got any others?* ◇ *Some of my friends went to university, others didn't.* ◇ *She doesn't care what other people think.* **2** (after *the, my, your, his, her*, etc. with a singular noun) the

second of two people or things, when the first has already been mentioned: *I can only find one sock. Have you seen the other one?* **3** (after *the, my, your, his, her,* etc. with a plural noun) the rest of a group or number of people or things: *Their youngest son still lives with them but their other children have left home.* ◇ *I'll have to wear this shirt because all my others are dirty.* ◇ *Mick and I got a taxi there, the others walked.*
IDM **every other** → EVERY
in other words used for saying sth in a different way: *My boss said she would have to let me go. In other words, she sacked me.*
one after another/the other → ONE[1]
other than (usually after a negative) apart from; except (for): *The plane was a little late, but other than that the journey was fine.*
the other day/morning/week recently, not long ago: *An old friend rang me the other day.*
the other way round → ROUND[2]
sb/sth/somewhere or other → OR

otherwise /ˈʌðəwaɪz/ ***adv., conj.*** **1** (used for stating what will happen if you do not do sth or if sth does not happen) if not: *You have to press the red button, otherwise it won't work.* **2** apart from that: *I'm a bit tired but otherwise I feel fine.* **3** in a different way to the way mentioned; differently

otitis /əʊˈtaɪtɪs/ ***noun*** [U] (**HEALTH**) a painful swelling of the ear, caused by an infection

otter /ˈɒtə(r)/ ***noun*** [C] a river animal with brown fur that eats fish

ouch /aʊtʃ/ ***exclamation*** used when reacting to a sudden feeling of pain

oud /uːd/ ***noun*** [C] (**MUSIC**) a musical instrument similar to a LUTE played mainly in Arab countries

ought to /ˈɔːt tə/ (before vowels and in final position /ˈɔːt tu)/ ***modal verb*** (*negative* **ought not to**; *short form* **oughtn't to** /ˈɔːtnt tə/ (before vowels and in final position /ˈɔːtnt tu)/) **1** used to say what sb should do: *You ought to visit your parents more often.* ◇ *She oughtn't to make private phone calls in work time.* ◇ *He oughtn't to have been driving so fast.* **2** used to say what should happen or what you expect: *She ought to pass her test.* ◇ *They ought to be here by now. They left at six.* ◇ *There ought to be more buses in the rush hour.* **3** used for asking for and giving advice about what to do: *You ought to read this book. It's really interesting.*

ounce /aʊns/ ***noun*** **1** [C] (*abbr.* **oz**) a measure of weight; 28.35 grams. There are 16 **ounces** in a pound: *For this recipe you need four ounces of flour.* **2** [sing.] **an ~ of sth** (usually in negative statements) a very small amount of sth: *He hasn't got an ounce of imagination.*

our /ɑː(r); ˈaʊə(r)/ ***det.*** of or belonging to us: *Our house is at the bottom of the road.* ◇ *This is our first visit to Britain.*

ours /ɑːz; ˈaʊəz/ ***pronoun*** the one or ones belonging to us: *Their garden is quite nice but I prefer ours.*

ourselves /ɑːˈselvz; ˌaʊəˈs-/ ***pronoun*** **1** used when you and another person or other people together cause and are affected by an action: *Let's relax and enjoy ourselves.* ◇ *They asked us to wait so we sat down and made ourselves comfortable.* **2** used to emphasize sth: *Do you think we should paint the flat ourselves?* (= or should we ask sb else to do it for us?)
IDM **(all) by ourselves 1** alone: *Now that we're by ourselves, could I ask you a personal question?* **2** without help: *We managed to move all our furniture into the new flat by ourselves.*

oust /aʊst/ ***verb*** [T] (*written*) **~ sb (from/as sth)** to force sb out of a job or position of power, especially in order to take their place: *He was ousted as chairman.*

out[1] /aʊt/ ***adv., prep.*** **1** away from the inside of a place: *He opened the drawer and took a fork out.* ◇ *She opened the window and put her head out.* ◇ *Can you show me the way out?* ➲ look at **out of 2** not at home or in your place of work: *The manager was out when she called.* ◇ *I'd love a night out – I'm bored with staying at home.* **3** a long distance away from a place, for example from land or your country: *The current is quite strong so don't swim too far out.* **4** (used about the sea) when the water is furthest away from the land: *Don't swim when the tide is on the way out.* **5** used for showing that sth is no longer hidden: *I love the spring when all the flowers are out.* ◇ *The secret's out now. There's no point pretending any more.* **6** made available to the public; published: *There'll be a lot of controversy when her book comes out next year.* **7** in a loud voice; clearly: *She cried out in pain.* **8** not in fashion: *Short skirts are out this season.* **9** (*spoken*) not possible or acceptable: *I'm afraid Friday is out. I've got a meeting that day.* **10** (used about a player in a game or sport) not allowed to continue playing: *If you get three answers wrong, you're out.* **11** (**SPORT**) (used about a ball, etc.) not inside the playing area and therefore not allowed **12** (used when you are calculating sth) making or containing a mistake; wrong: *My guess was only out by a few centimetres.* **13** (used about a light or a fire) not on; not burning: *The lights are out. They must be in bed.* ◇ *Once the fire was completely out, experts were sent in to inspect the damage.*
IDM **be out for sth**; **be out to do sth** to try hard to get or do sth: *I'm not out for revenge.*
be/come out to tell family, friends, etc. that you are a HOMOSEXUAL
out-and-out complete: *It was out-and-out war between us.*
out loud = ALOUD

out[2] /aʊt/ ***verb*** [T] to say publicly that sb is a homosexual, especially when they would rather keep it a secret: *The politician was eventually outed by a tabloid newspaper.*

out- /aʊt/ ***prefix*** **1** (used in verbs) greater, better, further, longer, etc.: *outdo* ◇ *outrun* **2** (used in nouns and adjectives) outside; away from: *outbuildings* ◇ *outpatient*

the outback /ˈaʊtbæk/ ***noun*** [sing.] (**GEOGRAPHY**) the part of a country (especially Australia) which is a long way from the coast and towns, where few people live

outboard motor /ˌaʊtbɔːd ˈməʊtə(r)/ ***noun*** [C] an engine that can be fixed to a boat

outbound /ˈaʊtbaʊnd/ ***adj.*** (*formal*) (**TOURISM**) travelling from a place rather than arriving in it: ***outbound flights/passengers*** OPP **inbound**

ˈout box ***noun*** [C] (*AmE*) = OUT TRAY

outbox /ˈaʊtbɒks/ ***noun*** [C] (**COMPUTING**) the place on a computer where new email messages that you write are stored before you send them ➲ look at **inbox**

outbreak /ˈaʊtbreɪk/ ***noun*** [C] the sudden start of sth unpleasant (especially a disease or violence): *an outbreak of cholera/fighting*

outbuilding /ˈaʊtbɪldɪŋ/ ***noun*** [C] a building such as a SHED or STABLE that is built near to, but separate from, a large building: *a large farmhouse with several outbuildings*

outburst /'aʊtbɜːst/ ***noun*** [C] a sudden expression of a strong feeling, especially anger: *Afterwards, she apologized for her outburst.*

outcast /'aʊtkɑːst/ ***noun*** [C] a person who is no longer accepted by society or by a group of people: *a social outcast*

outclass /ˌaʊt'klɑːs/ ***verb*** [T] (often passive) to be much better than sb/sth, especially in a game or competition

outcome AW /'aʊtkʌm/ ***noun*** [C] the result or effect of an action or an event ➲ note at **effect**[1]

outcrop /'aʊtkrɒp/ ***noun*** [C] (GEOGRAPHY) a large mass of rock that stands above the surface of the ground

outcry /'aʊtkraɪ/ ***noun*** [C, usually sing.] (*pl.* **outcries**) a strong protest by a large number of people because they disagree with sth: *The public outcry forced the government to change its mind about the new tax.*

outdated /ˌaʊt'deɪtɪd/ ***adj.*** not useful or common any more; old-fashioned: *A lot of the computer equipment is getting outdated.*

outdo /ˌaʊt'duː/ ***verb*** [T] (*pres. part.* **outdoing**; *3rd person sing. pres.* **outdoes** /-'dʌz/; *pt* **outdid** /-'dɪd/; *pp* **outdone** /-'dʌn/) to do sth better than another person; to be more successful than sb else: ***Not to be outdone*** (=not wanting anyone else to do better), *she tried again.*

outdoor 🔑 /'aʊtdɔː(r)/ ***adj.*** (only *before* a noun) happening, done, or used outside, not in a building: *an outdoor swimming pool* ◇ *outdoor clothing/activities* OPP **indoor**

outdoors 🔑 /ˌaʊt'dɔːz/ ***adv.*** outside a building: *It's a very warm evening so why don't we eat outdoors?* SYN **out of doors** OPP **indoors** ➲ look at **outside**

outer 🔑 /'aʊtə(r)/ ***adj.*** (only *before* a noun) **1** on the outside of sth: *the outer layer of skin on an onion* **2** far from the inside or the centre of sth: *the outer suburbs of a city* OPP **inner**

outermost /'aʊtəməʊst/ ***adj.*** (only *before* a noun) furthest from the inside or centre; most DISTANT OPP **innermost**

ˌouter 'space = SPACE[1] (2)

outfit /'aʊtfɪt/ ***noun*** [C] a set of clothes that are worn together for a particular occasion or purpose: *I'm going to buy a whole new outfit for the party.*

outflow /'aʊtfləʊ/ ***noun*** [C] **~ (of sth/sb) (from sth)** the movement of a large amount of money, liquid, people, etc. out of a place: *a steady outflow of oil from the tank*

outgoing /'aʊtgəʊɪŋ/ ***adj.*** **1** friendly and interested in other people and new experiences **2** (only *before* a noun) leaving a job or a place: *the outgoing president/government* ◇ *Put all the outgoing mail in a pile on that table.* OPP **incoming**

outgoings /'aʊtgəʊɪŋz/ ***noun*** [pl.] (*BrE*) (FINANCE) an amount of money that you spend regularly, for example every week or month OPP **income**

outgrow /ˌaʊt'grəʊ/ ***verb*** [T] (*pt* **outgrew** /-'gruː/; *pp* **outgrown** /-'grəʊn/) to become too old or too big for sth

outing /'aʊtɪŋ/ ***noun*** [C] a short trip for pleasure: *to* ***go on an outing*** *to the zoo*

outlandish /aʊt'lændɪʃ/ ***adj.*** very strange or unusual: *outlandish clothes*

outlast /ˌaʊt'lɑːst/ ***verb*** [T] to continue to exist or to do sth for a longer time than sb/sth

outlaw[1] /'aʊtlɔː/ ***verb*** [T] (LAW) to make sth illegal

outlaw[2] /'aʊtlɔː/ ***noun*** [C] (HISTORY) (used in past times) a person who has done sth illegal and is hiding to avoid being caught

outlay /'aʊtleɪ/ ***noun*** [C, usually sing.] **~ (on sth)** (FINANCE) money that is spent, especially in order to start a business or project

outlet /'aʊtlet/ ***noun*** [C] **an ~ (for sth) 1** a way of expressing and making good use of strong feelings, ideas or energy: *Gary found an outlet for his aggression in boxing.* **2** (BUSINESS) a shop, business, etc. that sells goods made by a particular company or of a particular type: *fast food/retail outlets* **3** a pipe through which a gas or liquid can escape

outline[1] 🔑 /'aʊtlaɪn/ ***noun*** [C] **1** a description of the most important facts or ideas about sth: *a brief outline of Indian history* **2** a line that shows the shape or outside edge of sb/sth: *She could see the outline of a person through the mist.*

outline[2] 🔑 /'aʊtlaɪn/ ***verb*** [T] **~ sth (to sb)** to give the most important facts or ideas about sth

outlive /ˌaʊt'lɪv/ ***verb*** [T] to live or exist longer than sb/sth

outlook /'aʊtlʊk/ ***noun*** [C] **1 an ~ (on sth)** your attitude to or feeling about life and the world: *an optimistic outlook on life* **2 ~ (for sth)** what will probably happen: *The outlook for the economy is not good.*

outlying /'aʊtlaɪɪŋ/ ***adj.*** (only *before* a noun) far from the centre of a town or city: *The bus service to the outlying villages is very poor.*

outmoded /ˌaʊt'məʊdɪd/ ***adj.*** (only *before* a noun) no longer common or fashionable

outnumber /ˌaʊt'nʌmbə(r)/ ***verb*** [T] (often passive) to be greater in number than an enemy, another team, etc.: *The demonstrators were heavily outnumbered by the police.* ◇ *The enemy troops outnumbered us by three to one.*

'out of ***prep.*** **1** (used with verbs expressing movement) away from the inside of sth: *She took her purse out of her bag.* ◇ *to get out of bed* OPP **into** **2** away from or no longer in a place or situation: *He's out of the country on business.* ◇ *The doctors say she's* ***out of danger.*** **3** at a distance from a place: *We live a long way out of London.* **4** used for saying which feeling causes you to do sth: *I was only asking out of curiosity.* **5** used for saying what you use to make sth else: *What is this knife* ***made out of****?* ◇ *to be made out of wood/metal/plastic/gold* **6** from among a number or set: *Nine out of ten people prefer this model.* **7** from; having sth as its source: *I copied the recipe out of a book.* ◇ *I paid for it out of the money I won on the lottery.* **8** used for saying that you no longer have sth: *to be out of milk/sugar/tea* ◇ *He's been* ***out of work*** *for months.* **9** used for saying that sth is not as it should be: *My notes are all* ***out of order*** *and I can't find the right page.*

IDM **be/feel out of it** to be/feel lonely and unhappy because you are not included in sth: *I don't speak French so I felt rather out of it at the meeting.*

out of bounds → BOUNDS

out of order → ORDER[1]

ˌout-of-'work ***adj.*** unable to find a job; unemployed: *an out-of-work actor*

outpace /ˌaʊt'peɪs/ ***verb*** [T] to go, rise, improve, etc. faster than sb/sth: *He easily outpaced the other runners.*

outpatient /ˈaʊtpeɪʃnt/ ***noun*** [C] (HEALTH) a person who goes to a hospital for treatment but who does not stay there during the night

outplay /ˌaʊtˈpleɪ/ ***verb*** [T] (SPORT) to play much better than sb you are competing against: *We were totally outplayed and lost 106–74.*

outpost /ˈaʊtpəʊst/ ***noun*** [C] **1** a small military camp away from the main army, used for watching an enemy's movements, etc. **2** a small town or group of buildings in a lonely part of a country

output¹ 🔑 AW /ˈaʊtpʊt/ ***noun*** [U, C] **1** the amount that a person or machine produces **2** (COMPUTING) the information that a computer produces ➲ look at **input 3** (PHYSICS) the power, energy, etc. produced by a piece of equipment: *an output of 100 watts* **4** (PHYSICS) the place where power, energy, etc. leaves a system

output² /ˈaʊtpʊt/ ***verb*** [T] (**outputting**; **output**; **output**) (COMPUTING) to supply or produce information, results, etc.: *Computers can now output data much more quickly.* ➲ look at **input**

outrage /ˈaʊtreɪdʒ/ ***noun*** **1** [C] something that is very bad or wrong and that causes you to feel great anger: *It's an outrage that such poverty should exist in the 21st century.* **2** [U] great anger: *a feeling of outrage* ▶ **outrage** ***verb*** [T]

outrageous /aʊtˈreɪdʒəs/ ***adj.*** that makes you very angry or shocked: *outrageous behaviour/prices* ▶ **outrageously** ***adv.***

outright /ˈaʊtraɪt/ ***adj., adv.*** **1** open and direct; in an open and direct way: *She told them outright what she thought about it.* **2** complete and clear; completely and clearly: *an outright victory* ◇ *to win outright* **3** not gradually; immediately: *They were able to buy the house outright.*

outrun /ˌaʊtˈrʌn/ ***verb*** [T] (*pres. part.* **outrunning**; *pt* **outran** /-ˈræn/; *pp* **outrun**) to run faster or further than sb/sth: *He couldn't outrun his pursuers.*

outset /ˈaʊtset/ ***noun***

IDM **at/from the outset (of sth)** at/from the beginning (of sth)

outside¹ 🔑 /ˌaʊtˈsaɪd/ ***adv., prep.*** **1** in, at or to a place that is not in a room or not in a building: *Please wait outside for a few minutes.* ◇ *Leave your muddy boots outside the door.* **2** (*AmE also* **outside of**) not in: *You may do as you wish outside office hours.* ◇ *a small village just outside Stratford*

outside² 🔑 /ˈaʊtsaɪd/ ***adj.*** (only *before* a noun) **1** of or on the outer side or surface of sth: *the outside walls of a building* **2** not part of the main building: *an outside toilet* **3** not connected with or belonging to a particular group or organization: *We can't do all the work by ourselves. We'll need outside help.* **4** (used about a chance or possibility) very small

IDM **the outside world** people, places, activities, etc. that are away from the area where you live and your own experience of life

outside³ 🔑 /ˌaʊtˈsaɪd/ ***noun*** **1** [C, usually sing.] the outer side or surface of sth: *There is a list of all the ingredients on the outside of the packet.* **2** [sing.] the area that is near or round a building, etc.: *We've only seen the church from the outside.* **3** [sing.] the part of a road, a track, etc. that is away from the side that you usually drive on, run on, etc.: *The other runners all overtook him on the outside.* OPP **inside**

IDM **at the outside** at the most: *It will take us 3 days at the outside.*

outsider /ˌaʊtˈsaɪdə(r)/ ***noun*** [C] **1** a person who is not accepted as a member of a particular group **2** (SPORT) a person or animal in a race or competition that is not expected to win OPP **favourite**

outsize /ˈaʊtsaɪz/ ***adj.*** (often used about clothes) larger than usual

outskirts /ˈaʊtskɜːts/ ***noun*** [pl.] the parts of a town or city that are furthest from the centre: *They live **on the outskirts** of Athens.*

outsource /ˈaʊtsɔːs/ ***verb*** [T,I] (BUSINESS) to arrange for sb outside a company to do work or provide goods for that company: *We outsource all our computing work.* ▶ **outsourcing** ***noun*** [U]

outspoken /aʊtˈspəʊkən/ ***adj.*** saying exactly what you think or feel although you may shock or upset other people: *Linda is very outspoken in her criticism.*

outstanding 🔑 /aʊtˈstændɪŋ/ ***adj.*** **1** extremely good; excellent: *The results in the exams were outstanding.* ◇ *an area of **outstanding natural beauty*** **2** not yet paid, done or dealt with: *Some of the work is still outstanding.* ◇ *outstanding debts/issues*

outstandingly /aʊtˈstændɪŋli/ ***adv.*** extremely; very well: *outstandingly good*

outstretched /ˌaʊtˈstretʃt/ ***adj.*** reaching as far as possible: *He came towards her with his arms outstretched.*

ˈout tray (*AmE also* **ˈout box**) ***noun*** [C] (in an office) a container on your desk for letters or documents that are waiting to be sent out or passed to sb else ➲ look at **in tray**

outward /ˈaʊtwəd/ ***adj.*** (only *before* a noun) **1** on the outside: *Despite her cheerful outward appearance, she was in fact very unhappy.* **2** (TOURISM) (used about a journey) going away from the place that you will return to later OPP **return** **3** away from the centre or from a particular point: *outward movement/pressure* OPP **inward** ▶ **outwardly** ***adv.***: *He remained outwardly calm so as not to frighten the children.*

outwards /ˈaʊtwədz/ (*especially AmE* **outward**) ***adv.*** towards the outside or away from the place where you are: *This door opens outwards.*

outweigh /ˌaʊtˈweɪ/ ***verb*** [T] to be more in amount or importance than sth: *The advantages outweigh the disadvantages.*

outwit /ˌaʊtˈwɪt/ ***verb*** [T] (**outwitting**; **outwitted**) to gain an advantage over sb by doing sth clever

oval /ˈəʊvl/ ***adj., noun*** [C] shaped like an egg; a shape like that of an egg

ˈoval window ***noun*** [C] (ANATOMY) an opening covered by a MEMBRANE (= a thin layer of skin) between the middle ear and the inner ear, through which sound VIBRATIONS pass ➲ look at **round window** ➲ picture at **ear**

ovary /ˈəʊvəri/ ***noun*** [C] (*pl.* **ovaries**) **1** (ANATOMY) one of the two parts of the female body that produce eggs **2** (BIOLOGY) the part of a plant that produces seeds ➲ picture at **flower**

ovation /əʊˈveɪʃn/ ***noun*** [C] an enthusiastic reaction given by an audience when it likes sb/sth very much. The people in the audience CLAP (= make a noise with their hands) and CHEER (= shout) and often stand up: *The dancers got **a standing ovation** at the end of the performance.*

oven 🔑 /ˈʌvn/ ***noun*** [C] the part of a cooker that has a door. You put things inside an oven to cook them: *Cook in a hot oven for 50 minutes.* ◇ *a microwave oven*

over[1] /ˈəʊvə(r)/ ***adv.*, *prep.*** **1** straight above sth, but not touching it: *There's a painting over the bookcase.* ◇ *We watched the plane fly over.* ➲ look at **above 2** covering sth: *He was holding a towel over the cut.* ◇ *She hung her coat over the back of the chair.* **3** across to the other side of sth: *The horse jumped over the fence.* ◇ *a bridge over the river* **4** on or to the other side: *The student turned the paper over and read the first question.* **5** down or sideways from an UPRIGHT position: *He leaned over to speak to the woman next to him.* ◇ *I fell over in the street this morning.* **6** above or more than a number, price, etc.: *She lived in Athens for over ten years.* ◇ *suitable for children aged 10 and over* **7** used for expressing distance: *He's over in America at the moment.* ◇ *Sit down **over there**.* ◇ *Come **over here**, please.* **8** not used; still remaining: *There are a lot of cakes **left over** from the party.* **9** (used with *all*) everywhere: *There was blood **all over the place**.* ◇ *I can't find my glasses. I've looked all over for them.* **10** used for saying that sth is repeated: *You'll have to start **all over again*** (=from the beginning). ◇ *She kept saying the same thing **over and over again**.* **11** about; on the subject of: *We quarrelled over money.* **12** during: *We met several times over the Christmas holiday.*

over[2] /ˈəʊvə(r)/ ***adj.*** finished: *The exams are all over now.*

over- /ˈəʊvə(r)/ ***prefix*** (used in nouns, verbs, adjectives and adverbs) **1** more than usual; too much: *oversleep/overeat* ◇ *overcrowded/overexcited* **2** completely: *overjoyed* **3** upper, outer or extra: *overcoat* ◇ *overtime* **4** over; above: *overcast* ◇ *overhang*

overall[1] AW /ˌəʊvərˈɔːl/ ***adv.*, *adj.*** **1** including everything; total: *What will the overall cost of the work be?* **2** generally; when you consider everything: *Overall, I can say that we are pleased with the year's work.*

overall[2] AW /ˈəʊvərɔːl/ ***noun*** **1** [C] a piece of clothing like a coat that you wear over your clothes to keep them clean when you are working **2 overalls** (*AmE* **coveralls**) [pl.] a piece of clothing that covers your arms, legs and body that you wear over your clothes to keep them clean when you are working

overawe /ˌəʊvərˈɔː/ ***verb*** [T] (usually passive) to impress sb so much that they feel nervous or frightened

overbalance /ˌəʊvəˈbæləns/ ***verb*** [I] to lose your balance and fall

overbearing /ˌəʊvəˈbeərɪŋ/ ***adj.*** having an unpleasant way of telling other people what to do

overblown /ˌəʊvəˈbləʊn/ ***adj.*** that is made to seem larger, more impressive or more important than it really is SYN **exaggerated**

overboard /ˈəʊvəbɔːd/ ***adv.*** over the side of a boat or ship into the water

IDM **go overboard (on/about/for sb/sth)** to be too excited or enthusiastic about sb/sth

overcast /ˌəʊvəˈkɑːst/ ***adj.*** (used about the sky) covered with cloud

overcharge /ˌəʊvəˈtʃɑːdʒ/ ***verb*** [I,T] to ask sb to pay too much money for sth: *The taxi driver overcharged me.* ➲ look at **charge**

overcoat /ˈəʊvəkəʊt/ ***noun*** [C] a long thick coat that you wear in cold weather

overcome /ˌəʊvəˈkʌm/ ***verb*** [T] (*pt* **overcame** /-ˈkeɪm/; *pp* **overcome**) **1** to manage to control or defeat sb/sth: *She tried hard to overcome her fear of flying.* **2** (usually passive) to be extremely strongly affected by sth

overcook /ˌəʊvəˈkʊk/ ***verb*** [T] to cook food for too long OPP **undercook**

overcrowded /ˌəʊvəˈkraʊdɪd/ ***adj.*** (used about a place) with too many people inside

overdo /ˌəʊvəˈduː/ ***verb*** [T] (*pt* **overdid** /-ˈdɪd/; *pp* **overdone** /-ˈdʌn/) **1** to use or do too much of sth **2** to cook sth for too long: *The meat was overdone.*

IDM **overdo it/things** to work too hard: *Exercise is fine but don't overdo it.*

overdose /ˈəʊvədəʊs/ ***noun*** [C] (HEALTH) an amount of a drug or medicine that is too large and so is not safe: *to take an overdose* ➲ look at **dose**

overdraft /ˈəʊvədrɑːft/ ***noun*** [C] (FINANCE) an amount of money that you have spent that is greater than the amount you have in your bank account; an arrangement with your bank that allows you to spend more money than you have

overdrawn /ˌəʊvəˈdrɔːn/ ***adj.*** (FINANCE) having spent more money than you have in your bank account: *I checked my balance and discovered I was overdrawn.*

overdue /ˌəʊvəˈdjuː/ ***adj.*** late in arriving, happening, etc.: *an overdue library book* ◇ *Her baby is a week overdue.*

overeat /ˌəʊvərˈiːt/ ***verb*** [I] to eat more than is necessary or healthy

overestimate AW /ˌəʊvərˈestɪmeɪt/ ***verb*** [T] to guess that sb/sth is bigger, better, more important, etc. than they really are: *I overestimated how much we could paint in a day.* OPP **underestimate**
▶ **overestimate** /ˌəʊvərˈestɪmət/ ***noun*** [C]

overfishing /ˌəʊvəˈfɪʃɪŋ/ ***noun*** [U] (ENVIRONMENT) the process of taking so many fish from the sea, a river, etc. that the number of fish in it becomes very low

overflow /ˌəʊvəˈfləʊ/ ***verb*** **1** [I,T] **~ (with sth)** to be so full that there is no more space: *The tap was left on and the bath overflowed.* ◇ *The roads are overflowing with cars.* **2** [I] **~ (into sth)** to be forced out of a place or a container that is too full: *The crowd overflowed into the street.*

overgrazing /ˌəʊvəˈgreɪzɪŋ/ ***noun*** [U] (ENVIRONMENT, AGRICULTURE) allowing animals such as cows to eat the grass on an area of land for too long so that the grass disappears completely and the land can no longer be used

overgrown /ˌəʊvəˈgrəʊn/ covered with plants that have grown too big and untidy

overhang /ˌəʊvəˈhæŋ/ ***verb*** [I,T] (*pt, pp* **overhung** /ˌəʊvəˈhʌŋ/) to stick out above sth else: *The overhanging trees kept the sun off us.*

overhaul /ˌəʊvəˈhɔːl/ ***verb*** [T] to look at sth carefully and change or repair it if necessary: *to overhaul an engine* ▶ **overhaul** /ˈəʊvəhɔːl/ ***noun*** [C]

overhead /ˌəʊvəˈhed/ ***adv.*** /ˈəʊvəhed/ ***adj.*** above your head: *A helicopter flew overhead.* ◇ *overhead electricity cables*

overheads /ˈəʊvəhedz/ ***noun*** [pl.] (BUSINESS) money that a company must spend on things like heat, light, rent, etc.

overhear /ˌəʊvəˈhɪə(r)/ ***verb*** [T] (*pt, pp* **overheard** /-ˈhɜːd/) to hear what sb is saying by accident, when they are speaking to sb else and not to you

overjoyed /ˌəʊvəˈdʒɔɪd/ ***adj.*** (not before a noun) **~ (at sth/to do sth)** very happy

overland /ˈəʊvəlænd/ ***adj.*, *adv.*** not by sea or by air: *an overland journey* ◇ *We travelled overland to India.*

overlap AW /ˌəʊvəˈlæp/ *verb* [I,T] (**overlapping**; **overlapped**) **1** when two things **overlap**, part of one covers part of the other: *Make sure that the two pieces of material overlap.* **2** to be partly the same as sth: *Our jobs overlap to some extent.* ▶ **overlap** /ˈəʊvəlæp/ *noun* [C,U]

overlap

overlapping tiles

overleaf /ˌəʊvəˈliːf/ *adv.* on the other side of the page: *Full details are given overleaf.*

overload /ˌəʊvəˈləʊd/ *verb* [T] **1** (often passive) to put too many people or things into or onto sth: *an overloaded vehicle* **2** ~ **sb (with sth)** to give sb too much of sth: *to be overloaded with work/information* **3** to put too much electricity through sth: *If you use too many electrical appliances at one time you may overload the system.*

overlook /ˌəʊvəˈlʊk/ *verb* [T] **1** to fail to see or notice sth: *to overlook a spelling mistake* ◇ *She felt that her opinion had been completely overlooked.* **2** to see sth wrong but decide to forget it: *I will overlook your behaviour this time but don't let it happen again.* **3** to have a view over sth: *My room overlooks the sea.*

overnight /ˌəʊvəˈnaɪt/ *adj.*, *adv.* **1** for one night: *an overnight bag* ◇ *We stayed overnight in Hamburg.* **2** (happening) very suddenly: *She became a star overnight.*

overpass /ˈəʊvəpɑːs/ (*AmE*) = FLYOVER

overpay /ˌəʊvəˈpeɪ/ *verb* [T] (*pt*, *pp* **overpaid**) (usually passive) to pay sb too much; to pay sb more than their job is worth: *He is grossly overpaid for what he does.* OPP **underpay**

overpopulated /ˌəʊvəˈpɒpjuleɪtɪd/ *adj.* (used about a country or city) with too many people living in it ▶ **overpopulation** /ˌəʊvəˌpɒpjuˈleɪʃn/ *noun* [U]

overpower /ˌəʊvəˈpaʊə(r)/ *verb* [T] to be too strong for sb: *The fireman was overpowered by the heat and smoke.* ▶ **overpowering** *adj.*: *an overpowering smell*

overpriced /ˌəʊvəˈpraɪst/ *adj.* too expensive; costing more than it is worth

overproduce /ˌəʊvəprəˈdjuːs/ *verb* [T,I] (BUSINESS) to produce more of sth than is wanted or needed ▶ **overproduction** /ˌəʊvəprəˈdʌkʃn/ *noun* [U]

overprotective /ˌəʊvəprəˈtektɪv/ *adj.* too anxious to protect sb from being hurt, in a way that restricts their freedom: *overprotective parents*

overrate /ˌəʊvəˈreɪt/ *verb* [T] (often passive) to think that sth/sb is better than they really are OPP **underrate**

overreact /ˌəʊvəriˈækt/ *verb* [I] ~ **(to sth)** to react too strongly, especially to sth unpleasant ▶ **overreaction** /-ˈækʃn/ *noun* [U,C]

override /ˌəʊvəˈraɪd/ *verb* [T] (*pt* **overrode** /-ˈrəʊd/; *pp* **overridden** /-ˈrɪdn/) **1** to use your authority to reject sb's decision, order, etc.: *They overrode my protest and continued with the meeting.* **2** to be more important than sth **3** to stop sth being done automatically in order to control it yourself: *You need a special password to override the safety lock.*

overriding /ˌəʊvəˈraɪdɪŋ/ *adj.* (only *before* a noun) more important than anything else: *Our overriding concern is safety.*

overrule /ˌəʊvəˈruːl/ *verb* [T] (LAW) to use your authority to change what sb else has already decided or done: *The Appeal Court overruled the judge's decision.*

overrun /ˌəʊvəˈrʌn/ *verb* (*pt* **overran** /-ˈræn/; *pp* **overrun**) **1** [T] (often passive) to spread all over an area in great numbers: *The city was overrun by rats.* **2** [I,T] to use more time or money than expected: *The meeting overran by 30 minutes.*

overseas AW /ˌəʊvəˈsiːz/ *adj.* (only *before* a noun) *adv.* in, to or from another country that you have to cross the sea to get to: *overseas students studying in Britain* ◇ *Frank has gone to live overseas.*

oversee /ˌəʊvəˈsiː/ *verb* [T] (*pt* **oversaw** /-ˈsɔː/; *pp* **overseen** /-ˈsiːn/) to watch sth to make sure that it is done properly

overshadow /ˌəʊvəˈʃædəʊ/ *verb* [T] **1** to cause sb/sth to seem less important or successful: *Connor always seemed to be overshadowed by his sister.* **2** to cause sth to be less enjoyable

oversight /ˈəʊvəsaɪt/ *noun* [C,U] something that you do not notice or do that you should have noticed or done

oversimplify /ˌəʊvəˈsɪmplɪfaɪ/ *verb* [I,T] (*pres. part.* **oversimplifying**; *3rd person sing. pres.* **oversimplifies**; *pt*, *pp* **oversimplified**) to explain sth in such a simple way that its real meaning is lost

oversleep /ˌəʊvəˈsliːp/ *verb* [I] (*pt*, *pp* **overslept** /-ˈslept/) to sleep longer than you should have done: *I overslept and was late for school.* ➲ look at **lie in**, **sleep in**

overstate /ˌəʊvəˈsteɪt/ *verb* [T] to say sth in a way that makes it seem more important than it really is OPP **understate**
▶ **overstatement** /ˈəʊvəsteɪtmənt/ *noun* [C,U]: *It is not an overstatement to say a crisis is imminent.* OPP **understatement**

overstep /ˌəʊvəˈstep/ *verb* [T] (*pres. part.* **overstepping**; *pt*, *pp* **overstepped**) to go further than an acceptable limit

overt /ˈəʊvɜːt/ *adj.* (usually *before* a noun) (*formal*) done in an open way and not secretly OPP **covert** ▶ **overtly** *adv.*

overtake /ˌəʊvəˈteɪk/ *verb* [I,T] (*pt* **overtook** /-ˈtʊk/; *pp* **overtaken** /-ˈteɪkən/) to go past another person, car, etc. because you are moving faster: *The lorry overtook me on the bend.*

overthrow /ˌəʊvəˈθrəʊ/ *verb* [T] (*pt* **overthrew** /-ˈθruː/; *pp* **overthrown** /-ˈθrəʊn/) (POLITICS) to remove a leader or government from power, by using force ▶ **overthrow** /ˈəʊvəθrəʊ/ *noun* [sing.]

overtime /ˈəʊvətaɪm/ *noun* [U] (BUSINESS) time that you spend at work after your usual working hours; the money that you are paid for this: *Betty did ten hours' overtime last week.* ▶ **overtime** *adv.*: *I have been working overtime for weeks.*

overtone /ˈəʊvətəʊn/ *noun* [C, usually pl.] something that is suggested but not expressed in an obvious way: *Some people claimed there were racist overtones in the advertisement.*

overture /ˈəʊvətʃʊə(r); -tjʊə(r)/ *noun* **1** [C] (MUSIC) a piece of music that is the introduction to a musical play (such as an OPERA or a BALLET) **2** [C, usually pl.] (*formal*) an act of being friendly towards sb, especially because you want to be friends, to start a business relationship, etc.

overturn /ˌəʊvə'tɜːn/ ***verb*** **1** [I,T] to turn over so that the top is at the bottom: *The car overturned but the driver escaped unhurt.* **2** [T] to officially decide that a decision is wrong and change it

overview /'əʊvəvjuː/ ***noun*** [C] a general description of sth without any details

overweight /ˌəʊvə'weɪt/ ***adj.*** too heavy or fat: *I'm a bit overweight – I think I might go on a diet.* **OPP** **underweight**

overwhelm /ˌəʊvə'welm/ ***verb*** [T] (usually passive) **1** to cause sb to feel such a strong emotion that they do not know how to react: *The new world champion was overwhelmed by all the publicity.* **2** to be so powerful, big, etc., that sb cannot deal with it: *The television company was overwhelmed by complaints.* ◇ *He overwhelmed his opponent with his superb technique.*

overwhelming /ˌəʊvə'welmɪŋ/ ***adj.*** extremely great or strong: *Anna had an overwhelming desire to return home.* ▶ **overwhelmingly** ***adv.***

overwork /ˌəʊvə'wɜːk/ ***verb*** [T] to make sb work too hard: *The staff are overworked and underpaid.* ▶ **overwork** ***noun*** [U]

overwrought /ˌəʊvə'rɔːt/ ***adj.*** very worried and upset; excited in a nervous way **SYN** **distraught**

oviparous /əʊ'vɪpərəs/ ***adj.*** (BIOLOGY) (used about animals) producing eggs rather than live babies ➲ look at **viviparous**

ovulate /'ɒvjuleɪt/ ***verb*** [I] (BIOLOGY) (used about a woman or female animal)to produce an egg (**ovum**) ▶ **ovulation** /ˌɒvju'leɪʃn/ ***noun*** [U] ➲ picture at **fertilize**

ovule /'ɒvjuːl/ ***noun*** [C] (BIOLOGY) (in plants that produce seeds) the part of the OVARY that contains the female cell that becomes the seed ➲ picture at **flower**

ovum /'əʊvəm/ ***noun*** [C] (*pl.* **ova** /'əʊvə/) (BIOLOGY) an egg produced by a woman or female animal ➲ picture at **fertilize**

ow /aʊ/ ***exclamation*** used when reacting to a sudden feeling of pain

owe 🔑 /əʊ/ ***verb*** [T] **1** ~ **sth (to sb)**; ~ **sb for sth** to have to pay money to sb for sth that they have done or given: *I owe Katrina a lot of money.* ◇ *I owe a lot of money to Katrina.* ◇ *I still owe you for that bread you bought yesterday.* **2** to feel that you should do sth for sb or give sth to sb, especially because they have done sth for you: *Claudia owes me an explanation.* ◇ *I owe you an apology.* **3** ~ **sth to sb/sth** to have sth for the reason given: *She said she owes her success to hard work and determination.*

owing /'əʊɪŋ/ ***adj.*** (not before a noun) ~ **(to sb)** not yet paid

'owing to ***prep.*** because of: *The match was cancelled owing to bad weather.*

owl /aʊl/ ***noun*** [C] a bird with large eyes that hunts small animals at night ➲ picture on **page 28**

own[1] 🔑 /əʊn/ ***adj.***, ***pronoun*** **1** used to emphasize that sth belongs to a particular person: *I saw him do it with **my own** eyes.* ◇ *This is **his own** house.* ◇ *This house is his own.* ◇ *Rachel would like her own room/a room **of her own**.* **2** used to show that sth is done or made without help from another person: *The children are old enough to get their own breakfast.*

IDM **come into your own** to have the opportunity to show your special qualities

hold your own (against sb/sth) to be as strong, good, etc. as sb/sth else

(all) on your own 1 alone: *John lives all on his own.* **2** without help: *I managed to repair the car all on my own.*

get/have your own back (on sb) (*informal*) to hurt sb who has hurt you

own[2] 🔑 /əʊn/ ***verb*** [T] to have sth belonging to you; to possess sth: *We don't own the house. We just rent it.* ◇ *a privately owned company*

PHR V **own up (to sth)** (*informal*) to tell sb that you have done sth wrong: *None of the children owned up to breaking the window.*

owner 🔑 /'əʊnə(r)/ ***noun*** [C] a person who owns sth: *a house/dog owner*

ownership /'əʊnəʃɪp/ ***noun*** [U] the state of owning sth: *in private/public **ownership***

ox /ɒks/ ***noun*** [C] (*pl.* **oxen** /'ɒksn/) a male cow that has been CASTRATED (=had part of its sex organs removed). **Oxen** are used in some places for pulling or carrying heavy loads. ➲ look at **bull**

oxbow /'ɒksbəʊ/ ***noun*** [C] (GEOGRAPHY) a bend in a river that almost forms a full circle; a lake that forms when this bend is separated from the river

oxbow lake

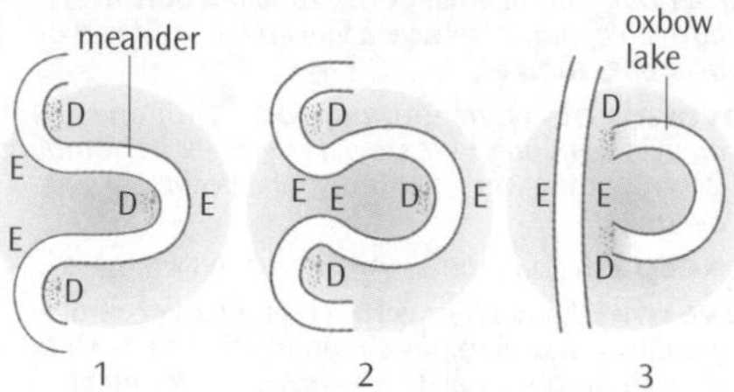

1 Erosion (E) and deposition (D) around a meander.
2 Increased erosion during flood conditions. The meander becomes exaggerated.
3 The river breaks through during a flood. Further deposition causes the old meander to become an oxbow lake.

oxford /'ɒksfəd/ ***noun*** **1 oxfords** [pl.] (*especially AmE*) leather shoes that fasten with LACES **2** [U] thick cotton material: *an oxford shirt*

oxide /'ɒksaɪd/ ***noun*** [C,U] (CHEMISTRY) a combination of OXYGEN and another chemical element: *iron oxide*

oxidize (also **-ise**) /'ɒksɪdaɪz/ ***verb*** [I,T] (CHEMISTRY) to remove one or more ELECTRONS from a substance, or to combine or make sth combine with OXYGEN, especially when this causes metal to become covered with RUST ➲ look at **reduce** ▶ **oxidation** /ˌɒksɪ'deɪʃn/ ***noun*** [U] ➲ look at **reduction**

oxygen /'ɒksɪdʒən/ ***noun*** [U] (*symbol* **O**) (CHEMISTRY) a gas that you cannot see, taste or smell. Plants and animals cannot live without **oxygen**. ℹ For more information on the periodic table of elements, look at pages R34-5.

oxygenate /'ɒksɪdʒəneɪt/ ***verb*** [T] (CHEMISTRY) to add OXYGEN to sth

oxymoron /ˌɒksɪ'mɔːrɒn/ ***noun*** [C] (LITERATURE) a phrase that combines two words that seem to be the opposite of each other, such as *a deafening silence*

oyster /'ɔɪstə(r)/ ***noun*** [C] a SHELLFISH that we eat. Some **oysters** produce PEARLS.

oz ***abbr.*** ounce(s): *Add 4oz flour.*

ozone /ˈəʊzəʊn/ ***noun*** [U] (**CHEMISTRY**) a poisonous gas which is a form of OXYGEN ➲ picture at **acid rain**

ˌozone-ˈfriendly ***adj.*** (**ENVIRONMENT**) (used about cleaning products, etc.) not containing chemicals that could harm THE OZONE LAYER

the ˈozone layer ***noun*** [sing.] (**ENVIRONMENT**, **SCIENCE**) the layer of OZONE high up in the atmosphere that helps to protect the earth from the dangerous RAYS of the sun: *a hole in the ozone layer* ➲ look at **CFC** ➲ picture at **atmosphere**

P p

P, p¹ /piː/ ***noun*** [C,U] (*pl.* **P's**; **p's** /piːz/) the sixteenth letter of the English alphabet: *'Pencil' begins with (a) 'P'.*

p² ⊶ ***abbr.*** **1** (*pl.* **pp**) page: *See p94.* ◇ *pp 63-96* **2** (*BrE, informal*) penny, pence: *a 27p stamp* **3 P** (on a road sign) parking

PA /ˌpiː ˈeɪ/ ***abbr.***, ***noun*** [C] **1** = PUBLIC ADDRESS SYSTEM: *Announcements were made over the PA.* **2** (*especially BrE*) (**BUSINESS**) = PERSONAL ASSISTANT: *She's the Managing Director's PA.*

p.a. ***abbr.*** per annum; in or for a year: *salary £15000 p.a.*

PAC /ˌpiː ei ˈsiː/ ***abbr.*** (**POLITICS**) = POLITICAL ACTION COMMITTEE

pace¹ ⊶ /peɪs/ ***noun*** **1** [U, sing.] ~ (**of sth**) the speed at which you walk, run, etc. or at which sth happens: *to run at a steady/gentle pace* ◇ *I can't stand the pace of life in London.* ◇ *Students are encouraged to work at their own pace* (= as fast or as slowly as they like). **2** [C] the distance that you move when you take one step: *Take two paces forward and then stop.*
IDM **keep pace (with sb/sth)** to move or do sth at the same speed as sb/sth else; to change as quickly as sth else is changing: *Wages are not keeping pace with inflation.*
set the pace to move or do sth at the speed that others must follow: *Pinto set the pace for the first three miles.*

pace² /peɪs/ ***verb*** [I,T] to walk up and down in the same area many times, especially because you are nervous or angry

pacemaker /ˈpeɪsmeɪkə(r)/ ***noun*** [C] **1** (**HEALTH**) a machine that helps to make a person's heart beat regularly or more strongly **2** (**SPORT**) a person in a race who sets the speed that the others must follow

pachyderm /ˈpækɪdɜːm/ ***noun*** [C] (**BIOLOGY**) a type of animal with a very thick skin, for example an ELEPHANT

pachyderms

hippopotamus

rhinoceros

pacifier /ˈpæsɪfaɪə(r)/ (*AmE*) = DUMMY (3)

pacifism /ˈpæsɪfɪzəm/ ***noun*** [U] the belief that all wars are wrong and that you should not fight in them ▶ **pacifist** /-ɪst/ ***noun*** [C]

pacify /ˈpæsɪfaɪ/ ***verb*** [T] (*pres. part.* **pacifying**; *3rd person sing. pres.* **pacifies**; *pt, pp* **pacified**) to make sb who is angry or upset be calm or quiet

pack¹ ⊶ /pæk/ ***noun*** [C] **1** a set of things that are supplied together for a particular purpose: *an information pack* ◇ *These batteries are sold in packs of four.* ◇ (*figurative*) *Everything she told me was **a pack of lies**.* ➲ look at **package**, **packet**, **parcel** **2** (*AmE*) = PACKET (1) **3** a bag that you carry on your back SYN **rucksack**, **backpack** **4** [with sing. or pl. verb] a group of wild animals that hunt together: *a pack of dogs/wolves* **5** a large group of similar people or things, especially one that you do not like or approve of: *a pack of journalists* **6** (*AmE* **deck**) a complete set of playing cards

pack² ⊶ /pæk/ ***verb*** **1** [I,T] (**TOURISM**) to put your things into a suitcase, etc. before you go away or go on holiday: *I'll have to pack in the morning.* ◇ *Have you packed your toothbrush?* OPP **unpack** **2** [I,T] to put things into containers so they can be stored, transported or sold: *I packed all my books into boxes.* OPP **unpack** **3** [I] (often passive) (*informal*) to fill with people or things until crowded or full: *The train was absolutely packed.* ◇ *The book is **packed with** useful information.* ◇ *People packed the pavements, waiting for the president to arrive.*
PHR V **pack sth in** (*informal*) to stop doing sth: *I've packed in my job.* ◇ *I've had enough of you boys arguing – just pack it in, will you!*
pack sth in/into sth to do a lot in a short time: *They packed a lot into their three days in Rome.*
pack sth out (usually passive) to fill sth with people: *The bars **are packed out** every night.*
pack up (*informal*) **1** to finish working or doing sth: *There was nothing else to do so we packed up and went home.* **2** (used about a machine, engine, etc.) to stop working: *My old car packed up last week so now I cycle to work.*

package ⊶ /ˈpækɪdʒ/ ***noun*** [C] **1** (*BrE*) something, or a number of things, covered in paper or in a box: *There's a large package on the table for you.* ➲ look at **pack¹**, **packet**, **parcel** **2** a number of things that must be bought or accepted together: *a word-processing package* ◇ *a financial aid package* **3** (*AmE*) = PACKET (1) and PARCEL ▶ **package** ***verb*** [T]: *Goods that are attractively packaged sell more quickly.*

ˈpackage tour (*BrE also* **ˈpackage holiday**) ***noun*** [C] (**TOURISM**) a holiday that is organized by a company at a fixed price and that includes the cost of travel, hotels, etc.

packaging ⊶ /ˈpækɪdʒɪŋ/ ***noun*** [U] all the materials (boxes, bags, paper, etc.) that are used to cover or protect goods before they are sold

ˌpacked ˈlunch ***noun*** [C] food that you prepare at home and take with you to eat at work or school

packer /ˈpækə(r)/ ***noun*** [C] a person, company or machine that puts goods, especially food, into boxes, plastic, paper, etc. to be sold

packet ⊶ /ˈpækɪt/ ***noun*** **1** (*AmE* **pack**; **package**) [C] a small box, bag, etc. in which things are packed to be sold in a shop: ***a packet of*** *sweets/biscuits/crisps* ◇ *a cigarette packet* ➲ look at **pack¹**, **package**, **parcel** **2** [sing.] (*spoken*) a large amount of money: *That new kitchen must have cost them a packet.* **3** [C] (**COMPUTING**) an amount of data that is sent through a computer NETWORK

packing /ˈpækɪŋ/ ***noun*** [U] **1** (**TOURISM**) the act of putting your clothes, possessions, etc. into boxes or cases in order to take or send them somewhere: *We're going on holiday tomorrow so I'll **do my packing** tonight.* **2** (*BrE*) soft material that you use to stop things from being damaged or broken when you are sending them somewhere: *The price of the book includes **postage and packing**.*

'packing case ***noun*** [C] a wooden box that you put things in before they are sent somewhere or stored

pact /pækt/ ***noun*** [C] a formal agreement between two or more people, groups or countries

pad[1] /pæd/ ***noun*** [C] **1** a thick piece of soft material, used for cleaning or protecting sth or to make sth a different shape: *Remove eye make-up with cleanser and a cotton wool pad.* ◇ *a jacket with shoulder pads* **2** a number of pieces of paper that are fastened together at one end: *a notepad* **3** the place where a SPACECRAFT takes off: *a launch pad* **4** the soft part on the bottom of the feet of some animals, for example dogs and cats

pad[2] /pæd/ ***verb*** (**padding**; **padded**) **1** [T] **~ sth (with sth)** (usually passive) to fill or cover sth with soft material in order to protect it, make it larger or more comfortable, etc.: *All the sharp corners were padded with foam.* **2** [I] **~ about, along, around, etc.** to walk quietly, especially because you are not wearing shoes: *He got up and padded into the bathroom.*
PHR V **pad sth out** to make a book, speech, etc. longer by adding things that are not necessary

padding /'pædɪŋ/ ***noun*** [U] soft material that is put inside sth to protect it or to make it larger, more comfortable, etc.

paddle[1] /'pædl/ ***noun*** [C] a short pole that is flat and wide at one or both ends and that you use for moving a small boat through water ➲ picture at **canoe**

paddle[2] /'pædl/ ***verb*** **1** [I,T] to move a small boat through water using a short pole that is flat and wide at one or both ends: *We paddled down the river.* ➲ look at **row** **2** [I] to walk in water that is not very deep: *We paddled in the stream.*

'paddle steamer (*AmE*) (*BrE also* **paddleboat**) ***noun*** [C] an old-fashioned type of boat driven by steam and moved forward by a large wheel or wheels at the side

paddock /'pædək/ ***noun*** [C] a small field where horses are kept

paddy /'pædi/ (*also* **'paddy field**) ***noun*** [C] (*pl.* **paddies**) (AGRICULTURE) a field that is covered with water in which rice is grown

padlock /'pædlɒk/ ***noun*** [C] a type of lock that you can use for fastening gates, bicycles, etc. ▶ **padlock** ***verb*** [T] **~ sth (to sth)**: *I padlocked my bicycle to a post.*

paed- (*AmE* **ped-**) /piːd/ ***prefix*** (used in nouns and adjectives) connected with children: *paediatrics*

paediatrician (*AmE* **pediatrician**) /ˌpiːdiə'trɪʃn/ ***noun*** [C] (HEALTH) a doctor who deals with the diseases of children

paediatrics (*AmE* **pediatrics**) /ˌpiːdi'ætrɪks/ ***noun*** [U] (HEALTH) the area of medicine connected with the diseases of children ▶ **paediatric** (*AmE* **pediatric**) ***adj.***

paedophile (*AmE* **pedo-**) /'piːdəʊfaɪl/ ***noun*** [C] a person who is sexually attracted to children

paedophilia (*AmE* **pedo-**) /ˌpiːdə'fɪliə/ ***noun*** [U] the condition of being sexually attracted to children; sexual activity with children

paella /paɪ'elə/ ***noun*** [U, C] a Spanish dish made with rice, meat, fish and vegetables

pagan /'peɪgən/ ***adj.*** (RELIGION) having religious beliefs that do not belong to any of the main religions ▶ **pagan** ***noun*** [C]

page[1] ⊶ /peɪdʒ/ ***noun*** [C] **1** (*abbr.* **p**) one or both sides of a piece of paper in a book, magazine, etc.: *The letter was three pages long.* ◇ *Turn over the page.* ◇ *Turn to page 12 of your book.* ◇ ***the front page*** *of a newspaper* **2** (COMPUTING) a section of data or information that can be shown on a computer screen at any one time ➲ look at **home page**

page[2] /peɪdʒ/ ***verb*** [T] to call sb by sending a message to a PAGER, or by calling their name publicly through a LOUDSPEAKER (= a device fixed to the wall)

pageant /'pædʒənt/ ***noun*** [C] **1** (HISTORY) a type of public entertainment at which people dress in clothes from past times and give outdoor performances of scenes from history **2** (*AmE*) = BEAUTY CONTEST

pageantry /'pædʒəntri/ ***noun*** [U] the feeling and appearance of a big, colourful ceremony: *Millions of people enjoyed the pageantry of the Olympic opening ceremony on television.*

pager /'peɪdʒə(r)/ ***noun*** [C] a small machine that you carry, that makes a sound when sb sends you a message **SYN** **bleeper**

pagoda /pə'gəʊdə/ ***noun*** [C] (RELIGION) a religious building (**temple**) in India or East Asia in the form of a tall tower with several levels, each of which has its own roof

pagoda

paid[1] past tense, past participle of **pay[2]**

paid[2] /peɪd/ ***adj.*** **1** for which people receive money: *Neither of them is currently in paid employment.* ◇ *a well-paid job* **2** receiving money for doing work: *Men still outnumber women in the paid workforce.* **OPP** **unpaid**

'paid-up ***adj.*** (only *before* a noun) having paid all the money that you owe, for example to become a member of a club: *He's a fully paid-up member of Friends of the Earth.*

pail /peɪl/ (*AmE* or *old-fashioned*) = BUCKET

pain[1] ⊶ /peɪn/ ***noun*** **1** [C,U] the unpleasant feeling that you have when a part of your body has been hurt or when you are ill: *to **be in pain*** ◇ *He screamed with pain.* ◇ *chest pains*

> **WHICH WORD?**
>
> We use **ache** for a long, continuous pain and **pain** for sudden, short, sharp periods of pain.
>
> Therefore we usually say: *I've got earache/backache/toothache/a headache* but: *He was admitted to hospital with pains in his chest.*
>
> For the use of 'a' or 'an' with **ache**, look at the note at **ache**.

2 [U] sadness that you feel because sth bad has happened: *the pain of losing a parent*
IDM **a pain (in the neck)** (*spoken*) a person, thing or situation that makes you angry or annoyed

pain[2] /peɪn/ ***verb*** [T] (*formal*) to make sb feel sad or upset: ***It pains me*** *to think how much money we've wasted.*

pained /peɪnd/ ***adj.*** showing that you are sad or upset: *a pained expression*

painful ⊶ /'peɪnfl/ ***adj.*** **~ (for sb) (to do sth)** **1** that causes pain or hurts: *A wasp sting can be very painful.* **2** making you feel upset or embarrassed:

The break-up of their marriage was very painful for the children. ▶ **painfully** /-fəli/ ***adv.***

painkiller /ˈpeɪnkɪlə(r)/ ***noun*** [C] (**HEALTH**) a drug that is used for reducing pain

painless /ˈpeɪnləs/ ***adj.*** that does not cause pain: *The animals' death is quick and painless.* ▶ **painlessly** ***adv.***

pains /peɪnz/ ***noun***
IDM **be at/take pains to do sth; take pains (with/over sth)** to make a special effort to do sth well: *He was at pains to hide his true feelings.*

painstaking /ˈpeɪnzteɪkɪŋ/ ***adj.*** very careful and taking a long time: *The painstaking search of the wreckage gave us clues as to the cause of the crash.* ▶ **painstakingly** ***adv.***

paint[1] **⊶** /peɪnt/ ***noun*** **1** [U] coloured liquid that you put onto a surface to decorate or protect it: *green/orange/yellow paint ◇ The door will need another* ***coat of paint****.* **2** [U] (**ART**) coloured liquid that you can use to make a picture: *oil paint ◇ watercolour paint* **3 paints** [pl.] (**ART**) a collection of tubes or blocks of paint that an artist uses for painting pictures

paint[2] **⊶** /peɪnt/ ***verb*** [I,T] **1** to put paint onto a surface or an object: *We painted the fence. ◇ The walls were painted pink.* **2** (**ART**) to make a picture of sb/sth using paints: *We painted some animals on the wall.*

paintbox /ˈpeɪntbɒks/ ***noun*** [C] (**ART**) a box that contains blocks or tubes of paint of many colours

paintbrush /ˈpeɪntbrʌʃ/ ***noun*** [C] (**ART**) a brush that you use for painting with

painter **⊶** /ˈpeɪntə(r)/ ***noun*** [C] **1** a person whose job is to paint buildings, walls, etc. **2** (**ART**) a person who paints pictures

painting **⊶** /ˈpeɪntɪŋ/ ***noun*** (**ART**) **1** [C] a picture that sb has painted: *a famous painting by Van Gogh* ❶ A **drawing** is similar to a **painting**, but is done using pencils, pens or crayons instead of paints. **2** [U] the act of painting pictures or buildings: *She studies Indian painting.*

paintwork /ˈpeɪntwɜːk/ ***noun*** [U] a painted surface, especially on a vehicle

pair[1] **⊶** /peə(r)/ ***noun*** [C] **1** two things of the same type that are used or worn together: *a pair of shoes/gloves/earrings* **2** a thing that consists of two parts that are joined together: *a pair of scissors/glasses/trousers* **3** [with pl. verb] two people or animals that are doing sth together: *These boxers have fought several times, and tonight the pair meet again.*
IDM **in pairs** two at a time: *These earrings are only sold in pairs. ◇ The students were working in pairs.*

pair[2] /peə(r)/ ***verb***
PHR V **pair (sb/sth) off (with sb)** to come together, especially to form a romantic relationship; to bring two people together for this purpose: *She's always trying to pair me off with her brother.*
pair up (with sb) to join together with another person or group to work, play a game, etc.: *I paired up with another student and we did the project together.*

pairing /ˈpeərɪŋ/ ***noun*** **1** [C] two people or things that work together or are placed together; the act of placing them together: *Tonight they take on a Chinese pairing in their bid to reach the final tomorrow.* **2** [U] (**POLITICS**) (in the British Parliament) the practice of an MP agreeing with an MP of a different party that neither of them will vote in a debate so that they do not need to attend the debate

paisley /ˈpeɪzli/ ***noun*** [U] a detailed pattern of curved shapes that look like feathers: *a paisley tie*

pajamas (*AmE*) = PYJAMAS

palace **⊶** /ˈpæləs/ ***noun*** [C] a large house that is or was the home of a king or queen

Palaeolithic (*AmE usually* **Paleolithic**) /ˌpæliəˈlɪθɪk/ ***adj.*** (**HISTORY**) from or connected with the early part of the STONE AGE (= the very early period of human history) ➲ look at **Neolithic**

palaeontologist (*AmE* **paleo-**) /ˌpæliɒnˈtɒlədʒɪst; ˌpeɪl-/ ***noun*** [C] (**GEOLOGY**) a person who studies very old dead animals or plants in FOSSILS

palaeontology (*AmE* **paleo-**) /ˌpæliɒnˈtɒlədʒi; ˌpeɪl-/ ***noun*** [U] (**GEOLOGY**) the scientific study of FOSSILS

palatable /ˈpælətəbl/ ***adj.*** **1** (used about food or drink) having a pleasant or acceptable taste **2 ~ (to sb)** pleasant or acceptable to sb

palate /ˈpælət/ ***noun*** [C] (**ANATOMY**) the top part of the inside of your mouth ➲ picture at **digestive system**

pale **⊶** /peɪl/ ***adj.*** **1** (used about a person or their face) having skin that is light in colour, often because of fear or illness: *She has a pale complexion. ◇ I felt myself* ***go/turn pale*** *with fear.* ➲ noun **pallor** ➲ look at **pallid** **2** not bright or strong in colour: *a pale yellow dress* OPP **dark** ▶ **pale** ***verb*** [I]

ˈpalette /ˈpælət/ ***noun*** [C] (**ART**) a thin board with a hole in it for the thumb to go through, used by an artist for mixing colours when painting

ˌpalisade /ˌpælɪˈseɪd/ ***noun*** [C] (**HISTORY**) (in past times) a fence made of strong wooden or metal posts that are pointed at the top, especially used to protect a building: *a wooden palisade*

pall /pɔːl/ ***verb*** [I] to become less interesting or important: *After a few months, the excitement of his new job began to pall.*

palladium /pəˈleɪdiəm/ ***noun*** [U] (*symbol* **Pd**) (**CHEMISTRY**) a chemical element. **Palladium** is a rare silver-white metal that looks like PLATINUM. ❶ For more information on the periodic table of elements, look at pages R34-5.

palliative /ˈpæliətɪv/ ***noun*** [C] **1** (**HEALTH**) a medicine or medical treatment that reduces pain without curing its cause: *Aromatherapy can be used as a palliative.* **2** (*formal*) an action, a decision, etc. that is designed to make a difficult situation seem better without actually solving the cause of the problems ▶ **palliative** ***adj.***: *palliative care/treatment*

pallid /ˈpælɪd/ ***adj.*** (used about a person or their face) light in colour, especially because of illness: *His pallid complexion made him look unhealthy.*

pallor /ˈpælə(r)/ ***noun*** [U] pale colouring of the face, especially because of illness or fear

palm[1] /pɑːm/ ***noun*** [C] **1** the flat, inner surface of your hand: *She held the coins tightly in the palm of her hand.* ➲ picture on **page 80** **2** (*also* **ˈpalm tree**) a tall straight type of tree that grows in hot countries. **Palms** have a lot of large leaves at the top but no branches. ➲ picture at **plant**

palm[2] /pɑːm/ ***verb***
PHR V **palm sb off (with sth)** (*informal*) to persuade sb to believe sth that is not true in order to stop them asking questions or complaining
palm sth off (on sb) to persuade sb to accept sth

that they do not want: *She's always palming off the worst jobs on her assistant.*

ˈpalm oil *noun* [U] oil that we get from the fruit of a PALM TREE that is used in cooking and in making soap, CANDLES, etc.

palmtop /ˈpɑːmtɒp/ *noun* [C] (COMPUTING) a very small computer that can be held on the PALM (= the flat inner surface) of one hand ➲ look at **Blackberry**, **desktop**, **laptop**

palpate /pælˈpeɪt/ *verb* [T] (HEALTH) to examine part of the body by touching it

palsy /ˈpɔːlzi/ → CEREBRAL PALSY

paltry /ˈpɔːltri/ *adj.* too small to be considered important or useful: *a paltry sum of money*

the pampas /ˈpæmpəs/ *noun* [sing.] (GEOGRAPHY) the large area of land in South America that has no trees and is covered in grass

pamper /ˈpæmpə(r)/ *verb* [T] to take care of sb very well and make them feel as comfortable as possible

pamphlet /ˈpæmflət/ *noun* [C] a very thin book with a paper cover containing information about a particular subject

pan ⊷ /pæn/ *noun* [C] **1** a metal container with a handle or handles that is used for cooking food in; the contents of a pan: *Cook the spaghetti in a large pan of boiling water.* ➲ look at **frying pan**, **saucepan** **2** either of the dishes on a pair of SCALES (= a piece of equipment that is used for weighing sth) that you put things into in order to weigh them

pan- /pæn/ *prefix* (used in adjectives and nouns) including all of sth; connected with the whole of sth: *pan-African*

pancake /ˈpænkeɪk/ *noun* [C] a type of very thin round cake that is made by frying a mixture of flour, milk and eggs (**batter**)

ˈPancake Day (*also* ˌ**Shrove ˈTuesday**) *noun* [U,C] (*informal*) a Tuesday in February when people in Britain traditionally eat PANCAKES ❶ PANCAKE DAY is the day before the period of LENT begins.

pancreas /ˈpæŋkriəs/ *noun* [C] (ANATOMY) an organ near the stomach that produces INSULIN (= the substance that controls the amount of sugar in the blood) and which helps your body to deal with (**digest**) the food you eat ➲ picture at **digestive system** ▶ **pancreatic** /ˌpæŋkriˈætɪk/ *adj.*

panda /ˈpændə/ *noun* [C] a large black and white bear that comes from China

pandemic /pænˈdemɪk/ *noun* [C] (HEALTH) a disease that spreads over a whole country or the whole world ▶ **pandemic** *adj.* ➲ look at **endemic**, **epidemic**

pandemonium /ˌpændəˈməʊniəm/ *noun* [U] a state of great noise and confusion

pander /ˈpændə(r)/ *verb*
PHRV **pander to sb/sth** to do or say exactly what sb wants, especially when this is not reasonable: *He refuses to pander to his boss's demands.*

p. and p. *abbr.* (*BrE*) postage and packing: *price: £29 incl. p. and p.*

pane /peɪn/ *noun* [C] a piece of glass in a window, etc.: *a windowpane*

panel ⊷ AW /ˈpænl/ *noun* [C] **1** a square or RECTANGULAR piece of wood, metal or glass that forms part of a door or wall **2** (ARTS AND MEDIA) [with sing. or pl. verb] a group of people who give their advice or opinions about sth; a group of people who discuss topics of interest on television or radio: *a panel of judges* (= in a competition) ◇ *a panel game* (= a TV game show with two teams) **3** (TECHNICAL) a flat surface that contains the equipment for controlling a vehicle, machine, etc.: *a control/display panel* ➲ picture at **energy**

panelling (*AmE* **paneling**) /ˈpænəlɪŋ/ *noun* [U] square or RECTANGULAR pieces of wood used to cover and decorate walls, ceilings, etc.

panellist (*AmE* **panelist**) /ˈpænəlɪst/ *noun* [C] (ARTS AND MEDIA) a member of a PANEL (2)

pang /pæŋ/ *noun* [C, usually pl.] a sudden strong feeling of emotional or physical pain: *hunger pangs* ◇ *a pang of jealousy*

panic /ˈpænɪk/ *noun* [C,U] a sudden feeling of fear that cannot be controlled and stops you from thinking clearly: *People fled **in panic** as the fire spread.* ◇ *There was a mad panic when the alarm went off.* ▶ **panic** *verb* [I] (**panicking**; **panicked**): *Stay calm and don't panic.*

panicky /ˈpænɪki/ *adj.* (*informal*) anxious about sth; feeling or showing PANIC

ˈpanic-stricken /ˈpænɪk strɪkn/ *adj.* very frightened in a way that stops you from thinking clearly

panorama /ˌpænəˈrɑːmə/ *noun* [C] a view over a wide area of land ▶ **panoramic** /ˌpænəˈræmɪk/ *adj.*

pant /pænt/ *verb* [I] to breathe quickly, for example after running or because it is very hot ▶ **pant** *noun* [C]

panther /ˈpænθə(r)/ *noun* [C] a large wild animal of the cat family with black fur ➲ picture at **lion**

panties /ˈpæntiz/ (*especially AmE*) = KNICKERS

pantomime /ˈpæntəmaɪm/ *noun* [C,U] **1** (ARTS AND MEDIA) (also *informal* **panto** /ˈpæntəʊ/) (*BrE*) a type of play for children, with music, dancing and jokes, that is usually performed at Christmas. **Pantomimes** are based on traditional children's stories (**fairy tales**). **2** (*AmE*) = MIME

pantry /ˈpæntri/ *noun* [C] (*pl.* **pantries**) a small room where food is kept SYN **larder**

pants ⊷ /pænts/ *noun* [pl.] **1** (*BrE*) = UNDERPANTS **2** (*AmE*) = TROUSERS

pantyhose /ˈpæntihəʊz/ (*AmE*) = TIGHTS

paparazzi /ˌpæpəˈrætsi/ *noun* [pl.] photographers who follow famous people around in order to get pictures of them to sell to a newspaper or magazine

papaya /pəˈpaɪə/ (*also* **pawpaw** /ˈpɔːpɔː/) *noun* [C] a large tropical fruit which is sweet and orange inside and has small black seeds

paper ⊷ /ˈpeɪpə(r)/ *noun* **1** [U] a material made in thin sheets that you use for writing or drawing on, covering things, etc.: *a piece/sheet of paper* ◇ *a paper handkerchief* **2** [C] = NEWSPAPER (1): *Where's today's paper?* **3 papers** [pl.] important letters or pieces of paper that have information written on them: *The document you want is somewhere in the pile of papers on her desk.* **4** [C] (EDUCATION) the written questions or the written answers in an exam: *The history exam is divided into three papers.* **5** [C] (EDUCATION) a piece of writing on a particular subject that is written for specialists: *At the conference, the Professor presented a paper on Sri Lankan poetry.*
IDM **on paper 1** in writing: *I've had nothing on paper to say that I've been accepted.* **2** as an idea, but not in a real situation; in theory: *The scheme seems fine on paper, but would it work in practice?*

paperback /ˈpeɪpəbæk/ *noun* [C,U] a book that has a paper cover: *The novel is available **in paperback**.* ➲ look at **hardback**

ˈ**paper boy** *noun* [C] a boy who takes newspapers to people's houses

ˈ**paper clip** *noun* [C] a small piece of bent wire that is used for holding pieces of paper together

ˈ**paper girl** *noun* [C] a girl who takes newspapers to people's houses

paperless /ˈpeɪpələs/ *adj.* using computers, telephones, etc. rather than paper to exchange information: *the paperless office*

paperweight /ˈpeɪpəweɪt/ *noun* [C] a small heavy object that you put on top of loose papers to keep them in place

paperwork /ˈpeɪpəwɜːk/ *noun* [U] **1** the written work that is part of a job, such as writing letters and reports and filling in forms, etc.: *I hate doing paperwork.* **2** documents that need to be prepared, collected, etc. in order for a piece of business to be completed: *Some of the paperwork is missing from this file.*

papier mâché /ˌpæpieɪ ˈmæʃeɪ/ *noun* [U] (**ART**) paper mixed with glue or flour and water, that is used to make decorative objects

paprika /ˈpæprɪkə/ *noun* [U] a red powder made from a sweet red pepper that you can use in cooking

papyrus /pəˈpaɪrəs/ *noun* (*pl.* **papyri** /pəˈpaɪriː/) **1** [U] a tall plant with a thick STEM (=the main central part of the plant) that grows in water **2** [U] (**HISTORY**) paper made from the STEMS of the **papyrus** plant, used in ancient Egypt for writing and drawing on **3** [C] a document or piece of paper made of **papyrus**

par /pɑː(r)/ *noun* [U] (in GOLF) the standard number of times a player should hit the ball in order to complete a particular hole or series of holes

IDM **below par** (*informal*) not as good or as well as usual

on a par with sb/sth of an equal level, standard, etc. to sb/sth else

par. (*also* **para.**) *abbr.* PARAGRAPH

para- /ˈpærə/ *prefix* (used in nouns and adjectives) **1** beyond: *paranormal* **2** similar to but not official or not fully qualified: *a paramedic* ◇ *paramilitary*

parable /ˈpærəbl/ *noun* [C] (**RELIGION**) a short story that teaches a lesson, especially one told by Jesus in the Bible

parabola /pəˈræbələ/ *noun* [C] (**GEOMETRY**) a curve like the path of an object that is thrown through the air and falls back to earth ➲ picture at **conic**
▶ **parabolic** /ˌpærəˈbɒlɪk/ *adj.*: *parabolic curves*

parachute /ˈpærəʃuːt/ *noun* [C] a piece of equipment that opens and lets a person fall to the ground slowly when they jump from a plane
▶ **parachute** *verb* [IT]

parade /pəˈreɪd/ *noun* [C] an occasion when a group of people stand or walk in a line so that people can look at them: *a military parade* ◇ *a fashion parade*

paradigm AW /ˈpærədaɪm/ *noun* [C] **1** *formal* or *technical*) a typical example or pattern of sth: *a paradigm for students to copy* ◇ *The war was a paradigm of the destructive side of human nature.* **2** (**LANGUAGE**) a set of all the different forms of a word: *verb paradigms*

paradise /ˈpærədaɪs/ *noun* **1** (often **Paradise**) [U] the perfect place where some people think that good people go after they die SYN **heaven** **2** [C] a perfect place: *This beach is a paradise for windsurfers.*

paradox /ˈpærədɒks/ *noun* [C] a situation or statement with two or more parts that seem strange or impossible together: *It's a paradox that some countries produce too much food while in other countries people are starving.* ▶ **paradoxical** /ˌpærəˈdɒksɪkl/ *adj.* ▶ **paradoxically** /ˌpærəˈdɒksɪkli/ *adv.*

paraffin /ˈpærəfɪn/ (*AmE* **kerosene**) *noun* [U] (**CHEMISTRY**) a type of oil that is burned to produce heat or light ➲ picture at **fractional distillation**

paragraph AW /ˈpærəgrɑːf/ *noun* [C] (**LANGUAGE**) a part of a piece of writing that consists of one or more sentences. A **paragraph** always starts on a new line.

parakeet /ˈpærəkiːt/ *noun* [C] a small bird, usually with green feathers and a long tail, that lives in hot countries

paralegal /ˌpærəˈliːgl/ *noun* [C] (*AmE*) (**LAW**) a person who is trained to help a lawyer ▶ **paralegal** *adj.*

parallel[1] 🔑 AW /ˈpærəlel/ *adj.*, *adv.* **1** ~ (to sth) (used about two lines, etc.) with the same distance between them for all their length: *parallel lines* ◇ *The railway runs parallel to the road.* ➲ picture at **line** **2** similar and happening at the same time: *The two brothers followed parallel careers in different companies.*

parallel[2] AW /ˈpærəlel/ *verb* [T] **1** to be similar to sth; to happen at the same time as sth: *Their legal system parallels our own.* **2** to be as good as sth SYN **equal**: *a level of achievement that has never been paralleled*

parallel[2] AW /ˈpærəlel/ *noun* [C,U] a person, thing or situation that is similar to another one in a different situation, place or time: *The government's huge election victory is* **without parallel** *this century.*

ˌ**parallel ˈbars** *noun* [pl.] two bars on posts that are used for doing GYMNASTIC exercises ➲ picture at **asymmetric bars**

parallelograms

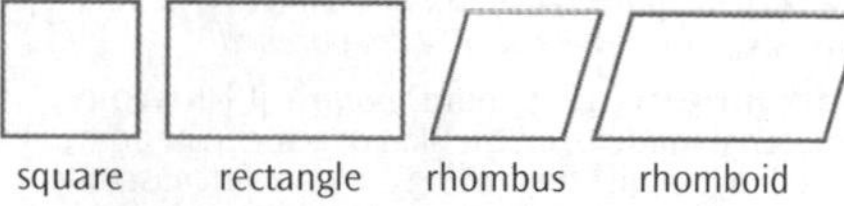

parallelogram /ˌpærəˈleləgræm/ *noun* [C] (**MATHEMATICS**) a flat shape with four straight sides. The opposite sides are parallel and equal to each other.

Paralympics /ˌpærəˈlɪmpɪks/ *noun* [pl.] (**SPORT**) an international ATHLETICS competition for people who are disabled

paralyse (*AmE* **paralyze**) /ˈpærəlaɪz/ *verb* [T] **1** (**HEALTH**) to make a person unable to move their body or a part of it: *Miriam is paralysed from the waist down.* **2** to make sb/sth unable to work in a normal way ▶ **paralysis** /pəˈræləsɪs/ *noun* [U]: *The disease can cause paralysis or even death.* ◇ *There has been complete paralysis of the railway system.*

paramedic /ˌpærəˈmedɪk/ *noun* [C] (**HEALTH**) a person who has had special training in treating people who are hurt or ill, but who is not a doctor or nurse

parameter AW /pəˈræmɪtə(r)/ *noun* [C, usually pl.] (*formal*) something that decides or limits the way in which sth can be done: *to set/define the parameters* ◇ *We had to work within the parameters that had already been established.*

paramilitary /ˌpærəˈmɪlətri/ ***adj.*** organized in the same way as, but not belonging to, an official army: *a paramilitary group*

paramount /ˈpærəmaʊnt/ ***adj.*** (*formal*) most important: *Safety is paramount in car design.*

paranoia /ˌpærəˈnɔɪə/ ***noun*** [U] **1** (**HEALTH**) a type of mental illness in which you wrongly believe that other people want to harm you **2** (*informal*) a feeling of fear and suspicion of other people

paranoid /ˈpærənɔɪd/ ***adj.*** wrongly believing that other people are trying to harm you or are saying bad things about you

paraphernalia /ˌpærəfəˈneɪliə/ ***noun*** [U] a large number of different objects that you need for a particular purpose

paraphrase /ˈpærəfreɪz/ ***verb*** [T] (**LANGUAGE**) to express sth again using different words so that it is easier to understand ▶ **paraphrase** ***noun*** [C]

paraplegia /ˌpærəˈpliːdʒə/ ***noun*** [U] (**HEALTH**) PARALYSIS (= loss of control or feeling) in the legs and lower body

paraplegic /ˌpærəˈpliːdʒɪk/ ***noun*** [C] (**HEALTH**) a person who suffers from PARAPLEGIA

parasite /ˈpærəsaɪt/ ***noun*** [C] (**BIOLOGY**) a plant or an animal that lives in or on another plant or animal and gets its food from it. **Parasites** sometimes cause disease. ▶ **parasitic** /ˌpærəˈsɪtɪk/ ***adj.***

parasol /ˈpærəsɒl/ ***noun*** [C] an umbrella that you use to protect yourself from the sun

paratroops /ˈpærətruːps/ ***noun*** [pl.] soldiers who are trained to jump from planes using a PARACHUTE (= a piece of equipment that opens to help them fall slowly)

parcel /ˈpɑːsl/ (*AmE also* **package**) ***noun*** [C] something that is covered in brown paper and sent to sb ➲ look at **pack**[1], **package**, **packet**

parched /pɑːtʃt/ ***adj.*** very hot and dry, or very thirsty: *Can I have a drink? I'm parched!*

parchment /ˈpɑːtʃmənt/ ***noun*** **1** [U] (**HISTORY**) material made from the skin of a sheep or GOAT, used in the past for writing on: *parchment scrolls* **2** [U] a thick yellowish type of paper

pardon[1] /ˈpɑːdn/ (*also* ˌ**pardon ˈme**) ***exclamation*** **1** used for asking sb to repeat what they have just said because you did not hear or understand it **2** used by some people to mean *sorry* or *excuse me*

pardon[2] /ˈpɑːdn/ ***noun*** [C,U] (**LAW**) an official decision not to punish sb for a crime ▶ **pardon** ***verb*** [T] **~ sb (for sth/doing sth)**

pare /peə(r)/ ***verb*** [T] **1 ~ sth (off/away)** to remove the thin outer layer of sth: *First, pare the rind from the lemon.* ◇ *She pared the apple.* **2 ~ sth (back/down)** to gradually reduce the size or amount of sth: *The training budget has been pared back to a minimum.* ◇ *The workforce has been* ***pared to the bone*** (= reduced to the lowest possible level). **3** (*especially BrE*) to cut away the edges of sth, especially your nails, in order to make them smooth

parent 🔑 /ˈpeərənt/ ***noun*** [C] **1** a person's mother or father ℹ A **single parent** is a mother or father who is bringing up his/her child or children alone, without the other parent. A **foster parent** is a person who looks after a child who is not legally his/her own. **2** a company that owns smaller companies of the same type: *a parent company*

parentage /ˈpeərəntɪdʒ/ ***noun*** [U] (*formal*) the origin of a person's parents and who they are: *a young American of German parentage* ◇ *Nothing is known of her parentage and background.*

parental /pəˈrentl/ ***adj.*** (only *before* a noun) of a parent or parents: *parental support/advice*

parenthesis /pəˈrenθəsɪs/ ***noun*** [C] (*pl.* **parentheses** /pəˈrenθəsiːz/) **1** a word, sentence, etc. that is added to a speech or piece of writing, especially in order to give extra information. In writing, it is separated from the rest of the text using brackets, commas or DASHES **2** [usually pl.] (*AmE* or *formal*) = BRACKET[1] (1): *Irregular forms are given* ***in parentheses***

parenthood /ˈpeərənthʊd/ ***noun*** [U] the state of being a parent

parenting /ˈpeərəntɪŋ/ ***noun*** [U] the process of caring for your child or children

ˌ**parent-ˈteacher association** = PTA

parish /ˈpærɪʃ/ ***noun*** [C] (**RELIGION**) an area or a district which has its own church; the people who live in this area: *the parish church* ▶ **parishioner** /pəˈrɪʃənə(r)/ ***noun*** [C]

ˌ**parish ˈcouncil** ***noun*** [C, with sing. or pl. verb] (**POLITICS**) a division of local government which looks after the interests of a very small area, especially a village

parity /ˈpærəti/ ***noun*** [U] **1** (*formal*) **~ (with sb/sth)**; **~ (between A and B)** the state of being equal, especially the state of having equal pay or position: *Prison officers are demanding pay parity with the police force.* **2** (**ECONOMICS**) (in finance) the fact of the units of money of two different countries being equal: *to achieve parity with the dollar*

park[1] 🔑 /pɑːk/ ***noun*** [C] **1** an open area in a town, often with grass or trees, where people can go to walk, play, etc.: *Let's go for a walk in the park.* **2** (in compounds) a large area of land that is used for a special purpose: *a national park* ◇ *a business park* ◇ *a theme park*

park[2] 🔑 /pɑːk/ ***verb*** [I,T] to leave the vehicle that you are driving somewhere for a period a time: *You can't park in the centre of town.* ◇ *Somebody's parked their car in front of the exit.*

parka /ˈpɑːkə/ ***noun*** [C] a warm jacket or coat with a part for covering your head (**hood**)

ˌ**park and ˈride** ***noun*** [C] a system designed to reduce traffic in towns in which people park their cars on the edge of a town and then take a special bus or train to the town centre; the area where people park their cars before taking the bus: *Use the park and ride.* ◇ *I've left my car in the park and ride.*

parking /ˈpɑːkɪŋ/ ***noun*** [U] the action of leaving a car, lorry, etc. somewhere for a time: *The sign said 'No Parking'.*

ˈ**parking garage** ***noun*** [C] (*AmE*) = MULTI-STOREY CAR PARK

ˈ**parking lot** (*AmE*) = CAR PARK

ˈ**parking meter** ***noun*** [C] a metal post that you put coins into to pay for parking a car in the space beside it for a period of time

ˈ**parking ticket** ***noun*** [C] a piece of paper that orders you to pay money (**a fine**) for parking your car where it is not allowed

Parkinson's disease /ˈpɑːkɪnsnz dɪziːz/ ***noun*** [U] (**HEALTH**) a disease that gets worse over a period of time and causes the muscles to become weak and the arms and legs to shake

parliament ⊶ /ˈpɑːləmənt/ ***noun*** (POLITICS) **1** [C] the group of people who are elected to make and change the laws of a country **2 Parliament** [sing.] the parliament of the United Kingdom: *a Member of Parliament (MP)*

CULTURE

Parliament

The UK Parliament consists of **the House of Lords**, whose members have been appointed rather than elected, and **the House of Commons**, whose members have been elected by the people to represent areas of the country (called **constituencies**).

parliamentary /ˌpɑːləˈmentri/ ***adj.*** (only *before* a noun) (POLITICS) connected with parliament

parody /ˈpærədi/ ***noun*** [C,U] (*pl.* **parodies**) (LITERATURE) a piece of writing, speech or music that copies the style of sb/sth in a funny way: *a parody of a spy novel* ▶ **parody** ***verb*** [T] (*pres. part.* **parodying**; *3rd person sing. pres.* **parodies**; *pt, pp* **parodied**)

parole /pəˈrəʊl/ ***noun*** [U] (LAW) permission that is given to a prisoner to leave prison early on the condition that they behave well: *He's going to be released **on parole**.*

parrot /ˈpærət/ ***noun*** [C] a type of tropical bird with a curved beak and usually with very bright feathers. **Parrots** that are kept as pets can be trained to copy what people say.

ˈparrot-fashion ***adv.*** without understanding the meaning of sth: *to learn sth parrot-fashion*

parsley /ˈpɑːsli/ ***noun*** [U] a plant with small leaves that are used in cooking and for food decoration as a HERB

parsnip /ˈpɑːsnɪp/ ***noun*** [C] a long thin white vegetable, that grows under the ground

part¹ ⊶ /pɑːt/ ***noun*** **1** [C,U] (a) ~ **(of sth)** one of the pieces, areas, periods, things, etc. that together with others forms the whole of sth; some, but not all of sth: *Which part of Spain do you come from?* ◇ *The film is good **in parts**.* ◇ ***spare parts** for a car* ◇ *a part of the body* ◇ *Part of the problem is lack of information.* ◇ *I enjoy being part of a team.* **2** [C] (ARTS AND MEDIA) a role or character in a play, film, etc.: *He played the part of Macbeth.* ◇ *I had a small part in the school play.* **3 parts** [pl.] a region or an area: *Are you from **these parts**?* **4** (ARTS AND MEDIA) [C] a section of a book, television series, etc.: *You can see part two of this programme at the same time next week.* **5** [C] an amount or quantity (of a liquid or substance): *Use one part cleaning fluid to ten parts water.*

IDM **the best/better part of sth** most of sth; more than half of sth, especially a period of time: *They've lived here for the best part of forty years.*

for the most part usually or mostly

for my/his/their, etc. part speaking for myself, himself, etc.; personally

have/play a part (in sth) to be involved in sth

in part not completely: *The accident was, in part, the fault of the driver.*

on the part of sb/on sb's part made, done or felt by sb: *There is concern on the part of the teachers that class sizes will increase.* ◇ *I'm sorry. It was a mistake on my part.*

take part (in sth) to join with other people in an activity: *Everybody took part in the discussion.*

part² /pɑːt/ ***verb*** **1** [I,T] (*formal*) ~ **(sb) (from sb)** to leave or go away from sb; to separate people or things: *We exchanged telephone numbers when we parted.* ◇ *He hates being parted from his children for long.* **2** [I,T] to move apart; to make things or people move apart: *Her lips were slightly parted.* **3** [T] to separate the hair on the head with a COMB in order to make a clear line: *She parts her hair in the middle.* ➲ look at **parting**

IDM **part company (with sb/sth)** to go different ways or to separate after being together

PHR V **part with sth** to give or sell sth to sb: *When we went to live in Italy, we had to part with our horses.*

part³ /pɑːt/ ***adv.*** not completely one thing and not completely another: *She's part Russian and part Chinese.*

ˌpart exˈchange ***noun*** [U] a way of buying sth, such as a car, in which you give your old one as some of the payment for a more expensive one

partial /ˈpɑːʃl/ ***adj.*** **1** not complete: *The project was only a partial success.* **2** (*old-fashioned*) ~ **to sth** liking sth very much: *He's very partial to ice cream.*
▶ **partially** ***adv.***

partiality /ˌpɑːʃiˈæləti/ ***noun*** [U] (*formal*) unfair support for one person, team, etc. above another: *The referee was accused of partiality towards the home team.* OPP **impartiality**

participant AW /pɑːˈtɪsɪpənt/ ***noun*** [C] a person who takes part in sth

participate AW /pɑːˈtɪsɪpeɪt/ ***verb*** [I] ~ **(in sth)** to take part or become involved in sth: *Students are encouraged to participate in sporting activities.*
▶ **participation** AW /pɑːˌtɪsɪˈpeɪʃn/ ***noun*** [U]
▶ **participatory** AW /pɑːˌtɪsɪˈpeɪtəri/ ***adj.***: *Ordinary people had no participatory role in the Government.*

participle /ˈpɑːtɪsɪpl; ˌpɑːˈtɪsɪpl/ ***noun*** [C] (LANGUAGE) a word that is formed from a verb and that ends in *-ing* (present participle) or *-ed*, *-en*, etc. (past participle). **Participles** are used to form TENSES of the verb, or as adjectives: *'Hurrying' and 'hurried' are the present and past participles of 'hurry'.*

particle /ˈpɑːtɪkl/ ***noun*** [C] **1** a very small piece; a bit: *dust particles* **2** (PHYSICS) a very small piece of matter, such as an ELECTRON or PROTON, that is part of an atom ➲ look at **alpha particle**, **elementary particle** **3** (LANGUAGE) a small word that is not as important as a noun, verb or adjective: *In the phrasal verb 'break down', 'down' is an adverbial particle.*

particular ⊶ /pəˈtɪkjələ(r)/ ***adj.*** **1** (only *before* a noun) used to emphasize that you are talking about one person, thing, time, etc. and not about others: *Is there any particular dish you enjoy making?* **2** (only *before* a noun) greater than usual; special: *This article is of particular interest to me.* **3** connected with one person or thing and not with others: *Everybody has their own particular problems.* **4** ~ **(about/over sth)** (not before a noun) difficult to please: *Some people are extremely particular about what they eat.* ➲ look at **fussy**

IDM **in particular** especially: *Is there **anything in particular** you'd like to do this weekend?*

particularly ⊶ /pəˈtɪkjələli/ ***adv.*** especially; more than usual or more than others: *I'm particularly interested in Indian history.* ◇ *The match was excellent, particularly the second half.*

particulars /pəˈtɪkjələz/ ***noun*** [pl.] (*formal*) facts or details about sb/sth: *The police took down all the particulars about the missing child.*

parting /ˈpɑːtɪŋ/ ***noun*** **1** [C,U] saying goodbye to, or being separated from, another person (usually for quite a long time) **2** [C] the line in a person's hair

In the United States the main political parties are the **Republicans** and the **Democrats**.

where it is divided in two with a COMB: *a side/centre parting* ➲ look at **part²** (3)

partisan¹ /ˌpɑːtɪˈzæn; ˈpɑːtɪzæn/ *adj.* showing too much support for one person, group or idea, especially without considering it carefully: *Most newspapers are politically partisan.* ▶ **partisanship** *noun* [U]

partisan² /ˌpɑːtɪˈzæn; ˈpɑːtɪzæn/ *noun* [C] **1** (POLITICS) a person who strongly supports a particular leader, group or idea **2** (POLITICS) a member of an armed group that is fighting secretly against enemy soldiers who have taken control of its country

partition /pɑːˈtɪʃn/ *noun* **1** [C] something that divides a room, office etc. into two or more parts, especially a thin or temporary wall **2** [U] (POLITICS) the division of a country into two or more countries ▶ **partition** *verb* [T]: *to partition a country/room*

partly 🔑 /ˈpɑːtli/ *adv.* not completely: *She was only partly responsible for the mistake.*

partner 🔑 AW /ˈpɑːtnə(r)/ *noun* [C] **1** the person that you are married to or live with as if you are married **2** (BUSINESS) one of the people who owns a business: *business partners* **3** a person that you are doing an activity with as a team, for example dancing or playing a game **4** (POLITICS) a country or an organization that has an agreement with another ▶ **partner** *verb* [T]: *Hales partnered his brother in the doubles, and they won the gold medal.*

partnership 🔑 AW /ˈpɑːtnəʃɪp/ *noun* **1** [U] (BUSINESS) the state of being a partner in business: *Simona went into partnership with her sister and opened a shop in Rome.* **2** [C] a relationship between two people, organizations, etc.: *Marriage is a partnership for life.* **3** [C] (BUSINESS) a business owned by two or more people

ˌpart of ˈspeech *noun* [C] (LANGUAGE) one of the groups that words are divided into, for example noun, verb, adjective, etc. SYN **word class**

partridge /ˈpɑːtrɪdʒ/ *noun* [C] a brown bird with a round body and a short tail, that people hunt for sport or food

ˌpart-ˈtime *adj., adv.* for only a part of the working day or week: *She's got a part-time job.* ➲ look at **full-time**

party 🔑 /ˈpɑːti/ *noun* [C] (*pl.* **parties**) **1** a social occasion to which people are invited in order to eat, drink and enjoy themselves: *When we've moved into our new house we're going to **have a party**.* ◇ *a birthday/dinner party* **2** (*also* **Party**) (POLITICS) a group of people who have the same political aims and ideas and who are trying to win elections to parliament, etc. **3** (often in compounds) a group of people who are working, travelling, etc. together: *a party of tourists* **4** (*formal*) (LAW) one of the people or groups of people involved in a legal case: *the guilty/innocent party* ➲ look at **third party**

ˌparty ˈpolitics *noun* [U, with sing. or pl. verb] (POLITICS) political activity that involves political parties: *The President should stand above party politics.* ◇ *Many people think that party politics should not enter into local government.*

CULTURE

The two main political parties in Great Britain are the **Labour Party** (left-wing) and the **Conservative** (or **Tory**) **Party** (right-wing). There is also a centre party called the **Liberal Democrats** and some other smaller parties.

pass¹ 🔑 /pɑːs/ *verb* **1** [I,T] to move past or to the other side of sb/sth: *The street was crowded and the two buses couldn't pass.* ◇ *I passed him in the street but he didn't say hello.* **2** [I,T] ~ (sth) **along, down, through, etc.** (sth) to go or move, or make sth move, in the direction mentioned: *A plane passed overhead.* ◇ *We'll have to pass the wire through the window.* **3** [T] ~ **sth (to sb)** to give sth to sb: *Could you pass (me) the salt, please?* **4** [I,T] ~ (**sth**) (**to sb**) (SPORT) (in some sports) to kick, hit or throw the ball to sb on your own team **5** [I] (used about time) to go by: *At least a year has passed since I last saw them.* ◇ *It was a long journey but the time passed very quickly.* **6** [T] to spend time, especially when you are bored or waiting for sth: *I'll have to think of something to do to **pass the time** in hospital.* **7** [I,T] (EDUCATION) to achieve the necessary standard in an exam, test, etc.: *Good luck in the exam! I'm sure you'll pass.* OPP **fail** **8** [T] (EDUCATION) to test sb/sth and say that they are good enough: *The examiner passed most of the students.* **9** [T] (LAW) to officially approve a law, etc. by voting: *One of the functions of Parliament is to **pass new laws**.* **10** [T] ~ **sth (on sb/sth)** to give an opinion, a judgement, etc.: *The judge **passed sentence** on the young man* (= said what his punishment would be). **11** [I] to be allowed or accepted: *I didn't like what they were saying but I **let it pass**.*

IDM **pass the buck (to sb)** to make sb else responsible for a difficult situation

pass water (*formal*) (HEALTH) to get rid of waste liquid from your body

PHR V **pass away** used as a polite way of saying 'die'

pass by (sb/sth) to go past: *I pass by your house on the way to work.*

pass sth down to give or teach sth to people who will live after you have died

pass for sb/sth to be accepted as sb/sth that you are not: *His mother looks so young she'd pass for his sister.*

pass sb/sth off (as sb/sth) to say that a person or a thing is sth that he/she/it is not: *He tried to pass the work off as his own.*

pass sth on (to sb) to give sth to sb else, especially after you have been given it or used it yourself: *Could you pass the message on to Mr Roberts?*

pass out (HEALTH) to become unconscious SYN **faint** OPP **come round/to**

pass² /pɑːs/ *noun* [C] **1** (EDUCATION) a successful result in an exam: *The pass mark is 50%.* ◇ *Grades A, B and C are passes.* OPP **fail** **2** an official piece of paper that gives you permission to enter or leave a building, travel on a bus or train, etc.: *Show your student pass when you buy a ticket.* **3** (SPORT) the act of kicking, hitting or throwing the ball to sb on your own team in some sports **4** a road or way over or through mountains: *a mountain pass*

passable /ˈpɑːsəbl/ *adj.* **1** good enough but not very good: *My French is not brilliant but it's passable.* **2** (not before a noun) (used about roads, rivers, etc.) possible to use or cross; not blocked OPP **impassable**

passage 🔑 /ˈpæsɪdʒ/ *noun* **1** [C] (*also* **passageway**) a long, narrow way with walls on either side that connects one place with another: *a secret underground passage* **2** [C] (BIOLOGY) a tube in your body which air, liquid, etc. can pass through: *the nasal passages* **3** [C] (ARTS AND MEDIA) a short part of a book, a speech or a piece of music: *The students were given a passage from the novel to study.* **4** [sing.] the process of passing: *His painful memories faded with **the passage of time**.*

passenger ⊶ /ˈpæsɪndʒə(r)/ ***noun*** [C] a person who is travelling in a car, bus, train, plane, etc. but who is not driving it or working on it

ˌpasser-ˈby ***noun*** [C] (*pl.* **passers-by**) a person who is walking past sb/sth

passing[1] ⊶ /ˈpɑːsɪŋ/ ***adj.*** (only *before* a noun) **1** lasting for only a short time; brief: *a passing phase/thought/interest* **2** going past: *I stopped a passing car and asked for help.*

passing[2] ⊶ /ˈpɑːsɪŋ/ ***noun*** [U] the process of going by: *the passing of time*

IDM **in passing** done or said quickly, while you are thinking or talking about sth else: *He mentioned the house in passing but he didn't give any details.*

passion /ˈpæʃn/ ***noun*** **1** [C,U] (a) very strong feeling, especially of love, hate or anger: *He was a violent man, controlled by his passions.* **2** [sing.] **a ~ (for sb)** very strong sexual love or attraction: *He longed to tell Sashi of his passion for her.* **3** [sing.] **a ~ for sth** a very strong liking for or interest in sth: *He has a passion for history.*

passionate /ˈpæʃənət/ ***adj.*** **1** showing or caused by very strong feelings: *The President gave a passionate speech about crime.* **2** showing or feeling very strong love or sexual attraction: *a passionate kiss* ▸ **passionately** ***adv.***: *He believes passionately in democracy.*

ˈpassion fruit ***noun*** [C,U] (*pl.* **passion fruit**) a small tropical fruit with a thick purple skin and many seeds inside

passive[1] AW /ˈpæsɪv/ ***adj.*** **1** showing no reaction, feeling or interest; not active: *Some people prefer to play a passive role in meetings.* **2** (LANGUAGE) used about the form of a verb or a sentence when the subject of the sentence is affected by the action of the verb: *In the sentence 'He was bitten by a dog', the verb is passive.* ➲ look at **active** ▸ **passively** ***adv.***

passive[2] AW (*also* **ˌpassive ˈvoice**) ***noun*** [sing.] (LANGUAGE) the form of a verb used when the subject is affected by the action of the verb ➲ look at **active**

ˌpassive ˈsmoking ***noun*** [U] (HEALTH) the act of breathing in smoke from other people's cigarettes

Passover /ˈpɑːsəʊvə(r)/ ***noun*** [U,C] (RELIGION) the Jewish religious festival and holiday in memory of the escape of the Jews from Egypt

passport ⊶ /ˈpɑːspɔːt/ ***noun*** [C] **1** an official document that identifies you as a citizen of a particular country and that you have to show when you enter or leave a country: *a valid passport* ◇ *a South African passport* ◇ *I was stopped as I went through* ***passport control.*** ❶ You **apply for** or **renew** your passport at the **passport office**. This office **issues** new passports. **2 a ~ to sth** a thing that makes it possible to achieve sth: *a passport to success*

password /ˈpɑːswɜːd/ ***noun*** [C] **1** a secret word or phrase that you need to know in order to be allowed into a place **2** (COMPUTING) a series of letters or numbers that you must type into a computer or computer system in order to be able to use it: *Please enter your password.*

past[1] ⊶ /pɑːst/ ***adj.*** **1** already gone; belonging to a time before the present: *in past centuries/times* ◇ *I'd rather forget some of my past mistakes.* **2** (only *before* a noun) just finished; last: *He's had to work very hard during the past year.*

past[2] ⊶ /pɑːst/ ***prep., adv.*** **1** (used when telling the time) after; later than: *It's ten (minutes) past three.* ◇ *It was past midnight when we got home.* **2** from one side to the other of sb/sth; further than or on the other side of sb/sth: *He walked straight past me.* ◇ *She looked right past me without realizing who I was.* **3** above or further than a certain point, limit or age: *Unemployment is now past the 2 million mark.* ◇ *I'm so tired that I'm* ***past caring*** (= I don't care any more) *what we eat.*

IDM **not put it past sb** to think sb is capable of doing sth bad: *I wouldn't put it past him to do a thing like that.*

past it (*informal*) too old

past[3] ⊶ /pɑːst/ ***noun*** **1 the past** [sing.] the time that has gone by; the things that happened before now: *in the recent/distant past* ◇ *The art of writing letters seems to be* ***a thing of the past.*** **2** [C] a person's life and career before now: *We know nothing about his past.* **3** (LANGUAGE) **the past** [sing.] = THE PAST TENSE

pasta /ˈpæstə/ ***noun*** [U] an Italian food made from flour, eggs and water, formed into different shapes, cooked, and usually served with a sauce

paste[1] /peɪst/ ***noun*** **1** [C,U] a soft, wet mixture, usually made of a powder and a liquid and sometimes used for sticking things: *wallpaper paste* ◇ *Mix the flour and milk into a paste.* **2** [U] (usually used in compound nouns) a soft mixture of food that you can spread onto bread, etc.: *fish/chicken paste*

paste[2] /peɪst/ ***verb*** [T] **1** to stick sth to sth else using **paste** or a similar substance (**glue**): *He pasted the picture into his book.* **2** (COMPUTING) to copy or move text into a document from somewhere else: *This function allows you to* ***cut and paste*** *text.*

pastel /ˈpæstl/ ***noun*** **1** [U] (ART) soft coloured CHALK, used for drawing pictures: *drawings in pastel* **2 pastels** [pl.] (ART) small sticks of CHALK: *a box of pastels* **3** [C] (ART) a picture drawn with **pastels** **4** [C] a pale delicate colour: *The whole house was painted in soft pastels.*

pasteurized (also **-ised**) /ˈpɑːstʃəraɪzd/ ***adj.*** (BIOLOGY) (used about milk or cream) free from bacteria because it has been heated and then cooled

pastiche /pæˈstiːʃ/ ***noun*** (*written*) **1** (ART, LITERATURE) [C] a work of art, piece of writing, etc. that is created by deliberately copying the style of sb/sth else: *a pastiche of the classic detective story* **2** [C] (ART) a work of art, etc. that consists of a variety of different styles **3** [U] (ART) the art of creating a **pastiche**

pastime /ˈpɑːstaɪm/ ***noun*** [C] something that you enjoy doing when you are not working SYN **hobby**

pastoral /ˈpɑːstərəl/ ***adj.*** **1** (connected with the work of a priest or a teacher) giving help and advice on personal matters rather than on matters of religion or education **2** connected with pleasant country life

ˌpast parˈticiple → PARTICIPLE

the ˌpast ˈperfect (*also* **the pluperfect**) ***noun*** [sing.] (LANGUAGE) the tense of a verb that describes an action that was finished before another event happened

pastry /ˈpeɪstri/ ***noun*** (*pl.* **pastries**) **1** [U] a mixture of flour, fat and water that is rolled out flat and cooked as a base or covering for pies, etc. **2** [C] a small cake made with **pastry**

the ˌpast ˈtense (*also* **the past**) ***noun*** [sing.] (LANGUAGE) the form of a verb used to describe actions in the past: *The past (tense) of the verb 'come' is 'came'.*

pasture /ˈpɑːstʃə(r)/ ***noun*** [C,U] (AGRICULTURE) a field or land covered with grass, where cows, etc. can feed

pasty /ˈpæsti/ ***noun*** [C] (*pl.* **pasties**) (*BrE*) a small pie containing meat and/or vegetables

pat¹ /pæt/ ***verb*** [T] (**patting**; **patted**) to touch sb/sth gently with a flat hand, especially as a sign of friendship, care, etc.

pat² /pæt/ ***noun*** [C] a gentle friendly touch with a flat hand: *He gave her knee an affectionate pat.*
IDM **a pat on the back (for sth/doing sth)** approval for sth good that a person has done: *She deserves a pat on the back for all her hard work.*

pat³ /pæt/ ***adj.***, ***adv.*** (only *before* a noun) (used about an answer, comment, etc.) said in a quick or simple way that does not sound natural or realistic

patch¹ /pætʃ/ ***noun*** [C] **1 a ~ (of sth)** a part of a surface that is different in some way from the area around it: *Drive carefully. There are patches of ice on the roads.* ◇ *a bald patch* **2** a piece of material that you use to cover a hole in clothes, etc.: *I sewed patches on the knees of my jeans.* **3** a small piece of material that you wear over one eye, usually because the eye is damaged **4** a small piece of land, especially for growing vegetables or fruit: *a vegetable patch*
IDM **go through a bad patch** (*especially BrE, informal*) to experience a difficult or unhappy period of time
not a patch on sb/sth (*especially BrE, informal*) not nearly as good as sb/sth: *Her new book isn't a patch on her others.*

patch² /pætʃ/ ***verb*** [T] to cover a hole in clothes, etc. with a piece of material in order to repair it: *patched jeans*
PHR V **patch sth up 1** to repair sth, especially in a temporary way by adding a new piece of material **2** to stop arguing with sb and to be friends again: *Have you tried to* ***patch things up*** *with her?*

patchwork /ˈpætʃwɜːk/ ***noun*** [U] (ART) a type of sewing in which small pieces of cloth of different colours and patterns are sewn together

patchy /ˈpætʃi/ ***adj.*** **1** existing or happening in some places but not others: *patchy fog/clouds/rain* **2** not complete; good in some parts but not in others: *My knowledge of German is rather patchy.*

pâté /ˈpæteɪ/ ***noun*** [U] food that is made by making meat, fish or vegetables into a smooth, thick mixture that is served cold and spread on bread, etc.: *liver pâté*

patella /pəˈtelə/ (ANATOMY) = KNEECAP ➲ picture on **page 80**

patent¹ /ˈpeɪtnt/ ***adj.*** (*formal*) clear; obvious: *a patent lie* ▶ **patently** ***adv.***

patent² /ˈpætnt; ˈpeɪtnt/ ***noun*** [C,U] (BUSINESS) the official right to be the only person to make, use or sell a product or an invention; the document that shows this is your right ▶ **patent** ***verb*** [T]

ˌpatent ˈleather ***noun*** [U] a type of leather with a hard, shiny surface, used especially for making shoes and bags

paternal /pəˈtɜːnl/ ***adj.*** (only *before* a noun) **1** behaving as a father would behave; connected with being a father **2** related through the father's side of the family: *my paternal grandparents* ➲ look at **maternal**

paternalism /pəˈtɜːnəlɪzəm/ ***noun*** [U] the system in which a government or an employer protects the people who are governed or employed by providing them with what they need, but does not give them any responsibility or freedom of choice
▶ **paternalistic** /pəˌtɜːnəˈlɪstɪk/ (*also* **paternalist**) ***adj.***: *a paternalistic employer/state*

paternity /pəˈtɜːnəti/ ***noun*** [U] the fact of being the father of a child: *paternity leave* (= time that the father of a new baby is allowed to have away from work) ➲ look at **maternity**

path 🔑 /pɑːθ/ ***noun*** [C] **1** (*also* **pathway**) a way across a piece of land that is made by or used by people walking: *the garden path* ◇ *There was a narrow pathway leading down the cliff.* ➲ look at **footpath 2** the line along which sb/sth moves; the space in front of sb/sth as they move: *He threw himself* ***into the path of*** *an oncoming vehicle.* ➲ look at **flight path**

pathetic /pəˈθetɪk/ ***adj.*** **1** causing you to feel pity or sadness: *the pathetic cries of the hungry children* **2** (*informal*) very bad, weak or useless: *What a pathetic performance! The team deserved to lose.*
▶ **pathetically** /-kli/ ***adv.***

paˌthetic ˈfallacy ***noun*** [U, sing.] (ART, LITERATURE) the act of describing animals and things as having human feelings

patho- /ˈpæθəʊ/ ***prefix*** (used in nouns, adjectives and adverbs) (BIOLOGY) connected with disease: *pathology*

pathogen /ˈpæθədʒən/ ***noun*** [C] (HEALTH) a thing that causes disease

pathological /ˌpæθəˈlɒdʒɪkl/ ***adj.*** **1** caused by feelings that you cannot control; not reasonable or sensible: *He's a pathological liar* (= he cannot stop lying). ◇ *pathological fear/hatred/violence* **2** (HEALTH) caused by or connected with disease or illness: *pathological depression* **3** (HEALTH) connected with PATHOLOGY ▶ **pathologically** /-kli/ ***adv.***

pathologist /pəˈθɒlədʒɪst/ ***noun*** [C] (HEALTH) a doctor who is an expert in PATHOLOGY, and examines dead bodies to find out why people have died

pathology /pəˈθɒlədʒi/ ***noun*** [U] (HEALTH) the scientific study of diseases of the body

pathos /ˈpeɪθɒs/ ***noun*** [U] (LITERATURE) the power of a performance, description, etc. to produce feelings of sadness or pity

pathway /ˈpɑːθweɪ/ ***noun*** [C] = PATH (1)

patience 🔑 /ˈpeɪʃns/ ***noun*** [U] **1 ~ (with sb/sth)** the quality of being able to stay calm and not get angry, especially when there is a difficulty or you have to wait a long time: *I've got no patience with people who don't even try.* ◇ *to* ***lose patience*** *with sb*
OPP **impatience 2** (*AmE* **solitaire**) a card game for only one player

patient¹ 🔑 /ˈpeɪʃnt/ ***adj.*** **~ (with sb/sth)** able to stay calm and not get angry, especially when there is a difficulty or you have to wait a long time: *She's very patient with young children.* OPP **impatient** ▶ **patiently** ***adv.***: *to wait patiently*

patient² 🔑 /ˈpeɪʃnt/ ***noun*** [C] (HEALTH) a person who is receiving medical treatment: *a hospital patient* ◇ *He's one of Dr Waters' patients.*

patio /ˈpætiəʊ/ ***noun*** [C] (*pl.* **patios** /-əʊz/) a flat, hard area, usually behind a house, where people can sit, eat, etc. outside ➲ look at **balcony**, **veranda**, **terrace**

patois /ˈpætwɑː/ ***noun*** [C] (*pl.* **patois** /ˈpætwɑːz/) (LANGUAGE) a form of a language, spoken by people in a particular area, that is different from the standard language of the country

patriarch /ˈpeɪtriɑːk/ ***noun*** [C] a man who is the head of a family or social group ➲ look at **matriarch**

patriarchal /ˌpeɪtriˈɑːkl/ ***adj.*** (used about a society or system) (**SOCIAL STUDIES**) controlled by men rather than women; passing power, property, etc. from father to son rather than from mother to daughter ➲ look at **matriarchal**

patriarchy /ˈpeɪtriɑːki/ ***noun*** [C,U] (*pl.* **patriarchies**) (**SOCIAL STUDIES**) a social system that gives power and control to men rather than women ➲ look at **matriarchy**

patricide /ˈpætrɪsaɪd/ ***noun*** [U] (*formal*) (**LAW**) the crime of killing your father ➲ look at **matricide**

patrimony /ˈpætrɪməni/ ***noun*** [sing.] (*formal*) (**LAW**) **1** property that is given to sb when their father dies **SYN** **inheritance** **2** the works of art and TREASURES of a nation, church, etc. **SYN** **heritage**

patriot /ˈpeɪtriət; ˈpæt-/ ***noun*** [C] a person who loves their country and is ready to defend it against an enemy ▶ **patriotism** /ˈpeɪtriətɪzəm; ˈpæt-/ ***noun*** [U]

patriotic /ˌpeɪtriˈɒtɪk; ˌpæt-/ ***adj.*** having or showing great love for your country ▶ **patriotically** /-kli/ ***adv.***

patrol¹ /pəˈtrəʊl/ ***verb*** [I,T] (**patrolling**; **patrolled**) to go round an area, a building, etc. at regular times to make sure that it is safe and that nothing is wrong

patrol² /pəˈtrəʊl/ ***noun*** **1** [C,U] the act of going round an area, building, etc. at regular times to make sure that it is safe and that nothing is wrong: *a police car **on patrol** in the area* **2** [C] a group of soldiers, vehicles, etc. that **patrol** sth: *a naval/police patrol ◇ a patrol car/boat*

patron /ˈpeɪtrən/ ***noun*** [C] **1** (**ARTS AND MEDIA**) a person who gives money and support to artists, writers and musicians: *a patron of the arts* **2** a famous person who supports an organization such as a charity and whose name is used in advertising it ➲ look at **sponsor** **3** (*formal*) a person who uses a particular shop, theatre, restaurant, etc.: *This car park is for patrons only.*

patronage /ˈpætrənɪdʒ; ˈpeɪt-/ ***noun*** [U] (*formal*) **1** the support, especially financial, that is given to a person or an organization by a PATRON: *Patronage of the arts comes mainly from businesses and private individuals.* **2** the system by which an important person gives help or a job to sb in return for their support **3** (*especially AmE*) the support that a person gives a shop, restaurant, etc. by spending money there

patronize (also **-ise**) /ˈpætrənaɪz/ ***verb*** [T] **1** to treat sb in a way that shows that you think you are better, more intelligent, experienced, etc. than they are **2** (*formal*) to be a regular customer of a shop, restaurant, etc. ▶ **patronizing** (also **-ising**) ***adj.***: *I really hate that patronizing smile of hers.* ▶ **patronizingly** (also **-isingly**) ***adv.***

ˌpatron ˈsaint ***noun*** [C] (**RELIGION**) a religious being who is believed by Christians to protect a particular place or people doing a particular activity

patter /ˈpætə(r)/ ***noun*** **1** [sing.] the sound of many quick light steps or knocks on a surface: *the patter of the children's feet on the stairs* **2** [U, sing.] fast continuous talk by sb who is trying to sell you sth or entertain you: *sales patter* ▶ **patter** ***verb*** [I]

pattern 🔑 /ˈpætn/ ***noun*** [C] **1** the way in which sth happens, develops, or is done: *Her days all seemed to follow the same pattern. ◇ changing patterns of behaviour/work/weather* **2** (**ART**) an arrangement of lines, shapes, colours, etc. as a design: *a shirt with a floral pattern on it* **SYN** **design** **3** a design, a set of instructions or a shape to cut around that you use in order to make sth

patterned /ˈpætənd/ ***adj.*** decorated with a PATTERN (2)

pause¹ 🔑 /pɔːz/ ***noun*** **1** [C] a ~ (**in sth**) a short period of time during which sb stops talking or stops what they are doing: *He continued playing for twenty minutes without a pause.* **2** (*also* **ˈpause button**) [U] a control on a DVD player, etc. that allows you to stop playing or recording for a short time

pause² 🔑 /pɔːz/ ***verb*** [I] ~ (**for sth**) to stop talking or doing sth for a short time before continuing

pave /peɪv/ ***verb*** [T] ~ **sth** (**with sth**) (often passive) to cover an area of ground with flat stones (**paving stones**) or bricks

pavement /ˈpeɪvmənt/ ***noun*** [C] **1** (*AmE* **sidewalk**) a hard flat area at the side of a road for people to walk on **2** (**GEOLOGY**) a large flat area of bare rock ➲ picture at **limestone**

pavilion /pəˈvɪliən/ ***noun*** [C] (*BrE*) a building at a sports ground where players can change their clothes

ˈpaving stone ***noun*** [C] a flat piece of stone that is used for covering the ground

paw¹ /pɔː/ ***noun*** [C] (**BIOLOGY**) the foot of animals such as dogs, cats, bears, etc. ➲ picture at **lion**

paw² /pɔː/ ***verb*** [I,T] ~ (**at**) **sth** (used about an animal) to touch or scratch sb/sth several times with a **paw**: *The dog pawed at my sleeve.*

pawn¹ /pɔːn/ ***noun*** [C] **1** (in the game of CHESS) one of the eight pieces that are of least value and importance **2** a person who is used or controlled by other more powerful people

pawn² /pɔːn/ ***verb*** [T] to leave a valuable object with a PAWNBROKER in return for money. If you cannot pay back the money after a certain period, the object can be sold or kept.

pawnbroker /ˈpɔːnbrəʊkə(r)/ ***noun*** [C] a person who lends money to people when they leave sth of value with them

pay¹ 🔑 /peɪ/ ***verb*** (*pt, pp* **paid**) **1** [I,T] ~ (**sb**) (**for sth**); ~ (**sb**) **sth** (**for sth**) to give sb money for work, goods, services, etc.: *She is very **well paid**. ◇ The work's finished but we haven't paid for it yet. ◇ We paid the dealer £3000 for the car.* ➲ note at **income** **2** [T] ~ **sth** (**to sb**) to give the money that you owe for sth: *Have you paid her the rent yet? ◇ to pay a bill/fine* **3** [I,T] to make a profit; to be worth doing: *It would pay you to get professional advice before making a decision.* **4** [I] ~ (**for sth**) to suffer or be punished because of your beliefs or actions: *You'll pay for that remark!*

IDM **be paid in arrears** → ARREARS

pay attention (**to sb/sth**) to listen carefully to or to take notice of sb/sth

pay sb a compliment; **pay a compliment to sb** to say that you like sth about sb

pay your respects (**to sb**) (*formal*) to visit sb as a sign of respect: *Hundreds came to pay their last respects to her* (= came to her funeral).

pay tribute to sb/sth to say good things about sb/sth and show your respect for sb/sth

put paid to sth to destroy or finish sth: *The bad weather put paid to our picnic.*

PHR V **pay sth back** (**to sb**) to give money back to sb that you borrowed from them: *Can you lend me £5? I'll pay you back/I'll pay it back to you on Friday.*

pay sb back (**for sth**) to punish sb for making you or

sb else suffer: *What a mean trick! I'll pay you back one day.*
pay off (*informal*) to be successful: *All her hard work has paid off! She passed her exam.*
pay sth off to pay all the money that you owe for sth: *to pay off a debt/mortgage*
pay up (*informal*) to pay the money that you owe: *If you don't pay up, we'll take you to court.*

RELATED VOCABULARY

Pay is the general word for money that you get regularly for work that you have done.

Wages are paid weekly or daily in cash.

A **salary** is paid monthly, directly into a bank account.

You pay a **fee** for professional services, for example to a doctor, lawyer, etc.

Payment is money for work that you do once or not regularly. Your **income** is all the money you get regularly, both for work you have done, and as interest on money you have saved.

pay² ⊶ /peɪ/ ***noun*** [U] money that you get regularly for work that you have done

payable /ˈpeɪəbl/ ***adj.*** that should or must be paid: *A 10% deposit is payable in advance.* ◇ *Make the cheque* ***payable to*** *Pauline Nolan.*

PAYE /ˌpiː eɪ waɪ ˈiː/ ***abbr.*** pay as you earn; a British system of paying tax in which money is taken from the money you earn by your employer and paid to the government

payee /ˌpeɪˈiː/ ***noun*** [C] (*written*) a person that money, especially a cheque, is paid to

payment ⊶ /ˈpeɪmənt/ ***noun*** ~ **(for sth) 1** [U] the act of paying sb or of being paid: *I did the work last month but I haven't had any payment for it yet.* ➲ note at **pay² 2** [C] an amount of money that you must pay: *They asked for a payment of £100 as a deposit.*

ˌpay-per-ˈview ***noun*** [U] (ARTS AND MEDIA) a system of television broadcasting in which you pay an extra sum of money to watch a particular programme, such as a film or a sports event

payphone /ˈpeɪfəʊn/ ***noun*** [C] a telephone, usually in a public place, that is operated using coins or a card

payroll /ˈpeɪrəʊl/ ***noun*** **1** [C] a list of people employed by a company showing the amount of money to be paid to each of them: *There are 70 people* ***on the payroll***. **2** [C, usually sing.] the total amount paid by a company to its employees

PC /ˌpiː ˈsiː/ ***abbr.*** **1** (COMPUTING) personal computer; a computer that is designed for one person to use at work or at home **2** = POLICE CONSTABLE **3** = POLITICALLY CORRECT

PDA /ˌpiː diː ˈeɪ/ ***noun*** [C] (COMPUTING) **personal digital assistant**; a very small computer that is used for storing personal information and creating documents, and that may include other functions such as telephone, FAX, connection to the Internet, etc.

PDF /ˌpiː diː ˈef/ (*also* ˌ**PDˈF file**) ***noun*** [C] (COMPUTING) **Portable Document Format**; a type of computer file that can contain words or pictures. It can be read using any system, can be sent from one computer to another, and will look the same on any computer: *I'll send it to you as a PDF.*

PE /ˌpiː ˈiː/ ***abbr.*** (EDUCATION) physical education: *a PE lesson*

pea /piː/ ***noun*** [C] a small round green seed that is eaten as a vegetable. A number of **peas** grow together in a long thin case (**a pod**).

peace ⊶ /piːs/ ***noun*** [U] **1** a situation or a period of time in which there is no war or violence in a country or area: *The two communities now manage to live* ***in peace*** *together.* ◇ *A UN force has been sent in to* ***keep the peace***. **2** the state of being calm or quiet: *He longed to escape from the city to the* ***peace and quiet*** *of the countryside.*

peaceful ⊶ /ˈpiːsfl/ ***adj.*** **1** not wanting or involving war, violence or argument: *a peaceful protest/demonstration/solution* **2** calm and quiet: *a peaceful village* ▸ **peacefully** /-fəli/ ***adv.***: *The siege ended peacefully.* ▸ **peacefulness** ***noun*** [U]

peacekeeping /ˈpiːskiːpɪŋ/ ***adj.*** (only *before* a noun) (POLITICS) intended to help keep the peace and prevent war or violence in a place where this is likely: *a United Nations peacekeeping force*

peacemaker /ˈpiːsmeɪkə(r)/ ***noun*** [C] (POLITICS) a person who tries to persuade people or countries to stop arguing or fighting and to make peace ▸ **peacemaking** ***noun*** [U], ***adj.***

peacetime /ˈpiːstaɪm/ ***noun*** [U] a period when a country is not at war

peach /piːtʃ/ ***noun*** **1** [C] a soft round fruit with orange-red skin and a large stone in the centre. **2** [U] a pinkish-orange colour

peacock /ˈpiːkɒk/ ***noun*** [C] a large bird with beautiful long blue and green tail feathers that it can lift up and spread out

peak¹ ⊶ /piːk/ ***noun*** [C] **1** the point at which sth is the highest, best, strongest, etc.: *a man* ***at the peak of*** *his career* **2** (GEOGRAPHY) the pointed top of a mountain: *snow-covered peaks* ➲ picture at **glacial 3** the front part of a cap that sticks out above your eyes

peak² /piːk/ ***verb*** [I] to reach the highest point or value: *Sales peak just before Christmas.* ◇ *Unemployment peaked at 17%.*

peak³ /piːk/ ***adj.*** (only *before* a noun) used to describe the highest level of sth, or a time when the greatest number of people are doing or using sth: *Summer is the* ***peak period*** *for most hotels.* ◇ *The athletes are all in* ***peak condition***. ◇ *We need extra help during the* ***peak season***. ➲ look at **off-peak**

peal /piːl/ ***noun*** [C] the loud ringing of a bell or bells: (*figurative*) *peals of laughter* ▸ **peal** ***verb*** [I]

peanut /ˈpiːnʌt/ ***noun*** **1** (*also* **groundnut**) [C] a nut that grows underground in a thin shell **2 peanuts** [pl.] (*informal*) a very small amount of money: *We get paid peanuts for doing this job.*

pear /peə(r)/ ***noun*** [C] a fruit that has a yellow or green skin and is white inside. **Pears** are thinner at the top than at the bottom.

pearl /pɜːl/ ***noun*** [C] a small, hard, round, white object that is used as jewellery. **Pearls** grow inside the shells of OYSTERS (sea creatures): *pearl earrings*

peasant /ˈpeznt/ ***noun*** [C] (used especially in past times) a person who owns or rents a small piece of land on which they grow food and keep animals in order to feed their family

peat /piːt/ ***noun*** [U] (AGRICULTURE) a soft black or brown natural substance that is formed from dead plants just under the surface of the ground in cool, wet places. It can be burned as a fuel or put on land to make plants grow better.

pebble /'pebl/ ***noun*** [C] a smooth round stone that is found in or near water

pecan /'pi:kən/ ***noun*** [C] a type of nut that we eat

peck /pek/ ***verb*** [I,T] **1** ~ **(at) sth** (used about a bird) to eat or bite sth with its beak **2** (*informal*) to kiss sb quickly and lightly: *She pecked him on the cheek and then left.* ▶ **peck** ***noun*** [C]

peckish /'pekɪʃ/ ***adj.*** (*informal*) hungry

pectoral /'pektərəl/ ***adj.*** (BIOLOGY) on or connected with the chest or breast of a fish or animal: *pectoral fins* ➲ look at **dorsal**, **ventral**

pectorals /'pektərəlz/ (also *informal* **pecs** /peks/) ***noun*** [pl.] (ANATOMY) the muscles of the chest

peculiar /pɪ'kju:liə(r)/ ***adj.*** **1** unusual or strange: *There's a very peculiar smell in here.* SYN **odd** **2** ~ **to sb/sth** only belonging to one person or found in one place: *a species of bird peculiar to South East Asia*

peculiarity /pɪˌkju:li'ærəti/ ***noun*** (*pl.* **peculiarities**) **1** [C] a strange or unusual characteristic, quality or habit: *There are some peculiarities in her behaviour.* **2** [C] a characteristic or a quality that only belongs to one particular person, thing or place: *the cultural peculiarities of the English* **3** [U] the quality of being strange or unusual

peculiarly /pɪ'kju:liəli/ ***adv.*** **1** in a strange and unusual way: *Luke is behaving very peculiarly.* **2** especially; very: *Lilian's laugh can be peculiarly annoying.* **3** in a way that is especially typical of one person, thing or place: *a peculiarly French custom*

ped- (*AmE*) = PAED-

pedagogical /ˌpedə'gɒdʒɪkl/ ***adj.*** (EDUCATION) connected with ways of teaching

pedagogy /'pedəgɒdʒi/ ***noun*** [U] (EDUCATION) the study of teaching methods

pedal /'pedl/ ***noun*** [C] the part of a bicycle or other machine that you push with your foot in order to make it move or work ➲ picture at **piano** ▶ **pedal** ***verb*** [I,T] (**pedalling**; **pedalled**: *AmE* **pedaling**; **pedaled**): *She had to pedal hard to get up the hill.*

pedantic /pɪ'dæntɪk/ ***adj.*** too worried about rules or details ▶ **pedantically** /-kli/ ***adv.***

pedestal /'pedɪstl/ ***noun*** [C] the base on which a column, statue, etc. stands

pedestrian /pə'destriən/ ***noun*** [C] a person who is walking in the street (not travelling in a vehicle) ➲ look at **motorist**

peˌdestrian 'crossing (*AmE* **crosswalk**) ***noun*** [C] a place for people to cross the road ➲ look at **zebra crossing**

pedestrianize (also -ise) /pə'destriənaɪz/ ***verb*** [T] to make a street or part of a town into an area that is only for people who are walking, not for vehicles: *Most of the city streets have been pedestrianized.*

pediatrician (*AmE*) = PAEDIATRICIAN

pediatrics (*AmE*) = PAEDIATRICS

pedigree[1] /'pedɪgri:/ ***noun*** [C] **1** an official record of the parents, grandfather, grandmother, etc. from which an animal has been bred ➲ look at **mongrel** **2** a person's family history, especially when this is impressive

pedigree[2] /'pedɪgri:/ ***adj.*** (only *before* a noun) (used about an animal) of high quality because the parents, grandfather, grandmother, etc. are all of the same breed and specially chosen

pediment /'pedɪmənt/ ***noun*** [C] (ARCHITECTURE) the part in the shape of a triangle above the entrance of a building in the ancient Greek style

pedophile (*AmE*) = PAEDOPHILE

pee /pi:/ ***verb*** [I] (*informal*) to get rid of waste water from your body; to URINATE ▶ **pee** ***noun*** [U, sing.]

peek /pi:k/ ***verb*** [I] (*informal*) ~ **(at sth)** to look at sth quickly and secretly because you should not be looking at it: *No peeking at your presents before your birthday!* ▶ **peek** ***noun*** [sing.]: *to have a quick peek*

peel[1] /pi:l/ ***verb*** **1** [T] to take the skin off a fruit or vegetable: *Could you peel the potatoes, please?* **2** [I,T] ~ **(sth) (off/away/back)** to come off or to take sth off a surface in one piece or in small pieces: *I peeled off the price label before handing her the book.*

IDM **keep your eyes peeled/skinned (for sb/sth)** → EYE[1]

peel[2] /pi:l/ ***noun*** [U] the skin of a fruit or vegetable: *apple/potato peel* ➲ look at **rind**, **skin**

peeler /'pi:lə(r)/ ***noun*** [C] a special knife for taking the skin off fruit and vegetables: *a potato peeler*

peep[1] /pi:p/ ***verb*** [I] **1** ~ **(at sth)** to look at sth quickly and secretly, especially through a small opening **2** to be in a position where a small part of sb/sth can be seen: *The moon peeped out from behind the clouds.*

peep[2] /pi:p/ ***noun*** [sing.] (*informal*) **1** a quick look: *Have a peep in the bedroom and see if the baby is asleep.* **2** a sound: *There hasn't been a peep out of the children for hours.*

peer[1] /pɪə(r)/ ***noun*** [C] (SOCIAL STUDIES) **1** a person who is of the same age or position in society as you: *Children hate to look stupid in front of their peers.* **2** (*BrE*) a member of the top level of society (**the nobility**)

peer[2] /pɪə(r)/ ***verb*** [I] ~ **(at sb/sth)** to look closely or carefully at sb/sth, for example because you cannot see very well: *He peered at the photo, but it was blurred.*

peerage /'pɪərɪdʒ/ ***noun*** **1** [with sing. or pl. verb] all the PEERS[1] (2) as a group **2** [C] the social position (**rank**) of a PEER[1] (2)

'peer group ***noun*** [C] (SOCIAL STUDIES) a group of people who are all of the same age and social position

ˌpeer-to-'peer ***adj.*** (COMPUTING) in which each computer can act as a SERVER for the others, allowing data to be shared without the need for a central SERVER

peeved /pi:vd/ ***adj.*** (*informal*) quite angry or annoyed

peevish /'pi:vɪʃ/ ***adj.*** annoyed by things that are not important ▶ **peevishly** ***adv.***

peg[1] /peg/ ***noun*** [C] **1** a piece of wood, metal, etc. on a wall or door that you hang your coat on **2** (*also* **tent peg**) a piece of metal that you push into the ground to keep one of the ropes of a tent in place **3** (*also* **clothes peg**, *AmE* **clothes pin**) a type of small wooden or plastic object used for fastening wet clothes to a clothes line

peg[2] /peg/ ***verb*** [T] (**pegging**; **pegged**) **1** ~ **sth (out)** to fix sth with a **peg** **2** ~ **sth (at/to sth)** to fix or keep sth at a certain level: *Wage increases were pegged at 5%.*

pelican /'pelɪkən/ ***noun*** [C] a large bird that lives near water in warm countries. A **pelican** has a large beak that it uses for catching and holding fish.

pellet /'pelɪt/ ***noun*** [C] **1** a small hard ball of any substance, often of soft material that has become hard **2** a very small metal ball that is fired from a gun: *shotgun pellets*

pelt /pelt/ ***verb*** **1** [T] to attack sb/sth by throwing things **2** [I] ~ **(down)** (used about rain) to fall very heavily: *It's absolutely pelting down.* **3** [I] (*informal*) to run very fast: *Some kids pelted past us.*

pelvis /'pelvɪs/ ***noun*** [C] (*pl.* **pelvises**) (ANATOMY) the set of wide bones at the bottom of your back, to which your leg bones are joined ➲ picture on **page 80** ▶ **pelvic** /'pelvɪk/ ***adj.***

pen 🔑 /pen/ ***noun*** [C] **1** an object that you use for writing in ink: *a ballpoint/felt-tip/marker/fountain pen* **2** (AGRICULTURE) a small piece of ground with a fence around it that is used for keeping animals in

penal /'piːnl/ ***adj.*** (only *before* a noun) (LAW) connected with punishment by law: *the penal system*

penalize (also **-ise**) /'piːnəlaɪz/ ***verb*** [T] **1** (LAW) to punish sb for breaking a law or rule **2** to cause sb to have a disadvantage: *Children should not be penalized because their parents cannot afford to pay.*

penalty /'penəlti/ ***noun*** [C] (*pl.* **penalties**) **1** (LAW) a punishment for breaking a law, rule or contract: *the death penalty ◇ What's the maximum penalty for smuggling drugs?* **2** a disadvantage or sth unpleasant that happens as the result of sth: *I didn't work hard enough and I* ***paid the penalty****: I failed all my exams.* **3** (SPORT) a punishment for one team and an advantage for the other team because a rule has been broken: *The referee awarded a penalty to the home team.*

'penalty area (*BrE also* **'penalty box**) ***noun*** [C] (SPORT) the marked area in front of the goal in football

'penalty box ***noun*** [C] (SPORT) **1** (*BrE*) = PENALTY AREA **2** (in ice hockey) an area next to the ice where a player who has broken the rules must wait for a short time

penance /'penəns/ ***noun*** [C,U] a punishment that you give yourself to show you are sorry for doing sth wrong

pence 🔑 plural of **penny**

pencil[1] 🔑 /'pensl/ ***noun*** [C,U] an object that you use for writing or drawing. Pencils are usually made of wood and contain a thin stick of a black or coloured substance: *Bring a pencil and paper with you. ◇ Write* ***in pencil****, not ink.*

pencil[2] /'pensl/ ***verb*** [T] (**pencilling**; **pencilled**: *AmE* **penciling**; **penciled**) to write or draw sth with a pencil

PHRV **pencil sth/sb in** to write down the details of an arrangement that might have to be changed later: *Shall we pencil the next meeting in for 14th May?*

'pencil case ***noun*** [C] a small bag or box that you keep pens, pencils, etc. in

'pencil sharpener ***noun*** [C] an instrument that you use for making pencils sharp

pendant /'pendənt/ ***noun*** [C] a small attractive object that you wear on a chain around your neck

pending /'pendɪŋ/ ***adj.***, ***prep.*** (*formal*) **1** waiting to be done or decided: *The judge's decision is still pending.* **2** until sth happens: *He took over the leadership pending the elections.*

'Pen drive™ ***noun*** [C] (COMPUTING) a small device that you can carry around with you which is used for storing and moving data onto a computer SYN **Memory Stick™**, **USB drive™**

pendulum /'pendjələm/ ***noun*** [C] **1** a chain or stick with a heavy weight at the bottom that moves regularly from side to side to work a clock **2** a way of describing a situation that changes from one thing to its opposite: *Since last year's election, the pendulum of public opinion has swung against the government.*

penetrate /'penɪtreɪt/ ***verb*** **1** [I,T] to go through or into sth, especially when this is difficult: *The knife penetrated ten centimetres into his chest.* **2** [T] to manage to understand sth difficult: *Scientists have still not penetrated the workings of the brain.* **3** [I,T] to be understood or realized: *I was back at home when the meaning of her words finally penetrated.*
▶ **penetration** /ˌpenɪ'treɪʃn/ ***noun*** [U]

penetrating /'penɪtreɪtɪŋ/ ***adj.*** **1** (used about sb's eyes or expression) making you feel uncomfortable; seeming to know what you are thinking: *a penetrating look/stare/gaze ◇ penetrating blue eyes* **2** showing that you have understood sth completely and quickly: *a penetrating question/comment* **3** that can be heard, felt, smelled, etc. a long way away

penfriend /'penfrend/ (*especially AmE* **'pen pal**) ***noun*** [C] a person that you become friendly with by exchanging letters, often a person that you have never met

penguin /'peŋgwɪn/ ***noun*** [C] a black and white SEABIRD that cannot fly and that lives in the Antarctic

penicillin /ˌpenɪ'sɪlɪn/ ***noun*** [U] (HEALTH) a medicine (**antibiotic**) that is used for preventing and treating diseases and infections caused by bacteria

peninsula /pə'nɪnsjələ/ ***noun*** [C] (GEOGRAPHY) an area of land that is almost surrounded by water

penis /'piːnɪs/ ***noun*** [C] (ANATOMY) the male sex organ that is used for getting rid of waste liquid and having sex

penitent /'penɪtənt/ ***adj.*** (*formal*) sorry for having done sth wrong

penitentiary /ˌpenɪ'tenʃəri/ ***noun*** [C] (*pl.* **penitentiaries**) (*AmE*) a prison

penknife /'pennaɪf/ ***noun*** [C] (*pl.* **penknives**) a small knife with one or more BLADES (= parts used for cutting) that fold down into the handle when not being used

penniless /'peniləs/ ***adj.*** having no money; poor

penny 🔑 /'peni/ ***noun*** [C] (*pl.* **pence** /pens/ or **pennies**) **1** (*abbr.* **p**) a small brown British coin. There are a hundred pence in a pound: *a fifty-pence piece/coin* **2** (*AmE*) a cent

pension[1] 🔑 /'penʃn/ ***noun*** [C] money that is paid regularly by a government or company to sb who has stopped working (**retired**) because of old age or who cannot work because they are ill ➲ look at **pension**[2] ▶ **pensioner** = OLD-AGE PENSIONER

pension[2] /'penʃn/ ***verb***

PHRV **pension sb off** (*especially BrE*) to allow or force sb to retire and to pay them a pension: *He was pensioned off and his job given to a younger man.*

pension[3] /'pɒ̃sjɒ̃/ ***noun*** [C] (TOURISM) a small, usually cheap, hotel in some European countries, especially France ➲ look at **pension**[1]

penta- /'pentə/ ***prefix*** (used in nouns, adjectives and adverbs) five; having five: *pentathlon*

pentagon /'pentəgən/ ***noun*** **1** [C] (GEOMETRY) a shape that has five straight and equal sides **2 the Pentagon** [sing.] (POLITICS) a large government building near Washington DC in the US that contains the main offices of the US military forces; the military officials who work there

pentameter /pen'tæmɪtə(r)/ ***noun*** [C, U] (**LITERATURE**) a line of poetry with five stressed syllables; the rhythm of poetry with five stressed syllables to a line

pentathlon /pen'tæθlən/ ***noun*** [C] (**SPORT**) a sports competition in which you have to take part in five different events

pentatonic /ˌpentə'tɒnɪk/ ***adj.*** (**MUSIC**) related to or based on a SCALE (=a series) of five notes

penthouse /'penthaʊs/ ***noun*** [C] an expensive flat at the top of a tall building

pent-up /ˌpent 'ʌp/ ***adj.*** (only *before* a noun) (used about feelings) that you hold inside and do not express: *pent-up anger*

penultimate /pen'ʌltɪmət/ ***adj.*** (in a series) the one before the last one: *'Y' is the penultimate letter of the alphabet.*

penumbra /pə'nʌmbrə/ ***noun*** [C] **1** the outer part of a SHADOW, that is less dark than the central part **2** (**ASTRONOMY**) a dark area on the earth caused by the moon, or a dark area on the moon caused by the earth, during a PARTIAL ECLIPSE (=a time when the moon comes between the earth and the sun, or when the earth comes between the moon and the sun) ➲ look at **umbra** ➲ picture at **shadow**

people ⊶ /'pi:pl/ ***noun*** **1** [pl.] more than one person: *How many people are coming to the party?* **2** [C] (*pl.* **peoples**) (*formal*) all the men, women and children who belong to a particular place or race: *The President addressed the American people.* ◇ *the French-speaking peoples of the world* **3** [pl.] men and women who work in a particular activity: *business/sports people* **4 the people** [pl.] the ordinary citizens of a country: *The President is popular because he listens to the people.*

'**people carrier** (*AmE* **minivan**) ***noun*** [C] a large car, like a van, designed to carry up to eight people **SYN** **MPV**

pepper¹ ⊶ /'pepə(r)/ ***noun*** **1** [U] a black or white powder with a hot taste that is used for flavouring food: *salt and pepper* **2** [C] a green, red or yellow vegetable that is almost empty inside

pepper² /'pepə(r)/ ***verb*** [T] ~ **sb/sth with sth** (usually passive) to hit sb/sth with a series of small objects, especially bullets: *The wall had been peppered with bullets.*

peppercorn /'pepəkɔ:n/ ***noun*** [C] a dried BERRY from a tropical plant, that is pressed into small pieces or powder to make pepper

peppermint /'pepəmɪnt/ ***noun*** **1** [U] a natural substance with a strong fresh flavour that is used in sweets and medicines **2** (*also* **mint**) [C] a sweet with a peppermint flavour ➲ look at **spearmint**

pepsin /'pepsɪn/ ***noun*** [U] (**BIOLOGY**) the main ENZYME in the stomach that breaks down PROTEIN (=a natural substance found in meat, eggs, fish, etc. that the body needs to grow and be healthy)

pep talk /'pep tɔ:k/ ***noun*** [C] (*informal*) a speech that is given to encourage people or to make them work harder

per ⊶ /pə(r) *strong form* pɜ:(r)/ ***prep.*** for each: *The speed limit is 110 kilometres per hour.* ◇ *Rooms cost 60 dollars per person per night.*

per capita /pə 'kæpɪtə/ ***adj.*** (**BUSINESS**) for each person: *Per capita income rose sharply last year.* ▸ **per capita** ***adv.***: *average earnings per capita*

perceive **AW** /pə'si:v/ ***verb*** [T] (*formal*) **1** to notice or realize sth: *Scientists failed to perceive how dangerous the level of pollution had become.* **2** to understand or think of sth in a particular way: *I perceived his comments as a criticism.* ➲ note at **regard¹** ➲ noun **perception**

> **WORD FAMILY**
> **perceive** *verb*
> **perception** *noun*
> **perceptive** *adj.*
> **perceptible** *adj.* (≠ **imperceptible**)

per cent **AW** (*AmE* **percent**) /pə'sent/ ***adj.***, ***adv.***, ***noun*** [C, with sing. or pl. verb] (*pl.* **per cent**) (*symbol* %) (**MATHEMATICS**) in or of each hundred; one part in every hundred: *You get 10% off if you pay cash.* ◇ *90% of the population owns a television.* ◇ *The price of bread has gone up* ***by 50 per cent*** *in two years.*

percentage **AW** /pə'sentɪdʒ/ ***noun*** [C, with sing. or pl. verb] (**MATHEMATICS**) the number, amount, rate, etc. of sth, expressed as if it is part of a total which is a hundred; a part or share of a whole: *What percentage of people voted in the last election?*

perceptible /pə'septəbl/ ***adj.*** (*formal*) that can be seen or felt: *a barely perceptible change in colour* **OPP** **imperceptible** ▸ **perceptibly** /-əbli/ ***adv.***

perception **AW** /pə'sepʃn/ ***noun*** **1** [U] the ability to notice or understand sth **2** [C] a particular way of looking at or understanding sth; an opinion: *What is your perception of the situation?* ➲ verb **perceive**

perceptive /pə'septɪv/ ***adj.*** (*formal*) quick to notice or understand things ▸ **perceptively** ***adv.***

perch¹ /pɜ:tʃ/ ***verb*** **1** [I] (used about a bird) to sit on a branch, etc. **2** [I,T] to sit or be put on the edge of sth: *The house was perched on the edge of a cliff.*

perch² /pɜ:tʃ/ ***noun*** [C] a branch (or a bar in a CAGE) where a bird sits

percolate /'pɜ:kəleɪt/ ***verb*** **1** [I] (used about a liquid, gas, etc.) to move gradually through a surface that has very small holes or spaces in it: *Water had percolated down through the rocks.* **2** [I,T] to make coffee in a PERCOLATOR; to be made in this way ▸ **percolation** /pɜ:kə'leɪʃn/ ***noun*** [U]

percolator /'pɜ:kəleɪtə(r)/ ***noun*** [C] a pot for making coffee, in which boiling water is forced up a central tube and then comes down again through the coffee ➲ look at **cafetière**

percussion /pə'kʌʃn/ ***noun*** [U] (**MUSIC**) drums and other instruments that you play by hitting them

perennial¹ /pə'reniəl/ ***adj.*** **1** that happens often or that lasts for a very long time: *a perennial problem* **2** (**BIOLOGY**) (used about plants) living for two years or more

perennial² /pə'reniəl/ ***noun*** [C] (**BIOLOGY**) any plant that lives for more than two years ➲ look at **annual**, **biennial**

perfect¹ ⊶ /'pɜ:fɪkt/ ***adj.*** **1** completely good; without faults or weaknesses: *The car is two years old but it is still in perfect condition.* **OPP** **imperfect** **2** ~ (**for sb/sth**) exactly suitable or right: *Ken would be perfect for the job.* **3** (only *before* a noun) complete; total: *What he was saying made perfect sense to me.* ◇ *a perfect stranger* **4** (**LANGUAGE**) used to describe the tense of a verb that is formed with *has/have/had* and the past participle ▸ **perfectly** ***adv.***: *He played the piece of music perfectly.*

perfect² /pə'fekt/ ***verb*** [T] to make sth perfect: *Vinay is spending a year in France to perfect his French.*

perfection /pə'fekʃn/ ***noun*** [U] the state of being perfect or without fault: *The steak was cooked* ***to perfection***.

perfectionist /pəˈfekʃənɪst/ ***noun*** [C] a person who always does things as well as he/she possibly can and who expects others to do the same

the ˌperfect ˈtense (*also* **the perfect**) ***noun*** [sing.] (LANGUAGE) the tense of a verb that is formed with *has/have/had* and the past participle: *'I've finished' is in the present perfect tense.*

perforate /ˈpɜːfəreɪt/ ***verb*** [T] to make a hole or holes in sth

perforation /ˌpɜːfəˈreɪʃn/ ***noun*** **1** [C] a series of small holes in paper, etc. that make it easy for you to tear **2** [U] the action of making a hole or holes in sth

perform /pəˈfɔːm/ ***verb*** **1** [T] (*formal*) to do a piece of work or sth that you have been ordered to do: *to perform an operation/an experiment/a task* **2** [I,T] (ARTS AND MEDIA) to take part in a play or to sing, dance, etc. in front of an audience: *She is currently performing at the National Theatre.* **3** [I] ~ **(well/badly/poorly)** to work or function well or badly: *The company has not been performing well recently.*

IDM **work/perform miracles** → MIRACLE

performance /pəˈfɔːməns/ ***noun*** **1** [C] the act of performing sth in front of an audience; something that you perform: *What time does the performance start?* **2** [C] (ARTS AND MEDIA) the way a person performs in a play, concert, etc.: *His moving performance in the film won him an Oscar.* **3** [C] the way in which you do sth, especially how successful you are: *The company's performance was disappointing last year.* **4** [U] (used about a machine, etc.) the ability to work well: *This car has a high performance engine.* **5** [U, sing.] (*formal*) the act or process of doing a task, an action, etc.: *the performance of your duties*

perˈformance art ***noun*** [U] (ART) an art form in which an artist gives a performance, rather than producing a physical work of art

performer /pəˈfɔːmə(r)/ ***noun*** [C] **1** (ARTS AND MEDIA) a person who performs for an audience **2** a person or thing that behaves or works in the way mentioned: *Diana is a poor performer in exams.*

COLLOCATIONS AND PATTERNS

Performing arts

A **composer** writes **a song/a musical/an opera.** A **playwright** writes **plays.**
He's written a new musical.

A group **presents/performs/produces/puts on/stages** a play, show, etc.
The drama group is putting on a show at the local school.
We are proud to present Arthur Miller's 'The Crucible'.

A **director directs** a play, show, etc.
The theatre has got a new director.
She is directing Mozart's 'Figaro' at La Scala.

A performer, actor, etc. **acts/appears/performs/sings/stars in** a play, show, etc..
She's appearing in 'The Seagull' at the New Theatre.
He starred in the musical 'Guys and Dolls'.

A performer, actor, etc. **rehearses (for)** a play, show, etc..
She had 3 weeks to rehearse for the concert.

perˌforming ˈarts ***noun*** [pl.] (ARTS AND MEDIA) arts such as music, dance and drama which are performed for an audience

perfume /ˈpɜːfjuːm/ ***noun*** [C,U] **1** (*BrE also* **scent**) a liquid with a sweet smell that you put on your body to make yourself smell nice: *Are you wearing perfume?* **2** a pleasant, often sweet, smell

perhaps /pəˈhæps; præps/ ***adv.*** (used when you are not sure about sth) possibly; maybe: *Perhaps he's forgotten.* ◇ *She was, perhaps, one of the most famous writers of the time.*

STYLE

Perhaps and **maybe** are similar in meaning. They are often used to make what you are saying sound more polite: *Perhaps I could borrow your book, if you're not using it?* ◇ *Maybe I'd better explain...*

pericardium /ˌperiˈkɑːdiəm/ ***noun*** [C,U] (*pl.* **pericardia** /ˌperiˈkɑːdiə/) (ANATOMY) the MEMBRANE (=layer of skin or tissue) that surrounds the heart

peril /ˈperəl/ ***noun*** (*written*) **1** [U] great danger: *A lack of trained nurses is putting patients' lives* ***in peril.*** **2** [C] sth that is very dangerous: *the perils of drug abuse* ▶ **perilous** /ˈperələs/ ***adj.***

perimeter /pəˈrɪmɪtə(r)/ ***noun*** [C] the outside edge or limit of an area of land: *the perimeter fence of the army camp*

period AW /ˈpɪəriəd/ ***noun*** [C] **1** a length of time: *The scheme will be introduced for a six-month trial period.* ◇ *Her son is going through a difficult period at the moment.* ◇ *What period of history are you most interested in?* **2** (EDUCATION) a lesson in school: *We have five periods of English a week.* **3** (HEALTH) the time every month when a woman loses blood from her body **4** (*AmE*) = FULL STOP

periodic AW /ˌpɪəriˈɒdɪk/ (*also* **periodical** /-kl/) ***adj.*** happening fairly regularly: *We have periodic meetings to check on progress.* ▶ **periodically** /-kli/ ***adv.***: *All machines need to be checked periodically.*

periodical AW /ˌpɪəriˈɒdɪkl/ ***noun*** [C] (*formal*) (ARTS AND MEDIA) a magazine that is produced regularly

the ˌperiodic ˈtable ***noun*** [sing.] (CHEMISTRY) a list of all the chemical elements, arranged according to the number of PROTONS (=parts with a positive electric charge) that they each have in their centre (**nucleus**)

peripheral¹ /pəˈrɪfərəl/ ***adj.*** **1** (*formal*) ~ **(to sth)** not as important as the main aim, part, etc. of sth **2** connected with the outer edge of a particular area: *the peripheral nervous system* ◇ *peripheral vision* **3** (COMPUTING) (used about equipment) connected to a computer: *a peripheral device* ▶ **peripherally** /pəˈrɪfərəli/ ***adv.***

peripheral² /pəˈrɪfərəl/ ***noun*** [C] (COMPUTING) a piece of equipment that is connected to a computer, for example a PRINTER

periphery /pəˈrɪfəri/ ***noun*** [C, usually sing.] (*pl.* **peripheries**) (*formal*) **1** the outer edge of a particular area: *industrial development* ***on the periphery of*** *town* **2** the less important part of sth, for example of a particular activity or of a social or political group: *minor parties* ***on the periphery of*** *American politics*

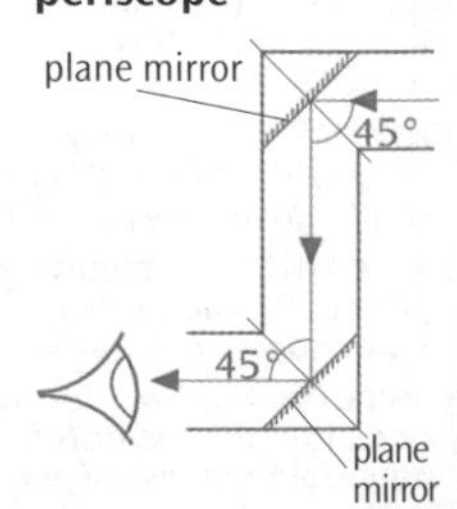

periscope /ˈperɪskəʊp/ ***noun*** [C] a device like a long tube, containing mirrors which allow you to see over the top of sth, used especially in a SUBMARINE (=a ship that can operate underwater), to see above the surface of the sea

perish /'perɪʃ/ ***verb*** [I] (*written*) to die or be destroyed: *Thousands perished in the war.*

perishable /'perɪʃəbl/ ***adj.*** (used about food) that will go bad quickly OPP **non-perishable**

peristalsis /ˌperɪ'stælsɪs/ ***noun*** [U] (BIOLOGY) the movements that the large tubes inside the body make automatically to push sth out or along

perjury /'pɜːdʒəri/ ***noun*** [U] (*formal*) (LAW) the act of telling a lie in a court of law ▶ **perjure** /'pɜːdʒə(r)/ ***verb*** [T] ~ **yourself**: *She admitted that she had perjured herself while giving evidence.*

perk¹ /pɜːk/ ***verb***

PHR V **perk (sb/sth) up** to become or make sb become happier and have more energy

perk² /pɜːk/ ***noun*** [C] (*informal*) something extra that you get from your employer in addition to money: *Travelling abroad is one of the perks of the job.*

perm /pɜːm/ ***noun*** [C] the treatment of hair with special chemicals in order to make it curly ⇨ look at **wave** ▶ **perm *verb*** [T]: *She has had her hair permed.*

permafrost /'pɜːməfrɒst/ ***noun*** [U] (GEOGRAPHY) a layer of soil that is permanently frozen, in very cold regions of the world

permanent ⊶ /'pɜːmənənt/ ***adj.*** lasting for a long time or for ever; that will not change: *The accident left him with a permanent scar.* ◇ *Are you looking for a permanent or a temporary job?* ▶ **permanently *adv.***: *Has she left permanently?* ▶ **permanence *noun*** [U]

permeable /'pɜːmiəbl/ ***adj.*** allowing a liquid or gas to pass through: *A frog's skin is permeable to water.* OPP **impermeable** ▶ **permeability** /ˌpɜːmiə'bɪləti/ ***noun*** [U]

permissible /pə'mɪsəbl/ ***adj.*** (*formal*) ~ **(for sb) (to so sth)** that is allowed by law or by a set of rules: *They have been exposed to radiation above the permissible level.*

permission ⊶ /pə'mɪʃn/ ***noun*** [U] ~ **(for sth)**; ~ **(for sb) (to do sth)** the act of allowing sb to do sth, especially when this is done by sb in a position of authority: *I'm afraid you can't leave **without permission**.* ◇ *to **ask/give permission** for sth*

permissive /pə'mɪsɪv/ ***adj.*** having, allowing or showing a lot of freedom that many people do not approve of, especially in sexual matters

permit¹ ⊶ /pə'mɪt/ ***verb*** (**permitting**; **permitted**) **1** [T] (*formal*) to allow sb to do sth or to allow sth to happen: *You are not permitted to smoke in the hospital.* ◇ *His visa does not permit him to work.* **2** [I,T] to make sth possible: *There will be a barbecue on Saturday, **weather permitting**.*

permit² /'pɜːmɪt/ ***noun*** [C] an official document that says you are allowed to do sth, especially for a limited period of time: *Next month I'll have to apply for a new **work permit**.*

peroxide /pə'rɒksaɪd/ (*also* ˌ**hydrogen pe'roxide**) ***noun*** [U] (CHEMISTRY) a colourless liquid that is used to kill bacteria and to make hair a lighter colour

perpendicular /ˌpɜːpən'dɪkjələ(r)/ ***adj.*** **1** (GEOMETRY) at an angle of 90° to sth: *Are the lines perpendicular to each other?* ➊ look at **horizontal**, **vertical** **2** pointing straight up: *The path was almost perpendicular* (= it was very steep).

perpetrate /'pɜːpətreɪt/ ***verb*** [T] (*formal*) ~ **sth (against/upon/on sb)** (LAW) to commit a crime or do sth wrong or evil: *to perpetrate a crime/fraud/massacre* ◇ *violence perpetrated against women and children* ▶ **perpetration** /ˌpɜːpə'treɪʃn/ ***noun*** [U]

perpetual /pə'petʃuəl/ ***adj.*** **1** continuing for a long period of time without stopping: *They lived in perpetual fear of losing their jobs.* **2** frequently repeated in a way which is annoying: *How can I work with these perpetual interruptions?* ▶ **perpetually** /-tʃuəli/ ***adv.***

perpetuate /pə'petʃueɪt/ ***verb*** [T] (*formal*) to cause sth to continue for a long time: *to perpetuate an argument*

perplexed /pə'plekst/ ***adj.*** not understanding sth; confused

persecute /'pɜːsɪkjuːt/ ***verb*** [T] **1** ~ **sb (for sth)** (often passive) to treat sb in a cruel and unfair way, especially because of race, religion or political beliefs **2** to deliberately annoy sb and make their life unpleasant ▶ **persecution** /ˌpɜːsɪ'kjuːʃn/ ***noun*** [C,U]: *the persecution of minorities* ▶ **persecutor** /'pɜːsɪkjuːtə(r)/ ***noun*** [C]

persevere /ˌpɜːsɪ'vɪə(r)/ ***verb*** [I] ~ **(at/in/with sth)** to continue trying to do or achieve sth that is difficult: *The treatment is painful but I'm going to persevere with it.* ▶ **perseverance *noun*** [U]

persist AW /pə'sɪst/ ***verb*** [I] **1** ~ **(in sth/doing sth)** to continue doing sth even though other people say that you are wrong or that you cannot do it: *If you persist in making so much noise, I shall call the police.* **2** to continue to exist: *If your symptoms persist you should consult your doctor.* ▶ **persistence** AW ***noun*** [U]: *Finally her persistence was rewarded and she got what she wanted.*

persistent AW /pə'sɪstənt/ ***adj.*** **1** determined to continue doing sth even though people say that you are wrong or that you cannot do it: *Some salesmen can be very persistent.* **2** lasting for a long time or happening often: *a persistent cough* ▶ **persistently *adv.***

person ⊶ /'pɜːsn/ ***noun*** [C] (*pl.* **people** or, especially in formal use, **persons**) **1** a man or woman; a human being: *I would like to speak to the person in charge.* **2 -person** (used to form compound nouns) a person doing the job mentioned: *a salesperson/spokesperson* **3** (LANGUAGE) one of the three types of pronoun in grammar. *I/we* are the first person, *you* is the second person and *he/she/it/they* are the third person.

IDM **in person** seeing or speaking to sb face to face (not speaking on the telephone or writing a letter)

personal ⊶ /'pɜːsənl/ ***adj.*** **1** (only *before* a noun) of or belonging to one particular person: *personal belongings* ◇ *Judges should not let their **personal feelings** influence their decisions.*
2 concerning your feelings, health or relationships with other people: *I should like to speak to you in private. I have something personal to discuss.* ◇ *Do you mind if I ask you a **personal question**?* **3** not connected with a person's job or official position: *Please keep personal phone calls to a minimum.* ◇ *I try not to let work interfere with my **personal life**.* **4** (only *before* a noun) done by a particular person rather than by sb who is acting for them: *The Prime Minister made a personal visit to the victims in hospital.*
5 (only *before* a noun) made or done for one particular person rather than for a large group of people or people in general: *We offer a personal service to all our customers.* **6** speaking about sb's

appearance or character in an unpleasant or unfriendly way: *It started as a general discussion but then people started to **get personal** and an argument began.* **7** (only *before* a noun) connected with the body: *personal hygiene* ◊ *She's always worrying about her personal appearance.*

ˌpersonal asˈsistant *noun* [C] (*abbr.* **PA**) (BUSINESS) a person who works as a secretary or an assistant for one person

ˌpersonal comˈputer = PC (1)

personality ⊶ /ˌpɜːsəˈnæləti/ *noun* (*pl.* **personalities**) **1** [C,U] the different qualities of a person's character that make them different from other people: *Joe has a kind personality.* **2** [U] the quality of having a strong, interesting and attractive character: *A good entertainer needs a lot of personality.* **3** [C] (ARTS AND MEDIA) a famous person (especially in sport, on television, etc.): *a television personality*

personalize (also **-ise**) /ˈpɜːsənəlaɪz/ *verb* [T] (usually passive) to mark sth with your name, etc. to show that it belongs to you: *a car with a personalized number plate*

personally ⊶ /ˈpɜːsənəli/ *adv.* **1** used to show that you are expressing your own opinion: *Personally, I think that nurses deserve more money.* **2** done by you yourself, not by sb else acting for you: *I will deal with this matter personally.* **3** in a way that is connected with one particular person rather than a group of people: *I wasn't talking about you personally – I meant all teachers.* **4** in a way that is intended to offend: *Please don't **take it personally**, but I would just rather be alone this evening.* **5** in a way that is connected with sb's private life, rather than their job

ˌpersonal ˈpronoun *noun* [C] (LANGUAGE) any of the pronouns *I, me, she, her, he, him, we, us, you, they, them*

ˌpersonal ˈstereo *noun* [C] a small machine that plays CDs that you can carry round with you and listen to through EARPHONES

ˌpersonal ˈtrainer *noun* [C] (SPORT) a person who is paid by sb to help them exercise, especially by deciding what types of exercise are best for them

persona non grata /pɜːˌsəʊnə nɒn ˈɡrɑːtə/ *noun* [U] (POLITICS) a person who is not welcome in a particular place because of sth they have said or done, especially one who is told to leave a country by the government

personification /pəˌsɒnɪfɪˈkeɪʃn/ *noun* **1** [C, usually sing.] **~ of sth** a person who has a lot of a particular quality or characteristic SYN **epitome**: *She was the personification of elegance.* **2** [U, C] (LITERATURE, ART) the practice of representing objects, qualities, etc. as humans; an object, quality, etc. that is represented in this way: *the personification of autumn in Keats's poem*

personify /pəˈsɒnɪfaɪ/ *verb* [T] (*pres. part.* **personifying**; *3rd person sing. pres.* **personifies**; *pt, pp* **personified**) **1** to be an example in human form of a particular quality: *She is kindness personified.* **2** (LITERATURE) to describe an object or a feeling as if it were a person, for example in a poem

personnel /ˌpɜːsəˈnel/ *noun* **1** [pl.] the people who work for a large organization or one of the armed forces: *sales/medical/technical personnel* **2** (*also* **personˈnel department**) [U, with sing. or pl. verb] (BUSINESS) the department of a large company or organization that deals with employing and training people: *Personnel is/are currently reviewing pay scales.*

perspective AW /pəˈspektɪv/ *noun* **1** [U] the ability to think about problems and decisions in a reasonable way without exaggerating them: *Hearing about others' experiences often helps to **put** your own problems **into perspective*** (= makes them seem less important then you thought). ◊ *Try to **keep** these issues **in perspective*** (= do not exaggerate them). **2** [C] your opinion or attitude towards sth: *Try and look at this **from my perspective**.* **3** [U] (ART) the art of drawing on a flat surface so that some objects appear to be farther away than others

Perspex™ /ˈpɜːspeks/ *noun* [U] a strong transparent plastic material that is often used instead of glass

perspire /pəˈspaɪə(r)/ *verb* [I] (*formal*) (BIOLOGY) to lose liquid through your skin when you are hot SYN **sweat** ▶ **perspiration** /ˌpɜːspəˈreɪʃn/ *noun* [U] SYN **sweat**

persuade ⊶ /pəˈsweɪd/ *verb* [T] **1 ~ sb (to do sth); ~ sb (into sth/doing sth)** to make sb do sth by giving them good reasons: *It was difficult to persuade Louise to change her mind.* ◊ *We eventually persuaded Sanjay into coming with us.* OPP **dissuade** **2** (*formal*) **~ sb that...; ~ sb (of sth)** to make sb believe sth: *She had persuaded herself that she was going to fail.* ◊ *The jury was not persuaded of her innocence.* ➲ look at **convince**

persuasion /pəˈsweɪʒn/ *noun* **1** [U] the act of persuading sb to do sth or to believe sth: *It took a lot of persuasion to get Alan to agree.* **2** [C] (*formal*) a religious or political belief: *politicians of all persuasions*

persuasive /pəˈsweɪsɪv/ *adj.* able to persuade sb to do or believe sth: *the persuasive power of advertising* ▶ **persuasively** *adv.* ▶ **persuasiveness** *noun* [U]

pertinent /ˈpɜːtɪnənt/ *adj.* (*formal*) closely connected with the subject being discussed: *to ask a pertinent question*

perturb /pəˈtɜːb/ *verb* [T] (*formal*) to make sb worried or upset ▶ **perturbed** *adj.*

peruse /pəˈruːz/ *verb* [T] (*formal*) to read sth, especially in a careful way ▶ **perusal** /pəˈruːzl/ *noun* [U, sing.]: *The agreement was signed after careful perusal.*

pervade /pəˈveɪd/ *verb* [T] (*formal*) to spread through and be noticeable in every part of sth: *A sadness pervades most of her novels.*

pervasive /pəˈveɪsɪv/ *adj.* that is present in all parts of sth: *a pervasive mood of pessimism*

perverse /pəˈvɜːs/ *adj.* (*formal*) liking to behave in a way that is not acceptable or reasonable or that most people think is wrong: *Derek gets perverse pleasure from shocking his parents.* ▶ **perversely** *adv.* ▶ **perversity** *noun* [U]

perversion /pəˈvɜːʃn/ *noun* [U, C] **1** sexual behaviour that is not considered normal or acceptable by most people **2** the action of changing sth from right to wrong or from good to bad: *That statement is a perversion of the truth.*

pervert¹ /pəˈvɜːt/ *verb* [T] **1** to change a system, process, etc. in a bad way: *to pervert the course of justice* (= to deliberately prevent the police from finding out the truth about a crime) **2** to cause sb to think or behave in a way that is not moral or acceptable

pervert² /ˈpɜːvɜːt/ *noun* [C] a person whose sexual behaviour is not thought to be natural or normal by most people

pessimism /ˈpesɪmɪzəm/ *noun* [U] ~ **(about/over sth)** the state of expecting or believing that bad things will happen and that sth will not be successful OPP **optimism** ▶ **pessimistic** /ˌpesɪˈmɪstɪk/ *adj.* OPP **optimistic** ▶ **pessimistically** /-kli/ *adv.* OPP **optimistically**

pessimist /ˈpesɪmɪst/ *noun* [C] a person who always thinks that bad things will happen or that sth will not be successful OPP **optimist**

pest /pest/ *noun* [C] **1** (AGRICULTURE, BIOLOGY) an insect or animal that destroys plants, food, etc. **2** (*informal*) a person or thing that annoys you

ˈ**PEST analysis** (*also* ˈ**STEP analysis**) *noun* [C,U] (BUSINESS) **political, economic, social and technological analysis**; an examination of a situation to see how it is affecting a company and its products

pester /ˈpestə(r)/ *verb* [T] ~ **sb (for sth)**; ~ **sb (to do sth)** to annoy sb, for example by asking them sth many times: *to pester sb for money* ◇ *The kids kept pestering me to take them to the park.*

pesticide /ˈpestɪsaɪd/ *noun* [C,U] (AGRICULTURE) a chemical substance that is used for killing insects and other creatures that eat food crops ➲ look at **insecticide**

pestle /ˈpesl/ *noun* [C] a small heavy tool with a round end used for crushing food or other substances into powder in a special bowl (**mortar**) ➲ picture at **laboratory**

pet 🔑 /pet/ *noun* [C] **1** an animal or bird that you keep in your home for pleasure rather than for food or work: *a pet dog/cat/hamster* ◇ *a pet shop* **2** a person who is treated as a favourite: *teacher's pet*

petal /ˈpetl/ *noun* [C] (BIOLOGY) one of the thin soft coloured parts of a flower ➲ picture at **flower**

peter /ˈpiːtə(r)/ *verb*

PHR V **peter out** to slowly become smaller, quieter, etc. and then stop

ˌ**pet** ˈ**hate** *noun* [C] sth that you particularly do not like: *Filling in forms is one of my pet hates.*

pethidine /ˈpeθədiːn/ *noun* [U] (HEALTH) a drug used to reduce severe pain, for example for women giving birth

petition /pəˈtɪʃn/ *noun* [C] (POLITICS) a written document, signed by many people, that asks a government, etc. to do or change sth: *More than 50 000 people signed the petition protesting about the new road.* ▶ **petition** *verb* [I,T]

Petri dish /ˈpetri dɪʃ; ˈpiːtri/ *noun* [C] (SCIENCE) a covered dish that is not very deep, used for growing bacteria, etc. in ➲ picture at **laboratory**

petrified /ˈpetrɪfaɪd/ *adj.* very frightened

petro- /ˈpetrəʊ/ *prefix* (used in nouns, adjectives and adverbs) **1** (GEOLOGY) connected with rocks: *petrology* **2** (SCIENCE) connected with petrol: *petrochemical*

petrochemical /ˌpetrəʊˈkemɪkl/ *noun* [C] (CHEMISTRY) any chemical substance obtained from petrol or natural gas

petrol 🔑 /ˈpetrəl/ (*AmE* **gas**; **gasoline**) *noun* [U] liquid that is used as fuel for vehicles such as cars and motorbikes ➲ look at **diesel** ➲ picture at **fractional distillation**

petroleum /pəˈtrəʊliəm/ *noun* [U] (CHEMISTRY) mineral oil that is found under the ground or sea and is used to make petrol, plastic and other types of chemical substances ➲ picture at **fractional distillation**

ˈ**petrol station** (*AmE* ˈ**gas station**) *noun* [C] a place where you can buy petrol and other things for your car ➲ look at **garage**

petroleum formation

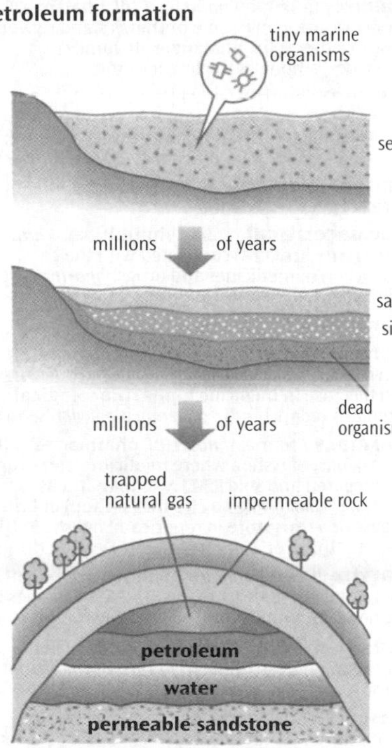

petticoat /ˈpetɪkəʊt/ *noun* [C] (*old-fashioned*) a piece of women's underwear like a thin dress or skirt, worn under a dress or skirt

petty /ˈpeti/ *adj.* **1** small and unimportant: *He didn't want to get involved with the petty details.* ◇ *petty crime/theft* (= that is not very serious) **2** unkind or unpleasant to other people (for a reason that does not seem very important): *petty jealousy/revenge* ◇ *Don't be so petty!*

ˌ**petty** ˈ**cash** *noun* [U] a small amount of money kept in an office for small payments

pew /pjuː/ *noun* [C] (RELIGION) one of the long wooden seats in a church

pewter /ˈpjuːtə(r)/ *noun* [U] a grey metal that is made from TIN and LEAD, used especially in the past for making cups, dishes, etc.; objects made from this metal

PG /ˌpiː ˈdʒiː/ *abbr.* (*BrE*) (ARTS AND MEDIA) (used about films in which there are scenes that are not suitable for children) parental guidance

PGCE /ˌpiː dʒiː siː ˈiː/ *noun* [C] (EDUCATION) **Postgraduate Certificate in Education**; a British teaching qualification taken by people who have a university degree

pH /ˌpiː ˈeɪtʃ/ *noun* [sing.] (CHEMISTRY) a measurement of the level of acid or ALKALI in a substance ❶ A **pH** value of below 7 shows an acid and a value of above 7 shows an alkali.

phagocyte /ˈfæɡəsaɪt/ *noun* [C] (BIOLOGY) a type of cell in the body that can surround smaller cells or small pieces of material and take them into itself

phalanx /ˈfælæŋks/ ***noun*** [C] **1** (*pl.* **phalanxes**) (*formal*) a group of people or things standing very close together **2** (*pl.* **phalanges** /fəˈlændʒiːz/) (ANATOMY) a bone of the finger or toe

phantom /ˈfæntəm/ ***noun*** [C] **1** (*written*) the spirit of a dead person that is seen or heard by sb who is still living SYN **ghost 2** something that you think exists, but that is not real: *phantom fears/illnesses*

pharaoh /ˈfeərəʊ/ ***noun*** [C] (HISTORY) a ruler of ancient Egypt

pharmaceutical /ˌfɑːməˈsjuːtɪkl; -ˈsuː-/ ***adj.*** (CHEMISTRY, HEALTH) connected with the production of medicines and drugs: *pharmaceutical companies*

pharmacist /ˈfɑːməsɪst/ = CHEMIST (1)

pharmacology /ˌfɑːməˈkɒlədʒi/ ***noun*** [U] (CHEMISTRY, HEALTH) the scientific study of drugs and their use in medicine ▶ **pharmacological** /ˌfɑːməkəˈlɒdʒɪkl/ ***adj.***: *pharmacological research*

pharmacy /ˈfɑːməsi/ ***noun*** (*pl.* **pharmacies**) **1** [C] a shop or part of a shop where medicines and drugs are prepared and sold HELP A shop that sells medicine is also called **a chemist's (shop)** in British English or a **drugstore** in American English. **2** [U] (HEALTH) the preparation of medicines and drugs

pharynx /ˈfærɪŋks/ ***noun*** [C] (BIOLOGY) the soft area at the top of the throat where the passages to the nose and mouth connect with the throat

phase[1] ⊶ AW /feɪz/ ***noun*** [C] a stage in the development of sth: *Julie went through a difficult phase when she started school.*

phase[2] AW /feɪz/ ***verb*** [T] (usually passive) to arrange to do sth gradually in stages over a period of time: *Closure of the hospitals was phased over a three-year period.*

PHR V **phase sth in** to introduce or start using sth gradually in stages over a period of time: *The metric system was phased in over several years.*

phase sth out to stop using sth gradually in stages over a period of time: *The older machines are gradually being phased out and replaced by new ones.*

PhD /ˌpiː eɪtʃ ˈdiː/ ***abbr.*** (EDUCATION) Doctor of Philosophy; an advanced university degree that you receive when you complete a piece of research into a special subject: *She has a PhD in History.* SYN **DPhil**

pheasant /ˈfeznt/ ***noun*** [C] (*pl.* **pheasants** or **pheasant**) a type of bird with a long tail. The males have brightly coloured feathers. **Pheasants** are often shot for sport and eaten. ➲ picture on **page 28**

phenomenal AW /fəˈnɒmɪnl/ ***adj.*** very great or impressive: *phenomenal success* ▶ **phenomenally** /-nəli/ ***adv.***

phenomenon AW /fəˈnɒmɪnən/ ***noun*** [C] (*pl.* **phenomena** /-ɪnə/) a fact or an event in nature or society, especially one that is not fully understood: *Acid rain is not a natural phenomenon. It is caused by pollution.*

phenotype /ˈfiːnətaɪp/ ***adj.***, ***noun*** [C] (BIOLOGY) the set of characteristics of a living thing, resulting from its combination of GENES (= units of information inside a cell which are passed from parents to children) and the effect of its environment ➲ look at **genotype**

phew /fjuː/ ***exclamation*** a sound which you make to show that you are hot, tired or happy that sth bad did not happen or has finished: *Phew, it's hot!* ◇ *Phew, I'm glad that interview's over!*

philanthropist /fɪˈlænθrəpɪst/ ***noun*** [C] a rich person who helps the poor and those in need, especially by giving money

philanthropy /fɪˈlænθrəpi/ ***noun*** [U] (*formal*) the practice of helping the poor and those in need, especially by giving money ▶ **philanthropic** /ˌfɪlənˈθrɒpɪk/ ***adj.***: *philanthropic work* ▶ **philanthropically** /ˌfɪlənˈθrɒpɪkli/ ***adv.***

-phile ***suffix*** (in nouns and adjectives) (LANGUAGE) a person who likes a particular thing or particular people: *Francophile* (= a person who likes France and its people) ◇ *bibliophile* (= a person who likes books) ➲ look at **-phobe**

philo- /ˈfɪləʊ/ ***prefix*** (used in nouns, adjectives, verbs and adverbs) (LANGUAGE) liking: *philanthropist*

philosopher AW /fəˈlɒsəfə(r)/ ***noun*** [C] a person who has developed a set of ideas and beliefs about the meaning of life

philosophical AW /ˌfɪləˈsɒfɪkl/ (*also* **philosophic**) ***adj.*** **1** of or concerning philosophy: *a philosophical debate* **2** ~ **(about sth)** staying calm and not getting upset or worried about sth bad that happens: *He is quite philosophical about failing the exam and says he will try again next year.* ▶ **philosophically** /-kli/ ***adv.***

philosophize (also **-ise**) AW /fəˈlɒsəfaɪz/ ***verb*** [I] ~ **(about/on sth)** to talk about sth in a serious way, especially when other people think this is boring: *He spent the evening philosophizing on the meaning of life.*

philosophy ⊶ AW /fəˈlɒsəfi/ ***noun*** (*pl.* **philosophies**) **1** [U] (EDUCATION) the study of ideas and beliefs about the meaning of life **2** [C] a set of beliefs that tries to explain the meaning of life or give rules about how to behave: *Her philosophy is 'If a job's worth doing, it's worth doing well'.*

phlegm /flem/ ***noun*** [U] (HEALTH) the thick substance that is produced in your nose and throat when you have a cold

phlegmatic /flegˈmætɪk/ ***adj.*** (*formal*) not easily made angry or upset; calm

pH

ACIDIC ⟵⟶ ALKALINE

pH 0	1	2	3	4	5	6	7	8	9	10	11	12	13	14
	strong acids		weak acids			neutral solutions			weak bases				strong bases	
e.g.	HCl		H2Co3				NaCl		NH3				NaOH	
colour of universal indicator		red		yellow			green				blue			violet

phloem /ˈfləʊem/ ***noun*** [U] (BIOLOGY) the material in a plant containing very small tubes that carry sugars and other substances down from the leaves ➲ picture at **flower**

-phobe (in nouns) ***suffix*** (LANGUAGE) a person who dislikes or is afraid of a particular thing or particular people: *Anglophobe* (=a person who dislikes the English) ◇ *xenophobe* (=a person who dislikes foreigners) ➲ look at **-phile**

phobia /ˈfəʊbiə/ ***noun*** [C] (often used in compounds) (PSYCHOLOGY) a very strong fear or hatred that you cannot explain: *arachnophobia* (=fear of spiders)

phone 🔑 /fəʊn/ ***noun*** (*informal*) **1** [U] =TELEPHONE (1): *a phone conversation* ◇ *You can book the tickets* ***over the/by phone***. **2** [C] =TELEPHONE (2): *The phone is ringing – could you answer it?* ▶ **phone** ***verb*** [I,T]: *Did anybody phone while I was out?* ◇ *Could you phone the restaurant and book a table?* SYN **ring, call**
IDM **on the phone/telephone 1** using the telephone **2** having a telephone in your home: *I'll have to write to her because she's not on the phone.*

ˈ**phone book** =TELEPHONE DIRECTORY

ˈ**phone box** =TELEPHONE BOX

phonecard /ˈfəʊnkɑːd/ ***noun*** [C] a small plastic card that you can use to pay for calls in a public telephone box

ˈ**phone-in** ***noun*** [C] (ARTS AND MEDIA) a radio or television programme during which you can ask a question or give your opinion by telephone

phoneme /ˈfəʊniːm/ ***noun*** [C] (LANGUAGE) any one of the set of smallest units of speech in a language that distinguish one word from another. In English, the *s* in *sip* and the *z* in *zip* represent two different phonemes. ▶ **phonemic** /fəˈniːmɪk/ ***adj.***

phonetic /fəˈnetɪk/ ***adj.*** (LANGUAGE) **1** connected with the sounds of human speech; using special symbols to represent these sounds: *the phonetic alphabet* ➲ look at **transcribe**
2 (used about spelling) having a close relationship with the sounds represented: *Spanish spelling is phonetic, unlike English spelling.* ▶ **phonetically** /-kli/ ***adv.***

phonetics /fəˈnetɪks/ ***noun*** [U] (LANGUAGE) the study of the sounds of human speech

phoney (*AmE* **phony**) /ˈfəʊni/ ***adj.*** not real; false: *She spoke with a phoney Russian accent.* ▶ **phoney** (*AmE* **phony**) ***noun*** [C]

phono- /ˈfəʊnəʊ/ ***prefix*** (used in nouns, adjectives and adverbs) (LANGUAGE) connected with sound or sounds: *phonetic* ◇ *phonics*

phonology /fəˈnɒlədʒi/ ***noun*** [U] (LANGUAGE) the speech sounds of a particular language; the study of these sounds

phosphate /ˈfɒsfeɪt/ ***noun*** [C,U] (AGRICULTURE, CHEMISTRY) any salt or COMPOUND containing PHOSPHORUS, used in industry or for helping plants to grow

phosphorus /ˈfɒsfərəs/ ***noun*** [U] (*symbol* **P**) a chemical element found in several different forms, including as a poisonous, pale yellow substance that shines in the dark and starts to burn as soon as it is placed in air ⓘ For more information on the periodic table of elements, look at pages R34-5.

photo 🔑 /ˈfəʊtəʊ/ ***noun*** [C] (*pl.* **photos** /-təʊz/) (*informal*) =PHOTOGRAPH

photo- /ˈfəʊtəʊ/ ***prefix*** (used in nouns, adjectives, verbs and adverbs) **1** (LANGUAGE) connected with light: *photosynthesis* **2** connected with photography: *photocopier*

photocell /ˈfəʊtəʊsel/ =PHOTOELECTRIC CELL

photocopier /ˈfəʊtəʊkɒpiə(r)/ ***noun*** [C] a machine that makes copies of documents by PHOTOGRAPHING them

photocopy 🔑 /ˈfəʊtəʊkɒpi/ ***noun*** [C] (*pl.* **photocopies**) a copy of a document, a page in a book, etc. that is made by a PHOTOCOPIER SYN **Xerox** ▶ **photocopy** ***verb*** [I,T] (*pres. part.* **photocopying**; *3rd person sing. pres.* **photocopies**; *pt, pp* **photocopied**)

photoelectric /ˌfəʊtəʊɪˈlektrɪk/ ***adj.*** (PHYSICS) using an electric current that is controlled by light

ˌ**photoelectric** ˈ**cell** (*also* **photocell**) ***noun*** [C] (PHYSICS) an electric device that uses a stream of light. When the stream is broken, it shows that sb/sth is present, and can be used to control alarms, machinery, etc.

photograph 🔑 /ˈfəʊtəgrɑːf/ (*also* **photo**) ***noun*** [C] a picture that is taken with a camera: *to take a photograph* ◇ *She looks younger in real life than she did* ***in the photograph***. ➲ look at **negative, slide** ▶ **photograph** ***verb*** [T]

photographer 🔑 /fəˈtɒgrəfə(r)/ ***noun*** [C] a person who takes photographs
➲ look at **cameraman**

photographic /ˌfəʊtəˈgræfɪk/ ***adj.*** connected with photographs or photography

photography 🔑 /fəˈtɒgrəfi/ ***noun*** [U] the skill or process of taking photographs

photomontage /ˌfəʊtəʊmɒnˈtɑːʒ/ ***noun*** [C,U] (ART) a picture which is made up of different photographs put together; the technique of producing these pictures

photon /ˈfəʊtɒn/ ***noun*** [C] (PHYSICS) a unit of ELECTROMAGNETIC ENERGY, for example light

photorealism /ˌfəʊtəʊˈriːəlɪzəm; -ˈrɪəl-/ ***noun*** [U] (ART) an artistic style that represents a subject in an accurate and detailed way, like a photograph

ˈ**photo shoot** ***noun*** [C] (ARTS AND MEDIA) an occasion when a photographer takes pictures of sb, for example a famous person, fashion model, etc. for use in a magazine, etc.: ***I went on a photo shoot to Rio with him.***

photosynthesis /ˌfəʊtəʊˈsɪnθəsɪs/ ***noun*** [U] (BIOLOGY) the process by which green plants turn CARBON DIOXIDE and water into food using energy from SUNLIGHT

photosynthesis

$6CO_2$ (carbon dioxide) + $6H_2O$ (water) —sunlight / chlorophyll→ $C_6H_{12}O_6$ (glucose) + $6O_2$ (oxygen)

phototropism /ˌfəʊtəʊˈtrəʊpɪzəm/ ***noun*** [U] (BIOLOGY) the action of a plant turning towards or away from light ▶ **phototropic** ***adj.***

phrasal verb /ˌfreɪzl ˈvɜːb/ ***noun*** [C] (LANGUAGE) a verb that is combined with an adverb or a preposition, or sometimes both, to give a new meaning, such as 'look after' or 'put sb off'

phrase[1] 🔑 /freɪz/ ***noun*** [C] (LANGUAGE) a group of words that are used together. A phrase does not contain a full verb: *'First of all' and 'a bar of chocolate' are phrases.* ➲ look at **sentence**

phrase² /freɪz/ ***verb*** [T] to express sth in a particular way: *The statement was phrased so that it would offend no one.*

'phrase book ***noun*** [C] (**TOURISM**) a book that gives common words and useful phrases in a foreign language. People often use phrase books when they travel to another country whose language they do not know.

phylum /'faɪləm/ ***noun*** [C] (*pl.* **phyla** /-lə/) (**BIOLOGY**) a group into which animals, plants, etc. are divided, smaller than a KINGDOM (2) and larger than a CLASS¹ (4) ➲ picture on **page 29**

physical ⊶ AW /'fɪzɪkl/ ***adj.*** **1** connected with your body rather than your mind: ***physical fitness/strength/disabilities*** **2** (only *before* a noun) connected with real things that you can touch, or with the laws of nature: ***physical geography*** (=the natural features on the face of the earth) **3** (only *before* a noun) (**PHYSICS**) connected with the study of PHYSICS and things that are not alive

ˌphysical edu'cation ***noun*** [U] (*abbr.* **PE**) (**EDUCATION**) sport and exercise that is taught in schools

physically ⊶ AW /'fɪzɪkli/ ***adv.*** **1** in a way that is connected with a person's body rather than their mind: *to be physically fit* ◇ *I don't find him physically attractive.* **2** according to the laws of nature or what is probable: *It's physically impossible to finish by the end of the week.*

physician /fɪ'zɪʃn/ (*AmE, formal*) =DOCTOR¹ (1)

physicist /'fɪzɪsɪst/ ***noun*** [C] (**PHYSICS**) a person who studies or is an expert in physics

physics ⊶ /'fɪzɪks/ ***noun*** [U] the scientific study of natural forces such as light, sound, heat, electricity, pressure, etc.

physio- /'fɪziəʊ/ ***prefix*** (used in nouns, adjectives and adverbs) **1** connected with nature **2** (**BIOLOGY**) connected with PHYSIOLOGY

physiologist /ˌfɪzi'ɒlədʒɪst/ ***noun*** [C] (**BIOLOGY**) a scientist who studies how living things function

physiology /ˌfɪzi'ɒlədʒi/ ***noun*** [U] (**BIOLOGY**) the way in which living things function, and the scientific study of this

physiotherapist /ˌfɪziəʊ'θerəpɪst/ ***noun*** [C] (**HEALTH**) a person who is trained to use PHYSIOTHERAPY

physiotherapy /ˌfɪziəʊ'θerəpi/ (*AmE* **ˌphysical 'therapy**) ***noun*** [U] (**HEALTH**) the treatment of disease or injury by exercise, light, heat, MASSAGE, etc.

physique /fɪ'ziːk/ ***noun*** [C] the size and shape of a person's body: *a strong muscular physique*

pi /paɪ/ ***noun*** [sing.] (**MATHEMATICS**) the symbol π used to show the relation between the CIRCUMFERENCE of a circle (=the distance around it) and its DIAMETER (=the distance across it) that is about 3.14159

pianist /'pɪənɪst/ ***noun*** [C] (**MUSIC**) a person who plays the piano

piano

piano ⊶ /pi'ænəʊ/ ***noun*** [C] (*pl.* **pianos** /-nəʊz/) (**MUSIC**) a large musical instrument that you play by pressing down black and white keys: *an upright piano* ◇ *a grand piano*

piccolo /'pɪkələʊ/ ***noun*** [C] (*pl.* **piccolos**) (**MUSIC**) a musical instrument like a small FLUTE (=an instrument like a pipe that you hold sideways and play by blowing over a hole at one side) that plays high notes

pick¹ ⊶ /pɪk/ ***verb*** [T] **1** to choose sb/sth from a group of people or things: *I was upset not to be picked for the team.* ◇ *Have I picked a bad time to visit?* **2** to take a flower, fruit or vegetable from the place where it is growing: *to pick flowers/grapes/cotton* **3** to remove a small piece or pieces of sth with your fingers: *Don't pick your nose!* ◇ *She picked a hair off her jacket.* **4** ~ **your way across, over, through, etc. sth** to walk carefully, choosing the best places to put your feet

IDM **have a bone to pick with sb** → BONE¹

pick a fight (with sb) to start a fight with sb deliberately

pick a lock to open a lock without using a key

pick and choose to choose only the things that you like or want very much

pick sb's pocket to steal money, etc. from sb's pocket or bag

PHR V **pick at sth 1** to eat only small amounts of food because you are not hungry **2** to touch sth many times with your fingers

pick on sb to behave unfairly or in a cruel way towards sb

pick sb/sth out to choose or recognize sb/sth from a number of people or things; identify: *I immediately picked Jean out in the photo.*

pick up to become better; to improve

pick sb up to collect sb, in a car, etc.: *We've ordered a taxi to pick us up at ten.*

pick sb/sth up 1 to take hold of and lift sb/sth: *Lucy picked up the child and gave him a cuddle.* **2** to receive an electronic signal, sound or picture: *In the north of France you can pick up English television programmes.*

pick sth up 1 to learn sth without formal lessons: *Joe picked up a few words of Spanish on holiday.* **2** to get or find sth: *I picked up this book at the market.* **3** to go and get sth; to collect sth: *I have to pick up my jacket from the cleaner's.*

pick² /pɪk/ ***noun*** **1** [sing.] the one that you choose; your choice: *You can have whichever cake you like. **Take your pick**.* **2** [sing.] the best of a group: *You can see **the pick of** the new films at this year's festival.* **3** (*also* **pickaxe** *AmE*) (**pickax** /'pɪkæks/) [C] a tool that consists of a curved iron bar with sharp points at both ends, fixed onto a wooden handle. **Picks** are used for breaking stones or hard ground. ➲ picture at **axe**

picket /'pɪkɪt/ ***noun*** [C] (**SOCIAL STUDIES**) a worker or group of workers who stand outside the entrance to a building to protest about sth, especially in order to stop people entering a factory, etc. during a strike ▸ **picket** ***verb*** [I,T]

pickle /'pɪkl/ ***noun*** **1** [C, usually pl.] (*BrE*) food such as fruit or vegetables that is put in salt water or VINEGAR (=a liquid with a strong sharp taste that is made from wine) so that it can be kept for a long time before being eaten **2** [U] a cold thick sauce with a strong flavour made from fruit and vegetables that have been boiled. **Pickle** is served with meat, cheese, etc. **3** [C] (*AmE*) =GHERKIN ▸ **pickle** ***verb*** [T]: *pickled onions*

pickpocket /'pɪkpɒkɪt/ ***noun*** [C] (**LAW**) a person who steals things from other people's pockets or bags in public places

pickup /ˈpɪkʌp/ (*also* **ˈpickup truck**) ***noun*** [C] a type of vehicle that has an open part with low sides at the back ➲ picture at **truck**

picky /ˈpɪki/ ***adj.*** (*informal*) (used about a person) liking only certain things and difficult to please ➲ look at **fussy**

picnic /ˈpɪknɪk/ ***noun*** [C] a meal that you take with you to eat outdoors: *We had a picnic on the beach.* ▸ **picnic** ***verb*** [I] (*pres. part.* **picnicking**; *pt, pp* **picnicked**)

Pict /pɪkt/ ***noun*** [C] (HISTORY) a member of an ancient race of people who lived in northern Scotland in Roman times ▸ **Pictish** ***adj.***

pictogram /ˈpɪktəgræm/ ***noun*** [C] **1** (LANGUAGE) a picture representing a word or phrase **2** (BUSINESS, MATHEMATICS) a diagram that uses pictures to represent amounts or numbers of a particular thing ➲ picture at **chart**

pictorial /pɪkˈtɔːriəl/ ***adj.*** expressed in pictures: *pictorial representations of objects*

picture[1] ⊶ /ˈpɪktʃə(r)/ ***noun*** [C] **1** (ART) a painting, drawing or photograph: *Who painted the picture in the hall?* ◇ *The teacher asked us to* ***draw a picture*** *of our families.* **2** an image on a television screen: *They showed pictures of the crash on the news.* **3** a description of sth that gives you a good idea of what it is like: *The police are trying to build up a picture of exactly what happened.*

picture[2] /ˈpɪktʃə(r)/ ***verb*** [T] **1** ~ **sb/sth (as sth)** to imagine sth in your mind: *I can't picture Ivan as a father.* **2** to make a picture of sb/sth: *She is pictured here with her parents.*

picturesque /ˌpɪktʃəˈresk/ ***adj.*** (usually used about an old building or place) attractive: *a picturesque fishing village*

pidgin /ˈpɪdʒɪn/ ***noun*** [U] (LANGUAGE) a simple form of a language, especially English, Portuguese or Dutch, with a limited number of words, that are used together with words from a local language. It is used when people who do not speak the same language need to talk to each other.

pie /paɪ/ ***noun*** [C,U] a type of food consisting of fruit, meat or vegetables inside a PASTRY case: *apple pie* ◇ *meat pie*

piece[1] ⊶ /piːs/ ***noun*** [C] **1** an amount or example of sth: *a piece of paper* ◇ *a piece of furniture* ◇ *a good piece of work* ◇ *a piece of advice/ information/news* **2** one of the parts that sth is made of: *We'll have to* ***take*** *the engine* ***to pieces*** *to find the problem.* **3** one of the parts into which sth breaks: *The plate fell to the floor and smashed* ***to pieces****.* ◇ *The vase lay* ***in pieces*** *on the floor.* **4** a ~ **(on/about sb/ sth)** an article in a newspaper or magazine: *There's a good piece on China in today's paper.* **5** a single work of art, music, etc.: *He played a piece by Chopin.* **6** one of the small objects that you use when you are playing games such as CHESS **7** a coin of the value mentioned: *a fifty-pence piece*

IDM **bits and pieces** → BIT[1]

give sb a piece of your mind to speak to sb angrily because of sth they have done

go to pieces to be no longer able to work or behave normally because of a difficult situation

in one piece not broken or injured: *I've only been on a motorbike once, and I was just glad to get home in one piece.*

a piece of cake (*informal*) something that is very easy

piece[2] /piːs/ ***verb***

PHR V **piece sth together 1** to discover the truth about sth from different pieces of information: *Detectives are trying to piece together the last few days of the man's life.* **2** to put sth together from several pieces

piecemeal /ˈpiːsmiːl/ ***adj.***, ***adv.*** done or happening a little at a time

ˈpiece rate ***noun*** [C] an amount of money paid for each thing or amount of sth that a worker produces

ˈpie chart ***noun*** [C] (MATHEMATICS) a diagram consisting of a circle divided into parts to show the size of particular parts in relation to the whole ➲ picture at **chart**

pier /pɪə(r)/ ***noun*** [C] **1** a large wooden or metal structure that is built out into the sea from the land. Boats can stop at **piers** so that people or goods can be taken on or off. **2** (in Britain) a large wooden or metal structure that is built out into the sea in holiday towns, where people can walk

pierce /pɪəs/ ***verb*** **1** [I] to make a hole in sth with a sharp point: *I'm going to* ***have my ears pierced****.* **2** [I,T] ~ **(through/into) sth** to manage to go through or into sth: *A scream pierced the air.*

piercing /ˈpɪəsɪŋ/ ***adj.*** **1** (used about the wind, pain, a loud noise, etc.) strong and unpleasant **2** (used about sb's eyes or a look) seeming to know what you are thinking

piety /ˈpaɪəti/ ***noun*** [U] (RELIGION) a way of behaving that shows a deep respect for God and religion ➲ adjective **pious**

pig[1] ⊶ /pɪg/ ***noun*** [C] **1** a fat pinkish animal with short legs and a short tail that is kept on farms for its meat (**pork**)

> **RELATED VOCABULARY**
>
> A male pig is a **boar**, a female pig is a **sow** and a young pig is a **piglet**.
>
> When they make a noise, pigs **grunt** and piglets **squeal**.

➲ note at **meat** **2** (*informal*) an unpleasant person or a person who eats too much

pig[2] /pɪg/ ***verb*** [T] (**pigging**; **pigged**) (*slang*) ~ **yourself** to eat too much

PHR V **pig out (on sth)** (*slang*) to eat too much of sth

pigeon /ˈpɪdʒɪn/ ***noun*** [C] a fat grey bird that often lives in towns

pigeonhole /ˈpɪdʒɪnhəʊl/ ***noun*** [C] one of a set of small open boxes that are used for putting papers or letters in

piggyback /ˈpɪgibæk/ ***noun*** [C] the way of carrying sb, especially a child, on your back: *to give sb a piggyback*

ˈpiggy bank ***noun*** [C] a small box, often shaped like a pig, that children save money in

ˌpig-ˈheaded ***adj.*** (*informal*) not prepared to change your mind or say that you are wrong ➲ look at **stubborn**, **obstinate**

ˈpig iron ***noun*** [U] (CHEMISTRY) a form of iron that is not pure

piglet /ˈpɪglət/ ***noun*** [C] a young pig

pigment /ˈpɪgmənt/ ***noun*** [C,U] (ART, BIOLOGY) a substance that gives colour to things: *The colour of your skin depends on the amount of pigment in it.*

pigsty /ˈpɪgstaɪ/ (*also* **sty**) (*AmE* **ˈpigpen**) ***noun*** [C] (*pl.* **pigsties**) (AGRICULTURE) a small building where pigs are kept

pigtail /ˈpɪgteɪl/ (*AmE* **braid**) ***noun*** [C] hair that is tied together in one or two thick pieces made by crossing three pieces of hair over each other (**plaiting**)

pilchard /ˈpɪltʃəd/ ***noun*** [C] a small sea fish that you can eat

pile¹ 🔑 /paɪl/ ***noun*** [C] **1** a number of things lying on top of one another, or an amount of sth lying in a mass: *a pile of books/sand* ◇ *He put the coins* ***in*** *neat* ***piles***. ◇ *She threw the clothes* ***in a pile*** *on the floor.* **2** (usually plural) (*informal*) **piles of sth** a lot of sth: *I've got piles of work to do this evening.* **3 piles** [pl.] = HAEMORRHOIDS

pile² 🔑 /paɪl/ ***verb*** [T] **1** ~ **sth (up)** to put things one on top of the other to form a pile: *We piled the boxes in the corner.* **2** ~ **A on(to) B**; ~ **B with A** to put a lot of sth on top of sth: *She piled the papers on the desk.* ◇ *The desk was piled with papers.*

PHR V **pile into, out of, off, etc. sth** (*informal*) to go into, out of, off, etc. sth quickly and all at the same time: *The children piled onto the bus.*

pile up (used about sth bad) to increase in quantity: *Our problems are really piling up.*

ˈ**pile-up** ***noun*** [C] a crash that involves several cars, etc.: *a multiple pile-up on the motorway*

pilgrim /ˈpɪlgrɪm/ ***noun*** [C] **1** (**RELIGION**) a person who travels a long way to visit a religious place: *Muslim pilgrims on their way to Mecca* **2 Pilgrim** (**HISTORY**) a member of the group of English people (**the Pilgrim Fathers**) who sailed to America on the ship (**The Mayflower**) in 1620 and started a COLONY in Massachusetts

pilgrimage /ˈpɪlgrɪmɪdʒ/ ***noun*** [C,U] (**RELIGION**) a long journey that a person makes to visit a religious place

pill 🔑 /pɪl/ ***noun*** **1** [C] (**HEALTH**) a small round piece of medicine that you swallow: *Take one pill, three times a day after meals.* ◇ *a sleeping pill* ➲ look at **tablet** ➲ picture at **health 2 the pill** [sing.] (**HEALTH**) a pill that some women take regularly so that they do not become pregnant: *She is* ***on the pill***.

pillar /ˈpɪlə(r)/ ***noun*** [C] **1** (**ARCHITECTURE**) a column of stone, wood or metal that is used for supporting part of a building **2** a person who has a strong character and is important to sb/sth: *Dave was a* ***pillar of strength*** *to his sister when she was ill.*

ˈ**pillar box** ***noun*** [C] (in Britain) a tall round red box in a public place into which you can post letters, which are then collected by sb from the post office ➲ look at **postbox**, **letter box**

pillion /ˈpɪliən/ ***noun*** [C] a seat for a passenger behind the driver on a motorbike ▶ **pillion** ***adv.***: *to ride pillion on a motorbike*

pillow /ˈpɪləʊ/ ***noun*** [C] a large CUSHION that you put under your head when you are in bed

pillowcase /ˈpɪləʊkeɪs/ ***noun*** [C] a thin soft cloth cover for a PILLOW

pilot¹ 🔑 /ˈpaɪlət/ ***noun*** [C] a person who flies an aircraft: *an airline pilot*

pilot² /ˈpaɪlət/ ***verb*** [T] **1** to operate the controls of a vehicle, especially an aircraft or a boat: *to pilot a ship* **2** to lead sb/sth through a difficult situation: *The booklet pilots you through the process of starting your own business.* **3** to be the first to test sth that will be used by everyone: *The new exam is being piloted in schools in Italy.*

pilot³ /ˈpaɪlət/ ***adj.*** (only *before* a noun) done as an experiment or to test sth that will be used by everyone: *The pilot scheme will run for six months.*

pimple /ˈpɪmpl/ ***noun*** [C] a small spot on your skin

PIN /pɪn/ (*also* ˈ**PIN number**) ***noun*** [C, usually sing.] (**FINANCE**) **personal identification number**; a number given to you by your bank so that you can use a plastic card to take out money from a cash machine

pin¹ 🔑 /pɪn/ ***noun*** [C] **1** a short thin piece of metal with a round head at one end and a sharp point at the other. Pins are used for fastening together pieces of cloth, paper, etc. **2** a thin piece of wood or metal that is used for a particular purpose: *a hairpin* ◇ *a two-pin plug* ➲ picture at **plug**

pin² 🔑 /pɪn/ ***verb*** [T] (**pinning**; **pinned**) **1** ~ **sth to/on sth**; ~ **sth together** to fasten sth with a pin or pins: *Could you pin this notice on the board, please?* **2** ~ **sb/sth against, to, under, etc. sth** to make sb/sth unable to move by holding or pressing down on them or it: *He caught his brother and pinned him to the floor.* ◇ *He was pinned under the fallen tree.*

IDM **pin (all) your hopes on sb/sth** to believe completely that sb/sth will help you or will succeed

PHR V **pin sb down 1** to hold sb so they cannot move **2** to force sb to decide sth or to say exactly what they are going to do

pin sth down to describe or explain exactly what sth is

pinafore /ˈpɪnəfɔː(r)/ ***noun*** [C] (*old-fashioned*) a piece of clothing or a dress that a woman can wear over her normal clothes to keep them clean when she is cooking or doing dirty jobs ➲ look at **apron**

pincer /ˈpɪnsə(r)/ ***noun*** **1 pincers** [pl.] a tool made of two crossed pieces of metal that is used for holding things, pulling nails out of wood, etc. **2** [C] (**BIOLOGY**) one of the two sharp, curved front legs of some SHELLFISH that are used for holding things ➲ picture on **page 29**

pinch¹ /pɪntʃ/ ***verb*** **1** [T] to hold a piece of sb's skin tightly between your thumb and first finger, especially in order to hurt them: *Paul pinched his brother and made him cry.* **2** [I,T] to hold sth too tight, often causing pain: *I've got a pinched nerve in my neck.* **3** [T] (*informal*) to steal: *Who's pinched my pen?*

pinch² /pɪntʃ/ ***noun*** [C] **1** the holding of sb's skin tightly between your finger and thumb: *She gave him a little pinch on the arm.* **2** the amount of sth that you can pick up with your thumb and first finger: *a pinch of salt*

IDM **at a pinch** used to say that sth can be done if it is really necessary: *We really need three cars but we could manage with two at a pinch.*

take sth with a pinch of salt to think that sth is probably not true or accurate

pinched /pɪntʃt/ ***adj.*** (used about sb's face) thin and pale because of illness or cold

pine¹ /paɪn/ ***noun*** **1** [C] (*also* ˈ**pine tree**) a tall EVERGREEN tree that has thin sharp leaves (**needles**) **2** [U] the wood from **pine** trees (which is often used for making furniture): *a pine table*

pine² /paɪn/ ***verb*** [I] ~ **(for sb/sth)** to be very unhappy because sb has died or gone away: *The dog sat outside, pining for its owner.*

pineapple /ˈpaɪnæpl/ ***noun*** [C,U] a large sweet fruit that is yellow inside and has a thick brown skin with sharp points. **Pineapples** grow in hot countries.

ˈ**pine nut** (*BrE also* ˈ**pine kernel**) ***noun*** [C] the white seed of some PINE trees, used in cooking

ping /pɪŋ/ ***noun*** [C] a short high noise that is made by a small bell or by a metal object hitting against sth: *The lift went ping and the doors opened.* ▶ **ping** ***verb*** [I]

ˈ**ping-pong** (*informal*) = TABLE TENNIS

pink 🔑 /pɪŋk/ ***adj.***, ***noun*** [U] (of) a pale red colour

pinna /ˈpɪnə/ ***noun*** [C] (*pl.* **pinnae** /-niː/) (**ANATOMY**) the outer part of the ear ➲ picture at **ear**

pinnacle /ˈpɪnəkl/ ***noun*** [C] **1** the most important or successful part of sth: *Celia is at the pinnacle of her career.* **2** (**GEOGRAPHY**) a high pointed rock on a mountain

pinpoint /ˈpɪnpɔɪnt/ ***verb*** [T] **1** to find the exact position of sth: *to pinpoint a place on the map* **2** to describe or explain exactly what sth is: *First we have to pinpoint the cause of the failure.*

ˌ**pins and ˈneedles** ***noun*** [pl.] a strange, sometimes painful feeling that you get in a part of your body after it has been in one position for too long and when the blood is returning to it

pinstripe /ˈpɪnstraɪp/ ***noun*** **1** [C] one of the white vertical lines printed on dark material that is used especially for making business suits **2** [C,U] dark material with white vertical lines printed on it; a suit made from this cloth

pint 🔑 /paɪnt/ ***noun*** [C] **1** (*abbr.* **pt**) a measure of liquid; 0.57 of a litre. There are 8 pints in a gallon: *a pint of milk* ℹ An American pint is 0.47 of a litre. **2** (*BrE, informal*) a pint of beer

ˈ**pin-up** ***noun*** [C] (*informal*) a picture of an attractive person, made to be put on a wall; a person who appears in these pictures

pioneer /ˌpaɪəˈnɪə(r)/ ***noun*** [C] **1 a ~ (in/of sth)** a person who is one of the first to develop an area of human knowledge, culture, etc.: *Yuri Gagarin was one of the pioneers of space exploration.* **2** a person who is one of the first to go and live in a particular area: *the pioneers of the American West* ▶ **pioneer** ***verb*** [T]: *a technique pioneered in the US*

pious /ˈpaɪəs/ ***adj.*** (**RELIGION**) having or showing a deep belief in religion ▶ **piously** ***adv.*** ➲ noun **piety**

pip /pɪp/ ***noun*** [C] (*BrE*) the small seed of an apple, a lemon, an orange, etc.

pipe¹ 🔑 /paɪp/ ***noun*** [C] **1** a tube that carries gas or liquid: *Waste water is carried away down the drainpipe.* **2** a tube with a small bowl at one end that is used for smoking TOBACCO: *to smoke a pipe* **3** (**MUSIC**) a simple musical instrument that consists of a tube with holes in it. You blow into it to play it.

pipe² /paɪp/ ***verb*** [T] to carry liquid or gas in pipes: *Water is piped to all the houses in the village.*

PHR V **pipe up** (*informal*) to suddenly say sth: *Suddenly Shirin piped up with a question.*

pipeline /ˈpaɪplaɪn/ ***noun*** [C] a line of pipes that are used for carrying liquid or gas over a long distance

IDM **in the pipeline** being planned or prepared

piper /ˈpaɪpə(r)/ ***noun*** [C] (**MUSIC**) a person who plays music on a pipe, or who plays the BAGPIPES (= a musical instrument that is typical in Scotland)

pipette /pɪˈpet/ ***noun*** [C] (**SCIENCE**) a narrow tube used in a LABORATORY for measuring or moving small amounts of liquids ➲ picture at **laboratory**

piracy /ˈpaɪrəsi/ ***noun*** [U] **1** (**LAW**) the crime of attacking ships in order to steal from them **2** (**LAW**) the illegal copying of books, video tapes, etc.

pirate¹ /ˈpaɪrət/ ***noun*** [C] **1** (usually in the past or in stories) a criminal who attacks ships in order to steal from them **2** (**LAW**) a person who copies books, video tapes, computer programs, etc. in order to sell them illegally

pirate² /ˈpaɪrət/ ***verb*** [T] (**LAW**) to make an illegal copy of a book, video tape, etc. in order to sell it

Pisces /ˈpaɪsiːz/ ***noun*** [U] the twelfth sign of the ZODIAC, the Fishes

pistachio /pɪˈstæʃiəʊ; -ˈstɑːʃiəʊ/ (*also* **piˈstachio nut**) ***noun*** [C] (*pl.* **pistachios**) the small green nut of an Asian tree

pistil /ˈpɪstɪl/ ***noun*** [C] (**BIOLOGY**) the female organs of a flower, which receive the POLLEN and produce seeds

pistol /ˈpɪstl/ ***noun*** [C] a small gun that you hold in one hand ➲ note at **gun**

piston /ˈpɪstən/ ***noun*** [C] (**PHYSICS, TECHNICAL**) a piece of metal in an engine, etc. that fits tightly inside a tube (**cylinder**). The **piston** is moved up and down inside the tube and causes other parts of the engine to move. ➲ picture at **hydraulic**

pit¹ /pɪt/ ***noun*** **1** [C] a large hole that is made in the ground: *They dug a large pit to bury the dead animals.* **2** [C] = COAL MINE **3 the pits** [pl.] (*AmE* **the pit** [C]) the place on a motor racing track where cars stop for fuel, new tyres, etc. during a race **4** [C] = ORCHESTRA PIT

IDM **be the pits** (*slang*) to be very bad: *The food in that restaurant is the pits!*

pit² /pɪt/ ***verb*** [T] (**pitting**; **pitted**) to make small holes in the surface of sth: *The front of the building was pitted with bullet marks.*

PHR V **pit A against B** to test one person or thing against another in a fight or competition: *The two strongest teams were pitted against each other in the final.*

pitch¹ 🔑 /pɪtʃ/ ***noun*** **1** [C] (*BrE*) (**SPORT**) a special area of ground where you play certain sports: *a football/hockey/cricket pitch* ➲ look at **court**, **field** **2** [sing.] the strength or level of feelings, activity, etc.: *The children's excitement almost reached fever pitch.* **3** [U] (**MUSIC**) how high or low a sound is, especially a musical note ➲ picture at **high-pitched** **4** [C] talk or arguments used by sb who is trying to sell sth or persuade sb to do sth: *a sales pitch* ◇ *to make a pitch for sth*

pitch² /pɪtʃ/ ***verb*** **1** [T] to set sth at a particular level: *The talk was pitched at people with far more experience than me.* **2** [I,T] to throw sth/sb; to be thrown: *Doug pitched his can into the bushes.* **3** [T] to put up a tent or tents: *They pitched their tents in the valley.* **4** [T] **~ sth (at sb)** to try to sell a product to a particular group of people or in a particular way: *This new breakfast cereal is being pitched at kids.*

PHR V **pitch in** (*informal*) to join in and work together with other people: *Everybody pitched in to clear up the flood damage.*

ˌ**pitch-ˈblack** ***adj.*** completely dark; with no light at all

pitcher /ˈpɪtʃə(r)/ ***noun*** [C] **1** a large container for holding and pouring liquids **2** (**SPORT**) (in BASEBALL) the player who PITCHES (= throws) the ball to a player from the other team, who tries to hit it

pitchfork /ˈpɪtʃfɔːk/ ***noun*** [C] (**AGRICULTURE**) a farm tool like a fork with a long handle and two or three sharp metal points. It is used for lifting and moving dried cut grass (**hay**).

piteous /ˈpɪtiəs/ ***adj.*** (*formal*) that makes you feel pity or sadness ▶ **piteously** ***adv.***

pitfall /ˈpɪtfɔːl/ ***noun*** [C] a danger or difficulty, especially one that is hidden or not obvious

pith /pɪθ/ ***noun*** [U] (BIOLOGY) the white substance inside the skin of an orange, lemon, etc.

pithy /ˈpɪθi/ ***adj.*** expressed in a clear, direct way: *a pithy comment*

piti·able /ˈpɪtiəbl/ ***adj.*** (*formal*) **1** deserving pity or causing you to feel pity: *The refugees were in a pitiable state.* **2** not deserving respect: *a pitiable lack of talent* ▸ **piti·ably** /-əbli/ ***adv.***

pitiful /ˈpɪtɪfl/ ***adj.*** causing you to feel pity or sadness: *the pitiful groans of the wounded soldiers* ▸ **pitifully** /-fəli/ ***adv.***

pitiless /ˈpɪtiləs/ ***adj.*** having or showing no pity for other people's suffering ▸ **pitilessly** ***adv.***

pituitary /pɪˈtjuːɪtəri/ (*also* **pi'tuitary gland**) ***noun*** [C] (*pl.* **pituitaries**) a small organ at the base of the brain that produces HORMONES (= substances that affect growth and sexual development) ➲ picture at **brain**

pity[1] 🔑 /ˈpɪti/ ***noun*** **1** [U] a feeling of sadness that you have for sb/sth that is suffering or in trouble: *The situation is his fault so I don't feel any pity for him.* **2** [sing.] something that makes you feel a little sad or disappointed: *'You're too late. Emily left five minutes ago.' 'Oh,* ***what a pity****!'* ◇ *It's a pity that Bina couldn't come.*

IDM **take pity on sb** to help sb who is suffering or in trouble because you feel sorry for them

> **WORD FAMILY**
> **pity** *noun, verb*
> **pitiful** *adj.*
> **pitiless** *adj.*
> **pitiable** *adj.*
> **piteous** *adj.*

pity[2] /ˈpɪti/ ***verb*** [T] (*pres. part.* **pitying**; *3rd person sing. pres.* **pities**; *pt, pp* **pitied**) to feel pity or sadness for sb who is suffering or in trouble

pivot[1] /ˈpɪvət/ ***noun*** [C] **1** (PHYSICS) the central point on which sth turns or balances SYN **fulcrum** **2** the central or most important person or thing: *West Africa was the pivot of the cocoa trade.*

pivot[2] /ˈpɪvət/ ***verb*** [I] to turn or balance on a central point

pixel /ˈpɪksl/ ***noun*** [C] (COMPUTING) any of the very small individual areas on a computer screen, which together form the whole image

pixelate (also **pixellate**) /ˈpɪksəleɪt/ ***verb*** [T] **1** (COMPUTING) to divide an image into PIXELS **2** (ARTS AND MEDIA) to show an image on television as a small number of large PIXELS, especially in order to hide sb's identity

pixie /ˈpɪksi/ ***noun*** [C] (in children's stories) a creature like a small person with pointed ears that has magic powers

pizza /ˈpiːtsə/ ***noun*** [C,U] an Italian dish consisting of a flat round bread base with vegetables, cheese, meat, etc. on top, which is cooked in an oven

pizzicato /ˌpɪtsɪˈkɑːtəʊ/ ***adj., adv.*** (MUSIC) using the fingers to pull the strings of a musical instrument, for example a VIOLIN, that you usually play with a BOW (= a long thin piece of wood with strings stretched tightly across it)

pl. ***abbr.*** (LANGUAGE) plural

placard /ˈplækɑːd/ ***noun*** [C] (SOCIAL STUDIES) a large written or printed notice that is put in a public place or carried on a stick in a protest march

placate /pləˈkeɪt/ ***verb*** [T] to make sb feel less angry about sth

place[1] 🔑 /pleɪs/ ***noun*** [C] **1** a particular position or area: *Show me the exact place where it happened.* ◇ *This would be a good place to sit down and have a rest.* ◇ *The wall was damaged in several places.* **2** a particular village, town, country, etc.: *Which places did you go to in Italy?* ◇ *Vienna is a very beautiful place.* **3** a building or an area that is used for a particular purpose: *The square is a popular* ***meeting place*** *for young people.* ◇ *The town is full of inexpensive eating places.* **4** a seat or position that can be used by sb/sth: *They went into the classroom and sat down in their places.* ◇ *Go on ahead and* ***save*** *me* ***a place*** *in the queue.* **5** [sing.] your position in society; your role: *I feel* ***it is not my place*** *to criticize my boss.* **6** an opportunity to study at a college, play for a team, etc.: *Abina has got a place to study law at Hull.* ◇ *Laila is now sure of a place on the team.* **7** the usual or correct position or occasion for sth: *The room was tidy. Everything had been put away* ***in its place****.* ◇ *A funeral is not the place to discuss business.* **8** (MATHEMATICS) the position of a number after the DECIMAL POINT: *Your answer should be correct to three decimal places.* **9** [sing.] (*spoken*) a person's home: *Her parents have got a place on the coast.* **10** [usually sing.] the position that you have at the end of a race, competition, etc.: *Cara finished* ***in second place****.*

IDM **all over the place** everywhere

change/swap places (with sb) to take sb's seat, position, etc. and let them have yours

fall/slot into place (used about sth that is complicated or difficult to understand) to become organized or clear in your mind: *After two weeks in my new job, everything suddenly started to fall into place.*

in my, your, etc. place/shoes in my, your, etc. situation or position: *If I were in your place I would wait a year before getting married.*

in place **1** in the correct or usual position: *Use tape to hold the picture in place.* **2** (used about plans or preparations) finished and ready to be used

in place of sb/sth; in sb/sth's place instead of sb/sth

in the first, second, etc. place (*informal*) used when you are giving a list of reasons for sth or explaining sth; FIRSTLY, SECONDLY, etc.

out of place **1** not suitable for a particular situation: *I felt very out of place among all those clever people.* **2** not in the correct or usual place

put sb in his/her place to show that sb is not as clever, important, etc. as they believe: *It really put her in her place when she failed to qualify for the race.*

put yourself in sb's place to imagine that you are in the same situation as sb else

take place (used about a meeting, an event, etc.) to happen: *The ceremony took place in glorious sunshine.*

place[2] 🔑 /pleɪs/ ***verb*** [T] **1** (*formal*) to put sth carefully or deliberately in a particular position: *The chairs had all been placed in neat rows.* ◇ *The poster was placed where everyone could see it.* **2** to put sb in a particular position or situation: *His behaviour placed me in a difficult situation.* ◇ *to place sb in charge* ◇ *Rhoda was placed third in the competition.* **3** used to express the attitude that sb has to sb/sth: *We placed our trust in you and you failed us.* ◇ *The blame for the disaster was placed firmly on the company.* **4** (usually in negative statements) to recognize sb/sth and be able to identify them or it: *Her face is familiar but I just can't place her.* **5** to give instructions about sth or to ask for sth to happen: *to place a bet on sth* ◇ *to place an order for sth*

placebo /pləˈsiːbəʊ/ ***noun*** [C] (*pl.* **placebos**) (HEALTH) a substance that has no physical effects, given to patients who do not need medicine but think that they do, or used when testing new drugs:

the **placebo effect** (=the effect of taking a placebo and feeling better)

ˈplace name ***noun*** [C] the name of a city, town, etc.

placenta /pləˈsentə/ ***noun*** [C] (**ANATOMY**) the material inside the WOMB (=the part of a woman's body where a baby grows) which protects the baby and supplies food through a tube (**umbilical cord**) ➲ picture at **fertilize**

placid /ˈplæsɪd/ ***adj.*** (used about a person or an animal) calm and not easily excited ▶ **placidly** ***adv.***

plagiarism /ˈpleɪdʒərɪzəm/ ***noun*** [U, C] the act of copying another person's ideas, words or work and pretending they are your own; sth that has been copied in this way ▶ **plagiarize** (also **-ise**) /ˈpleɪdʒəraɪz/ ***verb*** [T,I]

plague¹ /pleɪɡ/ ***noun*** **1** (**HEALTH**) [C,U] any infectious disease that spreads quickly and kills many people **2 the plague** [U] an infectious disease spread by RATS that causes swellings on the body, a very high temperature and often results in death **3** [C] **a ~ of sth** a large number of unpleasant animals or insects that come into an area at one time: *a plague of ants/locusts*

plague² /pleɪɡ/ ***verb*** [T] to cause sb/sth a lot of trouble: *The project was plagued by a series of disasters.*

plaice /pleɪs/ ***noun*** [C,U] (*pl.* **plaice**) a type of flat sea fish that we eat

plain¹ 🔑 /pleɪn/ ***adj.*** **1** easy to see, hear or understand; clear: *It was plain that he didn't want to talk about it.* ➲ note at **clear¹**: *She* ***made it plain that*** *she didn't want to see me again.* **2** (used about people, thoughts, actions, etc.) saying what you think; direct and honest: *I'll be plain with you. I don't like the idea.* **3** simple in style; not decorated or complicated: *My father likes plain English cooking.* **4** (only *before* a noun) all one colour; without a pattern on it: *a plain blue jumper* **5** (used especially about a woman or girl) not beautiful or attractive: *She's a rather plain child.*

plain² /pleɪn/ ***noun*** [C] (**GEOGRAPHY**) a large area of flat land with few trees

plain³ /pleɪn/ ***adv.*** (*spoken*) completely: *That's plain silly.*

ˌplain-ˈclothes ***adj.*** (used about a police officer) wearing ordinary clothes; not in uniform: *a plain-clothes detective* ▶ **ˌplain ˈclothes** ***noun*** [pl.]: ***officers in plain clothes***

ˌplain ˈflour ***noun*** [U] flour that does not contain a powder which makes cakes, etc. rise during cooking (**baking powder**) ➲ look at **self-raising flour**

plainly /ˈpleɪnli/ ***adv.*** **1** clearly: *He was plainly very upset.* **2** using simple words to say sth in a direct and honest way: *She told him plainly that he was not doing his job properly.* **3** in a simple way, without decoration: *She was plainly dressed and wore no make-up.*

plainsong /ˈpleɪnsɒŋ/ (*also* **plainchant**) ***noun*** [U] (**MUSIC**) a type of church music for voices alone, used since the Middle Ages

plaintiff /ˈpleɪntɪf/ ***noun*** [C] (**LAW**) a person who starts a legal action against sb in a court of law ➲ look at **defendant**

plaintive /ˈpleɪntɪv/ ***adj.*** sounding sad, especially in a weak complaining way ▶ **plaintively** ***adv.***

plait /plæt/ (*AmE* **braid**) ***verb*** [T] to cross three or more long pieces of hair, rope, etc. over and under each other to make one thick piece ▶ **plait** ***noun*** [C]

plan¹ 🔑 /plæn/ ***noun*** **1** [C] **a ~ (for sth/to do sth)** an idea or arrangement for doing or achieving sth in the future: *We usually* ***make*** *our holiday* ***plans*** *in January.* ◇ *The firm has no plans to employ more people.* ◇ *There has been* ***a change of plan*** *– we're meeting at the restaurant.* ◇ *If everything* ***goes according to plan*** (=happens as we planned) *we should be home by midnight.* **2** [C] a detailed map of a building, town, etc.: ***a street plan*** *of Berlin* **3 plans** [pl.] detailed drawings of a building, machine, road, etc. that show its size, shape and measurements: *We're getting an architect to* ***draw up*** *some* ***plans*** *for a new kitchen.* **4** [C] a diagram that shows how sth is to be organized or arranged: *Before you start writing an essay, it's a good idea to make a brief plan.*

plan² 🔑 /plæn/ ***verb*** (**planning**; **planned**) **1** [I,T] **~ (sth) (for sth)** to decide, organize or prepare for sth you want to do in the future: *to plan for the future* ◇ *You need to plan your work more carefully.* **2** [I,T] **~ (on sth/doing sth)**; **~ (to do sth)** to intend or expect to do sth: *I'm planning on having a holiday in July.* ◇ *We plan to arrive at about 4 o'clock.* ➲ note at **purpose** **3** [T] to make a diagram or a design of sth: *The new shopping centre is very badly planned.*

plane¹ 🔑 /pleɪn/ ***noun*** [C] **1** a vehicle that can fly through the air, with wings and one or more engines: *Has her plane landed yet?* **2** (**GEOMETRY**)

plane

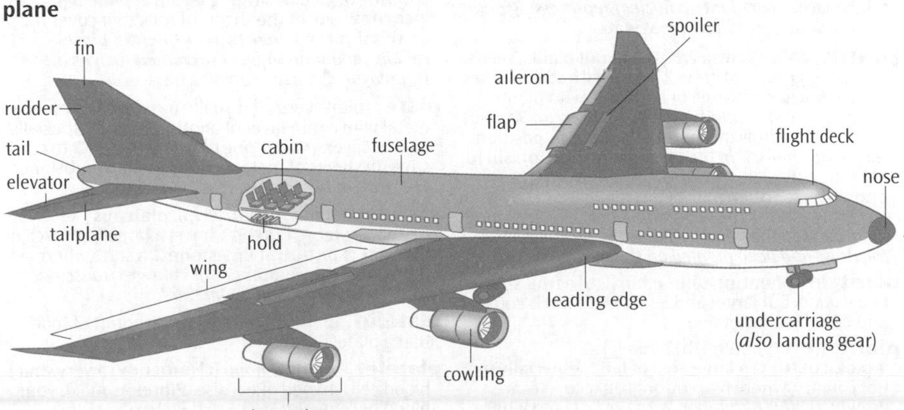

any flat or level surface, or an imaginary flat surface through or joining material objects: *the **horizontal/vertical plane*** **3** a tool used for making the surface of wood smooth by taking very thin pieces off it ➲ picture at **tool**

plane² /pleɪn/ *verb* [T] to make the surface of a piece of wood flat and smooth using a PLANE¹ (3)

plane³ /pleɪn/ *adj.* (only *before* a noun) completely flat; level: *a plane mirror*

planet 🔑 /ˈplænɪt/ *noun* **1** [C] (**ASTRONOMY**) a very large round object in space that moves around the sun or another star: *the planets of our solar system* **2 the planet** [sing.] (**ENVIRONMENT**) the world we live in; the Earth, especially when talking about the environment

planetarium /ˌplænɪˈteəriəm/ *noun* [C] (**ASTRONOMY**) a building with a curved ceiling that represents the sky at night. It is used for showing the positions and movements of the planets and stars for education and entertainment.

plank /plæŋk/ *noun* [C] a long flat thin piece of wood that is used for building or making things ➲ picture at **vice**

plankton /ˈplæŋktən/ *noun* [U, pl.] (**BIOLOGY**) the very small forms of plant and animal life that live in seas, rivers, lakes, etc.

ˌplanned eˈconomy (*also* **comˌmand eˈconomy**) *noun* [C] (**ECONOMICS**) an economy in which levels of pay, prices, production, etc. are decided by the government

planner /ˈplænə(r)/ *noun* [C] **1** (*also* **ˌtown ˈplanner**) a person whose job is to plan the growth and development of a town **2** a person who makes plans for a particular area of activity: *curriculum planners* **3** a book, computer program, etc. that contains dates and is used for recording information, arranging meetings, etc.

planning 🔑 /ˈplænɪŋ/ *noun* [U] **1** the act or process of making plans for sth: *financial planning* ◇ *The project requires careful planning.* **2** = TOWN PLANNING

plant¹ 🔑 /plɑːnt/ *noun* [C] **1** (**BIOLOGY**) a living thing that grows in the ground and usually has leaves, a long thin green central part (**a stem**) and roots: *a tomato plant* ◇ *a plant pot* (= a container for plants) ➲ picture at **flower 2** a factory or place where power is produced or an industrial process takes place: *a car plant* ◇ *a nuclear reprocessing plant* ➲ note at **factory** ➲ picture at **water**

plant² 🔑 /plɑːnt/ *verb* [T] **1** to put plants, seeds, etc. in the ground to grow **2 ~ sth (with sth)** to cover or supply a garden, area of land, etc. with plants: *The field's been planted with wheat this year.* **3** to put yourself/sth firmly in a particular place or position: *He planted himself in the best seat.* **4 ~ sth (on sb)** to hide sth, especially sth illegal, in sb's clothing, property, etc., often in order to make them seem guilty of a crime: *The police think that terrorists may have **planted the bomb**.* ◇ *The women claimed that the drugs had been planted on them.*

plantain /ˈplæntɪn; -teɪn/ *noun* [C,U] a fruit similar to a BANANA but larger and less sweet, that is cooked and eaten as a vegetable

plantation /plɑːnˈteɪʃn/ *noun* [C] **1** (**AGRICULTURE**) a large area of land, especially in a hot country, where tea, cotton, TOBACCO, etc. are grown: *a coffee plantation* **2** an area of land where trees are grown to produce wood

plaque /plɑːk/ *noun* **1** [C] a flat piece of stone or metal, usually with names and dates on it, that is fixed on a wall in memory of a famous person or event **2** [U] (**HEALTH**) a harmful substance that forms on your teeth

plasma /ˈplæzmə/ (*also* **plasm** /ˈplæzəm/) *noun* [U] (**BIOLOGY**) the colourless liquid part of blood, in which the blood cells, etc. float

ˌplasma ˈscreen *noun* [C,U] (**ARTS AND MEDIA**) a type of television or computer screen that is larger and thinner than most screens and produces a very clear image

plaster¹ /ˈplɑːstə(r)/ *noun* **1** [U] a mixture of a special powder and water that becomes hard when it is dry. **Plaster** is put on walls and ceilings to form a smooth surface. ➲ picture at **building 2** (*also* **ˈsticking plaster**) [C] (**HEALTH**) a small piece of sticky material that is used to cover a cut, etc. on the body ➲ picture at **health 3** (*also* **ˌplaster of ˈParis**) [U] (**HEALTH**) a white powder that is mixed with water and becomes hard when dry. It is used for putting round broken bones, etc. until they get better: *When Alan broke his leg it was **in plaster** for six weeks.* ➲ picture at **health**

plaster² /ˈplɑːstə(r)/ *verb* [T] **1** to cover a wall, etc. with **plaster¹**(1) to make the surface smooth **2 ~ sb/sth (in/with sth)** to cover sb/sth with a large amount of sth: *He plastered his walls with posters.*

ˈplaster cast *noun* [C] **1** (**HEALTH**) a case made of PLASTER¹ (3) that covers a broken bone and protects it ➲ picture at **health 2** a copy of sth, made using PLASTER: *They took a plaster cast of the teeth for identification purposes.*

plastic¹ 🔑 /ˈplæstɪk/ *noun* [C,U] (**CHEMISTRY**) a light, strong material that is made with chemicals and is used for making many different sorts of objects

plastic² 🔑 /ˈplæstɪk/ *adj.* made of plastic: *plastic cups* ◇ *a plastic bag*

ˌplastic ˈsurgery *noun* [U] (**HEALTH**) a medical operation to repair or replace damaged skin or to improve the appearance of a person's face or body ➲ look at **facelift**, **surgery**

plate¹ 🔑 /pleɪt/ *noun* **1** [C] a flat, usually round, dish for eating or serving food from: *a plastic/paper/china plate* ◇ *a plate of food* **2** [C] a thin flat piece of metal or glass: *a steel/metal plate* **3** [C] a flat piece of metal with sth written on it: *The brass plate beside the door said 'Dr Waters'.* **4** [U] metal that has a thin covering of gold or silver: *gold/silver plate* **5** [C] (**GEOLOGY**) one of the sheets of rock that cover the earth's surface: *Where two **continental plates** collide, mountain ranges are created such as the Himalayas.* ➲ picture on next page

plate² /pleɪt/ *verb* [T] (usually passive) **1** to cover a metal with a thin layer of another metal, especially gold or silver: *a silver ring plated with gold* **2** to cover sth with sheets of metal or another hard substance: *The walls of the vault were plated with steel.*

plateau /ˈplætəʊ/ *noun* [C] (*pl.* **plateaus** /-təʊz/ or **plateaux** /-təʊ/) **1** (**GEOGRAPHY**) a large high area of flat land ➲ picture at **limestone 2** a state where there is little development or change: *House prices seem to have **reached a plateau**.*

plateful /ˈpleɪtfʊl/ *noun* [C] the amount of food that a plate(1) can hold

platelet /ˈpleɪtlət/ *noun* [C] (**BIOLOGY**) a very small blood cell, shaped like a disc. **Platelets** make your blood become thicker so that it CLOTS (= stops flowing) when you cut yourself.

continental plates

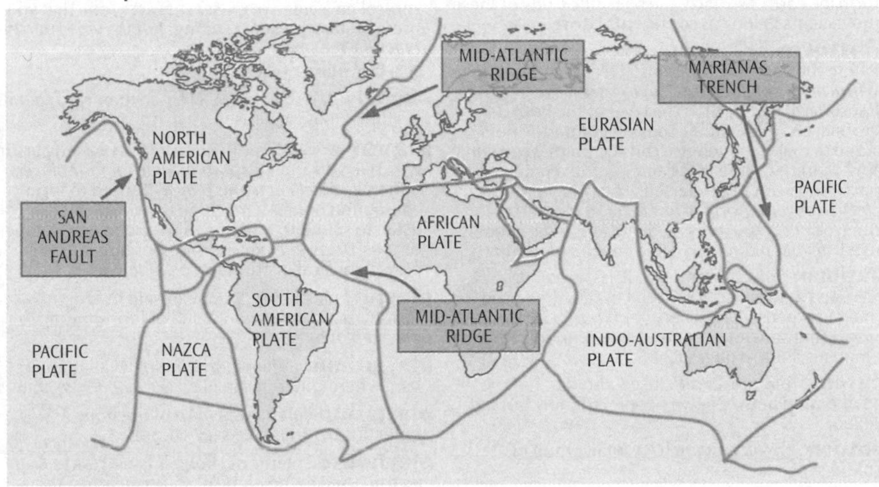

plate tectonics

plate boundaries

The point where two plates meet is called a **plate boundary**. Earthquakes are most likely to occur either on or near plate boundaries. There are three types of **plate boundaries**:

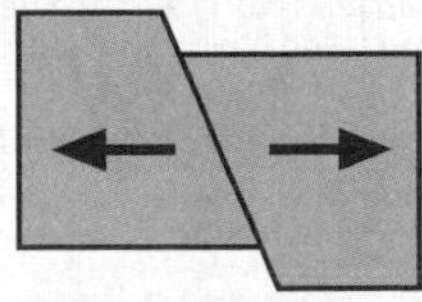

divergent boundary

At a **divergent boundary** the plates move apart. **Divergent boundaries** produce **rift valleys**, caused when two parallel cracks develop in the earth's surface and the land between them sinks. Volcanoes are often found along or near **rift valleys**. The **Great Rift Valley**, in the Middle East and Africa, is the most famous of these.

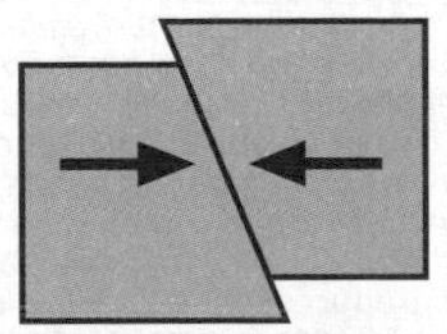

convergent boundary

At a **convergent boundary** the plates move towards each other and one plate is usually pushed up over the other plate. The Earth's biggest earthquakes, some measuring over 9 on the **Richter Scale**, occur at **convergent boundaries** and may cause tsunamis if the earthquake occurs underwater, as in the Asian tsunami disaster in December 2004.

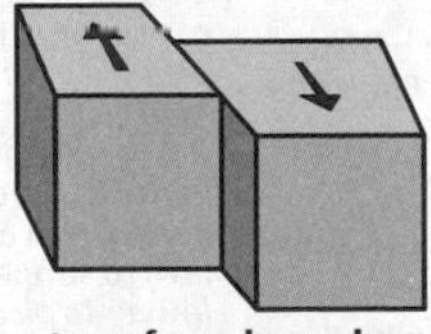

transform boundary

At a **transform boundary** plates slide and rub against each other along a **transform fault**. Most **transform boundaries** are found on the ocean floor. However, the most famous are found on land, for example the **San Andreas Fault** in California.

ˌplate tecˈtonics *noun* [U] (GEOLOGY) the movements of the large sheets of rock (**plates**) that form the earth's surface; the scientific study of these movements ➲ look at **continental drift**

platform 🔑 /ˈplætfɔːm/ *noun* [C] **1** the place where you get on or off trains at a railway station: *Which platform does the train to York leave from?* **2** a flat surface, higher than the level of the floor or ground, on which public speakers or performers stand so that the audience can see them **3** [usually sing.] (POLITICS) the ideas and aims of a political party who want to be elected: *They fought the election on a platform of low taxes.* **4** (COMPUTING) the type of computer system or the software that is used: *an IBM platform* ◊ *a multimedia platform*

platinum /ˈplætɪnəm/ *noun* [U] (*symbol* **Pt**) (CHEMISTRY) a silver-grey metal that is often used for making expensive jewellery: *a platinum wedding ring* ❶ For more information on the periodic table of elements, look at pages R34-5.

platonic /pləˈtɒnɪk/ *adj.* (used about a relationship between two people) friendly but not sexual

platoon /pləˈtuːn/ *noun* [C] a small group of soldiers

plausible /ˈplɔːzəbl/ *adj.* that you can believe; reasonable: *a plausible excuse* OPP **implausible**

play[1] 🔑 /pleɪ/ *verb* **1** [I] ~ (**with sb/sth**) to do sth to enjoy yourself; to have fun: *The children have been playing on the beach all day.* ◊ *Emma's found a new friend to play with.* **2** [I,T] (SPORT) to take part in a game or sport: *to play football/tennis/hockey* ◊ *I usually play against Bill.* ◊ *She played him at table tennis and won.* ◊ *Do you know how to play chess?* ◊ *Who's Brazil playing next in the World Cup?* **3** [I,T] ~ (**sth**) (**on sth**) (MUSIC) to use an instrument to make music: *to play the piano/guitar/trumpet* ◊ *My son's learning the piano. He plays very well.* ◊ *She played a few notes on the violin.* **4** [T] to turn on a video, tape, etc. so that it produces sound: *Shall I play the CD for you again?* **5** [I,T] (ARTS AND MEDIA) to act in a play, film, television programme, etc.; to act the role of sb: *Richard is going to play Romeo.* **6** ~ **a part/role in sth** [T] to have an effect on sth: *The media played an important part in the last election.* ◊ *John played a key role in organizing the protest.* **7** [I] (*formal*) to move quickly and lightly: *Sunlight played on the surface of the sea.*

PHR V **play at sth/being sth** to do sth with little interest or effort: *He's only playing at studying. He'd prefer to get a job now.* ◊ *What is that driver playing at* (=doing)?

play sth back (**to sb**) to turn on and watch or listen to a film, tape, etc. that you have recorded: *Play that last scene back to me again.*

play sth down to make sth seem less important than it really is: *to play down a crisis*

play A off against B to make people compete or argue with each other, especially for your own advantage: *I think she enjoys playing one friend off against another.*

play on sth to use and take advantage of sb's fears or weaknesses: *This advertising campaign plays on people's fears of illness.*

play (**sb**) **up** (*informal*) to cause sb trouble or pain: *The car always plays up in wet weather.*

play[2] 🔑 /pleɪ/ *noun* **1** [C] (ARTS AND MEDIA) a piece of writing performed by actors in the theatre, or on television or radio: *Would you like to see a play while you're in London?* ◊ *a radio/television play* ➲ note at **performing arts** **2** [U] (SPORT) the playing of a game or sport: *Bad weather stopped play yesterday.* **3** [U] activity done for enjoyment only, especially by children: *Young children learn through play.* ◊ *the happy sound of children* ***at play*** **4** [U] a control on a video or CASSETTE PLAYER, etc. that you press to start the tape running: *Put the video into the machine then* ***press play***.

IDM **fair play** → FAIR[1]

playboy /ˈpleɪbɔɪ/ *noun* [C] a rich man who spends his time enjoying himself

player 🔑 /ˈpleɪə(r)/ *noun* [C] **1** (SPORT) a person who plays a game or sport: *a game for four players* ◊ *She's an excellent tennis player.* **2** (used to form compound nouns) a machine on which you can listen to sound that has been recorded on CD, tape, etc.: *a CD/cassette player* **3** (MUSIC) a person who plays a musical instrument: *a piano player*

playful /ˈpleɪfl/ *adj.* **1** done or said in fun; not serious: *a playful remark* **2** full of fun; wanting to play: *a playful puppy*

playground /ˈpleɪgraʊnd/ *noun* [C] an area of land where children can play: *the school playground*

playgroup /ˈpleɪgruːp/ (*also* **playschool** /ˈpleɪskuːl/) (*BrE*) = NURSERY SCHOOL

playhouse /ˈpleɪhaʊs/ *noun* **1** [sing.] (ARTS AND MEDIA) used in the name of some theatres: *the Liverpool Playhouse* **2** [C] a model of a house for children to play in

ˈplaying card = CARD (4)

ˈplaying field *noun* [C] (SPORT) a large field used for sports such as CRICKET and football

IDM **a level playing field** → LEVEL[2]

ˈplay-off *noun* [C] (SPORT) a match between two teams or players who have equal scores to decide the winner

plaything /ˈpleɪθɪŋ/ *noun* [C] (*formal*) a toy

playtime /ˈpleɪtaɪm/ *noun* [C,U] a period of time between lessons when children at school can go outside to play

playwright /ˈpleɪraɪt/ *noun* [C] (ARTS AND MEDIA) a person who writes plays for the theatre, television or radio

plc (*also* **PLC**) /ˌpiː el ˈsiː/ *abbr.* (*BrE*) (BUSINESS) Public Limited Company

plea /pliː/ *noun* [C] **1** (*formal*) **a** ~ (**for sth**) an important and emotional request: *a plea for help* **2** **a** ~ **of sth** (LAW) a statement made by or for sb in a court of law: *a plea of guilty/not guilty*

plead /pliːd/ *verb* **1** [I] ~ (**with sb**) (**to do/for sth**) to ask sb for sth in a very strong and serious way: *She pleaded with him not to leave her.* ◊ *He pleaded for mercy.* **2** [I,T] (LAW) to state in a court of law that you did or did not do a crime: *The defendant* ***pleaded not guilty*** *to the charge of theft.* **3** [I,T] ~ (**sth**) (**for sb/sth**) (LAW) (used especially about a lawyer in a court of law) to support sb's case: *He needs the very best lawyer to plead (his case) for him.* **4** [T] to give sth as an excuse or explanation for sth: *He pleaded family problems as the reason for his lack of concentration.*

pleasant 🔑 /ˈpleznt/ *adj.* nice, enjoyable or friendly: *a pleasant evening/climate/place/view* ◊ *a pleasant smile/voice/manner* OPP **unpleasant**
▸ **pleasantly** *adv.*

please[1] 🔑 /pliːz/ *exclamation* used as a polite way of asking for sth or telling sb to do sth: *Come in, please.* ◊ *Please don't spend too much money.* ◊ *Sit down, please.* ◊ *Two cups of coffee, please.*

IDM **yes, please** used when you are accepting an offer of sth politely: *'Sugar?' 'Yes, please.'* OPP **no, thank you**

please² /pliːz/ *verb* **1** [I,T] to make sb happy; to satisfy: *There's just no pleasing some people* (=some people are impossible to please). **2** [I] (not used as the main verb in a sentence; used after words like *as, what, whatever, anything*, etc.) to want; to choose: *You can't always **do as you please**.* ◇ *She has so much money she can buy anything she pleases.*

IDM **please yourself** to be able to do whatever you want: *Without anyone else to cook for, I can please myself what I eat.*

pleased /pliːzd/ *adj.* (not before a noun) ~ **(with sb/sth)**; ~ **to do sth**; ~ **that...** happy or satisfied about sth: *John seems very pleased with his new car.* ◇ *Aren't you pleased to see me?* ◇ *We're **only too pleased*** (=very happy) *to help.* ◇ *I'm so pleased that you've decided to stay another week.* OPP **displeased**

pleasing /ˈpliːzɪŋ/ *adj.* giving you pleasure and satisfaction: *The exam results are very pleasing this year.* OPP **displeasing**

pleasurable /ˈpleʒərəbl/ *adj.* (*formal*) enjoyable: *a pleasurable experience*

pleasure /ˈpleʒə(r)/ *noun* **1** [U] the feeling of being happy or satisfied: *Parents **get a lot of pleasure out of** watching their children grow up.* ◇ ***It gives me great pleasure** to introduce our next speaker.* **2** [U] enjoyment (rather than work): *What brings you to Paris – business or pleasure?* **3** [C] an event or activity, that you enjoy or that makes you happy: *It's been a pleasure to work with you.* ◇ *'Thanks for your help.' **'It's a pleasure.'***

IDM **take (no) pleasure in sth/doing sth** to (not) enjoy (doing) sth

with pleasure used as a polite way of saying that you are happy to do sth: *'Could you give me a lift into town?' 'Yes, with pleasure.'*

pleat /pliːt/ *noun* [C] a permanent FOLD that is sewn or pressed into a piece of cloth: *a skirt with pleats at the front*

plebiscite /ˈplebɪsɪt; -saɪt/ *noun* [C] **a ~ (on sth)** (POLITICS) a vote by the people of a country or a region on a question that is very important: *to hold a plebiscite on the country's future system of government*

plectrum /ˈplektrəm/ *noun* [C] (MUSIC) a small piece of plastic, metal, etc., that you use to play the strings of a GUITAR or similar musical instrument instead of using your fingers

pledge /pledʒ/ *noun* [C] **a ~ (to do sth)** a formal promise or agreement ▶ **pledge** *verb* [T] ~ **(sth) (to sb/sth)**: *The Government has pledged £250 000 to help the victims of the crash.*

the ˌPledge of Alˈlegiance *noun* [sing.] a formal promise to be loyal to the US, which Americans make standing in front of the flag with their right hand on their heart

plenary /ˈpliːnəri/ *adj.* (used about meetings, etc.) that should be attended by everyone who has the right to attend: *The new committee holds its first **plenary session** this week.* ▶ **plenary** *noun* [C] (*pl.* **plenaries**): *the opening/final plenary of the conference*

plentiful /ˈplentɪfl/ *adj.* available in large amounts or numbers: *Fruit is plentiful at this time of year.* OPP **scarce**

plenty /ˈplenti/ *pronoun, adv.* **1** ~ **(of sb/sth)** as much or as many of sth as you need: *'Shall I get some more coffee?' 'No, we've still got plenty.'* ◇ *There's still plenty of time to get there.* ◇ *Have you brought plenty to drink?* **2** (before *more*) a lot: *There's plenty more ice cream.* **3** (*informal*) (with *big, long, tall*, etc. followed by *enough*) easily: *'This shirt's too small.' 'Well, it looks plenty big enough to me.'*

pleura /ˈplʊərə/ *noun* [C] (*pl.* **pleurae** /-riː/) (ANATOMY) one of the two MEMBRANES (=thin layers of skin or tissue) that surround the lungs

pleurisy /ˈplʊərəsi/ *noun* [U] (HEALTH) a serious illness that affects the inner covering of the chest and lungs, causing severe pain in the chest or sides

pliable /ˈplaɪəbl/ (*also* **pliant** /ˈplaɪənt/) *adj.* **1** easy to bend or shape **2** (used about a person) easy to influence

pliers /ˈplaɪəz/ *noun* [pl.] a tool made of two crossed pieces of metal with handles, that is used for holding things firmly and for cutting wire: *a pair of pliers* ➲ picture at **tool**

plight /plaɪt/ *noun* [sing.] (*formal*) a bad or difficult state or situation

plimsoll /ˈplɪmsəl/ (*also* **pump**, *AmE* **sneaker**) *noun* [C] a light shoe made of strong material (**canvas**) that is especially used for sports, etc.: *a pair of plimsolls* ➲ look at **trainer**

plinth /plɪnθ/ *noun* [C] a block of stone on which a column or statue stands

plod /plɒd/ *verb* [I] (**plodding**; **plodded**) ~ **(along/on)** **1** to walk slowly and in a heavy or tired way: *We plodded on through the rain for nearly an hour.* **2** to make slow progress, especially with difficult or boring work

plonk¹ /plɒŋk/ *verb* [T] (*spoken*) **1** ~ **sth (down)** to put sth down on sth, especially noisily or carelessly: *Just plonk your bag down anywhere.* **2** ~ **(yourself) (down)** to sit down heavily and carelessly: *He just plonked himself down in front of the TV.*

plonk² /plɒŋk/ *noun* [U] (*BrE, informal*) cheap wine: *Let's open a bottle of plonk!*

plop¹ /plɒp/ *noun* [C, usually sing.] a sound like that of a small object dropping into water

plop² /plɒp/ *verb* [I] (**plopping**; **plopped**) to fall making a PLOP: *The frog plopped back into the water.*

plot¹ /plɒt/ *noun* [C] **1** (LITERATURE) the series of events which form the story of a novel, film, etc.: *The play had a very weak plot.* ◇ *I can't follow the plot of this novel.* **2 a ~ (to do sth)** a secret plan made by several people to do sth wrong or illegal: *a plot to kill the president* **3** (AGRICULTURE) a small piece of land, used for a special purpose: *a plot of land*

plough

plot² 🔑 /plɒt/ *verb* (**plotting**; **plotted**) **1** [I,T] ~ **(with sb) (against sb)** to make a secret plan to do sth wrong or illegal: *They were accused of plotting against the government.* ◇ *The terrorists had been plotting this campaign for years.* **2** [T] to mark sth on a map, diagram, etc.: *to plot the figures on a graph*

plough (*AmE* **plow**) /plaʊ/ *noun* [C] (AGRICULTURE) a large farm tool which is pulled by a TRACTOR or by an animal. A **plough** turns the soil over ready for seeds to be planted. ➲ look at **snowplough** ▶ **plough** *verb* [I,T] (*figurative*): *The book was long and boring but I managed to plough through it* (=read it with difficulty).

ploy /plɔɪ/ *noun* [C] **a ~ (to do sth)** something that you say or do in order to get what you want or to persuade sb to do sth

pluck¹ /plʌk/ *verb* [T] **1** ~ **sth/sb (from sth/out)** to remove or take sth/sb from a place: *He plucked the letter from my hands.* **2** to pull the feathers out of a dead bird in order to prepare it for cooking **3** (MUSIC) to make the strings of a musical instrument play notes by moving your fingers across them

IDM **pluck up courage** to try to get enough courage to do sth

PHR V **pluck at sth** to pull sth gently several times

pluck² /plʌk/ *noun* [U] (*informal*) courage and determination ▶ **plucky** *adj.*

plug¹ 🔑 /plʌg/ *noun* [C] **1** a plastic or rubber object with two or three metal pins, which connects a piece of electrical equipment to the electricity supply **2** a round piece of rubber or plastic that you use to block the hole in a bath, etc. **3** a mention that sb makes of a new book, film, etc. in order to encourage people to buy or see it

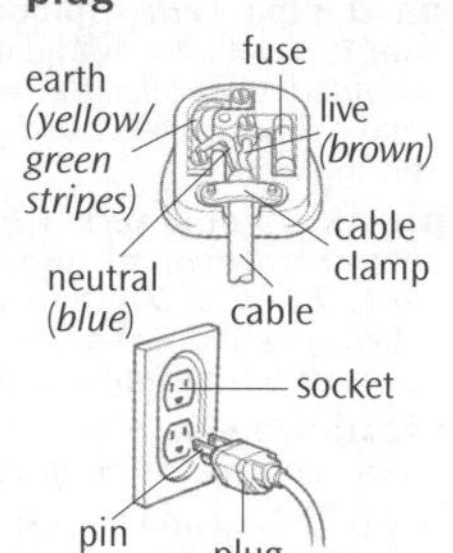

plug² /plʌg/ *verb* [T] (**plugging**; **plugged**) **1** to fill or block a hole with sth that fits tightly into it: *He managed to plug the leak in the pipe.* **2** (*informal*) to say good things about a new book, film, etc. in order to make people buy or see it: *They're really plugging that song on the radio at the moment.*

PHR V **plug sth in** to connect a piece of electrical equipment to the electricity supply or to another piece of equipment: *Is the microphone plugged in?* OPP **unplug**

plughole /ˈplʌghəʊl/ *noun* [C] (*BrE*) a hole in a bath, etc. where the water flows away

ˈ**plug-in¹** *adj.* **1** able to be connected using a plug: *a plug-in kettle* **2** (COMPUTING) able to be added to a computer system so that it can do more things: *a plug-in graphics card*

ˈ**plug-in²** *noun* [C] (COMPUTING) a piece of computer software that can be added to a system so that it can do more things

plum /plʌm/ *noun* [C] a soft, round fruit with red or yellow skin and a stone in the middle

plumage /ˈpluːmɪdʒ/ *noun* [U] the feathers covering a bird's body

plumber /ˈplʌmə(r)/ *noun* [C] a person whose job is to put in or repair water pipes, baths, toilets, etc.

plumbing /ˈplʌmɪŋ/ *noun* [U] **1** all the pipes, taps, etc. in a building **2** the work of a person who puts in and repairs water pipes, taps, etc.

plume /pluːm/ *noun* [C] **1** a quantity of smoke that rises in the air **2** a large feather or group of feathers, often worn as a decoration

plummet /ˈplʌmɪt/ *verb* [I] (*formal*) to fall suddenly and quickly from a high level or position: *Share prices plummeted to an all-time low.* ◇ *The jet plummeted into a row of houses.* SYN **plunge**

plump¹ /plʌmp/ *adj.* (used about a person or an animal) pleasantly fat: *the baby's plump cheeks*

plump² /plʌmp/ *verb*

PHR V **plump (yourself/sb/sth) down** to sit down or to put sb/sth down heavily: *She plumped herself down by the fire.*

plump for sb/sth (*BrE, informal*) to choose or decide to have sb/sth: *I think I'll plump for the roast chicken, after all.*

plunder /ˈplʌndə(r)/ *noun* [U] the action of stealing from people or places, especially during war or fighting; the goods that are stolen ▶ **plunder** *verb* [I,T]

plunge¹ /plʌndʒ/ *verb* **1** [I] ~ **(into sth/in)** to jump, drop or fall suddenly and with force: *He ran to the river and plunged in.* ◇ (*figurative*) *Share prices plunged overnight.* **2** [T] ~ **sth in/into sth** to push sth suddenly and with force into sth: *He plunged the knife into the table in anger.* **3** [T] to cause sb/sth to suddenly be in the state mentioned: *The country has been plunged into chaos by the floods.* **4** [I] ~ **into (doing) sth** to start doing sth with energy and enthusiasm: *Think carefully before you plunge into buying a house.*

plunge² /plʌndʒ/ *noun* [C] a sudden jump, drop or fall: *I slipped and took a plunge in the river.* ◇ *the plunge in house prices*

IDM **take the plunge** to decide to do sth difficult after thinking about it for quite a long time: *After going out together for five years, they took the plunge and got married.*

ˈ**plunge pool** *noun* [C] (GEOGRAPHY) an area of deep water that is formed by a WATERFALL (=water falling from above)

plunger /ˈplʌndʒə(r)/ *noun* [C] a part of a piece of equipment that can be pushed down, for example in a SYRINGE (=a device that is used for putting drugs into sb's body and for taking blood out) ➲ picture at **laboratory**

pluperfect /ˌpluːˈpɜːfɪkt/ =THE PAST PERFECT

plural /ˈplʊərəl/ *noun* [C] (LANGUAGE) the form of a noun, verb, etc. which refers to more than one person or thing: *The plural of 'boat' is 'boats'.* ◇ *The verb should be* ***in the plural***. ▶ **plural** *adj.* ➲ look at **singular**

pluralism /ˈplʊərəlɪzəm/ *noun* [U] (*formal*) (SOCIAL STUDIES) **1** the existence of many different groups of people in one society, for example people of different races or of different political or religious beliefs: *cultural pluralism* **2** the belief that it is possible and good for different groups of people to live together in peace in one society

plus¹ 🔑 AW /plʌs/ *prep.* **1** (MATHEMATICS) and; added to: *Two plus two is four (2 + 2 =4).* OPP **minus** **2** in addition to; and also: *You have to work five days a week plus every other weekend.*

plus² 🔑 AW /plʌs/ *noun* [C] **1** (MATHEMATICS) the sign (+) OPP **minus** **2** an advantage of a situation

plus³ 🔑 AW /plʌs/ ***adj.*** (only *after* a noun) **1** or more: *I'd say there were 30000 plus at the match.* **2** (EDUCATION) (used for marking work done by students) slightly above: *I got a B plus* (=B+) *for my homework.* OPP **minus**

plush /plʌʃ/ ***adj.*** comfortable and expensive: *a plush hotel*

Pluto /'plu:təʊ/ ***noun*** [sing.] (ASTRONOMY) the name of a large round object in space which ORBITS (=goes around) the sun

CULTURE

In August 2006, the International Astronomical Union declared that **Pluto** was to be called a **dwarf planet**, rather than a proper planet, because it has different characteristics from the other planets (**Mercury, Mars, Venus**, etc.) in our **solar system**. From 1930, when it was first discovered, until 2006, **Pluto** was known as the ninth planet in the **solar system** because of its position furthest from the sun.

plutonium /plu:'təʊniəm/ ***noun*** [U] (*symbol* **Pu**) (CHEMISTRY) a RADIOACTIVE substance used especially as a fuel in nuclear power stations ⓘ For more information on the periodic table of elements, look at pages R34-5.

ply /plaɪ/ ***verb*** (*pres. part.* **plying**; *3rd person sing. pres.* **plies**; *pt, pp* **plied**) [I,T] to try to sell services or goods to people, especially on the street: *Boat owners were **plying their trade** to passing tourists.* ◇ *to ply for business*

PHR V **ply sb with sth** to keep giving sb food and drink, or asking sb questions: *They plied us with food from the moment we arrived.*

plywood /'plaɪwʊd/ ***noun*** [U] board made by sticking several thin layers of wood together

p.m. 🔑 (*AmE* **P.M.**) /ˌpi: 'em/ ***abbr.*** after midday: *2 p.m.* (=2 o'clock in the afternoon) ◇ *11.30 p.m.* (=11.30 in the evening)

pneumatic /nju:'mætɪk/ ***adj.*** **1** filled with air: *a pneumatic tyre* **2** worked by air under pressure: *pneumatic tools*

pneuˌmatic 'drill (*AmE* **jackhammer**) ***noun*** [C] a large powerful tool, worked by air pressure, used especially for breaking up road surfaces

pneumonia /nju:'məʊniə/ ***noun*** [U] (HEALTH) a serious illness of the lungs which makes breathing difficult

PO /ˌpi: 'əʊ/ ***abbr.*** (used in compound nouns) Post Office: *a PO box*

poach /pəʊtʃ/ ***verb*** [T] **1** to cook food (especially fish or eggs) gently in a small amount of liquid **2** to hunt animals illegally on sb else's land **3** to take an idea from sb else and use it as though it is your own **4** to take members of staff from another company in an unfair way

poacher /'pəʊtʃə(r)/ ***noun*** [C] a person who hunts animals illegally on sb else's land

ˌP'O box ***noun*** [C] a place in a post office where letters, packages, etc. are kept until they are collected by the person they were sent to: *The address is PO Box 4287, Nairobi, Kenya.*

pocket¹ 🔑 /'pɒkɪt/ ***noun*** [C] **1** a piece of material like a small bag that is sewn inside or on a piece of clothing and is used for carrying things in: *He always walks with his hands in his trouser pockets.* ◇ *a pocket dictionary/calculator* (=one small enough to fit in your pocket) **2** a small bag or container that is fixed to the inside of a car door, suitcase, etc. and used for putting things in: *There are safety instructions in the pocket of the seat in front of you.* **3** used to talk about the amount of money that you have to spend: *They sell cars to suit every pocket.* ◇ *The school couldn't afford a CD player, so the teacher bought one **out of his own pocket**.* **4** a small area or group that is different from its surroundings: *pockets of warm water* ➲ look at **air pocket**

IDM **pick sb's pocket** → PICK¹

pocket² /'pɒkɪt/ ***verb*** [T] **1** to put sth in your pocket: *He took the letter and pocketed it quickly.* **2** to steal or win money

'pocket money (*AmE* **allowance**) ***noun*** [U] an amount of money that parents give a child to spend, usually every week

pod /pɒd/ ***noun*** [C] (BIOLOGY) the long, green part of some plants, such as PEAS and BEANS, that contains the seeds

podcast /'pɒdkɑ:st/ ***noun*** [C] (COMPUTING) a recording of sth such as a radio programme that you can DOWNLOAD (=copy onto your computer) from the Internet and listen to on your computer or on an MP3 PLAYER (=a small electronic device for playing sound files): *Click here to subscribe, and receive podcasts automatically each week.* ▶ **podcast** ***verb*** [T] (*pt, pp* **podcast**): *Part two will be podcast next week.*

podiatrist /pə'daɪətrɪst/ (*AmE*) = CHIROPODIST

podiatry /pə'daɪətri/ (*AmE*) = CHIROPODY

podium /'pəʊdiəm/ ***noun*** [C] a small platform for a speaker, a performer, etc. to stand on

poem 🔑 /'pəʊɪm/ ***noun*** [C] (LITERATURE) a piece of writing arranged in short lines. Poems try to express thoughts and feelings with the help of sound and rhythm.

poet /'pəʊɪt/ ***noun*** [C] (LITERATURE) a person who writes POEMS

poetic /pəʊ'etɪk/ (*also* **poetical** /-ɪkl/) ***adj.*** (LITERATURE) connected with POETS or like a poem ▶ **poetically** /-kli/ ***adv.***

poˌetic 'licence (*AmE* **poˌetic 'license**) ***noun*** [U] (LITERATURE) the freedom to change facts, the normal rules of language, etc. in a special piece of writing or speech in order to achieve a particular effect

Poet Laureate /ˌpəʊɪt 'lɒriət/ ***noun*** [C] (LITERATURE) **1** (especially in Britain) a person who has been officially chosen to write poetry for the country's important occasions **2** (*especially AmE*) a person whose poetry is considered to be the best, or most typical of their country or region.

poetry 🔑 /'pəʊətri/ ***noun*** [U] (LITERATURE) a collection of poems; poems in general: *Shakespeare's poetry and plays* ◇ *Do you like poetry?* ➲ look at **prose**

poignant /'pɔɪnjənt/ ***adj.*** causing sadness or pity: *a poignant memory* ▶ **poignancy** /-jənsi/ ***noun*** [U] ▶ **poignantly** ***adv.***

point¹ 🔑 /pɔɪnt/ ***noun*** **1** [C] a particular fact, idea or opinion that sb expresses: *You **make** some interesting **points** in your essay.* ◇ *I see your point but I don't agree with you.* ⓘ We can **bring up**, **raise**, **argue**, **emphasize** and **illustrate** a point.
2 the point [sing.] the most important part of what is being said; the main piece of information: *It makes no difference how much it costs — **the point is** we don't have any money!* ◇ *She always talks and talks and takes ages to **get to the point**.* **3** [C] an important idea or thought that needs to be considered. *'Have you checked what time the last bus back is?' 'That's a*

point – no I haven't.' **4** [C] a detail, characteristic or quality of sb/sth: *Make a list of your* ***strong points*** *and your* ***weak points*** (=good and bad qualities). **5** [sing.] **the ~ (of/in sth/doing sth)** the meaning, reason or purpose of sth: *She's said no, so* ***what's the point*** *of telephoning her again?* ◇ ***There's no point*** *in talking to my parents – they never listen.* ➲ note at **purpose** **6** [C] (often in compounds) a particular place, position or moment: *The library is a good* ***starting point*** *for that sort of information.* ◇ *He has reached the* ***high point*** *of his career.* ◇ *the boiling/ freezing point of water* ◇ *He waved to the crowd and it was* ***at that point*** *that the shot was fired.* ◇ ***At one point*** *I thought I was going to laugh.* **7** [C] the thin sharp end of sth: *the point of a pin/needle/pencil* **8** [C] a small round mark used when writing parts of numbers: *She ran the race in 11.2 (eleven point two) seconds.* **9** [C] (SPORT) a single mark in some games, sports, etc. that you add to others to get the score: *to score a point* ◇ *Rios needs two more points to win the match.* **10** [C] a unit of measurement for certain things: *The value of the dollar has fallen by a few points.*

IDM **be on the point of doing sth** just going to do sth: *I was on the point of going out when the phone rang.*

beside the point → BESIDE

have your, etc. (good) points to have some good qualities: *Bill has his good points, but he's very unreliable.*

make a point of doing sth to make sure you do sth because it is important or necessary: *I made a point of locking all the doors and windows before leaving the house.*

point of view a way of looking at a situation; an opinion: *From my point of view it would be better to wait a little longer.* SYN **viewpoint, standpoint**

prove your/the case/point → PROVE

a sore point → SORE[1]

sb's strong point → STRONG

take sb's point to understand and accept what sb is saying

to the point connected with what is being discussed; relevant: *His speech was short and to the point.*

up to a point partly: *I agree with you up to a point.*

point² 🔑 /pɔɪnt/ ***verb*** **1** [I] **~ (at/to sb/sth)** to show where sth is or to draw attention to sth using your finger, a stick, etc.: *'I'll have that one,' she said, pointing to a chocolate cake.* **2** [I,T] **~ (sth) (at/ towards sb/sth)** to aim (sth) in the direction of sb/ sth: *She pointed the gun at the target and fired.* **3** [I] to face in a particular direction or to show that sth is in a particular direction: *The sign pointed towards the motorway.* ◇ *Turn round until you're pointing north.* **4** [I] **~ to sth** to show that sth is likely to exist, happen or be true: *Research points to a connection between diet and cancer.*

PHR V **point sth out (to sb)** to make sb look at sth; to make sth clear to sb: *The guide pointed out all the places of interest to us on the way.* ◇ *I'd like to point out that we haven't got much time left.*

ˌpoint-ˈblank ***adj., adv.*** **1** (used about a shot) from a very close position: *He was shot in the leg* ***at point-blank range.*** **2** (used about sth that is said) very direct and not polite; not allowing any discussion: *He told her point-blank to get out of the house and never come back.*

pointed 🔑 /ˈpɔɪntɪd/ ***adj.*** **1** having a sharp end: *a pointed stick/nose* **2** (used about sth that is said) critical of sb in an indirect way: *She made a pointed comment about people who are always late.* ▶ **pointedly** ***adv.***

pointer /ˈpɔɪntə(r)/ ***noun*** [C] **1** a piece of helpful advice or information: *Could you* ***give*** *me some* ***pointers*** *on how best to tackle the problem?* **2** (COMPUTING) a small arrow on a computer screen that you move by moving the mouse **3** a stick that is used to point to things on a map, etc.

pointillism /ˈpɔɪntɪlɪzəm; ˈpwænt-/ ***noun*** [U] (ART) a style of painting that was developed in France in the late 19th century in which very small dots of colour are used to build up the picture ▶ **pointillist** /-lɪst/ ***adj., noun*** [C]

pointless /ˈpɔɪntləs/ ***adj.*** without any use or purpose: *It's pointless to try and make him agree.* ▶ **pointlessly** ***adv.*** ▶ **pointlessness** ***noun*** [U]

ˌpoint of ˈsale ***noun*** [sing.] (BUSINESS) the place where a product is sold: *More information on healthy foods should be provided* ***at the point of sale.***

poise /pɔɪz/ ***noun*** [U] a calm, confident way of behaving

poised /pɔɪzd/ ***adj.*** **1** not moving but ready to move: *'Shall I call the doctor or not?' he asked, his hand poised above the telephone.* **2 ~ (to do sth)** ready to act; about to do sth: *The government is poised to take action if the crisis continues.* **3** calm and confident

poison¹ 🔑 /ˈpɔɪzn/ ***noun*** [C,U] a substance that kills or harms you if you eat or drink it: *rat poison* ◇ *poison gas*

poison² 🔑 /ˈpɔɪzn/ ***verb*** [T] **1** to kill, harm or damage sb/sth with poison **2** to put poison in sth: *The cup of coffee had been poisoned.* **3** to spoil or ruin sth: *The quarrel had poisoned their relationship.* ▶ **poisoned** ***adj.***: *a poisoned drink*

poisoning /ˈpɔɪzənɪŋ/ ***noun*** [U] (HEALTH) the giving or taking of poison or a dangerous substance: *He got* ***food poisoning*** *from eating fish that wasn't fresh.*

poisonous 🔑 /ˈpɔɪzənəs/ ***adj.*** **1** causing death or illness if you eat or drink it **2** (used about animals, etc.) producing and using poison to attack its enemies: *He was bitten by a poisonous snake.* **3** very unpleasant and intended to upset sb: *She wrote him a poisonous letter criticizing his behaviour.*

poke /pəʊk/ ***verb*** **1** [T] to push sb/sth with a finger, stick or other long, thin object: *Be careful you don't poke yourself in the eye with that stick!* **2** [I,T] **~ (sth) into, through, out of, down, etc. sth** to move or to push sth quickly into sth or in a certain direction: *He poked the stick down the hole to see how deep it was.* ◇ *A child's head poked up from behind the wall.* ▶ **poke** ***noun*** [C]

IDM **poke fun at sb/sth** to make jokes about sb/sth, often in an unkind way

poke/stick your nose into sth → NOSE[1]

poker /ˈpəʊkə(r)/ ***noun*** **1** [U] a type of card game usually played to win money **2** [C] a metal stick for moving the coal or wood in a fire

poky /ˈpəʊki/ ***adj.*** (*BrE, informal*) (used about a house, room, etc.) too small: *a poky little office*

polar /ˈpəʊlə(r)/ ***adj.*** (only *before* a noun) (GEOGRAPHY) of or near the North or South Pole: *the polar regions*

ˈpolar bear ***noun*** [C] a large white bear that lives in the area near the North Pole

polarize (also **-ise**) /ˈpəʊləraɪz/ ***verb*** **1** [I,T] (*formal*) to separate or make people separate into two groups with completely opposite opinions: *Public opinion has polarized on this issue.* **2** [T] (PHYSICS) to make waves of light, etc. VIBRATE (=move up and down with very small continuous movements) in a single direction **3** [T] (PHYSICS) to make sth have two poles(3) with opposite qualities: *to polarize a magnet* ▸ **polarization** (also **-isation**) /ˌpəʊləraɪˈzeɪʃn/ *noun* [U]

pole ⊶ /pəʊl/ *noun* [C] **1** a long, thin piece of wood or metal, used especially to hold sth up: *a flagpole* ◇ *a tent pole* **2** (GEOGRAPHY) either of the two points at the exact top and bottom of the earth: *the North/South Pole* ➲ picture at **earth 3** (PHYSICS) either of the two ends of a MAGNET, or the positive or negative points of an electric battery ➲ picture at **magnet 4** either of two opposite or contrasting extremes: *Their opinions were at opposite poles of the debate.*

the 'pole vault *noun* [sing.] (SPORT) a sporting event in which people try to jump over a high bar, using a long pole to push themselves off the ground

police[1] ⊶ /pəˈliːs/ *noun* [pl.] (LAW) the official organization whose job is to make sure that people obey the law, and to prevent and solve crime: *Dial 999 if you need to **call the police**.* ◇ *a police car* ◇ *the local **police station***

police[2] /pəˈliːs/ *verb* [T] to keep control in a place by using the police or a similar official group: *The cost of policing football games is extremely high.*

poˌlice 'constable (*also* **constable**) *noun* [C] (*BrF*) (*abbr.* **PC**) (LAW) a police officer of the lowest position (**rank**)

po'lice force *noun* [C] (LAW) the police organization of a country, district or town: *Kamal wants to join the police force when he finishes school.*

po'lice officer (*also* **officer**, **po'liceman**; **po'licewoman**) *noun* [C] (LAW) a member of the police

po'lice state *noun* [C] (POLITICS) a country where people's freedom, especially to travel and to express political opinions, is controlled by the government, with the help of the police

policy ⊶ AW /ˈpɒləsi/ *noun* (*pl.* **policies**) **1** [C,U] ~ **(on sth)** a plan of action agreed or chosen by a government, a company, etc.: *Labour has a new set of policies on health.* ◇ *It is company policy not to allow smoking in meetings.* **2** [C,U] a way of behaving that you think is best in a particular situation: *It's my policy only to do business with people I like.* **3** [C] a document that shows an agreement that you have made with an insurance company: *an insurance policy*

polio /ˈpəʊliəʊ/ *noun* [U] (HEALTH) a serious disease which can cause you to lose the power in certain muscles

polish[1] ⊶ /ˈpɒlɪʃ/ *verb* [T] to make sth shine by rubbing it and often by putting a special cream or liquid on it: *to polish your shoes/a table*
PHR V **polish sth off** (*informal*) to finish sth, especially food, quickly: *The two of them polished off a whole chicken for dinner!*

polish[2] ⊶ /ˈpɒlɪʃ/ *noun* **1** [U] a cream, liquid, etc. that you put on sth to clean it and make it shine: *a tin of shoe polish* **2** [sing.] the action of polishing sth: *I'll **give** the glasses **a polish** before the guests arrive.*

polished /ˈpɒlɪʃt/ *adj.* **1** shiny because of polishing: *polished wood floors* **2** (used about a performance, etc.) of a high standard: *Most of the actors gave **a polished performance**.*

politburo /ˈpɒlɪtbjʊərəʊ/ *noun* [C] (*pl.* **politburos**) (POLITICS) the most important committee of a Communist party, with the power to decide on policy

polite ⊶ /pəˈlaɪt/ *adj.* having good manners and showing respect for others: *The assistants in that shop are always very helpful and polite.* ◇ *He gave me a polite smile.* OPP **impolite**, **impertinent** ▸ **politeness** *noun* [U] ▸ **politely** *adv.*

political ⊶ /pəˈlɪtɪkl/ *adj.* **1** (POLITICS) connected with politics and government: *a political leader/debate/party* ◇ *She has very strong political opinions.* **2** (POLITICS) (used about people) interested in politics **3** concerned with the competition for power inside an organization: *I suspect he was dismissed for political reasons.*

poˌlitical 'action committee *noun* [C] (*abbr.* **PAC**) (POLITICS) (in the US) a group of people who collect money to support the candidates and policies that will help them achieve their political and social aims

poˌlitical a'sylum *noun* [U] (POLITICS) protection given by a state to a person who has left their own country for political reasons

poˌlitical cor'rectness *noun* [U] (SOCIAL STUDIES) the principle of avoiding language and behaviour that may offend particular groups of people

politically ⊶ /pəˈlɪtɪkli/ *adv.* (POLITICS) in a way that is connected with politics: *a politically sensitive issue* ◇ *It makes sense politically as well as economically.*

poˌlitically cor'rect *adj.* (*abbr.* **PC**) (SOCIAL STUDIES) used to describe language or behaviour that carefully avoids offending particular groups of people

politician ⊶ /ˌpɒləˈtɪʃn/ *noun* [C] (POLITICS) a person whose job is in politics, especially one who is a member of parliament or of the government: *Politicians of all parties supported the war.*

politics ⊶ /ˈpɒlətɪks/ *noun* **1** [U, with sing. or pl. verb] the work and ideas that are connected with governing a country, a town, etc.: *to go into politics.* ◇ *Politics has/have never been of great interest to me.* **2** [pl.] a person's political opinions and beliefs: *His politics are extreme.* **3** [U, with sing. or pl. verb] matters concerned with competition for power between people in an organization: *I never get involved in office politics.* **4** (*AmE* **Poˌlitical 'Science**) [U] the scientific study of government: *a degree in Politics*

'polka dot *noun* [C] one of many dots that together form a pattern, especially on material: *a polka-dot tie*

poll[1] /pəʊl/ *noun* [C] **1** (*also* **o'pinion poll**) a way of finding out public opinion by asking a number of people their views on sth: *This was voted best drama series in a viewers' poll.* **2** (POLITICS) the process of voting in a political election; the number of votes given: *The country will **go to the polls** (=vote) in June.*

poll[2] /pəʊl/ *verb* [T] **1** (POLITICS) to receive a certain number of votes in an election: *The Liberal Democrat candidate polled over 3000 votes.* **2** to ask members of the public their opinion on a subject: *Of those polled, only 20 per cent were in favour of changing the law.*

pollen /ˈpɒlən/ *noun* [U] (BIOLOGY) a fine, usually yellow, powder which is formed in flowers. It makes other flowers of the same type produce seeds when it is carried to them by the wind, insects, etc. ➲ picture at **flower**

'pollen count *noun* [C, usually sing.] (ENVIRONMENT) a number that shows how much POLLEN is in the air

'pollen tube *noun* [C] (BIOLOGY) a tube which grows when POLLEN lands on the top of the STIGMA (=the female part in the middle of a flower) to carry the male cell to the OVULE (=the part that contains the female cell) ➲ picture at **flower**

pollinate /'pɒləneɪt/ *verb* [T] (BIOLOGY) to put POLLEN into a flower or plant so that it produces seeds ▸ **pollination** /ˌpɒlə'neɪʃn/ *noun* [U]

polling /'pəʊlɪŋ/ *noun* [U] **1** (POLITICS) the activity of voting in an election: *Polling has been heavy since 8 o' clock this morning* **2** the act of asking questions in order to find out public opinion

'polling booth (*AmE usually* **'voting booth**) *noun* [C] (POLITICS) a small, partly ENCLOSED place where you stand to mark your card in order to vote in an election

'polling day *noun* [U, C] (*BrE*) (POLITICS) a day on which people vote in an election

'polling station *noun* [C] (*especially BrE*) (POLITICS) a building where you go to vote in an election

pollutant /pə'lu:tənt/ *noun* [C] (ENVIRONMENT) a substance that POLLUTES air, rivers, etc.

pollute /pə'lu:t/ *verb* [T] (ENVIRONMENT) to make air, rivers, etc. dirty and dangerous: *Traffic fumes are polluting our cities.* ◇ *The beach has been polluted with oil.*

pollution ⊶ /pə'lu:ʃn/ *noun* [U] (ENVIRONMENT) **1** the action of making the air, water, etc. dirty and dangerous: *Major steps are being taken to control the pollution of beaches.* **2** substances that POLLUTE: *The rivers are full of pollution.*

polo /'pəʊləʊ/ *noun* [U] (SPORT) a game for two teams of horses and riders. The players try to score goals by hitting a ball with long wooden hammers.

'polo neck *noun* [C] a high COLLAR on a piece of clothing that is rolled over and that covers most of your neck; a piece of clothing with this type of COLLAR

polonium /pə'ləʊniəm/ *noun* [U] (*symbol* **Po**) (CHEMISTRY) a chemical element. **Polonium** is a RADIOACTIVE metal that is present in nature when URANIUM decays. ❶ For more information on the periodic table of elements, look at pages R34-5.

poly- /'pɒli/ *prefix* (used in nouns, adjectives and adverbs) many: *polygamy*

polyester /ˌpɒli'estə(r)/ *noun* [U] an artificial material that is used for making clothes, etc.

polyethylene /ˌpɒli'eθəli:n/ (*AmE*) =POLYTHENE

polygamy /pə'lɪgəmi/ *noun* [U] the custom of having more than one wife at the same time ➲ look at **bigamy, monogamy** ▸ **polygamous** /pə'lɪgəməs/ *adj.*: *a polygamous society*

polygon /'pɒlɪgən/ *noun* [C] (GEOMETRY) a flat shape with at least three, and usually five or more, angles and straight sides ▸ **polygonal** /pə'lɪgənl/ *adj.*

polyhedron /ˌpɒli'hi:drən; -'hed-/ *noun* [C] (*pl.* **polyhedra** /-'hi:drə; -'hed-/ or **polyhedrons**) (GEOMETRY) a solid shape with many flat sides, usually more than six

polymer /'pɒlɪmə(r)/ *noun* [C] (CHEMISTRY) a natural or artificial substance consisting of large MOLECULES (=groups of atoms) that are made from combinations of small simple MOLECULES

polymerize (also -**ise**) /'pɒlɪməraɪz/ *verb* [I,T] (CHEMISTRY) to combine, or to make units of a chemical combine, to make a POLYMER: *The substance polymerizes to form a hard plastic.* ▸ **polymerization** /ˌpɒlimərаɪ'zeɪʃn/ *noun* [U]

polyp /'pɒlɪp/ *noun* [C] **1** (HEALTH) a small lump that grows inside the body, especially in the nose. It is caused by disease but is usually harmless. **2** (BIOLOGY) a small and very simple sea creature with a body shaped like a tube

polypropylene /ˌpɒli'prəʊpəli:n/ *noun* [U] a strong plastic often used for objects such as toys or chairs that are made in a MOULD

polystyrene /ˌpɒli'staɪri:n/ *noun* [U] a light firm plastic substance that is used for packing things so that they do not get broken

polytheism /'pɒliθiɪzəm/ *noun* [U] (RELIGION) the belief that there is more than one god ➲ look at **monotheism**

polythene /'pɒlɪθi:n/ (*AmE* **polyethylene** /ˌpɒli'eθəli:n/) *noun* [U] a type of very thin plastic material often used to make bags for food, etc. or to keep things dry

polyunsaturated /ˌpɒliʌn'sætʃəreɪtɪd/ *adj.* (CHEMISTRY, HEALTH) (used about fats and oils) having the type of chemical structure that is thought to be good for your health: *polyunsaturated margarine* ➲ look at **saturated, unsaturated**

pomegranate /'pɒmɪgrænɪt/ *noun* [C] a round fruit with thick smooth skin that is red inside and full of seeds

pommel /'pɒml/ *noun* [C] **1** the higher front part of a SADDLE (=a leather seat) on a horse **2** the round part on the end of the handle of a SWORD (=a long sharp metal weapon)

pommel horse

'pommel horse *noun* [C] (SPORT) a large object on legs with two handles on top, which GYMNASTS put their hands on and swing their body and legs around

pomp /pɒmp/ *noun* [U] the impressive nature of a large official occasion or ceremony

pompous /'pɒmpəs/ *adj.* showing that you think you are more important than other people, for example by using long words that sound impressive

pond /pɒnd/ *noun* [C] an area of water that is smaller than a lake

ponder /'pɒndə(r)/ *verb* [I,T] ~ (**on/over sth**) to think about sth carefully or for a long time

pong /pɒŋ/ *noun* [C] (*BrE, slang*) a strong unpleasant smell ▸ **pong** *verb* [I]

pony /'pəʊni/ *noun* [C] (*pl.* **ponies**) a small horse

ponytail /'pəʊniteɪl/ *noun* [C] long hair that is tied at the back of the head and that hangs down in one piece

'pony-trekking (*AmE* **'trail riding**) *noun* [U] the activity of riding horses for pleasure in the country

poodle /'pu:dl/ *noun* [C] a type of dog with thick curly fur that is sometimes cut into a special pattern

pooh /pu:/ *exclamation* (*BrE, informal*) said when you smell sth unpleasant

pool[1] /puːl/ ***noun*** **1** [C] a ~ (of sth) a small amount of liquid lying on a surface: *There's a huge pool of water on the kitchen floor.* **2** [C] a small area of light: *a pool of light* **3** [C] = SWIMMING POOL: *He swam ten lengths of the pool.* **4** [C] a quantity of money, goods, etc. that is shared between a group of people: *There is a pool of cars that anyone in the company can use.* **5** [U] a game that is played on a table with 16 coloured and numbered balls. Two players try to hit these balls into pockets at the edge of a large table with long thin sticks (**cues**). ➲ look at **billiards, snooker** ➲ picture at **sport 6 the pools** [pl.] = FOOTBALL POOLS

pool[2] /puːl/ ***verb*** [T] to collect money, ideas, etc. together from a number of people: *If we pool our ideas we should come up with a good plan.*

poor /pɔː(r)/ ***adj.*** **1** not having enough money to have a comfortable life: *The family was too poor to buy new clothes.* ◇ *Richer countries could do more to help poorer countries.* OPP **rich 2 the poor** ***noun*** [pl.] people who do not have enough money to have a comfortable life **3** of low quality or in a bad condition: *Paul is in very poor health.* ◇ *The industry has a poor safety record.* **4** used when you are showing that you feel sorry for sb: *Poor Dan! He's very upset!*

poorly[1] /ˈpɔːli/ ***adv.*** not well; badly: *a poorly paid job*

poorly[2] /ˈpɔːli/ ***adj.*** (*BrE, informal*) not well; ill: *I'm feeling a bit poorly.*

POP /ˌpiː əʊ ˈpiː/ ***abbr.*** (COMPUTING) **Post Office Protocol**; a set of rules that enables you to receive emails on your computer ➲ look at **SMTP**

pop[1] /pɒp/ ***verb*** (**popping**; **popped**) **1** [I,T] to make a short sudden sound like a small explosion; to cause sth to do this: *The balloon popped.* ◇ *He popped the balloon.* **2** [I] ~ **across, down, out, etc.** to come or go somewhere quickly or suddenly: *I'm just popping out to the shops.* **3** [T] ~ **sth in, into, etc. sth** to put or take sth somewhere quickly or suddenly: *She popped the note into her bag.*

PHR V **pop in** to make a quick visit: *Why don't you pop in for a cup of tea?*

pop out to come out (of sth) suddenly or quickly: *Her eyes nearly popped out of her head in surprise.*

pop up (*informal*) to appear or happen when you are not expecting it

pop[2] /pɒp/ ***noun*** **1** [U] (*also* **ˈpop music**) (MUSIC) modern music that is most popular among young people: *a pop group* ➲ look at **jazz, rock, classical 2** [C] a short sudden sound like a small explosion: *There was a loud pop as the champagne cork came out of the bottle.*

pop. ***abbr.*** population: *pop. 12m*

ˈpop art (also **ˈPop Art**) ***noun*** [U] (ART) a style of art, developed in the 1960s, that was based on popular culture and used material such as advertisements, film images, etc.

popcorn /ˈpɒpkɔːn/ ***noun*** [U] a type of CORN that is heated until it bursts and forms light whitish balls that are eaten with salt or sugar on them

pope /pəʊp/ ***noun*** [C] (RELIGION) the head of the Roman Catholic Church

poplar /ˈpɒplə(r)/ ***noun*** [C] a tall straight tree with soft wood

popper /ˈpɒpə(r)/ (*also* **ˈpress stud**) (*AmE* **snap**) ***noun*** [C] two round pieces of metal or plastic that you press together in order to fasten a piece of clothing

poppy /ˈpɒpi/ ***noun*** [C] (*pl.* **poppies**) a bright red wild flower that has small black seeds

Popsicle™ /ˈpɒpsɪkl/ ***noun*** [C] (*AmE*) = ICE LOLLY

popular /ˈpɒpjələ(r)/ ***adj.*** **1** ~ (with sb) liked by many people or by most people in a group: *a popular holiday resort* ◇ *He's always been very popular with his pupils.* OPP **unpopular 2** made for the tastes and knowledge of ordinary people: *The popular newspapers seem more interested in scandal than news.* **3** (only *before* a noun) of or for a lot of people: *The programme is being repeated* ***by popular demand.***

popularity /ˌpɒpjuˈlærəti/ ***noun*** [U] the quality or state of being liked by many people: *The band's popularity is growing.*

popularize (also **-ise**) /ˈpɒpjʊləraɪz/ ***verb*** [T] to make a lot of or most people like sth: *The film did a lot to popularize her novels.*

popularly /ˈpɒpjələli/ ***adv.*** by many people; generally: *The Conservatives are popularly known as the Tories.*

populate /ˈpɒpjuleɪt/ ***verb*** [T] (usually passive) (GEOGRAPHY) to fill a particular area with people: *Parts of the country are very thinly populated.*

population /ˌpɒpjuˈleɪʃn/ ***noun*** **1** [C,U] (GEOGRAPHY) the number of people who live in a particular area, city or country: *What is the population of your country?* ◇ *an increase/a fall in population* **2** [C] all the people who live in a particular place or all the people or animals of a particular type that live somewhere: *the local population* ◇ *the male/female population* ◇ *The prison population has increased in recent years.*

popuˈlation explosion ***noun*** [C] (GEOGRAPHY) a sudden large increase in the number of people in an area

ˈpop-up ***adj.*** (COMPUTING) appearing on a computer screen quickly to show a list of choices, an advertisement, etc. while you are working on another document: *Select an item from the pop-up dialog box.* ▸ **pop-up** ***noun*** [C]: *The software automatically blocks annoying pop-ups.*

porcelain /ˈpɔːsəlɪn/ ***noun*** [U] a hard white substance that is used for making expensive cups, plates, etc.

porch /pɔːtʃ/ ***noun*** [C] **1** (*BrE*) a small covered area at the entrance to a house or church **2** (*AmE*) = VERANDA

porcupine /ˈpɔːkjupaɪn/ ***noun*** [C] an animal covered with long thin sharp parts (**quills**) which it can lift up to protect itself when it is attacked

pore[1] /pɔː(r)/ ***noun*** [C] one of the small holes in your skin through which sweat can pass

pore[2] /pɔː(r)/ ***verb***

PHR V **pore over sth** to study or read sth very carefully

pork /pɔːk/ ***noun*** [U] meat from a pig ➲ look at **bacon, ham** ➲ note at **meat**

ˈpork barrel ***noun*** [U] (*AmE, slang*) (POLITICS) local projects that are given a lot of government money in order to win votes; the money that is used: *pork-barrel projects/spending/politics* ▸ **ˈpork-barrelling** ***noun*** [U]

pornography /pɔːˈnɒɡrəfi/ (also *informal* **porn** /pɔːn/) ***noun*** [U] books, magazines, films, etc. that describe or show sexual acts in order to cause sexual excitement ▸ **pornographic** /ˌpɔːnəˈɡræfɪk/ ***adj.***

porous /ˈpɔːrəs/ ***adj.*** allowing liquid or air to pass through slowly: *porous rock* OPP **non-porous**

porpoise /ˈpɔːpəs/ ***noun*** [C] a sea animal with a pointed nose that lives in groups. **Porpoises** are similar to DOLPHINS but smaller.

porridge /ˈpɒrɪdʒ/ ***noun*** [U] a soft, thick white food that is made from a type of grain (**oats**) boiled with milk or water and eaten hot

port[1] /pɔːt/ ***noun*** **1** [C,U] an area where ships stop to let goods and passengers on and off: *a fishing port* ◇ *The damaged ship reached port safely.* **2** [C] a town or city that has a large area of water where ships load CARGO, etc.: *Hamburg is a major port.* **3** [U] a strong sweet red wine **4** [U] the side of a ship that is on your left when you are facing towards the front of the ship OPP **starboard** **5** [C] (COMPUTING) a place on a computer where you can attach another piece of equipment, often using a cable: *the modem port* ◇ *a USB port*

port[2] /pɔːt/ ***verb*** [T] (COMPUTING) to copy software from one system or machine to another: *The software can be ported to an IBM RS/6000.*

portable /ˈpɔːtəbl/ ***adj.*** that can be moved or carried easily: *a portable television* ➲ look at **movable**, **mobile**

portal /ˈpɔːtl/ ***noun*** [C] (COMPUTING) a website that is used as a point of entry to the Internet, where information has been collected that will be useful to a person interested in particular kinds of things: *a business/health/children's portal*

ˌportal ˈvein (*also* **heˌpatic ˌportal ˈvein**) ***noun*** [C] (ANATOMY) a VEIN that takes blood from the stomach and other organs near the stomach to the LIVER (= the large organ in your body that cleans your blood)

portcullis /pɔːtˈkʌlɪs/ ***noun*** [C] (*pl.* **portcullises**) a strong, heavy iron gate that can be raised or let down at the entrance to a castle

porter /ˈpɔːtə(r)/ ***noun*** [C] **1** a person whose job is to carry suitcases, etc. at a railway station, airport, etc. **2** a person whose job is to be in charge of the entrance of a hotel or other large building

portfolio /pɔːtˈfəʊliəʊ/ ***noun*** [C] (*pl.* **portfolios**) **1** a thin flat case used for carrying documents, drawings, etc. **2** (ART) a collection of photographs, drawings, etc. that you use as an example of your work, especially when applying for a job **3** (BUSINESS) a set of shares owned by a particular person or organization: *an **investment/share portfolio***

porthole /ˈpɔːthəʊl/ ***noun*** [C] a small round window in a ship

portico /ˈpɔːtɪkəʊ/ ***noun*** [C] (*pl.* **porticoes** or **porticos**) (*formal*) (ARCHITECTURE) a roof that is supported by columns, especially one that forms the entrance to a large building

portico

portion AW /ˈpɔːʃn/ ***noun*** [C] **a ~ (of sth)** **1** a part or share of sth: *What portion of your salary goes on tax?* ◇ *We must both accept a portion of the blame.* **2** an amount of food for one person (especially in a restaurant): *Could we have two extra portions of chips, please?* ➲ look at **helping**

portrait /ˈpɔːtreɪt/ ***noun*** [C] **1** (ART) a picture, painting or photograph of a person: *to paint sb's portrait* **2** a description of sb/sth in words

portray /pɔːˈtreɪ/ ***verb*** [T] **1** to show sb/sth in a picture; to describe sb/sth in a piece of writing: *Zola portrayed life in 19th-century France.* **2 ~ sb/sth as sth** to describe sb/sth in a particular way: *In many of his novels life is portrayed as being hard.* **3** to act the part of sb in a play or film: *In this film she portrays a very old woman.* ▶ **portrayal** /pɔːˈtreɪəl/ ***noun*** [C]

pose[1] AW /pəʊz/ ***verb*** **1** [T] to create sth for or give sth to sb that they have to deal with: *to pose a problem/threat/challenge/risk* ◇ *to pose* (= ask) *a question* **2** [I] to sit or stand in a particular position for a painting, photograph, etc.: *After the wedding we all posed for photographs.* **3** [I] **~ as sb/sth** to pretend to be sb/sth: *The robbers got into the house by posing as telephone engineers.* **4** [I] to behave in a way that is intended to impress people who see you: *They hardly swam at all. They just sat posing at the side of the pool.*

pose[2] AW /pəʊz/ ***noun*** [C] **1** a position in which sb stands, sits, etc. especially in order to be painted or photographed **2** a way of behaving that is intended to impress people who see you

posh /pɒʃ/ ***adj.*** (*informal*) **1** fashionable and expensive: *We went for a meal in a really posh hotel.* **2** (*BrE*) (used about people) belonging to or typical of a high social class

position[1] /pəˈzɪʃn/ ***noun*** **1** [C,U] the place where sb/sth is or should be: *Are you happy with the position of the chairs?* ◇ *All the dancers were **in position** waiting for the music to begin.* **2** [C,U] the way in which sb/sth sits or stands, or the direction that sth is pointing in: *My leg hurts when I **change position**.* ◇ *Turn the switch to the off position.* **3** [C, usually sing.] the state or situation that sb/sth is in: *I'm in a very **difficult position**.* ◇ *I'm sorry, I'm not **in a position** to help you financially.* ➲ note at **situation** **4** [C] **a ~ (on sth)** what you think about sth; your opinion: *What is your position on smoking?* **5** [C,U] the place or level of a person, company, team, etc. compared to others: *the position of women in society* ◇ *Max finished the race in second position.* ◇ *Wealth and position are very important to some people.* **6** [C] a job: *There have been over a hundred applications for the position of Sales Manager.* SYN **post** **7** [C] (SPORT) the part you play in a team game: *Danny can play any position except goalkeeper.*

position[2] /pəˈzɪʃn/ ***verb*** [T] to put sb/sth in a particular place or position: *Mary positioned herself near the door so she could get out quickly.*

positive AW /ˈpɒzətɪv/ ***adj.*** **1** thinking or talking mainly about the good things in a situation, in a way that makes you or sb else feel HOPEFUL and confident: *Their reaction to my idea was generally positive.* ◇ *I **feel** very **positive** about our team's chances this season.* ◇ ***Positive thinking** will help you to succeed.* OPP **negative** **2 ~ (about sth/that...)** certain; sure: *Are you positive that this is the woman you saw?* ➲ note at **sure** **3** clear; definite: *There is no positive evidence that he is guilty.* ◇ *to take positive action* **4** (HEALTH) (used about a medical or scientific test) showing that sth has happened or is present: *The result of the pregnancy test was positive.* ◇ *Two athletes tested positive for steroids.* OPP **negative** **5** (MATHEMATICS) (used about a number) more than zero OPP **negative**

ˌpositive disˌcriminˈation (*AmE* **reˌverse disˌcrimiˈnation**) (*also* **afˌfirmative ˈaction**) ***noun*** [U] (SOCIAL STUDIES) the practice or policy of making sure that a particular number of jobs, etc. are given to people from groups that are often treated unfairly because of their race, sex, etc.

positively AW /'pɒzətɪvli/ *adv.* **1** with no doubt; firmly: *I was positively convinced that I was doing the right thing.* **2** in a way that shows you are thinking about the good things in a situation, not the bad: *Thinking positively helps many people deal with stress.* **3** (used about a person's way of speaking or acting) in a confident and HOPEFUL way: *The team played cautiously for the first ten minutes, then continued more positively.* **4** (*informal*) (used for emphasizing sth) really; extremely: *He wasn't just annoyed – he was positively furious!*

possess /pə'zes/ *verb* [T] (not used in the continuous tenses) **1** (*formal*) to have or own sth: *They lost everything they possessed in the fire.* ◇ *Paola possesses a natural ability to make people laugh.* **2** to influence sb or to make sb do sth: *What possessed you to say a thing like that!*

possession /pə'zeʃn/ *noun* **1** [U] the state of having or owning sth: *The gang were caught **in possession of** stolen goods.* ◇ *Enemy forces managed to **take possession of** the town.* **2** [C, usually pl.] something that you have or own: *Bud packed all his possessions and left.*

possessive /pə'zesɪv/ *adj.* **1** ~ **(of/about sb/sth)** not wanting to share sb/sth: *Dan is so possessive with his toys – he won't let other children play with them.* **2** (LANGUAGE) used to describe words that show who or what a person or thing belongs to: *'My', 'your' and 'his' are possessive adjectives.* ◇ *'Mine', 'yours' and 'his' are possessive pronouns.*

possessor /pə'zesə(r)/ *noun* [C] a person who has or owns sth

possibility /ˌpɒsə'bɪləti/ *noun* (*pl.* **possibilities**) **1** [U, C] (a) ~ **(of sth/doing sth)**; (a) ~ **that...** the fact that sth might exist or happen, but is not likely to: *There's not much possibility of the letter reaching you before Saturday.* ◇ *There is **a strong possibility** that the fire was started deliberately.* **2** [C] one of the different things that you can do in a particular situation or in order to achieve sth: *There is a wide range of possibilities open to us.*

possible /'pɒsəbl/ *adj.* **1** that can happen or be done: *I'll phone you back **as** soon **as possible**.* ◇ *Could you give me your answer today, **if possible**?* ◇ *The doctors did **everything possible** to save his life.* ◇ *You were warned of all the possible dangers.* OPP **impossible** **2** that may be suitable or acceptable: *There are four possible candidates for the job.* ➲ look at **probable** **3** used after adjectives to emphasize that sth is the best, worst, etc. of its type: *Alone and with no job or money, I was in the worst possible situation.*

possibly /'pɒsəbli/ *adv.* **1** perhaps; maybe: *'Will you be free on Sunday?' 'Possibly.'* **2** (used for emphasizing sth) according to what is possible: *I will leave as soon as I possibly can.*

post[1] /pəʊst/ *noun* **1** (*especially AmE* **mail**) [U] the system or organization for collecting and dealing with letters, packages, etc.: *The document is too valuable to send **by post**.* ◇ *If you hurry you might **catch the post*** (= post it before everything is collected). **2** (*AmE* **mail**) [U] letters, packages, etc. that are collected or brought to your house: *Has the post come yet this morning?* ◇ *There wasn't any post for you.* **3** [C] a job: *The post was advertised in the local newspaper.* SYN **position** **4** [C] a place where sb is on duty or is guarding sth: *The soldiers had to remain at their posts all night.* **5** [C] an UPRIGHT piece of metal or wood that is put in the ground to mark a position or to support sth: *a goal post* ◇ *Can you see a signpost anywhere?*

IDM **by return (of post)** → RETURN[2]

post[2] /pəʊst/ *verb* [T] **1** (*especially AmE* **mail**) to send a letter, package, etc. by post: *This letter was posted in Edinburgh yesterday.* **2** to send sb to go and work somewhere: *After two years in London, Rosa was posted to the Tokyo office.* **3** to put sb on guard or on duty in a particular place: *Policemen were posted outside the building.* **4** (often passive) to put a notice where everyone can see it: *The exam results will be posted on the main noticeboard.* ◇ *The results will be posted on the Internet.*

post- /pəʊst/ *prefix* (used in nouns, verbs and adjectives) after: *postgraduate* ◇ *post-war* ➲ look at **ante-**, **pre-**

postage /'pəʊstɪdʒ/ *noun* [U] the amount that you must pay to send a letter, package etc.

'postage stamp = STAMP[1] (1)

postal /'pəʊstl/ *adj.* connected with the sending and collecting of letters, packages, etc.

'postal order *noun* [C] a piece of paper that you can buy at a post office that represents a certain amount of money. A **postal order** is a safe way of sending money by post.

postbox /'pəʊstbɒks/ (*also* **'letter box**, *AmE* **mailbox**) *noun* [C] a box in a public place where you put letters, etc. that you want to send ➲ look at **pillar box**

postcard /'pəʊstkɑːd/ *noun* [C] (TOURISM) a card that you write a message on and send to sb. **Postcards** have a picture on one side and are usually sent without an envelope.

postcode /'pəʊstkəʊd/ (*AmE* **ZIP code**) *noun* [C] a group of letters and/or numbers that you put at the end of an address

poster /'pəʊstə(r)/ *noun* [C] **1** a large printed picture or a notice in a public place, often used to advertise sth **2** a large picture printed on paper that is put on a wall for decoration

posterity /pɒ'sterəti/ *noun* [U] the future and the people who will be alive then: *We should look after our environment for the sake of posterity.*

postgraduate /ˌpəʊst'grædʒuət/ *noun* [C] (EDUCATION) a person who is doing further studies at a university after taking their first degree ➲ look at **graduate**, **undergraduate**

posthumous /'pɒstjʊməs/ *adj.* given or happening after sb has died: *a posthumous medal for bravery* ▶ **posthumously** *adv.*

ˌpost-Im'pressionism *noun* [U] (ART) the work or style of a group of artists in the late 19th century and early 20th century that came after and reacted against IMPRESSIONISM (= a style of painting in late 19th century France) ▶ **ˌpost-Im'pressionist** *noun* [C], *adj.*

posting /'pəʊstɪŋ/ *noun* [C] **1** (*especially BrE*) an act of sending sb to a particular place to do their job, especially for a limited period of time **2** (COMPUTING) a message sent to a discussion group on the Internet

'Post-it™ (*also* **'Post-it note**) *noun* [C] a small piece of coloured, sticky paper that you use for writing a note on, and that can be easily removed

postman /'pəʊstmən/ (*AmE* **mailman**) *noun* [C] (*pl.* **-men** /-mən/) a person whose job is to collect letters, packages, etc. and take them to people's houses

postmark /'pəʊstmɑːk/ *noun* [C] an official mark over a stamp on a letter, package, etc. that says when and where it was posted

postmodern /ˌpəʊstˈmɒdn/ ***adj.*** (**ART, ARTS AND MEDIA**) connected with or influenced by POSTMODERNISM: *postmodern architecture*

postmodernism /ˌpəʊstˈmɒdənɪzəm/ ***noun*** [U] (**ART, ARTS AND MEDIA**) a style and movement in art, ARCHITECTURE, literature, etc. in the late 20th century that reacts against modern styles, for example by mixing features from traditional and modern styles ➲ look at **modernism** ▶ **postmodernist** ***noun*** [C], ***adj.***

post-mortem /ˌpəʊst ˈmɔːtəm/ ***noun*** [C] (**HEALTH, LAW**) a medical examination of a dead body to find out how the person died

post-natal /ˌpəʊst ˈneɪtl/ ***adj.*** (only *before* a noun) (**HEALTH**) connected with the period after the birth of a baby ➲ look at **antenatal**

ˈ**post office** ***noun*** [C] **1** a place where you can buy stamps, post packages, etc. **2 the Post Office** the national organization that is responsible for collecting and dealing with letters, packages, etc.

postpone /pəˈspəʊn/ ***verb*** [T] to arrange that sth will happen at a later time than the time you had planned; to delay: *The match was postponed because of water on the pitch.* ➲ look at **cancel** ▶ **postponement** ***noun*** [C,U]

postscript /ˈpəʊstskrɪpt/ ***noun*** [C] an extra message or extra information that is added at the end of a letter, note, etc. ➲ look at **PS**

posture /ˈpɒstʃə(r)/ ***noun*** [C,U] the way that a person sits, stands, walks, etc.: *Poor posture can lead to backache.*

ˌ**post-ˈwar** ***adj.*** existing or happening in the period after the end of a war, especially the Second World War

pot[1] 🔑 /pɒt/ ***noun*** [C] **1** a round container that is used for cooking food in **2** a container that you use for a particular purpose: *a flowerpot* ◇ *a pot of paint* **3** the amount that a pot contains: *We drank two pots of tea.*

pot[2] /pɒt/ ***verb*** [T] (**potting**; **potted**) **1** to put a plant into a pot filled with soil **2** (**SPORT**) to hit a ball into one of the pockets in the table in the game of POOL, BILLIARDS or SNOOKER: *He potted the black ball into the corner pocket.*

potable /ˈpəʊtəbl/ ***adj.*** (*formal*) (used about water) safe to drink

potassium /pəˈtæsiəm/ ***noun*** [U] (*symbol* **K**) (**CHEMISTRY**) a soft silver-white metal that exists mainly in mixtures (**compounds**) which are used in industry and farming ❶ For more information on the periodic table of elements, look at pages R34-5.

potato 🔑 /pəˈteɪtəʊ/ ***noun*** [C,U] (*pl.* **potatoes**) a round vegetable that grows under the ground with a brown, yellow or red skin. Potatoes are white or yellow inside: *mashed potato* ◇ *to peel potatoes*

potato ˈcrisp (*AmE* **poˈtato chip**) = CRISP²

potent /ˈpəʊtnt/ ***adj.*** strong or powerful: *a potent drug/drink* ▶ **potency** /-nsi/ ***noun*** [U]

potential[1] 🔑 AW /pəˈtenʃl/ ***adj.*** (only *before* a noun) that may possibly become sth, happen, be used, etc.: *Wind power is a potential source of energy.* ◇ *potential customers* ▶ **potentially** AW /-ʃəli/ ***adv.***

potential[2] 🔑 AW /pəˈtenʃl/ ***noun*** [U] the qualities or abilities that sb/sth has but that may not be fully developed yet: *That boy **has great potential** as an athlete.*

poˌtential ˈenergy ***noun*** [U] (**PHYSICS**) the form of energy that an object gains as it is lifted ➲ picture at **energy**

pothole /ˈpɒthəʊl/ ***noun*** [C] **1** a hole in the surface of a road that is formed by traffic and bad weather **2** (**GEOLOGY**) a deep hole in rock that is formed by water over thousands of years and often leads to underground rooms (**caves**)

potholing /ˈpɒthəʊlɪŋ/ ***noun*** [U] (**SPORT**) the sport of climbing down inside POTHOLES(2), walking through underground tunnels, etc.: *to go potholing*

ˈ**pot plant** ***noun*** [C] (*BrE*) a plant that you keep indoors

potter[1] /ˈpɒtə(r)/ (*AmE* **putter**) ***verb*** [I] ~ (**about/around**) to spend your time doing small jobs or things that you enjoy without hurrying

potter[2] /ˈpɒtə(r)/ ***noun*** [C] a person who makes POTTERY

pottery /ˈpɒtəri/ ***noun*** (*pl.* **potteries**) **1** [U] pots, dishes, etc. that are made from baked CLAY **2** [U] the activity or skill of making dishes, etc. from CLAY: *a pottery class* ➲ look at **ceramic 3** [C] a place where CLAY pots and dishes are made

potty[1] /ˈpɒti/ ***adj.*** (*BrE*, *informal*) **1** crazy or silly **2** ~ **about sb/sth** liking sb/sth very much: *Penny's potty about Mark.*

potty[2] /ˈpɒti/ ***noun*** [C] (*pl.* **potties**) a plastic bowl that young children use when they are too small to use a toilet

pouch /paʊtʃ/ ***noun*** [C] **1** a small leather bag **2** a pocket of skin on the stomach of some female animals, for example KANGAROOS, in which they carry their babies ➲ picture on **page 28**

poultice /ˈpəʊltɪs/ ***noun*** [C] (**HEALTH**) a soft substance that you spread on a cloth and put on the skin to reduce pain or swelling

poultry /ˈpəʊltri/ ***noun* 1** [pl.] (**AGRICULTURE**) birds, for example chickens, DUCKS, etc. that are kept for their eggs or their meat ➲ picture on **page 28 2** [U] the meat from these birds

pounce /paʊns/ ***verb*** [I] ~ (**on sb/sth**) to attack sb/sth by jumping suddenly on them or it: (*figurative*) *He was quick to pounce on any mistakes I made.*

pound[1] 🔑 /paʊnd/ ***noun* 1** [C] (*also* ˌ**pound ˈsterling**) (*symbol* **£**) the unit of money in Britain; one hundred pence (100p): *Melissa earns £16000 a year.* ◇ *Can you change a ten-pound note?* ◇ *a pound coin* **2** [sing.] **the pound** the value of the British pound on international money markets: *The pound has fallen against the dollar.* ◇ *How many yen are there **to the pound**?* **3** [C] (*abbr.* **lb**) a measurement of weight, equal to 0.454 of a kilogram: *The carrots cost 30p a pound.* ◇ *Half a pound of mushrooms, please.* **4** [C] (**LAW**) a place where vehicles that have been parked illegally are kept until their owners pay to get them back **5** [C] a place where dogs that have been found in the street without their owners are kept until their owners claim them

pound[2] /paʊnd/ ***verb* 1** [I] ~ (**at/against/on sth**) to hit sth hard many times making a lot of noise: *She pounded on the door with her fists.* **2** [I] ~ **along, down, up, etc.** to walk with heavy, noisy steps in a particular direction: *Jason went pounding up the stairs three at a time.* **3** [I] (used about your heart, blood, etc.) to beat quickly and loudly: *Her heart was pounding with fear.* **4** [T] to hit sth many times to break it into smaller pieces

pour 🔑 /pɔː(r)/ ***verb* 1** [T] to make a liquid or other substance flow steadily out of or into a container: *Pour the sugar into a bowl.* **2** [I] (used about a liquid, smoke, light, etc.) to flow out of or into sth quickly and steadily, and in large quantities: *Tears were pouring down her cheeks.* ◇ *She opened the curtains and sunlight poured into the room.* **3** [T] ~ **sth (out)** to serve a drink to sb by letting it flow from a container into a cup or glass: *Have you poured out the tea?* **4** [I] ~ **(down) (with rain)** to rain heavily: *The rain poured down all day long.* ◇ *I'm not going out. It's pouring with rain.* **5** [I] to come or go somewhere continuously in large numbers: *People were pouring out of the station.*

IDM **pour your heart out (to sb)** to tell sb all your personal problems, feelings, etc.

PHR V **pour sth out** to speak freely about what you think or feel about sth that has happened to you: *to pour out all your troubles*

pout /paʊt/ *verb* [I] to push your lips, or your bottom lip, forward to show that you are annoyed about sth or to look sexually attractive ▶ **pout** *noun* [C]

poverty /ˈpɒvəti/ *noun* [U] the state of being poor: *There are millions of people in this country who are living* ***in poverty.***

the ˈpoverty line (*especially AmE* **the ˈpoverty level**) *noun* [sing.] (FINANCE) the official level of income (= money that you earn) that is necessary to be able to buy the basic things you need such as food and clothes and to pay for somewhere to live: *A third of the population is living* ***at or below the poverty line.***

poverty-stricken /ˈpɒvəti strɪkən/ *adj.* very poor

POW /ˌpiː əʊ ˈdʌbljuː/ *abbr.* prisoner of war

powder ⊶ /ˈpaʊdə(r)/ *noun* [U, C] a dry substance that is in the form of very small grains: *washing powder* ◇ *Grind the spices into a fine powder.* ▶ **powder** *verb* [T]

powdered /ˈpaʊdəd/ *adj.* (used about a substance that is usually liquid) dried and made into powder: *powdered milk/soup*

power¹ ⊶ /ˈpaʊə(r)/ *noun* **1** [U] ~ **(over sb/sth)**; ~ **(to do sth)** the ability to control people or things or to do sth: *The aim is to give people more power over their own lives.* ◇ *to have sb* ***in your power*** ◇ ***It's not in my power*** (= I am unable) *to help you.* **2** [U] (POLITICS) political control of a country or area: *When did this government* ***come to power?*** ◇ *to take/seize power* **3** [C] **the** ~ **(to do sth)** the right or authority to do sth: *Do the police have the power to stop cars without good reason?* **4** [C] a country with a lot of influence in world affairs or that has great military strength: *a military/economic power* ➲ look at **superpower**, **world power** **5** **powers** [pl.] a particular ability of the body or mind: *He has great powers of observation.* ◇ *She had to use all her powers of persuasion on him.* **6** [U] the energy or strength that sb/sth has: *The ship was helpless against the power of the storm.* ◇ *I've lost all power in my right arm.* **7** [U] energy that can be collected and used for operating machines, making electricity, etc.: *nuclear/wind/solar power* ◇ *This car has power steering.* **8** [C, usually sing.] (MATHEMATICS) the number of times that an amount is to be multiplied by itself: *4* ***to the power of*** *3 is* 4^3 (= $4 \times 4 \times 4 = 64$). **9** [U] (PHYSICS) the amount by which a LENS can make objects appear larger: *the power of a microscope/telescope*

power² /ˈpaʊə(r)/ *verb* [T] to supply energy to sth to make it work: *What powers the motor in this machine?* ▶ **-powered** *adj.*: *a solar-powered calculator* ◇ *a high-powered engine*

ˈpower cut *noun* [C] a time when the supply of electricity stops, for example during a storm

powerful ⊶ /ˈpaʊəfl/ *adj.* **1** having a lot of control or influence over other people: *a powerful nation* ◇ *He's one of the most powerful directors in Hollywood.* **2** having great strength or force: *a powerful car/engine/telescope* ◇ *a powerful swimmer* **3** having a strong effect on your mind or body: *The Prime Minister made a powerful speech.* ◇ *a powerful drug* ▶ **powerfully** /-fəli/ *adv.*

powerless /ˈpaʊələs/ *adj.* **1** without strength, influence or control **2** ~ **to do sth** completely unable to do sth: *I stood and watched him struggle, powerless to help.*

ˌpower of atˈtorney *noun* [U,C] (*pl.* **powers of attorney**) (LAW) the right to act as the representative of sb in business or financial matters; a document that gives sb this right

ˈpower point (*BrE*) = SOCKET (1)

ˈpower station (*AmE* **ˈpower plant**) *noun* [C] a place where electricity is made (**generated**)

pp *abbr.* **1 pp.** pages: *See pp. 100–178.* **2** (*also* **p.p.**) (before a signature) used to mean 'on behalf of': *pp Mike Holland* (= from Mike Holland but signed by sb else because he is away)

PR /ˌpiː ˈɑː(r)/ *abbr.* **1** public relations **2** proportional representation

practicable /ˈpræktɪkəbl/ *adj.* (used about an idea, a plan or a suggestion) able to be done successfully: *The scheme is just not practicable.* OPP **impracticable**

practical¹ ⊶ /ˈpræktɪkl/ *adj.* **1** concerned with actually doing sth rather than with ideas or thought: *Have you got any* ***practical experience*** *of working on a farm?* ➲ look at **theoretical** **2** that is likely to succeed; right or sensible: *We need to find a practical solution to the problem.* OPP **impractical** **3** very suitable for a particular purpose; useful: *a practical little car, ideal for the city* OPP **impractical** **4** (used about people) making sensible decisions and good at dealing with problems: *We must be practical. It's no good buying a house we cannot afford.* OPP **impractical** **5** (used about a person) good at making and repairing things

practical² /ˈpræktɪkl/ *noun* [C] (*BrE, informal*) (EDUCATION) a lesson or an exam where you do or make sth rather than just writing: *He passed the theory paper but failed the practical.*

practicality /ˌpræktɪˈkæləti/ (*pl.* **practicalities**) *noun* **1** [U] the quality of being suitable and realistic, or likely to succeed: *I am not convinced of the practicality of the scheme.* **2** [pl.] the real facts rather than ideas or thoughts: *Let's look at the practicalities of the situation.*

ˌpractical ˈjoke *noun* [C] a trick that you play on sb that makes them look silly and makes other people laugh

practically ⊶ /ˈpræktɪkli/ *adv.* **1** (*spoken*) almost; very nearly: *My essay is practically finished now.* **2** in a realistic or sensible way

practice ⊶ /ˈpræktɪs/ *noun* **1** [U] action rather than ideas or thought: *the* ***theory and practice*** *of language teaching* ◇ *I can't wait to* ***put*** *what I've learnt* ***into practice.*** **2** [C,U] (*formal*) the usual or expected way of doing sth in a particular organization or situation; a habit or custom: *It is standard practice not to pay bills until the end of the month.* **3** [C,U] (a period of) doing an activity many times or training regularly so that you become good at it: *piano/football practice* ◇ *His accent should improve* ***with practice.*** **4** [U] the work of a doctor or lawyer: *Dr Roberts doesn't work in a hospital. He's in **general practice*** (=he's a family doctor). **5** [C] the business of a doctor, dentist or lawyer: *a successful medical/dental practice*

IDM **be/get out of practice** to find it difficult to do sth because you have not done it for a long time: *I'm not playing very well at the moment. I'm really out of practice.*

in practice in reality: *Prisoners have legal rights, but in practice these rights are not always respected.*

practise ⊶ (*AmE* practice) /ˈpræktɪs/ **verb** [I,T] **1** to do an activity or train regularly so that you become very good at sth: *If you want to play a musical instrument well, you must practise every day.* ◇ *He always wants to **practise** his English **on** me.* **2** to do sth or take part in sth regularly or publicly: *a practising Catholic/Jew/Muslim* **3** ~ **(sth/as sth)** to work as a doctor or lawyer: *She's practising as a barrister in Leeds.* ◇ *He was banned from practising medicine.*

practised (*AmE* **practiced**) /ˈpræktɪst/ **adj.** ~ **(in sth)** very good at sth, because you have done it a lot or often: *He was practised in the art of inventing excuses.*

practitioner AW /prækˈtɪʃənə(r)/ **noun** [C] (*formal*) **1** a person who works as a doctor, dentist or lawyer ➲ look at **GP 2** a person who regularly does a particular activity, especially one that requires skill: *one of the greatest practitioners of science fiction*

pragmatic /prægˈmætɪk/ **adj.** dealing with problems in a practical way rather than by following ideas or principles

pragmatism /ˈprægmətɪzəm/ **noun** [U] (*formal*) thinking about solving problems in a practical and sensible way rather than by having fixed ideas ▸ **pragmatist** /-tɪst/ **noun** [C]: *Most successful teachers are pragmatists and realists.*

prairie /ˈpreəri/ **noun** [C] (GEOGRAPHY) a very large area of flat land covered in grass with few trees (especially in North America)

praise[1] ⊶ /preɪz/ **verb** [T] ~ **sb/sth (for sth)** to say that sb/sth is good and should be admired: *The fireman was praised for his courage.*

praise[2] ⊶ /preɪz/ **noun** [U] what you say when you are expressing admiration for sb/sth: *The survivors were full of praise for the paramedics.*

praiseworthy /ˈpreɪzwɜːði/ **adj.** that should be admired and recognized as good

pram /præm/ (*AmE* **ˈbaby carriage**) **noun** [C] a small vehicle on four wheels for a young baby, pushed by a person on foot

prance /prɑːns/ **verb** [I] to move about with quick, high steps, often because you feel proud or pleased with yourself

prank /præŋk/ **noun** [C] a trick that is played on sb as a joke: *a childish prank*

praseodymium /ˌpreɪziəʊˈdɪmiəm/ **noun** [U] (*symbol* **Pr**) (CHEMISTRY) a chemical element. **Praseodymium** is a soft silver-white metal used in ALLOYS and to colour glass. ❶ For more information on the periodic table of elements, look at pages R34-5.

prat /præt/ **noun** [C] (*BrE, slang*) a stupid person: *What a prat!*

prawn /prɔːn/ (*AmE* **shrimp**) **noun** [C] a small SHELLFISH that we eat and that becomes pink when cooked ➲ look at **shrimp** ➲ picture on **page 29**

pray ⊶ /preɪ/ **verb** [I,T] ~ **(to sb) (for sb/sth)** (RELIGION) to speak to God or a god in order to give thanks or to ask for help: *They knelt down and prayed for peace.*

prayer ⊶ /preə(r)/ **noun** (RELIGION) **1** [C] a ~ **(for sb/sth)** the words that you use when you speak to God or a god: *Let's **say a prayer** for all the people who are ill.* ◇ *a prayer book* **2** [U] the act of speaking to God or a god: *to kneel **in prayer***

pre- /priː/ **prefix** (used in verbs, nouns and adjectives) before: *prepay* ◇ *preview* ◇ *pre-war* ➲ look at **ante-**, **post-**

preach /priːtʃ/ **verb 1** [I,T] (RELIGION) to give a talk (**a sermon**) on a religious subject, especially in a church **2** [T] to say that sth is good and persuade other people to accept it: *I always preach caution in situations like this.* **3** [I] to give sb advice on how to behave, on what is considered morally acceptable, etc., in a way that they find boring or annoying: *I'm sorry, I didn't mean to preach.*

preacher /ˈpriːtʃə(r)/ **noun** [C] (RELIGION) a person who gives religious talks (**sermons**), for example in a church

precarious /prɪˈkeəriəs/ **adj.** not safe or certain; dangerous ▸ **precariously** **adv.**

precaution /prɪˈkɔːʃn/ **noun** [C] a ~ **(against sth)** something that you do now in order to avoid danger or problems in the future: *You should always **take the precaution of** locking your valuables in the hotel safe.* ◇ *precautions against fire/theft* ▸ **precautionary** /prɪˈkɔːʃənəri/ **adj.**

precede AW /prɪˈsiːd/ **verb** [I,T] (*written*) to happen, come or go before sb/sth: *Look at the table on the preceding page.*

precedence AW /ˈpresɪdəns/ **noun** [U] ~ **(over sb/sth)** the right that sb/sth has to come before sb/sth else because they or it are more important: *In business, making a profit seems to **take precedence** over everything else.*

precedent AW /ˈpresɪdənt/ **noun** [C,U] an official action or decision that has happened in the past and that is considered as an example or rule to follow in the same situation later: *We don't want to **set a precedent** by allowing one person to come in late or they'll all want to do it.* ◇ *Such protests are **without precedent** in recent history.* ➲ look at **unprecedented**

precinct /ˈpriːsɪŋkt/ **noun 1** [C] (*BrE*) a special area of shops in a town where cars are not allowed: *a shopping precinct* **2** [C] (*AmE*) a part of a town that has its own police station **3 precincts** [pl.] (*formal*) the area near or around a building: *the hospital and its precincts*

precious /ˈpreʃəs/ **adj. 1** of great value (usually because it is rare or difficult to find): *In overcrowded Hong Kong, every small piece of land is precious.* **2** loved very much: *The painting was very precious to her.*

ˌprecious ˈmetal **noun** [C] a metal which is very rare and valuable and often used in jewellery: *Gold and silver are precious metals.*

ˌprecious ˈstone (*also* **stone**) **noun** [C] a stone which is very rare and valuable and often used in jewellery: *diamonds and other precious stones*

precipice /ˈpresəpɪs/ **noun** [C] (GEOGRAPHY) a very steep side of a high mountain or CLIFF

precipitate[1] /prɪˈsɪpɪteɪt/ **verb** [T] (*formal*) **1** to make sth, especially sth bad, happen suddenly or sooner than it should **2** ~ **sb/sth into sth** to suddenly force sb/sth into a particular state or condition: *The* *president's assassination precipitated the country into war.*

precipitate² /prɪˈsɪpɪtət/ ***adj.*** (*formal*) (used about an action or a decision) happening very quickly or suddenly and usually without enough care and thought ▶ **precipitately** ***adv.***

precipitate³ /prɪˈsɪpɪteɪt/ ***noun*** [C] (CHEMISTRY) a solid substance that has been separated from a solution in a chemical process

precipitation /prɪˌsɪpɪˈteɪʃn/ ***noun*** **1** [U] (GEOGRAPHY) rain, snow, etc. that falls; the amount of this that falls **2** [U, C] (CHEMISTRY) a chemical process in which solid material is separated from a solution (=a liquid in which it has been dissolved)

precis /ˈpreɪsiː/ ***noun*** [C,U] (*pl.* **precis** /-siːz/) a short version of a speech or written text that contains only the most important points SYN **summary**

precise 🔑 AW /prɪˈsaɪs/ ***adj.*** **1** clear and accurate: *precise details/instructions/measurements* ◇ *He's in his forties – well, forty-four,* ***to be precise.*** ◇ *She couldn't be very precise about what her attacker was wearing.* ➲ note at **true** OPP **imprecise** **2** (only *before* a noun) exact; particular: *I'm sorry. I can't come just* ***at this precise moment.*** **3** (used about a person) taking care to get small details right: *He's very precise about his work.*

precisely 🔑 AW /prɪˈsaɪsli/ ***adv.*** **1** exactly: *The time is 10.03 precisely.* SYN **exactly** **2** used to emphasize that sth is very true or obvious: *It's precisely because I care about you that I got so angry when you stayed out late.* **3** (*spoken*) (used for agreeing with a statement) yes, that is right: *'So, if we don't book now, we probably won't get a flight?' 'Precisely.'*

precision AW /prɪˈsɪʒn/ ***noun*** [U] the quality of being clear or exact: *The plans were drawn with great precision.* ▶ **precision** ***adj.***: *precision instruments/tools*

preclude /prɪˈkluːd/ ***verb*** [T] (*formal*) **~ sth; ~ sb from doing sth** to prevent sth from happening or sb from doing sth; to make sth impossible: *Lack of time precludes any further discussion.* ◇ *His religious beliefs precluded him/his serving in the army.*

precocious /prɪˈkəʊʃəs/ ***adj.*** (used about children) having developed certain abilities and ways of behaving at a much younger age than usual: *a precocious child who started her acting career at the age of 5*

preconceived /ˌpriːkənˈsiːvd/ ***adj.*** (only *before* a noun) (used about an idea or opinion) formed before you have enough information or experience

preconception /ˌpriːkənˈsepʃn/ ***noun*** [C] an idea or opinion that you have formed about sb/sth before you have enough information or experience

precondition /ˌpriːkənˈdɪʃn/ ***noun*** [C] (*written*) a **~ (for/of sth)** something that must happen or exist before sth else can exist or be done SYN **prerequisite**

precursor /priːˈkɜːsə(r)/ ***noun*** [C] **~ (of/to sth)** (*formal*) a person or thing that comes before sb/sth similar and that leads to or influences its development

predator /ˈpredətə(r)/ ***noun*** [C] (BIOLOGY) an animal that kills and eats other animals

predatory /ˈpredətri/ ***adj.*** **1** (used about an animal) (BIOLOGY) living by killing and eating other animals **2** (*written*) (used about a person) using weaker people for their own financial or sexual advantage

predecessor /ˈpriːdɪsesə(r)/ ***noun*** [C] **1** the person who was in the job or position before the person who is in it now **2** a thing such as a machine, that has been followed or replaced by sth else ➲ look at **successor**

predicament /prɪˈdɪkəmənt/ ***noun*** [C] an unpleasant and difficult situation that is hard to get out of

predicative /prɪˈdɪkətɪv/ ***adj.*** (LANGUAGE) (used about an adjective) not used before a noun: *You cannot say 'an asleep child' because 'asleep' is a predicative adjective.*

RELATED VOCABULARY

An adjective that *can* be used before a noun is called **attributive**. Many adjectives, for example 'big', can be either **predicative** or **attributive**: *The house is big.* ◇ *It's a big house.*

▶ **predicatively** ***adv.***: *'Asleep' can only be used predicatively.*

predict 🔑 AW /prɪˈdɪkt/ ***verb*** [T] to say that sth will happen in the future: *Scientists still cannot predict exactly when earthquakes will happen.*

predictable AW /prɪˈdɪktəbl/ ***adj.*** **1** that was or could be expected to happen: *The match had a predictable result.* **2** (used about a person) always behaving in a way that you would expect and therefore rather boring: *I knew you were going to say that – you're so predictable.* ▶ **predictably** ***adv.***

prediction AW /prɪˈdɪkʃn/ ***noun*** [C,U] saying what will happen; what sb thinks will happen: *The exam results confirmed my predictions.*

predilection /ˌpriːdɪˈlekʃn/ ***noun*** [usually sing.] **~ (for sth)** (*formal*) if you **have a predilection for** sth, you like it very much SYN **liking, preference**

predispose /ˌpriːdɪˈspəʊz/ ***verb*** [T] (*formal*) **1 ~ sb to sth/to do sth** to influence sb so that they are likely to think or behave in a particular way: *He believes that some people are predisposed to criminal behaviour.* **2 ~ sb to sth** (HEALTH) to make it likely that you will suffer from a particular illness: *Stress can predispose people to heart attacks.*

predisposition /ˌpriːdɪspəˈzɪʃn/ ***noun*** [C,U] **~ (to/towards sth)** (*formal*) (HEALTH) a condition that makes sb/sth likely to behave in a particular way or to suffer from a particular disease: *a genetic predisposition to liver disease*

predominance AW /prɪˈdɒmɪnəns/ ***noun*** [sing.] the state of being more important or greater in number than other people or things: *There is a predominance of Japanese tourists in Hawaii.*

predominant AW /prɪˈdɒmɪnənt/ ***adj.*** most noticeable, powerful or important: *The predominant colour was blue.*

predominantly AW /prɪˈdɒmɪnəntli/ ***adv.*** mostly; mainly: *The population of the island is predominantly Spanish.*

predominate AW /prɪˈdɒmɪneɪt/ ***verb*** [I] (*formal*) **~ (over sb/sth)** to be most important or greatest in number: *Private interest was not allowed to predominate over public good.*

pre-empt /priˈempt/ ***verb*** [T] (*formal*) **1** to prevent sth from happening by taking action to stop it: *Her departure pre-empted any further questions.* ◇ *A good training course will pre-empt many problems.* **2** to do or say sth before sb else does: *She was just about to apologize when he pre-empted her.*

ˌ**pre-eˈxist** *verb* [I] to exist from an earlier time: *a pre-existing medical condition*

preface /ˈprefəs/ ***noun*** [C] a written introduction to a book that explains what it is about or why it was written

prefect /ˈpriːfekt/ ***noun*** [C] (*BrE*) (EDUCATION) an older girl or boy in a school who has special duties and responsibilities. **Prefects** often help to make sure that the younger schoolchildren behave properly.

prefer ⊶ /prɪˈfɜː(r)/ ***verb*** [T] (**preferring; preferred**) ~ **sth (to sth)**; ~ **to do sth**; ~ **doing sth** (not used in the continuous tenses) to choose sth rather than sth else; to like sth better: *Would you prefer tea or coffee?* ◇ *Marianne prefers not to walk home on her own at night.* ◇ *My parents would prefer me to study law at university.*

preferable /ˈprefrəbl/ ***adj.*** ~ **(to sth/doing sth)** better or more suitable: *Going anywhere is preferable to staying at home for the weekend.*

preferably /ˈprefrəbli/ ***adv.*** used to show which person or thing would be better or preferred, if you are given a choice: *Give me a ring tonight – preferably after 7 o'clock.*

preference ⊶ /ˈprefrəns/ ***noun*** **1** [C, U] a ~ **(for sth)** an interest in or desire for one thing more than another: *What you wear is entirely a matter of* ***personal preference****.* ◇ *Please list your choices* ***in order of preference*** (= put the things you want most first on the list). **2** [U] special treatment that you give to one person or group rather than to others: *When allocating accommodation, we will* ***give preference to*** *families with young children.*

preferential /ˌprefəˈrenʃl/ ***adj.*** (only *before* a noun) giving or showing special treatment to one person or group rather than to others: *I don't see why he should get* ***preferential treatment*** *– I've worked here just as long as he has!*

prefix /ˈpriːfɪks/ ***noun*** [C] (LANGUAGE) a letter or group of letters that you put at the beginning of a word to change its meaning ➲ look at **affix**[2], **suffix**

pregnancy /ˈpregnənsi/ ***noun*** (*pl.* **pregnancies**) [U, C] (HEALTH) the state of being pregnant

pregnant ⊶ /ˈpregnənt/ ***adj.*** (HEALTH) (used about a woman or female animal) having a baby developing in her body: *Liz is five months pregnant.* ◇ *to get pregnant*

prehensile /prɪˈhensaɪl/ ***adj.*** (BIOLOGY) (used about part of an animal's body) able to hold things: *the monkey's prehensile tail* ➲ picture on **page 28**

prehistoric /ˌpriːhɪˈstɒrɪk/ ***adj.*** (HISTORY) from the time in history before events were written down

prejudice[1] /ˈpredʒudɪs/ ***noun*** [C,U] ~ **(against sb/sth)** a strong unreasonable feeling of not liking or trusting sb/sth, especially when it is based on their or its race, religion or sex: *a victim of* ***racial prejudice***

prejudice[2] /ˈpredʒudɪs/ ***verb*** [T] **1** ~ **sb (against sb/sth)** to influence sb so that they have an unreasonable or unfair opinion about sb/sth: *The newspaper stories had prejudiced the jury against him.* **2** to have a harmful effect on sb/sth: *Continuing to live with her violent father may prejudice the child's welfare.*

prejudiced /ˈpredʒədɪst/ ***adj.*** not liking or trusting sb/sth for no other reason than their race, religion or sex

preliminary[1] AW /prɪˈlɪmɪnəri/ ***adj.*** coming or happening before sth else that is more important

preliminary[2] AW /prɪˈlɪmɪnəri/ ***noun*** [C, usually pl.] (*pl.* **preliminaries**) an action or event that is done before and in preparation for another event

prelude /ˈpreljuːd/ ***noun*** [C] **1** (MUSIC) a short piece of music, especially an introduction to a longer piece **2** (*written*) ~ **(to sth)** an action or event that happens before sth else or that forms an introduction to sth

premature /ˈpremətʃə(r); ˌpreməˈtʃʊə(r)/ ***adj.*** **1** happening before the normal or expected time: *Her baby was premature* (= born before the expected time). **2** acting or happening too soon: *I think our decision was premature. We should have thought about it for longer.* ▶ **prematurely** ***adv.***

premeditated /ˌpriːˈmedɪteɪtɪd/ ***adj.*** (LAW) (used about a crime) planned in advance

premier[1] /ˈpremiə(r)/ ***adj.*** (only *before* a noun) most important; best: *a premier chef* ◇ *the Premier Division* (= in football)

premier[2] /ˈpremiə(r)/ ***noun*** [C] (POLITICS) (used especially in newspapers) the leader of the government of a country (**prime minister**)

premiere /ˈpremieə(r)/ ***noun*** [C] (ARTS AND MEDIA) the first public performance of a play, film, etc.

premises ⊶ /ˈpremɪsɪz/ ***noun*** [pl.] the building and the land around it that a business owns or uses: *Smoking is not allowed* ***on the premises****.* ➲ note at **building**

premium /ˈpriːmiəm/ ***noun*** [C] **1** an amount of money that you pay regularly to a company for insurance against accidents, damage, etc.: *a monthly premium of £25* **2** an extra payment: *You must pay a premium for express delivery.*

premolar /priːˈməʊlə(r)/ ***noun*** [C] (ANATOMY) one of the eight teeth near the back of your mouth between the MOLARS and the CANINES ➲ look at **canine**, **incisor**, **molar** ➲ picture at **tooth**

premonition /ˌpriːməˈnɪʃn; ˌprem-/ ***noun*** [C] a ~ **(of sth)** a feeling that sth unpleasant is going to happen in the future: *a premonition of disaster*

prenatal /ˌpriːˈneɪtl/ ***adj.*** (*especially AmE*) = ANTENATAL ➲ look at **post-natal**

preoccupation /priˌɒkjuˈpeɪʃn/ ***noun*** [U, C] ~ **(with sth)** the state of thinking and/or worrying continuously about sth: *She was irritated by his preoccupation with money.*

preoccupied /priˈɒkjupaɪd/ ***adj.*** ~ **(with sth)** not paying attention to sb/sth because you are thinking or worrying about sb/sth else ➲ look at **occupied**

preoccupy /priˈɒkjupaɪ/ ***verb*** [T] (*pres. part.* **preoccupying**; *3rd person sing. pres.* **preoccupies**; *pt, pp* **preoccupied**) to fill sb's mind so that they do not think about anything else; to worry

ˌ**pre-ˈpacked** (*also* ˌ**pre-ˈpackaged**) ***adj.*** (used about goods, especially food) put into packages before being sent to shops to be sold: *pre-packed sandwiches*

prepaid /ˌpriːˈpeɪd/ ***adj.*** paid for in advance: *a prepaid envelope is enclosed* (= so you do not have to pay the cost of sending a letter)

preparation ⊶ /ˌprepəˈreɪʃn/ ***noun*** **1** [U] getting sb/sth ready: *The team has been training hard* ***in preparation for*** *the big game.* ◇ *exam preparation* **2** [C, usually pl.] ~ **(for sth/to do sth)** something that you do to get ready for sth: *We started to* ***make preparations*** *for the wedding six months ago.*

preparatory /prɪˈpærətri/ ***adj.*** done in order to get ready for sth

pre'paratory school (*also* **'prep school**) ***noun*** [C] (EDUCATION) **1** (in Britain) a private school for children between the ages of 7 and 13 ➲ look at **public school 2** (in the US) a school, usually a private one, that prepares students for college

prepare ⊶ /prɪ'peə(r)/ ***verb*** [I,T] ~ (sb/sth) (for sb/sth) to get ready or to make sb/sth ready: *Bo helped me prepare for the exam.* ◇ *The course prepares foreign students for studying at university.* ◇ *to prepare a meal*

IDM **be prepared for sth** to be ready for sth difficult or unpleasant

be prepared to do sth to be ready and happy to do sth: *I am not prepared to stay here and be insulted.*

preponderance /prɪ'pɒndərəns/ ***noun*** [sing.] if there is a **preponderance** of one type of people or things in a group, there are more of them than others SYN **predominance**

preponderant /prɪ'pɒndərənt/ ***adj.*** (*formal*) (usually used *before* a noun) larger in number or more important than other people or things in a group

preposition /ˌprepə'zɪʃn/ ***noun*** [C] (LANGUAGE) a word or phrase that is used before a noun or pronoun to show place, time, direction, etc.: *'In', 'for', 'to' and 'out of' are all prepositions.*

preposterous /prɪ'pɒstərəs/ ***adj.*** silly; ridiculous; not to be taken seriously

'prep school ***noun*** [C] = PREPARATORY SCHOOL

prerequisite /ˌpriː'rekwəzɪt/ ***noun*** [C] **a ~ (for/of sth)** something that is necessary for sth else to happen or exist

prerogative /prɪ'rɒgətɪv/ ***noun*** [C] a special right that sb/sth has: *It is the Prime Minister's prerogative to fix the date of the election.*

Pres. ***abbr.*** President

prescribe /prɪ'skraɪb/ ***verb*** [T] **1** (HEALTH) to say what medicine or treatment sb should have: *Can you prescribe something for my cough please, doctor?* **2** (*formal*) (used about a person or an organization with authority) to say that sth must be done: *The law prescribes that the document must be signed in the presence of two witnesses.*

prescription /prɪ'skrɪpʃn/ ***noun*** [C,U] (HEALTH) a paper on which a doctor has written the name of the medicine that you need. You take your **prescription** to the CHEMIST'S and get the medicine there: *a prescription for sleeping pills* ◇ *Some medicines are only available* ***on prescription*** (= with a prescription from a doctor).

presence ⊶ /'prezns/ ***noun*** **1** [U] the fact of being in a particular place: *He apologized to her* ***in the presence of*** *the whole family.* ◇ *an experiment to test for the presence of oxygen* OPP **absence 2** [sing.] a number of soldiers or police officers who are in a place for a special reason: *There was a huge police presence at the demonstration.*

present¹ ⊶ /'preznt/ ***adj.*** **1** (only *before* a noun) existing or happening now: *We hope to overcome our present difficulties very soon.* **2** (not before a noun) being in a particular place: *There were 200 people present at the meeting.* OPP **absent**

IDM **the present day** modern times: *In some countries traditional methods of farming have survived to the present day.*

present² ⊶ /'preznt/ ***noun*** **1** [C] something that you give to sb or receive from sb SYN **gift**: *a birthday/wedding/leaving/Christmas present* **2** (usually **the present**) [sing.] the time now: *We live* ***in the present*** *but we must learn from the past.* ◇ *I'm rather busy* ***at present****. Can I call you back later?* **3 the present** [sing.] = THE PRESENT TENSE

IDM **for the moment/present** → MOMENT

present³ ⊶ /prɪ'zent/ ***verb*** [T] **1** ~ **sb with sth**; ~ **sth (to sb)** to give sth to sb, especially at a formal ceremony: *All the dancers were presented with flowers.* ◇ *Flowers were presented to all the dancers.* **2** ~ **sth (to sb)** to show sth that you have prepared to people: *Good teachers try to present their material in an interesting way.* **3** ~ **sb with sth**; ~ **sth (to sb)** to give sb sth that has to be dealt with: *Learning English presented no problem to him.* ◇ *The manager presented us with a bill for the broken chair.* **4** (ARTS AND MEDIA) to introduce a television or radio programme **5** (ARTS AND MEDIA) to show a play, etc. to the public: *The Theatre Royal is presenting a new production of 'Ghosts'.* **6** ~ **sb (to sb)** to introduce sb to a person in a formal ceremony: *The teams were presented to the President before the game.*

presentable /prɪ'zentəbl/ ***adj.*** good enough to be seen by people you do not know well

presentation ⊶ /ˌprezn'teɪʃn/ ***noun*** **1** [C,U] the act of giving or showing sth, especially a new product or idea, or a piece of work, to sb: *The head will now* ***make a presentation*** *to the winners of the competition.* **2** [U] the way in which sth is shown, explained, offered, etc. to people: *Untidy presentation of your work may lose you marks.* **3** [C] a meeting at which sth, especially a new product or idea, or piece of work, is shown or explained to a group of people: *Each student has to* ***give a*** *short* ***presentation*** *on a subject of his/her choice.* **4** [C] a formal ceremony at which a prize, etc. is given to sb

the ˌpresent 'day ***noun*** [sing.] the situation that exists in the world now, rather than in the past or the future: *a study of European drama, from Ibsen* ***to the present day*** ▶ **ˌpresent-'day** ***adj.*** (only *before* a noun): *present-day fashions* ◇ *present-day America*

presenter /prɪ'zentə(r)/ ***noun*** [C] (ARTS AND MEDIA) a person who introduces a television or radio programme

presently /'prezntli/ ***adv.*** **1** soon; shortly: *I'll be finished presently.* **2** (*written*) after a short time: *Presently I heard the car door shut.* **3** (*especially AmE*) now; currently: *The management are presently discussing the matter.*

ˌpresent 'participle ***noun*** [C] (LANGUAGE) the form of the verb that ends in *-ing*

the ˌpresent 'perfect ***noun*** [sing.] (LANGUAGE) the form of a verb that expresses an action done in a time period from the past to the present, formed with the present tense of *have* and the past participle of the verb: *'I've finished', 'She hasn't arrived' and 'I've been studying' are all* ***in the present perfect***.

the ˌpresent 'tense ***noun*** [C] (*also* **the present** [sing.]) (LANGUAGE) the tense of the verb that you use when you are talking about what is happening or what exists now

preservative /prɪ'zɜːvətɪv/ ***noun*** [C,U] a substance that is used for keeping food, etc. in good condition

preserve ⊶ /prɪ'zɜːv/ ***verb*** [T] to keep sth safe or in good condition: *They've managed to preserve most of the wall paintings in the caves.* ▶ **preservation** /ˌprezə'veɪʃn/ ***noun*** [U]

preside /prɪ'zaɪd/ ***verb*** [I] to be in charge of a discussion, meeting, etc.

PHR V **preside over sth** to be in control of or responsible for sth

presidency /ˈprezɪdənsi/ ***noun*** (*pl.* **presidencies**) **1 the presidency** [sing.] (POLITICS) the position of being president **2** [C] the period of time that sb is president

president ⊶ /ˈprezɪdənt/ ***noun*** [C] **1** (*also* **President**) (POLITICS) the leader of a REPUBLIC: *the President of France ◇ the US President* **2** the person with the highest position in some organizations ▶ **presidential** /ˌprezɪˈdenʃl/ ***adj.***: *presidential elections*

press[1] ⊶ /pres/ ***noun*** **1** (usually **the press**) [sing., with sing. or pl. verb] (ARTS AND MEDIA) newspapers and the journalists who work for them: *The story has been reported on TV and* ***in the press****. ◇ the local/national press ◇ The press support/supports government policy.* **2** [sing., U] (ARTS AND MEDIA) what or the amount that is written about sb/sth in newspapers: *This company has had* ***a bad press*** *recently. ◇ The strike got very little press.* **3** [C,U] a machine for printing books, newspapers, etc.; the process of printing them: *All details were correct at the time of* ***going to press****.* **4** [C] a business that prints books, etc.: *Oxford University Press* **5** [C] an act of pushing sth firmly: ***Give that button a press*** *and see what happens.*

press[2] ⊶ /pres/ ***verb*** **1** [I,T] to push sth firmly: *Just press that button and the door will open. ◇ He pressed the lid firmly shut.* **2** [T] to put weight onto sth, for example in order to get juice out of it: *to press grapes* **3** [T] to make a piece of clothing smooth by using an iron: *This shirt needs pressing.* **4** [T] to hold sb/sth firmly in a loving way: *She pressed the photo to her chest.* **5** [I] **~ across, against, around, etc. (sth)** (used about people) to move in a particular direction by pushing: *The crowd pressed against the wall of policemen.* **6** [I,T] **~ (sb) (for sth/to do sth)** to try to persuade or force sb to do sth: *I pressed them to stay for dinner. ◇ to press sb for an answer* **7** [T] to express or repeat sth in an urgent way: *I don't want to press the point, but you still owe me money.*

IDM **be hard pressed/pushed/put to do sth** → HARD[2]

be pressed for sth to not have enough of sth: *I must hurry. I'm really pressed for time.*

bring/press charges (against sb) → CHARGE[1]

PHR V **press ahead/forward/on (with sth)** to continue doing sth even though it is difficult or hard work: *They pressed on with the building work in spite of the bad weather.*

ˈ**press conference** ***noun*** [C] (ARTS AND MEDIA) a meeting when a famous or important person answers questions from newspaper and television journalists: *to hold a press conference*

pressing /ˈpresɪŋ/ ***adj.*** that must be dealt with immediately; urgent

ˈ**press release** ***noun*** [C] (ARTS AND MEDIA) an official statement made to journalists by a large organization, a political party or a government department: *The company issued a press release to end speculation about its future.*

ˈ**press stud** ***noun*** [C] = POPPER

ˈ**press-up** (*AmE* ˈ**push-up**) ***noun*** [C] a type of exercise in which you lie on your front on the floor and push your body up with your arms: *I do 50 press-ups every morning.* ➲ picture at **sit-up**

pressure ⊶ /ˈpreʃə(r)/ ***noun*** **1** [U] the force that is produced when you press on or against sth: *Apply pressure to the cut and it will stop bleeding. ◇ The pressure of the water caused the dam to crack.* **2** [C,U] (PHYSICS) the force that a gas or liquid has when it is contained inside sth: *high/low blood pressure ◇ You should check your tyre pressures regularly.* **3** [C,U] worries or difficulties that you have because you have too much to deal with; stress: *financial pressures ◇ I find it difficult to cope with pressure at work.* ▶ **pressure** ***verb*** [T] = PRESSURIZE

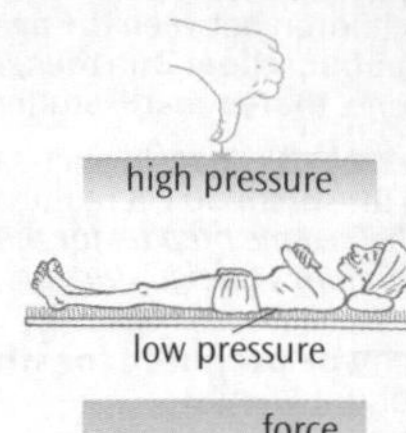

pressure = $\frac{\text{force}}{\text{area}}$

IDM **put pressure on sb (to do sth)** to force sb to do sth: *The press is putting pressure on him to resign.*

under pressure 1 being forced to do sth: *Anna was under pressure from her parents to leave school and get a job.* **2** worried or in difficulty because you have too much to deal with: *I perform poorly under pressure, so I hate exams.* **3** (used about liquid or gas) contained inside sth or sent somewhere using force: *Water is forced out through the hose under pressure.*

ˈ**pressure cooker** ***noun*** [C] a strong metal pot with a tight lid, that cooks food quickly using steam under high pressure

ˈ**pressure group** ***noun*** [C, with sing. or pl. verb] (POLITICS) a group of people who are trying to influence what a government or other organization does

pressurize (also **-ise**) /ˈpreʃəraɪz/ (*also* **pressure**) ***verb*** [T] **~ sb (into sth/doing sth)** to use force or influence to make sb do sth: *Some workers were pressurized into taking early retirement.*

pressurized (also **-ised**) /ˈpreʃəraɪzd/ ***adj.*** (used about air in an aircraft) kept at the pressure at which people can breathe

prestige /preˈstiːʒ/ ***noun*** [U] the respect and admiration that people feel for a person because they have a high social position or have been very successful ▶ **prestigious** /preˈstɪdʒəs/ ***adj.***: *a prestigious prize/school/job*

presumably ⊶ AW /prɪˈzjuːməbli/ ***adv.*** I imagine; I suppose: *Presumably this rain means the match will be cancelled?*

presume AW /prɪˈzjuːm/ ***verb*** [T] to think that sth is true even if you do not know for sure; to suppose: *The house looks empty so I presume they are away on holiday.* ▶ **presumption** AW /prɪˈzʌmpʃn/ ***noun*** [C]

presumptuous /prɪˈzʌmptʃuəs/ ***adj.*** confident that sth will happen or that sb will do sth without making sure first, in a way that annoys people

presuppose /ˌpriːsəˈpəʊz/ ***verb*** [T] (*formal*) **1** to accept sth as true or existing and act on that basis, before it has been shown to be true: *Teachers sometimes presuppose a fairly high level of knowledge by the students.* SYN **presume 2** to depend on sth in order to exist or be true: *His argument presupposes that it does not matter who is in power.*

pretence (*AmE* **pretense**) /prɪˈtens/ ***noun*** [U, sing.] an action that makes people believe sth that is not true: *She was unable to keep up the pretence that she loved him.*

IDM **on/under false pretences** → FALSE

pretend ⊶ /prɪˈtend/ ***verb*** [I,T] **1** to behave in a particular way in order to make other people believe sth that is not true: *You can't just pretend* *that the problem doesn't exist.* ◇ *Paul's not really asleep. He's just pretending.* **2** (used especially about children) to imagine that sth is true as part of a game: *The kids were under the bed pretending to be snakes.*

pretentious /prɪˈtenʃəs/ ***adj.*** trying to appear more serious or important than you really are

pretext /ˈpriːtekst/ ***noun*** [C] a reason that you give for doing sth that is not the real reason: *Tariq left* ***on the pretext of*** *having an appointment at the dentist's.* ➲ note at **reason[1]**

pretty[1] 🔑 /ˈprɪti/ ***adj.*** (**prettier**; **prettiest**) attractive and pleasant to look at or hear: *a pretty girl/smile/dress/garden/name* ▶ **prettily** ***adv.***: *The room is prettily decorated.* ▶ **prettiness** ***noun*** [U]

pretty[2] 🔑 /ˈprɪti/ ***adv.*** (*informal*) quite; fairly: *The film was pretty good but not fantastic.* ◇ *I'm pretty certain that Alex will agree.* ➲ note at **rather**

IDM **pretty much/nearly/well** almost; very nearly: *I won't be long. I've pretty well finished.*

prevail /prɪˈveɪl/ ***verb*** [I] **1** to exist or be common in a particular place or at a particular time **2** (*formal*) ~ (**against/over sb/sth**) to win or be accepted, especially after a fight or discussion: *In the end justice prevailed and the men were set free.*

prevailing /prɪˈveɪlɪŋ/ ***adj.*** (only *before* a noun) **1** existing or most common at a particular time: *the prevailing climate of opinion* **2** (GEOGRAPHY) (used about the wind) most common in a particular area: *The prevailing wind is from the south-west.*

prevalent /ˈprevələnt/ ***adj.*** (*formal*) most common in a particular place at a particular time: *The prevalent atmosphere was one of fear.* ▶ **prevalence** /-əns/ ***noun*** [U]

prevent 🔑 /prɪˈvent/ ***verb*** [T] ~ **sb/sth (from) (doing sth)** to stop sth happening or to stop sb doing sth: *This accident could have been prevented.* ◇ *Her parents tried to prevent her from going to live with her boyfriend.* ▶ **prevention** ***noun*** [U]: *accident/crime prevention*

preventable /prɪˈventəbl/ ***adj.*** that can be prevented: *Many accidents are preventable.*

preventive /prɪˈventɪv/ (*also* **preventative** /prɪˈventətɪv/) ***adj.*** intended to stop or prevent sth from happening: *preventative medicine*

preview /ˈpriːvjuː/ ***noun*** [C] (ARTS AND MEDIA) a chance to see a play, film, etc. before it is shown to the general public

previous 🔑 AW /ˈpriːviəs/ ***adj.*** coming or happening before or earlier: *Do you have previous experience of this type of work?* ▶ **previously** AW ***adv.***: *Before I moved to Spain I had previously worked in Italy.*

prey[1] /preɪ/ ***noun*** [U] an animal or bird that is killed and eaten by another animal or bird: *The eagle is a bird of prey* (=it kills and eats other birds or small animals).

prey[2] /preɪ/ ***verb***

IDM **prey on sb's mind** to cause sb to worry or think about sth: *The thought that he was responsible for the accident preyed on the train driver's mind.*

PHR V **prey on sth** (used about an animal or bird) to kill and eat other animals or birds: *Owls prey on mice and other small animals.*

COLLOCATIONS AND PATTERNS

A charge is the amount of money that you must pay for using something.
Is there a charge for parking here?
admission charges

You use **cost** when you are talking about paying for services or about prices in general, without mentioning an actual sum of money.
The cost of electricity is going up.
a steady rise in the cost of living

The **price** of something is the amount of money that you must pay in order to buy it.
A shop may **raise/increase, reduce/bring down** or **freeze** its prices.
The prices **rise/go up** or **fall/go down.**

price[1] 🔑 /praɪs/ ***noun*** **1** [C] the amount of money that you must pay in order to buy sth: *What's the price of petrol now?* ◇ *We can't afford to buy the car at that price.* ◇ *There's no price on* (=written on) *this jar of coffee.* **2** [sing.] unpleasant things that you have to experience in order to achieve sth or as a result of sth: *Sleepless nights are a small price to pay for having a baby.*

IDM **at a price** costing a lot of money or involving sth unpleasant

at any price even if the cost is very high or if it will have unpleasant results: *Richard was determined to succeed at any price.*

not at any price never; under no CIRCUMSTANCES

price[2] /praɪs/ ***verb*** [T] to fix the price of sth or to write the price on sth: *The books were all priced at between £5 and £10.* ▶ **pricing** ***noun*** [U]: *competitive pricing* ◇ *pricing policy*

priceless /ˈpraɪsləs/ ***adj.*** of very great value: *priceless jewels and antiques* ➲ look at **worthless**, **valuable**, **invaluable**

ˈ**price list** ***noun*** [C] a list of the prices of the goods that are on sale

pricey /ˈpraɪsi/ ***adj.*** (*informal*) expensive

prick[1] /prɪk/ ***verb*** [T] to make a small hole in sth or to cause sb pain with a sharp point: *She pricked her finger on a needle.*

IDM **prick up your ears** (used about an animal) to hold up the ears in order to listen carefully to sth: (*figurative*): *Mike pricked up his ears when he heard Emma's name mentioned.*

prick[2] /prɪk/ ***noun*** [C] the sudden pain that you feel when sth sharp goes into your skin

prickle[1] /ˈprɪkl/ ***noun*** [C] one of the sharp points on some plants and animals: *Hedgehogs are covered in prickles.* ➲ look at **spine**

prickle[2] /ˈprɪkl/ ***verb*** [I,T] to have or make sb/sth have an uncomfortable feeling on the skin: *His skin prickled with fear.*

prickly /ˈprɪkli/ ***adj.*** **1** covered with sharp points: *a prickly bush* **2** causing an uncomfortable feeling on the skin **3** (*informal*) (used about a person) easily made angry

pride[1] 🔑 /praɪd/ ***noun*** **1** [U, sing.] ~ (**in sth/doing sth**) the feeling of pleasure that you have when you or people who are close to you do sth good or own sth good: *I* ***take a*** *great* ***pride*** *in my work.* ◇ *Her parents watched with pride as Milena went up to collect her prize.* ◇ *You should* ***feel pride*** *in your achievement.* **2** [U] the respect that you have for yourself: *You'll hurt his pride if you refuse to accept the present.* **3** [U] the feeling that you are better than other people **4** [sing.] **the ~ of sth/sb** a person or thing that is very important or of great value to sth/sb: *The new stadium was the pride of the whole town.* ➲ adjective **proud**

IDM **sb's pride and joy** a thing or person that gives sb great pleasure or satisfaction

pride² /praɪd/ *verb*
PHRV **pride yourself on sth/doing sth** to feel pleased about sth good or clever that you can do: *Fabio prides himself on his ability to cook.*

priest /priːst/ *noun* [C] (RELIGION) a person who performs religious ceremonies in some religions

prim /prɪm/ *adj.* (used about a person) always behaving in a careful or formal way and easily shocked by anything that is rude ▶ **primly** *adv.*

primacy AW /ˈpraɪməsi/ *noun* (*formal*) **1** [U] the fact of being the most important person or thing: *a belief in the primacy of the family* **2** [C] (*pl.* **-ies**) (RELIGION) the position of an ARCHBISHOP

prima donna /ˌpriːmə ˈdɒnə/ *noun* [C] **1** (ARTS AND MEDIA) the main woman singer in an OPERA performance or an OPERA company **2** a person who thinks they are very important because they are good at sth, and who behaves badly when they do not get what they want

primal /ˈpraɪml/ *adj.* (only *before* a noun) (*formal*) connected with the earliest origins of life; very basic SYN **primeval**: *the primal hunter-gatherer*

primarily AW /ˈpraɪmərəli; praɪˈmerəli/ *adv.* more than anything else; mainly: *The course is aimed primarily at beginners.*

primary¹ AW /ˈpraɪməri/ *adj.* **1** most important; main: *Smoking is one of the primary causes of lung cancer.* **2** (*especially BrE*) (EDUCATION) connected with the education of children between about five and eleven years old: *primary teachers* ➲ look at **primary school**

primary² AW /ˈpraɪməri/ (*also* **primary eˈlection**) *noun* [C] (*pl.* **primaries**) (*AmE*) (POLITICS) an election in which people from a particular area vote to choose a CANDIDATE (=a person who will represent the party) for a future important election

ˌprimary ˈcolour *noun* [C] any of the colours red, yellow or blue. You can make any other colour by mixing primary colours in different ways.

ˈprimary school *noun* [C] (*BrE*) (EDUCATION) a school for children between the ages of 5 and 11 ➲ look at **secondary school**

ˈprimary source *noun* [C] a document, etc. that contains information obtained by research or observation, not taken from other books, etc. ➲ look at **secondary source**

primate /ˈpraɪmeɪt/ *noun* [C] (BIOLOGY) any animal that belongs to the group that includes humans, MONKEYS and APES ➲ picture on **page 28**

prime¹ AW /praɪm/ *adj.* (only *before* a noun) **1** main; the first example of sth that sb would think of or choose: *She is a prime candidate as the next team captain.* ➲ note at **main¹** **2** of very good quality; best: *prime pieces of beef* **3** having all the typical qualities: *That's* ***a prime example*** *of what I was talking about.*

prime² AW /praɪm/ *noun* [sing.] the time when sb is strongest, most beautiful, most successful, etc.: *Several of the team are* ***past their prime.*** ◇ ***In his prime,*** *he was a fine actor.* ◇ *to be* ***in the prime of life***

prime³ AW /praɪm/ *verb* [T] ~ **sb (for/with sth)** to give sb information in order to prepare them for sth: *The politician had been well primed with all the facts before the interview.*

ˌprime ˈminister (also **ˌPrime ˈMinister**) *noun* [C] (*abbr.* **PM**) (POLITICS) the main minister and leader of the government in some countries

ˌprime ˈnumber *noun* [C] (MATHEMATICS) a number that can be divided exactly only by itself and 1, for example 7, 17 and 41

primeval (also **primaeval**) /praɪˈmiːvl/ *adj.* (HISTORY) from the earliest period of the history of the world, very ancient

primitive /ˈprɪmətɪv/ *adj.* **1** very simple and not developed: *The washing facilities in the camp were very primitive.* **2** (only *before* a noun) connected with a very early stage in the development of humans or animals: *Primitive man lived in caves and hunted wild animals.*

primitivism /ˈprɪmɪtɪvɪzəm/ *noun* [U] (ARTS AND MEDIA) a belief that simple forms and ideas are the most valuable, expressed as a philosophy or in art or literature

primrose /ˈprɪmrəʊz/ *noun* [C] a yellow spring flower

prince /prɪns/ *noun* [C] **1** a son or other close male relative of a king or queen **2** (POLITICS) the male ruler of a small country

princess /ˌprɪnˈses/ *noun* [C] **1** a daughter or other close female relative of a king or queen **2** the wife of a prince

principal¹ AW /ˈprɪnsəpl/ *adj.* (only *before* a noun) most important; main: *the principal characters in a play* ➲ note at **main¹** ▶ **principally** AW /-pli/ *adv.*: *Our products are designed principally for the European market.*

principal² AW /ˈprɪnsəpl/ *noun* [C] (EDUCATION) the head of some schools, colleges, etc.

principality /ˌprɪnsɪˈpæləti/ *noun* [C] (*pl.* **principalities**) (GEOGRAPHY) a country that is ruled by a prince: *the principality of Andorra*

principle AW /ˈprɪnsəpl/ *noun* **1** [C,U] a rule for good behaviour, based on what a person believes is right: *He doesn't eat meat* ***on principle.*** ◇ *She refuses to wear fur. It's* ***a matter of principle*** *with her.* **2** [C] a basic general law, rule or idea: *The system works* ***on the principle that*** *heat rises.* ◇ *The course teaches the basic principles of car maintenance.*
IDM **in principle** in general, but possibly not in detail: *His proposal sounds fine in principle, but there are a few points I'm not happy about.*

principled AW /ˈprɪnsəpld/ *adj.* **1** having strong beliefs about what is right and wrong; based on strong beliefs: *a principled woman* OPP **unprincipled** **2** based on rules or truths: *a principled approach to language teaching*

print¹ /prɪnt/ *verb* **1** [I,T] to put words, pictures, etc. onto paper by using a special machine: *How much did it cost to print the posters?* **2** [T] to produce books, newspapers, etc. in this way: *50 000 copies of the textbook were printed.* **3** [T] to include sth in a book, newspaper, etc.: *The newspaper should not have printed the photographs of the crash.* **4** [T] to make a photograph from a piece of negative film **5** [I,T] to write with letters that are not joined together: *Please print your name clearly at the top of the paper.* **6** [T] to put a pattern onto cloth, paper, etc.
PHRV **print (sth) out** to print information from a computer onto paper: *I'll just print out this file.*

print² /prɪnt/ *noun* **1** [U] the letters, words, etc. in a book, newspaper, etc.: *The print is too small for me to read without my glasses.* **2** [U] used to refer to the business of producing newspapers, books, etc.: *the print unions/workers* **3** [C] a mark that is made by sth pressing onto sth else: *The police are searching the room for fingerprints.* ◇ *footprints in the* *snow* **4** [C] a picture that was made by printing **5** [C] a photograph (when it has been printed from a negative): *I ordered an extra set of prints for my friends.*

IDM **in print 1** (used about a book) still available from the company that published it **2** (used about a person's work) published in a book, newspaper, etc. **out of print** (used about a book) no longer available from the company that published it; not being printed any more

printer /'prɪntə(r)/ ***noun*** [C] **1** a person or company that prints books, newspapers, etc. **2** (COMPUTING) a machine that prints out information from a computer onto paper: *a laser printer*

printing /'prɪntɪŋ/ ***noun*** **1** [U] the act of producing letters, pictures, patterns, etc. on sth by pressing a surface covered with ink against it: *the invention of printing* ◇ *colour printing* **2** [C] the act of printing a number of copies of a book at one time: *The book is in its sixth printing.* **3** [U] a type of writing when you write all the letters separately and do not join them together

'**printing press** (*also* **press**) ***noun*** [C] a machine that is used for printing books, newspapers, etc.

printmaking /'prɪntmeɪkɪŋ/ ***noun*** [U] (ART) the art of making pictures or designs by pressing a surface covered with ink onto paper or other material

printout /'prɪntaʊt/ ***noun*** [C,U] (COMPUTING) information from a computer that is printed onto paper

prior AW /'praɪə(r)/ ***adj.*** (only *before* a noun) coming before or earlier

prioritize (also **-ise**) AW /praɪ'ɒrətaɪz/ ***verb*** **1** [I,T] to put tasks, problems, etc. in order of importance, so that you can deal with the most important first: *You should make a list of all the jobs you have to do and prioritize them.* **2** [T] (*formal*) to treat sth as being more important than other things: *The organization was formed to prioritize the needs of older people.*

priority AW /praɪ'ɒrəti/ ***noun*** (*pl.* **priorities**) **1** [U] ~ (**over sb/sth**) the state of being more important than sb/sth or of coming before sb/sth else: *We **give priority** to families with small children.* ◇ *Emergency cases **take priority** over other patients in hospital.* **2** [C] something that is most important or that you must do before anything else: *Our **top priority** is to get food and water to the refugee camps.* ◇ *I'll **make it** my **priority** to sort out your problem.*

'**prior to** ***prep.*** (*formal*) before: *Passengers are asked to report to the check-in desk prior to departure.*

prise /praɪz/ (*especially AmE* **prize**, **pry**) ***verb*** [T] ~ **sth off, apart, open, etc.** to use force to open sth, remove a lid, etc.: *He prised the door open with an iron bar.*

prism /'prɪzəm/ ***noun*** [C] **1** (GEOMETRY) a solid object with ends that are parallel and of the same size and shape, and with sides whose opposite edges are equal and parallel ➲ picture at **solid 2** (PHYSICS) a transparent glass or plastic object which separates light that passes through it into the seven different colours

prison /'prɪzn/ (*also* **jail**) ***noun*** [C,U] (LAW) a building where criminals are kept as a punishment: *The terrorists were **sent to prison** for twenty-five years.* ◇ *He will be **released from prison** next month.* ➲ look at **imprison**, **jail**

prisoner /'prɪznə(r)/ ***noun*** [C] (LAW) a person who is being kept in prison: *a political prisoner*

prisms

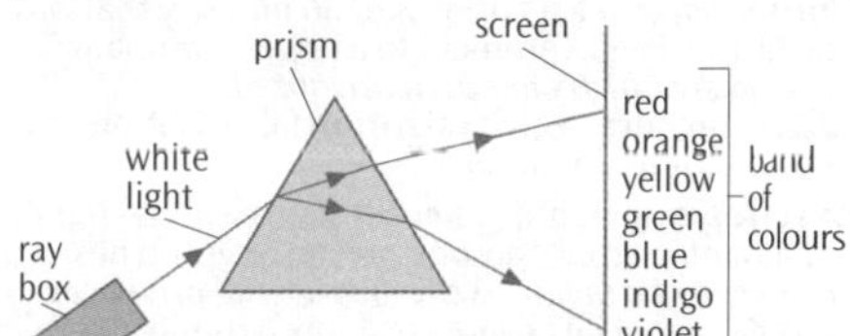

white light can be split into its components using a prism

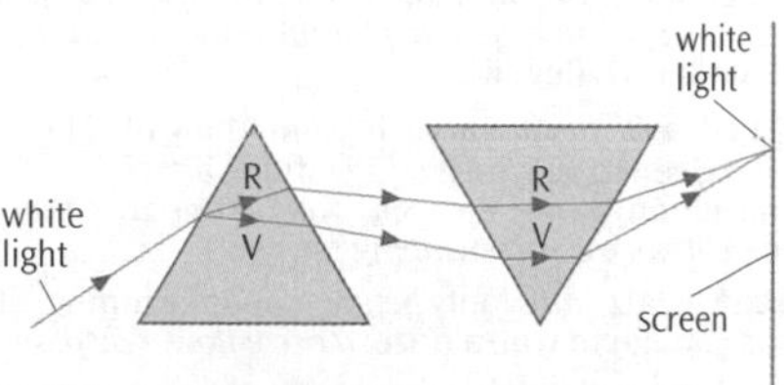

splitting and recombining the colours in white light

R = red V = violet

ˌ**prisoner of 'war** ***noun*** [C] (*pl.* **prisoners of war**) (*abbr.* **POW**) a soldier, etc. who is caught by the enemy during a war and who is kept in prison until the end of the war

privacy /'prɪvəsi/ ***noun*** [U] **1** the state of being alone and not watched or disturbed by other people: *There is not much privacy in large hospital wards.* **2** the state of being free from the attention of the public: *The actress claimed that the photographs were an **invasion of privacy**.*

private¹ /'praɪvət/ ***adj.*** **1** belonging to or intended for one particular person or group and not to be shared by others: *This is private property. You may not park here.* ◇ *a private letter/conversation* **2** not connected with work or business: *He never discusses his **private life** with his colleagues at work.* **3** owned, done or organized by a person or company, and not by the government: *a private hospital/school* (=you pay to go there) ◇ *a private detective* (=one who is not in the police) ➲ look at **public 4** with no one else present: *I would like a private interview with the personnel manager.* **5** not wanting to share thoughts and feelings with other people: *He's a very private person.* **6** (used about classes, lessons, etc.) given by a teacher to one student or a small group for payment: *Claire gives private English lessons at her house.* ▶ **privately** ***adv.***

private² /'praɪvət/ ***noun*** [C] a soldier of the lowest level

IDM **in private** with no one else present: *May I speak to you in private?*

ˌ**private 'school** (*also* **indeˌpendent 'school**) ***noun*** [C] (EDUCATION) a school that receives no money from the government and where the education of the students is paid for by their parents ➲ look at **public school**, **state school**

the ˌprivate 'sector ***noun*** [sing.] (ECONOMICS) the part of the economy of a country that is not under the direct control of the government: *to work in the private sector* ➲ look at **the public sector**

privatize (also **-ise**) /ˈpraɪvɪtaɪz/ *verb* [T] (BUSINESS) to sell a business or an industry that was owned by the government to a private company: *The water industry has been privatized.* OPP **nationalize** ▶ **privatization** (also **-isation**) /ˌpraɪvɪtaɪˈzeɪʃn/ *noun* [U]

privilege /ˈprɪvəlɪdʒ/ *noun* **1** [C,U] a special right or advantage that only one person or group has: *Prisoners who behave well* ***enjoy special privileges****.* **2** [sing.] a special advantage or opportunity that gives you great pleasure: *It was a great privilege to hear her sing.*

privileged /ˈprɪvəlɪdʒd/ *adj.* having an advantage or opportunity that most people do not have: *Only a* ***privileged few*** *are allowed to enter this room.* ◇ *I feel very privileged to be playing for the national team.* OPP **underprivileged**

prize¹ 🔑 /praɪz/ *noun* [C] something of value that is given to sb who is successful in a race, competition, game, etc.: *She won* ***first prize*** *in the competition.* ◇ *a prizewinning novel*

prize² /praɪz/ *adj.* (only *before* a noun) winning, or good enough to win, a prize: *a prize flower display*

prize³ /praɪz/ *verb* [T] to consider sth to be very valuable: *This picture is one of my most prized possessions.*

prize⁴ /praɪz/ (*especially AmE*) = PRISE

pro /prəʊ/ *noun* [C] (*pl.* **pros**) (*informal*) **1** (SPORT) a person who plays or teaches a sport for money: *a golf pro* **2** a person who has a lot of skill and experience SYN **professional**

IDM **the pros and cons** the reasons for and against doing sth: *We should consider all the pros and cons before reaching a decision.*

pro- /prəʊ/ *prefix* (used in adjectives) in favour of; supporting: *pro-democracy* ◇ *pro-European*

proactive /ˌprəʊˈæktɪv/ *adj.* controlling a situation by making things happen rather than waiting for things to happen and then reacting to them ➲ look at **reactive** ▶ **proactively** *adv.*

probability /ˌprɒbəˈbɪləti/ *noun* (*pl.* **probabilities**) **1** [U, sing.] how likely sth is to happen: *At that time there seemed little probability of success.* **2** [C] something that is likely to happen: *Closure of the factory now seems a probability.* **3** [C, U] (MATHEMATICS) a RATIO (= the relation between two numbers which shows how much bigger one quantity is than another) showing the chances that a particular thing will happen: *There is a 60% probability that the population will be infected with the disease.*

THESAURUS

Notice that **probable** and **likely** mean the same but are used differently: ***It's probable that*** *he will be late.* ◇ *He* ***is likely to*** *be late.*

probable 🔑 /ˈprɒbəbl/ *adj.* that you expect to happen or to be true; likely OPP **improbable** ➲ look at **possible**

probably 🔑 /ˈprɒbəbli/ *adv.* almost certainly: *I will phone next week, probably on Wednesday.*

probation /prəˈbeɪʃn/ *noun* [U] **1** (LAW) a system that allows sb who has committed a crime not to go to prison if they go to see an official (**a probation officer**) regularly for a fixed period of time: *Jamie is* ***on probation*** *for two years.* **2** a period of time at the start of a new job when you are tested to see if you are suitable: *a three-month probation period*

probe¹ /prəʊb/ *verb* [I,T] **1** ~ **(into sth)** to ask questions in order to find out secret or hidden information: *The newspapers are now probing into the President's past.* **2** to examine or look for sth, especially with a long thin instrument: *The doctor probed the cut for pieces of broken glass.* ▶ **probing** *adj.*: *to ask probing questions*

probe² /prəʊb/ *noun* [C] **1** the process of asking questions, collecting facts, etc. in order to find out hidden information about sth: *a police probe into illegal financial dealing* **2** (*also* **ˈspace probe**) (ASTRONOMY) a SPACECRAFT without people on board which obtains information and sends it back to earth **3** (HEALTH) a long thin metal tool used by doctors for examining inside the body **4** (TECHNICAL) a small device put inside sth and used by scientists to test sth or record information

problem 🔑 /ˈprɒbləm/ *noun* [C] **1** a thing that is difficult to deal with or to understand: *social/family/financial/technical problems* ◇ *You won't* ***solve the problem*** *if you ignore it.* ◇ *The company will* ***face problems*** *from unions if it sacks workers.* ◇ *It's going to* ***cause problems*** *if Donna brings her husband.* ◇ *I can't play because I've got* ***a problem with*** *my knee.* ◇ *'Can you fix this for me?' '****No problem.****'* ◇ *It's a great painting —* ***the problem is*** *I've got nowhere to put it.* **2** a question that you have to solve by thinking about it: *a maths/logic problem*

problematic /ˌprɒbləˈmætɪk/ (*also* **problematical** /-ɪkl/) *adj.* difficult to deal with or to understand; full of problems; not certain to be successful: *Finding replacement parts for such an old car could be problematic.* OPP **unproblematic**

pro bono /ˌprəʊ ˈbəʊnəʊ/ *adj.* (FINANCE) done without asking for payment

procaryote = PROKARYOTE

procedure 🔑 AW /prəˈsiːdʒə(r)/ *noun* **1** [C,U] the usual or correct way for doing sth: *What's the procedure for making a complaint?* **2** [C] (HEALTH) a medical operation: *to perform a routine surgical procedure* ▶ **procedural** AW /prəˈsiːdʒərəl/ *adj.* (*formal*): *procedural rules*

proceed 🔑 AW /prəˈsiːd/ *verb* [I] **1** (*formal*) to continue doing sth; to continue being done: *The building work was proceeding according to schedule.* **2** (*formal*) ~ **(with sth/to do sth)** to start doing the next thing after finishing the last one: *Once he had calmed down he proceeded to tell us what had happened.*

proceeding AW /prəˈsiːdɪŋ/ *noun* (*formal*) **1** [usually pl.] ~ **(against sb/for sth)** (LAW) the process of using a court to settle a disagreement or to deal with a complaint: *to start divorce proceedings* ◇ *to bring* ***legal proceedings*** *against sb* **2 proceedings** [pl.] an event or a series of actions: *The Mayor will open the proceedings at the City Hall tomorrow.*

proceeds AW /ˈprəʊsiːdz/ *noun* [pl.] ~ **(of/from sth)** money that you get when you sell sth: *The proceeds from the sale will go to charity.*

process¹ 🔑 AW /ˈprəʊses/ *noun* [C] **1** a series of actions that you do for a particular purpose: *We've just begun the complicated process of selling the house.* **2** a series of changes that happen naturally: *Mistakes are part of the learning process.*

IDM **in the process** while you are doing sth else: *We washed the dog yesterday – and we all got very wet in the process.*

in the process of sth/doing sth in the middle of doing sth: *They are in the process of moving house.*

process² 🔑 AW /ˈprəʊses/ ***verb*** [T] **1** to treat sth, for example with chemicals, in order to keep it, change it, etc.: *Cheese is processed so that it lasts longer.* ◇ *I sent two rolls of film away to be processed.* **2** to deal with information, for example on a computer: *It will take about ten days to process your application.* ◇ *data processing*

procession /prəˈseʃn/ ***noun*** [C,U] a number of people, vehicles, etc. that move slowly in a line, especially as part of a ceremony: *to walk* ***in procession*** ◇ *a funeral procession*

processor /ˈprəʊsesə(r)/ ***noun*** [C] **1** a machine or a person that processes things ➲ look at **food processor**, **word processor 2** (COMPUTING) a part of a computer that controls all the other parts of the system

proclaim /prəˈkleɪm/ ***verb*** [T] (*written*) to make sth known officially or publicly: *The day was proclaimed a national holiday.* ▶ **proclamation** /ˌprɒkləˈmeɪʃn/ ***noun*** [C,U]: *to make a proclamation of war*

procrastinate /prəʊˈkræstɪneɪt/ ***verb*** [I] (*formal*) to delay doing sth that you should do, usually because you do not want to do it ▶ **procrastination** /prəʊˌkræstɪˈneɪʃn/ ***noun*** [U]

procreate /ˈprəʊkrieɪt/ ***verb*** [I] (*formal*) (BIOLOGY) to produce children or baby animals SYN **reproduce** ▶ **procreation** /ˌprəʊkriˈeɪʃn/ ***noun*** [U]

procure /prəˈkjʊə(r)/ ***verb*** [T] (*written*) ~ **sth (for sb)** to obtain sth, especially with difficulty: *I managed to procure two tickets for the match.*

prod /prɒd/ ***verb*** [I,T] (**prodding**; **prodded**) to push or press sb/sth with your finger or a pointed object: (*figurative*) *Ruth works quite hard but she does need prodding occasionally.* ▶ **prod** ***noun*** [C]: *to give the fire a prod with a stick* ▶ **prodding** ***noun*** [U]

prodigious /prəˈdɪdʒəs/ ***adj.*** very large or powerful and surprising: *He seemed to have a prodigious amount of energy.*

prodigy /ˈprɒdədʒi/ ***noun*** [C] (*pl.* **prodigies**) a child who is unusually good at sth: *Mozart was a* ***child prodigy***. ➲ look at **genius**

produce¹ 🔑 /prəˈdjuːs/ ***verb*** [T] **1** to make sth to be sold, especially in large quantities: *The factory produces 20 000 cars a year.* SYN **manufacture** **2** to make sth by a natural process; to grow sth: *This region produces most of the country's wheat.* ◇ (*figurative*) *He's the greatest athlete this country has produced.* **3** to create sth using skill: *The children have produced some beautiful pictures for the exhibition.* ➲ note at **make¹** **4** to cause a particular effect or result: *Her remarks produced roars of laughter.* **5** to show sth so that sb else can look at or examine it: *to produce evidence in court* **6** (ARTS AND MEDIA) to be in charge of preparing a film, play, etc. so that it can be shown to the public: *She is producing 'Romeo and Juliet' at the local theatre.*

> WORD FAMILY
> **produce** *verb*
> **produce** *noun*
> **producer** *noun*
> **production** *noun*
> **productive** *adj.*
> (≠ **unproductive**)

produce² /ˈprɒdjuːs/ ***noun*** [U] food, etc. that is grown on a farm and sold: *fresh farm produce*

producer 🔑 /prəˈdjuːsə(r)/ ***noun*** [C] **1** (AGRICULTURE) a person, company or country that makes or grows sth: *Brazil is a major producer of coffee.* **2** (ARTS AND MEDIA) a person who deals with the business side of organizing a play, film, etc. **3** (ARTS AND MEDIA) a person who arranges for sb to make a programme for television or radio, or a record **4** (BIOLOGY) a living thing such as a green plant that makes its own food by PHOTOSYNTHESIS and is itself eaten as food by other living things ➲ picture at **food chain**

> **THESAURUS**
>
> **product**
>
> **goods • commodity • merchandise • produce • wares**
> These are all words for things that are produced to be sold.
> **product**: *to create/develop/launch a new product*
> **goods**: *electrical/leather goods*
> **commodity**: *rice, flour and other basic commodities*
> **merchandise**: *official Olympic merchandise*
> **produce**: *fresh local produce*
> **wares**: *traders displaying their wares*

product 🔑 /ˈprɒdʌkt/ ***noun*** [C] **1** something that is made in a factory or that is formed naturally: *dairy/meat/pharmaceutical/software products* ◇ *Carbon dioxide is one of the waste products of this process.* **2** ~ **of sth** the result of sth: *The industry's problems are the product of government policy.* **3** (MATHEMATICS) the amount that you get if you multiply one number by another: *The product of three and five is fifteen.*

production 🔑 /prəˈdʌkʃn/ ***noun*** **1** [U] (BUSINESS) the making or growing of sth, especially in large quantities: *The latest model will be* ***in production*** *from April.* ◇ *This farm specializes in the production of organic vegetables.* ◇ *mass production* **2** [U] the amount of sth that is made or grown: *a rise/fall in production* ◇ *a high level of production* **3** [C] (ARTS AND MEDIA) a play, film or programme that has been made for the public
IDM **on production of sth** when you show sth: *You can get a ten per cent discount on production of your membership card.*

productive /prəˈdʌktɪv/ ***adj.*** **1** that makes or grows sth, especially in large quantities: *The company wants to sell off its less productive factories.* **2** useful (because results come from it): *a productive discussion* ▶ **productivity** /ˌprɒdʌkˈtɪvəti/ ***noun*** [U]

ˌproduct ˈplacement ***noun*** [C,U] (BUSINESS) the use of particular products in films or television programmes in order to advertise them

Prof. ***abbr.*** (*written*) (EDUCATION) Professor

profess /prəˈfes/ ***verb*** [T] (*formal*) **1** to say that sth is true or correct, even when it is not: *Marianne professed to know nothing at all about it, but I did not believe her.* **2** to state honestly that you have a particular belief, feeling, etc.: *He professed his hatred of war.*

profession 🔑 /prəˈfeʃn/ ***noun*** [C] **1** a job that needs a high level of training and/or education: *the medical/legal/teaching profession* ◇ *She's thinking of entering the nursing profession.* ➲ note at **work¹** **2 the ... profession** [with sing. or pl. verb] all the people who work in a particular profession: *The legal profession is/are trying to resist the reforms.*
IDM **by profession** as your job: *George is an accountant by profession.*

professional¹ 🔑 AW /prəˈfeʃənl/ ***adj.*** **1** (only *before* a noun) connected with a job that needs a high level of training and/or education: *Get professional advice from your lawyer before you take any action.* **2** doing sth in a way that shows skill, training or care: *The police are trained to deal with* *every situation in a calm and professional manner.* ◇ *Her application was neatly typed and looked very professional.* OPP **unprofessional 3** doing a sport, etc. as a job or for money; (used about a sport, etc.) done by people who are paid: *He's planning to* ***turn professional*** *after the Olympics.* ◇ *professional football* OPP **amateur**

> **COLLOCATIONS AND PATTERNS**
>
> **Professionals**
>
> If you work in law or architecture or one of the medical professions, you **practise** your profession or you **practise as** a lawyer, an architect, etc.
> *He's a practising child psychiatrist.*
> *She practised as a barrister for years.*
>
> If you want a professional to work for you, you **appoint** or **engage** them.
> *A lawyer was appointed to represent the child.*
> *He engaged a sports psychologist to motivate his team.*
>
> When you need help, you can **consult/get advice from/see** a professional.
> *She consulted her financial adviser.*
> *We were advised to seek legal advice.*
> *You ought to see a doctor about that cough.*
>
> A solicitor or lawyer can **act for/defend** or **represent** sb.
> *a lawyer acting for a major company*

professional² 🔑 AW /prəˈfeʃənl/ ***noun*** [C] **1** a person who works in a job that needs a high level of training and/or education **2** (also *informal* **pro**) (SPORT) a person who plays or teaches a sport, etc. for money **3** (also *informal* **pro**) a person who has a lot of skill and experience

proˌfessional ˈfoul ***noun*** [C] (*BrE*) (SPORT) (in sport, especially football) a rule that sb breaks deliberately so that their team can gain an advantage, especially to prevent a player from the other team from scoring a goal

professionalism AW /prəˈfeʃənəlɪzəm/ ***noun*** [U] a way of doing a job that shows great skill and experience: *We were impressed by the professionalism of the staff.*

professionally AW /prəˈfeʃənəli/ ***adv.*** **1** in a way that shows great skill and experience **2** for money; by a professional person: *Rob plays the saxophone professionally.*

professor 🔑 /prəˈfesə(r)/ ***noun*** [C] (*abbr.* **Prof.**) (EDUCATION) **1** (*BrE*) a university teacher of the highest level: *She's professor of English at Bristol University.* **2** (*AmE*) a teacher at a college or university

proficient /prəˈfɪʃnt/ ***adj.*** ~ **(in/at sth/doing sth)** able to do a particular thing well; skilled: *We are looking for someone who is proficient in French.* ▶ **proficiency** ***noun*** [U] ~ **(in sth/doing sth)**: *a certificate of proficiency in English*

profile¹ /ˈprəʊfaɪl/ ***noun*** [C] **1** a person's face or head seen from the side, not the front: *I did a sketch of him* ***in profile***. **2** a short description of sb/sth that gives useful information: *We're building up a profile of our average customer.*

IDM **a high/low profile** a way of behaving that does/does not attract other people's attention: *I don't know much about the subject – I'm going to keep a low profile at the meeting tomorrow.*

profile² /ˈprəʊfaɪl/ ***verb*** [T] to give or write a description of sb/sth that gives the most important information: *His career is profiled in this month's journal.*

profiling /ˈprəʊfaɪlɪŋ/ ***noun*** [U] the act of collecting useful information about sb/sth so that you can give a description of them or it: *customer profiling*

profit¹ 🔑 /ˈprɒfɪt/ ***noun*** [C,U] (ECONOMICS) the money that you make when you sell sth for more than it cost you: *Did you* ***make a profit on*** *your house when you sold it?* ◇ *I'm hoping to sell my shares* ***at a profit.*** ➲ look at **loss**

profit² /ˈprɒfɪt/ ***verb*** [I,T] (*formal*) ~ **(from/by sth)** to get an advantage from sth; to give sb an advantage: *Who will profit most from the tax reforms?*

profitable /ˈprɒfɪtəbl/ ***adj.*** **1** that makes money: *a profitable business* ➲ note at **successful 2** helpful or useful: *We had a very profitable discussion yesterday.* ▶ **profitably** ***adv.***: *to spend your time profitably* ▶ **profitability** /ˌprɒfɪtəˈbɪləti/ ***noun*** [U]

ˌprofit and ˈloss account ***noun*** [C] (FINANCE) a written record of the amounts of money that a business or organization earns and spends in a particular period

profiterole /prəˈfɪtərəʊl/ ***noun*** [C] a small cake in the shape of a ball, made of light PASTRY, filled with cream and usually with chocolate on top

ˈprofit margin (*also* **margin**) ***noun*** [C] (FINANCE) the difference between the cost of buying or producing sth and the price that it is sold for: *a profit margin of 20%*

profligate /ˈprɒflɪgət/ ***adj.*** (*formal*) using money, time, materials, etc. in a careless way SYN **wasteful**: *profligate spending*

pro forma /ˌprəʊ ˈfɔːmə/ ***adj.*** (usually *before* a noun) (TECHNICAL) **1** (used especially about a document) prepared in order to show the usual way of doing sth or to provide a standard method: *a pro-forma letter* ◇ *pro-forma instructions* **2** (used about a document) sent in advance: *a pro-forma invoice* (= a document that gives details of the goods being sent to a customer) ▶ **pro forma** ***noun*** [C]: *I enclose a pro forma for you to complete, sign and return.*

profound /prəˈfaʊnd/ ***adj.*** **1** very great; that you feel very strongly: *The experience had a profound influence on her.* **2** needing or showing a lot of knowledge or thought: *He's always making profound statements about the meaning of life.* ▶ **profoundly** ***adv.***: *I was profoundly relieved to hear the news.*

profuse /prəˈfjuːs/ ***adj.*** (*formal*) given or produced in great quantity: *profuse apologies* ▶ **profusely** ***adv.***: *She apologized profusely for being late.*

profusion /prəˈfjuːʒn/ ***noun*** [sing., with sing. or pl. verb, U] (*formal*) a very large quantity of sth: *a profusion of colours/flowers* ◇ *Roses grew* ***in profusion*** *against the old wall.*

progesterone /prəˈdʒestərəʊn/ ***noun*** [U] (BIOLOGY) a (**hormone**) produced in the bodies of women and female animals which prepares the body to become pregnant ➲ look at **oestrogen**, **testosterone**

prognosis /prɒgˈnəʊsɪs/ ***noun*** [C] (*pl.* **prognoses** /-siːz/) **1** (HEALTH) an opinion, based on medical experience, of the likely development of a disease or an illness **2** (*formal*) a judgement about how sth is likely to develop in the future: *The prognosis is for more people to work part-time in the future.*

program¹ ⊶ /ˈprəʊɡræm/ ***noun*** [C] **1** (COMPUTING) a set of instructions that you give to a computer so that it will do a particular task: *to write a program* **2** (*AmE*) = PROGRAMME¹: *the university's graduate programs* ◇ *a TV program*

program² ⊶ /ˈprəʊɡræm/ ***verb*** [I,T] (**programming; programmed**) (COMPUTING) to give a set of instructions to a computer, etc. to make it perform a particular task

programme¹ ⊶ (*AmE* program) /ˈprəʊɡræm/ ***noun*** [C] **1** (ARTS AND MEDIA) a show or other item that is sent out on the radio or television: *a TV/radio programme* ◇ *We've just missed an interesting programme on elephants.* **2** a plan of things to do; a scheme: *What's (on) your programme today?* (=what are you going to do today?) ◇ *The leaflet outlines the government's programme of educational reforms.* **3** a little book or piece of paper which you get at a concert, a sports event, etc. that gives you information about what you are going to see **4** (*AmE*) (EDUCATION) a course of study: *a school programme*

programme² /ˈprəʊɡræm/ (*AmE* **program**) ***verb*** [T] (**programming; programmed**: *AmE also* **programing; programed**) **1** to plan for sth to happen at a particular time: *The road is programmed for completion next May.* **2** to make sb/sth work or act automatically in a particular way: *The lights are programmed to come on as soon as it gets dark.*

programmer /ˈprəʊɡræmə(r)/ ***noun*** [C] (COMPUTING) a person whose job is to write programs for a computer

programming /ˈprəʊɡræmɪŋ/ ***noun*** [U] **1** (COMPUTING) the process of writing and testing programs for computers: *a high-level programming language* **2** (ARTS AND MEDIA) the planning of which television or radio programmes to broadcast: *politically balanced programming*

progress¹ ⊶ /ˈprəʊɡres/ ***noun*** [U] **1** movement forwards or towards achieving sth: *Anna's* ***making progress*** *at school.* ◇ *to make slow/steady/rapid/good progress* **2** change or improvement in society: *scientific progress*
IDM **in progress** happening now: *Silence! Examination in progress.*

progress² ⊶ /prəˈɡres/ ***verb*** [I] **1** to become better; to develop (well): *Medical knowledge has progressed rapidly in the last twenty years.* **2** to move forward; to continue: *I got more and more tired as the evening progressed.*

progression /prəˈɡreʃn/ ***noun*** [C,U] (a) ~ **(from sth) (to sth)** movement forward or a development from one stage to another: *You've made the progression from beginner to intermediate level*

progressive /prəˈɡresɪv/ ***adj.*** **1** using modern methods and ideas: *a progressive school* **2** happening or developing steadily: *a progressive reduction in the number of staff*

progressively /prəˈɡresɪvli/ ***adv.*** steadily; a little at a time: *The situation became progressively worse.*

the pro,gressive 'tense ***noun*** [sing.] (LANGUAGE) = THE CONTINUOUS TENSE

prohibit AW /prəˈhɪbɪt/ ***verb*** [T] (*formal*) ~ **sb/sth (from doing sth)** to say that sth is not allowed by law; to FORBID: *English law prohibits children under 16 from buying cigarettes.*

prohibition AW /ˌprəʊɪˈbɪʃn/ ***noun*** (LAW) **1** [C] (*formal*) **a ~ (on/against sth)** a law or rule that FORBIDS sth: *There is a prohibition on the carrying of knives.* **2** [U] the action of stopping sth being done or used, especially by law: *the prohibition of alcohol in the 1920s*

prohibitive AW /prəˈhɪbətɪv/ ***adj.*** (used about a price or cost) so high that it prevents people from buying sth or doing sth: *The price of houses in the centre of town is prohibitive.* ▶ **prohibitively** ***adv.***

project¹ ⊶ AW /ˈprɒdʒekt/ ***noun*** [C] **1** a piece of work, often involving many people, that is planned and organized carefully: *a major project to reduce pollution in our rivers* **2** (EDUCATION) a piece of school work in which the student has to collect information about a certain subject and then write about it: *Our group chose to do a project on rainforests.*

project² ⊶ AW /prəˈdʒekt/ ***verb*** **1** [T] (usually passive) to plan sth that will happen in the future: *the band's projected world tour* **2** [T] (usually passive) to guess or calculate the size, cost or amount of sth: *a projected increase of 10%* **3** [T] ~ **sth (on/onto sth)** to make light, a picture from a film, etc. appear on a flat surface or screen **4** [T] to show or represent sb/sth/yourself in a certain way: *The government is trying to project a more caring image.* **5** [I] (*formal*) to stick out: *The balcony projects one metre out from the wall.* **6** [T] to send or throw sth upwards or away from you: *Actors have to learn to project their voice.*

projectile /prəˈdʒektaɪl/ ***noun*** [C] (*formal*) **1** an object, such as a bullet, that is fired from a gun or other weapon **2** any object that is thrown as a weapon

projection AW /prəˈdʒekʃn/ ***noun*** **1** [C] a guess about a future amount, situation, etc. based on the present situation: *sales projections for the next five years* **2** [U] the act of making light, a picture from a film, etc. appear on a surface

projector /prəˈdʒektə(r)/ ***noun*** [C] a piece of equipment that projects pictures or films onto a screen or wall: *a film/slide/overhead projector*

prokaryote (also **procaryote**) /prəʊˈkæriəʊt/ ***noun*** [C] (BIOLOGY) an ORGANISM (=a very small living thing) consisting of just one cell that does not have a clear NUCLEUS (=central part). Most **prokaryotes** are bacteria. ➲ look at **eukaryote** ▶ **prokaryotic** /ˌprəʊkæriˈɒtɪk/ ***adj.***

proliferate /prəˈlɪfəreɪt/ ***verb*** [I] (*formal*) to increase quickly in number ▶ **proliferation** /prəˌlɪfəˈreɪʃn/ ***noun*** [U]

prolific /prəˈlɪfɪk/ ***adj.*** (used especially about a writer, artist, etc.) producing a lot: *a prolific goal scorer*

prologue /ˈprəʊlɒɡ/ ***noun*** [C] (LITERATURE) a piece of writing or a speech that introduces a play, poem, etc. ➲ look at **epilogue**

prolong /prəˈlɒŋ/ ***verb*** [T] to make sth last longer

prolonged /prəˈlɒŋd/ ***adj.*** continuing for a long time: *There was a prolonged silence before anybody spoke.*

prom /prɒm/ ***noun*** [C] **1** (especially in the US) a formal dance, especially one that is held at a HIGH SCHOOL: *the senior prom* **2** (*BrE, informal, old-fashioned*) = PROMENADE **3** (*BrE*) (MUSIC) a concert at which many of the audience stand up or sit on the floor: *the last night of the proms*

promenade /ˌprɒməˈnɑːd/ (also *informal* **prom**) ***noun*** [C] (*BrE, old-fashioned*) a public place for walking, usually a wide path beside the sea

promethium /prəˈmiːθiəm/ ***noun*** [U] (*symbol* **Pm**) (CHEMISTRY) a chemical element. **Promethium** is a RADIOACTIVE metal that was first produced artificially in a nuclear REACTOR and is found in small amounts in nature. ❶ For more information on the periodic table of elements, look at pages R34-5.

prominent /ˈprɒmɪnənt/ ***adj.*** **1** important or famous: *a prominent political figure* **2** noticeable; easy to see: *The church is the most prominent feature of the village.* ▶ **prominence** ***noun*** [U]: *The newspaper gave the affair great prominence.* ▶ **prominently** ***adv.***

promiscuous /prəˈmɪskjuəs/ ***adj.*** having sexual relations with many people ▶ **promiscuity** /ˌprɒmɪsˈkjuːəti/ ***noun*** [U]

promise[1] 🔑 /ˈprɒmɪs/ ***verb*** **1** [I,T] ~ **(to do sth)**; ~ **(sb) that...** to say definitely that you will do or not do sth or that sth will happen: *She promised to write every week.* ◇ *She promised (me) that she would write every week.* ◇ *She promised not to forget to write.* **2** [T] ~ **sth (to sb)**; ~ **sb sth** to say definitely that you will give sth to sb: *Can you promise your support?* ◇ *My dad has promised me a bicycle.* ◇ *You have to give him the money if you promised it to him.* **3** [T] to show signs of sth, so that you expect it to happen: *It promises to be an exciting occasion.*

promise[2] 🔑 /ˈprɒmɪs/ ***noun*** **1** [C] a ~ **(to do sth/that...)** a written or spoken statement or agreement that you will or will not do sth: *I want you to **make a promise** that you won't do that again.* ◇ *Make sure you **keep** your **promise** to always do your homework.* ◇ *You should never **break a promise**.* ◇ *I **give** you my **promise** that I won't tell anyone.* **2** [U] signs that you will be able to do sth well or be successful: *He **showed** great **promise** as a musician.*

promising /ˈprɒmɪsɪŋ/ ***adj.*** showing signs of being very good or successful: *a promising young writer*

promontory /ˈprɒməntri/ ***noun*** [C] (*pl.* **-ies**) (GEOGRAPHY) a long narrow area of high land that goes out into the sea: *a rocky promontory overlooking the bay*

promote 🔑 AW /prəˈməʊt/ ***verb*** [T] **1** to encourage sth; to help sth to happen or develop: *to promote good relations between countries* **2** ~ **sth (as sth)** to advertise sth in order to increase its sales or make it popular: *The new face cream is being promoted as a miracle cure for wrinkles.* **3** ~ **sb (from sth) (to sth)** (often passive) to give sb a higher position or more important job: *He's been promoted from assistant manager to manager.* OPP **demote**

promoter AW /prəˈməʊtə(r)/ ***noun*** [C] a person who organizes or provides the money for an event

promotion 🔑 AW /prəˈməʊʃn/ ***noun*** **1** [C,U] ~ **(to sth)** a move to a higher position or more important job: *The new job is a promotion for her.* OPP **demotion** **2** [U, C] things that you do in order to advertise a product and increase its sales: *It's all part of a special promotion of the new book.* ➲ note at **ad** **3** [U] (*formal*) ~ **(of sth)** the activity of trying to make sth develop or become accepted by people: *We need to work on the promotion of health, not the treatment of disease.*

promotional /prəˈməʊʃənl/ ***adj.*** connected with advertising: *promotional material*

prompt[1] 🔑 /prɒmpt/ ***adj.*** **1** immediate; done without delay: *We need a prompt decision on this matter.* **2** ~ **(in doing sth/to do sth)** (not before a noun) (used about a person) quick; acting without delay: *We are always prompt in paying our bills.* ◇ *She was prompt to point out my mistake.*

prompt[2] 🔑 /prɒmpt/ ***verb*** **1** [T] to cause sth to happen; to make sb decide to do sth: *What prompted you to give up your job?* **2** [I,T] to encourage sb to speak by asking questions or to remind an actor of their words in a play: *The speaker had to be prompted several times.* ▶ **prompting** ***noun*** [U]: *He apologized without any prompting.*

prompt[3] 🔑 /prɒmpt/ ***noun*** [C] **1** (ARTS AND MEDIA) a word or words said to an actor to remind them of what to say next: *When she forgot her lines I had to give her a prompt.* **2** (COMPUTING) a sign on a computer screen that shows that the computer has finished what it was doing and is ready for more instructions: *Wait for the prompt to come up then type in your password.*

promptly 🔑 /ˈprɒmptli/ ***adv.*** **1** immediately; without delay: *I invited her to dinner and she promptly accepted.* **2** (*also* **prompt**) at exactly the time that you have arranged; PUNCTUALLY: *We arrived promptly at 12 o'clock.* ◇ *I'll pick you up at 7 o'clock prompt.*

prone /prəʊn/ ***adj.*** ~ **to sth/to do sth** likely to suffer from sth or to do sth bad: *prone to infection/injury/heart attacks* ◇ *Working without a break makes you more prone to error.* ◇ *to be **accident-prone*** (= to have a lot of accidents)

prong /prɒŋ/ ***noun*** [C] **1** each of the two or more long pointed parts of a fork **2** each of the separate parts of an attack, argument, etc. that sb uses to achieve sth **3 -pronged** (used to form compound adjectives) having the number or type of **prongs** mentioned: *a three-pronged attack*

pronoun /ˈprəʊnaʊn/ ***noun*** [C] (LANGUAGE) a word that is used in place of a noun or a phrase that contains a noun: *'He', 'it', 'hers', 'me', 'them', etc. are all pronouns.* ➲ look at **personal pronoun**

pronounce 🔑 /prəˈnaʊns/ ***verb*** **1** [T] (LANGUAGE) to make the sound of a word or letter in a particular way: *You don't pronounce the 'b' at the end of 'comb'.* ◇ *How do you pronounce your surname?* ➲ noun **pronunciation** **2** [T] (*formal*) to say or give sth formally, officially or publicly: *The judge will pronounce sentence today.* **3** [I,T] (*formal*) ~ **(on sth)** to give your opinion on sth, especially formally: *The play was pronounced 'brilliant' by all the critics.*

> WORD FAMILY
> **pronounce** *verb*
> **pronunciation** *noun*
> **unpronounceable** *adj.*
> **mispronounce** *verb*

pronounced /prəˈnaʊnst/ ***adj.*** very noticeable; obvious: *His English is excellent although he speaks with a pronounced French accent.*

pronunciation 🔑 /prəˌnʌnsiˈeɪʃn/ ***noun*** **1** [U, C] (LANGUAGE) the way in which a language or a particular word or sound is said: *American pronunciation* ➲ verb **pronounce** **2** [U] a person's way of speaking a language: *His grammar is good but his pronunciation is awful!*

proof 🔑 /pruːf/ ***noun*** **1** [U] ~ **(of sth)**; ~ **that...** information, documents, etc. which show that sth is true: *'We need some **proof of identity**,' the shop assistant said.* ◇ *You've got no proof that John took the money.* ➲ verb **prove**
2 [C, usually pl.] a first copy of printed material that is produced so that mistakes can be corrected

-proof /pruːf/ ***suffix*** (used to form compound adjectives) able to protect against the thing mentioned: *a soundproof room* ◇ *a waterproof/windproof jacket* ◇ *bulletproof glass*

prop[1] /prɒp/ ***verb*** [T] (**propping**; **propped**) to support sb/sth or keep sb/sth in position by putting them or it against or on sth: *I'll use this book to prop the window open.* ◇ *He propped his bicycle against the wall.*

PHR V **prop sth up** to support sth that would otherwise fall

prop[2] /prɒp/ ***noun*** [C] **1** a stick or other object that you use to support sth or to keep sth in position: *Rescuers used props to stop the roof of the tunnel collapsing.* **2** [usually pl.] (ARTS AND MEDIA) an object that is used in a play, film, etc.: *He's responsible for all the stage props, machinery and lighting.*

propaganda /ˌprɒpəˈɡændə/ ***noun*** [U] (POLITICS) information and ideas that may be false or exaggerated, which are used to gain support for a political leader, party, etc.

propagate /ˈprɒpəɡeɪt/ ***verb*** [I,T] (AGRICULTURE) to produce new plants from a parent plant ▶ **propagation** /ˌprɒpəˈɡeɪʃn/ ***noun*** [U]

propane /ˈprəʊpeɪn/ ***noun*** [U] (CHEMISTRY) a colourless gas that is found in natural gas and petrol and that we use as a fuel for cooking and heating

propel /prəˈpel/ ***verb*** [T] (**propelling**; **propelled**) to move, drive or push sb/sth forward or in a particular direction

propeller /prəˈpelə(r)/ ***noun*** [C] (TECHNICAL) a device with several flat metal parts (**blades**) which turn round very fast in order to make a ship or a plane move

propensity /prəˈpensəti/ ***noun*** [C] (*pl.* **propensities**) (*formal*) **a ~ (for sth); a ~ (for doing sth); a ~ (to do sth)** a habit of behaving in a particular way: *He showed a propensity for violence.* ◇ *She has a propensity to exaggerate.*

proper ⊶ /ˈprɒpə(r)/ ***adj.*** **1** (*especially BrE*) (only *before* a noun) right, suitable or correct: *If you're going skiing you must have the proper clothes.* ◇ *I've got to get these pieces of paper in the proper order.* **2** (only *before* a noun) that you consider to be real or good enough: *I didn't see much of the flat yesterday. I'm going to go today and have a proper look.* **3** (*formal*) socially and morally acceptable: *I think it would be only proper for you to apologize.* OPP **improper** **4** (only *after* a noun) real or main: *We travelled through miles of suburbs before we got to the city proper.*

ˌ**proper ˈfraction** ***noun*** [C] (MATHEMATICS) a FRACTION that is less than one, with the bottom number greater than the top number, for example ¼ or ⅝ ➲ look at **improper fraction**

properly ⊶ /ˈprɒpəli/ ***adv.*** **1** (*especially BrE*) correctly; in an acceptable way: *The teacher said I hadn't done my homework properly.* ◇ *These shoes don't fit properly.* **2** in a way that is socially and morally acceptable; politely: *If you two children can't behave properly then we'll have to go home.* OPP **improperly**

ˌ**proper ˈname** (*also* ˌ**proper ˈnoun**) ***noun*** [C] (LANGUAGE) a word which is the name of a particular person or place and begins with a CAPITAL LETTER: *'Mary' and 'Rome' are proper names.*

property ⊶ /ˈprɒpəti/ ***noun*** (*pl.* **properties**) **1** [U] a thing or things that belong to sb: *The sack contained **stolen property**.* ◇ *Is this bag your property?* ◇ *This file is government property.* ➲ look at **lost property** **2** [U] land and buildings: *Property prices vary enormously from area to area.* ➲ note at **building** **3** [C] one building and the land around it: *There are a lot of empty properties in the area.* **4** [C, usually pl.] (*formal*) a special quality or characteristic that a substance, etc. has: *Some plants have healing properties.* ◇ *Compare the physical properties of the two substances.*

prophecy /ˈprɒfəsi/ ***noun*** [C] (*pl.* **prophecies**) a statement about what is going to happen in the future: *to fulfil a prophecy* (=to make it come true)

prophesy /ˈprɒfəsaɪ/ ***verb*** [T] (*pres. part.* **prophesying**; *3rd person sing. pres.* **prophesies**; *pt, pp* **prophesied**) to say what you think will happen in the future: *to prophesy disaster/war*

prophet /ˈprɒfɪt/ ***noun*** [C] **1** (*also* **Prophet**) (RELIGION) (in the Christian, Jewish and Muslim religions) a person who is sent by God to teach the people and give them messages from God **2** a person who says what will happen in the future ▶ **prophetic** /prəˈfetɪk/ ***adj.***

prophylactic[1] /ˌprɒfɪˈlæktɪk/ ***adj.*** (HEALTH) done or used in order to prevent a disease: *prophylactic treatment*

prophylactic[2] /ˌprɒfɪˈlæktɪk/ ***noun*** [C] (*formal*) (HEALTH) a medicine, device or course of action that prevents disease

proportion ⊶ AW /prəˈpɔːʃn/ ***noun*** **1** [C] (MATHEMATICS) a part or share of a whole: *A large proportion of the earth's surface is covered by sea.* **2** [U] **~ (of sth to sth)** the relationship between the size or amount of two things: *The proportion of men to women in the college has changed dramatically over the years.* **3 proportions** [pl.] the size or shape of sth: *a room of odd proportions* ◇ *Political unrest is reaching alarming proportions.*

IDM **in proportion** the right size in relation to other things: *to draw sth in proportion* ◇ *She's so upset that it's hard for her to keep the problem in proportion* (=to her it seems more important or serious than it really is).

in proportion to sth **1** by the same amount or number as sth else; relative to: *Salaries have not risen in proportion to inflation.* **2** compared with: *In proportion to the number of students as a whole, there are very few women.*

out of proportion (to sth) **1** too big, small, etc. in relation to other things **2** too great, serious, important, etc. in relation to sth: *His reaction was completely out of proportion to the situation.*

proportional AW /prəˈpɔːʃənl/ ***adj.*** **~ (to sth)** of the right size, amount or degree compared with sth else: *Salary is proportional to years of experience.* ▶ **proportionally** ***adv.***

proˌportional ˌrepresenˈtation ***noun*** [U] (*abbr.* **PR**) (POLITICS) a system that gives each political party in an election a number of representatives in parliament in direct relation to the number of votes its CANDIDATES (=people who want to be elected) receive ➲ look at **representation**

proportionate AW /prəˈpɔːʃənət/ ***adj.*** **~ (to sth)** (*formal*) increasing or decreasing in size, amount or degree according to changes in sth else SYN **proportional**: *The number of accidents is proportionate to the increased volume of traffic.* OPP **disproportionate**

proposal ⊶ /prəˈpəʊzl/ ***noun*** [C] **1 a ~ (for/to do sth); a ~ that...** a plan that is formally suggested: *a new proposal for raising money* ◇ *a proposal to build more student accommodation* ◇ *May I **make a proposal** that we all give an equal amount?* **2** an act of formally asking sb to marry you

propose ⊶ /prəˈpəʊz/ ***verb*** **1** [T] to formally suggest sth as a possible plan or action: *At the meeting a new advertising campaign was proposed.*

2 [T] to intend to do sth; to have sth as a plan: *What do you propose to do now?* **3** [I,T] ~ **(to sb)** to ask sb to marry you: *to propose marriage* **4** [T] ~ **sb for/as sth** to suggest sb for an official position: *I'd like to propose Anna Marsland as Chairperson.*

proposition /ˌprɒpəˈzɪʃn/ ***noun*** [C] **1** (**BUSINESS**) an idea, a plan or an offer, especially in business; a suggestion: *I'd like to put a business proposition to you.* ◇ *She was trying to make it look like an* ***attractive proposition***. **2 also Proposition** (**POLITICS**) (in the US) a suggested change to the law that people can vote on: *How did you vote on Proposition 8?* **3** (*formal*) an idea or opinion that sb expresses about sth: *That's a very interesting proposition. Are you sure you can prove it?* **4** (**MATHEMATICS**) a statement of a THEOREM (=a rule or principle in mathematics that can be shown to be true), and an explanation of how it can be proved

proprietor /prəˈpraɪətə(r)/ ***noun*** [C] (*feminine* **proprietress** /prəˈpraɪətres/) (**BUSINESS**) the owner of a business, a hotel, etc.

propulsion /prəˈpʌlʃn/ ***noun*** [U] (**PHYSICS**) the force that drives sth forward: ***wind/steam/jet propulsion*** ➲ look at **propel**

pro rata /ˌprəʊ ˈrɑːtə/ ***adj.*** (*formal*) (**FINANCE**) calculated according to how much of sth has been used, the amount of work done, etc.: *If costs go up, there will be a pro rata increase in prices.* ▶ **pro rata** ***adv.***: *Prices will increase pro rata.*

proscenium /prəˈsiːniəm/ ***noun*** [C] (**ARTS AND MEDIA**) the part of the stage in a theatre that is in front of the curtain: *a traditional theatre with a* ***proscenium arch*** (=one that forms a frame for the stage where the curtain is opened).

prose /prəʊz/ ***noun*** [U] (**LITERATURE**) written or spoken language that is not poetry: *to write* ***in prose*** ➲ look at **poetry**

prosecute /ˈprɒsɪkjuːt/ ***verb*** [I,T] ~ **sb (for sth)** (**LAW**) to officially charge sb with a crime and try to show that they are guilty, in a court of law: *the prosecuting counsel/lawyer/attorney* ◇ *He was prosecuted for theft.* ➲ look at **defend**

prosecution /ˌprɒsɪˈkjuːʃn/ ***noun*** **1** [U, C] (**LAW**) the process of officially charging sb with a crime and of trying to show that they are guilty, in a court of law: *to bring a prosecution against sb* ◇ *Failure to pay your parking fine will result in prosecution.* **2 the prosecution** [sing., with sing. or pl. verb] (**LAW**) a person or group of people who try to show that sb is guilty of a crime in a court of law: *The prosecution claim/claims that Lloyd was driving at 100 miles per hour.* ➲ look at **defence**

prosecutor /ˈprɒsɪkjuːtə(r)/ ***noun*** [C] **1** (**LAW**) a public official who charges sb with a crime and tries to show that they are guilty in a court of law: *the public/state prosecutor* **2** (**LAW**) a lawyer who leads the case against the accused person (**the defendant**) in a court of law

prosody /ˈprɒsədi/ ***noun*** [U] (**LITERATURE**) the patterns of sounds and rhythms in poetry and speech; the study of this

prospect 🔑 AW /ˈprɒspekt/ ***noun*** **1** [U, sing.] ~ **(of sth/of doing sth)** the possibility that sth will happen: *There's little prospect of better weather before next week.* **2** [sing.] ~ **(of sth/of doing sth)** a thought about what may or will happen in the future: *The prospect of becoming a father filled James with horror.* **3 prospects** [pl.] chances of being successful in the future: *good job/career/promotion prospects*

prospective AW /prəˈspektɪv/ ***adj.*** likely to be or to happen; possible: *prospective changes in the law*

prospectus /prəˈspektəs/ ***noun*** [C] (**EDUCATION, BUSINESS**) a small book which gives information about a school, college or business in order to advertise it

prosper /ˈprɒspə(r)/ ***verb*** [I] to develop in a successful way; to be successful, especially with money

prosperity /prɒˈsperəti/ ***noun*** [U] the state of being successful, especially with money: *Tourism has brought prosperity to many parts of Spain.*

prosperous /ˈprɒspərəs/ ***adj.*** rich and successful

prostate /ˈprɒsteɪt/ (*also* **ˈprostate gland**) ***noun*** [C] (**ANATOMY**) a small organ in a man's body near the BLADDER (=the organ where waste liquid collects), that produces a liquid in which SPERM is carried

prostitute /ˈprɒstɪtjuːt/ ***noun*** [C] a person, especially a woman, who earns money by having sex with people

prostitution /ˌprɒstɪˈtjuːʃn/ ***noun*** [U] working as a PROSTITUTE

prostrate /prɒˈstreɪt/ ***adj.*** lying flat on the ground, facing downwards

protactinium /ˌprəʊtækˈtɪniəm/ ***noun*** [U] (*symbol* **Pa**) (**CHEMISTRY**) a chemical element. **Protactinium** is a RADIOACTIVE metal found naturally when URANIUM decays. ℹ For more information on the periodic table of elements, look at pages R34-5.

protagonist /prəˈtæɡənɪst/ ***noun*** [C] (*formal*) (**LITERATURE**) the main character in a play, film or book

protease /ˈprəʊtieɪz/ ***noun*** [U] (**BIOLOGY**) an ENZYME that breaks down PROTEIN (=a natural substance found in meat, eggs, fish, etc. that the body needs to grow and be healthy)

protect 🔑 /prəˈtekt/ ***verb*** [T] ~ **sb/sth (against/from sth)** to keep sb/sth safe; to defend sb/sth: *Parents try to protect their children from danger as far as possible.* ◇ *Bats are a* ***protected species*** (=they must not be killed).

protection 🔑 /prəˈtekʃn/ ***noun*** [U] ~ **(against/from sth)** the act of keeping sb/sth safe so that they or it are not harmed or damaged: *Vaccination gives protection against diseases.* ◇ *After the attack he was put* ***under*** *police* ***protection***.

protectionism /prəˈtekʃənɪzəm/ ***noun*** [U] (**ECONOMICS**) the principle or practice of protecting a country's own industry by taxing foreign goods ▶ **protectionist** /-ʃənɪst/ ***adj.***: *protectionist measures/policies*

protective /prəˈtektɪv/ ***adj.*** **1** (only *before* a noun) that prevents sb/sth from being damaged or harmed: *In certain jobs workers need to wear protective clothing.* **2** ~ **(of/towards sb/sth)** wanting to keep sb/sth safe: *Female animals are very protective of their young.*

protector /prəˈtektə(r)/ ***noun*** [C] a person, an organization or a thing that protects sb/sth: *I regarded him as my friend and protector.* ◇ *Hard hats and ear protectors are provided.*

protectorate /prəˈtektərət/ ***noun*** [C] (**POLITICS**) a country that is controlled and protected by a more powerful country

protein /'prəʊtiːn/ ***noun*** [C,U] (**BIOLOGY**) a substance found in food such as meat, fish, eggs and BEANS. It is important for helping people and animals to grow and be healthy.

protest[1] /'prəʊtest/ ***noun*** [U, C] ~ **(against sth)** a statement or action that shows that you do not like or approve of sth: *He resigned* ***in protest*** *against the decision.* ◇ *The union organized a protest against the redundancies.*

IDM **under protest** not happily and after expressing disagreement: *Fiona agreed to pay in the end but only under protest.*

protest[2] /prə'test/ ***verb*** **1** [I,T] ~ **(about/ against/at sth)** to say or show that you do not approve of or agree with sth, especially publicly: *Students have been protesting against the government's decision.* ❶ In American English **protest** is used without a preposition: *They protested the government's handling of the situation.* **2** [T] to say sth firmly, especially when others do not believe you: *She has always* ***protested*** *her* ***innocence.***
▶ **protester** ***noun*** [C]: *Protesters blocked the road outside the factory.*

Protestant /'prɒtɪstənt/ ***noun*** [C] (**RELIGION**) a member of the Christian church that separated from the Catholic church in the 16th century
▶ **Protestant** ***adj.***: *a Protestant church* ➲ look at **Roman Catholic**

proto- /'prəʊtəʊ/ ***prefix*** (used in nouns and adjectives) original; from which others develop: *prototype*

protocol AW /'prəʊtəkɒl/ ***noun*** **1** [U] (*formal*) (**POLITICS**) a system of fixed rules and formal behaviour used at official meetings, usually between governments: *a breach of protocol* ◇ *the protocol of diplomatic visits* **2** [C] (**POLITICS**) the first or original version of a written agreement, especially one between countries; an extra part added to a written agreement: *the first Geneva Protocol* ◇ *It is set out in a legally binding protocol which forms part of the treaty.* **3** [C] (**COMPUTING**) a set of rules that control the way information is sent between computers **4** [C] (**HEALTH**) a plan for carrying out a scientific experiment or medical treatment

proton /'prəʊtɒn/ ***noun*** [C] (**CHEMISTRY, PHYSICS**) one of the three types of PARTICLES that form all atoms. **Protons** have a positive electric charge. ➲ look at **electron, neutron**

protoplasm /'prəʊtəplæzəm/ ***noun*** [U] (**BIOLOGY**) a clear substance like jelly which forms the living part of an animal or plant cell ➲ look at **cytoplasm**

prototype /'prəʊtətaɪp/ ***noun*** [C] the first model or design of sth from which other forms will be developed

protozoan /ˌprəʊtə'zəʊən/ ***noun*** [C] (*pl.* **protozoans** or **protozoa** /-'zəʊə/) (**BIOLOGY**) a very small living thing, usually with only one cell, that can only be seen using a special piece of equipment that makes it look bigger (**a microscope**)

protractor /prə'træktə(r)/ ***noun*** [C] (**GEOMETRY**) an instrument for measuring and drawing angles, usually made from a HALF-CIRCLE of clear plastic with degrees (0° to 180°) marked on it

protrude /prə'truːd/ ***verb*** [I] ~ **(from sth)** to stick out from a place or surface: *protruding eyes/teeth*

protrusion /prə'truːʒn/ ***noun*** [C,U] (*formal*) a thing that sticks out from a place or surface; the fact of doing this: *a protrusion on the rock face*

protuberance /prə'tjuːbərəns/ ***noun*** [C] (*formal*) a round part that sticks out from a surface: *The diseased trees have protuberances on their trunks.*

proud /praʊd/ ***adj.*** **1** ~ **(of sb/sth)**; ~ **to do sth/that...** feeling pleased and satisfied about sth that you own or have done: *They are very proud of their new house.* ◇ *I feel very proud to be part of such a successful organization.* ◇ *You should feel very proud that you have been chosen.* **2** feeling that you are better and more important than other people: *Now she's at university she'll be much too proud to talk to us!* **3** having respect for yourself and not wanting to lose the respect of others: *He was too proud to ask for help.* ➲ noun **pride**

proudly /'praʊdli/ ***adv.*** in a way that shows that sb is proud of sth: *'I did all the work myself,' he said proudly.*

prove /pruːv/ ***verb*** (*pp* **proved**: *AmE* **proven**) **1** [T] ~ **sth (to sb)** to use facts and evidence to show that sth is true: *It will be difficult to prove that she was lying.* ◇ *She tried to prove her innocence to the court.* ◇ *He felt he needed* ***to prove a point*** (=show other people that he was right). ➲ noun **proof**
2 ***linking verb*** to show a particular quality over a period of time: *The job proved more difficult than we'd expected.* **3** [T] ~ **yourself (to sb)** to show other people how good you are at doing sth and/or that you are capable of doing sth: *He constantly feels that he has to prove himself to others.*

> WORD FAMILY
> **prove** *verb* (≠ **disprove**)
> **proof** *noun*
> **proven** *adj.* (≠ **unproven**)

proven /'prəʊvn; 'pruːvn/ ***adj.*** that has been shown to be true: *a proven fact*

proverb /'prɒvɜːb/ ***noun*** [C] (**LANGUAGE**) a short well-known sentence or phrase that gives advice or says that sth is generally true in life: *'Too many cooks spoil the broth,' is a proverb.* ➲ look at **saying**

proverbial /prə'vɜːbiəl/ ***adj.*** **1** (only *before* a noun) used to show you are referring to a well-known phrase (**a proverb**): *Let's not count our proverbial chickens.* **2** well known and talked about by a lot of people

provide /prə'vaɪd/ ***verb*** [T] ~ **sb (with sth)**; ~ **sth (for sb)** to give sth to sb or make sth available for sb to use; to supply sth: *This book will provide you with all the information you need.* ◇ *We are able to provide accommodation for two students.* ➲ noun **provision**

PHR V **provide for sb** to give sb all that they need to live, for example food and clothing

provide for sth to make preparations to deal with sth that might happen in the future: *We did not provide for such a large increase in prices.*

provided /prə'vaɪdɪd/ (*also* **providing**) ***conj.*** ~**/providing (that)** only if; on condition that: *She agreed to go and work abroad provided (that) her family could go with her.*

provider /prə'vaɪdə(r)/ ***noun*** [C] (**BUSINESS**) a person or an organization that supplies sb with sth they need or want: *training providers* ◇ *The eldest son is the family's sole provider* (=the only person who earns money). ➲ look at **service provider**

province /'prɒvɪns/ ***noun*** **1** [C] (**POLITICS**) one of the areas that some countries are divided into with its own local government: *Canada has ten provinces.* ➲ look at **county, state 2 the provinces** [pl.] (*BrE*) (**GEOGRAPHY**) the part of a country that is outside the most important city (**the capital**)

provincial /prə'vɪnʃl/ ***adj.*** **1** (POLITICS) (only *before* a noun) connected with one of the large areas that some countries are divided into: *provincial governments/elections* **2** (GEOGRAPHY) connected with the parts of a country that do not include its most important city: *a provincial town/newspaper* **3** (used about a person or their ideas) not wanting to consider new or different ideas or fashions: *provincial attitudes*

provision /prə'vɪʒn/ ***noun*** **1** [U] the giving or supplying of sth to sb or making sth available for sb to use: *The council is responsible for the provision of education and social services.* **2** [U] ~ **for sb/sth** preparations that you make to deal with sth that might happen in the future: *She **made provision for*** (=planned for the financial future of) *the children in the event of her death.* **3 provisions** [pl.] (*formal*) supplies of food and drink, especially for a long journey ➲ verb **provide**

provisional /prə'vɪʒənl/ ***adj.*** only for the present time, that is likely to be changed in the future: *The provisional date for the next meeting is 18 November.* ◇ *a **provisional driving licence*** (=that you use when you are learning to drive) ▶ **provisionally** /-nəli/ ***adv.***: *I've only repaired the bike provisionally – we'll have to do it properly later.*

proviso /prə'vaɪzəʊ/ ***noun*** [C] (*pl.* **provisos**) a condition that must be accepted before an agreement can be made: *He agreed to the visit **with the proviso that** they should stay no longer than a week.*

provocation /ˌprɒvə'keɪʃn/ ***noun*** [U, C] doing or saying sth deliberately to try to make sb angry or upset; sth that is said or done to cause this: *You should never hit children, even **under** extreme **provocation**.* ➲ verb **provoke**

provocative /prə'vɒkətɪv/ ***adj.*** **1** intended to make sb angry or upset or to cause an argument: *He made a provocative remark about a woman's place being in the home.* **2** intended to cause sexual excitement ▶ **provocatively** ***adv.***

provoke /prə'vəʊk/ ***verb*** [T] **1** to cause a particular feeling or reaction: *an article intended to provoke discussion* **2** ~ **sb (into sth/into doing sth)** to say or do sth that you know will make a person angry or upset: *The lawyer claimed his client was provoked into acts of violence.* ➲ noun **provocation**

prow /praʊ/ ***noun*** [C] the front part of a ship or boat ➲ look at **stern**

prowess /'praʊəs/ ***noun*** [U] (*formal*) great skill at doing sth: *academic/sporting prowess*

prowl /praʊl/ ***verb*** [I,T] ~ **(about/around)** (used about an animal that is hunting or a person who is waiting for a chance to steal sth or do sth bad) to move around an area quietly so that you are not seen or heard: *I could hear someone prowling around outside so I called the police.* ▶ **prowler** ***noun*** [C]: *The police arrested a prowler outside the hospital.*

proximity /prɒk'sɪməti/ ***noun*** [U] (*formal*) ~ **(of sb/sth) (to sb/sth)** the state of being near to sb/sth in distance or time: *An advantage is the proximity of the new offices to the airport.*

proxy /'prɒksi/ ***noun*** [U] the authority that you give to sb to act for you if you cannot do sth yourself: *to vote **by proxy***

prude /pru:d/ ***noun*** [C] a person who is easily shocked by anything connected with sex ▶ **prudish** ***adj.***

prudent /'pru:dnt/ ***adj.*** (*formal*) sensible and careful when making judgements and decisions; avoiding unnecessary risks: *It would be prudent to get some more advice before you invest your money.* **OPP imprudent** ▶ **prudence** ***noun*** [U] ➲ note at **care**[1] ▶ **prudently** ***adv.***

prune[1] /pru:n/ ***noun*** [C] a dried PLUM (=a small soft fruit that grows on trees)

prune[2] /pru:n/ ***verb*** [T] (AGRICULTURE) to cut branches or parts of branches off a tree or bush in order to make it a better shape

pry /praɪ/ ***verb*** (*pres. part.* **prying**; *3rd person sing. pres.* **pries**; *pt, pp* **pried**) **1** [I] ~ **(into sth)** to try to find out about other people's private affairs: *I'm sick of you prying into my personal life.* **2** [T] (*especially AmE*) =PRISE

PS (*also* **ps**) /ˌpi: 'es/ ***abbr.*** (used for adding sth to the end of a letter) postscript: *Love Tessa. PS I'll bring the car.*

pseudo- /'su:dəʊ; 'sju:-/ ***prefix*** (used in nouns, adjectives and adverbs) not genuine; false or pretended: *pseudonym* ◇ *pseudo-science*

pseudocode /'su:dəʊkəʊd; 'sju:-/ ***noun*** [C] (COMPUTING) a very simple form of computer language used in program design

pseudonym /'su:dənɪm; 'sju:-/ ***noun*** [C] a name used by sb, especially a writer, instead of their real name

psych /saɪk/ ***verb***

PHR V psych yourself up (*informal*) to prepare yourself in your mind for sth difficult: *I've got to psych myself up for this interview.*

psyche /'saɪki/ ***noun*** [C] (*formal*) (PSYCHOLOGY) the mind; your deepest feelings and attitudes: *the human/female/national psyche*

psychedelic /ˌsaɪkə'delɪk/ ***adj.*** (used about art, music, clothes, etc.) having bright colours or patterns or strange sounds

psychiatrist /saɪ'kaɪətrɪst/ ***noun*** [C] (HEALTH) a doctor who is trained to treat people with mental illness

psychiatry /saɪ'kaɪətri/ ***noun*** [U] (HEALTH) the study and treatment of mental illness ➲ look at **psychology** ▶ **psychiatric** /ˌsaɪki'ætrɪk/ ***adj.***: *a psychiatric hospital/unit/nurse*

psychic /'saɪkɪk/ ***adj.*** (used about a person or their mind) having unusual powers that cannot be explained, for example knowing what sb else is thinking or being able to see into the future

psycho /'saɪkəʊ/ =PSYCHOPATH

psycho- /'saɪkəʊ/ (*also* **psych-**) ***prefix*** (used in nouns, adjectives and adverbs) connected with the mind: *psychology* ◇ *psychiatrist*

psychoanalysis /ˌsaɪkəʊə'næləsɪs/ (*also* **analysis**) ***noun*** [U] (PSYCHOLOGY) a method of treating sb with a mental illness by asking about their past experiences, feelings, dreams, etc. in order to find out what is making them ill ▶ **psychoanalyse** (*AmE* **-yze**) /ˌsaɪkəʊ'ænəlaɪz/ ***verb*** [T]

psychoanalyst /ˌsaɪkəʊ'ænəlɪst/ ***noun*** [C] (PSYCHOLOGY) a person who treats sb with a mental illness by using PSYCHOANALYSIS

psycholinguistics /ˌsaɪkəʊlɪŋ'gwɪstɪks/ ***noun*** [U] (LANGUAGE) the study of how the mind processes and produces language ▶ **psycholinguistic** /ˌsaɪkəʊlɪŋ'gwɪstɪk/ ***adj.***

psychological AW /ˌsaɪkə'lɒdʒɪkl/ ***adj.*** **1** (PSYCHOLOGY) connected with the mind or the way that it works: *Has her ordeal caused her long-term psychological damage?* **2** (PSYCHOLOGY) connected with the study of the mind and the way people behave (**psychology**) ▶ **psychologically** /-kli/ **adv.**: *Psychologically, it was a bad time to be starting a new job.*

psychologist AW /saɪˈkɒlədʒɪst/ **noun** [C] (PSYCHOLOGY) a scientist who studies the mind and the way that people behave

psychology AW /saɪˈkɒlədʒi/ **noun 1** [U] the scientific study of the mind and the way that people behave: *child psychology* ➲ look at **psychiatry** **2** [sing.] the type of mind that a person or group of people has: *If we understood the psychology of the killer we would have a better chance of catching him.*

psychopath /ˈsaɪkəpæθ/ (also *spoken* **psycho**) **noun** [C] (HEALTH) a person who has a serious mental illness that may cause them to hurt or kill other people

psychosis /saɪˈkəʊsɪs/ **noun** [C,U] (*pl.* **psychoses** /-siːz/) (HEALTH) a very serious mental illness that affects your whole personality ▶ **psychotic** /saɪˈkɒtɪk/ **adj., noun** [C]: *a psychotic patient/individual*

psychosomatic /ˌsaɪkəʊsəˈmætɪk/ **adj.** (HEALTH) (of an illness) caused by mental problems rather than physical problems

psychotherapy /ˌsaɪkəʊˈθerəpi/ (*also* **therapy**) **noun** [U] (HEALTH, PSYCHOLOGY) the treatment of mental illness by discussing sb's problems with them rather than by giving them drugs ▶ **psychotherapist** /-pɪst/ (*also* **therapist**) **noun** [C]

PT /ˌpiː ˈtiː/ **abbr.** (EDUCATION) physical training

pt ⊶ (*pl.* **pts**) **abbr. 1** pint: *2 pts milk* **2** (in a game or competition) point: *Laura 5 pts, Arthur 4 pts*

PTA /ˌpiː tiː ˈeɪ/ **noun** [C] (EDUCATION) **parent-teacher association**; a group run by parents and teachers in a school that organizes social events and helps the school in different ways

PTO (*also* **pto**) /ˌpiː tiː ˈəʊ/ **abbr.** (at the bottom of a page) please turn over

pub ⊶ /pʌb/ (also *formal* ˌ**public** ˈ**house**) **noun** [C] (*BrE*) a place where people go to buy and drink alcohol that also often serves food

puberty /ˈpjuːbəti/ **noun** [U] (BIOLOGY) the time when a child's body is changing and becoming physically like that of an adult

pubic /ˈpjuːbɪk/ **adj.** (BIOLOGY) of the area around the sexual organs: *pubic hair*

public[1] ⊶ /ˈpʌblɪk/ **adj. 1** (only *before* a noun) connected with ordinary people in general, not those who have an important position in society: ***Public opinion*** *was in favour of the war.* ◇ *How much public support is there for the government's policy?* **2** provided for the use of people in general; not private: *a public library/telephone* ◇ *public spending* (= money that the government spends on education, health care, etc.) **3** known by many people: *We're going to* ***make*** *the news* ***public*** *soon.* ➲ look at **private** ▶ **publicly** **adv.**: *The company refused to admit publicly that it had acted wrongly.*

IDM **be common/public knowledge** → KNOWLEDGE

go public 1 to tell people about sth that is a secret: *The sacked employee went public with his stories of corruption inside the company.* **2** (used about a company) to start selling shares to the public

in the public eye often appearing on television, in magazines, etc.

public[2] ⊶ /ˈpʌblɪk/ **noun** [sing., with sing. or pl. verb] **1 the public** people in general: *The university swimming pool is* ***open to the public*** *in the evenings.* ◇ *The police have asked for help from* ***members of the public.*** ◇ *The public is/are generally in favour of the new law.* **2** a group of people who are all interested in sth or who have sth in common: *the travelling public*

IDM **in public** when other people are present: *This is the first time that Miss Potter has spoken about her experience in public.*

ˌ**public adˈdress system** **noun** [C] (*abbr.* **PA system**) an electronic system that uses MICROPHONES and LOUDSPEAKERS to make music, voices, etc. louder so that they can be heard by everyone in a particular place or building

publican /ˈpʌblɪkən/ **noun** [C] a person who owns or manages a pub

publication ⊶ AW /ˌpʌblɪˈkeɪʃn/ **noun 1** [U] the act of printing a book, magazine, etc. and making it available to the public: *His latest book has just been accepted for publication.* **2** [C] a book, magazine, etc. that has been published **3** [U] the action of making sth known to the public: *the publication of exam results*

ˌ**public ˈcompany** (*also* ˌ**public** ˌ**limited** ˈ**company**) **noun** [C] (*BrE*) (*abbr.* **plc**) (BUSINESS) a large company that sells shares in itself to the public

ˌ**public conˈvenience** **noun** [C] (*BrE*) a toilet in a public place that anyone can use

ˌ**public ˈholiday** **noun** [C] a day on which most of the shops, businesses and schools in a country are closed, often to celebrate a particular event ➲ look at **bank holiday**

ˌ**public ˈhouse** (*formal*) = PUB

publicity ⊶ /pʌbˈlɪsəti/ **noun** [U] **1** (ARTS AND MEDIA) notice or attention from the newspapers, television, etc.: *to seek/avoid publicity* **2** the business of attracting people's attention to sth/sb; advertising: *There has been a lot of publicity for this film.*

publicize (also **-ise**) /ˈpʌblɪsaɪz/ **verb** [T] to attract people's attention to sth: *The event has been well publicized and should attract a lot of people.*

ˌ**public reˈlations** **noun** (*abbr.* **PR**) **1** [pl.] (BUSINESS) the state of the relationship between an organization and the public: *Giving money to local charities is good for public relations.* **2** [U] the job of making a company, organization, etc. popular with the public: *a Public Relations Officer*

ˌ**public ˈschool** **noun** [C] (EDUCATION) **1** (in Britain, especially in England) a private school for children aged between 13 and 18, whose parents pay for their education. The children often live at the school while they are studying. ➲ look at **preparatory school, private school** **2** ˈ**public school** (in the US, Australia, Scotland and other countries) a free local school paid for by the government ➲ look at **state school**

the ˌ**public ˈsector** **noun** [sing.] (ECONOMICS) the part of the economy of a country that is owned or controlled by the government ➲ look at **the public sector**

ˌ**public-ˈspirited** **adj.** always ready to help other people and the public in general

ˌ**public ˈtransport** **noun** [U] (the system of) buses, trains, etc. that run according to a series of planned times and that anyone can use: *to travel by/on public transport*

publish ⊶ AW /ˈpʌblɪʃ/ **verb 1** [I,T] (ARTS AND MEDIA) to prepare and print a book, magazine, etc. and make it available to the public: *This dictionary was published by Oxford University Press.* **2** [T] (ARTS AND MEDIA) (used about a writer, etc.) to have your work put in a book, magazine, etc.: *Dr Wreth has published several articles on the subject.* **3** [T] to make sth known to the public: *Large companies must publish their accounts every year.*

publisher AW /ˈpʌblɪʃə(r)/ ***noun*** [C] (ARTS AND MEDIA) a person or company that publishes books, magazines, etc.

publishing 🔑 AW /ˈpʌblɪʃɪŋ/ ***noun*** [U] the business of preparing books, magazines, etc. to be printed and sold: *She's aiming for a career in publishing.*

puck /pʌk/ ***noun*** [C] (SPORT) a hard flat rubber disc that is used as a ball in ICE HOCKEY

pudding /ˈpʊdɪŋ/ ***noun*** [C,U] (*BrE*) **1** any sweet food that is eaten at the end of a meal: *What's for pudding today?* ➲ look at **sweet 2** a type of sweet food that is made from bread, flour or rice with eggs, milk, etc.: *rice pudding*

puddle /ˈpʌdl/ ***noun*** [C] a small pool of water or other liquid, especially rain, that has formed on the ground

puff[1] /pʌf/ ***verb* 1** [I,T] (used about air, smoke, wind, etc.) to blow or come out in clouds: *Smoke was puffing out of the chimney.* **2** [I,T] to smoke a cigarette, pipe, etc.: *to puff on a cigarette* **3** [I] to breathe loudly or quickly, for example when you are running: *He was puffing hard as he ran up the hill.* **4** [I] **~ along, in, out, up, etc.** to move in a particular direction with loud breaths or small clouds of smoke: *The train puffed into the station.*

PHR V **puff sth out/up** to cause sth to become larger by filling it with air: *The trumpet player was puffing out his cheeks.*

puff up (used about part of the body) to become swollen: *Her arm puffed up when she was stung by a wasp.*

puff[2] /pʌf/ ***noun*** [C] **1** a small amount of air, smoke, wind, etc. that is blown or sent out: *a puff of smoke* **2** one breath that you take when you are smoking a cigarette or pipe: *to take/have a puff on a cigarette*

puffed /pʌft/ (*also* ˌ**puffed ˈout**) ***adj.*** finding it difficult to breathe, for example because you have been running

puffin /ˈpʌfɪn/ ***noun*** [C] a North Atlantic SEABIRD with a large brightly-coloured beak ➲ picture on **page 28**

puffy /ˈpʌfi/ ***adj.*** (used about a part of a person's body) looking soft and swollen: *Your eyes look a bit puffy. Have you been crying?*

puke /pjuːk/ ***verb*** [I,T] (*slang*) (HEALTH) to be sick; to VOMIT ▶ **puke *noun*** [U]

pull[1] 🔑 /pʊl/ ***verb* 1** [I,T] to use force to move sb/sth towards yourself: *I pulled on the rope to make sure that it was secure.* ◇ *to pull the trigger of a gun* ◇ *I felt someone pull at my sleeve and turned round.* ◇ *They managed to pull the child out of the water just in time.* **2** [T] **~ sth on, out, up, down, etc.** to move sth in the direction that is described: *She pulled her sweater on/She pulled on her sweater.* ◇ *He pulled up his trousers/He pulled his trousers up.* ◇ *I switched off the TV and pulled out the plug.* **3** [T] to hold or be fastened to sth and move it along behind you in the direction that you are going: *That cart is too heavy for one horse to pull.* **4** [I,T] to move your body or a part of your body away with force: *She pulled away as he tried to kiss her.* ◇ *I pulled back my fingers just as the door slammed.* **5** [T] (HEALTH) to damage a muscle, etc. by using too much force: *I've **pulled a muscle** in my thigh.* ➲ note at **injure**

IDM **make/pull faces/a face (at sb)** → FACE[1]

pull sb's leg (*informal*) to play a joke on sb by trying to make them believe sth that is not true

pull out all the stops (*informal*) to make the greatest possible effort to achieve sth

pull your punches (*informal*) (usually used in negative sentences) to be careful what you say or do in order not to shock or upset anyone: *The film pulls no punches in its portrayal of urban violence.*

pull strings to use your influence to gain an advantage

pull your weight to do your fair share of the work

PHR V **pull away (from sb/sth)** to start moving forward, leaving sb/sth behind: *We waved as the bus pulled away.*

pull sth down to destroy a building

pull in (to sth); **pull into sth 1** (used about a train) to enter a station **2** (used about a car, etc.) to move to the side of the road and stop

pull sth off (*informal*) to succeed in sth: *to pull off a business deal*

pull out (used about a car, etc.) to move away from the side of the road: *I braked as a car suddenly pulled out in front of me.*

pull out (of sth) (used about a train) to leave a station

pull (sb/sth) out (of sth) (to cause sb/sth) to leave sth: *The Americans have pulled their forces out of the area.* ◇ *We've pulled out of the deal.*

pull sth out to take sth out of a place suddenly or with force: *She walked into the bank and pulled out a gun.*

pull over (used about a vehicle or its driver) to slow down and move to the side of the road: *I pulled over to let the ambulance past.*

pull through (sth) to survive a dangerous illness or a difficult time

pull together to do sth or work together with other people in an organized way and without fighting

pull yourself together to control your feelings and behave in a calm way: *Pull yourself together and stop crying.*

pull up (to cause a car, etc.) to stop

pull[2] 🔑 /pʊl/ ***noun* 1** [C] **a ~ (at/on sth)** the action of moving sb/sth towards you using force: *I gave a pull on the rope to check it was secure.* **2** [sing.] a physical force or an attraction that makes sb/sth move in a particular direction: *the earth's gravitational pull* ◇ *He couldn't resist the pull of the city.* **3** [sing.] the act of taking a breath of smoke from a cigarette

ˌ**pull-down ˈmenu** ***noun*** [C] = DROP-DOWN MENU

pulley /ˈpʊli/ ***noun*** [C] a piece of equipment, consisting of a wheel and a rope, that is used for lifting heavy things ➲ picture at **block and tackle**

pullover /ˈpʊləʊvə(r)/ ***noun*** [C] a knitted WOOLLEN piece of clothing for the upper part of the body, with long sleeves and no buttons

pulmonary /ˈpʌlmənəri/ ***adj.*** (ANATOMY) connected with the lungs: *the pulmonary artery* ➲ picture at **heart**

pulp /pʌlp/ ***noun* 1** [sing., U] a soft substance that is made especially by pressing sth: *Mash the beans to a pulp.* ➲ look at **wood pulp 2** [U] the soft inner part of some fruits or vegetables **3** [U] (ANATOMY) the soft, sensitive TISSUE in the inside of a tooth

ˈ**pulp cavity** ***noun*** [C] (ANATOMY) the area inside a tooth where the PULP is ➲ picture at **tooth**

pulpit /ˈpʊlpɪt/ ***noun*** [C] (RELIGION) a raised platform in a church where the priest stands when he or she is speaking

pulsar /ˈpʌlsɑː(r)/ ***noun*** [C] (**ASTRONOMY**) a star that cannot be seen but that sends out fast regular radio signals ➲ look at **quasar**

pulsate /pʌlˈseɪt/ ***verb*** [I] to move or shake with strong regular movements: *a pulsating rhythm*

pulse¹ /pʌls/ ***noun* 1** [C, usually sing.] (**BIOLOGY**) the regular beating in your body as blood is pushed around it by your heart. You can feel your **pulse** at your wrist, neck, etc.: *Your pulse rate increases after exercise.* ◇ *to feel/take sb's pulse* (= to count how many times it beats in one minute) **2 pulses** [pl.] the seeds of some plants such as BEANS and PEAS that are cooked and eaten as food

pulse² /pʌls/ ***verb*** [I] to move with strong regular movements

pulverize (also **-ise**) /ˈpʌlvəraɪz/ ***verb*** [T] (*formal*) to crush sth into a fine powder: *pulverized bones*

puma /ˈpjuːmə/ (*AmE* **cougar** or **ˈmountain lion**) ***noun*** [C] a large American wild animal of the cat family, with yellowish-brown or greyish fur

pumice /ˈpʌmɪs/ (*also* **ˈpumice stone**) ***noun*** [U] a type of grey stone that is very light in weight. It is used as a powder for cleaning and polishing, and in larger pieces for rubbing on the skin to make it softer.

pump¹ /pʌmp/ ***verb* 1** [T] to force a gas or liquid to go in a particular direction: *Your heart pumps blood around your body.* **2** [I] (used about a liquid) to flow in a particular direction as if forced by a PUMP: *Blood was pumping out of the wound.* **3** [I,T] to be moved or to move sth very quickly up and down or in and out: *He pumped his arms up and down to keep warm.*

PHRV pump sth into sth/sb to put a lot of sth into sth/sb: *He pumped all his savings into the business.*

pump sth up to fill sth with air, for example by using a PUMP: *to pump up a car tyre*

pump² /pʌmp/ ***noun*** [C] **1** a machine that is used for forcing a gas or liquid in a particular direction: *Have you got a bicycle pump?* ◇ *a petrol pump* **2** [usually pl.] a flat woman's shoe with no fastening: *ballet pumps*

ˈpump-action ***adj.*** (used about a machine or device) that you operate using a PUMPING action of your hand or arm: *a pump-action spray/shotgun*

pumpkin /ˈpʌmpkɪn/ ***noun*** [C,U] a very large round fruit with thick orange-coloured skin that is cooked and eaten as a vegetable

pun /pʌn/ ***noun*** [C] (**LANGUAGE**) an amusing use of a word that can have two meanings or of different words that sound the same

punch¹ 🔑 /pʌntʃ/ ***verb*** [T] **1 ~ sb (in/on sth)** to hit sb/sth hard with your closed hand (**fist**): *to punch sb on the nose* ◇ *He punched the air when he heard the good news.* **2** to make a hole in sth with a special tool (**a punch**): *He punched a hole in the ticket.*

punch² 🔑 /pʌntʃ/ ***noun* 1** [C] a hard hit with your closed hand (**fist**) **2** [C] a machine or tool that you use for making holes in sth: *a ticket punch* ◇ *a hole punch* **3** [U] a drink made from wine, fruit juice and sugar

IDM pull your punches → PULL¹

punchline /ˈpʌntʃlaɪn/ ***noun*** [C] the last and most important words of a joke or story

ˈpunch-up ***noun*** [C] (*BrE, informal*) a fight in which people hit each other

punctual /ˈpʌŋktʃuəl/ ***adj.*** doing sth or happening at the right time; not late: *It is important to be punctual for your classes.* ▶ **punctuality** /ˌpʌŋktʃuˈæləti/ ***noun*** [U]: *Japanese trains are famous for their punctuality.* ▶ **punctually** ***adv.***

punctuate /ˈpʌŋktʃueɪt/ ***verb* 1** [T] **~ sth (with sth)** to interrupt sth many times: *Her speech was punctuated with bursts of applause.* **2** [I,T] (**LANGUAGE**) to divide writing into sentences and phrases by adding full stops, question marks, etc.

punctuation /ˌpʌŋktʃuˈeɪʃn/ ***noun*** [U] the marks used for dividing writing into sentences and phrases: ***Punctuation marks*** *include full stops, commas and question marks.*

puncture /ˈpʌŋktʃə(r)/ ***noun*** [C] a small hole made by a sharp point, especially in a bicycle or car tyre ▶ **puncture** ***verb*** [I,T]

pungent /ˈpʌndʒənt/ ***adj.*** (used about a smell) very strong

punish 🔑 /ˈpʌnɪʃ/ ***verb*** [T] **~ sb (for sth/for doing sth)** to make sb suffer because they have done sth bad or wrong: *The children were severely punished for telling lies.*

punishable /ˈpʌnɪʃəbl/ ***adj.*** **~ (by sth)** (**LAW**) (used about a crime, etc.) that you can be punished for doing: *a punishable offence* ◇ *In some countries drug smuggling is punishable by death.*

punishing /ˈpʌnɪʃɪŋ/ ***adj.*** that makes you very tired or weak: *The Prime Minister had a punishing schedule, visiting five countries in five days.*

punishment 🔑 /ˈpʌnɪʃmənt/ ***noun*** [C,U] the action or way of punishing sb: *He was excluded from school for a week as a punishment.* ◇ ***capital punishment*** (= punishment by death)

punitive /ˈpjuːnətɪv/ ***adj.*** (*formal*) **1** intended as a punishment: *to take punitive measures against sb* **2** very HARSH and that people find difficult to pay: *punitive taxation*

punk /pʌŋk/ ***noun* 1** [U] (**MUSIC**) a type of loud music that was popular in Britain in the late 1970s and early 1980s. **Punk** deliberately tried to offend people with traditional views and behaviour. **2** [C] a person who likes punk music and often has brightly-coloured hair and unusual clothes

punt /pʌnt/ ***noun*** [C] a long narrow boat with a flat bottom and square ends which is moved by pushing a long pole against the bottom of a river ▶ **punt** ***verb*** [I,T]: *to go punting*

puny /ˈpjuːni/ ***adj.*** very small and weak

pup /pʌp/ ***noun*** [C] **1** = PUPPY **2** (**BIOLOGY**) the young of some animals, for example SEALS

pupa /ˈpjuːpə/ ***noun*** [C] (*pl.* **pupae** /-piː/) (**BIOLOGY**) an insect in the stage of development before it becomes an adult insect ➲ look at **larva** ❶ The pupa of a butterfly or moth is called a **chrysalis**.

pupil 🔑 /ˈpjuːpl/ ***noun*** [C] **1** (**EDUCATION**) a child in school: *There are 28 pupils in my class.* **2** (**ARTS AND MEDIA**) a person who is taught artistic, musical, etc. skills by an expert: *He was a pupil of Liszt.* ➲ look at **student 3** (**ANATOMY**) the round black hole in the middle of your eye ➲ picture at **eye**

puppet /ˈpʌpɪt/ ***noun*** [C] **1** (**ARTS AND MEDIA**) a model of a person or an animal that you can move by pulling the strings which are tied to it or by putting your hand inside it and moving your fingers **2** a person or an organization that is controlled by sb else: *The occupying forces set up a puppet government.*

puppetry /ˈpʌpɪtri/ ***noun*** [U] (**ARTS AND MEDIA**) the art and skill of making and using PUPPETS

puppy /ˈpʌpi/ ***noun*** [C] (*pl.* **puppies**) (*also* **pup**) a young dog

purchase ⊶ AW /ˈpɜːtʃəs/ ***noun*** (*formal*) **1** [U] the action of buying sth: *to take out a loan for the purchase of a car* **2** [C] something that you buy: *These shoes were a poor purchase – they're falling apart already.* ◇ *to make a purchase* ▶ **purchase *verb*** [T]: *Many employees have the opportunity to purchase shares in the company they work for.*

purchaser /ˈpɜːtʃəsə(r)/ ***noun*** [C] (*formal*) a person who buys sth: *The purchaser of the house agrees to pay a deposit of 10%.* ➲ look at **vendor**

pure ⊶ /pjʊə(r)/ ***adj.*** **1** not mixed with anything else: *pure orange juice/silk/alcohol* **2** clean and not containing any harmful substances: *pure air/water* OPP **impure 3** (only *before* a noun) complete and total: *We met by pure chance.* **4** (used about a sound, colour or light) very clear; perfect: *She was dressed in pure white.* **5** (only *before* a noun) (used about an area of learning) concerned only with increasing your knowledge rather than having practical uses: *pure mathematics* OPP **applied 6** not doing or knowing anything evil or anything that is connected with sex: *a young girl still pure in mind and body* OPP **impure**

purée /ˈpjʊəreɪ/ ***noun*** [C,U] a food that you make by cooking a fruit or vegetable and then pressing and mixing it until it is smooth and liquid: *apple/tomato purée*

purely ⊶ /ˈpjʊəli/ ***adv.*** only or completely: *It's not purely a question of money.*

purge /pɜːdʒ/ ***verb*** [T] **~ sth (of sb); ~ sb (from sth)** to remove people that you do not want from a political party or other organization ▶ **purge *noun*** [C]: *The General carried out a purge of his political enemies.*

purify /ˈpjʊərɪfaɪ/ ***verb*** [T] (*pres. part.* **purifying**; *3rd person sing. pres.* **purifies**; *pt, pp* **purified**) to remove dirty or harmful substances from sth: *purified water* ➲ picture at **water**

puritan /ˈpjʊərɪtən/ ***noun*** [C] a person who thinks that it is wrong to enjoy yourself ▶ **puritan** (*also* **puritanical** /ˌpjʊərɪˈtænɪkl/) ***adj.***: *a puritan attitude to life*

purity /ˈpjʊərəti/ ***noun*** [U] the state of being pure: *to test the purity of the air* ➲ look at **impurity**

purl /pɜːl/ ***noun*** [U] a simple STITCH used in knitting

purple ⊶ /ˈpɜːpl/ ***adj., noun*** [U] (of) a reddish-blue colour: *His face was purple with rage.*

purport /pəˈpɔːt/ ***verb*** [I] (*formal*) to give the impression of being sth or of having done sth, when this may not be true: *The book does not purport to be a true history of the period.*

> **THESAURUS**
>
> **purpose**
>
> **aim • intention • plan • point • idea**
> These are all words for talking about what sb/sth intends to do or achieve.
>
> **purpose**: *Our purpose is to raise money.*
>
> **aim**: *Her aim was to find a job in London.*
>
> **intention**: *I have no intention of going to the party.*
>
> **plan**: *There are plans to build new offices.*
>
> **point** (*informal*): *What's the point of all this violence?*
>
> **idea** (*informal*): *The idea was to meet her new boyfriend.*

purpose ⊶ /ˈpɜːpəs/ ***noun*** **1** [C] the aim or intention of sth: *The main purpose of this meeting is to decide what we should do next.* ◇ *You may only use the telephone for business purposes.* **2 purposes** [pl.] what is needed in a particular situation: ***For the purposes of*** *this demonstration, I will use model cars.* **3** [U] a meaning or reason that is important to you: *A good leader inspires people with a* ***sense of purpose***. **4** [U] the ability to plan sth and work hard to achieve it: *I was impressed by his* ***strength of purpose***.

IDM **to/for all intents and purposes** → INTENT[2]

on purpose not by accident; with a particular intention: *'You've torn a page out of my book!' 'I'm sorry, I didn't do it on purpose.'* SYN **deliberately**

purposeful /ˈpɜːpəsfl/ ***adj.*** having a definite aim or plan: *Greg strode off down the street looking purposeful.* ▶ **purposefully** /-fəli/ ***adv.***

purposely /ˈpɜːpəsli/ ***adv.*** with a particular intention: *I purposely waited till everyone had gone so that I could speak to you in private.* SYN **deliberately**

purr /pɜː(r)/ ***verb*** [I] (used about a cat) to make a continuous low sound that shows pleasure ➲ look at **miaow**

purse[1] /pɜːs/ ***noun*** [C] **1** a small bag made of leather, etc., for carrying coins and often also paper money, used especially by women ➲ look at **wallet 2** (*AmE*) = HANDBAG

purse[2] /pɜːs/ ***verb***

IDM **purse your lips** to press your lips together to show that you do not like sth

purser /ˈpɜːsə(r)/ ***noun*** [C] the person on a ship who looks after the accounts and deals with passengers' problems

pursue ⊶ AW /pəˈsjuː/ ***verb*** [T] (*formal*) **1** to follow sb/sth in order to catch them or it SYN **chase**: *The robber ran off pursued by two policemen.* **2** to try to achieve sth or to continue to do sth over a period of time: *to pursue a career in banking* ◇ *She didn't seem to want to pursue the discussion so I changed the subject.*

pursuer /pəˈsjuːə(r)/ ***noun*** [C] a person who is following and trying to catch sb/sth

pursuit AW /pəˈsjuːt/ ***noun*** **1** [U] the action of trying to achieve or get sth: *the pursuit of pleasure* **2** [C] an activity that you do either for work or for pleasure: *outdoor/leisure pursuits*

IDM **in hot pursuit** → HOT[1]

in pursuit (of sb/sth) trying to catch or get sb/sth: *He neglected his family in pursuit of his own personal ambitions.*

pus /pʌs/ ***noun*** [U] (**HEALTH**) a thick yellowish liquid that may form in a part of your body that has been hurt

push[1] ⊶ /pʊʃ/ ***verb*** **1** [I,T] to use force to move sb/sth forward or away from you: *She pushed him into the water.* ◇ *to push a pram* ◇ *She pushed the door shut with her foot.* **2** [I,T] to move forward by pushing sb/sth: *John pushed his way through the crowd.* ◇ *to push past sb* ◇ *People were* ***pushing and shoving*** *to try to get to the front.* **3** [I,T] to press a switch, button, etc., for example in order to start a machine: *Push the red button if you want the bus to stop.* **4** [T] **~ sb (to do sth /into doing sth); ~ sb (for sth)** to try to make sb do sth that they do not want to do: *My friend pushed me into entering the competition.* ◇ *Ella will not work hard unless you push her.* **5** [T] (*informal*) to try to make sth seem attractive, for example so that people will buy it: *They are launching a major publicity campaign to push their new product.*

IDM be hard pressed/pushed/put to do sth → HARD[2]
be pushed for sth (*informal*) to not have enough of sth: *Hurry up. We're really* ***pushed for time****.*
push your luck; **push it/things** (*informal*) to take a risk because you have successfully avoided problems in the past: *You didn't get caught last time, but don't push your luck!*
PHR V push sb about/around to give orders to sb in a rude and unpleasant way: *Don't let your boss push you around.*
push ahead/forward (with sth) to continue with sth
push for sth to try hard to get sth: *Jim is pushing for a pay rise.*
push in to join a line of people waiting for sth by standing in front of others who were there before you
push on to continue a journey: *Although it was getting dark, we decided to push on.*
push sb/sth over to make sb/sth fall down by pushing them or it

push² ⊶ /pʊʃ/ ***noun*** [C] an act of pushing: *Can you help me* ***give*** *the car* ***a push*** *to get it started?* ◇ *The car windows opened at the push of a button.*
IDM at a push (*informal*) if it is really necessary (but only with difficulty): *We can get ten people round the table at a push.*
give sb the push to tell sb you no longer want them in a relationship, or in a job

'push-button ***adj.*** (only *before* a noun) (used about a machine, etc.) that you work by pressing a button: *a radio with push-button controls*

pushchair /'pʊʃtʃeə(r)/ (*BrE also* **buggy**) ***noun*** [C] a chair on wheels that you use for pushing a young child in

pusher /'pʊʃə(r)/ ***noun*** [C] a person who sells illegal drugs

pushover /'pʊʃəʊvə(r)/ ***noun*** [C] (*informal*) **1** something that is easy to do or win **2** a person who is easy to persuade to do sth

'push technology ***noun*** [U] (COMPUTING) a service that allows Internet users to keep receiving the particular type of information that they describe by completing a form

'push-up (*AmE*) = PRESS-UP ➲ picture at **sit-up**

pushy /'pʊʃi/ ***adj.*** (*informal*) (used about a person) trying hard to get what you want, in a way that seems rude

put ⊶ /pʊt/ ***verb*** [T] (*pres. part.* **putting**; *pt, pp* **put**) **1** to move sb/sth into a particular place or position: *She put the book on the table.* ◇ *Did you put sugar in my tea?* ◇ *When do you put the children to bed?* **2** to fix sth to or in sth else: *Can you put (=sew) a button on this shirt?* ◇ *We're going to put a picture on this wall.* **3** to write sth: *12.30 on Friday? I'll put it in my diary.* ◇ *What did you put for question 2?* **4** ~ **sb/sth in/into sth** to bring sb/sth into the state or condition mentioned: *This sort of weather always puts me in a bad mood.* ◇ *I was* ***put in charge*** *of the project.* ◇ *It was time to* ***put*** *our ideas* ***into practice****.* **5** to make sb/sth feel sth or be affected by sth: *This will* ***put pressure on*** *them to finish the job quickly.* ◇ *Don't* ***put the blame on*** *me!* ◇ *The new teacher soon* ***put a stop to*** *cheating in tests.* **6** to give or fix a particular value or importance to sb/sth: *We'll have to* ***put a limit on*** *how much we spend.* ◇ *I'd put him in my top five favourite writers.* **7** to say or express sth: *I don't know exactly how to put this, but...* ◇ ***To put it another way****, you're sacked.* ◇ ***Put simply****, he just wasn't good enough.*
IDM put it to sb that... (*formal*) to suggest to sb that sth is true: *I put it to you that this man is innocent.*
put together (used after a noun or nouns referring to a group of people or things) combined; in total: *You got more presents than the rest of the family put together.*
PHR V put sth/yourself across/over to say what you want to say clearly, so that people can understand it: *He didn't put his ideas across very well at the meeting.*
put sth aside 1 to save sth, especially money, to use later **2** to ignore or forget sth: *We agreed to put aside our differences and work together.*
put sb away (*informal*) to send sb to prison
put sth away 1 to put sth where you usually keep it because you have finished using it: *Put the tools away if you've finished with them.* **2** to save money to spend later
put sth back 1 to return sth to its place: *to put books back on the shelf* **2** to move sth to a later time: *The meeting's been put back until next week.* **OPP bring sth forward 3** to change the time shown on a clock to an earlier time: *We have to put the clocks back tonight.* **OPP put sth forward**
put sb/sth before/above sb/sth to treat sb/sth as more important than sb/sth else: *He puts his children before anything else.*
put sth by to save money to use later: *Her grandparents had put some money by for her wedding.*
put sb down 1 (*informal*) to say things to make sb seem stupid or FOOLISH **2** to put a baby to bed
put sth down 1 to stop holding sth and put it on the floor, a table, etc.: *The policeman persuaded him to put the gun down.* **2** to write sth: *I'll put that down in my diary.* **3** to pay part of the cost of sth: *We put down a 10% deposit on a car.* **4** (used about a government, an army or the police) to stop sth by force: *to put down a rebellion* **5** to kill an animal because it is old, sick or dangerous: *The dog was put down after it attacked a child.*
put sth down to sth to believe that sth is caused by sth: *I put his bad exam results down to laziness rather than a lack of ability.*
put yourself/sb forward to suggest that you or another person should be considered for a job, etc.: *His name was put forward for the position of chairman.*
put sth forward 1 to change the time shown on a clock to a later time: *We put the clocks forward in spring.* **OPP put sth back 2** to suggest sth: *She put forward a plan to help the homeless.*
put sth in 1 to fix equipment or furniture in position so that it can be used: *We're having a shower put in.* **SYN install 2** to include a piece of information, etc. in sth that you write **3** to ask for sth officially: *to put in an invoice/request*
put sth in; **put sth into sth/into doing sth** to spend time, etc. on sth: *She puts all her time and energy into her business.*
put sb off (sb/sth/doing sth) 1 to make sb not like sb/sth or not want to do sth: *The accident put me off driving for a long time.* **2** to say to a person that you can no longer do what you had agreed: *They were coming to stay last weekend but I had to put them off at the last moment.* **3** to make sb unable to give their attention to sth: *Don't stare at me – you're putting me off!*
put sth off to turn or switch a light off: *She put off the light and went to sleep.*
put sth off; **put off doing sth** to move sth to a later time; to delay doing sth: *She put off writing her essay until the last minute.*
put sth on 1 to dress yourself in sth: *Put on your coat!* ◇ *I'll have to put my glasses on.* **2** to cover an area of your skin with sth: *You'd better put some sun*

cream on. **3** to switch on a piece of electrical equipment: *It's too early to put the lights on yet.* **4** to make a tape, a CD, etc. begin to play: *Let's put some music on.* **5** to become heavier, especially by the amount mentioned: *I* ***put on weight*** *very easily.* OPP **lose 6** to organize or prepare sth for people to see or use: *The school is putting on 'Macbeth'.* ◇ *They put on extra trains in the summer.* **7** to pretend to be feeling sth; to pretend to have sth: *He's not angry with you really: he's just putting it on.*

put sth on sth 1 to add an amount of money, etc. to the cost or value of sth: *The government want to put more tax on the price of a packet of cigarettes.* **2** to bet money on sth: *He put all his money on a horse.* SYN **bet**

put sb out 1 to give sb trouble or extra work: *He put his hosts out by arriving very late.* **2** to make sb upset or angry: *I was quite put out by their selfish behaviour.*

put sth out 1 to make sth stop burning: *to put out a fire* SYN **extinguish 2** to switch off a piece of electrical equipment: *They put out the lights and locked the door.* **3** to take sth out of your house and leave it: *to put the rubbish out* **4** to give or tell the public sth, often on the television or radio or in newspapers: *The police put out a warning about the escaped prisoner.*

put yourself out (*informal*) to do sth for sb, even though it brings you trouble or extra work: *'I'll give you a lift home.' 'I don't want you to put yourself out. I'll take a taxi.'*

put sth/yourself over → PUT STH/YOURSELF ACROSS/OVER

put sb through sth to make sb experience sth unpleasant

put sb/sth through to make a telephone connection that allows sb to speak to sb: *Could you put me through to Jeanne, please?*

put sth to sb to suggest sth to sb; to ask sb sth: *I put the question to her.*

put sth together to build or repair sth by joining its parts together: *The furniture comes with instructions on how to put it together.* ➲ note at **build**[1]

put sth towards sth to give money to pay part of the cost of sth: *We all put a pound towards a leaving present for Joe.*

put sb up to give sb food and a place to stay: *She had missed the last train home, so I offered to put her up for the night.*

put sth up 1 to lift or hold sth up: *Put your hand up if you know the answer.* **2** to build sth: *to put up a fence/tent* ➲ note at **build**[1] **3** to fix sth to a wall, etc. so that everyone can see it: *to put up a notice* **4** to increase sth: *Some shops put up their prices just before Christmas.*

put up sth to try to stop sb attacking you: *The old lady put up a struggle against her attacker.*

put up with sb/sth to suffer sb/sth unpleasant and not complain about it: *I don't know how they put up with this noise.*

putrid /'pju:trɪd/ ***adj.*** **1** (used about dead animals and plants) smelling bad after being dead for some time **2** (*informal*) very unpleasant: *The food there was putrid.*

putt /pʌt/ ***verb*** [I,T] (**SPORT**) (used in GOLF) to hit the ball gently when it is near the hole

putter /'pʌtə(r)/ (*AmE*) = POTTER[1]

putty /'pʌti/ ***noun*** [U] a soft substance that is used for fixing glass into windows that becomes hard when dry

puzzle[1] /'pʌzl/ ***noun*** [C] **1** [usually sing.] something that is difficult to understand or explain; a mystery: *The reasons for his actions have remained a puzzle to historians.* **2** a game or toy that makes you think a lot: *a crossword/jigsaw puzzle* ◇ *I like to* ***do puzzles****.*

puzzle[2] /'pʌzl/ ***verb*** **1** [T] to make sb feel confused because they do not understand sth: *Her strange illness puzzled all the experts.* **2** [I] ~ **over sth** to think hard about sth in order to understand or explain it: *to puzzle over a mathematical problem*

PHR V **puzzle sth out** to find the answer to sth by thinking hard

puzzled /'pʌzld/ ***adj.*** not able to understand or explain sth: *a puzzled expression*

PVC /ˌpi: vi: 'si:/ ***noun*** [U] (**CHEMISTRY**) a strong plastic material used to make clothing, pipes, floor COVERINGS, etc.

pygmy[1] (also **pigmy**) /'pɪgmi/ ***noun*** [C] (*pl.* **pygmies**; **pigmies**) **1 Pygmy** a member of a race of very small people living in parts of Africa and SE Asia **2** a very small person or thing or one that is weak in some way

pygmy[2] (also **pigmy**) /'pɪgmi/ ***adj.*** (only *before* a noun) (**BIOLOGY**) used to describe a plant or SPECIES (= type) of animal that is much smaller than other similar kinds: *a pygmy shrew*

pyjamas (*AmE* **pajamas**) /pə'dʒɑ:məz/ ***noun*** [pl.] loose trousers and a loose jacket or T-SHIRT that you wear in bed

pylon /'paɪlən/ ***noun*** [C] a tall metal tower that supports heavy electrical wires

pyramid /'pɪrəmɪd/ ***noun*** [C] (**GEOMETRY**) a shape with a flat base and three or four sides in the shape of triangles ➲ picture at **solid** ▸ **pyramidal** /'pɪrəmɪdl/ ***adj.***

Pythagoras' theorem /paɪˌθægərəs 'θɪərəm/ ***noun*** [sing.] (**GEOMETRY**) the rule that, in a RIGHT-ANGLED TRIANGLE, the SQUARE[1] (3) (= the number that you get when you multiply another number by itself) of the HYPOTENUSE (= the side opposite the right angle) is equal to the SQUARES[1] (3) of the other two sides added together

python /'paɪθən/ ***noun*** [C] a large snake that kills animals by squeezing them very hard

Q q

Q, q[1] /kju:/ ***noun*** [C,U] (*pl.* **Q's**; **q's** /kju:z/) the seventeenth letter of the English alphabet: *'Queen' begins with (a) 'Q'.*

Q[2] ***abbr.*** question: *Qs 1-5 are compulsory.*

QC /ˌkju: 'si:/ ***noun*** [C] (**LAW**) the highest level of BARRISTER (= a type of lawyer) who can speak for the government in a court of law in Britain. **QC** is an abbreviation for 'Queen's Counsel' and is used when there is a queen in Britain. ➲ look at **KC** ➲ note at **lawyer**

qt ***abbr.*** quart(s)

quack /kwæk/ ***noun*** [C] the sound that a DUCK makes ▸ **quack** ***verb*** [I]

quad /kwɒd/ **1** = QUADRANGLE **2** (*informal*) = QUADRUPLET

quad- /kwɒd/ ***prefix*** (used in nouns, adjectives, verbs and adverbs) four; having four: *quadruple*

quad bike /'kwɒd baɪk/ (*AmE* ˌ**four-'wheeler**) ***noun*** [C] a motorbike with four large wheels, used for riding over rough ground, often for fun

quadrangle /ˈkwɒdræŋɡl/ (*also* **quad**) *noun* [C] a square open area with buildings round it in a school, college, etc.

quadrant /ˈkwɒdrənt/ *noun* [C] **1** (**GEOMETRY**) a quarter of a circle or of its CIRCUMFERENCE (= the distance around it) ➲ picture at **circle 2** an instrument for measuring angles, especially to check your position at sea or to look at stars

quadratic /kwɒˈdrætɪk/ *adj.* (**MATHEMATICS**) involving an unknown quantity that is multiplied by itself once only: *a quadratic equation*

quadri- /ˈkwɒdri/ *prefix* (used in nouns, adjectives, verbs and adverbs) four; having four: *quadrilateral*

quadrilateral /ˌkwɒdrɪˈlætərəl/ *noun* [C] (**GEOMETRY**) a flat shape with four straight sides ▸ **quadrilateral** *adj.*

quadruped /ˈkwɒdruped/ *noun* [C] (**BIOLOGY**) any creature with four feet ➲ look at **biped**

quadruple /kwɒˈdruːpl/ *verb* [I,T] (**MATHEMATICS**) to multiply or be multiplied by four

quadruplet /ˈkwɒdrʊplət/ (also *informal* **quad**) *noun* [C] (**BIOLOGY**) one of four children or animals that are born to one mother at the same time

quail /kweɪl/ *noun* **1** [C] a small brown bird whose meat and eggs we eat **2** [U] the meat of this bird

quaint /kweɪnt/ *adj.* attractive or unusual because it seems to belong to the past

quake¹ /kweɪk/ *verb* [I] (used about a person) to shake: *to quake with fear*

quake² /kweɪk/ (*informal*) = EARTHQUAKE

qualification 🔑 /ˌkwɒlɪfɪˈkeɪʃn/ *noun* **1** [C] (**EDUCATION**) an exam that you have passed or a course of study that you have completed: *to **have a** teaching/nursing **qualification*** ◇ *She left school at 16 with no formal qualifications.* **2** [C] a skill or quality that you need to do a particular job: *Is there a height qualification for the police force?* **3** [C,U] something that limits the meaning of a general statement or makes it weaker: *I can recommend him for the job **without qualification**.* ◇ *She accepted the proposal with only a few qualifications.* **4** [U] the fact of doing what is necessary in order to be able to do a job, play in a competition, etc.

qualified 🔑 /ˈkwɒlɪfaɪd/ *adj.* **1** ~ **(for sth/to do sth)** having passed an exam or having the knowledge, experience, etc. in order to be able to do sth: *Edward is well qualified for this job.* ◇ *a fully qualified doctor* ◇ *I don't feel qualified to comment – I know nothing about the subject.* **2** not complete; limited: *My boss gave only qualified approval to the plan.* OPP **unqualified**

qualify 🔑 /ˈkwɒlɪfaɪ/ *verb* (*pres. part.* **qualifying**; *3rd person sing. pres.* **qualifies**; *pt, pp* **qualified**) **1** [I] ~ **(as sth)** to pass the examination that is necessary to do a particular job; to have the qualities that are necessary for sth: *It takes five years to qualify as a vet.* ◇ *A cup of coffee and a sandwich doesn't really qualify as a meal.* **2** [I,T] ~ **(sb) (for sth/ to do sth)** to have or give sb the right to have or do sth: *How many years must you work to qualify for a pension?* ◇ *This exam will qualify me to teach music.* **3** [I] ~ **(for sth)** to win the right to enter a competition or continue to the next part: *Our team has qualified for the final.* **4** [T] to limit the meaning of a general statement or make it weaker

qualitative AW /ˈkwɒlɪtətɪv/ *adj.* (*formal*) connected with how good sth is, rather than with how much of it there is: *qualitative analysis/research* ◇ *There are qualitative differences between the two products.*

quality¹ 🔑 /ˈkwɒləti/ *noun* (*pl.* **qualities**) **1** [U, sing.] how good or bad sth is: *This paper isn't very good quality.* ◇ *to be of good/poor/top quality* ◇ *goods of a high quality* ◇ *high-quality goods* ◇ *the **quality of life** in our cities* **2** [U] a high standard or level: *Aim for quality rather than quantity in your writing.* **3** [C] something that is typical of a person or thing: *Vicky has all the qualities of a good manager.*

quality² /ˈkwɒləti/ *adj.* (only *before* a noun) used especially by people trying to sell goods or services to say that sth is of a high quality: *quality service at a competitive price*

ˈ**quality control** *noun* [U] (**BUSINESS**) the practice of checking goods as they are being produced, to make sure that they are of a high standard

qualm /kwɑːm/ *noun* [C, usually pl.] a feeling of doubt or worry that what you are doing may not be morally right: *I don't **have any qualms about** asking them to lend us some money.*

quandary /ˈkwɒndəri/ *noun* (*pl.* **quandaries**) [C, usually sing.] a state of not being able to decide what to do; a difficult situation: *I'm **in a quandary** – should I ask her or not?*

quango /ˈkwæŋɡəʊ/ *noun* [C] (*pl.* **quangos**) (**POLITICS**) (in Britain) an organization dealing with public matters, started by the government, but working independently and with its own legal powers

quantify /ˈkwɒntɪfaɪ/ *verb* [T] (*pres. part.* **quantifying**; *3rd person sing. pres.* **quantifies**; *pt, pp* **quantified**) to describe or express sth as an amount or a number ▸ **quantifiable** /ˈkwɒntɪfaɪəbl/ *adj.* ▸ **quantification** /ˌkwɒntɪfɪˈkeɪʃn/ *noun* [U]

quantitative /ˈkwɒntɪtətɪv/ *adj.* (*formal*) connected with the amount or number of sth rather than with how good it is: *quantitative analysis/ research* ◇ *There is no difference between the two in quantitative terms.*

quantity 🔑 /ˈkwɒntəti/ *noun* (*pl.* **quantities**) [C,U] **1** a number or an amount of sth: *Add a small quantity of salt.* ◇ *It's cheaper to buy goods **in large quantities**.* **2** a large number or amount of sth: *It's cheaper to buy goods **in quantity**.*
IDM **an unknown quantity** → UNKNOWN¹

ˈ**quantity surveyor** *noun* [C] (*BrE*) a person whose job is to calculate the quantity of materials needed for building sth, how much it will cost and how long it will take

quantum /ˈkwɒntəm/ *noun* [C] (*pl.* **quanta** /-tə/) (**PHYSICS**) a very small quantity of ELECTROMAGNETIC energy (= energy that is made up of electricity and magnetism)

ˈ**quantum theory** *noun* [U] (**PHYSICS**) a theory based on the idea that energy exists in units that cannot be divided

quarantine /ˈkwɒrəntiːn/ *noun* [U] (**HEALTH**) a period of time when a person or animal that has or may have an infectious disease must be kept away from other people or animals

quarrel¹ /ˈkwɒrəl/ *noun* [C] **1 a** ~ **(about/over sth)** an angry argument or disagreement: *We sometimes **have a quarrel** about who should do the washing-up.* ➲ look at **argument**, **fight²** (3) **2 a** ~ **with sb/sth** a reason for complaining about or disagreeing with sb/sth: *I have no quarrel with what has just been said.*

quarrel² /ˈkwɒrəl/ *verb* [I] (**quarrelling**; **quarrelled**: *AmE* **quarreling**; **quarreled**) **1** ~ **(with sb) (about/over sth)** to have an angry argument or disagreement: *The children are always quarrelling!*

◇ *I don't want to quarrel with you about it.* ➲ look at **argue**, **fight**[1] (4) **2 ~ with sth** to disagree with sth

quarrelsome /ˈkwɒrəlsəm/ ***adj.*** (used about a person) liking to argue with other people

quarry[1] /ˈkwɒri/ ***noun*** (*pl.* **quarries**) **1** [C] a place where sand, stone, etc. is dug out of the ground ➲ look at **mine 2** [sing.] a person or animal that is being hunted

quarry[2] /ˈkwɒri/ ***verb*** [I,T] (*pres. part.* **quarrying**; *3rd person sing. pres.* **quarries**; *pt, pp* **quarried**) to dig, stone, sand, etc. out of the ground: *to quarry for marble*

quart /kwɔːt/ ***noun*** [C] (*abbr.* **qt**) a measure of liquid; 1.14 litres. There are 2 pints in a quart. ❶ An American quart is 0.94 of a litre.

quarter 🔑 /ˈkwɔːtə(r)/ ***noun*** **1** [C] (MATHEMATICS) one of four equal parts of sth: *The programme lasts for three quarters of an hour.* ◇ *a mile and a quarter* ◇ *to cut an apple into quarters* **2** [sing.] 15 minutes before or after every hour: *I'll meet you at **(a) quarter past** six.* ◇ *It's **(a) quarter to** three.* ❶ In American English you say '(a) quarter **after**' and '(a) quarter **of**': *I'll meet you at (a) quarter after six.* ◇ *It's a quarter of three.*
3 [C] a period of three months: *You get a gas bill every quarter.* **4** [C, usually sing.] a part of a town, especially a part where a particular group of people live: *the Chinese quarter* ◇ *the historic quarter of the city* **5** [C] a person or group of people who may give help or information or who have certain opinions **6** [C] (in the US or Canada) a coin that is worth 25 cents (¼ dollar) **7 quarters** [pl.] a place that is provided for people, especially soldiers, to live in **8** [C] four OUNCES of sth; ¼ of a pound: *a quarter of mushrooms*
IDM **at close quarters** → CLOSE[3]

ˌquarter-ˈfinal ***noun*** [C] one of the four matches between the eight players or teams left in a competition ➲ look at **semi-final**

quarterly /ˈkwɔːtəli/ ***adj., adv.*** (produced or happening) once every three months: *a quarterly magazine*

ˈquarter note (*AmE*) = CROTCHET

quartet /kwɔːˈtet/ ***noun*** [C] (MUSIC) **1** four people who sing or play music together **2** a piece of music for four people to sing or play together

quartz /kwɔːts/ ***noun*** [U] (GEOLOGY) a type of hard rock that is used in making very accurate clocks or watches

quasar /ˈkweɪzɑː(r)/ ***noun*** [C] (ASTRONOMY) a large object like a star, that is far away and that shines very brightly and sometimes sends out strong radio signals ➲ look at **pulsar**

quash /kwɒʃ/ ***verb*** [T] (*formal*) **1** to say that an official decision is no longer true or legal **2** to stop or defeat sth by force: *to quash a rebellion*

quasi- /ˈkweɪzaɪ; -saɪ/ ***prefix*** (used in adjectives and nouns) **1** that appears to be sth but is not really so: *a quasi-scientific explanation* **2** partly; almost: *a quasi-official body*

quatrain /ˈkwɒtreɪn/ ***noun*** [C] (LITERATURE) a poem or VERSE of a poem that has four lines

quaver /ˈkweɪvə(r)/ (*AmE* **ˈeighth note**) ***noun*** [C] (MUSIC) a type of note ➲ note at **crotchet** ➲ picture at **music**

quay /kiː/ ***noun*** [C] a platform where goods and passengers are loaded on and off boats

quayside /ˈkiːsaɪd/ ***noun*** [sing.] the area of land that is near a QUAY

queasy /ˈkwiːzi/ ***adj.*** feeling sick; wanting to VOMIT (= bring up food from your stomach)

queen 🔑 /kwiːn/ ***noun*** [C] **1** (*also* **Queen**) (POLITICS) the female ruler of a country: *Queen Elizabeth II* (= the second) ➲ look at **king**, **prince**, **princess 2** (*also* **Queen**) the wife of a king **3** (BIOLOGY) the largest and most important female in a group of insects: *the queen bee* **4** one of the four playing cards in a pack with a picture of a queen: *the queen of hearts* **5** (in CHESS) the most powerful piece, that can move any distance and in all directions

queer /kwɪə(r)/ ***adj.*** (*old-fashioned*) strange or unusual: *His face was a queer pink colour.*

quell /kwel/ ***verb*** [T] (*formal*) to end sth

quench /kwentʃ/ ***verb*** [T] to satisfy your feeling of THIRST by drinking liquid: *He drank some juice to quench his thirst.*

query /ˈkwɪəri/ ***noun*** [C] (*pl.* **queries**) a question, especially one asking for information or expressing a doubt about sth: *Does anyone have any queries?* ➲ note at **ask** ▶ **query** ***verb*** [T] (*pres. part.* **querying**; *3rd person sing. pres.* **queries**; *pt, pp* **queried**): *We queried the bill but were told it was correct.*

quest /kwest/ ***noun*** [C] (*formal*) a long search for sth that is difficult to find: *the quest for happiness/knowledge/truth*

question[1] 🔑 /ˈkwestʃən/ ***noun*** **1** [C] **a ~ (about/on sth)** a sentence or phrase that asks for an answer: *Put up your hand if you want to **ask a question**.* ◇ *In the examination, you must **answer** five **questions** in one hour.* ◇ *What's the answer to Question 5?* **2** [C] a problem or difficulty that needs to be discussed or dealt with: *The resignations **raise the question** of who will take over.* ◇ ***The question is**, how are we going to raise the money?* **3** [U] doubt or UNCERTAINTY: *There is no question about Brenda's enthusiasm for the job.* ◇ *His honesty is **beyond question**.* ◇ *The results of the report were accepted **without question**.*
IDM **(be) a question of sth/of doing sth** a situation in which sth is needed: *It's not difficult – it's just a question of finding the time to do it.*
in question that is being considered or talked about: *The lawyer asked where she was on the night in question.*
no question of no possibility of: *There is no question of him leaving hospital yet.*
out of the question impossible: *A new car is out of the question. It's just too expensive.*

question[2] 🔑 /ˈkwestʃən/ ***verb*** [T] **1 ~ sb (about/on sth)** to ask sb a question or questions: *The police questioned him for several hours.* **2** to express or feel doubt about sth: *She told me she was from the council so I didn't question her right to be there.* ◇ *to question sb's sincerity/honesty*

questionable /ˈkwestʃənəbl/ ***adj.*** **1** that you have doubts about; not certain: *It's questionable whether we'll be able to finish in time.* **2** likely to be dishonest or morally wrong: *questionable motives*
OPP **unquestionable**

ˈquestion mark ***noun*** [C] (LANGUAGE) the sign (?) that you use when you write a question

questionnaire /ˌkwestʃəˈneə(r)/ ***noun*** [C] a list of questions that are answered by many people. A **questionnaire** is used to collect information about a particular subject: *to complete/fill in a questionnaire*

ˈquestion tag (*also* **tag**; **ˈtag question**) ***noun*** [C] (LANGUAGE) a short phrase such as 'isn't it?' or 'did you?' at the end of a sentence that changes it into a question and is often used to ask sb to agree with you

queue /kjuː/ (*AmE* **line**) ***noun*** [C] a line of people, cars, etc. that are waiting for sth or to do sth: *We had to **wait in a queue** for hours to get tickets.* ◇ *to **join** the end of **a queue*** ◇ *We were told to **form a queue** outside the doors.* ▸ **queue** ***verb*** [I] ~ **(up) (for sth)**: *to queue for a bus*

IDM jump the queue → JUMP[1]

quiche /kiːʃ/ ***noun*** [C,U] a type of food made of PASTRY filled with a mixture of eggs and milk with cheese, onion, etc. and cooked in the oven. You can eat **quiche** hot or cold.

quick[1] 🔑 /kwɪk/ ***adj.*** **1** done with speed; taking or lasting a short time: *May I make a quick telephone call?* ◇ *This dish is quick and easy to make.* ◇ *His quick thinking saved her life.* ◇ *We need to make a quick decision.* **2** ~ **(to do sth)** doing sth at speed or in a short time: *It's quicker to travel by train.* ◇ *Nicola is a quick worker.* ◇ *She was quick to point out all the mistakes I had made.* **3** used to form compound adjectives: *quick-thinking* ◇ *quick-drying paint*

IDM (as) quick as a flash very quickly

quick/slow on the uptake → UPTAKE

quick[2] /kwɪk/ ***adv.*** (*informal*) quickly: *Come over here quick!*

quicken /ˈkwɪkən/ ***verb*** [I,T] (*written*) **1** to become quicker or make sth quicker: *She felt her heartbeat quicken as he approached.* ◇ *He quickened his pace to catch up with them.* **2** (*written*) to become more active; to make sth more active: *His interest quickened as he heard more about the plan.*

quickly 🔑 /ˈkwɪkli/ ***adv.*** fast; in a short time: *He quickly undressed and got into bed.* ◇ *I'd like you to get here as quickly as possible.*

quicksand /ˈkwɪksænd/ ***noun*** [U] (*also* **quicksands** [pl.]) deep wet sand that you sink into if you walk on it

quid /kwɪd/ ***noun*** [C] (*pl.* **quid**) (*BrE, informal*) a pound (in money); £1: *Can you lend me a couple of quid until tomorrow?*

quid pro quo /ˌkwɪd prəʊ ˈkwəʊ/ ***noun*** [sing.] a thing given in return for sth else

quiet[1] 🔑 /ˈkwaɪət/ ***adj.*** **1** with very little or no noise: *Be quiet!* ◇ *His voice was quiet but firm.* ◇ *Go into the library if you want to work. It's much quieter in there.* **OPP loud** **2** without much activity or many people: *The streets are very quiet on Sundays.* ◇ *Business is quiet at this time of year.* ◇ *a quiet country village* ◇ *We lead a quiet life.* **3** (used about a person) not talking very much: *You're very quiet today. Is anything wrong?* ◇ *He's very quiet and shy.* ▸ **quietly** ***adv.***: *Try and shut the door quietly!* ▸ **quietness** ***noun*** [U]

IDM keep quiet about sth; keep sth quiet to say nothing about sth

quiet[2] /ˈkwaɪət/ ***noun*** [U] the state of being calm and without much noise or activity: *the **peace and quiet** of the countryside*

IDM on the quiet secretly: *She's given up smoking but she still has an occasional cigarette on the quiet.*

quieten /ˈkwaɪətn/ ***verb*** [T] to make sb/sth quiet

PHR V quieten (sb/sth) down to become quiet or to make sb/sth quiet: *When you've quietened down, I'll tell you what happened.*

quill /kwɪl/ ***noun*** [C] **1** (*also* **ˈquill feather**) a large feather from the wing or tail of a bird **2** (*also* **ˌquill ˈpen**) a pen made from a **quill** feather **3** one of the long, thin, sharp points on the body of a PORCUPINE

quilt /kwɪlt/ ***noun*** [C] a cover for a bed that has a thick warm material, for example feathers, inside it ➲ look at **duvet**

quinine /kwɪˈniːn/ ***noun*** [U] (**HEALTH**) a drug made from the BARK of a South American tree, used in the past to treat a tropical disease (**malaria**)

quintessential /ˌkwɪntɪˈsenʃl/ ***adj.*** being the perfect example of sth: *He was the quintessential tough guy.* ▸ **quintessence** /kwɪnˈtesns/ ***noun*** [sing.]: *It was the quintessence of an English manor house.* ▸ **quintessentially** /-ʃəli/ ***adv.***: *a sense of humour that is quintessentially British*

quintet /kwɪnˈtet/ ***noun*** [C] (**MUSIC**) **1** a group of five people who sing or play music together **2** a piece of music for five people to sing or play together

quintuplet /ˈkwɪntʊplət/ ***noun*** [C] (**BIOLOGY**) one of five children or animals that are born to one mother at the same time

quirk /kwɜːk/ ***noun*** [C] **1** an aspect of sb's character or behaviour that is strange: *You'll soon get used to the boss's little quirks.* **2** a strange thing that happens by chance: *By **a strange quirk of fate** they met again several years later.* ▸ **quirky** ***adj.***: *Some people don't like his quirky sense of humour.*

quit 🔑 /kwɪt/ ***verb*** (*pres. part.* **quitting**; *pt, pp* **quit**) **1** [I,T] ~ **(as sth)** to leave a job, etc. or to go away from a place: *She quit as manager of the volleyball team.* **2** [T] (*especially AmE, informal*) to stop doing sth: *to quit smoking* **3** [I,T] (**COMPUTING**) to close a computer program

quite 🔑 /kwaɪt/ ***adv.*** **1** not very; to a certain degree; rather: *The film's quite good.* ◇ *It's quite a good film.* ◇ *I quite enjoy cooking.* ◇ *They had to wait quite a long time.* ◇ *It's quite cold today.* ◇ *We still meet up quite often.* ➲ note at **rather** **2** (used for emphasizing sth) completely; very: *Are you quite sure you don't mind?* ◇ *I quite agree – you're quite right.* ◇ *To my surprise, the room was quite empty.* **3** used for showing that you agree with or understand sth: *'He'll find it difficult.' 'Well, quite* (= I agree).*'*

IDM not quite used for showing that there is almost enough of sth, or that it is almost suitable: *There's not quite enough bread for breakfast.* ◇ *These shoes don't quite fit.*

quite a used for showing that sth is unusual: *It's quite a climb to the top of the hill.*

quite a few; quite a lot (of) a fairly large amount or number: *We've received quite a few enquiries.*

quite enough used for emphasizing that no more of sth is wanted or needed: *I've had quite enough of listening to you two arguing!* ◇ *That's quite enough wine, thanks.*

quits /kwɪts/ ***adj.***

IDM be quits (with sb) (*informal*) if two people are quits, it means that neither of them owes the other anything: *You buy me a drink and then we're quits.*

quiver /ˈkwɪvə(r)/ ***verb*** [I] to shake slightly: *to quiver with rage/excitement/fear* **SYN tremble**

quiz[1] /kwɪz/ ***noun*** [C] (*pl.* **quizzes**) a game or competition in which you have to answer questions: *a quiz programme on TV* ◇ *a general knowledge quiz*

quiz[2] /kwɪz/ (*3rd person sing. pres.* **quizzes**; *pres. part.* **quizzing**; *pt, pp* **quizzed**) ***verb*** [T] to ask sb a lot of questions in order to get information

quizzical /ˈkwɪzɪkl/ ***adj.*** (used about a look, smile, etc.) seeming to ask a question ▸ **quizzically** /-kli/ ***adv.***

quorum /ˈkwɔːrəm/ ***noun*** [sing.] the smallest number of people that must be at a meeting before it can make official decisions

quota /ˈkwəʊtə/ ***noun*** [C] the number or amount of sth that is allowed or that you must do: *We have a fixed quota of work to get through each day.*

quotation AW /kwəʊˈteɪʃn/ (also *informal* **quote**) ***noun*** [C] **1** (LITERATURE) a phrase from a book, speech, play, etc. that sb repeats because it is interesting or useful: *a quotation from Shakespeare* **2** (BUSINESS) a statement that says how much a piece of work will probably cost: *You should get quotations from three different builders.* ➲ look at **estimate**

quoˈtation marks (*also* **ˈspeech marks**, (*informal*) **quotes**, *BrE also* **inˌverted ˈcommas**) ***noun*** [pl.] (LANGUAGE) the signs '...' or "..." that you put around a word, a sentence, etc. to show that it is what sb said or wrote, that it is a title, or that you are using it in a special way

quote[1] ⊶ AW /kwəʊt/ ***verb*** **1** [I,T] ~ (sth) (from sb/sth) to repeat exactly sth that sb else has said or written before: *The minister asked the newspaper not to quote him.* **2** [T] to give sth as an example to support what you are saying ➲ note at **mention** **3** [I,T] (BUSINESS) to say what the cost of a piece of work, etc. will probably be

quote[2] AW /kwəʊt/ ***noun*** [C] **1** = QUOTATION (1): *The essay was full of quotes.* **2** = QUOTATION (2): *Their quote for the job was way too high.* **3 quotes** (LANGUAGE) [pl.] = QUOTATION MARKS: *If you take text from other sources, place it **in quotes**.*

quotient /ˈkwəʊʃnt/ ***noun*** [C] (MATHEMATICS) a number which is the result when one number is divided by another ➲ look at **IQ**

R r

R, r[1] /ɑː(r)/ ***noun*** [C,U] (*pl.* **R's; r's** /ɑːz/) the eighteenth letter of the English alphabet: *'Rabbit' begins with an 'R'.*

R[2] ***abbr.*** river: *R Thames*

rabbi /ˈræbaɪ/ ***noun*** [C] (*pl.* **rabbis**) (RELIGION) a Jewish religious leader and teacher of Jewish law

rabbit /ˈræbɪt/ ***noun*** [C] a small animal with long ears: *a wild rabbit* ◇ *a rabbit hutch* (= a cage for rabbits)

ˈrabbit warren ***noun*** [C] a system of holes and underground tunnels where wild RABBITS live

rabble /ˈræbl/ ***noun*** [C] a noisy crowd of people who are or may become violent

rabies /ˈreɪbiːz/ ***noun*** [U] (HEALTH) a very dangerous disease that a person can get if they are bitten by an animal that has the disease

race[1] ⊶ /reɪs/ ***noun*** **1** [C] a ~ (against/with sb/sth); a ~ **for sth/to do sth** a competition between people, animals, cars, etc. to see which is the fastest or to see which can achieve sth first: *to run/win/lose a race* ◇ *to come first/second/last **in a race*** ◇ *the race for the presidency* ◇ *the race to find a cure for Aids* ◇ *Rescuing victims of the earthquake is now **a race against time**.* **2 the races** [pl.] (*BrE*) (SPORT) an occasion when a number of horse races are held in one place **3** [C,U] one of the groups into which people can be divided according to the colour of their skin, their hair type, the shape of their face, etc. ➲ look at **human race** **4** [C] a group of people who have the same language, customs, history, etc.

IDM **the rat race** → RAT

race[2] ⊶ /reɪs/ ***verb*** **1** [I,T] ~ (against/with sb/sth); ~ **sb/sth** to have a competition with sb/sth to find out who is the fastest or to see who can do sth first: *I'll race you home.* **2** [I,T] to go very fast or to move sb/sth very fast: *We raced up the stairs.* ◇ *The child had to be raced to hospital.* **3** [T] (SPORT) to make an animal or a vehicle take part in a race

racecourse /ˈreɪskɔːs/ (*AmE* **racetrack**) ***noun*** [C] (SPORT) a place where horse races take place

racehorse /ˈreɪshɔːs/ ***noun*** [C] (SPORT) a horse that is trained to run in races

ˌrace reˈlations ***noun*** [pl.] the relations between people of different races who live in the same town, area, etc.

racetrack /ˈreɪstræk/ ***noun*** [C] **1** (SPORT) a track for races between runners, cars, bicycles, etc. **2** (*AmE*) = RACECOURSE

racial /ˈreɪʃl/ ***adj.*** connected with people's race; happening between people of different races: *racial tension/discrimination* ▶ **racially** /-ʃəli/ ***adv.***: *a racially mixed school*

racing ⊶ /ˈreɪsɪŋ/ ***noun*** [U] **1** = HORSE RACING **2** (SPORT) the sport of taking part in races: *motor racing* ◇ *a racing driver/car*

racism /ˈreɪsɪzəm/ ***noun*** [U] (SOCIAL STUDIES) the belief that some races of people are better than others; unfair ways of treating people that show this belief: *to take measures to combat racism* ▶ **racist** /ˈreɪsɪst/ ***noun*** [C], ***adj.***: *He's a racist.* ◇ *racist beliefs/views/remarks*

rack[1] /ræk/ ***noun*** [C] (often in compounds) a piece of equipment, usually made of bars, that you can put things in or on: *I got on the train and put my bags up in the luggage rack.* ◇ *We need a roof rack on the car for all this luggage.* ➲ picture at **laboratory**

IDM **go to rack and ruin** to be in or get into a bad state because of a lack of care

rack[2] /ræk/ ***verb***

IDM **rack your brains** to try hard to think of sth or remember sth

racket /ˈrækɪt/ ***noun*** **1** [sing.] (*informal*) a loud noise: *Stop making that terrible racket!* **2** [C] (LAW) an illegal way of making money: *a drugs racket* **3** (also **racquet**) [C] (SPORT) a piece of sports equipment that you use to hit the ball with in sports such as TENNIS and BADMINTON ➲ picture at **sport**

racy /ˈreɪsi/ ***adj.*** (used especially about speech and writing) having a style that is exciting and amusing, often in a way that is connected with sex: *a racy novel*

radar /ˈreɪdɑː(r)/ ***noun*** [U] a system that uses radio waves for finding the position of moving objects, for example ships and planes: *This plane is hard to detect by radar.* ➲ look at **sonar**

ˈradar trap ***noun*** [C] = SPEED TRAP

radial /ˈreɪdiəl/ ***adj.*** having a pattern of lines, etc. that go out from a central point towards the edge of a circle

radiant /ˈreɪdiənt/ ***adj.*** **1** showing great happiness: *a radiant smile* **2** sending out light or heat: *the radiant heat/energy of the sun*

radiate /ˈreɪdieɪt/ ***verb*** **1** [T] (used about people) to clearly show a particular quality or emotion in your appearance or behaviour: *She radiated self-confidence in the interview.* **2** [T] (PHYSICS) to send out light or heat **3** [I] to go out in all directions from a central point: *Narrow streets radiate from the village square.*

radiation /ˌreɪdiˈeɪʃn/ ***noun*** [U] **1** (CHEMISTRY, PHYSICS) powerful and very dangerous RAYS that are sent out from certain substances. You cannot see or feel **radiation** but it can cause serious illness or death ➲ look at **radioactive 2** (PHYSICS) heat, light or energy that is sent out from sth: *ultraviolet radiation* **3** (HEALTH) (*also* **radiation therapy**) the treatment of cancer and other diseases using **radiation** ➲ look at **chemotherapy**, **radiotherapy**

radiator /ˈreɪdieɪtə(r)/ ***noun*** [C] **1** a piece of equipment that is usually fixed to the wall and is used for heating a room. **Radiators** are made of metal and filled with hot water. **2** a piece of equipment that is used for keeping a car engine cool

radical[1] AW /ˈrædɪkl/ ***adj.*** **1** (used about changes in sth) very great; complete: *The tax system needs radical reform.* ◇ *radical change* **2** wanting great social or political change: *to have radical views* ➲ look at **moderate[1]** (2) ▶ **radically** /-kli/ ***adv.***: *The First World War radically altered the political map of Europe.*

radical[2] AW /ˈrædɪkl/ ***noun*** [C] a person who wants great social or political change ➲ look at **moderate[3]**, **extremist**

radii plural of **radius**

radio ⊶ /ˈreɪdiəʊ/ ***noun*** (*pl.* **radios**) **1** (often **the radio**) [U, sing.] (ARTS AND MEDIA) the activity of sending out programmes for people to listen to; the programmes that are sent out: *I always* ***listen to the radio*** *in the car.* ◇ *I heard an interesting report* ***on the radio*** *this morning.* ◇ *a radio station/programme* ◇ *national/local radio* **2** [C] a piece of equipment that is used for receiving and/or sending radio messages or programmes (on a ship, plane, etc. or in your house) **3** [U] the sending or receiving of messages through the air by electrical signals: *to keep in radio contact* ◇ *radio signals/waves* ▶ **radio** ***verb*** [I,T] (*pt, pp* **radioed**)

radio- /ˈreɪdiəʊ/ ***prefix*** (used in nouns, adjectives and adverbs) **1** connected with radio waves or BROADCASTING (= the activity of sending out radio or television programmes): *a radio-controlled car* **2** (PHYSICS) connected with RADIOACTIVITY (= powerful and very dangerous rays that are produced when atoms are broken up): *radiographer*

radioactive /ˌreɪdiəʊˈæktɪv/ ***adj.*** (CHEMISTRY, PHYSICS) sending out powerful and very dangerous RAYS that are produced when atoms are broken up. These RAYS cannot be seen or felt but can cause serious illness or death: *the problem of the disposal of* ***radioactive waste*** *from power stations* ➲ look at **radiation** ▶ **radioactivity** /ˌreɪdiəʊækˈtɪvəti/ ***noun*** [U]

radiographer /ˌreɪdiˈɒɡrəfə(r)/ ***noun*** [C] (HEALTH) a person who is trained to take pictures of your bones, etc. (**X-rays**) in a hospital or to use them for the treatment of certain illnesses

radiology /ˌreɪdiˈɒlədʒi/ ***noun*** [U] (HEALTH) the study and use of different types of RADIATION in medicine, for example to treat diseases

radiotherapy /ˌreɪdiəʊˈθerəpi/ ***noun*** [U] (HEALTH) the treatment of disease by RADIATION (= powerful and very dangerous rays that are sent out from certain substances): *a course of radiotherapy* ➲ look at **chemotherapy** ▶ **radiotherapist** ***noun*** [C]

ˈradio wave ***noun*** [C] (PHYSICS) a low-energy ELECTROMAGNETIC wave, used especially for long-distance communication ➲ picture at **wavelength**

radish /ˈrædɪʃ/ ***noun*** [C] a small red vegetable that is white inside with a strong taste. You eat **radishes** in salads.

radium /ˈreɪdiəm/ ***noun*** [U] (*symbol* **Ra**) (CHEMISTRY) a chemical element. **Radium** is a white RADIOACTIVE metal used in the treatment of some serious diseases ❶ For more information on the periodic table of elements, look at pages R34-5.

radius /ˈreɪdiəs/ ***noun*** [C] (*pl.* **radii**) /-diaɪ/ **1** (MATHEMATICS) the distance from the centre of a circle to the outside edge ➲ look at **diameter**, **circumference** ➲ picture at **circle** **2** a circular area that is measured from a point in its centre: *The wreckage of the plane was scattered over a radius of several miles.* **3** (HEALTH) the shorter bone of the two bones in the lower part of your arm between your wrist and your elbow ➲ look at **ulna** ➲ picture on **page 80**

radon /ˈreɪdɒn/ ***noun*** [U] (*symbol* **Rn**) (CHEMISTRY) a chemical element. **Radon** is a colourless RADIOACTIVE gas used in the treatment of some serious diseases ❶ For more information on the periodic table of elements, look at pages R34-5.

RAF /ˌɑːr eɪ ˈef; ræf/ ***abbr.*** (*BrE*) **the Royal Air Force**

raffle /ˈræfl/ ***noun*** [C] a way of making money for a charity or a project by selling tickets with numbers on them. Later some numbers are chosen and the tickets with these numbers on them win prizes.

raft /rɑːft/ ***noun*** [C] **1** a flat structure made of pieces of wood tied together and used as a boat or a floating platform **2** a small boat made of rubber or plastic that is filled with air: *an inflatable raft* ➲ picture at **rafting**

rafter /ˈrɑːftə(r)/ ***noun*** [C] one of the long pieces of wood that support a roof

rafting

rafting /ˈrɑːftɪŋ/ ***noun*** [U] (SPORT) the sport or activity of travelling down a river on a RAFT: *We went* ***white-water rafting*** *on the Colorado River.*

rag /ræɡ/ ***noun*** **1** [C,U] a small piece of old cloth that you use for cleaning **2 rags** [pl.] clothes that are very old and torn

raga /ˈrɑːɡə/ ***noun*** [C] (MUSIC) a traditional pattern of notes used in Indian music; a piece of music based on one of these patterns

rage[1] /reɪdʒ/ ***noun*** [C,U] a feeling of violent anger that is difficult to control: *He was trembling with rage.* ◇ *to fly into a rage*

rage[2] /reɪdʒ/ ***verb*** [I] **1** ~ **(at/against/about sb/sth)** to show great anger about sth, especially by shouting: *He raged against the injustice of it all.* **2** (used about a battle, disease, storm, etc.) to continue with great force: *The battle raged for several days.* ▸ **raging** *adj.* (only *before* a noun): *a raging headache*

ragged /ˈrægɪd/ *adj.* **1** (used about clothes) old and torn **2** not straight; untidy: *a ragged edge/coastline*

ragtime /ˈrægtaɪm/ *noun* [U] (MUSIC) an early form of JAZZ, especially for the piano, first played by African American musicians in the early 1900s

raid /reɪd/ *noun* [C] **a ~ (on sth) 1** a short surprise attack on an enemy by soldiers, ships or aircraft: *an air raid* **2** (LAW) a surprise visit by the police looking for criminals or illegal goods **3** a surprise attack on a building in order to steal sth: *a bank raid* ▸ **raid** *verb* [T]: *Police raided the club at dawn this morning.*

rail 🔑 /reɪl/ *noun* **1** [C] a wooden or metal bar fixed to a wall, which you can hang things on: *a towel/curtain/picture rail* **2** [C] a bar which you can hold to stop you from falling (on stairs, from a building, etc.) **3** [C, usually pl.] each of the two metal bars that form the track that trains run on **4** [U] the railway system; trains as a means of transport: *rail travel/services/fares*

railcard /ˈreɪlkɑːd/ *noun* [C] (*BrE*) a special card that allows you to buy train tickets at a lower price if you are an old person, student, etc.

railing /ˈreɪlɪŋ/ *noun* [C, usually pl.] a fence (around a park, garden, etc.) that is made of metal bars

railway 🔑 /ˈreɪlweɪ/ (*AmE* ˈ**railroad**) *noun* [C] **1** (*BrE* ˈ**railway line**) the metal lines on which trains travel between one place and another **2** the whole system of tracks, the trains and the organization and people needed to operate them: *He works on the railways.* ◇ *a railway engine/company*

ˈ**railway station** = STATION[1] (1)

rain[1] 🔑 /reɪn/ *noun* **1** [U] the water that falls from the sky: *Take your umbrella, **it looks like rain*** (= as if it is going to rain). ◇ *It's **pouring with rain*** (= the rain is very heavy). ➲ look at **shower** (3), **acid rain** ➲ note at **weather 2 rains** [pl.] (in tropical countries) the time of the year when there is a lot of rain

IDM **(as) right as rain** → RIGHT[1]

rain[2] 🔑 /reɪn/ *verb* **1** [I] (used with *it*) to fall as rain: *Oh no! **It's raining again!*** ◇ *Is it **raining hard**?* ◇ *We'll go out when it stops raining.* **2** [I,T] **~ (sth) (down) (on sb/sth)** to fall or make sth fall on sb/sth in large quantities: *Bombs rained down on the city.*

PHR V **be rained off** to be cancelled or to have to stop because it is raining

rainbow /ˈreɪnbəʊ/ *noun* [C] an ARCH of many colours that sometimes appears in the sky when the sun shines through rain

ˈ**rain check** *noun* (*especially AmE*)

IDM **take a rain check on sth** (*spoken*) to refuse an invitation or offer but say that you might accept it later

raincoat /ˈreɪnkəʊt/ *noun* [C] a long light coat which keeps you dry in the rain

raindrop /ˈreɪndrɒp/ *noun* [C] a single drop of rain

rainfall /ˈreɪnfɔːl/ *noun* [U, sing.] (GEOGRAPHY) the total amount of rain that falls in a particular place during a month, year, etc.

rainforest /ˈreɪnfɒrɪst/ *noun* [C] (GEOGRAPHY) a thick forest in tropical parts of the world that have a lot of rain: *the Amazon rainforest* ➲ picture at **ecosystem**

rainwater /ˈreɪnwɔːtə(r)/ *noun* [U] water that has fallen as rain

rainy /ˈreɪni/ *adj.* having or bringing a lot of rain: *a rainy day* ◇ *the rainy season*

IDM **keep/save sth for a rainy day** to save sth, especially money, for a time when you really need it

raise[1] 🔑 /reɪz/ *verb* [T] **1** to lift sth up: *If you want to leave the room raise your hand.* ◇ *He raised himself up on one elbow.* OPP **lower 2 ~ sth (to sth)** to increase the level of sth or to make sth better or stronger: *to raise taxes/salaries/prices* ◇ *The hotel needs to **raise** its **standards**.* ◇ *There's no need to **raise your voice*** (= speak loudly or angrily). OPP **lower 3** to get money from people for a particular purpose: *We are doing a sponsored walk to **raise money** for charity.* ◇ *a **fund-raising** event* **4** to introduce a subject that needs to be talked about or dealt with: *I would like to **raise the subject** of money.* ◇ *This **raises the question** of why nothing was done before.* **5** to cause a particular reaction or emotion: *The neighbours **raised the alarm*** (= told everybody there was a fire/an emergency) *when they saw smoke coming out of the window.* ◇ *to **raise hopes/fears/suspicions** in people's minds* **6** to look after a child or an animal until they are an adult: *You can't **raise a family** on what I earn.* ➲ look at **bring sb up 7** to breed animals or grow a particular plant for a special purpose

IDM **raise your eyebrows** to show that you are surprised or that you do not approve of sth

raise[2] 🔑 /reɪz/ *noun* [C] (*AmE*) = RISE[1] (2)

raisin /ˈreɪzn/ *noun* [C] a dried GRAPE, used in cakes, etc. ➲ look at **sultana**

Raj /rɑːdʒ; rɑːʒ/ *noun* [sing.] (HISTORY) British rule in India before 1947

rake /reɪk/ *noun* [C] (AGRICULTURE) a garden tool with a long handle and a row of metal teeth, used for collecting leaves or making the earth smooth ➲ picture at **agriculture** ▸ **rake** *verb* [T]: *to rake up the leaves*

PHR V **rake sth in** (*informal*) to earn a lot of money, especially when it is done easily: *She's been **raking it in** since she got promoted.*

rake sth up to start talking about sth that it would be better to forget: *Don't rake up all those old stories again.*

rallentando /ˌrælənˈtændəʊ/ *noun* [C,U] (*pl.* **rallentandos**) (MUSIC) a gradual slowing down in a piece of music

rally[1] /ˈræli/ *noun* [C] (*pl.* **rallies**) **1** (POLITICS) a large public meeting, especially one held to support a political idea **2** (SPORT) (*BrE*) a race for cars or motorbikes on public roads **3** (SPORT) (used in TENNIS and similar sports) a series of hits of the ball before a point is won **4** [sing.] (SPORT, BUSINESS) an act of returning to a strong position after a period of difficulty or weakness SYN **recovery**: *After a furious late rally, they finally scored.* ◇ *a rally in shares on the stock market*

rally[2] /ˈræli/ *verb* (*pres. part.* **rallying**; *3rd person sing. pres.* **rallies**; *pt, pp* **rallied**) **1** [I,T] **~ (sb/sth) (around/behind/to sb)** to come together or to bring people together in order to help or support sb/sth: *The cabinet rallied behind the Prime Minister.* **2** [I] to get stronger, healthier, etc. after an illness or a period of weakness

PHR V **rally round** to come together to help sb: *When I was in trouble my family all rallied round.*

RAM /ræm/ *abbr.* (COMPUTING) **random-access memory**; computer memory in which data can be changed or removed and can be looked at in any order: *32 megabytes of RAM*

ram¹ /ræm/ ***noun*** [C] a male sheep ➲ note at **sheep** ➲ picture at **sheep**

ram² /ræm/ ***verb*** [T] (**ramming**; **rammed**) to crash into sth or push sth with great force

Ramadan /ˈræmədæn; ˌræməˈdæn/ ***noun*** [C,U] (**RELIGION**) a period of a month when, for religious reasons, Muslims do not eat anything from early morning until the sun goes down in the evening ➲ look at **Eid**

ramble¹ /ˈræmbl/ ***verb*** [I] **1** to walk in the countryside for pleasure: *to go rambling* **2** ~ **(on)** **(about sth)** to talk for a long time in a confused way

ramble² /ˈræmbl/ ***noun*** [C] a long, organized walk in the country for pleasure

rambler /ˈræmblə(r)/ ***noun*** [C] **1** (*especially BrE*) a person who walks in the countryside for pleasure, especially as part of an organized group **2** a plant that grows up walls, fences, etc.

rambling /ˈræmblɪŋ/ ***adj.*** **1** (used about speech or writing) very long and confused **2** (used about a building) spreading in many directions: *a rambling old house*

ramp /ræmp/ ***noun*** [C] **1** a path going up or down which you can use instead of steps or stairs to get from one place to a higher or lower place: *There are ramps at both entrances for wheelchair access.* **2** (*AmE*) = SLIP ROAD: *a freeway exit ramp*

rampage¹ /ræmˈpeɪdʒ/ ***verb*** [I] to move through a place in a violent group, usually breaking things and attacking people: *The football fans rampaged through the town.*

rampage² /ˈræmpeɪdʒ/ ***noun***
IDM **be/go on the rampage** to move through a place in a violent group, usually breaking things and attacking people

rampant /ˈræmpənt/ ***adj.*** (used about sth bad) existing or spreading everywhere in a way that is very difficult to control: *Car theft is rampant in this town.*

ramshackle /ˈræmʃækl/ ***adj.*** (usually used about a building) old and needing repair

ran past tense of **run¹**

ranch /rɑːntʃ/ ***noun*** [C] (**AGRICULTURE**) a large farm, especially in the US or Australia, where cows, horses, sheep, etc. are kept

rancid /ˈrænsɪd/ ***adj.*** if food containing fat is **rancid**, it tastes or smells unpleasant because it is no longer fresh: *rancid butter*

R & B /ˌɑːr ən ˈbiː/ ***abbr.*** (**MUSIC**) = RHYTHM AND BLUES

R & D /ˌɑːr ən ˈdiː/ ***abbr.*** = RESEARCH AND DEVELOPMENT

random AW /ˈrændəm/ ***adj.*** chosen by chance: *For the opinion poll they interviewed **a random selection** of people in the street.* ▶ **randomly** ***adv.***
IDM **at random** without thinking or deciding in advance what is going to happen: *The competitors were chosen at random from the audience.*

ˌrandom-ˌaccess ˈmemory ***noun*** [U] (**COMPUTING**) = RAM

randy /ˈrændi/ ***adj.*** (*BrE, informal*) sexually excited

rang past tense of **ring²**

range¹ 🔑 AW /reɪndʒ/ ***noun*** **1** [C, usually sing.] a ~ **(of sth)** a variety of things that belong to the same group: *The course will cover a **whole range** of topics.* ◇ *This shop has a very **wide range** of clothes.* **2** [C] the limits between which sth can vary: *That car is outside my **price range**.* ◇ *I don't think this game is suitable for all **age ranges**.* **3** [C,U] the distance that it is possible for sb/sth to travel, see, hear, etc.: *Keep **out of range of** the guns.* ◇ *The gunman shot the policeman **at close range**.* ◇ *They can pick up signals **at a range of** 400 metres.* **4** [C] (**GEOGRAPHY**) a line of mountains or hills **5** [C] (**MATHEMATICS**) the difference between the largest and smallest number in a set. To find the **range**, subtract the lowest number from the highest number in the set. **6** [C] (*AmE*) = COOKER

range² AW /reɪndʒ/ ***verb*** [I] **1** ~ **between A and B**; ~ **from A to B** to vary between two amounts, sizes, etc., including all those between them: *The ages of the students range from 15 to 50.* **2** ~ **(from A to B)** to include a variety of things in addition to those mentioned

rank¹ 🔑 /ræŋk/ ***noun*** **1** [C,U] the position, especially a high position, that sb has in an organization such as the army, or in society: *General is one of the highest ranks in the army.* ◇ *She's much higher in rank than I am.* **2** [C] a group or line of things or people: *a taxi rank* **3 the ranks** [pl.] the ordinary soldiers in the army; the members of any large group: *At the age of 43, he was forced to **join the ranks of** the unemployed.*
IDM **the rank and file** the ordinary soldiers in the army; the ordinary members of an organization

rank² 🔑 /ræŋk/ ***verb*** [I,T] ~ **(sb/sth)** **(as sth)** (not used in the continuous tenses) to give sb/sth a particular position on a scale according to importance, quality, success, etc.; to have a position of this kind: *She's ranked as one of the world's top players.* ◇ *a high-ranking police officer* ▶ **ranking** ***noun*** [C]: *She has retained her No.1 world ranking.*

ransack /ˈrænsæk/ ***verb*** [T] ~ **sth (for sth)** to search a place, making it untidy and causing damage, usually because you are looking for sth: *The house had been ransacked by burglars.*

ransom /ˈrænsəm/ ***noun*** [C,U] the money that you must pay to free sb who has been captured illegally and who is being kept as a prisoner: *The kidnappers demanded a ransom of $500 000 for the boy's release.*
IDM **hold sb to ransom** (**LAW**) to keep sb as a prisoner and say that you will not free them until you have received a certain amount of money ➲ look at **hostage**

rap¹ /ræp/ ***noun*** **1** [C] a quick, sharp hit or knock on a door, window, etc.: *There was a sharp rap on the door.* **2** [C,U] (**MUSIC**) a style or a piece of music with a fast strong rhythm, in which the words are spoken fast, not sung

rap² /ræp/ ***verb*** (**rapping**; **rapped**) **1** [I,T] to hit a hard object or surface several times quickly and lightly, making a noise: *She rapped angrily on/at the door.* **2** [T] (*informal*) (used mainly in newspaper HEADLINES) to criticize sb strongly: *Minister raps police over rise in crime.* **3** [I] (**MUSIC**) to speak the words of a RAP¹

rape¹ /reɪp/ ***verb*** [T] (**LAW**) to force a person to have sex when they do not want to, using threats or violence

rape² /reɪp/ ***noun*** **1** [U, C] (**LAW**) the crime of forcing sb to have sex when they do not want to: *to commit rape* **2** [sing.] (*written*) **the** ~ **(of sth)** the destruction of sth beautiful **3** (*also* ˌ**oilseed ˈrape**) [U] (**AGRICULTURE**) a plant with bright yellow flowers, that farmers grow as food for farm animals and for its seeds, which are used to make oil: *a field of rape* ◇ *rape oil/seed*

rapid 🔑 /ˈræpɪd/ ***adj.*** happening very quickly or moving with great speed: *She made rapid progress and was soon the best in the class.*

▸ **rapidity** /rəˈpɪdəti/ ***noun*** [U] (*formal*): *The rapidity of change has astonished most people.*
▸ **rapidly** ***adv.***

rapids /ˈræpɪdz/ ***noun*** [pl.] (**GEOGRAPHY**) a part of a river where the water flows very fast over rocks

rapist /ˈreɪpɪst/ ***noun*** [C] (**LAW**) a person who forces sb to have sex when they do not want to

rappel /ræˈpel/ (*AmE*) = ABSEIL

rapport /ræˈpɔː(r)/ ***noun*** [sing., U] (a) ~ (**with sb**); (a) ~ (**between A and B**) a friendly relationship in which people understand each other very well: *She understood the importance of establishing a close rapport with clients.* ◇ *Honesty is essential if there is to be good rapport between patient and therapist.*

rapt /ræpt/ ***adj.*** (*written*) so interested in one particular thing that you do not notice anything else: *a rapt audience* ◇ *She listened to the speaker with rapt attention.*

rapture /ˈræptʃə(r)/ ***noun*** [U] a feeling of extreme happiness
IDM **go into raptures (about/over sb/sth)** to feel and show that you think that sb/sth is very good: *I didn't like the film much but my boyfriend went into raptures about it.*

rapturous /ˈræptʃərəs/ ***adj.*** (usually *before* a noun) expressing extreme pleasure or enthusiasm for sb/sth: *rapturous applause*

rare 🔑 /reə(r)/ ***adj.*** **1** ~ (**for sb/sth to do sth**); ~ (**to do sth**) not done, seen, happening, etc. very often: *a rare bird/flower/plant* **2** (used about meat) not cooked for very long so that the inside is still red: *a rare steak* ➲ look at **medium**, **well done**

rarefied /ˈreərɪfaɪd/ ***adj.*** **1** understood or experienced by only a very small group of people who share a particular area of knowledge or activity **2** (**ENVIRONMENT**) (used about air) containing less OXYGEN than usual: *Climbers may experience difficulty breathing in the rarefied air at high altitudes.*

rarely 🔑 /ˈreəli/ ***adv.*** not very often: *People rarely live to be 100 years old.* ◇ *She is rarely seen in public nowadays.*

raring /ˈreərɪŋ/ ***adj.*** ~ **to do sth** wanting to start doing sth very much: *They were raring to try out the new computer.*

rarity /ˈreərəti/ ***noun*** (*pl.* **rarities**) **1** [C] a thing or a person that is unusual and is therefore often valuable or interesting: *Women lorry drivers are still quite a rarity.* **2** [U] the quality of being rare: *The rarity of this stamp increases its value a lot.*

rascal /ˈrɑːskl/ ***noun*** [C] a person, especially a child, who shows a lack of respect for other people and enjoys playing tricks on them

rash¹ /ræʃ/ ***noun*** **1** [C, usually sing.] (**HEALTH**) an area of small red spots that appear on your skin when you are ill or have a reaction to sth: *He* ***came out in a rash*** *where the plant had touched him.* **2** [sing.] **a** ~ (**of sth**) a series of unpleasant events of the same kind happening close together

rash² /ræʃ/ ***adj.*** (used about people) doing things that might be dangerous or bad without thinking about the possible results first; (used about actions) done in this way: *a rash decision/promise*
▸ **rashly** ***adv.***

rasher /ˈræʃə(r)/ ***noun*** [C] (*BrE*) a slice of BACON (= meat from a pig)

raspberry /ˈrɑːzbəri/ ***noun*** [C] (*pl.* **raspberries**) a small, soft, red fruit which grows on bushes: *raspberry jam*

rasterize (also **rasterise**) /ˈræstəraɪz/ (*also* **rip**) ***verb*** [T] (**COMPUTING**) to change text or images into a form in which they can be printed

rat /ræt/ ***noun*** [C] an animal like a large mouse
IDM **rat race** the way of life in which everyone is only interested in being better or more successful than everyone else

ratchet /ˈrætʃɪt/ ***noun*** [C] a wheel or bar with teeth along the edge and a metal piece that fits between the teeth, allowing movement in one direction only

ratchet

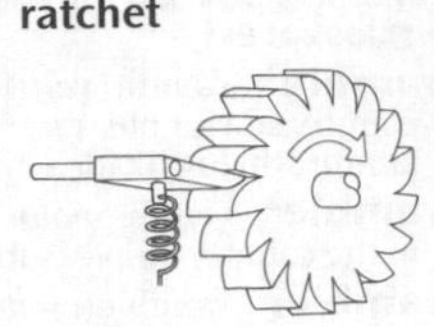

rate¹ 🔑 /reɪt/ ***noun*** [C] **1** a measurement of the speed at which sth happens or the number of times sth happens or exists during a particular period: *The* ***birth rate*** (= the number of children born each year) *is falling.* ◇ *The* ***death rate*** *from lung cancer is far higher among smokers.* ◇ *The population is increasing* ***at the rate of*** *less than 0.5% a year.* ◇ *an* ***exchange rate*** *of one pound to ten francs* **2** (**FINANCE**) a fixed amount of money that sth costs or that sb is paid: *The basic* ***rate of pay*** *is £10 an hour.* ◇ *We offer special reduced rates for students.* ➲ look at **first-rate**, **second-rate**
IDM **at any rate** (*spoken*) **1** used when you are giving more exact information about sth: *He said that they would be here by ten. At any rate, I think that's what he said.* **2** whatever else might happen: *Well, that's one good piece of news at any rate.*
the going rate (for sth) → GOING²

rate² 🔑 /reɪt/ ***verb*** (not used in the continuous tenses) **1** [I,T] to say how good you think sb/sth is: *She's rated among the best tennis players of all time.* ◇ *The match rated as one of their worst defeats.* **2** [T] to be good, important, etc. enough to be treated in a particular way: *The accident wasn't very serious – it didn't rate a mention in the local newspaper.*

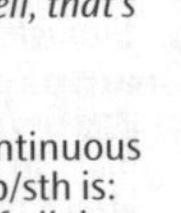

THESAURUS

rather

fairly • quite • pretty

These words can all mean 'to some extent'. **Rather** and **pretty** *(informal)* are the strongest and **fairly** is the weakest.

Fairly and **quite** are mostly used with words that are positive.

Rather is used with a negative word when you are criticizing sb/sth. If you use **rather** with a positive word, it sounds as if you are surprised and pleased

rather: *This room's rather untidy.* ◇ *The new teacher is actually rather nice, though he doesn't look very friendly.*

fairly: *The car was fairly clean.*

quite: *He plays the guitar quite well.*

pretty: *The game was pretty good.*

rather 🔑 /ˈrɑːðə(r)/ ***adv.*** quite; to some extent: *It was a rather nice day.* ◇ *It was rather a nice day.* ◇ *It cost rather a lot of money.* ◇ *I was rather hoping that you'd be free on Friday.*
IDM **or rather** used as a way of correcting sth you have said, or making it more exact: *She lives in London, or rather she lives in a suburb of London.*
rather than instead of; in place of: *I think I'll just have a sandwich rather than a full meal.*
would rather... (than) would prefer to: *I'd rather go to the cinema than watch television.*

ratify /'rætɪfaɪ/ ***verb*** [T] (*pres. part.* **ratifying**; *3rd person sing. pres.* **ratifies**; *pt, pp* **ratified**) to make an agreement officially acceptable by voting for or signing it ▶ **ratification** /ˌrætɪfɪ'keɪʃn/ ***noun*** [U]: *The agreement is subject to ratification by the Senate.*

rating /'reɪtɪŋ/ ***noun*** [C] **1** a measurement of how popular, important, good, etc. sth is **2** (usually **the ratings**) a set of figures showing the number of people who watch a particular television programme, etc., used to show how popular the programme is

ratio AW /'reɪʃiəʊ/ ***noun*** [C] ~ **(of A to B)** (MATHEMATICS) the relation between two numbers which shows how much bigger one quantity is than another: *The ratio of boys to girls in this class is three to one* (= there are three times as many boys as girls).

ration /'ræʃn/ ***noun*** [C] a limited amount of food, petrol, etc. that you are allowed to have when there is not enough for everyone to have as much as they want ▶ **ration** ***verb*** [T]: *In the desert water is strictly rationed.* ▶ **rationing** ***noun*** [U]

rational AW /'ræʃnəl/ ***adj.*** **1** (used about a person) able to use logical thought rather than emotions to make decisions OPP **irrational** **2** based on reason; sensible or logical: *There must be a rational explanation for why he's behaving like this.* ▶ **rationally** ***adv.***

rationale /ˌræʃə'nɑːl/ ***noun*** [C] (*formal*) **the ~ (behind/for/of sth)** the principles or reasons which explain a particular decision, course of action, belief, etc.: *What is the rationale behind these new exams?*

rationalism AW /'ræʃnəlɪzəm/ ***noun*** [U] the belief that all behaviour, opinions, etc. should be based on reason rather than on emotions or religious beliefs

rationalize (also **-ise**) AW /'ræʃnəlaɪz/ ***verb*** **1** [I,T] to find reasons that explain why you have done sth (perhaps because you do not like the real reason) **2** [T] to make a business or a system better organized ▶ **rationalization** (also **-isation**) /ˌræʃnəlaɪ'zeɪʃn/ ***noun*** [C,U]

rattle¹ /'rætl/ ***verb*** **1** [I,T] to make a noise like hard things hitting each other or to shake sth so that it makes this noise: *The windows were rattling all night in the wind.* ◇ *He rattled the money in the tin.* **2** [T] (*informal*) to make sb suddenly become worried: *The news of his arrival really rattled her.*

PHR V **rattle sth off** to say a list of things you have learned very quickly: *She rattled off the names of every player in the team.*

rattle² /'rætl/ ***noun*** [C] **1** a toy that a baby can shake to make a noise **2** a noise made by hard things hitting each other

rattlesnake /'rætlsneɪk/ ***noun*** [C] a poisonous American snake that makes a noise by moving the end of its tail quickly when it is angry or afraid

raucous /'rɔːkəs/ ***adj.*** (used about people's voices) loud and unpleasant

ravage /'rævɪdʒ/ ***verb*** [T] to damage sth very badly; to destroy sth

rave¹ /reɪv/ ***verb*** [I] **1** (*informal*) ~ **(about sb/sth)** to say very good things about sb/sth: *Everyone's raving about her latest record!* **2** to speak angrily or wildly

rave² /reɪv/ ***noun*** [C] (*BrE*) (MUSIC) a large party held outside or in an empty building, at which people dance to fast electronic music

raven /'reɪvn/ ***noun*** [C] a large black bird that has an unpleasant voice

ravenous /'rævənəs/ ***adj.*** very hungry ▶ **ravenously** ***adv.***

ˌrave re'view ***noun*** [C] (ARTS AND MEDIA) an article in a newspaper, etc. that says very good things about a new book, film, play, etc.

ravine /rə'viːn/ ***noun*** [C] (GEOGRAPHY) a narrow deep valley with steep sides

raving /'reɪvɪŋ/ ***adj.***, ***adv.*** (*informal*) (used about a person) talking or behaving in a way that shows they are crazy: *The man's a raving lunatic.* ◇ *Have you gone raving mad?*

raw ⊶ /rɔː/ ***adj.*** **1** not cooked: *Raw vegetables are good for your teeth.* **2** in its natural state; not yet changed, used or made into sth else: *raw sugar* **3** (HEALTH) used about an injury where the skin has come off from being rubbed

ˌraw ma'terial ***noun*** [C,U] (BUSINESS) a basic material that is used to make a product: *We have had problems with the supply of raw materials to the factory.* ◇ *These trees provide the raw material for high-quality paper.*

ray /reɪ/ ***noun*** [C] (PHYSICS) a line of light, heat or energy: *the sun's rays* ◇ *ultraviolet rays* ➲ look at **X-ray**

IDM **a ray of hope** a small chance that things will get better

razor /'reɪzə(r)/ ***noun*** [C] a sharp instrument which people use to cut off the hair from their skin (**shave**): *an electric razor* ◇ *a disposable razor*

'razor blade ***noun*** [C] the thin sharp piece of metal that you put in a RAZOR

Rd ***abbr.*** road: *21 Hazel Rd*

re /riː/ ***prep.*** (*written*) used at the beginning of a business letter, etc. to introduce the subject that it is about: *Re: travel expenses*

re- /riː/ ***prefix*** (used in verbs and related nouns, adjectives and adverbs) again: *rebuild* ◇ *reappearance*

reach¹ ⊶ /riːtʃ/ ***verb*** **1** [T] to arrive at a place or condition that you have been going towards: *We won't reach Dover before 12.* ◇ *The two sides hope to **reach an agreement** sometime today.* ◇ *Sometimes the temperature reaches 45°C.* ◇ *The team reached the semi-final last year.* ◇ *to reach a decision/conclusion/compromise* **2** [I,T] ~ **(out) (for sb/sth)**; ~ **(sth) (down)** to stretch out your arm to try and touch or get sth: *The child reached out for her mother.* ◇ *She reached into her bag for her purse.* **3** [I,T] to be able to touch sth: *Can you get me that book off the top shelf? I can't reach.* ◇ *He couldn't reach the light switch.* ◇ *I need a longer ladder. This one won't reach.* **4** [T] to communicate with sb, especially by telephone; contact: *You can reach me at this number.*

reach² /riːtʃ/ ***noun*** [U] the distance that you can stretch your arm

IDM **beyond/out of (sb's) reach** **1** outside the distance that you can stretch your arm: *Keep this medicine out of the reach of children.* **2** not able to be got or done by sb: *A job like that is beyond his reach.*

within (sb's) reach **1** inside the distance that you can stretch your arm **2** able to be achieved by sb: *We were one goal ahead with ten minutes left and so could sense that victory was within our reach.*

within (easy) reach of sth not far from sth

react ⊶ AW /ri'ækt/ ***verb*** [I] **1** ~ **(to sth) (by doing sth)** to do or say sth because of sth that has happened or been said: *He reacted to the news by jumping up and down and shouting.* ◇ *The players reacted angrily to the decision.* **2** ~ **(to sth)** (HEALTH) to become ill after eating, breathing, etc. a particular substance **3** ~ **(with sth/together)**

(CHEMISTRY) (used about a chemical substance) to change after coming into contact with another substance

PHR V **react against sb/sth** to behave or talk in a way that shows that you do not like the influence of sb/sth (for example authority, your family, etc.)

reactant /ri'æktənt/ ***noun*** [C] (CHEMISTRY) a substance that takes part in and is changed by a chemical reaction

reaction 🔑 AW /ri'ækʃn/ ***noun*** **1** [C,U] (a) ~ **(to sb/sth)** something that you do or say because of sth that has happened: *Could we have your reaction to the latest news, Prime Minister?* ◇ *I shook him to try and wake him up but there was no reaction.* **2** [C,U] (a) ~ **(against sb/sth)** behaviour that shows that you do not like the influence of sb/sth (for example authority, your family, etc.) **3** [C] **a** ~ **(to sth)** (HEALTH) a bad effect that your body experiences because of sth that you have eaten, touched or breathed: *She had an* ***allergic reaction*** *to something in the food.* **4** [C, usually pl.] the physical ability to act quickly when sth happens: *If the other driver's reactions hadn't been so good, there would have been an accident.* **5** [C,U] (CHEMISTRY) a chemical change produced by two or more substances coming into contact with each other

reactionary AW /ri'ækʃənri/ ***noun*** [C] (*pl.* **reactionaries**) (POLITICS, SOCIAL STUDIES) a person who tries to prevent political or social change ▶ **reactionary** ***adj.***: *reactionary views/politics/groups*

reactivate AW /ri'æktɪveɪt/ ***verb*** [T] to make sth start working or happening again after a period of time

reactive AW /ri'æktɪv/ ***adj.*** **1** (*formal*) showing a reaction or response ➲ look at **proactive** **2** (CHEMISTRY) having chemical characteristics that will change when mixed with another substance OPP **unreactive**

reactivity /ˌri:æk'tɪvəti/ ***noun*** [U] (CHEMISTRY) the degree to which a substance shows chemical change when mixed with another substance

reactor AW /ri'æktə(r)/ = NUCLEAR REACTOR

read[1] 🔑 /ri:d/ ***verb*** (*pt, pp* **read** /red/) **1** [I,T] to look at words or symbols and understand them: *He never learnt to read and write.* ◇ *Have you read any good books lately?* ◇ *Can you read music?* **2** [I,T] ~ **(sb) (sth)**; ~ **sth (to sb)** to say written words to sb: *My father used to read me stories when I was a child.* ◇ *I hate reading out loud.* **3** [T] to be able to understand sth from what you can see: *A man came to read the gas meter.* ◇ *Profoundly deaf people train to* ***read lips.*** ◇ *I've no idea what he'll say – I can't* ***read*** *his* ***mind!*** **4** [T] to show words or a sign of sth: *The sign read 'Keep Left'.* **5** [T] (*formal*) (EDUCATION) to study a subject at university: *She read Modern Languages at Cambridge.*

PHR V **read sth into sth** to think that there is a meaning in sth that may not really be there

read on to continue reading; to read the next part of sth

read sth out to read sth to other people

read sth through to read sth to check details or to look for mistakes: *I read my essay through a few times before handing it in.*

read up on sth to find out everything you can about a subject

read[2] /ri:d/ ***noun*** [sing.] (*informal*) a period or the action of reading: *Her detective novels are usually* ***a good read.***

readable /'ri:dəbl/ ***adj.*** **1** able to be read: *machine-readable data* ➲ look at **legible** **2** easy or interesting to read

reader 🔑 /'ri:də(r)/ ***noun*** [C] **1** a person who reads sth (a particular newspaper, magazine, type of book, etc.): *She's an avid reader of science fiction.* **2** (with an adjective) a person who reads in a particular way: *a fast/slow reader* **3** (EDUCATION) a book for practising reading

readership /'ri:dəʃɪp/ ***noun*** [sing.] the number of people who regularly read a particular newspaper, magazine, etc.: *The newspaper has a readership of 200000.*

readily /'redɪli/ ***adv.*** **1** easily, without difficulty: *Most vegetables are* ***readily available*** *at this time of year.* **2** without pausing; without being forced: *He readily admitted that he was wrong.*

readiness /'redinəs/ ***noun*** [U] **1** ~ **(for sth)** the state of being ready or prepared **2** ~ **(to do sth)** the state of being prepared to do sth without arguing or complaining: *The bank have indicated their readiness to lend him the money.*

reading 🔑 /'ri:dɪŋ/ ***noun*** **1** [U] what you do when you read: *I haven't had time to do much reading lately.* ◇ *Her hobbies include painting and reading.* **2** [U] (ARTS AND MEDIA, LITERATURE) books, articles, etc. that are intended to be read: *The information office gave me a pile of* ***reading matter*** *to take away.* **3** [C] the particular way in which sb understands sth: *What's your reading of the situation?* **4** [C] the number or measurement that is shown on an instrument: *a reading of 20°*

readjust AW /ˌri:ə'dʒʌst/ ***verb*** **1** [I] ~ **(to sth)** to get used to a different or new situation: *After her divorce, it took her a long time to readjust to being single again.* **2** [T] to change or move sth slightly ▶ **readjustment** ***noun*** [C,U]

ˌread-only 'memory ***noun*** [U] (COMPUTING) = ROM

ready 🔑 /'redi/ ***adj.*** **1** ~ **(for sb/sth)**; ~ **(to do sth)** prepared and able to do sth or to be used: *The car will be ready for you to collect on Friday.* ◇ *He isn't ready to take his driving test – he hasn't had enough lessons.* ◇ *I'm meeting him at 7, so I don't have long to* ***get ready.*** ◇ *I'll go and* ***get*** *the dinner* ***ready.*** ◇ ***Have*** *your money* ***ready*** *before you get on the bus.* **2** ~ **to do sth**; ~ **(with/for sth)** prepared and happy to do sth: *You know me – I'm always ready to help.* ◇ *Charlie's always ready with advice.* ◇ *The men were angry and ready for a fight.* ◇ *I know it's early, but I'm* ***ready for bed.*** **3** ***adv.*** (used to form compound adjectives) that has already been made or done; not done especially for you: *ready-prepared meals*

ˌready-'made ***adj.*** prepared in advance so that you can eat or use it immediately: *ready-made pastry*

reagent /ri'eɪdʒənt/ ***noun*** [C] (CHEMISTRY) a substance used to cause a chemical reaction, especially in order to find out if another substance is present

real[1] 🔑 /'ri:əl; rɪəl/ ***adj.*** **1** actually existing, not imagined: *The film is based on real life.* ◇ *This isn't a real word, I made it up.* ◇ *We have a real chance of winning.* ◇ *Closure of the factory is a very real danger.* **2** actually true; not only what people think is true: *The name he gave to the police wasn't his real name.* **3** (only *before* a noun) having all, not just some, of the qualities necessary to really be sth: *She was my first real girlfriend.* **4** natural, not false or artificial: *This shirt is real silk.* **5** (only *before* a noun) (used to emphasize a state, feeling or quality) strong or big:

Money is a real problem for us at the moment. ◇ *He made a real effort to be polite.*
IDM **for real** genuine or serious: *Her tears weren't for real.* ◇ *Was he for real when he offered you the job?* **the real thing** something genuine, not a copy: *This painting is just a copy. The real thing is in a gallery.* ◇ *She's had boyfriends before but this time she says it's the real thing* (= real love).

real² /'ri:əl; rɪəl/ *adv.* (*AmE, informal*) very; really

'real estate *noun* [U] property in the form of land and buildings

'real estate agent (*AmE*) = ESTATE AGENT

realism /'ri:əlɪzəm (*BrE also* 'rɪə-)/ *noun* [U] **1** behaviour that shows that you accept the facts of a situation and are not influenced by your feelings ➲ look at **idealism 2** (ART, LITERATURE) showing things as they really are

realist /'ri:əlɪst (*BrE also* 'rɪə-)/ *noun* [C] **1** a person who accepts the facts of a situation, and does not try to pretend that it is different: *I'm a realist – I don't expect the impossible.* **2** (ART, LITERATURE) an artist or writer who shows things as they really are

realistic 🔑 /ˌri:ə'lɪstɪk (*BrE also* ˌrɪə-)/ *adj.* **1** sensible and understanding what it is possible to achieve in a particular situation: *We have to be realistic about our chances of winning.* **2** showing things as they really are: *a realistic drawing/description* **3** not real but appearing to be real: *The monsters in the film were very realistic.* ▶ **realistically** /-kli/ *adv.*

reality 🔑 /ri'æləti/ *noun* (*pl.* **realities**) **1** [U] the way life really is, not the way it may appear to be or how you would like it to be: *I enjoyed my holiday, but now it's back to reality.* ◇ *We have to **face reality** and accept that we've failed.* **2** [C] a thing that is actually experienced, not just imagined: *Films portray war as heroic and exciting, but the reality is very different.*
IDM **in reality** in fact, really (not the way sth appears or has been described): *People say this is an exciting city but in reality it's rather boring.*

reˌality T'V *noun* [U] (ARTS AND MEDIA) television shows that are based on real people (not actors) in real situations, presented as entertainment

realize 🔑 (also -ise) /'rɪəlaɪz/ *verb* [T] **1** to know and understand that sth is true or that sth has happened: *I'm sorry I mentioned it, I didn't realize how much it upset you.* ◇ *Didn't you realize (that) you needed to bring money?* **2** to become conscious of sth or that sth has happened, usually some time later: *When I got home, I realized that I had left my keys at the office.* **3** to make sth that you imagined become reality: *His worst fears were realized when he saw the damage caused by the fire.* ▶ **realization** (also -isation) /ˌrɪəlaɪ'zeɪʃn/ *noun* [U]

ˌreal-'life *adj.* actually happening or existing in life, not in books, stories or films: *a novel based on real-life events* ◇ *a real-life Romeo and Juliet* OPP **fictional**

really 🔑 /'rɪəli/ *adv.* **1** actually; in fact: *I couldn't believe it was really happening.* ◇ *He said he was sorry but I don't think he really meant it.* ◇ *She wasn't really angry, she was only pretending.* ◇ *Is it really true?* **2** very; very much: *I'm really tired.* ◇ *Are you really sure?* ◇ *I really hope you enjoy yourself.* ◇ *I really tried but I couldn't do it.* **3** used as a question for expressing surprise, interest, doubt, etc.: *'She's left her husband.' 'Really? When did that happen?'* **4** used in negative sentences to make what you are saying less strong: *I don't really agree with that.* **5** used in questions when you are expecting sb to answer 'No': *You don't really expect me to believe that, do you?*

ˌreal 'time *noun* [U] (COMPUTING) the fact that there is only a very short time between a computer system receiving information and dealing with it: *To make the training realistic the simulation operates **in real time**.* ◇ *real-time missile guidance systems*

Realtor™ /'ri:əltə(r)/ (*AmE*) = ESTATE AGENT

reap /ri:p/ *verb* [T] (AGRICULTURE) to cut and collect a crop (CORN, WHEAT, etc.): (*figurative*) *Work hard now and you'll **reap the benefits** later on.*

reappear /ˌri:ə'pɪə(r)/ *verb* [I] to appear again or be seen again ▶ **reappearance** /-rəns/ *noun* [C,U]

reappraisal /ˌri:ə'preɪzl/ *noun* [C,U] the new examination of a situation, way of doing sth, etc. in order to decide if any changes are necessary

rear¹ 🔑 /rɪə(r)/ *noun* [sing.] **1 the rear** the back part: *Smoking is only permitted at the rear of the bus.* **2** the part of your body that you sit on; bottom ▶ **rear** *adj.*: *the rear window/lights of a car*
IDM **bring up the rear** to be the last one in a race, a line of people, etc.

rear² /rɪə(r)/ *verb* **1** [T] to look after and educate children: *This generation of children will be reared without fear of war.* **2** [T] (AGRICULTURE) to breed and look after animals on a farm, etc.: *to rear cattle/poultry* **3** [I] ~ **(up)** (used about horses) to stand only on the back legs

rearm /ri'ɑ:m/ *verb* [I,T] to obtain, or supply sb with, new or better weapons, armies, etc.: *The country was forbidden to rearm under the terms of the treaty.* ◇ *Rebel troops were being rearmed.* ▶ **rearmament** /ri'ɑ:məmənt/ *noun* [U]

rearrange /ˌri:ə'reɪndʒ/ *verb* [T] **1** to change the position or order of things **2** to change a plan, meeting, etc. that has been fixed: *The match has been rearranged for next Wednesday.*

ˌrear-view 'mirror *noun* [C] a mirror in which a driver can see the traffic behind

THESAURUS

reason

grounds • excuse • motive • need • justification • cause • pretext

These are all words for a cause or an explanation for sth that has happened or that sb has done.

reason: *What's your reason for being so late?*
grounds (*formal*): *He had no grounds for complaint.*
excuse: *The rain gave her an excuse to take the car.*
motive: *There didn't seem to be any motive for the murder.*
need: *There's no need to ask permission.*
justification (*formal*): *There's no justification for the tax rises.*
cause: *There's no cause for alarm.*
pretext (*formal*): *He left the party early on the pretext of having to finish some work.*

reason¹ 🔑 /'ri:zn/ *noun* **1** [C] **a ~ (for sth/for doing sth); a ~ why.../that...** a cause or an explanation for sth that has happened or for sth that sb has done: *Is there any reason why you couldn't tell me this before?* ◇ *He said he couldn't come but he didn't **give a reason**.* ◇ *The reason (that) I'm phoning you is to ask a favour.* ◇ ***For some reason** they can't give us an answer until next week.* ◇ *She left the job for personal reasons.* **2** [C,U] **(a) ~ (to do sth); (a) ~ (for sth/for doing sth)** something that shows that it is right or fair to do sth: *I **have reason** to believe that you've been lying.* ◇ *I think we have reason for complaint.*

◇ *You* ***have every reason*** (=you are completely right) *to be angry, considering how badly you've been treated.* **3** [U] the ability to think and to make sensible decisions: *Only human beings are capable of reason.* **4** [U] what is right or acceptable: *I tried to persuade him not to drive but he just wouldn't* ***listen to reason.*** ◇ *I'll pay anything* ***within reason*** *for a ticket.*
IDM **it stands to reason** (*informal*) it is obvious if you think about it

reason² /'riːzn/ ***verb*** [I,T] to form a judgement or an opinion, after thinking about sth in a logical way
PHR V **reason with sb** to talk to sb in order to persuade them to behave or think in a more reasonable way

reasonable ⊷ /'riːznəbl/ ***adj.*** **1** fair, practical and sensible: *I think it's reasonable to expect people to keep their promises.* ◇ *I tried to be reasonable even though I was very angry.* **2** acceptable and appropriate in a particular situation: *He made us a reasonable offer for the car.* OPP **unreasonable** **3** (used about prices) not too expensive: *We sell good quality food at reasonable prices.* **4** quite good, high, big, etc. but not very: *His work is of a reasonable standard.*

reasonably ⊷ /'riːznəbli/ ***adv.*** **1** fairly or quite (but not very): *The weather was reasonably good but not brilliant.* **2** in a sensible and fair way

reasoning /'riːzənɪŋ/ ***noun*** [U] the process of thinking about sth and making a judgement or decision: *What's the reasoning behind his sudden decision to leave?*

reassemble /ˌriːə'sembl/ ***verb*** [T] to fit the parts of sth together again after it has been taken apart

reassess AW /ˌriːə'ses/ ***verb*** [T] to think again about sth to decide if you need to change your opinion of it

reassurance /ˌriːə'ʃɔːrəns/ ***noun*** [U, C] advice or help that you give to sb to stop them worrying or being afraid: *I need some reassurance that I'm doing things the right way.*

reassure /ˌriːə'ʃɔː(r)/ ***verb*** [T] to say or do sth in order to stop sb worrying or being afraid: *The mechanic reassured her that the engine was fine.* ▸ **reassuring** ***adj.*** ▸ **reassuringly** ***adv.***

rebate /'riːbeɪt/ ***noun*** [C] (FINANCE) a sum of money that is given back to you because you have paid too much: *to get a tax rebate*

rebel¹ /'rebl/ ***noun*** [C] **1** (POLITICS) a person who fights against their country's government because they want things to change **2** a person who refuses to obey people in authority or to accept rules: *At school he had a reputation as a rebel.*

rebel² /rɪ'bel/ ***verb*** [I] (**rebelling**; **rebelled**) ~ **(against sb/sth)** to fight against authority, society, a law, etc.: *She rebelled against her parents by marrying a man she knew they didn't approve of.*

rebellion /rɪ'beljən/ ***noun*** [C,U] **1** (POLITICS) an occasion when some of the people in a country try to change the government, using violence **2** the action of fighting against authority or refusing to accept rules: *Voting against the leader of the party was an act of open rebellion.*

rebellious /rɪ'beljəs/ ***adj.*** not doing what authority, society, etc. wants you to do: *rebellious teenagers*

rebirth /ˌriː'bɜːθ/ ***noun*** [U, sing.] a period of new life, growth or activity: *the seasonal cycle of death and rebirth*

reboot /ˌriː'buːt/ ***verb*** [T,I] (COMPUTING) if you **reboot** a computer or if it **reboots**, you turn it off and then turn it on again immediately

rebound /rɪ'baʊnd/ ***verb*** [I] ~ **(from/off sth)** to hit sth/sb and then go in a different direction: *The ball rebounded off a defender and went into the goal.* ▸ **rebound** /'riːbaʊnd/ ***noun*** [C]

rebrand /ˌriː'brænd/ ***verb*** [I,T] (BUSINESS) to change the image of a company or an organization or one of its products or services, for example by changing its name or by advertising it in a different way: *In the 1990s the Labour Party* ***rebranded*** *itself as New Labour.* ▸ **rebranding** ***noun*** [sing., U]: *a rebranding exercise* ◇ *a £5 million rebranding*

rebuff /rɪ'bʌf/ ***noun*** [C] an unkind refusal of an offer or suggestion ▸ **rebuff** ***verb*** [T]

rebuild /ˌriː'bɪld/ ***verb*** [T] (*pt, pp* **rebuilt** /ˌriː'bɪlt/) to build sth again: *Following the storm, a great many houses will have to be rebuilt.*

rebuke /rɪ'bjuːk/ ***verb*** [T] (*formal*) to speak angrily to sb because they have done sth wrong ▸ **rebuke** ***noun*** [C]

recall ⊷ /rɪ'kɔːl/ ***verb*** [T] **1** to remember sth (a fact, event, action, etc.) from the past: *I don't recall exactly when I first met her.* ◇ *She couldn't recall meeting him before.* **2** to order sb to return; to ask for sth to be returned: *The company has recalled all the fridges that have this fault.*

recap /'riːkæp/ (**recapping**; **recapped**) (*spoken*) (also *written* **recapitulate** /ˌriːkə'pɪtʃuleɪt/) ***verb*** [I,T] to repeat or look again at the main points of sth to make sure that they have been understood: *Let's quickly recap what we've done in today's lesson.*

recapture /ˌriː'kæptʃə(r)/ ***verb*** [T] **1** to win back sth that was taken from you by an enemy or a COMPETITOR: *Government troops have recaptured the city.* **2** to catch a person or animal that has escaped **3** to create or experience again sth from the past: *The film brilliantly recaptures life in the 1930s.*

recede /rɪ'siːd/ ***verb*** [I] **1** to move away and begin to disappear: *The coast began to recede into the distance.* **2** (used about a hope, fear, chance, etc.) to become smaller or less strong **3** (used about a man's hair) to fall out and stop growing at the front of the head: *He's got a* ***receding hairline.***

receipt ⊷ /rɪ'siːt/ ***noun*** **1** [C] a ~ **(for sth)** a piece of paper that is given to show that you have paid for sth: *Keep the receipt in case you want to exchange the shirt.* **2** [U] (*formal*) ~ **(of sth)** the act of receiving sth

receive ⊷ /rɪ'siːv/ ***verb*** [T] **1** ~ **sth (from sb/sth)** to get or accept sth that sb sends or gives to you: *I received a letter from an old friend last week.* ◇ *to receive a phone call/a prize* **2** to experience a particular kind of treatment or injury: *We received a warm welcome from our hosts.* ◇ *He received several cuts and bruises in the accident.* **3** (often passive) to react to sth new in a particular way: *The film has been well received by the critics.*

reˌceived pronunci'ation = RP

receiver /rɪ'siːvə(r)/ ***noun*** [C] **1** (*also* **handset**) the part of a telephone that is used for listening and speaking **2** a piece of television or radio equipment that changes electronic signals into sounds or pictures **3** (LAW) a person who is chosen by a court to be in charge of a company that is BANKRUPT (=does not have enough money to pay its debts): *to call in the receivers*

receivership /rɪˈsiːvəʃɪp/ ***noun*** [U] (LAW) the state of a business being controlled by an official RECEIVER because it has no money: *Five hundred jobs were lost last year when the company* ***went into receivership****.*

recent ⊶ /ˈriːsnt/ ***adj.*** that happened or began only a short time ago: ***In recent years*** *there have been many changes.* ◇ *This is a recent photograph of my daughter.*

recently ⊶ /ˈriːsntli/ ***adv.*** not long ago: *She worked here until quite recently.* ◇ *Have you seen Paul recently?*

receptacle /rɪˈseptəkl/ ***noun*** [C] **1 a** ~ **(for sth)** (*formal*) a container for putting sth in **2** (BIOLOGY) the rounded area at the top of a STEM that supports the head of a flower ➲ picture at **flower**

reception ⊶ /rɪˈsepʃn/ ***noun*** **1** [U] the place inside the entrance of a hotel or office building where guests or visitors go when they first arrive: *Leave your key* ***at /in reception*** *if you go out, please.* ◇ *the reception desk* **2** [C] a formal party to celebrate sth or to welcome an important person: *Their* ***wedding reception*** *was held at a local hotel.* ◇ *There will be an official reception at the embassy for the visiting ambassador.* **3** [sing.] the way people react to sth: *The play got a mixed reception* (=some people liked it, some people didn't). **4** [U] the quality of radio or television signals: *TV reception is very poor where we live.*

receptionist /rɪˈsepʃənɪst/ ***noun*** [C] a person who works in a hotel, office, etc. answering the telephone and dealing with visitors and guests when they arrive: *a hotel receptionist*

receptive /rɪˈseptɪv/ ***adj.*** ~ **(to sth)** ready to listen to new ideas, suggestions, etc.

receptor /rɪˈseptə(r)/ ***noun*** [C] (ANATOMY) a sense organ or nerve ending in the body that reacts to changes such as heat or cold and makes the body react in a particular way

recess /rɪˈses/ ***noun*** **1** [C,U] a period of time when Parliament, committees, etc. do not meet **2** [U] (LAW) a short break during a trial in a court of law **3** [C] (*AmE*) =BREAK² (3) **4** [C] part of a wall that is further back than the rest, forming a space **5** [C] a part of a room that receives very little light

recession /rɪˈseʃn/ ***noun*** [C,U] (ECONOMICS) a period when the business and industry of a country is not successful: *The country is now* ***in recession****.* ◇ *How long will the recession last?*

recessive /rɪˈsesɪv/ ***adj.*** (BIOLOGY) a recessive physical characteristic only appears in a child if they have two GENES for this characteristic, one from each parent. ➲ look at **dominant**

recharge /ˌriːˈtʃɑːdʒ/ ***verb*** [T,I] (PHYSICS) to fill a battery with electrical power; to fill up with electrical power: *He plugged the drill in to recharge it.* ➲ look at **charge** ▶ **rechargeable** ***adj.***: *rechargeable batteries*

recipe /ˈresəpi/ ***noun*** [C] **1 a** ~ **(for sth)** the instructions for cooking or preparing sth to eat. A **recipe** tells you what to use (**the ingredients**) and what to do: *a recipe for chocolate cake* **2 a** ~ **for sth** the way to get or produce sth: *Putting Dave in charge of the project is* ***a recipe for disaster****.*

recipient /rɪˈsɪpiənt/ ***noun*** [C] (*formal*) a person who receives sth

reciprocal /rɪˈsɪprəkl/ ***adj.*** involving two or more people or groups who agree to help each other or to behave in the same way towards one another: *The arrangement is reciprocal. They help us and we help them.*

reciprocate /rɪˈsɪprəkeɪt/ ***verb*** **1** [T,I] (*formal*) ~ **(sth) (with sth)** to behave or feel towards sb in the same way as they behave or feel towards you: *Her passion for him was not reciprocated.* ◇ *They wanted to reciprocate the kindness that had been shown to them.* ◇ *He smiled but his smile was not reciprocated.* **2** [I] to move backwards and forwards in a straight line: *a reciprocating action/movement* ▶ **reciprocation** /rɪˌsɪprəˈkeɪʃn/ ***noun*** [U]

recital /rɪˈsaɪtl/ ***noun*** [C] (LITERATURE, MUSIC) a formal public performance of music or poetry: *a piano recital* ➲ look at **concert**

recitative /ˌresɪtəˈtiːv/ ***noun*** [C,U] (MUSIC) a passage in an OPERA or ORATORIO that is sung in the rhythm of ordinary speech with many words on the same note

recite /rɪˈsaɪt/ ***verb*** [I,T] (LITERATURE) to say aloud a piece of writing, especially a poem or a list, from memory

reckless /ˈrekləs/ ***adj.*** not thinking about possible bad or dangerous results that could come from your actions: *reckless driving* ▶ **recklessly** ***adv.***

reckon ⊶ /ˈrekən/ ***verb*** [T] (*informal*) **1** to think; to have an opinion about sth: *She's very late now. I reckon (that) she isn't coming.* ◇ *I think she's forgotten. What do you reckon?* **2** to calculate sth approximately: *I reckon the journey will take about half an hour.* **3** to expect to do sth: *I wasn't reckoning to pay so much.*

PHR V **reckon on sth** to expect sth to happen and therefore to base a plan or action on it: *I didn't book in advance because I wasn't reckoning on tickets being so scarce.*

reckon (sth) up to calculate the total amount or number of sth

reckon with sb/sth to think about sb/sth as a possible problem

reckoning /ˈrekənɪŋ/ ***noun*** **1** [U, C] the act of calculating sth, especially in a way that is not very exact **2** [C, usually sing., U] (*formal*) a time when sb's actions will be judged to be right or wrong and they may be punished: *In the* ***final reckoning*** *truth is rewarded.* ◇ *Officials concerned with environmental policy predict that* ***a day of reckoning*** *will come.*

IDM **in/into/out of the reckoning** (*especially BrE*) (especially in sport) among/not among those who are likely to win or be successful: *Greene is fit again and should come into the reckoning.*

reclaim /rɪˈkleɪm/ ***verb*** [T] **1** ~ **sth (from sb/sth)** to get back sth that has been lost or taken away: *Reclaim your luggage after you have been through passport control.* **2** to get back useful materials from waste products **3** (ENVIRONMENT) to make wet land suitable for use ▶ **reclamation** /ˌrekləˈmeɪʃn/ ***noun*** [U]

recline /rɪˈklaɪn/ ***verb*** [I] to sit or lie back in a relaxed and comfortable way ▶ **reclining** ***adj.***: *The car has* ***reclining seats*** *at the front.*

recluse /rɪˈkluːs/ ***noun*** [C] a person who lives alone and likes to avoid other people ▶ **reclusive** /rɪˈkluːsɪv/ ***adj.***: *a reclusive millionaire*

recognition ⊶ /ˌrekəgˈnɪʃn/ ***noun*** **1** [U] the fact that you can identify sb/sth that you see: *When I arrived no sign of recognition showed on her face at all.* **2** [U, sing.] the act of accepting that sth exists, is true or is official **3** [U] a public show of respect for sb's work or actions: *She has* ***received*** *public* ***recognition*** *for her services to charity.* ◇ *Please accept this gift* ***in recognition of*** *the work you have done.*

recognizable (also **-isable**) /ˈrekəgnaɪzəbl; ˌrekəgˈnaɪzəbl/ ***adj.*** ~ **(as sb/sth)** that can be identified as sb/sth: *He was barely recognizable with his new short haircut.* ▶ **recognizably** (also **-isably**) /-əbli/ ***adv.***

recognize 🔑 (also -ise) /ˈrekəgnaɪz/ ***verb*** [T] **1** to know again sb/sth that you have seen or heard before: *I recognized him but I couldn't remember his name.* **2** to accept that sth is true **3** to accept sth officially: *My qualifications are not recognized in other countries.* **4** to show officially that you think sth that sb has done is good

recoil /rɪˈkɔɪl/ ***verb*** [I] to quickly move away from sb/sth unpleasant: *She recoiled in horror at the sight of the corpse.*

recollect /ˌrekəˈlekt/ ***verb*** [I,T] to remember sth, especially by making an effort: *I don't recollect exactly when it happened.*

recollection /ˌrekəˈlekʃn/ ***noun*** **1** [U] ~ **(of sth/doing sth)** the ability to remember: ***I have no recollection** of promising to lend you money.* **2** [C, usually pl.] something that you remember: *I have only vague recollections of the town where I spent my early years.*

THESAURUS

recommend

advise • advocate • urge

These words all mean to tell sb what you think they should do in a particular situation.

recommend: *Early booking is recommended.*

advise: *I'd advise you not to tell him.*

advocate (*formal*): *The group does not advocate the use of violence.*

urge (*formal*): *The UN is urging caution in this dangerous situation.*

recommend 🔑 /ˌrekəˈmend/ ***verb*** [T] **1** ~ **sb/sth (to sb) (for/as sth)** to say that sb/sth is good and that sb should try or use them or it: *Which film would you recommend?* ◇ *Could you recommend me a good hotel?* ◇ *We hope that you'll recommend this restaurant to all your friends.* ◇ *Doctors don't always recommend drugs as the best treatment for every illness.* **2** to tell sb what you strongly believe they should do: *I recommend that you get some legal advice.* ◇ *I wouldn't recommend (your) travelling on your own. It could be dangerous.* ➲ look at **suggest**

recommendation /ˌrekəmenˈdeɪʃn/ ***noun*** **1** [C,U] saying that sth is good and should be tried or used: *I visited Seville **on a friend's recommendation** and I really enjoyed it.* **2** [C] a statement about what should be done in a particular situation: *In their report on the crash, the committee **make** several **recommendations** on how safety could be improved.*

recompense /ˈrekəmpens/ ***verb*** [T] (*formal*) ~ **sb (for sth)** to give money, etc. to sb for special efforts or work or because you are responsible for a loss they have suffered: *The airline has agreed to recompense us for the damage to our luggage.*
▶ **recompense** ***noun*** [sing., U]: *Please accept this cheque **in recompense for** our poor service.*

reconcile /ˈrekənsaɪl/ ***verb*** [T] **1** ~ **sth (with sth)** to find a way of dealing with two ideas, situations, statements, etc. that seem to be opposite to each other: *She finds it difficult to reconcile her career ambitions with her responsibilities to her children.* **2** (often passive) ~ **sb (with sb)** to make people become friends again after an argument: *After years of not speaking to each other, she and her parents were eventually reconciled.* **3** ~ **yourself to sth** to accept an unpleasant situation because there is nothing you can do to change it ▶ **reconciliation** /ˌrekənsɪliˈeɪʃn/ ***noun*** [sing., U]: *The negotiators are hoping to bring about a reconciliation between the two sides.*

reconnaissance /rɪˈkɒnɪsns/ ***noun*** [C,U] the study of a place or area for military reasons: *The plane was shot down while on a reconnaissance mission over enemy territory.*

reconsider /ˌriːkənˈsɪdə(r)/ ***verb*** [I,T] to think again about sth, especially because you may want to change your mind

reconstruct AW /ˌriːkənˈstrʌkt/ ***verb*** [T] **1** to build again sth that has been destroyed or damaged **2** to get a full description or picture of sth using the facts that are known: *The police are trying to reconstruct the victim's movements on the day of the murder.* ▶ **reconstruction** AW /-ˈstrʌkʃn/ ***noun*** [C,U]: *a reconstruction of the crime using actors*

record[1] 🔑 /ˈrekɔːd/ ***noun*** **1** [C] a ~ **(of sth)** a written account of what has happened, been done, etc.: *The teachers **keep records** of the children's progress.* ◇ *medical records* **2** [sing.] the facts, events, etc. that are known (and sometimes written down) about sb/sth: *The police said that the man had **a criminal record** (=he had been found guilty of crimes in the past).* ◇ *This airline has a bad safety record.* **3** [C] (*also* **album**) (MUSIC) a thin, round piece of plastic which can store music so that you can play it when you want **4** [C] the best performance or the highest or lowest level, etc. ever reached in sth, especially in sport: *Who **holds the world record for** high jump?* ◇ *She's hoping to **break the record** for the 100 metres.* ◇ *He did it **in record time** (=very fast).*

IDM **be/go on (the) record (as saying...)** to say sth publicly or officially so that it may be written down and repeated: *He didn't want to go on the record as either praising or criticizing the proposal.*

off the record if you tell sb sth off the record, it is not yet official and you do not want it to be repeated publicly: *She told me off the record that she was going to resign.*

put/set the record straight to correct a mistake by telling sb the true facts

record[2] 🔑 /rɪˈkɔːd/ ***verb*** **1** [T] to write down or film facts or events so that they can be referred to later and will not be FORGOTTEN: *He recorded everything in his diary.* ◇ *At the inquest the coroner **recorded a verdict** of accidental death.* **2** [I,T] to put music, a film, a programme, etc. onto a CD or CASSETTE so that it can be listened to or watched again later: *Quiet, please! We're recording.* ◇ *The band has recently recorded a new album.* ◇ *There's a concert I would like to record from the radio this evening.*

ˈ**record-breaker** ***noun*** [C] (SPORT) a person or thing that achieves a better result or higher level than has ever been achieved before

ˈ**record-breaking** ***adj.*** (only *before* a noun) the best, fastest, highest, etc. ever: *He won the race in record-breaking time.*

recorder /rɪˈkɔːdə(r)/ ***noun*** [C] **1** a machine for recording sound and/or pictures: *a tape/cassette/video recorder* **2** (MUSIC) a type of musical instrument that is often played by children. You play it by blowing through it and covering the holes in it with your fingers. ➲ picture on **page 465**

ˈ**record holder** ***noun*** [C] (SPORT) a person who has achieved the best result that has ever been achieved in a sport

recording ⊶ /rɪˈkɔːdɪŋ/ *noun* **1** [C] sound or pictures that have been put onto a CASSETTE, CD, film, etc.: *the Berlin Philharmonic's recording of Mahler's sixth symphony* **2** [U] the process of making a CASSETTE, record, film, etc.: *a recording session/studio*

ˈrecord player *noun* [C] a machine that you use for playing records

recount /rɪˈkaʊnt/ *verb* [T] (*formal*) to tell a story or describe an event

recourse /rɪˈkɔːs/ *noun* [C] (*formal*) having to use sth or ask sb for help in a difficult situation: *She made a complete recovery* ***without recourse to*** *surgery.*

recover ⊶ AW /rɪˈkʌvə(r)/ *verb* **1** [I] ~ (**from sth**) to become well again after you have been ill: *It took him two months to recover from the operation.* **2** [I] ~ (**from sth**) to get back to normal again after a bad experience, etc.: *The old lady never really recovered from the shock of being mugged.* **3** [T] ~ **sth** (**from sb/sth**) to find or get back sth that was lost or stolen: *Police recovered the stolen goods from a warehouse in South London.* **4** [T] to get back the use of your senses, control of your emotions, etc.

recovery AW /rɪˈkʌvəri/ *noun* **1** [usually sing., U] ~ (**from sth**) a return to good health after an illness or to a normal state after a difficult period of time: *to* ***make a*** *good/quick/speedy/slow* ***recovery*** ◇ *She's* ***on the road to recovery*** (= getting better all the time) *now.* ◇ *the prospects of* ***economic recovery*** **2** [U] ~ (**of sth/sb**) getting back sth that was lost, stolen or missing

recreate AW /ˌriːkriˈeɪt/ *verb* [T] to make sth that existed in the past exist or seem to exist again: *The movie recreates the glamour of 1940s Hollywood.*

recreation /ˌrekriˈeɪʃn/ *noun* [U, sing.] enjoying yourself and relaxing when you are not working; a way of doing this: *the need to improve facilities for leisure and recreation* ▶ **recreational** /ˌrekriˈeɪʃənl/ *adj.*: *recreational activities*

ˌrecreational ˈvehicle *noun* [C] (*AmE*) (*abbr.* **RV**) = CAMPER (2)

recrimination /rɪˌkrɪmɪˈneɪʃn/ *noun* [C, usually pl., U] an angry statement accusing sb of sth, especially in answer to a similar statement from them: *bitter recriminations*

recruit[1] /rɪˈkruːt/ *noun* [C] a person who has just joined the army or another organization

recruit[2] /rɪˈkruːt/ *verb* [I,T] to find new people to join a company, an organization, the armed forces, etc. ▶ **recruitment** *noun* [U]

rectal /ˈrektəl/ → RECTUM

rectangle /ˈrektæŋgl/ *noun* [C] (GEOMETRY) a shape with four straight sides and four angles of 90 degrees (**right angles**). Two of the sides are longer than the other two. SYN **oblong** ➲ picture at **parallelogram** ▶ **rectangular** /rekˈtæŋgjələ(r)/ *adj.*

rectify /ˈrektɪfaɪ/ *verb* [T] (*pres. part.* **rectifying**; *3rd person sing. pres.* **rectifies**; *pt, pp* **rectified**) (*formal*) to correct sth that is wrong

rectum /ˈrektəm/ *noun* [C] (ANATOMY) the end section of the tube through which solid waste leaves the body ➲ picture on **page 80** ▶ **rectal** *adj.*

recuperate /rɪˈkuːpəreɪt/ *verb* [I] (*formal*) ~ (**from sth**) (HEALTH) to get well again after an illness or injury ▶ **recuperation** /rɪˌkuːpəˈreɪʃn/ *noun* [U]

recur /rɪˈkɜː(r)/ *verb* [I] (**recurring**; **recurred**) to happen again or many times: *a recurring problem/illness/nightmare* ▶ **recurrence** /rɪˈkʌrəns/ *noun* [C,U] ▶ **recurrent** /rɪˈkʌrənt/ *adj.*

reˌcurring ˈdecimal *noun* [C] (MATHEMATICS) a DECIMAL FRACTION in which the same figure or group of figures is repeated for ever, for example 3.999...: *The recurring decimal 3.999...is also described as 3.9 recurring.*

recycle /ˌriːˈsaɪkl/ *verb* [T] (ENVIRONMENT) **1** to put used objects and materials through a process so that they can be used again: *recycled paper* ◇ *Aluminium cans can be recycled.* **2** to keep used objects and materials and use them again: *Don't throw away your plastic carrier bags – recycle them!* ▶ **recyclable** *adj.*: *Most plastics are recyclable.* ▶ **recycling** *noun* [U]: *the recycling of glass* ◇ *a recycling plant*

red ⊶ /red/ *noun* [C,U], *adj.* (**redder**; **reddest**) **1** (of) the colour of blood: *red wine* ◇ *She was dressed in red.* **2** a colour that some people's faces become when they are embarrassed, angry, shy, etc.: *He went bright red when she spoke to him.* ◇ *to turn/be/go red in the face* **3** (used about a person's hair or an animal's fur) (of) a colour between red, orange and brown: *She's got red hair and freckles.*

IDM **be in the red** (FINANCE) to have spent more money than you have in the bank, etc.: *I'm £500 in the red at the moment.* OPP **be in the black**

catch sb red-handed → CATCH[1]

a red herring an idea or a subject which takes people's attention away from what is really important

see red (*informal*) to become very angry

ˌred ˈcard *noun* [C] (SPORT) (in football) a card that is shown to a player who is being sent off the field for doing sth wrong ➲ look at **yellow card**

the ˌred ˈcarpet *noun* [sing.] a piece of red carpet that is put outside to receive an important visitor; a special welcome for an important visitor: *I didn't expect to be given the red carpet treatment!*

the ˌRed ˈCross *noun* [sing.] (HEALTH, POLITICS) an international organization that takes care of people who are suffering because of war or natural disasters. Its full name is 'the International Movement of the Red Cross and the Red Crescent'.

redcurrant /ˌredˈkʌrənt/ *noun* [C] a small red BERRY that you can eat: *redcurrant jelly*

redden /ˈredn/ *verb* [I,T] to become red or to make sth red

reddish /ˈredɪʃ/ *adj.* fairly red in colour

redecorate /ˌriːˈdekəreɪt/ *verb* [I,T] to put new paint and/or paper on the walls of a room or house

redeem /rɪˈdiːm/ *verb* [T] **1** to prevent sth from being completely bad: *The* ***redeeming feature*** *of the job is the good salary.* **2** ~ **yourself** to do sth to improve people's opinion of you, especially after you have done sth bad

redemption /rɪˈdempʃn/ *noun* [U] (RELIGION) (according to the Christian religion) the action of being saved from evil

IDM **beyond redemption** too bad to be saved or improved

redesign /ˌriːdɪˈzaɪn/ *verb* [T] to design sth again, in a different way

redevelop /ˌriːdɪˈveləp/ *verb* [T] to build or arrange an area, a town, a building, etc. in a different and more modern way: *They're redeveloping the city centre.* ▶ **redevelopment** *noun* [U]

redhead /ˈredhed/ *noun* [C] a person, usually a woman, who has red hair

ˌred-ˈhot *adj.* (used about a metal) so hot that it turns red

redial /ˌriːˈdaɪəl/ ***verb*** [I,T] (on a telephone) to call the same number that you have just called

redistribute AW /ˌriːdɪˈstrɪbjuːt; ˌriːˈdɪs-/ ***verb*** [T] to share sth out among people in a different way from before
▶ **redistribution** AW /ˌriːdɪstrɪˈbjuːʃn/ ***noun*** [U]

ˌred-ˈletter day ***noun*** [C] an important day, or a day that you will remember, because of sth good that happened then

ˌred-ˈlight district ***noun*** [C] a part of a town where there are a lot of people, especially women, who earn money by having sex with people

redo /ˌriːˈduː/ ***verb*** [T] (*3rd person sing. pres.* **redoes** /-ˈdʌz/; *pt* **redid** /-ˈdɪd/; *pp* **redone** /-ˈdʌn/) to do sth again or differently: *A whole day's work had to be redone.* ◇ *We've just redone the bathroom* (=decorated it differently).

ˌred ˈpepper ***noun*** [C] =PEPPER[1] (2)

redress[1] /rɪˈdres/ ***verb*** [T] (*formal*) to correct sth that is unfair or wrong: *to redress an injustice*

redress[2] /rɪˈdres; ˈriːdres/ ***noun*** [U] ~ **(for/against sth)** (LAW) (*formal*) payment, etc. that you should get for sth wrong that has happened to you or harm that you have suffered SYN **compensation**: *to seek legal redress for unfair dismissal*

ˌred ˈtape ***noun*** [U] official rules that must be followed and papers that must be filled in, which seem unnecessary and often cause delay and difficulty in achieving sth

ˈred-top ***noun*** [C] (*BrE, informal*) (ARTS AND MEDIA) a British TABLOID newspaper (=a newspaper with small pages, a lot of pictures and stories about famous people, often thought of as less serious than other newspapers), whose name is in red at the top of the front page

reduce 🔑 /rɪˈdjuːs/ ***verb*** [T] **1** ~ **sth (from sth) (to sth)**; ~ **sth (by sth)** to make sth less or smaller in quantity, price, size, etc.: *The sign said 'Reduce speed now'.* OPP **increase** **2** ~ **sb/sth (from sth) to sth** (often passive) to force sb/sth into a particular state or condition, usually a bad one: *One of the older boys* ***reduced*** *the small child* ***to tears.*** **3** (CHEMISTRY) to add one or more ELECTRONS to a substance or to remove OXYGEN from a substance ➲ look at **oxidize**

reduction 🔑 /rɪˈdʌkʃn/ ***noun*** **1** [C,U] ~ **(in sth)** the action of becoming or making sth less or smaller: *a sharp reduction in the number of students* **2** [C] the amount by which sth is made smaller, especially in price: *There were massive reductions in the June sales.* **3** (CHEMISTRY) [U] the fact of adding one or more ELECTRONS to a substance or of removing OXYGEN from a substance ➲ look at **oxidation**

redundant /rɪˈdʌndənt/ ***adj.*** **1** (used about employees) no longer needed for a job and therefore out of work: *When the factory closed 800 people were* ***made redundant.*** **2** not necessary or wanted ▶ **redundancy** /-dənsi/ ***noun*** [C,U] (*pl.* **redundancies**): *redundancy pay*

reed /riːd/ ***noun*** [C] **1** a tall plant, like grass, that grows in or near water **2** (MUSIC) a thin piece of wood at the end of some musical instruments which produces a sound when you blow through it ➲ picture on **page 465**

reef /riːf/ ***noun*** [C] (GEOGRAPHY) a long line of rocks, plants, etc. just below or above the surface of the sea: *a coral reef*

reek /riːk/ ***verb*** [I] ~ **(of sth)** to smell strongly of sth unpleasant: *His breath reeked of tobacco.* ▶ **reek** ***noun*** [sing.]

reel[1] /riːl/ ***noun*** [C] a round object that thread, wire, film for cameras, etc. is put around: *a cotton reel* ◇ *a reel of film* ➲ look at **spool** ➲ picture at **agriculture**

reel[2] /riːl/ ***verb*** **1** [I] to walk without being able to control your legs, for example because you are drunk or you have been hit **2** [I] to feel very shocked or upset about sth: *His mind was still reeling from the shock of seeing her again.* **3** [T] ~ **sth in/out** to pull sth towards you or move it away from you by turning a REEL: *to reel in a fish*

PHR V **reel sth off** to say or repeat sth from memory quickly and without having to think about it: *She reeled off a long list of names.*

ˌre-ˈentry ***noun*** [U] **re-entry (into sth) 1** the act of returning to a place or an area of activity that you used to be in: *She feared she would not be granted re-entry into Britain.* **2** (ASTRONOMY) the return of a SPACECRAFT into the earth's atmosphere: *The capsule gets very hot on re-entry.*

ref. ***abbr.*** reference: *ref. no. 3456*

refectory /rɪˈfektri/ ***noun*** [C] (*pl.* **refectories**) a large room in which meals are served, especially in a religious institution and in some schools and colleges in Britain

refer 🔑 /rɪˈfɜː(r)/ ***verb*** (**referring**; **referred**) **1** [I] ~ **to sb/sth (as sth)** to mention or talk about sb/sth: *When he said 'some students', do you think he was referring to us?* ◇ *She always referred to Ben as 'that nice man'.* ➲ note at **mention** **2** [I] ~ **to sb/sth** to describe or be connected with sb/sth: *The term 'adolescent' refers to young people between the ages of 12 and 17.* **3** [I] ~ **to sb/sth** to find out information by asking sb or by looking in a book, etc.: *If you don't understand a word you may refer to your dictionaries.* **4** [T] ~ **sb/sth to sb/sth** to send sb/sth to sb/sth else for help or to be dealt with: *The doctor has referred me to a specialist.*

referee /ˌrefəˈriː/ ***noun*** [C] **1** (also *informal* **ref**) (SPORT) the official person in sports such as football who controls the match and prevents players from breaking the rules ➲ look at **umpire** **2** (*BrE*) a person who gives information about your character and ability, usually in a letter, for example when you are hoping to be chosen for a job: *Her teacher agreed to* ***act as her referee.*** ▶ **referee** ***verb*** [I,T]

reference 🔑 /ˈrefrəns/ ***noun*** **1** [C,U] (a) ~ **(to sb/sth)** a written or spoken comment that mentions sb/sth: *The article* ***made a direct reference to*** *a certain member of the royal family.* **2** [U] looking at sth for information: *The guidebook might be useful* ***for future reference.*** **3** [C] (LITERATURE) a note, especially in a book, that tells you where certain information came from or can be found **4** [C] (*abbr.* **ref.**) (used on business letters, etc.) a special number that identifies a letter, etc.: *Please quote our reference when replying.* **5** [C] a statement or letter describing a person's character and ability that is given to a possible future employer: *My boss gave me a good reference.*

IDM **with reference to sb/sth** (*formal*) about or concerning sb/sth: *I am writing with reference to your letter of 10 April...*

ˈreference book ***noun*** [C] a book that you use to find a piece of information: *dictionaries, encyclopedias and other reference books*

referendum /ˌrefəˈrendəm/ ***noun*** [C,U] (*pl.* **referendums** or **referenda** /-də/) (POLITICS) an occasion when all the people of a country can vote on a particular political question: *to hold a referendum*

refill /ˌriːˈfɪl/ ***verb*** [T] to fill sth again: *Can I refill your glass?* ▶ **refill** /ˈriːfɪl/ ***noun*** [C]: *a refill for a pen*

refine AW /rɪˈfaɪn/ ***verb*** [T] **1** to make a substance pure and free from other substances: *to refine sugar/oil* **2** to improve sth by changing little details: *to refine a theory*

refined AW /rɪˈfaɪnd/ ***adj.*** **1** (used about a substance) that has been made pure by having other substances taken out of it: *refined sugar/oil/flour* OPP **unrefined** **2** (used about a person) polite; having very good manners OPP **unrefined** **3** improved and therefore producing a better result

refinement AW /rɪˈfaɪnmənt/ ***noun*** **1** [C] a small change that improves sth: *The new model has electric windows and other refinements.* **2** [U] good manners and polite behaviour

refinery /rɪˈfaɪnəri/ ***noun*** [C] (*pl.* **refineries**) a factory where a substance is made pure by having other substances taken out of it: *an oil/sugar refinery*

reflect 🔑 /rɪˈflekt/ ***verb*** **1** [T] (PHYSICS) to send back light, heat or sound from a surface: *The windows reflected the bright morning sunlight.* **2** [T] ~ **sb/sth (in sth)** (usually passive) to show an image of sb/sth on the surface of sth such as a mirror, water or glass: *She caught sight of herself reflected in the shop window.* **3** [T] to show or express sth: *His music reflects his interest in African culture.* **4** [I] ~ **(on/upon sth)** to think, especially deeply and carefully, about sth

PHR V **reflect (well, badly, etc.) on sb/sth** to give a particular impression of sb/sth: *It reflects badly on the whole school if some of its pupils misbehave in public.*

reflection

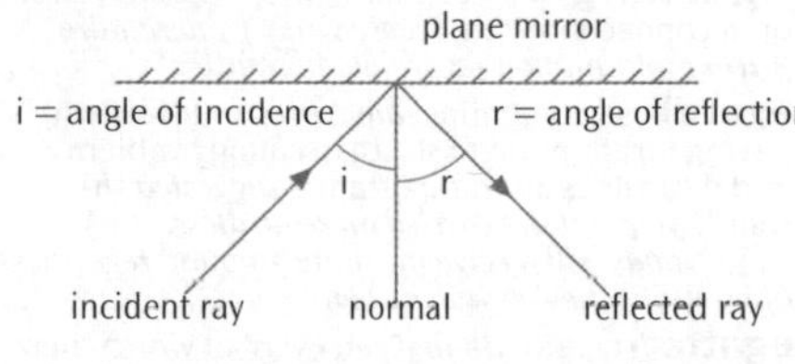

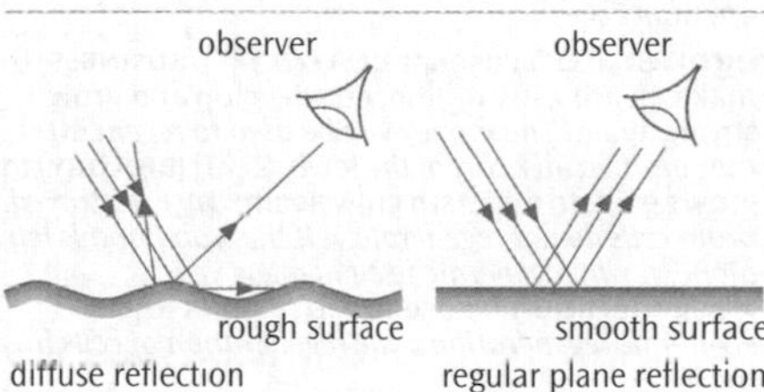

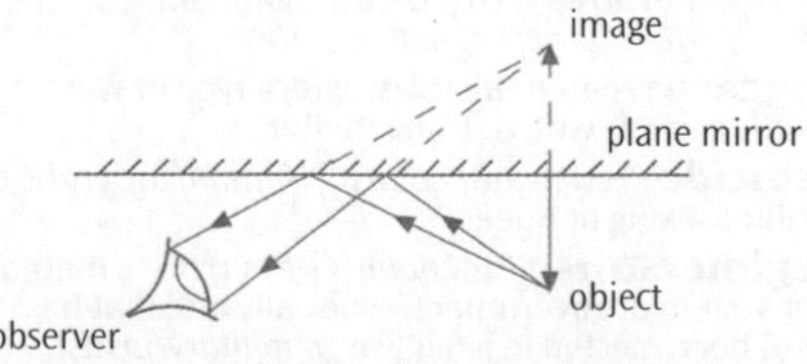

reflection (*BrE also* **reflexion**) /rɪˈflekʃn/ ***noun*** **1** [C] an image that you see in a mirror, in water or on a shiny surface: *He admired his reflection in the mirror.* **2** [U] (PHYSICS) the sending back of light, heat or sound from a surface **3** [C] a thing that shows what sb/sth is like: *Your clothes are a reflection of your personality.* **4** [sing.] **a ~ on/upon sb/sth** something that causes people to form a good or bad opinion about sb/sth: *Parents often feel that their children's behaviour is a reflection on themselves.* **5** [U, C] careful thought about sth: *a book of his* ***reflections on*** *fatherhood*

IDM **on reflection** after thinking again: *I think, on reflection, that we were wrong.*

reflective /rɪˈflektɪv/ ***adj.*** **1** (*written*) (used about a person, mood, etc.) thinking deeply about things: *a reflective expression* **2** (used about a surface) sending back light or heat: *Wear reflective strips when you're cycling at night.* **3** ~ **(of sth)** showing what sth is like

reflector /rɪˈflektə(r)/ ***noun*** [C] **1** a surface that REFLECTS light, heat or sound that hits it **2** a small piece of glass or plastic on a bicycle or on clothing that can be seen at night when light shines on it

reflex /ˈriːfleks/ ***noun*** [C] (BIOLOGY) an action or a movement of your body that happens naturally in response to sth and that you cannot control; sth that you do without thinking: *The doctor tested his reflexes.* ◇ *She put her hands out as a* ***reflex action*** *to stop her fall.* ◇ *A good tennis player needs to have excellent reflexes.*

ˌreflex ˈangle ***noun*** [C] (MATHEMATICS) an angle of more than 180° ➲ look at **acute angle**, **obtuse angle**, **right angle** ➲ picture at **angle**

reflexion (*BrE*) = REFLECTION

reflexive /rɪˈfleksɪv/ ***adj.***, ***noun*** [C] (LANGUAGE) (a word or verb form) showing that the person who performs an action is also affected by it: *In 'He cut himself', 'himself' is a* ***reflexive pronoun***.

reflux /ˈriːflʌks/ ***noun*** [U] **1** (CHEMISTRY) the process of boiling a liquid so that any VAPOUR (= very small drops of liquid in the air, such as steam) which rises up from it, is changed to liquid again and falls back down into the bottle or container **2** (HEALTH) the flowing back of a liquid inside the body, such as acid from the stomach into the OESOPHAGUS: *acid reflux*

reform 🔑 /rɪˈfɔːm/ ***verb*** **1** [T] to change a system, the law, etc. in order to make it better **2** [I,T] to improve your behaviour; to make sb do this: *Our prisons aim to reform criminals, not simply to punish them.* ▶ **reform** ***noun*** [C,U]

reformation /ˌrefəˈmeɪʃn/ ***noun*** **1** [U] (*formal*) the act of improving or changing sb/sth **2 the Reformation** [sing.] (HISTORY, RELIGION) new ideas in religion in 16th century Europe that led to changes in the Roman Catholic Church and the forming of the Protestant Churches; the period in history when these changes were taking place

reformer /rɪˈfɔːmə(r)/ ***noun*** [C] (SOCIAL STUDIES) a person who tries to change society and make it better

refract /rɪˈfrækt/ ***verb*** [T] (PHYSICS) (used about water, glass, etc.) to make a RAY of light change direction when it goes through at an angle ▶ **refraction** ***noun*** [U]

refraction

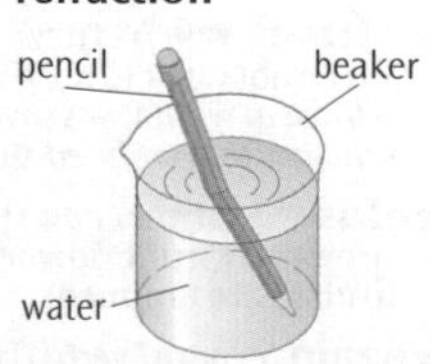

refrain[1] /rɪˈfreɪn/ ***verb*** [I] (*formal*) ~ **(from sth/from doing sth)** to stop yourself doing sth; to not do sth: *Please refrain from smoking in the hospital.*

refrain² /rɪˈfreɪn/ ***noun*** [C] (*formal*) (**MUSIC**) a part of a song which is repeated, usually at the end of each VERSE **SYN** **chorus**

refresh /rɪˈfreʃ/ ***verb*** **1** [T] to make sb/sth feel less tired or less hot and full of energy again: *He looked refreshed after a good night's sleep.* **2** [T,I] (**COMPUTING**) to get the most recent information, for example on an Internet page, by clicking on a button on the screen: *Click here to refresh this document.* ◇ *The page refreshes automatically.*

IDM **refresh your memory (about sb/sth)** to remind yourself about sb/sth: *Could you refresh my memory about what we said on this point last week?*

refreshing /rɪˈfreʃɪŋ/ ***adj.*** **1** pleasantly new or different: *It makes **a refreshing change** to meet somebody who is so enthusiastic.* **2** making you feel less tired or hot: *a refreshing swim/shower/drink*

refreshment /rɪˈfreʃmənt/ ***noun*** **1 refreshments** [pl.] light food and drinks that are available at a cinema, theatre or other public place **2** [U] (*formal*) the fact of making sb feel stronger and less tired or hot; food or drink that helps to do this

refrigerant /rɪˈfrɪdʒərənt/ ***noun*** [C] (**CHEMISTRY**) a substance used for cooling

refrigerate /rɪˈfrɪdʒəreɪt/ ***verb*** [T] to make food, etc. cold in order to keep it fresh ▶ **refrigeration** /rɪˌfrɪdʒəˈreɪʃn/ ***noun*** [U]

refrigerator 🔑 /rɪˈfrɪdʒəreɪtə(r)/ ***noun*** [C] *formal* or *AmE*) =FRIDGE: *This dessert can be served straight from the refrigerator.*

refuge /ˈrefjuːdʒ/ ***noun*** [C,U] **~ (from sb/sth)** protection from danger, trouble, etc.; a place that is safe: *We had to **take refuge** under a tree while it rained.* ◇ *a refuge for the homeless*

refugee /ˌrefjuˈdʒiː/ ***noun*** [C] (**POLITICS**) a person who has been forced to leave their country for political or religious reasons, or because there is a war, not enough food, etc.: *a refugee camp* ➲ look at **fugitive**, **exile**

refund /ˈriːfʌnd/ ***noun*** [C] (**FINANCE**) a sum of money that is paid back to you, especially because you have paid too much or you are not happy with sth you have bought: *to claim/demand/get a refund* ▶ **refund** /rɪˈfʌnd; ˈriːfʌnd/ ***verb*** [T] ▶ **refundable** ***adj.***: *The deposit is not refundable.*

refurbish /riːˈfɜːbɪʃ/ ***verb*** [T] to clean and decorate a room, building, etc. in order to make it more attractive, more useful, etc. ▶ **refurbishment** ***noun*** [U, C]: *The hotel is now closed for refurbishment.*

refusal 🔑 /rɪˈfjuːzl/ ***noun*** [U, C] (a) **~ (of sth)**; (a) **~ (to do sth)** saying or showing that you will not do, give or accept sth: *I can't understand her refusal to see me.*

refuse¹ 🔑 /rɪˈfjuːz/ ***verb*** [I,T] to say or show that you do not want to do, give, or accept sth: *He refused to listen to what I was saying.* ◇ *My application for a grant has been refused.* **OPP** **agree**

refuse² /ˈrefjuːs/ ***noun*** [U] (*formal*) things that you throw away; rubbish: *the refuse collection* (=when dustbins are emptied)

regain /rɪˈɡeɪn/ ***verb*** [T] to get sth back that you had lost: *to regain consciousness*

regal /ˈriːɡl/ ***adj.*** very impressive; typical of or suitable for a king or queen

THESAURUS

regard

consider • see • view • perceive

These words all mean to think about sb/sth in a particular way.

regard: *He seems to regard the whole thing as a joke.*

consider: *Who do you consider responsible?*

see: *Try to see things from her point of view.*

view: *How do you view your position here?*

perceive (*formal*): *The discovery was perceived as a major breakthrough in scientific research.*

regard¹ 🔑 /rɪˈɡɑːd/ ***verb*** [T] **1 ~ sb/sth as sth**; **~ sb/sth (with sth)** to think of sb/sth (in the way mentioned): *Do you regard this issue as important?* ◇ *Her work is highly regarded* (=people have a high opinion of it). ◇ *In some villages newcomers are regarded with suspicion.* **2** (*formal*) to look at sb/sth for a while

IDM **as regards sb/sth** (*formal*) in connection with sb/sth: *What are your views as regards this proposal?*

regard² 🔑 /rɪˈɡɑːd/ ***noun*** **1** [U] **~ to/for sb/sth** attention to or care for sb/sth: *He shows little regard for other people's feelings.* **2** [U, sing.] (a) **~ (for sb/sth)** a feeling of admiration for sb/sth: respect: *She obviously **has** great **regard** for your ability.* **3 regards** [pl.] (used especially to end a letter politely) kind thoughts; best wishes: *Please **give my regards to** your parents.*

IDM **in/with regard to sb/sth**; **in this/that/one regard** (*formal*) about sb/sth; connected with sb/sth: *With regard to the details – these will be finalized later.*

regarding 🔑 /rɪˈɡɑːdɪŋ/ ***prep.*** (*formal*) about or in connection with: *Please write if you require further information regarding this matter.*

regardless /rɪˈɡɑːdləs/ ***adv.***, ***prep.*** **~ (of sb/sth)** paying no attention to sb/sth; treating problems and difficulties as unimportant: *I suggested she should stop but she **carried on regardless**.* ◇ *Everybody will receive the same amount, regardless of how long they've worked here.*

regatta /rɪˈɡætə/ ***noun*** [C] an event at which there are boat races

regenerate /rɪˈdʒenəreɪt/ ***verb*** **1** [T] (**BUSINESS**) to make an area, institution, etc. develop and grow strong again: *The money will be used to regenerate the commercial heart of the town.* **2** [I,T] (**BIOLOGY**) to grow again; to make sth grow again: *Once destroyed, brain cells do not regenerate.* ◇ *If the woodland is left alone, it will regenerate itself in a few years.* ▶ **regeneration** /rɪˌdʒenəˈreɪʃn/ ***noun*** [U]: *economic regeneration* ◇ *the regeneration of cells in the body* ▶ **regenerative** /rɪˈdʒenərətɪv/ ***adj.***: *the regenerative powers of nature*

reggae /ˈreɡeɪ/ ***noun*** [U] (**MUSIC**) a type of West Indian music with a strong rhythm

regicide /ˈredʒɪsaɪd/ ***noun*** [U] (*formal*) the crime of killing a king or queen

regime **AW** /reɪˈʒiːm/ ***noun*** [C] (**POLITICS**) a method or system of government, especially one that has not been elected in a fair way: *a military/fascist regime*

regiment /ˈredʒɪmənt/ [C, with sing. or pl. verb] a group of soldiers in the army who are commanded by a particular officer (**a colonel**) ▶ **regimental** /ˌredʒɪˈmentl/ ***adj.***

regimented /ˈredʒɪmentɪd/ ***adj.*** (*formal*) (too) strictly controlled

region ⊶ AW /'ri:dʒən/ ***noun*** [C] **1** (GEOGRAPHY) a part of the country or the world; a large area of land: *desert/tropical/polar regions* ◇ *This region of France is very mountainous.* **2** an area of your body
IDM **in the region of sth** about or approximately: *There were somewhere in the region of 30000 people at the rally.*

regional ⊶ AW /'ri:dʒənl/ ***adj.*** (GEOGRAPHY) connected with a particular region: *regional accents* ➲ look at **local**, **international**, **national**

register[1] ⊶ AW /'redʒɪstə(r)/ ***verb*** **1** [I,T] to put a name on an official list: *You should register with a doctor nearby.* ◇ *All births, deaths and marriages must be registered.* **2** [I,T] to show sth or to be shown on a measuring instrument: *The thermometer registered 32°C.* ◇ *The earthquake registered 6.4 on the Richter scale.* **3** [T] to show feelings, opinions, etc.: *Her face registered intense dislike.* **4** [I,T] (often used in negative sentences) to notice sth and remember it; to be noticed and remembered: *He told me his name but it didn't register.* **5** [T] to send a letter or package by REGISTERED POST

register[2] ⊶ AW /'redʒɪstə(r)/ ***noun*** **1** [C] an official list of names, etc. or a book that contains this kind of list: *The teacher calls the register first thing in the morning.* ◇ *the electoral register* (= of people who are able to vote in an election) **2** [C,U] (LANGUAGE) the type of language (formal or informal) that is used in a piece of writing

ˌregistered 'post ***noun*** [U] (*BrE*) a way of sending things by post that you pay extra for. If your letter or package is lost the post office will make a payment to you.

ˌregistered 'trademark ***noun*** [C] (*symbol* ®) the sign or name of a product, etc. that is officially recorded and protected so that nobody else can use it

'register office = REGISTRY OFFICE

registrar /ˌredʒɪ'strɑ:(r); 'redʒɪstrɑ:(r)/ ***noun*** [C] **1** a person whose job is to keep official lists, especially of births, marriages and deaths **2** (EDUCATION) a person who is responsible for keeping information about the students at a college or university

registration AW /ˌredʒɪ'streɪʃn/ ***noun*** [U] putting sb/sth's name on an official list: *Registration for evening classes will take place on 8 September.*

ˌregi'stration number ***noun*** [C] the numbers and letters on the front and back of a vehicle that are used to identify it

registry /'redʒɪstri/ ***noun*** [C] (*pl.* **registries**) a place where official lists are kept

'registry office (*also* **register office**) ***noun*** [C] an office where a marriage can take place and where births, marriages and deaths are officially written down

regress /rɪ'gres/ ***verb*** [I] ~ **(to sth)** (*formal*) (PSYCHOLOGY) to return to an earlier or less advanced form or way of behaving ▶ **regression** /rɪ'greʃn/ ***noun*** [U,C]: *He began to show signs of regression to his childhood.*

regressive /rɪ'gresɪv/ ***adj.*** becoming or making sth less advanced: *The policy has been condemned as a regressive step.*

regret[1] ⊶ /rɪ'gret/ ***verb*** [T] (**regretting**; **regretted**) **1** to feel sorry that you did sth or that you did not do sth: *I hope you won't regret your decision later.* ◇ *Do you regret not taking the job?* **2** (*formal*) used as a way of saying that you are sorry for sth: *I regret to inform you that your application has been unsuccessful.*

regret[2] ⊶ /rɪ'gret/ ***noun*** [C,U] a feeling of sadness about sth that cannot now be changed: *Do you* ***have any regrets*** *that you didn't go to university?* ▶ **regretful** /-fl/ ***adj.***: *a regretful look/smile* ▶ **regretfully** /-fəli/ ***adv.***

regrettable /rɪ'gretəbl/ ***adj.*** that you should feel sorry or sad about: *It is regrettable that the police were not informed sooner.* ▶ **regrettably** /-əbli/ ***adv.***

regular[1] ⊶ /'regjələ(r)/ ***adj.*** **1** having the same amount of space or time between each thing or part: *a regular heartbeat* ◇ *Nurses checked her blood pressure* ***at regular intervals.*** ◇ *The fire alarms are tested* ***on a regular basis.*** ◇ *We have regular meetings every Thursday.* OPP **irregular** **2** done or happening often: *The doctor advised me to take regular exercise.* ◇ *Accidents are* ***a regular occurrence*** *on this road.* **3** going somewhere or doing sth often: *a regular customer* ◇ *We're regular visitors to Britain.* **4** normal or usual: *Who is your regular dentist?* **5** not having any individual part that is different from the rest: *regular teeth/features* ◇ *a regular pattern* OPP **irregular** **6** fixed or permanent: *a regular income/job* ◇ *a regular soldier/army* **7** (*especially AmE*) standard, average or normal: *Regular or large fries?* **8** (LANGUAGE) (used about a noun, verb, etc.) having the usual or expected plural, verb form, etc.: *'Walk' is a regular verb.* OPP **irregular** ▶ **regularity** /ˌregju'lærəti/ ***noun*** [U, C]: *Aircraft passed overhead with monotonous regularity.*

regular[2] /'regjələ(r)/ ***noun*** [C] **1** (*informal*) a person who goes to a particular shop, bar, restaurant, etc. very often **2** a person who usually does a particular activity or sport **3** a permanent member of the army, navy, etc.

regularly ⊶ /'regjələli/ ***adv.*** **1** at regular intervals or times: *We meet regularly to discuss the progress of the project.* **2** in an even or balanced way: *The plants were spaced regularly, about 50 cm apart.*

regulate AW /'regjuleɪt/ ***verb*** [T] **1** to control sth by using laws or rules **2** to control a machine, piece of equipment, etc.: *You can regulate the temperature in the car with this dial.*

regulation ⊶ AW /ˌregju'leɪʃn/ ***noun*** **1** [C, usually pl.] an official rule that controls how sth is done: *to observe/obey the safety regulations* ◇ *The plans must comply with EU regulations.* **2** [U] the control of sth by using rules: *state regulation of imports and exports*

regulator AW /'regjuleɪtə(r)/ ***noun*** [C] **1** (BUSINESS) a person or an organization that officially controls an area of business or industry and makes sure that it is operating fairly **2** (PHYSICS) a device that automatically controls sth such as speed, temperature or pressure

regulatory AW /'regjələtəri/ ***adj.*** having the power to control an area of business or industry and make sure that it is operating fairly: ***regulatory authorities/bodies***

regurgitate /rɪ'gɜ:dʒɪteɪt/ ***verb*** [T] **1** (*formal*) (BIOLOGY) to bring food that has been swallowed back up into the mouth again: *The bird regurgitates half-digested fish to feed its young.* **2** to repeat sth you have heard or read without really thinking about it or understanding it: *He's just regurgitating what his father says.*

rehabilitate /ˌriːəˈbɪlɪteɪt/ ***verb*** [T] to help sb to live a normal life again after an illness, being in prison, etc. ▶ **rehabilitation** /ˌriːəˌbɪlɪˈteɪʃn/ ***noun*** [U]: *a rehabilitation centre for drug addicts*

rehearsal /rɪˈhɜːsl/ ***noun*** [C,U] (ARTS AND MEDIA, MUSIC) the time when you practise a play, dance, piece of music, etc. before you perform it to other people: *a dress rehearsal* (=when all the actors wear their stage clothes) ▶ **rehearse** /rɪˈhɜːs/ ***verb*** [I,T]

rehouse /ˌriːˈhaʊz/ ***verb*** [T] to provide sb with a different home to live in: *Thousands of earthquake victims are still waiting to be rehoused.*

reign /reɪn/ ***verb*** [I] **1** ~ **(over sb/sth)** (POLITICS) (used about a king or queen) to rule a country: (*figurative*) *the reigning world champion* **2** ~ **(over sb/sth)** to be in charge of a business or an organization **3** to be present as the most important quality of a particular situation: *Chaos reigned after the first snow of the winter.* ▶ **reign** ***noun*** [C]

reimburse /ˌriːɪmˈbɜːs/ ***verb*** [T] (*formal*) (FINANCE) to pay money back to sb: *The company will reimburse you in full for your travelling expenses.*

rein /reɪn/ ***noun*** [C, usually pl.] a long thin piece of leather that is held by the rider and used to control a horse's movements

reincarnation /ˌriːɪnkɑːˈneɪʃn/ ***noun*** (RELIGION) **1** [U] the belief that people who have died can live again in a different body: *Do you believe in reincarnation?* **2** [C] a person or animal whose body is believed to contain the soul of a dead person: *He believes he is the reincarnation of an Egyptian princess.* ➲ look at **incarnation**

reindeer /ˈreɪndɪə(r)/ ***noun*** [C] (*pl.* **reindeer**) a type of large brownish wild animal that eats grass and lives in Arctic regions

reinforce AW /ˌriːɪnˈfɔːs/ ***verb*** [T] to make sth stronger: *Concrete can be reinforced with steel bars.*

reinforcement AW /ˌriːɪnˈfɔːsmənt/ ***noun*** **1** [U] making sth stronger: *The sea wall is weak in places and needs reinforcement.* **2 reinforcements** [pl.] extra people who are sent to make an army, navy, etc. stronger

reinstate /ˌriːɪnˈsteɪt/ ***verb*** [T] **1** ~ **sb (in/as sth)** to give back a job or position that was taken from sb: *He was cleared of the charge of theft and reinstated as Head of Security.* **2** to return sth to its former position or role ▶ **reinstatement** ***noun*** [U]

reinvest AW /ˌriːɪnˈvest/ ***verb*** [T,I] (FINANCE) to put profits that have been made on an investment back into the same investment or into a new one

reissue /ˌriːˈɪʃuː/ ***verb*** [T] ~ **sth (as sth)** to publish or produce again a book, record, etc. that has not been available for some time: *old jazz recordings reissued on CD*

reject[1] ⊶ AW /rɪˈdʒekt/ ***verb*** [T] to refuse to accept sb/sth: *The plan was rejected as being impractical.* ▶ **rejection** AW ***noun*** [C,U]: *Gargi got a rejection from Leeds University.* ◇ *There has been total rejection of the new policy.*

reject[2] AW /ˈriːdʒekt/ ***noun*** [C] a person or thing that is not accepted because they or it are not good enough: *Rejects are sold at half price.*

rejoice /rɪˈdʒɔɪs/ ***verb*** [I] (*formal*) ~ **(at/over sth)** to feel or show great happiness ▶ **rejoicing** ***noun*** [U]: *There were scenes of rejoicing when the war ended.*

rejoin /ˌriːˈdʒɔɪn/ ***verb*** [T,I] to join sb/sth again after leaving them or it

rejuvenate /rɪˈdʒuːvəneɪt/ ***verb*** [T] (often passive) to make sb/sth feel or look younger ▶ **rejuvenation** /rɪˌdʒuːvəˈneɪʃn/ ***noun*** [U]

relapse /rɪˈlæps/ ***verb*** [I] to become worse again after an improvement: *He relapsed into his old bad habits* ▶ **relapse** /ˈriːlæps/ ***noun*** [C]: *The patient had a relapse and then died.*

relate ⊶ /rɪˈleɪt/ ***verb*** [T] **1** ~ **A to/with B** to show or make a connection between two or more things: *The report relates heart disease to high levels of stress.* **2** (*formal*) ~ **sth (to sb)** to tell a story to sb: *He related his side of the story to a journalist.*

PHR V **relate to sb/sth 1** to be concerned or involved with sth **2** to be able to understand how sb feels: *Some teenagers find it hard to relate to their parents.*

related ⊶ /rɪˈleɪtɪd/ ***adj.*** ~ **(to sb/sth)** **1** connected with sb/sth: *The rise in the cost of living is directly related to the price of oil.* **2** of the same family: *We are related by marriage.*

relation ⊶ /rɪˈleɪʃn/ ***noun*** **1 relations** [pl.] **relations (with sb); relations (between A and B)** the way that people, groups, countries, etc. feel about or behave towards each other: *The police officer stressed that good relations with the community were essential.* **2** [U] ~ **(between sth and sth)**; ~ **(to sth)** the connection between two or more things: *There seems to be little relation between the cost of the houses and their size.* ◇ *Their salaries* ***bear no relation*** *to the number of hours they work.* **3** [C] a member of your family: *a close/distant relation* SYN **relative**

IDM **in/with relation to sb/sth 1** concerning sb/sth: *Many questions were asked, particularly in relation to the cost of the new buildings.* **2** compared with: *Prices are low in relation to those in other parts of Europe.*

relationship ⊶ /rɪˈleɪʃnʃɪp/ ***noun*** [C] **1** a ~ **(with sb/sth)**; a ~ **(between A and B)** the way that people, groups, countries, etc. feel about or behave towards each other: *The relationship between the parents and the school has improved greatly.* **2** a ~ **(with sb)**; a ~ **(between A and B)** a friendly or loving connection between people: *to* ***have a relationship*** *with sb* ◇ *He'd never been* ***in a*** *serious* ***relationship*** *before he got married.* ◇ *The film describes the relationship between a young man and an older woman.* ◇ *Do you have a close relationship with your brother?* **3** a ~ **(to sth)**; a ~ **(between A and B)** the way in which two or more things are connected: *Is there a relationship between violence on TV and the increase in crime?* **4** a ~ **(to sb)**; a ~ **(between A and B)** a family connection: *'What is your relationship to Bruce?' 'He's married to my cousin.'*

relative[1] ⊶ /ˈrelətɪv/ ***adj.*** **1** ~ **(to sth)** when compared to sb/sth else: *the position of the earth relative to the sun* ◇ *They live in relative luxury.* **2** (LANGUAGE) referring to an earlier noun, sentence or part of a sentence: *In the phrase 'the lady who lives next door', 'who' is a* ***relative pronoun*** *and 'who lives next door' is a* ***relative clause****.*

relative[2] ⊶ /ˈrelətɪv/ ***noun*** [C] a member of your family: *a close/distant relative* SYN **relation**

relatively ⊶ /ˈrelətɪvli/ ***adv.*** to quite a large degree, especially when compared to others: *Spanish is a relatively easy language to learn.*

relativity /ˌreləˈtɪvəti/ ***noun*** [U] (PHYSICS) Einstein's belief that all movement is affected by space, light, time and GRAVITY (=the force that makes things fall to the ground)

relax 🗝 AW /rɪˈlæks/ *verb* **1** [I] to rest while you are doing sth enjoyable, especially after work or effort: *This holiday will give you a chance to relax.* ◇ *They spent the evening relaxing in front of the television.* **2** [I] to become calmer and less worried: *Relax – everything's going to be OK!* **3** [I,T] to become or make sb/sth become less hard or tight: *A hot bath will relax you after a hard day's work.* ◇ *Don't relax your grip on the rope!* **4** [T] to make rules or laws less strict

relaxation AW /ˌriːlækˈseɪʃn/ *noun* **1** [C,U] something that you do in order to rest, especially after work or effort: *Everyone needs time for rest and relaxation.* **2** [U] making sth less strict, tight or strong

relaxed 🗝 /rɪˈlækst/ *adj.* not worried or TENSE: *The relaxed atmosphere made everyone feel at ease.*

relaxing 🗝 /rɪˈlæksɪŋ/ *adj.* pleasant, helping you to rest and become less worried: *a quiet relaxing holiday*

relay[1] /rɪˈleɪ; ˈriːleɪ/ *verb* [T] (*pt, pp* **relayed**) **1** to receive and then pass on a signal or message: *Instructions were relayed to us by phone.* **2** (*BrE*) to put a programme on the radio or television

relay[2] /ˈriːleɪ/ (*also* **ˈrelay race**) *noun* [C] (**SPORT**) a race in which each member of a team runs, swims, etc. one part of the race

release[1] 🗝 AW /rɪˈliːs/ *verb* [T] **1** ~ **sb/sth (from sth)** to allow sb/sth to be free: *He's been released from prison.* ◇ (*figurative*) *His firm released him for two days a week to go on a training course.* **2** to stop holding sth so that it can move, fly, fall, etc. freely: *1000 balloons were released at the ceremony.* ◇ (*figurative*) *Crying is a good way to release pent-up emotions.* **3** to move sth from a fixed position: *He released the handbrake and drove off.* **4** to allow sth to be known by the public: *The identity of the victim has not been released.* **5** to make a film, record, etc. available so the public can see or hear it: *Their new single is due to be released next week.*

release[2] 🗝 AW /rɪˈliːs/ *noun* [C,U] **1** (a) ~ **(of sth) (from sth)** the freeing of sth or the state of being freed: *The release of the hostages took place this morning.* ◇ *I had a great feeling of release when my exams were finished.* **2** (**ARTS AND MEDIA, LITERATURE**) a book, film, record, piece of news, etc. that has been made available to the public; the act of making sth available to the public: *a press release* ◇ *The band played their latest release.* ◇ *The film won't* ***be/go on release*** *until March.*

relegate /ˈrelɪɡeɪt/ *verb* [T] to put sb/sth into a lower level or position: *The team finished bottom and were relegated to the second division.* ▶ **relegation** /ˌrelɪˈɡeɪʃn/ *noun* [U]

relent /rɪˈlent/ *verb* [I] **1** to finally agree to sth that you had refused: *Her parents finally relented and allowed her to go to the concert.* **2** to become less determined, strong, etc.: *The heavy rain finally relented and we went out.*

relentless /rɪˈlentləs/ *adj.* not stopping or changing: *the relentless fight against crime* ▶ **relentlessly** *adv.*: *The sun beat down relentlessly.*

relevant 🗝 AW /ˈreləvənt/ *adj.* ~ **(to sb/sth)** **1** connected with what is happening or being talked about: *Much of what was said was not directly relevant to my case.* **2** important and useful: *Many people feel that poetry is no longer relevant in today's world.* OPP **irrelevant** ▶ **relevance** *noun* [U]: *I honestly can't see the relevance of what he said.*

reliable AW /rɪˈlaɪəbl/ *adj.* that you can trust: *Japanese cars are usually very reliable.* ◇ *Is he a reliable witness?* OPP **unreliable** ➲ verb **rely** ▶ **reliability** /rɪˌlaɪəˈbɪləti/ *noun* [U] ▶ **reliably** /-əbli/ *adv.*: *I have been reliably informed that there will be no trains tomorrow.*

reliance AW /rɪˈlaɪəns/ *noun* [U] ~ **on sb/sth** **1** being able to trust sb/sth: *Don't* ***place*** *too much* ***reliance*** *on her promises.* **2** not being able to live or work without sb/sth; being DEPENDENT on sb/sth ➲ verb **rely**

reliant AW /rɪˈlaɪənt/ *adj.* ~ **on sb/sth** not being able to live or work without sb/sth: *They are totally reliant on the state for financial support.* ➲ verb **rely** ➲ look at **self-reliant**

relic /ˈrelɪk/ *noun* [C] (**HISTORY**) an object, tradition, etc. from the past that still survives today

relief 🗝 /rɪˈliːf/ *noun* **1** [U, sing.] ~ **(from sth)** the feeling that you have when sth unpleasant stops or becomes less strong: ***What a relief!*** *That awful noise has stopped.* ◇ *It was a great relief to know they were safe.* ◇ *to breathe* ***a sigh of relief*** ◇ ***To my relief,*** *he didn't argue with my suggestion at all.* **2** [U] the removal or reduction of pain, worry, etc.: *These tablets provide pain relief for up to four hours.* **3** [U] (**POLITICS**) money or food that is given to help people who are in trouble or difficulty: *disaster relief for the flood victims* **4** [U] (**FINANCE**) a reduction in the amount of tax you have to pay **5** [U, C] (**ART**) a way of decorating wood, stone, etc. by cutting designs into the surface of it so that some parts stick out more than others; a design that is made in this way: *The column was decorated* ***in high relief*** (= with designs that stick out a lot) *with scenes from Greek mythology.* ➲ look at **bas-relief**

reˈlief map *noun* [C] (**GEOGRAPHY**) a map that uses different colours to show the different heights of hills, valleys, etc.

relieve /rɪˈliːv/ *verb* [T] to make an unpleasant feeling or situation stop or get better: *This injection should* ***relieve the pain.*** ◇ *We played cards to relieve the boredom.*

PHR V **relieve sb of sth** (*formal*) to take sth away from sb: *to relieve sb of responsibility*

relieved /rɪˈliːvd/ *adj.* pleased because your fear or worry has been taken away: *I was very relieved to hear that you weren't seriously hurt.*

COLLOCATIONS AND PATTERNS

Religion

Six of the main world **religions** or **faiths** are **Buddhism, Christianity, Hinduism, Islam, Judaism** and **Sikhism.**
He's a follower of Sikhism.

Followers of these religions are called **Buddhists, Christians, Hindus, Muslims, Jews** and **Sikhs.**
She's a Hindu.
He's a Muslim.

You can **turn to/embrace** religion.
Elly turned to religion after her father's death.

You can **convert to/reject** a faith.
He converted to Judaism when he got married.

A follower of a religion **preaches, teaches** or **proclaims** its **beliefs.**
Buddha came to preach his first sermon near Varanasi.

We can talk about the **rise/spread** of religion.
He described the rise of Christianity in the first century.
Islam spread rapidly through North Africa.

religion /rɪˈlɪdʒən/ **noun 1** [U] the belief in a god or gods and the activities connected with this **2** [C] one of the systems of beliefs that is based on a belief in a god or gods: *Representatives of all the major world religions were present at the talks.*

religious /rɪˈlɪdʒəs/ **adj.** (RELIGION) **1** connected with religion: *religious faith* **2** having a strong belief in a religion: *a deeply religious person*

religiously /rɪˈlɪdʒəsli/ **adv. 1** very carefully or regularly: *She stuck to the diet religiously.* **2** (RELIGION) in a religious way

relinquish /rɪˈlɪŋkwɪʃ/ **verb** [T] (*formal*) to stop having or doing sth SYN **give up**

relish¹ /ˈrelɪʃ/ **verb** [T] to enjoy sth or to look forward to sth very much: *I don't* ***relish the prospect*** *of getting up early tomorrow.*

relish² /ˈrelɪʃ/ **noun 1** [U] (*written*) great enjoyment: *She accepted the award with obvious relish.* **2** [U, C] a thick, cold sauce made from fruit and vegetables

relive /ˌriːˈlɪv/ **verb** [T] to remember sth and imagine that it is happening again

reload /ˌriːˈləʊd/ **verb** [I,T] to put sth into a machine again: *to reload a gun* ◇ *to reload a disk into a computer*

relocate AW /ˌriːləʊˈkeɪt/ **verb** [I,T] (BUSINESS) (used especially about a company or workers) to move or to move sb/sth to a new place to work or operate: *The firm may be forced to relocate from New York to Stanford.* ▶ **relocation** /ˌriːləʊˈkeɪʃn/ **noun** [U]: *relocation costs*

reluctant AW /rɪˈlʌktənt/ **adj.** ~ **(to do sth)** not wanting to do sth because you are not sure it is the right thing to do ▶ **reluctance** AW **noun** [U]: *Tony left* ***with obvious reluctance.*** ▶ **reluctantly adv.**

rely AW /rɪˈlaɪ/ **verb** [I] (*pres. part.* **relying**; *3rd person sing. pres.* **relies**; *pt, pp* **relied**) ~ **on/upon sb/sth (to do sth) 1** to need sb/sth and not be able to live or work properly without them or it: *The old lady had to rely on other people to do her shopping for her.* **2** to trust sb/sth to work or behave well: *Can I rely on you to keep a secret?* ➲ note at **trust²** ➲ noun **reliance** ➲ Look at **reliable** and **reliant**.

WORD FAMILY
rely *verb*
reliable *adj.* (≠ **unreliable**)
reliability *noun* (≠ **unreliability**)
reliance *noun*

remain /rɪˈmeɪn/ **verb 1** ***linking verb*** to stay or continue in the same place or condition: *to remain silent/standing/seated* **2** [I] to be left after other people or things have gone: *Josef went to live in America but his family remained behind in Europe.* ◇ *They spent the remaining two days of their holiday relaxing on the beach.* **3** [I] to still need to be done, said or dealt with: ***It remains to be seen*** (=we do not know yet) *whether we've made the right decision.* ◇ *Although he seems very pleasant,* ***the fact remains*** *that I don't trust him.*

remainder /rɪˈmeɪndə(r)/ **noun** [sing., with sing. or pl. verb] (usually **the remainder**) the people, things, etc. that are left after the others have gone away or been dealt with; the rest

remains /rɪˈmeɪnz/ **noun** [pl.] **1** what is left behind after other parts have been used or taken away: *The builders found the remains of a Roman mosaic floor.* **2** (*formal*) a dead body (sometimes one that has been found somewhere a long time after death): *Human remains were discovered in the wood.*

remand /rɪˈmɑːnd/ **noun** [U] (*BrE*) (LAW) the time before a prisoner's trial takes place: *a remand prisoner* ▶ **remand verb** [T]: *The man was* ***remanded in custody*** (=sent to prison until the trial).

IDM **on remand** (used about a prisoner) waiting for the trial to take place

remark /rɪˈmɑːk/ **verb** [I,T] ~ **(on/upon sb/sth)** to say or write sth; to comment: *A lot of people have remarked on the similarity between them.* ➲ note at **comment²** ▶ **remark noun** [C] ➲ note at **statement**

remarkable /rɪˈmɑːkəbl/ **adj.** unusual and surprising in a way that people notice: *That is a remarkable achievement for someone so young.* ▶ **remarkably** /-əbli/ **adv.**

remedial /rɪˈmiːdiəl/ **adj. 1** aimed at improving or correcting a situation **2** (EDUCATION) helping people who are slow at learning sth: *remedial English classes*

remedy¹ /ˈremədi/ **noun** [C] (*pl.* **remedies**) **a ~ (for sth) 1** (HEALTH) something that makes you better when you are ill or in pain: *Hot lemon with honey is a good remedy for colds.* **2** a way of solving a problem: *There is no easy remedy for unemployment.* **3 ~ (against sth)** (LAW) a way of dealing with a problem, using the processes of the law SYN **redress**: *Holding copyright provides the only legal remedy against unauthorized copying.*

remedy² /ˈremədi/ **verb** [T] (*pres. part.* **remedying**; *3rd person sing. pres.* **remedies**; *pt, pp* **remedied**) to change or improve sth that is wrong or bad

remember /rɪˈmembə(r)/ **verb** [I,T] **1 ~ (sb/sth)**; **~ (doing sth)**; **~ that...** to have sb/sth in your mind or to bring sb/sth back into your mind: *We arranged to go out tonight – remember?* ◇ ***As far as I can remember,*** *I haven't seen him before.* ◇ *I'm sorry. I don't remember your name.* ◇ *Do you remember the night we first met?* ◇ *Remember that we're having visitors tonight.* ◇ *Can you remember when we bought the stereo?* **2 ~ (sth/to do sth)** to not forget to do what you have to do: *I remembered to buy the coffee.* ◇ *Remember to turn the lights off before you leave.* **3** [T] to give money, etc. to sb/sth: *to remember sb in your will* **4** (*formal*) to think about and show respect for sb who is dead

IDM **remember me to sb** used when you want to send good wishes to a person you have not seen for a long time: *Please remember me to your wife.*

remembrance /rɪˈmembrəns/ **noun** [U] (*formal*) thinking about and showing respect for sb who is dead: *a service* ***in remembrance of*** *those killed in the war*

remind /rɪˈmaɪnd/ **verb** [T] **1 ~ sb (about/of sth)**; **~ sb (to do sth/that...)** to help sb to remember sth, especially sth important that they have to do: *Can you remind me of your address?* ◇ *He reminded the children to wash their hands.* ◇ *Remind me what we're supposed to be doing tomorrow.* **2 ~ sb of sb/sth** to cause sb to remember sb/sth: *That smell reminds me of school.* ◇ *You remind me of your father.*

reminder /rɪˈmaɪndə(r)/ **noun** [C] something that makes you remember sth: *We received a reminder that we hadn't paid the electricity bill.*

reminisce /ˌremɪˈnɪs/ **verb** [I] **~ (about sb/sth)** to talk about pleasant things that happened in the past

reminiscent /ˌremɪˈnɪsnt/ ***adj.*** (not before a noun) that makes you remember sb/sth; similar to: *His suit was reminiscent of an old army uniform.*

remit[1] /ˈriːmɪt; rɪˈmɪt/ ***noun*** [usually sing.] ~ **(of sb/sth)**; ~ **(to do sth)** (*BrE*) the area of activity over which a particular person or group has authority, control or influence: *Such decisions are* ***outside the remit*** *of this committee.*

remit[2] /rɪˈmɪt/ ***verb*** [T] (**remitting**; **remitted**) (*formal*) **1** ~ **sth (to sb)** (FINANCE) to send money, etc. to a person or place: *to remit funds* ◇ *Payment will be remitted to you in full.* **2** (LAW) to cancel or free sb from a debt, duty, punishment, etc. **SYN** **cancel**: *to remit a fine* ◇ *to remit a prison sentence*
PHR V **remit sth to sb** (LAW) to send a matter to an authority so that a decision can be made: *The case was remitted to the Court of Appeal.*

remnant /ˈremnənt/ ***noun*** [C] a piece of sth that is left after the rest has gone: *These few trees are the remnants of a huge forest.*

remorse /rɪˈmɔːs/ ***noun*** [U] ~ **(for sth/doing sth)** a feeling of sadness because you have done sth wrong: *She was filled with remorse for what she had done.* ▶ **remorseful** /-fl/ ***adj.***

remorseless /rɪˈmɔːsləs/ ***adj.*** **1** showing no pity **2** not stopping or becoming less strong: *a remorseless attack on sb* ▶ **remorselessly** ***adv.***

remote 🔑 /rɪˈməʊt/ ***adj.*** **1** ~ **(from sth)** far away from where other people live: *a remote island in the Pacific* **2** far away in time: *the remote past/future* **3** not very great: *I haven't* ***the remotest*** *idea who could have done such a thing.* ◇ *a remote possibility* **4** not very friendly or interested in other people: *He seemed rather remote.* ▶ **remoteness** ***noun*** [U]

reˌmote conˈtrol ***noun*** **1** [U] a system for controlling sth from a distance: *The doors can be opened by remote control.* **2** (*also* **remote**) [C] a piece of equipment for controlling sth from a distance

remotely /rɪˈməʊtli/ ***adv.*** (used in negative sentences) to a very small degree; at all: *I'm not remotely interested in your problems.*

removable AW /rɪˈmuːvəbl/ ***adj.*** (usually *before* a noun) that can be taken off or out of sth **SYN** **detachable**

removal 🔑 AW /rɪˈmuːvl/ ***noun*** **1** [U] the action of taking sb/sth away: *the removal of restrictions/regulations/rights* **2** [C,U] the activity of moving from one house to live in another: *a removal van*

remove[1] 🔑 AW /rɪˈmuːv/ ***verb*** [T] (*formal*) **1** ~ **sb/sth (from sth)** to take sb/sth off or away: *Remove the saucepan from the heat.* ◇ *This washing powder will remove most stains.* ◇ *to remove doubts/fears/problems* ◇ *I would like you to remove my name from your mailing list.* ◇ *He had an operation to remove the tumour.* **2** ~ **sb (from sth)** to make sb leave their job or position

remove[2] AW /rɪˈmuːv/ ***noun*** [C,U] (*formal*) an amount by which two things are separated: *Jane seemed to be living* ***at one remove*** *from reality.*

removed /rɪˈmuːvd/ ***adj.*** (not before a noun) far or different from sth: *Hospitals today are* ***far removed from*** *what they were fifty years ago.*

remover /rɪˈmuːvə(r)/ ***noun*** [C,U] a substance that cleans off paint, dirty marks, etc.: *make-up remover*

the Renaissance /rɪˈneɪsns/ ***noun*** [sing.] (ARTS AND MEDIA, HISTORY) the period in Europe during the 14th, 15th and 16th centuries when people became interested in the ideas and culture of ancient Greece and Rome and used them in their own art, literature, etc.: *Renaissance art/drama/music*

renal /ˈriːnl/ ***adj.*** (ANATOMY) involving or connected to your KIDNEYS (=the two organs in your body which separate waste liquid from your blood): *renal failure*

rename /ˌriːˈneɪm/ ***verb*** [T] to give sb/sth a new name: *to rename a street* ◇ *Leningrad was renamed St Petersburg.*

render /ˈrendə(r)/ ***verb*** [T] (*written*) **1** to cause sb/sth to be in a certain condition: *She was rendered speechless by the attack.* **2** to give help, etc. to sb: *to render sb a service/render a service to sb*

rendezvous /ˈrɒndɪvuː; -deɪ-/ ***noun*** [C] (*pl.* **rendezvous** /-vuːz/) **1** a ~ **(with sb)** a meeting that you have arranged with sb: *He had a secret rendezvous with Daniela.* **2** a place where people often meet: *The cafe is a popular rendezvous for students.*

rendition /renˈdɪʃn/ ***noun*** [C] the performance of sth, especially a song or piece of music; the particular way in which it is performed

renegade /ˈrenɪɡeɪd/ ***noun*** [C] (*formal*) **1** (often used as an adjective) a person who leaves one political, religious, etc. group to join another that has very different views **2** a person who decides to live outside a group or society because they have different opinions: *teenage renegades*

renew /rɪˈnjuː/ ***verb*** [T] **1** to start sth again: *renewed outbreaks of violence* ◇ *to renew a friendship* **2** to give sb new strength or energy: *After a break he set to work with renewed enthusiasm.* **3** to make sth valid for a further period of time: *to renew a contract/passport/library book* ▶ **renewal** /-ˈnjuːəl/ ***noun*** [C,U]: *When is your passport due for renewal?*

renewable /rɪˈnjuːəbl/ ***adj.*** **1** (ENVIRONMENT) (used about sources of energy) that will always exist: *renewable resources such as wind and solar power* ◇ *10 percent of the nation's electricity must come from renewable energy sources by 2020.*
OPP **non-renewable** **2** that can be continued or replaced with a new one for another period of time: *The work permit is not renewable.*

renounce /rɪˈnaʊns/ ***verb*** [T] (*formal*) to say formally that you no longer want to have sth or to be connected with sth ➲ noun **renunciation**

renovate /ˈrenəveɪt/ ***verb*** [T] to repair an old building and put it back into good condition ▶ **renovation** /ˌrenəˈveɪʃn/ ***noun*** [C,U]: *The house is in need of complete renovation.*

renown /rɪˈnaʊn/ ***noun*** [U] (*formal*) fame and respect that you get for doing sth especially well ▶ **renowned** ***adj.*** ~ **(for/as sth)**: *The region is renowned for its food.*

rent[1] 🔑 /rent/ ***noun*** [U, C] (FINANCE) money that you pay regularly for the use of land, a house or a building: *a high/low rent* ◇ *She was allowed to live there* ***rent-free*** *until she found a job.* ◇ *Is this house* ***for rent*** (=available to rent)?

rent[2] 🔑 /rent/ ***verb*** [T] **1** ~ **sth (from sb)** to pay money for the use of land, a building, a machine, etc.: *Do you own or rent your television?* ◇ *to rent a flat* **2** ~ **sth (out) (to sb)** to allow sb to use land, a building, a machine, etc. for money: *We could rent out the small bedroom to a student.* ➲ look at **hire[1]**

rental /ˈrentl/ ***noun*** [C,U] **1** the amount of money that you pay to use sth for a particular period of time: *Telephone charges include line rental.* **2** [U] the act of renting sth or an arrangement to rent sth: *the* *world's largest car rental company ◇ video rental* ➲ look at **hire 3** [C] (*especially AmE*) a house, car, or piece of equipment that you can rent: *'Is this your own car?' 'No, it's a rental.'*

renunciation /rɪˌnʌnsi'eɪʃn/ ***noun*** [U] (*formal*) saying that you no longer want sth or believe in sth ➲ verb **renounce**

reorganize (also **-ise**) /ri'ɔːgənaɪz/ ***verb*** [I,T] to organize sth again or in a new way ▶ **reorganization** (also **-isation**) /riˌɔːgənaɪ'zeɪʃn/ ***noun*** [C,U]

Rep. ***abbr.*** (POLITICS) (in the US) **1** Representative (in Congress) **2** Republican (Party)

rep /rep/ (*informal*) (*also* **representative** /ˌreprɪ'zentətɪv/) ***noun*** [C] (BUSINESS) a person whose job is to travel round a particular area and visit companies, etc., to sell the products of the firm for which they work: *a sales rep*

repair¹ 🔑 /rɪ'peə(r)/ ***verb*** [T] to put sth old or damaged back into good condition: *These cars can be expensive to repair. ◇ How much will it cost to have the TV repaired?* SYN **fix, mend** ➲ look at **irreparable**

repair² 🔑 /rɪ'peə(r)/ ***noun*** [C,U] something that you do to fix sth that is damaged: *The school is closed for repairs to the roof. ◇ The road is **in need of repair**. ◇ The bridge is **under repair**. ◇ The bike was damaged **beyond repair** so I threw it away.*
IDM **in good, bad, etc. repair** in a good, bad, etc. condition

reparation /ˌrepə'reɪʃn/ ***noun*** (*formal*) **1** [pl.] (POLITICS) money that is paid by a country that has lost a war, for the damage, injuries, etc. that it has caused **2** [U] (LAW) the act of giving sth to sb or doing sth for them in order to show that you are sorry for suffering that you have caused: *Offenders should be forced to **make reparation to** the community.*

repatriate /ˌriː'pætrieɪt/ ***verb*** [T] (POLITICS) to send sb back to their own country ▶ **repatriation** /ˌriːˌpætri'eɪʃn/ ***noun*** [C,U]

repay /rɪ'peɪ/ ***verb*** [T] (*pt, pp* **repaid** /rɪ'peɪd/) **1** ~ **sth (to sb)**; ~ **(sb) sth** to pay back money that you owe to sb: *to repay a debt/loan ◇ When will you repay the money to them? ◇ When will you repay them the money?* **2** ~ **sb (for sth)** to give sth to sb in return for help, kindness, etc.: *How can I ever repay you for all you have done for me?*

repayable /rɪ'peɪəbl/ ***adj.*** (FINANCE) that you can or must pay back: *The loan is repayable over three years.*

repayment /rɪ'peɪmənt/ ***noun*** **1** [U] paying sth back: *the repayment of a loan* **2** [C] money that you must pay back to sb/sth regularly: *I make monthly repayments on my loan.*

repeal /rɪ'piːl/ ***verb*** [T] (*formal*) (LAW) to officially make a law no longer valid

repeat¹ 🔑 /rɪ'piːt/ ***verb*** **1** [I,T] ~ **(sth/yourself)** to say, write or do sth again or more than once: *Could you repeat what you just said? ◇ The essay is quite good, but you repeat yourself several times. ◇ Raise and lower your left leg ten times, then repeat with the right.* **2** [T] ~ **sth (to sb)** to say or write sth that sb else has said or written or that you have learnt: *Please don't repeat what you've heard here to anyone. ◇ Repeat each sentence after me.* ➲ noun **repetition**

> WORD FAMILY
> **repeat** *verb, noun*
> **repeatable** *adj.* (≠ **unrepeatable**)
> **repeated** *adj.*
> **repetition** *noun*
> **repetitive** *adj.*
> **repetitious** *adj.*

repeat² /rɪ'piːt/ ***noun*** [C] something that is done, shown, given, etc. again: *I think I've seen this programme before – it must be a repeat.*

repeatable /rɪ'piːtəbl/ ***adj.*** **1 of a comment, etc.** (usually in negative sentences) polite and not offensive: *His reply was not repeatable.* **2** that can be repeated OPP **unrepeatable**

repeated 🔑 /rɪ'piːtɪd/ ***adj.*** (only *before* a noun) done or happening many times: *There have been repeated accidents on this stretch of road.* ▶ **repeatedly** ***adv.***: *I've asked him repeatedly not to leave his bicycle there.*

repel /rɪ'pel/ ***verb*** [T] (**repelling; repelled**) **1** to send or push sb/sth back or away **2** to make sb feel disgusted: *The dirt and smell repelled her.* **3** (PHYSICS) if one thing **repels** another, or if two things **repel** each other, an electrical or MAGNETIC force pushes them apart: *Like poles repel each other.* OPP **attract** ➲ noun **repulsion**

repellent¹ /rɪ'pelənt/ ***noun*** [C,U] a chemical substance that is used to keep insects, etc. away

repellent² /rɪ'pelənt/ ***adj.*** causing a strong feeling of disgust: *a repellent smell*

repent /rɪ'pent/ ***verb*** [I,T] (*formal*) ~ **(sth)**; ~ **of sth** to feel and show that you are sorry about sth bad that you have done: *to repent of your sins ◇ He repented his hasty decision.* ▶ **repentance** ***noun*** [U] /-əns/ ▶ **repentant** /-ənt/ ***adj.***

repercussion /ˌriːpə'kʌʃn/ ***noun*** [C, usually pl.] an unpleasant effect or result of sth you do: *His resignation will **have** serious **repercussions**.* ➲ note at **effect¹**

repertoire /'repətwɑː(r)/ ***noun*** [C] **1** (ARTS AND MEDIA, MUSIC) all the plays or music that an actor or a musician knows and can perform: *He must have sung every song in his repertoire last night.* **2** all the things that a person is able to do

repetition /ˌrepə'tɪʃn/ ***noun*** [U, C] doing sth again; sth that you do or that happens again: *to learn by repetition ◇ Let's try to avoid a repetition of what happened last Friday.* ➲ verb **repeat**

repetitious /ˌrepə'tɪʃəs/ ***adj.*** involving sth that is often repeated: *a long and repetitious speech* ▶ **repetitiously** ***adv.*** ▶ **repetitiousness** ***noun***

repetitive /rɪ'petətɪv/ (*also* **repetitious** /ˌrepə'tɪʃəs/) ***adj.*** not interesting because the same thing is repeated many times

rephrase /ˌriː'freɪz/ ***verb*** [T] to say or write sth using different words in order to make the meaning clearer

replace 🔑 /rɪ'pleɪs/ ***verb*** [T] **2** ~ **sb/sth (as/with sb/sth)** to take the place of sb/sth; to use sb/sth in place of another person or thing: *Teachers will never be replaced by computers in the classroom.* **2** ~ **sb/sth (with sb/sth)** to exchange sb/sth for sb/sth that is better or newer: *We will replace any goods that are damaged.* **3** to put sth back in the place where it was before: *Please replace the books on the shelves when you have finished with them.*

replaceable /rɪ'pleɪsəbl/ ***adj.*** that can be replaced OPP **irreplaceable**

replacement /rɪ'pleɪsmənt/ ***noun*** **1** [U] exchanging sb/sth for sb/sth that is better or newer: *The carpets are in need of replacement.* **2** [C] a person or thing that will take the place of sb/sth

replay¹ /'riːpleɪ/ ***noun*** [C] **1** (*BrE*) (SPORT) a sports match that is played again because neither team won the first time **2** something on the television, on a film or a CASSETTE TAPE that you watch or listen to again: *Now let's see **an action replay** of that tremendous goal!*

replay² /ˌriːˈpleɪ/ ***verb*** [T] **1** (SPORT) to play a sports match, etc. again because neither team won the first time **2** to play again sth that you have recorded: *They kept replaying the goal over and over again.*

replenish /rɪˈplenɪʃ/ ***verb*** [T] **replenish sth (with sth)** (*formal*) to make sth full again by replacing what has been used: *to replenish food and water supplies*

replete /rɪˈpliːt/ ***adj.*** ~ **(with sth)** (*formal*) filled with sth; with a full supply of sth: *literature replete with drama and excitement*

replica /ˈreplɪkə/ ***noun*** [C] **a ~ (of sth)** an exact copy of sth

replicate /ˈreplɪkeɪt/ [T] (*formal*) to copy sth exactly ▸ **replication** /ˌreplɪˈkeɪʃn/ ***noun*** [U, C]

reply 🔑 /rɪˈplaɪ/ ***verb*** [I,T] (*pres. part.* **replying**; *3rd person sing. pres.* **replies**; *pt, pp* **replied**) ~ **(to sb/sth) (with sth)** to say, write or do sth as an answer to sb/sth: *I wrote to Sue but she hasn't replied.* ◇ *'Yes, I will,' she replied.* ◇ *to reply to a question* ▸ **reply *noun*** [C,U] (*pl.* **replies**): *Al nodded **in reply to** my question.*

report¹ 🔑 /rɪˈpɔːt/ ***verb*** **1** [I,T] ~ **(on sb/sth) (to sb/sth)**; ~ **sth (to sb)** to give people information about what you have seen, heard, done, etc.: *Several people reported seeing/having seen the boy.* ◇ *Several people reported that they had seen the boy.* ◇ *The company reported huge profits last year.* ◇ *Call me if you have anything new to report.* **2** [I,T] ~ **(on) sth** (in a newspaper or on the television or radio) to write or speak about sth that has happened: *The paper sent a journalist to report on the events.* **3** [T] ~ **sb (to sb) (for sth)** (LAW) to tell a person in authority about an accident, a crime, etc. or about sth wrong that sb has done: *All accidents must be reported to the police.* ◇ *The boy was reported missing early this morning.* **4** [I] ~ **(to sb/sth) for sth** to tell sb that you have arrived: *On your arrival, please report to the reception desk.* **5** [T] (*formal*) **be reported to be/as sth** used to say that you have heard sth said, but you are not sure if it is true: *The 70 year-old actor is reported to be/as being comfortable in hospital.*

PHR V **report back (on sth) (to sb)** to give information to sb about sth that they have asked you to find out about: *One person in each group will then report back to the class on what you've decided.*

report to sb (not used in the continuous tenses) to have sb as your manager in the company or organization that you work for

report² 🔑 /rɪˈpɔːt/ ***noun*** [C] **1** a ~ **(on/of sth)** a written or spoken description of what you have seen, heard, done, studied, etc.: *newspaper reports* ◇ *a report on the company's finances* ◇ *a first-hand report* (=from the person who saw what happened) **2** (EDUCATION) a written statement about the work of a student at school, college, etc.: *to get a good/bad report*

reportedly /rɪˈpɔːtɪdli/ ***adv.*** (*written*) according to what some people say: *The band have reportedly decided to split up.*

reˌported 'speech = INDIRECT SPEECH

reporter /rɪˈpɔːtə(r)/ ***noun*** [C] (ARTS AND MEDIA) a person who writes about the news in a newspaper or speaks about it on the television or radio ➲ look at **journalist**

represent 🔑 /ˌreprɪˈzent/ ***verb*** **1** [T] to act or speak in the place of sb else; to be the representative of a group or country: *You will need a lawyer to represent you in court.* ◇ *It's an honour for an athlete to represent his or her country.* **2 *linking verb*** to be equal to sth; to be sth: *These results represent a major breakthrough in our understanding of cancer.* **3** [T] to be a picture, sign, example, etc. of sb/sth: *The yellow lines on the map represent minor roads.* **4** [T] to describe sb/sth in a particular way

representation /ˌreprɪzenˈteɪʃn/ ***noun*** **1** [U, C] the way that sb/sth is shown or described; something that shows or describes sth: *The article complains about the representation of women in advertising.* **2** [U] (*formal*) having sb to speak for you ➲ look at **proportional representation**

representative¹ 🔑 /ˌreprɪˈzentətɪv/ ***adj.*** ~ **(of sb/sth)** typical of a larger group to which sb/sth belongs: *Tonight's audience is not representative of national opinion.*

representative² 🔑 /ˌreprɪˈzentətɪv/ ***noun*** [C] **1** a person who has been chosen to act or speak for sb else or for a group **2** (also *informal* **rep**) (BUSINESS) a person who works for a company and travels around selling its products: *a sales representative* ◇ *She's our representative in France.* **3 Representative** (*abbr.* **Rep.**) (POLITICS) (in the US) a member of the House of Representatives, the Lower House of Congress; a member of the House of Representatives in the lower house of a state parliament

repress /rɪˈpres/ ***verb*** [T] **1** to control an emotion or to try to prevent it from being shown or felt: *She tried to repress her anger.* **2** (POLITICS) to limit the freedom of a group of people ▸ **repression** /rɪˈpreʃn/ ***noun*** [U]: *protests against government repression*

repressed /rɪˈprest/ ***adj.*** **1** (used about a person) having emotions and desires that they do not show or express **2** (used about an emotion) that you do not show: *repressed anger/desire*

repressive /rɪˈpresɪv/ ***adj.*** (POLITICS) that limits people's freedom: *a repressive government*

reprieve /rɪˈpriːv/ ***verb*** [T] (LAW) to stop or delay the punishment of a prisoner who was going to be punished by death ▸ **reprieve *noun*** [C]: *The judge granted him a last-minute reprieve.*

reprimand /ˈreprɪmɑːnd/ ***verb*** [T] ~ **sb (for sth)** to tell sb officially that they have done sth wrong ▸ **reprimand *noun*** [C]: *a severe reprimand*

reprisal /rɪˈpraɪzl/ ***noun*** [C,U] punishment, especially by military force, for harm that one group of people does to another

reproach /rɪˈprəʊtʃ/ ***verb*** [T] ~ **sb (for/with sth)** to tell sb that they have done sth wrong; to blame sb: *You've nothing to reproach yourself for. It wasn't your fault.* ▸ **reproach *noun*** [C,U]: *His behaviour is **beyond reproach*** (=cannot be criticized). ◇ *Alison felt his reproaches were unjustified.* ▸ **reproachful** /-fl/ ***adj.***: *a reproachful look* ▸ **reproachfully** /-fəli/ ***adv.***

reproduce 🔑 /ˌriːprəˈdjuːs/ ***verb*** **1** [T] to produce a copy of sth: *It is very hard to reproduce a natural environment in the laboratory.* **2** [I] (BIOLOGY) (used about people, animals and plants) to produce young

reproduction /ˌriːprəˈdʌkʃn/ ***noun*** **1** [U] (BIOLOGY) the process of producing babies or young: *sexual reproduction* **2** [U] the production of copies of sth: *Digital recording gives excellent sound reproduction.* **3** [C] (ART) a copy of a painting, etc.

reproductive /ˌriːprəˈdʌktɪv/ ***adj.*** (BIOLOGY) connected with the production of young animals, plants, etc.: *the male reproductive organs*

reproof /rɪ'pruːf/ ***noun*** [C,U] (*formal*) something that you say to sb when you do not approve of what they have done

reptile /'reptaɪl/ ***noun*** [C] an animal that has cold blood and a skin covered in scales, and whose young come out of eggs, for example CROCODILES and snakes ➲ look at **amphibian** ➲ picture on **page 29**

republic /rɪ'pʌblɪk/ ***noun*** [C] (POLITICS) a country that has an elected government and an elected leader (**president**): *the Republic of Ireland* ➲ look at **monarchy**

republican /rɪ'pʌblɪkən/ ***noun*** [C] (POLITICS) **1** a person who supports the system of an elected government and leader **2 Republican** a member of the Republican Party ➲ look at **Democrat** ▸ **republican *adj.***

the Re'publican Party ***noun*** [sing.] (POLITICS) one of the two main political parties of the US ℹ The other party is the Democratic Party, whose members are called **Democrats**.

repudiate /rɪ'pjuːdieɪt/ ***verb*** [T] to say that you refuse to accept or believe sth: *to repudiate a suggestion/an accusation* ▸ **repudiation** /rɪˌpjuːdi'eɪʃn/ ***noun*** [U]

repugnant /rɪ'pʌɡnənt/ ***adj.*** (not usually before a noun) (*formal*) ~ **(to sb)** making you feel disgust: *We found his suggestion absolutely repugnant.* ◇ *The idea of eating meat was repugnant to her.*

repulsion /rɪ'pʌlʃn/ ***noun*** [U] **1** a strong feeling of not liking sth that you find extremely unpleasant **2** (PHYSICS) the force by which objects push each other away: *the forces of attraction and repulsion* ➲ verb **repel** ➲ picture at **magnet**

repulsive /rɪ'pʌlsɪv/ ***adj.*** that causes a strong feeling of disgust ➲ verb **repel**

reputable /'repjətəbl/ ***adj.*** that is known to be good OPP **disreputable**

reputation 🔑 /ˌrepju'teɪʃn/ ***noun*** [C] a ~ **(for/as sth)** the opinion that people in general have about what sb/sth is like: *to **have a good /bad reputation*** ◇ *Adam has a reputation for being late.* SYN **name**

repute /rɪ'pjuːt/ ***noun*** [U] (*formal*) the opinion that people have of sb/sth: *I know him only by repute.* ◇ *She is a writer of international repute.* SYN **reputation**

reputed /rɪ'pjuːtɪd/ ***adj.*** generally said to be sth, although it is not certain: *He's reputed to be the highest-paid sportsman in the world.* ▸ **reputedly *adv.***

request[1] 🔑 /rɪ'kwest/ ***noun*** [C,U] ~ **(for sth/ that...)** an act of asking for sth: *a request for help* ◇ *I'm going to **make a request** for a larger desk.* ◇ *to grant/ turn down a request* ◇ *Single rooms are available **on request**.*

request[2] 🔑 /rɪ'kwest/ ***verb*** [T] (*formal*) ~ **sth (from/of sb)** to ask for sth: *Passengers are requested not to smoke on this bus.* ◇ *to request a loan from the bank*

require 🔑 AW /rɪ'kwaɪə(r)/ ***verb*** [T] **1** to need sth: *a situation that requires tact and diplomacy* **2** (often passive) to officially demand or order sth: *Passengers are required by law to wear seat belts.* ➲ note at **demand**[2]

requirement 🔑 AW /rɪ'kwaɪəmənt/ ***noun*** [C] something that you need or that you must do or have: *university entrance requirements*

requisite /'rekwɪzɪt/ ***adj.*** (only *before* a noun) (*formal*) necessary for a particular purpose: *She lacks the requisite experience for the job.* ▸ **requisite *noun*** [C] **a ~ (for/of sth)**: *toilet requisites* ◇ *A university degree has become a requisite for entry into most professions.* ➲ look at **prerequisite**

reschedule AW /ˌriː'ʃedjuːl/ ***verb*** [T] **1** ~ **sth (for/ to sth)** to change the time at which sth has been arranged to happen, especially so that it takes place later: *The meeting has been rescheduled for next week.* **2** (FINANCE) to arrange for sb to pay back money that they have borrowed at a later date than was originally agreed: *to reschedule a loan*

rescind /rɪ'sɪnd/ ***verb*** [T] (*formal*) (LAW) to officially state that a law, contract, decision, etc. is no longer valid

rescue 🔑 /'reskjuː/ ***verb*** [T] ~ **sb/sth (from sb/ sth)** to save sb/sth from a situation that is dangerous or unpleasant: *He rescued a child from drowning.* ▸ **rescue *noun*** [C,U]: *Ten fishermen were saved in a daring sea rescue.* ◇ *Blow the whistle if you're in danger, and someone should **come to** your **rescue**.* ◇ *rescue workers/boats/helicopters* ▸ **rescuer *noun*** [C]

research 🔑 AW /rɪ'sɜːtʃ/ ***noun*** [U] ~ **(into/on sth)** a detailed and careful study of sth to find out more information about it: *to do research into sth* ◇ *scientific/medical/historical research* ◇ *We are carrying out **market research** to find out who our typical customer is.* ▸ **research *verb*** [I,T] ~ **(into/in/ on sth)**: *They're researching into ways of reducing traffic in the city centre.*

reˌsearch and de'velopment ***noun*** [U] (*abbr.* **R & D**) (BUSINESS) (in industry, etc.) work that tries to find new products and processes or to improve existing ones

researcher /rɪ'sɜːtʃə(r)/ ***noun*** [C] a person who does research

resemble /rɪ'zembl/ ***verb*** [T] to be or look like sb/ sth else: *Laura resembles her brother.* ▸ **resemblance** /rɪ'zembləns/ ***noun*** [C,U] **(a) ~ (between A and B)**; **(a) ~ (to sb/sth)**: *a family resemblance* ◇ *The boys **bear** no **resemblance** to their father.*

resent /rɪ'zent/ ***verb*** [T] to feel angry about sth because you think it is unfair: *I resent his criticism.* ◇ *Louise bitterly resented being treated differently from the men.* ▸ **resentful** /-fl/ ***adj.*** ▸ **resentment *noun*** [sing., U]: *to feel resentment towards sb/sth*

reservation 🔑 /ˌrezə'veɪʃn/ ***noun*** **1** [C] (TOURISM) a seat, table, room, etc. that you have booked: *We have reservations in the name of Petrovic.* ◇ *I'll phone the restaurant to **make a reservation**.* **2** [C,U] a feeling of doubt about sth (such as a plan or an idea): *I **have** some **reservations** about letting Julie go out alone.*

reserve[1] 🔑 /rɪ'zɜːv/ ***verb*** [T] ~ **sth (for sb/sth)** **1** to keep sth for a special reason or to use at a later time: *The car park is reserved for hotel guests only.* **2** to ask for a seat, table, room, etc. to be available at a future time; to book: *to reserve theatre tickets*

reserve[2] 🔑 /rɪ'zɜːv/ ***noun*** **1** [C, usually pl.] something that you keep for a special reason or to use at a later date: *The US has huge oil reserves.* **2** [C] (ENVIRONMENT) an area of land where the plants, animals, etc. are protected by law: *a nature reserve* ◇ *He works as a warden on a **game reserve** in Kenya.* **3** [U] the quality of being shy or keeping your feelings hidden: *It took a long time to break down her reserve and get her to relax.* **4** [C] (SPORT) a person who will play in a game if one of the usual members of the team cannot play

IDM **in reserve** that you keep and do not use unless you need to: *Keep some money in reserve for emergencies.*

reserved /rɪ'zɜːvd/ *adj.* shy and keeping your feelings hidden OPP **unreserved**

reservoir /'rezəvwɑː(r)/ *noun* [C] (GEOGRAPHY) a large lake where water is stored to be used by a particular area, city, etc.

reshuffle /ˌriː'ʃʌfl/ *verb* [I,T] to change around the jobs that a group of people do, for example in the British Government ▶ **reshuffle** /'riːʃʌfl/ *noun* [C]: *a Cabinet reshuffle*

reside AW /rɪ'zaɪd/ *verb* [I] (*formal*) ~ **(in/at…)** to have your home in or at a particular place

residence AW /'rezɪdəns/ *noun* **1** [U] the state of having your home in a particular place: *The family applied for permanent residence in the United States.* ◇ *a* ***hall of residence*** *for college students* ◇ *Some birds have taken up residence in our roof.* **2** [C] = RESIDENCY (4)

residency /'rezɪdənsi/ *noun* (*pl.* **residencies**) (*formal*) **1** [U, C] = RESIDENCE (1): *She has been granted permanent residency in Britain.* **2** [U, C] (ARTS AND MEDIA) the period of time that an artist, a writer or a musician spends working for a particular institution **3** [U, C] (*especially AmE*) (HEALTH) the period of time when a doctor working in a hospital receives special advanced training **4** (*also* **residence**) [C] (*formal*) the official house of sb important in the government, etc.

resident ⊶ AW /'rezɪdənt/ *noun* [C] **1** a person who lives in a place: *local residents* **2** (TOURISM) a person who is staying in a hotel: *The hotel bar is open only to residents.* **3** (HEALTH) a doctor working in a hospital in the US who is receiving special advanced training ▶ **resident** *adj.*

residential AW /ˌrezɪ'denʃl/ *adj.* **1** (used about a place or an area) that has houses rather than offices, large shops or factories: *They live in a quiet residential area.* **2** that provides a place for sb to live: *This home provides residential care for the elderly.*

residual /rɪ'zɪdjuəl/ *adj.* (only *before* a noun) (*formal*) left at the end of a process: *There are still a few residual problems with the computer program.*

residue /'rezɪdjuː/ *noun* [C, usually sing.] (*formal*) what is left after the main part of sth is taken or used: *The washing powder left a white residue on the clothes.*

resign /rɪ'zaɪn/ *verb* **1** [I,T] ~ **(from/as) (sth)** to leave your job or position: *He's resigned as chairman of the committee.* **2** [T] ~ **yourself to sth/doing sth** to accept sth that is unpleasant but that you cannot change: *Jamie resigned himself to the fact that she was not coming back to him.*

resignation /ˌrezɪg'neɪʃn/ *noun* **1** [C,U] ~ **(from sth)** a letter or statement that says you want to leave your job or position: *to hand in your resignation* ◇ *a letter of resignation* **2** [U] the state of accepting sth unpleasant that you cannot change

resigned /rɪ'zaɪnd/ *adj.* ~ **(to sth/doing sth)** accepting sth that is unpleasant but that you cannot change: *Ben was resigned to the fact that he would never be an athlete.*

resilient /rɪ'zɪliənt/ *adj.* strong enough to deal with illness, a shock, change, etc. ▶ **resilience** *noun* [U]

resin /'rezɪn/ *noun* [U] **1** a sticky substance that is produced by some trees and is used in making VARNISH (= a liquid that you paint onto hard surfaces to protect them), medicine, etc. **2** an artificial substance that is used in making plastics

resist ⊶ /rɪ'zɪst/ *verb* **1** [I,T] to try to stop sth happening or to stop sb from doing sth; to fight back against sth/sb: *The government are resisting pressure to change the law.* ◇ *to resist arrest* **2** [T] to stop yourself from having or doing sth that you want to have or do: *I couldn't resist telling Nadia what we'd bought for her.*

resistance ⊶ /rɪ'zɪstəns/ *noun* **1** [U] ~ **(to sb/sth)** trying to stop sth from happening or to stop sb from doing sth; fighting back against sb/sth: *The government troops overcame the resistance of the rebel army.* **2** [U] ~ **(to sth)** (HEALTH) the power in a person's body not to be affected by disease **3** [C,U] (*symbol* **R**) (PHYSICS) the fact of a substance not CONDUCTING heat or electricity (= not allowing heat or electricity to flow through it); a measurement of this

resistant /rɪ'zɪstənt/ *adj.* ~ **(to sth) 1** not wanting sth and trying to prevent sth happening: *resistant to change* **2** not harmed or affected by sth: *This watch is water-resistant.*

resistor

Resistance is measured in ohms (Ω). A resistor of 100 Ω is a much greater obstacle to the flow of current than a resistor of 10 Ω.

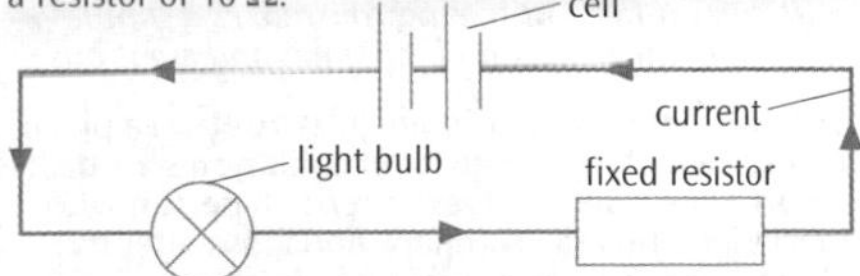

Variable resistors have values that can be altered so it is possible to adjust the current flowing in the circuit

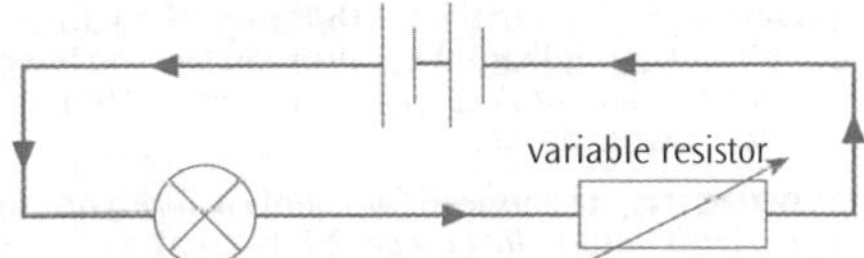

resistor /rɪ'zɪstə(r)/ *noun* [C] (PHYSICS) a device that does not allow electric current to flow through it freely in a CIRCUIT

resolute /'rezəluːt/ *adj.* having or showing great determination SYN **determined**: *a resolute refusal to change* ▶ **resolutely** *adv.*

resolution AW /ˌrezə'luːʃn/ *noun* **1** [U] the quality of being firm and determined **2** [U] solving or settling a problem, DISPUTE, etc. **3** [C] (POLITICS) a formal decision that is taken after a vote by a group of people: *The UN resolution condemned the invasion.* **4** [C] a firm decision to do or not to do sth **5** [U, sing.] (COMPUTING) the power of a computer screen, printer, etc. to give a clear image, depending on the size of the dots that make up the image: *high-resolution graphics*

resolve[1] ⊶ AW /rɪ'zɒlv/ *verb* (*formal*) **1** [T] to find an answer to a problem: *Most of the difficulties have been resolved.* **2** [I,T] to decide sth and be determined not to change your mind: *He resolved never to repeat the experience.*

resolve[2] AW /rɪ'zɒlv/ *noun* [U] ~ **(to do sth)** (*formal*) strong determination to achieve sth: *The difficulties in her way merely strengthened her resolve.*

resonance /ˈrezənəns/ ***noun*** **1** [U] (*formal*) (used about sound) the quality of being RESONANT: *the strange and thrilling resonance of her voice* **2** [C,U] (**PHYSICS**) the sound produced in an object by sound of a similar FREQUENCY from another object **3** [U, C] (*formal*) (**ARTS AND MEDIA, LITERATURE, MUSIC**) (in a piece of writing, music, etc.) the power to bring images, feelings, etc. into the mind of the person reading or listening; the images, etc. produced in this way

resonant /ˈrezənənt/ ***adj.*** **1** (used about a sound) deep, clear and continuing for a long time: *a deep resonant voice* **2** causing sounds to continue for a long time: *resonant frequencies* **3** having the power to bring images, feelings, memories, etc. into your mind: *a poem filled with resonant imagery*

resonate /ˈrezəneɪt/ ***verb*** [I] (*formal*) **1** (used about a voice, an instrument, etc.) to make a deep, clear sound that continues for a long time: *Her voice resonated through the theatre.* **2** ~ **(with sth)** (**MUSIC**) (used about a place) to be filled with sound; to make a sound continue longer: *The room resonated with the chatter of 100 people.* **3** ~ **(with sb/sth)** to remind sb of sth; to be similar to what sb thinks or believes: *These issues resonated with the voters.*

PHR V **resonate with sth** (*formal*) to be full of a particular quality or feeling: *She makes a simple story resonate with complex themes and emotions.*

resort¹ /rɪˈzɔːt/ ***noun*** [C] (**TOURISM**) a place where a lot of people go to on holiday: *a* ***seaside/ski resort*** ◇ *She works as a* ***resort rep*** (= a person who works for a holiday company and looks after its clients when they are away on holiday).

IDM **in the last resort; (as) a last resort** → LAST¹

resort² /rɪˈzɔːt/ ***verb*** [I] ~ **to sth/doing sth** to do or use sth bad or unpleasant because you feel you have no choice: *After not sleeping for three nights I finally resorted to sleeping pills.*

resounding /rɪˈzaʊndɪŋ/ ***adj.*** (only *before* a noun) **1** very loud: *resounding cheers* **2** very great: *a resounding victory/win/defeat/success*

resource¹ **AW** /rɪˈsɔːs; -ˈzɔːs/ ***noun*** [C, usually pl.] a supply of sth, a piece of equipment, etc. that is available for sb to use: *Russia is rich in* ***natural resources*** *such as oil and minerals.*

resource² **AW** /rɪˈsɔːs; -ˈzɔːs/ ***verb*** [T] to provide sth with the money or equipment that is needed: *Schools in the area are still inadequately resourced.*

resourceful **AW** /rɪˈzɔːsfl; -ˈsɔːs-/ ***adj.*** good at finding ways of doing things and solving problems, etc. ▸ **resourcefully** /-fəli/ ***adv.*** ▸ **resourcefulness** ***noun*** [U]

respect¹ /rɪˈspekt/ ***noun*** **1** [U] ~ **(for sb/sth)** the feeling that you have when you admire or have a high opinion of sb/sth: *I* ***have little respect for*** *people who are arrogant.* ◇ *to win/lose sb's respect* ➲ look at **self-respect** **2** [U] ~ **(for sb/sth)** polite behaviour or care towards sb/sth that you think is important: *We should all treat older people with more respect.* **OPP** **disrespect** **3** [C] a detail or point: ***In what respects*** *do you think things have changed in the last ten years?* ◇ *Her performance was brilliant* ***in every respect.***

IDM **with respect to sth** (*formal*) about or concerning sth

pay your respects → PAY¹

respect² /rɪˈspekt/ ***verb*** [T] **1** ~ **sb/sth (for sth)** to admire or have a high opinion of sb/sth: *I respect him for his honesty.* **2** to show care for or pay attention to sb/sth: *We should respect other people's cultures and values.* ▸ **respectful** /-fl/ ***adj.*** ~ **(to/towards sb)**: *The crowd listened in respectful silence.* **OPP** **disrespectful** ▸ **respectfully** /-fəli/ ***adv.***

respectable /rɪˈspektəbl/ ***adj.*** **1** considered by society to be good, proper or correct: *a respectable family* ◇ *He combed his hair and tried to look respectable for the interview.* **2** quite good or large: *a respectable salary* ▸ **respectability** /rɪˌspektəˈbɪləti/ ***noun*** [U]

respective /rɪˈspektɪv/ ***adj.*** (only *before* a noun) belonging separately to each of the people who have been mentioned: *They all left for their respective destinations.*

respectively /rɪˈspektɪvli/ ***adv.*** in the same order as sb/sth that was mentioned: *Rhoda Jones and Robbie Vaccaro, aged 17 and 19 respectively*

respiration /ˌrespəˈreɪʃn/ ***noun*** [U] **1** (*formal*) (**HEALTH**) breathing **2** (**BIOLOGY**) a process by which living things produce energy from food. **Respiration** usually needs OXYGEN.

respirator /ˈrespəreɪtə(r)/ ***noun*** [C] **1** (**HEALTH**) a piece of equipment that makes it possible for sb to breathe over a long period when they are unable to do so naturally: *She was put on a respirator.* **2** a device worn over the nose and mouth to allow sb to breathe in a place where there is a lot of smoke, gas, etc.

respiratory /rəˈspɪrətri; ˈrespərətri/ ***adj.*** (**HEALTH**) connected with breathing: *the respiratory system* ◇ *respiratory diseases*

respire /rɪˈspaɪə(r)/ ***verb*** [I] (**BIOLOGY**) to breathe

respite /ˈrespaɪt/ ***noun*** [sing., U] ~ **(from sth)** a short period of rest from sth that is difficult or unpleasant: *There was a brief respite from the fighting.*

respond **AW** /rɪˈspɒnd/ ***verb*** [I] **1** (*formal*) ~ **(to sb/sth) (with/by sth)** to say or do sth as an answer or reaction to sth: *He responded to my question with a nod.* ◇ *Owen responded to the manager's criticism by scoring two goals.* **SYN** **reply**

respiration

aerobic respiration

$C_6H_{12}O_6$ (glucose) + $6O_2$ → $6CO_2$ + $6H_2O$ + energy — about 3000 kJ for every molecule of glucose

anaerobic respiration

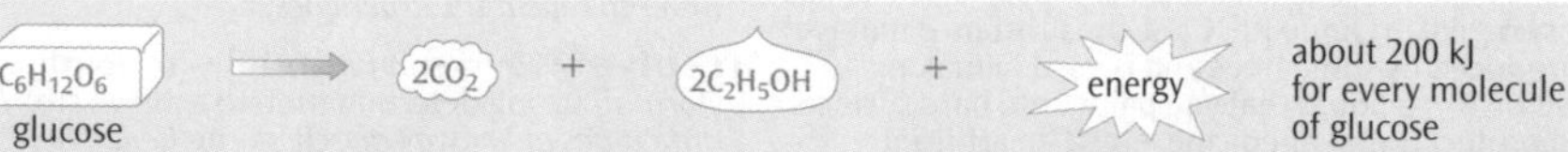

2 ~ **(to sb/sth)** to have or show a good or quick reaction to sb/sth: *The patient did not respond well to the new treatment.*

respondent AW /rɪˈspɒndənt/ ***noun*** [C] **1** a person who answers questions, especially in a survey: *60% of the respondents agreed with the suggestion* **2** (LAW) a person who is accused of sth

response 🔑 AW /rɪˈspɒns/ ***noun*** [C,U] (a) ~ **(to sb/sth)** an answer or reaction to sb/sth: *I've sent out 20 letters of enquiry but I've had no responses yet.* ◇ *The government acted **in response to** economic pressure.*

responsibility 🔑 /rɪˌspɒnsəˈbɪləti/ ***noun*** (*pl.* **responsibilities**) **1** [U, C] ~ **(for sb/sth)**; ~ **(to do sth)** a duty to deal with sth so that it is your fault if sth goes wrong: *I refuse to **take responsibility** if anything goes wrong.* ◇ *It is John's responsibility to make sure the orders are sent out on time.* ◇ *I feel that I **have a responsibility** to help them – after all, they did help me.* ◇ *Who **has responsibility** for the new students?* **2** [U] the fact of sth being your fault; blame: *No group has yet admitted responsibility for planting the bomb.*
IDM **shift the blame/responsibility (for sth) (onto sb)** → SHIFT[1]

responsible 🔑 /rɪˈspɒnsəbl/ ***adj.*** **1** (not before a noun) ~ **(for sb/sth)**; ~ **(for doing sth)** having the job or duty of dealing with sb/sth, so that it is your fault if sth goes wrong: *The school is responsible for the safety of the children in school hours.* ◇ *The manager is responsible for making sure the shop is run properly.* **2** (not before a noun) ~ **(for sth)** being the person whose fault sth is: *Who was responsible for the accident?* **3** (not before a noun) ~ **(to sb/sth)** having to report to sb/sth with authority, or to sb who you are working for, about what you are doing: *Members of Parliament are responsible to the electors.* **4** (used about a person) that you can trust to behave well and in a sensible way: *Marisa is responsible enough to take her little sister to school.* OPP **irresponsible** **5** (used about a job) that is important and that should be done by a person who can be trusted

responsibly /rɪˈspɒnsəbli/ ***adv.*** in a sensible way that shows that you can be trusted: *They can be relied on to act responsibly.*

responsive AW /rɪˈspɒnsɪv/ ***adj.*** paying attention to sb/sth and reacting in a suitable or positive way: *By being responsive to changes in the market, the company has had great success.*

rest[1] 🔑 /rest/ ***verb*** **1** [I] to relax, sleep or stop after a period of activity or because of illness: *We've been walking for hours. Let's rest here for a while.* **2** [T] to not use a part of your body for a period of time because it is tired or painful: *Your knee will get better as long as you rest it as much as you can.* **3** [I,T] ~ **(sth) on/against sth** to place sth in a position where it is supported by sth else; to be in such a position: *She rested her head on his shoulder and went to sleep.*
IDM **let sth rest** to not talk about sth any longer
PHR V **rest on sb/sth** to depend on sb/sth or be based on sth: *The whole theory rests on a very simple idea.*

rest[2] 🔑 /rest/ ***noun*** **1** [C,U] a period of relaxing, sleeping or doing nothing: *I can't walk any further! I need a rest.* ◇ *I'm going upstairs to **have a rest** before we go out.* ◇ *Try not to worry now. **Get some rest** and think about it again tomorrow.* ◇ *I sat down to **give** my bad leg **a rest**.* **2 the** ~ **(of sb/sth)** [sing., with sing. or pl. verb] the part that is left; the ones that are left: *We had lunch and spent the rest of the day on the beach.* ◇ *She takes no interest in what happens in the rest of the world.* ◇ *They were the first people to arrive. The rest came later.* ◇ *The rest of our bags are still in the car.* **3** [C,U] (MUSIC) a period of silence between notes; a sign for this ➲ picture at **music**
IDM **at rest** not moving: *At rest the insect looks like a dead leaf.*
come to rest to stop moving: *The car crashed through a wall and came to rest in a field.*
put/set your/sb's mind at rest → MIND[1]

restate /ˌriːˈsteɪt/ ***verb*** [T] (*formal*) to say sth again or in a different way, especially so that it is more clearly or strongly expressed

restaurant 🔑 /ˈrestrɒnt/ ***noun*** [C] a place where you can buy and eat a meal: *a fast food/hamburger restaurant* ◇ *a Chinese/an Italian/a Thai restaurant* ➲ look at **cafe**, **takeaway**

restful /ˈrestfl/ ***adj.*** giving a relaxed, peaceful feeling: *I find this piece of music very restful.*

restitution /ˌrestɪˈtjuːʃn/ ***noun*** [U] ~ **(of sth) (to sb/sth)** **1** (*formal*) the act of giving back sth that was lost or stolen to its owner **2** (LAW) payment, usually money, for some harm or wrong that sb has suffered

restless /ˈrestləs/ ***adj.*** **1** unable to relax or be still because you are bored, nervous or impatient: *The children always get restless on long journeys.* **2** (used about a period of time) without sleep or rest ▶ **restlessly** ***adv.***

restoration AW /ˌrestəˈreɪʃn/ ***noun*** **1** [C,U] the return of sth to its original condition; the things that are done to achieve this: *The house is in need of restoration.* **2** [U] the return of sth to its original owner: *the restoration of stolen property to its owner*

restore 🔑 AW /rɪˈstɔː(r)/ ***verb*** [T] **1** ~ **sb/sth (to sb/sth)** to put sb/sth back into their or its former condition or position: *She restores old furniture as a hobby.* ◇ *In the recent elections, the former president was restored to power.* **2** ~ **sth to sb** (*formal*) to give sth that was lost or stolen back to sb

restrain AW /rɪˈstreɪn/ ***verb*** [T] ~ **sb/sth (from sth/doing sth)** to keep sb or sth under control; to prevent sb or sth from doing sth: *I had to restrain myself from saying something rude.*

restrained /rɪˈstreɪnd/ ***adj.*** not showing strong feelings

restraint AW /rɪˈstreɪnt/ ***noun*** **1** [U] the quality of behaving in a calm or controlled way: *It took a lot of restraint on my part not to hit him.* ◇ *Soldiers have to exercise **self-restraint** even when provoked.* **2** [C] a ~ **(on sb/sth)** a limit or control on sb/sth: *Are there any restraints on what the newspapers are allowed to publish?* ➲ note at **limit**

restrict 🔑 AW /rɪˈstrɪkt/ ***verb*** [T] ~ **sb/sth (to sth/doing sth)** to put a limit on sb/sth: *There is a plan to restrict the use of cars in the city centre.*

restricted 🔑 AW /rɪˈstrɪktɪd/ ***adj.*** controlled or limited: *There is only restricted parking available.*

restriction 🔑 AW /rɪˈstrɪkʃn/ ***noun*** ~ **(on sth)** **1** [C] something (sometimes a rule or law) that limits the number, amount, size, freedom, etc. of sb/sth: *parking restrictions in the city centre* ◇ *The government is to **impose** tighter **restrictions** on the number of immigrants permitted to settle in this country.* ➲ note at **limit** **2** [U] the action of limiting the freedom of sb/sth: *This ticket permits you to travel anywhere, without restriction.*

restrictive AW /rɪˈstrɪktɪv/ ***adj.*** limiting; preventing people from doing what they want

restroom /ˈrestruːm/ ***noun*** [C] (*AmE*) a public toilet in a hotel, shop, restaurant, etc.

restructure AW /ˌriːˈstrʌktʃə(r)/ *verb* [T,I] (BUSINESS) to organize sth such as a system or a company in a new and different way ▶ **restructuring** *noun* [U, C, usually sing.]: *The company is undergoing a major restructuring.*

result[1] /rɪˈzʌlt/ *noun* **1** [C] something that happens because of sth else; the final situation at the end of a series of actions: *The traffic was very heavy and **as a result** I arrived late.* ◇ *This wasn't really the result that I was expecting.* ➲ note at **effect**[1] **2** [C,U] a good effect of an action: *He has tried very hard to find a job, until now without result.* ◇ *The treatment is beginning to show results.* **3** [C] the score at the end of a game, competition or election: *Have you heard today's football results?* ◇ *The results of this week's competition will be published next week.* ◇ *The result of the by-election was a win for the Liberal Democrats.* **4** [C, usually pl.] (EDUCATION) the mark given for an exam or test: *When do you **get** your exam **results**?* **5** [C] (HEALTH) something that is discovered by a medical test: *I'm still waiting for the result of my X-ray.* ◇ *The result of the test was negative.*

result[2] /rɪˈzʌlt/ *verb* [I] ~ **(from sth)** to happen or exist because of sth: *Ninety per cent of the deaths resulted from injuries to the head.*
PHR V **result in sth** to cause sth to happen; to produce sth as an effect: *There has been an accident on the motorway, resulting in long delays.*

resume /rɪˈzuːm; -ˈzjuː-/ *verb* [I,T] to begin again or continue after a pause or interruption: *Normal service will resume as soon as possible.*

résumé /ˈrezjumeɪ/ (*AmE*) = CV

resumption /rɪˈzʌmpʃn/ *noun* [sing., U] (*written*) beginning again or continuing after a pause or interruption

resurgence /rɪˈsɜːdʒəns/ *noun* [C, usually sing.] (*formal*) the return and growth of an activity that had stopped: *a resurgence of interest in the artist's work*

resurrect /ˌrezəˈrekt/ *verb* [T] to bring back sth that has not been used or has not existed for a long time

resurrection /ˌrezəˈrekʃn/ *noun* **1** [U] bringing back sth that has not existed or not been used for a long time **2 the Resurrection** [sing.] (RELIGION) (in Christianity) the return to life of Jesus Christ

resuscitate /rɪˈsʌsɪteɪt/ *verb* [T] (HEALTH) to bring sb who has stopped breathing back to life: *Unfortunately, all efforts to resuscitate the patient failed.* ▶ **resuscitation** /rɪˌsʌsɪˈteɪʃn/ *noun* [U]: *mouth-to-mouth resuscitation*

retail[1] /ˈriːteɪl/ *noun* [U] (BUSINESS) the selling of goods to the public in shops, etc. ➲ look at **wholesale** ▶ **retail** *adv.*: *to **buy/sell retail*** (= in a shop)

retail[2] /ˈriːteɪl/ *verb* (BUSINESS) **1** [T] to sell goods to the public, usually through shops: *The firm manufactures and retails its own range of sportswear.* **2** [I] ~ **at/for sth** to be sold at a particular price: *The book retails at £14.95.* ▶ **retailing** *noun* [U]: *career opportunities in retailing*

retailer /ˈriːteɪlə(r)/ *noun* [C] a person or company who sells goods to the public in a shop ➲ look at **wholesaler**

retain AW /rɪˈteɪn/ *verb* [T] (*formal*) to keep or continue to have sth; not to lose: *Despite all her problems, she has managed to retain a sense of humour.* ➲ noun **retention**

retainer AW /rɪˈteɪnə(r)/ *noun* [C] **1** (FINANCE) a sum of money that is paid to sb to make sure they will be available to do work when they are needed **2** (*BrE*) (FINANCE) a small amount of rent that you pay for a room, etc. when you are not there in order to keep it available for your use **3** (*old-fashioned*) a servant, especially one who has been with a family for a long time

retaliate /rɪˈtælieɪt/ *verb* [I] ~ **(against sb/sth)** to react to sth unpleasant that sb does to you by doing sth unpleasant in return ▶ **retaliation** /rɪˌtæliˈeɪʃn/ *noun* [U] ~ **(against sb/sth) (for sth)**: *The terrorist group said that the shooting was **in retaliation** for the murder of one of its members.*

retarded /rɪˈtɑːdɪd/ *adj.* slower to develop than normal

retch /retʃ/ *verb* [I] (HEALTH) to make sounds and movements as if you are going to VOMIT, but without bringing any food up from your stomach

retention AW /rɪˈtenʃn/ *noun* [U] the action of keeping sth or of being kept ➲ verb **retain**

retentive AW /rɪˈtentɪv/ *adj.* (used about the memory) able to store facts and remember things easily

rethink /ˈriːθɪŋk; ˌriːˈθɪŋk/ *verb* [I,T] (*pt, pp* **rethought** /-ˈθɔːt/) to think about sth again because you probably need to change it: *The government has been forced to rethink its economic policy.*

reticent /ˈretɪsnt/ *adj.* ~ **(about sth)** not wanting to tell people about things: *He is extremely reticent about his personal life.* ▶ **reticence** *noun* [U]

retina /ˈretɪnə/ *noun* [C] (ANATOMY) the area at the back of your eye that is sensitive to light and sends an image of what is seen to your brain ➲ picture at **eye**

retire /rɪˈtaɪə(r)/ *verb* [I] **1** ~ **(from sth)** to leave your job and stop working, usually because you have reached a certain age: *Most people in the company retire at 60.* ◇ *Injury forced her to retire from professional athletics.* **2** (*formal*) to leave and go to a quiet or private place

retired /rɪˈtaɪəd/ *adj.* having stopped work permanently: *a retired teacher*

retirement /rɪˈtaɪəmənt/ *noun* **1** [C,U] the act of stopping working permanently: *She has decided to **take early retirement**.* ◇ *The former world champion has announced his retirement from the sport.* **2** [sing., U] the situation or period after retiring from work: *We all wish you a long and happy retirement.*

RELATED VOCABULARY

A **pension** is the regular money received by somebody who has retired. It comes from the government, his/her former employer or both. A **pensioner** or an **old-age pensioner** is a person who has retired because of age.

retiring /rɪˈtaɪərɪŋ/ *adj.* (used about a person) shy and quiet

retort[1] /rɪˈtɔːt/ *verb* [T] to reply quickly to what sb says, in an angry or amusing way: *'Who asked you for your opinion?' she retorted.*

retort[2] /rɪˈtɔːt/ *noun* [C] **1** a quick, angry or amusing reply: *an angry retort* **2** (CHEMISTRY) a closed bottle with a long narrow bent SPOUT (= a tube through which liquid comes out) that is used in a LABORATORY (= a room used for scientific experiments) for heating chemicals ➲ picture at **laboratory**

retrace /rɪ'treɪs/ ***verb*** [T] to repeat a past journey, series of events, etc.: *If you* ***retrace your steps****, you might see where you dropped the ticket.*

retract /rɪ'trækt/ ***verb*** [I,T] (*formal*) to say that sth you have said is not true: *When he appeared in court, he retracted the confession he had made to the police.*

retreat¹ /rɪ'triːt/ ***verb*** [I] **1** (used about an army, etc.) to move backwards in order to leave a battle or in order not to become involved in a battle: *The order was given to retreat.* OPP **advance 2** to move backwards; to go to a safe or private place: (*figurative*) *She seems to retreat into a world of her own sometimes.*

retreat² /rɪ'triːt/ ***noun*** **1** [C,U] the action of moving backwards, away from a difficult or dangerous situation: *The invading forces are now in retreat.* OPP **advance 2** [C] a private place where you can go when you want to be quiet or to rest: *a country retreat*

retrial /ˌriː'traɪəl/ ***noun*** [C, usually sing.] (LAW) a new trial for a person whose criminal offence has already been judged once in a court of law: *The judge ordered a retrial because new evidence had appeared.*

retribution /ˌretrɪ'bjuːʃn/ ***noun*** [U] (*written*) ~ **(for sth)** (LAW) punishment for a crime

retrieve /rɪ'triːv/ ***verb*** [T] **1** ~ **sth (from sb/sth)** to get sth back from the place where it was left or lost: *Police divers retrieved the body from the canal.* **2** (COMPUTING) to find information that has been stored: *The computer can retrieve all the data about a particular customer.* **3** to make a bad situation or a mistake better; to put sth right: *The team was losing two–nil at half-time but they managed to* ***retrieve the situation*** *in the second half.* ▶ **retrieval** /-vl/ ***noun*** [U]

retro- /'retrəʊ/ ***prefix*** (used in nouns, adjectives and adverbs) back or backwards: *retrospective*

retrograde /'retrəgreɪd/ ***adj.*** (*formal*) (used about an action) making a situation worse or returning to how sth was in the past: *The closure of the factory is a* ***retrograde step****.*

retrospect /'retrəspekt/ ***noun***
IDM **in retrospect** thinking about sth that happened in the past, often seeing it differently from the way you saw it at the time: *In retrospect, I can see what a stupid mistake it was.*

retrospective /ˌretrə'spektɪv/ ***adj.*** **1** looking again at the past: *a retrospective analysis of historical events* **2** (used about laws, decisions, payments, etc.) intended to take effect from a date in the past: *Is this new tax law retrospective?* ▶ **retrospectively** ***adv.***

return¹ ⊶ /rɪ'tɜːn/ ***verb*** **1** [I] ~ **(to/from…)** to come or go back to a place: *I leave on 10 July and return on 6 August.* ◇ *I shall be returning to this country in six months.* ◇ *When did you return from Italy?* ◇ *He left his home town when he was 18 and never returned.* **2** [I] ~ **(to sth/doing sth)** to go back to the former or usual activity, situation, condition, etc.: *The strike is over and they will* ***return to work*** *on Monday.* ◇ *It is hoped that train services will* ***return to normal*** *soon.* **3** [I] to come back; to happen again: *If the pain returns, make another appointment to see me.* **4** [T] ~ **sth (to sb/sth)** to give, send, put or take sth back: *I've stopped lending him things because he never returns them.* ◇ *Application forms must be returned by 14 March.* **5** [T] to react to sth that sb does, says or feels by doing, saying or feeling sth similar: *I've phoned them several times and left messages but they haven't returned any of my calls.* ◇ *We'll be happy to return your hospitality if you ever come to our country.* **6** [T] (SPORT) (in TENNIS) to hit or throw the ball back

return² ⊶ /rɪ'tɜːn/ ***noun*** **1** [sing.] a ~ **(to/from…)** coming or going back to a place or to a former activity, situation or condition: *I'll contact you* ***on*** *my* ***return*** *from holiday.* ◇ *He has recently made a return to form* (=started playing well again). **2** [U] giving, sending, putting or taking sth back: *I demand the immediate return of my passport.* **3** [C] (SPORT) (in TENNIS) the act of hitting or throwing the ball back: *She hit a brilliant return.* **4** [C,U] (a) ~ **(on sth)** (BUSINESS) the profit from a business, etc.: *This account offers high returns on all investments.* **5** [C] (*BrE also* **reˌturn 'ticket**, *AmE* **ˌround 'trip**; **ˌround ˌtrip 'ticket**) a ticket to travel to a place and back again: *A* ***day return*** *to Oxford, please.* ◇ *Is the* ***return fare*** *cheaper than two singles?* OPP **single**, **one-way 6** (*also* **the re'turn key**) [sing.] (COMPUTING) the button on a computer that you press when you reach the end of a line or of an instruction
IDM **by return (of post)** (*BrE*) immediately; by the next post
in return (for sth) as payment or in exchange (for sth); as a reaction to sth: *Please accept this present in return for all your help.*

returnable /rɪ'tɜːnəbl/ ***adj.*** that can or must be given or taken back: *a non-returnable deposit*

reunion /riː'juːniən/ ***noun*** **1** [C] a party or occasion when friends or people who worked together meet again after they have not seen each other for a long time: *The college holds an annual reunion for former students.* **2** [C,U] **a ~ (with sb/between A and B)** coming together again after being apart: *The released hostages had an emotional reunion with their families at the airport.*

reunite /ˌriːju'naɪt/ ***verb*** [I,T] ~ **(A with/and B)** to come together again; to join two or more people, groups, etc. together again: *The missing child was found by the police and reunited with his parents.*

reusable /ˌriː'juːzəbl/ ***adj.*** that can be used again: *reusable plastic bottles*

reuse /ˌriː'juːz/ ***verb*** [T] to use sth again: *Please reuse your envelopes.* ▶ **reuse** /ˌriː'juːs/ ***noun*** [U]

Rev. ***abbr.*** Reverend

rev¹ /rev/ ***verb*** [I,T] (**revving**; **revved**) ~ **(sth) (up)** when an engine **revs** or when you **rev** it, it turns quickly and noisily

rev² /rev/ ***noun*** [C] (*informal*) (used when talking about an engine's speed) one complete turn: *4000 revs per minute* ➲ look at **revolution**

reveal ⊶ AW /rɪ'viːl/ ***verb*** [T] **1** ~ **sth (to sb)** to make sth known that was secret or unknown before: *He refused to reveal any names to the police.* **2** to show sth that was hidden before: *The X-ray revealed a tiny fracture in her right hand.*

revealing AW /rɪ'viːlɪŋ/ ***adj.*** **1** allowing sth to be known that was secret or unknown before: *This book provides a revealing insight into the world of politics.* **2** allowing sth to be seen that is usually hidden, especially sb's body: *a very revealing swimsuit*

revel /'revl/ ***verb*** (**revelling**; **revelled**: *AmE* **reveling**; **reveled**)
PHR V **revel in sth/doing sth** to enjoy sth very much: *He likes being famous and revels in the attention he gets.*

revelation AW /ˌrevə'leɪʃn/ ***noun*** **1** [C] something that is made known, that was secret or unknown before, especially sth surprising: *This magazine is full of revelations about the private lives of the stars.*

2 [sing.] a thing or a person that surprises you and makes you change your opinion about sb/sth

revenge /rɪˈvendʒ/ ***noun*** [U] ~ **(on sb) (for sth)** something that you do to punish sb who has hurt you, made you suffer, etc.: *He made a fool of me and now I want to* ***get my revenge****.* ◇ *He wants to* ***take revenge*** *on the judge who sent him to prison.* ◇ *The shooting was* ***in revenge*** *for an attack by the nationalists.* ➲ look at **vengeance** ▶ **revenge** ***verb*** [T] ~ **yourself on sb**: *She revenged herself on her enemy.* ➲ look at **avenge**

revenue AW /ˈrevənjuː/ ***noun*** [U] (*also* **revenues** [pl.]) (FINANCE) money regularly received by a government, company, etc.: *Revenue from income tax rose last year.*

reverberate /rɪˈvɜːbəreɪt/ ***verb*** [I] **1** (used about a sound) to be repeated several times as it comes off different surfaces: *Her voice reverberated around the hall.* SYN **echo 2** ~ **(with/to sth)** (used about a place) to seem to shake because of a loud noise: *The hall reverberated with the sound of music and dancing.*

revere /rɪˈvɪə(r)/ ***verb*** [T] (usually passive) (*formal*) ~ **sb/sth (as sth)** to feel great respect or admiration for sb/sth: *He is revered as one of the greatest musicians of his generation.*

reverence /ˈrevərəns/ ***noun*** [U] (*formal*) ~ **(for sb/sth)** a feeling of great respect

reverend (*also* **Reverend**) /ˈrevərənd/ ***adj.*** (*abbr.* **Rev.**) (RELIGION) the title of a Christian priest

reverent /ˈrevərənt/ ***adj.*** (*formal*) showing respect

reversal AW /rɪˈvɜːsl/ ***noun*** [U, C] the action of changing sth to the opposite of what it was before; an occasion when this happens: *The government insists that there will be no reversal of policy.* ◇ *The decision taken yesterday was a complete reversal of last week's decision.*

reverse¹ 🔑 AW /rɪˈvɜːs/ ***verb*** **1** [T] to put sth in the opposite position to normal or to how it was before: *Today's results have reversed the order of the top two teams.* **2** [T] to exchange the positions or functions of two things or people: *Jane and her husband have reversed roles – he stays at home now and she goes to work.* **3** [I,T] to go backwards in a car, etc.; to make a car go backwards: *It might be easier to reverse into that parking space.* ◇ *He reversed his brand new car into a wall.*

IDM **reverse (the) charges** (*BrE*) to make a telephone call that will be paid for by the person who receives it: *Phone us when you get there, and reverse the charges.* ◇ *a reverse charge call* ❶ The American English expression is to **call collect**.

reverse² 🔑 AW /rɪˈvɜːs/ ***noun*** **1** [sing.] **the ~ (of sth)** the complete opposite of what was said just before, or of what is expected: *Of course I don't dislike you – quite the reverse* (= I like you very much). ◇ *This course is the exact reverse of what I was expecting.* **2** (*also* **reˌverse ˈgear**) [U] the control in a car, etc. that allows it to move backwards: *Leave the car* ***in reverse*** *while it's parked on this hill.* ◇ *Where's reverse in this car?*

IDM **in reverse** in the opposite order, starting at the end and going backwards to the beginning

reverse³ AW /rɪˈvɜːs/ ***adj.*** opposite to what is expected or has just been described

IDM **in/into reverse order** starting with the last one and going backwards to the first one: *The results will be announced in reverse order.*

reˌverse disˌcriminˈation ***noun*** [U] = POSITIVE DISCRIMINATION

reversible AW /rɪˈvɜːsəbl/ ***adj.*** **1** (used about clothes) that can be worn with either side on the outside: *a reversible coat* **2** (used about a process, an action or a disease) that can be changed so that sth returns to its original state or situation OPP **irreversible**

revert /rɪˈvɜːt/ ***verb*** [I] ~ **(to sth)** to return to a former state or activity: *The land will soon revert to jungle if it is not farmed.* ◇ *If the experiment is unsuccessful we will revert to the old system.*

review¹ 🔑 /rɪˈvjuː/ ***noun*** **1** [C,U] the examining or considering again of sth in order to decide if changes are necessary: *There will be a review of your contract after the first six months.* ◇ *The system is in need of review.* ➲ note at **examine 2** [C] a look back at sth in order to check, remember, or be clear about sth: *a review of the major events of the year* **3** [C] (ARTS AND MEDIA) a newspaper or magazine article, or an item on television or radio, in which sb gives an opinion on a new book, film, play, etc.: *The film got bad reviews.*

review² 🔑 /rɪˈvjuː/ ***verb*** [T] **1** to examine or consider sth again in order to decide if changes are necessary: *Your salary will be reviewed after one year.* **2** to look at or think about sth again to make sure that you understand it: *Let's review what we've done in class this week.* **3** (ARTS AND MEDIA) to write an article or to talk on television or radio, giving an opinion on a new book, film, play, etc.: *In this week's edition our film critic reviews the latest films.*

reviewer /rɪˈvjuːə(r)/ ***noun*** [C] (ARTS AND MEDIA) a person who writes about new books, films, etc.

revise 🔑 AW /rɪˈvaɪz/ ***verb*** **1** [T] to make changes to sth in order to correct or improve it: *The book has been revised for this new edition.* ◇ *I revised my opinion of him when I found out that he had lied.* **2** [I,T] (*BrE*) ~ **(for sth)** (EDUCATION) to read or study again sth that you have learnt, especially when preparing for an exam: *I can't come out tonight. I'm revising for my exam.* ◇ *None of the things I had revised came up in the exam.*

revision 🔑 AW /rɪˈvɪʒn/ ***noun*** **1** [C,U] the changing of sth in order to correct or improve it: *It has been suggested that the whole system is in need of revision.* **2** [U] (*BrE*) (EDUCATION) the work of reading or studying again sth you have learnt, especially when preparing for an exam: *I'm going to have to* ***do*** *a lot of* ***revision*** *for History.*

revitalize (also **-ise**) /ˌriːˈvaɪtəlaɪz/ ***verb*** [T] to make sth stronger, more active or more healthy: *measures to revitalize the inner cities*

revival /rɪˈvaɪvl/ ***noun*** **1** [C,U] the act of becoming or making sth strong or popular again: *economic revival* ◇ *a revival of interest in traditional farming methods* **2** [C] (ARTS AND MEDIA) a new performance of a play that has not been performed for some time: *a revival of the musical 'The Sound of Music'*

revive /rɪˈvaɪv/ ***verb*** [I,T] **1** to become or to make sb/sth strong or healthy again; to come or to bring sb back to life or CONSCIOUSNESS: *Hopes have revived for an early end to the fighting.* ◇ *I'm very tired but I'm sure a cup of coffee will revive me.* ◇ *Attempts were made to revive him but he was already dead.* **2** to become or to make sth popular again; to begin to do or use sth again: *Public interest in athletics has revived now that the national team is doing well.* ◇ *to revive an old custom*

revoke /rɪˈvəʊk/ ***verb*** [T] (*formal*) to officially cancel sth so that it is no longer valid

revolt /rɪˈvəʊlt/ ***verb*** **1** [I] ~ **(against sb/sth)** to protest in a group, often violently, against the person or people in power: *A group of generals* *revolted against the government.* **2** [T] to make sb feel disgusted or ill: *The sight and smell of the meat revolted him.* ➲ noun **revulsion** ▸ **revolt** *noun* [C,U]: *The people rose* ***in revolt*** *against the corrupt government.*

revolting /rɪˈvəʊltɪŋ/ ***adj.*** extremely unpleasant; disgusting

revolution ⊶ AW /ˌrevəˈluːʃn/ ***noun*** **1** [C,U] (**POLITICS**) action taken by a large group of people to try to change the government of a country, especially by violent action: *the French Revolution of 1789* ◇ *a country on the brink of revolution* **2** [C] a ~ (**in sth**) a complete change in methods, opinions, etc., often as a result of progress: *the Industrial Revolution* **3** [C,U] a movement around sth; one complete turn around a central point (for example in a car engine): *400 revolutions per minute* ➲ look at **rev**[2]

revolutionary[1] AW /ˌrevəˈluːʃənəri/ ***adj.*** **1** (**POLITICS**) connected with or supporting political revolution: *the revolutionary leaders* **2** producing great changes; very new and different: *a revolutionary new scheme to ban cars from the city centre*

revolutionary[2] AW /ˌrevəˈluːʃənəri/ ***noun*** [C] (*pl.* **revolutionaries**) (**POLITICS**) a person who starts or supports action to try to change the government of a country, especially by using violent action

revolutionize (also -ise) AW /ˌrevəˈluːʃənaɪz/ ***verb*** [T] to change sth completely, usually improving it: *a discovery that could revolutionize the treatment of mental illness*

revolve /rɪˈvɒlv/ ***verb*** [I] to move in a circle around a central point: *The earth revolves around the sun.* PHR V **revolve around sb/sth** to have sb/sth as the most important part: *Her life revolves around the family.*

revolver /rɪˈvɒlvə(r)/ ***noun*** [C] a type of small gun with a container for bullets that turns round

revolving /rɪˈvɒlvɪŋ/ ***adj.*** that goes round in a circle: *revolving doors*

revulsion /rɪˈvʌlʃn/ ***noun*** [U] a feeling of disgust (because sth is extremely unpleasant) ➲ verb **revolt**

reward[1] ⊶ /rɪˈwɔːd/ ***noun*** ~ (**for sth/doing sth**) **1** [C,U] something that you are given because you have done sth good, worked hard, etc.: *Winning the match was* ***just reward*** *for all the effort.* **2** [C] an amount of money that is given in exchange for helping the police, returning sth that was lost, etc.: *Police are offering a reward for information leading to a conviction.*

reward[2] ⊶ /rɪˈwɔːd/ ***verb*** [T] ~ **sb** (**for sth/for doing sth**) (often passive) to give sth to sb because they have done sth good, worked hard, etc.: *Eventually her efforts were rewarded and she got a job.*

rewarding /rɪˈwɔːdɪŋ/ ***adj.*** (used about an activity, job, etc.) giving satisfaction; making you happy because you think it is important, useful, etc.

rewind /ˌriːˈwaɪnd/ ***verb*** [T] (*pt, pp* **rewound**) to make a video or CASSETTE TAPE go backwards: *Please rewind the tape at the end of the film.* ▸ **rewind** ***noun*** [U] ➲ look at **fast forward**

rewrite /ˌriːˈraɪt/ ***verb*** [T] (*pt* **rewrote** /-ˈrəʊt/; *pp* **rewritten** /-ˈrɪtn/) to write sth again in a different or better way

rhenium /ˈriːniəm/ ***noun*** [U] (*symbol* **Re**) (**CHEMISTRY**) a chemical element. **Rhenium** is a rare silver-white metal that exists naturally in the ORES of MOLYBDENUM and some other metals. ❶ For more information on the periodic table of elements, look at pages R34-5.

rhetoric /ˈretərɪk/ ***noun*** [U] (*formal*) a way of speaking or writing that is intended to impress or influence people but is not always sincere ▸ **rhetorical** /rɪˈtɒrɪkl/ ***adj.*** ▸ **rhetorically** /-kli/ ***adv.***

rheˌtorical ˈquestion ***noun*** [C] (**LANGUAGE**) a question that does not expect an answer

rheumatism /ˈruːmətɪzəm/ ***noun*** [U] (**HEALTH**) an illness that causes pain in muscles and where your bones join together (**the joints**)

rheumatology /ˌruːməˈtɒlədʒi/ ***noun*** [U] (**HEALTH**) the study of the diseases of joints and muscles, such as RHEUMATISM and ARTHRITIS

rhino /ˈraɪnəʊ/ (*pl.* **rhinos**) (*informal*) = RHINOCEROS

rhinoceros /raɪˈnɒsərəs/ ***noun*** [C] (*pl.* **rhinoceros** or **rhinoceroses**) a large animal from Africa or Asia, with a thick skin and with one or two horns on its nose ➲ picture at **pachyderm**

rhodium /ˈrəʊdiəm/ ***noun*** [U] (*symbol* **Rh**) (**CHEMISTRY**) a chemical element. **Rhodium** is a hard silver-white metal that is usually found with PLATINUM. ❶ For more information on the periodic table of elements, look at pages R34-5.

rhomboid /ˈrɒmbɔɪd/ ***noun*** [C] (**GEOMETRY**) a flat shape with four straight sides, with only the opposite sides and angles equal to each other ➲ picture at **parallelogram**

rhombus /ˈrɒmbəs/ ***noun*** [C] (**GEOMETRY**) a flat shape with four equal sides and four angles which are not 90° ➲ picture at **parallelogram**

rhubarb /ˈruːbɑːb/ ***noun*** [U] a plant with long red parts (**stalks**) that can be cooked and eaten as fruit

rhyme[1] /raɪm/ ***noun*** **1** [C] a word that has the same sound as another **2** [C] a short piece of writing, or sth spoken, in which the word at the end of each line sounds the same as the word at the end of the line before it ➲ look at **nursery rhyme** **3** [U] the use of words in a poem or song that have the same sound, especially at the ends of lines: *All of his poetry was written* ***in rhyme.***

rhyme[2] /raɪm/ ***verb*** **1** [I] ~ (**with sth**) to have the same sound as another word; to contain lines that end with words that sound the same: *'Tough' rhymes with 'stuff'.* **2** [T] ~ **sth** (**with sth**) to put together words that have the same sound

rhythm ⊶ /ˈrɪðəm/ ***noun*** [C,U] (**MUSIC**) a regular repeated pattern of sound or movement: *I'm not keen on the tune but I love the rhythm.* ◇ *He's a terrible dancer because he has no* ***sense of rhythm.*** ◇ *He tapped his foot* ***in rhythm*** *with the music.* ▸ **rhythmic** /ˈrɪðmɪk/ (*also* **rhythmical** /ˈrɪðmɪkl/) ***adj.***: *the rhythmic qualities of African music* ▸ **rhythmically** /-kli/ ***adv.***

ˌrhythm and ˈblues ***noun*** [U] (*abbr.* **R & B**) (**MUSIC**) a type of music that is a mixture of BLUES and JAZZ and has a strong rhythm

ria /ˈriːə/ ***noun*** [C] (**GEOGRAPHY**) a long narrow area of water formed when a river valley floods

rib /rɪb/ ***noun*** [C] (**ANATOMY**) one of the curved bones that go round your chest: *He's so thin that you can see his ribs.* ➲ picture on **page 80**

ribbon /ˈrɪbən/ ***noun*** [C,U] a long, thin piece of material that is used for tying or decorating sth

ˈribbon lake ***noun*** [C] (**GEOGRAPHY**) a long narrow lake ➲ picture at **glacial**

ribcage /ˈrɪbkeɪdʒ/ ***noun*** [C] (**ANATOMY**) the structure of curved bones (**ribs**) that surrounds and protects the chest ➲ picture on **page 80**

rice ⊶ /raɪs/ ***noun*** [U] short, thin, white or brown grain from a plant that grows on wet land in hot countries. We cook and eat rice: *boiled/fried/ steamed rice* ➲ picture at **cereal**

rich ⊶ /rɪtʃ/ ***adj.*** **1** having a lot of money or property; not poor: *a rich family/country* ◇ *one of the richest women in the world* ➲ look at **wealthy** OPP **poor 2 the rich** ***noun*** [pl.] people with a lot of money or property **3** ~ **in sth** containing a lot of sth: *Oranges are rich in vitamin C.* **4** (used about food) containing a lot of fat, oil, sugar or cream and making you feel full quickly: *a rich chocolate cake* **5** (used about soil) containing the substances that make it good for growing plants in **6** (used about colours, sounds or smells) strong and deep ▶ **richness** ***noun*** [U]

riches /ˈrɪtʃɪz/ ***noun*** [pl.] (*formal*) a lot of money or property SYN **wealth**

richly /ˈrɪtʃli/ ***adv.*** **1** in a generous way: *She was richly rewarded for her hard work.* **2** in a way that people think is right: *His promotion was richly deserved.*

the Richter scale /ˈrɪktə skeɪl/ ***noun*** [sing.] (GEOLOGY, GEOGRAPHY) a system for measuring movements of the earth's surface (**earthquakes**): *an earthquake measuring 7* ***on the Richter scale***

rickets /ˈrɪkɪts/ ***noun*** [U] (HEALTH) a disease of children caused by a lack of good food that makes the bones become soft and badly formed, especially in the legs

rickety /ˈrɪkəti/ ***adj.*** likely to break; not strongly made: *a rickety old fence* ◇ *rickety furniture*

rickshaw /ˈrɪkʃɔː/ ***noun*** [C] (TOURISM) a small light vehicle with two wheels used in some Asian countries to carry passengers. The **rickshaw** is pulled by a person walking or riding a bicycle.

ricochet /ˈrɪkəʃeɪ/ ***verb*** [I] (*pt, pp* **ricocheted** /-ʃeɪd/) ~ **(off sth)** (used about a moving object) to fly away from a surface after hitting it: *The bullet ricocheted off the wall and grazed his shoulder.*

rid ⊶ /rɪd/ ***verb*** [T] (*pres. part.* **ridding**; *pt, pp* **rid**) (*formal*) ~ **yourself/sb/sth of sb/sth** to make yourself/sb/sth free from sb/sth that is unpleasant or not wanted: *He was unable to rid himself of his fears and suspicions.* ◇ (*BrE*) *He was a nuisance and we're* ***well rid*** *of him* (=it will be much better without him).

IDM **get rid of sb/sth** to make yourself free of sb/sth that is annoying you or that you do not want; to throw sth away: *Let's get rid of that old chair and buy a new one.*

riddance /ˈrɪdns/ ***noun***

IDM **good riddance (to sb/sth)** (*spoken*) used for expressing pleasure or satisfaction that sb/sth that you do not like has gone

ridden[1] past participle of **ride**[1]

ridden[2] /ˈrɪdn/ ***adj.*** (*formal*) (usually in compound adjectives) full of: *She was guilt-ridden.* ◇ *She was ridden with guilt.*

riddle /ˈrɪdl/ ***noun*** [C] **1** a difficult question that you ask people for fun that has a clever or amusing answer **2** a person, thing or event that you cannot understand or explain

riddled /ˈrɪdld/ ***adj.*** ~ **with sth** full of sth, especially sth unpleasant: *This essay is riddled with mistakes.*

ride[1] ⊶ /raɪd/ ***verb*** (*pt* **rode** /rəʊd/; *pp* **ridden** /ˈrɪdn/) **1** [I,T] (SPORT) to sit on a horse, etc. and control it as it moves: *We rode through the woods and over the moor.* ◇ *Which horse is Dettori riding in the next race?* **2** [I,T] to sit on a bicycle, motorbike, etc. and control it as it moves: *She jumped onto her motorbike and rode off* (=went away). ◇ *Can John ride a bike yet?* **3** [I] (*especially AmE*) (TOURISM) to travel as a passenger in a bus, car, etc.

ride[2] ⊶ /raɪd/ ***noun*** [C] **1** a short journey on a horse or bicycle, or in a car, bus, etc.: *It's only a short bus/train ride into Warwick.* ◇ *We went for a bike ride on Saturday.* **2** used to describe what a journey or trip is like: *a smooth/bumpy/comfortable ride* **3** a large machine at an AMUSEMENT PARK which you pay to go on for amusement or excitement; an occasion when you go on one of these: *My favourite* ***fairground ride*** *is the roller coaster.*

IDM **take sb for a ride** (*informal*) to cheat or trick sb

rider ⊶ /ˈraɪdə(r)/ ***noun*** [C] **1** a person who rides a horse, bicycle or motorcycle: *She's an experienced rider.* ◇ *a motorcycle dispatch rider* **2** ~ **(to sth)** (LAW) an extra piece of information that is added to an official document

ridge /rɪdʒ/ ***noun*** [C] **1** (GEOGRAPHY) a long, narrow piece of high land along the top of hills or mountains **2** (GEOMETRY) a line where two surfaces meet at an angle

ridicule /ˈrɪdɪkjuːl/ ***noun*** [U] unkind LAUGHTER or behaviour that is intended to make sb/sth appear silly: *He had become an object of ridicule.* ▶ **ridicule** ***verb*** [T]: *The idea was ridiculed by everybody present.*

ridiculous ⊶ /rɪˈdɪkjələs/ ***adj.*** very silly or unreasonable: *They're asking a ridiculous* (=very high) *price for that house.* ▶ **ridiculously** ***adv.***

riding ⊶ /ˈraɪdɪŋ/ (*AmE* **ˈhorseback riding**) ***noun*** [U] (SPORT) the sport or hobby of riding a horse: *riding boots* ◇ *a riding school*

rife /raɪf/ ***adj.*** (not *before* a noun) (*formal*) (used about bad things) very common: *Rumours are rife that his wife has left him.*

rifle[1] /ˈraɪfl/ ***noun*** [C] a long gun that you hold against your shoulder to shoot with

rifle[2] /ˈraɪfl/ ***verb*** [I,T] ~ **(through sth)** to search sth usually in order to steal from it: *I caught him rifling through the papers on my desk.*

rift /rɪft/ ***noun*** [C] **1** a serious disagreement between friends, groups, etc. that stops their relationship from continuing: *a growing rift between the brothers* **2** (GEOGRAPHY, GEOLOGY) a very large crack or opening in the ground, a rock, etc. ➲ picture at **plate tectonics**

ˈrift valley ***noun*** [C] (GEOGRAPHY) a valley with steep sides formed when two parallel cracks develop in the earth's surface and the land between them sinks

rig[1] /rɪɡ/ ***verb*** [T] (**rigging**; **rigged**) to arrange or control an event, etc. in an unfair way, in order to get the result you want: *They claimed that the competition had been rigged.*

PHRV **rig sth up** to make sth quickly, using any materials you can find: *We tried to rig up a shelter using our coats.*

rig[2] /rɪɡ/ =OIL RIG

rigging /ˈrɪɡɪŋ/ ***noun*** [U] the ropes, etc. that support a ship's sails

right[1] ⊶ /raɪt/ ***adj.*** **1** correct; true: *I'm afraid that's not the right answer.* ◇ *Have you got* ***the right time****?* ◇ *You're quite right – the film does start at 7 o'clock.* ◇ *You were right about the weather – it did rain.* ◇ *'You're Chinese, aren't you?' 'Yes,* ***that's right****.'* ➲ note at **true** OPP **wrong 2** ~ **(for sb/sth)** best; most suitable: *I hope I've made* ***the right decision****.* ◇ *I am sure we've chosen* ***the right person*** *for the job.* ◇ *I would help you to wash the car, but I'm not wearing* *the right clothes.* OPP **wrong 3** (used about behaviour, actions, etc.) fair; morally and socially correct: *It's not right to pay people so badly.* ◇ *What do you think is* ***the right thing*** *to do?* OPP **wrong 4** healthy or normal; as it should be: *The car exhaust doesn't sound right – it's making a funny noise.* ◇ *I don't feel quite right today* (= I feel ill). **5** on or of the side of the body that faces east when a person is facing north: *Most people write with their right hand.* ◇ *He's blind in his right eye.* OPP **left 6** (*BrE, spoken*) (used for emphasizing sth bad) real or complete: *I'll look a right idiot in that hat!* ▸ **rightness** ***noun*** [U]

IDM **get/start off on the right/wrong foot (with sb)** → FOOT[1]

get on the right/wrong side of sb → SIDE[1]

on the right/wrong track → TRACK[1]

put/set sth right to correct sth or deal with a problem: *There's something wrong with the lawnmower. Do you think you'll be able to put it right?*

right (you are)! (*spoken*) yes, I will or yes, I agree; OK: *'See you later.' 'Right you are!'*

(as) right as rain completely healthy and normal

right² ⊶ /raɪt/ ***adv.*** **1** exactly; directly: *The train was right on time.* ◇ *He was sitting right beside me.* **2** correctly; in the way that it should happen or should be done: *Have I spelt your name right?* ◇ *Nothing seems to be going right for me at the moment.* OPP **wrong 3** all the way; completely: *Did you watch the film right to the end?* ◇ *There's a high wall that goes right round the house.* **4** to the right side: *Turn right at the traffic lights.* OPP **left 5** immediately: *Wait here a minute – I'll* ***be right back.*** **6** (*spoken*) (used for preparing sb for sth that is about to happen) get ready; listen: *Have you got your seat belts on? Right, off we go.*

IDM **right/straight away** → AWAY

right now at this moment; exactly now: *We can't discuss this right now.*

serve sb right → SERVE

right³ ⊶ /raɪt/ ***noun*** **1** [U] what is morally good and fair: *Does a child of four really understand the difference between right and wrong?* ◇ *You* ***did right*** *to tell me what happened.* OPP **wrong 2** [sing.] the right side or direction: *We live in the first house* ***on the right.*** ◇ *Take the first right and then the second left.* OPP **left 3** [U, C] **the ~ (to sth/to do sth)** a thing that you are allowed to do according to the law; a moral authority to do sth: *Freedom of speech is one of the basic* ***human rights.*** ◇ ***civil rights*** (= the rights each person has to political and religious freedom, etc.) ◇ *animal rights campaigners* ◇ *Everyone has the right to a fair trial.* ◇ *You have no right to tell me what to do.* **4 the Right** [sing., with sing. or pl. verb] (POLITICS) the people or political parties who are against social change

IDM **be in the right** to be doing what is correct and fair: *You don't need to apologize. You were in the right and he was in the wrong.*

by rights according to what is fair or correct: *By rights, half the profit should be mine.*

in your own right because of what you are yourself and not because of other people

within your rights (to do sth) acting in a reasonable or legal way: *You are quite within your rights to demand to see your lawyer.*

right⁴ /raɪt/ ***verb*** [T] to put sb/sth/yourself back into a normal position: *The boat tipped over and then righted itself again.*

IDM **right a wrong** to do sth to correct an unfair situation or sth bad that you have done

'right angle ***noun*** [C] (GEOMETRY) an angle of 90°: *A square has four right angles.* ➲ look at **acute angle, obtuse angle, reflex angle** ➲ picture at **angle**

ˌright-angled 'triangle (*AmE usually* **ˌright 'triangle**) ***noun*** [C] (GEOMETRY) a triangle with a RIGHT ANGLE: *a right-angled triangle* ➲ picture at **triangle**

righteous /ˈraɪtʃəs/ ***adj.*** (*formal*) that you think is morally good or fair: *righteous anger/indignation* ➲ look at **self-righteous**

rightful /ˈraɪtfl/ ***adj.*** (only *before* a noun) (*formal*) legally or morally correct; fair ▸ **rightfully** /-fəli/ ***adv.***

'right-hand ***adj.*** (only *before* a noun) of or on the right of sb/sth: *The postbox is on the right-hand side of the road.* ◇ *in the top right-hand corner of the screen*

ˌright-'handed ***adj.*** using the right hand for writing, etc. and not the left

ˌright-hand 'man ***noun*** [sing.] the person you depend on most to help and support you in your work: *the President's right-hand man*

rightly ⊶ /ˈraɪtli/ ***adv.*** correctly or fairly: *He's been sacked and* ***quite rightly****, I believe.*

ˌright of 'way ***noun*** (*pl.* **rights of way**) **1** [C,U] (*especially BrE*) (LAW) a path across private land that the public may use; legal permission to go into or through another person's land: *Walkers have right of way through the farmer's field.* **2** [U] (used in road traffic) the fact that a vehicle in a particular position is allowed to drive into or across a road before another vehicle in a different position: *He should have stopped – I had the right of way.*

ˌright 'triangle ***noun*** [C] (*AmE*) = RIGHT-ANGLED TRIANGLE

ˌright 'wing ***noun*** [sing., with sing. or pl. verb] (POLITICS) the people in a political party who are against social change ▸ **right-wing** ***adj.***: *a right-wing government* OPP **left-wing**

rigid AW /ˈrɪdʒɪd/ ***adj.*** **1** not able or not wanting to change or be changed **2** difficult to bend; stiff: *a rucksack with a rigid frame* ◇ *She was rigid with fear.* ▸ **rigidity** /rɪˈdʒɪdəti/ ***noun*** [U] ▸ **rigidly** ***adv.***: *The speed limit must be rigidly enforced.*

rigor mortis /ˌrɪgə ˈmɔːtɪs/ ***noun*** [U] (HEALTH) the process by which the body becomes difficult to bend or move after death

rigorous /ˈrɪgərəs/ ***adj.*** done very carefully and with great attention to detail: *Rigorous tests are carried out on the drinking water.* ▸ **rigorously** ***adv.***

rigour (*AmE* **rigor**) /ˈrɪgə(r)/ ***noun*** (*formal*) **1** [U] doing sth carefully with great attention to detail: *The tests were carried out with rigour.* **2** [U] the quality of being strict: *the full rigour of the law* **3** [C, usually pl.] difficult conditions

rim /rɪm/ ***noun*** [C] an edge at the top or outside of sth that is round: *the rim of a cup*

rind /raɪnd/ ***noun*** [C,U] the thick hard skin on the outside of some fruits, some types of cheese, meat, etc.

ring¹ ⊶ /rɪŋ/ ***noun*** **1** [C] a piece of jewellery that you wear on your finger: *a gold/diamond/wedding ring* ◇ *an engagement ring* **2** [C] (usually in compound nouns) a round object of any material with a hole in the middle: *curtain rings* ◇ *a key ring* (= for holding keys) **3** [C] a round mark or shape: *The coffee cup left a ring on the table top.* ◇ *Stand in a ring and hold hands.* **4** [C] the space with seats all around it where a performance, BOXING match, etc. takes place: *a circus/boxing ring* **5** (*AmE* **burner**) [C] one of the round parts on the top of an electric or gas cooker on which you can put pans **6** [C] a number of people who are involved in sth that is secret or not legal: *a spy/drugs ring* **7** [C] the sound made by a bell; the action of ringing a bell: *There was a ring at the door.* **8** [sing.] a ~ **of sth** a particular quality that words or sounds have: *What the man said **had a ring of truth** about it* (=sounded true).

IDM **give sb a ring** (*BrE, informal*) to telephone sb: *I'll give you a ring in the morning.*

ring² ⊶ /rɪŋ/ *verb* (*pt* **rang** /ræŋ/; *pp* **rung** /rʌŋ/) **1** [I,T] (*especially AmE* **call**) ~ **(sb/sth) (up)** to telephone sb/sth: *What time will you ring tomorrow?* ◇ *I rang up yesterday and booked the hotel.* ◇ *Ring the station and ask what time the next train leaves.* SYN **phone 2** [I,T] to make a sound like a bell or to cause sth to make this sound: *Is that the phone ringing?* ◇ *We rang the door bell but nobody answered.* **3** [I] ~ **(for sb/sth)** to ring a bell in order to call sb, ask for sth, etc.: *'Did you ring, sir?' asked the stewardess.* ◇ *Could you ring for a taxi, please?* **4** [I] (used about words or sounds) to have a certain effect when you hear them: *Her words didn't **ring true*** (=you felt that you could not believe what she said). **5** [I] ~ **(with sth)** to be filled with loud sounds: *The music was so loud it made my ears ring.* **6** [T] (*pt, pp* **ringed**) (often passive) to surround sb/sth **7** [T] (*AmE* **circle**) (*pt, pp* **ringed**) to draw a circle around sth

IDM **ring a bell** to sound familiar or to remind you, not very clearly, of sb/sth: *'Do you know Chris Oliver?' 'Well, the name rings a bell.'*

PHR V **ring (sb) back** (*BrE*) to telephone sb again or to telephone sb who has telephoned you: *I can't talk now – can I ring you back?*

ring in (*BrE*) to telephone a television or radio show, or the place where you work: *Mandy rang in sick this morning.*

ring out to sound loudly and clearly

'ring binder *noun* [C] a file for holding papers, in which metal rings go through the edges of the pages, holding them in place

ringleader /'rɪŋliːdə(r)/ *noun* [C] a person who leads others in crime or in causing trouble: *The ringleaders were jailed for 15 years.*

'ring pull (*AmE* **'pull tab**) *noun* [C] a small piece of metal with a ring which you pull to open cans of food, drink, etc.

'ring road *noun* [C] (*BrE*) a road that is built all around a town so that traffic does not have to go into the town centre ➲ look at **bypass¹**

ringtone /'rɪŋtəʊn/ *noun* [C] the sound that your telephone (especially a mobile phone) makes when sb is calling you. RINGTONES are often short tunes.

ringworm /'rɪŋwɜːm/ *noun* [U] (HEALTH) a skin disease that produces round red areas, especially on the head or the feet

rink /rɪŋk/ =SKATING RINK

rinse /rɪns/ *verb* [T] to wash sth in water in order to remove soap or dirt: *Rinse your hair thoroughly after each shampoo.* ▶ **rinse** *noun* [C]

riot /'raɪət/ *noun* [C] a situation in which a group of people behave in a violent way in a public place, often as a protest ▶ **riot** *verb* [I]: *There is a danger that the prisoners will riot if conditions do not improve.* ▶ **rioter** *noun* [C]

IDM **run riot 1** to behave in a wild way without any control: *At the end of the football match, the crowd ran riot.* **2** (used about your imagination, feelings, etc.) to allow sth to develop and continue without trying to control it

riotous /'raɪətəs/ *adj.* **1** wild or violent; lacking in control **2** wild and full of fun

RIP /ˌɑːr aɪ 'piː/ *abbr.* (used on graves) rest in peace

rip¹ /rɪp/ *verb* (**ripping**; **ripped**) **1** [I,T] to tear or be torn quickly and suddenly: *Oh no! My dress has ripped!* ◇ *He **ripped** the letter **in half/two** and threw it in the bin.* ◇ *The blast of the bomb ripped the house apart.* **2** [T] to remove sth quickly and violently, often by pulling it: *He ripped the poster from the wall.* **3** [T] (COMPUTING) =RASTERIZE

PHR V **rip through sth** to move very quickly and violently through sth: *The house was badly damaged when fire ripped through the first floor.*

rip sb off (*informal*) to cheat sb by charging too much money for sth

rip sth up to tear sth into small pieces

rip² /rɪp/ *noun* [C] a long tear (in material, etc.)

ripe /raɪp/ *adj.* **1** (AGRICULTURE) (used about fruit, grain, etc.) ready to be picked and eaten **2** ~ **(for sth)** ready for sth or in a suitable state for sth ▶ **ripen** /-ən/ *verb* [I,T]

'rip-off *noun* [C, usually sing.] (*informal*) something that costs a lot more than it should

ripple /'rɪpl/ *noun* [C] **1** a very small wave or movement on the surface of water **2** [usually sing.] **a** ~ **(of sth)** a sound that gradually becomes louder and then quieter again; a feeling that gradually spreads through a person or a group of people: *a ripple of laughter* ▶ **ripple** *verb* [I,T]

rise¹ ⊶ /raɪz/ *noun* **1** [C] **a** ~ **(in sth)** an increase in an amount, a number or a level: *There has been a **sharp rise** in the number of people out of work.* OPP **drop, fall 2** [C] (*AmE* **raise**) (FINANCE) an increase in the money you are paid for the work you do: *I'm hoping to **get a rise** next April.* ◇ *a 10% **pay rise*** **3** [sing.] **the** ~ **(of sth)** the process of becoming more powerful or important: *The rise of fascism in Europe.* ◇ *her meteoric **rise to fame/power***

IDM **give rise to sth** (*formal*) to cause sth to happen or exist

THESAURUS

rise

grow • increase • climb • go up • escalate

These are all words that can be used when an amount, level or number of sth gets bigger or higher.

rise: *We are all concerned by rising divorce rates.*

grow: *There is growing opposition to the latest proposals.*

increase: *The population has increased from 1.2 million to 1.8 million.*

climb: *The temperature has been climbing all week.*

go up (*spoken*): *The price of bread has gone up again.*

escalate (*formal*): *The fighting escalated into a full-scale war.*

rise² ⊶ /raɪz/ *verb* [I] (*pt* **rose** /rəʊz/; *pp* **risen** /'rɪzn/) **1** to move upwards, to become higher, stronger or to increase: *Smoke was rising from the chimney.* ◇ *The temperature has risen to nearly 40°.* OPP **fall 2** (*written*) to get up from a chair, bed, etc.: *The audience rose and applauded the singers.* **3** (used about the sun, moon, etc.) to appear above the HORIZON: *The sun rises in the east and sets in the west.* OPP **set 4** to become more successful, powerful, important, etc.: *He **rose through the ranks** to become managing director.* ◇ *She **rose to power** in the 90s.* **5** to be seen above or higher than sth else **6** to come from: *Shouts of protest rose from the crowd.*

7 ~ **(up)** **(against sb/sth)** to start fighting against your ruler, government, etc. ▶ **rising** ***adj.***: *the rising cost of living ◇ a rising young rock star*

IDM **rise to the occasion, challenge, task, etc.** to show that you are able to deal with a problem, etc. successfully

risk¹ 🔑 /rɪsk/ ***noun*** **1** [C,U] (a) ~ **(of sth/that...)**; (a) ~ **(to sb/sth)** a possibility of sth dangerous or unpleasant happening; a situation that could be dangerous or have a bad result: *Don't **take any risks** when you're driving. ◇ You could drive a car without insurance, but it's **not worth the risk**. ◇ Scientists say these pesticides **pose a risk** to wildlife. ◇ If we don't leave early enough we **run the risk** of missing the plane. ◇ Small children are most **at risk** from the disease.* **2** [sing.] a person or thing that might cause danger: *If he knows your real name he's a security risk.*

IDM **at your own risk** having the responsibility for whatever may happen: *This building is in a dangerous condition – enter at your own risk.*

at the risk of sth/doing sth even though there could be a bad effect: *At the risk of showing my ignorance, how exactly does the Internet work?*

risk² 🔑 /rɪsk/ ***verb*** [T] **1** to take the chance of sth unpleasant happening: *If you don't work hard now you risk failing your exams.* **2** to put sth or yourself in a dangerous position: *The man had to **risk** his **life** to save the little boy.*

risky /ˈrɪski/ ***adj.*** (**riskier**; **riskiest**) involving the possibility of sth bad happening; dangerous

rite /raɪt/ ***noun*** [C] (RELIGION) a ceremony performed by a particular group of people, often for religious purposes

ritual /ˈrɪtʃuəl/ ***noun*** [C,U] (RELIGION) an action, ceremony or process which is always done the same way: *(a) religious ritual* ▶ **ritual** ***adj.*** ▶ **ritually** ***adv.***

rival¹ 🔑 /ˈraɪvl/ ***noun*** [C] a person, company, or thing that competes with another in sport, business, etc.: *It seems that we're rivals for the sales manager's job. ◇ The two teams have always been rivals.*

rival² 🔑 /ˈraɪvl/ ***verb*** [T] (**rivalling**; **rivalled**: *AmE* **rivaling**; **rivaled**) ~ **sb/sth (for/in sth)** to be as good as sb/sth: *Nothing rivals skiing for sheer excitement.*

rivalry /ˈraɪvlri/ ***noun*** [C,U] (*pl.* **rivalries**) ~ **(with sb)**; ~ **(between A and B)** competition between people, groups, etc.: *There was a lot of rivalry between the sisters.*

river 🔑 /ˈrɪvə(r)/ ***noun*** [C] (GEOGRAPHY) a large, natural flow of water that goes across land and into the sea: *the River Nile ◇ He sat down on the bank of the river to fish.* ❶ A river **flows** into the sea. Where it joins the sea is the river **mouth**. A boat sails **on** the river. We walk, sail, etc. **up** or **down river**.

riverbank /ˈrɪvəbæŋk/ ***noun*** [C] (GEOGRAPHY) the ground at the side of a river: *on the riverbank*

ˈriver bed ***noun*** [C] (GEOGRAPHY) the area of ground over which a river usually flows: *a dried-up river bed*

riverside /ˈrɪvəsaɪd/ ***noun*** [sing.] (GEOGRAPHY) the land next to a river: *a riverside hotel*

rivet¹ /ˈrɪvɪt/ ***noun*** [C] a metal pin for fastening two pieces of metal together

rivet² /ˈrɪvɪt/ ***verb*** [T] **1** (usually passive) to keep sb very interested: *I was riveted by her story.* **2** to fasten sth with RIVETS: *The steel plates were riveted together.*

rm ***abbr.*** room

RNA /ˌɑːr en ˈeɪ/ ***noun*** [U] (BIOLOGY) a chemical present in all living cells; like ➲ note at **DNA** it is a type of NUCLEIC ACID

roach /rəʊtʃ/ (*AmE*) = COCKROACH

road 🔑 /rəʊd/ ***noun*** **1** [C] a way between places, with a hard surface which cars, buses, etc. can drive along: *Turn left off the **main road**. ◇ road signs* **2 Road** (*abbr.* **Rd**) [sing.] used in names of roads, especially in towns: *60 Marylebone Road, London*

IDM **by road** in a car, bus, etc.: *It's going to be a terrible journey by road – let's take the train.*

on the road travelling: *We were on the road for 14 hours.*

roadblock /ˈrəʊdblɒk/ ***noun*** [C] a barrier put across a road by the police or army to stop traffic

ˈroad rage ***noun*** [U] a situation in which a driver becomes extremely angry or violent with the driver of another car because of the way they are driving

roadside /ˈrəʊdsaɪd/ ***noun*** [C, usually sing.] the edge of a road: *a roadside cafe*

ˈroad sign ***noun*** [C] a sign near a road giving information or instructions to drivers

ˈroad tax ***noun*** [C,U] (*BrE*) a tax which the owner of a vehicle has to pay to be allowed to drive it on public roads

the roadway /ˈrəʊdweɪ/ ***noun*** [sing.] the part of the road used by cars, etc.; not the side of the road

roadworks /ˈrəʊdwɜːks/ ***noun*** [pl.] work that involves repairing or building roads

roadworthy /ˈrəʊdwɜːði/ ***adj.*** (used about a vehicle) in good enough condition to be driven on the road ▶ **roadworthiness** ***noun*** [U]

roam /rəʊm/ ***verb*** [I,T] to walk or travel with no particular plan or aim: *Gangs of youths were roaming the streets looking for trouble.*

roaming /ˈrəʊmɪŋ/ ***noun*** [U] the process by which a mobile phone connects to a different company's network, for example when you are in a different country: *international roaming charges*

roar /rɔː(r)/ ***verb*** **1** [I] to make a loud, deep sound: *She **roared with laughter** at the joke. ◇ The lion opened its huge mouth and roared.* **2** [I,T] to shout sth very loudly **3** [I] ~ **along, down, past, etc.** to move in the direction mentioned, making a loud, deep sound: *A motorbike roared past us.* ▶ **roar** ***noun*** [C]: *the roar of heavy traffic on the motorway ◇ roars of laughter*

roaring /ˈrɔːrɪŋ/ ***adj.*** **1** making a very loud noise **2** (used about a fire) burning very well **3** very great: *a roaring success*

roast¹ /rəʊst/ ***verb*** **1** [I,T] to cook or be cooked in an oven or over a fire: *a smell of roasting meat ◇ to roast a chicken* ➲ note at **cook** **2** [T] to heat and dry sth: *roasted peanuts* ▶ **roast** ***adj.*** (only *before* a noun): *roast beef/potatoes/chestnuts*

roast² /rəʊst/ ***noun*** **1** [C,U] a piece of meat that has been cooked in an oven **2** [C] (*especially AmE*) an outdoor meal at which food is cooked over a fire ➲ look at **barbecue**

rob 🔑 /rɒb/ ***verb*** [T] (**robbing**; **robbed**) ~ **sb/sth (of sth)** **1** (LAW) to take money, property, etc. from a person or place illegally: *to rob a bank* **2** to take sth away from sb/sth that they or it should have: *His illness robbed him of the chance to play for his country.*

robber /ˈrɒbə(r)/ ***noun*** [C] (LAW) a person who steals from a place or a person, especially using violence or threats ➲ note at **thief**

robbery /ˈrɒbəri/ ***noun*** [C,U] (*pl.* **robberies**) (LAW) the crime of stealing from a place or a person, especially using violence or threats: *They were found guilty of **armed robbery*** (=using a weapon).

robe /rəʊb/ ***noun*** [C] **1** a long, loose piece of clothing, especially one worn at ceremonies **2** (*AmE*) =DRESSING GOWN

robin /ˈrɒbɪn/ ***noun*** [C] a small brown bird with a bright red chest

robot /ˈrəʊbɒt/ ***noun*** [C] a machine that works automatically and can do some tasks that a human can do: *These cars are built by robots.*

robust /rəʊˈbʌst/ ***adj.*** strong and healthy

rock[1] /rɒk/ ***noun*** **1** [U] (GEOGRAPHY, GEOLOGY) the hard, solid material that forms part of the surface of the earth: *layers of rock formed over millions of years* **2** [C, usually pl.] (GEOGRAPHY) a large mass of rock that sticks out of the sea or the ground: *The ship hit the rocks and started to sink.* **3** [C] a single large piece of rock: *The beach was covered with rocks that had broken away from the cliffs.* **4** [C] (*AmE*) a small piece of rock that can be picked up; a stone: *The boy threw a rock at the dog.* **5** (*also* ˈ**rock music**) [U] (MUSIC) a type of pop music with a very strong beat, played on electric GUITARS, etc.: *I prefer jazz to rock.* ◇ *a rock singer/band* ➲ look at **classical**, **jazz**, **pop** **6** [U] (*BrE*) a type of hard sweet made in long, round sticks

IDM **on the rocks 1** (used about a marriage, business, etc.) having problems and likely to fail **2** (used about drinks) served with ice but no water: *whisky on the rocks*

rock[2] /rɒk/ ***verb*** **1** [I,T] to move backwards and forwards or from side to side; to make sb/sth do this: *boats rocking gently on the waves* ◇ *He rocked the baby in his arms to get her to sleep.* **2** [T] to shake sth violently: *The city was rocked by a bomb blast.* **3** [T] to shock sb

IDM **rock the boat** to do sth that causes problems or upsets people

ˌ**rock and** ˈ**roll** (*also* **rock 'n' roll**) ***noun*** [U] (MUSIC) a type of music with a strong beat that was most popular in the 1950s

ˌ**rock** ˈ**bottom** ***noun*** [U] the lowest point: *He **hit rock bottom** when he lost his job and his wife left him.* ◇ *rock-bottom prices*

ˈ**rock climbing** ***noun*** [U] (SPORT) the sport of climbing rocks and mountains with ropes, etc.

rocket[1] /ˈrɒkɪt/ ***noun*** [C] **1** (ASTRONOMY) a vehicle that is used for travel into space: *a space rocket* ◇ *to launch a rocket* **2** a weapon that travels through the air and that carries a bomb SYN **missile** **3** a FIREWORK that shoots high into the air and explodes in a beautiful way

rocket[2] /ˈrɒkɪt/ ***verb*** [I] to increase or rise very quickly: *Prices have rocketed recently.*

rocky /ˈrɒki/ ***adj.*** covered with or made of rocks: *a rocky road/coastline*

rococo (also **Rococo**) /rəˈkəʊkəʊ/ ***adj.*** (ARCHITECTURE, ARTS AND MEDIA) used to describe a style of ARCHITECTURE, furniture, etc. that has a lot of decoration, especially in the shape of curls; used to describe a style of literature or music that has a lot of detail and decoration. The **rococo** style was popular in the 18th century.

rod /rɒd/ ***noun*** [C] (often in compounds) a thin straight piece of wood, metal, etc.: *a fishing rod* ➲ picture at **laboratory**

rode past tense of **ride[1]**

rodent /ˈrəʊdnt/ ***noun*** [C] a type of small animal, with strong sharp front teeth. Mice and RATS are **rodents**.

rodeo /ˈrəʊdiəʊ; rəʊˈdeɪəʊ/ ***noun*** [C] (*pl.* **rodeos**) a competition or performance in which people show their skill in riding wild horses, catching cows, etc.

roe /rəʊ/ ***noun*** [U,C] the mass of eggs inside a female fish, used as food

rogue /rəʊg/ ***adj.*** (only *before* a noun) behaving differently from other similar people or things, often causing damage: *a rogue gene/program*

role AW /rəʊl/ ***noun*** [C] **1** the position or function of sb/sth in a particular situation: *Parents **play a** vital **role** in their children's education.* **2** a person's part in a play, film, etc.: *She was chosen to **play the role** of Cleopatra.* ◇ *a **leading role** in the film*

ˈ**role-play** ***noun*** [C,U] an activity, used especially in teaching, in which a person acts a part

the rock cycle

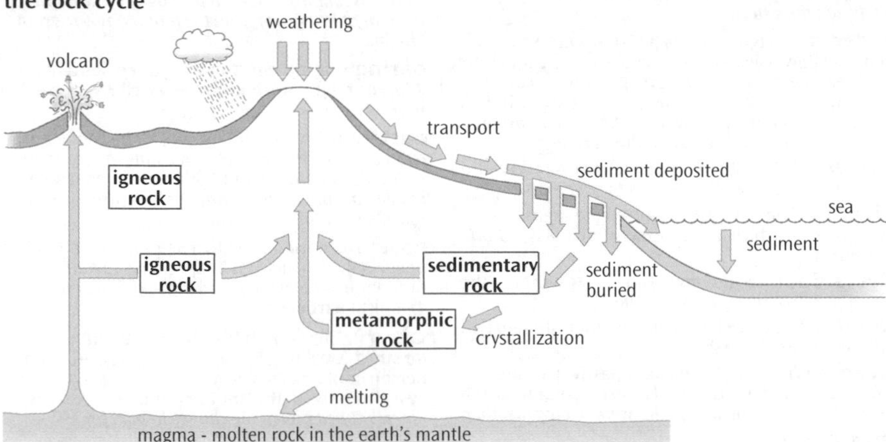

roll[1] 🔑 /rəʊl/ ***noun*** [C] **1** something made into the shape of a tube by turning it round and round itself: *a roll of film/wallpaper* **2** bread baked in a round shape for one person to eat **3** moving or making sth move by turning over and over: *Everything depended on one roll of the dice.* **4** an official list of names: *the electoral roll* (= the list of people who can vote in an election) **5** a long, low sound: *a roll of drums* **6** a movement from side to side

roll[2] 🔑 /rəʊl/ ***verb*** **1** [I,T] to move by turning over and over; to make sth move in this way: *The apples fell out of the bag and rolled everywhere.* ◇ *Delivery men were rolling barrels across the yard.* **2** [I] to move smoothly, often on wheels: *The car began to roll back down the hill.* ◇ *Tears were rolling down her cheeks.* **3** [I,T] ~ **(sth) (over)** to turn over and over; to make sth do this: *The horse was rolling in the dirt.* ◇ *The car rolled over in the crash.* ◇ *We rolled the log over to see what was underneath.* **4** [I,T] ~ **(sth) (up)** to make sth into the shape of a ball or tube: *He was rolling himself a cigarette.* ◇ *The insect rolled up when I touched it.* OPP **unroll** **5** [T] ~ **sth (out)** to make sth become flat by moving sth heavy over it: *Roll out the pastry thinly.* **6** [I] to move from side to side: *The ship began to roll in the storm.*

IDM **be rolling in money/in it** (*slang*) to have a lot of money

PHR V **roll in** (*informal*) to arrive in large numbers or amounts: *Offers of help have been rolling in.*

roll up (*informal*) (used about a person or a vehicle) to arrive, especially late

roller /ˈrəʊlə(r)/ ***noun*** [C] **1** a piece of equipment or part of a machine that is shaped like a tube and used, for example, to make sth flat or to help sth move: *a roller blind on a window* **2** [usually pl.] a small plastic tube that you roll hair around in order to make the hair curly

Rollerblade™ /ˈrəʊləbleɪd/ ***noun*** [C] a boot with one row of narrow wheels on the bottom: *a pair of Rollerblades* ▶ **rollerblade** ***verb*** [I] ▶ **rollerblading** ***noun*** [U]

ˈroller coaster ***noun*** [C] a narrow metal track at a FAIRGROUND that goes up and down and round tight bends, and that people ride on in a special vehicle for fun

ˈroller skate (*also* **skate**) ***noun*** [C] a type of shoe with small wheels on the bottom: *a pair of roller skates* ▶ **ˈroller skate** ***verb*** [I] ▶ **ˈroller skating** ***noun*** [U]

rolling /ˈrəʊlɪŋ/ ***adj.*** (only *before* a noun) **1** (used about hills or the countryside) having gentle slopes **2** done in regular stages or at regular intervals over a period of time: *a rolling programme of reform*

ˈrolling pin ***noun*** [C] a piece of wood, etc. in the shape of a tube, that you use for making PASTRY flat and thin before cooking

ROM /rɒm/ ***noun*** [U] (**COMPUTING**) **read-only memory**; computer memory that contains instructions or data that cannot be changed or removed ➲ look at **CD-ROM**

Roman /ˈrəʊmən/ ***adj.*** **1** (**HISTORY**) connected with ancient Rome or the Roman Empire: *Roman coins* ◇ *the Roman invasion of Britain* **2** **roman** ordinary printing type which does not lean forward: *Definitions in this dictionary are printed in roman type.* ➲ look at **italic** **3** connected with the modern city of Rome ▶ **Roman** ***noun*** [C]

the ˌRoman ˈalphabet ***noun*** [sing.] (**LANGUAGE**) the letters A to Z, used especially in Western European languages

ˌRoman ˈCatholic (*also* **Catholic**) ***noun*** [C], ***adj.*** (**RELIGION**) (a member) of the Christian Church which has the Pope as its head: *She's (a) Roman Catholic.* ➲ look at **Protestant**

ˌRoman Caˈtholicism (*also* **Catholicism**) ***noun*** [U] (**RELIGION**) the beliefs of the Roman Catholic Church

Romance /rəʊˈmæns; ˈrəʊmæns/ ***adj.*** (**LANGUAGE**) **Romance** languages, such as French, Italian and Spanish, are languages that developed from Latin

romance /rəʊˈmæns/ ***noun*** **1** [C] a love affair: *The film was about a teenage romance.* **2** [U] a feeling or atmosphere of love or of sth new, special and exciting **3** [C] (**LITERATURE**) a novel about a love affair: *historical romances*

Romanesque /ˌrəʊməˈnesk/ ***adj.*** (**ARCHITECTURE**) used to describe a style of building that was popular in western Europe from the 10th to the 12th centuries and that had round ARCHES, thick walls and tall PILLARS ➲ look at **Norman**

ˌRoman ˈnumeral ***noun*** [C] (**HISTORY**, **MATHEMATICS**) one of the letters used by the ancient Romans to represent numbers and still used today, in some situations. In this system I = 1, V = 5, X = 10, L = 50, C = 100, D = 500, M = 1000 and these letters are used in combinations to form other numbers: *Henry VIII*

romantic[1] 🔑 /rəʊˈmæntɪk/ ***adj.*** **1** having a quality that strongly affects your emotions or makes you think about love; showing feelings of love: *a romantic candlelit dinner* ◇ *He isn't very romantic – he never says he loves me.* **2** involving a love affair: *Reports of a romantic relationship between the two film stars have been strongly denied.* **3** having or showing ideas about life that are emotional rather than real or practical: *He has a romantic idea that he'd like to live on a farm in Scotland.* ▶ **romantically** /-kli/ ***adv.***

romantic[2] /rəʊˈmæntɪk/ ***noun*** [C] a person who has ideas that are not based on real life or that are not very practical

romanticism /rəʊˈmæntɪsɪzəm/ ***noun*** [U] (**ARTS AND MEDIA**) (also **Romanticism**) a style and movement in art, music and literature in the late 18th and early 19th century, in which strong feelings, imagination and a return to nature were more important than reason, order and INTELLECTUAL ideas ➲ look at **realism**

romanticize (also **-ise**) /rəʊˈmæntɪsaɪz/ ***verb*** [I,T] to make sth seem more interesting, exciting, etc. than it really is

romp /rɒmp/ ***verb*** [I] (used about children and animals) to play in a happy and noisy way ▶ **romp** ***noun*** [C]

IDM **romp home/to victory** to win easily: *United romped to a 4-0 victory over Juventus.*

rondo /ˈrɒndəʊ/ ***noun*** [C] (*pl.* **rondos**) (**MUSIC**) a piece of music in which the main tune is repeated several times, sometimes forming part of a longer piece

roof 🔑 /ruːf/ ***noun*** [C] (*pl.* **roofs**) **1** (**ARCHITECTURE**) the part of a building, vehicle, etc. which covers the top of it: *a flat/sloping/tiled roof* ◇ *the roof of a car* ◇ *The library and the sports hall are* ***under one roof*** (= in the same building). **2** the highest part of the inside of sth: *The roof of the cave had collapsed.* ◇ *The soup burned the roof of my mouth.*

IDM **a roof over your head** somewhere to live: *I might not have any money, but at least I've got a roof over my head.*

'roof rack *noun* [C] a structure that you fix to the roof of a car and use for carrying luggage or other large objects

rooftop /'ru:ftɒp/ *noun* [C, usually pl.] the outside of the roofs of buildings: *From the tower we looked down over the rooftops of the city.*

room ⊶ /ru:m; rʊm/ *noun* **1** [C] a part of a house or building that has its own walls, floor and ceiling: *a sitting/dining/living room* ◇ *I sat down in the waiting room until the doctor called me.* ◇ *I'd like to book a double room for two nights.* **2** [U] ~ (**for sb/ sth**); ~ (**to do sth**) space; enough space: *These chairs **take up** too much **room**.* ◇ *How can we **make room** for all the furniture?* ◇ *There were so many people that there wasn't any room to move.* ➲ look at **space 3** [U] ~ for sth the opportunity or need for sth: *There's **room for improvement** in your work* (=it could be much better). ◇ *The lack of time gives us very little **room for manoeuvre**.*

roomful /'ru:mfʊl; 'rʊm-/ *noun* [C] a large number of people or things in a room

'room-mate *noun* **1** a person that you share a room with, especially at a college or university **2** (also *informal* **roomie**) (*AmE*) = FLATMATE

'room service *noun* [U] (TOURISM) a service provided in a hotel, by which guests can order food and drink to be brought to their rooms: *He ordered coffee from room service.*

'room temperature *noun* [U] the normal temperature inside a building: *Serve the wine **at room temperature**.*

roomy /'ru:mi/ *adj.* (**roomier**; **roomiest**) having plenty of space: *a roomy house/car*

roost /ru:st/ *noun* [C] a place where birds rest or sleep ▶ **roost** *verb* [I]

rooster /'ru:stə(r)/ (*AmE*) = COCK[1] (1)

root[1] ⊶ /ru:t/ *noun* **1** [C] the part of a plant that grows under the ground and takes in water and food from the soil: *The deep roots of these trees can cause damage to buildings.* ◇ ***root vegetables** such as carrots and parsnips* ➲ picture at **flower 2** [C] the part of a hair or tooth that is under the skin and that holds it in place on the body **3 roots** [pl.] the feelings or connections that you have with a place because you have lived there or your family came from there: *She's proud of her Italian roots.* **4** [C] the basic cause or origin of sth: *Let's try and get to the **root of the problem**.* ➲ look at **square root**

root[2] /ru:t/ *verb*

PHR V **root about/around (for sth)** to search for sth by moving things: *What are you rooting around in my desk for?*

root for sb to give support to sb who is in a competition, etc.

root sth out to find sth bad and destroy it completely

rope[1] ⊶ /rəʊp/ *noun* [C,U] very thick, strong string that is used for tying or lifting heavy things, climbing up, etc.: *We need some rope to tie up the boat with.*

IDM **show sb/know/learn the ropes** to show sb/ know/learn how a job should be done

rope[2] /rəʊp/ *verb* [T] ~ **A to B**; ~ **A and B together** to tie sb/sth with a rope

PHR V **rope sb in (to do sth)** (*informal*) to persuade sb to help in an activity, especially when they do not want to

rope sth off to put ropes round or across an area in order to keep people out of it

rosary /'rəʊzəri/ *noun* [C] (*pl.* **rosaries**) (RELIGION) a string of small round pieces of wood, etc. used by some Roman Catholics for counting prayers

rose[1] past tense of **rise**[2]

rose[2] /rəʊz/ *noun* [C] a flower with a sweet smell, that grows on a bush that usually has sharp points (**thorns**) growing on it

rosé /'rəʊzeɪ/ *noun* [U] pink wine

rosebud /'rəʊzbʌd/ *noun* [C] the flower of a ROSE before it is open

rosemary /'rəʊzməri/ *noun* [U] a plant with small narrow leaves that have a sweet smell and are used in cooking as a HERB

rosette /rəʊ'zet/ *noun* [C] a decoration made from long pieces of coloured material (**ribbons**) that you wear on your clothes. **Rosettes** are given as prizes or worn to show that sb supports a particular political party.

roster /'rɒstə(r)/ (*especially AmE*) = ROTA

rostrum /'rɒstrəm/ *noun* [C] a platform that sb stands on to make a public speech, etc.

rosy /'rəʊzi/ *adj.* (**rosier**; **rosiest**) **1** pink and pleasant in appearance: *rosy cheeks* **2** full of good possibilities: *The future was looking rosy.*

rot /rɒt/ *verb* [I,T] (**rotting**; **rotted**) to go bad or make sth go bad as part of a natural process: *Too many sweets will rot your teeth!* SYN **decay** ▶ **rot** *noun* [U]

rota /'rəʊtə/ (*AmE also* **roster**) *noun* [C] a list of people who share a certain job or task and the times that they are each going to do it: *We organize the cleaning **on a rota**.*

rotary /'rəʊtəri/ *adj.* moving in circles around a central point

rotate /rəʊ'teɪt/ *verb* [I,T] **1** to turn in circles round a central point; to make sth do this: *The earth rotates on its axis.* **2** to happen in turn or in a particular order; to make sth do this: *We rotate the duties so that nobody is stuck with a job they don't like.*

rotation /rəʊ'teɪʃn/ *noun* [C,U] **1** movement in circles around a central point: *one rotation every 24 hours* **2** the act of regularly changing the thing that is being used in a particular situation, or of changing the person who does a particular job: *The company is chaired by all the members **in rotation**.* ➲ look at **crop rotation**

rotor /'rəʊtə(r)/ *noun* [C] (TECHNICAL) a part of a machine that turns around a central point: *rotor blades on a helicopter*

rotten /'rɒtn/ *adj.* **1** (used about food and other substances) old and not fresh enough or good enough to use: *rotten vegetables* **2** (*informal*) very unpleasant: *That was a rotten thing to say!* **3** (*spoken*) used to emphasize that you are angry: *You can keep your rotten job!*

rouge /ru:ʒ/ *noun* [U] (*old-fashioned*) a red powder or cream used for giving more colour to the cheeks ➲ look at **blusher**

rough[1] ⊶ /rʌf/ *adj.* **1** not smooth, soft or level: *rough ground* **2** violent; not calm or gentle: *You can hold the baby, but don't be rough with him.* ◇ *The sea was rough and half the people on the boat were seasick.* **3** made or done quickly or without much care; approximate: *a rough estimate* ◇ *Can you give me a rough idea of what time you'll be arriving?* **4** (*informal*) looking or feeling ill: *You look a bit*

rough – are you feeling all right? ▶ **roughness** *noun* [U]
IDM **be rough (on sb)** be unpleasant or bad luck for sb

rough² /rʌf/ *noun*
IDM **in rough** done quickly without worrying about mistakes, as a preparation for the finished piece of work or drawing
take the rough with the smooth to accept difficult or unpleasant things in addition to pleasant things

rough³ /rʌf/ *adv.* in a rough way: *One of the boys was told off for playing rough.*
IDM **live/sleep rough** to live or sleep outdoors, usually because you have no home or money

rough⁴ /rʌf/ *verb*
IDM **rough it** to live without all the comfortable things that you usually have: *You have to rough it a bit when you go camping.*

roughage /ˈrʌfɪdʒ/ *noun* [U] the types or parts of food that help food to pass through your body

roughen /ˈrʌfn/ *verb* [T] to make sth less smooth or soft

roughly ⊶ /ˈrʌfli/ *adv.* **1** in a violent way; not gently: *He grabbed her roughly by her arm.* **2** not exactly; approximately: *It took roughly three hours, I suppose.*

roulette /ruːˈlet/ *noun* [U] a game in which a ball is dropped onto a moving wheel that has holes with numbers on them. The players bet on which hole the ball will be in when the wheel stops.

round¹ ⊶ /raʊnd/ *adj.* having the shape of a circle or a ball: *a round table*
IDM **in round figures/numbers** given to the nearest 10, 100, 1000, etc.; not given in exact numbers

round² ⊶ /raʊnd/ *adv., prep.* **1** in a circle or curve; on all sides of sth: *He had a bandage right round his head.* ◇ *We sat round the table, talking late into the night.* ◇ *We were just talking about Ravi and he came* ***round the corner****.* ◇ *How long would it take to walk round the world?* ◇ *(figurative) It wasn't easy to see a way round the problem* (= a way of solving it). **2** in a full circle: *The wheels spun* ***round and round*** *but the car wouldn't move.* **3** turning to look or go in the opposite direction: *Don't* ***look round*** *but the teacher's just come in.* ◇ *She* ***turned*** *the car* ***round*** *and drove off.* **4** from one place, person, etc. to another: *Pass the photographs* ***round*** *for everyone to see.* ◇ *I've been rushing round all day.* **5** in or to a particular area or place: *Do you live round here?* ◇ *I'll come round to see you at about 8 o'clock.* **6** in or to many parts of sth: *Let me* ***show you round*** *the house.* ◇ *He spent six months travelling round Europe.*
IDM **round about (sth)** in the area near a place; approximately: *We hope to arrive round about 6.*
the other way round in the opposite way or order: *My appointment's at 3 and Lella's is at 3.15 – or was it the other way round?*

round³ ⊶ /raʊnd/ *noun* [C] **1** a number or series of events, etc.: *a further round of talks with other European countries* **2** a regular series of visits, etc., often as part of a job: *The postman's round takes him about three hours.* ◇ *Dr Adamou is on his daily round of the wards.* **3** a number of drinks (one for all the people in a group): *It's my round* (= it's my turn to buy the drinks). **4** (SPORT) one part of a game or competition: *Parma will play Real Madrid in the next round.* **5** (SPORT) (in GOLF) one game, usually of 18 holes: *to play a round of golf* **6** a bullet or a number of bullets, fired from a gun: *He fired several rounds at us.* **7** a short, sudden period of loud noise: *The last speaker got the biggest* ***round of applause****.* **8** (MUSIC) a song for two or more voices in which each sings the same tune but starts at a different time

round⁴ /raʊnd/ *verb* [T] to go around sth: *The police car rounded the corner at high speed.*
PHR V **round sth off** to do sth that completes a job or an activity: *We rounded off the meal with coffee and chocolates.*
round sb/sth up to bring sb/sth together in one place: *The teacher rounded up the children.*
round sth up/down to increase/decrease a number, price, etc. to the nearest whole number

roundabout¹ /ˈraʊndəbaʊt/ *noun* [C] **1** a circle where several roads meet, that all the traffic has to go round in the same direction **2** a round platform made for children to play on. They sit or stand on it and sb pushes it round. **3** = MERRY-GO-ROUND

roundabout² /ˈraʊndəbaʊt/ *adj.* longer than is necessary or usual; not direct: *We got lost and came by a rather roundabout route.*

rounders /ˈraʊndəz/ *noun* [U] (SPORT) a British game that is similar to BASEBALL

ˌround ˈtrip *noun* [C] **1** a journey to a place and back again: *It's a four-mile round trip to the centre of town.* **2** (*AmE*) = RETURN² (5)

ˈround window *noun* [C] (ANATOMY) an opening covered by a MEMBRANE (= a thin layer of skin) between the middle ear and the inner ear ➲ look at **oval window** ➲ picture at **ear**

roundworm /ˈraʊndwɜːm/ *noun* [C] a WORM (= a small creature with a soft body and no legs) that lives inside the bodies of pigs, humans and some other animals

rouse /raʊz/ *verb* [T] **1** (*formal*) to make sb wake up: *She was sleeping so soundly that I couldn't rouse her.* **2** to make sb/sth very angry, excited, interested, etc.

rousing /ˈraʊzɪŋ/ *adj.* exciting and powerful: *a rousing speech*

rout /raʊt/ *verb* [T] to defeat sb completely ▶ **rout** *noun* [C]

route ⊶ AW /ruːt/ *noun* [C] **1 a ~ (from A) (to B)** a way from one place to another: *What is the most direct route from Bordeaux to Lyon?* ◇ *I got a leaflet about the bus routes from the information office.* **2 a ~ to sth** a way of achieving sth: *Hard work is the only route to success.* **3** used before the number of a main road in the US: *Route 66* ▶ **route** *verb* [T] (*pres. part.* **routing** or **routeing**; *pt, pp* **routed**): *Satellites route data all over the globe.*

router /ˈruːtə(r) (*AmE also* ˈraʊt-)/ *noun* [C] (COMPUTING) a device which sends data to the appropriate parts of a computer network

routine¹ ⊶ /ruːˈtiːn/ *noun* **1** [C,U] the usual order and way in which you regularly do things: *Make exercise part of your daily routine.* **2** [U] tasks that have to be done again and again and so are boring **3** [C] a series of movements, jokes, etc. that are part of a performance: *a dance/comedy routine* **4** [C] (COMPUTING) a list of instructions that make a computer able to perform a particular task

routine² ⊶ /ruːˈtiːn/ *adj.* **1** normal and regular; not unusual or special: *The police would like to ask you some routine questions.* **2** boring; not exciting: *It's a very routine job, really.*

routinely /ruːˈtiːnli/ *adv.* regularly; as part of a routine: *The machines are routinely checked every two months.*

row¹ 🔑 /rəʊ/ *noun* [C] **1** a line of people or things: *a row of books* ◇ *The children were all standing* ***in a row*** *at the front of the class.* **2** a line of seats in a theatre, cinema, etc.: *Our seats were in the back row.* ◇ *a front-row seat*

IDM **in a row** one after another; without a break: *It rained solidly for four days in a row.*

row² /rəʊ/ *verb* **1** [I,T] (SPORT) to move a boat through the water using OARS (=poles with flat ends): *We often* ***go rowing*** *on the lake.* **2** [T] to carry sb/sth in a boat that you row: *Could you row us over to the island?* ➲ look at **paddle** ▶ **row** *noun* [sing.]

row³ /raʊ/ *noun* **1** [C] a ~ **(about/over sth)** a noisy argument or serious disagreement between two or more people, groups, etc.: *When I* ***have a row*** *with my girlfriend, I always try to make up as soon as possible.* ◇ *A row has broken out between the main parties over education.* **2** [sing.] a loud noise: *What a row! Could you be a bit quieter?* ▶ **row** *verb* [I] ~ **(with sb) (about/over sth)**: *Pete and I are always rowing about money!*

rowdy /ˈraʊdi/ *adj.* noisy and likely to cause trouble: *a rowdy group of football fans* ◇ *rowdy behaviour* ▶ **rowdily** *adv.* ▶ **rowdiness** *noun* [U]

ˈrowing boat (*AmE* **rowboat** /ˈrəʊbəʊt/) *noun* [C] a small boat that you move through the water using OARS (=poles with flat ends)

royal 🔑 /ˈrɔɪəl/ *adj.* (POLITICS) **1** connected with a king or queen or a member of their family: *the royal family* **2** (used in the names of organizations) supported by a member of the royal family

▶ **royal** *noun* [C] (*informal*): *the Queen, the Princes and other royals*

ˌRoyal ˈHighness *noun* [C] **His/Her/Your Royal Highness** used when you are speaking to or about a member of the royal family

royalty /ˈrɔɪəlti/ *noun* (*pl.* **royalties**) **1** [U] members of the royal family **2** [C] (ARTS AND MEDIA, MUSIC, LITERATURE) an amount of money that is paid to the person who wrote a book, piece of music, etc. every time their work is sold or performed: *The author earns a 2% royalty on each copy sold.*

RP /ˌɑː ˈpiː/ *noun* [U] (LANGUAGE) received pronunciation; the standard form of British pronunciation

rpm /ˌɑː piː ˈem/ *abbr.* (PHYSICS) revolutions per minute: *an engine speed of 2500 rpm*

RSI /ˌɑːr es ˈaɪ/ *noun* [U] (HEALTH) repetitive strain injury; pain and swelling, especially in the wrists and hands, caused by doing the same movement many times in a job or an activity

RSVP /ˌɑːr es viː ˈpiː/ *abbr.* (used on invitations) please reply

Rt Hon *abbr.* (POLITICS) Right Honourable: a title used in Britain for Cabinet ministers in the government and some other people in important positions

rub 🔑 /rʌb/ *verb* (**rubbing**; **rubbed**) **1** [I,T] to move your hand, a cloth, etc. backwards and forwards on the surface of sth while pressing firmly: *Ralph rubbed his hands together to keep them warm.* ◇ *The cat rubbed against my leg.* **2** [T] ~ **sth in (to sth)** to put a cream, liquid, etc. onto a surface by rubbing: *Apply a little of the lotion and rub it into the skin.* **3** [I,T] ~ **(on/against sth)** to press on/against sth, often causing pain or damage: *These new shoes are rubbing my heels.* ▶ **rub** *noun* [C]

IDM **rub salt into the wound/sb's wounds** to make a situation that makes sb feel bad even worse

rub shoulders with sb to meet and spend time with famous people: *As a journalist you rub shoulders with the rich and famous.*

PHR V **rub it in** to remind sb of sth embarrassing that they want to forget: *I know it was a stupid mistake, but there's no need to rub it in!*

rub off (on/onto sb) (used about a good quality) to be passed from one person to another: *Let's hope some of her enthusiasm rubs off onto her brother.*

rub sth off (sth) to remove sth from a surface by rubbing: *He rubbed the dirt off his boots.*

rub sth out to remove the marks made by a pencil, CHALK, etc. using a rubber, cloth, etc.: *That answer is wrong. Rub it out.*

rubber 🔑 /ˈrʌbə(r)/ *noun* **1** [U] a strong substance that can be stretched and does not allow water to pass through it, used for making tyres, boots, etc. **Rubber** is made from the juice of a tropical tree or is produced using chemicals: *a rubber ball* ◇ *rubber gloves* ◇ *foam rubber* **2** [C] (*especially AmE* **eraser**) a small piece of rubber that you use for removing pencil marks from paper; soft material used for removing CHALK marks or pen marks from a board

ˌrubber ˈband (*also* **eˌlastic ˈband**) *noun* [C] a thin circular piece of rubber that is used for holding things together: *Her hair was tied back with a rubber band.*

ˌrubber ˈstamp *noun* [C] **1** a small tool that you hold in your hand and use for printing the date, the name of an organization, etc. on a document **2** a person or group who gives official approval to sth without thinking about it first ▶ **ˌrubber-ˈstamp** *verb* [T]: *The committee have no real power – they just rubber-stamp the chairman's ideas.*

rubbery /ˈrʌbəri/ *adj.* like rubber: *This meat is rubbery.*

rubbish 🔑 /ˈrʌbɪʃ/ (*AmE* **garbage**; **trash**) *noun* [U] **1** things that you do not want any more; waste material: *The dustmen collect the rubbish every Monday.* ◇ *a rubbish bin* ◇ *It's only rubbish – throw it away.* ➲ look at **waste** **2** something that you think is bad, silly or wrong: *I thought that film was absolute rubbish.* ◇ *Don't talk such rubbish.*

ˈrubbish tip = TIP¹ (4)

rubble /ˈrʌbl/ *noun* [U] pieces of broken brick, stone, etc., especially from a damaged building

rubella /ruːˈbelə/ = GERMAN MEASLES

rubidium /rʊˈbɪdiəm/ *noun* [U] (*symbol* **Rb**) (CHEMISTRY) a chemical element. **Rubidium** is a rare soft silver-coloured metal that reacts strongly with water and burns when it is brought into contact with air. ❶ For more information on the periodic table of elements, look at pages R34-5.

rubric /ˈruːbrɪk/ *noun* [C] (*formal*) a title or set of instructions written in a book, an exam paper, etc.

ruby /ˈruːbi/ *noun* [C] (*pl.* **rubies**) a type of PRECIOUS STONE that is red

ˌruby ˈwedding *noun* [C] the 40th anniversary of a wedding ➲ look at **diamond wedding**, **golden wedding**, **silver wedding**

rucksack /ˈrʌksæk/ *noun* [C] (*BrE*) a bag that you use for carrying things on your back SYN **backpack**, **pack** ➲ picture at **luggage**

rudder /ˈrʌdə(r)/ *noun* [C] a piece of wood or metal that is used for controlling the direction of a boat or plane ➲ picture at **plane**

rude 🔑 /ruːd/ *adj.* **1** ~ **(to sb) (about sb/sth)** not polite: *She was very rude to me about my new jacket.* ◇ *It's rude to interrupt when people are speaking.* ◇ *I think it was rude of them not to phone and say that* *they weren't coming.* SYN **impolite 2** connected with sex, using the toilet, etc. in a way that might offend people: *a rude joke/word/gesture* **3** (*written*) sudden and unpleasant: *If you're expecting any help from him, you're in for a rude shock.* ▶ **rudeness** *noun* [U]

rudely 🔑 /ˈruːdli/ *adv.* **1** in a way that shows a lack of respect for other people and their feelings: *They brushed rudely past us.* ◇ *'What do you want?' she asked rudely.* **2** in a way that is sudden, unpleasant and unexpected: *I was rudely awakened by the phone ringing.*

rudimentary /ˌruːdɪˈmentri/ *adj.* (*formal*) very basic or simple

rudiments /ˈruːdɪmənts/ *noun* [pl.] **the ~ (of sth)** (*formal*) the most basic or important facts of a particular subject, skill, etc.

ruffle /ˈrʌfl/ *verb* [T] **1 ~ sth (up)** to make sth untidy or no longer smooth: *to ruffle sb's hair* **2** (often passive) to make sb annoyed or confused

rug /rʌg/ *noun* [C] **1** a piece of thick material that covers a small part of a floor ➲ look at **carpet**, **mat** **2** a large piece of thick cloth that you put over your legs or around your shoulders to keep warm, especially when travelling

rugby /ˈrʌgbi/ *noun* [U] (SPORT) a form of football that is played by two teams of 13 or 15 players with an OVAL ball that can be carried, kicked or thrown ⓘ **Rugby League** is played with 13 players in a team, **Rugby Union** with 15 players.

rugged /ˈrʌgɪd/ *adj.* **1** (used about land) rough, with a lot of rocks and not many plants **2** (used about a man) strong and attractive **3** strong and made for difficult conditions

ruin¹ 🔑 /ˈruːɪn/ *verb* [T] **1** to damage sth so badly that it loses all its value, pleasure, etc.: *a ruined building* ◇ *The bad news ruined my week.* ◇ *That one mistake ruined my chances of getting the job.* **2** to cause sb to lose all their money, hope of being successful, etc.: *The cost of the court case nearly ruined them.*

ruin² 🔑 /ˈruːɪn/ *noun* **1** [U] the state of being destroyed or very badly damaged: *The city was in a state of ruin.* **2** [U] the cause or state of having lost all your money, hope of being successful, etc.: *Many small companies are facing* ***financial ruin.*** **3** [C] the parts of a building that are left standing after it has been destroyed or badly damaged: *the ruins of the ancient city of Pompeii*

IDM **go to rack and ruin** → RACK¹

in ruins badly damaged or destroyed: *After the accident her life seemed to be in ruins.*

ruinous /ˈruːɪnəs/ *adj.* causing serious problems, especially with money

rule¹ 🔑 /ruːl/ *noun* **1** [C] an official statement that tells you what you must or must not do in a particular situation or when playing a game: *to* ***obey /break a rule*** ◇ *Do you know the rules of chess?* ◇ *It's* ***against the rules*** *to smoke in this area.* ◇ *The company have strict* ***rules and regulations*** *governing employees' dress.* **2** [C] a piece of advice about what you should do in a particular situation: *When you run a marathon, the* ***golden rule*** *is: don't start too fast.* **3** [sing.] what is usual: *Large families are the exception rather than the rule nowadays.* ◇ ***As a general rule****, women live longer than men.* ◇ *I don't read much* ***as a rule****.* **4** [C] (LANGUAGE) a description of what is usual or correct: *What is the rule for forming the past tense?* **5** [U] government; control: *The country is* ***under military rule****.*

IDM **bend the rules** → BEND¹

a rule of thumb a simple piece of practical advice, not involving exact details or figures

work to rule to follow the rules of your job in a very strict way in order to cause delay, as a form of protest against your employer or your working conditions ➲ look at **work-to-rule**

rule² 🔑 /ruːl/ *verb* [I,T] **1 ~ (over sb/sth)** (POLITICS) to have the power over a country, group of people, etc.: *Julius Caesar ruled over a vast empire.* ◇ (*figurative*) *His whole life was ruled by his ambition to become President.* **2 ~ (on sth); ~ (in favour of/ against sb/sth); ~ (that...)** to make an official decision: *The judge will rule on whether or not the case can go ahead.*

PHR V **rule sb/sth out** to say that sb/sth is not possible, cannot do sth, etc.; to prevent sth: *The government has ruled out further increases in train fares next year.*

ruler 🔑 /ˈruːlə(r)/ *noun* [C] **1** (POLITICS) a person who rules a country, etc. **2** (MATHEMATICS) a straight piece of wood, plastic, etc. marked in CENTIMETRES or INCHES, that you use for measuring sth or for drawing straight lines

ruling¹ /ˈruːlɪŋ/ *adj.* (only *before* a noun) with the most power in an organization, country, etc.: *the ruling political party*

ruling² /ˈruːlɪŋ/ *noun* [C] an official decision

rum /rʌm/ *noun* [C,U] a strong alcoholic drink that is made from the juice of SUGAR CANE (=a plant from which sugar is made)

rumble /ˈrʌmbl/ *verb* [I] to make a deep heavy sound: *I was so hungry that my stomach was rumbling.* ▶ **rumble** *noun* [sing.]: *a rumble of thunder*

ruminant /ˈruːmɪnənt/ *noun* [C] (BIOLOGY) any animal that brings back food from its stomach and CHEWS it (=breaks it up in its mouth with its teeth) again: *Cows and sheep are both ruminants.* ▶ **ruminant** *adj.*

rummage /ˈrʌmɪdʒ/ *verb* [I] to move things and make them untidy while you are looking for sth: *Nina rummaged through the drawer looking for the tin-opener.*

rumour¹ 🔑 (*AmE* **rumor**) /ˈruːmə(r)/ *noun* [C,U] **(a) ~ (about/of sb/sth)** (a piece of) news or information that many people are talking about but that is possibly not true: *I didn't start the rumour about Barry's operation.* ◇ ***Rumour has it*** (=people are saying) *that Lena has resigned.* ◇ ***to confirm/deny a rumour*** (=to say that it is true/not true)

rumour² (*AmE* **rumor**) /ˈruːmə(r)/ *verb* [T] (always passive) **be rumoured** to be reported as a rumour and possible not true: ***It's widely rumoured that*** *they are getting divorced.* ◇ *They are rumoured to be getting divorced.*

rump /rʌmp/ *noun* [C] the back end of an animal: *rump steak* (=meat from the rump)

run¹ 🔑 /rʌn/ *verb* [I,T] (*pres. part.* **running**; *pt* **ran** /ræn/; *pp* **run**) **1** [I,T] to move using your legs, going faster than a walk: *I had to run to catch the bus.* ◇ *I often* ***go running*** *in the evenings* (=as a hobby). ◇ *I ran nearly ten kilometres this morning.* **2** [I,T] to move, or move sth, quickly in a particular direction: *I've been running around after the kids all day.* ◇ *The car ran off the road and hit a tree.* ◇ *She ran her finger down the list of passengers.* **3** [I] to lead from one place to another; to be in a particular position: *The road runs along the side of a lake.* **4** [T] to organize or be in charge of sth; to provide a service: *She runs a restaurant.* ◇ *They run English courses all the year round.* **5** [I,T] to operate or function; to make sth do this: *The engine is running very smoothly now.* ◇ *We're running a new computer program today.* **6** [I] to operate at a particular time: *All the trains are* ***running late*** *this morning.* ◇ *We'd better hurry up – we're running behind schedule.* **7** [T] to use and pay for a vehicle: *It costs a lot to run a car.* **8** [I] to continue for a time: *My contract has two months left to run.* ◇ *The play ran for nearly two years in a London theatre.* **9** [I,T] (used about water or other liquid) to flow; to make water flow: *When it's really cold, my nose runs.* ◇ *I can hear a tap running somewhere.* ◇ *to run a bath/a tap* **10** [I] ~ **with sth** to be covered with flowing water: *My face was running with sweat.* **11** [I] (used about the colour in material, etc.) to spread, for example when the material is washed: *Don't put that red shirt in the washing machine. It might run.* **12** [I] ~ **(for sth)** (POLITICS) to be a CANDIDATE (=one of the people hoping to be chosen) in an election: *He's running for president.* **13** [T] (ARTS AND MEDIA) to publish sth in a newspaper or magazine: *'The Independent' is running a series of articles on pollution.* **14** [T] ~ **a test/check (on sth)** to do a test or check on sth: *They're running checks on the power supply to see what the problem is.*

IDM **be running at** to be at a certain level

run for it to run in order to escape

PHR V **run across sb/sth** to meet or find sb/sth by chance

run after sb/sth to try to catch sb/sth

run away to escape from somewhere: *He's run away from home.*

run sb/sth down 1 to hit a person or an animal with your vehicle: *She was run down by a bus.* **2** to criticize sb/sth: *He's always running her down in front of other people.*

run (sth) down to stop functioning gradually; to make sth do this: *Turn the lights off or you'll run the battery down.*

run into sb to meet sb by chance

run into sth to have difficulties or a problem: *If you run into any problems, just let me know.*

run (sth) into sb/sth to hit sb/sth with a car, etc.: *He ran his car into a brick wall.*

run sth off to copy sth, using a machine

run off with sth to take or steal sth

run out (of sth) to finish your supply of sth; to come to an end: *We've run out of coffee.* ◇ *Time is running out.* ◇ *My passport runs out next month.*

run sb/sth over to hit a person or an animal with your vehicle: *The child was run over as he was crossing the road.*

run through sth to discuss or read sth quickly: *She ran through the names on the list.*

run[2] ⊶ /rʌn/ ***noun* 1** [C] (SPORT) an act of running on foot: ***I go for a*** *three-mile* ***run*** *every morning.* ◇ *The prisoner tried to* ***make a run for it*** (=to escape on foot). **2** [C] a journey by car, train, etc.: *The bus driver was picking up kids on the school run.* **3** [sing.] a series of similar events or sth that continues for a very long time: *We've had a run of bad luck recently.* **4** [sing.] **a ~ on sth** a sudden great demand for sth **5** [C] (SPORT) a point in the games of BASEBALL and CRICKET

IDM **in the long run** → LONG[1]

on the run hiding or trying to escape from sb/sth: *The escaped prisoner is still on the run.*

runaway[1] /ˈrʌnəweɪ/ ***adj.* 1** out of control: *a runaway horse/car/train* **2** happening very easily: *a runaway victory*

runaway[2] /ˈrʌnəweɪ/ ***noun*** [C] a person, especially a child, who has left or escaped from somewhere

ˌrun-ˈdown ***adj.* 1** (used about a building or place) in bad condition: *a run-down block of flats* **2** very tired and not healthy

rung[1] /rʌŋ/ ***noun*** [C] one of the bars that form the steps of a LADDER

rung[2] past participle of **ring**[2]

runner ⊶ /ˈrʌnə(r)/ ***noun*** [C] **1** (SPORT) a person or an animal that runs, especially in a race: *a long-distance runner* **2** (LAW) a person who takes guns, drugs, etc. illegally from one country to another

ˌrunner-ˈup ***noun*** [C] (*pl.* **runners-up**) the person or team that finished second in a race or competition

running[1] ⊶ /ˈrʌnɪŋ/ ***noun*** [U] **1** the action or sport of running: *How often do you* ***go running****?* ◇ *running shoes* **2** the process of managing a business or other organization: *She's not involved in the day-to-day running of the office.* ◇ *the* ***running costs*** *of a car* (=petrol, insurance, repairs, etc.)

IDM **in/out of the running (for sth)** (*informal*) having/not having a good chance of getting or winning sth

running[2] /ˈrʌnɪŋ/ ***adj.* 1** used after a number and a noun to say that sth has happened a number of times in the same way without a change: *Our school has won the competition for four years running.* **2** (only *before* a noun) (used about water) flowing or available from a tap: *There is no running water in the cottage.* **3** (only *before* a noun) not stopping; continuous: *a running battle between two rival gangs*

ˌrunning ˈcommentary ***noun*** [C] a spoken description of sth while it is happening

ˈrunning mate ***noun*** [C] (POLITICS) (in the US) a person who is chosen by a CANDIDATE (=the person who wants to be elected) in an election, especially an election for a president, to support them and to have the next highest political position if they win

runny /ˈrʌni/ ***adj.*** (*informal*) **1** containing more liquid than is usual or than you expected: *runny jam* **2** (used about your eyes or nose) producing too much liquid: *Their children always seem to have runny noses.* ► **runniness** ***noun*** [U]

ˌrun-of-the-ˈmill ***adj.*** ordinary, with no special or interesting characteristics: *a run-of-the-mill job*

ˈrun-up ***noun*** [sing.] **1** the period of time before a certain event: *the run-up to the election* **2** (SPORT) a run that people do in order to be going fast enough to do an action

runway /ˈrʌnweɪ/ ***noun*** [C] **1** a long piece of ground with a hard surface where aircraft take off and land at an airport **2** (*AmE*) =CATWALK

rupture /ˈrʌptʃə(r)/ ***noun*** [C,U] **1** a sudden bursting or breaking **2** (*formal*) the sudden ending of good relations between two people or groups ► **rupture** ***verb*** [I,T]: *Her appendix ruptured and she had to have emergency surgery.*

rural ⊶ /ˈrʊərəl/ ***adj.*** (GEOGRAPHY) connected with the country, not the town ➲ look at **urban**, **rustic**

ruse /ruːz/ ***noun*** [C] a trick or clever plan

rush[1] ⊶ /rʌʃ/ ***verb* 1** [I,T] to move or do sth with great speed, often too fast: *I rushed back home when I got the news.* ◇ *Don't rush off – I want to talk to you.* ◇ *We had to rush our meal.* ◇ *The public rushed to buy shares in the new company.* **2** [T] to take sb/sth to a place very quickly: *He suffered a heart attack and* ***was rushed to hospital****.* **3** [I,T] ~ **(sb) (into sth/into doing sth)** to do sth or make sb do sth without thinking about it first: *Don't let yourself be rushed into marriage.* ◇ *Don't rush me – I'm thinking!*

IDM **be rushed/run off your feet** → FOOT[1]

rush[2] /rʌʃ/ ***noun* 1** [sing.] a sudden quick movement: *At the end of the match there was a rush for the exits.* ◇ *I was so nervous, all my words came out **in a rush**.* **2** [sing., U] a situation in which you are in a hurry and need to do things quickly: *I can't stop now. I'm **in a** terrible **rush**.* ◇ *Don't hurry your meal. There's no rush.* **3** [sing.] a ~ (on sth) a time when many people try to get sth: *There's been a rush to buy petrol before the price goes up.* **4** [sing.] a time when there is a lot of activity and people are very busy: *We'll leave early to avoid the rush.* **5** [C] a type of tall grass that grows near water

'rush hour ***noun*** [C] the times each day when there is a lot of traffic because people are travelling to or from work: *Try to avoid travelling in the rush-hour.*

rust /rʌst/ ***noun*** [U] (CHEMISTRY) a reddish-brown substance that forms on the surface of iron, etc., caused by the action of air and water ▶ **rust** ***verb*** [I,T]: *Some parts of the car had rusted.*

rustic /'rʌstɪk/ ***adj.*** typical of the country or of country people; simple: *The whole area is full of rustic charm.* ➲ look at **rural**, **urban**

rustle /'rʌsl/ ***verb*** [I,T] to make a sound like dry leaves or paper moving: *There was a rustling noise in the bushes.* ▶ **rustle** ***noun*** [sing.]

PHR V **rustle sth up (for sb)** (*informal*) to make or find sth quickly for sb and without planning: *Shall I rustle something up for our lunch?*

rusty /'rʌsti/ ***adj.* 1** (used about metal objects) covered with RUST: *rusty tins* **2** (used about a skill) not as good as it was because you have not used it for a long time: *My French is rather rusty.*

rut /rʌt/ ***noun*** [C] a deep track that a wheel makes in soft ground

IDM **be in a rut** to have a boring way of life that is difficult to change

ruthenium /ru:'θi:niəm/ ***noun*** [U] (*symbol* **Ru**) (CHEMISTRY) a chemical element. **Ruthenium** is a hard silver-white metal that breaks easily and is found in PLATINUM ORES. ❶ For more information on the periodic table of elements, look at pages R34-5.

ruthless /'ru:θləs/ ***adj.*** (used about people and their behaviour) hard and cruel; determined to get what you want and showing no pity to others: *a ruthless dictator* ▶ **ruthlessly** ***adv.*** ▶ **ruthlessness** ***noun*** [U]

RV /ˌɑ: 'vi:/ ***noun*** [C] (*AmE*) = CAMPER (2)

rye /raɪ/ ***noun*** [U] (AGRICULTURE) a plant that is grown in colder countries for its grain, which is used to make flour and also an alcoholic drink (**whisky**) ➲ picture at **cereal**

S s

S, s[1] /es/ ***noun*** [C,U] (*pl.* **S's**; **s's** /'esɪz/) the nineteenth letter of the English alphabet: *'Sam' begins with (an) 'S'.*

S[2] ***abbr.* 1** small (size) **2** (*AmE* **So**) (GEOGRAPHY) south(ern): *S Yorkshire*

sabbath /'sæbəθ/ **the Sabbath** ***noun*** [sing.] (RELIGION) the day of the week for rest and prayer in certain religions (Sunday for Christians, Saturday for Jews)

sabotage /'sæbətɑ:ʒ/ ***noun*** [U] damage that is done on purpose and secretly in order to prevent an enemy or a COMPETITOR being successful, for example by destroying machinery, roads, bridges, etc.: *industrial/economic/military sabotage* ▶ **sabotage** ***verb*** [T]

sabre (*AmE* **saber**) /'seɪbə(r)/ ***noun*** [C] **1** a heavy SWORD with a curved blade **2** (SPORT) a light SWORD with a thin blade used in the sport of FENCING

saccharin /'sækərɪn/ ***noun*** [U] (CHEMISTRY) a very sweet chemical substance that can be used instead of sugar

sachet /'sæʃeɪ/ ***noun*** [C] a small plastic or paper packet that contains a small amount of liquid or powder: *a sachet of shampoo/sugar/coffee*

sack[1] /sæk/ ***noun*** [C] a large bag made from a rough heavy material, paper or plastic, used for carrying or storing things: *sacks of flour/potatoes*

IDM **get the sack** (*BrE*) to be told by your employer that you can no longer continue working for them (usually because you have done sth wrong): *Tony got the sack for poor work.*

give sb the sack (*BrE*) to tell an employee that they can no longer continue working for you (because of bad work, behaviour, etc.): *Tony's work wasn't good enough and he was given the sack.*

sack[2] /sæk/ (*especially AmE* **fire**) ***verb*** [T] to tell an employee that they can no longer work for you (because of bad work, bad behaviour, etc.): *Her boss has threatened to sack her if she's late again.*

sackcloth /'sækklɒθ/ (*also* **sacking** /'sækɪŋ/) ***noun*** [U] a rough cloth that is used for making SACKS[1]

sacred /'seɪkrɪd/ ***adj.* 1** (RELIGION) connected with God, a god or religion: *The Koran is the sacred book of Muslims.* **2** too important and special to be changed or harmed: *a sacred tradition*

sacrifice[1] /'sækrɪfaɪs/ ***noun*** [U, C] **1** giving up sth that is important or valuable to you in order to get or do sth that seems more important; sth that you give up in this way: *If we're going to have a holiday this year, we'll have to **make** some **sacrifices**.* **2** ~ **(to sb)** the act of offering sth to a god, especially an animal that has been killed in a special way; an animal, etc. that is offered in this way

sacrifice[2] /'sækrɪfaɪs/ ***verb* 1** [T] **~ sth (for sb/sth)** to give up sth that is important or valuable to you in order to get or do sth that seems more important: *She is not willing to sacrifice her career in order to have children.* **2** [I,T] (RELIGION) to kill an animal and offer it to a god, in order to please the god

sacrilege /'sækrəlɪdʒ/ ***noun*** [U, sing.] (RELIGION) treating a religious object or place without the respect that it deserves

sad /sæd/ ***adj.*** (**sadder**; **saddest**) **1** ~ (to do sth); ~ (that...) unhappy or causing sb to feel unhappy: *We are very sad to hear that you are leaving.* ◇ *I'm very sad that you don't trust me.* ◇ *That's one of the saddest stories I've ever heard!* ◇ *a sad poem/song/film* **2** bad or unacceptable: *It's a sad state of affairs when your best friend doesn't trust you.* ▶ **sadden** /'sædn/ ***verb*** [T] (*formal*): *The news of your father's death saddened me greatly.*

saddle /'sædl/ ***noun*** [C] **1** a seat, usually made of leather, that you put on a horse so that you can ride it **2** a seat on a bicycle or motorbike ▶ **saddle** ***verb*** [T]

PHR V **saddle sb with sth** to give sb a responsibility or task that they do not want

saddlebag /'sædlbæg/ ***noun*** [C] **1** one of a pair of bags put over the back of a horse **2** a bag attached to the back of a bicycle or motorcycle

sadism /ˈseɪdɪzəm/ ***noun*** [U] getting pleasure, especially sexual pleasure, from hurting other people ➲ look at **masochism**

sadist /ˈseɪdɪst/ ***noun*** [C] a person who gets pleasure, especially sexual pleasure, from hurting other people ▶ **sadistic** /səˈdɪstɪk/ ***adj.*** ▶ **sadistically** /-kli/ ***adv.***

sadly ⊶ /ˈsædli/ ***adv.*** **1** unfortunately: *Sadly, after eight years of marriage they had grown apart.* **2** in a way that shows unhappiness **3** in a way that is wrong: *If you think that I've forgotten what you did, you're **sadly mistaken**.*

sadness ⊶ /ˈsædnəs/ ***noun*** **1** [U, sing.] the feeling of being sad: *memories tinged with sadness* ◇ *I felt a deep sadness.* **2** [C, usually pl.] something which makes you sad: *our joys and sadnesses*

sae /ˌes eɪ ˈiː/ ***abbr.*** stamped addressed envelope

safari /səˈfɑːri/ ***noun*** [C,U] (*pl.* **safaris**) a trip to see or hunt wild animals, especially in east or southern Africa: *to be/go **on safari***

safe[1] ⊶ /seɪf/ ***adj.*** **1** (not before a noun) ~ (**from sb/sth**) free from danger; not able to be hurt: *She didn't **feel safe** in the house on her own.* ◇ *Do you think my car will be safe in this street?* ◇ *Keep the papers where they will be safe from fire.* **2** ~ (**to do sth**); ~ (**for sb**) not likely to cause danger, harm or risk: *Don't sit on that chair, it isn't safe.* ◇ *I left my suitcase in a **safe place** and went for a cup of coffee.* ◇ *Is this drug safe for children?* ◇ *She's a very safe driver.* ◇ *It's not safe to walk alone in the streets at night here.* ◇ *Is it safe to drink the water here?* ◇ *I think **it's safe to say** that the situation is unlikely to change for some time.* **3** (not before a noun) not hurt, damaged or lost: *After the accident he checked that all the passengers were safe.* ◇ *After five days the child was found, **safe and sound**.* **4** based on good evidence: *a safe verdict*

IDM **in safe hands** with sb who will take good care of you

on the safe side not taking risks; being very careful

safe[2] /seɪf/ ***noun*** [C] a strong metal box or cupboard with a special lock that is used for keeping money, jewellery, documents, etc. in

safeguard /ˈseɪfɡɑːd/ ***noun*** [C] **a** ~ (**against sb/sth**) something that protects against possible dangers ▶ **safeguard** ***verb*** [T]: *to safeguard sb's interests/rights/privacy*

safely ⊶ /ˈseɪfli/ ***adv.*** **1** without being harmed, damaged or lost: *The plane landed safely.* ◇ *I rang my parents to tell them I had arrived safely.* **2** in a way that does not cause harm or that protects sb/sth from harm: *The bomb has been safely disposed of.* ◇ *The money is safely locked in a drawer.* **3** without much possibility of being wrong: *We can **safely say** that he will accept the job.*

safety ⊶ /ˈseɪfti/ ***noun*** [U] the state of being safe; not being dangerous or in danger: *In the interests of safety, smoking is forbidden.* ◇ ***road safety*** (=the prevention of road accidents) ◇ *New **safety measures** have been introduced on trains.*

ˈ**safety belt** =SEAT BELT

ˈ**safety net** ***noun*** [C] **1** a net that is placed to catch sb who is performing high above the ground if they fall **2** an arrangement that helps to prevent disaster (usually with money) if sth goes wrong

ˈ**safety pin** ***noun*** [C] a metal pin with a point that is bent back towards the head, which is covered so that it cannot be dangerous.

safety symbols

harmful

emergency stop

toxic

first aid post

oxidizing

danger

irritant

electrical shock - 230V

corrosive

highly flammable

laser

ˈ**safety valve** ***noun*** [C] a device in a machine that allows steam, gas, etc. to escape if the pressure becomes too great

saffron /ˈsæfrən/ ***noun*** [U] **1** a bright yellow powder from a flower (**crocus**), that is used in cooking to give colour to food **2** a bright orange-yellow colour ▶ **saffron** ***adj.***

sag /sæɡ/ ***verb*** [I] (**sagging**; **sagged**) to hang or to bend down, especially in the middle

saga /ˈsɑːɡə/ ***noun*** [C] (**LITERATURE**) a very long story; a long series of events

sage /seɪdʒ/ ***noun*** [U] a plant with flat green leaves that have a strong smell and are used in cooking as a HERB: *duck with sage and onion stuffing*

Sagittarius /ˌsædʒɪˈteəriəs/ ***noun*** [U] (**ASTRONOMY**) the ninth sign of the ZODIAC, the Archer

sago /ˈseɪɡəʊ/ ***noun*** [U] hard white grains made from the soft inside of a PALM tree, often cooked with milk to make a sweet dish: *sago pudding*

said[1] past tense, past participle of **say**[1]

said[2] /sed/ ***adj.*** =AFOREMENTIONED

sail[1] ⊶ /seɪl/ ***verb*** **1** [I] (used about a boat or ship and the people on it) to travel on water in a ship or boat of any type: *I stood at the window and watched the ships sailing by.* ◇ *to sail round the world* **2** [I,T] (**SPORT**) to travel in and control a boat with sails, especially as a sport: *My father is teaching me to sail.* ◇ *I've never sailed this kind of yacht before.* **3** [I] to begin a journey on water: *When does the ship sail?* ◇ *We sail for Santander at six o'clock tomorrow morning.* **4** [I] to move somewhere quickly in a smooth or proud way: *The ball sailed over the fence and into the neighbour's garden.* ◇ *Mary sailed into the room, completely ignoring all of us.*

IDM **sail through (sth)** to pass a test or exam easily

sail[2] ⊶ /seɪl/ ***noun*** **1** [C] a large piece of strong material that is fixed onto a ship or boat. The wind blows against the sail and moves the ship along. **2** [sing.] a trip on water in a ship or boat with a sail **3** [C] any of the long parts that the wind moves round that are fixed to a WINDMILL ➲ picture at **windmill**

IDM **set sail** → SET[1]

sailboard /ˈseɪlbɔːd/ =WINDSURFER (1)

sailing ⊶ /ˈseɪlɪŋ/ ***noun*** [U] (**SPORT**) the sport of being in, and controlling, small boats with sails

ˈsailing boat (*AmE* **sailboat** /ˈseɪlbəʊt/) ***noun*** [C] a boat with a sail or sails

sailor ⊶ /ˈseɪlə(r)/ ***noun*** [C] a person who works on a ship or a person who sails a boat

saint /seɪnt; snt/ ***noun*** [C] **1** (**RELIGION**) a very good or religious person who is given special respect after death by the Christian church **2** a very good, kind person

sake /seɪk/ ***noun*** [C]

IDM **for goodness'/Heaven's/pity's, etc. sake** (*spoken*) used to emphasize that it is important to do sth or to show that you are annoyed: *For goodness' sake, hurry up!* ◇ *Why have you taken so long, for pity's sake?*

for the sake of sb/sth; **for sb's/sth's sake** in order to help sb/sth: *Don't go to any trouble for my sake.* ◇ *They only stayed together for the sake of their children/for their children's sake.*

for the sake of sth/of doing sth in order to get or keep sth; for the purpose of sth: *She gave up her job for the sake of her health.*

salad ⊶ /ˈsæləd/ ***noun*** [C,U] a mixture of raw vegetables such as LETTUCE and tomato, usually served with other food as part of a meal: *All main courses are served with chips or salad.*

salamander /ˈsæləmændə(r)/ ***noun*** [C] a small thin animal with four legs and a long tail, of the type that lives both on land and in water (**amphibian**). **Salamanders** often have bright colours on their skin. ➲ look at **lizard** ➲ picture on **page 28**

salary ⊶ /ˈsæləri/ ***noun*** [C,U] (*pl.* **salaries**) (**BUSINESS**) the money that a person receives (usually every month) for the work they have done: *My salary is paid directly into my bank account.* ◇ *a high/low salary* ➲ note at **income**, **pay²**

sale ⊶ /seɪl/ ***noun*** **1** [C,U] the action of selling or being sold; the occasion when sth is sold: *The sale of alcohol to anyone under the age of 18 is forbidden.* ◇ *a sale of used toys* **2** **sales** [pl.] the number of items sold: *Sales of personal computers have increased rapidly.* ◇ *The company reported excellent sales figures.* **3** **sales** [U] (*also* **ˈsales department**) (**BUSINESS**) the part of a company that deals with selling its products: *Jodie works in sales/in the sales department.* ◇ *a sales representative/sales rep* **4** [C] a time when shops sell things at prices that are lower than usual: *The sale starts on December 28th.* ◇ *I got several bargains **in the sales**.* ➲ look at **car boot sale**, **jumble sale**

IDM **for sale** offered for sb to buy: *This painting is not for sale.* ◇ *I see our neighbours have **put** their house **up for sale**.*

on sale **1** available for sb to buy, especially in shops: *This week's edition is on sale now at your local newsagents.* **2** (*AmE*) offered at a lower price than usual

ˈsales clerk (*also* **clerk**) (*AmE*) = SHOP ASSISTANT

salesman /ˈseɪlzmən/ **saleswoman** /ˈseɪlzwʊmən/ ***noun*** [C] (*pl.* **-men** /-mən/) (*pl.* **-women** /-wɪmɪn/) a person whose job is selling things to people

salesperson /ˈseɪlzpɜːsn/ ***noun*** [C] (*pl.* **salespeople** /ˈseɪlzpiːpl/) a person whose job is selling things to people, especially in a shop

ˈsales representative (also *informal* **ˈsales rep**; **rep**) ***noun*** [C] (**BUSINESS**) an employee of a company who travels around a particular area selling the company's goods to shops, etc.

salient /ˈseɪliənt/ ***adj.*** (only *before* a noun) most important or noticeable

saline /ˈseɪlaɪn/ ***adj.*** (**CHEMISTRY**) containing salt: *a saline solution*

saliva /səˈlaɪvə/ ***noun*** [U] (**BIOLOGY**) the liquid that is produced in the mouth ➲ look at **spit**

salivary /səˈlaɪvəri; ˈsælɪvəri/ ***adj.*** (**BIOLOGY**) of or producing SALIVA: *salivary glands* ➲ picture at **digestive system**

salivate /ˈsælɪveɪt/ ***verb*** [I] (*formal*) (**BIOLOGY**) to produce more SALIVA in your mouth than usual, especially when you see or smell food

sallow /ˈsæləʊ/ ***adj.*** (**HEALTH**) (used about a person's skin or face) having a slightly yellow colour that does not look healthy

salmon /ˈsæmən/ ***noun*** [C,U] (*pl.* **salmon**) a large fish with silver skin and pink meat that we eat: *smoked salmon*

salmonella /ˌsælməˈnelə/ ***noun*** [U] (**HEALTH**) a type of bacteria that causes food poisoning

salon /ˈsælɒn/ ***noun*** [C] a shop where you can have beauty or hair treatment or where you can buy expensive clothes

saloon /səˈluːn/ (*AmE* **sedan**) ***noun*** [C] a car with a fixed roof and a separate area (**boot**) for luggage

salt¹ ⊶ /sɔːlt (*BrE also* sɒlt)/ ***noun*** **1** [U] a common white substance that is found in sea water and the earth. Salt is used in cooking for flavouring food: *Season with **salt and pepper**.* ◇ *Add a pinch* (= a small amount) *of salt.* **2** [C] (**CHEMISTRY**) a chemical mixture (**compound**) of a metal and an acid ▶ **salt** ***adj.***: *salt water*

IDM **rub salt into the wound/sb's wounds** → RUB

take sth with a pinch of salt → PINCH²

salt² /sɔːlt (*BrE also* sɒlt)/ ***verb*** [T] (usually passive) to put salt on or in sth: *salted peanuts*

ˈsalt cellar ***noun*** [C] (*AmE* **ˈsalt shaker**) a small container for salt, usually with one hole in the top, that is used at the table

saltwater /ˈsɔːltwɔːtə(r)/ ***adj.*** living in the sea: *a saltwater fish* ➲ look at **freshwater**

salty ⊶ /ˈsɒlti/ ***adj.*** having the taste of or containing salt: *I didn't like the meat, it was too salty.*

salutation /ˌsæljuˈteɪʃn/ ***noun*** **1** [C, U] (*formal*) something that you say to welcome or say hello to sb; the action of welcoming or saying hello to sb: *He raised his hand in salutation.* **2** [C] (*technical*) the words that are used in a letter to address the person you are writing to, for example 'Dear Sir'

salute /səˈluːt/ ***noun*** [C] **1** an action that a soldier, etc. does to show respect, by holding their hand to their head: *to give a salute* **2** something that shows respect for sb: *The next programme is **a salute to** one of the world's greatest film stars.* ▶ **salute** ***verb*** [I,T]: *The soldiers saluted as they marched past the general.*

salvage¹ /ˈsælvɪdʒ/ ***noun*** [U] saving things that have been or are likely to be lost or damaged, especially in an accident or a disaster; the things that are saved: *a salvage operation/company/team*

salvage² /ˈsælvɪdʒ/ ***verb*** [T] ~ **sth (from sth)** to manage to rescue sth from being lost or damaged; to rescue sth or a situation from disaster: *They salvaged as much as they could from the house after the fire.*

salvation /sælˈveɪʃn/ ***noun*** **1** [U] (RELIGION) (in Christianity) being saved from the power of evil **2** [U, sing.] a thing or person that rescues sb/sth from danger, disaster, etc.

samarium /səˈmeəriəm/ ***noun*** [U] (*symbol* **Sm**) (CHEMISTRY) a chemical element. **Samarium** is a hard silver-white metal used in making strong MAGNETS. ❶ For more information on the periodic table of elements, look at pages R34-5.

same ⊶ /seɪm/ ***adj., adv., pronoun*** **1 the same... (as sb/sth); the same...that...** not different, not another or other; exactly the one or ones that you have mentioned before: *My brother and I had the same teacher at school.* ◇ *They both said the same thing.* ◇ *I'm going to wear the same clothes as/that I wore yesterday.* ◇ *This one looks **exactly the same** as that one.* **2 the same... (as sb/sth); the same...that...** exactly like the one already mentioned: *I wouldn't buy the same car again* (=the same model of car). ◇ *We treat all the children in the class the same.* ◇ *I had the same experience as you some time ago.* ◇ *All small babies look the same.* ◇ *Is there another word that means the same as this?*

IDM **all/just the same** in spite of this/that; anyway: *I understand what you're saying. All the same, I don't agree with you.* ◇ *I don't need to borrow any money but thanks all the same for offering.*

at the same time 1 together; at one time: *I can't think about more than one thing at the same time.* **2** on the other hand; however: *It's a very good idea but at the same time it's rather risky.*

much the same → MUCH

on the same wavelength able to understand sb because you have similar ideas and opinions

(the) same again (*spoken*) a request to be served or given the same drink as before

same here (*spoken*) the same thing is also true for me: *'I'm bored.' 'Same here.'*

(the) same to you (*spoken*) used as an answer when sb says sth rude to you or wishes you sth: *'You idiot!' 'Same to you!'* ◇ *'Have a good weekend.' 'The same to you.'*

sample ⊶ /ˈsɑːmpl/ ***noun*** [C] **1** a number of people or things taken from a larger group and used in tests to provide information about the group: *The interviews were given to a **random sample** of shoppers.* **2** a small amount of a substance taken from a larger amount and tested in order to obtain information about the substance: *to take a blood sample* ◇ *Samples of the water contained pesticide.* **3** a small amount or example of sth that can be looked at or tried to see what it is like: *a free sample of shampoo* **4** (MUSIC) a piece of recorded music or sound that is used in a new piece of music ▶ **sample** ***verb*** [T]: *You are welcome to sample any of our wines before making a purchase.*

sampling /ˈsɑːmplɪŋ/ ***noun*** [U] **1** the process of taking a sample: *statistical sampling* **2** (MUSIC) the process of copying and recording parts of a piece of music in an electronic form so that they can be used in a different piece of music

sanatorium /ˌsænəˈtɔːriəm/ (*AmE also* **sanitarium** /ˌsænəˈteəriəm/) ***noun*** [C] (HEALTH) a type of hospital where patients who need a long period of treatment for an illness can stay

sanction¹ /ˈsæŋkʃn/ ***noun*** **1** [C, usually pl.] **sanctions (against sb)** (LAW, POLITICS) an official order that limits business, contact, etc. with a particular country, in order to make it do sth, such as obeying international law: *Economic sanctions were imposed on any country that refused to sign the agreement.* ◇ *The sanctions against those countries have now been lifted.* **2** [U] (*formal*) official permission to do or change sth **3** [C] a punishment for breaking a rule or law

sanction² /ˈsæŋkʃn/ ***verb*** [T] to give official permission for sth

sanctuary /ˈsæŋktʃuəri/ ***noun*** (*pl.* **sanctuaries**) **1** [C] a place where birds or animals are protected and encouraged to breed: *a wildlife sanctuary* **2** [U] safety and protection, especially for people who are being chased or attacked: *to take sanctuary in a place* **3** [C] a safe place, especially one where people who are being chased or attacked can stay and be protected **4** [C] a holy building or the part of it that is considered the most holy

sand ⊶ /sænd/ ***noun*** (GEOGRAPHY) **1** [U] a powder consisting of very small grains of rock, found in deserts and on beaches: ***a grain of sand*** ◇ *Concrete is a mixture of sand and cement.* **2** [U,C, usually pl.] a large area of sand on a beach: *We went for a walk along the sand.* ◇ *children playing on the sand* ◇ *miles of golden sands*

sandal /ˈsændl/ ***noun*** [C] a type of light, open shoe that people wear when the weather is warm

sandalwood /ˈsændlwʊd/ ***noun*** [U] a type of oil with a sweet smell that comes from a hard tropical wood and is used to make pleasant smelling liquid (**perfume**)

sandbank /ˈsændbæŋk/ ***noun*** [C] (GEOGRAPHY) an area of sand that is higher than the sand around it in a river or the sea

sandbar /ˈsændbɑː(r)/ ***noun*** [C] (GEOGRAPHY) a long mass of sand at the point where a river meets the sea that is formed by the movement of the water

sandcastle /ˈsændkɑːsl/ ***noun*** [C] a pile of sand that looks like a castle, made by children playing on a beach

ˈsand dune = DUNE

sandpaper /ˈsændpeɪpə(r)/ ***noun*** [U] strong paper with sand on it that is used for rubbing surfaces in order to make them smooth

sandstone /ˈsændstəʊn/ ***noun*** [U] (GEOLOGY) a type of stone that is formed of grains of sand tightly pressed together and that is used in building

sandstorm /ˈsændstɔːm/ ***noun*** [C] a storm in a desert in which sand is blown into the air by strong winds

sandwich¹ /ˈsænwɪdʒ/ ***noun*** [C] two slices of bread with food between them: *a ham/cheese sandwich*

sandwich² /ˈsænwɪdʒ/ ***verb*** [T] ~ **sb/sth (between sb/sth)** to place sb/sth in a very narrow space between two other things or people

ˈsandwich course ***noun*** [C] (*BrE*) (EDUCATION) a course of study which includes periods of working in business or industry

sandy /ˈsændi/ ***adj.*** covered with or full of sand

sane /seɪn/ ***adj.*** **1** (used about a person) having a normal healthy mind; not mentally ill: *No sane person would do anything like that.* **2** sensible and reasonable: *the sane way to solve the problem* OPP **insane** ➲ noun **sanity**

sang past tense of **sing**

sanitarium /ˌsænəˈteəriəm/ (*AmE*) = SANATORIUM

sanitary /ˈsænətri/ ***adj.*** (HEALTH) connected with the protection of health, for example how human waste is removed: *Sanitary conditions in the refugee camps were terrible.* ➲ look at **insanitary**

ˈsanitary towel (*AmE* **ˈsanitary napkin**) ***noun*** [C] (**HEALTH**) a thick piece of soft material that women use to take in and hold blood lost during their period (3) ➲ look at **tampon**

sanitation /ˌsænɪˈteɪʃn/ ***noun*** [U] the equipment and systems that keep places clean, especially by removing human waste

sanity /ˈsænəti/ ***noun*** [U] **1** the state of having a normal healthy mind **2** the state of being sensible and reasonable OPP **insanity** ➲ adjective **sane**

sank past tense of **sink**[1]

Santa Claus /ˈsæntə klɔːz/ = FATHER CHRISTMAS

sap[1] /sæp/ ***noun*** [U] (**BIOLOGY**) the liquid in a plant or tree

sap[2] /sæp/ ***verb*** [T] (**sapping**; **sapped**) ~ **(sb of) sth** to make sb/sth weaker; to destroy sth gradually: *Years of failure have sapped (him of) his confidence.*

sapling /ˈsæplɪŋ/ ***noun*** [C] (**BIOLOGY**) a young tree ➲ picture at **tree**

sapphire /ˈsæfaɪə(r)/ ***noun*** [C,U] a bright blue PRECIOUS STONE

sarcasm /ˈsɑːkæzəm/ ***noun*** [U] the use of words or expressions to mean the opposite of what they actually say. People use **sarcasm** in order to criticize other people or to make them look silly. ➲ look at **ironic** ▸ **sarcastic** /sɑːˈkæstɪk/ ***adj.***: *a sarcastic comment* ▸ **sarcastically** /-kli/ ***adv.***

sardine /ˌsɑːˈdiːn/ ***noun*** [C] a type of small silver-coloured fish that we cook and eat: *a tin of sardines*

sari /ˈsɑːri/ ***noun*** [C] a dress that consists of a long piece of cloth that women, particularly Indian women, wear around their bodies

sarong /səˈrɒŋ/ ***noun*** [C] a long piece of material folded around the body from the waist or the chest, worn by Malaysian and Indonesian men and women

SARS /sɑːz/ ***noun*** [U] (**HEALTH**) **severe acute respiratory syndrome**; an illness that is easily spread from person to person, which affects the lungs and can sometimes cause death: *No new SARS cases have been reported in the region.*

sash /sæʃ/ ***noun*** [C] a long piece of material that is worn round the waist or over the shoulder, often as part of a uniform

SAT ***noun*** [C] (**EDUCATION**) **1 SAT™** /ˌes eɪ ˈtiː/ (in the US) **Scholastic Aptitude Test**; a test taken by HIGH SCHOOL students who want to go to a college or university: *to take the SAT* ◇ *I scored 1050 on the SAT.* ◇ *an SAT score* **2** /sæt/ (in Britain) **Standard Assessment Task**; now called National Curriculum Test (NCT)

Sat. ***abbr.*** Saturday: *Sat. 2 May*

sat past tense, past participle of **sit**

Satan /ˈseɪtn/ ***noun*** [sing.] (**RELIGION**) a name for the DEVIL

satchel /ˈsætʃəl/ ***noun*** [C] a bag, often carried over the shoulder, used by schoolchildren for taking books to and from school

satellite /ˈsætəlaɪt/ ***noun*** [C] **1** an electronic device that is sent into space and moves around the earth or another planet for a particular purpose: *a weather/communications satellite* **2** (**ASTRONOMY**) a natural object that moves round a bigger object in space

ˈsatellite dish (*also* **dish**) ***noun*** [C] a large, circular piece of equipment that people have on the outside of their houses so that they can receive SATELLITE TELEVISION

ˌsatellite ˈtelevision (*also* **ˌsatellite TˈV**) ***noun*** [U] television programmes that are sent out using a SATELLITE (1)

satin /ˈsætɪn/ ***noun*** [U] a type of cloth that is smooth and shiny: *a satin dress/ribbon*

satire /ˈsætaɪə(r)/ ***noun*** **1** [U] the use of humour to attack a person, an idea, or behaviour that you think is bad or silly **2** [C] **a ~ (on sb/sth)** (**LITERATURE, ARTS AND MEDIA**) a piece of writing or a play, film, etc. that uses **satire**: *a satire on political life* ▸ **satirical** /səˈtɪrɪkl/ ***adj.***: *a satirical magazine* ▸ **satirically** /-kli/ ***adv.***

satirize (also **-ise**) /ˈsætəraɪz/ ***verb*** [T] to use SATIRE to show the faults in a person, an organization, a system, etc.

satisfaction 🔑 /ˌsætɪsˈfækʃn/ ***noun*** [U, C] the feeling of pleasure that you have when you have done, got, or achieved what you wanted; sth that gives you this feeling: *Roshni stood back and looked at her work with a sense of satisfaction.* ◇ *We finally found a solution that was **to everyone's satisfaction**.* ◇ *She was about to **have the satisfaction of** seeing her book in print.* OPP **dissatisfaction**

satisfactory /ˌsætɪsˈfæktəri/ ***adj.*** good enough for a particular purpose; acceptable: *This piece of work is not satisfactory. Please do it again.* OPP **unsatisfactory** ▸ **satisfactorily** /-tərəli/ ***adv.***: *Work is progressing satisfactorily.*

satisfied 🔑 /ˈsætɪsfaɪd/ ***adj.*** ~ **(with sb/sth)** pleased because you have achieved sth or because sth that you wanted to happen has happened: *a satisfied smile* ◇ *a satisfied customer* OPP **dissatisfied**

satisfy 🔑 /ˈsætɪsfaɪ/ ***verb*** [T] (*pres. part.* **satisfying**; *3rd person sing. pres.* **satisfies**; *pt, pp* **satisfied**) **1** to make sb pleased by doing or giving them what they want: *Nothing satisfies him – he's always complaining.* **2** to have or do what is necessary for sth: *Make sure you **satisfy** the entry **requirements** before you apply to the university.* ◇ *I had a quick look inside the parcel just to **satisfy** my **curiosity**.* **3** ~ **sb (that...)** to show or give proof to sb that sth is true or has been done: *Once the police were satisfied that they were telling the truth, they were allowed to go.*

satisfying 🔑 /ˈsætɪsfaɪɪŋ/ ***adj.*** pleasing; giving satisfaction: *I find it satisfying to see people enjoying something I've cooked.*

satnav /ˈsætnæv/ ***noun*** [U,C] **satellite navigation**; a system or device in your vehicle that tells you how to find your way somewhere while you are driving

satsuma /sætˈsuːmə/ ***noun*** [C] a type of small orange

saturate /ˈsætʃəreɪt/ ***verb*** [T] **1** to make sth extremely wet **2** to fill sth so completely that it is impossible to add any more: *The market is saturated with cheap imports.* ▸ **saturation** /ˌsætʃəˈreɪʃn/ ***noun*** [U]

saturated /ˈsætʃəreɪtɪd/ ***adj.*** **1** completely wet **2** (**CHEMISTRY, HEALTH**) (used about fats in food) that are not easily dealt with by the body because of their chemical structure ➲ look at **polyunsaturated**, **unsaturated**

ˌsatuˈration point ***noun*** [U, sing.] **1** the stage at which no more of sth can be accepted or added because there is already too much of it or too many of them: *The market for mobile phones is reaching saturation point.* **2** (**CHEMISTRY**) the stage at which no more of a substance can be absorbed by a liquid or VAPOUR

Saturday /'sætədeɪ; -di/ ***noun*** [C,U] (*abbr.* **Sat.**) the day of the week after Friday

Saturn /'sætɜːn; -tən/ ***noun*** [sing.] (**ASTRONOMY**) the planet that is sixth in order from the sun and that has rings around it ➲ picture at **solar system**

sauce 🔑 /sɔːs/ ***noun*** [C,U] a thick hot or cold liquid that you eat on or with food: *The chicken was served in a delicious sauce.* ◇ *ice cream with chocolate sauce* ➲ look at **gravy**

saucepan /'sɔːspən/ ***noun*** [C] a round metal pot with a handle that is used for cooking things on top of a cooker

saucer /'sɔːsə(r)/ ***noun*** [C] a small round plate that you put under a cup

sauna /'sɔːnə/ ***noun*** [C] a period of time in which you sit or lie in a small room (also called a **sauna**) which has been heated to a very high temperature by burning coal or wood. Some **saunas** involve the use of steam: *to have a sauna* ◇ *a hotel with a swimming pool and sauna*

saunter /'sɔːntə(r)/ ***verb*** [I] to walk without hurrying

sausage /'sɒsɪdʒ/ ***noun*** [C,U] a mixture containing meat and spices that is made into a long thin shape. Some **sausages** are eaten cold in slices; other types are cooked and then served whole: *garlic/liver sausage* ◇ *We had sausages and chips for lunch.*

savage[1] /'sævɪdʒ/ ***adj.*** very cruel or violent: *He was the victim of a savage attack.* ◇ *The book received savage criticism.* ▶ **savagely** ***adv.*** ▶ **savagery** /'sævɪdʒri/ ***noun*** [U]

savage[2] /'sævɪdʒ/ ***verb*** [T] (used about an animal) to attack sb violently, causing serious injury: *The boy died after being savaged by a dog.*

savannah (also **savanna**) /sə'vænə/ ***noun*** [U] (**GEOGRAPHY**) a wide flat open area of land, especially in Africa, that is covered with grass but has few trees ➲ picture at **ecosystem**

save[1] 🔑 /seɪv/ ***verb*** **1** [T] ~ **sb/sth (from sth/from doing sth)** to keep sb/sth safe from death, harm, loss, etc.: *to **save** sb's **life*** ◇ *to save sb from drowning* ◇ *We are trying to save the school from closure.* **2** [I,T] ~ **(sth) (up) (for sth)** to keep or not spend money so that you can use it later: *I'm saving up for a new bike.* ◇ *Do you manage to save any of your wages?* **3** [T] to keep sth for future use: *I'll be home late so please save me some dinner.* ◇ *Save that box. It might come in useful.* ◇ *If you get there first, please save me a seat.* **4** [I,T] ~ **(sb) (sth) (on) sth** to avoid wasting time, money, etc.: *It will save you twenty minutes on the journey if you take the express train.* ◇ *You can save on petrol by getting a smaller car.* ◇ *This car will save you a lot on petrol.* **5** [T] ~ **(sb) sth/doing sth** to avoid, or make sb able to avoid, doing sth unpleasant or difficult: *If you make an appointment it will save you waiting.* **6** [T] (**COMPUTING**) to store information in a computer: *Don't forget to save the file before you close it.* **7** [T] (**SPORT**) to stop a goal being scored in sports such as football, HOCKEY, etc.

IDM **save sth for a rainy day** → RAINY

save face to prevent yourself losing the respect of other people

save[2] /seɪv/ ***noun*** [C] (**SPORT**) (in football, etc.) the action of preventing a goal from being scored: *The goalkeeper made a great save.*

saver /'seɪvə(r)/ ***noun*** [C] **1** a person who saves money for future use: *The rise in interest rates is good news for savers.* **2** (often used in compounds) a thing that helps you save time, money, or the thing mentioned: *Their new model of dishwasher is a great water and energy saver.*

saving 🔑 /'seɪvɪŋ/ ***noun*** **1** [C] a ~ **(of sth) (on sth)** an amount of time, money, etc. that you do not have to use or spend: *The sale price represents a saving of 25% on the usual price.* **2 savings** [pl.] money that you have saved for future use: *All our savings are in the bank.*

saviour (*AmE* **savior**) /'seɪvjə(r)/ ***noun*** [C] **1** a person who rescues sb/sth from a dangerous or difficult situation **2 the Saviour** (**RELIGION**) used in the Christian religion as another name for Jesus Christ

savoury (*AmE* **savory**) /'seɪvəri/ ***adj.*** (used about food) having a taste that is not sweet ➲ look at **sweet**

saw[1] past tense of **see**

saw[2] /sɔː/ ***noun*** [C] a tool that is used for cutting wood, etc. A saw has a long flat metal part (**a blade**) with sharp teeth on it, and a handle at one or both ends. ➲ picture at **tool**

saw[3] /sɔː/ ***verb*** [I,T] (*pt* **sawed**; *pp* **sawn** /sɔːn/) to use a SAW to cut sth: *to saw through the trunk of a tree* ◇ *He sawed the log up into small pieces.* ℹ In American English the past participle is **sawed**.

sawdust /'sɔːdʌst/ ***noun*** [U] very small pieces of wood that fall like powder when you are cutting a large piece of wood

saxophone /'sæksəfəʊn/ (also *informal* **sax**) ***noun*** [C] (**MUSIC**) a metal musical instrument that you play by blowing into it. **Saxophones** are especially used for playing modern music, for example JAZZ: *This track features Dexter Gordon on sax.* ➲ picture on **page 465**

say[1] 🔑 /seɪ/ ***verb*** [T] (*3rd person sing. pres.* **says** /sez/; *pt, pp* **said** /sed/) **1** ~ **sth (to sb)**; ~ **that...**; ~ **sth (about sb)** to speak or tell sb sth, using words: *'Please come back,' she said.* ◇ *The teacher said we should hand in our essays on Friday.* ◇ *I said goodbye to her at the station.* ◇ *We can ask him, but I'm sure he'll say no.* ◇ *He said to his mother that he would phone back later.* ◇ *She said nothing to me about it.* ◇ *They just sat there without saying anything.* ◇ *'This isn't going to be easy,' she said to herself* (=she thought). ◇ *'What time is she coming?' 'I don't know – she didn't say.'* ◇ ***It is said that*** *cats can sense the presence of ghosts.* **2** to express an opinion on sth: *I wouldn't say she's unfriendly – just shy.* ◇ *What is the artist trying to say in this painting?* ◇ *Well,* ***what do you say****? Do you think it's a good idea?* ◇ *It's* ***hard to say*** *what I like about the book.* ◇ *'When will it be finished?'* ***'I couldn't say*** (=I don't know)'. **3** (used about a book, notice, etc.) to give information: *What time does it say on that clock?* ◇ *The map says the hotel is just past the railway bridge.* ◇ *The sign clearly says 'No dogs'.* **4** ~ **sth (to sb)** to show a feeling, a situation, etc. without using words: *His angry look said everything about the way he felt.* **5** to imagine or guess sth about a situation; to suppose: *We will need, say, £5000 for a new car.* ◇ *Say you don't get a place at university, what will you do then?*

IDM **go without saying** to be clear, so that you do not need to say it: *It goes without saying that the children will be well looked after at all times.*

have a lot, nothing, etc. to say for yourself to have a lot, nothing, etc. to say in a particular situation: *Late again! What have you got to say for yourself?*

I must say (*spoken*) used to emphasize your opinion: *I must say, I didn't believe him at first.*

I wouldn't say no (*spoken*) used to say that you would like sth: *'Coffee?' 'I wouldn't say no.'*

Say when (*spoken*) used to tell sb to say when you

have poured enough drink in their glass or put enough food on their plate

that is to say... which means...: *We're leaving on Friday, that's to say in a week's time.*

say² /seɪ/ ***noun*** [sing., U] (a) ~ **(in sth)** the authority or right to decide sth: *I'd like to have some say in the arrangements for the party.*

IDM **have your say** to express your opinion: *Thank you for your comments. Now let somebody else have their say.*

saying /ˈseɪɪŋ/ ***noun*** [C] a well-known phrase that gives advice about sth or says sth that many people believe is true: *'Love is blind' is an old saying.* ➲ look at **proverb**

scab /skæb/ ***noun*** [C,U] (HEALTH) a mass of dried blood that forms over a part of the body where the skin has been cut or broken ➲ look at **scar**

scabies /ˈskeɪbiːz/ ***noun*** [U] (HEALTH) a skin disease that causes small red spots and makes your skin feel uncomfortable so that you want to rub or scratch it

scaffold /ˈskæfəʊld/ ***noun*** [C] a platform on which criminals were killed in past times by hanging

scaffolding /ˈskæfəldɪŋ/ ***noun*** [U] long metal poles and wooden boards that form a structure which is put next to a building so that people who are building, painting, etc. can stand and work on it

scalar /ˈskeɪlə(r)/ ***adj.*** (MATHEMATICS) (used about a measurement or a quantity) having size but no direction ▶ **scalar** ***noun*** [C] ➲ note at **vector**

scald /skɔːld/ ***verb*** [T] to burn sb/sth with very hot liquid: *I scalded my arm badly when I was cooking.* ▶ **scald** ***noun*** [C]

scalding /ˈskɔːldɪŋ/ ***adj.*** hot enough to SCALD: *scalding water*

scale¹ 🔑 /skeɪl/ ***noun*** **1** [C,U] the size of sth, especially when compared to other things: *We shall be making the product* ***on a large scale*** *next year.* ◇ *At this stage it is impossible to estimate* ***the full scale of*** *the disaster.* **2** [C] (MATHEMATICS, SCIENCE) a series of marks on a tool or piece of equipment that you use for measuring sth: *The ruler has one scale in centimetres and one scale in inches.* **3** [C] a series of numbers, amounts, etc. that are used for measuring or fixing the level of sth: *The earthquake measured 6.5 on the Richter scale.* ◇ *the new pay scale for nurses* ➲ look at **the Beaufort scale, the Richter scale** **4** [C] (GEOGRAPHY, MATHEMATICS) the relationship between the actual size of sth and its size on a map or plan: *The map has a scale of one centimetre to a kilometre.* ◇ *a scale of 1: 50000* (=one to fifty thousand) ◇ *We need a map with a larger scale.* ◇ *a scale model* **5 scales** [pl.] a piece of equipment that is used for weighing sb/sth: *I weighed it on the kitchen scales.* **6** [C] (MUSIC) a series of musical notes which go up or down in a fixed order. People play or sing scales to improve their technical ability: *the scale of C major* **7** [C] (BIOLOGY) one of the small flat pieces of hard material that cover the body of some fish and animals: *the scales of a snake* ➲ picture on **page 28**

scale² /skeɪl/ ***verb*** [T] to climb up a high wall, steep CLIFF, etc.

PHRV **scale sth up/down** to increase/decrease the size, number, importance, etc. of sth: *Police have scaled up their search for the missing boy.*

scalene triangle /ˌskeɪliːn ˈtraɪæŋɡl/ ***noun*** [C] (GEOMETRY) a triangle whose sides are all of different lengths ➲ picture at **triangle**

scallop /ˈskɒləp/ ***noun*** [C] a SHELLFISH that we eat, with two flat round shells that fit together

scalp /skælp/ ***noun*** [C] the skin on your head that is under your hair

scalpel /ˈskælpəl/ ***noun*** [C] (HEALTH) a small knife that is used by doctors (**surgeons**) when they are doing operations

scaly /ˈskeɪli/ ***adj.*** (**scalier**; **scaliest**) covered with SCALES (7), or hard and dry, with small pieces that come off

scamper /ˈskæmpə(r)/ ***verb*** [I] (used especially about a child or small animal) to run quickly

scan¹ /skæn/ ***verb*** [T] (**scanning**; **scanned**) **1** to look at or read every part of sth quickly until you find what you are looking for: *Vic scanned the list until he found his own name.* **2** (used about a machine) to examine what is inside a person's body or inside an object such as a suitcase: *Machines scan all the luggage for bombs and guns.* **3** ~ **sth (into sth)**; ~ **sth (in)** (COMPUTING) to copy words or pictures using a SCANNER: *Text and pictures can be scanned into the computer.*

scan² /skæn/ ***noun*** **1** [C] (HEALTH) a medical test in which a machine produces a picture of the inside of a person's body on a computer screen: *to do/have a brain scan* **2** [C] (HEALTH) a medical test for pregnant women in which a machine uses ULTRASOUND to produce a picture of a baby inside its mother's body: *The scan showed the baby was in the normal position.* **3** [sing.] the act of looking quickly through sth written or printed, usually in order to find sth: *a scan of the newspapers*

scandal /ˈskændl/ ***noun*** **1** [C,U] an action, a situation or behaviour that shocks people; the public feeling that is caused by such behaviour: *The chairman resigned after being involved in a financial scandal.* ◇ *There was no suggestion of scandal in his private life.* ◇ *The poor state of school buildings is a real scandal.* **2** [U] talk about sth bad that sb has done or may have done: *to spread scandal about sb*

scandalize (also **-ise**) /ˈskændəlaɪz/ ***verb*** [T] to cause sb to feel shocked, by doing sth that they think is bad or wrong

scandalous /ˈskændələs/ ***adj.*** very shocking or wrong: *It is scandalous that so much money is wasted.*

Scandinavia /ˌskændɪˈneɪviə/ ***noun*** [sing.] (GEOGRAPHY) the group of countries in northern Europe that consists of Denmark, Norway and Sweden. Sometimes Finland and Iceland are also said to be part of **Scandinavia**. ▶ **Scandinavian** ***adj.***, ***noun*** [C]

scandium /ˈskændiəm/ ***noun*** [U] (*symbol* **Sc**) (CHEMISTRY) a chemical element. **Scandium** is a silver-white metal found in various minerals. ❶ For more information on the periodic table of elements, look at pages R34-5.

scanner /ˈskænə(r)/ ***noun*** [C] an electronic machine that can look at, record or send images or electronic information: *The scanner can detect cancer at an early stage.* ◇ *I used the scanner to send the document by email.*

scant /skænt/ ***adj.*** (only *before* a noun) not very much; not as much as necessary

scanty /ˈskænti/ ***adj.*** **1** too little in amount for what is needed: *Details of his life are scanty.* **2** (used about clothes) very small and not covering much of your body: *a scanty bikini* ▶ **scantily** ***adv.***: *scantily dressed models*

scapegoat /ˈskeɪpɡəʊt/ ***noun*** [C] a person who is blamed for sth bad that sb else has done or for some failure: *She felt she had been made a scapegoat for her boss's incompetence.*

scapula /ˈskæpjʊlə/ (*formal*) = SHOULDER BLADE ➲ picture on **page 80**

scar /skɑː(r)/ *noun* [C] **1** (HEALTH) a mark on the skin that is caused by a cut that skin has grown over: *The operation didn't leave a very big scar.* ➲ look at **scab** **2** (GEOGRAPHY) an area of a hill or CLIFF where there is rock with nothing covering it and no grass: *a mile-long limestone scar* ➲ picture at **limestone** ▶ **scar** *verb* [I,T] (**scarring**; **scarred**): *William's face was **scarred for life** in the accident.*

scarce /skeəs/ *adj.* not existing in large quantities; hard to find: *Food for birds and animals is scarce in the winter.* OPP **plentiful** ▶ **scarcity** /ˈskeəsəti/ *noun* [C,U] (*pl.* **scarcities**): *(a) scarcity of food/jobs/resources*

scarcely /ˈskeəsli/ *adv.* **1** only just; almost not: *There was scarcely a car in sight.* ◇ *She's not a friend of mine. I scarcely know her.* ➲ look at **hardly** **2** used to suggest that sth is not reasonable or likely: *You can scarcely expect me to believe that after all you said before.*

scare[1] 🔑 /skeə(r)/ *verb* **1** [T] to make a person or an animal frightened: *The sudden noise scared us all.* ◇ *It scares me to think what might happen.* **2** [I] to become frightened: *I don't scare easily, but when I saw the gun I was terrified.*

PHR V **scare sb/sth away/off** to make a person or animal leave or stay away by frightening them

scare[2] 🔑 /skeə(r)/ *noun* [C] **1** a feeling of being frightened: *It wasn't a serious heart attack but it gave him a scare.* **2** a situation where many people are afraid or worried about sth: *Last night there was a **bomb scare** in the city centre.*

scarecrow /ˈskeəkrəʊ/ *noun* [C] (AGRICULTURE) a very simple model of a person that is put in a field to frighten away the birds

scared 🔑 /skeəd/ *adj.* ~ (**of sb/sth**); ~ (**of doing sth/to do sth**) frightened: *Are you scared of the dark?* ◇ *She's scared of walking home alone.* ◇ *Everyone was too scared to move.*

scarf /skɑːf/ *noun* [C] (*pl.* **scarves** /skɑːvz/ or **scarfs** /skɑːfs/) **1** a long thin piece of cloth that you wear around your neck to keep warm **2** a square piece of cloth that women wear around their neck or shoulders or over their heads

scarlet /ˈskɑːlət/ *adj.*, *noun* [U] (of) a bright red colour

ˌscarlet ˈfever *noun* [U] (HEALTH) a serious disease that is passed from one person to another and that makes sb very hot and get red marks on the skin

scarp /skɑːp/ *noun* [C] (GEOGRAPHY) a very steep piece of land

scary /ˈskeəri/ *adj.* (**scarier**; **scariest**) (*informal*) frightening: *a scary ghost story* ◇ *It was a bit scary driving in the mountains at night.*

scat /skæt/ *noun* [U] (MUSIC) a style of JAZZ singing in which the voice is made to sound like a musical instrument

scathing /ˈskeɪðɪŋ/ *adj.* expressing a very strong negative opinion about sb/sth; very critical: *a scathing attack on the new leader* ◇ *scathing criticism*

scatter /ˈskætə(r)/ *verb* **1** [I] (used about a group of people or animals) to move away quickly in different directions **2** [T] to drop or throw things in different directions over a wide area: *The wind scattered the papers all over the room.*

ˈscatter diagram (*also* **scattergram** /ˈskætəgræm/) *noun* [C] (MATHEMATICS) a diagram that shows the relationship between two VARIABLES by creating a pattern of dots ➲ picture at **chart**

scattered /ˈskætəd/ *adj.* spread over a large area or happening several times during a period of time: *There will be sunny intervals with scattered showers today.*

scavenge /ˈskævɪndʒ/ *verb* [I,T] to look for food, etc. among waste and rubbish ▶ **scavenger** *noun* [C]: *Scavengers steal the food that the lion has killed.*

SCE /ˌes siː ˈiː/ *abbr.* (EDUCATION) Scottish Certificate of Education. Students in Scotland take the SCE at Standard grade at the age of about 16 and at Higher grade at about 17.

scenario AW /səˈnɑːriəʊ/ *noun* [C] (*pl.* **scenarios**) **1** one way that things may happen in the future: *A likely scenario is that the company will get rid of some staff.* **2** (ARTS AND MEDIA) a description of what happens in a play or film

scene 🔑 /siːn/ *noun* **1** [C] the place where sth happened: *the scene of a crime/an accident* ◇ *An ambulance was **on the scene** in minutes.* **2** [C] an occasion when sb expresses great anger or another strong emotion in public: *There was quite a scene when she refused to pay the bill.* **3** [C] (LITERATURE, ARTS AND MEDIA) one part of a book, play, film, etc. in which the events happen in one place: *The first scene of 'Hamlet' takes place on the castle walls.* **4** [C,U] what you see around you in a particular place: *a delightful rural scene* ◇ *They went abroad for **a change of scene*** (= to see and experience new surroundings). **5 the scene** [sing.] the way of life or the present situation in a particular area of activity: *The political scene in Eastern Europe is very confused.* ◇ *the fashion scene*

IDM **behind the scenes** **1** (ARTS AND MEDIA) in the part of a theatre, etc. that the public does not usually see: *The students were able to go behind the scenes to see how programmes are made.* **2** in a way that people in general are not aware of: *A lot of negotiating has been going on behind the scenes.* ◇ *behind-the-scenes work*

set the scene (for sth) **1** to create a situation in which sth can easily happen or develop: *His arrival set the scene for another argument.* **2** to give sb the information and details that they need in order to understand what comes next: *The first part of the programme was just setting the scene.*

scenery /ˈsiːnəri/ *noun* [U] **1** the natural beauty that you see around you in the country: *The scenery is superb in the mountains.* **2** (ARTS AND MEDIA) the furniture, painted cloth, boards, etc. that are used on the stage in a theatre: *The scenery is changed during the interval.*

scenic /ˈsiːnɪk/ *adj.* having beautiful SCENERY (1)

scent /sent/ *noun* **1** [C,U] a pleasant smell: *This flower has no scent.* **2** [C,U] the smell that an animal leaves behind and that some other animals can follow **3** [U] (*especially BrE*) a liquid with a pleasant smell that you wear on your skin to make it smell nice SYN **perfume** **4** [sing.] the feeling that sth is going to happen: *The scent of victory was in the air.* ▶ **scent** *verb* [T]: *The dog scented a rabbit and shot off.* ▶ **scented** *adj.*

sceptic (*AmE* **skeptic**) /ˈskeptɪk/ *noun* [C] a person who doubts that sth is true, right, etc. ▶ **sceptical** (*AmE* **skeptical**) /-kl/ *adj.* ~ (**of/about sth**): *Many doctors are sceptical about the value of alternative medicine.*

scepticism (*AmE* **skepticism**) /ˈskeptɪsɪzəm/ *noun* [U] a general feeling of doubt about sth; a feeling that you are not likely to believe sth

schedule[1] **AW** /ˈʃedjuːl/ ***noun*** **1** [C,U] a plan of things that will happen or of work that must be done: *Max has a busy schedule for the next few days.* ◇ *to be ahead of/behind schedule* (=to have done more/less than was planned) **2** (*AmE*) =TIMETABLE

schedule[2] **AW** /ˈʃedjuːl/ ***verb*** [T] ~ **sth (for sth)** to arrange for sth to happen or be done at a particular time: *We've scheduled the meeting for Monday morning.* ◇ *The train was scheduled to arrive at 10.07.*

ˌscheduled ˈflight ***noun*** [C] (**TOURISM**) a plane service that leaves at a regular time each day or week ➲ look at **charter flight**

schematic **AW** /skiːˈmætɪk/ ***adj.*** **1** in the form of a diagram that shows the main features or relationships but not the details: *a schematic diagram* **2** according to a fixed plan or pattern: *The play has a very schematic plot.*

scheme[1] **AW** /skiːm/ ***noun*** [C] **1** a ~ **(to do sth/for doing sth)** an official plan or system for doing or organizing sth: *a new scheme to provide houses in the area* ◇ *a local scheme for recycling newspapers* **2** a clever plan to do sth: *He's thought of a new scheme for making money fast.* ➲ look at **colour scheme**

scheme[2] **AW** /skiːm/ ***verb*** [I,T] to make a secret or dishonest plan: *She felt that everyone was scheming to get rid of her.*

scherzo /ˈskeətsəʊ/ ***noun*** [C] (*pl.* **-os**) (**MUSIC**) a short, lively piece of music that is often part of a longer piece

schist /ʃɪst/ ***noun*** [U] (**GEOLOGY**) a type of rock formed of layers of different minerals, that breaks naturally into thin flat pieces

schizophrenia /ˌskɪtsəˈfriːniə/ ***noun*** [U] (**HEALTH**) a serious mental illness in which a person confuses the real world and the world of the imagination and often behaves in strange and unexpected ways ▶ **schizophrenic** /ˌskɪtsəˈfrenɪk/ ***adj.***, ***noun*** [C]

scholar /ˈskɒlə(r)/ ***noun*** [C] (**EDUCATION**) **1** a person who studies and has a lot of knowledge about a particular subject **2** a person who has passed an exam or won a competition and has been given a SCHOLARSHIP to help pay for their studies: *a British Council scholar* ➲ look at **student**

scholarly /ˈskɒləli/ ***adj.*** (**EDUCATION**) **1** (used about a person) spending a lot of time studying and having a lot of knowledge about an academic subject **2** connected with academic study

scholarship /ˈskɒləʃɪp/ ***noun*** (**EDUCATION**) **1** [C] an amount of money that is given to a person who has passed an exam or won a competition, in order to help pay for their studies: *to win a scholarship to Yale* **2** [U] serious study of an academic subject

school /skuːl/ ***noun*** **1** [C] (**EDUCATION**) the place where children go to be educated: *They're building a new school in our area.* ◇ *Was your school co-educational* (=for boys and girls) *or single-sex?* **2** [U] (**EDUCATION**) (used without *the* or *at*) the time you spend at a school; the process of being educated in a school: *Where did you **go to school**?* ◇ *Their children are still **at school**.* ◇ *Children **start school** at 5 years old in Britain and can **leave school** at 16.* ◇ *School starts at 9 o'clock and finishes at about 3.30.* ◇ *After school we usually have homework to do.* **3** [sing., with sing. or pl. verb] (**EDUCATION**) all the students and teachers in a school: *The whole school cheered the winner.* **4** (**EDUCATION**) (used to form compounds) connected with school: *Do you have to wear **school uniform**?* ◇ *children **of school age*** ◇ *The bus was full of **schoolchildren**.* ◇ *It is getting increasingly difficult for **school-leavers** to find jobs.* ◇ *I don't have many good memories of my **schooldays**.* **5** [C] (**EDUCATION**) a place where you go to learn a particular subject: *a language/driving/drama/business school* **6** [C] (*AmE*) (**EDUCATION**) a college or university **7** [C] (**EDUCATION**) a department of a university that teaches a particular subject: *the school of geography at Leeds University* **8** [C] (**ART, LITERATURE**) a group of writers, painters, etc. who have the same ideas or style: *the Flemish school of painting* **9** [C] (**BIOLOGY**) a large group of fish swimming together

IDM **a school of thought** the ideas or opinions that one group of people share: *There are various schools of thought on this matter.*

schoolboy /ˈskuːlbɔɪ/ ***noun*** [C] (**EDUCATION**) a boy who goes to school

schoolgirl /ˈskuːlɡɜːl/ ***noun*** [C] (**EDUCATION**) a girl who goes to school

schooling /ˈskuːlɪŋ/ ***noun*** [U] (**EDUCATION**) the time that you spend at school; your education

schoolmaster /ˈskuːlmɑːstə(r)/ **schoolmistress** /ˈskuːlmɪstrəs/ ***noun*** (*old-fashioned*) (*especially BrE*) (**EDUCATION**) a teacher in a school, especially a private school ➲ look at **master**

schoolteacher /ˈskuːltiːtʃə(r)/ ***noun*** [C] (**EDUCATION**) a person whose job is teaching in a school

schooner /ˈskuːnə(r)/ ***noun*** [C] **1** a sailing ship with two or more MASTS (=posts that support the sails) **2** a tall glass for beer or SHERRY (=strong wine)

schwa /ʃwɑː/ ***noun*** [C] (**LANGUAGE**) a VOWEL sound in parts of words that are not emphasized (**stressed**), for example the 'a' in 'about' or the 'e' in 'moment'; the symbol that represents this sound, /ə/

science /ˈsaɪəns/ ***noun*** **1** [U] the study of and knowledge about the physical world and natural laws: *Modern science has discovered a lot about the origin of life.* ◇ *Fewer young people are studying science at university.* ➲ look at **arts** **2** [C] (**EDUCATION**) one of the subjects into which science can be divided: *Biology, chemistry and physics are all sciences.* ➲ look at **social science**

ˌscience ˈfiction (*also* **ˈsci-fi**) ***noun*** [U] (**ARTS AND MEDIA, LITERATURE**) books, films, etc. about events that take place in the future, often involving travel in space

scientific /ˌsaɪənˈtɪfɪk/ ***adj.*** **1** (**SCIENCE**) connected with or involving science: *We need more funding for scientific research.* ◇ *scientific instruments* **2** (used about a way of thinking or of doing sth) careful and logical: *a scientific study of the way people use language* ▶ **scientifically** /-kli/ ***adv.***: *Sorting out the files won't take long if we do it scientifically.*

scientist /ˈsaɪəntɪst/ ***noun*** [C] (**SCIENCE**) a person who studies or teaches science, especially biology, chemistry or physics

sci-fi /ˈsaɪ faɪ/ (*informal*) =SCIENCE FICTION

scintillating /ˈsɪntɪleɪtɪŋ/ ***adj.*** very clever, amusing and interesting: *The lead actor gave a scintillating performance.*

scissors /ˈsɪzəz/ ***noun*** [pl.] a tool for cutting things that consists of two long, flat, sharp pieces of metal that are joined together: *a pair of scissors*

scoff /skɒf/ ***verb* 1** [I] **~ (at sb/sth)** to speak about sb/sth in a way that shows you think that they are stupid or ridiculous **2** [T] (*BrE, informal*) to eat a lot of sth quickly

scold /skəʊld/ ***verb*** [I,T] **~ sb (for sth/for doing sth)** to speak angrily to sb because they have done sth bad or wrong

scone /skɒn; skəʊn/ ***noun*** [C] a small, simple cake, usually eaten with butter on

scoop[1] /sku:p/ ***noun*** [C] **1** a tool like a spoon used for picking up ice cream, flour, grain, etc. **2** the amount that one scoop contains **3** an exciting piece of news that is reported by one newspaper, television or radio station before it is reported anywhere else

scoop[2] /sku:p/ ***verb*** [T] **1 ~ sth (out/up)** to move or lift sth with a SCOOP or sth like a SCOOP: *Scoop out the middle of the pineapple.* **2 ~ sb/sth (up)** to move or lift sb/sth using a continuous action: *He scooped up the child and ran.* **3** to win a big or important prize: *The film has scooped all the awards this year.* **4** (**ARTS AND MEDIA**) to get a story before all other newspapers, television stations, etc.

scooter /ˈsku:tə(r)/ ***noun*** [C] **1** a light motorbike with a small engine **2** a child's toy with two wheels that you stand on and move by pushing one foot against the ground

scope AW /skəʊp/ ***noun* 1** [U] **~ (for sth/to do sth)** the chance or opportunity to do sth: *The job offers plenty of scope for creativity.* **2** [sing.] the variety of subjects that are being discussed or considered: *The government was unwilling to extend the scope of the inquiry.*

scorch /skɔ:tʃ/ ***verb*** [T] to burn sth so that its colour changes but it is not destroyed: *I scorched my blouse when I was ironing it.*

scorching /ˈskɔ:tʃɪŋ/ ***adj.*** very hot: *It was absolutely scorching on Tuesday.*

score[1] 🔑 /skɔ:(r)/ ***noun* 1** [C] the number of points, goals, etc. that sb/sth gets in a game, competition, exam, etc.: *What was the final score?* ◇ *The score is 3-2 to Liverpool.* ◇ *The top score in the test was 80%.* **2 scores** [pl.] very many: *Scores of people have written to offer their support.* **3** [C] (**MUSIC**) the written form of a piece of music **4** [C] (*pl.* **score**) a set or group of 20 or approximately 20
IDM **on that score** as far as that is concerned: *Alan will be well looked after. Don't worry on that score.*

score[2] 🔑 /skɔ:(r)/ ***verb*** [I,T] (**SPORT**) to get points, goals, etc. in a game, competition, exam, etc.: *The team still hadn't scored by half-time.* ◇ *Louise scored the highest marks in the exam.*

scoreboard /ˈskɔ:bɔ:d/ ***noun*** [C] (**SPORT**) a large board that shows the score during a game, competition, etc.

scorn[1] /skɔ:n/ ***noun*** [U] **~ (for sb/sth)** the strong feeling that you have when you do not respect sb/sth

scorn[2] /skɔ:n/ ***verb*** [T] **1** to feel or show a complete lack of respect for sb/sth: *The President scorned his critics.* **2** to refuse to accept help or advice, especially because you are too proud: *The old lady scorned all offers of help.* ▶ **scornful** /-fl/ ***adj.***: *a scornful look/smile/remark* ▶ **scornfully** /-fəli/ ***adv.***

Scorpio /ˈskɔ:piəʊ/ ***noun*** [U] (**ASTRONOMY**) the eighth sign of the ZODIAC, the Scorpion

scorpion /ˈskɔ:piən/ ***noun*** [C] a small creature which has a long curved tail with a poisonous sting in it. ➲ picture on **page 28**

Scot /skɒt/ ***noun*** [C] a person who comes from Scotland

Scotch /skɒtʃ/ ***noun*** [U, C] a strong alcoholic drink (**whisky**) that is made in Scotland; a glass of this

ˈScotch tape™ (*AmE*) = SELLOTAPE

Scots /skɒts/ ***adj.*** of or connected with people from Scotland

Scottish /ˈskɒtɪʃ/ ***adj.*** of or connected with Scotland, its people, culture, etc.

scoundrel /ˈskaʊndrəl/ ***noun*** [C] (*old-fashioned*) a man who behaves very badly towards other people, especially by being dishonest

scour /ˈskaʊə(r)/ ***verb*** [T] **1** to clean sth by rubbing it hard with sth rough: *to scour a dirty pan* **2** to search a place very carefully because you are looking for sb/sth

scourge /skɜ:dʒ/ ***noun*** [C] a person or thing that causes a lot of trouble or suffering: *Raul was the scourge of the United defence.*

scout /skaʊt/ ***noun*** [C] **1 the Scouts** [pl.] an organization, originally for boys, which trains young people in practical skills and does a lot of activities with them, for example camping: *to join the Scouts* **2** [C] (*BrE*) a boy or girl who is a member of the **Scouts** ➲ look at **Guide 3** a soldier who is sent on in front of the rest of the group to find out where the enemy is or which is the best route to take

scowl /skaʊl/ ***noun*** [C] a look on your face that shows you are angry or in a bad mood
▶ **scowl** ***verb*** [I]

scrabble /ˈskræbl/ ***verb*** [I] to move your fingers or feet around quickly, trying to find sth or get hold of sth: *She scrabbled about in her purse for some coins.*

scramble /ˈskræmbl/ ***verb*** [I] **1** to climb quickly up or over sth using your hands to help you; to move somewhere quickly: *He scrambled up the hill and over the wall.* ◇ *He* ***scrambled to his feet*** (= off the ground) *and ran off into the trees.* ◇ *The children scrambled into the car.* **2 ~ (for sth/to do sth)** to fight or move quickly to get sth which a lot of people want: *People stood up and began scrambling for the exits.* ◇ *Everyone was scrambling to get the best bargains.* ▶ **scramble** ***noun*** [sing.]

ˌscrambled ˈegg ***noun*** [U] (*also* **ˌscrambled ˈeggs** [pl.]) eggs mixed together with milk and then cooked in a pan

scrap[1] /skræp/ ***noun* 1** [C] a small piece of sth: *a scrap of paper/cloth* ◇ *scraps of food* **2** [U] something that you do not want any more but that is made of material that can be used again: *The old car was sold* ***for scrap****.* ◇ *scrap paper* **3** [C] (*informal*) a short fight or argument

scrap[2] /skræp/ ***verb*** [T] (**scrapping**; **scrapped**) to get rid of sth that you do not want any more: *I think we should scrap that idea.*

scrapbook /ˈskræpbʊk/ ***noun*** [C] a large book with empty pages that you can stick pictures, newspaper articles, etc. in

scrape[1] /skreɪp/ ***verb* 1** [T] **~ sth (down/out/off)** to remove sth from a surface by moving a sharp edge across it firmly: *Scrape all the mud off your boots before you come in.* **2** [T] **~ sth (against/along/on sth)** to damage or hurt sth by rubbing it against sth rough or hard: *Mark fell and scraped his knee.* ◇ *Sunita scraped the car against the wall.* **3** [I,T] **~ (sth) against/along/on sth** to rub (sth) against sth and make a sharp unpleasant noise: *The branches scraped against the window.* **4** [T] to manage to get or win sth with difficulty: *I just scraped a pass in the maths exam.*
PHR V **scrape by** to manage to live on the money

you have, but with difficulty: *We can just scrape by on my salary.*
scrape through (sth) to succeed in doing sth with difficulty: *to scrape through an exam* (=just manage to pass it)
scrape sth together/up to get or collect sth together with difficulty

scrape² /skreɪp/ ***noun*** [C] **1** the action or unpleasant sound of one thing rubbing against another **2** damage or an injury caused by rubbing against sth rough: *I got a nasty scrape on my knee.* **3** (*informal*) a difficult situation that was caused by your own stupid behaviour

'scrap heap ***noun*** [C] a large pile of objects, especially metal, that are no longer wanted
IDM **on the scrap heap** not wanted any more: *Many of the unemployed feel that they are on the scrap heap.*

scrappy /'skræpi/ ***adj.*** not organized or tidy and so not pleasant to see: *a scrappy essay/football match*

scratch¹ /skrætʃ/ ***verb*** **1** [I,T] ~ (at sth) to rub your skin with your nails, especially because it is irritating you (**itching**): *Don't scratch at your insect bites or they'll get worse.* ◇ *Could you scratch my back for me?* ◇ *She sat and scratched her head as she thought about the problem.* **2** [I,T] to make a mark on a surface or a slight cut on a person's skin with sth sharp: *The cat will scratch if you annoy it.* ◇ *The table was badly scratched.* **3** [I] to make a sound by rubbing a surface with sth sharp: *The dog was scratching at the door to go outside.* **4** [T] to use sth sharp to make or remove a mark: *He scratched his name on the top of his desk.* ◇ *I tried to scratch the paint off the table.*

scratch² /skrætʃ/ ***noun*** **1** [C] a cut, mark or sound that was made by sb/sth sharp rubbing a surface: *There's a scratch on the car door.* **2** [sing.] an act of scratching part of the body because it is irritating you (**itching**): *The dog had a good scratch.*
IDM **from scratch** from the very beginning: *I'm learning Spanish from scratch.*
(be/come) up to scratch (*informal*) (to be/become) good enough

scrawl /skrɔːl/ ***verb*** [I,T] to write sth quickly in an untidy and careless way: *He scrawled his name across the top of the paper.* ► **scrawl** ***noun*** [sing.]: *Her signature was just a scrawl.* SYN **scribble**

scrawny /'skrɔːni/ ***adj.*** (**scrawnier**; **scrawniest**) very thin in a way that is not attractive

scream¹ /skriːm/ ***verb*** [I,T] ~ (sth) (out) (at sb) to cry out loudly in a high voice because you are afraid, excited, angry, in pain, etc.: *She saw a rat and screamed out.* ◇ *'Don't touch that,' he screamed.* ◇ *She screamed at the children to stop.* ◇ *He screamed with pain.* ◇ *He clung to the edge of the cliff, screaming for help.* ➲ look at **shout**

scream² /skriːm/ ***noun*** **1** [C] a loud cry in a high voice: *a scream of pain* **2** [sing.] (*informal*) a person or thing that is very funny: *Sharon's a real scream.*

scree /skriː/ ***noun*** [U, C] (**GEOGRAPHY**) a steep area of small loose stones, especially on a mountain

screech /skriːtʃ/ ***verb*** [I,T] to make an unpleasant loud, high sound: *'Get out of here,' she screeched at him.* ➲ look at **shriek** ► **screech** ***noun*** [sing.]: *the screech of brakes*

screen¹ /skriːn/ ***noun*** **1** [C] a flat vertical surface that is used for dividing a room or keeping sb/sth out of sight: *The nurse pulled the screen round the bed.* **2** [C] (**COMPUTING, ARTS AND MEDIA**) the surface of a television or computer where the picture or information appears ➲ picture at **computer** **3** [C] (**ARTS AND MEDIA**) the large flat surface on which films are shown **4** [sing., U] (**ARTS AND MEDIA**) films or television in general: *Some actors look better in real life than on screen.*

screen² /skriːn/ ***verb*** [T] **1** ~ **sb/sth (off) (from sb/sth)** to hide or protect sb/sth from sb/sth else: *The bed was screened off while the doctor examined him.* ◇ *to screen your eyes from the sun* **2** ~ **sb (for sth)** (**HEALTH**) to examine or test sb to find out if they have a particular disease or if they are suitable for a particular job: *All women over 50 should be screened for breast cancer.* ◇ *The Ministry of Defence screens all job applicants.* **3** (**ARTS AND MEDIA**) to show sth on television or in a cinema **4** to check sth to see if it is suitable or if you want it: *I use my answerphone to screen my phone calls.* ➲ picture at **water**

'screen-print ***verb*** [T,I] (**ART**) to produce a picture by forcing ink or metal onto a surface through a screen of silk or artificial material ► **'screen print** ***noun*** [C]

'screen saver ***noun*** [C] (**COMPUTING**) an image that appears on your computer screen when you are not using it; the program that produces the image

screw¹ /skruː/ ***noun*** [C] a thin pointed piece of metal used for fixing two things, for example pieces of wood, together. You turn a screw with a special tool (**a screwdriver**). ➲ picture at **bolt**

screw² /skruː/ ***verb*** **1** [T] ~ **sth (on, down, etc.)** to fasten sth with a screw or screws: *The bookcase is screwed to the wall.* ◇ *The lid is screwed down so you can't remove it.* **2** [I,T] to fasten sth, or to be fastened, by turning: *The legs screw into holes in the underside of the seat.* ◇ *Make sure that you screw the top of the jar on tightly.* **3** ~ **sth (up) (into sth)** to squeeze sth, especially a piece of paper, into a tight ball: *He screwed the letter up into a ball and threw it away.*
PHR V **screw (sth) up** (*slang*) to make a mistake and cause sth to fail: *You'd better not screw up this deal.*
screw your eyes, face, etc. up to change the expression on your face by nearly closing your eyes, because you are in pain or because the light is strong

screwdriver /'skruːdraɪvə(r)/ ***noun*** [C] a tool that you use for turning screws ➲ picture at **tool**

scribble /'skrɪbl/ ***verb*** [I,T] **1** to write sth quickly and carelessly: *to scribble a note down on a pad* SYN **scrawl** **2** to make marks with a pen or pencil that are not letters or pictures: *The children had scribbled all over the walls.* ► **scribble** ***noun*** [C,U]

script /skrɪpt/ ***noun*** **1** [C] (**LITERATURE, ARTS AND MEDIA**) the written form of a play, film, speech, etc.: *Who wrote the script for the movie?* **2** [C,U] (**LANGUAGE**) a system of writing: *Arabic/Cyrillic/Roman script*

scripture /'skrɪptʃə(r)/ ***noun*** [U] (*also* **the scriptures** [pl.]) (**RELIGION**) books of religious importance for particular religions, such as the Bible for Christians

scroll¹ /skrəʊl/ ***noun*** [C] **1** (**LITERATURE**) a long roll of paper with writing on it **2** (**ARCHITECTURE**) a decoration cut in stone or wood with a curved shape like a roll of paper

scroll² /skrəʊl/ ***verb*** [I] ~ **(up/down)** (**COMPUTING**) to move text on a computer screen up or down or from side to side so that you can read different parts of it

'scroll bar *noun* [C] (COMPUTING) a tool on a computer screen that you use to move the text up and down or side to side

scrotum /'skrəʊtəm/ ***noun*** [C] (ANATOMY, BIOLOGY) the bag of skin that contains the two male sex organs (**testicles**)

scrounge /skraʊndʒ/ ***verb*** [I,T] (*informal*) ~ **(sth) (from/off sb)** to get sth by asking another person to give it to you instead of making an effort to get it for yourself: *Lucy is always scrounging money off her friends.*

scrub[1] /skrʌb/ ***verb*** [I,T] (**scrubbing**; **scrubbed**) **1** ~ **(sth) (down/out)** to clean sth with soap and water by rubbing it hard, often with a brush: *to scrub (down) the floor/walls* **2** ~ **(sth) (off/out)**; ~ **(sth) (off sth/out of sth)** to remove sth or be removed by **scrubbing**: *to scrub the dirt off the walls* ◇ *I hope these coffee stains will scrub out.*

scrub[2] /skrʌb/ ***noun*** **1** [sing.] an act of cleaning sth by rubbing it hard, often with a brush: *This floor needs a good scrub.* **2** [U] (GEOGRAPHY) small trees and bushes that grow in an area that has very little rain **3** (*also* **'scrubland** /'skrʌblənd/) [U] (GEOGRAPHY) an area of dry land covered with small bushes and trees

scruff /skrʌf/ ***noun***
IDM **by the scruff (of the/your neck)** roughly holding the back of an animal's or person's neck

scruffy /'skrʌfi/ ***adj.*** dirty and untidy: *He always looks so scruffy.* ◇ *scruffy jeans*

scrum /skrʌm/ ***noun*** [C] (SPORT) the part of a game of RUGBY when several players put their heads down in a circle and push against each other to try to get the ball

scruples /'skru:plz/ ***noun*** [pl.] a feeling that stops you from doing sth that you think is morally wrong: *I've got no scruples about asking them for money* (=I don't think it's wrong).

scrupulous /'skru:pjələs/ ***adj.*** **1** very careful or paying great attention to detail: *a scrupulous investigation into the causes of the disaster* **2** careful to do what is right or honest OPP **unscrupulous** ▶ **scrupulously** ***adv.***: *scrupulously clean/honest/tidy*

scrutinize (also **-ise**) /'skru:tɪnaɪz/ ***verb*** [T] to look at or examine sth carefully: *The customs official scrutinized every page of my passport.* ▶ **scrutiny** /'skru:təni/ ***noun*** [U]: *The police kept all the suspects **under close scrutiny**.*

scuba-diving /'sku:bə daɪvɪŋ/ ***noun*** [U] swimming under water using special equipment for breathing: *to go scuba-diving*

scuff /skʌf/ ***verb*** [T] to make a mark on your shoes or with your shoes, for example by kicking sth or by rubbing your feet along the ground

scuffle /'skʌfl/ ***noun*** [C] a short, not very violent fight

sculptor /'skʌlptə(r)/ ***noun*** [C] (ART) a person who makes SCULPTURES (2)

sculpture /'skʌlptʃə(r)/ ***noun*** (ART) **1** [U] the art of making figures or objects from stone, wood, CLAY, etc. **2** [C,U] a work or works of art that are made in this way

scum /skʌm/ ***noun*** [U] **1** a dirty or unpleasant substance on the surface of a liquid **2** (*slang*) an insulting word for people that you have no respect for: *Drug dealers are scum.*

scurry /'skʌri/ ***verb*** [I] (*pres. part.* **scurrying**; *3rd person sing. pres.* **scurries**; *pt, pp* **scurried**) to run quickly with short steps; to hurry

scurvy /'skɜ:vi/ ***noun*** [U] (HEALTH) a disease caused by a lack of VITAMIN C

scuttle /'skʌtl/ ***verb*** [I] to run quickly with short steps or with the body close to the ground: *The spider scuttled away when I tried to catch it.*

scythe /saɪð/ ***noun*** [C] (AGRICULTURE) a tool with a long handle and a long, curved BLADE (=a piece of metal with a very sharp edge). You use a **scythe** to cut long grass, CORN, etc. ➲ picture at **agriculture**

SE ***abbr.*** (GEOGRAPHY) south-east(ern): *SE Asia*

sea ⊶ /si:/ ***noun*** **1** (often **the sea**) [U] (GEOGRAPHY) the salt water that covers large parts of the surface of the earth: *The sea is quite calm/rough today.* ◇ *Do you live **by the sea**?* ◇ *to travel **by sea*** ◇ *There were several people swimming **in the sea**.* **2** (often **Sea**) [C] (GEOGRAPHY) a particular large area of salt water. A sea may be part of the ocean or may be surrounded by land: *the Mediterranean Sea* ◇ *the Black Sea* ➲ look at **ocean** **3** [sing.] (*also* **seas** [pl.]) (GEOGRAPHY) the state or movement of the waves of the sea: *The boat sank in **heavy*** (=rough) ***seas** off the Scottish coast.* **4** [sing.] a large amount of sb/sth close together: *a sea of people*
IDM **at sea 1** sailing in a ship: *They spent about three weeks at sea.* **2** not understanding or not knowing what to do

'sea anemone *noun* [C] a small, brightly-coloured sea creature that lives on rocks and looks like a flower ➲ look at **anemone**

the seabed /'si:bed/ ***noun*** [sing.] (GEOGRAPHY) the floor of the sea ➲ picture at **wave**

seabird /'si:bɜ:d/ ***noun*** [C] any bird that lives close to the sea and gets its food from it ➲ look at **waterbird** ➲ picture on **page 28**

seafood /'si:fu:d/ ***noun*** [U] fish and SHELLFISH from the sea that can be eaten

the 'sea front *noun* [sing.] the part of a town facing the sea: *The hotel is right **on the sea front**.* ◇ *to walk **along the sea front***

seagull /'si:gʌl/ =GULL

seal[1] ⊶ /si:l/ ***noun*** [C] **1** a grey animal with short fur that lives in and near the sea and that eats fish. **Seals** have no legs and swim with the help of short flat arms (**flippers**). **2** an official design or mark that is put on a document, an envelope, etc. to show that it is genuine or that it has not been opened **3** a small piece of paper, metal, plastic, etc. on a packet, bottle, etc. that you must break before you can open it **4** something that stops air or liquid from getting in or out of something: *The seal has worn and oil is escaping.*

seal[2] ⊶ /si:l/ ***verb*** [T] **1** ~ **sth (up/down)** to close or fasten a package, envelope, etc.: *The parcel was sealed with tape.* ◇ *to seal (down) an envelope* **2** ~ **sth (up)** to fill a hole or cover sth so that air or liquid does not get in or out: *The food is packed in sealed bags to keep it fresh.* **3** (*formal*) to make sth sure, so that it cannot be changed or argued about: *to seal an agreement*
PHR V **seal sth off** to stop any person or thing from entering or leaving an area or building: *The building was sealed off by the police.*

'sea level *noun* [U] (GEOGRAPHY) the average level of the sea, used for measuring the height of places on land: *The town is 500 metres above sea level.*

'sea lion *noun* [C] a type of large animal that lives in the sea and on land and uses two flat arms (**flippers**) to move through the water

seam /siːm/ ***noun*** [C] **1** the line where two pieces of cloth are sewn together **2** (GEOGRAPHY) a layer of coal under the ground

seaman /ˈsiːmən/ ***noun*** [C] (*pl.* **-men** /-mən/) a sailor

seamless /ˈsiːmləs/ ***adj.*** with no spaces or pauses between one part and the next: *a seamless flow of talk* ▶ **seamlessly** ***adv.***

seance (also **séance**) /ˈseɪɒ̃s/ ***noun*** [C] a meeting at which people try to talk to the spirits of dead people

seaplane /ˈsiːpleɪn/ (*AmE also* **hydroplane**) ***noun*** [C] a plane that can take off from and land on water

search[1] /sɜːtʃ/ ***verb*** [I,T] ~ **(sb/sth) (for sb/sth)**; ~ **(through sth) (for sth)** to examine sb/sth carefully because you are looking for sth; to look for sth that is missing: *The men were arrested and searched for drugs.* ◇ *Were your bags searched at the airport?* ◇ *They are still searching for the missing child.* ◇ *She searched through the papers on the desk, looking for the letter.* ◇ *I started searching the Web for interesting sites.*

search[2] /sɜːtʃ/ ***noun*** **1** [C,U] an act of trying to find sb/sth, especially by looking carefully for them or it: *the search for the missing boy* ◇ *She walked round for hours* ***in search of*** (= looking for) *her missing dog.* **2** [C] (COMPUTING) an act of looking for information: *to do a search on the Internet*

ˈsearch engine ***noun*** [C] (COMPUTING) a computer program that searches the Internet for information

searcher /ˈsɜːtʃə(r)/ ***noun*** [C] **1** a person who is looking for sb/sth **2** (COMPUTING) a program that allows you to look for particular information on a computer

searching /ˈsɜːtʃɪŋ/ ***adj.*** (used about a look, question, etc.) trying to find out the truth: *The customs officers asked a lot of searching questions about our trip.*

searchlight /ˈsɜːtʃlaɪt/ ***noun*** [C] a powerful lamp that can be turned in any direction, used, for example, for finding people or vehicles at night

ˈsearch party ***noun*** [C] a group of people who look for sb who is lost or missing

ˈsearch warrant ***noun*** [C] an official piece of paper that gives the police the right to search a building, etc.

seascape /ˈsiːskeɪp/ ***noun*** [C] (ART) a picture or view of the sea: *a vast, sweeping seascape of sky, waves and sand* ➲ look at **landscape**[1] (2)

seashell /ˈsiːʃel/ ***noun*** [C] the empty shell of a small animal that lives in the sea

seashore /ˈsiːʃɔː(r)/ (usually **the seashore**) ***noun*** [sing.] (GEOGRAPHY) the part of the land that is next to the sea: *We were looking for shells* ***on the seashore***.

seasick /ˈsiːsɪk/ ***adj.*** (HEALTH) feeling sick or VOMITING because of the movement of a boat or ship: *to feel/get/be seasick* ➲ look at **airsick**, **carsick**, **travel-sick**

seaside /ˈsiːsaɪd/ ***noun*** (often **the seaside**) [sing.] (TOURISM) an area on the coast, especially one where people go on holiday: *to go to the seaside* ◇ *a seaside town*

season[1] /ˈsiːzn/ ***noun*** [C] **1** one of the periods of different weather into which the year is divided: *In cool countries the four seasons are spring, summer, autumn and winter.* ◇ *the dry/rainy season* ➲ look at **high season**, **low season**, **off season** **2** the period of the year when sth is common or popular or when sth usually happens or is done: *the holiday/football season*

IDM **in season** **1** (used about fresh foods) available in large quantities **2** (BIOLOGY) (used about a female animal) ready to have sex

out of season **1** (used about fresh foods) not available in large quantities **2** (TOURISM) (used about a place where people go on holiday) at the time of year when it is least popular with tourists

the seasons

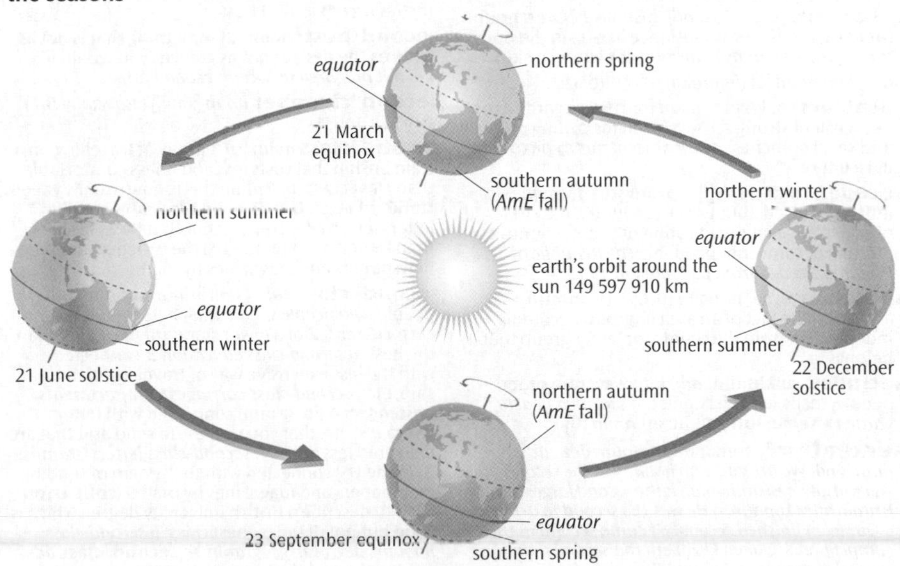

season² 🔑 /'si:zn/ ***verb*** [T] to add salt, pepper, spices, etc. to food in order to make it taste better ▶ **seasoning** ***noun*** [C,U]: *Add seasoning to the soup and serve with bread.*

seasonal /'si:zənl/ ***adj.*** happening or existing at a particular time of the year: *There are a lot of seasonal jobs in the summer.*

seasoned /'si:znd/ ***adj.*** having a lot of experience of sth: *a seasoned traveller*

'season ticket ***noun*** [C] a ticket that allows you to make a particular journey by bus, train, etc. or to go to a theatre or watch a sports team as often as you like for a fixed period of time

seat¹ 🔑 /si:t/ ***noun*** [C] **1** something that you sit on: *Please* ***take a seat*** (=sit down). ◇ *the back/driving/passenger seat of a car* **2** the part of a chair, etc. that you sit on **3** a place in a theatre, on a plane, etc. where you pay to sit: *There are no seats left on that flight.* **4** a place on a council or in a parliament that you win in an election: *to win/lose a seat*
IDM **be in the driving seat** to be the person, group, etc. that has the most powerful position in a particular situation
take a back seat → BACK²

seat² /si:t/ ***verb*** [T] **1** (often passive) (*formal*) to give sb a place to sit; to sit down in a place: *Please be seated.* **2** to have seats or chairs for a particular number of people: *The theatre seats 750 people.*

'seat belt (*also* **'safety belt**) ***noun*** [C] a STRAP that is fixed to the seat in a car or plane and that you wear around your body so that you are not thrown forward if there is an accident: *to fasten/unfasten your seat belt* ➲ look at **belt**

seating /'si:tɪŋ/ ***noun*** [U] the seats or chairs in a place or the way that they are arranged: *The conference hall has seating for 500 people.*

'sea turtle (*AmE*) =TURTLE (1)

seaweed /'si:wi:d/ ***noun*** [U] a plant that grows in the sea. There are many different types of **seaweed**.

seaworthy /'si:wɜ:ði/ ***adj.*** (used about a ship) in a suitable condition to sail ▶ **seaworthiness** ***noun*** [U]

sebaceous /sɪ'beɪʃəs/ ***adj.*** (usually *before* a noun) (**HEALTH**) producing a substance like oil in the body: *the sebaceous glands in the skin* ➲ picture at **skin**

sec /sek/ ***noun*** [C] (*informal*) =SECOND² (2)

secateurs /ˌsekə'tɜ:z/ ***noun*** [pl.] (*BrE*) a garden tool like a pair of strong scissors, used for cutting plants and small branches: *a pair of secateurs* ➲ picture at **agriculture**

secede /sɪ'si:d/ ***verb*** [I] ~ **(from sth)** (*formal*) (**POLITICS**) (used about a state, country, etc.) to officially leave an organization of states, countries, etc. and become independent: *The Republic of Panama seceded from Colombia in 1903.*

secession /sɪ'seʃn/ ***noun*** [U, C] ~ **(from sth)** (**POLITICS**) the fact of an area or group becoming independent from the country or larger group that it belongs to

secluded /sɪ'klu:dɪd/ ***adj.*** far away from other people, roads, etc.; very quiet: *a secluded beach/garden* ▶ **seclusion** /sɪ'klu:ʒn/ ***noun*** [U]

second¹ 🔑 /'sekənd/ ***pronoun, det., adv., noun*** 2nd: *We are going on holiday in the second week in July.* ◇ *Birmingham is the second largest city in Britain after London.* ◇ *He was the second to arrive.* ◇ *Our team finished second.* ◇ ***I came second*** *in the competition.* ◇ *Queen Elizabeth the Second* ◇ ***the second of*** *January* ◇ *January* ***the second***
IDM **second nature (to sb)** something that has become a habit or that you can do easily because you have done it so many times: *With practice, typing becomes second nature.*
second thoughts a change of mind or opinion about sth; doubts that you have when you are not sure if you have made the right decision: ***On second thoughts****, let's go today, not tomorrow.* ◇ *I'm starting to* ***have second thoughts*** *about accepting their offer.*

second² 🔑 /'sekənd/ ***noun*** **1** [C] one of the 60 parts into which a minute is divided **2** (also *informal* **sec**) [C] a short time: *Wait a second, please.* **3** [U] the second of the four or five speeds (**gears**) that a car can move forward in: *Once the car's moving, put it* ***in second****.* **4** [C] something that has a small fault and that is sold at a lower price: *The clothes are all seconds.* **5** [C] (*formal*) a ~ **(in sth)** (**EDUCATION**) the second-best result in a British university degree: *to get an upper/a lower second in physics*

second³ /'sekənd/ ***verb*** [T] to support sb's suggestion or idea at a meeting so that it can then be discussed or voted on

second⁴ /sɪ'kɒnd/ ***verb*** [T] ~ **sb (from sth) (to sth)** to move sb from their job for a fixed period of time to do another job: *Our teacher has been seconded to another school for a year.* ▶ **secondment** ***noun*** [U, C]: *to be on secondment*

secondary 🔑 /'sekəndri/ ***adj.*** **1** less important than sth else: *Other people's opinions are secondary – it's my opinion that counts.* **2** caused by or developing from sth else **3** (*BrE*) (only *before* a noun) (**EDUCATION**) at, or connected with SECONDARY SCHOOL: *secondary students*

'secondary colour ***noun*** [C] a colour made by mixing two primary colours

'secondary school ***noun*** [C] (*BrE*) (**EDUCATION**) a school for children aged from 11 to 18

'secondary source ***noun*** [C] a book or other source of information where the writer has taken the information from some other source and not collected it himself or herself ➲ look at **primary source**

ˌsecond 'best¹ ***adj.*** not quite the best but the next one after the best: *the second-best time in the 100 metres race* ➲ look at **best**

ˌsecond 'best² ***noun*** [U] something that is not as good as the best, or not as good as you would like: *I'm not prepared to accept second best.*

ˌsecond 'chamber ***noun*** [sing.] (*especially BrE*) =UPPER HOUSE

ˌsecond 'class ***noun*** [U] **1** a way of travelling on a train or ship that costs less and is less comfortable than FIRST CLASS. In Britain this is now usually called **standard class**. **2** (in Britain) the way of sending letters, etc. that is cheaper but that takes longer than FIRST CLASS **3** (in the US) the system of sending newspapers and magazines by mail

ˌsecond-'class ***adj.*** **1** less important than other people: *Old people should not be treated as* ***second-class citizens****.* **2** of a lower standard or quality than the best: *a second-class education* **3** connected with the less expensive way of travelling on a train, ship, etc.: ***second-class carriages/compartments/passengers*** **4** (in Britain) connected with letters, packages, etc. that you pay less to send and that are delivered less quickly: ***second-class letters/stamps*** **5** (in the US) connected with the system of sending newspapers and magazines by mail **6** (**EDUCATION**) used to describe a British university degree which is good but not of the highest class: *a second-class honours degree in geography* ▶ **ˌsecond 'class** ***adv.***: *to travel second class* ◇ *to send a letter second class*

ˌsecond ˈcousin *noun* [C] the child of your mother's or father's COUSIN

ˌsecond-deˈgree *adj.* (only *before* a noun) **1** (*especially AmE*) (**LAW**) (used about murder) not of the most serious kind **2** (**HEALTH**) (used about burns) of the second most serious of three kinds, causing the skin to form bubbles (**blisters**) but not leaving any permanent marks ➲ look at **first-degree**, **third-degree**

ˌsecond ˈfloor *noun* [C] the floor in a building that is two floors above the lowest floor: *I live on the second floor.* ◇ *a second-floor flat* ❶ In American English the second floor is next above the lowest.

ˈsecond hand *noun* [C] the hand on some clocks and watches that shows seconds

ˌsecond-ˈhand *adj.*, *adv.* **1** already used or owned by sb else: *a second-hand car* ◇ *I bought this camera second-hand.* ➲ look at **old 2** (used about news or information) that you heard from sb else, and did not see or experience yourself ➲ look at **hand**

ˌsecond ˈlanguage *noun* [C] (**LANGUAGE**) a language that is not the language that you learned first, as a child, but which you learn because it is used, often for official purposes, in your country: *French is the second language of several countries in Africa.*

secondly /ˈsekəndli/ *adv.* (used when you are giving your second reason or opinion) also: *Firstly, I think it's too expensive and secondly, we don't really need it.*

ˈsecond name *noun* [C] (*especially BrE*) **1** = SURNAME **2** a second personal name: *His second name is Prabhakar, after his father.*

the ˌsecond ˈperson *noun* [sing.] (**LANGUAGE**) the set of pronouns and verb forms that you use when you talk to sb: *In the phrase 'you are', the verb 'are' is in the second person and the word 'you' is a second-person pronoun.* ➲ look at **the first person**, **the third person**

ˌsecond-ˈrate *adj.* of poor quality: *a second-rate poet*

secrecy /ˈsiːkrəsi/ *noun* [U] being secret or keeping sth secret: *I must stress the importance of secrecy in this matter.*

secret[1] 🔑 /ˈsiːkrət/ *noun* **1** [C] something that is not or must not be known by other people: *to* ***keep a secret*** ◇ *to let sb in on/tell sb a secret* ◇ *I can't tell you where we're going – it's a secret.* ◇ ***It's no secret that*** *they don't like each other* (= everybody knows). **2** [sing.] the only way or the best way of doing or achieving sth: *What is the secret of your success* (= how did you become so successful)?

IDM **in secret** without other people knowing: *to meet in secret*

secret[2] 🔑 /ˈsiːkrət/ *adj.* **1** ~ (**from sb**) that is not or must not be known by other people: *We have to* ***keep*** *the party* ***secret*** *from Carmen.* ◇ *a secret address* ◇ *a secret love affair* **2** used to describe actions that you do not tell anyone about: *a secret drinker* ◇ *She's got a secret admirer.* ▶ **secretly** *adv.*: *The government secretly agreed to pay the kidnappers.*

ˌsecret ˈagent (*also* **agent**) *noun* [C] a person who tries to find out secret information, especially about the government of another country ➲ look at **spy**

secretarial /ˌsekrəˈteəriəl/ *adj.* involving or connected with the work that a secretary does: *secretarial skills/work*

secretariat /ˌsekrəˈteəriət/ *noun* [C] (**POLITICS**) the department of a large international or political organization, especially the office of a SECRETARY GENERAL, that manages the way the organization is run

secretary 🔑 /ˈsekrətri/ *noun* [C] (*pl.* **secretaries**) **1** a person who works in an office. A secretary types letters, answers the telephone, keeps records, etc.: *the director's personal secretary* **2** an official of a club or society who is responsible for keeping records, writing letters, etc. **3** (*AmE*) (**POLITICS**) the head of a government department, chosen by the President **4** (*BrE*) = SECRETARY OF STATE (1)

ˌSecretary ˈGeneral *noun* [C] the person who is in charge of the department which runs a large international or political organization

ˌSecretary of ˈState *noun* [C] **1** (*also* **Secretary**) (**POLITICS**) (in Britain) the head of one of the main government departments: *the Secretary of State for Defence* **2** (in the US) the head of the government department that deals with foreign affairs

secrete /sɪˈkriːt/ *verb* [T] **1** (used about a part of a plant, animal or person) to produce a liquid **2** (*formal*) to hide sth in a secret place

secretion /sɪˈkriːʃn/ *noun* (*formal*) [C,U] a liquid that is produced by a plant or an animal; the process by which the liquid is produced: *The frog covers itself in a poisonous secretion for protection.*

secretive /ˈsiːkrətɪv/ *adj.* liking to keep things secret from other people: *Wendy is very secretive about her private life.* ▶ **secretively** *adv.* ▶ **secretiveness** *noun* [U]

ˌsecret poˈlice *noun* [C, with sing. or pl. verb] (**POLITICS**) a police force that works secretly to make sure that people behave as their government wants

the ˌsecret ˈservice *noun* [sing., with sing. or pl. verb] (**POLITICS**) the government department that tries to find out secret information about other countries and governments

sect /sekt/ *noun* [C] (**POLITICS**, **RELIGION**) a group of people who have a particular set of religious or political beliefs. A **sect** has often broken away from a larger group.

sectarian /sekˈteəriən/ *adj.* (**RELIGION**) connected with the differences that exists between religious groups: *sectarian violence*

section[1] 🔑 AW /ˈsekʃn/ *noun* [C] **1** one of the parts into which sth is divided: *the string section of an orchestra* ◇ *the financial section of a newspaper* ◇ *The library has an excellent reference section.* **2** a drawing or diagram of sth as it would look if it were cut from top to bottom or from one side to the other: *The illustration shows a section through a leaf.* **3** (**HEALTH**) the act of cutting or separating sth in an operation: *The surgeon performed a section* (= made a cut) *on the vein.* ➲ look at **Caesarean**

section[2] AW /ˈsekʃn/ *verb* [T] **1** (**HEALTH**) to divide body TISSUE by cutting **2** (**BIOLOGY**) to cut animal or plant TISSUE into thin slices in order to look at it under a MICROSCOPE **3** (**HEALTH**) (*BrE*) to officially order a mentally ill person to go and receive treatment in a PSYCHIATRIC hospital, using a law that can force them to stay there until they are successfully treated

sector 🔑 AW /ˈsektə(r)/ *noun* [C] **1** a part of the business activity of a country: *The manufacturing sector has declined in recent years.* ➲ look at **the private sector**, **the public sector** **2** a part of an area or of a large group of people: *the Christian sector of* *the city* **3** (MATHEMATICS) a part of a circle that is between two straight lines drawn from the centre to the edge ➲ picture at **circle**

secular /'sekjələ(r)/ ***adj.*** (RELIGION) not concerned with religion or the church

secure¹ 🔑 AW /sɪ'kjʊə(r)/ ***adj.*** **1** free from worry or doubt; confident: *Children need to **feel secure**.* ◇ *to be financially secure* OPP **insecure** **2** not likely to be lost; safe: *Business is good so his job is secure.* ◇ *a secure investment* **3** not likely to fall or be broken; firmly fixed: *That ladder doesn't look very secure.* **4** ~ **(against/from sth)** well locked or protected: *Check that the house is secure against intruders.* ▶ **securely** AW ***adv.***: *All doors and windows must be securely fastened.*

secure² 🔑 AW /sɪ'kjʊə(r)/ ***verb*** [T] **1** ~ **sth (to sth)** to fix or lock sth firmly: *The load was secured with ropes.* ◇ *Secure the rope to a tree or a rock.* **2** ~ **sth (against/from sth)** to make sth safe: *The sea wall needs strengthening to secure the town against flooding.* **3** to obtain or achieve sth, especially by having to make a big effort: *The company has secured a contract to build ten planes.*

security 🔑 AW /sɪ'kjʊərəti/ ***noun*** (*pl.* **securities**) **1** [U] the state of feeling safe and being free from worry; protection against the difficulties of life: *Children need the security of a stable home environment.* ◇ *financial/job security* OPP **insecurity** **2** [U] things that you do to protect sb/sth from attack, danger, thieves, etc.: *Security was tightened at the airport before the president arrived.* ◇ *The robbers were caught on the bank's **security cameras**.* **3** [U] (BUSINESS) the section of a large company or organization that deals with the protection of buildings, equipment and staff: *If you see a suspicious bag, contact airport security immediately.* **4** [C,U] (FINANCE) something of value that you use when you borrow money. If you cannot pay the money back then you lose the thing you gave as security **6** **securities** [pl.] (BUSINESS) documents proving that sb is the owner of shares, etc. in a particular company: *government securities*

sedan /sɪ'dæn/ ***noun*** [C] (*AmE*) = SALOON

sedate¹ /sɪ'deɪt/ ***adj.*** quiet, calm and well behaved

sedate² /sɪ'deɪt/ ***verb*** [T] (HEALTH) to give sb a drug or medicine to make them feel calm or want to sleep: *The lion was sedated and treated by a vet.* ▶ **sedation** /sɪ'deɪʃn/ ***noun*** [U]: *The doctor put her **under sedation**.*

sedative /'sedətɪv/ ***noun*** [C] (HEALTH) a drug or medicine that makes you feel calm or want to sleep ➲ look at **tranquillizer**

sedentary /'sedntri/ ***adj.*** involving a lot of sitting down; not active: *a sedentary lifestyle/job*

sediment /'sedɪmənt/ ***noun*** [U,C] **1** (CHEMISTRY) the thick substance that forms at the bottom of a liquid **2** (GEOLOGY) sand, stones, mud, etc. carried by water or wind and left, for example, on the bottom of a lake, river, etc. ➲ picture at **rock**

sedimentary /ˌsedɪ'mentri/ ***adj.*** (GEOLOGY) (used about rocks) formed from the sand, stones, mud, etc. that are at the bottom of lakes, rivers, etc. ➲ look at **igneous**, **metamorphic** ➲ picture at **rock**

sedimentation /ˌsedɪmen'teɪʃn/ ***noun*** [U] (GEOLOGY) the process of leaving SEDIMENT, for example on the bottom of a lake, river, etc. ➲ picture at **water**

sedition /sɪ'dɪʃn/ ***noun*** [U] (*formal*) (POLITICS) the use of words or actions that are intended to encourage people to be or act against a government ▶ **seditious** ***adj.***

seduce /sɪ'dju:s/ ***verb*** [T] **1** ~ **sb (into sth/doing sth)** to persuade sb to do sth they would not usually agree to do: *Special offers seduce customers into spending their money.* **2** to persuade sb to have sex with you ▶ **seduction** /sɪ'dʌkʃn/ ***noun*** [C,U]

seductive /sɪ'dʌktɪv/ ***adj.*** **1** sexually attractive: *a seductive smile* **2** attractive in a way that makes you want to have or do sth: *a seductive argument/opinion* (= one which you want to agree with)

see 🔑 /si:/ ***verb*** (*pt* **saw** /sɔ:/; *pp* **seen** /si:n/) **1** [I,T] to become conscious of sth, using your eyes; to use the power of sight: *It was so dark that we couldn't see.* ◇ *On a clear day you can see for miles.* ◇ *Have you seen my wallet anywhere?* ◇ *I've just seen a mouse run under the cooker.* ◇ *He looked for her but couldn't see her in the crowd.* **2** [T] to look at or watch a film, play, television programme, etc.: *Did you see that programme on sharks last night?* ◇ *Have you seen Spielberg's latest film?* **3** [T] to find out sth by looking, asking or waiting: ***Go and see** if the postman has been yet.* ◇ *We'll **wait and see** what happens before making any decisions.* ◇ *'Can we go swimming today, Dad?' 'I'll see.'* ◇ *I saw in the paper that they're building a new theatre.* **4** [T] to spend time with sb; to visit sb: *I saw Alan at the weekend; we had dinner together.* ◇ *You should see a doctor about that cough.* **5** [I,T] to understand sth; to realize sth: *Do you **see what I mean**?* ◇ *She doesn't **see the point in** spending so much money on a car.* ◇ *'You have to key in your password first.' 'Oh, **I see**.'* ➲ note at **regard¹** **6** [T] to have an opinion about sth: *How do you see the situation developing?* **7** [T] to imagine sth as a future possibility: *I can't see her changing her mind.* **8** [T] to do what is necessary in a situation; to make sure that sb does sth: *I'll **see that** he gets the letter.* **9** [T] to go with sb, for example to help or protect them: *He asked me if he could see me home, but I said no.* ◇ *I'll see you to the door.* **10** [T] to be the time when an event happens: *Last year saw huge changes in the education system.* **11** [T] to have a romantic relationship with sb: *Is Frank seeing anybody at the moment?*

IDM **as far as I can see** → FAR²

as far as the eye can see → FAR²

let me see; let's see → LET

see eye to eye (with sb) to agree with sb; to have the same opinion as sb: *We don't always see eye to eye on political matters.*

see if... to try to do sth: *I'll see if I can find time to do it.* ◇ *See if you can undo this knot.*

see you around (*informal*) used for saying goodbye to sb you have made no arrangement to see again

see you (later) used for saying goodbye to sb you expect to see soon or later that day

you see used for giving a reason: *She's very unhappy. He was her first real boyfriend, you see.*

PHR V **see about sth/doing sth** to deal with sth: *I've got to go to the bank to see about my traveller's cheques.*

see sb off to go with sb to the railway station, the airport, etc. in order to say goodbye to them

see through sb/sth to be able to see that sb/sth is not what he/she/it appears: *The police immediately saw through his story.*

see to sb/sth to do what is necessary in a situation; to deal with sb/sth: *I'll see to the travel arrangements and you book the hotel.*

seed 🔑 /si:d/ ***noun*** **1** [C,U] (BIOLOGY) the small hard part of a plant from which a new plant of the same kind can grow: *a packet of sunflower seeds* **2** [C] the start of a feeling or event that continues to grow **3** [C] a player in a sports competition, especially TENNIS, who is expected to finish in a high position

seeded /'si:dɪd/ ***adj.*** (SPORT) (used about a player or a team) expected to finish in a high position

seedless /'si:dləs/ ***adj.*** (used about fruit) having no seeds: *seedless grapes*

seedling /'si:dlɪŋ/ ***noun*** [C] (BIOLOGY) a very young plant or tree that has grown from a seed

seedy /'si:di/ ***adj.*** dirty and unpleasant; possibly connected with illegal or immoral activities: *a seedy hotel/neighbourhood*

seeing /'si:ɪŋ/ (*also* **seeing that**; **seeing as**) ***conj.*** (*informal*) because; as: *Seeing as we're going the same way, I'll give you a lift.*

ˌSeeing 'Eye dog ***noun*** [C] = GUIDE DOG

seek 🔑 AW /si:k/ ***verb*** [T] (*pt, pp* **sought** /sɔ:t/) (*formal*) **1** to try to find or get sth: *Politicians are still seeking a peaceful solution.* **2 ~ sth (from sb)** to ask sb for sth: *You should seek advice from a solicitor about what to do next.* **3 ~ (to do sth)** to try to do sth: *They are still seeking to find a peaceful solution to the conflict.* **4 -seeking** (used to form compound adjectives) looking for or trying to get the thing mentioned: *attention-seeking behaviour* ◇ *a heat-seeking missile*

seeker /'si:kə(r)/ ***noun*** [C] (often used in compounds) a person who is trying to find or get the thing mentioned: *an attention seeker* ◇ *asylum seekers*

seem 🔑 /si:m/ ***linking verb*** **~ (to sb) (to be) sth; ~ (like) sth** (not in the continuous tenses) to give the impression of being or doing sth; to appear: *Emma seems (like) a very nice girl.* ◇ *Emma seems to be a very nice girl.* ◇ *It seems to me that we have no choice.* ◇ *You seem happy today.* ◇ *This machine doesn't seem to work.*

seeming /'si:mɪŋ/ ***adj.*** (only *before* a noun) appearing to be sth: *Despite her seeming enthusiasm, Sandra didn't really help much.* ▶ **seemingly** ***adv.***: *a seemingly endless list of complaints*

seen past participle of **see**

seep /si:p/ ***verb*** [I] (used about a liquid) to flow very slowly through sth: *Water started seeping in through small cracks.*

'see-saw ***noun*** [C] an outdoor toy for children that consists of a long piece of wood that is balanced in the middle. One child sits on each end of the **see-saw** and one goes up while the other goes down.

seethe /si:ð/ ***verb*** [I] **1** to be very angry: *She seethed silently in the corner.* **2 ~ (with sth)** to be very crowded: *The streets were seething with people.*

segment /'segmənt/ ***noun*** [C] **1** a section or part of sth: *I've divided the sheet of paper into three segments.* ◇ *a segment of the population* ➲ picture at **circle 2** one of the sections of an orange, a lemon, etc. **3** (MATHEMATICS) a part of a circle separated from the rest by a single line ▶ **segment** /seg'ment/ ***verb*** [T]: *Market researchers often segment the population on the basis of age and social class.*

segmentation /ˌsegmen'teɪʃn/ ***noun*** [U, C] the act of dividing sth into different parts; one of these parts: *the segmentation of social classes* ➲ look at **market segmentation**

segregate /'segrɪgeɪt/ ***verb*** [T] **~ sb/sth (from sb/sth)** (SOCIAL STUDIES) to separate one group of people or things from the rest: *The two groups of football fans were segregated to avoid trouble.* ➲ look at **integrate** ▶ **segregation** /ˌsegrɪ'geɪʃn/ ***noun*** [U]: *racial segregation* (= separating people of different races)

segregationist /ˌsegrɪ'geɪʃənɪst/ ***adj.*** (POLITICS) supporting the separation of people according to their sex, race or religion: *segregationist policies* ▶ **segregationist** ***noun*** [C]

seismic waves

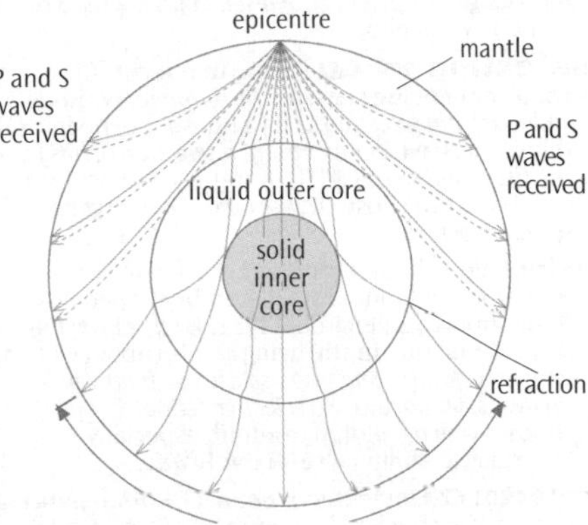

seismic /'saɪzmɪk/ ***adj.*** (GEOLOGY) connected with or caused by movements in the earth's surface (**earthquakes**)

seismograph /'saɪzməgrɑ:f/ ***noun*** [C] (GEOLOGY) an instrument that measures and records information about movements in the earth's surface (**earthquakes**)

seismology /saɪz'mɒlədʒi/ ***noun*** [U] (GEOLOGY) the scientific study of movements in the earth's surface (**earthquakes**)

seize /si:z/ ***verb*** [T] **1** to take hold of sth suddenly and firmly; to grab sth: *The thief seized her handbag and ran off with it.* ◇ (*figurative*) *to seize a chance/an opportunity* **2** to take control or possession of sb/sth: *The police seized 50 kilos of illegal drugs.* **3** (usually passive) (used about an emotion) to affect sb suddenly and very strongly: *I felt myself seized by panic.*

PHR V **seize (on/upon) sth** to make use of a good and unexpected chance: *He seized on a mistake by the goalkeeper and scored.*

seize up (used about a machine) to stop working because it is too hot, does not have enough oil, etc.

seizure /'si:ʒə(r)/ ***noun*** **1** [U] using force or legal authority to take control or possession of sth: *the seizure of 30 kilos of heroin by police* **2** [C] (HEALTH) a sudden strong attack of an illness, especially one affecting the brain

seldom /'seldəm/ ***adv.*** not often: *There is seldom snow in Athens.* ◇ *I very seldom go to the theatre.* SYN **rarely**

select[1] 🔑 AW /sɪ'lekt/ ***verb*** [T] to choose sb/sth from a number of similar things: *The best candidates will be selected for interview.* HELP **Select** is more formal than **choose** and suggests that a lot of care is taken when making the decision.

select² AW /sɪ'lekt/ ***adj.*** (*formal*) **1** carefully chosen as the best of a group: *A university education is no longer the privilege of* ***a select few.*** **2** used or owned by rich people

select² AW /sɪ'lekt/ ***adj.*** (*formal*) **1** carefully chosen as the best of a group: *A university education is no longer the privilege of* ***a select few.*** **2** used or owned by rich people

selection 🔑 AW /sɪ'lekʃn/ ***noun*** **1** [U] choosing or being chosen: *The manager is responsible for team selection.* **2** [C] a number of people or things that have been chosen: *a selection of hits from the fifties and sixties* **3** [C] a number of things from which you can chose: *This shop has a very good selection of toys.*

selective AW /sɪ'lektɪv/ ***adj.*** **1** affecting or concerned with only a small number of people or things from a larger group: *the* ***selective breeding*** *of cattle* **2** ~ **(about/in sth)** being careful about what or who you choose: *She's very selective about who she invites to her parties.* ◇ *a selective school* (=one that chooses which children to admit, especially according to ability) ▶ **selectively** ***adv.***

selector AW /sɪ'lektə(r)/ ***noun*** [C] **1** (*BrE*) (SPORT) a person who chooses the members of a particular sports team **2** a device in an engine, a piece of machinery, etc. that allows you to choose a particular function

selenium /sə'liːniəm/ ***noun*** [U] (*symbol* **Se**) (CHEMISTRY) a chemical element. **Selenium** is a grey substance that is used in making electrical equipment and coloured glass. A lack of **selenium** in the human body can lead to illnesses such as DEPRESSION. ❶ For more information on the periodic table of elements, look at pages R34-5.

self 🔑 /self/ ***noun*** [C] (*pl.* **selves** /selvz/) a person's own nature or qualities: *It's good to see you back to* ***your old self*** *again* (=feeling well or happy again). ◇ *Her spiteful remark revealed her* ***true self*** (=what she was really like).

self- ***prefix*** (used in nouns and adjectives) of, to, or by yourself or itself: *self-control* ◇ *self-addressed* ◇ *self-taught*

ˌself-'access ***noun*** [U] (EDUCATION) a method of learning in which students choose their materials and use them to study on their own: ***a self-access centre/library***

ˌself-addressed 'envelope = STAMPED ADDRESSED ENVELOPE

ˌself-as'sured ***adj.*** = ASSURED ▶ **ˌself-as'surance** ***noun*** [U] = ASSURANCE (2)

ˌself-'catering ***adj.*** (*BrE*) (TOURISM) (used about a holiday or a place to stay) where meals are not provided for you so you cook them yourself

ˌself-'centred (*AmE* **self-centered**) ***adj.*** thinking only about yourself and not about other people ➲ look at **selfish**

ˌself-con'fessed ***adj.*** admitting that you are sth or do sth that most people consider to be bad: *a self-confessed chocolate addict*

ˌself-'confident ***adj.*** feeling sure about your own value and abilities ➲ look at **confident** ▶ **ˌself-'confidence** ***noun*** [U]: *Many women lack the self-confidence to apply for senior jobs.*

ˌself-'conscious ***adj.*** too worried about what other people think about you ▶ **ˌself-'consciously** ***adv.*** ▶ **ˌself-'consciousness** ***noun*** [U]

ˌself-con'tained ***adj.*** (*BrE*) (used about a flat, etc.) having its own private entrance, kitchen and bathroom

ˌself-con'trol ***noun*** [U] the ability to control your emotions and appear calm even when you are angry, afraid, excited, etc.: *to lose/keep your self-control*

ˌself-de'fence (*AmE* **ˌself de'fense**) ***noun*** [U] the use of force to protect yourself or your property: *Lee is learning karate for self-defence.* ◇ *to shoot sb* ***in self-defence*** (=because they are going to attack you)

ˌself-des'truct ***verb*** [I] (used especially about a machine, etc.) to destroy itself, usually by exploding ▶ **self-destructive** ***adj.*** ▶ **self-destruction** ***noun*** [U]

ˌself-deˌtermi'nation ***noun*** [U] (POLITICS, SOCIAL STUDIES) the right of a country and its people to be independent and to choose their own government and political system
SYN **independence**

ˌself-'discipline ***noun*** [U] the ability to make yourself do sth difficult or unpleasant: *It takes a lot of self-discipline to give up smoking.*

ˌself-em'ployed ***adj.*** working for yourself and earning money from your own business

ˌself-es'teem ***noun*** [U] a good opinion of your own character and abilities: *a man with high/low self-esteem*

ˌself-'evident ***adj.*** that does not need any proof or explanation; clear

ˌself-ex'planatory ***adj.*** clear and easy to understand; not needing to be explained: *The book's title is self-explanatory.*

ˌself-im'portant ***adj.*** thinking that you are more important than other people ▶ **ˌself-im'portance** ***noun*** [U] ▶ **ˌself-im'portantly** ***adv.***

ˌself-in'dulgent ***adj.*** allowing yourself to have or do things you enjoy (sometimes when it would be better to stop yourself)
▶ **ˌself-in'dulgence** ***noun*** [C,U]

ˌself-'interest ***noun*** [U] thinking about what is best for you rather than for other people

selfish /'selfɪʃ/ ***adj.*** thinking only about your own needs or wishes and not about other people's: *a selfish attitude* ◇ *I'm sick of your selfish behaviour!*
OPP **unselfish, selfless** ➲ look at **self-centred**
▶ **selfishly** ***adv.*** ▶ **selfishness** ***noun*** [U]

selfless /'selfləs/ ***adj.*** thinking more about other people's needs or wishes than your own

ˌself-'made ***adj.*** having become rich or successful by your own efforts: *a self-made millionaire*

ˌself-'pity ***noun*** [U] the state of thinking too much about your own problems or troubles and feeling sorry for yourself

ˌself-'portrait ***noun*** [C] (ART) a picture that you draw or paint of yourself

ˌself-raising 'flour (*AmE* **ˌself-'rising flour**) ***noun*** [U] flour that contains BAKING POWDER (a powder that makes cakes, etc. rise during cooking) ➲ look at **plain flour**

ˌself-re'liant ***adj.*** not depending on help from anyone else ➲ look at **reliant**

ˌself-re'spect ***noun*** [U] a feeling of confidence and pride in yourself: *Old people need to keep their dignity and self-respect.* ➲ look at **respect**
▶ **ˌself-re'specting** ***adj.*** (often in negative sentences): *No self-respecting language student* (=nobody who is serious about learning a language) *should be without this book.*

ˌ**self-re'straint** *noun* [U] the ability to stop yourself doing or saying sth, because you know it is better not to do or say it: *She* ***exercised*** *all her* ***self-restraint*** *and kept quiet.*

ˌ**self-'righteous** *adj.* believing that you are always right and other people are wrong, so that you are better than other people ➲ look at **righteous** ▶ **self-righteously** *adv.* ▶ **self-righteousness** *noun* [U]

ˌ**self-'rising flour** (*AmE*) = SELF-RAISING FLOUR

ˌ**self-'sacrifice** *noun* [U] giving up what you need or want, in order to help others

ˌ**self-'satisfied** *adj.* too pleased with yourself or with what you have done **SYN smug**

ˌ**self-'service** *adj.* (used about a shop, restaurant, etc.) where you serve yourself and then pay at a special desk (**cash desk**)

ˌ**self-'study** *noun* [U] (EDUCATION) the activity of learning about sth without a teacher to help you ▶ **self-study** *adj.*

ˌ**self-'styled** *adj.* (only *before* a noun) using a name or title that you have given yourself, especially when you do not gave the right to do it: *the self-styled king of fashion*

ˌ**self-suf'ficient** *adj.* able to produce or provide everything that you need without help from or having to buy from others

sell ⊶ /sel/ *verb* (*pt, pp* **sold** /səʊld/) **1** [I,T] ~ **(sb) (sth) (at/for sth)**; ~ **(sth) (to sb) (at/for sth)** to give sth to sb who pays for it and is then the owner of it: *We are going to sell our car.* ◇ *I sold my guitar to my neighbour for £200.* ◇ *Would you sell me your ticket?* ◇ *I offered them a lot of money but they wouldn't sell.* **2** [T] to offer sth for people to buy: *Excuse me, do you sell stamps?* ◇ *to sell insurance/advertising space* **3** [I,T] to be bought by people in the way or in the numbers mentioned; to be offered at the price mentioned: *These watches sell at £1000 each in the shops but you can have this one for £500.* ◇ *Her books sell well abroad.* ◇ *This newspaper sells over a million copies a day.* **4** [T] to make people want to buy sth: *They rely on advertising to sell their products.* ➲ noun for senses **1** to **4** is **sale**
5 [T] ~ **sth/yourself to sb** to persuade sb to accept sth; to persuade sb that you are the right person for a job, position, etc.: *Now we have to try and sell the idea to the management.*
IDM be sold on sth (*informal*) to be very enthusiastic about sth
PHR V sell sth off to sell sth in order to get rid of it, often at a low price: *The shops sell their remaining winter clothes off in the spring sales.*
sell out; be sold out (used about tickets for a concert, football game, etc.) to be all sold: *All the tickets sold out within two hours* ◇ *The concert was sold out weeks ago.*
sell out (of sth); be sold out (of sth) to sell all of sth so that no more is available to be bought: *I'm afraid we've sold out of bread.*
sell up to sell everything you own, especially your house, your business, etc. (in order to start a new life, move to another country, etc.)

'**sell-by date** *noun* [C] (*BrE*) the date printed on food containers after which the food should not be sold: *This milk is past its sell-by date.*

seller /'selə(r)/ *noun* [C] **1** (often in compounds) a person or business that sells: *a bookseller* ◇ *a flower seller* **2** something that is sold, especially in the amount or way mentioned: *This magazine is a big seller in the 25-40 age group.* ➲ look at **best seller**

'**selling price** *noun* [C] (FINANCE) the price at which sth is sold ➲ look at **asking price**, **cost price**

Sellotape™ /'seləteɪp/ (*AmE* '**Scotch tape™**) *noun* [U] a type of clear tape that is sold in rolls and used for sticking things ➲ look at **tape** ▶ **sellotape** *verb* [T]

'**sell-out** *noun* [C, usually sing.] a play, concert, etc. for which all the tickets have been sold: *Next week's final is likely to be a sell-out.* ◇ *The band are on a sell-out tour.*

selves plural of **self**

semantic /sɪ'mæntɪk/ *adj.* (LANGUAGE) connected with the meaning of words and sentences ▶ **semantically** /-kli/ *adv.*

semantics /sɪ'mæntɪks/ *noun* [U] (LANGUAGE) **1** the study of the meanings of words and phrases **2** the meaning of words and phrases: *the semantics of the language*

semblance /'sembləns/ *noun* [sing., U] (*formal*) **(a) ~ of sth** the appearance of being sth or of having a certain quality

semen /'si:men/ *noun* [U] (BIOLOGY) the liquid that is produced by the male sex organs, containing the seed (**sperm**) necessary for producing babies or young

semester /sɪ'mestə(r)/ *noun* [C] (EDUCATION) (especially in the US) one of the two periods that the school or college year is divided into: *the spring/fall semester* ➲ look at **term**[1] (4), **trimester**

semi /'semi/ *noun* [C] (*pl.* **semis** /'semiz/) (*BrE, informal*) a house that is joined to another house with a shared wall on one side

semi- /'semi/ *prefix* (used in adjectives and nouns) half; partly: *semicircular* ◇ *semi-final*

ˌ**semi-'arid** *adj.* (GEOGRAPHY) (used about land or climate) dry; with little rain

semibreve /'semibri:v/ (*AmE* **whole note**) *noun* [C] (MUSIC) a type of note ➲ note at **crotchet** ➲ picture at **music**

semicircle /'semisɜ:kl/ *noun* [C] one half of a circle; something that is arranged in this shape: *I want you all to sit* ***in a semicircle.*** ➲ picture at **circle** ▶ **semicircular** /ˌsemi'sɜ:kjələ(r)/ *adj.*

ˌ**semiˌcircular ca'nals** *noun* [pl.] (ANATOMY) three SEMICIRCULAR tubes in the inner ear, which are filled with liquid and are connected together. The **semicircular canals** are important for the body's balance. ➲ picture at **ear**

semicolon /ˌsemi'kəʊlən/ *noun* [C] (LANGUAGE) a mark (;) used in writing for separating parts of a sentence or items in a list

semiconductor /ˌsemikən'dʌktə(r)/ *noun* [C] (PHYSICS) a solid substance that allows heat or electricity to pass through it or along it in particular conditions ➲ look at **conductor**

ˌ**semi-de'tached** *adj.* (used about a house) joined to another house with a shared wall on one side

ˌ**semi-'final** *noun* [C] (SPORT) one of the two games in a sports competition which decide which players or teams will play each other in the final ➲ look at **quarter-final**, **final** ▶ ˌ**semi-'finalist** *noun* [C]

seminar /'semɪnɑ:(r)/ *noun* [C] **1** (EDUCATION) a class at a university, college, etc. in which a small group of students discuss or study a subject with a teacher: *Teaching is by lectures and seminars.* ◇ *a graduate seminar* ◇ *a seminar room* **2** (BUSINESS) a meeting for business people in which working methods, etc. are taught or discussed: *a one-day management seminar*

semiquaver /ˈsemikweɪvə(r)/ (*AmE* **sixteenth note**) *noun* [C] (MUSIC) a type of note ➲ note at **crotchet** ➲ picture at **music**

ˌ**semi-ˈskilled** *adj.* (used about workers) having some special training or QUALIFICATIONS, but less than skilled people

semitone /ˈsemitəʊn/ (*AmE* **half step**; **half-tone**) *noun* [C] (MUSIC) the shortest step between notes in a musical scale, for example between C♯ and D, or B♭ and B ➲ look at **tone**

semolina /ˌseməˈliːnə/ *noun* [U] large hard grains of WHEAT used for making sweet dishes and PASTA

Sen. *abbr.* (POLITICS) (in the US) Senator

senate ⊶ /ˈsenət/ *noun* (often **the Senate**) [C, with sing. or pl. verb] (POLITICS) one of the two groups of elected politicians who make laws in the government in some countries, for example the US ➲ look at **Congress**, **House of Representatives**

senator ⊶ /ˈsenətə(r)/ *noun* (often **Senator**) (*abbr.* Sen.) [C] (POLITICS) a member of THE SENATE: *Senator McCarthy*

send ⊶ /send/ *verb* [T] (*pt, pp* **sent** /sent/) **1** ~ **sth (to sb/sth)**; ~ **(sb) sth** to make sth go or be taken somewhere, especially by mail, radio, etc.: *to send a letter/parcel/message/fax to sb* ◇ *Don't forget to send me a postcard.* **2** to tell sb to go somewhere or to do sth; to arrange for sb to go somewhere: *My company is sending me on a training course next month.* ◇ *She* ***sent*** *the children* ***to bed*** *early.* ◇ ***to send sb to prison*** ◇ *I'll send someone round to collect you at 10.00.* **3** to cause sb/sth to move in a particular direction, often quickly or as a reaction that cannot be prevented: *I accidentally pushed the table and* ***sent*** *all the drinks* ***flying.*** **4** ~ **sb (to/into sth)** to make sb have a particular feeling or enter a particular state: *The movement of the train* ***sent*** *me* ***to sleep.***

IDM **give/send sb your love** → LOVE[1]

PHR V **send for sb/sth** to ask for sb to come to you; to ask for sth to be brought or sent to you: *Quick! Send for an ambulance!*

send sth in to send sth to a place where it will be officially dealt with: *I sent my application in three weeks ago but I still haven't had a reply.*

send off (for sth); **send away (to sb) (for sth)** to write to sb and ask for sth to be sent to you: *Let's send off for some holiday brochures.*

send sb off (SPORT) to order a player who has broken a rule to leave the field and not to return

send sth off to post sth: *I'll send the information off today.*

send sth out 1 to send sth to a lot of different people or places: *We sent out the invitations two months before the wedding.* **2** to produce sth, for example light, heat, sound, etc.

send sb/sth up (*BrE, informal*) to make sb/sth look ridiculous or silly, especially by copying them in a way that is intended to be amusing

sender /ˈsendə(r)/ *noun* [C] a person who sends sth: *The sender's name appears at the top of the email.*

senile /ˈsiːnaɪl/ *adj.* (HEALTH) behaving in a confused and strange way, and unable to remember things because of old age: *I think she's* ***going senile.*** ▶ **senility** /səˈnɪləti/ *noun* [U]

senior[1] ⊶ /ˈsiːniə(r)/ *adj.* **1** ~ **(to sb)** having a high or higher position in a company, organization, etc.: *a senior lecturer/officer/manager* ◇ *He's senior to me.* **2** (often **Senior**) (*abbr.* **Snr**; **Sr**) (*especially AmE*) used after the name of a man who has the same name as his son, to avoid confusion **3** (*BrE*) (EDUCATION) (used in schools) older **4** (*AmE*) (EDUCATION) connected with the final year in a HIGH SCHOOL or college ➲ look at **junior[1]** (4)

senior[2] ⊶ /ˈsiːniə(r)/ *noun* [C] **1** somebody who is older or of a higher position (than one or more other people): *My oldest sister is* ***ten years my senior.*** ◇ *She felt undervalued, both by her colleagues and her seniors.* **2** (*BrE*) (EDUCATION) one of the older students at a school **3** (*AmE*) (EDUCATION) a student in the final year of school, college or university: *high school seniors* ➲ look at **junior[2]**

ˌ**senior ˈcitizen** = OLD-AGE PENSIONER

ˌ**senior ˈhigh school** (*also* ˌ**senior ˈhigh**) *noun* [C,U] (EDUCATION) (in the US) a school for young people between the ages of 14 and 18 ➲ look at **junior high school**

seniority /ˌsiːniˈɒrəti/ *noun* [U] the position or importance that a person has in a company, organization, etc. in relation to others: *The names are listed below* ***in order of seniority.***

sensation /senˈseɪʃn/ *noun* **1** [C] a feeling that is caused by sth affecting your body or part of your body: *a pleasant/unpleasant/tingling sensation* **2** [U] the ability to feel when touching or being touched: *For some time after the accident he had no sensation in his legs.* **3** [C, usually sing.] a general feeling or impression that is difficult to explain: *I had the peculiar sensation that I was floating in the air.* **4** [C, usually sing.] great excitement, surprise or interest among a group of people; sb/sth that causes this excitement: *The young American* ***caused a sensation*** *by beating the top player.*

sensational /senˈseɪʃənl/ *adj.* **1** causing, or trying to cause, a feeling of great excitement, surprise or interest among people: *This magazine specializes in sensational stories about the rich and famous.* **2** (*informal*) extremely good or beautiful; very exciting ▶ **sensationally** /-nəli/ *adv.*

sensationalism /senˈseɪʃənəlɪzəm/ *noun* [U] a way of getting people's interest by using shocking words or by presenting facts and events as worse or more shocking than they really are ▶ **sensationalist** /-ʃənəlɪst/ *adj.*: *sensationalist headlines*

sense[1] ⊶ /sens/ *noun* **1** [U] the ability to think or act in a reasonable or sensible way; good judgement: *At least he* ***had the sense*** *to stop when he realized he was making a mistake.* ◇ *I think there's a lot of sense in what you're saying.* ➲ look at **common sense 2** [U, sing.] the ability to understand sth; the ability to recognize what sth is or what its value is: *She seems to have lost all* ***sense of reality.*** ◇ *I like him – he's got a great* ***sense of humour.*** ◇ *I'm always getting lost. I've got absolutely no* ***sense of direction.*** **3** [U] ~ **(in doing sth)** the reason for doing sth; purpose: *There's no sense in going any further – we're obviously lost.* ◇ ***What's the sense*** *in making things more difficult for yourself?* **4** [U, sing.] a natural ability to do or produce sth well: *Good* ***business sense*** *made her a millionaire.* ◇ *He's got absolutely no* ***dress sense*** (=he dresses very badly). **5** [sing.] a feeling of sth: *I felt a tremendous* ***sense of relief*** *when the exams were finally over.* ◇ *She only visits her family out of a* ***sense of duty.*** **6** [C] (BIOLOGY) one of the five natural physical powers of sight, hearing, smell, taste and touch, that people and animals have: *I've got a cold and I've lost my* ***sense of smell.*** ◇ *Dogs have an acute* ***sense of hearing.*** **7** [C] (LANGUAGE) (used about a word, phrase, etc.) a meaning: *This word has two senses.*

IDM **come to your senses** to finally realize that you should do sth because it is the most sensible thing to do

in a sense in one particular way but not in other ways; partly: *In a sense you're right, but there's more to the matter than that.*
make sense 1 to be possible to understand; to have a clear meaning: *What does this sentence mean? It doesn't make sense to me.* **2** (used about an action) to be sensible or logical: *I think it would make sense to wait for a while before making a decision.*
make sense of sth to manage to understand sth that is not clear or is difficult to understand: *I can't make sense of these instructions.*
talk sense → TALK[1] (6)

sense² /sens/ ***verb*** [T] (not used in the continuous tenses) to realize or become conscious of sth; to get a feeling about sth even though you cannot see it, hear it, etc.: *He sensed her unease.* ◇ *I **sensed that** something was wrong as soon as I went in.*

senseless /ˈsensləs/ ***adj.*** **1** having no meaning or purpose **2** unconscious: *He was beaten senseless.*

sensibility /ˌsensəˈbɪləti/ ***noun*** (*pl.* **sensibilities**) **1** [U, C] the ability to understand and experience deep feelings, for example in art, literature, etc. **2 sensibilities** [pl.] a person's feelings, especially when they are easily offended

sensible 🔑 /ˈsensəbl/ ***adj.*** (used about people and their behaviour) able to make good judgements based on reason and experience; practical: *a sensible person/decision/precaution* ◇ *Stop joking and give me a sensible answer.* ◇ *I think it would be sensible to leave early, in case there's a lot of traffic.* OPP **silly, foolish** ▶ **sensibly** /-əbli/ ***adv.***: *Let's sit down and discuss the matter sensibly.*

sensitive 🔑 /ˈsensətɪv/ ***adj.*** **1** ~ (to sth) showing that you are conscious of and able to understand people's feelings, problems, etc.: *It wasn't very sensitive of you to keep mentioning her boyfriend. You know they've just split up.* ◇ *to be sensitive to sb's feelings/wishes* OPP **insensitive 2** ~ (about/to sth) easily upset, offended or annoyed, especially about a particular subject: *She's still a bit sensitive about her divorce.* ◇ *He's very sensitive to criticism.* **3** (used about a subject, a situation, etc.) needing to be dealt with carefully because it is likely to cause anger or trouble: *This is a sensitive period in the negotiations between the two countries.* **4** ~ (to sth) easily hurt or damaged; painful, especially if touched: *a new cream for sensitive skin* ◇ *My teeth are very sensitive to hot or cold food.* **5** (used about a scientific instrument, a piece of equipment, etc.) able to measure very small changes ▶ **sensitively** ***adv.***: *The investigation will need to be handled sensitively.* ▶ **sensitivity** /ˌsensəˈtɪvəti/ ***noun*** [U]: *I think your comments showed a complete lack of sensitivity.*

sensor /ˈsensə(r)/ ***noun*** [C] (PHYSICS) a device that can react to light, heat, pressure, etc. in order to make a machine, etc. do sth or show sth: *security lights with an infrared sensor* (= that come on when a person is near them)

sensory /ˈsensəri/ ***adj.*** (usually *before* a noun) (BIOLOGY) connected with your physical senses: *sensory organs* ◇ *sensory deprivation*

sensual /ˈsenʃuəl/ ***adj.*** connected with physical or sexual pleasure: *the sensual rhythms of Latin music* ▶ **sensuality** /ˌsenʃuˈæləti/ ***noun*** [U]

sensuous /ˈsenʃuəs/ ***adj.*** giving pleasure to the mind or body through the senses: *the sensuous feel of pure silk* ▶ **sensuously** ***adv.*** ▶ **sensuousness** ***noun*** [U]

sent past tense, past participle of **send**

sentence¹ 🔑 /ˈsentəns/ ***noun*** [C] **1** (LANGUAGE) a group of words containing a subject and a verb, that expresses a statement, a question, etc. When a sentence is written it begins with a big (**capital**) letter and ends with a full stop. ➲ look at **phrase 2** (LAW) the punishment given by a judge to sb who has been found guilty of a crime: *20 years in prison was a very harsh sentence.*

sentence² /ˈsentəns/ ***verb*** [T] ~ **sb (to sth)** (LAW) (used about a judge) to tell sb who has been found guilty of a crime what the punishment will be: *The judge sentenced her to three months in prison for shoplifting.*

sentiment /ˈsentɪmənt/ ***noun*** **1** [C,U] (often plural) (*formal*) an attitude or opinion that is often caused or influenced by emotion: *Public sentiment is against any change to the law.* **2** [U] feelings such as pity, romantic love, sadness, etc. that influence sb's action or behaviour (sometimes in situations where this is not appropriate): *There's no room for sentiment in business.*

sentimental /ˌsentɪˈmentl/ ***adj.*** **1** producing or connected with emotions such as romantic love, pity, sadness, etc. which may be too strong or not appropriate: *How can you be sentimental about an old car!* ◇ *a sentimental love song* **2** connected with happy memories or feelings of love rather than having any financial value: *The jewellery wasn't worth much but it had great **sentimental value** to me.* ▶ **sentimentality** /ˌsentɪmenˈtæləti/ ***noun*** [U] ▶ **sentimentally** /-təli/ ***adv.***

sentry /ˈsentri/ ***noun*** [C] (*pl.* **sentries**) a soldier who stands outside a building and guards it

sepal /ˈsepl/ ***noun*** [C] (BIOLOGY) a part of a flower, like a leaf, that lies under and supports the PETALS (= the coloured parts that make up the head of the flower) ➲ look at **calyx** ➲ picture at **flower**

separable /ˈsepərəbl/ ***adj.*** able to be separated OPP **inseparable**

separate¹ 🔑 /ˈseprət/ ***adj.*** **1** ~ (from sth/sb) apart; not together: *You should always keep your cash and credit cards separate.* **2** different; not connected: *We stayed in separate rooms in the same hotel.*

separate² 🔑 /ˈsepəreɪt/ ***verb*** **1** [I,T] ~ (sb/sth) (from sb/sth) to stop being together; to cause people or things to stop being together: *I think we should separate into two groups.* ◇ *The friends separated at the airport.* ◇ *I got separated from my friends in the crowd.* **2** [T] ~ sb/sth (from sb/sth) to keep people or things apart; to be between people or things with the result that they are apart: *The two sides of the city are separated by the river.* **3** [I] to stop living together as a couple with your wife, husband or partner: *His parents separated when he was still a baby.*

separated 🔑 /ˈsepəreɪtɪd/ ***adj.*** not living together as a couple any more: *My wife and I are separated.*

separately 🔑 /ˈseprətli/ ***adv.*** apart; not together: *Shall we pay separately or all together?*

separation 🔑 /ˌsepəˈreɪʃn/ ***noun*** **1** [C,U] the action of separating or being separated; a situation or period of being apart **2** [C] an agreement where a couple decide not to live together any more: *a trial separation*

Sept. ***abbr.*** September: *2 Sept. 1920*

sept- /sept/ ***prefix*** (used in nouns, adjectives and adverbs) seven; having seven: *septet* ◇ *septennial*

September /sep'tembə(r)/ ***noun*** [U, C] (*abbr.* **Sept.**) the ninth month of the year, coming after August

septet /sep'tet/ ***noun*** [C] (MUSIC) **1** a group of seven musicians or singers **2** [C] a piece of music for seven musicians or singers

septic /'septɪk/ ***adj.*** (HEALTH) infected with poisonous bacteria: *The wound **went septic**.*

septicaemia (*AmE* **septicemia**) /ˌseptɪ'si:miə/ ***noun*** [U] (HEALTH) infection of the blood by poisonous bacteria SYN **blood poisoning**

sequel /'si:kwəl/ ***noun*** [C] **a ~ (to sth)** **1** (LITERATURE, ARTS AND MEDIA) a book, film, etc. that continues the story of the one before **2** something that happens after, or is the result of, an earlier event

sequence[1] AW /'si:kwəns/ ***noun*** [C] **1** a number of things (actions, events, etc.) that happen or come one after another: *Complete the following sequence: 1, 4, 8, 13, ...* **2** [U] the order in which a number of things happen or are arranged: *The photographs are **in sequence**.*

sequence[2] /'si:kwəns/ [T] **1** (TECHNICAL) to arrange things into a SEQUENCE **2** (BIOLOGY) to identify the order in which a set of GENES or parts of MOLECULES are arranged: *The human genome has now been sequenced.* ▶ **sequencing** AW ***noun*** [U]: *a gene sequencing project*

sequential AW /sɪ'kwenʃl/ ***adj.*** (*formal*) following in order of time or place: *sequential data processing* ▶ **sequentially** /-ʃəli/ ***adv.***: *data stored sequentially on the computer*

sequin /'si:kwɪn/ ***noun*** [C] a small shiny round piece of metal or plastic that is sewn onto clothing as decoration ▶ **sequinned** ***adj.***

serenade /ˌserə'neɪd/ ***noun*** [C] (MUSIC) **1** a song or tune played or sung at night by a lover outside the window of the woman he loves **2** a gentle piece of music in several parts, usually for a small group of instruments ▶ **serenade** ***verb*** [T]: *We were serenaded by a string quartet.*

serene /sə'ri:n/ ***adj.*** calm and peaceful: *a serene smile* ▶ **serenely** ***adv.*** ▶ **serenity** /sə'renəti/ ***noun*** [U]

sergeant /'sɑ:dʒənt/ ***noun*** [C] (*abbr.* **Sgt**) **1** an officer with a low position in the army or air force **2** an officer with a middle position in the police force

serial /'sɪəriəl/ ***noun*** [C] (ARTS AND MEDIA) a story in a magazine or on television or radio that is told in a number of parts over a period of time: *the first part of a six-part drama serial* ▶ **serialize** (also **-ise**) /-rɪəlaɪz/ ***verb*** [T]

ˌserial 'killer ***noun*** [C] (LAW) a person who murders several people one after the other in a similar way

'serial number ***noun*** [C] the number marked on sth to identify it and to distinguish it from other things of the same type

series ⚿ AW /'sɪəri:z/ ***noun*** [C] (*pl.* **series**) **1** a number of things that happen one after another and are of the same type or connected: *a series of events* ◇ *There has been a series of burglaries in this district recently.* **2** (ARTS AND MEDIA) a number of programmes on radio or television which have the same main characters and each tell a complete story

serious ⚿ /'sɪəriəs/ ***adj.*** **1** bad or dangerous: *a serious accident/illness/offence* ◇ *Pollution is a very serious problem.* ◇ *Her condition is serious and she's likely to be in hospital for some time.* **2** needing to be treated as important; not just for fun: *Don't laugh, it's a serious matter.* ◇ *a serious discussion* **3 ~ (about sth/about doing sth)** (used about a person) not joking; thinking about things in a careful and sensible way: *Are you serious about starting your own business* (=are you really going to do it)? ◇ *He's terribly serious. I don't think I've ever seen him laugh.* ◇ *You're looking very serious. Was it bad news?* ▶ **seriousness** ***noun*** [U]

seriously ⚿ /'sɪəriəsli/ ***adv.*** **1** in a serious way: *Three people were seriously injured in the accident.* ◇ *My mother is seriously ill.* ◇ *It's time you started to think seriously about the future.* **2** used at the beginning of a sentence for showing that you are not joking or that you really mean what you are saying: *Seriously, I do appreciate all your help.* ◇ *Seriously, you've got nothing to worry about.* **3** used for expressing surprise at what sb has said and asking if it is really true: *'I'm 40 today.' 'Seriously? You look a lot younger.'*

IDM **take sb/sth seriously** to treat sb or sth as important: *You take everything too seriously! Relax and enjoy yourself.*

sermon /'sɜ:mən/ ***noun*** [C] (RELIGION) a speech on a religious or moral subject that is given as part of a service in church

serpent /'sɜ:pənt/ ***noun*** [C] a snake, especially a large one

serrated /sə'reɪtɪd/ ***adj.*** having a row of points in V-SHAPES along the edge: *a knife with a **serrated edge***

serum /'sɪərəm/ ***noun*** (*pl.* **sera** /-rə/ or **serums**) **1** [U] (HEALTH) the thin liquid that is left after blood has CLOTTED (=formed thick lumps) **2** [U, C] (HEALTH) a liquid that is taken from the blood of an animal and given to people to protect them from disease, poison, etc.

servant ⚿ /'sɜ:vənt/ ***noun*** [C] a person who is paid to work in sb's house, doing work such as cooking, cleaning, etc. ➲ look at **civil servant**

serve ⚿ /sɜ:v/ ***verb*** **1** [T] to give food or drink to sb during a meal; to take an order and then bring food or drink to sb in a restaurant, bar, etc.: *Breakfast is served from 7.30 to 9.00 am.* **2** [T] (used about an amount of food) to be enough for a certain number of people: *According to the recipe, this dish serves four.* **3** [I,T] (in a shop) to take a customer's order; to give help, sell goods, etc.: *There was a long queue of people waiting to be served.* **4** [I,T] to be useful or suitable for a particular purpose: *The judge said the punishment would serve as a warning to others.* ◇ *It's an old car but it will **serve our purpose** for a few months.* **5** [I,T] to perform a duty or provide a service for the public or for an organization: *During the war, he served in the Army.* ◇ *She became a nurse because she wanted to serve the community.* **6** [T] (LAW) to spend a period of time in prison as a punishment: *He is currently **serving a** ten-year **sentence** for fraud.* **7** [I,T] (SPORT) (in TENNIS and similar sports) to start play by hitting the ball

IDM **first come, first served** → FIRST[2]

serve sb right used when sth unpleasant happens to sb and you do not feel sorry for them because you think it is their own fault: *'I feel sick.' 'It serves you right for eating so much.'*

server /'sɜ:və(r)/ ***noun*** [C] (COMPUTING) a computer that stores information that a number of computers can share ➲ look at **client**

service[1] ⊷ /ˈsɜːvɪs/ ***noun*** **1** [C] a system or organization that provides the public with sth that it needs; the job that an organization does: *There is a regular bus service to the airport.* ◇ *the postal service* ◇ *the National Health Service* ➲ look at **Civil Service** **2** [C,U] (BUSINESS) a business whose work involves doing sth for customers but not producing goods; the work that such a service does: *financial/banking/insurance services* ◇ *the* ***service sector*** (=the part of the economy involved in this type of business) ➲ look at **service industry** **3** [U] (*also* **the services** [pl.]) (POLITICS) the armed forces; the army, navy or air force; the work done by the people in them: *They both joined the services when they left school.* ◇ *Do you have to do* ***military service*** *in your country?* **4** [U, C] work done for sb; help given to sb: *He left the police force after thirty years' service.* **5** [U] (BUSINESS) the work or the quality of work done by sb when serving a customer: *I enjoyed the meal but the service was terrible.* ◇ *Is service included in the bill?* ➲ look at **service charge** **6** [C] the checks, repairs, etc. that are necessary to make sure that a machine is working properly: *We take our car for a service every six months.* **7** [C] (RELIGION) a religious ceremony, usually including prayers, singing, etc.: *a funeral service* **8** [C] (SPORT) (in TENNIS and similar sports) the first hit of the ball at the start of play; a player's turn to serve (7) **9 services** [pl.] a place at the side of a motorway where there is a petrol station, a shop, toilets and a restaurant

service[2] /ˈsɜːvɪs/ ***verb*** [T] to examine and, if necessary, repair a car, machine, etc.: *All cars should be serviced at regular intervals.*

ˈ**service charge** ***noun*** [C] **1** (BUSINESS) an amount of money that is added to a bill, as an extra charge for a service: *That will be $50, plus a service charge of $2.50.* **2** (*BrE*) (BUSINESS) an amount of money that is added to a bill in a restaurant, for example 10% of the total, that goes to pay for the work of the staff **3** an amount of money that is paid to the owner of an apartment building for services such as putting out rubbish, cleaning the stairs, etc.

ˈ**service industry** ***noun*** [U, C] (BUSINESS) =TERTIARY INDUSTRY

serviceman /ˈsɜːvɪsmən/ **servicewoman** /ˈsɜːvɪswʊmən/ ***noun*** [C] (*pl.* **-men** /-mən/) (*pl.* **-women** /-wɪmɪn/) a member of the armed forces

ˈ**service provider** ***noun*** [C] (BUSINESS, COMPUTING) a business company that provides a service to customers, especially one that connects customers to the Internet: *an Internet service provider*

ˈ**service station** =SERVICE[1] (9)

serviette /ˌsɜːviˈet/ ***noun*** [C] a square of cloth or paper that you use when you are eating to keep your clothes clean and to clean your mouth or hands on **SYN** **napkin**

sesame /ˈsesəmi/ ***noun*** [U] a tropical plant grown for its seeds and oil, both of which are used in cooking: *sesame seeds*

session ⊷ /ˈseʃn/ ***noun*** **1** [C] a period of doing a particular activity: *The whole tape was recorded in one session.* ◇ *She has a session at the gym every week.* **2** [C,U] (POLITICS, LAW) a formal meeting or series of meetings of a court of law, parliament, etc.

set[1] ⊷ /set/ ***verb*** (*pres. part.* **setting**; *pt, pp* **set**) **1** [T] to put sb/sth or to cause sb/sth to be in a particular place or position: *I set the box down carefully on the floor.* **2** [T] (often passive) (ARTS AND MEDIA, LITERATURE) to make the action of a book, play, film, etc. take place in a particular time, situation, etc.: *The film is set in 16th century Spain.* **3** [T] to cause a particular state or event; to start sth happening: *The new government* ***set*** *the prisoners* ***free***. ◇ *The rioters* ***set*** *a number of cars* ***on fire***. **4** [T] to prepare or arrange sth for a particular purpose: *I set my alarm for 6.30.* ◇ *to set the table* (=put the plates, knives, forks, etc. on it) **5** [T] to decide or arrange sth: *Can we* ***set a limit*** *of two hours for the meeting?* ◇ *They haven't* ***set the date*** *for their wedding yet.* **6** [T] to do sth good that people have to try to copy or achieve: *Try to* ***set a good example*** *to the younger children.* ◇ *He has* ***set a*** *new world* ***record***. ◇ *They set high standards of customer service.* **7** [T] to give sb a piece of work or a task: *We've been* ***set a lot of homework*** *this weekend.* ◇ *I've* ***set*** *myself* ***a target*** *of four hours' study every evening.* **8** [I] to become firm or hard: *The concrete will* ***set solid /hard*** *in just a few hours.* **9** [T] to fix a PRECIOUS STONE, etc. in a piece of jewellery **10** [T] (HEALTH) to fix a broken bone in the correct position so that it can get better: *The doctor set her broken leg.* **11** [I] (used about the sun) to go down below the HORIZON in the evening **OPP** **rise**

IDM **set eyes on sb/sth** to see sb/sth: *He loved the house the moment he set eyes on it.*

set foot (in/on sth) to visit, enter or arrive at/in a place: *No woman has ever set foot in the temple.*

set your heart on sth; have your heart set on sth → HEART

put/set your/sb's mind at rest → MIND[1]

put/set sth right → RIGHT[1]

set sail to begin a journey by sea: *Columbus set sail for India.*

set the scene (for sth) → SCENE

PHR V **set about sth** to start doing sth, especially dealing with a problem or task: *How would you set about tackling this problem?*

set sth aside to keep sth to use later: *I try to set aside part of my wages every week.*

set sb/sth back to delay sb/sth: *The bad weather has set our plans back six weeks.*

set forth (*formal*) to start a journey

set sth forth (*formal*) to show or tell sth to sb or to make sth known

set in to arrive and stay for a period of time: *I'm afraid that the bad weather has set in.*

set off to leave on a journey: *We set off at 3 o'clock this morning.*

set sth off to do sth which starts a reaction: *When this door is opened, it sets off an alarm.*

set on/upon sb to attack sb suddenly: *He was set upon by a gang of youths on his way home.*

set out to leave on a journey

set out to do sth to decide to achieve sth: *He set out to prove that his theory was right.*

set (sth) up to start a business, organization, system, etc.

set[2] ⊷ /set/ ***noun*** [C] **1 a ~ (of sth)** a number of things that belong together: *a set of kitchen knives* ◇ *In the first set of questions, you have to fill in the gap.* ◇ *a spare set of keys* ◇ *a chess set* **2** [with sing. or pl. verb] a group of people who have similar interests and spend a lot of time together socially ➲ look at **the jet set** **3** (ARTS AND MEDIA) a piece of equipment for receiving television or radio signals: *a television set* **4** (ARTS AND MEDIA) the SCENERY that is made for a play or film: *a set designer* **5** (SPORT) (used in games such as tennis and volleyball) a group of games forming part of a match: *She won* ***in straight sets*** (=without losing a set). **6** (MATHEMATICS) a group of things that have a shared quality **7** (EDUCATION) (*BrE*) a group of school students with a similar ability who work together in a particular subject

set³ /set/ ***adj.*** **1** placed in a particular position: *deep-set eyes ◇ Our house is quite set back from the road.* **2** planned or fixed and not changing: *There are no set hours in my job.* **3** (EDUCATION) (used about a book, text, etc.) that everyone must study for an exam: *We have to study three set texts for French.* **4** (only *before* a noun) (used about a meal in a restaurant) having a fixed price and a limited choice of dishes: *a* ***set dinner/lunch/meal*** *◇ Shall we have the* ***set menu****?* **5** ~ **(for sth)**; ~ **(to do sth)** ready, prepared or likely to do sth: *Okay, I'm set – let's go! ◇ I was all set to leave when the phone rang. ◇ The Swiss team look set for victory.*

IDM **be set against sth/doing sth** to be determined that sth will not happen or that you will not do sth

be set in your ways to be unable to change your habits, attitudes, etc.

be set on sth/doing sth to be determined to do sth: *She's set on a career in acting.*

setback /ˈsetbæk/ ***noun*** [C] a difficulty or problem that stops you progressing as fast as you would like: *She suffered a major setback when she missed the exams through illness.*

ˈset square (*AmE* **triangle**) ***noun*** [C] (GEOMETRY) an instrument for drawing straight lines and angles, made from a flat piece of plastic or metal in the shape of a triangle with one angle of 90°

settee /seˈtiː/ ***noun*** [C] a long soft seat with a back and arms that more than one person can sit on SYN **sofa**

setting /ˈsetɪŋ/ ***noun*** [C] **1** the position sth is in; the place and time in which sth happens: *The hotel is in a beautiful setting, close to the sea.* **2** one of the positions of the controls of a machine: *Cook it in the oven on a moderate setting.*

settle ⊶ /ˈsetl/ ***verb*** **1** [I,T] to put an end to an argument or disagreement: *They settled the dispute without going to court. ◇ They settled out of court. ◇ We didn't speak to each other for years, but we've* ***settled our differences*** *now.* **2** [T] to decide or arrange sth finally: *Everything's settled. We leave on the nine o'clock flight on Friday.* **3** [I] to go and live permanently in a new country, area, town, etc.: *A great many immigrants have settled in this country.* **4** [I,T] to put yourself or sb else into a comfortable position: *I settled in front of the television for the evening. ◇ She settled herself beside him on the sofa.* **5** [I,T] to become or to make sb/sth calm or relaxed: *The baby wouldn't settle.* **6** [T] to pay money that you owe: *to settle a bill/a debt* **7** [I] to land on a surface and stop moving: *A flock of birds settled on the roof.*

PHR V **settle down** **1** to get into a comfortable position, sitting or lying **2** to start having a quieter way of life, especially by staying in the same place or getting married: *She had a number of jobs abroad before she eventually settled down.* **3** to become calm and quiet: *Settle down! It's time to start the lesson.*

settle down to sth to start doing sth which involves all your attention: *Before you settle down to your work, could I ask you something?*

settle for sth to accept sth that is not as good as what you wanted: *We're going to have to settle for the second prize.*

settle in/into sth to start feeling comfortable in a new home, job, etc.: *How are the children settling in at their new school?*

settle on sth to choose or decide sth after considering many different things

settle up (with sb) to pay money that you owe to sb

settled /ˈsetld/ ***adj.*** **1** not changing or not likely to change: *More settled weather is forecast for the next few days.* **2** comfortable; feeling that you belong (in a home, a job, a way of life, etc.): *We feel very settled here.*

settlement /ˈsetlmənt/ ***noun*** [C,U] **1** an official agreement that ends an argument; the act of reaching an agreement: *a divorce settlement ◇ the settlement of a dispute* **2** (GEOGRAPHY) a place that a group of people have built and live in, where few or no people lived before; the process of people starting to live in a place: *There is believed to have been a prehistoric settlement on this site. ◇ the settlement of the American West*

settler /ˈsetlə(r)/ ***noun*** [C] (GEOGRAPHY) a person who goes to live permanently in a place where not many people live: *the first white settlers in Australia*

seven /ˈsevn/ ***number*** **1** 7 ➲ note at **six** **2** (used to form compound adjectives) having seven of the thing mentioned: *a seven-sided coin*

seventeen /ˌsevnˈtiːn/ ***number*** 17 ➲ note at **six**

seventeenth /ˌsevnˈtiːnθ/ ***ordinal number*** 17th ➲ note at **sixth¹**

seventh¹ /ˈsevnθ/ ***noun*** [C] the FRACTION 1/7; one of seven equal parts of sth

seventh² /ˈsevnθ/ ***ordinal number*** 7th ➲ note at **sixth¹**

seventieth /ˈsevntiəθ/ ***ordinal number*** 70th ➲ note at **sixth¹**

seventy /ˈsevnti/ ***number*** **1** 70 **2** **the seventies** [pl.] numbers, years or temperatures from 70 to 79 ➲ note at **sixty**

sever /ˈsevə(r)/ ***verb*** [T] (*formal*) **1** to cut sth into two pieces; to cut sth off: *The builders accidentally severed a water pipe. ◇ His hand was almost severed in the accident.* **2** to end a relationship or communication with sb: *He has severed all links with his former friends.*

several ⊶ /ˈsevrəl/ ***pronoun, det.*** more than two but not very many: *It took her several days to recover from the shock. ◇ There were lots of applications for the job – several of them from very well-qualified people. ◇ I don't think it's a good idea for several reasons.*

severance /ˈsevərəns/ ***noun*** [sing., U] **1** the act of ending a connection or relationship: *the severance of diplomatic relations* **2** (BUSINESS) the act of ending sb's work contract: *severance pay/terms*

severe ⊶ /sɪˈvɪə(r)/ ***adj.*** **1** causing sb to suffer, be upset or have difficulties: *Such terrible crimes deserve the severest punishment. ◇ I think your criticism of her work was too severe.* **2** extremely bad or serious: *The company is in severe financial difficulty. ◇ He suffered severe injuries in the fall. ◇ severe weather conditions* ▶ **severely** ***adv.***: *The roof was severely damaged in the storm. ◇ The report severely criticizes the Health Service.* ▶ **severity** /sɪˈverəti/ ***noun*** [U]: *I don't think you realize the severity of the problem.*

sew ⊶ /səʊ/ ***verb*** [I,T] (*pt* **sewed**; *pp* **sewn** /səʊn/ or **sewed**) ~ **(sth) (on)** to join pieces of cloth, or to join sth to cloth, using a needle and thread and forming STITCHES: *I can't sew. ◇ A button's come off my shirt – I'll have to sew it back on.*

PHR V **sew sth up** **1** to join two things by sewing; to repair sth by sewing two things together: *The surgeon sewed up the wound.* **2** to arrange sth so that it is certain to happen or be successful

sewage /ˈsuːɪdʒ/ ***noun*** [U] the waste material from people's bodies that is carried away from their homes in SEWERS

sewer /'su:ə(r)/ ***noun*** [C] an underground pipe that carries human waste to a place where it can be treated

sewing /'səʊɪŋ/ ***noun*** [U] **1** using a needle and thread to make or repair things: *I always take a sewing kit when I travel.* ◇ *a **sewing machine*** **2** something that is being sewn

sewn past participle of **sew**

sex AW /seks/ ***noun* 1** [U] (BIOLOGY) the state of being either male or female: *Applications are welcome from anyone, regardless of sex or race.* ◇ *Do you mind what sex your baby is?* SYN **gender 2** [C] (SOCIAL STUDIES) one of the two groups consisting of all male people or all female people: *the male/ female sex* ◇ *He's always found it difficult to get on with **the opposite sex*** (=women). **3** (also *formal* **coitus; intercourse; ˌsexual 'intercourse**) [U] (BIOLOGY) the physical act in which the sexual organs of two people touch and which can result in a woman having a baby: *to **have sex** with somebody* ◇ *sex education in schools*

sexism AW /'seksɪzəm/ ***noun*** [U] (SOCIAL STUDIES) the unfair treatment of people, especially women, because of their sex; the attitude that causes this ▸ **sexist** /'seksɪst/ ***adj.***: *a sexist attitude to women* ◇ *sexist jokes*

'sex life ***noun*** [C] a person's sexual activities: *ways to improve your sex life*

sextet /seks'tet/ ***noun*** [C] (MUSIC) **1** a group of six musicians or singers who play or sing together **2** [C] a piece of music for six musicians or singers

sextuplet /'sekstʊplət; sek'stju:plət; -'stʌp-/ ***noun*** [C] one of six children or animals that are born to one mother at the same time

sexual AW /'sekʃuəl/ ***adj.*** connected with sex: *sexual problems* ◇ *the sexual organs* ◇ *sexual reproduction* ◇ *a campaign for sexual equality* (=to get fair and equal treatment for both men and women) ▸ **sexually** /'sekʃəli/ ***adv.***: *to be sexually attracted to sb*

ˌsexual 'intercourse (*formal*) =SEX (3)

sexuality AW /ˌsekʃu'æləti/ ***noun*** [U] the nature of sb's sexual activities or desires

sexy /'seksi/ ***adj.*** (**sexier**; **sexiest**) sexually attractive or exciting: *Do you find the lead singer sexy?* ◇ *a sexy dress*

SFX /ˌes ef 'eks/ ***abbr.*** (ARTS AND MEDIA) =SPECIAL EFFECTS

Sgt ***abbr.*** =SERGEANT

sh /ʃ/ ***exclamation*** used to tell sb to stop making noise: *Sh! People are trying to sleep in here.*

shabby /'ʃæbi/ ***adj.* 1** in bad condition because of having been used or worn too much: *a shabby suit* **2** (used about people) dressed in an untidy way; wearing clothes that are in bad condition **3** (used about the way that sb is treated) unfair; not generous ▸ **shabbily** /-ɪli/ ***adv.***: *a shabbily-dressed man* ◇ *She felt she'd been treated shabbily by her employers.*

shack /ʃæk/ ***noun*** [C] a small building, usually made of wood or metal, that has not been built well

shade¹ /ʃeɪd/ ***noun* 1** [U] an area that is out of direct SUNLIGHT and is darker and cooler than areas in the sun: *It was so hot that I had to go and sit **in the shade**.* **2** [C] something that keeps out light or makes it less bright: *a lampshade* **3 shades** [pl.] (*informal*) =SUNGLASSES **4** [C] **a ~ (of sth)** a type of a particular colour: *a shade of green* **5** [C] a small difference in the form or nature of sth: *a word with various shades of meaning* **6** [sing.] **a ~** a little bit

shade² /ʃeɪd/ ***verb*** [T] **1** to protect sth from direct light; to give shade to sth: *The sun was so bright that I had to shade my eyes.* **2 ~ sth (in)** to make an area of a drawing darker, for example with a pencil: *The trees will look more realistic once you've shaded them in.*

types of shadow

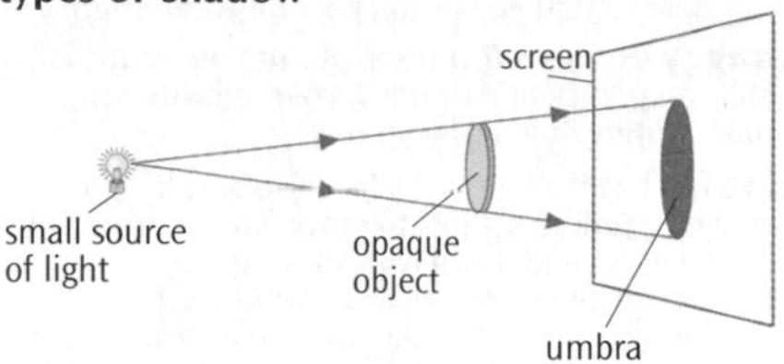

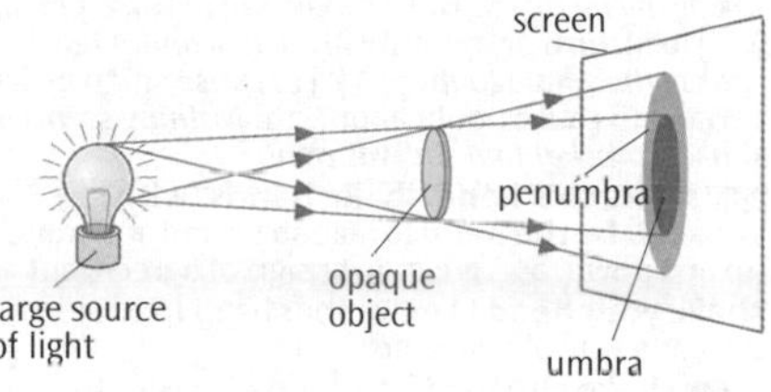

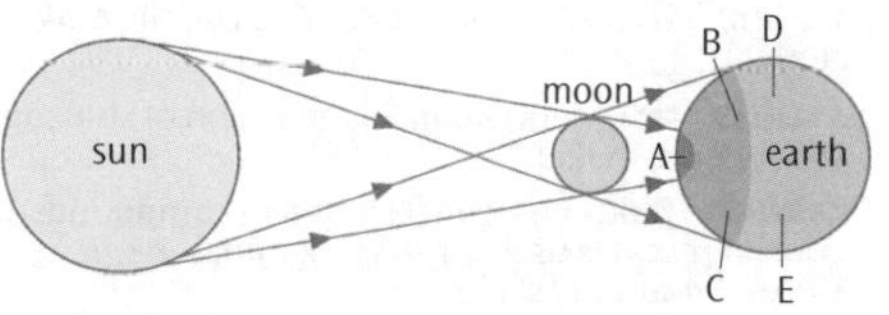

A	umbra - total eclipse
B+C	penumbra - partial eclipse
D+E	no shadow - no eclipse

shadow¹ /'ʃædəʊ/ ***noun* 1** [C] a dark shape on a surface that is caused by sth being between the light and that surface: *The dog was chasing its own shadow.* ◇ *The shadows lengthened as the sun went down.* ➲ look at **penumbra**, **umbra** **2** [U] an area that is dark because sth prevents direct light from reaching it: *His face was **in shadow**.* **3** [sing.] a very small amount of sth: *I know without **a shadow of doubt** that he's lying.*

IDM **cast a shadow (across/over sth)** → CAST¹

shadow² /'ʃædəʊ/ ***verb*** [T] to follow and watch sb: *The police shadowed the suspect for three days.*

shadow³ /'ʃædəʊ/ ***adj.*** (only *before* a noun) (POLITICS) (in Britain) belonging to the biggest political party that is not in power, with special responsibility for a particular subject, for example education or defence. **Shadow** ministers would probably become government ministers if their party won the next election: *the shadow Cabinet*

shadowy /'ʃædəʊi/ ***adj.* 1** dark and full of shadows: *a shadowy forest* **2** difficult to see because there is not much light: *A shadowy figure was coming towards me.* **3** that not much is known about; mysterious

shady /ˈʃeɪdi/ *adj.* **1** giving shade; giving protection from the sun: *I found a shady spot under the trees and sat down.* **2** (*informal*) not completely honest or legal

shaft /ʃɑːft/ *noun* [C] **1** a long, narrow hole in which sth can go up and down or enter or leave: *a lift shaft* ◇ *a mine shaft* **2** a bar that connects parts of a machine so that power can pass between them

shaggy /ˈʃæɡi/ *adj.* **1** (used about hair, material, etc.) long, thick and untidy **2** covered with long, thick, untidy hair: *a shaggy dog*

shake¹ 🔑 /ʃeɪk/ *verb* (*pt* **shook** /ʃʊk/; *pp* **shaken** /ˈʃeɪkən/) **1** [I,T] to move (sb/sth) from side to side or up and down with short, quick movements: *I was so nervous that I was shaking.* ◇ *The whole building shakes when big lorries go past.* ◇ (*figurative*) *His voice shook with emotion as he described the accident.* ◇ *Shake the bottle before taking the medicine.* ◇ *She shook him to wake him up.* **2** [T] to disturb or upset sb/sth: *The scandal has shaken the whole country.* **3** [T] to cause sth to be less certain; to cause doubt about sth: *Nothing seems to shake her belief that she was right.*

IDM **shake sb's hand/shake hands (with sb)**; **shake sb by the hand** to take sb's hand and move it up and down, as a greeting or sign of agreement

shake your head to move your head from side to side, as a way of saying no

PHR V **shake sb/sth off** to get rid of sb/sth; to remove sth by shaking: *I don't seem to be able to shake off this cold.* ◇ *Shake the crumbs off the tablecloth.*

shake² 🔑 /ʃeɪk/ *noun* [C] the action of shaking sth or being shaken

ˈshaker /ˈʃeɪkə(r)/ *noun* [C] (often in compounds) a container that is used for shaking things: *a salt shaker* ◇ *a cocktail shaker*

ˈshake-up *noun* [C] a complete change in the structure or organization of sth

shaky /ˈʃeɪki/ *adj.* (**shakier**; **shakiest**) **1** shaking or feeling weak because you are frightened or ill **2** not firm; weak or not very good: *The table's a bit shaky so don't put anything heavy on it.* ◇ *They've had a* ***shaky start*** *to the season losing most of their games.* ▸ **shakily** /-ɪli/ *adv.*

shale /ʃeɪl/ *noun* [U] (GEOGRAPHY, GEOLOGY) a type of soft stone that splits easily into thin flat layers

shall 🔑 /ʃəl *strong form* ʃæl/ *modal verb* (*negative* **shall not**; *short form* **shan't** /ʃɑːnt/) **1** used for asking for information or advice: *What time shall I come?* ◇ *Where shall we go for our holiday?* **2** used for offering to do sth: *Shall I help you carry that box?* ◇ *Shall we drive you home?* **3 shall we** used for suggesting that you do sth with the person or people that you are talking to: *Shall we go out for a meal this evening?* **4** (*formal*) used with 'I' and 'we' in FUTURE TENSES, instead of 'will': *I shall be very happy to see him again.* ◇ *We shan't be arriving until ten o'clock.* ◇ *At the end of this year, I shall have been working here for five years.* **5** (*formal*) used for saying that sth must happen or will definitely happen: *In the rules it says that a player shall be sent off for using bad language.*

shallot /ʃəˈlɒt/ *noun* [C] a vegetable like a small onion with a very strong taste

shallow 🔑 /ˈʃæləʊ/ *adj.* **1** not deep; with not much distance between top and bottom: *The sea is very shallow here.* ◇ *a shallow dish* **2** not having or showing serious or deep thought: *a shallow person/book* OPP **deep** ▸ **shallowness** *noun* [U]

shame¹ 🔑 /ʃeɪm/ *noun* **1** [U] the unpleasant feeling of GUILT and embarrassment that you get when you have done sth stupid or morally wrong; the ability to have this feeling: *She was* ***filled with shame*** *at the thought of how she had lied to her mother.* ◇ *His actions have* ***brought shame on*** *his whole family.* ◇ *He doesn't care how he behaves in public. He's got no shame!* ➲ adjective **ashamed** **2 a shame** [sing.] a fact or situation that makes you feel disappointed: ***It's a shame*** *about Adam failing his exams, isn't it?* ◇ ***What a shame*** *you have to leave so soon.* ◇ *It would be a shame to miss an opportunity like this.*

shame² /ʃeɪm/ *verb* [T] to make sb feel shame for sth bad that they have done

shameful /ˈʃeɪmfl/ *adj.* which sb should feel bad about; shocking: *a shameful waste of public money* ▸ **shamefully** /-fəli/ *adv.*

shameless /ˈʃeɪmləs/ *adj.* not feeling embarrassed about doing sth bad; having no shame: *a shameless display of greed and bad manners* ▸ **shamelessly** *adv.*

shampoo /ʃæmˈpuː/ *noun* **1** [C,U] a liquid that you use for washing your hair; a similar liquid for cleaning carpets, cars, etc.: *shampoo for greasy/dry/normal hair* **2** [C] the action of washing sth with shampoo ▸ **shampoo** *verb* [T] (*pres. part.* **shampooing**; *3rd person sing. pres.* **shampoos**; *pt, pp* **shampooed**)

shamrock /ˈʃæmrɒk/ *noun* [C,U] a plant with three leaves, which is the national symbol of Ireland

shandy /ˈʃændi/ *noun* [C,U] (*pl.* **shandies**) a drink that is a mixture of beer and LEMONADE (1)

shan't short for SHALL NOT

shanty /ˈʃænti/ *noun* (*pl.* **shanties**) **1** a small house, built of pieces of wood, metal and cardboard, where very poor people live, especially on the edge of a big city **2** (*also* **ˈsea shanty**, *AmE* **chanty**, **chantey**) (MUSIC) a song that sailors traditionally used to sing while pulling ropes, etc.

shanty town /ˈʃænti taʊn/ *noun* [C] an area, usually on the edge of a big city, where poor people live in bad conditions in buildings that they have made themselves

shape¹ 🔑 /ʃeɪp/ *noun* **1** [C,U] the form of the outer edges or surfaces of sth; an example of sth that has a particular form: *a round/square/rectangular shape* ◇ *a cake* ***in the shape of*** *a heart* ◇ *clothes to fit people of* ***all shapes and sizes*** ◇ *Squares, circles and triangles are all different shapes.* ◇ *I could just make out a dark shape in the distance.* ◇ *The country is roughly square* ***in shape***. **2** [U] the physical condition of sb/sth; the good or bad state of sb/sth: *She was* ***in*** *such bad* ***shape*** (=so ill) *that she had to be taken to hospital.* ◇ *I go swimming regularly to keep* ***in shape***. **3** [sing.] **the ~ (of sth)** the organization, form or structure of sth

IDM **out of shape 1** not in the usual or correct shape: *My sweater's gone out of shape now that I've washed it.* **2** (HEALTH) not physically fit: *You're out of shape. You should get more exercise.*

take shape to start to develop well: *Plans to expand the company are beginning to take shape.*

shape² 🔑 /ʃeɪp/ *verb* [T] **1 ~ sth (into sth)** to make sth into a particular form: *Shape the mixture into small balls.* **2** to influence the way in which sth develops; to cause sth to have a particular form or nature: *His political ideas were shaped by his upbringing.*

shaped ⊶ /ʃeɪpt/ ***adj.*** having the type of shape mentioned: *a huge balloon **shaped like** a cow* ◇ *almond-shaped eyes* ◇ *an L-shaped room*

shapeless /ˈʃeɪpləs/ ***adj.*** not having a clear shape: *a shapeless dress*

share[1] ⊶ /ʃeə(r)/ ***verb*** **1** [T] ~ **sth (out)** to divide sth between two or more people: *We shared the pizza out between the four of us.* **2** [I,T] ~ **(sth) (with sb)** to have, use, do or pay sth together with another person or other people: *I share a flat with four other people.* ◇ *Children should learn to share.* ◇ *We share the same interests.* **3** [T] ~ **sth (with sb)** to tell sb about sth; to allow sb to know sth: *Sometimes it helps to share your problems.*

share[2] ⊶ /ʃeə(r)/ ***noun*** **1** [sing.] ~ **(of sth)** a part or amount of sth that has been divided between several people: *We each pay a share of the household bills.* ◇ *I'm willing to **take** my **share** of the blame.* **2** [C, usually pl.] ~ **(in sth)** (ECONOMICS, BUSINESS) one of many equal parts into which the value of a company is divided, that can be sold to people who want to own part of the company

IDM **the lion's share (of sth)** → LION
(more than) your fair share of sth → FAIR[1]

shareholder /ˈʃeəhəʊldə(r)/ ***noun*** [C] (ECONOMICS, BUSINESS) an owner of shares in a company

shareware /ˈʃeəweə(r)/ ***noun*** [U] (COMPUTING) software that is available free for a user to test, after which they must pay if they want to continue using it ➲ look at **freeware**

shark /ʃɑːk/ ***noun*** [C] a large, often dangerous, sea fish that has a lot of sharp teeth

sharp[1] ⊶ /ʃɑːp/ ***adj.*** **1** having a very thin but strong edge or point; able to cut or make a hole in sth easily: *a sharp knife* ◇ *sharp teeth* OPP **blunt** **2** (used about a change of direction or level) very great and sudden: *a sharp rise/fall in inflation* ◇ *This is a sharp bend so slow down.* **3** clear and definite: *the sharp outline of the hills* ◇ *a sharp contrast between the lives of the rich and the poor* **4** able to think, act, understand, see or hear quickly: *a sharp mind* ◇ *You must have sharp eyes if you can read that sign from here.* **5** (used about actions or movements) quick and sudden: *One short sharp blow was enough to end the fight.* **6** (used about words, comments, etc.) said in an angry way; intended to upset sb or be critical **7** (used about pain) very strong and sudden: *a sharp pain in the chest* OPP **dull** **8** (used about sth that affects the senses) strong; not mild or gentle, often causing an unpleasant feeling: *a sharp taste* ◇ *a sharp wind* **9** (*symbol* ♯) (MUSIC) half a note higher than the stated note: *in the key of C sharp minor* ➲ look at **flat**[1] (5) **10** (MUSIC) slightly higher than the correct note: *That last note was sharp. Can you sing it again?* ➲ look at **flat**[1] (6) ▶ **sharply** ***adv.***: *The road bends sharply to the left.* ◇ *Share prices fell sharply this morning.* ▶ **sharpness** ***noun*** [U]

sharp[2] /ʃɑːp/ ***adv.*** **1** (used about a time) exactly, PUNCTUALLY: *Be here at three o'clock sharp.* **2** turning suddenly: *Go to the traffic lights and turn sharp right.* **3** (MUSIC) slightly higher than the correct note ➲ look at **flat**[1] (6)

sharp[3] /ʃɑːp/ ***noun*** [C] (*symbol* ♯) (MUSIC) a note that is half a note higher than the note with the same letter ➲ look at **flat**[2] (2) ➲ picture at **music**

sharpen /ˈʃɑːpən/ ***verb*** [I,T] to become or to make sth sharp or sharper: *to sharpen a knife* ◇ *The outline of the trees sharpened as it grew lighter.*

sharpener /ˈʃɑːpnə(r)/ ***noun*** [C] an object or a tool that is used for making sth sharp: *a pencil/knife sharpener*

sharply ⊶ /ˈʃɑːpli/ ***adv.*** **1** in a critical, rough or severe way: *'Is there a problem?' he asked sharply.* **2** suddenly and by a large amount: *The road bends sharply to the left.* ◇ *Share prices fell sharply this morning.* **3** in a way that clearly shows the differences between two things: *Their experiences contrast sharply with those of other children.* **4** quickly and suddenly or loudly: *She moved sharply across the room to block his exit.*

shatter /ˈʃætə(r)/ ***verb*** **1** [I,T] (used about glass, etc.) to break or make sth break into very small pieces: *I dropped the glass and it shattered on the floor.* ◇ *The force of the explosion shattered the windows.* **2** [T] to destroy sth completely: *Her hopes were shattered by the news.*

shattered /ˈʃætəd/ ***adj.*** **1** very shocked and upset **2** (*informal*) very tired: *I'm absolutely shattered.*

shave[1] ⊶ /ʃeɪv/ ***verb*** [I,T] ~ **(sth) (off)** to remove hair from the face or another part of the body with an extremely sharp piece of metal (**a razor**): *I cut myself shaving this morning.* ◇ *When did you shave off your moustache?* ◇ *to shave your legs*

PHR V **shave sth off (sth)** to cut a very small amount from sth

shave[2] /ʃeɪv/ ***noun*** [C, usually sing.] the action of shaving: *to have a shave* ◇ *I need a shave.*

IDM **a close shave/thing** → CLOSE[3]

shaven /ˈʃeɪvn/ ***adj.*** having been shaved: *clean-shaven* (= not having a beard or moustache)

shaver /ˈʃeɪvə(r)/ (*also* **electric razor**) ***noun*** [C] an electric tool that is used for removing hair from the face or another part of the body

shavings /ˈʃeɪvɪŋz/ ***noun*** [pl.] thin pieces cut from a piece of wood, etc. using a sharp tool, especially a PLANE (= a tool used for making the surface of wood smooth by taking very thin pieces off it): *wood shavings*

shawl /ʃɔːl/ ***noun*** [C] a large piece of cloth that is worn by a woman round her shoulders or head or that is put round a baby

she ⊶ /ʃiː/ ***pronoun*** (LANGUAGE) (the subject of a verb) the female person who has already been mentioned: *'What does your sister do?' 'She's a dentist.'* ◇ *I asked her a question but she didn't answer.*

shear /ʃɪə(r)/ ***verb*** [T] (*pt* **sheared**; *pp* **shorn** /ʃɔːn/ or **sheared**) (AGRICULTURE) to cut the wool off a sheep

shears /ʃɪəz/ ***noun*** [pl.] a tool that is like a very large pair of scissors and that is used for cutting things in the garden: *a pair of shears* ➲ picture at **agriculture**

sheath /ʃiːθ/ ***noun*** [C] (*pl.* **sheaths** /ʃiːðz/) a cover for a knife or other sharp weapon ➲ picture at **weapon**

shed[1] /ʃed/ ***noun*** [C] a small building that is used for keeping things or animals in: *a garden shed* ◇ *a bicycle shed* ◇ *a cattle shed*

shed[2] /ʃed/ ***verb*** [T] (*pres. part.* **shedding**; *pt, pp* **shed**) **1** to lose sth because it falls off: *This snake sheds its skin every year.* ◇ *Autumn is coming and the trees are beginning to shed their leaves.* **2** to get rid of or remove sth that is not wanted

IDM **shed blood** (*written*) to kill or injure people
shed light on sth to make sth clear and easy to understand
shed tears to cry

she'd /ʃiːd/ short for SHE HAD, SHE WOULD

sheep

sheep /ʃiːp/ ***noun*** [C] (*pl.* **sheep**) an animal that is kept on farms and used for its wool or meat

> **RELATED VOCABULARY**
>
> A male sheep is a **ram**, a female sheep is a **ewe** and a young sheep is a **lamb**.
>
> When sheep make a noise, they **bleat**. This is written as **baa**.
>
> The meat from sheep is called **lamb** or **mutton**.

➲ note at **meat**

sheepdog /ˈʃiːpdɒɡ/ ***noun*** [C] (AGRICULTURE) a dog that has been trained to control sheep

sheepish /ˈʃiːpɪʃ/ ***adj.*** feeling or showing embarrassment because you have done sth silly: *a sheepish grin* ▶ **sheepishly** ***adv.***

sheepskin /ˈʃiːpskɪn/ ***noun*** [U, C] the skin of a sheep, including the wool, from which coats, etc. are made: *a sheepskin rug/jacket*

sheer /ʃɪə(r)/ ***adj.*** **1** (only *before* a noun) used to emphasize the size, degree or amount of sth: *It's sheer stupidity to drink and drive.* ◇ *It was* ***sheer luck*** *that I happened to be in the right place at the right time.* ◇ *Her success is due to sheer hard work.* ◇ *I only agreed out of sheer desperation.* **2** very steep; almost vertical: *Don't walk near the edge. It's* ***a sheer drop*** *to the sea.*

sheet /ʃiːt/ ***noun*** [C] **1** a large piece of material used on a bed **2** a piece of paper that is used for writing, printing, etc. on: *a sheet of notepaper* ◇ *Write each answer on a separate sheet.* ➲ look at **balance sheet** **3** a flat, thin piece of any material, especially a square or RECTANGULAR one: *a sheet of metal/glass* **4** a wide, flat area of sth: *The road was covered with* ***a sheet of ice.***

ˌ**sheet ˈlightning** ***noun*** [U] LIGHTNING (=flashes of light in the sky when there is a storm) that appears as a broad area of light in the sky ➲ look at **forked lightning**

ˈ**sheet music** ***noun*** [U] (MUSIC) music printed on separate pieces of paper rather than in a book

sheikh (*also* **sheik**) /ʃeɪk; ʃiːk-/ ***noun*** [C] (POLITICS) an Arab ruler

sheikhdom /ˈʃeɪkdəm; ˈʃiːk-/ ***noun*** [C] (POLITICS) an area of land ruled by a SHEIKH

shelf /ʃelf/ ***noun*** [C] (*pl.* **shelves** /ʃelvz/) a long flat piece of wood, glass, etc. that is fixed to a wall or in a cupboard, used for putting things on: *I put up a shelf in the kitchen.* ◇ *I reached up and took down the book from the top shelf.* ◇ *a bookshelf*

ˈ**shelf life** ***noun*** [usually sing.] the length of time that food, etc. can be kept before it is too old to be sold or used

shell[1] /ʃel/ ***noun*** **1** [C,U] (BIOLOGY) a hard covering that protects eggs, nuts and some animals: *Some children were collecting shells on the beach.* ◇ *a piece of eggshell* ◇ *Tortoises have a hard shell.* ➲ picture on **page 28** **2** [C] the walls or hard outer structure of sth: *The body shell of the car is made in another factory.* **3** [C] a metal container that explodes when it is fired from a large gun

IDM **come out of your shell** to become less shy and more confident when talking to other people

go, retreat, etc. into your shell to suddenly become shy and stop talking

shell[2] /ʃel/ ***verb*** [T] **1** to take the SHELL[1] (1) off a nut or other kind of food: *to shell peas* **2** to fire SHELLS[1] (3) full of EXPLOSIVES from a large gun

she'll /ʃiːl/ short for SHE WILL

shellfish /ˈʃelfɪʃ/ ***noun*** (*pl.* **shellfish**) **1** [C] a type of animal that lives in water and has a shell ➲ picture on **page 28** **2** [U] these animals eaten as food

shelter[1] /ˈʃeltə(r)/ ***noun*** **1** [U] ~ **(from sth)** protection from danger or bad weather: *to give somebody food and shelter* ◇ *We looked around for somewhere to* ***take shelter*** *from the storm.* **2** [C] a small building that gives protection, for example from bad weather or attack: *a bus shelter* ◇ *an air-raid shelter*

shelter[2] /ˈʃeltə(r)/ ***verb*** **1** [I] ~ **(from sth)** to find protection or a safe place: *Let's shelter from the rain under that tree.* **2** [T] ~ **sb/sth (from sb/sth)** to protect sb/sth; to provide a safe place away from harm or danger: *The trees shelter the house from the wind.*

sheltered /ˈʃeltəd/ ***adj.*** **1** (used about a place) protected from bad weather **2** protected from unpleasant things in your life: *We had a sheltered childhood, living in the country.*

shelve /ʃelv/ ***verb*** [T] to decide not to continue with a plan, either for a short time or permanently: *Plans for a new motorway have been shelved.*

shelves plural of **shelf**

shelving /ˈʃelvɪŋ/ ***noun*** [U] a set of shelves

shepherd[1] /ˈʃepəd/ ***noun*** [C] (AGRICULTURE) a person whose job is to look after sheep

shepherd[2] /ˈʃepəd/ ***verb*** [T] to guide and look after people so that they do not get lost

sherbet /ˈʃɜːbət/ ***noun*** [U] (*BrE*) a flavoured powder that makes bubbles when you put it in your mouth and is eaten as a sweet

sheriff /ˈʃerɪf/ ***noun*** [C] (LAW) an officer of the law in a US county

sherry /ˈʃeri/ ***noun*** [C,U] (*pl.* **sherries**) a type of strong Spanish wine; a glass of this wine

she's /ʃiːz; ʃiz/ short for SHE IS, SHE HAS

shield[1] /ʃiːld/ ***noun*** [C] **1** (in past times) a large piece of metal or wood that soldiers carried to protect themselves **2** (*also* **riot shield**) a piece of equipment made of strong plastic, that the police use to protect themselves from angry crowds **3** a person or thing that is used to protect sb/sth especially by forming a barrier: *The metal door acted as a shield against the explosion.* **4** an object or drawing in the shape of a **shield**, sometimes used as a prize in a sports competition

shield[2] /ʃiːld/ ***verb*** [T] ~ **sb/sth (against/from sb/sth)** to protect sb/sth from danger or damage: *I shielded my eyes from the bright light with my hand.*

shift[1] AW /ʃɪft/ ***verb*** [I,T] **1** to move or be moved from one position or place to another: *She shifted uncomfortably in her chair.* ◇ *He shifted his desk closer to the window.* **2** to change your opinion of or attitude towards sth: *Public attitudes towards marriage have shifted over the years.*

IDM **shift the blame/responsibility (for sth)**

(onto sb) to make sb else responsible for sth you should do or for sth bad you have done

shift² 🔑 AW /ʃɪft/ ***noun*** **1** [C] a ~ **(in sth)** a change in your opinion of or attitude towards sth: *There has been a shift in public opinion away from war.* **2** [C] (in a factory, etc.) one of the periods that the working day is divided into: *to work **in shifts*** ◇ *shift work/workers* ◇ *to be on the day/night shift* **3** [C, with sing. or pl. verb] the workers who work a particular shift: *The night shift has/have just gone off duty.* **4** [U] (COMPUTING) one of the keys on a KEYBOARD that allows you to write a CAPITAL (=big) letter: *the shift key*

ˌshifting ˌculti'vation ***noun*** [U] (AGRICULTURE) a way of farming in some tropical countries in which farmers use an area of land until it cannot be used for growing plants any more, then move on to a new area of land

shifty /'ʃɪfti/ ***adj.*** (used about a person or their appearance) giving the impression that you cannot trust them: *shifty eyes*

shilling /'ʃɪlɪŋ/ ***noun*** [C] (FINANCE) **1** the basic unit of money in some countries, for example Kenya **2** a British coin worth five pence that was used in past times

shimmer /'ʃɪmə(r)/ ***verb*** [I] to shine with a soft light that seems to be moving: *Moonlight shimmered on the sea.*

shin /ʃɪn/ ***noun*** [C] (ANATOMY) the front part of your leg from your knee to your foot
➲ picture on **page 80**

'shin bone =TIBIA

shine¹ 🔑 /ʃaɪn/ ***verb*** (*pt, pp* **shone** /ʃɒn/) **1** [I] to send out or to send back (**reflect**) light; to be bright: *I could see a light shining in the distance.* ◇ *The sea shone in the light of the moon.* **2** [T] to direct a light at sb/sth: *The policeman shone a torch on the stranger's face.* **3** [I] ~ **(at/in sth)** to be very good at a school subject, a sport, etc.: *She has always shone at languages.*

shine² /ʃaɪn/ ***noun*** [sing.] **1** a bright effect caused by light hitting a polished surface **2** the act of polishing sth so that it shines

shingle /'ʃɪŋgl/ ***noun*** [U] (GEOLOGY, GEOGRAPHY) small pieces of stone lying in a mass on a beach

shingles /'ʃɪŋglz/ ***noun*** [U] (HEALTH) a disease that affects the NERVES (=long thin threads in the body that carry messages to and from the brain) and produces a band of painful spots on the skin

'shin pad ***noun*** [C] (SPORT) a thick piece of material used to protect the SHIN (=the front part of your leg from your knee to your foot) when playing some sports

shiny 🔑 /'ʃaɪni/ ***adj.*** (**shinier**; **shiniest**) causing a bright effect when in the sun or in light: *The shampoo leaves your hair soft and shiny.* ◇ *a shiny new car*

ship¹ 🔑 /ʃɪp/ ***noun*** [C] a large boat used for carrying passengers or CARGO by sea: *to travel **by ship*** ◇ *to launch a ship*

ship² /ʃɪp/ ***verb*** [T] (**shipping**; **shipped**) to send or carry sth by ship or by another type of transport

shipbuilder /'ʃɪpbɪldə(r)/ ***noun*** [C] a person or company who makes or builds ships
▶ **shipbuilding** ***noun*** [U]

shipment /'ʃɪpmənt/ ***noun*** **1** [U] the carrying of goods from one place to another **2** [C] a quantity of goods that are sent from one place to another

shipping /'ʃɪpɪŋ/ ***noun*** [U] **1** ships in general or considered as a group **2** the carrying of goods from one place to another: *a shipping company*

shipwreck /'ʃɪprek/ ***noun*** [C,U] an accident at sea in which a ship is destroyed by a storm, rocks, etc. and sinks ➲ A person or a ship that has suffered such an accident has been **shipwrecked**.

shipyard /'ʃɪpjɑːd/ ***noun*** [C] a place where ships are repaired or built

shirk /ʃɜːk/ ***verb*** [I,T] to avoid doing sth that is difficult or unpleasant, especially because you are too lazy: *to shirk your responsibilities*

shirt 🔑 /ʃɜːt/ ***noun*** [C] a piece of clothing made of cotton, etc., worn on the upper part of the body

shiver /'ʃɪvə(r)/ ***verb*** [I] to shake slightly, especially because you are cold or frightened: *shivering with cold/fright* ▶ **shiver** ***noun*** [C]: *The thought sent a shiver down my spine.*

shoal /ʃəʊl/ ***noun*** [C] a large group of fish that feed and swim together

shock¹ 🔑 /ʃɒk/ ***noun*** **1** [C,U] the feeling that you get when sth unpleasant happens suddenly; the situation that causes this feeling: *The sudden noise **gave him a shock**.* ◇ *The bad news **came as a shock** to her.* ◇ *I'm still suffering from shock at the news.* ◇ *His mother is **in a state of shock**.* **2** [U] (HEALTH) a serious medical condition of extreme weakness caused by damage to the body: *He **was in/went into shock** after the accident.* **3** [C] a violent shaking movement (caused by a crash, explosion, etc.) **4** [C] =ELECTRIC SHOCK

shock² 🔑 /ʃɒk/ ***verb*** **1** [T] to cause an unpleasant feeling of surprise in sb: *We were shocked by his death.* ◇ *I'm sorry, I didn't mean to shock you when I came in.* **2** [I,T] to make sb feel disgusted or offended: *These films deliberately set out to shock.* ▶ **shocked** ***adj.***: *a shocked expression/look*

'shock absorber ***noun*** [C] a device that is fitted to each wheel of a vehicle in order to reduce the effects of travelling over rough ground, so that passengers can be more comfortable

shocking 🔑 /'ʃɒkɪŋ/ ***adj.*** **1** that offends or upsets people; that is morally wrong: *a shocking accident* ◇ *shocking behaviour/news* **2** (*especially BrE, informal*) very bad

'shock wave ***noun*** [C] a movement of very high air pressure that is caused by an explosion, an EARTHQUAKE (=a sudden movement of the earth's surface), etc.

shod past tense, past participle of **shoe²**

shoddy /'ʃɒdi/ ***adj.*** **1** made carelessly or with poor quality materials: *shoddy goods* **2** dishonest or unfair ▶ **shoddily** ***adv.***

shoe¹ 🔑 /ʃuː/ ***noun*** [C] **1** a type of covering for the foot, usually made of leather or plastic: *a pair of shoes* ◇ *running shoes* ◇ *What size are your shoes/What is your shoe size?* ◇ *I tried on a nice pair of shoes but they didn't fit.* **2** =HORSESHOE
IDM **in my, your, etc. place/shoes** → PLACE¹

shoe² /ʃuː/ ***verb*** [T] (*pt, pp* **shod** /ʃɒd/) to fit a shoe on a horse

shoehorn /'ʃuːhɔːn/ ***noun*** [C] a curved piece of plastic or metal that you use to help the back of your foot go into your shoe

shoelace /ˈʃuːleɪs/ (*especially AmE* **shoestring**) ***noun*** [C] a long thin piece of material like string used to fasten a shoe: *to tie/untie a shoelace*

shoestring /ˈʃuːstrɪŋ/ ***noun*** [sing.] (*especially AmE*) =SHOELACE

IDM **on a shoestring** using very little money: *to live on a shoestring*

shone past tense, past participle of **shine**[1]

shoo[1] /ʃuː/ ***verb*** [T] (*pt, pp* **shooed**) **~ sb/sth away, off, out, etc.** to make sb/sth go away by saying '**shoo**' and waving your hands: *She shooed the children out of the kitchen.*

shoo[2] /ʃuː/ ***exclamation*** used to tell a child or an animal to go away

shook past tense of **shake**[1]

shoot[1] 🔑 /ʃuːt/ ***verb*** (*pt, pp* **shot** /ʃɒt/) **1** [I,T] **~ (sth) (at sb/sth)** to fire a gun or another weapon: *Don't shoot! ◇ She shot an arrow at the target, but missed it.* **2** [T] to injure or kill sb/sth with a gun: *The policeman was shot in the arm. ◇ The soldier was* ***shot dead***. **3** [I,T] (SPORT) to hunt and kill birds and animals with a gun as a sport: *He* ***goes shooting*** *at the weekends.* ➲ look at **hunting** **4** [I,T] to move somewhere quickly and suddenly; to make sth move in this way: *The car shot past me at 100 miles per hour.* **5** [I] (HEALTH) (of pain) to go very suddenly along part of your body: *The pain shot up my leg. ◇ shooting pains in the chest* **6** [I,T] (ARTS AND MEDIA) to make a film or photograph of sth: *They shot the scene ten times.* **7** [I] **~ (at sth)** (SPORT) (in football, etc.) to try to kick or hit the ball into the goal: *He should have shot instead of passing.* ➲ noun **shot**

PHR V **shoot sb/sth down** to make sb/sth fall to the ground by shooting them or it: *The helicopter was shot down by a missile.*

shoot up to increase by a large amount; to grow very quickly: *Prices have shot up in the past year.*

shoot[2] /ʃuːt/ ***noun*** [C] (BIOLOGY) a new part of a plant or tree ➲ picture at **flower**

ˌ**shooting ˈstar** ***noun*** [C] (ASTRONOMY) a small piece of rock in space (**a meteor**) that travels very fast and burns with a bright light as it enters the earth's atmosphere

shop[1] 🔑 /ʃɒp/ (*AmE* **store**) ***noun*** [C] a building or part of a building where things are bought and sold: *a cake/shoe shop ◇ a corner shop* (=a local shop, usually at the corner of a street) *◇ When do the shops open?*

IDM **talk shop** → TALK[1]

shop[2] 🔑 /ʃɒp/ ***verb*** [I] (**shopping**; **shopped**) **~ (for sth)** to go to a shop or shops in order to buy things: *He's shopping for some new clothes.* ▶ **shopper** ***noun*** [C]

PHR V **shop around (for sth)** to look at the price and quality of an item in different shops before you decide where to buy it

shopaholic /ˌʃɒpəˈhɒlɪk/ ***noun*** [C] (*informal*) a person who enjoys shopping very much and spends too much time or money doing it

ˈ**shop assistant** (*also* **assistant**, *AmE* ˈ**sales clerk**; **clerk**) ***noun*** [C] a person whose job is to serve customers in a shop

ˌ**shop ˈfloor** ***noun*** [sing.] (*BrE*) **1** an area of a factory where the goods are made by the workers: *to work* ***on the shop floor*** **2** the workers in a factory, not the managers

shopkeeper /ˈʃɒpkiːpə(r)/ (*AmE* **storekeeper**) ***noun*** [C] a person who owns or manages a small shop

shoplifter /ˈʃɒplɪftə(r)/ ***noun*** [C] (LAW) a person who steals sth from a shop while pretending to be a customer ➲ note at **thief**

shoplifting /ˈʃɒplɪftɪŋ/ ***noun*** [U] (LAW) the crime of stealing goods from a shop while pretending to be a customer: *He was arrested for shoplifting.* ➲ look at **lift**[1] (6)

shopping 🔑 /ˈʃɒpɪŋ/ ***noun*** [U] **1** the activity of going to the shops and buying things: *We always* ***do the shopping*** *on a Friday night. ◇ a shopping basket/bag/trolley* **2** (*especially BrE*) the things that you have bought in a shop

ˈ**shopping centre** (*AmE* ˈ**shopping mall**; **mall**) ***noun*** [C] a place where there are many shops, either outside or in a covered building

ˈ**shopping mall** (*also* **mall**) ***noun*** [C] (*especially AmE*) a large building or covered area that has many shops, restaurants, etc. inside it ➲ look at **arcade**

shore[1] /ʃɔː(r)/ ***noun*** [C,U] (GEOGRAPHY) the land at the edge of a sea or lake: *The sailors* ***went on shore*** (=on land). ➲ look at **ashore**

shore[2] /ʃɔː(r)/ ***verb***

PHR V **shore sth up 1** to support part of a building or other large structure by placing large pieces of wood or metal against or under it so that it does not fall down **2** to help support sth that is weak or going to fail: *The measures were aimed at shoring up the economy.*

shoreline /ˈʃɔːlaɪn/ ***noun*** [C, usually sing.] (GEOGRAPHY) the edge of the sea, the ocean or a lake: *a rocky shoreline*

shorn past participle of **shear**

short[1] 🔑 /ʃɔːt/ ***adj., adv.*** **1** not measuring much from one end to the other: *a short line/distance/dress ◇ This essay is rather short. ◇ short hair* OPP **long** ➲ verb **shorten** **2** less than the average height: *a short, fat man* OPP **tall** **3** not lasting a long time; brief: *a short visit/film ◇ She left a short time ago. ◇ to have a short memory* (=to only remember things that have happened recently) OPP **long** ➲ verb **shorten** **4 ~ (of/on sth)** not having enough of what is needed: *Because of illness, the team is two players short. ◇ Good secretaries are* ***in short supply*** (=there are not enough of them). *◇ We're a bit short of money at the moment. ◇ Your essay is a bit short on detail.* ➲ noun **shortage** **5** suddenly: *She* ***stopped short*** *when she saw the accident.* **6 ~ for sth** used as a shorter way of saying sth or as an abbreviation: *'Bill' is short for 'William'.* **7 ~ (with sb)** (used about a person) speaking in an impatient and angry way to sb ➲ adverb **shortly** ▶ **shortness** ***noun*** [U]: *She suffered from shortness of breath.*

IDM **cut sth/sb short** to not allow sb to finish speaking; to interrupt

fall short (of sth) to not be enough; to not reach sth: *The pay rise fell short of the workers' demands.*

for short as a short form: *She's called 'Diana', or 'Di' for short.*

go short (of sth) to be without enough (of sth): *He made sure his family never went short of food.*

in the long/short term → TERM[1]

in short in a few words; briefly

run short (of sth) to have used up most of sth so there is not much left: *We're running short of coffee.*

short of sth/doing sth apart from; except for: *Nothing short of a miracle will save the business now.*

stop short of sth/doing sth → STOP[1]

short² /ʃɔːt/ ***noun*** [C] **1** (*informal*) = SHORT CIRCUIT **2** (*especially BrE*) a small strong alcoholic drink: *I prefer wine to shorts.*

shortage /ˈʃɔːtɪdʒ/ ***noun*** [C] a situation where there is not enough of sth: *a food/housing/water shortage* ◇ *a shortage of trained teachers*

shortbread /ˈʃɔːtbred/ ***noun*** [U] a sweet biscuit made with sugar, flour and butter

ˌshort ˈcircuit (also *informal* **short**) ***noun*** [C] (**PHYSICS**) a bad electrical connection that causes a machine to stop working ▶ **ˌshort-ˈcircuit** ***verb*** [I,T]: *The lights short-circuited.*

shortcoming /ˈʃɔːtkʌmɪŋ/ ***noun*** [C, usually pl.] a fault or weakness

ˌshort ˈcut ***noun*** [C] a quicker, easier or more direct way to get somewhere or to do sth: *He **took a short cut** to school through the park.*

shorten /ˈʃɔːtn/ ***verb*** [I,T] to become shorter or to make sth shorter

shortfall /ˈʃɔːtfɔːl/ ***noun*** [C] ~ **(in sth)** the amount by which sth is less than you need or expect

shorthand /ˈʃɔːthænd/ ***noun*** [U] (**LANGUAGE**) a method of writing quickly that uses signs or short forms of words: *to write **in shorthand*** ◇ *a shorthand typist* ➲ look at **longhand**

ˈshort-haul ***adj.*** (**TOURISM**) that involves transporting people or goods over short distances, especially by plane: *short-haul flights* OPP **long-haul**

shortlist /ˈʃɔːtlɪst/ ***noun*** [C, usually sing.] a list of the best people for a job, etc. who have been chosen from all the people who want the job: *She's one of the four people on the shortlist.* ▶ **shortlist** ***verb*** [T]: *Six candidates were shortlisted for the post.*

ˌshort-ˈlived ***adj.*** lasting only for a short time

shortly 🔑 /ˈʃɔːtli/ ***adv.*** **1** soon; not long: *The manager will see you shortly.* **2** in an impatient, angry way

shorts /ʃɔːts/ ***noun*** [pl.] **1** a type of short trousers ending above the knee that you wear in hot weather, while playing sports, etc. **2** (*AmE*) = BOXER SHORTS

ˌshort-ˈsighted ***adj.*** **1** (*especially AmE* **ˌnear-ˈsighted**) (**HEALTH**) able to see things clearly only when they are very close to you SYN **myopic**: *I have to wear glasses because I'm short-sighted.* OPP **long-sighted** **2** not considering what will probably happen in the future: *a short-sighted attitude/policy* ▶ **ˌshort-ˈsightedness** ***noun*** [U]

ˌshort-ˈstaffed ***adj.*** (used about an office, a shop, etc.) not having enough people to do the work

ˌshort ˈstory ***noun*** [C] (**LITERATURE**) a piece of writing that is shorter than a novel

ˌshort-ˈterm ***adj.*** lasting for a short period of time from the present: *short-term plans/memory*

ˈshort wave ***noun*** [C,U] (*abbr.* **SW**) (**ARTS AND MEDIA, PHYSICS**) a system for sending radio signals: *Short wave is a radio wave of frequency greater than 3 MHz.* ➲ look at **long wave, medium wave**

shot¹ 🔑 /ʃɒt/ ***noun*** [C] **1** a ~ **(at sb/sth)** an act of firing a gun, etc., or the noise that this makes: *to **take a shot** at the target* ◇ *The policeman fired **a warning shot** into the air.* **2** (**SPORT**) (in sport) the action of kicking, throwing or hitting a ball in order to score a point or a goal: *Owen scored with a low shot into the corner of the net.* ◇ *Good shot!* **3** (**ARTS AND MEDIA**) a photograph or a picture in a film: *I got some good shots of the runners as they crossed the line.* **4** [usually sing.] (*informal*) **a ~ (at sth/at doing sth)** a try at doing sth; an attempt: *Let me **have a shot at it*** (= let me try to do it). ◇ *Just **give it your best shot*** (= try as hard as you can). **5** (**HEALTH**) a small amount of a drug that is put into your body using a needle **6** (often **the shot**) (**SPORT**) a heavy metal ball that is thrown in THE SHOT-PUT

IDM **a long shot** → LONG¹

call the shots/tune → CALL¹

like a shot (*informal*) very quickly; without stopping to think about it: *If someone invited me on a free holiday, I'd go like a shot.*

shot² past tense, past participle of **shoot¹**

shotgun /ˈʃɒtɡʌn/ ***noun*** [C] a long gun that is used for shooting small animals and birds

the ˈshot-put ***noun*** [sing.] (**SPORT**) the event or sport of throwing a heavy metal ball as far as possible

should 🔑 /ʃəd; *strong form* ʃʊd/ ***modal verb*** (*negative* **should not**; *short form* **shouldn't** /ˈʃʊdnt/) **1** (used for saying that it is right or appropriate for sb to do sth, or for sth to happen) ought to: *The police should do something about street crime in this area.* ◇ *Children shouldn't be left on their own.* ◇ *I'm tired. I shouldn't have gone to bed so late/I should have gone to bed earlier.* **2** used for giving or for asking for advice: *You should try that new restaurant.* ◇ *Do you think I should phone him?* ◇ *What should I do?* **3** used for saying that you expect sth is true or will happen:

short-sighted / long-sighted

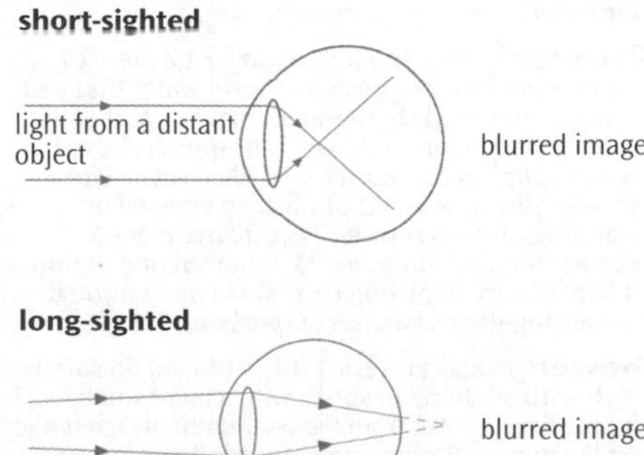

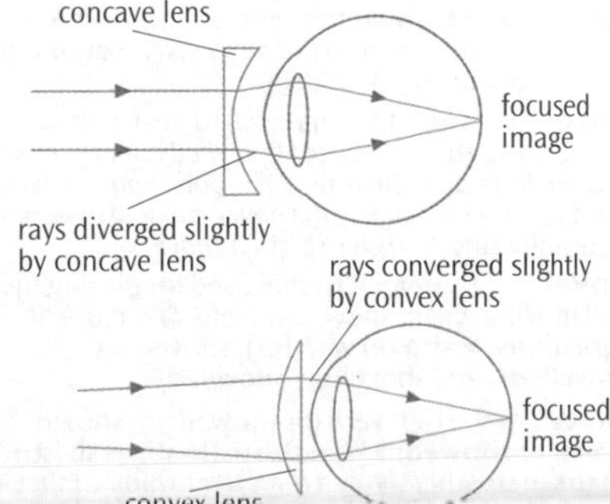

It's 4.30. They should be in New York by now. ◇ *It should stop raining soon.* **4** (*BrE, formal*) used with 'I/we' instead of 'would' in 'if' sentences: *I should be most grateful if you could send me...* **5** (*formal*) used to refer to a possible event or situation: ***In case/If you should** decide to accept, please phone us.* ◇ ***Should you** decide to accept, please phone us.* **6** used as the past tense of 'shall' when we report what sb says: *He asked me if he should come today* (=he asked 'Shall I come today?'). **7** **I ~ imagine, say, think, etc.** used to give opinions that you are not certain about

shoulder[1] ⊶ /'ʃəʊldə(r)/ ***noun*** **1** [C] (ANATOMY, BIOLOGY) the part of your body between your neck and the top of your arm: *I asked him why he'd done it but he just **shrugged his shoulders*** (=raised his shoulders to show that he did not know or care). ◇ *She fell asleep with her head on his shoulder.* ➲ picture on **page 80** **2** **-shouldered** (used to form compound adjectives) having the type of shoulders mentioned: *a broad-shouldered man* **3** [C] a part of a dress, coat, etc. that covers the shoulders ➲ look at **hard shoulder**

IDM **a shoulder to cry on** used to describe a person who listens to your problems and understands how you feel

have a chip on your shoulder → CHIP[1]

rub shoulders with sb → RUB

shoulder[2] /'ʃəʊldə(r)/ ***verb*** [T] **1** to accept the responsibility for sth: *to **shoulder the blame/responsibility** for sth* **2** to push sb/sth with your shoulder

'**shoulder bag** ***noun*** [C] a type of bag that you carry over one shoulder with a long STRAP

'**shoulder blade** ***noun*** [C] (ANATOMY) either of the two large flat bones on each side of your back, below your shoulders SYN **scapula** ➲ picture on **page 80**

'**shoulder strap** ***noun*** [C] **1** a narrow piece of material on a dress or other piece of clothing that goes over your shoulder from the front to the back **2** a long narrow piece of material, leather, etc. that is part of a bag so that you can carry it over your shoulder

shout ⊶ /ʃaʊt/ ***verb*** **1** [I] **~ (at/to sb); ~ out** to speak or cry out in a very loud voice: *There's no need to shout – I can hear you.* ◇ *The teacher shouted angrily at the boys.* ◇ *to shout out in pain/excitement* **2** [T] **~ sth (at/to sb); ~ sth out** to say sth in a loud voice: *'Careful,' she shouted.* ◇ *The students kept shouting out the answers, so we stopped playing in the end.* ◇ *The captain shouted instructions to his team.* ➲ look at **scream** ▶ **shout** ***noun*** [C]

PHR V **shout sb down** to shout so that sb who is speaking cannot be heard: *The speaker was shouted down by a group of protesters.*

shove /ʃʌv/ ***verb*** [I,T] (*informal*) to push with a sudden, rough movement: *Everybody in the crowd was **pushing and shoving**.* ◇ *The policeman shoved the thief into the back of the police car.* ▶ **shove** ***noun*** [C, usually sing.]: *to give sb/sth a shove*

shovel /'ʃʌvl/ ***noun*** [C] a tool used for picking up and moving earth, snow, sand, etc. ➲ picture at **agriculture** ▶ **shovel** ***verb*** [I,T] (**shovelling**; **shovelled**: *AmE* **shoveling**; **shoveled**)

show[1] ⊶ /ʃəʊ/ ***verb*** (*pt* **showed**; *pp* **shown** /ʃəʊn/ or **showed**) **1** [T] **~ sb/sth (to sb); ~ sb (sth)** to let sb see sb/sth: *I showed the letter to him.* ◇ *I showed him the letter.* ◇ *She showed me what she had bought.* ◇ *They're showing his latest film at our local cinema.* ◇ *She was showing signs of stress.* ◇ *This white T-shirt really shows the dirt.* ◇ *The picture showed him arguing with a photographer.* **2** [T] to make sth clear; to give information about sth: *Research shows that most people get too little exercise.* ◇ *This graph shows how prices have gone up in the last few years.* **3** [I] to be able to be seen; to appear: *I tried not to let my disappointment show.* **4** [T] to help sb to do sth by doing it yourself; to explain sth: *Can you show me how to put the disk in the computer?* **5** [T] to lead sb to or round a place; to explain how to go to a place: *I'll come with you and show you the way.* ◇ *Shall I show you to your room?* ◇ *A guide showed us round the museum.*

PHR V **show (sth) off** (*informal*) to try to impress people by showing them how clever you are or by showing them sth that you are proud of: *John was showing off by driving his new car very fast.* ➲ noun **show-off**

show up (*informal*) to arrive, especially when sb is expecting you: *I thought you'd never show up.*

show (sth) up to allow sth to be seen: *The sunlight shows up those dirty marks on the window.*

show sb up (*informal*) to make sb embarrassed by your behaviour or appearance: *His criticisms showed her up in front of the boss.*

show[2] ⊶ /ʃəʊ/ ***noun*** **1** [C] (ARTS AND MEDIA) a type of entertainment performed for an audience: *a TV comedy show* ◇ *a quiz show* **2** [C,U] an occasion when a collection of things is brought together for people to look at: *a dog show* ◇ *a fashion show* ◇ *Paintings by local children will be **on show** at the town hall next week.* **3** [C,U] something that a person does or has in order to make people believe sth that is not true: *Although she hated him, she **put on a show of** politeness.* ◇ *His bravery is **all show*** (=he is not as brave as he pretends to be). **4** [sing.] an occasion when you let sb see sth: *a show of emotion/gratitude/temper*

'**show business** (also *informal* **showbiz** /'ʃəʊbɪz/) ***noun*** [U] (ARTS AND MEDIA) the business of entertaining people, in the theatre, in films, on television, etc.: *He's been **in show business** since he was five years old.*

showcase /'ʃəʊkeɪs/ ***noun*** [C, usually sing.] **~ (for sb/sth)** an event that presents sb's abilities or the good qualities of sth in an attractive way: *The festival was a showcase for young musicians.* ▶ **showcase** ***verb*** [T]: *Jack found a film role that showcased all his talents.*

showdown /'ʃəʊdaʊn/ ***noun*** [C] a final argument, meeting or fight at the end of a long disagreement: *The management are preparing for a showdown with the union.*

shower[1] ⊶ /'ʃaʊə(r)/ ***noun*** [C] **1** a piece of equipment that produces a spray of water that you stand under to wash; the small room or part of a room that contains a shower: *The shower doesn't work.* ◇ *She's in the shower.* ◇ *I'd like a room with a shower, please.* **2** an act of washing yourself by standing under a shower: *I'll just **have a** quick **shower** then we can go out.* **3** a short period of rain **4** a lot of very small objects that fall or fly through the air together: *a shower of sparks/broken glass*

shower[2] /'ʃaʊə(r)/ ***verb*** **1** [I,T] **~ (down) on sb/sth; ~ sb with sth** to cover sb/sth with a lot of small falling objects: *Ash from the volcano showered down on the town.* ◇ *People suffered cuts after being showered with broken glass.* **2** [I] to wash yourself under a shower: *I came back from my run, showered and got changed.*

showing /ˈʃəʊɪŋ/ *noun* **1** [C] (ARTS AND MEDIA) an act of showing a film, etc.: *The second showing of the film begins at 8 o'clock.* **2** [sing.] how sb/sth behaves; how successful sb/sth is: *On its present showing, the party should win the election.*

showjumping /ˈʃəʊdʒʌmpɪŋ/ *noun* [U] (SPORT) a competition in which a person rides a horse over a series of fences (**jumps**)

shown past participle of **show**[1]

ˈshow-off *noun* [C] a person who tries to impress others by showing them how clever they are, or by showing them sth they are proud of: *She's such a show-off, always boasting about how good she is at this and that.*

showroom /ˈʃəʊruːm; -rʊm/ *noun* [C] a type of large shop where customers can look at goods such as cars, furniture and electrical items that are on sale

shrank past tense of **shrink**

shrapnel /ˈʃræpnəl/ *noun* [U] small pieces of metal that fly around when a bomb explodes

shred[1] /ʃred/ *noun* **1** [C] a small thin piece of material that has been cut or torn off: *His clothes were torn to shreds by the rose bushes.* **2 a ~ of sth** [sing.] (in negative sentences) a very small amount of sth: *There wasn't a shred of truth in her story.*

shred[2] /ʃred/ *verb* [T] (**shredding**; **shredded**) to tear or cut sth into **shreds**: *shredded cabbage*

shrew /ʃruː/ *noun* [C] **1** a small animal like a mouse with a long nose **2** (*old-fashioned*) a bad-tempered unpleasant woman

shrewd /ʃruːd/ *adj.* able to make good decisions because you understand a situation well: *a shrewd thinker/decision* ▶ **shrewdly** *adv.*

shriek /ʃriːk/ *verb* **1** [I] to make a short, loud, noise in a high voice: *She shrieked in fright.* ◇ *The children were shrieking with laughter.* **2** [T] to say sth loudly in a high voice: *'Stop it!' she shrieked.* ➲ look at **screech** ▶ **shriek** *noun* [C]

shrill /ʃrɪl/ *adj.* (used about a sound) high and unpleasant: *a shrill cry*

shrimp /ʃrɪmp/ *noun* [C] **1** a small sea creature with a shell and a lot of legs that turns pink when you cook it **2** (*AmE*) = PRAWN ➲ picture on **page 28**

shrine /ʃraɪn/ *noun* [C] (RELIGION) a place that is important to a particular person or group of people for religious reasons or because it is connected with a special person

shrink /ʃrɪŋk/ *verb* (*pt* **shrank** /ʃræŋk/ or **shrunk** /ʃrʌŋk/; *pp* **shrunk**) **1** [I,T] to become smaller or make sth smaller: *My T-shirt shrank in the wash.* ◇ *Television has shrunk the world.* ◇ *The rate of inflation has shrunk to 4%.* **2** [I] to move back because you are frightened or shocked: *We shrank back against the wall when the dog appeared.*

PHR V **shrink from sth/doing sth** to not want to do sth because you find it unpleasant

ˌshrink-ˈwrapped *adj.* covered tightly in a thin sheet of plastic: *The books are shrink-wrapped so you can't open them in the shop.*

shrivel /ˈʃrɪvl/ *verb* [I,T] (**shrivelling**; **shrivelled**: *AmE* **shriveling**; **shriveled**) ~ **(sth) (up)** to become smaller, especially because of dry conditions: *The plants shrivelled up and died in the hot weather.*

shroud[1] /ʃraʊd/ *noun* [C] a cloth or sheet that is put round a dead body before it is buried

shroud[2] /ʃraʊd/ *verb* [T] ~ **sth (in sth)** (usually passive) to cover or hide sth

Shrove Tuesday /ˌʃrəʊv ˈtjuːzdeɪ; -di/ *noun* [C] (RELIGION) the day before a period of 40 days (**Lent**) during which some Christians do not eat certain foods

shrub /ʃrʌb/ *noun* [C] a small bush

shrubbery /ˈʃrʌbəri/ *noun* [C] (*pl.* **shrubberies**) an area where a lot of small bushes have been planted

shrug /ʃrʌg/ *verb* [I,T] (**shrugging**; **shrugged**) to lift your shoulders as a way of showing that you do not know sth or are not interested: *'Who knows?' he said and shrugged.* ◇ *'It doesn't matter to me,' he said, **shrugging his shoulders**.* ▶ **shrug** *noun* [C, usually sing.]: *I asked him if he was sorry and he just answered with a shrug.*

PHR V **shrug sth off** to not allow sth to affect you in a bad way: *An actor has to learn to shrug off criticism.*

shrunk past tense, past participle of **shrink**

shudder /ˈʃʌdə(r)/ *verb* [I] to suddenly shake hard, especially because of an unpleasant feeling or thought: *Just to think about the accident makes me shudder.* ◇ *The engine shuddered violently and then stopped.* ▶ **shudder** *noun* [C]

shuffle[1] /ˈʃʌfl/ *verb* **1** [I] to walk by sliding your feet along instead of lifting them off the ground **2** [I,T] to move your body or feet around because you are uncomfortable or nervous: *The audience were so bored that they began to shuffle in their seats.* **3** [I,T] to mix a pack of playing cards before a game: *It's your turn to shuffle.* ◇ *She shuffled the cards carefully.*

shuffle[2] /ˈʃʌfl/ *noun* [C, usually sing.] **1** a way of walking without lifting your feet off the ground **2** an act of **shuffling** cards

shun /ʃʌn/ *verb* [T] (**shunning**; **shunned**) (*written*) to avoid sb/sth; to keep away from sb/sth: *She was shunned by her family when she married him.*

shunt /ʃʌnt/ *verb* [T] **1** to move a railway train from one track to another **2** to make sb go from one place to another: *He was shunted around from one hospital to another.*

shut[1] ⊶ /ʃʌt/ *verb* (*pres. part.* **shutting**; *pt, pp* **shut**) **1** [I,T] to make sth close; to become closed: *Could you shut the door, please?* ◇ *I can't shut my suitcase.* ◇ *Shut your books, please.* ◇ *He shut his eyes and tried to go to sleep.* ◇ *This window won't shut properly.* ◇ *The doors open and shut automatically.* **2** [I,T] (used about a shop, restaurant, etc.) to stop doing business for the day; to close: *What time do the shops shut on Saturday?* **3** [T] to prevent sb/sth from leaving a place; to close a door on sth: *She shut herself in her room and refused to come out.* ◇ *Tony shut his fingers in the door of the car.*

PHR V **shut sb/sth away** to keep sb/sth in a place where people cannot find or see them or it

shut (sth) down (used about a factory, etc.) to close for a long time or for ever: *Financial problems forced the business to shut down.*

shut sb/sth off (from sth) to keep sb/sth apart from sth: *He shuts himself off from the rest of the world.*

shut sb/sth out to keep sb/sth out: *He tried to shut out all thoughts of the accident.*

shut (sb) up (*informal*) **1** to stop talking; to be quiet: *I wish you'd shut up!* **2** to make sb stop talking

shut sb/sth up (in sth) to put sb/sth somewhere and stop them or it leaving: *He was shut up in prison for nearly ten years.*

shut[2] ⊶ /ʃʌt/ *adj.* (not before a noun) **1** in a closed position: *Make sure the door is shut properly before you leave.* **2** not open to the public: *The* *restaurant was shut so we went to one round the corner.*

IDM **keep your mouth shut** → MOUTH¹

shutter /ˈʃʌtə(r)/ ***noun*** [C] **1** a wooden or metal cover that is fixed outside a window and that can be opened or shut. A shop's **shutter** usually slides down from the top of the shop window. **2** the part at the front of a camera that opens for a very short time to let light in so that a photograph can be taken ➲ picture at **camera**

shuttle /ˈʃʌtl/ ***noun*** [C] **1** a plane, bus or train that travels regularly between two places: *We run a shuttle service between the hotel and the airport.* **2** a pointed tool used in making cloth (**weaving**) to pull a thread between the other threads that pass along the length of the cloth ➲ picture at **loom**

shuttlecock /ˈʃʌtlkɒk/ ***noun*** [C] (**SPORT**) (in the sport of BADMINTON) the small, light object that is hit over the net ➲ picture at **sport**

shy¹ ⊷ /ʃaɪ/ ***adj.*** **1** nervous and uncomfortable about meeting and speaking to people; showing that sb feels like this: *She's very shy with strangers.* ◇ *a shy smile* **2** ~ **(of/about sth/doing sth)** frightened to do sth or to become involved in sth: *She's not shy of telling people what she thinks.* ▶ **shyly *adv.***
▶ **shyness *noun*** [U]

shy² /ʃaɪ/ ***verb*** (*pres. part.* **shying**; *3rd person sing. pres.* **shies**; *pt, pp* **shied**) [I] (used about a horse) to suddenly move back or sideways in fear

PHRV **shy away from sth/from doing sth** to avoid doing sth because you are afraid

SI /ˌes ˈaɪ/ ***abbr.*** (used to describe units of measurement) International System (from French 'Système International'): *SI units* ℹ For more information about **SI units**, look at the **Expressions using numbers** section on pages R36-40 in this dictionary.

Siamese twin /ˌsaɪəmiːz ˈtwɪn/ (*also* **conˌjoined ˈtwin**) ***noun*** [C] (**HEALTH**) one of two people who are born with their bodies joined together in some way, sometimes sharing the same organs

sibling /ˈsɪblɪŋ/ ***noun*** [C] (*formal*) (**BIOLOGY**) a brother or a sister

sic /sɪk; siːk/ ***adv.*** (**LANGUAGE**) (written after a word that you have copied from somewhere, to show that you know that the word is wrongly spelled or wrong in some other way): *In the letter to parents it said: 'The school is proud of it's [sic] record of excellence'.*

sick¹ ⊷ /sɪk/ ***adj.*** **1** (**HEALTH**) not well; ill: *a sick child* ◇ *Do you get paid for days when you're **off sick*** (= from work)? ◇ *You're too ill to work today – you should **phone in sick**.* **2 the sick** (**HEALTH**) ***noun*** [pl.] people who are ill **3** (**HEALTH**) feeling ill in your stomach so that you may VOMIT (= bring up food through your mouth): *I feel sick – I think it was that fish I ate.* ◇ *Don't eat any more or you'll make yourself sick.* ➲ look at **airsick**, **carsick**, **nausea**, **seasick**, **travel-sick** **4** ~ **of sb/sth** feeling bored or annoyed because you have had too much of sb/sth: *I'm sick of my job.* ◇ *I'm sick of tidying up your mess!* **5** ~ **(at/about sth)** very annoyed or disgusted by sth: *He felt sick at the sight of so much waste.* **6** (*informal*) mentioning disease, suffering, death, etc. in a cruel or disgusting way: *He offended everyone with a sick joke about blind people.*

IDM **be sick** (**HEALTH**) to bring up food from the stomach; VOMIT

make sb sick to make sb very angry: *Oh, stop complaining. You make me sick!*

sick to death of sb/sth feeling tired of or annoyed by sb/sth: *I'm sick to death of his grumbling.*

sick² /sɪk/ ***noun*** [U] (**HEALTH**) food that sb has brought up from their stomach; VOMIT: *There was sick all over the car seat.*

ˌsick ˈbuilding syndrome ***noun*** [U] (**HEALTH**) a condition that affects people who work in large offices, making them feel tired and causing headaches, sore eyes and breathing problems, thought to be caused by, for example, the lack of fresh air or by chemicals in the air

sicken /ˈsɪkən/ ***verb*** [T] to make sb feel disgusted: *The sight of people fighting sickens me.* ▶ **sickening *adj.***: *His head made a sickening sound as it hit the road.*

sickle /ˈsɪkl/ ***noun*** [C] (**AGRICULTURE**) a tool with a short handle and a long, curved BLADE (= a metal part with a sharp edge) that is used for cutting long grass, CORN, etc. ➲ picture at **agriculture**

ˈsick leave ***noun*** [U] (**BUSINESS**) a period spent away from work, etc. because of illness: *Mike's been off **on sick leave** since March.*

ˌsickle-cell aˈnaemia (*also* **ˈsickle-cell disease**) ***noun*** [U] (**HEALTH**) a serious medical condition in which the red blood cells are damaged and change shape

sickly /ˈsɪkli/ ***adj.*** **1** (used about a person) weak and often ill: *a sickly child* **2** unpleasant; causing you to feel ill: *the sickly smell of rotten fruit*

sickness /ˈsɪknəs/ ***noun*** (**HEALTH**) **1** [U] the state of being ill: *A lot of workers are absent because of sickness.* **2** [U] a feeling in your stomach that may make you bring up food through your mouth: *Symptoms of the disease include sickness and diarrhoea.* **3** [C,U] a particular type of illness: *pills for seasickness* ➲ look at **sleeping sickness**

ˈsick pay ***noun*** [U] (**HEALTH**, **BUSINESS**) pay given to an employee who is away from work because of illness

side¹ ⊷ /saɪd/ ***noun*** [C] **1** one of the flat outer surfaces of sth: *A cube has six sides.* **2 -sided** (used to form compound adjectives) having the number of sides mentioned: *a six-sided coin* **3** one of the surfaces of sth except the top, bottom, front or back: *I went round to the side of the building.* ◇ *The side of the car was damaged.* **4** the edge of sth, away from the middle: *Make sure you stay **at the side** of the road when you're cycling.* ◇ *We moved **to one side** to let the doctor get past.* **5** the area to the left or right of sth; the area in front of or behind sth: *We live (on) **the other side** of the main road.* ◇ *It's more expensive to live on the north side of town.* ◇ *In Japan they drive on **the left-hand side** of the road.* ◇ *She sat at the side of his bed/at his bedside.* **6** either of the two flat surfaces of sth thin: *Write on both sides of the paper.* **7** the right or the left part of your body, especially from under your arm to the top of your leg: *She lay on her side.* ◇ *The soldier stood with his hands by his sides.* **8** either of two or more people or groups who are fighting, playing, arguing, etc. against each other: *The two sides agreed to stop fighting.* ◇ *the winning/losing side* ◇ *Whose side are you on?* (= Who do you want to win?) **9** what is said by one person or group that is different from what is said by another: *I don't know whose **side of the story** to believe.* **10** your mother's or your father's family: *There is no history of illness **on** his mother's **side**.*

IDM **get on the right/wrong side of sb** to please/annoy sb: *He tried to get on the right side of his new boss.*

look on the bright side → LOOK¹

on/from all sides; **on/from every side** in/from all directions

on the big, small, high, etc. side (*informal*) slightly too big, small, high, etc.

on the safe side → SAFE[1]
put sth on/to one side; leave sth on one side to leave or keep sth so that you can use it or deal with it later: *You should put some money to one side for the future.*
side by side next to each other; close together: *They walked side by side along the road.*
take sides (with sb) to show that you support one person rather than another in an argument: *Parents should never take sides when their children are quarrelling.*

side² /saɪd/ *verb*
PHR V side with sb (against sb) to support sb in an argument

sideboard /ˈsaɪdbɔːd/ *noun* [C] a type of low cupboard about as high as a table, that is used for storing plates, etc. in a room that is used for eating (**dining room**)

sideburns /ˈsaɪdbɜːnz/ *noun* [pl.] hair that grows down a man's face in front of his ears

ˈside effect *noun* [C] **1** (**HEALTH**) the unpleasant effect that a drug may have in addition to its useful effects: *Side effects of the drug include nausea and dizziness.* **2** an unexpected effect of sth that happens in addition to the intended effect: *One of the side effects when the chemical factory closed was that fish returned to the river.* ➲ look at **after-effect**, **effect**

sideline /ˈsaɪdlaɪn/ *noun* **1** [C] something that you do in addition to your regular job, especially to earn extra money: *He's an engineer, but he repairs cars* ***as a sideline.*** **2 sidelines** [pl.] the lines that mark the two long sides of the area used for playing sports such as football, TENNIS, etc.; the area behind this
IDM on the sidelines not involved in an activity; not taking part in sth

sidelong /ˈsaɪdlɒŋ/ *adj.* directed from the side; sideways: *a sidelong glance*

ˈside road *noun* [C] a small road which joins a bigger main road

sidestep /ˈsaɪdstep/ *verb* (**sidestepping**; **sidestepped**) **1** [T] to avoid answering a question or dealing with a problem: *Did you notice how she neatly sidestepped the question?* **2** [T,I] to avoid sth, for example being hit, by stepping to one side

ˈside street *noun* [C] a narrow or less important street near a main street

sidetrack /ˈsaɪdtræk/ *verb* [T] (usually passive) to make sb forget what they are doing or talking about and start doing or talking about sth less important

sidewalk /ˈsaɪdwɔːk/ (*AmE*) = PAVEMENT

sideways 🔑 /ˈsaɪdweɪz/ *adv., adj.* **1** to, towards or from one side: *He jumped sideways to avoid being hit.* **2** with one of the sides at the top: *We'll have to turn the sofa sideways to get it through the door.*

siding /ˈsaɪdɪŋ/ *noun* [C, usually pl.] a short track at the side of a main railway line where trains go when they are not being used

sidle /ˈsaɪdl/ *verb* [I] ~ **up/over (to sb/sth)** to move towards sb/sth in a nervous way, as if you do not want anyone to notice you

siege /siːdʒ/ *noun* [C,U] a situation in which an army surrounds a town for a long time or the police surround a building so that nobody can get in or out
IDM lay siege to sth 1 to begin a **siege** of a town, building, etc.: *The crusaders laid siege to Lisbon.* **2** to surround a building, especially in order to speak to or question the person or people living or working there

siesta /siˈestə/ *noun* [C] a short sleep or rest that people take in the afternoon, especially in hot countries

sieve /sɪv/ *noun* [C] a type of kitchen tool that has a metal or plastic net, used for separating solids from liquids or very small pieces of food from large pieces: *Pour the soup through a sieve to get rid of any lumps.* ▶ **sieve** *verb* [T]: *to sieve flour*

sift /sɪft/ *verb* **1** [T] to pass flour, sugar or a similar substance through a SIEVE in order to remove any lumps: *to sift flour/sugar* **2** [I,T] ~ **(through) sth** to examine sth very carefully: *It took weeks to sift through all the evidence.*

sigh /saɪ/ *verb* **1** [I] to let out a long, deep breath that shows you are tired, sad, disappointed, etc.: *She sighed with disappointment at the news.* **2** [T] to say sth with a **sigh**: *'I'm so tired,' he sighed.*
▶ **sigh** *noun* [C]
IDM heave a sigh → HEAVE[1]

sight¹ 🔑 /saɪt/ *noun* **1** [U] (**HEALTH**) the ability to see: *He lost his sight in the war* (= he became blind). ◇ *My grandmother has very poor sight.* **2 -sighted** (used to form compound adjectives) able to see in the way mentioned: *a partially sighted child* ➲ look at **long-sighted**, **short-sighted** **3** [sing.] **the ~ of sb/sth** the act of seeing sb/sth: *I feel ill* ***at the sight of*** *blood.* **4** [U] a position where sb/sth can be seen: *They waited until the plane was* ***in /within sight*** *and then fired.* ◇ *When we get over this hill the town should* ***come into sight.*** ◇ *She didn't let the child* ***out of her sight.*** **5** [C] something that you see: *The burned-out building was a terrible sight.* **6 sights** [pl.] (**TOURISM**) places of interest that are often visited by tourists: *When you come to New York I'll show you the sights.* **7 a sight** [sing.] (*informal*) a person or thing that looks strange or amusing **8** [C, usually pl.] the part of a gun that you look through in order to aim it
IDM at first glance/sight → FIRST[1]
catch sight/a glimpse of sb/sth → CATCH[1]
in sight likely to happen or come soon: *A peace settlement is in sight.*
lose sight of sb/sth → LOSE
on sight as soon as you see sb/sth: *The soldiers were ordered to shoot the enemy on sight.*

sight² /saɪt/ *verb* [T] to see sb/sth, especially after looking out for them or it

sighting /ˈsaɪtɪŋ/ *noun* [C] an occasion when sb/sth is seen: *the first sighting of a new star*

sightseeing /ˈsaɪtsiːɪŋ/ *noun* [U] (**TOURISM**) visiting the sights of a city, etc. as a tourist: *We did some sightseeing in Rome.*

sightseer /ˈsaɪtsiːə(r)/ *noun* [C] (**TOURISM**) a person who visits the sights of a city, etc. as a tourist ➲ look at **tourist**

THESAURUS

sign

indication • symptom • symbol • indicator • signal
These are all words for an event, action or fact that shows that sth exists, is happening or may happen in the future.
sign: *Headaches may be a sign of stress.*
indication: *She gave no indication of being tired.*
symptom: *Symptoms include a sore throat.*
symbol: *The dove is a symbol of peace.*
indicator (*formal*): *early economic indicators*
signal: *Her smile was a signal of a new start.*

sign[1] ⊶ /saɪn/ ***noun*** [C] **1** ~ (of sth) something that shows that sb/sth is present, exists or may happen: *The patient was* ***showing*** *some* ***signs*** *of improvement.* ◇ *As we drove into the village there wasn't a sign of life anywhere* (=we couldn't see anyone). ➲ note on page 645 **2** a piece of wood, paper, etc. that has writing or a picture on it that gives you a piece of information, an instruction or a warning: *What does that sign say?* ◇ *a road sign* ◇ *Follow the signs to Banbury.* **3** a movement that you make with your head, hands or arms that has a particular meaning: *I* ***made a sign*** *for him to follow me.* ◇ *I'll* ***give you a sign*** *when it's time for you to speak.* **4** a type of shape, mark or symbol that has a particular meaning: *In mathematics, a cross is a plus sign.* **5** (*also* ˌ**sign of the 'zodiac**) one of the twelve divisions or symbols of the ZODIAC: *'What sign are you?' – 'Taurus.'* ◇ *I'm a Leo. What sign are you?*

sign[2] ⊶ /saɪn/ ***verb*** **1** [I,T] to write your name on a letter, document, etc. to show that you have written it or that you agree with what it says: *'Could you sign here, please?'* ◇ *I forgot to sign the cheque.* ◇ *The two presidents signed the treaty.* ➲ noun **signature**

2 [T] ~ **sb (up)** to get sb to sign a contract to work for you: *Real Madrid have signed two new players.* **3** [I] (LANGUAGE) to communicate using sign language

PHRV **sign in/out** to write your name to show you have arrived at or left a hotel, club, etc.

sign up (for sth) to agree formally to do sth: *I've signed up for evening classes.*

signal ⊶ /'sɪɡnəl/ ***noun*** [C] **1** a sign, action or sound that sends a particular message: *When I give (you) the signal, run!* **2** an event, action or fact that shows that sth exists or is likely to happen: *The fall in unemployment is a clear signal that the economy is improving.* SYN **sign**[1] **3** a set of lights used to give information to train drivers **4** a series of radio waves, etc. that are sent out or received: *a signal from a satellite* ▸ **signal *verb*** [I,T] (**signalling**; **signalled**: *AmE* **signaling**; **signaled**): *She was signalling wildly that something was wrong.*

signatory /'sɪɡnətri/ ***noun*** [C] (*pl.* **signatories**) ~ **(to sth)** one of the people or countries that sign an agreement, etc.

signature ⊶ /'sɪɡnətʃə(r)/ ***noun*** [C] a person's name, written by that person and always written in the same way ➲ verb **sign**

significance /sɪɡ'nɪfɪkəns/ ***noun*** [U] the importance or meaning of sth: *Few people realized the significance of the discovery.*

significant ⊶ AW /sɪɡ'nɪfɪkənt/ ***adj.*** **1** important or large enough to be noticed: *Police said that the time of the murder was extremely significant.* ◇ *There has been a significant improvement in your work.* **2** having a particular meaning: *It could be significant that he took out life insurance shortly before he died.*

significantly ⊶ AW /sɪɡ'nɪfɪkəntli/ ***adv.*** **1** in a way that is large or important enough to have an effect on sth or to be noticed: *Profits have increased significantly over the past few years.* ◇ *Attitudes have changed significantly since the 1960s.* **2** in a way that has a particular meaning: *Significantly, he did not deny that there might be an election.* **3** in a way that has a special or secret meaning: *She paused significantly before she answered.*

signify AW /'sɪɡnɪfaɪ/ ***verb*** [T] (*pres. part.* **signifying**; *3rd person sing. pres.* **signifies**; *pt, pp* **signified**) (*formal*) **1** to be a sign of sth; to mean: *What do those lights signify?* **2** to express or indicate sth: *They signified their agreement by raising their hands.*

'sign language ***noun*** [U] (LANGUAGE) a language used especially by people who cannot hear or speak, using the hands to make signs instead of spoken words

signpost /'saɪmpəʊst/ ***noun*** [C] a sign at the side of a road that gives information about directions and distances to towns

Sikh /siːk/ ***noun*** [C] (**RELIGION**) a member of one of the religions of India (**Sikhism**) that developed from Hinduism but teaches that there is only one god ▸ **Sikh *adj.*** ▸ **Sikhism** /'siːkɪzəm/ ***noun*** [U]

silage /'saɪlɪdʒ/ ***noun*** [U] (**AGRICULTURE**) grass or other green plants that are stored without being dried and are used to feed farm animals in winter

silence ⊶ /'saɪləns/ ***noun*** **1** [U] no noise or sound at all: *There must be silence during examinations.* **2** [C,U] a period when nobody speaks or makes a noise: *My question was met with an awkward silence.* ◇ *We ate* ***in silence***. **3** [U] not making any comments about sth ▸ **silence *verb*** [T]

silencer /'saɪlənsə(r)/ (*AmE* **muffler**) ***noun*** [C] **1** a device which is fixed to the EXHAUST PIPE (=the long tube under a vehicle) to reduce the noise made by the engine **2** the part of a gun that reduces the noise when it is fired

silent ⊶ /'saɪlənt/ ***adj.*** **1** where there is no noise; making no noise; very quiet: *The house was empty and silent.* **2** ~ **(on/about sth)** refusing to speak about sth: *The policeman told her she had the right to* ***remain silent***. **3** not using spoken words: *a silent prayer/protest* **4** (of a letter) not pronounced: *The 'b' in 'comb' is silent.* ▸ **silently *adv.***

silhouette /ˌsɪlu'et/ ***noun*** [C] the dark solid shape of sb/sth seen against a light background ▸ **silhouetted *adj.***

silica /'sɪlɪkə/ ***noun*** [U] (*symbol* **SiO_2**) (**CHEMISTRY**) a chemical COMPOUND of SILICON found in sand and in rocks such as QUARTZ, used in making glass and CEMENT

silicon /'sɪlɪkən/ ***noun*** [U] (*symbol* **Si**) (**CHEMISTRY**) a substance that exists as a grey solid or as a brown powder and is found in rocks and sand. It is used in making glass. ℹ For more information on the periodic table of elements, look at pages R34-5.

ˌ**silicon 'chip** ***noun*** [C] (**COMPUTING**) a very small piece of SILICON that is used to carry a complicated electronic CIRCUIT

silk ⊶ /sɪlk/ ***noun*** [U] the soft smooth cloth that is made from threads produced by a SILKWORM: *a silk shirt/dress*

silkworm /'sɪlkwɜːm/ ***noun*** [C] a small creature with a soft body and legs (**a caterpillar**) that produces SILK

silky /'sɪlki/ ***adj.*** smooth, soft and shiny; like silk: *silky hair*

sill /sɪl/ ***noun*** [C] a shelf that is at the bottom of a window, either inside or outside: *a window sill*

silly ⊶ /'sɪli/ ***adj.*** (**sillier**; **silliest**) **1** not showing thought or understanding; FOOLISH: *a silly mistake* ◇ *Don't be so silly!* OPP **sensible** **2** appearing ridiculous, so that people will laugh: *I'm not wearing that hat – I'd look silly in it.* ▸ **silliness *noun*** [U]

silo /ˈsaɪləʊ/ *noun* [C] (AGRICULTURE) **1** a tall tower on a farm used for storing grain, etc. **2** an underground place where grass or other green plants are made into SILAGE (= a substance that is stored until winter to feed the farm animals)

silt /sɪlt/ *noun* [U] (GEOGRAPHY) sand, soil or mud that collects at the sides or on the bottom of a river ➲ picture at **flood plain**

silver[1] /ˈsɪlvə(r)/ *noun* [U] **1** (*symbol* **Ag**) (CHEMISTRY) a valuable grey-white metal that is used for making jewellery, coins, etc.: *a silver spoon/necklace* ◇ *That's a nice ring. Is it silver?* ❶ For more information on the periodic table of elements, look at pages R34-5. **2** (FINANCE) coins made from silver or sth that looks like silver **3** objects that are made of silver, for example knives, forks, spoons, dishes: *The thieves stole some jewellery and some valuable silver.* IDM **every cloud has a silver lining** → CLOUD[1]

silver[2] /ˈsɪlvə(r)/ *adj.* having the colour of silver: *a silver sports car*

ˌsilver ˈmedal (*also* **silver**) *noun* [C] (SPORT) a small flat round piece of silver that is given to the person or team that comes second in a sports competition: *to win a silver medal at the Olympic Games* ➲ look at **gold medal, bronze medal** ▶ **ˌsilver ˈmedallist** *noun* [C]

ˌsilver ˈservice *noun* [U] a style of serving food at formal meals in which the person serving uses a silver fork and spoon

silverware /ˈsɪlvəweə(r)/ *noun* [U] **1** objects that are made of or covered with silver, especially knives, forks, dishes, etc. that are used for eating and serving food: *a piece of silverware* **2** (*AmE*) = CUTLERY

ˌsilver ˈwedding *noun* [C] the 25th anniversary of a wedding ➲ look at **golden wedding, diamond wedding**

silvery /ˈsɪlvəri/ *adj.* having the appearance or colour of silver: *an old lady with silvery hair*

SIM card /ˈsɪm kɑːd/ *noun* [C] a plastic card inside a mobile phone that stores personal information about the person using the phone

similar AW /ˈsɪmələ(r)/ *adj.* ~ **(to sb/sth)**; ~ **(in sth)** like sb/sth but not exactly the same: *Our houses are very similar in size.* ◇ *Your handwriting is very similar to mine.* OPP **different, dissimilar**

similarity AW /ˌsɪməˈlærəti/ *noun* (*pl.* **similarities**) **1** [U, sing.] ~ **(to sb/sth)**; ~ **(in sth)** the state of being like sb/sth but not exactly the same: *She **bears a remarkable/striking similarity** to her mother.* **2** [C] a ~ **(between A and B)**; a ~ **(in/of sth)** a characteristic that people or things have which makes them similar: *Although there are some similarities between the two towns, there are a lot of differences too.* ◇ *similarities in/of style*

similarly AW /ˈsɪmələli/ *adv.* **1** in almost the same way: *Husband and wife were similarly successful in their chosen careers.* **2** used to say that two facts, actions, statements, etc. are like each other: *The plural of 'shelf' is 'shelves'. Similarly, the plural of 'wolf' is 'wolves'.*

simile /ˈsɪməli/ *noun* [C,U] (LANGUAGE, LITERATURE) a word or phrase that compares sth to sth else, using the words 'like' or 'as', for example '*a face like a mask*' or '*as white as snow*'; the use of such words and phrases ➲ look at **metaphor**

simmer /ˈsɪmə(r)/ *verb* [I,T] to cook gently in a liquid that is almost boiling

simple /ˈsɪmpl/ *adj.* **1** easy to understand, do or use; not difficult or complicated: *This dictionary is written in simple English.* ◇ *a simple task/method/solution* ◇ *I can't just leave the job. It's not as simple as that.* **2** without decoration or unnecessary extra things; plain and basic: *a simple black dress* ◇ *The food is simple but perfectly cooked.* **3** used for saying that the thing you are talking about is the only thing that is important or true: *I'm not going to buy it **for the simple reason that*** (= only because) *I haven't got enough money.* **4** (used about a person or a way of life) natural and not complicated: *a simple life in the country* **5** not intelligent; slow to understand **6** (LANGUAGE) used to describe the present or past tense of a verb that is formed without using an AUXILIARY verb, as in '*She loves him*' and '*He arrived late.*': *the simple present/past tense*

ˌsimple ˈinterest *noun* [U] (FINANCE) interest that is paid only on the original amount of money that you invested, and not on any interest that it has earned ➲ look at **compound interest**

simplicity /sɪmˈplɪsəti/ *noun* [U] **1** the quality of being easy to understand, do or use: *We all admired the simplicity of the plan.* **2** the quality of having no decoration or unnecessary extra things; being natural and not complicated: *I like the simplicity of her paintings.*

simplify /ˈsɪmplɪfaɪ/ *verb* [T] (*pres. part.* **simplifying**; *3rd person sing. pres.* **simplifies**; *pt, pp* **simplified**) to make sth easier to do or understand; to make sth less complicated: *The process of applying for visas has been simplified.* ▶ **simplification** /ˌsɪmplɪfɪˈkeɪʃn/ *noun* [C,U]

simplistic /sɪmˈplɪstɪk/ *adj.* making a problem, situation, etc. seem less difficult and complicated than it really is

simply /ˈsɪmpli/ *adv.* **1** used to emphasize how easy or basic sth is: *Simply add hot water and stir.* **2** (used to emphasize an adjective) completely; absolutely: *That meal was simply excellent.* **3** in a way that makes sth easy to understand: *Could you explain it more simply?* **4** in a simple, basic way; without decoration or unnecessary extra things: *They live simply, with very few luxuries.* **5** only; just: *There's no need to get angry. The whole problem is simply a misunderstanding.*

simulate AW /ˈsɪmjuleɪt/ *verb* [T] to create certain conditions that exist in real life using computers, models, etc., usually for study or training purposes: *The astronauts trained in a machine that simulates conditions in space.* ▶ **simulation** AW /ˌsɪmjuˈleɪʃn/ *noun* [C,U]: *a computer simulation of a nuclear attack*

simulator /ˈsɪmjuleɪtə(r)/ *noun* [C] a piece of equipment that artificially creates a particular set of conditions in order to train sb to deal with a situation that they may experience in reality: *a flight simulator*

simultaneous /ˌsɪmlˈteɪniəs/ *adj.* happening or done at exactly the same time as sth else ▶ **simultaneously** *adv.*

sin /sɪn/ *noun* [C,U] (RELIGION) an action or way of behaving that is not allowed by a religion: *He believes it is a sin for two people to live together without being married.* ▶ **sin** *verb* [I] (**sinning**; **sinned**) ▶ **sinner** *noun* [C]

since /sɪns/ *adv., conj., prep.* **1** from a particular time in the past until a later time in the past or until now: *My parents bought this house in 1975 and we've been living here ever since.* ◇ *I've been working in a bank ever since I left school.* ◇ *It was the first time they'd won since 1974.* ◇ *I haven't seen him since last Tuesday.* ◇ *She has had a number of jobs since leaving university.* **2** at a time after a particular time in the past: *We were divorced two years ago and she has since married someone else.* **3** because; as: *Since they've obviously forgotten to phone me, I'll have to phone them.*

sincere 🔑 /sɪn'sɪə(r)/ ***adj.*** **1** (used about a person) really meaning or believing what you say; not pretending: *Do you think she was being sincere when she said she admired me?* **2** (used about a person's feelings, beliefs or behaviour) true; showing what you really mean or feel: *Please accept our sincere thanks/apologies.* OPP **insincere**
▶ **sincerity** /sɪn'serəti/ ***noun*** [U] OPP **insincerity**

sincerely 🔑 /sɪn'sɪəli/ ***adv.*** in a way that shows what you really feel or think about sb/sth: *I am sincerely grateful to you for all your help.* ◇ *'I won't let you down.' 'I sincerely hope not.'*
IDM **Yours sincerely**; (*AmE*) **Sincerely (yours)** used at the end of a formal letter before you sign your name, when you have addressed sb by their name: *Yours sincerely, ...*

sine /saɪn/ ***noun*** [C] (*abbr.* **sin**) (MATHEMATICS) the RATIO of the length of the side opposite one of the angles in a RIGHT-ANGLED triangle (= a triangle with one angle of 90°) to the length of the longest side ➲ look at **cosine**, **tangent**

sinew /'sɪnjuː/ ***noun*** [C, U] (ANATOMY) a strong band of substance that joins a muscle to a bone

sinful /'sɪnfl/ ***adj.*** (RELIGION) breaking a religious law; immoral

sing 🔑 /sɪŋ/ ***verb*** [I,T] (*pt* **sang** /sæŋ/; *pp* **sung** /sʌŋ/) (MUSIC) to make musical sounds with your voice: *He always sings when he's in the bath.* ◇ *The birds were singing outside my window.* ◇ *She sang all her most popular songs at the concert.*

singe /sɪndʒ/ ***verb*** [I,T] (*pres. part.* **singeing**) to burn the surface of sth slightly, usually by accident; to be burned in this way

singer 🔑 /'sɪŋə(r)/ ***noun*** [C] (MUSIC) a person who sings, or whose job is singing, especially in public: *an opera singer*

singing 🔑 /'sɪŋɪŋ/ ***noun*** [U] (MUSIC) the activity of making musical sounds with your voice: *There was singing and dancing all night.* ◇ *singing lessons*

single[1] 🔑 /'sɪŋgl/ ***adj.*** **1** (only *before* a noun) only one: *He gave her a single red rose.* ◇ *I managed to finish the whole job in a single afternoon.* ➲ look at **single-sex** **2** (only *before* a noun) used to emphasize that you are talking about each individual item of a group or series: *You answered **every single** question correctly. Well done!* **3** not married: *Are you married or single?* ◇ *a single man/woman* **4** (only *before* a noun) for the use of only one person: *I'd like to book a single room, please.* **5** (*also* **one-way**) (only *before* a noun) (used about a ticket or the price of a ticket) for a journey to a particular place, but not back again: *How much is the single fare to Rome?* ➲ look at **return**[2] (5)
IDM **in single file** → FILE[1]

single[2] /'sɪŋgl/ ***noun*** **1** [C] a ticket for a journey to a particular place, but not back again: *Two singles to Hull, please.* ➲ look at **return**[2] (5) **2** [C] (MUSIC) a CD, tape, etc. that has only one song on each side; the main song on this tape or CD: *U2's best-selling single* ➲ look at **album** **3** [C] a bedroom for one person in a hotel, etc. ➲ look at **double**[3] (5) **4 singles** [pl.] people who are not married and do not have a romantic relationship with sb else **5 singles** [U] (SPORT) a game of TENNIS, etc. in which one player plays against one other player ➲ look at **doubles**

single[3] /'sɪŋgl/ ***verb***
PHR V **single sb/sth out (for sth)** to give special attention or treatment to one person or thing from a group: *She was singled out for criticism.*

ˌsingle-'breasted ***adj.*** (used about a jacket or a coat) having only one row of buttons that fasten in the middle ➲ look at **double-breasted**

ˌsingle-'decker ***noun*** [C] a bus with only one level ➲ picture at **bus**

ˌsingle-'handed ***adj.***, ***adv.*** on your own with nobody helping you

ˌsingle-'minded ***adj.*** having one clear aim or goal which you are determined to achieve
▶ **ˌsingle-'mindedness** ***noun*** [U]

ˌsingle 'parent ***noun*** [C] a person who looks after their child or children without a husband, wife or partner: *a single-parent family*

ˌsingle-'sex ***adj.*** (EDUCATION) (used about a school) for boys only or girls only: *She went to a single-sex secondary school.* OPP **co-educational**, **mixed**

singlet /'sɪŋglət/ ***noun*** [C] a piece of clothing without sleeves, worn under or instead of a shirt, often worn by runners, etc.

singly /'sɪŋgli/ ***adv.*** one at a time SYN **individually**: *You can buy the tapes either singly or in packs of three.*

singular /'sɪŋgjələ(r)/ ***adj.*** **1** (LANGUAGE) in the form that is used for talking about one person or thing only: *'Table' is a singular noun; 'tables' is a plural noun.* ➲ look at **plural** **2** (*written*) unusual ▶ **singular** ***noun*** [sing.] (LANGUAGE): *The word 'clothes' has no singular.* ◇ *What's the singular of 'people'?*

singularly /'sɪŋgjələli/ ***adv.*** (*formal*) very; in an unusual way: *The government has been singularly unsuccessful in its policy against terrorism.*

sinister /'sɪnɪstə(r)/ ***adj.*** seeming evil or dangerous; making you feel that sth bad will happen: *There's something sinister about him. He frightens me.*

sink[1] 🔑 /sɪŋk/ ***verb*** (*pt* **sank** /sæŋk/; *pp* **sunk** /sʌŋk/) **1** [I,T] to go down or make sth go down under the surface of liquid or a soft substance: *If you throw a stone into water, it sinks.* ◇ *My feet sank into the mud.* **2** [I] (used about a person) to move downwards, usually by falling or sitting down: *I came home and sank into a chair, exhausted.* **3** [I] to get lower; to fall to a lower position or level: *We watched the sun sink slowly below the horizon.* **4** [I] to decrease in value, number, amount, strength, etc.
IDM **your heart sinks** → HEART
PHR V **sink in** (used about information, an event, an experience, etc.) to be completely understood or realized: *It took a long time for the terrible news to sink in.*
sink in; sink into sth (used about a liquid) to go into sth solid; to be absorbed

sink[2] /sɪŋk/ ***noun*** [C] a large open container in a kitchen, with taps to supply water, where you wash things ➲ look at **washbasin**

sinus /'saɪnəs/ ***noun*** [C] (often plural) (ANATOMY) one of the spaces in the bones of your face that are connected to your nose: *I've got a terrible cold and my sinuses are blocked.* ◇ *a sinus infection*

sip /sɪp/ ***verb*** [I,T] (**sipping**; **sipped**) to drink, taking only a very small amount of liquid into your mouth at a time: *We sat in the sun, sipping lemonade.* ▶ **sip** ***noun*** [C]

siphon (*also* **syphon**) /'saɪfn/ ***verb*** [T] **1** ~ **sth into/out of sth**; ~ **sth off/out** (CHEMISTRY) to remove a liquid from a container, often into another container, through a tube **2 ~ sth off; ~ sth (from/ out of sb/sth)** (LAW) to take money from a company illegally over a period of time

sir ⊶ /sɜː(r)/ ***noun*** **1** [sing.] used as a polite way of speaking to a man whose name you do not know, for example in a shop or restaurant, or to show respect: *I'm afraid we haven't got your size, sir.* ➲ look at **madam 2** [C] used at the beginning of a formal letter to a male person or male people: *Dear Sir... ◇ Dear Sirs...* ➲ look at **Madam 3** /sə(r)/ [sing.] the title that is used in front of the name of a man who has received one of the highest British honours

siren /ˈsaɪrən/ ***noun*** [C] **1** a device that makes a long, loud sound as a warning or signal: *an air-raid siren ◇ Three fire engines raced past, sirens wailing.* **2** (LITERATURE) (in ancient Greek stories) any of a group of sea creatures that were part woman and part bird, or part woman and part fish, whose beautiful singing made sailors sail towards them into rocks or dangerous waters

sirloin /ˈsɜːlɔɪn/ (*also* ˌ**sirloin ˈsteak**) ***noun*** [U, C] good quality meat that is cut from a cow's back

sirocco /sɪˈrɒkəʊ/ (*pl.* **siroccos**) ***noun*** [C] a hot wind that blows from Africa into Southern Europe

sisal /ˈsaɪsl/ ***noun*** [U] strong thin threads made from the leaves of a tropical plant and used for making rope, floor COVERINGS, etc.

sister ⊶ /ˈsɪstə(r)/ ***noun*** [C] **1** a girl or woman who has the same parents as another person: *I've got one brother and two sisters. ◇ We're sisters.* ➲ look at **half-sister, stepsister 2** (often **Sister**) (*BrE*) (HEALTH) a female hospital nurse in a high position **3 Sister** (RELIGION) a member of certain female religious groups; a NUN **4** (usually used as an adjective) a thing that belongs to the same type or group as sth else: *We have a sister company in Japan.* **5** (*informal*) a woman who you feel close to because she is a member of the same society, group, etc. as you

ˈ**sister-in-law** ***noun*** [C] (*pl.* **sisters-in-law**) **1** the sister of your husband or wife **2** the wife of your brother

sit ⊶ /sɪt/ ***verb*** (*pres. part.* **sitting**; *pt, pp* **sat** /sæt/) **1** [I] to rest your weight on your bottom, for example in a chair: *We sat in the garden all afternoon. ◇ She was sitting on the sofa, talking to her mother.* **2** [T] **~ sb (down)** to put sb into a sitting position; make sb sit down: *He picked up his daughter and sat her down on a chair. ◇ She sat me down and offered me a cup of tea.* **3** [I] to be in a particular place or position: *The letter sat on the table for several days before anybody opened it.* **4** [T] (*BrE*) (EDUCATION) to take an exam: *If I fail, will I be able to* ***sit the exam*** *again?* **5** [I] (*formal*) (used about an official group of people) to have a meeting or series of meetings

IDM **sit on the fence** to avoid saying which side of an argument you support

PHR V **sit about/around** (*informal*) to spend time doing nothing active or useful: *We just sat around chatting all afternoon.*

sit back to relax and not take an active part in what other people are doing: *Sit back and take it easy while I make dinner.*

sit down to lower your body into a sitting position: *He sat down in an armchair.*

sit sth out 1 to stay in a place and wait for sth unpleasant or boring to finish **2** to not take part in a dance, game, etc.

sit through sth to stay in your seat until sth boring or long has finished

sit up 1 to move into a sitting position when you have been lying down or to make your back straight: *Sit up straight and concentrate!* **2** to not go to bed although it is very late: *We sat up all night talking.*

sitar /sɪˈtɑː(r); ˈsɪtɑː(r)/ ***noun*** [C] (MUSIC) a musical instrument from India like a GUITAR, with a long neck and two sets of metal strings

sitcom /ˈsɪtkɒm/ (*also formal* ˌ**situation ˈcomedy**) ***noun*** [C,U] (ARTS AND MEDIA) a funny programme on television that shows the same characters in different amusing situations each week

site ⊶ AW /saɪt/ ***noun*** [C] **1** a piece of land where a building was, is or will be SITUATED: *a building/ construction site ◇ The company is looking for a site for its new offices.* **2** a place where sth has happened or that is used for sth: *the site of a famous battle* **3** (COMPUTING) a place on the Internet where a company, an organization, a university, etc. puts information ➲ look at **website** ▶ **site** ***verb*** [T] (*written*): *They met to discuss the siting of the new school.*

sitting /ˈsɪtɪŋ/ ***noun*** [C] **1** (LAW) a period of time during which a court of law or a parliament meets and does its work **2** a time when a meal is served in a school, hotel, etc. to a number of people at the same time: *Dinner will be in two sittings.*

ˈ**sitting room** (*BrE*) = LIVING ROOM

situate /ˈsɪtʃueɪt/ ***verb*** [T] **1** to build or place sth in a particular position **2** to consider how an idea, event, etc. is related to other things that influence your view of it: *Let me try and situate the events in their historical context.*

situated /ˈsɪtʃueɪtɪd/ ***adj.*** in a particular place or position: *The hotel is conveniently situated close to the beach.*

THESAURUS

situation

circumstances • position • conditions

These are all words for the conditions and facts that are connected with and affect the way things are.

situation: *the present economic situation*

circumstances: *The ship sank in mysterious circumstances.*

position: *She was in a position of power.*

conditions: *They had to work outside in freezing conditions.*

situation ⊶ /ˌsɪtʃuˈeɪʃn/ ***noun*** [C] **1** the things that are happening in a particular place or at a particular time: *The situation in the north of the country is extremely serious. ◇ Tim is* ***in a*** *difficult* ***situation*** *at the moment. ◇ the economic/financial/ political situation* **2** (*written*) the position of a building, town, etc. in relation to the area around it **3** (*written, old-fashioned*) a job: *Situations Vacant* (= the part of a newspaper where jobs are advertised)

sit-up

press-up (*AmE* push-up) sit-up

'sit-up ***noun*** [C] an exercise for the stomach muscles in which you lie on your back with your legs bent, then lift the top half of your body from the floor: *to do sit-ups* ➲ picture on previous page

six /sɪks/ ***number*** **1** 6 HELP Note how numbers are used in sentences: *The answers are on page six.* ◇ *There are six of us for dinner tonight.* ◇ *They have six cats.* ◇ *My son is six (years old) next month.* ◇ *She lives at 6 Elm Drive.* ◇ *a birthday card with a big 6 on it* **2 six-** (in compounds) having six of the thing mentioned: *She works a six-day week.* ℹ For more information about numbers in dates, measurements, prices, etc., look at the special section on numbers on pages R36-40 in this dictionary.

sixteen /ˌsɪks'tiːn/ ***number*** 16 ➲ note at **six**

sixteenth /ˌsɪks'tiːnθ/ ***ordinal number, noun*** [C] 16th ➲ note at **sixth¹**

ˌsix'teenth note (*AmE*) = SEMIQUAVER

sixth¹ /sɪksθ/ ***ordinal number*** 6th HELP Note how ordinal numbers are used in sentences: *Today is the sixth of March.* ◇ *Today is March the sixth.* ◇ *My office is on the sixth floor.* ◇ *This is the sixth time I've tried to phone him.* ◇ *It was Olivia's sixth birthday.* ℹ For more information about numbers in dates, measurements, prices, etc., look at the **Expressions using numbers** section on pages R36-40 in this dictionary.

sixth² /sɪksθ/ ***noun*** [C] the FRACTION ⅙; one of six equal parts of sth

'sixth form ***noun*** [C, usually sing., with sing. or pl. verb] (*BrE*) (EDUCATION) the final two years at secondary school for students from the age of 16 to 18 who are studying for A level exams ▶ **'sixth-former** ***noun*** [C]

ˌsixth-form 'college ***noun*** [C] (EDUCATION) (in Britain) a school for students over the age of 16

sixtieth /'sɪkstiəθ/ ***ordinal number, noun*** [C] 60th ➲ note at **sixth¹**

sixty /'sɪksti/ ***number*** **1** 60 HELP Note how numbers are used in sentences: *Sixty people went to the meeting.* ◇ *There are sixty pages in the book.* ◇ *He retired **at sixty**.* **2 the sixties** [pl.] the numbers, years or temperatures between 60 and 69; the 60s: *I don't know the exact number of members, but it's in the sixties.* ◇ *The most famous pop group of the sixties was The Beatles.* ◇ *The temperature tomorrow will be in the high sixties.*

IDM **in your sixties** between the age of 60 and 69: *I'm not sure how old she is but I should think she's in her sixties.* ◇ *in your **early/mid/late sixties*** ℹ For more information about numbers in dates, measurements, prices, etc., look at the special section on numbers on page R36-40.

size¹ 🔑 /saɪz/ ***noun*** **1** [U] how big or small sth is: *I was surprised at the size of the hotel. It was enormous!* ◇ *The planet Uranus is about four times the size of* (= as big as) *Earth.* **2** [C] one of a number of fixed measurements in which sth is made: *Have you got this dress **in a** bigger **size**?* ◇ *I'm a size 12.* ◇ *What size pizza would you like? Medium or large?* **3 -sized** (*also* -size) (used to form compound adjectives) of the size mentioned: *a medium-sized flat* ◇ *a king-size bed*

size² /saɪz/ ***verb***

PHR V **size sb/sth up** to form an opinion or judgement about sb/sth

sizeable (also **sizable**) /'saɪzəbl/ ***adj.*** quite large: *a sizeable sum of money*

sizzle /'sɪzl/ ***verb*** [I] to make the sound of food frying in hot fat

skate¹ /skeɪt/ ***noun*** [C] **1** (*also* **'ice skate**) (SPORT) a boot with a thin sharp metal part on the bottom that is used for moving on ice **2** = ROLLER SKATE **3** a large flat sea fish that can be eaten

skate² /skeɪt/ ***verb*** [I] **1** (*also* **'ice-skate**) to move on ice wearing ICE SKATES: *Can you skate?* ◇ *They skated across the frozen lake.* **2** = ROLLER SKATE ▶ **skater** ***noun*** [C]

skateboard /'skeɪtbɔːd/ ***noun*** [C] a short narrow board with small wheels at each end that you can stand on and ride as a sport ▶ **skateboarder** ***noun*** [C] ▶ **skateboarding** ***noun*** [U]: *When we were children we used to **go skateboarding** in the park.*

skating /'skeɪtɪŋ/ ***noun*** [U] **1** (*also* **'ice skating**) the activity or sport of moving on ice wearing special boots: *Would you like to **go skating** this weekend?* **2** = ROLLER SKATING

'skating rink (*also* **ice rink; rink**) ***noun*** [C] a large area of ice, or a building containing a large area of ice, that is used to SKATE on

skeletal /'skelətl/ ***adj.*** **1** (ANATOMY) connected with the SKELETON of a person or an animal: *Skeletal remains of the earliest dinosaurs are rare.* **2** looking like a SKELETON; very thin

skeleton¹ /'skelɪtn/ ***noun*** [C] (ANATOMY, BIOLOGY) the structure formed by all the bones in a human or animal body: *the human skeleton* ◇ *a dinosaur skeleton* ➲ picture on **page 80**

skeleton² /'skelɪtn/ ***adj.*** (used about an organization, a service, etc.) having the smallest number of people that is necessary for it to operate

skeptic, skeptical, skepticism (*AmE*) = SCEPTIC, SCEPTICAL, SCEPTICISM

sketch /sketʃ/ ***noun*** [C] **1** (ART) a simple, quick drawing without many details: *He drew a **rough sketch** of the new building on the back of an envelope.* **2** (ARTS AND MEDIA) a short funny scene on television, in the theatre, etc.: *The drama group did a sketch about a couple buying a new house.* **3** a short description without any details ▶ **sketch** ***verb*** [I,T]: *I sat on the grass and sketched the castle.*

sketchy /'sketʃi/ ***adj.*** not having many or enough details

skewer /'skjuːə(r)/ ***noun*** [C] a long thin pointed piece of metal or wood that is pushed through pieces of meat, vegetables, etc. to hold them together while they are cooking ▶ **skewer** ***verb*** [T]

ski¹ /skiː/ ***verb*** [I] (*pres. part.* **skiing**; *pt, pp* **skied**) to move over snow on SKIS: *When did you learn to ski?* ◇ *They **go skiing** every year.* ▶ **ski** ***adj.***: *a ski resort/instructor/slope/suit* ▶ **skiing** ***noun*** [U]: *Alpine/downhill/cross-country skiing*

ski² /skiː/ ***noun*** [C] one of a pair of long, flat, narrow pieces of wood or plastic that are fastened to boots and used for sliding over snow: *a pair of skis*

skid /skɪd/ ***verb*** [I] (**skidding**; **skidded**) (usually used about a vehicle) to suddenly slide forwards or sideways without any control: *I skidded on a patch of ice and hit a tree.* ▶ **skid** ***noun*** [C]: *The car went into a skid and came off the road.*

skier /'skiːə(r)/ ***noun*** [C] a person who SKIS: *Mina's a good skier.*

skilful 🔑 (*AmE* **skillful**) /'skɪlfl/ ***adj.*** **1** (used about a person) very good at doing sth: *a skilful painter/politician* ◇ *He's very skilful with his hands.* **2** done very well: *skilful guitar playing* ▶ **skilfully** /-fəli/ ***adv.***

skill 🔑 /skɪl/ ***noun*** **1** [U] the ability to do sth well, especially because of training, practice, etc.: *It takes great skill to make such beautiful jewellery.* ◇ *This is an easy game to play. No skill is required.* **2** [C] an ability that you need in order to do a job, an activity, etc. well: *The course will help you to develop your reading and listening skills.* ◇ *management skills* ◇ *Typing is a skill I have never mastered.*

skilled 🔑 /skɪld/ ***adj.*** **1** (used about a person) having skill; skilful: *a skilled worker* **2** (used about work, a job, etc.) needing skill or skills; done by people who have been trained: *a highly skilled job* ◇ *Skilled work is difficult to find in this area.* OPP **unskilled**

skillet /ˈskɪlɪt/ (*AmE*) = FRYING PAN

skim /skɪm/ ***verb*** (**skimming**; **skimmed**) **1** [T] ~ **sth (off/from sth)** to remove sth from the surface of a liquid: *to skim the cream off the milk* **2** [I,T] to move quickly over or past sth, almost touching it or touching it slightly: *The plane flew very low, skimming the tops of the buildings.* **3** [I,T] ~ **(through/over) sth** to read sth quickly in order to get the main idea, without paying attention to the details and without reading every word: *I usually just skim through the newspaper in the morning.*

ˌskimmed ˈmilk ***noun*** [U] milk from which the cream has been removed

skimp /skɪmp/ ***verb*** [I] ~ **(on sth)** to use or provide less of sth than is necessary

skimpy /ˈskɪmpi/ ***adj.*** using or having less than is necessary; too small or few

skin¹ 🔑 /skɪn/ ***noun*** [C,U] **1** (ANATOMY, BIOLOGY) the natural outer covering of a human or animal body: *to have (a) fair/dark/sensitive skin* ◇ *skin cancer* **2 -skinned** (used to form compound adjectives) having the type of skin mentioned: *My sister's very dark-skinned.* **3** (often in compounds) the skin of a dead animal, with or without its fur, used for making things: *a sheepskin jacket* ◇ *a bag made of crocodile skin* **4** the natural outer covering of some fruits or vegetables; the outer covering of a SAUSAGE: *(a) banana/tomato skin* **5** the thin solid surface that can form on a liquid: *A skin had formed on top of the milk.*

IDM **by the skin of your teeth** (*informal*) (used to show that sb almost failed to do sth) only just: *I ran into the airport and caught the plane by the skin of my teeth.*

have a thick skin → THICK¹

skin-deep (used about a feeling or an attitude) not as important or as strongly felt as it appears to be; SUPERFICIAL: *I knew his concern about me was only skin-deep.*

skin² /skɪn/ ***verb*** [T] (**skinning**; **skinned**) to remove the skin from sth

IDM **keep your eyes peeled/skinned (for sb/sth)** → EYE¹

skinhead /ˈskɪnhed/ ***noun*** [C] a young person with shaved or extremely short hair

skinny /ˈskɪni/ ***adj.*** (used about a person) too thin

skint /skɪnt/ ***adj.*** (*BrE, informal*) (FINANCE) having no money

ˌskinˈtight ***adj.*** (used about a piece of clothing) fitting very tightly and showing the shape of the body

skip¹ /skɪp/ ***verb*** (**skipping**; **skipped**) **1** [I] to move along quickly and lightly in a way that is similar to dancing, with little jumps and steps, from one foot to the other: *A little girl came skipping along the road.* ◇ *Lambs were skipping about in the field.* **2** [I] to jump over a rope that you or two other people hold at each end, turning it round and round over the head and under the feet: *Some girls were skipping in the playground.* **3** [T] to not do sth that you usually do or should do: *I got up rather late, so I skipped breakfast.* **4** [T] to miss the next thing that you would normally read, do, etc.: *I accidentally skipped one of the questions in the test.*

skip² /skɪp/ ***noun*** [C] **1** a small jumping movement **2** a large, open metal container for rubbish, often used during building work

structure of the skin

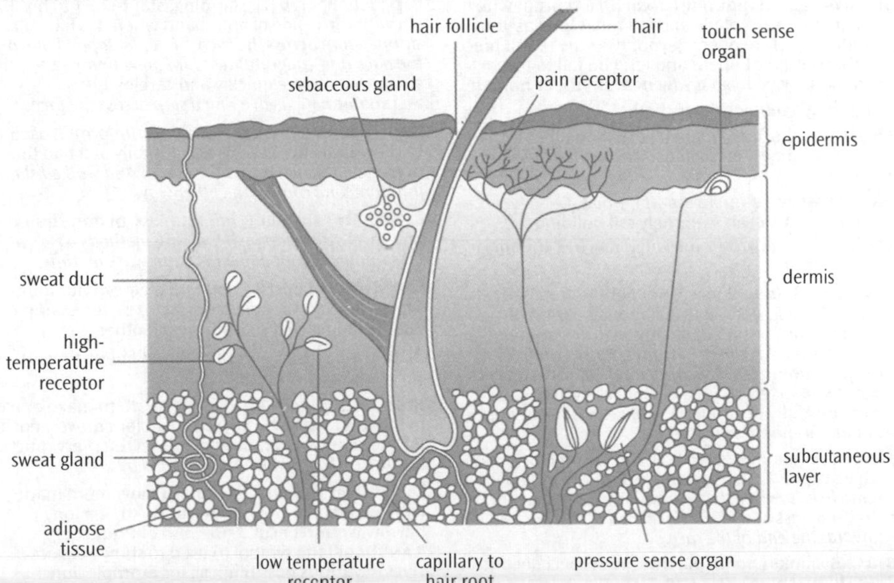

skipper /ˈskɪpə(r)/ *noun* [C] (*informal*) the captain of a boat or ship, or of a sports team

ˈ**skipping rope** *noun* [C] a rope, often with handles at each end, that you turn over your head and then jump over, for fun or for exercise

skirmish /ˈskɜːmɪʃ/ *noun* [C] a short fight between groups of people

skirt¹ ⊶ /skɜːt/ *noun* [C] **1** a piece of clothing that is worn by women and girls and that hangs down from the waist ➲ look at **culottes** **2** an outer covering or protective part for the base of a vehicle or machine: *the rubber skirt around the bottom of a hovercraft*

skirt² /skɜːt/ *verb* [I,T] to go around the edge of sth
PHR V **skirt round sth** to avoid talking about sth in a direct way: *The manager skirted round the subject of our pay increase.*

skirting board /ˈskɜːtɪŋ bɔːd/ (*also* **skirting**, *AmE* **baseboard**) *noun* [C,U] a narrow piece of wood that is fixed along the bottom of the walls in a house

skittles /ˈskɪtlz/ *noun* [U] a game in which players try to knock down as many bottle-shaped objects (**skittles**) as possible by throwing or rolling a ball at them

skive /skaɪv/ *verb* [I] (*BrE, informal*) ~ **(off)** to not work when you should

skulk /skʌlk/ *verb* [I] to stay somewhere quietly and secretly, hoping that nobody will notice you, especially because you are planning to do sth bad

skull /skʌl/ *noun* [C] (ANATOMY) the bone structure of a human or animal head: *She suffered a fractured skull in the fall.* ➲ picture on **page 80**

sky ⊶ /skaɪ/ *noun* [C, usually sing., U] (*pl.* **skies**) the space that you can see when you look up from the earth, and where you can see the sun, moon and stars: *a cloudless/clear blue sky* ◇ *I saw a bit of blue sky between the clouds.* ◇ *I saw a plane high up* ***in the sky***.

skydiving /ˈskaɪdaɪvɪŋ/ *noun* [U] a sport in which you jump from a plane and fall for as long as you safely can before opening your PARACHUTE (=a piece of thin cloth that opens and lets you fall to the ground slowly): *to go skydiving* ▸ **skydiver** *noun* [C]

ˌ**sky-ˈhigh** *adj.*, *adv.* very high

skyline /ˈskaɪlaɪn/ *noun* [C] the shape that is made by tall buildings, etc. against the sky: *the Manhattan skyline*

skyscraper /ˈskaɪskreɪpə(r)/ *noun* [C] (ARCHITECTURE) an extremely tall building

slab /slæb/ *noun* [C] a thick, flat piece of sth: *huge concrete slabs*

slack /slæk/ *adj.* **1** loose; not tightly stretched: *Leave the rope slack.* **2** (used about a period of business) not busy; not having many customers: *Trade is very slack here in winter.* **3** not carefully or properly done: *Slack security made terrorist attacks possible.* **4** (used about a person) not doing your work carefully or properly: *You've been rather slack about your homework lately.*

slacken /ˈslækən/ *verb* [I,T] **1** to become or make sth less tight: *The rope slackened and he pulled his hand free.* **2** ~ **(sth)** **(off)** to become or make sth slower or less active: *He slackened off his pace towards the end of the race.*

slacks /slæks/ *noun* [pl.] trousers (especially not very formal ones): *a pair of slacks*

slag¹ /slæg/ *verb*
PHR V **slag sb off** (*informal*) to say cruel or critical things about sb

slag² /slæg/ *noun* [U] the waste material that is left after metal has been removed from rock

ˈ**slag heap** *noun* [C] a hill made of SLAG

slain past participle of **slay**

slalom /ˈslɑːləm/ *noun* [C] (in SKIING, CANOEING, etc.) a race along a course on which COMPETITORS have to move from side to side between poles

slam /slæm/ *verb* (**slamming**; **slammed**) **1** [I,T] to shut or make sth shut very loudly and with great force: *I heard the front door slam.* ◇ *She slammed her book shut and rushed out of the room.* **2** [T] to put sth somewhere very quickly and with great force: *He slammed the book down on the table and stormed out.* ➲ look at **grand slam**

slander /ˈslɑːndə(r)/ *noun* [C,U] (LAW) a spoken statement about sb that is not true and that is intended to damage the good opinion that other people have of them; the legal offence of making this kind of statement ▸ **slander** *verb* [T]
▸ **slanderous** /-dərəs/ *adj.*

slang /slæŋ/ *noun* [U] (LANGUAGE) very informal words and expressions that are more common in spoken language. **Slang** is sometimes used only by a particular group of people (for example students, young people, criminals) and often stays in fashion for a short time. Some **slang** is not polite: *'Fag' is slang for 'cigarette' in British English.*

slant¹ /slɑːnt/ *verb* **1** [I] to be at an angle, not vertical or horizontal: *My handwriting slants backwards.* **2** [T] (usually passive) to describe information, events, etc. in a way that supports a particular group or opinion ▸ **slanting** *adj.*: *She has beautiful slanting eyes.*

slant² /slɑːnt/ *noun* **1** [sing.] a position at an angle, not horizontal or vertical: *The sunlight fell on the table* ***at a slant***. **2** [C] a way of thinking, writing, etc. about sth, that sees things from a particular point of view

slap¹ /slæp/ *verb* [T] (**slapping**; **slapped**) **1** to hit sb/sth with the inside of your hand when it is flat: *She slapped him* ***across the face***. ◇ *People slapped him on the back and congratulated him on winning.* **2** to put sth onto a surface quickly and carelessly
▸ **slap** *noun* [C]: *I gave him a slap across the face.*

slap² /slæp/ (*also* ˌ**slap ˈbang**) *adv.* (*informal*) used to show that sth happens accidentally at a bad time or place: *I hurried round the corner and walked slap into someone coming the other way.*

slapdash /ˈslæpdæʃ/ *adj.* careless, or done quickly and carelessly: *slapdash building methods* ◇ *He's a bit slapdash about doing his homework on time.*

slapstick /ˈslæpstɪk/ *noun* [U] a type of humour that is based on simple physical jokes, for example people falling over or hitting each other

ˈ**slap-up** *adj.* (*BrE, informal*) (used about a meal) very large and very good

slash¹ /slæʃ/ *verb* **1** [I,T] ~ **(at)** **sb/sth** to make or try to make a long cut in sth with a violent movement **2** [T] to reduce an amount of money, etc. very much: *The price of coffee has been slashed by 20%.*

slash² /slæʃ/ *noun* [C] **1** a sharp movement made with a knife, etc. in order to cut sb/sth **2** a long narrow wound or cut **3** (*BrE also* **oblique**) (LANGUAGE) the symbol (/) used to show ALTERNATIVES (=various possibilities), for example 'lunch and/or dinner', and also to write FRACTIONS, as in '⅙'
➲ look at **backslash**, **forward slash**

ˌ**slash-and-ˈburn** *adj.* **1** (AGRICULTURE) relating to a method of farming in which existing plants, crops, etc. are cut down and burned before new seeds are planted: *slash-and-burn agriculture* **2** aggressive and causing a lot of harm or damage: *a slash-and-burn takeover*

slat /slæt/ *noun* [C] one of a series of long, narrow pieces of wood, metal or plastic, used in furniture, fences, etc.

slate /sleɪt/ *noun* **1** [U] (GEOLOGY) a type of dark grey rock that can easily be split into thin flat pieces **2** [C] one of the thin flat pieces of **slate** that are used for covering roofs

slaughter /ˈslɔːtə(r)/ *verb* [T] **1** to kill an animal, usually for food **2** to kill a large number of people at one time, especially in a cruel way: *Men, women and children were slaughtered and whole villages destroyed.* ➲ note at **kill** ▶ **slaughter** *noun* [U]

slaughterhouse /ˈslɔːtəhaʊs/ (*BrE* **abattoir**) *noun* [C] a place where animals are killed for food

slave¹ /sleɪv/ *noun* [C] (SOCIAL STUDIES) (in past times) a person who was owned by another person and had to work for them ▶ **slavery** *noun* [U]: *the abolition of slavery in America*

slave² /sleɪv/ *verb* [I] ~ **(away)** to work very hard

slay /sleɪ/ *verb* [T] (*pt* **slew** /sluː/; *pp* **slain** /sleɪn/) (*old-fashioned*) to kill violently; to murder

sleazy /ˈsliːzi/ *adj.* (used about a place or a person) unpleasant and probably connected with immoral activities: *a sleazy nightclub*

sledge /sledʒ/ (*AmE also* **sled** /sled/) *noun* [C] a vehicle without wheels that is used for travelling on snow. Large **sledges** are often pulled by dogs, and smaller ones are used for going down hills, for fun or as a sport ➲ look at **bobsleigh, toboggan** ▶ **sledge** *verb* [I]

sledgehammer /ˈsledʒhæmə(r)/ *noun* [C] a large heavy hammer with a long handle

sleek /sliːk/ *adj.* **1** (used about hair or fur) smooth and shiny because it is healthy **2** (used about a vehicle) having an elegant, smooth shape: *a sleek new sports car*

sleep¹ 🔑 /sliːp/ *noun* **1** [U] the natural condition of rest when your eyes are closed and your mind and body are not active or conscious: *Most people need at least seven hours' sleep every night.* ◇ *I didn't get much sleep last night.* ◇ *Do you ever talk in your sleep?* ◇ *I couldn't* **get to sleep** *last night.* **2** [sing.] a period of sleep: *You'll feel better after a good night's sleep.* ◇ *I sometimes have a short sleep in the afternoon.*

IDM **go to sleep 1** to start sleeping: *He got into bed and soon went to sleep.* **2** (used about an arm, a leg, etc.) to lose the sense of feeling in it

put (an animal) to sleep to kill an animal that is ill or injured because you want to stop it suffering

sleep² 🔑 /sliːp/ *verb* (*pt, pp* **slept** /slept/) **1** [I] to rest with your eyes closed and your mind and body not active: *Did you sleep well?* ◇ *I only slept for a couple of hours last night.* ◇ *I slept solidly from 10 last night till 11 this morning.* **2** [T] (used about a place) to have enough beds for a particular number of people

IDM **sleep/live rough** → ROUGH³

PHRV **sleep in** to sleep until later than usual in the morning because you do not have to get up ➲ look at **oversleep**

sleep together; sleep with sb to have sex with sb (usually when you are not married to or living with that person)

sleeper /ˈsliːpə(r)/ *noun* [C] **1** (with an adjective) a person who sleeps in a particular way. If you are a light **sleeper** you wake up easily: *a light/heavy sleeper* **2** a bed on a train; a train with beds

ˈ**sleeping bag** *noun* [C] a large soft bag that you use for sleeping in when you go camping, etc.

ˈ**sleeping car** (*also* **sleeper**) *noun* [C] a railway CARRIAGE (= part of a train) with beds for people to sleep in

ˈ**sleeping pill** *noun* [C] (HEALTH) a medicine in solid form that you swallow to help you sleep

ˌ**sleeping poˈliceman** *noun* [C] (*BrE, informal*) = SPEED BUMP

ˈ**sleeping sickness** *noun* [U] (HEALTH) a tropical disease carried by a TSETSE FLY that makes you want to go to sleep and usually causes death

sleepless /ˈsliːpləs/ *adj.* (used about a period, usually the night) without sleep ▶ **sleeplessness** *noun* [U] ➲ look at **insomnia**

sleepwalk /ˈsliːpwɔːk/ *verb* [I] to walk around while you are asleep

sleepy /ˈsliːpi/ *adj.* **1** tired and ready to go to sleep: *These pills might make you feel a bit sleepy.* **2** (used about a place) very quiet and not having much activity ▶ **sleepily** *adv.*

sleet /sliːt/ *noun* [U] a mixture of rain and snow ➲ note at **weather**

sleeve 🔑 /sliːv/ *noun* [C] **1** one of the two parts of a piece of clothing that cover the arms or part of the arms: *a blouse with long sleeves* **2 -sleeved** (used to form compound adjectives) with sleeves of a particular kind: *a short-sleeved shirt*

sleeveless /ˈsliːvləs/ *adj.* without sleeves: *a sleeveless sweater*

sleigh /sleɪ/ *noun* [C] a vehicle without wheels that is used for travelling on snow and that is usually pulled by horses ➲ look at **bobsleigh**

sleight of hand /ˌslaɪt əv ˈhænd/ *noun* [U] skilful movements of your hand that other people cannot see: *The trick is done simply by sleight of hand.*

slender /ˈslendə(r)/ *adj.* **1** (used about a person or part of sb's body) thin in an attractive way: *long slender fingers* **2** smaller in amount or size than you would like: *My chances of winning are very slender.*

slept past tense, past participle of **sleep²**

slew past tense of **slay**

slice¹ 🔑 /slaɪs/ *noun* [C] **1** a flat piece of food that is cut from a larger piece: *a thick/thin slice of bread* ◇ *Cut the meat into thin slices.* **2** a part of sth: *The directors have taken a large slice of the profits.*

slice² 🔑 /slaɪs/ *verb* **1** [T] to cut into thin flat pieces: *Peel and slice the apples.* ◇ *a loaf of sliced bread* **2** [I,T] to cut sth easily with sth sharp: *He sliced through the rope with a knife.* ◇ *The glass sliced into her hand.* **3** [T] (in ball sports) to hit the ball on the bottom or side so that it does not travel in a straight line

slick¹ /slɪk/ *adj.* **1** done smoothly and well, and seeming to be done without any effort **2** clever at persuading people but perhaps not completely honest

slick² /slɪk/ = OIL SLICK

slide¹ 🔑 /slaɪd/ *verb* (*pt, pp* **slid** /slɪd/) **1** [I,T] to move or make sth move smoothly along a surface: *She fell over and slid along the ice.* ◇ *The doors slide open automatically.* **2** [I,T] to move or make sth move quietly without being noticed: *I slid out of the room when nobody was looking.* ◊ *She slid her hand into her pocket and took out a gun.* **3** [I] (used about prices, values, etc.) to go down slowly and continuously **4** [I] to move gradually towards a worse situation: *The company slid into debt and eventually closed.*

slide² /slaɪd/ ***noun*** [C] **1** (SCIENCE) a small piece of glass that you put sth on when you want to examine it under a MICROSCOPE (=a piece of equipment that makes things appear much bigger) ➲ picture at **laboratory** **2** a large toy consisting of a LADDER and a long piece of metal, plastic, etc. Children climb up the ladder then slide down the other part. **3** a continuous slow fall, for example of prices, values, levels, etc. **4** a small piece of PHOTOGRAPHIC film in a plastic or cardboard frame ➲ look at **transparency**

'slide rule ***noun*** [C] (MATHEMATICS) a long narrow instrument like a ruler, with a middle part that slides backwards and forwards, used for calculating numbers

ˌsliding 'scale ***noun*** [C] a system in which the rate at which sth is paid varies according to particular conditions: *Fees are calculated **on a sliding scale** according to income* (=richer people pay more).

slight 🔑 /slaɪt/ ***adj.*** **1** very small; not important or serious: *I've got a slight problem, but it's nothing to get worried about.* ◊ *a slight change/difference/increase/improvement* ◊ *I haven't the slightest idea* (=no idea at all) *what you're talking about.* **2** (used about a person's body) thin and light: *His slight frame is perfect for a long-distance runner.*

IDM **not in the slightest** not at all: *'Are you angry with me?' 'Not in the slightest.'*

slightly 🔑 /'slaɪtli/ ***adv.*** **1** a little: *I'm slightly older than her.* **2** a **slightly-built** person is small and thin

slim¹ /slɪm/ ***adj.*** (**slimmer**; **slimmest**) **1** thin in an attractive way: *a tall, slim woman* **2** not as big as you would like: *Her chances of success are very slim.*

slim² /slɪm/ ***verb*** [I] (**slimming**; **slimmed**) to become or try to become thinner and lighter by eating less food, taking exercise, etc. ➲ look at **diet**

slime /slaɪm/ ***noun*** [U] a thick unpleasant liquid: *The pond was covered with slime and had a horrible smell.*

slimy /'slaɪmi/ ***adj.*** **1** covered with SLIME **2** (used about a person) pretending to be friendly, in a way that you do not trust or like

sling¹ /slɪŋ/ ***noun*** [C] **1** (HEALTH) a piece of cloth that you put under your arm and tie around your neck to support a broken arm, wrist, etc.: *She had her arm **in a sling**.* **2** a device consisting of a band, ropes, etc. for holding and lifting heavy objects: *The engine was lifted in a sling of steel rope.* **3** a device like a bag for carrying a baby on your back or in front of you **4** (in the past) a simple weapon made from a band of leather, etc., used for throwing stones SYN **catapult**

▸ **slinger** ***noun*** [C]

sling² /slɪŋ/ ***verb*** [T] (*pt, pp* **slung**) **1** to put or throw sth somewhere in a rough or careless way **2** to put sth into a position where it hangs loosely

slingback /'slɪŋbæk/ ***noun*** [C] a woman's shoe that is open at the back with a STRAP around the heel

slingshot /'slɪŋʃɒt/ (*AmE*) =CATAPULT¹

slink /slɪŋk/ ***verb*** [I] (*pt, pp* **slunk**) to move somewhere slowly and quietly because you do not want anyone to see you, often when you feel guilty or embarrassed

slip¹ 🔑 /slɪp/ ***verb*** (**slipping**; **slipped**) **1** [I] ~ (over); ~ (on sth) to slide accidentally and fall or nearly fall: *She slipped over on the wet floor.* ◊ *His foot slipped on the top step and he fell down the stairs.* **2** [I] to slide accidentally out of the correct position or out of your hand: *This hat's too big. It keeps slipping down over my eyes.* ◊ *The glass slipped out of my hand and smashed on the floor.* **3** [I] to move or go somewhere quietly, quickly, and often without being noticed: *While everyone was dancing we slipped away and went home.* **4** [T] ~ sth (to sb); ~ (sb) sth to put sth somewhere or give sth to sb quietly and often without being noticed: *She picked up the money and slipped it into her pocket.* **5** [I,T] ~ into/out of sth; ~ sth on/off to put on or take off a piece of clothing quickly and easily: *I slipped off my shoes.* **6** [I] to fall a little in value, level, etc.

IDM **let sth slip** → LET

slip your mind to be FORGOTTEN: *I'm sorry, the meeting completely slipped my mind.*

PHR V **slip out** to accidentally say sth or tell sb sth: *I didn't intend to tell them. It just slipped out.*

slip up (*informal*) to make a mistake

slip² /slɪp/ ***noun*** [C] **1** a small mistake, usually made by being careless or not paying attention: *to make a slip* **2** a small piece of paper: *I made a note of her name on **a slip of paper**.* ◊ (*BrE*) *There seems to be a mistake on my **payslip*** (=the piece of paper from your employer each month showing how much money you have been paid and how much tax, etc. has been taken off). **3** an act of sliding accidentally and falling or nearly falling **4** a thin piece of clothing that is worn by a woman under a dress or skirt

IDM **give sb the slip** (*informal*) to escape from sb who is following or trying to catch you

a slip of the tongue something that you say that you did not mean to say

ˌslipped 'disc ***noun*** [C] (HEALTH) a painful injury caused when one of the DISCS in your SPINE (=the bones of your back) moves out of its correct position

slipper /'slɪpə(r)/ ***noun*** [C] a light soft shoe that is worn inside the house: *a pair of slippers*

slippery /'slɪpəri/ (also *informal* **slippy**) ***adj.*** (used about a surface or an object) difficult to walk on or hold because it is smooth, wet, etc.: *a slippery floor*

'slip road (*AmE* **ramp**) ***noun*** [C] a road that leads onto or off a motorway

slipway /'slɪpweɪ/ ***noun*** [C] a track leading down to water, on which ships are built or pulled up out of the water for repairs, or from which they are LAUNCHED (=put into the water)

slit¹ /slɪt/ ***noun*** [C] a long narrow cut or opening: *a long skirt with a slit up the back*

slit² /slɪt/ ***verb*** [T] (**slitting**; *pt, pp* **slit**) to make a long narrow cut in sth: *She slit the envelope open with a knife.*

slither /'slɪðə(r)/ ***verb*** [I] to move by sliding from side to side along the ground like a snake: *I saw a snake slithering down a rock.*

slob /slɒb/ ***noun*** [C] (*informal*) (used as an insult) a very lazy or untidy person

slog¹ /slɒg/ ***verb*** [I] (**slogging**; **slogged**) **1** (*informal*) ~ (away) (at sth); ~ (through sth) to work hard for a long period at sth difficult or boring: *I've been slogging away at this homework for hours.* **2** ~ **down, up, along, etc.** to walk or move in a certain direction with a lot of effort

slog² /slɒg/ ***noun*** [sing.] a period of long, hard, boring work or a long, tiring journey

slogan /ˈsləʊɡən/ *noun* [C] (POLITICS) a short phrase that is easy to remember and that is used in politics or advertising: *Anti-government slogans had been painted all over the walls.* ◇ *an advertising slogan*

sloop /sluːp/ *noun* [C] a small sailing ship with one MAST (=a post to support the sails)

slop /slɒp/ *verb* [I,T] (**slopping**; **slopped**) (used about a liquid) to pour over the edge of its container; to make a liquid do this: *He filled his glass too full and beer slopped onto the table.*

slope /sləʊp/ *noun* **1** [C] a surface or piece of land that goes up or down: *The village is built **on a slope**.* ◇ *a steep/gentle slope* ◇ *The best **ski slopes** are in the Alps.* **2** [sing.] the amount that a surface is not level; the fact of not being level ▶ **slope** *verb* [I]: *The road slopes down to the river.* ◇ *a sloping roof*

sloppy /ˈslɒpi/ *adj.* **1** that shows lack of care, thought or effort; untidy: *a sloppy worker/writer/dresser* ◇ *a sloppy piece of work* **2** (used about clothes) not tight and without much shape **3** (*BrE*, *informal*) showing emotions in a silly embarrassing way SYN **sentimental**: *I can't stand sloppy love songs.*

slosh /slɒʃ/ *verb* (*informal*) **1** [I] (used about a liquid) to move around noisily inside a container **2** [T] to pour or drop liquid somewhere in a careless way

sloshed /slɒʃt/ *adj.* (*slang*) drunk

slot[1] /slɒt/ *noun* [C] **1** a straight narrow opening in a machine, etc.: *Put your money into the slot and take the ticket.* **2** a place in a list, system, organization, etc.: *The single has occupied the Number One slot for the past two weeks.*

slot[2] /slɒt/ *verb* [I,T] (**slotting**; **slotted**) to put sth into a particular space that is designed for it; to fit into such a space: *He slotted a tape into the VCR.* ◇ *The video slotted in easily.*

IDM **fall/slot into place** → PLACE[1]

ˈslot machine *noun* [C] a machine with an opening for coins that sells drinks, cigarettes, etc. or on which you can play games

slouch /slaʊtʃ/ *verb* [I] to sit, stand or walk in a lazy way, with your head and shoulders hanging down

slovenly /ˈslʌvnli/ *adj.* (*old-fashioned*) lazy, careless and untidy

slow[1] /sləʊ/ *adj.*, *adv.* **1** moving, doing sth or happening without much speed; not fast: *The traffic is always very slow in the city centre.* ◇ *Haven't you finished your homework yet? You're being very slow!* ◇ *Progress was slower than expected.* ◇ *a slow driver/walker/reader* OPP **fast** **2** ~ **to do sth**; ~ **(in/about) doing sth** not doing sth immediately: *She was rather slow to realize what was going on.* ◇ *They've been rather slow in replying to my letter!* **3** not quick to learn or understand: *He's the slowest student in the class.* **4** not very busy; with little action: *Business is very slow at the moment.* **5** (not before a noun) (used about watches and clocks) showing a time that is earlier than the real time: *That clock is five minutes slow* (=it says it is 8.55 when the correct time is 9.00). OPP **fast** ▶ **slowness** *noun* [U]

IDM **quick/slow on the uptake** → UPTAKE

slow[2] /sləʊ/ *verb* [I,T] to start to move, do sth or happen at a slower speed; to cause sth to do this: *He slowed his pace a little.*

PHRV **slow (sb/sth) down/up** to start to move, do sth or happen at a slower speed; to cause sb/sth to do this: *Can't you slow down a bit? You're driving much too fast.* ◇ *These problems have slowed up the whole process.*

slowdown /ˈsləʊdaʊn/ *noun* [C] (BUSINESS) a reduction in speed or activity: *a slowdown in economic growth*

slowly /ˈsləʊli/ *adv.* at a slow speed; not quickly: *He walked slowly along the street.*

ˌslow ˈmotion *noun* [U] (ARTS AND MEDIA) (in a film or on television) a method of making action appear much slower than in real life: *They showed the winning goal again, this time **in slow motion**.*

ˈslow-worm *noun* [C] a small brownish animal with no legs, like a snake, that is found in Europe and Asia

sludge /slʌdʒ/ *noun* [U] a thick, soft unpleasant substance; mud

slug /slʌɡ/ *noun* [C] a small black or brown animal with a soft body and no legs, that moves slowly along the ground and eats garden plants ➲ picture on **page 29**

sluggish /ˈslʌɡɪʃ/ *adj.* moving or working more slowly than normal in a way that seems lazy

sluice /sluːs/ (*also* **ˈsluice gate**) *noun* [C] a type of gate that you can open or close to control the flow of water out of or into a CANAL, etc.

slum /slʌm/ *noun* [C] (GEOGRAPHY, SOCIAL STUDIES) an area of a city where living conditions are extremely bad, and where the buildings are dirty and have not been repaired for a long time

slumber /ˈslʌmbə(r)/ *verb* [I] (*old-fashioned*) to be deeply asleep ▶ **slumber** *noun* [C]

slump[1] /slʌmp/ *verb* [I] **1** (ECONOMICS) (used about economic activity, prices, etc.) to fall suddenly and by a large amount: *Shares in the bank **slumped** 33p **to** 181p yesterday.* ◇ *The newspaper's circulation has **slumped by** 30%.* ➲ note at **fall**[1] **2** to fall or sit down suddenly when your body feels heavy and weak, usually because you are tired or ill

slump[2] /slʌmp/ *noun* [C] **1 a** ~ **(in sth)** a sudden large fall in sales, prices, the value of sth, etc.: *a slump in house prices* **2** (ECONOMICS) a period when a country's economy is doing very badly and a lot of people do not have jobs

slung past tense, past participle of **sling**[2]

slunk past tense, past participle of **slink**

slur[1] /slɜː(r)/ *verb* [T] (**slurring**; **slurred**) to pronounce words in a way that is not clear, often because you are drunk

slur[2] /slɜː(r)/ *noun* [C] **a** ~ **(on sb/sth)** an unfair comment or an insult that could damage people's opinion of sb/sth

slurp /slɜːp/ *verb* [I,T] (*informal*) to drink noisily

slurry /ˈslʌri/ *noun* [U] (AGRICULTURE) a thick liquid consisting of water mixed with animal waste that farmers use on their fields to make plants grow better

slush /slʌʃ/ *noun* [U] **1** partly melted snow that is usually dirty **2** (*informal*) films, books, feelings, etc. that are considered to be silly because they are too romantic and emotional ▶ **slushy** *adj.*

ˈslush fund *noun* [C] (POLITICS) an amount of money that is kept to pay people illegally to do things, especially in politics

sly /slaɪ/ *adj.* **1** (used about a person) acting or done in a secret or dishonest way, often intending to trick people SYN **cunning** **2** (used about an action) suggesting that you know sth secret: *a sly smile/look* ▶ **slyly** *adv.*

smack /smæk/ ***verb*** [T] to hit sb with the inside of your hand when it is flat, especially as a punishment: *I never smack my children.* ▶ **smack** ***noun*** [C]: *You're going to get a smack if you don't do as I say!*
PHR V **smack of sth** to make you think that sb/sth has an unpleasant attitude or quality

small 🔑 /smɔːl/ ***adj.*** **1** not large in size, number, amount, etc.: *a small car/flat/town* ◇ *a small group of people* ◇ *a small amount of money* ◇ *That dress is too small for you.* **2** young: *He has a wife and three small children.* ◇ *When I was small we lived in a big old house.* **3** not important or serious; slight: *Don't worry. It's only a small problem.* ▶ **small** /smɔːl/ ***adv.***: *She's painted the picture far too small.*
IDM **in a big/small way** → WAY[1]

ˌsmall ˈads ***noun*** [pl.] (*BrE, informal*) = CLASSIFIED ADVERTISEMENTS

ˈsmall arms ***noun*** [C, pl.] small light weapons that you can carry in your hands

ˌsmall ˈchange ***noun*** [U] (FINANCE) coins that have a low value

smallholder /ˈsmɔːlhəʊldə(r)/ ***noun*** [C] (AGRICULTURE) a person who owns or rents a small piece of land for farming

smallholding /ˈsmɔːlhəʊldɪŋ/ ***noun*** [C] (AGRICULTURE) a small piece of land that is used for farming

the ˈsmall hours ***noun*** [pl.] the early morning hours soon after midnight

smallpox /ˈsmɔːlpɒks/ ***noun*** [U] (HEALTH) a serious infectious disease that causes a high temperature and leaves marks on the skin. In past times many people died from **smallpox**.

the ˈsmall print (*AmE* **the ˈfine print**) ***noun*** [U] (LAW) the important details of a legal document, contract, etc. that are usually printed in small type and are therefore easy to miss: *Make sure you read the small print before you sign anything.*

ˌsmall-ˈscale ***adj.*** (used about an organization or activity) not large; limited in what it does

ˈsmall talk ***noun*** [U] polite conversation, for example at a party, about unimportant things: *We had to **make small talk** for half an hour.*

smart[1] 🔑 /smɑːt/ ***adj.*** **1** (*especially BrE*) (used about a person) having a clean and tidy appearance: *You look smart. Are you going somewhere special?* **2** (*especially BrE*) (used about a piece of clothing, etc.) good enough to wear on a formal occasion: *a smart suit* **3** clever; intelligent: *He's not smart enough to be a politician.* **4** (*especially BrE*) fashionable and usually expensive: *a smart restaurant/hotel* **5** (used about a movement or action) quick and usually done with force **6** (COMPUTING) (used about a device, especially a weapon) controlled by a computer, so that it appears to act in an intelligent way: *smart bombs* ▶ **smartly** ***adv.***: *She's always smartly dressed.*

smart[2] /smɑːt/ ***verb*** [I] **1** ~ **(from sth)** to feel a stinging pain in your body **2** ~ **(from/over sth)** to feel upset or offended because of a criticism, failure, etc.

ˈsmart card ***noun*** [C] (COMPUTING) a plastic card, for example a CREDIT CARD, on which information can be stored in electronic form

smarten /ˈsmɑːtn/ ***verb*** (*especially BrE*)
PHR V **smarten (yourself/sb/sth) up** to make yourself/sb/sth look tidy and more attractive

smash[1] 🔑 /smæʃ/ ***verb*** **1** [I,T] to break sth, or to be broken violently and noisily into many pieces: *The glass smashed into a thousand pieces.* ◇ *The police had to smash the door open.* **2** [I,T] ~ **(sth) against, into, through, etc.** to move with great force in a particular direction; to hit sth very hard: *The car smashed into a tree.* ◇ *He smashed his fist through the window.* **3** [T] ~ **sth (up)** to crash a vehicle, usually causing a lot of damage **4** [T] (SPORT) (in TENNIS) to hit a ball that is high in the air downwards very hard over the net

smash[2] 🔑 /smæʃ/ ***noun*** **1** [sing.] the action or the noise of sth breaking violently **2** [C] (SPORT) (in TENNIS, etc.) a way of hitting a ball that is high in the air downwards and very hard over the net **3** (*also* **smash ˈhit**) [C] (*informal*) (ARTS AND MEDIA) a song, play, film, etc. that is very successful

smashing /ˈsmæʃɪŋ/ ***adj.*** (*BrE, informal*) extremely good; wonderful

smear[1] /smɪə(r)/ ***verb*** [T] ~ **sth on/over sth/sb; ~ sth/sb with sth** to spread a sticky substance across sth/sb: *Her face was smeared with blood.*

smear[2] /smɪə(r)/ ***noun*** [C] **1** a dirty mark made by spreading a substance across sth **2** something that is not true that is said or written about an important person and that is intended to damage people's opinion about them, especially in politics: *He was the victim of a **smear campaign**.*

smell[1] 🔑 /smel/ ***verb*** (*pt, pp* **smelt** /smelt/ or **smelled** /smeld/) **1** [I] ~ **(of sth)** to have a particular smell: *Dinner smells good!* ◇ *This perfume smells of roses.* ◇ *His breath smelt of whisky.* **2** [I] to have a bad smell: *Your feet smell.* **3** [T] to notice or recognize sb/sth by using your nose: *He could smell something burning.* ◇ *Can you smell gas?* ◇ *I could still smell her perfume in the room.* **4** [T] to put your nose near sth and breathe in so that you can discover or identify its smell: *I smelt the milk to see if it had gone off.* **5** [I] to be able to smell: *I can't smell properly because I've got a cold.*

smell[2] 🔑 /smel/ ***noun*** **1** [C] the impression that you get of sth by using your nose; the thing that you smell: *What's that smell?* ◇ *a sweet/musty/fresh/sickly smell* ◇ *a strong/faint smell of garlic* **2** [sing.] an unpleasant smell: *Ugh! What's that smell?* **3** [U] the ability to sense things with the nose: *Dogs have a very good **sense of smell**.* **4** [C] the action of putting your nose near sth to smell it: *Have a smell of this milk; is it all right?*

smelly /ˈsmeli/ ***adj.*** (*informal*) having a bad smell: *smelly feet*

smelt[1] /smelt/ ***verb*** [T] to heat and melt rock containing ORE in order to get the metal out

smelt[2] past tense, past participle of **smell**

smile[1] 🔑 /smaɪl/ ***noun*** [C] an expression on your face in which the corners of your mouth turn up, showing happiness, pleasure, etc.: *to have a smile on your face* ◇ *'It's nice to see you,' he said with a smile.* ➲ look at **beam**, **grin**, **smirk**

smile[2] 🔑 /smaɪl/ ***verb*** **1** [I] ~ **(at sb/sth)** to make a smile appear on your face: *to smile sweetly/faintly/broadly* ◇ *She smiled at the camera.* **2** [T] to say or express sth with a smile: *I smiled a greeting to them.*

smiley /ˈsmaɪli/ ***noun*** [C] **1** a simple picture of a smiling face that is drawn as a circle with two eyes and a curved mouth **2** (COMPUTING) a simple picture or series of keyboard symbols :-) that represents a smiling face. The symbols are used, for example, in email or text messages to show that the person sending the message is pleased or joking.

smirk /smɜːk/ ***noun*** [C] an unpleasant smile which you have when you are pleased with yourself or think you are very clever ▶ **smirk *verb*** [I]

smock /smɒk/ ***noun*** [C] **1** a loose comfortable piece of clothing like a long shirt, worn especially by women **2** a long loose piece of clothing worn over other clothes to protect them from dirt, etc.: *an artist's smock* ◇ *Smocks were formerly worn by farm workers.*

smog /smɒg/ ***noun*** [U] (ENVIRONMENT, GEOGRAPHY) dirty, poisonous air that can cover a whole city ➲ note at **weather**

smoke[1] /sməʊk/ ***noun*** **1** [U] the grey, white or black gas that you can see in the air when sth is burning: *Thick smoke poured from the chimney.* ◇ *a room full of cigarette smoke* **2** [C, usually sing.] an action of smoking a cigarette, etc.

smoke[2] /sməʊk/ ***verb*** **1** [I,T] to breathe in smoke through a cigarette, etc. and let it out again; to use cigarettes, etc. in this way, as a habit: *Do you mind if I smoke?* ◇ *I used to smoke 20 cigarettes a day.* **2** [I] to send out smoke: *The oil in the pan started to smoke.* ▶ **smoker *noun*** [C]: *She's a* ***chain smoker*** (=she finishes one cigarette and then immediately lights another). OPP **non-smoker**

smoked /sməʊkt/ ***adj.*** (used of certain types of food) given a special taste by being hung for a period of time in smoke from wood fires: *smoked salmon/ham/cheese*

smoking /'sməʊkɪŋ/ ***noun*** [U] (HEALTH) the activity or habit of smoking cigarettes, etc.: ***No Smoking*** (=for example, on a notice) ◇ *Would you like* ***smoking or non-smoking****?* (=for example in a restaurant) ◇ *He's trying to* ***give up smoking****.*

smoky /'sməʊki/ ***adj.*** **1** full of smoke; producing a lot of smoke: *a smoky room/fire* **2** with the smell, taste or appearance of smoke

smolder (*AmE*) =SMOULDER

smooth[1] /smuːð/ ***adj.*** **1** having a completely flat surface with no lumps or holes or rough areas: *smooth skin* ◇ *a smooth piece of wood* OPP **rough** **2** (of a liquid mixture) without lumps: *Stir the sauce until it is smooth.* OPP **lumpy** **3** without difficulties: *The transition from the old method to the new has been very smooth.* **4** (of a journey in a car, etc.) with an even, comfortable movement: *You get a very smooth ride in this car.* OPP **bumpy** **5** too pleasant or polite to be trusted
▶ **smoothness *noun*** [U]
IDM **take the rough with the smooth** → ROUGH[2]

smooth[2] /smuːð/ ***verb*** [T] **~ sth (away, back, down, out, etc.)** to move your hands in the direction mentioned over a surface to make it smooth

smoothie /'smuːði/ ***noun*** [C] **1** (*informal*) a man who dresses well and talks very politely in a confident way, but who is often not honest or sincere **2** a drink made of fruit or fruit juice, sometimes mixed with milk or ice cream

smoothly /'smuːðli/ ***adv.*** without any difficulty: *My work has been going quite smoothly.*

smother /'smʌðə(r)/ ***verb*** [T] **1** **~ sb (with sth)** to kill sb by covering their face so that they cannot breathe: *She was smothered with a pillow.* **2** **~ sth/sb in/with sth** to cover sth/sb with too much of sth **3** to stop a feeling, etc. from being expressed **4** to stop sth burning by covering it: *to smother the flames with a blanket*

smoulder (*AmE* **smolder**) /'sməʊldə(r)/ ***verb*** [I] to burn slowly without a flame: *a cigarette smouldering in an ashtray*

SMS /ˌes em 'es/ ***abbr.*** **short message service**; a system for sending short written messages from one mobile phone to another ➲ look at **text message**

SMTP /ˌes em tiː 'piː/ ***abbr.*** (COMPUTING) **Simple Mail Transfer Protocol**; a set of rules that enables you to send emails from your computer ➲ look at **POP**

smudge /smʌdʒ/ ***verb*** **1** [T] to make sth dirty or untidy by touching it: *Leave your painting to dry or you'll smudge it.* **2** [I] to become untidy, without a clean line around it: *Her lipstick smudged when she kissed him.* ▶ **smudge *noun*** [C]

smug /smʌg/ ***adj.*** too pleased with yourself: *Don't look so smug.* ▶ **smugly *adv.***: *He smiled smugly as the results were announced.* ▶ **smugness *noun*** [U]

smuggle /'smʌgl/ ***verb*** [T] (LAW) to take things into or out of a country secretly in a way that is not allowed by the law; to take a person or a thing secretly into or out of a place: *The drugs had been smuggled through customs.* ▶ **smuggler *noun*** [C]: *a drug smuggler*

snack /snæk/ ***noun*** [C] food that you eat quickly between main meals: *I had a snack on the train.*
▶ **snack *verb*** [I] (*informal*) **~ on sth**

'snack bar *noun* [C] a type of small CAFE where you can buy a small quick meal like a sandwich

snag[1] /snæg/ ***noun*** [C] a small difficulty or disadvantage that is often unexpected or hidden: *His offer is very generous – are you sure there isn't a snag?*

snag[2] /snæg/ ***verb*** [T] (**snagging**; **snagged**) to catch a piece of clothing, etc. on sth sharp and tear it

snail /sneɪl/ ***noun*** [C] a type of animal with a soft body and no legs that is covered by a shell. **Snails** move very slowly. ➲ picture on **page 29**

'snail mail *noun* [U] (*informal*) used by people who use email to describe the system of sending letters by ordinary post

snake[1] /sneɪk/ ***noun*** [C] a type of long thin animal with no legs that slides along the ground by moving its body from side to side

snake[2] /sneɪk/ ***verb*** [I] (*written*) to move like a snake in long curves from side to side

snap[1] /snæp/ ***verb*** (**snapping**; **snapped**) **1** [I,T] to break or be broken suddenly, usually with a sharp noise: *The top has snapped off my pen.* ◇ *The branch snapped.* ◇ *I snapped my shoelace when I was tying it.* **2** [I,T] to move or be moved into a particular position, especially with a sharp noise: *She snapped the bag shut and walked out.* **3** [I,T] **~ (sth) (at sb)** to speak or say sth in a quick angry way: *Why do you always snap at me?* **4** [I] to try to bite sb/sth: *The dog snapped at the child's hand.* **5** [I,T] (*informal*) to take a quick photograph of sb/sth: *A tourist snapped the plane as it crashed.* **6** [I] to suddenly be unable to control your feelings any longer: *Suddenly something just snapped and I lost my temper with him.*
IDM **snap your fingers** to make a sharp noise by moving your middle finger quickly against your thumb, especially when you want to attract sb's attention
PHR V **snap sth up** to buy or take sth quickly, especially because it is very cheap

snap[2] /snæp/ ***noun*** **1** [C] a sudden sharp sound of sth breaking **2** (*also* **snapshot** /'snæpʃɒt/) [C] a photograph that is taken quickly and in an informal way **3** [U] (*BrE*) a card game where players call out '**Snap**' when two cards that are the same are put down by different players

snap³ /snæp/ ***adj.*** (*informal*) (only *before* a noun) done quickly and suddenly, often without any careful thought: *a snap decision/judgement*

snare /sneə(r)/ ***noun*** [C] a TRAP used to catch birds or small animals ▶ **snare** ***verb*** [T]

snarl /snɑːl/ ***verb*** [I,T] ~ **(sth) (at sb)** (used about an animal) to make an angry sound while showing the teeth: *The dog snarled at the stranger.* ▶ **snarl** ***noun*** [C, usually sing.]

snatch¹ /snætʃ/ ***verb*** **1** [I,T] to take sth with a quick rough movement: *A boy snatched her handbag and ran off.* **SYN** **grab 2** [T] to take or get sth quickly using the only time or chance that you have: *I managed to snatch some sleep on the train.*

PHR V **snatch at sth** to try to take hold of sth suddenly: *The man snatched at my wallet but I didn't let go of it.*

snatch² /snætʃ/ ***noun*** **1** [sing.] a sudden movement that sb makes when trying to take hold of sth **2** [C, usually pl.] a short part or period of something: *I heard snatches of conversation from the next room.*

sneak¹ /sniːk/ ***verb*** (*pt, pp* **sneaked** (*informal, especially AmE* **snuck**) **1** [I] ~ **into, out of, past, etc. sth**; ~ **in, out, away, etc.** to go very quietly in the direction mentioned, so that no one can see or hear you: *The prisoner sneaked past the guards.* ◇ *Instead of working, he sneaked out to play football.* **2** [T] (*informal*) to do or take sth secretly: *I tried to **sneak a look** at the test results in the teacher's bag.*

PHR V **sneak up (on sb/sth)** to go near sb very quietly, especially so that you can surprise them

sneak² /sniːk/ ***noun*** [C] (*informal*) a person, especially a child, who tells sb about the bad things sb has done

sneaker /ˈsniːkə(r)/ (*AmE*) = PLIMSOLL, TRAINER (1) ➲ picture at **sport**

sneaking /ˈsniːkɪŋ/ ***adj.*** (used about feelings) not expressed; secret: *I've a sneaking suspicion that he's lying.*

sneer /snɪə(r)/ ***verb*** [I] ~ **(at sb/sth)** to show that you have no respect for sb/sth by the expression on your face or the way that you speak: *She sneered at his attempts to speak French.* ▶ **sneer** ***noun*** [C]

sneeze /sniːz/ ***verb*** [I] (**HEALTH**) to make air come out of your nose suddenly and noisily in a way that you cannot control, for example because you have a cold: *Dust makes me sneeze.* ▶ **sneeze** ***noun*** [C]

snide /snaɪd/ ***adj.*** (used about an expression or comment) critical in an unpleasant way

sniff /snɪf/ ***verb*** **1** [I] to breathe air in through the nose in a way that makes a sound, especially because you have a cold or you are crying: *Stop sniffing and blow your nose.* **2** [I,T] ~ **(at) sth** to smell sth by **sniffing**: *'I can smell gas,' he said, sniffing the air.* ◇ *The dog sniffed at the bone.* ▶ **sniff** ***noun*** [C]: *Have a sniff of this milk and tell me if it's still OK.*

sniffle /ˈsnɪfl/ ***verb*** [I] to make noises by breathing air suddenly up your nose, especially because you have a cold or you are crying

snigger /ˈsnɪɡə(r)/ ***verb*** [I] ~ **(at sb/sth)** to laugh quietly and secretly in an unpleasant way ▶ **snigger** ***noun*** [C]

snip¹ /snɪp/ ***verb*** [I,T] (**snipping**; **snipped**) ~ **(sth) (off, out, in, etc.)** to cut using scissors, with a short quick action: *He sewed on the button and snipped off the ends of the cotton.* ◇ *to snip a hole in sth*

snip² /snɪp/ ***noun*** [C] **1** a small cut made with scissors **2** (*BrE, informal*) something that is much cheaper than expected

sniper /ˈsnaɪpə(r)/ ***noun*** [C] a person who shoots at sb from a hidden position

snippet /ˈsnɪpɪt/ ***noun*** [C] a small piece of sth, especially information or news

snivel /ˈsnɪvl/ ***verb*** [I] (**snivelling**; **snivelled**: *AmE* **sniveling**; **sniveled**) to keep crying quietly in a way that is annoying

snob /snɒb/ ***noun*** [C] a person who thinks they are better than sb of a lower social class and who admires people who have a high social position ▶ **snobbish** ***adj.*** ▶ **snobbishly** ***adv.*** ▶ **snobbishness** ***noun*** [U]

snobbery /ˈsnɒbəri/ ***noun*** [U] behaviour or attitudes typical of people who think they are better than other people in society, for example because they have more money, better education, etc.

snog /snɒɡ/ ***verb*** [I,T] (**snogging**; **snogged**) (*BrE, informal*) (used about a couple) to kiss each other for a long period of time ▶ **snog** ***noun*** [sing.]

snooker /ˈsnuːkə(r)/ ***noun*** [U] a game in which two players try to hit a number of coloured balls into pockets at the edges of a large table using a long stick (**cue**): *to play snooker* ➲ look at **billiards**, **pool** ➲ picture at **sport**

snoop /snuːp/ ***verb*** [I] ~ **(around)**; ~ **(on sb)** to look around secretly and without permission in order to find out information, etc.: *She suspected that her neighbours visited just to snoop on her.*

snooty /ˈsnuːti/ ***adj.*** (*informal*) acting in a rude way because you think you are better than other people

snooze /snuːz/ ***verb*** [I] (*informal*) to have a short sleep, especially during the day ▶ **snooze** ***noun*** [C, usually sing.]: *I had a bit of a snooze on the train.* ➲ look at **nap**

snore /snɔː(r)/ ***verb*** [I] to breathe noisily through your nose and mouth while you are asleep ▶ **snore** ***noun*** [C]: *He's got the loudest snore I've ever heard.*

snorkel /ˈsnɔːkl/ ***noun*** [C] a tube that you can breathe air through when you are swimming under the surface of the water

snorkelling (also **snorkeling**) /ˈsnɔːkəlɪŋ/ ***noun*** [U] the sport or activity of swimming underwater with a SNORKEL: *to go snorkelling*

snort /snɔːt/ ***verb*** [I] **1** (used about animals) to make a noise by blowing air through the nose and mouth **2** (used about people) to blow out air noisily as a way of showing that you do not like sth, or that you are impatient ▶ **snort** ***noun*** [C]

snot /snɒt/ ***noun*** [U] (*informal*) (**HEALTH**) the liquid produced by the nose

snout /snaʊt/ ***noun*** [C] (**BIOLOGY**) the long nose of certain animals: *a pig's snout* ➲ picture on **page 28**

snow¹ 🔑 /snəʊ/ ***noun*** [U] small, soft, white pieces of frozen water that fall from the sky in cold weather: *Three centimetres of snow fell during the night.* ◇ *The snow melted before it could settle* (= stay on the ground). ➲ note at **weather**

snow² 🔑 /snəʊ/ ***verb*** [I] (used about snow) to fall from the sky: *It snowed all night.*

snowball¹ /ˈsnəʊbɔːl/ ***noun*** [C] a lump of snow that is pressed into the shape of a ball and used by children for playing

snowball² /ˈsnəʊbɔːl/ ***verb*** [I] to quickly grow bigger and bigger or more and more important

snowboard /ˈsnəʊbɔːd/ *noun* [C] a type of board that you fasten to both your feet and use for moving down mountains that are covered with snow ▶ **snowboarder** *noun* [C] ▶ **snowboarding** *noun* [U]: *Have you ever been snowboarding?*

snowdrift /ˈsnəʊdrɪft/ *noun* [C] a deep pile of snow that has been made by the wind: *The car got stuck in a snowdrift.*

snowdrop /ˈsnəʊdrɒp/ *noun* [C] a type of small white flower that appears at the end of winter

ˌsnowed ˈin *adj.* not able to leave home or travel because the snow is too deep

ˌsnowed ˈunder *adj.* with more work, etc. than you can deal with

snowfall /ˈsnəʊfɔːl/ *noun* **1** [C] the snow that falls on one occasion: *heavy snowfalls* **2** [U] the amount of snow that falls in a particular place

snowflake /ˈsnəʊfleɪk/ *noun* [C] one of the small, soft, white pieces of frozen water that fall together as snow

snowman /ˈsnəʊmæn/ *noun* [C] (*pl.* **-men** /-men/) the figure of a person made out of snow

snowplough (*AmE* **snowplow**) /ˈsnəʊplaʊ/ *noun* [C] a vehicle that is used to clear snow away from roads or railways ➲ look at **plough**

snowy /ˈsnəʊi/ *adj.* with a lot of snow: *snowy weather* ◇ *a snowy scene*

Snr (also **Sr**) *abbr.* (*especially AmE*) Senior

snub /snʌb/ *verb* [T] (**snubbing**; **snubbed**) to treat sb rudely, for example by refusing to look at or speak to them ▶ **snub** *noun* [C]

snuck /snʌk/ (*informal*) (*especially AmE*) past tense, past participle of **sneak**[1]

snuff /snʌf/ *noun* [U] (especially in past times) TOBACCO which people breathe up into the nose in the form of a powder

snuffle /ˈsnʌfl/ *verb* [I] (used about people and animals) to make a noise through your nose

snug /snʌg/ *adj.* **1** warm and comfortable: *a snug little room* ◇ *The children were snug in bed.* **2** fitting sb/sth closely: *Adjust the safety belt to give a snug fit.* ▶ **snugly** *adv.*

snuggle /ˈsnʌgl/ *verb* [I] ~ **(up to sb)**; ~ **(up/down)** to get into a position that makes you feel safe, warm and comfortable, usually next to another person: *She snuggled up to her mother.* ◇ *I snuggled down under the blanket to get warm.*

so[1] 🔑 /səʊ/ *adv.* **1** used to emphasize an adjective or adverb, especially when this produces a particular result: *She's so ill (that) she can't get out of bed.* ◇ *He was driving so fast that he couldn't stop.* ◇ *You've been so kind. How can I thank you?* **2** used in negative sentences for comparing people or things: *She's not so clever as we thought.* **3** used in place of something that has been said already, to avoid repeating it: *Are you coming by plane? If so,* (= if you are coming by plane) *I can meet you at the airport.* ◇ *'I failed, didn't I?' 'I'm afraid so.'* **4** (not with verbs in the negative) also, too: *He's a teacher and* **so is** *his wife.* ◇ *'I've been to New York.'* **'So have I.'** ◇ *I like singing* **and so does** *Helen.* ➲ look at **neither 5** used to show that you agree that sth is true, especially when you are surprised: *'It's getting late.' 'So it is. We'd better go.'* **6** (*formal*) (used when you are showing sb sth) in this way; like this: *It was a black insect, about so big* (= using your hands to show the size). ◇ *Fold the paper in two diagonally,* **like so**.

IDM **and so on (and so forth)** used at the end of a list to show that it continues in the same way: *They sell pens, pencils, paper and so on.*

I told you so used to tell sb that they should have listened to your advice: *'I missed the bus.' 'I told you so. I said you needed to leave earlier.'*

it (just) so happens (used to introduce a surprising fact) by chance: *It just so happened that we were going the same way, so he gave me a lift.*

just so → JUST[1]

or so (used to show that a number, time, etc. is not exact) approximately; about: *A hundred or so people came to the meeting.*

so as to do sth with the intention of doing sth; in order to do sth

so much for used for saying that sth was not helpful or successful: *So much for that diet! I didn't lose any weight at all.*

that is so (*formal*) that is true

so[2] 🔑 /səʊ/ *conj.* **1** with the result that; therefore: *She felt very tired so she went to bed early.* **2** ~ **(that)** with the purpose that; in order that: *She wore dark glasses so (that) nobody would recognize her.* **3** used to show how one part of a story follows another: *So what happened next?*

IDM **so what?** (*informal*) (showing that you think sth is not important) Who cares?: *'It's late.' 'So what? We don't have to go to school tomorrow.'*

soak /səʊk/ *verb* **1** [I,T] to become or make sth completely wet: *Leave the dishes to soak for a while.* ◇ *The dog came out of the river and shook itself, soaking everyone.* **2** [I] ~ **into/through sth**; ~ **in** (used about a liquid) to pass into or through sth: *Blood had soaked through the bandage.*

PHRV **soak sth up** to take sth in (especially a liquid): *I soaked the water up with a cloth.*

soaked /səʊkt/ *adj.* (not before a noun) extremely wet: *I got* **soaked** *waiting for my bus in the rain.*

soaking /ˈsəʊkɪŋ/ (*also* **ˌsoaking ˈwet**) *adj.* extremely wet

ˈso-and-so *noun* [C] (*pl.* **so-and-sos**) (*informal*) **1** a person who is not named: *Imagine a Mrs So-and-so telephones. What would you say?* **2** a person that you do not like: *He's a bad-tempered old so-and-so.*

soap 🔑 /səʊp/ *noun* **1** [U] a substance that you use for washing and cleaning: *He washed his hands with soap.* ◇ *a bar of soap* ◇ *soap powder* (= for washing clothes) **2** [C] (*informal*) = SOAP OPERA ▶ **soapy** *adj.*

ˈsoap opera (also *informal* **soap**) *noun* [C] (ARTS AND MEDIA) a story about the lives and problems of a group of people which continues several times a week on television or radio

soar /sɔː(r)/ *verb* [I] **1** to fly high in the air **2** to rise very fast: *Prices are soaring because of inflation.*

soaraway /ˈsɔːrəweɪ/ *adj.* (*BrE*) (used especially about success) very great; growing very quickly

sob /sɒb/ *verb* [I] (**sobbing**; **sobbed**) to cry while taking in sudden, sharp breaths; to speak while you are crying: *The child was sobbing because he'd lost his toy.* ▶ **sob** *noun* [C]: *It was heartbreaking to listen to her sobs.*

sober[1] /ˈsəʊbə(r)/ *adj.* **1** (of a person) not affected by alcohol: *He'd been drunk the first time he'd met her, but this time he was* **stone-cold sober**. **2** not funny; serious: *a sober expression* ◇ *Her death is a sober reminder of just how dangerous drugs can be.* **3** (of a colour) not bright or likely to be noticed: *a sober grey suit*

sober[2] /ˈsəʊbə(r)/ *verb*

PHRV **sober (sb) up** to become or make sb become normal again after being affected by alcohol: *I need* *a cup of black coffee to sober me up.* ◇ *There's no point talking to him until he's sobered up.*

sobering /ˈsəʊbərɪŋ/ ***adj.*** making you feel serious: *It is **a sobering thought** that over 25 million people have been killed in car accidents.*

Soc. ***abbr.*** Society: *Amateur Dramatic Soc.*

ˌso-ˈcalled AW ***adj.*** **1** used to show that the words you describe sb/sth with are not correct: *Her so-called friends only wanted her money.* **2** used to show that a special name has been given to sb/sth

soccer /ˈsɒkə(r)/ (*especially AmE*) = FOOTBALL (1)

sociable /ˈsəʊʃəbl/ ***adj.*** enjoying being with other people; friendly

social ⊶ /ˈsəʊʃl/ ***adj.*** **1** (SOCIAL STUDIES) connected with society and the way it is organized: *social problems/issues/reforms* **2** (SOCIAL STUDIES) concerning the position of people in society: *We share the same social background.* **3** connected with meeting people and enjoying yourself: *a social club* ◇ *She has a busy **social life**.* ◇ *Children have to develop their **social skills** when they start school.* **4** (used about animals) living in groups ▸ **socially** /-ʃəli/ ***adv.***: *We work together but I don't know him socially.*

ˌsocial deˈmocracy ***noun*** [U, C] (POLITICS) a political system that combines the principles of one system (**socialism**) with the greater personal freedom of another system (**democracy**); a country that has this political system of government ▸ **ˌsocial ˈdemocrat** ***noun*** [C]

socialism /ˈsəʊʃəlɪzəm/ ***noun*** [U] (POLITICS) the political idea that is based on the belief that all people are equal and that money and property should be equally divided ➲ look at **communism**, **Marxism**, **capitalism** ▸ **socialist** ***adj.***, ***noun*** [C]: *socialist beliefs/policies/writers* ◇ *Tony was a socialist when he was younger.*

ˌsocialist ˈrealism ***noun*** [U] (ARTS AND MEDIA, ART, LITERATURE) a theory that was put into practice in some COMMUNIST countries, especially in the Soviet Union under Stalin, that art, music and literature should be used to show people the principles of a SOCIALIST society and encourage them to support it

socialization (also **-isation**) /ˌsəʊʃəlaɪˈzeɪʃn/ ***noun*** [U] (*formal*) (SOCIAL STUDIES) the process by which sb, especially a child, learns to behave in a way that is acceptable in their society

socialize (also **-ise**) /ˈsəʊʃəlaɪz/ ***verb*** **1** [I] ~ (**with sb**) to meet and spend time with people in a friendly way, in order to enjoy yourself: *I enjoy socializing with the other students.* **2** [T] (*formal*) (SOCIAL STUDIES) to teach people to behave in ways that are acceptable to their society

ˈsocial life ***noun*** [C] (SOCIAL STUDIES) the part of your life you spend going out and enjoying yourself with other people

ˌsocial ˈscience ***noun*** [C,U] (SOCIAL STUDIES) the study of people in society

ˌsocial seˈcurity (*AmE* **welfare**) ***noun*** [U] (POLITICS, FINANCE, SOCIAL STUDIES) money paid regularly by the government to people who are poor, old, ill, or who have no job: *to live on social security*

ˌsocial ˈservices ***noun*** [pl.] (POLITICS, SOCIAL STUDIES) a group of services organized by local government to help people who have money or family problems

ˈsocial work ***noun*** [U] (SOCIAL STUDIES) paid work that involves giving help and advice to people living in the community who have financial or family problems

ˈsocial worker ***noun*** [C] (SOCIAL STUDIES) a person whose job is SOCIAL WORK

society ⊶ /səˈsaɪəti/ ***noun*** (*pl.* **societies**) **1** [C,U] (SOCIAL STUDIES) the people in a country or area, thought of as a group, who have shared customs and laws: *a civilized society* ◇ *Society's attitude to women has changed considerably this century.* ◇ *The role of men **in society** is changing.* **2** [C] an organization of people who share a particular interest or purpose; a club: *a drama society*

socio- /ˈsəʊsiəʊ/ ***prefix*** (used in nouns, adjectives and adverbs) (SOCIAL STUDIES) connected with society or the study of society: *socio-economic* ◇ *sociolinguistics*

sociolinguistics /ˌsəʊsiəʊlɪŋˈgwɪstɪks/ ***noun*** [U] (LANGUAGE) the study of the way language is affected by differences in social class, region, sex, etc. ▸ **sociolinguistic** /ˌsəʊsiəʊlɪŋˈgwɪstɪk/ ***adj.***

sociologist /ˌsəʊsiˈɒlədʒɪst/ ***noun*** [C] (SOCIAL STUDIES) a student of or an expert in SOCIOLOGY

sociology /ˌsəʊsiˈɒlədʒi/ ***noun*** [U] (SOCIAL STUDIES) the study of human societies and social behaviour ▸ **sociological** /ˌsəʊsiəˈlɒdʒɪkl/ ***adj.***

sock ⊶ /sɒk/ ***noun*** [C] a piece of clothing that you wear on your foot and lower leg, inside your shoe: *a pair of socks*

IDM **pull your socks up** (*BrE*) to start working harder or better than before

socket /ˈsɒkɪt/ ***noun*** [C] **1** (*also* **ˈpower point**; *informal* **plug**) a place in a wall where a piece of electrical equipment can be connected to the electricity supply ➲ picture at **plug** **2** a hole in a piece of electrical equipment where another piece of equipment can be connected **3** a hole that sth fits into: *your eye socket*

soda /ˈsəʊdə/ ***noun*** **1** (*also* **ˈsoda water**) [U] water that has bubbles in it and is usually used for mixing with other drinks: *a whisky and soda* **2** [C] (*AmE*) = FIZZY DRINK ➲ look at **caustic soda**

sodium /ˈsəʊdiəm/ ***noun*** [U] (*symbol* **Na**) (CHEMISTRY) a soft silver-white metal that is found naturally only in chemical mixtures (**compounds**), such as salt ❶ For more information on the periodic table of elements, look at pages R34-5.

ˌsodium biˈcarbonate (*also* **biˌcarbonate of ˈsoda**; **ˈbaking soda**) ***noun*** [U] (*symbol* **$NaHCO_3$**) (CHEMISTRY) a white powder that is used in baking to make cakes, etc. rise and become light

ˌsodium ˈcarbonate (*also* **ˈwashing soda**) ***noun*** [U] (*symbol* **Na_2CO_3**) (CHEMISTRY) a chemical COMPOUND in the form of white CRYSTALS or powder that is used in making glass, soap and paper, and for making hard water soft

ˌsodium ˈchloride ***noun*** [U] (*symbol* **NaCl**) (CHEMISTRY) common salt (a chemical COMPOUND of SODIUM and CHLORINE)

sofa /ˈsəʊfə/ ***noun*** [C] a comfortable seat with a back and arms for two or more people to sit on: *a sofa bed* (= a sofa that you can open out to make a bed) SYN **settee**

soft ⊶ /sɒft/ ***adj.*** **1** not hard or firm: *a soft bed/seat* ◇ *The ground is very soft after all that rain.* OPP **hard** **2** smooth and pleasant to touch; not rough: *soft skin/hands* ◇ *a soft towel* OPP **rough** **3** (used about sounds, voices, words, etc.) quiet or gentle; not loud or angry: *She spoke in a soft whisper.* OPP **loud**, **harsh** **4** (used about light, colours, etc.) gentle

and pleasant: *The room was decorated in soft pinks and greens.* OPP **bright** **5** (used about people) kind and gentle, sometimes too much so: *A good manager can't afford to be too soft.* OPP **hard**, **strict** **6** (used about water) not containing mineral salts and therefore good for washing as soap will make a lot of bubbles OPP **hard** ▶ **softness** ***noun*** [U]
IDM **have a soft spot for sb/sth** (*informal*) to have good or loving feelings towards sb/sth

ˌsoft ˈdrink ***noun*** [C] a cold drink that contains no alcohol

ˌsoft ˈdrug ***noun*** [C] (LAW) an illegal drug, such as CANNABIS, that some people take for pleasure, that is not considered very harmful or likely to cause ADDICTION ➲ look at **hard drug**

soften /ˈsɒfn/ ***verb*** **1** [I, I] to become softer or gentler; to make sb/sth softer or gentler: *a lotion to soften the skin* **2** [T] to make sth less strong and unpleasant: *Her letter sounded too angry so she softened the language.* ◇ *The air bag softened the impact of the crash.*

ˌsoft ˈfruit ***noun*** [C,U] small fruits without a large seed inside or hard skin: *raspberries, strawberries and other soft fruits*

ˌsoft-ˈhearted ***adj.*** kind and good at understanding other people's feelings OPP **hard-hearted**

softly 🔑 /ˈsɒftli/ ***adv.*** in a soft way: *She closed the door softly behind her.* ◇ *'I missed you,' he said softly.*

ˌsoft ˈoption ***noun*** [C] the easier thing to do of two or more possibilities, but not the best one: *The government has taken the soft option of agreeing to their demands.*

ˌsoft-ˈspoken ***adj.*** having a gentle, quiet voice: *He was a kind, soft-spoken man.*

software 🔑 /ˈsɒftweə(r)/ ***noun*** [U] (COMPUTING) the programs and other operating information used by a computer: *There's a lot of new educational software available now.* ➲ look at **hardware**

softwood /ˈsɒftwʊd/ ***noun*** [U, C] wood that is cheap to produce and can be cut easily: *Pine is a softwood.* ➲ look at **hardwood**

soggy /ˈsɒgi/ ***adj.*** very wet and soft and so unpleasant

soil¹ 🔑 /sɔɪl/ ***noun*** **1** [C,U] (AGRICULTURE, GEOLOGY) the substance that plants, trees, etc. grow in; earth: *poor/dry/acid/sandy soil* ➲ note at **ground¹** **2** [U] (*written*) the land that is part of a country

soil² /sɔɪl/ ***verb*** [T] (*formal*) (often passive) to make sth dirty

solace /ˈsɒləs/ ***noun*** [U, sing.] (*written*) ~ **(in sth)** a person or thing that makes you feel better or happier when you are sad or disappointed: *to find/seek solace in sb/sth*

solar /ˈsəʊlə(r)/ ***adj.*** (only *before* a noun) **1** (ASTRONOMY) connected with the sun: *a solar eclipse* (=when the sun is blocked by the moon) **2** (ENVIRONMENT) using the sun's energy: *solar heating/power* ➲ picture at **energy**

ˌsolar ˈcell ***noun*** [C] (PHYSICS, SCIENCE, ENVIRONMENT) a device that converts light and heat energy from the sun into electricity

solarium /səˈleəriəm/ ***noun*** [C] a room whose walls are mainly made of glass, or which has special lamps, where people go to get a SUNTAN (=make their skin go brown) using light from the sun or artificial light

ˌsolar ˈpanel ***noun*** [C] (ENVIRONMENT) a piece of equipment on a roof that uses light and heat energy from the sun to produce hot water and electricity

the ˈsolar system ***noun*** [sing.] (ASTRONOMY) the sun and the planets that move around it

ˌsolar ˈyear ***noun*** [C] (ASTRONOMY) the time it takes the earth to go around the sun once, approximately 365¼ days

sold past tense, past participle of **sell**

solder /ˈsəʊldə(r); ˈsɒldə(r)/ ***verb*** [T] ~ **sth (to/onto sth)**; ~ **(A and B together)** to join pieces of metal or wire together using a mixture of metals which is heated and melted ▶ **solder** ***noun*** [U] ➲ look at **weld**

ˈsoldering iron ***noun*** [C] a tool that is heated and used for joining metals and wires by SOLDERING them

soldier 🔑 /ˈsəʊldʒə(r)/ ***noun*** [C] a member of an army: *The soldiers marched past.*

sole¹ AW /səʊl/ ***adj.*** (only *before* a noun) **1** only; single: *His sole interest is football.* **2** belonging to one person only; not shared ▶ **solely** AW ***adv.***: *I agreed to come solely because of your mother.*

sole² AW /səʊl/ ***noun*** **1** [C] the bottom surface of your foot ➲ picture on **page 80** **2** [C] the part of a shoe or sock that covers the bottom surface of your foot **3** [C,U] (*pl.* **sole**) a flat sea fish that we eat

the solar system

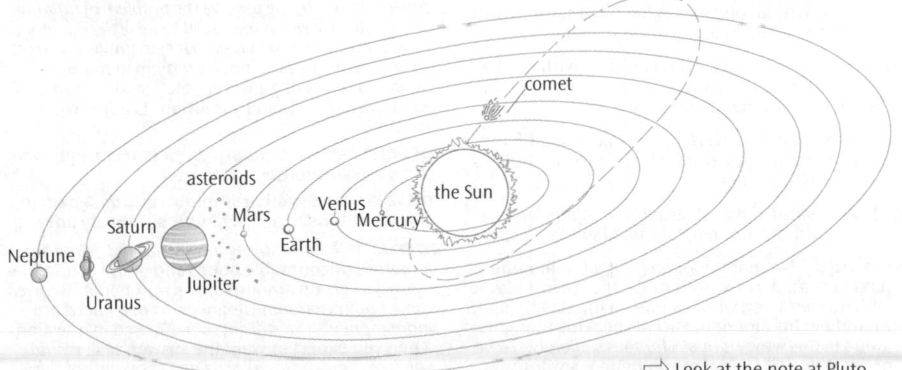

⇨ Look at the note at Pluto.

solemn /'sɒləm/ ***adj.*** **1** (used about a person) very serious; not happy or smiling: *Her solemn face told them that the news was bad.* **2** sincere; done or said in a formal way: *to make a solemn promise* ▸ **solemnity** /sə'lemnəti/ ***noun*** [U] ▸ **solemnly** ***adv.***: *'I have something very important to tell you,' she began solemnly.*

solicit /sə'lɪsɪt/ ***verb*** **1** [T] (*formal*) to ask sb for money, help, support, etc.: *They tried to solicit support for the proposal.* **2** [I,T] (used about a woman who has sex for money) to go to sb, especially in a public place, and offer sex in return for money

solicitor /sə'lɪsɪtə(r)/ ***noun*** [C] (*BrE*) (LAW) a lawyer whose job is to give legal advice, prepare legal documents and arrange the buying and selling of land, etc. ➲ note at **lawyer**

solid[1] 🔑 /'sɒlɪd/ ***adj.*** **1** hard and firm; not in the form of liquid or gas: *It was so cold that the village pond had* ***frozen solid***. **2** having no holes or empty spaces inside; not hollow: *a solid mass of rock* **3** strong, firm and well made: *a solid little car* ◇ (*figurative*) *They built up a solid friendship over the years.* **4** of good enough quality; that you can trust: *The police cannot make an arrest without solid evidence.* **5** (only *before* a noun) made completely of one substance, both on the inside and outside: *a* ***solid gold*** *chain* **6** (*spoken*) without a break or pause: *I was so tired that I slept for twelve solid hours/twelve hours solid.* ▸ **solidity** /sə'lɪdəti/ ***noun*** [U]

solids

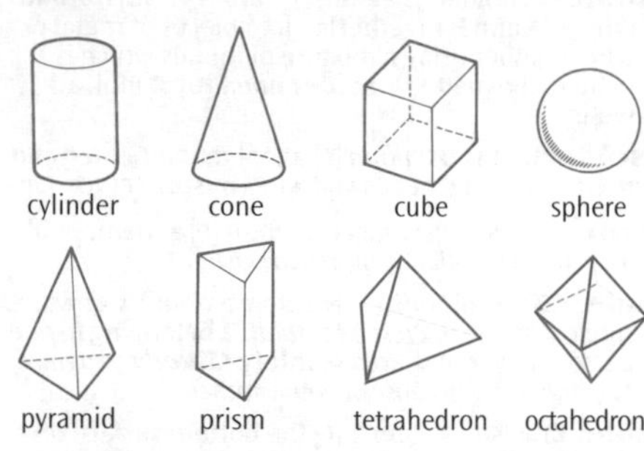

solid[2] 🔑 /'sɒlɪd/ ***noun*** [C] **1** a substance or object that is hard; not a liquid or gas: *Liquids become solids when frozen.* ◇ *The baby is not yet on solids* (=solid food). ➲ picture at **state**[1] **2** (GEOMETRY) an object that has length, width and height, not a flat shape: *A cube is a solid.*

solidarity /ˌsɒlɪ'dærəti/ ***noun*** [U] ~ (**with sb**) the support of one group of people for another, because they agree with their aims

solidify /sə'lɪdɪfaɪ/ ***verb*** [I] (*pres. part.* **solidifying**; *3rd person sing. pres.* **solidifies**; *pt, pp* **solidified**) to become hard or solid

solidly /'sɒlɪdli/ ***adv.*** **1** strongly: *a solidly built house* **2** without stopping: *It rained solidly all day.*

soliloquy /sə'lɪləkwi/ ***noun*** [C,U] (*pl.* **soliloquies**) (LITERATURE, ARTS AND MEDIA) a speech in a play in which a character, who is alone on the stage, speaks their thoughts aloud; the act of speaking thoughts aloud in this way: *Hamlet's famous soliloquy, 'To be or not to be...'* ➲ look at **monologue** ▸ **soliloquize** (also **-ise**) /sə'lɪləkwaɪz/ ***verb*** [I]

solitaire /ˌsɒlɪ'teə(r)/ ***noun*** [U] **1** a game for one person in which you remove pieces from a special board by moving other pieces over them until you have only one piece left **2** (*AmE*) = PATIENCE (2)

solitary /'sɒlətri/ ***adj.*** **1** done alone, without other people: *Writing novels is a solitary occupation.* **2** (used about a person or an animal) enjoying being alone; frequently spending time alone: *She was always a solitary child.* **3** (only *before* a noun) one on its/his/her own with no others around: *a solitary figure walking up the hillside* SYN **lone** **4** (only *before* a noun) (usually in negative sentences or questions) only one; single: *I can't think of a solitary example* (=not even one).

ˌsolitary con'finement ***noun*** [U] (LAW) a punishment in which a person in prison is kept completely alone in a separate cell away from the other prisoners

solitude /'sɒlɪtjuːd/ ***noun*** [U] the state of being alone, especially when you find this pleasant: *She longed for peace and solitude.* ➲ look at **loneliness**, **isolation**

solo[1] /'səʊləʊ/ ***noun*** [C] (*pl.* **solos**) (MUSIC) a piece of music for only one person to play or sing ➲ look at **duet** ▸ **soloist** ***noun*** [C]

solo[2] /'səʊləʊ/ ***adj.***, ***adv.*** **1** (done) alone; by yourself: *a solo flight* ◇ *to fly solo* **2** connected with or played as a musical **solo**: *a solo artist* (=a singer who is not part of a group)

solstice /'sɒlstɪs/ ***noun*** [C] (ASTRONOMY) either of the two times of the year at which the sun reaches its highest or lowest point in the sky at midday, marked by the longest and shortest days: *the summer/winter solstice* ➲ look at **equinox** ➲ picture at **season**

soluble /'sɒljəbl/ ***adj.*** **1** (SCIENCE) ~ (**in sth**) that will dissolve in liquid: *These tablets are soluble in water.* **2** (*formal*) (used about a problem, etc.) that has an answer; that can be solved OPP **insoluble**

solute /'sɒljuːt/ ***noun*** [C] (SCIENCE) a substance that has dissolved in a SOLVENT and become part of the liquid so that together they form a solution

solution 🔑 /sə'luːʃn/ ***noun*** **1** [C] **a** ~ (**to sth**) a way of solving a problem, dealing with a difficult situation, etc.: *a solution to the problem of unemployment* **2** [C] **the** ~ (**to sth**) the answer (to a game, competition, etc.): *The solution to the quiz will be published next week.* **3** [C,U] (a) liquid in which sth solid has been dissolved: *saline solution* **4** (SCIENCE) [U] the process of dissolving a solid or gas in a liquid: *the solution of glucose in water* ➲ picture at **erode**

solve 🔑 /sɒlv/ ***verb*** [T] **1** to find a way of dealing with a problem or difficult situation: *The government is trying to solve the problem of inflation.* ◇ *The police have not managed to solve the crime.* ◇ *to solve a mystery* **2** (MATHEMATICS) to find the correct answer to a competition, a problem in mathematics, a series of questions, etc.: *to solve a puzzle/equation/riddle* ➲ noun **solution** ➲ adjective **soluble**

solvent /'sɒlvənt/ ***noun*** [C,U] (SCIENCE) a liquid that can dissolve another substance

sombre (*AmE* **somber**) /'sɒmbə(r)/ ***adj.*** **1** dark in colour; dull **2** sad and serious ▸ **sombrely** ***adv.***

some 🔑 /səm *strong form* sʌm/ ***det.***, ***pronoun*** **1** (before uncountable nouns and plural countable nouns) a certain amount of or a number of: *We need some butter and some potatoes.* ◇ *I don't need any more money – I've still got some.* **2** used in questions when you expect or want the answer 'yes': *Would you like some more cake?* ◇ *Can I take some of this paper?* **3** ~ (**of sb/sth**) used when you are referring to certain members of a group or certain types of a thing, but not all of them: *Some pupils enjoy this kind of work, some don't.* ◇ *Some of his books are very exciting.* ◇ *Some of us are going to the park.* **4** used with SINGULAR COUNTABLE nouns for talking about a person or thing without saying any details: *I'll see you again some time, I expect.* ◇ *There must be some mistake.* ◇ *I read about it in **some** newspaper **or other**.*

somebody 🔑 /'sʌmbədi/ (*also* **someone**) ***pronoun*** a person who is not known or not mentioned by name: *How are you? Somebody said that you'd been ill.* ◇ *She's getting married to someone she met at work.* ◇ *There's somebody at the door.* ◇ *I think you should talk to **someone else*** (=another person) *about this problem.*

'some day (*also* **someday**) ***adv.*** at a time in the future that is not yet known: *I hope you'll come and visit me some day.*

somehow 🔑 /'sʌmhaʊ/ ***adv.*** **1** in a way that is not known or certain: *The car's broken down but I'll get to work somehow.* ◇ *Somehow we had got completely lost.* **2** for a reason you do not know or understand: *I somehow get the feeling that I've been here before.*

someone 🔑 /'sʌmwʌn/ =SOMEBODY

someplace /'sʌmpleɪs/ (*AmE*) =SOMEWHERE

somersault /'sʌməsɔːlt/ ***noun*** [C] a movement in which you roll right over with your feet going over your head

something 🔑 /'sʌmθɪŋ/ ***pronoun*** **1** a thing that is not known or not named: *I've got something in my eye.* ◇ *Wait a minute – I've forgotten something.* ◇ *Would you like **something else*** (=another thing) *to drink?* **2** a thing that is important, useful or worth considering: *There's **something in** what your mother says.* ◇ *I think you've got something there – I like that idea.* **3** (*informal*) used to show that a description, an amount, etc. is not exact: *a new comedy series aimed at **thirty-somethings*** (=people between thirty and forty years old).

IDM **or something** (*informal*) used for showing that you are not sure about what you have just said: *'What's his job?' 'I think he's a plumber, or something.'*

something like similar to: *A loganberry is something like a raspberry.*

something to do with connected or involved with: *The programme's something to do with the environment.*

sometime (*also* **'some time**) /'sʌmtaɪm/ ***adv.*** at a time that you do not know exactly or have not yet decided: *I'll phone you sometime this evening.* ◇ *I must go and see her sometime.*

sometimes 🔑 /'sʌmtaɪmz/ ***adv.*** on some occasions; now and then: *Sometimes I drive to work and sometimes I go by bus.* ◇ *I sometimes watch television in the evenings.*

somewhat 🔑 AW /'sʌmwɒt/ ***adv.*** rather; to some degree: *We missed the train, which was somewhat unfortunate.*

somewhere 🔑 /'sʌmweə(r)/ (*AmE also* **someplace**) ***adv.*** **1** at, in, or to a place that you do not know or do not mention by name: *I've seen your glasses somewhere downstairs.* ◇ *'Have they gone to France?' 'No, I think they've gone **somewhere else*** (=to another place) *this year.'* **2** used when you do not know an exact time, number, etc.: *Your ideal weight should probably be **somewhere around** 70 kilos.*

sommelier /sə'melɪeɪ; 'sɒməljeɪ/ ***noun*** [C] (TOURISM) a person who works in a restaurant serving wine and helping customers to decide which wine to choose SYN **wine waiter**

son 🔑 /sʌn/ ***noun*** [C] a male child ➲ look at **daughter**

sonar

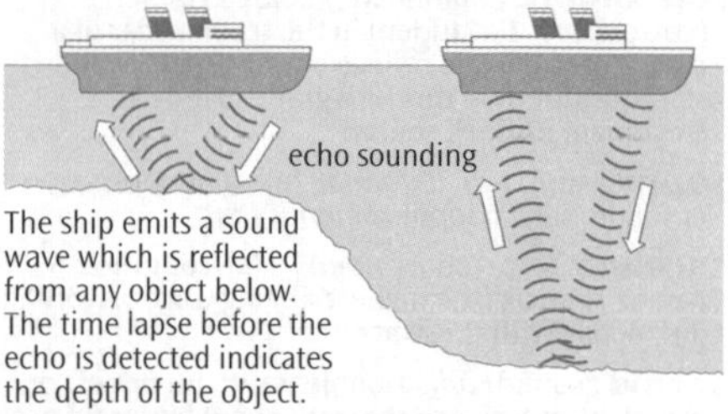

The ship emits a sound wave which is reflected from any object below. The time lapse before the echo is detected indicates the depth of the object.

sonar /'səʊnɑː(r)/ ***noun*** [U] (PHYSICS) equipment or a system for finding objects under water using sound waves ➲ look at **radar**

sonata /sə'nɑːtə/ ***noun*** [C] (MUSIC) a piece of music written for the piano, or for another instrument together with the piano

song 🔑 /sɒŋ/ ***noun*** **1** [C] (MUSIC) a piece of music with words that you sing: *a folk/love/pop song* **2** [U] (MUSIC) songs in general; music for singing: *to burst/break into song* (=to suddenly start singing) **3** [U, C] the musical sounds that birds make: *birdsong*

songbird /'sɒŋbɜːd/ ***noun*** [C] a bird that has a musical call, for example a BLACKBIRD or a THRUSH

songwriter /'sɒŋraɪtə(r)/ ***noun*** [C] (MUSIC) a person whose job is to write songs

sonic /'sɒnɪk/ ***adj.*** (PHYSICS) connected with sound waves

'son-in-law ***noun*** [C] (*pl.* **sons-in-law**) the husband of your daughter

sonnet /'sɒnɪt/ ***noun*** [C] (LITERATURE) a poem that has 14 lines, each usually containing 10 SYLLABLES, and a fixed pattern of RHYME (=lines with the same sound at the end as other lines)

soon 🔑 /suːn/ ***adv.*** **1** in a short time from now; a short time after sth else has happened: *It will soon be dark.* ◇ *He left soon after me.* ◇ *We should arrive at your house soon after twelve.* ◇ (*spoken*) *See you soon.* **2** early; quickly: *Don't leave so soon. Stay for tea.* ◇ *How soon can you get here?*

IDM **as soon as** at the moment (that); when: *Phone me as soon as you hear some news.* ◇ *I'd like your reply **as soon as possible*** (=at the earliest possible moment).

no sooner...than (*written*) immediately when or after: *No sooner had I shut the door than I realized I'd left my keys inside.*

sooner or later at some time in the future; one day

soot /sʊt/ ***noun*** [U] black powder that comes from burning things and collects in CHIMNEYS

soothe /suːð/ ***verb*** [T] **1** to make sb calmer or less upset; to comfort sb **2** to make a part of the body or a feeling less painful: *The doctor gave me some skin cream to soothe the irritation.* ► **soothing** ***adj.***: *soothing music* ◇ *a soothing massage*
► **soothingly** ***adv.***

sophisticated /səˈfɪstɪkeɪtɪd/ ***adj.*** **1** having or showing a lot of experience of the world and social situations; knowing about fashion, culture, etc. **2** (used about machines, systems, etc.) advanced and complicated **3** able to understand difficult or complicated things: *Voters are much more sophisticated these days.* ▶ **sophistication** /səˌfɪstɪˈkeɪʃn/ ***noun*** [U]

sophomore /ˈsɒfəmɔː(r)/ ***noun*** [C] (*AmE*) (EDUCATION) **1** a student in the second year of a course of study at a college or university **2** a HIGH SCHOOL student in the 10th grade ➲ look at **freshman**, **junior²**, **senior²**

soppy /ˈsɒpi/ ***adj.*** (*informal*) full of unnecessary emotion; silly: *a soppy romantic film*

soprano /səˈprɑːnəʊ/ ***noun*** [C] (*pl.* **sopranos** /-nəʊz/) (MUSIC) the highest singing voice; a woman, girl, or boy with this voice

sordid /ˈsɔːdɪd/ ***adj.*** **1** unpleasant; not honest or moral: *We discovered the truth about his sordid past.* **2** very dirty and unpleasant

sore¹ 🗝 /sɔː(r)/ ***adj.*** (HEALTH) (used about a part of the body) painful, especially when touched: *to have a sore throat* ◇ *My feet were sore from walking so far.* ▶ **soreness** ***noun*** [U]: *a cream to reduce soreness and swelling*

IDM **a sore point** a subject that is likely to make sb upset or angry when mentioned

stand/stick out like a sore thumb to be extremely obvious, especially in a negative way: *A big new office block would stand out like a sore thumb in the old part of town.*

sore² /sɔː(r)/ ***noun*** [C] (HEALTH) a painful, often red place on your body where the skin is cut or infected ➲ look at **cold sore**

sorely /ˈsɔːli/ ***adv.*** (*formal*) very much; seriously: *You'll be **sorely missed** when you leave.*

sorority /səˈrɒrəti/ ***noun*** [C] (*pl.* **sororities**) (EDUCATION) a club for a group of women students at an American college or university ➲ look at **fraternity**

sorrow /ˈsɒrəʊ/ ***noun*** (*formal*) **1** [U] a feeling of great sadness because sth bad has happened **2** [C] a very sad event or situation ▶ **sorrowful** ***adj.*** ▶ **sorrowfully** ***adv.***

sorry¹ 🗝 /ˈsɒri/ ***adj.*** (**sorrier**; **sorriest**) **1** (not before a noun) ~ (**to see, hear, etc.**); ~ **that...** sad or disappointed: *I was sorry to hear that you've been ill.* ◇ *I am sorry that we have to leave so soon.* ◇ *'Simon's mother died last week.' 'Oh, I am sorry.'* **2** (not before a noun) ~ (**for/about sth**); ~ (**to do sth/that...**) used for excusing yourself for sth that you have done: *I'm awfully sorry for spilling that coffee.* ◇ *I'm sorry I've kept you all waiting.* ◇ *I'm sorry to disturb you so late in the evening, but I wonder if you can help me.* **3** (not before a noun) used for politely saying 'no' to sth, disagreeing with sth or introducing bad news: *'Would you like to come to dinner on Friday?' 'I'm sorry, I'm busy that evening.'* ◇ *I'm sorry, I don't agree with you. I think we should accept the offer.* ◇ *I'm sorry to tell you that your application has been unsuccessful.* **4** (only *before* a noun) very bad: *The house was in a **sorry state** when we first moved in.* ◇ *They were a **sorry sight** when they finally got home.*

IDM **be/feel sorry for sb** to feel sadness or pity for sb: *I feel very sorry for the families of the victims.* ◇ *Stop feeling sorry for yourself!*

sorry² /ˈsɒri/ ***exclamation*** **1** used for making excuses, apologizing, etc.: *Sorry, I didn't see you standing behind me.* ◇ *Sorry I'm late – the bus didn't come on time.* ◇ *He didn't even **say sorry*** (=apologize)! **2** (*especially BrE*) (used for asking sb to repeat sth that you have not heard correctly): *'My name's Dave Harries.' 'Sorry? Dave who?'* **3** (used for correcting yourself when you have said sth wrong): *Take the second turning, sorry, the third turning on the right.*

sort¹ 🗝 /sɔːt/ ***noun*** **1** [C] **a ~ of sb/sth** a type or kind: *What sort of music do you like?* ◇ *She's got **all sorts of** problems at the moment.* ◇ *There were snacks – peanuts, olives, **that sort of thing**.* **2** [sing.] (*especially BrE*) a particular type of character; a person SYN **kind**

IDM **a sort of sth** (*informal*) a type of sth; sth that is similar to sth: *Can you hear a sort of ticking noise?*

sort of (*spoken*) rather; in a way: *'Do you see what I mean?' 'Sort of.'* ◇ *I'd sort of like to go, but I'm not sure.*

sort² 🗝 /sɔːt/ ***verb*** [T] **1** ~ **sth (into sth)** to put things into different groups or places, according to their type, etc.; to separate things of one type from others: *I'm just sorting these papers into the correct files.* **2** (*especially BrE, informal*) (often passive) to find an answer to a problem or difficult situation; to organize sth/sb: *I'll have more time when I've **got things sorted** at home.*

PHR V **sort sth out 1** to find an answer to a problem; to organize sth: *I haven't found a flat yet but I hope to sort something out soon.* **2** to tidy or organize sth: *The toy cupboard needs sorting out.*

sort through sth to look through a number of things, in order to find sth that you are looking for or to put them in order

ˌso-ˈso ***adj.***, ***adv.*** (*informal*) all right but not particularly good/well: *'How are you?' 'So-so.'*

soufflé /ˈsuːfleɪ/ ***noun*** [C,U] a type of food made mainly from egg whites, flour and milk, beaten together and baked until it rises

sought past tense, past participle of **seek**

ˈsought after ***adj.*** that people want very much, because it is of high quality or rare

soul 🗝 /səʊl/ ***noun*** **1** [C] (RELIGION) the spiritual part of a person that is believed to continue to exist after the body is dead **2** [C,U] the inner part of a person containing their deepest thoughts and feelings: *There was a feeling of restlessness deep in her soul.* ➲ look at **spirit** **3** [C] (*old-fashioned*) (used with adjectives) a particular type of person: *She's a kind soul.* **4** [sing.] (in negative statements) a person: *There wasn't a soul in sight* (=there was nobody). ◇ *Promise me you won't tell a soul.* **5** (*also* ˈ**soul music**) [U] (MUSIC) a type of popular African American music: *a soul singer*

IDM **heart and soul** → HEART

soulful /ˈsəʊlfl/ ***adj.*** having or showing deep feeling: *a soulful expression*

soulless /ˈsəʊlləs/ ***adj.*** without feeling, warmth or interest: *soulless industrial towns*

sound¹ 🗝 /saʊnd/ ***noun*** **1** [C,U] something that you hear or that can be heard: *the sound of voices* ◇ *a clicking/buzzing/scratching sound* ◇ *After that, he didn't **make a sound**.* ◇ *She opened the door without a sound.* ◇ *Light travels faster than sound.* ◇ *sound waves* ➲ picture at **amplitude** **2** [U] what you can hear coming from a television, radio, etc.: *Can you turn the sound up/down?*

IDM **by the sound of it/things** judging from what sb has said or what you have read about sb/sth: *She must be an interesting person, by the sound of it.*

sound² ⊷ /saʊnd/ *verb* **1** *linking verb* (not usually in the continuous tenses) to give a particular impression when heard or read about; to seem: *That* ***sounds like*** *a child crying.* ◇ *She sounded upset and angry on the phone.* ◇ *You sound like your father when you say things like that!* ◇ *He sounds a very nice person from his letter.* ◇ *Does she sound like the right person for the job?* ◇ *It doesn't* ***sound as if/though*** *he's very reliable.* **2 -sounding** (used to form compound adjectives) seeming to be of the type mentioned, from what you have heard or read: *a Spanish-sounding surname* **3** [T] to cause sth to make a sound; to give a signal by making a sound: *to sound the horn of your car* ◇ *A student on one of the upper floors* ***sounded the alarm.*** **4** [I,T] to measure the depth of the sea or a lake by using a line with a weight on it, or an electronic instrument

PHR V **sound sb out (about sth)** to ask sb questions in order to find out what they think or intend

sound³ /saʊnd/ *adj.* **1** sensible; that you can depend on and that will probably give good results: *sound advice* ◇ *a sound investment* **2** healthy and strong; in good condition: *The structure of the bridge is basically sound.* OPP **unsound**
▶ **soundness** *noun* [U]

sound⁴ /saʊnd/ *adv.*

IDM **be sound asleep** to be deeply asleep

the 'sound barrier *noun* [sing.] (PHYSICS) the point at which an aircraft's speed is the same as the speed of sound: *to break the sound barrier* (=to travel faster than the speed of sound)

'sound effect *noun* [C, usually pl.] (ARTS AND MEDIA) a sound that is made artificially, for example the sound of the wind, and used in a play, film or computer game to make it more realistic

soundly /'saʊndli/ *adv.* completely or deeply: *The children were sleeping soundly.*

soundproof /'saʊndpru:f/ *adj.* made so that no sound can get in or out: *a soundproof room*

soundtrack /'saʊndtræk/ *noun* [C] (ARTS AND MEDIA, MUSIC) the recorded sound and music from a film or computer game ➲ look at **track**

soup ⊷ /su:p/ *noun* [U, C] liquid food made by cooking meat, vegetables, etc. in water: *a tin of chicken soup*

sour ⊷ /'saʊə(r)/ *adj.* **1** having a sharp taste like that of a lemon: *This sauce is quite sour.* **2** (used especially about milk) tasting or smelling unpleasant because it is no longer fresh: *This cream has* ***gone sour.*** **3** (used about people) angry and unpleasant: *a sour expression* ◇ *a* ***sour-faced*** *old woman* ▶ **sour** *verb* [T] (*formal*): *The disagreement over trade tariffs has soured relations between the two countries.* ▶ **sourly** *adv.* ▶ **sourness** *noun* [U]

IDM **go/turn sour** to stop being pleasant or friendly: *Their relationship turned sour after a few months.*

sour grapes pretending to not want sth that in fact you secretly want, because you cannot have it

source¹ ⊷ AW /sɔ:s/ *noun* [C] a place, person or thing where sth comes or starts from or where sth is obtained: *Britain's oil reserves are an important* ***source of income.*** ◇ *This word has its source in Greek.* ◇ *The television is a great source of entertainment.* ◇ *Police have refused to reveal the source of their information.*

source² AW /sɔ:s/ *verb* [T] ~ **sth (from...)** (BUSINESS) to get sth from a particular place: *We source all the meat sold in our stores from British farms.*

'source code *noun* [U] (COMPUTING) a computer program written in text form that must be translated into MACHINE CODE before it can run on a computer

sous-chef /'su: ʃef/ *noun* [C] a person who is the second most senior cook in a restaurant ➲ look at **chef, commis**

south¹ ⊷ /saʊθ/ (*also* **the south**) *noun* [sing.] (*abbr.* S) **1** (GEOGRAPHY) the direction that is on your right when you watch the sun rise; one of the points of the COMPASS (=the four main directions that we give names to): *warm winds from the south* ◇ *Which way is south?* ◇ *We live to the south of* (=further south than) *London.* ➲ picture at **compass 2 the South** the southern part of any country, city, region or the world: *Nice is in the South of France.* ➲ look at **north, east, west**

south² ⊷ /saʊθ/ *adj., adv.* **1** (*also* **South**) (only *before* a noun) (GEOGRAPHY) in the south: *the south coast of Cornwall* **2** to or towards the south: *The house faces south.* ◇ *We live just south of Birmingham.* **3** (used about a wind) coming from the south

southbound /'saʊθbaʊnd/ *adj.* (GEOGRAPHY) travelling or leading towards the south

ˌsouth-'east¹ (*also* **the South-East**) *noun* [sing.] (*abbr.* **SE**) (GEOGRAPHY) the direction or a region that is halfway between south and east ➲ picture at **compass**

ˌsouth-'east² *adj., adv.* (GEOGRAPHY) in, from or to the south-east of a place or country: *the south-east coast of Spain*

ˌsouth-'easterly *adj.* **1** (GEOGRAPHY) towards the south-east: *in a south-easterly direction* **2** (used about a wind) coming from the south-east

ˌsouth-'eastern *adj.* (only *before* a noun) (GEOGRAPHY) connected with the south-east of a place or country: *the south-eastern states of the US*

ˌsouth-'eastward(s) *adv.* (GEOGRAPHY) towards the south-east

southerly /'sʌðəli/ *adj.* (GEOGRAPHY) **1** to, towards or in the south: *Keep going in a southerly direction.* **2** (used about a wind) coming from the south

southern ⊷ (*also* **Southern**) /'sʌðən/ *adj.* (GEOGRAPHY) of, in or from the south of a place: *a man with a southern accent* ◇ *Greece is in Southern Europe.*

southerner (*also* **Southerner**) /'sʌðənə(r)/ *noun* [C] a person who was born in or lives in the southern part of a country OPP **northerner**

the ˌSouthern 'Lights *noun* [pl.] (*also* **aurora australis**) (ASTRONOMY) bands of coloured light that are sometimes seen in the sky at night in the most southern countries of the world

the ˌSouth 'Pole *noun* [sing.] (GEOGRAPHY) the point on the earth's surface which is furthest south ➲ picture at **earth**

ˌsouth-south-'east *noun* [sing.] (*abbr.* **SSE**) (GEOGRAPHY) the direction halfway between south and south-east

ˌsouth-south-'west *noun* [sing.] (*abbr.* **SSW**) (GEOGRAPHY) the direction halfway between south and south-west

southward /'saʊθwəd/ (*also* **southwards**) *adj., adv.* (GEOGRAPHY) towards the south

ˌsouth-ˈwest¹ (*also* **the South-West**) **noun** [sing.] (*abbr.* **SW**) (**GEOGRAPHY**) the direction or region halfway between south and west ➲ picture at **compass**

ˌsouth-ˈwest² *adj.*, *adv.* (**GEOGRAPHY**) in, from or to the south-west of a place or country: *the south-west coast of France* ◇ *Our garden faces south-west.*

ˌsouth-ˈwesterly *adj.* (**GEOGRAPHY**) **1** towards the south-west: *in a south-westerly direction* **2** (used about a wind) coming from the south-west

ˌsouth-ˈwestern *adj.* (only *before* a noun) (**GEOGRAPHY**) connected with the south-west of a place or country

ˌsouth-ˈwestward(s) *adv.* (**GEOGRAPHY**) towards the south-west: *Follow the B409 south-westward for twenty miles.*

souvenir /ˌsuːvəˈnɪə(r)/ **noun** [C] (**TOURISM**) something that you keep to remind you of somewhere you have been on holiday or of a special event: *I brought back a menu as a souvenir of my trip.*

sovereign¹ /ˈsɒvrɪn/ **noun** [C] (**POLITICS**) a king or queen

sovereign² /ˈsɒvrɪn/ *adj.* **1** (**POLITICS**) (used about a country) not controlled by any other country; independent **2** having the highest possible authority

sovereignty /ˈsɒvrənti/ **noun** [U] (**POLITICS**) the power that a country has to control its own government

sow¹ /saʊ/ **noun** [C] (**AGRICULTURE**) an adult female pig ➲ note at **pig**

sow² /səʊ/ **verb** [T] (*pt* **sowed**; *pp* **sown** /səʊn/ or **sowed**) **~ A (in B)**; **~ B (with A)** (**AGRICULTURE**) to plant seeds in the ground: *to sow seeds in pots* ◇ *to sow a field with wheat*

soya /ˈsɔɪə/ (*AmE* **soy** /sɔɪ/) **noun** [U] a plant on which SOYA BEANS grow; the food obtained from those BEANS: *soya flour/milk/oil*

ˈsoya bean (*AmE* **ˈsoy bean**) **noun** [C] a type of BEAN that can be cooked and eaten or used to make many different kinds of food, for example flour, oil and a sort of milk

ˌsoy ˈsauce (*also* **ˌsoya ˈsauce**) **noun** [U] a thin dark brown sauce that is made from SOYA BEANS and has a salty taste, used in Chinese and Japanese cooking

spa /spɑː/ **noun** [C] a place where mineral water comes out of the ground and where people go to drink this water because it is considered to be healthy

space¹ 🔑 /speɪs/ **noun** **1** [C,U] **~ (for sb/sth) (to do sth)** a place or an area that is empty or not used: *Is there enough space for me to park the car there?* ◇ *Shelves would* **take up** *less* **space** *than a cupboard.* ◇ *a parking space* ◇ *We're a bit short of space.* ◇ *There's a space here for you to write your name.* ◇ *Leave a space after the comma.* ➲ look at **room** **2** [U] (*also* **ˌouter ˈspace**) (often used to form compound nouns) (**ASTRONOMY**) the area which surrounds the planet Earth and the other planets and stars: *space travel* ◇ *a spaceman/spacewoman* (=a person who travels in space) **3** [C, usually sing.] a period of time: *Priti had been ill three times* **in /within the space of** *four months.* ◇ *He's achieved a lot in* **a short space of time**. **4** [U] time and freedom to think and do what you want: *I need some space to think.*

space² /speɪs/ **verb** [T] **~ sth (out)** to arrange things so that there are empty spaces between them

spacecraft /ˈspeɪskrɑːft/ **noun** [C] (*pl.* **spacecraft**) (**ASTRONOMY**) a vehicle that travels in space

ˌspaced ˈout *adj.* (*informal*) not completely conscious of what is happening around you, often because of taking drugs

ˈspace probe **noun** [C] = PROBE

spaceship /ˈspeɪsʃɪp/ **noun** [C] (**ASTRONOMY**) a vehicle that travels in space, carrying people

ˈspace shuttle **noun** [C] (**ASTRONOMY**) a vehicle that can travel into space and land like a plane when it returns to Earth

spacesuit /ˈspeɪssuːt/ **noun** [C] (**ASTRONOMY**) a special suit that covers the whole body and has a supply of air, allowing sb to survive and move around in space

spacewalk /ˈspeɪswɔːk/ **noun** [C] (**ASTRONOMY**) a period of time that an ASTRONAUT spends in space outside a SPACECRAFT

spacious /ˈspeɪʃəs/ *adj.* having a lot of space; large in size ▸ **spaciousness** **noun** [U]

spade /speɪd/ **noun** **1** [C] a tool that you use for digging ➲ picture at **agriculture** **2** **spades** [pl.] the group (**suit**) of playing cards with pointed black symbols on them: *the king of spades* **3** [C] one of the cards from this suit: *Have you got a spade?*

spaghetti /spəˈgeti/ **noun** [U] a type of PASTA (=Italian food made from flour, eggs and water) that looks like long strings: *How long does spaghetti take to cook?*

spam /spæm/ **noun** [U] (*informal*) (**COMPUTING**) advertising material sent by email to people who have not asked for it: *There are filters to block spam from your inbox.* ➲ look at **junk mail**
▸ **spam** *verb* [I,T] (**spamming**; **spammed**) (*informal*)
▸ **spamming** **noun** [U] (*informal*)

span¹ /spæn/ **noun** [C] **1** the length of sth from one end to the other: *the wingspan of a bird* **2** the length of time that sth lasts or continues: *Young children have a short attention span.*

span² /spæn/ **verb** [T] (**spanning**; **spanned**) **1** to form a bridge over sth **2** to last or continue for a particular period of time

spank /spæŋk/ **verb** [T] to hit a child on their bottom with an open hand as a punishment

spanner /ˈspænə(r)/ (*AmE* **wrench**) **noun** [C] a metal tool with an end shaped for turning NUTS and BOLTS that are used for holding things together ➲ look at **adjustable spanner** ➲ picture at **tool**

spare¹ 🔑 /speə(r)/ *adj.* **1** not needed now but kept because it may be needed in the future: *The spare tyre is kept in the boot.* ◇ *a spare room* **2** not used for work: *What do you do in your* **spare time**? **3** not being used; free: *There were no seats spare so we had to stand.* ▸ **spare** **noun** [C]: *The fuse has blown. Where do you keep your spares?*

spare² /speə(r)/ **verb** [T] **1** **~ sth (for sb)**; **~ (sb) sth** to be able to give sth to sb: *I suppose I can spare you a few minutes.* **2** **~ sb (from) sth/doing sth** to save sb from having an unpleasant experience: *You could spare yourself waiting if you book in advance.* **3** **~ no effort, expense, etc.** to do sth as well as possible without limiting the money, time, etc. involved: *No expense was spared at the wedding.* ◇ *He spared no effort in trying to find a job.* **4** **~ sb/sth (from sth)** to not hurt or damage sb/sth

IDM **to spare** more than is needed: *There's no time to spare. We must leave straight away.*

ˌspare ˈpart **noun** [C] a part for a machine, engine, etc. that you can use to replace an old part which is damaged or broken

ˌ**spare 'rib** ***noun*** [C] a bone (**rib**) of meat from a pig (**pork**) with most of the meat cut off

sparing /'speərɪŋ/ ***adj.*** (*formal*) using only a little of sth; careful ▶ **sparingly** ***adv.***

spark¹ /spɑːk/ ***noun*** **1** [C] a very small bright piece of burning material: *A spark set fire to the carpet.* **2** [C] a flash of light that is caused by electricity: *A spark ignites the fuel in a car engine.* **3** [C,U] an exciting quality that sb/sth has

spark² /spɑːk/ ***verb***
PHR V **spark sth off** to cause sth: *Eric's comments sparked off a tremendous argument.*

sparkle /'spɑːkl/ ***verb*** [I] to shine with many small points of light: *The river sparkled in the sunlight.* ▶ **sparkle** ***noun*** [C,U]

sparkling /'spɑːklɪŋ/ ***adj.*** **1** shining with many small points of light: *sparkling blue eyes* **2** (used about a drink) containing bubbles of gas: *sparkling wine/mineral water*

'**spark plug** ***noun*** [C] a small piece of equipment in an engine that produces a SPARK to make the fuel burn and start the engine

sparrow /'spærəʊ/ ***noun*** [C] a small brown and grey bird that is common in many parts of the world

sparse /spɑːs/ ***adj.*** small in quantity or amount: *a sparse crowd* ◇ *He just had a few sparse hairs on his head.* ▶ **sparsely** ***adv.***: *a sparsely populated area* ▶ **sparseness** ***noun*** [U]

spartan /'spɑːtn/ ***adj.*** (*formal*) very simple and not comfortable: *spartan living conditions*

spasm /'spæzəm/ ***noun*** [C,U] (**HEALTH**) a sudden movement of a muscle that you cannot control: *He had painful muscular spasms in his leg.*

spat past tense, past participle of **spit¹**

spate /speɪt/ ***noun*** [sing.] a large number or amount of sth happening at one time: *There has been a spate of burglaries in the area recently.*

spatial /'speɪʃl/ ***adj.*** (*formal*) connected with the size or position of sth

spatter /'spætə(r)/ ***verb*** [T] ~ **sb/sth (with sth)**; ~ **sth (on sb/sth)** to cover sb/sth with small drops of sth wet

spatula /'spætʃələ/ ***noun*** [C] a tool with a wide flat part used in cooking for mixing and spreading things

speak 🔑 /spiːk/ ***verb*** (*pt* **spoke** /spəʊk/; *pp* **spoken** /'spəʊkən/) **1** [I] ~ **(to sb) (about sb/sth)**; ~ **(of sth)** to talk or say things: *I'd like to speak to the manager, please.* ◇ *Could you speak more slowly?* ◇ *I was so angry I could hardly speak.* **2** [T] (not used in the continuous tenses) to know and be able to use a language: *Does anyone here speak German?* ◇ *She speaks (in) Greek to her parents.* ◇ *a French-speaking guide* **3** [I] ~ **(on/about sth)** to make a speech to a group of people **4** [I] (*informal*) **be speaking (to sb)** to be friendly with sb again after an argument
IDM **be on speaking terms (with sb)** to be friendly with sb again after an argument: *Thankfully they are back on speaking terms again.*
so to speak used when you are describing sth in a way that sounds strange: *She turned green, so to speak, after watching a television programme about the environment.*
speak for itself to be very clear so that no other explanation is needed: *The statistics speak for themselves.*
speak/talk of the devil → DEVIL
speak your mind to say exactly what you think, even though you might offend sb
PHR V **speak for sb** to express the thoughts or opinions of sb else
speak out (against sth) to say publicly that you think sth is bad or wrong
speak up to speak louder

speaker 🔑 /'spiːkə(r)/ ***noun*** [C] **1** a person who makes a speech to a group of people: *Tonight's speaker is a well-known writer and journalist.* **2** a person who speaks a particular language: *She's a fluent Russian speaker.* **3** = LOUDSPEAKER (1) ➲ picture at **computer**

spear /spɪə(r)/ ***noun*** [C] a long pole with a sharp point at one end, used for hunting or fighting ➲ picture at **weapon**

spearhead /'spɪəhed/ ***noun*** [C, usually sing.] a person or group that begins or leads an attack ▶ **spearhead** ***verb*** [T]

spearmint /'spɪəmɪnt/ ***noun*** [U] a type of leaf with a strong fresh taste that is used in sweets, etc.: *spearmint chewing gum* ➲ look at **peppermint**

special¹ 🔑 /'speʃl/ ***adj.*** **1** not usual or ordinary; important for some particular reason: *a special occasion* ◇ *Please take special care of it.* ◇ *Are you doing anything special tonight?* **2** (only *before* a noun) for a particular purpose: *Andy goes to a special school for the deaf.* ◇ *There's a special tool for doing that.*

special² /'speʃl/ ***noun*** [C] something that is not of the usual or ordinary type: *an all-night election special on TV* ◇ *I'm going to cook one of my specials tonight.*

ˌ**special ef'fects** (*also* **SFX**) ***noun*** [pl.] (**ARTS AND MEDIA**) unusual or exciting pieces of action in films or television programmes, that are created by computers or clever photography to show things that do not normally exist or happen

specialist 🔑 /'speʃəlɪst/ ***noun*** [C] a person with special or deep knowledge of a particular subject: *She's a specialist in diseases of cattle.* ◇ *I have to see a heart specialist.* ◇ *to give specialist advice*

speciality /ˌspeʃi'æləti/ ***noun*** [C] (*pl.* **specialities**) (*AmE* **specialty**; *pl.* **specialties**) **1** (**EDUCATION**) an area of study or a subject that you know a lot about **2** something made by a person, place, business, etc. that is very good and that they or it are known for: *The cheese is a speciality of the region.*

specialize (also **-ise**) /'speʃəlaɪz/ ***verb*** [I] ~ **(in sth)** to give most of your attention to one subject, type of product, etc.: *This shop specializes in clothes for taller men.* ▶ **specialization** (also **-isation**) /ˌspeʃəlaɪ'zeɪʃn/ ***noun*** [U]

specialized (also **-ised**) /'speʃəlaɪzd/ ***adj.*** **1** to be used for a particular purpose: *a specialized system* **2** having or needing deep or special knowledge of a particular subject: *We have specialized staff to help you with any problems.*

specially 🔑 /'speʃəli/ (*also* **especially**) ***adv.*** **1** for a particular purpose or reason: *I made this specially for you.* **2** particularly; very; more than usual: *The restaurant has a great atmosphere but the food is not specially good.* ◇ *It's not an especially difficult exam.*

ˌ**special 'needs** ***noun*** [pl.] (*especially BrE*) (**HEALTH, EDUCATION**) needs that a person has because of mental or physical problems: *She teaches children with special needs.*

ˌ**special 'offer** ***noun*** [C,U] (**BUSINESS**) a product that is sold at less than its usual price, especially in order to persuade people to buy it; the act of offering goods in this way: *French wine is **on special offer** this week.*

specialty /ˈspeʃəlti/ (*AmE*) = SPECIALITY

species /ˈspiːʃiːz/ ***noun*** [C] (*pl.* **species**) (**BIOLOGY**) a group of plants or animals that are all the same and that can breed together: *This conservation group aims to protect endangered species.* ◇ *a rare species of frog* ➲ picture on **page 29**

specific 🔑 AW /spəˈsɪfɪk/ ***adj.*** **1** ~ (**about sth**) detailed or exact: *You must give the class specific instructions on what they have to do.* ◇ *Can you be more specific about what the man was wearing?* **2** particular; not general: *Everyone has been given a specific job to do.*

specifically 🔑 AW /spəˈsɪfɪkli/ ***adv.*** **1** in a detailed and exact way: *I specifically told you not to go near the water!* **2** connected with or intended for one particular thing only: *a play written specifically for radio*

specification AW /ˌspesɪfɪˈkeɪʃn/ ***noun*** [C,U] detailed information about how sth is or should be built or made

specify AW /ˈspesɪfaɪ/ ***verb*** [T] (*pres. part.* **specifying**; *3rd person sing. pres.* **specifies**; *pt, pp* **specified**) to say or name sth clearly or in detail: *The fire regulations specify the maximum number of people allowed in.*

specimen /ˈspesɪmən/ ***noun*** [C] **1** (**SCIENCE**) an example of a particular type of thing, especially intended to be studied by experts or scientists ➲ note at **example 2** (**HEALTH**) a small amount of sth that is tested for medical or scientific purposes: *Specimens of the patient's blood were tested in the hospital laboratory.*

speck /spek/ ***noun*** [C] a very small spot or mark: *a speck of dust/dirt*

specs /speks/ (*informal*) = GLASSES

spectacle /ˈspektəkl/ ***noun*** [C] something that is impressive or shocking to look at

spectacles /ˈspektəklz/ (*formal*) = GLASSES

spectacular /spekˈtækjələ(r)/ ***adj.*** very impressive to see: *The view from the top of the hill is quite spectacular.* ▶ **spectacularly** ***adv.***

spectator /spekˈteɪtə(r)/ ***noun*** [C] a person who is watching an event, especially a sporting event

specˈtator sport ***noun*** [C] (**SPORT**) a sport that many people watch; a sport that is interesting to watch

spectre (*AmE* **specter**) /ˈspektə(r)/ ***noun*** [C] **1** something unpleasant that people are afraid might happen in the future: *the spectre of unemployment* **2** (*old-fashioned*) = GHOST

spectroscopy /spekˈtrɒskəpi/ ***noun*** [U] (**CHEMISTRY, PHYSICS**) the study of forming and looking at SPECTRA

spectrum /ˈspektrəm/ ***noun*** [C, usually sing.] (*pl.* **spectra** /ˈspektrə/) **1** (**PHYSICS**) the set of seven colours into which white light can be separated: *You can see the colours of the spectrum in a rainbow.* **2** all the possible varieties of sth: *The speakers represented the whole spectrum of political opinions.*

speculate /ˈspekjuleɪt/ ***verb*** **1** [I,T] ~ (**about/on sth**); ~ **that...** to make a guess about sth: *to speculate about the result of the next election* **2** [I] (**BUSINESS**) to buy and sell with the aim of making money but with the risk of losing it: *to speculate on the stock market* ▶ **speculator** ***noun*** [C]

speculation /ˌspekjuˈleɪʃn/ ***noun*** **1** [U,C] ~ (**that...**); ~ (**about/over sth**) the act of forming opinions about what has happened or what might happen without knowing all the facts: *There was widespread speculation that she was going to resign.* **2** [U,C] ~ (**in sth**) (**BUSINESS**) the activity of buying and selling goods or shares in a company in the hope of making a profit, but with the risk of losing money: *speculation in oil*

speculative /ˈspekjələtɪv/ ***adj.*** **1** based on guessing without knowing all the facts; showing that you are trying to guess sth: *a speculative look/glance* **2** (**BUSINESS**) done with the aim of making money but also with the risk of losing it: *speculative investment*

speculum /ˈspekjələm/ ***noun*** [C] (**HEALTH**) a metal instrument that is used to make a hole or tube in the body wider so it can be examined

sped past tense, past participle of **speed²**

speech 🔑 /spiːtʃ/ ***noun*** **1** [C] a formal talk that you give to a group of people: *The Chancellor is going to **make a speech** to city businessmen.* **2** [U] the ability to speak: *He lost the **power of speech** after the accident.* ◇ *freedom of speech* (= being allowed to express your opinions openly) **3** [U] the particular way of speaking of a person or group of people: *She's doing a study of children's speech.* **4** [C] (**ARTS AND MEDIA, LITERATURE**) a group of words that one person must say in a play

speechless /ˈspiːtʃləs/ ***adj.*** not able to speak, for example because you are shocked, angry, etc.

ˈspeech marks = QUOTATION MARKS

speed

$$\text{speed} = \frac{\text{distance travelled}}{\text{time taken}}$$

This arrow travels 50m each second it is in flight. Its speed is 50m/s.

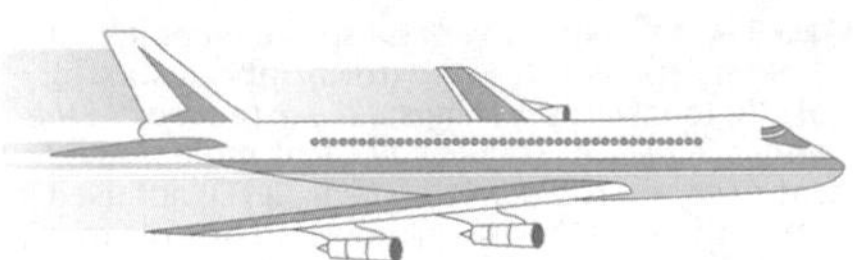

This aeroplane travels 1000km each hour it is in flight. Its speed is 1000km/h.

speed¹ 🔑 /spiːd/ ***noun*** **1** [U] fast movement: *The bus began to **pick up speed** down the hill.* ◇ *The bus was travelling **at speed** when it hit the wall.* **2** [C,U] (**PHYSICS**) the rate at which sb/sth moves or travels: *The car was travelling **at a speed of** 140 kilometres an hour.* ◇ *to travel **at top/high/full/maximum speed**.*

speed² /spiːd/ ***verb*** [I] (*pt, pp* **sped** /sped/) **1** to go or move very quickly: *He sped round the corner on his bicycle.* **2** (only used in the continuous tenses) to drive a car, etc. faster than the legal speed limit: *The police said she had been speeding.*

PHR V **speed (sth) up** (*pt, pp* **speeded**) to go or make sth go faster: *The new computer system should speed up production in the factory.*

speedboat /ˈspiːdbəʊt/ ***noun*** [C] a small fast boat with an engine

ˈ**speed bump** (*AmE and BrE also* ˈ**speed hump**, *BrE also, informal* ˌ**sleeping poˈliceman**) ***noun*** [C] a raised area across a road that is put there to make traffic go slower

ˈ**speed camera** ***noun*** [C] (*BrE*) (LAW) a machine which takes pictures of vehicles that are being driven too fast. The pictures are then used as evidence so that the drivers can be punished.

ˈ**speed hump** ***noun*** [C] = SPEED BUMP

speeding /ˈspiːdɪŋ/ ***noun*** [U] (LAW) driving a car, etc. faster than the legal speed limit

ˈ**speed limit** ***noun*** [C, usually sing.] (LAW) the highest speed that you may drive without breaking the law on a particular road: *He was going way* ***over the speed limit*** *when the police stopped him.*

speedometer /spiːˈdɒmɪtə(r)/ ***noun*** [C] a piece of equipment in a vehicle that tells you how fast you are travelling

ˈ**speed trap** (*BrE also* ˈ**radar trap**) ***noun*** [C] (LAW) a place on a road where police use special equipment to catch drivers who are going too fast

speedway /ˈspiːdweɪ/ ***noun*** [U] the sport of racing motorbikes around a track

speedy /ˈspiːdi/ ***adj.*** fast; quick: *a speedy response/reply* ▶ **speedily** ***adv.*** ▶ **speediness** ***noun*** [U]

spell¹ 🔑 /spel/ ***verb*** (*pt, pp* **spelled** /speld/ or **spelt** /spelt/) **1** [I,T] (LANGUAGE) to write or say the letters of a word in the correct order: *I could never spell very well at school.* ◇ ***How do you spell*** *your surname?* ◇ *His name is spelt P-H-I-L-I-P.* **2** [T] (used about a set of letters) to form a particular word: *If you add an 'e' to 'car' it spells 'care'.* **3** [T] to mean sth; to have sth as a result: *Another poor harvest would* ***spell disaster*** *for the region.*

PHR V **spell sth out 1** to write or say the letters of a word or name in the correct order: *I have an unusual name, so I always have to spell it out to people.* **2** to express sth in a very clear and direct way

spell² 🔑 /spel/ ***noun*** [C] **1** a short period of time: *a spell of cold weather* **2** (especially in stories) magic words or actions that cause sb to be in a particular state or condition

spellcheck /ˈspeltʃek/ ***verb*** [I,T] (COMPUTING) to use a computer program to check your writing to see if your spelling is correct ▶ **spellcheck** ***noun*** [C]

spellchecker /ˈspeltʃekə(r)/ (*also* **spellcheck**) ***noun*** [C] (COMPUTING) a computer program that checks your writing to see if your spelling is correct

spelling 🔑 /ˈspelɪŋ/ ***noun*** **1** [C,U] (LANGUAGE) the way that letters are arranged to make a word: *'Center' is the American spelling of 'centre'.* **2** [U] the ability to write the letters of a word correctly: *Roger is very poor at spelling.*

spelt past tense, past participle of **spell¹**

spend 🔑 /spend/ ***verb*** (*pt, pp* **spent** /spent/) **1** [I,T] ~ (**sth**) (**on sth**) to give or pay money for sth: *How much do you spend on food each week?* ◇ *You shouldn't go on spending like that.* **2** [T] ~ **sth** (**on sth/doing sth**) to pass time: *I spent a whole evening writing letters.* ◇ *I'm spending the weekend at my parents' house.* ◇ *He spent two years in Rome.* ◇ *I don't want to spend too much time on this project.*

spending /ˈspendɪŋ/ ***noun*** [U] the amount of money that is spent by a government or an organization

sperm /spɜːm/ ***noun*** (BIOLOGY) **1** [C] (*pl.* **sperm** or **sperms**) a cell that is produced in the sex organs of a male and that can join with a female egg to produce young ➲ picture at **fertilize 2** [U] the liquid that contains **sperms**

sphere AW /sfɪə(r)/ ***noun*** [C] **1** (GEOMETRY) any round object shaped like a ball ➲ picture at **solid 2** an area of interest or activity ▶ **spherical** AW /ˈsferɪkl/ ***adj.***

spheroid /ˈsfɪərɔɪd/ ***noun*** [C] (GEOMETRY) a solid object that is approximately the same shape as a SPHERE

sphincter /ˈsfɪŋktə(r)/ ***noun*** [C] (BIOLOGY, ANATOMY) a ring of muscle that surrounds an opening in the body and that can become tighter in order to close the opening: *the anal sphincter*

sphinx /sfɪŋks/ ***noun*** [C] (HISTORY) an ancient Egyptian stone statue of a creature with a human head and the body of a LION lying down

spice¹ 🔑 /spaɪs/ ***noun*** **1** [C,U] a substance, especially a powder, that is made from a plant and used to give flavour to food: *I use a lot of herbs and spices in my cooking.* ◇ *Pepper and paprika are two common spices.* ➲ look at **herb 2** [U] excitement and interest: *to* ***add spice*** *to a situation*

spice² /spaɪs/ ***verb*** [T] ~ **sth** (**up**) (**with sth**) **1** to add spice to food: *He always spices his cooking with lots of chilli powder.* **2** to add excitement to sth

spicy 🔑 /ˈspaɪsi/ ***adj.*** **1** (used about food) having a strong taste because spices have been used to flavour it: *Do you like spicy food?* **2** (*informal*) (used about a story, piece of news, etc.) exciting and slightly shocking

spider 🔑 /ˈspaɪdə(r)/ ***noun*** [C] a type of small animal like an insect with eight legs. Spiders spin WEBS to catch insects for food.
➲ picture on **page 29**

spike /spaɪk/ ***noun*** [C] a piece of metal, wood, etc. that has a sharp point at one end

spill /spɪl/ ***verb*** (*pt, pp* **spilt** /spɪlt/ or **spilled**) **1** [I,T] (used especially about a liquid) to accidentally come out of a container; to make a liquid, etc. do this: *The bag split, and sugar spilled everywhere.* ◇ *Some water had spilled out of the bucket onto the floor.* ◇ *I've spilt some coffee on the desk.* **2** [I] ~ **out, over, into, etc.** to come out of a place suddenly and go in different directions: *The train stopped and everyone spilled out.* ▶ **spill** ***noun*** [C]: *Many seabirds died as a result of the oil spill.*

IDM **spill the beans** (*informal*) to tell a person about sth that should be a secret

spin¹ 🔑 /spɪn/ ***verb*** (**spinning**; *pt, pp* **spun** /spʌn/) **1** [I,T] ~ (**sth**) (**round**) to turn or to make sth turn round quickly: *Mary spun round when she heard someone call her name.* ◇ *to spin a ball/coin/wheel* **2** [I,T] to make thread from a mass of wool, cotton, etc.: *A spider spins a web.* **3** [T] to remove water from clothes that have just been washed by turning them round and round very fast in a machine

PHR V **spin sth out** to make sth last as long as possible

spin² /spɪn/ ***noun*** [C,U] **1** an act of making sth spin: *She* ***put a lot of spin on*** *the ball.* **2** (POLITICS) a way of talking publicly about a difficult situation, a mistake, etc. that makes it sound positive for you

IDM **go/take sb for a spin** to go/take sb out in a car or other vehicle

spinach /ˈspɪnɪtʃ; -ɪdʒ/ ***noun*** [U] a plant with large dark green leaves that can be cooked and eaten as a vegetable

sporadic /spəˈrædɪk/ ***adj.*** not done or happening regularly ▶ **sporadically** /-kli/ ***adv.***

spore /spɔː(r)/ ***noun*** [C] (BIOLOGY) one of the very small cells like seeds that are produced by some plants and that develop into new plants

sport 🔑 /spɔːt/ ***noun*** **1** [U] physical games or activity that you do for exercise or because you enjoy it: *John **did a lot of sport** when he was at school.* ◇ *Do you like sport?* **2** [C] a particular game or type of sport: *What's your favourite sport?* ◇ ***winter sports*** (=skiing, skating, etc.) ▶ **sporting** ***adj.***: *a major sporting event*

ˈ**sports car** ***noun*** [C] a low, fast car often with a roof that you can open

sportsman /ˈspɔːtsmən/ **sportswoman** /ˈspɔːtswʊmən/ ***noun*** [C] (*pl.* **-men** /-mən/) (*pl.* **-women** /-wɪmɪn/) (SPORT) a person who does a lot of sport or who is good at sport: *a keen sportsman*

sportsmanlike /ˈspɔːtsmənlaɪk/ ***adj.*** behaving in a fair, generous and polite way when you are playing a game or doing sport

sportsmanship /ˈspɔːtsmənʃɪp/ ***noun*** [U] the quality of being fair, generous and polite when you are playing a game or doing sport

sportswear /ˈspɔːtsweə(r)/ ***noun*** [U] clothes that are worn for playing sports or in informal situations

sporty /ˈspɔːti/ ***adj.*** (**sportier**; **sportiest**) (*informal*) (*especially BrE*) (SPORT) liking or good at sport: *I'm not very sporty.*

spot¹ 🔑 /spɒt/ ***noun*** [C] **1** a small round mark on a surface: *Leopards have dark spots.* ◇ *a blue skirt with red spots on it* ➲ adjective **spotted** **2** a small dirty mark on sth: *grease/rust spots* **3** (HEALTH) a small red or yellow lump that appears on your skin: *Many teenagers **get spots**.* ➲ adjective **spotty** **4** a particular place or area: *a quiet/lonely/secluded spot* **5** [usually sing.] a ~ **of sth** (*BrE, informal*) a small amount of sth **6** = SPOTLIGHT (1)

IDM **have a soft spot for sb/sth** → SOFT

on the spot **1** immediately: *Paul was caught stealing money and was dismissed on the spot.* **2** at the place where sth happened or where sb/sth is needed: *The fire brigade were on the spot within five minutes.*

put sb on the spot to make sb answer a difficult question or make a difficult decision without having much time to think

spot² /spɒt/ ***verb*** [T] (**spotting**; **spotted**) (not used in the continuous tenses) to see or notice sb/sth, especially suddenly or when it is not easy to do: *I've spotted a couple of spelling mistakes.*

ˌ**spot** ˈ**check** ***noun*** [C] a check that is made suddenly and without warning on a few things or people chosen from a group

spotless /ˈspɒtləs/ ***adj.*** perfectly clean

spotlight /ˈspɒtlaɪt/ ***noun*** **1** (*also* **spot**) [C] (ARTS AND MEDIA) a lamp that can send a single RAY of bright light onto a small area. **Spotlights** are often used in theatres. **2 the spotlight** [sing.] the centre of public attention or interest: ***to be in the spotlight***

ˌ**spot** ˈ**on** ***adj.*** (*BrE, informal*) (not before a noun) exactly right: *Your estimate was spot on.*

spotted /ˈspɒtɪd/ ***adj.*** (used about clothes, cloth, etc.) covered with round shapes of a different colour: *a spotted blouse*

spotty /ˈspɒti/ ***adj.*** (HEALTH) having SPOTS (=small red or yellow lumps on your skin): *a spotty teenager*

spouse /spaʊs/ ***noun*** [C] (*written*) your husband or wife

spout¹ /spaʊt/ ***noun*** [C] a tube or pipe through which liquid comes out: *the spout of a teapot*

spout² /spaʊt/ ***verb*** [I,T] **1** to send out a liquid with great force; to make a liquid do this **2** (*informal*) ~ **(on/off) (about sth)** to say sth, using a lot of words, in a way that is boring or annoying

sprain /spreɪn/ ***verb*** [T] (HEALTH) to injure part of your body, especially your wrist or your ankle by suddenly bending or turning it: *to sprain your ankle* ➲ note at **injure** ▶ **sprain** ***noun*** [C]

sprang past tense of **spring²**

sprawl /sprɔːl/ ***verb*** [I] **1** to sit or lie with your arms and legs spread out in an untidy way: *People lay sprawled out in the sun.* **2** to cover a large area of land ▶ **sprawling** ***adj.***: *the sprawling city suburbs*

spray¹ 🔑 /spreɪ/ ***noun*** **1** [U] liquid in very small drops that is sent through the air: *clouds of spray from the waves* **2** [C,U] liquid in a special container (**an aerosol**) that is forced out under pressure when you push a button: *hairspray*

spray² 🔑 /spreɪ/ ***verb*** [I,T] (used about a liquid) to be forced out of a container or sent through the air in very small drops; to send a liquid out in this way: *The crops are regularly sprayed with pesticide.*

spread¹ 🔑 /spred/ ***verb*** (*pt, pp* **spread**) **1** [I,T] to affect a larger area or a bigger group of people; to make sth do this: *The fire spread rapidly because of the strong wind.* ◇ *Rats and flies **spread disease**.* ◇ *to **spread rumours** about sb* **2** [T] ~ **sth (out) (on/over sth)** to open sth that has been folded so that it covers a larger area; to move things so that they cover a larger area: *Spread the map out on the table so we can all see it!* **3** [T] ~ **A on/over B**; ~ **B with A** to cover a surface with a layer of a soft substance: *to spread jam on bread* ◇ *to spread bread with jam* **4** [T] ~ **sth**

sports equipment

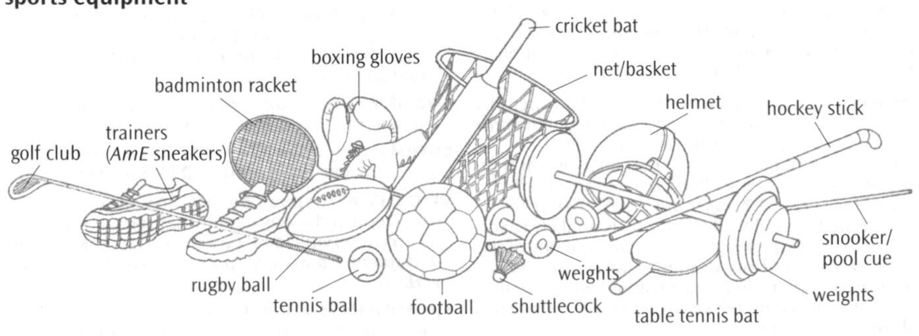

(out) (over sth) to separate sth into parts and divide them between different times or people: *You can spread your repayments over a period of three years.*
PHR V **spread (sb/yourself) out** to move away from the others in a group of people in order to cover a larger area: *The police spread out to search the whole area.*

spread² /spred/ ***noun*** **1** [U] an increase in the amount or number of sth that there is, or in the area that is affected by sth: *Dirty drinking water encourages **the spread of disease**.* **2** [C,U] a soft food that you put on bread **3** [C] (ARTS AND MEDIA) a newspaper or magazine article that covers one or more pages: *a double-page spread*

spreadsheet /ˈspredʃiːt/ ***noun*** [C] (COMPUTING) a computer program for working with rows of numbers, used especially for doing accounts

spree /spriː/ ***noun*** [C] (*informal*) a short time that you spend doing sth you enjoy, often doing too much of it: *to **go on a** shopping/spending **spree***

sprig /sprɪɡ/ ***noun*** [C] a small piece of a plant with leaves on it

spring

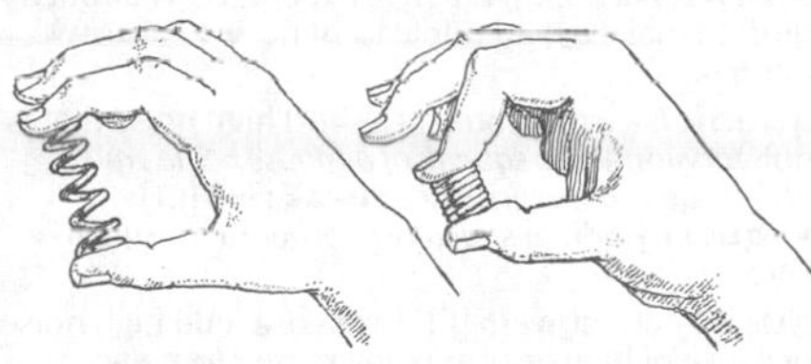

spring¹ ⊶ /sprɪŋ/ ***noun*** **1** [C,U] the season of the year between winter and summer when the weather gets warmer and plants begin to grow: *Daffodils bloom **in spring**.* ➲ picture at **season** **2** [C] a long piece of thin metal or wire that is bent round and round. After you push or pull a spring it goes back to its original shape and size: *bed springs* **3** [C] (GEOGRAPHY) a place where water comes up naturally from under the ground: *a hot spring* **4** [C] a sudden jump upwards or forwards

spring² /sprɪŋ/ ***verb*** [I] (*pt* **sprang** /spræŋ/; *pp* **sprung** /sprʌŋ/) **1** to jump or move quickly: *When the alarm went off, Ray sprang out of bed.* ◇ *to spring to your feet* (=stand up suddenly) ◇ (*figurative*) *to spring to sb's defence/assistance* (=to quickly defend or help sb) **2** (used about an object) to move suddenly and violently: *The branch sprang back and hit him in the face.* **3** to appear or come somewhere suddenly: *Tears sprang to her eyes.* ◇ *Where did you just spring from?*
IDM **come/spring to mind** → MIND¹
PHR V **spring from sth** (*written*) to be the result of: *The idea for the book sprang from an experience she had while travelling in India.*
spring sth on sb (*informal*) to do or say sth that sb is not expecting
spring up to appear or develop quickly or suddenly

ˈspring balance ***noun*** [C] (*BrE*) a device that uses a hook on a spring to measure the weight of things

springboard /ˈsprɪŋbɔːd/ ***noun*** [C] **1** a low board that bends and that helps you jump higher, for example before you jump into a swimming pool **2 a ~ (for/to sth)** something that helps you start an activity, especially by giving you ideas

ˌspring-ˈclean ***verb*** [T] to clean a house, room, etc. very well, including the parts that you do not usually clean

ˌspring ˈonion ***noun*** [C,U] a type of small onion with a long green central part and leaves

springtime /ˈsprɪŋtaɪm/ ***noun*** [U] (*written*) the season of spring

springy /ˈsprɪŋi/ ***adj.*** going quickly back to its original shape or size after being pushed, pulled, etc.: *soft springy grass*

sprinkle /ˈsprɪŋkl/ ***verb*** [T] **~ A (on/onto/over B)**; **~ B (with A)** to throw drops of liquid or small pieces of sth over a surface: *to sprinkle sugar on a cake* ◇ *to sprinkle a cake with sugar*

sprinkler /ˈsprɪŋklə(r)/ ***noun*** [C] a device with holes in it that sends out water in small drops. **Sprinklers** are used in gardens, to keep the grass green, and in buildings, to stop fires from spreading.

sprint /sprɪnt/ ***verb*** [I,T] (SPORT) to run a short distance as fast as you can ▶ **sprint** ***noun*** [C] ▶ **sprinter** ***noun*** [C]

sprocket /ˈsprɒkɪt/ ***noun*** [C] **1** (*also* **ˈsprocket wheel**) a wheel with a row of teeth around the edge that connect with the holes of a bicycle chain or with holes in a film, etc. in order to turn it **2** one of the teeth on such a wheel

sprout¹ /spraʊt/ ***verb*** [I,T] (BIOLOGY) (used about a plant) to begin to grow or to produce new leaves: *The seeds are sprouting.*

sprout² /spraʊt/ ***noun*** [C] **1** = BRUSSELS SPROUT **2** a new part that has grown on a plant

spruce /spruːs/ ***verb***
PHR V **spruce (sb/yourself) up** to make sb/yourself clean and tidy

sprung past participle of **spring²**

spud /spʌd/ ***noun*** [C] (*informal*) a potato

spun past participle of **spin¹**

spur¹ /spɜː(r)/ ***noun*** [C] **1** a piece of metal that a rider wears on the back of their boots to encourage the horse to go faster **2 a ~ (to sth)** something that encourages you to do sth or that makes sth happen more quickly **3** (GEOGRAPHY) a part of a hill that sticks out from the rest, often with lower ground around it
IDM **on the spur of the moment** without planning; suddenly

spur² /spɜː(r)/ ***verb*** [T] (**spurring**; **spurred**) **~ sb/sth (on/onto sth)** to encourage sb or make them work harder or faster: *The letter spurred me into action.* ◇ *We were spurred on by the positive feedback from customers.*

spurn /spɜːn/ ***verb*** [T] (*formal*) to refuse sth that sb has offered to you: *to spurn an offer of friendship*

spurt /spɜːt/ ***verb*** **1** [I,T] (used about a liquid) to come out quickly with great force; to make a liquid do this: *Blood spurted from the wound.* **2** [I] to suddenly increase your speed or effort ▶ **spurt** ***noun*** [C]

spy¹ /spaɪ/ ***noun*** [C] (*pl.* **spies**) a person who tries to get secret information about another country, person or organization

spy² /spaɪ/ ***verb*** (*pres. part.* **spying**; *3rd person sing. pres.* **spies**; *pt, pp* **spied**) **1** [I] to try to get secret information about sb/sth ➲ look at **espionage** **2** [T] (*formal*) to see
IDM **spy on sb/sth** to watch sb/sth secretly: *The man next door is spying on us.*

spyhole /ˈspaɪhəʊl/ ***noun*** [C] a small hole in a door for looking at the person on the other side before deciding to let them in

sq *abbr.* **1** =SQUARE² (6): *10 sq cm* **2 Sq.** =SQUARE¹ (2): *6 Hanover Sq.*

squabble /ˈskwɒbl/ *verb* [I] ~ **(over/about sth)** to argue in a noisy way about sth that is not very important ▶ **squabble** *noun* [C]

squad /skwɒd/ *noun* [C, with sing. or pl. verb] a group of people who work as a team: *He's a policeman with the drugs squad.*

squadron /ˈskwɒdrən/ *noun* [C, with sing. or pl. verb] a group of military aircraft or ships

squalid /ˈskwɒlɪd/ *adj.* very dirty, untidy and unpleasant: *squalid housing conditions*

squall /skwɔːl/ *noun* [C] a sudden storm with strong winds

squalor /ˈskwɒlə(r)/ *noun* [U] the state of being very dirty, untidy or unpleasant: *to live **in squalor***

squander /ˈskwɒndə(r)/ *verb* [T] ~ **sth (on sth)** to waste time, money, etc.: *He squanders his time on TV and computer games.*

square¹ 🔑 /skweə(r)/ *noun* [C] **1** (GEOMETRY) a shape that has four sides of the same length and four RIGHT ANGLES (=angles of 90°): *There are 64 squares on a chess board.* ➲ picture at **parallelogram** **2** (*also* Square) (*abbr.* Sq.) an open space in a town or city that has buildings all around it: *Protesters gathered in the town square.* ◇ *Trafalgar Square* **3** (MATHEMATICS) the number that you get when you multiply another number by itself: *Four is the square of two.* ➲ look at **squared**, **square root**

square² 🔑 /skweə(r)/ *adj., adv.* **1** having four straight sides of the same length and corners of 90°: *a square tablecloth* **2** shaped like a square or forming an angle of about 90°: *a square face* ◇ *square shoulders* **3** (not before a noun) not owing any money: *Here is the money I owe you. Now we're (all) square.* **4** (not before a noun) having equal points (in a game, etc.): *The teams were **all square** at half-time.* **5** fair or honest, especially in business matters: *a square deal* **6** (*abbr.* sq) used for talking about the area of sth: *If a room is 5 metres long and 4 metres wide, its area is 20 square metres.* **7** (used about sth that is square in shape) having sides of a particular length: *The picture is twenty centimetres square* (=each side is twenty centimetres long). **8** (*also* squarely) in an obvious and direct way: *to look sb square in the eye* ◇ *I think the blame falls squarely on her.*

IDM **a square meal** a good meal that makes you feel satisfied

square³ /skweə(r)/ *verb* [I,T] ~ **(sth) with sb/sth** to agree with sth; to make sure that sb/sth agrees with sth: *Your conclusion doesn't really square with the facts.* ◇ *If you want time off you'll have to square it with the boss.*

PHR V **square up (with sb)** to pay sb the money that you owe them

squared /skweəd/ *adj.* (MATHEMATICS) (used about a number) multiplied by itself: *Four squared is sixteen.* ➲ look at **square root**

ˌsquare ˈroot *noun* [C] (MATHEMATICS) a number that produces another particular number when it is multiplied by itself: *The square root of sixteen is four.* ➲ look at **cube root**

squash¹ /skwɒʃ/ *verb* **1** [T] to press sth so that it is damaged, changes shape or becomes flat: *The fruit at the bottom of the bag will **get squashed**.* ◇ *Move up – you're squashing me!* **2** [I,T] to go into a place, or move sb/sth to a place, where there is not much space: *We all squashed into the back of the car.* **3** [T] to destroy sth because it is a problem: *to squash sb's suggestion/plan/idea*

squash² /skwɒʃ/ *noun* **1** [C, sing.] a lot of people in a small space: *We can get ten people around the table, but it's **a bit of a squash**.* **2** [U, C] (*BrE*) a drink that is made from fruit juice and sugar. You add water to **squash** before you drink it: *orange squash* **3** [U] (SPORT) a game for two people, played on a COURT (=a special room). You play **squash** by hitting a small rubber ball against any one of the walls of the room: *a squash racket* **4** [C, U] (*pl.* **squash**) a type of vegetable that grows on the ground with hard skin and orange flesh inside, or soft yellow or green skin and white flesh inside

squat¹ /skwɒt/ *verb* [I] (**squatting**; **squatted**) **1** to rest with your weight on your feet, your legs bent and your bottom just above the ground **2** to go and live in an empty building without permission from the owner

squat² /skwɒt/ *adj.* short and fat or thick: *a squat ugly building*

squatter /ˈskwɒtə(r)/ *noun* [C] a person who is living in an empty building without the owner's permission

squawk /skwɔːk/ *verb* [I] (used especially about a bird) to make a loud unpleasant noise ▶ **squawk** *noun* [C]

squeak /skwiːk/ *noun* [C] a short high noise that is not very loud: *the squeak of a mouse* ◇ *She gave a little squeak of surprise.* ▶ **squeak** *verb* [I,T] ▶ **squeaky** *adj.*: *a squeaky floorboard* ◇ *a squeaky voice*

squeal /skwiːl/ *verb* [I,T] to make a loud high noise because of pain, fear or enjoyment: *The baby squealed in delight at the new toy.* ▶ **squeal** *noun* [C]

squeamish /ˈskwiːmɪʃ/ *adj.* easily upset by unpleasant sights, especially blood

squeeze¹ 🔑 /skwiːz/ *verb* **1** [T] ~ **sth (out)**; ~ **sth (from/out of sth)** to press sth hard for a particular purpose: *She squeezed his hand as a sign of affection.* ◇ *to squeeze a tube of toothpaste* ◇ *Squeeze a lemon/the juice of a lemon into a glass.* ◇ *I squeezed the water out of the cloth.* **2** [I,T] ~ **(sb/sth) into, through, etc. sth**; ~ **(sb/sth) through, in, past, etc.** to force sb/sth into or through a small space: *We can squeeze another person into the back of the car.* ◇ *There was just room for the bus to squeeze past.*

squeeze² 🔑 /skwiːz/ *noun* **1** [C] an act of pressing sth firmly: *He gave her hand a squeeze and told her he loved her.* **2** [C] the amount of liquid that you get from squeezing an orange, a lemon, etc.: *a squeeze of lemon* **3** [sing.] a situation where there is not much space: *It was **a tight squeeze** to get everybody around the table.* **4** [C, usually sing.] an effort to use less money, time, etc., especially with the result that there is not enough

squelch /skweltʃ/ *verb* [I] to make the sound your feet make when you are walking in deep wet mud

squid /skwɪd/ *noun* [C,U] (*pl.* **squid** or **squids**) a sea animal that we eat with a long soft body and ten TENTACLES

squid

squiggle /ˈskwɪgl/ *noun* [C] (*informal*) a quickly drawn line that goes in all directions

squint /skwɪnt/ *verb* [I] **1** ~ **(at sth)** to look at sth with your eyes almost closed: *to squint in bright sunlight* **2** to have eyes that appear to look in different directions at the same time ▶ **squint** *noun* [C]

squirm /skwɜːm/ ***verb*** [I] to move around in your chair because you are nervous, uncomfortable, etc.

squirrel /ˈskwɪrəl/ ***noun*** [C] a small red or grey animal with a long thick tail that lives in trees and eats nuts ➲ picture on **page 28**

squirt /skwɜːt/ ***verb*** [I,T] If a liquid **squirts** or if you **squirt** it, it is suddenly forced out of sth in a particular direction: *I cut the orange and juice squirted out.* ◇ *She squirted water on the flames.* ◇ *He squirted me with water.* ▶ **squirt** ***noun*** [C]: *a squirt of lemon juice*

Sr ***abbr.*** = SNR

SSE ***abbr.*** (GEOGRAPHY) south-south-east

SSW ***abbr.*** (GEOGRAPHY) south-south-west

St ***abbr.*** **1** = SAINT: *St Peter* **2** = STREET: *20 Swan St* **3** st (*BrE*) stone; a measure of weight

stab[1] /stæb/ ***verb*** [T] (**stabbing**; **stabbed**) to push a knife or other pointed object into sb/sth: *The man had been stabbed in the back.* ◇ *He stabbed a potato with his fork.*

stab[2] /stæb/ ***noun*** [C] **1** an injury that was caused by a knife, etc.: *He received stab wounds to his neck and back.* **2** (HEALTH) a sudden sharp pain

IDM **have a stab at sth/doing sth** (*informal*) to try to do sth

stabbing[1] /ˈstæbɪŋ/ ***noun*** [C] an occasion when sb is injured or killed with a knife or other sharp object

stabbing[2] /ˈstæbɪŋ/ ***adj.*** (only *before* a noun) (used about a pain) sudden and strong

stability AW /stəˈbɪləti/ ***noun*** [U] the state or quality of being steady and not changing: *After so much change we now need a period of stability.* ◇ *The ladder is slightly wider at the bottom for greater stability.* OPP **instability** ➲ adjective **stable**

stabilize (also -ise) AW /ˈsteɪbəlaɪz/ ***verb*** [I,T] to become or to make sth firm, steady and unlikely to change: *The patient's condition has stabilized.* ➲ look at **destabilize**

stabilizer (also -ise) /ˈsteɪbəlaɪzə(r)/ ***noun*** [C] **1** a device that keeps sth steady, especially one that stops an aircraft or a ship from rolling to one side **2** (TECHNICAL) a chemical that is sometimes added to food or paint to stop the various substances in it from becoming separate

stable[1] ⊶ AW /ˈsteɪbl/ ***adj.*** steady, firm and unlikely to change: *This ladder doesn't seem very stable.* ◇ *The patient is **in a stable condition**.* OPP **unstable** ➲ noun **stability**

> **WORD FAMILY**
> **stable** *adj.* (≠ **unstable**)
> **stability** *noun*
> (≠ **instability**)
> **stabilize** *verb*

stable[2] ⊶ AW /ˈsteɪbl/ ***noun*** [C] (AGRICULTURE) a building where horses are kept

staccato /stəˈkɑːtəʊ/ ***adj.*** (MUSIC) with each note played separately in order to produce short, sharp sounds OPP **legato** ▶ **staccato** ***adv.***

stack[1] /stæk/ ***noun*** [C] **1** a tidy pile of sth: *a stack of plates/books/chairs* **2** (*informal*) (often plural) a lot of sth: *I've still got stacks of work to do.* **3** (GEOGRAPHY) a tall thin part of a CLIFF that has been separated from the land and stands on its own in the sea ➲ picture at **erode**

stack[2] /stæk/ ***verb*** [T] **~ sth (up)** to put sth into a tidy pile: *Could you stack those chairs for me?*

stacked /stækt/ ***adj.*** full of piles of things: *The room was stacked high with books.*

stadium /ˈsteɪdiəm/ ***noun*** [C] (*pl.* **stadiums** or **stadia** /-diə/) a large structure, usually with no roof, where people can sit and watch sport

staff ⊶ /stɑːf/ ***noun*** [C, usually sing., U] **1** the group of people who work for a particular organization: *hotel/library/medical staff* ◇ *Two **members of staff** will accompany the students on the school trip.* ◇ *The hotel has over 200 people **on its staff**.* ◇ *full-time/part-time staff* ◇ *a staffroom* (= in a school) **2** (*AmE*) = STAVE[1] (2) ▶ **staff** ***verb*** [T] (usually passive): *The office is staffed 24 hours a day.*

staffroom /ˈstɑːfruːm/ ***noun*** [C] (*BrE*) (EDUCATION) a room in a school where teachers can go when they are not teaching

stag /stæg/ ***noun*** [C] the male of a DEER

stage[1] ⊶ /steɪdʒ/ ***noun*** **1** [C] one part of the progress or development of sth: *The first stage of the course lasts for three weeks.* ◇ *I suggest we do the journey **in two stages**.* ◇ ***At this stage** it's too early to say what will happen.* **2** [C] (ARTS AND MEDIA) a platform in a theatre, concert hall, etc. on which actors, musicians, etc. perform **3** [sing., U] (ARTS AND MEDIA) the world of theatre; the profession of acting: *Her parents didn't want her to **go on the stage**.* ◇ *an actor of stage and screen*

stage[2] /steɪdʒ/ ***verb*** [T] **1** (ARTS AND MEDIA) to organize a performance of a play, concert, etc. for the public **2** to organize an event: *They have decided to stage a 24-hour strike.*

stagehand /ˈsteɪdʒhænd/ ***noun*** [C] (ARTS AND MEDIA) a person whose job is to help move furniture, SCENERY, etc. in a theatre, to prepare the stage for the next play or the next part of a play

ˌstage ˈmanager ***noun*** [C] (ARTS AND MEDIA) the person who is responsible for the stage, lights, SCENERY, etc. during a theatre performance

stagger /ˈstægə(r)/ ***verb*** [I] to walk with short steps as if you could fall at any moment, for example because you are ill, drunk or carrying sth heavy: *He staggered across the finishing line and collapsed.*

staggered /ˈstægəd/ ***adj.*** **1** (*informal*) very surprised: *I was absolutely staggered when I heard the news.* **2** (used about a set of times, payments, etc.) arranged so that they do not all happen at the same time: *staggered working hours* (= when people start and finish work at different times)

staggering /ˈstægərɪŋ/ ***adj.*** that you find difficult to believe ▶ **staggeringly** ***adv.***

stagnant /ˈstægnənt/ ***adj.*** **1** (used about water) not flowing and therefore dirty and having an unpleasant smell **2** (BUSINESS) not active; not developing: *a stagnant economy*

stagnate /stægˈneɪt/ ***verb*** [I] **1** to stop developing, changing or being active: *a stagnating economy* **2** (used about water) to be or become STAGNANT ▶ **stagnation** /stægˈneɪʃn/ ***noun*** [U]

ˈstag night (*also* **ˈstag party**) ***noun*** [C] a party for men only that is given for a man just before his wedding day ➲ look at **hen party**

staid /steɪd/ ***adj.*** serious, old-fashioned and rather boring

stain /steɪn/ ***verb*** [I,T] to leave a coloured mark that is difficult to remove: *Don't spill any of that red wine – it'll stain the carpet.* ▶ **stain** ***noun*** [C]: *The blood had left a stain on his shirt.*

ˌstained ˈglass ***noun*** [U] (ARCHITECTURE) pieces of coloured glass that are put together to make windows, especially in churches: *a magnificent medieval **stained glass window***

ˌ**stainless ˈsteel** ***noun*** [U] a type of steel that does not RUST (= change colour or get damaged by water): *a stainless steel pan*

stair 🔑 /steə(r)/ ***noun*** **1 stairs** [pl.] a series of steps inside a building that lead from one level to another: ***a flight of stairs*** ◇ *I heard somebody coming* ***down the stairs.*** ◇ *She ran* ***up the stairs.*** ➲ look at **downstairs**, **upstairs** **2** [C] (**ARCHITECTURE**) one of the steps in a series inside a building

staircase /ˈsteəkeɪs/ (*also* **stairway** /ˈsteəweɪ/) ***noun*** [C] a set of stairs with rails on each side that you can hold on to ➲ look at **escalator** ➲ picture at **spiral**

stairlift /ˈsteəlɪft/ ***noun*** [C] a piece of equipment in the form of a seat that sb can sit on to be moved up and down stairs, used by people who find it difficult to walk up and down stairs without help

stake[1] /steɪk/ ***noun*** **1** [C] a wooden or metal pole with a point at one end that you push into the ground **2** [C] (**BUSINESS**) a part of a company, etc. that you own, usually because you have put money into it: *Foreign investors now* ***have a 20% stake in*** *the company.* **3 stakes** [pl.] the things that you might win or lose in a game or in a particular situation: *We play cards for money, but never for very high stakes.*
IDM **at stake** in danger of being lost; at risk: *He thought very carefully about the decision because he knew his future was at stake.*

stake[2] /steɪk/ ***verb*** [T] ~ **sth (on sth)** to put your future, etc. in danger by doing sth, because you hope that it will bring you a good result: *He is staking his political reputation on this issue.*
IDM **stake a/your claim (to sth)** to say that you have a right to have sth
PHR V **stake sth out 1** to clearly mark an area of land that you are going to use **2** to make your position, opinion, etc. clear to everyone: *In his speech, the President staked out his position on tax reform.* **3** (**LAW**) to watch a place secretly for a period of time: *The police had been staking out the house for months.*

stalactite /ˈstæləktaɪt/ ***noun*** [C] (**GEOGRAPHY**, **GEOLOGY**) a long thin piece of rock hanging down from the roof of a CAVE ➲ picture at **limestone**

stalagmite /ˈstæləgmaɪt/ ***noun*** [C] (**GEOGRAPHY**, **GEOLOGY**) a thin piece of rock pointing upwards from the floor of a CAVE ➲ picture at **limestone**

stale /steɪl/ ***adj.*** **1** (used about food or air) old and not fresh any more: *The bread will* ***go stale*** *if you don't put it away.* **2** not interesting or exciting any more ➲ look at **fresh**

stalemate /ˈsteɪlmeɪt/ ***noun*** [sing., U] **1** a situation in an argument in which neither side can win or make any progress **2** (in CHESS) a position in which a game ends without a winner because neither side can move

stalk[1] /stɔːk/ ***noun*** [C] (**BIOLOGY**) one of the long thin parts of a plant which the flowers, leaves or fruit grow on ➲ picture at **tree**

stalk[2] /stɔːk/ ***verb*** **1** [T] to move slowly and quietly towards an animal in order to catch or kill it: *a lion stalking its prey* **2** [T] to follow a person over a period of time in a frightening or annoying way: *The actress claimed the man had been stalking her for two years.* **3** [I] to walk in an angry way

stall[1] /stɔːl/ ***noun*** **1** [C] a small shop with an open front or a table with things for sale: *a market stall* ◇ *a bookstall at the station* **2 stalls** [pl.] (**ARTS AND MEDIA**) the seats nearest the front in a theatre or cinema **3** [C, usually sing.] a situation in which a vehicle's engine suddenly stops because it is not receiving enough power: *The plane went into a stall and almost crashed.*

stall[2] /stɔːl/ ***verb*** [I,T] **1** (used about a vehicle) to stop suddenly because the engine is not receiving enough power; to make a vehicle do this accidentally: *The bus often stalls on this hill.* ◇ *I kept stalling the car.* **2** to avoid doing sth or to try to stop sth happening until a later time

stallion /ˈstæliən/ ***noun*** [C] an adult male horse, especially one that is kept for breeding ➲ note at **horse**

stalwart /ˈstɔːlwət/ ***adj.*** always loyal to the same organization, team, etc.: *a stalwart supporter of the club* ► **stalwart** ***noun*** [C]

stamen /ˈsteɪmən/ ***noun*** [C] (**BIOLOGY**) a small thin male part in the middle of a flower that produces a fine powder (**pollen**) ➲ picture at **flower**

stamina /ˈstæmɪnə/ ***noun*** [U] the ability to do sth that involves a lot of physical or mental effort for a long time: *You need a lot of stamina to run long distances.*

stammer /ˈstæmə(r)/ ***verb*** [I,T] to speak with difficulty, repeating sounds and pausing before saying things correctly: *He stammered an apology and left quickly.* ► **stammer** ***noun*** [sing.]: *to have a stammer*

stamp[1] 🔑 /stæmp/ ***noun*** [C] **1** (also *formal* ˈ**postage stamp**) a small piece of paper that you stick onto a letter or package to show that you have paid for it to be posted: *a first-class/second-class stamp* ◇ *Barry's hobby is collecting stamps.* **2** a small object that prints some words, a design, the date, etc. when you press it onto a surface: *a date stamp* **3** the mark made by stamping sth onto a surface: *Have you got any visa stamps in your passport?* ◇ (*figurative*) *The government has given the project its* ***stamp of approval.*** **4 the ~ of sth** [usually sing.] something that shows a particular quality or that sth was done by a particular person

stamp[2] 🔑 /stæmp/ ***verb*** **1** [I,T] ~ **(on sth)** to put your foot down very heavily and noisily: *He stamped on the spider and squashed it.* ◇ *It was so cold that I had to stamp my feet to keep warm.* ◇ *She stamped her foot in anger.* **2** [I] to walk with loud heavy steps: *She stamped around the room, shouting angrily.* **3** [T] ~ **A (on B)**; ~ **B (with A)** to print some words, a design, the date, etc. by pressing a STAMP onto a surface: *to stamp a passport*
PHR V **stamp sth out** to put an end to sth completely: *The police are trying to stamp out this kind of crime.*

ˈ**stamp duty** ***noun*** [U] (**LAW**, **FINANCE**) a tax in Britain on some legal documents

ˌ**stamped addressed ˈenvelope** (*also* ˌ**self-addressed ˈenvelope**) ***noun*** [C] (*abbr.* **sae**) an empty envelope with your own name and address and a stamp on it that you send to a company, etc. when you want sth sent back to you

stampede /stæmˈpiːd/ ***noun*** [C] a situation in which a large number of animals or people start running in the same direction, for example because they are frightened or excited ► **stampede** ***verb*** [I]

stance /stæns; stɑːns/ ***noun*** [C, usually sing.] **1** ~ **(on sth)** the opinions that sb expresses publicly about sth: *the Prime Minister's stance on foreign affairs* **2** the position in which sb stands, especially when playing a sport

stand[1] 🔑 /stænd/ ***verb*** [I,T] (*pt, pp* **stood** /stʊd/) **1** [I] to be on your feet, not sitting or lying down; to be UPRIGHT: *He was standing near the window.*

◇ ***Stand still** – I'm trying to take a photo of you!* ◇ *Only a few houses were left standing after the earthquake.* **2** [I] ~ **(up)** to rise to your feet from another position: *He stood up when I entered the room.* **3** [T] to put sb/sth in a particular place or position: *We stood the mirror against the wall while we decided where to hang it.* **4** [I] to be or to stay in a particular position or situation: *The castle stands on a hill.* ◇ *The house has stood empty for ten years.* **5** [I] (used about an offer, a decision, etc.) to stay the same as before, without being changed: *Does your decision still stand?* ◇ *The world record has stood for ten years.* **6** [I] ~ **(at) sth** to be of a particular height, level, amount, etc.: *The world record stands at 6.59 metres.* ◇ *The building stands nearly 60 metres high.* **7** [I] ~ **(on sth)** to have an opinion or view about sth **8** [I] ~ **to do sth** to be in a situation where you are likely to do sth: *If he has to sell the company, he stands to lose a lot of money.* **9** [I] ~ **(for/as sth)** to be a CANDIDATE (=one of the people hoping to be chosen) in an election: *She's standing for the European Parliament.* **10** [T] (in negative sentences and questions, with *can't/couldn't*) to not like sb/sth at all; to hate sb/sth: *I **can't stand** that woman – she's so rude.* ◇ *I couldn't **stand the thought of** waiting another two hours so I went home.* SYN **bear** **11** [T] (used especially with *can/could*) to be able to survive difficult conditions: *Camels can stand extremely hot and cold temperatures.* SYN **take**

PHR V **stand around** to stand somewhere not doing anything: *A lot of people were just standing around outside.*

stand aside to move to one side: *People stood aside to let the police pass.*

stand back to move back: *The policeman told everybody to stand back.*

stand by 1 to be present, but do nothing in a situation: *How can you stand by and let them treat their animals like that?* **2** to be ready to act: *The police are standing by in case there's trouble.*

stand for sth 1 to be a short form of sth: *What does BBC stand for?* **2** to support sth (such as an idea or opinion): *I hate everything that the party stands for.*

stand in (for sb) to take sb's place for a short time

stand out to be easily seen or noticed

stand up to be or become vertical: *You'll look taller if you stand up straight.*

stand sb up (*informal*) to not appear when you have arranged to meet sb, especially a boyfriend or girlfriend

stand up for sb/sth to say or do sth which shows that you support sb/sth: *I admire him. He really stands up for his rights.*

stand up to sb/sth to defend yourself against sb/sth who is stronger or more powerful

stand[2] 🔑 /stænd/ ***noun*** [C] **1** a table or an object that holds or supports sth, often so that people can buy it or look at it: *a newspaper/hamburger stand* ◇ *a company stand at a trade fair* **2** a large structure where people can watch sport from seats arranged in rows that are low near the front and high near the back **3 a** ~ **(on/against sth)** a strong effort to defend yourself or sth that you have a strong opinion about: *The workers have decided to **take /make a stand** against further job losses.* **4** [usually sing.] =WITNESS BOX: *He **took the stand** as the first witness.*

'stand-alone ***adj.*** (COMPUTING) (used about computer machinery or programs) able to operate without any other machinery or programs

standard[1] 🔑 /'stændəd/ ***noun*** [C] **1** a level of quality: *We complained about the low standard of service in the hotel.* ◇ *This work is not **up to** your usual **standard**.* **2** a level of quality that you compare sth else with: ***By** European **standards** this is a very expensive city.* ◇ *He is a brilliant player **by any standard**.* **3** [usually pl.] a level of behaviour that is morally acceptable: *Many people are worried about falling standards in modern society.* **4** a flag that is used during official ceremonies, especially one connected with a particular military group

standard[2] 🔑 /'stændəd/ ***adj.*** **1** normal or average; not special or unusual: *He's got long arms, so standard sizes of shirt don't fit him.* **2** that people generally accept as normal and correct: *standard English*

standardize (also **-ise**) /'stændədaɪz/ ***verb*** [T] to make things that are different the same: *Safety tests on old cars have been standardized throughout Europe.* ▶ **standardization** (also **-isation**) /stændədaɪ'zeɪʃn/ ***noun*** [U]

ˌstandard of 'living ***noun*** [C] (SOCIAL STUDIES) a measure of how comfortable the life of a particular person or group is: *There is a higher standard of living in the north than in the south.*

standby /'stændbaɪ/ ***noun*** **1** [C] (*pl.* **standbys**) a thing or person that can be used if needed, for example if sb/sth is not available or in an emergency **2** [U] the state of being ready to do sth immediately if needed or if a ticket becomes available: *Ambulances were **on standby** along the route of the marathon.* ◇ *We were **put on standby** for the flight to Rome.* ▶ **standby** ***adj.*** (only *before* a noun): *a standby ticket/passenger*

'stand-in ***noun*** [C] **1** a person who does sb's job for a short time when they are not available **2** a person who replaces an actor in some scenes in a film, especially dangerous ones

standing[1] /'stændɪŋ/ ***noun*** [U] **1** the position that sb/sth has, or how people think of them or it: *The agreement has no legal standing.* SYN **status** **2** the amount of time during which sth has continued to exist

standing[2] /'stændɪŋ/ ***adj.*** that always exists; permanent

ˌstanding 'order ***noun*** [C] (FINANCE) an instruction to your bank to make a regular payment to sb from your account

standpoint /'stændpɔɪnt/ ***noun*** [C] a particular way of thinking about sth SYN **point of view**

standstill /'stændstɪl/ ***noun*** [sing.] a situation when there is no movement, progress or activity: *The traffic **is at /has come to a complete standstill**.*

IDM **grind to a halt/standstill** → GRIND[1]

stank past tense of **stink**

stanza /'stænzə/ ***noun*** [C] (LITERATURE) a group of lines in a repeated pattern that form a unit in some types of poem SYN **verse**

stapes /'steɪpiːz/ ***noun*** [C] (*pl.* **stapes**) (*also* **stirrup**) (ANATOMY) a small bone in the middle ear, which sends sound VIBRATIONS from the INCUS to the inner ear ➲ picture at **ear**

staple /'steɪpl/ ***noun*** [C] a small thin piece of bent wire that you push through pieces of paper using a special tool (**stapler**) in order to fasten them together ▶ **staple** ***verb*** [T]: *Staple the letter to the application form.* ▶ **stapler** ***noun*** [C]

ˌstaple 'diet ***noun*** [C, usually sing.] the main food that a person or animal normally eats: *a staple diet of rice and fish*

star[1] 🔑 /stɑː(r)/ ***noun*** **1** [C] (ASTRONOMY) a large ball of burning gas in outer space that you see as a small point of light in the sky at night: *It was a clear* *night and the stars were shining brightly.* **2** [C] a shape, decoration, mark, etc. with five or six points sticking out in a regular pattern: *I've marked the possible candidates on the list with a star.* **3** [C] (TOURISM) a mark that is used for telling you how good sth is, especially a hotel or restaurant: *a five-star hotel* **4** [C] (ARTS AND MEDIA, MUSIC, SPORT) a famous person in acting, music or sport: *a pop/rock/film/movie star* ◇ *a football/tennis star* **5 stars** [pl.] =HOROSCOPE

star² /stɑ:(r)/ *verb* (**starring**; **starred**) **1** [I] ~ (in sth) (ARTS AND MEDIA) to be one of the main actors in a play, film, etc.: *Gwyneth Paltrow is to star in a new romantic comedy.* **2** [T] (ARTS AND MEDIA) to have sb as a star: *The film stars Kate Winslet.*

starboard /'stɑ:bəd/ *noun* [U] the side of a ship that is on the right when you are facing towards the front of it OPP **port**

starch /stɑ:tʃ/ *noun* [C,U] **1** (BIOLOGY, CHEMISTRY) a white substance that is found in foods such as potatoes, rice and bread **2** a substance that is used for making cloth STIFF

stardom /'stɑ:dəm/ *noun* [U] the state of being a famous person in acting, music or sport: *She **shot to stardom** in a Broadway musical.*

stare /steə(r)/ *verb* [I] ~ (at sb/sth) to look at sb or sth for a long time because you are surprised, shocked, etc.: *Everybody stared at his hat.* ◇ *He didn't reply, he just stared into the distance.*

starfish /'stɑ:fɪʃ/ *noun* [C] (*pl.* **starfish**) a flat sea animal in the shape of a star with five or more arms

starfruit /'stɑ:fru:t/ *noun* [C] (*pl.* **starfruit**) a green or yellow tropical fruit with a shape like a star

stark¹ /stɑ:k/ *adj.* **1** very empty and without decoration and therefore not attractive: *a stark landscape* **2** unpleasant and impossible to avoid: *He now faces the **stark reality** of life in prison.* **3** very different to sth in a way that is easy to see

stark² /stɑ:k/ *adv.* completely; extremely: *stark naked* ◇ *Have you gone stark raving mad?*

starlight /'stɑ:laɪt/ *noun* [U] (ASTRONOMY) the light that is sent out by stars in the sky

starling /'stɑ:lɪŋ/ *noun* [C] a common bird with dark shiny feathers and a noisy call

starry /'stɑ:ri/ *adj.* (ASTRONOMY) full of stars: *a starry night*

start¹ /stɑ:t/ *verb* **1** [I,T] ~ (sth/to do sth/doing sth) to begin doing sth: *Turn over your exam papers and start now.* ◇ *We'll have to start* (=leave) *early if we want to be in Dover by 10.00* ◇ *Prices start at £5.* ◇ *After waiting for an hour, the customers started to complain.* ◇ *She started playing the piano when she was six.* ◇ *What time do you have to **start work** in the morning?* **2** [I,T] to begin or to make sth begin to happen: *What time does the concert start?* ◇ *I'd like to start the meeting now.* ◇ *The police think a young woman may have started the fire.* **3** [I,T] ~ (sth) (up) (used about a machine, etc.) to begin to work; to make an engine, a car, etc. begin to work: *The car won't start.* ◇ *We heard an engine starting up in the street.* ◇ *He got onto his motor bike, started the engine and rode away.* **4** [I,T] ~ (sth) (up) (BUSINESS) to create a company, an organization, etc.; to begin to exist: *They've decided to start their own business.* ◇ *There are a lot of new companies starting up in that area now.* **5** [I] to make a sudden, quick movement because you are surprised or afraid: *A loud noise outside made me start.*

IDM **get/start off on the right/wrong foot (with sb)** → FOOT¹

to start (off) with 1 used for giving your first reason for sth: *'Why are you so angry?' 'Well, to start off with, you're late, and secondly you've lied to me.'* **2** in the beginning; at first

set/start the ball rolling → BALL

PHR V **start off** to begin in a particular way: *I'd like to start off by welcoming you all to Leeds.*

start on sth to begin doing sth that needs to be done

start out to begin your life, career, etc. in a particular way that changed later: *She started out as a teacher in Glasgow.*

start over (*AmE*) to begin again

start² /stɑ:t/ *noun* **1** [C, usually sing.] the point at which sth begins: *The chairman made a short speech **at the start of** the meeting.* ◇ *I told you it was a bad idea **from the start**.* **2** [C, usually sing.] the action or process of starting: *to make a fresh start* (=do sth again in a different way) **3 the start** [sing.] (SPORT) the place where a race begins: *The athletes are now lining up at the start.* **4** [C, usually sing.] an amount of time or distance that you give to a weaker person at the beginning of a race, game, etc. ➲ look at **head start 5** [C, usually sing.] a sudden quick movement that your body makes because you are surprised or afraid: *She woke up **with a start**.*

IDM **for a start** (*spoken*) (used to emphasize your first reason for sth): *'Why can't we go on holiday?' 'Well, for a start we can't afford it...'*

get off to a good, bad, etc. start to start well, badly, etc.

get off to a flying start → FLYING

starter /'stɑ:tə(r)/ (*AmE usually* **appetizer**) *noun* [C] a small amount of food that is served before the main course of a meal

'starting point *noun* [C] **starting point (for sth) 1** an idea or a topic that you use to begin a discussion with **2** the place where you begin a journey

startle /'stɑ:tl/ *verb* [T] to surprise sb/sth in a way that slightly shocks or frightens them or it: *The gunshot startled the horses.* ▶ **startled** *adj.* ▶ **startling** /'stɑ:tlɪŋ/ *adj.*

'start-up *noun* (BUSINESS) **1** [U] the action or process of making sth start: *They announced the start-up of a new pension scheme.* ◇ ***On start-up**, the computer asks for a password.* **2** [C] a new company: *This region has the highest level of start-ups in the country.* ▶ **start-up** *adj.* (only *before* a noun): *The venture failed because of high start-up costs.* ◇ *a start-up company*

starvation /stɑ:'veɪʃn/ *noun* [U] (HEALTH) suffering or death because there is not enough food: *to die of starvation*

starve /stɑ:v/ *verb* [I,T] (HEALTH) to suffer or die because you do not have enough food to eat; to make sb/sth suffer or die in this way: *Millions of people are starving in the poorer countries of the world.* ◇ *That winter many animals **starved to death**.*

IDM **be starved of sth** to suffer because you are not getting enough of sth that you need: *The children had been starved of love and affection for years.*

be starving (*informal*) to be extremely hungry

state¹ /steɪt/ *noun* **1** [C] the mental, emotional or physical condition that sb/sth is in at a particular time: *the state of the economy* ◇ *He is in a **state of shock**.* ◇ *The house is in a terrible state.* **2** [C] (SCIENCE) the physical condition of sth according to its internal or MOLECULAR structure: *water in a liquid state* ◇ *the three **states of matter*** (=liquid, solid and gas) **3** (*also* **State**) [C] (POLITICS) a country considered as an organized political community controlled by one government: *Pakistan has been an independent state since 1947.* ➲ note at **country 4** (especially **the State**) [U] (POLITICS) the government of a country: *affairs/matters of state* ◇ *the relationship between the Church and the State* ◇ *a state-owned company* ◇ *She went to a state school.* ◇ *heads of State* (=government leaders) **5** (*also* **State**) [C] (POLITICS) an organized political community forming part of a country: *the southern States of the US* ➲ look at **county, province 6** [U] (POLITICS) the formal ceremonies connected with high levels of government or with the leaders of countries: *The Queen is going on **a state visit** to China.* **7 the States** [pl.] (*informal*) the United States of America: *We lived in the States for about five years.*

IDM **be in/get into a state** (*especially BrE, informal*) to be or become very nervous or upset: *Now don't get into a state! I'm sure everything will be all right.*
state of affairs a situation: *This state of affairs must not be allowed to continue.*
state of mind mental condition: *She's in a very confused state of mind.*

state² /steɪt/ *verb* [T] to say or write sth, especially formally: *Your letter states that you sent the goods on 31 March, but we have not received them.* ➲ note at **declare**

stateless /ˈsteɪtləs/ *adj.* (LAW, SOCIAL STUDIES) not officially a citizen of any country: *The children of illegal immigrants will in many cases be born stateless.*

stately /ˈsteɪtli/ *adj.* formal and impressive: *a stately old building*

ˌstately ˈhome *noun* [C] (*BrE*) a large old house that has historical interest and can be visited by the public

statement /ˈsteɪtmənt/ *noun* [C] **1** something that you say or write, especially formally: *The Prime Minister will **make a statement** about the defence cuts today.* **2** = BANK STATEMENT ➲ note at **bill¹**

ˌstate of the ˈart *adj.* using the most modern or advanced methods; as good as it can be at the present time: *The system was state of the art.* ◇ *a state-of-the-art system*

ˈstate school *noun* [C] (EDUCATION) **1** (*BrE*) (*AmE* **ˈpublic school**) a school that is paid for by the government and provides free education ➲ look at **private school, public school 2** (*AmE*) = STATE UNIVERSITY

states of matter

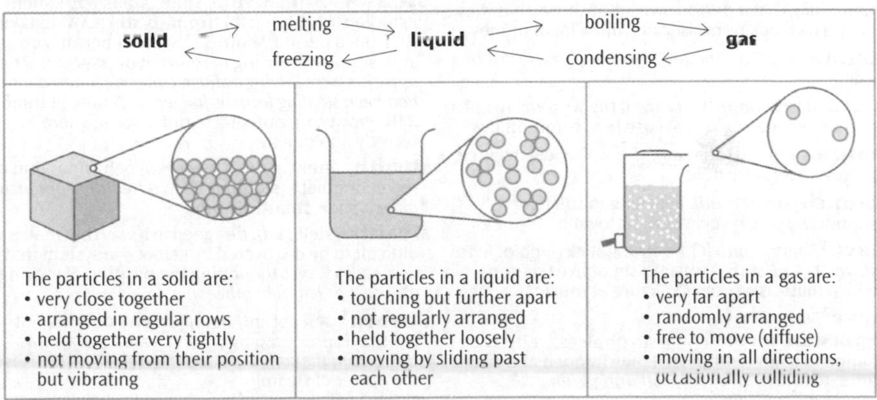

THESAURUS

statement

comment • announcement • remark • declaration • observation

These are all words for sth that you say or write, especially sth that gives information or an opinion.
statement: *The police issued a statement.*
comment: *She made helpful comments on his work.*
announcement: *the announcement of a peace agreement*
remark: *He made rude remarks about her cooking.*
declaration (*formal*): *a declaration of war*
observation (*formal*): *He began with a few general observations about the report.*

statesman /ˈsteɪtsmən/ *noun* [C] (*pl.* **-men** /-mən/) (POLITICS) an important and experienced politician who has earned public respect

ˈstate university (*also* **ˈstate school**) *noun* [C] (*AmE*) (EDUCATION) a university that is managed by a state of the US

static¹ /ˈstætɪk/ *adj.* **1** not moving, changing or developing: *House prices are static.* **2** (PHYSICS) (used about a force) acting as a weight but not producing movement: *static pressure* OPP **dynamic**

static² /ˈstætɪk/ *noun* [U] **1** sudden noises that disturb radio or television signals, caused by electricity in the atmosphere **2** (*also* **ˌstatic elecˈtricity**) electricity that collects on a surface: *My hair gets full of static when I brush it.*

station¹ /ˈsteɪʃn/ *noun* [C] **1** (*also* **ˈrailway station**) a building on a railway line where trains stop so that passengers can get on and off **2** (usually in compound nouns) a building from which buses begin and end journeys **3** (usually in compound nouns) a building where a particular service or activity is based: *a police/fire station* ◇ *a petrol station* ◇ *a power station* (=where electricity is generated) **4** (often in compound nouns) (ARTS AND MEDIA) a radio or television company and the programmes it sends out: *a local radio/TV station* ◇ *He tuned in to another station.* ➲ look at **channel**

station² /ˈsteɪʃn/ ***verb*** [T] (often passive) to send sb, especially members of the armed forces, to work in a place for a period of time

stationary /ˈsteɪʃənri/ ***adj.*** not moving: *He crashed into the back of a stationary vehicle.*

stationer's /ˈsteɪʃənəz/ ***noun*** [sing.] a shop that sells writing equipment, such as paper, pens, envelopes, etc.

stationery /ˈsteɪʃənri/ ***noun*** [U] writing equipment, for example pens, pencils, paper, envelopes

ˈstation wagon (*AmE*) = ESTATE CAR

statistic AW /stəˈtɪstɪk/ ***noun*** **1 statistics** (also *informal* **stats**) [pl.] a collection of information shown in numbers: *Statistics indicate that 90% of homes in this country have a television.* ◇ *crime statistics* **2 statistics** (also *informal* **stats**) [U] (MATHEMATICS) the science of collecting and studying these numbers: *There is a compulsory course in statistics.* **3** [C] a piece of information shown in numbers: *I felt I was no longer being treated as a person but as a statistic.*
▶ **statistical** /stəˈtɪstɪkl/ ***adj.***: *statistical analysis*
▶ **statistically** /-kli/ ***adv.***

statistician AW /ˌstætɪˈstɪʃn/ ***noun*** [C] a person who studies or works with STATISTICS

statue 🔑 /ˈstætʃuː/ ***noun*** [C] (ART) a figure of a person or animal that is made of stone or metal and usually put in a public place

statuette /ˌstætʃuˈet/ ***noun*** [C] (ART) a small statue

stature /ˈstætʃə(r)/ ***noun*** [U] (*written*) **1** the importance and respect that sb has because people have a high opinion of their skill or of what they have done **2** the height of a person: *He's quite small **in stature**.*

status 🔑 AW /ˈsteɪtəs/ ***noun*** **1** [U] the legal position of a person, group or country: *Please indicate your name, age and **marital status*** (= whether you are married or single). ◇ *They were granted refugee status.* **2** [sing.] your social or professional position in relation to other people: *Teachers don't have a very high status in this country.* SYN **standing** **3** [U] a high social position: *The new job gave him much more status.*

the status quo /ˌsteɪtəs ˈkwəʊ/ ***noun*** [sing.] the situation as it is now, or as it was before a recent change

ˈstatus symbol ***noun*** [C] (SOCIAL STUDIES) something that a person owns that shows that they have a high position in society and a lot of money

statute /ˈstætʃuːt/ ***noun*** [C] (*formal*) (LAW) a law or a rule

ˈstatute law ***noun*** [U] (LAW) all the written laws of a parliament, etc. ➲ look at **case law**, **common law**

statutory /ˈstætʃətri/ ***adj.*** (*formal*) (LAW) decided by law: *a statutory right*

staunch /stɔːntʃ/ ***adj.*** believing in sb/sth or supporting sb/sth very strongly; loyal

stave¹ /steɪv/ ***noun*** [C] **1** a strong stick or pole: *fence staves* **2** (*AmE* **staff**) (MUSIC) a set of five lines on which music is written ➲ picture at **music**

stave² /steɪv/ ***verb***
PHR V **stave sth off** to stop sth unpleasant from happening now, although it may happen at a later time; to delay sth: *to stave off hunger/illness/inflation/bankruptcy*

stay¹ 🔑 /steɪ/ ***verb*** [I] **1** to continue to be somewhere and not go away: *Patrick stayed in bed until 11 o'clock.* ◇ *I can't stay long.* ◇ *Stay on this road until you get to Wells.* ◇ *Pete's staying late at the office tonight.* **2** to continue to be in a particular state or situation without change: *I can't **stay awake** any longer.* ◇ *I don't know why they stay together* (= continue to be married or in a relationship). **3** to live in a place temporarily as a visitor or guest: *We stayed with friends in France.* ◇ *Which hotel are you **staying at**?* ◇ *Can you stay for lunch?* ◇ *Why don't you **stay the night**?*
IDM **stay put** (*informal*) to continue in one place; to not leave
PHR V **stay behind** to not leave a place after other people have gone: *I'll stay behind and help you wash up.*
stay in to be at home and not go out: *I'm going to stay in and watch TV.*
stay on (at…) to continue studying, working, etc. somewhere for longer than expected or after other people have left
stay out to continue to be away from your house, especially late at night
stay up to go to bed later than usual: *I'm going to stay up to watch the late film.*

stay² 🔑 /steɪ/ ***noun*** [C] a period of time that you spend somewhere as a visitor or guest: *Did you enjoy your stay in Crete?*

STD /ˌes tiː ˈdiː/ ***abbr.*** **1** (*BrE*) subscriber trunk dialling; the system by which you can make long-distance telephone calls direct **2** (HEALTH) sexually transmitted disease

steady¹ 🔑 /ˈstedi/ ***adj.*** (**steadier**; **steadiest**) **1** developing, growing or happening gradually and at a regular rate: *a steady increase/decline* **2** staying the same; not changing and therefore safe: *a steady job/income* **3** firmly fixed, supported or balanced; not shaking or likely to fall down: *You need **a steady hand** to take good photographs.* ◇ *He held the ladder steady as she climbed up it.* ▶ **steadily** ***adv.***: *Unemployment has risen steadily since April 2005.*

steady² /ˈstedi/ ***verb*** [I,T] (*pres. part.* **steadying**; *3rd person sing. pres.* **steadies**; *pt, pp* **steadied**) to stop yourself/sb/sth from moving, shaking or falling; to stop moving, shaking or falling: *She thought she was going to fall, so she put out a hand to steady herself.* ◇ *He had to **steady** his **nerves/voice** before beginning his speech.*

steak /steɪk/ ***noun*** [C,U] a thick flat piece of meat or fish: *a piece of steak* ◇ *a cod/salmon steak* ➲ look at **chop²**

steal 🔑 /stiːl/ ***verb*** (*pt* **stole** /stəʊl/; *pp* **stolen** /ˈstəʊlən/) **1** [I,T] ~ **(sth) (from sb/sth)** (LAW) to take sth from a person, shop, etc. without permission and without intending to return it or pay for it: *The terrorists were driving a stolen car.* ◇ *We found out she had been stealing from us for years.* ➲ note at **thief** **2** [I] ~ **away, in, out, etc.** to move somewhere secretly and quietly

stealth¹ /stelθ/ ***noun*** [U] (*formal*) behaviour that is secret or quiet ▶ **stealthy** ***adj.***: *a stealthy approach/movement* ▶ **stealthily** ***adv.***

stealth² /stelθ/ ***adj.*** designed in a way that makes it difficult to be discovered by RADAR (= a system that uses radio waves for finding the position of moving objects): *a stealth bomber*

steam¹ 🔑 /stiːm/ ***noun*** [U] (PHYSICS) the hot gas that is produced by boiling water: *Steam was rising from the coffee.* ◇ *a **steam engine*** (= that uses the power of steam)
IDM **let off steam** (*informal*) to get rid of energy or

express strong feeling by behaving in a noisy or wild way
run out of steam to gradually lose energy or enthusiasm

steam² /stiːm/ ***verb*** **1** [I] to send out steam: *a bowl of steaming hot soup* **2** [I,T] to place food over boiling water so that it cooks in the steam; to cook in this way: *steamed vegetables/fish* ◇ *Leave the potatoes to steam for 30 minutes.*
IDM **be/get steamed up** (*informal*) to be or become very angry or worried about sth
PHR V **steam (sth) up** to cover sth or become covered with steam: *My glasses have steamed up.*

steamer /ˈstiːmə(r)/ ***noun*** [C] **1** a ship that is driven by steam **2** a metal container with small holes in it, that is placed over a pan of boiling water in order to cook food in the steam

steamroller /ˈstiːmrəʊlə(r)/ ***noun*** [C] a big heavy vehicle with wide heavy wheels that is used for making the surface of a road flat

steel¹ 🔑 /stiːl/ ***noun*** [U] (CHEMISTRY) a very strong metal that is made from iron mixed with CARBON. Steel is used for making knives, tools, machines, etc.

steel² /stiːl/ ***verb*** [T] ~ **yourself** to prepare yourself to deal with sth difficult or unpleasant: *Steel yourself for a shock.*

ˌsteel ˈband ***noun*** [C] (MUSIC) a group of musicians who play music on drums that are made from empty metal oil containers. **Steel bands** originally came from the West Indies.

ˌsteel ˈdrum (*also* ˌsteel ˈpan) ***noun*** [C] (MUSIC) a musical instrument used in West Indian music, made from a metal oil container which is hit in different places with two sticks to produce different notes

ˌsteel ˈwool (*also* ˌwire ˈwool) ***noun*** [U] a mass of fine steel threads that you use for cleaning pots and pans, making surfaces smooth, etc.

steelworks /ˈstiːlwɜːks/ ***noun*** [C, with sing. or pl. verb] (*pl.* **steelworks**) a factory where steel is made

steep 🔑 /stiːp/ ***adj.*** **1** (used about a hill, mountain, street, etc.) rising or falling quickly; at a sharp angle: *I don't think I can cycle up that hill. It's too steep.* **2** (used about an increase or fall in sth) very big **3** (*informal*) too expensive ▸ **steeply** ***adv.***: *House prices have risen steeply this year.*
▸ **steepness** ***noun*** [U]

steeped /stiːpt/ ***adj.*** ~ **in sth** having a lot of; full of sth: *a city steeped in history*

steeple /ˈstiːpl/ ***noun*** [C] (ARCHITECTURE) a tower on the roof of a church, often with a pointed top (spire)

steer 🔑 /stɪə(r)/ ***verb*** **1** [I,T] to control the direction that a vehicle is going in: *Can you push the car while I steer?* ◇ *to steer a boat/ship/bicycle/motorbike* **2** [T] to take control of a situation and try to influence the way it develops: *She tried to steer the conversation away from the subject of money.*
IDM **keep/stay/steer clear (of sb/sth)** → CLEAR²

steering /ˈstɪərɪŋ/ ***noun*** [U] the parts of a vehicle that control the direction that it moves in: *a car with power steering*

ˈsteering wheel (*also* **wheel**) ***noun*** [C] the wheel that the driver turns in a vehicle to control the direction that it moves in

stellar /ˈstelə(r)/ ***adj.*** (only *before* a noun) (ASTRONOMY) connected with the stars

stem¹ /stem/ ***noun*** [C] **1** (BIOLOGY) the main long thin part of a plant above the ground from which the leaves or flowers grow ➲ picture at **flower**
2 (LANGUAGE) the main part of a word onto which other parts are added: *'Writ-' is the stem of the words 'write', 'writing', 'written' and 'writer'.*

stem² /stem/ ***verb*** [T] (**stemming**; **stemmed**) to stop sth that is increasing or spreading
PHR V **stem from sth** (not used in the continuous tenses) to be the result of sth

ˈstem cell ***noun*** [C] (BIOLOGY) a basic type of cell which can divide and develop into cells with particular functions. All the different kinds of cells in the human body develop from **stem cells**: *Tests suggest that stem cells could be used to regenerate damaged body parts.* ◇ *Stem cell research is the essential first step for cloning.*

stench /stentʃ/ ***noun*** [C, sing.] a very unpleasant smell

stencil /ˈstensl/ ***noun*** [C] (ART) a thin piece of metal, plastic or card with a design cut out of it, that you put onto a surface and paint over, so that the design is left on the surface; the pattern or design that is produced in this way ▸ **stencil** ***verb*** [T] (**stencilling**; **stencilled**: *AmE* **stenciling**; **stenciled**)

step¹ 🔑 /step/ ***noun*** [C] **1** the action of lifting one foot and putting it down in a different place: *Nick **took a step** forward and then stopped.* ◇ *I heard steps outside the window.* ◇ *We were obviously lost so we decided to **retrace our steps*** (= go back the way we had come). **2** one action in a series of actions that you take in order to achieve sth: *This will not solve the problem completely, but it is **a step in the right direction**.* **3** one of the surfaces on which you put your foot when you are going up or down stairs: *on the top/bottom step*
IDM **in/out of step (with sb/sth)** moving/not moving your feet at the same time as other people when you are marching, dancing, etc.
step by step (used for talking about a series of actions) moving slowly and gradually from one action or stage to the next: *clear step-by-step instructions*
take steps to do sth to take action in order to achieve sth
watch your step 1 to be careful about where you are walking **2** to be careful about how you behave

step² 🔑 /step/ ***verb*** [I] (**stepping**; **stepped**) **1** to lift one foot and put it down in a different place when you are walking: *Be careful! Don't step in the mud.* ◇ *to step forward/back* ◇ *Ouch! You stepped on my foot!* **2** to move a short distance; to go somewhere: *Could you step out of the car please, sir?* ◇ *I stepped outside for a minute to get some air.*
PHR V **step down** to leave an important job or position and let sb else take your place
step in to help sb in a difficult situation or to become involved in a DISPUTE
step sth up to increase the amount, speed, etc. of sth: *The Army has decided to step up its security arrangements.*

step- /step-/ ***prefix*** (used in compound nouns) related as a result of one parent marrying again

ˈSTEP analysis ***noun*** [C,U] = PEST ANALYSIS

stepbrother /ˈstepbrʌðə(r)/ ***noun*** [C] the son from an earlier marriage of sb who has married your mother or father ➲ look at **half-brother**

stepchild /ˈsteptʃaɪld/ ***noun*** [C] (*pl.* **stepchildren**) the child from an earlier marriage of your husband or wife

stepdaughter /ˈstepdɔːtə(r)/ ***noun*** [C] the daughter from an earlier marriage of your husband or wife

stepfather /ˈstepfɑːðə(r)/ ***noun*** [C] the man who has married your mother when your parents are divorced or your father is dead

stepladder /ˈsteplædə(r)/ ***noun*** [C] a short LADDER with two parts, one with steps, that are joined together at the top so that it can stand on its own and be folded up when you are not using it.

stepmother /ˈstepmʌðə(r)/ ***noun*** [C] the woman who has married your father when your parents are divorced or your mother is dead

steppe /step/ ***noun*** [C, usually pl., U] (**GEOGRAPHY**) a large area of land with grass but few trees, especially in south-east Europe and Siberia

ˈstepping stone ***noun*** [C] **1** one of a line of flat stones that you can step on in order to cross a river **2** something that allows you to make progress or helps you to achieve sth

stepsister /ˈstepsɪstə(r)/ ***noun*** [C] the daughter from an earlier marriage of sb who has married your mother or father ➲ look at **half-sister**

stepson /ˈstepsʌn/ ***noun*** [C] the son from an earlier marriage of your husband or wife

stereo /ˈsteriəʊ/ (*pl.* **stereos**) ***noun*** **1** (*also* **ˈstereo system**) [C] a machine that plays CDs or CASSETTES, or a radio, that has two SPEAKERS so that you hear separate sounds from each: *a car/personal stereo* **2** [U] the system for playing recorded music, speech etc. in which the sound is divided in two parts: *This programme is broadcast **in stereo**.* ➲ look at **mono** ▸ **stereo *adj.***: *a stereo television*

stereotype /ˈsteriətaɪp/ ***noun*** [C] a fixed idea about a particular type of person or thing, which is often not true in reality ▸ **stereotype *verb*** [T]: *In advertisements, women are often stereotyped as housewives.*

sterile /ˈsteraɪl/ ***adj.*** **1** (**HEALTH**) not able to produce young animals or babies **2** (**HEALTH**) completely clean and free from bacteria: *All equipment used during a medical operation must be sterile.* **3** not producing any useful result: *a sterile discussion/argument* ▸ **sterility** /stəˈrɪləti/ ***noun*** [U]

sterilize (also **-ise**) /ˈsterəlaɪz/ ***verb*** [T] (**HEALTH**) **1** to make sb/sth completely clean and free from bacteria **2** (usually passive) to perform an operation on a person or an animal so that they or it cannot have babies ▸ **sterilization** (also **-isation**) /ˌsterəlaɪˈzeɪʃn/ ***noun*** [U]

sterling[1] /ˈstɜːlɪŋ/ ***noun*** [U] (**FINANCE, ECONOMICS**) the system of money that is used in Britain, that uses the pound as its basic unit

sterling[2] /ˈstɜːlɪŋ/ ***adj.*** of very high quality: *sterling work*

stern[1] /stɜːn/ ***adj.*** very serious; not smiling: *a stern expression/warning* ▸ **sternly *adv.***

stern[2] /stɜːn/ ***noun*** [C] the back end of a ship or boat ➲ look at **bow**[2]

sternum /ˈstɜːnəm/ ***noun*** [C] (*formal*) (**ANATOMY**) the long flat bone in the middle of your chest that the seven top pairs of curved bones (**ribs**) are connected to SYN **breastbone** ➲ picture on **page 80**

steroid /ˈsterɔɪd/ ***noun*** [C] (**HEALTH**) a chemical substance produced naturally in the body. There are several different types of **steroids**. They can be used to treat various diseases and are also sometimes used illegally by people playing sports to improve their performance. ➲ look at **anabolic steroid**

stethoscope /ˈsteθəskəʊp/ ***noun*** [C] (**HEALTH**) the piece of equipment that a doctor uses for listening to your breathing and heart

stew /stjuː/ ***noun*** [C,U] a type of food that you make by cooking meat and/or vegetables in liquid for a long time ▸ **stew *verb*** [I,T]

steward /ˈstjuːəd/ ***noun*** [C] **1** a man whose job is to look after passengers on an aircraft, a ship or a train **2** (*BrE*) a person who helps to organize a large public event, for example a race

stewardess /ˌstjuːəˈdes; ˈstjuːə-/ ***noun*** [C] **1** a woman whose job is to look after passengers on an aircraft SYN **air hostess** **2** a woman who looks after the passengers on a ship or train

stick[1] 🔑 /stɪk/ ***verb*** (*pt, pp* **stuck** /stʌk/) **1** [I,T] ~ **(sth) in/into (sth)** to push a pointed object into sth; to be pushed into sth: *Stick a fork into the meat to see if it's ready.* **2** [I,T] to fix sth to sth else by using a special substance (**glue**); to become fixed to sth else: *I stuck a stamp on an envelope.* **3** [T] (*informal*) to put sth somewhere, especially quickly or carelessly: *Stick your bags in the bedroom.* ◇ *Just at that moment James stuck his head round the door.* **4** [I] ~ **(in sth)** (used about sth that can usually be moved) to become fixed in one position so that it cannot be moved: *The car was stuck in the mud.* ◇ *This drawer keeps sticking.* **5** [T] (*informal*) (often in negative sentences and questions) to stay in a difficult or unpleasant situation: *I can't stick this job much longer.*

IDM **poke/stick your nose into sth** → NOSE[1]
stick/put your tongue out → TONGUE

PHR V **stick around** (*informal*) to stay somewhere, waiting for sth to happen or for sb to arrive
stick at sth (*informal*) to continue working at sth even when it is difficult
stick by sb (*informal*) to continue to give sb help and support even in difficult times
stick out (*informal*) to be very noticeable and easily seen: *The new office block really sticks out from the older buildings around it.*
stick (sth) out to be further out than sth else; to push sth further out than sth else: *The boy's head was sticking out of the window.*
stick it/sth out (*informal*) to stay in a difficult or unpleasant situation until the end
stick to sth (*informal*) to continue with sth and not change to anything else
stick together (*informal*) (used about a group of people) to stay friendly and loyal to each other
stick up to point upwards: *You look funny. Your hair's sticking up!*
stick up for yourself/sb/sth (*informal*) to support or defend yourself/sb/sth: *Don't worry. I'll stick up for you if there's any trouble.*

stick[2] 🔑 /stɪk/ ***noun*** [C] **1** a small thin piece of wood from a tree **2** (*especially BrE*) = WALKING STICK **3** (in HOCKEY and some other sports) a long thin piece of wood that you use for hitting the ball: *a hockey stick* ➲ look at **bat**, **club**, **racket** ➲ picture at **sport** **4** a long thin piece of sth: *a stick of celery/dynamite*

sticker /ˈstɪkə(r)/ ***noun*** [C] a piece of paper with writing or a picture on one side that you can stick onto sth

sticky 🔑 /ˈstɪki/ ***adj.*** (**stickier**; **stickiest**) **1** used for describing a substance that easily becomes joined to things that it touches, or sth that is covered with this kind of substance: *These sweets are very sticky.* ◇ *sticky tape* **2** (*informal*) (used about a situation) difficult or unpleasant

stiff[1] 🔑 /stɪf/ ***adj.*** **1** (used about material, paper, etc.) firm and difficult to bend or move: *My new shoes feel rather stiff.* ◇ *The door handle is stiff and I can't turn it.* **2** (used about parts of the body) not easy to move: *My arm feels really stiff after playing tennis yesterday.* **3** (used about a liquid) very thick; almost solid: *Beat the egg whites until they are stiff.* **4** more difficult or stronger than usual: *The firm faces stiff competition from its rivals.* ◇ *a stiff breeze/wind* **5** (used about sb's behaviour) not relaxed or friendly; formal **6** (used about an alcoholic drink) strong: *a stiff whisky* ▶ **stiffness** ***noun*** [U]

stiff[2] /stɪf/ ***adv.*** (*informal*) extremely: *to be bored/frozen/scared/worried stiff*

stiffen /ˈstɪfn/ ***verb*** **1** [I] (used about a person) to suddenly stop moving and hold your body very straight, usually because you are afraid or angry **2** [I,T] to become RIGID; to make sth RIGID so that it will not bend

stiffly 🔑 /ˈstɪfli/ ***adv.*** in an unfriendly formal way: *He smiled stiffly.*

stifle /ˈstaɪfl/ ***verb*** **1** [T] to stop sth happening, developing or continuing: *Her strict education had stifled her natural creativity.* ◇ *to stifle a yawn/cry/giggle* **2** [I,T] to be or to make sb unable to breathe because it is very hot and/or there is no fresh air: *Richard was almost stifled by the smoke.* ▶ **stifling** /ˈstaɪflɪŋ/ ***adj.***: *The heat was stifling.*

stigma /ˈstɪgmə/ ***noun*** **1** [C,U] bad and often unfair feelings that people in general have about a particular illness, way of behaving, etc.: *There is still a lot of stigma attached to being unemployed.* **2** [C] (**BIOLOGY**) the top of the CARPEL (=the female part in the middle of a flower) where POLLEN is received ➲ picture at **flower**

stiletto /stɪˈletəʊ/ ***noun*** [C] a women's shoe with a very high narrow heel; the heel on such a shoe

still[1] 🔑 /stɪl/ ***adv.*** **1** continuing until now or until the time you are talking about and not finishing: *Do you still live in London?* ◇ *It's still raining.* ◇ *I've eaten all the food but I'm still hungry.* ◇ *In 1997 Zoran was still a student.* **2** in addition; more: *There are still ten days to go until my holiday.* **3** in spite of what has just been said: *He had a bad headache but he still went to the party.* **4** used for making a COMPARATIVE adjective stronger: *It was very cold yesterday, but today it's colder still.* ◇ *There was still more bad news to come.*

still[2] 🔑 /stɪl/ ***adj.***, ***adv.*** **1** not moving: *Stand still! I want to take a photograph!* ◇ *Children find it hard to* ***keep/stay still*** *for long periods.* **2** quiet or calm: *The water was perfectly still.* **3** (used about a drink) not containing gas: *still mineral water* ➲ look at **fizzy**, **sparkling** ▶ **stillness** ***noun*** [U]

still[3] /stɪl/ ***noun*** [C] (**ARTS AND MEDIA**) a single photograph that is taken from a film or video

stillborn /ˈstɪlbɔːn/ ***adj.*** (**HEALTH**) (used about a baby) dead when it is born

ˌstill ˈlife ***noun*** [U,C] (*pl.* **still lifes**) (**ART**) the art of painting or drawing arrangements of objects such as flowers, fruit, etc.; a painting, etc. like this: *a still life in oils*

stilt /stɪlt/ ***noun*** [C] **1** one of two long pieces of wood, with places to rest your feet on, on which you can walk above the ground: *Have you tried walking* ***on stilts****?* **2** one of a set of poles that support a building above the ground or water

stilted /ˈstɪltɪd/ ***adj.*** (used about a way of speaking or writing) not natural or relaxed; too formal

stimulant /ˈstɪmjələnt/ ***noun*** [C] a drug or medicine that makes you feel more active

stimulate /ˈstɪmjuleɪt/ ***verb*** [T] **1** to make sth active or more active: *Exercise stimulates the blood circulation.* ◇ *The government has decided to cut taxes in order to stimulate the economy.* **2** to make sb feel interested and excited about sth: *The lessons don't really stimulate him.* ▶ **stimulation** /ˌstɪmjuˈleɪʃn/ ***noun*** [U]

stimulating /ˈstɪmjuleɪtɪŋ/ ***adj.*** interesting and exciting: *a stimulating discussion*

stimulus /ˈstɪmjələs/ ***noun*** [C,U] (*pl.* **stimuli** /-laɪ/) something that causes activity, development or interest: *Books provide children with ideas and a stimulus for play.*

sting[1] 🔑 /stɪŋ/ ***verb*** [I,T] (*pt, pp* **stung** /stʌŋ/) **1** (**HEALTH**) (used about an insect, a plant, etc.) to make a person or an animal feel a sudden pain by pushing sth sharp into their skin and sending poison into them: *Ow! I've been stung by a bee!* ◇ *Be careful. Those plants sting.* **2** to make sb/sth feel a sudden, sharp pain: *Soap stings if it gets in your eyes.* **3** to make sb feel very hurt and upset because of sth you say

sting[2] 🔑 /stɪŋ/ ***noun*** [C] **1** the sharp pointed part of some insects and animals that is used for pushing into the skin of a person or an animal and putting in poison ➲ picture on **page 29** **2** the pain that you feel when an animal or insect pushes its sting into you: *I got a wasp sting on the leg.* **3** (**HEALTH**) a sharp pain that feels like a sting

stink /stɪŋk/ ***verb*** [I] (*pt* **stank** /stæŋk/ or **stunk** /stʌŋk/; *pp* **stunk**) (*informal*) ~ **(of sth)** **1** to have a very strong and unpleasant smell: *It stinks in here – open a window!* ◇ *to stink of fish* **2** to seem to be very bad, unpleasant or dishonest: *The whole business stinks of corruption.* ▶ **stink** ***noun*** [C]

stint /stɪnt/ ***noun*** [C] a fixed period of time that you spend doing sth: *He did a brief stint in the army after leaving school.*

stipulate /ˈstɪpjuleɪt/ ***verb*** [T] (*formal*) to say exactly and officially what must be done: *The law stipulates that all schools must be inspected every three years.* ▶ **stipulation** /ˌstɪpjuˈleɪʃn/ ***noun*** [C,U]

stir[1] 🔑 /stɜː(r)/ ***verb*** (**stirring; stirred**) **1** [T] to move a liquid, etc. round and round, using a spoon, etc.: *She stirred her coffee with a teaspoon.* **2** [I,T] to move or make sb/sth move slightly: *She heard the baby stir in the next room.* **3** [T] to make sb feel a strong emotion: *The story stirred Carol's imagination.* ◇ *a stirring speech*

PHR V **stir sth up** to cause problems, or to make people feel strong emotions: *He's always trying to* ***stir up trouble****.* ◇ *The article stirred up a lot of anger among local residents.*

stir[2] /stɜː(r)/ ***noun*** **1** [C] the action of stirring: *Give the soup a stir.* **2** [sing.] something exciting or shocking that everyone talks about

ˈstir-fry[1] ***verb*** [T] to cook thin strips of vegetables or meat quickly by stirring them in very hot oil: *stir-fried chicken*

ˈstir-fry[2] ***noun*** [C] a hot dish made by STIR-FRYING small pieces of meat, fish and/or vegetables

stirring /ˈstɜːrɪŋ/ ***adj.*** causing strong feelings; exciting: *a stirring performance*

stirrup /ˈstɪrəp/ ***noun*** [C] **1** one of the two metal objects that you put your feet in when you are riding a horse **2** (also *technical* **stapes**) (**ANATOMY**) a small bone in the middle ear which is shaped like a **stirrup**

stitch¹ /stɪtʃ/ *noun* [C] **1** one of the small lines of thread that you can see on a piece of material after it has been sewn **2** (HEALTH) one of the small pieces of thread that a doctor uses to sew your skin together if you cut yourself very badly, or after an operation: *How many stitches did you have in your leg?* **3** one of the small circles of wool that you put round a needle when you are knitting **4** [usually sing.] (HEALTH) a sudden pain that you get in the side of your body when you are running

IDM **in stitches** (*informal*) laughing so much that you cannot stop

stitch² /stɪtʃ/ *verb* [I,T] to sew

stock¹ ⊶ /stɒk/ *noun* **1** [U, C] the supply of things that a shop, etc. has for sale: *We'll have to order extra stock if we sell a lot more this week.* ◇ *I'm afraid that book's* ***out of stock*** *at the moment. Shall I order it for you?* ◇ *I'll see if we have your size* ***in stock***. **2** [C] an amount of sth that has been kept ready to be used: *Food stocks in the village were very low.* **3** [C,U] (BUSINESS) a share that sb has bought in a company, or the value of a company's shares: *to invest in stocks and shares* **4** [C,U] a liquid that is made by boiling meat, bones, vegetables, etc. in water, used especially for making soups and sauces

IDM **take stock (of sth)** to think about sth very carefully before deciding what to do next ➲ note at **examine**

stock² /stɒk/ *verb* [T] **1** (usually used about a shop) to have a supply of sth: *They stock food from all over the world.* **2** to fill a place with sth: *a well-stocked library*

PHR V **stock up (on/with sth)** to collect a large supply of sth for future use: *to stock up with food for the winter*

stock³ /stɒk/ *adj.* (only *before* a noun) (used for describing sth that sb says) used so often that it does not have much meaning: *He always gives the same stock answers.*

stockbroker /ˈstɒkbrəʊkə(r)/ (*also* **broker**) *noun* [C] a person whose job it is to buy and sell shares in companies for other people

ˈstock exchange *noun* [C, usually sing.] (BUSINESS) a place where shares in companies are bought and sold; all of the business activity involved in doing this: *the Tokyo Stock Exchange* ◇ *to lose money on the stock exchange*

stocking /ˈstɒkɪŋ/ *noun* [C] one of a pair of thin pieces of clothing that fit tightly over a woman's feet and legs: *a pair of stockings* ➲ look at **tights**

stockist /ˈstɒkɪst/ *noun* [C] a shop that sells goods made by a particular company

ˈstock market (*also* **market**) *noun* [C] (BUSINESS) the business of buying and selling shares in companies and the place where this happens; a STOCK EXCHANGE: *to make money on the stock market* ◇ *a stock market crash* (=when prices of shares fall suddenly and people lose money)

stockpile /ˈstɒkpaɪl/ *noun* [C] a large supply of sth that is kept to be used in the future if necessary ► **stockpile** *verb* [T]: *to stockpile food/fuel*

stocktaking /ˈstɒkteɪkɪŋ/ *noun* [U] the activity of counting the total supply of things that a shop or business has at a particular time: *They close for an hour a month to do the stocktaking.*

stocky /ˈstɒki/ *adj.* (used about a person's body) short but strong and heavy

stoic /ˈstəʊɪk/ (*also* **stoical** /-kl/) *adj.* (*formal*) suffering pain or difficulty without complaining ► **stoically** /-kli/ *adv.* ► **stoicism** /ˈstəʊɪsɪzəm/ *noun* [U]

stoke /stəʊk/ *verb* [T] **1 ~ sth (up) (with sth)** to add fuel to a fire, etc.: *to stoke up a fire with more coal* ◇ *to stoke a furnace* **2 ~ sth (up)** to make people feel sth more strongly: *to stoke up anger/envy* ◇ *The publicity was intended to stoke up interest in her music.*

PHR V **stoke up (on/with sth)** (*informal*) to eat or drink a lot of sth, especially so that you do not feel hungry later: *Stoke up for the day on a good breakfast.*

stole past tense of **steal**

stolen past participle of **steal**

stolid /ˈstɒlɪd/ *adj.* (used about a person) showing very little emotion or excitement ► **stolidly** *adv.*

stoma /ˈstəʊmə/ *noun* [C] (*pl.* **stomas** or **stomata** /ˈstəʊmətə/) **1** (BIOLOGY) any of the very small holes in the surface of a leaf or the STEM (=the main long thin part) of a plant that allow gases to pass in and out **2** (BIOLOGY) a small opening like a mouth in some simple creatures **3** (HEALTH) (in medicine) a hole that is made from the surface of the body to one of the tubes inside the body

stomach¹ ⊶ /ˈstʌmək/ (also *informal* **tummy**) *noun* [C] **1** (ANATOMY) the organ in your body where food goes after you have eaten it: *He went to the doctor with stomach pains.* ➲ picture at **digestive system** **2** the front part of your body below your chest and above your legs: *She turned over onto her stomach.*

stomach² /ˈstʌmək/ *verb* [T] (*informal*) (usually in negative sentences and questions) to be able to watch, listen to, accept, etc. sth that you think is unpleasant: *I can't stomach too much violence in films.*

ˈstomach ache *noun* [C,U] (HEALTH) a pain in your stomach: *I've got terrible stomach ache.* ➲ note at **ache**

stomp /stɒmp/ *verb* [I] (*informal*) to walk with heavy steps

stone ⊶ /stəʊn/ *noun* **1** [U] a hard solid substance that is found in the ground: *The house was built of grey stone.* ◇ *a stone wall* ➲ look at **cornerstone, foundation stone** **2** [C] (GEOLOGY) a small piece of rock: *The boy picked up a stone and threw it into the river.* **3** [C] =PRECIOUS STONE **4** [C] the hard seed inside some fruits, for example PEACHES, PLUMS, CHERRIES and OLIVES **5** [C] (*pl.* **stone**) a measure of weight; 6.35 kilograms. There are 14 pounds in a stone: *I weigh eleven stone two* (=2 pounds).

the ˈStone Age *noun* [sing.] (HISTORY) the very early period of human history when tools and weapons were made of stone

stoned /stəʊnd/ *adj.* (*slang*) not behaving or thinking normally because of drugs or alcohol

stonemason /ˈstəʊnmeɪsn/ *noun* [C] a person whose job is cutting and preparing stone for buildings

stonework /ˈstəʊnwɜːk/ *noun* [U] (ARCHITECTURE) the parts of a building that are made of stone

stony /ˈstəʊni/ *adj.* **1** (used about the ground) having a lot of stones in it, or covered with stones **2** not friendly: *There was a stony silence as he walked into the room.*

stood past tense, past participle of **stand¹**

stool /stuːl/ ***noun*** [C] **1** a seat that does not have a back or arms: *a piano stool* ➲ picture at **piano** **2** (HEALTH) a piece of solid waste from your body

stoop /stuːp/ ***verb*** [I] to bend your head and shoulders forwards and downwards: *He had to stoop to get through the low doorway.* ▶ **stoop** ***noun*** [sing.]: *to walk with a stoop*

PHR V **stoop to sth/doing sth** to do sth bad or wrong that you would normally not do

stop¹ ⊶ /stɒp/ ***verb*** (**stopping**; **stopped**) **1** [I,T] to finish moving or make sth finish moving: *He walked along the road for a bit, and then stopped.* ◇ *Does this train stop at Didcot?* ◇ *My watch has stopped.* ◇ *I stopped someone in the street to ask the way to the station.* **2** [I,T] to no longer continue or make sth not continue: *I think the rain has stopped.* ◇ *It's stopped raining now.* ◇ *Stop making that terrible noise!* ◇ *The bus service stops at midnight.* ◇ *We tied a bandage round his arm to stop the bleeding.* **3** [T] ~ **sb/sth (from) doing sth** to make sb/sth end or finish an activity; prevent sb/sth from doing sth: *They've built a fence to stop the dog getting out.* ◇ *I'm going to go and you can't stop me.* **4** [I,T] ~ **(for sth)**; ~ **(and do/to do sth)** to end an activity for a short time in order to do sth: *Shall we stop for lunch now?* ◇ *Let's stop and look at the map.* ◇ *We stopped work for half an hour to have a cup of coffee.*

IDM **stop at nothing** to do anything to get what you want, even if it is wrong or dangerous

stop short of sth/doing sth to almost do sth, but then decide not to do it at the last minute

PHR V **stop off (at/in...)** to stop during a journey to do sth

stop over (at/in...) to stay somewhere for a short time during a long journey

stop² ⊶ /stɒp/ ***noun*** [C] **1** an act of stopping or state of being stopped: *Our first stop will be in Edinburgh.* ◇ *Production at the factory will* ***come to a stop*** *at midnight tonight.* ◇ *I managed to* ***bring*** *the car* ***to a stop*** *just in time.* **2** the place where a bus, train, etc. stops so that people can get on and off: *a bus stop* ◇ *I'm getting off at the next stop.*

IDM **pull out all the stops** → PULL¹

put a stop to sth to prevent sth bad or unpleasant from continuing

stopgap /ˈstɒpɡæp/ ***noun*** [C] a person or a thing that does a job for a short time until sb/sth permanent can be found

stopover /ˈstɒpəʊvə(r)/ ***noun*** [C] a short stop in a journey

stoppage /ˈstɒpɪdʒ/ ***noun*** [C] **1** a situation in which people stop working as part of a protest **2** (in sport) an interruption in a game for a particular reason

stopper /ˈstɒpə(r)/ ***noun*** [C] an object that you put into the top of a bottle in order to close it ➲ picture at **Thermos**

stopwatch /ˈstɒpwɒtʃ/ ***noun*** [C] a watch which can be started and stopped by pressing a button, so that you can measure exactly how long sth takes

storage /ˈstɔːrɪdʒ/ ***noun*** [U] the keeping of things until they are needed; the place where they are kept: *This room is being used for storage at the moment.* ➲ look at **cold storage**

store¹ ⊶ /stɔː(r)/ ***noun*** [C] **1** a large shop: *She's a sales assistant in a large department store.* ◇ *a furniture store* ➲ look at **chain store** **2** (*AmE*) = SHOP¹ (1) **3** a supply of sth that you keep for future use; the place where it is kept: *a good store of food for the winter* ◇ *Police discovered a weapons store in the house.*

IDM **in store (for sb/sth)** going to happen in the future: *There's a surprise in store for you when you get home!*

set...store by sth to consider sth to be important: *Nick sets great store by his mother's opinion.*

store² ⊶ /stɔː(r)/ ***verb*** [T] to keep sth or a supply of sth for future use: *to store information on a computer*

storekeeper /ˈstɔːkiːpə(r)/ (*AmE*) = SHOPKEEPER

storeroom /ˈstɔːruːm; -rʊm/ ***noun*** [C] a room where things are kept until they are needed

storey (*AmE* **story**) /ˈstɔːri/ ***noun*** [C] (*pl.* **storeys**: *AmE* **stories**) one floor or level of a building: *The building will be five storeys high.* ◇ *a two-storey house* ◇ *a multi-storey car park*

stork /stɔːk/ ***noun*** [C] a large white bird with a long beak, neck and legs. **Storks** often make their homes (**nests**) on the top of buildings.

RELATED VOCABULARY

Storm is the general word for very bad weather.

A very strong wind is a **gale**. A storm with very strong winds is a **hurricane**. A storm with a very strong circular wind is called a **cyclone**, **tornado**, **typhoon** or **whirlwind**.

A very bad snowstorm is a **blizzard**.

storm¹ ⊶ /stɔːm/ ***noun*** [C] very bad weather, with a lot of rain, strong winds, etc.: *Look at those black clouds. I think there's going to be a storm.* ◇ *a hailstorm/snowstorm/sandstorm/thunderstorm*

storm² /stɔːm/ ***verb*** **1** [I] to enter or leave somewhere in a very angry and noisy way: *He threw down the book and stormed out of the room.* **2** [T] to attack a building, town, etc. suddenly and violently in order to take control of it

stormy /ˈstɔːmi/ ***adj.*** **1** used for talking about very bad weather, with strong winds, heavy rain, etc.: *a stormy night* ◇ *stormy weather* **2** involving a lot of angry argument and strong feeling: *a stormy relationship*

story ⊶ /ˈstɔːri/ ***noun*** [C] (*pl.* **stories**) **1** a ~ **(about sb/sth)** (LITERATURE, ARTS AND MEDIA) a description of people and events that are not real: *I'll* ***tell*** *you* ***a story*** *about the animals that live in that forest.* ◇ *I always read the children* ***a bedtime story****.* ◇ *a detective/fairy/ghost/love story* **2** an account, especially a spoken one, of sth that has happened: *The police didn't believe his story.* **3** a description of true events that happened in the past: *He's writing his life story.* **4** (ARTS AND MEDIA) an article or report in a newspaper or magazine: *The plane crash was the front-page story in most newspapers.* **5** (*AmE*) = STOREY

stout /staʊt/ ***adj.*** **1** (used about a person) rather fat **2** strong and thick: *stout walking boots*

stove ⊶ /stəʊv/ ***noun*** [C] **1** a piece of equipment that can burn various fuels and is used for heating rooms: *a gas/wood-burning stove* **2** (*especially AmE*) = COOKER: *She put a pan of water on the stove.*

stow /stəʊ/ ***verb*** [T] ~ **sth (away)** to put sth away in a particular place until it is needed

stowaway /ˈstəʊəweɪ/ ***noun*** [C] a person who hides in a ship or plane so that they can travel without paying

straddle /ˈstrædl/ ***verb*** [T] **1** (used about a person) to sit or stand with your legs on each side of sb/sth: *to straddle a chair* **2** (used about a building, bridge, etc.) to cross, or exist on both sides of, a river, a road or an area of land

straggle /'strægl/ ***verb*** [I] **1** to walk, etc. more slowly than the rest of the group: *The children straggled along behind their parents.* **2** to grow, spread or move in an untidy way or in different directions: *Her wet hair straggled across her forehead.* ▶ **straggler** ***noun*** [C] ▶ **straggly** ***adj.***: *long straggly hair*

straight¹ /streɪt/ ***adj.*** **1** with no bends or curves; going in one direction only: *a straight line* ◇ *He's got dark, straight hair.* ◇ *Keep your back straight!* ◇ *He was so tired he couldn't walk* ***in a straight line****.* ➲ picture at **line** **2** (not before a noun) in an exactly horizontal or vertical position: *That picture isn't straight.* **3** honest and direct: *Politicians never give* ***a straight answer****.* ◇ *Are you being straight with me?* **4** tidy or organized as it should be: *It took ages to* ***put*** *the room* ***straight*** *after we'd decorated it.* **5** (*informal*) attracted to people of the opposite sex SYN **heterosexual** OPP **gay** **6** (*informal*) used to describe a person who you think is too serious and boring

IDM **get sth straight** to make sure that you understand sth completely

keep a straight face to stop yourself from smiling or laughing

put/set the record straight → RECORD¹

straight² /streɪt/ ***adv.*** **1** not in a curve or at an angle; in a straight line: *Go* ***straight on*** *for about two miles until you come to some traffic lights.* ◇ *He was looking* ***straight ahead****.* ◇ *to sit up straight* (=with a straight back) **2** without stopping; directly: *I took the children straight home after school.* ◇ *to walk straight past sb/sth* ◇ *I'm going straight to bed when I get home.* ◇ *He joined the army straight from school.* **3** in an honest and direct way: *Tell me straight, doctor – is it serious?*

IDM **go straight** to become honest after being a criminal

right/straight away → AWAY

straight out in an honest and direct way: *I told Asif straight out that I didn't want to see him any more.*

'straight angle ***noun*** [C] (MATHEMATICS) an angle of 180° ➲ picture at **angle**

straighten /'streɪtn/ ***verb*** [I,T] ~ **(sth) (up/out)** to become straight or to make sth straight: *The road straightens out at the bottom of the hill.* ◇ *to straighten your tie*

PHR V **straighten sth out** to remove the confusion or difficulties from a situation

straighten up to make your body straight and vertical

straightforward AW /ˌstreɪt'fɔːwəd/ ***adj.*** **1** easy to do or understand; simple: *straightforward instructions* **2** honest and open: *a straightforward person*

strain¹ /streɪn/ ***noun*** **1** [U] pressure that is put on sth when it is pulled or pushed by a physical force: *Running downhill puts strain on the knees.* ◇ *The rope finally broke* ***under*** *the* ***strain****.* **2** [C,U] worry or pressure caused by having too much to deal with: *to be* ***under*** *a lot of* ***strain*** *at work* **3** [C] something that makes you feel worried and tense: *I always find exams a terrible strain.* **4** [C,U] (HEALTH) an injury to part of your body that is caused by using it too much ➲ note at **injure** **5** [C] (BIOLOGY) one type of animal, plant or disease that is slightly different from the other types

strain² /streɪn/ ***verb*** **1** [I,T] to make a great mental or physical effort to do sth: *I was straining to see what was happening.* ◇ *She strained her ears* (=listened very hard) *to catch what they were saying.* ◇ *Bend down as far as you can without straining.* **2** [T] (HEALTH) to injure a part of your body by using it too much: *Don't read in the dark. You'll strain your eyes.* ◇ *I think I've strained a muscle in my neck.* **3** [T] to put a lot of pressure on sth: *Money problems have strained their relationship.* **4** [T] to separate a solid and a liquid by pouring them into a special container with small holes in it: *to strain tea/vegetables/spaghetti*

strained /streɪnd/ ***adj.*** **1** not natural or friendly: *Relations between the two countries are strained.* **2** worried because of having too much to deal with: *Martin looked tired and strained.*

strait /streɪt/ ***noun*** **1** [C, usually pl.] (GEOGRAPHY) a narrow piece of sea that joins two larger seas: *the straits of Gibraltar* **2** **straits** [pl.] a very difficult situation, especially one caused by having no money: *The company is in financial straits.*

IDM **be in dire straits** → DIRE

straitjacket (also **straightjacket**) /'streɪtdʒækɪt/ ***noun*** [C] a piece of clothing like a jacket with long arms which is put on people who are considered dangerous to prevent them from behaving violently

strand /strænd/ ***noun*** [C] **1** a single piece of cotton, wool, hair, etc. **2** one part of a story, situation or idea

stranded /'strændɪd/ ***adj.*** left in a place that you cannot get away from: *We were left stranded when our car broke down in the mountains.*

strange /streɪndʒ/ ***adj.*** **1** unusual or unexpected: *A very strange thing happened to me on the way home.* ◇ *a strange noise* **2** that you have not seen, visited, met, etc. before: *a strange town* ◇ *My mother told me not to talk to strange men.*
▶ **strangeness** ***noun*** [U]

strangely /'streɪndʒli/ ***adv.*** in an unusual or surprising way: *She's been acting very strangely lately.* ◇ ***Strangely enough****, I don't feel at all nervous.*

stranger /'streɪndʒə(r)/ ***noun*** [C] **1** a person that you do not know: *I had to ask a* ***complete stranger*** *to help me with my suitcase.* **2** a person who is in a place that they do not know: *I'm a stranger to this part of the country.*

strangle /'stræŋgl/ ***verb*** [T] **1** to kill sb by squeezing their neck or throat with your hands, a rope, etc. SYN **throttle** ➲ look at **choke** **2** to prevent sth from developing

strap /stræp/ ***noun*** [C] a long narrow piece of leather, cloth, plastic, etc. that you use for carrying sth or for keeping sth in position: *I managed to fasten my watch strap but now I can't undo it.* ▶ **strap** ***verb*** [T] (**strapping**; **strapped**): *The racing driver was securely strapped into the car.*

strapping /'stræpɪŋ/ ***noun*** [U] (HEALTH) sticky material that is wrapped round a part of the body that is injured

strata plural of **stratum**

strategic AW /strə'tiːdʒɪk/ (*also* **strategical** /-dʒɪkl/) ***adj.*** **1** helping you to achieve a plan; giving you an advantage: *They made a strategic decision to sell off part of the company.* **2** connected with a country's plans to achieve success in a war or in its defence system **3** (used about bombs and other weapons) intended to be fired at the enemy's country rather than be used in battle
▶ **strategically** /-kli/ ***adv.***: *The island is strategically important.*

strategist AW /'strætədʒɪst/ ***noun*** [C] a person who is skilled at planning things, especially military activities

strategy ⊶ AW /'strætədʒi/ ***noun*** (*pl.* **strategies**) **1** [C] a plan that you use in order to achieve sth **2** [U] the action of planning how to do or achieve sth: *military strategy*

stratification /ˌstrætɪfɪ'keɪʃn/ ***noun*** [U] the division of sth into different layers or groups: *social stratification*

stratosphere /'strætəsfɪə(r)/ ***noun*** [sing.] **the stratosphere** (GEOGRAPHY) the layer of the earth's atmosphere between about 10 and 50 kilometres above the surface of the earth ➲ picture at **atmosphere** ▶ **stratospheric** /ˌstrætə'sferɪk/ ***adj.***: *stratospheric clouds/ozone*

stratum /'strɑːtəm/ ***noun*** [C] (*pl.* **strata** /-tə/) (GEOGRAPHY) a layer or set of layers of rock, earth, etc. in the ground

stratus /'streɪtəs; 'strɑːtəs/ ***noun*** [U] (GEOGRAPHY) a type of cloud that forms a continuous grey sheet covering the sky ➲ picture at **cloud**

straw /strɔː/ ***noun*** **1** [U] (AGRICULTURE) the STEMS (=long, straight, central parts) of plants, for example WHEAT, that are dried and then used for animals to sleep on or for making BASKETS, covering a roof, etc.: *a straw hat* **2** [C] one piece of **straw** **3** [C] a long plastic or paper tube that you can use for drinking through
IDM **the last/final straw** the last in a series of bad things that happen to you that makes you decide that you cannot accept the situation any longer

strawberry /'strɔːbəri/ ***noun*** [C] (*pl.* **strawberries**) a small soft red fruit with small white seeds on it: *strawberries and cream*

stray¹ /streɪ/ ***verb*** [I] **1** to go away from the place where you should be: *The sheep had strayed onto the road.* **2** to not keep to the subject you should be thinking about or discussing: *My thoughts strayed for a few moments.*

stray² /streɪ/ ***noun*** [C] a dog, cat, etc. that does not have a home ▶ **stray** ***adj.*** (only *before* a noun): *a stray dog*

streak¹ /striːk/ ***noun*** [C] **1** ~ **(of sth)** a thin line or mark: *The cat had brown fur with streaks of white in it.* **2** a part of a person's character that sometimes shows in the way they behave: *Vesna's a very caring girl, but she does have a selfish streak.* **3** a continuous period of bad or good luck in a game of sport: *The team is **on a losing /winning streak** at the moment.*

streak² /striːk/ ***verb*** [I] (*informal*) to run fast

streaked /striːkt/ ***adj.*** ~ **(with sth)** having lines of a different colour: *black hair streaked with grey*

stream¹ ⊶ /striːm/ ***noun*** [C] **1** (GEOGRAPHY) a small river: *I waded across the shallow stream.* **2** the continuous movement of a liquid or gas: *a stream of blood* **3** a continuous movement of people or things: *a stream of traffic* **4** a large number of things which happen one after another: *a stream of letters/telephone calls/questions*

stream² /striːm/ ***verb*** [I] **1** (used about a liquid, gas or light) to flow in large amounts: *Tears were streaming down his face.* ◇ *Sunlight was streaming in through the windows.* **2** (used about people or things) to move somewhere in a continuous flow: *People were streaming out of the station.*

streamer /'striːmə(r)/ ***noun*** [C] a long piece of coloured paper that you use for decorating a room before a party, etc.

streamline /'striːmlaɪn/ ***verb*** [T] **1** to give a vehicle, etc. a long smooth shape so that it will move easily through air or water **2** to make an organization, process, etc. work better by making it simpler ▶ **streamlined** ***adj.***

ˌstream of 'consciousness ***noun*** [U] (LITERATURE) a continuous flow of ideas, thoughts and feelings, as they are experienced by a person; a style of writing that expresses this without using the usual methods of description and conversation

street ⊶ /striːt/ ***noun*** [C] **1** a road in a town, village or city that has shops, houses, etc. on one or both sides: *to walk **along /down the street*** ◇ *to **cross the street*** ◇ *I met Karen **in the street** this morning.* ◇ *a narrow street* ◇ *a street map of Rome* **2 Street** (*abbr.* **St**) [sing.] used in the names of streets: *64 High Street* ◇ *The post office is in Sheep Street.*
IDM **the man in the street** → MAN¹
streets ahead (of sb/sth) (*informal*) much better than sb/sth
(right) up your street (*informal*) (used about an activity, subject, etc.) exactly right for you because you know a lot about it, like it very much, etc.

street cred /'striːt kred/ (*also* **'street credibility**) ***noun*** [U] (SOCIAL STUDIES) a way of behaving and dressing that is acceptable to young people, especially those who live in cities: *Those clothes do nothing for your street cred.*

streetwise /'striːtwaɪz/ (*AmE also* **'street-smart**) ***adj.*** (*informal*) having the knowledge and experience that is needed to deal with the difficulties and dangers of life in a big city

strength ⊶ /streŋθ/ ***noun*** **1** [U] the quality of being physically strong; the amount of this quality that you have: *He pulled with all his strength but the rock would not move.* ◇ *I didn't have the strength to walk any further.* **2** [U] the ability of an object to hold heavy weights or not to break or be damaged easily: *All our suitcases are tested for strength before they leave the factory.* **3** [U] the power and influence that sb has: *Germany's economic strength* **4** [U] how strong a feeling or opinion is **5** [C,U] a good quality or ability that sb/sth has: *His greatest strength is his ability to communicate with people.* ◇ *the strengths and weaknesses of a plan* OPP **weakness**
IDM **at full strength** (used about a group) having all the people it needs or usually has: *Nobody is injured, so the team will be at full strength for the game.*
below strength (used about a group) not having the number of people it needs or usually has
on the strength of as a result of information, advice, etc.

strengthen /'streŋθn/ ***verb*** [I,T] to become stronger or to make sth stronger: *exercises to strengthen your muscles* OPP **weaken**

strenuous /'strenjuəs/ ***adj.*** needing or using a lot of effort or energy: *Don't do **strenuous exercise** after eating.* ◇ *She's making a **strenuous effort** to be on time every day.* ▶ **strenuously** ***adv.***

streptococcus /ˌstreptə'kɒkəs/ ***noun*** [C] (*pl.* **-cocci** /-'kɒkaɪ/) (BIOLOGY, HEALTH) a type of bacteria, some types of which can cause serious infections and illnesses

stress¹ ⊶ AW /stres/ ***noun*** **1** [C,U] (HEALTH) worry and pressure that is caused by having too much to deal with: *He's been **under** a lot of **stress** since his wife went into hospital.* ◇ ***stress-related** illnesses* ➲ look at **trauma** **2** [U,C] ~ **(on sth)** (HEALTH) pressure put on sth that can damage it or make it lose its shape: *When you have an injury you start putting stress on other parts of your body.* ◇ *a **stress fracture** of the foot* (=one caused by such pressure) **3** [U] ~ **(on sth)** the special attention that you give to sth because you think it is important: *We should **put** more **stress** on preventing crime.* **4** [C,U] (a) ~ **(on sth)** (LANGUAGE) the force that you put on a particular word or part of a word when you speak: *In the word 'dictionary' the stress is on the first syllable, 'dic'.*

stress² 🔑 AW /stres/ ***verb*** [T] to give sth special force or attention because it is important: *The minister stressed the need for a peaceful solution.* ◇ *Which syllable is stressed in this word?* SYN **emphasize**

stressed AW /strest/ ***adj.*** (not before a noun) **1** (*informal*) (*also* ˌ**stressed 'out**) too anxious and tired to be able to relax: *He was feeling very stressed and tired.* **2** (LANGUAGE) (used about a syllable) pronounced with emphasis OPP **unstressed** **3** (TECHNICAL) that has had a lot of physical pressure put on it: *stressed metal*

stressful AW /'stresfl/ ***adj.*** causing worry and pressure: *a stressful job*

'stress mark ***noun*** [C] (LANGUAGE) a mark used to show which part of a particular word or SYLLABLE is pronounced with more force than others

stretch¹ 🔑 /stretʃ/ ***verb*** **1** [I,T] to pull sth so that it becomes longer or wider; to become longer or wider in this way: *The artist stretched the canvas tightly over the frame.* ◇ *My T-shirt stretched when I washed it.* **2** [I,T] ~ **(sth) (out)** to push out your arms, legs, etc. as far as possible: *He switched off the alarm clock, yawned and stretched.* ◇ *She stretched out on the sofa and fell asleep.* ◇ *She stretched out her arm to take the book.* **3** [I] to cover a large area of land or a long period of time: *The long white beaches stretch for miles along the coast.* **4** [T] to make use of all the money, ability, time, etc. that sb has available for use: *The test has been designed to really stretch students' knowledge.*

IDM **stretch your legs** to go for a walk after sitting down for a long time

stretch² /stretʃ/ ***noun*** [C] **1 a** ~ **(of sth)** an area of land or water: *a dangerous stretch of road* **2** [usually sing.] the action of making the muscles in your arms, legs, back, etc. as long as possible: *Stand up, everybody, and have a good stretch.*

IDM **at a stretch** without stopping: *We travelled for six hours at a stretch.*

at full stretch → FULL¹

stretcher /'stretʃə(r)/ ***noun*** [C] (HEALTH) a piece of cloth supported by two poles that is used for carrying a person who has been injured

stretchy /'stretʃi/ ***adj.*** (**stretchier**; **stretchiest**) that can easily be made longer or wider without tearing or breaking: *stretchy fabric*

strict 🔑 /strɪkt/ ***adj.*** **1** not allowing people to break rules or behave badly: *Samir's very strict with his children.* ◇ *I went to a very strict school.* **2** that must be obeyed completely: *I gave her strict instructions to be home before 9.00.* **3** exactly correct; accurate: *a strict interpretation of the law*

strictly 🔑 /'strɪktli/ ***adv.*** in a strict way: *Smoking is strictly forbidden.*

IDM **strictly speaking** to be exactly correct or accurate: *Strictly speaking, the tomato is not a vegetable. It's a fruit.*

stride¹ /straɪd/ ***verb*** [I] (*pt* **strode** /strəʊd/) (not used in the perfect tenses) to walk with long steps, often because you feel very confident or determined: *He strode up to the house and knocked on the door.*

stride² /straɪd/ ***noun*** [C] a long step

IDM **get into your stride** to start to do sth in a confident way and well after an uncertain beginning

make great strides to make very quick progress

take sth in your stride to deal with a new or difficult situation easily and without worrying

strident /'straɪdnt/ ***adj.*** (used about a voice or a sound) loud and unpleasant

strife /straɪf/ ***noun*** [U] (*written*) trouble or fighting between people or groups

strike¹ 🔑 /straɪk/ ***noun*** [C] **1** a period of time when people refuse to go to work, usually because they want more money or better working conditions: *a one-day strike* ◇ *Union members voted to **go on strike**.* **2** a sudden military attack, especially by aircraft

strike² 🔑 /straɪk/ ***verb*** (*pt, pp* **struck** /strʌk/) **1** [T] (*formal*) to hit sb/sth: *The stone struck her on the head.* ◇ *The boat struck a rock and began to sink.* **2** [I,T] to attack and harm sb/sth suddenly: *The earthquake struck Kobe in 1995.* ◇ *The building had been **struck by lightning**.* **3** [I] to stop work as a protest: *The workers voted to strike for more money.* **4** [T] ~ **sb (as sth)** to give sb a particular impression: *Does anything here strike you as unusual?* ◇ *He strikes me as a very caring man.* **5** [T] (used about a thought or an idea) to come suddenly into sb's mind: *It suddenly struck me that she would be the ideal person for the job.* **6** [T] to produce fire by rubbing sth, especially a match, on a surface: *She struck a match and lit her cigarette.* **7** [I,T] (used about a clock) to ring a bell so that people know what time it is: *The clock struck eight* (= 8 o'clock). **8** [T] to discover gold, oil, etc. in the ground

IDM **strike a balance (between A and B)** to find a middle way between two extremes

strike a bargain (with sb) to make an agreement with sb

within striking distance near enough to be reached or attacked easily

PHR V **strike back** to attack sb/sth that has attacked you

strike up sth (with sb) to start a conversation or friendship with sb

striker /'straɪkə(r)/ ***noun*** [C] **1** a person who has stopped working as a protest **2** (SPORT) (in football) a player whose job is to score goals

striking 🔑 /'straɪkɪŋ/ ***adj.*** very noticeable; making a strong impression: *There was a striking similarity between the two men.* ▶ **strikingly** ***adv.***

string¹ 🔑 /strɪŋ/ ***noun*** **1** [C,U] a piece of long, strong material like very thin rope, that you use for tying things: *a ball/piece/length of string* ◇ *The key is hanging on a string.* **2** [C] (MUSIC) one of the pieces of thin wire, etc. that produce the sound on some musical instruments: *A guitar has six strings.* ➲ picture on **page 465** **3** [C] one of the tightly stretched pieces of NYLON, etc. in a RACKET (= the thing that you use to hit the ball in tennis and other sports) **4 the strings** [pl.] (MUSIC) the instruments in an ORCHESTRA that have strings **5** [C] **a** ~ **of sth** a line of things that are joined together on the same piece of thread: *a string of beads* **6** [C] **a** ~ **of sth** a series of people, things or events that follow one after another: *a string of visitors* **7** [C] (COMPUTING) a series of letters, numbers, words, etc.

IDM **(with) no strings attached**; **without strings** with no special conditions

pull strings → PULL¹

string² /strɪŋ/ ***verb*** [T] (*pt, pp* **strung** /strʌŋ/) ~ **sth (up)** to hang up a line of things with a piece of string, etc.

PHR V **string sb/sth out** to make people or things

form a line with spaces between each person or thing

string sth together (LANGUAGE) to put words or phrases together to make a sentence, speech, etc.

stringed instrument /ˌstrɪŋd ˈɪnstrəmənt/ ***noun*** [C] (MUSIC) any musical instrument with strings that you play with your fingers or with a BOW

stringent /ˈstrɪndʒənt/ ***adj.*** (used about a law, rule, etc.) very strict

strip[1] /strɪp/ ***noun*** [C] a long narrow piece of sth: *a strip of paper*

strip[2] /strɪp/ ***verb*** (**stripping**; **stripped**) **1** [I,T] ~ **(sth) (off)** to take off your clothes; to take off sb else's clothes: *The doctor asked him to strip to the waist.* ◇ *I was stripped and searched at the airport by two customs officers.* **2** [T] ~ **sb/sth (of sth)** to take sth away from sb/sth: *They stripped the house of all its furniture.* **3** [T] ~ **sth (off)** to remove sth that is covering a surface: *to strip the paint off a door* ◇ *to strip wallpaper*

stripe /straɪp/ ***noun*** [C] a long narrow line of colour: *Zebras have black and white stripes.*

striped /straɪpt/ (*BrE also, informal* **stripy**) ***adj.*** marked with a pattern of stripes: *a red and white striped dress*

stripper /ˈstrɪpə(r)/ ***noun*** [C] a person whose job is to take off their clothes in order to entertain people

striptease /ˈstrɪptiːz/ ***noun*** [C,U] entertainment in which sb takes off their clothes, usually to music

stripy /ˈstraɪpi/ ***adj.*** (*informal*, *BrE*) = STRIPED: *a stripy jumper*

strive /straɪv/ ***verb*** [I] (*pt* **strove** /strəʊv/; *pp* **striven** /ˈstrɪvn/) (*formal*) ~ **(for sth/to do sth)** to try very hard to do or get sth: *to strive for perfection*

strode past tense of **stride[1]**

stroke[1] /strəʊk/ ***noun*** [C] **1** (ART) one of the movements that you make when you are writing or painting: *a brush stroke* **2** (SPORT) one of the movements that you make when you are swimming, rowing, playing GOLF, etc.: *Woods won by three strokes* (= hits of the ball in golf). **3** (also used in compounds) (SPORT) a style of swimming: *Butterfly is the only stroke I can't do.* ➲ look at **backstroke**, **breaststroke** **4** (HEALTH) a sudden illness which attacks the brain and can leave a person unable to move part of their body, speak clearly, etc.: *to* ***have a stroke*** **5** [sing.] a ~ **of sth** a single successful or unsuccessful action or event: *It was* ***a stroke of luck*** *finding your ring on the beach, wasn't it?* **6** each of the sounds made by a clock or bell giving the hours: *At the first stroke it will be 9 o'clock exactly.* ◇ ***on the stroke of*** *three* (= at 3 o'clock exactly)

IDM **at a/one stroke** with a single action
not do a stroke (of work) to not do any work at all

stroke[2] /strəʊk/ ***verb*** [T] **1** to move your hand gently over sb/sth: *She stroked his hair affectionately.* ◇ *to stroke a dog* **2** to move sth somewhere with a smooth movement: *She stroked away his tears.*

stroll /strəʊl/ ***noun*** [C] a slow walk for pleasure: *to* ***go for a stroll*** *along the beach* ▶ **stroll** ***verb*** [I]

strong /strɒŋ/ ***adj.*** **1** (used about a person) physically powerful; able to lift or carry heavy things: *I need someone strong to help me move this bookcase.* ◇ *to have strong arms/muscles* **2** (used about an object) not easily broken or damaged: *That chair isn't strong enough for you to stand on.* **3** (used about a natural force) powerful: *strong winds/currents/sunlight* **4** having a big effect on the mind, body or senses: ***a strong smell*** *of garlic* ◇ *strong coffee* ◇ *a strong drink* (= with a lot of alcohol in it) ◇ *I have the* ***strong impression*** *that they don't like us.* **5** (used about opinions and beliefs) very firm; difficult to fight against: *There was* ***strong opposition*** *to the idea.* ◇ ***strong support*** *for the government's plan* **6** powerful and likely to succeed: *She's a strong candidate for the job.* ◇ *a strong team* **7** (used after a noun) having a particular number of people ➲ noun **strength** for all senses **8** (LANGUAGE) used to describe the way some words are pronounced when they are emphasized. For example, the strong form of *and* is /ænd/.
▶ **strongly** ***adv.***: *The directors are strongly opposed to the idea.* ◇ *to feel very strongly about sth*

IDM **going strong** (*informal*) continuing, even after a long time: *The company was formed in 1851 and is still going strong.*
sb's strong point something that a person is good at: *Maths is not my strong point.*

stronghold /ˈstrɒŋhəʊld/ ***noun*** [C] **1** (POLITICS) an area in which there is a lot of support for a particular belief or group of people, especially a political party: *a Republican stronghold/a stronghold of Republicanism* **2** (HISTORY) a castle or a place that is strongly built and difficult to attack **3** an area where there are a large number of a particular type of animal: *This valley is one of the last strongholds of the Siberian tiger.*

ˌstrong-ˈminded ***adj.*** having firm ideas or beliefs

strontium /ˈstrɒntiəm; ˈstrɒnʃ-/ ***noun*** [U] (*symbol* **Sr**) (CHEMISTRY) a soft silver-white metal ❶ For more information on the periodic table of elements, look at pages R34-5.

stroppy /ˈstrɒpi/ ***adj.*** (*BrE*, *slang*) (used about a person) easily annoyed and difficult to deal with

strove past tense of **strive**

struck past tense, past participle of **strike[2]**

> **THESAURUS**
>
> **structure**
>
> **framework • composition • construction • fabric • make-up**
>
> These are all words for the way the different parts of sth combine together or the way that sth has been made.
>
> **structure**: *the structure of the human body*
> **framework**: *The report provides a framework for further research.*
> **composition**: *changes in the composition of the workforce*
> **construction**: *ships of steel construction*
> **fabric**: *the fabric of society*
> **make-up**: *the genetic make-up of plants*

structure[1] AW /ˈstrʌktʃə(r)/ ***noun*** **1** [C,U] the way that the parts of sth are put together or organized: *the political and social structure of a country* ◇ *the grammatical structures of a language* **2** [C] a building or sth that has been built or made from a number of parts: *The old office block had been replaced by a modern glass structure.* ➲ note at **building** ▶ **structural** AW /ˈstrʌktʃərəl/ ***adj.***

structure[2] AW /ˈstrʌktʃə(r)/ ***verb*** [T] to arrange sth in an organized way: *a carefully-structured English course*

struggle[1] /ˈstrʌɡl/ ***verb*** [I] **1** ~ **(with sth/for sth/to do sth)** to try very hard to do sth, especially when it is difficult: *We struggled up the stairs with our* *heavy suitcases.* ◇ *Maria was struggling with her English homework.* ◇ *The country is struggling for independence.* **2** ~ **(with sb/sth)**; ~ **(against sth)** to fight in order to prevent sth or to escape from sb: *He shouted and struggled but he couldn't get free.* ◇ *A passer-by was struggling with one of the robbers on the ground.* ◇ *He has been struggling against cancer for years.*

PHR V **struggle on** to continue to do sth although it is difficult: *I felt terrible but managed to struggle on to the end of the day.*

struggle² ⊶ /ˈstrʌgl/ ***noun*** [C] **1** a fight in which sb tries to do or get sth when this is difficult: *All countries should join together in the struggle against terrorism.* ◇ *He will not give up the presidency without a struggle.* ◇ *a struggle for independence* ➲ note at **campaign¹** **2** [usually sing.] sth that is difficult to achieve: *It will be a struggle to get there on time.*

strum /strʌm/ ***verb*** [I,T] (**strumming**; **strummed**) (MUSIC) to play a GUITAR by moving your hand up and down over the strings

strung past tense, past participle of **string²**

strut /strʌt/ ***verb*** [I] (**strutting**; **strutted**) to walk in a proud way

strychnine /ˈstrɪkniːn/ ***noun*** [U] (HEALTH) a poisonous substance that can be used in very small amounts as a medicine

stub /stʌb/ ***noun*** [C] the short piece of a cigarette or pencil that is left after the rest of it has been used

stubble /ˈstʌbl/ ***noun*** [U] **1** (AGRICULTURE) the short parts of CORN, WHEAT, etc. that are left standing after the rest has been cut **2** the short hairs that grow on a man's face when he has not shaved for some time

stubborn /ˈstʌbən/ ***adj.*** not wanting to do what other people want you to do; refusing to change your plans or decisions: *She's too stubborn to apologize.* SYN **obstinate** ➲ look at **pig-headed** ▶ **stubbornly** ***adv.***: *He stubbornly refused to apologize so he was sacked.* ▶ **stubbornness** ***noun*** [U]

stuck¹ past tense, past participle of **stick²**

stuck² /stʌk/ ***adj.*** **1** not able to move: *This drawer's stuck. I can't open it at all.* ◇ *We were stuck in traffic for over two hours.* **2** not able to continue with an exercise, etc. because it is too difficult: *If you* ***get stuck****, ask your teacher for help.*

stud /stʌd/ ***noun*** **1** [C] a small piece of metal that sticks out from the rest of the surface that it is fixed to: *a black leather jacket with studs all over it* **2** [C] a small, round, solid piece of metal that you wear through a hole in your ear or other part of the body **3** [C] one of the pieces of plastic or metal that stick out from the bottom of football, etc. boots and that help you stand up on wet ground **4** [C,U] (AGRICULTURE) a number of high quality horses or other animals that are kept for breeding young animals; the place where these horses, etc. are kept: *a stud farm*

studded /ˈstʌdɪd/ ***adj.*** **1** covered or decorated with STUDS **2** ~ **(with sth)** containing a lot of sth

student ⊶ /ˈstjuːdnt/ ***noun*** [C] (EDUCATION) a person who is studying at a college or university: *Paola is a medical student at Bristol University.* ◇ *a full-time/part-time student* ◇ *a postgraduate/research student* ➲ look at **pupil**, **scholar**, **graduate**, **undergraduate**

studied /ˈstʌdid/ ***adj.*** (*formal*) carefully planned or done, especially when you are trying to give a particular impression

studio ⊶ /ˈstjuːdiəʊ/ ***noun*** [C] (*pl.* **studios**) **1** (ART) a room where an artist or photographer works **2** (ARTS AND MEDIA, MUSIC) a room or building where films or television programmes are made, or where music, radio programmes, etc. are recorded: *a film/TV/recording studio*

studious /ˈstjuːdiəs/ ***adj.*** (used about a person) spending a lot of time studying

studiously /ˈstjuːdiəsli/ ***adv.*** with great care

study¹ ⊶ /ˈstʌdi/ ***noun*** (*pl.* **studies**) **1** [U] (EDUCATION) the activity of learning about sth: *One hour every afternoon is left free for individual study.* ◇ *Physiology is the study of how living things work.* **2 studies** [pl.] (EDUCATION) the subjects that you study: *business/media/Japanese studies* **3** [C] (EDUCATION) a piece of research that examines a question or a subject in detail: *They are doing a study of the causes of heart disease.* ➲ note at **examine** **4** [C] a room in a house where you go to read, write or study

COLLOCATIONS AND PATTERNS

Studying and exams

When you study a subject, you need to **do your homework,** and then **give/hand it in.**
Have you done your physics homework?
Hand in your essays on Friday.

You **revise/study for** a **test** or an **exam.**
He revised for four hours a day for his chemistry exam.

You **have/take a test** or **take/sit an exam** to see how well you know sth.
They have a vocabulary test every Monday.
He took the TOEFL exam last week.

The **results** tell you your **marks/grades** or **score.**
Have you had your results yet?
He was thrilled when he got top/full marks for history.
She got good grades for all five subjects.
They achieved the necessary IELTS scores.

If you have been successful, you have **passed.** If you have been unsuccessful, you have **failed.**
She was delighted when she passed her maths exam.
He failed his driving test twice.

The **pass mark** (= the number of marks that you need to pass an exam) is usually given as a percentage.
The pass mark is 65%.

study² ⊶ /ˈstʌdi/ ***verb*** (*pres. part.* **studying**; *3rd person sing. pres.* **studies**; *pt, pp* **studied**) **1** [I,T] ~ **(sth/for sth)** (EDUCATION) to spend time learning about sth: *to study French at university* ◇ *Leon has been studying hard for his exams.* **2** [T] to look at sth very carefully: *to study a map*

stuff¹ ⊶ /stʌf/ ***noun*** [U] (*informal*) **1** used to refer to sth without using its name: *What's that green stuff at the bottom of the bottle?* ◇ *The shop was burgled and a lot of stuff was stolen.* ◇ *They sell stationery and stuff (like that).* ◇ *I'll put the swimming stuff in this bag.* **2** used to refer in general to things that people do, say, think, etc.: *I've got lots of stuff to do tomorrow so I'm going to get up early.* ◇ *I don't believe all that stuff about him being robbed.* ◇ *I like reading and stuff.*

stuff² /stʌf/ ***verb*** **1** [T] ~ **sth (with sth)** to fill sth with sth: *The pillow was stuffed with feathers.* ◇ *red peppers stuffed with rice* **2** [T] (*informal*) ~ **sth into sth** to put sth into sth else quickly or carelessly: *He quickly stuffed a few clothes into a suitcase.* **3** [T] (*informal*) ~ **sb/yourself (with sth)** to eat too much of sth; to give sb too much to eat: *Barry just sat there stuffing himself with sandwiches.* ◇ *Don't stuff the kids with chocolate before their dinner.* **4** [T] to fill the body of a dead bird or animal with special material so that it looks as if it is alive: *They've got a stuffed crocodile in the museum.*

stuffing /ˈstʌfɪŋ/ ***noun*** [U] **1** a mixture of small pieces of food that you put inside a chicken, vegetable, etc. before you cook it **2** the material that you put inside CUSHIONS, soft toys, etc.

stuffy /ˈstʌfi/ ***adj.*** **1** (used about a room) too warm and having no fresh air **2** (*informal*) (used about a person) formal and old-fashioned

stumble /ˈstʌmbl/ ***verb*** [I] **1** ~ **(over/on sth)** to hit your foot against sth when you are walking or running and almost fall over **2** ~ **(over/through sth)** (**LANGUAGE**, **MUSIC**) to make a mistake when you are speaking, playing music, etc.: *The newsreader stumbled over the name of the Russian tennis player.*
PHR V **stumble across/on sb/sth** to meet or find sb/sth by chance

ˈ**stumbling block** *noun* [C] something that causes trouble or a difficulty, so that you cannot achieve what you want: *Money is still the stumbling block to settling the dispute.*

stump¹ /stʌmp/ ***noun*** [C] **1** the bottom part of a tree left in the ground after the rest has fallen or been cut down **2** the end of sth or the part that is left after the main part has been cut, broken off or worn away ➲ picture at **erode** **3** (**HEALTH**) the short part of sb's leg or arm that is left after the rest has been cut off **4** [usually pl.] (**SPORT**) (in the game of CRICKET) one of the set of three vertical wooden sticks that form the WICKET: *The ball went past the batsman and hit **the stumps**.*

stump² /stʌmp/ ***verb*** [T] (*informal*) to cause sb to be unable to answer a question or find a solution for a problem: *I was completely stumped by question 14.*

stun /stʌn/ ***verb*** [T] (**stunning**; **stunned**) **1** to make a person or animal unconscious or confused, especially by hitting them or it on the head **2** to make a person very surprised by telling them some unexpected news: *His sudden death stunned his friends and colleagues.* ▸ **stunned** ***adj.***

stung past tense, past participle of **sting¹**

stunk past participle of **stink**

stunning /ˈstʌnɪŋ/ ***adj.*** (*informal*) very attractive, impressive or surprising: *a stunning view*

stunt¹ /stʌnt/ ***noun*** [C] **1** something that you do to get people's attention: *a publicity stunt* **2** (**ARTS AND MEDIA**) a very difficult or dangerous thing that sb does to entertain people or as part of a film: *Some actors do their own stunts, others use a stuntman.*

stunt² /stʌnt/ ***verb*** [T] to stop sb/sth growing or developing properly: *A poor diet can stunt a child's growth.*

stuntman /ˈstʌntmæn/ **stuntwoman** /ˈstʌntwʊmən/ ***noun*** [C] (*pl.* **-men** /-men/) (*pl.* **-women** /-wɪmɪn/) (**ARTS AND MEDIA**) a person whose job is to do dangerous things in place of an actor in a film, etc.; a person who does dangerous things in order to entertain people

stupendous /stjuːˈpendəs/ ***adj.*** very large or impressive: *a stupendous achievement*

stupid ⊶ /ˈstjuːpɪd/ ***adj.*** **1** not intelligent or sensible: *Don't be so stupid, of course I'll help you!* ◇ *He was stupid to trust her.* ◇ *a stupid mistake/suggestion/question* **2** (only *before* a noun) (*informal*) used to show that you are angry or do not like sb/sth: *I'm tired of hearing about his stupid car.*
▸ **stupidity** /stjuːˈpɪdəti/ ***noun*** [U] ▸ **stupidly** ***adv.***

stupor /ˈstjuːpə(r)/ ***noun*** [sing., U] the state of being nearly unconscious or being unable to think properly

sturdy /ˈstɜːdi/ ***adj.*** (**sturdier**; **sturdiest**) strong and healthy; that will not break easily: *sturdy legs* ◇ *sturdy shoes* ▸ **sturdily** ***adv.*** ▸ **sturdiness** ***noun*** [U]

stutter /ˈstʌtə(r)/ ***verb*** [I,T] (**LANGUAGE**) to have difficulty when you speak, so that you keep repeating the first sound of a word ▸ **stutter** ***noun*** [C]: *to have a stutter*

sty (also **stye**) /staɪ/ ***noun*** [C] (*pl.* **sties** or **styes**) **1** (**HEALTH**) a painful spot on the EYELID (= the skin that covers the eye) **2** = PIGSTY

style¹ ⊶ **AW** /staɪl/ ***noun*** **1** [C,U] the way that sth is done, built, etc.: *a new style of architecture* ◇ *The writer's style is very clear and simple.* ◇ *an American-style education system* **2** [C,U] the fashion, shape or design of sth: *We stock all the latest styles.* ◇ *I like your new hairstyle.* **3** [U] the ability to do things in a way that other people admire: *He's got no sense of style.* **4** [C] (**BIOLOGY**) the long thin part of the CARPEL (= the female part in the middle of a flower) that supports the STIGMA ➲ picture at **flower**

style² **AW** /staɪl/ ***verb*** [T] to design, make or shape sth in a particular way: *He'd had his hair styled at an expensive salon.*
PHR V **style sth/yourself on sth/sb** to copy the style, manner or appearance of sb/sth **SYN** **model**: *a coffee bar styled on a Parisian cafe*

stylish **AW** /ˈstaɪlɪʃ/ ***adj.*** fashionable and attractive: *She's a stylish dresser.*

stylistic /staɪˈlɪstɪk/ ***adj.*** (**ART**) connected with the style an artist uses in a particular piece of art, writing or music: *stylistic analysis* ◇ *stylistic features*
▸ **stylistically** /-kli/ ***adv.***

stylized (also **-ised**) **AW** /ˈstaɪlaɪzd/ ***adj.*** (**ART**, **LITERATURE**) drawn, written, etc. in a way that is not natural or realistic: *a stylized drawing of a house*

stylus /ˈstaɪləs/ ***noun*** [C] (*pl.* **styluses** or **styli** /ˈstaɪlaɪ/) **1** a device on a RECORD PLAYER that looks like a small needle and is placed on the record in order to play it **2** (**COMPUTING**) a special pen used to write text or draw an image on a special computer screen

stymie /ˈstaɪmi/ ***verb*** [T] (*pres. part.* **stymieing** or **stymying**; *3rd person sing. pres.* **stymies**; *pt, pp* **stymied**) (*informal*) to prevent sb from doing sth that they have planned or want to do; to prevent sth from happening **SYN** **foil²**

suave /swɑːv/ ***adj.*** (usually used about a man) confident, elegant and polite, sometimes in a way that does not seem sincere

sub- /sʌb/ ***prefix*** **1** (used in nouns and adjectives) below; less than: *sub-zero temperatures* ◇ *a subtropical* (= almost tropical) *climate* ◇ *a sub lieutenant* **2** (used in nouns and adjectives) under: *subway* ◇ *submarine* **3** (used in verbs and nouns) making a smaller part of sth: *subdivide* ◇ *subset*

subconscious /ˌsʌbˈkɒnʃəs/ (*also* **unconscious**) ***noun*** [sing.] (**PSYCHOLOGY**) **the subconscious** the hidden part of your mind that can affect the way that you behave without you realizing ▸ **subconscious** ***adj.***: *the subconscious mind* ◇ *Many advertisements work at a subconscious level.* ▸ **subconsciously** ***adv.***

subcontinent /ˌsʌbˈkɒntɪnənt/ ***noun*** [sing.] (GEOGRAPHY) a large land mass that forms part of a continent, especially the part of Asia that includes India, Pakistan and Bangladesh

subcontract /ˌsʌbkənˈtrækt/ ***verb*** [T] ~ **sth (to sb)** (BUSINESS) to pay a person or company to do some of the work that you have been given a contract to do

subcutaneous /ˌsʌbkjuˈteɪniəs/ ***adj.*** (usually *before* a noun) (ANATOMY) under the skin: *a subcutaneous injection* ➲ picture at **skin**

subdivide /ˌsʌbdɪˈvaɪd/ ***verb*** [I,T] to divide or be divided into smaller parts ▸ **subdivision** /ˈsʌbdɪvɪʒn/ ***noun*** [C,U]

subdue /səbˈdjuː/ ***verb*** [T] to defeat sb/sth or bring sb/sth under control

subdued /səbˈdjuːd/ ***adj.*** **1** (used about a person) quieter and with less energy than usual **2** not very loud or bright: *subdued laughter/lighting*

COLLOCATIONS AND PATTERNS

Studying subjects at college or university

A student can **do/study** a **course/subject** at college or university.
Rhodri did history at Exeter University.
Lucy did a course in art and design.
She's studying health and psychology at Witney College.
(BrE, formal) He read Classics at Cambridge.

A **lecturer/tutor** teaches in a **department** of a college or university.
She's an economics lecturer.
Dr Scragg was my history tutor at university.
The anthropology department is expanding.

A **professor** is a **lecturer** at the highest level in a university.
He's professor of linguistics at Bangor University.

A student **attends/goes to lectures, seminars** and **tutorials.**
She went to a seminar on Wittgenstein with Professor Brown.
The genetics lectures are on a different campus.

At the end of a course a student is awarded with **a degree** or **a diploma.**
a sociology degree
a diploma in food hygiene

An **undergraduate** is a student studying for their first degree, a **graduate** is sb who has got a university degree and a **postgraduate** already holds a first degree and is doing further study or research.
Good science graduates are always in demand.
She completed a postgraduate course in journalism.

subject¹ 🔑 /ˈsʌbdʒɪkt/ ***noun*** [C] **1** a person or thing that is being considered, shown or talked about: *What subject is the lecture on?* ◇ *What are your views on this subject?* ◇ *I've tried several times to* ***bring up /raise the subject*** *of money.* **2** (EDUCATION) an area of knowledge that you study at school, university, etc.: *My favourite subjects at school are Biology and French.* **3** (ART) a person or thing that is the main feature of a picture or photograph, or that a work of art is based on: *Focus the camera on the subject.* ◇ *Classical landscapes were a popular subject with many 18th century painters.* **4** (LANGUAGE) the person or thing that does the action described by the verb in a sentence: *In the sentence 'The cat sat on the mat', 'the cat' is the subject.* ➲ look at **object** **5** (POLITICS) a person from a particular country, especially one with a king or queen; a citizen: *a British subject*
IDM **change the subject** → CHANGE¹

subject² /səbˈdʒekt/ ***verb***
PHR V **subject sb/sth to sth** to make sb/sth experience sth unpleasant: *He was subjected to verbal and physical abuse from the other boys.*

subject³ /ˈsʌbdʒɪkt/ ***adj.*** **1** ~ **to sth** likely to be affected by sth: *The area is subject to regular flooding.* ◇ *Smokers are more subject to heart attacks than non-smokers.* **2** ~ **to sth** depending on sth as a condition: *The plan for new housing is still subject to approval by the minister.* **3** controlled by or having to obey sb/sth

subjective /səbˈdʒektɪv/ ***adj.*** based on your own tastes and opinions instead of on facts OPP **objective** ▸ **subjectively** ***adv.***

ˈ**subject matter** ***noun*** [U] (ART, ARTS AND MEDIA, LITERATURE) the ideas or information contained in a book, speech, painting, etc.

subjunctive /səbˈdʒʌŋktɪv/ ***noun*** [sing.] (LANGUAGE) the form of a verb in certain languages that expresses doubt, possibility, a wish, etc. ▸ **subjunctive** ***adj.***

sublet /ˌsʌbˈlet/ ***verb*** [T,I] (*pres. part.* **subletting**; *pt, pp* **sublet**) ~ **(sth) (to sb)** (FINANCE) to rent to sb else all or part of a property that you rent from the owner

sublime¹ /səˈblaɪm/ ***adj.*** (*formal*) of extremely high quality that makes you admire sth very much ▸ **sublimely** ***adv.***

sublime² /səˈblaɪm/ (also **sublimate** /ˈsʌblɪmeɪt/) ***verb*** [I] (CHEMISTRY) (used about a solid substance) to change into a gas when heated and back into a solid after cooling, without first becoming a liquid ▸ **sublimation** /ˌsʌblɪˈmeɪʃn/ ***noun*** [U]

subliminal /ˌsʌbˈlɪmɪnl/ ***adj.*** affecting your mind even though you are not aware of it: *subliminal advertising* ▸ **subliminally** ***adv.***

submarine /ˌsʌbməˈriːn/ ***noun*** [C] a type of ship that can travel under the water as well as on the surface

submerge /səbˈmɜːdʒ/ ***verb*** [I,T] to go or make sth go under water: *The fields were submerged by the floods.* ▸ **submerged** ***adj.***

submersible¹ ***adj.*** (*AmE also* **submergible** /səbˈmɜːdʒəbl/) that can be used underwater: *a submersible camera*

submersible² ***noun*** [C] a SUBMARINE (= a ship that can travel underwater) that goes underwater for short periods

submission AW /səbˈmɪʃn/ ***noun*** **1** [U] the accepting of sb else's power or control because they have defeated you **2** [U, C] the action of giving a plan, document, etc. to an official organization so that it can be studied and considered; the plan, document, etc. that you send

submissive /səbˈmɪsɪv/ ***adj.*** ready to obey other people and do whatever they want

submit AW /səbˈmɪt/ ***verb*** (**submitting**; **submitted**) **1** [T] ~ **sth (to sb/sth)** to give a plan, document, etc. to an official organization so that it can be studied and considered: *to submit an application/complaint/claim* **2** [I] ~ **(to sb/sth)** to accept sb/sth's power or control because they have defeated you

subordinate[1] AW /sə'bɔːdɪnət/ *adj.* ~ **(to sb/sth)** having less power or authority than sb else; less important than sth else ▶ **subordinate** *noun* [C]: *the relationship between superiors and their subordinates*

subordinate[2] AW /sə'bɔːdɪneɪt/ *verb* [T] to treat one person or thing as less important than another

su,bordinate 'clause *noun* [C] (LANGUAGE) a group of words that is not a sentence but that adds information to the main part of the sentence: *In the sentence 'We left early because it was raining', 'because it was raining' is the subordinate clause.*

subpoena /sə'piːnə/ *noun* [C,U] (LAW) a written order to attend a court of law to give evidence: *She is appearing today* ***under subpoena*** (=she has been given a subpoena to appear in court). ▶ **subpoena** *verb* [T]: *The court subpoenaed her to appear as a witness.*

subscribe /səb'skraɪb/ *verb* [I] **1** ~ **(to sth)** (ARTS AND MEDIA) to pay for a newspaper or magazine to be sent to you regularly **2** (*formal*) ~ **to sth** to agree with an idea, belief, etc.: *I don't subscribe to the view that all war is wrong.*

subscriber /səb'skraɪbə(r)/ *noun* [C] (ARTS AND MEDIA) a person who pays to receive a newspaper or magazine regularly or to use a particular service: *subscribers to satellite and cable television*

subscription /səb'skrɪpʃn/ *noun* [C] (ARTS AND MEDIA) an amount of money that you pay, usually once a year, to receive a newspaper or magazine regularly or to belong to an organization

subsequent AW /'sʌbsɪkwənt/ *adj.* (*formal*) (only *before* a noun) coming after or later: *I thought that was the end of the matter but subsequent events proved me wrong.* ▶ **subsequently** AW *adv.*: *The rumours were subsequently found to be untrue.*

subservient /səb'sɜːviənt/ *adj.* **1** ~ **(to sb/sth)** too ready to obey other people **2** (*formal*) ~ **(to sth)** considered to be less important than sth else ▶ **subservience** *noun* [U]

subset /'sʌbset/ *noun* [C] (TECHNICAL) a smaller group of people or things formed from the members of a larger group

subside /səb'saɪd/ *verb* [I] **1** to become calmer or quieter: *The storm seems to be subsiding.* **2** (used about land, a building, etc.) to sink down into the ground ▶ **subsidence** /'sʌbsɪdns; səb'saɪdns/ *noun* [U]

subsidiarity /səb,sɪdi'ærɪti; ,sʌbsɪdi-/ *noun* [U] (POLITICS) the principle that a central authority should not be very powerful, and should only control things which cannot be controlled by local organizations

subsidiary[1] AW /səb'sɪdiəri/ *adj.* connected with sth but less important than it

subsidiary[2] /səb'sɪdiəri/ *noun* [C] (*pl.* **subsidiaries**) a business company that belongs to and is controlled by another larger company

subsidize (also **-ise**) AW /'sʌbsɪdaɪz/ *verb* [T] (ECONOMICS) (used about a government, etc.) to give money in order to keep the cost of a service low: *Public transport should be subsidized.*

subsidy AW /'sʌbsədi/ *noun* [C,U] (*pl.* **subsidies**) (ECONOMICS) money that the government, etc. pays to help an organization or to keep the cost of a service low: *agricultural/state/housing subsidies*

subsist /səb'sɪst/ *verb* [I] (*formal*) ~ **(on sth)** to manage to live with very little food or money ▶ **subsistence** /səb'sɪstəns/ *noun* [U]

sub'sistence crop *noun* [C] (AGRICULTURE) plants that people grow to eat or use themselves, not to sell ➲ look at **cash crop**

subsoil /'sʌbsɔɪl/ *noun* [U] (GEOGRAPHY) the layer of soil between the surface of the ground and the hard rock underneath it ➲ look at **topsoil**

substance ⊶ /'sʌbstəns/ *noun* **1** [C] a solid or liquid material: *poisonous substances* ◇ *The cloth is coated in a new waterproof substance.* **2** [U] importance, value or truth: *The commissioner's report* ***gives substance to*** *these allegations.* **3** [U] the most important or main part of sth: *What was the substance of his argument?*

substandard /,sʌb'stændəd/ *adj.* of poor quality; not as good as usual or as it should be

substantial ⊶ /səb'stænʃl/ *adj.* **1** large in amount: *The storms caused substantial damage.* ◇ *a substantial sum of money* **2** large or strong OPP **insubstantial**

substantially ⊶ /səb'stænʃəli/ *adv.* **1** very much; greatly: *House prices have fallen substantially.* **2** generally; in most points

substantiate /səb'stænʃieɪt/ *verb* [T] (*formal*) to provide information or evidence to prove that sth is true: *They made accusations which could not be substantiated.*

substitute ⊶ AW /'sʌbstɪtjuːt/ *noun* [C] a ~ **(for sb/sth)** a person or thing that takes the place of sb/sth else: *One player was injured so the substitute was sent on to play.* ▶ **substitute** *verb* [T] ~ **sb/sth (for sb/sth)**: *You can substitute margarine for butter.* ▶ **substitution** AW /,sʌbstɪ'tjuːʃn/ *noun* [C,U]

'substitute teacher (*AmE*) =SUPPLY TEACHER

subterranean /,sʌbtə'reɪniən/ *adj.* (usually *before* a noun) (*formal*) (GEOGRAPHY) under the ground: *a subterranean cave/passage/tunnel*

subtitle /'sʌbtaɪtl/ *noun* [C, usually pl.] (ARTS AND MEDIA) the words at the bottom of the picture on television or at the cinema. The **subtitles** translate the words of a foreign film or programme, or show the words that are spoken, to help people with hearing problems: *a Polish film with English subtitles* ➲ look at **dub(2)** ▶ **subtitle** *verb* [T] (usually passive): *a Spanish film subtitled in English*

subtle /'sʌtl/ *adj.* **1** not very noticeable; not very strong or bright: *subtle colours* ◇ *I noticed a subtle difference in her.* **2** very clever; and using indirect methods to achieve sth: *Advertisements persuade us to buy things in very subtle ways.* ▶ **subtlety** /'sʌtlti/ *noun* [C,U] (*pl.* **subtleties**) ▶ **subtly** /'sʌtli/ *adv.*

subtotal /'sʌbtəʊtl/ *noun* [C] (MATHEMATICS) the total of a set of numbers which is then added to other totals to give a final number

subtract /səb'trækt/ *verb* [T] ~ **sth (from sth)** (MATHEMATICS) to take one number or quantity away from another: *If you subtract five from nine you get four.* OPP **add** ▶ **subtraction** /səb'trækʃn/ *noun* [C,U]

subtropical /,sʌb'trɒpɪkl/ *adj.* (GEOGRAPHY) in or connected with regions that are near tropical parts of the world: *subtropical forests*

suburb /'sʌbɜːb/ *noun* [C] (GEOGRAPHY) an area where people live that is outside the central part of a town or city: *Most people live* ***in the suburbs*** *and work in the centre of town.* ▶ **suburban** /sə'bɜːbən/ *adj.* ❶ People often think of life in the suburbs as dull, so **suburban** sometimes means 'dull and uninteresting'. ▶ **suburbia** /sə'bɜːbiə/ *noun* [U]

subversive /səb'vɜːsɪv/ ***adj.*** trying to destroy or damage a government, religion or political system by attacking it secretly and in an indirect way ▸ **subversive** ***noun*** [C] ▸ **subversion** /səb'vɜːʃn/ ***noun*** [U]

subvert /səb'vɜːt/ ***verb*** [T] to try to destroy or damage a government, religion or political system by attacking it secretly and in an indirect way

subway /'sʌbweɪ/ ***noun*** [C] **1** a tunnel under a busy road or railway that is for people who are walking (**pedestrians**) **2** (*AmE*) = UNDERGROUND³

succeed 🔑 /sək'siːd/ ***verb*** **1** [I] ~ **(in sth/doing sth)** to manage to achieve what you want; to do well: *Our plan succeeded.* ◇ *A good education will help you succeed in life.* ◇ *to succeed in passing an exam* OPP **fail** ➲ noun **success** **2** [I,T] to have a job or important position after sb else: *Who succeeded Kennedy as president?* ➲ noun **succession**

success 🔑 /sək'ses/ ***noun*** **1** [U] the fact that you have achieved what you want; doing well and becoming famous, rich, etc.: *Hard work is **the key to** success.* ◇ *Her attempts to get a job for the summer have not **met with** much **success*** (= she hasn't managed to do it). ◇ *What's the secret of your success?* **2** [C] the thing that you achieve; sth that becomes very popular: *He really tried to **make a success of** the business.* ◇ *The film 'Titanic' was a huge success.* OPP **failure**

THESAURUS

successful

profitable • commercial • lucrative • economic

These words all describe sb/sth that is making or is likely to make money.

successful: *The company has had another successful year.*

profitable: *a highly profitable business*

commercial: *The film was not a commercial success* (= made no profit).

lucrative: *They do a lot of business in lucrative overseas markets.*

economic: *Local shops stop being economic when supermarkets open.*

successful 🔑 /sək'sesfl/ ***adj.*** having achieved what you wanted; having become popular, rich, etc.: *a successful attempt to climb Mount Everest* ◇ *a successful actor* ▸ **successfully** /-fəli/ ***adv.***

succession AW /sək'seʃn/ ***noun*** **1** [C] a number of people or things that follow each other in time or order; a series: *a succession of events/problems/visitors* **2** [U] the act of taking over an official position or title; the right to take over an official position or title, especially to become the king or queen of a country: *She's third **in order of succession** to the throne.* ➲ verb **succeed**

IDM **in succession** following one after another: *There have been three deaths in the family in quick succession.*

successive AW /sək'sesɪv/ ***adj.*** (only *before* a noun) following immediately one after the other SYN **consecutive**: *This was their fourth successive win.*

successor AW /sək'sesə(r)/ ***noun*** [C] a person or thing that comes after sb/sth else and takes their/its place ➲ look at **predecessor**

succinct /sək'sɪŋkt/ ***adj.*** said clearly, in a few words ▸ **succinctly** ***adv.***

succulent /'sʌkjələnt/ ***adj.*** (used about fruit, vegetables and meat) containing a lot of juice and tasting very good

succumb /sə'kʌm/ ***verb*** [I] (*formal*) ~ **(to sth)** to stop fighting against sth

such 🔑 /sʌtʃ/ ***det., pronoun*** **1** (used for referring to sb/sth that you mentioned earlier) of this or that type: *I don't believe in ghosts. There's **no such thing**.* ◇ *The economic situation is such that we all have less money to spend.* **2** used for emphasizing the degree of sth: *It was such a fascinating book that I couldn't put it down.* ◇ *It seems such a long time since we last met.*

GRAMMAR

You use **such** before a noun or before a noun that has an adjective in front of it: *Simon is such a bore!* ◇ *Susan is such a boring woman.* You use **so** before an adjective that is used without a noun: *Don't be so boring.* Compare: *It was so cold we stayed at home.* ◇ *It was such a cold night that we stayed at home.*

3 used to describe the result of sth: *The statement was worded **in such a way that** it did not upset anyone.*

IDM **as such** as the word is usually understood; exactly: *It's not a promotion as such, but it will mean more money.*

such as for example: *Fatty foods such as chips are bad for you.*

suck 🔑 /sʌk/ ***verb*** **1** [I,T] to pull a liquid into your mouth: *to suck milk up through a straw* **2** [I,T] to have sth in your mouth and keep touching it with your tongue: *He was noisily sucking (on) a sweet.* **3** [T] to pull sth in a particular direction, using force: *Vacuum cleaners suck up the dirt.*

sucker /'sʌkə(r)/ ***noun*** [C] **1** (*informal*) a person who believes everything that you tell them and who is easy to trick or persuade to do sth **2** (BIOLOGY) a part of some plants, animals or insects that is used for helping them stick onto a surface ➲ picture on **page 29**

sucrose /'suːkrəʊz; -krəʊs/ ***noun*** [U] the form of sugar that comes from SUGAR CANE or SUGAR BEET, and which is used to make food sweet ➲ look at **dextrose**, **fructose**, **glucose**, **lactose**

suction /'sʌkʃn/ ***noun*** [U] the action of removing air or liquid from a space or container so that sth else can be pulled into it or so that two surfaces can stick together: *A vacuum cleaner works by suction.*

sudden 🔑 /'sʌdn/ ***adj.*** done or happening quickly, or when you do not expect it: *a sudden decision/change* ▸ **suddenness** ***noun*** [U]

IDM **all of a sudden** quickly and unexpectedly: *All of a sudden the lights went out.*

sudden death (SPORT) a way of deciding who wins a game where the score is equal by playing one more point or game

suddenly 🔑 /'sʌdənli/ ***adv.*** quickly and unexpectedly: *I suddenly realized what I had to do.* ◇ *It all happened so suddenly.*

sudoku /su'dəʊkuː/ ***noun*** [U, C] a number game with 81 squares in which you have to write the numbers 1 to 9 in a particular pattern: *Alison is addicted to sudoku.* ◇ *a sudoku puzzle*

suds /sʌdz/ ***noun*** [pl.] the bubbles that you get when you mix soap and water

sue /suː/ *verb* [I,T] ~ **(sb) (for sth)** (LAW) to go to a court of law and ask for money from sb because they have done sth bad to you, or said sth bad about you: *to sue sb for libel/breach of contract/damages*

suede /sweɪd/ *noun* [U] a type of soft leather which does not have a smooth surface and feels a little like cloth

suet /ˈsuːɪt/ *noun* [U] a type of hard animal fat that is used in cooking

suffer ⊶ /ˈsʌfə(r)/ *verb* **1** [I,T] ~ **(from sth)**; ~ **(for sth)** to experience sth unpleasant, for example pain, sadness, difficulty, etc.: *Mary often suffers from severe headaches.* ◇ *Our troops suffered heavy losses.* ◇ *He made a rash decision and now he's suffering for it.* **2** [I] to become worse in quality: *My work is suffering as a result of problems at home.* ▸ **sufferer** *noun* [C]: *asthma sufferers*

suffering ⊶ /ˈsʌfərɪŋ/ *noun* **1** [U] physical or mental pain: *Death finally brought an end to her suffering.* ◇ *This war has caused widespread human suffering.* **2 sufferings** [pl.] feelings of pain and unhappiness: *The hospice aims to ease the sufferings of the dying.*

sufficiency AW /səˈfɪʃnsi/ *noun* [sing.] ~ **(of sth)** (*formal*) an amount of sth that is enough for a particular purpose

sufficient ⊶ AW /səˈfɪʃnt/ *adj.* (*formal*) as much as is necessary; enough: *We have sufficient oil reserves to last for three months.* OPP **insufficient** ▸ **sufficiently** *adv.*

suffix /ˈsʌfɪks/ *noun* [C] (LANGUAGE) a letter or group of letters that you add at the end of a word, and that changes the meaning of the word or the way it is used: *To form the noun from the adjective 'sad', add the suffix 'ness'.* ➲ look at **affix**[2], **prefix**

suffocate /ˈsʌfəkeɪt/ *verb* [I,T] to die because there is no air to breathe; to kill sb in this way ▸ **suffocating** *adj.* ▸ **suffocation** /ˌsʌfəˈkeɪʃn/ *noun* [U]

suffrage /ˈsʌfrɪdʒ/ *noun* [U] (POLITICS) the right to vote in political elections: *universal suffrage* (= the right of all adults to vote) ◇ *women's suffrage*

suffragette /ˌsʌfrəˈdʒet/ *noun* [C] (HISTORY, POLITICS) a member of a group of women who, in Britain and the US in the early part of the 20th century, worked to get the right for women to vote in political elections

sugar ⊶ /ˈʃʊɡə(r)/ *noun* **1** [U] a sweet substance that you get from certain plants: *Do you* ***take sugar*** *in tea?* **2** [C] (in a cup of tea, coffee, etc.) the amount of sugar that a small spoon can hold; a lump of sugar **3** [C] any of various sweet substances that are found naturally in plants, fruit, etc.: *Glucose and fructose are sugars.*

ˈsugar beet (*BrE also* **beet**) *noun* [U] (AGRICULTURE) a plant with a large round root that sugar is made from

ˈsugar cane *noun* [U] (AGRICULTURE) a tall tropical plant with thick STEMS (= the long central parts that leaves grow on) that sugar is made from

ˈsugar cube *noun* [C] (*especially AmE*) = SUGAR LUMP

ˈsugar lump *noun* [C] (*BrE*) (*AmE and BrE also* **ˈsugar cube**) a small CUBE of sugar, used in cups of tea or coffee

sugary /ˈʃʊɡəri/ *adj.* very sweet

suggest ⊶ /səˈdʒest/ *verb* [T] **1** ~ **sth (to sb)**; ~ **doing sth**; ~ **that...** to mention a plan or an idea that you have for sb to discuss or consider: *Can anybody suggest ways of raising more money?* ◇ *Tony suggested going out for a walk.* ◇ *Tony suggested (that) we go out for a walk.* ◇ *Tony suggested a walk.* **2** ~ **sb/sth (for/as sth)** to say that a person, thing or place is suitable: *Who would you suggest for the job?* ➲ look at **recommend 3** to say or show sth in an indirect way: *Are you suggesting the accident was my fault?*

suggestion ⊶ /səˈdʒestʃən/ *noun* **1** [C] a plan or idea that sb mentions for sb else to discuss and consider: *May I* ***make a suggestion****?* ◇ *Has anyone got any suggestions for how to solve this problem?* **2** [U] putting an idea into a person's mind; giving advice about what to do **3** [sing.] a slight amount or sign of sth

suggestive /səˈdʒestɪv/ *adj.* **1** ~ **(of sth)** making you think of sth; being a sign of sth: *Your symptoms are more suggestive of an allergy than a virus.* **2** making you think about sex: *a suggestive dance/remark/posture* ▸ **suggestively** *adv.*

suicidal /ˌsuːɪˈsaɪdl/ *adj.* **1** (used about a person) wanting to kill himself/herself: *to be/feel suicidal* **2** likely to have a very bad result; extremely dangerous

suicide /ˈsuːɪsaɪd/ *noun* [U, C] the act of killing yourself deliberately: *Ben has tried to* ***commit suicide*** *several times.* ◇ *There have been three suicides by university students this year.*

suit[1] ⊶ /suːt/ *noun* [C] **1** a formal set of clothes that are made of the same material, consisting of a jacket and either trousers or a skirt: *He always wears a suit and tie to work.* **2** an article of clothing or set of clothes that you wear for a particular activity: *a tracksuit/swimsuit* **3** one of the four sets of 13 playing cards (**hearts, clubs, diamonds** and **spades**) that form a pack ➲ note at **card**

IDM **follow suit** → FOLLOW

suit[2] ⊶ /suːt/ *verb* [T] (not used in the continuous tenses) **1** to be convenient or useful for sb/sth: *Would Thursday at 9.30 suit you?* ◇ *He will help around the house, but only when it suits him.* **2** (used about clothes, colours, etc.) to make you look attractive: *That dress really suits you.*

suitable ⊶ /ˈsuːtəbl/ *adj.* ~ **(for sb/sth)**; ~ **(to do sth)** right or appropriate for sb/sth: *The film isn't suitable for children.* ◇ *I've got nothing suitable to wear for a wedding.* OPP **unsuitable** ▸ **suitability** /ˌsuːtəˈbɪləti/ *noun* [U] ▸ **suitably** *adv.*

suitcase ⊶ /ˈsuːtkeɪs/ (*also* **case**) *noun* [C] a box with a handle that you use for carrying your clothes, etc. in when you are travelling ➲ picture at **luggage**

suite /swiːt/ *noun* [C] **1** (TOURISM) a set of rooms, especially in a hotel: *the honeymoon/penthouse suite* ◇ *a suite of rooms/offices* ➲ look at **en suite 2** a set of two or more pieces of furniture of the same style or covered in the same material: *a three-piece suite* (= a sofa and two armchairs) **3** (MUSIC) a piece of music made up of three or more related parts, for example pieces from an OPERA: *Stravinsky's Firebird Suite* **4** (COMPUTING) a set of related computer programs: *a suite of software development tools*

suited ⊶ /ˈsuːtɪd/ *adj.* ~ **(for/to sb/sth)** appropriate or right for sb/sth

sulfur, sulfurous (*AmE*) = SULPHUR, SULPHUROUS

sulk /sʌlk/ *verb* [I] to refuse to speak or smile because you want people to know that you are angry about sth ▸ **sulky** *adj.* ▸ **sulkily** /-ɪli/ *adv.*

sullen /ˈsʌlən/ *adj.* looking bad tempered and not wanting to speak to people: *a sullen face/expression/glare* ▸ **sullenly** *adv.*

sulphide (*AmE* **sulfide**) /ˈsʌlfaɪd/ ***noun*** [C,U] (**CHEMISTRY**) a COMPOUND of SULPHUR with another chemical element

sulphur (*AmE* **sulfur**) /ˈsʌlfə(r)/ ***noun*** [U] (*symbol* **S**) (**CHEMISTRY**) a natural yellow substance with a strong unpleasant smell ❶ For more information on the periodic table of elements, look at pages R34-5. ▶ **sulphurous** (*AmE* **sulfurous**) /ˈsʌlfərəs/ ***adj.***: *sulphurous fumes*

ˌsulphur diˈoxide (*AmE* **ˌsulfur diˈoxide**) ***noun*** [U] (*symbol* SO_2) (**CHEMISTRY**) a poisonous gas with a strong smell, that is used in industry and causes air POLLUTION ➲ picture at **acid rain**

sulphuric acid (*AmE* **sulfuric acid**) /sʌlˌfjʊərɪk ˈæsɪd/ ***noun*** [U] (*symbol* H_2SO_4) (**CHEMISTRY**) a strong colourless acid

sultan (also **Sultan**) /ˈsʌltən/ ***noun*** [C] (**POLITICS**) the ruler in some Muslim countries

sultana /sʌlˈtɑːnə/ ***noun*** [C] a dried GRAPE with no seeds in it that is used in cooking ➲ look at **raisin**

sultry /ˈsʌltri/ ***adj.*** **1** (used about the weather) hot and uncomfortable **2** (used about a woman) behaving in a way that makes her sexually attractive

sum[1] 🔑 AW /sʌm/ ***noun*** [C] **1** an amount of money: *The industry has spent huge* ***sums of money*** *modernizing its equipment.* **2** [usually sing.] **the ~ (of sth)** (**MATHEMATICS**) the amount that you get when you add two or more numbers together: *The sum of two and five is seven.* **3** (**MATHEMATICS**) a simple problem that involves calculating numbers: ***to do sums*** *in your head*

sum[2] AW /sʌm/ ***verb*** (**summing**; **summed**)

PHR V **sum (sth) up** to describe in a few words the main ideas of what sb has said or written: ***To sum up****, there are three options here...*

sum sb/sth up to form an opinion about sb/sth: *He summed the situation up immediately.*

summary[1] 🔑 AW /ˈsʌməri/ ***noun*** [C] (*pl.* **summaries**) a short description of the main ideas or points of sth but without any details: *A brief summary of the experiment is given at the beginning of the report.* SYN **précis** ▶ **summarize** (also -ise) AW /ˈsʌməraɪz/ ***verb*** [I,T]: *Could you summarize the story so far?*

summary[2] AW /ˈsʌməri/ ***adj.*** (*formal*) done quickly and without taking time to consider whether it is the right thing to do or following the right process: *a summary judgment*

summation AW /sʌˈmeɪʃn/ ***noun*** [C] **1** [usually sing.] (*formal*) a summary of what has been done or said: *What he said was a fair summation of the discussion.* **2** (*formal*) a collection of different parts that forms a complete account or impression of sb/sth: *The exhibition presents a summation of the artist's career.* **3** (*AmE*) (**LAW**) a final speech that a lawyer makes near the end of a trial in court, after all the evidence has been given

summer 🔑 /ˈsʌmə(r)/ ***noun*** [C,U] one of the four seasons of the year, after spring and before autumn. Summer is the warmest season of the year: *Is it very hot here* ***in summer****? ◇ a summer's day* ➲ *picture at* **season** ▶ **summery** ***adj.***: *summery weather ◇ a summery dress*

ˈsummer school ***noun*** [C,U] (**EDUCATION**) courses that are held in the summer at a university or college

ˈsummer time (*AmE* **ˌdaylight ˈsaving time**) ***noun*** [U] (**GEOGRAPHY**) the period during which in some countries the clocks are put forward one hour, so that it is light for an extra hour in the evening

summertime /ˈsʌmətaɪm/ ***noun*** [U] the season of summer: *It's busy here in the summertime.*

ˌsumming-ˈup ***noun*** [C] (*pl.* **summings-up**) (**LAW**) a speech in which a judge gives a short description (**summary**) of what has been said in a court of law before a decision (**verdict**) is reached

summit /ˈsʌmɪt/ ***noun*** [C] **1** (**GEOGRAPHY**) the top of a mountain **2** (**POLITICS**) an important meeting or series of meetings between the leaders of two or more countries

summon /ˈsʌmən/ ***verb*** [T] **1** (*formal*) to order a person to come to a place: *The boys were summoned to the head teacher's office.* **2 ~ sth (up)** to find strength, courage or some other quality that you need even though it is difficult to do so: *She couldn't summon up the courage to leave him.*

summons /ˈsʌmənz/ ***noun*** [C] (*pl.* **summonses**) (**LAW**) an order to appear in a court of law

sumptuous /ˈsʌmptʃuəs/ ***adj.*** (*formal*) very expensive and looking very impressive: *We dined in sumptuous surroundings.* ▶ **sumptuously** ***adv.***

sun[1] 🔑 /sʌn/ ***noun*** **1 the sun** [sing.] the star that shines in the sky during the day and that gives the earth heat and light: *The sun rises in the east and sets in the west. ◇ the rays of the sun* ➲ picture at **solar system** **2** [sing., U] light and heat from the sun: *Don't sit* ***in the sun*** *too long. ◇ Too much sun can be harmful.*

IDM **catch the sun** → CATCH[1]

sun[2] /sʌn/ ***verb*** [T] (**sunning**; **sunned**) **~ yourself** sit or lie outside when the sun is shining in order to enjoy the heat

Sun. ***abbr.*** Sunday: *Sun. 5 April*

sunbathe /ˈsʌnbeɪð/ ***verb*** [I] to take off most of your clothes and sit or lie in the sun in order to make your skin go darker (**get a tan**) ➲ look at **bathe**

sunbeam /ˈsʌnbiːm/ ***noun*** [C] a RAY (=a line) of sunlight

sunburn /ˈsʌnbɜːn/ ***noun*** [U] (**HEALTH**) red painful skin caused by spending too long in the sun

sunburned /ˈsʌnbɜːnd/ (*also* **sunburnt** /ˈsʌnbɜːnt/) ***adj.*** **1** suffering from SUNBURN **2** (used about a person or his/her skin) (**HEALTH**) having an attractive brown colour from being in the sun

Sunday /ˈsʌndeɪ; -di/ ***noun*** [C,U] (*abbr.* **Sun.**) the day of the week after Saturday

sundial /ˈsʌndaɪəl/ ***noun*** [C] a type of clock used in past times that uses the shadow caused by a pointed piece of metal being between the sun and the clock surface to show what the time is

sundry /ˈsʌndri/ ***adj.*** (only *before* a noun) of various kinds that are not important enough to be named separately

IDM **all and sundry** (*informal*) everyone

sunflower /ˈsʌnflaʊə(r)/ ***noun*** [C] a very tall plant with large yellow flowers, often grown for its seeds and their oil, which is used in cooking

sung past participle of **sing**

sunglasses /ˈsʌŋɡlɑːsɪz/ (*also* **ˌdark ˈglasses**, *informal* **shades**) ***noun*** [pl.] a pair of glasses with dark glass in them to protect your eyes from bright SUNLIGHT

sunk past participle of **sink**[1]

sunken /'sʌŋkən/ ***adj.*** **1** below the water: *a sunken ship* **2** (used about cheeks or eyes) very far into the face as a result of illness or age **3** at a lower level than the surrounding area: *a sunken bath/garden*

sunlight /'sʌnlaɪt/ ***noun*** [U] the light from the sun

sunlit /'sʌnlɪt/ ***adj.*** having bright light from the sun: *a sunlit terrace*

sunny /'sʌni/ ***adj.*** (**sunnier**; **sunniest**) having a lot of light from the sun: *a sunny garden* ◇ *a sunny day*

sunrise /'sʌnraɪz/ ***noun*** [U,C] the time when the sun comes up in the morning: *to get up **at sunrise*** ➲ look at **dawn**, **sunset**

sunset /'sʌnset/ ***noun*** [C,U] the time when the sun goes down in the evening: *The park closes **at sunset**.* ◇ *a beautiful sunset*

sunshine /'sʌnʃaɪn/ ***noun*** [U] heat and light from the sun: *We sat down **in the sunshine** and had lunch.*

sunspot /'sʌnspɒt/ ***noun*** [C] (ASTRONOMY) a dark area that sometimes appears on the sun's surface

sunstroke /'sʌnstrəʊk/ ***noun*** [U] (HEALTH) an illness that is caused by spending too much time in very hot, strong SUNLIGHT: *Keep your head covered or you'll **get sunstroke**.*

suntan /'sʌntæn/ (*also* **tan**) ***noun*** [C] when you have a **suntan**, your skin is darker than usual because you have spent time in the sun: *to have/get a suntan* ◇ *suntan oil* ▶ **suntanned** (*also* **tanned**) ***adj.***

super /'su:pə(r)/ ***adj.*** (*informal, old-fashioned*) very good; wonderful: *We had a super time.* ▶ **super** ***adv.***: *He's been super understanding.*

super- /'su:pə(r)/ ***prefix*** **1** (used in adjectives, adverbs and nouns) extremely; more or better than normal: *super-rich* ◇ *superhuman* ◇ *superglue* **2** (used in nouns and verbs) above; over: *superstructure* ◇ *superimpose*

superb /su:'pɜ:b/ ***adj.*** extremely good, excellent ▶ **superbly** ***adv.***

superbug /'su:pəbʌg/ ***noun*** [C] (HEALTH) a type of bacteria that cannot easily be killed by ANTIBIOTICS (= medicine which is used for destroying bacteria and curing infections) ➲ look at **MRSA**

supercilious /ˌsu:pə'sɪliəs/ ***adj.*** showing that you think that you are better than other people: *a supercilious smile* ▶ **superciliously** ***adv.***

superconductor /'su:pəkəndʌktə(r)/ ***noun*** [C] (PHYSICS) a substance which, at very low temperatures, allows electricity to flow completely freely through it

supercrop /'su:pəkrɒp/ ***noun*** [C] (AGRICULTURE) a plant that has been grown from cells whose GENES have been changed artificially so that it does not get the diseases that ordinary crops get

superficial /ˌsu:pə'fɪʃl/ ***adj.*** **1** not studying or thinking about sth in a deep or complete way: *a superficial knowledge of the subject* **2** only on the surface, not deep: *a superficial wound/cut/burn* **3** (used about people) not caring about serious or important things: *He's a very superficial sort of person.* ▶ **superficiality** /ˌsu:pəˌfɪʃi'æləti/ ***noun*** [U] ▶ **superficially** /-ʃəli/ ***adv.***

superfluous /su:'pɜ:fluəs/ ***adj.*** more than is wanted; not needed

superhero /'su:pəhɪərəʊ/ ***noun*** [C] (*pl.* **-oes**) (ARTS AND MEDIA) a character in a story, film, etc. who has unusual strength or power and uses it to help people; a real person who has done sth unusually brave to help sb

superhuman /ˌsu:pə'hju:mən/ ***adj.*** greater than is usual for humans: *superhuman strength*

superimpose /ˌsu:pərɪm'pəʊz/ ***verb*** [T] ~ **sth (on sth)** to put sth on top of sth else so that what is underneath can still be seen: *The old street plan was superimposed on a map of the modern city.*

superintendent /ˌsu:pərɪn'tendənt/ ***noun*** [C] **1** (LAW) a police officer with a high position: *Detective Superintendent Waters* **2** a person who looks after a large building

superior[1] ⊶ /su:'pɪəriə(r)/ ***adj.*** **1** ~ (**to sb/sth**) better than usual or than sb/sth else: *He is clearly superior to all the other candidates.* OPP **inferior** **2** ~ (**to sb**) having a more important position: *a superior officer* **3** thinking that you are better than other people ▶ **superiority** /su:ˌpɪəri'ɒrəti/ ***noun*** [U]

superior[2] /su:'pɪəriə(r)/ ***noun*** [C] a person of higher position: *Report any accidents to your superior.* OPP **inferior**

superlative /su'pɜ:lətɪv/ ***noun*** [C] (LANGUAGE) the form of an adjective or adverb that expresses its highest degree: *'Most beautiful', 'best' and 'fastest' are all superlatives.*

supermarket ⊶ /'su:pəmɑ:kɪt/ ***noun*** [C] a very large shop that sells food, drink, goods used in the home, etc.

supermodel /'su:pəmɒdl/ ***noun*** [C] a very famous and highly paid fashion model

supernatural /ˌsu:pə'nætʃrəl/ ***adj.*** **1** that cannot be explained by the laws of science: *a creature with supernatural powers* **2 the supernatural** ***noun*** [sing.] events, forces or powers that cannot be explained by the laws of science: *I don't believe in the supernatural.*

supernova /ˌsu:pə'nəʊvə/ ***noun*** [C] (*pl.* **supernovae** /-vi:/ or **supernovas**) (ASTRONOMY) a star that suddenly becomes much brighter because it is exploding ➲ look at **nova**

superpower /'su:pəpaʊə(r)/ ***noun*** [C] (POLITICS) one of the countries in the world that has very great military or economic power and a lot of influence, for example the US ➲ look at **world power**

supersede /ˌsu:pə'si:d/ ***verb*** [T] to take the place of sb/sth which existed or was used before and which has become old-fashioned: *Steam trains were gradually superseded by electric trains.*

supersonic /ˌsu:pə'sɒnɪk/ ***adj.*** faster than the speed of sound

superstar /'su:pəstɑ:(r)/ ***noun*** [C] (ARTS AND MEDIA, MUSIC) a singer, film star, etc. who is very famous and popular

superstition /ˌsu:pə'stɪʃn/ ***noun*** [C,U] a belief that cannot be explained by reason or science: *According to superstition, it's unlucky to walk under a ladder.* ▶ **superstitious** /ˌsu:pə'stɪʃəs/ ***adj.***: *I never do anything important on Friday the 13th – I'm superstitious.*

superstore /'su:pəstɔ:(r)/ ***noun*** [C] a very large shop that sells food or a wide variety of one particular type of goods

supervise /'su:pəvaɪz/ ***verb*** [I,T] to watch sb/sth to make sure that work is being done properly or that people are behaving correctly: *Your job is to supervise the building work.* ▶ **supervision** /ˌsu:pə'vɪʒn/ ***noun*** [U]: *Children should not play here without supervision.* ▶ **supervisor** ***noun*** [C]

supper /'sʌpə(r)/ *noun* [C,U] (*old-fashioned*) the last meal of the day, either the main meal of the evening or a small meal that you eat quite late, not long before you go to bed

supple /'sʌpl/ *adj.* that bends or moves easily; not stiff: *Children are generally far more supple than adults.* ▶ **suppleness** *noun* [U]

supplement AW /'sʌplɪmənt/ *noun* [C] something that is added to sth else: *You have to pay a small supplement if you travel on a Saturday.* ▶ **supplement** /'sʌplɪment/ *verb* [T] ~ **sth (with sth)**: *to supplement your diet with vitamins* ▶ **supplementary** AW /ˌsʌplɪ'mentri/ *adj.*: *supplementary exercises at the back of the book*

supple͵mentary 'angle *noun* [C] (GEOMETRY, MATHEMATICS) either of two angles which together make 180° ➲ look at **complementary angle** ➲ picture at **angle**

supplier /sə'plaɪə(r)/ *noun* [C] a person or company that supplies goods

supply¹ 🔑 /sə'plaɪ/ *verb* [T] (*pres. part.* **supplying**; *3rd person sing. pres.* **supplies**; *pt, pp* **supplied**) ~ **sth (to sb)**; ~ **sb (with sth)** to give or provide sth: *The farmer supplies eggs to the surrounding villages.* ◇ *He supplies the surrounding villages with eggs.*

supply² 🔑 /sə'plaɪ/ *noun* [C] (*pl.* **supplies**) a store or amount of sth that is provided or available to be used: *The water supply was contaminated.* ◇ *Food supplies were dropped by helicopter.* ◇ *In many parts of the country water is* ***in short supply*** (= there is not much of it).

sup'ply chain *noun* [C, usually sing.] (BUSINESS) the series of processes involved in the production and supply of goods, from when they are first made, grown, etc. until they are bought or used

sup'ply teacher (*AmE* **'substitute teacher**) *noun* [C] (EDUCATION) a teacher employed to do the work of another teacher who is away because of illness, etc.

support¹ 🔑 /sə'pɔːt/ *verb* [T] **1** to help sb by saying that you agree with them or it, and sometimes giving practical help such as money: *Several large companies are supporting the project.* ◇ *Which political party do you support?* **2** to give sb the money they need for food, clothes, etc.: *Jim has to support two children from his previous marriage.* **3** to carry the weight of sb/sth: *Large columns support the roof.* **4** to show that sth is true or correct: *What evidence do you have to support what you say?* **5** to have a particular sports team as your favourite: *Which football team do you support?*

support² 🔑 /sə'pɔːt/ *noun* **1** [U] ~ **(for sb/sth)** help and encouragement that you give to a person or thing: *public support for the campaign* ◇ *Steve spoke* ***in support of*** *the proposal.* **2** [C,U] something that carries the weight of sb/sth or holds sth firmly in place: *a roof support* ◇ *She held on to his arm for support.* **3** [U] money to buy food, clothes, etc.: *She has no job, no home and no means of support.*
IDM **moral support** → MORAL¹

supporter 🔑 /sə'pɔːtə(r)/ *noun* [C] a person who supports a political party, sports team, etc.: *football supporters*

supportive /sə'pɔːtɪv/ *adj.* giving help or support to sb in a difficult situation: *Everyone was very supportive when I lost my job.*

suppose 🔑 /sə'pəʊz/ *verb* [T] **1** to think that sth is probable: *What do you suppose could have happened?* ◇ *I don't suppose that they're coming now.* **2** to pretend that sth will happen or is true: *Suppose you won the lottery. What would you do?* **3** used to make a suggestion, request or statement less strong: *I don't suppose you'd lend me your car tonight, would you?* **4** used when you agree with sth, but are not very happy about it: *'Can we give Andy a lift?' 'Yes, I suppose so, if we must.'*
IDM **be supposed to do sth 1** to be expected to do sth or to have to do sth: *The train was supposed to arrive ten minutes ago.* ◇ *This is secret and I'm not supposed to talk about it.* **2** (*informal*) to be considered or thought to be sth: *This is supposed to be the oldest building in the city.*

supposedly /sə'pəʊzɪdli/ *adv.* according to what many people believe

supposing /sə'pəʊzɪŋ/ *conj.* if sth happens or is true; what if: *Supposing the plan goes wrong, what will we do then?*

supposition /ˌsʌpə'zɪʃn/ *noun* [C,U] an idea that a person thinks is true but which has not been shown to be true

suppress /sə'pres/ *verb* [T] **1** to stop sth by using force **2** to stop sth from being seen or known: *to suppress the truth* **3** to stop yourself from expressing your feelings, etc.: *to suppress laughter/a yawn* ▶ **suppression** /sə'preʃn/ *noun* [U]

supremacy /suː'preməsi/ *noun* [U] ~ **(over sb/sth)** the state of being the most powerful

supreme /suː'priːm/ *adj.* the highest or greatest possible

Su͵preme 'Court (*also* ͵**High 'Court**) *noun* [sing.] (LAW) the highest court in a country or state

supremely /suː'priːmli/ *adv.* extremely

Supt *abbr.* (in the police force) Superintendent

surcharge /'sɜːtʃɑːdʒ/ *noun* [C] an extra amount of money that you have to pay for sth

> **THESAURUS**
>
> **sure**
>
> **confident • convinced • certain • positive**
>
> These words all describe sb who knows without doubt that sth is true or will happen.
>
> **sure**: *Are you sure that's the answer?*
>
> **confident**: *He was confident that he would pass the exam.*
>
> **convinced**: *I'm convinced she's innocent.*
>
> **certain**: *Are you absolutely certain about this?*
>
> **positive** (*informal*): *She was positive that he'd be there.*

sure 🔑 /ʃɔː(r)/ *adj.*, *adv.* **1** (not before a noun) having no doubt about sth; certain: *You must be sure of your facts before you make an accusation.* ◇ *I'm not sure what to do next.* ◇ *Craig was sure that he'd made the right decision.* ◇ *I think I had my bag when I got off the bus but I'm not sure.* **2** (not before a noun) ~ **of sth**; ~ **to do sth** that you will definitely get or do, or that will definitely happen: *If you go and see them you can be sure of a warm welcome.* ◇ *If you work hard you are sure to pass the exam.* ➲ note at **certain**
OPP **unsure 3** that you can be certain of: *A noise like that is a sure sign of engine trouble.* **4** (*informal*) used to say 'yes' to sb: *'Can I have a look at your newspaper?' 'Sure.'*
IDM **Be sure to do sth** Don't forget to do sth: *Be sure to write and tell me what happens.*
for sure without doubt: *Nobody knows for sure what happened.*

make sure 1 to find out whether sth is in a particular state or has been done: *I must go back and make sure I closed the window.* **2** to take the action that is necessary: *Make sure you are back home by 11 o'clock.*

sure enough as was expected: *I expected him to be early, and sure enough he arrived five minutes before the others.*

sure of yourself confident about your opinions, or about what you can do

sure (thing) (*AmE, informal*) yes: *'Can I borrow this book?' 'Sure thing.'*

surely ⊷ /ˈʃɔːli/ ***adv.*** **1** without doubt: *This will surely cause problems.* **2** used for expressing surprise at sb else's opinions, plans, actions, etc.: *Surely you're not going to walk home in this rain?* ◇ *'Meena's looking for another job.' 'Surely not.'* **3** (*AmE, informal*) yes; of course

surf[1] /sɜːf/ ***noun*** [U] (GEOGRAPHY) the white part on the top of waves in the sea

surf[2] /sɜːf/ ***verb*** [I] to stand or lie on a special board (**a surfboard**) and ride on a wave towards the beach IDM **surf the net** to use the Internet

surface[1] ⊷ /ˈsɜːfɪs/ ***noun*** **1** [C] the outside or top layer of sth: *Teeth have a hard surface called enamel.* ◇ *a broad leaf with a large **surface area*** ◇ *This tennis court has a very uneven surface.* **2** [C, usually sing.] the top layer of an area of water or land: *the earth's surface* ◇ *These plants float on the surface of the water.* **3** [C] the flat top part of a piece of furniture, used for working on: *a work surface* ◇ *kitchen surfaces* **4** [sing.] the qualities of sb/sth that you see or notice, that are not hidden: *Everybody seems very friendly but there are a lot of tensions **below /beneath the surface**.*

surface[2] /ˈsɜːfɪs/ ***verb*** **1** [I] to come up to the surface of water **2** [I] to suddenly appear again or become obvious after having been hidden for a while: *All the old arguments surfaced again in the discussion.* **3** [I] (*informal*) to wake up or get up after being asleep **4** [T] to cover the surface of sth, especially a road or a path

ˈsurface mail ***noun*** [U] letters, packages, etc. that go by road, rail or sea, not by air ➲ look at **airmail**

surfboard /ˈsɜːfbɔːd/ ***noun*** [C] a long narrow board used for SURFING

surfeit /ˈsɜːfɪt/ ***noun*** [sing.] (*written*) **a ~ (of sth)** too much of sth

surfer /ˈsɜːfə(r)/ ***noun*** [C] a person who rides on waves standing on a SURFBOARD

surfing /ˈsɜːfɪŋ/ ***noun*** [U] **1** the sport of riding on waves while standing on a SURFBOARD: *to go surfing* **2** (COMPUTING) the activity of looking at different things on the Internet in order to find sth interesting

surge /sɜːdʒ/ ***noun*** [C, usually sing.] **a ~ (of/in sth)** **1** a sudden strong movement in a particular direction by a large number of people or things: *a surge forward* ◇ *a surge* (=an increase) *in the demand for electricity* **2** a sudden strong feeling ▶ **surge *verb*** [I]: *The crowd surged forward.*

surgeon /ˈsɜːdʒən/ ***noun*** [C] (HEALTH) a doctor who performs medical operations (**surgery**): *a brain surgeon*

surgery /ˈsɜːdʒəri/ ***noun*** (*pl.* **surgeries**) **1** [U] (HEALTH) medical treatment in which your body is cut open so that part of it can be removed or repaired: *to undergo surgery* ➲ look at **plastic surgery, operation 2** [C,U] the place or time when a doctor or dentist sees patients: *Surgery hours are from 9.00 to 11.30.*

surgical /ˈsɜːdʒɪkl/ ***adj.*** (HEALTH) connected with medical operations: *surgical instruments* ▶ **surgically** /-kli/ ***adv.***

surly /ˈsɜːli/ ***adj.*** unfriendly and rude: *a surly expression*

surmount /səˈmaʊnt/ ***verb*** [T] to deal successfully with a problem or difficulty ➲ look at **insurmountable**

surname ⊷ /ˈsɜːneɪm/ (*also* **ˈlast name**) ***noun*** [C] the name that you share with other people in your family: *'What's your surname?' 'Jones.'*

surpass /səˈpɑːs/ ***verb*** [T] (*formal*) to do sth better than sb/sth else or better than expected: *The success of the film surpassed all expectations.*

surplus /ˈsɜːpləs/ ***noun*** [C,U] an amount that is extra or more than you need: *the food surplus in Western Europe* ▶ **surplus *adj.***: *They sell their surplus grain to other countries.*

surprise[1] ⊷ /səˈpraɪz/ ***noun*** **1** [U] the feeling that you have when sth happens that you do not expect: *They looked up **in surprise** when she walked in.* ◇ ***To my surprise** they all agreed with me.* **2** [C] something that you did not expect or know about: *What a pleasant surprise to see you again!* ◇ *The news came as a complete surprise.* ◇ *a surprise visit/attack/party*

IDM **take sb by surprise** to happen or do sth when sb is not expecting it

surprise[2] ⊷ /səˈpraɪz/ ***verb*** [T] **1** to make sb feel surprised: *It wouldn't surprise me if you get the job.* **2** to attack or find sb suddenly and unexpectedly

surprised ⊷ /səˈpraɪzd/ ***adj.*** feeling or showing surprise: *I was very surprised to see Cara there. I thought she was still abroad.*

surprising ⊷ /səˈpraɪzɪŋ/ ***adj.*** that causes surprise: *It's surprising how many adults can't read or write.* ▶ **surprisingly *adv.***: *Surprisingly few people got the correct answer.*

surreal /səˈriːəl/ (*also* **surrealistic** /səˌriːəˈlɪstɪk/) ***adj.*** very strange; with images mixed together in a strange way like in a dream: *a surreal film/painting/situation*

surrealism /səˈriːəlɪzəm/ ***noun*** [U] (ART, LITERATURE) a 20th century style and movement in art and literature in which images and events that are not connected are put together in a strange or impossible way, like a dream, to try to express what is happening deep in the mind ▶ **surrealist *adj.***, ***noun*** [C]: *a surrealist painter/painting* ◇ *the surrealist Salvador Dali*

surrender /səˈrendə(r)/ ***verb*** **1** [I,T] **~ (yourself) (to sb)** to stop fighting and admit that you have lost: *The hijackers eventually surrendered themselves to the police.* SYN **yield 2** [T] (*formal*) **~ sb/sth (to sb)** to give sb/sth to sb else: *The police ordered them to surrender their weapons.* ▶ **surrender *noun*** [C,U]

surreptitious /ˌsʌrəpˈtɪʃəs/ ***adj.*** done secretly: *I had a surreptitious look at what she was writing.* ▶ **surreptitiously *adv.***

surrogate /ˈsʌrəgət/ ***noun*** [C], ***adj.*** (a person or thing) that takes the place of sb/sth else: *a surrogate mother* (=a woman who has a baby and gives it to another woman who cannot have children)

surround ⊷ /səˈraʊnd/ ***verb*** [T] **~ sb/sth (by/with sth)** to be or go all around sb/sth: *The garden is surrounded by a high wall.* ◇ *Troops have surrounded the parliament building.*

surrounding ⊶ /sə'raʊndɪŋ/ ***adj.*** (only *before* a noun) that is near or around sth

surroundings ⊶ /sə'raʊndɪŋz/ ***noun*** [pl.] everything that is near or around you; the place where you live: *to live in pleasant surroundings* ◇ *animals living in their natural surroundings* (=not in zoos) ➲ look at **environment**

surveillance /sɜː'veɪləns/ ***noun*** [U] the careful watching of sb who may have done sth wrong: *The building is protected by surveillance cameras.*

survey[1] ⊶ AW /'sɜːveɪ/ ***noun*** [C] **1** a study of the opinions, behaviour, etc. of a group of people: *Surveys have shown that more and more people are getting into debt.* ◇ *to carry out/conduct/do a survey* **2** (GEOGRAPHY) the action of examining an area of land and making a map of it **3** the action of examining a building in order to find out if it is in good condition

survey[2] ⊶ AW /sə'veɪ/ ***verb*** [T] **1** to look carefully at the whole of sth: *We stood at the top of the hill and surveyed the countryside.* ➲ note at **examine 2** (GEOGRAPHY) to carefully measure and make a map of an area of land **3** to examine a building carefully in order to find out if it is in good condition

surveyor /sə'veɪə(r)/ ***noun*** [C] **1** a person whose job is to examine a building to make sure its structure is in good condition or to examine and record the details of a piece of land ➲ look at **quantity surveyor 2** (*BrE*) an official whose job is to check that sth is accurate, of good quality, etc.

survive ⊶ AW /sə'vaɪv/ ***verb*** **1** [I,T] to continue to live or exist in or after a difficult or dangerous situation: *More than a hundred people were killed in the crash and only five passengers survived.* ◇ *How can she survive on such a small salary?* ◇ *to survive a plane crash* ◇ *Not many buildings survived the bombing.* **2** [T] to live longer than sb/sth ▶ **survival** AW /sə'vaɪvl/ ***noun*** [U]: *A heart transplant was his only chance of survival.* ▶ **survivor** AW ***noun*** [C]: *There were five survivors of the crash.*

susceptibility /səˌseptə'bɪləti/ ***noun*** [U, sing.] ~ **(to sth)** the state of being very likely to be influenced, harmed or affected by sth: *susceptibility to disease*

susceptible /sə'septəbl/ ***adj.*** (not before a noun) ~ **to sth** very likely to be influenced, harmed or affected by sb/sth: *Some of these plants are more susceptible to frost damage than others*

suspect[1] ⊶ /sə'spekt/ ***verb*** [T] **1** to believe that sth may happen or be true, especially sth bad: *The situation is worse than we first suspected.* ◇ *Nobody suspected that she was thinking of leaving.* ➲ look at **unsuspecting 2** to not be sure that you can trust sb or believe sth: *I rather suspect his motives for offering to help.* **3** ~ **sb (of sth/of doing sth)** to believe that sb is guilty of sth: *I suspect Laura of taking the money.* ◇ *She strongly suspected that he was lying.* ➲ noun **suspicion**

suspect[2] ⊶ /'sʌspekt/ ***noun*** [C] a person who is thought to be guilty of a crime: *The suspects are being questioned by police.*

suspect[3] /'sʌspekt/ ***adj.*** possibly not true or not to be trusted: *to have suspect motives* ◇ *a suspect parcel* (=that may contain a bomb)

suspend AW /sə'spend/ ***verb*** [T] **1** ~ **sth (from sth) (by/on sth)** to hang sth from sth else **2** to stop or delay sth for a time: *Some rail services were suspended during the strike.* **3** ~ **sb (from sth)** to send sb away from their school, job, position, etc. for a period of time, usually as a punishment ➲ noun **suspension**

suˌspended 'sentence ***noun*** [C] (LAW) a punishment given to a criminal in court which means that they will only go to prison if they commit another crime within a particular period of time: *He was given an 18-month suspended sentence for theft.*

suspender /sə'spendə(r)/ ***noun*** **1** [C, usually pl.] (*BrE*) a short piece of ELASTIC that women use to hold up their STOCKINGS **2 suspenders** [pl.] (*AmE*) =BRACE[1] (2)

suspense /sə'spens/ ***noun*** [U] the feeling of excitement or worry that you have when you feel sth is going to happen, when you are waiting for news, etc.: *Don't keep us* ***in suspense****. Tell us what happened.*

suspension AW /sə'spenʃn/ ***noun*** **1** [C,U] (EDUCATION) not being allowed to do your job or go to school for a period of time, usually as a punishment: *suspension on full pay* **2** [U] delaying sth for a period of time ➲ verb **suspend 3 the suspension** [U] the parts that are connected to the wheels of a car, etc. that make it more comfortable to ride in **4** [C,U] (CHEMISTRY) a liquid with very small pieces of solid matter floating in it; the state of such a liquid

su'spension bridge ***noun*** [C] (ARCHITECTURE) a bridge that hangs from thick steel wires that are supported by towers at each end

suspicion ⊶ /sə'spɪʃn/ ***noun*** **1** [C,U] a feeling or belief that sth is wrong or that sb has done sth wrong: *I always treat smiling politicians with suspicion.* ◇ *She was arrested* ***on suspicion of*** *murder.* ◇ *He is* ***under suspicion*** *of being involved in drug smuggling.* **2** [C] a feeling that sth may happen or be true: *I have a suspicion that he's forgotten he invited us.* ➲ verb **suspect**

suspicious ⊶ /sə'spɪʃəs/ ***adj.*** **1** ~ **(of/about sb/sth)** feeling that sb has done sth wrong, dishonest or illegal: *We became suspicious of his behaviour and alerted the police.* **2** that makes you feel that sth is wrong, dishonest or illegal: *The old man died* ***in suspicious circumstances****.* ◇ *It's very suspicious that she was not at home on the evening of the murder.* ◇ *a suspicious-looking person* ▶ **suspiciously** ***adv.***: *to behave suspiciously*

sustain AW /sə'steɪn/ ***verb*** [T] **1** to keep sb/sth alive or healthy: *Oxygen sustains life.* **2** to make sth continue for a long period of time without becoming less: *It's hard to sustain interest for such a long time.* **3** (*formal*) to experience sth bad: *to sustain damage/ an injury/a defeat*

sustainable AW /sə'steɪnəbl/ ***adj.*** **1** (ENVIRONMENT) involving the use of natural products and energy in a way that does not harm the environment: *sustainable forest management* **2** that can continue or be continued for a long time **OPP** **unsustainable**
▶ **sustainability** /səˌsteɪnə'bɪləti/ ***noun*** [U]

sustenance AW /'sʌstənəns/ ***noun*** [U] (*formal*) **1** the food and drink that people, animals and plants need to live and stay healthy: *There's not much sustenance in a bowl of soup.* **2** the process of making sth continue to exist: *Elections are essential for the sustenance of parliamentary democracy.*

suture /'suːtʃə(r)/ ***noun*** [C] (HEALTH) a STITCH or STITCHES made when sewing up a wound, especially after an operation ▶ **suture** ***verb*** [T] (HEALTH): *The wound needs to be cleaned and then sutured.*

SW ***abbr.*** **1** =SHORT WAVE ➲ picture at **wavelength 2** (GEOGRAPHY) south-west(ern): *SW Australia*

swab /swɒb/ *noun* [C] **1** (HEALTH) a piece of soft material used by a doctor, nurse, etc. for cleaning a place where your body has been injured or cut, or for taking a substance from your body to test it **2** (HEALTH) an act of taking a substance from sb's body for testing, with a **swab**: *to take a throat swab* ▶ **swab** *verb* [T] (*pres. part.* **swabbing**; *pt, pp* **swabbed**)

swagger /ˈswæɡə(r)/ *verb* [I] to walk in a way that shows that you are too confident or proud ▶ **swagger** *noun* [sing.]

swallow¹ 🔑 /ˈswɒləʊ/ *verb* **1** [T] to make food, drink, etc. go down your throat to your stomach: *It's easier to swallow pills if you take them with water.* **2** [I] to make a movement in your throat, often because you are afraid or surprised, etc.: *She swallowed hard and tried to speak, but nothing came out.* **3** [T] to accept or believe sth too easily: *You shouldn't swallow everything they tell you!* **4** [T] to accept an insult, etc. without complaining: *I find her criticisms very hard to swallow.* **5** [T] ~ **sth (up)** to use all of sth, especially money: *The rent swallows up most of our monthly income.*
IDM **hard to swallow** → HARD¹

swallow² /ˈswɒləʊ/ *noun* [C] **1** a small bird with long pointed wings and a tail with two points, that spends the winter in Africa but flies to northern countries for the summer **2** an act of swallowing; an amount of food or drink that is swallowed at one time

ˈ**swallow hole** *noun* [C] (GEOGRAPHY) a large hole in the ground that a river flows into, created over a long period of time by water that has fallen as rain ➲ picture at **limestone**

swam past tense of **swim**

swamp¹ /swɒmp/ *noun* [C,U] (GEOGRAPHY) an area of soft wet land

swamp² /swɒmp/ *verb* [T] **1** to cover or fill sth with water: *The fishing boat was swamped by enormous waves.* **2** ~ **sb/sth (with sth)** (usually passive) to give sb so much of sth that they cannot deal with it: *We've been swamped with applications for the job.*
SYN **inundate**

swan /swɒn/ *noun* [C] a large, usually white, bird with a very long neck that lives on lakes and rivers

swap (*also* **swop**) /swɒp/ *verb* [I,T] (**swapping**; **swapped**) ~ **(sth) (with sb)**; ~ **A for B** to give sth for sth else; to exchange: *When we finish these books shall we swap* (=you have my book and I'll have yours)*?* ◇ *Would you swap seats with me?* ◇ *I'd swap my job for hers any day.* ▶ **swap** *noun* [sing.]: *Let's do a swap.*
IDM **change/swap places (with sb)** → PLACE¹

swarm¹ /swɔːm/ *noun* [C] **1** a large group of insects, especially BEES, moving around together: *a swarm of bees/locusts/flies* **2** a large number of people together

swarm² /swɔːm/ *verb* [I] to fly or move in large numbers
PHR V **swarm with sb/sth** to be too crowded or full

swash /swɒʃ/ *noun* [sing.] (GEOGRAPHY) the flow of water up the beach after a wave has broken ➲ look at **backwash** ➲ picture at **wave**

swat /swɒt/ *verb* [T] (**swatting**; **swatted**) to hit sth, especially an insect, with sth flat

sway /sweɪ/ *verb* **1** [I] to move slowly from side to side: *The trees were swaying in the wind.* **2** [T] to influence sb: *Many people were swayed by his convincing arguments.*

swear 🔑 /sweə(r)/ *verb* (*pt* **swore** /swɔː(r)/; *pp* **sworn** /swɔːn/) **1** [I] ~ **(at sb/sth)** to use rude or bad language: *He hit his thumb with the hammer and swore loudly.* ◇ *There's no point in swearing at the car just because it won't start!* ➲ look at **curse** **2** [I,T] ~ **(to do sth)**; ~ **that...** to make a serious promise: *When you give evidence in court you have to swear to tell the truth.* ◇ *Will you swear not to tell anyone?*
PHR V **swear by sth** to believe completely in the value of sth
swear sb in (usually passive) to make sb say officially that they will accept the responsibility of a new position: *The President will be sworn in next week.*

ˈ**swear word** (also *old-fashioned* **oath**) *noun* [C] (LANGUAGE) a word that is considered rude or bad and that may offend people

sweat 🔑 /swet/ *verb* [I] **1** to produce liquid through your skin because you are hot, ill or afraid **2** ~ **(over sth)** to work hard: *I've been sweating over that problem all day.* ▶ **sweat** *noun* [C,U]: *He stopped digging and wiped the sweat from his forehead.* ◇ *He woke up* ***in a sweat.*** ➲ look at **perspiration**
IDM **work/sweat your guts out** → GUT¹

sweater 🔑 /ˈswetə(r)/ *noun* [C] a warm piece of clothing with long sleeves, often made of wool, which you wear on the top half of your body

sweatpants /ˈswetpænts/ *noun* [pl.] loose warm trousers/pants, usually made of thick cotton and worn for relaxing or playing sports in

sweatshirt /ˈswetʃɜːt/ *noun* [C] a warm piece of cotton clothing with long sleeves, which you wear on the top half of your body

sweatshop /ˈswetʃɒp/ *noun* [C] (BUSINESS) a place where people work for low wages in poor conditions

sweatsuit /ˈswetsuːt/ *noun* [C] a SWEATSHIRT and SWEATPANTS worn together, for relaxing or playing sports in

sweaty /ˈsweti/ *adj.* **1** wet with sweat: *I was hot and sweaty after the match and needed a shower.* **2** causing you to sweat: *a hot sweaty day*

swede /swiːd/ *noun* [C,U] a large, round, yellow vegetable that grows under the ground

sweep¹ 🔑 /swiːp/ *verb* (*pt, pp* **swept** /swept/) **1** [I,T] to clean the floor, etc. by moving dust, dirt, etc. away with a brush: *to sweep the floor* ◇ *I'm going to sweep the leaves off the path.* **2** [T] to remove sth from a surface using your hand, etc.: *He swept the books angrily off the table.* **3** [I,T] to move quickly and smoothly over the area or in the direction mentioned: *Fire swept through the building.* **4** [T] to move or push sb/sth with a lot of force: *The huge waves swept her overboard.* ◇ *He was swept along by the huge crowd.* **5** [I] to move in a way that impresses or is intended to impress people: *Five big black Mercedes swept past us.* **6** [I,T] to move over an area, especially in order to look for sth: *The army were sweeping the fields for mines.* ◇ *His eyes swept quickly over the page.*
PHR V **sweep (sb/sth) aside** to not allow sb/sth to affect your progress or plans
sweep sth out to remove dirt and dust from the floor of a room or building using a brush
sweep over sb (used about a feeling) to suddenly affect sb very strongly
sweep (sth) up to remove dirt, dust, leaves, etc. using a brush

sweep² /swiːp/ *noun* [C] **1** [usually sing.] the action of moving dirt and dust from a floor or surface using a brush: *I'd better give the floor a sweep.* **2** a long, curving shape or movement: *He showed us which way to go with a sweep of his arm.* **3** a movement over an area, especially in order to look for sth **4** = CHIMNEY SWEEP

IDM a clean sweep → CLEAN[1]

sweeper /ˈswiːpə(r)/ ***noun*** [C] **1** a person or thing that cleans surfaces with a brush: *He's a road sweeper.* ◇ *Do you sell carpet sweepers?* **2** (**SPORT**) (in football) the defending player who plays behind the other defending players

sweeping /ˈswiːpɪŋ/ ***adj.*** **1** (used about statements, etc.) too general and not accurate enough: *He made a sweeping statement about all politicians being dishonest.* **2** having a great and important effect: *sweeping reforms*

sweet[1] /swiːt/ ***adj.*** **1** containing, or tasting as if it contains, a lot of sugar: *Children usually like sweet things.* ◇ *This cake's too sweet.* ➲ look at **savoury 2** (used especially about children and small things) attractive: *a sweet little kitten* ◇ *Isn't that little girl sweet?* **SYN cute 3** having or showing a kind character: *a sweet smile* ◇ *It's very sweet of you to remember my birthday!* **4** (used about a smell or a sound) pleasant ▶ **sweetness *noun*** [U]

IDM have a sweet tooth to like eating sweet things

sweet[2] /swiːt/ ***noun*** **1** [C, usually pl.] (*AmE* **candy** [U]) a small piece of boiled sugar, chocolate, etc., often sold in a packet: *He was sucking a sweet.* ◇ *a sweet shop* **2** [C,U] sweet food served at the end of a meal ➲ look at **pudding**, **dessert**

sweetcorn /ˈswiːtkɔːn/ (*AmE* **corn**) ***noun*** [U] yellow grains from a tall plant (**maize**) that taste sweet and are eaten as a vegetable

sweeten /ˈswiːtn/ ***verb*** [T] to make sth sweet by adding sugar, etc.

sweetener /ˈswiːtnə(r)/ ***noun*** [C,U] a substance used instead of sugar for making food or drink sweet: *artificial sweeteners*

sweetheart /ˈswiːthɑːt/ ***noun*** [C] **1** used when speaking to sb, especially a child, in a very friendly way: *Do you want a drink, sweetheart?* **2** (*old-fashioned*) a boyfriend or girlfriend

sweetly /ˈswiːtli/ ***adv.*** in an attractive, kind or pleasant way: *She smiled sweetly.* ◇ *sweetly-scented flowers*

ˌsweet poˈtato *noun* [C,U] a vegetable that grows under the ground and looks like a red potato, but is yellow inside and tastes sweet

swell[1] /swel/ ***verb*** (*pt* **swelled** /sweld/; *pp* **swollen** /ˈswəʊlən/ or **swelled**) **1** [I,T] ~ (**up**) to become or to make sth bigger, fuller or thicker: *After the fall her ankle began to swell up.* ◇ *Heavy rain had swollen the rivers.* **2** [I,T] to increase or make sth increase in number or size: *The crowd swelled to 600 by the end of the evening.* **3** [I] (*written*) (used about feelings or sound) to suddenly become stronger or louder: *Hatred swelled inside him.*

swell[2] /swel/ ***noun*** [sing.] the slow movement up and down of the surface of the sea

swelling /ˈswelɪŋ/ ***noun*** **1** [C] (**HEALTH**) a place on your body that is bigger or fatter than usual because of an injury or illness: *I've got a nasty swelling under my eye.* **2** [U] the process of becoming swollen: *The disease often causes swelling of the ankles and knees.*

sweltering /ˈsweltərɪŋ/ ***adj.*** (*informal*) much too hot: *It was sweltering in the office today.*

swept past tense, past participle of **sweep[1]**

swerve /swɜːv/ ***verb*** [I] to change direction suddenly: *The car swerved to avoid the child.* ▶ **swerve *noun*** [C]

swift /swɪft/ ***adj.*** happening without delay; quick: *a swift reaction/decision/movement* ◇ *a swift runner* ▶ **swiftly *adv.***

swig /swɪɡ/ ***verb*** [I,T] (**swigging**; **swigged**) (*informal*) to take a quick drink of sth, especially alcohol ▶ **swig *noun*** [C]

swill /swɪl/ ***verb*** [T] ~ **sth (out/down)** to wash sth by pouring large amounts of water, etc. into, over or through it

swimming strokes

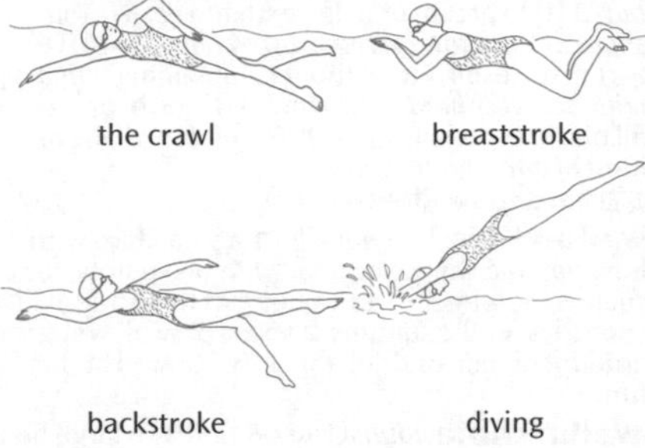

swim /swɪm/ ***verb*** (*pres. part.* **swimming**; *pt* **swam** /swæm/; *pp* **swum** /swʌm/) **1** [I,T] to move your body through water: *How far can you swim?* ◇ *Hundreds of tiny fish swam past.* **2** [I] **be swimming (in/with sth)** to be covered with a lot of liquid: *The salad was swimming in oil.* **3** [I] to seem to be moving or turning: *The floor began to swim before my eyes and I fainted.* **4** [I] (used about your head) to feel confused: *My head was swimming with so much new information.* ▶ **swim *noun*** [sing.]: *to go for /have a swim* ▶ **swimmer *noun*** [C]: *a strong/weak swimmer*

ˈswimming bath *noun* [C] (*also* **swimming baths** [pl.]) a public swimming pool, usually indoors

ˈswimming pool (*also* **pool**) ***noun*** [C] a pool that is built especially for people to swim in: *an indoor/outdoor/open-air swimming pool*

ˈswimming trunks *noun* [pl.] a piece of clothing like SHORTS that a man wears to go swimming: *a pair of swimming trunks*

swimsuit /ˈswɪmsuːt/ (*also* **ˈswimming costume**) ***noun*** [C] a piece of clothing that a woman wears to go swimming ➲ look at **bikini**

swindle /ˈswɪndl/ ***verb*** [T] ~ **sb/sth (out of sth)** to trick sb in order to get money, etc. ▶ **swindle *noun*** [C]: *a tax swindle*

swine /swaɪn/ ***noun*** **1** [C] (*informal*) a very unpleasant person **2** [pl.] (*old-fashioned*) (**AGRICULTURE**) pigs

swing[1] /swɪŋ/ ***verb*** (*pt, pp* **swung** /swʌŋ/) **1** [I,T] to move backwards and forwards or from side to side while hanging from sth; to make sb/sth move in this way: *The rope was swinging from a branch.* ◇ *She sat on the wall, swinging her legs.* **2** [I,T] to move or make sb/sth move in a curve: *The door swung open and Rudi walked in.* ◇ *He swung the child up onto his shoulders.* **3** [I] to move or change from one position or situation towards the opposite one: *She swung round when she heard the door open.* ◇ *His moods swing from one extreme to the other.* **4** [I,T] ~ **(sth) (at sb/sth)** to try to hit sb/sth

swing[2] 🔑 /swɪŋ/ ***noun*** **1** [sing.] a swinging movement or rhythm: *He took a swing at the ball.* **2** [C] a seat, a piece of rope, etc. that is hung from above so that you can swing backwards and forwards on it: *Some children were playing on the swings.* **3** [C] a change from one position or situation towards the opposite one
IDM **in full swing** → FULL[1]

swipe /swaɪp/ ***verb*** **1** [I,T] (*informal*) ~ **(at) sb/sth** to hit or try to hit sb/sth by moving your arm in a curve: *He swiped at the wasp with a newspaper but missed.* **2** [T] (*informal*) to steal sth **3** [T] to pass the part of a plastic card on which information is stored through a special machine for reading it: *The receptionist swiped my credit card and handed me the slip to sign.* ▶ **swipe** ***noun*** [C]: *She took a swipe at him with her handbag.*

'swipe card ***noun*** [C] a small plastic card on which information is stored which can be read by an electronic machine

swirl /swɜːl/ ***verb*** [I,T] to make or cause sth to make fast circular movements: *Her long skirt swirled round her legs as she danced.* ◇ *He swirled some water round in his mouth and spat it out.* ▶ **swirl** ***noun*** [C]

ˌSwiss 'roll ***noun*** [C] a thin flat cake that is spread with jam, etc. and rolled up

switch

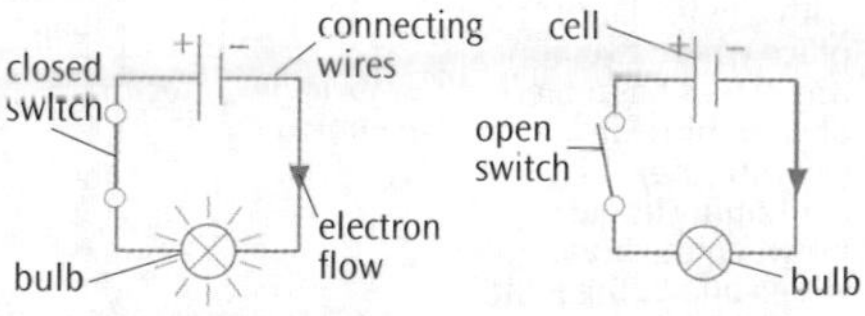

closed switch
connecting wires
cell
open switch
electron flow
bulb
bulb

complete circuit
- the charge flows
- the bulb is lit

incomplete circuit
- no flow of charge
- the bulb is not lit

switch[1] 🔑 /swɪtʃ/ ***noun*** [C] **1** a small button or sth similar that you press up or down in order to turn on electricity: *a light switch* **2** a sudden change: *a switch in policy*

switch[2] 🔑 /swɪtʃ/ ***verb*** [I,T] **1** ~ **(sth) (over) (to sth)**; ~ **(between A and B)** to change or be changed from one thing to another: *I'm fed up with my glasses – I'm thinking of switching over to contact lenses.* ◇ *Press these two keys to switch between documents on screen.* ◇ *The match has been switched from Saturday to Sunday.* **2** ~ **(sth) (with sb/sth)**; ~ **(sth) (over/round)** to exchange positions, activities, etc.: *This week you can have the car and I'll go on the bus, and next week we'll switch over.* ◇ *Someone switched the signs round and everyone went the wrong way.*
PHR V **switch (sth) off/on** to press a switch in order to start/stop electric power: *Don't forget to switch off the cooker.*
switch (sth) over to change to a different television programme

switchboard /'swɪtʃbɔːd/ ***noun*** [C] the place in a large company, etc. where all the telephone calls are connected

swivel /'swɪvl/ ***verb*** [I,T] (**swivelling; swivelled**: *AmE* **swiveling; swiveled**) ~ **(sth) (round)** to turn around a central point; to make sth do this: *She swivelled round to face me.* ◇ *He swivelled his chair towards the door.*

swollen[1] 🔑 past participle of **swell**[1]

swollen[2] 🔑 /'swəʊlən/ ***adj.*** thicker or wider than usual: *Her leg was badly swollen after the accident.*

swoop /swuːp/ ***verb*** [I] **1** to fly or move down suddenly: *The bird swooped down on its prey.* **2** (used especially about the police or the army) to visit or capture sb/sth without warning: *Police swooped at dawn and arrested the man.*
▶ **swoop** ***noun*** [C] **a** ~ **(on sb/sth)**

swop = SWAP

sword /sɔːd/ ***noun*** [C] a long, very sharp metal weapon, like a large knife ➲ picture at **weapon**

swordfish /'sɔːdfɪʃ/ ***noun*** [C,U] (*pl.* **swordfish**) a large sea fish that you can eat, with a very long thin sharp upper JAW

swore past tense of **swear**

sworn past participle of **swear**

swot[1] /swɒt/ ***verb*** [I,T] (**swotting; swotted**) (*informal*) ~ **(up) (for/on sth)**; ~ **sth up** (EDUCATION) to study sth very hard, especially to prepare for an exam: *She's swotting for her final exams.*

swot[2] /swɒt/ ***noun*** [C] (*informal*) (EDUCATION) a person who studies too hard

'SWOT analysis ***noun*** [C] (BUSINESS) a study done by an organization in order to find its strengths and weaknesses, and what problems or opportunities it should deal with. **SWOT** is formed from the initial letters of 'strengths', 'weaknesses', 'opportunities' and 'threats'.

swum past participle of **swim**

swung past tense, past participle of **swing**[1]

syllable /'sɪləbl/ ***noun*** [C] (LANGUAGE) a word or part of a word which contains one VOWEL sound: *'Mat' has one syllable and 'mattress' has two syllables.* ◇ *The stress in 'international' is on the third syllable.*

syllabus /'sɪləbəs/ ***noun*** [C] (*pl.* **syllabuses**) (EDUCATION) a list of subjects, etc. that are included in a course of study ➲ look at **curriculum**

symbiosis /ˌsɪmbaɪ'əʊsɪs/ ***noun*** [U,C] (*pl.* **symbioses** /-'əʊsiːz/) **1** (BIOLOGY) the relationship between two different living creatures that live close together and depend on each other in particular ways, each getting particular benefits from the other: *The birds live in symbiosis with the cattle, picking insects from their skin to eat.* **2** a relationship between people, companies, etc. that is to the advantage of both
▶ **symbiotic** /-'ɒtɪk/ ***adj.***: *a symbiotic relationship*
▶ **symbiotically** /ˌsɪmbaɪ'ɒtɪkli/ ***adv.***

symbol 🔑 AW /'sɪmbl/ ***noun*** [C] **1** a ~ **(of sth)** a sign, object, etc. which represents sth: *The cross is the symbol of Christianity.* ➲ note at **sign**[1] **2** a ~ **(for sth)** a letter, number or sign that has a particular meaning: *O is the symbol for oxygen.*

symbolic AW /sɪm'bɒlɪk/ (*also* **symbolical** /-kl/) ***adj.*** used or seen to represent sth: *The white dove is symbolic of peace.* ▶ **symbolically** ***adv.*** /-kli/

symbolism AW /'sɪmbəlɪzəm/ ***noun*** [U] (ART, LITERATURE) **1** the use of symbols to represent things, especially in art and literature **2** (also **Symbolism**) a style in painting and poetry developed in France and Belgium in the late 19th century which uses images and symbols to express ideas and emotions ▶ **symbolist** ***noun*** [C], ***adj.***

symbolize (also **-ise**) AW /'sɪmbəlaɪz/ ***verb*** [T] to represent sth: *The deepest notes in music are often used to symbolize danger or despair.*

symmetrical /sɪ'metrɪkl/ (*also* **symmetric** /sɪ'metrɪk/) ***adj.*** having two halves that match each other exactly in size, shape, etc. OPP **asymmetric**
▶ **symmetrically** /-kli/ ***adv.***

symmetry /ˈsɪmətri/ ***noun*** [U] the state of having two halves that match each other exactly in size, shape, etc. ➲ picture at **axis**

sympathetic 🔑 /ˌsɪmpəˈθetɪk/ ***adj.*** **1** ~ **(to/towards sb)** showing that you understand other people's feelings, especially their problems: *When Suki was ill, everyone was very sympathetic.* ◇ *I felt very sympathetic towards him.* **2** ~ **(to sb/sth)** being in agreement with or supporting sb/sth: *I explained our ideas but she wasn't sympathetic to them.* OPP **unsympathetic** ▶ **sympathetically** /-kli/ ***adv.***

sympathize (also **-ise**) /ˈsɪmpəθaɪz/ ***verb*** [I] ~ **(with sb/sth) 1** to feel sorry for sb; to show that you understand sb's problems: *I sympathize with her, but I don't know what I can do to help.* **2** to support sb/sth: *I find it difficult to sympathize with his opinions.*

sympathizer (also **-iser**) /ˈsɪmpəθaɪzə(r)/ ***noun*** [C] a person who agrees with and supports an idea or aim

sympathy 🔑 /ˈsɪmpəθi/ ***noun*** (*pl.* **sympathies**) **1** [U] ~ **(for/towards sb)** an understanding of other people's feelings, especially their problems: *Everyone **feels** great **sympathy** for the victims of the attack.* ◇ *I don't expect any sympathy from you.* ◇ *I **have no sympathy** for Mark – it's his own fault.* **2 sympathies** [pl.] feelings of support or agreement

IDM **in sympathy (with sb/sth)** in agreement, showing that you support or approve of sb/sth: *Train drivers stopped work in sympathy with the striking bus drivers.*

symphony /ˈsɪmfəni/ ***noun*** [C] (*pl.* **symphonies**) (MUSIC) a long piece of music written for a large ORCHESTRA

symptom /ˈsɪmptəm/ ***noun*** [C] **1** (HEALTH) a change in your body that is a sign of illness: *The symptoms of flu include a headache, a high temperature and aches in the body.* **2** a sign (that sth bad is happening or exists) ➲ note at **sign**[1] ▶ **symptomatic** /ˌsɪmptəˈmætɪk/ ***adj.***

synagogue /ˈsɪnəɡɒɡ/ ***noun*** [C] (RELIGION) a building where Jewish people go to pray or to study their religion

synapse /ˈsaɪnæps; ˈsɪn-/ ***noun*** [C] (BIOLOGY) a connection between two nerve cells ▶ **synaptic** /saɪˈnæptɪk; sɪn-/ ***adj.***: *the synaptic membranes*

sync (also **synch**) /sɪŋk/ ***noun*** [U] (*informal*)

IDM **in sync** moving or working at exactly the same time and speed as sb/sth else: *The soundtrack is **not in sync** with the music.*

out of sync not moving or working at exactly the same time and speed as sb/sth else

synchronize (also **-ise**) /ˈsɪŋkrənaɪz/ ***verb*** [T] to make sth happen or work at the same time or speed: *We synchronized our watches to make sure we agreed what the time was.*

syncline /ˈsɪŋklaɪn/ ***noun*** [C] (GEOLOGY) an area of ground where layers of rock in the earth's surface have been folded into a curve that is lower in the middle than at the ends ➲ look at **anticline**

syncopated /ˈsɪŋkəpeɪtɪd/ ***adj.*** (MUSIC) in **syncopated** rhythm the strong beats are made weak and the weak beats are made strong ▶ **syncopation** /ˌsɪŋkəˈpeɪʃn/ ***noun*** [U]

syndicate[1] /ˈsɪndɪkət/ ***noun*** [C] (BUSINESS) a group of people or companies that work together in order to achieve a particular aim

syndicate[2] /ˈsɪndɪkeɪt/ ***verb*** [T] (usually passive) (BUSINESS) to sell an article, a photograph, a television programme, etc. to several different newspapers, etc.: *His column is syndicated throughout the world.*

syndrome /ˈsɪndrəʊm/ ***noun*** [C] **1** (HEALTH) a group of signs or changes in the body that are typical of an illness: *Down's syndrome* ◇ *Acquired Immune Deficiency Syndrome (Aids)* **2** a set of opinions or a way of behaving that is typical of a particular type of person, attitude or social problem

synergy /ˈsɪnədʒi/ ***noun*** [U,C] (*pl.* **-ies**) (*technical*) the extra energy, power, success, etc. that is achieved by two or more people or companies working together, instead of on their own

synonym /ˈsɪnənɪm/ ***noun*** [C] (LANGUAGE) a word or phrase that has the same meaning as another word or phrase in the same language: *'Big' and 'large' are synonyms.* ➲ look at **antonym** ▶ **synonymous** /sɪˈnɒnɪməs/ ***adj.*** ~ **(with sth)**

synopsis /sɪˈnɒpsɪs/ ***noun*** [C] (*pl.* **synopses** /-siːz/) (ARTS AND MEDIA, LITERATURE) a SUMMARY (= a short description of the main points without any details) of a piece of writing, a play, etc. ▶ **synoptic** /sɪˈnɒptɪk/ ***adj.*** (*formal*)

synovial /saɪˈnəʊviəl/ ***adj.*** (ANATOMY) connected with a type of JOINT (= a place where two bones meet) that has a piece of very thin skin (**membrane**) containing liquid between the bones, which allows the joint to move freely: *a synovial joint/membrane*

synovial joint

syntax /ˈsɪntæks/ ***noun*** [U] (LANGUAGE) the system of rules for the structure of a sentence in a language

synthesis /ˈsɪnθəsɪs/ ***noun*** (*pl.* **syntheses** /-siːz/) **1** [U, C] **(a)** ~ **(of sth)** the act of combining separate ideas, beliefs, styles, etc.; a mixture or combination of ideas, beliefs, styles, etc.: *the synthesis of traditional and modern values* ◇ *a synthesis of art with everyday life* **2** [U] (SCIENCE) the natural chemical production of a substance in animals and plants: *protein synthesis* **3** [U] (SCIENCE) the artificial production of a substance that is present naturally in animals and plants: *the synthesis of penicillin* **4** [U] (MUSIC) the production of sounds, music or speech by electronic means: *digital/sound/speech synthesis*

synthesize (also **-ise**) /ˈsɪnθəsaɪz/ ***verb*** [T] **1** (SCIENCE) to produce a substance by artificial means **2** (MUSIC) to produce sounds, music or speech using electronic equipment **3** to combine separate ideas, beliefs, styles, etc.

synthesizer (also **-iser**) /ˈsɪnθəsaɪzə(r)/ ***noun*** [C] (MUSIC) an electronic musical instrument that can produce a wide variety of different sounds

synthetic /sɪnˈθetɪk/ ***adj.*** made by a chemical process; not natural: *synthetic materials/fibres* ➲ note at **artificial** ▶ **synthetically** /-kli/ ***adv.***

syphilis /ˈsɪfɪlɪs/ ***noun*** [U] (HEALTH) a serious disease that passes from one person to another by sexual contact

syphon = SIPHON

syringe /sɪˈrɪndʒ/ ***noun*** [C] **1** (HEALTH) a plastic or glass tube with a needle that is used for taking a small amount of blood out of the body or for putting drugs into the body ➲ picture at **health** **2** a plastic or glass tube with a rubber part at the end, used for sucking up liquid and then pushing it out ➲ picture at **laboratory**

syrup /ˈsɪrəp/ ***noun*** [U] a thick sweet liquid, often made by boiling sugar with water or fruit juice: *peaches in syrup* ➲ look at **treacle**

system 🔑 /ˈsɪstəm/ ***noun*** **1** [C] a set of ideas or rules for organizing sth; a particular way of doing sth: *We have a new computerized system in the library.* ◇ *The government is planning to reform the education system.* **2** [C] a group of things or parts that work together: *a central heating system* ◇ *a transport system* **3** [C] the body of a person or animal; parts of the body that work together: *the central nervous system* **4 the system** [sing.] (*informal*) the traditional methods and rules of a society: *You can't **beat the system*** (=you must accept these rules).

IDM **get sth out of your system** (*informal*) to do sth to free yourself of a strong feeling or emotion

systematic /ˌsɪstəˈmætɪk/ ***adj.*** done using a fixed plan or method: *a systematic search* ▶ **systematically** /-kli/ ***adv.***

systemic /sɪˈstemɪk; sɪˈstiːmɪk/ ***adj.*** **1** affecting or connected with the whole of sth, especially the human body **2 systemic** chemicals or drugs, which are used to treat diseases in plants or animals, enter the body of the plant or animal and spread to all parts of it: *systemic weedkillers* ▶ **systemically** /-kli/ ***adv.***

ˈ**systems analyst** ***noun*** [C] (COMPUTING) a person whose job is to look carefully at the needs of a business company or an organization and then design the best way of working and completing tasks using computer programs

systole /ˈsɪstəli/ ***noun*** [C] (HEALTH) the part of the heart's rhythm when the heart PUMPS blood ➲ look at **diastole** ▶ **systolic** /ˌsɪsˈtɒlɪk/ ***adj.***: *systolic blood pressure*

Tt

T, t¹ /tiː/ ***noun*** [C,U] (*pl.* **T's**; **t's** /tiːz/) the twentieth letter of the English alphabet: *'Table' begins with (a) 'T'.*

t² (*AmE also* **tn**) ***abbr.*** ton(s), tonne(s): *5t coal*

ta /tɑː/ ***exclamation*** (*BrE, informal*) thank you

tab /tæb/ ***noun*** [C] **1** a small piece of cloth, metal or paper that is fixed to the edge of sth to help you open, hold or identify it: *You open the tin by pulling the metal tab.* **2** the money that you owe for food, drink, etc. in a bar, CAFE or restaurant; the bill ➲ note at **bill¹**

IDM **keep tabs on sb/sth** (*informal*) to watch sb/sth carefully; to check sth

tabla /ˈtæblə; ˈtʌb-/ ***noun*** [C] (MUSIC) a pair of small drums played with the hands and used in S Asian music, usually to accompany other instruments

table 🔑 /ˈteɪbl/ ***noun*** [C] **1** a piece of furniture with a flat top supported by legs: *a dining/bedside/coffee/kitchen table* ◇ *Could you **lay/set the table** for lunch?* (=put the knives, forks, plates, etc. on it) ◇ *Let me help you **clear the table*** (=remove the dirty plates, etc. at the end of a meal). **2** a list of facts or figures, usually arranged in rows and columns down a page: *Table 3 shows the results.*

tablecloth /ˈteɪblklɒθ/ ***noun*** [C] a piece of cloth that you use for covering a table, especially when having a meal

ˈ**table manners** ***noun*** [pl.] behaviour that is considered correct while you are having a meal at a table with other people

tablespoon /ˈteɪblspuːn/ ***noun*** [C] **1** a large spoon used for serving or measuring food **2** (*also* ˈ**tablespoonful**) the amount that a **tablespoon** holds: *Add two tablespoons of sugar.*

tablet 🔑 /ˈtæblət/ ***noun*** [C] (HEALTH) a small amount of medicine in solid form that you swallow: *Take two **tablets** every four hours.* ➲ picture at **health**

ˈ**table tennis** (also *informal* **ping-pong**) ***noun*** [U] (SPORT) a game with rules like TENNIS in which you hit a light plastic ball across a table with a small round BAT

ˌ**tablet ˌPˈC** ***noun*** [C] (COMPUTING) a very small computer that you can carry with you and that has a screen that you touch with a special pen (**stylus**) so that you do not have to use a mouse or a KEYBOARD

tabloid /ˈtæblɔɪd/ ***noun*** [C] (ARTS AND MEDIA) a newspaper with small pages, a lot of pictures and short articles

taboo /təˈbuː/ ***noun*** [C] (*pl.* **taboos**) something that you must not say or do because it might shock, offend or make people embarrassed ▶ **taboo** ***adj.***: *a taboo subject/word*

tabular /ˈtæbjələ(r)/ ***adj.*** (usually *before* a noun) presented or arranged in a TABLE (=in rows and columns): *tabular data* ◇ *The results are presented **in tabular form**.*

tabulate /ˈtæbjuleɪt/ ***verb*** [T] to arrange facts or figures in columns or lists so that they can be read easily ▶ **tabulation** /ˌtæbjuˈleɪʃn/ ***noun*** [U, C]

tacit /ˈtæsɪt/ ***adj.*** (*formal*) understood but not actually said ▶ **tacitly** ***adv.***

tack¹ /tæk/ ***noun*** **1** [sing.] a way of dealing with a particular situation: *If people won't listen we'll have to try a different tack.* **2** [C] a small nail with a sharp point and a flat head

tack² /tæk/ ***verb*** [T] **1** to fasten sth in place with **tacks¹**(2) **2** to fasten cloth together temporarily with long STITCHES that can be removed easily

PHR V **tack sth on (to sth)** to add sth extra on the end of sth

tackle¹ 🔑 /ˈtækl/ ***verb*** **1** [T] to make an effort to deal with a difficult situation or problem: *The government must tackle the problem of rising unemployment.* ◇ *Firemen were brought in to tackle the blaze.* **2** [I,T] (SPORT) (used in football, etc.) to try to take the ball from sb in the other team **3** [T] to stop sb running away by pulling them down **4** [T] ~ **sb about sth** to speak to sb about a difficult subject: *I'm going to tackle him about the money he owes me.*

tackle² /ˈtækl/ ***noun*** **1** [C] the action of trying to get the ball from another player in football, etc. **2** [U] the equipment you use in some sports, especially fishing: *fishing tackle*

tacky /ˈtæki/ ***adj.*** (*informal*) **1** cheap and of poor quality and/or not in good taste: *a shop selling tacky souvenirs* **2** (used about paint, etc.) not quite dry; sticky

tact /tækt/ ***noun*** [U] the ability to deal with people without offending or upsetting them: *She handled the situation with great tact and diplomacy.*

tactful /ˈtæktfl/ ***adj.*** careful not to say or do things that could offend people ▶ **tactfully** /-fəli/ ***adv.***

tactic /ˈtæktɪk/ ***noun*** **1** [C, usually pl.] the particular method you use to achieve sth: *We must decide what our tactics are going to be at the next meeting.* ◇ *I don't think this tactic will work.* **2 tactics** [pl.] the skilful arrangement and use of military forces in order to win a battle

tactical /ˈtæktɪkl/ ***adj.*** **1** connected with the particular method you use to achieve sth: *a tactical error* ◇ *tactical discussions/planning* **2** designed to bring a future advantage: *a tactical decision* ▶ **tactically** /-kli/ ***adv.***

ˌtactical ˈvoting ***noun*** [U] (*BrE*) (**POLITICS**) the act of voting for a particular person or political party, not because you support them, but in order to prevent sb else from being elected

tactless /ˈtæktləs/ ***adj.*** saying and doing things that are likely to offend and upset other people: *It was rather tactless of you to ask her how old she was.* ▶ **tactlessly** ***adv.***

tadpole /ˈtædpəʊl/ ***noun*** [C] a young form of a FROG when it has a large black head and a long tail ➲ picture on **page 29**

tae kwon do /ˌtaɪ ˌkwɒn ˈdəʊ/ ***noun*** [U] (**SPORT**) a Korean system of fighting without weapons, similar to KARATE

tag[1] /tæg/ ***noun*** [C] **1** (often used to form compound nouns) a small piece of card, material, etc. fastened to sth to give information about it; a label: *How much is this dress? There isn't a* ***price tag*** *on it.* **2** (**LANGUAGE**) = QUESTION TAG

tag[2] /tæg/ ***verb*** [T] (**tagging**; **tagged**) to fasten a **tag** onto sb/sth

PHR V **tag along** to follow or go somewhere with sb, especially when you have not been invited

ˈtag question ***noun*** [C] (**LANGUAGE**) = QUESTION TAG

t'ai chi ch'uan /ˌtaɪ tʃiː ˈtʃwɑːn/ (*also* **ˌt'ai ˈchi**) ***noun*** [U] (**SPORT**) a Chinese system of exercises consisting of sets of very slow controlled movements

tail[1] 🔑 /teɪl/ ***noun*** **1** [C] the part at the end of the body of an animal, bird, fish, etc.: *The dog barked and wagged its tail.* ➲ picture on **page 28** **2** [C] the back part of an aircraft, SPACECRAFT, etc. ➲ picture at **plane** **3 tails** [pl.] a man's formal coat that is short at the front but with a long, divided piece at the back, worn especially at weddings **4 tails** [pl.] the side of a coin that does not have the head of a person on it: *'We'll toss a coin to decide,' said my father.* ***'Heads or tails?'*** **5** [C] (*informal*) a person who is sent to follow sb secretly to get information about them

IDM **make head or tail of sth** → HEAD[1]

tail[2] /teɪl/ ***verb*** [T] to follow sb closely, especially to watch where they go

PHR V **tail away/off** (*especially BrE*) to become smaller and weaker

tailback /ˈteɪlbæk/ ***noun*** [C] a long line of traffic that is moving slowly or not moving at all, because sth is blocking the road in front

tailgate[1] /ˈteɪlgeɪt/ ***noun*** [C] **1** (*also* **tailboard**) a door at the back of a lorry that opens downwards and that you can open or remove when you are loading or unloading the vehicle **2** the door that opens upwards at the back of a HATCHBACK (= a car that has three or five doors)

tailgate[2] /ˈteɪlgeɪt/ ***verb*** **1** [I,T] (*informal*) (*especially AmE*) to drive too closely behind another vehicle **2** [I] (*AmE*) to eat food and drinks outdoors, served from the TAILGATE of a car

tailor[1] /ˈteɪlə(r)/ ***noun*** [C] a person whose job is to make clothes, especially for men

tailor[2] /ˈteɪlə(r)/ ***verb*** [T] (usually passive) **1 ~ sth to/for sb/sth** to make or design sth for a particular person or purpose: *programmes tailored to the needs of specific groups* **2** to make clothes: *a well-tailored coat*

ˌtailor-ˈmade ***adj.*** **tailor-made (for sb/sth)** made for a particular person or purpose and therefore very suitable

tailplane /ˈteɪlpleɪn/ ***noun*** [C] a small horizontal wing at the back of an aircraft ➲ picture at **plane**

tailwind /ˈteɪlwɪnd/ ***noun*** [C] a wind that blows from behind a moving vehicle, a runner, etc. ➲ look at **headwind**

taint /teɪnt/ ***noun*** [C, usually sing.] (*formal*) the effect of sth bad or unpleasant that spoils the quality of sb/sth: *the taint of corruption.* ▶ **taint** ***verb*** [T] (usually passive): *Her reputation was tainted by the scandal.*

take 🔑 /teɪk/ ***verb*** [T] (*pt* **took** /tʊk/; *pp* **taken** /ˈteɪkən/) **1** to carry or move sb/sth; to go with sb from one place to another: *Take your coat with you – it's cold.* ◇ *Could you take this letter home to your parents?* ◇ *The ambulance took him to hospital.* ◇ *I'm taking the children swimming this afternoon.* **2** to put your hand round sth and hold it (and move it towards you): *She held out the keys, and I took them.* ◇ *He took a sweater out of the drawer.* ◇ *She* ***took*** *my* ***hand*** */me by the hand.* **3** to remove sth from a place or a person, often without permission: *Who's taken my pen?* ◇ *My name had been taken off the list.* ◇ *The burglars took all my jewellery.* **4** to accept or receive sth: *If you* ***take*** *my* ***advice*** *you'll forget all about him.* ◇ *Do you take credit cards?* ◇ *What coins does the machine take?* ◇ *I'm not going to* ***take the blame*** *for the accident.* ◇ *She's not going to* ***take the job***. **5** to capture a place by force; to get control of sb/sth: *The state will* ***take control of*** *the company.* **6** to understand sth or react to sth in a particular way: *She took what he said as a compliment.* ◇ *I wish you would* ***take*** *things more* ***seriously***. **7** to get a particular feeling from sth: *He* ***takes*** *great* ***pleasure in*** *his grandchildren.* ◇ *When she failed the exam she* ***took comfort from*** *the fact that it was only by a few marks.* **8** to be able to deal with sth difficult or unpleasant: *I can't take much more of this heat.* SYN **stand** **9** to need sth/sb: *It took three people to move the piano.* ◇ *How long did the journey take?* ◇ *It took a lot of courage to say that.* **10** to swallow sth: ***Take*** *two* ***tablets*** *four times a day.* ◇ *Do you* ***take sugar*** *in tea?* **11** to write or record sth: *She* ***took notes*** *during the lecture.* ◇ *The police officer took my name and address.* **12** to photograph sth: *I* ***took*** *some nice* ***photos*** *of the wedding.* **13** to measure sth: *The doctor* ***took*** *my* ***temperature*** */pulse/blood pressure.* **14** (not used in the continuous tenses) to have a certain size of shoes or clothes: *What size shoes do you take?* **15** (not used in the continuous tenses) to have enough space for sb/sth: *How many passengers can this bus take?* **16** used with nouns to say that sb is performing an action: ***Take a look*** *at this article* (= look at it). ◇ *We have to* ***take a decision*** (= decide). **17** (**EDUCATION**) to study a subject for an exam; to do an exam: *I'm taking the advanced exam this summer.* **18 ~ sb (for sth)** (**EDUCATION**) to give lessons to sb: *Who takes you for English* (= who is your teacher)? **19** to use a form of transport; to use a particular route: *I always* ***take the train*** *to York.*

◇ *Which road do you take to Hove?* ◇ *Take the second turning on the right.* **20** (not used in the continuous tenses) (LANGUAGE) to have or need a word to go with it in a sentence or other structure: *The verb 'depend' takes the preposition 'on'.*

IDM **be taken with sb/sth** to find sb/sth attractive or interesting

I take it (that...) (used to show that you understand sth from a situation, even though you have not been told) I imagine; I guess; I suppose: *I take it that you're not coming?*

take it from me believe me

take a lot out of sb to make sb very tired

take a lot of/some doing to need a lot of work or effort

PHR V **take sb aback** → ABACK

take after sb (not used in the continuous tenses) to look or behave like an older member of your family, especially a parent

take sth apart to separate sth into the different parts it is made of

take sth away 1 to cause a feeling, etc. to disappear: *These aspirins will take the pain away.* **2** to buy cooked food at a restaurant, etc. and carry it out to eat somewhere else, for example at home ➲ noun takeaway

take sb/sth away (from sb) to remove sb/sth: *She took the scissors away from the child.*

take sth back 1 to return sth to the place that you got it from **2** to admit that sth you said was wrong

take sth down 1 to remove a structure by separating it into the pieces it is made of: *They took the tent down and started the journey home.* **2** to write down sth that is said

take sb in 1 to make sb believe sth that is not true: *I was completely taken in by her story.* **2** to invite sb who has no home to live with you

take sth in to understand what you see, hear or read: *There was too much in the museum to take in at one go.*

take off 1 (used about an aircraft) to leave the ground and start flying OPP **land 2** (used about an idea, a product, etc.) to become successful or popular very quickly or suddenly

take sb off to copy the way sb speaks or behaves in an amusing way

take sth off 1 to remove sth, especially clothes: *Come in and take your coat off.* **2** to have the period of time mentioned as a holiday: *I'm going to take a week off.*

take sb on to start to employ sb: *The firm is taking on new staff.*

take sth on to accept a responsibility or decide to do sth: *He's taken on a lot of extra work.*

take sb out to go out with sb (for a social occasion): *I'm taking Sarah out for a meal tonight.*

take sth out to remove sth from inside your body: *He's having two teeth taken out.*

take sth out (of sth) to remove sth from sth: *He took a notebook out of his pocket.* ◇ *I need to take some money out of the bank.*

take it out on sb to behave badly towards sb because you are angry or upset about sth, even though it is not this person's fault

take (sth) over to get control of sth or responsibility for sth: *The firm is being taken over by a large company.* ◇ *Who's going to take over as assistant when Tim leaves?*

take to sb/sth to start liking sb/sth

take to sth/doing sth to begin doing sth regularly as a habit

take sth up to start doing sth regularly (for example as a hobby): *I've taken up yoga recently.*

take up sth to use or fill an amount of time or space: *All her time is taken up looking after the new baby.* SYN **occupy**

take sb up on sth 1 to say that you disagree with sth that sb has just said, and ask them to explain it: *I must take you up on that last point.* **2** (*informal*) to accept an offer that sb has made

take sth up with sb to ask or complain about sth: *I'll take the matter up with my MP.*

takeaway /ˈteɪkəweɪ/ (*AmE* **takeout** /ˈteɪkaʊt/; **ˈcarry-out**) *noun* [C] **1** a restaurant that sells food that you can eat somewhere else **2** the food that such a restaurant sells: *Let's have a takeaway.*

ˈtake-off *noun* [U, C] the moment when an aircraft leaves the ground and starts to fly: *The plane is ready for take-off.* OPP **landing**

takeover /ˈteɪkəʊvə(r)/ *noun* [C] the act of taking control of sth: *They made a takeover bid for the company.* ◇ *a military takeover of the government*

takings /ˈteɪkɪŋz/ *noun* [pl.] (FINANCE) the amount of money that a shop, theatre, etc. gets from selling goods, tickets, etc.

talcum powder /ˈtælkəm paʊdə(r)/ (*also* **talc** /tælk/) *noun* [U] a soft powder which smells nice. People often put it on their skin after a bath.

tale /teɪl/ *noun* [C] **1** (LITERATURE) a story about events that are not real: *fairy tales* **2** a report or description of sb/sth that may not be true: *I've heard tales of people seeing ghosts in that house.*

talent /ˈtælənt/ *noun* [C,U] (a) ~ (**for sth**) a natural skill or ability: *She has a talent for painting.* ◇ *His work shows great talent.* ▶ **talented** *adj.*: *a talented musician*

talk¹ 🔑 /tɔːk/ *verb* **1** [I] ~ (**to/with sb**) (**about/of sb/sth**) to say things; to speak in order to give information or to express feelings, ideas, etc.: *I could hear them talking downstairs.* ◇ *Can I talk to you for a minute?* ◇ *Nasreen is not an easy person to talk to.* ◇ *We need to talk about the plans for the weekend.* ◇ *He's been talking of going to Australia for some time now.* ◇ *Dr Hollis will be talking about Japanese art in her lecture.* **2** [I,T] to discuss sth serious or important: *We can't go on like this. We need to talk.* ◇ *Could we **talk business** after dinner?* **3** [I] to discuss people's private lives: *His strange lifestyle started the local people talking.* SYN **gossip 4** [I] to give information to sb, especially when you do not want to

IDM **know what you are talking about** → KNOW¹

talk sense to say things that are correct or sensible: *He's the only politician who talks any sense.*

talk/speak of the devil → DEVIL

talk shop to talk about your work with the people you work with, outside working hours

PHR V **talk down to sb** to talk to sb as if they are less intelligent or important than you

talk sb into/out of doing sth to persuade sb to do/not to do sth: *She tried to talk him into buying a new car.*

talk sth over (with sb) to discuss sth with sb, especially in order to reach an agreement or make a decision

talk² 🔑 /tɔːk/ *noun* **1** [C] a ~ (**with sb**) (**about sth**) a conversation or discussion: *Tim and I had a long talk about the problem.* **2 talks** [pl.] (POLITICS) formal discussions between governments: *The Foreign Ministers of the two countries will meet for talks next week.* ◇ *arms/pay/peace talks* **3** [C] a ~ (**on sth**) a formal speech on a particular subject: *He's giving a talk on 'Our changing world'.* SYN **lecture 4** [U] (*informal*) things that people say that are not based on facts or reality: *He says he's going to resign but it's just talk.* ➲ look at **small talk**

talkative /'tɔːkətɪv/ ***adj.*** liking to talk a lot

tall 🔑 /tɔːl/ ***adj.*** **1** (used about people or things) of more than average height; not short: *a tall young man* ◇ *a tall tree/tower/chimney* OPP **short 2** used to describe the height of sb/sth: *Claire is five feet tall.* ◇ *How tall are you?* ◇ *Nick is taller than his brother.* ➲ noun **height**

tally[1] /'tæli/ ***noun*** [C] (*pl.* **tallies**) a record of the number or amount of sth, especially one that you can keep adding to: *He hopes to improve on his tally of three goals in the past nine games.*

tally[2] /'tæli/ ***verb*** (*3rd person sing. pres.* **tallies**; *pres. part.* **tallying**; *pt, pp* **tallied**) **1** [I] ~ **(with sth)** to be the same as or to match another person's account of sth, another set of figures, etc.: *Her report of what happened tallied exactly with the story of another witness.* **2** [T] ~ **sth (up)** to calculate the total number, cost, etc. of sth

talon /'tælən/ ***noun*** [C] a long sharp curved nail on the feet of some birds, especially ones that kill other animals and birds for food ➲ picture on **page 28**

tambourine /ˌtæmbə'riːn/ ***noun*** [C] (MUSIC) a musical instrument that has a circular frame covered with plastic or skin, with metal discs round the edge. To play it, you hit it or shake it with your hand. ➲ picture on **page 465**

tame[1] /teɪm/ ***adj.*** **1** (used about animals or birds) not wild or afraid of people: *The birds are so tame they will eat from your hand.* **2** boring; not interesting or exciting: *After the big city, you must find village life very tame.*

tame[2] /teɪm/ ***verb*** [T] to bring sth wild under your control; to make sth **tame**

tamper /'tæmpə(r)/ ***verb***

PHR V **tamper with sth** to make changes to sth without permission, especially in order to damage it

tampon /'tæmpɒn/ ***noun*** [C] (HEALTH) a TIGHTLY-ROLLED piece of cotton material that a woman puts inside her body to take in and hold the blood that she loses once a month ➲ look at **sanitary towel**

tan[1] /tæn/ ***noun*** **1** [C] = SUNTAN **2** [U] a colour between yellow and brown ▶ **tan** ***adj.***

tan[2] /tæn/ ***verb*** [I,T] (**tanning**; **tanned**) (used about a person's skin) to become or make sth brown as a result of spending time in the sun: *Do you tan easily?* ▶ **tanned** ***adj.***: *You're looking very tanned – have you been on holiday?*

tandem /'tændəm/ ***noun*** [C] a bicycle with seats for two people, one behind the other

IDM **in tandem (with sb/sth)** working together with sth/sb else; happening at the same time as sth else

tangent /'tændʒənt/ ***noun*** [C] **1** (MATHEMATICS) a straight line that touches a curve but does not cross it ➲ picture at **circle 2** (MATHEMATICS) (*abbr.* **tan**) the RATIO of the length of the side opposite an angle in a RIGHT-ANGLED triangle (= a triangle with one angle of 90°) to the length of the side next to it ➲ look at **cosine**, **sine**

IDM **go off at a tangent**; (*AmE*) **go off on a tangent** to suddenly start saying or doing sth that seems to have no connection with what has gone before

tangerine /ˌtændʒə'riːn/ ***noun*** **1** [C] a fruit like a small sweet orange with a skin that is easy to take off **2** [U], ***adj.*** (of) a deep orange colour

tangible /'tændʒəbl/ ***adj.*** that can be clearly seen to exist: *There are tangible benefits in the new system.* OPP **intangible**

tangle /'tæŋgl/ ***noun*** [C] a confused mass, especially of threads, hair, branches, etc. that cannot easily be separated from each other: *My hair's full of tangles.* ◇ *This string's* ***in a tangle.*** ▶ **tangled** ***adj.***: *The wool was all tangled up.*

tango /'tæŋgəʊ/ ***noun*** [C] (*pl.* **tangos**) a fast South American dance with a strong rhythm, in which two people hold each other closely; a piece of music for this dance ▶ **tango** ***verb*** [I] (*pres. part.* **tangoing**; *pt, pp* **tangoed**)

tank 🔑 /tæŋk/ ***noun*** [C] **1** a container for holding liquids or gas; the amount that a tank will hold: *a water/fuel/petrol/fish tank* ◇ *We drove there and back on one tank of petrol.* **2** a large, heavy military vehicle covered with strong metal and armed with guns, that moves on special wheels

tanker /'tæŋkə(r)/ ***noun*** [C] a ship or lorry that carries oil, petrol, etc. in large amounts: *an oil tanker*

Tannoy™ /'tænɔɪ/ ***noun*** [C] a system used for giving spoken information in a public place: *They announced* ***over the tannoy*** *that our flight was delayed.*

tantalizing (also **-ising**) /'tæntəlaɪzɪŋ/ ***adj.*** making you want sth that you cannot have or do; TEMPTING: *A tantalizing aroma of cooking was coming from the kitchen.* ▶ **tantalizingly** (also **-isingly**) ***adv.***

tantalum /'tæntələm/ ***noun*** [U] (*symbol* **Ta**) (CHEMISTRY) a chemical element. **Tantalum** is a hard silver-grey metal used in the production of electronic parts and of metal plates and pins for connecting broken bones. ❶ For more information on the periodic table of elements, look at pages R34-5.

tantrum /'tæntrəm/ ***noun*** [C] a sudden explosion of anger, especially by a child

tap[1] 🔑 /tæp/ ***verb*** (**tapping**; **tapped**) **1** [I,T] ~ **(at/on sth)**; ~ **sb/sth (on/with sth)** to touch or hit sb/sth quickly and lightly: *Their feet were tapping in time to the music.* ◇ *She tapped me on the shoulder.* **2** [I,T] ~ **(into) sth** to make use of a source of energy, knowledge, etc. that already exists: *to tap the skills of young people* **3** [T] to fit a device to sb's telephone so that their calls can be listened to secretly

tap[2] 🔑 /tæp/ ***noun*** [C] **1** (*AmE* **faucet**) a type of handle that you turn to let water, gas, etc. out of a pipe or container: *Turn the hot/cold tap on/off.* **2** a light hit with your hand or fingers **3** a device that is fitted to sb's telephone so that their calls can be listened to secretly

'tap dance ***noun*** [C] a style of dancing in which you tap the rhythm of the music with your feet, wearing special shoes with pieces of metal on them ▶ **'tap-dance** ***verb*** [I]

tape[1] 🔑 AW /teɪp/ ***noun*** **1** [U] (ARTS AND MEDIA) a thin band of plastic material used for recording sound, pictures or information: *I've got the whole concert* ***on tape*** (= recorded). **2** [C] (ARTS AND MEDIA, MUSIC) a CASSETTE which is used for recording or playing music, videos, etc.: ***a blank tape*** (= a tape which is empty) ◇ *to rewind a tape* **3** [U] a long narrow band of plastic, etc. with a sticky substance on one side that is used for sticking things together, covering electric wires, etc.: *sticky/adhesive tape* ➲ look at **insulating tape**, **Sellotape** **4** [C,U] a narrow piece of cloth that is used for tying things together or as a label ➲ look at **red tape** **5** [C] a piece of material stretched across a race track to mark where the race finishes

tape² AW /teɪp/ ***verb*** [T] **1** (ARTS AND MEDIA, MUSIC) to record sound, music, television programmes, etc. using a CASSETTE **2** ~ **sth (up)** to fasten sth by sticking or tying sth with tape¹(3)

'tape deck ***noun*** [C] the part of a music system (**stereo**) on which you play CASSETTES or tapes

'tape measure (*also* **'measuring tape**) ***noun*** [C] a long thin piece of plastic, cloth or metal with centimetres, etc. marked on it. It is used for measuring things. ➲ look at **tape**

'tape recorder ***noun*** [C] a machine that is used for recording and playing sounds on tape

tapescript /'teɪpskrɪpt/ ***noun*** [C] a written or printed copy of words that are spoken on a CD, a DVD, etc.

tapestry /'tæpəstri/ ***noun*** [C,U] (*pl.* **tapestries**) a piece of heavy cloth with pictures or designs sewn on it in coloured thread

tapeworm /'teɪpwɜːm/ ***noun*** [C] a flat WORM (=a long creature with a soft body and no legs) that lives in the INTESTINES (=the tube that carries food out of the stomach) of humans and animals

tapioca /ˌtæpi'əʊkə/ ***noun*** [U] hard white grains obtained from a CASSAVA plant often cooked with milk to make a sweet dish

'tap water ***noun*** [U] water that comes through pipes and out of taps, not water sold in bottles

tar /tɑː(r)/ ***noun*** [U] **1** a thick black sticky liquid that becomes hard when it is cold. **Tar** is obtained from coal and is used for making roads, etc. ➲ look at **Tarmac 2** a similar substance formed by burning TOBACCO: *low-tar cigarettes*

tarantula /tə'ræntʃələ/ ***noun*** [C] a large hairy spider that lives in hot countries. Some **tarantulas** are poisonous.

THESAURUS

target

objective • goal • object • end

These are all words for sth that you are trying to achieve.

target: *attainment targets*

objective: *the main objective of the project*

goal: *He pursued his goal of becoming an actor.*

object: *The object is to educate people about health.*

end: *He joined the group for political ends.*

target¹ 🔑 AW /'tɑːɡɪt/ ***noun*** [C] **1** a result that you try to achieve: *Our target is to finish the job by Friday.* ◇ *So far we're right* ***on target*** (=making the progress we expected). ◇ *a target area/audience/group* (=the particular area, audience, etc. that a product, programme, etc. is aimed at) **2** a person, place or thing that you try to hit when shooting or attacking: *Doors and windows are* ***an easy target*** *for burglars.* **3** a person or thing that people criticize, laugh at, etc.: *The education system has been the target of heavy criticism.* **4** an object, often a round board with circles on it, that you try to hit in shooting practice: *to aim at/hit/miss a target*

target² AW /'tɑːɡɪt/ ***verb*** [T] (usually passive) ~ **sb/sth**; ~ **sth at/on sb/sth** to try to have an effect on a particular group of people; to try to attack sb/sth: *The product is targeted at teenagers.*

tariff /'tærɪf/ ***noun*** [C] **1** (ECONOMICS) a tax that has to be paid on goods coming into a country **2** a list of prices, especially in a hotel

Tarmac™ /'tɑːmæk/ ***noun*** **1** [U] a black material used for making the surfaces of roads ➲ look at **tar 2 the tarmac** [sing.] an area covered with a **Tarmac** surface, especially at an airport

tarn /tɑːn/ ***noun*** [C] (GEOGRAPHY) a small lake in the mountains

tarnish /'tɑːnɪʃ/ ***verb*** **1** [I,T] (used about metal, etc.) to become or to make sth less bright and shiny **2** [T] to spoil the good opinion people have of sb/sth

tarpaulin /tɑː'pɔːlɪn/ ***noun*** [C,U] strong material that water cannot pass through, which is used for covering things to protect them from the rain

tarragon /'tærəɡən/ ***noun*** [U] a plant with leaves that have a strong taste and are used in cooking to flavour food

tarsal /'tɑːsl/ ***noun*** [C] (ANATOMY) one of the small bones in the ankle and upper foot ➲ picture on **page 80**

tart¹ /tɑːt/ ***noun*** **1** [C,U] an open pie filled with sweet food such as fruit or jam **2** [C] (*BrE, informal*) a woman who dresses or behaves in a way that people think is immoral

tart² /tɑːt/ ***verb***

PHR V **tart sb/sth up** (*BrE, informal*) to decorate and improve the appearance of sb/sth

tartan /'tɑːtn/ ***noun*** [U, C] **1** a traditional Scottish pattern of coloured squares and lines that cross each other **2** material made from wool with this pattern on it

task 🔑 AW /tɑːsk/ ***noun*** [C] a piece of work that has to be done, especially an unpleasant or difficult one: *Your first task will be to type these letters.* ◇ *to perform/carry out/undertake a task* ▶ **task** /tɑːsk/ ***verb*** [T] (usually passive) ~ **sb (with sth)** (*formal*): *NATO troops were tasked with keeping the peace.*

tassel /'tæsl/ ***noun*** [C] a group of threads that are tied together at one end and hang from CUSHIONS, curtains, clothes, etc. as a decoration

taste¹ 🔑 /teɪst/ ***noun*** **1** [sing.] the particular quality of different foods or drinks that allows you to recognize them when you put them in your mouth; flavour: *I don't like the taste of this coffee.* ◇ *a sweet/bitter/sour/salty taste* **2** [U] the ability to recognize the flavour of food or drink: *I've got such a bad cold that I seem to have lost my sense of taste.* **3** [C, usually sing.] a ~ **(of sth)** a small amount of sth to eat or drink that you have in order to see what it is like: *Have a taste of this cheese to see if you like it.* **4** [sing.] a short experience of sth: *That was my* ***first taste*** *of success.* **5** [U] the ability to decide if things are suitable, of good quality, etc.: *He has excellent* ***taste in*** *music.* **6** [sing.] a ~ **(for sth)** what a person likes or prefers: *She has developed a taste for modern art.*

IDM **(be) in bad, poor, etc. taste** (used about sb's behaviour) (to be) unpleasant and not suitable: *Some of his comments were in very bad taste.*

taste² 🔑 /teɪst/ ***verb*** **1** ***linking verb*** ~ **(of sth)** to have a particular flavour: *The pudding tasted of oranges.* ◇ *to taste sour/sweet/delicious* **2** [T] to notice or recognize the flavour of food or drink: *Can you taste the garlic in this soup?* **3** [T] to try a small amount of food and drink; to test the flavour of sth: *Can I taste a piece of that cheese to see what it's like?*

'taste bud ***noun*** [C, usually pl.] (ANATOMY) one of the small cells on your tongue that allow you to recognize the flavours of food and drink

tasteful /ˈteɪstfl/ ***adj.*** (used especially about clothes, furniture, decorations, etc.) attractive and well chosen: *tasteful furniture* OPP **tasteless** ▸ **tastefully** /-fəli/ ***adv.***

tasteless /ˈteɪstləs/ ***adj.*** **1** having little or no flavour: *This sauce is rather tasteless.* OPP **tasty** **2** likely to offend people: *His joke about the funeral was particularly tasteless.* **3** (used especially about clothes, furniture, decorations, etc.) not attractive; not well chosen OPP **tasteful**

tasty /ˈteɪsti/ ***adj.*** (**tastier**; **tastiest**) having a good flavour: *spaghetti with a tasty mushroom sauce*

tattered /ˈtætəd/ ***adj.*** old and torn; in bad condition: *a tattered coat*

tatters /ˈtætəz/ ***noun***
IDM **in tatters** badly torn or damaged; ruined: *Her dress was in tatters.*

tattoo /təˈtuː/ ***noun*** [C] (*pl.* **tattoos**) a picture or pattern that is marked permanently on sb's skin ▸ **tattoo *verb*** [T] (**tattooing**; **tattooed**): *She had his name tattooed on her left hand.*

tatty /ˈtæti/ ***adj.*** (*comparative* **tattier**; *superlative* **tattiest**) (*informal*) in bad condition: *tatty old clothes*

taught past tense, past participle of **teach**

taunt /tɔːnt/ ***verb*** [T] to try to make sb angry or upset by saying unpleasant or cruel things ▸ **taunt *noun*** [C]

Taurus /ˈtɔːrəs/ ***noun*** [U] (ASTRONOMY) the second sign of the ZODIAC, the Bull

taut /tɔːt/ ***adj.*** (used about rope, wire, etc.) stretched very tight; not loose

tautology /tɔːˈtɒlədʒi/ ***noun*** [U, C] (LANGUAGE) a statement in which you say the same thing twice in different words, when this is unnecessary, for example 'They spoke in turn, one after the other.' ▸ **tautological** /ˌtɔːtəˈlɒdʒɪkl/ ***adj.***

tavern /ˈtævən/ ***noun*** [C] (*old-fashioned*) a pub

tax 🔑 /tæks/ ***noun*** [C,U] (a) ~ (**on sth**) (ECONOMICS) the money that you have to pay to the government so that it can provide public services: *income tax* ◇ *There used to be a tax on windows.* ▸ **tax *verb*** [T] (often passive): *Alcohol, cigarettes and petrol are heavily taxed.*

taxable /ˈtæksəbl/ ***adj.*** on which you have to pay tax: *taxable income*

taxation /tækˈseɪʃn/ ***noun*** [U] **1** (ECONOMICS, POLITICS) the system by which a government takes money from people so that it can pay for public services: *direct/indirect taxation* **2** (ECONOMICS) the amount of money that people have to pay in tax: *to increase/reduce taxation* ◇ *high/low taxation*

ˌtax-ˈfree ***adj.*** on which you do not have to pay tax

ˈtax haven ***noun*** [C] (FINANCE) a place where taxes are low and where people choose to live or officially register their companies because taxes are higher in their own countries

taxi[1] 🔑 /ˈtæksi/ (*also* ˈ**taxicab**; *especially AmE* **cab**) ***noun*** [C] a car with a driver whose job is to take you somewhere in exchange for money: *Shall we go by bus or* ***get /take a taxi****?*

taxi[2] /ˈtæksi/ ***verb*** [I] (used about an aircraft) to move slowly along the ground before or after flying

taxing /ˈtæksɪŋ/ ***adj.*** difficult; needing a lot of effort: *a taxing exam* ➲ note at **difficult**

ˈtaxi rank ***noun*** [C] a place where taxis park while they are waiting for passengers

taxonomist /tækˈsɒnəmɪst/ ***noun*** [C] (SCIENCE) a scientist who arranges things into groups

taxonomy /tækˈsɒnəmi/ ***noun*** **1** [U] (SCIENCE) the scientific process of arranging things into groups ➲ picture on **page 29** **2** [C] (*pl.* **taxonomies**) one particular system of groups that things have been arranged in

taxpayer /ˈtækspeɪə(r)/ ***noun*** [C] (ECONOMICS) a person who pays tax to the government, especially on the money that they earn

TB /ˌtiː ˈbiː/ ***abbr.*** (HEALTH) = TUBERCULOSIS

tbsp ***abbr.*** tablespoonful(s): *Add 3 tbsp sugar.*

TCP/IP /ˌtiː siː ˌpiː aɪ ˈpiː/ ***abbr.*** (COMPUTING) **transmission control protocol/Internet protocol**; a system that controls the connection of computers to the Internet

tea 🔑 /tiː/ ***noun*** **1** [U, C] a hot drink made by pouring boiling water onto the dried leaves of the tea plant or of some other plants; a cup of this drink: *a cup/pot of tea* ◇ *weak/strong tea* ◇ *herb/mint/camomile tea* ◇ *Two teas and one coffee, please.* **2** [U] the dried leaves that are used for making tea: *a packet of tea* **3** [C,U] (*especially BrE*) a small afternoon meal of SANDWICHES, cakes, etc. and tea to drink, or a cooked meal eaten at 5 or 6 o'clock: *The kids have their tea as soon as they get home from school.*
IDM **(not) sb's cup of tea** → CUP[1]

ˈtea bag ***noun*** [C] a small paper bag with tea leaves in it, that you use for making tea

teach 🔑 /tiːtʃ/ ***verb*** (*pt, pp* **taught** /tɔːt/) **1** [I,T] ~ **sb (sth/to do sth)**; ~ **sth (to sb)** (EDUCATION) to give sb lessons or instructions so that they know how to do sth: *My mother taught me to play the piano.* ◇ *Jeremy is teaching us how to use the computer.* ◇ *He teaches English to foreign students.* ◇ *I teach in a primary school.* **2** [T] to make sb believe sth or behave in a certain way: *The story teaches us that history often repeats itself.* ◇ *My parents taught me always to tell the truth.* **3** [T] to make sb have a bad experience so that they are careful not to do the thing that caused it again: *All the seats are taken. That'll teach you to turn up half an hour late.*
IDM **teach sb a lesson** to make sb have a bad experience so that they will not do the thing that caused it again

teacher 🔑 /ˈtiːtʃə(r)/ ***noun*** [C] (EDUCATION) a person whose job is to teach, especially in a school or college: *He's a teacher at a primary school.* ◇ *a maths/chemistry/music teacher* ➲ look at **head**[1] (6)

teaching 🔑 /ˈtiːtʃɪŋ/ ***noun*** **1** [U] (EDUCATION) the work of a teacher: *My son went into teaching and my daughter became a doctor.* ◇ *teaching methods* **2** [C, usually pl.] ideas and beliefs that are taught by sb/sth: *the teachings of Gandhi*

ˈtea cloth (*BrE*) = TEA TOWEL

teacup /ˈtiːkʌp/ ***noun*** [C] a cup that you drink tea from

teak /tiːk/ ***noun*** [U] the strong hard wood of a tall Asian tree, used especially for making furniture

ˈtea leaves ***noun*** [pl.] the small leaves that are left in a cup after you have drunk the tea

team[1] 🔑 AW /tiːm/ ***noun*** [C] **1** (SPORT) a group of people who play a sport or game together against another group: *a football team* ◇ *Are you* ***in /on the team****?* **2** a group of people who work together: *a team of doctors*

team[2] AW /tiːm/ ***verb***
PHRV **team up (with sb)** to join sb in order to do sth together: *I teamed up with Elena to plan the project.*

teamwork /ˈtiːmwɜːk/ ***noun*** [U] the ability of people to work together: *Teamwork is a key feature of the training programme.*

teapot /ˈtiːpɒt/ ***noun*** [C] a container that you use for making tea in and for serving it

tear[1] **0** /tɪə(r)/ ***noun*** [C, usually pl.] a drop of water that comes from your eye when you are crying, etc.: *I was* ***in tears*** (=crying) *at the end of the film.* ◇ *The little girl* ***burst into tears*** (=suddenly started to cry).

IDM **shed tears** → SHED[2]

tear[2] **0** /teə(r)/ ***verb*** (*pt* **tore** /tɔː(r)/; *pp* **torn** /tɔːn/) **1** [I,T] to damage sth by pulling it apart or into pieces; to become damaged in this way: *I tore my shirt on that nail.* ◇ *She tore the letter in half.* ◇ *I tore a page out of my notebook.* ◇ *This material doesn't tear easily.* **2** [T] to remove sth by pulling violently and quickly: *Paul tore the poster down from the wall.* ◇ *He tore the bag out of her hands.* **3** [T] to make a hole in sth by force **4** [I] ~ **along, up, down, past, etc.** to move very quickly in a particular direction: *An ambulance went tearing past.* ▶ **tear** ***noun*** [C]: *You've got a tear in the back of your trousers.*

IDM **wear and tear** → WEAR[2]

PHR V **tear sth apart 1** to pull sth violently into pieces **2** to destroy sth completely: *The country has been torn apart by the war.*

tear yourself away (from sb/sth) to make yourself leave sb/sth or stop doing sth

be torn between A and B to find it difficult to choose between two things or people

tear sth down (used about a building) to destroy it: *They tore down the old houses and built a shopping centre.*

tear sth up to pull sth into pieces, especially sth made of paper: *'I hate this photograph,' she said, tearing it up.*

tearful /ˈtɪəfl/ ***adj.*** crying or nearly crying

tear gas /ˈtɪə gæs/ ***noun*** [U] a type of gas that hurts the eyes and throat, and is used by the police, etc. to control large groups of people

tease /tiːz/ ***verb*** [I,T] to laugh at sb either in a friendly way or in order to upset them: *Don't pay any attention to those boys. They're only teasing.* ◇ *They teased her about being fat.*

teaspoon /ˈtiːspuːn/ ***noun*** [C] **1** a small spoon used for putting sugar in tea, coffee, etc. **2** (*also* **teaspoonful** /-fʊl/) the amount that a teaspoon can hold

teat /tiːt/ ***noun*** [C] **1** the rubber part at the end of a baby's bottle that the baby sucks in order to get milk, etc. from the bottle **2** one of the parts of a female animal's body that the babies drink milk from

ˈ**tea towel** (*also* **tea cloth**) ***noun*** [C] a small towel that is used for drying plates, knives, forks, etc.

tech /tek/ ***noun*** [C] (*BrE, informal*) =TECHNICAL COLLEGE

technetium /tekˈniːʃɪəm/ ***noun*** [U] (*symbol* **Tc**) (CHEMISTRY) a chemical element. **Technetium** is found naturally as a product of URANIUM or made artificially from MOLYBDENUM. ❶ For more information on the periodic table of elements, look at pages R34-5.

technical **0** AW /ˈteknɪkl/ ***adj.*** **1** connected with the practical use of machines, methods, etc. in science and industry: *The train was delayed owing to a technical problem.* **2** connected with the skills involved in a particular activity or subject: *This computer magazine is too technical for me.*

ˈ**technical college** (*BrE also, informal* **tech**) ***noun*** [C] (EDUCATION) a college where students can study mainly practical subjects

technicality /ˌteknɪˈkæləti/ ***noun*** [C] (*pl.* **technicalities**) one of the details of a particular subject or activity

technically AW /ˈteknɪkli/ ***adv.*** **1** according to the exact meaning, facts, etc.: *Technically, you should pay by May 1st, but it doesn't matter if it's a few days late.* **2** in a way that involves detailed knowledge of the machines, etc. that are used in industry or science: *The country is technically not very advanced.* **3** used about sb's practical ability in a particular activity: *He's a technically brilliant dancer.*

technician /tekˈnɪʃn/ ***noun*** [C] a person whose work involves practical skills, especially in industry or science: *a laboratory technician*

technique **0** AW /tekˈniːk/ ***noun*** **1** [C] a particular way of doing sth: *new techniques for teaching languages* ◇ *marketing/management techniques* **2** [U] the practical skill that sb has in a particular activity: *He's a naturally talented runner, but he needs to work on his technique.*

techno /ˈteknəʊ/ ***noun*** [U] (MUSIC) a style of modern popular music with a regular rhythm for dancing, that makes use of technology to produce the sound

techno- /ˈteknəʊ/ ***prefix*** (used in nouns, adjectives and adverbs) connected with technology: *technophobe* (=a person who is afraid of technology)

technocrat /ˈteknəkræt/ ***noun*** [C] (POLITICS) an expert in science, engineering, etc. who has a lot of power in politics and/or industry

technology **0** AW /tekˈnɒlədʒi/ ***noun*** [C,U] (*pl.* **technologies**) the scientific knowledge and/or equipment that is needed for a particular industry, etc.: *developments in computer technology* ▶ **technological** AW /ˌteknəˈlɒdʒɪkl/ ***adj.***: *technological developments* ▶ **technologist** /tekˈnɒlədʒɪst/ ***noun*** [C]: *Technologists are developing a computer that can perform surgery.*

technophile /ˈteknəʊfaɪl/ ***noun*** [C] a person who is enthusiastic about new technology

technophobe /ˈteknəʊfəʊb/ ***noun*** [C] a person who is afraid of, dislikes or avoids new technology

tectonic /tekˈtɒnɪk/ ***adj.*** (GEOLOGY) connected with the structure of the earth's surface ➲ look at **plate tectonics**

teddy /ˈtedi/ (*also* ˈ**teddy bear**) ***noun*** [C] (*pl.* **teddies**) a toy for children that looks like a bear

tedious /ˈtiːdiəs/ ***adj.*** boring and lasting for a long time: *a tedious train journey*

tee /tiː/ ***noun*** [C] (SPORT) **1** a flat area on a GOLF COURSE from which players hit the ball **2** a small piece of plastic or wood that you stick in the ground to support a GOLF ball before you hit it

teem /tiːm/ ***verb*** [I] ~ **with sth** (used about a place) to have a lot of people or things moving about in it: *The streets were teeming with people.*

teenage /ˈtiːneɪdʒ/ ***adj.*** (only *before* a noun) **1** between 13 and 19 years old: *teenage children* **2** typical of or suitable for people between 13 and 19 years old: *teenage magazines/fashion*

teenager /ˈtiːneɪdʒə(r)/ ***noun*** [C] a person aged between 13 and 19 years old: *Her music is very popular with teenagers.* ➲ look at **adolescent**

teens /tiːnz/ ***noun*** [pl.] the period of a person's life between the ages of 13 and 19: *to be **in your** early/ late **teens***

ˈ**tee shirt** = T-SHIRT

teeth plural of **tooth**

teethe /tiːð/ ***verb*** [I] (usually **be teething**) (used about a baby) to start growing its first teeth

ˈ**teething problems** (*also* ˈ**teething troubles**) ***noun*** [pl.] the problems that can develop when a person, system, etc. is new: *We've just installed this new software and are having a few teething problems with it.*

teetotal /ˌtiːˈtəʊtl/ ***adj.*** (not before a noun) (used about a person) never drinking alcohol ▸ **teetotaller** (*AmE* **teetotaler**) /-tlə(r)/ ***noun*** [C]

TEFL /ˈtefl/ ***abbr.*** (EDUCATION) Teaching English as a Foreign Language

tel. ***abbr.*** telephone (number): *tel. 01865 56767*

tele- /ˈteli/ ***prefix*** (used in nouns, verbs, adjectives and adverbs) **1** over a long distance; far: *telepathy* ◇ *telescopic* **2** connected with television: *teletext* **3** done using a telephone: *telesales*

telebanking /ˈtelibæŋkɪŋ/ ***noun*** [U] = TELEPHONE BANKING

telecommunications /ˌtelikəˌmjuːnɪˈkeɪʃnz/ ***noun*** [pl.] the technology of sending signals, images and messages over long distances by radio, telephone, television, etc.

telecommute /ˌtelikəˈmjuːt/ ***verb*** [I] (BUSINESS) to work from home, communicating with your office, customers and others by telephone, email, etc. ▸ **telecommuter** ***noun*** [C] SYN **teleworker** ▸ **telecommuting** ***noun*** [U] SYN **teleworking**

teleconference /ˈtelikɒnfərəns/ ***noun*** [C] (BUSINESS) a conference or discussion at which members are in different places and speak to each other using telephone and video connections ▸ **teleconference** *verb* [I]

telegraph /ˈtelɪɡrɑːf/ ***noun*** [U] a method of sending messages over long distances, using wires that carry electrical signals

ˈ**telegraph pole** ***noun*** [C] a tall wooden pole that is used for supporting telephone wires

telemarketing /ˈtelimɑːkɪtɪŋ/ = TELESALES

telepathy /təˈlepəθi/ ***noun*** [U] the communication of thoughts between people's minds without using speech, writing or other normal methods

telephone 🔑 /ˈtelɪfəʊn/ (also *informal* **phone**) ***noun*** **1** [U] an electrical system for talking to sb in another place by speaking into a special piece of equipment: *Can I contact you **by telephone**?* ◇ *to **make a telephone call*** ◇ *What's your **telephone number**?* **2** [C] the piece of equipment that you use when you talk to sb by telephone: *Could I use your telephone?* ◇ ***a mobile phone*** (= one that you can carry around) ◇ *a public telephone*

▸ **telephone** (*also* **phone**) ***verb*** [I,T]: *Sarah phoned. She's going to be late.* ◇ *I'll phone you later.*

IDM **on the phone/telephone** → PHONE

ˌ**telephone** ˈ**banking** (*also* ˈ**telebanking**) ***noun*** [U] (FINANCE) activities relating to your bank account, which you do using the telephone

ˈ**telephone box** (*also* ˈ**phone box**; ˈ**call box**) ***noun*** [C] a small covered place in a street, etc. that contains a telephone for public use

> **RELATED VOCABULARY**
>
> **Telephones**
>
> When you make a telephone call, you first **dial** the number. The telephone **rings** and the person at the other end **answers** it. If they are already using the telephone, it is **engaged**.
>
> When you finish speaking, you **hang up** or **put the phone down**.
>
> Calling from a **mobile phone/cellphone** can be more convenient than from a **landline** (= a normal telephone) because **mobiles/cells** can be used anywhere where there is a signal.
>
> The number that you dial before the telephone number if you are telephoning a different area or country is called the **code**: *'What's the code for Spain?'*

ˈ**telephone directory** (also *informal* ˈ**phone book**) ***noun*** [C] a book that gives a list of the names, addresses and telephone numbers of the people in a particular area

ˈ**telephone exchange** (*also* **exchange**) ***noun*** [C] a place where telephone calls are connected so that people can speak to each other

teleprompter /ˈteliprɒmptə(r)/ ***noun*** [C] (*especially AmE*) = AUTOCUE™

telesales /ˈteliseɪlz/ (*also* **telemarketing**) ***noun*** [U] (BUSINESS) a method of selling things by telephone: *He works in telesales.*

telescope /ˈtelɪskəʊp/ ***noun*** [C] (ASTRONOMY, PHYSICS) an instrument in the shape of a tube with special pieces of glass (**lenses**) inside it. You look through it to make things that are far away appear bigger and nearer. ➲ picture at **binoculars**

teletext /ˈtelitekst/ ***noun*** [U] (ARTS AND MEDIA) a service that provides news and other information in written form on television

televise /ˈtelɪvaɪz/ ***verb*** [T] (ARTS AND MEDIA) to show sth on television: *a televised concert*

television 🔑 /ˈtelɪvɪʒn/ (*also* **TV**; *BrE, informal* **telly**) ***noun*** **1** (*also* ˈ**television set**) [C] a piece of electrical equipment in the shape of a box. It has a glass screen which shows programmes with moving pictures and sounds: *to turn the television on/off* **2** [U] the programmes that are shown on a television set: *Paul's watching television.* **3** [U] the electrical system and business of sending out programmes so that people can watch them on their television sets: *a television presenter/series/ documentary* ◇ *cable/satellite/terrestrial/digital television* ◇ *She works in television.*

IDM **on television** being shown by television; appearing in a television programme: *What's on television tonight?*

teleworking /ˈteliwɜːkɪŋ/ ***noun*** [U] (*BrE*) (BUSINESS) the practice of working from home, communicating with your office, customers and others by telephone, email, etc. SYN **telecommuting** ▸ **teleworker** ***noun*** [C] SYN **telecommuter**

tell 🔑 /tel/ ***verb*** (*pt, pp* **told** /təʊld/) **1** [T] ~ **sb (sth/that...)**; ~ **sb (about sth)**; ~ **sth to sb** to give information to sb by speaking or writing: *She told me her address but I've forgotten it.* ◇ *He wrote to tell me that his mother had died.* ◇ *Tell us about your holiday.* ◇ *to **tell the truth /a lie*** ◇ *to **tell a story*** ◇ *Excuse me, could you tell me where the station is?* ◇ *He tells that story to everyone he sees.* **2** [T] ~ **sb to do sth** to order or advise sb to do sth: *The policewoman told us to get out of the car.* **3** [I,T] to know, see or judge (sth) correctly: *'What do you think Jenny will do next?' '**It's hard to tell.**'* ◇ *I could tell that he had enjoyed the evening.* ◇ ***You can never tell** what he's going to say next.* ◇ *I can't **tell the difference between** Dan's sisters.* **4** [T] (used about a thing) to give information to sb: *This book will tell you all you need to know.* **5** [I] to not keep a secret: *Promise you won't tell!* **6** [I] ~ **(on sb/sth)** to have a noticeable effect: *I can't run as fast as I could – my age is beginning to tell!*

IDM **all told** with everyone or everything counted and included

(I'll) tell you what (*informal*) used to introduce a suggestion: *I'll tell you what – let's ask Diane to take us.*

I told you (so) (*informal*) I warned you that this would happen

tell A and B apart → APART

tell the time to read the time from a clock or watch

PHR V **tell sb off (for sth/for doing sth)** to speak to sb angrily because they have done sth wrong: *The teacher told me off for not doing my homework.*

tell on sb to tell a parent, teacher, etc. about sth bad that sb has done

telling /'telɪŋ/ ***adj.*** **1** showing, without intending to, what sb/sth is really like: *The number of homeless people is a telling comment on today's society.* **2** having a great effect: *That's quite a telling argument.*

telltale /'telteɪl/ ***adj.*** giving information about sth secret or private: *He said he was fine, but there were telltale signs of worry on his face.*

tellurium /te'ljʊəriəm/ ***noun*** [U] (*symbol* **Te**) (CHEMISTRY) a chemical element. **Tellurium** is a shiny silver-white substance that breaks easily, found in SULPHIDE ORES. ❶ For more information on the periodic table of elements, look at pages R34-5.

telly /'teli/ (*pl.* **tellies**) (*BrE, informal*) = TELEVISION

telnet /'telnet/ ***noun*** [U] (COMPUTING) a computer system which allows you to use data and programs on another computer; a connection made using this system ▶ **telnet** ***verb*** (**telnetting**; **telnetted**) [T]

temp[1] /temp/ ***noun*** [C] (*informal*) a temporary employee, especially in an office, who works somewhere for a short period of time when sb else is ill or on holiday ▶ **temp** ***verb*** [I]

temp[2] ***abbr.*** temperature: *temp 15 °C*

temper /'tempə(r)/ ***noun*** **1** [C,U] If you have a **temper** you get angry very easily: *Be careful of Paul. He's got quite a temper!* ◇ *You must learn to control your temper.* **2** [C] the way you are feeling at a particular time: *It's no use talking to him when he's **in a bad temper**.* SYN **mood**

IDM **in a temper** feeling very angry and not controlling your behaviour

keep/lose your temper to stay calm/to become angry ➲ look at **bad-tempered**

temperament /'temprəmənt/ ***noun*** [C,U] a person's character, especially as it affects the way they behave and feel: *to have an artistic/a fiery/a calm temperament*

temperamental /ˌtemprə'mentl/ ***adj.*** often and suddenly changing the way you behave or feel

temperate /'tempərət/ ***adj.*** (used about a climate) not very hot and not very cold

temperature 🔑 /'temprətʃə(r)/ ***noun*** **1** [C,U] how hot or cold sth is: *Heat the oven to a temperature of 200°C.* ◇ *a high/low temperature* ◇ *an increase in temperature* **2** [C] how hot or cold a person's body is

IDM **have a temperature** (HEALTH) (used about a person) to be hotter than normal because you are ill

take sb's temperature (HEALTH) to measure the temperature of sb's body with a special instrument (**a thermometer**)

template /'templeɪt/ ***noun*** [C] **1** a shape cut out of a hard material, used as a model for producing exactly the same shape many times in another material **2** a thing that is used as a model for producing other similar examples: *If you need to write a lot of similar letters, set up a template on your computer.*

temple /'templ/ ***noun*** [C] **1** (RELIGION) a building where people pray to a god or gods: *a Buddhist/Hindu temple* **2** (ANATOMY) one of the flat parts on each side of your FOREHEAD ➲ picture on **page 80**

tempo /'tempəʊ/ ***noun*** (*pl.* **tempos** /'tempəʊz/) **1** [sing., U] the speed of an activity or event **2** [C,U] (MUSIC) the speed of a piece of music: *a fast/slow tempo*

temporary 🔑 AW /'temprəri/ ***adj.*** lasting for a short time; not permanent: *a temporary job* ◇ *This arrangement is only temporary.* ▶ **temporarily** /'temprərəli/ ***adv.***

tempt /tempt/ ***verb*** [T] ~ **sb (into sth/into doing sth)**; ~ **sb (to do sth)** to try to persuade or attract sb to do sth, even if it is wrong: *His dream of riches had tempted him into a life of crime.* ◇ *She was tempted to stay in bed all morning.*

temptation /temp'teɪʃn/ ***noun*** **1** [U] a feeling that you want to do sth, even if you know that it is wrong: *I managed to **resist the temptation** to tell him what I really thought.* ◇ *She wanted a cigarette badly, but didn't **give in to temptation**.* **2** [C] a thing that attracts you to do sth wrong or silly: *All that money is certainly a big temptation.*

tempting /'temptɪŋ/ ***adj.*** attractive in a way that makes you want to do or have sth: *a tempting offer*

ten /ten/ ***number*** 10

tenacious /tə'neɪʃəs/ ***adj.*** not likely to give up or let sth go; determined ▶ **tenacity** /tə'næsəti/ ***noun*** [U]

tenancy /'tenənsi/ ***noun*** [C,U] (*pl.* **tenancies**) the use of a room, flat, building or piece of land, for which you pay rent to the owner: *a six-month tenancy* ◇ *It says in the tenancy agreement that you can't keep pets.*

tenant /'tenənt/ ***noun*** [C] a person who pays money (**rent**) to the owner of a room, flat, building or piece of land so that they can live in it or use it: *They had evicted their tenants for non-payment of rent.* ◇ *tenant farmers* (= ones who do not own their own farms) ➲ look at **landlady, landlord**

tend 🔑 /tend/ ***verb*** **1** [I] ~ **to do sth** to usually do or be sth: *Women tend to live longer than men.* ◇ *There tends to be a lot of heavy traffic on that road.* ◇ *My brother tends to talk a lot when he's nervous.* **2** [I] used for giving your opinion in a polite way: *I **tend to think** that we shouldn't interfere.* **3** [I,T] (*formal*) ~ **(to) sb/sth** to look after sb/sth: *Paramedics tended (to) the injured.*

tendency 🔑 /'tendənsi/ ***noun*** [C] (*pl.* **tendencies**) a ~ **(to do sth/towards sth)** something that a person or thing usually does; a way of behaving: *They both **have a tendency** to be late for appointments.* ◇ *The dog began to show vicious tendencies.* ◇ *She seems to have a tendency towards depression.*

tender[1] /'tendə(r)/ ***adj.*** **1** kind and loving: *tender words/looks/kisses* **2** (used about food) soft and easy to cut or bite; not tough: *The meat should be nice and* *tender.* **3** (used about a part of the body) painful when you touch it ▶ **tenderly** *adv.* ▶ **tenderness** *noun* [U]

IDM **at a tender age; at the tender age of...** when still young and without much experience: *She went to live in London at the tender age of 15.*

tender² /'tendə(r)/ ***noun*** [C] a formal offer to supply goods or do work at a stated price: *Several firms submitted a tender for the catering contract.*

tender³ /'tendə(r)/ ***verb*** **1** [I] ~ **(for sth)** to make a formal offer to supply goods or do work at a stated price: *Local firms were invited to tender for the building contract.* **2** [T] ~ **sth (to sb)** (*formal*) to offer or give sth to sb: *He has **tendered his resignation** to the Prime Minister.*

tendon /'tendən/ ***noun*** [C] (ANATOMY) a strong, thin part inside your body that joins a muscle to a bone ➲ picture at **arm**

tendril /'tendrəl/ ***noun*** [C] (BIOLOGY) a long thin part that grows from a climbing plant. A plant uses **tendrils** to fasten itself to a wall, etc.

tenement /'tenəmənt/ ***noun*** [C] a large building that is divided into small flats, especially in a poor area of a city

tenner /'tenə(r)/ ***noun*** [C] (*BrE, informal*) a ten-pound note; £10

tennis /'tenɪs/ ***noun*** [U] (SPORT) a game for two or four players who hit a ball over a net using a piece of equipment (**a racket**) that is held in one hand: *Let's play tennis.* ◇ *to have a game of tennis* ◇ *a tennis match* ❶ In tennis you can play **singles** (a game between two people) or **doubles** (a game between two teams of two people).

tenor /'tenə(r)/ ***noun*** [C] (MUSIC) a fairly high singing voice for a man; a man with this voice: *Pavarotti is a famous Italian tenor.* ❶ Tenor is between **alto** and **baritone**. ▶ **tenor** *adj.* (only *before* a noun): *a tenor saxophone/trombone*

tenpin bowling /,tenpɪn 'bəʊlɪŋ/ ***noun*** [U] a game in which you roll a heavy ball towards ten objects (**tenpins**) and try to knock them down

tense¹ AW /tens/ ***adj.*** **1** (used about a person) not able to relax because you are worried or nervous: *She looked pale and tense.* **2** (used about a muscle or a part of the body) tight; not relaxed **3** (used about an atmosphere or a situation) in which people feel worried and not relaxed

tense² AW /tens/ ***verb*** [I,T] ~ **(up)** to have muscles that have become hard and not relaxed

tense³ AW /tens/ ***noun*** [C,U] (LANGUAGE) a form of a verb that shows if sth happens in the past, present or future

tension 🔑 AW /'tenʃn/ ***noun*** **1** [U] the condition of not being able to relax because you are worried or nervous: *I could hear the tension in her voice as she spoke.* **2** [C,U] bad feeling and lack of trust between people, countries, etc.: *There are signs of growing tensions between the two countries.* **3** [U] (used about a rope, muscle, etc.) the state of being stretched tight; how tightly sth is stretched: *The massage relieved the tension in my neck.*

tent 🔑 /tent/ ***noun*** [C] a small structure made of cloth that is held up by poles and ropes. You use a tent to sleep in when you go camping: *to put up/take down a tent*

tentacle /'tentəkl/ ***noun*** [C] one of the long thin soft parts like legs that some sea animals have: *An octopus has eight tentacles.* ➲ picture at **jellyfish**

tentative /'tentətɪv/ ***adj.*** **1** (used about plans, etc.) uncertain; not definite **2** not behaving or done with confidence: *a tentative smile/suggestion* ▶ **tentatively** *adv.*

tenterhooks /'tentəhʊks/ ***noun*** [pl.]

IDM **(be) on tenterhooks** (to be) in a very nervous or excited state because you are waiting to find out what is going to happen

tenth¹ /tenθ/ ***ordinal number*** 10th ➲ note at **sixth¹**

tenth² /tenθ/ ***noun*** [C] the FRACTION 1/10; one of ten equal parts of sth

tenuous /'tenjuəs/ ***adj.*** very weak or uncertain: *The connection between Joe's story and what actually happened was tenuous.*

tenure /'tenjə(r)/ ***noun*** [U] a legal right to live in a place, hold a job, use land, etc. for a certain time

tepid /'tepɪd/ ***adj.*** (used about liquids) only slightly warm

terbium /'tɜːbiəm/ ***noun*** [U] (*symbol* **Tb**) (CHEMISTRY) a chemical element. **Terbium** is a silver-white metal used in LASERS, X-RAYS and television TUBES. ❶ For more information on the periodic table of elements, look at pages R34-5.

term¹ 🔑 /tɜːm/ ***noun*** **1** [C] (LANGUAGE) a word or group of words with a particular meaning: *What exactly do you mean by the term 'racist'?* ◇ *a technical term in computing* **2** (*AmE also* **trimester**) [C] (EDUCATION) (especially in Britain) one of the three periods in the year during which classes are held in schools, universities, etc.: *the autumn/spring/summer term* ◇ *an end-of-term test* ➲ look at **semester** **3 terms** [pl.] **in terms of...; in...terms** used for showing which particular way you are thinking about sth or from which point of view: *The flat would be ideal in terms of size, but it is very expensive.* **4** [C] a period of time for which sth lasts: *The US President is now in his second term of office.* **5 terms** [pl.] the conditions of an agreement: ***Under the terms of** the contract you must give a week's notice.* ◇ *Both sides agreed to the peace terms.* **6** [C] (MATHEMATICS) each of the various parts in a series, an EQUATION etc.

IDM **be on equal terms (with sb)** → EQUAL¹

be on good, friendly, etc. terms (with sb) to have a friendly relationship with sb

come to terms with sth to accept sth unpleasant or difficult

in the long/short term over a long/short period of time in the future

term² /tɜːm/ ***verb*** [T] to describe sb/sth by using a particular word or expression: *the period of history that is often termed the 'Dark Ages'* ➲ note at **language**

terminal¹ AW /'tɜːmɪnl/ ***adj.*** (HEALTH) (used about an illness) slowly causing death: *terminal cancer* ▶ **terminally** /-nəli/ ***adv.***: *a terminally ill patient*

terminal² AW /'tɜːmɪnl/ ***noun*** [C] **1** a large railway station, bus station or building at an airport where journeys begin and end: *the bus terminal* ◇ *Which terminal are you flying from?* **2** (COMPUTING) the computer that one person uses for getting information from a central computer or for putting information into it

terminate AW /'tɜːmɪneɪt/ ***verb*** [I,T] (*formal*) to end or to make sth end: *to terminate a contract/an agreement* ▶ **termination** AW ***noun*** [U, C]

terminology /,tɜːmɪ'nɒlədʒi/ ***noun*** [U] the special words and expressions that are used in a particular profession, subject or activity ➲ note at **language**

terminus /ˈtɜːmɪnəs/ ***noun*** [C] (*pl.* **terminuses** /-nəsɪz/) the last stop or station at the end of a bus route or railway line

termite /ˈtɜːmaɪt/ ***noun*** [C] a small insect that lives in large groups, mainly in hot countries. **Termites** eat the wood of trees and buildings.

ternary form /ˈtɜːnəri fɔːm/ ***noun*** [U] (MUSIC) the structure of a piece of music in three sections, in which the third section is the same as the first

terrace /ˈterəs/ ***noun*** **1** (*BrE*) [C] (ARCHITECTURE) a line of similar houses that are all joined together in one block: *12 Albert Terrace* **2** [C] a flat area of stone next to a restaurant or large house where people can have meals, sit in the sun, etc.: *a sun terrace* ◇ *All rooms have a balcony or terrace.* ➲ look at **patio** **3** [C, usually pl.] (AGRICULTURE) one of a series of flat areas of ground that are cut into the side of a hill like steps so that crops can be grown there ➲ picture at **flood plain** **4 terraces** [pl.] (*BrE*) (SPORT) the wide steps that people stand on to watch a football match

terraced /ˈterəst/ ***adj.*** **1** (*BrE*) (used about a house) forming part of a line of similar houses that are all joined together **2** (AGRICULTURE) (used about a hill) having steps cut out of it so that crops can be grown there

terracotta /ˌterəˈkɒtə/ ***noun*** [U] reddish-brown CLAY that has been baked but not GLAZED (=covered in a shiny transparent substance), and is used for making pots, etc.

terrain /təˈreɪn/ ***noun*** [U] (GEOGRAPHY) land of the type mentioned: *mountainous/steep/rocky terrain*

terrestrial /təˈrestriəl/ ***adj.*** **1** (BIOLOGY) (used about animals and plants) living on the land or on the ground, rather than in water, in trees or in the air **2** (ASTRONOMY) connected with the planet Earth: *terrestrial life* ➲ look at **celestial, extraterrestrial** **3** (ARTS AND MEDIA) (used about television and broadcasting systems) operating on earth rather than from a SATELLITE (=an electronic device that is sent into space)

terrible 🔑 /ˈterəbl/ ***adj.*** **1** very unpleasant; causing great shock or injury: *a terrible accident* ◇ *terrible news* ◇ *What a terrible thing to do!* **2** ill or very upset: *I **feel terrible**. I think I'm going to be sick.* ◇ *He felt terrible when he realized what he had done.* **3** very bad; of poor quality: *a terrible hotel/book/memory/driver* **4** (only *before* a noun) used to emphasize how bad sth is: *in terrible pain/trouble* ◇ *The room was in a terrible mess.*

terribly 🔑 /ˈterəbli/ ***adv.*** **1** very: *I'm terribly sorry.* **2** very badly: *I played terribly.* ◇ *The experiment went terribly wrong.*

terrier /ˈteriə(r)/ ***noun*** [C] a type of small dog

terrific /təˈrɪfɪk/ ***adj.*** **1** (*informal*) extremely nice or good; excellent: *You're doing a terrific job!* **2** (only *before* a noun) very great: *I've got a terrific amount of work to do.* ▶ **terrifically** /-kli/ ***adv.***: *terrifically expensive*

terrified /ˈterɪfaɪd/ ***adj.*** ~ **(of sb/sth)** very afraid: *I'm absolutely terrified of snakes.* ◇ *What's the matter? You look terrified.*

terrify /ˈterɪfaɪ/ ***verb*** [T] (*pres. part.* **terrifying**; *3rd person sing. pres.* **terrifies**; *pt, pp* **terrified**) to frighten sb very much

territorial /ˌterəˈtɔːriəl/ ***adj.*** (only *before* a noun) connected with the land or area of sea that belongs to a country

ˌterritorial ˈwaters ***noun*** [pl.] the parts of a sea or an ocean which are near a country's coast and are legally under its control

territory /ˈterətri/ ***noun*** (*pl.* **territories**) **1** [C,U] (POLITICS) an area of land that belongs to one country: *to fly over enemy territory* **2** [C,U] an area that an animal has as its own **3** [U] an area of knowledge or responsibility: *Computer programming is Frank's territory.*

terror /ˈterə(r)/ ***noun*** **1** [U] very great fear: *He screamed **in terror** as the rats came towards him.* **2** [C] a person or thing that makes you feel afraid: *the terrors of the night* **3** [U] (POLITICS) violence and the killing of ordinary people for political purposes: *a campaign of terror* **4** [C] a person or animal, especially a child, that is difficult to control: *Joey's a little terror.*

terrorism /ˈterərɪzəm/ ***noun*** [U] the killing of ordinary people for political purposes: *an act of terrorism* ▶ **terrorist** /ˈterərɪst/ ***noun*** [C], ***adj.***

terrorize (also **-ise**) /ˈterəraɪz/ ***verb*** [T] to make sb feel frightened by using or threatening to use violence against them: *The gang has terrorized the neighbourhood for months.*

terse /tɜːs/ ***adj.*** said in few words and in a not very friendly way: *a terse reply*

tertiary /ˈtɜːʃəri/ ***adj.*** third in order, rank or importance: *the **tertiary sector*** (=the area of industry that deals with services rather than materials or goods) ◇ (*BrE*) ***tertiary education*** (=at university or college level) ➲ look at **primary, secondary**

ˈtertiary industry (*also* **ˈservice industry**) ***noun*** [U, C] (ECONOMICS) the part of a country's economy that provides services

TESL /ˈtesl/ ***abbr.*** (LANGUAGE, EDUCATION) Teaching English as a Second Language

tessellated /ˈtesəleɪtɪd/ ***adj.*** (*technical*) made from small flat pieces arranged in a pattern

test[1] 🔑 /test/ ***noun*** [C] **1** (EDUCATION) a short exam to measure sb's knowledge or skill in sth: *We have a spelling test every Friday.* **2** (HEALTH) a short medical examination of a part of your body: *to have an eye test* **3** an experiment to find out if sth works or to find out more information about it: *Tests show that the new drug is safe and effective.* ◇ *to carry out/perform/do a test* **4** a situation or an event that shows how good, strong, etc. sb/sth is

IDM **put sb/sth to the test** to do sth to find out how good, strong, etc. sb/sth is

test[2] 🔑 /test/ ***verb*** **1** [I,T] to find out how much sb knows, or what they can do by asking them questions or giving them activities to perform: *We're being tested on irregular verbs this morning.* ◇ *Schools use various methods of testing.* **2** ~ **sb/sth (for sth)** [T] (HEALTH) to examine the blood, a part of the body, etc. to find out what is wrong with a person, or to check the condition of their health: *to have your eyes tested* ◇ *The doctor tested him for hepatitis.* **3** ~ **sth (for sth)**; ~ **sth (on sb/sth)** [T] to use or try a machine, substance, etc. to find out how well it works or to find out more information about it: *These cars have all been tested for safety.* ◇ *Do you think drugs should be tested on animals?*

testament /ˈtestəmənt/ ***noun*** [C, usually sing.] (*written*) **a** ~ **(to sth)** something that shows that sth exists or is true ➲ look at **the New Testament, the Old Testament**

ˈtest drive ***noun*** [C] an occasion when you drive a vehicle that you are thinking of buying so that you can see how well it works and if you like it ▶ **ˈtest-drive** ***verb*** [T]

testes plural of **testis**

testicle /ˈtestɪkl/ ***noun*** [C] one of the two ROUNDISH male sex organs that produce the male cells (**sperm**) that are needed for making young

testify /ˈtestɪfaɪ/ ***verb*** [I,T] (*pres. part.* **testifying**; *3rd person sing. pres.* **testifies**; *pt, pp* **testified**) (**LAW**) to make a formal statement that sth is true, especially in a court of law

testimony /ˈtestɪməni/ ***noun*** (*pl.* **testimonies**) **1** [C,U] (**LAW**) a formal statement that sth is true, especially one that is made in a court of law **2** [U, sing.] (*formal*) something that shows that sth else exists or is true

testis /ˈtestɪs/ (*pl.* **testes** /-tiːz/) = TESTICLE

testosterone /teˈstɒstərəʊn/ ***noun*** [U] (**BIOLOGY**) a HORMONE produced in men's bodies that makes them develop male physical and sexual characteristics ➲ look at **oestrogen**, **progesterone**

ˈ**test tube** ***noun*** [C] (**SCIENCE**) a thin glass tube that is used in chemical experiments ➲ picture at **laboratory**

tetanus /ˈtetənəs/ ***noun*** [U] (**HEALTH**) a serious disease that makes your muscles, especially the muscles of your face, hard and impossible to move. You can get **tetanus** by cutting yourself on sth dirty.

tether[1] /ˈteðə(r)/ ***verb*** [T] to tie an animal to sth with a rope, etc.

tether[2] /ˈteðə(r)/ ***noun***
IDM **at the end of your tether** → END[1]

tetrahedron /ˌtetrəˈhiːdrən/ ***noun*** [C] (**GEOMETRY**) a solid shape with four flat sides that are triangles ➲ picture at **solid**

text[1] AW /tekst/ ***noun*** **1** [U] (**ARTS AND MEDIA**, **LITERATURE**) the main printed part of a book or magazine, not the notes, pictures, etc.: *My job is to lay out the text and graphics on the page.* **2** [U] any form of written material: *a computer that can process text* **3** [C] = TEXT MESSAGE **4** [C] the written form of a speech, a play, an article, etc.: *The newspaper printed the complete text of the interview.* **5** [C] (**LITERATURE**) a book, play, etc., especially one studied for an exam: *a literary text* ◇ (*BrE*) *'Macbeth' is a* ***set text*** *this year.*

text[2] AW /tekst/ ***verb*** [T] to send sb a written message using a MOBILE PHONE: *Text me when you're ready.*

textbook /ˈtekstbʊk/ ***noun*** [C] (**EDUCATION**) a book that teaches a particular subject and that is used especially in schools: *a history textbook*

textile /ˈtekstaɪl/ ***noun*** **1** [C] any kind of cloth made in a factory: *cotton textiles* ◇ *the textile industry* **2** **textiles** [pl.] the industry that makes cloth: *He got a job in textiles.*

ˈ**text message** (*also* **text**) ***noun*** [C] a written message that is sent from one mobile phone to another ▶ ˈ**text messaging** ***noun*** [U]

textual AW /ˈtekstʃuəl/ ***adj.*** connected with or contained in a TEXT[1]: *textual errors* ◇ *textual analysis*

texture /ˈtekstʃə(r)/ ***noun*** [C,U] the way that sth feels when you touch it: *a rough/smooth/coarse texture* ◇ *This cheese has a very creamy texture.*

thalamus /ˈθæləməs/ ***noun*** [C] (*pl.* **thalami** /ˈθæləmaɪ; -mi/) (**ANATOMY**) either one of the two parts of the brain that control pain and feeling ➲ picture at **brain**

thallium /ˈθæliəm/ ***noun*** [U] (*symbol* **Tl**) (**CHEMISTRY**) a chemical element. **Thallium** is a soft silver-white metal whose COMPOUNDS are very poisonous. ℹ For more information on the periodic table of elements, look at pages R34-5.

than /ðən *strong form* ðæn/ ***conj.***, ***prep.*** **1** used when you are comparing two things: *He's taller than me.* ◇ *He's taller than I am.* ◇ *London is more expensive than Madrid.* ◇ *You speak French much better than she does/than her.* **2** used with 'more' and 'less' before numbers, expressions of time, distance, etc.: *I've worked here for more than three years.* **3** used after 'would rather' to say that you prefer one thing to another: *I'd rather play tennis than football.*

thank /θæŋk/ ***verb*** [T] ~ **sb (for sth/for doing sth)** to tell sb that you are grateful: *I'm writing to thank you for the present you sent me.* ◇ *I'll go and thank him for offering to help.*
IDM **thank God/goodness/heavens** used for expressing happiness that sth unpleasant has stopped or will not happen: *Thank goodness it's stopped raining.*

thankful /ˈθæŋkfl/ ***adj.*** ~ **(for sth/to do sth/that...)** (not before a noun) pleased and grateful: *I was thankful to hear that you got home safely.* ◇ *I was thankful for my thick coat when it started to snow.*

thankfully /ˈθæŋkfəli/ ***adv.*** **1** used for expressing happiness that sth unpleasant did not or will not happen SYN **fortunately**: *Thankfully, no one was injured in the accident.* **2** in a pleased or grateful way: *I accepted her offer thankfully.*

thankless /ˈθæŋkləs/ ***adj.*** involving hard work that other people do not notice or thank you for

thanks /θæŋks/ ***exclam***, ***noun*** [pl.] words which show that you are grateful: *I'd like to express my thanks to all of you for coming here today.*
IDM **thanks to sb/sth** because of sb/sth: *We're late, thanks to you!*
a vote of thanks → VOTE[1]
IDM **thanks to sb/sth** because of sb/sth: *We're late, thanks to you!*
a vote of thanks → VOTE[1]

Thanksgiving (Day) /ˌθæŋksˈɡɪvɪŋ deɪ/ ***noun*** [U, C] a public holiday in the US and in Canada

CULTURE ℹ

Thanksgiving Day is on the fourth Thursday in November in the US and on the second Monday in October in Canada. It was originally a day when people thanked God for the **harvest** (= the amount of crops gathered on a farm each year).

ˈ**thank you** ***exclam***, ***noun*** [C] an expression of thanks

that /ðæt/ ***det.***, ***pronoun***, ***conj.***, ***adv.*** **1** (*pl.* **those** /ðəʊz/) used to refer to a person or thing, especially when they are not near the person speaking: *I like that house over there.* ◇ *What's that in the road?* ◇ *'Could you pass me the book?' 'This one?' 'No, that one over there.'* **2** (*pl.* **those** /ðəʊz/) used for talking about a person or thing already known or mentioned: *That was the year we went to Spain, wasn't it?* ◇ *Can you give me back that money I lent you last week?* **3** /ðət *strong form* ðæt/ (used for introducing a relative clause) the person or thing already mentioned: *I'm reading the book that won the Booker prize.* ◇ *The people that live next door are French.* **4** /ðət *strong form* ðæt/ used after certain verbs, nouns and adjectives to introduce a new part of the sentence: *She told me that she was leaving.* ◇ *I hope that you feel better soon.* ◇ *I'm certain that he will come.* ◇ *It's funny that you should say that.*

5 (used with adjectives, adverbs) as much as that: *30 miles? I can't walk that far.*

IDM **that is (to say)** used when you are giving more information about sb/sth: *I'm on holiday next week. That's to say, from Tuesday.*

that's that there is nothing more to say or do: *I'm not going and that's that.*

thatched /θætʃt/ ***adj.*** (used about a building) having a roof made of REEDS, dried STRAW or a similar material

thaw /θɔː/ ***verb*** [I,T] ~ **(sth) (out)** to become or to make sth become soft or liquid again after freezing: *Is the snow thawing?* ◇ *Always thaw chicken thoroughly before you cook it.* ➲ look at **melt** ▸ **thaw** ***noun*** [C, usually sing.]

the ⊷ /ðə; ði *strong form* ðiː/ ***def. article*** **1** used for talking about a person or thing that is already known or that has already been mentioned: *I took the children to the dentist.* ◇ *We met the man who bought your house.* ◇ *The milk is in the fridge.* **2** used when there is only one of sth: *The sun is very strong today.* ◇ *Who won the World Cup?* ◇ *the government* **3** used with numbers and dates: *This is the third time I've seen this film.* ◇ *Friday the thirteenth* ◇ *I grew up in the sixties.* **4** used with adjectives to name a group of people: *the French* ◇ *the poor* **5** (*formal*) used with a SINGULAR noun when you are talking generally about sth: *The dolphin is an intelligent animal.* **6** with units of measurement, meaning 'every': *Our car does forty miles to the gallon.* **7** with musical instruments: *Do you play the piano?* **8** the well-known or important one: *'My best friend at school was Tony Blair.' 'You mean **the** Tony Blair?'* **9 the...the...** used for saying that the way in which two things change is connected: *The more you eat, the fatter you get.*

theatre ⊷ (*AmE* **theater**) /ˈθɪətə(r)/ ***noun*** **1** [C] (**ARTS AND MEDIA**) a building where you go to see plays, shows, etc.: *How often do you **go to the theatre**?* **2** [U] (**ARTS AND MEDIA**) plays in general; drama: *He's studying modern Russian theatre.* **3** [sing., U] (**ARTS AND MEDIA**) the work of acting in or producing plays: *He's worked in (the) theatre for thirty years.* **4** (**HEALTH**) [C, U] = OPERATING THEATRE

theatregoer (*AmE* **theatergoer**) /ˈθɪətəɡəʊə(r)/ ***noun*** [C] (**ARTS AND MEDIA**) a person who goes regularly to the theatre

theatrical /θiˈætrɪkl/ ***adj.*** **1** (only *before* a noun) connected with the theatre **2** (used about behaviour) dramatic and exaggerated because you want people to notice it

theft /θeft/ ***noun*** [C,U] (**LAW**) the crime of stealing sth: *There have been a lot of thefts in this area recently.* ◇ *The woman was arrested for theft.* ➲ note at **thief**

their ⊷ /ðeə(r)/ ***det.*** **1** of or belonging to them: *The children picked up their books and walked to the door.* **2** (*informal*) used instead of *his* or *her*: *Has everyone got their book?*

theirs ⊷ /ðeəz/ ***pronoun*** of or belonging to them: *Our flat isn't as big as theirs.*

them ⊷ /ðəm *strong form* ðem/ ***pronoun*** (the object of a verb or preposition) **1** the people or things mentioned earlier: *I'll phone them now.* ◇ *'I've got the keys here.' 'Oh good. Give them to me.'* ◇ *We have students from several countries but **most of them** are Italian.* ◇ *They asked for your address so I gave it to them.* **2** (*informal*) him or her: *If anyone phones, tell them I'm busy.*

thematic AW /θɪˈmætɪk; θiː-/ ***adj.*** connected with the subject or subjects of sth: *the thematic structure of a text* ▸ **thematically** /-kli/ ***adv.***: *The books have been grouped thematically.*

theme ⊷ AW /θiːm/ ***noun*** [C] (**ART, LITERATURE**) the subject of a talk, a piece of writing or a work of art: *The theme of today's discussion will be 'Our changing cities'.*

ˈtheme park ***noun*** [C] a park with a lot of things to do, see, ride on, etc., which are all based on a single idea

themselves ⊷ /ðəmˈselvz/ ***pronoun*** **1** used when the people or things who do an action are also affected by it: *Helen and Sarah seem to be enjoying themselves.* ◇ *People often talk to themselves when they are worried.* **2** used to emphasize 'they': *They themselves say that the situation cannot continue.* ◇ *Did they paint the house themselves?* (= or did sb else do it for them?)

IDM **(all) by themselves 1** alone: *The boys are too young to go out by themselves.* **2** without help: *The children cooked the dinner all by themselves.*

then ⊷ /ðen/ ***adv.*** **1** (at) that time: *In 1990? I was at university then.* ◇ *I spoke to him on Wednesday, but I haven't seen him **since then**.* ◇ *They met in 1941 and remained close friends **from then on**.* ◇ *I'm going tomorrow. Can you wait **until then**?* ◇ *Phone me tomorrow – I will have decided **by then**.* **2** next; after that: *I'll have a shower and get changed, then we'll go out.* ◇ *There was silence for a minute. Then he replied.* **3** used to show the logical result of a statement or situation: *'I don't feel at all well.' 'Why don't you go to the doctor then?'* ◇ *If you don't do any work then you'll fail the exam.* **4** (*spoken*) (used after words like *now, okay, right*, etc. to show the beginning or end of a conversation or statement): *Now then, are we all ready to go?* ◇ *Right then, I'll see you tomorrow.*

IDM **then/there again** → AGAIN

there and then; then and there → THERE

thence /ðens/ ***adv.*** (*old-fashioned*) from there

theo- /ˈθiːəʊ/ ***prefix*** (used in nouns, adjectives and adverbs) (**RELIGION**) connected with God or a god: *theology*

theodolite /θiˈɒdəlaɪt/ ***noun*** [C] (**GEOMETRY**) a piece of equipment that is used for measuring angles

theologian /ˌθiːəˈləʊdʒən/ ***noun*** [C] (**RELIGION**) a person who studies THEOLOGY

theology /θiˈɒlədʒi/ ***noun*** [U] (**RELIGION**) the study of religion ▸ **theological** /ˌθiːəˈlɒdʒɪkl/ ***adj.***

theorem /ˈθɪərəm/ ***noun*** [C] (**MATHEMATICS**) a rule or principle, especially in mathematics, that can be shown to be true: *Pythagoras' theorem*

theoretical AW /ˌθɪəˈretɪkl/ ***adj.*** **1** based on ideas and principles, not on practical experience: *A lot of university courses are still too theoretical these days.* **2** that may possibly exist or happen, although it is unlikely: *There is a theoretical possibility that the world will end tomorrow.* ➲ look at **practical** ▸ **theoretically** AW /-kli/ ***adv.***

theorist AW /ˈθɪərɪst/ (*also* **theoretician** /ˌθɪərəˈtɪʃn/) ***noun*** [C] a person who develops ideas and principles about a particular subject in order to explain why things happen or exist

theory ⊷ AW /ˈθɪəri/ ***noun*** (*pl.* **theories**) **1** [C] an idea or set of ideas that tries to explain sth: *the theory about how life on earth began* **2** [U] the general idea or principles of a particular subject: *political theory* ◇ *the theory and practice of language* *teaching* **3** [C] an opinion or a belief that has not been shown to be true

IDM **in theory** as a general idea which may not be true in reality: *Your plan sounds fine in theory, but I don't know if it'll work in practice.*

therapeutic /ˌθerəˈpjuːtɪk/ ***adj.*** **1** helping you to relax and feel better: *I find listening to music very therapeutic.* **2** (HEALTH) helping to cure an illness: *therapeutic drugs*

therapy /ˈθerəpi/ ***noun*** (HEALTH) **1** [U,C] treatment to help or cure a mental or physical illness, usually without drugs or medical operations: *to have/ undergo therapy* **2** [U] = PSYCHOTHERAPY: *She's* ***in therapy.*** ▶ **therapist** /ˈθerəpɪst/ ***noun*** [C]: *a speech therapist*

there 🔑 /ðeə(r)/ ***adv., pronoun*** **1** used as the subject of 'be', 'seem', 'appear', etc. to say that sth exists: *Is there a god?* ◇ *There's a man at the door.* ◇ *There wasn't much to eat.* ◇ *There's somebody singing outside.* ◇ *There seems to be a mistake here.* **2** in, at or to that place: *Could you put the table there, please?* ◇ *I like Milan. My husband and I met there.* ◇ *Have you been to Bonn? We're going there next week.* ◇ *Have you looked under there?* **3** used for calling attention to sth: *Oh look, there's Kate!* ◇ *Hello there! Can anyone hear me?* **4** at that point (in a conversation, story, etc.): *Could I interrupt you there for a minute?* **5** available if needed: *Her parents are always there if she needs help.*

IDM **be there for sb** to be available to help and support sb when they have a problem: *Whenever I'm in trouble, my sister is always there for me.*

then/there again → AGAIN

there and then; then and there immediately; at that time and place

there you are 1 used when you give sth to sb: *There you are. I've bought you a newspaper.* **2** used when you are explaining sth to sb: *Just press the switch and there you are!*

thereabouts /ˌðeərəˈbaʊts/ (*AmE* **thereabout** /ˌðeərəˈbaʊt/) ***adv.*** (usually after *or*) somewhere near a number, time or place: *There are 100 students, or thereabouts.* ◇ *She lives in Sydney, or thereabouts.*

thereafter /ˌðeərˈɑːftə(r)/ ***adv.*** (*written*) after that

thereby AW /ˌðeəˈbaɪ/ ***adv.*** (*written*) in that way

therefore 🔑 /ˈðeəfɔː(r)/ ***adv.*** for that reason: *The new trains have more powerful engines and are therefore faster.* SYN **thus**

thermometers

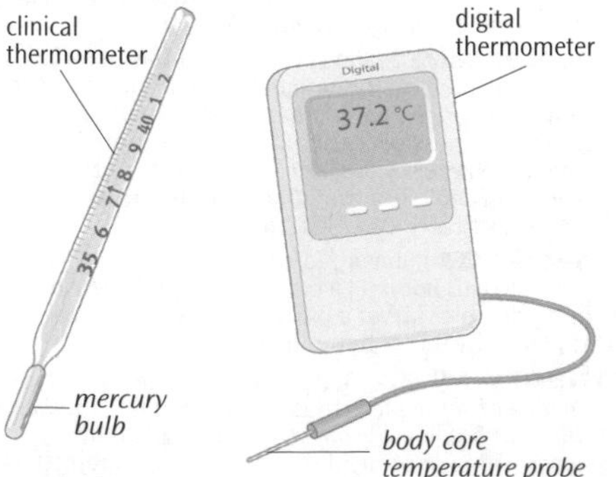

therein /ˌðeərˈɪn/ ***adv.*** (*written*) because of sth that has just been mentioned

thereupon /ˌðeərəˈpɒn/ ***adv.*** (*written*) immediately after that and often as the result of sth

therm /θɜːm/ ***noun*** [C] a unit of heat, used in Britain for measuring a gas supply

thermal¹ /ˈθɜːml/ ***adj.*** **1** (SCIENCE) connected with heat: *thermal energy* **2** (used about clothes) made to keep you warm in cold weather: *thermal underwear*

thermal² /ˈθɜːml/ ***noun*** **1 thermals** [pl.] clothes, especially underwear, made to keep you warm in cold weather **2** [C] (GEOGRAPHY) a flow of rising warm air

thermo- /ˈθɜːməʊ/ ***prefix*** (used in nouns, adjectives and adverbs) connected with heat: *thermonuclear*

thermometer /θəˈmɒmɪtə(r)/ ***noun*** [C] an instrument for measuring temperature

thermoplastic /ˌθɜːməʊˈplæstɪk/ ***noun*** [U] (TECHNICAL) a plastic material that can be easily shaped and bent when it is heated, and that becomes hard when it is cooled ➲ look at **thermoset**

Thermos™ /ˈθɜːməs/ (*also* **'Thermos flask**) ***noun*** [C] a type of VACUUM FLASK (= a container used for keeping a liquid hot or cold)

Thermos™

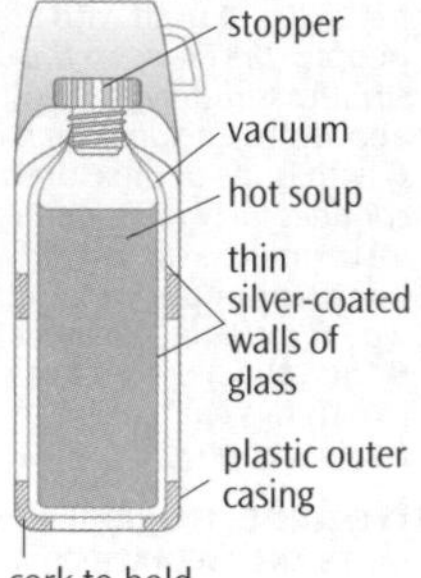

thermoset /ˈθɜːməʊset/ ***noun*** [C] (CHEMISTRY) a substance which becomes permanently hard when it is heated ➲ look at **thermoplastic** ▶ **thermosetting** /ˈθɜːməʊsetɪŋ/ ***adj.***

thermosphere /ˈθɜːməsfɪə(r)/ ***noun*** [sing.] **the thermosphere** (GEOGRAPHY) the region of the atmosphere above the MESOSPHERE, and where the temperature increases with height ➲ picture at **atmosphere**

thermostat /ˈθɜːməstæt/ ***noun*** [C] a device that controls the temperature in a house or machine by switching the heat on and off as necessary

thermostat

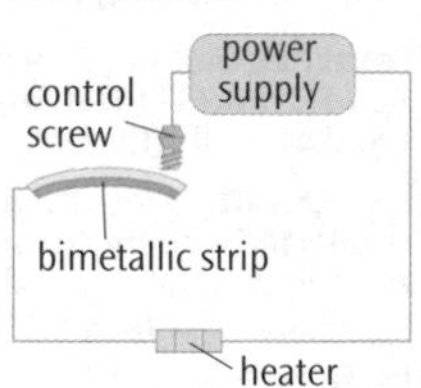

thesaurus /θɪˈsɔːrəs/ ***noun*** [C] (*pl.* **thesauruses**) (LANGUAGE) a book that contains lists of words and phrases with similar meanings

these → THIS

thesis AW /ˈθiːsɪs/ ***noun*** [C] (*pl.* **theses** /ˈθiːsiːz/) **1** a long piece of writing on a particular subject that you do as part of a university degree: *He did his thesis on Japanese investment in Europe.* ➲ look at **dissertation** **2** an idea that is discussed and presented with evidence in order to show that it is true

they 🔑 /ðeɪ/ ***pronoun*** (the subject of a verb) **1** the people or things that have been mentioned: *We've got two children. They're both boys.* ◇ *'Have you seen my keys?' 'Yes, they're on the table.'* **2** people in general or people whose identity is not known or stated: *They say it's going to be a mild winter.* **3** (*informal*) used instead of *he* or *she*: *Somebody phoned for you but they didn't leave their name.*

they'd /ðeɪd/ short for THEY HAD, THEY WOULD

they'll /ðeɪl/ short for THEY WILL

they're /ðeə(r)/ short for THEY ARE

they've /ðeɪv/ short for THEY HAVE

thick¹ /θɪk/ *adj.* **1** (used about sth solid) having a large distance between its opposite sides; not thin: *a thick black line* ◇ *a thick coat/book* ◇ *These walls are very thick.* OPP **thin** **2** used for saying what the distance is between the two opposite sides of something: *The ice was six centimetres thick.* OPP **thin** **3** having a lot of things close together: *a thick forest* ◇ *thick hair* OPP **thin** **4** (used about a liquid) that does not flow easily: *thick cream* ◇ *This paint is too thick.* OPP **thin** **5** (used about FOG, smoke, etc.) difficult to see through: *There'll be a thick fog tonight.* ◇ *thick clouds of smoke* OPP **thin** **6** ~ **(with sth)** containing a lot of sth/sb close together: *The air was thick with dust.* ◇ *The streets were thick with shoppers.* **7** (used about sb's accent) very strong **8** (*informal*) slow to learn or understand; stupid ▶ **thick** *adv.*: *Snow lay thick on the ground.*

IDM **have a thick skin** to be not easily upset or worried by what people say about you

thick² /θɪk/ *noun*

IDM **in the thick of sth** in the most active or crowded part of sth; very involved in sth

through thick and thin through difficult times and situations

thicken /ˈθɪkən/ *verb* [I,T] to become or to make sth thicker

thickener /ˈθɪkənə(r)/ *noun* [C] a substance used to make a liquid thicker: *paint thickeners*

thickly /ˈθɪkli/ *adv.* **1** in a way that produces a wide piece or deep layer of sth: *Spread the butter thickly.* ◇ *thickly sliced bread* **2** ~ **wooded, populated, etc.** having a lot of trees, people, etc. close together: *a thickly wooded area* **3** in a deep voice that is not as clear as normal, especially because of illness or emotion

thickness /ˈθɪknəs/ *noun* [C,U] the quality of being thick or how thick sth is

ˌ**thick-ˈskinned** *adj.* not easily worried or upset by what other people say about you

thief /θiːf/ *noun* [C] (*pl.* **thieves** /θiːvz/) (LAW) a person who steals things from another person

RELATED VOCABULARY

Stealing

A **thief** is a general word for a person who steals things, usually secretly and without violence. The name of the crime is **theft**.

A **robber** steals from a bank, shop, etc. and often uses violence or threats. A **burglar** steals things by breaking into a house, shop, etc., often at night, and a **shoplifter** goes into a shop when it is open and takes things without paying. A **mugger** steals from sb in the street and uses violence or threats.

thigh /θaɪ/ *noun* [C] (ANATOMY) the top part of your leg, above your knee ➲ picture on **page 80**

ˈ**thigh bone** *noun* [C] (ANATOMY) the large thick bone in the top part of your leg above your knee SYN **femur** ➲ picture on **page 80**

thimble /ˈθɪmbl/ *noun* [C] a small metal or plastic object that you wear on the end of your finger to protect it when you are sewing

thin¹ /θɪn/ *adj.* (**thinner**; **thinnest**) **1** (used about sth solid) having a small distance between the opposite sides; not thick: *a thin book/shirt* ◇ *a thin slice of meat* OPP **thick** **2** having very little fat on the body: *You need to eat more. You're too thin!* OPP **fat** **3** (used about a liquid) that flows easily; not thick: *a thin sauce* OPP **thick** **4** (used about MIST, smoke, etc.) not difficult to see through OPP **thick** ▶ **thin** *adv.*: *Don't slice the onion too thin.* ▶ **thinly** *adv.*: *thinly sliced bread* ◇ *thinly populated areas*

IDM **thin on the ground** → GROUND¹

through thick and thin → THICK²

vanish, etc. into thin air to disappear completely

wear thin → WEAR¹

thin² /θɪn/ *verb* [I,T] (**thinning**; **thinned**) ~ **(sth) (out)** to become thinner or fewer in number; to make sth thinner: *The trees thin out towards the edge of the forest.* ◇ *Thin the sauce by adding milk.*

thing /θɪŋ/ *noun* **1** [C] an object that is not named: *What's that red thing on the table?* ◇ *A pen is a thing you use for writing with.* ◇ *I need to get a few things at the shops.* **2** [C] a quality or state: *There's* ***no such thing as*** *a ghost* (=it doesn't exist). ◇ *The best thing about my job is the way it changes all the time.* **3** [C] an action, event or statement: *When I get home the first thing I do is have a cup of tea.* ◇ *A strange thing happened to me yesterday.* ◇ *What a nice thing to say!* **4** [C] a fact, subject, etc.: *He told me a few things that I didn't know before.* **5 things** [pl.] clothes or tools that belong to sb or are used for a particular purpose: *I'll just go and pack my things.* ◇ *We keep all the cooking things in this cupboard.* **6 things** [pl.] the situation or conditions of your life: *How are things with you?* **7** [C] used for expressing how you feel about a person or an animal: *You've broken your finger? You poor thing!* **8 the thing** [sing.] exactly what is wanted or needed: *That's just the thing I was looking for!*

IDM **a close shave/thing** → CLOSE³

be a good thing (that) to be lucky that: *It's a good thing you remembered your umbrella.*

do your own thing to do what you want to do, independently of other people

first/last thing as early/late as possible: *I'll telephone her first thing tomorrow morning.* ◇ *I saw him last thing on Friday evening.*

for one thing used for introducing a reason for something: *I think we should go by train. For one thing it's cheaper.*

have a thing about sb/sth (*informal*) to have strong feelings about sb/sth

to make matters/things worse → WORSE

take it/things easy → EASY²

THESAURUS

think

believe • feel • be under the impression • be of the opinion

These words all mean to have an idea that sth is true or possible or to have a particular opinion about sb/sth.

think: *Do you think he'll like it?*

believe: *The police believe that the man may be armed.*

feel: *We felt we were unlucky to lose.*

be under the impression: *I was under the impression that she had finished the work.*

be of the opinion (*formal*): *We are of the opinion that this matter deserves your full attention.*

think /θɪŋk/ ***verb*** (*pt, pp* **thought** /θɔːt/) **1** [I,T] ~ (sth) (of/about sb/sth); ~ that... to have a particular idea or opinion about sth/sb; to believe: *'Do you think (that) we'll win?' 'No, I* ***don't think so****.'* ◇ *'Sue's coming tomorrow, isn't she?' 'Yes, I* ***think so****.'* ◇ *I think (that) they've moved to York but I'm not sure.* ◇ *What did you think of the film?* ◇ *What do you think about going out tonight?* ◇ *Gary's on holiday, I think.* **2** [I] ~ (about sth) to use your mind to consider sth or to form connected ideas: *Think before you speak.* ◇ *What are you thinking about?* ◇ *He had to think hard* (= a lot) *about the question.* **3** [I] ~ of/about doing sth; ~ that... to intend or plan to do sth: *We're thinking of moving house.* ◇ *I think I'll go for a swim.* **4** [T] to form an idea of sth; to imagine sth: ***Just think*** *what we could do with all that money!* **5** [I] ~ about/of sb to consider the feelings of sb else: *She never thinks about anyone but herself.* **6** [T] to remember sth; to have sth come into your mind: *Can you think where you left the keys?* ◇ *I didn't think to ask him his name.* **7** [T] to expect sth: *The job took longer than we thought.* **8** [I] to think in a particular way: *If you want to be successful, you have to* ***think big****.* ◇ *We've got to* ***think positive****.* ▶ **think** ***noun*** [sing.]: *I'm not sure. I'll have to* ***have a think*** *about it.*

IDM **think better of (doing) sth** to decide not to do sth; to change your mind

think highly, a lot, not much, etc. of sb/sth to have a good, bad, etc. opinion of sb/sth: *I didn't think much of that film.*

think the world of sb to love and admire sb very much

PHR V **think of sth** to create an idea in your imagination: *Who first thought of the plan?*

think sth out to consider carefully all the details of a plan, idea, etc.: *a well-thought-out scheme*

think sth over to consider sth carefully: *I'll think your offer over and let you know tomorrow.*

think sth through to consider every detail of sth carefully: *He made a bad decision because he didn't think it through.*

think sth up to create sth in your mind; to invent: *to think up a new advertising slogan*

thinker /ˈθɪŋkə(r)/ ***noun*** [C] **1** a person who thinks about serious and important subjects **2** a person who thinks in a particular way: *a quick/creative/clear thinker*

thinking[1] /ˈθɪŋkɪŋ/ ***noun*** [U] **1** using your mind to think about sth: *We're going to have to do some quick thinking.* **2** ideas or opinions about sth: *This accident will make them change their thinking on safety matters.* ➲ look at **wishful thinking**

thinking[2] /ˈθɪŋkɪŋ/ ***adj.*** intelligent and using your mind to think about important subjects

ˈ**think tank** ***noun*** [C] (POLITICS) a group of experts who provide advice and ideas on political, social or economic issues

third[1] /θɜːd/ ***ordinal number*** 3rd ➲ note at **sixth[1]**

third[2] /θɜːd/ ***noun*** [C] **1** the FRACTION ⅓; one of three equal parts of sth **2** (*BrE*) a result in final university exams, below first and second class degrees

ˌ**third** ˈ**class** ***noun*** **1** [U, sing.] (TOURISM) (especially in the past) the cheapest and least comfortable part of a train, ship, etc. **2** [U] (in the US) the class of mail used for sending advertisements, etc. **3** [U, sing.] (EDUCATION) the lowest standard of degree given by a British university

ˈ**third-class** ***adj.*** **1** (TOURISM) (especially in the past) connected with the cheapest and least comfortable way of travelling on a train, ship, etc. **2** (in the US) connected with the class of mail used to send advertisements, etc. **3** (EDUCATION) used to describe the lowest standard of degree given by a British university **4** less important than other people: *They are treated as* ***third-class citizens****.* ▶ ˌ**third** ˈ**class** ***adv.***: *to travel third class*

ˌ**third-de**ˈ**gree** ***adj.*** (only *before* a noun) **1** (*especially AmE*) (LAW) used to describe the least serious of three kinds of murder **2** (HEALTH) used to describe the most serious of three kinds of burn, affecting the flesh under the skin and leaving permanent marks ➲ look at **first-degree, second-degree**

thirdly /ˈθɜːdli/ ***adv.*** used to introduce the third point in a list: *We have made savings in three areas: firstly, defence, secondly, education and thirdly, health.*

ˌ**third** ˈ**party** ***noun*** [C] a person who is involved in a situation in addition to the two main people involved

the ˌ**third** ˈ**person** ***noun*** [sing.] **1** (LANGUAGE) the set of pronouns and verb forms used by a speaker to refer to other people and things: *'They are' is the third person plural of the verb 'to be'.* **2** (LANGUAGE) the style of writing a novel, telling a story, etc. as the experience of sb else, using third person forms: *a book written* ***in the third person*** ➲ look at **the first person, the second person**

ˌ**Third** ˈ**World** ***noun*** [sing.] (GEOGRAPHY, SOCIAL STUDIES) a way of referring to the poor or developing countries of Africa, Asia and Latin America, which is sometimes considered offensive: *the causes of poverty and injustice in the Third World* ◇ *Third-World debt* ➲ look at **First World**

thirst /θɜːst/ ***noun*** **1** [U, sing.] the feeling that you have when you want or need a drink: *Cold tea really quenches your thirst.* ◇ *to die of thirst* **2** [sing.] **a ~ for sth** a strong desire for sth ➲ look at **hunger**

thirsty /ˈθɜːsti/ ***adj.*** (**thirstier**; **thirstiest**) wanting or needing a drink: *I'm thirsty. Can I have a drink of water, please?* ➲ look at **hungry** ▶ **thirstily** ***adv.***

thirteen /ˌθɜːˈtiːn/ ***number*** 13 ➲ note at **six**

thirteenth /ˌθɜːˈtiːnθ/ ***ordinal number, noun*** [C] 13th ➲ note at **sixth[1]**

thirtieth /ˈθɜːtiəθ/ ***ordinal number, noun*** [C] 30th ➲ note at **sixth[1]**

thirty /ˈθɜːti/ ***number*** **1** 30 **2 the thirties** [pl.] numbers, years or temperatures from 30 to 39 ➲ note at **sixty**

this /ðɪs/ ***det., pronoun*** (*pl.* **these** /ðiːz/) **1** used for talking about sb/sth that is close to you in time or space: *Have a look at this photo.* ◇ *These boots are really comfortable. My old ones weren't.* ◇ *Is this the book you asked for?* ◇ *These are the letters to be filed, not those over there.* ◇ *This chair's softer than that one, so I'll sit here.* **2** used for talking about sth that was mentioned or talked about earlier: *Where did you hear about this?* **3** used for introducing sb or showing sb sth: *This is my wife, Claudia, and these are our children, David and Vicky.* ◇ *It's easier if you do it like this.* **4** (used with days of the week or periods of time) of today or the present week, year, etc.: *Are you busy this afternoon?* ◇ *this Friday* (= the Friday of this week) **5** (*informal*) (used when you are telling a story) a certain: *Then this woman said...* ▶ **this** ***adv.***: *The road is not usually this busy.*

IDM **this and that; this, that and the other** various things: *We chatted about this and that.*

thistle /ˈθɪsl/ ***noun*** [C] a wild plant with purple flowers and sharp points (**prickles**) on its leaves

thong /θɒŋ/ (*AmE*) = FLIP-FLOP

thorax /ˈθɔːræks/ ***noun*** [C] **1** (ANATOMY) the middle part of your body between your neck and your waist **2** (BIOLOGY) the middle section of an insect's body, to which the legs and wings are connected ➲ picture on **page 80** ➲ look at **abdomen** ▸ **thoracic** /θɔːˈræsɪk/ ***adj.***

thorium /ˈθɔːriəm/ ***noun*** [U] (*symbol* **Th**) (CHEMISTRY) a chemical element. **Thorium** is a white RADIOACTIVE metal used as a source of nuclear energy. ❶ For more information on the periodic table of elements, look at pages R34-5.

thorn /θɔːn/ ***noun*** [C] one of the hard sharp points on some plants and bushes, for example on ROSE bushes ➲ picture at **flower**

thorny /ˈθɔːni/ ***adj.*** **1** causing difficulty or disagreement: *a thorny problem/question* **2** having THORNS

thorough 🔑 /ˈθʌrə/ ***adj.*** **1** careful and complete: *The police made a thorough search of the house.* **2** doing things in a very careful way, making sure that you look at every detail: *Pam is slow but she is very thorough.* ▸ **thoroughness** ***noun*** [U]

thoroughbred /ˈθʌrəbred/ ***noun*** [C] an animal, especially a horse, of high quality, that has parents that are both of the same type ▸ **thoroughbred** ***adj.***

thoroughly 🔑 /ˈθʌrəli/ ***adv.*** **1** in a careful and complete way: *to study a subject thoroughly* **2** completely; very much: *We thoroughly enjoyed our holiday.*

those plural of **that**

though 🔑 /ðəʊ/ ***conj.***, ***adv.*** **1** in spite of the fact that; although: *Though he had very little money, Alex always managed to dress smartly.* ◇ *She still loved him **even though** he had treated her so badly.* **2** but: *I'll come as soon as I can, though I can't promise to be on time.* **3** (*informal*) however: *I quite like him. I don't like his wife, though.*

IDM **as if** → AS

as though → AS

thought¹ past tense, past participle of **think**

thought² 🔑 /θɔːt/ ***noun*** **1** [C] an idea or opinion: *What are your thoughts on this subject?* ◇ *The thought of living alone filled her with fear.* ◇ *I've just had a thought* (= an idea). **2** [U] the power or process of thinking: *I need to **give** this problem **some thought**.* **3 thoughts** [pl.] a person's mind and all the ideas that are in it: *You are always **in my thoughts**.* **4** [sing.] a feeling of care or worry: *They sent me flowers. What a kind thought!* **5** [U] particular ideas or a particular way of thinking: *a change in medical thought on the subject*

IDM **deep in thought/conversation** → DEEP¹

a school of thought → SCHOOL

second thoughts → SECOND¹

thoughtful /ˈθɔːtfl/ ***adj.*** **1** thinking deeply: *a thoughtful expression* **2** thinking about what other people want or need: *It was very thoughtful of you to send her some flowers.* ▸ **thoughtfully** /-fəli/ ***adv.*** ▸ **thoughtfulness** ***noun*** [U]

thoughtless /ˈθɔːtləs/ ***adj.*** not thinking about what other people want or need or what the result of your actions will be SYN **inconsiderate** ▸ **thoughtlessly** ***adv.*** ▸ **thoughtlessness** ***noun*** [U]

thousand /ˈθaʊznd/ ***number*** 1000 ❶ For examples of how to use numbers in sentences, look at **six**. For more information about numbers look at the special section on numbers on pages R36-41.

thousandth¹ /ˈθaʊznθ/ ***ordinal number*** 1000th

thousandth² /ˈθaʊznθ/ ***noun*** [C] the FRACTION 1/1000; one of a thousand equal parts of sth

thrash /θræʃ/ ***verb*** **1** [T] to hit sb/sth many times with a stick, etc. as a punishment **2** [I,T] ~ **(sth)** **(about/around)** to move or make sth move wildly without any control **3** [T] to defeat sb easily in a game, competition, etc.

PHR V **thrash sth out** to talk about sth with sb until you reach an agreement

thrashing /ˈθræʃɪŋ/ ***noun*** [C] **1** the action of hitting sb/sth many times with a stick, etc. as a punishment **2** (*informal*) a bad defeat in a game

thread¹ 🔑 /θred/ ***noun*** **1** [C,U] a long thin piece of cotton, wool, etc. that you use for sewing or making cloth: *a needle and thread* **2** [C] the connection between ideas, the parts of a story, etc.: *I've lost the thread of this argument.* **3** [C] (COMPUTING) a series of connected messages on a MESSAGE BOARD on the Internet which have been sent by different people **4** [C] the raised line that runs around the length of a screw and that allows it to be fixed in place by twisting ➲ picture at **bolt**

thread² /θred/ ***verb*** [T] **1** to put sth long and thin, especially thread, through a narrow opening or hole: *to thread a needle* ◇ *He threaded the belt through the loops on the trousers.* **2** to join things together by putting them onto a string, etc.

IDM **thread your way through sth** to move through sth with difficulty, going around things or people that are in your way

threadbare /ˈθredbeə(r)/ ***adj.*** (used about material or clothes) old and very thin

threat 🔑 /θret/ ***noun*** **1** [C] a warning that sb may hurt, kill or punish you if you do not do what they want: *to **make threats** against sb* ◇ *He keeps saying he'll resign, but he won't **carry out** his **threat**.* **2** [U, sing.] the possibility of trouble or danger: *The forest is **under threat** from building developments.* **3** [C] a person or thing that may damage sth or hurt sb; something that indicates future danger

threaten 🔑 /ˈθretn/ ***verb*** **1** [T] ~ **sb (with sth)**; ~ **(to do sth)** to warn that you may hurt, kill or punish sb if they do not do what you want: *The boy threatened him with a knife.* ◇ *She was threatened with dismissal.* ◇ *The man threatened to kill her if she didn't tell him where the money was.* **2** [I,T] to seem likely to do sth unpleasant: *The wind was threatening to destroy the bridge.*

threatening 🔑 /ˈθretnɪŋ/ ***adj.*** **1** expressing a threat of harm or violence: *threatening letters* ◇ *threatening behaviour* **2** (used about the sky, clouds, etc.) showing that bad weather is likely: *The sky was dark and threatening.* ▸ **threateningly** ***adv.***: *He glared at her threateningly.*

three /θriː/ ***number*** **1** 3 **2** (used to form compound adjectives) having three of the thing mentioned: *a three-legged stool* ➲ look at **third**

ˌthree-ˈD (also **3-D**) ***noun*** [U] the quality of having, or appearing to have, length, width and depth (= three dimensions): *These glasses allow you to see the film in three-D.* ◇ *a three-D image*

ˌthree-diˈmensional (*also* **ˌ3-ˈD**) ***adj.*** having or appearing to have length, width and depth: *a three-dimensional model* ➲ look at **two-dimensional**

ˈthree-star ***adj.*** (TOURISM) having three stars in a system that measures quality. The highest standard is usually represented by four or five stars: *a three-star hotel*

thresh /θreʃ/ *verb* [T] (AGRICULTURE) to separate grains of CORN, rice, etc. from the rest of the plant using a machine or, especially in the past, by hitting it with a special tool ▸ **threshing** *noun* [U]: *a threshing machine*

threshold /ˈθreʃhəʊld/ *noun* [C] **1** the ground at the entrance to a room or building **2** the level at which sth starts to happen: *Young children have a low boredom threshold.* **3** the time when you are just about to start sth or find sth: *We could be **on the threshold of** a scientific breakthrough.*

threw past tense of **throw**

thrift /θrɪft/ *noun* [U] the quality of being careful not to spend too much money ▸ **thrifty** *adj.*

ˈ**thrift shop** (*also* ˈ**thrift store**) *noun* [C] (*AmE*) = CHARITY SHOP

thrill /θrɪl/ *noun* [C] a sudden strong feeling of pleasure or excitement ▸ **thrill** *verb* [T]: *His singing thrilled the audience.* ▸ **thrilled** *adj.*: *He was absolutely thrilled with my present.* ▸ **thrilling** *adj.*

thriller /ˈθrɪlə(r)/ *noun* [C] (ARTS AND MEDIA, LITERATURE) a play, film, book, etc. with a very exciting story, often about a crime

thrive /θraɪv/ *verb* [I] (*pt* **thrived** or (*old-fashioned*) **throve** /θrəʊv/; *pp* **thrived**) to grow or develop well ▸ **thriving** *adj.*: *a thriving industry*

throat 🔑 /θrəʊt/ *noun* [C] **1** the front part of your neck: *The attacker grabbed the man by the throat.* ➲ picture on **page 80** **2** (ANATOMY) the back part of your mouth and the passage down your neck through which air and food pass: *She got a piece of bread stuck in her throat.* ◇ *I've got a sore throat.*

IDM **clear your throat** → CLEAR[3]

have/feel a lump in your throat → LUMP[1]

throb /θrɒb/ *verb* [I] (**throbbing**; **throbbed**) to make strong regular movements or noises; to beat strongly: *Her finger throbbed with pain.* ▸ **throb** *noun* [C]

thrombosis /θrɒmˈbəʊsɪs/ *noun* [C,U] (*pl.* **thromboses** /-siːz/) (HEALTH) a serious medical condition caused by a CLOT (= a lump of thick blood) forming in a BLOOD VESSEL (= tube) or in the heart

throne /θrəʊn/ *noun* **1** [C] the special chair where a king or queen sits **2 the throne** [sing.] the position of being king or queen

throng[1] /θrɒŋ/ *noun* [C] (*written*) a large crowd of people

throng[2] /θrɒŋ/ *verb* [I,T] (*written*) (used about a crowd of people) to move into or fill a particular place

throttle[1] /ˈθrɒtl/ *verb* [T] to hold sb tightly by the throat and stop them breathing SYN **strangle**

throttle[2] /ˈθrɒtl/ *noun* [C] the part in a vehicle that controls the speed by controlling how much fuel goes into the engine

through 🔑 /θruː/ *prep., adv.* **1** from one end or side of sth to the other: *We drove through the centre of London.* ◇ *to look through a telescope* ◇ *She cut through the rope.* ◇ *to push through a crowd of people* **2** from the beginning to the end of sth: *Food supplies will not last through the winter.* ◇ *We're halfway through the book.* ◇ *He read the letter through and handed it back.* **3** past a limit, stage or test: *He lifted the rope to let us through.* ◇ *She didn't get through the first interview.* **4** because of; with the help of: *Errors were made through bad organization.* ◇ *David got the job through his uncle.* **5** (also **thru**) (*AmE*) until, and including: *They are staying Monday through Friday.* **6** (*BrE*) connected by telephone: *Can you put me through to extension 5678, please?*

PHR V **be through (with sb/sth)** to have finished with sb/sth

throughout 🔑 /θruːˈaʊt/ *adv., prep.* **1** in every part of sth: *The house is beautifully decorated throughout.* ◇ *The match can be watched live on television throughout the world.* **2** from the beginning to the end of sth: *We didn't enjoy the holiday because it rained throughout.*

throve past tense of **thrive**

throw 🔑 /θrəʊ/ *verb* (*pt* **threw** /θruː/; *pp* **thrown** /θrəʊn/) **1** [I,T] ~ (sth) (to/at sb); ~ sb sth to send sth from your hand through the air by moving your hand or arm quickly: *How far can you throw?* ◇ *Throw the ball to me.* ◇ *Throw me the ball.* ◇ *Don't throw stones at people.* **2** [T] to put sth somewhere quickly or carelessly: *He threw his bag down in a corner.* ◇ *She threw on a sweater and ran out of the door.* **3** [T] to move your body or part of it quickly or suddenly: *Jenny threw herself onto the bed and sobbed.* ◇ *Lee threw back his head and roared with laughter.* **4** [T] to cause sb to fall down quickly or violently: *The bus braked and we were thrown to the floor.* **5** [T] to put sb in a particular (usually unpleasant) situation: *We were thrown into confusion by the news.* **6** [T] (*informal*) to make sb feel upset, confused or surprised: *The question threw me and I didn't know what to reply.* **7** [T] to send light or shade onto sth: *The tree threw a long shadow across the lawn.* ▸ **throw** *noun* [C]: *It's your throw* (= it's your turn to throw the dice in a board game, etc.). ◇ *a throw of 97 metres*

PHR V **throw sth away 1** (*also* **throw sth out**) to get rid of rubbish or sth that you do not want: *I threw his letters away.* **2** to waste or not use sth useful: *to throw away a good opportunity*

throw sth in (*informal*) to include sth extra without increasing the price

throw sb out to force sb to leave a place

throw sth out 1 to decide not to accept sb's idea or suggestion **2** = THROW STH AWAY (1)

throw up (*informal*) (HEALTH) to VOMIT; to be sick

throw sth up 1 (HEALTH) to VOMIT food **2** to produce or show sth **3** to leave your job, career, studies, etc.

throwaway /ˈθrəʊəweɪ/ *adj.* (only *before* a noun) **1** used to describe sth that you say quickly without careful thought, sometimes in order to be funny: *a throwaway line/remark/comment* **2** (BUSINESS) (used about goods, etc.) produced at a low cost and intended to be thrown away as rubbish after being used: *throwaway products* SYN **disposable**: *We live in a throwaway society* (= a society in which things are not made to last a long time)

thru (*AmE*) = THROUGH (5)

thrush /θrʌʃ/ *noun* **1** [C] a bird with a brown back and brown spots on its chest: *a song thrush* **2** (*AmE* ˈ**yeast infection**) [U] (HEALTH) an infection that affects a person's VAGINA or mouth

thrust[1] /θrʌst/ *verb* [I,T] (*pt, pp* **thrust**) **1** to push sb/sth suddenly or violently; to move quickly and suddenly in a particular direction: *The man thrust his hands deeper into his pockets.* ◇ *She thrust past him and ran out of the room.* **2** to make a sudden forward movement with a knife, etc.

PHR V **thrust sb/sth upon sb** to force sb to accept or deal with sb/sth

thrust[2] /θrʌst/ *noun* **1 the thrust** [sing.] the main part or point of an argument, policy, etc. **2** [C] a sudden strong movement forward

thud /θʌd/ ***noun*** [C] the low sound that is made when a heavy object hits sth else: *Her head hit the floor with a dull thud.* ▶ **thud** ***verb*** [I] (**thudding**; **thudded**)

thug /θʌg/ ***noun*** [C] a violent person who may harm other people

thulium /ˈθuːliəm (*BrE also* ˈθjuː-)/ ***noun*** [U] (*symbol* **Tm**) (CHEMISTRY) a chemical element. **Thulium** is a soft silver-white metal. ❶ For more information on the periodic table of elements, look at pages R34-5.

thumb¹ 🔑 /θʌm/ ***noun*** [C] **1** the short thick finger at the side of each hand ➲ picture on **page 80** **2** the part of a glove, etc. that covers your **thumb**

IDM **a rule of thumb** → RULE¹

stand/stick out like a sore thumb → SORE¹

the thumbs up/down a sign or an expression that shows approval/disapproval

under sb's thumb (used about a person) completely controlled by sb: *She's got him under her thumb.*

thumb² /θʌm/ ***verb*** [I,T] ~ **(through) sth** to turn the pages of a book, etc. quickly

IDM **thumb a lift** to hold out your thumb to cars going past, to ask sb to give you a free ride

thumbtack /ˈθʌmtæk/ (*AmE*) = DRAWING PIN

thump /θʌmp/ ***verb*** **1** [T] to hit sb/sth hard with sth, usually your closed hand (**fist**): *He started coughing and Jo thumped him on the back.* **2** [I,T] to make a loud sound by hitting sth or by beating hard: *His heart was thumping with excitement.* ▶ **thump** ***noun*** [C]

thunder¹ /ˈθʌndə(r)/ ***noun*** [U] the loud noise in the sky that you can hear when there is a storm and that usually comes after a flash of light (**lightning**): *a clap/crash/roll of thunder*

thunder² /ˈθʌndə(r)/ ***verb*** [I] **1** (used with *it*) to make a loud noise in the sky during a storm: *The rain poured down and it started to thunder.* **2** to make a loud deep noise like THUNDER: *Traffic thundered across the bridge.*

thunderbolt /ˈθʌndəbəʊlt/ ***noun*** [C] (*written*) a flash of LIGHTNING that comes at the same time as the noise of THUNDER and that hits sth

thunderclap /ˈθʌndəklæp/ ***noun*** [C] a loud crash made by THUNDER

thunderstorm /ˈθʌndəstɔːm/ ***noun*** [C] a storm with THUNDER and flashes of light in the sky (**lightning**)

Thur. (*also* **Thurs.**) ***abbr.*** Thursday: *Thur. 26 June*

Thursday /ˈθɜːzdeɪ; -di/ ***noun*** [C,U] (*abbr.* **Thur.**; **Thurs.**) the day of the week after Wednesday

thus 🔑 /ðʌs/ ***adv.*** (*formal*) **1** like this; in this way: *Thus began the series of incidents which changed her life.* **2** because of or as a result of this SYN **therefore**

thwart /θwɔːt/ ***verb*** [T] ~ **sth**; ~ **sb (in sth)** to stop sb doing what they planned to do; to prevent sth happening: *to thwart sb's plans/ambitions/efforts* ◇ *She was thwarted in her attempt to gain control.*

thyme /taɪm/ ***noun*** [U] a plant with small leaves that have a sweet smell and are used in cooking as a HERB

thymine /ˈθaɪmiːn/ ***noun*** [U] (BIOLOGY) one of the four COMPOUNDS that make up DNA and RNA ➲ picture at **DNA**

thyroid /ˈθaɪrɔɪd/ (*also* ˈ**thyroid gland**) ***noun*** [C] (ANATOMY) a small organ at the front of your neck that produces HORMONES that control the way in which your body grows and works

tibia /ˈtɪbiə/ ***noun*** [C] (ANATOMY) the inner and larger bone of the two bones in the lower part of the leg between your knee and foot SYN **shin bone** ➲ look at **fibula** ➲ picture on **page 80**

tic /tɪk/ ***noun*** [C] (HEALTH) a sudden quick movement of a muscle, especially in your face or head, that you cannot control: *He has a nervous tic.*

tick¹ /tɪk/ ***verb*** **1** [I] (used about a clock or watch) to make regular short sounds **2** (*AmE* **check**) [T] to put a mark (✓) next to a name, an item on a list, etc. to show that sth has been dealt with or chosen, or that it is correct: *Please tick the appropriate box.*

IDM **what makes sb/sth tick** the reasons why sb behaves or sth works in the way he/she/it does: *He has a strong interest in people and what makes them tick.*

PHR V **tick away/by** (used about time) to pass

tick sb/sth off to put a mark (✓) next to a name, an item on a list, etc. to show that sth has been done or sb has been dealt with

tick over (*informal*) (usually used in the continuous tenses) **1** (used about an engine) to run slowly while the vehicle is not moving **2** to keep working slowly without producing or achieving very much

tick² /tɪk/ ***noun*** [C] **1** (*AmE* **check mark**; **check**) a mark (✓) next to an item on a list that shows that sth has been done or is correct: *Put a tick after each correct answer.* **2** (*also* **ticking**) the regular short sound that a watch or clock makes when it is working **3** (*BrE, informal*) a moment **4** a small animal with eight legs, like an insect, that bites humans and animals and sucks their blood ➲ picture on **page 29**

ticket 🔑 /ˈtɪkɪt/ ***noun*** [C] **1** a ~ **(for/to sth)** a piece of paper or card that shows you have paid for a journey, or that allows you to enter a theatre, cinema, etc.: *two tickets for the Cup Final* ◇ *a single/return ticket to London* ◇ *a ticket office/machine/collector* ➲ look at **season ticket** **2** a piece of paper or a label in a shop that shows the price, size, etc. of sth that is for sale **3** (LAW) an official piece of paper that you get when you have parked illegally or driven too fast telling you that you must pay money as a punishment (**a fine**): *a parking ticket*

IDM **just the job/ticket** → JOB

ˈ**ticket tout** ***noun*** [C] (*BrE*) = TOUT

tickle /ˈtɪkl/ ***verb*** **1** [T] to touch sb lightly with your fingers or with sth soft so that they laugh: *She tickled the baby's toes.* **2** [I,T] to produce or to have an uncomfortable feeling in a part of your body: *My nose tickles/is tickling.* ◇ *The woollen scarf tickled her neck.* **3** [T] (*informal*) to amuse and interest sb: *That joke really tickled me.* ▶ **tickle** ***noun*** [C]

ticklish /ˈtɪklɪʃ/ ***adj.*** if a person is **ticklish**, they laugh when sb touches them in a sensitive place: *Are you ticklish?*

tidal /ˈtaɪdl/ ***adj.*** (GEOGRAPHY) connected with the TIDES

ˈ**tidal wave** ***noun*** [C] (GEOGRAPHY) a very large wave in the sea which destroys things when it reaches the land, and is often caused by an EARTHQUAKE (= a sudden movement of the earth's surface) SYN **tsunami**

tidbit /ˈtɪdbɪt/ (*AmE*) = TITBIT

tide¹ /taɪd/ ***noun*** [C] **1** (GEOGRAPHY) the regular change in the level of the sea caused by the moon and the sun. At **high tide** the sea is closer to the land, at **low tide** it is farther away and more of the beach can be seen: *The tide is **coming in /going out**.* ➲ look at **ebb 2** [usually sing.] the way that most people think or feel about sth at a particular time: *It appears that **the tide has turned** in the government's favour.*

tide² /taɪd/ ***verb***
PHR V **tide sb over** to give sb sth to help them through a difficult time

tidy¹ 🔑 /ˈtaɪdi/ ***adj.*** (**tidier**; **tidiest**) **1** (*especially BrE*) arranged with everything in good order: *If you keep your room tidy it is easier to find things.* **2** (used about a person) liking to keep things in good order: *Mark is a very tidy boy.* SYN **neat** OPP **untidy** ▶ **tidily** ***adv.*** ▶ **tidiness** ***noun*** [U]

tidy² 🔑 /ˈtaɪdi/ ***verb*** [I,T] (*pres. part.* **tidying**; *3rd person sing. pres.* **tidies**; *pt, pp* **tidied**) ~ (**sb/sth/yourself**) (**up**) to make sb/sth/yourself look in order and well arranged: *We must tidy this room up before the visitors arrive.*
PHR V **tidy sth away** to put sth into the drawer, cupboard, etc. where it is kept so that it cannot be seen

tie¹ 🔑 /taɪ/ ***noun*** [C] **1** (*AmE also* **necktie**) a long thin piece of cloth worn round the neck, especially by men, with a knot at the front. A tie is usually worn with a shirt: *a striped silk tie* ➲ look at **bow tie 2** [usually pl.] a strong connection between people or organizations: *personal/emotional ties* ◇ *family ties* **3** something that limits your freedom **4** a situation in a game or competition in which two or more teams or players get the same score: *There was a tie for first place.* **5** (MUSIC) a curved line written over notes of the same PITCH (= how high or low a note is) to show that they should be played or sung as one note ➲ picture at **music**

tie² 🔑 /taɪ/ ***verb*** (*pres. part.* **tying**; *3rd person sing. pres.* **ties**; *pt, pp* **tied**) **1** [T] to fasten sb/sth or fix sb/sth in position with rope, string, etc.; to make a knot in sth: *The prisoner was tied to a chair.* ◇ *Kay tied her hair back with a ribbon.* ◇ *to tie sth in a knot* ◇ *to tie your shoelaces* OPP **untie 2** [T] ~ **sb** (**to sth/to doing sth**) (usually passive) to limit sb's freedom and make them unable to do everything they want to: *I don't want to be tied to staying in this country permanently.* **3** [I] ~ (**with sb**) (**for sth**) to have the same number of points as another player or team at the end of a game or competition: *England tied with Italy for third place.*
IDM **your hands are tied** → HAND¹
PHR V **tie sb/yourself down** to limit sb's/your freedom: *Having young children really ties you down.*
tie in (**with sth**) to agree with other facts or information that you have; to match: *The new evidence seems to tie in with your theory.*
tie sb/sth up 1 to fix sb/sth in position with rope, string, etc.: *The dog was tied up in the back garden.* **2** (usually passive) to keep sb busy: *Mr Jones is tied up in a meeting.*

tier /tɪə(r)/ ***noun*** [C] one of a number of levels

tiger /ˈtaɪɡə(r)/ ***noun*** [C] a large wild cat that has yellow fur with black lines (**stripes**). **Tigers** live in parts of Asia. ❶ A female **tiger** is called a **tigress** and a baby is called a **cub**. ➲ picture at **lion**

tight 🔑 /taɪt/ ***adj.***, ***adv.*** **1** fixed firmly in position and difficult to move or remove: *a tight knot* ◇ *Keep a **tight grip/hold** on this rope.* ◇ ***Hold tight** so that you don't fall off.* **2** (used about clothes) fitting very closely in a way that is often uncomfortable: *These shoes hurt. They're too tight.* ◇ *a tight-fitting skirt* OPP **loose 3** controlled very strictly and firmly: *Security is very tight at the airport.* **4** stretched or pulled hard so that it cannot be stretched further: *The rope was stretched tight.* **5** not having much free time or space: *My schedule this week is very tight.* **6 -tight** (used to form compound adjectives) not allowing sth to get in or out: *an airtight/watertight container* ▶ **tightness** ***noun*** [U]

tighten /ˈtaɪtn/ ***verb*** [I,T] ~ (**sth**) (**up**) to become or to make sth tight or tighter: *His grip on her arm tightened.* ◇ *He tightened the screws as far as they would go.*
IDM **tighten your belt** to spend less money because you have less than usual available
PHR V **tighten up (on) sth** to cause sth to become stricter: *to tighten up security/a law*

tightly 🔑 /ˈtaɪtli/ ***adv.*** closely and firmly; in a tight manner: *Her eyes were tightly closed.* ◇ *He held on tightly to her arm.*

tightrope /ˈtaɪtrəʊp/ ***noun*** [C] a rope or wire that is stretched high above the ground on which people walk, especially as a form of entertainment

tights /taɪts/ (*AmE* **pantyhose**) ***noun*** [pl.] a piece of thin clothing, usually worn by women, that fits tightly from the waist over the legs and feet: *a pair of tights* ➲ look at **stocking**

tilapia /tɪˈleɪpiə; -ˈlæpiə/ ***noun*** [C] an African fish that lives in fresh water and that we can eat

tilde /ˈtɪldə/ ***noun*** [C] (LANGUAGE) the mark (~) placed over letters in some languages and some vowels in the International Phonetic Alphabet to show how they should be pronounced, as in *España*, *São Paulo* and *croissant* /ˈkrwæsɒ̃/

tile /taɪl/ ***noun*** [C] one of the flat, square objects that are arranged in rows to cover roofs, floors, bathroom walls, etc. ➲ picture at **building** ▶ **tile** ***verb*** [T]: *a tiled bathroom*

till /tɪl/ ***verb*** [T] (*old-fashioned*) (AGRICULTURE) to prepare and use land for growing crops

till¹ 🔑 /tɪl/ (*informal*) = UNTIL

till² /tɪl/ (*also* **ˈcash register**) ***noun*** [C] the machine or drawer where money is kept in a shop, etc.: *Please pay at the till.*

tilt /tɪlt/ ***verb*** [I,T] to move, or make sth move, into a position with one end or side higher than the other: *The front seats of the car tilt forward.* ◇ *She tilted her head to one side.* ▶ **tilt** ***noun*** [sing.]

timber /ˈtɪmbə(r)/ ***noun*** **1** (*especially AmE* **lumber**) [U] wood that is going to be used for building **2** [C] a large piece of wood: *roof timbers*

timbre /ˈtæmbə(r)/ ***noun*** [C] (*formal*) (MUSIC) the quality of sound that is produced by a particular voice or musical instrument

time¹ 🔑 /taɪm/ ***noun*** **1** [U, sing.] a period of minutes, hours, days, etc.: *As time passed and there was still no news, we got more worried.* ◇ *You're **wasting time** – get on with your work!* ◇ *I'll go by car to **save time**.* ◇ *free/spare time* ◇ *We haven't got time to stop now.* ◇ *I've been waiting **a long time**.* ◇ *Learning a language **takes time**.* **2** [U, C] ~ (**to do sth**); ~ (**for sth**) the time in hours and minutes shown on a clock; the moment when sth happens or should happen: *What's the time?/What time is it?* ◇ *Can you tell me the times of trains to Bristol, please?* ◇ *It's time to go home.* ◇ ***By the time** I get home, Alex will have cooked the dinner.* ◇ ***This time tomorrow** I'll be on the plane.* ◇ *It's time for lunch.* **3** [U, sing.] a system for measuring time in a particular part of the world: *eleven o'clock **local time*** **4** [C] an occasion when you do sth or when sth happens: *I phoned them three times.* ◇ *I'll do it better* ***next time.*** ◇ ***Last time*** *I saw him, he looked ill.* ◇ ***How many times*** *have I told you not to touch that?* **5** [C] an event or an occasion that you experience in a certain way: ***Have a good time*** *tonight.* ◇ *We had a terrible time at the hospital.* **6** [C] a period in the past; a part of history: *In old times, few people could read.* ◇ *The 19th century was a time of great industrial change.* **7** [C,U] the number of minutes, etc., taken to complete a race or an event: *What was his time in the hundred metres?*

IDM **(and) about time (too); (and) not before time** (*spoken*) used to say that sth should already have happened

ahead of your time → AHEAD

all the time/the whole time during the period that sb was doing sth or that sth was happening: *I searched everywhere for my keys and they were in the door all the time.*

at the same time → SAME

at a time on each occasion: *The lift can hold six people at a time.* ◇ *She ran down the stairs two at a time.*

at one time in the past; previously

at the time at a particular moment or period in the past; then: *I agreed at the time but later changed my mind.*

at times sometimes; occasionally: *At times I wish we'd never moved house.*

before your time before you were born

behind the times not modern or fashionable

bide your time → BIDE

buy time → BUY[1]

for the time being just for the present; not for long

from time to time sometimes; not often

give sb a hard time → HARD[1]

have a hard time doing sth → HARD[1]

have no time for sb/sth to not like sb/sth: *I have no time for lazy people.*

have the time of your life to enjoy yourself very much

in the course of time → COURSE

in good time early; at the right time

in the nick of time → NICK[1]

in time (for sth/to do sth) not late; with enough time to be able to do sth: *Don't worry. We'll get to the station in time for your train.*

it's about/high time (*spoken*) used to say that you think sb should do sth very soon: *It's about time you told him what's going on.*

kill time, an hour, etc. → KILL[1]

once upon a time → ONCE

on time not too late or too early; PUNCTUAL: *The train left the station on time.*

one at a time → ONE[1]

take your time to do sth without hurrying

tell the time → TELL

time after time, time and (time) again again and again; repeatedly

time² /taɪm/ ***verb*** [T] **1** (often passive) to arrange to do sth or arrange for sth to happen at a particular time: *Their request was badly timed* (= it came at the wrong time). ◇ *She timed her arrival for shortly after three.* **2** to measure how long sb/sth takes: *Try timing yourself when you write your essay.*

'time-consuming ***adj.*** that takes or needs a lot of time

timekeeper /'taɪmkiːpə(r)/ ***noun*** [C] a person who records the time that is spent doing sth, for example at work or at a sports event

'time lag = LAG²

timeless /'taɪmləs/ ***adj.*** (*formal*) that does not seem to be changed by time or affected by changes in fashion

'time limit ***noun*** [C] a time during which sth must be done: *We have to* ***set a time limit*** *for the work.*

timeline /'taɪmlaɪn/ ***noun*** [C] a horizontal line that is used to represent time, with the past towards the left and the future towards the right

timely /'taɪmli/ ***adj.*** happening at exactly the right time

timeout /taɪm'aʊt/ ***noun*** [C] (*AmE*) (SPORT) a short period of rest during a sports game

timer /'taɪmə(r)/ ***noun*** [C] a person or machine that measures time: *an oven timer*

times¹ /taɪmz/ ***prep.*** (*symbol* ×) (MATHEMATICS) used when you are multiplying one figure by another: *Three times four is twelve.*

times² /taɪmz/ ***noun*** [pl.] used for comparing things: *Tea is* ***three times as /more*** *expensive in Spain as/than in England.*

timeshare /'taɪmʃeə(r)/ ***noun*** (TOURISM) **1** (*also* **'time-sharing**) [U] an arrangement in which several people own a holiday home together and each uses it at a different time of the year: *timeshare apartments* **2** [C] a holiday home that you own in this way: *They have a timeshare in Italy.*

'time signature ***noun*** [C] (MUSIC) a sign at the start of a piece of music, usually in the form of numbers, showing the number of beats in each BAR (= each of the equal units of time into which music is divided) ➲ picture at **music**

timetable 🔑 /'taɪmteɪbl/ (*AmE* **schedule**) ***noun*** [C] a list that shows the times at which sth happens: *a bus/train/school timetable*

'time zone ***noun*** [C] (GEOGRAPHY) one of the 24 areas that the world is divided into, each with its own time that is one hour earlier than that of the **time zone** immediately to the east

timid /'tɪmɪd/ ***adj.*** easily frightened; shy and nervous ▶ **timidity** ***noun*** [U] ▶ **timidly** ***adv.***

timing /'taɪmɪŋ/ ***noun*** [U] **1** the time when sth is planned to happen: *The manager was very careful about the timing of his announcement.* **2** the skill of doing sth at exactly the right time: *The timing of her speech was perfect.*

timpani /'tɪmpəni/ ***noun*** [pl.] (MUSIC) a set of large metal drums (also called KETTLEDRUMS) ▶ **timpanist** /-nɪst/ ***noun*** [C]

tin 🔑 /tɪn/ ***noun*** **1** [U] (*symbol* **Sn**) (CHEMISTRY) a soft silver-white metal that is often mixed with other metals ❶ For more information on the periodic table of elements, look at pages R34-5.
2 (*also* ˌ**tin 'can**; *especially AmE* **can**) [C] a closed metal container in which food, paint, etc. is stored and sold; the contents of one of these containers: *a tin of peas/beans/soup* ◇ *a tin of paint/varnish* **3** [C] a metal container with a lid for keeping food in: *a biscuit/cake tin* ▶ **tinned** ***adj.***: *tinned peaches/peas/soup*

tinfoil /'tɪnfɔɪl/ = FOIL¹

tinge /tɪndʒ/ ***noun*** [C, usually sing.] a small amount of a colour or a feeling: *a tinge of sadness* ▶ **tinged** ***adj.*** ~ **(with sth)**: *Her joy at leaving was tinged with regret.*

tingle /'tɪŋgl/ ***verb*** [I] (used about a part of the body) to feel as if a lot of small sharp points are pushing into it: *His cheeks tingled as he came in from the cold.* ▶ **tingle** ***noun*** [C, usually sing.]: *a tingle of excitement/anticipation/fear*

tinker /'tɪŋkə(r)/ ***verb*** [I] ~ **(with sth)** to try to repair or improve sth without having the proper skill or knowledge

tinkle /'tɪŋkl/ ***verb*** [I] to make a light high ringing sound, like that of a small bell ▶ **tinkle** ***noun*** [C, usually sing.]

tinnitus /'tɪnɪtəs/ ***noun*** [U] (HEALTH) an unpleasant condition in which sb hears ringing in their ears

'tin-opener (*especially AmE* **can-opener**) ***noun*** [C] a tool that you use for opening a tin of food

tinsel /'tɪnsl/ ***noun*** [U] long strings of shiny coloured paper, used as a decoration to hang on a Christmas tree

tint /tɪnt/ ***noun*** [C] a shade or a small amount of a colour: *white paint with a pinkish tint* ▶ **tint** ***verb*** [T]: *tinted glasses* ◇ *She had her hair tinted.*

tiny 🔑 /'taɪni/ ***adj.*** (**tinier**; **tiniest**) very small: *the baby's tiny fingers*

tip¹ 🔑 /tɪp/ ***noun*** [C] **1** the thin or pointed end of sth: *the tips of your toes/fingers* ◇ *the tip of your nose* ◇ *the southernmost tip of South America* **2** a ~ **(on/for sth/doing sth)** a small piece of useful advice about sth practical: *useful tips on how to save money* **3** a small amount of extra money that you give to sb who serves you, for example in a restaurant: *to leave a tip for the waiter* ◇ *I gave the porter a $5 tip.* **4** (*BrE*) (*also* **'rubbish tip**) a place where you can take rubbish and leave it SYN **dump 5** (*BrE, informal*) a place that is very dirty or untidy

IDM **(have sth) on the tip of your tongue** to be sure you know sth but to be unable to remember it for the moment

the tip of the iceberg only a small part of a much larger problem

tip² 🔑 /tɪp/ ***verb*** (**tipping**; **tipped**) **1** [I,T] ~ **(sth) (up)** to move so that one side is higher than the other; to make sth move in this way: *When I stood up, the bench tipped up and the person on the other end fell off.* **2** [T] to make sth come out of a container by holding or lifting it at an angle: *Tip the dirty water down the drain.* ◇ *The child tipped all the toys onto the floor.* **3** [I,T] to give a WAITER, etc. a small amount of extra money (in addition to the normal charge) to thank them: *She tipped the taxi driver generously.* **4** [T] ~ **sb/sth (as sth/to do sth)** to think or say that sb/sth is likely to do sth: *This horse is tipped to win the race.* ◇ *He is widely tipped as the next Prime Minister.*

PHR V **tip sb off** to give sb secret information

tip (sth) up/over to fall or turn over; to make sth do this: *An enormous wave crashed into the little boat and it tipped over.*

'tip-off ***noun*** [C] (LAW) secret information that sb gives, for example to the police, about an illegal activity that is going to happen: *Acting on a tip-off, the police raided the house.*

Tippex™ /'tɪpeks/ ***noun*** [U] (*BrE*) a liquid, usually white, that you use to cover mistakes that you make when you are writing or typing, and that you can write on top of; a type of CORRECTION FLUID ▶ **tippex** ***verb*** [T] ~ **sth (out)**: *I tippexed out the mistakes.*

tiptoe¹ /'tɪptəʊ/ ***noun***

IDM **on tiptoe** standing or walking on the ends of your toes with your heels off the ground, in order not to make any noise or to reach sth high up

tiptoe² /'tɪptəʊ/ ***verb*** [I] to walk on your toes with your heels off the ground

tire¹ 🔑 /'taɪə(r)/ ***verb*** [I,T] to feel that you need to rest or sleep; to make sb feel like this

PHR V **tire of sth/sb** to become bored or not interested in sth/sb any more

tire sb/yourself out to make sb/yourself very tired; to EXHAUST sb/yourself: *The long walk tired us all out.*

tire² 🔑 (*AmE*) = TYRE

tired 🔑 /'taɪəd/ ***adj.*** feeling that you need to rest or sleep: *She was tired after a hard day's work.* ◇ *I was completely **tired out*** (= exhausted) *after all that.* ▶ **tiredness** ***noun*** [U]

IDM **be tired of sb/sth/doing sth** to be bored with or annoyed by sb/sth/doing sth: *I'm tired of this game. Let's play something else.* ◇ *I'm **sick and tired** of listening to the same thing again and again.*

tireless /'taɪələs/ ***adj.*** putting a lot of hard work and energy into sth over a long period of time without stopping or losing interest

tiresome /'taɪəsəm/ ***adj.*** (*formal*) that makes you angry or bored; annoying

tiring 🔑 /'taɪərɪŋ/ ***adj.*** making you want to rest or sleep: *a tiring journey/job*

tissue /'tɪʃuː; 'tɪsjuː/ ***noun*** **1** [U] (*also* **tissues** [pl.]) (ANATOMY, BIOLOGY) the mass of cells that form the bodies of humans, animals and plants: *muscle/brain/nerve/scar tissue* ◇ *Radiation can destroy the body's tissues.* **2** [C] a thin piece of soft paper that you use to clean your nose and throw away after you have used it: *a box of tissues* **3** (*also* **'tissue paper**) [U] thin soft paper that you use for putting around things that may break

tit /tɪt/ ***noun*** [C] a small European bird that eats insects and seeds. There are several types of **tit**.

IDM **tit for tat** something unpleasant that you do to sb because they have done sth to you

titanium /tɪ'teɪniəm/ ***noun*** [U] (*symbol* **Ti**) (CHEMISTRY) a hard silver-grey metal that is combined with other metals to make strong, light materials that do not easily RUST (= react with air over a period of time) ❶ For more information on the periodic table of elements, look at pages R34-5.

titbit /'tɪtbɪt/ (*AmE* **tidbit**) ***noun*** [C] **1** a small but very nice piece of food **2** an interesting piece of information

title 🔑 /'taɪtl/ ***noun*** [C] **1** (ARTS AND MEDIA, LITERATURE) the name of a book, play, film, picture, etc.: *I know the author's name but I can't remember the title of the book.* **2** a word that shows a person's position, profession, etc.: *'Lord', 'Doctor', 'Reverend', 'Mrs' and 'General' are all titles.* **3** the position of being the winner of a competition, especially a sports competition: *Sue is playing this match to defend her title* (= to remain champion).

titled /'taɪtld/ ***adj.*** having a word, for example 'Duke', 'Lady', etc. before your name that shows that your family has an important position in society

'title-holder ***noun*** [C] the person or team who won a sports competition the last time it took place; the current CHAMPION

'title role ***noun*** [C] (ARTS AND MEDIA, LITERATURE) the main character in a film, book, etc. whose name is the same as the title

titration /taɪ'treɪʃn/ ***noun*** [U] (CHEMISTRY) the process of finding out how much of a particular substance is in a liquid by measuring how much of another substance is needed to react with it

titter /'tɪtə(r)/ ***verb*** [I] to laugh quietly, especially in an embarrassed or nervous way ▶ **titter** ***noun*** [C]

'T-junction ***noun*** [C] a place where two roads join to form the shape of a T

tn ***abbr.*** (*AmE*) = T²

TNT /ˌtiː en 'tiː/ ***noun*** [U] a highly EXPLOSIVE substance

to ⊶ /tə; *before vowels* tu; *strong form* tuː/ ***prep.***, ***adv.*** **1** in the direction of; as far as: *She's going to London.* ◇ *Turn to the left.* ◇ *Pisa is to the west of Florence.* ◇ *He has gone to school.* **2** used to show the end or limit of a series of things or period of time: ***from*** *Monday* ***to*** *Friday* ◇ *from beginning to end* **3** used to show the person or thing that receives sth: *Give that to me.* ◇ *I am very grateful to my parents.* ◇ *What have you done to your hair?* ◇ *Sorry, I didn't realize you were talking to me.* **4** (nearly) touching sth; directed towards sth: *He put his hands to his ears.* ◇ *They sat back to back.* ◇ *She made no reference to her personal problems.* **5** reaching a particular state: *The meat was cooked to perfection.* ◇ *His speech reduced her to tears* (=made her cry). **6** used to introduce the second part of a comparison: *I prefer theatre to opera.* **7** (used for expressing quantity) for each unit of money, measurement, etc.: *How many dollars are there to the euro?* **8** (used to say what time it is) before: *It's ten to three* (=ten minutes before three o'clock). **9** used to express sb's opinion or feeling about sth: *To me, it was the wrong decision.* ◇ *It sounded like a good idea to me.* ◇ *I don't think our friendship means anything to him.* **10** used for expressing a reaction or attitude to sth: *To my surprise, I saw two strangers coming out of my house.* ◇ *His paintings aren't really to my taste.* **11** used with verbs to form the INFINITIVE: *I want to go home now.* ◇ *Don't forget to write.* ◇ *I didn't know what to do.* **12** /tuː/ (used about a door) in or into a closed position: *Push the door to.*

IDM **to and fro** backwards and forwards

toad /təʊd/ ***noun*** [C] a small cold-blooded animal that has a rough skin and lives both on land and in water ➲ picture on **page 29**

toadstool /'təʊdstuːl/ ***noun*** [C] a type of small wild plant (**a fungus**) that is usually poisonous, with a round top and a thin supporting part ➲ look at **mushroom**, **fungus**

toast /təʊst/ ***noun*** **1** [U] a thin piece of bread that is heated on both sides to make it brown: *a piece/slice of toast* **2** [C] **a ~ (to sb/sth)** an occasion at which a group of people wish sb happiness, success, etc., by drinking a glass of wine, etc. at the same time: *I'd like to* ***propose a toast to*** *the bride and groom.* ➲ look at **drink** ▶ **toast** ***verb*** [T]

toaster /'təʊstə(r)/ ***noun*** [C] an electrical machine for making bread turn brown by heating it on both sides

tobacco /tə'bækəʊ/ ***noun*** [U] the substance that people smoke in cigarettes and pipes (the dried leaves of the **tobacco** plant)

tobacconist /tə'bækənɪst/ ***noun*** **1** [C] a person who sells cigarettes, matches, etc. **2** (*also* **the tobacconist's**) [sing.] a shop where you can buy cigarettes, matches, etc.

toboggan /tə'bɒgən/ ***noun*** [C] a type of flat board with flat pieces of metal underneath, that people use for travelling down hills on snow for fun SYN **sledge** ➲ look at **bobsleigh**

toccata /tə'kɑːtə/ ***noun*** [C] (MUSIC) a piece of music for a keyboard instrument which includes difficult passages designed to show the player's skill

today ⊶ /tə'deɪ/ ***noun*** [U], ***adv.*** **1** (on) this day: *Today is Monday.* ◇ *What shall we do today?* ◇ *School ends* ***a week today*** (=on this day next week). ◇ *Where is today's paper?* **2** (in) the present age; these days: *Young people today have far more freedom.* SYN **nowadays**

toddle /'tɒdl/ ***verb*** [I] **1** to walk with short steps like a very young child **2** (*informal*) to walk or go somewhere

toddler /'tɒdlə(r)/ ***noun*** [C] a young child who has only just learnt to walk

toe[1] ⊶ /təʊ/ ***noun*** [C] **1** (ANATOMY) one of the small parts like fingers at the end of each foot: *the big/little toe* (=the largest/smallest toe) ➲ picture on **page 80** **2** the part of a sock, shoe, etc. that covers your toes

toe[2] /təʊ/ ***verb*** (*pres. part.* **toeing**; *pt, pp* **toed**)

IDM **toe the (party) line** to do what sb in authority tells you to do, even if you do not agree with them

TOEFL™ /'təʊfl/ ***abbr.*** (EDUCATION, LANGUAGE) **Test of English as a Foreign Language**; a test of a person's level of English that is taken in order to go to a university in the US

TOEIC™ /'təʊɪk/ ***abbr.*** (EDUCATION, LANGUAGE) **Test of English for International Communication**; a test that measures your ability to read and understand English if it is not your first language

toenail /'təʊneɪl/ ***noun*** [C] one of the hard flat parts that cover the end of your toes ➲ picture on **page 80**

toffee /'tɒfi/ ***noun*** [C,U] a hard sticky sweet that is made by cooking sugar and butter together

toga /'təʊgə/ ***noun*** [C] (HISTORY) a loose outer piece of clothing worn by the citizens of ancient Rome

together[1] ⊶ /tə'geðə(r)/ ***adv.*** **1** with or near each other: *Can we have lunch together?* ◇ *They walked home together.* ◇ *I'll get all my things together tonight because I want to leave early.* ◇ *Stand with your feet together.* **2** so that two or more things are mixed or joined to each other: *Mix the butter and sugar together.* ◇ *Tie the two ends together.* ◇ *Add these numbers together to find the total.* **3** at the same time: *Don't all talk together.*

IDM **get your act together** → ACT[2]

together with in addition to; as well as: *I enclose my order together with a cheque for £15.*

together[2] /tə'geðə(r)/ ***adj.*** (*informal*) (used about a person) organized, capable: *I'm not very together this morning.*

togetherness /'tə'geðənəs/ ***noun*** [U] a feeling of friendship

toggle /'tɒgl/ ***noun*** [C] **1** a short piece of wood, plastic, etc. that is put through a LOOP of thread to fasten sth, such as a coat or bag, instead of a button **2** (*also* **'toggle switch**) (COMPUTING) a key on a computer that you press to change from one style or operation to another, and back again

toggle[2] ***verb*** [I,T] (COMPUTING) to press a key or set of keys on a computer keyboard in order to turn a feature on or off, or to move from one program, etc. to another: *He toggled between the two windows.*

toil /tɔɪl/ ***verb*** [I] (*formal*) to work very hard or for a long time at sth ▶ **toil** ***noun*** [U]

toilet ⊶ /'tɔɪlət/ ***noun*** [C] a large bowl with a seat, connected to a water pipe, that you use when you need to get rid of waste material from your body; the room containing this: *I need to* ***go to the toilet*** (=use the toilet).

'toilet bag (*also* **sponge bag**) ***noun*** [C] a bag that you use when travelling to carry TOILETRIES

ˈ**toilet paper** (*also* ˈ**toilet tissue**) ***noun*** [U] soft, thin paper that you use to clean yourself after going to the toilet

toiletries /ˈtɔɪlətriz/ ***noun*** [pl.] things such as soap or TOOTHPASTE that you use for washing, cleaning your teeth, etc.

ˈ**toilet roll** ***noun*** [C] a long piece of toilet paper rolled round a tube

token[1] /ˈtəʊkən/ ***noun*** [C] **1** a round piece of metal, plastic, etc. that you use instead of money to operate some machines or as a form of payment **2** (*BrE*) a piece of paper that you can use to buy sth of a certain value in a particular shop. **Tokens** are often given as presents: *a £10 book/CD/gift token* ➲ look at **voucher 3** something that represents or is a symbol of sth: *Please accept this gift **as a token of** our gratitude.*

token[2] /ˈtəʊkən/ ***adj.*** (only *before* a noun) **1** done, chosen, etc. in a very small quantity, and only in order not to be criticized: *There is a token woman on the board of directors.* **2** small, but done or given to show that you are serious about sth and will keep a promise or an agreement: *a token payment*

told past tense, past participle of **tell**

tolerable /ˈtɒlərəbl/ ***adj.*** **1** quite good, but not of the best quality **2** of a level that you can accept or deal with, although unpleasant or painful: *Drugs can reduce the pain to a tolerable level.*
OPP **intolerable**

tolerant /ˈtɒlərənt/ ***adj.*** ~ **(of/towards sb/sth)** able to allow or accept sth that you do not like or agree with **OPP** **intolerant** ▶ **tolerance** *noun* [U] ~ **(of/for sb/sth)**: *religious/racial tolerance* **OPP** **intolerance**

tolerate /ˈtɒləreɪt/ ***verb*** [T] **1** to allow or accept sth that you do not like or agree with: *In a democracy we must tolerate opinions that are different from our own.* **2** to accept or be able to deal with sb/sth unpleasant without complaining: *The noise was more than she could tolerate.* ▶ **toleration** /ˌtɒləˈreɪʃn/ ***noun*** [U]

toll /təʊl/ ***noun*** **1** [C] money that you pay to use a road or bridge: *motorway tolls* ◇ *a toll bridge* **2** [C, usually sing.] the amount of damage done or the number of people who were killed or injured by sth: *The official death toll has now reached 5000.*
IDM **take a heavy toll/take its toll (on sth)** to cause great loss, damage, suffering, etc.

tom /tɒm/ = TOMCAT

tomato 🔑 /təˈmɑːtəʊ/ ***noun*** [C] (*pl.* **tomatoes**) a soft red fruit that is often eaten without being cooked in salads, or cooked as a vegetable: *tomato juice/soup/sauce*

tomb /tuːm/ ***noun*** [C] a large place, usually built of stone under the ground, where the body of an important person is buried: *the tombs of the Pharaohs* ➲ look at **grave**

tomboy /ˈtɒmbɔɪ/ ***noun*** [C] a young girl who likes the games and activities that are traditionally considered to be for boys

tombstone /ˈtuːmstəʊn/ ***noun*** [C] a large flat stone that lies on or stands at one end of a GRAVE (= the place where a person is buried) and shows the name, dates, etc. of the dead person ➲ look at **gravestone, headstone**

tomcat /ˈtɒmkæt/ (*also* **tom**) ***noun*** [C] a male cat

tomorrow 🔑 /təˈmɒrəʊ/ ***noun*** [U], ***adv.*** **1** (on) the day after today: *Today is Friday so tomorrow is Saturday.* ◇ *See you tomorrow.* ◇ *I'm going to bed. I've got to get up early tomorrow morning.* ◇ *a week tomorrow* (= a week from tomorrow) **2** the future: *The schoolchildren of today are tomorrow's workers.*

ton 🔑 /tʌn/ ***noun*** **1** [C] a measure of weight; 2240 pounds **2 tons** [pl.] (*informal*) a lot: *I've got tons of homework to do.*

tone[1] 🔑 /təʊn/ ***noun*** **1** [C,U] the quality of a sound or of sb's voice, especially expressing a particular emotion: *'Do you know each other?' she asked in a casual tone of voice.* **2** [sing.] the general quality or style of sth: *The tone of the meeting was optimistic.* **3** [C] a shade of a colour: *warm tones of red and orange* **4** [C] a sound that you hear on the telephone: *Please speak after the tone* (= an instruction on an answering machine). **5** [C] (MUSIC) one of the longer steps between the notes in a musical scale, for example between C and D, or between E and F♯
➲ look at **semitone**

tone[2] /təʊn/ ***verb*** [T] ~ **sth (up)** to make your muscles, skin, etc. firmer, especially by doing exercise
PHR V **tone sth down** to change sth that you have said, written, etc., to make it less likely to offend

ˌ**tone-ˈdeaf** ***adj.*** (MUSIC) not able to sing or hear the difference between notes in music

ˈ**tone poem** ***noun*** [C] (MUSIC) a piece of music that is intended to describe a place or express an idea

tongs /tɒŋz/ ***noun*** [pl.] a tool that looks like a pair of scissors but that you use for holding or picking things up ➲ picture at **laboratory**

tongue 🔑 /tʌŋ/ ***noun*** **1** [C] (ANATOMY) the soft part inside your mouth that you can move. You use your tongue for speaking, tasting things, etc. ➲ picture on **page 80** **2** [C,U] the tongue of some animals, cooked and eaten **3** [C] (*formal*) (LANGUAGE) a language: *your **mother tongue*** (= the language you learned as a child)
IDM **on the tip of your tongue** → TIP[1]
put/stick your tongue out to put your tongue outside your mouth as a rude sign to sb
a slip of the tongue → SLIP[2]
(with) tongue in cheek done or said as a joke; not intended seriously

ˈ**tongue-tied** ***adj.*** not saying anything because you are shy or nervous

ˈ**tongue-twister** ***noun*** [C] (LANGUAGE) a phrase or sentence with many similar sounds that is difficult to say correctly when you are speaking quickly

tonic /ˈtɒnɪk/ ***noun*** **1** (*also* ˈ**tonic water**) [U, C] a type of water with bubbles in it and a rather bitter taste that is often added to alcoholic drinks: *a gin and tonic* **2** [C,U] a medicine or sth you do that makes you feel stronger, healthier, etc., especially when you are very tired: *A relaxing holiday is a wonderful tonic.*

tonight 🔑 /təˈnaɪt/ ***noun*** [U], ***adv.*** (on) the evening or night of today: *Tonight is the last night of our holiday.* ◇ *What's on TV tonight?* ◇ *We are staying with friends tonight and travelling home tomorrow.*

tonne 🔑 /tʌn/ (*also* ˌ**metric ˈton**) ***noun*** [C] (*pl.* **tonnes** or **tonne**) a measure of weight; 1000 kilograms ➲ look at **ton**

tonsil /ˈtɒnsl/ ***noun*** [C] (ANATOMY) one of the two soft lumps in your throat at the back of your mouth: *She had to **have her tonsils out*** (= removed in a medical operation). ➲ picture on **page 80**

tonsillitis /ˌtɒnsəˈlaɪtɪs/ ***noun*** [U] (HEALTH) an illness in which the TONSILS become very sore and swollen

too 🔑 /tuː/ ***adv.*** **1** (used before adjectives and adverbs) more than is good, allowed, possible, etc.: *These boots are too small.* ◇ *It's far too cold to go out without a coat.* ◇ *It's too long a journey for you to make alone.* **2** (not with negative statements) in addition; also: *Red is my favourite colour but I like blue, too.* ◇ *Phil thinks you're right and I do too.* **3** used to add sth which makes a situation even worse: *Her purse was stolen. And on her birthday too.* **4** (usually used in negative sentences) very: *The weather is not too bad today.*

took past tense of **take**

tool

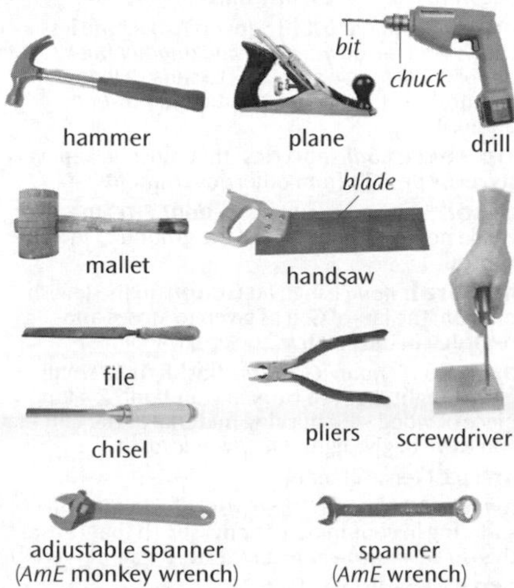

tool 🔑 /tuːl/ ***noun*** [C] a piece of equipment such as a hammer, that you hold in your hand(s) and use to do a particular job: *Hammers, screwdrivers and saws are all carpenter's tools.* ◇ ***garden tools*** ◇ ***a tool kit*** (=a set of tools in a box or a bag) =TOOLBOX

RELATED VOCABULARY

Tools

A **tool** is usually something you can hold in your hand, for example a spanner or hammer.

An **implement** is often used outside, for example for farming or gardening.

A **machine** has moving parts and works by electricity, with an engine, etc.

An **instrument** is often used for technical or delicate work: *a dentist's instruments.*

A **device** is a more general word for a piece of equipment that you consider to be useful and that is designed to do one particular task: *The machine has a safety device which switches the power off if there is a fault.*

toolbar /ˈtuːlbɑː(r)/ ***noun*** [C] (COMPUTING) a row of symbols on a computer screen that show the different things that the computer can do

toolbox /ˈtuːlbɒks/ ***noun*** [C] a box with a lid for keeping tools in

toot /tuːt/ ***noun*** [C] the short high sound that a car horn makes ▶ **toot** ***verb*** [I,T]: *Toot your horn to let them know we're here.*

tooth 🔑 /tuːθ/ ***noun*** [C] (*pl.* **teeth** /tiːθ/) **1** (ANATOMY) one of the hard white things in your mouth that you use for biting: *She's got beautiful teeth.*

tooth

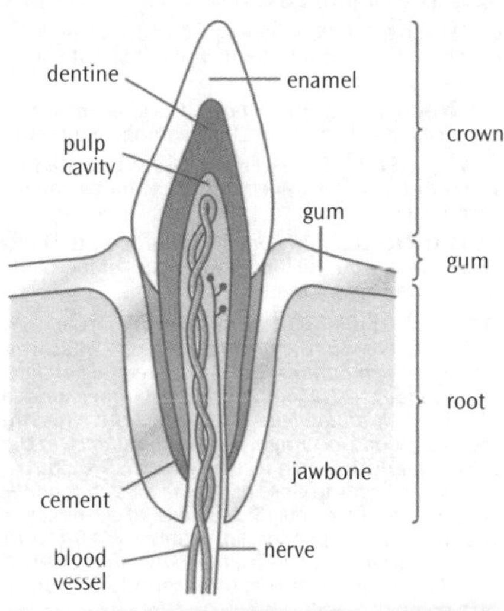

structure of a tooth

tooth

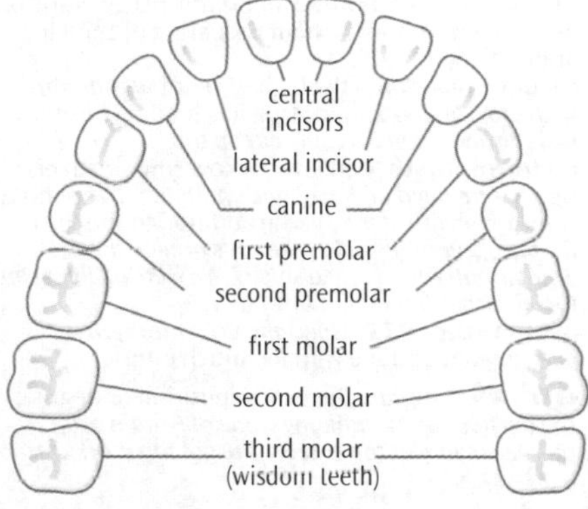

permanent teeth in a human adult

RELATED VOCABULARY

Teeth

You **brush/clean** your teeth with a **toothbrush**. You clean between your teeth with special string called **dental floss**.

If you have **toothache** (=pain in your teeth) or **tooth decay** (=a tooth that has gone bad), you should see a dentist. You might need a **filling**, or the tooth might have to be **taken out/extracted**.

People with no teeth can have **false teeth/ dentures**.

➲ look at **wisdom tooth** **2** one of the long narrow pointed parts of an object such as a COMB

IDM **by the skin of your teeth** → SKIN[1]

gnash your teeth → GNASH

grit your teeth → GRIT[2]
have a sweet tooth → SWEET[1]

toothache /ˈtuːθeɪk/ ***noun*** [U, C, usually sing.] (**HEALTH**) a pain in your tooth or teeth ➲ note at **ache**

toothbrush /ˈtuːθbrʌʃ/ ***noun*** [C] a small brush with a handle that you use for cleaning your teeth

toothpaste /ˈtuːθpeɪst/ ***noun*** [U] a substance that you put on your TOOTHBRUSH and use for cleaning your teeth

toothpick /ˈtuːθpɪk/ ***noun*** [C] a short pointed piece of wood that you use for getting pieces of food out from between your teeth

top[1] 🔑 /tɒp/ ***noun*** **1** [C] the highest part or point of sth: *The flat is **at the top of** the stairs.* ◇ *Snow was falling on the mountain tops.* ◇ *Start reading at the top of the page.* OPP **foot 2** [C] the flat upper surface of sth: *a desk/table/bench top* **3** [sing.] **the ~ (of sth)** the highest or most important position: *to be at the top of your profession* **4** [C] the cover that you put onto sth in order to close it: *Put the tops back on the pens or they will dry out.* **5** [C] a piece of clothing that you wear on the upper part of your body: *a tracksuit/bikini/pyjama top* ◇ *I need a top to match my new skirt.* **6** [C] a child's toy that turns round very quickly on a point
IDM **at the top of your voice** as loudly as possible
get on top of sb (*informal*) to be too much for sb to manage or deal with: *I've got so much work to do. It's really getting on top of me.*
off the top of your head (*informal*) just guessing or using your memory without preparing or thinking about sth first
on top 1 on or onto the highest point: *a mountain with snow on top* **2** in control; in a leading position: *Josie always seems to come out on top.*
on top of sb/sth 1 on, over or covering sb/sth else: *Books were piled on top of one another.* ◇ *The remote control is on top of the TV.* **2** in addition to sb/sth else: *On top of everything else, the car's broken down.* **3** (*informal*) very close to sb/sth: *We were all living on top of each other in that tiny flat.*
over the top; **OTT** (*especially BrE, informal*) exaggerated or done with too much effort

top[2] 🔑 /tɒp/ ***adj.*** highest in position or degree: *the top floor of the building* ◇ *one of Britain's top businessmen* ◇ *at top speed* ◇ *She got top marks for her essay.*

top[3] 🔑 /tɒp/ ***verb*** [T] (**topping**; **topped**) **1** to be higher or greater than a particular amount **2** to be in the highest position on a list because you are the most important, successful, etc. **3 ~ sth (with sth)** (usually passive) to put sth on the top of sth: *cauliflower topped with cheese sauce*
PHR V **top (sth) up** to fill sth that is partly empty

topaz /ˈtəʊpæz/ ***noun*** [C,U] (**GEOLOGY**) a clear yellow precious stone

ˌtop-ˈclass ***adj.*** of the highest quality or standard: *a top-class performance*

ˌtop ˈhat ***noun*** [C] the tall black or grey hat that men sometimes wear on formal occasions

ˌtop-ˈheavy ***adj.*** heavier at the top than the bottom and likely to fall over

topic 🔑 AW /ˈtɒpɪk/ ***noun*** [C] a subject that you talk, write or learn about

topical AW /ˈtɒpɪkl/ ***adj.*** connected with sth that is happening now; that people are interested in at the present time

topless /ˈtɒpləs/ ***adj.***, ***adv.*** (used about a woman) not wearing any clothes on the upper part of the body so that her breasts are not covered

topmost /ˈtɒpməʊst/ ***adj.*** (only *before* a noun) highest: *the topmost branches of the tree*

ˌtop-ˈnotch ***adj.*** (*informal*) excellent; of the highest quality

topography /təˈpɒgrəfi/ ***noun*** [U] (**GEOGRAPHY**) the physical characteristics of an area of land, especially the position of its rivers, mountains, etc.

topping /ˈtɒpɪŋ/ ***noun*** [C,U] something such as cream or a sauce that is put on the top of food to decorate it or make it taste nicer

topple /ˈtɒpl/ ***verb*** **1** [I] **~ (over)** to become less steady and fall down: *Don't add another book to the pile or it will topple over.* **2** [T] to cause a leader of a country, etc. to lose their position of power or authority

ˌtop ˈsecret ***adj.*** (**POLITICS**) that must be kept very secret, especially from other governments

topsoil /ˈtɒpsɔɪl/ ***noun*** [U] (**GEOGRAPHY**) the layer of soil nearest the surface of the ground ➲ look at **subsoil**

the Torah ***noun*** [sing.] (**RELIGION**) (in the Jewish religion) the law of God as given to Moses and recorded in the first five books of the Bible

torch /tɔːtʃ/ ***noun*** [C] **1** (*AmE* **flashlight**) a small electric light that you carry in your hand **2** a long piece of wood with burning material at the end that you carry to give light: *the Olympic torch*

tore past tense of **tear**[2]

torment /ˈtɔːment/ ***noun*** [U, C] great pain and suffering in your mind or body; sb/sth that causes this: *to be **in torment*** ▶ **torment** /tɔːˈment/ ***verb*** [T]

torn past participle of **tear**[2]

tornado /tɔːˈneɪdəʊ/ ***noun*** [C] (*pl.* **tornadoes**) (**GEOGRAPHY**) a violent storm with a very strong wind that blows in a circle ➲ note at **storm**

torpedo /tɔːˈpiːdəʊ/ ***noun*** [C] (*pl.* **torpedoes**) a bomb, shaped like a long narrow tube, that is fired from a SUBMARINE (= a type of ship that travels under the water) and explodes when it hits another ship

torque /tɔːk/ ***noun*** [U] (**PHYSICS**) a force that causes machinery, etc. to turn round (**rotate**): *The more torque an engine has, the bigger the load it can pull in the same gear.*

torrent /ˈtɒrənt/ ***noun*** [C] a strong fast flow of sth, especially water: *The rain was coming down **in torrents**.*

torrential /təˈrenʃl/ ***adj.*** (used about rain) very great in amount

torsion /ˈtɔːʃn/ ***noun*** [U] (**PHYSICS**) the action of TWISTING sth, especially one end of sth while the other end is held fixed

torso /ˈtɔːsəʊ/ ***noun*** [C] (*pl.* **torsos**) the main part of your body, not your head, arms and legs

tort /tɔːt/ ***noun*** [C,U] (**LAW**) something wrong that sb does to sb else that is not criminal, but that can lead to action in a CIVIL court

tortilla /tɔːˈtiːə/ ***noun*** [C] a type of very thin, round Mexican bread made with eggs and flour. It is usually eaten hot and filled with meat, cheese etc.

tortoise /ˈtɔːtəs/ (*AmE* **turtle**) ***noun*** [C] a small animal with a hard shell that moves very slowly. A **tortoise** can pull its head and legs into its shell to protect them. ➲ picture on **page 28**

tortuous /ˈtɔːtʃuəs/ ***adj.*** **1** complicated, not clear and simple **2** (used about a road, etc.) with many bends

torture /ˈtɔːtʃə(r)/ ***noun*** [U, C] **1** the action of causing sb great pain either as a punishment or to make them say or do sth: *His confession was extracted* ***under torture***. **2** mental or physical suffering: *It's torture having to sit here and listen to him complaining for hours.* ▶ **torture** ***verb*** [T]: *Most of the prisoners were tortured into making a confession.* ◇ *She was tortured by the thought that the accident was her fault.* ▶ **torturer** ***noun*** [C]

Tory /ˈtɔːri/ ***noun*** [C], ***adj.*** (*pl.* **Tories**) (POLITICS) a member or supporter of the British Conservative Party; connected with this party: *the Tory Party conference* ➲ note at **party**

toss /tɒs/ ***verb*** **1** [T] to throw sth lightly and carelessly: *Bob opened the letter and tossed the envelope into the bin.* **2** [I,T] to move, or to make sb/sth move up and down or from side to side: *He lay* ***tossing and turning*** *in bed, unable to sleep.* ◇ *The ship was tossed about by huge waves.* **3** [T] to move your head back quickly especially to show you are annoyed or impatient: *I tried to apologize but she just* ***tossed*** *her* ***head*** *and walked away.* **4** [I,T] ~ **(up)** **(for sth)** to throw a coin into the air in order to decide sth, by guessing which side of the coin will land facing upwards: *to toss a coin* ▶ **toss** ***noun*** [C]
IDM **win/lose the toss** to guess correctly/wrongly which side of a coin will face upwards when it lands: *Ms Hingis won the toss and chose to serve first.*

tot¹ /tɒt/ ***noun*** [C] **1** (*informal*) a very small child **2** (*especially BrE*) a small glass of a strong alcoholic drink

tot² /tɒt/ ***verb*** (**totting**; **totted**)
PHR V **tot (sth) up** (*informal*) to add numbers together to form a total

total¹ ⊶ /ˈtəʊtl/ ***adj.*** being the amount after everyone or everything is counted or added together; complete: *What was the total number of people there?* ◇ *a total failure* ◇ *They ate in total silence.*

total² ⊶ /ˈtəʊtl/ ***noun*** [C] the number that you get when you add two or more numbers or amounts together ▶ **total** ***verb*** [T] (**totalling**; **totalled**: *AmE* **totaling**; **totaled**): *His debts totalled more than £10000.*
IDM **in total** when you add two or more numbers or amounts together: *The appeal raised £4 million in total.*

totalitarian /təʊˌtæləˈteəriən/ ***adj.*** (POLITICS) in which there is only one political party that has complete power and control over the people ▶ **totalitarianism** /-ɪzəm/ ***noun*** [U]

totally ⊶ /ˈtəʊtəli/ ***adv.*** completely: *I totally agree with you.*

totter /ˈtɒtə(r)/ ***verb*** [I] to stand or move in a way that is not steady, as if you are going to fall, especially because you are drunk, ill or weak

toucan /ˈtuːkæn/ ***noun*** [C] a tropical American bird with bright feathers and a very large beak

touch¹ ⊶ /tʌtʃ/ ***verb*** **1** [T] to put your hand or fingers onto sb/sth: *Don't touch that plate – it's hot!* ◇ *He touched her gently on the cheek.* ◇ *The police asked us not to touch anything.* **2** [I,T] (used about two or more things, surfaces, etc.) to be or move so close together that there is no space between them: *They were sitting so close that their shoulders touched.* ◇ *This bicycle is too big. My feet don't* ***touch the ground***. **3** [T] to make sb feel sad, sorry for sb, grateful, etc. ➲ look at **touched** **4** [T] (in negative sentences) to be as good as sb/sth in skill, quality, etc.: *He's a much better player than all the others. No one else can touch him.*
IDM **touch wood**; **knock on wood** → WOOD
PHR V **touch down** (used about an aircraft) to land
touch on/upon sth to mention or refer to a subject for only a short time

touch² ⊶ /tʌtʃ/ ***noun*** **1** [C, usually sing.] the action of putting your hands or fingers onto sb/sth: *I felt the touch of her hand on my arm.* **2** [U] the way sth feels when you touch it: *Marble is cold* ***to the touch***. **3** [U] one of the five senses: the ability to feel things and know what they are like by putting your hands or fingers on them: *The* ***sense of touch*** *is very important to blind people.* **4** [C] a small detail that is added to improve sth: *The flowers in our room were* ***a nice touch***. ◇ *She's just* ***putting the finishing touches to*** *the cake.* **5** [sing.] a way or style of doing sth: *She prefers to write her letters by hand for a more* ***personal touch***. **6** [sing.] a ~ **(of sth)** a small amount of sth
IDM **in/out of touch (with sb)** being/not being in contact with sb by speaking or writing to them: *During the year she was abroad, they* ***kept in touch*** *by letter.*
in/out of touch with sth having/not having recent information about sth: *We're out of touch with what's going on.*
lose touch → LOSE
lose your touch → LOSE

touchdown /ˈtʌtʃdaʊn/ ***noun*** **1** [C,U] the moment when a plane or SPACECRAFT lands SYN **landing** **2** [C] (SPORT) (in the game of RUGBY) an act of scoring points by putting the ball down on the area of ground behind the other team's GOAL LINE **3** [C] (SPORT) (in the game of AMERICAN FOOTBALL) an act of scoring points by crossing the other team's GOAL LINE while carrying the ball, or receiving the ball when you are over the other team's GOAL LINE

touched /tʌtʃt/ ***adj.*** (not before a noun) ~ **(by sth)**; ~ **that...** made to feel sad, sorry for sb, grateful, etc.: *We were very touched by the plight of the refugees.* ◇ *I was touched that he offered to help.*

touching /ˈtʌtʃɪŋ/ ***adj.*** that makes you feel sad, sorry for sb, grateful, etc.

touchline /ˈtʌtʃlaɪn/ ***noun*** [C] (SPORT) a line that marks the side of the playing field in football, RUGBY, etc.

ˈtouch screen ***noun*** [C] (COMPUTING) a computer screen which shows information when you touch it

ˈTouch-Tone™ ***adj.*** (used about a telephone or telephone system) producing different sounds when different numbers are pushed

touchy /ˈtʌtʃi/ ***adj.*** **1** ~ **(about sth)** easily upset or made angry: *He's a bit touchy about his weight.* **2** (used about a subject, situation, etc.) that may easily upset people or make them angry: *Don't mention the exam. It's a very touchy subject.*

tough ⊶ /tʌf/ ***adj.*** **1** difficult; having or causing problems: *It will be a tough decision to make.* ◇ *He's had* ***a tough time of it*** (= a lot of problems) *recently.* **2** ~ **(on/with sb/sth)** strict; not feeling sorry for anyone: *The government plans to* ***get tough with*** *people who drink and drive.* ◇ *Don't be too tough on them – they were only trying to help.* **3** strong enough to deal with difficult conditions or situations: *You need to be tough to go climbing in winter.* **4** (used especially about meat) difficult to cut and eat **5** not easily broken, torn or cut; very strong: *a tough pair of boots* **6** (*informal*) ~ **(on sb)** unfortunate for sb in a way that seems unfair: *It's tough on her that she lost her job.* ▶ **toughness** ***noun*** [U]

toughen /ˈtʌfn/ ***verb*** [I,T] ~ **(sb/sth) (up)** to become or to make sb/sth tough

toupee /ˈtuːpeɪ/ *noun* [C] a small section of artificial hair, worn by a man to cover an area of his head where hair no longer grows

tour 🔑 /tʊə(r)/ *noun* **1** [C] a ~ (of/round/around sth) (TOURISM) a journey that you make for pleasure during which you visit many places: *to **go on a** ten-day coach **tour** of/around Scotland ◇ a sightseeing tour* ➲ look at **tour operator** ➲ note at **travel** **2** [C] (TOURISM) a short visit around a city, famous building, etc.: *a **guided tour** round St Paul's Cathedral* **3** [C,U] (MUSIC, SPORT) an official series of visits that singers, musicians, sports players, etc. make to different places to perform, play, etc.: *The band is currently **on tour** in America. ◇ a concert/cricket tour* ▶ **tour** *verb* [I,T]: *We toured southern Spain for three weeks.*

tourism /ˈtʊərɪzəm/ *noun* [U] (SOCIAL STUDIES) the business of providing and arranging holidays and services for people who are visiting a place: *The country's economy relies heavily on tourism.*

tourist 🔑 /ˈtʊərɪst/ *noun* [C] (SOCIAL STUDIES, TOURISM) a person who visits a place for pleasure ➲ look at **sightseer**

ˈ**tourist board** *noun* [C] (TOURISM) an organization in a town, city or country that provides services and information for tourists

ˈ**tourist class** *noun* [U] (TOURISM) the cheapest type of ticket or accommodation that is available on a plane or ship or in a hotel

ˈ**tourist trap** *noun* [C] (*informal*) (TOURISM) a place that attracts a lot of tourists and where food, drink, entertainment, etc. is more expensive than normal

tournament /ˈtɔːnəmənt/ *noun* [C] (SPORT) a competition in which many players or teams play games against each other

tourniquet /ˈtʊənɪkeɪ/ *noun* [C] (HEALTH) a piece of cloth, etc. that is tied tightly around an arm or a leg to stop a cut or an injury from BLEEDING

ˈ**tour operator** *noun* [C] (TOURISM) a person or company that organizes tours

tousled /ˈtaʊzld/ *adj.* (used about hair) untidy, often in an attractive way

tout /taʊt/ *verb* **1** [T] ~ **sb/sth (as sth)** to try to persuade people that sb/sth is important or valuable by praising them/it: *She's being touted as the next leader of the party.* **2** [I,T] ~ **(for sth)** (*especially BrE*) (BUSINESS) to try to persuade people to buy your goods or services, especially by going to them and asking them directly: *the problem of unlicensed taxi drivers touting for business at airports* **3** [I,T] (*BrE*) to sell tickets for a popular event illegally, at a price that is higher than the official price, especially outside a theatre, STADIUM, etc. ▶ **tout** *noun* [C] (*also* ˈ**ticket tout**) (*BrE*): *Touts are selling concert tickets at three times their original price.*

tow /təʊ/ *verb* [T] to pull a car or boat behind another vehicle, using a rope or chain: *My car was towed away by the police.* ▶ **tow** *noun* [sing., U]
IDM **in tow** (*informal*) following closely behind: *He arrived with his wife and five children in tow.*

towards 🔑 /təˈwɔːdz/ (*also* **toward** /təˈwɔːd/) *prep.* **1** in the direction of sb/sth: *I saw Ken walking towards the station. ◇ She had her back towards me. ◇ a first step towards world peace* **2** near or nearer a time or date: *It gets cool towards evening. ◇ The shops get very busy towards Christmas.* **3** (used when you are talking about your feelings about sb/sth) in relation to: *Patti felt very protective towards her younger brother. ◇ What is your attitude towards this government?* **4** as part of the payment for sth: *The money will **go towards** the cost of a new minibus.*

towel 🔑 /ˈtaʊəl/ *noun* [C] a piece of cloth or paper that you use for drying sb/sth/yourself: *a bath/hand/beach towel ◇ kitchen/paper towels* ➲ look at **sanitary towel**, **tea towel**

towelling (*AmE* **toweling**) /ˈtaʊəlɪŋ/ *noun* [U] a thick soft cotton cloth that is used especially for making bath towels

tower 🔑 /ˈtaʊə(r)/ *noun* [C] (ARCHITECTURE) a tall narrow building or part of a building such as a church or castle: *the Eiffel Tower ◇ a church tower*

ˈ**tower block** *noun* [C] (*BrE*) a very tall building consisting of flats or offices

town 🔑 /taʊn/ *noun* **1** [C] (GEOGRAPHY) a place with many streets and buildings. A town is larger than a village but smaller than a city: *Romsey is a small market town. ◇ After ten years away, she decided to move back to her **home town*** (= the town where she was born and spent her childhood). **2 the town** [sing.] all the people who live in a town: *The whole town is talking about it.* **3** [U] the main part of a town, where the shops, etc. are: *I've got to go into town this afternoon.*
IDM **go to town (on sth)** (*informal*) to do sth with a lot of energy and enthusiasm; to spend a lot of money on sth
(out) on the town (*informal*) going to restaurants, theatres, clubs, etc., for entertainment, especially at night

ˌ**town** ˈ**council** *noun* [C] (*BrE*) (POLITICS) a group of people who are responsible for the local government of a town

ˌ**town** ˈ**hall** *noun* [C] a large building that contains the local government offices and often a large room for public meetings, concerts, etc. ➲ look at **hall**

ˌ**town** ˈ**planning** (*also* **planning**) *noun* [U] the control of the development of towns and their buildings, roads, etc. so that they can be pleasant and convenient places for people to live in; the subject that studies this

townspeople /ˈtaʊnzpiːpl/ (*also* **townsfolk** /ˈtaʊnsfəʊk/) *noun* [pl.] people who live in towns, not in the countryside; the people who live in a particular town

ˈ**tow truck** (*AmE*) = BREAKDOWN TRUCK

toxic /ˈtɒksɪk/ *adj.* (CHEMISTRY, HEALTH) poisonous

toxicity /tɒkˈsɪsəti/ *noun* (CHEMISTRY, HEALTH) **1** [U] the quality of being poisonous; the degree to which sth is poisonous: *substances with high/low levels of toxicity* **2** [C] the effect that a poisonous substance has: *Minor toxicities of this drug include nausea and vomiting.*

toxicology /ˌtɒksɪˈkɒlədʒi/ *noun* [U] (SCIENCE) the scientific study of poisons ▶ **toxicological** /ˌtɒksɪkəˈlɒdʒɪkl/ *adj.* ▶ **toxicologist** /ˌtɒksɪˈkɒlədʒɪst/ *noun* [C]

toxin /ˈtɒksɪn/ *noun* [C] (CHEMISTRY, HEALTH) a poisonous substance, especially one that is produced by bacteria in plants and animals

toy[1] 🔑 /tɔɪ/ *noun* [C] an object for a child to play with: *The little boy continued playing with his toys. ◇ a toy car/farm/soldier ◇ a toyshop*

toy[2] /tɔɪ/ *verb*
PHR V **toy with sth** **1** to think about doing sth, perhaps not very seriously: *She's **toying with the idea of** going abroad for a year.* **2** to move sth about without thinking about what you are doing, often because you are nervous or upset: *He toyed with his food but hardly ate any of it.*

trace[1] 🔑 AW /treɪs/ ***noun*** **1** [C,U] a mark, an object or a sign that shows that sb/sth existed or happened: *traces of an earlier civilization* ◇ *The man* ***disappeared/vanished without trace***. **2** [C] a ~ **(of sth)** a very small amount of sth: *Traces of blood were found under her fingernails.*

trace[2] 🔑 AW /treɪs/ ***verb*** [T] **1** ~ **sb/sth (to sth)** to find out where sb/sth is by following marks, signs or other information: *The wanted man was traced to an address in Amsterdam.* **2** ~ **sth (back) (to sth)** to find out where sth came from or what caused it; to describe the development of sth: *She traced her family tree back to the 16th century.* **3** to make a copy of a map, plan, etc. by placing a piece of TRACING PAPER (= transparent paper) over it and drawing over the lines

ˈ**trace element** ***noun*** [C] **1** (**CHEMISTRY**) a chemical substance that is found in very small amounts **2** (**BIOLOGY**) a chemical substance that living things, especially plants, need only in very small amounts to be able to grow well

tracery /ˈtreɪsəri/ ***noun*** [U] (**ARCHITECTURE**) a pattern of lines and curves in stone on the top part of some church windows

trachea /trəˈkiːə/ ***noun*** [C] (*pl.* **tracheae** /-kiːiː/ or **tracheas**) (**HEALTH, ANATOMY**) the tube in your throat that carries air to the lungs SYN **windpipe** ➲ picture on **page 80** ➲ picture at **lung**

tracheotomy /ˌtrækiˈɒtəmi/ ***noun*** [C] (*pl.* **-ies**) (**HEALTH**) a medical operation to cut a hole in sb's TRACHEA so that they can breathe

tracing AW /ˈtreɪsɪŋ/ ***noun*** [C] (**ART**) a copy of a map, drawing, etc. that you make by drawing on a piece of transparent paper placed on top of it

ˈ**tracing paper** ***noun*** [U] strong transparent paper that is placed on top of a drawing, etc. so that you can follow the lines with a pen or pencil in order to make a copy of it

track[1] 🔑 /træk/ ***noun*** **1** [C] a natural path or rough road: *Follow the dirt track through the wood.* **2** [C, usually pl.] marks that are left on the ground by a person, an animal or a moving vehicle: *The hunter followed the tracks of a deer.* ◇ *tyre tracks* ➲ look at **footprint** **3** [C,U] the two metal rails on which a train runs: *The train stopped because there was a tree across the track.* **4** [C] a piece of ground, often in a circle, for people, cars, etc. to have races on: *a running track* **5** [C] (**MUSIC**) one song or piece of music on a CASSETTE, CD or record: *the first track from her latest album* ➲ look at **soundtrack**

IDM **keep/lose track of sb/sth** to have/not have information about what is happening or where sb/sth is

off the beaten track → BEAT[1]

on the right/wrong track having the right/wrong idea about sth: *That's not the answer but you're on the right track.*

track[2] /træk/ ***verb*** [T] to follow the movements of sb/sth: *to track enemy planes on a radar screen*

PHR V **track sb/sth down** to find sb/sth after searching for them or it

ˈ**track event** ***noun*** [C] (**SPORT**) a sports event that consists of running round a track in a race, rather than throwing sth or jumping ➲ look at **field event**

ˈ**track record** ***noun*** [sing.] all the past successes or failures of a person or an organization

tracksuit /ˈtræksuːt/ ***noun*** [C] a warm pair of soft trousers and a matching jacket that you wear for sports practice

tract /trækt/ ***noun*** [C] (**ANATOMY**) a system of organs or tubes in the body that are connected and that have a particular purpose: *the respiratory/digestive tract*

traction /ˈtrækʃn/ ***noun*** [U] **1** the action of pulling sth along a surface; the power that is used for doing this: *diesel/electric/steam traction* **2** (**HEALTH**) a way of treating a broken bone in the body that involves using special equipment to pull the bone gradually back into its correct place: *He spent six weeks* ***in traction*** *after he broke his leg.* **3** the force that stops sth, for example the wheels of a vehicle, from sliding on the ground

tractor /ˈtræktə(r)/ ***noun*** [C] (**AGRICULTURE**) a large vehicle that is used on farms for pulling heavy pieces of machinery

tractor

trade[1] 🔑 /treɪd/ ***noun*** **1** [U] (**ECONOMICS, SOCIAL STUDIES**) the buying or selling of goods or services between people or countries: *an international trade agreement* ◇ *Trade is not very good* (= not many goods are sold) *at this time of year.* **2** [C] a particular type of business: *the tourist/building/retail trade* **3** [C,U] a job for which you need special skill, especially with your hands: *Jeff is a plumber* ***by trade***. ◇ *to learn a trade* ➲ note at **work**

trade[2] 🔑 /treɪd/ ***verb*** **1** [I] ~ **(in sth) (with sb)** (**ECONOMICS, SOCIAL STUDIES**) to buy or sell goods or services: *to trade in luxury goods* ◇ *to trade in stocks and shares* ◇ *We no longer trade with that country.* **2** [T] ~ **sth (for sth)** to exchange sth for sth else: *He traded his CD player for his friend's bicycle.*

PHR V **trade sth in (for sth)** to give sth old in part payment for sth new or newer: *We traded in our old car for a van.*

ˈ**trade balance** = BALANCE OF TRADE

trademark /ˈtreɪdmɑːk/ ***noun*** [C] (*abbr.* **TM**) a special symbol, design or name that a company puts on its products and that cannot be used by any other company

ˈ**trade name** ***noun*** [C] = BRAND NAME

trader /ˈtreɪdə(r)/ ***noun*** [C] (**ECONOMICS, SOCIAL STUDIES**) a person who buys and sells things, especially goods in a market or company shares

ˈ**trade route** ***noun*** [C] (**HISTORY**) (in the past) the route that people buying and selling goods used to take across land or sea

ˌ**trade ˈsecret** ***noun*** [C] a piece of information, for example about how a particular product is made, that is known only to the company that makes it

tradesman /ˈtreɪdzmən/ ***noun*** [C] (*pl.* **-men** /-mən/) a person who brings goods to people's homes to sell them or who has a shop

ˌ**trade ˈunion** (*also* ˌ**trades ˈunion**; **union**) ***noun*** [C] (**POLITICS, SOCIAL STUDIES**) an organization for people who all do the same type of work. Trade unions try to get better pay and working conditions for their members.

ˌ**trade ˈunionist** (also ˌ**trades ˈunionist; unionist**) ***noun*** [C] (**POLITICS, SOCIAL STUDIES**) a member of a TRADE UNION

'trade wind *noun* [C] (GEOGRAPHY) a strong wind that blows all the time towards the EQUATOR (=the imagined line around the middle of the earth) and then to the west

trading 🔑 /'treɪdɪŋ/ *noun* [U] (BUSINESS) the activity of buying and selling things: *new laws on* ***Sunday trading*** (=shops being open on Sundays) ◇ *Shares worth $8 million changed hands during a day of hectic trading.*

tradition 🔑 AW /trə'dɪʃn/ *noun* [C,U] (SOCIAL STUDIES) a custom, belief or way of doing sth that has continued from the past to the present: ***religious/cultural/literary traditions*** ◇ ***By tradition****, the bride's family pays the costs of the wedding.*

traditional 🔑 AW /trə'dɪʃənl/ *adj.* **1** (SOCIAL STUDIES) being part of the beliefs, customs or way of life of a particular group of people, that have not changed for a long time: *It is traditional in Britain to eat turkey at Christmas.* **2** following older methods and ideas rather than modern or different ones: *traditional methods of teaching* ▶ **traditionally** /-ʃənəli/ *adv.*: *Housework has traditionally been regarded as women's work.*

traditionalist AW /trə'dɪʃənəlɪst/ *noun* [C] a person who prefers tradition to modern ideas or ways of doing things ▶ **traditionalist** *adj.*

traffic 🔑 /'træfɪk/ *noun* [U] **1** all the vehicles that are on a road at a particular time: *heavy/light traffic* ◇ *We got stuck* ***in traffic*** *and were late for the meeting.* **2** the movement of ships, aircraft, etc.: *air traffic control* **3** ~ (in sth) (LAW) the illegal buying and selling of sth: *the traffic in drugs/firearms* ▶ **traffic** *verb* [I] (*pres. part.* **trafficking**; *pt, pp* **trafficked**) ~ (in sth): *He was arrested for trafficking in drugs.* ◇ *human trafficking* ▶ **trafficker** *noun* [C]: *a drugs trafficker*

'traffic calming *noun* [U] (*BrE*) ways of making roads safer, especially for people who are walking or riding bicycles, by building raised areas, etc. to make cars go more slowly

'traffic island (*also* **island**) *noun* [C] a higher area in the middle of the road, where you can stand and wait for the traffic to pass when you want to cross

'traffic jam *noun* [C] a long line of cars, etc. that cannot move or that can only move very slowly: *to be stuck in a traffic jam.*

'traffic light *noun* [C, usually pl.] a sign with three coloured lights (**red, amber** and **green**) that is used for controlling the traffic where two or more roads meet

'traffic warden *noun* [C] (*BrE*) a person whose job is to check that cars are not parked in the wrong place or for longer than is allowed

tragedy /'trædʒədi/ *noun* (*pl.* **tragedies**) **1** [C,U] a very sad event or situation, especially one that involves death: *It's a tragedy that he died so young.* **2** [C] (ARTS AND MEDIA, LITERATURE) a serious play that has a sad ending: *Shakespeare's 'King Lear' is a tragedy.* ➲ look at **comedy**

tragic /'trædʒɪk/ *adj.* **1** that makes you very sad, especially because it involves death: *It's tragic that she lost her only child.* ◇ *a tragic accident* **2** (*written*) (LITERATURE) (only *before* a noun) in the style of TRAGEDY: *a tragic actor/hero* ▶ **tragically** /-kli/ *adv.*

trail[1] /treɪl/ *noun* [C] **1** a series of marks in a long line that is left by sb/sth as they or it move: *a trail of blood/footprints* **2** a track, sign or smell that is left behind and that you follow when you are hunting sb/sth: *The dogs ran off* ***on the trail of*** *the fox.* **3** a path through the country

trail[2] /treɪl/ *verb* **1** [I,T] to pull or be pulled along behind sb/sth: *The skirt was too long and trailed along the ground.* **2** [I] to move or walk slowly behind sb/sth else, usually because you are tired or bored: *It was impossible to do any shopping with the kids trailing around after me.* **3** [I,T] ~ (**by/in sth**) (usually used in the continuous tenses) to be in the process of losing a game or a competition: *At half-time Liverpool were trailing by two goals to three.* **4** [I] (used about plants or sth long and thin) to grow over sth and hang downwards; to lie across a surface: *Computer wires trailed across the floor.*

PHR V **trail away/off** (used about sb's voice) to gradually become quieter and then stop

trailer /'treɪlə(r)/ *noun* [C] **1** a truck, or a container with wheels, that is pulled by another vehicle: *a car towing a trailer with a boat on it* **2** (*AmE*) (*BrE* ˌ**mobile 'home**) a vehicle without an engine, that can be pulled by a car or truck or used as a home or an office when it is parked: *a* ***trailer park*** (=an area where trailers are parked and used as homes) **3** (*AmE*) =MOBILE HOME (1) **4** (*especially BrE*) (ARTS AND MEDIA) a series of short pieces taken from a film and used to advertise it ➲ look at **clip** ➲ note at **ad**

train[1] 🔑 /treɪn/ *noun* [C] **1** a type of transport that is pulled by an engine along a railway line. A train is divided into sections for people (**carriages** and **coaches**) and for goods (**wagons**): *a passenger/goods/freight train* ◇ *a fast/slow/express train* ◇ *to catch/take/get the train to London* ◇ *the 12 o'clock train to Bristol* ◇ *to get on/off a train* ◇ *Hurry up or we'll* ***miss the train****.* ◇ *You have to* ***change trains*** *at Reading.* **2** [usually sing.] a series of thoughts or events that are connected: *A knock at the door interrupted my* ***train of thought****.*

train[2] 🔑 /treɪn/ *verb* **1** [T] ~ sb (as sth/to do sth) to teach a person to do sth which is difficult or which needs practice: *The organization trains guide dogs for the blind.* ◇ *There is a shortage of trained teachers.* **2** [I,T] ~ (as/in sth) (to do sth) (EDUCATION) to learn how to do a job: *She trained as an engineer.* ◇ *He's not trained in anything.* ◇ *He's training to be a doctor.* **3** [I,T] ~ (**for sth**) to prepare yourself, especially for a sports event, by practising; to help a person or an animal to do this: *I'm training for the London Marathon.* ◇ *to train racehorses* **4** [T] ~ **sth (at/on sb/sth)** to point a gun, camera, etc. at sb/sth

trainee /ˌtreɪ'niː/ *noun* [C] a person who is being taught how to do a particular job

trainer /'treɪnə(r)/ *noun* [C] **1** (*AmE* **sneaker**) [usually pl.] a shoe that you wear for doing sport or as informal clothing ➲ look at **plimsoll** ➲ picture at **sport** **2** a person who teaches people or animals how to do a particular job or skill well, or to do a particular sport: *teacher trainers* ◇ *a racehorse trainer*

training 🔑 /'treɪnɪŋ/ *noun* [U] **1** ~ (in sth/in doing sth) the process of learning the skills that you need to do a job: *staff training* ◇ *a training course* **2** the process of preparing to take part in a sports competition by doing physical exercises: *to be* ***in training*** *for the Olympics*

'training college *noun* [C] (*BrE*) (EDUCATION) a college that trains people for a job or profession: *a police training college*

trainspotter /'treɪnspɒtə(r)/ *noun* [C] (*BrE*) **1** a person who collects the numbers of railway engines as a hobby **2** a person who has a boring hobby or who is interested in the details of a subject that other people find boring ▶ **trainspotting** *noun* [U]

trait /treɪt/ ***noun*** [C] a quality that forms part of your character or personality

traitor /'treɪtə(r)/ ***noun*** [C] **a ~ (to sb/sth)** a person who is not loyal to their country, friends, etc. ❶ A traitor **betrays** his/her friends, country, etc. and the crime against his/her country is called **treason**.

trajectory /trə'dʒektəri/ (*pl.* **-ies**) ***noun*** [C] (TECHNICAL) the curved path of sth that has been fired, hit or thrown into the air: *a missile's trajectory*

tram /træm/ (*AmE* **streetcar**; **trolley**) ***noun*** [C] a type of bus that works by electricity and that moves along special rails in the road

tramp¹ /træmp/ ***noun*** **1** [C] a person who has no home or job and who moves from place to place **2** [sing.] the sound of people walking with heavy or noisy steps

tramp² /træmp/ ***verb*** [I,T] to walk with slow heavy steps, especially for a long time

trample /'træmpl/ ***verb*** [I,T] **~ on/over sb/sth** to walk on sb/sth and damage or hurt them or it: *The boys trampled on the flowers.*

trampoline /'træmpəli:n/ ***noun*** [C] (SPORT) a piece of equipment for jumping up and down on, made of a piece of strong material fixed to a metal frame by springs ▶ **trampoline** ***verb*** [I] ▶ **trampolining** ***noun*** [U]

trance /trɑ:ns/ ***noun*** [C] a mental state in which you do not notice what is going on around you: *to go/fall into a trance*

tranquil /'træŋkwɪl/ ***adj.*** (*formal*) calm and quiet

tranquillize (also **-ise**; *AmE* **tranquilize**) /'træŋkwəlaɪz/ ***verb*** [T] (HEALTH) to make a person or an animal calm or unconscious, especially by giving them or it a drug

tranquillizer (also **-iser**; *AmE also* **tranquilizer**) /'trænkwəlaɪzə(r)/ ***noun*** [C] (HEALTH) a drug that is used for making people feel calm or to help them sleep ➲ look at **sedative**

trans- /trænz; træns/ ***prefix*** **1** (used in adjectives) across; beyond: *transatlantic* ◇ *transcontinental* **2** (used in verbs) into another place or state: *transplant* ◇ *transform*

transaction /træn'zækʃn/ ***noun*** [C] (BUSINESS) a piece of business that is done between people: *financial transactions*

transatlantic /,trænzət'læntɪk/ ***adj.*** to or from the other side of the Atlantic Ocean; across the Atlantic: *a transatlantic flight/voyage*

transcend /træn'send/ ***verb*** [T] (*formal*) to go further than the usual limits of sth

transcribe /træn'skraɪb/ ***verb*** [T] **1 ~ sth (into sth)** to record thoughts, speech or data in a written form, or in a different written form from the original: *Clerks transcribe everything that is said in court.* ◇ *The interview was recorded and then transcribed.* **2** (LANGUAGE) to show the sounds of speech using a special PHONETIC alphabet ➲ look at **phonetic** **3 ~ sth (for sth)** (MUSIC) to write a piece of music in a different form so that it can be played by another musical instrument or sung by another voice: *a piano piece transcribed for the guitar*

transcript /'trænskrɪpt/ (*also* **tran'scription**) ***noun*** [C] a written or printed copy of what sb has said: *a transcript of the interview/trial*

transcription /træn'skrɪpʃn/ ***noun*** **1** [U] the act or process of representing sth in a written or printed form: *errors made in transcription* ◇ *phonetic transcription* **2** [C] = TRANSCRIPT: *The full transcription of the interview is attached.* **3** [C] something that is represented in writing: *This dictionary gives phonetic transcriptions of all headwords.* **4** [C] (MUSIC) a change in the written form of a piece of music so that it can be played on a different instrument or sung by a different voice

transducer /,trænz'dju:sə(r)/ ***noun*** [C] (PHYSICS) a device for producing an electrical signal from another form of energy such as pressure

transept /'trænsept/ ***noun*** [C] (ARCHITECTURE) either of the two wide parts of a church shaped like a cross, that are built at RIGHT ANGLES to the main central part ➲ look at **nave**

transfer¹ 🔑 AW /træns'fɜ:(r)/ ***verb*** (**transferring**; **transferred**) **1** [I,T] **~ (sb/sth) (from...) (to...)** to move, or to make sb/sth move, from one place to another: *He's transferring to our Tokyo branch next month.* ◇ *I'd like to transfer £1000 from my deposit account* (=in a bank). ◇ *Transfer the data onto a disk.* **2** [T] to officially arrange for sth to belong to, or be controlled by, sb else: *She transferred the property to her son.* ▶ **transferable** /-'fɜ:rəbl/ ***adj.***: *This ticket is not transferable* (=may only be used by the person who bought it).

transfer² 🔑 AW /'trænsfɜ:(r)/ ***noun*** **1** [C,U] moving or being moved from one place, job or state to another: *Paul is not happy here and has asked for a transfer.* **2** [U] changing to a different vehicle or route during a journey: *The travel company will arrange **airport transfer**.* **3** [C] (*AmE*) a ticket that allows you to continue your journey on another bus or train **4** [C] (*especially BrE*) a piece of paper with a picture or writing on it that you can stick onto another surface by pressing or heating it

transference AW /'trænsfərəns/ ***noun*** [U] (TECHNICAL) the process of moving sth from one place, person or use to another: *the transference of heat from the liquid to the container*

transfigure /træns'fɪgə(r)/ ***verb*** [T] (often passive) (*written*) to change the appearance of a person or thing so that they look more beautiful

transform 🔑 AW /træns'fɔ:m/ ***verb*** [T] **~ sb/sth (from sth) (into sth)** to change sb/sth completely, especially in a way which improves them or it ▶ **transformation** AW /,trænsfə'meɪʃn/ ***noun*** [C,U]

transformer /træns'fɔ:mə(r)/ ***noun*** [C] (PHYSICS) a device for reducing or increasing the electrical force (**voltage**) that goes into a piece of electrical equipment ➲ picture at **generator**

transfusion /træns'fju:ʒn/ ***noun*** [C] (HEALTH) the action of putting new blood into a person's body instead of their own because they are ill: *a blood transfusion*

transgenic /trænz'dʒenɪk/ ***adj.*** (BIOLOGY) (used about a plant or an animal) having GENETIC material introduced from another type of plant or animal: *transgenic crops* SYN **genetically modified**

transistor /træn'zɪstə(r); -'sɪst-/ ***noun*** [C] a small piece of electronic equipment that is used in computers, radios, televisions, etc.

transit AW /'trænzɪt; -'sɪt/ ***noun*** [U] **1** the act of being moved or carried from one place to another: *The goods had been damaged **in transit**.* **2** (TOURISM) the act of going through a place on the way to somewhere else: *the transit lounge at Singapore airport* ◇ ***a transit visa*** (=permission to pass through a country but not to stay there)

transition AW /træn'zɪʃn; -'sɪʃn/ ***noun*** [C,U] (a) **~ (from sth) (to sth)** a change from one state or form to another: *the transition from childhood to adolescence* ▶ **transitional** AW /-ʃənl/ ***adj.***: *a transitional stage/period*

tran'sition metal (*also* **tran'sition element**) ***noun*** [C] (**CHEMISTRY**) one of the group of metals in the centre of the PERIODIC TABLE (= a list of all the chemical elements). **Transition metals** are heavy, they melt only at high temperatures, they form coloured COMPOUNDS, they can combine with another element to form more than one COMPOUND, and they often act as a CATALYST (= a substance that makes a chemical reaction happen faster).

transitive /'trænsətɪv/ ***adj.*** (**LANGUAGE**) (used about a verb) that has a direct object: *In this dictionary transitive verbs are marked* [T]. **OPP** **intransitive**

transitory **AW** /'trænsətri/ ***adj.*** (*formal*) continuing for only a short time **SYN** **temporary**: *the transitory nature of his happiness*

translate ⊶ /træns'leɪt; trænz-/ ***verb*** [I,T] **1 ~ (sth) (from sth) (into sth)** (**LANGUAGE**) to change sth written or spoken from one language to another: *This book has been translated from Czech into English.* ➲ look at **interpret** **2 ~ (sth) (into sth)** to change sth, or to be changed into a different form: *I hope all the hard work will translate into profits.*

translation ⊶ /træns'leɪʃn; trænz-/ ***noun*** **1** [U] **~ (of sth) (into sth)**; **~ (from sth) (into sth)** the process of changing sth that is written or spoken into another language: *an error in translation* ◇ *The irony is* ***lost in translation***. **2** [C,U] a text or work that has been changed from one language into another: *a* ***rough translation*** (= not translating everything exactly) ◇ *a* ***literal translation*** (= following the original words exactly) ◇ *I have only read Tolstoy* ***in translation***. **3** [U] **~ (of sth) into sth** the process of changing sth into a different form: *the translation of theory into practice*

translator /træns'leɪtə(r); trænz-/ ***noun*** [C] a person who changes sth that has been written or spoken from one language to another ➲ look at **interpreter**

translucent /træns'lu:snt; trænz-/ ***adj.*** (*written*) allowing light to pass through but not transparent: *The sky was a pale translucent blue.* ◇ *His skin was translucent with age.* ▶ **translucence** /-sns/ (*also* **translucency** /-snsi/) ***noun*** [U]

transmission **AW** /træns'mɪʃn; trænz-/ ***noun*** **1** [U] sending sth out or passing sth on from one person, place or thing to another: *the transmission of television pictures by satellite* ◇ *the transmission of a disease/virus* **2** [C] (**ARTS AND MEDIA**) a television or radio programme **3** [U, C] the system in a car, etc. by which power is passed from the engine to the wheels

transmit **AW** /træns'mɪt; trænz-/ ***verb*** [T] (**transmitting**; **transmitted**) **1** (**ARTS AND MEDIA**) to send out television or radio programmes, electronic signals, etc.: *The match was transmitted live all over the world.* **2** to send or pass sth from one person or place to another: *a sexually transmitted disease*

transmitter /træns'mɪtə(r); trænz-/ ***noun*** [C] (**PHYSICS**) a piece of equipment that sends out electronic signals, television or radio programmes, etc.

transparency /træns'pærənsi/ ***noun*** [C] (*pl.* **transparencies**) a piece of plastic on which you can write or draw or that has a picture, etc. on it that you look at by putting it on a special machine (**projector**) and shining light through it: *a transparency for the overhead projector* ➲ look at **slide**² (4)

transparent ⊶ /træns'pærənt/ ***adj.*** that you can see through: *Glass is transparent.* **OPP** **opaque**

transpiration /ˌtrænspɪ'reɪʃn/ ***noun*** [U] (**BIOLOGY**) the process of water passing out from the surface of a plant or leaf

transpire /træn'spaɪə(r)/ ***verb*** [I] **1** (not usually used in the progressive tenses) to become known; to be shown to be true: ***It transpired that*** *the gang had had a contact inside the bank.* ◇ *This story, it later transpired, was untrue.* **2** to happen: *You're meeting him tomorrow? Let me know what transpires.* **3** (**BIOLOGY**) when plants or leaves **transpire**, water passes out from their surface ➲ picture at **water**

transplant¹ /træns'plɑ:nt; trænz-/ ***verb*** [T] **1** (**HEALTH**) to take out an organ or other part of sb's body and put it into another person's body **2** to move a growing plant and plant it somewhere else ➲ look at **graft**

transplant² /'trænsplɑ:nt; 'trænz-/ ***noun*** [C] (**HEALTH**) a medical operation in which an organ, etc. is taken out of sb's body and put into another person's body: *to have a heart/liver/kidney transplant*

transport ⊶ **AW** /'trænspɔ:t/ (*especially AmE* **transportation** /ˌtrænspɔ:'teɪʃn/) ***noun*** [U] **1** the action of carrying or taking people or goods from one place to another: *road/rail/sea transport* **2** vehicles that you travel in; a method of travel: *Do you have your own transport* (= for example a car)? ◇ *I travel to school by* ***public transport***. ◇ *His bike is his only* ***means of transport***. ▶ **transport** /træn'spɔ:t/ ***verb*** [T]

transpose /træn'spəʊz/ ***verb*** [T] (often passive) **1** (*formal*) to change the order of two or more things **SYN** **reverse** **2** (*formal*) to move or change sth to a different place or environment or into a different form **SYN** **transfer** **3** (**MUSIC**) to write or play a piece of music or a series of notes in a different key ▶ **transposition** /ˌtrænspə'zɪʃn/ ***noun*** [C,U]

transverse /'trænzvɜ:s; 'træns-/ ***adj.*** (usually *before* a noun) situated across sth: *A transverse bar joins the two posts.*

ˌtransverse 'wave ***noun*** [C] (**PHYSICS**) a wave that VIBRATES (= makes very small, fast movements from side to side) at an angle of 90° to the direction that it is moving in ➲ look at **longitudinal wave**

transvestite /trænz'vestaɪt; træns-/ ***noun*** [C] a person, especially a man, who enjoys dressing like a member of the opposite sex

trap¹ ⊶ /træp/ ***noun*** [C] **1** a piece of equipment that you use for catching animals: *a mousetrap* ◇ *The rabbit's leg was caught in the trap.* **2** a clever plan that is designed to trick sb: *She* ***walked straight into the trap***. **3** an unpleasant situation from which it is hard to escape ➲ look at **death trap**

trap² ⊶ /træp/ ***verb*** [T] (**trapping**; **trapped**) **1** (often passive) to keep sb in a dangerous place or a bad situation from which they cannot escape: *The door closed behind them and they were trapped.* ◇ *Many people are trapped in low-paid jobs.* **2** to catch and keep or store sth: *Special glass panels trap heat from the sun.* **3** to force sb/sth into a place or situation from which they or it cannot escape: *Police believe this new evidence could help trap the killer.* **4** to catch an animal, etc. in a trap **5 ~ sb (into sth/into doing sth)** to make sb do sth by tricking them: *She had been trapped into revealing her true identity.*

trapdoor /'træpdɔ:(r)/ ***noun*** [C] a small door in a floor or ceiling

trapeze /trəˈpiːz/ ***noun*** [C] a wooden or metal bar hanging from two ropes high above the ground, used by performers (**acrobats**)

trapezium /trəˈpiːziəm/ ***noun*** [C] (GEOMETRY) **1** (*AmE* **trapezoid**) a flat shape with four straight sides, one pair of opposite sides being parallel and the other pair not parallel **2** (*AmE*) = TRAPEZOID

trapezoid

trapezium (*AmE* trapezoid) trapezoid (*AmE* trapezium)

trapezoid /ˈtræpəzɔɪd; trəˈpiːzɔɪd/ ***noun*** [C] (GEOMETRY) **1** (*AmE* **trapezium**) a flat shape with four straight sides, none of which are parallel **2** (*AmE*) = TRAPEZIUM ▶ **trapezoidal** /ˌtræpɪˈzɔɪdl/ ***adj.***: *a trapezoidal window*

trappings /ˈtræpɪŋz/ ***noun*** [pl.] clothes, possessions, etc. which are signs of a particular social position

trash /træʃ/ (*AmE*) = RUBBISH

ˈtrash can (*AmE*) = DUSTBIN

trashy /ˈtræʃi/ ***adj.*** of poor quality: *trashy novels*

trauma /ˈtrɔːmə/ ***noun*** [C,U] (an event that causes) a state of great shock or sadness: *the trauma of losing your parents* ➲ look at **stress** ▶ **traumatic** /trɔːˈmætɪk/ ***adj.***

traumatize (also -ise) /ˈtrɔːmətaɪz/ ***verb*** [T] (usually passive) to shock and upset sb very much, often making them unable to think or work normally

travel¹ ⊶ /ˈtrævl/ ***verb*** (**travelling**; **travelled**: *AmE* **traveling**; **traveled**) **1** [I] to go from one place to another, especially over a long distance: *Charles travels a lot on business.* ◇ *to travel abroad* ◇ *to travel by sea/air/car* ◇ *to travel to work* ◇ *travelling expenses* **2** [T] to make a journey of a particular distance: *They travelled 60 kilometres to come and see us.*
IDM **travel light** to take very few things with you when you travel

travel² ⊶ /ˈtrævl/ ***noun*** **1** [U] the action of going from one place to another: *air/rail/space travel* ◇ *a travel bag/clock/iron* (= designed to be used when travelling) **2 travels** [pl.] time spent travelling, especially to places that are far away

RELATED VOCABULARY

Travel

Travel is an uncountable word and you can only use it to talk about the general activity of moving from place to place: *Foreign travel is very popular these days.*

When you talk about going from one particular place to another, you use **journey**. A journey can be long: *the journey across Canada*, or short, but repeated: *the journey to work*.

A **tour** is a circular journey or walk during which you visit several places. You may **go on a tour** round a country, city, place of interest, etc.: *a three-week tour around Italy* ◇ *a **guided tour** of the castle.*

You often use **trip** when you are thinking about the whole visit (including your stay in a place and the journeys there and back): *They're just back from a trip to Japan. They had a wonderful time.* (but: 'How was the journey back?' 'Awful – the plane was delayed!') A trip may be short: *a day trip*, or longer: *a trip round the world*, and can be for business or pleasure: *How about a shopping trip to London this weekend?* ◇ *He's on a business trip to New York to meet a client.*

An **excursion** is a short organized trip that you go on with a group of people: *The holiday includes a full-day excursion by coach to the capital.*

You **go on** a journey/tour/trip/excursion.

ˈtravel agency ***noun*** [C] (*pl.* **travel agencies**) (TOURISM) a company that makes travel arrangements for people (booking tickets, flights, hotels, etc.)

ˈtravel agent ***noun*** **1** [C] (TOURISM) a person whose job is to make travel arrangements for people **2 travel agent's** [sing.] (TOURISM) the shop where you can go to make travel arrangements, buy tickets, etc.

traveller ⊶ (*AmE* traveler) /ˈtrævələ(r)/ ***noun*** [C] **1** (TOURISM) a person who is travelling or who often travels **2** (*BrE*) a person who travels around the country in a large vehicle and does not have a permanent home anywhere ➲ look at **gypsy**

ˈtraveller's cheque (*AmE* **ˈtraveler's check**) ***noun*** [C] a cheque that you can change into foreign money when you are travelling in other countries

ˈtravel-sick ***adj.*** (HEALTH) feeling sick or VOMITING because of the movement of the vehicle you are travelling in ➲ look at **airsick**, **carsick**, **seasick**

trawl¹ /trɔːl/ ***verb*** [I,T] **1** ~ **(through sth) (for sth/sb)**; ~ **sth (for sth/sb)** to search through a large amount of information or a large number of people, places, etc. looking for a particular thing or person: *She trawled the shops for bargains.* ◇ *Major companies trawl the universities for potential employees.* ◇ *The police are trawling through their files for a similar case.* **2** ~ **(for sth)** to fish for sth by pulling a large net with a wide opening through the water

trawl² /trɔːl/ ***noun*** [C] **1** a search through a large amount of information, documents, etc.: *A trawl through the newspapers yielded two possible jobs.* **2** (*also* **ˈtrawl net**) a large net with a wide opening, that is pulled along the bottom of the sea by a boat in order to catch fish

trawler /ˈtrɔːlə(r)/ ***noun*** [C] a fishing boat that uses large nets that it pulls through the sea behind it

tray /treɪ/ ***noun*** [C] **1** a flat piece of wood, plastic, metal, etc. with slightly higher edges that you use for carrying food, drink, etc. on **2** a flat container with low edges in which you put papers, etc. on a desk

treacherous /ˈtretʃərəs/ ***adj.*** **1** (used about a person) that you cannot trust and who may do sth to harm you: *He was weak, cowardly and treacherous.* **2** dangerous, although seeming safe

treachery /ˈtretʃəri/ ***noun*** [U] the act of causing harm to sb who trusts you

treacle /ˈtriːkl/ (*AmE* **molasses**) ***noun*** [U] a thick, dark, sticky liquid that is made from sugar ➲ look at **syrup**

tread¹ /tred/ ***verb*** (*pt* **trod** /trɒd/; *pp* **trodden** /ˈtrɒdn/) **1** [I] ~ **(on/in/over sb/sth)** to put your foot down while you are walking: *Don't tread in the puddle!* ◇ *He trod on my foot and didn't even say sorry!* **2** [T] ~ **sth (in/into/down)** to press down on sth with your foot: *This wine is still made by treading grapes in the traditional way.*

tread² /tred/ ***noun* 1** [sing.] the sound you make when you walk; the way you walk **2** [C,U] the pattern on the surface of a tyre on a vehicle which is slightly higher than the rest of the surface

treason /ˈtriːzn/ ***noun*** [U] (LAW) the criminal act of causing harm to your country, for example by helping its enemies ➲ note at **traitor**

treasure¹ /ˈtreʒə(r)/ ***noun* 1** [U] a collection of very valuable objects, for example gold, silver, jewellery, etc.: *to find buried treasure* **2** [C] something that is very valuable

treasure² /ˈtreʒə(r)/ ***verb*** [T] to consider sb/sth to be very special or valuable: *I will treasure those memories forever.*

ˈtreasure hunt ***noun*** [C] a game in which people try to find a hidden prize by following special signs (**clues**) which have been left in different places

treasurer /ˈtreʒərə(r)/ ***noun*** [C] the person who looks after the money and accounts of a club or an organization

treasury /ˈtreʒəri/ ***noun*** (*pl.* **-ies**) **1 the Treasury** [sing.] (POLITICS) (in Britain, the US and some other countries) the government department that controls public money **2** [C] a place in a castle, etc. where valuable things are stored

treat¹ ⊶ /triːt/ ***verb*** [T] **1 ~ sb/sth (with/as/like sth)** to act or behave towards sb/sth in a particular way: *Teenagers hate being treated like children.* ◇ (*spoken*) *They* ***treat*** *their workers* ***like dirt*** (=very badly). ◇ *You should treat older people with respect.* ◇ *to treat sb badly/fairly/well* **2 ~ sth as sth** to consider sth in a particular way: *I decided to treat his comment as a joke.* **3** to deal with or discuss sth in a particular way: *The article treats this question in great detail.* **4 ~ sb/sth (for sth)** (HEALTH) to use medicine or medical care to try to make a sick or injured person well again: *The boy was treated for burns at the hospital.* **5 ~ sth (with sth)** to put a chemical substance onto sth in order to protect it from damage, clean it, etc. **6 ~ sb/yourself (to sth)** to pay for sth or give sb/yourself sth that is very special or enjoyable: *Clare treated the children to an ice cream* (=she paid for them).

treat² /triːt/ ***noun*** [C] something special or enjoyable that you pay for or give to sb/yourself: *I've brought some cream cakes as a treat.* ◇ *It's a real treat for me to stay in bed late.*

IDM **trick or treat** → TRICK

treatment ⊶ /ˈtriːtmənt/ ***noun* 1** [U, C] **~ (for sth)** (HEALTH) the use of medicine or medical care to cure an illness or injury; sth that is done to make sb feel and look good: *to require hospital/medical treatment* **2** [U] the way that you behave towards sb or deal with sth: *The treatment of the prisoners of war was very harsh.* **3** [U, C] **~ (for sth)** a process by which sth is cleaned, protected from damage, etc.

treaty /ˈtriːti/ ***noun*** [C] (*pl.* **treaties**) a written agreement between two or more countries: *to sign a peace treaty*

treble¹ /ˈtrebl/ ***verb*** [I,T] (MATHEMATICS) to become or to make sth three times bigger: *Prices have trebled in the past ten years.* ▶ **treble** ***det.***: *This figure is treble the number five years ago.*

treble² /ˈtrebl/ ***noun*** [C] (MUSIC) **1** [U] the high tones or part in music or a sound system: *to turn up the treble on the stereo* ➲ look at **bass 2** a child's high

tree

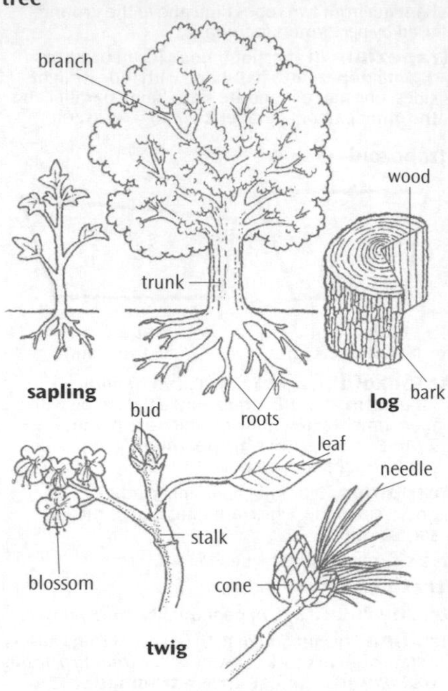

voice; a boy who has a high singing voice **3** [sing.] a musical part written for a **treble** voice

tree ⊶ /triː/ ***noun*** [C] (BIOLOGY) a tall plant that can live for a long time. Trees have a thick wooden central part from which branches grow: *an oak/apple/elm tree*

treeline /ˈtriːlaɪn/ ***noun*** [sing.] (GEOGRAPHY) the level of land, for example on a mountain, above which trees will not grow

trek /trek/ ***noun*** [C] **1** a long hard walk, lasting several days or weeks, usually in the mountains **2** (*informal*) a long walk: *It's quite a trek to the shops.* ▶ **trek** ***verb*** [I] (**trekking**; **trekked**)

trellis /ˈtrelɪs/ ***noun*** [C] a light frame made of long thin pieces of wood that cross each other, used to support climbing plants

tremble /ˈtrembl/ ***verb*** [I] **~ (with sth)** to shake, for example because you are cold, frightened, etc.: *She was pale and trembling with shock.* ◇ *His hand was trembling as he picked up his pen to sign.* ▶ **tremble** ***noun*** [C]

tremendous /trəˈmendəs/ ***adj.* 1** very large or great: *a tremendous amount of work* **2** (*informal*) very good: *It was a tremendous experience.*

tremendously /trəˈmendəsli/ ***adv.*** very; very much: *tremendously exciting* ◇ *Prices vary tremendously from one shop to another.*

tremolo /ˈtreməlaʊ/ ***noun*** [C] (*pl.* **tremolos**) (MUSIC) a special effect in singing or playing a musical instrument made by repeating the same note or two notes very quickly

tremor /ˈtremə(r)/ ***noun*** [C] a slight shaking movement: *an earth tremor* (=a small earthquake) ◇ *There was a tremor in his voice.*

trench /trentʃ/ ***noun*** [C] **1** a long narrow hole dug in the ground for water to flow along **2** a long deep hole dug in the ground for soldiers to hide in during enemy attacks **3** (*also* ˌ**ocean 'trench**) (GEOLOGY) a long deep narrow hole in the ocean floor ➲ picture at **plate tectonics**

'trench coat *noun* [C] a long loose coat, worn especially to keep off rain, with a belt and pockets in the style of a military coat

COLLOCATIONS AND PATTERNS

Describing economic trends

An amount can **be down/up (at)** or **be/remain unchanged (at).**
The share price is down at 234p.
The FT index was up 18.84 points.
The 100 Share Index remained unchanged at 5297.

Something can **stand at** or **reach** a figure or amount.
Second quarter sales stood at £18 billion.
Customer confidence reached a 30-year high.

A share can **gain** or **lose** an amount.
The share gained 19 cents to close at $4.38.

Markets, shares, profits, etc. **suffer** when there are economic problems.
Profit margins suffered when prices were lowered.

When amounts are **going up** they **climb, increase or rise.** When they go up suddenly, they **jump, rocket, shoot up** or **soar.**
Earnings per share climbed from 3.5p to 5.1p.
The pound increased in value relative to the euro.
Profits shot up by a staggering 25%.
Oil prices have rocketed.

When amounts are **going down** they **decline, drop or fall.** When they go down suddenly, they **crash, plummet, plunge** or **slump.**
Banana exports crashed nearly 50%.
The pound fell to a 14-year low against the dollar.
Net income plummeted to USD 3.7 million.
Sales have slumped by over 50%.

trend 🔑 AW /trend/ *noun* [C] a ~ **(towards sth)** a general change or development: *The current trend is towards smaller families.* ◇ *He always followed the latest trends in fashion.*
IDM **set a/the trend** to start a new style or fashion

trendy /'trendi/ *adj.* (*comparative* **trendier**; *superlative* **trendiest**) (*informal*) fashionable

trespass /'trespəs/ *verb* [I] to go onto sb's land or property without permission ▶ **trespasser** *noun* [C]

tri- /traɪ/ *prefix* (used in nouns and adjectives) three; having three: *tricycle* ◇ *triangular*

trial 🔑 /'traɪəl/ *noun* [C,U] **1** (LAW) the process in a court of law where a judge, etc. listens to evidence and decides if sb is guilty of a crime or not: *a fair trial* ◇ *He was* ***on trial for*** *murder.* **2** an act of testing sb/sth: *New drugs must go through extensive trials.* ◇ *a* ***trial period*** *of three months*
IDM **trial and error** trying different ways of doing sth until you find the best one

ˌ**trial 'run** *noun* [C] an occasion when you practise doing sth in order to make sure you can do it correctly later on

triangle 🔑 /'traɪæŋgl/ *noun* [C] **1** (GEOMETRY) a shape that has three straight sides: *a right-angled triangle* **2** (MUSIC) a metal musical instrument in the shape of a triangle that you play by hitting it with a metal stick ➲ picture on **page 465**

triangular /traɪ'æŋgjələ(r)/ *adj.* shaped like a triangle

triathlon /traɪ'æθlən/ *noun* [C] (SPORT) a sporting event in which people compete in three different sports, usually swimming, cycling and running ➲ look at **decathlon, pentathlon**

tribe /traɪb/ *noun* [C] (SOCIAL STUDIES) a group of people that have the same language and customs and that have a leader (**a chief**): *tribes living in the Amazonian rainforest* ▶ **tribal** /'traɪbl/ *adj.*: *tribal art*

tribulation /ˌtrɪbju'leɪʃn/ *noun* [C,U] (*written*) great trouble or suffering: *the tribulations of modern life*

tribunal /traɪ'bjuːnl/ *noun* [C] (LAW) a type of court with the authority to decide who is right in particular types of DISPUTE or disagreement: *an industrial tribunal*

tributary /'trɪbjətri/ *noun* [C] (*pl.* **tributaries**) (GEOGRAPHY) a small river that flows into a larger river

tribute /'trɪbjuːt/ *noun* **1** [C,U] ~ **(to sb)** something that you say or do to show that you respect or admire sb/sth, especially sb who has died: *A special concert was held as a tribute to the composer.* **2** [sing.] **a ~ (to sb/sth)** a sign of how good sb/sth is: *The success of the festival is a tribute to the organizers.*
IDM **pay tribute to sb/sth** → PAY[1]

triceps /'traɪseps/ *noun* [C] (*pl.* **triceps**) (ANATOMY) the large muscle at the back of the top part of your arm ➲ look at **biceps** ➲ picture at **arm**

trick[1] 🔑 /trɪk/ *noun* [C] **1** something that you do to make sb believe sth that is not true or a joke that you play to annoy sb: *The thieves used a trick to get past the security guards.* **2** something that confuses you so that you see, remember, understand, etc. things in the wrong way: *It was a* ***trick question*** (=one in which the answer looks easy, but actually is not) **3** an action that uses special skills to make people believe sth which is not true or real as a form of entertainment: *The magician* ***performed a trick*** *in which he made a rabbit disappear.* ◇ *a card trick* **4** [usually sing.] a clever or the best way of doing sth
IDM **do the job/trick** → JOB
play a joke/trick on sb → JOKE[1]
trick or treat (*especially AmE*) a tradition in which children dressed as GHOSTS, etc. go to people's houses on the evening of October 31st (**Hallowe'en**) and threaten to do sth bad to them if they do not give them sweets, etc.: *to go trick or treating*

trick[2] 🔑 /trɪk/ *verb* [T] to make sb believe sth that is not true: *I'd been tricked and I felt like a fool.* SYN **deceive**
PHR V **trick sb into sth/doing sth** to persuade sb to do sth by making them believe sth that is not true: *He tricked me into lending him money.*
trick sb out of sth to get sth from sb by making them believe sth that is not true: *Stella was tricked out of her share of the money.*

trickery /'trɪkəri/ *noun* [U] the use of dishonest methods to trick sb in order to get what you want

trickle /'trɪkl/ *verb* [I] **1** (used about a liquid) to flow in a thin line: *Raindrops trickled down the window.* **2** to go somewhere slowly and gradually ▶ **trickle** *noun* [C, usually sing.]: *a trickle of water*

tricky /'trɪki/ *adj.* (**trickier**; **trickiest**) difficult to do or deal with: *a tricky situation*

tricycle /'traɪsɪkl/ *noun* [C] a bicycle that has one wheel at the front and two at the back

trident /'traɪdnt/ *noun* [C] a weapon used in the past that looks like a long fork with three points

trifle /'traɪfl/ ***noun*** **1 a trifle** [sing.] (*formal*) slightly; rather **2** [C] something that is of little value or importance **3** [C,U] (*BrE*) a type of DESSERT made from cake and fruit covered with a sweet yellow sauce (**custard**) and cream

trifling /'traɪflɪŋ/ ***adj.*** very small or unimportant

trigger[1] AW /'trɪgə(r)/ ***noun*** [C] **1** the part of a gun that you press to fire it: *to pull the trigger* **2** the cause of a particular reaction or event, especially a bad one

trigger[2] AW /'trɪgə(r)/ ***verb*** [T] ~ **sth (off)** to make sth happen suddenly: *Her cigarette smoke had triggered off the fire alarm.*

trigonometry /ˌtrɪgə'nɒmətri/ ***noun*** [U] (**MATHEMATICS**) the type of mathematics that deals with the relationship between the sides and angles of triangles ▸ **trigonometric** /ˌtrɪgənə'metrɪk/ ***adj.*** ▸ **trigonometrical** /-kl/ ***adj.***

trill /trɪl/ ***noun*** [C] (**MUSIC**) the sound made when two notes next to each other in the musical SCALE are played or sung quickly several times one after the other

trillion /'trɪljən/ ***number*** one million million ❶ For examples of how to use numbers in sentences, look at **six**. For more information about numbers look at the special section on numbers on pages R36-41.

trilogy /'trɪlədʒi/ ***noun*** [C] (*pl.* **trilogies**) (**ARTS AND MEDIA, LITERATURE**) a group of three novels, plays, etc. that form a set

trim[1] /trɪm/ ***verb*** [T] (**trimming**; **trimmed**) **1** to cut a small amount off sth so that it is tidy: *to trim your hair/fringe/beard* ◇ *The hedge needs trimming.* **2** ~ **sth (off sth)** to cut sth off because you do not need it: *Trim the fat off the meat.* **3** ~ **sth (with sth)** to decorate the edge of sth with sth ▸ **trim** ***noun*** [C, usually sing.]: *My hair needs a trim.*

trim[2] /trɪm/ ***adj.*** **1** (used about a person) looking thin, healthy and attractive **2** well cared for; tidy

trimester /traɪ'mestə(r)/ ***noun*** [C] **1** (**HEALTH**) a period of three months during the time when a woman is pregnant: *the first trimester of pregnancy* **2** (*AmE*) = TERM[1] (4): *The school year is divided into three trimesters.* ➲ look at **semester**

trimming /'trɪmɪŋ/ ***noun*** **1 trimmings** [pl.] extra things which you add to sth to improve its appearance, taste, etc. **2** [C,U] material that you use for decorating the edge of sth

the Trinity /'trɪnəti/ ***noun*** [sing.] (**RELIGION**) (in Christianity) the three forms of God: the Father, Jesus the Son and the Holy Spirit

trinket /'trɪŋkɪt/ ***noun*** [C] a piece of jewellery or small object for decoration that is not worth much money

trio /'triːəʊ/ ***noun*** (*pl.* **trios**) (**MUSIC**) **1** [C, with sing. or pl. verb] a group of three people who play music or sing together **2** [C] a piece of music for three people to play or sing

trip[1] 🔑 /trɪp/ ***noun*** [C] a journey to a place and back again, either for pleasure or for a particular purpose: *How was your trip to Turkey?* ◇ *We had to make several trips to move all the furniture.* ◇ *to* ***go on a*** *business/shopping* ***trip*** ➲ note at **travel** ▸ **tripper** ***noun*** [C]: *Brighton was full of* ***day trippers*** (= people on trips that last for one day) *from London.*

trip[2] 🔑 /trɪp/ ***verb*** (**tripping**; **tripped**) **1** [I] ~ **(over/up)**; ~ **(over/on sth)** to catch your foot on sth when you are walking and fall or nearly fall: *Don't leave your bag on the floor. Someone might trip over it.* ◇ *She tripped up on a loose paving stone.* **2** [T] ~ **sb (up)** to catch sb's foot and make them fall or nearly fall: *Linda stuck out her foot and tripped Barry up.*

PHR V **trip (sb) up** to make a mistake; to make sb say sth that they did not want to say: *The journalist asked a difficult question to try to trip the politician up.*

tripartite /traɪ'pɑːtaɪt/ ***adj.*** (*formal*) having three parts or involving three people, groups, etc.: *tripartite discussions*

tripe /traɪp/ ***noun*** [U] **1** the inside part (**lining**) of a cow's or pig's stomach, which some people eat **2** (*informal*) something that sb says or writes that you think is nonsense or not of good quality

triple /'trɪpl/ ***adj.*** (only *before* a noun) having three parts, happening three times or containing three times as much as usual: *You'll receive triple pay if you work over the New Year.* ▸ **triple** ***verb*** [I,T]

'triple jump ***noun*** [sing.] (**SPORT**) a sporting event in which people try to jump as far forward as possible with three jumps. The first jump lands on one foot, the second on the other foot, and the third on both feet.

triplet /'trɪplət/ ***noun*** [C] one of three children or animals that are born to one mother at the same time ➲ look at **twin**

triplicate /'trɪplɪkət/ ***noun*** [U]

IDM **in triplicate 1** done three times: *Each sample was tested in triplicate.* **2** with three copies (for example of an official piece of paper) that are exactly the same: *Fill out the forms in triplicate.* ➲ look at **duplicate**

tripod /'traɪpɒd/ ***noun*** [C] a piece of equipment with three legs that you use for putting a camera, etc. on ➲ picture at **laboratory**

tripper /'trɪpə(r)/ ***noun*** [C] (*BrE*) (**TOURISM**) a person who is visiting a place for a short time for pleasure: *a day tripper*

triptych /'trɪptɪk/ ***noun*** [C] (**ART**) a picture that is painted or CARVED (= cut) on three pieces of wood placed side by side, especially one over an ALTAR (= the high table at the centre of a religious ceremony) in a church

triumph[1] /'traɪʌmf/ ***noun*** [C,U] a great success or victory; the feeling of happiness that you have because of this: *The team returned home* ***in triumph***. ◇ *The new programme was a triumph with the public.*

triumph[2] /'traɪʌmf/ ***verb*** [I] ~ **(over sb/sth)** to achieve success; to defeat sb/sth: *France triumphed over Brazil in the final.*

triumphal /traɪ'ʌmfl/ ***adj.*** (usually *before* a noun) done or made in order to celebrate a great success or victory

triumphant /traɪ'ʌmfənt/ ***adj.*** feeling or showing great happiness because you have won or succeeded at sth ▸ **triumphantly** ***adv.***

trivial /'trɪviəl/ ***adj.*** of little importance; not worth considering: *a trivial detail/problem* ▸ **triviality** /ˌtrɪvi'æləti/ ***noun*** [C,U] (*pl.* **trivialities**)

trivialize (also **-ise**) /'trɪviəlaɪz/ ***verb*** [T] to make sth seem less important, serious, etc. than it really is

trod past tense of **tread**[1]

trodden past participle of **tread**[1]

trolley /'trɒli/ ***noun*** [C] **1** (*AmE* **cart**) a piece of equipment on wheels that you use for carrying things: *a supermarket/shopping/luggage trolley* **2** (*BrE*) a small table with wheels that is used for carrying or serving food and drinks: *a tea/sweet/drinks trolley* **3** (*AmE*) = TRAM

trombone /trɒm'bəʊn/ ***noun*** [C] (**MUSIC**) a large BRASS musical instrument that you play by blowing into it and moving a long tube backwards and forwards ➲ picture on **page 465**

troop /tru:p/ ***noun*** **1 troops** [pl.] soldiers **2** [C] a large group of people or animals ▶ **troop** ***verb*** [I]: *When the bell rang everyone trooped into the hall.*

trope /trəʊp/ ***noun*** [C] (**LITERATURE**) a word or phrase that is used in a way that is different from its usual meaning in order to create a particular mental image or effect. METAPHORS and SIMILES are **tropes**.

trophic level /ˌtrɒfɪk 'levl/ ***noun*** [C] (**ENVIRONMENT**) each of several levels in an ECOSYSTEM (=all the plants and animals in a particular area and their relationship with their surroundings). Each level consists of living creatures that share the same function in the FOOD CHAIN and get their food from the same source. ➲ picture at **food chain**

trophy /'trəʊfi/ ***noun*** [C] (*pl.* **trophies**) a large silver cup, etc. that you get for winning a competition or race

tropic /'trɒpɪk/ ***noun*** (**GEOGRAPHY**) **1** [C, usually sing.] one of the two lines around the earth that are 23° 26′ north and south of the EQUATOR (=the line around the middle of the earth). The lines are called the Tropic of Cancer (=north) and the Tropic of Capricorn (=south) ➲ picture at **earth 2 the tropics** [pl.] the part of the world that is between these two lines, where the climate is hot and wet

tropical /'trɒpɪkl/ ***adj.*** (**GEOGRAPHY**) coming from, found in or typical of the parts of the world where the climate is hot and wet: *tropical fruit/fish ◇ a tropical island*

tropism /'trəʊpɪzəm; 'trɒp-/ ***noun*** [U] (**BIOLOGY**) the action of a living thing turning all or part of itself in a particular direction, towards or away from sth such as a source of light

tropopause /'trɒpəʊpɔ:z/ ***noun*** [sing.] (**GEOGRAPHY**) the part of the earth's atmosphere where the TROPOSPHERE meets the STRATOSPHERE (=the layer of the earth's atmosphere above the troposphere) ➲ picture at **atmosphere**

troposphere /'trɒpəsfɪə(r)/ ***noun*** [sing.] **the troposphere** (**GEOGRAPHY**) the lowest layer of the earth's atmosphere, between the surface of the earth and about 6 to 10 kilometres above the surface ➲ picture at **atmosphere**

trot[1] /trɒt/ ***verb*** (**trotting**; **trotted**) [I] **1** (used about a horse and its rider) to move forward at a speed that is faster than a walk ➲ look at **canter**, **gallop 2** (used about a person or an animal) to walk fast, taking short quick steps

PHR V trot sth out (*informal*) to repeat an old idea rather than thinking of sth new to say: *to trot out the same old story*

trot[2] /trɒt/ ***noun*** [sing.] a speed that is faster than a walk

IDM on the trot (*informal*) one after another; without stopping: *We worked for six hours on the trot.*

trotter /'trɒtə(r)/ ***noun*** [C] a pig's foot

trouble[1] /'trʌbl/ ***noun*** **1** [U, C] ~ **(with sb/sth)** (a situation that causes) a problem, difficulty or worry: *If I don't get home by 11 o'clock I'll* ***be in trouble****. ◇ I'm* ***having trouble*** *getting the car started. ◇ I'm having trouble with my car. ◇ financial troubles ◇ Marie is clever.* ***The trouble is*** *she's very lazy.* **2** [U] extra work or effort: *Let's eat out tonight. It will* ***save*** *you* ***the trouble*** *of cooking. ◇ Why don't you stay the night with us.* ***It's no trouble****. ◇ I'm sorry to* ***put you to*** *so much* ***trouble****.* **3** [C,U] a situation where people are fighting or arguing with each other: *There's often trouble in town on Saturday night after the bars have closed.* **4** [U] illness or pain: *back/heart trouble*

IDM ask for trouble → ASK

get into trouble to get into a situation which is dangerous or in which you may be punished

go to a lot of trouble (to do sth) to put a lot of work or effort into sth: *They went to a lot of trouble to make us feel welcome.*

take trouble over/with sth; **take trouble to do sth/doing sth** to do sth with care

take the trouble to do sth to do sth even though it means extra work or effort

trouble[2] /'trʌbl/ ***verb*** [T] **1** to make sb worried, upset, etc.: *Is there something troubling you?* **2** (*formal*) ~ **sb (for sth)** (used when you are politely asking sb for sth or to do sth) to disturb sb: *Sorry to trouble you, but would you mind answering a few questions?* **SYN bother**

troublemaker /'trʌblmeɪkə(r)/ ***noun*** [C] a person who often deliberately causes trouble

troubleshoot /'trʌblʃu:t/ ***verb*** [I] **1** (**BUSINESS**) to solve problems for an organization **2** to find and correct faults in an electronic system or a machine

troubleshooter /'trʌblʃu:tə(r)/ ***noun*** [C] (**BUSINESS**) a person who helps to solve problems in a company or an organization ▶ **troubleshooting** ***noun*** [U]

troublesome /'trʌblsəm/ ***adj.*** causing trouble, pain, etc. over a long period of time

trough /trɒf/ ***noun*** [C] **1** (**AGRICULTURE**) a long narrow container from which farm animals eat or drink **2** (**GEOGRAPHY**) a low area or point, between two higher areas ➲ picture at **glacial**

troupe /tru:p/ ***noun*** [C, with sing. or pl. verb] (**ARTS AND MEDIA**) a group of actors, singers, etc. who work together

trousers /'traʊzəz/ (*AmE* **pants**) ***noun*** [pl.] a piece of clothing that covers the whole of both your legs

trout /traʊt/ ***noun*** [C,U] (*pl.* **trout**) a type of fish that lives in rivers and that we eat

trowel /'traʊəl/ ***noun*** [C] **1** a small garden tool with a short handle and a curved part for lifting plants, digging small holes, etc. **2** a small tool with a short handle and a flat metal part used in building for spreading CEMENT, etc.

truant /'tru:ənt/ ***noun*** [C] (**LAW**) a child who stays away from school without permission ▶ **truancy** /-ənsi/ ***noun*** [U] ▶ **truant** ***verb*** [I]: *A number of pupils have been truanting regularly.*

IDM play truant; (*AmE*) **play hooky** to stay away from school without permission

trucks

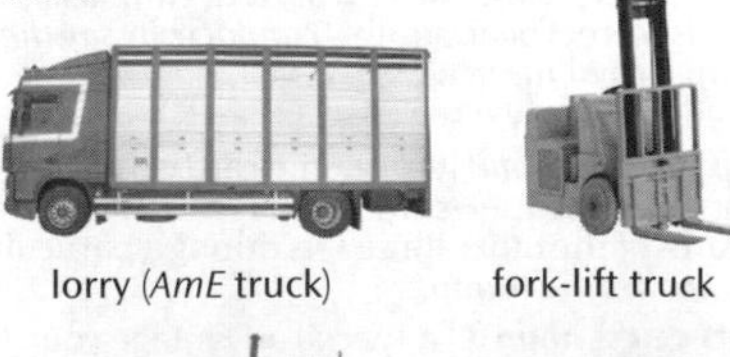

lorry (*AmE* truck) fork-lift truck

Jeep™ pickup / pickup truck

truce /truːs/ ***noun*** [C] an agreement to stop fighting for a period of time ➲ look at **ceasefire**

truck 🔑 /trʌk/ ***noun*** [C] **1** (*especially AmE*) = LORRY: *a truck driver* **2** (*BrE*) a section of a train that is used for carrying goods or animals: *a cattle truck*

trudge /trʌdʒ/ ***verb*** [I] to walk with slow, heavy steps, for example because you are very tired

THESAURUS

true

right • correct • exact • precise • accurate

These words all describe sth that cannot be doubted as fact and includes no mistakes.

true: *All the rumours turned out to be true.*

right: *That is the right answer.*

correct: *Check that the details are correct.*

exact: *The police need an exact description of the man.*

precise: *Give precise details.*

accurate: *Accurate records must be kept.*

true 🔑 /truː/ ***adj.*** **1** right or correct: *Is it true that Adam is leaving?* ◇ *I didn't think the film was at all* ***true to life*** (= it didn't show life as it really is). ◇ *Read the statements and decide if they are true or false.* OPP **untrue, false** **2** real or genuine, often when this is different from how sth seems: *The novel was based on* ***a true story***. OPP **false** **3** having all the typical qualities of the thing mentioned: *How do you know when you have found* ***true love***? **4** ~ (**to sb/sth**) behaving as expected or as promised: *He was* ***true to his word*** (= he did what he had promised). ◇ *She has been a true friend to me.* ➲ noun **truth**

WORD FAMILY
true *adj.* (≠ **untrue**)
truth *noun* (≠ **untruth**)
truthful *adj.* (≠ **untruthful**)
truly *adv.*

IDM **come true** to happen in the way you hoped or dreamed: *My dream has come true!*

too good to be true used to say that you cannot believe that sth/sb is as good as it or they seem

true to form typical; as usual

ˌ**true-ˈlife** ***adj.*** (LITERATURE) a **true-life** story is one that actually happened rather than one that has been invented

ˌ**true ˈnorth** ***noun*** [U] (GEOGRAPHY) north according to the earth's AXIS (= an imagined line that goes through the earth's centre from north to south) ➲ look at **magnetic north**

truly 🔑 /ˈtruːli/ ***adv.*** **1** (used to emphasize a feeling, statement) really; completely: *We are truly grateful to you for your help.* **2** used to emphasize that sth is correct or accurate: *I cannot truly say that I was surprised at the news.*

IDM **well and truly** → WELL[1]

trump /trʌmp/ ***noun*** [C] (in some card games) a card of the chosen set (**suit**) that has a higher value than cards of the other three sets during a particular game: *Spades are trumps.*

ˈ**trump card** ***noun*** [C] a special advantage you have over other people that you keep secret until you can surprise them with it: *It was time for her to play her* ***trump card***.

trumpet /ˈtrʌmpɪt/ ***noun*** [C] (MUSIC) a musical instrument made of BRASS that you play by blowing into it. There are three buttons on it which you press to make different notes. ➲ picture on **page 465**

truncate /trʌŋˈkeɪt/ ***verb*** [T] (usually passive) (*formal*) to make sth shorter, especially by cutting off the top or end

truncheon /ˈtrʌntʃən/ (*BrE*) (*also* **baton**) ***noun*** [C] (*old-fashioned*) (LAW) a short thick stick that a police officer carries as a weapon

trundle /ˈtrʌndl/ ***verb*** [I,T] to move, or make sth heavy move, slowly and noisily: *A lorry trundled down the hill.*

trunk /trʌŋk/ ***noun*** **1** [C] (BIOLOGY) the thick central part of a tree that the branches grow from ➲ picture at **tree** **2** [C] (*AmE*) = BOOT[1] (2) **3** [C] an ELEPHANT'S long nose ➲ picture on **page 28** **4 trunks** [pl.] = SWIMMING TRUNKS **5** [C] a large box that you use for storing or transporting things **6** [C, usually sing.] (ANATOMY) the main part of your body (not including your head, arms and legs)

trust[1] 🔑 /trʌst/ ***noun*** **1** [U] ~ (**in sb/sth**) the belief that sb is good, honest, sincere, etc. and will not try to harm or trick you: *Our marriage is based on love and trust.* ◇ *I should never have* ***put my trust in*** *him.* ➲ look at **distrust, mistrust** **2** [C,U] a legal arrangement by which a person or organization looks after money and property for sb else until that person is old enough to control it

IDM **take sth on trust** to believe what sb says without having proof that it is true: *I can't prove it. You must take it on trust.*

THESAURUS

trust

depend on • rely on • count on • believe in

These words all mean to believe that sb/sth will do what you hope or expect of them or that what they tell you is correct or true.

trust: *Can I trust you to keep a secret?*

depend on: *You can always depend on him for support.*

rely on: *You can't rely on anything you read in the newspapers.*

count on: *You can count on my help.*

believe in: *He's a leader they can believe in.*

trust[2] 🔑 /trʌst/ ***verb*** [T] ~ **sb (to do sth)**; ~ **sb (with sth)** to believe that sb is good, sincere, honest, etc. and that they will not trick you or try to harm you: *He said the car was safe but I just don't trust him.* ◇ *You can't trust her with money.* ◇ *I don't trust that dog. It looks dangerous.* ➲ look at **mistrust, distrust**

IDM **Trust sb (to do sth)** (*spoken*) it is typical of sb to do sth: *Trust Alice to be late. She's never on time!*

trustee /trʌˈstiː/ ***noun*** [C] a person who looks after money or property for sb else

trusting /ˈtrʌstɪŋ/ ***adj.*** believing that other people are good, sincere, honest, etc.

trustworthy /ˈtrʌstwɜːði/ ***adj.*** that you can depend on to be good, sincere, honest, etc.
▶ **trustworthiness** ***noun*** [U]

truth 🔑 /truːθ/ ***noun*** (*pl.* **truths** /truːðz/) **1 the truth** [sing.] what is true; the facts: *Please* ***tell me the truth***. ◇ *Are you telling me* ***the whole truth*** *about what happened?* ◇ ***The truth is****, we can't afford to live here any more.* **2** [U] the state or quality of being true: *There's a lot of truth in what she says.* **3** [C] a fact or an idea that is believed by most people to be true: *scientific/universal truths* ➲ adjective **true**

truthful /ˈtruːθfl/ ***adj.*** **1** ~ (**about sth**) (used about a person) who tells the truth; honest: *I don't think you're being truthful with me.* **2** (used about a statement) true or correct: *a truthful account*
▶ **truthfully** /-fəli/ ***adv.***

try[1] /traɪ/ *verb* (*pres. part.* **trying**; *3rd person sing. pres.* **tries**; *pt, pp* **tried**) **1** [I] ~ **(to do sth)** to make an effort to do sth: *I tried to phone you but I couldn't get through.* ◇ *She was* ***trying hard*** *not to laugh.* ◇ *She'll* ***try her best*** *to help you.* ◇ *I'm sure you can do it if you try.* **2** [T] ~ **(doing) sth** to do, use or test sth in order to see how good or successful it is: *'I've tried everything but I can't get the baby to sleep.' 'Have you tried taking her out in the car?'* ◇ *Have you ever tried raw fish?* ◇ *We tried the door but it was locked.* **3** [T] ~ **sb (for sth)** (LAW) to examine sb in a court of law in order to decide if they are guilty of a crime or not: *He was tried for murder.*
IDM **try your hand at sth** to do sth such as an activity or a sport for the first time
PHR V **try sth on** to put on a piece of clothing to see if it fits you properly: *Can I try these jeans on, please?*
try sb/sth out to test sb/sth to find out if they or it are good enough

try[2] /traɪ/ ***noun*** [C] (*pl.* **tries**) an occasion when you try to do sth; an attempt: *I don't know if I can move it by myself, but I'll* ***give it a try***.

trying /'traɪɪŋ/ ***adj.*** that makes you tired or angry: *a trying journey*

tsar (also **tzar**, **czar**) /zɑː(r)/ ***noun*** [C] the title of the EMPEROR (=the leader) of Russia in the past

tsarina (also **tzarina**, **czarina**) /zɑː'riːnə/ ***noun*** [C] the title of the EMPRESS of Russia in the past

tsetse /'tsetsi/ (*also* **'tsetse fly**) ***noun*** [C] an African fly that bites humans and animals and drinks their blood and can spread a serious disease (**sleeping sickness**)

'T-shirt (also **'tee shirt**) [C] a shirt with short sleeves and without buttons or a COLLAR

tsp ***abbr.*** teaspoonful(s): *Add 1 tsp salt.*

'T-square ***noun*** [C] a plastic or metal instrument in the shape of a T for drawing or measuring RIGHT ANGLES (=angles of 90°)

tsunami /tsuː'nɑːmi/ ***noun*** [C] (GEOGRAPHY, GEOLOGY) a very large wave in the sea which destroys things when it reaches the land, and is often caused by an EARTHQUAKE (=a violent movement under the surface of the earth) SYN **tidal wave**

tub /tʌb/ ***noun*** [C] **1** a large round container **2** a small plastic container with a lid that is used for holding food: *a tub of margarine/ice cream*

tuba /'tjuːbə/ ***noun*** [C] (MUSIC) a large musical instrument made of BRASS that makes a low sound ➲ picture on **page 465**

tube /tjuːb/ ***noun*** **1** [C] a long empty pipe: *Blood flowed along the tube into the bottle.* ◇ *the inner tube of a bicycle tyre* ➲ look at **test tube** **2** [C] a ~ **(of sth)** a long thin container made of soft plastic or metal with a lid at one end. Tubes are used for holding thick liquids that can be squeezed out of them: *a tube of toothpaste* **3 the tube** [sing.] (*BrE, informal*) =UNDERGROUND[3]

tuber /'tjuːbə(r)/ ***noun*** [C] (BIOLOGY) the short thick round part of some plants, such as potatoes, which grows under the ground

tuberculosis /tjuːˌbɜːkju'ləʊsɪs/ ***noun*** [U] (*abbr.* **TB**) (HEALTH) a serious disease that affects the lungs

tubing /'tjuːbɪŋ/ ***noun*** [U] a long piece of metal, rubber, etc. in the shape of a tube ➲ picture at **laboratory**

TUC /ˌtiː juː 'siː/ ***abbr.*** the Trades Union Congress; the association of British TRADES UNIONS

tuck /tʌk/ ***verb*** [T] **1** ~ **sth in, under, round, etc. (sth)** to put or fold the ends or edges of sth into or round sth else so that it looks tidy: *Tuck your shirt in – it looks untidy like that.* **2** to put sth into a small space, especially to hide it or to keep it safe: *The letter was tucked behind a pile of books.*
PHR V **tuck sth away 1** (only in the passive form) to be situated in a quiet place; to be hidden: *The house was tucked away among the trees.* **2** to hide sth somewhere; to keep sth in a safe place: *He tucked his wallet away in his inside pocket.*
tuck sb in/up to make sb feel comfortable in bed by pulling the covers up around them
tuck in; **tuck into sth** (*especially BrE, spoken*) to eat with pleasure

Tudor /'tjuːdə(r)/ ***adj.*** (HISTORY) connected with the time when kings and queens from the Tudor family ruled England (1485-1603): *Tudor architecture*

Tue. (*also* **Tues.**) ***abbr.*** Tuesday: *Tue. 9 March*

Tuesday /'tjuːzdeɪ; -di/ ***noun*** [C,U] (*abbr.* **Tue.**; **Tues.**) the day of the week after Monday

tuft /tʌft/ ***noun*** [C] a small amount of hair, grass, etc. growing together

tug[1] /tʌg/ ***verb*** [I,T] (**tugging**; **tugged**) ~ **(at/on sth)** to pull sth hard and quickly, often several times: *The little boy tugged at his father's trouser leg.*

tug[2] /tʌg/ ***noun*** [C] **1** a sudden hard pull: *She gave the rope a tug.* **2** (*also* **'tugboat**) a small powerful boat that is used for pulling ships into a port, etc.

tuition /tju'ɪʃn/ ***noun*** [U] ~ **(in sth)** (EDUCATION) teaching, especially to a small group of people: *private tuition in Italian* ◇ *tuition fees* (=the money that you pay to be taught, especially in a college or university)

tulip /'tjuːlɪp/ ***noun*** [C] a brightly-coloured flower, shaped like a cup, that grows in the spring

tumble /'tʌmbl/ ***verb*** [I] **1** to fall down suddenly but without serious injury: *He tripped and tumbled all the way down the steps.* **2** to fall suddenly in value or amount: *House prices have tumbled.* **3** to move in a particular direction in an untidy way: *She opened her suitcase and all her things tumbled out of it.*
► **tumble** ***noun*** [C]
PHR V **tumble down** to fall down; to collapse: *The walls of the old house were tumbling down.*

ˌtumble 'dryer (also **ˌtumble-'drier**) ***noun*** [C] (*BrE*) a machine that dries clothes by moving them about in hot air

tumbler /'tʌmblə(r)/ ***noun*** [C] a tall glass for drinking out of with straight sides and no handle

tummy /'tʌmi/ ***noun*** [C] (*pl.* **tummies**) (*informal*) =STOMACH[1]

tumour (*AmE* **tumor**) /'tjuːmə(r)/ ***noun*** [C] (HEALTH) a mass of cells that are not growing normally in the body as the result of a disease: *a brain tumour*

tumultuous /tjuː'mʌltʃuəs/ ***adj.*** very noisy, because people are excited: *tumultuous applause*

tuna /'tjuːnə/ (*also* **'tuna fish**) ***noun*** [C,U] (*pl.* **tuna**) a large sea fish that we eat: *a tin of tuna*

tundra /'tʌndrə/ ***noun*** [U] (GEOGRAPHY) the large flat Arctic regions of northern Europe, Asia and North America where no trees grow and where the soil below the surface of the ground is always frozen ➲ picture at **ecosystem**

tune[1] /tjuːn/ ***noun*** [C,U] (MUSIC) a series of musical notes that are sung or played to form a piece of music: *The children* ***played us a tune*** *on their recorders.*
IDM **call the shots/tune** → CALL[1]

change your tune → CHANGE[1]
in/out of tune 1 (MUSIC) at/not at the correct musical level (**pitch**): *You're singing out of tune.* **2** having/not having the same opinions, interests, feelings, etc. as sb/sth

tune² /tju:n/ *verb* **1** [T] (MUSIC) to make small changes to the sound a musical instrument makes so that it is at the correct musical level (**pitch**): *to tune a piano/guitar* **2** [T] to make small changes to an engine so that it runs well **3** [T] (usually passive) **~ sth (in) (to sth)** to move the controls on a radio or television so that you can receive a particular station: *The radio was tuned (in) to the BBC World Service.* ◇ (*spoken*) ***Stay tuned** for the latest news.*
PHR V **tune in (to sth)** to listen to a radio programme or watch a television programme
tune (sth) up (MUSIC) to make small changes to a group of musical instruments so that they sound pleasant when played together

tuneful /'tju:nfl/ *adj.* (used about music) pleasant to listen to

tungsten /'tʌŋstən/ *noun* [U] (*symbol* **W**) (CHEMISTRY) a very hard silver-grey metal, used especially in making steel and in FILAMENTS for LIGHT BULBS ❶ For more information on the periodic table of elements, look at pages R34-5.

tunic /'tju:nɪk/ *noun* [C] **1** a piece of women's clothing, usually without sleeves, that is long and not tight **2** (*BrE*) the jacket that is part of the uniform of a police officer, soldier, etc.

tunnel 🔑 /'tʌnl/ *noun* [C] a passage under the ground: *The train disappeared into a tunnel.*
▸ **tunnel** *verb* [I,T] (**tunnelling**; **tunnelled**: *AmE* **tunneling**; **tunneled**)

turban /'tɜ:bən/ *noun* [C] a covering for the head worn especially by Sikh and Muslim men. A **turban** is made by folding a long piece of cloth around the head.

turbine /'tɜ:baɪn/ *noun* [C] (PHYSICS) a machine or an engine that receives its power from a wheel that is turned by the pressure of water, air or gas ➲ look at **wind turbine** ➲ picture at **generator**

turbocharger /'tɜ:bəʊtʃɑ:dʒə(r)/ (*also* **'turbo** /'tɜ:bəʊ/) *noun* [C] (PHYSICS) a system in a car that sends a mixture of petrol and air into the engine at high pressure, making it more powerful

turbot /'tɜ:bət/ *noun* [C,U] (*pl.* **turbot** or **turbots**) a large flat European sea fish that some people eat

turbulent /'tɜ:bjələnt/ *adj.* **1** in which there is a lot of change, DISORDER and disagreement, and sometimes violence **2** (used about water or air) moving in a violent way ▸ **turbulence** *noun* [U]

turf¹ /tɜ:f/ *noun* [U, C] (a piece of) short thick grass and the layer of soil underneath it: *newly laid turf*

turf² /tɜ:f/ *verb* [T] to cover ground with **turf**
PHR V **turf sb out (of sth)** (*BrE*, *informal*) to force sb to leave a place

turkey /'tɜ:ki/ *noun* [C,U] a large bird that is kept on farms. **Turkeys** are usually eaten at Christmas in Britain and at Thanksgiving in the US. ➲ picture on page 28
IDM **cold turkey** → COLD[1]

turmoil /'tɜ:mɔɪl/ *noun* [U, sing.] a state of great noise or confusion: *His mind was **in (a) turmoil**.*

turn¹ 🔑 /tɜ:n/ *verb* **1** [I,T] to move or make sth move round a fixed central point: *The wheels turned faster and faster.* ◇ *She turned the key in the lock.* ◇ *Turn the steering wheel to the right.* **2** [I,T] to move your body, or part of your body, so that you are facing in a different direction: *He turned round when he heard my voice.* ◇ *She **turned** her **back on** me* (=she deliberately moved her body to face away from me). **3** [I,T] to change the position of sth: *I turned the box upside down.* ◇ *He turned the page and started the next chapter.* ◇ *Turn to page 33 in your books.* **4** [T] to point or aim sth in a particular direction: *She turned her attention back to the television.* **5** [I,T] to change direction when you are moving: *Go straight on and **turn left** at the church.* ◇ *The car **turned the corner**.* **6** [I,T] (to cause) to become: *He **turned** very **red** when I asked him about the money.* ◇ *These caterpillars will turn into butterflies.* **7** [T] (not used in the continuous tenses) to reach or pass a particular age or time: *It's turned midnight.*
PHR V **turn (sth) around/round** to change position or direction in order to face the opposite way, or to return the way you came: *This road is a dead end. We'll have to turn round and go back to the main road.* ◇ *He turned the car around and drove off.*
turn away to stop looking at sb/sth: *She turned away in horror at the sight of the blood.*
turn sb away to refuse to allow a person to go into a place
turn back to return the same way that you came: *We've come so far already, we can't turn back now.*
turn sb/sth down to refuse an offer, etc. or the person who makes it: *Why did you turn that job down?* ◇ *He asked her to marry him, but she turned him down.*
turn sth down to reduce the sound or heat that sth produces: *Turn the television down!*
turn off (sth) to leave one road and go on another
turn sth off to stop the flow of electricity, water, etc. by moving a switch, tap, etc.: *He turned the TV off.*
turn sth on to start the flow of electricity, water, etc. by moving a switch, tap, etc.: *to turn the lights on*
turn out (for sth) to be present at an event
turn out (to be sth) to be in the end: *The weather turned out fine.* ◇ *The house that they had promised us turned out to be a tiny flat.*
turn sth out to move the switch, etc. on a light or a source of heat to stop it: *Turn the lights out before you go to bed.*
turn over 1 to change position so that the other side is facing out or upwards: *He turned over and went back to sleep.* **2** (used about an engine) to start or to continue to run **3** (*BrE*) to change to another programme when you are watching television
turn sth over 1 to make sth change position so that the other side is facing out or upwards: *You may now turn over your exam papers and begin.* **2** to keep thinking about sth carefully: *She kept turning over what he'd said in her mind.*
turn to sb/sth to go to sb/sth to get help, advice, etc.
turn up 1 to arrive; to appear: *What time did they finally turn up?* **2** to be found, especially by chance: *I lost my glasses a week ago and they haven't turned up yet.*
turn sth up to increase the sound or heat that sth produces: *Turn the heating up – I'm cold.*

turn² 🔑 /tɜ:n/ *noun* [C] **1** the action of turning sb/sth round: *Give the screw another couple of turns to make sure it is really tight.* **2** a change of direction in a vehicle: *to make a **left/right turn*** ◇ *a **U-turn*** (=when you turn round in a vehicle and go back in the opposite direction) **3** (*BrE* **turning**) a bend or corner in a road, river, etc.: *Take the next turn on the left.* **4** [usually sing.] the time when sb in a group of people should or is allowed to do sth: *Please wait in the queue until it is your turn.* ◇ *Whose turn is it to do the cleaning?* SYN **go 5** an unusual or unexpected

change: *The patient's condition has* ***taken a turn for the worse*** (=suddenly got worse).
IDM **(do sb) a good turn** to do sth helpful for sb
in turn one after the other: *I spoke to each of the children in turn.*
take turns (at sth) to do sth one after the other to make sure it is fair
the turn of the century/year the time when a new century/year starts
wait your turn → WAIT[1]

turnaround /ˈtɜːnəraʊnd/ (*BrE also* **turnround**) *noun* [C, usually sing.] **1** (TOURISM) the amount of time it takes to unload a ship or plane at the end of one journey and load it again for the next one **2** the amount of time it takes to do a piece of work that you have been given and return it **3** a situation in which sth changes from bad to good: *a turnaround in the economy* **4** a complete change in sb's opinion, behaviour, etc.: *They remain suspicious about the government's turnaround on education policy.*

turning /ˈtɜːnɪŋ/ (*BrE*) (*also* **turn**) *noun* [C] a place where one road leads off from another: *We must have taken a wrong turning.*

ˈ**turning point** *noun* [C] **a turning point (in sth)** a time when an important change happens, usually a good one

turnip /ˈtɜːnɪp/ *noun* [C,U] a round white vegetable that grows under the ground

ˈ**turn-off** *noun* [C] the place where a road leads away from a larger or more important road: *This is the turn-off for York.*

turnout /ˈtɜːnaʊt/ *noun* [C, usually sing.] the number of people who go to a meeting, sports event, etc.

turnover /ˈtɜːnəʊvə(r)/ *noun* [sing.] **a ~ (of sth)** **1** the amount of business that a company does in a particular period of time: *The firm has an annual turnover of $50 million.* **2** the rate at which workers leave a company and are replaced by new ones: *a high turnover of staff*

turnpike /ˈtɜːnpaɪk/ (*also* **pike**) *noun* [C] (*AmE*) a wide road, where traffic can travel fast for long distances and that drivers must pay a TOLL (=a sum of money) to use

turnround /ˈtɜːnraʊnd/ *noun* [C] (*BrE*) =TURNAROUND

turnstile /ˈtɜːnstaɪl/ *noun* [C] a metal gate that moves round in a circle when it is pushed, and allows one person at a time to enter a place

turntable /ˈtɜːnteɪbl/ *noun* [C] **1** the round surface on a RECORD PLAYER that you place the record on to be played **2** a large round surface that is able to move in a circle and onto which a railway engine is driven in order to turn it to go in the opposite direction

ˈ**turn-up** *noun* [C] the bottom of the leg of a pair of trousers/pants that has been folded over on the outside

turpentine /ˈtɜːpəntaɪn/ *noun* [U] a clear liquid with a strong smell that you use for removing paint or for making paint thinner

turquoise /ˈtɜːkwɔɪz/ *adj., noun* **1** [C,U] (GEOLOGY) a blue or greenish-blue precious stone **2** [U] (of) a greenish-blue colour

turret /ˈtʌrət/ *noun* [C] (ARCHITECTURE) a small tower on the top of a large building ➲ picture at **castle**

turtle /ˈtɜːtl/ *noun* [C] **1** (*AmE also* ˈ**sea turtle**) a REPTILE with a thick shell that lives in the sea ➲ picture on **page 29** **2** (*AmE*) =TORTOISE

turtleneck /ˈtɜːtlnek/ *noun* [C] **1** a sweater with a high part fitting closely around the neck **2** =POLO NECK

tusk /tʌsk/ *noun* [C] (BIOLOGY) one of the two very long pointed teeth of an ELEPHANT, etc. **Tusks** are made of IVORY. ➲ picture on **page 28**

tussle /ˈtʌsl/ *noun* [C] (*informal*) **a ~ (for/over sth)** a fight, for example between two or more people who want to have the same thing

tut /tʌt/ (*also* ˌ**tut-**ˈ**tut**) *exclamation* the way of writing the sound that people make to show disapproval of sb/sth ▸ **tut** *verb* [I] (**tutting**; **tutted**)

tutor /ˈtjuːtə(r)/ *noun* (EDUCATION) [C] **1** a private teacher who teaches one person or a very small group **2** (*BrE*) a teacher who is responsible for a small group of students at school, college or university. A **tutor** advises students on their work or helps them if they have problems in their private life.

tutorial /tjuːˈtɔːriəl/ *noun* [C] (EDUCATION) a lesson at a college or university for an individual student or a small group of students

tuxedo /tʌkˈsiːdəʊ/ (*pl.* **tuxedos** /-dəʊz/) (*also informal* **tux**) (*AmE*) =DINNER JACKET

TV /ˌtiː ˈviː/ *abbr.* =TELEVISION

twang /twæŋ/ *noun* [C] the sound that is made when you pull a tight piece of string, wire or ELASTIC and then let it go suddenly ▸ **twang** *verb* [I,T]

tweed /twiːd/ *noun* [U] thick WOOLLEN cloth with a rough surface used for making clothes

tweezers /ˈtwiːzəz/ *noun* [pl.] a small tool consisting of two pieces of metal that are joined at one end. You use **tweezers** for picking up or pulling out very small things: *a pair of tweezers*

twelfth /twelfθ/ *ordinal number, noun* [C] 12th ➲ note at **sixth**[1]

twelve /twelv/ *number* 12 ➲ look at **dozen** ➲ note at **six**

twentieth /ˈtwentiəθ/ *ordinal number, noun* [C] 20th ➲ note at **sixth**[1]

twenty /ˈtwenti/ *number* **1** 20 **2 the twenties** [pl.] numbers, years or temperatures from 20 to 29 ➲ note at **sixty**

twice 🔑 /twaɪs/ *adv.* two times: *I've been to Egypt twice – once last year and once in 1994.* ◇ *The film will be shown twice daily.* ◇ *Take the medicine twice a day.* ◇ *Prices have risen twice as fast in this country as in Japan.*

twiddle /ˈtwɪdl/ *verb* [I,T] (*BrE*) **~ (with) sth** to keep turning or moving sth with your fingers, often because you are nervous or bored

twig /twɪg/ *noun* [C] a small thin branch on a tree or bush ➲ picture at **tree**

twilight /ˈtwaɪlaɪt/ *noun* [U] the time after the sun has set and before it gets completely dark ➲ look at **dusk**

twin 🔑 /twɪn/ *noun* [C] **1** one of two children or animals that are born to one mother at the same time: *They're very alike. Are they twins?* ◇ *a twin brother/sister* ◇ *identical twins* ➲ look at **Siamese twin, triplet** **2** one of a pair of things that are the same or very similar: *twin engines* ◇ *twin beds*

twinge /twɪndʒ/ *noun* [C] **1** (HEALTH) a sudden short pain: *He suddenly felt a twinge in his back.* **2 a ~ (of sth)** a sudden short feeling of an unpleasant emotion

twinkle /ˈtwɪŋkl/ ***verb*** [I] **1** to shine with a light that seems to go on and off: *Stars twinkled in the night sky.* **2** (used about your eyes) to look bright because you are happy ▶ **twinkle** ***noun*** [sing.]

ˌ**twin ˈtown** ***noun*** [C] one of two towns in different countries that have a special relationship: *Grenoble is Oxford's twin town.*

twirl /twɜːl/ ***verb*** [I,T] ~ **(sb/sth) (around/round)** to turn round and round quickly; to make sb/sth do this

twist[1] /twɪst/ ***verb*** **1** [I,T] to bend or turn sth into a particular shape, often one it does not go in naturally; to be bent in this way: *She twisted her long hair into a knot.* ◇ *Her face twisted in anger.* ◇ *He twisted his* ***ankle*** *while he was playing squash.* ➲ note at **injure** **2** [I,T] to turn a part of your body while the rest stays still: *She twisted round to see where the noise was coming from.* ◇ *He kept twisting his head from side to side.* **3** [T] to turn sth around in a circle with your hand: *She twisted the ring on her finger nervously.* ◇ *Most containers have twist-off caps.* **4** [I] (used about a road, etc.) to change direction often: *a narrow twisting lane* ◇ *The road* ***twists and turns*** *along the coast.* **5** [I,T] ~ **(sth) (round/around sth)** to put sth round another object; to be round another object: *The telephone wire has* ***got twisted*** *round the table leg.* **6** [T] to change the meaning of what sb has said: *Journalists often* ***twist*** *your* ***words****.*

IDM **twist sb's arm** (*informal*) to force or persuade sb to do sth

twist[2] /twɪst/ ***noun*** [C] **1** the action of turning sth with your hand, or of turning part of your body: *She killed the chicken with one twist of its neck.* **2** an unexpected change or development in a story or situation **3** a place where a road, river, etc. bends or changes direction: *the* ***twists and turns*** *of the river* **4** something that has become or been bent into a particular shape: *Straighten out the wire so that there are no twists in it.*

twit /twɪt/ ***noun*** [C] (*BrE, informal*) a stupid person

twitch /twɪtʃ/ ***verb*** [I,T] to make a quick sudden movement, often one that you cannot control; to cause sth to make a sudden movement: *The rabbit twitched and then lay still.* ◇ *He twitched his nose.* ▶ **twitch** ***noun*** [C]: *He has a nervous twitch.*

twitter /ˈtwɪtə(r)/ ***verb*** [I] (used about birds) to make a series of short high sounds

two /tuː/ ***number*** **1** 2 ➲ look at **second** ➲ note at **six** **2 two-** (used to form compound adjectives) having two of the thing mentioned: *a two-week holiday*

IDM **be in two minds (about sth/about doing sth)** → MIND[1]

in two in or into two pieces: *The plate fell on the floor and broke in two.*

ˌ**two-diˈmensional** (*also* ˌ**2-ˈD**) ***adj.*** (GEOMETRY) having or appearing to have length and width but no depth; flat ➲ look at **three-dimensional**

ˌ**two-ˈfaced** ***adj.*** (*informal*) not sincere; not acting in a way that supports what you say that you believe; saying different things to different people about a particular subject SYN **hypocritical**

ˈ**two-ply** ***adj.*** (used about wool, wood, etc.) with two threads or thicknesses

ˈ**two-star** ***adj.*** (TOURISM) having two stars in a system that measures quality. The highest standard is usually represented by four or five stars: *a two-star hotel*

ˌ**two-ˈway** ***adj.*** (usually before a noun) **1** moving in two different directions; allowing sth to move in two different directions: *two-way traffic* **2** (used about communication between people) needing equal effort from both people or groups involved: *Friendship is a two-way process.* **3** (used about radio equipment, etc.) used both for sending and receiving signals

tycoon /taɪˈkuːn/ ***noun*** [C] (BUSINESS) a person who is very successful in business or industry and who has become rich and powerful

type[1] /taɪp/ ***noun*** **1** [C] a ~ **(of sth)** a group of people or things that share certain qualities and that are part of a larger group; a kind or sort: *Which type of paint should you use on metal?* ◇ *Spaniels are a type of dog.* ◇ *You meet all types of people in this job.* ◇ *the first building of its type in the world* ◇ *I love this type/these types of movie.* **2** [C] a person of a particular kind: *He's the careful type.* ◇ *She's* ***not the type to*** *do anything silly.* ➲ look at **typical** **3** **-type** (used to form compound adjectives) having the qualities, etc. of the group, person or thing mentioned: *a ceramic-type material* ◇ *a police-type badge* **4** [U] letters that are printed or typed

type[2] /taɪp/ ***verb*** [I,T] to write sth by using a WORD PROCESSOR or TYPEWRITER: *Can you type?* ◇ *to type a letter* ▶ **typing** ***noun*** [U]: *typing skills*

typeface /ˈtaɪpfeɪs/ ***noun*** [C] a set of letters, numbers, etc. of a particular design, used in printing: *I'd like the heading to be in a different typeface from the text.*

typewriter /ˈtaɪpraɪtə(r)/ ***noun*** [C] a machine that you use for writing in print

typewritten /ˈtaɪprɪtn/ ***adj.*** written using a TYPEWRITER or computer

typhoid /ˈtaɪfɔɪd/ ***noun*** [U] (HEALTH) a serious disease that can cause death. People get **typhoid** from bad food or water.

typhoon /taɪˈfuːn/ ***noun*** [C] (GEOGRAPHY) a violent tropical storm with very strong winds ➲ note at **storm**

typical /ˈtɪpɪkl/ ***adj.*** ~ **(of sb/sth)** **1** having or showing the usual qualities of a particular person, thing or type: *a typical Italian village* ◇ *There's no such thing as a typical American* (=they are all different). OPP **untypical**, **atypical** **2** behaving in the way you expect: *It was absolutely typical of him not to reply to my letter.*

typically /ˈtɪpɪkli/ ***adv.*** **1** in a typical case; that usually happens in this way: *Typically it is the girls who offer to help, not the boys.* **2** in a way that shows the usual qualities of a particular person, type or thing: *typically British humour*

typify /ˈtɪpɪfaɪ/ ***verb*** [T] (*pres. part.* **typifying**; *3rd person sing. pres.* **typifies**; *pt, pp* **typified**) to be a typical mark or example of sb/sth: *This film typified the Hollywood westerns of that time.*

typist /ˈtaɪpɪst/ ***noun*** [C] a person who works in an office typing letters, etc.

typography /taɪˈpɒɡrəfi/ ***noun*** [U] the art or work of preparing books, etc. for printing, especially of designing how text will appear when it is printed ▶ **typographical** /ˌtaɪpəˈɡræfɪkl/ (*also* **typographic** /ˌtaɪpəˈɡræfɪk/) ***adj.***: *a typographical error* ◇ *typographic design* ▶ **typographically** /-kli/ ***adv.***

tyranny /ˈtɪrəni/ ***noun*** [U] (POLITICS) the cruel and unfair use of power by a person or small group to control a country or state ▶ **tyrannical** /tɪˈrænɪkl/ ***adj.***: *a tyrannical ruler* ▶ **tyrannize** (also **-ise**) /ˈtɪrənaɪz/ ***verb*** [I,T]

tyrant /ˈtaɪrənt/ ***noun*** [C] (POLITICS) a cruel ruler who has complete power over the people in their country ➲ look at **dictator**

tyre 🔑 (*AmE* **tire**) /ˈtaɪə(r)/ ***noun*** [C] the thick rubber ring that fits around the outside of a wheel: *a **flat tyre*** (= a tyre with no air in it)

tzar = TSAR

tzarina = TSARINA

U u

U, u[1] /juː/ ***noun*** [C,U] (*pl.* **U's**; **u's** /juːz/) the twenty-first letter of the English alphabet: *'Ulcer' begins with (a) 'U'.*

U[2] /juː/ ***abbr.*** (*BrE*) (used about films that are suitable for anyone, including children) universal

ubiquitous /juːˈbɪkwɪtəs/ ***adj.*** (usually *before* a noun) (*formal*) seeming to be everywhere or in several places at the same time; very common: *the ubiquitous bicycles of university towns* ◇ *the ubiquitous movie star, Tom Hanks* ▶ **ubiquitously** ***adv.*** ▶ **ubiquity** /juːˈbɪkwəti/ ***noun*** [U]

udder /ˈʌdə(r)/ ***noun*** [C] (AGRICULTURE) the part of a female cow, etc. that hangs under its body and produces milk ➲ picture at **goat**

UEFA /juˈeɪfə/ ***abbr.*** the Union of European Football Associations: *the UEFA cup*

UFD /ˌjuː ef ˈdiː/ ***noun*** [C] (COMPUTING) = USB FLASH DRIVE

UFO (*also* **ufo**) /ˌjuː ef ˈəʊ/ ***abbr.*** an unidentified flying object ➲ look at **flying saucer**

ugh /ɜː/ ***exclamation*** used in writing to express the sound that you make when you think sth is disgusting

ugly 🔑 /ˈʌɡli/ ***adj.*** (**uglier**; **ugliest**) **1** unpleasant to look at or listen to; not attractive: *The burn left an ugly scar on her face.* ◇ *an ugly modern office block* **2** (used about a situation) dangerous or threatening ▶ **ugliness** ***noun*** [U]

UHF /ˌjuː eɪtʃ ˈef/ ***abbr.*** ultra-high frequency; radio waves that move up and down at a particular speed and which are used to send out radio and television programmes ➲ picture at **wavelength**

UHT /ˌjuː eɪtʃ ˈtiː/ ***abbr.*** used about foods such as milk that are treated to last longer: *UHT milk*

UK /ˌjuː ˈkeɪ/ ***abbr.*** the United Kingdom; England, Scotland, Wales and N Ireland: *a UK citizen*

ulcer /ˈʌlsə(r)/ ***noun*** [C] (HEALTH) a painful area on your skin or inside your body. **Ulcers** may produce a poisonous substance and sometimes BLEED: *a mouth/stomach ulcer*

ulna /ˈʌlnə/ ***noun*** [C] (HEALTH, ANATOMY) the longer bone of the two bones in the lower part of your arm between your wrist and your elbow ➲ look at **radius** ➲ picture on **page 80**

ulterior /ʌlˈtɪəriə(r)/ ***adj.*** that you keep hidden or secret: *Why is he suddenly being so nice to me? He must have an **ulterior motive**.*

ultimate[1] 🔑 AW /ˈʌltɪmət/ ***adj.*** (only *before* a noun) **1** being or happening at the end; last or final: *Our ultimate goal is complete independence.* **2** the greatest, best or worst

ultimate[2] AW /ˈʌltɪmət/ ***noun*** [sing.] (*informal*) **the ~ (in sth)** the greatest or best: *This new car is the ultimate in comfort.*

ultimately 🔑 AW /ˈʌltɪmətli/ ***adv.*** **1** in the end: *Ultimately, the decision is yours.* **2** at the most basic level; most importantly

ultimatum /ˌʌltɪˈmeɪtəm/ ***noun*** [C] (*pl.* **ultimatums**) a final warning to sb that, if they do not do what you ask, you will use force or take action against them: *I gave him an ultimatum – either he paid his rent or he was out.*

ultra- /ˈʌltrə/ (in compounds) extremely: *ultra-modern*

ultrasonic /ˌʌltrəˈsɒnɪk/ ***adj.*** (usually before a noun) (PHYSICS) (used about sounds) higher than humans can hear: *ultrasonic frequencies/waves/signals*

ultrasound /ˈʌltrəsaʊnd/ ***noun*** **1** [U] (PHYSICS) sound that is higher than humans can hear **2** [U, C] (HEALTH) a medical process that produces an image of what is inside your body: *Ultrasound showed she was expecting twins.*

ultraviolet /ˌʌltrəˈvaɪələt/ ***adj.*** (*abbr.* **UV**) (PHYSICS) connected with or using ELECTROMAGNETIC waves that are just shorter than those of VIOLET light in the SPECTRUM and that cannot be seen: *ultraviolet rays* (= that cause the skin to go darker) ◇ *an ultraviolet lamp* ➲ look at **infrared** ➲ picture at **wavelength**

ultra vires /ˌʌltrə ˈvaɪriːz/ ***adv.*** (LAW) beyond your legal power or authority

umbilical cord /ʌmˌbɪlɪkl ˈkɔːd/ ***noun*** [C] (ANATOMY) the tube that connects a baby to its mother before it is born ➲ picture at **embryo**

umbra /ˈʌmbrə/ ***noun*** [C] **1** the central part of a SHADOW where it is completely dark **2** (ASTRONOMY) a completely dark area on the earth caused by the moon, or a completely dark area on the moon caused by the earth, during an ECLIPSE (= a time when the moon is between the earth and the sun, or when the earth is between the moon and the sun) ➲ look at **penumbra** ➲ picture at **shadow**

umbrella 🔑 /ʌmˈbrelə/ ***noun*** [C] an object that you open and hold over your head to keep yourself dry when it is raining: *to put an umbrella up/down*

umlaut /ˈʊmlaʊt/ ***noun*** [C] (LANGUAGE) the mark placed over a vowel in some languages to show how it should be pronounced, as over the *u* in the German word *für* ➲ look at **acute accent**, **circumflex**, **grave**[2], **tilde**

umpire /ˈʌmpaɪə(r)/ ***noun*** [C] (SPORT) a person who watches a game such as TENNIS or CRICKET to make sure that the players obey the rules ➲ look at **referee** ▶ **umpire** ***verb*** [I,T]

umpteen /ˌʌmpˈtiːn/ ***pronoun***, ***det.*** (*informal*) very many; a lot ▶ **umpteenth** /ˌʌmpˈtiːnθ/ ***pronoun***, ***det.***: *For the umpteenth time – phone if you're going to be late!*

UN /ˌjuː ˈen/ ***abbr.*** (POLITICS) the United Nations Organization

un- /ʌn/ ***prefix*** **1** (used in adjectives, adverbs and nouns) not; the opposite of: *unable* ◇ *unconsciously* ◇ *untruth* ◇ *un-American activities* (= against the interests of the US) **2** (used in verbs that describe the opposite of a process): *unlock* ◇ *undo* ◇ *unfold*

unabated /ˌʌnəˈbeɪtɪd/ ***adj.*** (*formal*) without becoming any less strong: *The rain **continued unabated**.*

unable ⊶ /ʌn'eɪbl/ ***adj.*** ~ **to do sth** not having the time, knowledge, skill, etc. to do sth; not able to do sth: *She lay there, unable to move.* ➲ noun **inability**

unacceptable ⊶ /ˌʌnək'septəbl/ ***adj.*** that you cannot accept or allow OPP **acceptable** ▸ **unacceptably** /-bli/ ***adv.***

unaccompanied AW /ˌʌnə'kʌmpənid/ ***adj.*** alone, without sb/sth else with you: *Unaccompanied children are not allowed in the bar.*

unaccustomed /ˌʌnə'kʌstəmd/ ***adj.*** (*formal*) ~ **to sth/to doing sth** not in the habit of doing sth; not used to sth: *He was unaccustomed to hard work.*

unadulterated /ˌʌnə'dʌltəreɪtɪd/ ***adj.*** **1** used to emphasize that sth is complete or total: *For me, the holiday was sheer unadulterated pleasure.* **2** not mixed with other substances: *unadulterated foods* SYN **pure**

unaffected AW /ˌʌnə'fektɪd/ ***adj.*** **1** not changed by sth **2** behaving in a natural way without trying to impress anyone OPP **affected**

unaided AW /ʌn'eɪdɪd/ ***adv.*** without any help

unalterable AW /ʌn'ɔːltərəbl/ ***adj.*** (*formal*) that cannot be changed: *the unalterable laws of the universe*

unambiguous AW /ˌʌnæm'bɪgjuəs/ ***adj.*** clear in meaning; that can only be understood in one way

unanimous /ju'nænɪməs/ ***adj.*** **1** (used about a group of people) all agreeing about sth: *The judges were unanimous in their decision.* **2** (used about a decision, etc.) agreed by everyone: *The jury reached a unanimous verdict of guilty.* ▸ **unanimously *adv.***

unanticipated AW /ˌʌnæn'tɪsɪpeɪtɪd/ ***adj.*** (*formal*) that you have not expected or predicted; that you have not anticipated

unapproachable AW /ˌʌnə'prəʊtʃəbl/ ***adj.*** (used about a person) unfriendly and not easy to talk to

unarmed /ˌʌn'ɑːmd/ ***adj.*** having no guns, knives, etc.; not armed OPP **armed**

unashamed /ˌʌnə'ʃeɪmd/ ***adj.*** not feeling sorry or embarrassed about sth bad that you have done OPP **ashamed** ▸ **unashamedly** /-'ʃeɪmɪdli/ ***adv.***

unassuming /ˌʌnə'sjuːmɪŋ/ ***adj.*** not wanting people to notice how good, important, etc. you are

unattached AW /ˌʌnə'tætʃt/ ***adj.*** **1** not connected to sb/sth else **2** not married; without a regular partner

unattainable AW /ˌʌnə'teɪnəbl/ ***adj.*** impossible to achieve or reach: *an unattainable goal* OPP **attainable**

unattended /ˌʌnə'tendɪd/ ***adj.*** not watched or looked after: *Do not leave children unattended.*

unattractive /ˌʌnə'træktɪv/ ***adj.*** **1** not attractive or pleasant to look at **2** not good, interesting or pleasant OPP **attractive**

unauthorized (also **-ised**) /ʌn'ɔːθəraɪzd/ ***adj.*** done without permission

unavailable AW /ˌʌnə'veɪləbl/ ***adj.*** (not usually before a noun) ~ **(to sb/sth) 1** that cannot be obtained: *Such luxury items were unavailable to ordinary people.* **2** not able or not willing to see, meet or talk to sb: *The minister was unavailable for comment.* OPP **available** ▸ **unavailability** /ˌʌnəˌveɪlə'bɪləti/ ***noun*** [U]

unavoidable /ˌʌnə'vɔɪdəbl/ ***adj.*** that cannot be avoided or prevented OPP **avoidable** ▸ **unavoidably** /-əbli/ ***adv.***

unaware AW /ˌʌnə'weə(r)/ ***adj.*** (not before a noun) ~ **(of sb/sth)** not knowing about or not noticing sb/sth: *She seemed unaware of all the trouble she had caused.* OPP **aware**

unawares /ˌʌnə'weəz/ ***adv.*** by surprise; without expecting sth or being prepared for it: *I was **taken** completely **unawares** by his suggestion.*

unbalanced /ˌʌn'bælənst/ ***adj.*** **1** (used about a person) slightly crazy **2** not fair to all ideas or sides of an argument OPP **balanced**

unbearable /ʌn'beərəbl/ ***adj.*** too unpleasant, painful, etc. for you to accept SYN **intolerable** OPP **bearable** ▸ **unbearably** /-əbli/ ***adv.***: *It was unbearably hot.*

unbeatable /ʌn'biːtəbl/ ***adj.*** that cannot be defeated or improved on: *unbeatable prices*

unbeaten /ʌn'biːtn/ ***adj.*** that has not been beaten or improved on

unbelievable /ˌʌnbɪ'liːvəbl/ ***adj.*** very surprising; difficult to believe OPP **believable** ➲ look at **incredible** ▸ **unbelievably** /-əbli/ ***adj.***: *His work was unbelievably bad.*

unbiased (also **unbiassed**) AW /ʌn'baɪəst/ ***adj.*** fair and not influenced by your own or sb else's opinions, desires, etc. SYN **impartial**: *an unbiased judge* OPP **biased**

unblemished /ʌn'blemɪʃt/ ***adj.*** not spoiled, damaged or marked in any way: *The new party leader has an unblemished reputation.*

unblock /ˌʌn'blɒk/ ***verb*** [T] to clean sth, for example a pipe, by removing sth that is blocking it

unborn /ˌʌn'bɔːn/ ***adj.*** not yet born

unbroken /ʌn'brəʊkən/ ***adj.*** **1** continuous; not interrupted: *a period of unbroken silence* **2** that has not been beaten: *His record for the 1500 metres remains unbroken.*

uncalled for /ʌn'kɔːld fɔː(r)/ ***adj.*** (used about behaviour or comments) not fair and not appropriate: *That comment was quite uncalled for.*

uncanny /ʌn'kæni/ ***adj.*** very strange; that you cannot easily explain: *an uncanny coincidence*

unceasing /ʌn'siːsɪŋ/ ***adj.*** (*written*) continuing all the time: *unceasing efforts* ◇ *the country's history of unceasing conflict and division* ▸ **unceasingly *adv.***: *The rain fell unceasingly.*

uncertain ⊶ /ʌn'sɜːtn/ ***adj.*** **1** ~ **(about/of sth)** not sure; not able to decide: *She was still uncertain of his true feelings for her.* **2** not known exactly or not decided: *He's lost his job and his future seems very uncertain.* OPP **certain** ▸ **uncertainly *adv.*** ▸ **uncertainty *noun*** [C,U] (*pl.* **uncertainties**): *Today's decision will put an end to all the uncertainty.* OPP **certainty**

unchanged /ʌn'tʃeɪndʒd/ ***adj.*** staying the same; not changed

uncharacteristic /ˌʌnˌkærəktə'rɪstɪk/ ***adj.*** not typical or usual OPP **characteristic** ▸ **uncharacteristically** /-kli/ ***adv.***

uncharted AW /ˌʌn'tʃɑːtɪd/ ***adj.*** **1** that has not been visited or investigated before; not familiar: *They set off into the country's uncharted interior.* ◇ (*figurative*) *The party is sailing in **uncharted waters*** (=a situation it has not been in before) **2** (GEOGRAPHY) not marked on a map: *The ship hit an uncharted rock.*

unchecked /ˌʌn'tʃekt/ *adj.* if sth harmful is **unchecked**, it is not controlled or stopped from getting worse: *The fire was allowed to burn unchecked.* ◇ *The rise in violent crime must not* ***go unchecked***. ◇ *The plant will soon choke ponds and waterways if* ***left unchecked***.

uncle ⊶ /'ʌŋkl/ ***noun*** [C] the brother of your father or mother; the husband of your aunt: *Uncle Steven*

unclear /ˌʌn'klɪə(r)/ ***adj.*** **1** not clear or definite; difficult to understand or be sure about: *His motives are unclear.* ◇ *Our plans are unclear at the moment.* ◇ *It is unclear whether there is any damage.* ◇ *Some of the diagrams are unclear.* **2 ~ (about sth); ~ (as to sth)** not fully understanding sth; uncertain about sth: *I'm unclear about what you want me to do.*

uncomfortable ⊶ /ʌn'kʌmftəbl/ ***adj.*** **1** not pleasant to wear, sit in, lie on, etc.: *uncomfortable shoes* **2** not able to sit, lie, etc. in a position that is pleasant **3** feeling or causing worry or embarrassment: *I felt very uncomfortable when they started arguing in front of me.* OPP **comfortable** ▸ **uncomfortably** /-əbli/ ***adv.***

uncommon /ʌn'kɒmən/ ***adj.*** unusual OPP **common**

uncompetitive /ˌʌnkəm'petətɪv/ ***adj.*** (BUSINESS) not cheaper or better than others and therefore not able to compete equally: *an uncompetitive industry* OPP **competitive**

uncompromising /ʌn'kɒmprəmaɪzɪŋ/ ***adj.*** refusing to discuss or change a decision

unconcerned /ˌʌnkən'sɜːnd/ ***adj.*** **~ (about/by/with sth)** not interested in sth or not worried about it OPP **concerned**

unconditional /ˌʌnkən'dɪʃənl/ ***adj.*** without limits or conditions: *an unconditional surrender* OPP **conditional** ▸ **unconditionally** /-ʃənəli/ ***adv.***

unconnected /ˌʌnkə'nektɪd/ ***adj.*** **~ (with/to sth)** not related or connected in any way: *The two crimes are apparently unconnected.*

unconscious ⊶ /ʌn'kɒnʃəs/ ***adj.*** **1** (HEALTH) in a state that is like sleep, for example because of injury or illness: *He was found lying unconscious on the kitchen floor.* **2 ~ of sb/sth** not knowing sth; not aware of sb/sth **3** (used about feelings, thoughts, etc.) existing or happening without your realizing; not deliberate: *The article was full of unconscious humour.* OPP **conscious** **4 the unconscious** ***noun*** [sing.] = SUBCONSCIOUS ▸ **unconsciously** ***adv.*** ▸ **unconsciousness** ***noun*** [U]

unconstitutional AW /ˌʌnˌkɒnstɪ'tjuːʃənl/ ***adj.*** (LAW) not allowed by the CONSTITUTION (= the basic laws or rules) of a country, a political system or an organization

uncontrollable /ˌʌnkən'trəʊləbl/ ***adj.*** that you cannot control: *I suddenly had an uncontrollable urge to laugh.* ▸ **uncontrollably** /-əbli/ ***adv.***

unconventional AW /ˌʌnkən'venʃənl/ ***adj.*** not following what is done or considered normal or acceptable by most people; different and interesting: *an unconventional approach to the problem* OPP **conventional** ▸ **unconventionally** /-ʃənəli/ ***adj.***

unconvinced /ˌʌnkən'vɪnst/ ***adj.*** not believing or not certain about sth despite what you have been told: *I* ***remain unconvinced*** *of the need for change.*

uncountable /ʌn'kaʊntəbl/ ***adj.*** (LANGUAGE) an **uncountable** noun cannot be counted and so does not have a plural. In this dictionary **uncountable** nouns are marked '[U]'. OPP **countable**

uncouth /ʌn'kuːθ/ ***adj.*** (used about a person or their behaviour) rude or socially unacceptable

uncover /ʌn'kʌvə(r)/ ***verb*** [T] **1** to remove the cover from sth OPP **cover** **2** to find out or discover sth: *Police have uncovered a plot to murder a top politician.*

undecided /ˌʌndɪ'saɪdɪd/ ***adj.*** **1** not having made a decision: *I'm still undecided about whether to take the job or not.* **2** without any result or decision OPP **decided**

undemanding /ˌʌndɪ'mɑːndɪŋ/ ***adj.*** not needing a lot of effort or thought: *an undemanding job*

undemocratic /ˌʌndemə'krætɪk/ ***adj.*** against or not acting according to the principles of DEMOCRACY (= a system which supports equal rights for all people) OPP **democratic**

undeniable AW /ˌʌndɪ'naɪəbl/ ***adj.*** clear, true or certain ▸ **undeniably** /-əbli/ ***adv.***

under ⊶ /'ʌndə(r)/ ***prep.***, ***adv.*** **1** in or to a position that is below sth: *We found him hiding under the table.* ◇ *The dog crawled under the gate and ran into the road.* **2** below the surface of sth; covered by sth: *Most of an iceberg is under the water.* ◇ *He was wearing a vest under his shirt.* **3** less than a certain number; younger than a certain age: *People working under 20 hours a week will pay no extra tax.* ◇ *Nobody under eighteen is allowed to buy alcohol.* **4** governed or controlled by sb/sth: *The country is now under martial law.* **5** according to a law, agreement, system, etc.: *Under English law you are innocent until you are proved guilty.* **6** experiencing a particular feeling, process or effect: *He was jailed for driving under the influence of alcohol.* ◇ *a building under construction* ◇ *The manager is* ***under pressure*** *to resign.* ◇ *I was* ***under the impression that*** *Bill was not very happy there.* **7** using a particular name: *to travel under a false name* **8** found in a particular part of a book, list, etc.: *You'll find some information on rugby under 'team sports'.*

under- /'ʌndə(r)/ ***prefix*** **1** (used in nouns and adjectives) below: *underground* ◇ *undergrowth* **2** (used in nouns) lower in age, level or position: *the under-fives* ◇ *an under secretary* **3** (used in adjectives and verbs) not enough: *undercooked food*

underarm[1] /'ʌndərɑːm/ ***adj.*** **1** (only *before* a noun) (ANATOMY) connected with a person's ARMPIT (= the part of the body under the arm where it joins the rest of the body): *underarm hair/deodorant/sweating* **2** an **underarm** throw of a ball is done with the hand kept below the level of the shoulder

underarm[2] /'ʌndərɑːm/ ***adv.*** if you throw, etc. **underarm**, you throw keeping your hand below the level of your shoulder

undercarriage /'ʌndəkærɪdʒ/ (*also* **'landing gear**) ***noun*** [C] the part of an aircraft, including the wheels, that supports it when it is landing and taking off ➲ picture at **plane**

underclothes /'ʌndəkləʊðz/ ***noun*** [pl.] = UNDERWEAR

undercook /ˌʌndə'kʊk/ ***verb*** [T] to not cook food for long enough OPP **overcook**

undercover /ˌʌndə'kʌvə(r)/ ***adj.*** working or happening secretly: *an undercover reporter/detective*

undercurrent /'ʌndəkʌrənt/ ***noun*** [C] **~ (of sth)** a feeling, especially a negative one, that is hidden but whose effects are felt: *I detect an undercurrent of resentment towards the new proposals.*

undercut /ˌʌndəˈkʌt/ *verb* [T] (*pres. part.* **undercutting**; *pt, pp* **undercut**) to sell sth at a lower price than other shops, etc.

undercutting /ˌʌndəˈkʌtɪŋ/ *noun* [U] (GEOGRAPHY) the destruction by water of a softer layer of rock below a hard top layer so that after a long period of time the top layer is not supported and falls down

underdeveloped /ˌʌndədɪˈveləpt/ *adj.* (GEOGRAPHY, ECONOMICS) (used about a country, society, etc.) having few industries and a low standard of living ➲ look at **developed**, **developing** ℹ 'A **developing country**' is now the usual expression. ▶ **underdevelopment** *noun* [U]

underdog /ˈʌndədɒg/ *noun* [C] a person, team, etc. who is weaker than others, and not expected to be successful: *San Marino were the underdogs, but managed to win the game 2-1.*

underestimate AW /ˌʌndərˈestɪmeɪt/ *verb* [T] **1** to guess that the amount, etc. of sth will be less than it really is **2** to think that sb/sth is not as strong, good, etc. as they really are: *Don't underestimate your opponent. He's a really good player.* OPP **overestimate** ▶ **underestimate** /-mət/ *noun* [C]

underfoot /ˌʌndəˈfʊt/ *adv.* under your feet; where you are walking: *It's very wet underfoot.*

underfunded /ˌʌndəˈfʌndɪd/ *adj.* (FINANCE) not having enough money to spend, with the result that it cannot function well

undergo AW /ˌʌndəˈgəʊ/ *verb* [T] (*pt* **underwent** /-ˈwent/; *pp* **undergone** /-ˈgɒn/) to have a difficult or unpleasant experience: *She underwent a five-hour operation.*

undergraduate /ˌʌndəˈgrædʒuət/ *noun* [C] (EDUCATION) a university student who has not yet taken their first degree ➲ look at **graduate**, **postgraduate**

underground[1] ⊶ /ˈʌndəgraʊnd/ *adj.* **1** under the surface of the ground: *an underground car park* **2** secret or illegal: *an underground radio station*

underground[2] ⊶ /ˌʌndəˈgraʊnd/ *adv.* **1** under the surface of the ground: *The cables all run underground.* **2** into a secret place: *She went underground to escape from the police.*

underground[3] /ˈʌndəgraʊnd/ (*AmE* **subway**) *noun* [sing.] a railway system under the ground

undergrowth /ˈʌndəgrəʊθ/ *noun* [U] bushes and plants that grow around and under trees

underhand /ˌʌndəˈhænd/ *adj.* secret or not honest

underlie AW /ˌʌndəˈlaɪ/ *verb* [T] (*pres. part.* **underlying**; *pt* **underlay** /-ˈleɪ/; *pp* **underlain** /-ˈleɪn/) (*formal*) to be the basis or cause of sth: *It is a principle that underlies all the party's policies.*

underline /ˌʌndəˈlaɪn/ (*especially AmE* **underscore**) *verb* [T] **1** to draw a line under a word, etc. **2** to show sth clearly or to emphasize sth: *This accident underlines the need for greater care.*

underlying AW /ˌʌndəˈlaɪɪŋ/ *adj.* important but hidden: *the underlying causes of the disaster*

undermine /ˌʌndəˈmaɪn/ *verb* [T] to make sth, especially sb's confidence or authority, gradually weaker or less effective: *The public's confidence in the government has been undermined by the crisis.*

the underneath /ˌʌndəˈniːθ/ *noun* [sing.] the bottom or lowest part of something: *There is a lot of rust on the underneath of the car.*

underneath ⊶ /ˌʌndəˈniːθ/ *prep., adv.* under; below: *The coin rolled underneath the chair.*

undernourished /ˌʌndəˈnʌrɪʃt/ *adj.* (HEALTH) in bad health because of not having enough food or enough of the right type of food

underpants /ˈʌndəpænts/ (*BrE also* **pants**) *noun* [pl.] a piece of clothing that men or boys wear under their trousers

underpass /ˈʌndəpɑːs/ *noun* [C] a road or path that goes under another road, railway, etc.

underpay /ˌʌndəˈpeɪ/ *verb* [T] (*pt, pp* **underpaid**) to pay sb too little OPP **overpay**

underperform /ˌʌndəpəˈfɔːm/ *verb* [I] to not be as successful as was expected

underpriced /ˌʌndəˈpraɪst/ *adj.* something that is **underpriced** is sold at a price that is too low and less than its real value

underprivileged /ˌʌndəˈprɪvəlɪdʒd/ *adj.* having less money, and fewer rights, opportunities, etc. than other people in society OPP **privileged**

underrate /ˌʌndəˈreɪt/ *verb* [T] to think that sb/sth is less clever, important, good, etc. than they or it really are OPP **overrate**

underscore /ˌʌndəˈskɔː(r)/ (*especially AmE*) = UNDERLINE

undershirt /ˈʌndəʃɜːt/ (*AmE*) = VEST (1)

underside /ˈʌndəsaɪd/ *noun* [C] the side or surface of sth that is underneath SYN **bottom**[1] (2)

understaffed /ˌʌndəˈstɑːft/ *adj.* (BUSINESS) not having enough people working and therefore not able to function well: *We're very understaffed at the moment.*

understand ⊶ /ˌʌndəˈstænd/ *verb* (*pt, pp* **understood** /-ˈstʊd/) **1** [I,T] to know or realize the meaning of sth: *I'm not sure that I really understand.* ◇ *I didn't understand the instructions.* ◇ *Please speak more slowly. I can't understand you.* ◇ *Do you understand what I'm asking you?* **2** [T] to know how or why sth happens or why it is important: *I can't understand why the engine won't start.* ◇ *As far as I understand it, the changes won't affect us.* **3** [T] to know sb's character and why they behave in a particular way: *It's easy to understand why she felt so angry.* **4** [T] (*formal*) to have heard or been told sth

IDM **give sb to believe/understand (that)** → BELIEVE

make yourself understood to make your meaning clear: *I can just about make myself understood in Russian.*

understandable /ˌʌndəˈstændəbl/ *adj.* that you can understand ▶ **understandably** /-əbli/ *adv.*: *She was understandably angry at the decision.*

understanding[1] ⊶ /ˌʌndəˈstændɪŋ/ *noun* **1** [U, sing.] the knowledge that sb has of a particular subject or situation: *A basic understanding of physics is necessary for this course.* ◇ *He has little understanding of how computers work.* **2** [C, usually sing.] an informal agreement: *I'm sure we can* ***come to /reach an understanding*** *about the money I owe him.* **3** [U] the ability to know why people behave in a particular way and to forgive them if they do sth wrong or bad **4** [U] the way in which you think sth is meant: *My understanding of the arrangement is that he will only phone if there is a problem.*

IDM **on the understanding that...** only if...; because it was agreed that...: *We let them stay in our house on the understanding that it was only for a short period.*

understanding² /ˌʌndəˈstændɪŋ/ ***adj.*** showing kind feelings towards sb; sympathetic

understate /ˌʌndəˈsteɪt/ ***verb*** [T] to say that sth is smaller or less important than it really is OPP **overstate**

understatement /ˈʌndəsteɪtmənt/ ***noun*** **1** [C] a statement that makes sth seem less important, impressive, serious, etc. than it really is: *'Is she pleased?' '**That's an understatement**. She's delighted.'* **2** [U] the practice of making things seem less impressive, important, serious, etc. than they really are: *He always goes for subtlety and understatement in his movies.* OPP **overstatement**

understudy /ˈʌndəstʌdi/ ***noun*** [C] (*pl.* **understudies**) (ARTS AND MEDIA) an actor who learns the role of another actor and replaces them if they are ill

undertake AW /ˌʌndəˈteɪk/ ***verb*** [T] (*pt* **undertook** /-ˈtʊk/; *pp* **undertaken** /-ˈteɪkən/) **1** to decide to do sth and start doing it: *The company is undertaking a major programme of modernization.* **2** to agree or promise to do sth

undertaker /ˈʌndəteɪkə(r)/ (*also* **ˈfuneral director**, *AmE also* **mortician**) ***noun*** [C] a person whose job is to prepare dead bodies to be buried and to arrange funerals

undertaking AW /ˌʌndəˈteɪkɪŋ/ ***noun*** [C, usually sing.] **1** a piece of work or business: *Buying the company would be a risky undertaking.* **2** ~ **(that.../to do sth)** a formal or legal promise to do sth

undertone /ˈʌndətəʊn/ ***noun*** [C] a feeling, quality or meaning that is not expressed in a direct way

IDM **in an undertone**; **in undertones** in a quiet voice

underused /ˌʌndəˈjuːzd/ ***adj.*** (also *formal* **underutilized** /ˌʌndəˈjuːtəlaɪzd/) not used as much as it could or should be

undervalue /ˌʌndəˈvæljuː/ ***verb*** [T] to place too low a value on sb/sth

underwater 🔑 /ˌʌndəˈwɔːtə(r)/ ***adj., adv.*** existing, happening or used below the surface of water: *underwater exploration* ◇ *an underwater camera* ◇ *Can you swim underwater?*

underwear 🔑 /ˈʌndəweə(r)/ ***noun*** [U] clothing that is worn next to the skin under other clothes SYN **underclothes**

underweight /ˌʌndəˈweɪt/ ***adj.*** weighing less than is normal or correct OPP **overweight**

the underworld /ˈʌndəwɜːld/ ***noun*** [sing.] (LAW) people who are involved in organized crime

underwrite /ˌʌndəˈraɪt/ ***verb*** [T] (*pt* **underwrote** /-ˈrəʊt/; *pp* **underwritten** /-ˈrɪtn/) to accept responsibility for an insurance policy by agreeing to pay if there is any damage or loss ▶ **underwriter** ***noun*** [C]

undesirable /ˌʌndɪˈzaɪərəbl/ ***adj.*** unpleasant or not wanted; likely to cause problems OPP **desirable**

undetectable /ˌʌndɪˈtektəbl/ ***adj.*** impossible to see or find: *The sound is virtually undetectable to the human ear.*

undid past tense of **undo**

undignified /ʌnˈdɪɡnɪfaɪd/ ***adj.*** causing you to look FOOLISH and to lose the respect of other people OPP **dignified**

undiminished AW /ˌʌndɪˈmɪnɪʃt/ ***adj.*** that has not become smaller or weaker: *They continued with undiminished enthusiasm.*

undisputed /ˌʌndɪˈspjuːtɪd/ ***adj.*** **1** that cannot be questioned or shown to be false; that cannot be argued against: *undisputed facts/evidence* **2** that everyone accepts or recognizes: *the undisputed champion of the world*

undisturbed /ˌʌndɪˈstɜːbd/ ***adj.*** **1** (not usually before a noun) not moved or touched by anyone or anything SYN **untouched** **2** not interrupted by anyone **3** (not usually before a noun) ~ **(by sth)** not affected or upset by sth SYN **unconcerned**: *He seemed undisturbed by the news of her death.*

undivided /ˌʌndɪˈvaɪdɪd/ ***adj.***

IDM **get/have sb's undivided attention** to receive all sb's attention

give your undivided attention (to sb/sth) to give all your attention to sb/sth

undo 🔑 /ʌnˈduː/ ***verb*** [T] (*3rd person sing. pres.* **undoes**; *pt* **undid**; *pp* **undone**) **1** to open sth that was tied or fastened: *to undo a knot/zip/button* **2** to destroy the effect of sth that has already happened: *His mistake has undone all our good work.*

undone /ʌnˈdʌn/ ***adj.*** **1** open; not fastened or tied: *I realized that my zip was undone.* **2** not done: *I left the housework undone.*

undoubted /ʌnˈdaʊtɪd/ ***adj.*** definite; accepted as being true ▶ **undoubtedly** ***adv.***

undress /ʌnˈdres/ ***verb*** **1** [I] to take off your clothes **2** [T] to take off sb's clothes OPP **dress** ▶ **undressed** ***adj.***

undue /ˌʌnˈdjuː/ ***adj.*** more than is necessary or reasonable: *The police try not to use undue force when arresting a person.* ▶ **unduly** ***adv.***: *She didn't seem unduly worried by their unexpected arrival.*

unearth /ʌnˈɜːθ/ ***verb*** [T] to dig sth up out of the ground; to discover sth that was hidden: *Archaeologists have unearthed a Roman tomb.*

unearthly /ʌnˈɜːθli/ ***adj.*** strange or frightening: *an unearthly scream*

IDM **at an unearthly hour** (*informal*) extremely early in the morning

unease /ʌnˈiːz/ (*also* **uneasiness**) ***noun*** [U] a worried or uncomfortable feeling OPP **ease**

uneasy /ʌnˈiːzi/ ***adj.*** **1** ~ **(about sth/doing sth)** worried; not feeling relaxed or comfortable **2** not settled; unlikely to last: *an uneasy compromise* ▶ **uneasily** ***adv.***

uneconomic /ˌʌniːkəˈnɒmɪk; ˌʌnek-/ ***adj.*** (BUSINESS) (used about a company, etc.) not making or likely to make a profit SYN **unprofitable** OPP **economic**

uneconomical AW /ˌʌniːkəˈnɒmɪkl; ˌʌnek-/ ***adj.*** wasting money, time, materials, etc. OPP **economical** ▶ **uneconomically** /-kli/ ***adv.***

unemployed 🔑 /ˌʌnɪmˈplɔɪd/ ***adj.*** **1** not able to find a job; out of work. *She has been unemployed for over a year.* SYN **jobless** OPP **employed** **2 the unemployed** ***noun*** [pl.] people who cannot find a job

unemployment 🔑 /ˌʌnɪmˈplɔɪmənt/ ***noun*** [U] **1** the situation of not being able to find a job: *The number of people claiming **unemployment benefit*** (=money given by the state) *has gone up.* OPP **employment** **2** the number of people who are unemployed: *The economy is doing very badly and unemployment is rising.* SYN **joblessness** ➲ look at **the dole**

unencumbered /ˌʌnɪnˈkʌmbəd/ ***adj.*** **1** not having or carrying anything heavy or anything that makes you go more slowly **2** (FINANCE) (used about property) not having any debts left to be paid

unending /ʌnˈendɪŋ/ ***adj.*** having or seeming to have no end

unequal /ʌnˈiːkwəl/ *adj.* **1** not fair or balanced: *an unequal distribution of power* **2** different in size, amount, level, etc. OPP **equal** ▶ **unequally** *adv.*

UNESCO (also **Unesco**) /juːˈneskəʊ/ *abbr.* (SOCIAL STUDIES) United Nations Educational, Scientific and Cultural Organization

unethical AW /ʌnˈeθɪkl/ *adj.* not morally acceptable: *unethical behaviour/conduct* OPP **ethical** ▶ **unethically** /-kli/ *adv.*

uneven /ʌnˈiːvn/ *adj.* **1** not completely smooth, level or regular: *The sign was painted in rather uneven letters.* OPP **even** **2** not always of the same level or quality ▶ **unevenly** *adv.*: *The country's wealth is unevenly distributed.*

unˌeven ˈbars *noun* [pl.] (*AmE*) = ASYMMETRIC BARS

unexceptional /ˌʌnɪkˈsepʃənl/ *adj.* not interesting or unusual ➲ look at **exceptional**

unexpected ⊶ /ˌʌnɪkˈspektɪd/ *adj.* not expected and therefore causing surprise ▶ **unexpectedly** *adv.*: *I got there late because I was unexpectedly delayed.*

unexploded /ˌʌnɪkˈspləʊdɪd/ *adj.* **of a bomb, etc.** that has not yet exploded

unexplored /ˌʌnɪkˈsplɔːd/ *adj.* **1** (GEOGRAPHY) (used about a country or an area of land) that nobody has investigated or put on a map; that has not been explored **2** (used about an idea, a theory, etc.) that has not yet been examined or discussed thoroughly

unfailing /ʌnˈfeɪlɪŋ/ *adj.* that you can depend on to always be there and always be the same: *unfailing devotion/support* ◇ *She fought the disease with unfailing good humour.* ▶ **unfailingly** *adv.*: *unfailingly loyal/polite*

unfair ⊶ /ˌʌnˈfeə(r)/ *adj.* **1** ~ **(on/to sb)** not dealing with people as they deserve; not treating each person equally: *This law is unfair to women.* ◇ *The tax is unfair on people with low incomes.* **2** not following the rules and therefore giving an advantage to one person, team, etc. OPP **fair** ▶ **unfairly** *adv.* ▶ **unfairness** *noun* [U]

unfaithful /ʌnˈfeɪθfl/ *adj.* ~ **(to sb/sth)** having a sexual relationship with sb who is not your husband, wife or partner OPP **faithful** ▶ **unfaithfulness** *noun* [U]

unfamiliar /ˌʌnfəˈmɪliə(r)/ *adj.* **1** ~ **(to sb)** that you do not know well: *an unfamiliar part of town* **2** ~ **(with sth)** not having knowledge or experience of sth: *I'm unfamiliar with this author.* OPP **familiar**

unfashionable /ʌnˈfæʃnəbl/ *adj.* not popular at a particular time: *unfashionable ideas/clothes* OPP **fashionable** ➲ look at **old-fashioned**

unfasten /ʌnˈfɑːsn/ *verb* [T] to open sth that was fastened: *to unfasten a belt/button/chain/lock* SYN **undo** OPP **fasten**

unfavourable (*AmE* **unfavorable**) /ʌnˈfeɪvərəbl/ *adj.* **1** showing that you do not like or approve of sb/sth **2** not good and likely to cause problems or make sth difficult OPP **favourable** ➲ look at **adverse** ▶ **unfavourably** (*AmE* **unfavorably**) /-əbli/ *adv.*: *In this respect, Britain* ***compares unfavourably*** *with other European countries.*

unfinished /ʌnˈfɪnɪʃt/ *adj.* not complete; not finished: *We have some* ***unfinished business*** *to settle.* ◇ *an unfinished drink/game/book*

unfit /ʌnˈfɪt/ *adj.* **1** ~ **(for sth/to do sth)** not suitable or not good enough for sth: *His criminal past makes him unfit to be a politician.* **2** not in good physical health, especially because you do not get enough exercise OPP **fit**

unfold /ʌnˈfəʊld/ *verb* [I,T] **1** to open out and become flat; to open out sth that was folded: *The sofa unfolds into a spare bed.* ◇ *I unfolded the letter and read it.* OPP **fold (up)** **2** to become known, or to allow sth to become known, a little at a time

unforeseen /ˌʌnfɔːˈsiːn/ *adj.* not expected: *an unforeseen problem*

unforgettable /ˌʌnfəˈɡetəbl/ *adj.* making such a strong impression that you cannot forget it

unforgivable /ˌʌnfəˈɡɪvəbl/ *adj.* if sb's behaviour is **unforgivable**, it is so bad or unacceptable that you cannot forgive the person SYN **inexcusable** OPP **forgivable** ▶ **unforgivably** /-əbli/ *adv.*

unfortunate ⊶ /ʌnˈfɔːtʃənət/ *adj.* **1** not lucky OPP **fortunate** **2** that you feel sorry about

unfortunately ⊶ /ʌnˈfɔːtʃənətli/ *adv.* used to say that a particular situation or fact makes you sad or disappointed, or gets you into a difficult position: *I'd like to help you but unfortunately there's nothing I can do.* ◇ *Unfortunately, I won't be able to attend the meeting.*

unfounded AW /ʌnˈfaʊndɪd/ *adj.* not based on or supported by facts: *unfounded allegations*

unfriendly ⊶ /ʌnˈfrendli/ *adj.* ~ **(to/towards sb)** unpleasant or not polite to sb OPP **friendly**

ungainly /ʌnˈɡeɪnli/ *adj.* moving in a way that is not smooth or elegant

ungrateful /ʌnˈɡreɪtfl/ *adj.* not feeling or showing thanks to sb OPP **grateful** ▶ **ungratefully** /-fəli/ *adv.*

unguarded /ʌnˈɡɑːdɪd/ *adj.* **1** not protected or guarded **2** saying more than you wanted to OPP **guarded**

unhappily /ʌnˈhæpɪli/ *adv.* **1** sadly **2** unfortunately OPP **happily**

unhappy ⊶ /ʌnˈhæpi/ *adj.* (**unhappier**; **unhappiest**) **1** ~ **(about sth)** sad: *She's terribly unhappy about losing her job.* ◇ *He had a very unhappy childhood.* **2** ~ **(about/at/with sth)** not satisfied or pleased; worried: *They're unhappy at having to accept a pay cut.* OPP **happy** ▶ **unhappiness** *noun* [U]

unharmed /ʌnˈhɑːmd/ *adj.* not injured or damaged; not harmed: *The hostages were released unharmed.*

UNHCR /ˌjuː en eɪtʃ siː ˈɑː(r)/ *abbr.* (POLITICS) **United Nations High Commission for Refugees**; an organization which exists to help and protect REFUGEES (= people who have been forced to leave their own country because of war, etc.) and to record what happens to them

unhealthy /ʌnˈhelθi/ *adj.* **1** (HEALTH) not having or showing good health: *He looks pale and unhealthy.* **2** likely to cause illness or poor health: *unhealthy conditions* **3** not natural: *an unhealthy interest in death* OPP **healthy**

unheard /ʌnˈhɜːd/ *adj.* (not before a noun) not listened to or given any attention: *My suggestions* ***went unheard***.

unˈheard-of *adj.* not known; never having happened before

unhelpful /ʌnˈhelpfl/ *adj.* not helpful or useful; not wanting to help sb: *an unhelpful response/reply* OPP **helpful** ▶ **unhelpfully** /-fəli/ *adv.*

unhurt /ʌn'hɜːt/ *adj.* (not before a noun) not injured or harmed: *He escaped from the crash unhurt.* SYN **unharmed** OPP **hurt**

uni- /'juːni/ *prefix* (used in nouns, adjectives and adverbs) one; having one: *uniform* ◇ *unilaterally*

UNICEF /'juːnɪsef/ *abbr.* (POLITICS) **United Nations Children's Fund**; an organization within the United Nations that helps to look after the health and education of children all over the world

unicellular /ˌjuːnɪ'seljələ(r)/ *adj.* (BIOLOGY) consisting of only one cell: *unicellular organisms*

unicorn /'juːnɪkɔːn/ *noun* [C] an animal that only exists in stories, that looks like a white horse with one horn growing out of its FOREHEAD

unidentified /ˌʌnaɪ'dentɪfaɪd/ *adj.* whose identity is not known: *An unidentified body has been found in the river.*

uniform¹ AW /'juːnɪfɔːm/ *noun* [C,U] the set of clothes worn at work by the members of certain organizations or groups and by some schoolchildren: *I didn't know he was a policeman because he wasn't* ***in uniform***. ▶ **uniformed** *adj.*

uniform² AW /'juːnɪfɔːm/ *adj.* not varying; the same in all cases or at all times ▶ **uniformity** AW /ˌjuːnɪ'fɔːməti/ *noun* [U]

unify AW /'juːnɪfaɪ/ *verb* [T] (*pres. part.* **unifying**; *3rd person sing. pres.* **unifies**; *pt, pp* **unified**) to join separate parts together to make one unit, or to make them similar to each other ▶ **unification** AW /ˌjuːnɪfɪ'keɪʃn/ *noun* [U]

unilateral /ˌjuːnɪ'lætrəl/ *adj.* done or made by one person who is involved in sth without the agreement of the other person or people: *a unilateral declaration of independence* ➲ look at **multilateral** ▶ **unilaterally** /-rəli/ *adv.*

unimaginable /ˌʌnɪ'mædʒɪnəbl/ *adj.* (*formal*) impossible to think of or to believe exists; impossible to imagine: *unimaginable wealth* ▶ **unimaginably** /-əbli/ *adv.*

unimportant /ˌʌnɪm'pɔːtnt/ *adj.* not important: *unimportant details* ◇ *relatively/comparatively unimportant* ◇ *They dismissed the problem as unimportant.*

uninhabitable /ˌʌnɪn'hæbɪtəbl/ *adj.* not possible to live in OPP **habitable**

uninhabited /ˌʌnɪn'hæbɪtɪd/ *adj.* (used about a place or a building) with nobody living in it OPP **inhabited**

uninhibited /ˌʌnɪn'hɪbɪtɪd/ *adj.* behaving in a free and natural way, without worrying what other people think of you OPP **inhibited**

unintelligible /ˌʌnɪn'telɪdʒəbl/ *adj.* impossible to understand OPP **intelligible**

unintended /ˌʌnɪn'tendɪd/ *adj.* an **unintended** effect, result or meaning is one that you did not plan or intend to happen

unintentional /ˌʌnɪn'tenʃənl/ *adj.* not done deliberately, but happening by accident: *Perhaps I misled you, but it was quite unintentional* (= I did not mean to). OPP **intentional** ▶ **unintentionally** /-ʃənəli/ *adv.*: *They had unintentionally provided wrong information.*

uninterested /ʌn'ɪntrəstɪd/ *adj.* ~ **(in sb/sth)** having or showing no interest in sb/sth: *She seemed uninterested in anything I had to say.* OPP **interested** ➲ look at **disinterested**

union /'juːniən/ *noun* **1** [U, sing.] the action of joining or the situation of being joined **2** [C] (POLITICS) a group of states or countries that have joined together to form one country or group: *the European Union* **3** = TRADE UNION **4** [C] an organization for a particular group of people: *the Athletics Union*

unionist /'juːniənɪst/ *noun* [C] (POLITICS) **1** = TRADE UNIONIST **2 Unionist** (POLITICS) a person who believes that Northern Ireland should stay part of the United Kingdom **3 Unionist** (HISTORY) a supporter of the Union during the Civil War in the US ▶ **unionism** /'juːniənɪzəm/ *noun* [U]

the ˌUnion 'Jack *noun* [sing.] the national flag of the United Kingdom, with red and white crosses on a dark blue background

unique AW /ju'niːk/ *adj.* **1** not like anything else; being the only one of its type: *Shakespeare made a unique contribution to the world of literature.* **2** ~ **to sb/sth** connected with only one place, person or thing: *This dance is unique to this region.* **3** very unusual

unisex /'juːnɪseks/ *adj.* designed for and used by both sexes: *unisex fashions*

unison /'juːnɪsn/ *noun*
IDM **in unison** saying, singing or doing the same thing at the same time as sb else: *'No, thank you,' they said in unison.*

unit /'juːnɪt/ *noun* [C] **1** a single thing which is complete in itself, although it can be part of sth larger: *The book is divided into ten units.* **2** (BUSINESS) a single item of the type of product that a company sells: *The game's selling price was $15 per unit.* ◇ *What's the* ***unit cost***? **3** a group of people who perform a certain function within a larger organization: *the intensive care unit of a hospital* **4** a fixed amount or number used as a standard of measurement: *a* ***unit of currency*** **5** a piece of furniture that fits with other pieces of furniture and has a particular use: *matching kitchen units* **6** a small machine that performs a particular task or that is part of a larger machine: *The heart of a computer is the central processing unit.* **7** (MATHEMATICS) any whole number from 0 to 9: *a column for the tens and a column for the units*

unitary /'juːnətri/ *adj.* **1** (POLITICS) consisting of a number of areas or groups that are joined together and are controlled by one government or group: *a single unitary state* ◇ (*BrE*) *a* ***unitary authority*** (= a type of local council, introduced in some areas from 1995 to replace existing local governments which consisted of county and district councils) **2** (*formal*) single; forming one unit

unite /ju'naɪt/ *verb* **1** [I,T] to join together and act in agreement; to make this happen: *Unless we unite, our enemies will defeat us.* **2** [I] ~ **(in sth/in doing sth)** to join together for a particular purpose: *We should all unite in seeking a solution to this terrible problem.*

united /ju'naɪtɪd/ *adj.* joined together by a common feeling or aim

the Uˌnited 'Kingdom *noun* [sing.] (*abbr.* **UK**) England, Scotland, Wales and Northern Ireland

CULTURE

The UK includes England, Scotland, Wales and Northern Ireland, but *not* the Republic of Ireland (Eire), which is a separate country.

Great Britain is England, Scotland and Wales only.

The British Isles include England, Scotland, Wales, Northern Ireland and the Republic of Ireland.

the U͵nited 'Nations *noun* [sing., with sing. or pl. verb] (*abbr.* **UN**) (POLITICS) the organization formed to encourage peace in the world and to deal with problems between countries

the U͵nited 'States (of A'merica) *noun* [sing., with sing. or pl. verb] (*abbr.* **US**; **USA**) a large country in North America made up of 50 states and the District of Columbia

unity /'ju:nəti/ *noun* [U] the situation in which people are in agreement and working together

universal /͵ju:nɪ'vɜ:sl/ *adj.* connected with, done by or affecting everyone in the world or everyone in a particular group ▸ **universally** /-səli/ *adv.*

͵uni͵versal 'indicator *noun* [C] (CHEMISTRY) a substance that changes to different colours according to whether another substance that touches it is an acid or an ALKALI ➲ picture at **pH**

the universe /'ju:nɪvɜ:s/ *noun* [sing.] (ASTRONOMY) everything that exists, including the planets, stars, space, etc.

university 🔑 /͵ju:nɪ'vɜ:səti/ *noun* [C] (*pl.* **universities**) (EDUCATION) an institution that provides the highest level of education, in which students study for degrees and in which academic research is done: *Which university did you go to?* ◇ *I did History* ***at university.*** ◇ *a university lecturer*

Unix™ /'ju:nɪks/ *noun* [U] (COMPUTING) an OPERATING SYSTEM (=a set of programs that controls the way a computer works and runs other programs) which can be used by many people at the same time

unjust /͵ʌn'dʒʌst/ *adj.* not fair or deserved: *an unjust accusation/law/punishment* ◇ *The system is corrupt and unjust.* OPP **just** ▸ **unjustly** *adv.*

unjustified AW /ʌn'dʒʌstɪfaɪd/ *adj.* not fair or necessary SYN **unwarranted** OPP **justified**

unkempt /͵ʌn'kempt/ *adj.* (used especially about sb's hair or general appearance) not well cared for; not tidy: *greasy, unkempt hair*

unkind 🔑 /͵ʌn'kaɪnd/ *adj.* unpleasant and not friendly: *That was an unkind thing to say.* ◇ *The zoo was accused of being unkind to its animals.* OPP **kind** ▸ **unkindly** *adv.* ▸ **unkindness** *noun* [U]

unknown¹ 🔑 /͵ʌn'nəʊn/ *adj.* **1** ~ **(to sb)** that sb does not know; without sb knowing: *Unknown to the boss, she went home early.* **2** not famous or familiar to other people: *an unknown actress* OPP **well known, famous**
IDM **an unknown quantity** a person or thing that you know very little about

unknown² /͵ʌn'nəʊn/ *noun* **1** (usually **the unknown**) [sing.] a place or thing that you know nothing about: *a fear of the unknown* **2** [C] a person who is not well known

unlawful /ʌn'lɔ:fl/ *adj.* (*formal*) (LAW) not allowed by the law SYN **illegal**

unleaded /͵ʌn'ledɪd/ *adj.* not containing lead: *unleaded petrol*

unleash /ʌn'li:ʃ/ *verb* [T] ~ **sth (on/upon sb/sth)** (*written*) to suddenly let a strong force, emotion, etc. be felt or have an effect: *The government's proposals unleashed a storm of protest in the press.*

unleavened /͵ʌn'levnd/ *adj.* (used about bread) made without any YEAST (=the substance that makes bread rise) and therefore flat and heavy

unless 🔑 /ən'les/ *conj.* if...not; except if: *I was told that unless my work improved, I would lose the job.* ◇ *'Would you like a cup of coffee?' 'Not unless you've already made some.'* ◇ *Unless anyone has anything else to say, the meeting is closed.* ◇ *Don't switch that on unless I'm here.*

unlicensed AW /ʌn'laɪsnst/ *adj.* without a licence: *an unlicensed vehicle* OPP **licensed**

unlike 🔑 /͵ʌn'laɪk/ *adj., prep.* **1** in contrast to; different from: *She's unlike anyone else I've ever met.* ◇ *He's extremely ambitious, unlike me.* ◇ *This is an exciting place to live, unlike my home town.* **2** not typical of; unusual for: *It's unlike him to be so rude – he's usually very polite.*

unlikely 🔑 /ʌn'laɪkli/ *adj.* (**unlikelier**; **unlikeliest**) **1** ~ **(to do sth/that...)** not likely to happen; not expected; not probable: *I suppose she might win but I think it's very unlikely.* ◇ *It's* ***highly unlikely*** *that I'll have any free time next week.* OPP **likely 2** difficult to believe: *an unlikely excuse* SYN **improbable**

unlimited /ʌn'lɪmɪtɪd/ *adj.* without limit; as much or as great as you want OPP **limited**

unload 🔑 /͵ʌn'ləʊd/ *verb* **1** [I,T] ~ **(sth) (from sth)** to take things that have been transported off or out of a vehicle: *We unloaded the boxes from the back of the van.* **2** [I,T] (used about a vehicle) to have the things removed that have been transported: *Parking here is restricted to vehicles that are loading or unloading.* OPP **load 3** [T] (*informal*) ~ **sb/sth (on/onto sb)** to get rid of sth you do not want or to pass it to sb else: *He shouldn't try and unload the responsibility onto you.*

unlock /͵ʌn'lɒk/ *verb* [I,T] to open the lock on sth using a key; to be opened with a key: *I can't unlock this door.* ◇ *This door won't unlock.* OPP **lock**

unlucky 🔑 /ʌn'lʌki/ *adj.* (**unluckier**; **unluckiest**) having or causing bad luck: *They were unlucky to lose because they played so well.* ◇ *Thirteen is often thought to be an unlucky number.* OPP **lucky** ▸ **unluckily** *adv.*

unmanageable /ʌn'mænɪdʒəbl/ *adj.* difficult or impossible to control or deal with

unmanned /͵ʌn'mænd/ *adj.* if a machine, vehicle or place is **unmanned**, it does not have or need a person to control or operate it

unmarried /͵ʌn'mærid/ *adj.* not married; single OPP **married**

unmistakable /͵ʌnmɪ'steɪkəbl/ *adj.* that cannot be confused with anything else; easy to recognize: *She had an unmistakable French accent.* ▸ **unmistakably** /-əbli/ *adv.*

unmoved /͵ʌn'mu:vd/ *adj.* not affected emotionally: *The judge was unmoved by the boy's sad story, and sent him to jail.*

unnatural /ʌn'nætʃrəl/ *adj.* different from what is normal or expected OPP **natural** ▸ **unnaturally** /-rəli/ *adv.*: *It's unnaturally quiet in here.*

unnecessary 🔑 /͵ʌn'nesəsəri/ *adj.* more than is needed or acceptable: *We should try to avoid all unnecessary expense.* ◇ *All this fuss is* ***totally unnecessary.*** OPP **necessary** ▸ **unnecessarily** /͵ʌn'nesəsərəli; ͵ʌn͵nesə'serəli/ *adv.*: *His explanation was unnecessarily complicated.*

unnerve /͵ʌn'nɜ:v/ *verb* [T] to make sb feel nervous or frightened or lose confidence: *His silence unnerved us.* ▸ **unnerving** *adj.*: *an unnerving experience* ▸ **unnervingly** *adv.*

unnoticed /͵ʌn'nəʊtɪst/ *adj.* not noticed or seen: *He didn't want his hard work to* ***go unnoticed.***

UNO /͵ju: en 'əʊ; 'ju:nəʊ/ *abbr.* (POLITICS) United Nations Organization

unobtainable AW /ˌʌnəbˈteɪnəbl/ *adv.* that cannot be bought or obtained

unobtrusive /ˌʌnəbˈtruːsɪv/ *adj.* avoiding being noticed; not attracting attention ▶ **unobtrusively** *adv.*: *He tried to leave as unobtrusively as possible.*

unofficial /ˌʌnəˈfɪʃl/ *adj.* not accepted or approved by a person in authority: *an unofficial strike* ◇ *Unofficial reports say that four people died in the explosion.* OPP **official** ▶ **unofficially** /-ʃəli/ *adv.*

unorthodox /ʌnˈɔːθədɒks/ *adj.* different from what is generally accepted, usual or traditional OPP **orthodox**

unpack /ˌʌnˈpæk/ *verb* [I,T] to take out the things that were in a bag, suitcase, etc.: *When we arrived at the hotel we unpacked and went to the beach.* OPP **pack**

unpaid /ˌʌnˈpeɪd/ *adj.* **1** not yet paid: *an unpaid bill* **2** not receiving money for work done: *an unpaid assistant* **3** (used about work) done without payment: *unpaid overtime*

unparalleled AW /ʌnˈpærəleld/ *adj.* (*formal*) used to emphasize that sth is bigger, better or worse than anything else like it: *The book has enjoyed a success unparalleled in recent publishing history.*

unpleasant 🔑 /ʌnˈpleznt/ *adj.* **1** causing you to have a bad feeling; not nice: *This news has come as an unpleasant surprise.* OPP **pleasant** **2** unfriendly; not polite: *There's no need to be unpleasant; we can discuss this in a friendly way.* ▶ **unpleasantly** *adv.*

unplug /ˌʌnˈplʌɡ/ *verb* [T] (**unplugging**; **unplugged**) to remove a piece of electrical equipment from the electricity supply: *Could you unplug the cassette recorder, please?* OPP **plug sth in**

unpopular /ʌnˈpɒpjələ(r)/ *adj.* ~ **(with sb)** not liked by many people: *Her methods made her very unpopular with the staff.* OPP **popular** ▶ **unpopularity** /ˌʌnˌpɒpjuˈlærəti/ *noun* [U]

unprecedented AW /ʌnˈpresɪdentɪd/ *adj.* never having happened or existed before ➲ look at **precedent**

unpredictable AW /ˌʌnprɪˈdɪktəbl/ *adj.* **1** that cannot be predicted because it changes a lot or depends on too many different things: *unpredictable weather* ◇ *The result is entirely unpredictable.* **2** if a person is **unpredictable**, you cannot predict how they will behave in a particular situation OPP **predictable** ▶ **unpredictability** /ˌʌnprɪˌdɪktəˈbɪləti/ *noun* [U]: *the unpredictability of the English weather* ▶ **unpredictably** *adv.*

unprincipled AW /ʌnˈprɪnsəpld/ *adj.* without moral principles SYN **dishonest**

unproductive /ˌʌnprəˈdʌktɪv/ *adj.* not producing very much; not producing good results: *an unproductive meeting* ◇ *I've had a very unproductive day.* OPP **productive** ▶ **unproductively** *adv.*

unprofessional /ˌʌnprəˈfeʃənl/ *adj.* not reaching the standard expected in a particular profession OPP **professional**

unpronounceable /ˌʌnprəˈnaʊnsəbl/ *adj.* of a word, especially a name too difficult to pronounce OPP **pronounceable**

unproven /ʌnˈpruːvn/ *adj.* not proved or tested: *unproven theories* OPP **proven**

unprovoked /ˌʌnprəˈvəʊkt/ *adj.* (used especially about an attack) not caused by anything the person who is attacked has said or done OPP **provoked**

unpublished AW /ʌnˈpʌblɪʃt/ *adj.* not published: *an unpublished novel*

unqualified /ˌʌnˈkwɒlɪfaɪd/ *adj.* **1** not having the knowledge or not having passed the exams that you need for sth: *I'm unqualified to offer an opinion on this matter.* OPP **qualified** **2** complete; absolute: *an unqualified success*

unquestionable /ʌnˈkwestʃənəbl/ *adj.* certain; that cannot be doubted OPP **questionable** ▶ **unquestionably** /-əbli/ *adv.*: *She is unquestionably the most famous opera singer in the world.*

unravel /ʌnˈrævl/ *verb* (**unravelling**; **unravelled**: *AmE* **unraveling**; **unraveled**) [I,T] **1** to remove the knots from a piece of string, thread, etc.; to come UNFASTENED in this way: *I unravelled the tangled string and wound it into a ball.* **2** (used about a complicated story, etc.) to become or to make sth become clear

unreactive /ˌʌnriˈæktɪv/ *adj.* (CHEMISTRY) having chemical characteristics that will not change when mixed with another substance OPP **reactive**

unreal /ˌʌnˈrɪəl/ *adj.* **1** very strange and seeming more like a dream than reality: *Her voice had an unreal quality about it* **2** not connected with reality: *Some people have unreal expectations of marriage.*

unrealistic /ˌʌnrɪəˈlɪstɪk/ *adj.* not showing or accepting things as they are: *unrealistic expectations* ◇ ***It is unrealistic to** expect them to be able to solve the problem immediately.* OPP **realistic** ▶ **unrealistically** /-kli/ *adv.*: *They're asking unrealistically high prices.*

unreasonable 🔑 /ʌnˈriːznəbl/ *adj.* unfair; expecting too much: *I think she is being totally unreasonable.* ◇ *He makes unreasonable demands on his staff.* OPP **reasonable** ▶ **unreasonably** /-əbli/ *adv.*

unregulated AW /ʌnˈreɡjuleɪtɪd/ *adj.* not controlled by means of rules

unrelated /ˌʌnrɪˈleɪtɪd/ *adj.* **1** not connected; not related to sth else: *The two events were totally unrelated.* **2** not belonging to the same family: *They have the same name but are, in fact, unrelated.* OPP **related**

unrelenting /ˌʌnrɪˈlentɪŋ/ *adj.* continuously strong, not becoming weaker or stopping

unreliable AW /ˌʌnrɪˈlaɪəbl/ *adj.* that cannot be trusted or depended on: *Trains here are notoriously unreliable.* ◇ *He's totally unreliable as a source of information.* OPP **reliable** ▶ **unreliability** /ˌʌnrɪˌlaɪəˈbɪləti/ *noun* [U]: *the unreliability of some statistics*

unrepeatable /ˌʌnrɪˈpiːtəbl/ *adj.* **1** too offensive or shocking to be repeated: *He called me several unrepeatable names.* **2** that cannot be repeated or done again: *an unrepeatable experience* OPP **repeatable**

unrequited /ˌʌnrɪˈkwaɪtɪd/ *adj.* (*formal*) (used about love) not returned by the person that you love

unreserved /ˌʌnrɪˈzɜːvd/ *adj.* **1** (used about seats in a theatre, etc.) not kept for the use of a particular person OPP **reserved** **2** without limit; complete: *The government's action received the unreserved support of all parties.* ▶ **unreservedly** /ˌʌnrɪˈzɜːvɪdli/ *adv.*

unresolved AW /ˌʌnrɪˈzɒlvd/ *adj.* (*formal*) (used about a problem or a question) not yet solved or answered; not having been resolved

unresponsive AW /ˌʌnrɪ'spɒnsɪv/ ***adj.*** ~ **(to sth)** (*formal*) not reacting to sb/sth; not giving the response that you would expect or hope for: *A number of patients were unresponsive to conventional treatments.*

unrest /ʌn'rest/ ***noun*** [U] a situation in which people are angry or not happy and likely to protest or fight: *social unrest*

unrestrained AW /ˌʌnrɪ'streɪnd/ ***adj.*** (*formal*) not controlled; not having been RESTRAINED

unrestricted AW /ˌʌnrɪ'strɪktɪd/ ***adj.*** not controlled or limited in any way SYN **unlimited**: *We have unrestricted access to all the facilities.* OPP **restricted**

unrivalled (*AmE* **unrivaled**) /ʌn'raɪvld/ ***adj.*** much better than any other of the same type: *His knowledge of Greek theology is unrivalled.*

unroll /ʌn'rəʊl/ ***verb*** [I,T] to open (sth) from a rolled position: *He unrolled the poster and stuck it on the wall.* OPP **roll (sth) (up)**

unruly /ʌn'ru:li/ ***adj.*** difficult to control; without discipline: *an unruly crowd* ▶ **unruliness** ***noun*** [U]

unsafe /ʌn'seɪf/ ***adj.*** **1** (used about a thing, a place or an activity) not safe; dangerous: *The roof was declared unsafe.* ◇ *It was considered unsafe to release the prisoners.* ◇ *unsafe sex* (=sex without protection against disease) **2** (used about people) in danger of being harmed: *He felt unsafe and alone.* **3** (LAW) (used about a decision in a court of law) based on evidence that may be false or is not good enough: *Their convictions were declared unsafe.* OPP **safe**

unsaid /ʌn'sed/ ***adj.*** (not before a noun) thought but not spoken: *Some things are better* ***left unsaid.***

unsatisfactory /ˌʌnˌsætɪs'fæktəri/ ***adj.*** not acceptable; not good enough SYN **unacceptable** ▶ **unsatisfactorily** /-tərəli/ ***adv.***

unsaturated /ʌn'sætʃəreɪtɪd/ ***adj.*** (CHEMISTRY, HEALTH) (used about fats in food) that are easily dealt with by the body because of their chemical structure ➲ look at **polyunsaturated**, **saturated**

unsavoury (*AmE* **unsavory**) /ʌn'seɪvəri/ ***adj.*** unpleasant; not morally acceptable: *His friends are all unsavoury characters.*

unscathed /ʌn'skeɪðd/ ***adj.*** not hurt, without injury: *He came out of the fight unscathed.*

unscheduled AW /ʌn'ʃedju:ld/ ***adj.*** that was not planned in advance: *The plane made an unscheduled stop in Fiji.*

unscrew /ˌʌn'skru:/ ***verb*** [T] **1** to remove the screws from sth **2** to open or remove sth by turning it: *Could you unscrew the top of this bottle for me?*

unscrupulous /ʌn'skru:pjələs/ ***adj.*** being dishonest, cruel or unfair in order to get what you want OPP **scrupulous**

unseeing /ˌʌn'si:ɪŋ/ ***adj.*** (*written*) not noticing or really looking at anything although your eyes are open

unseemly /ʌn'si:mli/ ***adj.*** (*old-fashioned* or *formal*) (used about behaviour, etc.) not polite; not right in a particular situation

unseen /ˌʌn'si:n/ ***adj.*** **1** that cannot be seen: *unseen forces/powers* ◇ *I managed to get out of the room unseen.* **2** not seen before: *unseen dangers/difficulties*

unsettle /ˌʌn'setl/ ***verb*** [T] to make sb feel upset or worried, especially because a situation has changed: *Changing schools might unsettle the kids.*

unsettled /ʌn'setld/ ***adj.*** **1** (used about a situation) that may change; making people uncertain about what might happen: *These were difficult and unsettled times.* ◇ *The weather has been very unsettled* (=it has changed a lot). **2** not calm or relaxed: *They all felt restless and unsettled.* **3** (used about an argument, etc.) that continues without any agreement being reached **4** (used about a bill, etc.) not yet paid

unsettling /ʌn'setlɪŋ/ ***adj.*** making you feel upset, nervous or worried

unshaven /ˌʌn'ʃeɪvn/ ***adj.*** not having shaved or been shaved recently: *He looked pale and unshaven.* ◇ *his unshaven face*

unsightly /ʌn'saɪtli/ ***adj.*** very unpleasant to look at; ugly: *an unsightly new building*

unskilled /ˌʌn'skɪld/ ***adj.*** not having or needing special skill or training: *an unskilled job/worker* OPP **skilled**

unsolicited /ˌʌnsə'lɪsɪtɪd/ ***adj.*** not asked for: *unsolicited praise/advice*

unsound /ˌʌn'saʊnd/ ***adj.*** **1** in poor condition; weak: *The building is structurally unsound.* **2** based on wrong ideas and therefore mistaken OPP **sound**

unspecified AW /ˌʌn'spesɪfaɪd/ ***adj.*** not stated clearly or definitely; not having been SPECIFIED: *The story takes place at an unspecified date.*

unspoiled /ˌʌn'spɔɪld/ (*also* **unspoilt** /ˌʌn'spɔɪlt/) ***adj.*** **1** (used about a place) beautiful because it has not been changed or built on **2** (used about a person) not made unpleasant, bad-tempered, etc. by being treated too well: *Despite being one of the best-known singers in the world, she has remained unspoiled.* OPP **spoilt**

unspoken /ˌʌn'spəʊkən/ ***adj.*** (*formal*) not stated; not said in words but understood or agreed between people: *an unspoken assumption*

unstable AW /ʌn'steɪbl/ ***adj.*** **1** likely to fall down or move; not firmly fixed **2** likely to change or fail: *a period of unstable government* **3** (used about a person's moods or behaviour) likely to change suddenly or often OPP **stable** ➲ noun **instability**

unsteady 🔑 /ʌn'stedi/ ***adj.*** **1** not completely in control of your movements so that you might fall: *She is still a little* ***unsteady on her feet*** *after the operation.* **2** shaking or moving in a way that is not controlled: *an unsteady hand/voice/step* OPP **steady** ▶ **unsteadily** /-ɪli/ ***adv.*** ▶ **unsteadiness** ***noun*** [U]

unstressed AW /ʌn'strest/ ***adj.*** (LANGUAGE) (used about a syllable) pronounced without emphasis OPP **stressed**

unstructured AW /ʌn'strʌktʃəd/ ***adj.*** without structure or organization

unstuck /ˌʌn'stʌk/ ***adj.*** no longer stuck together or stuck down: *The label on the parcel had* ***come unstuck.***

IDM **come unstuck** to fail badly; to be unsuccessful: *His plan came unstuck when he realized he didn't have enough money.*

unsubscribe /ˌʌnsəb'skraɪb/ ***verb*** [I,T] ~ **(from sth)** (COMPUTING) to remove your email address from an Internet MAILING LIST (=a list of the names and addresses of people to whom advertising material or information is regularly sent by a business or an organization)

unsuccessful 🔑 /ˌʌnsək'sesfl/ ***adj.*** not successful; not achieving what you wanted to: *His efforts to get a job proved unsuccessful.* ◇ *They were unsuccessful in meeting their objectives for the year.* ◇ *She made several unsuccessful attempts to see him.* ▶ **unsuccessfully** /-fəli/ ***adv.***

unsuitable /ʌn'su:təbl/ ***adj.*** not right or appropriate for sb/sth: *This film is unsuitable for children under 12.* OPP **suitable**

unsure /ˌʌn'ʃɔ:(r)/ ***adj.*** **1 ~ of yourself** not feeling confident about yourself: *He's young and still quite unsure of himself.* **2 ~ (about/of sth)** not certain; having doubts: *I didn't argue because I was unsure of the facts.* OPP **sure, certain**

unsurprising /ˌʌnsə'praɪzɪŋ/ ***adj.*** not causing surprise OPP **surprising** ▸ **unsurprisingly** ***adv.***: *Unsurprisingly, the plan failed.*

unsuspecting /ˌʌnsə'spektɪŋ/ ***adj.*** not realizing that there is danger ➲ look at **suspect, suspicious**

unsustainable AW /ˌʌnsə'steɪnəbl/ ***adj.*** (*written*) that cannot be continued at the same level, rate, etc. OPP **sustainable**

unsympathetic /ˌʌnˌsɪmpə'θetɪk/ ***adj.*** **1 ~ (towards sb)** not feeling or showing any SYMPATHY (=understanding of sb's problems) **2 ~ (to/towards sth)** not in agreement with sth; not supporting an idea, aim, etc.: *How can you trust a government that is unsympathetic to public opinion?* **3** (used about a person) not easy to like; unpleasant: *I found all the characters in the film unsympathetic.* OPP **sympathetic**

untangle /ˌʌn'tæŋgl/ ***verb*** [T] to separate threads which have become tied together in a confused way: *The wires got mixed up and it took me ages to untangle them.*

untapped /ˌʌn'tæpt/ ***adj.*** available but not yet used: *untapped reserves of oil*

unthinkable /ʌn'θɪŋkəbl/ ***adj.*** impossible to imagine or accept: *It was unthinkable that he would never see her again.*

unthinking /ʌn'θɪŋkɪŋ/ ***adj.*** done, said, etc. without thinking carefully ▸ **unthinkingly** ***adv.***

untidy 🔑 /ʌn'taɪdi/ ***adj.*** (**untidier; untidiest**) **1** not tidy or well arranged: *an untidy bedroom* ◇ *untidy hair* **2** (used about a person) not keeping things tidy or in good order: *My flatmate is so untidy!* OPP **tidy, neat** ▸ **untidily** /-ɪli/ ***adv.*** ▸ **untidiness** ***noun*** [U]

untie /ʌn'taɪ/ ***verb*** [T] (*pres. part.* **untying**, *3rd person sing. pres.* **unties**; *pt, pp* **untied**) to remove a knot; to free sb/sth that is tied by a rope, etc. OPP **tie up, fasten**

until 🔑 /ən'tɪl/ (*also* **till**) ***prep., conj.*** up to the time or the event mentioned: *The restaurant is open until midnight.* ◇ *Until that moment she had been happy.* ◇ *She waited until he had finished.* ◇ *We won't leave until the police get here* (=we won't leave before they come).

untold /ˌʌn'təʊld/ ***adj.*** very great; so big, etc. that you cannot count or measure it: *untold suffering*

untouched /ʌn'tʌtʃt/ ***adj.*** (not usually before a noun) **1 ~ (by sth)** not affected by sth, especially sth bad or unpleasant; not damaged: *The area has remained relatively untouched by commercial development.* ◇ *Some buildings had remained untouched by the explosion.* **2** (used about food or drink) not eaten or drunk: *She left her meal untouched.* **3** not changed in any way: *The final clause in the contract will be left untouched.*

untoward /ˌʌntə'wɔ:d/ ***adj.*** (used about an event, etc.) unexpected and unpleasant: *The security guard noticed* ***nothing untoward.***

untrue /ʌn'tru:/ ***adj.*** **1** not true; not based on facts: *These accusations are totally untrue.* ◇ *an untrue claim/statement* ◇ *It would be untrue to say that something like this could never happen again.* **2 ~ (to sb/sth)** (*written*) not loyal to sb/sth: *If he agreed to their demands, he would have to be untrue to his principles.* SYN **unfaithful**

untruth /ˌʌn'tru:θ/ ***noun*** [C] (*pl.* **untruths** /-'tru:ðz/) (*written*) something that is not true; a lie ▸ **untruthful** /-fl/ ***adj.***

untypical /ʌn'tɪpɪkl/ ***adj.*** not typical or usual: *an untypical example* OPP **typical** ➲ look at **atypical**

unused¹ /ˌʌn'ju:zd/ ***adj.*** that has not been used

unused² /ʌn'ju:st/ ***adj.*** **~ to sth/to doing sth** not having any experience of sth: *She was unused to getting such a lot of attention.*

unusual 🔑 /ʌn'ju:ʒuəl; -ʒəl/ ***adj.*** **1** not expected or normal: *It's unusual for Joe to be late.* OPP **usual 2** interesting because it is different: *What an unusual hat!*

unusually 🔑 /ʌn'ju:ʒuəli; -ʒəli/ ***adv.*** **1** in a way that is not normal or typical of sb/sth: *Unusually for her, she forgot his birthday.* **2** more than is common; extremely

unveil /ˌʌn'veɪl/ ***verb*** [T] to show sth new to the public for the first time: *The President unveiled a memorial to those who died in the war.*

unwanted /ˌʌn'wɒntɪd/ ***adj.*** not wanted: *an unwanted gift*

unwarranted /ʌn'wɒrəntɪd/ ***adj.*** that is not deserved or for which there is no good reason: *unwarranted criticism*

unwelcome /ʌn'welkəm/ ***adj.*** not wanted: *To avoid attracting unwelcome attention he spoke quietly.* OPP **welcome**

unwell /ʌn'wel/ ***adj.*** (not before a noun) (HEALTH) ill; sick: *to feel unwell*

unwieldy /ʌn'wi:ldi/ ***adj.*** difficult to move or carry because it is too big, heavy, etc.

unwilling 🔑 /ʌn'wɪlɪŋ/ ***adj.*** not wanting to do sth but often forced to do it by other people OPP **willing**

unwind /ˌʌn'waɪnd/ ***verb*** (*pt, pp* **unwound** /-'waʊnd/) **1** [I,T] if you **unwind** sth or if sth **unwinds**, it comes away from sth that it had been put round: *The bandage had unwound.* **2** [I] (*informal*) to relax, especially after working hard: *After a busy day, it takes me a while to unwind.* ➲ look at **wind³**

unwise /ˌʌn'waɪz/ ***adj.*** showing a lack of good judgement; FOOLISH: *It would be unwise to tell anyone about our plan yet.* OPP **wise** ▸ **unwisely** ***adv.***

unwitting /ʌn'wɪtɪŋ/ ***adj.*** not realizing sth; not intending to do sth: *an unwitting accomplice to the crime* ▸ **unwittingly** ***adv.***

unwrap /ʌn'ræp/ ***verb*** [T] (**unwrapping; unwrapped**) to take off the paper, etc. that covers or protects sth

unzip /ˌʌn'zɪp/ ***verb*** (**unzipping; unzipped**) **1** [I,T] if a bag, piece of clothing, etc. **unzips**, or you **unzip** it, you open it by pulling on the ZIP (=the device that fastens the opening) OPP **zip (up) 2** [T] (COMPUTING) to return a file to its original size after it has been COMPRESSED (=made smaller) SYN **decompress** OPP **zip**

up¹ 🔑 /ʌp/ ***prep., adv.*** **1** at or to a high or higher level or position: *The monkey* ***climbed up*** *the tree.* ◇ *I carried her suitcase up to the third floor.* ◇ ***Put your hand up*** *if you know the answer.* ◇ *I walked up the hill.* **2** in or into a vertical position: ***Stand up****, please.* ◇ *Is he up* (=out of bed) *yet?* **3** used for showing an increase in sth: *Prices have* ***gone up.*** ◇ *Turn the* *volume up.* **4** used with verbs of closing or covering: ***Do up** your coat. It's cold.* ◇ *She tied the parcel up with string.* ◇ *I found some wood to **cover up** the hole.* **5** to the place where sb/sth is: *She ran up to her mother and kissed her.* ◇ *A car drove up and two men got out.* **6** coming or being put together: *The teacher collected up our exam papers.* ◇ *Asif and Joe teamed up in the doubles competition.* **7** (used about a period of time) finished: *Stop writing. Your time's up.* **8** into pieces: *We chopped the old table up and used it for firewood.* ◇ *She **tore up** the letter and threw it away.* **9** used for showing that an action continues until it is completed: ***Eat up**, everybody, I want you to finish everything on the table.* ◇ *Can you help me **clean up** the kitchen?* **10** in a particular direction: *I live just **up the road**.* ◇ ***Move up** a little and let me sit down.* **11** in or to the north: *My parents have just moved **up north**.* ◇ *When are you going up to Scotland?* **12** (COMPUTING) working; in operation: *Are the computers back up yet?* **13** (*informal*) used for showing that sth is spoiled: *I really messed up when I told the interviewer I liked sleeping.*

IDM **be up for sth 1** to be available to be bought or chosen: *That house is up for sale.* ◇ *How many candidates are up for election?* **2** (*informal*) to be ready to do sth and enthusiastic about doing it: *Is anyone up for a swim?*

be up to sb to be sb's responsibility: *I can't take the decision. It's not up to me.*

not up to much (*informal*) not very good: *The programme wasn't up to much.*

up against sth/sb facing sth/sb that causes problems

up and down backwards and forwards, or rising and falling: *He was nervously walking up and down outside the interview room.*

up and running (used about sth new) working well

up to sth 1 as much/many as: *We're expecting up to 100 people at the meeting.* **2** as far as now: *Up to now, things have been easy.* **3** capable of sth: *I don't feel up to cooking this evening. I'm too tired.* **4** doing sth secret and perhaps bad: *What are the children up to? Go and see.*

what's up? (*informal*) what's the matter?

up² /ʌp/ ***noun***

IDM **ups and downs** the mixture of good and bad things in life or in a particular situation or relationship: *Every marriage has its ups and downs.*

up- /ʌp/ ***prefix*** (used in adjectives, verbs and nouns) higher; upwards; towards the top of sth: *upland* ◇ *upturned* ◇ *upgrade* ◇ *uphill*

upbeat /ˈʌpbiːt/ ***adj.*** (*informal*) positive and enthusiastic; making you feel that the future will be good SYN **optimistic**: *The tone of the speech was upbeat.*

upbringing /ˈʌpbrɪŋɪŋ/ ***noun*** [sing.] the way a child is treated and taught how to behave by their parents: *a strict upbringing*

update /ˌʌpˈdeɪt/ ***verb*** [T] **1** to make sth more modern **2** to put the latest information into sth; to give sb the latest information: *Our database of addresses is updated regularly.* ▶ **update** /ˈʌpdeɪt/ ***noun*** [C]: *an update on a news story* (= the latest information)

upgrade /ˌʌpˈgreɪd/ ***verb*** [T] **1** (COMPUTING) to make a piece of machinery, computer system, etc. more powerful and efficient: *Upgrading your computer software can be expensive.* **2 ~ sb (to sth)** to give sb a more important job **3 ~ sb (to sth)** (TOURISM) to give sb a better seat on a plane, room in a hotel, etc. than the one that they have paid for: *On the flight back, we were upgraded to business class.* **4** to improve the condition of a building, etc. in order to provide a better service: *to upgrade the town's leisure facilities* ➲ look at **downgrade** ▶ **upgrade** /ˈʌpgreɪd/ ***noun*** [C]: *Frequent flyers qualify for a free upgrade.*

upheaval /ʌpˈhiːvl/ ***noun*** [C,U] a sudden big change, especially one that causes a lot of trouble

uphill /ˌʌpˈhɪl/ ***adj., adv.*** **1** going towards the top of a hill OPP **downhill 2** needing a lot of effort: *It was an uphill struggle to find a job.*

uphold /ʌpˈhəʊld/ ***verb*** [T] (*pt, pp* **upheld** /-ˈheld/) to support a decision, etc. especially when other people are against it

upholstered /ʌpˈhəʊlstəd/ ***adj.*** (used about a chair, etc.) covered with a soft thick material

upholstery /ʌpˈhəʊlstəri/ ***noun*** [U] the thick soft materials used to cover chairs, car seats, etc.

upkeep /ˈʌpkiːp/ ***noun*** [U] **1** the cost or process of keeping sth in a good condition: *The landlord pays for the upkeep of the building.* **2** the cost or process of providing children or animals with what they need to live

upland /ˈʌplənd/ ***noun*** [C, usually pl.] (GEOGRAPHY) an area of high land that is situated away from the coast ▶ **upland** ***adj.*** (only *before* a noun): *upland agriculture*

uplifting /ˌʌpˈlɪftɪŋ/ ***adj.*** producing a feeling of hope and happiness: *an uplifting speech*

upload¹ /ˌʌpˈləʊd/ ***verb*** [T] (COMPUTING) to copy a computer file from a small computer system to a larger one OPP **download¹**

upload² /ˈʌpləʊd/ ***noun*** [U] (COMPUTING) the act or process of copying a computer file from a small computer system to a larger one ➲ look at **download²**

upon ⊶ /əˈpɒn/ ***prep.*** (*formal*) = ON

upper ⊶ /ˈʌpə(r)/ ***adj.*** (only *before* a noun) in a higher position than sth else; situated above sth: *He had a cut on his upper lip.* OPP **lower**

IDM **get, have, etc. the upper hand** to get into a stronger position than another person; to gain control over sb

ˌupper ˈcase ***noun*** [U] (LANGUAGE) letters that are written or printed in their large form; capital letters: *'BBC' is written in upper case.* OPP **lower case**

ˌupper ˈchamber ***noun*** [sing.] = UPPER HOUSE

the ˌupper ˈclass ***noun*** [sing.] (*also* **the ˌupper ˈclasses** [pl.]) (SOCIAL STUDIES) the group of people in a society who are considered to have the highest social position and who have more money and/or power than other people: *a member of the upper class/upper classes* ▶ **ˌupper ˈclass** ***adj.***: *They're upper class.* ◇ *an upper-class accent* ➲ look at **the middle class, the working class**

uppercut /ˈʌpəkʌt/ ***noun*** [C] (SPORT) (in boxing) a way of hitting sb on the chin, in which you bend your arm and move your hand upwards

ˌupper ˈhouse (*also* **ˌupper ˈchamber**, **ˌsecond ˈchamber**) ***noun*** [sing.] (POLITICS) one of the parts of a parliament in countries which have a parliament that is divided into two parts. In Britain it is the House of Lords and in the US it is the Senate. ➲ look at **lower house**

uppermost /ˈʌpəməʊst/ ***adj.*** in the highest or most important position: *Concern for her family was **uppermost in her mind**.*

upright /ˈʌpraɪt/ ***adj.***, ***adv.*** **1** in or into a vertical position: *I was so tired I could hardly stay upright.* **2** honest and responsible
IDM **bolt upright** → BOLT³

uprising /ˈʌpraɪzɪŋ/ ***noun*** [C] (POLITICS, SOCIAL STUDIES) a situation in which a group of people start to fight against the people in power in their country

uproar /ˈʌprɔː(r)/ ***noun*** [U, sing.] a lot of noise, confusion, anger, etc.; an angry discussion about sth: *The meeting ended* ***in uproar.***

uproot /ˌʌpˈruːt/ ***verb*** [T] to pull up a plant by the roots: *Strong winds had uprooted the tree.*

uprush /ˈʌprʌʃ/ ***noun*** [C] a sudden upward movement

upset¹ /ˌʌpˈset/ ***verb*** [T] (*pres. part.* **upsetting**; *pt, pp* **upset**) **1** to make sb worry or feel unhappy: *The pictures of starving children upset her.* **2** to make sth go wrong: *to upset someone's plans* **3** to knock sth over: *I upset a cup of tea all over the tablecloth.* **4** (HEALTH) to make sb ill in the stomach

upset² /ˌʌpˈset/ ***adj.*** **1** worried and unhappy: *She was looking very upset about something.* **2** (HEALTH) slightly ill: *I've got* ***an upset stomach.***

upset³ /ˈʌpset/ ***noun*** **1** [C,U] a situation in which there are unexpected problems or difficulties: *The company survived the recent upset in share prices.* **2** [C] a slight illness in your stomach: *a stomach upset* **3** [C,U] a situation that causes worry and sadness: *She's had a few upsets recently.* ◇ *It had been the cause of much emotional upset.*

upshot /ˈʌpʃɒt/ ***noun*** [sing.] **the ~ (of sth)** the final result, especially of a conversation or an event

upside down /ˌʌpsaɪd ˈdaʊn/ ***adv.***, ***adj.*** with the top part turned to the bottom: *You're holding the picture upside down.*
IDM **turn sth upside down** **1** to make a place untidy when looking for sth: *I had to turn the house upside down looking for my keys.* **2** to cause large changes and confusion in a person's life: *His sudden death turned her world upside down.*

upstairs /ˌʌpˈsteəz/ ***adv.*** to or on a higher floor of a building: ***to go upstairs*** ◇ *She's sleeping upstairs.* OPP **downstairs** ▶ **upstairs** /ˈʌpsteəz/ ***adj.***: *an upstairs window* ▶ **the upstairs** ***noun*** [sing.] (*informal*): *We're going to paint the upstairs.*

upstream /ˌʌpˈstriːm/ ***adv.***, ***adj.*** (GEOGRAPHY) in the direction that a river flows from: *He found it hard work swimming upstream.* OPP **downstream**

upsurge /ˈʌpsɜːdʒ/ ***noun*** [C, usually sing.] **an ~ (in sth)** a sudden increase of sth

uptake /ˈʌpteɪk/ ***noun***
IDM **quick/slow on the uptake** quick/slow to understand the meaning of sth: *I gave him a hint but he's slow on the uptake.*

upthrust /ˈʌpθrʌst/ ***noun*** [U] (PHYSICS) the force with which a liquid or gas pushes up against an object that is floating in it

uptight /ˌʌpˈtaɪt/ ***adj.*** (*informal*) nervous and not relaxed: *He gets uptight before an exam.*

ˌup to ˈdate ***adj.*** **1** modern **2** having the most recent information

ˌup-to-the-ˈminute ***adj.*** having the most recent information possible

upturn /ˈʌptɜːn/ ***noun*** [C] **an ~ (in sth)** an improvement in sth: *an upturn in support for the government* OPP **downturn**

upturned /ˌʌpˈtɜːnd/ ***adj.*** **1** pointing upwards: *an upturned nose* **2** turned upside down

upward /ˈʌpwəd/ ***adj.*** moving or directed towards a higher place: *an* ***upward trend*** *in exports* (=an increase) OPP **downward**

ˌupwardly ˈmobile ***adj.*** (SOCIAL STUDIES) moving towards a higher social position, usually in which you become richer: *an upwardly mobile lifestyle*

upwards /ˈʌpwədz/ (*also* **upward**) ***adv.*** **1** towards a higher place or position: *Place your hands on the table with the palms facing upwards.* **2** towards a higher amount or price: *Bad weather forced the price of fruit upwards.* **3 ~ of sth** more than the amount or number mentioned: *You should expect to pay upwards of $150 for a hotel room.*

ˈupwards of ***prep.*** more than the number mentioned: *They've invited upwards of a hundred guests.*

uranium /juˈreɪniəm/ ***noun*** [U] (*symbol* **U**) (CHEMISTRY) a metal that can be used to produce nuclear energy: *Uranium is highly radioactive.* ❶ For more information on the periodic table of elements, look at pages R34-5.

Uranus /ˈjʊərənəs; jʊˈreɪnəs/ ***noun*** [sing.] (ASTRONOMY) the planet that is seventh in order from the sun ➲ picture at **solar system**

urban /ˈɜːbən/ ***adj.*** (GEOGRAPHY) connected with a town or city: *urban development* ➲ look at **rural**, **urban morphology**

urbane /ɜːˈbeɪn/ ***adj.*** (*written*) (used especially about a man) good at knowing what to say and how to behave in social situations; appearing relaxed and confident ▶ **urbanely** ***adv.*** ▶ **urbanity** /ɜːˈbænəti/ ***noun*** [U]

urbanized (also **-ised**) /ˈɜːbənaɪzd/ ***adj.*** (GEOGRAPHY, ENVIRONMENT) (used about an area, a country, etc.) having a lot of towns, streets, factories, etc. rather than countryside ▶ **urbanization** (also **-isation**) /ˌɜːbənaɪˈzeɪʃn/ ***noun*** [U]

ˌurban morˈphology ***noun*** [U] (GEOGRAPHY) the study of the physical form of a city, which examines street patterns, the styles, sizes and shapes of buildings, the number of people who live there, what different areas of the city are used for, etc.

Urdu /ˈʊəduː; ˈɜːduː/ ***noun*** [U] (LANGUAGE) the official language of Pakistan, which is also spoken in parts of India

urea /jʊˈriːə/ ***noun*** [U] (BIOLOGY) a colourless substance that is found especially in URINE (=the liquid waste that is passed from your body when you go to the toilet)

ureter /juˈriːtə(r); ˈjʊərɪtə(r)/ ***noun*** [C] (ANATOMY, BIOLOGY) the tube that URINE (=waste liquid from the body) passes through to get from the KIDNEYS (=the two organs that produce urine from waste liquids in the blood) to the BLADDER (=the organ in which urine is held before being passed from the body)

urethra /jʊˈriːθrə/ ***noun*** [C] (ANATOMY) the tube that carries liquid waste out of the body. In men and male animals male seed (**sperm**) also flows along this tube. ▶ **urethral** ***adj.***

urge¹ /ɜːdʒ/ ***verb*** [T] **1 ~ sb (to do sth); ~ sth** to advise or try hard to persuade sb to do sth: *I urged him to fight the decision.* ◇ *Drivers are urged to take care on icy roads.* ◇ *Police urge caution on the icy roads.* ➲ note at **recommend** **2** to force sb/sth to go in a certain direction: *He urged his horse over the fence.*

PHR V **urge sb on** to encourage sb: *The captain urged his team on.*

urge² /ɜːdʒ/ ***noun*** [C] a strong need or desire: *sexual/creative urges*

urgent /ˈɜːdʒənt/ ***adj.*** needing immediate attention: *an urgent message* ▶ **urgency** /-dʒənsi/ ***noun*** [U]: *a matter of the greatest urgency* ▶ **urgently** ***adv.***: *I must see you urgently.*

urinal /jʊəˈraɪnl; ˈjʊərɪnl/ ***noun*** [C] a type of toilet for men that is attached to the wall; a room or building containing **urinals**

urinary /ˈjʊərɪnəri/ ***adj.*** (usually *before* a noun) (HEALTH) connected with URINE or the parts of the body through which it passes

urinate /ˈjʊərɪneɪt/ ***verb*** [I] (*formal*) (BIOLOGY, HEALTH) to pass URINE from the body

urine /ˈjʊərɪn; -raɪn/ ***noun*** [U] (BIOLOGY, HEALTH) the yellowish liquid that is passed from your body when you go to the toilet

URL /ˌjuː ɑːr ˈel/ ***abbr.*** (COMPUTING) uniform/universal resource locator (the address of a WORLD WIDE WEB page)

urn /ɜːn/ ***noun*** [C] **1** a special container, used especially to hold the powder (**ashes**) that is left when a dead person has been burnt (**cremated**) **2** a large metal container used for making a large quantity of tea or coffee and for keeping it hot

urology /jʊəˈrɒlədʒi/ ***noun*** [U] (HEALTH) the scientific study of the URINARY system ▶ **urological** /ˌjʊərəˈlɒdʒɪkl/ ***adj.*** ▶ **urologist** /jʊəˈrɒlədʒɪst/ ***noun*** [C]

US /ˌjuː ˈes/ ***abbr.*** the United States (of America)

us /əs; *strong form* ʌs/ ***pronoun*** (used as the object of a verb, or after *be*) me and another person or other people; me and you: *Come with us.* ◇ *Leave us alone.* ◇ *Will you write to us?*

USA /ˌjuː es ˈeɪ/ ***abbr.*** the United States of America

usable /ˈjuːzəbl/ ***adj.*** that can be used

usage /ˈjuːsɪdʒ/ ***noun*** **1** [U] the way that sth is used; the amount that sth is used **2** [C,U] (LANGUAGE) the way that words are normally used in a language: *a guide to English grammar and usage*

USB /ˌjuː es ˈbiː/ ***abbr.*** (COMPUTING) **universal serial bus**; the system for connecting other pieces of equipment to a computer: *All new PCs now have USB sockets.* ◇ *a USB port*

ˌUSB ˈFlash drive (*also* **ˌUSB ˈFlash disk**, **ˌUSˈB drive**; **ˌUSˈB stick**) ***noun*** [C] (*abbr.* **UFD**) (COMPUTING) a small device that you can carry around with you which is used for storing and moving data onto a computer SYN **Memory Stick™**, **Pen drive™**

use¹ /juːz/ ***verb*** [T] (*pres. part.* **using**; *pt, pp* **used** /juːzd/) **1** ~ **sth (as/for sth)**; ~ **sth (to do sth)** to do sth with a machine, an object, a method, etc. for a particular purpose: *Could I use your phone?* ◇ *The building was used as a shelter for homeless people.* ◇ *A gun is used for shooting with.* ◇ *What's this used for?* ◇ *We used the money to buy a house.* ◇ *Use your imagination!* ◇ *That's a word I never use.* **2** to need or to take sth: *Don't use all the milk.* **3** to treat sb/sth in an unfair way in order to get sth that you want

PHR V **use sth up** to use sth until no more is left

use² /juːs/ ***noun*** **1** [U] the action of using sth or of being used: *The use of computers is now widespread.* ◇ *She kept the money for use in an emergency.* **2** [C,U] the purpose for which sth is used: *This machine has many uses.* **3** [U] the ability or permission to use sth: *He lost the use of his hand after the accident.* ◇ *She offered them the use of her car.* **4** [U] the advantage of sth; how useful sth is: ***It's no use*** *studying for an exam at the last minute.* ◇ ***What's the use of*** *trying?* ◇ *Will this jumper* ***be of use to*** *you or should I get rid of it?*

IDM **come into/go out of use** to start/stop being used regularly or by a lot of people: *Email came into widespread use in the 1990s.*

make use of sth/sb to use sth/sb in a way that will give you an advantage

used ***adj.*** **1** /juːzd/ that has had another owner before SYN **second-hand**: *a garage selling used cars* **2** /juːst/ ~ **to sth/to doing sth** familiar with sth; ACCUSTOMED to sth: *He's used to the heat.* ◇ *I'll never* ***get used to*** *getting up so early.*

used to /ˈjuːst tə; *before a vowel and in final position* ˈjuːst tuː/ ***modal verb*** for talking about sth that happened often or continuously in the past or about a situation which existed in the past: *She used to live with her parents* (= but she doesn't now). ◇ *You used to live in Glasgow, didn't you?* ◇ *Did you use to smoke?* ◇ *He didn't use to speak to me.*

useful /ˈjuːsfl/ ***adj.*** having some practical use; helpful: *a useful tool* ◇ *useful advice* ▶ **usefully** /-fəli/ ***adv.*** ▶ **usefulness** ***noun*** [U]

IDM **come in useful** to be of practical help in a certain situation: *Don't throw that box away – it might come in useful for something.*

useless /ˈjuːsləs/ ***adj.*** **1** that does not work well, that does not achieve anything: *This new machine is useless.* ◇ *It's useless complaining/to complain – you won't get your money back.* **2** (*informal*) ~ (**at sth/at doing sth**) (used about a person) weak or not successful at sth: *I'm useless at sport.* ▶ **uselessly** ***adv.*** ▶ **uselessness** ***noun*** [U]

Usenet /ˈjuːznet/ ***noun*** [U] (COMPUTING) a service on the Internet used by groups of users who email each other because they share a particular interest

user /ˈjuːzə(r)/ ***noun*** [C] (often in compounds) a person who uses a service, machine, place, etc.: *users of public transport* ◇ *drug users*

ˌuser-ˈfriendly ***adj.*** (used about computers, books, machines, etc.) easy to understand and use ▶ **ˌuser-ˈfriendliness** ***noun*** [U]

ˈuser group ***noun*** [C] a group of people who use a particular thing and who share information about it, especially people who share information about computers on the Internet

username /ˈjuːzəneɪm/ ***noun*** [C] (COMPUTING) the name you use in order to be able to use a computer program or system: *Please enter your username.*

usher¹ /ˈʌʃə(r)/ ***noun*** [C] a person who shows people to their seats in a theatre, church, etc.

usher² /ˈʌʃə(r)/ ***verb*** [T] to take or show sb where to go: *I was ushered into an office.*

PHR V **usher sth in** to be the beginning of sth new or to make sth new begin: *The agreement ushered in a new period of peace for the two countries.*

USSR /ˌjuː es es ˈɑː(r)/ ***abbr.*** (until 1991) Union of Soviet Socialist Republics ➲ look at **CIS**

usual /ˈjuːʒuəl; -ʒəl/ ***adj.*** ~ (**for sb/sth**) (**to do sth**) happening or used most often: *It's usual for her to work at weekends.* ◇ *He got home later than usual.* ◇ *I sat in my usual seat.* OPP **unusual**

IDM **as usual** in the way that has often happened before: *Here's Dylan, late as usual!*

usually /ˈjuːʒuəli; -ʒəli/ ***adv.*** in the way that is usual; most often: *She's usually home by six.* ◇ *We usually go out on Saturdays.*

usurp /juːˈzɜːp/ ***verb*** [T] (*formal*) to take sb's position and/or power without having the right to do this ▶ **usurpation** /ˌjuːzɜːˈpeɪʃn/ ***noun*** [U, C] ▶ **usurper** ***noun*** [C]

utensil /juːˈtensl/ ***noun*** [C] a type of tool that is used in the home: *kitchen/cooking utensils*

uterus /ˈjuːtərəs/ ***noun*** [C] (*pl.* **uteruses** or, in scientific use, **uteri** /-raɪ/) (*formal*) (ANATOMY) the part of a woman or female animal where a baby develops before it is born SYN **womb** ➲ picture at **fertilize**

utility AW /juːˈtɪləti/ ***noun*** (*pl.* **utilities**) **1** [C] a service provided for the public, such as a water, gas or electricity supply: *the administration of* ***public utilities*** **2** [U] (*formal*) the quality of being useful **3** [C] (COMPUTING) a program or part of a program that does a particular task

u'tility room ***noun*** [C] a small room in some houses, often next to the kitchen, where people keep large pieces of kitchen equipment, such as a washing machine

utilize (also **-ise**) AW /ˈjuːtəlaɪz/ ***verb*** [T] (*formal*) to make use of sth: *to utilize natural resources*

utmost[1] /ˈʌtməʊst/ ***adj.*** (*formal*) (only *before* a noun) greatest: *a message* ***of the utmost importance***

utmost[2] /ˈʌtməʊst/ ***noun*** [sing.] the greatest amount possible: *Resources have been exploited* ***to the utmost.*** ◇ *I will* ***do my utmost*** (=try as hard as possible) *to help.*

utopia (also **Utopia**) /juːˈtəʊpiə/ ***noun*** [C,U] a place or state that exists only in the imagination, where everything is perfect ▶ **utopian** (also **Utopian**) /-piən/ ***adj.***

utter[1] /ˈʌtə(r)/ ***adj.*** (only *before* a noun) complete; total: *He felt an utter fool.* ▶ **utterly** ***adv.***: *It's utterly impossible.*

utter[2] /ˈʌtə(r)/ ***verb*** [T] to say sth or make a sound with your voice: *She did not* ***utter a word*** (=she did not say anything) *in the meeting.* ▶ **utterance** /ˈʌtərəns/ ***noun*** [C] (*formal*)

'U-turn ***noun*** [C] **1** a type of movement where a car, etc. turns round so that it goes back in the direction it came from **2** (*informal*) a sudden change from one plan or policy to a completely different or opposite one ➲ look at **about turn**

UV /ˌjuː ˈviː/ ***abbr.*** =ULTRAVIOLET: *UV radiation*

uvula /ˈjuːvjələ/ ***noun*** [C] (*pl.* **uvulae** /-liː/) (ANATOMY, BIOLOGY) a small piece of flesh that hangs from the top of the inside of the mouth just above the throat ➲ picture on **page 80**

V v

V, v[1] /viː/ ***noun*** [C,U] (*pl.* **V's; v's** /viːz/) **1** the twenty-second letter of the English alphabet: *'Velvet' begins with (a) 'V'.* **2** the shape of a V: *a V-neck sweater*

v[2] ***abbr.*** **1** (*also* **vs**) versus; against: *Liverpool v Everton* **2 V** volt(s): *a 9V battery* **3** verse **4** (*informal*) very: *v good*

vacancy /ˈveɪkənsi/ ***noun*** [C] (*pl.* **vacancies**) **1 a** ~ **(for sb/sth)** a job that is available for sb to do: *We have a vacancy for a secretary in our office.* **2** a room in a hotel, etc. that is available: *The sign outside the hotel said 'No Vacancies'.*

vacant /ˈveɪkənt/ ***adj.*** **1** (used about a house, hotel room, seat, etc.) not being used; empty **2** (used about a job in a company, etc.) that is available for sb to take: *the* ***'Situations Vacant'*** *page* (=the page of a British newspaper where jobs are advertised) **3** showing no sign of intelligence or understanding: *a vacant expression* ▶ **vacantly** ***adv.***: *She stared at him vacantly.*

vacate /veɪˈkeɪt; vəˈk-/ ***verb*** [T] (*formal*) to leave a building, a seat, a job, etc. so that it is available for sb else

vacation ⊶ /vəˈkeɪʃn/ ***noun*** **1** [C] (*BrE*) any of the periods of time when universities or courts of law are closed: *the Christmas/Easter vacation* **2** [C,U] (*AmE*) (a) holiday: *The boss is* ***on vacation***.

vaccinate /ˈvæksɪneɪt/ ***verb*** [T] ~ **sb (against sth)** (often passive) (HEALTH) to protect a person or an animal against a disease by giving them or it a mild form of the disease with a needle which is put under the skin (**an injection**): *Were you vaccinated against measles as a child?* ➲ look at **immunize, inoculate** ▶ **vaccination** /ˌvæksɪˈneɪʃn/ ***noun*** [C,U]

vaccine /ˈvæksiːn/ ***noun*** [C] (HEALTH) a mild form of a disease that is put (**injected**) into a person or an animal's blood using a needle (**an injection**) in order to protect the body against that disease

vacuole /ˈvækjuəʊl/ ***noun*** [C] (BIOLOGY) an empty space inside a living cell ➲ picture at **cell**

vacuum[1] /ˈvækjuəm/ ***noun*** [C] **1** (PHYSICS) a space that is completely empty of all substances, including air or other gases: *vacuum-packed foods* (=in a pack from which the air has been removed) **2** [usually sing.] a situation from which sth is missing or lacking **3** (*informal*) =VACUUM CLEANER **4** [usually sing.] the act of cleaning sth with a **vacuum cleaner**: *to give a room a quick vacuum*

vacuum[2] /ˈvækjuəm/ ***verb*** [I,T] to clean sth using a VACUUM CLEANER SYN **hoover**

'vacuum cleaner (also *informal* **vacuum**) ***noun*** [C] an electric machine that cleans carpets, etc. by sucking up dirt SYN **Hoover™** ➲ look at **cleaner**

'vacuum flask (*also* **flask**, *AmE* **'vacuum bottle**) ***noun*** [C] (PHYSICS) a container like a bottle with double walls with a VACUUM between them, used for keeping liquids hot or cold ➲ picture at **Thermos**

vagina /vəˈdʒaɪnə/ ***noun*** [C] (ANATOMY) the passage in the body of a woman or female animal that connects the outer sex organs to the WOMB (=the part where a baby grows)

vagrant /ˈveɪɡrənt/ ***noun*** [C] a person who has no home and no job, especially one who asks people for money

vague /veɪɡ/ ***adj.*** **1** not clear or definite: *He was very vague about how much money he'd spent.* ◇ *a vague shape in the distance* **2** (used about a person) not thinking or understanding clearly: *She looked vague when I tried to explain.* ▶ **vagueness** ***noun*** [U]

vaguely /ˈveɪɡli/ ***adv.*** **1** in a way that is not clear; slightly: *Her name is vaguely familiar.* **2** without thinking about what is happening: *He smiled vaguely and walked away.*

vain /veɪn/ ***adj.*** **1** useless; failing to produce the result you want: *She turned away* ***in a vain attempt*** *to hide her tears.* **2** (used about a person) too proud of your own appearance, abilities, etc.: *He's so vain – he looks in every mirror he passes.* ➲ noun **vanity** ▶ **vainly** ***adv.***

IDM **in vain** without success: *The firemen tried in vain to put out the fire.*

vale /veɪl/ ***noun*** [C] (GEOGRAPHY) a valley: *the Vale of York*

valency /ˈveɪlənsi/ ***noun*** [C,U] (*pl.* **valencies**) **1** (CHEMISTRY) a measurement of the power of an atom to combine with others, by the number of HYDROGEN atoms it can combine with or take the place of: *Carbon has a valency of 4.* **2** (LANGUAGE) the number of elements that a word, especially a verb, combines with in a sentence

valentine /ˈvæləntaɪn/ ***noun*** [C] **1** (*also* **ˈvalentine card**) a card that you send, usually without putting your name on it, to sb you love ❶ It is traditional to send these cards on **St Valentine's Day** (14 February).
2 the person you send this card to

valet[1] /ˈvæleɪ; ˈvælɪt/ (*AmE also* /væˈleɪ/) ***noun*** [C] **1** a man's personal servant who takes care of his clothes, serves his meals, etc. **2** (*BrE*) a hotel employee whose job is to clean the clothes of hotel guests **3** (*AmE*) a person who parks your car for you at a hotel or restaurant

valet[2] /ˈvælɪt/ ***verb*** **1** [T] (*BrE*) to clean a person's car thoroughly, especially on the inside: *a car valeting service* **2** [I] to perform the duties of a VALET

valiant /ˈvæliənt/ ***adj.*** (*formal*) full of courage and not afraid ▶ **valiantly** ***adv.***

valid 🔑 AW /ˈvælɪd/ ***adj.*** **1** ~ (for sth) that is legally or officially acceptable: *This passport is valid for one year only.* **2** based on what is logical or true; acceptable: *I could raise no valid objections to the plan.* ◇ *Jeff's making a perfectly valid point.* OPP **invalid** ▶ **validity** /vəˈlɪdəti/ ***noun*** [U]

validate AW /ˈvælɪdeɪt/ ***verb*** [T] (*formal*) **1** to show that sth is true: *to validate a claim/theory* OPP **invalidate** **2** to make sth legally valid: *to validate a contract* OPP **invalidate** **3** to state officially that sth is useful and of an acceptable standard: *Check that their courses have been validated by a reputable organization.* ▶ **validation** /ˌvælɪˈdeɪʃn/ ***noun*** [U]

valley 🔑 /ˈvæli/ ***noun*** [C] (GEOGRAPHY) the low land between two mountains or hills, which often has a river flowing through it ➲ look at **hanging valley**, **rift valley**

valour (*AmE* **valor**) /ˈvælə(r)/ ***noun*** [U] (*written, old-fashioned*) great courage and lack of fear, especially in war: *the soldiers' valour in battle*

valuable 🔑 /ˈvæljuəbl/ ***adj.*** **1** worth a lot of money: *Is this ring valuable?* **2** very useful: *a valuable piece of information* OPP **valueless**, **worthless**

valuables /ˈvæljuəblz/ ***noun*** [pl.] the small things that you own that are worth a lot of money, such as jewellery, etc.: *Please put your valuables in the hotel safe.*

valuation /ˌvæljuˈeɪʃn/ ***noun*** [C] (FINANCE) a professional judgement about how much money sth is worth

value[1] 🔑 /ˈvælju:/ ***noun*** **1** [U, C] (FINANCE) the amount of money that sth is worth: *The thieves stole goods with a total value of $10000.* ◇ *to go up/down in value* ➲ look at **face value** **2** [U] (*BrE*) how much sth is worth compared with its price: *The hotel was **good/excellent value*** (=well worth the money it cost). ◇ *Package holidays give the best **value for money**.* **3** [U] the importance of sth: *to be of great/little/no value to sb* ◇ *This bracelet is of great **sentimental value** to me.* **4 values** [pl.] beliefs about what is the right and wrong way for people to behave; moral principles: *a return to traditional values* ◇ *Young people have a different **set of values**.*

value[2] 🔑 /ˈvælju:/ ***verb*** [T] (*pres. part.* **valuing**) **1** ~ sb/sth (as sth) to think sb/sth is very important: *Sandra has always valued her independence.* ◇ *I really value her as a friend.* **2** (usually passive) ~ sth (at sth) to decide the amount of money that sth is worth: *The house was valued at $150000.*

ˌvalue added ˈtax ***noun*** [U] =VAT

valueless /ˈvælju:ləs/ ***adj.*** without value or use SYN **worthless** OPP **valuable**

valve /vælv/ ***noun*** [C] **1** (PHYSICS) a device in a pipe or tube which controls the flow of air, liquid or gas, letting it move in one direction only: *a radiator valve* ◇ *the valve on a bicycle tyre* **2** (ANATOMY) a structure in your heart or in a VEIN (=a tube that carries blood to the heart) that lets blood flow in one direction only ➲ picture at **heart**

vampire /ˈvæmpaɪə(r)/ ***noun*** [C] (in horror stories) a dead person who comes out at night and drinks the blood of living people

van 🔑 /væn/ ***noun*** [C] a road vehicle that is used for transporting things

vanadium /vəˈneɪdiəm/ ***noun*** [U] (*symbol* **V**) (CHEMISTRY) a hard grey metal, used in making special types of steel ❶ For more information on the periodic table of elements, look at pages R34-5.

vandal /ˈvændl/ ***noun*** [C] a person who damages sb else's property deliberately and for no purpose ▶ **vandalism** /-dəlɪzəm/ ***noun*** [U]: *acts of vandalism* ▶ **vandalize** (also **-ise**) /ˈvændəlaɪz/ ***verb*** [T] (usually passive): *All the phone boxes in this area have been vandalized.*

vanguard /ˈvæŋgɑ:d/ ***noun*** [sing.] (usually **the vanguard**) **1** the leaders of a movement in society, for example in politics, art, industry, etc.: *The company is proud to be **in the vanguard of** scientific progress.* **2** the part of an army, etc. that is at the front when moving forward to attack the enemy

vanilla /vəˈnɪlə/ ***noun*** [U] a substance from a plant that is used for giving flavour to sweet food: *vanilla ice cream*

vanish /ˈvænɪʃ/ ***verb*** [I] **1** to disappear suddenly or in a way that you cannot explain: *When he turned round, the two men had **vanished without trace**.* **2** to stop existing: *This species of plant is vanishing from our countryside.*

ˈvanishing point ***noun*** [C, usually sing.] (ART) the point in the distance at which parallel lines appear to meet

vanity /ˈvænəti/ ***noun*** [U] the quality of being too proud of your appearance or abilities ➲ adjective **vain**

vantage point /ˈvɑ:ntɪdʒ pɔɪnt/ ***noun*** [C] a place from which you have a good view of sth: (*figurative*) *From our modern vantage point, we can see why the Roman Empire collapsed.*

vaporize (also **-ise**) /ˈveɪpəraɪz/ ***verb*** [I,T] (CHEMISTRY, PHYSICS) to change into gas; to make sth change into gas ▶ **vaporization** (also **-isation**) /ˌveɪpəraɪˈzeɪʃn/ ***noun*** [U]

vapour (*AmE* **vapor**) /ˈveɪpə(r)/ ***noun*** [C,U] (SCIENCE) a mass of very small drops of liquid in the air, for example steam: *water vapour*

variable[1] AW /ˈveəriəbl/ ***adj.*** not staying the same; often changing ▶ **variability** /ˌveəriəˈbɪləti/ ***noun*** [U]

variable[2] AW /ˈveəriəbl/ ***noun*** [C] **1** a situation, number or quantity that can vary or be varied: *With so many variables to consider, it is difficult to calculate the cost.* ◇ *The temperature was kept constant throughout the experiment while pressure was a variable.* **2** (MATHEMATICS) a symbol that represents a quantity which can change in value during a calculation OPP **constant²**

variance AW /ˈveəriəns/ ***noun*** [U, C] (*formal*) the amount by which sth changes or is different from sth else: *variance in temperature/pay*
IDM **at variance (with sb/sth)** (*formal*) disagreeing with sb/sth

variant AW /ˈveəriənt/ ***noun*** [C] a slightly different form or type of sth

variation 🔑 AW /ˌveəriˈeɪʃn/ ***noun*** **1** [C,U] (a) ~ (**in sth**) a change or difference in the amount or level of sth: *There was a lot of variation in the examination results.* ◇ *There may be a slight variation in price from shop to shop.* **2** [C] a ~ (**on/of sth**) a thing that is slightly different from another thing in the same general group: *All her films are just variations on a basic theme.* **3** [C] ~ (**on sth**) (MUSIC) any of a set of short pieces of music based on a simple tune repeated in a different and more complicated form: *a set of variations on a theme by Mozart*

varicose vein /ˌværɪkəʊs ˈveɪn/ ***noun*** [C] (HEALTH) a VEIN (=a tube that carries blood around your body), especially one in the leg, which has become swollen and painful ➲ look at **deep vein thrombosis**

varied 🔑 AW /ˈveərid/ ***adj.*** having many different kinds of things or activities: *I try to make my classes as varied as possible.*

variety 🔑 /vəˈraɪəti/ ***noun*** (*pl.* **varieties**) **1** [sing.] a ~ (**of sth**) a number of different types of the same thing: *There is a* ***wide variety*** *of dishes to choose from.* **2** [U] the quality of not being or doing the same all the time: *There's so much variety in my new job. I do something different every day!* **3** [C] a ~ (**of sth**) a type of sth: *a new variety of apple called 'Perfection'* **4** [U] (ARTS AND MEDIA) a form of theatre or television entertainment that consists of a series of short performances, such as singing, dancing and funny acts: ***a variety show***

various 🔑 /ˈveəriəs/ ***adj.*** several different: *I decided to leave my job for various reasons.*

varnish /ˈvɑːnɪʃ/ ***noun*** [U] a clear liquid that you paint onto hard surfaces, especially wood, to protect them and make them shine ➲ look at **nail varnish** ▶ **varnish** ***verb*** [T]: *The doors are then stained and varnished.*

vary 🔑 AW /ˈveəri/ ***verb*** (*pres. part.* **varying**; *3rd person sing. pres.* **varies**; *pt, pp* **varied**) **1** [I] ~ (**in sth**) (used about a group of similar things) to be different from each other: *The hotel bedrooms vary in size from medium to very large.* **2** [I] ~ (**from...to...**) to be different or to change according to the situation, etc.: *The price of the holiday varies from £500 to £1200, depending on the time of year.* **3** [T] to make sth different by changing it often in some way: *I try to vary my work as much as possible so I don't get bored.*

vascular /ˈvæskjələ(r)/ ***adj.*** (BIOLOGY) (usually *before* a noun) of or containing VEINS (=the tubes that carry liquids around the bodies of animals and plants)

vas deferens /ˌvæs ˈdefərenz/ ***noun*** [C] (*pl.* **vasa deferentia** /ˌveɪsə defəˈrenʃiə/) (ANATOMY) the tube through which SPERM (=cells produced by the sex organs of a male) pass from the TESTIS on their way out of the body

vase /vɑːz/ ***noun*** a container that is used for holding cut flowers

vasectomy /vəˈsektəmi/ ***noun*** [C] (*pl.* **vasectomies**) (HEALTH) a medical operation to stop a man being able to have children

vassal /ˈvæsl/ ***noun*** [C] **1** (HISTORY) a man in the Middle Ages who promised to fight for and be loyal to a king or other powerful owner of land, in return for being given land to live on **2** (POLITICS) a country that depends on and is controlled by another country

vast 🔑 /vɑːst/ ***adj.*** extremely big: *a vast sum of money* ◇ *a vast country* ▶ **vastly** ***adv.***: *a vastly improved traffic system*

VAT (*also* **Vat**) /ˌviː eɪ ˈtiː; væt/ ***abbr.*** (FINANCE) **value added tax**; a tax that is added to the price of goods and services: *Prices include VAT.*

vaults

vault¹ /vɔːlt/ ***noun*** [C] **1** a room with a strong door and thick walls in a bank, etc. that is used for keeping money and other valuable things safe **2** (ARCHITECTURE) a room under a church where dead people are buried: *a family vault* **3** (ARCHITECTURE) a high roof or ceiling in a church, etc., made from a number of ARCHES joined together at the top **4** (SPORT) a jump made by VAULTING ➲ look at **pole vault**

vault² /vɔːlt/ ***verb*** [I,T] ~ (**over**) **sth** to jump over or onto sth in one movement, using your hands or a pole to help you

VCR /ˌviː siː ˈɑː(r)/ ***abbr.*** video cassette recorder

VD /ˌviː ˈdiː/ ***abbr.*** (HEALTH) venereal disease

VDU /ˌviː diː ˈjuː/ ***noun*** [C] (COMPUTING) visual display unit; a screen on which you can see information from a computer

veal /viːl/ ***noun*** [U] the meat from a young cow (**calf**) ➲ note at **meat**

vectors

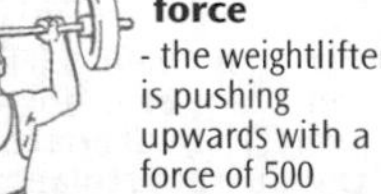

vector /ˈvektə(r)/ ***noun*** [C] **1** (MATHEMATICS) a measurement or a quantity that has both size and direction

RELATED VOCABULARY 

Scalars provide information about size (magnitude) such as distance, speed, mass, etc.

Vectors provide two pieces of information (magnitude and direction) such as velocity, acceleration, force, etc.

2 (HEALTH) an insect, etc. that carries a particular disease from one living thing to another: *Mosquitoes are the vectors in malaria.* **3** the course taken by an aircraft

veer /vɪə(r)/ ***verb*** [I] (used about vehicles) to change direction suddenly: *The car veered across the road and hit a tree.*

veg[1] /vedʒ/ ***noun*** [U] (*BrE, informal*) vegetables: *a fruit and veg stall*

veg[2] /vedʒ/ ***verb*** (*BrE, slang*)

PHR V **veg out** to relax and do nothing that needs thought or effort: *I'm just going to go home and veg out in front of the telly.*

vegan /'vi:gən/ ***noun*** [C] a person who does not eat meat or any other animal products at all ➲ look at **vegetarian** ▶ **vegan *adj.***

vegetable /'vedʒtəbl/ (also *informal* **veg**; **veggie**) ***noun*** [C] (BIOLOGY) a plant or part of a plant that we eat. Potatoes, BEANS and onions are vegetables: *vegetable soup*

vegetarian /,vedʒə'teəriən/ (*BrE, informal* **veggie**) ***noun*** [C] a person who does not eat meat or fish ➲ look at **vegan** ▶ **vegetarian *adj.***: *a vegetarian cookery book*

vegetation /,vedʒə'teɪʃn/ ***noun*** [U] (*formal*) plants in general; all the plants that are found in a particular place: *tropical vegetation*

veggie /'vedʒi/ ***noun*** [C] (*informal*) **1** (*BrE*) =VEGETARIAN **2** =VEGETABLE ▶ **veggie *adj.***: *a veggie burger*

vehement /'vi:əmənt/ ***adj.*** showing very strong (often negative) feelings, especially anger: *a vehement attack on the government*

vehicle AW /'vi:əkl/ ***noun*** [C] **1** something which transports people or things from place to place, especially on land, for example cars, bicycles, lorries and buses: *Are you the owner of this vehicle?* **2** something which is used for communicating particular ideas or opinions: *This newspaper has become a vehicle for Conservative opinion.*

vehicular /və'hɪkjələ(r)/ ***adj.*** (*formal*) intended for vehicles or consisting of vehicles: *vehicular access* ◇ *The road is closed to vehicular traffic.*

veil /veɪl/ ***noun*** [C] a piece of thin material for covering the head and face of a woman: *a bridal veil*

veiled /veɪld/ ***adj.*** **1** not expressed directly or clearly because you do not want your meaning to be obvious: *a **thinly veiled** threat/warning/criticism* **2** wearing a VEIL (=a piece of cloth that covers the face): *a veiled woman*

vein /veɪn/ ***noun*** **1** [C] (ANATOMY) one of the tubes which carry blood from all parts of your body to your heart ➲ look at **artery**, **jugular**, **varicose vein** ➲ picture at **circulation** **2** [sing., U] a particular style or quality: *After a humorous beginning, the programme continued in a more serious vein.*

Velcro™ /'velkrəʊ/ ***noun*** [U] a material for fastening parts of clothes together. **Velcro™** is made of a man-made material (**nylon**) and is used in small pieces, one rough and one smooth, that can stick together and be pulled apart.

veld /velt/ ***noun*** [U] (GEOGRAPHY) flat open land in South Africa with grass and no trees

vellum /'veləm/ ***noun*** [U] **1** material made from the skin of a sheep, GOAT or CALF, used for making book covers and, in the past, for writing on **2** smooth cream-coloured paper used for writing on

velocity /və'lɒsəti/ ***noun*** [U] (PHYSICS) the speed at which sth moves in a particular direction: *a high-velocity rifle/bullet* ➲ picture at **vectors**

velour /və'lʊə(r)/ ***noun*** [U] a kind of cloth with a thick soft surface similar to VELVET

velvet /'velvɪt/ ***noun*** [U] a kind of cloth made of SILK, cotton or other material, with a soft thick surface on one side only: *black velvet trousers*

vena cava /,vi:nə 'keɪvə/ ***noun*** [C] (*pl.* **venae cavae** /,vi:ni: 'keɪvi:/) (ANATOMY) a VEIN (=a tube that carries blood in the body) that takes blood without OXYGEN in it into the heart ➲ picture at **heart**

vendetta /ven'detə/ ***noun*** [C] a serious argument or DISPUTE between two people or groups which lasts for a long time

'vending machine ***noun*** [C] a machine from which you can buy drinks, cigarettes, etc. by putting coins in it

vendor /'vendə(r)/ ***noun*** [C] (*formal*) a person who is selling sth ➲ look at **purchaser**

veneer /və'nɪə(r)/ ***noun*** **1** [C,U] a thin layer of wood or plastic that is stuck onto the surface of a cheaper material, especially wood, to give it a better appearance **2** [sing.] (*formal*) **a ~ (of sth)** a part of sb's behaviour or of a situation which hides what it is really like underneath: *a thin veneer of politeness*

venereal disease /və,nɪəriəl dɪ'zi:z/ ***noun*** [C,U] (*abbr.* **VD**) (HEALTH) any disease caught by having sex with a person who has it

venetian blind /və,ni:ʃn 'blaɪnd/ ***noun*** [C] a covering for a window that is made of horizontal pieces of flat plastic, etc. which can be turned to let in as much light as you want

vengeance /'vendʒəns/ ***noun*** [U] (*written*) **~ (on sb)** the act of punishing or harming sb in return for sth bad they have done to you, your friends or family: *He felt a terrible desire for vengeance on the people who had destroyed his career.* ➲ look at **revenge**

IDM **with a vengeance** to a greater degree than is expected or usual: *After a week of good weather winter returned with a vengeance.*

venison /'venɪsn/ ***noun*** [U] the meat from a DEER (=a large wild animal)

Venn diagram

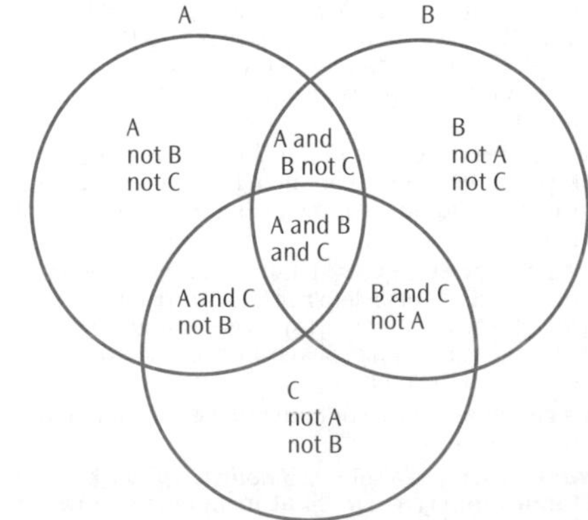

Venn diagram /ˈven daɪəɡræm/ ***noun*** [C] (**MATHEMATICS**) a picture showing SETS (=groups of things that have a shared quality) as circles that cross over each other, to show which qualities the different sets have in common

venom /ˈvenəm/ ***noun*** [U] **1** (**BIOLOGY**) the poisonous liquid that some snakes, spiders, etc. produce when they bite or sting you **2** extreme anger or hatred and a desire to hurt sb: *She shot him a look of pure venom.* ▸ **venomous** /ˈvenəməs/ ***adj.***

vent /vent/ ***noun*** [C] an opening in the wall of a room or machine which allows air to come in, and smoke, steam or smells to go out: *an air vent* ◇ *a heating vent* ➲ picture at **volcano**

ventilate /ˈventɪleɪt/ ***verb*** [T] to allow air to move freely in and out of a room or building: *The office is badly ventilated.* ▸ **ventilation** /ˌventɪˈleɪʃn/ ***noun*** [U]: *There was no ventilation in the room except for one tiny window.*

ventilator /ˈventɪleɪtə(r)/ ***noun*** [C] **1** a device or an opening that allows air to move freely in and out of a building, room, etc. **2** (**HEALTH**) a machine in a hospital that helps sb to breathe

ventral /ˈventrəl/ ***adj.*** (only *before* a noun) (**BIOLOGY**) on or connected with the under side of a fish or an animal ➲ look at **dorsal**, **pectoral** ➲ picture on **page 80**

ventricle /ˈventrɪkl/ ***noun*** (**ANATOMY**) [C] **1** either of the two lower spaces in the heart ➲ picture at **heart** **2** any space in the body that does not contain anything, especially one of the four main empty spaces in the brain

venture¹ ⊶ /ˈventʃə(r)/ ***noun*** [C] a project which is new and possibly dangerous, because you cannot be sure that it will succeed: *a business venture*

venture² ⊶ /ˈventʃə(r)/ ***verb*** [I] to do sth or go somewhere new and dangerous, when you are not sure what will happen: *He ventured out into the storm to look for the lost child.* ◇ *The company has decided to venture into computer production as well as design.*

ˈ**venture capital** ***noun*** [U] (**BUSINESS**) money that is invested in a new company to help it develop, which may involve a lot of risk ➲ look at **working capital**

venue /ˈvenjuː/ ***noun*** [C] the place where people meet for an organized event, for example a concert or a sporting event

Venus /ˈviːnəs/ ***noun*** [sing.] (**ASTRONOMY**) the planet that is second in order from the sun and nearest to the earth ➲ picture at **the solar system**

veranda (also **verandah**) /vəˈrændə/ (*AmE also* **porch**) ***noun*** [C] (**ARCHITECTURE**) a platform joined to the side of a house, with a roof and floor but no outside wall ➲ look at **balcony**, **patio**, **terrace**

verb /vɜːb/ ***noun*** [C] (**LANGUAGE**) a word or group of words that is used to indicate that sth happens or exists, for example *bring, happen, be, do.* ➲ look at **phrasal verb**

verbal /ˈvɜːbl/ ***adj.*** (*formal*) **1** connected with words, or the use of words: *verbal skills* **2** spoken, not written: *a verbal agreement/warning* **3** (**LANGUAGE**) connected with verbs, or the use of verbs ▸ **verbally** /ˈvɜːbəli/ ***adv.***

verbatim /vɜːˈbeɪtɪm/ ***adj.***, ***adv.*** exactly as it was spoken or written: *a verbatim report* ◇ *He reported the speech verbatim.*

verdict /ˈvɜːdɪkt/ ***noun*** [C] **1** (**LAW**) the decision that is made by a specially chosen group of people (**the jury**) in a court of law, which states if a person is guilty of a crime or not: *The jury **returned a verdict** of 'not guilty'.* ◇ *Has the jury **reached a verdict**?* **2 a** ~ **(on sb/sth)** a decision that you make or an opinion that you give after testing sth or considering sth carefully: *The general verdict was that the restaurant was too expensive.*

verge¹ /vɜːdʒ/ ***noun*** [C] (*BrE*) the narrow piece of land at the side of a road, path, etc. that is usually covered in grass

IDM **on the verge of sth/doing sth** very near to doing sth, or to sth happening: *He was on the verge of a nervous breakdown.* ◇ *Scientists are on the verge of discovering a cure.*

verge² /vɜːdʒ/ ***verb***

PHR V **verge on sth** to be very close to an extreme state or condition: *What they are doing verges on the illegal.*

verify /ˈverɪfaɪ/ ***verb*** [T] (*pres. part.* **verifying**; *3rd person sing. pres.* **verifies**; *pt, pp* **verified**) (*formal*) to check or state that sth is true: *to verify a statement* ▸ **verification** /ˌverɪfɪˈkeɪʃn/ ***noun*** [U]

veritable /ˈverɪtəbl/ ***adj.*** (only *before* a noun) (*formal*) a word used to emphasize that sb/sth can be compared to sb/sth else that is more exciting, more impressive, etc.: *The meal was a veritable banquet.*

vermilion /vəˈmɪliən/ ***adj.*** bright red in colour ▸ **vermilion** ***noun*** [U]

vermin /ˈvɜːmɪn/ ***noun*** [pl.] small wild animals (for example RATS) that carry disease and destroy plants and food

vernacular /vəˈnækjələ(r)/ ***noun*** [C] (usually **the vernacular**) [sing.] (**LANGUAGE**) the language spoken in a particular area or by a particular group of people, especially one that is not the official or written language

vernal /ˈvɜːnl/ ***adj.*** (only *before* a noun) (*formal*) (**GEOGRAPHY**) connected with the season of spring: *the vernal equinox*

versatile /ˈvɜːsətaɪl/ ***adj.*** **1** (used about an object) having many different uses: *a versatile tool that drills, cuts or polishes* **2** (used about a person) able to do many different things: *She's so versatile! She can dance, sing, act and play the guitar!*

verse /vɜːs/ ***noun*** **1** [U] writing arranged in lines which have a definite rhythm and often finish with the same sound (**rhyme**): *He wrote his valentine's message in verse.* **2** [C] a group of lines which form one part of a song or poem: *This song has five verses.* SYN stanza

version ⊶ AW /ˈvɜːʃn/ ***noun*** [C] **1** a thing which has the same basic contents as sth else but which is presented in a different way: *Have you heard the live version of this song?* **2** a person's description of sth that has happened: *The two drivers gave very different versions of the accident.*

versus /ˈvɜːsəs/ ***prep.*** **1** (*abbr.* **v**, **vs**) used in sport for showing that two teams or people are playing against each other: *England versus Argentina* **2** used for showing that two ideas or things are opposite to each other, especially when you are trying to choose one of them: *It's a question of quality versus price.*

vertebra /ˈvɜːtɪbrə/ ***noun*** [C] (*pl.* **vertebrae** /-breɪ/ /-briː/) (**ANATOMY**, **BIOLOGY**) any of the small bones that are connected together to form the SPINE (=the column of bones down the middle of your back) ➲ picture on **page 80** ▸ **vertebral** ***adj.***

vertebrate /ˈvɜːtɪbrət/ ***noun*** [C] (BIOLOGY) an animal, bird or fish that has a BACKBONE **OPP invertebrate**

vertex /ˈvɜːteks/ ***noun*** [C] (*pl.* **vertices** /-tɪsiːz/ or **vertexes**) **1** (MATHEMATICS) a point where two lines meet to form an angle, especially the point of a triangle or CONE opposite the base **2** (TECHNICAL) the highest point or top of sth

vertical /ˈvɜːtɪkl/ ***adj.*** (GEOMETRY) going straight up at an angle of 90° from the ground: *a vertical line* ◇ *The cliff was almost vertical.* ➲ look at **horizontal, perpendicular** ➲ picture at **line** ▶ **vertically** /-kli/ ***adv.***

verve /vɜːv/ ***noun*** [U, sing.] (*written*) energy, excitement or enthusiasm: *It was a performance of verve and vitality.*

very[1] /ˈveri/ ***adv.*** (used to emphasize an adjective or an adverb) extremely; in a high degree: *very small* ◇ *very slowly* ◇ *I don't like milk very much.* ◇ *'Are you hungry?' 'Not very.'*

very[2] /ˈveri/ ***adj.*** (only *before* a noun) **1** used to emphasize that you are talking about a particular thing or person and not about another: *Those were his very words.* ◇ *You're the very person I wanted to talk to.* **2** extreme: *We climbed to the very top of the mountain.* **3** used to emphasize a noun: *The* ***very thought of*** *drink made her feel sick.*
IDM before sb's very eyes → EYE[1]

vesicle /ˈvesɪkl/ ***noun*** [C] **1** (BIOLOGY) a small bag or hollow structure in the body of a plant or an animal **2** (HEALTH) a small swelling filled with liquid under the skin

vessel /ˈvesl/ ***noun*** [C] **1** (*written*) a ship or large boat **2** (*old-fashioned*) a container for liquids, for example a bottle, cup or bowl: *ancient drinking vessels*

vest /vest/ ***noun*** [C] **1** (*AmE* **undershirt**) a piece of clothing that you wear under your other clothes, on the top part of your body **2** (*AmE*) = WAISTCOAT

vested interest /ˌvestɪd ˈɪntrest/ ***noun*** [C] a strong and often secret reason for doing sth that will bring you an advantage of some kind, for example more money or power

vestige /ˈvestɪdʒ/ ***noun*** [C] a small part of sth that is left after the rest of it has gone: *the last vestige of the old system* **SYN trace**

vet[1] /vet/ (also *formal* **ˈveterinary surgeon**, *AmE* **veterinarian**) ***noun*** [C] a doctor for animals: *We took the cat to the vet/to the vet's.*

vet[2] /vet/ ***verb*** [T] (**vetting**; **vetted**) to do careful and secret checks before deciding if sb/sth can be accepted or not: *All new employees at the Ministry of Defence are carefully vetted* (= somebody examines the details of their past lives).

veteran /ˈvetərən/ ***noun*** [C] **1** a person who has served in the army, navy or air force, especially during a war **2** a person who has very long experience of a particular job or activity

veterinarian /ˌvetərɪˈneəriən/ (*AmE*) = VET[1]

veterinary /ˈvetnri/ ***adj.*** connected with the medical treatment of sick or injured animals: *a veterinary practice* ➲ look at **vet**

veto /ˈviːtəʊ/ ***verb*** [T] (*pres. part.* **vetoing**; *3rd person sing. pres.* **vetoes**; *pt, pp* **vetoed**) to refuse to give official permission for an action or plan, when other people have agreed to it: *The Prime Minister vetoed the proposal to reduce taxation.* ▶ **veto** ***noun*** [C,U] (*pl.* **vetoes**): *the right of veto*

vexed /vekst/ ***adj.*** causing difficulty, worry, and a lot of discussion: *the vexed question of our growing prison population*

VHF /ˌviː eɪtʃ ˈef/ ***abbr.*** (PHYSICS) very high frequency; a band of radio waves used for sending out a high quality signal: *a VHF transmitter* ➲ picture at **wavelength**

via AW /ˈvaɪə/ ***prep.*** **1** going through a place: *We flew from Paris to Sydney via Bangkok.* **2** by means of sth; using sth: *These pictures come to you via our satellite link.*

viable /ˈvaɪəbl/ ***adj.*** that can be done; that will be successful: *I'm afraid your idea is just not commercially viable.* ▶ **viability** /ˌvaɪəˈbɪləti/ ***noun*** [U]

viaduct /ˈvaɪədʌkt/ ***noun*** [C] a long, high bridge which carries a railway or road across a valley

vibrant /ˈvaɪbrənt/ ***adj.*** **1** full of life and energy; exciting: *a vibrant city/atmosphere/personality* **2** (used about colours) bright and strong

vibrate /vaɪˈbreɪt/ ***verb*** [I] to make continuous very small and fast movements from side to side: *When a guitar string vibrates it makes a sound.* ▶ **vibration** /vaɪˈbreɪʃn/ ***noun*** [C,U]

vibrato /vɪˈbrɑːtəʊ/ ***noun*** [U, C] (*pl.* **vibratos**) (MUSIC) a shaking effect in singing or playing a musical instrument, made by making a note slightly higher and lower many times very quickly

vicar /ˈvɪkə(r)/ ***noun*** [C] (RELIGION) a priest of the Church of England. A **vicar** looks after a church and the people in the surrounding area (**parish**). ➲ look at **minister**

vicarage /ˈvɪkərɪdʒ/ ***noun*** [C] (RELIGION) the house where a VICAR lives

vicarious /vɪˈkeəriəs/ ***adj.*** (only *before* a noun) felt or experienced by watching or reading about sb else doing sth, rather than by doing it yourself: *He got a vicarious thrill out of watching his son score the winning goal.*

vice

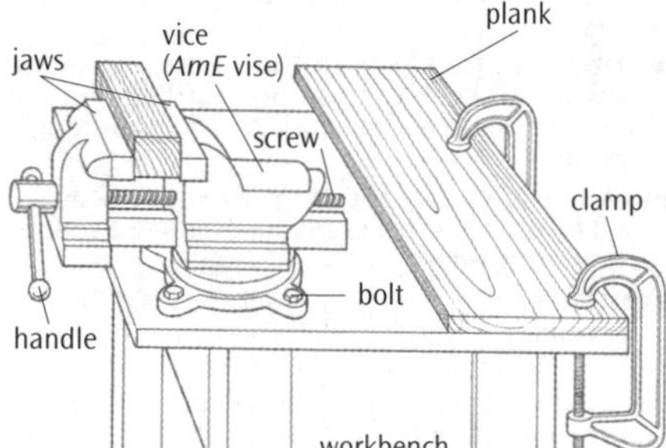

vice /vaɪs/ ***noun*** **1** [U] (LAW) criminal activities involving sex or drugs **2** [C] a moral weakness or bad habit: *Greed and envy are terrible vices.* ◇ *My only vice is smoking.* ➲ look at **virtue 3** (*AmE* **vise**) [C] a tool that you use to hold a piece of wood, metal, etc. firmly while you are working on it: (*figurative*) *He held my arm in a vice-like* (= very firm) *grip.*

vice- /vaɪs/ (used to form compound nouns) having a position second in importance to the position mentioned: *Vice-President* ◇ *the vice-captain*

ˌvice ˈchancellor ***noun*** [C] (EDUCATION) the head of a university in Britain who is in charge of the work of running the university ℹ Compare **vice chancellor** with **chancellor**, who is the official head of a university, but only has duties at various ceremonies.

ˌvice-'president *noun* [C] (*abbr.* **VP**) **1** (POLITICS) the person below the president of a country in rank, who takes control of the country if the president is not able to **2** (*AmE*) (BUSINESS) a person in charge of a particular part of a business company: *the vice-president of sales*

vice versa /ˌvaɪs 'vɜːsə/ *adv.* in the opposite way to what has just been said: *Anna ordered fish and Maria chicken – or was it vice versa?*

vicinity /və'sɪnəti/ *noun*
IDM **in the vicinity (of sth)** (*formal*) in the surrounding area: *There's no bank in the immediate vicinity.*

vicious /'vɪʃəs/ *adj.* **1** cruel; done in order to hurt sb/sth: *a vicious attack* **2** (used about an animal) dangerous; likely to hurt sb ▶ **viciously** *adv.*
IDM **a vicious circle** a situation in which one problem leads to another and the new problem makes the first problem worse

victim /'vɪktɪm/ *noun* [C] a person or animal that is injured, killed or hurt by sb/sth: *a murder victim* ◇ *The children are often the innocent victims of a divorce.*

victimize (also **-ise**) /'vɪktɪmaɪz/ *verb* [T] to punish or make sb suffer unfairly ▶ **victimization** (also **-isation**) /ˌvɪktɪmaɪ'zeɪʃn/ *noun* [U]

victor /'vɪktə(r)/ *noun* [C] (*formal*) the person who wins a game, competition, battle, etc.

Victorian /vɪk'tɔːriən/ *adj.* (HISTORY) **1** connected with the time of the British queen Victoria (1837-1901): *Victorian houses* **2** having attitudes that were typical in the time of Queen Victoria ▶ **Victorian** *noun* [C]

victory /'vɪktəri/ *noun* [C,U] (*pl.* **victories**) success in winning a battle, game, competition, etc.: *Keane led his team to victory in the final.* ▶ **victorious** /vɪk'tɔːriəs/ *adj.*: *the victorious team*
IDM **romp home/to victory** → ROMP

video /'vɪdiəʊ/ *noun* (*pl.* **videos**) **1** [U] the system of recording moving pictures and sound by using a camera, and showing them using a VIDEO CASSETTE RECORDER: *We recorded the wedding **on video**.* ◇ *The film is coming out **on video** in May.* **2** (also ˌ**video cas'sette**, **videotape**) [C] a tape or CASSETTE on which you record moving pictures and sound, or on which a film or television programme has been recorded: *Would you like to see the video we made on holiday?* ◇ *to rent a video* **3** =VIDEO RECORDER ▶ **video** *verb* [T] (*3rd person sing. pres.* **videos**; *pres. part.* **videoing**; *pt, pp* **videoed**): *We hired a camera to video the school play.*

ˌ**video cas'sette recorder** (*also* **video**; **'video recorder**) *noun* [C] (*abbr.* **VCR**) (ARTS AND MEDIA) a machine that is connected to a television on which you can record or play back a film or television programme

videoconferencing /'vɪdiəʊkɒnfərənsɪŋ/ *noun* [U] a system that allows people in different parts of the world to have a meeting by watching and listening to each other using video screens

videophone /'vɪdiəʊfəʊn/ *noun* [C] (ARTS AND MEDIA) a type of telephone with a screen that allows you to see the person you are talking to

videotape /'vɪdiəʊteɪp/ *noun* [C] =VIDEO (2) ▶ **videotape** *verb* [T] (*formal*) =VIDEO: *a videotaped interview*

videotex /'vɪdiəʊteks/ *noun* [U] (*AmE*) =VIEWDATA

view[1] /vjuː/ *noun* **1** [C] a ~ (about/on sth) an opinion or a particular way of thinking about sth: *He expressed the view that standards were falling.* ◇ ***In my view**, she has done nothing wrong.* ◇ *She has **strong views** on the subject.* ➲ note at **regard**[1] **2** [U] the ability to see sth or to be seen from a particular place: *The garden was hidden from view behind a high wall.* ◇ *Just then, the sea **came into view**.* ◇ *to disappear from view* **3** [C] what you can see from a particular place, especially beautiful natural SCENERY: *There are **breathtaking views** from the top of the mountain.* ◇ *a room with **a sea view***
IDM **have, etc. sth in view** (*formal*) to have sth as a plan or idea in your mind
in full view (of sb/sth) → FULL[1]
in view of sth because of sth; as a result of sth: *In view of her apology we decided to take no further action.*
a point of view → POINT[1]
with a view to doing sth (*formal*) with the aim or intention of doing sth

view[2] /vjuː/ *verb* [T] (*formal*) **1** ~ sth (as sth) to think about sth in a particular way: *She viewed holidays as a waste of time.* **2** to watch or look at sth: *Viewed from this angle, the building looks much taller than it really is.*

viewdata /'vjuːdeɪtə/ (*AmE also* **videotex**) *noun* [U] (COMPUTING) an information system in which computer data is sent along telephone lines and shown on a television screen

viewer /'vjuːə(r)/ *noun* [C] a person who watches television

viewpoint /'vjuːpɔɪnt/ *noun* [C] a way of looking at a situation; an opinion: *Let's look at this problem from the customer's viewpoint.* SYN **point of view**

vigil /'vɪdʒɪl/ *noun* [C,U] a period when you stay awake all night for a special purpose: *All night she **kept vigil** over the sick child.*

vigilant /'vɪdʒɪlənt/ *adj.* (*formal*) careful and looking out for danger ▶ **vigilance** /-əns/ *noun* [U]

vigilante /ˌvɪdʒɪ'lænti/ *noun* [C] (LAW) a member of a group of people who try to prevent crime or punish criminals in a community, especially because they believe the police are not doing this

vigour (*AmE* **vigor**) /'vɪgə(r)/ *noun* [U] strength or energy: *After the break we started work again with renewed vigour.* ▶ **vigorous** /'vɪgərəs/ *adj.*: *vigorous exercise* ▶ **vigorously** *adv.*

Viking /'vaɪkɪŋ/ *noun* [C] (HISTORY) a member of a race of Scandinavian people who attacked and sometimes settled in parts of NW Europe, including Britain, in the 8th to the 11th centuries

vile /vaɪl/ *adj.* very bad or unpleasant: *She's in a vile mood.* ◇ *a vile smell*

villa /'vɪlə/ *noun* [C] **1** (TOURISM) a house that people rent and stay in on holiday **2** a large house in the country, especially in Southern Europe

village /'vɪlɪdʒ/ *noun* **1** [C] (GEOGRAPHY) a group of houses with other buildings, for example a shop, school, etc., in a country area. A village is smaller than a town: *a small fishing village* ◇ *the village shop* **2** [sing., with sing. or pl. verb] all the people who live in a village: *All the village is/are taking part in the carnival.*

villager /'vɪlɪdʒə(r)/ *noun* [C] a person who lives in a village

villain /'vɪlən/ *noun* [C] **1** an evil person, especially in a book or play: *In most of his films he has played villains, but in this one he's a good guy.* ➲ look at **hero**

2 (*informal*) (LAW) a criminal: *The police caught the villains who robbed the bank.*

villus /ˈvɪləs/ ***noun*** [C] (*pl.* **villi** /ˈvɪlaɪ; -liː/) (BIOLOGY) any one of the many small thin parts that stick out from some surfaces on the inside of the body (for example in the INTESTINE). **Villi** increase the area of these surfaces so that substances can be taken into the body more easily.

vindicate /ˈvɪndɪkeɪt/ ***verb*** [T] (*formal*) **1** to prove that sth is true or that you were right to do sth, especially when other people had a different opinion: *I have every confidence that this decision will be fully vindicated.* **2** to prove that sb is not guilty when they have been accused of doing sth wrong or illegal: *New evidence emerged, vindicating him completely.*

vindictive /vɪnˈdɪktɪv/ ***adj.*** wanting or trying to hurt sb without good reason: *a vindictive comment/person* ▶ **vindictiveness** ***noun*** [U]

vine /vaɪn/ ***noun*** [C] (BIOLOGY) the plant that GRAPES grow on

vinegar /ˈvɪnɪɡə(r)/ ***noun*** [U] a liquid with a strong sharp taste that is made from wine. **Vinegar** is often mixed with oil and put onto salads.

vineyard /ˈvɪnjəd/ ***noun*** [C] (AGRICULTURE) a piece of land where GRAPES are grown

vintage¹ /ˈvɪntɪdʒ/ ***noun*** [C] the wine that was made in a particular year: *1999 was an excellent vintage.*

vintage² /ˈvɪntɪdʒ/ ***adj.*** (only *before* a noun) **1 vintage** wine is of very good quality and has been stored for several years: *vintage champagne/port/wine* **2** (used about a vehicle) made between 1917 and 1930 and admired for its style and interest **3** typical of a period in the past and of high quality; the best work of the particular person: *a vintage performance by Robert De Niro*

vinyl /ˈvaɪnl/ ***noun*** [C,U] a strong plastic that can bend easily and is used for making wall and floor covers, etc.

viola /viˈəʊlə/ ***noun*** [C] (MUSIC) a musical instrument with strings, that you hold under your chin and play with a BOW (=a long thin stick made of wood and hair): *A viola is like a large violin.* ➲ picture on **page 465**

violate AW /ˈvaɪəleɪt/ ***verb*** [T] (*formal*) **1** to break a rule, an agreement, etc.: *to violate a peace treaty* **2** to not respect sth; to spoil or damage sth: *to violate sb's privacy/rights* ▶ **violation** AW /ˌvaɪəˈleɪʃn/ ***noun*** [C,U]: *(a) violation of human rights*

violence 🔑 /ˈvaɪələns/ ***noun*** [U] **1** behaviour which harms or damages sb/sth physically: *They threatened to* ***use violence*** *if we didn't give them the money.* ◇ *an* ***act of violence*** **2** great force or energy: *the violence of the storm*

violent 🔑 /ˈvaɪələnt/ ***adj.*** **1** using physical strength to hurt or kill sb; caused by this behaviour: *The demonstration started peacefully but later turned violent.* ◇ *a violent death* ◇ ***violent crime*** **2** very strong and impossible to control: *He has a violent temper.* ◇ *a violent storm/collision*

violently 🔑 /ˈvaɪələntli/ ***adv.*** **1** with great energy or strong movement, especially caused by a strong emotion such as fear or hatred: *She shook her head violently.* ◇ *to shiver violently* **2** very strongly or severely: *He was violently sick.* ◇ *They are violently opposed to the idea.* **3** in a way that involves physical violence: *The crowd reacted violently.*

violet /ˈvaɪələt/ ***noun*** **1** [C] a small plant that grows wild or in gardens and has purple or white flowers and a pleasant smell **2** [U] a bluish purple colour ▶ **violet** ***adj.***

violin /ˌvaɪəˈlɪn/ ***noun*** [C] (MUSIC) a musical instrument with strings, that you hold under your chin and play with a BOW (=a long thin stick made of wood and hair) ➲ picture on **page 465**

VIP /ˌviː aɪ ˈpiː/ ***abbr.*** (*informal*) very important person: *the VIP lounge at the airport* ◇ *give someone the VIP treatment* (=treat sb especially well)

viper /ˈvaɪpə(r)/ ***noun*** [C] a small poisonous snake

viral → VIRUS

ˈviral marketing ***noun*** [U] (BUSINESS) a way of advertising in which information about a company's products or services is sent by email to people who then send it on by email to other people they know

virgin¹ /ˈvɜːdʒɪn/ ***noun*** [C] **1** a person who has never had sex **2 the (Blessed) Virgin** [sing.] (RELIGION) the Virgin Mary, mother of Jesus Christ

virgin² /ˈvɜːdʒɪn/ ***adj.*** in its original pure or natural condition and not changed, touched or spoiled: *virgin forest/land/territory*

virginity /vəˈdʒɪnəti/ ***noun*** [U] the state of never having had sex: *to lose your virginity*

Virgo /ˈvɜːɡəʊ/ ***noun*** [U] the sixth sign of the ZODIAC, the Virgin

virile /ˈvɪraɪl/ ***adj.*** (used about a man) strong and having great sexual energy

virility /vəˈrɪləti/ ***noun*** [U] a man's sexual power and energy

virtual AW /ˈvɜːtʃuəl/ ***adj.*** (only *before* a noun) **1** being almost or nearly sth: *The country is in a state of virtual civil war.* **2** (COMPUTING) made to appear to exist by the use of computer software, for example on the Internet: *New technology has enabled development of an online 'virtual library'.*

virtually 🔑 AW /ˈvɜːtʃuəli/ ***adv.*** **1** almost, or very nearly, so that any slight difference is not important: *The building is virtually finished.* **2** (COMPUTING) by the use of computer programs, etc. that make sth appear to exist: *Check out our new hotel rooms virtually by visiting our website at ...*

ˌvirtual ˈmemory (*also* **ˌvirtual ˈstorage**) ***noun*** [U] (COMPUTING) extra memory that is automatically created when all the normal memory is being used

ˌvirtual reˈality ***noun*** [U] (COMPUTING) images created by a computer that appear to surround the person looking at them and seem almost real

virtue /ˈvɜːtʃuː/ ***noun*** **1** [U] behaviour which shows high moral standards: *to lead a life of virtue* SYN **goodness** **2** [C] a good quality or habit: *Patience is a great virtue.* ➲ look at **vice** **3** [C,U] **the ~ (of sth/of being/doing sth)** an advantage or a useful quality of sth: *This new material* ***has the virtue*** *of being strong as well as very light.*

IDM **by virtue of sth** (*formal*) by means of sth or because of sth

virtuoso /ˌvɜːtʃuˈəʊsəʊ/ ***noun*** [C] (*pl.* **virtuosos** or **virtuosi** /-siː; -ziː/) (MUSIC) a person who is extremely skilful at sth, especially playing a musical instrument

virtuous /ˈvɜːtʃuəs/ ***adj.*** behaving in a morally good way

virulent /ˈvɪrələnt; ˈvɪrjələnt/ ***adj.*** **1** (HEALTH) (used about a poison or a disease) very strong and dangerous: *a particularly virulent form of influenza* **2** (*formal*) very strong and full of anger: *a virulent attack on the leader*

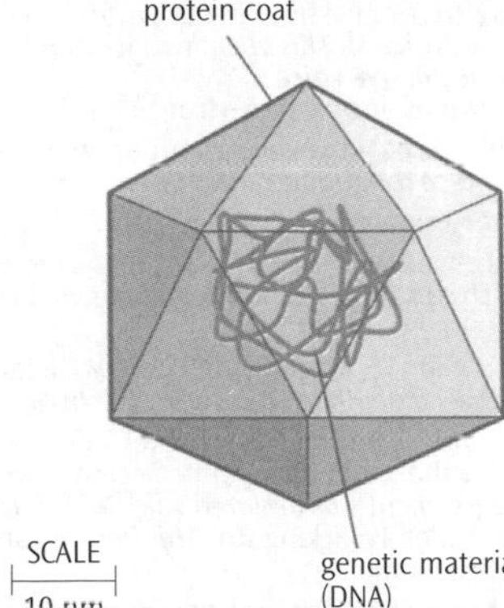

virus 🔑 /ˈvaɪrəs/ ***noun*** [C] (*pl.* **viruses**) **1** (BIOLOGY, HEALTH) a living thing, too small to be seen without a special instrument (**microscope**), that causes disease in people, animals and plants: *HIV, the virus that is thought to cause Aids* ◇ *to catch a virus* ◇ *the flu virus* ➲ look at **bacteria**, **germ** (1) **2** (COMPUTING) instructions that are put into a computer program in order to stop it working properly and destroy information ▶ **viral** /ˈvaɪrəl/ ***adj.***: *a viral infection*

visa /ˈviːzə/ ***noun*** [C] an official mark or piece of paper that shows you are allowed to enter, leave or travel through a country: *His passport was full of visa stamps.* ◇ *a tourist/work/student visa*

viscous /ˈvɪskəs/ ***adj.*** (used about liquids) thick and sticky; not flowing easily ▶ **viscosity** /vɪˈskɒsəti/ ***noun*** [U]

vise (*AmE*) = VICE (3)

visibility AW /ˌvɪzəˈbɪləti/ ***noun*** [U] the distance that you can see in particular light or weather conditions: *In the fog visibility was down to 50 metres.* ◇ *poor/good visibility*

visible 🔑 AW /ˈvɪzəbl/ ***adj.*** that can be seen or noticed: *The church tower was visible from the other side of the valley.* ◇ *a visible improvement in his work* OPP **invisible** ▶ **visibly** AW /-əbli/ ***adv.***: *Rosa was visibly upset.*

Visigoth /ˈvɪzɪgɒθ/ ***noun*** [C] (HISTORY) a member of an ancient race of people who fought against the Roman Empire in between the 3rd and 5th centuries AD and ruled much of Spain until 711, when the Moors took control

vision 🔑 AW /ˈvɪʒn/ ***noun*** **1** [U] (HEALTH) the ability to see; sight: *to have good/poor/normal/perfect vision* **2** [C] a picture in your imagination: *They have a vision of a world without weapons.* ◇ *I **had visions of** being left behind, but in fact the others had waited for me.* **3** [C] a dream or similar experience often connected with religion **4** [U] the ability to make great plans for the future: *a leader of great vision* **5** [U] the picture on a television or cinema screen: *a temporary loss of vision*

visionary /ˈvɪʒənri/ ***adj.*** (*pl.* **-ies**) having great plans for the future: *a visionary leader* ▶ **visionary** ***noun*** [C] (*pl.* **visionaries**)

visit 🔑 /ˈvɪzɪt/ ***verb*** [I,T] to go to see a person or place for a period of time: *I don't live here. I'm just visiting.* ◇ *We often visit relatives at the weekend.* ◇ *She's going to visit her son in hospital.* ◇ *When you go to London you must visit the Science Museum.* ▶ **visit** ***noun*** [C]: *The Prime Minister is **on a visit** to Germany.* ◇ *We had **a flying** (=very short) **visit** from Richard on Sunday.* ◇ *I decided it was time to **pay** him **a visit**.*

visiting /ˈvɪzɪtɪŋ/ ***adj.*** (only *before* a noun) (EDUCATION) a **visiting** professor or LECTURER is one who is teaching for a fixed period at a particular university or college, but who normally teaches at another one

visitor 🔑 /ˈvɪzɪtə(r)/ ***noun*** [C] a person who visits a person or a place: *She's a frequent visitor to the US.* ◇ *How can we attract more visitors to our website?*

visor /ˈvaɪzə(r)/ ***noun*** [C] **1** the part of a hard hat (**a helmet**) that you can pull down to protect your eyes or face **2** a piece of plastic, cloth, etc. on a hat or in a car, which stops the sun shining into your eyes

vista /ˈvɪstə/ ***noun*** [C] (*written*) **1** a beautiful view, for example of the countryside, a city, etc. **2** a variety of things that might happen or be possible in the future: *This job could open up whole new vistas for her.*

visual AW /ˈvɪʒuəl/ ***adj.*** connected with seeing: *the visual arts* (=painting, sculpture, cinema, etc.) ▶ **visually** AW ***adv.***: *The film is visually stunning.*

ˌvisual ˈaid ***noun*** [C] (EDUCATION) a picture, film, map, etc. that helps a student to learn sth

visualize (also **-ise**) AW /ˈvɪʒuəlaɪz/ ***verb*** [T] to imagine or have a picture in your mind of sb/sth: *It's hard to visualize what this place looked like before the factory was built.*

vital 🔑 /ˈvaɪtl/ ***adj.*** **1** very important or necessary: *Practice is vital if you want to speak a language well.* ◇ *vital information* ➲ note at **essential** **2** full of energy; lively ▶ **vitally** /ˈvaɪtəli/ ***adv.***: *vitally important*

vitality /vaɪˈtæləti/ ***noun*** [U] the state of being full of energy

vitamin /ˈvɪtəmɪn/ ***noun*** [C] (HEALTH) one of several substances that are found in certain types of food and that are important for growth and good health

ˌvitamin ˈA ***noun*** [U] (HEALTH) a VITAMIN found in cheese, eggs, fish oils and milk that is essential for healthy growth and sight

ˌvitamin ˈB ***noun*** [U] (HEALTH) any one of a group of VITAMINS found in foods such as CEREAL grains, meat and fish that are essential for the blood and the nervous system and for processing the food we eat

ˌvitamin ˈC (*also* **asˌcorbic ˈacid**) ***noun*** [U] (HEALTH) a VITAMIN found in fruits such as oranges and lemons, and in green vegetables. **Vitamin C** is essential for healthy skin and CONNECTIVE TISSUE. A lack of **vitamin C** can cause SCURVY: *Oranges are rich in vitamin C.*

ˌvitamin ˈD ***noun*** [U] (HEALTH) a VITAMIN found in meat such as LIVER, fish oils and eggs, which is essential for healthy bones and teeth. **Vitamin D** is also produced by the action of the sun on the skin. A lack of **vitamin D** can cause RICKETS.

vivacious /vɪˈveɪʃəs/ ***adj.*** (used about a person, usually a woman) full of energy; lively and happy

vivid /ˈvɪvɪd/ ***adj.*** **1** having or producing a strong, clear picture in your mind: *vivid dreams/memories* **2** (used about light or a colour) strong and very bright: *the vivid reds and yellows of the flowers* ▶ **vividly** ***adv.***

viviparous /vɪˈvɪpərəs/ ***adj.*** (BIOLOGY) (used about animals) that produce live babies from their bodies rather than eggs ➲ look at **oviparous**

vivisection /ˌvɪvɪˈsekʃn/ ***noun*** [U] doing scientific experiments on live animals

vixen /ˈvɪksn/ ***noun*** [C] a female FOX (= a type of reddish wild dog)

viz. /vɪz/ ***abbr.*** (often read out as 'namely') that is to say; in other words

ˈV-neck ***noun*** [C] an opening for the neck in a piece of clothing shaped like the letter V; a piece of clothing with a **V-neck**: *I went out and bought a navy V-neck*

vocabulary 🔑 /vəˈkæbjələri/ ***noun*** (*pl.* **vocabularies**) (LANGUAGE) **1** [C,U] all the words that sb knows or that are used in a particular book, subject, etc.: *He has an amazing vocabulary for a five-year-old.* ◇ *There are many ways to increase your English vocabulary.* **2** [sing.] all the words in a language: *New words are always coming into the vocabulary.* ➲ note at **language**

vocal /ˈvəʊkl/ ***adj.*** **1** (only *before* a noun) connected with the voice **2** expressing your ideas or opinions loudly or freely: *a small but vocal group of protesters*

ˌvocal ˈcords ***noun*** [C] (ANATOMY) the thin bands of muscle in the back of your throat that move to produce the voice

vocalist /ˈvəʊkəlɪst/ ***noun*** [C] (MUSIC) a singer, especially in a band: *a lead/backing vocalist*

vocally /ˈvəʊkəli/ ***adv.*** **1** in a way that uses the voice: *to communicate vocally* **2** by speaking in a loud and confident way: *They protested vocally.*

vocation /vəʊˈkeɪʃn/ ***noun*** [C,U] a type of work or a way of life that you believe to be especially suitable for you: *Peter has finally found his vocation in life.*

vocational /vəʊˈkeɪʃənl/ ***adj.*** connected with the skills, knowledge, etc. that you need to do a particular job: *vocational training*

voˈcational school ***noun*** [C, U] (EDUCATION) (in the US and some other countries) a school that teaches skills that are necessary for particular jobs

vocative /ˈvɒkətɪv/ ***noun*** [C] (LANGUAGE) (in some languages) the form of a noun, a pronoun or an adjective used when addressing a person or thing ▶ **vocative** ***adj.***: *the vocative case* ➲ look at **accusative**, **dative**, **genitive**, **nominative**

vociferous /vəˈsɪfərəs/ ***adj.*** (*formal*) expressing your opinions or feelings in a loud and confident way ▶ **vociferously** ***adv.***

vodka /ˈvɒdkə/ ***noun*** [C,U] a strong clear alcoholic drink originally from Russia

vogue /vəʊg/ ***noun*** [C,U] **a ~ (for sth)** a fashion for sth: *a vogue for large cars* ◇ *That hairstyle is **in vogue** at the moment.*

voice[1] 🔑 /vɔɪs/ ***noun*** **1** [C] the sounds that you make when you speak or sing; the ability to make these sounds: *He had a bad cold and **lost** his **voice*** (= could not speak for a period of time). ◇ *to speak in a loud/soft/low/hoarse voice* ◇ *to lower/raise your voice* (= speak more quietly/loudly) ◇ *Shh! **Keep your voice down!*** ◇ *Alan is 13 and his **voice is breaking*** (= becoming deep and low like a man's). **2 -voiced** (used to form compound adjectives) having a voice of the type mentioned: *husky-voiced* **3** [sing.] **a ~ (in sth)** (the right to express) your ideas or opinions: *The workers want more of a voice in the running of the company.* **4** [C] a particular feeling, attitude or opinion that you have or express: *You should listen to the voice of reason and apologize.* **5** [sing.] (LANGUAGE) the form of a verb that shows if a sentence is ACTIVE or PASSIVE: *'Keats wrote this poem' is in the **active voice**.* ◇ *'This poem was written by Keats' is in the **passive voice**.*

IDM **at the top of your voice** → TOP[1]

voice[2] /vɔɪs/ ***verb*** [T] to express your opinions or feelings: *to voice complaints/criticisms*

ˈvoice box = LARYNX

voicemail /ˈvɔɪsmeɪl/ ***noun*** [U] an electronic system which can store telephone messages, so that sb can listen to them later

void[1] /vɔɪd/ ***noun*** [C, usually sing.] (*formal*) a large empty space: *Her death left a void in their lives.*

void[2] /vɔɪd/ ***adj.*** **1** (used about a ticket, contract, decision, etc.) that can no longer be accepted or used: *The agreement was declared void.* **2** (*formal*) **~ (of sth)** completely lacking sth: *This book is totally void of interest for me.*

vol. ***abbr.*** **1** (*pl.* **vols.**) (LITERATURE) volume (of a book): *The Complete Works of Byron, Vol. 2* **2** (MATHEMATICS, PHYSICS) volume: *vol. 333 ml*

volatile /ˈvɒlətaɪl/ ***adj.*** **1** that can change suddenly and unexpectedly: *a highly volatile situation which could easily develop into rioting* ◇ *a volatile personality* **2** (CHEMISTRY) (used about a substance) that can easily change into a gas ▶ **volatility** /ˌvɒləˈtɪləti/ ***noun*** [U]

volcano

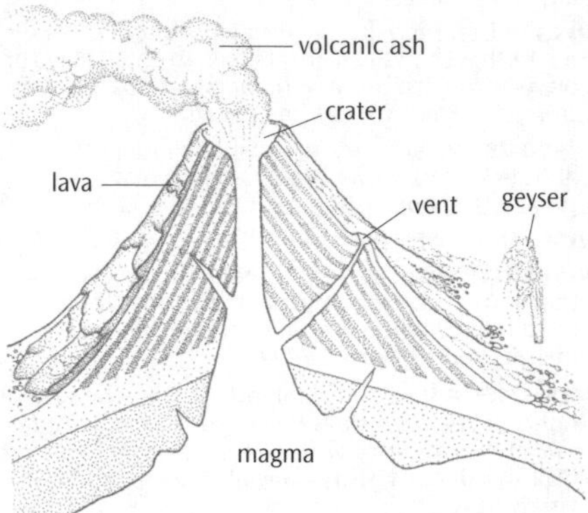

volcano /vɒlˈkeɪnəʊ/ ***noun*** [C] (*pl.* **volcanoes**; **volcanos**) (GEOLOGY) a mountain with a hole (**crater**) at the top through which steam, hot melted rock (**lava**), fire, etc. sometimes come out: *an active/dormant/extinct volcano* ◇ *When did the volcano last erupt?* ▶ **volcanic** /vɒlˈkænɪk/ ***adj.***: *volcanic rock/ash*

volcanology /ˌvɒlkəˈnɒlədʒi/ (*also* **vulcanology**) ***noun*** [U] (GEOLOGY) the scientific study of VOLCANOES

vole /vəʊl/ ***noun*** [C] a small animal like a mouse or RAT that lives in fields or near rivers

volition /vəˈlɪʃn/ ***noun*** [U] (*formal*) the power to choose sth freely or to make your own decisions: *They left entirely **of their own volition*** (= because they wanted to).

volley /ˈvɒli/ ***noun*** [C] **1** (in TENNIS FOOTBALL, etc.) a hit or kick of the ball before it touches the ground: *a forehand/backhand volley* **2** a number of stones, bullets, etc. that are thrown or shot at the same time: *The soldiers fired a volley over the heads of the crowd.* **3** a lot of questions, insults, etc. that are directed at one person very quickly, one after the other: *a volley of abuse* ▶ **volley** *verb* [I,T]: *Rios volleyed the ball into the net.*

volleyball /ˈvɒlibɔːl/ *noun* [U] (SPORT) a game in which two teams of six players hit a ball over a high net with their hands while trying not to let the ball touch the ground on their own side

volt /vəʊlt/ *noun* [C] (*abbr.* **V**) (PHYSICS) a unit for measuring electrical force

voltage /ˈvəʊltɪdʒ/ *noun* [C,U] (PHYSICS) an electrical force measured in VOLTS

volte-face /ˌvɒlt ˈfæs/ *noun* [sing.] (*formal*) a complete change of opinion or plan SYN **about-turn**

voltmeter /ˈvəʊltmiːtə(r)/ *noun* [C] (PHYSICS) an instrument for measuring voltage

volume 🔑 AW /ˈvɒljuːm/ *noun* **1** [U, C] (*abbr.* vol.) (MATHEMATICS, PHYSICS) the amount of space that sth contains or fills: *What is the volume of this sphere?* ➲ look at **area** (2) **2** [C,U] the large quantity or amount of sth: *the **sheer volume*** (= the large amount) *of traffic on the roads* **3** [U, sing.] (MUSIC) how loud a sound is: *to turn the volume on a radio up/down* ◇ *a low/high volume* **4** [C] (*abbr.* vol.) (LITERATURE) a book, especially one of a set or series: *The dictionary comes in three volumes.*

voluminous /vəˈluːmɪnəs/ *adj.* (*formal*) **1** (used about clothing) very large; having a lot of cloth: *a voluminous skirt* **2** (used about a piece of writing, a book, etc.) very long and detailed **3** (used about a container, piece of furniture, etc.) very large: *a voluminous armchair*

voluntary AW /ˈvɒləntri/ *adj.* **1** done or given because you want to do it, not because you have to do it: *He took **voluntary redundancy** and left the firm last year.* OPP **compulsory 2** done or working without payment: *She does some **voluntary work** at the hospital.* **3** (used about movements of the body) that you can control OPP **involuntary** ▶ **voluntarily** AW /ˈvɒləntrəli; ˌvɒlənˈterəli/ *adv.*: *She left the job voluntarily; she wasn't sacked.*

volunteer¹ AW /ˌvɒlənˈtɪə(r)/ *noun* [C] **1** a person who offers or agrees to do sth without being forced or paid to do it: *Are there any volunteers to do the washing up?* **2** a person who joins the armed forces without being ordered to ➲ look at **conscript²**

volunteer² AW /ˌvɒlənˈtɪə(r)/ *verb* **1** [I,T] ~ **(sth)**; ~ **(to do sth)** to offer sth or to do sth which you do not have to do or for which you will not be paid: *They volunteered their services free.* ◇ *She frequently volunteers for extra work because she really likes her job.* ◇ *One of my friends volunteered to take us all in his car.* **2** [I] ~ **(for sth)** to join the armed forces without being ordered **3** [T] to give information, etc. or to make a comment or suggestion without being asked to: *I volunteered a few helpful suggestions.*

vomit /ˈvɒmɪt/ *verb* [I,T] (HEALTH) to bring food, etc. up from the stomach and out of the mouth ▶ **vomit** *noun* [U]

voracious /vəˈreɪʃəs/ *adj.* (*written*) **1** eating or wanting large amounts of food: *a voracious eater* ◇ *to have a **voracious appetite*** **2** wanting a lot of new information and knowledge: *a voracious reader* ▶ **voraciously** *adv.* ▶ **voracity** /vəˈræsəti/ *noun* [U]

vortex /ˈvɔːteks/ *noun* [C] (*pl.* **vortexes** or **vortices** /-tɪsiːz/) (PHYSICS) a mass of air, water, etc. that turns around very fast and pulls things into its centre

vote¹ 🔑 /vəʊt/ *noun* **1** [C] a ~ **(for/against sb/sth)** (POLITICS) a formal choice in an election or at a meeting, which you show by holding up your hand or writing on a piece of paper: *The votes are still being counted.* ◇ *There were 10 **votes for**, and 25 **against** the motion.* **2** [C] a ~ **(on sth)** a method of deciding sth by asking people to express their choice and finding out what most people want: *The democratic way to decide this would be to **take a vote**.* ◇ *Let's **have a vote**/**put it to the vote**.* **3 the vote** [sing.] (POLITICS) the total number of votes in an election: *She obtained 30% of the vote.* **4 the vote** [sing.] (POLITICS) the legal right to vote in political elections: *Women did not get the vote in this country until the 1920s.*

IDM **cast a/your vote** → CAST¹

a vote of thanks a short speech to thank sb, usually a guest, at a meeting, dinner, etc.: *The club secretary proposed a vote of thanks to the guest speaker.*

vote² 🔑 /vəʊt/ *verb* **1** [I,T] ~ **(for/against sb/sth)**; ~ **(on sth)**; ~ **to do sth** to show formally a choice or opinion by marking a piece of paper or by holding up your hand: *Who did you vote for in the last general election?* ◇ *46% **voted in favour of*** (= for) *the proposed change.* ◇ *Very few MPs voted against the new law.* ◇ *After the debate we'll vote on the motion.* ◇ *They voted to change the rules of the club.* ◇ *I voted Liberal Democrat.* **2** [T] (usually passive) to choose sb for a particular position or prize: *He was voted best actor at the Oscars.* ▶ **voter** *noun* [C]

vouch /vaʊtʃ/ *verb*

PHR V **vouch for sb/sth** to say that a person is honest or good or that sth is true or genuine: *I can vouch for her ability to work hard.*

voucher /ˈvaʊtʃə(r)/ *noun* [C] (*BrE*) a piece of paper that you can use instead of money to pay for all or part of sth ➲ look at **token**

vow /vaʊ/ *noun* [C] a formal and serious promise (especially in a religious ceremony): *to keep/break your **marriage vows*** ▶ **vow** *verb* [T]: *We vowed never to discuss the subject again.*

vowel /ˈvaʊəl/ *noun* [C] (LANGUAGE) any of the sounds represented in English by the letters a, e, i, o, or u ➲ look at **consonant**

voyage /ˈvɔɪɪdʒ/ *noun* [C] a long journey by sea or in space: *a voyage to Jupiter* ▶ **voyager** *noun* [C]

VPN /ˌviː piː ˈen/ *abbr.* (COMPUTING) **virtual private network**; a system that allows you to connect to a private computer network over a public network such as the Internet

VSO /ˌviː es ˈəʊ/ *abbr.* (*BrE*) **Voluntary Service Overseas**; an organization that arranges for people to go to work in developing countries

VTOL /ˌviː tiː əʊ ˈel/ *abbr.* **vertical take-off and landing**; used to refer to an aircraft that can take off and land by going straight up or straight down

vulcanized (also **-ised**) /ˈvʌlkənaɪzd/ *adj.* (TECHNICAL) treated with SULPHUR at great heat to make it stronger: *vulcanized rubber*

vulcanology /ˌvʌlkəˈnɒlədʒi/ *noun* [U] = VOLCANOLOGY

vulgar /ˈvʌlgə(r)/ *adj.* **1** not having or showing good judgement about what is attractive or appropriate; not polite or well behaved: *vulgar furnishings* ◇ *a vulgar man/woman* **2** rude or likely to offend people: *a vulgar joke* ▶ **vulgarity** /vʌlˈgærəti/ *noun* [C,U] (*pl.* **vulgarities**)

ˌvulgar ˈfraction *noun* [C] (*BrE*) (MATHEMATICS) a FRACTION (= a number less than one) that is shown as numbers above and below a line: *¾ and ⅝ are vulgar fractions.* ➲ look at **decimal fraction**

vulnerable /ˈvʌlnərəbl/ *adj.* ~ **(to sth/sb)** weak and easy to hurt physically or emotionally: *Poor organization left the troops vulnerable to enemy* *attack.* OPP **invulnerable** ▶ **vulnerability** /ˌvʌlnərəˈbɪləti/ ***noun*** [U]

vulture /ˈvʌltʃə(r)/ ***noun*** [C] a large bird with no feathers on its head or neck that eats dead animals ➲ picture on **page 28**

W w

W, w¹ /ˈdʌbljuː/ ***noun*** [C,U] (*pl.* **W's; w's** /ˈdʌbljuːz/) the twenty-third letter of the English alphabet: *'Water' begins with (a) 'W'.*

W² ***abbr.*** **1** watt(s): *a 60W light bulb* **2** west(ern): *W Cumbria*

wacky (also **whacky**) /ˈwæki/ ***adj.*** (*informal*) amusing or funny in a slightly crazy way

wad /wɒd/ ***noun*** [C] **1** a large number of papers, paper money, etc. folded or rolled together: *He pulled a wad of £20 notes out of his pocket.* **2** a mass of soft material that is used for blocking sth or keeping sth in place: *The nurse used a wad of cotton wool to stop the bleeding.*

waddle /ˈwɒdl/ ***verb*** [I] to walk with short steps, moving the weight of your body from one side to the other, like a DUCK

wade /weɪd/ ***verb*** [I] to walk with difficulty through fairly deep water, mud, etc.
PHR V **wade through sth** to deal with or read sth that is boring and takes a long time

wadi /ˈwɒdi/ ***noun*** [C] (GEOGRAPHY) a valley or passage in the Middle East and North Africa that is dry except when it rains

wafer /ˈweɪfə(r)/ ***noun*** [C] a very thin, dry biscuit often eaten with ice cream

waffle¹ /ˈwɒfl/ ***noun*** **1** [C] a flat cake with a pattern of squares on it that is often eaten warm with a sweet sauce (**syrup**) **2** [U] (*BrE, informal*) language that uses a lot of words but that does not say anything important or interesting: *The last two paragraphs of your essay are just waffle.*

waffle² /ˈwɒfl/ ***verb*** [I] (*BrE, informal*) ~ **(on) (about sth)** to talk or write for much longer than necessary without saying anything important or interesting

waft /wɒft/ ***verb*** [I,T] to move, or make sth move, gently through the air: *The smell of her perfume wafted across the room.*

wag /wæg/ ***verb*** [I,T] (**wagging**; **wagged**) to shake up and down or move from side to side; to make sth do this: *The dog wagged its tail.*

wage¹ 🔑 /weɪdʒ/ ***noun*** [sing.] (also **wages**; *pl.*) (FINANCE) the regular amount of money that you earn for a week's work: *a weekly wage of £200* ◇ *What's the national **minimum wage*** (= the lowest wage that an employer is allowed to pay by law)? ➲ note at **income**

wage² /weɪdʒ/ ***verb*** [T] ~ **sth (against/on sb/sth)** to begin and then continue a war, battle, etc.: *to wage war on your enemy*

waggle /ˈwægl/ ***verb*** [I,T] (*informal*) to move up and down or from side to side with quick, short movements; to make sth do this

wagon /ˈwægən/ ***noun*** [C] (*AmE* **ˈfreight car**) an open section of a railway train that is used for carrying goods or animals

waif /weɪf/ ***noun*** [C] a small thin person, usually a child, who seems to have nowhere to live

wail /weɪl/ ***verb*** **1** [I,T] to cry or complain in a loud, high voice, especially because you are sad or in pain **2** [I] (used about things) to make a sound like this: *sirens wailing in the streets outside* ▶ **wail** ***noun*** [C]

waist 🔑 /weɪst/ ***noun*** [C, usually sing.] **1** (ANATOMY) the narrowest part around the middle of your body: *She put her arms around his waist.* ➲ picture on **page 80** **2** the part of a piece of clothing that goes round the **waist**

waistband /ˈweɪstbænd/ ***noun*** [C] the narrow piece of material at the waist of a piece of clothing, especially trousers or a skirt

waistcoat /ˈweɪskəʊt/ (*AmE* **vest**) ***noun*** [C] a piece of clothing with buttons down the front and no sleeves that is often worn over a shirt and under a jacket as part of a man's suit

waistline /ˈweɪstlaɪn/ ***noun*** [C, usually sing.] **1** (used to talk about how fat or thin a person is) the measurement or size of the body around the waist **2** the place on a piece of clothing where your waist is

wait¹ 🔑 /weɪt/ ***verb*** [I] **1** ~ **(for sb/sth) (to do sth)** to stay in a particular place, and not do anything until sb/sth arrives or until sth happens: *Wait here. I'll be back in a few minutes.* ◇ *Have you been waiting long?* ◇ *If I'm a bit late, can you wait for me?* ◇ *I'm waiting to see the doctor.* **2** to be left or delayed until a later time: *Is this matter urgent or **can it wait**?*
IDM **can't wait/can hardly wait** used when you are emphasizing that sb is very excited and enthusiastic about doing sth: *The kids can't wait to see their father again.*
keep sb waiting to make sb wait or be delayed, especially because you arrive late
wait and see used to tell sb to be patient and to wait to find out about sth later
wait your turn to wait until the time when you are allowed to do sth
PHR V **wait behind** to stay in a place after others have left it: *She waited behind after class to speak to her teacher.*
wait in to stay at home because you are expecting sb to come or sth to happen
wait on sb to serve food, drink, etc. to sb, usually in a restaurant
wait up (for sb) to not go to bed because you are waiting for sb to come home

wait² /weɪt/ ***noun*** [C, usually sing.] **a ~ (for sth/sb)** a period of time when you wait
IDM **lie in wait (for sb)** → LIE²

waiter 🔑 /ˈweɪtə(r)/ ***noun*** [C] a man whose job is to serve customers at their tables in a restaurant, etc.

ˈwaiting list ***noun*** [C] a list of people who are waiting for sth, for example a service or medical treatment, that will be available in the future: *to put your name **on a waiting list***

ˈwaiting room ***noun*** [C] a room where people can sit while they are waiting, for example for a train, or to see a doctor

waitress 🔑 /ˈweɪtrəs/ ***noun*** [C] a woman whose job is to serve customers at their tables in a restaurant, etc.

waive /weɪv/ ***verb*** [T] (*formal*) to say officially that a rule, etc. need not be obeyed; to say officially that you no longer have a right to sth

waiver /ˈweɪvə(r)/ ***noun*** [C] (LAW) a situation in which sb gives up a legal right or claim; an official document stating this

wake[1] /weɪk/ *verb* [I,T] (*pt* **woke** /wəʊk/; *pp* **woken** /'wəʊkən/) ~ **(sb) (up)** to stop sleeping; to make sb stop sleeping: *I woke early in the morning and got straight out of bed.* ◇ *Wake up! It's nearly 8 o'clock!* ◇ *Could you wake me at 7.30, please?* ➲ adjective awake

PHR V **wake sb up** to make sb become more active or full of energy

wake up to sth to realize sth; to notice sth

wake[2] /weɪk/ *noun* [C] **1** an occasion before a funeral when people meet to remember the dead person, traditionally held at night to watch over the body before it is buried **2** the track that a moving ship leaves behind on the surface of the water

IDM **in the wake of sb/sth** following or coming after sb/sth: *The earthquake left a trail of destruction in its wake.*

wakeboarding /'weɪkbɔːdɪŋ/ *noun* [U] (SPORT) the sport of riding on a short wide board (**a wakeboard**) while being pulled along through the water by a fast boat ▶ **wakeboard** *verb* [I]

waken /'weɪkən/ *verb* [I,T] (*formal, old-fashioned*) to stop sleeping or to make sb/sth stop sleeping: *She wakened from a deep sleep.*

'**wake-up call** *noun* [C] **1** (TOURISM) a telephone call that you arrange to be made to you at a particular time, for example in a hotel, in order to wake you up: *I asked for a wake-up call at 6.30 a.m.* **2** an event that makes people realize that there is a problem that they need to do sth about: *These riots should be a wake-up call for the government.*

walk[1] /wɔːk/ *verb* **1** [I] to move or go somewhere by putting one foot in front of the other on the ground, but without running: *The door opened and Billy walked in.* ◇ *I walk to work every day.* ◇ *He walks with a limp.* ◇ *Are the shops **within walking distance** (=near enough to walk to)?* **2** [I] to move in this way for exercise or pleasure **3** [T] to go somewhere with sb/sth on foot, especially to make sure they get there safely: *I'll **walk you home** if you don't want to go on your own.* ◇ *He walked me to my car.* **4** [T] to take a dog out for exercise: *I'm just going to **walk the dog**.* ▶ **walker** *noun* [C]: *She's a fast walker.* ◇ *This area is very popular with walkers.*

PHR V **walk off with sth 1** to win sth easily: *She walked off with all the prizes.* **2** to steal sth; to take sth that does not belong to you by mistake

walk out (of sth) to leave suddenly and angrily: *She walked out of the meeting in disgust.*

walk out on sb (*informal*) to leave sb for ever: *He walked out on his wife and children after 15 years of marriage.*

walk (all) over sb (*informal*) **1** to treat sb badly, without considering their needs or feelings **2** to defeat sb completely: *He played brilliantly and walked all over his opponent.*

walk up (to sb/sth) to walk towards sb/sth, especially in a confident way

walk[2] /wɔːk/ *noun* **1** [C] going somewhere on foot for pleasure, exercise, etc.: *We went for a walk in the country.* ◇ *I'm just going to take the dog for a walk.* ◇ *The beach is five minutes' walk/a five-minute walk from the hotel.* **2** [C] a path or route for walking for pleasure: *From here there's a lovely walk through the woods.* **3** [sing.] a way or style of walking: *He has a funny walk.* **4** [sing.] the speed of walking: *She slowed to a walk.*

IDM **a walk of life** a person's job or position in society

walkie-talkie /ˌwɔːki 'tɔːki/ *noun* [C] (*informal*) a small radio that you can carry with you to send or receive messages

'**walking stick** (*also* **stick**) *noun* [C] a stick that you carry and use as a support to help you walk ➲ look at **crutch**

walkover /'wɔːkəʊvə(r)/ *noun* [C] an easy win or victory in a game or competition

wall /wɔːl/ *noun* [C] **1** a solid, vertical structure made of stone, brick, etc. that is built round an area of land to protect it or to divide it: *There is a high wall all around the prison.* **2** one of the sides of a room or building joining the ceiling and the floor: *He put the picture up **on the wall**.*

IDM **up the wall** (*informal*) crazy or angry: *That noise is driving me up the wall.*

wallaby /'wɒləbi/ *noun* [C] (*pl.* **wallabies**) an Australian animal that moves by jumping on its strong back legs and keeps its young in a pocket of skin (**pouch**) on the front of the mother's body. A **wallaby** looks like a small KANGAROO.

walled /wɔːld/ *adj.* surrounded by a wall

wallet /'wɒlɪt/ (*AmE* **billfold**) *noun* [C] a small, flat, folding case in which you keep paper money, plastic cards, etc. ➲ look at **purse**

wallop /'wɒləp/ *verb* [T] (*informal*) to hit sb/sth very hard

wallow /'wɒləʊ/ *verb* [I] ~ **(in sth) 1** (used about people and large animals) to lie and roll around in water, etc. in order to keep cool or for pleasure: *I spent an hour wallowing in the bath.* **2** to take great pleasure in sth (a feeling, situation, etc.): *to wallow in self-pity* (=to think about your unhappiness all the time and seem to be enjoying it)

wallpaper /'wɔːlpeɪpə(r)/ *noun* [U] paper that you stick to the walls of a room to decorate or cover them ▶ **wallpaper** *verb* [I,T]

ˌ**wall-to-'wall** *adj.* (only *before* a noun) (used especially about a carpet) covering the floor of a room completely

wally /'wɒli/ *noun* [C] (*pl.* **wallies**) (*BrE, slang*) a silly person; a FOOL

walnut /'wɔːlnʌt/ *noun* **1** [C] a nut that we eat, with a hard brown shell that is in two halves **2** (*also* **walnut tree**) [C] the tree on which these nuts grow **3** [U] the wood of the **walnut** tree, used in making furniture

walrus /'wɔːlrəs/ *noun* [C] a large animal that lives in or near the sea in Arctic regions. It is similar to a SEAL, but the **walrus** has two long outer teeth (**tusks**).

waltz[1] /wɔːls/ *noun* [C] (MUSIC) an elegant dance that you do with a partner, to music which has a rhythm of three beats; the music for this dance: *a Strauss waltz*

waltz[2] /wɔːls/ *verb* **1** [I,T] to dance a WALTZ: *They waltzed around the floor.* ◇ *He waltzed her round the room.* **2** [I] (*informal*) to go somewhere in a confident way: *You can't just waltz in and expect your meal to be ready for you.*

WAN /wæn/ *abbr.* (COMPUTING) **wide area network**; a system in which computers in different places are connected, usually over a large area ➲ look at **LAN**

wan /wɒn/ *adj.* looking pale and ill or tired

wand /wɒnd/ *noun* [C] a thin stick that people hold when they are doing magic tricks: *I wish I could **wave a magic wand** and make everything better.*

wander /'wɒndə(r)/ *verb* **1** [I,T] to walk somewhere slowly with no particular sense of direction or purpose: *We spent a pleasant day* *wandering around the town.* ◇ *He was found in a confused state, wandering the streets.* **2** [I] ~ **(away/off) (from sb/sth)** to walk away from a place where you ought to be or the people you were with: *We must stay together while visiting the town so I don't want anybody to wander off.* **3** [I] (used about sb's mind, thoughts, etc.) to stop paying attention to sth; to be unable to stay on one subject: *The lecture was so boring that my attention began to wander.*

wane[1] /weɪn/ ***verb*** [I] **1** (*written*) to become gradually weaker or less important: *My enthusiasm was waning rapidly.* **2** (ASTRONOMY) (used about the moon) to appear slightly smaller each day after being full and round OPP **wax[2]**

wane[2] /weɪn/ ***noun***
IDM **on the wane** (*written*) becoming smaller, less important or less common

wangle /ˈwæŋgl/ ***verb*** [T] (*informal*) to get sth that you want by persuading sb or by having a clever plan: *Somehow he wangled a day off to meet me.*

wanna /ˈwɒnə/ a way of writing 'want to' or 'want a', which is considered to be bad style, to show that sb is speaking in an informal way: *I wanna go home now.*

wannabe /ˈwɒnəbi/ ***noun*** [C] (*informal*) a person who behaves, dresses, etc. like a famous person because they want to be like them

want[1] ⊶ /wɒnt/ ***verb*** [T] (not used in the continuous tenses) **1** ~ **sth (for sth)**; ~ **(sb) to do sth**; ~ **sth (to be) done** to have a desire or a wish for sth: *He wants a new bike.* ◇ *What do they want for breakfast?* ◇ *I don't want to discuss it now.* ◇ *I want you to stop worrying about it.* ◇ *The boss wants this letter typed.* ◇ *I don't want Emma going out on her own at night.* ◇ *They want Bhanot as captain.*
2 (*informal*) used to say that sth needs to be done: *The button on my shirt wants sewing on.* ◇ *The house wants a new coat of paint.* **3** (*informal*) (used to give advice to sb) should or ought to: *He wants to be more careful about what he tells people.* **4** (usually passive) to need sb to be in a particular place or for a particular reason: *Mrs Lewis, you are wanted on the phone.* ◇ *She is **wanted by the police*** (= the police are looking for her because she is suspected of committing a crime). **5** to feel sexual desire for sb

want[2] /wɒnt/ ***noun*** (*formal*) **1 wants** [pl.] sth you need or want: *All our wants were satisfied.* **2** [sing.] a lack of sth: *He's suffering due to a want of care.*
IDM **for (the) want of sth** because of a lack of sth; because sth is not available: *I took the job for want of a better offer.*

wanting /ˈwɒntɪŋ/ ***adj.*** (*formal*) ~ **(in sth)** (not before a noun) **1** not having enough of sth; lacking: *The children were certainly not wanting in enthusiasm.* **2** not good enough: *The new system **was found wanting**.*

wanton /ˈwɒntən/ ***adj.*** (*formal*) (used about an action) done in order to hurt sb or damage sth for no good reason: *wanton vandalism*

WAP /wæp/ ***abbr.*** (COMPUTING) **wireless application protocol**; a technology that connects devices such as mobile phones to the Internet. It consists of rules for changing Internet information so that it can be shown on a very small screen: *a WAP phone*

war ⊶ /wɔː(r)/ ***noun*** **1** [U, C] a state of fighting between different countries or groups within countries using armies and weapons: *The Prime Minister announced that the country was **at war**.* ◇ *to **declare war on** another country* (= announce that a war has started) ◇ *When **war broke out** (= started), thousands of men volunteered for the army.* ◇ ***a civil war*** (= fighting between different groups in one country) ◇ *to **go to war** against sb* ◇ *to fight a war*
2 [C,U] very aggressive competition between groups of people, companies, countries, etc.: *a price war among oil companies* **3** [U, sing.] ~ **(against/on sb/sth)** efforts to end or get rid of sth: *We seem to be winning the war against organized crime.* ➲ note at **campaign[1]**

ˈwar crime ***noun*** [C] (LAW) a cruel act that is committed during a war and that is against the international rules of war

ward[1] /wɔːd/ ***noun*** [C] **1** (HEALTH) a separate part or room in a hospital for patients with the same kind of medical condition: *the maternity/psychiatric/surgical ward* **2** (*BrE*) (POLITICS) one of the sections into which a town is divided for elections **3** (LAW) a child who is under the protection of a court of law; a child whose parents are dead and who is cared for by another adult (**guardian**): *The child was made a ward of court.*

ward[2] /wɔːd/ ***verb***
PHR V **ward sb/sth off** to protect or defend yourself against danger, illness, attack, etc.

warden /ˈwɔːdn/ ***noun*** [C] **1** a person whose job is to check that rules are obeyed or to look after the people in a particular place: *a **traffic warden*** (= a person who checks that cars are not parked in the wrong place) **2** (*especially AmE*) (LAW) the person in charge of a prison

warder /ˈwɔːdə(r)/ ***noun*** [C] (*BrE*) (LAW) a person whose job is to guard prisoners ➲ look at **guard**

wardrobe /ˈwɔːdrəʊb/ ***noun*** [C] **1** a large cupboard in which you can hang your clothes **2** a person's collection of clothes: *I need a new summer wardrobe.*

ware /weə(r)/ ***noun*** **1** [U] (used in compounds) objects made from a particular type of material or suitable for a particular use: *glassware* ◇ *kitchenware*
2 wares [pl.] (*old-fashioned*) goods offered for sale ➲ note at **product**

warehouse /ˈweəhaʊs/ ***noun*** [C] a building where large quantities of goods are stored before being sent to shops

warfare /ˈwɔːfeə(r)/ ***noun*** [U] methods of fighting a war; types of war: *guerrilla warfare*

warhead /ˈwɔːhed/ ***noun*** [C] the EXPLOSIVE part of a MISSILE (= a powerful exploding weapon)

warily, wariness → WARY

warlike /ˈwɔːlaɪk/ ***adj.*** liking to fight or good at fighting: *a warlike nation*

warm[1] ⊶ /wɔːm/ ***adj.*** **1** having a pleasant temperature that is fairly high, between cool and hot: *It's quite warm in the sunshine.* ◇ *I jumped up and down to keep my feet warm.* ➲ note at **cold[1]**
2 (used about clothes) preventing you from getting cold: *Take plenty of warm clothes.* **3** friendly, kind and pleasant: *I was given a very warm welcome.*
4 creating a pleasant, comfortable feeling: *warm colours* ▶ **the warm** ***noun*** [sing.]: *It's awfully cold out here – I want to go back into the warm.* ▶ **warmly** ***adv.***: *warmly dressed* ◇ *She thanked him warmly for his help.*

warm[2] ⊶ /wɔːm/ ***verb*** [I,T] ~ **(sb/sth) (up)** to become or to make sb/sth become warm or warmer: *It was cold earlier but it's beginning to warm up now.* ◇ *I sat in front of the fire to warm up.*
PHR V **warm to/towards sb** to begin to like sb that you did not like at first
warm to sth to become more interested in sth

warm up to prepare to do an activity or sport by practising gently: *The team warmed up before the match.*

ˌwarm-ˈblooded *adj.* (BIOLOGY) (used about animals) having a blood temperature that does not change if the temperature of the surroundings changes OPP **cold-blooded**

ˌwarm-ˈhearted *adj.* kind and friendly

warmonger /ˈwɔːmʌŋɡə(r)/ *noun* [C] (*formal*) a person, especially a politician or leader, who wants to start a war or encourages people to start a war ▶ **warmongering** *noun* [U]

warmth /wɔːmθ/ *noun* [U] **1** a fairly high temperature or the effect created by this, especially when it is pleasant: *She felt the warmth of the sun on her face.* **2** the quality of being kind and friendly: *I was touched by the warmth of their welcome.*

ˈwarm-up *noun* [usually sing.] **1** a short practice or a series of gentle exercises that you do to prepare yourself for doing a particular sport or activity **2** (ARTS AND MEDIA) a short performance of music, comedy, etc. that is intended to prepare the audience for the main show

warn /wɔːn/ *verb* [T] **1** ~ **sb** (**of sth**); ~ **sb** (**about sb/sth**) to tell sb about sth unpleasant or dangerous that exists or might happen, so that they can avoid it: *When I saw the car coming I tried to warn him, but it was too late.* ◊ *The government is warning the public of possible terrorist attacks.* ◊ *He warned me about the danger of walking home alone at night.* **2** ~ (**sb**) **against doing sth**; ~ **sb** (**not to do sth**) to advise sb not to do sth: *The radio warned people against going out during the storm.* ◊ *I warned you not to trust him.*

warning /ˈwɔːnɪŋ/ *noun* [C,U] something that tells you to be careful or tells you about sth, usually sth bad, before it happens: *Your employers can't dismiss you **without warning**.* ◊ *You could have given me some warning that your parents were coming to visit.*

warp[1] /wɔːp/ *verb* **1** [I,T] to become bent into the wrong shape, for example as a result of getting hot or wet; to make sth become like this: *The window frame was badly warped and wouldn't shut.* **2** [T] to influence sb so that they start behaving in an unusual or shocking way: *His experiences in the war had warped him.* ▶ **warped** *adj.*

warp[2] /wɔːp/ *noun* **the warp** [sing.] (TECHNICAL) the threads on a LOOM (= a frame or machine for making cloth) that other threads are passed over and under in order to make cloth ➲ look at **weft**

warpath /ˈwɔːpɑːθ/ *noun*
IDM **(be/go) on the warpath** (*informal*) to be very angry and want to fight or punish sb

warrant[1] /ˈwɒrənt/ *noun* [C] an official written statement that gives sb permission to do sth: *a search warrant* (= a document that allows the police to search a house)

warrant[2] /ˈwɒrənt/ *verb* [T] (*formal*) to make sth seem right or necessary; to deserve sth: *I don't think her behaviour warrants such criticism.*

warranty /ˈwɒrənti/ *noun* [C,U] (*pl.* **warranties**) a written statement that you get when you buy sth, which promises to repair or replace it if it is broken or does not work: *Fortunately my stereo is still **under warranty**.* ➲ look at **guarantee**

warren /ˈwɒrən/ = RABBIT WARREN

warrior /ˈwɒriə(r)/ *noun* [C] (*old-fashioned*) a person who fights in a battle; a soldier

warship /ˈwɔːʃɪp/ *noun* [C] a ship for use in war

wart /wɔːt/ *noun* [C] (HEALTH) a small hard dry lump that sometimes grows on the face or body

warthog /ˈwɔːthɒɡ/ *noun* [C] an African wild pig with two large outer teeth (**tusks**) and lumps on its face

wartime /ˈwɔːtaɪm/ *noun* [U] a period of time during which there is a war

wary /ˈweəri/ *adj.* ~ (**of sb/sth**) careful because you are uncertain or afraid of sb/sth: *Since becoming famous, she has grown wary of journalists.* ➲ note at **care**[1] ▶ **warily** /-rəli/ *adv.* ▶ **wariness** /ˈweərinəs/ *noun* [U, sing.]

was /wəz *strong form* wɒz/ → BE

wash[1] /wɒʃ/ *verb* **1** [I,T] to clean sb/sth/yourself with water and often soap: *to wash your hands/face/hair* ◊ *That shirt needs washing.* ◊ *Wash and dress quickly or you'll be late!* ◊ *I'll wash* (= wash the dishes), *you dry.* **2** [I,T] (used about water) to flow or carry sth/sb in the direction mentioned: *I let the waves wash over my feet.* ◊ *The current washed the ball out to sea.* **3** [I] to be able to be washed without being damaged: *Does this material wash well, or does the colour come out?*
IDM **wash your hands of sb/sth** to refuse to be responsible for sb/sth any longer: *They washed their hands of their son when he was sent to prison.*
PHR V **wash sb/sth away** (used about water) to carry sb/sth away: *The floods had washed away the path.*
wash (sth) off to (make sth) disappear by washing: *The writing has washed off and now I can't read it.* ◊ *Go and wash that make-up off!*
wash out to be removed from a material by washing: *These grease marks won't wash out.*
wash sth out to wash sth or the inside of sth in order to remove dirt: *I'll just wash out this bowl and then we can use it.*
wash (sth) up 1 (*BrE*) to wash the plates, knives, forks, etc. after a meal: *Whose turn is it to wash up?* **2** (*AmE*) to wash your face and hands: *Go and wash up quickly and put on some clean clothes.* **3** (often passive) (used about water) to carry sth to land and leave it there: *Police found the girl's body washed up on the beach.*

wash[2] /wɒʃ/ *noun* **1** [C, usually sing.] an act of cleaning or being cleaned with water: *I'd better go and **have a wash** before we go out.* **2** [sing.] the waves caused by the movement of a ship through water
IDM **in the wash** (used about clothes) being washed: *'Where's my red T-shirt?' 'It's in the wash.'*

washable /ˈwɒʃəbl/ *adj.* that can be washed without being damaged

washbasin /ˈwɒʃbeɪsn/ (*also* **basin**) *noun* [C] a large bowl for water that has taps and is fixed to a wall, in a bathroom, etc. ➲ look at **sink**

ˌwashed ˈout *adj.* tired and pale: *They arrived looking washed out after their long journey.*

washer /ˈwɒʃə(r)/ *noun* [C] a small flat ring made of rubber, metal or plastic placed between two surfaces to make a connection tight ➲ picture at **bolt**

washing /ˈwɒʃɪŋ/ *noun* [U] **1** clothes that need to be washed or are being washed: *Could you put the washing in the machine?* ◊ *a pile of dirty washing* **2** the act of cleaning clothes, etc. with water: *I usually **do the washing** on Mondays.*

ˈwashing machine *noun* [C] an electric machine for washing clothes

ˈwashing powder *noun* [U] soap in the form of powder for washing clothes

ˌ**washing-ˈup** *noun* [U] **1** the work of washing the plates, knives, forks, etc. after a meal: *I'll **do the washing-up**.* ◇ *washing-up liquid* **2** plates, etc. that need washing after a meal: *Put the washing-up next to the sink.*

washout /ˈwɒʃaʊt/ *noun* [C] (*informal*) an event that is a complete failure, especially because of rain

washroom /ˈwɒʃruːm; -rʊm/ *noun* [C] (*AmE*) a toilet, especially in a public building

wasn't /ˈwɒznt/ → BE

Wasp (also **WASP**) /wɒsp/ *noun* [C] (*especially AmE*) (SOCIAL STUDIES) **White Anglo-Saxon Protestant**; a white American whose family originally came from northern Europe and is therefore thought to be from the most powerful section of society: *a privileged Wasp background*

wasp /wɒsp/ *noun* [C] a small black and yellow flying insect that can sting ➲ look at **hornet** ➲ picture on **page 29**

wastage /ˈweɪstɪdʒ/ *noun* [U] (*formal*) using too much of sth in a careless way; the amount of sth that is wasted

waste[1] ⊶ /weɪst/ *verb* [T] **1** ~ sth (on sb/sth); ~ sth (in doing sth) to use or spend sth in a careless way or for sth that is not necessary: *She wastes a lot of money on cigarettes.* ◇ *He wasted his time at university because he didn't work hard.* ◇ *She wasted no time in decorating her new room* (=she did it immediately). **2** (usually passive) to give sth to sb who does not value it: *Expensive wine is wasted on me. I don't even like it.*

waste[2] ⊶ /weɪst/ *noun* **1** [sing.] a ~ (of sth) using sth in a careless and unnecessary way: *The seminar was **a waste of time** – I'd heard it all before.* ◇ *It seems a waste to throw away all these old newspapers.* **2** [U] material, food, etc. that is not needed and is therefore thrown away: *nuclear waste* ◇ *A lot of household waste can be recycled and reused.* ➲ look at **rubbish 3 wastes** [pl.] (*formal*) (GEOGRAPHY) large areas of land that are not lived in and not used: *the wastes of the Sahara desert*

IDM **go to waste** to not be used and so thrown away and wasted: *I can't bear to see good food going to waste!*

waste[3] ⊶ /weɪst/ *adj.* (only *before* a noun) **1** (used about land) not used or not suitable for use; not looked after: *There's an area of waste ground outside the town where people dump their rubbish.* **2** no longer useful; that is thrown away: *waste paper* ◇ *waste material*

wasted /ˈweɪstɪd/ *adj.* **1** not necessary or successful: *a wasted journey* **2** very thin, especially because of illness **3** (*slang*) suffering from the effects of drugs or alcohol

wasteful /ˈweɪstfl/ *adj.* using more of sth than necessary; causing waste

wasteland /ˈweɪstlænd/ *noun* [U, C] (GEOGRAPHY) an area of land that cannot be used or that is no longer used for building or growing things on

ˌ**waste-ˈpaper basket** *noun* [C] a BASKET, etc. in which you put paper, etc. which is to be thrown away

watch[1] ⊶ /wɒtʃ/ *verb* **1** [I,T] to look at sb/sth for a time, paying attention to what happens: *I **watched in horror** as the car swerved and crashed.* ◇ *I'm watching to see how you do it.* ◇ *We **watch television** most evenings.* ◇ *Watch what she does next.* ◇ *I watched him open the door and walk away.* **2** [T] to take care of sth for a short time: *Could you watch my bag for a second while I go and get a drink?* **3** [T] ~ sb/sth (for sth) to be careful about sb/sth; to pay careful attention to sth/sb: *You'd better **watch what you say** to her. She gets upset very easily.* ◇ *Watch those two boys – they're acting suspiciously.*

IDM **watch your step** → STEP[1]

PHR V **watch out** to be careful because of possible danger or trouble: *Watch out! There's a car coming.* ◇ *If you don't watch out you'll lose your job.*

watch out for sb/sth to look carefully and be ready for sb/sth: *Watch out for snakes if you walk through the fields.*

watch over sb/sth to look after or protect sb/sth: *For two weeks she watched over the sick child.*

watch[2] ⊶ /wɒtʃ/ *noun* **1** [C] a type of small clock that you usually wear around your wrist: *a digital watch* ◇ *My watch is a bit fast/slow* (=shows a time that is later/earlier than the correct time). ➲ look at **clock 2** [sing., U] the action of watching sb/sth in case of possible danger or problems: *Tour companies have to **keep a close watch on** the political situation in the region.*

watchdog /ˈwɒtʃdɒg/ *noun* [C] a person or group whose job is to make sure that large companies respect people's rights: *a consumer watchdog*

watchful /ˈwɒtʃfl/ *adj.* careful to notice things

watchtower /ˈwɒtʃtaʊə(r)/ *noun* [C] a tall tower from which soldiers, etc. watch when they are guarding a place

COLLOCATIONS AND PATTERNS

The water cycle – describing a cycle

The water cycle is the constant circulation of water between the **atmosphere,** the **land** and the **sea. Evaporation** from oceans, lakes and plants produces **water vapour** which forms **clouds** in the **atmosphere.**

The water in the clouds then falls to the ground as **rain** or **snow.** Some drains off the surface into **rivers** and **lakes**, and some goes through the soil to **underground streams.**

Eventually, all this water drains back into the **sea** and the cycle begins again.

water purification

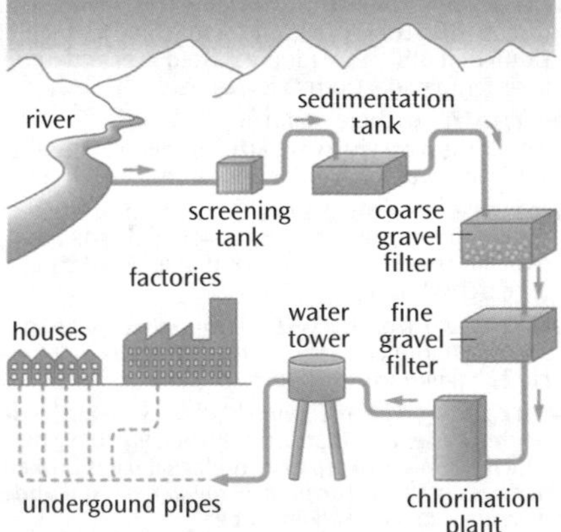

water[1] ⊶ /ˈwɔːtə(r)/ *noun* **1** [U] the clear liquid that falls as rain and is in rivers, seas and lakes: *a glass of water* ◇ *All the rooms have hot and cold running water.* ◇ *drinking water* ◇ *tap water*

RELATED VOCABULARY

When water is heated to 100° Celsius, it **boils** and becomes **steam**.

When steam touches a cold surface, it **condenses** and becomes water again.

When water is cooled below 0° Celsius, it **freezes** and becomes **ice**.

2 [U] a large amount of water, especially the water in a lake, river or sea: *Don't go too near the edge or you'll fall in the water!* ◇ *After the heavy rain several fields were* ***under water***. **3** [U] the surface of an area of water: *Can you swim* ***under water***? ◇ *I can see my reflection in the water.* **4 waters** [pl.] (GEOGRAPHY) the water in a particular sea, lake, etc. or near a particular country: *The ship was still in British waters.*

IDM **keep your head above water** → HEAD¹
pass water → PASS¹

water² /ˈwɔːtə(r)/ ***verb*** **1** [T] to give water to plants **2** [I] (used about the eyes or mouth) to fill with liquid: *The smoke in the room was starting to* ***make my eyes water***. ◇ *These menus will really* ***make your mouth water***.

PHRV **water sth down 1** to add water to a liquid in order to make it weaker **2** to change a statement, report, etc. so that the meaning is less strong or direct

waterbird /ˈwɔːtəbɜːd/ ***noun*** [C] a bird that lives near and walks or swims in water, especially rivers or lakes ➲ look at **seabird**

waterborne /ˈwɔːtəbɔːn/ ***adj.*** spread or carried by water: *cholera and other waterborne diseases* ➲ look at **airborne**

ˈwater buffalo ***noun*** [C] a large animal of the cow family, used for pulling vehicles and farm equipment in Asia

watercolour (*AmE* **watercolor**) /ˈwɔːtəkʌlə(r)/ ***noun*** (ART) **1 watercolours** [pl.] paints that are mixed with water, not oil **2** [C] a picture that has been painted with **watercolours**

watercourse /ˈwɔːtəkɔːs/ ***noun*** [C] (GEOGRAPHY) a small river (**stream**) or an artificial passage for water

watercress /ˈwɔːtəkres/ ***noun*** [U] a water plant with small round green leaves which have a strong taste and are often eaten in salads

waterfall /ˈwɔːtəfɔːl/ ***noun*** [C] (GEOGRAPHY) a river that falls down from a CLIFF, rock, etc. ➲ picture at **glacial**

waterfront /ˈwɔːtəfrʌnt/ ***noun*** [C, usually sing.] (GEOGRAPHY) a part of a town or an area that is next to the sea, a river or a lake

waterhole /ˈwɔːtəhəʊl/ (*also* **ˈwatering hole**) ***noun*** [C] a place in a hot country where animals go to drink

ˈwatering can ***noun*** [C] a container with a long tube on one side which is used for pouring water on plants ➲ picture at **agriculture**

ˈwatering hole = WATERHOLE

ˈwater lily ***noun*** [C] a plant that floats on the surface of water, with large round flat leaves and white, yellow or pink flowers

waterlogged /ˈwɔːtəlɒgd/ ***adj.*** **1** (used about the ground) extremely wet: *Our boots sank into the waterlogged ground.* **2** (used about a boat) full of water and likely to sink

watermark /ˈwɔːtəmɑːk/ ***noun*** [C] a symbol or design in some types of paper, which can be seen when the paper is held against the light

watermelon /ˈwɔːtəmelən/ ***noun*** [C,U] a large, round fruit with a thick, green skin. It is pink or red inside with a lot of black seeds.

ˈwater polo ***noun*** [U] (SPORT) a game played by two teams of people swimming in a swimming pool. Players try to throw a ball into the other team's goal.

waterproof /ˈwɔːtəpruːf/ ***adj.*** that does not let water go through: *a waterproof jacket*

watershed /ˈwɔːtəʃed/ ***noun*** [C] an event or time which is important because it marks the beginning of sth new or different

waterside /ˈwɔːtəsaɪd/ ***noun*** [sing.] (GEOGRAPHY) the area at the edge of a river, lake, etc.: *They strolled down to the waterside.* ◇ *a waterside cafe*

waterski /ˈwɔːtəskiː/ ***verb*** [I] (SPORT) to move across the surface of water standing on narrow boards (**waterskis**) and being pulled by a boat

ˈwater sports ***noun*** [pl.] (SPORT) sports that are done on or in water, for example sailing and WATER-SKIING

the ˈwater table ***noun*** [sing.] (GEOGRAPHY) the level at and below which water is found in the ground

watertight /ˈwɔːtətaɪt/ ***adj.*** **1** made so that water cannot get in or out: *a watertight container* **2** (used about an excuse, opinion, etc.) impossible to show

water cycle

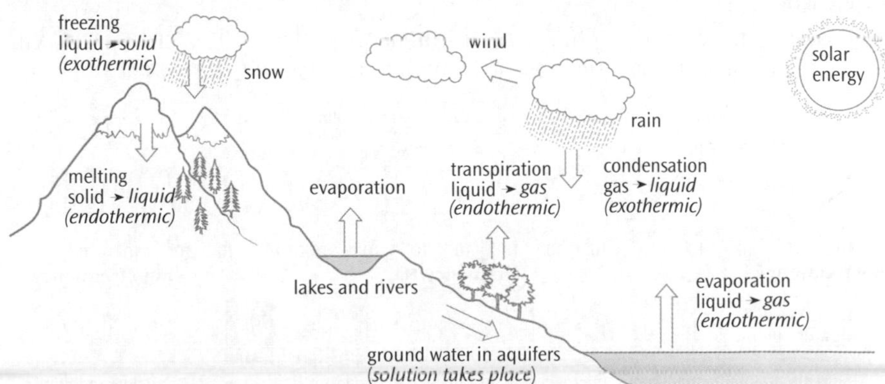

to be wrong; without any faults: *His alibi was absolutely watertight.*

'water tower *noun* [C] a tall structure with a tank of water at the top from which water is supplied to buildings in the area around it ➲ picture at **water**

waterway /'wɔːtəweɪ/ *noun* [C] (GEOGRAPHY) a canal, river, etc. along which boats can travel

watery /'wɔːtəri/ *adj.* **1** containing mostly water: *watery soup* ◇ *A watery liquid came out of the wound.* **2** weak and pale: *watery sunshine* ◇ *a watery smile*

watt /wɒt/ *noun* [C] (*abbr.* **W**) a unit of electrical power: *a 60-watt light bulb*

waves

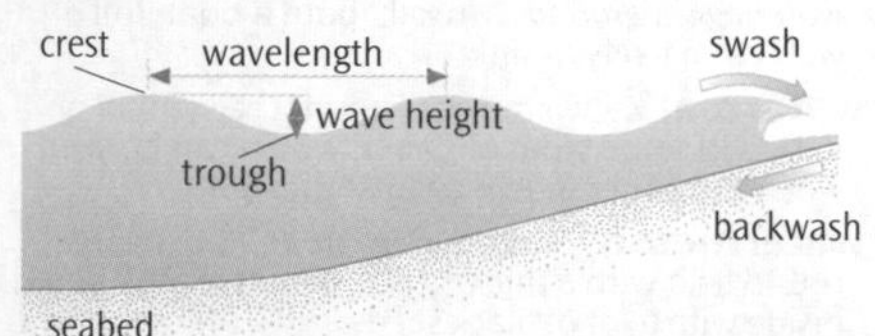

wave¹ /weɪv/ *noun* [C] **1** (GEOGRAPHY) a line of water moving across the surface of water, especially the sea, that is higher than the rest of the surface: *We watched the waves roll in and break on the shore.* ➲ picture at **diffract** ➲ look at **tidal wave** **2** a sudden increase or spread of a feeling or type of behaviour: *There has been a wave of sympathy for the refugees.* ◇ *a* ***crime wave*** ◇ *The pain came* ***in waves.*** ➲ look at **heatwave** **3** a large number of people or things suddenly moving or appearing somewhere: *There is normally a wave of tourists in August.* **4** a movement of sth, especially your hand, from side to side in the air: *With a wave of his hand, he said goodbye and left.* **5** (PHYSICS) the form that some types of energy such as sound, light, heat, etc. take when they move: *sound waves* ➲ look at **long wave, medium wave, short wave** **6** a gentle curve in your hair ➲ look at **perm**

wave² /weɪv/ *verb* **1** [I,T] to move your hand from side to side in the air, usually to attract sb's attention or as you meet or leave sb: *She waved to me as the train left the station.* ◇ *I leant out of the window and* ***waved goodbye*** *to my friends.* **2** [T] ~ **sth (at sb)**; ~ **sth (about)** to hold sth in the air and move it from side to side: *The crowd waved flags as the President came out.* ◇ *She was talking excitedly and waving her arms about.* **3** [T] ~ **sb/sth away, on, through, etc.** to move your hand in a particular direction to show sb/sth which way to go: *There was a policeman in the middle of the road, waving us on.* **4** [I] to move gently up and down or from side to side: *The branches of the trees waved gently in the breeze.*

PHR V **wave sth aside** to decide not to pay attention to sb/sth because you think they or it are not important

wave sb off to wave to sb who is leaving

waveband /'weɪvbænd/ *noun* [C] a set of radio waves of similar length

,wave-cut 'platform *noun* [C] (GEOGRAPHY) an area of land between the CLIFFS and the sea which is covered by water when the sea is at its highest level

wavelength /'weɪvleŋθ/ *noun* [C] **1** (PHYSICS) the distance between two similar points on a wave of energy, such as light or sound ➲ picture at **amplitude** **2** the size of a radio wave that is used by a particular radio station, etc. for sending signals or broadcasting programmes

IDM **on the same wavelength** → SAME

waver /'weɪvə(r)/ *verb* [I] **1** to become weak or uncertain, especially when making a decision or choice: *He never wavered in his support for her.* **2** to move in a way that is not firm or steady: *His hand wavered as he reached for the gun.*

wavy /'weɪvi/ *adj.* having curves; not straight: *wavy hair* ◇ *a wavy line* ➲ picture at **line**

wax¹ /wæks/ *noun* [U] **1** a substance made from fat or oil that melts easily and is used for making CANDLES, polish, etc. **2** (BIOLOGY) a yellow substance that is found in your ears

wax² /wæks/ *verb* **1** [T] to polish sth with WAX **2** [T] (often passive) to remove hair from a part of the body using WAX: *to wax your legs/have your legs waxed* **3** [I] (used about the moon) (ASTRONOMY) to seem to get gradually bigger until its full form can be seen OPP **wane**

'wax paper (*AmE*) = GREASEPROOF PAPER

waxwork /'wækswɜːk/ *noun* [C] **1** a model of sb/sth, especially of a famous person, made of WAX **2 waxworks** [sing.] a place where WAX models of famous people are shown to the public

way¹ /weɪ/ *noun* **1** [C] a ~ **(to do sth/of doing sth)** a particular method, style or manner of doing sth: *What is* ***the best way*** *to learn a language?* ◇ *I've discovered a brilliant way of saving paper!* ◇ *They'll have to find the money* ***one way or another.*** ◇ *He*

wavelength

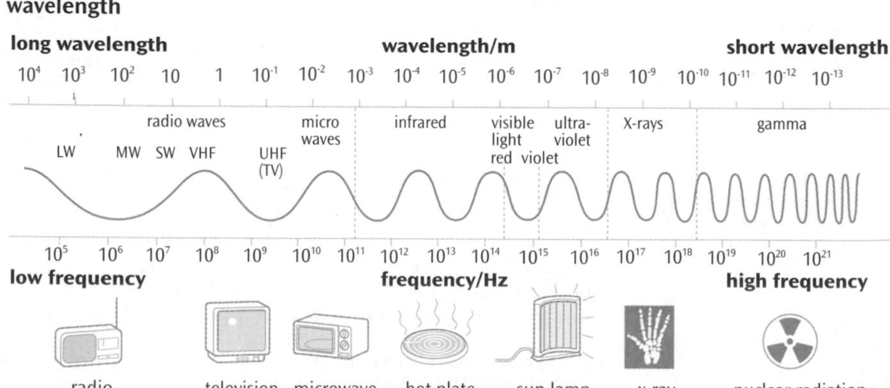

always **does things his own way**. ◇ She smiled **in a friendly way**. **2** [C, usually sing.] the route you take to reach somewhere; the route you would take if nothing were stopping you: *Can you tell me **the way to** James Street?* ◇ *Which way should I go to get to the town centre?* ◇ *If you **lose your way**, phone me.* ◇ *We stopped **on the way to** Leeds for a meal.* ◇ *Can I drive you home? It's **on my way**.* ◇ *Get out of my way!* ◇ *Can you move that box – it's **in my /the way**.* **3** [sing.] a direction or position: *Look this way!* ◇ *That painting is **the wrong way up*** (=with the wrong edge at the top). ◇ *Shouldn't you be wearing that hat **the other way round**?* (=facing in the other direction) ◇ *He thought I was older than my sister but in fact it's **the other way round*** (=the opposite of what he thought). ➲ look at **back to front** **4** [C] a path, road, route, etc. that you can travel along ➲ look at **highway**, **motorway**, **railway** **5** [sing.] a distance in space or time: ***It's a long way from** London to Edinburgh.* ◇ *The exams are still **a long way off**.* ◇ *We came all this way to see him and he's not at home!*

IDM **be set in your ways** → SET[3]

by the way (used for adding sth to the conversation) on a new subject: *Oh, by the way, I saw Mario in town yesterday.*

change your ways → CHANGE[1]

get/have your own way to get or do what you want, although others may want sth else

give way to break or fall down: *The branch of the tree suddenly gave way and he fell.*

give way (to sb/sth) 1 to stop or to allow sb/sth to go first: *Give way to traffic coming from the right.* **2** to allow sb to have what they want although you did not at first agree with it: *We shall not give way to the terrorists' demands.*

go a long way → LONG[1]

go out of your way (to do sth) to make a special effort to do sth

have a long way to go → LONG[1]

the hard way → HARD[1]

in a/one/any way; in some ways to a certain degree but not completely: *In some ways I prefer working in a small office.*

in a big/small way used for expressing the size or importance of an activity: *'Have you done any acting before?' 'Yes, but in a very small way'* (=not very much).'

in the way 1 blocking the road or path: *I can't get past. There's a big lorry in the way.* **2** not needed or wanted: *I felt rather in the way at my daughter's party.*

learn the hard way → LEARN

no way (*informal*) definitely not: *'Can I borrow your car?' 'No way!'*

under way having started and making progress: *Discussions between the two sides are now under way.*

a/sb's way of life the behaviour and customs that are typical of a person or group of people

way[2] /weɪ/ ***adv.*** (*informal*) very far; very much: *I finally found his name way down at the bottom of the list.* ◇ *Matt's got way more experience than me.*

WC /ˌdʌblju: ˈsi:/ ***abbr.*** toilet

we 🔑 /wi:/ ***pronoun*** the subject of a verb; used for talking about the speaker and one or more other people: *We're going to the cinema.* ◇ *We are both very pleased with the house.*

weak 🔑 /wi:k/ ***adj.*** **1** (used about the body) having little strength or energy; not strong: *The child was weak with hunger.* ◇ *Her legs felt weak.* **2** that cannot support a lot of weight; likely to break: *That bridge is too weak to take heavy traffic.* **3** not having economic success: *a weak currency/economy/market* **4** easy to influence; not firm or powerful: *He is too weak to be a good leader.* ◇ *a weak character* **5** (used about an argument, excuse, etc.) not easy to believe: *She made some weak excuse about washing her hair tonight.* **6** not easy to see or hear; not definite or strong: *a weak voice* ◇ *She gave a weak smile.* **7** (used about liquids) containing a lot of water, not strong in taste: *weak coffee* ◇ *I like my tea quite weak.* **8** ~ **(at/in/on sth)** not very good at sth: *He's weak at maths.* ◇ *His maths is weak.* ◇ *a weak team* OPP **strong**
▶ **weakly** ***adv.***

weaken /ˈwi:kən/ ***verb*** [I,T] **1** to become less strong; to make sb/sth less strong: *The illness had left her weakened.* ◇ *The building had been weakened by the earthquake.* OPP **strengthen** **2** to become less certain or firm about sth: *She eventually weakened and allowed him to stay.*

ˈweak form ***noun*** [C] (LANGUAGE) a way of pronouncing a word when it is not emphasized

weakness 🔑 /ˈwi:knəs/ ***noun*** **1** [U] the state of being weak: *He thought that crying was a sign of weakness.* OPP **strength** **2** [C] a fault or lack of strength, especially in a person's character: *It's important to know your own strengths and weaknesses.* OPP **strength** **3** [C, usually sing.] **a ~ for sth/sb** a particular and often FOOLISH liking for sth/sb: *I have a weakness for chocolate.*

wealth 🔑 /welθ/ ***noun*** **1** [U] (FINANCE) a lot of money, property, etc. that sb owns; the state of being rich: *They were a family of enormous wealth.* SYN **riches** **2** [sing.] **a ~ of sth** a large number or amount of sth: *a wealth of information/experience/talent*

wealthy /ˈwelθi/ ***adj.*** (**wealthier**; **wealthiest**) having a lot of money, property, etc. SYN **rich**

wean /wi:n/ ***verb*** [T] to gradually stop feeding a baby or young animal with its mother's milk and start giving it solid food

weapons

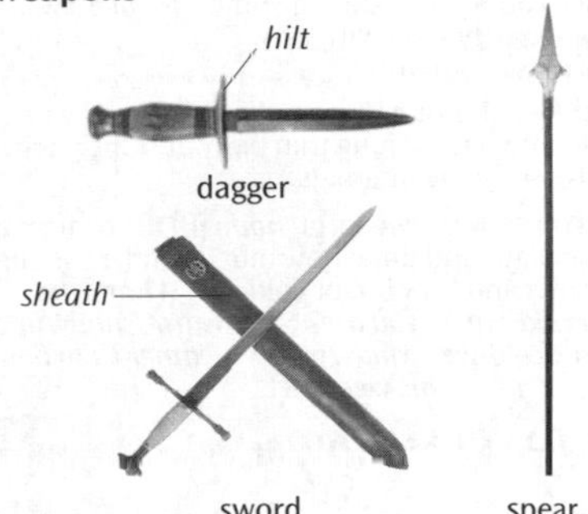

weapon 🔑 /ˈwepən/ ***noun*** [C] an object which is used for fighting or for killing people, such as a gun, knife, bomb, etc.

ˌweapon of ˌmass deˈstruction ***noun*** [C] (*abbr.* **WMD**) a weapon such as a nuclear weapon, a CHEMICAL WEAPON or a BIOLOGICAL WEAPON that can cause a lot of destruction and kill many people

wear[1] 🔑 /weə(r)/ ***verb*** (*pt* **wore** /wɔ:(r)/; *pp* **worn** /wɔ:n/) **1** [T] to have clothes, jewellery, etc. on your body: *He was wearing a suit and tie.* ◇ *I wear glasses for reading.* **2** [T] to have a certain look on your face: *His face wore a puzzled look.* **3** [I,T] to become or make sth become thinner, smoother or weaker because of being used or rubbed a lot: *These tyres are badly worn.* ◇ *The soles of his shoes had worn* *smooth.* **4** [T] to make a hole, path, etc. in sth by rubbing, walking, etc.: *I'd worn a hole in my sock.* **5** [I] to last for a long time without becoming thinner or damaged: *This material wears well.*

IDM **wear thin** to have less effect because of being used too much: *We've heard that excuse so often that it's beginning to wear thin.*

PHR V **wear (sth) away** to damage sth or to make it disappear over a period of time, by using or touching it a lot; to disappear or become damaged in this way: *The wind had worn the soil away.*

wear (sth) down to become or to make sth smaller or smoother: *The heels on these shoes have worn right down.*

wear sb/sth down to make sb/sth weaker by attacking, persuading, etc.: *They wore him down with constant arguments until he changed his mind.*

wear off to become less strong or to disappear completely: *The effects of the drug wore off after a few hours.*

wear (sth) out to become too thin or damaged to use any more; to cause sth to do this: *Children's shoes wear out very quickly.*

wear sb out to make sb very tired: *She wore herself out walking home with the heavy bags.* ➲ look at **worn-out**

wear[2] /weə(r)/ ***noun*** [U] **1** wearing or being worn; use as clothing: *You'll need jeans and jumpers for everyday wear.* **2** (usually in compounds) used especially in shops to describe clothes for a particular purpose or occasion: *casual/evening wear* ◇ *children's wear* **3** long use which damages the quality or appearance of sth: *The engine is checked regularly for signs of wear.*

IDM **wear and tear** the damage to objects, furniture, etc. that is the result of normal use

the worse for wear → WORSE

weary /'wɪəri/ ***adj.*** very tired, especially after you have been doing sth for a long time: *He gave a weary smile.* ▶ **wearily** /'wɪərəli/ ***adv.*** ▶ **weariness** ***noun*** [U]

weasel /'wi:zl/ ***noun*** [C] a small wild animal with reddish-brown fur, a long thin body and short legs. **Weasels** eat smaller animals.

weather[1] ⊶ /'weðə(r)/ ***noun*** [U] the climate at a certain place and time, how much wind, rain, sun, etc. there is and how hot or cold it is: ***What's the weather like*** *where you are?* ◇ *hot/warm/sunny/fine weather* ◇ *cold/wet/windy/wintry weather* ◇ *I'm not going for a run* ***in this weather****!*

RELATED VOCABULARY

weather

Rain is drops of water that fall from the clouds.

Snow is frozen rain. It is soft and white and often settles on the ground.

Sleet is rain that is not completely frozen.

Hail is rain frozen to ice.

When it is only raining very slightly it is **drizzling**. When it is raining very hard it is **pouring**.

Fog is like a cloud at ground level. It makes it difficult to see very far ahead. **Mist** is a thin type of fog. **Haze** is caused by heat. **Smog** is caused by pollution.

➲ note at **storm**

IDM **make heavy weather of sth** → HEAVY

under the weather (*informal*) not very well

weather[2] /'weðə(r)/ ***verb*** **1** [I,T] (GEOGRAPHY, GEOLOGY) to change or make sth change in appearance because of the effect of the sun, air or wind: *This stone weathers to a warm pinkish-brown colour.* ➲ picture at **erode 2** [T] to come safely through a difficult time or experience: *Their company managed to weather the recession and recover.*

'**weather-beaten** ***adj.*** (used especially about a person's face or skin) made rough and damaged by the sun and wind

'**weather forecast** (*also* **forecast**) ***noun*** [C] a description of the weather that is expected for the next day or next few days ➲ look at **weather**

weathering /'weðərɪŋ/ ***noun*** [U] (GEOLOGY) the action of sun, rain or wind on rocks, making them change shape or colour

weathervane /'weðəveɪn/ ***noun*** [C] a metal object on the roof of a building that turns easily in the wind and shows which direction the wind is blowing from ➲ picture at **vector**

weave /wi:v/ ***verb*** [I,T] (*pt* **wove** /wəʊv/ or in sense 2 **weaved**; *pp* **woven** /'wəʊvn/ or in sense 2 **weaved**) **1** to make cloth, etc. by passing threads under and over a set of threads that is fixed to a frame (**loom**): *woven cloth* **2** to change direction often when you are moving so that you are not stopped by anything: *The cyclist weaved in and out of the traffic.*

web ⊶ /web/ ***noun*** **1** [C] a type of fine net that a spider makes in order to catch small insects: *A spider spins webs.* ➲ look at **cobweb 2** (COMPUTING) (usually **the Web**) [sing.] = WORLD WIDE WEB: *a Web browser*

webbed /webd/ ***adj.*** (BIOLOGY) (of the feet of a bird or an animal) having pieces of skin between the toes ➲ picture on **page 28**

webcam (*AmE* **Webcam™**) /'webkæm/ ***noun*** [C] (COMPUTING) a video camera that is connected to a computer so that what it records can be seen on a website as it happens

webcast /'webkɑ:st/ ***noun*** [C] (COMPUTING) a live broadcast that is sent out on the Internet

webhead /'webhed/ ***noun*** [C] (COMPUTING) a person who uses the Internet a lot

webliography /ˌwebli'ɒgrəfi/ ***noun*** [C] (*pl.* **-ies**) (COMPUTING) a list of websites or electronic works about a particular subject that have been used by a person writing an article, etc.: *a selected webliography on new Irish poetry*

weblog /'weblɒg/ ***noun*** [C] (COMPUTING) a website that belongs to a particular person and where they write about things that interest them and list other websites that they think are interesting ➲ look at **blog**

webmaster /'webmɑ:stə(r)/ ***noun*** [C] (COMPUTING) a person who is responsible for particular pages of information on the WORLD WIDE WEB

'**web page** ***noun*** [C] (COMPUTING) a document that is connected to the World Wide Web and that anyone with an Internet connection can see, usually forming part of a website: *We learned how to create and register a new web page.*

website ⊶ /'websaɪt/ ***noun*** [C] (COMPUTING) a place connected to the Internet, where a company, organization, etc. puts information that can be found on the WORLD WIDE WEB

webzine /'webzi:n/ ***noun*** [C] (COMPUTING) a magazine published on the Internet, not on paper

Wed. ***abbr.*** Wednesday: *Wed. 4 May*

we'd /wi:d/ short for WE HAD, WE WOULD

wedding ⊶ /ˈwedɪŋ/ ***noun*** [C] a marriage ceremony and often the meal or party that follows it (**the reception**): *I've been invited to their wedding.* ◇ *a wedding dress/guest/present* ◇ *a wedding ring* (=one that is worn on the third finger to show that a person is married)

wedge[1] /wedʒ/ ***noun*** [C] a piece of wood, etc. with one thick and one thin pointed end that you can push into a small space, for example to keep things apart: *The door was kept open with a wedge.*

wedge[2] /wedʒ/ ***verb*** [T] **1** to force sth apart or to prevent sth from moving by using a **wedge**: *to wedge a door open* **2** to force sth/sb to fit into a small space: *The cupboard was wedged between the table and the door.*

Wednesday /ˈwenzdeɪ; -di/ ***noun*** [C,U] (*abbr.* **Wed.**) the day of the week after Tuesday

wee /wiː/ (*also* **ˈwee-wee**) ***noun*** [C,U] (*informal*) (used by young children or when you are talking to them) water that you pass from your body **SYN** **urine** ▸ **wee** ***verb*** [I]

weed[1] /wiːd/ ***noun*** **1** [C] a wild plant that is not wanted in a garden because it prevents other plants from growing properly **2** [U] a mass of very small green plants that floats on the surface of an area of water

weed[2] /wiːd/ ***verb*** [I,T] to remove **weeds** from a piece of ground, etc.

PHR V **weed sth/sb out** to remove the things or people that you do not think are good enough: *He weeded out all the letters with spelling mistakes in them.*

weedy /ˈwiːdi/ ***adj.*** (*informal*) small and weak: *a small weedy man*

week ⊶ /wiːk/ ***noun*** [C] **1** a period of seven days, especially from Monday to Sunday or from Sunday to Saturday: *We arrived* ***last week.*** ◇ *He left two weeks ago.* ◇ *I haven't seen her for a week.* ◇ *I go there twice a week.* ◇ *They'll be back in a week/in a week's time.* **2** the part of the week when people go to work, etc., usually from Monday to Friday: *She works hard during the week so that she can enjoy herself at the weekend.* ◇ *I work a 40-hour week.*

IDM **today, tomorrow, Monday, etc. week** seven days after today, tomorrow, Monday, etc.

week in, week out every week without a rest or change: *He's played for the same team week in, week out for 20 years.*

a week yesterday, last Monday, etc. seven days before yesterday, Monday, etc.

weekday /ˈwiːkdeɪ/ ***noun*** [C] any day except Saturday or Sunday: *I only work on weekdays.*

weekend ⊶ /ˌwiːkˈend/ ***noun*** [C] Saturday and Sunday (*BrE*): *The office is closed* ***at the weekend.*** ◇ (*especially AmE*) *The office is closed* ***on the weekend.*** ◇ *Have a good weekend!*

weekly[1] ⊶ /ˈwiːkli/ ***adj.***, ***adv.*** happening or appearing once a week or every week: *a weekly report* ◇ *We are paid weekly.*

weekly[2] /ˈwiːkli/ ***noun*** [C] (*pl.* **weeklies**) a newspaper or magazine that is published every week

weep /wiːp/ ***verb*** [I,T] (*pt, pp* **wept** /wept/) (*formal*) to let tears fall because of strong emotion; to cry: *She wept at the news of his death.*

weft /weft/ ***noun*** [sing.] (TECHNICAL) the threads that are twisted under and over the threads that are held on a LOOM (=a frame or machine for making cloth) ➲ look at **warp**

weigh ⊶ /weɪ/ ***verb*** **1** [T] to measure how heavy sth is, especially by using a machine (**scales**): *I weigh myself every week.* ◇ *Can you weigh this parcel for me, please?* **2** ***linking verb*** to have or show a certain weight: *I weigh 56 kilos.* ◇ *How much does this weigh?* **3** [T] ~ **sth (up)** to consider sth carefully: *You need to weigh up your chances of success.* **4** [T] ~ **sth (against sb/sth)** to consider if one thing is better, more important, etc. than another or not: *We shall weigh the advantages of the plan against the risks.* **5** [I] ~ **against sb/sth** to be considered as a disadvantage when sb/sth is being judged: *She didn't get the job because her lack of experience weighed against her.*

PHR V **weigh sb down** to make sb feel worried and sad: *He felt weighed down by all his responsibilities.*

weigh sb/sth down to make it difficult for sb/sth to move (by being heavy): *I was weighed down by heavy shopping.*

weigh on sb/sth to make sb worry: *The problem has been* ***weighing on my mind*** (=I have felt worried about it).

weigh sb/sth up to consider sb/sth carefully and form an opinion: *I weighed up my chances and decided it was worth applying.*

weight[1] ⊶ /weɪt/ ***noun*** **1** [U] how heavy sth/sb is; the fact of being heavy: *The doctor advised him to* ***lose weight*** (=become thinner and less heavy). ◇ *He's* ***put on weight*** (=got fatter). ◇ *The weight of the snow broke the branch.* **2** [C] a heavy object: *The doctor has told me not to lift heavy weights.* **3** [C] a piece of metal that weighs a known amount that can be used to measure an amount of sth, or that can be lifted as a form of exercise: *a 500-gram weight* ◇ *She lifts weights in the gym as part of her daily training.* ➲ picture at **sport** **4** [sing.] something that you are worried about: *Telling her the truth took* ***a weight off his mind.***

IDM **carry weight** → CARRY

pull your weight → PULL[1]

weight[2] /weɪt/ ***verb*** [T] **1** ~ **sth (down) (with sth)** to hold sth down with a heavy object or objects: *to weight down a fishing net* **2** (usually passive) to organize sth so that a particular person or group has an advantage/disadvantage: *The system is* ***weighted in favour of/against*** *people with children.*

weightless /ˈweɪtləs/ ***adj.*** having no weight, for example when travelling in space ▸ **weightlessness** ***noun*** [U]

weightlifting /ˈweɪtlɪftɪŋ/ ***noun*** [U] (SPORT) the sport or activity of lifting heavy metal objects ▸ **weightlifter** ***noun*** [C]

ˈweight training ***noun*** [U] the activity of lifting WEIGHTS as a form of exercise: *I* ***do weight training*** *to keep fit.*

weighty /ˈweɪti/ ***adj.*** (**weightier**; **weightiest**) serious and important: *a weighty question*

weir /wɪə(r)/ ***noun*** [C] a type of wall that is built across a river to stop or change the direction of the flow of water

weird /wɪəd/ ***adj.*** strange and unusual: *a weird noise/experience* ▸ **weirdly** ***adv.***

welcome[1] ⊶ /ˈwelkəm/ ***verb*** [T] **1** to be friendly to sb when they arrive somewhere: *Everyone came to the door to welcome us.* **2** to be pleased to receive or accept sth: *I've no idea what to do next, so I'd welcome any suggestions.* ▸ **welcome** ***noun*** [C]: *Let's give a warm welcome to our next guest.*

welcome² ⊶ /ˈwelkəm/ ***adj.*** **1** received with pleasure; giving pleasure: *You're always welcome here.* ◇ *welcome news* OPP **unwelcome** **2** ~ **to sth/to do sth** allowed to do sth: *You're welcome to use my bicycle.* **3** used to say that sb can have sth that you do not want yourself: *Take the car if you want. You're welcome to it. It's always breaking down.* ▶ **welcome** ***exclamation***: *Welcome to London!* ◇ *Welcome home!*
IDM **make sb welcome** to receive sb in a friendly way
you're welcome (*spoken*) used as a polite reply when sb thanks you for sth: *'Thank you for your help.' 'You're welcome.'*

weld /weld/ ***verb*** [I,T] to join pieces of metal by heating them and pressing them together ➲ look at **solder**

welfare AW /ˈwelfeə(r)/ ***noun*** [U] **1** the general health and happiness of a person, an animal or a group: *The doctor is concerned about the child's welfare.* **2** (SOCIAL STUDIES) the help and care that is given to people who have problems with health, money, etc.: *education and welfare services* **3** (*AmE*) = SOCIAL SECURITY

ˌwelfare ˈstate ***noun*** [sing.] (SOCIAL STUDIES) a system organized by a government to provide free services and money for people who have no job, who are ill, etc.; a country that has this system

well¹ ⊶ /wel/ ***adv.*** (**better**; **best**) **1** in a good way: *You speak English very well.* ◇ *I hope your work is* ***going well****.* ◇ *You passed your exam!* ***Well done****!* ◇ *He took it well when I told him he wasn't on the team.* OPP **badly** **2** completely or fully: *Shake the bottle well before opening.* ◇ *How well do you know Henry?* **3** very much: *They arrived home well past midnight.* ◇ *She says she's 32 but I'm sure she's well over 40.* ◇ *This book is* ***well worth*** *reading.* **4** (used with *can, could, may* or *might*) probably or possibly: *He might well be right.* **5** (used with *can, could, may* or *might*) with good reason: *I can't very well refuse to help them after all they've done for me.* ◇ *'Where's Bill?' 'You may well ask* (= I don't know either)*!'*
IDM **as well (as sb/sth)** in addition to sb/sth: *Can I come as well?* ◇ *He's worked in Japan as well as Italy.*
augur well/ill for sb/sth → AUGUR
bode well/ill (for sb/sth) → BODE
do well 1 to be successful: *Their daughter has done well at university.* **2** to be getting better after an illness: *Mr Singh is doing well after his operation.*
do well to do sth used to say that sth is the right and sensible thing to do: *He would do well to check the facts before accusing people.*
may/might (just) as well used for saying that sth is the best thing you can do in the situation, even though you may not want to do it: *I may as well tell you the truth – you'll find out anyway.*
mean well → MEAN¹
well and truly completely: *We were well and truly lost.*
well/badly off → OFF¹

well² ⊶ /wel/ ***adj.*** (*comparative* **better**; *superlative* **best**) (not before a noun) **1** (HEALTH) in good health: *'How are you?' 'I'm very well, thanks.'* ◇ *This medicine will make you* ***feel better****.* ◇ ***Get well soon*** (= written in a card that you send to somebody who is ill). **2** in a good state: *I hope all is well with you.*
IDM **all very well (for sb)** (*informal*) used for showing that you are not happy or do not agree with sth: *It's all very well for her to criticize* (= it's easy for her to criticize) *but it doesn't help the situation.*
(just) as well (to do sth) sensible; a good idea: *It would be just as well to ask his permission.*

well³ ⊶ /wel/ ***exclamation*** **1** used for showing surprise: *Well, thank goodness you've arrived.* **2** used for expressing UNCERTAINTY: *'Do you like it?' 'Well, I'm not really sure.'* **3** used when you begin the next part of a story or when you are thinking about what to say next: *Well, the next thing that happened was...* ◇ *Well now, let me see...* **4** used to show that you are waiting for sb to say sth: *Well? Are you going to tell us what happened?* **5** used to show that you want to finish a conversation: *Well, it's been nice talking to you.* **6** (*also* **oh well**) used for showing that you know there is nothing you can do to change a situation: *Oh well, there's nothing we can do about it.*

well⁴ /wel/ ***noun*** [C] **1** a deep hole in the ground from which water is obtained: *to draw water from a well* **2** = OIL WELL

well⁵ /wel/ ***verb*** [I] ~ **(out/up)** (used about a liquid) to come to the surface: *Tears welled up in her eyes*

we'll /wiːl/ short for WE SHALL, WE WILL

ˌwell adˈjusted ***adj.*** able to deal with people, problems and life in general in a normal, sensible way ➲ look at **maladjusted**

ˌwell ˈbalanced ***adj.*** **1** (used about a person) calm and sensible **2** (used about a meal, etc.) containing enough of the healthy types of food your body needs: *a well-balanced diet*

ˌwell beˈhaved ***adj.*** behaving in a way that most people think is correct

ˈwell-being ***noun*** [U] a state of being healthy and happy

ˌwell ˈdone ***adj.*** (used about meat, etc.) cooked for a long time ➲ look at **rare**, **medium**

ˌwell ˈdressed ***adj.*** wearing attractive and fashionable clothes

ˌwell ˈearned ***adj.*** that you deserve, especially because you have been working hard: *a well-earned holiday*

ˌwell ˈfed ***adj.*** having good food regularly

ˌwell inˈformed ***adj.*** knowing a lot about one or several subjects

wellington /ˈwelɪŋtən/ (*also informal* **welly** /ˈweli/) ***noun*** [C] (*pl.* **wellingtons**; **wellies**) (*BrE*) one of a pair of long rubber boots that you wear to keep your feet and the lower part of your legs dry: *a pair of wellingtons*

ˌwell ˈkept ***adj.*** looked after very carefully so that it has a tidy appearance: *a well-kept garden*

ˌwell ˈknown ***adj.*** known by a lot of people; famous OPP **unknown**

ˌwell ˈmeaning ***adj.*** (used about a person) wanting to be kind or helpful, but often not having this effect

ˌwell ˈmeant ***adj.*** intended to be kind or helpful but not having this result

ˌwell ˈread ***adj.*** having read many books and therefore having a lot of knowledge

ˌwell-to-ˈdo ***adj.*** having a lot of money, property, etc. SYN **rich**

ˈwell-wisher ***noun*** [C] somebody who hopes that a person or thing will be successful: *She received lots of letters from well-wishers before the competition.*

Welsh /welʃ/ ***adj.*** from Wales ❶ For more information, look at the section on geographical names at the back of this dictionary.

went past tense of **go¹**

wept past tense, past participle of **weep**

were /wə(r)/ → BE

we're /wɪə(r)/ short for WE ARE

west¹ ⊶ /west/ ***noun*** [sing.] (GEOGRAPHY) (*abbr.* W) **1** (*also* **the west**) the direction you look towards in order to see the sun go down; one of the points of the COMPASS (=the four main directions that we give names to): *Which way is west?* ◇ *Rain is spreading from the west.* ◇ *There's a road **to the west of** here.* ➲ picture at **compass 2 the west**; **the West** the part of any country, city, etc. that is further to the west than other parts: *I live in the west of Scotland.* ◇ *The climate in the West is much wetter than the East.* **3 the West** the countries of North America and Western Europe ➲ look at **north**, **south**, **east**

west² ⊶ /west/ ***adj.***, ***adv.*** (GEOGRAPHY) in, to or towards the west: *The island is five miles west of here.* ◇ *to travel west* ◇ *West London*

westbound /'westbaʊnd/ ***adj.*** travelling or leading towards the west: *the westbound carriageway of the motorway*

the 'West Country ***noun*** [U] (GEOGRAPHY) the south-west part of Britain

the ˌWest 'End ***noun*** [U] (GEOGRAPHY) the western part of central London where there are many shops, theatres, cinemas, etc.

westerly /'westəli/ ***adj.*** (GEOGRAPHY) **1** to, towards or in the west: *in a westerly direction* **2** (used about winds) coming from the west

western¹ ⊶ (*also* **Western**) /'westən/ ***adj.*** (GEOGRAPHY) **1** in or of the west: *western France* **2** from or connected with the western part of the world, especially Europe or North America

western² /'westən/ ***noun*** [C] (ARTS AND MEDIA, LITERATURE) a film or book about life in the past in the west of the United States

westerner /'westənə(r)/ ***noun*** [C] (GEOGRAPHY) a person who was born or who lives in the western part of the world, especially Europe or North America: *Westerners arriving in China usually experience culture shock.*

westernize (also **-ise**) /'westənaɪz/ ***verb*** [T] (usually passive) (SOCIAL STUDIES) to bring ideas or ways of life that are typical of western Europe and N America to other countries ► **westernized** (also **-ised**) ***adj.***: *a westernized society*

the West Indies /ˌwest 'ɪndɪz; -diːz/ ***noun*** [pl., with sing. or pl. verb] (GEOGRAPHY) a group of islands between the Caribbean and the Atlantic, that includes the Antilles and the Bahamas ► **ˌWest 'Indian *noun*** [C]: *The West Indians won their match against Australia.* ► **ˌWest 'Indian *adj.***

ˌwest-north-'west ***noun*** [sing.] (GEOGRAPHY) (*abbr.* WNW) the direction halfway between west and north-west

ˌwest-south-'west ***noun*** [sing.] (GEOGRAPHY) (*abbr.* WSW) the direction halfway between west and south-west

westward /'westwəd/ ***adj.*** (GEOGRAPHY) towards the west: *in a westward direction* ► **westward** (*also* **westwards**) ***adv.***: *to fly westwards*

wet¹ ⊶ /wet/ ***adj.*** (**wetter**; **wettest**) **1** covered in a liquid, especially water: *wet clothes/hair/grass/roads* ◇ *Don't **get** your feet **wet**.* OPP **dry 2** (used about the weather, etc.) with a lot of rain: *a wet day* OPP **dry 3** (used about paint, etc.) not yet dry or hard: *The ink is still wet.* OPP **dry 4** (*informal*) (used about a person) without energy or enthusiasm ► **the wet *noun*** [sing.]: *Come in out of the wet* (=the rainy weather).

IDM **a wet blanket** (*informal*) a person who spoils other people's fun, especially because he or she refuses to take part in sth

wet through extremely wet

wet² /wet/ ***verb*** [T] (*pres. part.* **wetting**; *pt, pp* **wet** or **wetted**) **1** to make sth wet **2** (used especially of young children) to make yourself or your bed, clothes, etc. wet by URINATING

wetland /'wetlənd/ ***noun*** [C] (*also* **wetlands** [pl.]) (GEOGRAPHY) an area of land that is always wet

wetsuit /'wetsuːt/ ***noun*** [C] a rubber suit that covers the whole of the body, used by people doing sports in the water or swimming under the water

we've /wiːv/ short for WE HAVE

whack /wæk/ ***verb*** [T] (*informal*) to hit sb/sth hard

whacky =WACKY

whale /weɪl/ ***noun*** [C] a very large animal that lives in the sea and looks like a very large fish ➲ picture on **page 28**

whaling /'weɪlɪŋ/ ***noun*** [U] the hunting of WHALES

wharf /wɔːf/ ***noun*** [C] (*pl.* **wharves** /wɔːvz/) a platform made of stone or wood at the side of a river where ships and boats can be tied up

what ⊶ /wɒt/ ***det.***, ***pronoun*** **1** used for asking for information about sb/sth: *What time is it?* ◇ *What kind of music do you like?* ◇ *She asked him what he was doing.* ◇ *What's their phone number?* **2** the thing or things that have been mentioned or said: *What he says is true.* ◇ *I haven't got much, but you can borrow what money I have.* **3** used for emphasizing sth: *What strange eyes she's got!* ◇ *What a kind thing to do!* **4** used to express surprise or to tell sb to say or repeat sth: *'I've asked Alice to marry me.' 'What!'*

IDM **how/what about...?** → ABOUT²

what for for what purpose or reason: *What's this little switch for?* ◇ *What did you say that for* (=why did you say that)?

what if...? what would happen if...?: *What if the car breaks down?*

whatever ⊶ /wɒt'evə(r)/ ***det.***, ***pronoun***, ***adv.*** **1** any or every; anything or everything: *You can say whatever you like.* ◇ *He took whatever help he could get.* **2** used to say that it does not matter what happens or what sb does, because the result will be the same: *I still love you, whatever you may think.* ◇ *Whatever she says, she doesn't really mean it.* **3** (used for expressing surprise or worry) what: *Whatever could have happened to them?* **4** (*also* **whatsoever**) at all: *I've no reason whatever to doubt him.* ◇ *'Any questions?' 'None whatsoever.'*

IDM **or whatever** (*informal*) or any other or others of a similar kind: *You don't need to wear anything smart – jeans and a sweater or whatever.*

whatever you do used to emphasize that sb must not do sth: *Don't touch the red switch, whatever you do.*

wheat /wiːt/ ***noun*** [U] **1** a type of grain which can be made into flour **2** (AGRICULTURE) the plant which produces this grain: *a field of wheat* ➲ picture at **cereal**

wheel¹ ⊶ /wiːl/ ***noun*** [C] **1** one of the circular objects under a car, bicycle, etc. that turns when it moves: *His favourite toy is a dog on wheels.* ◇ *By law, you have to carry a spare wheel in your car.* **2** [usually sing.] =STEERING WHEEL: *Her husband was **at the wheel*** (=he was driving) *when the accident happened.*

wheel² /wiːl/ ***verb*** **1** [T] to push along an object that has wheels; to move sb about in/on a vehicle with wheels: *He wheeled his bicycle up the hill.* ◇ *She was wheeled back to her bed on a trolley.* **2** [I] to fly round in circles: *Birds wheeled above the ship.* **3** [I] to turn round suddenly: *Eleanor wheeled round, with a look of horror on her face.*

wheelbarrow /ˈwiːlbærəʊ/ (*also* **barrow**) ***noun*** [C] a type of small open container with one wheel and two handles that you use outside for carrying things ➲ picture at **agriculture**

wheelchair /ˈwiːltʃeə(r)/ ***noun*** [C] a chair with large wheels that a person who cannot walk can move or be pushed about in

ˈwheel clamp (*BrE*) = CLAMP¹ (2)

wheeze /wiːz/ ***verb*** [I] (**HEALTH**) to breathe noisily, for example if you have a chest illness

when 🔑 /wen/ ***adv., conj.*** **1** at what time: *When did she arrive?* ◇ *I don't know when she arrived.* **2** used for talking about the time at which sth happens or happened: *Sunday is the day when I can relax.* ◇ *I last saw her in May, when she was in London.* ◇ *He jumped up when the phone rang.* **3** since; as; considering that: *Why do you want more money when you've got enough already?*

whence /wens/ ***adv.*** (*old-fashioned*) (from) where: *They returned whence they came.*

whenever 🔑 /wenˈevə(r)/ ***conj., adv.*** **1** at any time; no matter when: *You can borrow my car whenever you want.* ◇ *Don't worry. You can give it back the next time you see me, or whenever.* **2** (used when you are showing that you are surprised or impatient) when: *Whenever did you find time to do all that cooking?*

where 🔑 /weə(r)/ ***adv., conj.*** **1** in or to what place or position: *Where can I buy a newspaper?* ◇ *I asked him where he lived.* **2** in or to the place or situation mentioned: *the town where you were born* ◇ *She ran to where they were standing.* ◇ *Where possible, you should travel by bus, not taxi.* ◇ *We came to a village, where we stopped for lunch.* ◇ ***Where** maths **is concerned**, I'm hopeless.*

whereabouts¹ /ˌweərəˈbaʊts/ ***adv.*** where; in or near what place: *Whereabouts did you lose your purse?*

whereabouts² /ˈweərəbaʊts/ ***noun*** [pl.] the place where sb/sth is: *The whereabouts of the stolen painting are unknown.*

whereas 🔑 AW /ˌweərˈæz/ ***conj.*** used for showing a fact that is different: *He eats meat, whereas she's a vegetarian.* SYN **while**

whereby AW /weəˈbaɪ/ ***adv.*** (*written*) by which; because of which: *These countries have an agreement whereby foreign visitors can have free medical care.*

whereupon /ˌweərəˈpɒn/ ***conj.*** (*written*) after which: *He fell asleep, whereupon she walked quietly from the room.*

wherever 🔑 /weərˈevə(r)/ ***conj., adv.*** **1** in or to any place: *You can sit wherever you like.* ◇ *She comes from Desio, wherever that is* (=I don't know where it is). **2** everywhere, in all places that: *Wherever I go, he goes.* **3** used for showing surprise: *Wherever did you learn to cook like that?*

IDM **or wherever** or any other place: *The students might be from Sweden, Denmark or wherever.*

whet /wet/ ***verb*** (**whetting**; **whetted**)

IDM **whet sb's appetite** to make sb want more of sth: *Our short stay in Dublin whetted our appetite to spend more time there.*

whether 🔑 /ˈweðə(r)/ ***conj.*** **1** (used after verbs like 'ask', 'doubt', 'know', etc.) if: *He asked me whether we would be coming to the party.* **2** used for expressing a choice or doubt between two or more possibilities: *I can't make up my mind **whether** to go **or not**.*

IDM **whether or not** used to say that sth will be true in either of the situations that are mentioned: *We shall play on Saturday whether it rains or not.* ◇ *Whether or not it rains, we shall play on Saturday.*

whey /weɪ/ ***noun*** [U] the thin liquid that is left from sour milk after the solid parts (**curds**) have been removed

which 🔑 /wɪtʃ/ ***det., pronoun*** **1** used in questions to ask sb to be exact, when there are a number of people or things to choose from: *Which hand do you write with?* ◇ *Which is your bag?* ◇ *She asked me which book I preferred.* ◇ *I can't remember which of the boys is the older.* **2** used for saying exactly what thing or things you are talking about: *Cars which use unleaded petrol are more eco-friendly.* ◇ (*formal*) *The situation **in which** he found himself was very difficult.* **3** used for giving more information about a thing or animal: *My first car, which I bought as a student, was a Renault.* **4** used for making a comment on what has just been said: *We had to wait 16 hours for our plane, which was really annoying.*

whichever /wɪtʃˈevə(r)/ ***det., pronoun*** **1** any person or thing; it does not matter which one you choose: *You can choose whichever book you want.* **2** (used for expressing surprise) which: *You're very late. Whichever way did you come?*

whiff /wɪf/ ***noun*** [C, usually sing.] **a ~ (of sth)** a smell, especially one which only lasts for a short time: *He **caught a whiff** of her perfume.*

while¹ 🔑 /waɪl/ (*also formal* **whilst** /waɪlst/) ***conj.*** **1** during the time that; when: *He always phones while we're having lunch.* **2** at the same time as: *He always listens to the radio while he's driving to work.* **3** (*formal*) used when you are contrasting two ideas: *Some countries are rich, while others are extremely poor.* SYN **whereas**

while² 🔑 /waɪl/ ***noun*** [sing.] a (usually short) period of time: *Let's sit down here for a while.*

IDM **once in a while** → ONCE

worth sb's while → WORTH¹

while³ /waɪl/ ***verb***

PHRV **while sth away** to pass time in a lazy or relaxed way: *We whiled away the evening chatting and listening to music.*

whim /wɪm/ ***noun*** [C] a sudden idea or desire to do sth (often sth that is unusual or not necessary): *We bought the house **on a whim**.*

whimper /ˈwɪmpə(r)/ ***verb*** [I] to cry softly, especially with fear or pain ▶ **whimper** ***noun*** [C]

whine /waɪn/ ***verb*** **1** [I,T] to complain about sth in an annoying, crying voice: *The children were whining all afternoon.* **2** [I] to make a long high unpleasant sound because you are in pain or unhappy: *The dog is whining to go out.* ▶ **whine** ***noun*** [C]

whip¹ /wɪp/ ***noun*** [C] **1** a long thin piece of leather, etc. with a handle, that is used for making animals go faster and for hitting people as a punishment: *He **cracked the whip** and the horse leapt forward.* **2** (**POLITICS**) (in Britain and the US) an official of a political party who makes sure that all members vote on important matters: *the chief whip*

whip² /wɪp/ ***verb*** (**whipping**; **whipped**) **1** [T] to hit a person or an animal hard with a **whip**, as a punishment or to make them or it go faster or work harder **2** [I] (*informal*) to move quickly, suddenly or violently: *She whipped round to see what had made the noise behind her.* **3** [T] to remove or pull sth quickly and suddenly: *He whipped out a pen and made a note of the number.* **4** [T] ~ **sth (up)** to mix the white part of an egg or cream until it is light and thick: *whipped cream* **5** [T] (*BrE, informal*) to steal sth: *Who's whipped my pen?*

PHR V **whip through sth** (*informal*) to do or finish sth very quickly

whip sb/sth up to deliberately try to make people excited or feel strongly about sth: *to whip up excitement*

whip sth up (*informal*) to prepare food quickly: *to whip up a quick snack*

whir (*especially AmE*) = WHIRR

whirl[1] /wɜːl/ ***verb*** [I,T] to move, or to make sb/sth move, round and round very quickly in a circle: *The dancers whirled round the room.* ◇ (*figurative*) *I couldn't sleep. My mind was whirling after all the excitement.*

whirl[2] /wɜːl/ ***noun*** [sing.] **1** the action or sound of sth moving round and round very quickly: *the whirl of the helicopter's blades* **2** a state of confusion or excitement: *My head's **in a whirl** – I'm so excited.* **3** a number of events or activities happening one after the other: *The next few days passed in a whirl of activity.*

IDM **give sth a whirl** (*informal*) to try sth to see if you like it or can do it

whirlpool /ˈwɜːlpuːl/ ***noun*** [C] (**GEOGRAPHY**) a place in a river or the sea where currents in the water move very quickly round in a circle

whirlwind /ˈwɜːlwɪnd/ ***noun*** [C] (**GEOGRAPHY**) a very strong circular wind that forms a tall column of air moving round and round in a circle as it travels across the land or the sea ➲ note at **storm**

whirr (*especially AmE* **whir**) /wɜː(r)/ ***verb*** [I] to make a continuous low sound like the parts of a machine moving: *The noise of the fan whirring kept me awake.* ▶ **whirr** (*especially AmE* **whir**) ***noun*** [C, usually sing.]

whisk[1] /wɪsk/ ***noun*** [C] a tool that you use for beating eggs, cream, etc. very fast

whisk[2] /wɪsk/ ***verb*** [T] **1** to beat or mix eggs, cream, etc. very fast using a fork or a WHISK: *Whisk the egg whites until stiff.* **2** to take sb/sth somewhere very quickly: *The prince was whisked away in a black limousine.*

whisker /ˈwɪskə(r)/ ***noun*** [C] (**BIOLOGY**) one of the long thick hairs that grow near the mouth of some animals such as a mouse, cat, etc. ➲ picture at **lion**

whisky (*AmE* **whiskey**) /ˈwɪski/ ***noun*** (*pl.* **whiskies**; **whiskeys**) **1** [U] a strong alcoholic drink that is made from grain and is sometimes drunk with water and/ or ice: *Scotch whisky* **2** [C] a glass of **whisky**

whisper ⊶ /ˈwɪspə(r)/ ***verb*** [I,T] to speak very quietly into sb's ear, so that other people cannot hear what you are saying ▶ **whisper** ***noun*** [C]: *to speak **in a whisper***

whistle[1] ⊶ /ˈwɪsl/ ***noun*** [C] **1** a small metal or plastic tube that you blow into to make a long high sound: *The referee blew his whistle to stop the game.* **2** the sound made by blowing a whistle or by blowing air out between your lips: *United scored just moments before **the final whistle**.* ◇ *He gave a low whistle of surprise.*

whistle[2] ⊶ /ˈwɪsl/ ***verb*** **1** [I,T] to make a musical or a high sound by forcing air out between your lips or by blowing a whistle: *He whistled a tune to himself.* **2** [I] to move somewhere quickly making a sound like a whistle: *A bullet whistled past his head.*

white[1] ⊶ /waɪt/ ***adj.*** **1** of the very light colour of fresh snow or milk: *a white shirt* ◇ *white coffee* (=with milk) **2** (used about a person) belonging to or connected with a race of people who have pale skin **3** ~ **(with sth)** (used about a person) very pale because you are ill, afraid, etc.: *to be white with shock/anger/fear* ◇ *She went **white as a sheet** when they told her.*

IDM **black and white** → BLACK[1]

white[2] ⊶ /waɪt/ ***noun*** **1** [U] the very light colour of fresh snow or milk: *She was dressed **in white**.* **2** [C, usually pl.] a member of a race of people with pale skin **3** [C,U] the part of an egg that surrounds the yellow part (**yolk**) and that becomes white when it is cooked: *Beat the whites of four eggs.* **4** [C] the white part of the eye

IDM **in black and white** → BLACK[2]

whitebait /ˈwaɪtbeɪt/ ***noun*** [pl.] very small young fish of several types that are fried and eaten whole

whiteboard /ˈwaɪtbɔːd/ ***noun*** [C] a large board with a smooth white surface that teachers, etc. write on with special pens ➲ look at **blackboard**, **interactive whiteboard**

ˌwhite-ˈcollar ***adj.*** (**SOCIAL STUDIES**) working in an office, rather than in a factory, etc.; connected with work in offices: *white-collar workers* ◇ *a white-collar job* ➲ look at **blue-collar**

ˌwhite ˈelephant ***noun*** [sing.] something that you no longer need and that is not useful any more, although it cost a lot of money

ˈwhite goods ***noun*** [pl.] large pieces of electrical equipment in the house, such as WASHING MACHINES, etc. ➲ look at **brown goods**

ˌwhite-ˈhot ***adj.*** (of sth burning) so hot that it looks white

the ˈWhite House ***noun*** [sing.] (**POLITICS**) **1** the large building in Washington D.C. where the US president lives and works **2** the US president and the other people in the government who work with him or her

ˌwhite ˈlie ***noun*** [C] a lie that is not very harmful or serious, especially one that you tell because the truth would hurt sb

ˌwhite ˈlight ***noun*** [U] (**PHYSICS**) ordinary light that is colourless ➲ picture at **prism**

whitewash[1] /ˈwaɪtwɒʃ/ ***noun*** [U] **1** a white liquid that you use for painting walls **2** [sing.] trying to hide unpleasant facts about sb/sth: *The opposition claimed the report was a whitewash.*

whitewash[2] /ˈwaɪtwɒʃ/ ***verb*** [T] **1** to paint WHITEWASH onto a wall **2** to try to hide sth bad or wrong that you have done

ˌwhite ˈwater ***noun*** [U] (**GEOGRAPHY**) **1** a part of a river that looks white because the water is moving very fast over rocks: *a stretch of white water* ◇ *to **go white-water rafting*** **2** a part of the sea or ocean that looks white because it is very rough and the waves are high

whizz[1] (*especially AmE* **whiz**) /wɪz/ ***verb*** [I] (*informal*) to move very quickly, often making a high continuous sound: *The racing cars went whizzing by.*

whizz[2] (*especially AmE* **whiz**) /wɪz/ ***noun*** [sing.] (*informal*) a person who is very good and successful at sth: *She's a whizz at crosswords.* ◇ *He's our new marketing **whizz-kid*** (=a young person who is very good at sth).

WHO /ˌdʌblju: eɪtʃ ˈəʊ/ ***abbr.*** (HEALTH) **World Health Organization**; an international organization that tries to fight and control disease

who /hu:/ ***pronoun*** **1** used in questions to ask sb's name, identity, position, etc.: *Who was on the phone?* ◇ *Who's that woman in the grey suit?* ◇ *She wondered who he was.* **2** used for saying exactly which person or what kind of person you are talking about: *I like people who say what they think.* ◇ (*informal*) *That's the man who I met at Ann's party.* ◇ *The woman who I work for is very nice.* **3** used for giving extra information about sb: *My mother, who's over 80, still drives a car.* ❶ The extra information you give is separated from the main clause by commas.

who'd /hu:d/ short for WHO HAD, WHO WOULD

whodunnit (*AmE*) (*BrE also* **whodunit**) (*informal*) (ARTS AND MEDIA, LITERATURE) a story, play, etc. about a murder in which you do not know who did the murder until the end

whoever /hu:ˈevə(r)/ ***pronoun*** **1** the person or people who; any person who: *I want to speak to whoever is in charge.* **2** it does not matter who: *I don't want to see anybody – whoever it is.* **3** (used for expressing surprise) who: *Whoever could have done that?*

whole¹ /həʊl/ ***adj.*** **1** complete; full: *I drank a whole bottle of water.* ◇ *Let's just forget* ***the whole thing***. ◇ *She wasn't telling me the* ***whole truth***. **2** not broken or cut: *Snakes swallow their prey whole* (= in one piece). ➲ adverb **wholly**

whole² /həʊl/ ***noun*** [sing.] **1** a thing that is complete or full in itself: *Two halves make a whole.* **2 the ~ of sth** all that there is of sth: *I spent the whole of the morning cooking.*

IDM **as a whole** as one complete thing or unit and not as separate parts: *This is true in Britain, but also in Europe as a whole.*

on the whole generally, but not true in every case: *On the whole I think it's a very good idea.*

wholefood /ˈhəʊlfu:d/ ***noun*** [U] **wholefoods** [pl.] food that is considered healthy because it does not contain artificial substances and is produced as naturally as possible

wholehearted /ˌhəʊlˈhɑ:tɪd/ ***adj.*** complete and enthusiastic: *to give sb your wholehearted support* ▶ **wholeheartedly** ***adv.***

wholemeal /ˈhəʊlmi:l/ (*also* **wholewheat**) ***adj.*** (made from) flour that contains all the grain including the outside layer (**husk**): *wholemeal bread/flour*

ˈ**whole note** (*AmE*) = SEMIBREVE

wholesale /ˈhəʊlseɪl/ ***adv.***, ***adj.*** (adjective only *before* a noun) **1** (BUSINESS) connected with buying and selling goods in large quantities, especially in order to sell them again and make a profit: *They get all their building materials wholesale.* ◇ *wholesale goods/prices* ➲ look at **retail** **2** (usually about sth bad) very great; on a very large scale: *the wholesale slaughter of wildlife*

wholesaler /ˈhəʊlseɪlə(r)/ ***noun*** [C] (BUSINESS) a person or business that buys goods in large quantities and sells them to businesses, so they can be sold again to make a profit ➲ look at **retailer**

wholesome /ˈhəʊlsəm/ ***adj.*** **1** good for your health: *simple wholesome food* **2** having a moral effect that is good: *clean wholesome fun*

who'll /hu:l/ short for WHO WILL

wholly /ˈhəʊlli/ ***adv.*** completely; fully: *George is not wholly to blame for the situation.*

whom /hu:m/ ***pronoun*** (*formal*) used instead of 'who' as the object of a verb or preposition: *Whom did you meet there?* ◇ *He asked me whom I had met.* ◇ *To whom am I speaking?*

whooping cough /ˈhu:pɪŋ kɒf/ ***noun*** [U] (HEALTH) a serious disease, especially of children, which makes them cough loudly and not be able to breathe easily

whoops /wʊps/ ***exclamation*** used when you have, or nearly have, a small accident: *Whoops! I nearly dropped the cup.*

whoosh /wʊʃ/ ***noun*** [C, usually sing.] the sudden movement and sound of air or water going past very fast ▶ **whoosh** ***verb*** [I]

who're /ˈhu:ə(r)/ short for WHO ARE

who's /hu:z/ short for WHO IS, WHO HAS

whose /hu:z/ ***det.***, ***pronoun*** **1** (used in questions to ask who sth belongs to) of whom?: *Whose car is that?* ◇ *Whose is that car?* ◇ *Those are nice shoes – I wonder whose they are.* **2** (used to say exactly which person or thing you mean, or to give extra information about a person or thing) of whom; of which: *That's the boy whose mother I met.* ◇ *My neighbours, whose house is up for sale, are splitting up.*

who've /hu:v/ short for WHO HAVE

why /waɪ/ ***adv.*** **1** for what reason: *Why was she so late?* ◇ *I wonder why they went.* ◇ *'I'm not staying any longer.' 'Why not?'* **2** used for giving or talking about a reason for sth: ***The reason why*** *I'm leaving you is obvious.* ◇ *I'm tired and* ***that's why*** *I'm in such a bad mood.*

IDM **why ever** used to show that you are surprised or angry: *Why ever didn't you phone?*

why not? used for making or agreeing to a suggestion: *Why not phone her tonight?* ◇ *'Shall we go out tonight?' 'Yes, why not?'*

wick /wɪk/ ***noun*** [C] the piece of string that burns in the middle of a CANDLE

wicked /ˈwɪkɪd/ ***adj.*** **1** morally bad; evil **2** (*informal*) slightly bad but in a way that is amusing and/or attractive: *a wicked sense of humour* **3** (*slang*) very good: *This song's wicked.* ▶ **wickedly** ***adv.*** ▶ **wickedness** ***noun*** [U]

wicker /ˈwɪkə(r)/ ***noun*** [U] long thin sticks of wood that are used to make BASKETS, furniture, etc.

wicket /ˈwɪkɪt/ ***noun*** [C] (SPORT) **1** (in cricket) either of the two sets of three upright sticks with pieces of wood lying across the top. **2** the area of ground between the two **wickets**

wide¹ /waɪd/ ***adj.*** **1** measuring a lot from one side to the other: *The road was not wide enough for two cars to pass.* ◇ *a wide river* OPP **narrow** ➲ noun **width** **2** measuring a particular distance from one side to the other: *The box was only 20 centimetres wide.* ◇ *How wide is the river?* **3** including a large number or variety of different people or things; covering a large area: *You're the nicest person in* ***the whole wide world!*** ◇ *a* ***wide range/choice/variety*** *of goods* ◇ *a manager with wide experience of industry* **4** fully open: *The children's eyes were wide with excitement.* **5** not near what you wanted to touch or hit: *His first serve was wide* (= the ball did not land inside the tennis court).

wide² /waɪd/ ***adv.*** as far or as much as possible; completely: *Open your mouth wide.* ◇ *It was late but she was still* ***wide awake***. ◇ *The front door was* ***wide open***.

widely ⊶ /ˈwaɪdli/ *adv.* **1** by a lot of people; in or to many places: *a widely held belief* ◇ *He has travelled widely in Asia.* ◇ *He's an educated, **widely-read** man* (=he has read a lot of books). **2** to a large degree; a lot: *Standards vary widely.*

widen /ˈwaɪdn/ *verb* [I,T] to become wider; to make sth wider: *The road widens just up ahead.*

ˌwide-ˈranging *adj.* covering a large area or many subjects: *a wide-ranging discussion*

widespread AW /ˈwaɪdspred/ *adj.* found or happening over a large area; affecting a large number of people: *The storm has caused widespread damage.*

widow /ˈwɪdəʊ/ *noun* [C] a woman whose husband has died and who has not married again ▸ **widowed** /ˈwɪdəʊd/ *adj.*: *She's been widowed for ten years now.*

widower /ˈwɪdəʊə(r)/ *noun* [C] a man whose wife has died and who has not married again

width ⊶ /wɪdθ; wɪtθ/ *noun* **1** [C,U] the amount that sth measures from one side or edge to the other: *The room is eight metres **in width**.* ◇ *The carpet is available in two different widths.* ➲ adjective **wide** ➲ picture at **dimension 2** [C] the distance from one side of a swimming pool to the other ➲ look at **length**, **breadth**

wield /wiːld/ *verb* [T] **1** to have and use power, authority, etc.: *She wields enormous power in the company.* **2** to hold and be ready to use a weapon: *Some of the men were wielding knives.*

wiener /ˈwiːnə(r)/ (*AmE*) = FRANKFURTER

wife ⊶ /waɪf/ *noun* [C] (*pl.* **wives** /waɪvz/) the woman to whom a man is married

Wi-Fi /ˈwaɪ faɪ/ *noun* [U] (COMPUTING) **Wireless Fidelity**; a system for sending data over computer networks using radio waves instead of wires

wig /wɪg/ *noun* [C] a covering made of real or false hair that you wear on your head

wiggle /ˈwɪgl/ *verb* [I,T] (*informal*) to move from side to side with small quick movements; to make sth do this: *You have to wiggle your hips in time to the music.* ▸ **wiggle** *noun* [C]

wiggly /ˈwɪgli/ *adj.* (of a line) having many curves in it ➲ picture at **line**

wigwam /ˈwɪgwæm/ *noun* [C] a type of tent that was used by some Native Americans in past times

wiki /ˈwɪki/ *noun* [C] (COMPUTING) a type of website that allows visitors to easily add and remove information and change the content if they want to

wild¹ ⊶ /waɪld/ *adj.* **1** (used about animals or plants) living or growing in natural conditions, not looked after by people: *wild animals/flowers/strawberries* **2** (used about an area of land) in its natural state; not changed by people: *wild moorland* **3** (used about a person or their behaviour or emotions) without control or discipline; slightly crazy: *The crowd **went wild** with excitement.* ◇ *They let their children **run wild*** (=behave in an uncontrolled way). **4** not carefully planned; not sensible or accurate: *She made **a wild guess**.* ◇ *wild accusations/rumours* **5** (*informal*) ~ (**about sb/sth**) liking sb/sth very much: *I'm not wild about their new house.* **6** (used about the weather) with strong winds; STORMY: *It was a wild night last night.* ▸ **wildness** *noun* [U]

wild² /waɪld/ *noun* **1 the wild** [sing.] (ENVIRONMENT) a natural environment that is not controlled by people: *the thrill of seeing elephants **in the wild*** **2 the wilds** [pl.] places that are far away from towns, where few people live: *They live somewhere out in the wilds.*

wilderness /ˈwɪldənəs/ *noun* [C, usually sing.] **1** a large area of land that has never been used for building on or for growing things: *The Antarctic is the world's last great wilderness.* **2** a place that people do not take care of or control: *Their garden is a wilderness.*

wildlife /ˈwaɪldlaɪf/ *noun* [U] birds, plants, animals, etc. that are wild and live in a natural environment

wildly ⊶ /ˈwaɪldli/ *adv.* **1** in a way that is not controlled: *She looked wildly around for an escape.* ◇ *His heart was beating wildly.* **2** extremely; very: *The story had been wildly exaggerated.*

wilful (*AmE also* **willful**) /ˈwɪlfl/ *adj.* **1** done deliberately although the person doing it knows that it is wrong: *wilful damage/neglect* **2** doing exactly what you want, no matter what other people think or say: *a wilful child* ▸ **wilfully** /-fəli/ *adv.*

will¹ ⊶ /wɪl/ *modal verb* (*short form* **'ll**; *negative* **will not**; *short form* **won't** /wəʊnt/) **1** used in forming the FUTURE TENSES: *He'll be here soon.* ◇ *I'm sure you'll pass your exam.* ◇ *I'll be sitting on the beach this time next week.* ◇ *Next Sunday, they'll have been in England for a year.* **2** used for showing that sb is offering sth or wants to do sth, or that sth is able to do sth: *'We need some more milk.' 'OK, I'll get it.'* ◇ *Why won't you tell me where you were last night?* ◇ *My car won't start.* **3** used for asking sb to do sth: *Will you sit down, please?* **4** used for ordering sb to do sb: *Will you all be quiet!* **5** used for saying that you think sth is probably true: *That'll be the postman at the door.* ◇ *He'll have left work by now, I suppose.* **6** (only in positive sentences) used for talking about sth annoying that sb always or very often does

PRONUNCIATION

You must put extra stress on 'will' and the short form cannot be used when you want to show that you are annoyed: *He **will** keep interrupting me when I'm trying to work.*

will² ⊶ /wɪl/ *noun* **1** [C,U] the power of the mind to choose what to do; a feeling of strong determination: *Both her children have got very strong wills.* ◇ *My father seems to have lost **the will to live**.* **2 -willed** (used to form compound adjectives) having the type of will mentioned: *a strong-willed/weak-willed person* **3** [sing.] what sb wants to happen in a particular situation: *My mother doesn't want to sell the house and I don't want to **go against her will**.* **4** [C] (LAW) a legal document in which you write down who should have your money and property after your death: *You really ought to **make a will**.* ◇ *Gran left us some money **in her will**.*

IDM **of your own free will** → FREE¹

will³ /wɪl/ *verb* [T] to use the power of your mind to do sth or to make sth happen: *He willed himself to carry on to the end of the race.*

willing ⊶ /ˈwɪlɪŋ/ *adj.* **1** ~ (**to do sth**) (not before a noun) happy to do sth; having no reason for not doing sth: *Are you willing to help us?* ◇ *She's **perfectly willing** to lend me her car.* ◇ *I'm not willing to take any risks.* **2** ready or pleased to help and not needing to be persuaded; enthusiastic: *a willing helper/volunteer* OPP **unwilling** ▸ **willingness** *noun* [U, sing.] ▸ **willingly** *adv.*

willow /ˈwɪləʊ/ (*also* **ˈwillow tree**) *noun* [C] a tree with long thin branches that hang down which grows near water

willpower /ˈwɪlpaʊə(r)/ ***noun*** [U] determination to do sth; strength of mind: *It takes a lot of willpower to give up smoking.*

willy-nilly /ˌwɪli ˈnɪli/ ***adv.*** (*informal*) **1** in a careless way without planning: *Don't spend your money willy-nilly.* **2** if you want to or not

wilt /wɪlt/ ***verb*** [I] (**BIOLOGY**) (used about a plant or flower) to bend and start to die, because of heat or a lack of water

wily /ˈwaɪli/ ***adj.*** clever at getting what you want **SYN cunning**

wimp /wɪmp/ ***noun*** [C] (*informal*) a weak person who has no courage or confidence ▶ **wimpish** ***adj.***

win ⊶ /wɪn/ ***verb*** (*pres. part.* **winning**; *pt, pp* **won** /wʌn/) **1** [I,T] to be the best, first or strongest in a race, game, competition, etc.: *to win a game/match/championship* ◇ *I never win at table tennis.* ◇ *Which party do you think will win the next election?* **2** [T] to get money, a prize, etc. as a result of success in a competition, race, etc.: *We won a trip to Australia.* ◇ *Who won the gold medal?* ◇ *He won the jackpot in the lottery.* **3** [T] to get sth by hard work, great effort, etc.: *Her brilliant performance won her a great deal of praise.* ◇ *to win support for a plan* ▶ **win** ***noun*** [C]: *We have had two wins and a draw so far this season.*

IDM win/lose the toss → TOSS

you can't win (*informal*) there is no way of being completely successful or of pleasing everyone: *Whatever you do you will upset somebody. You can't win.*

PHR V win sb over/round (to sth) to persuade sb to support or agree with you: *They're against the proposal at the moment, but I'm sure we can win them over.*

wince /wɪns/ ***verb*** [I] to make a sudden quick movement (usually with a part of your face) to show you are feeling pain or embarrassment

winch /wɪntʃ/ ***noun*** [C] a machine that lifts or pulls heavy objects using a thick chain, rope, etc. ▶ **winch** ***verb*** [T]: *The injured climber was winched up into a helicopter.*

wind[1] ⊶ /wɪnd/ ***noun*** **1** [C,U] (**GEOGRAPHY**) air that is moving across the surface of the earth: *There was a strong wind blowing.* ◇ *A* ***gust of wind*** *blew his hat off.* ◇ *gale-force/strong/high winds* **2** [U] the breath that you need for doing exercise or playing a musical instrument: *She stopped running to get her wind back.* **3** [U] (**HEALTH**) gas that is formed in your stomach: *The baby cries when he has wind.* **4** [U] (**MUSIC**) the group of instruments in an ORCHESTRA that you blow into to produce the sound

IDM get wind of sth (*informal*) to hear about sth that is secret

wind[2] /wɪnd/ ***verb*** [T] **1** to cause sb to have difficulty in breathing: *The punch in the stomach winded her.* **2** to help a baby get rid of painful gas in the stomach by rubbing or gently hitting its back

wind[3] ⊶ /waɪnd/ ***verb*** (*pt, pp* **wound** /waʊnd/) **1** [I] (used about a road, path, etc.) to have a lot of bends or curves in it: *The path winds down the cliff to the sea.* **2** [T] to put sth long round sth else several times: *She wound the bandage around his arm.* **3** [T] to make sth work or move by turning a key, handle, etc.: *He wound the car window down.* ◇ *Wind the tape on a bit to the next song.*

PHR V wind down (about a person) to rest and relax after a period of hard work, worry, etc. ➲ look at **unwind**

wind up to find yourself in a place or situation that you did not intend to be in: *We got lost and wound up in a dangerous-looking part of town.*

wind sb up to annoy sb until they become angry

wind sth up to finish, stop or close sth

wind-blown /ˈwɪnd bləʊn/ ***adj.*** **1** carried from one place to another by the wind **2** made untidy by the wind: *wind-blown hair*

wind chill /ˈwɪnd tʃɪl/ ***noun*** [U] (**GEOGRAPHY**) the effect of low temperature combined with wind on sb/sth: *Take the* ***wind-chill factor*** *into account.*

windfall /ˈwɪndfɔːl/ ***noun*** [C] an amount of money that you win or receive unexpectedly

wind farm /ˈwɪnd fɑːm/ ***noun*** [C] (**ENVIRONMENT**) an area of land on which there are a lot of WINDMILLS or WIND TURBINES for producing electricity

winding /ˈwaɪndɪŋ/ ***adj.*** with bends or curves in it: *a winding road through the hills*

ˈwind instrument ***noun*** [C] (**MUSIC**) a musical instrument that you play by blowing through it

windmill

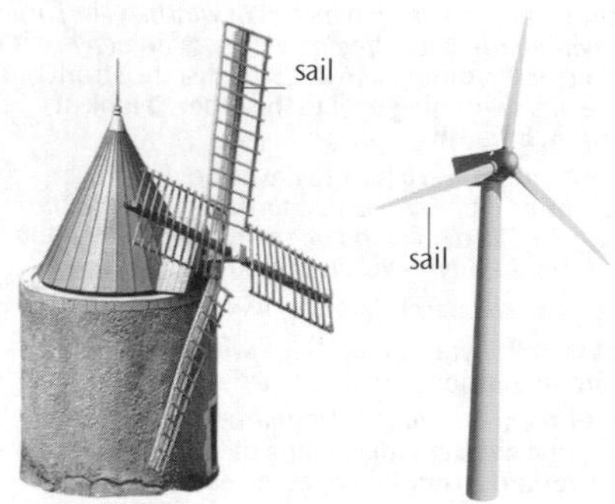

windmill /ˈwɪndmɪl/ ***noun*** [C] a tall building or structure with SAILS (=long parts that turn in the wind). In past times **windmills** were used for making flour from grain, but now they are used mainly for producing electricity.

window ⊶ /ˈwɪndəʊ/ ***noun*** [C] **1** the opening in a building, car, etc. that you can see through and that lets light in. A window usually has glass in it: *Open the window. It's hot in here.* ◇ *a shop window* ◇ *These windows need cleaning.* **2** (**COMPUTING**) an area inside a frame on a computer screen, that has a particular program operating in it, or shows a particular type of information: *to create/open/close a window* **3** a time when you have not arranged to do anything and so are free to meet sb, etc.

windowpane /ˈwɪndəʊpeɪn/ ***noun*** [C] one piece of glass in a window

ˈwindow-shopping ***noun*** [U] looking at things in shop windows without intending to buy anything

windowsill /ˈwɪndəʊsɪl/ (*also* **ˈwindow ledge**) ***noun*** [C] the narrow shelf at the bottom of a window, either inside or outside

windpipe /ˈwɪndpaɪp/ ***noun*** [C] (**ANATOMY**) the tube that takes air from your throat to the lungs **SYN trachea** ➲ picture on **page 80**

windscreen /ˈwɪndskriːn/ (*AmE* **windshield** /ˈwɪndʃiːld/) ***noun*** [C] the window in the front of a vehicle

ˈwindscreen wiper (*also* **wiper** *AmE* **ˈwindshield wiper**) ***noun*** [C] one of the two moving arms (**blades**) that remove water, snow, etc. from a WINDSCREEN

windsurf /ˈwɪndsɜːf/ ***verb*** [I] to move over water standing on a special board with a sail ▸ **windsurfing** ***noun*** [U]

windsurfer /ˈwɪndsɜːfə(r)/ ***noun*** [C] **1** (*also* **sailboard**) a board with a sail that you stand on as it moves over the surface of the water, pushed by the wind **2** a person who rides on a board like this

windswept /ˈwɪndswept/ ***adj.*** **1** (used about a place) that often has strong winds: *a windswept coastline* **2** looking untidy because you have been in a strong wind: *windswept hair*

wind turbine /ˈwɪnd tɜːbaɪn/ ***noun*** [C] (ENVIRONMENT) a type of modern WINDMILL used for producing electricity ➲ picture at **windmill**

windward /ˈwɪndwəd/ ***adj.*** on the side of a hill, building, etc. towards which the wind is blowing ➲ look at **lee**, **leeward**

windy /ˈwɪndi/ ***adj.*** (**windier**; **windiest**) with a lot of wind: *a windy day*

wine 🔑 /waɪn/ ***noun*** [C,U] an alcoholic drink that is made from GRAPES, or sometimes other fruit: *sweet/dry wine* ◇ *German wines*

winegrower /ˈwaɪngrəʊə(r)/ ***noun*** [C] (AGRICULTURE) a person who grows GRAPES (= green or purple fruit) for making wine

winemaker /ˈwaɪnmeɪkə(r)/ ***noun*** [C] a person who produces wine ▸ **winemaking** /ˈwaɪnmeɪkɪŋ/ ***noun*** [U]

ˈ**wine waiter** ***noun*** [C] (TOURISM) a person who works in a restaurant serving wine and helping customers to decide which wine to choose **SYN** **sommelier**

wing 🔑 /wɪŋ/ ***noun*** **1** [C] (BIOLOGY) one of the two parts that a bird, insect, etc. uses for flying: *The chicken ran around flapping its wings.* ➲ picture on **page 28** **2** [C] one of the two long parts that stick out from the side of a plane and support it in the air ➲ picture at **plane** **3** [C] a part of a building that sticks out from the main part or that was added on to the main part: *the maternity wing of the hospital* **4** (*AmE* **fender**) [C] the part of the outside of a car that covers the top of the wheels: *a wing mirror* (= fixed to the side of the car) **5** [C, usually sing.] (POLITICS) a group of people in a political party that have particular beliefs or opinions: *the right wing of the Conservative Party* ➲ look at **left-wing**, **right-wing** **6** [C] (SPORT) (in football, etc.) the part at each side of the area where the game is played: *to play on the wing* **7** (*also* **winger**) [C] (in football, etc.) a person who plays in an attacking position at one of the sides of the field **8 the wings** [pl.] (ARTS AND MEDIA) (in a theatre) the area at the sides of the stage where you cannot be seen by the audience

IDM **take sb under your wing** to take care of and help sb who has less experience than you

wingspan /ˈwɪŋspæn/ ***noun*** [C] the distance between the end of one wing and the end of the other when the wings are fully stretched

wink /wɪŋk/ ***verb*** [I] ~ **(at sb)** to close and open one eye very quickly, usually as a signal to sb ➲ look at **blink** ▸ **wink** ***noun*** [C]: *He smiled and gave the little girl a wink.* ◇ *I didn't sleep a wink* (= not at all).

IDM **forty winks** → FORTY

winner 🔑 /ˈwɪnə(r)/ ***noun*** [C] **1** a person or animal that wins a competition, game, race, etc.: *The winner of the competition will be announced next week.* **2** (*informal*) something that is likely to be successful: *I think your idea is a winner.* **3** (SPORT) a goal that wins a match, a hit that wins a point, etc.: *Anelka scored the winner in the last minute.*

winning[1] 🔑 → WIN

winning[2] 🔑 /ˈwɪnɪŋ/ ***adj.*** **1** that wins or has won sth, for example a race or competition: *The winning ticket is number 65.* ◇ *the winning horse* **2** attractive in a way that makes other people like you: *a winning smile*

winnings /ˈwɪnɪŋz/ ***noun*** [pl.] money that sb wins in a competition, game, etc.

winter 🔑 /ˈwɪntə(r)/ ***noun*** [C,U] the coldest season of the year between autumn and spring: *It snows a lot here* ***in winter***. ◇ *a cold winter's day* ◇ *We went skiing in France last winter.* ➲ picture at **season** ▸ **wintry** /ˈwɪntri/ ***adj.***: *wintry weather*

ˌ**winter** ˈ**sports** ***noun*** [pl.] sports which take place on snow or ice, for example SKIING and SKATING

wintertime /ˈwɪntətaɪm/ ***noun*** [U] the period or season of winter

wipe[1] /waɪp/ ***verb*** [T] **1** to clean or dry sth by rubbing it with a cloth, etc.: *She stopped crying and wiped her eyes with a tissue.* ◇ *Could you wipe the table, please?* **2** ~ **sth from/off sth**; ~ **sth away/off/up** to remove sth by rubbing it: *He wiped the sweat from his forehead.* ◇ *Wipe up the milk you spilled.* **3** ~ **sth (off) (sth)** to remove sound, information or images from sth: *I accidentally wiped the tape.* ◇ *I tried to wipe the memory from my mind.*

PHR V **wipe sth out** to destroy sth completely: *Whole villages were wiped out in the bombing raids.*

wipe[2] /waɪp/ ***noun*** [C] **1** the action of **wiping**: *He gave the table a quick wipe.* **2** a piece of paper or thin cloth that has been made wet with a special liquid and is used for cleaning sth: *a box of baby wipes*

wiper /ˈwaɪpə(r)/ = WINDSCREEN WIPER

wire[1] 🔑 /ˈwaɪə(r)/ ***noun*** [C,U] **1** metal in the form of thin thread; a piece of this: *a piece of wire* ◇ *Twist those two wires together.* ◇ *a wire fence* **2** (PHYSICS) a piece of wire that is used to carry electricity: *telephone wires* ➲ picture at **cable**

wire[2] /ˈwaɪə(r)/ ***verb*** [T] **1** ~ **sth (up) (to sth)** (PHYSICS) to connect sth to a supply of electricity or to a piece of electrical equipment by using wires: *to wire a plug* ◇ *The microphone was wired up to a loudspeaker.* **2** ~ **sth (to sb)**; ~ **sb sth** (FINANCE) to send money to sb's bank account using an electronic system: *The bank's going to wire me the money.* **3** to join two things together using wire

wireless /ˈwaɪələs/ ***adj.*** (COMPUTING) not using wires: *wireless technology/communications*

ˌ**wire** ˈ**wool** = STEEL WOOL

wiring /ˈwaɪərɪŋ/ ***noun*** [U] the system of wires that supplies electricity to rooms in a building

wiry /ˈwaɪəri/ ***adj.*** (used about a person) small and thin but strong

wisdom /ˈwɪzdəm/ ***noun*** [U] the ability to make sensible decisions and judgements because of your knowledge or experience: *I don't see the wisdom of this plan* (= I do not think that it is a good idea). ➲ adjective **wise**

ˈ**wisdom tooth** ***noun*** [C] (ANATOMY) one of the four teeth at the back of your mouth that appear when you are about 20 years old ➲ picture at **tooth**

wise 🔑 /waɪz/ ***adj.*** having the knowledge or experience to make good and sensible decisions and judgements: *a wise choice* ◇ *It would be wiser to wait for a few days.* ▸ **wisely** ***adv.***

wish[1] 🔑 /wɪʃ/ ***verb*** **1** [I] ~ **(that)** (often with a verb in the past tense) to want sth that cannot now happen or that probably will not happen: *I wish I* *had listened more carefully.* ◇ *I wish that I knew what was going to happen.* ◇ *I wish I was taller.* ◇ *I wish I could help you.* **2** [I] ~ **for sth** to say to yourself that you want sth that can only happen by good luck or chance: *She wished for her mother to get better.* **3** [I,T] (*formal*) ~ (**to do sth**) to want to do sth: *I wish to make a complaint about one of the doctors.* **4** [T] to say that you hope sb will have sth: *I rang him up to* ***wish*** *him* ***a happy birthday***. ◇ *We* ***wish*** *you* ***all the best*** *for your future career.*

wish² ⊶ /wɪʃ/ ***noun* 1** [C] a feeling that you want to have sth or that sth should happen: *I have no wish to see her ever again.* ◇ *Doctors should respect the patient's wishes.* **2** [C] a try at making sth happen by thinking hard about it, especially in stories when it often happens by magic: *Throw a coin into the fountain and* ***make a wish***. ◇ *My wish came true* (= I got what I asked for). **3 wishes** [pl.] a hope that sb will be happy or have good luck: *Please* ***give*** *your parents* ***my best wishes***. ◇ *Best wishes* (= at the end of a letter)

ˌ**wishful ˈthinking** ***noun*** [U] ideas that are based on what you would like, not on facts

wisp /wɪsp/ ***noun*** [C] **1** a few pieces of hair that are together **2** a small amount of smoke ▶ **wispy** ***adj.***

wistful /ˈwɪstfl/ ***adj.*** feeling or showing sadness because you cannot have what you want: *a wistful sigh* ▶ **wistfully** /-fəli/ ***adv.***

wit /wɪt/ ***noun*** [U] **1** the ability to use words in a clever and amusing way ➲ adjective **witty** **2 -witted** (used to form compound adjectives) having a particular type of intelligence: *quick-witted* ◇ *slow-witted* **3** (*also* **wits** [pl.]) the fact of being clever; intelligence: *The game of chess is essentially* ***a battle of wits***.

> **WORD FAMILY**
> **wit** *noun*
> **witty** *adj.*
> **witticism** *noun*
> **outwit** *verb*

IDM **at your wits' end** not knowing what to do or say because you are very worried

keep your wits about you to be ready to act in a difficult situation

witch /wɪtʃ/ ***noun*** [C] (in past times and in stories) a woman who is thought to have magic powers ➲ look at **wizard**

witchcraft /ˈwɪtʃkrɑːft/ ***noun*** [U] the use of magic powers, especially evil ones

ˈ**witch-hunt** ***noun*** [C] the activity of trying to find and punish people who hold opinions that are thought to be unacceptable or dangerous to society

with ⊶ /wɪð; wɪθ/ ***prep.* 1** in the company of sb/sth; in or to the same place as sb/sth: *I live with my parents.* ◇ *Are you coming with us?* ◇ *I talked about the problem with my tutor.* **2** having or carrying sth: *a girl with red hair* ◇ *a house with a garden* ◇ *the man with the suitcase* **3** using sth: *Cut it with a knife.* ◇ *I did it with his help.* **4** used for saying what fills, covers, etc. sth: *Fill the bowl with water.* ◇ *His hands were covered with oil.* **5** in competition with sb/sth; against sb/sth: *He's always arguing with his brother.* ◇ *I usually play tennis with my sister.* **6** towards, concerning or compared with sb/sth: *Is he angry with us?* ◇ *There's a problem with my visa.* ◇ *Compared with Canada, England has mild winters.* **7** including sth: *The price is for two people with all meals.* **8** used to say how sth happens or is done: *Open this parcel with care.* ◇ *to greet sb with a smile* **9** because of sth; as a result of sth: *We were shivering with cold.* ◇ *With all the problems we've got, we're not going to finish on time.* **10** in the care of sb: *We left the keys with the neighbours.* **11** agreeing with or supporting sb/sth: *We've got everybody with us on this issue.* OPP **against** **12** at the same time as sth: *I can't concentrate with you watching me all the time.*

IDM **be with sb** to be able to follow what sb is saying: *I'm not quite with you. Say it again.*

withdraw ⊶ /wɪðˈdrɔː/ ***verb*** (*pt* **withdrew** /-ˈdruː/; *pp* **withdrawn** /-ˈdrɔːn/) **1** [I,T] ~ (**sb/sth**) (**from sth**) to move or order sb to move back or away from a place: *The troops withdrew from the town.* **2** [T] to remove sth or take sth away: *to withdraw an offer/a statement* **3** [T] to take money out of a bank account: *How much would you like to withdraw?* ➲ look at **deposit** **4** [I] to decide not to take part in sth: *Jackson withdrew from the race at the last minute.*

withdrawal /wɪðˈdrɔːəl/ ***noun* 1** [C,U] moving or being moved back or away from a place: *the withdrawal of troops from the war zone* **2** [C] taking money out of your bank account; the amount of money that you take out: *to* ***make a withdrawal*** **3** [U] the act of stopping doing sth, especially taking a drug: *When he gave up alcohol he suffered severe* ***withdrawal symptoms***.

withdrawn /wɪðˈdrɔːn/ ***adj.*** (used about a person) very quiet and not wanting to talk to other people

wither /ˈwɪðə(r)/ ***verb* 1** [I,T] ~ (**sth**) (**away**) (used about plants) to become dry and die; to make a plant do this: *The plants withered in the hot sun.* **2** [I] ~ (**away**) to become weaker then disappear: *This type of industry will wither away in the years to come.*

withering /ˈwɪðərɪŋ/ ***adj.*** done to make sb feel silly or embarrassed: *a withering look*

withhold /wɪðˈhəʊld/ ***verb*** [T] (*pt, pp* **withheld** /-ˈheld/) (*formal*) ~ **sth** (**from sb/sth**) to refuse to give sth to sb: *to withhold information from the police*

within ⊶ /wɪˈðɪn/ ***prep., adv.* 1** in a period not longer than a particular length of time: *I'll be back within an hour.* ◇ *She got married, found a job and moved house, all within a week.* **2** ~ **sth** (**of sth**) not further than a particular distance from sth: *The house is within a kilometre of the station.* **3** not outside the limits of sb/sth: *Each department must keep within its budget.* **4** (*formal*) inside sb/sth: *The anger was still there deep within him.*

without ⊶ /wɪˈðaʊt/ ***prep., adv.* 1** not having or showing sth: *Don't go out without a coat on.* ◇ *He spoke without much enthusiasm.* ◇ *If there's no salt we'll have to manage without.* **2** not using or being with sb/sth: *I drink my coffee without milk.* ◇ *Can you see without your glasses?* ◇ *Don't leave without me.* **3** used with a verb in the *-ing* form to mean 'not': *She left without saying goodbye.* ◇ *I used her phone without her knowing.*

withstand /wɪðˈstænd/ ***verb*** [T] (*pt, pp* **withstood** /-ˈstʊd/) (*formal*) to be strong enough not to break, give up, be damaged, etc.: *These animals can withstand very high temperatures.*

witness¹ ⊶ /ˈwɪtnəs/ ***noun*** [C] **1** (*also* **eyewitness**) a ~ (**to sth**) a person who sees sth happen and who can tell other people about it later: *There were two witnesses to the accident.* **2** (LAW) a person who appears in a court of law to say what they have seen or what they know about sb/sth: *a witness for the defence/prosecution* **3** (LAW) a person who sees sb sign an official document and who then signs it himself/herself

IDM **bear witness (to sth)** → BEAR²

witness² ⊶ /ˈwɪtnəs/ ***verb*** [T] **1** to see sth happen and be able to tell other people about it later: *to witness a murder* **2** (LAW) to see sb sign an official document and then sign it yourself: *to witness a will*

'witness box (*AmE* **'witness-stand**, *BrE and AmE also* **stand**) ***noun*** [C] (LAW) the place in court where people stand to give evidence

witticism /'wɪtɪsɪzəm/ ***noun*** a clever and amusing remark

witty /'wɪti/ ***adj.*** (**wittier**; **wittiest**) clever and amusing; using words in a clever way: *a very witty speech* ➲ noun **wit**

wives plural of **wife**

wizard /'wɪzəd/ ***noun*** [C] (in stories) a man who is believed to have magic powers ➲ look at **witch**, **magician**

wk ***abbr.*** (*pl.* **wks**) week

WMD /ˌdʌblju: em 'di:/ ***abbr.*** =WEAPON OF MASS DESTRUCTION

WNW ***abbr.*** west-north-west

wobble /'wɒbl/ ***verb*** [I,T] to move from side to side in a way that is not steady; to make sb/sth do this: *Put something under the leg of the table. It's wobbling.* ◇ *Stop wobbling the desk. I can't write.* ▶ **wobbly** /'wɒbli/ ***adj.***

woe /wəʊ/ ***noun*** (*formal*) **1 woes** [pl.] the problems that sb has **2** [U] (*old-fashioned*) great unhappiness
IDM **woe betide sb** used as a warning that there will be trouble if sb does/does not do a particular thing: *Woe betide anyone who yawns while the boss is talking.*

wok /wɒk/ ***noun*** [C] a large pan that is shaped like a bowl and used for cooking Chinese food

woke past tense of **wake**[1]

woken past participle of **wake**[1]

wolf /wʊlf/ ***noun*** [C] (*pl.* **wolves** /wʊlvz/) a wild animal that looks like a dog and that lives and hunts in a group (**pack**)

woman 🔑 /'wʊmən/ ***noun*** [C] (*pl.* **women** /'wɪmɪn/) **1** an adult female person: *men, women and children* ◇ *Would you prefer to see a woman doctor?* **2 -woman** (in compounds) a woman who does a particular activity: *a businesswoman*

womanhood /'wʊmənhʊd/ ***noun*** [U] the state of being a woman

womanly /'wʊmənli/ ***adj.*** having qualities considered typical of a woman

womb /wu:m/ ***noun*** [C] (ANATOMY) the part of a woman or female animal where a baby grows before it is born SYN **uterus** ➲ picture at **embryo**

won past tense, past participle of **win**

wonder[1] 🔑 /'wʌndə(r)/ ***verb*** **1** [I,T] ~ (about sth) to want to know sth; to ask yourself questions about sth: *I wonder what the new teacher will be like.* ◇ *Vesna's been gone a long time – I wonder if she's all right.* ◇ *It was something that she had been wondering about for a long time.* **2** [T] used as a polite way of asking a question or of asking sb to do sth: *I wonder if you could help me.* ◇ *I was wondering if you'd like to come to dinner at our house.* **3** [I,T] ~ (**at sth**) to feel great surprise or admiration: *We wondered at the speed with which he worked.* ◇ *'She was very angry.' 'I don't wonder* (=I'm not surprised). *She had a right to be.'*

wonder[2] /'wʌndə(r)/ ***noun*** **1** [U] a feeling of surprise and admiration: *The children just stared* ***in wonder*** *at the acrobats.* **2** [C] something that causes you to feel surprise or admiration: *the wonders of modern technology*
IDM **do wonders (for sb/sth)** to have a very good effect on sb/sth: *Working in Mexico did wonders for my Spanish.*
it's a wonder (that)... it's surprising that...: *It's a wonder we managed to get here on time, with all the traffic.*
no wonder it is not surprising: *You've been out every evening this week. No wonder you're tired.*

wonderful 🔑 /'wʌndəfl/ ***adj.*** extremely good; FANTASTIC: *What wonderful weather!* ◇ *It's wonderful to see you again.* ▶ **wonderfully** /-fəli/ ***adv.***

won't short for WILL NOT

wood 🔑 /wʊd/ ***noun*** **1** [U, C] the hard substance that trees are made of: *He chopped some wood for the fire.* ◇ *Pine is a softwood.* ➲ picture at **tree** **2** [C] (often plural) (GEOGRAPHY) an area of land that is covered with trees. A wood is smaller than a forest: *a walk in the woods*
IDM **touch wood**; (*AmE*) **knock on wood** an expression that people use (often while touching a piece of wood) to prevent bad luck: *I've been driving here for 20 years and I haven't had an accident yet – touch wood!*

woodcut /'wʊdkʌt/ ***noun*** [C] (ART) a print that is made from a pattern cut in a piece of wood

wooded /'wʊdɪd/ ***adj.*** (GEOGRAPHY) (used about an area of land) having a lot of trees growing on it

wooden 🔑 /'wʊdn/ ***adj.*** made of wood

woodland /'wʊdlənd/ ***noun*** [C,U] (GEOGRAPHY) land that has a lot of trees growing on it: *The village is surrounded by woodland.* ◇ *woodland birds*

woodlouse /'wʊdlaʊs/ ***noun*** [C] (*pl.* **woodlice** /'wʊdlaɪs/) (BIOLOGY) a small grey creature like an insect, with a hard shell, that lives in decaying wood or damp soil ➲ picture on **page 29**

'wood pulp ***noun*** [U] wood that has been broken into small pieces and pressed until it is soft. It is used for making paper.

woodwind /'wʊdwɪnd/ ***noun*** [sing., with sing. or pl. verb] (MUSIC) the set of musical instruments that you play by blowing into them

woodwork /'wʊdwɜ:k/ ***noun*** [U] **1** the parts of a building that are made of wood such as the doors, stairs, etc. **2** the activity or skill of making things out of wood

woodworm /'wʊdwɜ:m/ ***noun*** **1** [C] a small, soft, fat creature, the young form of a BEETLE, that eats wood, making a lot of small holes in it **2** [U] the damage to wood caused by these creatures

woof /wʊf/ ***noun*** [C] (*informal*) used for describing the sound that a dog makes (**a bark**)

wool 🔑 /wʊl/ ***noun*** [U] **1** the soft thick hair of sheep **2** thick thread or cloth that is made from **wool**: *The sweater is 50% wool and 50% acrylic.* ➲ look at **cotton wool**

woollen (*AmE* **woolen**) /'wʊlən/ ***adj.*** made of wool: *a warm woollen jumper*

woolly (*AmE* **wooly**) /'wʊli/ ***adj.*** like wool or made of wool: *The dog had a thick woolly coat.* ◇ *long woolly socks*

word[1] 🔑 /wɜ:d/ ***noun*** **1** [C] (LANGUAGE) a sound or letter or group of sounds or letters that expresses a particular meaning: *What's the Greek word for 'mouth'?* ◇ *What does this word mean?* **2** [C] a thing that you say; a short statement or comment: *Could I* ***have a word*** *with you in private?* ◇ *Don't say a word about this to anyone.* **3** [sing.] a promise: *I* ***give you***

my word that I won't tell anyone. ◇ *I'll **keep my word** to her and lend her the money.* ◇ *You'll just have to trust him not to **go back on his word**.*

IDM **a dirty word** → DIRTY[1]
not breathe a word (of/about sth) (to sb) → BREATHE
not get a word in edgeways to not be able to interrupt when sb else is talking so that you can say sth yourself
have, etc. the last word → LAST[1]
in other words → OTHER
lost for words → LOST[2]
put in a (good) word for sb to say sth good about sb to sb else: *If you could put in a good word for me I might stand a better chance of getting the job.*
take sb's word for it to believe what sb says without any proof
word for word 1 repeating sth exactly: *Sharon repeated word for word what he had told her.* **2** (LANGUAGE) translating each word separately, not looking at the general meaning: *a word-for-word translation*

word[2] /wɜːd/ ***verb*** [T] (often passive) (LANGUAGE) to write or say sth using particular words: *The statement was carefully worded so that nobody would be offended by it.*

'word class ***noun*** [C] (LANGUAGE) one of the classes into which words are divided according to their grammar, such as noun, verb, adjective, etc. SYN **part of speech**

wording /ˈwɜːdɪŋ/ ***noun*** [sing.] (LANGUAGE) the words that you use to express sth: *The wording of the contract was vague.* ➲ note at **language**

,word-'perfect ***adj.*** able to say sth that you have learnt from memory, without making a mistake

'word processing ***noun*** [U] (COMPUTING) the use of a computer to write, store and print a piece of text: *I mainly use the computer for word processing.*

,word 'processor ***noun*** [C] (COMPUTING) a type of small computer that you can use for writing letters, reports, etc. You can correct or change what you have written before you print it out.

wore past tense of **wear[1]**

work[1] ⊶ /wɜːk/ ***verb* 1** [I,T] ~ (as sth) (for sb); ~ (at/on sth); ~ (to do sth) to do sth which needs physical or mental effort, in order to earn money or to achieve sth: *She's working for a large firm in Glasgow.* ◇ *I'd like to work as a newspaper reporter.* ◇ *Doctors often work extremely long hours.* ◇ *My teacher said that I wouldn't pass the exam unless I worked harder.* ◇ *I hear she's working on a new novel.* ◇ *I'm going to stay in tonight and work at my project.* **2** [T] to make yourself/sb work, especially very hard: *The coach works the players very hard in training.* **3** [I,T] (used about a machine, etc.) to function; to make sth function; to operate: *Our telephone hasn't been working for several days.* ◇ *We still don't really understand how the brain works.* ◇ *Can you show me how to work the photocopier?* **4** [I] to have the result or effect that you want; to be successful: *Your idea sounds good but I don't think it will really work.* ◇ *The heat today could work in favour of the African runners.* **5** [I,T] to move gradually to a new position or state: *Engineers check the plane daily, because nuts and screws can **work loose**.* ◇ *I watched the snail **work its way** up the wall.* **6** [I,T] to use materials to make a model, a picture, etc.: *He worked the clay into the shape of a horse.* ◇ *She usually works in/with oils or acrylics.*

IDM **work/perform miracles** → MIRACLE
work/sweat your guts out → GUT[1]
work to rule → RULE[1]

PHR V **work out 1** to develop or progress, especially in a good way: *I hope things work out for you.* **2** to do physical exercises in order to keep your body fit: *We work out to music at my exercise class.*
work out (at) to come to a particular result or total after everything has been calculated: *If we divide the work between us it'll work out at about four hours each.*
work sb out to understand sb: *I've never been able to work her out.*
work sth out 1 to find the answer to sth; to solve sth: *I can't work out how to do this.* **2** (MATHEMATICS) to calculate sth: *I worked out the total cost.* **3** to plan sth: *Have you worked out the route through France?*
work up to sth to develop or progress to sth: *Start with 15 minutes' exercise and gradually work up to 30.*
work sth up to develop or improve sth with effort: *I'm trying to work up the energy to go out.*
work sb/yourself up (into sth) to make sb/yourself become angry, excited, upset, etc.: *He had worked himself up into a state of anxiety about his interview.*

work[2] ⊶ /wɜːk/ ***noun* 1** [U] the job that you do, especially in order to earn money; the place where you do your job: *It is very difficult to **find work** in this city.* ◇ *He's been **out of work*** (=without a job) *for six months.* ◇ *When do you **start work**?* ◇ *I'll ask if I can **leave work** early today.* ◇ *I **go to work** at 8 o'clock.* ◇ *The people **at work** gave me some flowers for my birthday.* ◇ *Police work is not as exciting as it looks on TV.*

> **RELATED VOCABULARY**
>
> **work**
>
> **Work** is an uncountable noun. In some contexts we have to use **job**: *I've found work at the hospital.* ◇ *I've got a new job at the hospital.*
>
> **Employment** is the state of having a paid job and is more formal and official than **work** or **job**: *Many married women are in part-time employment.*
>
> **Occupation** is the word used on forms to ask what you are or what job you do: *Occupation: student. Occupation: bus driver.*
>
> A **profession** is a job that needs special training and higher education: *the medical profession.*
>
> A **trade** is a job that you do with your hands and that needs special skill: *He's a carpenter by trade.*

2 [U] something that requires physical or mental effort that you do in order to achieve sth: *Her success is due to sheer **hard work**.* ◇ *I've got a lot of work to do today.* ◇ *We hope to **start work on** the project next week.* **3** [U] something that you are working on or have produced: *a piece of written work* ◇ *The teacher marked their work.* ◇ *Is this all your own work?* **4** [C] (ARTS AND MEDIA, LITERATURE) a book, painting, piece of music, etc.: *an early work by Picasso* ◇ *the complete works of Shakespeare* **5 works** [pl.] the act of building or repairing sth: *The roadworks are causing long traffic jams.* **6 works** [C, with sing. or pl. verb] (often in compounds) a factory: *The steelworks is/are closing down.* ➲ note at **factory 7** [U] the use of force to produce movement

IDM **get/go/set to work (on sth)** to begin; to make a start (on sth)

workable /ˈwɜːkəbl/ ***adj.*** that can be used successfully; practical: *a workable plan/solution*

workaholic /ˌwɜːkəˈhɒlɪk/ ***noun*** [C] a person who loves work and does too much of it

workbench /ˈwɜːkbentʃ/ *noun* [C] a long heavy table used for doing practical jobs, working with tools, etc. ➲ picture at **vice**

workbook /ˈwɜːkbʊk/ *noun* [C] (EDUCATION) a book with questions and exercises in it that you use when you are studying sth

workday /ˈwɜːkdeɪ/ *noun* [C] **1** (*AmE*) = WORKING DAY (1): *an 8-hour workday* **2** = WORKING DAY (2): *workday traffic*

worker 🔑 /ˈwɜːkə(r)/ *noun* [C] **1** (often in compounds) a person who works, especially one who does a particular kind of work: *factory/office/farm workers ◇ skilled/manual workers* **2** a person who is employed to do physical work rather than organizing things or managing people: *Workers' representatives will meet management today to discuss the pay dispute.* **3** a person who works in a particular way: *a slow/fast worker*

workforce /ˈwɜːkfɔːs/ *noun* [C, with sing. or pl. verb] **1** (ECONOMICS) the total number of people who work in a company, factory, etc. **2** (SOCIAL STUDIES) the total number of people in a country who are able to work: *Ten per cent of the workforce is/are unemployed.*

working 🔑 /ˈwɜːkɪŋ/ *adj.* (only *before* a noun) **1** employed; having a job: *the problems of childcare for working mothers* **2** connected with your job: *He stayed with the same company for the whole of his **working life**. ◇ The company offers excellent working conditions.* **3** good enough to be used, although it could be improved: *We are looking for someone with **a working knowledge** of French.*
IDM **in working order** → ORDER[1]

ˌ**working ˈcapital** *noun* [U] (BUSINESS) the money that is needed to run a business rather than the money that is used to buy buildings and equipment when starting the business ➲ look at **venture capital**

the ˌworking ˈclass *noun* [sing.] (*also* **the ˌworking ˈclasses** [pl.]) (SOCIAL STUDIES) the group of people in a society who do not have much money or power and who usually do physical work, especially in industry: *unemployment among the working class*
▶ ˌ**working ˈclass** *adj.*: *They're working class. ◇ a working-class family* ➲ look at **the middle class**, **the upper class**

ˌ**working ˈday** *noun* [C] (*BrE*) **1** (*AmE* **workday**) the part of a day during which you work: *I spend most of my working day sitting at a desk.* **2** (*also* **workday**) a day on which you usually work or on which most people usually work: *Sunday is a normal working day for me. ◇ Allow two working days* (= not Saturday or Sunday) *for delivery.*

workings /ˈwɜːkɪŋz/ *noun* [pl.] the way in which a machine, an organization, etc. operates: *It's very difficult to understand the workings of the legal system.*

ˌ**working ˈweek** (*AmE* **workweek** /ˈwɜːkwiːk/) *noun* [C] the total amount of time that you spend at work during the week: *a 40-hour working week*

workload /ˈwɜːkləʊd/ *noun* [C] the amount of work that you have to do: *She often gets home late when she has a **heavy workload**.*

workman /ˈwɜːkmən/ *noun* [C] (*pl.* **-men** /-mən/) a man who works with his hands, especially at building or making things

workmanlike /ˈwɜːkmənlaɪk/ *adj.* done, made, etc. very well, but not original or exciting: *The leading actor gave a workmanlike performance.*

workmanship /ˈwɜːkmənʃɪp/ *noun* [U] the skill with which sth is made

ˌ**work of ˈart** *noun* [C] (*pl.* **works of art**) (ART, LITERATURE, MUSIC) a very good painting, book, piece of music, etc. ➲ look at **art**

workout /ˈwɜːkaʊt/ *noun* [C] a period of physical exercise, for example when you are training for a sport or keeping fit: *She does a twenty-minute workout every morning.*

workplace /ˈwɜːkpleɪs/ *noun* [sing.] **the workplace** the office, factory, etc. where people work: *the introduction of new technology into the workplace*

worksheet /ˈwɜːkʃiːt/ *noun* [C] (EDUCATION) a piece of paper with questions or exercises on it that you use when you are studying sth

workshop /ˈwɜːkʃɒp/ *noun* [C] **1** a place where things are made or repaired ➲ note at **factory** **2** a period of discussion and practical work on a particular subject, when people share their knowledge and experience: *a drama/writing workshop*

workstation /ˈwɜːksteɪʃn/ *noun* [C] (COMPUTING) the desk and computer that a person works at; one computer that is part of a NETWORK

worktop /ˈwɜːktɒp/ (*also* **ˈwork surface**) *noun* [C] a flat surface in a kitchen, etc. that you use for preparing food, etc. on

ˌ**work-to-ˈrule** *noun* [usually sing.] a situation in which workers refuse to do any work that is not in their contracts, in order to protest about sth

world 🔑 /wɜːld/ *noun* **1 the world** [sing.] (GEOGRAPHY) the earth with all its countries and people: *a map of the world ◇ the most beautiful place **in the world** ◇ I took a year off work to travel **round the world**. ◇ She is famous **all over the world**.*
2 [sing.] (GEOGRAPHY) a particular part of the earth or group of countries: *the western world ◇ the Arab world ◇ the Third World* **3** [sing.] the life and activities of people; their experience: *It's time you learned something about the real world! ◇ the modern world* **4** [C] (often in compounds) a particular area of activity or group of people or things: *the world of sport/fashion/politics ◇ the medical/business/animal/natural world* **5** [sing.] the people in the world: ***The whole world** seemed to know the news before me!* **6** [C] a planet with life on it: *Do you believe there are other worlds out there, like ours?*
IDM **do sb a/the world of good** (*informal*) to have a very good effect on sb: *The holiday has done her the world of good.*
in the world used to emphasize what you are saying: *Everyone else is stressed but he doesn't seem to have a care in the world. ◇ There's no need to rush – we've got all the time in the world. ◇ What in the world are you doing?*
the outside world → OUTSIDE[2]
think the world of sb/sth → THINK

the ˌWorld ˈBank *noun* [sing.] (ECONOMICS) an international organization that lends money to countries who are members at times when they are in danger or difficulty and need more money

ˌ**world ˈEnglish** *noun* [U] (LANGUAGE) the English language, used throughout the world for international communication, including all of its regional varieties, such as Australian, Indian and South African English

ˌ**world-ˈfamous** *adj.* known all over the world

ˌ**World ˈHeritage Site** *noun* [C] (GEOGRAPHY) a natural or MAN-MADE place that is recognized as having great international importance and is therefore protected

worldly /ˈwɜːldli/ ***adj.*** **1** connected with ordinary life, not with the spirit: *He left all his worldly possessions to his nephew.* **2** having a lot of experience and knowledge of life and people: *a sophisticated and worldly man*

ˈworld music ***noun*** [U] (**MUSIC**) a type of pop music that includes influences from different parts of the world, especially Africa and Asia

ˌworld ˈpower ***noun*** [C] (**POLITICS**) a powerful country that has a lot of influence in international politics ➲ look at **power**, **superpower**

ˌworld ˈwar ***noun*** [C] a war that involves a lot of different countries: *the Second World War ◇ World War One*

worldwide /ˌwɜːldˈwaɪd/ ***adv.*** /ˈwɜːldwaɪd/ ***adj.*** (happening) in the whole world: *The product will be marketed worldwide. ◇ The situation has caused worldwide concern.*

the ˌWorld Wide ˈWeb (*also* **the Web**) ***noun*** [sing.] (*abbr.* **WWW**) (**COMPUTING**) the international system of computers that makes it possible for you to see information from around the world on your computer: *a Web browser/page* ➲ look at **the Internet**

worm[1] /wɜːm/ ***noun*** [C] **1** a small animal with a long thin body and no eyes, bones or legs: *an earthworm* **2 worms** [pl.] (**HEALTH**) one or more **worms** that live inside a person or an animal and may cause disease: *He's got worms.* **3** [C] (**COMPUTING**) a computer program that is a type of virus and that spreads across a network by copying itself

worm[2] /wɜːm/ ***verb*** [T] **~ your way/yourself along, through, etc.** to move slowly or with difficulty in the direction mentioned: *I managed to worm my way through the crowd.*

PHR V **worm your way/yourself into sth** to make sb like you or trust you, in order to dishonestly gain an advantage for yourself

worn past participle of **wear[1]**

ˌworn ˈout ***adj.*** **1** too old or damaged to use any more: *My shoes are completely worn out.* **2** extremely tired: *I'm absolutely worn out. I think I'll go to bed early.* ➲ look at **wear**

worried 🔑 /ˈwʌrid/ ***adj.*** ~ **(about sb/sth)**; ~ **(that...)** thinking that sth bad might happen or has happened: *Don't look so worried. Everything will be all right. ◇ I'm **worried sick** about the exam. ◇ We were **worried stiff*** (=extremely worried) *that you might have had an accident.*

worry[1] 🔑 /ˈwʌri/ ***verb*** (*pres. part.* **worrying**; *3rd person sing. pres.* **worries**; *pt, pp* **worried**) **1** [I] ~ **(about sb/sth)** to think that sth bad might happen or has happened: *Don't worry – I'm sure everything will be all right. ◇ There's nothing to worry about. ◇ He worries if I don't phone every weekend.* **2** [T] ~ **sb/yourself (about sb/sth)** to make sb/yourself think that sth bad might happen or has happened: *What worries me is how are we going to get home? ◇ She worried herself sick when he was away in the army.* **3** [T] ~ **sb (with sth)** to disturb sb; to bother sb: *I'm sorry to worry you with my problems but I really do need some advice.*

IDM **not to worry** it is not important; it doesn't matter

worry[2] 🔑 /ˈwʌri/ ***noun*** (*pl.* **worries**) **1** [U] the state of worrying about sth: *His son has caused him a lot of worry recently.* **2** [C] something that makes you worry; a problem: *Crime is a real worry for old people. ◇ financial worries*

worrying 🔑 /ˈwʌriɪŋ/ ***adj.*** that makes you worry: *a worrying development ◇ It is particularly worrying that nobody seems to be in charge. ◇ It's been a **worrying time** for us all.* ▶ **worryingly** ***adv.***: *worryingly high levels of radiation*

worse 🔑 /wɜːs/ ***adj.***, ***adv.*** (the comparative of *bad* or of *badly*) **1** not as good or as well as sth else: *My exam results were **far/much worse** than I thought they would be. ◇ She speaks German **even worse** than I do.* **2** (not before a noun) more ill; less well: *If you **get** any **worse** we'll call the doctor.* ▶ **worse** ***noun*** [U]: *The situation was already bad but there was worse to come.*

IDM **to make matters/things worse** to make a situation, problem, etc. even more difficult or dangerous than before

none the wiser/worse → NONE[2]

the worse for wear (*informal*) damaged; not in good condition: *This suitcase looks a bit the worse for wear.*

worse luck! (*spoken*) unfortunately: *The dentist says I need three fillings, worse luck!*

worsen /ˈwɜːsn/ ***verb*** [I,T] to become worse or to make sth worse: *Relations between the two countries have worsened.*

worship[1] 🔑 /ˈwɜːʃɪp/ ***verb*** (**worshipping**; **worshipped**: *AmE* **worshiping**; **worshiped**) **1** [I,T] (**RELIGION**) to pray to and show respect for God or a god: *People travel from all over the world to worship at this shrine.* **2** [T] to love or admire sb/sth very much: *She worshipped her husband.* ▶ **worshipper** ***noun*** [C]

worship[2] 🔑 /ˈwɜːʃɪp/ ***noun*** [U] **1** (**RELIGION**) the practice of showing respect for God or a god, by saying prayers, singing with others, etc.; a ceremony for this: ***an act/a place of worship*** **2** a strong feeling of love and respect for sb/sth **3 His, Your, etc. Worship** [C] (*formal*) (**LAW**) a polite way of addressing or referring to a MAGISTRATE or MAYOR

worst[1] 🔑 /wɜːst/ ***adj.***, ***adv.*** (the superlative of *bad* or of *badly*) the least pleasant or suitable; the least well: *It's been the worst winter that I can remember. ◇ A lot of the children behaved badly but my son behaved worst of all!*

worst[2] /wɜːst/ ***noun*** [sing.] something that is as bad as it can be: *My parents always expect the worst if I'm late.*

IDM **at (the) worst** if the worst happens or if you consider sb/sth in the worst way: *The problem doesn't look too serious. At worst we'll have to make a few small changes.*

if the worst comes to the worst if the worst possible situation happens

worth[1] 🔑 /wɜːθ/ ***adj.*** **1** having a particular value (in money): *How much do you think that house is worth?* **2** ~ **doing, etc.** used as a way of recommending or advising: *That museum's **well worth** visiting if you have time. ◇ The library closes in 5 minutes – it's not worth going in.* **3** enjoyable or useful to do or have, even if it means extra cost, effort, etc.: *It takes a long time to walk to the top of the hill but it's worth the effort. ◇ Don't bother cooking a big meal. It isn't **worth it** – we're not hungry.*

IDM **get your money's worth** → MONEY

worth sb's while helpful, useful or interesting to sb

worth[2] /wɜːθ/ ***noun*** [U] **1** the value of sb/sth; how useful sb/sth is: *She has proved her worth as a member of the team.* **2** the amount of sth that the money mentioned will buy: *ten pounds' worth of* *petrol* **3** the amount of sth that will last for the time mentioned: *two days' worth of food*

worthless /ˈwɜːθləs/ ***adj.*** **1** having no value or use: *It's worthless – it's only a bit of plastic!* **2** (used about a person) having bad qualities ➲ look at **priceless**, **valuable**, **invaluable**

worthwhile /ˌwɜːθˈwaɪl/ ***adj.*** enjoyable, useful or satisfying enough to be worth the cost or effort: *Working for so little money just isn't worthwhile.*

worthy /ˈwɜːði/ ***adj.*** (**worthier**; **worthiest**) **1** ~ **of sth/to do sth** good enough for sth or to have sth: *He felt he was not worthy to accept such responsibility.* **2** that should receive respect, support or attention: *a worthy leader* ◇ *a worthy cause*

would 🔑 /wəd/ *strong form* /wʊd/ ***modal verb*** (*short form* **'d**; *negative* **would not**; *short form* **wouldn't** /ˈwʊdnt/) **1** used when talking about the result of an event that you imagine: *He would be delighted if you went to see him.* ◇ *She'd be stupid not to accept.* ◇ *I would have done more, if I'd had the time.* **2** used for asking sb politely to do sth: *Would you come this way, please?* **3** used with 'like' or 'love' as a way of asking or saying what sb wants: ***Would you like** to come with us?* ◇ ***I'd love** a piece of cake.* **4** to agree or be ready to do sth: *She just wouldn't do what I asked her.* **5** used as the past form of 'will' when you report what sb says or thinks: *They said that they would help us.* ◇ *She didn't think that he would do a thing like that.* **6** used after 'wish': *I wish the sun would come out.* **7** used for talking about things that often happened in the past: *When he was young he would often walk in these woods.* **8** used for commenting on behaviour that is typical of sb: *You would say that. You always support him.* **9** used when you are giving your opinion but are not certain that you are right: *I'd say she's about 40.*

ˈwould-be ***adj.*** (only *before* a noun) used to describe sb who is hoping to become the type of person mentioned: *advice for would-be parents*

wound[1] 🔑 /wuːnd/ ***noun*** [C] (HEALTH) an injury to part of your body, especially a cut, often one received in fighting: *a bullet wound* ➲ note at **injure**

IDM **rub salt into the wound/sb's wounds** → RUB

wound[2] 🔑 /wuːnd/ ***verb*** [T] (usually passive) **1** (HEALTH) to injure sb's body with a weapon: *He was wounded in the leg during the war.* ➲ note at **hurt** **2** (*formal*) to hurt sb's feelings deeply: *I was wounded by his criticism.*

wound[3] past tense, past participle of **wind**[3]

wounded 🔑 /ˈwuːndɪd/ ***adj.*** **1** (HEALTH) injured by a weapon, for example in a war: *wounded soldiers* ◇ *He was **seriously wounded**.* **2** feeling emotional pain because of sth unpleasant that sb has said or done: *wounded pride* **3 the wounded** ***noun*** [pl.] (HEALTH) people who are wounded, for example in a war: *Paramedics tended to the wounded at the scene of the explosion.*

wove past tense of **weave**

woven past participle of **weave**

wow /waʊ/ ***exclamation*** (*informal*) used for saying that you are very impressed and surprised by sth: *Wow! What a fantastic boat!*

WP ***abbr.*** (COMPUTING) word processing; word processor

wrangle /ˈræŋgl/ ***noun*** [C] a noisy or complicated argument: *The company is involved in **a legal wrangle** over copyrights.* ▶ **wrangle** ***verb*** [I]

wrap 🔑 /ræp/ ***verb*** [T] (**wrapping**, **wrapped**) **1** ~ **sth (up) (in sth)** to put paper or cloth around sb/sth as a cover: *to wrap up a present* ◇ *The baby was found wrapped in a blanket.* **2** ~ **sth round/around sb/sth** to tie sth such as paper or cloth around an object or a part of the body: *The man had a bandage wrapped round his head.*

IDM **be wrapped up in sth** to be very involved and interested in sb/sth: *They were completely wrapped up in each other. They didn't notice I was there.*

PHR V **wrap (sb/yourself) up** to put warm clothes on sb/yourself

wrapper /ˈræpə(r)/ ***noun*** [C] the piece of paper or plastic which covers sth when you buy it: *a sweet/chocolate wrapper*

wrapping 🔑 /ˈræpɪŋ/ ***noun*** [C,U] paper, plastic, etc. that is used for covering sth in order to protect it: *Remove the wrapping before heating the pie.*

ˈwrapping paper ***noun*** [U] paper which is used for putting round presents

wrath /rɒθ/ ***noun*** [U] (*written*) very great anger

wreak /riːk/ ***verb*** [T] (*formal*) ~ **sth (on sb/sth)** to cause great damage or harm to sb/sth: *Fierce storms **wreak havoc** at this time of year.*

wreath /riːθ/ ***noun*** [C] (*pl.* **wreaths** /riːðz/) a circle of flowers and leaves, especially one that you give to the family of sb who has died

wreck /rek/ ***noun*** [C] **1** a ship that has sunk or been badly damaged at sea: *Divers searched the wreck.* **2** a car, plane, etc. which has been badly damaged, especially in an accident: *The car was a wreck but the lorry escaped almost without damage.* **3** [usually sing.] (*informal*) a person or thing that is in a very bad condition: *He drove so badly I was **a nervous wreck** when we got there.* ▶ **wreck** ***verb*** [T]: *Vandals had wrecked the school hall.* ◇ *The strike wrecked all our holiday plans.*

wreckage /ˈrekɪdʒ/ ***noun*** [U] the broken pieces of sth that has been destroyed: *Investigators searched the wreckage of the plane for evidence.*

wrench[1] /rentʃ/ ***verb*** [T] **1** ~ **sb/sth (away, off, etc.)** to pull or turn sb/sth strongly and suddenly: *They had to wrench the door off the car to get the driver out.* ◇ (*figurative*) *The film was so exciting that I could hardly wrench myself away.* **2** to injure part of your body by turning it suddenly

wrench[2] /rentʃ/ ***noun*** **1** [C] a sudden, violent pull or turn: *With a wrench I managed to open the door.* **2** [sing.] the sadness you feel because you have to leave sb/sth **3** [C] (*especially AmE*) = SPANNER ➲ look at **monkey wrench**, **adjustable spanner** ➲ picture at **tool**

wrestle /ˈresl/ ***verb*** [I] **1** ~ **(with) sb** (SPORT) to fight by trying to get hold of your opponent's body and throw them to the ground. People **wrestle** as a sport: *He managed to wrestle the man to the ground and take the knife from him.* **2** ~ **(with sth)** to try hard to deal with sth that is difficult

wrestling /ˈreslɪŋ/ ***noun*** [U] (SPORT) a sport in which two people fight and try to throw each other to the ground: *a wrestling match* ▶ **wrestler** ***noun*** [C]

wretch /retʃ/ ***noun*** [C] (*old-fashioned*) a poor, unhappy person: *The poor wretch was clearly starving.*

wretched /ˈretʃɪd/ ***adj.*** **1** very unhappy **2** (*informal*) used for expressing anger: *That wretched dog has chewed up my slippers again!*

wriggle /ˈrɪɡl/ ***verb*** [I,T] **1** ~ **(sth) (about/around)** to move about, or to move a part of your body, with short, quick movements, especially from side to side: *The baby was wriggling around on my lap.* ◇ *She wriggled her fingers about in the hot sand.* **2** to move in the direction mentioned by making quick turning movements: *The worm wriggled back into the soil.*
PHR V **wriggle out of sth/doing sth** (*informal*) to avoid sth by making clever excuses: *It's your turn to wash up – you can't wriggle out of it this time!*

wring /rɪŋ/ ***verb*** [T] (*pt, pp* **wrung** /rʌŋ/) ~ **sth (out)** to press and squeeze sth in order to remove water from it

wrinkle¹ /ˈrɪŋkl/ ***noun*** [C] a small line in sth, especially one on the skin of your face which you get as you grow older: *She's got fine wrinkles around her eyes.* ◇ *Smooth out the wrinkles in the fabric.* ➲ look at **furrow**

wrinkle² /ˈrɪŋkl/ ***verb*** [I,T] ~ **(sth) (up)** to form small lines and folds in sth: *She wrinkled her nose at the nasty smell.* ◇ *My skirt had wrinkled up on the journey.* ▶ **wrinkled** /ˈrɪŋkld/ ***adj.***

wrist ⊶ /rɪst/ ***noun*** [C] (ANATOMY) the narrow part at the end of your arm where it joins your hand ➲ picture on **page 80**

wristwatch /ˈrɪstwɒtʃ/ ***noun*** [C] a watch on a STRAP which you wear round your arm near your hand

writ /rɪt/ ***noun*** [C] (LAW) a legal order to do or not to do sth, given by a court of law

write ⊶ /raɪt/ ***verb*** (*pt* **wrote** /rəʊt/; *pp* **written** /ˈrɪtn/) **1** [I,T] to make words, letters, etc., especially on paper using a pen or pencil: *I can't write with this pen.* ◇ *Write your name and address on the form.* **2** [T] (LITERATURE) to create a book, story, song, etc. in written form for people to read or use: *Tolstoy wrote 'War and Peace'.* ◇ *He wrote his wife a poem.* ◇ *Who wrote the music for that film?* **3** [I,T] ~ **(sth) (to sb)**; ~ **(sb) sth** to write and send a letter, etc. to sb: *I've written a letter to my son./I've written my son a letter.* ◇ *I've written to him.* ◇ *She wrote that they were all well and would be home soon.* ◇ *She phones every week and writes occasionally.* **4** [T] ~ **sth (out) (for sb)** to fill or complete a form, cheque, document, etc. with the necessary information: *I wrote out a cheque for £10.*
PHR V **write back (to sb)** to send a reply to sb
write sth down to write sth on paper, especially so that you can remember it
write in (to sb/sth) (for sth) to write a letter to an organization, etc. to ask for sth, give an opinion, etc.
write off/away (to sb/sth) (for sth) to write a letter to an organization, etc. to order sth or ask for sth
write sb/sth off to accept or decide that sb/sth will not be successful or useful: *Don't write him off yet. He could still win.*
write sth off to accept that you will not get back an amount of money you have lost or spent: *to write off a debt*
write sth out to write the whole of sth on paper: *Can you write out that recipe for me?*
write sth up to write sth in a complete and final form, often using notes that you have made

ˈwrite-off ***noun*** [C] a thing, especially a vehicle, that is so badly damaged that it is not worth repairing

writer ⊶ /ˈraɪtə(r)/ ***noun*** [C] (LITERATURE) a person who writes, especially one whose job is to write books, stories, etc.

writhe /raɪð/ ***verb*** [I] to turn and roll your body about: *She was writhing in pain.*

writing ⊶ /ˈraɪtɪŋ/ ***noun*** **1** [U] words that have been written or printed; the way a person writes: *This card's got no writing inside. You can put your own message.* ◇ *I can't read your writing, it's too small.* **2** [U] (EDUCATION) the skill or activity of writing words: *He had problems with his reading and writing at school.* **3** [U] (LITERATURE) the activity or job of writing books, etc.: *It's difficult to earn much money from writing.* **4** [U] (LITERATURE) the books, etc. that sb has written or the style in which sb writes: *Love is a common theme in his early writing.* **5 writings** [pl.] (LITERATURE) a group of pieces of writing, especially by a particular person on a particular subject: *the writings of Hegel*
IDM **in writing** in written form: *I'll confirm the offer in writing next week.*

ˈwriting paper ***noun*** [U] paper for writing letters on

written¹ ⊶ past participle of **write**

written² ⊶ /ˈrɪtn/ ***adj.*** expressed on paper; not just spoken: *a written agreement*

wrong¹ ⊶ /rɒŋ/ ***adj.***, ***adv.*** **1** not correct; in a way that is not correct: *the wrong answer* ◇ *I always pronounce that word wrong.* ◇ *You've got the wrong number* (=on the telephone). ◇ *I think you're wrong about Nicola – she's not lazy.* OPP **right 2** not the best; not suitable: *That's the wrong way to hold the bat.* ◇ *I think she married the wrong man.* ◇ *I like him – I just think he's wrong for the job.* OPP **right 3** (not before a noun) ~ **(with sb/sth)** causing problems or difficulties; not as it should be: *You look upset. Is something wrong?* ◇ ***What's wrong** with the car this time?* ◇ *She's got something wrong with her leg.* **4** ~ **(to do sth)** not morally right or honest: *It's wrong to tell lies.* ◇ *The man said that he had done nothing wrong.*
IDM **get on the right/wrong side of sb** → SIDE¹
get sb wrong (*informal*) to not understand sb: *Don't get me wrong! I don't dislike him.*
go wrong 1 to make a mistake: *I'm afraid we've gone wrong. We should have taken the other road.* **2** to stop working properly or to stop developing well: *My computer's gone wrong and I've lost all my work.*
get/start off on the right/wrong foot (with sb) → FOOT¹
on the right/wrong track → TRACK¹

wrong² /rɒŋ/ ***noun*** **1** [U] things that are morally bad or dishonest: *Children quickly learn the difference between **right and wrong**.* **2** [C] an action or situation which is not fair: *A terrible wrong has been done. Those men should never have gone to prison.*
IDM **in the wrong** (used about a person) having made a mistake; whose fault sth is

wrong³ /rɒŋ/ ***verb*** [T] to do sth to sb which is bad or unfair: *I wronged her when I said she was lying.*

ˌwrong-ˈfoot ***verb*** [T] (*BrE*) to put sb in a difficult or embarrassing situation by doing sth that they do not expect

wrongful /ˈrɒŋfl/ ***adj.*** (*formal*) (only *before* a noun) not fair, not legal or not moral: *He sued the company for wrongful dismissal.*

wrongly ⊶ /ˈrɒŋli/ ***adv.*** in a wrong or mistaken way: *He was wrongly accused of stealing money.*

wrote past tense of **write**

wrought iron /ˌrɔːt ˈaɪən/ ***noun*** [U] a type of iron that is used for making fences, gates, etc.
▶ **ˈwrought-iron** ***adj.***: *wrought-iron gates*

wrung past tense, past participle of **wring**

wry /raɪ/ ***adj.*** expressing both disappointment and AMUSEMENT: *'Never mind,' she said with a wry grin. 'At least we got one vote.'* ▶ **wryly** ***adv.***

WSW ***abbr.*** west-south-west

wt ***abbr.*** weight: *net wt 500g*

WTO /ˌdʌbljuː tiː ˈəʊ/ ***abbr.*** (**ECONOMICS**) the World Trade Organization; an organization that encourages economic development and international TRADE (= buying and selling between different countries)

WWW /ˌdʌbljuː dʌbljuː ˈdʌbljuː/ ***abbr.*** the World Wide Web

X, x /eks/ ***noun*** **1** [C,U] (*pl.* **X's**; **x's** /ˈeksɪz/) the twenty-fourth letter of the English alphabet: *'Xylophone' begins with (an) 'X'.* **2** [U] (**MATHEMATICS**) used to represent a number whose value is not mentioned: *The equation is impossible for any value of x greater than 2.* **3** [U] a person, a number, an influence, etc. that is not known or not named: *Let's suppose X knows what Y is doing.*

ˈX chromosome ***noun*** [C] (**BIOLOGY**) a SEX CHROMOSOME. Two **X chromosomes** exist in the cells of human females. In human males each cell has one **X chromosome** and one Y CHROMOSOME.

xenon /ˈziːnɒn; ˈzen-/ ***noun*** [U] (*symbol* **Xe**) (**CHEMISTRY**) a gas that is present in air and that is sometimes used in electric lamps ❶ For more information on the periodic table of elements, look at pages R34-5.

xenophobia /ˌzenəˈfəʊbiə/ ***noun*** [U] (**SOCIAL STUDIES**) a fear or hatred of foreign people and cultures ▶ **xenophobe** /ˈzenəfəʊb/ ***noun*** [C] ▶ **xenophobic** /ˌzenəˈfəʊbɪk/ ***adj.***

Xerox™ /ˈzɪərɒks/ ***noun*** [C] **1** a machine that produces copies of letters, documents, etc. **2** a copy produced by such a machine **SYN** **photocopy**
▶ **xerox** ***verb*** [T]

XL ***abbr.*** extra large (size)

Xmas /ˈkrɪsməs; ˈeksməs/ ***noun*** [C,U] (*informal*) (used as a short form in writing) Christmas

XML /ˌeks em ˈel/ ***abbr.*** (**COMPUTING**) **Extensible Mark up Language**; a system used for marking the structure of text on a computer, for example when creating website pages

ˈX-ray ***noun*** [C] **1** [usually pl.] (**HEALTH, PHYSICS**) a kind of light that makes it possible to see inside solid objects, for example the human body, so that they can be examined and a photograph of them can be made **2** (**HEALTH**) a photograph that is made with an **X-ray** machine: *The X-ray showed that the bone was not broken.* ➲ look at **ray** ➲ picture at **wavelength**
▶ **X-ray** ***verb*** [T]: *She had her chest X-rayed.*

xylem /ˈzaɪləm/ ***noun*** [U] (**BIOLOGY**) the material in plants that carries water and food upwards from the root ➲ picture at **flower**

xylophone /ˈzaɪləfəʊn/ ***noun*** [C] (**MUSIC**) a musical instrument that usually consists of two rows of wooden bars of different lengths. You play it by hitting these bars with two small hammers.
➲ picture on **page 465**

Y, y /waɪ/ ***noun*** **1** [C,U] (*pl.* **Y's**; **y's** /waɪz/) the twenty-fifth letter of the English alphabet: *'Yawn' begins with (a) 'Y'.* **2** [U] (**MATHEMATICS**) used to represent a number whose value is not mentioned: *Can the value of y be predicted from the value of x?* **3** [U] a person, a number, an influence, etc. that is not known or not named: *Let's suppose X knows what Y is doing.* ➲ look at **Y chromosome**

yacht /jɒt/ ***noun*** [C] **1** a boat with sails used for pleasure: *a yacht race* **2** a large boat with a motor, used for pleasure ➲ look at **dinghy**

yachting /ˈjɒtɪŋ/ ***noun*** [U] the activity or sport of sailing or racing YACHTS

yachtsman /ˈjɒtsmən/ **yachtswoman** /ˈjɒtswʊmən/ ***noun*** [C] (*pl.* **-men** /-mən/) (*pl.* **-women** /-wɪmɪn/) a person who sails a YACHT in races or for pleasure

yak /jæk/ ***noun*** [C] an animal of the cow family, with long horns and long hair, that lives in central Asia

yam /jæm/ ***noun*** [C,U] the large brownish root of a tropical plant that is cooked as a vegetable

yank /jæŋk/ ***verb*** [I,T] (*informal*) to pull sth suddenly, quickly and hard ▶ **yank** ***noun*** [C]

yap /jæp/ ***verb*** [I] (**yapping**; **yapped**) (used about dogs, especially small ones) to make short, loud noises in an excited way

yard 🔑 /jɑːd/ ***noun*** [C] **1** (*BrE*) an area outside a building, usually with a hard surface and a wall or fence around it: *a school/prison yard* ➲ look at **courtyard, churchyard** **2** (*AmE*) = GARDEN[1] (1) **3** (usually in compounds) an area, usually without a roof, used for a particular type of work or purpose: *a shipyard/boatyard* ◇ *a builder's yard* ➲ note at **factory** **4** (*abbr.* **yd**) a measure of length; 0.914 of a metre. There are 3 feet in a yard: *Our house is 100 yards from the supermarket.*

yardstick /ˈjɑːdstɪk/ ***noun*** [C] a standard with which things can be compared: *Exam results should not be the only yardstick by which pupils are judged.*

yarn /jɑːn/ ***noun*** **1** [U] thread (usually of wool or cotton) that has been prepared (**spun**) and is used for knitting, etc. **2** [C] (*informal*) a long story that sb tells, especially one that is invented or exaggerated

yashmak /ˈjæʃmæk/ ***noun*** [C] a piece of material covering most of the face, worn by some Muslim women

yawn 🔑 /jɔːn/ ***verb*** [I] to open your mouth wide and breathe in deeply, especially when you are tired or bored ▶ **yawn** ***noun*** [C]: *'How much longer will it take?' he said with a yawn.*

yaws /jɔːz/ ***noun*** [U] (**HEALTH**) a tropical skin disease that causes large red swellings

ˈY chromosome ***noun*** [C] (**BIOLOGY**) a SEX CHROMOSOME. In human males each cell has one X CHROMOSOME and one **Y chromosome**. In human females there is never a **Y chromosome**.

yd (*pl.* **yds**) ***abbr.*** yard, a measure of length

yeah 🔑 /jeə/ ***exclamation*** (*informal*) yes

year ⊶ /jɪə(r); jɜː(r)/ *noun* **1** [C] (*also* **'calendar year**) the period from 1 January to 31 December, 365 or 366 days divided into 12 months or 52 weeks: *last year/this year/next year* ◇ *The population of the country will be 70 million by the year 2010.* ◇ *Interest is paid on this account once a year.* ◇ *a* ***leap year*** (=one that has 366 days) ◇ *the* ***New Year*** (=the first days of January) **2** [C] any period of 12 months, measured from any date: *She worked here for twenty years.* ◇ *He left school just over a year ago.* ◇ *In a year's time, you'll be old enough to vote.* **3** [C] a period of 12 months in connection with schools, the business world, etc.: *the academic/school year* ◇ *the tax/financial year* **4** [C] (*especially BrE*) (used in schools, universities, etc.) the level that a particular student is at: *My son is in year ten now.* ◇ *The first years* (=students in their first year at school/university, etc.) *do French as a compulsory subject.* ◇ *He was a year below me at school.* ➲ note at **form**[1] (4) **5** [C, usually pl.] (used in connection with the age of sb/sth) a period of 12 months: *He's ten years old today.* ◇ *a six-year-old daughter* ◇ *This car is nearly five years old.* ◇ *The company is now in its fifth year.* **6 years** [pl.] a long time: *It happened years ago.* ◇ *I haven't seen him for years.*

IDM **all year round** for the whole year

donkey's years → DONKEY

year after year; **year in year out** every year for many years

yearly /'jɪəli; 'jɜːli/ ***adj.***, ***adv.*** (happening) every year or once a year: *The conference is held yearly.*

yearn /jɜːn/ *verb* [I] (*written*) ~ **(for sb/sth)**; ~ **(to do sth)** to want sb/sth very much, especially sth that you cannot have ▶ **yearning** *noun* [C,U]

yeast /jiːst/ *noun* [U] a substance used for making bread rise and for making beer, wine, etc.

'yeast infection (*AmE*) =THRUSH

yell /jel/ *verb* [I,T] ~ **(out) (sth)**; ~ **(sth) (at sb/sth)** to shout very loudly, often because you are angry, excited or in pain: *She yelled out his name.* ▶ **yell** *noun* [C]

yellow ⊶ /'jeləʊ/ *noun* [C,U], ***adj.*** (of) the colour of lemons or butter: *a pale/light yellow dress* ◇ *a bright shade of yellow* ◇ *the yellows and browns of the autumn leaves*

,yellow 'card *noun* [C] (SPORT) (used in football) a card that is shown to a player as a warning that they will be sent off the field if they behave badly again ➲ look at **red card**

,yellow 'fever *noun* [U] (HEALTH) a tropical disease that is passed from one person to another and that makes the skin turn yellow and often causes death

yellowish /'jeləʊɪʃ/ ***adj.*** (*also* **yellowy** /'jeləʊi/) slightly yellow in colour

,yellow 'line *noun* [C] (*BrE*) a yellow line at the side of a road to show that you can only park there for a limited time: ***double yellow lines*** (=you must not park there at all)

,Yellow 'Pages™ *noun* [pl.] a telephone book (on yellow paper) that lists all the business companies, etc. in a certain area in sections according to the goods or services they provide

yelp /jelp/ *verb* [I] to give a sudden short cry, especially of pain ▶ **yelp** *noun* [C]

yes ⊶ /jes/ *exclamation* **1** used to give a positive answer to a question, for saying that sth is true or correct or for saying that you want sth: *'Are you having a good time?' 'Yes, thank you.'* ◇ *'You're married, aren't you?' 'Yes, I am.'* ◇ *'May I sit here?' 'Yes, of course.'* ◇ *'More coffee?' 'Yes, please.'* **2** used for showing you have heard sb or will do what they ask: *'Waiter!' 'Yes, madam.'* **3** used when saying that a negative statement that sb has made is not true: *'You don't care about anyone but yourself.' 'Yes I do.'* OPP **no** ▶ **yes** *noun* [C] (*pl.* **yeses** /'jesɪz/): *Was that a yes or a no?*

yesterday ⊶ /'jestədeɪ; 'jestədi/ ***adv.***, ***noun*** [C,U] (on) the day before today: *Did you watch the film on TV yesterday?* ◇ *yesterday morning/afternoon/evening* ◇ *I posted the form* ***the day before yesterday*** (=if I am speaking on Wednesday, I posted it on Monday). ◇ *Have you still got yesterday's paper?* ◇ *I spent the whole of yesterday walking round the shops.*

yet ⊶ /jet/ ***adv.***, ***conj.*** **1** used with negative verbs or in questions for talking about sth that has not happened but that you expect to happen: *Has it stopped raining yet?* ◇ *I haven't seen that film yet.* ❶ In American English you can say: ***I didn't*** *see that film yet.* **2** (used with negative verbs) now; as early as this: *You don't have to leave yet – your train isn't for another hour.* **3** from now until the period of time mentioned has passed: *She isn't that old; she'll live for years yet.* **4** (used especially with *may* or *might*) at some time in the future: *With a bit of luck, they may yet win.* **5** (used with SUPERLATIVES) until now/until then; so far: *This is her best film yet.* **6** used with COMPARATIVES to emphasize an increase in the degree of sth: *a recent and yet more improbable theory* **7** but; in spite of that: *He seems pleasant, yet there's something about him I don't like.*

IDM **as yet** until now: *As yet little is known about the disease.*

yet again (used for expressing surprise or anger that sth happens again) once more; another time: *I found out that he had lied to me yet again.*

yet another used for expressing surprise that there is one more of sth: *They're opening yet another fast food restaurant in the square.*

yet to do, etc. that has not been done and is still to do in the future: *The final decision has yet to be made.*

yew /juː/ (*also* **'yew tree**) *noun* [U] a small tree with dark green leaves and small red BERRIES; the wood of this tree

YHA /,waɪ eɪtʃ 'eɪ/ ***abbr.*** **Youth Hostels Association**; an organization that exists in many countries and provides cheap simple accommodation

yield[1] /jiːld/ *verb* **1** [T] (AGRICULTURE, BUSINESS) to produce or provide crops, profits or results: *How much wheat does each field yield?* ◇ *Did the experiment yield any new information?* **2** [I] ~ **(to sb/sth)** (*formal*) to stop refusing to do sth or to obey sb SYN **give in**: *The government refused to yield to the hostage takers' demands.* **3** [T] ~ **sb/sth (up) (to sb/sth)** to allow sb to have control of sth that you were controlling: *The army has yielded power to the rebels.* **4** [I] (*formal*) to move, bend or break because of pressure SYN **give way**: *The dam finally yielded under the weight of the water.* **5** [I] (*AmE*) ~ **(to sb/sth)** to allow other vehicles on a bigger road to go first SYN **give way**: *You have to yield to traffic from the left here.*

PHR V **yield to sth** (*formal*) to be replaced by sth, especially sth newer: *Old-fashioned methods have yielded to new technology.*

yield[2] /jiːld/ *noun* [C,U] (AGRICULTURE, BUSINESS) the total amount of crops, profits, etc. that are produced: *Wheat yields were down 5% this year.* ◇ *This will give a yield of 10% on your investment.*

yo /jəʊ/ ***exclamation*** (*especially AmE, slang*) used by some people when they see a friend; hello

yob /jɒb/ ***noun*** [C] (*BrE, slang*) (SOCIAL STUDIES) a boy or young man who is rude, loud and sometimes violent or aggressive ➲ look at **lout**, **hooligan**

yoga /ˈjəʊɡə/ ***noun*** [U] a system of exercises for the body that helps you control and relax both your mind and your body

yoghurt (also **yogurt**) /ˈjɒɡət/ ***noun*** [C,U] a slightly sour, thick liquid food made from milk: *plain/banana/strawberry yoghurt*

yoke /jəʊk/ ***noun*** **1** [C] (AGRICULTURE) a long piece of wood fixed across the necks of two animals so that they can pull heavy loads together **2** [sing.] something that limits your freedom and makes your life difficult

yolk /jəʊk/ ***noun*** [C,U] the yellow part in the middle of an egg

yonks /jɒŋks/ ***noun*** [U] (*slang*) a very long time: *I haven't been to the theatre for yonks.*

you 🔑 /jə; juː/ ***pronoun*** **1** used as the subject or object of a verb, or after a preposition to refer to the person or people being spoken or written to: *You can play the guitar, can't you?* ◇ *I've told you about this before.* ◇ *Bring your photos with you.* **2** used with a noun, adjective or phrase when calling sb sth: *You idiot! What do you think you're doing?* **3** used for referring to people in general: *The more you earn, the more tax you pay.*

you'd /juːd/ short for YOU HAD, YOU WOULD

you'll /juːl/ short for YOU WILL

young[1] 🔑 /jʌŋ/ ***adj.*** (**younger** /ˈjʌŋɡə(r)/, **youngest** /ˈjʌŋɡɪst/) not having lived or existed for very long; not old: *They have two young children.* ◇ *I'm a year younger than her.* ◇ *My father was the youngest of eight children.* ◇ *my younger brothers* OPP **old**

IDM **young at heart** behaving or thinking like a young person, although you are old

young[2] /jʌŋ/ ***noun*** [pl.] **1** young animals: *Swans will attack to protect their young.* **2 the young** (SOCIAL STUDIES) young people considered as a group: *The young of today are more ambitious than their parents.*

youngish /ˈjʌŋɪʃ/ ***adj.*** quite young

youngster /ˈjʌŋstə(r)/ ***noun*** [C] a young person

your 🔑 /jə(r); jɔː(r)/ ***det.*** **1** of or belonging to the person or people being spoken to: *What's your flat like?* ◇ *Thanks for all your help.* ◇ *How old are your children now?* **2** belonging to or connected with people in general: *When your life is as busy as mine, you have little time to relax.* **3** (*informal*) used for saying that sth is well known to people in general: *So this is your typical English pub, is it?* **4** (*also* **Your**) used in some titles: *your Highness*

you're /jɔː(r); jʊə(r)/ short for YOU ARE

yours 🔑 /jɔːz/ ***pronoun*** **1** of or belonging to you: *Is this bag yours or mine?* ◇ *I was talking to a friend of yours the other day.* **2 Yours** used at the end of a letter: *Yours sincerely.../faithfully...* ◇ *Yours...*

yourself 🔑 /jɔːˈself; jəˈself/ ***pronoun*** (*pl.* **yourselves** /-ˈselvz/) **1** used when the person or people being spoken to do an action and are also affected by it: *Be careful or you'll hurt yourself.* ◇ *Here's some money. Buy yourselves a present.* ◇ *You're always talking about yourself!* **2** used to emphasize sth: *You yourself told me there was a problem last week.* ◇ *Did you repair the car yourselves?* (= or did sb else do it for you?) **3** you: *'How are you?' 'Fine, thanks. And yourself?'* **4** in your normal state; healthy: *You don't look yourself today.*

IDM **(all) by yourself/yourselves 1** alone: *Do you live by yourself?* **2** without help: *You can't cook dinner for ten people by yourself.*

youth 🔑 /juːθ/ ***noun*** (*pl.* **youths** /juːðz/) **1** [U] the period of your life when you are young, especially the time before a child becomes an adult: *He was quite a good sportsman **in his youth**.* **2** [U] the fact or state of being young: *I think that her youth will be a disadvantage in this job.* **3** [C] (SOCIAL STUDIES) a young person (usually a young man, and often one that you do not have a good opinion of): *a gang of youths* **4 the youth** [U] (SOCIAL STUDIES) young people considered as a group: *the youth of today* ➲ look at **age**, **old age**

ˈyouth club ***noun*** [C] (in Britain) a club where young people can meet each other and take part in various activities

youthful /ˈjuːθfl/ ***adj.*** **1** typical of young people: *youthful enthusiasm* **2** seeming younger than you are: *She's a youthful fifty-year-old.*

ˈyouth hostel ***noun*** [C] a cheap and simple place to stay, especially for young people, when they are travelling

you've /juːv/ short for YOU HAVE

ˈYo Yo™ (*also* **ˈyo-yo**) ***noun*** [C] (*pl.* **Yo Yos**; **yo-yos**) a toy which is a round piece of wood or plastic with a string round the middle. You put the string round your finger and can make the **yo-yo** go up and down it.

yr (*pl.* **yrs**) ***abbr.*** year

ytterbium /ɪˈtɜːbiəm/ ***noun*** [U] (*symbol* **Yb**) (CHEMISTRY) a chemical element. **Ytterbium** is a silver-white metal used to make steel stronger and in some X-RAY machines. ❶ For more information on the periodic table of elements, look at pages R34-5.

yttrium /ˈɪtriəm/ ***noun*** [U] (*symbol* **Y**) (CHEMISTRY) a chemical element. **Yttrium** is a grey-white metal used in MAGNETS. ❶ For more information on the periodic table of elements, look at pages R34-5.

yuck /jʌk/ ***exclamation*** (*informal*) used for saying that you think sth is disgusting or very unpleasant: *It's filthy! Yuck!* ▶ **yucky** ***adj.***: *What a yucky colour!*

yummy /ˈjʌmi/ ***adj.*** (*informal*) tasting very good; DELICIOUS: *a yummy cake*

yuppie (also **yuppy**) /ˈjʌpi/ ***noun*** [C] (*pl.* **yuppies**) (SOCIAL STUDIES) a successful young professional person who lives in a city, earns a lot of money and spends it on fashionable things

Z z

Z, z /zed/ ***noun*** [C,U] (*pl.* **Z's**; **z's** /zedz/) the twenty-sixth letter and last letter of the English alphabet: *'Zero' begins with (a) 'Z'.*

zany /ˈzeɪni/ ***adj.*** funny in an unusual and crazy way: *a zany comedian*

zap /zæp/ ***verb*** (**zapping**; **zapped**) (*informal*) **1** [T] ~ **sb/sth (with sth)** to destroy, hit or kill sb, usually with a gun or other weapon: *It's a computer game where you have to zap aliens with a laser.* **2** [I,T] to change television programmes very quickly using an electronic device (**remote control**)

zeal /ziːl/ ***noun*** [U] (*written*) great energy or enthusiasm: *religious zeal*

zealous /ˈzeləs/ ***adj.*** using great energy and enthusiasm ▸ **zealously** ***adv.***

zebra /ˈzebrə/ ***noun*** [C] (*pl.* **zebra** or **zebras**) an African wild animal that looks like a horse, with black and white STRIPES all over its body

ˌzebra ˈcrossing ***noun*** [C] (*BrE*) a place where the road is marked with black and white lines and people can cross safely because cars must stop to let them do this ➲ look at **pedestrian crossing**

Zen /zen/ ***noun*** [U] (RELIGION) a Japanese form of Buddhism

zenith /ˈzenɪθ/ ***noun*** [sing.] (ASTRONOMY) the highest point that the sun or moon reaches in the sky, directly above you SYN **peak** OPP **nadir**

THESAURUS

The figure **0** has several different names in *BrE*.

Zero is most commonly used in scientific or technical contexts.

Nil is most commonly used in scores in sport, especially football (when spoken).

Nought is used when referring to the figure **0** as part of a larger number: *a million is one, followed by six noughts.*

O (pronounced '**oh**') is most commonly used when saying numbers such as telephone or flight numbers.

zero /ˈzɪərəʊ/ ***noun*** **1** [C] (MATHEMATICS) 0 **2** [U] (PHYSICS) freezing point; 0°C: *The temperature is likely to fall to five degrees* ***below zero*** (= −5°C). **3** [U] the lowest possible amount or level; nothing at all: *zero growth/inflation/profit*

ˌzero ˈtolerance ***noun*** [U] (LAW) the act of following the law very strictly so that people are punished even when what they have done wrong is not very serious

zest /zest/ ***noun*** [U, sing.] ~ **(for sth)** a feeling of enjoyment, excitement and enthusiasm: *She has a great* ***zest for life.***

zigzag /ˈzɪgzæg/ ***noun*** [C], ***adj.*** (GEOMETRY) (consisting of) a line with left and right turns, like a lot of letter W's, one after the other: *The skier came down the slope in a series of zigzags.* ◇ *a zigzag pattern/line* ➲ picture at **line** ▸ **zigzag** ***verb*** [I] (**zigzagging**; **zigzagged**)

zinc /zɪŋk/ ***noun*** [U] (*symbol* **Zn**) (CHEMISTRY) a whitish metal, often put on the surface of iron and steel as protection against water ℹ For more information on the periodic table of elements, look at pages R34-5.

zip¹ /zɪp/ (*AmE* **zipper** /ˈzɪpə(r)/) ***noun*** [C] a device for fastening clothes, bags, etc.: *to do up/undo a zip*

zip² /zɪp/ ***verb*** [T] (**zipping**; **zipped**) **1** ~ **sth (up)** to fasten clothes, bags, etc. with a ZIP: *There was so much in the bag that it was difficult to zip it up.* OPP **unzip** **2** (COMPUTING) to COMPRESS a computer file (= make it smaller) OPP **unzip**

ˈzip code (*also* **ZIP code**) (*AmE*) = POSTCODE

zirconium /zɜːˈkəʊniəm/ ***noun*** [U] (*symbol* **Zr**) (CHEMISTRY) a chemical element. **Zirconium** is a hard silver-grey metal that does not CORRODE very easily. ℹ For more information on the periodic table of elements, look at pages R34-5.

zither /ˈzɪðə(r)/ ***noun*** [C] (MUSIC) a musical instrument with a lot of metal strings stretched over a flat wooden box, that you play with your fingers or a PLECTRUM (= a small piece of plastic, metal, etc., that you use to play the strings of a musical instrument instead of using your fingers)

the zodiac /ˈzəʊdiæk/ ***noun*** [sing.] (ASTRONOMY) a diagram of the positions of the sun, moon and planets, which is divided into twelve equal parts, each with a special name and symbol (**the signs of the zodiac**)

zone¹ /zəʊn/ ***noun*** [C] **1** an area or a region with a particular feature or use: ***a war zone*** ◇ ***an earthquake/danger, etc. zone*** ◇ ***a pedestrian zone*** (= where vehicles may not go) **2** one of the areas that a larger area is divided into for the purpose of organization: *postal charges to countries in zone 2* **3** (GEOGRAPHY) one of the parts that the earth's surface is divided into by imaginary lines that are parallel to the EQUATOR: *the northern/southern temperate zone*

zone² /zəʊn/ ***verb*** [T] (usually passive) **1** ~ **sth (for sth)** to keep an area of land to be used for a particular purpose: *The town centre was zoned for office development.* **2** to divide an area of land into smaller areas ▸ **zoning** ***noun*** [U]

zoo /zuː/ ***noun*** [C] (*pl.* **zoos**) a park where many kinds of wild animals are kept so that people can look at them and where they are bred, studied and protected

zoology /zəʊˈɒlədʒi; zuˈɒl-/ ***noun*** [U] (BIOLOGY) the scientific study of animals ➲ look at **botany, biology** ▸ **zoological** /ˌzəʊəˈlɒdʒɪkl; ˌzuːəˈl-/ ***adj.*** ▸ **zoologist** /zəʊˈɒlədʒɪst; zuˈɒl-/ ***noun*** [C]

zoom /zuːm/ ***verb*** [I] to move or go somewhere very fast

PHR V **zoom in (on sb/sth)** (used in photography) to give a closer view of the object/person being photographed by fixing a ZOOM LENS to the camera: *The camera zoomed in on the actor's face.*

ˌzoom ˈlens ***noun*** [C] a device on a camera that can make an object being photographed appear gradually bigger or smaller so that it seems to be getting closer or further away

zucchini /zuˈkiːni/ ***noun*** [C] (*pl.* **zucchini** or **zucchinis**) (*especially AmE*) = COURGETTE

zygote /ˈzaɪgəʊt/ ***noun*** [C] (BIOLOGY) a cell that starts the process of forming a baby person or animal, formed by the joining together of a male and a female GAMETE (= a cell that is provided by each parent)

KEY TO EXERCISES

Dictionary quiz (page ix)

1 dried fruit, nuts, sugar (but no meat)
2 a doctor
3 tells a story or explains what is happening in a play, film, etc.
4 dial the number
5 dishonest
6 chase
7 commence (*informal* start or begin)
8 adjective
9 uncountable
10 broadcast
11 factories
12 occurring
13 the "p"
14 **tourist** board
15 Kill time, an hour, etc, Kill two birds with one stone
16 burn down, burn sth down, burn sth off, burn (sth) out, burn yourself out, burn (sth) up
17 elegance
18 jealously
19 Norwegian
20 one thousand

Using your dictionary for CLIL
(page R2–R5)

A Spidergrams
Bulb:
Filament, alloy wires, wires, cap, plastic insulator, contact, fuses, glass

B Concept maps
i) Body
Body: Head, shoulder, upper arm, leg, knee, shin, knuckle, bottom, hip, thigh, etc.
Skeleton: Skull, spine, scapula, humerus, coccyx, patella, clavicle, sternum, vertebrae, etc.
Internal Organs: Brain, lung, oesophagus, kidney, appendix, heart, colon, bladder, liver etc.
Face: Temple, forehead, eyelid, eyebrow, cheek, lip, tongue, gums, chin, jaw, teeth, etc.

ii) Plate tectonics
Continental plates: Pacific, Nazca, North American, South American, African, Indo-European, Eurasian
Plate boundaries: convergent, divergent, transform
Natural disasters caused by plate movement: earthquakes, tsunamis
Geographical features caused by plate movement: rift valleys, transform faults

Exercise 2
Example

LABORATORY APPARATUS

Containers	Non containers
slide	microscope
petri dish	objective lens
evaporating dish	eyepiece
crucible	stand
mortar	clamp
beaker	tripod
flask	gauze
funnel	stopper
retort	pestle
filter paper	tongs
test tube	glass rod
syringe	spatula
burette	plunger
pipette	cover
	test tube rack

Exercise 3
Example *(depending on words/phrases chosen)*
Circulation
Circulation refers to the movement of blood around the body. The main **artery** moves blood **away** from the heart around the body through the digestive system, the kidneys, the arms, legs and head while the main **vein** moves blood **back** to the heart through the same parts. The blood moves through the liver in the system via the hepatic portal vein.

Exercise 4
Example *(depending on words/phrases chosen)*
Subject
Works of Art
Vocabulary
artist/painter/sculptor; studio; pictures; portraits/landscapes/abstracts; watercolour/acrylic/oil painting; sculptures; masterpiece; exhibition; art gallery/public gallery
Collocations
a painter paints; a sculptor makes figures or objects; people collect works of art; works of art are on display/on show; galleries have permanent collections; sculptures are made in marble/bronze

Exercise 9
Example *(answers may vary, depending on chosen words/phrases)*
Cell
Plant cells have walls which are made of cellulose, whereas animal cells do not have walls. Plant cells have their nucleus at the edge of the cell, whereas animal cells have the nucleus anywhere, but often at the centre. Chloroplasts are present in many plant cells but never in animal cells. In plant cells there is a thin lining of cytoplasm against the wall of the cell, whereas in the animal cell cytoplasm is present throughout. In a plant cell there is often one large central vacuole, whereas in an animal cell there are small vacuoles throughout the cytoplasm.

Practice for IELTS (page R6–9)

Reading test 1
1 v
2 viii
3 xi
4 ii
5 iv
6 ix
7 i
8 xii
9 vii
10 A
11 C
12 B
13 D

Reading test 2
14 industry
15 labour
16 service
17 decentralisation
18 entertainment
19 beautification
20 T
21 F
22 NG
23 T
24 T
25 NG
26 F

Essay writing (page R15–17)

Exercise 1

paragraph 1 nowadays, recently
paragraph 2 as a result, consequently, therefore
paragraph 3 furthermore, in addition, moreover
paragraph 4 nevertheless, on the other hand, while, however
paragraph 5 in conclusion, to sum up, finally

Exercise 2

compared with	in comparison with
obviously	clearly
affect sth drastically	have a devastating impact on sth
in particular	especially
appreciate	value
moreover	furthermore
whereas	while
is a significant factor	plays an important role
in contrast	on the other hand
a cross section	a representative group
as a result	consequently
grave difficulties	serious problems

Exercise 3

suggested plan:

paragraph 1 recent advances in science; new possibilities
paragraph 2 unknown dangers; interfering with nature; can't go back
paragraph 3 religious concerns; designer babies; cloning humans; political purposes
paragraph 4 new cures for illnesses; banning impractical; impossible to regulate
paragraph 5 benefits and challenges

Exercise 4

Recently; As a result; Furthermore; On the other hand; In conclusion

Interpreting graphs (page R18–20)

Exercise 1

1 peaked
2 1997 and 1999
3 plummeted
4 January and August
5 levelled out
6 1999
7 increased/rose
8 declined/decreased/dropped/fell

Exercise 2

suggested answers:

1 Sales increased/rose dramatically/sharply.
2 Sales decreased rapidly.
3 Sales increased gradually.
4 Sales fell steadily.
5 Sales rose moderately.
6 Sales increased slightly.

1 There was a dramatic increase in sales from 1997 to 1999.
2 There was a rapid decrease in sales from 1999 to 2001.
3 There was a gradual increase in sales between 2001 and 2004.
4 There was a steady fall in sales from 2004 to 2006.
5 Between July and August 2006 there was a moderate rise in sales.
6 There was a slight increase in sales from November to December 2006.

Exercise 3

1 of
2 From, to, to
3 at, in, to
4 at, of
5 at, of
6 by, by

Exercise 4

well over
just over
exactly
almost/nearly
just under
well under

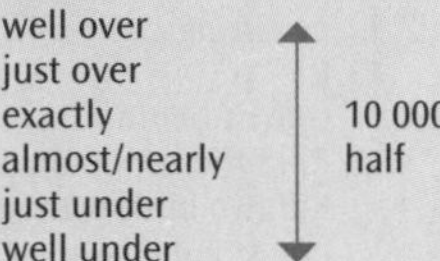

10 000
half

Exercise 5

text with suggested corrections:

Family A's biggest expenditure each month is the mortgage. Family A spends far more on their mortgage than they do on anything else (32%). This is exactly double what they spend on entertainment each month. Their food budget (19%) is slightly higher than their entertainment budget, while they spend just under 10% each month on clothes. Family B's clothes budget is a little less (5%). Family B's entertainment budget is considerably less than Family A's, at just 9%. In contrast, Family B spends much more on bills each month, nearly a quarter of the whole monthly budget. This is compensated for by their mortgage, which is much less than Family A's, at only 24%. Just under 15% of their monthly budget goes on the car, significantly more than the 9% that Family A spends each month. In general. Family B spends more on necessary items such as bills, food and car, while Family A allows significantly more money for entertainment and clothes.

Letter writing page (page R23–25)

Exercise 1

a 6
b 9
c 14
d 3
e 12
f 8
g 13
h 2
i 11
j 5
k 4
l 10
m 1
n 7

Exercise 2

1 d
2 e
3 f
4 b
5 a
6 c

Exercise 3

1 d
2 h
3 c
4 f
5 b
6 i
7 a
8 e
9 g

Taking notes (page R26–27)

Exercise 1

	symbol	meaning
1	*	this is an important point
2	≈	is approximately equal to
3	≠	is not, does not equal
4	+	and, plus
5	=	is, equals
6	∵	because
7	@	at
8	>	is more than
9	<	is less than
10	♂	male
11	♀	female

12 ∴ therefore, so
13 & and
14 " the same word as above

Exercise 2

vol.	volume	**sing.**	singular
ex.	example	**approx.**	approximately
usu.	usually	**incl.**	including, inclusive
diffs.	differences		

Exercise 3

i.e.	that is	**c**	about, approximately
e.g.	for example	**cf.**	compare/contrast
no.	number	**pp**	pages

Exercise 5

Energy – *Suggested notes:*

Most energy for heat , light, machs., etc. ← fossil fuels. Will run out.

∴ a) need altern. srcs – e.g. wind, solar pwr. Renew.; not poll. air.

b) don't waste: - use less elec. + wtr.
- insul. houses.

IRREGULAR VERBS

In this list you will find the infinitive form of the irregular verb followed by the past tense and the past participle. Where two forms are given, look up the verb in the main part of the dictionary to see whether there is a difference in the meaning.

Infinitive	Past Tense	Past Participle
arise	arose	arisen
awake	awoke	awoken
be	was/were	been
bear	bore	borne
beat	beat	beaten
become	became	become
befall	befell	befallen
begin	began	begun
bend	bent	bent
beseech	beseeched, besought	beseeched, besought
beset	beset	beset
bet	bet, betted	bet, betted
bid	bid	bid
bind	bound	bound
bite	bit	bitten
bleed	bled	bled
blow	blew	blown
break	broke	broken
breastfeed	breastfed	breastfed
breed	bred	bred
bring	brought	brought
broadcast	broadcast	broadcast
browbeat	browbeat	browbeaten
build	built	built
burn	burnt, burned	burnt, burned
burst	burst	burst
bust	bust, busted	bust, busted
buy	bought	bought
cast	cast	cast
catch	caught	caught
choose	chose	chosen
cling	clung	clung
come	came	come
cost	cost	cost
creep	crept	crept
cross-breed	cross-bred	cross-bred
cut	cut	cut
deal	dealt /delt/	dealt /delt/
dig	dug	dug
dive	dived; (*AmE* dove)	dived
do	did	done
draw	drew	drawn
dream	dreamt /dremt/, dreamed /dri:md/	dreamt /dremt/, dreamed /dri:md/
drink	drank	drunk
drive	drove	driven
dwell	dwelt, dwelled	dwelt, dwelled
eat	ate	eaten
fall	fell	fallen
feed	fed	fed
feel	felt	felt
fight	fought	fought
find	found	found
fit	fitted; (*AmE usually* fit)	fitted; (*AmE usually* fit)

Infinitive	Past Tense	Past Participle
flee	fled	fled
fling	flung	flung
fly	flew	flown
forbid	forbade	forbidden
forecast	forecast	forecast
foresee	foresaw	foreseen
forget	forgot	forgotten
forgive	forgave	forgiven
forgo	forwent	forgone
forsake	forsook	forsaken
freeze	froze	frozen
get	got	got; (*AmE*) gotten
give	gave	given
go	went	gone
grind	ground	ground
grow	grew	grown
hang	hung, hanged	hung, hanged
have	had	had
hear	heard /hɜːd/	heard /hɜːd/
hide	hid	hidden
hit	hit	hit
hold	held	held
hurt	hurt	hurt
input	input, inputted	input, inputted
keep	kept	kept
kneel	knelt (*especially AmE* kneeled)	knelt; (*especially AmE* kneeled)
know	knew	known
lay	laid	laid
lead	led	led
lean	leant /lent/, leaned /liːnd/	leant /lent/, leaned /liːnd/
leap	leapt /lept/, leaped /liːpt/	leapt /lept/, leaped /liːpt
learn	learnt, learned	learnt, learned
leave	left	left
lend	lent	lent
let	let	let
lie	lay	lain
light	lit, lighted	lit, lighted
lip-read	lip-read /ˈlɪpred/	lip-read /ˈlɪpred/
lose	lost	lost
make	made	made
mean	meant /ment/	meant /ment/

Infinitive	Past Tense	Past Participle
meet	met	met
mislay	mislaid	mislaid
mislead	misled	misled
misread	misread /ˌmɪsˈred/	misread /ˌmɪsˈred/
misspell	misspelt, misspelled	misspelt, misspelled
mistake	mistook	mistaken
misunderstand	misunderstood	misunderstood
mow	mowed	mown, mowed
outdo	outdid	outdone
outgrow	outgrew	outgrown
outrun	outran	outrun
overcome	overcame	overcome
overdo	overdid	overdone
overhang	overhung	overhung
overhear	overheard /ˌəʊvəˈhɜːd/	overheard /ˌəʊvəˈhɜːd/
overpay	overpaid	overpaid
override	overrode	overridden
overrun	overran	overrun
oversee	oversaw	overseen
oversleep	overslept	overslept
overtake	overtook	overtaken
overthrow	overthrew	overthrown
pay	paid	paid
prove	proved	proved, proven
put	put	put
quit	quit, quitted	quit, quitted
read	read /red/	read /red/
rebuild	rebuilt	rebuilt
redo	redid	redone
repay	repaid	repaid
rethink	rethought	rethought
rewind	rewound	rewound
rewrite	rewrote	rewritten
rid	rid	rid
ride	rode	ridden
ring	rang	rung
rise	rose	risen
run	ran	run
saw	sawed	sawn; (*AmE* sawed)
say	said	said
see	saw	seen
seek	sought	sought

Infinitive	Past Tense	Past Participle
sell	sold	sold
send	sent	sent
set	set	set
sew	sewed	sewn, sewed
shake	shook	shaken
shear	sheared	shorn, sheared
shed	shed	shed
shine	shone	shone
shoe	shod	shod
shoot	shot	shot
show	showed	shown, showed
shrink	shrank, shrunk	shrunk
shut	shut	shut
sing	sang	sung
sink	sank	sunk
sit	sat	sat
slay	slew	slain
sleep	slept	slept
slide	slid	slid
sling	slung	slung
slink	slunk	slunk
slit	slit	slit
smell	smelt, smelled	smelt, smelled
sneak	sneaked; (*informal, especially AmE* snuck)	sneaked; (*informal, especially AmE* snuck)
sow	sowed	sown, sowed
speak	spoke	spoken
speed	sped, speeded	sped, speeded
spell	spelt, spelled	spelt, spelled
spend	spent	spent
spill	spilt, spilled	spilt, spilled
spin	spun	spun
spit	spat, (*AmE also* spit)	spat, (*AmE also* spit)
split	split	split
spoil	spoilt, spoiled	spoilt, spoiled
spread	spread	spread
spring	sprang	sprung
stand	stood	stood
steal	stole	stolen
stick	stuck	stuck
sting	stung	stung
stink	stank, stunk	stunk
stride	strode	—
strike	struck	struck
string	strung	strung
strive	strove	striven
swear	swore	sworn
sweep	swept	swept
swell	swelled	swollen, swelled
swim	swam	swum
swing	swung	swung
take	took	taken
teach	taught	taught
tear	tore	torn
tell	told	told
think	thought	thought
thrive	thrived; (*old-fashioned* throve)	thrived
throw	threw	thrown
thrust	thrust	thrust
tread	trod	trodden, trod
undercut	undercut	undercut
undergo	underwent	undergone
underpay	underpaid	underpaid
understand	understood	understood
undertake	undertook	undertaken
underwrite	underwrote	underwritten
undo	undid	undone
unwind	unwound	unwound
uphold	upheld	upheld
upset	upset	upset
wake	woke	woken
wear	wore	worn
weave	wove, weaved	woven, weaved
weep	wept	wept
wet	wet, wetted	wet, wetted
win	won	won
wind[3]	wound	wound
withdraw	withdrew	withdrawn
withhold	withheld	withheld
withstand	withstood	withstood
wring	wrung	wrung
write	wrote	written

PRONUNCIATION

If two pronunciations for one word are given, both are acceptable. The first form given is considered to be more common.

/ - / A hyphen is used in alternative pronunciations when only part of the pronunciation changes. The part that remains the same is replaced by the hyphen.
accent /ˈæksent: -sənt/

/ ˈ / This mark shows that the syllable after it is said with more force (stress) than other syllables in the word or group of words. For example **any** /ˈeni/ has a stress on the first syllable; **depend** /dɪˈpend/ has a stress on the second syllable.

/ ˌ / This mark shows that a syllable is said with more force than other syllables in a word but with a stress that is not as strong as for those syllables marked /ˈ/. So in the word **pronunciation** /prəˌnʌnsiˈeɪʃn/ the main stress is on the syllable /ˈeɪ/ and the secondary stress is on the syllable /ˌnʌn/.

Strong and weak forms

Some very common words, for example **an**, **as**, **that**, **of**, have two or more pronunciations: a **strong** form and one or more **weak** forms. In speech the weak forms are more common. For example **from** is /frəm/ in **He comes from Spain**. The strong form occurs when the word comes at the end of a sentence or it is given special emphasis. For example **from** is /frɒm/ in **Where are you from?** and in **The present ís not from John; it's for him**.

Weak vowels /i/ and /u/

The sounds represented by /iː/ and /ɪ/ must always be made different, as in **heat** /hiːt/ compared with **hit** /hɪt/.

The symbol /i/ represents a vowel that can be sounded as either /iː/ or /ɪ/, or as a sound which is a compromise between them.

When /i/ is followed by /ə/ the sequence can also be pronounced as /jə/. So the word **dubious** can be either /ˈdjuːbiəs/ or /djuːbjəs/.

In the same way the two vowels represented by /uː/ and /ʊ/ must be made different, but /u/ represents a weak vowel that varies between them. If /u/ is followed directly by a consonant sound, it can also be pronounced as /ə/. So **stimulate** can be /ˈstɪmjuleɪt/ or /ˈstɪmjəleɪt/.

Pronunciation in derivatives and compounds

Many **derivatives** are formed by adding a suffix to the end of a word. These are pronounced by simply saying the suffix after the word. For example **slowly** /ˈsləʊli/ is said by adding the suffix **-ly** /li/ to the word **slow** /sləʊ/.

However, where there is doubt about how a derivative is pronounced, the phonetic spelling is given. The part that remains the same is represented by a hyphen.

accidental /ˌæksɪˈdentl/; **accidentally** /-təli/

In **compounds** (made up of two or more words) the pronunciation of the individual words is not repeated. The dictionary shows how the compound is stressed using the marks /ˈ/ and /ˌ/. In **ˈair steward** the stress is on the first word. In **ˌair ˌtraffic conˈtroller** there are secondary stresses on **air** and on the first syllable of **traffic**, and the main stress is on the second syllable of **controller**.